THE ROUGH GUIDE TO

Germ

before

There are more than two hundred Rough Guide titles
covering destinations from Alaska to Zimbabwe
and subjects from Acoustic Guitar to Travel Health

Forthcoming travel guides include

Chicago • Corfu • First-Time Round the World
Grand Canyon • Philippines • Skiing & Snowboarding in North America
South America • The Gambia • Walks Around London

Forthcoming reference guides include

Chronicles series: China, England,
France, India • Night Sky

Rough Guides Online
www.roughguides.com

ROUGH GUIDE CREDITS

Text editor: Judith Bamber
Series editor: Mark Ellingham
Editorial: Martin Dunford, Jonathan Buckley, Jo Mead, Kate Berens, Ann-Marie Shaw, Paul Gray, Helena Smith, Orla Duane, Olivia Eccleshall, Ruth Blackmore, Geoff Howard, Claire Saunders, Gavin Thomas, Alexander Mark Rogers, Polly Thomas, Joe Staines, Richard Lim, Duncan Clark, Peter Buckley, Sam Thorne, Lucy Ratcliffe, Clifton Wilkinson, David Glen, Alison Murchie, Matthew Teller (UK); Andrew Rosenberg, Stephen Timblin, Yuki Takagaki, Richard Koss (US)
Production: Susanne Hillen, Andy Hilliard, Link Hall, Helen Prior, Julia Bovis, Michelle Draycott, Katie

Pringle, Mike Hancock, Zoë Nobes, Rachel Holmes, Andy Turner
Cartography: Melissa Baker, Maxine Repath, Ed Wright, Katie Lloyd-Jones
Picture research: Louise Boulton, Sharon Martins
Online: Kelly Cross, Anja Mutić-Blessing, Jennifer Gold, Audra Epstein, Suzanne Welles (US)
Finance: John Fisher, Gary Singh, Edward Downey, Mark Hall, Tim Bill
Marketing & Publicity: Richard Trillo, Niki Smith, David Wearn, Chloë Roberts, Birgit Hartmann, Claire Southern (UK); Simon Carloss, David Wechsler, Kathleen Rushforth (US)
Administration: Tania Hummel, Demelza Dallow, Julie Sanderson

ACKNOWLEDGEMENTS

Very special thanks are due to the editor, Judith Bamber, who has been an unfailing source of encouragement and good humour throughout the long and painstaking process of preparing this much-altered new edition; and to Janice and Steve Hopwood, who since 1994 have provided an annual home from home in Munich.

Thanks also to the cartographers Mandy Muggridge, The Map studio and Maxine Repath for a fine new set

of maps; to Mike Hancock and the production team; to Jennifer Speake for proofreading; to Natascha Norton, for her contributions to previous editions; to regular correspondent Dr Stephen v. Paczynski for so many useful tips; to Richard Mead for the box on The Beatles (p.727); to Hedda Manhard, Vicky Weller, Astrid Ganssen, Karin Storz, Helen McLachlan and Ian McLachlan for all sorts of advice and help; and to the readers who wrote in.

PUBLISHING INFORMATION

This fifth edition published June 2001 by
  Rough Guides Ltd, 62–70 Shorts Gardens,
  London WC2H 9AH. Reprinted June 2002
Distributed by the Penguin Group:
Penguin Books Ltd, 80 Strand, London, WC2R ORL
Penguin Putnam, Inc. 375 Hudson Street, NY 10014, USA
Penguin Books Australia Ltd, 487 Maroondah Highway,
  PO Box 257, Ringwood, Victoria 3134, Australia
Penguin Books Canada Ltd, 10 Alcorn Avenue, Toronto,
  Ontario, Canada M4V 1E4
Penguin Books (NZ) Ltd, 182–190 Wairau Road,
  Auckland 10, New Zealand
Typeset in Linotron Univers and Century Old Style to an
  original design by Andrew Oliver.
Printed in England by Clays Ltd, St Ives PLC.
Illustrations in Part One and Part Three by Edward Briant.

Illustrations on p.1 & p.1061 by Mike Hancock
© Gordon McLachan 2001
No part of this book may be reproduced in any form
  without permission from the publisher except for the
  quotation of brief passages in reviews.
1152pp – Includes index
A catalogue record for this book is available from the
  British Library
ISBN 1-85828-706-5

The publishers and authors have done their best to
  ensure the accuracy and currency of all the information
  in *The Rough Guide to Germany*, however, they can
  accept no responsibility for any loss, injury, or
  inconvenience sustained by any traveller as a result of
  information or advice contained in the guide.

THE ROUGH GUIDE TO

Germany

written and researched by

Gordon McLachan

with additional research by

John Gawthorp, Jack Holland and Andrew Roth

ROUGH
GUIDES

TRAVEL GUIDES • PHRASEBOOKS • MUSIC AND REFERENCE GUIDES

 We set out to do something different when the first Rough Guide was published in 1982. Mark Ellingham, just out of university, was travelling in Greece. He brought along the popular guides of the day, but found they were all lacking in some way. They were either strong on ruins and museums but went on for pages without mentioning a beach or taverna. Or they were so conscious of the need to save money that they lost sight of Greece's cultural and historical significance. Also, none of the books told him anything about Greece's contemporary life – its politics, its culture, its people, and how they lived.

So with no job in prospect, Mark decided to write his own guidebook, one which aimed to provide practical information that was second to none, detailing the best beaches and the hottest clubs and restaurants, while also giving hard-hitting accounts of every sight, both famous and obscure, and providing up-to-the-minute information on contemporary culture. It was a guide that encouraged independent travellers to find the best of Greece, and was a great success, getting shortlisted for the Thomas Cook travel guide award, and encouraging Mark, along with three friends, to expand the series.

The Rough Guide list grew rapidly and the letters flooded in, indicating a much broader readership than had been anticipated, but one which uniformly appreciated the Rough Guide mix of practical detail and humour, irreverence and enthusiasm. Things haven't changed. The same four friends who began the series are still the caretakers of the Rough Guide mission today: to provide the most reliable, up-to-date and entertaining information to independent-minded travellers of all ages, on all budgets.

We now publish more than 150 titles and have offices in London and New York. The travel guides are written and researched by a dedicated team of more than 100 authors, based in Britain, Europe, the USA and Australia. We have also created a unique series of phrasebooks to accompany the travel series, along with an acclaimed series of music guides, and a best-selling pocket guide to the Internet and World Wide Web. We also publish comprehensive travel information on our Web site:

www.roughguides.com

HELP US UPDATE

We've gone to a lot of effort to ensure that the fifth edition of *The Rough Guide to Germany* is accurate and up-to-date. However, things change – places get "discovered", opening hours are notoriously fickle, restaurants and rooms raise prices or lower standards. If you feel we've got it wrong or left something out, we'd like to know, and if you can remember the address, the price, the time, the phone number, so much the better.

We'll credit all contributions, and send a copy of the next edition (or any other Rough Guide if you prefer) for the best letters. Please mark letters: "Rough Guide Germany Update" and send to:
Rough Guides, 62–70 Shorts Gardens, London WC2H 9AH, or Rough Guides, 4th Floor, 345 Hudson St, New York, NY 10014.
Or send email to: mail@roughguides.co.uk
Online updates about this book can be found on Rough Guides' Web site at **www.roughguides.com**

Will you have enough stories to tell your grandchildren?

©2000 Yahoo! Inc.

Yahoo! Travel

THE AUTHOR

Gordon McLachlan first became fascinated by Germany while studying modern European history at school and university in his native Edinburgh. In the 1980s, when the Iron Curtain was still firmly in place, he researched and wrote most of the inaugural *Rough Guide to Germany*. He has updated every subsequent edition, monitoring closely the country's transformation from a divided to a united nation. In the process he has travelled to every corner of the country, visiting all of the main monuments and museums, and sampling hundreds of hotels, restaurants, cafés and bars. He has also written books on Berlin and Germany's Romantic Road, and on two countries immediately to Germany's east – Poland and Lithuania.

READERS' LETTERS

Thanks to readers of the last edition who wrote in with helpful comments and suggestions:

Darius Baghernajad, John R.T. Bailey, Diane Belfield, Chris Burrell, Phil Carey, Jin Chin, Damian Connolly, Martin Cottam, Richard Czepukojc, Gisela Dimond, Chris Elliott, Ronald Gee, Bruce Gilsen, Elizabeth Hodkinson, Frank Henk Hoekstra, Gordon Kadatz, Andrew Lee, Ian Miller, John D. Norman, Stuart and Dorothy Nattrass, Patrick O'Beirne, R. Piggott, Ben Pollard, Jonathan Rodgers, Peter Schuller, Doug Shearer, H. Smithson, Ian Stafford, Tom Wagener, John D. Wallace, Mike Weeks, Marilyn Welker, Stephen Wicks, Mark Worledge.

Apologies to any reader whose name has been omitted inadvertently or spelt incorrectly.

CONTENTS

Introduction x

PART THREE CONTEXTS 1061

LIST OF MAPS

MAP SYMBOLS

▬▬▬	International boundary	▲	Peak
▬ ▬	State boundary	⌃⌃	Mountains
▬ ▬ ▬	Chapter division boundary	◆	Point of interest
▬▬	Railway	▮	Tower
⊞⊞⊞⊞	Furnicular	ⓘ	Tourist office
▬▬	Motorway	⊠	Post office
▬▬	Road	✡	Synagogue
▬▬	Pedestrianized street	▮	Building
- - - -	Footpath	⊞	Church
▬ ▬	Ferry route	₊†₊	Cemetery
▬▬	Waterway	⌐⌐	Jewish cemetery
Ⓧ	Campsite	▨	Park
Ⓤ	U-Bahn	▨	National park
Ⓢ	S-Bahn	⠰⠤	Forest

INTRODUCTION

Germany has always been the problem child of Europe. For over a millennium it was no more than a loose confederation of separate states and territories, whose number at times topped the thousand mark. When unification belatedly came about in 1871, it was achieved almost exclusively by military might; as a direct result of this, the new nation was consumed by a thirst for power and expansion abroad. Defeat in World War I only led to a desire for revenge, the consequence of which was the Third Reich, a regime bent on mass genocide and on European, indeed world, domination. It took another tragic global war to crush this system and its people. When the victors quarrelled over how to prevent Germany ever again becoming dominant, they divided it into two hostile states; the parts held by the Western powers were developed into the **Federal Republic of Germany**, while the eastern zone occupied by the Soviets became the **German Democratic Republic**.

The contest between the two was an unequal one – the GDR, never able to break free from being a client state of the Soviet Union and forced to adopt a Communist system at odds with the national character, had fallen so far behind its rival in living standards that in 1961 the authorities constructed the notorious electrified barbed-wire frontier, with the **Berlin Wall** as its lynchpin, to halt emigration – the first time in the history of the world that a fortification system had been erected by a regime against its own people. Thereafter, the society settled down, but the GDR was a grey, cheerless place whose much trumpeted economic success was a mirage, and bought at the price of terrible pollution problems.

On the other hand, the Federal Republic – which was seen as the natural successor to the old Reich, if only on account of its size – had not only picked itself up by the bootstraps, but developed into what many outsiders regarded as a **model modern society**. A nation with little in the way of a liberal tradition, and even less of a democratic one, quickly developed a degree of political maturity that put other countries to shame. In atonement for past sins, the new state committed itself to providing a haven for foreign refugees and dissidents. It also became a multiracial and multicultural society – even if the reason for this was less one of penance than the self-interested need to acquire extra cheap labour to fuel the economic boom. A delicate balance was struck between the old and the new. Historic town centres were immaculately restored, while the corporate skyscrapers and well-stocked department stores represented a commitment to a modern consumer society. Vast sums of money were lavished on preserving the best of the country's cultural legacy, yet equally generous budgets were allocated to encouraging all kinds of contemporary expression in the arts.

Officially, the Federal Republic was always a "provisional" state, biding its time before national reunification occurred. Yet there was a realization that nobody outside Germany was really much in favour of this. "I love Germany so much I'm glad there are two of them", scoffed the French novelist François Mauriac, articulating the unspoken gut reactions of the powers on both sides of the Iron Curtain. German division may have been cruel, but at least it had provided a lasting solution to the German "problem". Such thinking was rendered obsolete by the unstoppable momentum of events in the wake of the **Wende**, the peaceful revolution that toppled the Communist regime in the GDR in 1989, leading to the full union of the two Germanys less than a year later. Yet initial euphoria has been quickly replaced by concern about the myriad problems facing the new nation as it attempts to integrate the bankrupt social and economic system of the GDR into the successful framework of the Federal Republic. While Germany may officially be one again, it will certainly continue to look and feel like two separate countries until the end of the century – and probably well beyond. Moreover, international pressure has ensured that, far from being a re-creation of the old Reich, it can be no more than the nineteenth-century concept of a *Kleines Deutschland* ("little Germany"), excluding not only Austria but also the "lost" Eastern Territories, which are now part of Poland, the Czech Republic and the Russian Federation.

In total contrast to Germany's intrinsic fascination as the country which has played such a determining role in the history of the twentieth century is its otherwise predominantly **romantic image**. This is the land of fairy-tale castles, of thick dark forests, of the legends collected by the Brothers Grimm, of perfectly preserved timber-framed medieval towns, and of jovial locals swilling from huge foaming mugs of beer. As always, there *is* some truth in these stereotypes, though most of them stem from the southern part of the country, particularly **Bavaria**, which, as a predominantly rural and Catholic area, stands apart from the urbanized Protestant north which engineered the unity of the nation last century and thereafter dominated its affairs.

Regional characteristics, indeed, are a strong feature of German life, and there are many hangovers from the days when the country was a political patchwork, even though some historical provinces have vanished from the map and others have merged. More detail on each of the current Länder, as the constituent states are now known, can be found in the chapter introductions. **Hamburg** and **Bremen**, for example, retain their age-old status as free cities. The imperial capital, **Berlin**, also stands apart, as an island in the midst of the erstwhile GDR where the liberalism of the West was pushed to its extreme, sometimes decadent, always exciting. In polar opposition to it, and as a corrective to the normal view of the Germans as an essentially serious race, is the **Rhineland**, where the great river's majestic sweep has spawned a particularly rich fund of legends and folklore, and where the locals are imbued with a Mediterranean-type sense of fun. The five **new Länder** which have supplanted the GDR, and in particular the small towns and rural areas, are in many ways the ones which best encapsulate the feel and appearance of Germany as it was before the war and the onset of foreign influences which were an inevitable consequence of defeat.

Where and when to go

There's enough variety within all but the smallest Länder to fill several weeks of travel, and you may prefer to confine your trip to just one or two regions. Among the **scenic highlights** are the Bavarian Alps, the Bodensee, the Black Forest, the valleys of the Rhine and Mosel, the Baltic island of Rügen, the Harz, and Saxon Switzerland. However, you may prefer one of the many less spectacular areas of natural beauty, which can be found in every province – these are the places the Germans themselves love the most, and where they spend their holidays and weekends. Several of the cities have the air of capitals, though **Bonn** has lost the role it "temporarily" carried for fifty years. Nearby **Cologne**, on the other hand, is one of the most characterful cities in the country, and the richest in historic monuments. Bavaria's capital, **Munich**, is another obvious star and boasts of having the best the country has to offer – whether in museums, beer, fashion or sport. **Nürnberg** reflects on its bygone years of glory, while **Frankfurt** looks on itself as the "real" capital of the country, and **Stuttgart** and **Düsseldorf** compete for the title of champion of German postwar success. In the east, **Dresden** is making a comeback as one of the world's great cultural centres, while **Leipzig** is returning to its role as one of the continent's main trading centres. However, as all these cities have suffered to a considerable extent from bomb damage and ugly postwar redevelopment, the smaller places in many respects offer a more satisfying experience. Chief among these is the university city of **Heidelberg**, star and guiding light of the Romantic movement. Trier, Bamberg, Regensburg, Rothenburg and

Marburg in the west, and Potsdam, Meissen and Quedlinburg in the east, are some of the many towns which deserve to be regarded among the most outstanding in Europe.

The best **times to go** are between April and October. Germany has a fairly volatile climate, not so different from that of Britain or New England. Summers are usually warm, but not overpoweringly so; good weather may come at an unexpected time, while it's not uncommon to have several abrupt changes in temperature within a single day. Rain occurs fairly regularly throughout the year. Unless you're intending to go skiing, winter travel can't really be recommended, other than for seeing the cities stripped of tourist hordes. Otherwise, there's a chance of snow at any time from November onwards. In the really popular areas, the claustrophobic effect of masses of organized tour groups is a factor to be taken into account between mid-June and mid-September: best avoid such places altogether then, and head for the many less spoiled alternatives. All things considered, however, the ideal times for visiting Germany are late spring and early autumn.

AVERAGE TEMPERATURES (°F)		Berlin	Frankfurt	Hamburg	Munich
January	Max	48	50	36	35
	Min	10	14	28	23
February	Max	52	54	37	38
	Min	10	16	28	23
March	Max	63	66	44	48
	Min	19	25	31	30
April	Max	72	75	55	56
	Min	28	32	38	38
May	Max	82	84	64	64
	Min	36	37	46	45
June	Max	86	88	69	70
	Min	43	45	51	51
July	Max	90	91	73	74
	Min	48	50	55	36
August	Max	88	90	72	73
	Min	46	48	54	55
September	Max	82	82	66	67
	Min	39	41	49	54
October	Max	70	70	55	62
	Min	30	32	43	48
November	Max	55	59	45	56
	Min	25	27	37	40
December	Max	50	52	39	44
	Min	16	19	31	33

To convert °Fahrenheit into °Centigrade, subtract 32 and multiply by 5/9
Rainfall is consistent throughout the year for all the above cities, at 2–3 inches per month; only Munich exceeds this, with an average 4–6 inches per month in summer

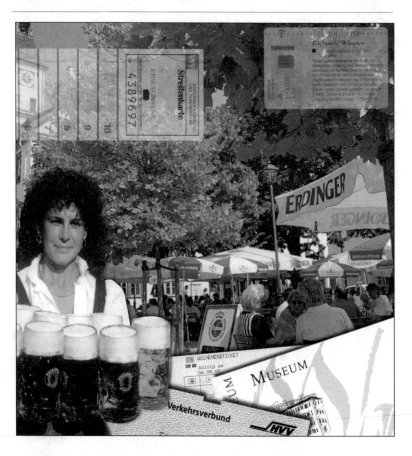

GETTING THERE FROM BRITAIN

The most convenient and usually best-value way to get to Germany is to fly – flights from London to Frankfurt take little over an hour and to Berlin around an hour and a half. Travelling by train through the Channel Tunnel makes a pleasant alternative, and journey times have improved recently: from London to Frankfurt via Brussels and Cologne takes just under eight hours. Getting over to Germany with your car is also fairly easy with the Eurotunnel Shuttle. If you're heading for north Germany or destinations in the former GDR you can cut down on the driving by taking the ferry from Harwich to Hamburg.

BY PLANE

Most major west German cities have numerous daily links with London (Heathrow and Gatwick), as well as with several regional UK airports. Flight times are around 1hr to 1hr 30min. Often you'll find that the lowest fares and the most frequent flights are to **Frankfurt**, very much at the centre of German air routes. To fly to other German cities costs slightly more, while **Berlin** and the former GDR cities are the most expensive of all to reach.

The main airlines that fly to Germany from the UK are **British Airways** and **Lufthansa**. Their standard scheduled fares are expensive, but they have numerous special offers throughout the year. In January 2001, for example, Lufthansa was offering a return fare of £72.30 from London Stansted to Frankfurt. Usually,

these tickets come with various restrictions and have to be booked well in advance. BA and Lufthansa also offer **fly-drive deals** and **open-jaw flights**, which allow you to fly into one airport and back from another.

Extremely competitive fares are also offered by the **low-cost airlines**, Ryanair and Buzz. Both operate regular flights to Frankfurt from London Stansted. **Ryanair**'s lowest fare is £47 return, excluding airport tax; they also fly for £66 (again minus taxes) from Glasgow Prestwick to the misleadingly named Frankfurt-Hahn airport – not the city's main airport, but a tiny former military airport 60km to the west and connected by special buses to Frankfurt, and by scheduled buses to nearby Bingen. **Buzz**'s fares to Frankfurt from Stansted start at £87, and they also fly to Berlin for £89, both fares including tax.

Another source of cheap tickets are **discount flight agents**. The ones listed in the box on p.4 make a good starting point. Particularly worth trying is the **German Travel Centre**, which specializes in flights to Germany. Other agents can be found on the pages of the Sunday or local evening papers, regional listings magazines and, in London, *Time Out*. If you're a student or under 26, you're best off contacting the independent travel specialists **STA Travel** and **Usit Campus** (see box on p.4 for addresses), which offer discounted fares to young people. They are also worth calling even if you aren't a student, as they offer a good range of budget fares.

Typical fares **from London** available from discount agents are £112 to Frankfurt, £122 to Hamburg, £132 to Munich and £150 to Berlin. You can fly direct **from Birmingham** to Frankfurt for around £112, to Munich for £127 and to Berlin for £150. **From Manchester** you're looking at £122 to Frankfurt, £178 to Munich and £155 to Berlin via Frankfurt. The cheapest flights from **Edinburgh and Glasgow** to Frankfurt and Munich tend to be with KLM and involve a change in Amsterdam. Prices are around £118 to Frankfurt and £143 to Munich. From Edinburgh you can get a direct flight to Berlin for around £139, but from Glasgow your cheapest option is with KLM, again via Amsterdam, with a fare of around £153. Note that all the above prices are exclusive of **airport tax**: this is usually somewhere between £20 and £30. You'll also need to

British Airways ☎0345/222111, www.britishairways.com

Buzz ☎0870/240 7070, www.buzzaway.com

Lufthansa ☎0845/773 7747, www.lufthansa.com

Ryanair ☎0541/569569, www.ryanair.com

DISCOUNT FLIGHT AGENTS

German Travel Centre, German House, 403–09 Rayners Lane, Pinner, Middlesex HA5 5ER (☎020/8429 2900, www.german-travel-uk.com). Discount flight specialists. They can also arrange accommodation.

North South Travel, Moulsham Mill, Parkway, Chelmsford, Essex CM2 7PX (☎01245/608291, www.northsouthtravel.co.uk). Friendly, competitive travel agency, offering discounted fares worldwide – profits are used to support projects in the developing world, especially the promotion of sustainable tourism.

STA Travel, 86 Old Brompton Rd, London SW7 3LH; 117 Euston Rd, London NW1 2SX; 38 Store St, London WC1E 7BZ; and 11 Goodge St, London W1P 1FU (all ☎020/7361 6161); 25 Queen's Rd, Bristol BS8 1QE (☎0117/929 4399); 38 Sidney St, Cambridge CB2 3HX (☎01223/366966); 75 Deansgate, Manchester M3 2BW (☎0161/834 0668); 36 George St, Oxford OX1 2OJ (☎01865/792800). Web site: www.statravel.co.uk. Independent travel specialists; discounted flights.

Trailfinders, 215 Kensington High St, London W6 6BD (☎020/7937 5400); 1 Threadneedle St, London EC2R 8JX (☎020/7628 7628); 58 Deansgate, Manchester M3 2FF (☎0161/839 6969); 254–284 Sauchiehall St, Glasgow G2 3EH (☎0141/353 2224); 22–24 The Priory Queensway, Birmingham B4 6BS (☎0121/236 1234); 48 Corn St, Bristol BS1 1HQ (☎0117/929 9000). Web site: www.trailfinders.co.uk. One of the best-informed and most efficient agents for independent travellers.

Usit CAMPUS Travel, 52 Grosvenor Gardens, London SW1W 0AG (☎0870/240 1010); 541 Bristol Rd, Selly Oak, Birmingham B29 6AU (☎0121/414 1848); 39 Queen's Rd, Clifton, Bristol BS8 1QE (☎0117/929 2494); 5 Emmanuel St, Cambridge CB1 1NE (☎01223/324283); 53 Forest Rd, Edinburgh EH1 2QP (☎0131/668 3303); 166 Deansgate, Manchester M3 3FE (☎0161/273 1721); 105–6 St Aldates, Oxford OX1 1DO (☎01865/242067); also in YHA shops and on university campuses throughout Britain. Web site: www.usitcampus.co.uk. Youth/student specialist.

bear in mind that these tickets usually come with certain **conditions**: you'll probably have to stay for a minimum of three nights, one of which will be a Saturday, and once the tickets are booked, they tend to be non-refundable and the dates non-changeable.

Ceefax is also an extremely good source of discounted flights. In addition, **Web-based companies** such as www.lastminute.com, www.cheapflights.co.uk and www.deckchair.com can offer some of the best discounted fares and last-minute deals available.

BY TRAIN

The introduction of high-speed InterCityExpress trains on major routes in Germany has helped to reduce journey times **by train** from the UK. Using the high-speed Eurostar services direct from London Waterloo to Brussels, with connecting trains onwards to Cologne, it's now possible to

reach Germany in less than seven hours. Prices are fairly reasonable, too, compared with flights. London to Cologne is £89, Frankfurt is £129, Heidelberg £139 and Stuttgart, Munich, Berlin or Dresden £159. Rates are for a return journey in second class, including Eurostar, and with a stay of at least three nights or a Saturday night. For the longer journeys you might want to consider an overnight sleeper service, which costs around £60 extra.

You can get through ticketing – including the tube journey to Waterloo – from mainline stations in Britain; typical add-on prices are £28 from Edinburgh or Glasgow, £19 from Manchester and £14 from Birmingham.

RAIL PASSES

If you plan to travel extensively in Germany by train, there are better-value options than simply buying a return ticket. You might consider invest-

TRAIN AND BUS INFORMATION

Eurolines, 52 Grosvenor Gardens (opposite Victoria train station), London SW1W 0AU (☎0870/240 8079, *www.eurolines.co.uk*). Coach services to over 460 European destinations.

Eurostar, Eurostar House, Waterloo Station, London SE1 8SE (☎0345 /881881, *www.eurostar.com*). Train services from London to Paris and Brussels via the Channel Tunnel.

Eurotunnel, PO Box 300, Dept 302, Folkestone, Kent CT19 4QD (☎0870/535 3535, *www .eurotunnel.com*). Shuttle train via the Channel Tunnel for passengers and their vehicles.

German Rail, 18 Conduit St, London W1R 9TD (☎0870/243 5363, *www.bahn.de*). German rail tickets and passes.

Rail Europe, 179 Piccadilly, London W1V 0BA (☎0870/5848 848, *www.raileurope.co.uk*). European rail tickets and passes.

ing in an **InterRail** pass, available from Rail Europe or any travel agent; the only restriction on purchase is that you must have been resident in Europe for at least six months. The pass comes in two forms. The **InterRail Global** pass is valid for one month's unlimited travel in 26 European countries, including Germany, and costs £219 if you're under 26, and £309 for over-26s. The other option is an **InterRail Zonal** pass: the 26 countries are split into seven zones and you choose which zone you want the pass to be valid for. A one-zone card valid for 22 days is £129/£179; any two contiguous zones, valid for one month, £169/235; any three, also for one month, £195/269. Germany is in the same zone as Austria, Switzerland and Denmark. The two adjoining zones are France, Belgium, Netherlands and Luxembourg; and the Czech Republic, Slovakia, Poland, Hungary, Bulgaria and Croatia. Note that InterRail passes do not include travel between Britain and the Continent, although InterRail pass-holders are eligible for discounts on rail travel in the UK, on the London–Paris Eurostar service and on cross-Channel ferries.

Be prepared to pay extra supplements on some German trains, especially on InterCityExpress services. There are also some private lines, including east Germany's narrow-gauge steam rail lines, on which passes are not valid.

Specific **passes for travel in Germany only** can be bought before you go from Rail Europe or the DER Travel Service (see box on p.7) and other agents – for a full list of national passes contact **German Rail** (see box above).

If you're 60 or over and have a British Rail Senior Card (£18 from any train station), you can get a **Rail Europe Senior Card** for £5, which gives discounts of approximately 30 percent on

cross-border train and sea travel in Germany and most of western Europe; both are valid for one year.

BY BUS

Travelling to Germany **by bus** won't bring any major savings over the cheapest air fares, and the journey will be long and uncomfortable, interrupted every three to four hours by stops at highway services. The one advantage is that you can have an open return at no extra cost.

The main operator is **Eurolines** (see box above for details). Summer frequencies, timings and return fares from London to the major cities are: Cologne (daily, 12hr) £70; Frankfurt (daily, 14hr 45min) £81; Hamburg (2 weekly, 20hr 30min) £77; Berlin (4 weekly, 23hr 30min) £91; Munich (daily, 23hr 30min) £91. Winter departures are only slightly fewer and fares are usually the same as during the summer. There are small reductions (£2–10) for students, youths and senior citizens, slightly more substantial ones for children.

Tickets can be booked through most major travel agents; Eurolines sells tickets and through transport to London at all National Express bus terminals.

BY CAR, SHUTTLE TRAIN AND FERRY

Travelling by **car**, your route across to the Continent will be largely determined by which part of Germany you're heading for. For the Rhineland and south Germany, you're best off going to France or Belgium. One of the easiest ways to cross the Channel is via the Eurotunnel Shuttle train. The alternative is one of the time-honoured ferry crossings. For northern Germany or Berlin and the former GDR, you'll save on driving time by taking a boat to Holland or direct to Hamburg.

FERRY COMPANIES

DFDS, Scandinavia House, Parkeston Quay, Harwich, Essex CO12 4QG (☎0807/533 3000, *www.dfdsseaways.co.uk*). Harwich to Hamburg.

Hoverspeed, International Hoverport, Dover, Kent (☎0870/524 0241, *www.hoverspeed.co.uk*). Dover to Calais and Ostend; Folkestone to Boulogne.

P&O North Sea Ferries, King George Dock, Hedon Rd, Hull HU9 5QA (☎01482/377177,

www.ponsf.com). Hull to Rotterdam and Zeebrugge.

P&O Stena Line, Channel House, Channel View Rd, Dover CT17 9TJ (☎0870/598 0980, *www.posl.com*). Dover to Calais.

Sea France, Eastern Docks, Dover CT16 1JA (☎0870/571 1711, *www.seafrance.com*). Dover to Calais.

Once across, particularly if you drive through Holland or Belgium – less so in France – you'll rarely be travelling on anything but highways all the way to any German city. From Calais and the other Channel ports allow about three hours to Cologne or Düsseldorf, six to seven to Hamburg or Frankfurt and twelve to Munich or Berlin. For practical details on driving in Germany see pp.33–4.

SHUTTLE TRAIN

Probably the most convenient way of taking your car across to the Continent is to drive down to the Channel Tunnel, load your car on the **Shuttle train**, and be whisked under the Channel in 35 minutes. The tunnel entrance is off the M20 at Junction 11A, just outside Folkestone; at the other end, you emerge just outside Calais. The Shuttle train operates services round the clock, 365 days a year. Trains run three times an hour during the day and once hourly at night. Tickets can be bought on arrival, but advance booking (by phone or via the Internet) is advised at peak times. The recommended check-in time is thirty minutes beforehand. Prices are charged per vehicle, with no extra charge for passengers. Return trips made within five days entitle you to mini-break fares starting from £95, while return trips of more than five days start at £159. You can book online or over the Internet (see box on p.5 for details).

CROSS-CHANNEL FERRIES

Regular crossings by boat or hovercraft operate from Dover, Folkestone and Ramsgate to Boulogne or Calais in France, and to Ostend or Zeebrugge in Belgium – any of which will leave you with a drive of only two to three hours to the German border. Any travel agent in the UK should be able to provide details of crossings and make

bookings for you. To get the cheapest tickets you'll need to book well in advance.

Sea France runs regular services from Dover to **Calais**. The cheapest fare is £119 for a car plus up to nine passengers. A standard return in high season for a car and up to two passengers starts at £269.

P&O Stena Line plies the same route and offers similar fares. Their cheapest tickets start at £89 for a car and up to nine passengers for a five-day return or £129 for a flexible return.

Hoverspeed operates a hovercraft service from Dover to Calais (35min), as well as a Seacat service from Folkestone to Boulogne (55min) and from Dover to Ostend (2hr). All three cost £218 for a standard return fare for a car and two passengers and £48 for a foot passenger. If you book well in advance, however, you'll pay as little as £129 return for a car and up to five passengers.

Handy if you're heading for northern Germany or the former GDR is the **Channel crossing** from **Harwich to the Hook of Holland** (3hr 40min) with Stena Line. Ferries run twice daily and in the daytime only. Five-day returns for a medium-sized car plus driver, travelling over the weekend, are £219 in high-season (July and August), and £149 in low season – with extra passengers charged at £22 each; travelling midweek brings the price down to £165 and £119 respectively. Standard midweek returns, which don't have a time limit and include up to four passengers, are £249 in high season and £189 in low, though frequent special offers can bring prices down to under £100.

From the **north of England**, there's a routing from Hull to Zeebrugge or Rotterdam with **P&O North Sea Ferries**. The service runs daily throughout the year and takes thirteen and a half hours. Summer passenger fares are £81 return, and a further £129 for a car. There are also five-day excursion fares, which must include a Saturday night away; these are £52 per person, £84 for a car.

FERRIES TO HAMBURG

DFDS operates ferries around three to four times a week throughout the year from Harwich **to Hamburg**. The crossing takes about nineteen hours and passengers are required to book at least a couchette berth. The cheapest fare is the excursion fare, which is for a return journey of six nights or fewer, including two nights on the ship. It must be booked 21 days in advance and costs £64 in the low season (Jan to mid-April & Nov–Dec), rising to £109 in the peak period of July to August. Prices are inclusive of accommodation in an economy cabin. The excursion rate for a car is £68 in low season, rising to a maximum of £108 in summer. For longer stays in Germany, the best option is the Seapex return, which likewise needs to be booked 21 days in advance: the cheapest rates are £74 per person in the low season, rising to £134 in the high season. If you're travelling in a group, the All in a Car ticket is even better value. Covering up to four people plus a car, prices range from £269 in winter to £469 in July and August; the ticket has to be booked at least 42 days in advance.

PACKAGE AND CITY BREAKS

Most travel agents have brochures detailing the many **package holidays** to Germany. The most common type of package, and also the best value, is **motoring holidays**, where you drive your own car to Germany and stay in pre-arranged accommodation in hotels or guesthouses in several locations. The price also includes travel by Eurotunnel or ferry, insurance, and sometimes meals. The pick of these are operated by **DER Travel Service** (see box below), which has a wide selection of packages all over Germany. The same company offers **fly-drive packages**, where you fly to a German city and pick up a rental car there.

Short **city breaks** are offered by most major travel agents. If you don't want the hassle of booking the flight and finding accommodation yourself, these can be very convenient, and, especially out of season, you can get some good bargains. Adding extra nights or upgrading your hotel is possible. The prices always include return flights, transfers and bed and breakfast in a

---

SELECTED TOUR OPERATORS

Bents, The Blue Cross, Orleton, Ludlow, Shropshire SY8 4HN (☎01568/780800). Cycling and walking tours. Their ten-day cycling tour of Bavaria starts at £629.

DER Travel Service, 18 Conduit St, London W1R 9TD (☎020/7290 1111, *www.dertravel.co.uk*). The national German travel agency offering a full range of tours, as well as accommodation service and rail passes. A seven-night self-drive holiday with half-board, in the Black Forest starts from £390.

Martin Randall Travel, 10 Barley Mow Passage, Chiswick, London W4 4PH (☎020/8742 3355, *info@martinrandall.co.uk*). Small-group cultural tours, led by experts on art, music or archeology. Tours include "Handel in Halle", "Easter Music in Berlin" and "German Gothic". Prices range from £880 to £1750.

Moswin's, 21 Church St, Oadby, Leicester LE2 5DB (☎0116/271 4982, *www.moswin.com*). A specialist in Germany, with a wide variety of air, rail and self-drive package holidays. A three-night stay in Bavaria, including flights, starts at £348.

Peter Deilmann, Albany House, Suite 404, 324/326 Regent St, London W1R 5AA (☎020/7436 2931, *info@peterdeilmanncruises.co.uk*). Elbe, Rhine and Mosel cruises, from £764.

Ramblers Holidays, PO Box 43, Longcroft House, Frethern Rd, Welwyn Garden City, Herts AL8 6PQ (☎01707/320226). A long-established and reputable walking holiday specialist, offering organized trips to the Black Forest and Allgäu Alps. Prices start at £398.

Taber Holidays, 30a Bingley Rd, Saltaire, Shipley, West Yorkshire BD18 4RS (☎0870/747 9042, *www.taberhols.co.uk*). German specialists, offering city breaks, cruises and self-catering holidays. Three nights in Regensburg or Nürnberg cost £300 and upwards. Rhineland cruises start at £647.

Waymark Holidays, 44 Windsor Rd, Slough SL1 2EJ (☎01753/516477). Walking holidays in the Black Forest and winter cross-country skiing trips to Oberammergau. Prices from £465 for seven nights.

centrally located hotel. Again, ask your travel agent for the best deal, and check the specialists in the box on p.7. If you want an all-inclusive trip to the **Oktoberfest** arranged for you, you're looking at around £349 for three nights, and again DER is the best operator to try. Other companies with a good choice of holidays throughout Germany are Moswin's and Taber (see box on p.7). Organized **cruises** on the Rhine and Mosel,

Danube or Elbe are offered by several operators (see box on p.7), though these are usually expensive.

Several companies offer guided **walking tours**. Recommended operators include Ramblers Holidays, Bents and Waymark Holidays. This last also offers cross-country skiing trips to Oberammergau. See box on p.7 for contact details.

GETTING THERE FROM IRELAND

Given the time and inconvenience of getting a ferry over to Britain and then crossing the Channel, travelling by plane is by far the simplest way of getting to Germany from Ireland. Depending on where you're flying from and which city you want to fly into, it won't necessarily work out any more expensive either.

BY PLANE

Only Aer Lingus operates direct flights **from Dublin** to Germany. Fares to Frankfurt and Düsseldorf cost £IR167/€212 in low season and £IR188/€239 in high season. Berlin via Amsterdam is £IR269/€342 all year round, though you might be able to undercut this by flying with Aer Lingus to London for around IR£80/€101 or with one of the newer, cheaper outfits like Ryanair (IR£49/€62), and picking up an onward flight (see p.3). All the above prices

are exclusive of airport tax, which is another IR£16–30/€20–38.

If you're heading for Frankfurt or Berlin and are able to fly **from Shannon**, you can pick up some cheap fares with Ryanair and Virgin Express. Ryanair operates a direct service to Frankfurt for a bargain £IR54/€69, including airport tax, though the ticket comes with strict booking conditions. Virgin Express runs a service to Berlin, with a stopover at London Stansted, for IR£200–240 (€250–305) in high season.

There are no direct flights **from Belfast** to Germany. The main operators are British Airways and British Midland. BA's flights are routed via London, Manchester or Birmingham. Their cheapest flight from Belfast to Frankfurt is £159, and to Berlin, £200, both exclusive of tax – around £30 extra. British Midland flights all go via London Heathrow or East Midlands airport. Their cheapest fare to Frankfurt, excluding tax, is £209, to Hamburg and Düsseldorf £159, and to Munich £199. Other options involve switching carriers for the second leg of your journey. You can fly with Sabena for example, from Belfast via Brussels to Frankfurt for £163 and to Berlin for £175, excluding tax. Discount flight agents, listed in the box on p.4, will be able to advise you on the cheapest options.

The best discount deals on flights for **students** and anyone under 26 are usually to be had from the independent travel specialists UsitNOW (see box opposite for outlets).

BY TRAIN

The **train** journey from Ireland to Germany is a long one and won't bring you any major savings over the

USEFUL ADDRESSES IN IRELAND

AIRLINES

Aer Lingus Northern Ireland ☎0845/973 7747; Eire ☎01/705 3994. Web site: *www.aerlingus.ie*.

British Airways Northern Ireland: reservations ☎0345/222111, bookings and travel agency services ☎0345/326566. BA doesn't have a Dublin office; for reservations from Eire, call ☎0141/222 2345. Web site: *www. britishairways.com*.

British Midland Northern Ireland ☎0870/607 0555; Eire ☎01/283 8833. Web site: *www.britishmidland.com*.

Lufthansa Northern Ireland ☎0845/773 7747; Eire ☎01/844 5544. Web site: *www.lufthansa.com*.

Ryanair Northern Ireland ☎0870/517 1717; Eire ☎01/609 7800. Web site: *www.ryanair.com*.

Virgin Express Northern Ireland & Eire ☎020/7744 0004. Web site: *www.virginexpress.com*.

DISCOUNT FLIGHT AND TRAVEL AGENTS

Fahy Travel, 3 Bridge St, Galway (☎091/563055, *fahytrav@iol.ie*). Travel agents, specializing in last-minute bargains.

Joe Walsh Ltd, 8–11 Baggot St, Dublin 2 (☎01/676 3053); 117 St Patrick St, Cork (☎021/427 7959). Travel and general budget fares agent.

Sunway Travel, 63 Mary St, Dublin 1 ☎01/872 8055.

Thomas Cook, 11 Donegal Place, Belfast BT1 5AJ (☎028/9024 0833); 118 Grafton St, Dublin 2 (☎01/677 1360). Package-holiday and flight agent, with occasional discount offers.

Twohigs Travel, 8 Burgh Quay, Dublin 2 (☎01/677 2666); 13 Duke St, Dublin 2 (☎01/670 9750). General budget fares agent.

Trailfinders, 4–5 Dawson St, Dublin 2 (☎01/677 7888). Competitive fares out of all Irish airports, as well as deals on hotels, insurance, tours and car rental worldwide.

UsitNOW, Fountain Centre, College St, Belfast BT1 6ET (☎028/9032 4073); 66 Oliver Plunkett St, Cork (☎021/427 0900); 4 Shipquay Place, Derry (☎028/7137 1888); 19 Aston Quay, Dublin 2 (☎01/602 1600); 16 Mary St, Galway (☎091/565177); Central Buildings, 51 O'Connell St, Limerick (☎061/415064); 36–37 Georges St, Waterford (☎051/872601). Student and youth specialists for flights and trains.

RAIL INFORMATION AND PASSES

Continental Rail Desk, Irish Rail (Euro Rail Desk), 35 Lower Abbey St, Dublin 1 (☎01/703 4095). InterRail agents.

NIR Travel, 28–30 Great Victoria Street Station, Belfast BT2 7UB (☎028/9023 0671). InterRail agents.

FERRY COMPANIES

Brittany Ferries Tourist House, 42 Grand Parade, Cork (Enquiries ☎021/427 7801, reservations and information ☎021/427 7705, fax 021/427 7262). Routes: Cork to Roscoff (March–Oct only).

Irish Ferries, 2–4 Merrion Row, Dublin 2 (☎01/638 3333, 24hr information ☎01/661 0715); St Patrick's Bldgs, Cork (☎021/4551 995). For reservations from Northern Ireland, call ☎0345/171 717. Web site: *www.irishferries.com*. Ferries from Rosslare to Cherbourg and Roscoff.

cheapest flights. A standard return from Dublin to Frankfurt is £IR255/€324. The route takes you from Dublin to Rosslare, Rosslare to Cherbourg, Cherbourg to Paris and Paris to Frankfurt. If you plan to travel extensively in Germany, you're much better off paying a bit more for an **InterRail** pass. A global InterRail pass for under-26s costs £IR266.50/€338 and for the over-26s it's £IR367.50/€467. For a three-zone pass, which would cover you for travel across the UK and France or Belgium to Germany, valid for a month, you'll pay £IR228/€289 if you're under 26, and £IR321/€408 if you're over 26. For more details see "Getting There from Britain" (pp.4–5). Agents are listed in the box on p.9.

BY FERRY

There are no direct **ferries** to Germany. The nearest they get is the northwest of France. Irish Ferries runs services from Rosslare to Cherbourg (18hr) and Roscoff (16hr) on alternate days all year round. Prices start at £IR280/ €427 return for a car and two passengers.

Brittany Ferries operates a weekly crossing April to September from Cork to Roscoff (14hr). Prices for a car and two passengers start at £IR280/€427 return.

PACKAGE HOLIDAYS

Package holidays and city breaks are mostly routed via London, with an add-on fare for the connection from Ireland. Any travel agent should be able to give details of the best deals.

GETTING THERE FROM NORTH AMERICA

Fares between North America and Germany are among the cheapest transatlantic crossings. Frankfurt, Germany's largest airport, handles most international flights, from where you can get onward connections to other major cities. Lufthansa, Germany's national airline, has the most direct flights to Germany from the US and Canada, flying nonstop to Frankfurt, Munich and Düsseldorf from fourteen North American cities.

Though it may be more interesting, it's not usually cheaper to stop over in **another European country** and make your way to Germany from there. You may find cheap flights to **Paris** or **Amsterdam**, but the most common deals available through the seat consolidators are on scheduled airlines plying long-haul routes to the Gulf states, almost all of which stop in **London**. From mainland Europe, **trains** are the

cheapest and easiest way to make the final leg to Germany – a Eurail pass (see p.14) is useful, especially if you are on a longer European trip, as you can use it to get from any part of Europe to Germany. From England, flying is often as cheap if not cheaper than ground travel.

SHOPPING FOR TICKETS

On busy routes, discount ticket outlets – advertised in the Sunday newspaper travel sections such as the *New York Times* – are usually your best bet for cheap tickets. They come in several forms. **Consolidators** buy up blocks of tickets that airlines don't think they'll be able to sell at their published fares, and unload them at a discount. Many advertise fares on a one-way basis, enabling you to fly into one city and out from another without penalty. Consolidators normally don't impose advance purchase requirements (although in busy times you should book ahead just to be sure of getting a ticket), but they do often charge very stiff fees for date changes. Also these companies' profit margins are pretty tiny, so they make their money by dealing in volume – don't expect them to entertain lots of questions. **Discount agents** also deal in blocks of tickets offloaded by the airlines, but they typically offer a range of other travel-related services like insurance, rail passes, youth- and student-ID cards, car rentals and tours. These agencies tend to be most worthwhile for students and under-26s, who can benefit from special fares and deals. **Travel clubs** are another option – most charge an annual membership fee, which may be worth it for their discounts on air tickets and

DISCOUNT TRAVEL COMPANIES IN NORTH AMERICA

Air Brokers International, 150 Post St, Ste 620, San Francisco, CA 94108-4707 (☎1-800/883-3273, *www.airbrokers.com*). Consolidator and round-the-world specialist.

Air Courier Association, 15000 W 6th Ave, Suite 203, Golden, CO 80401 (☎1-800/282 1202 or 303/215 9000, *www.aircourier.org*). Courier flight broker.

Council Travel, Head Office: 205 E 42nd St, New York, NY 10017 (☎212/822-2700, *www.counciltravel.com*). Student travel organization with branches (among others) in San Francisco, Washington DC, Boston, Austin, Seattle, Chicago and Minneapolis.

Educational Travel Center, 438 N Frances St, Madison, WI 53703 (☎1-800/747-5551, *www.edtrav.com*). Student/youth discount agent.

Encore Travel Club, 4501 Forbes Blvd, Lanham, MD 20706 (☎1-800/444-9800, *www.preferredtraveller.com*). Discount travel club.

Interworld Travel, 800 Douglass Rd, Miami, FL 33134 (☎1-800/468-3796; 305/443-4929, *www.interworldtravel.com*). Consolidator.

Last Minute Travel, 100 Sylvan Rd, Woburn, MA 01801 (☎1-800/LAST MIN, *www.lastminutetravel.com*). Offers discount airfares and vacation packages.

New Frontiers/Nouvelles Frontières, Head offices: 6 E 46th St, New York, NY 10017 (☎1-800/366-6387, *www.newfrontiers.com*); 1001 Sherbrook East, Suite 720, Montréal, H2L 1L3 (☎514/526-8444). French discount travel and tour operator. Other branches in Los Angeles, San Francisco and Québec City.

STA Travel, 10 Downing St, New York, NY 10014, with 150 offices worldwide (☎1-800/777-0112, *www.sta-travel.com*). Worldwide discount travel agency specializing in student and youth travel.

Travac, Head office: 989 6th Ave, New York, NY 10018 (☎1-800/872-8800, *www.thetravelsite.com*). Consolidator; has another branch in Orlando.

Travel CUTs, Head office: 187 College St, Toronto, ON M5T 1P7 (☎1-800/667-2887 from within Canada only, otherwise call ☎416/979-2406, *www.travelcuts.com*). Canadian student travel organization specializing in student fares, IDs and other travel services with many branches all over Canada (mostly on, or near, university campuses).

UniTravel, 11737 Administration Drive, St Louis, MO 63146 (☎1-800/325-2222, *www.flightsforless.com*). Consolidator.

Worldwide Discount Travel Club, 11601 Biscayne Blvd, Suite 310, Nr Miami, FL 33181 (☎305/895 2082). Discount travel club.

car rental. Some agencies specialize in **charter flights**, which may be even cheaper than anything available on a scheduled flight, but again there's a trade-off: departure dates are fixed, and withdrawal penalties are high (check the refund policy).

For destinations not handled by discounters you'll have to deal with airlines' published fares. The cheapest way to go is with an **APEX** (Advance Purchase Excursion) ticket. This carries certain restrictions: you have to book – and pay – at least twenty one days before departure and spend at least seven days abroad (maximum stay three months), and you're liable to penalties if you change your schedule. There are also winter **Super APEX** tickets, sometimes known as "Eurosavers" – slightly cheaper than an ordinary APEX, but limiting your stay to between seven and twenty one days. Some airlines also issue **Special APEX** tickets to those under 24, often extending the maximum stay to a year.

Note that fares are heavily dependent on **season**, and are highest from early June to the end of September; they drop during the "shoulder" seasons, April, May and October, and you'll get the best deals during the low season, November to the end of March (excluding Christmas). Note that flying on weekends ordinarily adds $60 to the return fare; prices quoted in the sections below assume midweek travel.

FLIGHTS FROM THE US

You can usually find **direct flights** from the major gateway cities of New York JFK, Newark, Atlanta, Boston, Washington DC, Miami, Chicago and Los Angeles to either **Frankfurt** or **Berlin**, with connections to Hamburg, Stuttgart, Munich and Düsseldorf.

FARES

There are constant fare wars raging between the airlines on flights to Germany. On average, the

AIRLINES IN NORTH AMERICA

Air Canada Canada: ☎1-800/776-3000; US ☎1-888/247 22, *www.aircanada.ca*. Flies nonstop from Toronto, Montréal and Vancouver to Frankfurt with connections to other German cities.

Air France US ☎1-800/237-2747; Canada ☎1-800/667-2747, *www.airfrance.com*. Flies from eleven US cites including Miami, Los Angeles, San Francisco, New York and Washington to nine German cities, including Berlin and Munich, all via Paris.

American Airlines ☎1-800/433-7300, *www.aa.com*. Flies nonstop from Chicago to Frankfurt.

British Airways US ☎1-800/247-9297; Canada ☎1-800/668-1059, *www.britishairways.com*. Flies from most major North American cities to London, with extensive connections to nine German cities including Frankfurt, Munich, Stuttgart, Berlin and Hamburg.

Continental Airlines ☎1-800/231-0856, *www.continental.com*. Flies from Newark to Frankfurt and Düsseldorf nonstop, with connections to other German cities.

Delta Airlines ☎1-800/241-4141, *www.delta.com*. Nonstop flights from Cincinnati and Atlanta to Frankfurt; from New York and Atlanta to Munich; and from Atlanta to Stuttgart.

LTU ☎1-800/888-0200, *www.ltu.com*. Flies nonstop from Miami, Orlando, Florida and Ft Myers to Düsseldorf with connecting flights to most major German cities.

Lufthansa ☎1-800/645-3880, *www.lufthansa.com*. Flies from fourteen North American gateways nonstop to Frankfurt, Munich and Düsseldorf with connecting flights to all major German cities.

Northwest Airlines/KLM Airlines ☎1-800/447 4747, *www.nwa.com*. Flies nonstop from Detroit to Frankfurt. Also flies from ten US cities including Miami, Seattle and New York to eleven German cities including Munich and Berlin all via Amsterdam.

Sabena ☎1-800/955-2000, *www.sabena.com*. Flies from seven US cities including Chicago, New York and Atlanta to twelve German cities via Brussels.

Singapore Airlines ☎1-800/742-3333, *www.singaporeair.com*. Flies nonstop from New York to Frankfurt.

Swissair ☎1-800/221-4750, *www.swissair.com*. Flies from nine US cities including New York, Washington and Miami to seven German cities including Munich and Berlin all via Zürich.

United Airlines ☎1-800/538-2929, *www.ual.com*. Flies from five US cities including Chicago and Washington Dulles nonstop to Frankfurt.

US Air ☎1-800/622-1015, *www.usairways.com*. Flies nonstop from Pittsburgh and Charlotte to Frankfurt and nonstop from Philadelphia to Munich, with connections to other German cities.

European airlines offer some of the lowest fares and best connection possibilities, and many nonstop flights have been added lately. There is no great change in price between any of the German hub cities from the US and you'll find airport tax to be the main factor in price difference.

Typical flights from the **east coast** to Germany can start as low as $350 with restrictions during low season, and rise up to $1100 during high season. From the **midwest** flights to Germany start at around $400 low season but prices can rise to over $1400 high season. Flying direct from the **west coast** isn't that much more expensive than flying out of New York, with average fares to Germany being around $500 in low season and $1100 in high season. You can usually get direct flights from the **main gateways** of Los Angeles, San Francisco and Seattle.

Many airlines also offer special **discounts** and offers from their **Web sites** so they are always worth checking out as are the Internet-based companies such as *www.cheaptickets.com*, *www.travelocity.com* or *www.lastminute.com*.

It is also worth looking out for **courier flights** as these can be exceptionally good value. In return for shepherding a parcel through customs and possibly giving up your baggage allowance, you can expect to pay something around $300 for a return ticket (see box on p.11).

FLIGHTS FROM CANADA

Flying from **Canada**, you have fewer direct options than from the US, though again European carriers such as British Airways, Lufthansa, Northwest/KLM and Swissair offer the most choices with a stopover in Europe. The best selections are out of

Toronto and **Montréal** – direct fares with Air Canada to Frankfurt range from CDN$800 (low season) to CDN$1500 (high season) – and from Vancouver to Frankfurt, starting at CDN$1000 and rising up to CDN$2000. In most cases you will find cheaper fares with a travel agent or by travelling to **New York** and picking up a flight from there. With reduced options, it's worth considering getting a discount fare to a city like London, Amsterdam or Paris and travelling on from there.

PACKAGES AND ORGANIZED TOURS

Package tours may not sound like your kind of travel, but don't dismiss the idea out of hand. If your trip is geared around special interests, packages can work out cheaper than the same arrangements made on arrival. A package trip can also be great for your peace of mind, if only to ensure a worry-free first week while you're finding your feet on a longer tour. The **German**

TOUR OPERATORS IN NORTH AMERICA

Abercrombie & Kent, 1520 Kensington Rd, Oak Brook, IL 60523 (☎1-800/323-7308, *www .abercrombiekent.com*). General tour operator. Offer three independent travel tours and one escorted tour of Germany.

Adventure Tours, 815 North Rd, Westfield, MA 01085 (☎1-800/628-9655, *www.advonskis .com*). Ski vacation packages in Garmisch-Partenkirchen.

Angersbach International Tours, 170 Main St, Manasquan, NJ 08736 (☎1-800/526-2358, *www.angersbach.com*). Specialists in all-inclusive packages. Tours of Germany including escorted motor-coach sightseeing tours, *Oktoberfest* and Christmas.

Brendan Tours, 15137 Califa St, Van Nuys, CA 91411-3021 (☎1-800/421-8446, *www .brendantours.com*). Offers four escorted all-inclusive tours, ranging between ten and fifteen days, of Germany's major cities. Tours are between April and October only.

CBT College Bicycle Tours, Inc 2506 N Clark St, Suite 150, Chicago, IL 60614 (☎1-800/736-BIKE, *www.biketrip.net*). Affordable tours, May to September only usually one week long taking in various German cities via bike.

Danube Cruises Inc, 4365 McLauthlin, Unit 16, Los Angeles, CA 90060 (☎1-800/999-0226, *www.nnsconnections.com*). Organizes cruises on the Rhine, Danube and Elbe from late March to late October on seven different boats of varying sizes. Also arranges fly-drive and hotel packages.

Delta Vacations, PO Box 1525, Fort Lauderdale, FL 33302 (☎1-800/221-6666, *www .deltavacations.com*). Organizes package deals to Berlin, Munich and Frankfurt.

DER Tours, 9501 W Devon Ave, Rosemont, IL 60018 (☎1-888/337 7350, *www.dertravel.com*). Specialists in German travel. Can arrange flights,

car rental, rail passes, custom tours, group tours and an extensive range of packages including *Oktoberfest* and city tours.

Euro Bike/Euro-Walking Tours, PO Box 990, De Kalb, IL 60115 (☎1-800/252-1990). Offers two six-day cycling tours of Germany, including one along the Mosel aimed at families. Also offers one eight-day walking tour along the Alps of Bavaria taking in historic sights. All tours operate from April to October.

Euro-Connection, 7500 212th St SW, Suite 103, Admonds, WA 98026 (☎1-800/645-3876, *www.euro-connections.com*). Customized package specialists.

KD River Cruises of Europe, 2500 Westchester Ave, Purchase, NY 10577 (☎1-800/346-6525, *www.rivercruises.com*). Organizes cruises on the Rhine, Elbe, Danube, Main and Mosel rivers. Arranges hotel packages in conjunction with cruises.

Maupintour, 1421 Research Park Drive, #300, Lawrence, KS 66049 (☎1-800/255-6162, *www.maupintour.com*). Arranges customized city-break tours and has two escorted tours of Germany: the "Highlights of Germany" and "Oktoberfest" tours.

Snow Search Ski Tours, 209 Delmar, Suite 206, San Clemente, CA 92672 (☎1-800/628-8884, *www.snowsearchski tours.com*). Ski vacation packages in Garmisch-Partenkirchen.

Trafalgar Tours, 11 E 26th St, New York, NY 10010 (☎1-800/854 0103, *www.trafalgartours .com*). Offers two escorted city-tours of Germany between April and October. Also offers multi-country tours including Germany.

United Vacations, PO Box 24580, Milwaukee, WI 53224 (☎1-800/328 6877, *www .unitedvacations.com*). Offers escorted and independent tours of Germany. Also arranges fly/drive deals, hotel packages and car rental.

National Tourist Office is your best starting-off point for gathering information, and the airlines are all good sources for deals. Delta and some other airlines have city and **fly-drive packages**. Delta, for example, can arrange hotel stays in Munich, Frankfurt, Berlin, Heidelberg, Dresden, Cologne and Nürnberg. Most of the tour operators listed in the box arrange similar city packages and fly-drives as well as trips to the **Oktoberfest**. Other specialist companies offer skiing, cycling and river **cruises**. Cruises generally start at around $900.

RAIL PASSES

A **Eurail pass** is not likely to pay for itself if you're planning to stick to Germany. The pass, which must be purchased before arrival in Europe, allows unlimited free train travel in Germany and sixteen other countries. Several options are available. For example, you can have a **Eurail Flexipass** for $654, allowing ten travel days in two months, ($458 for those under 26), which is valid in seventeen European countries, so may prove useful for those including Germany as part of a larger trip. Slightly cheaper is the **Eurail pass**, which costs $554 ($388 for under 26s) for fifteen days of travel in two months, but which is valid in Germany only. With a **Euro Adult pass** or **Euro Youth pass**, you can travel for any five days in a two-month period for $348 and $233 respectively, and for fifteen days in the same period for $728/$513.

Finally, you should remember that North Americans are also eligible to purchase more specific passes valid for travel in Germany only, for details of which see "Getting Around", p.30. The more common European passes can be purchased through most travel agents or try the agents listed in the box above.

GETTING THERE FROM AUSTRALIA AND NEW ZEALAND

There is a good choice of scheduled flights from Australia and New Zealand to German destinations chiefly via Southeast Asian cities and Frankfurt. Some stopovers will be only a few hours, while with other flights you have to change planes or break your journey en route. Charter flights are hard to come by as there is little cargo traffic flying directly to Germany, and as there's little to be saved in terms of cost, they're not really worth considering. Similarly, while travel agents can organize fly-drive deals these rarely offer enormous savings; generally, it is cheaper to buy a scheduled flight and rent the car on arrival in Germany.

One thing that is worth considering before you leave home is a **rail pass** – these can offer substantial savings on basic rail fares, and are of particular value if your trip includes Germany as part of a wider European tour.

DISCOUNT AND SPECIALIST AGENTS AND OPERATORS

There is very little in the way of organized tours to Germany from Australia or New Zealand, and you are better off making arrangements once you're in Europe.

Anywhere Travel, 345 Anzac Parade, Kingsford, Sydney 2032 (☎02/9663 0411). Can arrange flight, accommodation and car rental deals.

Budget Travel, 66 Wyndham St, Auckland, plus branches around the city (☎09/307 1888). As well as good standard package deals, they can arrange tailor-made deals for the independent traveller.

European Travel Office, 122 Rosslyn St, West Melbourne 3000 (☎03/9329 8844); 89 York St, Sydney 2000 (☎02/9299 9177); 407 Great South Rd, Auckland (☎09/525 3074). Tourist to five-star accommodation, city stays, car rental and cultural tours throughout Germany.

Flight Centres, 82 Elizabeth St, Sydney 2000, plus branches nationwide (☎13 1600); 205 Queen St, Auckland (☎09/309 6171), plus branches nationwide. Good fare discounts worldwide.

Rail Tickets, Level 6, 310 King St, Melbourne, 3000 (☎1300/360 823, www.railtickets.com.au).

STA Travel, Australia: 702 Harris St, Ultimo, Sydney 2007; 256 Flinders St, Melbourne 3000; other offices in state capitals and major universities (nearest branch ☎13 1776, fastfare telesales ☎1300/360 960); 10 High St, Auckland (☎09/309 0458, fastfare telesales ☎09/366 6673), plus branches in Wellington, Christchurch, Dunedin, Palmerston North, Hamilton and at major universities. Web site: www.statravelaus.com.au. Discounts for students and under-26s. Also arranges Eurail passes.

Thomas Cook, 175 Pitt St, Sydney; 257 Collins St, Melbourne 3000; plus branches in other state capitals (local branch ☎13 1771, telesales ☎1800/063 913); 191 Queen St, Auckland (☎09/359 5200). Travellers' cheques, bus and rail passes as well as general travel arrangements.

Walkabout Gourmet Adventures, PO Box 52, Dinner Plain, Melbourne 3888 (☎03/5159 5556). Classy food, wine and walking tours from Kassel and Munich.

YHA Travel Centre, 422 Kent St, Sydney 2000 (☎02/9261 1111); 83 Hardware Lane, Melbourne 3000 (☎03/9670 9611); 38 Stuart St, Adelaide 5000 (☎08/8231 5583); 154 Roma St, Brisbane 4000 (☎07/3236 1680); 236 William St, Perth 6003 (☎08/9227 5122); 69 Mitchell St, Darwin 800 (☎08/8981 2560); 28 Criterion St, Hobart 7000 (☎03/6234 9617); 36 Customs House, Auckland (☎09/379 4224). Organizes budget accommodation and travel throughout Germany for YHA members.

AIRLINES IN AUSTRALIA AND NEW ZEALAND

Aeroflot, 24/44 Market St, Sydney 2000 (☎02/9262 2233). No NZ office. Twice-weekly flights from Sydney to Moscow, with connections to Berlin, Munich and Frankfurt.

Air France, 64 York St, Sydney 2000 (☎02/9244 2400); 6/229 Queen St, Auckland (☎09/379 4457). Sydney to Paris daily via Tokyo or Singapore, with connections to several destinations in Germany.

Air New Zealand, 5 Elizabeth St, Sydney 2000 (☎13/2476); 139 Queen St, Auckland (☎09/336 2424). Auckland to Frankfurt via Los Angeles three times a week.

Alitalia, 64 York St, Sydney 2000 (☎02/9244 2400); 6/229 Queen St, Auckland (☎09/379 4457). Sydney to Rome several times a week, with connections to Frankfurt, Düsseldorf, Berlin, Hamburg and Cologne.

British Airways, 26/201 Kent St, Sydney 2000 (☎02/9258 3200); 154 Queen St, Auckland (☎09/356 8690). Daily from major Australasian cities to London via Singapore or Hong Kong, onward connections to destinations in Germany.

Canadian Airlines, 117 York St, Sydney 2000 (☎1300/655 767); 15/44 Emily Place, Auckland (☎09/309 0735). Daily from Sydney to Frankfurt via a transfer in Vancouver and Munich via Toronto.

Garuda, 55 Hunter St, Sydney 2000 (☎02/9334 9944 or 1-800/800 873); 120 Albert St, Auckland (☎09/366 1855). Sydney to Frankfurt four times a week, via either a transfer or stopover in Jakarta or Denpasar.

Japan Air Lines, 14/201 Sussex St, Sydney 2000 (☎02/9272 1111); 12/120 Albert St, Auckland (☎09/379 3202). Daily from Sydney to Frankfurt with a night's accommodation in either Tokyo or Osaka included in the fare.

KLM, 5 Elizabeth St, Sydney 2000 (☎02/9231 6333 or 1800/505 747); 369 Queen St, Auckland (☎09/309 1782). Sydney to Amsterdam via Kuala Lumpur twice a week, with connections to various German cities.

Lauda Air, 11/143 Macquarie St, Sydney 2000 (☎02/9241 4277). Sydney to destinations in Germany via Vienna and Kuala Lumpur four times a week, and three times a week from Melbourne.

Lufthansa, 143 Macquarie St, Sydney 2000 (☎02/9367 3888); 109 Queen St, Auckland (☎09/303 1529). Sydney to Frankfurt daily via a transfer in Bangkok, with connections to all German airports.

Malaysia Airlines, 16 Spring St, Sydney 2000 (☎13 2627); 12/12 Swanson St, Auckland (☎09/373 2741). Several flights weekly from Sydney, Melbourne, Brisbane, Perth and Auckland to Frankfurt and Munich via Kuala Lumpur.

Philippine Airlines, 49 York St, Sydney 2000 (☎02/9262 3333). No NZ office. Several flights weekly from Sydney to Frankfurt via either a transfer or stopover in Manila.

Qantas, 70 Hunter St, Sydney 2000 (☎13 1313); 154 Queen St, Auckland (☎09/357 8900 or 800/808 767). Daily flights from major Australasian cities to Frankfurt via Bangkok and Singapore.

Singapore Airlines, 17 Bridge St, Sydney 2000 (☎13/1011); cnr Albert St and Fanshawe St, Auckland (☎09/379 3209). Several flights a week to Frankfurt from major Australian and New Zealand cities via Singapore.

Thai Airways, 75 Pitt St, Sydney 2000 (☎02/9251 1922); cnr Albert St and Fanshawe St, Auckland (☎09/379 3209). Sydney, Brisbane, Perth and Auckland to Frankfurt several times a week via Bangkok, with onward connections to other destinations in Germany.

United, 10 Barrack St, Sydney 2000 (☎13/1777); 7 City Rd, Auckland (☎09/379 3800). Sydney to Frankfurt via Los Angeles and either Chicago, Washington or New York, with onward connections to Hamburg, Munich and Stuttgart.

FLIGHTS

As destinations in Europe are "common-rated" – you pay the same fare whatever your destination – some airlines offer free flight coupons, car rental or accommodation if you arrange these extras with your ticket. Choose carefully, though, as these perks are impossible to alter later. Alternatively, you could buy the cheapest possible flight to anywhere in Europe and make your way to Germany by stand-by flight, train or bus, but this rarely works out as cheaply as buying a discounted airfare all the way; however, if you intend to take in Germany as part of a wider European trip it's worth checking out the many rail passes that are available.

For extended trips, a **round-the-world** (RTW) ticket can work out very good value – especially from New Zealand, where airlines offer fewer bonuses to fly with them. Currently the best deals on offer are Cathay Pacific/United's "Globetrotter", Air New Zealand/KLM/ Northwest's "World Navigator", Qantas/BA's "Global Explorer" tickets: all allow six stopovers worldwide with limited backtracking and open-jaw travel, from A$2499 and NZ$3199.

Fares are seasonally adjusted with high season mid-May to August (the European summer) and December to mid-January, shoulder seasons March to mid-May and September, and low season the rest of the year. Seasons vary slightly depending on the airline. Tickets purchased direct from the airlines tend to be expensive. Travel agents offer much better deals and have the latest information on limited specials and stopovers, with the best discounts being through Flight Centres and STA, who can also advise on visa regulations. Students and under-26s are usually able to get at least 10 percent off published prices.

FROM AUSTRALIA

Most of the major airlines quote the same fare from all the eastern cities (ie they are common-rated), with flights from Perth via Asia and Africa around $200 less and via the Americas about $400 more. The cheapest scheduled flights **via Asia** (these generally involve a transfer in the carrier's Asian hub city) are with Philippine Airlines and Garuda for around $1600 in low season and $1999 in high season. In the mid range, JAL, Malaysia Airlines, Thai Airways, and Singapore Airlines all fly to Frankfurt for around AUS$1899–2599. If you're after a bit more comfort, British Airways and Qantas both quote published fares from AUS$2399 in low season up to AUS$3199 in high season.

Flights are pricier **via North America**, with United Airlines offering the cheapest deal via LA and either New York, Washington or Chicago for AUS$2299–2899, while Air New Zealand via Auckland and LA and Canadian Airlines via Toronto or Vancouver are both around AUS$2499–3099.

FROM NEW ZEALAND

From Auckland fares are all similar so it depends on which route you prefer. The lowest are to Frankfurt with Garuda NZ$1899 low season, NZ$2499 high season and Thai Airways NZ$2099–2599, while Malaysia Airlines, Singapore Airlines, Air New Zealand, Lufthansa and JAL charge around NZ$2199–2999. United Airlines fly via LA from NZ$2599.

RED TAPE AND VISAS

Citizens of most EU countries (and of Norway and Iceland) need only a valid national identity card to enter Germany. Since Britain has no identity card system, however, British citizens do have to take a passport.

US, Canadian, Australian and New Zealand passport holders can also enter the country for ninety days (in any one year) for a tourist visit without a visa. However, you're strongly advised, if you know your stay will be longer than this, to apply for an extension visa from the local German embassy before you go. In order to extend a stay once in the country, all visitors should contact the *Ausländeramt* (Alien

Authorities) in the nearest large town: addresses are in the phone books.

EU nationals are also entitled to **work in Germany**, but anyone else has to have secured a job **before** arrival in order to get a work permit, for which they should apply to their local German consulate or embassy. For casual labour jobs during harvests or in the hotel and catering trades, nobody is going to ask too many questions, but wages are accordingly low and the work tough.

CUSTOMS

EU nationals can take goods for personal consumption across EU borders without incurring duty, as long as they've paid the local tax at the place of purchase. **Duty-free shopping** no longer exists. However, there are still personal allowance limits on what were once duty-free goods – alcohol, tobacco and perfume – bought in EU countries. Each person is allowed up to 800 cigarettes, 400 cigarillos, 200 cigars, 1kg of smoking tobacco, 90 litres of wine (no more than 60 litres of which can be sparkling wine), 10 litres of spirits, 20 litres of fortified wine and 110 litres of beer.

Residents of the US and Canada can take up to 200 cigarettes and one litre of spirits home, as can **Australian** citizens, while **New Zealanders** must confine themselves to 200 cigarettes, 4.5 litres of beer or wine and just over one litre of spirits.

GERMAN EMBASSIES ABROAD

Australia 119 Empire Circuit, Yarralumla, Canberra, ACT 2600 (☎02/6270 1911, *consugerma .sydney@bigpond.com*).

Britain 23 Belgrave Square, London SW1X 8PZ (☎020/7824 1300, *www.german-embassy.org.uk*).

Canada 1 Waverly St, Ottawa, Ont. K2P 0T8 (☎613/232-1101, *www .germanembassyottawa.org*).

Ireland 31 Trimelston Ave, Booterstown, Blackrock, Co. Dublin (☎01/269 3011).

New Zealand 90–2 Hobson St, Thorndon, Wellington (☎04/473 6063).

US 4645 Reservoir Rd NW, Washington 20007 (☎202/298 8140, *www.germany-info.org*).

COSTS, MONEY AND BANKS

Despite the cost of unification, Germany is still one of the world's most industrialized and wealthiest consumer societies, and its currency, the Deutschmark (DM) was one by which international financial standards were set. However, since 1999 it has been tied to the euro, which will replace it and ten other European currencies in 2002 (see box below). Although a pet German project, the new currency has failed to win the confidence of the international financial markets, and the once mighty Deutschmark has spent its final years declining steadily in value. Another point to note is that Germany is a cash society: people carry money with them, rather than rely on credit cards. Outside the major cities, it's a surprisingly affordable country to travel in, with the reasonable price of food and accommodation in popular holiday areas helping keep costs down.

COSTS

If you're prepared to cut every corner by staying in youth hostels or campsites, and never eating out, you could get by on as little as DM70/€35 (just over £20/$30) per day, though DM100–150/€50–75 is a more realistic budget on which to enjoy yourself properly. Should you have the means to spend a bit more than that, you will be able to live really well. Bear in mind that visiting cities will cost far more than staying in the countryside – a gap that is widening – and that a trip to Berlin is guaranteed to knock a large hole in any budget. If you intend to base yourself mainly in one or two rural areas – even ones as famous as the Alps or Black Forest – as opposed to travelling around a lot, you should be able to reduce the above figures by a quarter.

Accommodation costs per person can be confined to an average of about DM25–30/€12.50–15 per day for youth hostels, around DM30–40/€15–20 for rooms in private houses and around DM40–60/€20–30 for guesthouses, pensions and the more basic hotels: double rooms cost on average a bit less than twice the above rates. **Food** prices in shops are slightly lower than in Britain, and eating out is markedly cheaper at every level – except for the scarcity of bargain lunches. North Americans, however, will find prices slightly higher than at home, as will Australians and New Zealanders. Snack bars abound, and for around

THE EURO

Germany is one of twelve European Union countries which have changed over to a single currency, the **euro** (€). The transition period, which began on January 1, 1999, is however lengthy: euro notes and coins are not scheduled to be issued until January 1, 2002, with Deutschmarks remaining in place for cash transactions until that date, at which point they will be scrapped entirely – although you will be able to exchange Deutschmarks for euros in any bank or post office until 28 February, 2002.

Even before euro cash appears in 2002, you can opt to pay in euros by credit card and you can get travellers' cheques in euros – you should

not be charged commission for changing them in any of the twelve countries in the euro zone (also known as "Euroland"), nor for changing from any of the old Euroland currencies to any other (French francs to Deutschmarks, for example).

All prices in this book are given in Deutschmarks and the approximate equivalent in euros. When the new currency takes over completely, prices are likely to be rounded off – and if decimalization in the UK is anything to go by, rounded up.

Euro notes will be issued in **denominations** of 5, 10, 20, 50, 100, 200 and 500 euros, and coins in denominations of 1, 2, 5, 10, 20 and 50 cents and 1 and 2 euros.

DM10–15/€5–7.50 you can put together a very filling meal. DM25–30/€12.50–15 should buy a hearty German meal plus drink in a traditional Gaststätte, while a decent dinner in a more upmarket restaurant can be had for around DM35–40/€17.50–20. Drink is marginally more expensive than in Britain, Australia or the US, but the quality, especially of the beer, is significantly higher.

Though seldom a major expense, **admission charges for museums** vary markedly, and tend to reflect whether the relevant authority regards them as a social service or an exploitable asset, rather than their intrinsic quality. Moreover, temporary exhibitions do not always have separate entrance fees: often the normal cost of admission (which is quoted throughout the *Guide*) is bumped up instead. The free museum, which was quite common in western Germany a decade ago, is now a rarity. Historic monuments tend to charge around DM3–10/€1.50–5, comparing favourably with similar places in Britain, Australia and the US. Wherever you go, a **student card** usually brings a reduction in admission costs, often substantial. It's always worth asking about combination tickets or museum passes to several sights in the same city, which bring substantial savings.

Public transport is the one area where prices are likely to present a problem. A single fare within a city, for example, is generally around DM3/€1.50, while a sample single train fare from Munich to Frankfurt would be DM147/€73.50. The only ways in which you can soften these costs are to use rail and other passes, confine your travel to a limited area or make use of the organized hitching alternative, the *Mitfahrzentralen* (see p.35).

CURRENCY AND THE EXCHANGE RATE

The German currency is the **Deutschmark**, which comes in **notes** of DM5 (rarely encountered), DM10, DM20, DM50, DM100, DM200, DM500 and DM1000; and **coins** of DM0.01 (one Pfennig), DM0.02, DM0.05, DM0.10, DM0.50, DM1, DM2 and DM5. The exchange rate for the Deutschmark is fixed at DM1.96 to the **euro**.

Throughout the *Guide*, prices are given in both Deutschmarks and euros, using a straight two to one conversion. However, it is fair to anticipate that the introduction of the new currency will lead to prices being rounded upwards far more often than downwards, so expect to pay a bit more than the amounts quoted after January 2002.

CREDIT CARDS, CHANGING MONEY AND BANKS

Unusually, for such a consumer-oriented society, **credit cards** are little used in Germany, at least by British, American or Australian standards. Though they are growing in popularity, plenty of shops and restaurants still do not accept them.

Where they do come into their own, however, is for obtaining **cash advances**, and this is now by far the quickest and most convenient means of changing money. Provided you have a Personal Identification Number (PIN), there's no longer any need to go to a bank counter to make this transaction, as ATM machines accepting a wide range of credit cards are now ubiquitous features of German shopping streets, even in quite small towns. Mostly, they are just holes-in-the-wall outside banks, though some are located in secure areas which require a swipe of the card to gain admission. The machines invariably offer the option of instructions in German or English, and sometimes other languages as well. Typically, you are offered a choice of sums of money which can be withdrawn; the upper limit is normally DM500/€250 or DM600/€300, though there is often the possibility of requesting more. **American Express** card holders can take advantage of the full range of that company's facilities in the major cities.

In comparison to credit cards, **travellers' cheques** now seem a cumbersome option, though they remain a safe and reliable way of carrying money. Theoretically, they can be cashed in any bank or exchange office, though banks in small towns can be very choosy about which travellers' cheques they will accept, often refusing even some of the best-known names. In contrast to the United States, very few stores accept them in lieu of cash.

Banking hours are Monday to Friday 9am to noon and 1.30 to 3.30pm, with late opening on Thursday until 6pm. In the cities, these hours are often extended and you'll always find at least one bank open on a Saturday morning, as well as the *Postbank* in the main post office. If you're on a tight budget, it may be worth shopping around several banks (including the savings banks or *Sparkassen*), as the amount of commission deducted varies. Commission tends to be charged at a flat rate, meaning that small-scale transactions are not cost-effective.

Exchange facilities for cash and travellers' cheques can be found in virtually all high street banks as well as in commercial exchange shops called *Wechselstuben*, usually located near stations and airports, though often also in city centres, on the main shopping street. The *Reisebank* has branches in the train stations of most main cities; these are generally open seven days a week, and until quite late in the evening.

INSURANCE AND HEALTH

A typical travel insurance policy usually provides cover for the loss of baggage, tickets and – up to a certain limit – cash or cheques, as well as cancellation or curtailment of your journey. Most of them exclude so-called dangerous sports unless an extra premium is paid: in Germany this can mean climbing, skiing and whitewater rafting. Read the small print and benefits tables of prospective policies carefully; coverage can vary wildly for roughly similar premiums. Many policies can be chopped and changed to exclude coverage you don't need – for example, sickness and accident benefits can often be excluded or included at will. If you do take medical coverage, ascertain whether benefits will be paid as treatment proceeds or only after return home, and whether there is a 24-hour medical emergency number. When securing baggage cover, make sure the per-article limit – typically under £500 equivalent – will cover your most valuable possession. If you need to make a claim, you should keep receipts for medicines and medical treatment, and in the event you have anything stolen, you must obtain an official statement (*Aussage*) from the police. Bank and credit cards often have certain levels of medical or other insurance included and you may automatically get travel insurance if you use a major credit card to pay for your trip.

ROUGH GUIDES TRAVEL INSURANCE

Rough Guides now offers its own **travel insurance**, customized for our readers by a leading UK broker and backed by a Lloyds underwriter. It's available for anyone, of any nationality, travelling anywhere in the world.

There are two main Rough Guide insurance plans: **Essential**, for basic, no-frills cover, starting at £11.75 (European) and £23.03 (worldwide) for two weeks; and **Premier** – with more generous and extensive benefits – starting at £12.50 (European) and £28.79 (worldwide). Alternatively, you can take out annual **multi-trip insurance**, which covers you for any number of trips throughout the year (with a maximum of sixty days for any one trip), starting at £47.26 (European) and £83.99 (worldwide). Unlike many policies, the Rough Guides schemes are calculated by the day, so if you're travelling for 27 days rather than a month, that's all you pay for. If you intend to be away for the whole year, the **Adventurer** policy will cover you for 365 days from £90 (Europe), £160 (worldwide excluding US and Canada), and £200 (worldwide including US and Canada). Each plan can be supplemented with a "Hazardous Activities Premium" if you plan to indulge in sports considered dangerous, such as skiing, scuba-diving or trekking. Rough Guides also does good deals for older travellers, and will insure you up to any age, at prices comparable to SAGA's.

For a **policy quote**, call the Rough Guides Insurance Line on UK freefone 0800015 0906, or, if you're calling from outside Britain on (44/1243 621 046). Alternatively, get an online quote at *www.roughguides.com/insurance*.

Although covered for reciprocal health care while in Germany (see below), citizens of **Britain** and **Ireland** would still do well to take out an insurance policy before travelling to cover against cancellation, loss and theft – and these will generally give you some kind of health cover, too. Travel agents and tour operators are likely to require some sort of insurance when you book a package holiday, though under UK law they can't make you buy their own (other than a £1 premium for "schedule airline failure"). If you have a good all-risks home insurance policy it *may* cover your possessions against loss or theft even when overseas. Note also, that many private medical schemes such as BUPA or PPP also offer coverage plans for abroad, including baggage loss, cancellation or curtailment and cash replacement as well as sickness or accident.

Americans and **Canadians** should also check that they're not already covered. Canadian provincial health plans usually provide partial cover for medical mishaps overseas. Holders of official student/teacher/youth cards are entitled to meagre accident coverage and hospital in-patient benefits. Students will often find that their student health coverage extends during the vacations and for one term beyond the date of last enrolment. Homeowners' or renters' insurance often covers theft or loss of documents, money and valuables while overseas, though conditions and maximum amounts vary from company to company.

HEALTH

Citizens of all EU countries are entitled to free medical care in Germany on production of a **form** E111, available over the counter from main post offices. Without this form you'll have to pay in full for all medical treatment, which is expensive – currently a minimum of DM40/€20 for a visit to the doctor. The scheme does not cover you for dental charges. Whether or not you are eligible for an E111, it's sensible to take out some form of **health insurance** and remember that to make claims you will need to keep copies of receipts and prescriptions.

In the case of an **emergency**, such as a broken leg, the fastest way (though it is not free of charge) to contact an ambulance is to call ☎19222; information on which GPs or specialists are on duty at night and at weekends is also available via this number. The free but slower alternative is ☎112, which covers rescue services as well as medical emergencies. For **minor ailments**, you'll need to visit a GP (*Arzt für Allgemeinmedizin*) in his surgery; these are usually open on weekday mornings, and on afternoons other than Wednesday. German doctors usually speak English, but if you want to be certain, your consulate can provide a list of English-speaking doctors in the major cities, which also have a GP on call for out-of-hours emergencies (*Ärztlicher Notdienst*). Finally, the national **AIDS** help organization, Deutsche AIDS-Hilfe e.V (D.A.H.), is at Dieffenbachstr. 33, Berlin (☎0 30/6 90 08 70).

To get a prescription made up, go to a **pharmacy** (*Apotheke*). German pharmacists are well trained and often speak English. *Apotheken* serving **international prescriptions** can be found in most large cities, and a rota of late-opening or 24-hour places in larger towns is posted on all *Apotheken* doors.

TRAVELLERS WITH DISABILITIES

You'll find that ease of access and facilities are good in Germany and plenty of information is available. All ICE, IC and EC trains (see p.27) are adapted for wheelchair access, as are all IR trains and regional double-deckers and many of the suburban S-Bahns; on the ICE, IC and EC trains there's also a mandatory right to a free seat reservation. Within cities, modern trams and U-Bahns tend to have low entrance platforms and are thus suitable for wheelchairs. Sometimes, old and modern trams alternate on the same routes, and it is common practice to identify the latter on the timetables posted beside stops: the key word to look out for is *Niedrig* (low), hence *Neidrigeingang* (low entrance). Help within stations is available if requested in advance. Museums and public buildings are usually equipped with ramps.

The **Touristik Union International** (TUI), 3000 Hannover 61 (☎05 11/56 70), has a centralized information bank on many German hotels, pensions and resorts that cater to the needs of disabled travellers or those with specific dietary requirements – not in specially

CONTACTS FOR TRAVELLERS WITH DISABILITIES

BRITAIN

Access Travel, 6 The Hillock, Astley, Lancashire M29 7GW (☎01942/888844, fax 891811, *www.access.co.uk*). Tour operator that can arrange flights, transfer and accommodation.

Holiday Care, 2nd Floor, Imperial Building, Victoria Rd, Horley, Surrey RH6 7PZ (☎01293/774535). Information on all aspects of travel. Web site: *www.holidaycare.org.uk*.

RADAR, 12 City Forum, 250 City Rd, London EC1V 8AF (☎020/7250 3222). A good source of advice on holidays and travel abroad. Web site: *www.radar.org.uk*.

Tripscope, Alexandra House, Albany Rd, Brentford, Middlesex TW8 0NE (☎08457/585 641, fax 020/8580 7022, *www.justmobility.co.uk/tripscope*). A national telephone-information service offering free transport and travel advice.

IRELAND

Disability Action Group, 2 Annadale Ave, Belfast BT7 3JH (☎028/9029 7880). Web site: *www.disabilityaction.org*.

Irish Wheelchair Association, Blackheath Drive, Clontarf, Dublin 3 (☎01/833 8241, fax 833 3873, email *iwa@iol.ie*).

NORTH AMERICA

Directions Unlimited, 123 Greenlane, Bedford Hills, NY 10507 (☎914/241 1700). Travel agency specializing in custom tours for people with disabilities.

Mobility International USA, PO Box 10767, Eugene, OR 97440 (Voice and TDD: ☎541/343 1284, *www.miusa.org*). Information and referral services, access guides, tours and exchange programmes. Annual membership $35 (incl quarterly newsletter).

Society for the Advancement of Travel for the Handicapped (SATH), 347 5th Ave, New York, NY 10016 (☎212/447-7284, *sathtravel@aol.com*). Non profit-making travel industry referral service that passes queries on to its members as appropriate (allow plenty of time for a response).

Travel Information Service (☎215/456 9600). Telephone-only information and referral service.

Twin Peaks Press, Box 129, Vancouver, WA 98666 (☎360/694 2462 or 1-800/637 2256). Publisher of the *Directory of Travel Agencies for the Disabled* ($19.95), listing more than 370 agencies worldwide; *Travel for the Disabled* ($19.95); the *Directory of Accessible Van Rentals* ($9.95) and *Wheelchair Vagabond* ($14.95), loaded with personal tips.

AUSTRALIA AND NEW ZEALAND

ACROD (Australian Council for Rehabilitation of the Disabled), PO Box 60, Curtin, ACT 2605 (☎02/6282 4333).

Disabled Persons Assembly, 173–5 Victoria St, Wellington (☎04/801 9100).

designed and separate establishments, but within the mainstream of German tourist facilities. The TUI can also book you onto a package tour or organize rooms according to individual itineraries, taking into account each customer's needs, which are gauged from a questionnaire filled out before booking arrangements commence. Their services also include such details as providing suitable wheelchairs for train travel, the transportation of travellers' own wheelchairs, and the provision of transport at airports and stations.

INFORMATION AND MAPS

Before you leave, it's worth contacting the German National Tourist Office, which has extensive information on campsites, youth hostels, hotels, train timetables and many glossy brochures besides. It also has an extensive English-language Web site (*www.germany-tourism.de*).

TOURIST OFFICES

In **Germany**, you'll find **tourist offices** everywhere, even in tiny villages – addresses are listed in the *Guide*. They're almost universally friendly and very efficient, providing large amounts of free literature, maps and glossy bumf in a selection of languages. Most publish an annual accommodation price list (which

MAP OUTLETS

BRITAIN

Maps are available by **mail order** from Stanfords (☎020/7836 1321, *www.stanfords.co.uk*) and the Amazon Web site (*www.amazon.co.uk*).

Bristol Stanfords, 29 Corn St, BS1 1HT (☎0117/929 9966, *www.stanfords.co.uk*).

Cambridge Heffers Map and Travel, 20 Trinity St, CB2 1TJ (☎01223/586 586, *www.heffers.co.uk*).

Cardiff Blackwell's, 13–17 Royal Arcade, CF1 2PR (☎029/2039 5036, *www.blackwell.co.uk*).

Edinburgh James Thin, 53–59 South Bridge, EH1 1YS (☎0131/556 6743, *www.jthin.co.uk*); Waterstone's, 128 Princes St, EH2 4AD (☎0131/226 2666, *www.waterstones.co.uk*).

Glasgow John Smith & Son, 50 Couper St, Townhead, G4 0DL (☎0141/559 5450).

Inverness James Thin Melven's Bookshop, 29 Union St, IV1 1QA (☎01463/23350, *www.jthin.co.uk*).

London Daunt Books, 83 Marylebone High St, W1M 3DE (☎020/7224 2295); National Map Centre, 22–24 Caxton St, SW1H 0QU (☎020/7222 2466, *www.mapsnmc.co.uk*); Stanfords, 12–14 Long Acre, WC2E 9LP (☎020/7836 1321, *www.stanfords.co.uk*); The Travel Bookshop, 13–15 Blenheim Crescent, W11 2EE (☎020/7229 5260, *www.thetravelbookshop.co.uk*).

Manchester Waterstone's, 91 Deansgate, M3 2BW (☎0161/837 3000, *www.waterstones.co.uk*).

Newcastle upon Tyne Newcastle Map Centre, 55 Grey St, NE1 6EF (☎0191/261 5622, *www.newtraveller.com*).

Oxford Blackwell's, 50 Broad St, OX1 3BQ (☎01865/792792, *www.blackwell.co.uk*).

IRELAND

Maps are available by **mail order** from Stanfords (☎020/7836 1321, *www.stanfords.co.uk*) and the Amazon Web site (*www.amazon.co.uk*).

Belfast Waterstone's Queens Bldg, 8 Royal Ave, BT1 1DA (☎028/9024 7355).

Cork 69 Patrick St (☎021/427 6522).

Dublin Easons Bookshop 40 O'Connell St, Dublin 1 (☎01/873 3811, *www.eason.ie*); Fred Hanna's Bookshop 27–29 Nassau St, Dublin 2 (☎01/677 1255); Hodges Figgis Bookshop 56–58 Dawson St, Dublin 2 (☎01/677 4754, *www.hodgesfiggis.com.*); 7 Dawson St, Dublin 2 (☎01/679 1415).

GERMAN NATIONAL TOURIST OFFICES

Australia c/o German-Australian Chamber of Industry and Commerce, PO Box A980, Sydney NSW 1235 (☎02/9267 8148).

Belgium Val d'Or 92,Gulledellelan, Brussels (☎02/245 9700).

Britain PO Box 2695, London W1A 3TN (☎020/7317 0908).

Canada 175 Bloor St East, North Tower, Suite 604, Toronto, Ontario (☎416/968 1570).

Denmark Vesterbrogade 6 D III, Copenhagen (☎33/436800).

Netherlands Hoogoorddreef 76, Amsterdam (☎020/697 8066).

Sweden PO Box 10147F, Stockholm (☎08/655 1882).

US 122 E 42nd St, 52nd floor, New York, NY 10168–0072 (☎212/661 7200).

becomes a glossy prospectus in resort towns); many also produce a monthly programme of events. The German word for a tourist office is *Fremdenverkehrsamt* (or just *Verkehrsamt*) though many sport a sign saying "Tourist Information". Another useful facility is that they can book a room for you, for which there may or may not be a small booking fee (see "Accommodation" p.36). An increasing number of tourist offices, particularly in major cities and resorts, have an after-hours computer-based service.

NORTH AMERICA

Maps are available **mail order** from Rand McNally, which has stores in two dozen North American cities (☎1-800/333-0136, *www.randmcnally.com*), and over the **Web** from Amazon.com (*www.amazon.com*).

Chicago Rand McNally, 444 N Michigan Ave, IL 60611 (☎312/321 1751, *www.randmcnally.com*).

Montreal Ulysses Travel Bookshop, 4176 St-Denis, PQ H2W 2M5 (☎514/843 9447, *www.ulyssesguides.com*).

New York The Complete Traveler Bookstore, 199 Madison Ave, NY 10016 (☎212/685 9007); Rand McNally, 150 E 52nd St, NY 10022 (☎212/758 7488). Web site: *www.randmcnally.com.*

Palo Alto Phileas Fogg's Books & Maps, #87 Stanford Shopping Center, CA 94304 (☎1-800/533 FOGG, *www.foggs.com*).

San Francisco Rand McNally, 595 Market St, CA 94105 (☎415/777 3131); Sierra Club Bookstore, 6014 College Ave, Oakland, CA 94618 (☎510/658 7470). Web site: *www.randmcnally.com.*

Santa Barbara Map Link, 30 S La Petera Lane, Unit #5, CA 93117 (☎805/692 6777, *www.maplink.com*).

Toronto Open Air Books and Maps, 25 Toronto St, ON M5R 2C1 (☎416/363 0719).

Vancouver International Travel Books and Maps, 552 Seymour St, BC V6B 3J5 (☎604/687 3320, *www.itmb.com*).

Vermont Adventurous Traveler Bookstore, 245 S Champlain St, PO Box 64769, Burlington, VT 05406 (☎1-800/282 3963, *www.adventuroustraveler.com*).

Washington DC The Map Store, 1636 1st St, DC 20006 (☎202/628 2608).

AUSTRALIA AND NEW ZEALAND

Adelaide The Map Shop, 2 Peel St, 5000 (☎08/8231 2033).

Brisbane Worldwide Maps and Guides 187 George St, 4000 (☎07/3221 4330, *www.worldwidemaps.com.au*).

Melbourne The Chart House, 372 Little Bourke St, 3000 (☎03/9670 4383, *www.mapland.com.au*).

Perth Perth Map Centre, 884 Hay St, 6000 (☎08/9322 5733, *www.perthmap.com.au*).

Sydney Travel Bookshop, 175 Liverpool St, 2000 (☎02/9261 8200).

Auckland Specialty Maps, 58 Albert St (☎09/307 2217).

Opening hours are given throughout the *Guide*, but beware that these are prone to change, especially in the case of resorts whose volume of tourism fluctuates according to the season. A weekend shutdown from Friday lunchtime is quite common during the off-season in many smaller towns. In major cities, offices are open virtually every day of the year from early morning until late at night.

The **German Travel Agency** is universally represented by the DER offices, generally to be found near train stations or next to tourist offices. They'll book your national and international train tickets, as well as provide general information about travel onwards from Germany. There is a DER office in London at 18 Conduit St, W1R 9TD (☎020/7408 0111) and in the States at 11933 Wiltshire Blvd, Los Angeles, CA 90025 (☎1-800/421-4343).

THE INTERNET

The **Internet** is now a major souce for tourist information material about Germany – though it has to be said that individual **Web sites** vary enormously in extent, quality and helpfulness; we've listed some of the best in the box below. Inevitably, many sites are in German only, though others offer a full or partial English translation. With very rare exceptions, each tourist office has a Web address, which is mentioned at the appropriate point in the *Guide*. Usually, this is a section of a larger site about the municipality, which also includes information about its economy, politics and local services. However, in some cases such sites are supplemented or replaced by ones devoted solely to tourist information. The best sites give up-to-the-minute information about opening times and prices, and comprehensive accommodation listings complete with on-line booking facilities. Others are little more than glorified advertisements inviting an email or phone call for the dispatch of the latest brochure. A fair number of museums, monuments and hotels also have their own individual sites, or else share a site with related institutions. Again, these are listed in the *Guide*, though it is fair to predict that many more will spring up over the next few years.

Other useful Web sites include those of the individual Länder, which can be accessed by keying in "www." followed by the German name, then ".de". When **surfing** for German names, remember that the Internet convention is that those of two or more words are either hyphenated (even when this is not the case in normal practice) or the names are run on (thus Bad Frankenhausen becomes bad-frankenhausen, and Bad Urach becomes badurach), and that the letters ä, ö and ü are rendered as ae, oe and ue respectively.

MAPS

German **maps** set international standards, and there's no shortage of excellent regional, motoring and hiking maps in most bookshops, newsagents and tourist offices. The best general maps are those printed by RV and Kümmerly & Frey, whose 1:500,000 map is the most detailed single sheet of the country available. Excellent A–Z city maps are published by Falk and ADAC, among others.

USEFUL WEB SITES

The following sites provide useful information and help for preparing a trip to Germany.

www.bahn.de The site of Deutsche Bahn, the national railway company, has a comprehensive timetabling service, enabling train journeys to be planned in advance in the minutest detail.

www.germany-info.org Run by the German Information Centre, this is packed with all sorts of official statistics about Germany.

www.germany-tourism.de The German National Tourist Office's site covers all matters connected with tourism.

www.goethe.de The site of the Goethe Institut, which runs language courses and cultural institutes throughout the world.

www.ltu.com Operated by the tourist arm of Lufthansa, the German national airline, this takes the form of a practical travel guide to the country.

Specialist maps marking cycling routes or Alpine hikes can be bought in the relevant regions and information on German **Alpine climbs and hikes** can be obtained from the Deutscher Alpenverein, Prater Insel 5, Munich. Other useful reference guides available are: *Fahrrad-Atlas*, the best for cycle routes in Germany; and *Mitfahrzentralen in Europa*, which is in three languages and lists all hiking agencies, their fees and regional accommodation options.

GETTING AROUND

While it may not be cheap, getting around Germany is spectacularly quick and easy. Barely a square kilometre of the country is untouched by an unfailingly reliable public transport system, and it's a simple matter to jump from train to bus on the integrated network. Driving is also a straightforward affair on what's probably the best road network on the continent. Costs can be offset by various discounts and passes available to visitors, and it's worth studying all the options outlined below before committing yourself.

TRAINS

By far the best means of public transport in Germany is the train. The **rail network**, operated by the privatized national company Deutsche Bahn (DB; *www.bahn.de*) – formed in 1994 from the union of the old West and East German networks – is far denser than that of any other comparable country in the world, and also has the most frequent service levels. It is particularly comprehensive in the former GDR, where there have hardly ever been any line closures, while an encouraging recent devolopment in the west has been the re-instatement of passenger trains to a number of towns cut off from the network since the 1970s. Where natural obstacles or a sparse population make rail routes unrealistic, the DB-associated buses, Bahnbusse, take over. North–south travel is particularly straightforward, while east–west journeys may require a change along the way. Everywhere services are very efficient, but relatively expensive. Up to 100km, a series of zone tariffs apply. Above that distance, the rates are calculated per kilometre: DM0.272/€0.136 second class, DM0.408/€0.204 first class.

On all intercity routes, even from one end of the country to another, the minimum **frequency** of service from early morning till late evening is one per hour, and in many cases is several times that. Between smaller towns, it's seldom worse than every two hours, and even the most isolated lines have several trains per day, although these are liable to cease in the early evening and be much reduced at weekends.

There are several **types of train**: most luxurious is the 280kph InterCityExpress (ICE), which is due to be upgraded to 330kph in 2002. It only operates on the most popular intercity routes, though these are gradually being extended. On top of the normal fare, there's a supplement to be paid on these trains, increasing according to the distance travelled up to a maximum of DM50/€25. Otherwise, the fastest and most comfortable trains are those designated InterCity (IC) and EuroCity (EC); the only difference between them is that the ECs cross international borders. With these you can travel from one end of the country to the other – Hamburg to Munich, for example, takes six and a half hours. The only drawback is the supplement (*Zuschlag*) of DM9/€4.50 (or DM7/€3.50 if you buy it at the station before boarding the train), which is com-

RAIL LINES

N

pulsory unless you've already invested in a rail pass (see below). Slightly downscale from the ICs and ECs are the InterRegio (IR) trains offering a swift cross-country service along less heavily used routes – and charging a DM4/€2 supplement for journeys of under 50km. This also applies to the relatively cumbersome D-Zug or Schnellzug, which is now used primarily on evening and overnight routes. Of the more localized services, the RegionalExpress (RE) covers the most ground in the shortest time; the misleadingly named StadtExpress (SE) and, in particular, the RegionalBahn (RB) are prone to stop just about everywhere.

Around major cities, the **S-Bahn** is a commuter network on which all rail passes are valid; though these cannot be used on the underground **U-Bahn** system, or on municipally owned trams and buses.

The colossal national **timetable** (*Kursbuch*), which is published annually, can be bought from stations for DM25/€12.50, though it's too bulky to be easily portable. Otherwise, you can easily plan your route by picking up the many free leaflets detailing intercity services, available at any main train station, or by checking the company's Web site.

TICKET TYPES

Normal **tickets** (*Fahrkarten*) permit you to break the journey as often as you wish. For distances of up to 100km, they're valid for a day, and for further distances, for four days. Return tickets are valid for one month. Where automatic vending machines exist, tickets for journeys up to 50km can sometimes only be bought from them, and not from the counter. Prices are based on distance travelled and therefore a return will cost the same as two singles. Although it is usually possible to buy a ticket from the conductor (or the driver on some rural routes), you should make sure that you seek him or her out immediately on boarding. Otherwise, failure to produce a valid ticket results in a doubling of the normal fare, with a minimum charge of DM60/€30.

One useful bargain offer is the *Guten-Abend-Ticket*, which allows a journey of any length (including a return) to be made between 7pm and 3am for DM59/€29.50, or DM69/€34.50 if an ICE train is used. From Friday till Sunday, higher rates of DM74/€37 and DM84/€42 apply, though on Saturdays the ticket can be used from 2pm. If you're making a lot of rail journeys, it's extremely sensible to buy a **rail pass**.

RAIL PASSES

InterRail (see p.5) and **Eurail** (see p.14) passes are valid on all trains but you will have to pay supplements on ICE trains (and, in the case of an InterRail pass, on IC and EC trains as well, though conductors do not always enforce this). If you're using the trains extensively in Germany, there are other passes which may make train travel cheaper.

The broadest-ranging pass, available to all EU citizens, is the **EuroDomino**, which entitles the holder to unlimited travel on all trains and Bahnbusses; on the buses which ply the tourist-oriented "**scenic routes**" such as the Burgenstrasse (Castle Road), the Romantische Strasse (Romantic Road) and the Schwarzwald Hochstrasse (Black Forest Highway); and the K-D Linie steamers on the Mosel and on the Rhine between Cologne and Mainz (see "Boats" on p.32). With prices ranging from £112 for three days to £195 for eleven days (not necessarily consecutive) within the period of a month, it can be excellent value, especially as no further supplements are payable, except on ICE trains.

All the passes mentioned above must be bought **before entering Germany**. They are available from agents throughout Europe and the US (for addresses, see boxes on pp.5 &14).

Should you be staying in Germany for an extended period it's worth considering the **BahnCard** which gives half-price travel for a full year on virtually all trains. This costs DM260/€130 for standard second class, half that for over-60s, those aged 18–22, students up to 26 and spouses or partners of holders of a full-price BahnCard. In all cases, the price is double for first class. There's also a **BahnCard Familie**, which costs from DM130/€65 for up to three children, and a further DM10/€5 and DM20/€10 respectively for each subsequent child. With this, 12–17 year-olds are charged half the adult fare, 6–11 year-olds half the child fare.

Another possibility is the somewhat complicated **Ferienticket**, which is available for twelve popular holiday regions, and can only be purchased in conjunction with a normal return ticket (whether international or domestic) to the same area costing a minimum of DM199/€99.50 or its equivalent. The *Ferienticket* itself costs DM50/€25 for one person for a week; accompanying travellers (up to a maximum of four) pay DM25/€12.50 each. For an extra DM25/€12.50 (DM13/€6.50 for those accompanying), the ticket can be extended for a further week (up to a maximum of two weeks); for the same prices, it can cover the adjacent holiday region as well. The *Ferienticket* is valid from 9am to 3am on weekdays, all day long on weekends and holidays.

GROUP TRAVEL, CHILDREN AND OVERNIGHT TRAVEL

By far the best bargain DB offers is the DM35/€17.50 **Schönes-Wochenend-Ticket**, which allows up to five people travelling together to use any local trains (RE, RB, SE and S-Bahn) on either a Saturday or a Sunday. (Until 1999, it covered the entire weekend, but the old name, which now seems rather misleading, has been retained.) Even for a single traveller, this soon pays for itself, and it can make astronomical savings if used to make a long cross-country journey – which it can easily do, albeit in short and slowish stages. The introduction of this ticket has had the desired effect of filling up previously little-patronized services, though there are periodic threats to withdraw it because of widespread abuses (many people sell or give away their tickets after they have finished using them, others tag along for free with perfect strangers).

The nearest weekday equivalents are the **Ländertickets**, which likewise cover up to five people travelling together (with the alternative of one or both parents accompanied by any or all of their own children aged 17 or under) on the local trains. All are valid on Mondays to Fridays from 9am until 4pm and from 6pm until 3am the following day; in some of the Länder, and on public holidays which fall on weekdays they can be used the whole day. These tickets are sponsored by the Land governments, and in 2001 were available for all the Länder except the three city states (where they are obviously not relevant) plus Hesse, North Rhine-Westphalia and Saxony, which will hopefully join the scheme in due course. A combined ticket for Rhineland-Palatinate and Saarland is currently DM30/€15; in Saxony-Anhalt and Thuringia the ticket costs DM35/€17.50; in all the other Länder it is DM40/€20.

There are various other possibilities for several people travelling together. For medium-distance return journeys, there's the **Mitfahrer-Fahrpreis**,

whereby the first adult pays the full fare (which must be at least DM54/€27 second class, DM82/€41 first class), then up to four other adults may travel at half price and one child at quarter price. Similarly, the *Sparpreis* and *Supersparpreis* fares for up to five people making a long-distance return journey can bring massive savings, in the most extreme cases reducing costs to less than a third of the normal rates. **Sparpreis** tickets require that the outward and return journeys are separated by at least a weekend, or that one or the other is made on a Saturday or Sunday. They cost a fixed DM249/€124.50 in second class, DM374/€187 in first class for the first person, rising to DM299/€145.50 and DM499/€249.50 if an ICE train is used. As with the *Mitfahrer-Fahrpreis*, up to four accompanying adults are charged half-fare, a child quarter-fare. **Supersparpreis** tickets work on the same principle, but cannot be used on Fridays and Sundays. The first person pays DM199/€99.50 second class, DM299/€149.50 first class, or DM249/€124.50 and DM374/€187 if an ICE train is taken.

If **travelling with kids**, note that the under-6s travel free, while those aged between 6 and 11 travel for half the adult price. Long-distance trains generally have a special compartment, designated a *Kinderabteilung*, for mother and toddlers.

On long journeys, such as from the North Sea coast to Bavaria, it's worth considering **travelling overnight**. If aiming to sit up, note that conditions can be very cramped on Fridays and Sundays; on other nights you should manage to find an empty or near-empty compartment. However, this can be a dangerous option, as there are professional gangs "working" such trains; their favourite technique is to spray gas into compartments through air ducts, thereby ensuring that the passengers inside remain asleep while they are robbed. Couchettes, which cost upwards of DM24/€12, are far safer. Better still are the sleepers available on international services and the new InterCity Night (ICN) trains, though at DM90/€45 or more they are comparable in price with an upmarket hotel room.

PRIVATE RAILWAYS

A large number of short stretches of railway line lie outside the DB network. They have their own special ticketing arrangements, and rail passes are often not valid. Those in this category include the famous **narrow-gauge lines** in Saxony, the Harz and the coast of Mecklenburg-Lower Pomerania which were, prior to the creation of the new DB in 1994, an integral part of the old East German system. Their privatization has brought much higher fares and led to plenty of protests, though at least their long-term future now seems totally secure. **Steam engines** are still used regularly on these lines, though modern diesels frequently take their place.

There's a much larger number of lines no longer used for regular passenger services where DB allows a local preservation society to run special excursions, usually with historic locomotives, throughout the summer. In some cases, such as the spectacular *Wutachtalbahn* in the Black Forest, these are quite frequent; more typically, they take place only once or twice a month, invariably at weekends or on public holidays.

The most interesting private railways are all described in the *Guide*. Full operational details, including the exact dates of excursion services, can be found in DB's *Kursbuch*.

BUSES

At such rare times as you have to forsake the trains for **buses**, you'll find no decline in the standard of efficiency. Most buses are run in association with DB and are known as Bahnbusse. They're organized into regional associations, which offer **runabout passes** for a variety of periods; these can be quite remarkable value, particularly if you're making an extended stay in a scenic area such as the Alps or the Black Forest. There are also some privately operated routes outside this system.

You're most likely to need buses in remote rural areas – or along the designated "scenic routes" mentioned earlier (see "Rail Passes", p.30). On these routes, buses are luxury class, often packed with tourists, and pause long enough by the major points of scenic or historic interest for passengers to hop out and take a couple of photographs. Although expensive to use without a railcard (EuroDomino holders travel free and InterRail cards get a 50 percent reduction), these buses are usually the only way to visit certain locales if you don't have your own transport or the patience to zigzag around on the slow local buses.

A point to watch out for in the remoter country areas is punctuality. Unlike trains, buses are allowed to run ahead of their timetable – and

often do if they have few passengers to pick up. It's therefore prudent to be at the stop at least ten minutes before the bus is due to arrive.

Finally, although there are some long-distance bus routes undercutting the railways, these are on a very small scale in comparison with Britain, the US or Australia. Many link major holiday resorts and the big population centres, and are clearly targeted at the latter's less affluent residents.

BOATS

Travelling by **boat** is another option, though more for relaxation than covering large distances. All along the major rivers, and in particular the **Rhine** and **Mosel**, there are innumerable local boats waiting to ferry you across or around the waters. For a longer trip, K-D Linie steamers sail on the Rhine between Cologne and Mainz, and on the Mosel between Koblenz and Cochem, every day from April to October inclusive. On these routes, possession of a EuroDomino or Eurail pass will get you free passage, while InterRail brings a 50 percent reduction.

The steamers call at many riverside villages and you can get on or off wherever you want. The fare, as you'd expect, depends on how far you travel; Cologne to Koblenz, for example, costs DM59.80/€29.90 single, DM66.40/€33.20 for a day return (DM90/€45 and DM118/€59 respectively by fast boat). Several smaller companies also operate short-haul services along both the Rhine and Mosel, and along most other main navigable rivers as well. In the former GDR, there are especially beautiful cruises to be had on the Elbe, particularly the stretch from Dresden south into the Czech Republic.

Germany's biggest lake, an enormous bulge in the Rhine called the **Bodensee**, is also a prime spot for water-borne travel, either for a direct journey or a lazy cruise to explore the nooks and crannies of its shoreline, which spans Austria and Switzerland as well as Germany; full details are on p.302. Cruise boats also ply many of Bavaria's Alpine and pre-Alpine lakes.

MUNICIPAL PUBLIC TRANSPORT

Municipal public transport in most German cities (though western Berlin and Hamburg are notable exceptions) is still centred on **trams**. Increasingly, these are sleek modern vehicles capable of moving at a fair speed between stops. They often have an underground stretch in the city centre, where they're known as the **U-Bahn**. This is often a source of confusion; it's important to remember that Berlin, Hamburg, Munich and Nürnberg have a much more extensive U-Bahn system using tube trains as distinct from trams, while in cities with trams only you may have to look both above and below ground in the central area to find the stop for the service you want. In some cities, old boneshaker trams are still the mainstay of the public transport system, though these are gradually being replaced. Wherever the trams and U-Bahns do not go, you can be sure that there will be a **bus** to fill the void.

Tickets, which can be bought from automatic vending machines or the driver, are valid on all the different forms of transport – which include the S-Bahn and mainline **trains** as well in all the major conurbations – and you can change from one to another, with no supplement for transfers. This means that, if making a train journey between two places within the same public transport authority, you are entitled to have what are in effect free rides on the local public transport systems at either end, provided these are made within the allowed time periods. Normal **single** fares are relatively expensive – DM3/€1.50 is the standard rate in many cities, though there's generally a special lower tariff for short journeys (*Kurzstrecke*).

If you're planning to make several journeys, it's advisable either to buy in **blocks** (usually offering a total saving of around 30 percent), or invest in a **fixed time period** (generally 24hr) ticket. The latter, which can be bought for the city itself or the whole of the regional network, can be a tremendous bargain – in some cities, up to two adults and two children are covered by the ticket, for an outlay of around DM8/€4 for the city only and DM15/€7.50 for the regional network. Even better value are the cards which, for a minimal extra outlay, include free or reduced admission to the main museums and monuments. Details of these are given throughout the *Guide*, but note that exact conditions are particularly prone to change.

Finally, note that the purchase of tickets functions largely on the honour system, and spot checks by plain-clothes inspectors are fairly rare. However, they do take place rather more frequently than was once the case, and result in an automatic DM60/€30 **fine** for anyone caught without a valid ticket.

PLANES

While **domestic flights** are numerous and quick between the major cities, they are also expensive. Single fares are available in business class only, and are far more expensive than the cheapest returns, which include Frankfurt–Berlin for DM220/€110, Frankfurt–Hamburg for DM260/€130. If you're in a desperate rush, it's worth trying to obtain one of these tickets, even if it means destroying the return portion. Student and youth fares are 25 percent less than normal rates. Any tourist office or Lufthansa agent will be able to provide full details of the current offers. If you definitely want to fly between German cities and are starting and finishing your journey in the UK, it's cheaper to book all the flights together, although this usually means that dates of travel cannot be changed. The same applies for travellers from North America, Australia and New Zealand.

DRIVING AND VEHICLE RENTAL

Foreigners may drive in Germany for one year with a national or international driving licence (for more than a year you must have a German licence). At least third-party **insurance** is mandatory (normal third-party insurance in Britain does not cover foreign travel, although more extensive policies do). It's not necessary to carry a green card, but some other form of proof of insurance is essential.

Seatbelts are compulsory for all passengers as well as the driver, and **children under 12** years must sit in the back. Understanding **right of way** can be problematic: if no right of way is indicated, priority is always with vehicles coming from the right. In cities, be aware that **trams** always have the right of way. Unfamiliarity with the traffic system means that unwary visiting drivers are prone to cut in front of turning trams at junctions – a frightening and potentially lethal error. Also, when trams halt at their designated stops it's forbidden to overtake until the tram starts moving, to allow passengers time to cross the road and board.

Germany's highways, or **Autobahnen**, are the most extensive and efficient network in Europe, though those in the north can sometimes be only two lanes. Fuel stations, roadside restaurants and motels are located every 30–40km, and every city and virtually all the towns are within simple striking distance, using equally high-quality secondary

CAR RENTAL AGENCIES

AUSTRALIA
Avis ☎13 6333, *www.avis.com*
Budget ☎13 2727, *www.budget.com*
Hertz ☎13 3039, *www.hertz.com*

BRITAIN
Autos Abroad ☎0207/287 6000,
www.autosabroad.co.uk
Avis ☎0870/606 0100, *www.avis.com*
Budget ☎0800/181181,
www.budgetrentacar.com
Europcar ☎0345/222 525, *www.europcar.com*
Hertz ☎0870/844 8844, *www.hertz.com*
Holiday Autos ☎0870/400 0011, *www*
.holidayautos.com
Thrifty ☎01494/442 110, *www.thrifty.com*

IRELAND
Avis Eire ☎01/8745844; Northern Ireland
☎0990/900500. Web site: *www.avis.com*
Budget Rent-A-Car Eire ☎0800/973 159;
Northern Ireland ☎0800/181181. Web site:
www.budgetrentacar.com
Europcar Eire ☎01/874 5844; Northern Ireland
☎0345/222525. Web site: *www.europcar.com*

Hertz Eire ☎01/676 7476; Northern Ireland
☎0990/996699. Web site: *www.hertz.com*
Holiday Autos Eire ☎01/872 9366366; Northern
Ireland ☎0990/300400. Freefax ☎1800/729366,
info@holidayautos.ie; Web site: *www*
.holidayautos.com

NORTH AMERICA
Alamo ☎1-800/522-9696, *www.goalamo.com*
Auto Europe ☎1-800/223-5555,
www.world.com
Avis ☎1-800/331-1084, *www.avis.com*
Budget ☎1-800/527-0700,
www.budgetrentacar.com
Europe by Car ☎1-800/223-1516,
www.ebcar.com
Hertz US ☎1-800/654-3001, Canada ☎1-
800/263-0600. Web site: *www.hertz.com.*
Holiday Autos ☎1-800/422 7737,
www.kemwel.com

NEW ZEALAND
Avis ☎09/379 2650, *www.avis.com*
Budget ☎0800/650 700, *www.budget.com*
Hertz ☎09/364 6350, *www.hertz.com*

roads to link them to the Autobahnen. A huge amount of work has been done in the former GDR to bring its road system up to western standards, though many minor routes still remain in a poor state of repair.

There are no legally enforced **speed limits** on the Autobahnen although there is a recommended limit of 130kmph. The official speed limit on country roads is 100kmph, and in built-up areas 50kmph, unless a lower figure is indicated.

Note that there are **on-the-spot fines** for speeding and other offences. For speeding these are charged on a sliding scale from about DM20–50/€10–25; after a cut-off point of roughly 25km above the limit, you're charged and taken to court.

CAR RENTAL

Car rental (*Autovermietung*) is available at most airports and major train stations, and regional tourist offices will always be able to inform you of the nearest car-rental firm. Although the major

companies like Avis, Budget or Hertz are easy to find, smaller local companies often offer better rates. Rates tend to be higher than in the UK and Australia, and markedly higher than in the US (upwards of DM400/€200 for a small hatchback for a week). You'll need to be 21 or over to rent a car in Germany.

Fly-drive deals can be good value if you know in advance that you want to rent a car, but you'll often get a better deal through someone who deals with local agents. Some of the best rates are offered by **Autos Abroad** (see box above for contact details): weekly rates for a small car in Germany, including the collision damage waiver and unlimited mileage, start at £119 between November and March, £125 from April to October. If you're going in high season, you're advised to book well in advance.

TAXIS

In cities and towns, taking into account the high cost of local public transport, several people sharing a cab may actually save money over using a local bus or train. **Taxis** (nearly all of which are Mercedes) have a sign on the roof which is illuminated if they are free. Hail one from the street, or wait at the taxi stands – alternatively there are always plenty hovering around train stations and big hotels.

MITFAHRZENTRALEN

As in most other countries today, casual **hitching** is not recommended as a safe method of getting around Germany.

However, the Germans have developed an institutionalized form of hitching called **Mitfahrzentralen**, located in most large cities and listed throughout the *Guide*. (Beware that their addresses and phone numbers tend to change rapidly, so it's always worth checking the local directory.) These are agencies that put drivers and travellers in touch with each other for a nominal fee, and then it's up to the participants to work out an agreeable fuel contribution, usually a simple two-way split, although the agency does suggest a reasonable sum. There's a valuable safety factor in this system, since all drivers have to notify the agencies of their addresses and car registration numbers. There are also a few **women-only agencies**, known as *Frauenmitfahrzentralen*.

CYCLING

Cyclists are well catered for in Germany – at least in comparison with the UK, US or Australia – though sensibly they're banned from the *Autobahnen*. Many smaller roads have marked cycle-paths, and bike-only lanes are a common sight in cities and towns. Fairly hassle-free **long-distance cycling** is possible all over the country, but obviously you'll need a strong pair of legs and a sturdy, reliable machine to get much joy out of the Bavarian Alps. To take your own **bike on a train**, you need to purchase a *Fahrrad-Karte* (bicycle ticket), which costs DM6/€3 for up to 100km, and DM12/€6 otherwise. On express services, you have to take the bike to the luggage van; on S-Bahn and regional trains, there are

marked carriages where cyclists can stay with their bikes.

Between April and October, the best place to **rent a bike** is from a train station participating in the Fahrrad am Bahnhof scheme (most of the main stations), whereby a bike costs from DM10–20/€5–10 per day. You can return it to any other participating station and EuroDomino or InterRail card-holders get a 50 percent discount. This is obviously perfect for splitting train travel with pedalling as and when the mood, terrain or weather takes you. During the rest of the year, or in an area where there's no suitable station, simply look in the phone book under *Fahrradverleih* to find the address of a local bike rental outlet. Renting this way, however, means you'll have to leave a deposit, usually around DM50/€25.

WALKING AND HIKING

The German countryside is laced with colour-coded **hiking trails**, most of which are suitable for a Sunday afternoon stroll, though many trails are actually sections of much longer hikes. Very few hikes pass through remote or isolated areas and there's always a village, campsite or youth hostel fairly close by so you can make a trek of just a few hours or of several days' duration without much trouble. The best of the trails are described in the *Guide* and the local tourist offices have masses of **information and maps** (*Wanderkarten*) relating to the walks in their area. Because the hikes are so easy, you won't need any specialist equipment, but take a comfortable day-pack for carrying picnic provisions.

There are some **potential frustrations**, however. The prevalence of trees in all the scenic areas (with the exception of the Swabian Jura and the upper reaches of the Bavarian Alps) not only means that you're only occasionally rewarded with long-range views, but also ensures that there's seldom much chance to deviate from the regimentation of the marked paths. Don't let this rigidity fool you into skimping on proper maps: at times the trails can peter out or become confused, particularly when signs have become weather-worn or have been vandalized.

ACCOMMODATION

Be it high-rise city hotels or half-timbered guesthouses in the country, accommodation of all types is easy to find in Germany and can often be good value – especially in the growing number of rooms available in private houses. For those on a really tight budget, the youth hostels and campsites which proliferate over the entire country are a sound, cost-cutting alternative.

There are wide variations in the prices charged for similar types of accommodation. Predictably, Berlin is the most expensive destination in the country, with the likes of Munich, Hannover, Stuttgart, Cologne and Düsseldorf not too far behind. Yet other major cities, including Nuremberg, Augsburg and, to a lesser extent, Hamburg, Frankfurt and Dresden, are well-endowed with good-quality budget accommodation, whereas many far smaller towns are not.

Accommodation of all types in popular holiday areas – even ones as famous as the Bavarian Alps and the Black Forest – can be remarkably good value. Note that, in spas and other health resorts, there's a hidden extra charge in the form of the *Kurtaxe*, a **tax** levied on behalf of the municipality, which can be for anything up to DM7/€3.50 per day. In return, the guest is given a *Kurkarte*, which gives free or reduced entry to many local sights and facilities, sometimes including municipal buses. However, some proprietors do not bother implementing the system if a guest is only staying for a night or two.

The availability of **on-line booking facilities** for accommodation of all types is on the increase. Even when an establishment does not have an individual Web site or email address, it may still be possible to book on-line via the tourist office site.

HOTELS

Accommodation in Germany is subject to a somewhat complicated categorization system. The official classification of **Hotel** is not applied as widely as in many other countries, being confined in the main to mid-range and expensive establishments which have a manned reception desk and offer a full range of services, including a restaurant. Those of similar standing which serve no meals other than breakfast are classified as **Hotel Garni**. The designation **Gasthof** signifies a uniquely German institution, one roughly equivalent to the traditional English inn. More often than not, you have to ask for a room at its bar-cum-restaurant. The latter almost invariably has a regular local clientele, and often forms the mainstay of the business, with accommodation playing a secondary role.

Despite these different categories, the bedrooms on offer tend not to vary much: they're normally clean, comfortable and functional with conveniences like TV, phone and en-suite bathroom

---

ACCOMMODATION PRICE CODES

All the pensions and hotels in this book have been graded according to the following price categories. The codes quoted are for the cheapest available double room, except for establishments which have rooms costing widely different rates, when the most expensive price is given as well. Exact charges are given for youth hostels; in the case of the official DJH (HI) establishments, this is the lowest available rate. When two figures are quoted for these hostels, the first applies to juniors (ie under 27 years of age), the second to seniors (27 and above). In Bavaria, the hostel price applies to juniors only.

① less than DM60/€30	④ DM100–124/€50–62	⑦ DM200–249/€100–124
② DM60–79/€30–39	⑤ DM125–149/€63–74	⑧ DM250–299/€125–149
③ DM80–99/€40–49	⑥ DM150–199/€75–99	⑨ upwards of DM300/€150

usually taken for granted in the medium-range establishments upwards. Note that in the former GDR most hotels are either new or recently refurbished, and hence tend to be more expensive than their western counterparts. The listings in the *Guide* concentrate on the best options in all price categories from the points of view of convenience, character and value for money. However, it's always worth calling into the nearest **tourist office** to check any special deals which they may have with local establishments. This can result in you spending less than the figures quoted on the official **accommodation lists** which every tourist office provides. Many tourist offices charge DM3–10/€1.50–5 for finding you a room, but others perform the service free. In many of the principal cities, hotel prices are bumped up, often to double the normal rate, when there's a trade fair (*Messe*) taking place. During the biggest of these, all available rooms in the city and its hinterland are booked out months in advance.

In budget and medium-priced hotels, there's rarely any great saving to be made by two people sharing as opposed to one person travelling alone. In country areas, the least you'll have to spend is about DM35/€17.50 for a single, DM60/€30 for a double – at least DM10–20/ €5–10 extra for something similar in a city. Remember that any savings on accommodation costs that can be made by staying on the outskirts of a city may be offset by the price of public transport into the centre.

PENSIONS AND PRIVATE ROOMS

The official designation of **Pension** is applied to less formal establishments than hotels, though in some holiday areas – particularly in Bavaria – the term **Gästehaus** (guesthouse) is used instead. In such places, the rooms are usually within a private house or apartment block. Prices tend to be quite a bit lower than in hotels, though this is less marked in cities than in the countryside.

In busy holiday areas, an increasingly prevalent budget option is **bed and breakfast** accommodation in a private house (look for signs saying *Fremdenzimmer* or *Zimmer frei*): prices vary but are usually around DM30–45/€15–22.50 for a single, DM55–70/€27.50–35 for a double.

Very few west German cities have private rooms on offer other than to relieve congestion when there's a trade fair on; rates are then comparable with those of hotels. In the former GDR, on the other hand, thousands of householders

have opened up their **homes** to guests, in order to earn a bit of extra cash. This helped plug the huge shortfall in accommodation for travellers that would otherwise have existed in the years immediately following the *Wende*, and nowadays provides a budget alternative to the hotel sector, which in eastern Germany is now dominated by expensive business-class ventures. In the cities, many of the rooms are in high-rise apartment blocks, and thus impossible to locate under your own steam. You therefore need to go to the local tourist office or one of the **private agencies** (*Zimmervermittlung*), which are often open until late in the evening, to book a room. Usually, there's a charge similar to that made for booking hotels, but beware of any tourist office or agency which wants to levy a daily fee: in such cases, book for one night and then try to negotiate a longer stay with your hosts.

Farmhouse holidays (*Ferien auf dem Bauernhof*) are increasingly popular in Germany, and in many ways are the best bargains of all, with full board rates from as little as DM30/€15 per person per day. Full lists are available from local tourist offices; the major snag is that this option is really only feasible if you have your own transport.

Even more ubiquitous are **holiday homes** (*Ferienhäuser*) which you rent by the week, and these can be the cheapest option if you are travelling with a family or a group. Full lists are available from tourist offices in all main holiday areas. In major cities, it's well worth contacting one of the **flat- and room-letting agencies** (**Mitwohnzentralen**) if you intend to stay for an extended period. Some will only arrange accommodation for a minimum period of a month, but even if you leave early this may still undercut any other option.

YOUTH HOSTELS

In Germany, you're never far away from an official **youth hostel** (*Jugendherberge*) – the YH movement was born here, in fact, in 1909 – and these are likely to form the backbone of genuine budget travelling. Note, however, that at any time of the year they're liable to be block-booked by school groups – this is particularly likely on weekdays during the summer, and at weekends out of season. It's therefore advisable to make a reservation by phoning or writing to the hostel as far in advance as possible to be sure of a place – and be prepared to put up with marauding adolescents.

YOUTH HOSTEL ASSOCIATIONS

Australia Australian Youth Hostels Association, 422 Kent St, Sydney 2000 (☎02/9261 1111); 83 Harding Lane, Melbourne 3000 (☎03/9670 9611); 38 Stuart St, Adelaide 5000 (☎08/8231 5583); 154 Roma St, Brisbane 4000 (☎07/3236 1680); 236 William St, Perth 6003 (☎08/9227 5122); 69 Mitchell St, Darwin 800 (☎08/8981 2560); 28 Criterion St, Hobart (☎03/6234 9617). Web site: *www.yha.com.au*.

Canada Canadian Hostelling Association, Room 400, 205 Catherine St, Ottowa, ON K2P 1C3 (☎613/237-7884 or 1-800/663-5777, *www.hostellingintl.ca*).

England and Wales Youth Hostel Association (YHA), Trevelyan House, 8 St Stephen's Hill, St Albans, Herts AL1 2DY (☎01727/45047). London shop and information office: 14 Southampton St, London WC2 (☎020/7836 1036, *www.yha /england/wales.org.uk*).

Germany Deutsches Jugendherbergswerk, administration: Bad Meinberger Str. 1, 32760 Detmold (☎0 52 31/9 93 60); service: Bismarckstr. 8, 32756 Detmold (☎0 52 31/7 40 10).

New Zealand PO Box 436, Christchurch, (☎03/379 9970, www.*yhanz.org.nz*).

Northern Ireland Youth Hostel Association of Northern Ireland, 22–32 Donegal Rd, Belfast, BT12 5JN (☎028/9032 4733).

Scotland Scottish Youth Hostel Association, 7 Glebe Crescent, Stirling, FK8 2JA (☎01786/451181).

US Hostelling International-American Youth Hostels (HI-AYH), 733 15th St NW, Suite 840, Washington, DC 20005 (☎202/783-6161, *www.hiayh.org*).

Though most **wardens** and their staff are courteous and helpful, there's an unfortunate minority who seem to be leftovers from the leadership of the Hitler Youth, insisting on rigid regimentation and pedantic enforcement of the rules. You should be wary, too, of **age restrictions** (see below) and the fact that prices are slightly cheaper if you're under 27 years of age.

More than six hundred hostels are run by the German Youth Hostel Association (Deutsches Jugendherbergswerk; *www.djh.de*) and indicated by signs reading DJH. **Prices**, which start at around DM18/€9 in the most basic establishments, are inclusive bed and breakfast rates, and apply to HI members; non-members, if admitted at all, will be charged an extra DM4/€2 per night. If you're not a member and intend to use hostels for more than a couple of nights, it's wise to buy a year's HI **membership** from your own national association, before leaving home. You can buy the same thing at larger hostels in Germany but it's slightly more expensive.

German youth hostels do carry a number of other **rules** and restrictions. **Reservations** will only be held until 6pm unless you've informed the warden that you'll be arriving late. When things are busy, **priority** is given to people under 18, or hiking families travelling with children. Those **over 27**, if they've not made a reservation, are only supposed to get a place if the hostel is not

fully booked at 6pm – though this is by no means strictly applied. A more serious restriction for this age group is that they can't use the hostels in **Bavaria** at all, unless they are accompanying children. Elsewhere, they have to pay a slightly higher rate (usually an extra DM5/€2.50) at all but the hostels which bear the designation of **youth guesthouse** (*Jugendgästehaus*). These are more luxurious than the others, with accommodation in two- and four-bedded dorms and a wide range of facilities. However, at around DM40/€20 per head they can work out as a more expensive option than a guesthouse for two people sharing – and are almost invariably so for those travelling in a small group.

All hostels have a **curfew**, which can be as early as 10pm (and usually is in rural areas), but may be later (as is the case in all the big cities). The latest time you are able to check in is generally 10pm, too. **Length of stay** is officially limited to three days unless a longer period has been booked in advance. You can, however, stay longer – provided you're not going to deprive new arrivals from getting in. In **winter** many hostels close altogether and many more shut every other weekend; we have indicated months of closure throughout the *Guide*, but you should call ahead to check about odd closing days. Very few German hostels offer self-catering facilities, but most do provide meals.

Privately owned hostels are, in general, far more relaxed and less regimented than their official counterparts, dispensing with the more off-putting hostelling traditions such as lockouts, curfews and supplements for older guests. They are found mainly in the larger cities (Berlin and Munich both offer a wide choice of establishments) and are usually run by friendly, savvy young staff responsive to the needs of modern travellers.

Finally, the **Naturfreundehaus** association offers a variant on the hostel theme. Its establishments, often located in rural countryside close to towns and cities, are designed more for older people, with accommodation in singles, doubles or very small dorms.

CAMPING

Big, well-managed **campsites** are a feature of Germany, and they're located almost anywhere anybody could even think about wanting to camp. It's significant that sites are officially graded on a scale beginning at "good" and working up to "excellent". Even those in the lowest grade have toilet and washing facilities and a shop nearby on the site, while the grandest are virtually open-air hotels with swimming pools, supermarkets and various other comforts – though it must be said that camping purists find German sites rather too regimented. **Prices** are based on facilities and location, comprising a fee per person and per tent (each DM5–10/€2.50–5). There are extra fees for cars, caravans, etc, so you could easily spend quite a bit more than you might in other countries if there are several of you travelling in a car.

Bear in mind, too, that many sites, especially those in popular holiday areas, nearly always fill up from June to September, and you should arrive early in the afternoon for a good chance of getting in. Most campsites close down in the winter, but those in popular skiing areas remain open all year; months of closure, where they exist, are indicated throughout the *Guide*.

All the most useful sites are listed in the *Guide*, and you can also pick up the highly condensed **list of sites** which is available free from German National Tourist Offices. The complete official guide is available in bookshops throughout Germany, or direct from the German Camping Club, the DDC, at Mandlstr. 28, Munich. The motoring organization, ADAC, also produces a similar guide which includes Germany and much of northern and central Europe.

Rough camping on communally owned land is illegal – in the interests of protecting the environment – though a blind eye seems to be turned to camper vans: indeed stays ranging from 24 hours to three days are sometimes officially sanctioned. You can camp on private farmland by obtaining permission – which is often freely granted – from the owner.

EATING

German food is, as a rule, both good value and of high quality. However, it does help if you share the national penchant for solid, fatty food accompanied by compensatingly healthy fresh vegetables and salad. The pig is the staple element of the German menu – it's prepared in umpteen different ways, and just about every part of it is eaten. It also forms the main ingredient for sausages, which are not only the most popular snack, but are regarded as serious culinary fare – in Bavaria, there are even specialized *Wurstküchen* (sausage kitchens) which have gained Michelin ratings.

BREAKFAST

The vast majority of German hotels and guest-houses, and all youth hostels, include breakfast in the price of their accommodation. Although some places go in for the spartan French affair of rolls, jam and coffee, the normal German breakfast lies midway between this and the elaborate Scandinavian-style cold table, but the latter is catching on, particularly in middle- and upper-range hotels. Typically, you'll be offered a small platter of **cold meats** (usually sausage-based) and **cheeses**, along with a selection of marmalades, jams and honey. Muesli or another cereal is sometimes included as well. You're generally given a variety of **breads**, which are among the most distinctive features of German cuisine. Both brown and white rolls are popular; these are often given a bit of zap by the addition of a condiment, such as caraway, coriander, poppy or sesame seeds. The rich-tasting black rye bread, known as Pumpernickel, is a particular national favourite, as is the salted Brezel, which tastes nothing like any foreign imitation. **Coffee** (which is normally freshly brewed) is the usual accompaniment. **Drinking chocolate** is a common alternative, as are both herbal and plain **tea**. Tea is served black, often with optional lemon, but does not blend well with German milk. Fruit juice – almost invariably orange – is sometimes included as well.

If breakfast isn't included in your accommodation costs, you can usually do quite well by going to a local **baker's shop**, which generally opens from 7am, if not before. Most chain bakeries have an area set aside for breakfast, known as a *Stehcafé* (standing café), a practice taken up by some family establishments as well. The coffee and chocolate on offer tend to be of high quality, and there's the added bonus of being able to choose from the freshly made bakery on display; DM5–6/€2.50–3 should cover an adequate breakfast.

SNACKS AND FAST FOOD

Just as the English have their morning and afternoon tea, so the Germans have *Kaffee und Kuchen* (coffee and cakes). Though the elegant type of **café** serving a choice of espresso, capuccino and mocha to the accompaniment of cream cakes, pastries or handmade chocolates is indelibly associated with Austria, it's every bit as popular an institution in Germany. This hardly constitutes a cheap snack but is unlikely to be a rip-off – except in the most obvious tourist traps. An almost equally ubiquitous institution is the **ice-cream parlour** (*Eiscafé*). Almost invariably, these are run by Italian émigrés and offer a huge range of flavours and concoctions to choose from, which can either be eaten on the premises or taken away.

More substantial food is available from **butchers' shops**. Even in rural areas, you can generally choose from a variety of freshly roasted meats to make up a hot sandwich. It's also worth going to the open-air **markets** which are held anything from once to six times a week in the central square of most towns. With a bit of judicious shopping round the stalls, you should be able to

FOOD GLOSSARY

BASICS

Abendessen	supper, dinner	Gabel	fork	Öl	oil
Belegtes Brot	open sand-wich	Gemüse	vegetables	Pfeffer	pepper
		Glas	glass	Rechnung	bill
Biertieg	batter	Hauptgericht	main course	Reis	rice
Brot	bread	Honig	honey	Salz	salt
Brötchen	bread roll	Joghurt	yoghurt	Senf	mustard
Butter	butter	Käse	cheese	Sosse	sauce
Butterbrot	sandwich	Löffel	spoon	Spätzle	shredded pasta
Ei	egg	Marmelade	jam		
Eintopf	a soup–stew hybrid	Maultaschen	form of ravioli	Speisekarte	menu
		Messer	knife	Tasse	cup
Essig	vinegar	Mittagessen	lunch	Teller	plate
Fisch	fish	Nachspeise	dessert	Trinkgeld	tip
Fleisch	meat	Nudeln	noodles	Vorspeise	starter
Frühstück	breakfast	Obst	fruit	Zucker	sugar

SOUPS AND STARTERS

Bohnensuppe	bean soup	Lachsbrot	smoked salmon on bread
Erbsensuppe	pea soup	Leberknödelsuppe	clear soup with liver dumplings
Flädlesuppe, Pfannkuchensuppe	clear soup with pancake strips	Leberpastete	liver paté
Fleischsalat	sausage salad with onions	Linsensuppe	lentil soup
Fleischsuppe	clear soup and meat dumplings	Melone mit Schinken	melon and ham
		Ochsenschwanzsuppe	oxtail soup
Grüner Salat	mixed green salad	Schnittlauchbrot	chives on bread
Gulaschsuppe	thick soup in imitation of goulash	Sülze	jellied meat loaf
		Suppe	soup
Gurkensalat	cucumber salad	Würzfleisch	supreme of pork
Hühnersuppe	chicken soup	Zwiebelsuppe	onion soup

MEAT AND POULTRY

Aufschnitt	mixed slices of cold sausage	Gyros	kebab
		Hackbraten	mincemeat roast
Blutwurst	blood sausage, similar in taste to the British black pudding	Hackfleisch	mincemeat
		Hase	hare
		Herz	heart
Bockwurst	chunky boiled sausage	Hirn	brains
Bratwurst	grilled sausage	Hirsch, Reh	venison
Broiler	chicken	Huhn, Hähnchen	chicken
Currywurst	sausage served with piquant sauce	Innereien	innards
		Jägerschnitzel	cutlet in mushroom sauce
Eisbein	boiled knuckle of pig	Kanninchen	rabbit
Ente	duck	Kassler Rippchen	smoked and pickled pork chops
Fasan	pheasant		
Fleischpflanzerl	meatball (in Bavaria)	Kotelett	cutlet
Frikadelle	meatball	Krautwickerl	cabbage leaves filled with mincemeat
Froschschenkel	frogs' legs		
Gans	goose	Lamm	lamb
Geschnetzeltes	shredded meat, usually served with rice	Leber	liver
		Leberkäse	baked meatloaf

continued overleaf

continued from previous page

Lunge	lungs	*Schweinebraten*	roast pork
Nieren	kidneys	*Schweinefleisch*	pork
Ochsenschwanz	oxtail	*Schweinehaxe*	grilled knuckle of pig
Pferdefleich	horsemeat	*Spanferkel*	suckling pig
Rahmschnitzel	cutlet in cream sauce	*Speck*	bacon
Rinderroulade	beef olive	*Spiessbraten*	Skewered meat
Rindfleisch	beef	*Truthahn*	turkey
Sauerbraten	braised pickled beef	*Weisswurst*	white herb sausage
Saure Lunge	pickled lungs	*Wiener Schnitzel*	thin pork or veal cutlet in breadcumbs
Schaschlik	diced meat with piquant sauce	*Wild*	wild game
Schinken	ham	*Wildschwein*	wild boar
Schlachtplatte	mix of cured meats	*Wurst*	sausage
Schnecke	snail	*Zigeunerschnitzel*	cutlet in paprika sauce
Schnitzel Natur	uncoated cutlet (usually pork)	*Zunge*	tongue

FISH

Aal	eel	*Kaviar*	caviar	*Schellfisch*	haddock
Forelle	trout	*Krabben*	prawns	*Scholle*	plaice
Goldbarsch	redfish	*Lachs*	salmon	*Schwertfish*	swordfish
Hecht	pike	*Makrele*	mackerel	*Seezunge*	sole
Hering, Matjes	herring	*Muscheln*	mussels	*Skampi*	scampi
Hummer	lobster	*Rotbarsch*	rosefish	*Thunfisch*	tuna
Kabeljau	cod	*Sardellen*	anchovies	*Tintenfisch*	squid
Karpfen	carp	*Sardinen*	sardines	*Zander*	pike-perch

VEGETABLES

Blumenkohl	cauliflower	*Paprika*	green or red peppers
Bohnen	beans	*Pellkartoffeln*	jacket potatoes
Bratkartoffeln	sautée potatoes	*Pilze*	mushrooms
Champignons	button mushrooms	*Pommes frites*	fries
Erbsen	peas	*Reibekuchen*	potato cake
Grüne Bohnen	green beans	*Rosenkohl*	brussels sprouts
Gurke	cucumber	*Rote Rübe*	beetroot
Karotten, Möhren	carrots	*Rotkohl*	red cabbage
Kartoffelbrei	mashed potatoes	*Rübe*	turnip
Kartoffelpuree	creamed potatoes	*Salat*	salad
Kartoffelsalat	potato salad	*Salzkartoffeln*	boiled potatoes
Knoblauch	garlic	*Sauerkraut*	pickled cabbage
Knödel, Kloss	dumpling	*Spargel*	asparagus
Kopfsalat	lettuce	*Tomaten*	tomatoes
Lauche	leeks	*Weisskohl*	white cabbage
Maiskolben	corn on the cob	*Zwiebeln*	onions

make up an irresistible picnic for a modest outlay. Larger cities tend to have a daily indoor version of this, known as the *Markthalle*.

The easiest option for a quick snack, however, is to head for the ubiquitous **Imbiss** stands and shops. In the latter you have the option of eating in or taking away; the price is the same. These indigenous types of snack bar tend to serve a range of sausages, plus meatballs, hamburgers and chips; the better ones have soups, schnitzels, chops and salads as well. Spit-roasted chicken is usually recommendable and very cheap, at around DM5–6/€2.50–3 for half a bird. Mustard is usually available at no extra cost with all dishes, whereas small supplements are often levied for mayonnaise or ketchup. Most Imbiss places

FRUITS

Ananas	pineapple	*Mandarine*	tangerine
Apfel	apple	*Melone*	melon
Aprikose	apricot	*Obstsalat*	fruit salad
Banane	banana	*Orange*	orange
Birne	pear	*Pampelmuse*	grapefruit
Brombeeren	blackberries	*Pfirsich*	peach
Datteln	dates	*Pflaumen*	plums
Erdbeeren	strawberries	*Rosinen*	raisins
Feigen	figs	*Schwarze*	blackcurrants
Himbeeren	raspberries	*Johannisbeeren*	
Johannisbeeren	redcurrants	*Stachelbeeren*	gooseberries
Kirschen	cherries	*Trauben*	grapes
Kompott	stewed fruit or mousse	*Zitrone*	lemon

CHEESES AND DESSERTS

Emmentaler	Swiss Emmental	*Kaiserschmarrn*	shredded pancake served
Käseplatte	mixed selection of cheeses		with powdered sugar,
Schafskäse	sheep's cheese		jam and raisins
Weichkäse	cream cheese	*Käsekuchen*	cheesecake
Ziegenkäse	goat's cheese	*Keks*	biscuit
Apfelstrudel mit	apple strudel with fresh	*Krapfen*	doughnut
Sahne	cream	*Nüsse*	nuts
Berliner	jam doughnut	*Nusskuchen*	nut cake
Dampfnudel,	yeast dumpling, usually	*Obstkuchen*	fruit flan
Germknödel	served hot with vanilla	*Pfannkuchen*	pancake
	sauce	*Schokolade*	chocolate
Eis	ice cream	*Schwarzwälder*	Black Forest gateau
Eisbecher	ice-cream sundae	*Kirschtorte*	
Gebäck	pastries	*Torte*	gateau

COMMON TERMS

art	style of	*hausgemacht*	home-made
blau	rare	*heiss*	hot
eingelegte	pickled	*kalt*	cold
frisch	fresh	*neue deutsche*	German form of *nouvelle*
gebacken	baked	*Küche*	*cuisine*
gebraten	fried, roasted	*paniert*	coated in breadcrumbs,
gedämpft	steamed		then fried
gefüllt	stuffed	*schmoren*	casseroled, stewed
gegrillt	grilled	*vom heissen Stein*	raw meats you cook
gekocht	cooked		yourself on a red-hot
geräuchert	smoked		stone
gutbürgerliche Küche	traditional German cooking		

sell beer, but as many are unlicensed you may be forbidden from consuming it on the premises.

Among the fast-food **chains**, Kochlöffel stands out for cleanliness and good food. The speciality here is spit-roasted chicken; prices compare very favourably with the many American-owned hamburger joints. Another chain with decent food is Wienerwald, but its menu,

set-up and price structure are more comparable to a restaurant than a snack bar. The Bavarian butcher's chain Vincenz Murr sells full main courses to be eaten on your feet, costing DM5–12/€2.50–6; many smaller concerns throughout the country offer a similar service. Virtually the only places outside northern Germany where you can regularly find salt-water **fish** are the shops of the

Nordsee chain. These vary a lot in size and hence choice, and the pre-prepared dishes for consumption on the premises seldom look as appetising as the fish sold for cooking at home. Nonetheless, they are reliable choices for a quick lunch. By far the most innovative and original chain is that run by the Swiss company Mövenpick under the Restaurant Marché logo. Here, fresh market ingredients are the watchwords, whether in the enormous cold buffet selection from which you help yourself, or in the hot grill dishes cooked to order before your eyes. Because of the sheer scale of each operation, they're only to be found in the centres of major cities.

Ethnic snack bars are predominantly Italian, Greek or Turkish. The **pizzerias** are a major boon if you're on a tight budget. Either taking away or eating standing up, prices start at around DM5/€2.50 for a simple tomato and cheese pizza. Most pizzerias also serve pasta dishes, though these are usually less of a bargain. As always, the **kebab** houses adapt their technique to suit the national taste. The *Gyros* or *Döner* is based on real lamb meat and fat and served in bread, generally with tsatziki as a sauce, and costs DM4–6/€2–3.

MEALS AND RESTAURANTS

All **restaurants** display their menus and prices by the door, as well as their *Ruhetag*, the day they are closed. Hot meals are usually served throughout the day, but certainly where it says *durchgehend warme Küche*. The Gaststätte, Gasthaus, Gasthof, Brauhaus or Wirtschaft establishments, which are the nearest equivalents to old-fashioned English inns, mostly belong to a brewery and function as social meeting points, drinking havens and cheap restaurants combined. Their style of cuisine is known as **gutbürgerliche Küche**; this resembles hearty German home cooking (hence the comparatively low prices), and portions are almost invariably generous. Most of these places have a hard core of regular customers who sit at tables marked *Stammtisch*; unless invited to do so, it's not the done thing to sit there. However, don't be surprised if you're expected to share your table with strangers – in all but the poshest of restaurants, customers are often asked to give up free seats at their table at busy times. The bulk of the menu is the same all day long, though some establishments offer two- or three-course lunches at a bargain price. **Standards** are amazingly high: you're far less

likely to be served a dud meal in any German restaurant than in almost any other country.

Starters tend to be fairly unsophisticated – either a salad, pâté or cold meat dish, or, more commonly, soup. Choice for **soup** is fairly restricted, and tends to be based on an adaptation of foreign fare; prices are usually in the range of DM4–8/€2–4. Among the most popular are *Gulaschsuppe*, a liquidized version of the staple Magyar dish (despite often being dignified as "Ungarische", it's not something a Hungarian would recognize); *Bohnensuppe*, which is often quite spicy, and derived from the Serbian model; and *Zwiebelsuppe*, which is a direct copy of the famous French brown-onion soup, usually with floating cheese and croutons. In east Germany, you'll also find *Soljanka*, a spicy Ukrainian soup with sliced sausages. More authentically German are the clear soups with dumplings, of which the Bavarian *Leberknödelsuppe* is the best known.

Main courses in all German restaurants are overwhelmingly based on **pork**. As a rule, this is of noticeably higher quality than in Britain, and the variety in taste wrought by using different sauces (it's quite common to find a choice of up to twenty different types) and unexpected parts of the animal means that the predominance of the pig is far less tedious than might be supposed. As an alternative to the ubiquitous Schnitzel, try *Schweinehaxe* or *Eisbein*, respectively the grilled (or roasted) and boiled versions of pig's knuckles. **Sausages** regularly feature on the menu, with distinct regional varieties.

Whereas a main-course pork-based dish is likely to cost DM20/€10 or less, one with **beef** will cost a fair bit more. As is the case with snack bars, **chicken** dishes are comparatively cheap. Many restaurants have a **game** menu, with more exotic poultry such as duck or goose, along with venison, rabbit and hare; prices then tend to be DM25/€12.50 or more.

Outside northern Germany, where a wide variety of newly caught salt-water **fish** is readily available, you'll probably have to be content with fresh-water varieties if you want to eat fish – except in June and July, when restaurants all over the country offer special menus featuring herring (*Matjes*). Trout is by far the most popular fresh-water fish, though there's obviously a greater choice in places close to lakes and rivers. Where salt-water fish is generally available, the unfamiliar rosefish (*Rotbarsch*) – similar in taste to whiting – is generally the most reliable. Oddly enough, you're far more likely to encounter a choice of fresh fish in east Germany, where there remain many privatized survivors from the long-established Gastmahl des Meeres chain.

The main-course price invariably includes **vegetables**. Potatoes are usually sautéed, puréed or made into a cold salad. Boiled potatoes, often garnished with parsley, are increasingly popular, but baking, mashing and oven-roasting find little favour. **Dumplings** made from potatoes and flour are a common alternative. Cabbage is the other popular accompaniment – the green variety is pickled as **Sauerkraut**, whereas the red is normally cooked with apple as *Apfelrotkohl*. **Salads** of lettuce, cucumber, beetroot, carrots and gherkins are often included as a side-dish. From April to late June, when **asparagus** is in season, many restaurants have a special menu (*Spargelkarte*) of dishes – both vegetarian and carnivore – with this vegetable as a key ingredient. The noodles known as *Spätzle* and *Maultaschen* are a distinctive component of Swabian cuisine, occasionally adopted elsewhere.

Because so many Germans go to cafés (see p.40) for their daily helping of cakes, **desserts** in restaurants are an anticlimax, where they exist at all. The Bavarian *Dampfnudel* is one of the few distinctive dishes; otherwise there's just the usual selection of fresh and stewed fruits, cheeses and ice creams.

Germany has a wide variety of **ethnic restaurants**. The density of these is very much in line with the general Gastarbeiter influx, and there's a heavy southern European bias. Of these, the Italian are generally the best; there are also plenty offering Balkan, Greek and Turkish cuisines. Chinese restaurants are also ubiquitous and usually very consistent, with most offering good-value set lunches. On the other hand, Indian and Thai food is often toned down, largely because few Germans care for hot spices.

VEGETARIAN FOOD

Vegetarians will find Germany less than ideal – most menus are almost exclusively for carnivores, and even an innocent-sounding item like tomato soup might have small chunks of bacon floating around in it. However, it's usually easy enough to find such staples as salads, omelettes, pancakes, pasta and pizzas. Most cities also tend to have at least one specialist vegetarian and wholefood restaurant, and these are listed throughout the *Guide*. Many have self-service buffets where you pay for the items chosen according to their weight.

| *Ich bin Vegetarier* | I am a vegetarian |
| *Haben Sie etwas ohne Fleisch?* | Do you have anything without meat? |

DRINKING

The division between eating and drinking establishments in Germany is less demarcated than in the English-speaking world. Despite their inevitable connotations with beer and wine, the Brauhäuser and Weinstuben inevitably double as restaurants: the former usually offer a full range of *gutbürgerliche Küche*, whereas the latter tend to have shortish menus of rather lighter fare. There are also some purely drinking dens, generally known as Kneipen. Apart from beer and wine, there's nothing very distinctive about German beverages, save for Apfelwein, a variant of cider. The most popular spirits are the fiery *Korn* and after-dinner liqueurs, which are mostly fruit-based. Both hot and soft drinks are broadly the same as in Britain.

BEER

For serious **beer** drinkers, Germany is the ultimate paradise. Wherever you go, you can be sure of getting a product made locally, often brewed in a distinctive style. The country has well over 1200 breweries, with over half the total in Bavaria alone. By far the densest concentration is in Upper Franconia, where the traditional institution of the Hausbrauerei, a combination of a small brewery and a pub-restaurant (often offering accommodation as well) still survives in force. All German breweries voluntarily adhere to the *Reinheitsgebot* (Purity Law) of 1516, which

DRINKS GLOSSARY

Apfelsaft	apple juice	*Milchshake*	milk shake
Apfelwein	apple wine	*Mineralwasser*	mineral water
Bier	beer	*Orangensaft*	orange juice
Federweisser	new wine	*Roséwein*	rosé wine
Glühwein	hot mulled wine	*Rotwein*	red wine
Grog	hot rum	*Sekt*	sparkling wine
Herrengedeck	cocktail of beer and	*Tee*	tea
	Sekt	*Tomatensaft*	tomato juice
Kaffee	coffee	*Traubensaft*	grape juice
Kaffee mit Milch	coffee with milk	*Trinkschokolade*	drinking chocolate
Kakao	cocoa	*Wasser*	water
Korn	rye spirit	*Weinbrand*	brandy
Kräutertee,	herbal tea	*Weinschorle*	spritzer
Pflanzentee		*Weisswein*	white wine
Likör	liqueur	*Zitronenlimonade*	lemonade
Milch	milk	*Zitronentee*	lemon tea

lays down stringent standards of production, including a ban on chemical susbtitutes. Despite a growing trend towards takeovers and amalgamations, particularly among large and medium-sized brewers, the effect on consumer choice has been minimal. Often, production has been allowed to continue as before in different locations, though in others the brewing for several different labels has been consolidated in a single site. Another positive aspect has been the revival

BEER GLOSSARY

Alt	Literally, any beer made according to an old formula; particularly associated with the dark brown top-fermented barley malt beer of Düsseldorf (also made in Mönchengladbach and Münster)	*Doppelbock*	Extra-strong *Bock*, usually made specially for festivals
		Dunkel	Generic name for any dark beer
		Eisbock	"Ice beer", particularly associated with Kulmbach; the freezing process concentrates the alcohol
Altbierbowle	Glass of *Alt* with addition of a fresh fruit punch	*Export*	Originally, beers made to be exported. Now used to describe a premium beer, or in association with the brewing style of Dortmund, stronger than a *Pils* and lying midway between dry and sweet in taste
Berliner Weisse	Wheat beer from Berlin, usually served in a bowl-shaped glass, and with the addition of woodruff (*mit Grün*) or raspberry essence (*mit Schuss*)		
Bernstein	Amber-coloured beer		
Bock	Light or dark strong beer, originally from Einbeck, but particularly popular in Bavaria, containing at least 6.25 percent alcohol	*Fassbier, Schankbier*	Draught beer
		Flaschenbier	Bottled beer
		Hausbrauerei/ Gasthausbrauerei	"House brewery" (pub where beer is brewed on the premises)
Braunbier	Generic name for brown beer	*Hefe-Weizen*	Wheat beer given strong yeast boost

of long-forgotten techniques, often put into practice in new-generation Hausbrauereien. Usually subsidiaries of larger local or regional breweries, these are springing up all the time, and are deservedly very popular, often being the trendiest spot in town.

More generally, there's an encouraging continuation of old-fashioned **top-fermented** brewing styles. Until the nineteenth century, all beers were made this way, but the interaction of the yeasts with a hot atmosphere meant that brewing had to be suspended during the summer. It was the Germans who discovered that the yeast sank to the foot of the container when stored under icy conditions; thereafter, brewing took on a more scientific nature, and yeast strains were bred so that beer could be **bottom-fermented**, thus allowing its production all year round. The top-fermentation process, on the other hand, allows for a far greater individuality in the taste (often characterized by a distinct fruitiness), and can, of course, now be used throughout the year, thanks to modern temperature controls. All wheat beers use this process.

A quick beer tour of Germany would inevitably begin in **Munich**, which occupies third place in the world production league table. The city's beer gardens and beer halls are the most famous drinking dens in the country, offering a wide variety of premier products, from dark lagers through tart *Weizens* to powerful *Bocks*. Nearby **Freising** boasts the oldest brewery in the world, dating back to the eleventh century. In Upper Franconia, distinctive traditions are found in **Bamberg** (national champion for beer consumption per resident), **Kulmbach** and **Bayreuth**.

In Baden-Württemberg, the local brews are sweeter and softer, in order to appeal to palates accustomed to wine; **Stuttgart** and **Mannheim** are the main production centres. Central Germany is even more strongly wedded to wine, though there are odd pockets of resistance. Indeed, **Frankfurt**, the German cider metropolis, also has, in Binding, one of the country's largest breweries.

Further north, where it's too cold to grow grapes, the beer tradition returns with a vengeance. **Cologne** holds the world record for the number of city breweries, all of which produce

Hell, Helles	Generic names for light beers	*Münchener*	Brown-coloured lager; a style pioneered in Munich
Hofbräu	Brewery formerly belonging to a court; that in Munich is the most famous	*Ökobier*	Organically produced beer
		Pils	Bottom-fermented golden-coloured beer with a very high hop content
Klosterbräu	Brewery attached to a monastery		
Kölsch	Top-fermented pale-coloured beer peculiar to Cologne, invariably served in small glasses	*Radler, Alsterwasser*	Shandy
		Rauchbier	Aromatic beer from Bamberg made from smoked malt
Kellerbier, Kräusen, Zwickelbier	Unfiltered beers, each brewed to a slightly different formula	*Roggenbier*	Dark beer made with rye
		Schwarzbier	Generic name for black beer
Kristall-Weizen	Sparkling brew made from wheat: the beer answer to champagne	*Spezial*	Name given by breweries to their premium product, or to that made for special events
Leichtbier	Low-alcohol beer		
Maibock	Pale, high premium *Bock*, specially made to celebrate spring	*Starkbier*	Generic name for strong beer
		Urquell	Name used to identify the original of a particular brewing style
Malz	Unfermented black malt beer, similar to sweet stout		
		Vollbier	Standard medium-strong beer
Märzenbier	Strong beer made in March, but stored for later consumption; particularly associated with Munich's *Oktoberfest*	*Weihnachtsbier*	Special strong beer made for Christmas
		Weissbier, Weisse	Pale-coloured wheat beer
		Weizen	Light or dark wheat beer

the jealously guarded *Kölsch*. **Düsseldorf** again has its own distinctive brew, the dark *Alt*. **Dortmund** even manages to beat Munich for the title of European capital of beer production, and is particularly associated with *Export*. Equally good are the delicate brews of the **Sauerland** and **Siegerland**, made using the soft local spring water. One of these, the heavily promoted *Pils* produced by Warsteiner, is now Germany's best-selling beer, albeit with less than 5 percent of the total market.

Hannover, **Bremen** and **Hamburg** all have long brewing pedigrees, with many of their products widely available abroad. The most distinctive beers of the northernmost Länder, however, are those of **Einbeck** (the original home of *Bock*) and **Jever**. In contrast to these heady brews is the acidic *Weisse* of **Berlin**, which is completely transformed into a refreshing summer thirst-quencher by the addition of a dash of syrup.

East German brews are far less exciting, with the notable exception of *Köstrizer*, an outstanding black beer made in **Bad Köstritz** in the outskirts of Gera. **Leipzig** has managed a revival of its varied brewing tradition since the fall of Communism, but elsewhere there's seldom anything other than the standard fare of light beers and local variations of *Pils*, of which the best are from **Radeberg** near Dresden and those made from the soft water of the **Vogtland**.

WINE

Many people's knowledge of German wine starts and ends with *Liebfraumilch*, the medium-sweet easy-drinking wine. Sadly, its success has obscured the quality of other German wines, especially those made from the Riesling grape, and it's worth noting that the *Liebfraumilch* drunk in Germany tastes nothing like the bilge swilled back abroad.

The vast majority of German wine is white since the northern climate doesn't ripen red grapes regularly. If after a week or so you're pining for a glass of red, try a *Spätburgunder* (the *Pinot Noir* of Burgundy).

First step in any exploration of German wine should be to understand what's on the label: the predilection for Gothic script and gloomy martial crests makes this an uninviting prospect, but the division of categories is intelligent and helpful – if at first a little complex.

Like most EU wine, German wine is divided into two broad categories: *Tafelwein* ("table wine", for which read "cheap plonk") and *Qualitätswein* ("quality wine"), equivalent to the French *Appellation Contrôlée*.

TAFELWEIN

Tafelwein can be a blend of wines from any EU country; *Deutscher Tafelwein* must be 100 percent German. *Landwein* is a superior *Tafelwein*, equivalent to the French *Vin de Pays* and medium dry. Like all German wines, *Tafelwein* can be *trocken* (dry) or *halb-trocken* (medium dry).

QUALITÄTSWEIN

There are two basic subdivisions of *Qualitätswein*: **Qba** (*Qualitätswein eines bestimmten Anbaugebietes*) and **Qmp** (*Qualitätswein mit Prädikat*). *Qba* wines come from thirteen delimited regions and must pass an official tasting and analysis. *Qmp* wines are further divided into six grades:

Kabinett The first and lightest style.

Spätlese Must come from late-picked grapes, which result in riper flavours.

Auslese Made from a selected bunch of grapes, making a concentrated medium-sweet wine. If labelled as a *Trocken*, the wine will have lots of body and weight.

Beerenauslese Wine made from late-harvested, individually picked grapes. A rare wine, made only in the very best years, and extremely sweet.

Trockenbeerenauslese *Trocken* here means dry in the sense that the grapes have been left on the vine until some of the water content has evaporated. As with *Beerenauslese*, each grape will be individually picked. This is a very rare wine which is intensely sweet and concentrated.

Eiswein Literally "ice wine", this is made from Beerenauslese grapes – a hard frost freezes the water content of the grape, concentrating the juice. The flavour of an *Eiswein* is remarkably fresh tasting, due to its high acidity.

GRAPE VARIETIES

These often appear on wine labels and are a handy guide to judging a wine's flavour.

Riesling Germany's best grape variety. It can have a floral aroma when young, is often "honeyed" when ripe and develops interesting bouquets after five to seven years in the bottle.

Gewürztraminer *Gewürz* means spicy, and the wine has an intense aromatic nose, likened by some people to lychees and by others to Turkish delight.

Müller-Thurgau The most widely planted grape in Germany. Its flavour is less distinguished than Riesling but is generally fruity, has less acidity and a grapey, Muscat taste.

Silvaner Yields a fairly neutral wine, quite full-bodied and often blended with more aromatic varieties.

WINE REGIONS

Particularly at the *Qualitätswein* level, regional variations in climate produce markedly differing styles of wine.

Ahr Small area on both sides of the Ahr valley, devoted primarily to *Spätburgunder* and *Portugieser* red wines.

Baden The most southerly wine-growing region, extending almost continuously from Heidelberg to the Swiss border, with another area around the Bodensee. Its warm climate allows French grape varieties to be grown, and the majority of the wines are dry in flavour.

Franken (Franconia) Largely based around the Main valley, this produces high-quality wines which are easy to identify, as they always come in a distinctively dumpy, round-shouldered bottle known as a *Bocksbeutel*.

Hessische Bergstrasse (Hessian Mountain Road) The vineyards here are mainly minute operations run on a part-time basis producing wines similar to those of the more famous Rheingau.

Mittelrhein (Middle Rhine) Although the vineyards on the steep slopes of the Rhine gorge are

among Germany's most famous tourist sights, the wines, which are earthier than those of the nearby Rheingau, are mainly consumed locally.

Mosel-Saar-Ruwer The steep banks of the River Mosel and two of its tributaries enable the vines to catch long hours of sun, thus allowing grapes to ripen, despite the northerly latitude. Much Riesling is grown in the slatey soil, producing elegant wines in the best years. Thanks to a heavy export volume, they have come to be regarded as Germany's most characteristic wines.

Nahe Both geographically and stylistically between the Mosel-Saar-Ruwer and the Rheingau, this is a relatively small region whose acidic, fruity wines are often underrated.

Rheingau On the sloping northern bank of the Rhine as it flows between Hochheim and Assmannshausen, this is a prestigious region that produces wines slightly fuller than those from the Mosel region. The reds in particular are considered to be among the country's finest.

Rhein-Hessen (Rhine-Hesse) Germany's main producer of *Liebfraumilch* from large plantations of Müller-Thurgau and Silvaner grapes.

Rheinpfalz (Palatinate) A southern wine region that produces full-bodied, ripe wines, chiefly *Liebfraumilch* and *Riesling*.

Saale-Unstrut Around Naumburg is the country's most northerly wine-growing area, best known for its *Sekt*.

Sachsen (Saxony) *Sekt* is likewise a speciality of the vineyards in the vicinity of Meissen, the easternmost of the wine-growing regions.

Württemberg Centred on the Stuttgart conurbation, this is one of those regions characterized by smallholdings, which are best known for their red *Trollinger* wines.

COMMUNICATIONS

As one of the world's largest and most successful economies, it almost goes without saying that Germany has excellent postal and telecommunications services and a lively media, though its television coverage has to be regarded as something of a weak link.

POST OFFICES

Post offices (*Postämter*) are normally open Monday to Friday 8am to 6pm and Saturday 8am to noon. A restricted range of services is available beyond these hours at offices in or beside main train stations in large cities. Outbound mail should reach the UK within a few days, North America in one to two weeks and Australia over two weeks.

Poste restante services are available at the main post office (*Hauptpost*) in any given town (see listings in the *Guide* for addresses in the major cities): collect it from the counter marked *Postlagernde Sendungen* (always remember to take your passport). It's worth asking anyone writing to you to use this designation as well as, or instead of, poste restante. Incredible as it may seem in view of the country's reputation for superefficiency, many German post offices don't understand the international term and are likely to return a letter to the sender marked "address unknown". Bear in mind also that mail is usually only held for a couple of weeks. If you want your mail to be **registered**, ask for it to be sent *einschreiben*. **Fax** services are available at large post offices, usually at more favourable rates than in copy shops or hotels.

TELEPHONES

Telephoning is simple and most kiosks are equipped with basic instructions in several languages, including English. You can **call abroad** from all but those clearly marked "National". Calling **rates**, other than to some long-haul international destinations, vary according to the time of day. Within Germany, the first cheap period begins at 6pm, the next at 9pm, the last at 2am; within the EU, rates are reduced between 6pm and 8am. Some boxes are equipped with a ringing symbol to indicate that you can be called back on that phone. The major international codes are given in the box below; when using them, remember to omit the initial zero from the subscriber's number.

For **local calls**, you currently need to insert a minimum of DM0.20, which will last for a minimum of 90 seconds at the peak daytime rate. In the *Guide*, local codes are included with each telephone number.

At the time of writing, coins of DM0.10, DM1 and DM5 are accepted; only wholly unused ones are returned. However, a large percentage of pay phones in Germany accept **phone cards** only. These cost DM12/€6 or DM50/€25 from post offices or newsagents, and are well worth buying, especially if you're intending to call home. Another option is to use the **direct phone service** facility of the main post office: a phone booth will be allocated to you from the counter marked *Fremdgespräche*, which is also where you pay once you've finished.

INTERNATIONAL CALLS

From Germany dial ☎00 + IDD country code + area code minus first 0 + subscriber number

From Britain and Ireland to Germany dial ☎00 49 + area code minus first 0 + number

From North America to Germany dial ☎011 49 + area code minus first 0 + number

From Australia or New Zealand dial ☎0011 49 + area code minus first 0 + number

IDD CODES

Australia ☎ 61	Britain ☎44
Canada☎ 1	Ireland ☎ 353
New Zealand ☎ 64	US ☎1

USEFUL NUMBERS WITHIN GERMANY

Operator	☎03
Directory enquiries	☎11833
International directory enquiries	☎11834
Operator wake-up call	☎01141
Ambulance	☎112
Fire	☎112
Police	☎110

EMAIL AND THE INTERNET

The Germans have enthusiastically embraced the Internet as the recent proliferation of Web sites testifies. However, the institution of the **cyber-café** – which in so many other countries has been the principal means by which travellers maintain contact with home – has failed to secure much of a foothold. Such cafés do exist, especially in the larger cities, and are listed in the *Guide*, but their continued existence cannot be taken for granted, as many others have already come and gone. **Department stores**, curiously enough, are the most reliable places to obtain Internet access: the Karstadt chain, which has branches throughout the country, is particularly good in this respect, usually charging around DM5/€2.50 for thirty minutes. A small but increasing number of **hotels** in all price categories are wired up to the Net, and some of these allow guests to surf and send emails free of charge.

MEDIA

Germany is well supplied with **British newspapers**: in the larger cities it's relatively easy to pick up most of the London-printed editions on the same day, with the *Financial Times* having a particularly wide distribution. Some **US papers**, especially the *International Herald Tribune* and *USA Today*, are also readily obtainable.

With a few exceptions, **German newspapers** tend to be highly regionalized, mixing local and international news. Only the liberal *Frankfurter Rundschau* and Munich's *Süddeutsche Zeitung* are distributed much outside their own areas. Berlin produces two reputable organs: the *Tagespiegel*, a good left-wing read, and the

Greenish/alternative *Tageszeitung*, universally known as the *Taz*. Of the national daily papers, the two bestsellers come from the presses of the late, unlamented Axel Springer: *Die Welt* is a right-wing heavyweight, and the tabloid *Bild* a reactionary, sleazy and sensationalist rag. The *Frankfurter Allgemeine* is again conservative, appealing particularly to the business community, but follows a politically independent line.

Germany has more **magazines** than any other country in Europe. The leftish weekly news and current affairs magazine *Der Spiegel* is the most in-depth magazine for political analysis and investigative journalism. Unless your German is fluent, though, it's a heavy and often difficult read. Further to the right, *Die Zeit* is a wider-ranging (and to learners of the language, easier-to-read) alternative; *Focus* is another influential weekly with a conservative slant. *Stern* is the most popular current affairs magazine, though its prestige took a tumble following its publication of the forged Hitler diaries and, more than a decade later, has still not entirely recovered.

German **television** does not show the country at its best, though it has an undeniably varied output. Some of the more serious discussion programmes have a presentation style that is still reminiscent of the 1960s and early 1970s and might as well be broadcast on radio. Yet there are also plenty of derivatives of the banal game and chat shows characteristic of present-day American and British daytime TV, while in the late evenings pornography that leaves nothing to the imagination is often broadcast. There are two main national channels, **ARD** and **ZDF**, plus regional stations run by individual Länder and a number of commercial channels. The Austrian, Swiss, Dutch, Danish and Polish networks can be picked up in the areas they border. Many houses and hotels are equipped with **satellite** or **cable TV**; in such cases, you'll have access to a choice of British and American channels: CNN is particularly ubiquitous.

The only **English-speaking radio** channels are the BBC World Service (90.2FM), the British Forces station BFBS (98.8FM) and the dire American Armed Forces radio station AFN (87.6FM), which combines American music charts with military news. These should continue broadcasting for at least as long as the troops remain.

BUSINESS HOURS

Shopping hours in western Germany were strictly curtailed by a law passed in the 1950s in a bid to counter national workaholic tendencies. This measure remains in force, modified only by a limited reform, allowing slightly longer opening times, introduced in 1996. It is not strictly applied in Berlin and the five eastern Länder which formerly comprised the GDR.

All **shops** must close at 8pm on weekdays and at 4pm on Saturdays. In practice, many still adhere to the old deadlines of 6.30pm and 2pm, extending the latter only on the first Saturday of the month, the so-called *Langer Samstag*. Shops are closed all day Sunday (except for bakers, who may open between 11am and 3pm). **Pharmacists** can extend their opening hours on a strict basis of rotation. The only other exceptions are shops attached to filling stations and in and around train stations, which generally do stay open late and at weekends.

It has long been the custom in Germany for **museums** and **historic monuments** to close their doors to the public on Monday, unless it is a public holiday. Traditionally, there have only been a few exceptions to this rule, some of which take another day off instead. However, the frustration to visitors caused by this blanket Monday shutdown has at last been recognized in Bavaria, where in 2000 the traditional day of closure was abolished for many of the state-owned castles and palaces as part of a general extension of opening hours. It is to be hoped that this experiment will become permanent, and taken up elsewhere. Mondays apart, opening times (which are detailed in the *Guide*) are usually more generous than in other countries, with lunchtime closures rare. Many major civic museums are additionally open on at least one evening per week.

There's rarely any difficulty gaining access to **churches**, hence opening times are only listed in the *Guide* for ancillary attractions such as treasuries or towers, or when set times are both limited and rigidly enforced. Bear in mind that churches used for Protestant worship (predominantly in Swabia, Hesse, northern Germany and the former GDR) tend to keep office hours, whereas those in Catholic areas usually open earlier and close later.

Finally, it is worth noting that many sites of interest are open for shorter hours in winter – which in Germany is considered to be November to February, inclusive, plus any or all of March, April and October. Where opening or closing times differ only by these distinct **seasonal variations**, we have indicated these in the *Guide* with a slash: for example, Tues–Sun 10am–4/6pm.

FESTIVALS AND PUBLIC HOLIDAYS

Germany probably has more annual festivals than any other European country, with almost every village having its own summer fair, as well as a rich mixture of Christian and pagan festivals that have merged over the ages to fill the whole calendar.

These tend to flourish most in Bavaria, Baden-Württemberg and the Rhineland. In the former GDR, there are far fewer festivals – Communism is by no means entirely to blame for this, the roots lying in the puritanism which has long characterized the area. Since the *Wende*, a fair number of festivals have been initiated or reinstated.

The most famous German festival is undoubtedly the **Oktoberfest** in Munich, but **Carnival** and the **Christmas fairs** are other annual highlights, and take place all over the country. There's also a wealth of **music festivals**, ranging from opera seasons to open-air jazz and rock concerts. Main events are listed in the *Guide*, but below is a general overview.

January is a quiet month, though there are various events associated with the **Carnival season**, particularly the proclamation of the "Carnival King". Climax of the season comes in **February** or **March**, seven weeks before the date nominated for Easter. The Rhenish *Karneval* tends to have rather more gusto than its Bavarian counterpart, known as *Fasching*. Cologne has the most spectacular celebrations (detailed in the *Guide* on p.554–5), followed by those of Mainz and Düsseldorf; in each case, the *Rosenmontag* parade is the highpoint. Baden-Württemberg's *Fastnet* is a distinctive, very pagan, carnival tradition, best experienced in Rottweil. Another old pagan rite is the *Schäfertanz* held in Rothenburg in March and repeated on several subsequent occasions throughout the year. During Holy Week, and particularly on **Easter Day** (variable date in March/April), colourful church services are held throughout the country, particularly in rural Catholic areas. Another important **April** festival is the witches' sabbath of *Walpurgisnacht*, celebrated throughout the Harz region on the 30th of the month.

May marks the start of many of the **summer festivals**. Costume plays such as the *Rattenfängerspiele* in Hameln begin regular weekend performances, while there are classical concerts in historic buildings, notably the Schlosstheater in Schwetzingen. Every ten years (next in 2010), the famous *Passionspiele* in

PUBLIC HOLIDAYS

New Year's Day Jan 1

Epiphany Jan 6; only honoured in Bavaria and Baden-Württemberg

Good Friday

Easter Monday

May Day May 1

Ascension Day

Whit Monday

Corpus Christi early or mid-June; honoured only in Baden-Württemberg, Bavaria, Hesse, Rhineland-Palatinate, North Rhine-Westphalia and Saarland

Feast of the Assumption Aug 15; honoured only in Bavaria and Saarland

Day of German Unity Oct 3

All Saints' Day Nov 1; honoured only in Bavaria, Baden-Württemberg, Rhineland-Palatinate, North Rhine-Westphalia and Saarland

Christmas Dec 25 and 26

Oberammergau begins its run. On a lighter note, there's the *Stabenfest* in Nördlingen. **Whitsun** (variable date in May/June) sees distinctive religious festivals in many towns. On the same weekend, there are two celebrated reconstructions of historic events – the *Meistertrunk* drama in Rothenburg and the *Kuchen- und Brunnenfest* in Schwäbisch Hall. Shortly afterwards, *Corpus Christi* is celebrated in Catholic areas, and is best experienced in Cologne or Bamberg.

June sees important **classical music festivals**, with the *Bach-Woche* during the second weekend of the month in Lüneburg, the *Händel-Festspiele* in Göttingen and Halle, the *Schumann-Woche* in Zwickau and the *Europäische Wochen* in Passau, while there's a big festival of all kinds of music held under canvas in Freiburg. Throughout northern Germany, the shooting season is marked by *Schützenfeste*, the largest being Hannover's. Bad Wimpfen's *Talmarkt*, which begins at the end of the month, is a fair which can trace its history back a thousand years.

July is a particularly busy festival month, with summer fairs and both **wine** and **beer festivals** opening up every week; pick of the latter is that in Kulmbach. Dinkelsbühl's *Kinderzeche* and Ulm's *Schwörmontag* are the most famous folklore events at this time. The Bayreuth *Opernfest*, exclusively devoted to Wagner, begins its month-long run during late July, but note that all tickets are put on sale a year in advance and immediately snapped up. A more wide-ranging *Opernfest* takes place in Munich around the same time.

August is the main month for colourful displays of fireworks and illuminations, such as the *Schlossfest* in Heidelberg and *Der Rhein in Flammen* in Koblenz. There are a host of *Weinfeste* during the month in the Rhine-Mosel area, notably those in Rüdesheim and Mainz, while Straubing's *Gäubodenfest* is one of the country's largest beer festivals. Other important events at this time are the *Plärrer* city fair in Augsburg, the *Mainfest* in Frankfurt and the *Zissel* folk festival in Kassel.

Paradoxically, Munich's renowned *Oktoberfest* actually takes place mostly in **September** – it usually starts on the second last Saturday, but can be the third last (see box on p.89). This month sees many of the most bacchanalian festivals, such as Heilbronn's *Weindorf* and Bad Cannstatt's *Volksfest*. **October** sees things quietening down, though there's still the odd *Weinfest* in the Rhineland, along with the *Freimarkt* folk festival in Bremen, while in the Alpine region there are a number of religious festivals with an equestrian component; the *Colomansfest* in Schwangau is the most famous of these. In **November**, there's the month-long *Hamburger Dom* fair in Hamburg, while the *Martinsfest* on the 10th/11th of the month is celebrated in northern Baden and the Rhineland, most notably in Düsseldorf.

Finally, **December** is the month of the Christmas market (variably known as *Christkindelsmarkt* or *Weihnachtsmarkt*), which features stalls selling handmade goods of all kinds, from toys and leatherware to sweets and biscuits. Practically every town in the country has one; the most enjoyable are those, such as the ones at Nürnberg and Augsburg, which are most faithful to tradition.

SPORTS

Sports occupy a central position in German life: indeed it was the Germans who were chiefly responsible for developing sport towards its present key role in modern international society. This began with the introduction of gymnastics into schools as a means of pre-military training during the Napoleonic wars. It continued in an overtly political way with Hitler's exploitation of the 1936 Olympic Games and the GDR's nurturing – at great cost and by dubious means – of a sporting elite as a means of gaining international prestige. Facilities for both spectators and participants remain excellent in both parts of the united Germany, which seems likely to maintain its current leading position in a wide variety of sports, while doing its utmost to shed sinister undertones of the past.

Kaiserslautern, Bayer Leverkusen, Borussia Dortmund, and Schalke 04 – are based in industrial towns. Other well-known clubs are Werder Bremen, Hamburger SV, Hertha Berlin, FC Köln and VfB Stuttgart. Erstwhile GDR teams have struggled badly since unification, with only the hitherto unfashionable Hansa Rostock managing to hold down a regular place in the top flight. In 2000, it was joined in the elite division by an even more unlikely ex-GDR success story, Energie Cottbus, who pipped the venerable **Borussia Mönchengladbach**, once one of Europe's top teams, for the final promotion spot on the last day of the season. Among the erstwhile GDR sides now reduced to amateur status is **Dynamo Berlin** (now FC Berlin), the Stasi-sponsored outfit whose connections were a significant factor in its ten consecutive championship triumphs.

FOOTBALL

Football is the nearest Germany comes to having a national sport. The West German team's victory in the 1990 World Cup equalled the record (since surpassed by Brazil) of three wins in the competition while marking the end of separate representation for the two German states. Failure to produce a successful national team was always recognized as the biggest failure of the GDR's sports policy, though on the one occasion the two German states met in a tournament – in the 1974 World Cup – the East Germans scored what proved to be a hollow victory, as their victims subsequently went on to lift the trophy.

The **Bundesliga** elite division of eighteen clubs is fiercely competitive. As three teams are relegated each season, even some of the better-known names are liable to find themselves out of the top flight for a period. The German style of play, mirroring the national character, tends to be based on well-organized, methodical teamwork, rather than on the individual brilliance favoured in Latin countries. League matches are normally held on Saturday afternoons; European Cup games are usually on Wednesday evenings.

By far the most famous team is **Bayern München**, whose record down the years entitles it to be ranked among the world's top clubs. Given the game's working-class roots, it's not surprising that many of the other leading clubs –

TENNIS

Tennis has been a real German obsession ever since 1985, when the 17-year-old **Boris Becker** blasted all his opponents off the court to become the first unseeded and youngest-ever men's singles champion at Wimbledon. He did not quite fulfil his early promise, winning just five further Grand Slam tournaments – a smaller haul than someone of his talent and longevity might have expected. Nonetheless, he inspired a whole new generation of German players, one of whom, Michael Stich, became Wimbledon champion in 1991, but was thereafter persistently dogged by injury. Even more significant was the steamrolling success of **Steffi Graf**, who won all four Grand Slam tournaments at the age of 19 in 1988. For two years she carried an "invincible" tag, and although her form then fluctuated for several years, she was virtually unbeatable in 1996, by which time her career total of Grand Slam singles titles had risen to 21, the second highest on the all-time list. However, a spate of injuries in 1997 set her world ranking, never lower than no. 2 over the previous decade, into freefall. Against all the odds, she came back to win the French Open in 1999, leaving her just two short of equalling the Grand Slam record, but an unexpected defeat in the Wimbledon final a few weeks later prompted her immediate retirement. This brought a golden age of tennis in Germany to an end: the country now lacks a woman player likely to challenge for a Grand Slam title, and is left to pin future hopes on a small group of men who may or may not prove capable of doing so. Success-starved German tennis fans have meanwhile "adopted" the Brazilian Gustavo Kuerten, winner of the inaugral men's championship race in 2000, as his German ancestry means he has dual nationality.

Despite the leading position Germany has enjoyed in the game over the past two decades, the **tournaments** staged there are only second-string events on the international circuit. In early May, the Citizens' Cup for women is held in Hamburg; the German Open for men is held in the same city the next week, with the women's version following later that month in Berlin. Stuttgart hosts a men's event in October; Leipzig has a women's event at the same time.

ATHLETICS

The sport of **athletics** has had more than its share of controversy in recent years, and nowhere has that been more manifest than in Germany. Though West Germany did once in a while produce an outstanding individual athlete, it could never match the consistency of the GDR, which reaped a massive crop of golds at every Olympics; in women's events especially, it often ranked as the best team in the world. This consistency was always dogged by allegations of drug-taking, and it is now absolutely indubitable that the athletes were indeed specially "manufactured" by sports scientists using every means at their disposal. This huge state-sponsored scheme was in an altogether different league from the many cases of individual drug cheats (many of whom were never caught) in the free world. It subsequently came to haunt the combined German team, as witnessed by the disgrace of the star ex-GDR sprinter Kathrin Krabbe and others. To add to German discomfiture, there has been a growing demand from aggrieved rivals for all athletes who competed under the GDR flag to be stripped of their medals, with these being awarded instead to whoever finished immediately behind them.

The main annual grand prix **events** are all in the former West, with meets in early September in Cologne, Berlin and Koblenz.

OTHER SPORTS

Main venues for **motor sports** are Hockenheim near Heidelberg (where the German Formula 1 Grand Prix is held each July) and the venerable Nürburgring (which regained its status as a front-line venue in 1995, and has since been used for both the Luxembourg and European Grand Prix). The leading **equestrian events** are held consecutively in Hamburg and Aachen in June, while the celebrated dressage displays in Celle take place in September and October. Germany's **horse-racing** calendar is dominated by the spring and autumn season at Iffezheim near Baden-Baden and by the Derby week in Hamburg in late June.

WINTER SPORTS

From December to February, **winter sports** competitions, many associated with the skiing World Cup, are held in the southern part of the country. The main venues are Garmisch-Partenkirchen and Oberstdorf in Bavaria, and the Black Forest resorts of Todtmoos, Todtnau, Furtwangen and Schonach.

The German Alps offer some very attractive ski resorts, often overlooked in the rush to get to Austria, Switzerland and France. Everyone has heard of **Garmisch-Partenkirchen** (720–2966m), if only because of the 1936 Olympic runs still used by many professionals. Unfortunately it's an expensive – though well-equipped – resort. For equally excellent facilities, plenty of runs and lifts, affordable prices and a beautiful setting, **Oberstdorf** (700–2224m) is undoubtedly the all-round winner. Other, smaller resorts, which are high on picturesque views and ideally suited to novice and medium skiers, are **Bayrischzell** (800–1724m), **Mittenwald** (750–2385m), **Berchtesgaden** (550–1800m) and **Schliersee** (800–1693m). These are all traditional resorts, each with quite a few runs, good accommodation and plenty of activities other than skiing available. Families are especially well catered for, with resident ski schools to take care of the kids.

Travel to the German resorts is normally by plane to Munich, where trains connect with most skiing areas, the journey taking less than two hours in all cases. If you go on a package tour, a coach will normally pick you up from the airport, but check with your travel agent.

POLICE, CRIME AND PERSONAL SAFETY

The German police (*Polizei*) are not renowned for their friendliness, but they usually treat foreigners with courtesy. It's important to remember that you are expected to carry ID (your passport, or at least a student card or driving licence) at all times. Failure to do so could turn a routine police check into a drawn-out and unpleasant process.

Traffic offences or any other misdemeanours will result in a rigorous checking of documentation, and on-the-spot fines are best paid without argument. The police are generally very correct, and shouldn't subject you to any unnecessary chicanery.

Reporting thefts at local police stations is straightforward, but inevitably there'll be a great deal of bureaucratic bumf to wade through. All **drugs** are illegal in Germany, and anyone caught with them will face either prison or deportation: consulates will not be sympathetic towards those on drug charges. **Jaywalking** is illegal in Germany and you can, theoretically, be fined if caught. However, in the past few years increasing numbers of German pedestrians have abandoned the once prevalent habit of standing rigidly to attention – even when no car was in sight – until the lights changed in their favour.

The **GDR**'s claim that it was a crime-free state was a myth: there were always unsafe areas in the main cities, and particular problems with skinheads and football hooligans; these have, if anything, increased since unification. Bear in mind that the level of **theft** in the eastern part of Germany has – inevitably – increased dramatically in line with unemployment and the dashed hopes of the many who have found their dreams of quick riches unfulfilled. However, provided you take the normal precautions, there's certainly no particular cause for alarm.

Finally, thanks to the massive influx of *Gastarbeiter*, mainly from southern Europe, Germany is now firmly multicultural. However, there's no effective law against **racial discrimination**, and it's far from unknown for crankish pub landlords or nightclub proprietors to refuse entry on grounds of ethnicity. More seriously, a hard-core and sometimes violent racist element has arisen in the former GDR from the ranks of the disaffected.

> Throughout Germany the number to ring for the police is ☎110.

GAY GERMANY

Germany is one of the best countries in Europe in which to be gay (in German, *schwul*). The only real legal restriction is that the male age of consent is 18, and on the whole it's a tolerant place as far as attitudes go.

All the **big cities**, and especially Berlin, Hamburg, Munich, Cologne and Frankfurt, have thriving gay scenes, as do many medium-sized and even relatively small towns. The listings sections in the *Guide* give a run-down of the gay scene in the larger places.

Despite the Nazi interlude, when homosexuals were forced to wear pink triangles and lesbianism was deemed to be non-existent, Berlin in particular has a good record for tolerating an open and energetic gay and lesbian scene. As far back as the 1920s Christopher Isherwood and W.H. Auden

both came here, drawn to a city where, in sharp contrast with oppressive London, there was a gay community which did not live in fear of harassment and legal persecution.

Germany's most widely read gay **magazine** is *Männer*, which comes out bi-monthly; there are also numerous local publications.

Outside the major cities, Germany's **lesbian community** is perforce more muted than its male counterpart; being openly out in rural areas, particularly those where Roman Catholicism remains strong, is virtually impossible. Alternatively, *GAIA's Guide*, available from bookstores in Britain and Germany, lists lesbian bars and contact addresses throughout the country. Worth scanning while you're in Germany is *UKZ-Unsere Zeitung*, the monthly lesbian magazine.

DIRECTORY

ADDRESSES The street name is always written before the number. Strasse (street) is commonly abbreviated as Str., and often joined on to the end of the previous word. Other terms include Allee (avenue), Damm (embankment), Gasse (alley), Platz (square), Ring (ring road), Ufer (quay) and Weg (way). Note that when a town or village has been incorporated into the municipality of a larger neighbour, it assumes a double-barrelled name: thus Babelsberg appears in addresses as

Potsdam-Babelsberg, Bad Godesberg as Bonn-Bad Godesberg, Hohenschwangau as Schwangau-Hohenschwangau. One last point to note: the vast majority of streets in the former GDR have been stripped of their Communist names, though a number survive, with Karl Marx, in particular, hanging on in there in a surprising number of towns.

ELECTRIC CURRENT The supply is 220 volts, and anything requiring 240 volts (all UK appliances) will work. Sockets are of the two-pin variety, so a travel plug is useful.

EMBASSIES AND CONSULATES are listed under the relevant cities. Bear in mind that the level of help, other than in Berlin or Bonn, is likely to be variable – some cities keep up a fantasy diplomatic life, in which the honorary consul is a local businessman who has bought the title for the kudos it confers on him.

KIDS Travelling with youngsters shouldn't be a problem. Kids under 4 travel free on trains; those between 4 and 11 qualify for half-fare. On many municipal public transport tickets, kids travel free if accompanied by an adult. Similarly reduced rates are offered by hotels and guesthouses.

Most towns have crèche facilities: contact tourist offices for details. The best entertainments for kids are listed in the *Guide*.

LAUNDRY Laundries are not a very common sight in Germany, but they do exist – look under *Wäscherei* in the local Yellow Pages to find the nearest. Dry cleaners (*Reinigung*) are more frequent, but also quite expensive. Many youth hostels have washing machines in their basements.

LEFT LUGGAGE All main stations have a vast number of left-luggage lockers. The smallest and cheapest are large enough to hold all but the bulkiest rucksack or suitcase, and at DM2/€1 for 24 hours they make humping heavy luggage around town a false economy. At the time of writing, most lockers take any combination of DM0.50, DM1 and DM2 pieces, though occasionally there's a specific requirement: sometimes this is for two DM1 pieces, at other times for one DM2 piece. As yet, there are only a handful of stations with new computerized lockers which operate with codes rather than keys, though the advent of the euro is likely to lead to an increase in their number. Leaving bags with the station attendants costs DM4/€2 per item, but this is often the only option in small towns, where the hours of service are often very restricted.

STUDENT CARDS are worth carrying for the substantial reductions on entry fees they bring.

TIME Germany is one hour ahead of Britain and Ireland; nine hours ahead of US Pacific Standard Time and six hours ahead of Eastern Standard Time; and nine hours behind Sydney, and eleven hours behind Auckland. Clocks are turned an hour forward at the end of March, and an hour back in late October.

TIPPING This is seldom necessary in restaurants, as prices are almost invariably inclusive, but rounding up to at least the next DM/€ is expected – and even if you omit to say so, this will often be taken as read when change is given. In taxis, add a mark/euro or two to the total.

N

DENMARK

NORTH
SEA

BALTIC
SEA

CHAPTER 7
HAMBURG &
SCHLESWIG-
HOLSTEIN

CHAPTER 8
MECKLENBURG-
LOWER
POMERANIA

CHAPTER 6
BREMEN
&
LOWER SAXONY

CHAPTER 9
BERLIN &
BRANDENBURG

POLAND

NETHERLANDS

CHAPTER 10
SAXONY-ANHALT

CHAPTER 5
NORTH RHINE-
WESTPHALIA

CHAPTER 12
SAXONY

CHAPTER 11
THURINGIA

CHAPTER 3
HESSE

BELGIUM

CZECH
REPUBLIC

CHAPTER 4
RHINELAND-
PALATINATE
& SAARLAND

LUX.

CHAPTER 1
BAVARIA

FRANCE

CHAPTER 2
BADEN-
WÜRTTEMBERG

AUSTRIA

0   Metres   200

SWITZERLAND

CHAPTER ONE

BAVARIA

Bavaria (Bayern) is the original home of many of Germany's best-known clichés:
beer-swilling Lederhosen-clad men, sausage dogs, cowbells and Alpine villages,
Sauerkraut and Wurst and the fairy-tale castle of Neuschwanstein. Yet all this is
only a small part of the Bavarian picture, and one that's restricted to the southern areas in and around the Alps.

Historically and **politically**, Bavaria has always occupied a special position within
Germany. Although a wealthy duchy within the Holy Roman Empire, its rulers preferred artistic patronage to the territorial expansionism and dynastic feuding characteristic of the rest of the nation. A fundamental change in Bavaria's status occurred at
the beginning of the nineteenth century, when it profited from Napoleon's decision to
re-order the map of Germany: it was doubled in size, and promoted to the rank of a
kingdom. Thereafter, it retained much of its independence and its own monarch, even
after the union of Germany in 1871. Following the demise of the monarchy at the end
of World War I, Bavaria briefly became a free state, but quickly degenerated into a
hotbed of right-wing extremism where Hitler had his first successes. This reputation
for reactionary politics continues to the present day: Bavaria has continuously been
ruled since World War II by the ultra-conservative CSU, whose stranglehold on power
seems unshakeable.

Bavaria is made up of four distinct regions, each with its own identity and culture,
and its cities are equally varied in character. In **Munich** the Land has a cosmopolitan,
if conservative, capital that ranks as one of Germany's star attractions. The city lies at
the centre of **Upper Bavaria**, the state's heartland, a region that ranges from the snow-
capped peaks of the **Alps** to gentle hop-growing farmland. It's a traditional, deeply
Catholic area whose rural traditions continue in spite of the inroads of mass tourism.

West of here is **Bavarian Swabia**. Detached by Napoleon from the rest of its traditional province (thereafter officially known as Württemberg), it remains stubbornly
Swabian in culture – most obviously in its distinctive pasta-based cuisine. Even so, it is
home to the most outrageous of the Romantic castles which form such a crucial part of
the Bavarian stereotype. Outside of the mountainous **Allgäu** area in the south, this is a
region of undulating agricultural country, ideal for walking and cycling holidays. The

ACCOMMODATION PRICE CODES

All the pensions and hotels in this book have been graded according to the following
price categories. The codes quoted are for the cheapest available double room, except
for establishments which have rooms costing widely different rates, when the most
expensive price is given as well. Exact charges are given for youth hostels; in the case of
the official DJH (HI) establishments, this is the lowest available rate. When two figures
are quoted for these hostels, the first applies to juniors (ie under 27 years of age), the second to seniors (27 and above). In Bavaria, the hostel price applies to juniors only.

① less than DM60/€30   ④ DM100–124/€50–62   ⑦ DM200–249/€100–124
② DM60–79/€30–39   ⑤ DM125–149/€63–74   ⑧ DM250–299/€125–149
③ DM80–99/€40–49   ⑥ DM150–199/€75–99   ⑨ upwards of DM300/€150

pristine local capital of **Augsburg** has been a place of importance since the days of the Romans, and its resplendent Renaissance buildings give it a highly distinctive appearance.

To the north lies **Franconia**, which was likewise absorbed into Bavaria in 1803. The most obvious evidence of its distinctiveness can be seen in the wine-growing area around **Würzburg** in the northwest, where a culture quite at odds with the beer-loving rest of Bavaria exists. In the northeast of Franconia the difference can be seen most obviously in the elegantly plain Baroque architecture of the Lutheran strongholds of **Ansbach** and **Bayreuth**: the Reformation left Franconia more or less split down the middle along religious lines. **Nürnberg**, a place risen from the rubble of wartime destruction and restored to the splendour of its Middle Ages heyday, was another city which quickly embraced Protestantism. The same is true of **Rothenburg ob der Tauber**, the most famous of the medieval towns on the **Romantic Road**, one of Germany's most famous tourist routes. Yet **Bamberg**, whose magnificently varied architectural legacy is unsurpassed in all of Germany, remained, like Würzburg, staunchly Catholic.

Eastern Bavaria, incorporating the provinces of Lower Bavaria and the Upper Palatinate, is the state's backwater: a rustic, relatively poor region where life in the highlands revolves around logging and workshop industries such as traditional glass production. However, the region also has a number of urban attractions, most notably the wonderfully well-preserved medieval cities of **Regensburg** and **Landshut**, and the border town of **Passau**, which is notable for its harmonious Baroque layout.

Travel is made easy by a generally good network of trains and regional buses, though public transport is sometimes a little thin on the ground in Bavarian Swabia and Eastern Bavaria – having a car makes life easier here. Cycling is an excellent and very popular way to get around, and is facilitated by a great many marked cycling paths throughout the state. **Accommodation** is uniformly good; it's normally not too difficult to find a bed, though problems may occasionally be experienced in the mountain resorts and some of the more popular tourist towns. An unfortunate **restriction for travellers over 27** is that they're barred from using youth hostels, though reasonably priced private rooms in most places should compensate.

MUNICH (MÜNCHEN)

Pending Berlin's full recovery from its long period of division, **MUNICH** is the German city which most has the air of a capital about it. Even though it has never ruled over a territory any larger than the present-day Land, the grandiose palaces from Bavaria's era as an independent kingdom give it the appearance of a metropolis of great importance. When this is added to a remarkable postwar economic record (courtesy of such hi-tech giants as the car manufacturer BMW, the aerospace company MBB and the electronics group Siemens), and to its hard-won status as the national trendsetter in fashion matters, it's easy to see why Munich acts as a magnet to outsiders. Students flock here to study; the rich and jet-set like to live here, as do writers, painters, musicians and film-makers, while foreign nationals now make up more than a fifth of the population. Munich's other, more familiar face is of a homely city of provincially minded locals whose zest for drinking, seen at an extreme during the annual **Oktoberfest**, is kept up all year round in cavernous beer halls and spacious gardens.

The city is something of a late developer in German terms. It was founded in 1158 by Henry the Lion, the powerful Saxon duke who for a short time also ruled Bavaria, as a monastic village (*Mönchen* means monks) and toll-collection point on the River Isar, a Danube tributary. In 1180, it was allocated to the **Wittelsbachs**, who ruled the province continuously until 1918 – the longest period achieved by any of the nation's dynasties.

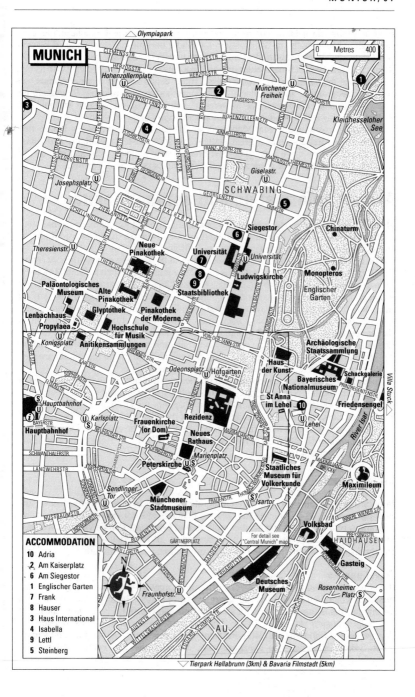

△ *Olympiapark*

MUNICH

0 Metres 400

Hohenzollernplatz

Münchener Freiheit

Kleinhesseloher See

Josephsplatz

Giselastr.

S C H W A B I N G

Siegestor

Chinaturm

Neue Pinakothek

Theresienstr.

Universität

Universität

Ludwigskirche

Monopteros

Paläontologisches Museum

Alte Pinakothek

Staatsbibliothek

Englischer Garten

Lenbachhaus

Glyptothek

Pinakothek der Moderne

Propylaea

Hochschule für Musik

Königsplatz

Anitikensammlungen

Archäologische Staatssammlung

Odeonsplatz *Hofgarten*

Haus der Kunst

Bayerisches Nationalmuseum

Schackgalerie

Villa Stuck ▷

Hauptbahnhof

Karlsplatz

St Anna im Lehel

Friedensengel

Rezidenz

Lehel

Hauptbahnhof

Frauenkirche (or Dom)

Neues Rathaus

Marienplatz

Peterskirche

Staatliches Museum für Volkerkunde

Maximilians-brücke

Maximileum

Sendlinger Tor

Münchener Stadtmuseum

Isartor

Volksbad

H A I D H A U S E N

Gärtnerplatz

For detail see "Central Munich" map

Gasteig

Fraunhofstr.

Deutsches Museum

Rosenheimer Platz S

A U

ACCOMMODATION

- 10 Adria
- 2 Am Kaiserplatz
- 6 Am Siegestor
- 1 Englischer Garten
- 7 Frank
- 8 Hauser
- 3 Haus International
- 4 Isabella
- 9 Lettl
- 5 Steinberg

▽ *Tierpark Hellabrunn (3km) & Bavaria Filmstadt (5km)*

Munich was initially overshadowed by Landshut, though it became the capital of the upper part of the divided duchy in 1255. Only in 1503 did it become capital of a united Bavaria, and it remained of relatively modest size until the nineteenth century, when it was expanded into a planned city of broad boulevards and spacious squares in accordance with its new role, granted by Napoleon, as a royal capital. Hitler began an even more ambitious construction programme in accordance with Munich's special role as *Hauptstadt der Bewegung* "Capital city of the (Nazi) Movement"; thankfully, only a part of it was built, surviving to this day as a reminder of this inglorious chapter in the city's history.

Despite its cosmopolitanism, Munich is small enough to be digestible in one visit, and has the added bonus of a great setting, the snow-dusted mountains and Alpine lakes just an hour's drive away. The best time of year to come is from June to early October, when all the beer gardens, street cafés and bars are in full swing.

Arrival, information and getting around

Munich's spankingly modern **airport**, Franz-Josef-Strauss-Flughafen, lies some 30km north of the city centre, to which it's linked by one of the two branches of S-Bahn #1, by S-Bahn #8 and by buses operated by the Lufthansa airline.

The **Hauptbahnhof** lies in a slightly seedy area at the western edge of the city centre. On its eastern side, at Bahnhofplatz 2, is one of the municipal **tourist offices** (Mon–Sat 9am–8pm, Sun 10am–6pm; ☎0 89/23 3 03 00, fax 23 33 02 33, *www.muenchen-tourist.de*). Although long queues are the norm in summer and during *Oktoberfest*, the staff are extremely helpful and will always assist you in finding a room. Within the station, alongside platform 11, is another very useful information office, EurAide (May to end of *Oktoberfest* daily 7.45am–noon & 1–6pm; ☎0 89/59 38 89). Specifically geared towards English-speaking travellers, this provides free train information and advice on preparing itineraries, books accommodation and runs excursions. Also within the station are plenty of shops and a bank, all of which stay open until late evening.

Another **tourist office** can be found in the heart of the city, in the Neues Rathaus on Marienplatz (Mon–Fri 10am–8pm, Sat 10am–4pm). The monthly English-language **magazine**, *Munich Found*, available from newsagents for DM5.50/€2.75, has useful listings and information, as well as articles about the city and Germany in general. Far more extensive (German-only) **listings** are to be found in the tourist office's *Offizielles Monatsprogramm* (DM3/€1.50) and the glossy *Prinz* (DM2/€1); the free *In München* is also worth consulting.

City transport

Munich's public transport system, an integrated network of **buses**, **trams** and **U- and S-Bahn trains**, is good, though the fare and ticketing system, despite attempts at simplification, remains by far the most complicated in Germany. **Prices** vary according to how many zones are crossed: the city is divided up into a series of concentric circles, clearly displayed on the transport maps at any station, tram or bus stop.

Travel passes

If you are intending to stay for a week or more, it may be worth investing in a **travel pass**, for which you'll need your passport and two photos. The most convenient office for buying this is the Hauptbahnhof's Zeitkartenstelle (Mon–Fri 9am–6pm), located in the hall opposite platforms 27–36. There are several other offices outside the Poccistrasse U-Bahn station (Mon–Fri 8am–6pm), and at the Ostbahnhof and various other S-Bahn stations. The cheapest pass, covering the city centre and most of

Schwabing, costs DM16.50/€8.25 for a week or DM63/€31.50 for a month. For the whole city, a weekly pass is DM38.50/€19.25, its monthly equivalent DM146/€73; the charges rise to DM68.50/€34.25 and DM260/€130 respectively if you also want to cover neighbouring places on the network, such as Dachau and the Ammersee. Note that weekly passes are only valid from one Monday to the next, so buying mid-week means losing out. Similarly, monthly passes are for calendar months only.

A worthwhile supplement to a travel pass is the DM30/€15 **Museum-Ticket**, which gives free access to most of the city's museums and monuments over a fourteen-day period. This can be bought at any of the participating venues.

Tickets

Other tickets for city transport are available from ticket machines in all U-Bahn stations, at some bus and tram stops and inside trams. If you're going to be making several journeys in the course of your stay it's not worth buying single tickets. Better value is a **strip ticket** (*Streifenkarte*), costing DM16/€8 for ten strips. You stamp two strips for every zone crossed except for journeys of up to four bus or tram stops or two S- or U-Bahn stops, when only one has to be cancelled. It's not necessary to cancel every strip: only the last needs to be punched. A child's strip ticket costs DM6.50/€3.25 for five strips; only one strip needs to be cancelled per journey, regardless of its length.

Various **day tickets** are also available. The *Single-Tageskarte* for individual travellers costs DM9/€4.50 for journeys within Munich, or DM18/€9 for the city and S-Bahn region. These charges rise to DM14/€7 and DM28/€14 respectively for the *Partner-Tageskarte*, which covers two adults and up to three children (though this limit is waived in the case of verifiable offspring). An enticing variant of this is the **München Welcome Card**, which can be purchased at the tourist offices. In addition to covering all public transport costs within Munich, this gives reductions of up to fifty percent on the entrance fees to the main museums and monuments. The *Single-Tageskarte* version of this costs DM12/€6 for one day, DM29/€14.50 for three days, while the *Partner-Tageskarte* is available, in the latter version only, for DM42/€21.

Accommodation

You'll find a good range of accommodation in the city. There are abundant **hotels** in every category from the basic to the hyper-luxury, and you'll even find several **hostels** in which the normal Bavarian restriction on those over 27 does not apply. Beware, however, that without advance booking it can be virtually impossible to find budget accommodation during the **Oktoberfest** beer festival/fair that usually runs from the last Saturday in September to the first Sunday in October: to be in with a chance, turn up very early in the day at the tourist office, and be prepared to queue for hours. On each of the three weekends, the only places likely to have free rooms are the most expensive hotels. If you're planning on an extended stay in Munich, contact one of the competing **Mitwohnzentralen** for a room or a flat.

Hotels and pensions

There are well over three hundred **hotels** and **pensions** scattered all over Munich. By far the densest concentration is around the Hauptbahnhof, particularly its southern side. Unfortunately, although there are many good-value establishments here, this area can feel a little rough after dark, despite being well policed. There are also plenty of places – mostly homely-type pensions – in Schwabing and the area around the university just to the south; these have the advantage of proximity to many of the best bars and restaurants. Provision in the city centre is sparser, but still adequate: most of the luxury establishments are located in this area.

Around the Hauptbahnhof

Alfa, Hirtenstr. 22 (☎0 89/5 45 95 30, fax 5 45 95 32 99, *www.hotel-alfa.de*). Located in one of the quieter streets to the north of the Hauptbahnhof. ④–⑨.

Central, Bayerstr. 55 (☎0 89/5 43 98 46, fax 5 43 98 47). Basic but perfectly acceptable hotel whose low prices make it a popular choice with young travellers from around the globe. ③–⑤.

Europäischer Hof, Bayerstr. 31 (☎0 89/55 15 10, fax 55 15 12 22, *www.heh.de*). Directly facing the Hauptbahnhof, and offering a very high overall standard; it's also one of the few hotels in the area with a restaurant. ④–⑨.

Excelsior, Schützenstr. 11 (☎0 89/55 13 70, fax 55 13 71 21, *Excelsior-Muenchen@t-online.de*). The most upmarket hotel in the vicinity of the Hauptbahnhof, with a renowned wine bar-restaurant, *Vinothek*. ⑨.

Haberstock, Schillerstr. 4 (☎0 89/55 78 55, fax 5 50 36 34). Right beside the Hauptbahnhof with basic, no-frills facilities, but it's good value nonetheless. ④–⑦.

Helvetia, Schillerstr. 6 (☎0 89/5 90 68 50, fax 59 06 85 70, *Hotel-Helvetia@t-online.de*). Offers some of the cheapest rooms in the area. ②–⑤.

Jedermann, Bayerstr. 95 (☎0 89/54 32 40, fax 54 32 41 11, *www.hotel-jedermann.de*). Located well away from any noise and seediness, five minutes' walk from the Hauptbahnhof in the opposite direction from the centre. It has a friendly English-speaking management, a wide choice of rooms of various degrees of luxury and an excellent breakfast buffet. Guests can surf the Internet and send email from the hotel computer free of charge. ③–⑧.

St Paul, St-Paul-Str. 7 (☎0 89/54 40 78 00, fax 53 46 52, *Hotel-St.Paul@t-online.de*). Family-run hotel located right beside the Theresienwiese U-Bahn station. It has well-appointed bedrooms and offers fine buffet breakfasts. ⑥–⑧.

Toskana, Schwanthalerstr. 42 (☎0 89/53 19 70, fax 5 32 82 40). Apartment-block hotel whose rooms all lack en-suite facilities and are correspondingly inexpensive. ③.

The city centre

Am Markt, Heiliggeiststr. 6 (☎0 89/22 50 14, fax 22 40 17). Pension with a fine setting overlooking the Viktualienmarkt. ④–⑥.

Bayerischer Hof, Promenadeplatz 6 (☎0 89/2 12 00, fax 2 12 09 06, *www.bayerischerhof.de*). An internationally celebrated hotel which has been run by four generations of the same family. The public rooms are beautifully furnished, while the facilities include a roof-garden swimming pool with sun terrace, a sauna, solarium and massage facilities. There are three restaurants: the moderately priced *Palais Keller*, the *Garden-Restaurant* with terrace and winter garden, and the renowned Polynesian-speciality *Trader Vic's* (evenings only). ⑨.

Blauer Bock, Sebastiansplatz 9 (☎0 89/23 17 80, fax 23 17 82 00). A recommended central hotel right beside the Stadtmuseum. ④–⑥.

Braunauer Hof, Frauenstr. 40 (☎0 89/22 36 13, fax 22 03 42). Best known for its restaurant, one of the more formal of Munich's traditional Gaststätten, this offers good-value rooms in a convenient location. ④.

Königshof, Karlsplatz 25 (☎0 89/55 13 60, fax 55 13 61 13, *Koenigshof-Muenchen@t-online.de*). Fine old privately owned hotel which has been going strong since the 1860s. Its restaurant, which boasts an outstanding wine list, is among the best in the city. ⑨.

Platzl, Sparkassenstr. 10 (☎0 89/23 70 30, fax 23 70 38 00). Recently modernized luxury hotel in the heart of the Altstadt. Its restaurant, *Pfistermühle*, in the adjoining sixteenth-century building, serves high-quality specialities from the different regions of Bavaria, and beers from the country brewery of Aying. ⑨.

Rafael, Neuturmstr. 1 (☎ 89/29 09 80, fax 22 25 39, *info@hotel-rafael.com*). Super-luxury establishment in a neo-Renaissance building of the 1880s. The bedrooms are individually decorated with antiques; there's also a roof terrace with swimming pool and a highly exclusive restaurant. ⑨.

Schlicker, Tal 8 (☎0 89/22 79 41, fax 29 60 59, *Schlicker-munich@t-online.de*). This hotel, which offers good breakfast buffets, has as an ideal setting just off Marienplatz. ⑥–⑧.

Vier Jahreszeiten, Maximilianstr. 17 (☎0 89/2 12 50, fax 21 25 20 00, *www.kempinski-vierjahreszeiten.de*). Grand hotel built at royal request in 1858 as an essential adornment to the latest showpiece boulevard. Now part of the Kempinski group, and fully refurbished a few years back, it maintains its reputation as one of the world's leading hotels. The facilities include a rooftop swimming pool, massage, a nightclub and three restaurants. ⑨.

Schwabing and the university area

Am Kaiserplatz, Kaiserplatz 12 (☎0 89/34 91 90). Very friendly pension in a good location. Wacky decor, with each room done in a different style – ranging from red satin to Bavarian rustic. ③.

Am Siegestor, Akademiestr. 5 (☎0 89/39 95 50, fax 34 30 50). Well-regarded pension just a stone's throw from the Siegestor and the main university building. ③.

Englischer Garten, Liebergesellstr. 8 (☎0 89/3 83 94 10, fax 38 39 41 33). This guesthouse occupies a fine old villa on the edge of the Englischer Garten, by the Kleinhesseloher See. ⑥.

Frank, Schellingstr. 24 (☎0 89/28 14 51, fax 2 80 09 10). Located midway between Ludwigstrasse and the Neue Pinakothek. Mainly frequented by young travellers. Lovely big rooms, and there's a fridge available to keep food in. ③.

Hauser, Schellingstr. 11 (☎0 89/2 86 67 50, fax 28 66 75 99, *Hotel-Hauser@Munich-info.de*). Unassuming hotel with a good location just off Ludwigstrasse and right beside the university. ⑥–⑧.

Isabella, Isabellastr. 35 (☎0 89/2 71 35 03, fax 2 71 29 03). Tiny pension with single and double rooms, but just twelve beds in all and one shared bathroom. ④.

Lettl, Amalienstr. 53 (☎0 89/2 86 69 70, fax 28 6 97 97, *Hotel-lettl-Munich@t-online.de*). Friendly hotel midway between Ludwigstrasse and the Neue Pinakothek. ⑥–⑧.

Steinberg, Ohmstr. 9 (☎0 89/33 10 11, fax 38 88 99 68). Pension with a nice atmosphere and a good location right by the university. ④.

Elsewhere in the city

Adria, Liebigstr. 8a (☎0 89/29 30 81, fax 22 70 15). Just two blocks south of the Englischer Garten and Prinzregentenstrasse museums. ⑥–⑧.

Galleria, Plinganserstr. 142 (☎0 89/7 23 30 01, fax 7 24 15 64). Set in a handsome Jugendstil villa in the suburb of Thalkirchen; take U-Bahn #3. ⑧–⑨.

Kriemhild, Guntherstr. 16 (☎0 89/1 71 11 70, fax 17 11 17 55, *www.kriemhild.de*). Although far from the centre, it's only a short walk from Schloss Nymphenburg and its beautiful park, and is good value at the price asked. ⑥.

Krone, Theresienhöhe 8 (☎0 89/5 08 08 00, fax 50 80 80 70). Classy hotel overlooking the Theresienwiese, setting of the *Oktoberfest*. ⑥–⑨.

Obermaier, Truderinger Str. 304b (☎0 89/42 90 21, fax 42 64 00, *HotelObermaier@t-online.de*). Way out in the eastern suburb of Trudering (reached by S-Bahn #5 or U-Bahn #2), this is a country-style Gasthaus, with beer garden and a restaurant serving its own home-grown produce. ⑥–⑨.

Stadt Rosenheim, Orleansplatz 6a (☎0 89/4 48 24 24, fax 48 59 87). Right by the Ostbahnhof and convenient for the bars and restaurants of Haidhausen, nowadays Munich's liveliest area by night. ⑨–⑦.

Mitwohnzentralen

City Mitwohnzentrale, Lämmerstr. 4 (☎0 89/1 94 30, fax 59 45 64, *www.mitwohnzentrale.de*). Located conveniently close to the Hauptbahnhof.

Mit-Wohn-Börse, Georgenstr. 45 (☎0 89/1 94 45, fax 2 71 20 19, *www.homecompany.de*). Part of a national network, this can find accommodation for any period from two nights upwards.

Mitwohnzentrale an der Uni, in Universität U-Bahn station (☎0 89/2 86 60 60, fax 28 66 06 24, *www.mrlodge.de*). Located by the Adalbertstrasse exit, this is staffed by English-speakers.

Mitwohnzentrale Mr Lodge, Kaulbachstr. 61 (☎0 89/3 40 82 30, fax 34 08 23 23). Deals only in stays of a month or longer.

Hostels

4 you münchen ökologisches Jugendgästehaus, Hirtenstr. 18 (☎0 89/5 52 16 60, fax 55 21 66 66, *www.the4you.de*). Modern, environmentally conscious hostel with vegetarian restaurant. Dorm beds DM34–40/€17–20, singles from DM64/€32, doubles from DM96/€48.

CVJM-Jugendgästehaus, Landwehrstr. 13 (☎0 89/5 52 14 10, fax 5 50 42 82, *info@cvjm-muenchen.org*). The local YMCA hostel, located a couple of blocks from the Hauptbahnhof and open to everyone. Beds in dorms DM42/€21, singles from DM53/€26.50, doubles from DM90/€45.

Haus International, Elisabethstr. 87 (☎0 89/12 00 60, fax 12 00 62 51). A no-age-limit youth hotel in Schwabing, complete with disco and swimming pool. Beds in small dorms from DM40/€20; also regular singles from DM55/€27.50, doubles from DM104/€52.

IN VIA Marienherberge, Goethestr. 9 (☎0 89/55 58 05, fax 55 02 82 60). Roman Catholic-run hostel near the Hauptbahnhof for women aged 25 or under. Beds in small dorms cost DM30/€15; there are also singles for DM40/€20, doubles for DM70/€35.

Jugendgästehaus München, Miesingstr. 4 (☎0 89/7 23 65 50, fax 7 24 25 67, *JGHMuenchen@djh-bayern.de*). This is the nicest and most expensive of the three HI establishments (see also the two following entries): all require a membership card, and are open only to those under 27, except for parents travelling with children. Take either U-Bahn #3 to Thalkirchen and then walk, or U-Bahn #6 or S-Bahn #7 to Harras then tram #16 to Boschetsriederstrasse. DM32.50/€16.25.

Jugendherberge München, Wendl-Dietrich-Str. 20 (☎0 89/13 11 56, fax 1 67 87 45, *JHMuenchen@djh-bayern.de*). This is the largest and most basic hostel, with beds in large, spartan dormitories. Take U-Bahn #1 to Rotkreuzplatz, from where it's a short walk down Wendl-Dietrich-Strasse. DM30/€15.

Jugendherberge Pullach, Burg Schwaneck, Burgweg 4–6, Pullach (☎0 89/7 93 06 43, fax 7 93 79 22). Atmospherically housed in an old castle by the River Isar, but a long way south of downtown Munich. Take S-Bahn #7 to Pullach, then follow the signs. DM23/€11.50.

Kolpinghaus St Theresia, Hanebergstr. 8 (☎0 89/12 60 50, fax 12 60 52 12, *www.Kolpinghaus-Muenchen.de*). Another Catholic hostel, this time open to everyone. Beds in dorms DM35/€17.50, singles DM50/€25, doubles from DM74/€37. Take U-Bahn #1 to Rotkreuzplatz; it's then a five-minute walk.

Campsites

Kapuzinerhölzl, Frank-Shrank-Strasse (☎0 89/1 41 43 00). Known as "The Tent" and municipally run, this is the cheapest place to stay during its period of operation (mid-June to early Sept), and is a fun place to be, despite the lack of privacy (it can accommodate up to 300 people). Young people only (preferably under 23) are admitted. Take tram #17 to Botanischer Garten, walk down Frank-Schrank-Strasse and turn left at the end of the road.

Langwieder See, Eschenrieder Str. 119 (☎ & fax 0 89/8 64 15 66). Small site in a quiet lakeside setting on the western fringe of the city. Open year-round, though notification must be given in advance from Nov to mid-March. Being off the U- and S-Bahn routes, it's really only practical if you've got your own transport.

Obermenzing, Lochhausener Str. 59 (☎0 89/8 11 22 35, fax 8 14 48 07). In a posh suburb, close to Schloss Nymphenburg. Take S-Bahn #2 to Obermenzing, then bus #75 to Lochhausener Strasse. Closed Nov to mid-March.

Thalkirchen, Zentralländstr. 49 (☎0 89/7 23 17 07, fax 7 24 31 77). Set in an attractive part of the Isar valley. Very popular during *Oktoberfest* because of its proximity to the fairground. Take U-Bahn #3 to Thalkirchen or U-Bahn #7 to Siemenswerke. Closed Nov to mid-March.

The City

Heart of the city and its Altstadt is **Marienplatz**; the pedestrian centre fans out from here in an approximate circle of one square kilometre. This is tourist and shopping land, with all the city's major department stores, the central market, the royal palace and the most important churches. North of Marienplatz, Ludwigstrasse and Leopoldstrasse run straight through the heart of **Schwabing**, Munich's entertainment quarter, full of *Schickies* (German yuppies) who frequent the many bars and pose in the street cafés. It's also close to the city's main park, the **Englischer Garten**. West of the Marienplatz–Schwabing axis is the main **museum quarter**, with many of the most

CENTRAL MUNICH

△ Schloss Nymphenburg (3km) △ Alte Pinakothek (and Neue Pinakothek) △ Alte Pinakothek and Neue Pinakothek △ Schwabing (1km)

Haus der Kunst
Staatskanzlei
Residenz
Hofgarten
Theatinerkirche
Feldherrnhalle
Erzbischöfliches Palais
Frauenkirche (or Dom)
Münze
Kammerspiele
Alter Hof
Hofbräuhaus
Heiliggeistkirche
Isartor
Neues Rathaus
Altes Rathaus
Peterskirche
Münchener Stadtmuseum
Viktualienmarkt
Dreifaltigkeitskirche
St. Michael
Augustinerkloster
Bürgersaal
Alte Akademie
Asamkirche
Sendlinger Tor
Karlsplatz
Karlstor
Alter Botanischer Garten
Amerikahaus
Hauptbahnhof
Theresienwiese

ACCOMMODATION

1 Alfa	7 Europäischer Hof	14 Platzl
18 Am Markt	5 Excelsior	15 Rafael
3 Bayerischer Hof	8 Haberstock	16 St Paul
21 Blauer Bock	11 Helvetia	19 Schlicker
20 Braunauer Hof	12 IN VIA	13 Toscana
6 Central	10 Marienherberge	4 Vier Jahreszeiten
17 CVJM-Jugendgästehaus	9 Jedermann	2 4 you München
	9 Königshof	

0 Metres 200

important of Munich's three dozen or so museums, including the world-famous Alte Pinakothek. Running the length of the eastern part of town is the River Isar, while **Nymphenburg**, with its palace and gardens, is the most enticing of the outer districts.

The Altstadt

Relatively little is left of medieval Munich, but three of the early fourteenth-century **gateways** remain to mark the boundaries of the Altstadt, now the heart of the modern city. Bounded by the **Odeonsplatz** and the **Sendlinger Tor** to the north and south, and the **Isartor** and **Karlstor** to the east and west, it's only a fifteen-minute walk from one end to the other. This doesn't mean you can see everything in a single day: there is so much packed into this area that two or three days are needed to explore it thoroughly.

Marienplatz and around

Marienplatz is the most central spot in the city. There's something almost cosy about it: street musicians and artists entertain the crowds and local youths lounge around the **Fischbrunnen** (Fish Fountain) and the **Mariensäule** – the latter being a column topped by a gilded statue of the Virgin Mary as Queen of Heaven, by **Hubert Gerhard**, a sixteenth-century Dutch-born sculptor whose work is an ubiquitous feature of the city.

At 11am and noon the square fills with tourists as the carillon in the **Neues Rathaus** jingles into action, displaying two events that happened on this spot: the marriage of Wilhelm V to Renata von Lothringen in 1568, and the first *Schäfflertanz* (coopers' dance) of 1517, intended to cheer people up during the plague. This dance is still held every seven years, next in 2005. The Neues Rathaus itself is a late nineteenth-century neo-Gothic monstrosity, whose redeeming feature is the view from its **tower** (ascent by elevator May–Oct Mon–Fri 9am–7pm, Sat & Sun 10am–7pm; Nov–April Mon–Thurs 9am–4pm, Fri 9am–1pm; DM3/€1.50). To the right is the Gothic tower of the **Altes Rathaus**, which was rebuilt to its original fifteenth-century form after being destroyed by lightning. Today it houses the **Spielzeugmuseum** (daily 10am–5.30pm; DM5/€2.50, kids DM1/€0.50), a fascinating collection of historic toys.

Just to the south is the **Peterskirche** (popularly known as Alter Peter), the oldest church within the bounds of the old city walls. Its distinctive **tower** (Mon–Sat 9am–5/8pm, Sun 10.15am–5/7pm according to season; DM2.50/€1.25) offers an even higher and better view than that from the Rathaus, and is far less busy. Originally a pillared Romanesque basilica, the church owes its present form to a fourteenth-century Gothic rebuilding following a fire. The original **high altar**, a collaboration between **Erasmus Grasser** and **Jan Polack**, respectively Munich's leading sculptor and painter in the fertile late Gothic period, is split up and distributed throughout the chancel, with the statue of St Peter centre stage in a theatrical Rococo extravaganza. However, your attention is most likely to be caught by the grizzly **shrine to St Munditia**, the patron saint of single women. Her skeletal relics are poised in a glass box on a side altar, including the skull wrapped in netting with two glass eyes gazing out from a deathly face.

Although only a block further east, the **Heiliggeistkirche**, which was originally the church of an infirmary and pilgrims' hostel, lay outside the city walls. Its Gothic hall church design is still clearly apparent, despite many modifications carried out down the centuries. The most significant of these was the sumptuous High Baroque interior decoration executed in the 1720s by the prolific **Asam brothers**, who modernized a host of medieval Bavarian churches in this way. Cosmas Damian Asam's spectacular ceiling frescoes include a depiction of the hospice's foundation.

Following Burgstrasse or Sparkassenstrasse from the Altes Rathaus, you soon come to the **Alter Hof**, a shady medieval courtyard which was the original palace of the

Wittelsbachs. To the north lie the **Postamt**, a Baroque palace transformed in the nine-teenth century to serve as the post office, and the Renaissance **Münze** (Mint). However, the prime attraction in this area is the **Hofbräuhaus** just to the east. This describes itself as "the most famous pub in the world", and is the epitome of the Munich beer hall, with its spacious chambers, hard benches, well-worn tables, crowds of rev-ellers and traditional oompah music. Originally the court brewery, it boasts an unin-terrupted tradition dating back to 1589, though the present building is some three cen-turies younger. A favourite haunt of Hitler in the days when he was struggling to estab-lish the Nazi Party, it still has a large hard-core local clientele, though in summer it is often overrun by tourists.

The Frauenkirche

The other great symbol of Munich is the **Frauenkirche** (or **Dom**), whose copper onion-domed **towers** (ascent by elevator April–Oct Mon–Sat 10am–5pm; DM4/€2) dominate the skyline. It stands in its own small square, just to the west of the Rathaus. Close up, the building, built as a parish church but now the seat of an archbishop, isn't really seen to its best advantage: its redbrick Gothic architecture is unrelievedly spare. The lofty whitewashed interior, however, has inspired the **legend of the Devil's foot-print**. Apparently the architect **Jerg von Halspach** (who also built most of the other surviving medieval monuments in the city) made a pact with the Devil. In order to get enough money to complete this church, he had to construct it without a single visible window. When the Devil came to inspect the completed church, he saw the high Gothic windows from a distance and thought he'd get the builder's soul. Once inside, he was led to a certain point from which not one window was visible, since all were hidden by pillars. Stamping his foot in rage the Devil stormed off, leaving his black hoofed foot-print in the pavement by the entrance hall. Rebuilding following war damage has meant the trick no longer quite works, but the footprint is still there.

In the first nave chapel to the south is the huge Mannerist **tomb of Ludwig IV**, a belated tribute, made over a hundred years after his death by Hubert Gerhard and oth-ers, to the first of only two Wittelsbachs who managed to get elected as Holy Roman Emperor. Some of the church's other artistic treasures have been destroyed, among them Erasmus Grasser's **choir stalls**, though the arresting wooden statues were saved and positioned on the modern replacements. There also remain beautiful stained-glass windows in the ambulatory chapels, notably the central Sakramentskapelle, which also has a fine painted altar, *The Virgin of the Protecting Cloak*, by Jan Polack.

West of Marienplatz

The almost straight line between Marienplatz and the Hauptbahnhof is the hub of the city's commercial activity; alongside the numerous department stores, some of the city's most famous beer halls are to be found, as well as a series of contrasting church-es. At the point where the pedestrianized Kaufingerstrasse changes its name to Neuhauser Strasse is the deconsecrated **Augustinerkloster**, whose ornate Rococo interior now houses the **Deutsches Jagd- und Fischerei Museum** (Mon & Thurs 9.30am–9pm, Tues, Wed & Fri–Sun 9.30am–5pm; DM6/€3), an array of hunting and fishing trophies and dioramas of animals in their natural environments.

A little further down the street, the Mannerist facade of **St Michael** stands in line with the street's other buildings. Built between 1583 and 1597 under the auspices of Wilhelm V, this Jesuit church – the first in northern Europe – was intended to symbol-ize the local victory of Catholicism over Lutherism. Hubert Gerhard's large bronze stat-ue between the two entrances shows the Archangel Michael fighting for the Faith and killing Evil in the shape of a satyr. The interior, with a barrel vault second only in size to St Peter's in Rome, is decorated in elegant white stucco. A huge Neoclassical monu-ment to Eugène de Beauharnais by Bertel Thorwaldsen can be seen in the transept. In the **crypt** (Mon–Fri 10am–1pm and 2–4.30pm, Sat 10am–3pm; DM2/€1) below are the tombs of the Wittelsbach dynasty, among them the famous castle-builder Ludwig II, whose coffin is permanently draped with flowers, a candle burning at its foot.

Alongside the church, forming a continuous architectural unit with it, is the **Alte Akademie**, the college where the Jesuits instilled their burning missionary ideals in the hearts and minds of their pupils. In front is the **Richard-Strauss-Brunnen**, a fountain in honour of the Munich-born composer. The reliefs show scenes from his opera *Salomé*, based on Oscar Wilde's play of the same name.

Continuing westwards, you soon arrive at the **Bürgersaal**, which was built for a Marian student congregation in the early eighteenth century. Pride of the upstairs oratory (Mon–Fri 11am–3pm) is a set of guardian angels under the organ gallery, carved by Ignaz Günther, Bavaria's greatest Rococo sculptor. However, it's the crypt at entrance level that is most visited, since **Rupert Mayer**, one of the city's main opponents of Nazism, is buried there and his grave has become something of a pilgrims' centre, particularly since his beatification in 1987. Father Mayer was the parish priest during the war and became such a nuisance to the authorities that he was shipped off to Sachsenhausen concentration camp. Because of his immense popularity and the bad press his death would have caused, he was transferred to house arrest in Kloster Ettal in the Alps. He survived to return to the Bürgersaal after the war, but died later the same year.

South of Marienplatz

Immediately south of Peterskirche is the **Viktualienmarkt**, the city's main marketplace for the last two hundred years. Delicious-looking fruit and vegetables, as well as all kinds of cheeses, meats and other foodstuffs can be bought there. Though not cheap, the quality is uniformly excellent. Right in the middle of all the bustle is a small beer garden, a good place to have a snack.

On St Jakobsplatz to the rear is the **Münchner Stadtmuseum** (Tues–Sun 10am–6pm; *www.stadtmuseum-online.de*; DM5/€2.50). This has fascinating permanent displays about the history of the city, supplemented by changing special exhibitions. On the ground floor are the **Waffenhalle**, containing a magnificent array of historic weapons, and the wonderfully contorted set of morris dancers, carved as adornments for the ballroom of the Altes Rathaus by **Erasmus Grasser**. The upper floors house specialist displays on photos and films, brewing, musical instruments and one of the largest collections of puppets in the world, from Indian and Chinese paper dolls to the large mechanical European variety.

To the west is Sendlinger Strasse, where at no. 62 you can see the small **Asamkirche** (officially known as **St-Johann-Nepomuk**), one of the most enchanting examples of the Bavarian Rococo style. Built between 1733 and 1746, it's the crowning effort of the partnership of the two Asam brothers, who here successfully achieved their goal of a building whose architecture was completely integrated with all aspects of its interior decoration. The younger brother, Egid Quirin Asam (who was the sculptor and stuccoist), bought the land and underwrote the cost of the whole enterprise, which was intended to serve as his private family church, and therefore one where he had the rare luxury of being able to put his artistic ideals into effect without the intervention of a patron. He added a Rococo facade to the sixteenth-century house next door and lived there for the rest of his life.

The southeastern boundary of the Altstadt is marked by the **Isartor**. This is the only one of the three gateways open to the public, its two octagonal towers being home to the **Valentin-Musäum** (Mon, Tues, Fri & Sat 11.01am–5.29pm, Sun 10.01am–5.29pm; DM2.99/€1.49). As its eccentric opening times and prices indicate, it's a whimsical institution, dedicated to the memory of the great local humourist Karl Valentin (1882–1948), his partner Liesl Karlstadt and the Munich folksinger tradition. On the top floor of one of the towers is a much-loved café, whose truly *gemütlich* interior features Jugendstil furniture from the famous Thonet factory.

North of Marienplatz

The smartest part of the city centre lies to the north of Marienplatz, where ritzy shops and expensive cafés line Theatinerstrasse, Maffeistrasse and Kardinal-Faulhaber-Strasse. At Theatinerstr. 15 is the **Kunsthalle der Hypo-Kulturstiftung** (Mon–Wed & Fri–Sun 10am–6pm, Thurs 10am–9pm; variable admission charge), which puts on a programme of international-class temporary exhibitions on artistic and archeological themes. Kardinal-Faulhaber-Strasse has the most ostentatious buildings of the lot, mostly one-time palaces of the rich which have been turned into banks and insurance houses. One which is still lived in is François Cuvilliés' **Erzbischöfliches-Palais**, the residence of the archbishop of Munich and Freising. West of here, on Parcellistrasse, a Carmelite church, the **Dreifaltigkeitskirche**, was one of the few historic buildings in Munich to come through the last war unscathed. It's a copybook example of Italianate Baroque by the Swiss architect Giovanni Antonio Viscardi (who was also responsible for the design of the Bürgersaal), with a vivacious dome fresco of *The Adoration of the Trinity* by Cosmas Damian Asam.

The Residenz

In the late fourteenth century, the Wittelsbachs moved their seat from the Alter Hof in the heart of the Altstadt to a new site at what was then the northeastern periphery of the town. Between 1570 and 1620, this fortress was replaced by a splendid Mannerist **Residenz**, constructed by a team of mostly Netherlandish architects and designers led by **Friedrich Sustris**. It was modified and expanded in the Baroque and Rococo periods, though the most significant additions were made, in accordance with its new function as a royal palace, by **Leo von Klenze**, the architect primarily responsible for giving Munich its nineteenth-century face: he added the rusticated Königsbau facing Max–Joseph-Platz to the south and the Festsaalbau on the garden side to the north. Extensively damaged in the last war, the Residenz was reconstructed in the 1950s and 1960s – and is still the subject of restoration work.

The Residenzmuseum

About half the palace, including all the most significant historical apartments, is open to the public as the **Residenzmuseum** (April to mid-Oct Mon–Wed & Fri–Sun 9am–6pm, Thurs 9am–8pm; mid-Oct to March daily 10am–4pm; DM8/€4, or DM14/€7 combined ticket with the Schatzkammer), entered from Max–Joseph-Platz. To see it all you have to visit twice, as part of it is open mornings only, with a different section open in the afternoons.

On both tours, you see the **Ahnengalerie** (Ancestors' Gallery), decorated in the richest Rococo style, which looks for all the world like a Hall of Mirrors, except that the glass is replaced by 121 (mostly imaginary) portraits of the Wittelsbachs, who tried to give their line the most prestigious roots possible by including tenuously linked predecessors like Charlemagne. The morning tour then procedes to the Mannerist **Grottenhof** (Grotto Court), whose centrepiece is a fountain with a statue of Perseus. Under the loggia is the grotto of tufa, crystal and coloured shells, framing a statue of Mercury. Alongside is the **Antiquarium**, the oldest and most original part of the palace. This long, cavernous chamber was built in 1571 to house the family's famous collection of antiquities. A generation later, its austere architecture was sharply modified in accordance with the new Mannerist craze to serve as a festive hall, and its tunnel vault covered with humanist-inspired frescoes. In the **Kurfürstenzimmer** (Rooms of the Elector), look out for three paintings by Bernardo Bellotto, who here applied to Munich the technique his uncle Canaletto had used so successfully to immortalize the Venice of his day. Other highlights are a passageway hung with a cycle of 25 views of Italy by the Munich Romantic painter Carl Rottmann, and a suite of rooms containing extensive collections of fourteenth- to nineteenth-century Chinese, Japanese and European porcelain.

The last stage of the morning tour can also be seen in the afternoon. This includes the eight appropriately named **Reiche Zimmer** (Rich Rooms) in the sumptuous Rococo style of François Cuvilliés, and the five **Nibelungensäle** (Halls of the Nibelungs), in which medieval Germany's most famous epic is depicted in a series of paintings by the Nazarene artist Julius Schnorr von Carolsfeld. Other rooms can be seen in the afternoon only, and include further displays of ceramics, along with the silverware collection and the sumptuous early Baroque **Goldener Saal** (Golden Hall). You can also see the ecclesiastical treasury and the two chapels, which were both built in the early years of the seventeenth century. The larger **Hofkapelle**, closely modelled on the town church of St Michael, was for general use, while the more lavish **Reichekapelle** was built for the private meditations of one of the most famous of the Wittelsbachs, Maximilian I. Another memento of Maximilian comes with the **Steinzimmer**, a suite of profusely furnished rooms with a complicated set of allegories illustrating the Elector's personal vision of the world and the afterlife.

The Schatzkammer

Sharing the same entrance but requiring a separate ticket is the **Schatzkammer** (same times; DM8/€4), which houses a really fabulous collection of treasures. Among the early items, look out for the late ninth-century **miniature ciborium** that belonged to King Arnulf of Carinthia, and the **cross** of Queen Gisela of Hungary. There's a spectacular array of **crowns** too, including that of Princess Blanche of England (daughter of Henry IV), but the star piece of the whole display, kept in a room of its own, is the **statuette of St George**, made in Munich around 1590 for Wilhelm V. This has a base of gold, silver and enamel, and is encrusted with diamonds, rubies, sapphires, emeralds and rock crystal. The outstanding German Renaissance tradition in the decorative arts can be seen in a host of chalices, tankards, caskets, pendants, clocks and portable altars; look out for the rock crystal dish with gold mount designed by Holbein. Faced with such competition, the Bavarian **crown jewels**, made in the early nineteenth century soon after the duchy was promoted to a kingdom, seem rather tame.

The rest of the complex

From the entrance on Residenzstrasse, you pass through the Kapellenhof into the elongated **Brunnenhof**, in the middle of which stands a large fountain in honour of the Wittelsbachs, replete with allegorical figures of the elements, river gods, tritons and dragons. At the far end is the entrance to the **Cuvilliéstheater** (same times; DM4/€2), a perfectly intact Rococo gem, dripping in gold and bristling with intricate carvings and delicate stucco. Formerly the Wittelsbachs' private theatre, it's now the jewel in the crown of the city's performing-arts venues. It's deservedly named after the man who built it, **François Cuvilliés** – a tenacious little Walloon who began his career in the debilitating role of court dwarf to Elector Max Emanuel, but proved that he was capable of greater things by designing defensive systems for the army he was precluded from joining. As a result, he was sent to Paris to study the latest architectural theories, and on his return developed the new Rococo style to its most extravagant limits in a series of stunningly original buildings.

The northwestern part of the Residenz, entered from Hofgartenstrasse, houses the **Staatliche Sammlung Ägyptischer Kunst** (Tues 9am–4pm & 7–9pm, Wed–Fri 9am–4pm, Sat & Sun 10am–5pm; DM5/€2.50, free Sun). As well as objects from all periods of Egyptian antiquity, this features displays of Coptic art and monumental reliefs from Assyria. Highlights include the copper statue of Amenemhet III, a masterpiece of royal portraiture from about 1800 BC; the gilded coffin mask of Queen Satdjehuti-Satibu of around 1575 BC; the gold treasure of the queen of Meroë; and Egyptian-style statues from the palace of Emperor Hadrian at Tivoli. The **Hofgarten** to the north, formerly the royal park, is an ideal place for a quiet stroll. At the far end, the bombed-out Armeemuseum was until recently left as an anti-war memorial, its contents having been transferred to Ingolstadt. It has since been rebuilt with modern wings as the **Staatskanzlei**, the Bavarian State Chancellery.

The nineteenth-century city

The nineteenth-century additions to the Residenz were merely one aspect of the changing face of Munich in line with its new royal status; the city was greatly expanded, particularly to the north, with a series of broad boulevards and spacious squares lined by grandiosely self-confident Neoclassical buildings.

Odeonsplatz

In 1817, Leo von Klenze began the project to link Munich with the outlying village of Schwabing to the north by constructing the **Odeonsplatz** at the far end of the Residenz. The southwest corner of this square, however, was already occupied by the Baroque **Theatinerkirche** (or **St Cajetan**), which ranks as one of Munich's most regal churches, its golden-yellow towers and green copper dome adding a welcome splash of colour to the city skyline. It was designed in the 1660s by the Bolognese Agostino Barelli, on the model of St Andrea della Valle in Rome, though many alterations to the original plan were made by Enrico Zuccalli, his successor as court architect, and it was only completed by Cuvilliés over a century later – hence the Rococo bravura of the facade.

Although other buildings in the square, including the **Odeon** itself (originally a music college, now a government office), are by Klenze, the building which finished it off, the **Feldherrnhalle** on the southern side, is by his rival **Friedrich von Gärtner**. The hall, closely modelled on the Loggia dei Lanzi in Florence, shelters statues of Bavaria's two greatest military heroes: Johann Tilly, the imperial field marshal in the Thirty Years War, and Karl Philipp von Wrede, the commander of the Bavarian corps originally allied with Napoleon, which changed sides in time to help defeat the French at the Battle of the Nations. Between the two is a memorial to the Bavarian dead of the Franco-Prussian War. It was here on November 9, 1923 that armed police stopped Hitler's Beer Hall Putsch in its tracks, opening fire on the future dictator's band of would-be revolutionaries as they stood at the head of the narrow Residenzstrasse, in the shadow of the Feldherrnhalle.

Ludwigstrasse

From Odeonsplatz, the dead straight **Ludwigstrasse** leads to Schwabing. Its name comes from King Ludwig I, who commissioned it; though it remained unfinished when he was forced to abdicate as a result of a scandal caused by his affair with a dancer, he continued to fund it from his private resources – a decision which later proved to have been a shrewd business investment, as he was able to let the buildings at enormous rates. The most southerly palaces, up to and including the **Bayerisches Hauptstaatsarchiv**, are in a style imitating the Italian Renaissance. Immediately to the north, and in a broadly similar style, is the **Bayerische Staatsbibliothek** (Mon–Fri 9am–7.30pm, Sat 9am–4.30pm; free); it houses one of Europe's richest libraries, the most famous treasure being the original of the great monastic collection of medieval songs and poems, *Carmina Burana*. There's usually a thematic exhibition on display, and you can always see the late sixteenth-century globes of the earth and the heavens made for Duke Albrecht V, which stand at the top of the stairway.

Beyond stands one of the country's most significant nineteenth-century churches, the inevitably named **Ludwigskirche**. It's an example of the peculiarly German architectural style known as *Rundbogenstil*, which took its cue from any previous form of building – whether classical, early Christian, Romanesque or Renaissance – using rounded arches; this appears to have been the invention of Ludwig as much as Gärtner. The chancel fresco of *The Last Judgement* by the Nazarene painter Peter Cornelius is one of the largest paintings in the world, and is a self-conscious (if ultimately unsuccessful) attempt to rival Michelangelo.

Further north is the main building of the **Ludwig-Maximilian-Universität**, which is now the biggest university in Germany. Although it's relatively young, only establishing itself in Munich in 1826, it has a distinguished academic record. The philosopher Friedrich Wilhelm von Schelling was an early luminary, while later professors have included such celebrated scientists as Georg Simon Ohm (discoverer of the law of magnetic resistance which bears his name), Justus von Liebig (father of scientific agriculture) and Wilhelm Conrad Röntgen (pioneer of the X-ray). Linking the university with the **Priesterseminar** (Seminary) opposite is a circular plaza known as Geschwister-Scholl-Platz. This is one of a large number of places in Germany dedicated to the memory of Hans Scholl and his sister Sophie, the Munich students who launched the Weisse Rose (White Rose) resistance movement to Hitler – an act of defiance which cost them their lives. There's now a small memorial and documentation centre, the **Denkstätte Weisse Rose** (Mon–Wed & Fri 10am–4pm, Thurs 10am–9pm; free), on the ground floor of the university building.

The final building on Ludwigstrasse, before it passes into Schwabing and becomes known as Leopoldstrasse, is the **Siegestor**, a triumphal arch balancing the Feldherrnhalle, this time exclusively dedicated to commemorating the Bavarian army's part in the wars against Napoleon between 1813 and 1815.

Königsplatz

West of Ludwigstrasse, a planned town was laid out on a strict geometrical pattern of huge squares. The focus of this is **Königsplatz**, which was intended as a sort of Bavarian Acropolis, with a grassy middle surrounded by showpiece public buildings. In the Nazi period, it was paved over to serve as a parade ground, and it has only recently been returned to its original form.

On the north side of the square is the **Glyptothek** (Tues, Wed & Fri–Sun 10am–5pm, Thurs 10am–8pm; DM6/€3, free Sun), built by Klenze to house Ludwig I's collection of Greek and Roman sculptures. At the heart of the display are the surviving parts from the front of the **temple of Aphaia on Aegina**, whose sculptures rank among the supreme masterpieces of Hellenistic art. As these were acquired under decidedly dubious circumstances, the Greeks would like them back: indeed they rank alongside the British Museum's Elgin Marbles at the top of Greece's shopping list in appeals for the return of the country's "looted" heritage. Other highlights of the museum are the tomb relief of Mnesarete, the daughter of Socrates; the famous **Barberini Faun**, a surpassingly beautiful carving of a sleeping satyr from about 220 BC; and a large collection of Roman busts, including one of the finest of more than two hundred extant portraits of Emperor Augustus.

Across the square, a later building contains the **Staatliche Antikensammlungen** (Tues & Thurs–Sun 10am–5pm, Wed 10am–8pm; DM6/€3, DM10/€5 for joint ticket with the Glyptothek, free Sun, but closed early 2002 for structural repairs), whose displays include Greek vases from the fifth and sixth centuries BC, as well as jewellery and small statues from Greek, Etruscan and Roman antiquity.

On the west side of the square is the **Propylaeum**, a severe twin-towered structure in an unashamedly derivative Grecian style. The reliefs show the Greek War of Independence against the Turks, whose successful conclusion led to the western powers forcing Prince Otto of Bavaria on the victors as their king. This didn't prove to be a happy match: Otto's authoritarian methods went down badly with his subjects, and he was eventually forced to abdicate. Before that had happened, however, this Propylaeum had already been built in his honour.

Just off Königsplatz, facing the Glyptothek in a picturesquely manicured garden, is the **Lenbachhaus** (Tues–Sun 10am–6pm; DM8/€4), the villa of nineteenth-century Bavarian painter **Franz von Lenbach**, an enormously successful high-society portraitist. Many of his paintings are displayed inside, in rooms furnished as he knew them. Works by other Munich painters down the centuries are also featured, with the highlight being those by Der Blaue Reiter (see p.1097), whose members included **Kandinsky**, **Klee**, **Marc** and **Macke**; the Kandinsky collection here is particularly outstanding. In recent years the museum has also concentrated on important contemporary German art, and is worth checking for special exhibitions.

Immediately to the north, at Richard-Wagner-Str. 10, is the **Paläontologisches Museum** (Mon–Thurs 8am–4pm, Fri 8am–2pm; free). Kids will love the display of prehistoric animal skeletons in the entrance hall, which include a sabre-toothed tiger from California, a giant deer from Ireland and an elephant found in Upper Bavaria which is calculated to be ten million years old. However, these are mere striplings in comparison to some of the skeletons upstairs, such as a fish and a crocodile found in Baden-Württemberg, both of which date back 190 million years.

The most sinister building in Munich stands on Arcisstrasse, opposite the Glyptothek. Now serving as a music academy known as the **Hochschule für Musik**, it was formerly the **Braunhaus**, the local Nazi headquarters, and the place where Neville Chamberlain made the infamous agreement to force Czechoslovakia to cede Hitler the Sudetenland, thereby making the very name of Munich synonymous in the English language with treachery.

The Alte Pinakothek

The **Alte Pinakothek** (Tues, Wed & Fri–Sun 10am–5pm, Thurs 10am–10pm; *www.pinakotheken-muenchen.de*; DM9/€4.50, free Sun), a Florentine-style palazzo by Klenze at Barer Str. 27, is one of the largest art galleries in Europe, housing an outstanding collection of paintings spanning the period from the fourteenth to the eighteenth century, including the finest representation of the German School to be found anywhere in the world (for more information on these artists, see Contexts p.1085). The ground floor covers fifteenth-century German painting in the left wing, and sixteenth- to seventeenth-century German, Flemish and Dutch painting in the right, while the first floor begins with fifteenth-century Netherlandish painting in the left wing, and then proceeds to German, Italian, Flemish, Dutch, French and Spanish art.

THE GERMAN SCHOOL

German painting of the fifteenth century had predominantly religious themes, and, in keeping with an age that believed art was for the greater glory of God, the names of many of the artists have not survived. Look out for the beautifully observed narrative cycle which has provided the nickname of **Master of the Life of the Virgin** for an unknown Cologne painter, and the idiosyncratic trompe l'oeil scenes of a Bavarian contemporary, **Master of the Tegernsee Altar**, whose panels are executed as if in imitation of a carved retable. From the following generation, the works of the Tyrolean **Michael Pacher** stand out. Though he's better known as a sculptor, his luxuriant altarpiece of *The Four Fathers of the Church*, an early attempt at fusing the rich late

Gothic style of southern Germany with the new approach of the Italian Renaissance, shows he was no less talented with the brush than the chisel.

Under the impact of the Renaissance, portraiture became increasingly popular, and **Dürer**'s *Self-Portrait* is one of the most famous paintings from this time, the artist looking out with a self-assured poise, his face framed by shoulder-length golden locks and his torso clad in a fur coat. The famous panels of *The Four Apostles* come from the very end of Dürer's career and are generally held to be his greatest achievement. Originally, they were meant as wings of an altarpiece dedicated to the Virgin, but the project was scrapped when the city of Nürnberg – with the artist himself an enthusiastic supporter – went over to Protestantism.

Another painting with a Reformation connection is **Grünewald**'s *Disputation of SS Erasmus and Maurice*. This was commissioned by the leading member of the conciliatory Catholic party, Cardinal Albrecht von Brandenburg. The gorgeously attired St Erasmus, who is shown arguing for the peaceful conversion of the world against the armed struggle favoured by the black warrior St Maurice, represents a double allusion to the contemporary approach favoured by the cardinal and his great friend, Erasmus of Rotterdam. As can be seen in the early *Mocking of Christ*, Grünewald himself was of a far more impassioned nature, and he became a supporter of the extreme wing of Protestantism. Strange as it seems, Cardinal Albrecht also patronized Luther's very own propagandist, **Lucas Cranach the Elder**, who took advantage of the new liberties of the age to introduce sensually explicit nudes – such as the full-lengths of *Lucretia* and *Venus and Cupid* – into German art for the first time. This approach was soon taken up and developed by **Hans Baldung**, as in the pair of allegorical female figures, perhaps representing Prudence and Music.

Albrecht Altdorfer's *Battle of Alexander*, depicting the victory of Alexander the Great over the Persian king Darius III in 333 BC, is a masterpiece of another new genre, that of history painting. Literally hundreds of soldiers are painted individually in minute detail, but at the same time represented as a heaving mass, dramatically giving the sense of a momentous battle. The artist often used identifiable landscapes in the Danube valley as backgrounds for his paintings; indeed, in *St George and the Dragon* the ostensible subject is really an excuse for a masterly nature study of the lush foliage of the beech trees which are a feature of the region.

THE FLEMISH AND DUTCH SCHOOLS

Among the fifteenth-century Flemish works, **Rogier van der Weyden**'s *Adoration of the Magi*, which was commissioned for St Kolumba in Cologne, is regarded as one of the greatest portrayals of this classic Christmas-card subject. It makes a fascinating contrast with the tiny house altar of the same scene (known as *The Pearl of Brabant* because of its highly polished sheen), by **Dieric Bouts**. Equally outstanding is **Memling**'s lyrical *Seven Joys of the Virgin*, which integrates all the scenes into a single dream-like fantasy of architecture and landscape. From the following century comes **Pieter Bruegel the Elder**'s *Land of Cockaigne*, depicting a seemingly utopian scene of plenty, where food cooks itself and pigs come ready-roasted; it's full of entertaining details, but, for all its humour, the real purpose of the work was actually to condemn gluttony and idleness. Very different in style is the exquisite small-scale art of his son **Jan Brueghel**, who is copiously represented here.

Centrepiece of the entire museum, and the main consideration in its architectural design, is the collection of works by the seventeeth-century Flemish painter **Rubens**. Sixty-two paintings display a wide range of the artist's prodigious output, including everything from the modellos the master made for the guidance of his large workshop to such massive finished altarpieces as *The Fall of the Rebel Angels* and *The Last Judgement* (which was commissioned for the Hofkirche in Neuburg an der Donau); from intimate portraits such as *Rubens and Isabella Brandt in the Honeysuckle Bower* (painted to celebrate his first marriage) to such boisterous mythological scenes as *Drunken Silenus*; and from the quiet beauty of *Landscape with a Rainbow* to the horrors of *The Massacre of the Innocents*.

Van Dyck, Rubens' most distinguished pupil, is also extensively represented, with portraits and religious scenes drawn from the main phases of his career. The small cabinet rooms beyond contain the largest collection of works in existence by **Adriaen Brouwer**, the most trenchant observer of the seamier side of life in seventeenth-century Flanders. There's also a haunting Passion cycle by **Rembrandt**, commissioned by the House of Orange as Reformed Protestant visions of Holy Week. In both *The Raising of the Cross* and *The Deposition*, the familiar figure of Rembrandt himself appears as a leading witness to the events.

THE ITALIAN, FRENCH AND SPANISH SCHOOLS

The Italian section begins with three little panels from a dispersed altarpiece by **Giotto**; other highlights include **Fra Filippo Lippi**'s classically inspired *The Annunciation*, **Botticelli**'s theatrical *Pietà*, **Raphael**'s tender *Holy Family* and a rare authenticated example of the young **Leonardo da Vinci**, *Madonna of the Carnation*. However, works by **Titian** steal the show here, notably the *Seated Portrait of Charles V*, which perfectly captures the self-confident poise of a man of destiny, and *Christ Crowned with Thorns*, dating from the end of the artist's very long life. Among later Italian works, **Tiepolo**'s *Adoration of the Magi*, a product of his Würzburg years, stands out. The French display includes **Poussin**'s *Lamentation over the Dead Christ* and several classical landscapes by **Claude**. There's also a room of seventeenth-century Spanish painting, including a *Portrait of a Young Man* by **Velázquez**, and genre pictures by **Murillo**; the latter were to have an enormous influence on French and English art of the following century.

The Neue Pinakothek

The **Neue Pinakothek** (Mon, Wed & Fri–Sun 10am–5pm, Thurs 10am–10pm; *www .pinakotheken-muenchen.de*; DM9/€4.50, free Sun) immediately to the north houses collections of eighteenth- and nineteenth-century painting and sculpture. After the wealth and variety of its neighbour, it can't help but seem a little thin on the ground, but it does have good examples of Neoclassical, Romantic and Realist art.

Cool, detached and precise, the portrait of *Marquise de Sourcy de Thélusson* by the French painter **David** is a beautiful example of the Neoclassical style. Of all the works from the mid-nineteenth century Romantic period, those by the Munich painter **Carl Spitzweg** are particularly entertaining. He painted scenes from everyday life, depicting human emotions and frailties with a wry sense of humour and cartoon-like style. *The Poor Poet*, *The Bookworm* and *The Childhood Friend* cover just some of his themes, which are always subtly observed and with a dig against pretension.

More controversial are the heroic visions of the city's mid-nineteenth century history painters. The sketches by **Wilhelm von Kaulbach** for the frescoes of the Neue Pinakothek's exterior are the only reminders left of this grandiose scheme, which was completely destroyed in the war. A monumental *Destruction of Jerusalem by Titus* by the same artist is remarkable for its scale and attention to detail, though the most celebrated example of this style is the far less bombastic *Seni with the Corpse of Wallenstein* by his pupil **Karl von Piloty**.

Of the works by French Impressionists and Post-Impressionists, **Manet**'s *Breakfast in the Studio* is probably the most famous; other highlights are one of **van Gogh**'s *Sunflowers* and **Gauguin**'s *Breton Farmwomen*. The main German exponent of this phase is **Max Liebermann**, whose *Boys by the Beach* beautifully captures a scene from life at the turn of the twentieth century. The museum rounds off with a small selection of Symbolism and Art Nouveau. **Franz von Stuck**'s *Sin* is the most striking piece, vice being represented as a lascivious woman exposing herself. Much more romantic and stylized is **Klimt**'s portrait of *Margarethe Stonborough-Wittgenstein*.

In 2000, some of the twentieth-century art formerly on display at the Haus der Kunst was temporarily put on display in the Neue Pinakothek. By the summer of 2002, this should be on view in the **Pinakothek der Moderne**, which is under construction on the plot immediately to the east. The most ambitious museum project in Bavaria since World War II, it is set to feature displays of design and applied art, architecture and graphics, in addition to the core collections of painting and sculpture.

Maximilianstrasse

Maximilian II, who succeeded his disgraced father in 1848, also wanted to have a show-piece boulevard named in his own honour; indeed, he had begun planning for it long before he came to the throne. The resultant **Maximilianstrasse** runs east from Max-Joseph-Platz in front of the Residenz, forming Munich's answer to the Champs-Elysées.

As with Odeonsplatz, there was already an extant building at the beginning of the street, this time Klenze's **Nationaltheater**, which maintains its reputation as one of Europe's most prestigious opera houses; almost completely destroyed by bombs in World War II, it was re-created at enormous expense in 1963. In many ways, it sets the tone for the rest of the street, which is a real theatre quarter, an almost equally prestigious venue being the Jugendstil **Münchener Kammerspiele** at no. 26. Across the road is the city's most exclusive address, the **Hotel Vierjahreszeiten**, while elsewhere are some two dozen commercial galleries and a seemingly endless number of luxury shops selling the latest fashions and trendiest designer goods.

Over the hideous ring road, at no. 42 on the street, is the **Staatliches Museum für Völkerkunde** (Tues–Sun 9.30am–4.30pm; DM6/€3), illustrating the art and history of non-European cultures in a series of excellently presented changing exhibitions. Further east is a huge bronze monument to Maximilian II. To the north, St-Anna-Strasse leads to the Franciscan church of **St Anna im Lehel**, designed by Johann Michael Fischer and decorated by the Asam brothers. Maximilianstrasse itself continues eastwards over the River Isar to the **Maximileum**, a grandiose palace by the Dresden architect Gottfried Semper. Intended as a cultural establishment, it's now home to the Bavarian parliament.

The Haus der Kunst

Another of Munich's great boulevards is **Prinzregentenstrasse**, which runs east from the Prinz-Carl-Palais at the far end of the Hofgarten. Laid out at the end of the nineteenth century and the beginning of the twentieth, its name comes from Prince Luitpold, who ruled as regent after the deposition of his nephew Ludwig II. Nowadays, it's the city's second main museum quarter. The **Haus der Kunst** (daily 10am–10pm; variable charge), the first building on the northern side, was built by the Nazis as a showcase for the sort of art they favoured. It's now used for temporary artistic exhibitions – usually two or three at a time, with at least one of international blockbuster status.

The Bayerisches Nationalmuseum and Archäologische Staatssammlung

Next door to the Haus der Kunst is the rambling pile of the **Bayerisches Nationalmuseum** (Tues–Sun 9.30am–5pm; *www.bayerisches-nationalmuseum.de*; DM6/€3, free Sun). For many years its magnificent collections were only partly accessible, but they can now be seen in their entirety as a result of structural repairs completed in time for the museum's jubilee in 2000. On the first floor, the exhibition halls are pastiches of the architectural style contemporary with the artefacts they display. The medieval sections feature the surviving sculptures from the original Kloster

Wessobrunn and *Der Kleine Dom*, a gorgeous miniature cathedral made by a fourteenth-century goldsmith. This is followed by a superb display of German wood sculpture at its fifteenth- and sixteenth-century peak. There are examples of **Tilman Riemenschneider's** art drawn from all phases of his career, ranging from the early *St Mary Magdalene Surrounded by Angels*, via a magnificently characterized set of Apostles made to adorn the Marienkapelle in Würzburg, to the serene late *St Barbara*. Many of his most talented contemporaries – Hans Multscher, Michel and Gregor Erhart, Hans Leinberger and Erasmus Grasser – are also well represented.

From the following generation is a statuette of *Judith with the Head of Holofernes* by **Conrad Meit**, one of the few major German sculptors to work in an Italianate style. There's also a miniature *Portrait of a 27-year-old Man* by **Hans Holbein the Younger**; this probably depicts Harry Maynert, a painter-colleague at the English court of Henry VIII and is one of only a dozen or so miniatures by Holbein to have survived. Look out also for the **map of Bavaria** drawn by the great geographer Philipp Apian in the 1560s and, from a decade later, the lovingly crafted **models** by Jacob Sandtner of the province's five courtly capitals. Despite the focus on Bavarian art, there's a decent Italian Renaissance section, which includes six magnificent bronze reliefs of the Passion by **Giambologna**, plus sculptures by Luca della Robbia and Antonio Rossellino. The late Renaissance section features the extraordinary costumes and jewellery retrieved from the tombs of members of the House of Pfalz-Neuburg. Bavarian Rococo art is copiously represented, notably by a number of impressive large-scale statues by **Ignaz Günther**.

Upstairs are displays of porcelain and musical instruments, plus a fascinating room devoted to **historic board games**, many of which are of great beauty. However, even these are overshadowed by the Rococo **dinner service** of the prince-bishops of Hildesheim, arguably the most spectacular example of Augsburg's long and proud silverware tradition. The museum's basement (closed noon–2pm) features Bavarian folk art and a really outstanding collection of **Christmas cribs** from Bavaria, Austria and Italy.

Just behind the Bayerisches Nationalmuseum, at Lerchenfeldstr. 2, is the **Archäologische Staatssammlung** (Tues–Sun 9am–4.30pm; DM5/€2.50, free Sun). This makes a good attempt at bringing alive Bavarian prehistory, the Roman occupation and early medieval life. Look out in particular for the Bronze Age golden cone from Ezelsdorf, the Roman treasure from Eining, the jewellery from tribal graves, the Carolingian choir screen and the surprising wheel-shaped Byzantine chandelier.

East along Prinzregentenstrasse

Further along the street from the Bayerisches Nationalmuseum is the former Prussian embassy, now housing the **Schackgalerie** (10am–5pm, closed Tues; DM5/€2.50). Count Schack was Munich's most important art patron during the nineteenth century, supporting struggling painters such as Franz von Lenbach, Marées, Böcklin and others until they achieved public acclaim. The museum, which preserves his collection intact, contains important examples of all those artists, plus other Romantic painters such as Feuerbach and Spitzweg.

Following Prinzregentenstrasse across the Isar over the Luitpoldbrücke, you come to the **Friedensengel**, a nineteenth-century monument to peace shining in gold splendour. Past Europaplatz at Prinzregentenstr. 60 is Munich's most eccentric nineteenth-century building, the **Villa Stuck** (Tues–Sun 10am–6pm; DM2/€1). This was the house of Franz von Stuck, the leader of the Munich Secession, and was designed by him – using a decidedly eclectic mix of styles, though showing distinct echoes of the city's Neoclassical palaces built earlier in the century – in his only attempt at architecture. Inside is a large collection of his paintings, plus other examples of *fin-de-siècle* art, with Jugendstil predominating.

Schwabing

Just north of the city centre lies the stylish district of **Schwabing**. During the Second Reich and the Weimar Republic it gained a reputation as a centre for radical bohemian chic. Its habitués included outcast revolutionary politicians, the young Lenin and Hitler among them, the artists of Der Blaue Reiter and writers such as Ibsen, the Mann brothers, Rilke, Brecht and Wedekind. Today, in contrast, Munich's real Latin Quarter has moved to Haidhausen, leaving Schwabing as the favourite haunt of the city's *Schickies*.

A much larger area than the city centre, Schwabing spreads untidily to the left and right of Leopoldstrasse, the northern continuation of Ludwigstrasse. The Englischer Garten makes up one pleasant border. Schwabing divides into three distinct areas. West of Leopoldstrasse, residential streets mix with wacky shops, student bars and restaurants. Along the centre line and to its right, trendy shops and café-bars ensure permanent crowds, day and night. Nightclubs are thick on the ground here too, especially around the Wedekindplatz near Münchener Freiheit. The far north of Schwabing is a tidily bourgeois residential area, uninteresting for visitors apart from the Olympiapark, which is way out, at the end of the U-Bahn line. For listings of the area's bars, restaurants and clubs see pp.91–98.

The Englischer Garten

The vast **Englischer Garten** takes its name from the eighteenth-century landscaping fashion which tried to create parks resembling untouched nature. Occupying what was formerly marshland, it was created at the instigation of Bavaria's most unlikely statesman, the American-born Benjamin Thompson, who was a leading minister under the garden-loving Elector Carl Theodor (see p.355).

When you've had enough of the city, the Eisbach meadow opposite the **Monopteros**, a Neoclassical temple by Klenze, is a good place to relax. It's the city's main playground: people come here to sunbathe, picnic, swim in the aptly named **Eisbach** (ice stream) or ride horses. Visitors often find the large-scale nudity a little unnerving – and it certainly wouldn't be acceptable in any other German city. Even "respectable" businessmen will pop over in the lunch hour, fold their suits in a neat pile and read the paper stark naked. There are rules on where exactly nude sunbathing is allowed, but the police have given up trying to enforce them.

One of the city's most famous beer gardens is around the **Chinesischer Turm** (known locally as the **Chinaturm**) to the north of the Monopteros. It's at its best (or worst) on Sunday afternoons, when a Bavarian band blares across the crowd from the heights of the Chinaturm itself. Two, more peaceful, beer gardens are not far off by the **Kleinhesseloher See**. Heading north from here, you get the feeling of being in the countryside rather than in a city park.

The Olympiapark and around

During the summer months of July and August the **Olympiapark** is the setting for open-air rock and pop concerts every weekend. Usually it's local bands of varying standards, but it doesn't cost anything and is worth checking out; the venue is a modern-day version of a Greek theatre, known as the **Theatron**, right next to the park's lake. The stadia all around were built for the 1972 Olympics and still have a somewhat futuristic look about them. In particular, the main **Olympiastadion** (daily 8.30am–6pm; DM3/€1.50) is a strange construction of steel poles and plexiglass expanses, looking rather like an overgrown tent. From the 290-metre-high **tower** (daily 9am–midnight; DM5/€2.50), there's a wonderful view over Munich and the Alps.

Just to the west rises another of Munich's most arresting modern buildings, the **BMW-Gebäude**, symbolically shaped as four tightly clustered cylindrical towers. The separate structure alongside houses the **BMW-Museum** (daily 9am–5pm;

DM5.50/€2.75). This has a certain novelty value in being laid out along a gently sloping ramp which you gradually ascend on your way round. A fair number of vintage models are on view, but essentially the presentation is a flash – and often none too subtle –
advert for the company and its products. If you'd like to see round the works, ask at the
reception (or better still, phone ☎0 89/38 95 33 06 as far in advance as possible); tours
(in English as well as German) are held regularly, but are often booked up weeks in
advance.

South along the River Isar

Wiener Platz, just of the east of the Maximileum, marks the beginning of **Haidhausen**.
Around here it's still more or less the working-class quarter that it always was, with its
own market and the large and shady beer garden of the Hofbräukeller. Until the early
1980s, Haidhausen was a run-down part of town that had become something of a
Turkish ghetto. The peeling squares and prewar houses have since been rediscovered,
and now trendy little health-food stores, alternative craftshops and hip bars have
sprouted like mushrooms. It's become *the* place to live, and spiralling rents have forced
out most of the original inhabitants.

Down towards the Isar on Rosenheimer Strasse is hidden one of Munich's real gems,
the **Volksbad** (daily 7.30am–11pm; prices range from DM5/€2.50 for a swim to
DM20/€10 for the full treatment of a Roman-Irish bath), a beautifully restored
Jugendstil indoor swimming hall. High stuccoed ceilings arch over two pools, with
mahogany changing cubicles surrounding each, and the sound of splashing water issuing from sculptured fountains makes the atmosphere perfect. There are a couple of
saunas and a traditional Turkish bath.

On an island spanned by Ludwigsbrücke is the **Deutsches Museum** (daily
9am–5pm; DM12/€6). Covering every conceivable aspect of technical endeavour,
from the first flint tools to the research labs of modern industry, this is the most compendious collection of its type in Europe. The sheer scale of the place is in itself
impressive – it's well worth spending the whole day there – and some of the large-
scale exhibits, such as biplanes and boats, are ranged in rooms the size of hangars.
Among the mould-breaking inventions on view in the engineering section on the
ground floor is the very first **diesel engine**, completed by Rudolf Diesel in 1897. The
chemistry department on the first floor features several notable historic displays,
including the monastic pharmacy from St Emmeram in Regensburg, and original
equipment from Justus von Liebig's Munich laboratory. Part of the second floor has
been converted into a replica of the Altamira caves while in the basement there's a
convincingly gloomy mock-up of a **coalmine**. Meticulously constructed large-scale
models are featured throughout, and the use of interactive displays makes them as
absorbing for kids as adults. Check the noticeboards for the times of the daily demonstrations given by museum staff; that of the historical **musical instruments** on the
first floor is particularly worth catching.

As a supplement, it's worth visiting the **Forum der Technik** (daily 9am–11pm) next
door. This boasts an ultra-modern Planetarium (various programmes from
DM12.50/€6.25) and a 400-square-metre screen for IMAX films (DM12.50/€6.25),
shown throughout the day.

From the Reichenbachbrücke onwards, paths follow the course of the Isar all the
way to the city's zoo, **Tierpark Hellabrunn** (daily: April–Sept 8am–6pm; Oct–March
9am–5pm; DM12/€6), which can be reached from the city centre by taking U-Bahn #3
to Thalkirchen. The east bank rises steeply around here and the river and canals are
completely hidden by thick woodland. Finally, if you want to see Bavaria's equivalent of
Hollywood, and Europe's largest film-making centre, join one of the guided tours
through **Bavaria Filmstadt** (March–Oct daily 9am–5pm; DM17/€8.50). It lies 2km

further south from the zoo and is reached by tram #25: this can be picked up on Grünwalder Strasse a block to the east of the zoo or at the Silberhorn U-Bahn station (lines #1 and #2 from the centre).

The Theresienwiese

Southwest of the Hauptbahnhof, reached by U-Bahn #4 or #5, lies a large egg-shaped fairground known as the **Theresienwiese**. For most of the year, this is an unremarkable meadow, but for sixteen days it's home to Germany's biggest annual event, the world-famous beer festival-cum-fair, the **Oktoberfest** (see box opposite). Until recently, it was also Munich's trade fair quarter, but this has moved to the suburb of Riem. The three redundant exhibition buildings which are under a protection order are currently being coverted to house the **Verkehrsmuseum**, which will house the land transport collections of the Deutsches Museum. This is currently scheduled to open in 2003.

Overlooking the field to the west is the colonnaded **Ruhmeshalle** (Hall of Fame), a Bavarian counterpart to the earlier Walhalla near Regensburg which was likewise paid for by Ludwig I and built by Leo von Klenze. In front stands the colossal bronze statue of **Bavaria** (April to mid-Oct Tues–Sun 9am–6pm; DM5/€2.50), a very Germanicized derivative of the art of classical Greece. Designed by Ludwig von Schwanthaler, it took all of six years to cast.

Nymphenburg

Schloss Nymphenburg (April to mid-Oct Mon–Wed & Fri–Sun 9am–6pm, Thurs 9am–8pm; mid-Oct to March daily 10am–4pm; DM 7/€3.50, or DM15/€7.50 including the Marstallmuseum and pavilions), which lies some 4km northwest of central Munich on the route of tram #17, was the summer residence of the Wittelsbachs. Its kernel is a small Italianate palace begun in 1664 by Agostino Barelli for the frivolous Electress Adelaide, who dedicated it to the pastoral pleasures of the goddess Flora and her nymphs – hence the name. Her son Max Emanuel commissioned an ingenious extension, whereby four pavilions were built to the side of the palace and connected to it by arcaded passages. Later, the palace itself was modified and much larger wings added, resulting in a remarkably unified whole, despite having been nearly a century in the making. By this time, an extensive French-style park had been laid out as an appropriate backdrop. In 1761 the famous porcelain factory was transferred to the site, but plans to establish a planned town on the model of Ludwigsburg in Württemberg came to nothing.

A resplendent Rococo festive hall, the **Grosser Saal** (or **Steinerner Saal**) forms the centrepiece of the interior. In its present form, it dates back to the 1750s and is a late work by one of the finest decorative artists of the period, Johann Baptist Zimmermann, whose gloriously coloured ceiling fresco incorporates a number of mythological scenes, including one of Flora receiving homage from her nymphs. Otherwise, the most celebrated room is the **Schönheitengalerie**, a collection of portraits by Joseph Stieler of beauties who caught King Ludwig I's eye between 1827 and 1850. Outsiders among the predominantly aristocratic line-up include the so-called Schöne Münchnerin, the daughter of a local shoemaker, and the dancer Lola Montez, who caused the king's downfall.

There is free access to the **Schlosskapelle**, which is cunningly concealed within one of the northern pavilions, with no outward sign of its ecclesiastical function. The ceiling frescoes by the Tyrolean Joseph Mölck illustrate the life of the chapel's patroness, St Mary Magdalene, while the high altar has a gilded tabernacle-cum-reliquary designed by Cuvilliés.

THE OKTOBERFEST

Munich's **Oktoberfest** has its origins in the marriage between the Bavarian Crown Prince Ludwig (the future King Ludwig I) and Princess Thérèse of Saxe-Hildburghausen on October 17, 1810. A massive fair was held on the fields now named after the princess, and it was such a popular event that it has been repeated annually ever since, and has spawned innumerable smaller imitations throughout Germany. Nowadays, it's quite simply an orgy of beer-drinking, with upwards of 50,000 hectolitres consumed, ensuring fabulous profits for the brewers – and the publicans lucky enough to be chosen as landlords. Each of the seven Munich breweries (Hacker-Pschorr counting as two for this purpose, even although Paulaner now makes all the beers which appear under the joint label) has its own huge **tent**, where in addition to beer, bretzels, chicken halves, sausages and pork knuckles are sold. Visitors sit ten to a bench, and after a few litres of beer half the hall is singing and dancing on the tables. There are also a number of smaller tents, which tend to be far less boisterous and not so overcrowded. The accompanying **fair** offers some great rides to churn your guts, some so hairy that they're banned in countries such as the US.

Despite its name, the *Oktoberfest* actually begins in September: it lasts for sixteen days, always ending on the first Sunday of October. The traditional **opening ceremonies** on the first Saturday revolve around the great horse-drawn brewery wagons arriving at the fairground at 11am to the sound of brass bands and much pomp and speech-making. That evening, a **folklore concert** is held in the Circus-Krone-Bau, Marsstr. 43, involving a selection of those taking part in the big **procession** the following day. It leaves from the centre of town at 10am, this time made up of hundreds of traditional folklore groups, marching bands, musicians, jesters, commercial floats and decorated horsemen that slowly converge on the fairground. A week later, a concert of all the *Oktoberfest* bands is held on the steps of the Bavaria statue at 11am, though this is postponed for a week if the weather is poor.

The proportions of the fair are so massive that the grounds are divided along four main **avenues**, creating a boisterous city of its own, heaving with revellers from morning till night. Ostensibly a family affair, with rides and stalls of every description jostling for customers, it attracts around seven million visitors. Over seventy percent of these come from Bavaria and its immediate vicinity; the rest are drawn from all over the world, with Australians, New Zealanders and Italians forming the largest foreign contingents. Things are fairly relaxed during daylight hours, and it's advisable to visit at lunchtime if you want to eat and drink in comfort, or to avoid long queues for the rides. However, the atmosphere gets increasingly wild as the evening wears on: many of the big tents are packed to overflowing, and at closing time (around 11pm) staff have the unenviable task of trying to eject hundreds of fighting drunks.

For **information** on the opening ceremonies and pageants, read the *Monatsmagazin* or contact the tourist office; advance **tickets** for the folklore concert are available from the organizers, Münchner Festring, Pestalozzistr. 3a (☎0 89/2 60 81 34). Even though entrance to the grounds is free, expect to spend lots of money. **Accommodation** prices during this time are often hiked up; on any of the three weekends you'll have trouble finding anything at all if you haven't booked in advance, while on weekdays only middle- and upper-range hotels are likely to have vacancies. Many Munich women choose to avoid the *Oktoberfest* altogether, and it's probably wise for unaccompanied women to proceed with caution after dark, avoiding the more raucous tents.

Housed within the Schloss's southern wing is the **Marstallmuseum** (same hours as Schloss; DM5/€2.50, or DM15/€7.50 combined ticket with Schloss), whose ground-floor halls display the elaborate **coaches** and **sleighs** of the Wittelsbachs. There are some magnificent Rococo pieces, notably the Paris-built coronation coach of Charles VII, the second and last of the Wittelsbachs to gain election as Holy Roman Emperor, and two racing sleighs carved in the workshop of the local court sculptor, Johann

Baptist Straub. Even more riotously ornate are the fairy-tale state and gala coaches made more than a century later for the ill-fated King Ludwig II. Upstairs is a comprehensive display of Nymphenburg **porcelain**, ranging from the early years of production to the twentieth century.

The Schlosspark

For all its splendours, the Schloss is overshadowed by the wonderful **Schlosspark** to the rear. Three of its four garden **pavilions**, which are all of a markedly different character, were designed by **Joseph Effner**, the innovative court architect who was also responsible for the harmonization of the Schloss. A short walk from the northern wing is the **Magdalenenklause** (April to mid-Oct Mon–Wed & Fri–Sun 9am–6pm, Thurs 9am–8pm; DM4/€2, or DM15/€7.50 combined ticket with Schloss), built to resemble a ruined hermitage, with a grotto and four simple cell-like rooms within. It's a very early example of the Historicism which was later to become a German obsession, borrowing elements from Roman, Gothic and even Moorish architecture. The Elector would come here when he wished to meditate – and he had not far to go if he tired of its peace and asceticism. Westwards through the park is the **Pagodenburg** (same times as Magdalenenklause, but closed since 1996 for restorations; DM4/€2, or DM15/€7.50 combined ticket with Schloss), which was used for the most exclusive parties thrown by the court. Effner's third building, the **Badenburg** (April to mid-Oct Mon–Wed & Fri–Sun 9am–6pm, Thurs 9am–8pm; DM4/€2, or DM15/€7.50 combined ticket with Schloss), lies on the opposite side of the canal, at the tip of the larger of the park's two lakes. It reflects contemporary interest in chinoiserie, though both the bathing room and the two-storey banqueting hall are in the richest Baroque tradition.

For all their charm, Effner's pavilions are overshadowed by the stunning **Amalienburg** (same times as Schloss; DM5/€2.50, or DM15/€7.50 combined ticket with Schloss), the hunting lodge built behind the south wing of the Schloss by his successor as court architect, **François Cuvilliés**. This is among the supreme expressions of the Rococo style, marrying a cunningly thought-out design – which makes the little building seem like a full-scale palace – with extravagant decoration. The entrance chamber, with its niches for the hunting dogs, must be the most tasteful kennel ever built, and the elaborately tiled kitchen is likewise without peer. However, the showpiece is the circular **Spiegelsaal** (Hall of Mirrors), best seen on a bright day when the light casts magical reflections on the pale blue walls and the silvery rocaille console tables, panelled garlands and stuccowork nymphs and putti, creating the uncanny illusion that the chamber forms a seemless whole with the landscape outside.

To the north of the Schloss, the **Botanischer Garten** (daily 9am–4.30/7pm, hothouses closed 11.45am–1pm; DM4/€2) hides all manner of plants in its steamy hothouses and landscaped herbarium.

Eating and drinking

Munich is awash with places to eat and drink, and you can find somewhere open at any time of the day or night. Though best known for its cavernous beer halls and leafy beer gardens, it also has a host of ethnic eateries as well as a lively café-bar culture which carries on well into the early hours. It's not difficult to eat well for relatively little money, with generous portions of heavy food being the norm in establishments which specialize in Bavarian cuisine.

Mensas are the cheapest places to get a good basic meal: you're supposed to have a valid student card to eat in them, but no one seems to check. The most central is at

Leopoldstr. 13a; another is at the technical university, Arcisstr. 17 (both 11am–2pm). Most **butchers' shops** sell bread rolls with various hot and cold fillings from as little as DM3/€1.50. Good places for this type of snack are the shops of the Vinzenz Murr chain, which can be found all over the city; they usually also serve hot daily specials which can be eaten within the shop.

Beer halls and beer gardens

The **beer cellar** (Bierkeller) and **beer garden** (Biergarten) are Munich's most characteristic institutions. Generally speaking the former are roomy halls (rather than cellars); often standing in leafy gardens, they serve strong, heady beer produced in a local brewery, plus hearty traditional Bavarian food. Although a few have become tainted by excessive tourism, they remain an essential and unmissable feature of the city.

City centre

Altes Hackerhaus, Sendlinger Str. 75. The city-centre beer hall of the Hacker-Pschorr brewery, jam-packed with bric-a-brac and with a minute beer garden.

Augustinerbräu, Neuhauser Str. 27. One of Munich's most celebrated beer halls, with an unusually long menu, a wonderfully evocative late nineteenth-century decor and an Italian garden to the rear.

Franziskaner Fuchsenstuben, Perusastr. 5. A good choice for either a full meal or a snack: it's said to serve Munich's best *Weisswurst*, the white sausage which traditionally should only be eaten before noon.

Hofbräuhaus, Platzl 9. The most famous one – which is consequently on the itinerary of just about every visitor to the city. Nonetheless, it's perfectly genuine, with plenty of regular customers, and the food and drink are fairly priced.

Löwenbräukeller, Nymphenburger Str. 2. Located a short distance west of Königsplatz, this serves excellent food and has a beer garden.

Spatenhaus, Residenzstr. 12. The most upmarket of Spaten's hostelries, with an interior decked out in traditional Alpine style, complete with a frescoed ceiling.

Spatenhofkeller, Neuhauser Str. 39. Offers hearty Bavarian cooking at lower than average prices, with bargain midday menus which sometimes feature quite innovative dishes.

Weisses Bräuhaus, Im Tal 10. This is the flagship of the Schneider brewery, a *Weissbier* specialist which moved its production base after the war from this site to Kelheim in Eastern Bavaria. Though it has a full menu, it's best known for its *Weisswurst*, which should preferably be eaten to the accompaniment of a *Weissbier*.

Elsewhere in the city

Augustinerkeller, Arnulfstr. 52. Near the S-Bahn stop Hackerbrücke, with a large, shady garden and hardly a tourist in sight.

Aumeister, Sondermeierstr. 1. At the far northern end of the Englischer Garten, this one is a good place for a daytime break.

Chinesischer Turm, Englischer Garten 3. Though worth a visit, this famous beer garden has become a real tourist trap.

Hirschgarten, Hirschgartenallee 1, Nymphenburg. Near Schloss Nymphenburg, this one, notwithstanding an estimated seating capacity of 8500, is rather civilized.

Hofbräukeller, Innere Wiener Str. 19, Haidhausen. Nestling under ancient chestnut trees, this is a very popular evening destination.

Menterschwaige, Menterschwaigstr. 4, Harlaching. One of Munich's best beer gardens. On the edge of the Isar valley, out in a southern suburb and near the route of tram #25, it's the place to bring a picnic to go with your beer.

Neue Schiess-Stätte, Zielstattstr. 6, Mittersendling. Located a short walk south of the Mittersendling S-Bahn station, this serves beers from Prince Luitpold of Bavaria's castle brewery at Kaltenberg to the west of Munich.

Paulanerkeller, Hochstr. 77, Au. Up on the Nockherberg, in the district immediately south of Haidhausen, this is the traditional venue for the spring *Starkbierfest*, and one of the oldest havens for serious beer drinkers. It was damaged by fire in 2000 but should now be open again.

Pschorrkeller, Theresienhöhe 7. On the heights above the Theresienwiese, with two cavernous halls and a front garden.

Seehaus, Kleinhesselohe 3. This has an excellent setting on the shores of the Kleinhesseloher See in the central area of the Englischer Garten. The standard of food served is a cut above that of most of the other beer gardens.

Zum Erdinger Weissbräu, Heiglhofstr. 13, Grosshadern. Beer hall and garden, reached by U-Bahn #6, which serves the products of the eponymous brewery in the small town of Erding north-east of Munich. It's well known for its wide range of wheat beers.

Zum Flaucher, Isarauen 2, Thalkirchen. Hiding amid the tall trees of the park on an island in the Isar, it does excellent fish dishes in summer.

Hausbrauereien

Predictably, Munich has played a pioneering role in the current craze for new Hausbrauereien, which represent a return to traditional methods by having a boutique brewery in or alongside the bar-restaurant where it is served, thereby ensuring the utmost freshness.

Braustübl der Forschungsbrauerei, Unterhachinger Str. 76, Altperlach. In a southeastern sub-urban setting with a garden, producing a fine dark beer, plus a *Bock* and a *Pils*. Reached by U-Bahn #8 or S-Bahn #2; closed Mon & mid-Oct to mid-March.

Flieger-Bräu, Sonnenstr. 2, Feldkirchen. In an eastern suburb, reached by S-Bahn #6, this is a sister establishment of the better-known Isar-Bräu.

Isar-Bräu, Kreuzeckstr. 23, Grosshesselohe. Located within the Grosshesselohe Isartalbahnhof on S-Bahn line #7, it makes a *Weissbier* and a dark *Spezial*, and also serves the products of its parent, the out-of-town Hofbräuhaus Traunstein.

Paulaner Bräuhaus, Kapuzinerplatz 5. Paulaner have opened this in the old Thomasbräu, whose name lives on in its non-alcoholic beer. Very trendy, particularly on Thurs, the day the new *Weissbier* is brewed.

Unionsbräu, Einsteinstr. 42, Haidhausen. The cellar has huge communal benches where you sit to sip the fine *Helles* made on the premises.

Restaurants

Munich has a wide selection of **restaurants**, and plenty of places offer good food at reasonable prices. As well as a good choice of ethnic eateries and several vegetarian specialists, there are many traditional Gaststätten which serve traditional Bavarian fare in a more intimate atmosphere than that of the beer halls listed above.

Gaststätten

Andechser am Dom, Weinstr. 7a. Despite its short menu, this restaurant is very "in"; it's also the only place in Munich serving the products of the monastic brewery at Andechs.

Asam-Schlössl, Maria-Einsiedel-Str. 45, Thalkirchen. The Rococo mansion of the painter Cosmas Damian Asam has been tastefully converted into a restaurant by the Augustiner brewery. It can be reached by U-Bahn #3 or bus #57.

Bamberger Haus, Brunnerstr. 2, Schwabing. Occupies a lovely Rococo mansion moved stone-by-stone from Bamberg to the Luitpoldpark, just east of the Olympiapark. Since Augustiner took it over, it no longer brews its own beer, but the food is excellent and there is the garden terrace which is a good place to relax when the weather is fine.

Burg Pappenheim, Baaderstr. 46. Fine old Gaststätte that's hugely popular with just about everyone. Evenings only.

Donisl, Weinstr. 1. A lively yet traditional establishment, with a pedigree dating back to the early eighteenth century.

MUNICH'S BEER CULTURE

Munich's **beer halls** have their origins in the Middle Ages, when brewers stored barrels indoors, planting chestnut trees around their premises to shade them from the heat of the sun. These days beer gardens remain popular with natives and visitors alike, really coming into their own in summer when tables and chairs are set up in the open. Beer is served in litre *Mass* measures, and the enduring image is that of the traditionally clad waitress sailing from table to table clutching several enormous, foaming glasses in each hand while the resident brass band plays a seemingly endless succession of oompah tunes. Many beer gardens serve up roasted half-chickens (always well salted to ensure a healthy customer thirst) with side orders of potato salad or French fries, while some have more extensive menus, and others allow you to bring your own food.

Munich ranks as the third largest producer of beer in the world, and it can legitimately claim to be both the most influential and the most varied in output: it pioneered wheat-based and brown-coloured beers, and adapted the original *Bock* of Einbeck to the form in which it's generally known today. The largest of the local **breweries** is **Paulaner**, which produces a full range of styles, generally with a drier flavour than those of its competitors; the dark and extremely powerful *Salvator-Doppelbock* is its star product. Paulaner has taken over **Hacker-Pschorr** (two formerly separate breweries which later united), whose product lines include an amber-coloured *Märzen* and *Pschorr-Weisse*, a very pale wheat beer. **Löwenbräu**, better known abroad through being a bigger exporter, produces a similarly wide variety of generally maltier beers, among which the *Pils* enjoys the highest reputation. Though it continues to operate as a separate entity, Löwenbräu is now owned by its erstwhile rival **Spaten**, which has the best amber and black beers – known respectively as *Ur-Märzen* and *Ludwig-Thoma-Dunkel* – but is equally known for its *Franziskaner Weissbier* (available in both light and dark versions) and *Maibock*. **Hofbräu**, the oldest of the breweries, makes the classic *Maibock* plus a number of contrasting wheat beers, though its standard line is an *Export*. The main strength of **Augustiner** is its pale (*Hell*) beer, but it produces several prestigious dark brews as well.

Fraunhofer, Fraunhoferstr. 9. A hugely popular traditional hostelry that usually gets packed early in the evening.

Haxnbauer, Münzstr. 6. Specializes in the delicious roasted pork knuckles that are such a high-point of German cuisine; the lamb version is no less tasty. The beers come not from Munich but from Dinkelacker in Stuttgart. There's another branch just a stone's throw away, at the corner of Sparkassenstrasse and Ledererstrasse.

Hundskugel, Hotterstr. 18. Munich's oldest surviving inn, established in 1440, has a cosy little interior. The dishes are lighter than in most rival establishments – which many will rate a positive advantage.

Lindwurmstüberl, Lindwurmstr. 32. A time-warped Munich institution, located beside the south-western entrance to the Goetheplatz U-Bahn station. It's renowned for its spit-roasted chicken, but serves a good range of dishes, including fried fish. Closed Sun.

Nürnberger Bratwurst-Glöckl, Frauenplatz 9. Standing in the shadow of the Dom, this is a transplant of the famous gourmet sausage restaurants of Nürnberg, with beer served straight from wooden barrels.

Ratskeller, Marienplatz 8. The cavernous cellars of the Neues Rathaus serve typically hearty meals. They also incorporate the *Fränkische Weinprobierstube*, where Franconian wines are served, as well as the informal *Frankenwein Vinothek*, where these vintages can be sampled from open bottles.

Sängerwarte, Pettenkoferstr. 48. Splendidly old-fashioned Gaststätte whose menu includes bargain set lunches, good-value duck dishes and fish from the Upper Bavarian lakes.

Schlosswirtschaft zur Schwaige, Eingang 30, Schloss Nymphenburg. A highly recommendable restaurant in its own right, and an ideal place to break for a meal when visiting Nymphenburg.

Zum Spöckmeier, Rosenstr. 9. Large and popular three-storey Gaststätte just off Marienplatz.

Non-German cuisine

Adria, Leopoldstr. 19, Schwabing. Popular late-night joint with excellent pizzas at reasonable prices.

Antalya, Bergmannstr. 50. West-end location and excellent Anatolian dishes.

Bangkok-House, Ledererstr. 17. Munich's most popular Thai restaurant. Evenings only, except in summer when it's open Wed & Thurs for set lunches.

Bella Italia, Herzog-Wilhelm-Str. 8. The most centrally sited of a small local chain of bargain-priced Italian restaurants.

Bernard & Bernard, Innere Wiener Str. 32, Haidhausen. Good choice for crêpes. Evenings only.

Bodega Dalí, Tengstr. 6, Schwabing. One of the best Spanish places in town, and with lower than average prices. Evenings only.

Cohen's, Theresienstr. 31. This serves Jewish cuisine in its various manifestations – Middle Eastern, Eastern European and American.

Dalmatiner Grill, Geibelstr. 10, Bogenhausen. The best bet in the district for affordable Balkan specialities.

Friulana, Zenettistr. 43. A homely local, much patronized by Italian expatriates; it's way off the usual tourist track, yet not too far from Theresienwiese.

Ganga, Baaderstr. 11. Offers a wide range of classic Indian dishes at reasonable prices. On weekdays, it has bargain menus at lunchtimes; on Sat & Sun it's open evenings only.

Il Falco, Falkenstr. 38, Au. Good-value Italian restaurant with changing daily specials, not far from the Deutsches Museum.

Klein Bukarest, Thalkirchner Str. 186, Sendling. Offers a rare chance to sample Romanian cuisine.

KUK Monarchie, Reichenbachstr. 22. This features dishes from throughout the old Austro-Hungarian Empire (Kaiserliche- und Königliche Monarchie), with separate Austrian, Magyar, Czech and Yugoslav menus. Evenings only.

Kyris Taverne, Sebastiansplatz 8. Crowded Greek taverna offering a changing daily selection of fresh fish flown in from the Mediterranean.

Matoi, Hans-Sachs-Str. 10. Japanese restaurant offering bargain lunches. Closed Sun.

Opatija, Viktualienmarkt 13 and Brienner Str. 41. Long-established Balkan favourites; the former has the benefit of a summertime patio, the latter is handy for the Königsplatz museums.

Shahrzad, Augustenstr. 1. Well placed for the Königsplatz museums, this is one of several Persian restaurants in the city, with bargain lunchtime menus.

Vegetarian restaurants

buxs, Frauenstr. 9. Has a mouth-watering cold buffet which you pay for according to weight. There's another branch in Schwabing, at Amalienstr. 38.

Gollier, Gollierstr. 83, Schwanthaler Höhe. Located to the northwest of Theresienwise, this serves excellent vegetarian food with organically produced drinks, and has lunchtime buffets on weekdays. Open evenings only on Sat.

Ignaz, Georgenstr. 67, Schwabing. Thanks to its location, this has a large student clientele. There are breakfast and lunch buffets Mon to Fri, and brunch buffets Sat and Sun.

Prinz Myshkin, Hackenstr. 2. Offers creative vegetarian dishes plus wholemeal pizzas.

Bars and café-bars

Much of the city's social life revolves around its bars and café-bars. Beer, coffee and snacks are served in most places, and while the roll-call of "in" and "out" bars is ever-changing, the ones listed below are of proven worth. *Schickies* hang out in **Schwabing** and hipsters head for **Haidhausen**, though things are pretty provincial in both areas. The city's bars suffer from limiting licensing laws (midnight closing at most places).

City centre

Am Eisbach, Marstallplatz 3. This modern glass palace, which makes an unlikely pair with Leo von Klenze's dignified Neoclassical Marstall (stables) alongside, is currently one of the hottest spots in town.

Havana Club, Herrnstr. 30. Great place for cocktails; so packed it's normally standing-room only.

Internet Café, Altheimer Eck 12. A conveniently central place in which to surf the Net: it's open daily 11am–1am, and serves pizzas and other Italian food. There's another branch at Nymphenburger Str. 145 which stays open until 4am.

Jodlerwirt, Altenhofstr. 4. There's a typical Gaststube on the ground floor which serves Aying beers, but the draw is the cramped little bar above, which is always jam-packed for the yodelling sessions: come along in the late evening and you'll immediately be sucked into the arm-linking singalong, a harmless piece of kitsch that's great fun.

Luigi Tambosi, Odeonsplatz 18. Something of a cross between a traditional café and a trendy café-bar, this is one of the most obvious places in the city in which to play at being seen. In summer, it spills over into Odeonsplatz and the Hofgarten.

Nachtcafé, Maximiliansplatz 5. Haunt of the true night owls, this is the place to see and be seen in the wee small hours. Open 7pm–5am.

Roma, Maximilianstr. 31. Hugely trendy new venture, popular with German film stars and other celebrities.

Schumann's, Maximilianstr. 36. Munich's movers and shakers congregate here, so this is the place to head for if you're looking to make contacts.

Schwabing

Alter Ofen, Zieblandstr. 41. Although a little worn about the edges this is still immensely popular with its student crowd.

Alter Simpl, Türkenstr. 57. Famous literary café and bistro which spawned the satirical magazine *Simplicissimus*; after a long period in the doldrums, it has become fashionable again. Open daily 5pm–3am, 4am at weekends.

CAU, Ludwigstr. 24. Very popular with students from the nearby university, and nearly always packed to the gills.

Cyber Ice-C@fé, Feilitzschstr. 15. An highly original combination of Internet café and ice-cream parlour.

Drugstore, Feilitzschstr. 12. A lively place that manages to avoid the usual Schwabing excess.

Schelling-Salon, Schellingstr. 54. A true golden oldie, having been run by the same family since 1872. It's a popular choice for breakfast, and has a wide range of board and table games on offer. Closed Tues & Wed.

Elsewhere in the city

Café im Hinterhof, Sedanstr. 29, Haidhausen. Café-bar which also offers health food for times when the beer and schnapps become too much.

Julep's, Breisacher Str. 18, Haidhausen. Recommended cocktail bar with a popular happy hour.

Paris Bar, Gravelottestr. 7, Haidhausen. Very trendy yuppie hangout.

Ruffini, Orffstr. 22, Neuhausen. Friendly *Szene* bar with roof terrace in the western part of the city; take U-Bahn #1 or #7 to Rotkreuzplatz.

Wirtshaus in der Au, Lilienstr. 51, Au. This place manages the difficult task of being a cross between a traditional beer hall and a modern café-bar.

Traditional cafés

Munich is no longer so well served by traditional *Kaffee und Küchen* establishments as most other large German cities, but some recommendable places do survive.

Café Frischhut, Prälat-Zeistl-Str. 8. A true original, popular with the local market traders and best known for the *Schmalznudel*, a deep-fried doughnut which can be eaten plain or sprinkled with sugar. Open Mon–Sat 5am–5pm.

Café Kreuzkamm, Maffeistr. 4. Delicious cakes, sweets and chocolates make this one of the best cafés in town. Closed Sun.

Café Luitpold, Brienner Str. 11. Still an extremely elegant café, despite losing its sumptuous neo-Rococo decoration during the war, save for a couple of huge statues now in the Bayerisches Nationalmuseum. It offers all-day breakfasts and also serves light meals. Closed Sun.

Café Monopteros, Königinstr. 43. Situated on the edge of the Englischer Garten, this offers hot daily specials, as well as a large choice of cakes from its own bakery.

Café Rottenhöfer, Residenzstr. 25–26. Founded in 1825, this is the café of the former court confectioners which makes a wonderful range of cakes and chocolates.

Café Schneller, Amalienstr. 59, Schwabing. A university location makes this popular with students rather than the antique lady contingent. It closes for the weekend at 2pm on Sat.

Wine bars

There's a limited choice of wine bars in this beer haven, though a wide geographical choice of vintages is on offer, particularly when the Ratskeller (see p.93) is added to those listed below.

Café Nymphenburg Sekt, Am Viktualienmarkt. Located alongside the fountain dedicated to Karl Valentin, this is a good place to sample Munich's own sparkling wine.

Pfälzer Weinprobierstuben, Residenzstr. 1. Wines and food from the Rhineland are served in a pleasant atmosphere in this wine bar in the Residenz.

Rolandseck, Viktoriastr. 23, Schwabing. This place has the best selection of Baden wines in town.

Weinhaus Neuner, Herzogspitalstr. 8. Nineteenth-century wine bar known for its gourmet food.

Weintrödler, Briennerstr. 10. This place is open daily 5pm–6am, and consequently tends to get packed in the early hours, when everywhere else is closed.

Music, nightlife and entertainment

Munich has a great deal to offer musically, whether you're into classical concerts or more modern fare. There's everything you'd expect to find in a cosmopolitan capital, and during the summer a glut of open-air music festivals takes place in or around the city. Several orchestras of international repute are based here, and the annual opera festival in July ranks with the Salzburg and Bayreuth festivals. Not that it's all highbrow: there's plenty of trash and tinsel as well, though perhaps the bars are more interesting than the discos. The various **listings** magazines (see p.68) are good sources of information on what's on.

Nightclubs, discos and live pop music

Munich has a thriving **nightclub** and **disco** scene, though in this city where money and appearances are everything, the snooty attitudes of many clubs can be rather off-putting. Most places are open 10pm–4am and entrance is about DM10/€5. During the summer there are **free rock concerts** by the lake in the Olympiapark, at the purpose-built stage known as the Theatron. There are also a few venues which have regular live music programmes throughout the year.

Crash, Ainmillerstr. 10, Schwabing. Heavy metal mecca and headbanger's delight.

Far Out, Neuturmstr. 5. Central venue where chart stuff, hip-hop and techno are the order of the evening.

Jackie O, Rosenkavalierplatz 12, Bogenhausen. Just about the strictest door policy in town, so unless you're loaded and look it, forget it.

Kaffee Giesing, Bergstr. 5, Untergiesing. Run by the singer Konstantin Wecker, and usually featuring small bands or solo artists.

Kunstpark-Ost, Grafinger Str. 6, Haidhausen. Though perennially under threat of closure, this mini-city of nightclubs, housed in a network of disused factories, is at the cutting edge of Munich's nightlife scene. All kinds of musical and social tastes are catered for.

Muffathalle, Zellstr. 4, Haidhausen. This converted waterworks is a major live music venue, often attracting well-known bands.

THE GAY SCENE

Deeply conservative Bavaria is not the best part of Germany in which to be gay. Nonetheless, Munich has one of Germany's most active and visible gay scenes, centred on the bars in and around Gärtnerplatz. The widely available *Columbia Fun Map* shows the main gay meeting-places; there's also a glossy monthly magazine for gays entitled *Our Munich* (despite its name, it's in German only). There's a shop of the same name at Müllerstr. 36–38, while the main information point, the Schwules Kommunikations- und Kulturzentrum, is at Müllerstr. 43 (☎0 89/60 30 56).

The Women's Centre, Frauenzentrum, Güllstr. 3 (☎0 89/7 25 42 71), runs a series of workshops and a café for all women, not just lesbians. On Tuesday between 1pm and 8pm, women from 13 to 20 years meet in the café, with Friday evenings specifically for lesbians. Cafés that cater predominantly for lesbians are *Inge's Karotte*, Baaderstr. 13, *Frauencafé im Kofra*, Baldestr. 8, and *Mädchenpower-Café*, Baldestr. 16. The only nightclub is *Mylord*, Ickstättstr. 2a (daily 6–9pm, 6pm–3am weekends).

Among the many gay men's bars, the following are the best known: *Colibri*, Utzschneiderstr. 8; *Juice*, Buthelmelcherstr. 2a; *Klimperkasten*, Maistr. 28; *Nil*, Hans-Sachs-Str. 2; and *Teddybar*, Hans-Sachs-Str. 1. *New York*, Sonnenstr. 25 (10pm–4am), is a gay disco offering chart and dance sounds, while *Ochsengarten*, Müllerstr. 47, is a leather bar. *Blue Moon*, Oberanger 38, caters for both gays and lesbians, as does the disco *Fortuna*, Maximiliansplatz 5. *Moriz*, Klenzestr. 47, is a recommendable gay-run restaurant that attracts plenty of straight customers.

Nachtwerk, Landsberger Str. 185, Laim. One of the city's best and most affordable nightlife possibilities. They put on occasional indie gigs here too.

Parkcafé, Sophienstr. 7. Ranks among Munich's most popular nightclubs; also has a nice beer garden.

Sugar Shack, Herzogspitalstr. 6. Standard central disco, but fun nevertheless.

Jazz

Munich has a monthly **jazz** magazine called *Münchener Jazz-Zeitung*, available in music shops and jazz venues. The city is corporate headquarters of the avant-garde jazz record label ECM, and club dates are accordingly more exciting than the German norm, attracting many big names on tour. The following venues play predominantly jazz, but check programmes for the latest details.

Alabamahalle, Domagkstr. 33, Schwabing. As you'd expect, this plays predominantly Dixieland fare.

Feierwerk, Hansastr. 39, Sendling. Has jazz, blues or rock every evening from 9pm.

Jam, Rosenheimer Str. 4, Haidhausen. A good bet for solid, reliable jazz, though don't expect any musical surprises. During the daytime, it's a regular café.

Mister B's, Herzog-Heinrich-Str. 38. Small jazz club with live music from 9.30pm. Closed Mon.

Unterfahrt, Einsteinstr. 42, Haidhausen. Munich's modern-jazz venue. Big names and unknowns play here, and the music is nearly always excellent. Closed Mon.

Folk

Predictably, the Munich folk scene is dominated by Germany's two favourite foreign imports – Irish and Country and Western.

Max–Emanuel-Brauerei, Adalbertstr. 33, Schwabing. For much of the time this is a normal Gaststätte, but it has tango evenings on Tues, salon music on Wed & Fri, and Fifties records on Sun. Entrance is upwards of DM10/€5.

Oklahoma, Schäftlarnstr. 156, Thalkirchen. Has live C&W Wed–Sun from 7pm.

Rattlesnake Saloon, Schneeglöckchenstr. 91, Moosach. There's either live C&W or blues every evening Thurs–Sun from 7pm.

Shamrock Irish Pub, Trautenwolfstr. 6, Schwabing. Live music, usually Irish folk, is played from 9pm each evening.

Shananigins, Ungererstr. 19, Schwabing. There are ceilidhs on Tuesdays, folk music or karaoke on other evenings.

Classical music

A number of resident **orchestras** and two **opera houses** cater to a very spoilt audience. The local radio orchestra, the Bayerisches-Rundfunk-Sinfonie-Orchester, is conducted by the American Lorin Maazel, who was lured here by what was probably the most lucrative contract ever offered to a conductor. For a quarter of a century, the Münchner Philharmoniker was directed by the Romanian Sergiu Celibidache, one of the great conductors of the century, a man who developed an aura by his stubborn refusal to make records. His death left a huge question mark over the orchestra's future status, which was resolved when another highly regarded American, James Levine, was secured as his successor. Yet another member of the conducting jet-set, the Indian Zubin Mehta, is musical director of a third full-sized body, the Bayerischer Staatsorchester, whose primary function is to play for the opera, which is managed by Britain's Sir Peter Jonas. A smaller ensemble, the Münchener Kammerorchester, has gained international standing for its interpretations of Baroque music and the Viennese classics. Among several distinguished **choirs**, Hanns-Martin Schneidt's Münchener-Bach-Chor has long been renowned for its performances, accompanied by the Münchener-Bach-Orchester, of Bach's church cantatas. Notwithstanding the irony of their championship of such overtly Protestant music in this stoutly Catholic city, this choir and orchestra hold a week-long *Bachfest* over a week in late May or early June each year. Finally, the **Münchener Opernfest**, an opera festival which takes place from the middle of July to the beginning of August, has a very high reputation. Classical concerts are also held at Schloss Nymphenburg and in the courtyard of the Residenz at this time of year.

Advance **tickets** for concerts can be bought at the relevant box offices or commercial ticket shops, such as München Ticket in the tourist office in the Neues Rathaus (Mon–Fri 10am–8pm, Sat 10am–4pm; ☎0 89/54 81 81 81, *www.muenchenticket.de*).

Venues

Bayerische Staatsoper (or **Nationaltheater**), Max-Joseph-Platz 1; advance booking office at Maximilianstr. 11 (☎0 89/21 85 19 20, *www.bayerische.staatsoper.de*). One of the world's most beautiful and distinguished opera houses, presenting both grand opera and ballet. Unsold and cheap standing tickets can be bought an hour before performance within the theatre itself.

Gasteig, Rosenheimer Str. 5 (☎0 89/48 09 80 or 54 81 81 81, *www.gasteig.de*). Modern concert hall complex in Haidhausen, built on the site of the *Bürgerbräukeller*, scene of Hitler's unsuccessful Munich Beer Hall Putsch of 1923. In addition to the main Philharmonie, where symphony orchestras perform, there's the Carl-Orff-Saal for chamber orchestras and the Kleiner Konzertsaal for soloists and small ensembles.

Hochschule für Musik, Arcisstr. 12 (☎0 89/28 92 74 42). The one-time Nazi Party headquarters, nowadays the local music academy, often stages high-quality solo instrumental and chamber music concerts, many of them free.

Olympiahalle, in the Olympiapark (☎0 89/54 81 81 81). The huge sports hall is frequently used for blockbuster all-star operas and concerts. High prices for even the worst seats.

Prinzregententheater, Prinzregentenplatz 12 (☎0 89/21 85 28 99, *www.prinzregententheater.de*); advance booking at Maximilianstr. 13 (☎0 89/29 16 14 14). Munich's main ballet venue, though other types of music are also featured.

Residenz, Residenzstr. 1 (☎0 89/29 06 72 63). There are two concert halls within the palace – the tapestry-lined Herkulessaal for orchestral music, and the Max-Joseph-Saal for chamber performances.
Staatstheater am Gärtnerplatz, Gärtnerplatz 3, advance booking office as for Staatsoper (☎0 89/2 01 67 67, *www.staatstheater-gaertnerplatz.de*). Presents operettas and the lighter fare of the operatic repertoire.

Theatre

Munich has a host of theatres and cabaret venues, all of which are listed in the official programmes and the local press. Almost all productions are exclusively in German.
Cirkus-Krone-Bau, Marsstr. 43 (☎0 89/55 81 66). Germany's only permanent circus tent, located close to the Hackerbrücke S-Bahn station.
Cuvilliéstheater (or **Altes Residenztheater**), Residenzstr. 1; advance tickets from Max-Joseph-Platz 1 (☎0 89/21 85 19 40, *www.staatstheater.bayern.de/schauspiel*). Munich's star venue for drama, this Rococo building saw the premiere of Mozart's *Idomeneo*.
Deutsches Theater, Schwanthalerstr. 13 (☎0 89/55 23 44 44, *www.deutsches-theater.de*). Features both home-grown and imported musicals.
Münchner Kammerspiele, Maximilianstr. 26 (☎0 89/2 33 37 00, *www.muenchner-kammerspiele.de*). An excellent venue, offering a wide variety of productions.
Münchner Lach- und Schiessgesellschaft, corner of Haimhauser Strasse and Ursulastrasse (☎0 89/39 19 97). The best known of a host of cabaret venues in the city.
Münchner Marionettentheater, Blumenstr. 32 (☎0 89/26 57 12). A puppet theatre – mainly for kids, though once a week the marionettes are put to more serious use in the performance of an opera or drama classic.
Münchner Theater für Kinder, Dachauer Str. 46 (☎0 89/59 54 54). Speciality children's venue.
Münchner Volkstheater, Am Stiglmaierplatz (☎0 89/5 23 46 55, *www.muenchner-volkstheater.de*). Plays predominantly modern drama. Christian Stückl, who won international acclaim for his direction of the Oberammergau Passion Play in 1990 and 2000, has recently assumed artistic control here.
Residenztheater, Max-Joseph-Platz 1 (☎0 89/21 85 19 40, *www.staatstheater.bayern.de/schauspiel*). Traditional dramatic fare in high-quality productions.
Schauburg am Elisabethplatz, Franz-Joseph-Str. 47 (☎0 89/23 33 71 71). Youth theatre venue.
Theater im Marstall, Marstallplatz; advance tickets from Max-Joseph-Platz 1 (☎0 89/21 85 19 40, *www.staatstheater.bayern.de/schauspiel*). An offshoot of the Residenztheater, specializing in experimental drama.

MUNICH'S FESTIVALS

Inevitably, all local **festivals** stand in the shadow of the **Oktoberfest** (see box on p.89), but there are plenty of other annual events. **Fasching**, Munich's Carnival, begins in earnest immediately after Epiphany with a week-long series of costume parades. Fancy-dress balls are held regularly up to and including Carnival Week, whose festivities come to a climax on Ash Wednesday with a ceremony of washing money bags at the Fischbrunnen in Marienplatz. A couple of weeks later begins **Starkbierzeit**, the period when strong beer is served in the taverns to help make the stringencies of Lent bearable. More specially brewed strong beer can be sampled at the **Maibock-Anstich** in May. Held in the Olympiapark during June and July, **Tollwood** is a world music festival which additionally features stalls selling a similarly international range of food and handicrafts.

The **Auer Dult** is a traditional market that takes place on the Mariahilfplatz during the last weeks of April, July and October each year. It has a combination of hardware, crafts and antiques, as well as a fairground for the kids. An annual Christmas market, known as the **Christkindlmarkt**, is held on the Marienplatz during the month of December, though the ones at the Münchener Freiheit, and around the Pariser Platz in Haidhausen, are less commercialized with more handmade crafts.

Listings

Airlines British Airways (☎01803/34 03 40); Lufthansa, Lenbachplatz 1 (☎0 89/55 25 50 21).

Airport information ☎0 89/97 52 13 13.

American Express Promenadeplatz 6 (Mon–Fri 9am–5.30pm, Sat 9.30am–12.30pm; ☎0 89/22 80 14 65).

Bike rental The most convenient place is Radius Touristik, located opposite platform 31 in the Hauptbahnhof. You can also rent bikes at many of the outlying S-Bahn stations, such as Aying, Dachau, Freising, Herrsching, Holzkirchen, Starnberg and Tutzing.

Bookstores Anglia English Bookshop, Schellingstr. 3, and Words'worth, Schellingstr. 21, have a good selection of paperbacks and English-language newspapers. Geobuch, Rosental 6, has the best selection of maps and guides, and there's a women's bookstore, Lillemors, at Barer Str. 30.

Car rental Avis, Nymphenburger Str. 61 (☎0 89/6 00 00); Hertz, Nymphenburger Str. 81 (☎0 89/1 29 50 01); there are also many competing offices in both the Hauptbahnhof and airport.

Consulates British, Bürkleinstr. 10 (☎0 89/21 10 90); Canadian, Tal 29 (☎0 89/2 19 95 70); Dutch, Nymphenburger Str. 1 (☎0 89/5 45 96 70); Irish, Mauerkircherstr. 1a (☎0 89/98 57 23); US, Königinstr. 5 (☎0 89/2 88 80).

Cultural institutes Amerikahaus, Karolinenplatz 3 (☎0 89/5 52 53 70); British Council, Rumfordstr. 7 (☎0 89/2 90 08 60).

Cultural societies The following run social functions advertised in the local press: Deutsch-Englische Gesellschaft (☎0 89/21 10 91 11); Deutsch-Kanadische Gesellschaft (☎0 89/3 07 33 45 or 3 14 84 10); Munich Scottish Association(☎0 89/39 12 53).

Medical emergencies ☎0 89/55 17 71.

Mitfahrzentralen City-Netz, Adalbertstr. 10–12 (☎0 89/1 94 44); McShare, Lämmerstr. 4 (☎0 89/19 44 40).

Pharmacy At the Internationale Apotheke, Neuhauser Str. 11, you can get your prescription no matter which country it comes from.

Post office The main post office is at Residenzstr. 2 (Mon–Fri 8am–6pm, Sat 8am–1pm); the longest hours are kept by the branch at Bahnhofplatz 1 (Mon–Fri 7am–8pm, Sat 8am–4pm, Sun 9am–3pm).

Sports FC Bayern München, Germany's most consistent football club, winner of many European trophies down the years, plays at the Olympiastadion in the Olympiapark, which is also the venue for major athletics meetings.

Taxis ☎0 89/1 94 10 or 2 16 10.

Travel agents Studiosus Reisen, Oberanger 6 (☎0 89/2 35 05 20); Thomas Cook, Petersplatz 10 (☎0 89/2 35 09 20).

UPPER BAVARIA

The name of **Upper Bavaria** (Oberbayern), Munich's own traditional province, is associated above all with the Alps. Quite simply, this is the most spectacular scenery Germany has to offer, a wonderfully contrasting array of glacial lakes and peaks commanding stunning panoramic views, with many dramatic castles and churches thrown in for good measure. Amid this picture-book scenery you'll find the Bavarian folklore and customs that are the subject of so many tourist brochures: men still wear Lederhosen and checked shirts, and women the traditional Dirndl dresses. Superficially it can all seem very kitsch, but beyond the packaged culture lies a fascinating mixture of Catholic and pagan rites that dominate the annual calendar – events usually accompanied by large amounts of eating and drinking.

Head for **Oberammergau** where the world-famous Passion Play is staged every ten years. From here it's only a few kilometres to the international ski resort of **Garmisch-Partenkirchen**, above which towers the **Zugspitze**, Germany's highest and most famous peak. The most dramatic heights of all are in the Berchtesgadener Land, an area that includes the town of **Berchtesgaden** as well as the marvellous peak of the **Watzmann**. The area is intensely geared towards tourism, as are the **Upper Bavarian lakes**, most of which lie in the glacial valleys of the Alpine foothills.

In contrast, other parts of the province are relatively little known, yet offer plenty of varied attractions. Between the Alps and the capital lie some equally enticing lakes and monasteries; to the east are the valleys of the **Inn** and **Salzach** rivers with the pilgrimage site of **Altötting** and the medieval towns of **Wasserburg** and **Burghausen**; while north of Munich are several wonderful old towns, most notable of which are the old metropolitan see of **Freising**, the former university and ducal capital of **Ingolstadt**, the planned residential seat of **Neuburg** and the little cathedral city of **Eichstätt**.

As if the scenery wasn't enough, manifold culinary delights are available in the wonderful old Gaststätten, often with beer gardens, where traditional Bavarian menus and innumerable regional beers are served. There are rail links to many destinations, and a network of connecting bus services between the Alpine towns, the only snag being that some of these only operate once or twice a day. **Accommodation** shouldn't be a major problem, except during July and August in the most sought-after destinations. There's a huge choice of rooms in private houses (identified by the *Zimmer frei* signs; contact the local tourist office if you want to make an advance booking) where prices are surprisingly reasonable (①–③) – even in major resorts such as Garmisch. Youth hostels (for the under-27s) and campsites are also plentiful.

North of Munich

North of Munich, making easy day-trips by the city's excellent S-Bahn network, are three sharply contrasting excursion possibilities. A visit to **Dachau** concentration camp is a harrowing experience, while **Freising** is one of Bavaria's most venerable and attractive towns, and **Oberschleissheim** has three impressive palaces to divert you.

Dachau

Situated on the S-Bahn #2 line, 17km north of Munich, **DACHAU** is a picturesque provincial town. It was formerly one of the seats of the Wittelsbachs, who built a Renaissance **Schloss** (April–Sept Tues–Sun 9am–6pm; Oct–March Tues–Sun 10am–4pm; DM3/€1.50) there in the sixteenth century. Three of the wings were pulled down by order of King Max I Joseph, leaving only the block with the main **Festsaal**, which features a spectacular coffered wooden vault and a frieze depicting mythological deities. It has excellent acoustics and concerts are regularly held there in summer. The **Schlossgarten** outside is a fine formal garden, while the *Schlosscafé* serves excellent cakes.

Despite tireless promotional efforts by the authorities, virtually none of the hordes of foreign visitors who come here venture into the town centre to experience its undoubted charms. Dachau's great misfortune is that its very name is synonymous with horrors that have been indelibly stamped on the consciousness of the modern mind, having been the site of Germany's **first concentration camp**, built on the outskirts of town in 1933, and the model for all others. Though not itself an extermination camp, many thousands were murdered here, and the motto that greeted new arrivals at the gates has taken its own chilling place in the history of Third Reich brutality: *Arbeit Macht Frei* – "Work Brings Freedom". The camp was mainly for political prisoners, and numbered among its inmates Pastor Martin Niemöller, the former French premier Léon Blum and Johann Elser, who tried to assassinate Hitler in 1939.

To reach the camp or **Konzentrationslager** (Tues–Sun 9am–5pm; free), take bus #724 or #726 from Dachau's Bahnhof. The rows of huts where prisoners lived were all torched by the Allies after the war, and neat windswept patches of rectangular gravel mark their former outlines. A replica of one of these huts gives some idea of the cramped conditions prisoners were cooped up in, but the only original buildings still standing are the gas chambers, never used, since the war ended before they could be set to work. Open ovens gape at you, and bright whitewashed walls almost distract from the ominous gas outlets set in the ceilings of the shower rooms. The stark wire perimeter fencing and watchtowers also remain. A permanent exhibition, with photographs and accompanying text in several languages including English, speaks for itself. Turn up at 11.30am or 3.30pm and you can also view the short, deeply disturbing documentary *KZ-Dachau* in English. Three small memorial churches – Catholic, Protestant and Orthodox – have been built within the complex, and the first two are normally kept open for visits.

Oberschleissheim

In the outskirts of the satellite town of **OBERSCHLEISSHEIM**, 14km north of Munich by S-Bahn #1, is the third major palace complex of the Wittelsbach dynasty (the first two being the Residenz in central Munich, see p77, and Nymphenburg, see p.88). All three palaces are located in **Park Schleissheim**, which is a ten-minute signposted walk from the Bahnhof.

The Renaissance **Altes Schloss Schleissheim** (Tues–Sun 9am–6pm; DM5/€2.50, free Sun) was built at the beginning of the seventeenth century as a spiritual retreat for the pious Duke Wilhelm V, who used only two of its forty-four rooms, going out every day to pray in the hermitages in the nearby woods. Suitably, therefore, the building, which was almost completely destroyed in World War II, has been rebuilt to house a museum of religious folk art entitled *Das Gottesjahr und seine Feste*. Assembled by a single collector, Gertrud Weinhold, the exhibits come predominantly from Eastern Europe, Latin America, Africa and Asia, and are displayed thematically. Most are from the Christian tradition, though other religions are represented in the final section on Paradise. The rooms on the opposite side of the entrance hall contain displays on the former German provinces of West and East Prussia.

A short distance to the east is the far larger and more significant **Neues Schloss Schleissheim** (April–Sept Tues–Sun 9am–6pm; Oct–March Tues–Sun 10am–4pm; DM3/€1.50), which was commissioned by Elector Max Emanuel in 1701. The project was initially riddled with bad luck: architect Enrico Zuccalli failed to establish sufficiently secure foundations for such an enormous building and, as a result, it had to be propped up with mounds of earth, spoiling the proportions and leaving the impression that it is built on quicksand. Work then had to be halted for ten years when the Elector was forced into exile as a result of his defeat in the War of the Spanish Sucession. However, building eventually resumed under the direction of Joseph Effner. Aided by such outstanding decorators as Ignaz Günther, Cosmas Damian Asam and Johann Baptist Zimmermann, he turned the seemingly ill-fated scheme into one of Germany's finest Baroque palaces. Of particular note are the monumental double **staircase** and the richly stuccoed **Festsaal**, where concerts are held every summer weekend. There's also a gallery of three hundred Baroque paintings, including works by Rubens, Van Dyck, Ribera and Guercino. This, like much of the rest of the palace, has not been accessible for many years, but restoration work is due to be completed in time for the 300th anniversary celebrations in 2001.

Prior to commissioning this extravaganza, Max Emanuel had asked Zuccalli to build **Schloss Lustheim** (same hours; DM5/€2.50, or DM6/€3 combined ticket with Neues Schloss Schleissheim), a small hunting and garden palace; this lies at the far end of the park, and is connected to the Neues Schloss by a landscaped canal. The architect created an Italianate masterpiece, which now contains an impressive collection of Meissen porcelain.

A short distance south of the park is the **Flugwerft Schleissheim** (daily 9am–5pm; DM6/€3, or DM14/€7 combined ticket with the Deutsches Museum in Munich), one of Germany's oldest airports, constructed in 1912–17. Nowadays an outstation of the Deutsches Museum, it displays early flying machines in the original hangar, later aeroplanes and helicopters in the modern exhibition hall.

Freising

FREISING, the terminus of one of the branches of S-Bahn #1, lies some 35km north of Munich, about halfway towards Landshut, and only 8km from the airport, to which it's linked by bus #635. One of Bavaria's oldest towns, it was the province's spiritual capital during its period as an episcopal see from 739 to 1803, and its name is retained in the title of the local archbishop, who now resides in Munich. Despite its proximity to the state capital, it gives no impression of belonging to commuter-belt land, retaining instead the very distinct atmosphere of a country town, particularly in the centre, where the picturesque **Markt** and **Hauptstrasse**, overlooked by the handsome Baroque tower of the Gothic **Stadtpfarrkirche St Georg**, are lined by colourful mansions of varying dates.

The hill between the River Isar and the centre is known as the Domberg and is a self-contained episcopal quarter centred on the twin-towered Romanesque **Dom**, whose exterior is covered with a startling coat of whitewash. After this, the interior comes as another surprise, the original architecture masked by a lavish decoration scheme carried out by the Asam brothers in an idiom which belongs to the final phase of Baroque. A few older furnishings, such as the late Gothic choir stalls with busts of the local prince-bishops and the *Lamentation* group by Erasmus Grasser in the apse of the north aisle, look rather incongruous amid this theatricality. Thankfully, the Asams didn't tamper with the **crypt**, the resting-place of St Korbinian, founder of the bishopric. Among the pillars supporting the vault of this beautiful chamber is the amazing *Bestiensäule*, which is festooned with carvings of fantastic animals. The **cloisters** built onto the east end of the Dom have Rococo decoration by Johann Baptist Zimmermann, as does François Cuvilliés' **Bibliotheksaal** (May–Oct Mon–Fri 2–3pm) alongside.

At the far end of the cloisters is the Gothic **Benediktuskirche**. A second and much larger church of the same period, the **Johanniskirche**, is built right against the front end of the Dom, and is in turn linked to the former **Residenz** of the prince-bishops, thereby creating a truly monumental complex of interconnected buildings. Occupying a former seminary at the western end of the Domberg is the **Diözesanmuseum** (Tues–Sun 10am–5pm; DM3/€1.50), the largest ecclesiastical museum in Germany. It features works by many of the leading Baroque and Rococo artists of Bavaria, though its most valuable treasure, gleaming in a dimly lit room, is a Byzantine icon known as the *Lukasbild*. There are also two magnificent paintings by **Rubens** of *The Adoration of the Shepherds* and *Pentecost*, which originally adorned the side altars of the Hofkirche in Neuburg an der Donau.

West of the town centre is another hill, on which stands **Kloster Weihenstephan**, a former monastery which is now home to the agricultural and brewing faculties of the technical university of Munich. Its main claim to fame is the **Weihenstephan-Brauerei**, which has been in operation since 1040, and is thus generally accepted as the oldest brewery in the world. Guided tours (DM3/€1.50) are run through the present ultra-modern premises from Monday to Thursday, but it's necessary to phone ahead (☎0 81 61/53 60) to join a group. Otherwise, you can content yourself with sampling the products – of which the wheat beers are the best known – in the *Bräustüberl* or its beer garden.

Ingolstadt

Even by German standards, **INGOLSTADT**, 60km due north of Munich, reeks of prosperity, courtesy of its four oil refineries, fed by pipelines from France and Italy, and the Audi car factory which migrated from Zwickau when the Iron Curtain went up. At least some of the wealth generated is used wisely, for the town spends more money on the upkeep of its historic monuments than anywhere else in Bavaria. For centuries one of Germany's most redoubtable fortresses, Ingolstadt is compact enough to be seen in a day, and has the benefit of being unspoiled by mass tourism.

The Town

All the notable monuments lie within the fortification system, and at present there's no need to wander any further afield. However, an Audi visitor centre is currently under construction in the company grounds in the north of town, and is likely to become a major local attraction when complete.

The fortifications

The Altstadt snuggles within its medieval horseshoe-shaped **Stadtmauer** on the north bank of the Danube, safely away from the industrial quarters. In the nineteenth century, an additional set of fortifications in a stern Neoclassical style was designed by Leo von Klenze to encase them, and to protect both sides of the bridgehead. Those on the south bank command a marvellous view of the whole skyline. They're centred on the **Reduit Tilly** (Tues–Sun 8.45am–4.30pm; DM5.50/€2.75, or DM7.50/€3.75 combined ticket with Bayerisches Armeemuseum), which contains displays about World War I.

Crossing over Konrad-Adenauer-Brücke, the most impressive stretch of the medieval walls lies just to the left; it's made yet more picturesque by the houses which were built directly on to it. This section is pierced by the **Taschenturm** (Pocket Tower), whose tall, whitewashed and gabled silhouette has a fairy-tale look about it, for all that it's perfectly genuine. Even it is eclipsed, however, by the **Kreuztor** which now stands like a pint-sized castle in splendid isolation further north. Nowadays, it seems hard to believe that such a lovingly crafted masterpiece of brickwork was built for purely military purposes.

Beyond, a green belt has been laid out round the huge polygonal fragments of the Neoclassical fortifications. One of these, the **Kavalier Hepp** to the northwest, now contains the **Stadtmuseum** (Tues–Sat 9am–4pm, Sun 10am–5pm; DM4/€2), whose exhibits range from a Celtic silver hoard via sculptures from the medieval city gates and the teaching stool of Johannes Eck, the Ingolstadt theologian who provided the (none-too-successful) frontline Catholic defence against Luther, to a stuffed horse said to have been King Gustavus Adolphus's mount during the Swedish siege in the Thirty Years War.

From here, you can continue all the way round the walls to the strongest point of the defences, the **Neues Schloss**, which sits in gleaming white splendour at the far end of the waterfront. The original structure with its distinctive angular towers was built in the fifteenth century during the short period when Ingolstadt was capital of an independent duchy; the imposing battlements were added a hundred years later. Built for the Francophile Duke Ludwig the Bearded, it looks completely un-German, resembling instead a French château. Part of the Schloss now houses the **Bayrisches Armeemuseum** (Tues–Sun 8.45am–4.30pm; DM5.50/€2.75), the most comprehensive collection of arms and armour in Germany. On the ground floor, the **Dürnitz**, the great banqueting hall, forms an appropriately grand setting for an outstanding section on the Thirty Years War. Highlight of the displays upstairs is the booty, including a magnificent golden helmet, captured from the Turks in 1682; here also is the finest room in the building, the **Schöner Saal**, whose vault springs from a graceful central pillar.

The Altstadt

The pedestrianized shopping streets lie west of the Neues Schloss. Along Hallstrasse, and now very much in the shadow of the huge modern Stadttheater, is the modestly sized **Altes Schloss**, built in the thirteenth century as a second residence for the Landshut dukes. Later prettified by the addition of ornate gables, it was demoted to serving as a granary when the Neues Schloss was built, but has found a new lease of life as the public library. Further along is the **Altes Rathaus**, created at the end of last century by knocking together several old burghers' houses. Behind is the Gothic **Stadtkirche St Moritz**, one of whose towers, the **Pfeifturm**, can be ascended on Saturday mornings for a view of the town. On Ludwigstrasse, a block to the north, is the **Ickstatthaus**, the most ornate of the town's many Rococo mansions.

From the Stadtkirche, Dollstrasse and Hoher Schulstrasse lead westwards to the **Hohe Schule**, built as a prebendary, but from 1472 until 1800 the main building of the University of Bavaria, one of the most famous in Germany and a leading centre of Counter-Reformation theology. Ingolstadt's academic tradition lay dormant until 1989, when an economics faculty was opened, but several reminders of its pre-eminence survive in this quarter. One of these is the **Alte Anatomie** at the end of Griesbadgasse to the southeast, a dignified, classically inspired Baroque building which was the place where Frankenstein created his monster in Mary Shelley's Gothic novel. The courtyard once again serves as a herb garden, while the interior contains the **Deutsches Medizinhistorisches Museum** (Tues–Sun 10am–noon & 2–5pm; DM4/€2), which shows the evolution of medical instruments from the ancient Egyptians to the present day.

To the north, and just east of the Kreuztor, is the huge **Liebfrauenmünster**, begun by Duke Ludwig as a sacred counterbalance to the Neues Schloss at the opposite end of town. The unfinished towers, set at startlingly oblique angles, are reminiscent of those of the castle, but otherwise this is a copybook German hall church, the plain brickwork outside brilliantly offset by the sweeping elevation of the gray and white interior. As work neared completion in the early sixteenth century, the masons created for the six nave chapels the most spectacularly ornate **vaults** in the entire history of European architecture. Here the delicately coloured filigree stonework has been twisted into such shapes as a crown of thorns, a giant insect and great flowering plants, which seem to sprout from the ceiling like huge jewels. The church served as the parish church of the university, whose centenary was commemorated by the commissioning of Hans Mielich's **high altar**: look out for the scenes on the reverse, showing cameos of the different faculties at work. On the north side of the ambulatory is the bronze epitaph to Johannes Eck; also of special note are the brilliantly coloured **stained-glass windows** of the east end, made from designs by Dürer and his followers.

A very different but equally dazzling church is the **Maria-de-Victoria-Kirche** (March–Nov Tues–Sun 9am–noon & 1–5pm; Dec–Feb Tues–Sun 10am–noon & 1–4pm; DM2.50/€1.25) immediately to the north on Konviktstrasse, an oratory built by the Asam brothers for the Jesuit-run Marian student congregation. Egid Quirin's simple little hall is little more than a stage-set for Cosmas Damian's colossal **ceiling fresco**, which was executed in just eight weeks. Its subject – a complicated allegory on the mystery of the Incarnation – hardly seems to matter, as you're likely to be completely mesmerized by its illusionistic tricks, in which everything appears to be in correct perspective, no matter what your vantage point. Ask the caretaker to let you see the **monstrance** depicting the Battle of Lepanto, another display of Rococo pyrotechnics, this time by an Augsburg goldsmith.

Directly opposite, at the corner of Johannesstrasse, stands the **Tillyhaus**, where Field Marshal Johann Tilly, the Catholic hero of the Thirty Years War, died in 1632. By then his awesome military reputation was in tatters, his once-invincible troops having been unequal to the challenge posed by the new fighting techniques of the Swedish army. The wounds of which he died were sustained in a vain attempt at preventing the Swedes crossing the Lech in their sweeping advance on Munich, though at least there was the compensation that Ingolstadt's fortifications proved strong enough to withstand the enemy siege. At the end of the street is a square dominated by the **Franziskanerkirche**, whose plain architecture is enlivened by a magnificent array of Gothic, Renaissance and Baroque epitaphs.

Practicalities

Ingolstadt's **Hauptbahnof**, a junction of the Munich–Nürnberg and Ulm–Regensburg lines, lies 2km south of the Altstadt, to which it's connected by buses #10, #11, #15, #16 and #44. The **tourist office** (Mon–Fri 8am–5pm, Sat 9am–noon; ☎08 41/3 05 10 98, fax 3 05 10 99, *www.ingolstadt.de*) is in the Altes Rathaus, Rathausplatz 2.

There are a couple of **pensions** fairly close to the Hauptbahnhof: *Bauer*, Hölzlstr. 2 (☎08 41/6 60 99 or 6 70 86; ③) is to the northeast; *Eisinger*, Dorfstr. 17a (☎08 41/97 36 60; ④) to the southwest. In the Altstadt there are four **hotels**: *Anker*, Tränktorstr. 1 (☎08 41/ 3 00 50; ⑤); *Adler*, Theresienstr. 22 (☎08 41/1 70 98 or 3 51 07; ⑤); *Bayerischer Hof*, Münzbergstr. 12 (☎08 41/93 40 60; ⑥); and *Rappensberger*, Harderstr. 3 (☎08 41/31 40; ⑥). The **youth hostel** is close to the Kreuztor at Friedhofstr. 41/2 (☎08 41/3 41 77, fax 91 01 78; DM21/€10.50). **Camping** facilities are available at Auwaldsee in the outskirts (☎08 41/9 61 16 16; closed Oct–March); take bus #60.

All the hotels listed above have **restaurants**, though the best place to eat is *Im Stadttheater*, Schlossländle 1. Also of special note is the flagship of one of the local breweries, *Weissbrauhaus zum Herrnbräu*, Dollstr. 3, a true old Bavarian tavern. Ingolstadt's main **festival** is the *Bürgenfest* on the first or second weekend of July.

Neuburg an der Donau

NEUBURG AN DER DONAU, 22km upstream from Ingolstadt on the rail line to Ulm, makes an enjoyable afternoon's outing or restful overnight stop. Perched on a chalk promontory overlooking the Danube, it was a strategic trading post in Roman times, but was thereafter an insignificant village until 1505, when it became the capital of the new Wittelsbach principality of Pfalz-Neuburg. Throughout the sixteenth and seventeenth centuries, it was developed into a proud Residenzstadt of elegant buildings, leafy squares and dreamy cobblestoned streets, presenting a Renaissance, Mannerist and Baroque architectural mix which has no counterpart elsewhere in Bavaria.

Neuburg's most significant and dominant building is the **Residenzschloss** (April–Sept Tues–Sun 9am–6pm; Oct–March Tues–Sun 10am–4pm; DM5/€2.50). The original Renaissance palace was erected between 1527 and 1545 by order of the first ruler of Pfalz-Neuburg, Ottheinrich, who later became Elector of the Palatinate and transformed the great Schloss in Heidelberg. This structure is dwarfed by the Baroque wing added in the 1660s, whose massive cylindrical towers give the complex its highly distinctive silhouette. On the ground floor of the northern tower is the **Grottenanlage**, a spectacular suite of artificial grottoes made from shells, tufa, glass and stucco. The first floor of the Schloss is devoted to the history of Pfalz-Neuburg and is particularly notable for the mementoes of Ottheinrich, including a sculpted portrait head, some of his clothes and two magnificent Brussels tapestries, one of which illustrates his pilgrimage to the Holy Land. On the second floor the region's pre- and early history is documented by means of the extensive archeological finds it has yielded, while the top storey features a display of religious art, including a wonderful group of Baroque embroideries woven at the local Ursuline convent. The **Schlosskapelle** by the courtyard entrance is the oldest custom-built Protestant church in Bavaria, and is adorned with a cycle of frescoes by the Salzburg artist Hans Bocksberger illustrating the Bible in line with the tenets of the new faith.

Uphill from the Residenzschloss, the central **Karlsplatz** is a particularly stylish example of town planning, despite having been built over a period of well over a hundred years. The two main buildings, the **Rathaus** on the north side and the **Hofkirche** on the east, were both begun in the first decade of the seventeenth century. At the time, the intention was that the latter should be the Protestant answer to the Jesuits' St Michael in Munich, but the House of Pfalz-Neuburg converted back to Catholicism during its construction, so it was finished off in a rather more elaborate manner than originally intended. The interior is – quite literally – covered with wonderfully ornate white stuccowork, with just a lick of gold highlighting to create a light and harmonious whole. Rubens was commissioned to paint three huge altarpieces for the church, but these were later replaced, and can now be seen in Munich's Alte Pinakothek and the Diözesanmuseum in Freising. Also on the square are mansions of noblemen and wealthy burghers, while the east side is closed by the **Provinzialbibliothek**, an early Rococo building with an imposing facade.

Practicalities

Neuburg's **Bahnhof** lies at the southern edge of town. The **tourist office** (May–Oct Mon–Fri 8am–noon & 2–5.30pm, Sat & Sun 10am–noon & 2–5pm; Nov–April Mon–Thurs 8am–noon & 2–4pm, Fri 8am–noon; ☎0 84 31/5 52 40, fax 5 52 42, *www.neuburg.net*) is at Residenzstr. A65. Here you can ask about rooms in **private houses** (②–③), of which there's a reasonable supply. The **campsite** is at Oskar-Wittmann-Str. 5 (☎0 84 31/94 73).

Hotels include *Kieferlbräu*, Eybstr. 239 (☎0 84 31/6 73 40, *Hotel.Kieferlbraeu.ND@t-online.de*; ③), *Neuwirt*, Färberstr. 88 (☎0 84 31/20 78; ③), *Bergbauer*, Fünfzehnerstr. 11 (☎0 84 31/4 70 95; ⑤), and *Am Fluss*, with a fine location by the Danube at Ingolstädter Str. 2 (☎0 84 31/6 76 80; ⑤). All but the last of these have **restaurants**: *Kiefelbräu* offers vegetarian as well as *bürgerliche* cuisine, while *Bergbauer*, open evenings only, is probably the best in town. One **café** particularly worth visiting is *Arco-Schlösschen*, which commands a wonderful view of the town from its riverside location 1km east of the centre.

In odd-numbered years, there's a Renaissance-style folklore **festival**, the *Schlossfest*, on the last weekend of June and the first weekend of July. There's also an annual festival of Baroque music in late September or early October in the Kongregationssaal, the former Jesuit oratory beside the Residenzschloss.

Eichstätt

EICHSTÄTT, which lies 27km northwest of Ingolstadt, is the gateway to Germany's largest *Naturpark*, the **Altmühl** valley. This Jurassic region was first inhabited by humans 100,000 years ago, and its soils have produced many yields of prehistoric fossils and minerals in a quite remarkable state of preservation. The town itself was for centuries a prince-bishopric at the junction of the three historic provinces of Bavaria, Franconia and Swabia, and was sufficiently prestigious for one of its rulers, Gebhard I, to gain election as Pope Victor II. Having been almost completely destroyed in the Thirty Years War, it was rebuilt in the eighteenth century by Italian Baroque architects, who gave it an incongruously Mediterranean appearance. Incorporated into Bavaria in the Napoleonic reforms, it thereafter sank into obscurity, but received a major boost in

1980, when its theological college was promoted to the status of a Catholic university – the only one in the German-speaking world.

The Town

The **Altstadt** is on the right bank of the Altmühl, while the great fortress of the prince-bishops, the **Willibaldsburg**, is high above on the opposite side of the river. Eichstätt presents an agreeable mixture of old and new: the university and its predecessor have been astute patrons of some of Germany's leading architectural practices, gaining much praise for the way they have augmented the historical heritage, which came through World War II virtually unscathed.

The Dom

Inevitably, the **Dom** is the focal point of the Altstadt. Its twin towers are Romanesque, but otherwise it's a fourteenth-century Gothic structure with a distinctive German accent, being a hall church with choirs at both ends of the building. It is especially notable for a number of outstanding works of art. Prominent among these is the **Pappenheim altar** in the north transept, an astonishing virtuoso carving of the Crucifixion, with each of the myriad figures carefully characterized, by a late Gothic carver known as Master VW from his cryptic signature. Fronting the western choir is the extraordinarily realistic seated **statue of St Willibald**, a memorial to the first Eichstätt bishop. Though dating from just a couple of decades after the altar, it is fully Renaissance in style and is by one of the few German sculptors to master this idiom, **Loy Hering**, who also carved the *Wolfsteinaltar* on the west wall of the nave and the crucifix in the Sakramentskapelle.

Off the west side of the cloisters is the **Mortuarium**, which is anything but the grim chamber its name suggests: it's a stately Gothic hall divided by a row of differently shaped columns, one of which is known as the Schöne Säule (Beautiful Pillar) from its profuse carvings. There's also a brilliantly coloured stained-glass window of *The Last Judgement*, designed by Holbein the Elder, and a *Crucifixion* group by Hering. Stairs lead up to the **Diözesanmuseum** (April–Oct Wed–Fri 10.30am–5pm, Sat & Sun 10am–5pm; free), whose exhibits include the Dom's treasury, the original sculptures from its north portal, the chasuble of St Willibald and a trio of fifteenth-century tapestries illustrating the life of his sister, St Walburga.

The rest of the Altstadt

Gabriel de Gabrieli, the most outstanding of the eighteenth-century architects who transformed Eichstätt, added a Baroque facade to the Dom in order that it could form an integral part of the new **Residenzplatz**, a truly monumental piece of urban design which is something of a hybrid between a crescent and the square its name suggests. One side is lined with the Baroque and Rococo palaces of the local Knights, canons and ecclesiastical administration, while in the centre is the cheerful **Mariensäule**. The **Residenz** (guided tours Mon–Thurs 11am & 3pm, Fri 11am, Sat & Sun 10.15–11.45am & 2–3.30pm; DM2/€1) itself, the former palace of the prince-bishops, is now occupied by municipal offices, but retains some splendid interiors, notably the grand staircase, the tiny **Hauskapelle** and the second-floor **Spiegelsaal**. In the last of these, stuccowork is present not only on the walls and ceiling, but on the mirrors themselves, a feature that is apparently unique.

Immediately east of Residenzplatz is a huge Jesuit church, the **Schutzengelkirche**. A short distance to the north, at the top end of Kardinal-Preysing-Platz, is the former **Kloster Notre Dame de Sacre Coeur**, whose domed church was designed by Gabrieli and frescoed by Johann Georg Bergmüller. Its conventual buildings now house the **Informationszentrum Naturpark Altmühltal** (April–Oct Mon–Sat 9am–5/6pm, Sun 10am–5/6pm; Nov–March Mon–Thurs 8am–noon & 2–4pm, Fri 8am–noon; free), with displays on the flora, fauna, geology, history and culture of the valley. Further east lies the **Hofgarten**, one of whose borders is taken up by the long frontage of the **Sommerresidenz**, formerly the second residence of the bishops, now the administrative headquarters of the Catholic university. Just beyond is the **Kapuzinerkirche**, which houses a twelfth-century **Holy Sepulchre**, one of the earliest and most accurate reproductions of the Jerusalem original, constructed with the help of descriptions supplied by crusaders who had been there.

To the north of the Dom, the commercial life of the town is centred on **Marktplatz**, another Baroque square whose central fountain bears a second Renaissance statue of St Willibald. On a prominent elevated site to the north is the huge complex of the **Kloster St Walburg**, a Benedictine convent with a richly decorated Baroque church and a Gothic crypt containing the tomb of St Walburga. Its terrace commands a fine view across the valley.

The Willibaldsburg

Occupying a dominant position high above the left bank of the Altmühl, best reached via Burgstrasse, is the **Willibaldsburg**. The earliest parts of this huge fortress date back to the mid-fourteenth century, but the most prominent part is the sumptuous palatial wing designed in the early seventeenth century by the great Augsburg architect, Elias Holl. This section now houses the **Jura-Museum** and the **Museum für Ur- und Frühgeschichte** (both April–Sept Tues–Sun 9am–6pm; Oct–March Tues–Sun 10am–4pm; DM6/€3). In the former, hi-tech display techniques are employed in the presentation of some of the many fossil finds made in the region. The rarest object is the skeleton (one of only seven yet discovered) of a prehistoric bird known as the archeopteryx. The latter museum is mostly devoted to archeological excavations, but also includes a four-metre-high, 60,000-year-old skeleton of a mammoth. One of the towers can be ascended for a view of the town and the valley, though a closer panorama of the former can be had from the **Bastionsgarten**, a recent re-creation of the Hortus Eystettensis, a famous Renaissance-era garden whose appearance had been documented in a meticulously accurate set of coloured engravings.

Practicalities

Eichstätt's **Bahnhof**, on the main line linking Ingolstadt with both Würzburg and Nürnberg, is in the middle of nowhere. Small diesels connect with all services, travelling along the 5km line to the **Stadtbahnhof**, which faces the Altstadt from the other side of the Altmühl. The **tourist office** (April–Oct Mon–Sat 9am–6pm, Sun 1–6pm; Nov–April Mon–Thurs 9am–noon & 2–4pm, Fri 9am–noon; ☎0 84 21/9 88 00, fax 98 80 30, *www.eichstaett.de*) is at Kardinal-Preysing-Platz 14.

There's a good range of central **hotels**, including *Gasthof Ratskeller*, Kardinal-Preysing-Platz 8 (☎0 84 21/90 12 58; ③), *Gasthof Trompete*, Ostenstr. 3 (☎0 84 21/9 81 70; ④), *Gasthof Sonne*, Buchtal 17 (☎0 84 21/67 91; ④), *Gasthof Klosterstuben*, Pedettistr. 26 (☎0 84 21/35 00; ④), and *Adler*, which occupies a Baroque mansion at Marktplatz 22–24 (☎0 84 21/67 67; ⑥). An excellent alternative is the *Burgschänke* in the Willibaldsburg, Burgstr. 19 (☎0 84 21/8 04 44; ④). There are also plenty of **private houses** offering rooms (①–②); the tourist office can supply a list. The **youth hostel** is midway between the Stadtbahnhof and the Willibaldsburg at Reichenaustr. 15 (☎0 84 21/9 80 40, fax 98 04 15, *JHEichstaett@djh-bayern.de*; DM25/€12.50).

All the hotels listed above, with the exception of *Adler*, have **restaurants**, and all are good and reasonably priced. Other enticing choices for a meal are *Zum Kavalier*, in the old theatre building at Residenzplatz 17, and *Krone*, Domplatz 3, which also has a beer garden. However, the top cuisine in town is at the pricey *Domherrenhof*, which occupies a Rococo mansion at Domplatz 5.

The Five Lakes Region (Fünf-Seen-Land)

The **Five Lakes Region** is a popular playground of the people of Munich, and it can easily be explored in day-trips from the city by S-Bahn. Three of the lakes are small and of minor interest, but the **Starnberger See** and **Ammersee**, which both offer boat trips, bear comparison with their Alpine counterparts.

The Starnberger See

Lying just to the southwest of the city and reached by S-Bahn #6, the largest lake of the group, the **Starnberger See**, is predominantly the domain of the city's rich and their weekend villas. The main resort is **STARNBERG** at the northernmost tip; here you'll find the local **tourist office** at Wittelsbacher Str. 2c (June–Sept Mon–Fri 8am–6pm, Sat 9am–1pm; rest of year Mon–Fri 8am–6pm; ☎0 81 51/9 06 00, fax 90 60 90), which will help with accommodation. The most bracing way to explore the lake is by boat;

Staatliche Schiffhart Starnberger See (☎0 81 51/1 20 23) charges DM24.50/€12.25 for a three-hour round trip, while journeys from one stop to the next cost DM8/€4.

The S-Bahn continues down the west coast as far as its terminus at Tutzing. This is the more commercialized side of the lake, with cafés and restaurants vying for your money; the main public **beach** is at Possenhofen. The eastern shore is lined with private properties and it's not always possible to get at the water, though there are some small public stretches between the villages of Berg, Leoni and Ammerland. The **Schloss** of the first (still a private residence of the Wittelsbachs and not open for visits) was where the ill-starred King Ludwig II was staying at the time of his mysterious death. Just to the south, a small **Votivkapelle**, modelled on the Church of the Holy Sepulchre in Jerusalem, has been erected in his memory.

Another tribute comes in the form of Germany's most popular long-distance footpath, the **King Ludwig Way** (*König-Ludwig-Weg*), covering the 120km between Starnberg and Füssen. It's easy to follow, being marked by signposts showing a blue K with a crown; although the scenery is imposing, the terrain is undemanding and is easily covered in a four- or five-day hike.

The Ammersee

The S-Bahn #5 line goes from Munich to the resort of **HERRSCHING** on the **Ammersee**; its three previous stops cover the remaining lakes of the group – Wessling is by the minute lake of the same name; Steinebach is on the west side of the deep blue Wörthsee; while Seefeld lies on the peaceful Pilsensee. Herrsching is a favourite place to go swimming and sailing and can get very crowded, particularly on summer weekends. There's a footpath along the water's edge to the west, where a few public beaches are slotted in between stretches of private property. The **tourist office** is at Bahnhofsplatz 3 (Mon–Fri 8.30am–noon & 2–5pm, Sat 10am–noon; ☎0 81 52/52 27, fax 4 05 19). **Boat trips** are run by Staatliche Schiffahrt Ammersee (☎0 81 43/2 29); three-hour cruises cost DM24/€12, though there are various cheaper options.

The village of **ANDECHS** sits atop the hill of the same name, Bavaria's "Holy Mountain". There's an attractive if strenuous walking trail from Herrsching which makes a viable alternative to using the regular bus service. A Benedictine **Kloster** was built in the late fourteenth century to celebrate the rediscovery of some relics brought to Andechs from Jerusalem by the local count in 952. Its Gothic church still survives, though its interior was completely remodelled in Rococo style in the eighteenth century. An additional enticement for the modern pilgrim is the delicious range of **beers** brewed by the monks, the most notable being a strong dark *Doppelbock*. These can be sampled in the *Bräustüberl* attached to the monastery; hearty local dishes and home-made cheese are also available.

Across the lake, on a rail line beyond the S-Bahn network, lies **DIESSEN**, a village whose population includes a sizeable artistic colony, with potters pre-eminent. Here you'll find a **tourist office** at Mühlstr. 4a (Mon–Wed 8am–noon & 2–5pm, Thurs 8am–noon & 2–6pm, Fri 8am–noon; ☎0 88 07/10 48, fax 44 59), plus a **campsite** (☎0 88 07/73 05). On the hill above is an Augustinian **Kloster**, which boasts one of Bavaria's finest Rococo churches: the design is by J.M. Fischer, the high altar by Cuvilliés, the ceiling frescoes by Johann Georg Bergmüller, while one of the side altars has a theatrical *Martyrdom of St Sebastian* by Tiepolo.

Landsberg am Lech and the Pfaffenwinkel

A staging-post on the Romantic Road (see bon on p.213), **Landsberg** lies less than 40km up the River Lech from Augsburg, and about 55km west of Munich. Like the latter, it was founded by Henry the Lion, and until the Napoleonic period it was Bavaria's westernmost outpost. It later became the site of a jail for high-profile political prisoners, and has the misfortune to have gone down in history as the place where Hitler, imprisoned following the botched Beer Hall Putsch, dictated to Rudolf Hess the insidious rantings of *Mein Kampf*. This unfortunate connection notwithstanding, it's a highly attractive town with easy access to the pre-Alpine countryside to the south. Known as the **Pfaffenwinkel** (literally, "Clerics' Corner"), this has no major towns, but – as the name suggests – is dotted with religious foundations. Two of the most famous of these lie within the borders of the little town of **Steingaden**. Be aware that the public transport network in this area is based primarily on buses, which operate very infrequently at weekends, particularly out of season. However, the Pfaffenwinkel is ideal walking country, and the King Ludwig Way (see p.111) cuts all the way through it.

Landsberg am Lech

As befits its long-time status as a border town, **LANDSBERG** was equipped with a formidable **Stadtmauer**, of which the southern, eastern and western ranges still survive. The most impressive part, situated high above the town centre, is the fifteenth-century

Bayertor (May–Sept daily 10am–noon & 2–5pm; DM2/€1), a mighty gateway consisting of an outer barbican and a 36-metre-high tower whose outer face is adorned with a monumental carving of the Crucifixion. On a clear day, the Alps can be seen from the top, though much of the Altstadt is out of view.

In spite of being sandwiched among a row of mansions, the **Rathaus** (May–Oct Mon–Fri 8am–6pm, Sat & Sun 10am–noon & 2–5pm; Nov–April Mon–Wed 8am–noon & 2–5pm, Thurs 8am–noon & 2–5.30pm, Fri 8am–12.30pm; DM2/€1) dominates the Hauptplatz, in large part because of its exuberant stuccowork facade. Together with the decoration of the main **Ratsstube** on the second floor, this was the only major secular commission undertaken by the great Rococo church-builder Dominikus Zimmermann, who did a stint as burgomaster of the town. He also created the **Johanniskirche** a short distance north on Vorderer Anger. Despite the minute size of the site, this is a wonderfully original design, with an oval nave preceding a horseshoe-shaped chancel filled with a theatrical high altar of the Baptism of Christ. The choir of the large Gothic **Stadtpfarrkirche Mariä Himmelfahrt** diagonally opposite contains another work by Zimmermann, a rosary altar made to shelter a beautiful *Madonna and Child* by the fifteenth-century Ulm sculptor Hans Multscher.

On the left bank of the Lech is the curious **Mutterturm** (Mother Tower; April–Jan Tues–Sun 2–5pm; DM2/€1), built by the Anglo-German artist Hubert von Herkomer as his Landsberg studio. Although now neglected, Herkomer was a leading light of Victorian society; a successful painter, film pioneer, early racing car promoter and occasional composer who was friendly with many of the greatest musicians of the day. The tower contains examples of his graphic work; portraits, landscapes and drawings can be seen in the adjacent **Herkomer-Museum** (same times and ticket), formerly the home of his parents.

Practicalities

Landsberg is now a dead-end for passenger trains; the **Bahnhof** is on the west side of the Lech, not far from the Mutterturm. The **tourist office** is in the Rathaus, Hauptplatz 1 (same hours, see above; ☎0 81 91/12 82 46, fax 12 81 60, *www.landsberg.de*). This is the best source for information about one of the biggest and most colourful **children's festivals** in Germany, the *Ruethenfest*, which takes place over a weekend in July every four years (next in 2003), and features two big processions plus recreations of military camps, a handicrafts market, street theatre and concerts.

Budget accommodation is in short supply: there are only a few **private rooms** (②–③) plus one small **guesthouse**, *Christine*, Galgenweg 4 (☎0 81 91/52 10, *www.gaestehaus-Christine.de*; ④). Otherwise, there are three good **hotels** to choose from: *Landsberger Hof*, Weilheimer Str. 5 (☎0 81 91/3 20 20; ④–⑤); *Gasthof Zum Mohren*, Hauptplatz 148 (☎0 81 91/4 22 10; ⑤); and *Goggl*, Herkomerstr. 19–20 (☎0 81 91/32 40; ⑥). There's also a **campsite**, *Romantik am Lech*, in a woodland setting by the Lech to the south of the Altstadt at Am Pössinger Wald (☎0 81 91/4 75 05). All the hotels listed above have **restaurants**, though strong competition comes from *Zederbräu*, Hauptplatz 155.

Steingaden

STEINGADEN, another stop on the Romantic Road, can be reached by bus from either Landsberg (this sometimes involves a change at Schongau) or Füssen (see p.238). The little town is centred on the **Welfenmünster**, the church of a former Premonstratensian monastery. It encompasses virtually the entire history of Bavarian ecclesiastical architecture: the exterior is one of the area's rare Romanesque survivors, the entrance porch and the frescoed Brunnenkapelle in the cloisters are Gothic, the choir stalls are Renaissance, the high altar and decoration of the chancel are Mannerist, while the nave was remodelled in Rococo style to celebrate the monastery's 600th anniversary, with refined stuccowork, a showy pulpit, and an outstanding set of ceiling frescoes of the life of the order's founder, St Norbert, by Johann Georg Bergmüller.

There are three **hotels**: *Gasthof Zur Post*, Marktplatz 1 (☎0 88 62/2 03; ②); *Gasthof Graf*, Schongauer Str. 15 (☎0 88 62/2 46; ②–④); and *Gasthof Lindenhof*, Schongauer Str. 35 (☎0 88 62/60 11; ③–⑤). Each has a **restaurant** serving homely Bavarian fare at moderate prices.

The Wieskirche

Within Steingaden's municipality, albeit tucked away in the countryside 5km southeast, is the **Wieskirche** (Meadow Church), the best-known pilgrimage church in Germany, and a UNESCO World Heritage Site. When the Steingaden monks discarded a statue of the suffering Christ which they formerly carried in their Holy Week processions, a farmer's wife found the figure crying. So many pilgrims flocked to the simple shrine her husband built that the abbot asked **Dominikus Zimmermann** to erect a worthy temple for the image. His carefully thought-out design, based on his earlier pilgrimage church in Steinhausen (see p.299), has an almost umbilical relationship with the mountains in the background.

The plain exterior belies the extravagance of the interior, which is crammed with furnishings displaying craftsmanship of the highest class. In a symbolic reference to the

THE PASSION PLAY

In 1632, the **plague**, whose spread was greatly facilitated by the famines caused by the Thirty Years War, struck the area around Oberammergau. So many people had died by the following July that the surviving inhabitants gathered and made a pledge that they and their descendants would forever stage a play on the Passion of Jesus if they would be rid of the plague. Even though some were already suffering from the first stages of the disease, there were to be no more deaths from it. In honour of the pledge, the first performance was staged; it has been revived (with few exceptions) every ten years since then. In due course, the years ending in zero were chosen as the normal performance years, though war and other factors have caused some variations.

Originally, there was just one **performance**, held at Easter. As the fame of the play spread, so did the number of performances increase, and in recent times there have been over ninety in the course of a season lasting from May until October. The **English-speaking world's infatuation** with the play began in earnest in 1871, when Thomas Cook first led organized groups from Britain, and the future King Edward VII paid what he vainly hoped would be an incognito visit. Jerome K. Jerome helped increase its popularity by writing a humorous travelogue of his journey to see the 1890 play. Nowadays, over 60 percent of the total audience of nearly half a million come from countries where English is the first language.

The somewhat bawdy and superstitious **text** of the early Passion Plays was replaced for the 1815 performances by one written by Othmar Weis, a monk from Ettal. This intersperses dramatic enactments of the main events of Holy Week with *tableaux vivants* illustrating Old Testament scenes which prefigure them. The local organist Rochus Dedler wrote a score to accompany this; clearly influenced by the great compositions of Haydn and Mozart, it has remained the main musical component ever since. A revised version of Weis's text, made in 1860 by his pupil Joseph Alois Daisenberger, the Oberammergau parish priest, was used with relatively little change up to 1990, but was heavily altered for the 2000 season. Then, the remaining anti-Semitic elements – which had for long been a source of protest – were removed completely, with Judas Iscariot characterized as a disappointed political zealot rather than a man consumed by greed. Modern performances last around six hours, excluding the two-hour lunch break, and visitors are forced to move on after two nights.

contrast between earth and heaven, the plain white pillars are offset by the gold-plated stucco ornamentation of the arches above and the bravura ceiling **fresco** by Johann Baptist Zimmermann (Dominikus's elder brother). Executed in glowing, pastel-like colours, this presents a radiant vision of the afterlife: the resurrected Christ sits on a rainbow in the centre, with the still unoccupied Throne of Judgement and the as yet unopened Gate to Eternity at either end.

Dominikus Zimmermann, a deeply pious man, built a house for himself alongside the church, and lived out his retirement there. Nowadays, it's a **restaurant**, *Schweiger*, serving marvellous Bavarian cuisine; *Moser*, which is down by the car park, also offers good food. If you fancy a quiet night in the countryside, try one of a couple of the nearby farmhouses offering **rooms** (①–②). Note that there are only three or four **buses** a day to and from Steingaden, though there's a very pleasant walking trail.

Oberammergau and Ettal

OBERAMMERGAU, the terminus of a branch rail line at the western edge of the Upper Bavarian Alps, is world-famous for the **Passion Play** (see box below) that the local villagers have been performing since 1634; the next performances will take place in the year 2010. Without the tradition of the play, it's likely that Oberammergau would

Only Oberammergau natives, or those who have resided in the village for at least five years, can become members of the **cast**. It is a major honour to be chosen for one of the leading roles, which are now alternated between two actors. However, with some one hundred and thirty speaking parts in all, and upwards of six hundred people on stage in some scenes, with a further fifty in both the choir and orchestra, almost any villager who so desires gets a chance to take part. Until 1980, the key roles were confined to Catholics, and women were not even allowed a bit part unless they were unmarried and under 35. However, in 1990 a mother-of-two was chosen to play the Virgin Mary, and a Protestant was given a prominent part. Discriminatory qualifications for women were abandoned completely for the 2000 production, and Protestants – who, as a result of internal migration, now account for nearly a quarter of the population of a village which was solidly Catholic until World War II – were allocated far more roles than hitherto.

All the **costumes** and other **props** are made locally. When the makers of these are added to the backstage staff, the shopkeepers, hoteliers and restaurateurs, almost the entire population of the village is directly involved in the Passion Play in some capacity. Local children are now groomed from an early age to play a role best suited to their talents, whether on or off stage. Thus, far from being an example of crude rural amateurism, the Passion Play has become a highly polished and **professional** operation in every way. As a dramatic spectacle, it is nothing short of awesome: no detail is spared in providing a historically accurate re-creation of the events, and the Judgement scene in particular, with its huge, baying mob, is positively spine-chilling. The unpredictable, fast-changing Alpine weather often adds to the drama (sometimes uncannily so, as when black clouds roll over during the Crucifixion scene), though the show always goes on, no matter what falls from the heavens onto the open-air stage.

For all its global fame and impact on the local economy, the Oberammergau Passion Play paradoxically remains at heart what it always has been, an act of **worship** signifying the villagers' continued commitment to the vow made by their seventeenth-century ancestors. Each performance of the play ends without applause and without curtain calls. Still photographs of all the scenes are taken during pre-season rehearsals, but the vast sums of money periodically offered by Hollywood for a Passion Play movie have always been firmly rebuffed, and no video record is ever made.

be stuck in relative obscurity, instead of being the tourist trap it has become, crammed with souvenir shops selling examples of the local **woodcarving** to the busloads of organized tour parties which roll up every summer. Nevertheless, it does preserve features genuinely characteristic of small Alpine communities. In particular, the facades of many of the houses are adorned with **frescoes**, which are either quaint or kitsch according to taste. This style of decoration, which is known as *Lüftlmalerei*, dates back to the mid-eighteenth century, and is a uniquely Catholic art. Thus the scenes depicted are usually based on biblical stories, making a highly distinctive transfer of a sacred art form to secular buildings.

Just north of the central axis, Dorfstrasse, is the huge **Passionspielhaus**, theatre where the Passion Play performances are held. It was custom-built in the 1890s to ensure that every member of the vast audience can see and hear all the action, and was modified in the 1930s and again in the late 1990s. Although a decidedly curious piece of architecture – the open-air stage is loosely modelled on the theatres of ancient Rome, while the covered auditorium resembles an aircraft hangar – it fulfils its purpose admirably. The backstage areas, including the collections of historic costumes and props, can be visited by **guided tour** (Sun–Fri at 2pm, Sat at 3.30pm; Dm4/€2).

The **Heimatmuseum** (mid-May to mid-Oct Tues–Sun 2–6pm; rest of year Sat 2–6pm only; DM4.50/€2.25) at Dorfstr. 8 contains extensive displays of folk art, particularly woodcarvings and paintings behind glass. There's a fine collection of historic cribs made from a variety of different materials; predictably, it's the wooden examples which are the most imposing. In the **Pilatushaus** (June–Oct Mon–Fri 1–6pm, Sat 10.30am–12.30pm; free), on Verlegergasse just to the south, you can watch some of the local craftsmen at work. The building itself is of special note for having been decorated by Franz Zwinck, Oberammergau's first and most celebrated *Lüftlmaler*. Beyond the far end of Dorfstrasse is the **Pfarrkirche St-Peter-und-Paul**, a splendid example of an Upper Bavarian village church. It was designed and built in 1736–49 by Joseph Schmuzer, a member of a prolific dynasty of architects and stuccoists, and embellished by several distinguished collaborators, notably the fresco painter Matthäus Günther and the sculptor Franz Xaver Schmädl.

For the best view of Oberammergau and its surroundings, take the cable car (DM14/€7 single, DM20/€10 return) from the eastern end of the village to the **Laber** (1683m).

Practicalities

Oberammergau's **Bahnhof** is on the west bank of the Ammer, just a few minutes' walk from the centre on the opposite side of the river. The **tourist office** is at Eugen-Papst-Str. 9a (Mon–Fri 8.30am–6pm, Sat 8.30am–noon; ☎0 88 22/9 23 10, fax 92 31 90, *www.oberammergau.de*). **Tickets** for the next performances of the Passion Play are unlikely to go on sale until 2008.

The village is well endowed with **private rooms** (①–③) and **pensions**, such as *Reiser*, In der Breitenau 6 (☎0 88 22/47 47; ②), *Dedlerhaus*, Ettaler Str. 8 (☎0 88 22/35 93, *www.dedlerhaus.de*; ②), and *Enzianhof*, Ettaler Str. 33 (☎0 88 22/2 15; ②). Among several classy **hotels** are *Alte Post*, Dorfstr. 19 (☎0 88 22/91 00, *www.ogau.de*; ④), *Wittelsbach*, Dorfstr. 21 (☎0 88 22/9 28 00, *www.hotelwittelsbach.de*; ⑤), and *Turmwirt*, Ettaler Str. 2 (☎0 88 22/9 26 00, *www.turmwirt.de*). The **youth hostel** is at the southwestern edge of the village at Mahlensteinweg 10 (☎0 88 22/41 14, fax 16 95; DM21/€10.50); the **campsite** is at the southern fringe at Ettaler Str. 54b (☎0 88 22/9 41 05).

As usual in resorts of this kind, the best **restaurants** are attached to hotels, and those listed above are as good as any, though *Wittelsbach* is open to residents only.

Ettal and Schloss Linderhof

The small health resort of **ETTAL**, 4km down the road, grew up around its Benedictine **Kloster**, which was founded in 1330 by Emperor Ludwig IV, and for several centuries wielded temporal (though not spiritual) jurisdiction over Oberammergau. A twelve-cornered design, based on the Church of the Holy Sepulchre in Jerusalem, was adopted for the original Gothic **Klosterkirche**, and this shape, along with much of the masonry, was preserved in the Baroque rebuilding carried out by Enrico Zuccalli and Joseph Schmuzer. Johann Straub carved the pulpit and assemblage of nave altars, while the fresco decoration of the vaults was entrusted to two Tyroleans, Johann Jakob Zeiller and Martin Knoller. A miraculous statue of the *Madonna and Child*, which the founder brought back from a journey to Italy, is the focus of the high altar. The monastery produces a variety of wonderful fruit liqueurs and brandies, plus some fine beers. A highly recommendable **hotel** with restaurant, *Ludwig der Bayer*, occupies the old monastic guesthouse at Kaiser-Ludwig-Platz 10–12 (☎0 88 22/91 50; ④).

Some 11km west of Ettal, but still within its municipal area, is **Schloss Linderhof** (guided tours April–Sept Mon–Wed & Fri–Sun 9am–6pm, Thurs 9am–8pm; DM11/€5.50 including pavilions; Oct–March daily 10am–4pm; DM8/€4), which can be reached by several buses daily. One of King Ludwig II's more restrained fantasies – and the only one that was actually completed – it was built as a private residence rather than a statement in royal architecture. From the garden terraces its creamy white walls and square shape make it look like a sparkling wedding cake. As you enter, it's impossible to miss a large bronze statue of one of Ludwig's heroes, Louis XIV, and, although this was a private retreat, Ludwig still had a reception room with gold-painted carvings, stucco ornamentation and a throne canopy draped in ermine curtains.

However, the top attraction is the delightful **Schlosspark**. The palace forms the axis of a cross-shaped design, which was laid out on the Italian Renaissance model of terraces, cascades and pools rising up in front and behind, while the shorter gardens to the right and left have strictly manicured lawns, hedges and flowerbeds. Initially, it's hard to tell that the surrounding "wild" scenery is actually a clever English garden design that gradually blends into the forests beyond. A number of romantic little buildings (open summer only, times as above) are dotted around the park, the most remarkable of which is the **Venus-Grotte**. It's supposed to be based on the set from the first act of Wagner's opera *Tannhäuser* and has an illuminated lake with an enormous golden conch floating on it in which the king would sometimes take rides. Equally outrageous is the **Maurischer Kiosk**, a mock-Moorish pavilion in which stands a throne with a backdrop of three huge peacocks crafted out of enamel and coloured glass. Also in the grounds is the *Schlosshotel* (☎0 88 22/7 90; ⑤), which offers **rooms** with balconies and a restaurant specializing in game dishes.

Garmisch-Partenkirchen and Mittenwald

GARMISCH-PARTENKIRCHEN, some 19km south of Oberammergau by road, is the most famous resort in the German Alps, partly because it's at the foot of the highest mountain – the **Zugspitze** – and partly because it hosted the fourth Winter Olympics back in 1936. Its location is marvellous, lying between the gentle Ammer mountains and the imposing peaks of the Wetterstein chain which form the frontier with Austria. During the winter months Garmisch is one of the foremost **skiing** bases, and it has excellent facilities for **skating** and other winter sports too. In summer, mountaineers and **hiking** enthusiasts come to explore the craggy heights, while there are cable cars for the less energetic.

The 1936 games quite literally put the town on the map; previously Garmisch and Partenkirchen had been separate villages, lying west and east of the River Partnach respectively. The area between them has now been built up, so that at first the town appears as a seamless whole, but closer acquaintance reveals that each part preserves its historic core and at least something of its old identity.

Garmisch's centre is the ritzier of the two, with plenty of fashionable shops and cafés. Its **Kurpark** (daily 9am–10pm; DM2/€1) has both formal and "natural" sections, and regularly hosts open-air concerts. Within the park is the **Kurhaus**, which contains the **Stiftung Aschenbrenner** (Tues–Fri 9am–noon & 3–6.30pm, Sat & Sun 10am–noon & 3–6.30pm; free), a delightful collection of Meissen porcelain and historic toys. A short distance to the west is the **Pfarrkirche St Martin**, a typical example of the work of Joseph Schmuzer. Further south is the **Alte Kirche**, which dates back to the time of Garmisch's foundation in the late thirteenth century, although the original Romanesque structure was partially modified in Gothic style. Inside are fourteenth- to sixteenth-century fresco cycles.

Partenkirchen's centre is characterized by the presence of many traditional painted houses, and one of these, the former merchant's residence at Ludwigstr. 47, contains the **Werdenfelser Heimatmuseum** (Tues–Fri 10am–1pm & 3–6pm; DM3/€1.50), which vividly brings the region's distinctive culture to life. Among the exhibits are sculptures by Ignaz Günther and the house's former owner, Joseph Wackerle, reconstructed interiors, Carnival masks, an eighteenth-century crib, costumes, glass paintings and furniture. Another church by Joseph Schmuzer, the Franciscan **Wallfahrtskirche St Anton**, lies in a rustic setting at the eastern edge of Partenkirchen, and is approached via a steepish path lined with ten pilgrimage chapels.

The peaks

From Garmisch, there are two possibilities for ascending the **Zugspitze** (2966m) by public transport; each costs DM44/€22 single, DM79/€39.50 return in summer, and DM36/€18 single, DM62/€31 return in winter. The electric train, the Zugspitzbahn, travels westwards to a forest lake, the **Eibsee**. Here you can either continue by the rack rail line, the Gletscherbahn, which goes up a winding tunnel carved through the interior of the mountain, or transfer to the Eibseebahn cable car. Whereas the latter goes straight to the summit, the former deposits you at the *Schneefernhaus* (2645m), which commands a huge skiing area. You can then ascend to the summit by the Gipfelbahn cable car, or walk via the tunnel to the customs point, the Zugspitzkamm (2805m), from where yet another cable car, the Tiroler Zugspitzbahn, runs to Ehrwald in Austria. The **views** from the top are all you'd expect, stretching from the Tyrolean High Alps to the Allgäu and the Bavarian lowlands.

Closer to Garmisch, the **Alpspitze** (2628m) is the highest peak in a range popular with serious hikers. In this case, the cable car, the Alpspitzbahn (DM27/€13.50 single, DM38/€19 return) does not go all the way to the summit, but terminates at the nearby **Osterfelderkopf** (2050m). The valley station is at the southwestern edge of Garmisch, reached by bus #2 from the centre; close by is the departure point of another cable car, which ascends to the **Kreuzeck** (1652m) for DM20/€10 single, DM28/€14 return. Two other peaks to the south of town, **Hausberg** (1350m) and **Eckbauer** (1236m) also have their own cable cars (DM15/€7.50 single, DM20/€10 return, and DM14/€7 single, DM19/€9.50 return respectively). A short walk south of the latter's valley station is the magnificent gorge known as the **Partnachklamm** (a DM3/€1.50 admission is levied throughout most of the day), which can be traversed by a circular path hewn out of the rock. East of Partenkirchen, the **Wank** (1780m) offers the best view of the basin in which the town is set, as well as a complete panorama of the Wetterstein chain. A cable car, whose valley station is served by buses #3, #4 and #5, goes to the summit for DM20/€10 single, DM29/€14.50 return.

Practicalities

Garmisch-Partenkirchen's **Bahnhof** is handily placed between the two constituent villages; immediately to its rear is the **Zugspitzbahnhof**, terminus of the mountain rail line. At the latter you can buy passes (a passport photograph is required) covering all the cable cars except those on the Zugspitze – something well worth considering if you're planning on doing a lot of hiking. During the summer season these cost DM64/€32 for adults, DM38/€19 for children for three days, rising to DM130/€65 and DM78/€39 respectively for a week, DM207/€103.50 and DM124/€62 for two weeks. Winter ski passes for the region are also available for a variety of periods, with the three-day versions costing DM144/€72. The **tourist office** (Mon–Sat 8am–6pm, Sun 10am–noon; ☎0 88 21/18 06, fax 18 07 55, *www.garmisch-partenkirchen.de*) is at Richard-Strauss-Platz 2, five minutes' walk south of the Bahnhof.

Budget accommodation options include the **youth hostel**, Jochstr. 10 (☎0 88 21/29 80, fax 5 85 36; DM21/€10.50) in the incorporated village of Burgrain, reached by bus #3, #4 or #5 from the Bahnhof, and the *Naturfreundehaus*, Schalmeiweg 21 (☎0 88 21/43 22) at the eastern edge of Partenkirchen. There's also a **campsite**, *Zugspitze* (☎0 88 21/31 80), ideally placed for the peaks, by the village of Grainau to the west. **Private rooms** (①–③), while on average marginally more expensive than elsewhere in the Alps, are still wonderful value, as are the many **guesthouses**, such as *Neuner*, Kreuzstr. 21 (☎0 88 21/5 62 91; ②), *Christina*, Burgstr. 61 (☎0 88 21/13 34 or 23 75, *www. gaestehaus-christina.de*; ②–④), and *Reiter*, Burgstr. 55 (☎0 88 21/22 33, *www.reiter-gap.de*; ②–④).

Among the town's **hotels**, *Berggasthof Panorama*, up from the Wank cable-car station at St Anton 3 (☎0 88 21/25 15, *www.garmisch-partenkirchen.com/berggasthof.panorama*; ⑤) offers the most spectacular views. A couple of medium-range alternatives in the heart of Partenkirchen are *Gasthof Zum Rassen*, Ludwigstr. 45 (☎0 88 21/20 89; ③–⑥), and *Gasthof Fraundorfer*, Ludwigstr. 24 (☎0 88 21/92 70, *www.gasthof-fraundorfer.de*; ⑤–⑦). There are many enticing luxury options, notably *Posthotel Partenkirchen*, Ludwigstr. 49 (☎0 88 21/9 36 30, *www.apzp.de*; ⑦), a marvellous old inn decked out in rustic style; *Reindl's Partenkircher Hof*, Bahnhofstr. 15 (☎0 88 21/5 80 25, *www.garmisch-partenkirchen.com/Reindl*; ⑦–⑨), which is furnished with antiques, has a swimming pool, fitness room, winter garden and balconies with panoramic views; and *Grand Hotel Sonnenbichl*, Burgstr. 97 (☎0 88 21/70 20, *www.sonnenbichl.de*; ⑧–⑨), which offers similar facilities, though if anything is even grander in style.

All the hotels listed above have recommendable **restaurants** open to non-residents. Among Garmisch's many enticing **cafés**, *Krönner*, Am Kurpark 5, and *Pavillon*, Am Kurpark 2, stand out.

Mittenwald

Just 20km southeast of Garmisch by road or rail, **MITTENWALD** could hardly be more different. In 1786 Goethe described it as a "living picture book", and so it remains, having the feel of a community and not just a resort. This is reflected in the carved pews with their family nameplates in the **Pfarrkirche St-Peter-und-Paul**. The church, yet another of Joseph Schmuzer's designs, is also notable for frescoes by Johann Georg Bergmüller, which give a deliberately prominent role to angel musicians, in recognition of the important role of music in the life of Mittenwald. In particular, the town has been an internationally renowned centre of violin making ever since **Matthias Klotz**, who is honoured by a statue outside the church, introduced this highly specialized craft to the village in the seventeenth century, thus raising it from the status of an impoverished backwater. Some of the finest work of the local craftsmen, from Klotz to the present day, can be seen in the **Geigenbaumuseum** (Mon–Fri 10–11.45am & 2–4.45pm, Sat & Sun 10–11.45am; closed Nov; DM3/€1.50), a short distance to the north at Ballenhausgasse 3. There's also a mock-up of Klotz's workshop, as well as a collection of festive masks and an impressive crib. To the west, on Im Gries, stand the oldest Mittenwald houses, with faded frescoes decorating their frontages.

Walks around town

Towering above Mittenwald is the **Karwendl** (2244m), one of the most popular climbs in Germany. The view from the top is exhilarating; a cable car will take you up for DM20/€10 single, DM32/€16 return. There are plenty of enticing but less demanding walks in the Isar valley below, including the **Leutaschklamm** (daily 9.30am–5.30pm; DM2/€1) 2km south of Mittenwald. Though technically in Austria, this dramatic narrow gorge with a 23-metre-high waterfall is inaccessible from that side of the border. To the west of town, two small lakes, the **Lautersee** and the **Ferchensee**, stand in the shadow of the mighty Wetterstein mountains; there are boats for rent and a good country Gasthaus at each. The path from Mittenwald, which starts just beyond the Kurpark, passes via a pretty waterfall, the **Laintalschlucht**.

Practicalities

Mittenwald's **Bahnhof** is at the eastern edge of the town centre; the **tourist office** is a short walk away at Dammkarstr. 3 (Mon–Fri 8am–noon & 1–5pm, Sat 10am–noon; ☎0 88 23/3 39 81, fax 0 88 23/27 01, *www.mittenwald.de*).

There are many good-value **guesthouses**, such as *Bergfrühling*, Dammkarstr. 12 (☎0 88 23/80 89; ②), *Franziska*, Innsbrucker Str. 24 (☎0 88 23/9 20 30, *www.franziska-tourismus.de*; ④), and *Sonnenbichl*, Klausnerweg 32 (☎0 88 23/9 22 30, *www.sonnenbichl-tourismus.de*; ④), the last of which is the place for a view. **Hotels** in the town centre include *Alpenrose*, Obermarkt 1 (☎0 88 23/9 27 00; ③–⑥), and *Post*, Obermarkt 9 (☎0 88 23/10 94, *www.TourOnline.de/posthotel/mittenwald*; ⑥). For an isolated setting, with the bonus of wonderful panoramas, there's *Alpengasthof Gröblalm* (☎0 88 23/91 10, *GroeblAlm@t-online.de*; ④–⑥), 2km north. The **youth hostel** at Buckelwiesen 7 (☎0 88 23/17 01, fax 29 07; DM21/€10.50) is an hour's walk from the Bahnhof, so isn't a very practical option for those without their own transport. However, the tourist office can fix you up with a room in a **private house** (①–③). The nearest **campsite**, the year-round *Am Isarhorn* (☎0 88 23/52 16), is 3km north, on the road to Garmisch.

All the hotels mentioned above have good **restaurants**. *Postkeller*, Innsbrucker Str. 13, the tap of the local brewery, is also recommendable, while *Arnspitze*, Innsbrucker Str. 68, is the best and most expensive in town.

The Tölzer Land

To the north of Mittenwald, the **Tölzer Land** offers altogether gentler scenery. Nonetheless, the area embraces two major lakes – the **Walchensee** and the **Kochelsee** – as well as **Benediktbeuern**, the oldest monastery in Upper Bavaria. It also has a rich folklore tradition of riflemen's festivals and costumed parades.

The Walchensee

Of the Tölzer Land's two lakes, the **Walchensee**, some 25km southwest of Bad Tölz, and 19km north of Mittenwald, is by far the more dramatic. Its depth is unknown and the water is so cold in the lower reaches that the many trees fallen from the mountainous shores haven't been able to sink completely; instead they've formed an impenetrable false bottom to the lake. Many people believe that the Nazis dumped their hoarded treasures here in the last days of the war. Plenty of divers have tried their luck and some have died, tangled in the branches.

Having said that, this is a good place to come if you're into **boats** and **windsurfing**, since it's never as crowded as the lowland lakes, and is cheaper too. A popular trip around here is the three-hour hike from **URFELD** at the northern tip of the lake to the summit of the **Herzogstand** (1731m). This commands a breathtaking panorama of the region's two lakes plus the snow-capped Austrian peaks to the south and the Bavarian plateau to the north. Alternatively, take the cable car (DM13/€6.50 single, DM24/€12 return) from the northern end of the scattered village of **WALCHENSEE** on the western shore.

The local **youth hostel** is at Mittenwalder Str. 17 (☎0 88 51/2 30, fax 10 22; DM23/€11.50) in Urfeld. Walchensee has several **guesthouses**, including *Seeblick*, Ringstr. 68a (☎0 88 58/2 28; ②), and *Edeltraut*, Seestr. 90 (☎0 88 58/2 62; ③). There are also two lakeside **hotels**: *Schwaigerhof*, Seestr. 42 (☎0 88 58/9 20 20; ③–⑤), and *Seehotel zur Post*, Seestr. 52 (☎0 88 58/4 64; ④–⑥). A full accommodation list can be had from the **tourist office** (mid-May to mid-Oct Mon–Fri 9am–noon & 1–5pm, Sat 10am–noon; mid-Oct to mid-May Mon–Thurs 9am–noon & 2–4pm, Fri 9am–noon; ☎0 88 58/4 11, *www.walchensee.de*) in the Rathaus.

The Kochelsee

A wonderful twisting nine-kilometre-long road links Urfeld with the **Kochelsee**. This lake combines lowland and highland attractions: to the north lies marshland while the craggy **Benediktenwand**, the first slopes in the Alpine chain, rise immediately from its southern shore. The shoreline has an agreeably empty feel to it, but a good deal of the immediate surrounding area is flat and rather dull. The village of **KOCHEL** on the northeastern side is the largest settlement; it's the terminus of a branch rail line which links up with the Munich S-Bahn network at Tutzing on the Starnberger See.

The Expressionist painter **Franz Marc** lived around here from 1908 until 1916, when he was killed in action in World War I at the age of 36. Unlike his friends in Der Blaue Reiter group such as Kandinsky and Macke, he preferred country life, and his pictures of horses and other animals are his most famous works. The **Franz-Marc-Museum** (April–Oct Tues–Sun 2–6pm; DM6/€3) at Herzogstandweg 43 contains a representative collection of his work, comprising about a hundred paintings, as well as examples of other members of Der Blaue Reiter.

Kochel's **tourist office** is at Kalmbachstr. 11 (Mon–Fri 8am–noon & 1–5pm; ☎0 88 51/3 38, fax 55 88, *www.kochel.de*). **Cruises**, costing DM10/€5 for a round trip (1hr 15min), are run between June and September by Motorschiffahrt Kochelsee (☎0 88 51/4 16). Accommodation possibilities include a **youth hostel** at Badstr. 2 (☎0 88 51/52 96, fax 70 19; DM21/€10.50) and the **campsites** *Kesselberg* (☎0 88 51/4 64) and *Renken* (☎0 88 51/57 76). There are also numerous **hotels**, including *Waltraud*, Bahnhofstr. 20 (☎0 88 51/3 33; ③), *Zur Post*, Schmied-von-Kochel-Platz 6 (☎0 88 51/9 24 10; ④), and the lakeside *Seehotel Grauer Bär*, Mittenwalder Str. 82–6 (☎0 88 51/9 25 00; ⑤), all of which have excellent **restaurants**.

Benediktbeuern

BENEDIKTBEUERN, 8km north of Kochel on the rail line to Munich, is a small health resort with its back to the Benediktenwand. Its **Kloster**, which dates back to 789, is chiefly famous for the manuscript known as *Carmina Burana*, which was compiled and illuminated there in the late thirteenth century, remaining in the monastery library until the Napoleonic secularization, when it was carted off to Munich. Although this anthology of eleventh- to thirteenth-century (mostly Latin) lyrics by itinerant scholars and monks contains some religious pieces, its primary concerns are decidedly earthly, with moral and satirical verses, ribald love laments, and bucolic drinking and gaming songs. In 1935 the Munich composer Carl Orff was inspired to write a technicolour choral and orchestral showpiece on some of the texts, and this remains one of the most popular of all twentieth-century compositions with the paying public – though not with the critics. At the time the cantata was written, the musical notation in the manuscript itself was thought to be indecipherable, but painstaking detective work by musicologists has enabled these hauntingly pure and simple songs to become mainstays of the repertoire of early music groups.

Nothing remains of the medieval Kloster, which was entirely rebuilt in the Baroque epoch. The **Klosterkirche** boasts a fresco cycle of the life of Christ by Hans Georg Asam (father of the famous architect-interior decorator brothers), but is rather overshadowed by the **Anastasiakapelle**, a separate chapel to the north, which is a miniature masterpiece by Johann Michael Fischer. In 1930, the monastic buildings were reoccupied by a congregation of Salesian monks, who have established a school and cultural centre. Concerts and exhibitions are regularly held there; also on the p remises are a fine **restaurant** with beer garden and a **youth hostel** (☎0 88 57/8 83 50, fax 8 83 51, *lichtenstern@don-bosco-jh.de*; DM25/€12.50).

The Tegernsee and beyond

The **Tegernsee**, which lies immediately east of the Tölzer Land, is among the most beautiful lakes in Bavaria. It has long been a favourite with the rich, who have built weekend homes along its privately owned sections, and a couple of the leading Alpine resorts can be found on its banks. To the east and southeast lies countryside that is far less well known, including two more lakes, the **Schliersee** and the **Spitzingsee**, and the most isolated section of the Bavarian Alps, the area around **Bayrischzell**. Trains throughout this area are now operated by a private company, Bayerische Oberlandbahn (BOB), though this currently accepts all DB and international rail passes.

Tegernsee

The little town of **TEGERNSEE** is on the east bank of the lake, at the end of a branch railway from Schaftlach on the main line to Munich. By the waterside towards the southern end of the resort is the former Benedictine **Kloster**, which was founded in 746 and flourished for over a millennium. A major centre for manuscript illumination and calligraphy, it once had a library considered superior to that of the Vatican. Following the Napoleonic secularization, Leo von Klenze converted the monastic buildings into a summertime **Schloss** for the Bavarian kings. He also added a twin-towered facade to the Baroque **Klosterkirche**, whose main body was designed by Enrico Zuccalli and frescoed by Hans Georg Asam.

The **tourist office** is in the Haus des Gastes, Hauptstr. 2 (Mon–Fri 8am–6pm, Sat & Sun 9am–noon & 3–5pm; ☎0 80 22/18 01 40, fax 37 58, *www.tegernsee.de*). Here you can pick up a list of **private rooms** and **guesthouses** (①–④). There are several lakeside **hotels**, the best being *Fischerstüberl am See*, Seestr. 51 (☎0 80 22/91 98 90; ④–⑥). *Leeberghof*, on a hillside to the south of town at Ellingerstr. 10 (☎0 80 22/39 66; ⑦), only has three bedrooms, but also has a superb restaurant with a panorama terrace. Tegernsee's top address is *Bayern*, uphill from the Bahnhof in the north of town at Neureuthstr. 23 (☎0 80 22/18 20; ⑦–⑨).

The north wing of the Schloss contains the *Bräustüberl* of the local **brewery**, the Herzogliches Bayerisches Brauhaus, which is still owned by the Wittelsbach family.

This is an extraordinary sight in the evening, when it's crammed full of local farmers trying to drink each other under the table. Only basic snacks are served there; for a full meal and a quieter atmosphere, go instead to the adjacent cellar **restaurant**, the *Schlossgaststätte*. Alternative places to eat can be found in all the hotels listed above. **Cruises** are run by Staatliche Schiffahrt Tegernsee (☎0 80 22/9 33 11), which charges DM13.50/€6.75 for an hour-long trip around the southern part of the lake, DM20/€10 for the complete circuit.

Rottach-Egern

At the southern end of the lake, reached by bus or boat from Tegernsee, is the double village of **ROTTACH-EGERN**. From there, you can take a cable car (DM12/€6 single, DM20/€10 return) up the **Wallberg** (1722m) for a grandstand view over the lake and the surrounding hills. There's a pleasant terrace **restaurant**, *Alpenwildpark*, at the valley station. Rottach-Egern has a few reasonably priced **hotels**, including *Reuther*, Salitererweg 6 (☎0 80 22/2 40 24; ⑤), and *Café Sonnenhof*, Sonnenmoosstr. 20 (☎0 80 22/ 58 12; ⑤). However, no matter how incongruous it may seem in this country setting, it's best known as a hangout of the chic, who favour such super-luxury establishments as *Park-Hotel Egerner Hof*, Aribostr. 19 (☎0 80 22/66 60; ⑨), whose *Dichterstub'n* is one of Bavaria's leading gourmet restaurants; and *Bachmair am See*, Seestr. 47 (☎0 80 22/27 20; ⑨), which comes complete with a glorious park and a high-fashion boutique.

The Schliersee

The next lake to the east, the **Schliersee**, has a more distinctively Alpine feel to it. At its northeast corner is the pretty village of **SCHLIERSEE**, which can be reached by bus from Tegernsee and Rottach-Egern or by the branch rail line from Munich (sometimes involving a change at Holzkirchen) which then backtracks and loops round the west side of the lake. Although a popular resort, it hasn't been annexed by the Porsche-driving set, instead preserving a traditional rural culture in which poaching was, until quite recently, an established feature. In the centre of the village stands the **Pfarrkirche St Sixtus**, which boasts frescoes and stuccowork by Johann Baptist Zimmermann and a painting of *The Madonna of Mercy* by Jan Polack. The nearby **Rathaus**, originally a courthouse, bristling with turrets and oriels, ranks among the most picturesque in the Alpine region.

From the east side of the village, cable-car gondolas (DM6/€3 single, DM10/€5 return) ascend to the **Schliersbergalm** (1061m), which commands the finest view over the area; in summer, those wanting the thrill of a helter-skelter descent can do so via the chute. **Cruises** on the lake are run between June and September by Motorschiffahrt Schliersee, and cost DM7.50/€3.75 for 35 minutes. There's a regular bus service up to the **Spitzingsee**, a much smaller mountain lake on whose eastern shore is the village of the same name, a popular winter-sports centre.

The **tourist office** (late May to Oct Mon–Fri 8am–6pm, Sat & Sun 10am–noon; reduced hours out of season; ☎0 80 26/6 06 50, fax 60 65 20, *www.schliersee.de*) is at Bahnhofstr. 11a. As usual, there's a wide provision of **private rooms** and **guesthouses** (②–④), as well as some splendid **hotels** – notably *Terofal*, Xaver-Terofal-Platz 2 (☎0 80 26/40 45; ④–⑥), and *Schlierseer Hof am See*, Seestr. 21 (☎0 80 26/94 00, *www.schlierseerhof.de*; ⑥–⑧). Both of these have superb **restaurants**, whose menus feature freshly caught fish from the lake. Among several colourful annual **festivals**, pride of place goes to the *Alt-Schlierseer-Kirchtag* on a Sunday in August, for which the locals don traditional costumes and sail across the lake in boats adorned with floral garlands.

Bayrischzell

BAYRISCHZELL, the terminus of the branch railway, is a small health and winter-sports resort in the enclosed setting of the upper valley of the River Leitzach, and has an appropriate end-of-the-line feel. Towering above is the rocky peak of the **Wendelstein** (1838m), one of the best-loved mountains in the Bavarian Alps, particularly with rock climbers. For the less energetic, there are two possible means of ascent to the summit, on which stand an eighteenth-century chapel, a meteorological station and an observatory with one of the most modern telescopes in Germany. Much the quicker of the two is the **cable car** (DM17.50/€8.75 single, DM30/€15 return) from the incorporated village of Osterhofen, 3km northwest of Bayrischzell. A far more atmospheric approach is the **rack railway** (DM26/€13 single, DM42/€21 return) up the eastern side of the mountain from Brannenburg, a town on the Munich–Innsbruck rail line (note that the valley terminus of the rack railway is a thirty-minute walk from the mainline Bahnhof). This was laid out in 1912, though the current trains date from 1991 and have halved the old journey time to thirty minutes. It's possible to ascend by cable car and descend via the rack railway, or vice versa; this costs DM42/€21, or DM44/€22 including use of the Wendelstein-Ringlinie, the circular bus service round the mountain.

Bayrischzell's **tourist office** is in the Kurverwaltung, Kirchplatz 2 (mid-May to mid-Oct Mon–Fri 8am–noon & 1–6pm, Sat 9am–noon; mid-Oct to mid-Dec & April to mid-May Mon–Fri 8am–noon & 1–5pm; mid-Dec to March Mon–Fri 8am–5pm, Sat & Sun 9am–noon; ☎0 80 23/6 48, fax 10 34, *www.bayrischzell.de*). In addition to numerous **private houses** and **guesthouses** (①–③), there are several fine **hotels**, including *Wendelstein*, Ursprungstr. 1 (☎0 80 23/8 08 90; ③), *Gasthof Zur Post*, Schulstr. 3 (☎0 80 23/2 26; ④), and *Alpenrose*, Schlierseer Str. 6 (☎0 80 23/9 06 50; ⑤), all of which have **restaurants**.

The Chiemsee and Chiemgau

The **Chiemgau** is a large Alpine and pre-Alpine region, stretching eastwards from the industrial town of Rosenheim, a major railway junction, all the way to the border with Austria along the River Salzach. At its western edge is the **Chiemsee**, Bavaria's largest lake, which is usually regarded as a separate region in its own right.

Prien am Chiemsee

The Chiemsee's main resort, well placed for visiting all the local beauty spots, is **PRIEN**, at the southwestern edge of the lake: it's easily accessible, as it lies on the main Munich–Salzburg rail line. In the town centre, set back 1.5km from the lake, is the Baroque **Pfarrkirche Mariä Himmelfahrt**, which has a spectacular illusionist ceiling fresco by Johann Baptist Zimmermann depicting the Christian naval victory over the Turks at the Battle of Lepanto. Though it's a pleasant enough walk down Seestrasse to the harbour district of **Stock**, it's far more fun to take the **narrow-gauge railway**, the Chiemseebahn (Easter–Sept only; DM3.50/€1.75 single, DM5.50/€2.75 return), which has been running since 1887 from its own little terminal alongside the Bahnhof, and is pulled by a steam engine at weekends and on public holidays. Stock is the hub of the watersports activities and of the **ferry** connections to the islands and the other resorts on the lake run by the Chiemseeschiffahrt (☎0 80 51/60 90).

The **tourist office** is in the Kurverwaltung at Alte Rathausstr. 11 (Mon–Fri 8.30am–6pm, Sat 9am–noon; ☎0 80 51/6 90 50, fax 69 05 40, *www.prien.chiemsee.de*). **Private houses** (①–③) with rooms to let can be found all over town; otherwise, the main concentration of accommodation is in and around Stock. Among the **hotels** here are *Seehotel Feldhütter*, Seestr. 101 (☎0 80 51/43 21; ④–⑥), *Gasthof Drexler*, Seestr. 95 (☎0 80 51/48 02; ⑤), *Neuer*, Seestr. 104 (☎0 80 51/60 99 60, *www. neuer-am-see.de*; ⑤), *Luitpold am See*, Seestr. 110 (☎0 80 51/60 91 00; ⑥), and *Reinhart*, Seestr. 117 (☎0 80 51/69 40; ⑥). There are a few other hotels in the town centre, including *Bayerischer Hof*, Bernauer Str. 3 (☎0 80 51/60 30, *www.telehotel.de*; ⑥). Just west of Stock and north of Seestrasse, at Carl-Braun-Str. 66, is the **youth hostel** (☎0 80 51/6 87 70, fax 68 77 15; DM25/€12.50). Two of the lake's many **campsites** are at the extreme southern edge of Prien: *Hofbauer* (☎0 80 51/41 36) is off the main road out of town, while *Harras* (☎0 80 51/25 15) is by the lakeside. All the hotels listed above have **restaurants**; another good place to eat and drink is *Weissbräu-Bräustuben*, Höhenbergstr. 6.

The Chiemsee islands

Just a few minutes by boat (DM10/€5 return) from Prien is the Chiemsee's largest island, **Herreninsel**, site of King Ludwig II's final monument to glorious absolutism and isolation: **Schloss Herrenchiemsee** (guided tours daily: April–Sept 9am–6pm; Oct–March 10am–4pm; DM11/€5.50). After saving the island – previously occupied by a monastery – from deforestation, Ludwig II set about building a complete replica of Versailles. Funds ran out in 1885 with only the central section – including a faithful copy of the Hall of the Mirrors – complete. For all the money squandered, the king only ever lived there for one week. The guided tours through the state apartments are very rushed, whereas you can see the **König-Ludwig-II-Museum** (same times and ticket) at leisure. This contains a fascinating collection of Ludwig memorabilia, including portraits, photographs, his christening and coronation robes, plans for unexecuted buildings and model backdrops for Wagner's operas. Herreninsel itself is a great place for walks, and by the landing stage there's a beer garden with a good view of the lake.

The neighbouring **Fraueninsel** (DM12.50/€6.25 return from Prien, which allows the journey to be broken at Herreninsel) is a much smaller island, built up with holiday homes, restaurants, cafés and an ancient, still-functioning Benedictine nunnery – hence the name. Its **Klosterkirche** preserves its original Romanesque form save for the fancy late Gothic vault and the onion dome crowning the freestanding belfry. An even rarer survival is the Carolingian gatehouse, or **Torhalle** (late May to early Oct daily 11am–6pm; DM3/€1.50), which features an upstairs chapel with ninth-century frescoes; reproductions of the church's Romanesque ceiling paintings – now concealed above the vaulting – are also on display.

Aschau im Chiemgau

A small railway, the Chiemgaubahn, runs from Prien up towards the Chiemgau Alps. It terminates at the mountain resort of **ASCHAU**, directly below the **Kampenwand** (1669m), one of the most popular hiking areas in the whole Alpine region. From the northern end of the village, a cable car (DM16/€8 single, DM24/€12 return) ascends to the summit; otherwise, it's a walk of about three and a half hours. Just east of the cable-car station, the immense **Schloss Hohenaschau** (guided tours May–Sept Tues–Fri at 9.30am, 10.30am & 11.30am; April & Oct Thurs only, same times; DM5/€2.50) rises above a hilltop. The interior includes a fine Baroque **Schlosskapelle** and the **Preysingsaal**, an extraordinary reception room covered in white stuccowork, with gigantic statues of the local dynasty's ancestors.

Aschau's **tourist office** is in the Kurverwaltung, Kampenwandstr. 38 (Feb–April Mon–Fri 8am–noon & 1.30–5pm, Sat 9am–noon; May to mid-Oct Mon–Fri 8am–noon & 2–6pm, Sat 9am–noon, Sun 10am–noon; mid-Oct to Jan Mon–Fri 8am–noon &

1.30–5pm; ☎0 80 52/90 49 37, fax 90 49 45, *www.aschau.de*). There are plenty of **private rooms** (①–③) and **hotels**; *Alpengasthof Brucker*, Schlossbergstr. 12 (☎0 80 52/49 87; ③) is a particular bargain, and it also has a good restaurant. *Residenz Heinz Winkler*, Kirchplatz 1 (☎0 80 52/1 79 90; ⑨), a supremely elegant modern hotel within in a historic coaching inn, is one of the top gourmet addresses in the whole of Germany.

Ruhpolding

East of Aschau are several more resorts, of which the most attractive is **RUHPOLDING**, at the end of a branch rail line from the junction of Traunstein. The town's dominant monument is the **Pfarrkirche St Georg**, a typical example of Bavarian Rococo, save for the fact that one of the side altars incorporates a rare Romanesque survivor in the little polychrome wood sculpture known as the *Ruhpolding Madonna*. Following the Weisse Traun 3km upstream brings you to the **Taubensee**, a secluded lake which is the valley station of the cable car (DM17/€8.50 single, DM28/€14 return) up the **Rauschberg** (1645m). The summit commands a marvellous view over the Chiemgau Alps, south into Austria and north to the Chiemsee. Ruhpolding's **tourist office** is in the Kurverwaltung, Hauptstr. 60 (Easter–Sept Mon–Fri 8am–noon & 2–6pm, Sat 9am–noon; Oct–Easter Mon–Fri 8am–noon & 2–6pm; ☎0 86 63/8 80 60, fax 88 06 20, *www.ruhpolding.de*). The town is choc-a-bloc with **private houses** offering rooms and **guesthouses** (①–③), and there are also good **hotels**, such as *Sonnenbichl*, Brandstätter Str. 48 (☎0 88 63/12 33; ④), *Diana*, Kurhausstr. 1 (☎0 88 63/97 05; ⑤), and *Ruhpoldinger Hof*, Hauptstr. 30 (☎0 88 63/12 12; ⑥), all of which have fine **restaurants**.

Bad Reichenhall

At the Chiemgau's far eastern end, just 19km from Salzburg, the old salt-producing town of **BAD REICHENHALL** lies in a majestic mountain-framed setting in the valley of the River Saalach. Its saline springs are the most concentrated in Europe, with a salt content of 24 percent. Their curative properties led to its nineteenth-century development into one of the country's classiest spas – a status it still holds – and the town is full of grand villas from this period.

The old saltworks, the **Alte Saline** (guided tours April–Oct daily 10–11.30am & 2–4pm; Nov–March Tues & Thurs 2–4pm; DM7/€3.50), are at the southern edge of the town centre. They were established in the sixteenth century, but remodelled in the 1830s by King Ludwig I according to the mock-medieval tastes then in vogue. All the equipment – including a pair of waterwheels thirteen metres in diameter and fifteen tonnes in weight – is in good working order and can be seen in action, but production has long since moved to larger and more practical premises a few blocks away.

Just to the north the elegant Ludwigstrasse, the town's main street, is lined with exclusive shops and spa hotels. At its far end is the **Kurpark**, a carefully tended park with mountain views and the principal spa buildings, the **Kurhaus** and the **Trinkhalle**; the latter regularly hosts concerts by the forty-strong Philharmonisches Orchester, the largest spa orchestra in Germany. The focal point of the park is the huge wooden **Gradierwerk**, whose function is to ensure that the air is kept as fresh and healthy as possible. Still further north, beyond Karlspark, is the basilica of **St Zeno**, built in the early thirteenth century in the Lombard Romanesque style. Although remodelled down the centuries, it preserves some of its original features, including the peaceful cloisters and the magnificent, very Italianate coloured-marble entrance portal complete with crouching lions and a tympanum showing the Madonna and Child adored by the church's patron and St Rupert, the Irish monk who became the first bishop of Salzburg.

Walks around town

Just south of the town centre, in the district of Kirchberg on the opposite side of the Saalach, is the valley station for the cable car (DM19/€9.50 single, DM30/€15 return) to the **Predigtstuhl** (1613m). From the upper station, follow the signs to the Aussichtskanzel belvedere, which gives a fine northwards view. For more extensive panoramas of the region, take the hiking trail to the nearby summits of **Hochschlegel** (1688m), **Karkopf** (1738m) and **Dreisesselberg** (1680m); a round trip will last about three hours.

Immediately north of Bad Reichenhall is a small massif whose main peak is **Hochstaufen** (1771m). The direct way up is not for the faint-hearted, as it involves ascents by fixed ladders, but there's also a normal path which swings round towards the summit from the west. For gentler walks, take bus #2 4km west to its terminus at **Thumsee**, a pretty little lake circumnavigated by a path. It has a couple of country Gaststätten, while at the roadside immediately to the east is an even smaller and equally picturesque stretch of water, the **Seerosen-Anlage**.

Practicalities

Bad Reichenhall's **Hauptbahnhof** lies west of St Zeno on the main outer axis. A second station, **Bahnhof Kirchberg**, is at the extreme southern end of town, on the opposite side of the river from the cable car. The **tourist office** is just to the south of the Hauptbahnhof, in the Kurgastzentrum at Wittelsbacherstr. 15 (Mon–Fri 8am–5/5.30pm, Sat 9am–noon; ☎0 86 51/60 63 03, fax 60 63 11, *www.bad-reichenhall.de*).

There are plenty of rooms in **private houses** and **guesthouses**; among the cheapest, a short walk north of St Zeno, are *Haus Rachl*, Salzburger Str. 44 (☎0 86 51/36 41; ②), and *Landhaus Kirchholz*, Salzburger Str. 44c (☎0 86 51/55 82; ②). The town has **hotels** to suit all tastes: *Hofwirt*, Salzburger Str. 21 (☎0 86 51/9 83 80; ④), is a renovated sixteenth-century inn; the environmentally conscious *Hansi*, Rinckstr. 3 (☎0 86 51/9 83 10, *www.hansi.de*; ⑤), occupies a town-centre villa and has a vegetarian restaurant for guests; while *Bürgerbräu*, Waaggasse 2 (☎0 86 51/60 89, *Hotel.Buergerbraeu@t-online.de*; ⑥), is the grand Wirtshaus of the local brewery. The two leading spa hotels are *Parkhotel Luisenbad*, Ludwigstr. 33 (☎0 86 51/60 40, *www.parkhotel.de*; ⑦–⑨), and *Axelmannstein*, Salzburger Str. 2–6 (☎0 86 51/77 70, *www.steigenberger.de*; ⑨). There's a **campsite** (☎0 86 51/21 34; closed Nov–March) at the north end of town, by the Saalach. All the hotels above have excellent **restaurants**, though the top gourmet address is *Kirchberg-Schlössl*, Thumseestr. 11. Among the many fine **cafés**, pride of place goes to *Café Reber*, Ludwigstr. 10, whose home-made chocolates, sold in the adjoining shop, are among the best known in Germany.

The Berchtesgadener Land

Almost entirely surrounded by mountains, the area south of Bad Reichenhall, the **Berchtesgadener Land**, gives the impression of being a separate little country. In fact this is exactly what it used to be: for centuries it was one of the smallest states in the Holy Roman Empire, ruled by an Augustinian prior. There's a magical atmosphere here, especially in the mornings, when mists rise from the lakes and swirl around lush valleys and rocky mountainsides. Not surprisingly the area is steeped in legends, often featuring the spiky peaks of the **Watzmann** (2713m), Germany's second highest mountain. A popular one has it that they're really the family of a tyrant king who ruled so mercilessly that God punished him and his by turning them all to stone. The entire southern half of the region has been declared the **Nationalpark Berchtesgaden**, and is thus under stricter environmental protection than any other part of the Bavarian Alps.

Berchtesgaden

The town of **BERCHTESGADEN** itself is 18km from Bad Reichenhall by rail or by either of two magnificent scenic roads, both of which are served by buses. At its heart is an attractive triangular square dominated by the **Schloss** (Mon–Fri 10am–1pm & 2–5pm; DM7/€3.50), which was originally the Augustinian priory. Following the Napoleonic secularization, when Berchtesgaden was incorporated into Bavaria, the complex was transformed into a sumptuous royal residence. After World War I, the deposed King Ludwig III fled here, and it remains the property of the family. Inside you can see the art treasures collected by his son, Crown Prince Ruprecht: medieval religious woodcarvings, sixteenth- and seventeenth-century Italian furniture and a fearsome collection of weaponry. Some parts of the medieval architecture still survive, notably the Romanesque cloister with its beautiful columns, and the graceful Gothic dormitory. Alongside the Schloss is the **Stiftskirche**, another Romanesque and Gothic mix, with elaborate choir stalls inside.

In the north of town, a twenty-minute walk from the centre along the valley of the Berchtesgadener Ache, is the saltmine, the **Salzbergwerk** (guided tours: May to mid-Oct daily 9am–5pm; mid-Oct to April Mon–Sat 12.30–3.30pm; tours last 1hr 30min; DM21/€10.50), which has been the region's source of wealth since 1515. Donning the traditional protective clothing, you're taken deep into the mountain astride a wooden train. Once underground, the tour passes all the machinery and processes of saltmining in disused shafts connected by wooden chutes, which everyone descends in groups, rather like at the fairground. There follows a raft trip across an underground salt lake, a ride back up towards the surface in the miners' elevator, before a final train journey to the exit. It's all great fun, so don't be deterred by the high entrance cost and the inevitable commercial trappings of the place. Be sure to arrive early, or else be prepared to queue.

Practicalities

Berchtesgaden's **Bahnhof** and **bus station** are at the southern end of town. The regional **tourist office** for the Berchtesgadener Land is directly opposite, in the Kurdirektion at Königsseer Str. 2 (late June to mid-Oct Mon–Fri 8am–6pm, Sat 8am–5pm, Sun 9am–3pm; rest of year Mon–Fri 8am–5pm, Sat 9am–noon; ☎0 86 52/96 70, fax 96 74 00, *www.berchtesgadener-land.de*). In the same building, there's an information point on Berchtesgaden Mini Bus Tours (☎0 86 52/6 49 71), which offers a variety of English-language trips, including a detailed exploration of the nearby Nazi sites. An **information centre** on the Nationalpark Berchtesgaden is in the heart of town at Franziskanerplatz 7 (Mon–Sat 9am–5pm; ☎0 86 52/6 43 43).

There are plenty of remarkably good-value **guesthouses**. The very friendly *Haus am Hang*, Göllsteinbichl 3 (☎0 86 52/43 59; ①), has bedrooms with balconies offering grandstand views of the surrounding mountains. Other inexpensive possibilities are *Hansererhäusl*, Hansererweg 8 (☎0 86 52/25 23; ①), *Gästehaus Alpina*, Ramsauer Str. 6 (☎0 86 52/25 17; ②), and *Haus Achental*, Ramsauer Str. 4 (☎0 86 52/45 49; ②). **Hotels** include *Watzmann*, Franziskanerplatz 2 (☎0 86 52/20 55; ②), *Vier Jahreszeiten*, Maximilianstr. 20 (☎0 86 52/95 20; ⑤–⑧), and *Fischer*, Königsseer Str. 51 (☎0 86 52/95 50; ⑥–⑧). All these hotels have **restaurants**, though there are plenty of other recommendable places to eat and drink. In the centre, *Neuhaus*, Marktplatz 1, is a good traditional Gaststätte, while *Da Noi*, Kälbersteinstr. 4, is an Italian restaurant in a villa built for King Maximilian II. On the way to the Salzbergwerk, at Bräuhausstr. 13, the *Bräustübl* of the adjoining brewery, the Hofbräuhaus Berchtesgaden, serves hearty Bavarian fare.

The only official **youth hostel** is in the village of Strub, 2.5km west of Berchtesgaden on the road to Ramsau, at Gebirgsjägerstr. 52 (☎0 86 52/9 43 70, fax 94 37 37;

DM22/€11). There are several **campsites** in the region, the nearest to town being *Allweglehen* (☎0 86 52/23 96) in Untersalzberg.

The Königssee

The focal point of the Nationalpark Berchtesgaden is the **Königssee**, Germany's highest lake, which lies 5km south of town and can be reached by bus. This bends around the foot of the Watzmann, rather like a Norwegian fjord, and the surrounding rock faces rise steeply and dramatically straight from the water. The northern tip of the lake, which is outside the, is crammed with cafés, restaurants and snack bars; to escape the crowds, follow the marked path to the Malerwinkel belvedere for an overall view. For a far more extensive panorama of the lake and the surrounding peaks, take the cable car up the **Jenner** (1874m); this costs DM26/€13 single, DM34/€17 return. This summit is also a useful starting point for an extended hike in the mountains.

Ferries, run by Motorschiffahrt Königssee, Seestr. 55 (☎0 86 52/40 26), make round trips to the far end of the Königssee and back. Although likewise rather expensive at DM22.50/€11.25 return, it's money well spent; the boats have been electric-powered since 1909, so the deep green waters are refreshingly clean and healthy. The boats stop at the lakeside church of **St Bartholomä**, whose appearance is familiar from its pictures in all the tourist brochures of the region. Romanesque by origin, it was remodelled in Baroque at the end of the seventeenth century by the addition of the projecting apses and onion-domed towers. Alongside is the former **Jagdschloss** of the Bavarian kings, which was converted into a restaurant almost immediately after the fall of the monarchy. There are some wonderful mountain hikes to be made from St Bartholomä; another good starting point is Salet at the far end of the Königssee, the only other place where the boats make a scheduled stop. This lies just a few minutes' walk from another, much smaller lake, the **Obersee**.

Obersalzberg

High above Berchtesgaden to the east is the scattered village of **OBERSALZBERG**, which can be reached from the town by cable car (DM7/€3.50 single, DM11/€ 5.50 return), or by a steep winding road. Hitler rented a home here which was later enlarged into the **Berghof**, a stately retreat where he could meet foreign dignitaries. With a final dramatic sweep of steps, its setting was expressly designed to awe visitors. Here, in 1938, British Prime Minister Neville Chamberlain journeyed to dissuade Hitler from attacking Czechoslovakia, the first in a series of meetings that ended with Chamberlain returning from Munich clutching the infamous piece of paper that would ensure "peace in our time" at the expense of Czechoslovakia. "He seemed a nice old man," smirked Hitler, "so I thought I would give him my autograph." Today the remains of the Berghof are almost entirely overgrown; what was left after wartime bombing was blown up by US troops in 1952 to avoid it becoming an object of pilgrimage for future Nazi generations. The only intact part of the complex is a **hotel**, *Zum Türken*, Hintereck 2 (☎0 86 52/24 28; ⑤), which pre-dated Hitler's appropriation of the site, and was afterwards returned to its rightful owners. Underneath it is the Nazi-era **Bunker** (daily 9am–5.30pm; DM5/€2.50).

One of the very few legacies of the Third Reich still looked upon with a large amount of pride is the 6.5-kilometre-long **Kehlsteinstrasse**, which rises from Obersalzberg in a series of curves before making a bold ascent up the northwest side of the **Kehlstein** (1834m). The road – generally considered the most spectacular in the country – is impassable because of snow for most of the year and permanently closed to normal traffic, but regular local buses (DM22/€11 return) make the ascent from the Hintereck stop between early May and mid-October. From the bus terminus, there's a long tunnel through the mountain to a lift (included in the ticket price), which covers the final 124m to the summit. Here is the **Kehlsteinhaus**, nowadays a restaurant, but originally Hitler's tea house, which became known as the "Eagle's Nest". The views across the Alps are stunning, and there's an enjoyable short trail round the summit which leads to very different vantage points, one offering a close-range perspective of the mighty **Hoher Göll** (2522m) to the southeast.

Another magnificent road from Obersalzberg, again served by regular buses, though also one on which you can take your own car (DM10/€5 toll), is the 21-kilometre-long **Rossfeld-Höhen-Ringstrasse**. This circular route passes through glacier country below the Hoher Göll, climbing to a height of 1604 metres, then for a time hugs the Austrian frontier, before making a return loop to Obersalzberg through the wooded Oberau valley.

Elsewhere in the Berchtesgadener Land

Two of the finest yet least demanding walks in the region are along gorges reachable from Berchtesgaden in just a few minutes by bus. The larger and more dramatic is the **Almbachklamm** (DM4/€2 admission levied throughout most of the day) 6km to the northeast, just off the road to Marktschellenberg. At the entrance to the gorge is the **Kugelmühle**, a mill for grinding marble which has been in operation since the seventeenth century.

The **Wimbachklamm** (DM2/€1 admission), a similar distance to the southwest, has the advantage of being a jumping-off point for various longer hikes in the region. It's certainly well worth continuing as far as the refreshment hut known as the Wimbachschloss, as the path passes through a dramatic rocky valley, where the Wimbach follows an underground course. The northern end of the Wimbachklamm is the starting point for the main **trail up the Watzmann**. After three to four hours walking, there's the *Watzmannhaus* refuge (☎0 86 52/13 10) at 1930m, where you can break the journey for the night; note that the final push to the summit requires mountaineering skills and has claimed many lives.

Some 3km west of the Wimbachklamm is the small resort of **RAMSAU**, the most popular base after Berchtesgaden for exploring the region. Continuing westwards through the enchanted forest of the **Zauberwald** brings you to the **Hintersee**, a beautiful lake commanding views towards the rugged precipices of the **Reiteralpe** and the icy blue **Hochkalter** (2608m), the most northerly glacier in the Alps.

The Inn-Salzachgau

The **Inn-Salzachgau** is the name given to the triangular area north of the Alps whose western and eastern boundaries are defined respectively by the mighty River Inn and its tributary, the Salzach. Inevitably, the landscapes of this rich farming country can't compete with those further south, but it's an unspoiled area preserving several fine old towns which well merit a detour from the established tourist circuits.

Wasserburg am Inn

The region's gateway is **WASSERBURG**, dramatically set on a promontory on a loop of the River Inn, 55km east of Munich. In the fifteenth and sixteenth centuries, the town became prosperous through shipping and its position on key salt-trade routes, but it fell into decay, never to recover. Today, it's a sleepy, somewhat dowdy little place of narrow streets and crooked medieval houses whose vaguely Italianate appearance is a direct consequence of the old trading links. You'll get the best views, showing the buildings rising abruptly from the Inn, by crossing over the river and walking uphill to the Schöne Aussicht belvedere.

Heart of the town is Marienplatz, dominated by the tall step gables of the **Rathaus** (guided tours Tues–Fri 10am, 11am, 2pm, 3pm & 4pm, Sat & Sun 10am & 11am, closed Aug; DM2/€1), whose first-floor **Ratssaal** is decorated with richly carved woodwork and painted panels. The disparate assortment of houses which complete the square makes a picturesque group, with arcades and oriels prominent; they range from the old toll-house, the **Altes Mauthaus**, which is Gothic with a Renaissance facade, to the fripperies of the **Kernhaus**, a Rococo patrician mansion with a facade by Johann Baptist Zimmermann. On the nearby Kirchplatz rises the parish church of **St Jakob**, whose nave is by Hans von Burghausen, an inspired Gothic architect who left a profound mark on the eastern regions of Bavaria. The chancel and tower were added later in the fifteenth century and show a somewhat abrupt change in building materials from brick to stone. Inside, the highlight of the furnishings is the elaborate late Renaissance pulpit.

Practicalities

Wasserburg's **Bahnhof**, on the Inn valley rail line linking the junctions of Mühldorf and Rosenheim, is 5km west of the town centre, to which it's connected by a somewhat irregular bus service aimed mainly at commuters. The **tourist office** in the Rathaus (Mon–Fri 9am–12.30pm; ☎0 80 71/1 05 22, fax 1 05 21, *www.wasserburg.de*) can supply a list of **private houses** (①–②) with rooms to let.

There are three central **hotels**: *Gasthof Hubertwirt*, on the south side of the Inn at Salzburger Str. 25 (☎0 80 71/74 33; ③); *Paulaner-Stuben*, in the aforementioned Kernhaus, Marienplatz 9 (☎0 80 71/39 03; ③); and *Fletzinger*, diagonally opposite at Fletzingergasse 1 (☎0 80 71/9 08 90, *www.hotel-fletzinger.de*; ⑤). All of these have **restaurants**; other good places to eat are *Herrenhaus*, occupying a fine Gothic mansion at Herrengasse 17, and *Weisses Rössl*, Herrengasse 1, which does bargain lunches.

Cruises on the Inn (☎0 80 71/47 93) depart daily at 2.15pm in summer; there are occasional off-season sailings as well.

Altötting

At Mühldorf, the rail line splits, with one branch line continuing eastwards to **ALTÖTTING**. This small town of spires and domes is one of the most venerable in Germany, having been a favourite residence of both the Carolingian emperors and the early Bavarian dukes, but for the past five hundred years it has chiefly been famous as the site of one of the most visited **shrines** in the country.

An immaculately tended square lined by dignified buildings, **Kapellplatz** forms the centre of the town. Its outsized dimensions really come into play at the time of the big pilgrimages: the most important is to celebrate the Feast of the Assumption (Aug 15); Corpus Christi (variable date in May/June) is next in order of rank, but there are many others throughout the year.

The goal of the believers is the **Gnadenkapelle** (or **Heilige-Kapelle**) in the centre of the square, a tiny octagonal chapel which offers a tantalizing reminder of Altötting's distinguished early history as it dates back to Carolingian times and may once have served as the baptistry of the imperial palace. In 1489, a 3-year-old local child who had drowned in the Inn was cured when her grief-stricken mother placed her in front of the **wooden statue** of the *Black Madonna* at the high altar. News of the miracle quickly spread, and the chapel was immediately extended by the erection of a nave and covered walkway. The sculpture seems to have been working cures relentlessly ever since, to judge from the thousands of **ex votos** – many of them outstanding examples of folk art – which now completely cover the walls. Since the seventeenth century, it has been housed in an elaborate silver shrine and is now generally to be seen draped in gorgeous robes which stand in stark contrast to the simplicity of the original carving. Opposite the altar are appropriately shaped urns containing the hearts of many of the Bavarian dukes, who thereby commended the most precious part of themselves to the special care of the Virgin.

Across from the Gnadenkapelle is the twin-towered **Stiftskirche**, a fine late Gothic church erected in the early years of the sixteenth century in order to cater for the ever-growing influx of pilgrims. Its **Schatzkammer** (April–Oct Tues-Sun 10am–noon & 2–4pm; DM3/€1.50) contains an excellent collection of treasury items. Particularly outstanding is the **Goldenes Rössl** (Golden Steed), a masterpiece by a Parisian goldsmith of the turn of the fifteenth century, commissioned by Isobel of Bavaria as a present for her husband, King Charles VI of France. Another exceptional piece is the **Füllkreuz**, a late sixteenth-century crucifix adorned with nineteen miniatures of the Passion painted on lapis lazuli. From the church's cloisters you can descend to the **Tilly-Gruft** (May–Oct daily 8–10am & 2–4pm; free) and peer into the coffin containing the gruesome skeleton of Field Marshal Johann Tilly, the Catholic hero of the Thirty Years War.

As the Stiftskirche eventually proved insufficiently large for the number of people who flocked here, a monstrous neo-Baroque **Basilika**, capable of accommodating six thousand worshippers at a time, was erected just off the square at the beginning of the twentieth century. Also from this period is the **Panorama** (March–Oct daily 9am–5pm; Nov–Feb Sat & Sun 11am–2pm; DM4.50/€2.25), a few minutes' walk to the east at Gebhard-Fugel-Weg 10. Housed in a custom-built rotunda, this monumental circular painting was a co-operative venture between Gebhard Fugel, who painted the figurative passages, notably the main scene of the Crucifixion, and Josef Krieger, who was responsible for the lovingly detailed background depiction of Jerusalem. Nearby, at Kreszentiaheimstr. 18, is the **Mechanische Krippe** (Mechanical Crib; daily 9am–5pm; DM2), which was made in the 1920s by woodcarvers from Oberammergau.

Altötting's **Bahnhof** is just south of the centre. The **tourist office** (May–Oct Mon–Fri 8am–noon & 2–5pm, Sat 9am–noon; Nov–April Mon–Thurs 8am–noon & 2–5pm, Fri 8am–noon; ☎0 86 71/80 68, fax 8 58 58, *www.altoetting-touristinfo.de*) is in the Rathaus, Kapellplatz 2a. Here you can book to stay in one of the many **private houses** (①–③) with rooms to let. There are also plenty of **hotels** in the heart of town, most of them very good value for what they offer. They include *Weissbräustuben*, Kapuzinerstr. 3b (☎0 86 71/55 11; ③), *Altöttinger Hof*, Mühldorfer Str. 1 (☎0 86 71/54 22; ④), *Zwölf Apostel*, Bruder-Konrad-Platz 3–4 (☎0 86 71/9 69 60; ⑤), *Plankl*, Schlotthamer Str. 4 (☎0 86 71/8 51 51; ⑤), and *Scharnagl*, Neuöttinger Str. 2 (☎0 86 71/69 83; ⑤). *Zur Post*, Kapellplatz 2 (☎0 86 71/50 40; ⑥–⑧), which has wonderful bathing facilities, is the best hotel in town. These hotels all have good **restaurants**. Other places to eat and drink are the taps of the two local breweries: *Altöttinger Bräustübl* is just to the north of the centre at Herrenmühlstr. 15, while *Weisses Brauhaus* is south of the Bahnhof at Graming 79; both have beer gardens.

Burghausen

At the terminus of the branch rail line 15km southeast of Altötting lies **BURGHAUSEN**, which for centuries ranked alongside Munich, Landshut, Ingolstadt and Straubing as one of the five residential towns of the Bavarian dukes. Nowadays, it's a modest-sized border town and an affluent centre for computer-based industries.

A tightly packed Altstadt nestles along the bank of the river and most of the buildings of note are found on the elongated **Stadtplatz**. On the eastern side are the colourful former ducal administrative buildings and the Rathaus. The south side is closed by the Gothic parish church of **St Jakob**, while at the opposite end stands the

Gymnasium established by the Jesuits, now serving once more as a school. An alley leads from the middle of the east side of the square to the finest local vantage point, the bridge over the Salzach to Austria.

From here, you get a great view of the **Burg** (April–Sept Mon–Wed & Fri–Sun 9am–6pm, Thurs 9am–8pm; Oct–March daily 10am–4pm; DM5/€2.50), which stands on a ridge high above the old town and between two stretches of water, the Salzach and the Wohrsee. Measuring 1030m from end to end, it ranks as the longest castle in Europe. With no fewer than six courtyards, it has the appearance of a complete upper town, rather than simply a fortress. The oldest surviving section of the fortifications dates back to the mid-thirteenth century, but much of what can be seen today is due to the expansion carried out at the end of the fifteenth century when there was fear of a Turkish invasion. Steps lead up from Stadtplatz to the main residential part of the palace, set in the last of the courtyards, but it's more fun to circle round and go up from the Wohrsee side, entering via the massive double gateway known as the **Georgstor** facing would-be attackers. The former ducal apartments contain the **Gemäldegalerie**, a collection of German paintings and furniture contemporary with the Burg itself, while the chambers of the duchess house the local history displays of the **Historisches Stadtmuseum**. Also included in the entrance fee is admission to the observation platform, which commands a splendid view over the fortress and the town.

Practicalities

Burghausen's **Bahnhof** is situated just over 1km north of the town centre, which is reached by following Marktler Strasse straight ahead. The **tourist office** (Mon–Wed 8am–noon & 2–4pm, Thurs 8am–noon & 2–6pm, Fri 8am–noon; ☎0 86 77/24 35, fax 88 71 55, *www.burghausen.de*) is in the Rathaus at Stadtplatz 112.

There are a couple of **pensions**: *Kaffeemühle*, Mautnerstr. 270 (☎0 86 77/6 19 65; ④); and *Salzburger Hof*, In den Grüben 190 ☎0 86 77/91 10 00; ④). **Hotels** include *Post*, Stadtplatz 39 (☎0 86 77/396 50; ⑤), *Glöcklhofer*, Ludwigsberg 4 (☎0 86 77/9 61 70; ⑥), and *Bayerische Alm*, Robert-Koch-Str. 211 (☎0 86 77/98 20; ⑥). The **youth hostel** is at Kapuzinergasse 235 (☎0 86 77/41 87, fax 91 13 18; DM21/€10.50).

All three hotels mentioned above have **restaurants** with beer gardens. Hottest nightspot is the *Jazzkeller* in the Mautnerschloss on Mautnerstrasse at the southern edge of the old town, which attracts the big names for periodic **jazz festivals**.

EASTERN BAVARIA

Eastern Bavaria (Ostbayern), which incorporates **Lower Bavaria** (Niederbayern) and the **Upper Palatinate** (Oberpfalz), two of the three provinces into which the medieval duchy was divided, is the least well-known region of the whole state, among Germans as well as visitors. Nonetheless, it includes both the cities that preceded Munich as capital of Bavaria. **Regensburg**, the main seat of power in the tribal days of the Dark Ages and nowadays capital of the Upper Palatinate, survived World War II rel-atively unscathed, and stands today as the most complete and one of the most beauti-ful medieval cities in Germany. In the region's southwestern corner is the wonderfully preserved town of **Landshut**, the capital of Lower Bavaria, which rivalled Munich in wealth and status during the fifteenth and sixteenth centuries. Downstream along the Danube from Regensburg are two other enticing old towns, **Straubing** and **Passau**. Most of the southeastern part of the region is taken up by the **Bavarian Forest**, part of the largest forested area in Central Europe and one that still retains much of its primeval character, as well as an unexpectedly vibrant cultural life, especially during the summer.

Landshut

One of Germany's most visually striking towns, **LANDSHUT** is set below wooded hills on the banks of the Isar 70km northeast of Munich. The Wittelsbachs established it as their main seat at the beginning of the thirteenth century, and it consistently outshone Munich, even when the latter became capital of the separate duchy of Upper Bavaria. When the local dukes died out in 1503 and Bavaria became a united province again, it lost its status as a capital, but nonetheless flourished as the second residence. However, it went into decline as a result of the Thirty Years War, never to recover. As a result, its showpiece centre was subject to few later alterations and remains wonderfully evocative of its fifteenth- and sixteenth-century heyday. Nowadays, it is the perfect backdrop for Germany's largest costumed festival, the Landshut Wedding (*Landshuter Hochzeit*).

Arrival, information and accommodation

Landshut's **Hauptbahnhof**, a major rail junction, is 2km northwest of the centre, which can be reached by buses #1, #2, #3, #4, #6 and #8. The **tourist office** at Altstadt 315 (Mon–Fri 9am–noon & 1.30–5pm, Sat 9am–noon; ☎08 71/92 20 50, fax 8 92 75, *www.landshut.de*) is the best place for details of the Landshut Wedding, which is held every four years (see also box opposite). Annual **festivals** include the *Fischerfest* and *Altstadtfest* on consecutive weekends in July, while the *Hofmusiktage*, featuring concerts of both old and new music, takes place in late June and early July in even-numbered years. The main year-round venue for cultural events of all kinds is the Stadttheater Landshut, Landtorplatz 2–5 (☎08 71/9 22 08 33).

There's a decent choice of **hotels**, most of them good value in terms of what they offer. The **youth hostel** is just south of Burg Trausnitz at Richard-Schirrmann-Weg 6 (☎08 71/2 34 49, fax 27 49 47, *stadt.landshut.jh@landshut.org*; DM21/€10.50), while the **campsite** (☎ & fax 08 71/5 33 66; closed Oct–March) is on the banks of the Isar at Breslauer Str. 122 in the northeastern district of Mitterwöhr.

Hotels

Bayerwald, Bayerwaldstr. 43 (☎08 71/1 25 36). This Alpine-style guesthouse to the north of the Hauptbahnhof has some of the cheapest rooms in town. ②–④.

Fürstenhof, Stethaimer Str. 3 (☎08 71/9 25 50, fax 92 55 44, *www.romantikhotels.com*). Delightful hotel in a gabled Romantic-era building just north of Abtei Seligenthal. Its two restaurants, *Herzogstüberl* and *Fürstenzimmer*, are of gourmet status. ⑥.

Goldene Sonne, Neustadt 520 (☎08 71/92530, fax 9 25 33 50, *www.goldenesonne.de*). Family-run hotel and restaurant in a splendid historic building which was first documented as an inn in the mid-fifteenth century. ⑥.

Lindner Hotel Kaiserhof, Papierstr. 2 (☎08 71/68 70, fax 68 74 03, *www.lindner.de*). Luxury modern hotel with restaurant, directly overlooking the Isar at the point where it splits into two arms. ⑥–⑧.

Park-Café, Papierstr. 36 (☎08 71/6 93 39, fax 63 03 07). This hotel and café (closed Sat), midway between the Hauptbahnhof and the historic centre, offers a choice of basic and well-appointed rooms. ③–⑤.

Schloss Schönbrunn, Schönbrunn 1 (☎08 71/9 52 20, fax 9 52 22 22, *www.hotel-schoenbrunn.de*). Hotel in a Historicist castle at the northeastern edge of town, 2km from the centre. It also has a beer garden and restaurant (closed Tues). ⑥.

Weinstube Heigl, Herrngasse 385 (☎08 71/8 91 32, fax 27 31 04). Hotel and wine bar (closed Sun) on one of the alleys linking Altstadt and Neustadt. ③.

Zur Insel, Badstr. 16 (☎08 71/92 31 60, fax 9 23 16 36). A high-quality Gasthof near the top of the island formed by the two arms of the Isar, offering fine views towards Burg Trausnitz. Its moderately priced restaurant, which has a riverside terrace, specializes in fish dishes. ④–⑤.

The Town

Many of Landshut's sights are concentrated on its main street, whose magnificence is immediately suggested by its name – **Altstadt**, the term normally used for the entire central part of a German city. Starting from the south bank of the southern arm of the Isar, it ascends in the direction of **Burg Trausnitz**, the old feudal fortress dominating the town, by means of a majestically sweeping curve.

Altstadt

Of an unusual width and spaciousness, **Altstadt** is lined with a resplendent series of colourful high-gabled mansions of widely varying design. Two very different hall churches stand at either end of the street; both were designed by Hans von Burghausen, one of Europe's most brilliant late Gothic architects. Overlooking the river is the **Heiliggeistkirche** (or Spitalkirche), which uses the same architectural methods as its earlier counterpart at the opposite end, but with each detail cleverly modified: the tower, for example, stands over the transept. Now deconsecrated, the church serves as the town's main space for temporary exhibitions, and is only open in conjunction with these. The hospital buildings it once served are across the road, but these were rebuilt in the Baroque period.

About halfway down Altstadt is the **Rathaus**, an assemblage of several burghers' mansions. Under the patronage of King Ludwig II, this was given a neo-Gothic facelift, starting with a new facade. A team of Romantic artists was then asked to decorate the main reception hall, the **Prunksaal** (Mon–Fri 2–3pm; free). They painted it with colourful scenes showing the 1475 wedding between the last duke of Lower Bavaria and Princess Jadwiga of Poland. Such a stir was caused by this work that the people of Landshut decided they would re-enact the event – and have continued to do so every four years (see box below).

Across from the Rathaus is the **Stadtresidenz** (guided tours April–Sept Tues–Sun 9am–6pm; Oct–March Tues–Sun 10am–4pm; DM4/€2). The front portion, the

---

THE LANDSHUT WEDDING

The spectacular costumed festival, the **Landshut Wedding** (*Landshuter Hochzeit*) has its origins in the marriage of Georg, son of Duke Ludwig the Rich and Princess Jadwiga of Poland. It was a spectacular society affair: the Archbishop of Salzburg conducted the ceremony, while all the leading German and Polish nobles were present, including the Holy Roman Emperor Friedrich III and his son, the future Maximilian I. Afterwards, the people of Landshut celebrated for a week at the expense of the bridegroom's father, and it is recorded that 40,000 chickens, 11,500 geese, 2700 lambs, nearly 700 pigs, 400 calves and over 300 oxen were consumed.

Needless to say, there is no such munificence in the modern re-creations of the event, which, with eyes firmly on the tourist market, have been moved from the original November date to high summer and go on for four weeks. Weekends are the best times to come: each Saturday at 9pm, the gathering of the guests is re-enacted, while at 2.30pm on Sundays, the wedding procession makes its way through the streets of the town, with a medieval-style tournament following at 4.30pm. Some two thousand participants are involved, each decked out in authentic reproductions of the costumes of the period. In addition to various impromptu events, there are also concerts of fifteenth-century music in the Stadtresidenz and Burg Trausnitz, while entertainments are held in the Rathaus; the latter are repeated on the evenings of Wednesday, Thursday and Friday.

Held every four years, the next **performances** will occur from June 30 to July 22, 2001. Tickets for the tournament and indoor events, and grandstand seats for the procession are available in advance from Landshut's tourist office

Deutscher Bau, was begun in 1536 as a relatively modest Renaissance palace for Ludwig X. However, later the same year the duke travelled to Italy, where he saw Giulio Romano's recently completed Palazzo Tè in Mantua, and was so impressed by this Mannerist masterpiece that he immediately decided to commission something similar for himself. The following year, a team of craftsmen who had worked on the Mantuan palace came to Landshut to construct the triple-winged **Italienischer Bau**, which was built onto the Deutscher Bau, with its own showpiece facade on Ländgasse to the rear and a magnificent arcaded inner courtyard which immediately evokes a sunny Mediterranean atmosphere. Of the showpiece apartments on the first floor, the most imposing is the **Italienischer Saal**, with its carved medallions of the Labours of Hercules and ceiling frescoes by the Salzburg artist Hans Bocksberger depicting the great personalities of the ancient world. Also of special note is the **Sternenzimmer**, whose remarkable coffered vault is covered with painted symbols of the planets and stars. Another chamber is devoted to the gods and goddesses of classical mythology, while Apollo, Venus and Diana each have a room in their honour.

Dominating Altstadt from the far end is Landshut's proudest adornment, the church of **St Martin**. In design alone, its **tower** (guided tours May–Nov first Sun in month at 11.15am; DM2/€1) is extraordinarily ingenious, beginning as a square shape, then narrowing and changing into an octagon. With a height of 131m, it's also the tallest brick structure in the world. The walls of the main body of the church are pierced by five portals richly decorated with terracotta sculptures, while on the south side is a memorial tablet to the architect Hans von Burghausen. The vertiginous **interior**, with slender pillars sweeping up to the lofty network vault, is hardly less impressive than the tower, the spareness of effect enhanced by the relative lack of furnishings. Nonetheless there are some notable works, such as the stone high altar and pulpit, Michel Erhart's impassioned triumphal cross and the elaborate choir stalls. Finest of all is the larger-than-life polychrome wood *Madonna and Child* in the south aisle, carved around 1520 by the local sculptor Hans Leinberger.

The rest of the lower town

A block to the south of Altstadt is **Neustadt**, which follows a roughly parallel course and offers even more dramatic views towards Burg Trausnitz. It also preserves a picturesque array of houses, many of which were rebuilt in the Baroque epoch. Closing the southern end of the street is the **Jesuitenkirche**, a towerless early seventeenth-century church by the Augsburg architect Johannes Holl. Its barrel-vaulted interior was decorated in the middle of the same century, and is one of the earliest examples of the highly distinctive south German Baroque style, featuring lavish stuccowork and an extravagant high altar showing Christ appearing to St Ignatius Loyola.

Regierungsplatz, which lies just east of the central part of Neustadt, is dominated by the former **Dominikanerkloster**, which was founded in the late thirteenth century. Its Gothic church of **St Blasius** was completely transformed in Rococo style by Johann Baptist Zimmermann, who was responsible for both the stuccowork and the illusionistic ceiling frescoes; subsequently, it was given a Neoclassical facade. Following the secularization of 1802, the conventual buildings became the seat of the University of Bavaria on its move from Ingolstadt, but this function ended in 1826, when the institution was transferred to Munich. Thirteen years later, the premises found another lease of life as the headquarters of the government of Lower Bavaria, a role retained to this day.

A huge, still-inhabited convent of Cistercian nuns, **Abtei Seligenthal**, lies ten minutes' walk north of the city centre, across both arms of the Isar. Founded a few decades before the Dominikanerkloster, it was likewise almost totally remodelled in the Rococo era, and the **Abteikirche** contains bravura frescoes and stucco by J.B. Zimmermann, including a depiction of the Coronation of the Virgin on the dome.

Burg Trausnitz

The most direct way of approaching **Burg Trausnitz** (guided tours April–Sept Mon–Wed & Fri–Sun 9am–6pm, Thurs 9am–8pm; Oct–March daily 10am–4pm; DM5/€2.50) is via the stone stairway from Alte Bergstrasse, which runs southeastwards from Dreifaltigkeitsplatz at the end of Altstadt. A more gentle ascent can be made via the expansive **Hofgarten**, which dates back to the mid-fifteenth century and is thus one of Bavaria's oldest landscaped gardens. The fortress itself was begun in the early thirteenth century, and much of the original castle – including the **Torbau** (entrance gateway), the keep, or **Wittelsbacher Turm**, and the **Palas** – still survives. In the fifteenth century, the defences were greatly strengthened, notably by the construction of a curtain wall with towers. The following century work began on converting the castle into a Renaissance palace; this came to a halt when Ludwig X decided to concentrate resources on the Stadtresidenz, but was revived again a generation later, reaching a climax with the construction of a new extension, the **Italienische Anbau**, and the remodelling of the inner courtyard into a graceful two-storey loggia.

Among the highlights of the tour of the interior is the late Romanesque **Burgkapelle St Georg**, which is visited first at ground level, then later from the Renaissance ducal oratory directly below the vault. The chapel's original polychromed decoration, which has no counterpart in Germany, survives almost intact: its main components are a stucco frieze on the balcony showing Christ and the Apostles, and a monumental Crucifixion group of carved oak suspended directly above. Among the later furnishings are three fifteenth-century winged altars. Another survivor from the original castle is the early Gothic **Alte Dürnitz**, a low hall reminiscent of monastic refectories of the period. From the first phase of Renaissance building comes the **Söller**, or balcony, which commands a marvellous panoramic view over Landshut's red-tiled roofs and church steeples, with St Martin prominent in the foreground. Sadly, many of the Mannerist interiors were stripped of their decoration by a fire in 1961, but a tantalizing reminder of what they must have looked like is provided by the **Narrentreppe** (Buffoons' Staircase), which is decorated with vivacious portrayals of characters from the *commedia dell'arte*.

Eating and drinking

Although most of the best restaurants are in the hotels (see p.134), there are several other eateries well worth seeking out.

Bernlochner, Ländtorplatz 2–5. Classy, fairly pricey theatre restaurant, which presents itself as a modern version of the traditional German tavern.

Burgschenke, Burg Trausnitz. The fifteenth-century cellars of the castle's Fürstenbau have been converted into a visitors' café-restaurant. Closed Nov–March.

Kochwirt, Altstadt 388. Occupying a splendid gabled house, this is the main tap of the Wittmann brewery, which makes a variety of light, dark and wheat beers. It also serves good-value meals.

Martinsklause, Kirchgasse 229. Situated to the rear of St Martin, this Gaststätte with beer garden owes allegiance to the Landshuter Brauhaus, which has a similar product range to its rival.

Residenzcafé, Altstadt 79. Traditional café in the Stadtresidenz.

Stegfellner, Altstadt 71. This wonderful delicatessen has a self-service snack counter in the shop itself, and a cosy daytime restaurant upstairs which serves high-quality meals, including moderately priced set lunches. Closed Sun.

Regensburg (Ratisbon)

"Regensburg surpasses every German city with its outstanding and vast buildings" drooled Emperor Maximilian I in 1517. The centre of **REGENSBURG** – nowadays a prosperous centre for hi-tech industries – has changed remarkably little since then, and gives a unique insight into the size and feel of a prosperous community of the Middle Ages. Founded as the military camp Castra Regina by the Romans, the city remained of importance during the Frankish period and was capital of the earliest Bavarian duchy. Most of the surviving architecture originates from the glory days between the thirteenth and sixteenth centuries, when it was a Free Imperial City, rich from trade with Europe, the Balkans and the Orient. Although other cities may have individual set-pieces which are more spectacular, none can match the satisfyingly integrated nature of the Regensburg townscape. When this is added to the stunning location on the banks of the Danube, and to the ample provision of Gaststätten and beer gardens – the favoured haunts of the large student population – there can be no doubt that it's a place well worth a visit of several days.

Arrival, information and accommodation

Regensburg's **Hauptbahnhof** is at the southern end of the city; follow Maximilianstrasse straight ahead to reach the centre. The **tourist office** (Mon–Fri 8.30am–6pm, Sat 9am–4pm, Sun 9.30am–2.30/4pm; ☎09 41/5 07 44 10, fax 5 07 44 19, *www.regensburg.de*) is in the Altes Rathaus, Rathausplatz 3. Mitfahrzentrale is at Prüfeninger Str. 13 (☎09 41/1 94 40).

There are plenty of good choices for **accommodation**, including several atmospheric places on islands in the Danube, though most of the top hotels are in the Altstadt. The **youth hostel** is about five minutes' walk from the heart of town at Wöhrdstr. 60 (☎09 41/5 74 02, fax 54 2 11; DM28/€14) on the island of Unterer Wöhrd, while the **campsite**, *Azur-Camping*, is about twenty minutes' walk from the centre, pleasantly situated next to the river at Weinweg 40 (☎09 41/27 00 25, fax 29 94 32).

Hotels

Altstadthotel Arch, Am Haidplatz 4 (☎09 41/5 86 60, fax 5 86 61 68, *www.regensburg-ringhotels.de*). One of Regensburg's very best hotels, occupying an eighteenth-century mansion. ⑥.

Am Peterstor, Fröhliche-Türken-Str. 12 (☎09 41/5 45 45, fax 5 45 42). By dispensing with extras and cutting services to a bare minimum, this hotel is able to offer modern, well-appointed bedrooms at minimal cost, though there's only a small discount for single occupancy. Optional breakfasts are served at the adjoining Italian restaurant, *L'Astice*, which also offers inexpensive set lunches and dinners. ②, ③ with breakfast.

Bischofshof, Krautermarkt 3 (☎09 41/5 84 60, fax 5 84 61 46, *www.hotel-bischofshof.de*). A grand hotel with tastefully furnished rooms in the former episcopal palace right beside the Dom. It has a fine restaurant and shady garden serving the diverse products of the brewery of the same name, which include five different wheat beers. ⑦.

Kaiserhof, Kramgasse 10-12 (☎09 41/58 53 50, fax 5 85 35 95, *www.Kaiserhof.germany.ms*). This hotel in a Gothic mansion has an ideal location, with its front rooms directly facing the Dom's facade. Breakfast is served to the accompaniment of classical music in the fourteenth-century house chapel. ⑤–⑦.

Münchner Hof, Tändlergasse 9 (☎09 41/5 84 40, fax 56 17 09, *www.muenchner-hof.de*). Comfortable mid-range family-owned hotel with restaurant in the pedestrianized heart of the Altstadt. ⑥.

Parkhotel Maximilian, Maximilianstr. 28 (☎09 41/5 68 50, fax 5 29 42, *www.maximilian-hotel.de*). This long-established luxury hotel occupies palatial neo-Rococo premises just north of the Hauptbahnhof. It also has a café plus a well-regarded Italian restaurant, *Locanda Botticelli* (closed Sun). ⑧.

Prösslbräu, Dominikanerinnenstr. 2, Adlersberg (☎0 94 04/18 22 or 8 08 36, fax 0 94 04/52 33). Occupying a former convent in the northwestern outskirts and reached by bus #12, this is the epitome of a country Gasthof. As well as inexpensive rooms, it has a restaurant (closed Mon) with a large shady beer garden serving the products of the small adjoining brewery (light and dark beers plus a powerful *Doppelbock*) and good, sensibly priced food. ③.

Schildbräu, Stadtamhof 24 (☎09 41/8 57 24). A real old-fashioned Gasthof in the village-like setting of the main street of one of the Danube islands. Its restaurant serves inexpensive local fare. ④.

Sorat Insel-Hotel, Müllerstr. 7 (☎09 41/8 10 40, fax 8 10 44 44, *www.sorat-hotels.com*). This new designer hotel, spanning an arm of the Danube and incorporating a former handicrafts factory, is now the most prestigious and expensive in the city. It also has a top-class restaurant, *Brandner*. ⑧.

Spitalgarten, St-Katharinen-Platz 1 (☎09 41/8 47 74, fax 8 90 31 68, *www.spitalgarten.de*). The cheapest rooms in Regensburg are at the Gasthof of the little Spital brewery (a *Helles* specialist), which is located right alongside. Its capacious beer garden, which commands a view across the Danube, is a great local favourite. ③.

Wiendl, Universitätsstr. 9 (☎09 41/92 02 70, fax 9 20 27 28, *www.hotelwiendl.de*). Pleasant and friendly middle-range hotel, sited immediately to the rear of the Hauptbahnhof, though it's a circuitous walk or drive to get there. It serves good buffet breakfasts, while the restaurant (closed all day Sat & Sun evening) has a strong line in fish dishes. ④–⑥.

Zum Fröhlichen Türken, Fröhliche-Türken-Str. 11 (☎09 41/5 36 51, fax 56 22 56). This reasonably priced hotel at the southern end of the Altstadt has bedrooms with and without private facilities. ③–⑤.

The City

Regensburg's medieval heart is quite extensive, even although it is only about twice the size of the original Roman fort. Some parts are pedestrianized, while others are only open to public transport, with the result that it's ideal for exploration on foot. With no fewer than 1300 buildings listed as being of historical interest, there are treasures at every turn.

Around the waterfront

One of the best views of Regensburg's medieval skyline is from the twelfth-century **Steinerne Brücke** (Stone Bridge), which spans the Danube by means of fifteen (originally sixteen) arches. At the time it was built, it was the only safe and fortified crossing along the entire length of the Danube, and thus had tremendous value for the city as a major international trading centre. It's a remarkable piece of engineering for its date, and its stability (it bore the full brunt of motorized traffic until 1997, and is still used by buses) is in large part attributable to its massive pier supports. These have protected it down the centuries from damage by water and ice, albeit at the cost of creating a very fast current, as the space the river is left to pass through is a third of its natural width. Legend has it that the bridge builder and the Dom's master mason laid a bet as to which of them would finish his project first. To ensure success, the former made a pact with the Devil to give him the first three souls who crossed the finished bridge. He duly completed his project in just eleven years and so won the wager. When the duke, the bishop and the leading local merchant came to lead the inspection of the newly finished bridge, the Devil turned up in the expectation of claiming them for himself, only to be foiled by the crafty builder, who shooed a dog, a cock and a hen across the bridge. Whereupon the Devil vainly tried to uproot the central arch, leaving it with a permanent hump.

The Steinerne Brücke crosses over an island in the Danube, **Oberer Wöhrd**. Together with the other island to the east, Unterer Wöhrd, which stretches to the confluence with the Regen, this traditionally belonged to Regensburg, the only municipality within the original Bavarian duchy which managed to establish independence from aristocratic or episcopal control. However, the next island to the north, **Stadtamhof**, always remained under the rule of the dukes, with the exception of the **St-Katharinen-Spital** at its southern end. The village which grew up beyond did not become part of Regensburg until 1924 and even now retains a distinctive character and atmosphere of its own. It has a broad main street lined with tall nineteenth-century houses, to the east of which is the elaborate Rococo church of **St Mang**, originally part of an Augustinian collegiate foundation.

Of the Steinerne Brücke's three original watchtowers, only the **Brückenturm** (daily 10am–5pm; DM3/€1.50), which guards the entrance to Regensburg's Altstadt, still survives. It has recently been made accessible to the public, though the views it offers are fairly restricted ones. The seven-storey building with the steeply pitched roof which adjoins it to the east is the seventeenth-century salt depot, the **Salzstadel**. A little further along the waterfront is the **Historische Wurstküche**, which is known to be at least five hundred years old and has been run by the same family for generations. Its menu is abbreviated, essentially consisting of potato soup and Regensburger sausages. The latter, which are traditionally served with sweet mustard and sauerkraut, are regarded by many aficionados as the ultimate German Wurst – though this is not an opinion shared by the rival sausage metropolis of Nürnberg. As the watermark on the outside wall shows, the building was almost washed away in 1988.

The Dom

The Altstadt's skyline is dominated by the **Dom**, Bavaria's most magnificent Gothic building. It replaced an earlier Romanesque cathedral, of which the **Eselsturm** (Donkey Tower) on the north side is the only remaining part above ground; this takes its name from the fact that donkeys were used to carry building materials up the ramp inside. Although begun around 1250, the Dom was still incomplete in 1525, when work was suspended as a result of the Reformation, with the city council eventually going over to the Lutheran side, while the bishopric remained Catholic. The upper parts of the twin towers, with their distinctively Germanic openwork spires, were belatedly erected in the mid-nineteenth century. An ambitious cleaning project, now nearing completion, has rid the exterior of its thick coat of grime, making it easy to distinguish the white limestone used by the medieval builders from the pale green sandstone of the neo-Gothic additions. The restoration has also had a revelatory effect on the small-scale **exterior sculptures**, which are iconographically highly unusual. Those on the facade include a depiction of St Peter, the Dom's patron, in his fishing boat, and representations of four of the great heathen rulers of the ancient world riding on wild beasts. Much controversy still surrounds a relief on one of the pillars on the Dom's south side, which, in a piece of calculated anti-Semitism, shows Jews suckling on a large sow.

More fine sculptures can be seen inside the Dom, the most outstanding being the expressive late thirteenth-century **Annunciation group** in the transept. Also of special note are the equestrian statues of St Martin and St George on the inner wall of the facade, and the quirky figures known as the **Devil** and the **Devil's grandmother** on either side of the main portal. The exact significance of the latter pair is disputed; they may have been placed in this position to remind the congregation that as soon as they left the safety of the church evil and temptation awaited. Other features from the medieval period are the **stained-glass windows** in the chancel, the five fifteenth-century **canopied altars** and the sixteenth-century crucifix on the south transept wall which, according to local legend, will herald Judgement Day when its real human hair grows to knee-length. Among the few later furnishings remaining in the Dom are the **tomb** of Cardinal Philipp Wilhelm by the Munich Mannerist sculptor Hans Krumper at the western end of the nave, and the **high altar**, an elaborate Baroque creation by Augsburg silversmiths. It's well worth trying to hear a concert or sung service (generally at 9am on Sunday) featuring the **Domspatzen** (Cathedral Sparrows), the most famous Catholic choir in Germany.

The **cloisters**, which are only accessible during guided tours (May–Oct Mon–Sat 10am, 11am & 2pm, Sun noon & 2pm; Nov–April Mon–Sat 11am, Sun noon; DM4/€2), have two interesting chapels, of which the **Allerheiligenkapelle** is a Romanesque gem, with many of the original twelfth-century frescoes surviving. Nearby, the eleventh-century **Stephanskapelle** was the bishop's private chapel, and though the frescoes have been lost, the altar is from the original building period.

The Domstadt

The dense complex of ecclesiastical buildings around the Dom is collectively known as the **Domstadt**. Much of the **Bischofshof**, the former episcopal palace, is now a hotel and restaurant (see p.139), but one of its wings, entered from the Dom's northern transept, contains the **Domschatzmuseum** (April–Oct Tues–Sat 10am–5pm, Sun noon–5pm; Dec–March Fri & Sat 10am–4pm, Sun noon–4pm; DM3/€1.50, DM5/€2.50 for joint ticket with Diözesanmuseum St Ulrich). This incorporates another chapel, the **Zwölfbotenkapelle**, which has fallen heir to a beautiful Renaissance retable made for the Obermünster, a convent church in the south of the Altstadt which was Regensburg's most serious loss to wartime bombs. Set in a red and white marble frame, its limestone reliefs were carved from designs by **Albrecht Altdorfer**, the city's greatest-ever artist. Among the highlights of the Dom's treasury displayed in the rooms alongside and upstairs are two thirteenth-century crosses, one containing a reliquary of St Andrew, the other a gift to the Dom from King Ottokar II of Bohemia; the so-called chalice of St Wolfgang, from the same century; and a fourteenth-century reliquary chest adorned with gilded miniatures. There are also several precious textiles, notably an eleventh-century chasuble traditionally but erroneously associated with St Wolfgang, and the thirteenth-century antependium of Bishop Heinrich von Rotteneck.

Treasures from elsewhere in the diocese are housed in the **Diözesanmuseum St Ulrich** (April–Oct Tues–Sun 10am–5pm; DM3/€1.50, DM5/€2.50 for joint ticket with Domschatzmuseum) immediately to the rear of the Dom. Constructed in the Transitional style between Romanesque and Gothic, the church itself is one of the most remarkable buildings in the city, featuring an unusual interior arrangement, with galleries on all four sides. This suggests that it was originally built as a court chapel, but when Regensburg gained the status of Free Imperial City in 1245 it became the Dom's parish church and served as such for nearly six centuries. Nowadays, it is the chapel of the Dom's chapter, notwithstanding the fact that it is fitted out as a museum. The displays begin with a number of Romanesque items, including a lion's head door knocker and a polychrome *Crucified Christ*, both from the Obermünster, and bishops' staffs which supposedly belonged to St Wolfgang and St Emmeram. In the Gothic section are a number of retables and the *Minnekästchen*, a beautiful painted casket used for storing documents or jewellery. Most of the gallery space is taken up by Baroque and Rococo artefacts, but pride of price is given to Altdorfer's *The Fair Virgin* altar.

A copy of the last-named can be seen in its original location, the former baptistery of **St Johannes**, at the western edge of the Domstadt. At the opposite end of the ecclesiastical complex is the **Niedermünster**, which has taken over St Ulrich's function as the Dom's parish church. Built as a collegiate foundation for noblewomen, it still preserves its Romanesque outline, including its austere twin towers, though it was remodelled internally in Baroque style.

The eastern Altstadt

On Pfauengasse, an alley leading south from Domplatz, is the tiny chapel popularly known as **Mariae-Laeng-Kapelle** after the seventeenth-century belief that the best way to get one's prayers heard was to write out prayer notes the same length (*laeng*) as the statue of Mary herself. The Church never accepted this idea, but people have come here ever since to pray to the Virgin and leave notes and gifts, examples of which can be seen at the back of the chapel.

A little further east is a large square, Alter Kornmarkt, at the northwestern end of which stands the much-altered Romanesque ducal palace, the **Herzogshof**, which is nowadays a cultural centre. It is linked by a covered passageway to the so-called **Römerturm** on the other side of the road. The latter was probably a treasury tower and, despite its name, its earliest masonry is Carolingian rather than Roman. On the south side of Alter Kornmarkt stands the **Alte Kapelle**, whose sober medieval exterior hardly prepares you for the riotous fricassee of Rococo decoration inside.

Just to the southwest, on Dachauplatz, the **Historisches Museum** (Tues–Sun 10am–4pm; DM4/€2) encompasses over one hundred rooms spread out on four floors of the former Minorite friary, one of several well-preserved monastic complexes in the city, and charts local cultural and artistic history from the Stone Age to the present day. The medieval department features the **tapestries** which formerly adorned the Altes Rathaus, and a fine collection of Gothic retables which includes a *Passion Altar* from St Ulrich, one of the few surviving works by **Rueland Frueauf the Elder**, the founding father of the Danube School. In the Renaissance section, the main focus is on **Albrecht Altdorfer**, who, apart from being one of Germany's greatest artists, was also a leading local politician, being involved in the decisions which saw the expulsion of the Jews and the introduction of the Reformation. The remains of the frescoes he painted for the bath house of the Bischofshof are on view, along with a panel showing *The Two St Johns*, which is set in a typically luxuriant Danube landscape. Among his etchings are two of the beautiful Romanesque–Gothic synagogue he helped destroy, which make a fascinating documentary record; these are displayed near the original wooden model (not by Altdorfer) of the huge pilgrimage church which was intended to replace it.

On the other side of the Domstadt, on the road known as Unter den Schibbögen, remains of the Roman fort are still visible at the corner of one of the houses. The **Porta Praetoria**, once the northern watchtower, was discovered during restoration work in 1887. From the end of the street, Ostengasse leads to the **Ostentor**, the only surviving gateway from the city's medieval defensive system. Overlooking the Danube in the little park to the north is the neo-Gothic **Königliche Villa**, which was built so that King Maximilian of Bavaria could have an appropriate place to stay and entertain guests on his rare visits to the city.

The merchant quarter

The streets west of the Dom were where the merchants who made Regensburg so prosperous in the Middle Ages had their homes. Unique for a German medieval town are the many **towers** built in the style of Italian fortified palaces; about twenty of these survive. Unlike their southern counterparts, however, they had no real defensive function; instead they were a statement of the competitive ethos that ruled their owners' lives: the higher the tower, the richer and more prestigious the occupier.

Directly facing the Dom is the **Haus Heuport**, a splendid patrician mansion in Venetian Gothic style, which boasts another of the city's jokey sculptures – a stone relief at the left-hand corner of the courtyard staircase representing the seduction of a careless virgin. One of the most beautiful of the fortified towers with high balconies is the **Baumburgerturm** in Watmarkt, just west of here. A block further north, on Goliathstrasse, is another notable example, the **Goliathhaus**, which takes its name from the huge re-touched sixteenth-century mural of an appropriately gargantuan Goliath about to face David in combat. On Wahlenstrasse to the southwest is the **Goldener Turm**, the town's highest remaining tower.

A handsome Gothic clock tower is the dominant external feature of the **Altes Rathaus** on Kohlenmarkt. Between 1663 and 1806 it served as the home of the so-called Perpetual Imperial Diet, Germany's first permanent parliament, and in honour of this role much of the interior is now designated the **Reichstagsmuseum** (guided tours in English May–Sept Mon–Sat at 3.15pm; guided tours in German year round Mon–Sat 9.30am–noon & 2–4pm, Sun 10am–noon; DM5/€2.50). Notable rooms include the **Kurfürstliches Nebenzimmer** (Electors' Antechamber), with its Renaissance panelling and fittings, and the **Blauer Saal** (Blue Hall), which has a glittering star-studded ceiling. Largest and most significant of all is the **Beratungszimmer der Reichsstände**, which was built as the municipal ballroom, but was later the setting for the full sessions of the Diet. The seating order was strictly defined by status: the emperor was enthroned on a dais with four steps; the Electors were placed on either side of him, two steps above the floor; the other princes sat on the benches along the walls one step lower, while the representatives of the Free Imperial Cities had to sit at the back and at floor level. Also included on the tour are the basement dungeons, which contain some gruesome instruments of torture.

Because the Altes Rathaus was allocated to the Diet, a new home was required for the municipal administration, and as a result a large Baroque building, the **Neues Rathaus**, was built on its eastern side. At the back of the Altes Rathaus is a tiny alleyway known as Roter Herzfleck (Red Heart Patch). It takes its name from the large Italianate mansion of **Zum Roten Herz**, which was formerly a Gasthaus, and reputedly once a brothel as well.

To the west lies the triangular-shaped Haidplatz. On its northern side is the **Thon-Dittmer-Palais**, whose arcaded courtyard is nowadays a regular summertime venue for plays and concerts. A little further along is the **Haus zum Goldenen Kreuz**, the town's main hotel between the sixteenth and nineteenth centuries and the site of its biggest scandal – the illicit meetings during the 1546 Diet of Emperor Charles V and a local girl named Barbara Blomberg. In the grand tradition of royal illegitimates, their son, John of Austria, became a great naval commander, winning the Battle of Lepanto against the Turks, and died governor of the Netherlands in 1578.

To the north, at Keplerstr. 5, the **Kepler-Gedächtnishaus** (April–Oct Tues–Sat 10am–noon & 2–4pm, Sun 10am–noon & 2–4pm; rest of year closed Sun afternoon; DM4/€2) occupies the merchant residence where the great astronomer Johannes Kepler, compiler of the *Rudolphine Tables* and author of *The Mystery of the Universe*, died in 1630, during a visit to the Diet. Although forced to waste his talents dabbling in astrology in order to earn his keep from the superstitious monarchs of the day, Kepler achieved ground-breaking advances in the study of both astronomy (proving the elliptical path of planetary movements) and optics (being the first to understand how the eye works). Among the exhibits are early editions of his publications, plus globes and other scientific instruments from his time, including a stone table with a perpetual calendar. The building itself is also of note as a prosperous mercantile home preserving many of its original fittings.

The southern Altstadt
In the southern part of the Altstadt are four notable churches, each markedly different in style. Oldest is the Romanesque **St Jakob** just off Bismarckplatz; this was first settled by Irish Benedictines, but is still generally known as the Schottenkirche in honour of the Scottish community which lived there from the sixteenth century until its dissolution in 1862, and which was subsequently re-established at Fort Augustus on Loch Ness. The magnificent **north portal**, which has suffered badly from pollution and was recently placed under a protective glass pavilion, features a mixture of pagan and Christian images and delicate decorative patterns. Just inside the doorway is an amusing sculpture of a monk named Rydan, who is depicted in a recumbent position with the key and the bar by which he secured the doorway every night. Other notable Romanesque carvings are the capitals of the pillars and the monumental triumphal cross above the beam at the entrance to the choir.

On Beraiterweg to the east stands the **Dominikanerkloster** (guided tours Easter–Oct Sat & Sun at 11am; DM5/€2.50), one of the earliest Gothic buildings in Germany. In the later stages of its construction period, its prior was St Albertus Magnus, who ranks among the most highly regarded scholars of medieval Europe, a man of unusually broad sympathies steeped in the works of his Jewish and Arab contemporaries. The priory church of **St Blasius** is a masterly example of the plain and pure architecture favoured by the mendicant orders: the facade portal with its statue of the patron is the sole exterior adornment. There are some notable Gothic furnishings inside, including murals, choir stalls, epitaphs and tombstones, though these are overshadowed by the majestic severity of the interior space. The guided tour also takes in the cloisters and the Albertuskapelle, which was partially remodelled in neo-Gothic style.

A few paces to the northeast, at the junction of Am Ölberg and Gesandtenstrasse, is the **Dreieinigkeitskirche** (Easter–Oct 10am–6pm, Sun 11am–6pm; DM3/€1.50), a typical example of Lutheran Baroque, the only decorative note in the galleried interior being the intricate star-shaped vault. The admission ticket gives access to the treasury in the west gallery, the secluded cemetery on the north side, with its row of elaborate tombstones, and to the tower, which commands what is by far the best aerial view of Regensburg generally accessible to the public.

Further east, in the centre of the recently pedestrianized Neupfarrplatz, is the **Neupfarrkirche**. This occupies the site of the old synagogue, and was intended to be a vast pilgrimage church dedicated to the Virgin as thanksgiving for deliverance from the Jewish "peril". However, the city council's cynical attempts to foster the bogus cult met with such apathy that the project was hastily dropped. When the council decided to adopt the Reformation a few years later, the church was completed in a much reduced form to serve as the city's Protestant flagship. Notwithstanding its unfortunate history, it's a dapper little building, with an unusual hexagonal nave.

The Abtei St Emmeram and Schloss Thurn und Taxis

A Benedictine foundation from around 700, the vast complex of the **Abtei St Emmeram**, named in honour of a martyred Regensburg bishop, lies south of the original city walls. For more than six centuries it was a quasi-independent state, subject only to the Holy Roman Emperor, and not to the local bishop or the authorities of the Free Imperial City. Following the Napoleonic secularization, the main church was transferred to parish use, while the monastic buildings were eventually donated to the Thurn und Taxis family (see box below) as partial compensation for the loss of their longstanding imperial postal monopoly. This dual arrangement has survived to the present day.

From Emmeramsplatz, which is lined by the Neoclassical headquarters of the government of the Upper Palatinate, a mid-thirteenth-century gateway leads into a little garden, where the detached **belfry**, a Renaissance building with a distinctively Italianate appearance, can be seen to the left. Ahead is a large sunken vestibule, whose eastern doorway gives access to the church of **St Rupert**, which served the local parish prior to secularization.

The former **Abteikirche St Emmeram** is entered from the same vestibule via a portal adorned with outstanding Romanesque sculptures of Christ, St Emmeram and St Dionysius. Inside, the original architecture of the main body of the church is smothered by the exuberant decorative scheme created by the Asam brothers, which includes two huge **ceiling frescoes**, one illustrating St Emmeram's martyrdom, the other the glorification of St Benedict. A **pantheon** of monuments to leading figures in

---

THE THURN UND TAXIS DYNASTY

Despite well-publicized financial problems in recent years, the **Thurn und Taxis** family may well still be the richest in Germany – as it undoubtedly was in the lifetime of Prince Johannes, who died in 1990, leaving his wife Gloria, 34 years his junior, as trustee of the fortune of their then 7-year-old son and heir. Originally known as Daxis and based in the Dolomite region between Austria and northern Italy, the dynasty came to prominence in the sixteenth century by developing a European-wide postal system, holding a monopoly within the Holy Roman Empire for some 250 years. In the process, they were raised to princely status, with a suitably grand palace in Frankfurt (a casualty of a World War II air raid) as their main seat. In 1748, Prince Alexander Ferdinand was appointed as Principal Commissioner (the personal representative of the Holy Roman Emperor) to the Perpetual Imperial Diet. This title became a hereditary possession, though the family was forbidden from acquiring property in the Free Imperial City of Regensburg, and was forced to live, admittedly in considerable style, in rented accommodation. However, after the Diet ratified Napoleon's dissolution of the Holy Roman Empire, including the secularization of the monasteries and an end to the independence of nearly all the city-states, the family seized the opportunity to acquire a new home and economic base to compensate for the loss of the postal monopoly, which came to an end with the empire itself. In time, they established ownership of nearly a fifth of Regensburg – a real irony, given the city's long independence from any kind of aristocratic control – as well as extensive tracts of land in the Bavarian Forest. The most visible sign of their varied business interests is the eponymous brewery, the largest one in Bavaria still in private hands.

early Bavarian history can be found at the eastern end of the two aisles: most notable are the grief-stricken Gothic tombstone to the executed Queen Hemma and its idealized counterpart to the legendary Blessed Aurelia. The church has several **crypts**, the oldest of which dates back to the eighth century, though the only one normally accessible to the public is that below the west choir; it bears a dedication to St Wolfgang, and preserves its original Romanesque form.

Following their acquisition of the monastic buildings, the Thurn and Taxis family (see box on p.145) set about converting them into the most modern residence of the day, with hot and cold running water, flushing toilets, central heating and, most luxurious of all, electricity. The resultant **Schloss Thurn und Taxis** (guided tours April–Oct Mon–Fri at 11am, 2pm, 3pm & 4pm, Sat & Sun at 10am, 11am, 2pm, 3pm & 4pm; Nov–March Sat & Sun at 10am, 11am, 2pm & 3pm; DM12/€6) is claimed as the largest aristocratic palace in Europe, surpassing all the Continent's royal residences in sheer scale. Most of it is kept firmly private, but the tour covers the main state rooms, which are still regularly used for lavish functions – whose guest lists usually feature international celebrities as well as nobility. The **Spiegelsalon**, which was transferred from one of the buildings on Emmeramsplatz, and the **Grüner Salon**, which is based on designs by Leo von Klenze, are both Neoclassical in style. Other rooms are clearly modelled on those of the Rococo palaces of Bavaria; among these is the **Thronsaal**, where a beautifully crafted Parisian easy-chair of the 1730s does service as the princely throne. Hung throughout the apartments are splendid seventeenth-century Brussels tapestries depicting the family's illustrious history.

St Emmeram's former **cloisters** (included in the tour, otherwise DM6/€3) offer a fascinating visual record of architectural development from the Romanesque of the mid-twelfth century via the Transitional and early Gothic styles to the High Gothic of the early fourteenth century. There is a good deal of fine decorative detail to be seen, not least in the pure Gothic **portal** which now gives the family its own private access to the church. Jutting into the cloister garth is their one significant addition, the neo-Gothic **Gruftkapelle**, whose vault contains 29 sarcophagi of members of the dynasty.

In the Neoclassical Marstall, or stables, are two museums that can be visited at leisure. The long-established **Marstallmuseum** (April–Oct Mon–Fri 11am–5pm, Sat & Sun 10am–5pm; DM7/€3.50, DM8/€4 for joint ticket with Thurn und Taxis Museum) holds a large collection of nineteenth- and early twentieth-century travelling and ceremonial coaches and winter sleighs. Curiously, all of these were for the family's own private use, none of the vehicles from the time of the postal monopoly having been retained by them. The new **Thurn und Taxis Museum** (Mon–Fri 11am–5pm, Sat & Sun 10am–5pm; DM6/€3, DM8/€4 for joint ticket with Marstallmuseum) represents a happy solution to the colossal death duties which became due on the death of Prince Johannes. In lieu of a monetary payment, the family made over to the Bavarian state several hundred *objets d'art*, together with rooms in which they could be displayed to the public to the best possible advantage. The artefacts are seventeenth to nineteenth century in date, and are mostly quite small-scale: indeed a highlight is what is probably the world's finest collection of snuffboxes. There are also some stunning pieces of jewellery, plus dinner services, silverware, glassware, clocks, furniture and weapons.

Eating and drinking

You're spoilt for choice when it comes to places to eat and drink in Regensburg; there's a bewildering variety of restaurants (including several of real curiosity value), bars, beer gardens and cafés, both traditional and modern. See also "Hotels" (p.139) for further recommendations.

Restaurants

Alte Münz, Fischmarkt 7. Top-class, moderately priced traditional restaurant with a special line in delicacies of the Upper Palatinate.

Dampfnudel-Uli, Watmarkt 4. Eccentric little restaurant in the former house chapel of the Baumburger Turm. It specializes in steamed dumplings with vanilla sauce, but serves a range of typically Bavarian main-course dishes as well. Open Tues–Fri 10.01am–6.01pm, Sat 10.01am–3.01pm.

David im Goliathhaus, Watmarkt 5. Its droll name notwithstanding, this is a serious culinary enterprise, with a wonderful location at the top of one of the city's great tower houses; it also has a roof terrace. Evenings only, closed Sun & Mon.

Fischerhaus, Untere Regenstr. 7. Speciality fish restaurant with a beer garden overlooking the right bank of the River Regen. Closed Mon.

Gänsbauer, Keplerstr. 10. Cosy and fairly pricey restaurant with a pretty inner courtyard. Evenings only.

Hagen's Auberge, Badstr. 54. Upmarket restaurant commanding a fine view across the Danube to the Altstadt. Its specialities are classic Mediterranean dishes and Black Angus steaks. Evenings only, closed Sun.

Historische Wurstküche, An der Steinernen Brücke. This famous sausage restaurant has become one of the essential sights of Regensburg. It has a truly *gemütlich* little dining room, though this is often closed off in summer, when tables are set up outside. Daily 8am–7pm.

Historisches Eck, Watmarkt 6. Regensburg's most renowned and expensive gourmet restaurant. Closed Sun & Mon.

Kneitinger, Arnulfsplatz 3. Excellent traditional Gaststätte, dating back to 1870s, of the eponymous local brewery, a charitable foundation which is best known for its dark beers.

Kneitinger-Keller, Galgenbergstr. 18. The brewery's other main outlet is in the southern part of the city, near the university and accordingly popular with students. It also has Regensburg's largest beer garden, with some 1200 seats.

Ratskeller, Rathausplatz 1. Moderately priced and typically reliable example of its kind, with a pleasant small courtyard.

Zur Brauschänke, Galgenbergstr. 3. The main Gaststätte of the princely Thurn und Taxis brewery, which makes a wide variety of beers, including a fine dark *Roggenbier*. Closed Sun.

Cafés and bars

Alt-Regensburger Weinkeller, Fischgässel 4. One of a group of wine bars clustered around Fischmarkt, which are particularly pleasant in summer when tables are set up outside. Evenings only, closed Mon.

Amapola, Am Römling 1. One of a number of trendy bars in the western part of the Altstadt.

Ambrosius, Brückstr. 5. A good choice for breakfast; open till 1am.

Brauhaus Johann Albrecht, Schwarze-Bären-Str. 6. Hausbrauerei with a predominantly young clientele; it brews both light and dark beers and serves full meals.

Felix, Fröhliche-Türken-Str. 6. *Szene* café-bar, and another popular breakfast choice.

Goldene Ente, Badstr. 32. Student Kneipe which serves a limited menu of hot dishes and has the benefit of a beer garden shaded by chestnut trees.

Kepler, Keplerstr. 3. A recently revamped bar with a beer garden in a quaint medieval courtyard overgrown with vines.

Netzblick, Am Römling 9. Internet café-bar. Open Tues–Sun 7pm–1am.

Palletti, Pustet Passage, Gesandtenstr. 9. An enduring haunt of the local in-crowd.

Prinzess, Rathausplatz 2. The oldest coffee house in Germany, founded in 1686, and still the best choice for handmade chocolates (especially pralines) and cakes. These can be bought in the downstairs shop, or eaten in the café or tea salon which occupy the two floors above.

Schlosscafé, Emmeramsplatz 5. Cosy little daytime café in a glass pavilion in the entrance courtyard of Schloss Thurn und Taxis. Closed Dec–March.

Schwedenkugel, Haaggasse 15. Another student favourite, with the unexpected bonus of a menu of Kurdish cuisine.

Entertainment and festivals

From Easter to late October, Regensburger Personenschiffahrt Klinger (☎09 41/5 21 04 or 5 53 59) runs hourly **cruises** (10am–4pm; DM11/€5.50) around the city, which include going through the rapids under the Steinerne Brücke. Throughout the same season, the company normally offers two daily trips along the Danube to Walhalla (DM11/€5.50 single, DM16/€8 return), plus occasional excursions to Straubing, Passau and the Altmühl valley via the Rhine-Main-Danube Canal. Tickets for all of these can be bought at the landing stage just east of the Historische Wurstküche.

Regensburg's main **theatre**, featuring a varied programme of drama, opera, musicals and concerts by the Philharmonisches Orchester der Stadt Regensburg, is the Stadttheater, Bismarckplatz 7 (☎09 41/5 07 44 12); pending its restoration, performances are being held at the Velodrom, Arnulfsplatz 4b. Other venues include the Theater am Haidplatz, the open-air courtyard of the Thon–Dittmer-Palais (☎09 41/5 07 44 12); the Turmtheater in the Goliathhaus at Watmarkt 5 (☎09 41/56 22 33); the cabaret STATT-Theater, Winklergasse 16 (☎09 41/5 33 02); and the marionette Figurentheater im Stadtpark, Dr-Johann-Maier-Str. 3 (☎09 41/2 83 28). The Kulturzentrum Alte Mälzerei, Galgenbergstr. 20 (☎09 41/7 57 49), presents all kinds of **live music** as well as cabaret and theatre; while the main jazz venue is Leerer Beutel, Bertoldstr. 9 (☎09 41/56 33 75). Among the many **discos**, the most enduringly popular are *Sudhaus*, Untere Bachgasse 8, and *Scala*, Gesandtenstr. 6.

Two big beer **festivals**, each lasting two weeks, take place annually – the *Maidult* in May, and the *Herbstdult* at the end of August and beginning of September. Another major folklore event is the *Brückenfest* in July. There is also a contrasting pair of music festivals each summer: the *Bach-Woche* in June and the *Bayerisches Jazz-Weekend* in July.

The Danube country around Regensburg

Within easy reach of Regensburg are some wonderful Danube landscapes, together with several spectacular historic monuments. While all the places described in this section are readily accessible by road, the cruise ships which run in summer are a far more atmospheric way to travel.

Kelheim

At the confluence of the Altmühl and the Danube about 20km southwest of Regensburg is **KELHEIM**, a little medieval town unusual for its time in having been laid out as a planned grid. In the centre, the most distinctive building is the **Herzogkasten** on Lederergasse, a fifteenth-century ducal tithe barn which now houses the **Archäologisches Museum** (April–Oct Tues–Sun 10am–4pm; DM5/€2.50), a collection of local finds ranging from prehistoric times to the early Bavarian era. Of particular note is a well-preserved group of vessels from around 1000 BC. Outside can be seen an original fragment of the ten-kilometre-long wall of the Celtic settlement of Oppidum Alkimoennis, together with a conjectural reconstruction of its original height.

Crowning the isolated Michelsberg above is the **Befreiungshalle** (Liberation Hall; daily: April–Sept 9am–5pm; Oct–March 10am–noon & 1–4pm; DM3/€1.50), one of two grandiose constructions on either side of Regensburg funded by King Ludwig I and built by Leo von Klenze. Designed in the manner of an early Christian rotunda, it commemorates the Bavarian dead in the wars against Napoleon. Its eighteen sides symbolize the fact that the key victories over the French – at Leipzig in 1813 and Waterloo in 1815 – both took place on the 18th of the month, and the massive figures atop the exterior buttresses represent eighteen different German peoples who took part in the battles. Around the perimeter of the interior stand 34 Victories, one for each of the German states that existed at the time. You can also climb up to the balconies, which command wonderful views over Kelheim and the Danube and Altmühl valleys.

Kelheim does not lie on a rail line, but **buses** connect with arrivals at Bahnhof Saal on the Donautalbahn between Regensburg and Ingolstadt; the most convenient stop is Wöhrdplatz, which lies between the town centre and the Danube jetty. The **tourist office** (Mon–Fri 9.30am–12.30pm & 2–5pm, Sat 2–5pm; ☎0 94 41/70 12 34, fax 70 12 07, *www.altmuehltal.de*) is in the Rathaus, Ludwigsplatz 14. Schneider, one of Bavaria's best-known **breweries**, decamped to Kelheim from Munich after World War II. It makes several classic wheat beers, including *Schneiderweisse Original* and *Aventinus-Starkbier*, which can be sampled in the rambling *Weisses Bräuhaus*, Emil-Ottl-Str. 3. Among the town's several **hotels**, two are attached to the other local breweries: *Gasthof Frischeisen*, which is midway between Bahnhof Saal and the town centre at Regensburger Str. 69 (☎0 94 41/5 04 90; ②); and *Gasthof Aukoferbräu*, at the north-western fringe of the centre at Alleestr. 27 (☎0 94 41/20 20; ④). Other central options include *Ehrnthaller*, Donaustr. 22 (☎0 94 41/33 33; ③), *Gasthof Weisses Lamm*, Ludwigstr. 12 (☎0 94 41/2 00 90; ④), and *Gasthof Stockhammer*, Am Oberen Zweck 2 (☎0 94 41/7 00 40; ④). All have recommendable **restaurants**, with the *Stockhammer*'s *Ratskeller* the pick of the bunch.

The Donaudurchbruch

From Easter until early October, there are between ten and twenty daily cruises (DM6.50/€3.25 single, DM11/€5.50 return) from Kelheim's Danube jetty (☎0 94 41/58 58) through the famous **Donaudurchbruch** gorge. Here the river washes past some very attractive wooded hillsides, and then dramatically cuts through white cliffs, becoming a fast current only 80m wide. The Danube took an estimated four thousand years to force its way through these rocks; once past the obstacle, it widens out into a broad sweep.

Situated on a bend of the river is the goal of the excursion boats, **Kloster Weltenburg**, Bavaria's oldest monastery, founded in the early seventh century by Benedictine monks. The complex was completely rebuilt in Baroque style, and the **Klosterkirche St Georg** is an early example of the collaborative skills of the Asam brothers. Despite its small size and plain exterior, it has a truly dazzling interior whose focal point is an illusionistic **high altar** with carved figures by Egid Quirin depicting the fight between St George and the dragon against a painted backdrop of *The Immaculate Conception* by Cosmas Damian. The latter, who was also the church's architect, covered the nave's cupola with an allegorical fresco, *The Triumph of the Church*, and filled the large niche on the south side with a depiction of the arrival of Benedictine monks in the American continent on Columbus's *Santa Maria*. On the balustrade above, he painted a half-length vignette of himself, bewigged and holding a brush and palette. In the *Klosterschenke*, a **restaurant** with beer garden, you can sample the dark **beers** (*Barock-Dunkel* and the strong *Asam-Bock*) made in the monastery's own brewery, the oldest of its type in the world.

Walhalla

Ludwig I's **Walhalla** (daily: April–Sept 9am–5.45pm; Oct 9am–4.45pm; Nov–March 10–11.45am & 1–3.45pm; DM3/€1.50) stands in splendid isolation high above the Danube 11km east of Regensburg, just beyond the village of Donaustauf. Self-consciously modelled on the Parthenon in Athens, the building takes its name from the Nordic mythological resting-place for warriors' souls, and contains a frieze illustrating the country's history, busts of 125 famous Germans and 64 plaques for older celebrities whose likenesses are unknown. The qualification adopted for being a German is a decidedly generous one, as Swiss, Austrian and even Dutch nationals are all deemed eligible; yet there are many unfathomable omissions along with others whose claim to everlasting fame now seems decidedly dubious. Busts continue to be added, normally every five to seven years, though there have been two very recent additions – St Maria Theresia (only the tenth woman to be admitted) and Konrad Adenauer. If the whole idea behind this project now seems slightly sinister, the view across the Danube valley is magnificent, and the surrounding park and forests are good places for picnics.

Straubing

About 30km downstream from Regensburg, **STRAUBING** is the main market town of the fertile Gäuboden region, one of the country's principal granaries. In 1353, as a result of a division of the Wittelsbach lands, it was united with the Netherlandish provinces of Holland, Zeeland, Friesland and Hainaut to form the Duchy of Straubing-Holland. Although this only survived until 1425, and although The Hague was the ducal capital, with Straubing the seat of a secondary court run by a relative of the ruling duke, it was nonetheless a true golden age for the town, and most of its finest monuments date from then. Nowadays, Straubing is best known for Bavaria's second largest **fair**, the *Gäubodenvolksfest*, which began in the early nineteenth century as a farmers' market but is nowadays a smaller-scale version of the *Oktoberfest* – albeit one that attracts over a million visitors.

The Town

A peculiarity of Straubing is that its largely pedestrianized historic centre is called the **Neustadt** (new town), this being a reflection of the fact that it is not the location of the original settlement. At its heart lie two contiguous elongated market squares, Theresienplatz and Ludwigsplatz, which are lined with a mixture of medieval, Baroque, Neoclassical, Historicist and Jugendstil houses. In the middle of the former stands the early eighteenth-century **Dreifaltigkeitssäule** (Holy Trinity Column); the latter has Baroque fountains dedicated to the local patrons, St James and St Tiburtius. Separating the two squares is the town's symbol, the **Stadtturm**, a picturesque Gothic tower crowned with five steeples. Alongside is the **Rathaus**, a fourteenth-century building (originally the local trading hall) with a neo-Gothic facade.

Rising just to the north, **St Jakob** is a majestic late Gothic hall church designed by the great fifteenth-century architect Hans von Burghausen, to which a slender tower was appended in the sixteenth century. It contains an extraordinary array of works of art of various periods. In the main body of the church are the carved and painted **high altar** from Nürnberg, which features six beautifully coloured panels by Dürer's master, Michael Wolgemut, and an extravagant Rococo **pulpit**. Despite their sober and regular external appearance, the side chapels are profusely furnished and decorated. The one immediately to the left of the central apsidal chapel contains the magnificent fifteenth-century **tomb slab** of Burgomaster Ulrich Kastenmayr, which is strikingly similar in style to the famous contemporary paintings of Jan van Eyck, who for a time was the Straubing-Holland court painter in The Hague. That on the other side of the apsidal chapel preserves its dazzling original **stained glass**, while the next in line was lavishly remodelled by the Asam brothers. The fifth chapel on the north side of the nave contains a touching *Madonna and Child* by Holbein the Elder.

A couple of blocks east of here, on Fraunhoferstrasse, is the **Gäubodenmuseum** (Tues–Sun 10am–4pm; DM4/€2, or DM6/€3 combined ticket with Sammlung Rudolf Kriss), which contains one of the most important hordes of **Roman treasures** ever found on German soil. This numbers 116 different pieces, ranging from iron and bronze tools and domestic ware to ornamental statuettes and beautifully crafted armour and masks for both soldiers and horses. The decorative nature of the horse masks, in which Oriental as well as Hellenistic influence is evident, suggests they were used for parades and exhibition games rather than war. Almost equally spectacular are the recently excavated **jewellery** and **glassware** from a graveyard of the early Bavarian period. The museum also has notable prehistoric displays, plus a collection of religious art ranging from Romanesque to Rococo.

A further block to the east is the **Karmelitenkirche**, another impressive design by Hans von Burghausen, albeit one given a heavy Baroque interior overlay by Wolfgang Dientzenhofer, a member of a prolific architectural dynasty active mainly in Franconia and Bohemia. It served as the pantheon of the local ducal family; appropriately enough, the most imposing tomb is that in the monks' choir to Albrecht II, who presided over the most brilliant flowering of the Straubing court. On Burggasse, the next alley to the east, is **St Ursula**, the last church the Asam brothers built and decorated together. Egid Quirin designed the building and executed the stuccowork and sculptures, including expressive statues of St Charles Borromeo and St Ignatius Loyola. Cosmas Damian, whose daughter became a member of the still-functioning Ursuline convent to which the church belongs, painted St Ursula's martyrdom in the vault above the organ, and filled the cupola with a fresco which combines the saint's glorification with an allegory of the continents.

Immediately to the north of here, overlooking the Danube, stands the somewhat austere fourteenth-century **Schloss**, which is guarded by formidable corner towers. Much of the complex is used as offices, but part houses an outstation of the Bayerisches Nationalmuseum, the **Sammlung Rudolf Kriss** (Tues–Sun 10am–4pm; DM4/€2). Named in honour of its founder, this collection of seventeenth- to twentieth-century religious folk art is displayed thematically in three sections: private devotions, major church festivals, and pilgrimages and votive offerings. The entrance ticket also gives admission to the heavily restored **Rittersaal**, the only one of the historic interiors generally open to the public.

Just over 1km to the east is the somnolent **Altstadt**, the former town of Strupinga, the predecessor of Straubing. Its twin-towered parish church, **St Peter**, is a real rarity for Bavaria, a pillared Romanesque basilica untouched by Baroque or Rococo decorators. It preserves two original **portals**, whose tympana show battles between a man and a dragon and between two imaginary beasts; inside, a polychrome crucifix survives from the same period.

The church stands within a walled cemetery which is unquestionably one of the most beautiful in Germany, preserving many historic tombstones, plus three Gothic chapels. A tragic story lies behind one of these, the **Agnes-Bernauer-Kapelle**. Following the extinction of the House of Straubing-Holland, Straubing passed to the Upper Bavarian duchy and became the residence of its heir, the future Albrecht III. At a tournament in Augsburg, he met and fell in love with a local barber's daughter named Agnes Bernauer; he subsequently married her in secret and took her to Straubing, where she presided over the life of the court. Scandalized by his son's union with a commoner, the reigning Duke Ernst tricked him into leaving town for a while, then had Agnes tried for witchcraft and drowned in the Danube. In expiation, he had this chapel erected in her memory, in which stands a marble epitaph with a poignant relief portrait of the deceased. Alongside is the ossuary, or **Totenkapelle**, which contains a lively cycle of paintings of *The Dance of Death* by the Rococo artist Felix Hölzl.

Practicalities

Straubing's **Hauptahnhof** lies just to the south of the Neustadt. The **tourist office** is in the Rathaus, Theresienplatz 20 (Mon–Wed & Fri 9am–5pm, Thurs 9am–6pm, Sat

9am–noon; ☎0 94 21/94 43 07, fax 94 41 03, *www.straubing.de*). There's a good range of town-centre **hotels**: *Bischofshof*, Fraunhoferstr. 16 (☎0 94 21/1 29 92; ③), *Gasthof Bayerischer Löwe*, Ludwigsplatz 24 (☎0 94 21/1 05 65; ④), *Röhrlbräu*, Theresienplatz 7 (☎0 94 21/9 90 80; ④), *Gäubodenhof*, Theresienplatz 8a (☎0 94 21/1 22 75; ④), *Wittelsbach*, Stadtgraben 25 (☎0 94 21/94 30; ④), *Seethaler*, Theresienplatz 25 (☎0 94 21/1 20 22; ⑤), and *Theresientor*, Theresienplatz 41 (☎0 94 21/84 90; ⑥–⑧). The **youth hostel** is a short walk east of the Hauptbahnhof at Friedhofstr. 12 (☎0 94 21/8 04 36, fax 1 20 94; DM17.50/€8.75), while the **campsite** (closed mid-Oct to April) is at the far northern edge of town at Wundermühlweg 9 (☎0 94 21/8 97 94).

All but the last of the hotels listed above have **restaurants**, of which the best is *Seethaler*. Inexpensive meals and local beers are available at the *Straubinger Weissbierhaus*, Theresienplatz 32, while *Spezerei*, Simon-Höller-Str. 8, is a daytime wholefood restaurant. The main **festivals** are the aforementioned *Gäubodenvolksfest*, which begins on the second Friday in August and lasts for ten days, and the *Agnes-Bernauer-Festspiele*, performances in the Schloss courtyard of a play about the eponymous local heroine, which are held every four years (next in July 2003).

Passau

"In all of Germany I never saw a town more beautiful" is how the marauding Napoleon Bonaparte is said to have reacted to **PASSAU**. Tucked away by the Austrian border, 90km downstream from Straubing, it's a place that the tourist brochures hail as the "Bavarian Venice". While that's a piece of hyperbole, the city does have a certain magic, and its character is very much defined by water, standing as it does at the confluence of the Danube, Inn and Ilz. For centuries, Passau was the seat of a powerful prince-bishopric, the largest in the Holy Roman Empire, and it was probably for this court that the national epic, the *Nibelungenlied* (see box on p.463), was written at the turn of the thirteenth century. Nowadays, it's a bustling town given a youthful edge by a university founded in 1978.

Arrival, information and accommodation

Passau's **Hauptbahnhof** is immediately west of the Altstadt. Outside, at Bahnhofstr. 36, is one of the **tourist offices** (Easter to mid-Oct Mon–Fri 9am–5pm, Sat & Sun 9am–1pm; rest of year Mon–Thurs 9am–5pm, Fri 9am–4pm; ☎08 51/95 59 80, fax 5 72 98, *www.passau.de*); the other is at Rathausplatz 3 (Easter to mid-Oct Mon–Fri 8.30am–6pm, Sat & Sun 9.30am–3pm; rest of year Mon–Thurs 8.30am–5pm, Fri 8.30am–4pm; ☎08 51/95 59 80, fax 3 51 07).

Passau has a good choice of **hotels** in all categories. The **youth hostel** (☎08 51/49 37 80, fax 4 93 78 20; DM23/€11.50) is within the Veste Oberhaus, while there's a **campsite**, *Zeltplatz Ilzstadt*, next to the River Ilz at Halserstr. 34 (☎08 51/4 14 57).

Hotels and pensions

Altstadthotel, Bräugasse 23–29 (☎08 51/33 70, fax 33 71 00, *www.altstadt-hotel.de*). Hotel and restaurant with a marvellous location at Dreiflusseck. ④–⑧.

Blauer Bock, Höllgasse 20 (☎08 51/3 46 37, fax 4 10 72). Historic Gasthof directly overlooking the Danube. ③–⑤.

Passauer Wolf, Rindermarkt 6 (☎08 51/93 15 10, fax 9 31 51 50). Elegant hotel in the central part of the Altstadt. Its restaurant (closed Sat lunchtime & Sun) is among the very best in Passau. ⑥–⑧.

Rosencafé, Donaustr. 23 (☎08 51/4 28 11, fax 4 10 72). Very good-value Gasthof on the north bank of the Danube, at the extreme eastern edge of the city. It can be reached from the centre by bus #1 or #3, though the walk is very pleasant. ②.

Rössner, Bräugasse 19 (☎08 51/93 13 50, fax 9 31 35 55, *www.passau.baynet.de*). An immaculately maintained pension in a restored mansion in the eastern part of the Altstadt. All rooms have private facilities. ③.

Rotel Inn, Donaulände (☎08 51/9 51 60, fax 9 51 61 00). Directly overlooking the Danube, just a stone's throw from the Hauptbahnhof, this building in the shape of a sleeping man is a patented hotel idea based on the sort of transportable accommodation used on long-haul safaris. The "rooms" are cabins measuring just 4m by 1.5m. Closed Oct–April. ①, ② with optional breakfast.

Schloss Ort, Im Ort 11 (☎08 51/3 40 72, fax 3 18 17). Well-appointed hotel overlooking the Inn near the Dreiflusseck. Its restaurant specializes in fish dishes and has a pleasant garden terrace. ⑤.

Weisser Hase, Ludwigstr. 23 (☎08 51/9 21 10, fax 9 21 11 00, *www.weisser-hase.de*). Historic hotel and restaurant (evenings only) in the very heart of the Altstadt, completely refurbished to a very high standard a few years back. ⑥–⑧.

Wienerwald, Grosse Klingergasse 17 (☎08 51/3 30 69, fax 3 30 60). Attached to the eponymous chain restaurant, this hotel offers good value at the price asked, particularly in view of its convenient Altstadt setting. ③.

Wilder Mann, Am Rathausplatz (☎08 51/3 50 71, fax 3 17 12). Passau's best-known hotel, occupying a former patrician mansion. Its accommodation ranges from relatively simple rooms to exquisitely furnished suites named after two former guests, King Ludwig II and Empress Susi. The latter also gives her name to the evenings-only gourmet restaurant, which draws on the world's largest collection of German-language cookery books for inspiration. The rooftop café-restaurant is open throughout the day. ⑥–⑨.

The City

Passau's **Altstadt** is crammed along the peninsula between the Danube and Inn. Even in medieval times, the city spilled across the rivers to form suburbs on each bank, the most important being **Oberhaus**, north of the Danube and west of the Ilz, and the **Innstadt** south of the Inn.

The Altstadt

Virtually the whole of the Altstadt burnt down in the seventeenth century, so the architectural picture features predominantly Baroque, Rococo and Neoclassical facades, which give the town a pleasingly elegant feel in spite of the tight squeeze of buildings. The enormous **Dom** is suitably enthroned at the highest point. Nearly all the original Gothic structure was destroyed by fire, to be replaced by a Baroque building designed by the Italian architect Carlo Lurago. His fellow countrymen, the stuccoist Giovanni Battista Carlone and the fresco painter Carpoforo Tencalla, were entrusted with the interior decoration, which is sumptuous in the extreme. The side altars were commisioned from other artists; of special note are the four by Austria's leading Baroque painter, Johann Michael Rottmayr, in the end chapels at either side of the nave. However, the most notable furnishing is the world's largest church **organ**, which has no fewer than 17,300 pipes and 231 separate registers. Recitals are given every weekday from May to October at noon (DM4/€2), with longer ones on Thursdays at 7.30pm (DM8/€4).

Residenzplatz, which is lined by the mansions of wealthy burgher families, is one of the very few open spaces in the tightly packed centre, and offers a fine view of the Dom's resplendent east end, the only significant section remaining from the Gothic period. It's named after the **Neue Residenz**, the Baroque town palace of the prince-bishops. Part of this houses the valuable treasures of the **Domschatz-und-Diözesanmuseum** (Easter–Oct Mon–Sat 10am–4pm; DM2/€1); the ticket also gives admission to the **Bibliotheksaal**, which is festooned with trompe l'oeil frescoes, and the magnificent main staircase.

Down towards the Danube is the **Rathaus**, a Gothic building with neo-Gothic accretions, notably the tall tower, where you can see the marks from the alarmingly high floods that have plagued the town. The main reception room, the **Rathaussaal**

(April–Oct daily 10am–4/5pm; DM3/€1.50), is lined with heroic nineteenth-century paintings illustrating key events in Passau's history. Directly opposite, the **Glasmuseum** (daily: March–Oct 10am–4pm; Nov–Feb 1–4pm; DM5/€2.50) in the Hotel Wilder Mann has a huge collection of glass – 30,000 exhibits in 35 rooms – ranging in style from Baroque to modern via Neoclassical, Empire, Biedermeier, Jugendstil and Art Deco. Products from nearby glass-blowers huts in the Bavarian and Bohemian forests (see opposite) feature prominently.

To the east, alleys and streets intertwine in picturesque disorder, offering a tantalizing reminder of how the medieval town must have looked. A restored patrician mansion at Bräugasse 17 contains the **Museum Moderner Kunst** (Tues, Wed & Fri–Sun 10am–6pm, Thurs 10am–8pm; DM8/€4), which has no permanent collection, staging instead highly ambitious temporary exhibitions, often of big names in the international art world. The tip of the peninsula is known as the **Dreiflusseck** (Three Rivers Corner), being the point where the Ilz, Danube and Inn all come together. Since the days of antiquity, the great combined river which flows east from here through three European capitals to the Black Sea has been known as the Danube. However, as can be seen clearly from this vantage point, the Inn is actually the major river: it is deeper, broader and faster-flowing, and has also travelled further to reach the place of convergence.

The Veste Oberhaus and the Innstadt

On the peninsula on the far side of the Danube is the **Veste Niederhaus**, a formidable-looking medieval fortress – nowadays in private hands and inaccessible to the public – which formed the outermost part of the defensive system of the castle of the prince-bishops, the **Veste Oberhaus**, high on the hill above. The steep walk up to the latter by the path along the southern side of the ramparts is enjoyable in its own right; alternatively, take one of the buses from Rathausplatz, which run every thirty minutes from 11.30am to 5pm between Easter and October. Much of the complex is given over to the **Kulturhistorisches Museum** (Mon–Fri 9am–5pm, Sat & Sun 10am–5pm; *www.oberhausmuseum.de*; DM7/€3.50), which contains displays on local and regional history, with informative sections on the medieval salt trade and on local sculptors and painters, the latter including Altdorfer's most talented follower, Wolf Huber. The museum circuit includes access to a section of the medieval fortifications, from where there's a wonderful picture-postcard view over the city and the confluence of the three rivers.

Itself a fine vantage point, the Innbrücke links the Altstadt with the **Innstadt** on the opposite side of the Inn. This suburb is dominated by the **Wallfahrtskirche Mariahilf**, a pretty twin-towered Baroque pilgrimage church approached via an extraordinary covered stairway with 321 steps. From the terrace, there's yet another wonderful panoramic view. A short walk west of the Innbrücke, at Ledergasse 43, is the **Römermuseum Kastell Boiotro** (March–Nov Tues–Sun 10am–noon & 1/2–4pm; DM2/€1). Outdoors, you can see the excavations of the eponymous Roman fort; the medieval house in the grounds contains archeological finds from the Passau region.

Eating and drinking

There's a wide range of enticing places to eat and drink in Passau, quite apart from the many fine hotel restaurants listed on p.152.

Bräustüberl Hacklberg, Bräuhausplatz 7. A highly atmospheric beer hall, complete with Passau's biggest beer garden. It's located alongside its brewery, a handsome Baroque building on the north side of the Danube (cross by the western of the two bridges, the Schanzlbrücke) which produces around a dozen different beers. Highly innovative meals are also served.

Bräustüberl Löwenbrauerei, Kleiner Exerzierplatz 17. The beer hall of Passau's Löwenbrauerei (no relation of its Munich namesake), which brews light, dark and wheat beers.

Café Add, Grosse Klingergasse 8. Internet café in the western part of the Altstadt.

Chesa Pressl, Römerplatz 3. Offers Swiss cuisine and fish specialities. Closed Tues.

Goldener Schiff, Unterer Sand 8. A good old-fashioned Gaststätte, popular with students and seasoned drinkers alike. The food is tasty and cheap; the beers come from the Peschl brewery.

Heilig-Geist-Stift-Schenke, Heilggeistgasse 4. Wonderful Weinstube in a fourteenth-century hospital building, serving wines from its own vineyard and some of the best meals in Passau, including fish dishes and Austrian pastries. In addition to the main dining rooms, its has intimate candlelit cellars and a peaceful rear garden. Closed Wed.

Innstadt Bräustüberl, Schmiedgasse 23. The beer hall of the nearby Innstadt brewery, offering good-value poultry dishes and other traditional fare. Closed Mon.

Oberhaus, Veste Oberhaus. Café-restaurant in the castle grounds, with a terrace offering a grandstand view over the city. Closed Nov–March.

Peschl-Terrasse, Rosstränke 4. Right alongside the Peschl brewery is its own terrace restaurant, commanding a fine view over the Danube. Closed Mon.

Stadtschreiber, Schustergasse 1. Popular student Kneipe, offering a choice of 101 different beers.

Cruises, festivals and entertainment

An excellent way to get an overall impression of the city is to take the 45-minute Dreiflüsse-Rundfahrt **cruise** (DM11/€5.50) offered by Wurm & Köck, Höllgasse 26 (☎08 51/92 92 92). From March to early November there are daily sailings from the quay at Rathausplatz, with departures every 20 to 30 minutes at the height of the season. Between May and mid-October, the same company also runs cruises (DM38/€19 single, DM46/€23 return) to Linz, the capital of Upper Austria, daily except Wednesdays.

The *Maidult* is a large and colourful market and beer **festival**, while during the *Europäische Wochen* in June, July and August, **concerts** are played by internationally renowned orchestras and musicians, and there's also ballet and opera. Passau's star **venue**, worth checking on throughout the year, is the eighteenth-century Theater im Fürstbischöflichen Opernhaus, Gottfried-Schäffer-Str. 2–4 (☎08 51/9 29 19 13). Scharfrichterhaus, Milchgasse 2 (☎08 51/3 59 00), has live music and cabaret, plus a cinema and a relaxed bar.

The Bavarian Forest

Poor, provincial and a bit out of the way, the **Bavarian Forest** (Bayerischer Wald) is part of Central Europe's largest woodland region, which also includes the Bohemian Forest on the other side of the Czech border. It's an area that retains a great deal of wilderness, plus much of its traditional culture. The craggy earth is full of rocks and barely fertile, and the inhabitants had to develop means of survival other than farming. Easy availability of firewood made glass-blowing a natural industry, and workers still tend to be employed in huts, working by hand in the heat of the furnaces. It's superb hiking country, with well-marked paths of varying length and difficulty throughout the region. There are also some wonderful popular **festivals**; see the box on p.156 for details of two of these.

Generally, prices are very low, and even during the height of summer finding accommodation is never a problem. **Private rooms** and small **guesthouses** (①–②) can be found everywhere and even cheaper accommodation is often available in farmhouses. **Public transport** is a bit fiddly. From Plattling, which lies between Straubing and Passau, a rail line, served by immaculate little diesels, cuts through the heart of the forest, terminating at Bayerisch Eisenstein on the Czech border. Along the way, at Zwiesel, there are short branch lines running northwest to Bodenmais and southeast to Grafenau. Another line travels from Schwandorf on the main route north of Regensburg

Furth im Wald, at the extreme northeastern edge of the Bavarian Forest, is home to one of Bavaria's largest and oldest popular festivals, the **Drachenstich** (literally, "Dragon Sticking"). This event, which goes back as far as 1431, begins on the second Sunday in August and ends a week later. Its central theme, the story of a maiden rescued by a gallant Knight from the clutches of a wicked dragon, is clearly rooted in the legend of St George, though it is also thought to have a symbolical reference to the Magyar invasions the area once suffered. A play based on this story is performed in the open air on several occasions throughout the duration of the festival. Lasting for about 75 minutes, it culminates in the grand and gory finale of the dragon's death, where the skewered monster spews blood over the street during its death throes. Tickets can be ordered in advance from *Drachenstichfestausschuss*, Stadtplatz 4 (☎0 99 73/93 08).

Kötzting, which lies at the foot of the Kaitersberg, one of the best hiking areas in the Bavarian Forest, hosts the **Pfingstritt** each Whit Monday. Although a religious festival, it probably has its origins in an ancient Germanic fertility rite; it involves the menfolk riding their richly adorned horses to a nearby pilgrimage church, and a symbolic wedding of a young couple elected as Whit bride and groom.

along the northern fringe of the forest to Furth im Wald. En route, at Cham, there are again two short branch lines, including one to Lam via Kötzting. Buses fill in the gaps in this network, though there are only a few services per day on most routes.

Frauenau

FRAUENAU, which lies on the Zwiesel–Grafenau rail line, is the best place to see the living crafts of glass-blowing and -cutting. Just off Bahnhofstrasse is the **Freiherr von Poschinger Kristallglasfabrik** (guided tours Mon–Sat 10am–1.15pm; free), the oldest glass-making factory in the world, which offers the opportunity to watch workers transform red molten lumps into glasses, plates and ornaments. For a technical history of glass production and representative work of each age, visit the **Glasmuseum** (mid-May to Oct Tues–Sun 9am–5pm; Nov to mid-May Tues–Sun 10am–4pm; DM3/€1.50) at Am Museumspark. Highlights of the collection are exquisite seventeenth- and eighteenth-century Venetian pieces and some anarchic Jugendstil vases. Local specialities, such as heavy cut crystal and delicate snuff bottles, are also included.

The **tourist office** (mid-May to mid-Oct Mon–Fri 8am–noon & 1.30–5pm, Sat 9.30–11.30am; rest of year Mon–Fri only; ☎0 99 26/9 41 00, fax 17 99) is at Hauptstr. 12. Here you can pick up a list of private rooms and guesthouses (①–②). **Hotels** include *Büchler*, Dörflstr. 18 (☎0 99 26/9 40 40; ④), and *Eibl-Brunner*, Hauptstr. 18 (☎0 99 26/95 10; ④–⑤). Both of these have good **restaurants**. The tiny **youth hostel** is at Hauptstr. 29a (☎ & fax 0 99 26/7 35; DM17.50/€8.75).

The Nationalpark Bayerischer Wald

Frauenau lies just outside the boundaries of the **Nationalpark Bayerischer Wald** (Bavarian Forest National Park), some 130 square kilometres of strictly protected countryside bounded to the east by the Czech frontier. The highest peak, the Rachel (1453m), is in the far north of the park, almost due east of Frauenau. Below it, the Rachelsee adds an isolated splash of blue to the landscape. Further south, stretches of moorland open out the forest.

An excellent **information centre** about the park is located in the *Hans-Eiesenmann-Haus* at Böhmstr. 35 (Mon–Sat 9am–5pm; ☎0 85 58/13 00) in the village of **NEUSCHÖNAU**, which lies at its southwestern edge and can be reached by bus from Grafenau. Some buses continue onwards to a **youth hostel**, *Waldhäuser* (☎0 85 53/60 00, fax 8 29; DM25/€12.50), located right in the heart of the Nationalpark. An ideal hiking base, this is the only accommodation available within the park itself.

Bodenmais

BODENMAIS, terminus of the other branch railway from Zwiesel, is the most popular resort in the Bavarian Forest, and can get quite busy in summer, though nothing like as crowded as its counterparts in the Alps. About 2km southeast of the centre is the **Silberberg** (955m), a mountain which was mined over the course of six centuries for its iron and silver deposits. It's riddled with horizontal mineshafts, some of which are now used for therapeutic treatments. The 600-metre-long gallery known as the **Barbarastollen** (guided tours Jan–March Tues–Fri 1–3pm; April–June, Sept & Oct daily 10am–4pm; July & Aug daily 9am–4.45pm; DM8/€4), which lies about halfway up, has been mothballed in the state it was in when mining ended. A **cable car** (DM5/€2.50 single, DM8/€4 return) runs to the summit, stopping en route at an intermediate station at the Barbarastollen (DM4/€2 return).

North of Bodenmais is the **Grosser Arber** (1456m), the highest peak in the region and, together with the nearby **Arbersee**, the only part prone to be overrun by tourist coaches. There's an exhilarating hiking trail up the mountain from the village, passing through the **Risslochschlucht**, a gorge with waterfalls, on the way. A **cable car** (DM9/€4.50 single, DM14/€7 return) goes up the other side.

The **tourist office** is in the Kurverwaltung, Bahnhofstr. 56 (Mon–Fri 8am–6pm, Sat 8am–noon, Sun 10am–noon; ☎0 99 24/77 81 35, fax 77 81 50, *www.bodenmais.de*). As well as the usual extensive provision of private rooms and pensions (①–③), there are plenty of good-value **hotels**, such as *Gasthof Zur Post*, Marktplatz 6 (☎0 99 24/9 19 35; ②), and *Adam-Bräu*, Bahnhofstr. 53 (☎0 99 24/2 78; ③); the latter is part of a large complex which includes a more upmarket sports hotel, the local brewery, a restaurant and café. Progressively more upmarket establishments include *Kurparkhotel*, Amselweg 1 (☎0 99 24/9 42 80; ④), *Hofbräuhaus*, Marktplatz 5 (☎0 99 24/77 70; ⑥), *Andrea*, Hölzlweg 10 (☎0 99 24/3 86 or 74 80; ⑥), and *Wald- und Sporthotel Riederin*, Riederin 1 (☎0 99 24/77 60; ⑦); the last two both include evening meals in the price of the room. The **youth hostel** (☎0 99 24/2 81; DM23/€11.50) is on the Kleiner Arber, some 45 minutes' walk from the Grosser Arber summit, and about twice that time from town.

FRANCONIA

Franconia (Franken) makes up the northern portion of Bavaria, bordering on Thuringia, Hesse and Baden-Württemberg. About half of it is covered by highland forest ranges, which span the entire width of the province, but the chief attractions are urban. **Nürnberg**, Bavaria's second city, is a particularly evocative place, with its heady reminders of the very best and the very worst of German culture. Within easy reach are **Erlangen**, with its famous university, and the courtly town of **Ansbach**, while to the north lie Wagner's **Bayreuth**, **Coburg**, the town from which the British royal family originally descended, and the artistic treasure chest of **Bamberg**. Further west are the old episcopal residential cities of **Aschaffenburg** and **Würzburg**. The latter is the starting point of Germany's most popular tourist route, the **Romantic Road**, whose highlights include the magnificently well-preserved medieval towns of **Rothenburg ob der Tauber** and **Dinkelsbühl**.

Franconia takes its name from the Frankish tribes of whose territory it formed a major part. In the tenth century it was made into a duchy which stretched all the way to the Rhine, but this was later split into two and the name retained only for the eastern half. Although the prince-bishops of Würzburg styled themselves dukes of Franconia, they ruled only a small part of its traditional territory: the ambitious Hohenzollern dynasty established two principalities on Franconian soil, while several of the towns, most significantly Nürnberg, became city-states. **Political fragmentation** later spawned a religious split within the old province, as the Hohenzollerns and the Free Imperial Cities became enthusiastic supporters of the Reformation, while the prince-bishoprics remained loyal to Catholicism. This division was in turn reflected in architecture, with the plain lines and sombre colours of Lutheran Baroque standing in potent contrast to the sumptuousness favoured in the Catholic lands. In 1803, the centuries of division came to an end when most of what was historically regarded as Franconia was absorbed into the new Bavarian kingdom. It was subsequently divided into three administrative provinces, which still exist today: Middle Franconia (Mittelfranken), Upper Franconia (Oberfranken) and Lower Franconia (Unterfranken).

Even after two centuries as part of Bavaria, the people still cling to their **regional heritage** and often only grudgingly see themselves as Bavarian. Certainly their dress, food and dialect are quite different. No one wears Lederhosen here, and Nürnberg is one of a very few cities in this conservative state with a strong socialist pedigree. Old divisions within Franconia linger on, not least in drinking habits, with the central and western areas staunch beer zones, while the district around Würzburg is very much a wine area.

Nürnberg (Nuremberg)

Nothing more magnificent or splendid is to be found in the whole of Europe. When one perceives this glorious city from afar, its splendour is truly dazzling. When one enters it, one's original impression is confirmed by the beauty of the streets and the comeliness of the houses. The burghers' dwellings seem to have been built for princes. In truth, the kings of Scotland would be glad to be housed so luxuriously as the ordinary citizen of Nürnberg.

This mid-fifteenth-century eulogy, written by the future Pope Pius II, shows the esteem in which medieval **NÜRNBERG** was held. As the favourite royal residence and seat of the first Diet called by each new emperor, the city then functioned as the unofficial capital of Germany. It was a status which had been achieved with remarkable speed, as Nürnberg was only founded in the eleventh century; thereafter, its position at the intersection of the north–south and east–west trading routes led to economic prosperity, and, as a corollary, political power. The arts flourished, too, though the most brilliant period was not to come until the late fifteenth and early sixteenth centuries, when the roll-call of citizens was led by **Albrecht Dürer**, Germany's most complete personification of Renaissance Man.

Like other wealthy European cities, Nürnberg went into gradual decline once the maritime trading routes to the Americas and Far East had been established; moreover, the official civic adoption of the Reformation cost the city the patronage of the Catholic emperors. It made a comeback in the nineteenth century, when it became the focus for the Pan-German movement, and the **Germanisches Nationalmuseum** – the most important and extensive collection of the country's arts and crafts – was founded at this time. This symbolic status was given a horrifying twist during the Third Reich; even today the city's image is marred by its association with the regime, a tangible reminder of which survives in the weather-beaten **Nazi architecture** of suburban Luitpoldhain, site of the mass rallies.

There's so much to see in Nürnberg that two or three days are probably the minimum necessary to get to know the place. It's especially enticing in the summer, when the

Altstadt is alive with street theatre and music, and there are open-air pop concerts in the parks and stadiums; but there's always a wide and varied range of nightlife. In winter, the renowned month-long **Christkindlesmarkt** (Christmas market) is held in the city.

Arrival, information and accommodation

Arriving at the **Hauptbahnhof**, you're just outside the medieval fortifications which still enclose the Altstadt. One of the **tourist offices** (Mon–Sat 9am–7pm; ☎09 11/2 33

61 31, fax 2 33 61 66, *www.nuernberg.de*) is currently housed in a pavilion in front, but may move back inside once the reconstruction of the station is complete; another branch (May–Sept Mon–Sat 9am–6pm, Sun 10am–1pm & 2–4pm; Oct–April Mon–Sat 9am–6pm; ☎09 11/2 33 61 35) is at Hauptmarkt 18 in the Altstadt. **Public transport**, though hardly necessary for the compact city centre, is provided by the U-Bahn (this is the smallest conurbation in Europe with a genuine tube train network), trams and buses, and the same tickets are valid on all three. A day-ticket costs DM6.60/€3.30 for individuals, DM10.50/€5.25 for up to two adults and four children. For DM29/€14.50, the **Nürnberg KulTour Ticket** covers two days' travel plus entrance to most of the museums and sights. The **airport** (☎09 11/3 50 62 00 for flight information) in the far north of the city is the terminus of U-Bahn #2. **Mitfahrzentrale** is at Strauchstr. 1 (☎09 11/1 94 40).

Hotels and pensions

There are plenty of mid-range hotels within the the Altstadt and this is also where you'll find Nürnberg's many excellent upmarket addresses. The majority of budget establishments are situated in the immediate vicinity of the Hauptbahnhof.

Agneshof, Agnesgasse 10 (☎09 11/21 44 40, fax 21 44 41 44, *www.hotel.net.de/agneshof*). Named in honour of one-time nearby resident Agnes Dürer (wife of Albrecht), this fine hotel boasts a sauna, solarium, whirlpool and garden terrace. ⑥–⑨.

Altstadt, Hintere Ledergasse 4 (☎09 11/22 61 02, fax 22 18 06). Small pension on an alley close to the Hauptmarkt. ③.

Am Jakobsmarkt, Schottengasse 5 (☎09 11/2 00 70, fax 2 00 72 00). Good mid-range hotel at the southwestern edge of the Altstadt. ⑥.

Burghotel, Lammsgasse 3 (☎09 11/20 44 14, fax 22 38 82). Pleasant hotel situated just below the Kaiserburg, offering a swimming pool, sauna and solarium. ⑥.

Burghotel Stammhaus, Schildgasse 14–16 (☎09 11/20 30 40, fax 22 65 03, *www.burghotel-stamm.de*). Another good medium-range hotel in the upper part of the Altstadt, and again with bathing facilities. ⑤.

Deutscher Hof, Frauentorgraben 29 (☎09 11/2 49 40, fax 22 76 34). Although outside the Altstadt, this has a handy enough location alongside the Opernhaus. It has a high-calibre, rustically decorated restaurant, *Weinstube Bocksbeutelkeller* (evenings only). ⑤–⑦.

Grand, Bahnhofstr. 1–3 (☎09 11/2 32 20, fax 2 32 24 44, *www.grand-hotel.de*). Nürnberg's leading hotel, now part of the Meridien chain, is a large and stylish Art Deco building directly opposite the Hauptbahnhof. It also has one of the city's leading restaurants, *Brasserie*. ⑨.

Melanchthon, Melanchthonplatz 1 (☎ & fax 09 11/41 26 26). Small pension a few minutes' walk to the southwest of the Hauptbahnhof. ②–④.

Pillhofer, Königstr. 78 (☎ & fax 09 11/22 63 22). Reasonably priced Gasthof at the southern end of one of the main pedestrian streets, with a restaurant offering Franconian specialties. ③–⑥.

Vater Jahn, Jahnstr. 13 (☎09 11/44 45 07, fax 4 31 52 36). Well-maintained, very good-value pension situated just west and to the rear of the Hauptbahnhof. ②–④.

Weinhaus Steichele, Knorrstr. 2–8 (☎09 11/20 22 80, fax 22 19 14). A member of the Flair group, this is probably Nürnberg's most atmospheric hotel, occupying an old wine house. Its restaurant (closed Sun) serves good and fairly priced meals. ⑥.

Zum Schwänlein, Hintere Sterngasse 11 (☎09 11/22 51 62, fax 2 41 90 08). Inexpensive and basic Altstadt Gasthof. ②.

Hostels and campsite

Jugendgästehaus, Burg 2 (☎09 11/2 30 93 60, fax 23 09 36 11). A top-class youth hostel located in the former stables of the Kaiserburg, the castle overlooking the Altstadt. It's a 20min walk from the Hauptbahnhof. DM30/€15.

Jugendhotel, Rathsbergstr. 300 (☎09 11/5 21 60 92, fax 5 21 69 54). A privately owned hostel without age restrictions, situated to the north of the city. The journey from the Hauptbahnhof by U-bahn

#2 to Herrenhütte and then bus #21 to Felsenkeller takes 20min. Dorm beds from DM28.50/€14.25, singles from DM45/€22.50, doubles from DM74/€37.
Campingplatz Nürnberg, Hans-Kalb-Str. 56 (☎ & fax 09 11/81 27 17). The campsite is beside the football stadium; take the U-Bahn #1 to Messezentrum. Closed Oct–April.

The city centre

On January 2, 1945 a storm of bombs reduced ninety percent of Nürnberg's city centre to ash and rubble. Yet walking through the **Altstadt** today, you'd never guess this had ever happened, so loving and effective was the postwar rebuilding. Covering about one square kilometres, the reconstructed medieval core is neatly split by the River Pegnitz and surrounded by the ancient **Stadtbefestigung**, which is guarded by eighty towers and pierced by four massive gateways. To walk from one end to the other takes about twenty minutes, but much of the centre, especially the area around the castle (known as the **Burgviertel**), is on a steep hill, and speedy walking is impractical. This makes wandering around all the more pleasurable, the rise and fall of the streets creating lop-sided views and houses squeezing together as if for comfort. The atmosphere is pleasantly relaxed as well; most of the area is pedestrianized, and there's little in the way of city rush within the fortifications. It's not all medieval pictures, however. Significant areas of modern architecture and open spaces are also prominent, thus ensuring a refreshing (and deliberate) mix of old and new.

The Kaiserburg

On one of the highest points of the city, and offering the best views, the **Kaiserburg** (guided tours of the interiors April–Sept Mon–Wed & Fri–Sun 9am–6pm, Thurs 9am–8pm; Oct–March daily 10am–4pm; DM10/€5) sits chunkily above all else. Scene of many imperial meetings from the eleventh to the sixteenth century, this castle was the "treasure chest of the German Empire", and, despite innumerable modifications and war damage down the centuries, it remains a key feature of the city's silhouette.

The earliest surviving part of the castle is the **Fünfeckturm** (Pentagonal Tower) on the eastern side, which dates back to the eleventh-century Salian epoch. A century later, Frederick Barbarossa decided to extend the castle to the west, using the Salian buildings as the first line of defence. From this period there remain several examples of the smooth ashlar structures characteristic of the Hohenstaufens. The **Sinwellturm** (Round Tower), built directly on the rock, can be ascended for the best of all the views. Another survivor is the two-storey **Kaiserkapelle**, a chapel whose high and airy upper level was reserved for the use of the emperor, with the courtiers confined to the squat and heavy lower tier. In a most unusual architectural arrangement, the bizarrely named **Heidenturm** (Heathens' Tower) was built over its chancel. At the extreme east end is the fourteenth-century **Luginslandturm**, which was erected by the city council to protect Nürnberg from the ambitious Hohenzollern family, who had acquired the old Salian part of the fortress and aimed to take control over local affairs. After a long war of attrition, the city emerged victorious, but most of the original castle was destroyed in the process.

Apart from the east wall, the Hohenstaufen residential quarters were demolished in the mid-fifteenth century and replaced by the late Gothic **Palais**, which retains its suite of halls. These now look rather plain and soulless, redeemed only by two eye-catching painted wooden ceilings, which were added the following century. At the end of the fifteenth century, the local authorities joined their Luginslandturm to the formerly hostile Fünfeckturm by building the vast **Kaiserstallung**, which today makes the perfect setting for a youth hostel (see p.160). During the sixteenth century the covered **Tiefer Brunnen** (Deep Well) was built and the defences strengthened by the erection of huge bastions on the north side.

The northwestern quarter

The area around the **Tiergärtner Tor** next to the Kaiserburg is one of the most attractive parts of the old town centre, and the open space inside the city gate is the main meeting point for summertime street vendors, artists and musicians. On warm evenings the surrounding pubs spill out onto the cobblestoned piazza, and the half-timbered houses form a picturesque backdrop for relaxed summer drinking.

A few minutes' walk away along Johannisstrasse lies the **Johannisfriedhof** (daily: April–Sept 7am–7pm; Oct–March 8am–5pm). This medieval cemetery, set outside the confines of the old city, is one of the country's most fascinating graveyards. The tombstones lie lengthwise above the graves, like so many coffins lined side by side, each simply decorated with a bowl of red-flowering plants. Look carefully on the "lids" – some show little scenes from the deceased person's life or trade chiselled into the stone.

Among the worthies buried in the graveyard is Albrecht Dürer. The **Albrecht-Dürer-Haus** (March–Oct Tues, Wed & Fri–Sun 10am–5pm, Thurs 10am–8pm; Nov–Feb Tues–Fri 1–5pm, Sat & Sun 10am–5pm; DM8/€4), where the versatile painter, engraver, scientist, writer, traveller and politician lived from 1509 to 1528, is virtually next door to the Tiergärtner Tor at Albrecht-Dürer-Str. 39. It's one of the very few original medieval houses still standing in the city, though there are many skilful reconstructions in the streets round about. Much of the furniture and decor dates back to the fifteenth century, giving a real sense of how people lived in the late Middle Ages. There's a fully functioning workshop from Dürer's time, where printing and other artistic techniques are demonstrated. A selection of the master's own graphic work is on display in the gallery beneath the eaves.

Southeast from here runs Bergstrasse, where at no. 19 you'll find the **Altstadthof**, a late sixteenth-century courtyard. Here you can visit the **Felsengänge** (guided tours daily at 11am, 1pm, 3pm & 5pm; DM7/€3.50), a series of sandstone storage cellars four floors deep which were used as shelters in World War II. There's also a museum-piece brewery, the **Altstadthof-Hausbrauerei**, which was put back into production a few years ago. Its main line is a wonderful unfiltered dark beer, though it also makes a light beer and various seasonal brews. These can be bought in bottles at the end of the tour, or sampled on draught in the adjoining bar (see p.170). At no. 52 on Obere Schmiedgasse, the next street to the north, is the entrance to another subterranean attraction, the **Historischer Kunstbunker** (guided tours April–Oct daily at 3pm; Jan–March Tues, Sat & Sun at 3pm; DM7/€3.50). The 24-metre-deep rock-cut cellars below the Kaiserburg were where the city's great art treasures were stored in moisture-proof cells during the war, thus saving them from the devastating effect the air raids had on the buildings where they were normally housed.

Proceeding southwards past the Weinmarkt, you come to the **Spielzeugmuseum** (Toy Museum; Tues & Thurs–Sun 10am–5pm, Wed 10am–9pm; DM5/€2.50) at Karlstr. 15. This celebrates Nürnberg's continuing role as the world metropolis of toy production by means of a thorough historical presentation of the craft. It's a must for kids – but is just as enjoyable for adults, who can enjoy a sentimental wallow in nostalgia. Further south, the huge half-timbered **Weinstadel**, a medieval wine depot, overlooks a particularly picturesque stretch of the Pegnitz, lined with weeping willows and spanned by the covered wooden walkway known as **Henkersteg** (Hangman's Bridge).

St Sebaldus

Nürnberg's oldest and most important church, the twin-towered **St Sebaldus**, lies just to the east of the Spielzeugmuseum via the quaint Weissgerbergasse. It was erected in the thirteenth century in the Transitional style, with choirs at each end of the building. A century later, the eastern choir was replaced by a soaring hall design. The exterior of the church drips with sculpture: on the south side are early fourteenth-century portals dedicated to the Last Judgement and to the Virgin Mary, while to the north is the slightly later Bridal Doorway, with its carvings of the Wise and Foolish Virgins.

An even more astonishing array of works of art can be found inside the church. Particularly striking is the bronze **shrine of St Sebald**, an early sixteenth-century masterpiece which combines late Gothic and Renaissance decoration and is heavy with religious symbols. **Peter Vischer the Elder**, aided by his two sons, took eleven years to complete this project. The figure of the master founder at work, dressed in skullcap and apron, has traditionally been assumed to be a self-portrait, but is now thought to be the work of Peter the Younger. On the pillar behind is an expressive *Crucifixion* scene (whose figures are taken from two separate groups, made two decades apart) by Nürnberg's most famous sculptor, Veit Stoss. The same artist also made the *St Andrew* and the three stone *Passion* reliefs on the end walls of the chancel.

The northeastern quarter

Immediately to the east of St Sebaldus is the **Altes Rathaus**, a self-confident late Renaissance building in the style of a Venetian *palazzo* which incorporates two older houses. If you're into the gorier side of medieval times, visit the torture chambers of its **Lochgefängnisse** (mid-April to mid-Oct Tues–Sun 10am–4.30pm; rest of year Tues-Fri at 4.30pm; DM4/€2). On a lighter note, go through to Rathausgasse to see one of the finest of the city's many fountains, the Renaissance **Gänsemännchen Brunnen**, which shows a farmer carrying two water-spouting geese to market.

Up the road at Burgstr. 15 is the **Stadtmuseum Fembohaus** (March–Oct Tues, Wed & Fri–Sun 10am–5pm, Thurs 10am–8pm; Nov–Feb Tues–Fri 1–5pm, Sat & Sun 10am–5pm; DM8/€4). Originally built at the end of the sixteenth century for a rich silk merchant, the mansion has truly startling interior decoration, featuring lurid colour schemes of pastel pink, yellow and green, with riotously ornate white stuccoed ceilings forming the icing on top. A number of interiors from other houses which failed to make it through the war have also been transferred here.

One of these comes from the **Pellerhaus** on the north side of nearby Egidienplatz. This was considered the finest patrician house in the city, but following almost total destruction by wartime bombs only the stately arcaded late Renaissance courtyard was rebuilt. Further along, in the shadow of the modern university buildings at Hirschelgasse 9–11, is the earlier **Tucherschlösschen** (Tues 10am–1pm, Thurs 10am–4pm, Sat & Sun 1–5pm; DM5/€2.50). This home of another (and, thanks to their beer, still prominent) Nürnberg dynasty survived in better shape, and was recently fully restored to serve as an illuminating illustration of the lifestyle enjoyed by its former owners. The exhibits include a portrait of Hans VI Tucher by Dürer's teacher Michael Wolgemut and a magnificent double goblet by Nürnberg's most distinguished silversmith of the Renaissance period, Wenzel Jamnitzer. At the northern end of the garden (not its original location), the **Hirsvogelsaal** (same times and ticket) was re-erected in 2000, having been in store since the war. Nürnberg's most spectacular patrician interior, it dates from the 1530s and is the work of two leading local artists: the sculptor Peter Flötner was responsible for the wall decoration, while Dürer's pupil Georg Pencz executed the colourful ceiling paintings.

The Hauptmarkt and around

Commercial heart of the city and main venue for the normal daily markets and the famous Christmas market, the **Hauptmarkt** lies just south of the Altes Rathaus, occupying the site of the Jewish quarter, which was razed to make way for it in a fourteenth-century pogrom. In the centre of the square stands a brightly coloured replica of the celebrated Gothic **Schöner Brunnen** (Beautiful Fountain). A tall stone pyramid chiselled out in filigree style and adorned with statues of the Electors accompanied by pagan, Jewish and Christian heroes, prophets, evangelists and Church Fathers, it has the dimensions of a great church spire rather than a mere fountain.

The Hauptmarkt's east side is bounded by the **Frauenkirche**. This little jewel of a church, commissioned by Emperor Charles IV as his court chapel, was one of the first buildings by the celebrated Parler family. Its facade, sheltering a porch with a delicately carved doorway dedicated to the Nativity, was enlivened in the early sixteenth century by the addition of a gable, an oriel and a clockwork mechanism known as the Männleinlaufen, which tinkles away each day at noon. The rather recondite story it tells is of the **Golden Bull** of 1356, whereby the church's founder established the identities of the seven Electors (here shown honouring him) on a permanent basis, as well as designating Nürnberg as the city in which every new emperor had to hold his first Imperial Diet. Among the works of art inside, pride of place goes to the *Tucher Altar* in the chancel, a late Gothic *Crucifixion* **triptych** painted by an unknown but highly expressive artist – now dubbed the Master of the Tucher Altar as a result – who was Nürnberg's finest painter of the period prior to Dürer.

Walking southwards from the Hauptmarkt, you cross the River Pegnitz by Museumsbrücke, which gives you a good view of the **Fleischbrücke** to the right (modelled on the Rialto Bridge in Venice) and the **Heilig-Geist-Spital** on the left. The latter – one of the largest hospitals built in the Middle Ages – stands on an islet, with two graceful arches spanning the water. Now a restaurant, it has an old-world inner courtyard with wooden galleries.

The southern quarter

Following Königstrasse south from the river, you shortly come to the parish church of **St Lorenz**. Its shape and ground plan are nearly identical to those of St Sebaldus, but this church of the southern of the two city-centre parishes is otherwise very different from its northern counterpart, with each of its constituent sections being about fifty years later in date. Thus the nave, complete with a majestic main portal and a resplendent rose window, is modelled on the High Gothic cathedrals in France, while the hall chancel, lit by a gleaming set of stained-glass windows, is in the Flamboyant style. Look out for the graceful late fifteenth-century **tabernacle** some 20m high, worked out of local sandstone by **Adam Kraft**, who depicted himself as a fiery, pensive figure crouching at the base. Equally spectacular is the larger-than-life polychrome wood

---

THE MASTERSINGERS OF NÜRNBERG

Nürnberg was only one of many homes of the distinctive form of lyric poetry known as **Meistergesang**, which flourished from the fourteenth century onwards, practised mainly by members of the skilled artisan class. The rules were highly pedantic, with words having to be fitted to *Töne* composed by thirteenth-century minstrels, and by the sixteenth century it had become a rather moribund art, despite a relaxation of the restrictions placed on the introduction of new *Töne*.

Nevertheless, it had a glorious final fling in Nürnberg, thanks above all to **Hans Sachs**. For a man who had to fit his literary activities into his spare time away from his trade of shoemaking, Sachs was unbelievably prolific, producing some six thousand works, including well over a hundred full-length plays which do not, however, show him at his best. Apart from some of the most accomplished *Meistergesänge*, Sachs wrote *Schwänke* (humorous stories told in doggerel verse) and *Fastnachtspiele* (dramatic interludes performed at Shrovetide). He was also a propagandist for the Reformation, coining Luther's proudly borne nickname of "the Nightingale of Wittenberg". That grandest of comic operas, Wagner's *The Mastersingers of Nürnberg*, is a celebration of the art of Sachs and his cronies; though historically rather wayward, it ranks as the most spectacular of the many tributes paid to the city by the Romantic movement.

Annunciation by **Veit Stoss** which is suspended from the ceiling above the high altar. It's set in a garland of roses and rosary beads and has seven small roundels illustrating the mysteries of this cult.

Outside the church is another wonderful fountain, the Mannerist **Tugendbrunnen**, in which water gushes from the breasts of the Seven Virtues and from the trumpets of the putti. Diagonally opposite is the oldest house in the city, the thirteenth-century **Nassauer Haus**. If you follow Karolinenstrasse west from here, you can see two notable modern additions to the city's tally of fountains. The **Peter-Henlein-Brunnen** on Hefnersplatz honours the local inventor who produced the first-ever pocket watch in the early sixteenth century. On Ludwigsplatz further west is the **Ehekarussell Brunnen**; illustrating a poem by the cobbler Hans Sachs (see box opposite), it displays six scenes from marriage, humorously alternating between bliss and nightmare.

Returning to Nassauer Haus and continuing down Königstrasse in the direction of the Hauptbahnhof you come to the massive and austere Renaissance **Mauthalle**, whose sloping roof is pierced by six tiers of windows. Formerly a granary and later a customs house, it now houses various stores plus another Hausbrauerei (see p.169). Beyond is the Gothic church of **St Martha**, the former hall of the Mastersingers.

The **Handwerkerhof** (mid-March to Dec 23 Mon–Fri 10am–6pm, Sat 10am–4pm; restaurants open till 10pm) by the Königstor, is an enclosed "medieval" village that brings to life historic Nürnberg trades such as handmade tin soldiers, dolls, brass objects and the famed *Lebkuchen* spice-cakes. Hot *Apfelstrudel* or the local delicacy of *Nürnberger Bratwürste* for sale in old-style taverns are very tasty.

Just outside the Altstadt to the west of here, at Lessingstr. 6, is the **Verkehrsmuseum** (Transport Museum; Tues–Sun 9am–5pm; DM6/€3). This actually contains two separate institutions – the **Museum für Post und Kommunikation**, which is devoted to the history of the postal services in Bavaria, and the **DB Museum**, the national railway museum. The latter has many ancient locomotives parked in its showrooms; these include a copy of the country's first train (named the *Adler* after Germany's eagle symbol) and the original of King Ludwig II's state train – which really does look like a miniature version on wheels of one of his fantasy castles. An instructive section on the role of rail during the Third Reich is also featured.

The Germanisches Nationalmuseum

The **Germanisches Nationalmuseum** (Tues & Thurs–Sun 10am–5pm, Wed 10am–9pm; *www.gnm.de*; DM6/€3, free Wed 6–9pm, when the museum is only partially open) on Kartäusergasse is one of the largest and most varied collections in the country. Its defining characteristic is that it is devoted exclusively to the German cultural tradition, which, in accordance with the perspective of its nineteenth-century founders, is taken to embrace Austria, Switzerland and the Netherlands. The museum occupies the late fourteenth-century **Karthaus** (Charterhouse) which is itself of considerable interest as one of the most complete examples of this type of monastery in Germany, though the modern galleries which have been added to provide badly needed extra display space seriously mar the effect.

On the **ground floor**, the first rooms contain the earliest items, ranging from a golden cone from the Bronze Age to the tenth-century *Echternach Gospels*. Immediately following is the section devoted to medieval **stone sculptures** from some of Nürnberg's most famous buildings (notably the Schöner Brunnen and the two parish churches), brought here for conservation, and replaced *in situ* with copies. You next enter the **Karthauskirche**, which still preserves the simple Gothic form favoured by the silent Carthusian monks. Exhibited here are the reliefs of the Seven Stations of the Cross by Adam Kraft, which originally lined the road to the Johannisfriedhof.

In the adjoining **cloister** are carvings by **Veit Stoss**, including an anguished *Crucifixion*, a light-hearted pair of *Tobias and the Archangel Raphael*, and the

Rosenkranztafel, a large wooden panel graphically portraying the drama of Judgement Day. A few sculptures by the other great woodcarver of the period, **Tilman Riemenschneider** – notably a noble figure of St Elizabeth – can be seen in the gallery beyond, which is chiefly devoted to fifteenth-century painting. The most important work here is *The Annunciation*, one of the best of the few surviving works of **Konrad Witz**, who played a crucial role in moving German painting towards a greater sense of realism: the perspective attempted in this panel is a world away from the flat backgrounds found in most of the other paintings here. Next comes an outstanding collection of historical **musical instruments**, which occupies the whole of the south wing.

German painting at its Renaissance peak dominates the north wing of the **first floor**, where you can see some **Dürer** originals. *Hercules Slaying the Stymphalian Birds* is a fairly early work, and the only mythological painting by the artist to have survived. The pair of imaginary portraits of *The Emperor Charlemagne* and *The Emperor Sigismund* were commissioned to adorn the room in which the imperial treasury (now in Vienna) was kept during the years it was displayed in Nürnberg; the actual crown, orb and sceptre are accurately depicted in the paintings. In contrast, *Emperor Maximilian I* and *Michael Wolgemut* are portraits made from life; the latter is a touching yet unsentimental portrayal of the artist's former teacher, by then a wrinkled old man of 82. Three panels from a dispersed series of *The Life of St Florian* by **Altdorfer** use the landscapes of the Danube valley to impressive effect; this same backdrop also occurs in **Baldung's** *Rest on the Flight into Egypt*. Most interesting of several works by **Cranach** is *King Christian II of Denmark*; the monarch had by then been deposed and had fled to Wittenberg, where he stayed as the artist's house guest.

The adjacent rooms focus on the diversity of Nürnberg's achievements during the Renaissance. There was a strong **goldsmith** tradition, shown to best effect in the superbly fashioned model of a three-masted ship. The city also played a leading role in the fast-developing science of geography, and you can see the first **globe** of the earth, made by Martin Behaim in 1491 – just before the discovery of America. From three-quarters of a century later is a globe of the heavens by Wenzel Jamnitzer. At the far end of the same wing is a collection of Dutch paintings, including a couple of small works by **Rembrandt**. This floor of the south wing and the storeys directly above it are entirely devoted to German **folklore**, in particular religious traditions which show the roots of customs still prevalent in rural areas.

The Nazi city

In virtually everyone's mind the word Nürnberg conjures up thoughts of Nazi rallies and the war-crime trials: in most peoples' memories are the scratchy black-and-white newsreels of fanatical crowds roaring *Sieg Heil*, and of Göring, Ribbentrop and other leaders standing in the dock a few years later. Nürnberg has the unenviable task of facing up to its historical role (see box opposite) more closely and openly than other cities, and the authorities, to their credit, are slowly but surely making positive moves towards helping visitors get to grips with the events of that time. For further background information, it's worth asking at the tourist office for the leaflet *Nürnberg 1933–1945*.

Luitpoldhain

The park known as the **Luitpoldhain** in the southeastern suburbs of the city, where many of the Nazi buildings still stand, has been dedicated to the memory of their victims, though it is also used for commercial and recreational purposes. If this seems a somewhat incongruous mix, it is in reality a case of history turning full circle, as the Luitpoldhain was originally laid out for the Bavarian Jubilee Exhibition of 1906, and was later a memorial for the dead of World War I before being commandeered by the Nazis.

NÜRNBERG UNDER THE NAZIS

As the present city council is eager to point out, the Nazis' choice of Nürnberg as the backdrop for their *Reichsparteitage* had little to do with local support of the "brown" ideology. Indeed, in marked contrast to Munich, the votes cast for them here in each of the elections before their assumption of power were derisory. The crucial factor was what the medieval city represented in German history: not only had it been the de facto capital, its rapid rise to prominence was seen as showing the nation's dynamism at its very peak. Also, the local police made it very easy for the NSDAP to gain the upper hand here, since they resented centralized Bavarian control and hoped to gain more independence if the Nazis took over.

The first of the **Nürnberg rallies** was held in 1927; between 1933 and 1938 they were an annual event, Hitler using the 1938 rally to raise world tension during the Munich crisis. As the most important display of Nazi power for home and foreign consumption, they were highly organized and ritualized mass demonstrations. Hitler's speeches formed the climax of the show, the intention being to underline his own unquestioned status as *Führer* and the total unity of purpose existing between the leadership and the led. Up to 250,000 people took part in these events, which were expertly stage-managed and totally hypnotic for the mass of participants. The sheer organizational skills which had to be brought to bear were themselves a form of preparation for war – and intended as a further warning to potential enemies. Leni Riefenstahl's film *Triumph of the Will*, a lyrical hymn to Nazism, is the best record of the week-long rallies.

There was no more fanatical proponent of the Nazis' anti-Semitic policies than the Franconian party chief, **Julius Streicher**, who strode around the city administering instant "justice" with his whip, and whose depravities reached such depths that even fellow party members felt sickened. His odious anti-Semitic newspaper, *Der Stürmer*, was specifically designed to stir up hysteria against the Jews, with its stories of their alleged child sacrifices and sexual perversities. The highlight of his career came with the passing of the so-called **Nürnberg Laws** in 1935, which deprived Jews of their citizenship and forbade relations between Jews and Gentiles. It was through these laws that the Nazis justified their extermination of six million Jews, ten thousand of whom came from Nürnberg – where the Jewish population was reduced to single figures by the end of the war.

So great was Nürnberg's identification with the proudest demonstrations of power of the Third Reich that it was deliberately chosen by the victorious Allies as the place for the **war-crime trials**, which are graphically recounted in Rebecca West's book *A Train of Powder*. The surviving leading players of the "Thousand Year Reich", before whom an entire nation had trembled for twelve years, now mostly appeared as broken men – and were shown up publicly as the ragbag of fanatics and misfits they had in reality always been. Ten of the most important Nazis – Ribbentrop, Keitel, Kaltenbrunner, Rosenberg, Frank, Frick, Streicher, Seyss-Inquart, Sauckel and Jodl – were successively hanged here at short intervals in the early hours of October 16, 1946. Former Reichsmarschall Hermann Göring committed suicide by swallowing a concealed cyanide pill two hours before his appointed execution. Of the rest, Hess, Funk and Raeder were confined to prison for life, while Speer, Schirach, Dönitz and Neurath were all given long-term sentences. Three men were acquitted: the propaganda officer Hans Fritzsche; Franz von Papen, the bungling ex-Chancellor who was more responsible than anyone else for Hitler's initial assumption of power; and Hjalmar Schacht, the financial guru who had managed the economic affairs of the Third Reich with the same enthusiasm, shrewdness and lack of political concern as he had shown when running the national economy in the days of the Weimar Republic.

At the northern entrance to the park, reached from the city centre by tram #9 or bus #36, is the **Luitpoldarena**, where parades of Nazi groups such as the SA and SS were held. Its grounds contained the former exhibition hall where the party conferences were held, but this was completely destroyed by bombing in 1945. The custom-built but unfinished **Kongressbau** behind, however, remains standing, and is the most chilling surviving visual reminder of the pretensions of the Third Reich. Built in the debased Neoclassical style beloved of modern totalitarian dictators, it self-consciously tries to present an updated, upstaging version of Rome's Colosseum. For decades, all attempts to find a suitable permanent use for this monstrosity came to naught – part of it was used as a store, and it was pressed into occasional service for crowd-pulling pop concerts – but from 2001 it should at last be open to the general public (see below).

To the rear, the **Grosse Strasse** leads over the artificial lake down to another parade ground, the **Märzfeld**. The dimensions of this road – 2km long and 60m wide – are awesome; the vista it opens up includes a distant view of the Kaiserburg, thus creating a visual reference to the symbolic union the Nazis wished to have with the medieval city. Nowadays, part of it is used as a car park by visitors to the modern trade fair buildings nearby. You can return to the Kongressbau by taking the path to the east. This passes firstly the **Stadion**, used for meetings of the Hitler Youth but now returned to its original purpose as a sports venue as home of the football club FC Nürnberg. Further north is the **Zeppelinfeld**, which was transformed by Albert Speer (Hitler's favourite architect, and subsequently armaments minister) into a stadium for the most important parades. The colonnaded tribunes, so familiar from old films, had to be dismantled for safety reasons, but the towers and terraces remain. Nowadays, the complex is used as a sports centre and for the celebrated **Norisring car races** in late June. (Information and tickets are available from MCN Motorsport-Club Nürnberg, Spittlertorgraben 47, ☎09 11/26 79 90.) At the back is the entrance to a multimedia presentation on the city's Nazi legacy, **Faszination und Gewalt** (Fascination and Force; May–Oct Tues–Sun 10am–6pm; DM2/€1). By autumn 2001, this is due to be replaced by a more extensive documentation centre in the Kongressbau.

The Landgericht Nürnberg-Fürth

In 2000, limited public access was belatedly introduced to the setting of the Nürnberg trials, the **Landgericht Nürnberg-Fürth** (guided tours Sat & Sun 1–4pm; free), a still-functioning courthouse at Fürther Str. 110 which can be reached by taking U-Bahn #1 or #11 to Bärenschanze. Courtroom 600 was specially reconstructed for the trials, which were mould-breaking both in the depth of evidence presented (240 witnesses were called and over 300,000 statements examined) and in introducing three new offences: crimes against peace, war crimes and crimes against humanity. As such, they have served as a model for all subsequent attempts at regulating international order by the force of law, though circumstances have seldom permitted repetitions of the clear-cut outcome that was achieved here.

Eating, drinking and entertainment

Nürnberg is the liveliest Bavarian city next to Munich, with a wealth of watering-holes and nightspots to suit all tastes and pockets. If the Bavarian's favourite snack is a *Weisswurst*, the Franconian's is a *Bratwurst* – a slim **pork sausage** roasted over wood fires and usually served at least six at a time, with a choice of sauerkraut, potato salad, onions or radishes as accompaniment. The most curious culinary feature of Nürnberg is that these sausages have been turned into an item of serious cuisine, best sampled in the highly rated speciality restaurants to the accompaniment of a glass of one of the wide variety of beers produced by the local Tucher or Lederer breweries. Equally ubiquitous are *Nürnberger Lebkuchen*, delicious **cakes** made from flour, nuts, honey, eggs and spices. Usually they're only eaten around Christmas, but here you can buy them all year round. The best-known maker is Lebkuchen Schmidt, which has shops in the

Handwerkerhof and by the southeastern corner of the Hauptmarkt at Plobenhofstr. 6. While many of the obviously recommendable places to eat and drink are in or near the Altstadt, it's also worth taking the U-Bahn to the grand nineteenth-century inner suburbs to the west, where there are some enticing alternatives.

Nürnberg hosts numerous festivals, as well as a predictably wide choice of entertainment all year round. For details of what's on, consult either the *Monatsmagazin* (DM2/€1), available from the tourist office, or *Plärrer* (DM4/€2), the city's **listings magazine**, on sale at any kiosk.

Sausage restaurants

Bratwurst-Friedl, Hallplatz 21. Offers a full, moderately priced menu in addition to the sausage specialities. Closed Sun.

Bratwurst-Glöcklein, Im Handwerkerhof. Despite its commercialized position in the crafts market, the food here can rival that of any of its competitors. Closed Sun.

Bratwurst-Häusle, Rathausplatz 1. With its huge chimney for grilling the sausages smoking over the main square, this is the most famous of the group: in spite of the restricted menu and frequent tourist hordes, it really shouldn't be missed. Closed Sun.

Bratwurst-Röslein, Obstmarkt 1. Has a wide-ranging menu in addition to the traditional sausage fare, and actively campaigns for low restaurant prices. Closed Mon.

Historische Bratwurstküche Zum Gulden Stern, Zirkelschmiedsgasse 26. Housed in a renovated fifteenth-century tavern, with a truly *gemütlich* atmosphere. Closed Sun.

Other restaurants

Barockhäusle, Johannisstr. 47. A multifunctional restaurant, café and beer garden in a Baroque house between the Kaiserburg and the Johannisfriedhof.

Böhms Herrenkeller, Theatergasse 19. Popular old wine bar-cum-restaurant. Closed Sun.

Essigbrätlein, Weinmarkt 3. One of the city's top restaurants for both international and traditional German cuisine. Very expensive; closed Sun & Mon.

Frankenstube, Pilotystr. 73. Situated north of the Altstadt, this combines reasonably priced food, including vegetarian dishes, with a good atmosphere.

Goldenes Posthorn, Glöckleinsgasse 2. A Gaststätte which has been on the go since the time of Dürer, and is still among the best in the city.

Heilig-Geist-Spital, Spitalgasse 12. Occupying the medieval hospital, this is arguably the city's most atmospheric restaurant; the food is outstanding too.

Ishihara, Schottengasse 3. Highly rated, fairly expensive Japanese restaurant.

Kettensteg, Maxplatz 35. Traditional Gasthaus with picturesque beer garden by the River Pegnitz.

Krakauer Turm, Vordere Insel Schütt 34. Polish restaurant and cultural centre (a spin-off of Nürnberg's twinning link with Kraków) in one of the medieval towers of the Stadtbefestigung.

Mount Lavinia, Jakobsplatz 22. The first and best Sinhalese restaurant in Germany; also serves Thai dishes. Bargain lunches are offered on weekdays; at weekends it's open evenings only.

Nassauer Keller, Karolinenstr. 2. Highly rated restaurant in the cellars of Nürnberg's oldest house.

Pele-Mele, Grossweidenmühlstr. 17. Bistro just west of the Altstadt which presents a choice of riverside beer garden or cool vaulted cellar in which to have your meal.

Tucherbräu am Opernhaus, Kartäusergasse 1. Gaststätte of the Tucher brewery, with a small beer garden perched directly over the city's ramparts.

Zum Schuldturm Heubrücke, Vordere Insel Schütt 4. Gaststätte with the nicest beer garden in the Altstadt, directly overlooking the Pegnitz.

Zum Sudhaus, Bergstr. 20. Well-regarded, fairly pricey restaurant with engagingly rustic decor.

Bars

Barfüsser, Hallplatz 2. Hausbrauerei in the cavernous cellars of the Mauthalle, whose walls are lined with pictures of film stars of the Fifties and Sixties. It brews a *Weisse* as well as light and dark beers; the food is inexpensive and typically hearty.

Landwehrkeller, Innere-Laufer-Gasse 11. Good choice for late-night drinking (and eating); also has occasional live music.

Lederer-Kulturbrauerei, Sielstr. 12. The tap of the adjacent Lederer brewery, whose main product is an olive-coloured beer known as *Krokodil*. It has a capacious beer garden and also serves very traditional Franconian fare. Take U-Bahn #1 or #11 to Bärenschanze.

O'Neill's, Bärenschanzstr. 121. The pick of the local Irish pubs is situated well off the beaten track; take U-Bahn #1 or #11 to Bärenschanze.

Palais Schaumburg, Kernstr. 46. Reached by taking U-Bahn #1 or #11 to Gostenhof, this has a beer garden, and also serves inexpensive meals, including an extensive vegetarian menu.

Schwarzer Bauer, Bergstr. 19. This small Kneipe is attached to the Altstadthof-Hausbrauerei mentioned on p.162. It also serves the products of its parent, the out-of-town Lammsbräu.

Werkstatt, Adam-Klein-Str. 87. A real oddity: features spare car parts for interior design, and beer served out of a petrol pump. Take U-Bahn #1 or #11 to Maximilianstrasse. On Sat it's open evenings only, on Sun it closes at 6pm.

Zig-Zag, Rohledererstr. 6. Serves excellent Spanish meals in a bar-type setting, a short distance northwest of the Altstadt.

Cafés and café-bars

Balazzo Brozzi, Hochstr. 2. Located just west of the Altstadt, this is a good place to start the day if you want a choice of cheap and decent breakfast dishes.

Café Dampfnudel-Bäcker, Johannisstr. 34. Old-fashioned café specializing in steamed dumplings.

Café Kroll, Hauptmarkt 6. The pick of the traditional *Kaffee und Kuchen* establishments, with a terrace overlooking the main square.

Meisengeige, Am Laufer Schlagturm 3. Tiny café-bar catering for a mixed and unpretentious crowd; there's also a small cinema attached that runs an off-beat selection of films you won't find in the commercial venues.

Mohr, Färberstr. 3. Candlelit café-bar in the western Altstadt.

Ruhestörung, Tetzelgasse 21. One of the main young and trendy watering-holes, with raucous music.

Wiener Spezialitäten Café, Kaiserstr. 1. As its name suggests, this is a Viennese-style coffee house.

Music bars and nightclubs

Bezirk 40, Humboldstr. 116. Cosy place offering TV, video games and pinball machines, which is popular with people who like going to nightclubs without having to make too much of an effort. Also serves food. Daily 7pm–1am.

Mach 1, Kaiserstr. 1–9. Currently the city's trendiest nightspot; the four different bars ensure variety, and there are some good lighting effects. Thurs–Sat 10pm–4am.

Rock-Café Brown Sugar, Königstorgraben 3. A couple of minutes' walk north of the Hauptbahnhof, this is the best of the city's seemingly endless number of heavy metal bars, with pinball machines and videos among the heady attractions.

Schmelztiegel, Bergstr. 21. Jazz bar which plays predominantly Dixieland.

Starclub, Maxtorgraben 33. Combination of a music bar and traditional beer haven, complete with garden.

Zabo-Linde, Zerzabelshofer Hauptstr. 28, Zerzabelshof. Both a traditional Gaststätte with beer garden and a regular venue for live music, ranging from rock to disco. Worth making the trip out for, if the evening's music programme appeals – check in the *Plärrer*, Nürnberg's listings magazine (see p.169). It's in an eastern suburb, reached by bus #43 or #44 to Zerzabelshof/Mitte.

Cultural venues

Die Bühne im Altstadthof, Bergstr. 19 (☎09 11/22 43 27). Small dramatic stage in the Altstadt.

Meistersingerhalle, Münchener Str. 21 (☎09 11/49 20 11). Located 2km southeast of the centre, this is the main venue for concerts by the Nürnberger Symphoniker, among others.

Opernhaus, Richard-Wagner-Platz 2 (☎09 11/2 31 38 08). Located in a grand Historicist building just west of the Hauptbahnhof, this presents operas, operettas and dance.

NÜRNBERG'S FESTIVALS

Nürnberg really comes alive in the summer when open-air music festivals and concerts abound. The season starts off in late May with *Musica Franconia*, a week-long series of concerts of old music played on period instruments. For a fortnight in June, the *Kulturzirkus*, an international theatre festival, is held. Towards the end of the same month begins the three-week-long *Internationale Orgelwoche*, featuring organ recitals in the city's churches and in the *Meistersingerhalle*; the office for information and tickets is at Bismarckstr. 46 (☎09 11/16 35 28). The *Bardentreffen* in the last week of July or first week of August is a popular annual event where singers and songwriters from Europe come together in free open-air concerts all over the city. An equally high status is enjoyed by the *Ost-West Jazzfestival* in the last week of October, which encompasses every jazz style and brings together musicians from around the world.

Prominent among folklore festivals is the *Altstadtfest* at the end of September, a local fair celebrating Franconian culture, with lots of food and drink, as well as river tournaments and a procession in traditional costumes. Finally, with a 400-year tradition, the Nürnberg *Christkindlesmarkt* (Christmas market) held on the Hauptmarkt from November 25 until December 24, is the largest and most popular in Germany, as well as being the founder of what has become very much a national institution, with derivatives found in every town of any size. It stands apart from its imitators by the wealth of handmade quality goods on sale, such as toys, brass utensils and tin soldiers, glass objects of all kinds, and, of course, the delicious *Lebkuchen*.

Schauspielhaus, Richard-Wagner-Platz 2 (☎09 11/2 31 38 08). Within the same complex as the Opernhaus, this has both large and small stages.

Erlangen

Just 20km north of Nürnberg, and now regarded as an integral part of its conurbation, **ERLANGEN** is nevertheless a town with its own distincitve history, traditions and appearance. Following the ending of religious toleration in France by the revocation of the Edict of Nantes in 1683, a large number of Huguenots settled here at the invitation of Margrave Christian Ernst of Bayreuth. A new **planned town** of regular streets and squares in the sober Baroque style then current in Protestant circles was built to accommodate them; this was extended to cover the whole of the city when the medieval Altstadt was destroyed by fire twenty years later. The Huguenots, skilled in textiles and leather crafts, established Erlangen's reputation as a major industrial centre, a tradition maintained today by electro-technics and power engineering. Indeed, Erlangen might be regarded almost as a company town of Siemens, were it not for the presence of the university, founded in 1743 and now shared with Nürnberg. The presence of so many students ensures an almost continuously lively atmosphere, and helps transform what might otherwise seem a place of specialist appeal.

The Town

Arriving at the Hauptbahnhof, at the western side of town, you're immediately confronted with the quarter of the original refugees. Across Bahnhofplatz stand the parish administration buildings of the **Hugenottenkirche**, which fronts the eponymous square on the far side. Outside, it appears as a plain box, enlivened only by the tower which was added a generation after the main body of the building. Inside, the wooden galleries have been arranged to give the illusion that the church is round in shape; otherwise, the pulpit provides the only decorative touch. Across Hugenottenplatz is the

Universitätskirche, which has a similar tower but is otherwise less austere, its double-galleried hall interior, in which pulpit and altar are combined in a single unit, being enlivened with rich stuccowork. A fine group of eighteenth-century houses, including the old pharmacy, stand around the church.

A couple of blocks to the north, divided by the pedestrian section of the central Hauptstrasse, are two more important squares. To the west is Marktplatz, on whose southern side is the **Stutterheimsches Palais**, formerly the Rathaus, now the public library and main local cultural centre. Across the road is Schlossplatz, in the centre of which stands a statue to Margrave Friedrich, the founder of the university. The **Schloss** itself, which takes up the entire eastern side of the square, now serves as the university's administrative headquarters. Despite Erlangen's association with technology, its academic tradition has been strongest in the humanities. Three of Germany's best-known nineteenth-century philosophers – Fichte, Schelling and Feuerbach – taught here. However, the most famous professor was the Orientalist **Friedrich Rückert**, who introduced poetry based on Persian, Sanskrit and Chinese models into the German language. Schubert and Brahms were among the composers who set his texts, while Mahler's kaleidoscopic song cycles *Rückert-Lieder* and *Kindertotenlieder* have raised his artistic standing to a level far beyond its purely literary merit.

Some compensation for the loss of the Schloss's original interiors in a nineteenth-century fire comes with the **Schlosspark** to the rear. The first part of this is a formal French garden, closed off by the horseshoe-shaped **Orangerie** to the north, and with the **Hugenottenbrunnen**, a large allegorical fountain, as centrepiece. Further reaches of the park are laid out in the English manner; tucked away in the middle is an equestrian memorial to Margrave Christian Ernst.

Immediately north of the Schloss is the **Wasserturm**, which served as the student prison for most of nineteenth century. Northeast of here is Theaterplatz, whose south side is lined by the three buildings primarily responsible for Erlangen's continued high standing in the dramatic field. The **Markgrafentheater**, indeed, is the town's finest feature, a part-Baroque part-Rococo jewel worthy of Bayreuth itself and still put to regular use. Alongside it stand the **Redoutensaal**, built as the main festival hall of the local Margraves, and the **Marstall** (stables), now the home of the experimental Theater in der Garage. North of here, at the top end of Hauptstrasse, the **Dreifaltigkeitskirche** was originally the parish church of the Altstadt, but rebuilt in the Lutheran Baroque style of its two counterparts in the new town. Once again the pulpit and altar blend seamlessly into one.

Beyond the built-up area are the ample open spaces of the **Burgberg**, the main public park. For eleven days up to and including Pentecost (variable date in May/June) each year, this is the site of the **Bergkirchweih**, one of Bavaria's leading folk festivals. It's rather like a smaller version of Munich's *Oktoberfest*, with orgies of beer drinking in massive tents, hairy funfair rides and performances of traditional and rock music. However, it is less blatantly commercialized and thus more authentically German, and all the attractions are concentrated in a manageable area.

Practicalities

The **tourist office** (May–Oct Mon–Fri 8am–6pm, Sat 10am–noon; Nov–April Mon–Thurs 8am–4.30pm, Fri 8am–12.30pm; ☎0 91 31/8 95 10, fax 89 51 51, *www. erlangen.de*) is beyond the southern end of Hauptstrasse at Rathausplatz 1. Budget **hotels** in the centre include *Gasthof Schwarzer Bär*, just south of the Hauptbahnhof at Innere-Brucker-Str. 19 (☎0 91 31/2 28 72; ③), and *Gasthof Oppelei*, Halbmondstr. 4 (☎0 91 31/2 15 62; ③). There are plenty of more upmarket options, including *Grauer Wolf*, Hauptstr. 80 (☎0 91 31/8 10 60; ⑤), *Altmann's Stube*, Theaterplatz 9 (☎0 91 31/8 91 60; ⑤), and *Rokokohaus*, Theaterplatz 13 (☎0 91 31/78 30; ⑥). The **youth hostel** is right in the heart of town at Südliche Stadtmauerstr. 35 (☎0 91 31/86 22 74, fax 86 21 19; DM21/€10.50), while the riverside **campsite**, *Naturfreunde*, is a short walk to the rear of the Hauptbahnhof at Wöhrmühle 6 (☎0 91 31/2 53 03).

All the hotels listed above, except for *Rokokohaus*, have **restaurants**. Good alternatives are *Grüner Markt*, just off Marktplatz at Einhornstr. 9; *Weinstube Kach*, Kirchenstr. 2; and *Bärengarten*, below the Burgberg at Rathsberger Str. 2. Plenty of student bars and discos can also be found dotted all over the town centre.

Ansbach

ANSBACH, 50km southwest of Nürnberg and less than a tenth of the size, is nevertheless the capital of the province of Middle Franconia. With only a relatively short interregnum, it has had capital status ever since 1331, when it became the seat of the first principality established by the Hohenzollerns. For most of its history, this was known as the Margravate of Brandenburg-Ansbach, though it was never the frontier district its name would suggest: the title was transferred from the dynasty's subsequent power base of Brandenburg after the latter was promoted to the rank of an Electorate of the Holy Roman Empire. The town wears a grand air which is quite disproportionate to its small size, and is well endowed with handsome buildings from a variety of architectural periods. It has also gone down in the annals of German history as the site of the unsolved murder of **Kaspar Hauser**, the notorious foundling.

The Town

The dominant building is the huge **Residenzschloss** (guided tours April–Sept Tues–Sun 9am–6pm; Oct–March Tues–Sun 10am–4pm; DM6/€3) at the southeastern edge of the Altstadt. It was originally a moated castle, and a Gothic hall which survives

---

THE MYSTERY OF KASPAR HAUSER

One day in 1828, a plainly dressed, bewildered-looking youth turned up in the streets of Nürnberg, carrying two letters addressed to the authorities. One was from a labourer who claimed to have guarded him for the past sixteen years, albeit in conditions of close confinement; the other purported to be from his natural mother, stating that his deceased father had been a cavalry officer. The boy gave his name as **Kaspar Hauser**, but he was unable to tell anyone where he came from, shunned all nourishment except for bread and water and seemed to lack all knowledge of external objects. His appearance caused an immediate sensation in the local press; this soon spread across Germany and beyond, fuelled by the burgeoning interest in psychology and the abnormal. There were all kinds of wild speculations as to his origins: one theory that was particularly popular was that he was the eldest son of Grand Duke Carl Ludwig of Baden, who had been kidnapped by order of his stepmother, though this seemed to be contradicted by evidence that the child in question had died in infancy, and was conclusively disproved by DNA tests carried out in 1997. In due course Kaspar was educated and proved to be highly intelligent and creative. He moved to Ansbach in 1831, becoming clerk to the president of the court of appeal. Two years later, just as he seemed to be falling out of the limelight, he met his violent death there. His murderer was never found, adding a final unsettling mystery to his life story: many suspected that he had died by his own hand. Much has been written about him since, little of it conclusive.

A highly effective fictionalization of the story by the Jewish author Jakob Wassermann, which was once among the most widely read German novels, is the most rewarding book on the subject.

from this contains the ticket office and a collection of locally made porcelain. In its present form, the complex dates almost entirely from a rebuilding undertaken between the late seventeenth and mid-eighteenth centuries. Initially, the work was carried out in a classicizing form of Baroque by the Italian Gabriel de Gabrieli, and the most striking feature of this is the inner **courtyard**, with its three tiers of open arcades. The last phase of construction was entrusted to the Rococo architect and interior designer Leopold Retti, who was responsible for the magnificent suite of 27 chambers on the first floor. With a single exception, these preserve their original decoration absolutely intact: the abdication of the last margrave in 1791 spelt an end to the building's function as a residential palace, and thus it was never modernized. The only room in the grand manner is the **Festsaal**, which has elaborate stuccowork and a ceiling fresco by Carlo Carlone glorifying the wise government of the patron, Margrave Carl Wilhelm Friedrich. All the other chambers are intimate in scale, and are grouped into three separate groups of apartments – for the margrave, the margravine and guests. Each has one highly idiosyncratic room: respectively these are the **Marmorkabinett** (Marble Cabinet), the **Spiegelkabinett** (Cabinet of Mirrors) and the **Gekachelter Saal** (Tiled Room), which is covered with 2800 delicately designed tiles made in the local factory.

Right in the heart of the Altstadt is the church of **St Gumbertus**. Originally it was part of a Romanesque collegiate foundation, but the only survivor from that period is the **crypt** (Fri–Sun 11am–noon & 3–5pm), which later served as the pantheon of the local margraves. Directly above is the Gothic chancel, which was converted to serve as the **Schwannenritterordenkapelle**, and shelters the elaborate epitaphs and death shields of members of the Order of the Swan, a lay foundation of Margrave Albrecht Achilles. The **nave** was remodelled in the eighteenth century into a vast preaching hall according to the restrained Lutheran tastes of the day. It's a classic among German Protestant churches – all slate grey and cream, without paintings or side altars, it presents a cool clarity, in which the focus is placed firmly on the small marble altar and the pulpit above.

To the rear of St Gumbertus is the **Beringershof**, a sixteenth-century mansion with a beautiful galleried courtyard, complete with a stair tower. On the west side of the church lies the sixteenth-century **Stadthaus**, the seat of the mayor and town council. Beyond is the main square, **Martin-Luther-Platz**, which is dominated by **St Johannis**, a large Gothic hall church built for parish use and containing an altar by the Nürnberg sculptor Peter Flötner. Just to the north, down Schaitbergerstrasse, is the **Markgrafenmuseum** (Tues–Sun 10am–noon & 2–5pm; DM2/€1). One part of this is devoted to the history of the margravate; the other, on the opposite side of the road, documents the life and times of **Kaspar Hauser** in a comprehensive fashion, though you'll need to have some German to get the most from the display. The exhibits include the bloodstained coat he was wearing when he was murdered, and it was a DNA sample taken from this which finally laid to rest the theory that he was an unwanted member of Baden's grand ducal family. For more on Hauser, see the box on p.173.

At the far southern end of the Altstadt is the **Herrieder Tor**, a medieval gateway refashioned in the Baroque period. On Rosenbadstrasse, a short distance to the northwest, is the **Synagoge**, which was built by Leopold Retti in the 1740s. It deserves to be considered as one of the most beautiful surviving Jewish temples in Germany, but its interior can unfortunately only be seen on guided tours of the town: these are held at 11am every Sunday between May and September and depart from **Anscavallo**, an avant-garde statue of a horse directly opposite the Residenzschloss.

Just to the southeast of the Altstadt is **Karlsplatz**, a monumental square planned in the late seventeenth century as the focal point of a Huguenot suburb. It was only completed in 1840, ironically enough with the building of the Neoclassical **Ludwigskirche**, the main Catholic church in this staunchly Protestant town. Further east lies the

Hofgarten, which contains both formal gardens and "natural" sections with centuries-old trees. Its **Orangerie** is a fine French-style Baroque building near which, at the spot where Kaspar Hauser received his fatal stab wounds, is a stone memorial with the inscription: "Here died a man unknown by means unknown."

Practicalities

Ansbach's **Bahnhof,** the junction of the Nürnberg–Stuttgart and Munich–Würzburg lines, is a few minutes' walk south of the centre. The **tourist office** (May–Oct Mon–Fri 9am–5pm, Sat 10am–1pm; Nov–April Mon–Fri 9am–12.30pm & 2–5pm; ☎09 81/5 12 43, fax 5 13 65, *www.ansbach.de*) is in the Stadthaus, Johann-Sebastian-Platz 1.

Of the centrally sited **hotels,** the lowest rates are at *Augustiner,* Karolinenstr. 30 (☎09 81/24 32; ③), and *Christl,* Richard-Wagner-Str. 39–41 (☎09 81/81 21; ④). There are several more upmarket options, including *Schwarzer Bock,* Pfarrstr. 31 (☎09 81/42 12 40; ⑤), *Der Platengarten,* Promenade 30 (☎09 81/97 14 20; ⑤–⑦); *Am DrechselsGarten,* Am Drechselsgarten 1 (☎09 81/8 90 20; ⑦), and *Bürger-Palais,* Neustadt 48 (☎09 81/9 51 31; ⑦), a beautifully renovated Baroque mansion. All these, except *Christl* and *Bürger-Palais,* have **restaurants,** which rank as the best in town; that of *Der Platengarten* also has the benefit of a beer garden. Another popular eatery with the same facility is *Zum Mohren,* Pfarrstr. 9.

A number of **festivals** take place in Ansbach, of which the best known is the *Bach-Woche,* which is held in the two civic churches at the end of July in even-numbered years. The *Ansbacher Rokokospiele* are period plays, music and dance events performed in the Residenzschloss and the local parks in late June and early July each year, while in early August various artistic events based around the story of the mysterious foundling are enacted under the title of the *Kaspar-Hauser-Festspiele.* Held every four years (next in 2002), the *Heimatfest* is a grand occasion where eighteenth-century music and dance play the most important part, but there's also a fair with plenty of regional delicacies.

Bayreuth

The capital of Upper Franconia, polished and respectable **BAYREUTH,** which lies some 80km northeast of Nürnberg, enjoys its reputation as one of the great cultural centres of Europe. Except for the five-week festival period beginning in the second half of July, it's a quiet provincial town, which was something of a late developer, only coming to prominence in 1603 when it displaced nearby Kulmbach as the seat of the second of the Hohenzollerns' Franconian principalities. Its subsequent fame is due to a series of imported creative spirits, two of whom played defining roles. The first of these was **Wilhelmine of Prussia,** Frederick the Great's elder sister, who was intended for the British royal throne, but was married off instead in 1732 to her amiable but dull kinsman, the future Margrave Friedrich of Brandenburg-Bayreuth. Instead of settling down to obscurity, Wilhelmine set about creating a vibrant courtly life, employing architects, painters, interior designers, landscape gardeners and musicians from all over Europe. The following century, **Richard Wagner** decided to settle in Bayreuth because the town offered to build him a stage large enough to put on his grand-scale opera productions, and the festival he founded, the *Richard-Wagner-Festspiele,* soon established itself as one of the great annual events of the music world. In common with everything else to do with Wagner, it was tarnished by association with Hitler's patronage and exploitation for propaganda purposes, but continues to flourish, with demand for tickets always exceeding supply many times over.

Arrival and accommodation

Bayreuth's **Hauptbahnhof** is a short walk north of the town centre. The **tourist office** is at Luitpoldplatz 9 (Mon–Fri 9am–6pm, Sat 9.30am–1pm; ☎09 21/8 85 88, fax 8 85 55, *www.bayreuth.de*). At DM17.50/€8.75 for three days, the **Bayreuth Card** is a good investment: it covers travel on the local buses (beware that some of these use different numbers for opposite directions of the same route) plus entrance to the local museums (but not the palaces and opera houses).

If visiting Bayreuth for the festival, you should reserve **accommodation** well in advance, preferably as soon as you receive your tickets, though it's normally possible to find a room at short notice. Note that **hotels**, of which the town has a plentiful supply in all categories, jack up their prices (usually by around 50 percent) for the duration of the festival. The **youth hostel** is in the southeastern part of town, almost next door to the university at Universitätsstr. 28 (☎09 21/25 12 62, fax 51 28 05; DM21/€10.50); bus #4 runs there regularly, though it's no more than a fifteen-minute walk from the centre.

Hotels

Bayerischer Hof, Bahnhofstr. 14 (☎09 21/7 86 00, fax 7 86 05 60, *hotel@bayerischer-hof.de*). One of several swanky hotels around the Hauptbahnhof; it also has a fine French-style bistro-restaurant. ⑦.

Eremitage, Eremitage 6 (☎09 21/79 99 70, fax 7 99 97 11). Located in the former stables of the Eremitage (see p.181), this has only six rooms, so should be booked well in advance. Its gourmet restaurant, *Cuvée* (evenings only, closed Sun), is among the very best in Bayreuth; in summer there's also a moderately priced daytime equivalent, complete with beer garden. ⑥.

Friedrichsthal, Laineck (☎09 21/9 25 10). Welcoming pension with restaurant in a rustic, very secluded riverside setting in the valley almost directly below the Friedrichsthal terminus of buses #1 and #3. ③.

Goldener Anker, Opernstr. 6 (☎09 21/6 50 51, fax 6 55 00). Old-fashioned hotel with restaurant (evenings only, closed Tues), run by the same family since 1753. It's close to the Opernhaus and has been much patronized by singers and conductors. ⑥.

Goldener Löwe, Kulmbacher Str. 30 (☎09 21/74 60 60, fax 4 77 77, *www.goldenerloewe.de*). Cosy Gasthof of the nearby Maisel brewery. Its restaurant (closed Sun evening) serves the full range of beers as well as excellent food. ⑤.

Hirsch, St Georgen 26 (☎09 21/2 67 14). Inexpensive Gasthof on the splendid main street of the St Georgen suburb, a short distance east of the Hauptbahnhof. Its restaurant is open Mon–Fri only. ②.

Kropf, Tristanstr. 8 (☎09 21/2 62 98). Good-value Gasthof in the north of town, near the Festspielhaus. ②–⑤.

Lohmühle, Badstr. 37 (☎09 21/5 30 60, fax 5 30 64 69, *www.hotel-lohmuehle.de*). Located in an old mill at the extreme east of the Altstadt, this has a top-notch restaurant (closed Sun evening) offering Franconian and international dishes plus fish specialities. ⑥.

Schlosshotel Thiergarten, Oberthiergärtner Str. 36, Wolfsbach (☎09 21/98 40, fax 9 84 29, *schlosshotel-thiergarten@t-online.de*). This former hunting lodge, which has only eight bedrooms, is 6km southeast of town near the terminus of bus #11. Its *Kaminrestaurant* (closed Sun evening & Mon) is one of Franconia's leading gourmet haunts; alternatively, there's the more affordable *Jägerstüberl*. ⑦.

Spiegelmühle, Kulmbacher Str. 28 (☎09 21/4 10 91, fax 4 73 20). A converted mill right alongside *Goldener Löwe*. It likewise has a recommendable restaurant (evenings only, closed Sun); the beers come from the rival Glenk brewery. ④.

Zum Brandenburger, St Georgen 9 (☎09 21/78 90 60, fax 78 90 62 40). Another Gasthof on St Georgen's main street, offering rooms with and without facilities. Its restaurant (closed all day Sat & Sun evening) has the benefit of a beer garden. ②–⑤.

Zum Herzog, Herzog 2 (☎09 21/4 13 34, fax 7 41 29 52). Located just off Kulmbacher Strasse, this Gasthof serves good-value meals and beers from both the Maisel and Bayreuther breweries. ③.

The Town

Bayreuth is a small place with many of the sights grouped together in the compact centre and the Hofgarten just beyond. Several other key attractions lie much further afield, but all can be reached by regular bus services.

The town centre

Margravine Wilhelmine's proudest legacy is the **Markgräfliches Opernhaus** (April–Sept Mon–Wed & Fri–Sun 9am–6pm, Thurs 9am–8pm; Oct–March daily 10am–4pm; DM7/€3.50 including audiovisual presentation, or DM10/€5 combined ticket with Neues Schloss) on Opernstrasse in the northern part of the town centre, which was erected in four years of concentrated activity in the 1740s. The exterior by the court architect, the Frenchman Joseph Saint-Pierre, is unusual in that it forms part of a terrace of buildings. Its sobriety stands in stark contrast to the glamorous interior, which was entrusted to Giuseppe and Carlo Galli da Bibiena, a father-and-son team from the great Bolognese dynasty of theatre-designers. Made entirely of wood, it is

RICHARD WAGNER (1813–83)

As the annual crowds to Bayreuth testify, no composer – with the possible exception of Mozart – has a more loyal, not to say adoring, following than **Richard Wagner**. His influence on musical history is also unsurpassed: his operas were revolutionary in their approach, using a recurring theme, or leitmotif, for programmatic purposes, and varying it to depict psychoanalytical developments. He expanded the orchestral palette (including the invention of the Wagner tuba) to create a more sumptuous sound than had ever previously been heard, and developed a new harmonic language in which rich chromaticism predominates. Apart from a few early works and occasional pieces, Wagner's output consists of lengthy "music dramas", all but one of them based on heroic love themes drawn from Germanic mythology. In these, he attempted to fuse all the arts: not only did he compose the music, he chose the plots and the associated symbolism, wrote the libretti and took an active role in staging.

Representing the Romantic approach to the arts at its most extreme, Wagner was a dreamer whose ambitions were only realized courtesy of the patronage of his equally unworldly soul-mate, King Ludwig II of Bavaria. For all his accomplishments, he was always a controversial figure, and even today he remains a composer whose stature is disputed far more than any other: despite the legions of adulators, many music lovers of otherwise catholic tastes listen only to fragments of his works, if they listen to them at all. This is not simply a question of Wagner's excessive nationalism and virulent anti-Semitism, which made the appropriation of his music by the Nazis inevitable. To all but the most initiated, his texts are mere doggerel, while his music is long-winded and repetitive, a point encapsulated in one of the famous asides made by the conductor Sir Thomas Beecham: "We've been playing for two solid hours and we're playing this bloody tune still!"

painted sea-green, highlighted with gold, white, yellow and red, and with the obligatory fresco of *Apollo and the Muses* on the ceiling. All the seats are in boxes on either side of the margravial loge, whose baldachin, like the proscenium arch opposite, is adorned with the coat of arms of Brandenburg-Bayreuth and the royal crown of Prussia. The stage, which preserves beautiful illusionistic scenery, is the same size as the auditorium, and remained the largest in Germany until the advent of Wagner. Although he found it too small for his purposes, it makes an ideal venue for eighteenth-century opera and vocal recitals, and is still a regular performance venue.

Immediately to the west stands the **Schlosskirche**, a Baroque church erected by Saint-Pierre during the following decade. Painted in a delicate pink and adorned with tasteful stuccowork, it's a typical example of Lutheran Baroque, though it has been Bayreuth's main Catholic church since 1813. In a vault beneath the organ are the tombs of Wilhelmine, her husband and their only child, Elisabeth Friederike Sophie. Alongside, dominated by its octagonal Renaissance tower, is the largely Baroque **Altes Schloss**. Much of this palace was accidentally burnt down in 1753 by the unfortunate Margrave Friedrich with a misplaced candle, but it was subsequently restored, and is now used as offices. The side facing the broad Maximilianstrasse (which is also known as the Markt) is decorated with vigorous late seventeenth-century medallions of deities and heroes of classical mythology.

Directly opposite, at the top end of Kanzleistrasse, is the new **Urweltmuseum Oberfranken** (July & Aug Mon–Wed & Fri–Sun 10am–5pm, Thurs 10am–8pm; rest of year Tues, Wed & Fri–Sun 10am–5pm, Thurs 10am–8pm; *www.Urwelt-Museum.de*; DM3/€1.50). This contains some remarkable local finds, including a number of very rare dinosaur bones (notably the only extant examples of the *Pistosaurus* and *Capitosaurus*) plus a collection of 200-million-year-old fossilized plants from the time when Upper Franconia was a tropical river delta. A few paces to the west along Maximilianstrasse, the **Altes Rathaus**, a Renaissance building with prominent oriels, has recently been converted into a cultural centre. Its focal point is the **Kunstmuseum** (same times; *www.kunstmuseum-bayreuth.de*; DM3/€1.50), its holdings of twentieth-century art displayed in rotating exhibitions. Also on Maximilianstrasse are three Baroque **fountains**, dedicated to Fame, Hercules and Neptune. At the far western end of the street is Saint-Pierre's **Spitalkirche**, which boasts a handsome sandstone facade and a typical galleried interior.

The narrow, twisting streets immediately south of Maximilianstrasse are medieval in origin, but lost most of their original buildings in two seventeenth-century fires. Among the casualties of the first of these, which occurred just two years after Bayreuth became a margravial residence, was the main civic church, the **Stadtkirche Heilig-Dreifaltigkeit**. It was immdiately rebuilt in a by then totally anachronistic Gothic style, the only authentically Baroque note being the steeple-crowned turrets above the twin towers, which are linked by a covered passageway. Inside are two notable furnishings from the same period as the rebuilding: the **font**, which has eight alabaster reliefs with a baptismal theme; and the **Kuffner'sche Epitaph**, which incorporates an older relief of *The Adoration of the Magi*, below which is a predella showing a distant view of Bayreuth.

On Kirchplatz to the side of the church is the **Alte Lateinschule**, the new home of the **Historisches Museum** (July & Aug Mon–Wed & Fri–Sun 10am–5pm, Thurs 10am–8pm; rest of year Tues, Wed & Fri–Sun 10am–5pm, Thurs 10am–8pm; DM3/€1.50), which presents well-thought-out displays on the town's past. The focus is firmly on the margravial period, with models illustrating Bayreuth's development, and an extensive collection of local porcelain, plus examples of the distinctive stoneware of the nearby village of Creussen. To its credit, the museum does not baulk at featuring the town's high-profile role during the Third Reich, and has on display an extensive photographic documentation of this period.

Friedrichstrasse, the southernmost of the central streets, is a splendid piece of eighteenth-century town planning, lined with Baroque palaces. Some were built as the homes of court officials, though others had a public function: that at no. 15 was the town's first university, while no. 14 was built as an orphanage, as the relief of a mother and child above the doorway indicates. About halfway down the street is a square, Jean-Paul-Platz, on which stands the monumental **Reiterhalle**, the former margravial riding hall, which has found a new lease of life as the **Stadthalle**, the town's exhibition and congress centre.

The Neues Schloss and the Hofgarten

South of the Altes Schloss is the replacement **Neues Schloss** (April–Sept Mon–Wed & Fri–Sun 9am–6pm, Thurs 9am–8pm; Oct–March daily 10am–4pm; DM5/€2.50), which was completed to plans by Saint-Pierre in 1755 after just two years' work. The building served as a residence only until 1769, when the male line of the House of Brandenburg-Bayreuth died out, and the territory passed to the Ansbach Hohenzollerns. This result-ed in the great state rooms being stripped of their furnishings, but the private apart-ments survive intact as testaments to Wilhelmine's very personal version of the Rococo style. Her own chambers, which are on the northern wing of the first floor, are hung with portraits by Antoine Pesne, court painter to Frederick the Great, plus a large num-ber of **pastels**, including some perfectly competent works by Wilhelmine herself. However, these are outclassed by the portraits of the margravine and her daughter by one of the greatest pastellists of all time, the Swiss Jean Étienne Liotard. Of the interi-ors themselves, the **Japanisches Zimmer** (Japanese Room) and the **Spiegelscherbenkabinett** (Broken Mirror Cabinet) stand out. The latter is lined from top to bottom with broken and uneven shapes, as if put together from several broken mirrors; based on a design by Wilhelmine, it's thought to be her comment on the false glamour of her age. Some highly individual examples of Rococo decoration can also be seen among the margrave's apartments in the southern wing, especially the **Palmenzimmer** (Palm Room), which is arranged as a trompe l'oeil grove of palm trees, and the **Spalierzimmer** (Trellis Room), which adopts a similar illusionistic technique. The ground-floor rooms are devoted to displaying products of the local **porcelain** factory.

Adjoining the Neues Schloss to the south is the **Italienisches Schlösschen**, which was built for Margrave Friedrich's second wife, Sophie Karoline of Braunschweig-Wolfenbüttel, by Carl von Gontard, who went on to pursue a highly successful career in Berlin. It has some fine interiors, though these can only be seen in conjunction with the **Archäologisches Museum** (April–Oct Sat 10am–3pm, first Sun of month 10am–noon; DM2/€1), a collection of local excavations. In the square in front of the Neues Schloss stands the swaggering late Baroque **Markgrafenbrunnen**, which was moved from its original location beside the Altes Schloss. The equestrian statue is of Margrave Christian Ernst in his role as Imperial Field Marshal in the wars against the Turks; around him are representations of the four continents. On the other side of the palace is the **Hofgarten**, which includes a formal parterre plus a far more extensive English-style landscape garden.

From the northern side of the Hofgarten, a pathway leads to a late nineteenth-century masonic lodge which now contains the national collections and library of the German Freemasons, the **Deutsches Freimaurer Museum** (Tues–Fri 10am–noon & 2–4pm, Sat 10am–noon; during the festival daily 10am–4pm; DM2/€1). Predictably, freemasonry is represented here as an international peace movement rather than anything sinister, though the ritual objects featured in the display are unlikely to win over any sceptics. It's revealing to see just how many well-known people were Freemasons, including Frederick the Great, Haydn, Mozart, Goethe, Dickens, Churchill, George Washington, Benjamin Franklin and Harry S. Truman.

A short walk to the east stands the sternly Neoclassical **Villa Wahnfried**, now the **Richard-Wagner-Museum** (April–Oct Mon, Wed & Fri–Sun 9am–5pm, Tues & Thurs 9am–8pm; Nov–March Mon–Wed & Fri–Sun 10am–5pm, Thurs 10am–8pm; DM4/€2). Wagner had this built to his own designs as his Bayreuth home: its enigmatic name literally means "peace from delusion". The large sitting-room-cum-concert-room, which was destroyed by a bomb in 1945 but rebuilt thirty years later to serve as a recital venue, was the setting for Wagner's famed soirées, attended by intellectuals, musicians and royalty alike. His wife Cosima was the daughter of another famous composer, Franz Liszt, and the combination of the couple's backgrounds and interests made the household an important focus of German cultural life. Theirs was also one of the most famous love stories of the nineteenth century (he lured her from her first husband, the conductor Hans von Bülow, who was sufficiently stoic about the affair to maintain his role as the leading contemporary interpreter of Wagner's music), and they lie buried together in the villa's garden. Wagner's life and the history of the festival are documented in the villa's other rooms, while the basement contains a collection of models of the stage-sets used in the latter's productions. Videos of the operas are screened in the now inter-connected Siegfried-Wagner-Haus alongside.

A block to the east, at Wahnfriedstr. 9, the **Franz-Liszt-Museum** (daily: July & Aug 10am–5pm; rest of year 10am–noon & 2–5pm; DM3/€1.50) has been set up in the forester's house where Wagner's father-in-law lodged on his visits to Bayreuth, and where he died in 1886. The displays illustrate the phases of his startlingly diverse career as a peripatetic concert virtuoso, the *Kappellmeister* of the Weimar court and as an abbé in a monastery in Rome.

The inner suburbs
A short walk west of the town centre, at Kulmbacher Str. 40, is the **Gebrüder-Maisel-Brauerei**, a splendid late nineteenth-century redbrick tower brewery which has been

mothballed as the **Brauerei- und Büttnerei-Museum** (guided tours Mon–Sat at 10am; DM5/€2.50), while production continues in the ultra-modern premises alongside. The brewery preserves its old equipment – including steam engines, coal-fired boilers and copper brewing kettles – in full working order, as well as its Büttnerei (coopers' workshop), where wooden beer barrels were made until the 1950s. The tour ends at the old bottling plant, now transformed into a saloon bar of the 1920s, where a half-litre glass of beer is served at no extra charge. The company is now primarily a *Weissbier* specialist, having abandoned production of the dark steam beer (*Dampfbier*) which was once its best-known line.

Bayreuth's most famous nineteenth-century building is the **Festspielhaus** (guided tours Tues–Sun at 10am, 10.45am, 2.15pm & 3pm; 10am & 10.45am only during the festival; closed Nov; DM3/€1.50), the custom-built theatre for the performance of Wagner's music dramas, which is set on a little hill in the far north of town, reached by following Bürgerreuther Strasse straight ahead from the Hauptbahnhof. Based on designs by Gottfried Semper, the leading German architect of the day and one of Wagner's comrades-in-arms on the Dresden barricades during the 1849 revolution, the theatre was inaugurated in 1876, when the *Ring* cycle was staged in its entirety for the first time. Ever since, nothing but Wagner's operas has been performed there. After the composer's death in 1882, his widow Cosima ensured that the annual festival continued, and various family members have been in charge ever since. It was during his English-born daughter-in-law Winifred's "reign" from 1931 to 1944 that the festival had the unfortunate honour of Hitler's patronage, and he stayed as her house-guest whenever he came to Bayreuth. Wagner buffs still argue over the extent to which she should be blamed for the misappropriation of Wagner's music during the Nazi era, and bitter quarrels within the Wagner family have continued to fuel the flames. Although externally prepossessing, the interior is spartan in the extreme, with the comfort of the audience (most of whom sit on hard wooden benches) and the orchestra (whose members have to endure their own high-decibel sound in the cramped, sweaty conditions of a deep pit) sacrificed for the sake of achieving the best possible acoustics.

A short distance to the southeast, immediately to the rear of the Hauptbahnhof, is **St Georgen**, a planned town founded in 1701 which was not incorporated into Bayreuth until after the the Bavarian takeover in 1810. Although never completed, it contains many fine Baroque buildings, including the **Schloss** of the courtly Roter-Adler-Orden (Red Eagle Order), a porcelain manufactory and two churches, the larger of which, the **Ordenskirche**, preserves an intact period-piece interior.

The Eremitage

Lying 4km east of town, and reached by bus #20 from Marktplatz, is the curious **Eremitage**, which has its origins in the eighteenth-century fad of the nobility for playing at asceticism by occasionally staying in sparse monks' cells and eating nothing but soup. When the original hermitage or **Altes Schloss** (guided tours April–Sept Mon–Wed & Fri–Sun 9am–6pm, Thurs 9am–8pm; DM5/€2.50) was given to Wilhelmine as a birthday present in 1735, the year her husband inherited the margravate, she proceeded to enlarge it into a glamorous summer hideaway in line with her own quirky vision of retreat as perfect indulgence. Thus some splendid Rococo chambers, notably the **Musikzimmer** and **Japanisches Kabinett**, are juxtaposed with the original bare cells. Between the two wings is the **Grotte**, featuring two hundred fountains grouped in three concentric circles which could be activated in various different ways to surprise or spray unwary guests.

Wilhelmine later commissioned a brand-new palace, the **Neues Schloss**, from Saint-Pierre and Gontard, and this was built just a short distance away. It is designed in a horseshoe shape, with mosaic-encrusted arcaded wings (which lost their interior decoration as a result of an artillery bombardment in the war) flanking a central rotunda known as the **Sonnentempel** after the gilded sculptural group of Apollo and his sun chariot on its roof. In the space between the wings is the **Obere Grotte**, whose **fountains** of tritons and fantastical creatures play on the hour between May and mid-October from 10am until 5pm. Ten minutes later, the jets are activated in the **Untere Grotte**, a nymphaeum with nymphs, putti, dolphins and sea-horses. Among the follies in the park is an open-air theatre built in the shape of a Roman ruin, where the margravine was wont to take to the stage, sometimes with her friend Voltaire.

Schloss Fantasie

Wilhelmine's daughter, Elisabeth Friederike Sophie, was considered one of the great beauties of her age, but her marriage to Duke Carl Eugen of Württemberg was a total mismatch, and after eight years the couple formally separated and she returned to Bayreuth. A new Rococo palace, **Schloss Fantasie** (April–Sept Tues–Sun 9am–6pm; DM5/€2), was built for her some 5km west of the town centre; it can be reached by local bus #5D and regional buses #8231, #8446 and #8449. Its most celebrated interior, the intarsia **Spindler-Kabinett**, is now the property of the Bayerisches Nationalmuseum in Munich, and is replaced *in situ* by a faithful copy; the only historic interior to survive, the main hall, or **Weisses Saal**, belongs to a partial Neoclassical remodelling carried out in the late eighteenth century. However, the rest of the palace has been put to effective use as the home of the **Gartenkunstmuseum**, which gives an entertaining overview of the entire history of landscape gardening in Germany, copiously illustrated with original paintings, drawings, prints and plans. In the immediate vicinity of the Schloss is Elisabeth Friederike Sophie's Rococo garden, complete with a graceful pavilion by Gontard, the so-called **Komödienhaus**, and a series of cascades centred on the **Neptunbrunnen**; beyond is an extensive English-style park.

Eating, drinking and entertainment

Bayreuth is awash with quality restaurants, many of the best choices being in the hotels (see p.117). As the home of several breweries, it's also a good place for a pub crawl.

Restaurants and cafés

Becher-Bräu, St-Nikolaus-Str. 25. Located to the west of the centre, this is Bayreuth's oldest brewery-owned Gaststätte, with a tradition going back more than two centuries. These days, however, the Becher label products (a *Pils*, a *Bock* and a *Dunkel*) are made under contract by the Schinner brewery. Closed Tues.

Brauereischänke am Markt, Maximilianstr. 56. A fairly genteel pub-restaurant on the main square, serving the beers of the Bayreuther brewery.

Braunbierhaus, Kanzleistr. 15. Occupying Bayreuth's oldest surviving house, this is the flagship of the Schinner brewery, and is named after the brown beer which is its principal product. There's a bar on the ground floor, a reasonably priced restaurant upstairs. Closed Mon.

Café an der Oper, Opernstr. 16. A supremely elegant café in the Redoutenhaus, the former court gardener's residence next door to the Opernhaus. Live classical music performances are sometimes featured.

Café Orangerie, Neues Schloss Eremitage. This café, which has indoor seating in the Orangerie and a terrace overlooking the fountains, is an attractive place for a break during a visit to the Eremitage.

Hansl's Holzofen Pizzeria, Friedrichstr. 13. This tiny place, which makes delicious pizzas in a wood-fired oven, is a favourite with local students.

Jean-Paul-Café, Friedrichstr. 10. A long-established family concern which is another good choice for *Kaffee und Kuchen*. Closed Mon.

Oskar, Maximilianstr. 33. Unusually trendy for a Rathaus restaurant; this gets packed for the Saturday breakfast buffets and Sunday brunches.

Podium, Gerberhaus, Gerberplatz 1. Bayreuth's jazz and blues bar; it serves Thai food and has a beer garden.

Porsch, Maximilianstr. 63. A time-warped Gaststätte, offering generous portions of inexpensive local fare plus beers from the rural Stöckel brewery.

Schützenhaus, Am Schiesshaus 2. Located to the northwest of the Festspielhaus, this serves inexpensive Franconian specialities and has a large beer garden. Closed Thurs.

Zur Sudpfanne, Oberkonnersreuther Str. 6, Oberkonnersreuth. Situated in an incorporated village 3km southeast of town (bus #11 stops at the door), this is the Gaststätte of the small Schaller brewery alongside, which produces a fine unfiltered beer, *Storchentrunk Zwickelbier*. Exquisite food is served in the large hall and the very formal *König-Ludwig-Saal*, more basic pub grub in the *Storchenkeller* beer garden. On Sat, it's only open in the evening.

Culture and festivals

Demand for **tickets** for the *Richard-Wagner-Festspiele* is so great that you need to write the year before you wish to visit to Kartenbüro, Festspielleitung Bayreuth, 95402 Bayreuth, but this only ensures entry into the lottery, and the normal waiting time for first-time individual applicants is between three and seven years. The various Wagner societies around the world receive special allocations, but the only other way you will realistically get to see a performance is to take an expensive package tour from abroad (see pp.7 & 13 for tour operators). Formal evening dress is the normal attire, but is not *de rigueur*. Note that it is necessary to pay more than one visit to see the entire Wagner canon (six different operas are normally staged in a season), and that each festival has a fair number of non-performance days. For the latest information, visit the festival Web site (*www.bayreuther-festspiele.de*).

Advance tickets for **opera**, **concerts** and **drama** performances in the Markgräflisches Opernhaus and other local venues can be bought from the box office in the tourist office premises at Luitpoldplatz 9 (☎09 21/6 90 01). Musical **festivals** by no means begin and end with the Wagner jamboree; in addition, there's the *Musica Bayreuth* in early May, the *Fränkische Festwoche* at the end of the same month and *Bayreuther Barock* in late September. Folklore events include *Maisels Weissbierfest* in mid-May, the *Volksfest* in early June and the *Bürgerfest* at the beginning of July.

Kulmbach

KULMBACH, which lies 22km northwest of Bayreuth on the banks of the Weisser (White) Main, just west of the point where it joins the Roter (Red) Main to form the River Main proper, is best-known for its **beer**, holding as it does two national records – the largest output per head of population and the strongest brew in regular production (*EKU 28*). Although the town was the capital of a Hohenzollern principality from 1398 until the court moved to Bayreuth in 1603, it preserves very few reminders of its medieval origins. The blame for this lies squarely with Margrave Albrecht Alcibiades of Brandenburg-Kulmbach, a megalomaniacal and unprincipled ruler who hoped to turn the great sixteenth-century religious divide to his own advantage by establishing control over the whole of the old Franconian duchy. Instead, he succeeded in uniting the Protestant city-state of Nürnberg and the Catholic prince-bishoprics of Bamberg and Würzburg in common cause against him, and in 1553, after a long siege, their combined forces captured the town and laid it to waste. The following year, the same fate befell the huge feudal fortress high above the eastern side of Kulmbach, whereupon Albrecht was deposed and forced into exile while a largely new town arose from the ashes of the old.

The Town

The original castle, the **Plassenburg**, was replaced almost immediately after its destruction with a splendid new Renaissance building of the same name, erected under the supervision of Caspar Vischer, a local architect who had recently worked on the great Schloss in Heidelberg. Within its formidable outer defences are two distinct entities. The lower castle, known as the **Niederburg** or **Kasernenhof**, has an austere silhouette of massive high walls, the only decorative note being the early seventeenth-century triumphal arch with an equestrian statue of Margrave Christian, who, ironically enough, was the man responsible for Kulmbach losing its capital status, largely because there was no room on this hill for the large residential palace he craved.

In contrast, the upper castle or **Hochburg** (guided tours of the interiors April–Sept Mon–Wed & Fri–Sun 9am–6pm, Thurs 9am–8pm; Oct–March daily 10am–4pm; DM5/€2.50, or DM12/€6 combined ticket with all the town's museums) ranks as one of the richest creations of the German Renaissance. Its four corner towers are evidence of its defensive status, but the arcaded courtyard, the **Schöner Hof**, has a true festive air, and makes an ideal open-air venue for concerts and theatre in the summer. On three of its four sides, virtually every square centimetre of the arches, pilasters and balustrades is festooned with carvings of foliage, mythological beasts, putti, vases, candelabra, scrollwork and medallion portraits of members of the Hohenzollern dynasty and their supposed ancient Roman ancestors. The tour takes in a suite of restored margravial chambers, which are decked out with period furniture, the most spectacular being the seventeenth-century four-poster bed, guarded by statues of Charity and Piety, of Margravine Maria. Most of the paintings on display are family portraits, but there is also a panel of *The Mysteries of the Rosary* by the town's most celebrated artist, Hans Suess von Kulmbach, a pupil of Dürer. Also included on the tour is the **Schlosskapelle**, one of the earliest custom-built Protestant chapels. Its three key focal points – the pulpit, altar and organ – are somewhat later than the structure itself, all dating from the early seventeenth century.

The same entrance ticket gives admission to the new **Armeemuseum Friedrich der Grosse**, which can be visited at leisure. This contains a wide range of exhibits illustrating the history of the legendary army of Frederick the Great and his predecessors, the primary force behind the rise of the Hohenzollern heartlands of Brandenburg and Prussia from rural backwaters to the dominant power in Europe. On display are arms and uniforms representing each of the component divisions of the army – regular infantry, artillery, riflemen, hussars, cuirassiers and dragoons. Also on view are nine original banners, the most precious being a blue silk dragoon standard of 1685.

Two other museums (with at least one more likely to be added in due course) can be found within the Hochburg. The **Landschaftsmuseum Obermain** (same times; DM4/€2) is an extensive and well-presented regional history museum. Among its exhibits are a fine nineteenth-century copy of the now-destroyed map of the world from the Lower Saxon convent of Ebstorf, which features a depiction of the original Plassenburg; a predella of *The Four Doctors of the Church*, painted by Hans Suess von Kulmbach for an altarpiece in the famous Mariacki church in the Polish city of Kraków; the Renaissance stone pulpit from Kulmbach's Petrikirche; the Pörbitsch treasure, a horde of goblets, tankards, dishes, bowls and cutlery by Nürnberg and Augsburg goldsmiths and silversmiths buried for safekeeping during the Thirty Years War and only rediscovered in 1912; and a collection of seven thousand historic cookbooks and a thousand associated samples from the foundation established by the spice company RAPS, a leading local employer.

Across the courtyard is the **Deutsches Zinnfigurenmuseum** (same times; DM4/€2), which contains the world's premier collection of tin figures, an art form taken very seriously in Germany. Dating from the eighteenth century onwards, there are 300,000 individual pieces on view, grouped in 150 different scenes illustrating historic and literary episodes. Among them is the largest diorama ever made, showing the 1553 siege of Kulmbach.

In comparison with the Plassenburg, the Altstadt is very low-key, with only a few historic buildings of note. Directly below the castle is the **Roter Turm**, a medieval tower with a half-timbered superstructure; nearby is the Renaissance **Kanzlei**, a gabled margravial administrative building. Further down and to the southeast, with a terrace commanding a fine view up to the Plassenburg, is the **Petrikirche**, a somewhat gaunt Gothic hall church containing the graves of members of the local margravial family. From there, Obere Stadt, an elongated former market square, swoops down to Marktplatz, on which stands the cheerful Rococo **Rathaus**.

On the opposite bank of the Main, about 2km northeast of Marktplatz, the town's brewing tradition is celebrated in the **Bayerisches Brauereimuseum Kulmbach** (Tues–Sun 10am–5pm; DM4/€2), which occupies the former Mönchshof brewery at Hofer Str. 20. The Mönchshof label, best-known for its coal-black *Schwarzbier*, still exists, as does the Kapuziner designation used for its wheat beers, though the brewery was one of two (the other being Sandlerbräu, whose name now has a very tenuous existence) taken over in the 1980s by the rival Reichelbräu, a *Pils* specialist whose highly regarded *Eisbock*, a powerful ice beer, is only available in winter. In 1996 Reichelbräu subsumed its one remaining local competitor, the better-known EKU; subsequently, it abolished its own name, adopting the new Kulmbacher label instead, and consolidated production of all the labels in one new hi-tech brewery.

Practicalities

Kulmbach's **Bahnhof**, which has regular direct services to both Bayreuth and Bamberg, is a few minutes' walk northwest of the Altstadt. The **tourist office** (May–Oct Mon–Fri 9am–1pm & 1.30–5.30pm, Sat 9.30am–1pm, Sun 11am–1pm; Nov–April Mon–Fri 9am–1pm & 1.30–5.30pm; ☎0 92 21/9 58 80, fax 95 88 44, *www.stadt-kulmbach.de*) is in the Stadthalle, Sutte 2. There are plenty of **hotels**, but only *Weisses Ross*, Marktplatz 12 (☎0 92 21/9 56 50; ③–⑤), and *Kronprinz*, Fischergasse 4 (☎0 92 21/9 21 80; ⑤–⑦), are in the Altstadt. However, there's a concentration around the Stadtpark to the west of the centre: *Ertl*, Hardenbergstr. 3 (☎0 92 21/97 40 00; ③–⑥); *Purucker*, Melkendorfer Str. 4 (☎0 92 21/9 02 00; ⑤); *Hansa*, Weltrichstr. 2a (☎0 92 21/6 00 90, *www.hansa-hotel-kulmbach.de*; ⑥–⑧); and *Astron*, Luitpoldstr. 2 (☎0 92 21/60 30; ⑦).

All the hotels around the Stadtpark have high-quality **restaurants**, while *Kronprinz* has a café. Tracking down the different local **beers** can be a time-consuming process. A good selection is offered by the *Stadtschänke* in the Burg, but most other restaurants remain loyal to a particular label. The Mönchshof Bräuhaus, in the same complex as the Brauereimuseum, has a huge beer garden and serves the full range of Mönchshof and Kapuziner products; these are also available in the town centre at the *Stadtschänke*, Holzmarkt 3, which has different themed-lunch menus each day. Kulmbacher beers are served at *Anno*, a bistro at Marktplatz 4; EKU beers at *Zunftstube*, Obere Stadt 4, and the pizzeria *EKU-Fässle*, Sutte 18. No local beer tour is complete without a visit to *Kulmbacher Kommunbräu*, Grünwehr 17, the town's only Hausbrauerei: it makes light and amber brews and serves hearty local dishes. Altogether different in style is a trendy French-style brasserie, *Alte Feuerwache*, Grabenstr. 4.

Special strong brews are served in litre measures in a huge tent set up beside the Stadthalle for the duration of the main local **festival**, the nine-day-long *Kulmbacher Bierfest*, which begins on the last Saturday of July. At the beginning of the same month is an annual folklore event, the *Altstadtfest*, while in the second week of August in odd-numbered years tin-figure enthusiasts descend on the town for the *Zinnfiguren-Börse*.

Coburg

A hugely imposing little town with a truly illustrious history and a mixed Franconian–Thuringian pedigree, **COBURG** lies about 50km northwest of Kulmbach. Following several changes of aristocratic ownership, it came into the hands of the powerful House of Wettin in 1353, and was initially regarded by them as a Saxon outpost within Franconia. In 1586, it was raised to the status of capital of one of the dynasty's splintered Saxon-Thuringian territories, the new Duchy of Saxe-Coburg. The ruling house proved to be masterly at self-promotion, particularly in the nineteenth century, when its clever dynastic marriage policy created ties with the royal families of Belgium, Bulgaria and Portugal as well as Great Britain, the last being achieved when **Albert of Saxe-Coburg-Gotha** married his first cousin, Queen Victoria, thus establishing the present British royal house, which tactfully renamed itself Windsor during World War I. This marriage in turn led to a union with Germany's ruling dynasty, the Hohenzollerns, when the couple's eldest child, Victoria, married the future Kaiser Friedrich III. In 1920, two years after the abdication of the last duke, the locals voted to join Bavaria – which proved a fortuitous choice, as it saved Coburg from the fate of all the other old Saxon-Thuringian principalities, which were incorporated into the GDR after World War II. As a virtual dead end, the town had a tough time economically during the decades of German division, but has recovered well.

Arrival, information and accommodation

Coburg's **Hauptbahnhof** is situated on the northwestern side of town; the quickest way to the centre is by going sharp right along Lossaustrasse. The **tourist office** is just off the Marktplatz at Herrngasse 4 (April–Oct Mon–Fri 9am–6.30pm, Sat 9am–1pm; Nov–March Mon–Fri 9am–5pm, Sat 9am–1pm; ☎0 95 61/7 41 80, fax 74 18 29, *www.coburg-tourist.de*).

Coburg has plenty of recommendable **hotels**, particularly in the middle-range category. There are a few **private houses** (②–③) with rooms to rent, bookable via the tourist office. The **youth hostel** occupies a redbrick neo-Gothic castle, Schloss Ketschendorf, 2km south of the centre at Parkstr. 2 (☎0 95 61/1 53 30, fax 2 86 53; DM23/€11.50); bus #1 stops outside.

Hotels

Blankenburg, Rosenauer Str. 30 (☎0 95 61/64 40, fax 64 19 99, *www.coburg-tourist.de/blankenburg*). This recently renovated hotel is in the north of town, beside the municipal swimming pool, which guests can use free of charge. It has a new rustic-style restaurant serving moderately priced local and international dishes, as well as the long-established gourmet favourite, *Kräutergarten*. ⑥.

Coburger Tor, Ketschendorfer Str. 22 (☎0 95 61/2 50 74, fax 2 88 74). Located across from the Rosengarten, this hotel prides itself on its breakfasts and even more on its evenings-only restaurant, *Schaller* (closed Sun), which has a summer garden and serves what is generally considered to be the finest cuisine in Coburg. ⑨.

Festungshof, Festungsberg 1 (☎0 95 61/8 02 90, fax 80 29 33, *hotelfestungshof@t-online.de*). The Veste Coburg's very own hotel, occuping a century-old building outside the fortifications. It also has a good restaurant, complete with café terrace and a large beer garden. ⑨–⑦.

Fink, Lützelbucher Str. 22, Lützelbuch (☎0 95 61/2 49 40, fax 2 72 40, *www.gasthof-fink.de*). A traditional Gasthof in an incorporated village 4km southeast of the Altstadt, reached by bus #4; it serves good buffet breakfasts and traditional cuisine. It has recently opened a new, slightly more upmarket offshoot, *Landhaus Fink*, at no. 25 on the same street. ③, ④ in *Landhaus*.

Goldene Sonne, Creidlitzer Str. 93, Creidlitz (☎ & fax 0 95 61/2 90 97). Inexpensive rooms with and without en-suite facilities are available at this Gasthof on the main street of an incorporated village 2km south of the Altstadt, reached by bus #1. Its own butcher's shop is the main source for the meals served in the restaurant. ②.

Goldene Traube, Am Viktoriabrunnen 2 (☎0 95 61/87 60, fax 87 62 22, *www.romantikhotels.com*). Grand hotel in the heart of the Altstadt; the facilities include a sauna and a cosmetic studio. Haute cuisine is served in the *Traube-Stuben*; less expensive fare in the rustic-style *Weinlaube*, which has a large selection of wines, available by the glass. ⑥–⑧.

Goldenes Kreuz, Herrengasse 1 (☎0 95 61/9 04 73, fax 9 05 02). An almost impossibly old-fashioned Gasthof at the corner of the Markt, with most of the bedrooms grouped round a quiet inner court-yard. Its restaurant has wonderfully evocative decor, and serves good low-cost local cuisine. ③.

Grosch, Oeslauer Str. 115, Rödental (☎0 95 63/75 00, fax 75 01 47). This Gasthof has a pedigree dat-ing back to 1425, and still preserves the traditional pattern of a hotel, restaurant and brewery all grouped together. It's located right alongside Bahnhof Rödental (two stops by train from the Hauptbahnhof), not far from Schloss Rosenau. ⑤.

Münchner Hofbräu, Kleine Johannisgasse 8 (☎0 95 61/7 50 49, fax 9 04 34). Small Altstadt Gasthof, whose restaurant serves Austrian as well as Franconian cuisine and has plenty of local wines as well as beers from Munich's Hofbräu. ④.

Stadt Coburg, Lossaustr. 12 (☎0 95 61/87 40, fax 87 42 22, *www.ringhotels.de*). A member of the Ringhotel group, this lies just across from the Hauptbahnhof. It has a fine restaurant, *Backstüble* (closed Sun), which specializes in dishes cooked on its open grill. ⑤.

The Town

Despite Coburg's modest size, its attractions are well spaced out: the great feudal cas-tle which gives the town its name lies high above the eastern side of the compact cen-tre, while there are two important palaces in the far outskirts.

The Veste Coburg

Towering 167 metres above the town and visible from miles around, the **Veste Coburg**, one of the largest surviving medieval fortresses in Germany, can be reached by bus #8 from the Markt, or by a steep thirty-minute walk. The oldest part, the **Blauer Turm** (Blue Tower), was built around 1230, but most of the present massive complex, which is enclosed by two rings of defensive walls, postdates a fire in 1499 which destroyed much of the earlier structure. In the early seventeenth century, four of the outer wall's roundels were replaced by bastions, including the protruding **Bärenbastei** to the northwest which, as its name suggests, contained a bear pit. Considerable restoration work was carried out on the fortress in the nineteenth and early twentieth centuries. Latterly, this was done in a scholarly rather than a romantic manner, and although not all the details are authentic, the Veste, in contrast to so many other German castles, still has a predominantly medieval silhouette.

Within the inner walls are two courtyards. That to the right is dominated by the impressive half-timbered facade of the residential **Fürstenbau**, which until recently was still in the possession of the descendants of the local dukes, with its main apart-ments open for guided tours. The family has now moved out, severing a link with the Veste of nearly six and a half centuries, and the building is likely to be under restora-tion and closed to the public for at least the next five years. Adjoining it to the east is the **Lutherkapelle**, a mid-nineteenth century structure on the site of its Romanesque predecessor. Its name commemorates the great reformer's five-and-a-half-month sojourn at the Veste under the protection of Elector John the Steadfast for the duration of the 1530 Diet of Augsburg, which, as an outlaw of the Holy Roman Empire, he was unable to attend. On the south side of the left-hand courtyard is the **Hohes Haus**, a tall building with a steeply pitched roof which was formerly an arsenal, and now con-tains the offices of the castle administration. Alongside is an elegant Renaissance **cistern**.

The three other edifices house one of Germany's most varied and remarkable museums, the **Kunstsammlungen der Veste Coburg** (April–Oct Tues–Sun 10am–5pm; Nov–March Tues–Sun 1–4pm; *www.kunstsammlungen-coburg.de*;

DM6/€3), whose exhibits are drawn predominantly, but by no means exclusively, from the ducal collections. Tickets are bought at the central building, the **Carl-Eduard-Bau**, the top two storeys of which house the largest department, the **Kupfestichkabinett**. Its 300,000-strong graphics collection is among the most important in the country, including as it does major examples of the work of Dürer, Cranach and Rembrandt. None of this is on permanent view, though temporary exhibitions are held at least a couple of times a year. In the same building are displays of decorative art, dominated by a fabulous **glass** section on the first floor, which includes many outstanding Venetian examples.

The **Steinerne Kemenate** (literally, Heated Stone Chamber) on the eastern side of the courtyard contains the **Lutherstube**, where the reformer progressed with his translation of the Bible and wrote no fewer than 26 works on issues arising from the Reformation. Adjoining it is a memorial room with portraits of the Saxon Electors Frederick the Wise and John the Steadfast by Cranach the Elder, and of Luther by Cranach the Younger. Also on view is an engraved Islamic drinking glass which once belonged to St Elisabeth and was later given as a present to Luther. Across the corridor is the **Grosse Hofstube**, containing a huge cast-iron stove of 1501, the oldest of its type in Germany, as well some splendid pieces of tournament armour, including items made for Emperors Maximilian I and Ferdinand I.

Upstairs is the **Jagdintarsienzimmer** (Marquetry Hunting Room), a chamber unlike any other in Germany. Completed in 1632, this extraordinary masterpiece of late Renaissance joinery originally adorned Schloss Ehrenburg in the town centre. On the walls are sixty highly detailed panels of inlaid coloured woods illustrating deer, boar and bear hunts, while the coffered ceiling has ornamental intarsia patterns and 72 human and animal heads. The huge sideboard in the passageway also formed part of the original furnishings. A small but highly distinguished display of old German masters, many on permanent loan from the Schäfer collection in Schweinfurt, can be seen in the rooms opposite. Of particular note are a very Italianate *Madonna and Child in a Landscape* by the young **Dürer**; a gorgeous painting of the same title by **Burgkmair**, featuring delicate depictions of flowers, plants and birds; two little panels of *The Last Supper* and *SS Dorothy and Agnes*, the earliest surviving works of **Grünewald**; *The Capture of Christ* by **Baldung**; and a dozen or so examples of the elder **Cranach**, including the very characteristic *Lucretia* and *Lot and his Daughters*, as well as a somewhat untypical *Last Judgement*. A few sculptures are displayed alongside, including a heartbreakingly intense Pietà by an anonymous local woodcarver of the second half of the fourteenth century.

Each floor of the **Herzoginbau** (Duchess Building) on the western side of the courtyard is devoted to a particular theme. One level contains historic **hunting weapons**, many of high artistic merit, another the **Rüstkammer**, which ranks among Europe's richest armouries. The armour of Johann Casimir, the first Duke of Saxe-Coburg, is displayed beside that of his dwarf, the cuirass of the Veste's commandant alongside the smaller swords of his children. There are also some rarities, such as a late sixteenth-century war chest, complete with coins, and an early seventeenth-century organ-pipe canon, so called because of its arrangement of 49 barrels in seven rows, each of which could be fired separately. The basement contains contemporary porcelain plus a large array of seventeenth- and eighteenth-century **stoneware tankards** from Creussen. Most remarkable of all is the floor devoted to **coaches** and **carousels**. Among the former are both of the oldest ceremonial coaches to have survived intact anywhere in Europe, those used at Johann Casimir's weddings in 1586 and 1599. Having been made in Braunschweig for the 1561 royal wedding in Copenhagen of the duke's parents-in-law, the latter is actually the older of the two. The thirteen carousels, which are all individually carved and painted, were used at tournament games staged by the ladies of the court in the seventeenth and eighteenth centuries.

Schloss Ehrenburg

In accordance with the fashion of the time, a new Renaissance palace, known as **Schloss Ehrenburg** (guided tours Tues–Sun: April–Sept 9am–6pm; Oct–March 10am–4pm; DM6/€3, or DM9/€4.50 combined ticket with Schloss Rosenau), was begun in the 1540s immediately to the east of the Altstadt, and the wing facing Steingasse is a survivor of this period. It was extended under Johann Casimir, and the inner courtyard largely dates from his reign. Following a fire in 1690, the palace was transformed in Baroque style by a team of decorators from northern Italy. Externally, there is little evidence of their work: the Schloss underwent extensive modifications throughout the course of the nineteenth century, and this included the remodelling of the front courtyard according to designs by the great Berlin architect Karl Friedrich Schinkel which were clearly inspired by the Tudor architecture of England.

For all its diversity, the palace is incredibly rich and sumptuous inside, crammed with paintings, furniture and tapestries, and with intricate parquet floors made to different designs in each room. The Baroque **Riesensaal** (Hall of Giants), the setting for festive events, takes its name from the 28 candelabra-bearing atlantes supporting the entablature, above which are 56 coats of arms of the various territories of the House of Wettin and a magnificent white stucco ceiling with allegorical paintings of the arts and sciences. Stuccowork of even greater virtuosity can be seen in the **Gobelinsaal**, where the foliage and garlands appear to hang down into the room in a naturalistic manner. Another fine interior by the Italian craftsmen is the **Hofkirche**, which is unusually ornate for a Lutheran church of the period, with stucco-framed ceiling frescoes illustrating the Book of Revelation. Its altar is based on Bernini's famous baldachin in St Peter's in Rome, subtly modified for Protestant worship by the insertion of a swallow's nest pulpit in the centre. The nineteenth-century chambers are influenced by the French Neoclassical and Empire styles; of particular importance is the **Thronsaal**, which is directly modelled on Napoleon's throne room in the Tuileries Palace in Paris. Many rooms are equipped with modern gadgets – the flushing mahogany toilet in the bedroom used by Queen Victoria is believed to be the first of its kind on the Continent.

As a supplement to the tour, it's well worth visiting the **Landesbibliothek** (Mon–Thurs 10am–5pm, Fri & Sat 10am–1pm; free), where five more of the Schloss's historic interiors are open to the public as reading and exhibition rooms. Among these is the Neoclassical **Silbersaal**, where temporary displays of the library's rich holdings of manuscripts, books, maps and engravings are regularly held.

The Altstadt

The boundaries of Coburg's Altstadt are still easily discernible, thanks to the survival of three now disembodied gateways. Crowned with an onion dome, the **Spitaltor** at the junction of Spitalgasse and Georgengasse served as the northern entrance; the **Judentor** on Judengasse and the **Ketschentor** on Ketschengasse were its western and southern counterparts.

At the heart of the Altstadt is the **Markt**, lined with handsome Renaissance buildings erected in the early years of the duchy, and with a statue of Prince Albert, paid for by his widow, in the middle. The **Rathaus** on the southern side was extensively rebuilt in Rococo style, but retains the characteristic two-storey oriel, plus the main hall on the second floor. Opposite stands the **Stadthaus**, the former government building, still in all its original splendour. On the eastern side, at the corner of Steingasse, the **Hofapotheke** is a mixture of Gothic and Renaissance elements, with an oriel in the older style. Leading off the square are several streets of half-timbered houses, the most grandiose being the **Münzmeisterhaus** (Mint Master's House) on Ketschengasse. Just to its east is another imposing Renaissance building, the **Gymnasium**

Casimirianum, founded with the intention of developing into a university, but which never rose beyond the status of a school.

Across from the Gymnasium is **St Moritz**, a fourteenth-century Gothic church with fifteenth-century towers which were intended to be identical but ended up with one much shorter than the other. Inside, the chamber under the south tower contains the only remaining medieval furnishing, the **tombstone** of a local fifteenth-century Knight, Albrecht von Bach. Towards the end of the sixteenth century, Johann Casimir had the chancel converted into his family mausoleum, and on the end wall stands the massive alabaster **epitaph to Johann Friedrich II**, the duke's father, by the Thuringian sculptor Nikolaus Bergner. In the foreground are statues of the deceased, his two wives and four sons; behind is an altar-like structure with polychromed Old and New Testament scenes. The largest of these, showing Joseph and his brothers escorting the coffin of their father Jacob from Egypt to Canaan, is an allegorical reference to the repatriation of the remains of Johann Friedrich, who was deposed as Duke of Saxony and spent the last 28 years of his life imprisoned in Austria. To the right of the monument are bronze **tombplates** with relief portraits of Johann Friedrich and his second wife, Elisabeth von der Pfalz. In contrastingly light mode is the **font** alongside, carved some six decades earlier with depictions of putti at play. The church's **nave** was remodelled in Lutheran Baroque style, with double galleries, a stuccoed ceiling and an organ (now with modern pipework).

A short distance north of the church, at Rückertstr. 2–3, is a large fifteenth-century mansion which for several years was the home of the poet and orientalist Friedrich Rückert, and now contains the **Coburger Puppenmuseum** (April–Oct daily 9am–5pm; Nov–March Tues–Sun 10am–5pm; DM3.50/€1.75, kids DM2/€1). Exhibited in 33 rooms arranged in chronological order are some nine hundred individual dolls and toys, plus over fifty dolls' houses dating from the beginning of the nineteenth century until the 1950s.

Schloss Callenberg

The descendants of the ducal family live 4km north of the Altstadt in **Schloss Callenberg** (guided tours April–Oct daily at 10am, 11am, noon, 2pm, 3pm & 4pm; Nov to early Jan, Feb & March Tues–Sun at 2pm, 3pm & 4pm; DM5/€2.50); this can be reached by bus #5, which only goes up to the entrance on Sundays, at other times depositing passengers at the foot of the hill. By origin the seat of the Knights of Callenberg, the medieval fortress later passed to the Wettins, and was rebuilt in the late sixteenth century in Mannerist style. It was given another major makeover under Dukes Ernst I and II, the father and elder brother of Prince Albert, acquiring an extravagant mock-medieval silhouette. Inside is the family's private collection of paintings and *objets d'art*, much of which was until recently on display in the Veste's Fürstenbau. Highlights are several paintings by Cranach; a drinking vessel, the *Vier-Becker-Wilkomm*, by the Nürnberg goldsmith Wenzel Jamnitzer; a silver model of a three-masted ship; and a valuable array of furniture by the celebrated Neoclassical cabinetmaker David Roentgen. The tour ends with a visit to the **Schlosskapelle**, which still preserves much of its Mannerist outline. A live music **festival**, the *Schlossfest*, is held in the grounds over a weekend in August.

Schloss Rosenau

Prince Albert was born in 1819 at **Schloss Rosenau** (guided tours April–Sept Tues–Sun 9am–6pm; Oct–March Tues–Sun 10am–4pm; DM5/€2.50), 7km to the northeast of the town centre; buses #8311 and #8312 stop nearby, otherwise it's a shortish walk from Bahnhof Rödental, two stops away from the Hauptbahnhof on a line served by hourly trains. This little palace is fifteenth century in origin, and was built as the home of the lords of Rosenau, who were Coburg's mint masters. In 1805 it was acquired by the ducal family and shortly afterwards remodelled as their summer residence to plans by

Schinkel; at the same time, the grounds were fashioned into a romantic English-style park. Half of the Schloss's ground floor is occupied by the **Marmorsaal**, which takes its name from its grey marble decoration. Alongside is the tiny eleven-sided **Bibliothek**, which was built to house a collection of chivalrous novels, and is decorated with paintings illustrating one of the genre, Friedrich de la Motte Fouquet's *The Travels of Thiodolf the Icelander*. Architecturally, it looks more like a chapel than a library, and indeed was used as such from 1890 by Duchess Maria, the daughter of the Russian Czar Alexander II. Upstairs, the private apartments, which are small and intimate in scale, are decked out with Biedermeier furniture from Vienna. Among the family heirlooms is a cradle which was probably once used by Prince Albert.

Eating, drinking and entertainment

All the leading **restaurants** are in the hotels, though there are plenty of good, cheaper alternatives, as well as some extremely enticing **cafés**. The favourite local **snack** is the *Coburger*, a long sausage given a distinctively sharp taste by being grilled over pine cones rather than the usual wood or charcoal; the stands on Marktplatz sell authentic examples. Coburg is also known for its dumplings, made according to a recipe combining the Thuringian and Franconian traditions by using both raw and cooked potatoes.

A varied programme of **operas, musicals, ballet** and **concerts** is performed at the former court **theatre**, a Neoclassical building of 1840 now known as the Landestheater, Schlossplatz 6 (☎0 95 61/9 27 42, *www.landestheater.coburg.de*).

Restaurants and cafés

Bratwurstglöckle, Kleine Johannisgasse 5. Inexpensive Altstadt Gaststätte, always with freshly made dumplings on the menu, as well as beers from the local Scheidmantel brewery, whose premier product is the dark *Cortendorfer Dunkel*.

Burgschänke, Veste Coburg 1b. The Veste's café-restaurant occupies a whimsical little building which was added during the early twentieth-century restorations. It also has a small beer garden.

Café Feyler Biedermeiercafé, Rosengasse 6–8. A lovely daytime café and cake shop which, as its name suggests, has Biedermeier decor. Its main specialities are *Lebkuchen* and *Coburger Schmätzchen* (Coburg Kisses), the latter being gingerbread decorated with gold leaf.

Café Schubart, Mohrenstr. 11. Another excellent traditional café, with a wide selection of homemade pralines.

Künstler-Klause, Theaterplatz 4a. *Gemütlich* little restaurant serving Franconian specialities. Tues–Sat from 4.30pm, Sun 11.30am–2pm.

Naturkostrestaurant Tie, Leopoldstr. 14. Primarily a wholefood specialist, though it also serves organic meat and fish dishes. Tues–Sun from 5pm.

Parkrestaurant Rosenau, Rosenau 5, Rödental. This occupies one of the outbuildings of Schloss Rosenau, and has a pleasant garden terrace. Closed Mon.

Ratskeller, Markt 1. Moderately priced restaurant in the Rathaus serving hearty Franconian and Bavarian fare.

Rosengarten, Berliner Platz 1. Classy restaurant in the Kongresshaus, with an international menu. Closed Mon.

Schmittners, Ahorner Str. 11. The main Gaststätte of the Sturm brewery, whose diverse products include a *Pils* named in honour of Prince Albert. Closed Wed.

Staffelstein

About 25km south of Coburg, almost exactly halfway towards Bamberg, two of Germany's most famous ecclesiastical complexes can be seen in exhilaratingly lofty positions on either side of the Main valley. Both lie within the scattered municipality of

STAFFELSTEIN, a recuperative health resort with a pretty half-timbered town centre. The main attraction of its Kurpark is the **Obermain Therme** (daily 8am–9pm), which offers some of the best and most up-to-date bathing facilities in Bavaria.

Kloster Banz

Kloster Banz, which stands on top of a hill to the west of the Main, directly above the incorporated village of Altenbanz, is about 3km from the town centre. The only buses which go there are school services, though it's a pleasant enough walk by a paved footpath. Benedictine monks first settled on the hilltop in the eleventh century, but the present Baroque buildings all date from the eighteenth century. Work was begun under Leonhard Dientzenhofer, the court architect in Bamberg, and was continued after his death by his brother Johann. It was brought to completion by Balthasar Neumann, who designed the buildings round the spacious entrance courtyard. After the Napoleonic secularization, the abbey was taken over by the Wittelsbachs as a summer residence.

Nowadays, the monastic buildings belong to a foundation and are used for seminars and conferences; the only part generally accessible to the public is the **Petrefakten Sammlung** (March–Oct Tues–Sun 10am–5pm; DM2/€1) by the main entrance. This contains a collection of fossils found locally, mostly in the first half of the nineteenth century. These are around 180 million years old, and are almost exclusively of maritime creatures, which suggests that the area was covered by a sea at the time. Of special note is the largest skull of a prehistoric fish ever found in Europe: it is more than two metres long and belonged to a reptile resembling a dolphin. Also on view are the artefacts accumulated by Duke Max of Bavaria on a voyage to Egypt in 1838: these include a 3000-year-old mummy and a stuffed crocodile he himself captured in the Nile.

The former abbey church of **St-Petrus-und-St-Dionysius** is now in parish use. It's normally only open as far as the grille: to penetrate further it's necessary to ring for a **guided tour** (May–Oct Mon–Sat 9am–noon & 2–5pm, Sun 10.15am–noon & 2–5pm; Nov–April Mon–Sat 9am–noon, Sun 10.15am–noon; donation requested). Designed and built by Johann Dientzenhofer, the church is a brilliant spatial composition based on a series of ovals. The **high altar** performs a crucial architectural function: it separates the choir, which was reserved for the use of the monks, from the main body of the church, while giving the congregation a framed view through to the choir altar, with its depiction of the martyrdom of St Dionysius. Among the abundant furnishings, the walnut **choir stalls** have pride of place; their backs are adorned with small illusionistic intarsia scenes of the life of St Benedict made from several different woods plus ivory, silver and mother-of-pearl. The nave **frescoes** by the Tyrolean Melchior Steidl are also of high artistic quality; the depiction of *Pentecost* on the dome is flanked by *The Conversion of Saul* and *The Last Supper*. At 11.30am on summer Sundays, recitals are held on the magnificent **organ**. Although the original pipework was removed from the case a century ago, another instrument by the same Baroque master, Johann Philipp Seuffert, has now taken its place.

Vierzehnheiligen

The pilgrimage church of **Vierzehnheiligen** on the opposite side of the Main lies 5km northeast of the centre of Staffelstein, and almost exactly the same distance southeast of the railway junction of Lichtenfels, the next town to the north. Some of the buses between the two towns pass via the church (check the posted timetables); additionally, there are two return services per day from Lichtenfels' Bahnhof. By foot, the way is clearly signposted from both towns, and the latter stages of these routes give some wonderful views up to the church and across the valley.

Vierzehnheiligen has its origins in three apparitions of the Christ Child in 1445–46 to a shepherd who worked for **Kloster Langheim**, a Cistercian monastery (nowadays occupied by Franciscans) high above Staffelstein. In the last of these, the Child was accompanied by fourteen smaller children who told the shepherd they were the auxiliary saints (those invoked by Roman Catholics for intercessory purposes in almost every sphere of life), and that they wished a chapel to be erected on the spot. A miraculous healing occurred shortly afterwards, and the site quickly became a popular place of pilgrimage – even although it lacked a tangible object, such as the relic of a saint or a miracle-working statue, which is normally a prerequisite for such a development. In the eighteenth century, as the pilgrimage became ever more popular and the chapel ever more dilapidated, thoughts turned to replacing it with a splendid new church. Initially, the project was complicated by disputes between the Langheim abbot and the Bamberg prince-bishop, but in 1743 **Balthasar Neumann** was given the task of turning his patrons' seemingly contradictory requirements into reality. Although he died ten years later with work far from complete, the result is in many ways his greatest achievement, one particularly admired by practising architects for the sheer complexity of its solutions.

The handsome twin-towered sandstone **facade** directly faces that of Banz, and is designed to appear like a great sentinel to pilgrims as they ascend the hill; the rest of the exterior consists of plain, straight walls. There could be no greater contrast with the **interior**, which is sumptuously decorated and imparts a restless sense of movement by dispensing with straight lines altogether, replacing them with curves. The groundplan is a development of that of Banz, being based on a series of intersecting oval rotundas; the fourteen piers symbolize the saints to whom the church is dedicated.

In the middle of the church stands the **Gnadenaltar**, a unique shrine-cum-altar which looks like a huge yet extremely fragile piece of porcelain; it was made by a large team of stuccowork artists led by one of Germany's greatest Rococo craftsmen, Johann Michael Feichtmayr. Statues of the fourteen intercessory saints, each carefully characterized, are grouped on and around the shrine; inside is a painting illustrating the shepherd's third miraculous vision. The same sculptors also made the high altar and the two large side altars; that on the north side contains the two most impressive figures of all – St Sebastian and the farmers' patron, St Wendelin. Unfortunately, the ceiling **frescoes** by the Italian Guiseppe Appiani were damaged by dampness in the nineteenth century, and their colours have faded badly. Nonetheless, their vivacity can still be appreciated: particularly effective is the scene above the Gnadenaltar, which shows the fourteen saints in the company of the patrons of the Bamberg diocese, Heinrich II and Kunigunde, adoring the Holy Trinity.

Practicalities

Staffelstein's **Bahnhof** is on the west side of town, close to the Kurpark; **taxis** are available at the rank outside for those who don't want to walk to Banz or wait for a bus to Vierzehnheiligen. Among the town's **hotels** are *Gasthof Grüner Baum*, Bamberger Str. 33 (☎0 95 73/2 93; ③), *Rödiger*, Zur Herrgottsmühle 2 (☎0 95 73/8 95; ⑤), and *Kurapparthotel*, Am Kurpark 7 (☎0 95 73/33 30; ⑥). Another option is *Haus Frankenthal* (☎0 95 73/92 60; ③), which is just a few paces from Vierzehnheiligen, though it is primarily a holiday retreat rather than a regular hotel. It adjoins the fifteenth-century *Gasthof Goldener Hirsch*, nowadays a daytime **restaurant**. A short walk uphill is the Alte Klosterbrauerei, a small brewery with a beer garden and bar, which also serves food; its main product is the dark *Nothelfer*. There are also good restaurants in each of the three hotels in town, while Kloster Banz has a daytime-only establishment, *Klosterschenke*.

Bamberg

There can be no doubt about the status of **BAMBERG** as one of the most beautiful small cities in Europe. Brought to prominence by the saintly eleventh-century Emperor Heinrich II, who wanted to turn it into a German metropolis to rival Rome, it never grew to be particularly big, but nonetheless has a sense of spacious grandeur which belies its actual size. Its relative geographical isolation, some 60km north of Nürnberg and 50km south of Coburg, has been a key factor in preserving its magnificent **artistic heritage** from the ravages of war. Every single European style from the Romanesque onwards has left its mark on the city, each bequeathing at least one outstanding building. For art lovers, there's the added bonus of one of the most marvellously diverse arrays of sculpture to be found in the country.

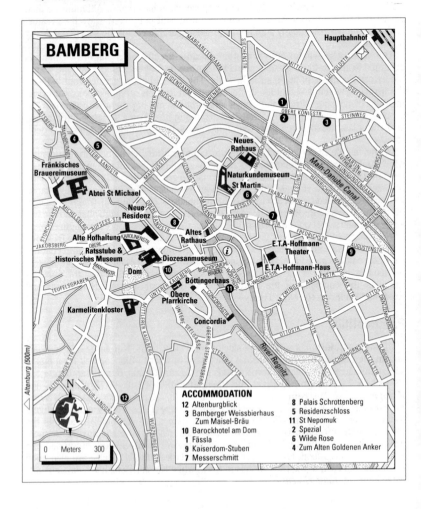

BAMBERG

Hauptbahnhof

Neues Rathaus

Fränkisches Brauereimuseum

Naturkundemuseum

St Martin

Abtei St Michael

Neue Residenz

Altes Rathaus

Alte Hofhaltung

E.T.A-Hoffmann-Theater

Ratsstube & Historisches Museum

Diozesanmuseum

E.T.A-Hoffmann-Haus

Dom

Böttingerhaus

Obere Pfarrkirche

Karmelitenkloster

Concordia

Altenburg (500m)

Main-Danube Canal

River Regnitz

0 Meters 300

ACCOMMODATION

12 Altenburgblick
3 Bamberger Weissbierhaus Zum Maisel-Bräu
10 Barockhotel am Dom
1 Fässla
9 Kaiserdom-Stuben
7 Messerschmitt
8 Palais Schrottenberg
5 Residenzschloss
11 St Nepomuk
2 Spezial
6 Wilde Rose
4 Zum Alten Goldenen Anker

Not the least of Bamberg's attractions is that, in contrast to some of Franconia's other picturesque old towns, it hasn't been mothballed into a museum-piece, being an animated city of modern industries which profits from the youthful presence of a university. It's also one of the country's great **beer** centres, holding the national record for consumption per inhabitant. Out of the 64 breweries the city had a century ago, nine still survive; all are traditional Hausbrauereien, and some have an in-house hotel as well as the obligatory restaurant. Together they make more than thirty different products, the most notable being the appropriately named *Rauchbier* (smoky beer): made from smoked malt according to a formula developed in the sixteenth century, it's as distinctive a local brew as you'll find in Germany, leaving its own very special lingering aftertaste.

Arrival, information and accommodation

Bamberg's **Hauptbahnhof** is about fifteen minutes' walk to the northeast of the Altstadt. From here, follow Luitpoldstrasse straight ahead, before turning into the third street on the right, Obere Königstrasse, cross the bridge over the Rhein-Main-Donau-Kanal and you're right in the heart of the lower town. The **tourist office** (Jan–April & Nov Mon–Fri 9am–6pm, Sat 9am–3pm; May–Oct & Dec Mon–Fri 9am–6pm, Sat 9am–3pm, Sun 10am–2pm; ☎09 51/87 11 61, fax 87 19 60, *www.tourismus.bamberg.de*) is on an island in the River Pegnitz at Geyerswörthstr. 3. Regnitz **cruises**, run by Personenschiffahrt Bamberg (☎09 51/2 66 79), depart from Am Kranen and cost DM10/€5 for an eighty-minute round trip.

Bamberg offers an exceptionally good choice of **hotels**, ranging from inexpensive brewery-owned inns (Brauereigasthöfe) to upmarket establishments in characterful historic buildings. The **youth hostel** is pleasantly situated on the bank of the Regnitz 2km south of the centre at Oberer Leinritt 70 (☎09 51/5 60 02, fax 5 52 11; DM21/€10.50); take bus #1 from the Hauptbahnhof to ZOB Promenade, then bus #18 to Regnitzufer. Another 2km further down the river is the *Insel* **campsite** (☎09 51/5 63 20).

Hotels

Altenburgblick, Panzerleite 59 (☎09 51/9 53 10, fax 9 53 14 44, *www.altenburgblick.de*). Run by the Greifenklau brewery, this is the pick of the panorama hotels in the hills in the southern part of Bamberg. The only meals it serves are breakfast buffets, but the associated Gaststätte (see p.201) is just a short walk away. ⑤.

Bamberger Weissbierhaus Zum Maisel-Bräu, Obere Königstr. 38 (☎ & fax 09 51/2 55 03). One of a trio of inexpensive Brauereigasthöfe on the street; unlike the other two, the brewery itself is elsewhere (see p.201). However, it does have a bar-restaurant (closed Sun), while the bedrooms are grouped in quiet seclusion around the inner courtyard. ③.

Barockhotel am Dom, Vorderer Bach 4 (☎09 51/5 40 31, fax 5 40 21). An aptly named hotel, offering good value at the price asked. ⑥.

Fässla, Obere Königstr. 21 (☎09 51/2 29 98 or 2 65 16, fax 20 19 89). Another Brauereigasthof, which recently celebrated 350 years in the same premises. It offers modernized bedrooms with private facilities, good buffet breakfasts and typically homely fare in the no-frills bar-restaurant (closed Sun after 1pm). Among its products is the city's strongest beer, the seasonal *Bambergator*. ③.

Kaiserdom, Gaustadter Hauptstr. 26 (☎09 51/96 51 40, fax 9 65 14 44, *www.kaiserdom.de*). The most upmarket of the Brauereigasthöfe, situated alongside Bamberg's largest brewery in an incorporated village 4km northwest of the Altstadt. It has an excellent restaurant (closed Mon) specializing in Franconian cuisine plus a large beer garden. There's a similarly priced offshoot, *Kaiserdom-Stuben*, much closer to the town centre at Urbanstr. 18 (☎09 51/98 07 30, fax 20 23 78). ④–⑤.

Messerschmitt, Lange Str. 41 (☎09 51/2 78 66, fax 2 61 41, *www.hotel-messerschmitt.de*). Part of the Romantik chain, this hotel and restaurant occupy a fine old Weinhaus with inner courtyard. ⑦.

Palais Schrottenburg, Kasernstr. 1 (☎09 51/95 58 80, fax 9 55 88 10, *www.palais-schrottenburg.de*). This hotel is in a splendid Baroque mansion on the west side of the Regnitz. Its restaurant has an elegant main dining room with a stucco ceiling. ⑥.

Residenzschloss, Untere Sandstr. 32 (☎09 51/6 09 10, fax 6 09 17 01, *www.hotel-residenzschloss.de*). Bamberg's leading hotel, a member of the Welcome chain, occupies a monumental Baroque hospital building. The facilities include a fitness centre, sauna, solarium, steam bath, whirlpool and two restaurants: *Orangerie* and *Fürst Bischof von Erthal*. The beautiful house chapel is a popular venue for weddings. ⑧–⑨.

Sankt Nepomuk, Obere Mühlbrücke 9 (☎09 51/9 84 20, fax 9 84 21 00, *www.hotel-nepomuk.de*). Classy hotel in a picturesque old mill on an islet in the Regnitz. It also has a fine restaurant which specializes in fish dishes. ⑦.

Spezial, Obere Königstr. 10 (☎09 51/2 43 04, fax 2 63 30). Cosy Brauereigasthof attached to one of the two producers of *Rauchbier*, and the only one which smokes all its brews. Its restaurant (closed Sat after 2pm) serves inexpensive local fare. ③.

Wilde Rose, Kesslerstr. 7 (☎09 51/98 18 20, fax 2 20 71). Good middle-range hotel in the east bank part of the lower town. The brewery from which it takes its name is no longer in operation, but its products are still made under licence and are available in the restaurant (closed Sun evening). ⑥.

Zum Alten Goldenen Anker, Untere Sandstr. 73 (☎09 51/6 65 05, fax 6 65 95). Historic Wirtshaus whose restaurant (closed Mon) has a vaulted interior and a tiny inner courtyard reached from upstairs. ③.

The City

Like Rome, on which it was very consciously modelled, Bamberg is built on seven hills, pocked with belvederes each of which offers a different perspective on the city. The Dom and related structures take up the entire crown of the main hill, towering high above the town centre to form the Domstadt, the headquarters of the prince-bishopric which ruled until the Napoleonic suppression, whereupon it gave way to the purely spiritual archbishopric still based here. Clinging to the lower slopes of the valley of the River Regnitz are the residential districts, which constitute an unusually complete Baroque townscape of picturesque corners, with the play of light on the river lending an extra sense of magic to the scene.

The Dom

Consecrated in 1012, the **Dom** (often dignified as the **Kaiserdom**) was burnt down twice in the following two centuries, and the present sandstone structure is the result of a slow rebuilding process that continued throughout the thirteenth century. During this period architectural tastes were beginning to change, but the ground plan follows the precedent of the imperial cathedrals of the Rhineland in having a choir at both ends of the building, each of which is flanked by twin towers. The east chancel is dedicated to the warrior St George, symbolizing the Empire, while its western counterpart bears a dedication to St Peter, representing the Papacy. These were the first and last parts of the Dom to be completed, and you can see that the rounded Romanesque arches and heavy vaults of the eastern choir had given way to the tall pointed windows and graceful ribs characteristic of early Gothic by the west end. In between, the nave was erected in the so-called Transitional style, offering insight into the way the original masons were experimenting with the new techniques.

What makes the Kaiserdom one of Europe's greatest cathedrals is the astonishing array of **sculptural decoration**. As with the architecture, this was initially executed in an orthodox Romanesque style, the best example being the **Fürstenportal** on the nave's north side, facing the main slope of the square. Its tympanum warns of the Last Judgement, while the progressively receding arches are each adorned with the figure of an apostle standing on the shoulders of an Old Testament prophet. Carvings in a similar style can be found on the **Marienportal** on the right-hand door to the east chancel, which shows the Madonna and Child adored by the Kaiserdom's patrons, founders and builders, and on the choir screen panels, also placing Apostles and prophets in juxtaposition.

Created by an unknown French-trained artist, the most famous of all this sculpture is the enigmatic **Bamberg Rider** (Bamberger Reiter) just inside the entrance doorway, one of the few equestrian statues which had been made since the days of classical antiquity. Nobody knows for sure who this noble figure is; the Romantics imagined it was an idealized portrait of a German emperor of the Hohenstaufen line. This was eagerly seized on by the Nazis, and during the Third Reich the statue was the national symbol of Germanic perfection, adorning every public hall and classroom. Two other **statues** to look out for are the female personifications of the Christian and Jewish faiths at the southeast end of the nave. The victory of Christianity over Judaism is highlighted by the women's contrasting countenances: the Christian is a beautiful woman clad in rich cloth, while the Jewess stands blindfolded holding a broken rod and wearing a plain tunic that emphasizes the outline of her fallen breasts. Even finer are the two figures of the Visitation group directly opposite. The Virgin Mary is young and bright, draped in a swirling dress; St Elizabeth is an ancient, haggard old crone whose expression speaks of an overwhelming sense of pathos.

As a perfect complement to the carvings associated with its construction, the Dom also contains a masterpiece by each of the two most famous sculptors of the early sixteenth century. Focus of the nave is the white limestone **tomb** of **Heinrich II and Kunigunde**, the canonized imperial couple, which stands slightly elevated as a result of the crypt built below. **Tilman Riemenschneider** laboured away for fourteen years on this sarcophagus, whose reliefs depict scenes taken from the life and times of the couple. The south transept contains **Veit Stoss**'s dark limewood **Nativity altar**, made when the artist was about 80 years old, as a result of a commission from his son, who was a Carmelite prior in Nürnberg. It was meant as a sort of artistic testament, executed without the usual studio assistance. Unfortunately, it's unfinished – the younger Stoss, a virulent anti-Protestant, was kicked out of Nürnberg when the city council adopted the Reformation, and the sculptor received no payment for his retable, which was soon afterwards moved to Bamberg.

Although it's not accessible to the public, it's worth knowing that the western choir holds the only **papal grave** in Germany, namely that of Pope Clement II. He was the local bishop before becoming pope, but died in 1047 after having enjoyed the papacy for a mere twelve months. Tomb slabs to the Dom's other bishops can be found scattered throughout the building. The most impressive, artistically speaking, is the **monument to Friedrich von Hohenlohe** in the south aisle, just before the transept. Dating from the latter half of the fourteenth century, it conveniently represents the period midway between the Bamberg Rider and the works of Riemenschneider and Stoss.

Entered from the southern aisle, the cloisters and associated buildings now house the **Diözesanmuseum** (Tues–Sun 10am–5pm; DM4/€2). On the walls of the cloister walks are lapidary fragments, most notably the six original statues from the **Adamportal**, the dogtooth doorway to the left of the east choir. Here the ubiquitous emperor and his wife turn up in the company of the Dom's two patrons, plus Adam and Eve. The last two are unashamedly sensual; covered only by fig-leaves, they come as near to erotic art as was ever dared in the Middle Ages. Upstairs, displayed under specially dimmed lights, is a collection of early medieval **vestments** – including the cloaks of Heinrich, Kunegunde and Pope Clement II – whose vibrant colours and intricate designs are quite amazingly well preserved. There are also some valuable treasury items, such as a twelfth-century ivory crucifix and the so-called staff of St Otto, as well as a magnificent tapestry of the Passion from around 1500.

Domplatz

Bamberg's **Domplatz** is lined with such a superb variety of buildings, which unfold like a great picture-book of architecture, and uses its spacious, sloping site to such dramatic advantage, that it has no possible rival for the title of Germany's finest square. The **Ratsstube** is a Renaissance gem, with elegantly tapering gables and an ornate oriel window. It now contains the **Historisches Museum** (Tues–Sun 9am–5pm; DM4/€2), which covers local and regional history from the Stone Age onwards, as well as Bamberg's rich artistic tradition. The exhibits include a tenth-century ivory Virgin *and Child* from Constantinople; an intricate late sixteenth-century clock; a typically idiosyncratic panel of *The Great Flood* by **Hans Baldung Grien**, who here tackled with relish a subject most painters shied away from; and Balthasar Neumann's original wooden model for Vierzehnheiligen.

Adjoining the Ratsstube is the **Reiche Tor**, in which Heinrich and Kunigunde appear once more; the model they carry is recognizably the Kaiserdom. This gate leads into the huge fifteenth-century courtyard of the **Alte Hofhaltung**, the former episcopal palace, which incorporates the remains of the eleventh-century hall of the Imperial Diet. The overhanging eaves of the huge sloping roof shelter two tiers of wooden galleries, and there's an unusual perspective on the towers of the Dom. One wing contains an annexe of the Historisches Museum.

Across the street is the building which supplanted it, the **Neue Residenz** (guided tours April–Sept Mon–Wed & Fri–Sun 9am–6pm, Thurs 9am–8pm; Oct–March daily 10am–4pm; DM6/€3). An early example of the passion for building huge new palaces in the Baroque style that was to sweep across the German principalities, it was erected at the turn of the eighteenth century to an L-shape plan by Leonhard Dientzenhofer. Inside, a suite of rooms designed expressly for occasions when the emperor stayed as guest culminates in the huge **Kaisersaal**, which is nowadays a regular concert venue. Its walls are entirely covered with rich stuccowork and colourful frescoes by Melchior Steidl, including portraits of the emperors of ancient Rome and a ceiling with an allegorical composition extolling the benefits of wise rule. The private apartments of the prince-bishops are far more homely in feel; the most original is the **Chinesische Kabinett**, a curious hybrid in which traditional Baroque decoration is mixed with chinoiserie.

Also included in the entrance ticket, but visited independently, is the **Staatsgalerie Bamberg** (same times), which occupies two suites of apartments. The first of these contains works by Bamberg painters of the Gothic and Renaissance periods, and by some of their German contemporaries, including the Master of the Life of the Virgin, Hans Suess von Kulmbach, Baldung and Cranach. In the second gallery, which is devoted to the Baroque era, the geographical scope is widened to include Dutch and Flemish paintings. The palace also houses the **Staatsbibliothek** (Mon–Fri 9am–5pm, Sat 9am–noon; free), and it's worth having at least a quick look at the elegant Baroque hall which serves as its reading room. It usually stages a couple of exhibitions per year; facsimiles of its most valuable treasures, including some stunning illuminated manuscripts, are on permanent view in the corridor. To the rear of the complex is the **Rosengarten**, a formal rose garden with playful Rococo statues. It commands marvellous views, particularly up to the Abtei St Michael.

The lower town

Below Domplatz is the lower town (*Unterstadt*), which is laid out on both sides of the Regnitz. From its islet position, the **Altes Rathaus**, which seems almost too picturesque for its own good, anchors together two of the connecting bridges, the Obere Brücke and Untere Brücke. Except for the half-timbered section overhanging the rapids, the original Gothic building was transformed in Rococo style, and its walls are

---

ERNST THEODOR AMADEUS HOFFMANN (1776–1822)

A native of the Prussian university city of Königsberg (now Kaliningrad, the capital of a stranded enclave of the Russian Federation), **Theodor Hoffmann** was a man of extraordinarily varied talents. For most of his life, he was employed by the civil service, but for the years he lived in Bamberg (1808–13) he tried to establish himself as a composer, conductor and theatre director, having previously failed as a painter. Music was his greatest passion, but, notwithstanding the fact that he was arguably the first truly Romantic composer, he came to realize that his genius lay with words. He developed into an unusually perspicacious music critic, then increasingly devoted himself to his real forte as an author of weird short stories that reflected his own rather schizophrenic nature. Appropriately enough, he was a constant source of inspiration to later composers: Offenbach portrayed his bizarre personality in the opera *The Tales of Hoffmann*, while his stories formed the basis for two of the great Romantic ballets, Delibes' *Coppélia* and Tchaikovsky's *The Nutcracker*. His finest works are the chillingly supernatural *The Golden Pot*, and the later *Mademoiselle de Scudéry*, which is now generally regarded as the first detective story.

---

busily tattooed with exuberant frescoes. Inside is the **Sammlung Ludwig** (Tues–Sun 9.30am–4.30pm; DM6/€3), a collection of Baroque porcelain and faience from all over Europe. On a much larger island to the south stands **Schloss GeyersWörth**, the Renaissance palace of the prince-bishops. The famous **Klein-Venedig** (Little Venice) of fishermen's houses is best seen from the Untere Brücke and presents one of the very few medieval scenes in the lower parts of town.

The bridges lead over to the elongated Grüner Markt, which is dominated by the facade of **St Martin**, a huge Jesuit church designed by the Dientzenhofer brothers. Within its former monastic buildings to the rear is the **Naturkundemuseum** (April–Sept Tues–Sun 9am–5pm; Oct–March Tues–Sun 10am–4pm; DM3/€1.50), which contains fossils found in the Franconian Jura as well as crystals and stuffed animals, including a rare quagga. However, the main attraction is what is described as a "museum within the museum", a beautiful Neoclassical exhibition hall still preserving its original display cabinets and their exhibits. The ground floor is entirely devoted to ornithology, and is divided equally between Central European and exotic species. In the upstairs galleries are small mammals, reptiles, fish, insects and shells.

Beyond Grüner Markt is the vast open space of **Maxplatz**, where daily markets are held. On its northern side is the vast **Neues Rathaus**, which was built by Balthasar Neumann, originally for use as a seminary. A smaller but prettier square on this side of the river is Schillerplatz to the southeast. Here, at no. 26, is the **E.T.A.-Hoffmann-Haus** (May–Oct Tues–Fri 4–6pm, Sat & Sun 10am–noon; DM2/€1), the home of one of the foremost figures of the Romantic movement (see box above). In addition to the expected memorabilia and documentation on his diverse career, it now contains contemporary artistic installations inspired by his stories.

Back on the west bank, the southern end of the lower town is dominated by the **Wasserschloss Concordia**, a riverside mansion built by Johann Dientzenhofer for the Franconian chargé d'affaires. The same patron had previously commissioned a grand Baroque palace, the **Böttingerhaus**, which lies a short walk to the north at Judenstr. 14.

The hills

On Unter Kaulberg, which sweeps uphill from Judenstrasse, is Bamberg's main parish church, the **Obere Pfarrkirche**. Architecturally, it's something of a hotchpotch, though the chancel and the **Brautportal** (Bridal Portal), whose carvings of the Wise and Foolish Virgins strike a suitable warning note, are distinguished productions of the famous fourteenth-century Parler family. The interior was remodelled in Baroque style, and contains a huge **high altar** of the period incorporating a much-venerated Gothic statue of the Virgin and Child. Other furnishings of special note include a highly elaborate late fourteenth-century **tabernacle**, now banished to one of the ambulatory chapels; an early sixteenth-century **font** with reliefs of the Sacraments; and a large painting of *The Assumption* by **Tintoretto**.

Further up the same hill is the **Karmelitenkloster**, whose Baroque church was designed by Leonhard Dientzenhofer. Of more interest are the surviving parts of the suppressed convent which formerly occupied the site: the Romanesque portal, guarded by lions, which is incongruously stranded in a walled-up position at the back of the present church, and the **cloister** (daily 8.30–11.30am & 2.30–5.30pm; free), the largest in Germany. The latter is now known to be late fourteenth century in date, though it was built in the long-superseded Romanesque style. Despite this anachronism, the column capitals were carved by masons possessed of fertile imagination: in addition to the biblical scenes, there's a fabulous bestiary, ranging from fearsome dragons to weird creepy-crawlies.

Crowning the hill to the north of the Dom is the **Abtei St Michael**, an eleventh-century Benedictine foundation. The **Abteikirche** still preserves some of its Romanesque masonry from the following century, though it was badly damaged by fire in 1610 and partially rebuilt in a tardy Gothic style. Also from this period are the **vault paintings**, which depict more than six hundred plants with medicinal properties, and the **organ gallery**, which is in the late Renaissance style then fashionable. The small crypt to the rear of the high altar contains the beautifully carved thirteenth-century **tomb of St Otto**, a Bamberg bishop of the previous century; there's also a polychrome portrait slab of him, made around the same time. In the nineteenth century, the grand tombs of the prince-bishops who ruled between the mid-sixteenth and late eighteenth centuries were moved here from the Dom, and placed in the aisles of the nave. Among the many large-scale furnishings added during the Baroque era, the finest are the gilded **pulpit**, which is topped by a dramatic composition of St Michael overcoming Satan, and the **choir stalls**, with their backs of inlaid wood. The part-stucco, part-painted depiction of the Dance of Death on the vault of the **Heilig-Grab-Kapelle** is from the same period.

Leonhard Dietzenhofer, who added a new facade to the church, also began the monumental complex of monastic buildings around the front courtyard; his work was continued by his brother Johann and Balthasar Neumann, among others. The cellars now house the **Fränkisches Brauereimuseum** (April–Sept Wed–Sun 1–5pm; DM3.50/€1.75), which displays all the equipment used in traditional brewing, as well as memorabilia of Bamberg breweries past and present. From the terrace beyond, there's a wonderful panorama of the town and the surrounding hills.

However, the most dramatic views of Bamberg's skyline are obtained from the footpath leading up to the **Altenburg**, a heavily restored feudal fortress at the southwestern edge of town. Dating back at least as far as the early twelfth century, it became the residence of the local prince-bishops a couple of hundred years later. During daylight hours, there's normally unrestricted access to the castle, whose ramparts command an extensive view over the surrounding countryside, but a far less satisfying one of the city itself than those en route.

Eating, drinking and entertainment

Many of Bamberg's best **restaurants** are in the hotels (see pp.195–6). The brewery-owned restaurants (Brauereigaststätten) and their associated **beer gardens** (some on site, others, usually much larger, on the hills above the town) are the obvious places for solid, good-value food accompanied by locally made beer. Note that, as well as those listed below, there are others which also incorporate a hotel and are therefore included in the hotel section. The city also hosts several worthwhile **festivals** and keeps up a strong **musical** and **theatrical** tradition.

Brewery restaurants and beer gardens

Greifenklau, Laurenziplatz 20. Beer cellar of Bamberg's smallest brewery, whose only year-round product is the golden amber *Lagerbier*. Its garden offers a view up to the Altenburg. Closes at 2pm on Sun.

Keesmann, Wunderburg 5. Another small operation, whose premier product is Bamberg's best *Pils*. It occupies a handsome building with a tree-shaded inner courtyard. Closed Sat after 3pm & Sun.

Klosterbräu, Obere Mühlbrücke 3. This picturesque riverside brewery, complete with inner courtyard and a medieval tithe barn where beer festivals are held in April and August, is the oldest in Bamberg, dating back to 1533. In accordance with its ecclesiastical origins, it's best known for its dark brews, *Braunbier* and *Schwärzla*. Closed Wed.

Mahrs-Bräu, Wunderburg 10. This decor of this Gaststätte has been preserved almost unaltered for more than a century; there's also a courtyard garden. The brewery alongside makes a range of predominantly pale-coloured beers.

Mahrs-Bräu-Keller, Oberer Stephansberg 36. Beer garden and restaurant of the eponymous brewery; the latter occupies a half-timbered building with a Jugendstil extension. Evenings only, except on Sun; closed Mon.

Maisel-Keller, Moosstr. 32. Bamberg's Maisel brewery (which is completely separate from its Bayreuth namesake) is a relative newcomer, being just over a century old, though it makes a wider variety of beers than its local rivals. There's a large garden on site.

Röckeleinskeller, Laurenzistr. 30. The year-round beer garden of the Kaiserdom brewery, which has a good portfolio of products, including a very dry *Pils* and three wheat beers.

Schlenkerla, Dominikanerstr. 6. Not to be missed: the seventeenth-century tavern of the Heller brewery, which makes what's generally regarded as the ultimate smoky beer, *Aecht Schlenkerla Rauchbier*: the standard version is a *Märzen*, though there's also a smoked *Weizen*. It also serves hearty local cuisine. Closed Tues.

Spezial-Keller, Oberer Stephansberg 47, entrance on Sternwartstrasse. Large and popular beer cellar-cum-garden, commanding a fine distant view of the city, of the other *Rauchbier* specialist. Open Tues–Sat from 3pm, Sun from 10am, closed Mon.

Wilde-Rose-Bräu-Keller, Obere Stephansberg 49. Beer garden, complete with pavilions, serving the products of a label which has survived the closure of the brewery itself. May–Sept only: weekdays from 4pm, weekends from 3pm.

Other restaurants

Alte Hofreit, Dominikanerstr. 10. Restaurant combining a traditional beer-hall atmosphere with wholefood dishes.

Brudermühle, Schranne 1. This restaurant specializes in trout, which is fresh daily, and game. It has a good selection of wines and also serves *Kaffee und Kuchen*.

Burggaststätte, Altenburg 1. Cosy restaurant in the Altenburg. Closed Sun evening & Mon.

Michaelsberg, Michaelsberg 10e. One of two restaurants in the abbey complex. It has a salad bar and a large terrace offering a wonderful view over Bamberg. Closed Tues.

Michaelsberg Benediktinerbräu, Michaelsberg 10f. This Gaststätte is in the same building as the Fränkisches Brauereimuseum; it also has a nineteenth-century glass pavilion extension, now under a protection order. Closed Mon.

Würzburger Weinstuben, Zinkenwörth 6. Classy wine bar-restaurant in a half-timbered building.

Bars and cafés

Bolero, Judenstr. 7. Popular tapas bar with a large beer garden.

Café im Rosengarten, Domplatz 1. A daytime café in a pavilion of the rose garden of the Neues Residenz; tables are also set up on the terrace outside. April–Oct only.

Downstairs, Lange Str. 16. Bamberg's best nightclub. Daily 10pm–4am.

Jazzkeller, Obere Sandstr. 18. Cellar bar with live jazz on Tues & Thurs.
Kaffeehaus Beckstein, Lange Str. 9. Viennese-style coffee house; also serves lunch dishes. Closed Sun.
Live-Club, Obere Sandstr. 7. Bar with live bands on Mon & Sat.

Culture

For its size, Bamberg has an amazingly vibrant cultural centre, especially for **classical music**. The Bamberger Symphoniker was actually the old Deutsches Orchester of Prague, which fled over the border at the time the Iron Curtain was going up. Now under the musical directorship of Britain's Jonathan Nott, the orchestra performs in a variety of venues, and is especially known for candle-lit concerts in the Neue Residenz. Tickets for most of the city's musical events can be obtained from the BVD Kartenservice, Lange Str. 22 (☎09 51/9 80 82 20). The principal **theatre**, not surprisingly, is the E.T.A. Hoffmann-Theater, Schillerplatz 7 (☎09 51/87 14 33); the resident company also holds an open-air season in June and July in the Alte Hofhaltung. Performances by the Marionettentheater Loose take place in a sixteen-seater puppet theatre of 1821 in the Staubsches Haus, Untere Sandstr. 30 (☎09 51/6 76 00).

Bamberg's most colourful religious **festival** is Corpus Christi (*Fronleichnam*; variable date in May/June), when an open-air Mass on Domplatz is followed by a procession in which devotional statues and ecclesiastical objects are carried through the streets of the town on stretchers adorned with magnificent floral garlands. In early summer, a couple of musical festivals are held in the Neues Residenz – the *Residenz Festival* and the *Tage Alter Musik*. A wine festival, the *Fränkisches Weinfest*, is held in Schloss Geyerswörth in late June, while the Fränkisches Brauereimuseum runs a beer festival, *Brauerei Nostalgiefest*, in early July. The main folklore event is the *Strassenfest* in late September.

The Steigerwald and the Hassberge

Within easy reach of Bamberg are two heavily wooded upland areas, the **Steigerwald** and **Hasseberge**, which are separated from each other by the serpentine course of the River Main. Both are popular hiking destinations, having exactly the sort of undemanding terrain the Germans favour for their weekend walks. There are also some important historic monuments, the most notable being in **Pommersfelden** and **Hassfurt**.

Pommersfelden

At the edge of the Steigerwald, about 20km south of Bamberg, the village of **POMMERSFELDEN** is dominated by **Schloss Weissenstein** (guided tours April–Oct Tues–Sun 9am–4pm; DM7/€3.50), the jewel in the crown of the enormous building programme that Prince-Bishop Lothar Franz von Schönborn funded from the sizeable fortune he assured himself by masterminding the election of Emperor Charles VI in 1711. Dating from around the same time as Germany's other great Baroque palaces such as Nymphenburg, Würzburg and the Neue Residenz in Bamberg itself, Weissenstein was built by Johann Dientzenhofer in equally ostentatious proportions. The entrance hall of the central pavilion takes up the full height of the three-storey palace, and the showpiece **double staircase** – which the prince-bishop designed himself after consulting with the great Viennese architect Lucas von Hildebrandt – swings up to galleries that encase the hall rather like great Italian courtyards. Its ceiling fresco uses clever perspective to depict the gods of Mount Olympus surrounded by scenes representing each of the four continents. Other highlights include the

Spiegelkabinett, which is decked out with oriental porcelain, and the collection of old masters, featuring works by Dürer, Titian and Rubens, among others. The obligatory ballroom, known as the **Marmorsaal** because of the stuccoed marble pillars that line its walls, has a ceiling fresco of *The Victory of the Virtues over the Vices* by Johann Michael Rottmayr.

From mid-July to mid-August each year, the Marmorsaal is used for the classical concerts of the *Collegium Musicum*, an international **festival** of young musicians. For information and tickets, contact the *Schlossverwaltung* (☎0 95 48/2 03). It's worth knowing that there's a fine **hotel** (☎0 95 48/6 80; ⑤) with restaurant in the Schloss. Unfortunately, the **bus** service is rather meagre, with only two or three per day to and from Bamberg.

Hassfurt

The pretty little town of **HASSFURT** lies on the north bank of the Main between the Steigerwald and the Hassberge, some 35km northwest of Bamberg on the looping rail line along the Main valley to Würzburg. For much of its history, it was a frontier post of the territory of the latter's prince-bishopric, and two massive medieval tower-gates, the **Oberes** (or **Bamberger**) **Tor** and **Unteres** (or **Würzburger**) **Tor**, still guard either end of Hauptstrasse. A third, the **Brückentorturm**, which formerly guarded the riverfront, was remodelled in Baroque style in the eighteenth century, probably by Balthasar Neumann. Alongside the Oberes Tor stand a number of official buildings from the time of the prince-bishopric, later adapted for municipal use – the tithe barn is now the **Stadthalle**, the offices the **Rathaus**. The latter has displaced a pinnacled Gothic building further down the street, facing Marktplatz to the north. On the other side of the square is the **Stadpfarrkirche St Kilian**, a modest twin-towered Gothic church whose high altar contains statues from the workshop of **Tilman Riemenschneider** of the eponymous Irish martyr and his companions, St Kolonat and St Totnan. These are surpasssed in quality by the *Hassfurt Madonna* at the end of the north aisle, an early work from the master's own hand, and the figure of St John the Baptist opposite, an example of his mature style.

Outside the fortifications, just east of the Oberes Tor, is **Marienkapelle**, popularly known as the **Ritterkapelle**, a splendid late Gothic chapel erected in the fifteenth century for a Marian brotherhood of priests and noblemen. Not only is this Hassfurt's finest building, it's the most important heraldic monument in all of Germany. The friezes decorating the exterior of the choir feature no fewer than 248 different **coats of arms**, principally of the Franconian and Swabian nobility. A further 28 can be seen inside, all but three of them on the choir vault. Above the facade doorway is a beautiful **tympanum** depicting the Journey and Adoration of the Magi in a lively narrative style, while the vault of the porch has a curious symbolic representation of the Four Virtues in the form of an almost naked man stretched out in the shape of a St Andrew's cross.

Hassfurt's **Bahnhof** is just a couple of minutes' walk north of the Oberes Tor. The **tourist office** (early May to Sept Mon–Wed 8am–noon & 2–4pm, Thurs 8am–noon & 2–5pm, Fri 8am–noon & 3.30–5.30pm, Sat 9–11.30am; rest of year Mon–Wed 8am–noon & 2–4pm, Thurs 8am–noon & 2–5pm, Fri 8am–noon; ☎0 95 21/68 82 27, fax 68 82 80, *www.hassfurt.de*) is in the Rathaus, Hauptstr. 5. There are three central **hotels**, all with **restaurants**: *Gasthof Mainaussicht*, Fischerrain 8 (☎0 95 21/14 09; ②), *Walfisch*, Vorstadt 8 (☎0 95 21/9 22 70; ③), and *Das Altstadthotel*, Pfarrgasse 2 (☎0 95 21/92 80; ⑤).

Schweinfurt

The former Free Imperial City of **SCHWEINFURT** lies 20km down the Main from Hassfurt, its Altstadt on the north bank of the river, a harbour and industrial district on the opposite side. For the past century, it has been known principally as a ball-bearing metropolis, and this ensured it was subject to severe aerial bombardment during World War II. Afterwards, the American forces, who established a large and still active base in the town, allowed the ball-bearing tycoon Georg Schäfer to return to his factory, and he had an enormously successful career, establishing subsidiary concerns all around the globe. Schäfer used his fortune to fund his passion for art, concentrating exclusively on the German-speaking world, and a few years after his death in 1975 his choice group of old masters was put on permanent display in Coburg. In the meantime, the nineteenth-century paintings and drawings which formed the core of his collection, rivalling and in many respects surpassing the holdings of this period in the great public galleries of Berlin, Hamburg and Munich, remained with his descendants, though selections were sometimes exhibited. The first steps towards making the works permanently accessible to the public were not taken until 1997, when a foundation was set up with the aim of giving Schweinfurt the major attraction it had hitherto lacked, yet desperately wanted, in its bid to become a tourist and conference centre.

The Town

After an almost miraculously short period of planning and construction work, the **Museum Georg Schäfer** (Tues, Wed & Fri–Sun 10am–5pm, Thurs 10am–9pm; *www.museumgeorgschaefer.de*; DM6/€3) opened in September 2000 at Brückenstr. 20 in the town centre. It has attracted rave reviews, not only for the quality of the exhibits, but also for the building by the Berlin architect Volker Staab, a satisfying blend of modernity and tradition, expertly lit and commanding fine views over the town from its top level, where about a third of the total stock of more than a thousand works is displayed in strict chronological order. The first room contains a wonderful group of canvases by **Friedrich**, ranging from a poetic nocturne, *Evening on the Baltic*, to a visionary masterpiece, *The Cathedral*. There are more than a hundred works in various media by **Menzel**, the most versatile German artist of the nineteenth century. These include historical vignettes of the court life of Frederick the Great and documentations of the contemporary court of Kaiser Wilhelm I, topographical views and scenes of the industrial world, as well as many superb portraits, including the artist Chodowiecki (depicted sketching on Jannowitzbrücke in Berlin), the author Paul Heyse, the so-called Rabbi of Baghdad, and a young girl, Friederike Arnold, drawn in gorgeous pastel colours. The Biedermeier artist **Spitzweg**, whose fun-poking yet never cruel humour is seen at its most effective in paintings such as *The Bookworm*, *The Cactus Lover* and *The Portraitist*, is even more copiously represented, by some 160 oils and 100 drawings, by far the largest collection of his work in existence, though much of it is usually in store. Other highpoints of the collection are an oval *Madonna and Child with St John* by **Overbeck**; the jewel-like *Sulamith and Maria* by his short-lived Nazarene colleague **Franz Pforr**; the salacious *Going for a Ride* by **Franz von Stuck**; and self-portraits by Wilhelm Busch (better-known as the father of the strip cartoon), Lenbach, Liebermann and Corinth. The first floor is devoted to themed exhibitions, which draw on the foundation's extensive collection of graphic art as well as its reserve of paintings.

Although the museum overshadows everything else in town, the Altstadt has some fine historic buildings, notably the **Rathaus**, which is at the top end of the same street. A mixture of Gothic and Renaissance elements, with a prominent tower-cum-oriel, the building was designed in the 1570s by the Saxon architect Nickel Hoffmann. It faces **Marktplatz**, where markets are held on Wednesday and Saturday mornings and Tuesday and Friday afternoons. In the centre of the square is a statue to Friedrich Rückert, who was born in the house with the commemorative plaque at the southeast corner.

On Martin-Luther-Platz, the next square to the north, is the church of **St Johannis**, which was built over the course of several centuries, and is thus a mixture of

Romanesque and both early and late Gothic elements. It also has a fine Renaissance chapel, the **Herrenkapelle**, on its north side, which was reserved for the use of the town councillors, and contains a valuable documentary painting illustrating the presentation of the basic Protestant creed, the Confession of Augsburg, to Emperor Charles V in 1530. The church's other furnishings include a fourteenth-century font which still preserves its original panel paintings, a carved and gilded Baroque pulpit and numerous funerary epitaphs.

Directly facing the Herrenkapelle is another handsome Renaissance building, the **Altes Gymnasium** (Tues–Fri 2–5pm, Sat & Sun 10am–1pm & 2–5pm; free). This now contains the local history museum, including memorabilia of Friedrich Rückert. It collections are supplemented by the Franconian paintings and sculptures housed in the **Alte Reichsvogtei** (same times; free), a plainer building of the period just a few paces to the east at Obere Str. 11.

Well to the northeast of the Altstadt, at Judithstr. 16, is the **Bibliothek Otto Schäfer** (same times; free), a valuable library donated to the town by Georg Schäfer's younger brother, who was also his business partner. Normally, four different exhibitions drawn from its holdings of printed books, manuscripts and graphics are staged each year.

Practicalities

Schweinfurt's **Hauptbahnhof**, a junction of the Würzburg-Bamberg line with that to Erfurt, lies 2km west of the Altstadt. Much closer to the centre, albeit a bit to the east, is the **Stadtbahnhof**, one stop away in the direction of Hassfurt. The **tourist office** (Mon–Wed & Fri–Sun 10am–5pm, Thurs 10am–7pm; ☎0 97 21/5 14 98, fax 5 16 05, *www.schweinfurt.de*) is on the ground floor of the Museum Georg Schäfer. Tickets can be bought there for Main **cruises**, which depart from the jetty at the western end of the Altstadt.

Hotels with a central location include *Gasthof Erdinger Weissbräu*, Obere Str. 21 (☎0 97 21/2 23 51; ③), *Gasthof Mangold*, Kornmarkt 13–15 (☎0 97 21/1 60 96; ③), *Panorama*, Am Oberen Marienbach 1 (☎0 97 21/20 40; ⑤), and the venerable *Ross*, Postplatz 9 (☎0 97 21/2 00 10, *www.swin.de/hotel-ross*; ⑥); a new top-of-the-range establishment is due to open in autumn 2001 as part of the conference centre on the Maininsel, the island opposite the Altstadt. The **youth hostel** is about 1km north of the Hauptbahnhof at Niederwerrner Str. 17 1/2 (☎0 97 21/2 14 04, fax 2 35 81; DM21/€10.50). All the hotels listed above except *Panorama* have **restaurants**, and that in *Ross* ranks as the best in town. There are also plenty of good places to eat and drink around the Markt, with outside tables in summer: *Brauhaus am Markt*, Markt 30, is the tap of the local brewery, Schweinfurter Brauhaus, while *Kunstcafé*, Markt 12, is an artists' **café** with regular exhibitions.

The main local **festivals** are the *Stadtmaifeste*, a series of markets held each May weekend; the two-week-long *Schweinfurter Volksfest* in late June and early July, and the *Strassenfest* in mid-September. All kinds of **music** and **theatre** are performed by visiting artistes at the *Theatre der Stadt*, Rossbrunnstr. 2 (☎0 97 21/5 14 75).

Aschaffenburg

King Ludwig I called **ASCHAFFENBURG**, which is situated on the River Main at the extreme northwestern corner of the state, about 80km due west of Schweinfurt, his "Bavarian Nice". Although the town has lost some of its charm since those days, the characterful historic centre and pleasant parks make it an agreeable place to spend a day or two, and it's also the obvious jumping-off point for exploring the unspoiled highland countryside of the Odenwald to the south. Once the preferred (though officially only secondary) residence of the powerful Archbishop-Electors of Mainz, Aschaffenburg is now mainly a dormitory town for Frankfurt.

The Town

Aschaffenburg's compact centre is dominated by **Schloss Johannisburg** (April–Sept Tues–Sun 9am–6pm; Oct–March Tues–Sun 10am–4pm; DM5/€2.50, or DM8/€4 combined ticket with Pompejanum), a very French-looking late Renaissance red sandstone pile built at the beginning of the seventeenth century for the Mainz Electors by the Strasbourg architect Georg Ridinger. It was the first purely residential princely palace ever erected in Germany, and the first to adopt symmetrical principles of a regular ground plan of four wings, though the keep of the previous medieval castle was retained as a fifth tower, counterbalancing those at the corners. The Schloss was badly damaged in World War II, and the surviving historic interiors, a suite of Neoclassical apartments on the second floor, are quite modest. A collection of eighteenth-century **ecclesiastical vestments**, which are displayed alongside liturgical objects and relief portraits of the archbishops, offers a more vivid evocation of the Mainz Electorate. However, these are overshadowed by the delectable collection of **cork models** of the monuments of ancient Rome, the earliest of which date back to the last decade of the eighteenth century and were made by the court pastry cook, Carl Joseph May. Even finer are the nine large models by his son, the civil engineer Georg Heinrich May, all of which are based on accurate on-the-spot measurements and observations.

Also within the Schloss, and covered by the same ticket, are two museums. The **Bayerische Staatsgalerie** on the first floor contains paintings by old German masters, including a large number by **Cranach** and his followers, **Baldung's** *Calvary* and the *Aschaffenburg Triptych* by the **Master of the Wendelin Altar**. There are also Dutch and Flemish works, including examples of Rubens, Van Dyck and Dou, as well as ten small but arresting scenes from a Passion cycle by **Arent de Gelder**, who continued the tradition of his master Rembrandt well into the eighteenth century. Upstairs, the **Städtische Sammlung** contains sculptures from the time of the Schloss's construction; products of the former stoneware factory in Damm, nowadays a suburb of Aschaffenburg; memorabilia of one-time local resident Clemens Brentano, the Romantic-era writer who jointly compiled the celebrated folk-poetry anthology *Des Knaben Wunderhorn*; and paintings by the Neue Sachlichkeit artist Christian Schad.

Within the palace's north wing is the **Schlosskirche**, though the only exterior clues as to its presence are the spire and the courtyard portal, above which is a relief of the Baptism of Christ. This is attributed to the early seventeenth-century court sculptor Hans Juncker, who made the church's pulpit and its alabaster and marble **high altar**, which stretches from the ceiling all the way to the vault and incorporates a dozen scenes from Jesus' life.

A few minutes' walk downstream along the Main is the **Pompejanum** (April–Sept Tues–Sun 9am–6pm; DM5/€2.50), a replica of the house of Castor and Pollux in Pompeii, built by Friedrich Gärtner for King Ludwig I. Its luxuriant gardens of Mediterranean trees and plants and its vineyard sloping down to the River Main make for an enjoyable stroll. The interior, which was badly damaged in the war, was only restored a few years ago, and now exhibits original Roman antiquities alongside the mock-classical decoration.

A walk down Pfaffengstrasse from Schloss Johannisburg takes you through the heart of the Altstadt, with its narrow streets of half-timbered houses, and leads to Stiftsplatz and Aschaffenburg's principal church, the **Stiftskirche St-Peter-und-Alexander**. Founded in the tenth century, it combines Romanesque, Gothic and Baroque features and it's this architectural identity crisis that gives it real visual impact. The furnishings are equally diverse: they include a pognant wooden crucifix which may date as far back as the tenth century, another pulpit by Juncker, and numerous **funerary monuments**. Of particular importance is the magnificent bronze memorial in the north transept to one of the leading Catholic figures of the Reformation era, Cardinal Albrecht von Brandenburg; this and the accompanying relief of the Virgin and Child were both cast in the famous Vischer workshop in Nürnberg. In the last chapel of the southern aisle is a small panel of *The Lamentation* by **Grünewald**, which appears to be truncated but is in fact complete. The same artist also painted *The Virgin of the Snows* altarpiece in the elevated Maria-Schnee-Kapelle opposite, but the original is now in Stuppach (see p.376) and has been replaced here with a copy by Christian Schad.

On the north side of the Stiftskirche are late Romanesque cloisters, and the buildings around them are home to the **Stiftsmuseum** (10am–1pm & 2–5pm, closed Tues; DM5/€2.50), which has wide-ranging collections, principally of archeology and sacred art. Especially intriguing are treasury items formerly belonging to Cardinal Albrecht, including a reliquary calendar in the shape of a book and Germany's oldest surviving chessboard; the latter dates from around 1300 and is a beautiful object made from wood, enamel, jasper, rock crystal, silver and clay. Among the sculptures are a panel of *The Nativity* by Riemenschneider and Juncker's imaginary portrait of Duke Otto of Swabia and Bavaria, the son of the founder of the Stiftskirche. Two remarkable mid-eighteenth-century painted panels mapping out the holdings of Kloster Himmelthal are the highlights of a room devoted to artefacts from Cistercian convents in the former Mainz Electorate. One of the museum's proudest possessions is the *Aschaffenburger Tafel*, a badly damaged but enormously powerful thirteenth-century painting of Christ as Judge which was once part of the Stiftskirche's high altar, but was later demoted to serve as a floorboard and only rediscovered during restoration work in 1986.

Just beyond the eastern end of the Altstadt is **Park Schöntal**, which features a lake with a ruined monastery. About 1km further east is the **Fasanerie** (Pheasantery): to get there, walk up Lindenallee, cross the rail bridge and continue along Bismarckallee, whose restaurants and beer gardens are popular destinations in summer. **Park Schönbusch**, on the western bank of the Main (reached by bus #4 from the Hauptbahnhof) is an eighteenth-century English-style landscape park, featuring a labyrinth of paths leading through woods and gardens past miniature temples and mazes. Here also is the pretty **Schlösschen Schönbusch** (guided tours April–Sept Tues–Sun 9am–6pm; DM5/€2.50), the Neoclassical summer palace of the Mainz Electors.

Finally, on the southern edge of town at Obernnauer Str. 125 (reached by bus #61 or #62 from the Hauptbahnhof), the **Rosso Bianco Collection** (April–Oct Tues–Sun 10am–6pm; Nov–March Sun 10am–6pm; DM10/€5) has the biggest array of racing cars in the world – some two hundred gleaming Porsches, Ferraris, Alfa Romeos and the like.

Practicalities

Aschaffenburg's **Hauptbahnhof** is just north of the Altstadt. The **tourist office** is in the Stadthalle, Schlossplatz 1 (Mon–Fri 9am–5pm, Sat 10am–1pm; ☎0 60 21/39 58 00, fax 39 58 02, *www.info-aschaffenburg.de*). Main **cruises** are run by Aschaffenburger Personenschiffahrt Sankt Martin, Ruhlandstr. 5 (☎0 60 21/8 72 88).

Of the **hotels** with a central location, the lowest rates are at *Central*, Steingasse 5 (☎0 60 21/2 33 11 or 2 33 92; ③), *Pape*, Würzburger Str. 16 (☎0 60 21/2 2 6 73; ③), and *Gasthof Goldener Karpfen*, Löherstr. 20 (☎0 60 21/4 43 69 70; ③). Two small, highly appealing middle-range choices, both further afield, are *Hofgut Fasanerie*, a former wine-producing estate at Bismarckallee 1 (☎0 60 21/3 17 30; ⑤), and *Schönbusch*, in the former court gardener's house at Kleine Schönbuschallee 1 (☎0 60 21/85 60; ⑤). More upmarket options include *Wilder Mann*, Löherstr. 51 (☎0 60 21/30 20; ⑥), and *Post*,

Goldbacher Str. 19–21 (☎0 60 21/33 40; ⑤). The **youth hostel** is in the southeastern outskirts at Beckerstr. 47 (☎0 60 21/93 07 63, fax 97 06 94; DM19/€9.50) and is reached by taking bus #5 or #41 to Schroberstrasse, from where it's a ten-minute walk. **Camping** is possible at Mainparksee (☎0 60 21/27 82 22) and in the suburb of Mainaschaff (☎0 60 21/27 82 22), fifteen minutes away by bus #44 from the Hauptbahnhof.

There are **restaurants** in all but the first two hotels listed above. Among other possibilities, *Zeughaus*, Bismarckallee 5, is particularly worth visiting in summer, when you can drink locally produced ciders in the shade of chestnut trees. Within Schloss Johannisburg is a recommendable wine bar-restaurant with its own vintages, *Schlossweinstuben*; the pick of the traditional beer taverns is *Wirtshaus Zum Fegerer*, Schlossgasse 14. *Klimperkasten* at Rossmarkt 21 is a lively, friendly bar with regular live music, while *Engelsberg* at Dalbergstr. 66 is a traditional but arty pub. The Neoclassical *Stadttheater*, Schlossgasse 8 (☎0 60 21/2 70 78) hosts **drama** and **concerts**.

The Odenwald

The Bavarian section of the **Odenwald**, a forest which straddles across into both Baden-Württemberg and Hesse (see also p406–409) consists of territory which, in common with Aschaffenburg, formerly belonged to the Archbishop-Electors of Mainz. It includes two small towns well worth making the object of a day-trip or overnight stay: being linked by rail, they are easily combined.

Miltenberg

MILTENBERG has a wonderfully photogenic setting, nestling tightly below wooded hills on a bend of the Main, 45km upstream from Aschaffenburg. Although its population has never numbered more than a few thousand, the Altstadt stretches for over 2.5km, its boundaries marked by two fourteenth-century gateways, the **Würzburger Tor** to the east and the **Mainzer Tor** to the west. Much of the area in between consists of a single street, Hauptstrasse, which is lined with the half-timbered buildings so characteristic of central Germany, as well as others of stone. One of the finest examples of the former is the **Gasthaus Zum Riesen** at no. 97, an inn with an uninterrupted tradition since the fifteenth century which assumed its present aspect at the end of the following century. A little further west, at no. 137, is the **Altes Rathaus**, a fourteenth-century Gothic sandstone building which was originally the municipal weigh house.

About halfway along its length, Hauptstrasse widens out to the south to form the triangular **Marktplatz**, which has a Renaissance fountain, the **Marktbrunnen**, and some of the finest houses, notably the **Weinhaus**, which is distinguished by a beautiful two-storey oriel, and the **Alte Amtskellerei** directly opposite. The latter now houses the **Museum der Stadt Miltenberg** (May–Oct Tues–Sun 11am–5pm; Nov–March Wed–Sun 11am–4pm; DM4/€2), which contains a distinguished collection of artefacts from the Roman period, notably an enigmatic five-metre-high monolith, the *Toutonenstein*. There's also a Jewish section: Miltenberg still preserves its tiny medieval synagogue, but it is marooned in the backyard of the Kalt-Loch brewery and seldom accessible to the public.

Just to the north of the square is the **Stadtpfarrkirche St Jakobus**, a Gothic church whose external appearance was sharply modified by the addition of two Neoclassical sandstone towers in the 1830s. Inside are a fifteenth-century relief of the Adoration of the Magi and a huge sixteenth-century crucifix. On its other side, Marktplatz slopes uphill to the outer defensive system of the **Mildenburg** (May–Oct Tues–Sun 11am–5.30pm; DM2/€1), the feudal frontier castle of the Mainz archbishops on the hill above. By its courtyard entrance is a late fourteenth-century residential building which was partially remodelled in Renaissance style a couple of hundred years later. Higher up is the keep, which formed part of the original fortress erected around 1200. It can be ascended for a grandstand view over the town and its surroundings.

Practicalities

Miltenberg's **Bahnhof**, a junction with lines to Aschaffenburg, Amorbach and Wertheim in Baden-Württemberg, is 1km north of the Altstadt, on the opposite side of the Main. The **tourist office** at Engelplatz 69 (May–Sept Mon–Fri 9am–noon & 2–5pm, Sat 9.30am–noon; Oct–April Mon–Fri 9am–noon & 2–5pm; ☎0 93 71/4 00 19, fax 40 41 05, *www.miltenberg.de*) can book private **rooms** (②–③). There's also a **campsite** (☎0 93 71/39 85), directly opposite the Altstadt, on either side of the Mainbrücke. However, it would be a pity not to stay in one of the lovely old Altstadt **hotels**. Two of these are sights in their own right: *Gasthaus Zum Riesen*, Hauptstr. 97 (☎0 93 71/36 44; ④), and *Weinhaus am Markt*, Marktplatz 185 (☎0 93 71/55 00; ④). Enticing alternatives are *Jagdhotel Rose*, Hauptstr. 280 (☎0 93 71/4 00 60; ⑤), *Brauerei Keller*, Hauptstr. 66–70 (☎0 93 71/50 80; ⑥), and *Altes Bannhaus*, Hauptstr. 211 (☎0 93 71/30 61; ⑥). With the exception of the first-named, each has a **restaurant**, and all are of high quality yet reasonably priced. As its name suggests, the *Weinhaus* offers a selection of its own vintages, while there are two still-functioning breweries on Hauptstrasse, Kalt-Loch and Faust. The former's *Bräustüble* is right alongside, at no. 201; the latter's tap, *Malzspeicher*, is just a short distance away at Löwengasse 3. Reederei Henneberger at Mainanlage (☎0 93 71/33 30) runs **cruises** to Aschaffenburg and Wertheim as well as shorter local trips. The big popular **festival** is the ten-day-long *Michaelis-Messe* in late August and early September; there's also a *Weinfest* in the Mildenburg in June and a folklore event, the *Altstadtfest*, at the end of the same month.

Amorbach

A further 10km south is **AMORBACH**, which is nowadays an official health resort. In the mid-seventeenth century the court architect Maximilian von Welsch was commissioned to transform its Romanesque **Abtei** into something more in keeping with the times. He responded with a design which is restrained by Bavarian standards – he went as far as preserving the original towers – yet which is none the worse for that, being a masterly exercise in late Baroque grandeur. Outstanding features of the **Abteikirche** are the ceiling frescoes, the wrought-iron screen dividing the nave from the transept and the sweet-toned organ. **Guided tours** (March Mon–Sat 9.40–11.40am & 1.40–5pm, Sun 1–5pm; April & Oct Mon–Sat 9.20am–noon & 1.20–5.20pm, Sun 11.20am–5.20pm; May–Sept Mon–Sat 9.20am–noon & 1.20–6pm, Sun 11.20am–6pm; DM4.50/€2.25) are run through the slightly later monastic buildings, which give a foretaste of the emergent Neoclassical style in such lovely interiors as the **Bibliotheksaal** and the **Grüner Saal**.

The **tourist office** (May–Oct Mon–Fri 9am–12.30pm & 3–6pm, Sat & Sun 10am–noon; Nov–April Mon–Fri 9am–noon & 3–5pm; ☎0 93 73/2 09 40, fax 2 09 33, *www.amorbach.de*) is in the Altes Rathaus on Marktplatz. **Private rooms** (①–②) can be booked here; otherwise there are several **hotels**, including *Weinstube Amorstüble*, Johannesturmstr. 6 (☎0 93 73/12 92; ④), *Post*, Schmiedgasse 2 (☎0 93 73/14 10; ⑥), and *Badischer Hof*, Am Stadttor 4 (☎0 93 73/95 05; ⑥). The **youth hostel** is well to the northwest of the centre at Kniebreche 4 (☎0 93 73/13 66, fax 71 40; DM19/€9.50).

Würzburg

Capital of Lower Franconia, local wine metropolis and northern terminus of Germany's most famous tourist route, the Romantic Road (see box on p.213), **WÜRZBURG** straddles the River Main some 80km southeast of Aschaffenburg and 50km southwest of Schweinfurt. During the night of March 16, 1945 it got the same treatment from Allied bombers that Nürnberg had received two months earlier. The 1200-year-old city had no important war industries but the presence of a busy rail junction provided a tenuous rationale for its destruction. Unfortunately, Würzburg has been less successful in rebuilding itself: gone is much of the Altstadt, leaving individual surprises of Baroque and Gothic beauty sandwiched between modern supermarkets and the new town. For all that, the city's location on both banks of the Main, a number of really outstanding sights and a marvellous range of places to eat and drink easily justify a visit of several days.

Würzburg has been one of Germany's most influential episcopal cities for many centuries, and some of the greatest architects and artists were employed by the prince-

ACCOMMODATION

7 Alter Kranen	2 Siegel
5 Amberger	1 Spehnkuch
6 Goldener Hahn	10 Till Eulenspiegel
9 Rebstock	11 Walfisch
8 Russ	12 Youth Hostel
4 Schönleber	3 Zur Stadt Mainz

0 Metres 200

bishops, bequeathing an exceptionally rich legacy. Prominent among them was the sculptor **Tilman Riemenschneider**, whose hauntingly characterized carvings, executed in the heady years leading up to the Reformation, decorate so many churches throughout Franconia. A later period saw patronage of **Balthasar Neumann**, who was then totally unknown and untried, but who duly developed here into the most inventive and accomplished architect of eighteenth-century Europe.

Arrival, information and accommodation

Würzburg's **Hauptbahnhof** is at the northern end of the city centre. The headquarters of the **tourist office** (Mon–Thurs 8.30am–5pm, Fri 8.30am–noon; ☎09 31/37 23 35, fax 37 36 52, *www.wuerzburg.de*) are at Am Congress Centrum, though the main public branch is in the Haus zum Falken on the Markt (Mon–Fri 10am–6pm, Sat 10am–2pm; April–Oct Sun 10am–2pm; ☎09 31/37 23 98). **Mitfahrzentrale's** office is on Bahnhofsvorplatz-Ost (☎09 31/1 94 48).

Though budget **accommodation** is fairly thin on the ground, Würzburg has plenty of good middle- and upper-range **hotels**. The **youth hostel**, Burkarderstr. 44 (☎09 31/4 25 90, fax 41 68 62; DM30/€15) is situated on the left bank of the Main below the Marienberg fortress; take tram #3 to Ludwigsbrücke from the Hauptbahnhof. There are several **campsites** in the outskirts, the most convenient being *Kalte Quelle*, Winterhäuser Str. 160 (☎09 31/6 55 98) in Heidingsfeld, about 4km south of the centre and best reached by taking bus #16 from Barbarossaplatz.

Hotels and pensions

Alter Kranen, Kärrnergasse 11 (☎09 31/3 51 80, fax 5 00 10, *www.hotel-alter-kranen.de*). Middle-range hotel with a lovely location right by the Main. ⑤.

Amberger, Ludwigstr. 17–21 (☎09 31/3 51 00, fax 3 51 08 00, *www.top-hotels.de/amberger*). High-class hotel situated just north of the Residenz. ⑦.

Goldener Hahn, Marktgasse 7 (☎09 31/5 19 41, fax 5 19 61). Gasthof located just off the Markt. It has basic singles which cost less than half the price of the doubles. ⑤.

Rebstock, Neubaustr. 7 (☎09 31/3 09 30, fax 3 09 31 00, *www.rebstock.com*). A splendid Rococo mansion in the university quarter, completely modernized inside. It serves wonderful buffet breakfasts, while full meals are available at either the reasonably priced *Fränkische Weinstube* (evenings only, closed Tues) or the pricey main restaurant (closed Sun evening). ⑧–⑨.

Russ, Wolfahrtsgasse 1 (☎09 31/5 00 16, fax 5 09 69, *www.hotel-russ.de*). Hotel with a well-regarded restaurant, handily located in the Altstadt. ④–⑥.

Schlosshotel Steinburg, Auf dem Steinberg (☎09 31/9 70 20, fax 9 71 21). Occupies a Romantic-era castle built on the foundations of its medieval predecessor on a hill 6km northwest of the centre. The facilities include a sauna, a swimming pool, a garden terrace commanding a grandstand view of the city, and a high-class wine restaurant. ⑥–⑧.

Schönleber, Theaterstr. 5 (☎09 31/1 20 68, fax 1 60 12). Pleasant, moderately priced hotel in the heart of the city. ④.

Siegel, Reisgrubengasse 7 (☎09 31/5 29 41 or 5 29 64, fax 5 29 67). Würzburg's cheapest pension, with a convenient location between the Hauptbahnhof and the centre of the city. ③.

Spehnkuch, Röntgenring 7 (☎09 31/5 47 52, fax 5 47 60). Small pension in a grand tenement directly facing the Hauptbahnhof. ③.

Till Eulenspiegel, Sanderstr. 1a (☎09 31/35 58 40, fax 3 55 84 30, *www.hotel-till-eulenspiegel.de*). Non-smoking hotel in the heart of the university quarter. It has a pleasant Weinstube plus a Bierkeller which is one of the liveliest nightspots in the district. ⑥–⑧.

Walfisch, Am Pleidenturm 5 (☎09 31/3 52 00, fax 3 52 05 00, *www.hotel-walfisch.com*). Upmarket hotel with restaurant commanding a wonderful view over the Main at its most picturesque spot. ⑦.

Zur Stadt Mainz, Semmelstr. 39 (☎09 31/5 31 55, fax 5 85 10). This is a real gem, a Franconian inn dating back to the fifteenth century, albeit with fully modern bedrooms. Its restaurant serves wonderful local dishes, including a couple from its own recipe book of 1850. The gargantuan breakfast buffet (also available to non-residents) must be a contender for the title of best in Germany. ⑤.

The City

The heart of the old city lies between the Main and the Residenz, roughly encompassed by the Juliuspromenade to the north and Neubaustrasse to the south. Most of the sights lie within this compact area, though you need to cross over to the right bank for a couple of major attractions – and the best views.

The Residenz

The **Residenz** (April to mid-Oct Mon–Wed & Fri–Sun 9am–6pm, Thurs 9am–8pm; mid-Oct to March daily 10am–4pm; DM8/€4) on the eastern edge of the town centre is a truly marvellous palace set in a park to match. It was intended to symbolize all the wealth and status of the Würzburg bishops, and to show they could hold their own with such great European courts as Versailles and Vienna – which, in artistic terms, they more than succeeded in doing. Construction was left largely in the hands of the prolific **Balthasar Neumann**, who had started off as a humble craftsman of church bells and weapons before working his way into the fine art of architecture. The palace is built in a great U-shape made up of a central pavilion and four equally proportioned two-storey courts. Its main facade and garden front are strongly contrasted, the former grand and ceremonial, heavily laden with sculptural decoration, while the latter has a playful, festive air. However, for all their impressive monumentality, they're rather overshadowed by the overwhelming magnificence of the interior.

As you enter the palace via the central wing, you're almost immediately confronted with the famed **staircase** which is covered by a single unsupported vault of audacious design. In response to jealous rivals who claimed this was bound to collapse, Neumann offered to have a battery of artillery fired under it. This experiment was never carried out, but full vindication of Neumann's faith in his design came in 1945, when the vault held firm against aerial bombardment. Its **fresco**, the largest in the world, thus miraculously survived unscathed. An allegory extolling the fame of the prince-bishops in the most immodest way imaginable, it was painted by the greatest decorator of the age, the Venetian **Giovanni Battista Tiepolo**. The four continents then known are depicted paying their respects to the ruler of Würzburg, Carl Philipp von Greiffenklau, who is transported to Heaven in triumph in the centre of the composition. Each continent is personified as a representative female character, Europe being a Greek goddess enthroned above a globe to symbolize this continent's status as ruler of the world. To her right, sitting on an old cannon, a reference to his original trade, Balthasar Neumann surveys the scene; behind him are Tiepolo and his fellow decorators.

The **Weisser Saal**, whose plain white stucco is a tasteful contrast to the staircase, gives the visitor a break before being hit by the opulence of the **Kaisersaal**, which is the centrepiece of the palace and the room reserved for the use of the emperor whenever he happened to be in the area. The marble, the gold-leaf stucco and the sparkling chandeliers combine to produce an effect of dazzling magnificence, but finest of all are more frescoes by Tiepolo, which dovetail with the architecture to absolute perfection. This time they glorify the concept of the Holy Roman Empire and Würzburg's part within it. On the ceiling, Beatrix of Burgundy is brought to the city as Frederick Barbarossa's betrothed: on the southern wall, the couple are married by the prince-bishop, who is invested with the title of duke of Franconia in the scene opposite. To the left and right are an array of **state rooms**, painstakingly re-created from the ashes with the help of photographs and old etchings. Look out in particular for the **Spiegelkabinett**, a unique work of its kind, the walls consisting entirely of glass panels decorated on the back.

THE ROMANTIC ROAD

Glibly named, but with many beautiful spots along it, the **Romantic Road** (Romantische Strasse) runs for 350km between Würzburg and Füssen in the Allgäu. The road gets its name from the fact that it passes gently rolling countryside, which is never very dramatic but instead pleasantly unspoilt and tranquil.

If pushed for time, taking the Europabus along the whole or part of the route is a good way to get a quick impression; both Eurail passes are valid, while InterRail and EuroDomino holders are entitled to a discount, but note that services run just once a day in each direction, and only during the summer. One snag is that stops are very short, which means that you only get a superficial impression unless you break your journey for a day or trust to the infrequent local buses. (Many places on the route are not served by rail.) It's essential to detour from the main drag to get a full impression of the area and to escape the tourists – exploring the regions alongside becomes much more rewarding with your own transport. A bike is an especially appropriate means of transport, as there's a waymarked cycling route, the Radroute Romantische Strasse, which utilizes a mixture of pre-existing and specially laid tracks, plus some minor roads. There's a fully comprehensive guide to this: *Germany's Romantic Road* by Gordon McLachlan (Cicerone Press).

For the first section of the Road after Würzburg – the Baden-Württemberg towns of Bad Mergentheim, Weikersheim and Creglingen – see pp.375–9. The stage after that, including Rothenburg and Dinkelsbühl, is described below, followed immediately by the Bavarian Swabia section between Nördlingen and Augsburg. For the next stretch, along the Lech valley via Landsberg and Steingaden, see pp.112–15. The southernmost staging posts, Schwangau and Füssen, are described on pp.238–9.

Built discreetly into the southwest corner of the palace in order not to spoil the symmetry, the **Hofkirche** (which you visit independently) is a brilliant early example of the spatial illusionism that was to become a Neumann speciality – the interior, based on a series of ovals, appears to be much larger than is actually the case. Both the side altars have paintings by Tieplo: *The Fall of the Rebel Angels* and *The Assumption*. Entered from within the main courtyard is the **Martin-von-Wagner-Museum** (Tues–Sat 9.30am–12.30pm & 2–5pm, Sun 9.30am–12.30pm; free). In the mornings and on alternate Sundays you see the gallery, featuring works by Riemenschneider and Tiepolo; at other times the collection of classical antiquities is on view. To the rear of the Residenz is the **Hofgarten**, a series of delightful terraced gardens enlivened by playful Rococo sculptures.

The episcopal and academic quarters

From the Residenz, it's only a short walk along Hofstrasse to the city's episcopal centre, in which the two main churches nestle side by side. The more northerly is the **Neumünster**, a Romanesque basilica partly rebuilt in the Baroque period, whose perfect symmetry is highlighted by a twin set of steps leading up to the elevated entrance from either side. In the **crypt**, a modern shrine contains the remains of St Kilian, an Irish missionary martyred on the spot in 689, together with his assistants St Kolonat and St Totnan, for trying to convert Franconia. The busts of the three martyrs on the church's high altar are copies of the originals by Riemenschneider, which were destroyed in 1945, but the statue of the Madonna and Child under the dome is a genuine work by the same sculptor.

Leaving the Neumünster by its northern exit, you come to the tiny **Lusamgärtchen** and the remains of the twelfth-century cloister. These days it's a romantically overgrown square, and at its centre is a commemorative block to the famous medieval minstrel **Walther von der Vogelweide**. He was the most popular poet and singer of the early thirteenth century, but also a valued political commentator of the Staufen rulers, which is why he was given a pension from the estate of this church and is assumed to have been buried in the cloister in 1230. His popularity still holds, and local residents always ensure that fresh flowers decorate his memorial stone, over 750 years after his death. To the northeast stand several fine old mansions, including the Renaissance **Hof Conti**, the present-day home of Würzburg's bishop.

The **Dom**, again consecrated to St Kilian, was one of the largest Romanesque churches in Germany, but was completely burnt out in 1945, and only the exterior is true to the original. Inside, the rich stucco embellishments of the eighteenth century have only been restored in the transept and chancel, and for the rest the walls are left plain white, with surviving **tombstones** of canons and prince-bishops lining the pillars: look out for those on the seventh and eighth bays of the north side, which are both by Riemenschneider. At the end of the northern transept, Balthasar Neumann's **Schönbornkapelle** holds the remains of four bishops from the House of Schönborn, the dynasty which specialized in collecting episcopal appointments and then building great palaces as spin-offs – Bamberg, Pommersfelden, Bruchsal and Würzburg itself being among their legacies. The **crypt** is fitted out as a museum of the Dom's history, with lapidary fragments from the eighth century onwards.

Immediately to the south, on Plattnerstrasse, the former workrooms of the **Marmelsteiner Hof**, a mansion by Balthasar Neumann, have been fitted out as the new home of the **Domschatz** (Thurs–Sun 2–5pm; DM4/€2). The most intriguing exhibits are the contents of the excavated graves of two medieval bishops, Berthold von Sternburg and Gerhard von Schwarzburg. Most of the collection of ecclesiastical treasure and vestments dates from the Baroque and Rococo periods, though there are a few older pieces, including a Byzantine reliquary.

A couple of blocks further south, the eastern end of Neubaustrasse is dominated by the huge Renaissance frontage of the **Alte Universität**, built in the late sixteenth century by order of one of the city's most enlightened prince-bishops, Julius Echter. The attached church also dates from this period, but the tower was added by Antonio Petrini, the seventeenth-century Italian architect who was responsible for transforming Würzburg into one of Germany's first Baroque cities.

Marktplatz, the hospitals and the waterfront

To the west of the episcopal quarter is the city's commercial heart, centred on **Marktplatz**, whose daily food market ensures that there's always a lively bustle. Just off the northeast side is the **Haus zum Falken**, the city's prize example of a Rococo mansion, bristling with white stucco decorations and perfectly restored to the very last curl. It now houses one of the city's tourist offices and the municipal library.

Overlooking Marktplatz is the **Marienkapelle**, an exceptionally graceful Gothic church of the fourteenth century, whose most interesting feature is the tympanum of the northern portal. The scene represented is the Annunciation, and if you look closely, you'll see that the artist has chosen to be very literal in his interpretation. There's the usual archangel with his scripted band indicating his speech to Mary, but another band leads from God the Father above to Mary's ear, and tucked away in the folds of this band, a little baby is sliding down towards her. Riemenschneider's sculptures for the southern side of the church, including the famous figures of Adam and Eve, have been replaced *in situ* by copies, but inside is an original work by the same sculptor, the touching sandstone tomb of the Knight Conrad von Schaumberg.

Eichhornstrasse leads eastwards from the Markt to Theaterstrasse, where you'll find the **Bürgerspital**, a charitable institution for the poor, old and sick established in the early fourteenth century by the wealthier citizens of the city. Its good works were funded from its vineyards, still among the largest in Germany; in accordance with the wishes of the founders, residents get a quarter of a litre of wine each day and double on

Sundays. The Gothic chapel remains from the initial complex, though other parts were rebuilt in the Baroque period. A short walk away on Juliuspromenade is the **Juliusspital**, a second and much larger institution of the same kind. It takes its name from its benefactor, Bishop Julius Echter, but again it was rebuilt in the Baroque period, partly by Petrini, who added the beautiful little pharmacy, which survives as an intact period-piece. It's best to visit the hospitals when you're in the mood for something to eat and drink, as they each incorporate a Weinstube (see p.216) where the products of their vineyards can be sampled. While walking between the two, it's worth making a short detour down Hauger Pfarrgasse to Petrini's strikingly Roman-looking **Stift Haug**, which contains a large painting of *The Crucifixion* by Tintoretto.

At the western end of Juliuspromenade, the eighteenth-century **Alte Kranen** (old cranes), used to unload shipping, stand guard over the Main. Further south stands the **Alte Mainbrücke**, the oldest bridge spanning this river. Built in 1133, it was often damaged over the centuries, most recently in 1945 when the Allies toppled the eighteenth-century statues of the town's bishops and saints into the river. However, some of the originals have been reinstated, joining with a number of copies to oversee the traffic once again. Just to the east is the **Grafeneckart** or **Rathaus**, a thirteenth-century Romanesque-Gothic building with a Renaissance extension.

The Marienberg

Towering high above the left bank of the Main, the **Festung Marienberg** was home to the prince-bishops from 1253 to 1719. Over this period, it evolved from a medieval castle into a Renaissance palace, which was fortified in the Baroque period, following its sacking at the hands of the Swedes, by the addition of a ring of bastions. At the entrance to the complex, the seventeenth-century **Zeughaus** houses the large **Mainfränkisches Museum** (April–Oct Tues–Sun 10am–6pm; Nov–March Tues–Sun 10am–4pm; DM5/€2.50). Pride of place among the collections is taken by a magnificent array of **Riemenschneider sculptures**, including the original stone-carvings from the Marienkapelle; there's also an impressive display of old wooden wine presses.

Within the courtyard is the round **Marienkirche**, Würzburg's original cathedral. This dates back to the eighth century and is claimed to be the oldest intact church in Germany, though it has been remodelled on several occasions. Another structure of special note is the Renaissance **Brunnenhaus**, an ornate octagonal structure sheltering the 105-metre well which was chiselled through rock in the early fourteenth century to ensure self-sufficiency in water. The eastern palace wing or **Fürstenbau** (April to mid-Oct Tues–Sun 9am–6pm; mid-Oct to March Tues–Sun 10am–4pm; DM5/€2.50) contains a historical museum whose exhibits include the thirteenth-century battle standard, the St Kilian banner, and the treasury of the prince-bishops. On the terrace below the palace is the **Fürstengarten**, a formal Baroque garden seen at its best when the roses are in bloom in summer, but always worth visiting for the sake of the wonderful view over the city.

Elsewhere on the left bank

Returning to the waterfront and heading south towards the youth hostel, you pass **St Burkhard**, whose late Gothic choir picturesquely straddles the street, forming a covered walkway. It's also worth a look inside to see a tender polychrome *Virgin and Child* by Riemenschneider.

During work on the Residenz, Balthasar Neumann took time off to build the **Käppele**, a twin-towered pilgrimage church crowned with onion domes, imperiously perched on the heights at the southwestern end of the city. Apart from the opportunity to see the interior, lavishly covered with frescoes and stucco, it's well worth visiting for the **view** from the terrace, which offers a frontal panorama of the Marienberg surrounded by its vineyards, with the city nestling in the valley below.

Eating, drinking and entertainment

Würzburg is one of Germany's leading gourmet cities. The best places to sample the local wines and traditional Franconian cooking are the famous Weinstuben, but the city is amply endowed with a wide range of restaurants (see the hotels section on pp.211–12 for more recommendations) and bars. There are also several annual festivals, which are the undoubted highpoints of local cultural life (see box below).

Weinstuben

Bürgerspital, Theaterstr. 19. The obvious place to sample the wines from the vineyards of the famous old hospital. Produces very dry *Riesling*, *Silvaner* and *Müller-Thurgau*; the food is almost equally excellent and surprisingly reasonably priced. Closed Tues.

Haus des Frankenweins, Kranenkai 1. A modern building by the Main with a shop selling the full range of Franconian wines, plus a restaurant, terrace and garden.

Juliusspital, Juliuspromenade 19. Full-bodied wines, with *Silvaner* being the most common type, are characteristic of this hospital's vineyards; they're matured in old oak casks to give a particularly strong flavour. Meals are also very good value here. Closed Wed.

Residenzgaststätten, Residenzplatz 1. The Hofkeller, the former court vineyard, maintains a modern rivalry to those of the two hospitals; their wide variety of wines can be enjoyed here in an outbuilding of the Residenz. Closed Mon.

Wirtshaus Zum Lämmle, Marienplatz 5. This has an evenings-only vaulted cellar, plus a ground-floor dining room open at lunchtime, with tables on the square outside during summer. Closed Sun.

Zum Stachel, Gressengasse 1. The city's oldest wine-drinking inn, it has a particularly picturesque courtyard for alfresco meals and does river-fish specialities, but is pricier than its rivals. Closed Sun.

Other restaurants

Backöfele, Ursulinergasse 2. Top-class traditional Gaststätte with a covered front courtyard. The specialities include steaks grilled in a wood-fired oven.

Burggaststätten, Festung Marienberg. The restaurant complex in the Marienberg includes a Weinstube (featuring wines from the Hofkeller), a beer garden (selling the local Hofbräu beers) and a traditional café; any of these is well worth patronizing when you're visiting the fortress.

Hofbräukeller, Höchberger Str. 28. In this wine stronghold, it's appropriate that the leading Bierkeller, whose garden can seat a thousand people, is way out of the centre on the western side of the city. An adventurous menu includes many vegetarian options as well as the expected Franconian dishes.

Kham, Burkardstr. 2-4. Innovative new restaurant serving a range of Asian cuisines.

WÜRZBURG'S FESTIVALS

Würzburg hosts several **wine festivals** throughout the year. The series begins with the *Würzburger Weindorf* in late May and early June, held in some forty little huts set up on the Markt. The Bürgerspital holds its *Weinfest* in late June; the Hofkeller has a similar event in the Hofgarten soon after. In September, the season ends with the *Würzburger Weinfest*, which is held in a huge tent.

The main **musical** event is the *Mozartfest* throughout June, in which Mozart concerts are held outdoors in the Hofgarten and indoors by candlelight in the opulent settings of the Weisser Saal and Kaisersaal of the Residenz. There's also a shorter festival devoted to Bach, the *Bachtage*, in late November and early December. At the beginning of July is the most important **popular** and **religious** festival, the fortnight-long *Kilianifest*. This consists for the most part of a huge funfair at the Talavera, a fairground on the left bank of the Main opposite the Congress-Centrum. However, it begins on a Saturday afternoon with a costumed pageant through the city; the following morning, there's a solemn religious procession followed by High Mass in the Dom.

Mal was anderes, Herzogenstr. 13. Würzburg's main vegetarian and wholefood specialist. Mon–Fri 8.15am–6pm, Sat 8.15am–3pm.

Ratskeller, Langgasse 1. Serves both Franconian and international dishes, and has an extensive wine list.

Schiffbäuerin, Katzengasse 7. Top choice for local fish specialities, with a fine selection of wines. Closed Sun evening & Mon.

Schützenhof Gutsschänke, Mainleitenweg 48. Terrace restaurant offering a beautiful view over the Main from its lofty position near the Käppele. Serves fruit wines and home-made cakes as well as Franconian dishes.

Bars and cafés

Brückenbäck, Zeller Str. 2. Coffee house which also serves light meals, and has the benefit of wonderful riverside views.

Café Uni, Neubaustr. 2. Trendy café-bar popular with local students.

Fränkisches Brauhaus Die Goldene Gans, Burkarderstr. 2–4. Cellar Hausbrauerei producing an unfiltered beer; it's primarily a drinking establishment but also serves light meals. Daily except Tues 8pm–1am.

Gehrings, Neubaustr. 24. Café-bistro right by the Alte Universität.

H@ckm@c, Sanderstr. 5. Internet café in the university quarter; there's another branch at Valentin-Becker-Str. 8.

Kult, Landwehrstr. 10. Student Kneipe serving a variety of breakfasts and vegetarian dishes.

Victoria, Neubaustr. 8. A good choice for *Kaffee und Kuchen*.

Entertainment

The main year-round **cultural** venue, with a varied programme of drama, opera, dance and music, is the Mainfranken Theater Würzburg, Theaterstr. 21 (☎09 31/3 90 81 24). From the Alter Kranen, **cruises** are run by two competing companies: Kurth und Schiebe (☎09 31/5 85 73) and Veitshöchhheimer Personenschiffahrt Heinrich Herbert (☎09 31/5 56 33). By far the most popular trip (DM9/€4.50 single, DM14/€7 return) is downstream to **Schloss Veitshöchheim** (guided tours April to mid-Oct Tues–Sun 9am–6pm; DM3/€1.50), the summer residence of the Würzburg prince-bishops, which is set in beautiful formal gardens. Upstream, there are occasional sailings to the fortified towns of Ochsenfurt and Sulzfeld.

Rothenburg ob der Tauber

ROTHENBURG OB DER TAUBER, which is some 60km south of Würzburg, is the most famous and most visited medieval town in Germany, and although it's very beautiful, it has been reduced to the ultimate museum-piece, with nearly half its working population employed in the tourist trade. Nonetheless, it should still merit at least one overnight stop: the only way to get this place to yourself is to stay the night and go out, either early in the morning or in the evening, when the crowds are absent.

Perched on a promontory 90m above the River Tauber, Rothenburg was a prosperous Free Imperial City in medieval times, but suffered a spectacular slump in its fortunes as it found itself cut off from the new trading routes and reduced to a very provincial market town. Without money to expand or erect new buildings, it vegetated until the nineteenth century, when its self-evident attraction for the Romantic movement led to the enforcement of preservation orders. In 1945, part of the town suffered severe damage in an American air raid. Thankfully, a civilian working for the US army, J.J. McCloy (later the High Commissioner to Germany), knew and loved Rothenburg, and lobbied successfully for it to be spared from further bombing. Money to pay for its restoration subsequently poured in from abroad, and it was soon returned to its former

ROTHENBURG OB DER TAUBER

0   250m

ACCOMMODATION

1 Altfränkische Weinstube
11 Café Gerberhaus
3 Eisenhut
10 Glocke
12 Goldene Rose
4 Goldener Greifen
9 Goldener Hirsch
2 Markusturm
8 Pöschel
7 Raidel
6 Roter Hahn
5 Then
13 Youth Hostels

appearance. Nowadays, its conservation policies are the strictest in Germany: even the biggest international chains are obliged to use traditional wrought-iron shop signs instead of corporate logos.

Arrival, information and accommodation

Rothenburg is the terminus of a branch rail line from Steinach on the stretch between Würzburg and Ansbach; buses sometimes supplant the trains on this route. From the **Bahnhof**, it's no more than a five-minute walk to the Rödertor. The **tourist office** (May–Oct Mon–Fri 9am–12.30pm & 1–6pm, Sat & Sun 10am–3pm; Nov–April Mon–Fri

9am–12.30pm & 1–5pm, Sat 10am–1pm; ☎0 98 61/4 04 92, fax 8 68 07, *www.rothenburg.de*)
is in the Ratsherrntrinkstube, Marktplatz 2.

Rothenburg offers a huge choice of **accommodation**, ranging from remarkably
cheap **pensions** to luxurious historic **hotels**. Despite the volume of tourism, there's
rarely any problem finding somewhere with vacancies. **Private rooms** (①–③) are
also in reasonable supply – look out for *Zimmer frei* signs. The two **youth hostels** are
in beautifully restored half-timbered houses off the bottom of the Spitalgasse:
Rossmühle, Mühlacker 1 (☎0 98 61/9 41 60, fax 94 16 20, *JHRothen@aol.com.de*;
DM23/€11.50), is the main building; the *Spitalhof* is its rather more spartan annexe.
Both **campsites** are in Detwang: *Tauber-Romantik* (☎0 98 61/61 91) and *Tauber-Idyll*
(☎0 98 61/31 77).

Hotels and pensions

Altfränkische Weinstube, Klosterhof 7 (☎0 98 61/64 04, fax 64 10). Small hotel attached to a wine
bar-restaurant. The local English Conversation Club meets in the latter every Wednesday at 8pm,
and invites all English-speaking visitors to the town to join them for a chat. ③–⑤.

Café Gerberhaus, Spitalgasse 25 (☎0 98 61/9 49 00, fax 8 65 55, *www.gerberhaus.rothenburg.de*).
Named after the old tannery it occupies, this offers modern hotel comforts at moderate prices. The
buffet breakfasts are outstanding. ④–⑥.

Eisenhut, Herrengasse 3–7 (☎0 98 61/70 50, fax 7 05 45, *www.eisenhut.com*). Rothenburg's leading
hotel occupies four patrician mansions on its most prestigious street. It is beautifully decorated with
furniture and antiques, has a garden terrace and a first-rate restaurant. ⑧–⑨.

Glocke, Am Plönlein 1 (☎0 98 61/95 89 90, fax 9 58 99 22, *www.ringhotels.de*). Fine old inn, now part
of the Ringhotel chain, situated at one of Rothenburg's most famous corners. Its restaurant,
Wirtshaus in Franken, has a strong line in fish dishes. ⑤.

Goldene Rose, Spitalgasse 28 (☎0 98 61/46 38, fax 8 64 17). Typical Franconian Gasthof, with a
variety of rooms, including tiny singles which are among the cheapest in town. ②.

Goldener Greifen, Obere Schmiedgasse 5 (☎0 98 61/22 81, fax 8 63 74). Gasthof with a quiet garden, and a good restaurant serving inexpensive Franconian specialities. ④.

Goldener Hirsch, Untere Schmiedgasse 16 (☎0 98 61/70 80, fax 70 81 00, *www*
.goldenerhirsch.rothenburg.de). One of the town's most luxurious hotels, with a renowned restaurant,
Die Blaue Terrasse, commanding a wonderful view over the Tauber valley. ⑥–⑨.

Markusturm, Rödergasse 1 (☎0 98 61/9 42 80, fax 26 92, *www.romantik.de*). Tastefully furnished
hotel with restaurant, part of the Romantik chain. Located at one of the town's most picturesque corners, it takes its name from the adjoining tower, a survivor of the original twelfth-century
Stadtmauer. ⑥–⑨.

Pöschel, Wenggasse 22 (☎0 98 61/34 30). Small family-run pension with immaculate, comfortable
bedrooms. ②.

Raidel, Wenggasse 3 (☎0 98 61/31 15, fax 93 52 55, *Gaestehaus-Raidel@t-online.de*). Another good-
value guesthouse, located in a 600-year-old half-timbered house. ②.

Roter Hahn, Obere Schmiedgasse 21 (☎0 98 61/97 40, fax 51 40, *www.roterhahn.com*). A famous
old hotel, formerly the home of Burgomaster Nusch. It has a good and reasonably priced restaurant. ⑥–⑧.

Then, Johannitergasse 8a (☎0 98 61/51 77, fax 8 60 14). Friendly pension with English-speaking
owners, located down a quiet side-street between the Bahnhof and the Rödertor. ②.

The Town

The best way to get your bearings and a first impression is to walk round the
fourteenth-century **Stadtmauer**, most of whose sentry walk survives. Tightly packed
within the walls, the town's houses get larger towards the middle where the local patri-
cians and merchants lived. Nearer the wall, tradesfolk and peasants lived in crooked little dolls' houses, half-timbered and with steeply pointed roofs. The plan of the town is
also highly distinctive, having a shape like a question mark, with an elongated south-

ern stalk. For a more elevated view, climb the eastern gateway, the **Rödertor** (April–Oct daily 9am–6pm; DM2/€1).

Marktplatz

The sloping central Marktplatz is dominated by the **Rathaus**, which is in two clearly defined parts. To the rear is the surviving half of the original Gothic building, the rest of which was destroyed by fire and replaced in the 1570s by a splendid new Renaissance structure, which was adorned with Baroque arcades a century later. Access to both parts of the Rathaus is via the stair turret which leads up to the wood-beamed **Kaisersaal** on the first floor, where festive events are held. From the landing above, a narrow staircase goes up to the top of the slender 60-metre **tower** (April–Oct daily 9.30am–12.30pm & 1–5pm; Nov–March Sat & Sun noon–3pm only; DM2/€1) of the Gothic Rathaus. It's the highest point in Rothenburg and provides the best view of the town and surrounding countryside. Back at street level, the inner courtyard between the two parts of the Rathaus gives access to the dungeons, the **Historiengewölbe** (mid-March to Oct daily 10am–5/6pm; DM3/€1.50) below, which were said to be more dreadful than any others of the day.

The other main tourist attraction on the Marktplatz is the pair of figures looking out from the windows on either side of the three clocks on the gable of the **Ratsherrntrinkstube** (Councillors' Tavern). Every day at 11am, noon, 1pm, 2pm, 3pm, 8pm, 9pm and 10pm, they re-enact a famous but apocryphal event. The story goes that in 1631, during the Thirty Years War, the imperial army, led by the fearsome Johann Tilly, captured the town and intended to destroy it as a punishment for its support of the Protestant cause. In a gesture of peace, the general was brought the huge civic tankard known as the Meistertrunk, which was filled with wine to its capacity of 3.25 litres, and was persuaded to accept the wager that Rothenburg should be spared if one of the councillors could down the contents in one go. The former burgomaster Georg Nusch duly obliged, taking ten minutes to accomplish the feat, after which he needed three days to sleep off the effects.

To the opposite side of the Marktplatz is Rothenburg's largest building, the Gothic parish church of **St Jakob** (daily Easter–Oct 9am–5.30pm; rest of year 10am–noon & 2–4pm; DM2.50/€1.25), whose main body and two towers rise above the sea of red roofs like a great ship, visible for miles around. The elevated west choir, built over an archway straddling the street, contains **Riemenschneider's** *Holy Blood Altar*, which is exquisitely carved in limewood, with a centrepiece showing the Last Supper. Also of note is the church's high altar, the *Twelve Apostles Altar*, by the Nördlingen artist Friedrich Herlin. The outer wings illustrate the legend of St James; the scene where the saint's dead body is carried to a medieval town features a depiction of fifteenth-century Rothenburg.

North of Marktplatz

Just to the northwest of St Jakob is the **Reichsstadtmuseum** (daily April–Oct 10am–5pm; Nov–March 1–4pm; DM5/€2.50) on Klosterhof. This occupies the former Dominican convent and is most interesting for the building's original medieval work-rooms, which include the oldest surviving kitchen in Germany. Other highlights are the *Rothenburg Passion*, a cycle of twelve pictures painted at the end of the fifteenth century by Martinus Schwarz, the abbot of the Franciscan friary, and the decorated glass vessel which inspired the Meistertrunk legend. Also of note is the collection on Jewish local history. In the thirteenth century Rothenburg had a large settlement of Jews, but their synagogue and ghetto were destroyed in the fifteenth-century pogroms.

You can see one surviving feature of their heritage, however, by going eastwards from here along Judengasse. At the end, built up against the twelfth-century **Weisser Turm** (White Tower), is the former Jewish dance hall, whose walls are embedded with gravestones. A couple of blocks to the south are the only other surviving parts of the original town wall: the hip-roofed **Markusturm** and the **Röderbogen**, to which a clock turret was later appended.

At the extreme northwestern end of town stands the late Gothic church of **St Wolfgang** (daily March–Oct 10am–1pm & 2–5pm; DM2.50/€1.25), whose austere northern wall, pierced only by embrasures, forms part of the Stadtmauer. Now deconsecrated, it was traditionally the parish of the local shepherds, and the sentry's house above the adjoining gateway appropriately contains a display on the *Schäfertanz* (see box on p.222). You can also descend to the casemates below the church, which have dungeons and gun emplacements.

West of Marktplatz

Herrngasse, which leads west from Marktplatz, is the widest street in Rothenburg. At its top end is **Käthe Wohlfahrt**, Europe's largest all-year-round Christmas store and the most obviously over-the-top of the many tourist-oriented shops which have lumbered the town with a reputation for kitsch. However, the street also has many outstanding patrician mansions, notably the **Staudtsches Haus**, where you can ring for a short guided tour (daily 9.30am–5pm; DM2/€1) which takes in the lobby, the kitchen and the remarkable wooden stairwell. Opposite is the severe early Gothic **Franziskanerkirche**, which still preserves the rood screen which divided the friars from the laity. Its walls and floor are covered with funerary monuments to local families, and there's a startlingly realistic retable, believed to be an early work by Riemenschneider, showing the Stigmatization of St Francis.

At the far end of Herrngasse is the tiny **Figurentheater** (☎0 98 61/73 54), which has gained international acclaim for the gentle humour and artistic integrity of its puppet shows. These take place at 8pm from Monday to Saturday; there are also shorter performances at 3pm on Saturday all year round, and on weekdays as well from June to September. Alongside is the **Burgtor**, the tallest of the town's gateways, which gives access to the immaculately tended **Burggarten**, from where there are wonderful views of the town's skyline and the Tauber valley below. In the early Middle Ages there was a castle belonging to the Hohenstaufen emperors here, but it was destroyed by a violent earthquake in 1356. Some of its masonry was used to construct the **Blasiuskapelle**, which is now a memorial to the dead of the two World Wars.

South of Marktplatz

At no. 13 on Hofbronnengasse, which leads off the southern side of Marktplatz, is the **Puppen- und Spielzeugmuseum** (daily: Jan & Feb 11am–5pm; March–Dec 9.30am–6pm; DM6/€3), Germany's largest private collection of toys and dolls. The exhibits date from 1780 to 1940 and are all beautifully displayed. Facing you across Burggasse at the end of the street is the fascinating **Mittelalterisches Kriminalmuseum** (daily: April–Oct 9.30am–6pm; Nov, Jan & Feb 2–3.30pm; Dec & March 10am–3.30pm; DM6/€3), which contains extensive collections of torture instruments and punishment devices – for example the beer barrels that drunks were forced to walk around in. An added attraction is that all exhibits are fully labelled and explained in English.

Schmiedgasse, which leads off the southeastern corner of Marktplatz, is lined with the most prestigious of all the mansions in town. The **Baumeisterhaus**, the finest house, was built by the same architect who designed the Rathaus, Leonhard Weidmann. The first floor is adorned with statues of the Seven Virtues; on the next level, the Seven Deadly Sins sound their warning notes. Burgomaster Nusch of Meistertrunk fame lived at no. 21, now a hotel called **Roter Hahn**. For an insight into how the medieval tradesfolk lived, it's worth making a short detour east along Alter

Stadtgarten to see the **Alt-Rothenburger Handwerkerhaus** (April–Oct daily 9am–6pm; Nov–March Sat & Sun 10am–4pm; DM4/€2), which is believed to be the oldest surviving house in town, dating back to 1270. Its eleven rooms are decked out in the style of centuries past.

At the far end of Schmiedgasse is the **Plönlein**, an outrageously picturesque little triangular square. Beyond lies the narrow southern stem of the town, which functioned as the hospital quarter. The **Spital** itself is a complex of various dates: the chapel is Gothic, the main building is by Weidmann. One of the town's two youth hostels occupies its former bakery; another is in the nearby **Rossmühle**, a sixteenth-century mill formerly powered by sixteen horses. To the east is the **Spitalbastei**, the strongest as well as most modern part of the fortification system, dating from the turn of the seventeenth century.

Outside the walls

From either Plönlein or the Spitalbastei, you can descend to the **Doppelbrücke**, a Gothic viaduct faithfully reconstructed after the war. From here, there's a superb long-range view of Rothenburg. More fine panoramas can be obtained by following the S-bend in the Tauber downstream to the **Topplerschlösschen** (Fri–Sun 1–4pm; DM3/€1.50), the summer and weekend retreat of Burgomaster Heinrich Toppler. This late fourteenth-century tower house has a bizarre top-heavy effect, with the upper storeys jutting out well over the stumpy base.

From here it's a 2km walk down the Tauber to **DETWANG**, a village which is actually older than Rothenburg, but has been part of its municipality since the thirteenth century. The Romanesque **Pfarrkirche** (April–Oct daily 8.30am–noon & 1.30–5/6pm; Nov–March Tues–Sun 10am–noon & 2–4pm; DM1/€0.50) contains another masterpiece by Riemenschneider, the *Holy Cross Altar*, featuring a central *Crucifixion* by the master, with wing reliefs of *The Agony in the Garden* and *The Resurrection* by his assistants.

Eating and drinking

The distinctive local **snowball** (*Schneebällchen*) is Rothenburg's best-known culinary speciality; this is made of dough, twisted into shape, then dipped in any one of several different coverings. For the best selection, visit *Diller* at Hofbronnengasse 16 or

---

ROTHENBURG'S FESTIVALS AND FOLKLORE

If you can stand the crowds and a certain sense of tweeness, it's worth trying to make your visit coincide with one of Rothenburg's many **festivals**. Each Whit Monday, the **Meistertrunk drama** is re-enacted – albeit with no more than a pretence at matching Nusch's feat. The preceding day sees one of the renditions of the historic **Schäfertanz** (Shepherds' Dance) in front of the Rathaus; this is repeated on selected Sundays in spring and summer. According to one tradition, the dance began as a thanksgiving for Rothenburg's deliverance from the plague; another theory asserts that it derives from the celebration of a discovery of hidden treasure by one of the shepherds. Also at Whitsun, and throughout July and August, there are costume performances of **plays by Hans Sachs**. The second weekend in September sees the **Freiereichstadtfest**, featuring pageants, historical tableaux and a fireworks display, as well as performances of the Meistertrunk and the *Schäfertanz*. Rothenburg, like neighbouring Dinkelsbühl and Nördlingen, is among the last towns in Europe still employing a **nightwatchman**. From April to October, he leads tours round the town, starting from the Rathaus; the 8pm tour is in English, the one at 9.30pm in German.

Hafengasse 4. Most of the town's many excellent **restaurants** are attached to hotels (see p.219), though there are a few other eateries worth a visit.

Altstadt-Café Alter Keller, Alter Keller 8. Offers Franconian food and wines, plus home-made cakes and gateaux. Closed Sun evening & Tues.

Baumeisterhaus, Obere Schmiedgasse 5. Provides a strong rivalry to its hotel counterparts for traditional German dishes. It's located in one of the town's most important Renaissance buildings, with a charming covered inner courtyard.

Café Toppler-Felsenkeller, Taubertalweg. Located near the Doppelbrücke, this café has a garden terrace commanding a spectacular view of the town.

Landsknechtstübchen, Galgengasse 21. Pleasant Gaststätte serving hearty Franconian cuisine.

Louvre, Klingengasse 15. Rothenburg's most creative restaurant, serving French-inspired cuisine and hosting changing art exhibitions. Evenings only, closed Sun & Mon.

Spätzle Schwob, Milchmarkt 6. Restaurant specializing in Swabian cuisine.

Dinkelsbühl

Some 40km southwards along the Romantic Road (see box on p.213) from Rothenburg is **DINKELSBÜHL**, which presents another immaculately preserved townscape from the Middle Ages. In contrast to its neighbour, it has managed to avoid being overrun by tourists and thus has a rather more authentic air.

The **Stadtmauer** survives almost intact, except for the sentry walk, of which only a small section remains. It's therefore best to begin your tour by walking round the outside of the walls via the pathway known as the Alte Promenade. Of the four gateways, the eastern **Wörnitz Tor** is part of the original thirteenth-century fortification system, though it was later prettified by the addition of a clock gable and a coating of orange paint. Proceeding southwards, you pass the most photogenic of the towers, the **Bäuerlinsturm**, whose projecting half-timbered upper storey was added when it passed into residential use. Beyond stands the late fourteenth-century **Nördlinger Tor**, again embellished with a Renaissance gable.

Alongside it is the **Stadtmühle**, perhaps the most formidable-looking mill ever built; because it lay outside the walls, it had to be fortified with corner towers and gun loops. It now houses the **Museum 3 Dimension** (April–Oct daily 10am–6pm; Nov–March Sat & Sun 11am–4pm; DM10/€5), an unexpected yet fascinating series of hands-on displays about three-dimensional effects. The western section of the Stadtmauer is pierced by a series of round towers, but its gateway, the **Segringer Tor**, is a decorative Baroque replacement for the one destroyed in the Thirty Years War. However, the northern **Rothenburger Tor** still preserves most of its medieval form, including a sturdy gatehouse.

Within the walls, the dominant monument is the church of **St Georg** on Weinmarkt. From the top of its **tower** (Easter–Sept Mon–Fri 9am–noon & 2–6pm, Sat 10am–noon & 1–5pm, Sun 1–5pm; DM3/€1.50), which survives from the original Romanesque church, there's a marvellous view of the town. The rest of the building is a textbook Gothic hall church from the second half of the fifteenth century, with an airily light interior of slender pillars and elaborate network vaults. In the north walk of the ambulatory is a didactic panel of *The Ten Commandments*, which pairs each scene with the consequences of failure to obey.

Facing the church are five magnificent mansions, of which the most notable are the half-timbered **Deutsches Haus**, now a hotel-restaurant, and the resplendently gabled **Schranne**, which contains the town's main festive hall. More fine houses can be seen down Segringer Strasse to the west: nos. 3 and 5 share a single gable, while no. 7 has a lovely arcaded, flower-strewn courtyard. In the opposite direction, the Altrathausplatz in the shadow of the Wörnitz Tor is another of the most picturesque corners, with the **Löwenbrunnen** (Lion Fountain) as its focal point.

DINKELSBÜHL FOLKLORE

In common with Rothenburg and Nördlingen, Dinkelsbühl still has a paid **nightwatch-man**. Decked out in cloak, breeches and felt hat, and carrying a halberd, horn and lantern, he sets out from St Georg at 9pm each evening from April to October (9.30pm in July and August), and does the rounds of the town's hotels. At each, he performs his song, and is thereupon presented with a glass of wine, which is passed round the tourists accompanying him.

The most famous piece of local folklore is the **Kinderzeche**, a ten-day-long festival held each July, the pivotal date being the third Monday of the month. This commemorates an event in the Thirty Years War which has obvious parallels with Rothenburg's Meistertrunk. This time it was the Swedes who were bent on destruction. According to the legend, when the town finally capitulated after a long siege, the Swedish commander was dissuaded from ransacking it by a deputation of local children. The events are re-enacted in plays performed in the Schranne, while on the Monday and each of the two Saturdays and Sundays there are costumed pageants through the streets. Music is provided by the *Knabenkapelle*; perhaps the best-known boys' band in Germany, its members are kitted out like little soldiers in red and white eighteenth-century uniform. In line with Bavarian taste, there are side-shows of open-air theatre, fireworks and the inevitable beer tents.

Practicalities

Dinkelsbühl lies on a rail line which used to provide a useful link with Nördlingen, the next stop on the Romantic Road some 30km south, but this has been superseded, except for occasional excursion steam trains in summer, by a **bus** service. Most departures are from the **Bahnhof**, a few minutes' walk east of the Altstadt, though the Europabus coaches travelling the Romantic Road leave from Schweinemarkt in the heart of town. The **tourist office** is on Marktplatz (April–Oct Mon–Fri 9am–6pm, Sat 10am–1pm & 2–4pm, Sun 10am–1pm; Nov–March Mon–Fri 9am–noon & 2–6pm, Sat 10am–1pm; ☎0 98 51/9 02 40, fax 9 02 79, *www.dinkelsbuehl.de*). Ask here if you're interested in staying in either a **private house** (①–②) or a neighbouring **farm** (①); provided you've got your own transport, the latter can be a tremendous bargain, particularly for stays of four days or more.

Otherwise, the cheapest rooms are at a small and homely Altstadt **pension**, *Lutz*, Schäfergässlein 4 (☎0 98 51/94 54; ②). There are numerous **hotels**, all of them in characterful old buildings, including *Gasthof Sonne und Palmengarten*, Weinmarkt 11 (☎0 98 51/5 76 70; ②–④), *Eisenkrug*, Dr-Martin-Luther-Str. 1 (☎0 98 51/5 77 00; ③–⑥), *Gasthof Goldene Krone*, Nördlinger Str. 24 (☎0 98 51/22 93; ④), *Weisses Ross*, Steingasse 12 (☎0 98 51/57 98 90; ⑤), *Goldene Rose*, Marktplatz 4 (☎0 98 51/5 77 50; ⑥); *Blauer Hecht*, Schweinemarkt 1 (☎0 98 51/58 10; ⑥), and *Deutsches Haus*, Weinmarkt 3 (☎0 98 51/60 59; ⑥). The **youth hostel** is housed in an old granary at Koppengasse 10 (☎0 98 51/95 09, fax 48 74; DM19/€9.50), while there's a **campsite** (☎0 98 51/78 17) to the northeast of the old town, just off the road from Rothenburg. Nearly all the hotels in the town centre have **restaurants**, and these are generally very good value.

BAVARIAN SWABIA

Approximately bordered by the rivers Iller and Lech, the southwestern part of Bavaria presents a landscape of rolling farmland dotted with quiet villages and picturesque medieval towns. The region is called **Bavarian Swabia** (Bayerisch-Schwaben) and used to form part of the medieval Duchy of Swabia, the rest of which became the separate state of Württemberg. Its capital is **Augsburg**, one of the greatest metropolises of sixteenth-century Europe and still an elegant city full of fine Renaissance architecture, largely unspoilt by later building.

North of here is the stretch of the **Romantic Road** immediately following on from the initial Franconian section; its main draws are **Nördlingen**, a well-preserved medieval walled town in a truly extraordinary natural setting, and fortified **Harburg**. South of Augsburg is the **Allgäu** region. The hilly pre-Alpine section includes the pretty town of **Kaufbeuren** and the health resort of **Ottobeuren**, whose Benedictine abbey should stun even the most jaded visitor of Baroque churches. Beyond here, everything is played against the dramatic backdrop of snow-capped mountains and sparkling lakes: highlights are the pair of fantasy castles near **Füssen**; **Oberstdorf**, a top-class resort set amid challenging peaks; and the island town of **Lindau** on the Bodensee.

An added pleasure of travelling through this region is the distinctive and excellent **food**: delicate handmade pasta and rich sauces quite different from the Italian kind, followed by sweets with irreverent names like *Nonnenfürzle* (Nun's Fart) and *Versoffene Jungfern* (Drunken Virgins).

Nördlingen and around

NÖRDLINGEN, together with 99 villages, lies in an enormous crater, known as the **Ries**, which was formed about 15 million years ago by a meteor which crashed to earth at a speed of about 100,000 kilometres per hour, and with a velocity 250,000 times that of the Hiroshima bomb. The initially transient crater spread to cover an almost circular area with a diameter of about 25km, in the process bringing a new type of rock, known as suevite, into existence. It's among the largest craters on earth, and presents one of the main locations for scientists to study stone formations similar to those on the Moon; it also provided ideal terrain for the Apollo 14 team to prepare for their lunar mission.

The Town

Along with Rothenburg and Dinkelsbühl, Nördlingen makes up the trio of towns on the Romantic Road which have almost completely retained their fortified medieval character. Of the three, it's the one which has made the most concessions to the modern commercial world, but the illusion remains. The fourteenth-century **Stadtmauer** forms an almost perfect circle, guarded by five gates, eleven towers and one bastion. You can traverse the covered sentry walk, the only one in Germany to survive intact, all the way round the 3km circuit. There is also the opportunity of ascending the eastern gateway, the **Löpsinger Tor** (April–Oct daily 10am–4.30pm; DM2/€1).

However, the best view – which shows clearly the distinctive shape and topography of the Ries – is from the 90-metre **Danielturm** (daily 9am–sundown; DM3/€1.50), the town's symbol, its highest building – and also the bull's-eye of the circular urban plan. The tower illustrates a gradual shift in architectural tastes from the late Gothic of its lower storeys to the full-blooded Renaissance of its cupola. A watchman still lives at the top of the tower, and sounds out the watch every half-hour from 10pm until midnight. The Danielturm actually forms part of the hall church of **St Georg**, the largest suevite building in the world, whose design closely resembles that of its namesake in Dinkelsbühl. At the high altar is an emotional polychrome wood *Crucifixion* by the great fifteenth-century Dutch sculptor Nicolaus Gerhaert von Leyden.

On the opposite side of the spacious Marktplatz lies the **Rathaus**, which has an entertaining little detail beside its ritzy outdoor stairway. The space underneath the steps used to hold the town's prisoners, and just by the wooden entrance is a medieval fool carved into the wall with an inscription saying *Nun sind unser zwey* – "Now there are two of us." Directly across is the half-timbered **Tanzhaus** (Dance Hall), bearing a statue of Emperor Maximilian I who had a special affinity with the town; he's depicted in the guise by which he most wanted to be remembered, that of a chivalrous Knight. Walking northwards from Marktplatz, you reach the curious building known as the **Klösterle** (Little Monastery), which has had a decidedly chequered history. Once the church of the bare-footed Franciscan friars, it was converted into a grain store after the Reformation, and is now the town's main festive hall.

Beyond, on Vordere Gerbergasse, is the **Spital**, an extensive medieval hospital complex complete with its own church, mill and stores. It now houses the **Stadtmuseum** (March–Oct Tues–Sun 10am–noon & 1.30–4.30pm; DM4/€2), whose main treasure is a colourful cycle of paintings of the Legend of St George by the fifteenth-century local master Friedrich Herlin. The local history section features terrible exhibits from the torture chambers used during the sixteenth-century witch-hunts: in Nördlingen alone, 35 women were put to death. There's also a diorama of the Battle of Nördlingen of 1634, the worst Protestant reverse in the Thirty Years War. On nearby Hintere Gerbergasse, a fifteenth-century barn has been converted to house the snazzy **Rieskrater-Museum** (Tues–Sun 10am–noon & 1.30–4.30pm; DM5/€2.50), which gives detailed information on the Ries crater's formation and geological history.

Practicalities

Nördlingen's **Bahnhof**, which lies on the slow route between Augsburg and Stuttgart via Schwäbisch Gmünd, is just to the east of the Altstadt. The **tourist office** is at Marktplatz 2 (Easter–Oct Mon–Thurs 9am–6pm, Fri 9am–4.30pm, Sat 9.30am–12.30pm; rest of the year Mon–Thurs 9am–5pm, Fri 9am–3.30pm; ☎0 90 81/43 80 or 8 41 16, fax 8 41 13, *www.noerdlingen.de*).

There are plenty of budget **hotels** within or beside the Stadtmauer, including *Gasthof Drei Mohren*, Reimlinger Str. 18 (☎0 90 81/31 13; ②), *Gasthof Walfisch*, Hallgasse 15 (☎0 90 81/31 07; ②–④), *Gasthof Zum Engel*, Wemdinger Str. 4 (☎0 90 81/31 67; ②–④), and *Café Altreuter*, Marktplatz 11 (☎0 90 81/43 19; ③–⑤). Two good upmarket choices are *Sonne*, Marktplatz 3 (☎0 90 81/50 67; ⑤–⑦), and *Klösterle*, Beim Klösterle 1 (☎0 90 81/8 70 80; ⑦). There's also a **youth hostel**, in an old half-timbered house just to the northwest of the Stadtmauer at Kaiserwiese 1 (☎ & fax 0 90 81/27 18 16; DM19/€9.50).

The **restaurants** of the last two hotels listed above are the best in town, while all the aforementioned Gasthöfe serve good and inexpensive Swabian cuisine. For a trendier atmosphere, try *Café Radlos*, Löpsinger Str. 8, which serves bistro-type food and has a wide range of guest beers on tap.

NÖRDLINGEN'S FESTIVALS

On the second Monday of May, the *Stabenfest* (Staff Festival) celebrates the arrival of spring with a children's procession. Trumpets sound the festival's beginning from the heights of the Danielturm and boys gather holding flags and poles decorated with flowers, the girls wearing costumes and crowns of flowers around their heads. At around 9am, the procession moves off accompanied by music and song until it reaches the Kaiserwiese, the fairground just to the north of the Stadtmauer, where the usual trappings of a Bavarian fair are set up around the beer tent. Another popular annual event is the *Scharlachrennen* in mid-July, whose origins lie in a horse race first held in 1438, with a piece of red cloth as a prize. Today, carriage events are also featured.

Harburg

From Nördlingen, it's only about 15km by road or rail to the next stop on the Romantic Road, the picturesquely sited little town of **HARBURG**. High above, dominating the valley of the River Wörnitz, is a huge **Schloss** (guided tours: mid-March to Sept Tues–Sun 9am–5pm; Oct Tues–Sun 9.30am–4.30pm; DM5/€2.50), which was founded in the twelfth century by the Hohenstaufen emperors, before passing to the counts of Oettingen, whose descendants still own it. Never taken in battle, its fortifications and residential buildings – which date from a variety of periods – survive in pretty good condition. The Renaissance Fürstenbau houses the **Kunstsammlung** (mid-March to Oct Tues–Sun 10am–noon & 2–5pm; DM5/€2.50), whose prize exhibit is a poignant, almost monumental ivory crucifix of the eleventh-century Ottonian period, a unique work of its kind. There are also several outstanding treasury items, notably a jewelled reliquary cross bearing the figures of the donor, Count Ludwig XII of Oettingen, and his family.

Gasthof Zum Straussen, Marktplatz 2 (☎0 90 80/13 98; ②), is one of the best-value **hotels** anywhere in Germany, and its **restaurant** serves king-sized portions of superb Swabian cuisine. Alternatives are *Gasthof Goldenes Lamm*, Marktplatz 15 (☎0 90 80/14 22; ②), and the *Fürstliche Burgschenke* in the Schloss (☎0 90 80/15 04, *www.ries-gastronomie.de*; ⑤).

Augsburg

Only 60km northwest of Munich, **AUGSBURG** certainly doesn't suffer from any inferiority complexes, despite being no more than a quarter of its size. Founded in 15 BC as Augusta Vindelicorum by two stepsons of Augustus, the city is one of the oldest in Germany. A Free Imperial City from 1276 and a frequent choice for meetings of the Diet, Augsburg had its heyday between the fifteenth and seventeenth centuries, when the **Fugger** and **Welser** dynasties made it Europe's most important centre of high finance. As a result it grew into one of the largest cities on the continent. It was the one major city in Germany to take the Renaissance style to its heart, and the highly individualistic buildings of **Elias Holl**, who served as municipal architect from 1602 until 1635, still dominate the townscape.

Local people have gone to vast expense to restore the numerous palaces and civic buildings to their original splendour. In fact civilian municipal life is the key to Augsburg's history. Trade and banking riches spawned a social conscience – in 1514 Augsburg built the world's first housing estate for the poor, the **Fuggerei**, an institution still in use today. Here too the revolutionary reforms of Martin Luther found their earliest support, as the city played a pivotal role in the Reformation and its aftermath. It became the model example of how different faiths could co-exist, making this visible by the curious practice of building new Protestant churches alongside existing Catholic ones.

Despite these associations, Augsburg is far from being a museum-piece. It has long been a leading centre for **new technologies**: here, for example, Rudolf Diesel invented the engine which has put his name into languages all round the world. There's also a lively cultural scene ranging from Mozart festivals to jazz and cabaret, and the local university means you'll find plenty of student bars and a thriving alternative culture.

Arrival, information and accommodation

The **Hauptbahnhof** lies just to the west of the Altstadt and is itself a remarkable sight, a mock *palazzo* of the 1840s which ranks as the longest-serving main station of any city in the world. Just down the road, at Bahnhofstr. 7, is the **tourist office** (Mon–Fri 9am–6pm; ☎08 21/50 20 70, fax 5 02 07 45, *www.regio-augsburg.de*). This has a small branch on Rathausplatz (Mon–Fri 9am–6pm, Sat 10am–1pm; May to mid-Oct Sun 10am–1pm). Its most useful leaflet is *Augsburg and its Sights*; this includes a trail round sixteen different craft workshops, which are mostly concentrated in the vicinity of the Lech canals. A day ticket on the **public transport** network is a good investment; it costs DM9/€4.50 for the city, DM19/€9.50 for the whole circuit.

Augsburg has a wide choice of **hotels** and **pensions**, with a surprisingly large number of eminently good budget options for such a major city. The **youth hostel** is centrally located, three minutes' walk from the Dom, at Beim Pfaffenkeller 3 (☎08 21/3 39 09, fax 15 11 49; DM21/E10.50); if you're coming from the Hauptbahnhof, take tram #2 to Stadtwerke. The nearest **campsite**, *Augusta*, is at highway exit Augsburg-Ost, next to the Autobahnsee (☎08 21/70 75 75), and reachable by bus #75.

Hotels and pensions

Altstadthotel Ulrich, Kapuzinergasse 6 (☎08 21/3 46 10, fax 3 46 13 46, *www.hotel-ulrich.de*). Excellent middle-range hotel handily located just off Maximilianstrasse. ⑤.

Augsburger Hof, Auf dem Kreuz 2 (☎08 21/34 30 50, fax 3 43 05 55, *www.augsburger-hof.de*). Part of the Romantik chain, this classy hotel and restaurant occupy a historic building in the northern Altstadt. ⑥.

Bayerischer Löwe, Linke Brandstr. 2, Lechhausen (☎08 21/70 28 70, fax 70 61 94). Good budget pension, situated in an inner suburb on the opposite side of the Lech from the city centre, a ten-minute ride away on tram #1. ③.

Dom-Hotel, Frauentorstr. 8 (☎08 21/34 39 30, fax 34 39 32 00, *www.domhotel-ausburg.de*). Attractive hotel occupying the former Domprobstei, the palace of the Dom's provost, in the heart of the quiet episcopal quarter. It has a garden terrace and an indoor swimming pool with sauna and solarium. ⑤–⑦.

Drei Mohren, Maximilianstr. 40 (☎08 21/5 03 60, fax 15 78 64, *www.steigenberger.de*). Run by the Steigenberger chain, this is one of Germany's most famous hotels, founded in 1723 and with an illustrious guest list which includes Mozart, Goethe, Napoleon and Wellington. Following wartime damage, it was rebuilt in a predominantly modern style, but is still very luxurious, with a lovely garden terrace and a moderately priced bistro as an alternative to the main restaurant. Substantial reductions in room rates are available from early July to mid-Sept, and at weekends throughout the year. ⑧–⑨.

Georgsrast, Georgenstr. 31 (☎08 21/50 26 10, fax 5 02 61 27). In the northwestern quarter of the Altstadt, this old-fashioned pension is one of the few inexpensive places you'll find in the area. ③.

Jakoberhof, Jakoberstr. 39–41 (☎08 21/51 00 30, fax 15 08 44). Good-value hotel with restaurant, located close to the Fuggerei. ④.

Lenzhalde, Thelottstr. 2 (☎08 21/52 07 45, fax 52 87 61). Greek-run hotel sited immediately behind the Hauptbahnhof, though it's a circuitous walk or drive to get here. In summer, its taverna spills out onto the shady beer garden in front. Breakfast is only served if requested in advance. ②.

Linderhof, Aspernstr. 38, Lechhausen (☎08 21/71 30 16, fax 71 67 66). Although on the other side of the Lech, this pension is only ten minutes from the centre by tram #1. ③.

Märkl, Schillstr. 20, Lechhausen (☎08 21/79 14 99, fax 72 19 87). This pension has the cheapest rooms in Augsburg, but is perfectly comfortable, with showers in every room. It's on the first street over the Lechbrücke; take tram #1. ②.

Ost am Kö, Fuggerstr. 4-6 (☎08 21/50 20 40, fax 5 02 04 44, *www.ostamkoe.de*). Fine hotel which is equally convenient for the commercial and historic parts of the city centre. A buffet breakfast is included in the room price. ⑤–⑦.

Riegele, Viktoriastr. 4 (☎08 21/50 90 00, fax 51 77 46). Nicely furnished hotel directly facing the Hauptbahnhof. It's named after Augsburg's largest brewery, but its restaurant, *Bräustüble*, is more formal and upmarket than the name would suggest, serving international as well as local dishes. ⑦.

The City

Augsburg is a remarkably easy city to get to grips with. The Altstadt is defined by the old fortifications, substantial parts of which still survive. Virtually everything you'll want to see is within walking distance of the central Maximilianstrasse, which makes a ready reference point for exploring the various quarters.

Rathausplatz

Heart of the city is the spacious cobbled **Rathausplatz**, which turns into a massive open-air café during the summer and a glittering Christmas market in December. At the baseline of this great semicircle stands the massive **Rathaus** built by Elias Holl, and generally regarded as Germany's finest example of a secular Renaissance building. The proportions and style of the elegantly plain exterior topped by two octagonal towers recall a Florentine palace rather than a town hall, a likeably overstated symbol of Augsburg's wealth and influence. What stands today is a painstaking reconstruction;

THE FUGGER DYNASTY

The Fugger family settled in Augsburg in the fourteenth century and were originally active in the linen trade. They gradually moved into the even more profitable business of money-lending, which they established throughout Germany and beyond, becoming the biggest banking outfit in Europe and reputedly five times richer than the Medici, their Italian counterparts. Although the youngest of seven brothers, **Jacob Fugger II** (1459–1525) became the head of the firm, and can legitimately be regarded as the first modern business tycoon.

He established the family interests as a public company, expanding its activities by gaining mining rights for copper and silver in the Tyrol and Silesia and entering the profitable spice trade. In addition, he safeguarded his prosperity by spreading his assets across a wide range of investments, including the acquisition of land – which brought the family into the ranks of the nobility. He also moved into big-time politics by initiating the long-running funding of the Habsburgs, whose goal of European domination seemed to have been achieved when Charles I of Spain won election in 1519 as the Holy Roman Emperor Charles V through outright bribes to the seven Electors with money largely supplied by the Fuggers.

The Reformation dealt a severe blow to the family, who lost key markets by remaining faithful to Catholicism, though the Habsburg connection was put to good use in the establishment of business interests in the burgeoning Spanish empire. Some four million ducats lent to the Habsburgs have never been repaid, but the Fuggers were able to sit back on the income from their landed holdings. To this day, the three branches of the family retain a high position in the German league-table of wealth – and they still own their own bank.

only the shell survived a 1944 air raid targeting the city's Messerschmidt aircraft factories. Not that you'd guess this from looking at the showpiece **Goldener Saal** (daily 10am–6pm; DM3/€1.50), which is once more resplendent with its gold-leaf pillars, marble floor and painted cedarwood ceiling.

Next to the Rathaus stands the **Perlachturm** (May–Oct daily 10am–6pm; DM2/€1), which was remodelled by Holl to its present height of just over 70m. A climb to the top gives a good vantage point from which to take in the whole city and get your bearings on Augsburg's main axis, neatly formed between the Dom to the north and the church of St-Ulrich-und-Afra at the far end of Maximilianstrasse to the south. The tower forms part of the Romanesque church of **St Peter am Perlach**, the oldest brick building in southern Germany, which preserves life-sized thirteenth-century murals of four saints. Opposite is the Mannerist **Augustusbrunnen**, by the Dutchman Hubert Gerhard, one of many grandiose fountains dotting the centre of the city, bearing a statue of the emperor and symbolic figures representing Augsburg's four rivers.

Maximilianstrasse
Maximilianstrasse is a true showpiece thoroughfare, lined with the headquarters of the leading corporate and municipal bodies, and the palatial residences of the richest merchant families who dominated their affairs. It's named in honour of the Habsburg Maximilian I, the last Holy Roman Emperor to preside over a unified empire and the man who set in motion his family's plans for European-wide domination. Augsburg was his favourite residence – no doubt partly because his political scheming was dependent on the backing of the city's bankers.

The first building of note is the fourteenth-century **Weberzunfthaus**, the guild hall of the linen weavers. Beyond, in the centre of the street, is the resplendent **Merkurbrunnen** by another Dutch-born Mannerist, Adrian de Vries, court sculptor to the Habsburgs. Soon after, the **Fuggerhäuser** stand proudly to the right. Built in 1515 by Jacob Fugger "the

Rich", these mansions remain in family hands (see box opposite), but you can walk through the main door to see the arcaded **Damenhof**, designed in Italian Renaissance style and often used for plays in the summer. In 1518 this courtyard was the venue for the meeting between Martin Luther and Cardinal Tommaso Cajetan, in which the great reformer attempted to justify his 95 theses against Catholic orthodoxy.

Continuing south down Maximilianstrasse, you come to Adrian de Vries's heroic **Herkulesbrunnen**, the most arresting of all the city's fountains. To the right is the **Schaezlerpalais** (Tues–Sun 10am–5pm; DM4/€2, or DM6/€3 combined day-ticket with Römisches Museum and Maximilianmuseum; free first Sun of month), the town's foremost Rococo building. Its sumptuous ballroom is in its original condition – right down to the candle-lit chandeliers that are still used during the annual Mozart concerts held in June and July. There's also a collection of sixteenth- to eighteenth-century German and Austrian paintings, plus a few works by foreigners, including Veronese and Tiepolo. Through the courtyard and included on the same entrance ticket, though currently closed for restoration, is the old Dominican nunnery, now housing the **Staatsgalerie**. This displays the work of the fifteenth- and sixteenth-century school of local painters – notably Hans Holbein the Elder and Hans Burgkmair – as well as Dürer's portrait of Jacob Fugger "the Rich", looking every bit the king-maker that he was.

Towards its end, Maximilianstrasse widens and sweeps up to the late Gothic basilica of **St-Ulrich-und-Afra**, whose Renaissance tower is crowned by the most famous of the city's characteristic onion domes. In the airily light interior are the tombs of the city's two patrons. St Afra, a Roman virgin martyr, is interred in a simple sarcophagus, whereas St Ulrich, the local prince-bishop whose army helped save the empire by turning back the rampaging Magyars at the Battle of Lechfeld in 955, is honoured by an ornate Rococo shrine. The three monumental gilded altars by Hans Degler in the choir are late Renaissance masterpieces belonging to the same brilliant artistic period as Holl's buildings. In the early eighteenth century, as a symbol of the religious tolerance of the time, the preaching hall on the north side of the basilica was rebuilt as the Lutheran church of **St Ulrich**, its cheerful Baroque facade making an effective foil to its much grander neighbour.

The eastern Altstadt

Just to the southeast of St-Ulrich-und-Afra is another distinctive landmark, the **Rotes Tor**, a fortified tower strengthened by Holl at the time of the Thirty Years War, whose courtyard is now used as an open-air theatre. The same architect's **Heilig-Geist-Spital** alongside is home to the celebrated Puppenkiste marionette theatre, which will open its own museum in autumn 2001. Following Bäckergasse and then Dominikanergasse back towards the city centre, you come to the former Dominican priory, which now houses the **Römisches Museum** (Tues–Sun 10am–5pm; DM4/€2, free first Sun of month), the city's collection of prehistoric and Roman remains. The richly stuccoed interior of the church makes an excellent setting for the artefacts, including a life-sized second-century bronze horse's head, which was probably part of a statue honouring Emperor Marcus Aurelius.

East of here is the most impressive surviving part of the medieval **Stadtmauer**, dominated by the fifteenth-century **Vogeltor**. Beyond lies the picturesque old artisans' quarter, laid out along the narrow canals of the Vorderer, Mittlerer and Unterer Lech. These back streets must have looked very similar a few hundred years ago, when they were populated with the tradesfolk and craftspeople who served the grand houses on Maximilianstrasse. At Vorderer Lech 20 the **Holbeinhaus** (Tues–Sun 11am–5pm; free) stands on the site of the original, which was destroyed in 1944. Here Hans the Younger, portraitist of the brilliant English court of Henry VIII, spent his childhood, his father having established himself as the city's leading painter. Changing exhibitions complement documentary material on the artists' lives.

Continuing northwards, you come to Elias-Holl-Platz to the rear of the Rathaus, on which stands a convent, **Kloster Maria Stern**. Originally built in the 1570s in late Gothic style by Johannes Holl, father of Elias, it was remodelled inside in the Baroque period. The slender brick belfry is crowned by the earliest example of the Welsche Haube, the distinctive onion dome that is a recurrent feature of the Augsburg skyline. A few paces on, fronting Schachthausgasse, is one of Elias Holl's finest buildings, the **Stadtmetzg**, the former guild hall and market of the butchers. Though its rusticated facade is the most visually impressive feature, it was also a technical *tour de force* in its day, harnessing the waters of the Lech canals which lie directly underneath for the cooling of meats and disposal of waste.

At Auf dem Rain 7, just to the north, is the **Bertolt-Brecht-Haus** (Tues–Sun 10am–5pm; DM2.50/€1.25), the birthplace of the great poet and playwright whose relationship with the city is far more problematic than that of any of its other famous sons. The embarrassing fact is that the people of Augsburg couldn't stand Brecht when he was alive – but then neither could he stomach his bourgeois home city. Today, however, all is forgiven, and the house presents a mainly photographic record of the writer, predictably concentrating on his early life in Augsburg. On Leonhardsberg immediately to the north is the luxuriant Jugendstil **Altes Stadtbad** (Mon & Tues 8am–7pm, Wed–Fri 8am–9pm, Sat 8am–8pm, Sun 8am–6pm; prices start at DM6.50/€3.25 for a swim, DM17/€8.50 for a full Roman-Irish bath), one of Germany's finest bathing halls.

The Fuggerei

One "Our Father", one "Hail Mary" and one "Credo" daily, plus DM1.72/€0.86 per annum, and good Catholics can retire to the **Fuggerei** at the age of 55. It's the world's oldest housing estate for the poor and must be one of the cleverest ploys ever devised for a place in Heaven – even if it now appears that Jacob Fugger's seeming generosity was at least partly inspired by the opportunities it offered for laundering part of his fortune. Entered via a gate which, in accordance with the still-enforced original regulations, is kept locked between 10pm and 5am, it's a town within a town, with two-storey ivy-covered houses lining six pedestrian-only streets. Originally intended for families with children, it has gradually evolved into a retirement colony, though residents must still be Roman Catholic, needy, free of a criminal record and citizens of Augsburg.

Behind the main gateway is the the Fuggerei's modest little church, the **Markuskirche**, which was built by Johannes Holl. The only other interior open to the public is that of Mittlere Gasse 13, which has been designated the **Fuggereimuseum** (March – Dec 23 daily 9am–6pm; DM1/€0.50), with furnishings vividly illustrating the lifestyle of the community's inhabitants of the seventeenth and eighteenth centuries. Another house from the time of the first settlement is no. 14 in the same street, which is where Mozart's great-grandfather lived in the late seventeenth century.

The western Altstadt

Exactly the other side of town, on Annastrasse, stands the Gothic church of **St Anna**, whose Renaissance tower was added by Elias Holl in an unconventional position above the body of the building, rather than on its own base. The chancel contains a number of devotional paintings, notably *Christ Blessing Children* by Cranach. Alongside is the **Goldschmiedkapelle** (Goldsmiths' Chapel), which preserves its original fresco cycle. In 1509, Ulrich and Jacob Fugger endowed a memorial chapel for themselves and their deceased brother Georg. The clout they wielded is shown by the fact that, against all convention, this formed an extension of the nave, instead of taking the humbler normal position off an aisle. The sumptuous **Fuggerkapelle** which resulted marks the belated German debut of the full-blooded Italian Renaissance style. An integrated, no-expenses-spared decorative scheme – marble pavement, an organ with painted shutters, stained glass, choir stalls, balustrade with putti, a monumental sculptural group of *The*

Lamentation over the Dead Christ, and memorial relief tablets made after woodcuts designed by Dürer – creates an effect of overwhelming richness. Now thought to have been the work of local rather than Italian craftsmen, its influence on Augsburg was profound, inspiring all subsequent building there for over a century.

St Anna is also celebrated for its role in the Reformation, when Luther found refuge with its Carmelite friars when he was summoned to meet the pope's legate Cardinal Cajetan, and today part of the former friary has been turned into the **Lutherstiege** (Tues–Sun 10am–noon & 3–5pm; free), a museum of the reformer's life and times. Along with extensive documentation on the events, you can see the **Lutherkammer**, the actual room where he stayed in 1518; the *Empore*, the old gallery for the Carmelites, shows the Bull of Excommunication which resulted from his refusal to retract his views.

Across from the friary, in a Renaissance mansion with sgraffito decoration at Philippine-Welser-Str. 24, is the **Maximilianmuseum** (Tues–Sun 10am–5pm; DM4/€2, free first Sun of month). Its courtyard has recently been covered with a glass roof in order that **original figures** from the city's three great Mannerist fountains can be displayed in natural light conditions, while protecting them from the elements. Also of special note is the collection of historic **wooden models** made by practising architects: that of the Gothic Rathaus makes for a fascinating comparison with the one Holl prepared in advance of his rebuilding project; there's another showing progress on the Perlachturm, which is shrouded under scaffolding. The museum has extensive displays of the wonderful Baroque and Rococo creations of the goldsmiths, silversmiths and watchmakers who made Augsburg one of Europe's leading producers of luxury goods. There are also collections of sculptures from Gothic to Rococo, porcelain and historic scientific instruments.

A couple of blocks further south, dominating the square named after it, is the **Zeughaus**, the first structure designed by Holl in his capacity as municipal architect. It's a brilliantly original composition whose facade is uncannily anticipatory of the Baroque style to come. Above its doorway is a striking monumental bronze group of *St Michael overcoming Satan*, the masterpiece of Hans Reichle, one of the few native German Mannerists.

The northern Altstadt

Dominating the northern part of the Altstadt is the **Dom**. Architecturally, it's a bit of a hotchpotch: in the fourteenth century, Gothic aisles were added to the original eleventh-century structure; a hundred years later, a lofty hall choir replaced its predecessor altogether. Entry is via the **portals** on the north and south sides of the chancel, which are dedicated to the Virgin Mary, and crowded with richly decorative Gothic sculptures. On the southern side of the nave's clerestory are five **stained-glass windows** showing the Old Testament figures of Moses, David, Hosea, Daniel and Jonah. The freshness of colour and the vibrancy of the design make it hard to believe they were made in the eleventh century: they're the oldest windows remaining *in situ* in any church in the world. Another Romanesque survivor is the **bishop's throne** in the west choir, imperiously perched on crouching lions. Look out also for the eight fine **altarpieces** by Hans Holbein the Elder, fixed to the pillars of the nave, of scenes from the life of the Virgin.

Housed in the chambers off the cloisters, but entered from Kornhausgasse to the north, is the new **Diözesanmuseum St Afra** (Tues–Sat 10am–5pm, Sun–5pm, first Fri in month 10am–9pm; DM4/€2). This is now home to the Dom's celebrated Romanesque **bronze doors**, which are decorated with 35 endearingly simple panels depicting Old Testament scenes and allegorical figures and animals. Also on view are the artefacts made for the funeral of Emperor Charles V, the most striking being a gilded helmet with a crown on top. Numerous monstrances, chalices, ciboria, reliquaries, altars and other liturgical artefacts illustrate the vitality of Augsburg's goldsmith tradition between the fifteenth and eighteenth centuries. Excavations of the Carolingian Dom of around 800 can also be seen.

Facing the Dom's facade is the **Fronhof**, the former palace of the prince-bishops. Only the tower remains of the medieval building where the Confession of Augsburg, the basic creed of Protestantism, was presented in 1530. The rest was rebuilt in Baroque style, and has served since 1817 as the regional government of Bavarian Swabia; the frescoed staircase and the main Festsaal are freely accessible, except when an official function is taking place.

Further west are the **Heilig-Kreuz-Kirchen**, another of the paired Catholic and Protestant churches, each with its own distinctive interpretation of the Welsche Haube. Originally an Augustinian collegiate foundation, the Gothic Catholic church contains an altarpiece of *The Assumption* by Rubens, but the seventeenth-century Protestant building alongside is the one which really catches the eye, not least because of the startlingly asymmetrical ground plan that resulted from the need to build the facade directly along the line of the street. It contains a large number of paintings, including a small panel of *The Baptism of Christ* by Tintoretto and several canvases by Johann Heinrich Schönfeld, notably the iconographically unusual *Christ Preaching from a Boat*.

North of the Dom, at Frauentorstr. 30, is the **Mozarthaus** (Tues–Sun 10am–5pm; DM2.50/€1.25), which documents the lives of Leopold and Wolfgang Amadeus and contains some of the original furnishings. This modest little house was the birthplace of Leopold, who moved to Salzburg long before his famous son was born. Notorious even in his day as a Svengali figure, he is now recognized as a highly competent composer in his own right, whose works include one of the best trumpet concertos ever written and two effective comic pieces, *A Musical Sleigh Ride* and the *Toy Symphony*. Guarding the extreme northern end of the Altstadt is the **Wertachbrucker Tor**, a fourteenth-century gateway to which Elias Holl appended two storeys, a pyramidal roof and a lantern.

Outside the Altstadt

Just outside the confines of the Altstadt is the **Synagoge** (Tues–Fri 9am–4pm, Sun 10am–5pm; DM3/€1.50) at Halderstr. 8, a few minutes' walk east of the Hauptbahnhof. This imposing Jugendstil complex, grouped round an open courtyard, was built during World War I as the main place of worship for what was one of Germany's largest and most liberal Jewish communities. Nowadays, the tiny orthodox sect that remains uses only the small prayer hall; the domed main temple (which you can only view from the gallery) and ancillary buildings (which house a surprisingly rich treasury) now serve as a museum of Swabian and Bavarian Jewish culture.

Beyond the southwestern fringe of the Altstadt, housed in the Industrie und Handelskammer at Stettenstr. 1–3, is the **Lettl-Atrium** or **Museum für Surreale Kunst** (Mon–Fri 8am–7.30pm, Sat 11am–4pm, Sun 11am–5pm; free). This contains well over a hundred canvases by the Augsburg Surrealist **Wolfgang Lettl**, whose work provides a refreshing corrective to the idea that Germans lack a sense of humour.

Eating, drinking and entertainment

In the food and drink field, Augsburg's main strengths are a wide range of restaurants offering hearty traditional fare, plus a large number of student pubs. In addition to the places listed below, and those in the hotels on p.229, it's worth knowing about the market and meat halls off Annastrasse, where you'll find several Imbiss stands which are the best bet for on-your-feet snacks. The city has a surprising dearth of discos and nightclubs, but is well-endowed with live music and theatrical venues.

AUGSBURG'S FESTIVALS

The main local **festival** is *Plärrer*, which is rather like a smaller version of Munich's *Oktoberfest*, except that it takes place twice annually, lasting for a fortnight on each occasion. The spring version, the *Frühjahrsplärrer*, begins on the Sunday after Easter; its autumn counterpart, the *Herbstplärrer*, takes place on the last week in August and the first in September. Other annual events are the *Jakober Kirchweih* at the end of July and beginning of August; the *Friedensfest* (Peace Festival) on August 8; the *Mozartsommer* in late August and early September; and the *Christkindlesmarkt*, whose opening on November 23 is marked by a colourful pageant, and which features live Christmas music each subsequent weekend.

Restaurants

Bräustüble Goldene Gans, Weite Gasse 11. The beer hall and garden of the eponymous brewery, which is located alongside. At lunchtime, it is transformed into a vegetarian specialist, with hot and cold buffet tables. Closed Sun.

Caruso, Karlstr. 9. Good, reasonably priced Italian restaurant.

Die Ecke, Elias-Holl-Platz 2. Famous old restaurant in the shadow of the Rathaus; among the most expensive, but also one of the most prestigious in the city.

Drei Königinnen, Meister-Veits-Gässchen 32. The Gasthaus and beer garden of the Augusta brewery, with a nicely varied menu; it also hosts regular literary and artistic events.

Fuggerei-Stube, Jakoberstr. 26. The "local" of the Fuggerei, serving some of the best food in town. Closed Mon.

Fuggerkeller, Maximilianstr. 38. Typically hearty German fare at reasonable prices is served up in the cellars of the Fuggerhäuser. Closed Sun evening.

Kaiser-Augustus-Weinstuben, Frauentorstr. 51. Historic wine cellar-cum-restaurant with summer terrace. Evenings only, closed Sun.

Welser-Kuche, Maximilianstr. 83 (☎08 21/9 61 10). Extremely gimmicky, but nonetheless a true original, this restaurant does nothing but Renaissance-style banquets using recipes from the cookery book of Philippine Welser. Meals start at 8pm and last for three hours; reservations essential.

Wirtshaus am Lech, Leipziger Str. 50, Lechhausen. Traditional Gasthaus with beer garden serving really excellent Swabian cooking. It's situated just over the Lechbrücke, and can be reached by tram #1.

Wirthaus am Wertachbrucker Tor, Wertachbrucker-Tor-Str. 9. The tap of the Thorbräu brewery alongside, though the cuisine served is mostly Spanish.

Zeughaus-Stuben, Zeughausplatz 4. Another good choice for local cuisine, in the historic setting of the Zeughaus itself; there's also a beer garden. Closed Sun evening.

Zum Weissen Hasen, Unter dem Bogen 4. The city centre Gaststätte of Hasenbräu, one of the big local breweries, offering cheap lunchtime specials.

Bars and cafés

Café Dichtl, Maximilianstr. 18. A modern variant on the theme of a traditional café.

Café Stadler, Bahnhofstr. 30. Another good choice, complete with winter garden, for *Kaffee und Kuchen* – and conveniently placed to while away the time waiting for a train. Closed Sun.

Caféhaus Eber, Philippine-Welser-Str. 6. Elegant coffee house which in summer sets up outside tables on Rathausplatz.

Charly-Bräu, Ulmer Str. 43, Oberhausen. Hausbrauerei with a predominantly young clientele, located near the Oberhausen S-Bahn station. It makes an amber-coloured *Weizen* and a very dark *Braunbier*.

Courage, Jakoberstr. 7. Trendy new Bertolt Brecht theme bar.

Feinkost Kahn, Annastr. 16. Café-cum-daytime restaurant attached to Augsburg's most mouthwatering delicatessen shop. Closed Sun.

Kappeneck, Kappeneck 30. Friendly, youthful café-bar with a wide range of drinks and snacks.

Kerosin, Gögginger Str. 26–28. Popular live music bar. Tues–Sat 9pm–1am.

König von Flandern, Karolinenstr. 12. Basement Hausbrauerei producing very mild-tasting light and dark beers. Also does basic meals, including cheap daily specials.

Sputnik, Stettenstr. 32. The leading late-nighter; open 9pm till 3am, 4am at weekends.

Striese, Kirchgasse 1. A student favourite, sometimes featuring theatre and live music. Daily 7pm–1am, also Sun 10am–1pm for breakfast.

Thorbräukeller, Heilig-Kreuz-Str. 20. Beer garden and Kneipe of the brewery of the same name.

Discos and nightclubs

Circus, Ludwigstr. 36. The most popular of the city's discos. Mon–Thurs & Sun 9pm–3am, Fri 9pm–5am, Sat 9pm–4am.

Hepcat Club, Maximilianstr. 56. Augsburg's swing club. Daily 6pm–2am, till 3am Fri & Sat.

Rockfabrik, Riedinger Str. 24. A meeting-place for heavy rock fans, located north of the city centre on bus route #26 from Königsplatz. Mon–Wed 8pm–3am, Thurs 9pm–3am, Fri 9pm–4am, Sat 9pm–5am.

Spectrum-Club, Ulmer Str. 234. Disco, party and live music venue. Thurs & Fri from 9pm, Sat & Sun from 8pm.

Classical music and theatre

abraxas, Sommestr. 30 (☎08 21/3 24 63 55). Arts centre with a varied theatrical programme, including performers from other continents.

Freilichtbühne, Am Roten Tor 5 (☎08 21/3 24 49 77). This mounts its open-air season of plays – with Brecht now featuring regularly – in June and July.

Kleiner Goldener Saal, Jesuitengasse 12 (☎08 21/3 24 49 80). A Baroque hall, formerly part of a Jesuit seminary, which makes a highly suitable venue for small-scale classical music concerts.

Komödie, Vorderer Lech 8 (☎08 21/3 24 49 78). Comedy playhouse in the eighteenth-century home and factory of a cotton manufacturer.

Kongresshalle, Göppinger Str. 10 (☎08 21/3 24 23 48). The usual venue for large-scale orchestral and choral concerts.

Kresslesmühle, Barfüsserstr. 4 (☎08 21/3 71 70). Another arts centre, offering both cabaret and experimental theatre.

Mozarthaus, Frauentorstr. 30 (☎08 21/51 85 88). Presents a regular season of chamber, instrumental and song recitals.

Puppenkiste, Spitalgasse 15 (☎08 21/43 44 40). This marionette theatre is Augsburg's most famous cultural venue and consequently tickets, which can only be booked in advance by telephone, are often hard to come by.

Theater Augsburg, Kennedyplatz 1 (☎08 21/32 49 00). The main municipal stage for opera and drama.

The Allgäu

The southwesternmost part of Bavaria is known as the **Allgäu**, and is as famed for its cheeses – which are the finest produced in Germany – as for its magnificent scenery. There are four constituent parts to the region. Closest to Augsburg is the **Lower Allgäu** (Unterallgäu or Allgäuer Voralpenland), a rolling pre-Alpine landscape punctuated by a few towns and villages, among which **Kaufbeuren** and **Ottobeuren** are particularly worth visiting. Prime attractions of the **Eastern Allgäu** (Ostallgäu) are the frivolous and extravagant but irresistible castles of **Hohenschwangau** and **Neuschwanstein**, which rather overshadow the neighbouring towns of **Füssen** and **Schwangau**. Jutting into Austria is the **Upper Allgäu** (Oberallgäu), a classic Alpine area dominated by the resort of **Oberstdorf**. Finally, there's the **Western Allgäu** (Westallgäu), part of which lies in Baden-Württemberg, though the Bavarian section includes the island town of **Lindau** on the shores of the **Bodensee**.

Ottobeuren

The star attraction of the Lower Allgäu is the small health resort of **OTTOBEUREN**, or more specifically the **Reichsabtei**, which stands on a gentle incline above the rest of the village. This still-functioning Benedictine abbey founded in 764 is one of the most imposing and grandiose monasteries north of the Alps. Its patron Charlemagne gave the abbot important rights, elevating him to the status of a prince of the Holy Roman Empire.

Architecturally the abbey has undergone many changes since its foundation. The present Baroque **Basilika** was created, after several false starts by other architects, by the Munich master Johann Michael Fischer in the eighteenth century. It's huge: physical details such as the 90-metre nave and 60-metre transept hardly convey the bombastic impression you get on entering. The wealth of altars, frescoes, paintings and stuccoed embellishments needs time to be appreciated fully, and yet there's nothing busy about the whole effect. Among the many treasures, a twelfth-century Romanesque *Crucifixion* is the most precious, but also special are the elaborate choir stalls and the three **organs**, considered among the most beautiful instruments in the world. At least one of them can be heard at the recitals held at 4pm every Saturday between February and November.

Apart from the church, there's also the **Museum der Benediktinerabtei** (daily 10am–noon & 2–5pm; DM4/€2), which is housed in a part of the abbot's palace. Highlights are the amazingly delicate seventeenth- and eighteenth-century inlaid furniture pieces and the beautiful Baroque library, which looks more like a ballroom than a place for contemplation, so rich is the decor of marble pillars and frescoed ceiling. Note also the theatre, which was an important element in the teaching of arts in any eighteenth-century Benedictine monastery.

Ottobeuren is not on a rail line, but has a regular **bus** link with Memmingen, a junction on the Munich–Lindau and Ulm–Oberstdorf lines, 11km to the northwest. Should you want to stay, there's a **youth hostel** at Kaltenbrunnweg 11 (☎0 83 32/3 68, fax 0 83 32/72 19; DM17.50/€8.75), along with plenty of **rooms** in private houses (①–③). Other than sanatoria, the only **hotels** in the village proper are *Hirsch*, Marktplatz 12 (☎0 83 32/79 90; ④), and *Am Mühlbach*, Luitpoldstr. 57 (☎0 83 32/9 20 50; ⑥). *Hirsch* also has the village's best **restaurant**, and is the main tap of the local brewery. The **tourist office** is in the Kurverwaltung, Marktplatz 14 (May–Oct Mon–Fri 8am–noon & 2–5pm, Sat 10am–noon; rest of year Mon–Fri only; ☎0 83 32/92 19 50, fax 92 19 92, *www.ottobeuren.de*).

Kaufbeuren

KAUFBEUREN, a former Free Imperial City some 55km southwest of Augsburg by road or rail, is in many ways reminiscent of the better-known and more heavily touristed medieval towns further north. The key difference is that it is larger and more industrialized, largely as a result of the creation of the suburb of **Neugablonz**, the only community set up after World War II by refugees from a single area of Eastern Europe (Gablonz in the Sudetenland) from which Germans had been expelled. An intact **Stadtmauer**, part of whose sentry walk survives, still surrounds the cobblestoned Altstadt. At its highest point, the northwestern corner, are a terrace commanding a bird's-eye view and the impressive fortified church of **St Blasius**, whose round tower has a decidedly military rather than ecclesiastical appearance. Ironically, the interior is a graceful Gothic hall, with an outstanding high altar featuring carvings by Jörg Lederer. The best time to visit the town is on the third Sunday of July when the highpoint of the main local **festival**, the *Tänzelfest*, occurs. This features a costumed procession performed by 1600 children, re-enacting a visit to the town by Emperor Maximilian I in 1497.

Kaufbeuren's **tourist office** is in the Rathaus, Kaiser-Max-Str. 1 (Mon–Fri 9am–6pm, Sat 9.30am–noon; ☎0 83 41/4 04 05, fax 7 39 62, *www.kaufbeuren.de*). If you need a **hotel**, one of the lowest priced is *Gasthof Leitner*, Neugablonzer Str. 68 (☎0 83 41/33 44; ③). In the Altstadt, choice is between *Am Turm*, Josef-Landes-Str. 1 (☎0 83 41/9 37 40; ⑤), and *Goldener Hirsch*, Kaiser-Max-Str. 39 (☎0 83 41/4 30 30; ⑤). Both *Leitner* and *Goldener Hirsch* also have good **restaurants**; otherwise the best place to eat is *Wärmflasch*, Am Hofanger 33.

Füssen

FÜSSEN, the southern terminus of the Romantic Road (see box on p.213), lies in a beautiful setting close to the Austrian border between the **Forggensee** reservoir and the **Ammer** mountains. Although used by most visitors merely as a jumping-off point for the two royal castles situated some 4km to the southeast, it's of far more than passing interest. Dominating the Lech valley from a position high above the Altstadt is the **Hohes Schloss**, which assumed its present late Gothic appearance at the turn of the sixteenth century, when the old fortress was rebuilt as a summer residence of the Augsburg prince-bishops. In an ingenious cost-saving device, the inner courtyard is adorned with illusionistic paintings showing elaborate door and window frames and oriels. Part of the north wing houses a branch of the **Bayerische Staatsgalerie** (April–Oct Tues–Sun 11am–4pm; Nov–March Tues–Sun 2–4pm; DM4/€2). Paintings by fifteenth- and sixteenth-century south German masters and members of the nineteenth-century Munich School are on view, but the chief attraction is the **Rittersaal**, which has a magnificent coffered vault.

Below the Schloss is the former **Kloster St Mang**, named in honour of the eighth-century "Apostle of the Allgäu". The present complex is almost entirely Baroque, but below the church, nowadays designated the **Stadtpfarrkirche**, is a Carolingian crypt containing the grave of the saint. This is only accessible on Sunday mornings, or by occasional guided tours, the times for which are posted in the porch. The monastic buildings house the **Museum der Stadt Füssen** (April–Oct Tues–Sun 11am–4pm; Nov–March Tues–Sun 2–4pm; DM5/€2.50), though the exhibits are overshadowed by the splendid Baroque interiors themselves, including the sumptuous **Festsaal**, which is still regularly used for concerts; the domed colloquium; and the oval refectory, which has an aperture in its ceiling looking up into the library above. Also of special note is the **Annakapelle**, the original monastic church, which was converted to serve as a funerary chapel and has a remarkable early seventeenth-century mural of *The Dance of Death*.

Practicalities

Füssen's dead-end **Bahnhof** is linked directly with Munich and Augsburg, with services departing on alternate hours. From outside, **buses** marked "Königsschlösser" leave at regular intervals for the castles. A couple of minutes' walk to the east, at Kaiser-Maximilian-Platz 1, is the **tourist office** (June–Aug Mon–Fri 8am–noon & 2–6pm, Sat 9.30am–12.30pm, Sun 10am–noon; Oct–May Mon–Fri 8am–noon & 2–6pm, Sat 10am–noon; ☎0 83 62/9 38 50, fax 93 85 20, *www.fuessen.de*).

Ask at the tourist office about **private rooms** (①–③), which can be surprisingly good value, though a stay of three nights may be required. There are plenty of **hotels** in town, including *Elisabeth*, Augustenstr. 10 (☎0 83 62/62 75; ③), *Zum Hechten*, Ritterstr. 6 (☎0 83 62/9 16 00; ④), *Sonne*, Reichenstr. 37 (☎0 83 62/90 80; ⑥), and *Hirsch*, Kaiser-Maximilian-Platz 7 (☎0 83 62/50 80; ⑥). The **youth hostel** is at the western edge of town at Mariahilferstr. 5 (☎0 83 62/77 54, fax 27 70; DM21/€10.50), while there's a **campsite** (☎0 83 62/74 31) by the Hopfensee to the north.

Füssen's best **restaurants** include that in the aforementioned *Zum Hechten* plus *Zum Schwanen*, Brotmarkt 4, and *Pulverturm* in the Kurhaus at the eastern edge of the town centre.

Schwangau

SCHWANGAU, 3km northeast of Füssen, to which it's connected by a frequent bus service, combines the roles of a traditional agricultural community and health resort. Its name literally means "Swan Country", and the presence of a sizeable colony of these aloof birds has cast a spell on rulers of the area down the centuries. As the decoration of their fantasy castles testifies, the nineteenth-century Bavarian kings Maximilian II and his son Ludwig II were obsessed by the swan motif and the medieval Grail legends associated with it.

The only historical monument of note in Schwangau itself is the Baroque **Wallfahrtskirche St Coloman**, which is set in isolation in the meadows north of town. Dedicated to an eleventh-century Irish martyr, it was designed and decorated by Johann Schmutzer. On the second Sunday of October, it's the setting for one of Germany's most picturesque and moving religious festivals, the **Colomansfest**. This features around three hundred horses and some beautifully decorated carriages, which process from the town centre to the surroundings of the church, where an open-air Mass is held. The horses are then ridden round the church three times for good luck, after which beer and food, the essential accompaniments to any Bavarian festival, are dispensed from the nearby tents.

Hohenschwangau

Within the Schwangau muncipality is the village of **HOHENSCHWANGAU**, 2km to the southeast. Consisting in the main of hotels, guesthouses, restaurants, snack bars and souvenir shops, not to mention five enormous car parks, it's the most rampantly commercialized place in the whole of Germany – though it's only fair to add that it's set in close proximity to some of the most spectacular scenery the country has to offer. To escape from the worst of the crowds, it's well worth taking a stroll along the footpaths encircling the two beautiful lakes which lie directly to the east. In summer, you can swim or sail in the larger lake, the **Alpsee**, whereas the **Schwansee** (literally, "Swan Lake") is a strict nature reserve surrounded by an English-style park offering wonderful framed vistas of the two royal castles.

The smaller of these, the golden yellow **Schloss Hohenschwangau** (guided tours daily April–Sept 8.39am–5pm; Nov–March 10am–4pm; DM14/€7, or DM26/€13 combined ticket with Schloss Neuschwanstein), rises directly above the Alpsee; note that there's free access to its lovely terraced garden, which commands wonderful views. Built in mock-Tudor style in the 1830s for Crown Prince Maximilian to replace a ruined feudal fortress, the Schloss still belongs to the Wittelsbach family, and feels like a lived-in private residence, crammed full of gifts from grateful subjects and fellow rulers. Several rooms are decorated with heroic **fresco cycles** illustrating German history and legends (including that of Lohengrin, the Swan Knight) painted from cartoons by Moritz von Schwind. In the **Hohenstaufensaal** is a square piano where Wagner would entertain **King Ludwig II** with themes from operas in progress. The latter's main contribution to the castle was to have the **ceiling** of his bedroom changed from a daytime to a night sky which could be illuminated by concealed spotlights.

Ludwig's own personal fantasy, the grey granite **Schloss Neuschwanstein** (guided tours: April–Sept Mon–Wed & Fri 9am–6pm, Thurs 9am–8pm; Oct–March daily 10am–4pm; DM14/€7), is a steep twenty-minute walk from the village. The ultimate storybook castle and Germany's most ubiquitous tourist icon, Neuschwanstein has become famous the world over through posters, cards and Disney films, not to mention the innumerable theme-park castles directly inspired by it. Begun in 1869 but never finished, it was intended as a tribute to medieval German chivalry and to Wagner, who had evoked this past so intoxicatingly in his vast music dramas, and as a symbol of Ludwig's belief in himself as a divinely chosen king. Plans were drawn by the theatre designer

Christian Jank, working in close collaboration with the king; professional architects were used only for supervising the actual construction. It undoubtedly looks far better from a distance than close up or inside. The architecture and decoration draw freely from different historical styles: Byzantine for the **Thronsaal**, Romanesque for the private apartments, Gothic for the showpiece **Sängersaal**.

A path behind Neuschwanstein leads to the **Marienbrücke**, a steel bridge that is a major feat of nineteenth-century engineering; it traverses the Poellat gorge, with its rushing waterfall. Continuing uphill by the steep marked footpath for about an hour, you reach the most celebrated vantage point over Neuschwanstein, in which the castle appears head-on from above, framed by the Alpsee, the Schwansee, the Ammergebirge and the Tyrolean Alps. The trail continues onwards to the top of the **Tegelberg** (1720m), a hike which normally takes a further two hours. This commands panoramas stretching as far as Munich on a clear day, and can also be reached by **cable car** (DM18/€9 single, DM25/€12.50 return) from Schwangau.

Practicalities

Schwangau's **tourist office** is in the Kurverwaltung, Münchener Str. 2 (Mon–Fri 7.30am–12.30pm & 1.30–5pm; ☎0 83 62/8 19 80, fax 81 98 25, *www.schwangau.de*). There's a reasonable supply of **private rooms** (①–②), as well as a few similarly inexpensive **pensions**, the most attractive being *Schlossblick*, Füssener Str. 48 (☎0 83 62/83 55; ②), with a view across to the castles. Among the **hotels** are *Gasthof Hanselewirt*, Mitteldorf 13 (☎0 83 62/82 37; ③), *Weinbauer*, Füssener Str. 3 (☎0 83 62/98 60; ④), and *Gasthof Zur Post*, Münchener Str. 5 (☎0 83 62/9 82 18; ⑤), all of which have good, reasonably priced **restaurants**.

If you'd prefer to be based in Hohenschwangau, there are several **pensions**, including *Haus Magdalena*, Schwangauer Str. 11 (☎0 83 62/8 11 26; ②), and *Weiher*, Hofwiesenweg 11 (☎0 83 62/8 11 61; ③). Alternatively, you can stay in style at one of the classy **hotels**, such as *Meier*, Schwangauer Str. 37 (☎0 83 62/8 11 52; ⑤), *Schlosshotel Lisl und Jägerhaus*, Neuschwansteinstr. 1–3 (☎0 83 62/88 70; ⑦), or *Müller*, Alpseestr. 16 (☎0 83 62/8 19 90; ⑧). Each of these has a top-notch **restaurant**; more basic fare is available at the *Schlosswirtschaft* just below Neuschwanstein. The only ready way of seeing any of Schloss Neuschwanstein at leisure is to attend one of the **concerts** in the *Sängersaal*; these are held over a week in mid- to late September, and tickets can be ordered in advance from the tourist office. In 2000, the Musical Theater Neuschwanstein (☎0 18 05/58 39 44) was inaugurated with a **musical** about the life of Ludwig II.

Oberstdorf

Imagine your ideal mountain resort and **OBERSTDORF** will almost certainly fit the picture. Tucked away about 50km southwest of Kaufbeuren by road or rail, amid magnificent Alpine mountains and valleys, the old village has grown discreetly, without any high-rise aberrations, but with excellent modern sports facilities, including swimming pools, a skating rink and an Olympic ski-jump. These co-exist with traditional farming life: there are open fields right on the outskirts of town.

The higher mountain valleys beyond Oberstdorf take you to lonely Alpine huts and the sort of views that give a surge of energy. Serious mountaineers will find the **Nebelhorn** (2224m) to the east of town the most challenging, while for less strenuous Alpine walking the **Fellhorn** (2039m) and **Söllereck** (1706m) to the south make good alternatives – the latter is especially gentle. All three peaks are also accessible by cable car (various rates, the maximum being DM40/€20 return to the Nebelhorn summit), and in winter form the heart of an excellent skiing range. Another worthwhile excursion is to the gorges of the **Breitachklamm**, some 6km southwest of Oberstdorf; these are best seen in late winter, when draped with ice.

A bit further south, the valley known as **Kleinwalsertal** is a real novelty. Once one of the most isolated corners of the Alps, it was settled by a hardy people known as the Walsers who gave their allegiance to the House of Habsburg. Today, it remains officially part of Austria, but it is only accessible by the road from Oberstdorf, which is served by regular buses.

Practicalities
Oberstdorf's **Bahnhof**, the southernmost train station in Germany, is at the northwestern edge of the town centre. It's the terminus of a branch line with regular services to Munich, Ulm and the Bodensee. If you need help with finding somewhere to stay, contact the **tourist office** (Mon–Fri 8.30am–noon & 2–6pm, Sat 9.30am–noon; ☎0 83 22/70 00, fax 70 02 36, *www.oberstdorf.de*), Marktplatz 7, or its Zimmervermittlung branch across from the Bahnhof (same times; ☎0 83 22/70 02 17).

There are any number of reasonably priced **private rooms** (①–③) and **guesthouses** near the town centre, so you shouldn't have too much difficulty finding something yourself. The latter include *Amman*, Weststr. 23 (☎0 83 22/29 61; ③), *Alpenglühn*, Wittelsbacherstr. 4 (☎0 83 22/46 92; ③), and *Buchenberg*, Lorettostr. 6 (☎0 83 22/23 15; ③). Among many excellent **hotels**, *Kurpark*, Prinzenstr. 1 (☎0 83 22/9 65 60; ⑥), has a fine setting, while *Haus Wiese*, Stillachstr. 4a (☎0 83 22/30 30; ⑥), and *Waldesruhe*, Alte Walserstr. 20 (☎0 83 22/40 61; ⑥), both offer outstanding views. At Haus no. 8 in the neighbouring village of Kornau, which can be reached by buses bound for Kleinwalsertal, you'll find the nearest **youth hostel** (☎0 83 22/22 25, fax 8 04 46; DM23/€11.50), while the all-year-round **campsite** (☎0 83 22/40 22) is just north of the Bahnhof.

The best and most expensive **restaurant** is *Maximilians*, Freibergstr. 21; *Bacchus-Stuben*, Freibergstr. 4, is a far more moderately priced alternative.

Lindau

At their most westerly point the Bavarian Alps descend to the waters of the **Bodensee** and the tiny island town of **LINDAU**, which is nowadays linked to the mainland by a road bridge and rail causeway. It's the starting point of the **German Alpine Road**, (Deutsche Alpenstrasse), a tourist route that runs the length of the German Alps, terminating 250km away in Berchtesgaden. In the Middle Ages, Lindau was a bustling trading post and city-state, and rich merchants built grand gabled houses on town squares that have a distinct Italian flavour. The half-timbered buildings lean over like stacks of dominoes, and narrow streets like Zitronengasse lead to quiet nooks and crannies.

At the southern end of the island is the **Hafen** (harbour), which, with its hazy views across the lake to the Alps, is the most popular spot in town. Its narrow entrance is guarded by two tall pillars, one a lighthouse, the other bearing the defiant Lion of Bavaria. The previous lighthouse, the **Mangturm** (variable opening hours; DM2/€1), stands in the middle of the sheltered port and was originally part of the medieval fortifications. Around it stand large hotels from an age when nineteenth-century travellers resided here in splendour. As soon as the summer sun comes out, the harbour promenade fills with coffee tables, giving a Mediterranean feel to the bustling waterfront. Several **ferries** operate on the lake (for full information, see box on p.302). All sorts of boats, canoes and windsurfers can be rented from the yacht marina east of the harbour.

On Reichsplatz, in the centre of the island, stands the Gothic **Altes Rathaus**; unfortunately the elaborate murals make it seem overdressed in comparison with the buildings around it. From here, you can walk west along the Maximilianstrasse, before turning north to see the **Diebsturm** (Brigands' Tower), the other surviving part of the fortifications. Alongside, Romanesque **St Peter**, now a war memorial, is the sole church in Lindau still in its medieval state. Hans Holbein the Elder's faded Passion cycle in the apse is his only surviving fresco.

The most stylish building in Lindau is the **Haus zum Cavazzen** (April–Oct Tues–Sun 10am–noon & 2–5pm; DM5/€2.50) on Marktplatz towards the eastern end of the island, whose three-storey Baroque facade is painted in subtle sandy-red tones, and which contains one of the most attractive local history museums of any town in Bavaria. There's an intriguing collection of seventeenth-century family trees painted on wooden panels that open up like a photo-album, to reveal little portraits and dates for each member, plus paintings of the same period, known as *Spottbilder*, mocking Luther. On the second and third floors are fine displays of furniture, ranging from items from the workshops of Lindau's former artisan guilds to beautifully inlaid Biedermeier furniture.

Should you only have time for one trip outside the island, take bus #7 to the suburb of Hoyren and walk up the **Hoyrenberg** for a stunning view of the lake and the Austrian and Swiss Alps. The villages and apple orchards around here seem very quiet after Lindau: Oberreitnau, Unterreitnau and Bodolz are especially pretty.

Practicalities

The **Hauptbahnhof** is at the southwestern corner of the island, right beside the harbour. Just across from the entrance, at Am Hauptbahnhof, is the **tourist office** (May–Sept Mon–Fri 9am–1pm & 2–6/7pm, Sat 9am–1pm; Oct–March Mon–Fri 9am–noon & 1–5pm; ☎0 83 82/26 00 30, fax 26 00 26, *www.lindau.de*).

Among the **guesthouses** and **pensions** on the island are *Lädine*, In der Grub 25 (☎0 83 82/53 26; ②), *Limmer*, In der Grub 16 (☎0 83 82/58 77; ②), and *Seerose*, Auf der Mauer 3 (☎0 83 82/2 41 20; ④). The many medium-range **hotels** include *Inselgraben*, Hintere Metzgergasse 4–6 (☎0 83 82/54 81; ④–⑤), *Alte Post*, Fischergasse 3 (☎0 83 82/9 34 60; ⑥), and *Insel-Hotel*, Maximilianstr. 42 (☎0 83 82/50 17; ⑥). Along Seepromenade are the four swankiest hotels, the most exclusive being *Bayerischer Hof* (☎0 83 82/91 50, *www.bayerischerhof-lindau.de*; ⑧–⑨). There are plenty of **rooms** in private houses (①–②), but most are on the mainland. The **youth hostel** is at Herbergsweg 11 (☎0 83 82/9 67 10, fax 9 67 50; DM29/€14.50) on mainland Lindau; take bus #1, #3 or #6 from the Hauptbahnhof. By the Austrian border at Fraunhoferstr. 20 (☎0 83 82/7 22 36) is the **campsite**, *Park-Camping Lindau am See*.

Inevitably, the leading **restaurants** are in the waterfront hotels, but there are plenty of excellent and far less expensive alternatives: *Zum Sünfzen*, Maximilianstr. 1, and the restaurant in *Alte Post* are both eminently recommendable. Even cheaper restaurants, plus a few bars, can be found in the suitably named In der Grub, a block north of Maximilianstrasse.

travel details

Trains

Munich to: Augsburg (every 20min; 30min); Cologne (hourly; 5hr 20min); Frankfurt (frequent; 4hr); Garmisch-Partenkirchen (hourly; 1hr 15min); Hamburg (hourly; 8hr); Ingolstadt (frequent; 45min); Innsbruck (hourly; 2hr 25min); Nürnberg (hourly; 1hr); Regensburg (hourly; 2hr); Salzburg (hourly; 2hr 30min); Strasbourg (6 daily; 5hr); Stuttgart (hourly; 2hr 15min); Ulm (hourly; 2hr 15min); Würzburg (hourly; 2hr 20min); Zürich (5 daily; 4hr 20min).

Nürnberg to: Ansbach (every 30min; 45min); Augsburg (hourly; 1hr); Bamberg (every 30min; 45min); Bayreuth (every 30min; 1hr 10min); Coburg (hourly; 1hr 35min); Frankfurt (hourly; 2hr); Passau (hourly; 2hr 20min).

Würzburg to: Cologne (hourly; 3hr 40min); Frankfurt (hourly; 1hr 20min); Stuttgart (hourly; 2hr).

CHAPTER TWO

BADEN-WÜRTTEMBERG

B aden-Württemberg only came into existence in 1952 as a result of the merger, approved by plebiscite, of three relatively small provinces established by the American and French occupying forces. Theodor Heuss, the first Federal president, saw it as "the model of German possibilities", and it hasn't disappointed, maintaining its ranking as the most prosperous part of the country. Being weak in natural resources, the area has had to rely on ingenuity to provide a spur to its industrial development, and ever since the motorcar was invented here in the late nineteenth century, it has been at the forefront of the world technology scene.

Ethnically, culturally and historically, the Land has two separate roots. **Baden**, the western part of the province, has been predominantly Catholic since the incorporation of the Breisgau region in the early nineteenth century, and its people are generally seen as being of a relaxed, almost carefree disposition. Their neighbours in **Württemberg** (or **Swabia**, as the locals still prefer to call it), on the other hand, are renowned for being hard-working, thrifty and house-proud, values instilled in them since the Reformation they embraced so openly. This stark division, however, has been much modified by the extensive influx of refugees from the Eastern Territories after World War II: along with their descendants, they now account for about a quarter of the total population.

For variety of scenery, Baden-Württemberg is rivalled only by Bavaria. The western and southern boundaries of the province are defined by the River Rhine and its bulge into Germany's largest lake, the **Bodensee**. Immediately beyond lies the **Black Forest**, one of Europe's main holiday areas. Here rises another of the continent's principal waterways, the **Danube**, which later forms a grandly impressive gorge at the foot of the **Swabian Jura**, the range in which the Neckar begins its increasingly sedate northerly course. At the eastern end of the province there's an even gentler valley, that of the **Tauber**.

Each of Baden-Württemberg's three largest cities – **Stuttgart**, **Mannheim** and **Karlsruhe** – was formerly a state capital (of Württemberg, the Palatinate and Baden respectively). All were extensively damaged in World War II and none could be called beautiful, though all have excellent museums and Stuttgart offers a wide variety of

---

ACCOMMODATION PRICE CODES

All the pensions and hotels in this book have been graded according to the following price categories. The codes quoted are for the cheapest available double room, except for establishments which have rooms costing widely different rates, when the most expensive price is given as well. Exact charges are given for youth hostels; in the case of the official DJH (HI) establishments, this is the lowest available rate. When two figures are quoted for these hostels, the first applies to juniors (ie under 27 years of age), the second to seniors (27 and above).

① less than DM60/€30   ④ DM100–124/€50–62   ⑦ DM200–249/€100–124
② DM60–79/€30–39   ⑤ DM125–149/€63–74   ⑧ DM250–299/€125–149
③ DM80–99/€40–49   ⑥ DM150–199/€75–99   ⑨ upwards of DM300/€150

nightlife. Unfortunately, the historic centres of **Freiburg im Breisgau** and **Ulm** were also bombed, but both their Münsters, which rank among Germany's greatest buildings, were spared. Other than this, Baden-Württemberg's lack of a heavy industrial base meant that it escaped the war relatively lightly. Germany's two most famous university cities, **Heidelberg** and **Tübingen**, were hardly touched, enabling the former to maintain its cherished role as the most romantic place in the entire country.

Almost equally enticing is the wealth of towns which stand as period-pieces of different epochs. **Bad Wimpfen** and **Schwäbisch Hall** each preserve the form and appearance of the Middle Ages, whereas **Rottweil** has medieval survivals amid streets which bridge the gap between Renaissance and Baroque, and **Haigerloch** is a varied confection enhanced by a superb natural setting. **Bruchsal**, **Ludwigsburg** and **Rastatt** are proud courtly towns in the full-blown Baroque manner, while **Schwetzingen** is a creation of pure Rococo fantasy and **Baden-Baden** remains wonderfully evocative of its nineteenth-century halcyon years as the favourite playground of European aristocracy. Another special historical feature of the province is the number of monasteries which have survived intact, among which **Maulbronn** ranks as the most complete and impressive in northern Europe.

A typically comprehensive **public transport** network means there's never any problem moving around, though waiting periods in rural areas not served by trains may be longer than is normal in Germany. Travelling is rendered particularly enjoyable by the profusion of scenic routes, of which the Schwarzwalder-Hochstrasse and the rail lines known as the Schwarzwaldbahn, the Höllentalbahn and the Donautalbahn are the most outstanding. There's the usual provision of **accommodation** in youth hostels and campsites, while the availability of lodgings in private houses is well above the national average. Only in the larger cities are you likely to encounter high prices.

SWABIA

Save for the small part of the province that Napoleon allocated to Bavaria, **Swabia** (Schwaben) has long ceased to exist as any form of political entity, yet such is the emotional attachment to the name that it stubbornly refuses to vanish from the map, far less from local consciousness. The rugged plateaux cutting right through the middle of the province continue to be known as the **Swabian Jura**, and two of many former Free Imperial Cities, **Schwäbisch Gmünd** and **Schwäbisch Hall**, have adopted their present forenames in order to show where their loyalties lie. Certainly, the name is far more popular than that of Württemberg, which is taken from the aristocratic family which established dominance over most of rural Swabia in the Middle Ages from their capital of **Stuttgart**. It remains something of a sore point that the Land of Baden-Württemberg was not designated as Swabia, on the grounds that to do so would have offended the people of Baden, which formed part of the province in the early medieval period, but later developed its own distinctive characteristics.

At the Reformation, the extreme wing of Protestantism – here known as **Pietism** – took firm root, bringing with it a commitment to the work ethic and a burning sense of individualism, tempered only by communal loyalties. There's no doubt that the intellectual rigour fostered in the province has led to its nurturing a gallery of inventors, philosophers and poets out of all proportion to its size.

If you despair of mastering the horrendous complexities of the German language, it's worth bearing in mind that the ingenious Swabians have developed a partial solution to the problem, put to everyday use in their own **dialect**. By adding -le to most nouns (which immediately become neuter), they don't have to worry about genders, while they omit the cumbersome ge- prefix from past participles and regularize the conjugation of verbs. The local **cuisine** is no less distinctive, with noodles as ubiquitous as in

Italian or Chinese cooking. Nearly every savoury dish comes with either *Spätzle*, a shredded pasta made from eggs and flour, or Maultaschen, which, with the exception of the sauces used to cover it, is broadly similar to ravioli. Equally popular are *Flädle* (pancakes) which turn up in both soups and desserts.

Stuttgart

STUTTGART breathes modern-day success. Düsseldorf and Hamburg may have more millionaires, but Baden-Württemberg's capital has the highest general standard of prosperity of any city in Germany, or, indeed, in Europe. Beaming out imperiously from its lofty station above the city centre is the local trademark, the three-pointed white star of Daimler-Benz – or Daimler-Chrysler as the corporation is now known, following its recent transatlantic tie-up. As Stuttgart is also home to Porsche and the almost equally celebrated electronics giant Robert Bosch, it has a secure place at the forefront of the global hi-tech industrial scene.

For all Stuttgart's present self-confidence, it was initially slow to develop. Founded around 950 as a stud farm (*Stutengarten* – hence the city's name), it only became a town in the fourteenth century, and lay in the shadow of its more venerable neighbours right up to the early nineteenth century, when Napoleon raised Württemberg to the status of a kingdom and placed the former Free Imperial Cities under its control. Though Stuttgart's standing as a royal capital was to last for only a century, the city has never looked back.

From the point of view of conventional sights, Stuttgart has relatively little to offer. On the other hand, it has a range of superb **museums** to appeal to all tastes, and a varied cultural and nightlife scene. It also has an enviable **setting** in a hollow surrounded by hills, which enables the cultivation of vineyards within a stone's throw of the centre, and the liberal endowment of parks and gardens successfully softens what would otherwise be a drab and unappealing cityscape.

Arrival and information

The **Hauptbahnhof** – an impressive example of railway architecture, built during the Weimar Republic – is plumb in the centre of the city. Immediately behind is the **bus station**. S-Bahn #2 and #3 offer a regular twenty-minute service between 5am and midnight between the Hauptbahnhof's underground terminal and the **airport** in the far south of the city. Across the road from the Hauptbahnhof at Königstr. 1a is the **tourist office**, i-Punkt (Mon–Fri 9.30am–8.30pm, Sat 9.30am–6pm, Sun 10.30am–6pm; ☎07 11/2 22 80 or 2 22 82 33, fax 2 22 82 33, *www.stuttgart-tourist.de*). The integrated **public transport** network, which covers nearby towns as well as the Stuttgart metropolitan area, enables you to switch among buses, trams, U-Bahns, mainline and S-Bahn trains and a rack railway. Note that all trams and U-Bahns travel both above and below ground; the former are older vehicles, and stop at the lower sections of underground station platforms, whereas their newer counterparts, whose numbers are prefaced by the letter U, halt at the upper parts. Given that the sights are very scattered, it may be worth investing in a DM21/€10.50 **day-ticket**; the exact conditions are prone to change but currently cover up to five people travelling together. However, for most visitors the drolly titled **StuttCard**, available from the tourist office and some hotels, is even better value. Costing DM25/€12.50 for three days, it covers all public transport in the city, admission to most museums and a range of reductions and numerous freebies, including drinks and food. There's a DM15/€7.50 variant called **StuttCard Light** giving the same benefits with the exception of public transport.

Accommodation

To some extent, the astronomical cost of rented accommodation in Stuttgart is reflected in **hotel** rates. However, there are bargains to be had, often with a decent location. The tourist office will always book you a room, and there's no charge for this service.

Hotels and pensions

Alte Mira, Büchsenstr. 24 (☎07 11/29 51 32, fax 2 10 91 55). This Croat-run Gasthof offers some of the best-value rooms in the city centre, as well as a decent restaurant. ③–⑤.

Alter Fritz am Killesberg, Feuerbacher Weg 101 (☎07 11/13 56 50, fax 1 35 65 65). Located in the north of the city, this is one of Stuttgart's more characterful upmarket hotels; there's also an innovative restaurant. Take U-Bahn #6 to Killesberg, then bus #43 or #50. ⑥.

Am Schlossgarten, Schillerstr. 23 (☎07 11/2 02 60, fax 2 02 68 88, *schlossgarten@t-online.de*). The pick of the luxury city-centre hotels, located just across from the Hauptbahnhof, with a terrace facing Oberer Schlossgarten. It has two restaurants, one of which, *Zirbelstube* (closed Sun & Mon), has gourmet status. ⑨.

Der Zauberlehrling, Rosenstr. 38 (☎07 11/2 37 77 70). Wonderful traditional Gasthof with a particularly well-regarded restaurant (closed Sat evening & Sun). Renovations are currently being carried out, so room prices are likely to rise. ③–⑤.

Eckel, Vorsteigstr. 10 (☎07 11/29 09 95, fax 2 23 81 23). Small pension just west of the centre.Take bus #40 to Hölderlinplatz. ③.

Ketterer, Marienstr. 3 (☎07 11/2 03 90, fax 2 03 96 00). City-centre business hotel in a relatively quiet street; has a very reasonably priced restaurant in the form of a traditional beer hall. ⑦–⑨.

Krehl's Linde, Obere Waiblinger Str. 113, Bad Cannstatt (☎07 11/52 75 67, fax 54 83 70). Located just to the southeast of the Kurpark, this hotel, which has been run by the same family since 1875, boasts a really outstanding restaurant (closed Sun & Mon). ⑥.

Kronen, Kronenstr. 48 (☎07 11/2 25 10, fax 2 25 14 04). High-class city-centre hotel, some of whose rooms have balconies. It serves a marvellous breakfast buffet, but no other meals. ⑧–⑨.

Lamm, Karl-Schurz-Str. 7 (☎07 11/2 62 23 54, fax 2 62 23 74). This hotel is handily located for the complex of parks and swimming pools to the east of the city centre. Take U-Bahn #1, #2 or #14 to Mineralbäder. ④.

Museum-Stube, Hospitalstr. 9. This Yugoslav-run Gasthof has decent, quiet rooms which are marginally cheaper than those of *Alte Mira*, which is just a few doors away. Also serves inexpensive meals. ③–⑤.

Schaich, Paulinenstr. 16 (☎07 11/60 26 79, fax 60 83 25). Pension in a tenement building just south of the centre. ④.

Solitude, Hohewartstr. 10, Feuerbach (☎07 11/85 49 19). Gasthof in a northern suburb. One of the cheapest places to stay in the city, especially for single travellers; unusually, single rooms are exactly half the price of doubles. Take U-Bahn #6 to Wilhelm-Geiger-Platz. ③.

Waldhotel Schatten, Magstadter Strasse, Büsnau (☎07 11/6 86 70, fax 6 86 79 99). Upmarket hotel in peaceful woodland setting within easy reach of the city centre. Also has a fine restaurant. Take S-Bahn #1, #2 or #3 to Vaihingen, then bus #92 to Schattengrund. ⑧–⑨.

Wörtz zur Weinsteige, Hohenheimer Str. 30 (☎07 11/2 36 70 00, fax 2 36 70 07, *www.Hotel -Woertz.de*). Popular hotel at the southeastern end of the city centre. Take U-Bahn #5, #6 or #7 to Dobelstrasse. It has a garden terrace and a prestigious wine restaurant (closed Sun & Mon). ⑥–⑧.

Youth hostels and campsites

Cannstatter Wasen, Mercedesstr. 40 (☎07 11/55 66 96, fax 55 74 54). The campsite is on the banks of the River Neckar in Bad Cannstatt.

IYHF Jugendherberge, Haussmannstr. 27 (☎07 11/24 15 83, fax 2 36 10 41). Stuttgart's official youth hostel is just fifteen minute walk east of the Hauptbahnhof. DM24/€12 or DM29/€14.50.

Jugendgästehaus Stuttgart, Richard-Wagner-Str. 2–4a (☎07 11/24 11 32, fax 23 66 11 10). Like *Tramper Point*, this place is intended for travellers aged between 16 and 27. Beds in dorms cost DM35/€17.50; there are also singles at DM55/€27.50. Take tram #15 to Budenbad.

Tramper Point, Wiener Str. 317 (☎07 11/8 17 74 76 or 2 37 28 15, fax 2 37 28 10). At DM13/€6.50 for a mattress and breakfast, this offers rock-bottom accommodation for young people between 16 and 27 only. To get there, take U-Bahn #6 to Sportpark Feuerbach. Closed early Sept to late June.

The City

One consequence of having been a late developer is that Stuttgart has one of the most manageable centres of any large German city. The exact opposite is true of the suburbs, where many of the leading attractions are scattered, though everything is readily accessible by the excellent integrated municipal transport network.

Schlossplatz

Königstrasse leads straight from the Hauptbahnhof past the modern Dom (a strong contender for the title of the dullest cathedral in Europe) to **Schlossplatz**. The vast open space here comes as a welcome relief after the hectic bustle of the neighbouring streets, but it does mean that it's the favourite spot of the tramps and alcoholics who form a noticeable sub-class amid the prosperity. On the eastern side of the square is the colossal Baroque **Neues Schloss**, now used for various state purposes by the government of Baden-Württemberg, and out of bounds to visitors except for the cellars which contain the **Römisches Lapidarium** (Sun 10am–5pm; free), a collection of stone fragments from Roman times. Particularly impressive are the surviving parts of a massive Jupitersäule erected around 200 AD in a settlement near Heilbronn. Opposite is the **Königsbau**, lined with shops all along its 135-metre facade and built in the late Neoclassical style much favoured in the city. Another example of this is the **Jubilaeumssäule**, erected in the centre of Schlossplatz to commemorate the twenty-fifth anniversary of the accession of King Wilhelm I of Württemberg.

On the north side of the square lies the Kunstgebäude, containing the **Galerie der Stadt Stuttgart** (Tues & Thurs–Sun 11am–6pm, Wed 11am–8pm; *www.swo/GalerieStuttgart*; free), though this is due to move to a new location in the near future. It owns some seminal works by **Otto Dix**, notably the luridly coloured *Metropolis* triptych, which perfectly conjures up the Weimar Republic's false sense of values and its smoky, decadent nightclub scene. The three leading Stuttgart painters of the twentieth century – Adolf Hölzel, Oskar Schlemmer and Willi Baumeister – are also well represented in the gallery's holdings.

The Altes Schloss

At the southern end of Schlossplatz is the **Altes Schloss**. A fortress was first built on this site in the tenth century to protect the stud farm; of the fourteenth-century moated castle which succeeded it one wing survives. In the 1550s, the rest of the building was replaced by a resplendent Renaissance palace with a majestic triple-tiered courtyard, designed by Aberlin Tretsch. This forms the perfect setting for nominally priced concerts of classical music put on there throughout the summer. The **Schlosskapelle** (Mon–Thurs 9am–12.30pm & 3–6pm, Sat 9–11.30am; free) disputes with its counterpart in Torgau the right to be regarded as the earliest-ever example of Protestant religious architecture, and its interior was specially designed in accordance with the tenets of the new faith, with an emphasis on preaching rather than the sacraments. It's a simple rectangular hall with galleries on three sides, and the elevated pulpit is given the same prominence as the altar.

Much of the Schloss, which was badly damaged in the war, is given over to the **Württemburgisches Landesmuseum** (Tues 10am–1pm, Wed–Sun 10am–5pm; *www.landesmuseum-stuttgart.de*; DM5/€2.50). It's one of the most richly varied museums in the country, and a particular highlight is the **Kunstkammer** of the House of Württemberg, displayed in one of the corner towers. The first floor has small bronze sculptures of predominantly Italian origin, while the second is laid out in the manner of a Renaissance curio cabinet, with the star exhibit being a beautiful set of Gothic playing cards. On the top storey are the nineteenth-century crown jewels, including a necklace with the 22-carat Harlequin diamond, and a Russian-made gold service.

Elsewhere, much of the display space is given over to **archeology**, with many locally excavated finds. A tiny head of a lion carved from the ivory of a mammoth is some 30,000 years old, and thus one of the oldest sculptures in existence. One room is devoted to the truly spectacular contents of the grave of the Celtic prince of Hochdorf, which include the surviving parts of a chariot, a harness for two horses, a bronze vessel, nine large bronze plates, a gilded drinking horn and various pieces of jewellery. Also of special note are the highly distinctive wooden objects discovered in an Alemannian cemetery.

There's also a large and important collection of Swabian devotional **wood sculptures**, arranged thematically rather than chronologically, thus offering inviting comparisons. Many of these are in a folk idiom, though others, such as the graceful Talheim Altar by an anonymous Ulm master and the Passion cycle for the original Münster in Zwiefalten by Jörg Syrlin the Younger, reveal a profound sense of pathos. The top floor is devoted to **decorative arts** and and **scientific instruments**. Of particular note are a stunning third-century cameo of Jupiter known as the Stuttgarter Stein (Stuttgart Stone); a wonderful array of clocks, including a sixteenth-century bear and ostrich automation timepiece from Augsburg; Philipp Matthäus Hahn's Weltmachine (World Machine) of the 1760s; and the so-called Württemberg sewing box of Czarina Feodorowna.

Schillerplatz and the Stiftskirche

To the west, the Altes Schloss overlooks **Schillerplatz**, Stuttgart's sole example of an old-world square. A pensive statue of Schiller himself by Bertel Thorwaldsen presides in the middle. Also here are three more Renaissance buildings – the **Prinzenbau**, the **Alte Kanzlei** (Old Chancellery) and the gabled **Fruchtkasten** (Granary; same hours and ticket as Landesmuseum). Behind its facade, the last-named preserves its original fourteenth-century core; this has now been converted to house the Landesmuseum's collection of historical musical instruments.

At the back of Schillerplatz is the **Stiftskirche**. Its present form is due to the prolific late fifteenth-century Stuttgart architect Aberlin Jerg, whose special skill, shown here to good effect, lay in welding old and new parts of buildings into a coherent whole. The western tower, an octagon on a square base, is Jerg's own work; unfortunately, the planned openwork steeple was never built. Inside the church, the choir is lined with one of the most important pieces of German Renaissance sculpture, an **ancestral gallery** of the counts and dukes of Württemberg. Each of the eleven swarthy figures is brilliantly characterized – a considerable feat of imagination on the part of the sculptor, Sem Schlör. Look out also for the gilded late Gothic pulpit, and the relief of *Christ Sheltering Humanity*.

The eastern boundary

A large modern boulevard, Konrad-Adenauer-Strasse, forms the eastern boundary of the city centre. At the southern end is the **Leonhardskirche**, another church re-worked by Aberlin Jerg. Its chancel houses the funerary monument to the celebrated Renaissance humanist and Hebrew scholar, Johannes Reuchlin. Just to the northeast lies the **Bohnenviertel** (Bean Quarter), whose name derives from the vegetable gardens kept by the artisans who formerly lived there. Nowadays, it is home to many of the city's famous Weinstuben (see p.256). Further north is the Neoclassical **Wilhelmspalais**, which was used by the last kings of Württemberg as their main residence and is now the main municipal archive and library.

Across the road, at the back of the Neues Schloss, lies the **Akadamiegarten**. This forms a southerly extension of the **Schlossgarten**, which stretches for 4km all the way to the banks of the Neckar. On the right is the straggling complex of the **Staatstheater** (see p.258) and, further on, close to the Hauptbahnhof, you'll find the **Carl-Zeiss-Planetarium** (sessions Tues & Thurs 10am & 3pm, Wed & Fri 10am, 3pm & 8pm, Sat & Sun 2pm, 4pm & 6pm; DM9/€4.50), whose projection equipment, made by Carl Zeiss, the famous Stuttgart optics company, ranks among the most modern in Europe.

The Staatsgalerie

Facing the Staatstheater from the other side of Konrad-Adenauer-Strasse is the **Staatsgalerie** (Tues, Wed & Fri–Sun 10am–6pm, Thurs 10am–9pm, first Sat in month 10am–midnight; *www.staatsgalerie.de*; DM9/€4.50). It's not often that an art gallery ranks as one of the most imposing buildings in a major city, but this is an exception. James Stirling, the most highly regarded British architect of his day, was commissioned to build an extension to the solid Neoclassical home of the city's magnificent collection of paintings, which was no longer big enough to accommodate the ever-growing acquisition of modern works. The result, completed in 1984, is an original masterpiece.

The displays begin upstairs in the old building. Of the medieval works, the earliest and most important is a **Bohemian School** altarpiece made in 1385 for a chapel on the outskirts of Stuttgart. You'll either see the inner part, in which Good King Wenceslas is flanked by St Vitus and Emperor Sigismund, or else the biblical scenes on the wings; the position is changed every fortnight. Among many examples of the fifteenth-century Swabian School, those by the Ulm painters **Bartolomäus Zeitblom** and the **Master of the Sterzing Altar** stand out, particularly the latter's courtly *Journey of the Magi*. The most startling work in the gallery is the huge, violently expressive *Herrenberg Altar* by **Jerg Ratgeb**, a man who knew all about violence himself in his other calling as a radical political leader. His reputation rests almost entirely on this single work, which cleverly compresses the Passion scenes into four panels and has an unusual reverse side, showing the apostles going out to preach the Word to all the corners of the earth.

The Italian section begins with two wonderfully stylized panels of *The Apocalypse* by a mid-fourteenth-century **Neapolitan** master, and continues with some excellent examples of the Venetian Renaissance, including works by Bellini, Carpaccio and Tintoretto. However, the gems of the display are several sketches by **Tiepolo**, notably a superbly compressed study for the central section of the great staircase fresco in Würzburg's Residenz. **Memling's** sensual *Bathsheba at her Toilet* kicks off the Low Countries section. The rare Mannerist **Joachim Wtewael** is represented by an animated cycle of portraits of *The Four Evangelists* and by an enamel-like *Adoration of the Shepherds*. There are two masterpieces by **Michael Sweerts**, another long-forgotten artist who has recently come to the fore: the pendants *Taste* and *Sight*, each characterized by an allegorical figure of a child. **Rembrandt** also treated the theme of sight in the tender *Tobit Healing his Father's Blindness*. It forms a sort of unofficial counterpart to the horrific *Blinding of Samson* in Frankfurt, which was painted the same year. One of his earliest works, *St Paul in Prison*, is also on show, along with important examples of Hals, Rubens and Ter Brugghen.

The biggest surprise of the gallery is a whole room devoted to **Edward Burne-Jones's** cycle of *The Legend of Perseus*. Commissioned by Arthur Balfour, the future British prime minister, this constitutes one of the finest achievements of the Pre-Raphaelite movement. Three of the eight scenes were never completed, but the full-scale cartoons shown here make ample substitutes. Other nineteenth-century highpoints are *Bohemian Landscape* and *The Cross in the Woods* by **Friedrich**, an impressive group of works by a local Neoclassical sculptor, **Johann Heinrich Dannecker**, and a decent cross-section of French Impressionism.

The modern extension features the seven vibrant figures made by **Oskar Schlemmer** for the kaleidoscopic *Triadschen Ballett* in 1922. Displayed high up on pedestals, they're arguably his most original creations. There are also monumental bronzes by **Matisse**, while examples of many of the century's leading sculptors can be found in the sculpture court downstairs or scattered throughout the galleries. A wooden group entitled *The Bathers* constitutes one of the main items in what's one of the two best **Picasso** collections in Germany. **Modigliani** is represented by *Portrait of Chaim Soutine* (the Russian-born painter) and *Reclining Nude*. The entire progress of German art this century is copiously traced: particularly outstanding are **Kirchner's** *Friedrichstrasse, Berlin*, **Marc's** *Horses*, **Dix's** *Matchstick Seller* and **Beckmann's** *Ascension* and *Self-Portrait with Red Scarf*. Avant-garde works occupy the end halls, while important temporary exhibitions are regularly featured downstairs.

The western quarters
The streets in the grid-plan western half of the city centre are given over almost entirely to shopping. Almost the only building of note is the **Hospitalkirche**, which is a rare example of Aberlin Jerg being allowed to design his own building from scratch. Unfortunately only the chancel has survived intact; it houses a monumental *Crucifixion* by the Heilbronn sculptor Hans Seyfer.

Further west, on Hegelplatz at the opposite end of the Stadtgarten, is the **Linden-Museum** (Tues & Thurs–Sun 10am–5pm, Wed 10am–8pm; *www.lindenmuseum.de*; free). This well-presented ethnology museum has displays covering the full gamut of non-European cultures, with Peru, Melanesia, Benin and the Congo being particularly well represented. A full-scale reproduction of an Islamic bazaar, using many original exhibits, is one of the most eye-catching features.

The Weissenhofsiedlung and the Rosensteinpark

Below the Killesberg hill to the northwest of the centre, reached by bus #43, is the **Weissenhofsiedlung**. This settlement was laid out in 1927, in conjunction with an exhibition of the Deutscher Werkbund. Sixteen well-known architects contributed to this Bauhaus scheme, among them Le Corbusier, Gropius and Mies van der Rohe. Badly bombed in the war, the houses have been restored, but with variable success, and it's only worth making a special trip here if you're passionately keen on modern architecture. The **Höhenpark Killesberg** immediately behind is a large, remarkably peaceful recreation area. It's equipped with scented gardens, a flamingo park and fields with donkeys, rabbits and sheep, making it a good place to take kids.

More generally enticing is the **Rosensteinpark** at the far end of the Schlossgarten; take U-Bahn #1, #2 or #14 to Mineralbäder. At the bottom end of the park is an artificial lake; a little way up the hill you'll find the ritzy **Schloss Rosenstein** (Tues–Fri 9am–5pm, Sat & Sun 10am–6pm; DM4/€2), the former country house of the kings of Württemberg, complete with rose garden, fountains and heroic statues. The interior now houses a natural history museum. Although this is fairly conventional in scope, the same cannot be said for the related collection in the modern **Museum am Löwentor** (same times and ticket) at the western end of the park, which has a magnificent display of dinosaur skeletons and fossils, including many recent finds from ongoing excavations in the Swabian Jura.

Bad Cannstatt

Immediately beyond the Rosensteinpark lies the old spa town of **BAD CANNSTATT**, whose favourable situation at a bend in the river meant that it initially outstripped Stuttgart. It gradually declined in importance and was incorporated into its erstwhile rival in 1905.

Bad Cannstatt's major attraction is the superbly landscaped **Wilhelma** (daily May–Aug 8.15am–6pm; rest of year closing time gradually reduces to 4pm; *www.wilhelma.de*; DM16/€8, kids DM8/€4), which adjoins the Rosensteinpark. Originally laid out as a Moorish garden in the mid-nineteenth century for King Wilhelm I, it's nowadays a combined botanical garden and zoo which adds a decidely exotic element to the cityscape. Despite losses to wartime bombs, some of the whimsical mock-Moorish pavilions still stand, and are surrounded by gardens which uncannily evoke those of Granada. Other botanical features include the largest magnolia grove in Europe, four thousand orchids and a large variety of azaleas and camelias. With around nine thousand animals, the zoo ranks among the most diverse in the country.

Bad Cannstatt is otherwise best known as the home of a huge beer festival (see box on p.258), and as the main sports and recreation area of the Stuttgart conurbation. However, it also preserves some of the faded elegance of a once-fashionable spa, and a great deal of self-confident late nineteenth- and early twentieth-century architecture remains in the town centre on the right bank of the Neckar, which can be reached directly from Stuttgart Hauptbahnhof by mainline train, or S-Bahn #1, #2 and #3. There are a few older buildings, too, such as the **Stadtkirche**, another Aberlin Jerg confection, retaining parts of earlier Romanesque and Gothic structures. The **Kurpark**, with its mineral-water springs and shady willow paths, is the most restful spot in Stuttgart.

Just south of the park at Taubenheimstr. 13 is the **Gottlieb-Daimler-Gedächtnisstätte** (Tues–Sun 10am–4pm; free). In 1882, Daimler, who was consumed by the dream of developing a new means of mechanical propulsion, gave up his highly successful corporate career, acquired a villa in Cannstatt (destroyed during the war), and carried out his top-secret experiments in an expanded version of its greenhouse, which somehow managed to escape the bombs. This humble, unpromising setting was where Daimler toiled away in obscurity for four years, aided only by his protégé Wilhelm Maybach. In their quest to create a light, fast-moving internal combustion engine which could power a moving vehicle, Daimler and Maybach invented the motorbike by 1885; the following year, the motorboat and four-wheeled motorcar had been added to their achievements. A year later, they established a factory in the town.

The Mercedes-Benz-Museum

By an extraordinary coincidence, another German, **Carl Benz**, invented a motorcar in the same year as Daimler, though neither was aware of the other's work. Both went on to run highly successful factories producing their inventions; these were united in 1926 (long after Daimler's death and Benz's retirement) and are now based at **Untertürkheim**, immediately south of Bad Cannstatt. In 1986, the **Mercedes-Benz-Museum** (Tues–Sun 9am–5pm; *www.mercedes-benz.com*; free) was set up to celebrate the centenary of the inventions. Unless you positively rue the day the car was invented, this museum is an absolute must. Even entering here is an experience – take S-Bahn #1 to Gottlieb-Daimler-Stadion, then walk straight ahead at the exit to the works entrance, or else go by bus #56 to Martin-Schrenk-Weg. In accordance with the company's obsession about industrial espionage, you then have to wait for a special sealed minibus to take you through the Daimler-Chrysler factory complex to the museum doors which are opened only in conjunction with these arrivals.

Over seventy **historical vehicles** are on display, all with their bodywork restored to pristine condition. The earliest exhibit is the *Daimler Reitwagen* of 1885, the first-ever motorbike, which was capable of 12kph. Benz's patent *Motorwagen* (a tricycle whose engine and bodywork are both his own design) from January the following year just beats the Daimler-Maybach *Motorkusche* (which was fitted into a four-wheeled horse-carriage) for the title of the world's first car. Both used one-cylinder engines and had a maximum speed of 16kph. The Daimler company's first *Mercedes* dates from 1902. This Spanish-sounding name was borrowed from the daughter of the firm's principal foreign agent, Emil Jellinek; it proved so successful a trademark that it replaced the recently deceased founder's name on all products.

The exhibits also include a fire engine, a motorboat, an aeroplane and a bus, but it's the **luxury cars** that steal the show – look out for the elite handmade *Grand Mercedes* models of the 1930s, including one used by the Japanese royal family, the official *300d* limousine of Konrad Adenauer, and the first of the "Popemobiles", the *Landaulet* of Paul VI. Equally impressive are the space-age vehicles specially designed for **world record attempts**; these look so futuristic it's hard to believe they were made more than half a century ago. In 1938, the *W125* achieved 437.7kph on the Frankfurt–Darmstadt Autobahn, still the fastest speed ever registered on a public road. The *T80* was designed for travel at 600kph – but World War II killed off this project, which was never subsequently revived.

Württemberg

Württemberg, the hill from which the province and its former ruling family take their name, rises up behind the incorporated village of **ROTENBERG**, which can be reached by bus #61 from Untertürkheim's S-Bahnhof. The route lies through wine-growing countryside that seems soporifically rural in appearance and atmosphere, and totally at odds with the thrusting, dynamic image with which Stuttgart is usually associated. It's a good place to look for examples of a distinctive local institution, the Besenwirtschaft (see p.256).

In 1083, the House of Württemberg began the construction of what was to become its ancestral castle on the top of the eponymous hill. This survived until 1819, when it was torn down by order of King Wilhelm I, and replaced by a sternly Neoclassical **Grabkapelle** (Burial Chapel; March–Oct Wed 10am–noon, Fri–Sun 10am–noon & 1–5pm; DM2.50/€1.25) for his recently deceased Russian-born queen, Katharina. On his death in 1864, Wilhelm was laid to rest beside her. From the terrace outside, there's a wonderful **view** over the vineyards to Bad Cannstatt and the city centre.

The Porsche-Museum

Based right beside the Bahnhof of the northern suburb of **Neuwirtshaus** (served by S-Bahn line #6), the **Porsche-Museum** (Mon–Fri 9am–4pm, Sat & Sun 9am–5pm; free) at Porschestr. 42 displays some fifty vehicles, illustrating all the company's models from the *356 Roadster* of 1948 to those currently in production. The Bohemian-born **Ferdinand Porsche** had already had a brilliant career when he set up in Stuttgart after World War II. As Austrian director of Daimler-Benz, he was responsible for the design of the handsome if underpowered *Pullman* saloons, and led the technical team involved with the world record attempts. His services had also been acquired by Hitler for the creation of the original *Volkswagen*, which was at the opposite end of the market from the vehicles Porsche concentrated on in his own enterprise.

The southern suburbs

Marienplatz, which lies just south of the centre on the route of U-Bahn #1 and #14, is the starting-point for a true curiosity of Stuttgart's public transport system, the **Zahnradbahn** or rack railway, popularly known as Zacke. Inaugurated in 1884, it climbs steeply to the suburb of Degerloch, and is a much-used local facility, one for which only a short journey ticket (*Kurzstrecke*) is required.

In the hills due south of the city centre, reached by U-Bahn #7 or tram #15 (the latter takes far longer, but offers a scenic woodland route), is the 217-metre-high **Fernsehturm** (daily 9am–midnight; DM6/€3 including ascent by lift). Completed in 1956, this was the first such television tower ever built and has been much imitated round the world, most of all in Germany itself, where it often became a civic obsession to acquire such an amenity. The **view** from the observation platform is much the best Stuttgart can offer, stretching over the Swabian Jura to the Black Forest and the Odenwald, with the Alps visible on clear days.

Bus #70 runs from here to **Schloss Hohenheim** in the far south of the municipal area. This Neoclassical palace was built between 1785 and 1797 to serve as the main seat of the Württemberg court, but since 1818 has been an agricultural college, nowadays with university status. The impressive entrance stairway and some of the interiors are freely accessible during normal working hours, even though the building is not a regular tourist sight. One of the outbuildings contains Stuttgart's most prestigious restaurant (see p.257), while the extensive grounds feature two landscaped gardens; of these, the **Botanischer Garten** is primarily a serious scientific institution, whereas the appropriately named **Exotischer Garten** is a colourful spot which makes a good place for a stroll.

Schloss Solitude

On a ridge in the hills to the west of the city centre, reached by bus #92, sits the appropriately named **Schloss Solitude** (April–Oct Tues–Sun 9am–noon & 1.30–5pm; Nov–March Tues–Sun 10am–noon & 1.30–4pm; DM4/€2). This exquisite oval pleasure palace, built in the 1760s, served for a couple of decades as the main summer residence of the Württemberg court. It ranks as the masterpiece of Pierre Louis Philippe de la Guêpière, one of the prime movers behind the introduction of the Louis XVI style (which marks the transition from Rococo to Neoclassicism) into Germany. A bonus here is that you're free to wander at leisure round its marbled and panelled apartments, which range from the grand festive hall, the **Weisser Saal**, to intimate chambers such as the **Marmorsaal** and the **Palmenzimmer**. The Kavaliersbau, one of the paired crescent-shaped buildings to the rear of the Schloss, contains the recently restored **Schlosskirche** and a high-class restaurant (see p.257).

Eating and drinking

Stuttgart's expensive reputation thankfully doesn't entirely extend to food and drink; though fancy restaurants abound, there are also any number of places offering traditional Swabian dishes at low cost, as well as plenty of ethnic eateries.

Local **wines** are almost equally divided between *Riesling* (white) and *Trollinger* (red) varieties. Demand for these within Stuttgart itself is often so high that they can't be obtained elsewhere. They can be sampled all year round in the city's many **Weinstuben**, cosy, homely establishments which are as well known for their solid cooking as for wine. Note that they're usually open evenings only and are all closed on Sundays. Rather harder to track down are the **Besenwirtschaften**, which are temporary wine bar-restaurants set up for one or two weeks each year by local vintners for the sampling of the latest vintages. To find out which ones are open, ask at the tourist office, consult the local press or simply look out for signs in the vine-growing areas.

A wide variety of **beers** is produced in Stuttgart as well. Under its own label, Dinkelacker produces a classic *CD-Pils*, plus a *Märzen*. It now owns Schwaben-Bräu, whose *Meister-Pils* has a far more bitter taste, as well as the former Sannwald brewery, whose name lives on in light and dark varieties of *Weizen*. The Hofbräu's *Herren-Pils* is gentler and sweeter, and geared towards palates weaned on wine rather than beer.

Weinstuben

Kachelofen, Eberhardstr. 10. The preferred haunt of the local bigwigs and the in-crowd. Open Mon–Sat 5pm–1am.

Klösterle, Marktstr. 71, Bad Cannstatt. A great favourite of the spa town, occupying a beautiful half-timbered medieval beguinage. Open Mon–Fri 5pm–midnight.

Schellenturm, Weberstr. 72. Housed in the only surviving tower of the Stadtbefestigung, with an appropriately cosy atmosphere. Open Mon–Sat 5pm–midnight.

Stuttgarter Stäffele, Buschlestr. 2a/b. In addition to unusually long opening hours, this has something of a museum character, with a cabinet of 250 wine rarities and a collection of corkscrews. Open Mon–Fri 11am–1am, Sat & Sun 6pm–1am.

Vetter, Bopserstr. 18. In summer this spills over into the square outside. Open Mon–Sat 5pm–1am.

Weinhaus Stetter, Rosenstr. 32. Offers the largest choice of wines: some six hundred in all. The meals are extraordinarily good value. Open Mon–Fri 3–11pm, Sat 10am–3pm.

Zur Kiste, Kanalstr. 2. The most famous of Stuttgart's Weinstuben, so it's fairly pricey and prone to get very crowded. Open Mon–Fri 5pm–midnight, Sat 11.30am–3.30pm.

Other restaurants

Alt Cannstatt, Königsplatz 1, Bad Cannstatt. Excellent traditional restaurant in the elegant setting of the spa town's Kursaal, with a large beer garden outside. Closed Mon.

Délice, Hauptstätter Str. 61. The leading gourmet restaurant in the city centre, housed in a cellar and featuring modern art exhibitions. Open Mon–Fri, evenings only.

Dinckelacker, Tübinger Str. 48. The Gaststätte of the eponymous brewery, decked out in rustic style. Closed Sun.

Fernsehturm, Jahnstr. 120. There are two high-class restaurants in the TV tower: *Webers Gourmet* at the top is very expensive and usually has to be booked far in advance (☎07 11/24 89 96 10); *Primafila* at the foot is far more affordable.

Iden, Schwabenzentrum, Eberhardstr. 1. The most interesting of the city's vegetarian restaurants, one where you pay for everything by weight. Open Mon–Fri 11am–9pm, Sat 10.30am–5pm.

Kicho, Jakobstr. 19. Japanese restaurant and sushi bar.

La Scala, Friedrichstr. 41. One of many fine Italian restaurants in Stuttgart. Closed Sun.

Litfass, Eberhardstr. 37. Serves both Swabian and Turkish dishes; very popular with students.

Max-und-Moritz, Geiss-Str. 3. Pizzeria mainly patronized by students.

Ochsen, Markgräflerstr. 6, Uhlbach. Popular Swabian Gasthaus that has been run by the same family for well over a century. It lies to the east of Untertürkheim, from where it can be reached by bus #62. Closed Mon & Tues.

Russische Datscha, Aachener Str. 23, Bad Cannstatt. Both Russian and Georgian dishes are on the menu in this restaurant, which is tastefully furnished with antiques. Evenings only, closed Mon.

Sannwald, Silberburgstr. 157. Gaststätte of the former brewery of the same name.

Schloss Restaurant, Haus no. 2, Schloss Solitude. Out to the west of the centre and a good place to eat if you're visiting the Schloss. It specializes in *neue deutsche Küche* and is fairly expensive. Closed Mon.

Speisemeisterei, Am Schloss Hohenheim (☎07 11/4 56 00 37). Located in the far south of the city, this is generally regarded as Stuttgart's best restaurant. Very expensive; reservations advisable. Open Tues–Sat 7–10.30pm, Sun noon–2pm.

Tauberquelle, Torstr. 19. Fine Swabian Gaststätte in the city centre. Evenings only, closed Sun.

TÜ8, Tübinger Str. 8. A complex of three restaurants that are hugely popular with the young crowd. *O'Mäxle* serves Swabian fare and brews its own *Pils* and *Weizen*; *Spaghetissimo* serves Italian cuisine, *Hacienda* Tex-Mex dishes.

Zum Paulaner, Calwer Str. 45. A Bavarian Bierkeller may seem an anomaly in Stuttgart, but this has been in existence since 1879 and includes Swabian dishes on its menu.

Bars, cafés and café-bars

Academie der schönensten Künste, Charlottenstr. 5. Trendy artists' café with regular exhibitions. Has good wine list, serves full meals and has the benefit of a courtyard garden. Closed Sat & Sun evenings.

Amadeus, Charlottenplatz 17. Situated in the former orphanage, this serves bistro-style dishes and has space for sevem hundred in its beer gardens.

Biergarten im Snhlossgarten, Canstatter Str. 18. A large beer garden serving hearty traditional cooking is set up in the Schlossgarten every summer.

Café Königsbau, Königstr. 28. One of the best places in Stuttgart for *Kaffee und Kuchen*.

Café KönigX, Esslinger Str. 22. A traditional café with modern touches, such as the inclusion of wholefood dishes on its menu.

Café Stella, Hauptstätter Str. 57. Popular café-bar that makes a good choice for breakfast or for late-night drinking.

Calwer-Eck-Bräu, Calwer Str. 31. Hausbrauerei serving good-value meals.

Exil di Nuovo, Filderstr. 61. Trendy bar which doubles as an Italian restaurant.

Hans im Glück, Geiss-Str. 8. Cocktail bar which also serves bistro food.

Jenseitz-Schwulencafé, Bebelstr. 25. Stuttgart's main gay café; predominantly male, and prone to become very crowded.

Merlin, Augustenstr. 72. Alternative café and arts centre which serves vegetarian food and organically produced beers, wines and fruit juices.

Sydney's, Calwer Str. 31. Australian theme bar directly underneath *Calwer-Eck-Bräu*.

Teehaus, Im Weissenburgpark. Outdoor city-centre venue that's predictably popular during hot summer days.

Entertainment

Local prosperity helps fund a highbrow cultural scene which is arguably richer and more diverse than that of any other city of comparable size in Europe. There's also a lively nightlife which takes place in various pockets throughout the city. The tourist office produces a monthly programme of events, *Stuttgarter Monatsspiegel*, for DM3.50/€1.75; two other useful listings magazines are *Prinz* (DM2/€1) and *Lift* (DM4.50/€2.25).

Nightclubs and live music

Classic Rock Café, Eberhardstr. 22. Plays both live and recorded rock music. German, American and vegetarian food available. Open daily from 5pm until 2 or 4am.

STUTTGART'S FESTIVALS

Stuttgart's main annual event is the sixteen-day **Cannstatter Volksfest**, held in the last week in September and the first in October. Founded in 1818 by King Wilhelm I of Württemberg, it's the second biggest beer festival in the world. In fact, most of the features are direct imitations of the larger *Oktoberfest* in Munich, although the beers on tap are Swabian. A more fundamental difference is that whereas *Oktoberfest* is relentlessly Bavarian, this festival has a wider outlook, with one recurrent feature being the *Französische Dorf*, a group of French-style brasseries.

If wine is your tipple, the **Stuttgarter Weindorf**, held in the city centre from the last Friday in August until the first Sunday in September, has over three hundred varieties available for tasting. Another big wine festival is the **Fellbacher Herbst**, held on the second weekend of October in Fellbach, which adjoins Bad Cannstatt to the east. The **Weihnachtsmarkt**, beginning in late November, has existed since the seventeenth century and is thus one of the oldest in the country, but the harlequins and tightrope walkers have unfortunately long gone, to be replaced by the standard offerings. Other notable events are the **Frühlingsfest**, lasting for a fortnight in late April/early May, and a **Sommerfest** in mid-August.

Jazzothek Rogers Kiste, Hauptstätter Str. 35. Jazz bar featuring live music every evening Mon–Thurs & Sun.

Laboratorium, Wagenburgstr. 147. Live music and cabaret venue that's been a favourite with Stuttgart's alternative set for the past two decades.

Perkins Park, Stresemannstr. 39. Stuttgart's most popular disco, particularly with those in their 20s and 30s. Open Wed & Thurs 9pm–4am, Fri & Sat 9pm–5am, Sun 7pm–2am.

Röhre, Wagenburgtunnel, Willy-Brandt-Str. 2/1. The celebrated "tunnel" nightclub occupies what was originally designed as a new rail line. Live bands play everything from jazz to punk; it's also a disco (Thurs–Sun 11pm–5am) patronized mainly by the most fashion-conscious locals.

Classical music

The five halls of the Liederhalle, Berliner Platz 1–3 (☎07 11/2 02 77 10) serve for concerts of all kinds. There are two full-sized symphony **orchestras**: the Stuttgarter Philharmoniker and the SWR Radio-Sinfonieorchester; the latter's chief conductor is Britain's Sir Roger Norrington. Additionally, there's a chamber-sized body, the Stuttgarter Kammerorchester, which is currently directed by the American Dennis Russell Davies. The smaller halls often feature performances by the local Melos-Quartett, one of Europe's finest string quartets. Stuttgart is, after Leipzig, the main centre for research into Bach performance practice, so any concerts by Helmut Rilling's Bach Collegium are worth looking out for. The city has more top-class **choirs** than anywhere else in Germany, the most celebrated being the Hymnus Chorknaben. Free concerts are often held in the churches – the Stiftskirche has a series at 7pm during the winter months. An annual international *Musikfest* features a different theme every year.

Theatre, ballet and opera

Stuttgart's leading highbrow venue is the **Staatstheater**, Oberer Schlossgarten 6 (☎07 11/20 20 90, *www.staatstheater.stuttgart.de*), a complex of three separate houses, with the resident **ballet** and **opera** companies alternating in the Grosses Haus. The former is one of the most famous in the world, with the great tradition established in the 1960s by the South African-born John Cranko (many of whose choreographies remain in the repertoire), continued by his protégé, the Brazilian Marcia Haydée, and now in the hands of Reid Anderson. In recent years, the opera company has risen to a similarly prestigious level; indeed, many critics rate it the best in Germany at the moment. **Plays** are performed in the Kleines Haus, while the James Stirling-designed Kammertheater is equipped with a moveable stage and seating, and puts on more experimental work. The city's other theatres include:

Altes Schauspielhaus, Kleine Königstr. 9 (☎07 11/2 26 55 05, *www.schauspielhaus-komoedie.de*). Specializes in nineteenth- and twentieth-century classics.

FITS Figuren Theater, Eberhardstr. 61D (☎07 11/24 15 41). A great place to take kids, this is the home of several puppet companies.

Friedrichsbau-Varieté, Friedrichstr. 24 (☎07 11/22 57 00). Stuttgart's spectacular new variety theatre.

Komödie in Marquardt, Bolzstr. 4–6 (☎07 11/2 27 70 22). A theatre specializing in comedies of all kinds.

Kruscheltunnel, Möhringer Str. 56 (☎07 11/2 36 14 81). Shows for the under-12s.

Makal-City-Theater, Marienstr. 12 (☎07 11/62 62 08). Traditional mime is the predominant fare here; there's a festival, too, each May.

Renitenz-Theater, Eberhardstr. 65 (☎07 11/29 70 75). The place to go for satirical cabaret; a good understanding of German is obviously needed for an appreciation.

Stella Erlebnis-Center, Plieninger Str. 100, Plieningen (☎07 11/2 22 82 43 or 5 44 44, *www.erlebniscenter.de*). Europe's biggest entertainment centre is centred on two theatres for blockbuster musicals. *Cats* and *Tanz der Vampire* (Dance of the Vampire) are currently playing, and likely to run for a while yet. Also on site are no fewer than nineteen theme restaurants (including a Hausbrauerei, *Schlossturm*), plus a casino, a fitness centre and a cinema complex.

Theaterhaus Stuttgart, Ulmer Str. 241, Wangen (☎07 11/40 20 70). This is the big venue for alternative events, including feminist work and visiting foreign groups, but it is due to move to another location.

Listings

Airport information ☎07 11/9 48 33 88.

Car rental Avis, Katharinenstr. 18 (☎07 11/23 93 20); Europcar, Im Hauptbahnhof (☎07 11/2 24 46 30); Hertz, Im Hauptbahnhof (☎07 11/2 26 29 21); Schlosstein, Hegelstr. 12 (☎07 11/29 38 44).

Consulates British, Breite Str. 2 (☎07 11/16 26 90); Canadian, Lange Str. 51 (☎07 11/2 23 96 78); US, Urbanstr. 7 (☎07 11/21 00 80).

Cruises Trips along the Neckar between April and Oct with Neckar-Käpt'n (NPS; ☎07 11/54 99 70 60); boats depart from opposite Wilhelma.

Dentist ☎07 11/7 80 02 66 or 7 87 77 11.

Doctor ☎07 11/2 62 80 12 or 28 02 11.

Markets The daily markets in the Jugendstil *Markthalle* on Schillerplatz are ideal for putting a picnic together. On Saturday mornings, a flower market is held on Schillerplatz itself, while there's also a flea market on Schlossplatz.

Mitfahrzentralen Hauptstätter Str. 154 (☎07 11/60 36 06); Lerchenstr. 65 (☎07 11/6 36 80 36).

Post office Main office is at the rear of the Königsbau on Schillerplatz, though this was only partially open in 2000, with the poste restante service moved to the branch in the Hauptbahnhof.

Sports The Gottlieb-Daimler-Stadion on Mercedesstrasse in Bad Cannstatt is the main stadium for outdoor events, including the matches of the leading local football team, VfB Stuttgart, one of the most consistent in Germany in recent seasons. Indoor events, including an international tennis tournament in November, are held at the Martin-Schleyer-Halle alongside it (☎07 11/56 15 65).

Swimming There are three main mineral baths: the venerable Leuze, Am Leuzebad 2–6 (daily 6am–9pm); Berg, Am Schwanenplatz 9 (Mon–Fri 6am–7.30pm, Sat 6am–8.30pm, Sun 6am–12.30pm); and Bad Cannstatt, Sulzerrainstr. 2 (Mon–Fri 9am–9.30pm, Sat 9am–9pm, Sun 9am–5pm). Expect to pay upwards of DM11.50/€5.75 for two hours.

Esslingen

If Stuttgart seems rather thin on historic monuments, ample compensation is provided by **ESSLINGEN**. Nowadays, this is virtually a southeastern suburb of the state capital, reached in fifteen minutes by S-Bahn #1, but for centuries it was a Free Imperial City and jealously guards its municipal independence. In the nineteenth century, it became an important centre of machine-tool manufacturing and is still ringed by ugly factories which provide a sharp contrast to the vineyard-clad hills above the town. However, the old centre has been preserved almost intact. With its winding streets, narrow alleys, spacious squares and dramatic views, it's one of the most visually pleasing – and most unexpected – places in this otherwise hi-tech dominated part of Baden-Württemberg.

The Town

The centre of town is separated from the Bahnhof by the Neckar canal. From the Bahnhof, go straight up the street of the same name and cross over the bridge. Two more bridges can be seen down to the right; the second of these, the fourteenth-century **Innere Brücke**, is outstanding, incorporating a graceful chapel which now serves as a memorial to the victims of the Third Reich.

Heart of the town is **Marktplatz**, scene of markets on Wednesday and Saturday mornings. Dominating the square is the Romanesque-Gothic **Stadtkirche St Dionys**, whose two towers are linked by a covered passageway, which served as a defensive look-out post. The church preserves its late Gothic rood screen, along with a soaring tabernacle and a font from the same period. In the chancel are glittering stained-glass windows, made in the late thirteenth and early fourteenth centuries. If you're keen on archeology, it's well worth coming here on a Wednesday between 2pm and 5pm, when you can view the extensive underground **excavations** for DM2/€1. These include Roman finds, plus the foundations of two previous churches on this spot – the first was erected around 720, the second throughout the first half of the following century.

Facing the back of the church is the **Speyrer Zehnthof**, a mid-sixteenth-century tithe barn. Since 1826, this has served as the headquarters of Sektkellerei Kessler, the oldest *Sekt* cellar in Germany. The **Spitalkelter**, a half-timbered structure on the north side of Marktplatz, is an earlier relic of the city's wine tradition, having been built as a wine-pressing factory, before later becoming a hospital.

Adjoining Marktplatz to the east is Rathausplatz. The **Altes Rathaus** began life in the early fifteenth century as a merchants' trading hall and tax collection point, but was taken over for municipal purposes at the end of the following century. It was then given a cheerful pink facade, much influenced by Dutch buildings of the time, and adorned with an astronomical clock. Opposite is the Baroque **Neues Rathaus**, originally a patrician palace. Beyond are a number of picturesque old streets, along with the Hafenmarkt, where you'll find the thirteenth-century **Gelbes Haus** (Yellow House), probably Germany's oldest surviving and most architecturally distinguished brothel. However, it hasn't served its original purpose since a fire devastated the town in 1701.

Just west of Marktplatz is the **Münster St Paul**, nowadays the main Catholic parish church but originally part of a Dominican priory consecrated by Albertus Magnus in 1268. It's of particular significance in marking the debut on German soil of the sober, unadorned Gothic architecture characteristic of the mendicant religious orders. In total contrast is the **Frauenkirche** on the brow of the hill behind, which represents the Gothic style at its most elaborate. The marked resemblance, albeit on a reduced scale, to the great Münster in Ulm is no coincidence: it shared the same master masons, members of the Ensinger and Böblinger families. There are two exquisite portals, showing the Life of the Virgin and the Last Judgement, while the hall church interior has lovely stained-glass windows made a generation after those in the Stadtkirche. However, as at Ulm, it's the highly decorated **tower**, crowned with an openwork spire, which provides the most memorable feature.

At the east end of the Frauenkirche is the **Blaubeurer Pfleghof**, the most impressive of about a dozen such institutions in Esslingen, which served as town headquarters and charitable institutions of rural monasteries. From here, you can ascend to the **Burg** along its own covered ramparts. Most of the thirteenth-century defensive system has disappeared, save for the walls themselves, the bulky **Hochwacht** (the corner tower where the fortifications stop climbing) and the **Dicker Turm** (Fat Tower) at the summit. This was restored last century in the Romantic manner, and is now an excellent upmarket restaurant. From here, there's a good **view** over the Neckar valley towards the Swabian Jura.

Practicalities

The **tourist office** (Mon–Fri 9am–6pm, Sat 10am–3pm; ☎07 11/35 12 31 77, fax 07 11/35 12 23 62, *www.esslingen.de*) is at Marktplatz 2. There's a reasonably priced **pension**, *Neckarhalde*, Mittelstr. 12 (☎07 11/9 32 59 69; ③); plus several **hotels**, the best and most convenient being *Am Schillerpark*, Neckarstr. 60 (☎07 11/93 13 30; ⑥), and *Am Schelztor*, Schelztorstr. 5 (☎07 11/3 96 96 40; ⑥). The **youth hostel** is a long way to the north of town at Neuffenstr. 65 (☎07 11/38 18 48, fax 38 88 86; DM22/€11 or DM27/€13.50).

The town centre abounds with places to **eat** and **drink**. *Palm'scher Bau*, Innere Brücke 2, is a Baroque palace with a beer garden; *Zum Schwanen*, Franziskanergasse 3, is a Hausbrauerei which serves bargain lunches; while *Rose*, Obere Beutau 1, is a vegetarian restaurant serving dishes from around the world.

Ludwigsburg and Marbach

On the S-Bahn network to the north of the Stuttgart are two nicely contrasted towns which make satisfying day-trips from the state capital: the Residenzstadt of **Ludwigsburg**, which has one of Germany's most impressive palace and park complexes, and the quaint half-timbered town of **Marbach**, which is mainly of note for its literary associations.

Ludwigsburg

The creation of **LUDWIGSBURG** began in 1697, when French troops destroyed an isolated hunting lodge of the House of Württemberg which lay some 15km north of Stuttgart and 35km south of Heilbronn. When Duke Eberhard Ludwig decided to rebuild the lodge, he found himself desiring something rather grander. By 1704, he hit on the idea of a planned town (named, needless to say, in his own honour); five years later, he had decided to make this his main residence and the duchy's new capital. To entice people to come to live there, he provided free land and building materials, plus exemption from taxes for fifteen years – an offer which duly found plenty of takers.

The Town
In contrast to Mannheim and Karlsruhe, the Schloss is not the epicentre of the Ludwigsburg plan; that distinction belongs to the outsized **Marktplatz**, which has churches for both the Catholic and Protestant faiths facing each other across the square. One of Ludwigsburg's main claims to fame is that it has nurtured rather more than its fair share of literary celebrities, and an obelisk in **Holzmarkt** immediately to the north commemorates four nineteenth-century writers who were born in the town – the Romantic poets Eduard Mörike and Justinus Kerner, and the realist philosophers Friedrich Theodor Vischer and David Friedrich Strauss. Schiller went to school in the town, while the revolutionary writer Friedrich Schubart did a six-year stint as organist of the Protestant church.

Ludwigsburg's complex of palaces and parks lies to the east of the town centre. The Baroque **Residenzschloss** (guided tours in German mid-March to mid-Oct daily 9am–noon & 1–5pm; mid-Oct to mid-March Mon–Fri at 10.30am, 11.45am, 1.30pm & 3pm, Sat & Sun 10am–noon & 1–4pm; guided tours in English Mon–Sat at 1.30pm, Sun 11am, 1.30pm & 3.15pm; DM7/€3.50) took thirty years to build under the direction of a whole team of architects, and was only completed in the year of the patron's death. By then, funds had completely dried up and much of the lavish interior decoration was put in place by his successors, who preferred to live in Stuttgart. There are 452 rooms in all, grouped in eighteen separate buildings arranged round three courtyards; some sixty of these are included in the compulsory tour, which normally lasts upwards of ninety minutes. Among the highlights are two chapels, the sumptuous **Schlosskapelle** and the somewhat stern **Ordenskapelle**, and the exquisite **Schlosstheater**, the first theatre in the world to be equipped with a revolving stage. The most opulent of the many large reception rooms is the **Ordenshalle** (throne room), which nowadays is a venue for the concerts which take place throughout the summer festival season.

Also housed in the Schloss, but visited separately, are two museums. The **Theatermuseum** (daily mid-March to early Nov 9am–5pm; rest of year 10am–4pm; free) occupies the rooms adjacent to the Schlosstheater, and includes a mock-up of its stage mechanism. Examples of the local porcelain, plus other courtly art of the Baroque era, are featured in a branch of the Württemburgisches Landesmuseum entitled **Höfische Kunst des Barock**, though this was closed in 2000 as part of the extensive programme of restoration work that is being carried out on the Residenzschloss.

The **Schlosspark** (daily 8am–8pm; DM12/€6, DM6/€3 after 6.30pm) is also known as **Blühendes Barock** after the huge floral festival held between mid-March and early November each year. To the front and rear of the Schloss, the formal Baroque sections have been re-created from old plans. To the east are upper and lower gardens laid out in a more naturalistic style, incorporating a range of attractions including an outlook tower, a rose garden, a rhododendron garden, a Japanese garden, a Sicilian garden, an aviary, a collection of historic fairground objects and a small vineyard with a rustic vintner's house. The entrance ticket also gives admission to the **Märchengarten** (daily 9am–6pm), a kitsch playground with huge model giants, witches and other fairy-tale figures, complete with sound effects.

Another good destination for a stroll is the Wildpark immediately to the north, in which stands **Schloss Favorite** (guided tours mid-March to mid-Oct daily 9am–noon & 1.30–5pm; mid-Oct to mid-March Tues–Sun 10am–noon & 1.30–4pm; DM4/€2), which was built as a resting-place for Ludwig and his cronies on their hunting trips. It has an appropriately playful-looking exterior, with little corner towers and prominent side pavilions. However, only one of the interiors survives in its original Baroque state; the others were partially or completely remodelled in mock-Pompeian style in the late eighteenth century. The third and last of Ludwig's palaces, **Seeschloss Monrepos**, is a thirty-minute walk away. This has a tranquil lakeside setting which is perfect for a picnic, but the building itself is in private hands and is normally closed to the public. Within the grounds is the town's top luxury hotel (see opposite).

Practicalities

Ludwigsburg's **Bahnhof** is just a short walk to the west of the town centre. As well as being on the main line between Stuttgart and Heilbronn, it's linked to the former by S-Bahn #4 and #5. The **tourist office** (Mon–Fri 9am–6pm, Sat 9am–2pm; ☎0 71 41/9 10 22 52, fax 9 10 27 74, *www.ludwigsburg.de*) is at Wilhelmstr. 10. Tickets for the *Ludwigsburger Schlossfestspiele*, the music and theatre **festival** held over three and a half months in the summer are available from the box office at Marstallstr. 5 (☎0 71 41/9 39 60, *www.festspiele.ludwigsburg.de*). The other big annual event is the *Pferdemarkt*, a horse fair held in May.

There are **hotels** in all price categories. At the budget end of the scale are *Kepler*, Keplerstr. 2 (☎0 71 41/92 38 87; ③), *Kronen-Stuben*, Kronenstr. 2 (☎0 71 41/9 62 50; ④), and *Pfauter*, Stresemannstr. 25 (☎0 71 41/9 50 60 10; ⑤). Pick of the upmarket options are *Favorit*, Gartenstr. 18 (☎0 71 41/97 67 70; ⑥;), *Nestor*, Stuttgarter Str. 35 (☎0 71 41/96 70, *www.nestor-hotels.de*; ⑦), and *Schlosshotel Monrepos*, Domäne Monrepos 22 (☎0 71 41/30 20, *www.schlosshotel-monrepos.de*; ⑧). The **youth hostel** is at Gemsenbergstr. 21 (☎0 71 41/5 15 64, fax 5 94 40; DM28/€14 or DM33/€16.50); take bus #422 from the Bahnhof to the Schlösslesfeld terminus.

Ludwigsburg has several good, inexpensive places to **eat** and **drink**, including two Hausbrauereien: *Sudhaus*, Bahnhofstr. 17, and *Zum Rossknecht*, Am Rathausplatz 21. *Württemberger Hof*, Bismarckstr. 24, offers a comprehensive vegetarian menu, alongside standard Swabian fare, while *Post-Cantz*, Eberhardstr. 6, is renowned for its home-made Maultaschen and other local specialities cooked in a historic steam oven. The last two hotels mentioned above both have excellent restaurants which are a good deal less expensive than the town's leading gourmet citadel, *Alte Sonne*, Bei der Katholische Kirche 3.

Marbach

Some 8km northeast of Ludwigsburg, at the terminus of S-Bahn #4, is **MARBACH**, a small town of half-timbered houses indelibly associated with **Friedrich Schiller** (see box below). The great poet, dramatist and historian was born in the house at Niklastorstr. 20, which is now designated the **Geburtshaus Schillers** (daily 9am–5pm; DM3/€1.50). It's a modest building, entirely typical of Marbach – the writer's mother had also been born in the town, and the family moved back to this rented property when his father retired from the army. As space is restricted here, a much grander memorial was created at the beginning of the twentieth century in the shape of the **Schiller-Nationalmuseum** (daily 9am–5pm; *www.dla-marbach.de*; DM4/€2), which is housed in a huge mock-Baroque castle perched above the Neckar valley. This contains mementoes not only of Schiller, but also of all the other leading Swabian writers.

Marbach's **tourist office** (Mon 9–11am & 4–6pm, Tues, Thurs & Fri 9–11am, Wed 2–4pm; ☎0 71 44/10 20, fax 10 23 00, *www.schillerstadt-marbach.de*) is in the Rathaus, Marktstr. 23. The *Stadthalle* near the museum has one of the best **restaurants** in town, offering the bonus of fine panoramic views from its terrace; *Goldener Löwe*, Niklastorstr. 39, is another good choice, occupying a nicely furnished seventeenth-century house. There's no hostel or campsite, but there are several **hotels**, including *Gasthof zum Bären*, Marktstr. 21 (☎0 71 44/54 55; ③), *Schillerhof*, Marktstr. 19 (☎0 71 44/66 86; ④), and *Parkhotel*, Schillerhöhe 14 (☎0 71 44/90 50; ⑥).

FRIEDRICH SCHILLER (1759–1805)

Considered in Germany to be one of the great lions of world literature, Schiller's fame elsewhere chiefly rests on a single poem, known in English as *Ode to Joy*, part of which was used by Beethoven for the choral finale of his titanic Ninth Symphony – the first time ever that words had been used in a symphonic composition. The strong liberal sentiments of this work are wholly characteristic of the output of Schiller, who was very much a product of the Age of Enlightenment. After his early Sturm und Drang period, he began to concentrate increasingly on large-scale historical problems, and was himself a practising historian, holding a chair at the University of Jena and writing a mammoth, Protestant-inspired account of the Thirty Years War. This research provided him with the raw material for his dramatic masterpiece, the *Wallenstein* trilogy. Rather bizarrely, Schiller is renowned for being unable to work without the aid of the smell of rotting apples and always had a bowl of festering fruit by his desk, much to the revulsion of visitors.

Maulbronn

MAULBRONN, whose famous Cistercian Kloster is the best-preserved medieval monastery north of the Alps, lies in the heart of the fertile Stromberg region. In 1557, just a couple of decades after the last monks had left, a Protestant school was established under the protection of the Dukes of Württemberg. As a result, Maulbronn never suffered as a target for iconoclasts and revolutionaries, and stands today as a complete monastic complex giving a unique insight into a way of life which exercised such enormous power and influence throughout the medieval period. A wonderfully evocative description of the monastery (thinly disguised as Mariabronn) in its heyday can be found in the picaresque novel *Narziss and Goldmund* by Hermann Hesse, one of the school's most famous old boys.

The Kloster

A characterless modern town has grown up on the slopes above the walled precincts of the **Kloster** (March–Oct daily 9am–5.30pm; Nov–Feb Tues–Sun 9.30am–5pm; DM8/€4), which was founded in 1147 in what was then the isolated valley of the River Salzach. This was exactly the sort of location favoured by the reforming Cistercian order, whose rule stressed both spirituality and the importance of manual labour. According to legend, the site was chosen when the monks stopped to water their mules – hence the name Maulbronn, meaning "Mule Well".

Entry to the complex is through the Romanesque **Klostertor**. Immediately to the right is a ruined chapel, in which early Masses were said; facing it is the priest's house, now converted into the **Klostermuseum** (April–Oct daily 9.30am–noon & 2–5pm; free). Beyond here, you pass into the spacious main **Klosterhof**, the first part of which is taken up by a jumble of predominantly late Gothic half-timbered buildings. These served as the storerooms and workshops, which were the province of the lay brothers of the monastery. They're now put to a variety of uses: the forge has been converted

JOHANNES FAUST AND THE FAUST LEGEND

Surprisingly little is known about the real-life Johannes Faust, though he seems to have been a celebrity in his day and the leading intellectuals of the time took him seriously, while regarding his practices as wholly evil. Unlike other leading practitioners of the occult, such as Nostradamus and Paracelsus, Faust left no tangible legacy, and his name would certainly have passed into oblivion had it not been for an unknown author who in 1587 published the *Faustbuch*, a pot-boiling collection of tales allegedly told by the magician, who had died nearly half a century before; this quickly became a best seller, despite the crudity of the text. It was the English playwright Christopher Marlowe who, just a few years afterwards, first realized the dramatic possibilities of the story, endowing the hero with a tragic dignity.

Ever since, the Faust legend – with its themes of absolute knowledge, absolute power and the relationship between the two – has ranked as one of the great subjects of the European literary tradition, one capable of a vast variety of interpretations and a convenient backdrop for the discussion of all kinds of issues. Lessing provided a happy ending, a lead followed by Goethe, whose vast two-part drama is the unchallenged summit of all German literature. It took him the best part of sixty years to write; in it, he explored the entire European cultural heritage. In the present century, the Faust themes are equally relevant, and Thomas Mann provided an appropriately updated version of the story in his novel of 1950, thus following in the footsteps of his son Klaus, whose *Mephisto*, a *roman à clef* about the Third Reich, was banned in Germany for several decades.

into a restaurant; the stables serve as the Rathaus. The stone-built mill, the oldest of the buildings, is linked to the passageway along the ramparts, at the end of which is the thirteenth-century **Haspelturm** (Witches' Tower).

At the southeast corner is the **Faustturm**, so called from having been the residence of the original Dr Faust (see box opposite), whose claim to be able to manufacture gold gained him employment for a time by an unscrupulous abbot who was willing to try anything to bolster the monastery's sagging finances. Within the corresponding corner to the north, the Dukes of Württemberg built a Renaissance **Jagdschloss** with fairy-tale corner turrets; it now forms the girls' section of the school they founded.

Facing the Klosterhof is the core of the monastery. The **Klosterkirche** was the first part to be built; it's in the severe, unadorned style laid down in the tenets of the order, with no tower and no decoration. Later generations were less enthusiastic about asceticism; in order to enliven their church they replaced the wooden roof with a lofty net vault, added a row of chapels with elaborate traceried windows to the south side and commissioned works of art. The fathers reserved the eastern part of the church for their own exclusive use, confining the lay brothers to the nave by the erection of a stone screen; members of the public weren't allowed into the church at all. Instead, a **porch** (or "Paradise"), enabling visitors to look in on the services, was built onto the facade of the church in 1220. This seems to be the earliest building in Germany to show awareness of the new Gothic style pioneered in France.

The same anonymous mason then began building the **cloister**, completing the southern wing plus the **monks' refectory** on the opposite side. Appropriately, the refectory is a masterpiece; it was the Cistercian custom to make the dining hall particularly splendid and luminous, in order to draw thoughts away from the frugality of the meals. The rest of the cloister, including the graceful **chapter house** on the east side, dates from around a century later; the use of elaborate tracery is the first visible sign of the dilution of the early Cistercian ideal of austerity. As a culmination, a striking polygonal **well-house** was added to house the fountain where the monks washed before each meal. Buildings continued to be added periodically – the long, narrow **parlatorium** (the room where conversations were held) beside the chapter house was built by a lay brother at the end of the fifteenth century, while the cloister was given a picturesque half-timbered upper storey soon after.

In the early sixteenth century, as the original Cistercian ideal of plain and unadorned architecture held ever less appeal, the most violently expressive of German artists, **Jerg Ratgeb**, was commissioned to execute a series of **fresco cycles**. He made a series of preliminary red-chalk drawings, which can still be seen; these include the depiction of the legend of the monastery's foundation in the well-house, and a number of allegorical subjects (incorporating a stern self-portrait) in the refectory. Completion of the project was interrupted by the Reformation when the painter abandoned art in favour of politics, serving as "War Councillor" and "Chancellor" of the Peasants' War in 1525. The failure of this rebellion led to Ratgeb's arrest; he was quartered in the Markt in Pforzheim a decade before his erstwhile patrons became very different casualties of the Reformation.

Practicalities

Maulbronn is slightly tricky to reach by public transport. It's best to come by **bus** from Mühlacker, which is a regular stop for trains between Stuttgart and Karlsruhe. There is a station, **Maulbronn West**, on the branch rail line to Bruchsal, but it's some 3km from the Kloster. The **tourist office** (Mon & Thurs 8am–noon & 1–5.30pm, Tues & Wed 8am–noon & 1–4.30pm, Fri 8am–1.30pm, Sat & Sun 11am–5pm; ☎0 70 43/1 03 12) is in the Rathaus, Klosterhof 31.

There are some **private rooms** (①–②) and a few **hotels**: *Ochsen*, Stuttgarter Str. 54 (☎0 70 43/73 14; ③), *Birkenhof*, Birkenplatz 1 (☎0 70 43/67 63; ⑤), and *Klosterpost*,

Frankfurter Str. 2 (☎0 70 43/10 80; ⑤); all have good restaurants. As an alternative to the excellent but expensive **restaurant** *Klosterkeller*, Klosterhof 32, *Scheffelhof*, just outside the gates at Frankfurter Str. 9, serves homely and hearty fare, including imaginative vegetarian dishes.

Heilbronn and the Swabian Forest

HEILBRONN, which lies in the Neckar valley just to the east of the Stromberg, 50km due north of Stuttgart, is deemed to mark the boundary of the mystical concept of Swabia – no true Schwob would live any further north. Today, it still boasts one of the richest folklore traditions in Germany and is also a leading centre for **wine** production – some five million litres, mostly *Riesling* and *Trollinger* varieties, are produced each year by the surrounding vineyards. Sadly, however, the old streets were almost razed to the ground in an air raid at the end of 1944. The rebuilding programme was unusual in that it concentrated on providing housing in the town centre, with most commercial activity banished to the suburbs. Only a few first-class monuments now remain, and it's best to time your visit to coincide with one of the many **festivals** which dot the calendar.

The Town

The surviving monuments are conveniently grouped closely together in the town centre. By far the most imposing is the Gothic hall church of **St Kilian**, on Kilianplatz, with its amazing later adjunct, the sixteenth-century **belfry** (daily 9.30am–4/6pm; DM1/€0.50), which can be climbed for a view of the town. One of the few examples of ecclesiastical architecture in northern Europe directly inspired by the Italian High Renaissance, its lower parts are richly decorated, much in the manner of the late Gothic style then still popular elsewhere in Germany, while the upper storeys are built in the manner of a miniature classical temple. At the summit, a copy of the *Männle* (a statue of an infantryman bearing the municipal coat of arms) lords it over the town. Inside the church is a wonderful retable of *The Virgin and Child with Saints* by a local man, **Hans Seyfer**, one of the seemingly endless number of virtuoso carvers active in late fifteenth-century Germany. Underneath the building is the Heiliger Brunnen, a well with supposedly miraculous properties, from which the town's name is derived.

HEILBRONN'S FESTIVALS

Foremost of the many local festivals is the *Heilbronner Herbst*, which begins with a procession through the streets on the first Saturday in September, and continues with a parade of lantern-bearing children and a fireworks display the next day. Later in the week, the *Weindorf* (Wine Village) is set up for nine days in the town centre, with the inevitable oompah bands to enliven the atmosphere. Nearly two hundred vintages are on offer at the various booths; in contrast to the inflated prices normally charged at German festivals, the rates are surprisingly reasonable – usually DM2/€1 per glass.

Heilbronn's other big event is the *Neckarfest*, featuring historical boat pageants, a flotilla of bizarre home-made "water transport" contraptions, aquatic tournaments and a serenade of lights. This takes place during June, but in even-numbered years only, as it alternates with the more orthodox *Stadtfest*. Other festivals are the huge *Pferdemarkt* (Horse Fair) in February and the *Unterländer Volksfest* in late July/early August; the latter sees beer take a rare centre-stage role in this wine stronghold.

Directly opposite St Kilian is the **Rathaus**, another amalgam of Gothic and Renaissance, whose facade is enlivened by a graceful balcony used for making public pronouncements and by an **astronomical clock**. The latter, which tells the day and the month as well as the time, was considered the ultimate municipal status symbol when it was installed in 1580. Its construction was entrusted to Isaak Habrecht, the finest horologist of the day, who was responsible for the clock inside Strasbourg cathedral. Sheltering under the Rathaus arcades is the original of the *Männle*.

Also on Marktplatz is the **Käthchenhaus**, a Gothic patrician mansion embellished with a Renaissance oriel. It takes its name from the legend of Käthchen of Heilbronn, best known through the play by Heinrich von Kleist. Käthchen was the product of a one-night stand between a German emperor and the wife of the blacksmith of Heilbronn. Her true identity was only revealed when, as a 15-year-old, she developed a mystical attraction to a count who had a premonition that he was going to marry an emperor's daughter. The town still gets a lot of mileage out of the story – every two years, a pretty local girl is designated as "Käthchen", to preside over all the festivals and to adorn the front cover of all the glossy promotional brochures.

In the pedestrian precinct south of Marktplatz is the **Deutschhof**, formerly belonging to the Teutonic Knights, which contains a Gothic church and Baroque administrative buildings. The **Städtisches Museum** (Tues & Thurs 10am–7pm, Wed & Fri–Sun 10am–5pm; free) is now housed in the latter, though its natural history department is in the Renaissance **Gerichtshaus** (Law Courts) across the street. There's also a third section, devoted to local wine production and shipping on the Neckar, in its own building at Frankfurter Str. 75, not far from the river itself. Up Obere Neckarstrasse from the Gerichtshaus is one of the few surviving parts of the medieval fortifications, the tower known as the **Götzenturm**. It's so called as a result of the daring escape made from it by the great iron-handed adventurer Götz von Berlichingen, who was held prisoner there in 1519.

Practicalities

The **Hauptbahnhof** is situated just to the west of the town centre, which is reached by following Bahnhofstrasse straight ahead. The **tourist office** (Mon–Fri 9am–5.30pm, Sat 9am–12.30pm; ☎0 71 31/1 94 33, fax 56 33 49, *www.heilbronn.de*) is in the Rathaus on Marktplatz. Conveniently located **hotels** include *Schlachthof*, Frankfurter Str. 83 (☎0 71 31/8 14 13; ②), *Grüner Kranz*, Lohtorstr. 9 (☎0 71 31/9 61 70; ⑤), *Burkhardt*, Lohtorstr. 7 (☎0 71 31/6 22 40, *www.ringhotels.de*; ⑥–⑧), and *Insel-Hotel*, Friedrich-Ebert-Brücke (☎0 71 31/63 00, *insel@insel-hotel.de*; ⑥–⑧). The **youth hostel** is at Schirrmannstr. 9 (☎0 71 31/7 29 61, fax 16 43 45; DM24/€12 or DM29/€14.50): take bus #1 to the Trappensee terminus.

All the hotels mentioned above have **restaurants**. Other good choices include *Am Stadtgarten*, Allee 28, *Haus des Handwerks*, Allee 76, and the *Ratskeller*, Marktplatz 7. *Barfüsser,* Allee 25, is a Hausbrauerei which serves full meals, including a pizza variant known as a *Brauerflade*. *Rawers*, Fischergasse 1, is a recommendable Weinstube, while *Dachpavilion*, on top of a row of shops at Kaiserstr. 25, is one of the most enticing **bars** in Heilbronn. Another lively hangout is *Bukowski*, Hafenstr. 36, which never seems to close at the weekend.

Classical music can be heard at the Harmonie concert hall on Allee; look out for performances by the Württembergisches Kammerorchester, one of the best chamber orchestras in Europe. On the same street, the spanking-new Stadttheater (☎0 71 31/56 30 01) presents all forms of **drama**. The booking office for **Neckar cruises**, which are run by Personenschiffahrt Stumpf (☎0 71 31/8 54 30) is beside Friedrich-Ebert-Brücke. There are generally at least a couple of sailings each day in summer to Gundelsheim; trips round the harbour are occasionally offered as an alternative.

The Swabian Forest (Schwäbischer Wald)

The **Swabian Forest** stretches over a neat, almost square geographical area between Heilbronn and Stuttgart in the west, and Schwäbisch Gmünd and Schwäbisch Hall in the east. To the north, it enters Franconia where it gives way to the flat plain of Hohenlohe. Stretching over some 900 square kilometres, the whole area is designated a *Naturpark*. Thickly wooded, it consists of three separate forest areas, plus two ranges of hills. Though there's little that's tremendously dramatic, the region offers the opportunity of escaping from the crowds, on weekdays at least. The old Roman **Limes-Wall**, some of whose towers have been restored to serve as vantage points, traverses the forest from north to south; and there's a marked trail along the entire route.

At the heart of the forest is the town of **MURRHARDT**, which lies on the rail line between Stuttgart and Schwäbisch Hall, and makes an obvious base from which to plan your explorations. The town boasts an outstanding monument in the **Walterichskapelle**, a tiny, highly ornamented late Romanesque chapel adjoining the fifteenth-century Stadtkirche. A number of half-timbered houses and a section of the Stadtmauer also survive.

The **tourist office** (Mon–Wed 8.30am–noon & 2–4pm, Thurs 8.30am–noon & 2–6pm, Fri 8.30am–noon; ☎0 71 92/21 30, fax 52 83, *www.murrhardt.de*) is in the Rathaus, Marktplatz 10. There are a couple of **hotels**: *Gasthof Zum Engel*, in a half-timbered sixteenth-century house at Hauptstr. 15 (☎0 71 92/52 32; ③), and the contrastingly modern *Sonne-Post*, Walterichsweg 1 (☎0 71 92/80 81; ④), both of which have **restaurants**. The only **youth hostel** in the region is at Karnsberger Str. 1 (☎0 71 92/75 01, fax 2 90 58; DM24/€12 or DM29/€14.50) at the northern end of town, while there's a **campsite**, *Am Waldsee*, in the incorporated village of Fornsbach (☎0 71 92/64 36).

Schwäbisch Hall

SCHWÄBISCH HALL, which lies just beyond the Swabian Forest and south of the Hohenlohe plain, 55km east of Heilbronn, was an important centre of minting, making the silver Häller (or Heller), the smallest unit of currency used in the Holy Roman Empire. Though now long out of circulation, the Heller's name lives on as a simile for worthlessness in many idiomatic expressions in modern German. Ultimately, the coin's name derives from the industry on which the local economy was originally based: Hall means "Place of Salt". Excavations show that the salt springs attracted Celtic tribes to establish a permanent settlement here; following the medieval revival, they served as the keystone of local prosperity, only going into decline in the nineteenth century with discoveries of richer deposits elsewhere. Subsequent attempts to develop a more modern industrial base failed, as did a bid to make Hall a bathing and health resort on the lines of so many other German spas. Coupled with the fact that bombing in World War II caused little more than superficial grazing, this means that the town preserves an unusually intact reminder of its medieval self, complete with tantalizing insights into the social and political preoccupations of the time.

Arrival, information and accommodation

Schwäbisch Hall's **Bahnhof**, which lies on a branch line from Heilbronn, is on the western bank of the Kocher; it's a ten-minute walk to the centre straight ahead via Bahnhofstrasse, then over the river. Trains continue along the valley to **Bahnhof Hessental**, a junction on the fast Stuttgart–Nürnberg line, which is 3km southeast of the Altstadt by road. The **bus station** is by the bank of the Kocher at the northern fringe of the town centre. From the eastern edge of the Altstadt, buses #1 and #4 run to Bahnhof Hessental via the incorporated village of Hessental, which lies 1km north of its station. The **tourist office** (May–Sept Mon–Fri 9am–6pm, Sat & Sun 10am–3pm; Oct–April Mon–Fri 9am–5pm; ☎07 91/75 12 46, fax 75 13 97, *www.schwaebischhall.de*) is at Am Markt 9.

Both the town centre and Hessental offer a good choice of **hotels**. The **youth hostel** is at Langenfelderweg 5 (☎07 91/4 0 50, fax 4 79 98; DM24/€12 or DM29/€14.50); from the rear of Marktplatz, follow Crailsheimer Strasse (the ring road) in an easterly direction, then turn left into Blutsteige. South of town, at Steinbacher See, is the **campsite** (☎07 91/29 84; closed mid-Oct to March); take bus #4.

Hotels

Blauer Bock, Lange Str. 51–53 (☎07 91/8 94 62, fax 85 61 15). Gasthof in a Baroque building on the west side of the Kocher. It offers four well-appointed bedrooms and one of the town's top restaurants (closed Mon), which is well known for its freshwater fish dishes and has a summertime beer garden. ⑤.

Der Adelshof, Am Markt 12–13 (☎07 91/7 58 90, fax 60 36). Although this hotel is in a prominent historical building, the facilities are modern and include a fitness centre with sauna and solarium. It incorporates the *Ratskeller* restaurant (closed Sun & Mon evenings). ⑥.

Die Krone, Wirtsgasse 1, Hessental (☎07 91/9 40 30, fax 94 03 84, *www.ringhotels.de*). A member of the Ringhotel chain, this hotel occupies a group of buildings, including a splendid Baroque palace. It has a fine restaurant and good bathing facilities, including steam baths. ⑥.

Goldener Adler, Am Markt 11 (☎07 91/61 68, fax 73 15). This graceful half-timbered building with a beautiful two-storey oriel has been an inn since the sixteenth century; the front rooms offer a grandstand view of the theatrical events and festivals enacted outside. It has a reasonably priced restaurant serving local specialities. ⑥.

Hirsch, Sulzdorfer Str. 14, Hessental (☎07 91/9 39 02 20, fax 93 90 22 11). A traditional family-run Gasthof offering remarkably good-value accommodation and meals. Unusually, the en-suite rooms cost only slightly more than those without facilities. ②.

Hohenlohe, Weilertor 14 (☎07 91/7 58 70, fax 75 87 84, *www.ringhotels.de*). The town's most expensive address, another member of the Ringhotel chain, is a large complex of red-roofed buildings on the west bank of the Kocher. Its facilities include a large thermal swimming pool, a sauna, a terrace and a panoramic restaurant. ⑦.

Krone, Klosterstr. 1 (☎07 91/60 22). Moderately priced Gasthof just to the rear of Marktplatz. ④.

Wolf, Karl-Kurz-Str. 2, Hessental (☎07 91/93 06 60, fax 93 06 61 10). This half-timbered building closed to Bahnhof Hessental offers good-quality accommodation, but is primarily known for its gourmet *Eisenbahn* restaurant (closed Sat lunchtime & Mon), the best and most expensive in Schwäbisch Hall. ⑤.

The Town

The **Altstadt** occupies a hilly site on the east side of the sedate River Kocher. There's a medieval suburb on the west bank, while the most important historic monument, the **Klosterburg Gross Comburg**, is one of several notable attractions in the outskirts.

Marktplatz

The steeply sloping **Marktplatz** at the heart of the **Altstadt** is lined by a series of handsome buildings which form an encyclopedia of German architecture. Its present character was largely determined during the late medieval period, at a time when the rampantly successful bourgeoisie had ousted the aristocracy from control of the council, forcing many of the latter to leave town. As a symbol of the self-confident spirit, it was decided to build a spectacular new church, to be approached by a monumental flight of 42 (now 54) steps. The dramatic possibilities of this backdrop were immediately evident, and the space was used for jousting and tournaments. Since 1926, the Marktplatz has been put to use every summer as a hugely impressive **open-air theatre** (see p.272).

The late Gothic **Stadtkirche St Michael** has a nave in the hall church style with slender pillars and wide vaults, contrasting with the much higher choir, which was only completed in 1525, the year that the authorities of Hall decided to go over to Protestantism. Luther's youthful protégé **Johannes Brenz** – a far more tolerant figure than most of the leading lights of the time – came from Heidelberg to be the new preacher. His portrait can be seen on one of the memorials in the nave. Another particularly interesting memorial tablet is in the fourth chapel from the left in the ambulatory; this was made for his own tomb by the sixteenth-century artist and calligrapher Thomas Schweicker, who, as the self-portrait shows, painted with his feet, having been born without hands or arms. The most striking work of art, however, is Michel Erhart's impassioned *Crucifixion*, placed above the Netherlandish Passion retable at the high altar. For the best aerial view of the town, climb the **tower** (March to mid-Nov Mon 2–5pm, Tues–Sat 9am–noon & 2–5pm, Sun 11am–noon & 2–5pm; mid-Nov to Feb Tues–Sun 11am–noon & 2–3pm; DM2/€1), a survivor of the previous Romanesque church.

Another embellishment to the square, erected at the same time as the Münster's chancel, is the **Fischbrunnen**, showing St Michael in the company of two other warriors against evil, Samson and St George. Rather bizarrely, the structure also incorporates the pillory, still preserving the manacles which bound the wrong-doers. The north side of the square is lined with a picturesque jumble of buildings, including what are now two of the best hotels in town (see p.269). Opposite is a series of houses which traditionally belonged to various religious and charitable bodies. The west side of the square seems to be jinxed – the church which formerly stood there was destroyed by fire in the eighteenth century, to be replaced by the **Rathaus**, which was in turn a rare casualty of the last war. However, it's been successfully restored, its ritzy curved facade and stately belfry giving it the look of a sumptuous Baroque palace.

The rest of the centre

South of Marktplatz runs a series of alleys – Untere Herrngasse, Obere Herrngasse and Pfarrgasse – which are all lined with superb old buildings often linked to one another by stairways. They all lead to the **Stadtbefestigung**, which survives in part all round the town, unfortunately shorn of most of the towers which were demolished after Hall was incorporated into Württemberg in the Napoleonic era. Rising high above the weakest part of the defensive system is the massive **Neubau**, which, in spite of its name, dates back to the time of the Reformation. It served as an arsenal and granary, and is now a concert hall.

The other dominant building at this side of town is the eight-storey **Keckenburg**, a tower-house from the Staufer period. Together with a series of now interconnected historic buildings nearby, it contains the **Hällisch-Fränkisches Museum** (Tues & Thurs–Sun 10am–5pm, Wed 10am–8pm; free), which features displays on local archeology, history, industry, geology, crafts and sacred sculpture. Among the highlights is a roomful of works by **Leonhard Kern**, a local man who was one of the most accomplished German sculptors of the late Renaissance period. He specialized in highly refined, small-scale figures, the serene *St Sebastian* and the enigmatic *Cannibal* being two characteristic examples of his art. There's also an important collection of painted **marksmen's shields**, all authentically pocked with bullet holes; around eighty of these date back to the eighteenth century. In 2001, a branch of the museum is due to open in the **Stadtmühle**, an old mill by the riverside. This will house sections on the nineteenth century and on local Jewish life, including the complete interior furnishings of an synagogue of the 1730s which formerly stood in a nearby village.

The banks of the Kocher are lined with weeping willows and a picturesque group of stone and wooden bridges reaching out to three islets. From the largest of these, **Unterwöhrd**, is the classic **view** of the Altstadt, which can be seen rising majestically in tiers. The left bank, which had its own set of walls and towers, was the artisans' district; it clusters around **St Katharina**, a Gothic church with gorgeous fourteenth-century stained-glass windows. At the northern end is a reproduction of the oldest of the bridges, **Henkersbrücke** (Hangman's Bridge), named after the house on it, in which the holder of the least coveted municipal office was forced to live.

The northern part of the Altstadt presents another characterful old quarter, beginning at the **Säumarkt** (Pig Market), a couple of minutes' walk due north of Marktplatz, which features the Neoclassical guardhouse of the Württemberg army and a sixteenth-century weigh-house, behind which is the late seventeenth-century tannery, whose arcades were used for drying skins until 1972. Leading off the square is Gelbinger Gasse, the longest and arguably the finest street in Hall, whose buildings cover the full gamut of styles from Gothic to Jugendstil. Look out in particular for no. 25, the **Engelhardbau**, the Baroque mansion of a town councillor; and for no. 47, the late Renaissance **Gräterhaus**, whose beam decoration includes the scraping tools of the tanners, an indication that the house was built by a prosperous member of that guild. About halfway along the street is the **Josenturm**, a fortified tower to which a picturesque half-timbered upper storey was appended in 1680.

Comburg

Perched magisterially on its hill a couple of kilometres south of the centre of Hall via the banks of the Kocher is the awesome **Klosterburg Gross Comburg**. Fortress-monasteries are common enough in Spain and the Middle East, but such blatant expressions of the Church Militant are extremely rare in Western Europe. In 1079 this collegiate foundation was endowed by the count of Comburg, Burkhard II, who, as a cripple, felt unable to perform the normal aristocratic duties and decided to retire to a monastic life. Much of the original Romanesque architecture survives intact, including the mighty ring wall with its defensive towers. The extensive additions to the complex made down the years included the progressive strengthening of the entrance, and you now pass through the Baroque Bastion and the Renaissance Zwingertor before arriving at the Romanesque **Michaelstor**, guarding a twelve-metre-long tunnel which served as the last line of defence. As the Baroque monastic buildings are now used as a college, there's normally unrestricted entry to the courtyard. Here you can see another Romanesque survival, the hexagonal **Ebehardskapelle**, which is ornamented with a graceful dwarf gallery. Its function is disputed, but it probably served as an ossuary.

The **Klosterkirche** (April–Oct Tues–Fri 10am–noon & 2–5pm, Sat & Sun 2–5pm; DM4/€2) retains the three imperious towers of the first church, but was otherwise rebuilt in the Würzburg Baroque style. Although the exterior retains much of the austerity of its predecessor, the interior, with its gleaming white stuccowork, comes in complete contrast. It still preserves, however, two stunning twelfth-century treasures made in the monastery's once-celebrated workshop: an enormous golden wheel-shaped **chandelier** (which is even larger and more impressive than those in Aachen and Hildesheim, the only others to have survived) and the gilded beaten-copper **antependium** (altar front), which has engravings of Christ surrounded by his disciples. A number of masterly tombs, including that of the founder, can be seen in the **chapter house**, which still preserves its Romanesque form.

It's also worth crossing over to the hill directly opposite, crowned by the **Klein Comburg**. This was founded as a convent about thirty years after its big brother and was also used for some time as a hospice. The church here was always very much the poor relation, but scores in the fact that it preserves its simple original form.

Wackershofen

Some 5km northwest of Hall is the incorporated village of **WACKERSHOFEN**, which has recently been made a train stop in order to improve visitor access to the **Hohenloher Freilandmuseum** (March & April Tues–Sun 10am–5pm; May, Oct & Nov Tues–Sun 9am–6pm; June–Aug daily 9am–6pm; *www.wackershofen.de*; DM9/€4.50).

This brings together redundant rural buildings from throughout the north of Baden-Württemberg, including the Tauber valley and the eastern Jura but concentrating on the Hohenlohe region. Ceramics, furniture-making and textiles are among the crafts demonstrated, while there's a *Backofenfest* on the last weekend in September. A historic inn, *Roter Ochsen*, is among the reconstructed buildings, providing a handy stopping-off point for lunch.

Eating and drinking

The leading **restaurants** are to be found in the hotels, but there are many other less expensive places to eat and drink.

Café Ableitner, Bahnhofstr. 5–7. Old-world café with a summer garden commanding a wonderful view over the Kocher to the Altstadt.

Café am Markt, Am Markt 9–10. Another good *Kaffee und Kuchen* establishment, offering the choice between imbibing in the handsome Baroque interior, or sitting outside on the square.

Dew Drop Inn, Klosterstr. 5. A genuine Irish pub, offering 21 different beers and live music on Fri & Sat evenings.

Salzsieder, Schulgasse 4. Brasserie which serves breakfast from 9am, typical Swabian cooking at lunchtime and in the evenings. Closed Sun.

Schuhbäck, Untere Herrngasse 1–3. Gaststätte serving inexpensive local dishes. Closed Tues.

Waldhorn, Untere Herrngasse 14. Italian restaurant with a wood-fired pizza oven in a prominent building at the top of the town.

Würth, Im Weiler 8–10. Weinstube with beer garden; also serves full meals.

Zum Alten Brauhaus, Mauerstr. 17. The main tap of the Haller Löwenbrauerei, which makes a range of beers, including a fine *Zwickelbier*. Also serves both German and Balkan cuisine.

Entertainment and festivals

Schwäbisch Hall has a strong **theatre** tradition, with pride of place taken by the *Freilichtspiele*, the open-air season on Marktplatz. This runs from late May to mid-August, and usually features a play by Shakespeare, a European classic and a modern work. Performances start at 8.30pm, but the scramble for the best seats begins as early as 6pm. Since 2000, the town has had a second, very different open-air stage, the wooden Haller-Globe-Theater on Unterwöhrd, a reproduction of Shakespeare's original Globe. Tickets for both venues can be purchased from the special counter in the tourist office (☎07 91/75 16 00), and cost DM10/€5 for standing room, DM20–50/€10–25 for seats. The town also has a prestigious Marionettentheater, which is near the left-bank quay at Im Lindbach 9 (☎07 91/4 85 36); it uses both historical and modern puppets and has shows for both children and adults.

The local salt heritage is celebrated each Whit weekend in one of Baden-Württemberg's most famous **festivals**, the *Kuchen- und Brunnenfest der Haller Salzsieder* (Cake and Fountain Festival of the Salt-Simmerers of Hall). This commemorates the occasion when the salt workers quenched a fire at the Stadtmühle. It features dancing and music on the Grasbödele (one of the islets) by the simmerers in their red, black and white historical costume, as well as a realistic simulation of the blaze. Additionally, historical tableau are re-enacted on Marktplatz, and there are processions through the streets of the Altstadt.

Schwäbisch Gmünd

SCHWÄBISCH GMÜND is 45km south of Schwäbisch Hall, and a similar distance east of Stuttgart on an almost dead straight rail line. The town lies in the heart of the

Stauferland, a countryside of castle-crowned conical hills, gentle slopes, lush meadows and juniper heathland straddling the northern end of the Swabian Jura and the southern edge of the Swabian Forest. It's named after its former feudal overlords, the Hohenstaufen dynasty, who were among the dominant forces of early medieval Germany and Italy.

The Town

Gmünd was founded by the first of the Hohenstaufen emperors, Conrad III, but after the family died out it became a Free Imperial City. Known in the Middle Ages for the luxury goods produced by its goldsmiths, silversmiths, jewellers, glass-blowers and watchmakers, today it's a lively provincial town with a compact Altstadt dominated by one of Germany's seminal churches.

The Heiligkreuzmünster

Around 1310, the citizens began the construction of the **Heiligkreuzmünster** as the centrepiece of their town. Some time later, Heinrich Parler arrived from Cologne and took charge of operations; he was later aided by his son Peter, who was soon after called to Prague, where he developed into one of the most brilliant and imaginative architects Europe ever produced. The Parler style – of which this church is recognized as the prototype – soon usurped France's long-standing architectural leadership and made its mark on a host of cities throughout central Europe. The celebrity status of the family is confirmed by the fact that, in contrast to the general anonymity of most of the masons who designed the great medieval cathedrals, they are relatively well documented. In spite of the lack of a tower, the Münster, whose exterior bristles with highly elaborate pinnacles, gables and gargoyles, floats high above the town. Its five entrance **portals** introduce the characteristic Parler sculpture, which aimed at a far greater sense of realism than had hitherto been in vogue. The figures are short and stocky, and are often placed in dramatic relationships to each other; they have lifelike facial expressions and wear contemporary dress, with heavy horizontal drapery folds.

However, there's no doubt that it's the **interior** which is the real show-stopper; it was the first hall church to be erected in southern Germany, and triumphantly gives the lie to the theory that this form of building is inherently dull and unvaried. Standing just inside the main western entrance, you're confronted by the majestic spectacle of 22 huge rounded pillars marching towards the choir. They support a coloured vault which grows ever richer, moving from a fanciful pattern of ribs in the nave to a rich tapestry of network and star shapes in the chancel which, contrary to normal practice, was the last part to be built. The ring of side chapels, cleverly placed between the buttresses so that their presence is not immediately apparent from outside, contains a wealth of late Gothic altarpieces, notably a *Tree of Jesse* in the baptistery. Above the seats of the Renaissance stalls stand animated figures of the apostles (on the left) and Old Testament prophets; a peculiarity is that each figure is carved twice and placed back-to-back, so that it faces the ambulatory as well as the choir.

The rest of the town

The original parish church, the octagonal-towered **Johanniskirche** (May–Oct Tues–Fri 10am–noon & 2–4pm, Sat 2–4pm, Sun 10am–noon & 2–4pm; DM1/€0.50) on the central Bocksgasse, is overshadowed by the Münster but is nevertheless a highly unusual building. It dates from the very end of the Romanesque period in the mid-thirteenth century and is extravagantly adorned all round its exterior with delicate reliefs of fantastic animals, fables, hunting scenes, flowers and foliage. The interior has nineteenth-century pastel murals and also serves as a repository for original lapidary fragments from the Münster and elsewhere.

Facing the west end of the Johanniskirche is the **Prediger**, a former Dominican friary which has been converted into a cultural centre, including the **Predigermuseum** (Tues, Wed & Fri 2–5pm, Thurs 2–7pm, Sat & Sun 11am–5pm; free) which contains good collections of medieval and Baroque sculpture, in addition to examples of the town's expertise in jewellery-making – the most notable being a fifteenth-century cross – and the usual local history displays. On the opposite side of the Johanniskirche, the **Marktplatz**, now largely Baroque in character, has several cheerful mansions and a rather saccharine fountain bearing a double-sided statue of the Madonna and Child. However, there are also a number of half-timbered houses from earlier periods, notably the **Amtshaus Spital** at the far end. A bit further east are four of the five remaining towers of the fourteenth-century city wall, with the highest of the group, the **Königsturm**, a short walk to the south.

Behind the Hauptbahnhof, there's a wonderful wooded uphill walk along Taubentalstrasse, past shrines dating as far back as the fifteenth century and a life-sized Calvary to the dark, secret **St-Salvator-Kapelle** at the top. This former hermit's cave and its adjoining stone-walled rooms are bedecked with candles, icons, statues and other religious paraphernalia.

Practicalities

The **Hauptbahnhof** is just to the northwest of the centre, which is reached by following Uferstrasse straight ahead, before turning into Bocksgasse. The **tourist office** (Mon–Fri 9am–5.30pm, Sat 9am–noon; ☎0 71 71/6 03 42 50, fax 6 03 42 99, *www. schwaebisch-gmuend.de*) is in the half-timbered former Kornhaus at Kornhausstr. 14.

Among the centrally placed **hotels**, cheapest are *Gasthof Weisser Ochsen*, Parlerstr. 47 (☎0 71 71/28 12; ②), and *Gasthaus Hopfensitz*, Klarenbergstr. 8 (☎0 71 71/24 08; ③). More upmarket choices include *Patrizier*, Kornhausstr. 25 (☎0 71 71/92 70 30; ④–⑥), *Einhorn*, Rinderbacher Gasse 10 (☎0 71 71/6 30 23; ⑤), and *Das Pelikan*, Türlensteg 9 (☎0 71 71/35 90; ⑥). The **campsite**, *Schurrenhof* (☎0 71 65/81 90), lies to the west of town.

All the hotels listed above have good **restaurants**, though there are plenty of recommendable alternatives. Best for traditional Swabian fare is the historic *Fuggerei*, Münstergasse 2, though it's on the expensive side. *Kübele*, Engelgasse 2, is a good, less pricey alternative; it's also the main tap for the local Aloisle beers, which are made with the soft spring-water of the Swabian Jura. Also very fine is the *Stadtgarten* restaurant in the eponymous park between the Hauptbahnhof and the centre, which has dining rooms in two adjacent buildings – a miniature Rococo palace and the Stadthalle, the town's main concert venue. Gmünd has some superb **cafés** including *Margrit*, Johannisplatz 10, which has delicious cakes, the long-established *Zieher*, Marktgässle 3, and *Spielplatz* at Münsterplatz 12, which often features exhibitions of contemporary international artists. Local **bars** include *Bierakademie*, Ledergasse 50, which serves what it claims are the fifteen best brews in the world, and *Taverne*, Kornhausstr. 13, which is the main concession to the American community, fitted out to resemble a saloon bar of the Fifties.

On the second Saturday in June, the *Schwabenalter* **festival** celebrates those who have passed their 40th birthday – the watershed year for the acquisition of true wisdom, according to Swabian custom. The following Saturday is devoted to 50-year-olds, the next to 60-year-olds, and so. Otherwise, *Fastnet* is the main event, reaching a climax on Shrove Tuesday.

Tübingen

"We have a town on our campus," runs a local saying in **TÜBINGEN**. No irony is intended – the **University** dominates the life of this city to an extent unparalleled even in

Schloss Neuschwanstein, Hohenschwangau

Ceiling fresco, the Wieskirche

Oktoberfest, Munich

Steamer on the Königssee

Corpus Christi procession, Bamberg

The Gebrûder-Maisel-Brauerei, Bayreuth

The Black Forest

The Residenz and Hofgarten, Würzburg

View of the city from the River Inn, Passau

Heidelberg from the Philosophenweg

The Kuchen- und Brunnenfest,
Schwäbisch Hall

The Rathaus facade, Ulm

The Neue Staatsgalerie, Stuttgart

Germany's other world-famous centres of learning, such as Heidelberg, Marburg and Göttingen. Over half the population of 70,000 is in some way connected with the university, and the current size of the town is due entirely to the twentieth-century boom in higher education – it was not until a hundred years ago that the number of inhabitants reached five figures, having remained static since the time of the university's foundation in 1477.

Tübingen's **setting**, on the gentle slopes above the willow-lined banks of the Neckar, some 50km upstream from Stuttgart, immediately sets the tone of the place. Upstream, the river follows a turbulent course, but here it's serene and placid, the perfect backdrop for the unhurried and unworldly groves of academe. With its students punting on the river on a balmy summer evening, the town is often described as a German counterpart of Oxford or Cambridge. Study is a very serious business here, however, with no nostalgic wallowings in ancient traditions – other than the small and discredited duelling *Verbindungen*. High jinks by the students are kept firmly in check and the prevailing atmosphere is of peace and quiet and of scholarly contemplation.

Arrival, information and accommodation

The **Hauptbahnhof** and **bus station** are side by side, just five minutes' walk from the Altstadt – turn right and follow Karlstrasse straight ahead. En route, at An der Neckarbrücke, is the **tourist office** (Easter–Sept Mon–Fri 9am–7pm, Sat 9am–5pm, Sun 2–5pm; rest of year closed Sun; ☎0 70 71/9 13 60, fax 3 50 70, *www.tuebingen-info .de*). **Mitfahrzentrale** is at Provenceweg 2 (☎0 70 71/1 94 40 or 50 81).

The tourist office has details of **private rooms** (①–③). There are **hotels** in all categories, though they are quite thin on the ground in the centre. The **youth hostel** is on the bank of the Neckar, a short walk to the right on the far side of the bridge at Gartenstr. 22/2 (☎0 70 71/2 30 02, fax 2 50 61; DM26/€13 or DM31/€15.50). To reach the **campsite**, also with a riverside setting, at Rappenberghalde (☎0 70 71/4 31 45), it's quicker to turn left from the Hauptbahnhof, and cross at Alleenbrücke.

Hotels and guesthouses

Am Bad, Am Freibad 2 (☎0 70 71/7 30 71, fax 7 53 36). Hotel backing onto a huge open-air swimming pool in a quiet park setting in the southwest of town, reached by bus #18 or #19. Its restaurant serves evening meals to guests only. ⑤.

Am Schloss, Burgsteige 18 (☎0 70 71/9 29 40, fax 92 94 10, *www.hotelamschloss.de*). Characterful hotel in a half-timbered building immediately below Schloss Hohentübingen; it also has more basic rooms in an annexe across the street. No fewer than 28 different kinds of Maultaschen are among the many different Swabian specialities on the menu of its restaurant *Mauganeschtle*. ④–⑦.

Barbarina, Wilhelmstr. 94 (☎0 70 71/2 60 48, fax 55 08 39). Fine middle-range hotel in the northeast of town, reached by bus #1, #2, #6 or #7. It also has a good restuarant, though this is open Mon–Fri evenings only. ⑥.

Hospiz, Neckarhalde 2 (☎0 70 71/92 40, fax 92 42 00). Medium-priced hotel in an imposing old building right in the heart of the Altstadt, with a good restaurant (Mon–Fri only). ⑥.

IB Gästehaus (Sprachinstitut Tübingen), Eugenstr. 71 (☎0 70 71/9 35 40, fax 3 84 57). This modern languages centre has a guesthouse geared mainly towards students taking their courses, but normally has rooms available for other visitors. ④.

Krone, Uhlandstr. 1 (☎0 70 71/1 33 10, fax 13 31 32). Tübingen's top hotel, situated just south of Eberhardsbrücke, has been in existence for well over a century, and remains strongly traditional. It has a similarly high-class restaurant. ⑦.

Kürner, Weizsäckerstr. 1 (☎0 70 71/2 27 35, fax 2 79 20). Moderately priced hotel with restaurant in the northeastern quarters; take bus #1, #4 or #7. ④.

Landhotel Hirsch, Schönbuchstr. 28, Bebenhausen (☎0 70 71/6 80 27, fax 60 08 03). Country house-style hotel and restaurant, reached by bus #826 or #828. ⑦.

Marianne, Johannesweg 14 (☎0 70 71/9 37 40, fax 93 74 99). Small guesthouse in the south of town, a ten-minute walk from the Hauptbahnhof. ③.

Sonne, Schönbuchstr. 15, Bebenhausen (☎0 70 71/6 74 01, fax 6 77 49). Good-value Gasthof, take bus #826 or #828. ④.

The Town

The Altstadt, having been spared the ravages of war, is a visual treat, a mixture of brightly painted half-timbered and gabled houses ranging from the fifteenth to the eighteenth century, grouped into twisting and plunging alleys. There are few truly outstanding buildings, but the whole ensemble is much more than the sum of its parts. Two large squares – **Holzmarkt** and the **Markt** – provide a setting for communal activities. The best **view** is from the Eberhardsbrücke over the Neckar, which embraces the Altstadt, the waterfront and the Platanenallee, the celebrated promenade along the man-made island in the river.

Holzmarkt

Dominating **Holzmarkt** is the **Stiftskirche St Georg**, an outwardly gaunt late Gothic church erected at the end of the fifteenth century, with a contrastingly stunning interior. Under the extravagant stellar vault of the nave, the pulpit is adorned with reliefs of the Madonna and the Four Doctors of the Church, and crowned by a tapering canopy. A triple-arched rood screen sheltering a painted retable by Hans Schäufelein, a pupil of Dürer, leads to the **chancel** (Easter–June, Sept & Oct Fri–Sun 11.30am–5pm; July & Aug daily 11.30am–5pm; DM2/€1). Here an outstanding series of stained-glass lancet windows, dating from the same period as the church's construction, cast their reflections on the pantheon of the House of Württemberg. In 1342 this family bought Tübingen, then no more than a village, from the local grandee; on the promotion of their territory to a duchy in 1495, they made the town their second residence. The thirteen **tombs** show the development of Swabian sculpture in the Gothic and Renaissance periods; finest is that of Countess Mechthild, made in the workshop of Hans Multscher of Ulm. Look out also for the monument to Duke Eberhard the Bearded, founder of the university. The **tower** (same hours and ticket) can be ascended for a view over the red roofs of Tübingen to the Neckar and the Swabian Jura.

Also on the square are the **Georgsbrunnen**, a fountain with a statue of St George, and the Buchhandlung Heckenhauer, where Hermann Hesse spent a four-year apprenticeship as a bookbinder and bookseller at the end of the last century, having dropped out of formal education.

On the far corner of Holzmarkt, which doubles as part of Munzgasse, is the original home of the university, the **Alte Aula**, rebuilt in Baroque style for celebrations marking the 300th anniversary of its foundation. Also here, at no. 15, is **Cottahaus**, the former headquarters of the famous company, now based in Stuttgart, which represented the high point of Tübingen's publishing tradition, begun soon after the foundation of the university. **Johann Friedrich Cotta**, who took over an ailing family company set up five generations previously, was an extremely astute and successful publisher; through friendship with Schiller, he came to know and publish all the leading figures of the German Enlightenment, and also set up the *Allgemeine Zeitung*, whose independence and liberal views came as a blast of fresh air in the context of the censored and despotically controlled press of the time. The **Studentenkarzer** (Students' Prison) at no. 20 in the same street is older than the one in Heidelberg and has more artistic graffiti, but unfortunately isn't so accessible (guided tours April–Oct Sat, Sun & holidays at 2pm; DM1/€0.50).

The Hölderlinturm and Evangelisches Stift

Overlooking the banks of the Neckar on Bursagasse, the street immediately below Holzmarkt, is the **Hölderlinturm** (Tues–Fri 10am–noon & 3–5pm, Sat & Sun 2–5pm; DM3/€1.50). Originally part of the medieval fortifications, it's now named after one of

Tübingen's most famous alumni, **Friedrich Hölderlin**, who lived here in the care of a carpenter's family, hopelessly but harmlessly insane, from 1807 until his death 36 years later. There's a collection of memorabilia of the poet, largely ignored in his lifetime, but now regarded as one of the greatest Germany ever produced. Just before the onset of his madness, he produced his most striking work, grandiose apocalyptic visions couched in complex language and original imagery, showing the anguished state of his own existence – "A son of earth I seem, born to love and suffer."

At the end of Bursagasse is the **Evangelisches Stift**, a Protestant seminary established in a former Augustinian monastery in 1547 as the theological faculty of the university. The great astronomer Johannes Kepler studied here at the end of the sixteenth century, and Hölderlin, who never managed to find the sense of belief to accompany his essentially religious outlook, was another of its students; he was joined by his classmates, Hegel and Schelling, subsequently the dominant figures of German philosophy. From here you can continue down Neckarhalde; at no. 24 is the birthplace of **Christoph Uhland**, the lyric poet and chronicler of old German legends.

The Markt, the Schloss and around

The **Markt**, heart of old Tübingen, is just a short walk uphill from the Stift. It preserves many of its Renaissance mansions, along with a fountain dedicated to Neptune, round which markets are held on Mondays, Wednesdays and Fridays. The **Rathaus**, originally fifteenth century but much altered down the years, is covered with historical frescoes, though these are hardly more than a hundred years old; other eye-catching features are the pulpit-like balcony for public announcements and the gabled pediment housing an astronomical clock made in 1511.

Burgsteige, one of the oldest and most handsome streets in town, climbs steeply from the corner of the Markt to **Schloss Hohentübingen**, the Renaissance successor to the original eleventh-century feudal castle. Entry is via a superb **gateway** in the form of a triumphal arch, made in 1604. It's adorned with the arms of the House of Württemberg and the riband of the Order of the Garter; the latter had recently been bestowed on Duke Friedrich by Queen Elizabeth I. A second, less ornate doorway leads to the heavily restored courtyard, which still needs time to mellow. One wing of this has recently been given over to the **Universitätsmuseum** (Wed–Sun 10am–6pm; DM4/€2). One of the largest university museums in the world, it features important archeology displays, notably from the Ice Age and ancient Egypt, as well as the collections of the history and ethnology departments. Weekend guided tours around the Schloss **prison**, and the **cellars** with a vat capable of holding 85,000 litres, have been available in the past, but are currently suspended, hopefully only temporarily.

The northwestern part of town, immediately below the Schloss, has traditionally been reserved for the non-academic community, particularly the *Gogen* (vine-growers) who are renowned for their rich fund of earthy humour. Here are some of the city's oldest and most spectacular half-timbered buildings, such as the municipal **Kornhaus** (Tues–Fri 3–6pm, Sat & Sun 11am–6pm; free) on the alley of the same name, which now contains the local history museum, and the **Fruchtschranne**, the storehouse for the yields of the ducal orchards, on Bachgasse.

The northeastern quarters

The quarter to the northeast of the Markt is once more dominated by the university. Down Collegiumsgasse is the **Wilhelmstift**, built in the late sixteenth century as the Collegium Illustre, an academy for members of the Protestant nobility, but since 1817 the site of the Catholic seminary. This building became the focus of worldwide media attention in the early 1970s when its leading theologian, the Swiss **Hans Küng**, published a series of articles and books attacking cherished doctrines, notably papal infallibility. The upshot was that he was stripped of his sacral offices, but he has remained in Tübingen as a professor (now with emeritus status), a celebrity, an ecumenical leader – and a Catholic. Crossing Lange Gasse and continuing along Metzgergasse, you come to the **Nonnenhaus**, most photogenic of the half-timbered houses, with its outside stairway and *Sprachhaus*.

Just outside the northeastern boundary of the old town is the **Alter Botanischer Garten**. This has been replaced by another complex (Mon–Fri 7.30am–4.45pm, Sat & Sun 10am–noon & 1.30–4.30pm; free), complete with arboretum and hothouses, located, along with most of the modern buildings of the university, a kilometre or so north by the ring road. The gardens serve as a reminder that botany has long been one of Tübingen's strong subjects. One of the leading lights in the academic life of the sixteenth century, Leonhard Fuchs (after whom the fuchsia is named), published an exhaustive and practical encyclopedia on plants and their medicinal properties. To the east, at Philosophenweg 76, the **Kunsthalle** (Tues–Sun variable hours and charges; *www.kunsthalle-tuebingen.de*) hosts tempting art exhibitions, sometimes of international standing.

Eating, drinking and entertainment

Predictably, Tübingen is awash with student **bars**, **cafés** and **discos**, and also has plenty of good **restaurants**. For highbrow **culture**, there's a choice between the traditional fare of plays and concerts at the Landestheater, Eberhardstr. 6 (☎0 70 71/9 31 31), and the experimental productions of the tiny Zimmertheater, Bursagasse 16 (☎0 70 71/9 27 30). **Rowing boats** and **punts** can be rented at Neckarbrücke. Throughout the summer, a number of companies offer **piloted punting** trips from the quayside beside the Hölderlinturm; these cost around DM10/€5 per person and leave as soon as there are enough passengers.

Restaurants

Forelle, Kronenstr. 8. *Gemütlich* old Weinstube in a listed nineteenth-century building, serving good fish and game specialities.

Krumme Brücke, Kornhausstr. 17. Tiny restaurant with kitsch decor and a varied menu including plenty of inexpensive Swabian dishes and vegetarian options.

Museum, Wilhelmstr. 3. Well-regarded restaurant at the corner of Alter Botanischer Garten; it's fairly pricey, but does good-value business lunches.

Ratskeller, Haaggasse 4. Cellar restaurant whose speciality is giant pancakes. Evenings only.

Rosenau, Rosenau 15. Expensive gourmet restaurant on the heights above the northern end of town, close to the Botanischer Garten. Closed Mon.

Waldhorn, Schönbuchstr. 49, Bebenhausen. An even more prestigious restaurant, generally agreed to be the best in Tübingen. Serves both international cuisine and traditional local dishes. Closed Mon & Tues.

Wurstküche, Am Lustnauer Tor 8. Cosy restaurant serving good Swabian fare.

Bars and Cafés

Bären, Schmiedtorstr. 3. Opens at 6am Mon–Sat and is consequently popular with both early risers and night owls finishing off the previous evening.

Café Lieb, Karlstr. 6. Traditional coffee house serving the best cakes in town.

Marktschenke, Am Markt 11. Lively student bar with jukebox.

Neckarbistro, Neckargasse 22. Modern-style bistro serving good breakfasts and snacks.

Neckarmüller, Gartenstr. 4. Hausbrauerei with a big beer garden on the north bank of the Neckar by Eberhardsbrücke. Makes light and dark *Weizen* beers; also serves full meals, including bargain lunches and a decent vegetarian selection.

Piccolo Sole d'Oro, Metzgergasse 39. Italian café which is one of the places to be seen. In summer you can sit outside on the so-called "Plaza Tübingen".

Discos and live music pubs

Cinderella, Düsseldorfer Str. 4. Big disco which plays chart and techno; particularly popular with younger punters. Open Wed–Sat.

Foyer an der Blauen Brücken, Friedrichstr. 12. Student disco in former French army cafeteria. Fri & Sat only.

Jazzkeller, Haaggasse 15/2. Discos on Mon, Thurs & Sat, live jazz or blues Wed.

Zentrum Zoo, Schleifmühleweg 86. Hugely popular live music pub with beer garden which features regular disco sessions.

Bebenhausen

Immediately to the north of the built-up area of Tübingen are the former hunting grounds of the dukes and kings of Württemberg, now re-stocked with deer and designated as the **Naturpark Schönbuch**. The main road to Stuttgart cuts right through this protected landscape, but its 150 square kilometres are virtually uninhabited – a welcome break from the urban area which encircles it. Within the park is the village of **BEBENHAUSEN**, just 5km north of the centre of Tübingen, of which it's now officially a part. It can be reached by bus #826 or #828, but it's far more fun to sample the park's scenery on foot. There's a choice of **trails** – you can either follow the course of the Goldersbach, parallel to the main road, or else set out from the Botanical Gardens in Tübingen and continue via Heuberger Tor and the path beside the Bettelbach.

In 1190, a group of Cistercian monks arrived in Bebenhausen, taking over from a Premonstratensian congregation which had settled there just a decade before. The **Abtei** (Tues–Fri 9am–noon & 2–6pm, Sat & Sun 9am–6pm; DM5/€2.50) is set in a walled enclosure with many half-timbered outbuildings matching those in the village; the main complex presents a cross-section of medieval European architecture. That the buildings survive in remarkably complete condition is due to the fact that they were converted into a (now defunct) Protestant seminary after the Reformation.

The best place to begin a tour is the **Abteikirche**. Built in the Transitional style between Romanesque and Gothic characteristic of the Cistercians, it was completed in 1228, but modernized a century later with the addition of the huge, airy east window, still with the original stained glass in between the tracery. At the beginning of the fifteenth century an eccentric crown-shaped tower topped with a miniature openwork steeple was built over the crossing. Unfortunately, the nave was truncated to a third of its original size after the suppression of the monastery, so the dimensions are now more those of a chapel.

A suite of rooms – the chapter house, *parlatorium* and lay brothers' hall – was built along the east walk of the present **cloister** in a pure early Gothic style after work had finished on the church. In the middle of the fourteenth century, the **summer refectory** was added to the southern side. Not only is this Bebenhausen's great glory, it's one of the finest Gothic buildings in Germany, a dining room like no other. Three central pillars stand like palm trees sprouting out their branches to form a vault of consummate grace and precision, which is painted with motifs of plants and birds. Later, the outer walls of the cloister were built, including a pretty **well-house**. This isn't quite symmetrical, as the mason himself realized, playfully confessing his guilt by adding a corbel of a fool holding up a mirror to show him where he had gone wrong.

Also in the monastery grounds is the **Jagdschloss** (guided tours on the hour: Tues–Fri 9–11am & 2–5pm, Sat & Sun 10am, 11am & 2–5pm; DM6/€3) of the kings of Württemberg. This was adapted from the monastery's former guesthouse and is luxuriantly furnished in nineteenth-century style, with many souvenirs of the chase. The building later did improbable service as a parliament, being the headquarters of the Land of South Württemberg-Hohenzollern (Südwürttemberg-Hohenzollern), which was set up by the French in 1945, but merged into the more viable province of Baden-Württemberg seven years later.

The Swabian Jura

The **Swabian Jura** (Schwäbische Alb) is the name given to the series of limestone plateaux forming the watershed between the valleys of the rivers Rhine, Neckar and Danube. It's a harsh, craggy landscape, with poor soils and a severe climate, though its appearance has mellowed thanks to the plantation of forests. Geological faults have meant that individual mountains have become detached from the main mass; these formed ideal natural defensive fortresses for feudal overlords, and many are still crowned by castles. The Jura has few towns and even less in the way of major sights; the area is primarily of note for its **hiking** possibilities. As usual in Germany, marked trails cross the countryside, and the views on offer have a majestic sweep, even if they're often rather monotonous. It's an area rich in **flora**, with thistles, daphnes, anemones and lady's slippers being particularly prominent. Highlights of the region are the beautiful little town of **Haigerloch**, the old ducal capital of **Bad Urach**, the relaxing resort of **Zwiefalten** and the fantasy castles outside **Lichtenstein** and **Hechingen**.

The following section describes the western and central parts of the Jura. For the southern and eastern border (which has much the grandest scenery of all), see p.288; while for the area to the north, where the Jura merges imperceptibly into the Stauferland, see p.273. **Public transport** in the area is slightly complicated. The rail lines tend to run parallel to each other, involving circuitous connections, while some of the bus companies are entirely in private hands.

Bad Urach

BAD URACH, some 30km east of Tübingen, is linked to Reutlingen, an industrial town on the main Stuttgart–Tübingen rail route, by the Ermstalbahn, a branch line recently reinstated after a quarter-century gap. Bad Urach is primarily a health resort and has a typical spa quarter at the western end of town. Nevertheless, the town centre has many half-timbered houses (otherwise a rarity in the Jura), including an impressive sixteenth-century group on **Marktplatz**, which also boasts a late Gothic fountain with a statue of St Christopher.

In 1442, when the county of Württemberg was partitioned, Urach became one of the two capitals and a new **Residenzschloss** (Tues–Sun 9am–noon & 1–4/5pm; DM5/€2.50), an unusually large-scale example of half-timbering, was built. The most impressive rooms are the Gothic **Türnitz** on the ground floor, and the **Goldener Saal** upstairs. Both were originally built by Eberhard the Bearded, who was born in the town and later reunited Württemberg as a duchy, but were sumptuously transformed at the end of the Renaissance epoch. Also on view is an impressive collection of Baroque sleighs formerly exhibited in the Landesmuseum in Stuttgart. Likewise associated with Eberhard is the **Stiftskirche** opposite, erected in late Gothic style by his court architect, Peter von Koblenz; the octagonal tower was, however, only completed in the nineteenth century.

Just to the west of town is the **Uracher Wasserfall**, set in beautiful secluded surroundings. Further into the hills are more waterfalls, a nature reserve and the ruined **Burg Hohenurach**, the original feudal castle, which is freely accessible at all times and commands a magnificent panoramic view over the town and the Jura. Continuing westwards, towards the tiny village of Glems, the scenery gets more and more luxuriant, brimming with wild flowers and foliage.

Practicalities

Bad Urach's unmanned dead-end **Bahnhof** is directly opposite the Residenzschloss; trains also stop at the **Kurgebiet-Wasserfall** halt at the western end of town. The **tourist office** is in the Kurverwaltung, Bei den Thermen 4 (Mon–Fri 9–11.45am &

2–4.45pm, Sat 9–11.45am; ☎0 71 25/9 43 20, fax 94 32 22, *www.badurach.de*); brochures can also be picked up from the Rathaus on Marktplatz during working hours. There are around a score of **private houses** (①–③) with rooms to let. Comparable rates are available at a number of **hotels**, including *Gasthof Weberbleiche*, Weberbleiche 11 (☎0 71 25/46 88 52; ②), *Krone*, Marktplatz 17 (☎0 71 25/81 48; ③), *Fanfarenhof*, Ulmer Str. 1 (☎0 71 25/4 06 63; ③), and *Gasthof Wilder Mann*, Pfählerstr. 7 (☎0 71 25/88 68; ③), which has its own small brewery, Quenzer, attached. More upmarket are *Buck*, Neue Str. 5–7 (☎0 71 25/9 49 40; ④–⑤); *Frank Vier Jahreszeiten*, which occupies a splendid timber-framed building at Stuttgarter Str. 5 (☎0 71 25/9 43 40; ⑤); and the spa hotel *Graf Eberhard*, Bei den Thermen 2 (☎0 71 25/14 80; ⑤–⑧). The **youth hostel** is at Burgstr. 45 (☎0 71 25/80 25, fax 4 03 58; DM22/€11 or DM26/€13) by the trailheads at the western side of town. Bad Urach has many elegant **cafés**, while there are high-class **restaurants** in each of the last three hotels, more homely ones in the others.

Lichtenstein and Sonnenbühl

LICHTENSTEIN is the designation given to a federation of villages 12km south of Reutlingen and 10km east of Tübingen. The name is taken from the **Schloss** (guided tours Feb, March & Nov Sat, Sun & holidays 9am–noon & 1–5pm; April–Oct Mon–Sat 9am–noon & 1–5pm; Sun 9am–5.30pm; DM6/€3), set on a high, narrow peak, and familiar through its appearance on the covers of all the tourist brochures to the region. Like many other castles in the area, it's a Romantic fantasy, erected in the 1840s as a replacement for one demolished in 1802. In the rebuilding, the architects were strongly influenced by the imaginary descriptions of its predecessor contained in the historical novel *Lichtenstein*, which was published in 1826. This was written by a remarkable author, Wilhelm Hauff, who died at the age of 25 but bequeathed a very considerable output, including many fairy stories which are still popular in Germany today. Inside the Schloss there's an excellent collection of arms and armour, while the chapel has Gothic stained-glass windows and a beautiful fifteenth-century altarpiece. It's a good thirty minutes' walk from Lichtenstein to the castle, but worth doing for the fantastic views across the Jura.

Within the neighbouring municipality of **SONNENBÜHL** are two of the most easily accessible caves in the Jura. The **Nebelhöhle** (Misty Cave; March & Nov Sat & Sun 9am–5pm; April–Oct daily 9am–5.30pm; DM5/€2.50), which can be reached by marked footpath from Schloss Lichtenstein, is an impressive stalactite grotto, some 380m in length. Although its full extent was only discovered in the nineteenth century, it had long been used as a refuge by the Württemberg dukes. You're allowed to wander around at leisure, instead of being subjected to a guided tour. A similar formation, the **Bärenhöhle** (Bears' Cave; same times; DM5/€2.50) is 3km south of Lichtenstein near Erpfingen, one of the villages which forms part of Sonnenbühl.

Zwiefalten

Continuing southeast, the peaceful health resort of **ZWIEFALTEN** lies in a valley at the edge of the Swabian Jura, just a few kilometres north of the Danube. Its name, meaning "duplicate waters", refers to the two streams which converge at this point. In the late eleventh century, a daughter church of Hirsau was established here. The huge Romanesque monastic complex survived until 1738 when, in preparation for its change in status to an Imperial Abbey, and in accordance with the passion for all things Baroque, it was demolished to make way for an entirely new set of buildings. This arrangement lasted for only a few decades. After the Napoleonic suppression, the church was given to the local Catholic parish and the outbuildings were converted into an asylum – a situation which persists to this day.

The **Münster**, the former monastic church, is a worthy rival to the great pilgrimage churches of Bavaria. Its highly original design, largely the work of **Johann Michael Fischer**, is already apparent from the outside, with its identical white towers and their green onion domes. Standing by the entrance grille, your eye is drawn down the enormous length of the church, yet is also diverted to the wavy lines of the side chapels; to the grey and rose marble columns with their gold-leaf capitals which shine like jewels against the pristine white walls; to the huge vault paintings glorifying the Virgin; and to the confessionals shaped like fantastic grottoes. At the far end, a statue of the fiery prophet Ezekiel set in an elaborate baldachin with depictions of the coming fall of Babylon faces the **pulpit**, whose base illustrates his visions of sin and death, while the sounding board depicts the triumphant power of the cross. The monks' choir is the most extravagantly sumptuous part of all, featuring a virtuoso set of walnut **stalls**, adorned with gilded limewood reliefs illustrating the life of the Virgin. Note that the entrance grille is generally closed between 11am and 1pm during the summer and all day through the week in winter, leaving you only with the sweeping initial view.

Following the Ach, one of Zwiefalten's rivers, for a couple of kilometres north of town, brings you to the **Friedrichshöhle** (or **Wimsener Höhle**), where it disappears underground. This is the only subterranean river in Germany which is readily accessible to the public; it's possible to penetrate a short way along the crystal-clear waters into the cave by **boat** (April–Oct daily 9am–5.30pm; DM4/€2) before the passage becomes too narrow.

Practicalities

The **tourist office** (Mon, Wed & Fri 8am–noon, Tues 8am–noon & 2–4pm, Thurs 8am–noon & 2–6pm; ☎0 73 73/20 5 20, fax 2 05 55,*www.zwiefalten.de*) is in the Rathaus, Marktplatz 3. In addition to **private rooms**, there's a largish **pension**, *Münsterblick*, Gustav-Werner-Str. 1 (☎0 73 73/3 69; ③), and a couple of good-value **hotels**: *Gasthof zum Hirsch*, Hauptstr. 2 (☎0 73 73/3 18; ③), and *Gasthof Zur Post*, Hauptstr. 44 (☎0 73 73/9 20 70; ③). The last-named has the best **restaurant** in town; the Gaststätte of the Klosterbräu, opposite the Münster at Hauptstr. 24, is also a good bet for food and makes an excellent variety of beers from its premises.

From Zwiefalten, it's only 13km to Riedlingen on the Danube and regular buses run there, connecting with the trains of the Donautalbahn (see pp.288–91).

Hechingen

The market town of **HECHINGEN** lies on and around a hill some 20km southwest of Tübingen on the rail line which travels across the western Jura, eventually linking up with the Donautalbahn. The main reason for visiting is to see the fabulous Romantic **Burg Hohenzollern**.

In the lower part of town, close to the Bahnhof, a pilgrims' route, complete with wayside shrines, leads to the **Franziskanerkirche St Luzen**. This late sixteenth-century church is rather plain-looking from the outside, but lusciously ornate within, containing richly decorated half-columns and pilasters, an elaborate vault with large polychrome keystones, and shell-shaped niches with statues of the apostles.

The upper town, which preserves a number of quaint, twisting streets, is entered via the bulky **Unterer Turm**. Built at the same time as St Luzen, this is now the only surviving part of the fortifications. Crowning the highest point of the hill is the **Stiftskirche**, erected in the grandly sombre Neoclassical Louis XVI style by the French architect Michel d'Inxard. Look out for the grave slab of Count Eitelfriedrich von Zollern, made by the doyen of German bronze-casters, Peter Vischer of Nürnberg. In the nearby Goldschmiedstrasse, which plunges back down the hill, is the Baroque **Synagoge**, immaculately restored to serve as a cultural centre.

There's no hostel or campsite in the vicinity, but there are several **hotels**, including *Mohren*, Schloss-Str. 18 (☎0 74 71/9 86 80; ③), *Gasthof Bären*, Gutleuthausstr. 3 (☎0 74 71/24 14; ③), and *Klaiber*, Obertorplatz 11 (☎0 74 71/22 57; ⑤), the last of which has the best **restaurant** in town. The **tourist office** (☎0 74 71/94 01 14, fax 94 01 08, *www.hechingen.de*) is in the Rathaus at Marktplatz 1.

Burg Hohenzollern

Rearing high above Hechingen, some 4km south of town on the most prominent of all the isolated rocks of the Swabian Jura, is **Burg Hohenzollern** (daily April–Oct 9am–5.30pm; Nov–March 9am–4.30pm; *www.burghohenzollern.de*; DM4/€2, or DM9/€4.50 including a guided tour of the interior), the ancestral seat of the most powerful family in Germany. From afar, the fortress, girded with intact battlements and bristling with a varied assortment of soaring towers, looks like the perfect incarnation of a vast medieval castle. Close up, however, it's soon apparent that the present complex is almost entirely a Romantic dreamland. It was commissioned by the most heritage-conscious of the clan, King Friedrich Wilhelm IV, and built by August Stüler, a pupil of the great Schinkel. Only the fifteenth-century **St-Michael-Kapelle** survives from the previous fortress; it has been retained for the use of the Roman Catholic branch of the family and preserves beautiful Gothic stained-glass windows, along with Romanesque reliefs from its own predecessor.

The **Schatzkammer** contains valuable heirlooms, notably the crown of Prussia, reconstructed in 1889 after the original was destroyed. There's also the snuffbox that

---

THE HOHENZOLLERN DYNASTY

Even in a country whose entire history is dominated by the rise and fall of powerful dynasties, there's nothing quite comparable to the story of the **Hohenzollerns**. Their path to national leadership seems like a carefully hatched master-strategy which took centuries to achieve, yet which had a certain remorseless inevitability about it. The barren, windswept territories they ruled in their capacity as Counts of Zollern hardly seemed an auspicious beginning, but their role as hereditary Burgraves of Nürnberg, a title conferred in 1192, gave them the opportunity to built up a territorial base in Franconia. In the fourteenth century, they established two small principalities, Ansbach and Kulmbach, but their attempts to seize control of Nürnberg – then the effective capital of the Holy Roman Empire – were soundly defeated by the city's independently minded burghers.

Frustrated in their quest for power at the heart of the empire, the Hohenzollerns turned to its periphery. In 1411, they were put in charge of the March of Brandenburg and were thus responsible for securing the country's eastern frontier; they also gained one of the seven seats on the imperial electoral college. Another important breakthrough came in 1525, when Albrecht von Hohenzollern, Grand Master of the Teutonic Knights, converted to Protestantism and secularized the order's holdings as the Duchy of Prussia, which paid nominal homage to the Polish crown, thereby giving the dynasty a power-base beyond the jurisdiction of the emperor.

From 1618, both Brandenburg and Prussia were held by the same branch of the family; in 1657 the latter was wrested from any vestige of Polish control and the two territories formally merged as Brandenburg-Prussia. Elector Friedrich III conferred royal status on himself in 1701 and renamed his country the Kingdom of Prussia. He and his successors, notably Frederick the Great, developed Prussia as a centralized military state which, by skilful warfare and diplomacy, became one of the great powers of Europe. The nineteenth century saw the completion of the jigsaw: as the Habsburgs increasingly turned their attentions towards the Balkans, the Hohenzollerns ousted them from German leadership, eventually excluding them from the unified nation they created by 1871. However, the family's reign was brief; Germany's defeat in World War I led to the collapse of the old aristocratic order and the abolition of the monarchy.

saved the life of Frederick the Great at the Battle of Kunersdorf by absorbing a bullet, which is still embedded in it.

Haigerloch

Unchallenged star of the western part of the Swabian Jura is **HAIGERLOCH**. Buses run from Hechingen, which is 17km east, and from Tübingen via Rottenburg, but the rail line is now used only for occasional steam-train jaunts in the summer months. One of the most outstanding small towns in Germany, Haigerloch's isolation means it's considerably less self-conscious than most of its rivals. Here there's a perfect blend of landscape and architecture, with an unorthodox setting, on rocks high above an S-bend on the River Eyach, playing a crucial role. The surrounding countryside is at its most luxuriant in May and June, when the **lilac** is in full, riotous bloom, but it's hard to be disappointed by the picture at whatever time of year you come.

The northern side of the river is dominated by the **Schloss**, a photogenic jumble of mostly Renaissance buildings which replaced a medieval fortress. Until a few years ago, it was in the possession of the Hohenzollern family, who were probably based in Haigerloch in the eleventh century. Nowadays, the Schloss serves as a hotel and arts centre. The **Schlosskirche**, lower down the hill, has an outwardly Gothic appearance, in spite of being built at the turn of the seventeenth century. The interior was given the full Rococo treatment 150 years later, with the addition of elaborate altars, frescoes and stuccowork. It's also worth walking eastwards through the woods from the Schloss courtyard; after a few minutes, you come to the **Kapf**, a belvedere with a large cross which commands a superb view over both parts of Haigerloch.

Underneath the Schloss's rock is the **Atomkeller-Museum** (May–Sept daily 10am–noon & 2–5pm; March, April, Oct & Nov same times Sat & Sun only; DM2/€1). Here, in March and April 1945, a distinguished group of German scientists carried out a series of experiments in nuclear fission. Throughout the war, the Allies had trembled at the prospect that Germany would be first to develop atomic weapons; thankfully, Hitler never took the project very seriously, while Himmler, who was nominally in charge of the scientists, constantly diverted the researchers into absurd pet projects of his own. When the Americans captured Haigerloch on April 23, they made a point of rounding up the scientists; the reactor was dismantled and shipped to the US in order to help with the successful testing of the atomic bomb just three months later.

Ironically, the American victory in this particular race owed a lot to Albert Einstein, who, as a Jew, had been forced to leave Germany in 1933. Haigerloch itself had been something of a Jewish stronghold until 1941. The **ghetto** can be seen at the western edge of the upper town; the synagogue and the rabbi's house still survive, though neither is used for its original purpose. There's also a Jewish cemetery, which (most unusually) is located well inside the municipal boundaries.

Further up is the pilgrimage church of **St Anna**, erected in the 1750s by the Swiss architect Tiberius Moosbrugger as an integrated ensemble with the monumental garden enclosure and the facing curate's house. The interior of the church has a sense of spaciousness out of all proportion to its small size and is filled with examples of Rococo workmanship of the highest class.

Outside the church is a belvedere offering the directly opposite panorama to that from the Kapf. Another fine view can be had from the **Römerturm** (April–Oct Sat & Sun 9am–6pm, variably on other days; DM1/€0.50) which dominates the centre of town. In spite of its name, it's of Romanesque, not Roman origin, and formed part of the citadel of the counts of Zollern. The nineteenth-century Protestant **Pfarrkirche** contains a meticulous copy of Leonardo da Vinci's *Last Supper*.

Practicalities

The **tourist office** (Mon–Wed & Fri 8am–noon, Thurs 8am–noon & 4–6pm; ☎0 74 74/6 97 27, fax 60 68, *www.haigerloch.de*) is in the Rathaus at Oberstadtstr. 11. Haigerloch, like so many places in the Jura, has no hostel or campsite. There are, however, a couple of cheapish **hotels**: *Gasthof Römer*, Oberstadtstr. 41 (☎0 74 74/10 15; ③), and *Krone*, Oberstadtstr. 47 (☎0 74 74/9 54 40; ④). At the opposite end of the scale, there are two special places to stay: the aforementioned *Gastschloss Haigerloch* in the Schloss (☎0 74 74/69 30; ⑥–⑧) and the seventeenth-century *Schwanen*, Marktplatz 5 (☎0 74 74/9 54 60; ⑥–⑨). All these hotels have **restaurants**; that of *Schwanen* is a true gourmet paradise renowned throughout southern Germany.

The chimney of the Schlossbräu brewery on the banks of the Eyach is the only sign of industry for miles around. An adventurous range of **beers** is made here – *Pils*, three varieties of *Weizen* and *Spezial*. The best place to sample these is its own *Gaststätte Schlössle*, Hechinger Str. 9, which also does good meals at reasonable prices.

Rottweil

In spite of the fact that the dog has put **ROTTWEIL**'s name into many foreign languages, this unhurried provincial market town is itself relatively little known. Lying between the Black Forest and the Swabian Jura, it's way off the beaten tourist track, with nothing of interest nearby and no overwhelming set-piece of its own to draw the crowds, yet the town is a visual marvel. Its isolation spared it from the horrors of modern warfare, and it has changed very little since the seventeenth century. Add to this highly original townscape a dramatic **setting**, a history as remarkable as that of any epic, one of the most impressive arrays of sculpture in Germany and a rich tradition of festivals, and you have what deserves to be considered one of the most enticing small towns in the country.

The Town

Rottweil is built on a strategically secure spur high above the still young River Neckar. This restricted area means that the buildings had to be packed tightly together, with no room for expansion. The town is approached via the **Hochbrücke**, which spans a deep gully. The site of Arae Flaviae lies just over 1km to the left down Königstrasse, and Roman baths have been excavated at the corner of what is now the cemetery.

ROTTWEIL'S DOGS

With its characteristic mixture of black and tan markings, stocky frame and stubby tail, the **Rottweiler** dog is now a familiar sight all over the world. When the Romans came on a road-building mission to southwestern Germany around 73 AD, they brought with them dogs to drive the livestock and defend the camp; in time, these were successfully bred with local species. The resultant crossbreed has survived down the centuries, named after Rottweil, the town which developed from the Roman settlement of Arae Flaviae, which stood at the intersection of the two main highways linking Strasbourg with Augsburg, and the Aargau region of Switzerland with the Middle Neckar. Local butchers trained the Rottweiler to pull their carts – hence its alternative name of Metzgerhund (butcher's dog) – but it's now used by the German police, army, customs and mountain rescue services, and as a guide for the blind.

Hochbrücktorstrasse and the Kapellenkirche

Immediately over the bridge, and named after the tower which once guarded it, is **Hochbrücktorstrasse**, the town's north–south axis. Here you'll see the brilliantly colourful **old houses** characteristic of Rottweil. These are mostly late Renaissance or Baroque in style, and are adorned with three-sided oriel windows, sometimes reaching up several storeys. Each balcony tries to outdo its neighbour in the profusion of carvings. These often illustrate the coat of arms of the original family or the emblem of the guild to which they belonged; others bear the imperial eagle, proud symbol of a Free Imperial City (a status this little town held for nearly six centuries). At the end of Hochbrücktorstrasse is the slender red sandstone **Marktbrunnen**, the most elaborate of the town's four Renaissance fountains. Built in tiers like a wedding cake, it's decorated with delicate statuettes made after woodcuts by Hans Burgkmair, and is crowned by a figure of a Swiss soldier, in commemoration of the "perpetual bond" between Rottweil and the Confederation of Switzerland.

Standing in a cramped square just behind is the **Kapellenkirche**, Gothic successor to an old pilgrimage chapel. It was begun in the early fourteenth century as a miniature version of the Münster in Freiburg, but money ran out with only the square lower part of the tower completed. Some 150 years later, the duke of Württemberg's architect, Aberlin Jerg, added a double octagonal storey to the tower, providing Rottweil with the dominant central monument it needed. The church's outstanding **sculptural decoration** is by several identifiable masters, with the mystical and gentle style of the so-called "Marienmeister" perfectly contrasting with the lively narrative approach of his successor, the "Christusmeister". These works have been replaced *in situ* by copies; the originals are now in the Lorenzkapelle (see opposite).

Hauptstrasse

From the northern side of the church, you pass into the resplendent main street, **Hauptstrasse**, which runs uphill by constantly changing gradients. It's lined by an even more impressive group of houses than those on the perpendicular Hochbrücktorstrasse. The oldest of these, no. 62, dates back to the thirteenth century, while the next two buildings, including the historic inn **Haus zum Sternen**, are in late Gothic style. To see the backs of these houses, whose half-timbering is uncharacteristic of Rottweil, go down to the massive viaduct, a notable piece of nineteenth-century engineering which carries the road out of town high over the valley. From here, there's also a sweeping view over the Swabian Jura.

In the upper half of Hauptstrasse, at no. 20, is the **Stadtmuseum** (Tues–Sat 10am–noon & 2–5pm, Sun 10am–noon; DM1/€0.50), whose star exhibit is the extraordinary **Pürschgerichtskarte** of 1564 – a *tour de force* of detail – proving how little Rottweil's overall appearance has altered. An adjoining room is devoted to the town's **Fastnet** celebrations (see box opposite), with wooden masks of the principal characters and a painstakingly executed cardboard cut-out of the *Narrensprung* – which makes an acceptable substitute if you don't manage to see the real thing.

Directly across the street, the **Apostelbrunnen**, with its figures of SS Peter, James and John, has been re-erected in front of the **Altes Rathaus**, whose simple Gothic architecture gives the street a rare touch of sobriety.

The top of Hauptstrasse is closed by the formidable **Schwarzes Tor** (Black Tower). Its lower section, with its rough masonry, dates back to 1230; the upper storeys were added around 1600 as a prison. Continuing uphill, you come to the **Hochturm** via the alley of the same name. This also belongs to the Staufian period and is a watchtower guarding Rottweil's vulnerable western flank, the only one to lack a natural defensive barrier. In the late eighteenth century, an octagon was added to the top to serve as a look-out gallery; it commands a superb view of the town and surrounding countryside. A plaque on the door tells you which family currently holds the key; otherwise, ask for it at the tourist office.

The rest of the town

Rathausgasse leads from the Rathaus to Münsterplatz, and the **Heilig-Kreuz-Münster**, a late Gothic basilica with a tall tower. Its most important furnishing is an anguished *Crucifixion* at the high altar, an early work by Veit Stoss. Proceeding down Bruderschaftsgasse at the eastern side of the Münster, you pass the **Dominikanerkirche**, a Gothic church with a sumptuous Baroque interior, and the last of the Renaissance fountains, the **Christophorusbrunnen**, with a relief of the city's coat of arms as well as a statue of St Christopher carrying the Christ Child.

Further north is the gleaming new building of the **Dominikanermuseum** (Tues–Sun 10am–1pm & 2–5pm; DM3/€1.50), a joint venture between the town and the Land of Baden-Württemberg in order that the former's remarkable collection of Swabian wood sculpture could be exhibited in its entirety. The museum also contains important excavations from Arae Flaviae, dominated by the second-century **Orpheus mosaic**. Made of some 570,000 coloured stones, this shows the mythical poet playing his lyre to the enchantment of the birds and beasts around him – among them a dog, who is doubtless an early Rottweiler.

At the end of Lorenzgasse is the **Lorenzkapelle** (Tues–Sun 2–5pm; DM1/€0.50), a late Gothic funerary chapel which is devoted to an array of **stone sculpture**. Pride of place here is given to the original carvings from the Kapellenkirche, including two reliefs by the "Marienmeister": *The Opening of the Book* symbolizes Knowledge, while the tender *Betrothal of the Knight* is an allegory of the marriage of Jesus to the Christian soul. A humorous figure, the *Weckenmännle*, probably served as the basis of the pulpit: it's thought to be a self-portrait of Anton Pilgram, who later became master mason at the Dom in Vienna. Outside the Lorenzkapelle is the **Pulverturm** (Powder Tower), one of the remaining vestiges of the fortifications.

Practicalities

Rottweil lies on the main rail line between Stuttgart and Tuttlingen, with onward connections to Switzerland; even international trains stop here. It can also be reached from various points in the Black Forest via the junction of Horb, 35km north. Arriving at the **Bahnhof**, turn right and walk straight uphill to the Hochbrücke. The **tourist office** (May–Oct Mon–Fri 9.30am–12.30pm & 2–6pm, Sat 9.30am–12.30pm; rest of year Mon–Fri only; ☎07 41/49 42 80, fax 49 43 73, *www.rottweil.de*) is in the Altes Rathaus, Hauptstr. 21.

The **youth hostel** has an ideal location in the centre of town at Lorenzgasse 8 (☎07 41/76 64, fax 76 04; DM22/€11 or DM27/€13.50). There's a large concentration of

---

THE ROTTWEIL FASTNET

Rottweil is at its most animated during the Carnival season, and its **Fastnet celebrations** – which are fifteenth century in origin and very different from those in the Rhineland – are arguably Baden-Württemberg's top popular festival. The action begins on the evening of the Thursday before Carnival Sunday (variable date Feb/March) with the *Schmotzige*, in which groups perform satirical revues of the previous year's events. On the Sunday, the mayor hands over control of the town for the duration of the festival, and the afternoon features a children's procession. The high point comes at 8am sharp the following morning with the *Narrensprung* (Parade of Fools), which is repeated on Shrove Tuesday at both 8am and 2pm. This features a cast of colourfully dressed characters in wooden masks. Their names are untranslatable; among them are the friendly Gschell, who represents the promise of summer, the fiery Biss and the vampire-like Federahannes, who both appear to symbolize the winter months, and Fransenkleid, a haughty aristocratic woman.

central **hotels**, including *Gasthof Goldenes Rad*, Hauptstr. 38 (☎07 41/74 12; ②), *Lamm*, Hauptstr. 45 (☎07 41/4 50 15; ④), *Bären*, Hochmaurenstr. 1 (☎07 41/17 46 00; ④), *Parkhotel*, Königstr. 21 (☎07 41/5 34 30; ⑤), *Johanniterbad*, Johannsergasse 12 (☎07 41/53 07 00; ⑤), and the aforementioned *Haus zum Sternen*, Hauptstr. 60 (☎07 41/5 33 00; ⑤–⑧), which is part of the Romantik chain.

Each of the hotels mentioned above has a recommendable **restaurant**; that in *Haus zum Sternen* is particularly good, with plenty of vegetarian options. However, the best place to eat is *Villa Duttenhofer*, Königstr. 1, which has an expensive restaurant, *L'Etoile* (evenings only) and a reasonably priced Weinstube. There's also a wide choice of genteel cafés around the town centre.

All **festivals** stand in the shadow of *Fastnet* (see box on p.287), but other folklore events include the week-long *Volksfest* in mid-August and the *Stadtfest* on the second weekend in September. On a more highbrow note, there's a series of **concerts** of Renaissance and Baroque music in late April/early May, and of chamber recitals later in the month, while for a fortnight in October a mixed programme of drama, cinema, exhibitions, jazz and classical music takes place.

The Upper Danube valley

For much of its course through Germany, the **Danube** gives little hint of the great river it is to become. Most of the famous landscapes with which it's associated lie in the Balkans, yet there's a short stretch early in its course which is equal to anything downstream. Known as the **Bergland Junge Donau** (Mountain country of the young Danube), this begins just beyond Donaueschingen and continues as far as Sigmaringen. The **rail** line to Ulm, the Donautalbahn, closely follows the mazy path of the river and ranks as one of the finest scenic routes in the country. There are services every couple of hours or so; the only snag is that there are relatively few stops.

The river valley forms the centrepiece of the **Naturpark Obere Donau**, which stretches northwards to the Heuberg, the highest range of the Swabian Jura; about half the area is forest, though a large amount is used for farming. It's superb country for **hiking**, particularly above the valley, where there are any number of belvederes offering wonderful views of the river's meandering course. If you've an interest in **flora**, note that springtime sees the countryside awash with snowdrops, narcissi and daphnes, while orchids and the tall Turk's-cap lily blossom at the end of the season. Autumn is if anything even more beautiful; the white limestone rocks of the valley are perfectly offset by the golden tones of the trees and shrubs lower down. Plenty of inexpensive accommodation makes the region ideal for a break away from the crowds.

Beuron and around

BEURON lies right in the heart of the Junge Donau at the point where the scenery is at its most dramatic, about 15km beyond Tuttlingen, where there's a junction between the Donautalbahn and the rail line between Stuttgart and Switzerland. It's immediately obvious that religion has loomed large in this place – one of the tall, seemingly impenetrable rocks on the opposite bank of the Danube is crowned by a large cross.

The village itself, laid out on a terrace above the river, nestles round the enormous **Kloster**. Completely rebuilt in the Baroque period, its size belies the fact that very few monks (sometimes no more than fifteen) ever actually lived there. Architecturally, the late seventeenth-century monastic buildings by Franz Beer are superior to the **Klosterkirche**, which dates from forty years later. By south German standards, it's fairly restrained, though the nave vaults are decorated with colourful frescoes; the legend of the monastery's foundation is sandwiched between scenes from the lives of its patron saints, Martin and Augustine. Sixty years after the Napoleonic suppression, the Kloster was taken over by a Benedictine congregation which played a leading role in the revitalization of European monasticism. They pioneered a simple style of architecture based on early Christian and Romanesque models; an example of this is the **Frauenkapelle** which they added to the north side of the Kloster's church to house a miracle-working fifteenth-century Swabian sculpture of the *Pietà*. Even more significant was their revival of the use of **Gregorian chant**, and the present-day monks remain among the world's leading executants of this stark, ethereally beautiful music, which can be heard at their main services (High Mass Mon–Sat 11.15am, Sun 10am; Vespers Mon–Sat 6pm, Sun 3pm).

Practicalities

Information on the walks in the *Naturpark* is available during normal working hours from the **tourist office** (☎0 74 66/2 14, *www.beuron.de*) in Beuron's Rathaus. Here you can also obtain a list of private houses with **rooms** to let (①–②). Otherwise, the cheapest place to stay is the pilgrims' *St-Gregorius-Haus* (☎0 74 66/2 02; ④) opposite the Kloster at Wolterstr. 9; the only **hotel** as such is *Pelikan*, Abteistr. 12 (☎0 74 66/4 06; ④). The nearest **campsite** (☎0 75 79/5 59) is in the incorporated village of Hausen im Tal to the north.

Hikes around Beuron

Among the many wonderful **hikes** which can be made around Beuron, two stand out. Back in the direction of Tuttlingen (but reached via the Holzbrücke, at the opposite side of town from the Bahnhof), you come after 6km to **Knopfmacherfelsen**, the finest of all the belvederes overlooking this stretch of the Danube. To the east, a similar distance away, is **Burg Wildenstein**, a feudal-castle stronghold dating back to the eleventh century in a stunningly precarious situation overlooking the Danube; part of it now houses a **youth hostel** (☎0 74 66/4 11, fax 4 17; DM24/€12 or DM29/€14.50).

Sigmaringen

Just beyond Hausen is the last stretch of high cliffs; between Thiergarten and Gutenstein, they are replaced by jagged rock needles. Thereafter the landscape is tamer, though there are exceptions, notably at **SIGMARINGEN**, next stop on the train line to Ulm, 20km from Beuron. This pint-sized princely capital came into the hands of the **Hohenzollern** dynasty in 1535, having at one time belonged to their rivals, the Habsburgs. The branch of the family who lived here remained Catholic and supplied the last ill-fated kings of Romania. They were very much junior relations of their Berlin cousins, but provided a useful south German foothold for the Prussians during their predatory takeover of the country in the nineteenth century.

The little town is completely dominated by its photogenic **Schloss** (guided tours daily Feb–April & Nov 9.30am–4.30pm; May–Oct 9am–4.45pm; *www.hohenzollern.com*; DM6/€3). This is essentially a product of the final phase of the Romantic movement, a sort of Swabian counterpart to "Mad" Ludwig's castles in Bavaria, which moves abruptly from one pastiche style to another. Only the towers remain from the medieval fortress, which was sacked in the Thirty Years War, then ravaged by fire in 1893. The **Waffenhalle**, with over 3000 pieces of arms and armour, is one of the best private collections in Europe; it's also a reminder of just how much the Hohenzollerns' rise to national leadership owed to their militarism. A dream-like neo-Gothic hall contains a good collection of south German paintings and sculptures of the fifteenth and sixteenth centuries, including works by the so-called **Master of Sigmaringen**, who was actually two people: the brothers Hans and Jacob Strüb. The entry ticket also covers admission to the **Kutschenmuseum**, a collection of historic coaches housed in the former stables.

Beside the Schloss is the Rococo **Johanniskirche**, containing the shrine of St Fidelio, a local man who became the first Capuchin martyr when he was murdered in 1622 by the fiercely Calvinist inhabitants of the Grisons region of Switzerland. In the town itself, there's nothing much to see, other than the usual array of half-timbered houses, mostly dating from the Baroque period.

Practicalities

The **tourist office** (May–Sept Mon 9.30am–1pm, Tues–Fri 9.30am–1pm & 2–5pm, Sat 10am–noon; Oct–April Mon–Wed 8.30am–noon & 2–4pm, Thurs 8.30am–noon & 2–6pm, Fri 8.30am–2pm; ☎0 75 71/10 62 23, fax 10 61 66, *www.sigmaringen.de*) is at Schwabstr. 1, between the Bahnhof and the Schloss. There's a **pension**, *Eichamt*, Donaustr. 15 (☎0 75 71/1 49 18; ④), plus several **hotels**: *Traube*, Fürst-Wilhelm-Str. 19 (☎0 75 71/6 45 10, *www.hotel-traube-sigmaringen.de*; ④); *Jägerhof*, Wentelstr. 4 (☎0 75 71/20 21, *www.jaegerhof-sigmaringen.de*; ④); and *Fürstenhof*, Zeppelinstr. 14 (☎0 75 71/7 20 60, *www.fuerstenhof-sig.de*; ⑤), the last of which has the leading **restaurant** in town. The **youth hostel** is at Hohenzollernstr. 31 (☎0 75 71/1 32 77, fax 6 11 59; DM22/€11 or DM27/€13.50) on the northeastern side of town and there's a **campsite** (☎0 75 71/54 79) by the Danube. Sigmaringen's main **festivals** are *Fastnet* and the *Donaufest*; the latter is held at the end of July and features a small-scale version of the fishermen's jousts made famous in Ulm.

Blaubeuren

Between the next two train stops, Mengen and Riedlingen, there's an extensive stretch of marshland on the right bank of the Danube, frequented by many species of waterfowl. After Ehingen, the Donautalbahn leaves the Danube and loops towards Ulm via **BLAUBEUREN**, which lies in a wonderful amphitheatre-like setting at the edge of the Swabian Jura. With its mix of natural and artistic attractions, this ranks as one of the most enticing places in the region and a good choice as a **hiking** base. The rocky hills above not only afford marvellous views over the red roofs of the spaciously laid-out little town and the wilder landscape beyond; they also offer constant surprises, such as labyrinths, caves, grottoes and ruined castles.

At the opposite end of town from the Bahnhof is the **Blautopf**, a shady pool formed during the glacial period; it's the source of the River Blau, the Danube tributary from which the town derives its name. In spite of its small size, the Blautopf is 20m deep, and its waters have a constant temperature of 9°C. The best time to see it is on a sunny but showery day. In bright weather, the pool is a deep rich blue, but the rain turns this successively to a lighter shade, then green, then a yellowish brown. Alongside is the **Hammerschmiede** (Palm Sunday to Oct daily 9am–6pm; rest of year Sat & Sun 11am–4pm; closed Dec; DM2/€1), a remarkable piece of industrial archeology. Built in the mid-eighteenth century as a water-mill, it was converted into a smithy at the beginning of the following century, before doing service as a mechanical workshop up until 1956, when it was finally retired – though the clanking machinery is still in full working order.

To the side of the Blautopf is the extensive complex of the former **Kloster**. Just 25 years after it had been completely rebuilt in late Gothic style, Württemberg went over to the Reformation; the monastery was disbanded and the buildings were put to use as a Protestant school. As in Maulbronn, with whose seminary Blaubeuren is now united, there's a remarkably complete picture of a monastic community, with a series of picturesque half-timbered workshops lining the courtyard. You can wander around and also in the cloister with its abutting lavabo and chapter house with tombs of the patrons.

The **Klosterkirche** (Jan & Feb Sat & Sun 11am–4pm; Palm Sunday to Oct daily 9am–6pm; rest of year daily 11am–4pm; DM3/€1.50) ingeniously preserves the tower of its Romanesque predecessor as a barrier separating the monks' choir from the nave. Only the former is kept open: it bristles with flamboyant works of art, among which the **high altar** – the only one of its kind to have escaped the iconoclasts – stands out. It's a co-operative work by at least two major Ulm studios – that of the sculptor **Michel Erhart** and his son **Gregor**, and of the painter **Bartholomäus Zeitblom**, who was assisted by **Bernhard Strigel** and at least one other pupil. When closed, it illustrates the Passion; the first opening shows scenes from the life of St John the Evangelist, patron of the Kloster. The carved heart of the retable has *The Virgin and Saints* flanked by reliefs of *The Adoration of the Shepherds* and *The Adoration of the Magi*. Originally, this part was only shown on the major feast days of the Church calendar. Nowadays, it can be seen any time a tour group is passing through, though the only guaranteed times are Sundays at 2.30pm and 3.30pm.

Also within the monastery walls is another survivor which is unique of its kind, the **Badhaus**, which was added to the amenities in 1510. It now houses the local museum (April–Oct Tues–Fri 10am–4pm, Sat & Sun 10am–5pm; DM1.50/€0.75), but the main interest is in the building itself – on the ground floor, you can see the baths and heating system, while upstairs is a room decorated with hunting frescoes. The archeological part of the collection is housed in the **Spital** (same times and ticket), the most imposing of the half-timbered houses in the town centre.

Practicalities

Tourist information is available at the Rathaus, Karlstr. 2 (☎0 73 44/13 17, *www.blaubeuren.de*) during office hours. For accommodation, there's a **youth hostel** at Auf dem Rucken 69 (☎0 73 44/64 44, fax 2 14 16; DM24/€12 or DM29/€14.50) on a hill at the eastern side of town, between the Bahnhof and the Blautopf. There are also several **hotels**, including *Gasthof zum Waldhorn*, Klosterstr. 21 (☎0 73 44/63 42; ②), *Löwen*, Marktstr. 1 (☎0 73 44/9 66 60; ③), *Ochsen*, Marktstr. 4 (☎0 73 44/96 98 90; ④), and *Adler*, Karlstr. 8 (☎0 73 44/50 27; ⑤). All of these have **restaurants**, with the last two having the edge over the others.

Ulm

Right on the border with Bavaria, **ULM** lies on the Danube, 18km downstream from Blaubeuren, and 85km southeast of Stuttgart. The city is famous for having the highest church spire in the world, and for being the birthplace of one of the all-time giants of science, **Albert Einstein**. Hermann Hesse, on a prewar visit, was entranced by its "ancient fishermen's homes tilted at an angle in the water, tiny houses on the city ramparts, stately burghers' residences in the alleys, an unusual gable here, a majestic doorway there".

Regrettably, some perseverance is now necessary for enjoyment of Ulm; a single air raid at the end of 1944 caused one of the worst devastations suffered by any German city, wiping out the vast majority of the historic centre. Much of this had to be rebuilt quickly. Try not to let this put you off; many of the finest streets escaped lightly and many painstaking restoration projects have been undertaken in recent years. Moreover, only superficial damage was inflicted on Ulm's magnificent centrepiece, the **Münster**.

Arrival, information and accommodation

Ulm's **Hauptbahnhof** lies to the west of the town centre; an unprepossessing shopping precinct leads straight to Münsterplatz. The **tourist office** (Mon–Fri 9am–6pm, Sat 9am–1pm; ☎ 07 31/1 61 28 30, fax 1 61 16 41, *www.ulm.de*) is housed in the Stadthaus, an audacious new building by the American architect Richard Meier at Münsterplatz 50. From May to mid-Oct there are fifty-minute **motorboat trips** (☎ 07 31/6 27 51) on the Danube every afternoon; these depart from the Metzgerturm and cost DM10/€5.

There's a good choice of **hotels** right in the city centre, while Ulm's **youth hostel** is 4km southwest of the centre at Grimmelfinger Weg 45 (☎ 07 31/38 44 55, fax 38 45 11; DM24/€12 or DM29/€14.50); take S-Bahn #1 to Ehinger Tor, then bus #4 or #8 to Schulzentrum.

Hotels

Bäumle, Kohlgasse 6 (☎ 07 31/6 22 87, fax 6 02 26 04). One of the few hotels in an old building, and one that is outstanding value at the price. Its restaurant (Mon–Fri evenings only) occupies two fine old rooms which have preserved their late nineteenth-century decoration. ③.

Goldener Bock, Bockgasse 25 (☎ 07 31/92 03 40, fax 9 20 34 30). Good middle-range hotel in the east of the Altstadt whose restaurant is one of the very best in the city. ⑤.

Rösch, Schwörhausgasse 18 (☎ 07 31/6 57 18, fax 6 02 25 84). Homely pension in the Fischerviertel. ④.

Roter Löwe, Ulmer Gasse 8 (☎ 07 31/6 20 31, fax 6 02 15 02, *www.akzent.de*). A member of the Akzent chain, this fine hotel is conveniently located midway between the Hauptbahnhof and the Münster. It also has a good restaurant (closed Sun). ⑥.

Schiefes Haus, Schwörhausgasse 6 (☎ 07 31/96 79 30, fax 9 67 93 33). Modern designer hotel in one of the city's most famous old houses. ⑧.

Ulmer Spatz, Münsterplatz 27 (☎ 07 31/6 80 81, fax 602 19 25). Classy hotel by the Münster with its own garden and a top-notch restaurant. ⑥.

Ulmer Stuben, Zinglerstr. 11 (☎ 07 31/96 22 00, fax 9 62 20 55). Middle-range hotel with restaurant, a few minutes' walk south of the Hauptbahnhof. ⑤.

Zum Anker, Rabengasse 2 (☎ 07 31/6 32 97). Very friendly and welcoming budget hotel, whose front rooms have a fantastic view of the Münster. Its lively and absolutely genuine Spanish wine bar-restaurant (closed Mon) is one of the most popular meeting-places in town. ③.

The city centre

In every way, the Münster dominates this city, dwarfing all the other buildings, not least those on Münsterplatz, the setting for markets on Wednesday and Saturday mornings. Nonetheless there are atmospheric quarters to the north and south between the natural boundaries of the hills and the Danube.

The Münster

From miles away, the massive west tower of the **Münster** acts as a beacon to the city. The 161-metre-high openwork **steeple** soars so high above everything else it seems to be a real-life fulfilment of those old master paintings which depict an imaginary Tower of Babel shooting through the clouds. In fact, the spire and upper storey of the tower were for centuries no more than a seemingly impossible dream and were only finished in 1890, faithfully following drawings made four hundred years before.

As you might expect, the tower offers a stupendous **view** from its platform (daily June–Aug 8am–6.45pm; times reduce seasonally to 9am–3.45pm; DM4/€2). A fair amount of puff is needed to climb the 768 steps, but you're rewarded with a panorama which stretches over the city and the Danube to the Swabian Jura and Black Forest, with the Swiss Alps visible on a clear day. On the final stage, there's also the rare opportunity to see the filigree architecture of an openwork spire at close quarters.

In accordance with Ulm's great sculptural tradition, there are no fewer than five superb **portals** to the Münster; that under the tower is appropriately the grandest. Above the doorway are scenes from the Book of Genesis, while the pillars have

---

THE BUILDING OF THE MÜNSTER

Work on the Münster began in the last quarter of the fourteenth century under the direction of the most famous master mason of the day, **Heinrich Parler**, and was continued by his descendants. Credit for its ultimate appearance, however, must go to the head of the succeeding dynasty, **Ulrich von Ensingen**, who altered the plans to make the church wider and loftier, and designed the lower part of the great tower. Despite the Münster's huge size, it was built as, and remains, no more than a parish church. An expression of a vain civic pride, its capacity of 20,000 was more than twice the population of the city, then one of the largest in Germany. At the end of the fifteenth century, when the structure was substantially complete, the architect **Matthäus Böblinger** made a drawing (which can be seen in the Ulmer Museum) for the completion of the tower, reaching to a height that had never previously been attempted. When he tried to build it, however, cracks appeared in the masonry and he fled in disgrace. As his successor's main problem was to repair the existing building, no more work was done on the tower, and the project was abandoned altogether when the city formally adopted the Reformation in 1530. It was only when the Romantic movement reawakened interest in the Middle Ages that steps were taken to finish it.

masterly statues of saints in the "Soft Style" of **Master Hartmann**, the first Ulm sculptor known by name. The ensemble is completed by a poignant *Man of Sorrows* (now replaced by a copy; the original can be seen inside), an early work by **Hans Multscher**, the founding father of the remarkable group of late Gothic and early Renaissance German sculptors.

The sense of massive space in the **interior** is as overwhelming as the tower's great height; the impression is aided by the simplicity of the design, which comprises a wide nave of five aisles culminating in a single chancel, with no intervening transept. The best time to come here is on a bright morning, when the sun's rays filter through the stained-glass windows onto the magnificent set of **choir stalls**: "a bold oaken outburst of three-dimensional humanism" was how Patrick Leigh Fermor described them. Made between 1469 and 1474 under the direction of two local men, **Jörg Syrlin the Elder** and **Michel Erhart**, the sheer profusion and originality of their carvings – particularly the vibrant life-sized busts – immediately grab your attention. They're a hymn of praise to the achievements of the antique as well as of the Christian world, with women, for once, given the same recognition as men.

Ulm's obsession with the steeple motif can be seen in the huge canopy covering the **font**, and in the sounding board added to the **pulpit** which includes, high up above the column capitals, a second pulpit inaccessible to a human preacher – a symbol that the sermon was really delivered by the Holy Ghost. It's seen even more spectacularly in the slender, tapering **tabernacle**, a structure of gossamer delicacy for all its towering height. In spite of its figurines of popes and bishops, this somehow survived the iconoclasm which denuded the Münster following the introduction of the Reformation. Over the triumphal arch leading to the chancel is a colossal crowded **fresco** of *The Last Judgement*, placed so that every member of the congregation could see it. As an antidote to the massiveness of the Münster, the **Besserer-Kapelle** to the right of the chancel is a small family chapel still retaining its beautifully drawn and coloured fifteenth-century stained-glass windows.

The Rathaus

That other self-conscious symbol of civic pride, the **Rathaus**, is situated just a block away from the Münster across Neue Strasse, the central arterial road. Even in a country as rich in picturesque town halls as Germany, there's none quite so photogenic as this disparate jumble of buildings, which has been restored to a pristine approximation of how it looked in 1540. In this year, the northern front was rebuilt in the Renaissance style and equipped with an arcaded passageway; the local painter **Martin Schaffner** was then let loose on the exterior walls, covering them with a series of brilliantly coloured **frescoes** of religious subjects, plus allegories of the Vices and Virtues. On the southern side of the building he painted battle scenes, along with a barge (symbolizing Ulm's dependence on the Danube), plus the coats of arms of the city's trading partners. Between the windows here are polychrome statues of six of the Electors, carved the previous century by Master Hartmann. Even more luxuriant is the eastern facade, with figures by Multscher of Charlemagne, the kings of Hungary and Bohemia, and two pages; there's also an elaborate astronomical clock made in 1520.

Inside the Rathaus, you can see a replica of the equipment used in 1811 by **Albrecht Berblinger**, "The Tailor of Ulm", in an ill-fated attempt to fly across the Danube; widely regarded in his own day as an eccentric fool, he's since been elevated to the status of a local hero. In 1944, the Rathaus formed an appropriately grand backdrop for the notorious state funeral of Field Marshal Erwin Rommel, who accepted this consolation prize, along with a draught of poison, rather than face trial and certain public execution for his alleged involvement in the July Plot against Hitler.

Marktplatz

To the rear of the Rathaus is the **Marktplatz**, preserving a few old houses but dominated by the brightly coloured **Fischkasten** (Fish Crate), finest of the many old fountains in the city. Made during the late fifteenth century in the workshop of Syrlin the Elder, it features statues of three saints attired as Knights, bearing the coats of arms of city and empire. In Taubenplätzle, just off the eastern end of the square, is the bronze **Delphinbrunnen**; a century younger, it was formerly part of a water-tower.

Behind stands a Renaissance mansion which has been adapted to house the **Ulmer Museum** (Tues–Sun 11am–5pm; *www.museum.ulm.de*; DM5/€2.50, free Fri). On the ground floor are choice examples of the city's artistic heritage; the **original figures** from the Rathaus and several of the fountains have been moved here. Alongside further works by Multscher and Erhart are carvings by **Daniel Mauch**, whose Italianate style represents the last flourish of Ulm's great sculptural tradition. The city's heritage in painting is far less rich, but Schaffner's *Eitel Besserer* (a descendant of the family who endowed the chapel in the Münster) is a masterpiece of Renaissance portraiture, and there are several works by an influential master of the previous generation, **Bartholomäus Zeitblom**. Highlight of the archeology department is the weird statuette of a *Woman with the Head of a Lioness*, which dates back to 30,000 BC. Upstairs, Ulm's history is extensively documented, with an illuminating section on the construction of the Münster.

The Neuer Bau and Schwörhaus

Westwards down Neuestrasse is the vast bulk of the **Neuer Bau**, a municipal warehouse built in the sixteenth century; its pentagonal courtyard contains a graceful staircase tower and a fountain with a statue of Hildegard, one of Charlemagne's wives. Turning left into Sattlergasse, you come to Weinhof, whose main building is the early seventeenth-century **Schwörhaus** (Oath House). Each year, the mayor addresses the citizens from the balcony, taking an oath according to the constitution of 1397 by which he must be "the same man to rich and poor alike in all common and honourable matters without discrimination or reservation". This was an advanced statement for its time, and is often taken as evidence that medieval Ulm was a democratic state. In fact, what the document signified was a passing of power from the patrician class to the guilds, who established an inbuilt majority for themselves on the council.

The Fischerviertel and southern quarters

One of the most interesting features of Ulm is the way the old patterns of settlement can still be clearly discerned. Between the Schwörhaus and the Danube is the celebrated **Fischerviertel** (Fishermen's Quarter), whose quaint scenes of half-timbered houses, waterways, courtyards and tiny bridges so delighted Hermann Hesse. This was actually the area where the artisan classes lived – the island on the Blau and the streets alongside were inhabited by tanners and millers, while on Fischergasse you can see a boatman's house at no. 18, a baker's at no. 22 and a fisherman's at no. 23. Look out for the **Schiefes Haus** (Crooked House), a hefty half-timbered building from about 1500 standing beside a remnant of the twelfth-century fortifications; it takes its name from its pronounced tilt over the river, into whose bed it's fastened by stilts. Another picturesque vista is on Fischerplätzle, which looks towards Häuslesbrücke and boasts the late fifteenth-century **Zunfthaus** (the fishermen's guildhall) and the seventeenth-century **Schönes Haus**, adorned with a scene of shipping on the Danube.

From here, you can walk high above the Danube along the medieval ramparts, now laid out as a shady promenade with a view over the backs of the Fisherviertel. Parallel with the Rathaus is the most impressive surviving gate, the **Metzgerturm** (Butchers'

Tower), locally dubbed "The Leaning Tower of Ulm" because it slants a good 2m from the vertical. Beyond Herdbrücke is the patrician **Reichenau Hof**, while Grünen Hof just to the north has the oldest intact buildings in Ulm – the Romanesque **Nikolauskapelle** (whose interior has Gothic frescoes), and a stone house of similar date. Nearby is the **Dreifaltigkeitskirche**, a plain Lutheran preaching house in the late Renaissance style, incorporating the Gothic chancel of the monastery which previously stood on the site. Only the older part of the building is now used as a church, the remainder having been converted into an ecumenical and cultural centre which often hosts worthwhile exhibitions. For a really superb **view** of Ulm, with the Münster rearing high up behind the houses of the Fischerviertel, cross over to the quays of Neue-Ulm, the city's southern extension but actually in neighbouring Bavaria.

The northern quarters

The merchants and craftsmen of medieval Ulm tended to live in the streets north of Neue Strasse. These aren't nearly so well preserved as other parts of the city, but some fine buildings remain. Just behind the Münster's east end is the sixteenth-century **Schuhhaus**, the guildhall of the shoemakers; it's now used for art exhibitions. Beyond is the Judenhof, the former ghetto; no. 10 seems to pre-date the pogrom of 1499. The streets immediately north of the Münster contain rows of simple houses once inhabited by skilled craft-workers, along with several stores, finest of which is the **Kornhaus**. In spite of its self-confident look and its current function as a concert hall, this was built as a panic measure at the end of the sixteenth century in the belief that there would soon be a famine. Look out also for Herrenkellergasse 12, whose turret served as an observation post for fathers trying to keep an eye on the evening jaunts of their eligible daughters.

Further north on Frauengrabben and Seelengrabben are terraces of soldiers' houses from the early seventeenth century, beyond which is the **Zeughaus** with a monumental Renaissance gateway and other surviving parts of the medieval fortifications. Ulm's military role reached a peak in the mid-nineteenth century with its transformation into a fortress of the German Confederation. This citadel was seventeen years in the making, but never once had to withstand a siege; the crumbling buildings are dotted all round the outer perimeter of the city. Finest is the **Wilhelmsburg**, an intact fort crowning the commanding heights of the Michelsberg at the extreme north of the city; it's well worth climbing up for the **view**. If you walk up via Frauenstrasse, you can see the **Pauluskirche**; built to serve the Protestant members of the garrison, it ranks as one of the finest Jugendstil churches in Germany.

Wiblingen

WIBLINGEN, 5km south of central Ulm and reached by bus #3 or #8, is now a large dormitory suburb but for centuries was no more than a hamlet clustered round the Benedictine **Abtei**. The present extensive complex was erected in a leisurely fashion throughout the eighteenth century. Only twenty years after completion, the abbey was secularized; the monastic quarters are now used by the University of Ulm.

Left of the entrance is the **Bibliothek** (April–Oct Tues–Sun 10am–noon & 2–5pm; Nov–March Sat & Sun 2–4pm; DM3/€1.50), lavishly adorned with stuccowork of shells, leaves and putti, columns painted pink and blue to resemble marble, large allegorical statues representing the Virtues and a colossal ceiling fresco glorifying wisdom, with subjects from the Bible and pagan mythology freely mixed together. The **Basilika St Martin**, which is later in date, shows a shift from Rococo self-indulgence towards the solemnity of Neoclassicism. On the flattened domes are masterly, highly theatrical trompe l'oeil frescoes by **Januarius Zick**, with a foreshortened *Last Supper* and a cycle illustrating *The Legend of the Cross*.

Eating, drinking and entertainment

Ulm has a wide range of good places to eat and drink, with the Fischerviertel and the streets north of the Münster both ideal areas for a pub crawl. There's also a decent choice of good entertainment.

Restaurants

Allgäuer Hof, Fischergasse 12. Pancakes are the main line here, with 42 varieties to choose from, but the usual hearty German fare is available as well.

Drei Kannen, Hafenbad 31/1. Traditional Gaststätte housed in an old Brauhaus with an adjoining Renaissance loggia and beer garden. Closed Mon.

Gerberhaus, Weinhofberg 9. Reasonably priced choice for high-quality Swabian fare. Closed Fri.

Herrenkeller, Herrenkellergasse 4. Gaststätte with a pedigree dating back to the seventeenth century, serving both Swabian and Bavarian dishes. Closed Sun.

Kornhäusle, Kornhausgasse 8. Small place specializing in salads and crêpes.

Pflugmerzler, Pfluggasse 6. High-quality restaurant offering regional cuisine. Closed Sat evening & Sun.

Weinkrüger, Weinhofberg 7. Excellent wine bar-cum-restaurant.

Zunfthaus der Schiffleute, Fischergasse 31. The old fishermen's guildhall, decked out as a cosy restaurant offering an excellent range of Swabian cuisine.

Zur Forelle, Fischergasse 25 (☎ 07 31/6 39 24). Arguably the best restaurant in Ulm, particularly for fish dishes. Limited capacity, so booking is advisable.

Zur Lochmühle, Gerbergasse 6. Occupies an old water-mill with a big beer garden, and serves both local and international cooking.

Bars and cafés

Alberts Café in EinsteinHaus, Kornhausplatz 5. Minimalist Internet café.

Barfüsser, Lautenberg 1. Hausbrauerei serving its own beer plus a good range of food.

Café Brettle, Rabengasse 10. Lively student bar.

Café Liquid, Münsterplatz 90. Café-bar in a strikingly modern pavilion overlooking the Münster, with outside seating in summer.

Café Lloyd, Herrenkellergasse 25. *Szene* café-bar.

Café Tröglen, Münsterplatz 5. One of a number of excellent traditional cafés grouped around the Münster. Closed Sun.

Entertainment

In 1641, Ulm became the first city in Germany to establish a permanent civic **theatre**; its modern successor, the Ulmer Theater, Olgastr. 73 (☎ 07 31/1 61 44 44) presents drama, opera, operetta, musicals and ballet. **Concert** tickets are available from the Stadthaus, Münsterplatz 50 (☎ 07 31/96 70 70). Orchestral and large-scale spectaculars are featured at the *Congress Centrum*, Basteistr. 40 (☎ 07 31/92 29 90); more intimate highbrow musical events are held in the Kornhaus on Kornhausplatz (☎ 07 31/1 61 76 70). Choral music is performed in the Münster every other Saturday, while the five-manual organ can be heard daily between 11am and noon. There's jazz most evenings at Sauschsdall, Prittwitzstr. 36 (☎ 07 31/9 26 61 46), and there are live rock bands and alternative film programmes at Charivari, Stuttgarter Str. 13 (☎ 07 31/1 61 54 42).

The main annual **popular festival** is *Schwörmontag* on the penultimate Monday of July; this begins at 11am in the Weinhof with the mayor's taking of the oath, and continues in the afternoon with a barge procession down the Danube. On the preceding Saturday evening there's the *Lichterserenade*, with thousands of illuminations. Each June, the *Stadtfest* is held in Münsterplatz. However, the most spectacular local tradition, *Fischerstechen* (Fishermen's Jousting), a colourful tournament with boats in place of horses, is only held at four-year intervals (next in July 2001). Prior to the competitions, there are processions and dances in the streets.

The Upper Swabian spas

Upper Swabia (Oberschwaben) is a triangular-shaped area of rich farmland to the south of the Danube; this is one of the least urbanized parts of the country, with no major cities and only a few medium-sized towns. In the heart of Upper Swabia is a group of health resorts, each specializing in mud bath (*Moorheilbad*) cures, and lying on both of the area's two tourist routes, the **Baroque Road** (Barockstrasse) and the **Spa Road** (Bäderstrasse). Any one of these is a good choice for a relaxing break, or as a base for exploring the whole region. Although the spa resorts and magnificent Baroque and Rococo monasteries are well known to the Germans themselves, they're little visited by foreigners.

Bad Schussenried

BAD SCHUSSENRIED lies some 60km southwest of Ulm on the rail line to the Bodensee; alternatively, it can be reached by bus from Riedlingen in the Danube valley via Bad Buchau, the least interesting of the four Upper Swabian spa towns. Ultramodern clinics now form a large part of its overall appearance, but the Baroque buildings of the huge former Premonstratensian **Kloster** at the northeastern edge of town retain their pre-eminence.

The monastic church, now the **Pfarrkirche St Magnus**, was built by a whole team of architects, including several members of the prolific Beer and Thumb families. Save for the single tower with its distinctive onion dome, it's rather plain on the outside, but the interior, set beneath Januarius Zick's **ceiling frescoes** of scenes from the life of St Norbert, the order's founder, is far more arresting. Highlight of the furnishings is the set of **choir stalls**, whose backs have limewood reliefs providing a complete illustrated Bible. However, the church is rather overshadowed by the **Bibliotheksaal** (April–Oct daily 10am–noon and 2–5pm; Nov–March Mon–Fri 2–5pm, Sat & Sun 10am–noon & 2–5pm; DM4.50/€2.25) in the former conventual buildings. There's no library in all of Germany to compare with this luxuriant creation, designed by **Dominikus Zimmermann** at the same time as he was working on the famous Wieskirche in Bavaria. It's a masterly balance of colour, light and shade, with the white porcelain statues contrasting with the pink marble columns and the ethereally blue bookcases with their trompe l'oeil volumes. The ceiling fresco, appropriately enough, is a glorification of Wisdom in both heavenly and earthly guises.

Bad Schussenried's **Bahnhof** is in Kürnbach, an incorporated village 1.5km south. To the rear of the station is the **Freilichtmuseum** (April & Oct Mon–Sat 10am–5pm, Sun 11am–5pm; May–Sept Tues–Sat 9am–6pm, Sun 11am–6pm; DM3/€1.50), a collection of redundant rural buildings from the surrounding area, though the centrepiece, a large seventeeth-century farmhouse, is original to the spot.

Practicalities

There are about thirty houses with **rooms** to let (①–③); the main concentrations are at the southern end of the main part of town, on Welfenstrasse, Blasius-Erler-Weg and Mozartstrasse. The best **hotels** are *Barbara*, Schulstr. 9 (☎0 75 83/2 65 03; ④), and *Amerika*, Zeppelinstr.13 (☎0 75 83/9 42 50; ④). A full list of places to stay is available from the **tourist office** (Easter–Sept Mon–Fri 9am–noon & 2–5pm, Sat 10am–noon; Oct–Easter Mon–Fri 9am–noon & 2–5pm; ☎0 75 83/94 01 71, fax 47 47, *www. bad-schussenried.de*) in the Kurverwaltung, Klosterhof 1.

Steinhausen

STEINHAUSEN, 5km northeast of Bad Schussenried, but always an integral part of the town, is well connected by bus. The settlement clusters round the **Wallfahrtskirche**, a building of the highest artistic importance, being generally accepted as the earliest church in the full-blown Rococo style where architecture, painting and decorations are all fused into an indivisible whole. This unity was made possible by the close collaboration between the **Zimmermann brothers**: Dominikus as architect, Johann Baptist as painter. The church consists of a large nave and a tiny chancel, both oval in shape; pristine white pillars, which look as if they're made of china, shoot up to the vault, whose **fresco**, an evocation of Heaven in limpid pastel colours, seems to be a continuation of the architecture. No less remarkable is the **stuccowork**, with its superbly crafted depictions of the animal, bird and plant kingdoms.

The main **pilgrimages** are on Good Friday and on the day of the patron saints, Peter and Paul (29 June). Across from the church is a **hotel**, *Landgasthof Linde* (☎0 75 83/23 81; ③) with a good restaurant; an even better place to eat is *Zur Barockkirche*, Dorfstr. 6.

Bad Waldsee

Some 15km southeast of Bad Schussenried, and reached either by bus or by a looping branch rail line, is **BAD WALDSEE**, which enjoys a pretty setting on an isthmus between two lakes, and which benefits from a rather more animated market-town feel than its soporific neighbour.

From just outside the Bahnhof, you get a fine view of the town over the Stadtsee, the larger of the lakes and a popular boating centre. Rising above everything else is the Baroque **Stiftskirche**, whose twin-facade towers are set at startling angles to one another. It's yet another church in which Dominikus Zimmermann had a hand: he created the multicoloured high altar, plus the smaller ones to the side. However, the greatest treasure is a resplendent early Renaissance bronze memorial to a local noble in the northern aisle, nicknamed Der eiserne Mann (The Iron Man).

In the medieval town centre are a number of half-timbered houses and step-gabled public buildings; the most notable are the **Kornhaus** and the **Rathaus**. Further west is the Renaissance and Baroque **Schloss** of the local grandees, the House of Waldburg-Waldsee. It's closed to the public, but you get a good view of the exterior by walking round the rustic-looking Schloss See, the smaller of the town's lakes.

Practicalities

The **tourist office** (Mon–Fri 8am–noon & 2–5pm, May–Sept also Sat 10am–noon; ☎0 75 24/94 13 42, fax 94 13 45, *www.badwaldsee.de*) is in the Kurverwaltung at Ravensburger Str. 1 beside the Rathaus and can provide a complete list of all the rooms available in **private houses** (①–③). There are also several **hotels**, including *Grüner Baum*, Hauptstr. 34 (☎0 75 24/9 79 00; ⑤), and *Altes Tor*, Hauptstr. 49 (☎0 75 24/9 71 90; ⑥); the former has one of the best **restaurants** in a town which is noticeably better off for places to eat and drink than the other spas in the region. The main local **festival** is the *Altstadt und Seenachtfest* in August, featuring a fireworks display over the Stadtsee.

Bad Wurzach

The last of the spas, **BAD WURZACH**, 12km further southeast, is very similar in feel to Bad Waldsee and there are regular bus services between the two towns. The best time to visit is on the second Friday in July, when Upper Swabia's most distinctive **festival**, the *Heilig-Blut-Fest*, takes place. Here it takes the form of a mounted pilgrimage to the Baroque church on the **Gottesberg**, the hill to the south; over 1500 horses take part, with their riders decked out in colourful costumes.

Dominating the main Marktstrasse is the dignified white **Schloss**, now a school run by Jesuits. Although the palace is mostly closed to the public, the main entrance is generally kept open to enable visitors to see the resplendent Baroque **staircase** and its gloriously profane ceiling fresco of *The Apotheosis of Hercules*. On Schulstrasse, the eastern continuation of the street, is the **Kloster Maria Rosengarten**, a functioning convent whose ornate Rococo chapel can be visited. However, the most intriguing monument is the half-timbered **Leprosenhaus** (Easter–Oct Fri, Sun & holidays 2–5pm; free) at the edge of town on the road southwest to Ravensburg; a leper colony existed there from the mid-fourteenth century until the end of the eighteenth century.

North of town is the **Wurzacher Ried**, fourteen square kilometres of moorland punctuated by woods and tarns with an extraordinarily rich indigenous flora and fauna. The whole area is a nature reserve and is listed by the Council of Europe as a landscape of outstanding botanical and geological importance.

Practicalities

The **tourist office** (Mon–Fri 9am–noon & 2–5pm, Easter–Nov Sat 9am–noon; ☎0 75 64/30 21 50, fax 30 21 54, *www.bad-wurzach.de*) is in the Kurverwaltung at Mühltorstr. 1. A generous number of **private rooms** (①–②) are available as in the other spas; prices if anything are slightly lower. Bad Wurzach is also the only one of the towns with a **campsite** (☎0 75 64/34 82); it's by the outlying village of Wiesen about a kilometre to the southeast. There are a couple of excellent **hotels**, both with restaurants, in the centre: *Adler*, Schloss-Str. 8 (☎0 75 64/9 30 30; ⑤), and *Rössle*, Schulstr. 12 (☎0 75 64/20 55; ⑤).

Weingarten and Ravensburg

Just over 30km south of Bad Schussenried on the main rail line to the Bodensee are two adjacent towns which are so close together as to be virtually one unit, yet which are very different in appearance and jealously guard their own municipal independence. Both are foundations of the Welf dynasty, one of the two most powerful families of early medieval Germany, and one which held sway in its later base in Lower Saxony right up to the twentieth century.

Weingarten

The town of **WEINGARTEN**, nowadays quite a bustling place, was originally no more than an adjunct to the huge hilltop Benedictine **Kloster** of the same name, which remains the sole monument of note. At the end of the seventeenth century, plans were drawn up to transform this, one of Germany's most famous medieval monasteries, into the principal centre of monasticism north of the Alps. Such an ambitious project was never fully realized, but the Baroque complex which was built is nonetheless the largest monastery in the country and an active centre of Roman Catholic education.

The **Basilika** is strikingly reminiscent of St Peter's in Rome and is a colossal structure, even if, both in its length and the height of its central dome, it's only about half the size of its great model. Inside, the vivacious **ceiling frescoes** by Cosmas Damian Asam glorify Christ, the Virgin and St Benedict; no less eye-catching are the **choir stalls**, Josef Anton Feichtmayr's first major commission. However, the most impressive feature of the furnishings is the **organ** by Josef Gabler, a particularly ingenious design, with the pipes housed in a series of towers specially constructed so as not to obscure the facade windows.

As in Bad Wurzach, the *Heilig-Blut-Fest* is the main **festival**; the monastery's most treasured relic is the focus of the procession. If you want to stay, there are several good **hotels**, including *Alt Ochsen*, Ochsengasse 5 (☎07 51/56 10 40; ④), and *Baren*, Kirchstr. 3 (☎07 51/56 12 00; ⑤), both of which have recommendable restaurants. Liveliest **bar** in town is *Schwinderhannes*, Liebfrauenstr. 37, which has a beer garden.

Ravensburg

If most of Upper Swabia seems too provincial and too relentlessly Baroque, then the regional "metropolis" of **RAVENSBURG** offers a refreshing antidote. This former Free Imperial City became, courtesy of the linen trade, one of the richest towns in Germany in the fifteenth century. Even if it lacks a spectacular centrepiece, its medieval core presents an unusually satisfying and well-preserved townscape, dominated by the towers and gates of the former fortifications, now laid out as a promenade encircling the heart of the old city.

The Town

Marienplatz, which is really a broad street rather than a square but which is used for outdoor markets, lies at the heart of the city, with a whole series of public buildings from the period when Ravensburg was at the height of its prosperity. An indication of the importance of commerce to the city is the fact that the **Rathaus** is overshadowed by the **Waaghaus** alongside; the latter had the weigh house and mint (Ravensburg was long a major centre for coin production) on the ground floor, with the trading hall upstairs. It was adorned in the mid-sixteenth century with the **Blaserturm**, a watchtower crowned by a Renaissance octagon which has become the symbol of the town.

Not far from the Bahnhof, on the corner of Charlottenstrasse and Untere Breite Strasse, is the **Vogthaus** (April–June & Oct Tues–Sat 3–5pm, Sun 10am–noon & 3–5pm; July & Aug also Mon 10am–noon; free), a half-timbered patrician residence of the fifteenth century. It's now the local museum, but the house itself, which includes rooms in Gothic, Renaissance and Baroque styles, is the main attraction. Further down the street is the **Zehntscheuer**, a large timber-framed building of the previous century which looks for all the world like a farmhouse; previously part of the leper hospital, it's now an arts centre. Behind it is part of the Stadtmauer, including the round **Wehrturm** and the tall square **Gemalter Turm** (Painted Tower), which preserves the jazzy decoration which was once a feature of all of Ravensburg's towers.

A few minutes' walk east is another corner of the wall, with the round **Grüner Turm** (Green Tower) and the step-gabled **Frauentor**. Another tower here doubles as the belfry of the **Liebfrauenkirche**, the town's parish church. From the original fourteenth-century building, there remains the beautiful portal tympanum with scenes from the life of the Virgin. The interior has often been remodelled but preserves some fine stained-glass windows in the chancel. It formerly contained one of the masterpieces of fifteenth-century German sculpture, Michel Erhart's *Ravensburg Madonna* (a haunting carving showing the Virgin sheltering humanity under her cloak), but this has been replaced by a copy, the original now being in the Skulpturensammlung in Berlin.

Bachstrasse leads southwest from Marienplatz to the **Untertor**, while Marktstrasse snakes up to the other main gateway, the **Obertor**. Continuing upwards, and therefore out of the boundaries of the old city, you come to the **Mehlsack** (Sack of Flour), a cylindrical tower erected by the independently minded city council in the sixteenth century as an extra line of defence against the expansionist designs of the aristocratic owners of the **Veitsburg**. A path climbs up steeply to this fortress, imperiously perched on the hill above; on the way you pass through the half-timbered **Burghaldentorkel**, the only surviving example of twenty buildings in the town where grapes were stored and pressed. The original Veitsburg has completely disappeared, leaving only some later workshop buildings, now modernized as the youth hostel, and a small Baroque pavilion which houses a restaurant. However, it's well worth going up for the sake of the wonderful **views** of the town you get on the way.

Practicalities

The **tourist office** (Mon 8am–noon, Tues–Fri 8am–5.30pm, Sat 9am–noon; ☎07 51/8 23 24, fax 8 24 66, *www.stadt-ravensburg.de*) is at Kirchstr. 16. Centrally sited **hotels** include *Gasthof Ochsen,* Eichelstr. 17 (☎07 51/2 54 80; ③), *Café Baur,* Marienplatz 1 (☎07 51/2 56 16; ④), *Obertor,* Marktstr. 67 (☎07 51/3 66 70; ⑥), and *Waldhorn,* Marionplatz 15 (☎07 51/3 61 20, *www.waldhorn.de*; ⑦–⑨). The **youth hostel** has an atmospheric location in the Veitsburg (☎07 51/2 53 63, fax 1 37 69; DM24/€12 or DM29/€14.50). Good choices for **eating** and **drinking** are *Räuberhöhle,* Burgstr. 14, *Ratstube,* Marienplatz 19, *Altes Lädele,* Seebruckstr. 2, *Brotlaube,* Gaspinstmarkt 25, and the Gaststätte in the Veitsburg. Best of all are the restaurants in the *Hotel Waldhorn*; one of these, the *Weinstube Rebleutehaus,* occupies a medieval guildhouse. *Fastnet* and the *Rutenfest* in July are the main **festivals**.

THE BODENSEE

The **Bodensee** (also know as Lake Constance, or the Schwäbisches Meer – the "Swabian Sea") is in reality an enormous bulge in the River Rhine, which enters it from the Austrian side to the east and leaves it again on the Swiss border to the west. It's the largest lake in Germany, 14km across at its widest point and about 65km long, and one of the country's most popular holiday destinations. Its main, eastern part is known as the Obersee, while the northern of the western forks is the Überlinger See, the south-

---

BOAT TRIPS ON THE BODENSEE

By far the largest operator of passenger ships on the lake is the DB-affiliated Bodensee-Schiffsbetriebe (BSB; *www.bsb-online.com*) whose main offices are: Seestr. 22, Friedrichshafen (☎0 75 41/20 13 89); Hafenstr. 6, Konstanz (☎0 75 31/28 13 98); and Am Hafen, Lindau (☎0 83 82/60 99). Fares are very reasonable, being calculated at similar rates to other forms of public transport, and various combination passes, which cover local buses and trains as well as the boats, are available. Bikes can be taken on board without extra charge. Frequency of services is very seasonal, but free current timetables are available at all the harbours, and are also posted on the company Web site. Excursion cruises are run in summer, though these offer few advantages over the main scheduled routes, which are:

- Friedrichshafen–Romanshorn (Switzerland). The only car ferry operated by the company.
- Kreuzlingen (Switzerland)– Konstanz–Reichenau–Schaffhausen (Switzerland). The most scenic of the routes, continuing along the Rhine and terminating at the Rheinfall.
- Konstanz –Reichenau–Rodolfzell
- Konstanz –Meersburg–Friedrichshafen–Lindau–Bregenz (Austria).
- Konstanz –Meersburg–Mainau–Überlingen.

Perhaps the most useful crossing of all, however, is the car ferry across the very heart of the lake between Konstanz and Meersburg. Run by the Stadtwerk Konstanz (☎0 75 31/80 30), it operates throughout the day and night, with frequencies ranging from fifteen minutes to one hour. In addition, various smaller companies offer excursions on the lake; check locally for the best deals.

ern the Untersee. Thanks to its balmy, dry climate the Bodensee has developed into the nearest the country comes to having a Riviera, though thankfully the shorelines have been preserved from high-rise developments. **Meersburg** and **Überlingen** on the northern side are two of Germany's most picturesque towns; across the water are Constance **(Konstanz)**, the most cosmopolitan centre in this whole region, and the contrasting islands of **Mainau** and **Reichenau**.

The north shore

Of the three countries bordering the Bodensee, Germany has the lion's share of the shoreline, including the entire northern side. Although the warm climate means that the sweeping views across to the Alps are often lost in haze, this is nevertheless one of the most beautiful parts of Germany, with a couple of the country's most outstanding small towns as added attractions. A **corniche road**, served by regular buses, runs all the way along the shore from the eastern end at Lindau (see p.241). This is far preferable to the rail line, which deviates inland, though the ferries (see box opposite) offer the best means of seeing the lake.

Friedrichshafen

Situated at the widest part of the Bodensee, 22km west of Lindau and 19km south of Ravensburg, **FRIEDRICHSHAFEN** is best known for its distinguished place in aviation history (see box below). Despite being the only industrial blot on the lake, it manages a decidedly curious double existence, taking full advantage of its setting to serve as a rather flashy resort.

The eastern part of the waterfront has been laid out as an attractive promenade with gardens. At the far end is the one historical monument of any note, the Baroque onion-towered **Schlosskirche**, built at the very end of the seventeenth century by Christian Thumb. Its monastic buildings were converted into a palace for the kings of Württemberg last century and are still in the hands of their descendants.

ZEPPELINS AND DORNIERS

Count Ferdinand von Zeppelin, a native of Konstanz, was intrigued by the use of hot-air balloons in the American Civil War, which he witnessed as an official observer. He developed the idea to build a rigid airship with a cigar-shaped trussed frame supported by gas cells; the first model, the LZ-1, was tested in Friedrichshafen (which thereafter became both the manufacturing and launch base) in 1900. These strange, silent machines, capable of going at no more than 35kph, were turned from their original peaceful purpose to undertake bombing missions in World War I. Afterwards, however, their potential for long-distance travel was realized, and in 1928 the new, specially built *Graf Zeppelin* made the first transatlantic passenger flight, then a round-the-world trip the following year. By 1937 it had made 590 flights, including 114 ocean crossings. Disaster then struck when the huge new airship *Hindenburg* went up in flames while landing in New Jersey, killing 36 passengers. No more flights were undertaken, and production was not resumed after the factory's destruction in the war, although by then a safe, noninflammable gas had been developed.

Claude Dornier, originally an employee of Zeppelin, used the Bodensee to test his "flying boats", but eventually moved into the production of fighter aircraft. His planes were deployed extensively in the Blitz, something which seems to have been a sore point with the French occupying forces in 1945, who systematically looted the factory. Unlike its counterpart, this was revived and is still in operation under the management of Daimler-Chrysler.

At the opposite end of town, in part of the Bauhaus-style Hafenbahnhof at Seestr. 22, is the **Zeppelin-Museum** (Tues–Sun 10am–5/6pm; DM12/€6). This contains a number of original aircraft, a reconstruction of a section of the famous *Hindenburg* (which can be boarded for inspection) and fascinating archive film (English soundtrack available) of the Zeppelins. There's also an art gallery, dominated by the works of the folksy school of painters based around the Bodensee in the fifteenth century.

Practicalities

Friedrichshafen has two train stations: the **Stadtbahnhof** near the promenade and the **Hafenbahnhof** further east by the commercial harbour. The **tourist office** (May–Sept Mon–Fri 8am–noon & 2–5pm; Oct–April Mon–Thurs 8am–noon & 2–5pm, Fri 8am–1pm; ☎0 75 41/3 00 10, fax 7 25 88, *www.friedrichshafen.de*) is just across from the former at Bahnhofplatz 2.

One of the cheapest accommodation options is a **pension**, *Wurster*, Georgstr. 14 (☎0 75 41/72 69 40; ②). **Hotels** include *Ailinger Hof*, Ailinger Str. 49 (☎0 75 41/2 27 88; ③), *City-Krone,* Schamstr. 7 (☎0 75 41/70 50, *www.hotel-city-krone.de*; ⑤), and *Buchhorner Hof,* Friedrichstr. 33 (☎0 75 41/20 50; ⑥–⑨). The **youth hostel** is in the eastern part of town at Lindauer Str. 3 (☎0 75 41/7 24 04, fax 7 49 86; DM26/€813 or DM31/€15.50); opposite, at Lindauer Str. 20, is the *Dimmler* **campsite** (☎0 75 41/7 34 21). Another campsite (☎0 75 41/4 20 59) can be found in the incorporated village of Fischbach to the west of town. The leading **restaurants** are those in the last two hotels mentioned above and the classy *Kurgartenrestaurant* in the *Graf-Zeppelin-Haus,* Olgastr. 20, which has a terrace overlooking the lake.

Meersburg

MEERSBURG, which clings to a steeply sloping site 16km from Friedrichshafen, is one of those places which perfectly fits the tourist-board image of Romantic Germany. It therefore usually swarms with an uncomfortably large number of day-trippers, but it's an atmospheric and picturesque little town well worth braving the hordes to see.

Arriving by the corniche road, which at this point passes high above the Bodensee, you enter the historic quarter via the dignified **Obertor**. It's then just a short walk down to the riotously picturesque **Marktplatz**, where three streets converge. Steigstrasse, lined on both sides with half-timbered houses, then plummets towards the lake; its west side, with a sloping ramp giving access to the houses, is particularly eye-catching.

All over town, you get tantalizing glimpses of its great pride and joy, the **Altes Schloss** (daily: March–Oct 9am–6.30pm; Nov–Feb 10am–6pm; *www.meersburg.com*; DM9/€4.50), whose round corner towers and gabled central block produce a distinctive silhouette. Founded by the Merovingian King Dagobert, it boasts of being the oldest surviving castle in Germany, a claim recently substantiated by the discovery that some sections of the masonry do actually appear to date back as far as the seventh century. For most of its history, it was a seat of the prince-bishops of Konstanz, who extensively rebuilt it throughout the medieval period, making it their main residence when they were bundled out of their city at the Reformation; since secularization, it has been in private ownership. Germany's greatest woman poet, **Annette von Droste-Hülshoff**, came to live here during the 1840s as guest of the then-owner, her brother-in-law, Baron von Lassberg. Her rooms, whose period furnishings are in stark contrast to the austerity of the medieval chambers, are still as they were in her day, and many of her most famous poems are exhibited on the walls.

The **Neues Schloss** (April–Oct daily 10am–1pm & 2–6pm; DM6/€3) above was built under the direction of Balthasar Neumann in the mid-eighteenth century, when the prince-bishops decided they warranted a more comfortable and modern residence.

It now houses a cultural centre and local museum, which includes displays on Claude Dornier and the fifteenth-century Cologne painter Stefan Lochner, who is thought to have been a native of the town. There's a wonderful view over the Bodensee from the gardens in front; an even better one can be had from the belvedere known as the **Känzele** a short walk to the east.

Practicalities

The Seepromenade below the Altes Schloss, lined with cafés and restaurants, many specializing in fresh fish from the lake, is the most popular rendezvous point. Here also is the **harbour** for the BSB ships; the terminal for the **car ferry** to Konstanz is some 700m west. **Buses** stop near the latter, as well as near the Obertor; Meersburg is not on the rail line. The **tourist office** (May–Sept Mon–Fri 9am–6.30pm, Sat 10am–2pm; Oct–April Mon–Fri 9am–noon & 2–4.30pm; ☎0 75 32/43 11 10, fax 43 11 20, *www. meersburg.de*) is at Kirchstr. 4 at the top of the town.

If you want to base yourself in only one resort while touring the Bodensee, Meersburg is probably the best choice, as its central location means that everywhere is within easy reach. There is no youth hostel or campsite, but plenty of **private rooms** (①–③) and small **pensions**, such as *Alpenblick*, Droste-Hülshoff-Weg 13 (☎0 75 32/66 77; ③), and *Am Hafen*, Spitalgasse 3–4 (☎0 75 32/70 69; ③). Among a host of enticing **hotels** are the two historic inns on Marktplatz: the seventeenth-century *Gasthof Zum Bären* at no. 11 (☎0 75 32/4 32 20; ④–⑥) and the fifteenth-century *Löwen* at no. 2 (☎0 75 32/4 30 40; ⑤–⑦). Pick of the lakeside hotels are *Seehotel Off*, Uferpromenade 51 (☎0 75 32/4 47 40; ⑥), and *Residenz am See*, Uferpromenade 11 (☎0 75 32/8 00 40; ⑦–⑨), which boasts a rose garden as well as a terrace. Of these, *Off* has an elegant **café**, while all the others have excellent **restaurants**.

Unteruhldingen and Birnau

Next resort along the lake, 7km away, is Uhldingen-Mühlhofen, a federation of several previously separate villages. Shoreside **UNTERUHLDINGEN** has the most unusual open-air museum in Germany, the **Pfahlbauten** (guided tours daily: April–Sept 8am–6pm; Oct daily 9am–5pm; March & Nov Sat & Sun 9am–5pm; DM6/€3), containing conjectural re-creations of Stone Age dwellings, remains of which were found here, built on huge wooden stilts driven into the bed of the lake. Come early as the queues are usually horrendous.

About twenty minutes' walk uphill is the Cistercian **Basilika Birnau**, whose wonderful, isolated setting is now marred by the proximity of the main road. Built in just four years, it's a collaboration by three of the finest Rococo artists – the architect Peter Thumb, the fresco painter Gottfried Bernard Göz and the sculptor Josef Anton Feichtmayr. The dazzling interior is a paean of praise to the Virgin Mary; its illusionistic tricks reach a climax in the cupola which incorporates a mirror to enhance its effects. Look out for the famous statuette known as the *Honigschlecker* (a cherub sucking the finger that has just been inside a bee's nest); it's placed beside an altar dedicated to St Bernard of Clairvaux, in honour of the claim that his words were as sweet as honey.

Überlingen

A further 5km on, the former Free Imperial City of **ÜBERLINGEN**, nowadays a specialist health resort, rises gently above the lake. For sheer good looks and polished appearance, it has few rivals in all of Germany: with its magnificent public buildings of a distinctive pale green stonework, picturesque alleys of half-timbered houses, glorious lakeward vistas and luxuriant gardens, it seems almost indecently favoured for a place whose population has never numbered more than a few thousand.

Dominating the town is the **Münster**, a huge Gothic structure which was constructed over a period of two hundred years. Its two towers make a fascinating pairing. The tall square clock tower to the south, which provides a landmark visible from far off, was specially heightened to serve as a watchtower, and crowned with an octagonal Renaissance lantern. In contrast, its stumpy northern counterpart which houses the huge *Osanna* bell, nestles under a steeply pitched wooden roof which looks as though it should belong on a barn rather than a church. The sobriety of the rest of the exterior sharply contrasts with the majestic interior, whose intricately vaulted nave of five aisles, built in the second half of the sixteenth century, shows the by then archaic Gothic style bowing out with a bang. Also marking the end of an era is the tiered main **altarpiece**, carved by Jörg Zürn in the early seventeenth century, which was the last of the great series of wooden retables illustrating biblical stories which adorn so many German churches; soon after, these were completely supplanted by more florid Baroque altars. Zürn also made the graceful tabernacle alongside, while he or members of his family carved four of the altars which adorn each of the fourteen nave chapels.

Across Münsterplatz, and backing onto Hofstatt, the market square, is the **Rathaus** (Mon–Fri 9am–noon & 2.30–5pm, Sat 9am–noon; free). Its first-floor **Ratsaal**, complete with panelled walls, projecting arches and a ribbed ceiling, is a masterpiece of late fifteenth-century design.

Climbing up either Krummebergstrasse or Luitzengasse on the northern side of Münsterplatz brings you to the **Reichlin-von-Meldegg-Haus** (Tues–Sat 9am–12.30pm & 2–5pm, Sun 10am–3pm; DM4/€2), another late fifteenth-century building, named after the wealthy doctor whose home it was. The interiors include a chapel and an ornate Rococo **Festsaal**, but most of the space is taken up by a surprisingly good **Heimatmuseum**, including the largest collection of dolls' houses in Germany, ranging from Renaissance to Jugendstil. From the balcony at the end of the gardens is the best **view** in Überlingen, showing the town etched out against the background of the Bodensee and Swiss Alps.

Above the northwest side of Münsterplatz is the **Franziskanerkirche**, with a spare, gaunt exterior typical of the mendicant orders. Its interior, however, was given the full Baroque treatment. More striking than the church is the late Gothic **Franziskanertor**, the northern entrance to the town. This is one of seven surviving gateways and towers of the **Stadtmauer**, which has now been laid out as a shady promenade.

The waterfront is dominated by the Neoclassical **Greth**, crowned with a huge slanting roof. Just to the west is the gabled Gothic **Zeughaus** (May–Sept Mon–Sat 10am–noon; DM2/€1), containing a private collection of arms and armour. At the end of the promenade are the **Kurpark** and spa quarters.

Practicalities

Überlingen's **Bahnhof** lies at the extreme western end of town, but **buses** stop on the one-way streets immediately south of the Münster. The **tourist office** (mid-March to April & Oct Mon–Fri 9am–1pm & 2–6pm; May–Sept Mon–Fri 9am–6pm, Sat 10am–1pm, Sun 2–5pm; Nov to mid-March Mon–Fri 9am–1pm & 2–5pm; ☎0 75 51/99 11 22, fax 99 11 35, *www.ueberlingen.de*) is housed in the Greth, Landungsplatz 14.

Among the numerous **pensions** are *Haus Klemm*, Zum Hecht 66 (☎0 75 51/6 37 49; ③), and *Gästehaus Mainaublick*, Zum Stichling 6 (☎0 75 51/6 34 74; ③). **Hotels** are mostly pricey by Bodensee standards, being geared to the lucrative spa market. The two best lakeside addresses are *Bad-Hotel*, Christophstr. 2 (☎0 75 51/83 70; ⑥–⑧), and *Seegarten*, Seepromenade 7 (☎0 75 51/6 34 98; ⑥–⑧). However, the finest views are from the town's most prestigious establishment, *Parkhotel St Leonhard*, which is set in its own park at Obere-St-Leonhard-Str. 71 (☎0 75 51/80 81 00; ⑧). Each of these has a recommendable **restaurant**. There's a large modern **youth hostel** at the eastern end of the waterside at Alte Nussdorfer Str. 26 (☎0 75 51/42 04 fax 12 77; DM26/€13 or DM31/€15.50), and four separate **campsites** in the vicinity: one (☎0 75 51/6 45 83) in the town itself, close to the Bahnhof, the others in Nussdorf a couple of kilometres down the lake.

Among the town's **festivals**, the most important is the *Schwedenprozession*, commemorating this Catholic town's successful defence of its independence against the Swedes in the Thirty Years War. This is performed twice annually: on the Sunday after May 16, and on the second Sunday in July. *Fastnacht* is also a big annual event and bizarrely features Bengali costumes.

Salem

SALEM, a group of villages 11km east of Überlingen, is centred on the great **Reichsabtei** (guided tours April–Oct Mon–Sat 9.30am–6pm, Sun 10.30am–6pm; *www.salem.de*; DM10/€5) of that name. Formerly a Cistercian monastery, and the mother house of Birnau, it was taken over on secularization by the Grand Dukes of Baden and remains in the possession of their descendants. Part of the complex is now occupied by one of Germany's most exclusive schools, founded by Kurt Hahn who later emigrated to Britain and established Gordonstoun.

The **Münster** is rarely used for public worship and hence has an inevitable coldness about it. Nonetheless, it's an outstanding example of the grandly sober Gothic architecture of the Cistercians, with their favoured characteristics of a large chancel terminating in a flat east end. In the eighteenth century, the church was littered with a series of altars and monuments in a very early Neoclassical style; the marriage of two very different kinds of artistic austerity works surprisingly well. Although originally the conventual part of the monastery, the **Schloss** indeed seems more like a palace, having been built in a luxuriant Baroque style following the destruction of the medieval buildings in a fire. The **Kaisersaal**, a richly decorated reception hall to accommodate any visiting imperial entourage, is particularly impressive.

Heiligenberg

Commanding a grandstand view over the whole Bodensee area on the heights above Salem and some 7km away by road, is the little health resort of **HEILIGENBERG**; unfortunately, there's no bus directly linking the two, though both have services to Überlingen. Its enormous **Schloss** (guided tours April to early July & mid-Aug to Oct daily 9.30am–noon & 1–5pm; DM7/€3.50) came into the possession of the House of Fürstenberg in the sixteenth century; they had the existing medieval castle radically rebuilt, creating a fine Renaissance palace. The **Rittersaal** is outstanding, especially its intricately carved coffered ceiling (which is suspended from the vault on steel rods to support its weight), and the glass paintings of coats of arms. Only marginally less impressive is the brightly painted **Schlosskapelle**, which is arranged more like a theatre than a chapel and has beautiful stained-glass windows brought from the former Dominican friary in Konstanz. You're allowed up into the family oratory to inspect the vault, with its seemingly inexhaustible series of angels in different guises, at close range. Between the Schloss and the village is the graceful **Glockenturm** (Bell Tower), built by Jerg Schwartzenberger, the principal architect of the Schloss.

There's a good **guesthouse**, *Haus Alpenblick*, Betenbrunner Str. 14 (☎07 5 54/3 55; ③), and a couple of enticing **hotels**: *Bayerischer Hof*, Röhrenbacher Str. 1 (☎0 75 54/2 17; ③), and *Berghotel Baader*, Salemer Str. 5 (☎0 75 54/80 21 00; ⑥). The last-named has a renowned gourmet **restaurant**, but even this faces strong competition from *Restaurant de Weiss im Hohenstein* at Postplatz 5, which doubles as an art gallery.

Konstanz (Constance)

By any standards, **KONSTANZ** has a remarkable geographical position. It's split in two by the Rhine, which re-emerges here from the Obersee (the main part of the Bodensee) as a channel for a brief stretch, before forming the Untersee, the arm from which it finally re-emerges as a river. The Altstadt is a tiny enclave on the otherwise Swiss side of the lake, a fact which was of inestimable benefit during the war when the Allies desisted from bombing it for fear of hitting neutral Switzerland. Curiously enough, the latter is one country to which Konstanz has never belonged: probably founded by the Romans, it has been a prince-bishopric and a Swabian Free Imperial City, then Austrian, before finally being allocated to Baden. Between 1414 and 1418, when the conclave met here to resolve the Great Schism, the city was the nerve-centre of European power politics. Nowadays, it contents itself with more modest roles as a resort town, frontier post and seat of a new university whose students help to give it a relaxed yet lively air all year round.

Arrival, information and accommodation

The **Deutscher Bahnhof**, the terminus of the line from the Black Forest, is right beside the Konzilgebäude; immediately south is its Swiss counterpart, the **Schweizer Bahnhof**, which is the departure point for most **bus** services beyond the urban area. In front of the former, at Bahnhofplatz 13, is the **tourist office** (April–Oct Mon–Fri 9am–6.30pm, Sat 9am–4pm, Sun 10am–1pm; Nov–March Mon–Fri 9.30am–12.30pm & 2–6pm; ☎0 75 31/13 30 30, fax 13 30 80, *www.konstanz.de*). For information on **boat trips**, see the box on p.302. Note that the car ferry to Meersburg is in the suburb of Staad; all other services leave from the harbour behind the Bahnhof. The main annual

---

THE COUNCIL OF 1414–1418

In 1409, the Council of Pisa elected Alexander V pope in an attempt to end the **Great Schism**, which had left rival claimants to the papacy in Rome and Avignon since 1378. Far from solving the problem, however, this left the world with three competing popes. Eventually, Emperor Sigismund forced Alexander's successor, John XXIII, to call an ecumenical council of ecclesiastical and secular rulers in Konstanz in 1414. This became one of the largest and most extraordinary gatherings in world history: the sittings lasted four years, during which time 72,000 visitors (more than seven times the number of the permanent population) flocked to the town. As well as reuniting the Church, the intention was also to reform it, as its institutions and practices, notably the rite of confession, the apostolic supremacy and the granting of indulgences, had come under attack from **Jan Hus**, the first Czech rector of Prague University, who had gained a large popular following in the process. Hus was guaranteed a safe return passage in order to defend his views, but was imprisoned, tried and condemned as a heretic, and handed over to the secular authorities for burning at the stake.

John XXIII, who realized he was likely to lose his position as pope, attempted to sabotage the council by withdrawing from it, whereupon it issued the highly dubious *Sacrosancta*, affirming its own superiority over the papacy. In 1417, both John and Gregory XII, his Roman rival, agreed to step down in favour of a compromise candidate; although the Avignon pope, Benedict XIII, stubbornly refused to do likewise, he found himself deserted by his supporters and was deposed. The way was therefore cleared for the election of Cardinal Oddo Colonna as Pope Martin V and an end to the schism. Various reforms, primarily financial, were then enacted, but the failure to undertake anything more radical – symbolized by the treatment of Hus – eventually led to a far more serious and lasting split in the Church with the Reformation exactly a century later.

festival is the *Seenachtsfest* in August, with a spectacular display of fireworks over the Bodensee, and classical music concerts, the *Konstanzer Internationale Musiktage*, are held throughout the summer.

There are **private rooms** (①–④) all over town. The **youth hostel** is at Zur Allmannshöhe 18 (☎0 75 31/3 22 60, fax 3 11 63; DM22/€11 or DM27/€13.50); take bus #4 from the Bahnhof to Jugendherberge, or bus #1 to Allmannsdorf-Post. Among the numerous **campsites** in the vicinity are *Klausehorn* (☎0 75 31/63 72) in the incorporated fishing village of Dingelsdorf and *Litzelstetten-Mainau* (☎0 75 31/94 30 30) near the island of Mainau; both can be reached by bus #4. Many of the more central **hotels** are in historic buildings and therefore somewhat expensive, though arguably worth it for the atmosphere.

Hotels and pensions

Barbarossa, Obermarkt 8–12 (☎0 75 31/2 20 21, fax 2 76 30). Fine middle-range hotel and restaurant in the heart of the Altstadt. ⑥.

Graf Zeppelin, Am Stephansplatz 15 (☎0 75 31/2 37 80, fax 1 72 26). A somewhat old-fashioned, archetypally German hotel and restaurant, conveniently located near the Münster. ③.

Gretel, Zollenstr. 6–8 (☎0 75 31/2 32 83). Altstadt pension run in tandem with a Weinstube, *Zum Guten Hirten*. ③.

Inselhotel, Auf der Insel (☎0 75 31/12 50, fax 2 64 02, *www.steigenberger.com*). Konstanz's most prestigious hotel is a notable historic landmark in its own right, and offers wonderful views over the Bodensee. It has two restaurants, *Dominikanerstube* being a bit less pricey than the showpiece *Seerestaurant*. ⑨

Schiff am See, William-Graf-Platz 2, Staad (☎0 75 31/3 10 41, fax 3 19 81, *www.ringhotels.de*). This fine waterfront hotel is handy for the car ferry. It also has a good restaurant (closed Mon & lunchtime Tues). ⑥–⑧.

Seehotel Silber, Seestr. 25 (☎0 75 31/6 30 44, fax 6 48 13). Located in a Jugendstil villa with a lakeside terrace, this is best known for its gourmet restaurant, generally considered the best in Konstanz. ⑨.

Seeschau, Zur Schiffslände 11, Dingelsdorf (☎0 75 31/51 90, fax 78 94). Lakeside Gasthaus in the far north of the urban area; take bus #4. ④.

Sonnenhof, Otto-Raggenbass-Str. 3 (☎0 75 31/2 22 57, fax 2 03 58). Reasonably priced hotel in the south of town, hard by the Swiss border. ④.

The Town

Nearly everything of interest in Konstanz lies in the Altstadt which stretches from the southern bank of the Rhine to the very abrupt border with Switzerland about 1km to the south.

The Münster

The famous conclave met in the **Münster**, suitably set on the highest point of the Altstadt. Its subsequent history has been less glorious: once the Reformation had taken hold, the local bishop was driven out of town, and after the see (which dated back at least as far as the seventh century) was dissolved in 1821, the church sank into insignificance. It was begun as a Romanesque pillared basilica – whose outline is still obvious – and building continued for six hundred years, so there are marked differences in style, particularly in the interior: the aisles and their chapels are Gothic, while the organ-case and gallery were built during the Renaissance, and the original ceiling was replaced by a vaulted Baroque one. The spot on which Hus is said to have stood during his trial is marked in the central aisle, by the twenty-fourth row.

Of the furnishings, the most remarkable are the vigorously carved fifteenth-century **choir stalls**, designed by Nicolaus Gerhaert, and the broadly contemporary and equally ornate **Schnegg**, a staircase in the northern transept. From here you descend to the **Konradikapelle**, named in honour of St Konrad, a tenth-century bishop of Konstanz, who is commemorated by a Gothic funerary slab and a golden shrine. The saint would probably still recognize the tiny **crypt** further on, the oldest surviving part of the building, whose walls are hung with remarkable gilded enamel medallions. Beyond are the Gothic cloisters, off which are several imposing chambers, notably the rotunda known as the Mauritiuskapelle, which houses a magnificent late thirteenth-century **Holy Sepulchre**, inspired by the original in Jerusalem. Next door is the Sylvesterkapelle, with a complete cycle of fifteenth-century frescoes of the life of Christ.

For a fine view of the town, climb up the **tower** (mid-April to mid-Oct Mon–Sat 10am–5pm, Sun 1–5pm; DM2/€1). The central lantern and openwork spire of this are nineteenth-century additions to the massive Gothic facade, whose three sections were, unusually, all of similar height, giving it a decidedly forbidding and unecclesiastical look.

Münsterplatz and the Niederburg

On Münsterplatz are a number of fine old mansions, including the **Haus zur Katz**, a fifteenth-century guildhouse which is the earliest example of rusticated stonework in Germany, and the **Haus zur Kunkel** (Tues–Fri 10am–noon & 2–4pm, Sat 10am–noon; free), formerly the residence of the sacristan. Behind the latter's Baroque exterior lurk some original thirteenth-century rooms, one of which features some beautiful early Gothic frescoes showing linen weavers at work; a sign tells you at which door to ring in order to see them.

Between here and the Rhine is the best-preserved part of town, the **Niederburg**, a quarter of twisting little alleys lined by old houses. Overlooking the river are two fragments of the fortifications – the **Pulverturm** and the **Rheintorturm**. The latter, hard by the modern Rheinbrücke which carries the main road and rail line into the heart of Konstanz, is particularly impressive; it dates back to the late twelfth century and preserves some scanty frescoes. Across the bridge is **Seestrasse**, a promenade of grandiosely elegant villas, one of which contains the **Casino**, a particular magnet to the Swiss.

At the southeast corner of the Rheinbrücke is the exclusive **Inselhotel**, occupying the old Dominican priory. Its cellars were used to imprison Hus, and it was also the birthplace of Ferdinand von Zeppelin, a statue to whom can be seen overlooking the main **harbour** – a bustle of colourful sails in the summer – just to the south. Behind it is the **Konzilgebäude**, a fourteenth-century storehouse with a prominent hipped roof. It owes its name to the disputed contention that it was the scene of the election of Pope Martin V; nowadays it has been restored to serve as a festival hall and a restaurant.

The rest of the centre

Konstanz's two market squares, Fischmarkt and Marktstätte, are respectively west and southwest of the Konzilgebäude. South of the latter, along the street of the same name, is the **Rosgartenmuseum** (currently closed for restoration; previously Tues–Thurs 10am–5pm, Fri–Sun 10am–4pm; DM3/€1.50), which has a good collection of local archeological finds, in particular from the Paleolithic period, and also art and craft exhibits from the Middle Ages. You might think from the name that the building must originally have had something to do with roses, but it's an old euphemism for the local horse abattoir: the German for horse was traditionally *Ross*, but by omitting one letter people could say *Rosgarten* and ignore its sorry purpose. At the end of the same street is the **Dreifaltigkeitskirche**, the church of the old Augustinian monastery. It was frescoed during the time of the Council with scenes from the history of the order, plus portraits of various personalities, among them Emperor Sigismund.

Returning to Marktstätte, Kanzleistrasse leads west past the Renaissance **Rathaus**, whose facade was jollied up by the addition of Romantic murals. At the end of the street is **Obermarkt**, which is lined with more colourful mansions; here, in 1411, the Hohenzollerns were invested with control over the March of Brandenburg, a crucial step in their drive, achieved four and a half centuries later, to unite the German nation under their control.

Hussenstrasse leads south from here to the **Schnetztor**, a fourteenth-century fortified gateway complete with outer courtyard. On the way you pass, at no. 64, the **Hus-Museum** (June–Sept Tues–Sun 10am–5pm; Oct–May Tues–Sun 10am–noon & 2–4pm; free). This half-timbered house, where the reformer stayed on his arrival in Konstanz, was bought by the Prague Museum Society in 1923 to turn it into a memorial to one of the Czechs' most important national heroes. Apart from his importance as a religious thinker, Hus had a major influence on the Czech sense of nationhood and he almost single-handedly established his country's national literature.

Eating and drinking

Konstanz is awash with good places to eat and drink, with plenty of alternatives to the excellent hotel restaurants mentioned on p.309.

Brauhaus Johann Albrecht, Konradigasse 2. Hausbrauerei which serves inexpensive meals.

Bürgerstuben, Bahnhofplatz 7. Café-restaurant featuring moderately priced Bodensee fish specialities.

Casino-Restaurant, Seestr. 21. A high-class, fairly expensive restaurant with panorama terrace. Evenings only.

Hafenhalle, Hafenstr. 10. Although the menu here has the expected fish dishes, game features as well.

Konzil-Gaststätten, Hafenstr. 2. The restaurant in the historic Konzilgebäude is reasonably priced considering its quality, and has the benefit of a terrace overlooking the harbour.

Rosgartencafé, Rosgartenstr. 9. Good traditional café.

St Stephanskeller, St-Stephans-Platz 43. A combined wine bar and restaurant; the latter is closed Sun & Mon.

Staader Fährhaus, Fischerstr. 30, Staad. One of the town's most creative restaurants, with a strong line in local fish dishes. Closed Tues and open evenings only on Wed.

The Bodensee islands

There are only two islands of any size in the Bodensee, and, notwithstanding the fact that both put their rich soils to good use, they could hardly be more different: **Mainau** is an exotic, scented floral isle which seems to have been wafted up from the Mediterranean, while **Reichenau**, which is mostly given over to the cultivation of fruit and vegetables, retains its three ancient monasteries as vivid reminders of its status as one of the cradles of German civilization. Ironically enough, the easiest way to reach either of the islands is by bus (causeways having been constructed to link them to the mainland), though it's obviously far more atmospheric to arrive by boat.

Mainau

Mainau (Easter to late Oct daily 7am–8pm; rest of year daily 9am–6pm; *www.mainau .de*; Easter to late Oct DM18.50/€9.25, kids DM6.50/3.25; rest of year free, though admission fees are levied for individual attractions), which lies in the Überlinger See, possesses an aura of immense grandeur, thanks to the riotous colours of the flowers and shrubs which bedeck it, and the exhilarating long-distance views over the lake across to the opposite shore, which are particularly spectacular at sunset. It's like a little tropical paradise – or it would be were it not for the relentless presence of thousands of visitors every day for at least six months of the year. With this in mind, try to come as early as possible: the crowds start to build up by mid-morning. Local bus #4 from the centre of Konstanz stops at the end of the causeway at the western approach to Mainau; ferries between Meersburg and Unteruhldingen call at the landing stage at the opposite side of the island.

For over five hundred years Mainau belonged to the Teutonic Knights, and the **Schloss** at the highest point of the island is a typical example of the Baroque architecture they favoured during the time they were based in Bad Mergentheim. It's now the residence of the island's flamboyant Swedish owner, Count Bernadotte, a descendant of the grand dukes of Baden who took possession of Mainau last century. Most of the interior is out of bounds to the public, though one hall is used for exhibitions, and the **Schlosskapelle**, with its frothy ceiling paintings and elaborate woodwork, is generally accessible.

The carefully manicured gardens, which occupy almost every available part of the island, are what everyone comes to see. A combination of the freak microclimate and the utilization of scientific techniques means that at least part of the garden is in bloom for half of the year; a unique feature is the presence of three-dimensional **floral sculptures**, which were specially created as diversions for the youngest visitors. **Spring** is the most delightful season here, with a big display of orchids in the Palmenhaus, along with an array of tulips, hyacinths, narcissi and primroses outside; azaleas and rhododendrons flower later. **Summer** sees the rose walk at its best, while palm trees, bananas, lemons and oranges also ripen then. **Autumn** features a dahlia show, after which the colour disappears, leaving only the year-round greenery of the cedars, sequoias and cypresses until the cycle starts again. A recent addition to the facilities is the **Schmetterlingshaus** (Butterfly House; daily: Easter to late Oct 10am–8pm; late Oct to Easter 11am–5pm), which has the largest collection of butterflies in the country.

As well as various snack bars, there's a classy **restaurant**, *Schwedenschenke,* located uphill by the Schloss. Note that, although you can stay on past the official closing time, you have to be off the island by midnight.

Reichenau

Reichenau, set in the Untersee 8km west of Konstanz, has a history almost as venerable as the city itself. Monastic life was established here in 724, and three monasteries, which all survive, were in place by the end of the ninth century. Many of the early abbots also held high positions in the Holy Roman Empire, and the island was a famous centre of scholarship, literature and painting, with the two arts combined in the great local speciality of manuscript illumination. However, by the twelfth century the monasteries were already in decline, and there was no more than a token monastic presence for several hundred years before the dissolution in 1803. Nowadays, two-thirds of the island's area is devoted to market gardens, giving it a character not dissimilar to the tulip-growing regions of Holland. Very quiet and sedate, it's a popular holiday resort with pensioners and families, who rent apartments around its coast.

Just 4.5km long and 1.5km wide, the layout of Reichenau is easy to grasp. There are three villages, each centred on a monastery. First up is **OBERZELL**, with the church of **St Georg**, the only one of the trio not completely reconstructed at a later date. The dignified Romanesque entrance hall was the sole significant addition made to the original, one of the most complete examples of Carolingian architecture to have survived anywhere in Europe. Inside is a wonderful set of Ottonian **frescoes**, which are about a century younger than the building and show the same style as the famed Reichenau miniatures, albeit on a monumental scale. The eight main scenes, whose colours have been vividly brought out in a recent restoration, illustrate the miracles of Christ – subjects which were mostly eschewed by later artists.

Little more than 1km further on is **MITTELZELL**, whose large **Münster** is the mother-church of Reichenau. Its present form, apart from the Gothic chancel, dates from the very beginning of the eleventh century and is an impressive sight, particularly when viewed from across the garden on its northern side. The **Schatzkammer** (May–Sept Mon–Sat 11am–noon & 3–4pm; DM1/€0.50) on the northern side of the chancel contains a carved fifth-century ivory pyx and a poignant Romanesque crucifix from St Georg, along with the usual array of reliquaries.

Towards the far end of the island is **NIEDERZELL**, with the twin-towered twelfth-century Romanesque church of **St-Peter-und-Paul**. This is the least distinctive of the three and is further marred by a fair amount of frivolous Baroque interior decoration, but a fresco of *The Last Judgement*, the final expression of the Reichenau school of painting, can be seen in the apse.

Practicalities

Reichenau's **tourist office** (March, April & Oct Mon–Fri 8.30am–noon & 2–5pm; May–Sept Mon–Fri 8.30am–noon & 2–6pm, Sat 9am–noon; Nov–Feb Mon–Fri 9am–noon; ☎0 75 34/9 20 70, fax 92 07 77, *www.reichenau.de*) is at Ergat 5 in Mittelzell. There's a **campsite** (☎0 75 34/73 84) on the shore in Niederzell, plus around a dozen **private houses** (①–③) with rooms to let. The most inexpensive **hotel** is *Kaiserpfalz*, Abt-Berno-Str. 1 (☎0 75 34/2 75; ③), in Mittelzell. In the same village are two highly prestigious lakeside establishments: *Strandhotel Löchnerhaus,* An der Schiffslände 12 (☎0 75 34/80 30; ⑤–⑧), and *Seeschau,* An der Schiffslände 8 (☎0 75 34/2 57; ⑦–⑨). Their **restaurants** are among the best in the Bodensee area.

Ferries between Konstanz and the Swiss city of Schaffhausen call at Reichenau. Otherwise, regular DB **buses** leave from outside the Bahnhof in Konstanz; less conveniently, there's a station near the island on the main rail line to the Black Forest.

THE BLACK FOREST REGION

Even in a country where woodland is so widespread as to exert a grip over such varied aspects of national life as folklore, literature and leisure activities, the **Black Forest** (Schwarzwald) stands out as a place with its own special mystique. Stretching 170km north to south, and up to 60km east to west, it's by far the largest German forest – and the most beautiful. Geographically speaking, it's a massif in its own right, but forms a pair with the broadly similar French Vosges on the opposite side of the Rhine valley, which demarcates the borders with both France and Switzerland. The name of the forest comes from the dark, densely packed fir trees on the upper slopes; oaks and beeches are characteristic of the lower ranges. With its houses sheltering beneath massive sloping straw roofs, its famous gateau, its cuckoo clocks and its colourful, often outrageous traditional dress, the Black Forest ranks second only to Bavaria as the font of stereotyped images of the country.

Even as late as the 1920s, much of this area was a rarely penetrated wilderness, forming a refuge for everything from boars to bandits. Romantics were drawn here by the wild beauty of watery gorges, dank valleys and exhilarating mountain views. Nowadays, most of the villages have been opened up as spa and health resorts, full of shops selling tacky souvenirs, while the old trails have become manicured gravel paths smoothed down for ramblers and strollers. Yet, for all that – and in spite of fears about the potentially disastrous effects of *Waldsterben*, which may have affected as many as half the trees – it remains a landscape of unique character, and by no means all the modernizations are drawbacks.

Accommodation, for example, is plentiful and generally excellent value. **Rail** fans will find several of the most spectacular lines in Europe, some of them brilliant feats of engineering. Note, though, that the trains tend to stick closely to the valleys, that **bus**

services are much reduced outside the tourist season, and that **walking** is undoubtedly the most satisfying way to get around.

Most of the Black Forest is associated with the Margravate (later Grand Duchy) of **Baden**, whose old capital of **Baden-Baden** – once the ultimate playground of the mega-rich – is at the northern fringe of the forest, in a fertile orchard and vineyard-growing area. This was later usurped by custom-built **Karlsruhe**, which is technically outside the Black Forest but best visited in conjunction with it. The only city actually surrounded by the forest is **Freiburg im Breisgau**, one of the most distinctive and enticing in the country. Nestling in the far southwestern corner of Germany, it lies just 30km from the French border and the gateway town of Breisach.

Freiburg im Breisgau

FREIBURG IM BREISGAU, "capital" of the Black Forest, basks in a laid-back atmosphere which seems completely un-German. As the seat of a university since 1457, it has an animated, youthful presence which, unlike so many other academic centres, is kept up all year round, with the help of a varied programme of festivals. It's a city of music, of street theatre and buskers, and a haunt of colourfully clad gypsies. Furthermore, the sun shines here more often, and there are more vineyards within the municipal area than in any other city in the country.

Freiburg's singularity is often attributed to the fact that it's really an Austrian city. Between 1368 and 1805, when it was allocated to the buffer state of Baden, it was almost continuously under the protection of the House of Habsburg. It's often claimed that the Austrians brought a touch of humanity to the German character, and that it was their eventual exclusion from the country's affairs which led to the triumph of militarism. The persistence here of the relaxed multicultural climate that was traditionally characteristic of Austria suggests that there's a grain of truth in this cliché.

Freiburg makes the most obvious base for visiting the Black Forest, with fast and frequent public transport connections to all the famous beauty spots. In its own right, it warrants a couple of days' exploration at least, and is renowned for its excellent mix of lively bars and restaurants. Even if you're only passing through, you should make a point of visiting Freiburg's lovely **Münster**. Although the city was extensively destroyed in a single air raid in 1944, no modern building has been allowed to challenge the supremacy of its magisterial tower, which the doyen of art historians, Jacob Burckhardt, described as "the greatest in Christendom".

Arrival, information and accommodation

Freiburg's **Hauptbahnhof**, with the **bus station** on its southern side, is about ten minutes' walk from the centre; follow Eisenbahnstrasse straight ahead. The **tourist office** is en route at Rotteckring 14 (June–Sept Mon–Fri 9.30am–8pm, Sat 9.30am–5pm, Sun 10am–noon; Oct–May Mon–Fri 9.30am–6pm, Sat 9.30am–2pm, Sun 10am–noon; ☎07 61/3 88 18 80, fax 3 88 18 87, *www.freiburg.de* & *freiburg-online.de*). **Mitfahrzentrale** is at Belfortstr. 55 (☎07 61/1 94 44). The main **post office** with poste restante is at Eisenbahnstr. 58–62.

The tourist office will find you a room free of charge; if you arrive after closing time, there's an electronic noticeboard equipped with a phone telling you which places have vacancies, though this is not an exhaustive service. For the best **budget hotels** you'll need to head out a little way from the centre, although if you are looking for a medium-priced place, Freiburg is one German city where a **luxury hotel** right in the centre of town might well be within your range. There are also plenty of **private houses** with rooms to let (①–④).

Freiburg has an excellent **youth hostel** and four **campsites**, although some of these are a bit out of the city. If you're staying far out, it makes sense to invest in a rover ticket on the **public transport** system. Prices for 24 hours are DM8/€4 for the city, DM16/€8 for the whole circuit; these rise to DM10/€5 and DM20/€10 respectively for two people travelling together.

Hotels and pensions

Colombi, Am Colombi-Park (☎07 61/2 10 60, fax 3 14 10, *www.columbi.de*). The city's leading hotel, well located at the western edge of the Altstadt and boasting all the luxuries including a swimming pool, steam baths, a sauna, solarium, fitness centre and a renowned gourmet restaurant. ⑨.

Dionysos, Hirschstr. 2 (☎07 61/2 93 53, fax 2 91 38). Greek-run hotel and ethnic restaurant in the south of the city, halfway towards Schauinsland; take tram #4. ②.

Haus Gisela, Am Vogelbach 27 (☎07 61/8 24 72, fax 8 11 52, *www.pensionhausgisela.here.de*). Homely, good-value pension in the northwestern suburbs, reached by bus #10. ③.

Markgräfler Hof, Gerberau 22 (☎07 61/29 64 90, fax 2 96 49 49). Occupies a fine fifteenth-century town palace. Its restaurant (closed Sun & Mon), one of the best in town, has a truly amazing wine list. ⑥–⑧.

Oberkirchs Weinstuben, Münsterplatz 22 (☎07 61/2 02 68 68, fax 2 02 68 69). Has an ideal location overlooking the Münster, and one of the city's best wine bar-restaurants (closed Sun). ⑦.

Rappen, Münsterplatz 13 (☎07 61/3 13 53, fax 38 22 52). Another hotel with many rooms overlooking the Münster; also has an excellent restaurant and a cosy Weinstube. ④–⑥.

Schemmer, Eschholzstr. 63 (☎07 61/20 74 90, fax 2 07 49 50). The lowest-priced central hotel, just south of the Hauptbahnhof on the opposite side of the tracks from the Altstadt. ③.

Schwarzwälder Hof, Herrenstr. 43 (☎07 61/3 80 30, fax 3 80 31 35). Hotel-cum-Weinstube in the heart of the Altstadt. ⑤.

Waldheim, Schauinslandstr. 20 (☎07 61/29 04 94). Budget hotel in the south of the city en route to Schauinsland; take tram #4. ③.

Zum Roten Bären, Oberlinden 12 (☎07 61/38 78 70, fax 3 87 87 17, *www.roter-baeren.de*). Germany's longest-functioning inn, part of the Ringhotel group, is in a house dated 1120. Nonetheless it offers everything that would be expected of a comfortable modern hotel, including a fine if expensive restaurant (closed Sun evenings & Mon). ⑧.

Youth hostel and campsites

Hirzberg, Kartäuserstr. 99 (☎07 61/3 50 54, fax 28 92 42, *www.freiburg-camping.de*). Not far from the youth hostel on the eastern outskirts of the city.

IYHF Jugendherberge, Karthäuserstr. 151 (☎07 61/6 76 56, fax 6 03 67). Freiburg's youth hostel is at the extreme eastern end of the city, ideally placed for walks in the hills or along the banks of the River Dreisam. Take tram #1 to Hasemannstrasse. DM26/€13 or DM31/€15.50.

Mösle-Park (☎ & fax 07 61/7 29 38). Situated south of the houses on the opposite side of the river and reached by tram #1. Closed late Oct to mid-March.

Silbersee, Seestr. 20 (☎0 76 65/23 46). Way to the north in the village of Hochdorf, this is the cheapest of the campsites.

Tunisee (☎0 76 65/22 49 or 12 49, fax 9 51 34). An enormous site likewise located in Hochdorf.

The City

As so often, most of what you'll want to see is in the Altstadt, and even here the main sights are concentrated on Münsterplatz and in the museum quarter to the south. However, it's also well worth venturing into the nearby hills for some wonderful views over the city and the Black Forest.

The Münster

Crafted out of a dark red sandstone quarried in one of the surrounding hills, the **Münster** (or **Dom**) is so magnificent and overpowering that it puts the rest of the city in the shade. Not the least remarkable fact about it is that, though it rivals any of the great European cathedrals, it was built as a mere parish church. No funds from the well-lined coffers of the ecclesiastical top brass were forthcoming for its construction – the costs were met entirely from the pockets of local citizens, to whom it was the ultimate symbol of municipal pride. In 1827, the Münster's artistic standing was given due recognition when it became the seat of the Upper Rhenish archbishopric.

Work on the present building began in about 1200, to replace a much simpler church dating from the time of the town's foundation eighty years before. The **transepts** were built first, in the picturesque late Romanesque style then still popular in Germany.

FREIBURG'S DRAINS

A peculiarity of Freiburg is the continuous visible presence throughout the old part of the city of its **sewerage system**, known as the *Bächle*. These are rivulets, fed by the River Dreisam, which run in deep gullies, serving as a trap for the unwary pedestrian or motorist. Formerly used for watering animals and as a sure precaution against the fire hazard which accounted for so many medieval towns, they have their purpose even today, helping to keep the city cool.

However, there was an abrupt change when the masons became aware of the structural advantages of Gothic, which the French had already mastered. At first, the same masons began building in this unfamiliar idiom; later, one of the architects of Strasbourg cathedral took over. He created a masterly **nave**, resplendent with flying buttresses, gargoyles and statues, already diverging from French models.

Further originality is evident in the west **porch**, begun around 1270. The figures, which still bear traces of colouring, are much the most important German works of their time. A sweetly carved *Madonna and Child* guards the door; above, the tympanum illustrates the entire New Testament. On the end walls, the *Wise and Foolish Virgins* confront each other, while deliberately shrouded on the west wall (at the point where the natural light is weakest) are the most striking figures: Satan as Prince of Darkness, beguilingly disguised as a youthful Knight, and Sensuality, who has toads and serpents writhing on her back.

The single **tower** (March–Nov Mon–Sat 9.30am–5pm, Sun 1–5pm; DM2.50/€1.25) above the porch was a unique design for its time, but was subsequently much imitated, most notably at Ulm. Though it seems to be an organic unity, it wasn't planned as a whole. The square plan of the lower storeys supports a soaring octagon, bearing animated statues of prophets and angels, which forms the stage above the bells. From the platform, you're rewarded with a fine panorama over the city and the Black Forest. However, the best view is of the lace-like tracery of the **openwork spire**, which rounds off the tower with a bravura flourish. The first of its kind, it was inspired by the mysticism of the time and symbolizes the human soul stretching out to receive divine knowledge. Many similar spires were planned for subsequent German churches, though most remained unbuilt until the nineteenth century. Exceptions are the two miniature versions which were immediately placed on Freiburg's own **Hahnentürme** (Cock Towers).

For the **chancel**, begun in the mid-fourteenth century (about 25 years after the completion of the spire), the authorities again struck lucky with their choice of architect, a man named Johannes of the famous Parler dynasty. His regular geometric layout marked a major advance on French models, and his two **portals**, particularly the northern one dedicated to the Creation, are adorned with superbly expressive sculptures – look out for the unusual depiction of God resting on the seventh day.

Inside, the transept is lit by luminous **stained-glass** windows of the early thirteenth century. Most of those in the nave date from a hundred years later and were donated by the local trades and guilds, who incorporated their coats of arms. Other items to look out for are a delicate late thirteenth-century *Madonna* on the west wall, a poignant fourteenth-century *Holy Sepulchre* in the south aisle, and the pulpit, an archaic Gothic work of the mid-sixteenth century with depictions of Freiburg personalities of the day. At the entrance to the chancel is a fine *Adoration of the Magi* by the leading local woodcarver of the late Gothic period, Hans Wydyz. This artist sometimes collaborated with the mercurial **Hans Baldung**, Dürer's most talented follower, whose high altar triptych of *The Coronation of the Virgin* – arguably his masterpiece – can be glimpsed from this point.

To see the chancel, and to get a better view of the Baldung triptych, you have to take a **guided tour** (Mon–Fri at 11am & 2.30pm; DM3/€1.50). In the Universitätskapelle, there are two wings of a curious **Holbein** retable. The portraits of the donor family are by Hans the Elder, but the main scenes of *The Nativity* and *Epiphany* are youthful works by his son, whose superior gifts are already in evidence. A *Rest on the Flight into Egypt* in the Kaiserkapelle has sculptures by Wydyz and a painted background by Baldung, who also designed many of the stained-glass windows in the chapels, though some of these have been replaced by copies. Hans Sixt von Staufen, another talented local sculptor of the time, carved the *Madonna of Mercy* in the Locherer Kapelle. In the Villinger Kapelle is a rare relic of the first Münster, a silver crucifix.

Münsterplatz

Until the war, the spacious **Münsterplatz** formed a fitting setting for the great church in its midst. However, the north side was flattened by bombs (which miraculously hardly touched the Münster itself) and only the late fifteenth-century **Kornhaus**, the municipal granary, has been rebuilt. The rest of the square has survived in much better shape and hosts an excellent daily market. There are also a couple of pretty fountains directly in front of the Münster – the **Georgsbrunnen** and the **Fischbrunnen** – along with three tall columns that bear statues of the local patron saints.

The south side of the square is dominated by the blood-red **Kaufhaus**, a sixteenth-century merchants' hall; its arcaded facade bears four statues by Sixt von Staufen of members of the House of Habsburg. On either side of the Kaufhaus are handsome Baroque palaces. To the west is the **Haus zum Ritter**, which was once the archbishop's palace but is now the Münster's song school. The **Wentzingerhaus** (Tues–Fri 9.30am–5pm, Sat & Sun 10.30am–5pm; DM4/€2 joint ticket with Augustinermuseum) to the east is named after the sculptor Christian Wentzinger who built it as his own residence. It features a resplendent Rococo staircase, complete with frescoed ceiling, while the back courtyard shelters huge allegorical statues of the Four Seasons by Wentzinger himself. The rest of the house is given over to displays on the history of Freiburg. Münsterplatz is closed on the far side by the canons' residences and the former **Hauptwache** (Guard House). The latter is now home to the Haus der Badischen Weine, where local vintages can be sampled and bought.

South of Münsterplatz

Following the main channel of the *Bächle* southwards, you come to the **Schwaben Tor**, one of two surviving towers of the medieval fortifications. On Oberlinden, just in front, is **Zum Roten Bären**, which is said to be Germany's oldest inn – a function it has held since 1311, although the building itself is two centuries older. The parallel **Konviktstrasse** has won conservation prizes for the restoration of its old houses.

Just to the west is Salzstrasse, which is lined with Baroque and Neoclassical mansions. Also here is the **Augustinermuseum** (Tues–Sun 10am–5pm; DM4/€2 joint ticket with Wentzingerhaus), which takes its name from the former monastery whose buildings it occupies. One of the most pleasing smaller collections in Germany, it makes an essential supplement to a visit to the Münster, containing as it does many works of art, such as gargoyles, statues and stained glass, which have been replaced *in situ* by copies to prevent further erosion. Also on show are examples of the religious art of the Upper Rhine, along with folklore displays on the Black Forest. There are also a few top-class old masters. Three panels of a Passion altar, including the central *Crucifixion*, constitute the most important surviving paintings by the great but mysterious draughtsman known as **Master of the Housebook**. *The Miracle of the Snow* by **Grünewald** is one of the wings of the altarpiece now in Stuppach: it depicts Pope Liberius laying the foundation stone of Santa Maria Maggiore in Rome, following a miraculous fall of snow on Midsummer's Day. As well as his stained glass, **Baldung** is represented by three typically unorthodox paintings, notably a *Cupid in Flight*, while there's a brightly coloured *Risen Christ* by **Cranach**.

South of here, on Marienstrasse, is the **Museum für Neue Kunst** (Tues–Sun 10am–5pm; free). Though it can't rival the richness of the parent collection, it does have a good cross-section of twentieth-century German painting. Beside it stands the Baroque **Adelhauserkirche**, retaining important works of art from its predecessor, notably a fourteenth-century crucifix. The former convent buildings now house the **Museum für Naturkunde** (Tues–Sun 10am–5pm; free), which has a dazzling display of gems, and the **Museum für Völkerkunde** (same hours; free) with exhibits drawn from all non-European cultures. From here, follow Fischerau, the former fishermen's street, and you come to the other surviving thirteenth-century tower, the **Martinstor**, which now stands in the middle of Freiburg's central axis, Kaiser-Joseph-Strasse.

The western quarters

Immediately west of here is the **Uni-Viertel** (university quarter), the liveliest part of the city during term-time and the best place to check out Freiburg's nightlife (see p.321). Alongside the inevitable modern buildings are several interesting older structures, including two Rococo mansions and a large Jugendstil lecture hall. On Bertoldstrasse, to the north, are the **Universitätskirche**, formerly the church of a Jesuit college, and the Baroque **Alte Universität**.

The **Neues Rathaus**, formed out of two separate Renaissance houses, one of which has an oriel adorned with a noble relief of *The Lady and the Unicorn*, was an earlier home of the university. It forms part of a shady chestnut tree-lined square whose other buildings include the **Altes Rathaus**, itself a fusion of several older buildings, and the plain Gothic Franciscan friary church of **St Martin**. A few minutes' walk to the west, in the Columbipark opposite the tourist office, is the **Columbischlössle**, a nineteenth-century villa built for a Spanish countess, which served after the war as parliament for the short-lived Land of South Baden (Südbaden). It now houses the **Museum für Ur- und Frühgeschichte** (Tues–Sun 10am–5pm; DM3.50/€1.75 donation requested), which has important archeological collections on the Black Forest region, particularly from the times of the Alemanni and the Franks; the treasury items in the basement are particularly worth seeing.

In the alley behind St Martin is the cheerful late Gothic facade of the **Haus zum Wallfisch**. For two years, this was the home of the great humanist **Desiderius Erasmus**, the most conciliatory and sympathetic of the leading figures of the Reformation period, who was forced to flee from his residence in Basel in the light of the turbulent religious struggles there. A late fifteenth-century palace nearby, on the main Kaiser-Joseph-Strasse, is known as the **Baseler Hof** as it served for nearly a century as the residence of the exiled cathedral chapter of the Swiss city.

Views of the city

It's well worth climbing one of the hills surrounding the city for the wonderful views they offer. The **Schlossberg** immediately to the east of the city centre is easily reached by a path from the Schwabentor. An alternative way up is by the **cable car** (DM3.50/€1.75 single, DM6/€3 return) from the Stadtgarten at the northeastern edge of the Altstadt. This summit also has the benefit of including close-range views of the Münster. For photography, it's best to come in the morning. To the south, the **Lorettoburg** (where the stone for the Münster was quarried) makes a good afternoon or evening alternative. Far higher, and thus with more spectacular panoramas than either of these, is the **Schauinsland** (1284m), still within the city boundaries but a good 15km southeast, reached by tram #4 to Günterstal, then bus #21. A series of marked nature trails comb the area, which is still inhabited by chamois, or you can ascend in fifteen minutes by **cable car** (DM13/€6.50 single, DM20/€10 return).

Eating, drinking and entertainment

Freiburg is a wonderful place for food and drink, with **restaurants** and **bars** to cater for all tastes and pockets, the liveliest concentration, as you'd expect, clustered around the university quarter. Many of the leading restaurants are in the hotels (see pp.316–17); for snacks the *Markthalle*, Kaiser-Joseph-Str. 237, is the best place to go. The city has a similarly eclectic choice of other entertainments.

FREIBURG'S FESTIVALS

The **Fastnet** celebrations are among the best in Baden-Württemberg; there are burning ceremonies on the evening of Shrove Tuesday, as well as parades of jesters the day before. Both the *Frühlingsfest* in May and the *Herbstsfest* in October last for ten days, and include spectacular fairground amusements. In late June and early July, the two-week *Internationales Zeltmusikfest* features all varieties of music, performed under canvas. Later in the month, five days are given over to a wine market known as the *Weintagen*. Mid-August has the nine-day-long *Weinkost*, a sampling session for wines produced in the Freiburg region.

Restaurants

Greiffenegg-Schlössle, Schlossbergring 3. A good terrace restaurant, accessible by elevator.

Grosser Meyerhof, Grünwälderstr. 7. Top-quality south German fare at eminently reasonable prices. Closed Mon & Tues.

Kleiner Meyerhof, Rathausgasse 27. Small and select south German restaurant with good-value set lunches.

Klösterle, Dreikönigstr. 8 (☎07 61/7 57 84). Small, highly regarded French restaurant southeast of the Altstadt, on the opposite side of the Dreisam; it specializes in organically raised beef and has a wide selection of Burgundy wines. Reservations necessary. Open Tues–Sat evenings only.

Milano, Schusterstr. 7. Bargain-priced trattoria.

Salatstuben, Schiffstr. 5–7 and Löwenstr. 1. Vegetarian restaurants with self-service salad bars. Both open Mon–Fri 10.15am–7pm, Sat 10.15am–4pm.

Schlossbergrestaurant Dattler, Am Schlossberg 1. First choice for alfresco eating, with a terrace on top of the Schlossberg commanding a superb view of Freiburg and the Kaiserstuhl. Closed Tues.

Tessiner Stuben, Bertoldstr. 17. Restaurant-cum-wine bar, complete with garden. Closed Sun.

Wolfshöhle, Konviktstr. 8. One of the best Italian restaurants in the country. Closed Sun.

Zur Traube, Schusterstr. 17. Quieter alternative to the wine bars on nearby Münsterplatz. Closed Mon lunchtime & Sun.

Bars, cafés and café-bars

Altstadt-Café, Gerberau 12. Good traditional café.

Café Atlantik, Schwabentorring 7. Run-down music pub serving very cheap food in the evenings.

Café Journal, Universitätsstr. 3. Popular if fairly expensive student hangout.

Dampfross, Löwenstr. 7. A student favourite, serving inexpensive meals.

Feierling, Gerberau 46. In addition to the fruity *Inselhopf* beer brewed on the premises, imaginative meals are served.

Kleines Freiburger Brauhaus, Moltkestr. 27. The smallest of the city's three Hausbrauereien produces an excellent *Roggenbier*.

Kornhaus Café, Münsterplatz 11. *Kaffee und Kuchen* establishment in the historic setting of the Kornhaus.

Martins Bräu, Fressgässle 1. Hausbrauerei which makes a blond beer and also has a short but eclectic menu.

Schlappen, Löwenstr. 2. Long-established but still very hip student pub.

Uni-Café, Niemensstr. 7. The trendiest café in Freiburg; serves a wide selection of coffees and has good snacks.

Discos

Agar, Löwenstr. 8. Themed nights each evening, playing music from mainly the 1980s and 1990s. Tues & Thurs 10pm–3am, Fri & Sat 11pm–4am, Sun 10pm–2.30am.

Exit, Kaiser-Joseph-Str. 248. One of Freiburg's most popular discos, with a predominantly young clientele.

Parabel Club, Universitätsstr. 3. Tiny disco. Tues–Sun 9pm–3am.

Theatre and concert venues

Freiburger Theater, Bertoldstr. 46 (☎07 61/3 48 74). The city's main theatre venue featuring drama, dance and opera; there are three auditoria plus the Theatercafé where late-night cabaret and variety shows are held.

Jazzhaus, Schnewlinstr. 1 (☎07 61/3 49 73). Freiburg now ranks as one of the leading German cities for jazz, thanks to this venue which has concerts every evening at 8.30pm.

Konzerthaus, Konrad-Adenauer-Platz 1 (☎07 61/8 85 81 30). State-of-the-art concert venue, with a large hall, the Grosser Saal, and a more intimate space, the Runder Saal. It regularly features performances by the renowned radio orchestra, the SWR Sinfonieorchester, as well as by the Freiburger Philharmonisches Orchester and the period-instrument Freiburger Barockorchester.

Theater in Marienbad, Marienstr. 4 (☎07 61/3 14 70). Children's and youth theatre, housed in a converted Jugendstil swimming pool.

Wallgrabentheater, Rathausgasse 5a (☎07 61/2 56 56). An intimate stage in the Altes Rathaus specializing in modern classics and the theatre of the absurd.

Breisach

BREISACH, whose historic heart is perched high above the Rhine on a promontory about 30km west of Freiburg, is an archetypal frontier post in what has been one of the most heavily disputed parts of Europe. Even if the river is now firmly established as a natural border and the town regarded as being indisputably German, the turbulent legacy of its past is still clearly visible. Breisach stands in the shadow of the **Kaiserstuhl**, an isolated volcanic mass in which Frederick Barbarossa, who died on his way to the Holy Land, is said to rest, waiting for his second coming – hence its name, which means "Emperor's Seat".

The Town

The lower town (*Unterstadt*) by the Rhine is modern – all the sights are located in the spacious, half-deserted upper town (*Oberstadt*), which is surrounded by the **Stadtbefestigung**, dating from the thirteenth century. The ramparts visible today bear the unmistakable stamp of the greatest of all military engineers, the Frenchman Sébastien Vauban, who was also responsible for laying out the town of Neuf Brisach on the opposite bank. Indeed, the monumental **Rheintor** at the northwest end of Breisach itself is as purely French a building as can be seen in Germany. Yet, just above it, the gabled medieval **Kapftor** could hardly be more German in feel, and the same applies to the earlier **Hagenbachtor** on the brow of the hill further south. Just beyond this is one of Breisach's many belvederes, offering grandstand views of France.

INTO FRANCE

Some 25km west of Breisach, and served by five buses per day, is the beautiful old Alsatian city of **COLMAR**. French since 1918, Colmar was German for much of its history, as is abundantly clear from its general appearance, and from the fact that most inhabitants are bilingual. It was the home town of medieval artist Martin Schongauer, and a good deal of his work can be seen there; it also possesses Grünewald's titanic *Isenheim Altarpiece*, generally regarded as the supreme masterpiece of German painting. A short train journey to the north is cosmopolitan **STRASBOURG**, specially chosen as home of the European Parliament in honour of its mixed Franco-German history. It was a free city of the Holy Roman Empire for three centuries and its magnificent cathedral is mostly the work of German masons.

The Münster

Looming high above all else is the **Münster**. From outside, it's no beauty, fashioned out of rough, diffuse stonework, and truncated on the southern side in order to squeeze into an irregular, constricted space. It was originally built in the late Romanesque period on the foundations of a Roman fortress; the nave, transept and the two "Cock" towers survive from this time. The upper parts of the southern tower were re-fashioned in Gothic style in the early fourteenth century, a period which also saw the construction of a new chancel (under which is an open crypt – apparently the only one of its kind in the world) and the stumpy facade, whose tympanum illustrates the life of the Münster's patron, St Stephen. At the end of the fifteenth century, it was decided to commission new decorations for the interior of the Münster rather than rebuild it; as a result, it came to acquire one of the most impressive arrays of **works of art** of any church in Germany, all created at the transitional point between Gothic and Renaissance.

Filling the three walls of the west end is a huge **fresco cycle** of *The Last Judgement*, sadly very faded, by **Martin Schongauer**, the father-figure of the golden age of German art. Contemporary with the frescoes is the filigree **rood screen**. In the chapel beside it is a silver **shrine** containing the relics of the early martyr-saints Gervase and Protase, which were swiped from Milan at the same time as those of the Three Magi (which were taken to Cologne), and allegedly arrived in Breisach by miraculous means, whereupon they became the joint patrons of the town. The reliefs on the lid include an illustration of this journey, complete with a depiction of fifteenth-century Breisach.

SS Gervase and Protase turn up again on the right wing of the main **retable**, while on the opposite side of the central *Coronation of the Virgin* are the martyred deacons, SS Stephen and Lawrence. This altarpiece is an astonishing piece of wholly eccentric yet hyper-skilled woodcarving. It may be late Gothic, but the entwined mass of cherubs, the swirling hair and drapery folds of the figures are uncannily anticipatory of the Baroque style of over a century later. Many attempts have been made to unmask the identity of the mysterious sculptor, known as **Master HL** after his cryptic signature, but to no conclusive effect. The sinuous upper part of the retable is by a more orthodox carver, but is still remarkable for the fact that it's actually higher than the ceiling, a trick achieved by means of a subtle slant.

Practicalities

Breisach's **Bahnhof** is at the southern end of town. The **tourist office** (May–Oct Mon–Fri 9am–6pm, Sat 10am–1pm, Sun 1–4pm; Nov–April Mon–Fri 9am–5pm, Sat 10am–1pm; ☎0 76 67/94 01 55, fax 94 01 58, *www.breisach.de*) at Marktplatz 16. Among the **hotels** are *Gasthof Bayrischer Hof*, Neutorstr. 25 (☎0 76 67/2 89; ③), *Kapuzinergarten*, Kapuzinergasse 26 (☎0 76 67/93000; ④–⑥), Kaiserstühler Hof, Richard-Müller-Str. 2 (☎0 76 67/8 30 60; ⑤–⑧), and *Am Münster*, Münsterbergstr. 23 (☎0 76 67/83 80; ⑤–⑧). All of these have good **restaurants**. The spanking-new **youth hostel** is by the river at Rheinuferstr. 12 (☎0 76 67/7665, fax 18 47; DM26/€13 or DM31/€15.50). Alternatively, there's a **campsite**, *Münsterblick* (☎0 76 67/9 39 30), in the village of Hochstetten 2km south.

The southern Black Forest

The southern part of the Black Forest is a mountainous region encompassed by the French border to the west and the Swiss border to the south, and gradually petering out towards the southeast, somewhat before the shores of the Bodensee. At the southern fringe of the region is a beautiful stretch of the Rhine, here dividing Germany from

Switzerland. Its landscape of forested hills is especially wonderful around the high points of the **Belchen** and the **Feldberg**. At 1414m and 1493m respectively, they're hardly mountains in the Alpine sense, but on clear days you get vast panoramas from their summits, reaching as far as the Swiss Alps and the western Rhine valley. While there are only two main highways heading from west to east (one following the Swiss border on the southern side of the region, and the road connecting Freiburg to Konstanz on the northern side), **travel** along the fringes of this area is easy and efficient by train. The interior, on the other hand, involves circuitous connections by infrequent bus services.

St Peter

Some 20km east of Freiburg, and connected by regular bus services, **ST PETER** is a tiny health resort clustering round a Benedictine **Kloster**. This was founded in the eleventh century, but the present complex belongs to a rebuilding begun in 1724. Peter Thumb built the striking twin-towered **Klosterkirche**, a classically inspired Baroque design of unusual width and spaciousness. The monastic buildings, now used as a seminary, are Rococo in style, dating from a generation later. Particularly eye-catching is the galleried library, the **Bibliotheksaal** (guided tours Mon–Wed & Sun at 11.30am, Thurs at 2.30pm; DM5/€2.50), gleaming with white stuccowork and frescoes. Colourful costumed **festivals** are held in the village on Corpus Christi and on the Sunday after the feast day of SS Peter and Paul (June 29).

Around Belchen

Belchen, surrounded by deep gorges some 20km south of Freiburg, is the most beautiful of the southern peaks, with wonderful views and quiet little villages in the valleys. The highlight of the region is the serene **Kloster St Trudpert**.

Münstertal

The **Münstertal** is a valley dotted with the characteristic low shingle roofs of traditional Black Forest farms, set among lush pastures clinging to the steep hillsides of the northern Belchen reaches. On the southwestern outskirts, near the village of Neuenweg, you'll find the **Nonnenmattweiher**, which is one of the oldest lakes of the region, formed during the receding Ice Age and an excellent place to combine hiking with fishing or simply picnicking. Be prepared for a lot of steep paths and deep furrows.

Some time in the seventh century, Irish missionaries came to Christianize this area: the most famous, St Trudpert, was murdered in 607 after only three years of missionary work. The **Kloster St Trudpert** in the upper Münstertal was founded about 250 years later, and the large Baroque complex you see today is the visual centre of the whole upper valley. It was a Benedictine monastery until secularization in 1806, but now it's home to the Josephschwestern order of nuns. The refreshingly plain Baroque interior of the church is considered architect Peter Thumb's masterpiece: white stucco decorations predominate, with only the ceiling frescoes and side altars adding discreet colour.

The Münstertal is awash with accommodation possibilities: look out for the *Zimmer frei* signs or you can book through the tourist office in Freiburg (see p.315). There's a **youth hostel** at Wieden (☎0 76 73/5 38, fax 5 04; DM22/€11 or DM27/€13.50): take the train from Freiburg to Münstertal, then the bus to Wieden.

Staufen

Following the Münstertal west, the foothills sink into the Rhine valley, the landscape quickly changing into gently rolling hills that make up some of Germany's most famous vineyards and provide a lucrative living to many small and ancient towns. Of these, **STAUFEN** is particularly attractive. Situated at the bottom of the Münstertal and surrounded by its vineyards, its idyllic location makes it a great base for relaxed hiking tours, while the cobbled streets and medieval houses mean it's worth a visit in its own right. The place also harbours a murky past in the shape of **Doktor Faustus** (Johannes Faust – see box on p.264). He came here in 1539 at the behest of Count Anton von Staufen, who was in serious debt and hoped to extricate himself by using the great necromancer's alleged ability to manufacture gold. However, Faust accidentally blew himself into small pieces when an experiment exploded in his room in the *Gasthaus zum Löwen*.

The **tourist office** is at Hauptstr. 53 (☎0 76 33/8 05 36, fax 5 05 93, *www.stadt -staufen.de*). You can stay in *Zum Löwen*, Hauptstr. 47, (☎0 76 33/70 78; ④–⑥) including Faust's room, no. 5 on the third floor. Other **hotels** are *Die Krone*, Hauptstr. 30 (☎0 76 33/58 40; ⑤), and *Kreuz-Post*, Hauptstr. 65 (☎0 76 33/9 53 20; ⑥). A few rooms in **private houses** (①–②) are also available and can be booked via the tourist office.

The annual *Sommerfest* is held during the last week in June, while the local *Weinfest* takes place on the first weekend in August. Star vineyards of the area are on the **Batzenberg** just north of town, and wine connoisseurs come from all over to go wine-tasting in the surrounding cellars. An even bigger *Weinfest* is held in nearby Schönberg in late April and early May.

Feldberg and around

Feldberg, the highest peak in the Black Forest, was, until last century, the heart of a remote and wild region, far away from human habitation. Nowadays, in contrast, the area is one of the most popular holiday destinations containing some spectacular scenery, notably the Höllental and the Wutachschlucht.

Höllental
The most atmospheric approach to Feldberg is by train from Freiburg. For the first leg of this, you pass through the narrow and formerly almost inaccessible **Höllental** (Hell Valley) gorge, which lies between Himmelreich and Hinterzarten. The track was first laid in 1887 by Robert Gerwig, who had earlier constructed the Schwarzwaldbahn (see box on p.330), and was an amazing technical achievement for the time, using a network of tunnels and viaducts. To appreciate both the scenery and the engineering, however, you really need to get out and walk along the footpath on the gorge's northern side; it takes about four hours to make a one-way trip.

Titisee, Schluchsee and Seebrugg
TITISEE, the next stop after Hinterzarten, lies on the glacial lake of the same name, which is encircled by a footpath. It's a highly commercialized and inordinately popular summer resort, particularly with holidaymakers around retirement age. Far preferable is **SCHLUCHSEE**, which lies on a larger glacial lake directly to the south. From Titisee, trains crawl up the side of the Feldberg towards Germany's highest station, **Feldberg-Bärental**, which is the place to alight if you want to walk all the way up the mountain. They then descend to Schluchsee, terminating a couple of kilometres further on at the hamlet of **SEEBRUGG**, which has a decent beach with sailing and windsurfing facilities. Motorized boats aren't allowed on the lake, a fact that makes for pleasant (and clean) swimming.

Titisee is awash with **accommodation** of all types, and you won't have trouble finding a hotel in Schluchsee either. There's also a **youth hostel** at Im Wolfsgrund 28 in Schluchsee (☎0 76 56/3 29, fax 92 37; DM24/€12 or DM29/€14.50), plus a **campsite**

(☎0 76 56/7739). Seebrugg also has a hostel, at Haus 9 (☎0 76 56/4 94, fax 1 89; DM24/€12 or DM29/€14.50).

Feldberg and the mountain resorts

In the eighteenth and nineteenth centuries, the rounded heights of the **Feldberg** itself (which can be reached more directly by bus from Freiburg than by the train connection) were denuded of forest and turned into highland pastures, so today the peak stands treeless above a sea of forest and isn't in itself particularly attractive. The TV tower and radio dishes plus the chairlift and gravel path to the top don't do the place any favours either, and the hotel and souvenir shop just about ruin it. Nonetheless, the area around is still an excellent hiking region, with many beautiful trails through uninhabited forests and gorges laced with a couple of romantic waterfalls and streams along the way. Even near the Feldberg, you'll find unspoilt and quiet places like the **Feldbergsee**, only accessible on foot, and the **Windgfällweiher**, another lake near the village of Altglasshütten a few kilometres southeast.

For keen hikers, **BERNAU**, 5km south of Feldberg, is a good place to stay. It's actually a collection of small villages and farms, ideal for groups looking for farmhouse accommodation or private holiday flats. Contact the **tourist office** in the Kurverwaltung at Rathausstr. 18 (☎0 76 75/16 00 30, fax 16 00 90) for accommodation lists.

The picturesque village of **TODTMOOS** is another centre for walking enthusiasts, offering all the facilities of Alpine villages. It is also an ideal base from which to explore the rarely visited **Hotzenwald**, which seamlessly extends south from the Black Forest, until dropping sharply towards the Rhine valley that marks the Swiss border. Accommodation lists are available from the **tourist office** (☎0 76 74/9 06 00, fax 90 60 25) in the Kurverwaltung, Wehratalstr. 19.

St Blasien

The most famous monastery of the southern Black Forest is in **ST BLASIEN**, some 20km southeast of the Feldberg. Burnt down a number of times, the **Klosterkirche** was given its present shape in 1768, when the local prince-abbot hired the Frenchman Michel d'Ixnard to design one of Germany's grandest classically inspired buildings; the great dome, carried by twenty Corinthian pillars, was modelled after St Peter's in Rome. Inside, the rotunda is a blaze of white marble, shining oppressively new and creating an atmosphere reminiscent of a cold, oversized bathroom.

For brochures and accommodation lists contact the **tourist office**, Am Kurgarten (Mon–Fri 9am–noon & 2–5pm, Sat 10am–noon; ☎0 76 72/9 30 90, fax 77 09, *www.st -blasien-menzenschwand.de*). The nearest **youth hostel** is in Menzenschwand, at Vorderdorferstr. 10 (☎0 76 75/3 26, fax 14 35; DM24/€12 or DM29/€14.50), which can be reached directly by bus from Seebrugg. This is a particularly beautiful hostel, located in one of the all-wood traditional farmhouses, 8km up the road from St Blasien.

Bonndorf and the Wutach valley

BONNDORF, on the eastern edges of the Black Forest, is an excellent hiking base, set among rich orchards. It's very close to the so-called "Grand Canyon" of the Black Forest, the **Wutachschlucht**, which is a small riverine gorge, very narrow in places, with gushing white-water shooting over mossy rocks and lined by ancient forest. About 10km long, it has been declared a nature reserve; a map of it is available from the **tourist office** (☎0 77 03/76 07, fax 75 07, *www.bonndorf.de*), Schloss-Str. 1. The local **youth hostel** is at Waldallee 19 (☎0 77 03/3 59, fax 6 86; DM22/€11 or DM27/€13.50).

Some 15km east of Bonndorf is **BLUMBERG**, departure point for another of the Black Forest's amazing rail lines, the Wutachtalbahn to **WEIZEN**. Although the two termini are less than 10km apart as the crow flies, the rail track stretches for a meandering 26km along the side of the River Wutach, and features numerous horseshoe curves, a bridge, three large viaducts and five tunnels, including the only spiral tunnel in Germany. The line closed as part of the normal network a couple of decades ago, and is now used for excursion services only, invariably pulled by steam engines. These run every Saturday and Sunday from May to September, and variably on Wednesdays to Fridays as well. Check locally, or in the DB timetable, for the current times.

The Upper Rhine valley

The **Upper Rhine valley** forms the southern boundary of the Black Forest, and – most of the time – the frontier with Switzerland as well. Though less famous than the Middle Rhine, it's a grandly beautiful landscape, easily appreciated from the train which closely follows the course of the river upstream towards the Bodensee. Along the way are many pretty small towns, usually directly facing their Swiss counterparts on the opposite bank.

Weil am Rhein

Just 8km north of Basel on the main rail line to Freiburg is the small industrial town of **WEIL AM RHEIN**, whose name is indelibly associated with Vitra, one of the leading players in contemporary international design. The company, which is based in a greenbelt site to the north of the centre, to which it is linked by bus #55, offers a major visitor attraction in the **Vitra Design Museum** (Tues–Sun 11am–6pm; *www.design -museum.de*; DM10/€5). This presents its diverse holdings of industrially produced furniture and other objects of the past two centuries in a series of changing exhibitions. However, in many ways the building itself is the main draw – it's a startlingly audacious construction by the Californian Frank O. Gehry, clearly anticipating his later commission for the Guggenheim Museum in Bilbao, which catapulted him to the status of the world's most fêted contemporary architect. **Guided tours** (Tues–Sun at noon & 2pm; DM13/€6.50, or DM21/€10.50 joint ticket with the museum) of the rest of the site take in various factory buildings by Gehry, Nicholas Grimshaw and Alvaro Siza, the conference pavilion by Tadao Ando and the fire station by Zaha Hadid. These depart from the museum entrance, last around two hours and are in German only.

Weil, or more precisely the incorporated wine village of Haltingen to the north, is a terminus of one more of the Black Forest's celebrated **railways**, the Kandertalbahn. This thirteen-kilometre-long line along the valley of the River Kander to the health resort of Kandern is served solely by excursion steam trains; these usually run every

---

INTO SWITZERLAND

It's easy enough to hop over into Switzerland from the Upper Rhine valley. In the case of the towns along the latter stretch, you simply need to walk over the appropriate bridge to the town on the opposite bank; customs officials often do not bother to check passports. However, the big draw is undoubtedly **BASEL**, Switzerland's second city, which straddles both sides of the Rhine at the point where the river makes a sharp north turn away from its previous east–west course. It's far more attractive than most of its German counterparts of similar size, Swiss neutrality having ensured it has not suffered in war. The Öffentliche Kunstsammlung, one of the oldest public museums in the world, has by far the largest collection of extant paintings by two of Germany's greatest artists, Konrad Witz and Hans Holbein the Younger.

One of Basel's two main stations, the Deutscher Bahnhof, is run by DB, using the Deutschmark/euro as currency. It's a junction of the lines south from Freiburg and east to the Bodensee and is also an official frontier crossing point.

Saturday from mid-May to mid-September, with occasional extra departures at other times. Timetable details are posted on the town's **Web site** (*www.weil-am-rhein.de*).

The centre of Weil is well equipped with **hotels**; among the best are the sixteenth-century *Zur Krone*, Hauptstr. 58 (☎0 76 21/7 11 64; ⑤), *Schwanen*, Hauptstr. 121 (☎0 76 21/9 78 60; ⑤–⑦), and *Adler*, Hauptstr. 139 (☎0 76 21/9 82 30; ⑦). There are also a couple of enticing alternatives in Haltingen: *Zur Krone*, Burgunderstr. 21 (☎0 76 21/6 22 03; ⑥), and *Rebstock*, Grosse Gasse 30 (☎0 76 21/96 49 60; ⑥). All of these have fine **restaurants**, with *Adler* being of gourmet status.

Bad Säckingen

The most attractive of the Upper Rhenish towns is **BAD SÄCKINGEN**, 30km upstream from Basel. Its name gained a certain international renown in the nineteenth century courtesy of the verse epic *The Trumpeter of Säckingen* by Joseph Victor von Scheffel, a work that is unjustly neglected nowadays. With a neat little Altstadt beside the Rhine and a plush modern spa quarter in the foothills to the north, Bad Säckingen is able to present two faces to visitors. By far the most impressive monument is the extraordinary **Rheinbrücke**, a covered wooden bridge which still provides a pedestrian link over the Rhine to the Swiss town of Stein. Thirteenth century by origin, it was rebuilt in the seventeenth and eighteenth centuries, and restored only a few years back. In the quiet shady park overlooking the river is the seat of the one-time local lords, **Schloss Schönau**, a miniature Renaissance palace with distinctive polygonal corner towers. It now houses the **Hochrheinmuseum** (Tues, Thurs & Sun 2–5pm; DM4/€2), the regional museum of the Upper Rhineland, featuring archeological finds, an array of Black Forest clocks and, in continued homage to the town's literary fame, what's claimed as the largest collection of historic trumpets in the world.

The **Bahnhof** lies between the Altstadt and the spa quarters; directly opposite, at Waldshuter Str. 20, is the **tourist office** (Mon–Fri 8am–noon & 2–5pm, Sat 9am–noon; ☎0 77 61/5 68 30, fax 56 83 17, *www.bad-saeckingen.de*). **Private rooms** (①–②) are in reasonable supply. There are a couple of enticing **hotels** in the Altstadt – *Kater Hiddigeigei*, Tanzenplatz 1 (☎0 77 61/40 55, *www.hotel-kater.de*; ⑥), and *Goldener Knopf*, Rathausplatz 9 (☎0 77 61/56 50; ⑥). Both of these have fine **restaurants**; they are rivalled by *Fuchshöhle*, Rheinbrückstr. 9, while *Margaretenschlössle*, Baltherplatz 1, is another good choice, whether for a full meal or *Kaffee und Kuchen*.

The central Black Forest

The central part of the Black Forest is the one most enshrined in popular imagination. This is the land of cuckoo clocks, of huge balconied farmsteads with hipped roofs, and of some of the world's most outrageous headgear: the *Schäppelkrone*, a "crown" made from hundreds of coloured glass beads and ribbons, and the *Bollenhut*, the woollen pom-pom hat whose colour indicates the wearer's marital status (red for unmarried, black for married). As a result, it's hardly surprising that this is the part of the forest which has gone in most for the tourist hard-sell, and is consequently the most spoiled, with a surfeit of tacky souvenir shops as well as an abundance of accommodation, and a highly developed network of trains and buses. Nonetheless, it's easy enough to escape from the organized tour groups, while the good communications make travel by public transport a pain-free experience.

Donaueschingen

Gateway to the central Black Forest is the rail junction of **DONAUESCHINGEN**, which lies some 50km northwest of the Bodensee on the windswept Baar plateau. Both

THE SOURCE OF THE DANUBE

In Donaueschingen's Schlosspark a grandiose early nineteenth-century fountain has been erected round the Donauquelle, a very unassuming spring. This flows eastwards through the grounds (at times invisibly below the surface), before joining the **Brigach**, a headstream which rises in the Black Forest and which has become a substantial river by the time it reaches this point. At the edge of town a couple of kilometres further on is the more substantial confluence with another and bigger Black Forest headstream, the **Breg**; from then on, the combined waters are known as the **Danube**. It's the longest river in Europe after the Volga, and the only important one to flow from west to east, following a course of some 2840km through seven different countries, eventually forming a labyrinth-like delta in Romania which feeds into the Black Sea. Whether or not the Donauquelle is really the ultimate source of this great river is a matter for dispute – the spring which feeds the Breg has a far better geological claim. However, given that the crucial merger occurs at Donaueschingen, it's easy to see why the town has been blessed with official recognition.

its name and fame are due to its status as the official source of one of the world's most celebrated rivers, the **Danube** (Donau), though it's also of note as a well-preserved example of a tinpot princely capital. Initially, the harsh climate militated against its growth – it was no more than a hamlet until the 1720s when Prince Joseph Wilhelm Ernst of the **Fürstenberg** dynasty descended from his feudal castle in the hills above to begin the planning of a new courtly town.

Between the town's Bahnhof and its centre is the Schlosspark, site of the source of the Danube. The **Schloss** (guided tours April–Sept Mon & Wed–Sun 9am–noon & 2–5pm; DM5/€2.50) itself is actually a fairly unassuming Baroque building at the far end of its park; much of the interior was modernized at the end of the nineteenth century. Its trappings are typical: Brussels tapestries, assorted *objets d'art* and family portraits. Among the last-named, there's one surprise – *Max Egon* was painted by the English artist Graham Sutherland. The sitter kept up the family tradition of musical patronage (Mozart and Liszt had both been guests) by establishing a **festival** now known as the *Donaueschinger Musiktage*. Held each October in the modern Donauhalle at the western end of town, this focuses on the work of contemporary composers. Many of twentieth century's leading musicians – Stravinsky, Hindemith, Boulez and Stockhausen – had works premiered there.

The main family treasures, known as the **Fürstenberg-Sammlungen** (March–Oct Tues–Sun 9am–noon & 1.30–5pm; Dec–Feb Tues–Sun 9am–noon & 1.30–4pm; DM5/€2.50), are housed in a building on Karlsplatz, a Baroque square situated over the main road directly behind the Schloss. Here various zoological and mineralogical collections are set out in the old-fashioned manner of cabinets of curiosities. There's also a room devoted to the history of the Fürstenbergs, complete with their ceremonial coach and sleighs. However, the main attraction is the outstanding second-floor display of south German and Swiss paintings and sculptures of the fifteenth and sixteenth centuries. Highlight is **Hans Holbein the Elder**'s *Grey Passion*, an expressive cycle of twelve pictures formerly in St-Ulrich-und-Afra in Augsburg. It takes its name from the idiosyncratic device of showing all the participants dressed in grey – until halfway through, when they change into white. There's also an important array of works by the enigmatic **Master of Messkirch**, one of Dürer's most distinctive followers, including parts of his eponymous work, and the jewel-like *Wildensteiner Altar*.

On a terrace to the side of the Schloss is the twin-towered **Johanniskirche**, whose restrained Baroque style is reminiscent of the churches then being built in Bohemia, rather than elsewhere in southern Germany. In the nave there's a wooden *Madonna* by the eccentric **Master HL** which predates the building by over two hundred years.

Other than these obvious attractions, all closely grouped together, Donaueschingen doesn't have much in the way of sights. However, several streets are good examples of period pieces. An example is **Josefstrasse**, linking the Bahnhof with the town centre, which is lined by stately Baroque and Neoclassical mansions. The outbuildings of the court are found on Haldenstrasse; the library here possesses one of the three original thirteenth-century manuscript versions of *The Nibelungenlied*. Though this street is now tucked away between the town centre and the Brigach, it's easily located by the chimneys of the **Fürstenberg-Brauerei**, one of the most famous breweries in Germany. In its present form it dates back to 1705, but the family's initial beer-making rights were granted in the thirteenth century.

Practicalities

The **tourist office** (Mon–Fri 8am–noon & 2–5/6pm, Sat 9am–noon; ☎07 71/85 72 21, fax 85 72 28, *www.donaueschingen.de*) is at Karlstr. 58. Here you can pick up a list of **private houses** (①–②) with rooms to let. Among the town's hotels are *Zum Hirschen*, Herdstr. 5 (☎07 71/8 98 55 80; ③–⑤), *Zur Sonne*, Karlstr. 38 (☎07 71/8 31 30; ⑤), and *Linde*, Karlstr. 18 (☎07 71/8 31 80; ⑥). Though there's no hostel, an HI card will bring a reduction at the *Naturfreundehaus*, Am Wolterdinger Str. 72 (☎07 71/29 85; ①), which has individual rooms rather than dorms. The **campsite** (☎07 71/55 11) is 8km away on the banks of the Riedsee. All the hotels mentioned above have good **restaurants**, though the obvious place to sample the products of the local brewery (whose *Pils* is one of Germany's best) is its *Bräustüble*, which is housed in a pink Baroque palace on Postplatz.

Villingen-Schwenningen

Created as recently as 1972, the double town of **VILLINGEN-SCHWENNINGEN**, some 15km north of Donaueschingen, is a decidedly curious union, as its two constituent parts belonged for centuries to different countries: Villingen, on the very fringe of the Black Forest, was Austrian before being allocated by Napoleon to Baden, while Schwenningen, set on the Baar plateau, was part of Württemberg. Villingen, much the more attractive of the two, really comes to life during the Shrovetide celebrations of **Fastnet**, which rival Rottweil's as the best in southern Germany.

At other times, Villingen is a busy enough market town, its pristine houses set behind the medieval **Stadtmauer**, of which several sections, including three towers and three impressive gates, survive. The huge **Münster** provides a central focus, particularly the two tall flamboyant towers of the late Gothic chancel, which was tacked on

---

THE SCHWARZWALDBAHN

Villingen is the terminus for one of the most spectacular rail lines in Europe, the Schwarzwaldbahn to Offenburg in the Rhine valley. Laid out between 1863 and 1873, this line successively follows the valleys of the Brigach, Gutach and Kinzig rivers, cutting through what had hitherto been impenetrable countryside, and was intended as a major prestige project by the Grand Duchy of Baden, which was always keen to present itself at the forefront of German progressiveness. It was built by the nation's most celebrated railway engineer, Robert Gerwig, who later went on to construct the St Gotthard route over the Alps, as well as another Black Forest line, the Höllentalbahn (see p.325). The nature of the terrain posed technical problems which had never previously been tackled, notably the need to climb a gradient of 448m in the short distance of 11km. To achieve this, Gerwig built 36 tunnels through the mountains, plus a series of daring hairpin bends. Two of these – the narrow, deep and rocky stages between St Georgen and Triberg, and between Triberg and Hornberg – involve the rail line virtually doubling back on itself to traverse the gradient.

to the Romanesque nave when its predecessor burned down. Unfortunately the interior was completely redecorated – none too successfully – in the eighteenth century, but compensation comes in the variety of colourful mansions which form Münsterplatz. These include the Romanesque **Rabenscheuer** to the north and the gabled Gothic **Altes Rathaus** (Tues, Wed & Fri–Sun 10am–noon, Thurs 10am–noon & 3–5pm; DM2/€1) to the west, where you can see both the main council chamber on the first floor and the former prison and torture room above, as well as a collection of fine medieval tapestries.

Also worth a visit is the **Franziskaner-Museum** (Tues–Sat 10am–noon & 1–5pm, Sun 1–5pm; DM5/€2.50) at Rietstr. 39 on the western edge of the Altstadt, which has comprehensive collections of material on the prehistory, archeology, folklore and crafts of the Black Forest. The adjoining buildings of the old friary give a good idea of the severely functional Gothic architecture that was favoured by the mendicant friars, and contain displays of sacred art.

Villingen's **Bahnhof** is just east of the Altstadt, on the opposite side of the River Brigach. The **tourist office** (Mon–Fri 8.30am–12.30pm & 1.30–5.30pm, Sat 8.30am–1.30pm; ☎0 77 21/82 23 40, fax 82 23 47, *www.villingen-schwenningen.de*) is at Rietstr. 8. There's a reasonable supply of **private rooms** (①–③) in the town. The **youth hostel** is in the very north of Villingen at St Georgener Str. 36 (☎0 77 21/5 41 49, fax 5 26 16; DM22/€11 or DM27/€13.50). Among **hotels**, the most central are *Gasthaus Zum Schlachthof*, Schlachthausstr. 11 (☎07721/9 82 90; ③), and *Bären*, Bärengasse 2 (☎0 77 21/5 55 41; ⑤). A good choice for **eating** is the *Ratskeller* in the Oberes Tor, which also has a beer garden.

Triberg

Heart of the central part of the Black Forest is the little town of **TRIBERG**, which lies at an altitude of 1000m, 25km northwest of Villingen. It's a renowned health resort, with the forest acting as a dust filter, ensuring particularly pure air. Some of the most imposing scenery in the region is nearby, and Triberg itself makes a good base for a day or two's relaxation. If you're travelling by train, arriving at the **Bahnhof** is a strange experience. As there's nothing but cliffs on either side of the narrow tracks it's easy to understand the derivation of the town's name, a corruption of "three mountains", after the peaks which surround it. It's a fifteen-minute walk uphill to the centre.

Prime attraction is the **Gutacher Wasserfall** at the top end of town. At 162m, it ranks as the highest waterfall in Germany and is undeniably impressive, even though it plunges in seven separate stages instead of a single dramatic dive. Unfortunately, in a reverse of the normal German penchant for unrestricted access to nature, it's sealed off, with a DM2.50/€1.25 levy for admission.

The **Schwarzwald-Museum** (daily 10am–5pm; DM6/€3) on Wallfahrtstrasse offers fascinating insights into the rural culture of the Black Forest as it was – and, to some extent, still is. There's a fine group of woodcarvings by the rustic local artist Karl Josef Fortwängler, who depicted the thick-set country bumpkins of the area in an idiosyncratic yet highly sympathetic manner. In addition, there's a large model of the Schwarzwaldbahn, while music boxes, clocks and examples of the traditional dress for carnivals and everyday wear complete the display. Further up the hill is the Baroque **Wallfahrtskirche St Maria in den Tannen**, whose painting of *The Virgin of the Pines* draws pilgrims for its allegedly miraculous qualities.

The **tourist office** (May–Sept Mon–Fri 8am–noon & 2–5pm, Sat 10am–noon; rest of year Mon–Fri only; ☎0 77 22/95 32 30, fax 95 32 36, *www.triberg.de*) in the Kurverwaltung, Luisenstr. 10. **Hotels** include *Central,* Hauptstr. 64 (☎0 77 22/43 60; ③), *Berg-Café*, Hermann-Schwer-Str. 6 (☎0 77 22/40 03; ④), *Adler,* Hauptstr. 52 (☎0 77 22/45 74; ⑤), and the top of the range *Parkhotel Wehrle,* Garbanstr. 24 (☎0 77 22/8 60 20; ⑦–⑨), which is set in its own park. It has a gourmet **restaurant** plus the more

---

CLOCK-MAKING IN THE BLACK FOREST

The first clocks to be seen in the Black Forest were mechanical contraptions brought by pedlars from Bohemia in the 1640s. Someone must have had the idea of reproducing them in wood, as a couple of decades later the first workshops had appeared. Originally, clock-making was an adjunct to farming and forestry, and was normally a co-operative venture involving several families, each of whom specialized in a different part of the business, such as woodcarving, painting or making the mechanism. The products were sold by itinerant hawkers, who gradually began to expand their operations abroad; by the end of the eighteenth century, demand was so great that clock-making became a lucrative full-time trade for many families and the single largest local industry. It has remained of key importance to the local economy to this day.

Although the cuckoo clock (*Kuckucksuhr*) is what most tourists want to buy, the alternative *Schilderuhr*, which has a hand-painted clockface, has a far longer and more prestigious tradition. Beautiful models designed to the customer's specification can be ordered throughout the Central Black Forest region; these contrast dramatically with the junk sold in the tackier souvenir shops.

---

affordable *Alta Schmieke*. The **youth hostel** is high in the hills at Rohrbacher Str. 35 (☎0 77 22/41 10, fax 66 62; DM24/€12 or DM29/€14.50); a bus will take you as far as the waterfall and then it's a very steep twenty-minute climb.

The Gutach valley

The **Gutach valley** north of Triberg is best known as the home of the traditional *Bollenhut* hat. At **HORNBERG**, the Schwarzwaldbahn emerges into a light and airy landscape again and traverses a huge viaduct. There's a fine view of the ensemble of town and rail line from the ruined Burg set high on a hill to the west.

A few kilometres north is the town of **GUTACH** itself, outside which is the **Schwarzwälder Freilichtmuseum** (April–Oct daily 8.30am–6pm; DM8/€4), a collection of buildings from the region. Centrepiece is what's probably the most famous house in the Black Forest, the late sixteenth-century **Vogtsbauernhof**. With its huge sloping roof and tiered facade, it's an outstanding example of the characteristic vernacular building style of the region. This was the original farmhouse on the site, whereas the various other exhibits have been moved in sfrom other locations. There are four more farmsteads, along with a wooden chapel and all kinds of workshops – smithies, granaries, a bakehouse, a distillery and various types of mills. Displays on the folklore and lifestyle of the region are also featured, and there are demonstrations of old crafts.

The Kinzig valley

At the next stop along the rail line, Hausach, the Gutach merges with the **Kinzig valley**; similarly, there's the junction of the Schwarzwaldbahn with the Kinzigtalbahn. **HASLACH**, an old market town and health resort just 8km from Hausach, is the most striking place on the Schwarzwaldbahn's stretch along the Kinzig towards the terminus at Offenburg. Its Rathaus is twely painted with depictions of locals in traditional dress, while the former Kapuzinerkloster is home to the **Trachtenmuseum** (April–Oct Tues–Sat 9am–5pm, Sun 10am–5pm; Nov–March Tues–Fri 1–5pm; DM3.50/€1.75), a huge collection of Black Forest costumes and folklore displays.

Following the Kinzigtalbahn eastwards from Hausach, the first stop is **WOLFACH**, situated at the point where the river after which the village is named joins the Kinzig.

SCHILTACH, a pretty, flower-lined place of half-timbered houses a further 10km east, is likewise set at the confluence of its river with the Kinzig.

ALPIRSBACH, 19km northeast of Schiltach, is grouped round the former **Kloster**. Begun in the late twelfth century, the **Klosterkirche**, which is now a Protestant parish church, preserves much of the simple, pure Romanesque form characteristic of the style of building championed at Hirsau (see p.336). The east end is especially notable – later Gothic masons ingeniously perched the chancel above the existing storey. Only one tower was built, however, and this was not finished until the Renaissance period, when it received an unusual gabled top. **Guided tours** (mid-March to Oct Mon–Sat at 9.30am–5.30pm, Sun 11am–5.30pm; DM4/€2) are run round the monastic buildings and the late Gothic cloisters which are often used for open-air concerts in summer.

Handsome half-timbered buildings decorate the centre of Alpirsbach, most notably the Rathaus; the town also makes a good centre for walks in the Kinzig valley. There are plenty of reasonably priced **pensions** (①–③), a **youth hostel** high on the Sulzberg at Reinerzauer Steige 80 (☎0 74 44/24 77, fax 13 04; DM24/€12 or DM29/€14.50), and two **campsites**. **Hotels** include *Löwen-Post,* Marktplatz 12 (☎0 74 44/23 93; ④), *Rössle,* Aischbachstr. 5 (☎0 74 44/22 81; ④), and *Gasthof Waldhorn,* Kranzgasse 4 (☎0 74 44/9 51 10; ④). A full accommodation list is available from the **tourist office** (☎0 74 44/9 51 62 81, fax 9 51 62 83, *www.alpirsbach.de*) in the Kurverwaltung, Hauptstr. 20. Alpirsbach's brewery, the Klosterbräu, produces a wide variety of excellent **beers**.

The northern Black Forest

To non-Germans, the northern stretch of the Black Forest, most of which belonged to Württemberg rather than Baden, is the least familiar part. Yet here are some of the most imposing landscapes – the forest really does look at its blackest and is cut by several deep, dark valleys which provide the strongest possible contrast to the long panoramic views from the hills. There are three main **touring routes**, each offering a widely varying choice of scenery: the Black Forest Highway, the Black Forest Valley Road and the circuitous Black Forest Spa Road. Walking or cycling are the best ways of **getting around**, but superb scenic rail lines, closely hugging the river valleys, enable all of the second and part of the third of these routes to be followed by even the most sedentary. Buses fill in the gaps, though the frequency of these varies considerably according to season, often drying up altogether in the winter months.

Freudenstadt

The hub of the transport system of the northern Black Forest is **FREUDENSTADT**, situated at high altitude on a plateau bordered by the rivers Murg and Kinzig. It's a polished, spick and span town and coupled with its extreme climate and arcaded streets, it has a feel reminiscent more of Switzerland than Germany. Its regularly built streets look gleamingly new, but it's new only in one sense, its history being dogged by an ill luck than contradicts its name, which means "town of joy".

Freudenstadt is still sufficiently singular to justify a look round, even if you aren't attracted to the leisure facilities or the excellent hiking opportunities in the neighbourhood. The **Marktplatz** must have seemed extraordinary when it was first built; it's an impressive sight even to the modern eye which is far more attuned to the large-scale, and it still ranks as much the biggest square in Germany. At diagonally opposite corners are the two main public buildings, the **Rathaus** and the **Stadtkirche**.

The Stadtkirche is particularly intriguing, built in an L-shape so that the men and women of the congregation could be segregated. Indeed, the arrangement meant they

---

THE CURIOUS HISTORY OF FREUDENSTADT

Freudenstadt was founded in 1599 by **Duke Friedrich I of Württemberg**. He had three main aims in establishing the new community: to give a much-needed boost to his ever-empty state coffers by exploiting the **silver mines** in the nearby Christophstal; to provide a home, at a time of high religious rivalry, for Protestant refugees from Austria; and to have a new, "secret" capital for Württemberg, which he dreamed of building up as an effective counterweight to France on the one hand and the Habsburg-dominated Holy Roman Empire on the other.

A highly talented Italian-trained architect, **Heinrich Schickhardt**, was accordingly charged with designing the first planned town in the province. He laid it out in the manner of a vast Roman camp, centred on a spaciously grandiose central square. In the middle, there was meant to be an even bigger Schloss than the one in Stuttgart but it was never built – the silver mines proved to be a mirage, and the town was devastated by **epidemic and fire** within 35 years of its birth, whereupon it lost all sense of importance. Something of a comeback was made in the nineteenth century with its development into one of the leading spas in the Black Forest. Two weeks before the end of World War II, **disaster struck again**: French artillery bombarded the town, and when it fell, the victors ran amok; only two streets survived the blaze intact. Within five years, however, Freudenstadt had been completely **rebuilt** to the old plans. This was regarded as a stunning achievement, even by the standards of German postwar reconstruction, but the undeniable effect – avoided in more painstaking restoration projects – is that the historic buildings look anachronistically modern.

---

could not even see each other – the better to keep their minds on the sermon. The church houses a magnificent polychrome wooden **lectern** made around 1150, which bears large statues of the Four Evangelists and their symbols. It's unique of its kind and one of the most important pieces of Romanesque church furniture to have survived. Along with the **font**, made half a century earlier and adorned with carvings of symbolical animals, it presumably came from one of the Black Forest monasteries.

Practicalities

There are two train stations: the **Stadtbahnhof**, on the Murgtalbahn, is just a few minutes' walk north of Marktplatz and has the **bus terminus** just outside, whereas the **Hauptbahnhof** is at the eastern edge of town, at a much lower altitude. The **tourist office** (April–Oct Mon–Fri 9am–6pm, Sat & Sun 10am–1/2pm; ☎0 74 41/86 47 30, fax 8 51 76, *www.freudenstadt.de*) is at Marktplatz 64.

Hotels and **pensions** are scattered all over town; for the lowest rates, try the concentration on Lauterbadstrasse. For something a bit more upmarket there's *Adler*, Forstr. 15–17 (☎0 74 41/9 15 20; ④), *Jägerstüble,* Marktplatz 12 (☎0 74 41/23 87; ⑤), *Zum Warteck*, Stuttgarter Str. 14 (☎0 74 41/74 18; ⑤), *Alte Kanzlei*, Strassburger Str. 6 (☎0 74 41/8 88 60; ⑤), and *Bären*, Lange Str. 33 (☎0 74 41/27 29; ⑥). Alternatively, the **youth hostel** is at Eugen-Nägele-Str. 69 (☎0 74 41/77 20, fax 8 57 88; DM23/€11.50 or DM28/€14), not far from the Stadtbahnhof, and a **campsite**, *Langenwald* (☎0 74 41/28 62), 3km to the west. All the hotels listed above have recommendable **restaurants:** *Jägerstüble* is perhaps the best value, while *Zum Warteck* scores for quality.

The Black Forest Highway (Schwarzwald-Hochstrasse)

The **Black Forest Highway**, linking Freudenstadt with Baden-Baden, is one of Germany's most famous roads. Up to five buses daily run in each direction in summer along this 60km stretch, which has no villages to speak of. However, there are plenty of **hotels**, many with spa facilities and nearly all on the expensive side. One of the most reasonably priced is *Berghotel Mummelsee* (☎0 78 2/10 88; ④–⑥). In addition, there's a single **youth hostel**, *Zuflucht* (☎0 78 04/6 11, fax 13 23; DM24/€12 or DM29/€14.50), located at a particularly scenic point just off the main road 19km north of Freudenstadt. It makes an excellent base for hiking in summer and for skiing in winter. Walking along the accompanying trail is really much the best way to see the area, which is pocked with belvederes offering vast panoramas towards the Rhine and the French Vosges.

Just beyond the hostel is the **Buhlbachsee**, the first of several tiny natural lakes along the highway. Before this, however, is a by-road leading west to Oppenau which joins with another fine scenic road running north to the valley of **Allerheiligen**, rejoining the Hochstrasse at Ruhestein. Allerheiligen has the ruins of a former Premonstratensian **Kloster**, the first Gothic building in southwest Germany, probably built by the same team of masons as Strasbourg cathedral. There's also an impressively curling stepped **waterfall** and a good restaurant, the *Klosterhof*, which makes its own fruit wines and liqueurs.

East of Ruhestein is the **Wildsee**, but the most celebrated of the lakes is the **Mummelsee** a further 8km north. It stands at the foot of the Hornigsrinde (1164m), the highest point in the Northern Black Forest, offering a particularly outstanding view. The Mummelsee itself, now a popular boating centre, is allegedly haunted by water-sprites and by the luckless King Ulmon, who was condemned by a sorceress to live for a thousand years, in spite of his continuous pleas to be released to join his friends in the afterlife. This legend has proved a potent inspiration for many German writers and formed the subject of one of Eduard Mörike's most evocative poems. It's often necessary to change buses here, particularly out of season when there are no through services.

The Murg valley

The **Murg valley** north of Freudenstadt is the second stage of the Black Forest Valley Road (Schwarzwald-Tälerstrasse). This is the only one of the three scenic routes which doesn't officially begin at Freudenstadt, its first stretch being the Kinzig valley from Alpirsbach.

What is arguably the most scenic of all the region's rail lines, the 60km Murgtalbahn line to Rastatt, follows a parallel course to the road. Though never more than a modest stretch of water, the River Murg cleaves an impressively grand valley in its downward journey towards its confluence with the Rhine. One of the best hikes which can be made from **BAIERSBRONN** (the first stop, 6km north of Freudenstadt) is west along the course of the young river towards its source in the shadow of the 1055-metre-high **Schliffkopf**.

All the little towns along the Murg have impressive settings, and make good bases for exploring an underrated part of the Black Forest. Particularly worthy of mention is **FORBACH**, about halfway along the line, which has a wonderful sixteenth-century single-span covered wooden bridge, the largest of its type in Europe. West of town is some fine countryside, with the artifical **Schwarzenbach Stausee**, a watersports centre, and the tiny **Herrenwieser See**. The latter lies below the **Badener Höhe**, whose TV tower commands an extensive view of the region. There's a **youth hostel** just to the north of Forbach at Birket 1 (☎0 72 28/24 27, fax 15 51; DM22/€11 or DM27/€13.50) and another out in the sticks at Haus no. 33 in Herrenwies (☎0 72 26/2 57, fax 13 18; DM24/€12 or DM29/€14.50). **Campsites** are also to be found in both locations, as well as a good number of cheap **pensions** (①–③).

Calw and the Nagold valley

Much the most impressive stretch of the Black Forest Spa Road (Schwarzwald-Bäderstrasse) is the wonderfully dark, secret **Nagold valley**. The Nagoldtalbahn, which runs most of the way alongside it, begins at the rail junction of Horb, which has connections to Stuttgart, Tübingen and Rottweil, but there's also a branch line to Freudenstadt which links up 6km further north, at Eutingen.

"The most beautiful town of all that I know," was how Hermann Hesse described **CALW**, the old textile centre which is the focal point of this valley. The eulogy needn't be taken too seriously – his judgement was more than a little bit coloured by the fact that he happened to have been born and bred there, though he eventually went into exile in Switzerland. Fans of Hesse's novels will certainly want to come here to see his birthplace at Marktplatz 30, now designated the **Hermann-Hesse-Museum** (Tues, Wed & Fri–Sun 11am–5pm, Thurs 11am–7pm; DM5/€2.50), and containing memorabilia of the writer.

Other than this, Calw boasts an impressive array of half-timbered houses, mostly dating from the late seventeenth and early eighteenth centuries, just after a fire had destroyed the medieval town. One of the few older monuments is the **Nikolausbrücke** from around 1400, which incorporates a picturesque little votive chapel. Hesse, true to form, considered the bridge and the square on its west bank to form an assemblage superior to the Piazza del Duomo in Florence.

HIRSAU, 2km downstream, is now a small health resort and officially part of Calw, but actually has a far longer history. Its Benedictine **Kloster**, indeed, was once the most powerful monastery in Germany, serving as mother-house to a host of dependent congregations and initiating a highly influential reform movement whose main effect was to free religious houses from the clutches of secular patrons, placing them instead under the direct control of the pope. The simple, original monastic church is tucked away in among a number of much later buildings, not far from the bridge over the Nagold. A ninth-century Carolingian structure, it was rebuilt in the mid-eleventh century, and now serves as the Catholic parish church of **St Aurelius**. To the rear is the new **Klostermuseum** (April–Oct Tues–Sun 2–5pm; Nov–March Sat & Sun 2–5pm; DM3/€1.50), which contains local finds plus documentation.

The eleventh-century complex, built in warm red sandstone, was directly modelled on the most famous and powerful European monastery of the day – that of Cluny in Burgundy – on sloping ground above the west bank of the Nagold. It was almost completely destroyed by the French in the War of the Palatinate Succession; only the **Eulenturm** (Owl Tower), originally one of a pair, survives from this epoch. However, there are also fragments from later building periods, notably the late fifteenth-century **cloisters**, the early sixteenth-century **Marienkapelle** (now restored to serve as the Protestant church) and the Renaissance **Jagdschloss** of the Dukes of Württemberg, who expelled the monks after the Reformation, taking over the land as pleasure and hunting grounds.

Practicalities

Calw's **tourist office** is at Marktbrücke (☎0 70 51/96 88 10, fax 96 88 77, *www.calw.de*). There are three **hotels** in the centre of Calw: *Alte Post*, Bahnhofstr. 1 (☎0 70 51/21 96; ③), *Rössle*, Hermann-Hesse-Platz 2 (☎0 70 51/7 90 00; ③), and *Ratsstube*, Marktplatz 12 (☎0 70 51/18 64; ⑤). Slightly more upmarket is *Kloster Hirsau*, Wildbadstr. 2 (☎0 70 51/9 67 40; ⑥) in Hirsau. Each of these, with the exception of the first-named, has a **restaurant**. **Campsites** are located at Eiselstätt (☎0 70 51/1 21 31 or 1 34 37) in the eastern part of town, and in the outlying villages of Stammheim (☎0 70 51/48 44) and Altburg (☎0 70 51/5 07 88).

Tiefenbronn

TIEFENBRONN, an unassuming-looking village situated at the extreme edge of the Black Forest in the peaceful valley of the River Würm 12km southeast of Pforzheim, has two claims to fame. First, it's a renowned gastronomic centre; people come from Stuttgart and beyond in order to eat at the *Ochsen-Post*, Franz-Josef-Gall-Str. 13 (☎0 72

34/9 54 50; ⑥), a **hotel** in a seventeenth-century timber-framed building. The main restaurant, one of the best in southern Germany, is expensive, but the *Bauernstuben*, open evenings only, is more affordable.

From the outside, there's little to suggest that there's anything remarkable about the steep-roofed fourteenth-century Gothic church of **St Maria Magdalena**. Architecturally, it's very ordinary indeed, yet it contains a magnificent array of **works of art** which put to shame those in most cathedrals. Jewel-like stained-glass windows, made in Strasbourg around 1370, illuminate the choir, and there are fifteenth-century wall-paintings throughout the church, including a depiction of the Last Judgement, a frieze of coats of arms and portraits of the family who provided the endowments. The high altar tells the story of the Passion and has panels of the Nativity on the reverse.

However, this is outclassed by the altar dedicated to the local patron saint, which is housed in the southern aisle. One of the most beautiful of all European Gothic paintings, it bears a curious inscription: "Weep, Art, weep and lament loudly, nobody nowadays wants you, so alas, 1432. Lucas Moser, painter of Wyl, master of this work, pray God for him." Nothing is known about the embittered **Lucas Moser**, whose style seems oddly modern for its day. The first German painting to try a realistic approach, including a sense of perspective, it still has all the grace and delicacy characteristic of the earlier Soft Style. It shows Mary Magdalene washing Christ's feet, her miraculous journey in a ship without sail or rudder to Marseille, her stay there and her last Communion in the cathedral of Aix-en-Provence.

Baden-Baden

It is an inane town, full of sham, and petty fraud, and snobbery, but the baths are good . . . I had had twinges of rheumatism unceasingly during three years, but the last one departed after a fortnight's bathing there, and I have never had one since. I fully believe I left my rheumatism in Baden-Baden. Baden-Baden is welcome to it. It was little, but it was all I had to give. I would have preferred to leave something that was catching, but it was not in my power.

Mark Twain, *A Tramp Abroad*

Mark Twain's ambivalent reactions to **BADEN-BADEN** – he actually seems to have revelled in the snob aspect, delighting in the fact that the little old woman he sat behind in church and had decided to foster, turned out to be the Empress of Germany – mirror the contrasting reactions of late nineteenth-century visitors to this town, then the glittering rendezvous of the wealthy and famous.

In the twentieth century, the idle rich classes who made Baden-Baden the "summer capital of Europe" were almost entirely wiped out. The Bolshevik Revolution accounted for the Russian landowners, while World War II took care of their counterparts in Prussia and the Balkans. Yet, if Baden-Baden isn't quite what it was, it has still maintained its image remarkably well; like Bath in England, it has a sense of style that no other spa in the country can quite match. This is in large measure thanks to the German infatuation with the concept of the spa cure, which is underpinned by an incredibly lenient health insurance system. Buoyed by the postwar economic prosperity, people flock here to enjoy a taste of a lifestyle their parents could only have dreamed about. It remains a place you're likely to either love or hate, but is somewhere which definitely should be experienced at first hand.

Arrival, information and accommodation

The **Bahnhof**, on the fast Freiburg to Karlsruhe line, is in the suburb of Oos, 4km northwest of the centre, which is reached by bus #201, #205 or #216. As the sights are

ACCOMMODATION
4 Am Friedrichsbad
5 Am Markt
3 Bad-Hotel Zum Hirsch
2 Badischer Hof
9 Brenner's Park-Hotel
8 Der Kleine Prinz
7 Holland Hotel Sophienpark
6 Rathausglöckel

BADEN-BADEN

scattered, it's well worth investing in a 24-hour ticket on the **public transport** network. This costs DM8.50/€4.25 for Baden-Baden or DM16/€8 for the whole region including Karlsruhe and covers two adults and two children travelling together. The **tourist office** is in the Trinkhalle on Kaiserallee (daily 10am-6.30pm; ☎0 72 21/27 52 00, fax 27 52 02, *www.baden-baden.de*).

Baden-Baden has **hotels** to suit every pocket, from the plain and serviceable to the super-luxury establishments frequented by aristocrats and oil sheikhs. There are a fair number of **private rooms** (②–④); the tourist office has a list but is unlikely to help with bookings. The **youth hostel** is between the Bahnhof and the centre at

Hardbergstr. 34 (☎0 72 21/5 22 23, fax 6 00 12; DM24/€12 or DM29/€14.50); take bus #201, #205 or #216 to Grosse-Dollen-Strasse, from where the way is signposted. **Camping** presents more of a problem, with no sites in the immediate vicinity. Nearest is in a large pleasure park named Oberbruch (☎0 72 23/2 31 94) in the outskirts of Bühl, 10km southwest and three stops away by slow train.

Hotels

Altes Schloss, Alter Schlossweg 10 (☎0 72 21/2 69 48, fax 39 17 75). A tiny hotel is run as an adjunct to the restaurant in Burg Hohenbaden. It only has two doubles and one single, so is best booked well in advance. ④.

Am Friedrichsbad, Gernsbacher Str. 31 (☎0 72 21/27 10 46, fax 3 83 10). Located directly opposite the Friedrichsbad, this has a Czech speciality restaurant, *Prager Stuben*, extravagantly decorated in the distinctive Art Nouveau style of Prague. ④–⑥.

Am Markt, Marktplatz 18 (☎0 72 21/2 70 40, fax 27 04 44). Well-regarded family-run hotel in the heart of the Altstadt. It serves evening meals (except on Wed & Sun) to house guests only. ④.

Bad-Hotel Zum Hirsch, Hirschstr. 1 (☎0 72 21/93 90, fax 3 81 48, *www.steigenberger.com*). Altstadt hotel in a 300-year-old building with some splendid public rooms, notably the *Ballsaal*. The bedrooms are nicely furnished, and some are supplied directly with thermal water. Evening meals are served to residents only. ⑧.

Badischer Hof, Lange Str. 47 (☎0 72 21/93 40, fax 93 44 70, *www.steigenberger.com*). This luxury hotel was founded in 1809 in the premises of a suppressed Capuchin friary. As well as sauna and massage facilities, it has its own thermal swimming pool, and some of the rooms have thermal water supplies. The restaurant is among the town's best. ⑨.

Brenner's Park-Hotel, An der Lichtentaler Allee (☎0 72 21/90 00, fax 3 87 72, *www.baden-baden.com*). Baden-Baden's most exclusive address is an enduring reminder of its halcyon years. Set in its own manicured private park, it boasts an extensive bathing complex with swimming pool, steam baths, sauna and solarium. Each room is individually decorated with chintz fabrics and antiques. There are two restaurants – the gourmet and very formal *Park Restaurant* and the more relaxed and slightly less expensive *Schwarzwald-Stube*. ⑨.

Der Kleine Prinz, Lichtentaler Str. 36 (☎0 72 21/34 64, fax 3 82 64, *www.romantik.de*). A flagship of the Romantik chain, exquisitely furnished and decorated throughout; a chief source of inspiration is Antoine de Saint Exupéry's illustrated children's novel *Le Petit Prince*, after which it is named. The restaurant (closed all day Mon & Tues lunchtime) is outstanding, albeit among the most expensive in town. ⑧–⑨.

Goldener Stern, Ooser Haupstr. 16 (☎0 72 21/6 15 09, fax 5 43 23). An archetypal German hotel and restaurant which offers the best value of the concentration near the Bahnhof in the suburb of Oos. ④.

Holland Hotel Sophienpark, Sophienstr. 14 (☎0 72 21/35 60, fax 35 61 21, *www.holland-hotel-sophienpark.de*). One of the least expensive of the town's luxury hotels, notwithstanding its setting in its own fine park. Set-price buffet lunches are served in its *Parkrestaurant*, an à la carte menu in the evening in the *Bauernstuben*. ⑨.

Rathausglöckel, Steinstr. 7 (☎0 72 21/9 06 10, fax 90 61 61). Historic hotel in a very quiet Altstadt street, just up from the Friedrichsbad. Its restaurant is worth seeking out in its own right for its inexpensive traditional fare. ⑤.

Waldhorn, Beuerner Str. 54 (☎0 72 21/7 21 88 or 7 22 88, fax 7 34 88). Two-hundred-year old Wirtshaus in the suburb of Oberbeuern, just beyond Lichtental. Its restaurant (closed Mon & Tues) is generally regarded as being among Baden-Baden's best. ⑤.

Wolfsschlucht, Ebersteinburgstr. 2 (☎0 72 21/2 23 82, fax 2 23 09). This hotel with café-restaurant is a good choice if you'd like to stay out of town. It's located by the main road on the outskirts of Ebersteinburg, at the junction of several hiking trails, one leading in a couple of minutes to the "Wolf's Glen" from which it takes its name. ③–⑤.

The Town

Although it's a relatively small town with a population of no more than 50,000, Baden-Baden is not a place to be seen in a hurry. The sights are spread out all over the valley

THE HISTORY OF THE SPA

The discovery of hot springs in the Florintinerberg, on the east side of the River Oos, was made by the Romans, who found in them cures for arthritis and rheumatism. They established a settlement at this point, known simply as Aquae (Waters). The vernacular form of this was later used not only for the town, but also for the Margravate established by the **Zähringen** family, who moved here in the eleventh century to rule their combined territories at the western frontiers of the Holy Roman Empire. In the sixteenth century, the Swiss alchemist and doctor Paracelsus utilized the springs to save the life of Margrave Philipp I. However, Baden-Baden's rise to international fame only came about as a result of Napoleon's creation of the buffer state of Baden in 1806, 35 years after it had lost its role as ducal capital to Karlsruhe. The grand dukes promoted their ancestors' old seat as a resort and began embellishing it with handsome new buildings, many designed by the Neoclassical architect Friedrich Weinbrenner.

A casino formed an integral part of the facilities from the beginning, though it only took off with the arrival from Paris in 1836 of the flamboyant impresario **Jacques Bénazet**, Le Roi de Bade. With gambling outlawed in France, he devoted all his energies to building up Baden-Baden as the gambling capital of Europe. Among the famous visitors was Dostoevsky, who became a compulsive addict, a theme he treated in his novella *The Gambler*. In 1872 Kaiser Wilhelm I – a faithful annual visitor to Baden-Baden over a period of forty years – abolished gambling throughout his newly united empire, forcing the town to concentrate on its spa facilities once more. However, the gaming tables were licensed again by Hitler in 1933, and have remained in operation ever since, save for the break caused by World War II.

of the River Oos and the hills around, while time is needed to bask in the varied spa attractions.

The Kurhaus

The **Kurhaus** was built in the 1820s by Weinbrenner as the focal point of the new spa quarter on the west side of the Oos. Its solemn, stately facade of eight Corinthian columns is now approached via an elegant shopping arcade of expensive shops. Bénazet's son Edouard, Le Duc de Zéro, added an opulent suite of gaming rooms to the Kurhaus, employing the same team of designers as had worked on the Paris Opéra; they married the contemporary style of the *belle époque* to the extravagant type of decor found at Versailles. Highlight is the **Wintergarten**, with its glass cupola, Chinese vases and pure gold roulette table, which is used only on Saturdays or for special guests. Almost equally striking is the **Roter Saal**, covered from top to bottom in red silk damask from Lyon, and with a glorious marbled fireplace and raised oval ceiling.

The easiest way to see these is to take a **guided tour** (daily: April–Sept 9.30am–noon; Oct–March 10am–noon; DM6/€3). However, it's far more fun to go when the action is on. A day-ticket for the **Casino**, which is housed in the Kurhaus, costs DM5/€2.50, with no obligation to participate. Formal dress (ie any kind of jacket and tie for men, skirt or dress for women) is a precondition of entry; access is officially forbidden to residents of Baden-Baden, anyone under 21 and students. Roulette is played daily from 2pm to 2am (until 3am on Saturday), black jack from 5pm to 1am Monday to Thursday, from 4pm to 1am Friday and Sunday, and from 4pm to 2am on Saturday, while baccarat is for the real night owls, running daily from 3pm to 6am. Minimum stake is DM5/€2.50; maximum is DM50,000/€25,000 though this limit is waived for baccarat.

Around Lichtentaler Allee

South of the Kurhaus runs Baden-Baden's most important thoroughfare, the **Lichtentaler Allee**. This was originally lined with oaks, but was transformed at the instigation of Edouard Bénazet into a landscape in the English style, with the addition of exotic trees and shrubs. It requires little effort of the imagination to visualize the procession of aristocratic carriages along this route; at Kettenbrücke, at the far end, an attempt was made on the life of Wilhelm I in 1861.

First of the buildings on Lichtentaler Allee is the Parisian-style **Theater** which opened in 1862 with the premiere of Berlioz's opera *Béatrice et Bénédict*. Next in line comes the **Internationaler Club**, built by Weinbrenner for a Swedish princess but now the headquarters of the big flat races which are held in Iffezheim, 12km northwest of Baden-Baden. There's a meeting in May, and a *Grosse Woche* in late August, which is the most important in the German calendar and now ranks as the high point of the Baden-Baden season. Further along is the **Kunsthalle** (Tues & Thurs–Sun 10am–6pm, Wed 10am–8pm; DM8/€4), which has no permanent collection but regularly hosts major loan exhibitions of twentieth-century art.

Immediately north of the Kurhaus, the **Trinkhalle** (Pump Room) was built by a follower of Weinbrenner, Heinrich Hübsch. Its arcades shelter fourteen large frescoes by the Romantic painter Jakob Götzenberger, illustrating legends about the town and the nearby countryside. Different varieties of spring water are dispensed from a modern mosaic fountain inside. Its interior was recently converted to house the tourist office along with a reading room and café.

The Michaelsberg, which rises behind the spa quarter, is named after the last Romanian Boyar of Moldavia, Michael Stourdza, who settled in Baden-Baden after he had been expelled from his homeland. In 1863, his teenage son was murdered in Paris; as a memorial, he commissioned the **Stourdzakapelle** to be built on the hill. Construction of this domed chapel, the most distinguished of the three nineteenth-century churches in Baden-Baden built for expatriate communities, was entrusted to the aged Leo von Klenze who had created so much of nineteenth-century Munich, but he died before it was complete. It's normally kept locked, but the priest, who lives in the house alongside, will open it on request.

The Altstadt

Little remains of the old town of Baden-Baden, which was almost completely destroyed in a single day in 1689, the result of a fire started by French troops. However, halfway up the Florintinerberg is the Marktplatz, where you'll find the **Rathaus**, formerly a Jesuit college but partially remodelled by Weinbrenner to serve as the original casino.

Opposite is the **Stiftskirche**, a Gothic hall church whose tower is an amalgam of the Romanesque lower storeys of the first church, a Gothic octagon and a Baroque cap. It may seem unexpected that Baden-Baden possesses one of the all-time masterpieces of European sculpture, but the Stiftkirche's 5.4-metre-high sandstone *Crucifixion*, depicting Christ as a noble giant triumphant over his suffering, certainly warrants such a rating. Carved in 1467, it stood for nearly five centuries in the Alter Friedhof, before being moved inside for conservation reasons. The work is signed by **Nicolaus Gerhaert von**

THE NAMING OF BADEN-BADEN

The division of the Margravate along Catholic and Protestant lines in 1525 is the source of the town's curious double-barrelled name. The Protestants moved to Durlach and founded the House of Baden-Durlach; the Catholic branch therefore became known as the House of Baden-Baden, following the usual practice, on the division of a state, of modifying the original name by adding that of its capital. Although this is also what the town itself has commonly been called ever since, the name was only officially adopted in 1931, more out of snobbery than anything else, in order to distinguish it from lesser spa towns named Baden in Austria and Switzerland.

Leyden, a mysterious, peripatetic sculptor of Dutch origin who pioneered a realist approach to art which was to have a profound influence on the German carvers of the next generation. The tabernacle was made about twenty years later by a mason who had clearly come under Gerhaert's spell, while there are also several impressive **tombs** of the margraves of Baden lining the chancel; particularly eye-catching is the Rococo monument to "Türkenlouis" (see also p.344 & p.348), replete with depictions of his trophies.

From Marktplatz you can climb the steep steps to the **Neues Schloss** whose terrace commands the best view over Baden-Baden, a dramatic mixture of rooftops, church spires and the Black Forest surroundings. The site served as the seat of the Margraves of Baden from 1437, and of the Catholic line of Baden-Baden when the House divided in 1525. Until recently, the main block was still a residence of the Zähringen family, but they have moved out and auctioned off many of the furnishings. However, one of the wings contains the archeology and toy departments of the **Stadtgeschichtliche Sammlungen** (Tues–Thurs noon–5pm, Fri–Sun 11am–5pm; DM2/€2.50).

The baths

Hidden underneath the Stiftskirche are the remains of the Roman imperial baths; the more modest **Römerbad** (previously Easter–Oct daily 10am–noon & 1.30–4pm; DM2.50/€1.25, but currently closed for restoration) just to the east on Römerplatz was probably for the use of soldiers.

Above the ruins is what must rank as one of the most magnificent bathing halls in the world, the **Friedrichsbad** (Mon–Sat 9am–10pm, Sun noon–8pm; DM36/€18, or DM46–56/€23–28 with massage treatment). Begun in 1869, it's as grandly sumptuous as a Renaissance palace. This elaborateness is at least partly due to the fact that, as gambling was outlawed while the building was under construction, the medicinal springs became even more crucial to local prosperity than they had been before. The red and white sandstone facade is crowned with sea-green cupolas, while inside the pools are surrounded by pillars, arches and classical-style tiles, giving a truly exotic atmosphere. Speciality of the house is a "Roman-Irish Bath", which consists of a two-hour programme of showers, hot air and steam baths, soap and brush massage, thermal bathing and a half-hour snooze in a specially designed rest room. The entire treatment is undertaken in the nude, with mixed bathing all day Wednesday and Friday.

The **Caracalla-Therme** (daily 8am–10pm; DM19/€9.50 for 2hr, DM25/€12.50 for 3hr, DM29/€14.50 for 4hr) on the same square is a vast complex, completed in 1985, as a replacement for the former Augustabad. There are seven pools, both indoors and out, which are all at different temperatures, along with a sauna, solarium and massage facility. In reality, it's no more than an upmarket swimming hall with thermal water springs, though it makes an ideal complement to the Friedrichsbad. Its humbler status is reflected in the considerably cheaper prices.

The Südstadt and Lichtental

The Südstadt, immediately south of the Florintinerberg, was traditionally the home of foreigners. Just off Bertholdsplatz is the onion-domed **Russische Kirche** (March–Dec daily 10am–1pm & 2–6pm; DM1/€0.50), while the neo-Gothic **Johanneskirche** on Bertholdstrasse was the place where Mark Twain had his encounter with the empress. Beyond the church is the **Gönneranlage**, a fine park with pergolas, fountains and a rose garden.

Further south is the incorporated village of **LICHTENTAL**, which can be reached by bus #201. The tranquil thirteenth-century **Kloster** is still occupied by Cistercian nuns, who keep up a long tradition of handicrafts, and also make several fiery liqueurs, which can be bought at their shop. There are two Gothic chapels: the larger one is used for services, while the other, the **Fürstenkapelle** (guided tours Tues–Sun at 3pm, closed first Sun in month; DM3/€1.50), served as the pantheon of the Margraves of Baden prior to the Stiftskirche. Particularly outstanding is the tomb of the foundress Irmengard, carved by a Strasbourg mason in the mid-fourteenth century.

Just down the road from here, at Maximilianstr. 85, is the **Brahms-Haus** (Mon, Wed & Fri 3–5pm, Sun 10am–1pm; DM3/€1.50), a tiny attic crammed with memorabilia, left exactly as when the great composer lived in it periodically during the years 1865 to 1874. This was the time when Brahms, ever conscious of his mantle as Beethoven's successor, was struggling to establish himself as a symphonist, only publishing his first, tormented essay in this form after he had passed his 40th birthday. Its elegaic successor was largely written during a later visit to Lichtental, while part of the massive *Ein Deutsches Requiem*, his most important choral work, was also composed here.

Other suburbs

The original castle of the margraves, **Burg Hohenbaden** (Tues–Sun 10am–10pm; free), is situated on the wooded slopes of the Battert, some 3km from the Neues Schloss, from which it's reached via Alter Schlossweg; alternatively, bus #215 goes there from the town centre. At one time, it boasted over a hundred rooms but is now ruinous, albeit still very much worth visiting for the sake of the sweeping views; there's also a good and reasonably priced restaurant. To the east, on the same bus route, lies the wine-growing village of **EBERSTEINBURG**, likewise dominated by a ruined fortress of the local rulers. Further south and reached from Ebersteinburg by footpath, or from the Bahnhof or centre by bus #205, is the **Merkur**, at 668 metres the highest hill in the Baden-Baden range. There's a choice of trails along it, or you can ascend to the summit by an unusually steep rack rail line (daily 10am–10pm; DM5/€2.50 single, DM7/€3.50 return). To obtain much of a view, you then need to climb the Jugendstil **Aussichtsturm**.

Eating and drinking

Most of the best restaurants in Baden-Baden are in the hotels (see p.339), though there are plenty of other enticing places to eat and drink.

Baden-Badener Weinkeller, Maria-Viktoria-Str. 2. Small wine bar-restaurant just south of the town centre. Evenings only, closed Sun.

Böckeler's Café, Lange Str. 40–42. Traditional café with a wonderful selection of cakes and sweets; also does light meals.

Café Hofmann, Lange Str. 39. Another fine *Kaffee und Kuchen* establishment on the main shopping street.

Eckberg, Eckhöfe 12. Baden-Baden's only Weingut, situated in the northern part of Lichtental, has an adjoining wine bar where you can sample its products. Full meals are also served. Open Wed & Thurs 3–10pm, Fri & Sat 3–11pm, Sun noon–10pm.

Kurhaus, Kaiserallee 1. Predictably classy restaurant attached to the casino.

Leo's, Luisenstr. 10. Trendy café-bar and, as such, something of a rarity in Baden-Baden.

Molkenkur, Quettigstr. 19. Gaststätte specializing in local dishes.

Münchner Löwenbräu, Gernsbacher Str. 9. This is like a little piece of Munich successfully transplanted to alien surroundings; it serves typically solid and inexpensive Bavarian fare, and is fronted by a small beer garden.

Papalangi, Lichtentaler Str. 13. Smart designer-style bistro with a courtyard terrace serving high-quality Italianate dishes, including good-value set lunches. Closed Sun & Mon.

Stahlbad, Augustaplatz 2. An extremely elegant and expensive restaurant with garden terrace. In both cuisine and decor it rivals any of the hotel restaurants. Closed Mon.

Warsteiner Brasserie, Kaiserallee 4. A popular rendezvous, particularly with the young. It serves a whole gamut of functions throughout the day, ranging from breakfast café to evening cocktail bar.

Entertainment

Baden-Baden maintains a prestigious highbrow cultural scene, which since 1998 has been centred on the Festspielhaus, Beim Alten Bahnhof 2 (☎0 72 21/3 01 31 01, *www.festspielhaus.de*), Europe's second largest **opera house**, a brash modernist structure built onto the plush neo-Renaissance station which had lacked a proper function since the closure of the branch line to Oos. This attracts a starry roster of visiting international artists for its ambitious opera, ballet and concert programmes. The town can also claim to be the smallest in the world to have two distinguished **symphony orchestras**, namely the recently retitled SWR Sinfonieorchester (which is now shared with Freiburg) and the Baden Badener Philharmonie, whose usual performing venue is the Kurhaus. Tickets for its concerts there, and for the **drama** at the nearby Theater on Goetheplatz (☎0 72 21/93 27 00), can be had from the Kurhaus box office (☎0 72 21/93 27 00).

Rastatt

In 1698, Margrave Ludwig, nicknamed "Türkenlouis" on account of his victories over the Turks, decided to shift his seat from Baden-Baden to **RASTATT**, then an insignificant village 15km to the north, just before the point where the River Murg flows into the Rhine. This move was partly precipitated by the dilapidated condition of the Neues Schloss after the War of the Palatinate Succession. However, it was also influenced by the courtly culture of the time, which had decided that hilltop fortresses were redundant and should be replaced by planned palatial towns on the model of Versailles.

Rastatt's town centre was planned in conjunction with its great Schloss but only finished in the mid-eighteenth century. Centrepiece is the elliptical Marktplatz, with several fountains, the **Rathaus** and the **Stadtkirche St Alexander**, the last-named already showing Neoclassical influence. Between here and the Schloss are a number of handsome courtiers' houses. One of these, Herrenstr. 11, houses the **Heimatmuseum** (Wed, Fri & Sun 10am–noon & 3–5pm; free), which traces the history of the town and includes displays of medieval art and souvenirs of Türkenlouis.

The massive red sandstone **Schloss** (guided tours Tues–Sun 10am–4/5pm; DM6/€3, or DM10/€5 combined ticket with Schloss Favorite) was built in just ten years to plans by an Italian architect, Domenico Rossi. It's approached via a spacious U-shaped courtyard, guarded by a balustrade with writhing Baroque statues, while the central wing is topped by a glistening figure of Jupiter, dubbed the Goldener Mann. In addition to the recently restored main reception rooms upstairs you can visit the **Wehrgeschichtliches Museum** (Tues–Sun 9.30am–5pm; DM3/€1.50) and the **Freiheitsmuseum** (Tues–Sun 9.30am–5pm; free) on the ground floor. The former shows weapons, uniforms and other military memorabilia from medieval times to the present day., while the latter traces the history of German liberalism – a slender theme. Rastatt was chosen as the venue for this museum because it was the last stronghold of the rebels in the revolutions of 1848–49, one of the few occasions when the authoritarian nature of German society was seriously challenged. In the north wing of the building, entered from Lyzeumstrasse, is the sumptuous **Schlosskirche**; it's generally kept locked but a notice will tell you where to get the key.

The most imposing part of the Schlossgarten is now unfortunately cut off by an arterial road to the south, though at least it does leave a peaceful corner at the edge of town. Here is the graceful **Einsiedelner Kapelle**, a miniaturized version of the great Swiss church of the same name. Türkenlouis' widow, Margravine Augusta Sibylla, went on pilgrimage there to pray for her son Ludwig Georg, who, at the age of 6, was still unable to speak; needless to say, her faith worked the trick. Later, the **Pagodenburg** was made as a play-house for the prince and his brother. This was modelled on its counterpart in Nymphenburg on the outskirts of Munich; like the chapel, it was built by the new court architect, Johann Michael Ludwig Rohrer. Behind is the Jugendstil **Wasserturm**, now a café.

Some 5km from the centre of Rastatt, on the way to Baden-Baden, is **Schloss Favorite** (guided tours mid-March to Sept 9am–5pm; Oct to mid-Nov 9am–4pm; DM8/€4), the summer residence of Augusta Sibylla in her years as regent. Here, J.M.L. Rohrer attempted to create the smaller-scale opulence characteristic of the Central European courts which the margravine preferred to the French-inspired grandeur favoured by her husband. Some of the interiors are riotously ornate, notably the **Spiegelkabinett** with its 330 mirrors, and the **Florentiner Zimmer**, lavishly adorned with coloured marbles, stucco, rare woods and semi-precious stones.

Practicalities

Rastatt's **Bahnhof** is at the eastern end of town; here the scenic Murgtalbahn from Freudenstadt connects with the express line down the Rhine. The **tourist office** (Mon 8.30am–6pm, Tues–Fri 8.30am–4.30pm; ☎0 72 22/97 24 62, fax 97 21 80, *www.rastatt.de*) is in the Schloss, Herrenstr. 18.

Reasonably priced **hotels** include *Zum Löwen*, Kaiserstr. 9 (☎0 72 22/3 45 56; ③), and *Kehler Hof*, Kehler Str. 43 (☎0 72 22/3 29 38; ③). For something more upmarket try *Zum Engel*, Kaiserstr. 65 (☎0 72 22/7 79 80; ④), *Zum Schiff*, Poststr. 2 (☎0 72 22/77 20; ⑤), or *Schwert*, in a Baroque mansion at Herrenstr. 3a (☎0 72 22/76 80, *www.ringhotels.de*; ⑦).

As can be seen from the smoking chimneys, Rastatt is a **beer** town in the middle of a wine region. The *Bräustübl* of Hofbräu Hatz is at Poststr. 12; the food here is very reasonably priced. Among the best **restaurants** are that in the aforementioned *Zum Engel*, *Sigi's* in *Hotel Schwert*, and *Zum Storchennest*, Karlstr. 24.

Karlsruhe

KARLSRUHE, which lies some 25km northeast of Rastatt, is the baby of German cities. It didn't exist at all until 1715, when **Carl Wilhelm**, Margrave of Baden-Durlach, began the construction of a retreat at the edge of the Hardter Wald. There he could escape from a wife who bored him, in order to pursue his cultural interests – and to enjoy the company of several mistresses. The planned town which subsequently grew up around the palace was given an appropriate appellation – "Carl's Rest". Initially modest in size, its growth was stimulated by its establishment as the capital of the reunited state of Baden in 1771 and by the subsequent elevation of its rulers to the title of grand dukes under Napoleon's reorganization of the European political map. Karlsruhe flourished throughout the nineteenth century, enjoying what was, by German standards, a remarkably liberal atmosphere and becoming a major centre for both science and art. In 1945, however, it finally lost its status as a regional capital; Baden was divided between the American and French occupation zones, and Stuttgart made the obvious choice as seat of government for the former's province, which went under the name of Württemberg-Baden. As if by way of compensation, Karlsruhe was nominated as the home of the two highest courts of the Federal Republic.

As a standard large industrial city, Karlsruhe is by no means the central target of anyone's travels, but it nonetheless has much to offer – to discerning eggheads at least. The city's own propaganda baldly proclaims that it occupies fifth place in the hierarchy of the country's cultural centres. Whether or not this self-estimation is accurate, the

KARLSRUHE

ACCOMMODATION
2 Am Markt
5 Am Zoo
4 Eden
7 Residenz
6 Schlosshotel
3 Stadtmitte
1 Youth Hostel

THE FAN TOWN

Looking at a map or an aerial photograph, Karlsruhe appears as an extraordinarily handsome city, thanks to its striking fan-shaped plan. As in an earlier purpose-built princely town, Mannheim, the hub of the system is the Schloss, here placed in isolation to the extreme north. Again this building is U-shaped, but thereafter the geometric patterns become far more imaginative and complex. The Schloss gardens are circular, with the outer half left in a natural state, while the inner is closed by a crescent of regular buildings; this forms a triangle with the Schloss which takes up exactly a quarter of the grounds. From here radiate nine dead-straight avenues (representing each of the Muses); the central axis, Karl-Friedrich-Strasse, runs in a vertical line from the palace's central pavilion, while the two end ones shoot outwards at angles of 45° from the wings, with the others placed at regular intervals in between.

---

museums (which are among the oldest public collections in Germany) are undeniably top class, the **Kunsthalle** alone being sufficient reason to justify a visit.

Arrival, information and accommodation

Karlsruhe's **Hauptbahnhof** is situated well to the south of the city centre. Directly facing the entrance at Bahnhofplatz 6 is the **tourist office** (Mon–Fri 9am–6pm, Sat 9am–12.30pm; ☎07 21/3 55 30, fax 35 53 43 99, *www.karlsruhe.de*). The 24-hour ticket on the **public transport** system is a bargain at DM8.50/€4.25 for the city, DM16/€8 for the whole circuit (including Baden-Baden and Bruchsal). Note that the regional S-Bahn is served by trams which run both on the main rail tracks and through the streets of the city. This can cause confusion, as their numbers duplicate those of normal trams serving completely different routes, except that they are also marked with the letter S. To reach the centre, you can either go from the eastwards-pointing stop with tram #3 to Marktplatz, or from the westward-pointing stop with tram #2 or #4 to Europaplatz. **Mitfahrzentrale** is at Rankestr. 14 (☎07 21/3 36 66). Between Easter and November, there's a varied choice of **Rhine cruises**, departing from the port at the western extremity of the city.

Centrally sited **hotels** are plentiful, but cater overwhelmingly for the business market; there are, however, a few bargains to be found. The **youth hostel** has a good location just five minutes' walk from the Schloss at Moltkestr. 2b (☎07 21/2 82 48, fax 2 76 47; DM24/€12 or DM29/€14.50). There's a **campsite**, *Turmbergblick*, Tiengerer Str. 40 (☎07 21/49 72 36, fax 49 72 37, *www.azur-camping.de*) 5km east in the incorporated town of Durlach.

Hotels and Pensions

Am Markt, Kaiserstr. 76 (☎07 21/91 99 80, fax 9 19 98 99). Of all the many business-class hotels in the city centre, this is the one with the best location. ⑥.

Am Zoo, Ettlinger Str. 33 (☎07 21/3 36 78). Pleasant small pension located a short walk north of the Hauptbahnhof. ④.

Beim Schupi, Durmersheimer Str. 6, Grünwinkel (☎07 21/5 59 40, fax 55 94 80). Highly characterful hotel in an inner suburb which doubles as the headquarters of a dialect theatre, the Volkstheater d'Badisch Bühn. The rooms are furnished in Black Forest style, while the restaurant serves traditional local dishes and has a beer garden. ⑤.

Eden, Bahnhofstr. 15–19 (☎07 21/1 81 80, fax 1 81 82 22, *www.hoteleden.de*). Large hotel just off the western side of the Stadtgarten, midway between the Hauptbahnhof and the city centre. Among the facilities are a good restaurant and a pleasant garden terrace. ⑥.

Residenz, Bahnhofplatz 14–16 (☎07 21/3 71 50, fax 3 71 51 13, *www.ringhotels.de*). Part of the Ringhotel chain, this fine hotel with restaurant is situated directly opposite the Hauptbahnhof. ⑦

Schlosshotel, Bahnhofplatz 2 (☎07 21/3 83 20, fax 3 83 23 33, *www.schlosshotel-karlsruhe.de*). Very grand and traditional hotel right beside the Hauptbahnhof. In addition to the expensive main restaurant, there's the more reasonably priced *Schwarzwaldstube*. ⑦–⑨.

Schwannen, Augustenburgstr. 10, Grötzingen (☎ & fax 07 21/46 34 96). This is located in an incorporated town immediately east of Durlach, and is easily reached by S-Bahn or mainline train. The rooms here, which form an adjunct to an Italian restaurant, are among the cheapest in Karlsruhe but nonetheless perfectly adequate. ③.

Stadtmitte, Zähringerstr. 72 (☎ & fax 07 21/38 96 37). Pension handily located in a city-centre apartment block. ④.

Steuermann, Hansastr. 13, Daxlanden (☎07 21/95 09 00, fax 9 50 90 50, *www.Hotel-Steuermann.de*). Good medium-range hotel and restaurant right by the Rhine harbour in the far west of the city, reached by tram #4 or #6. ⑥.

Zum Ochsen, Prinzstr. 64, Durlach (☎07 21/94 38 60, fax 9 43 86 43, *www.Ochsen-Durlach.de*). Seventeenth-century inn which has been refurbished in French country-house style. It only has six rooms, so is best booked well in advance. The gourmet restaurant, which continues the Gallic theme, is generally considered to be the best in Karlsruhe. ⑦.

The City

At ground level, the streets of the fan-shaped plan are rather less impressive than on a map, due largely to the fact that most of the original buildings have been supplanted by undistinguished successors, something for which war damage is partly, but by no means entirely, responsible. Nonetheless, outstanding architecture survives – including some of the finest **Neoclassical buildings** in Germany – though the Kunsthalle and the Landesmuseum are undoubtedly the city's prime attractions.

The Schloss and Schlosspark

Although the oldest surviving building, the **Schloss**, which is set in an extensive English-style park, is actually the second on the site, built in the French-influenced Baroque style of the 1750s. Sadly, it was completely gutted in the last war; the interior was later modernized to house the **Badisches Landesmuseum** (Tues–Sun 10am–6pm, *www.landesmuseum.de*; DM9/€4.50). To the left of the entrance is the **archeology** section. Highlights are the ivory treasure from the Assyrian city of Arslan Tash; a relief of two horsemen from Nineveh; a Sicilian statuette of the goddess Nike; and a carving of a gift bringer from Xerxes' palace in Persepolis. Further on are some impressive pieces of Roman sculpture, notably *Hanging Marsyas* from a villa near Rome; *Mithras Killing the Bull*, which came from near Heidelberg; and a relief of two underwater gods from a settlement not far from Karlsruhe. In the corresponding wing to the right of the entrance is the medieval and Renaissance section, which includes four stunningly bold stained-glass windows designed by **Baldung** for the Carthusian monastery in Freiburg and a polychrome limewood *Madonna and Child* by **Riemenschneider**.

Upstairs is a re-creation of the Schloss's **Thronsaal** and the crown jewels of the Grand Duchy of Baden. However, these are completely overshadowed by the **Turkish booty** (*Türkenbeute*), captured by Margrave Ludwig of Baden-Baden in his seventeenth-century campaigns against the Turks. Unique in western Europe, this includes embroidery, illuminated books, cutlery, jewellery, leather, woodwork, saddles and weapons of all types. From this floor a staircase leads up to the balcony of the **tower** which has recently been made accessible again following decades of closure. This is the only public place from which the city's famous fan shape can be seen to proper effect.

In a building immediately to the left of the Schloss is housed the highest judicial authority in the country, the **Bundesverfassungsgericht** (Federal Constitutional Court), though this will shortly move back to its prewar home in Leipzig. It is, in theory, an essential bulwark against the rise of any would-be Hitler, whose accession to power was greatly facilitated by the excessively liberal constitution of the Weimar Republic, which gave full rights to groups pledged to its destruction. The German "Basic Law" has been made much tougher; all political parties must now pledge themselves to the democratic process, or else be outlawed by this court.

The Staatliche Kunsthalle

At Hans-Thoma-Str. 2, the left side of the circular road round the Schlosspark, is the **Staatliche Kunsthalle** (Tues–Fri 10am–5pm, Sat & Sun 10am–6pm; *www.kunsthalle-karlsruhe.de*; DM5/€2.50), housed in the mid-nineteenth century Kunstakademie. The magnificent collection of old masters on the first floor is reached via a monumental staircase adorned with a huge fresco by **Moritz von Schwind**, *The Consecration of Freiburg Münster*. Focal point of the gallery is one of the world's greatest pictures, *The Crucifixion* by **Grünewald**. The last and most powerful of his four surviving versions of this scene, it conveys an almost unbearable feeling of tragic intensity. One of the most baffling aspects of Grünewald's art is its inconsistency, and *The Fall of Jesus*, which came from the same altarpiece, has far less emotional impact. Two small monochrome pictures, *St Elizabeth* and *St Lucy*, give a good idea of his early style.

A tiny *Christ with Symbols of the Passion* is a recently discovered **Dürer**; near it hangs a painted version of his famous woodcut *Knight, Death and the Devil* by one of his pupils. Other German paintings to look out for are **Burgkmair**'s *Portrait of Sebastian Brant* (the satirist), **Cranach**'s *Frederick the Wise Adoring the Virgin and Child* and several works by **Baldung**, among which is *Margrave Christoph I of Baden in Adoration*; Moritz von Schwind included a cameo of the artist painting this work in the stairway fresco. Among the gallery's rarities is *The Raising of Lazarus*, the sole extant painting by **Wendel Dietterlin**, author of a book of fantastical Mannerist engravings which was immensely influential with late sixteenth-century architects and decorators.

The representation of Flemish, Dutch and French painting is equally good. *St Jerome in the Desert* by **Patinir** is one of the few paintings definitely from the hand of this elusive Antwerp master of landscapes with fantastic rock formations. There are also important examples by three other rare painters – **Lucas van Leyden**'s *St Andrew*, **Wtewael**'s *Chicken Inspection* and **Sweerts**' *Roman Wrestling Match*. **Rembrandt** is represented by a middle-period oval *Self-Portrait*, while there are several examples of **Rubens**. One of **Claude**'s largest canvases, *Adoration of the Golden Calf*, is the star of the seventeenth-century French section, which also includes a diptych of *The Annunciation*, perhaps the only surviving painting by the great Mannerist engraver **Jacques Bellange**, and canvases by Poussin, Le Brun and the Le Nain brothers. From the following century are four still lifes by **Chardin**.

A notable array of nineteenth-century German painting is dominated by the work of **Hans Thoma**, who served as director of this gallery for twenty years. He was accomplished at both landscape and portraiture but had an unfortunate tendency to drift into sentimentality. **Menzel** and **Feuerbach** are represented by important works, but the gem of this section is **Friedrich**'s tiny *Rocky Reef by a Beach*.

The **Orangerie** (same hours and ticket) next door houses paintings by many of the established names of twentieth-century European art, along with a cross-section of nineteenth-century French schools, ranging from Delacroix and Courbet to the Impressionists and their followers. There's good representation of Der Blaue Reiter group, notably a couple of fine animal paintings by **Marc**. Another Expressionist masterpiece is **Kokoschka**'s *View of Mont Blanc from Chamonix*, while **Beckmann**'s *Transport of the Sphynxes* is an allegorical canvas alluding to France's liberation from Nazism.

The rest of the city centre

Few buildings from the same generation as the Schloss remain; an exception is the sole place of worship the town then possessed, the **Kleine Kirche** (Little Church) on the main horizontal street, Kaiserstrasse. The next phase of the building of Karlsruhe only occurred with Baden's promotion to an independent Grand Duchy. During the following 25 years, a remarkable local architect, **Friedrich Weinbrenner**, completely transformed the city into a worthy capital. As a young man, he had travelled to Rome; having assimilated the idiom of the ancient world, he employed its grand style in the creation of the great public buildings required by a modern city. Between the Schloss and the start of the central axis, he laid out the rectangular Marktplatz, at the far end of which is an austere red sandstone **Pyramid** containing the grave of Carl Wilhelm. The western side of the square is dominated by the long pink range of the **Rathaus**. Opposite, the Corinthian facade of the **Stadtkirche** looks like an updated version of a Roman temple. Its present interior is modern and functional, the dignified galleried original having been a casualty of wartime bombs.

Just off the northern side of the square at Karl-Friedrich-Str. 6 is the **Museum beim Markt** (Tues–Thurs 11am–5pm, Fri–Sun 10am–6pm; same ticket as for Landesmuseum). It's devoted to the applied and industrial arts of the twentieth century, featuring a good Art Nouveau/Jugendstil section, as well as works by members of the Bauhaus and other big names in international design.

Immediately south of Marktplatz is another square, Rondellplatz, this time circular in shape. It contains the **Palais** (now a bank), whose forms are almost identical to those of the Stadtkirche. In the centre of the square rises an **Obelisk** in honour of the Grand Duke Carl, celebrating his granting of a constitution to the citizens of Baden. West along Erbprinzstrasse is the **Museum am Friedrichsplatz** (Tues–Sat 10am–4pm, Sun 10am–6pm; DM5/€2.50), the original late Neoclassical home of the grand ducal collections. It's now entirely given over to natural history, mostly stuffed animals, but also includes an aquarium and an outstanding prehistoric section. The last-named features the only reasonably complete skeleton of a hipparion (a forerunner of the horse) yet discovered; a number of fossils from Messel (see p.406); and others from Peru, including a finback whale which is six to seven million years old. Alongside is the **Badische Landesbibliothek** (Mon–Wed & Fri 9am–6pm, Thurs 9am–8pm, Sat 9.30am–12.30pm; free), which displays its treasures – including many wonderful medieval illuminated manuscripts – in a series of temporary exhibitions.

Further evidence of the enlightened, tolerant nature of the young state of Baden is provided by the Catholic church of **St Stephan** directly opposite the Landesbibliothek. This was built by Weinbrenner, himself a Protestant, at the same time as he was working on the Stadtkirche for members of his own faith. The main body of the church is circular while the portico is Doric, the whole being a conscious reinterpretation of the great Pantheon in Rome. Down Ritterstrasse is a heavy late nineteenth-century palace formerly used by the heir to the Grand Duchy; it now houses the second most important law court in Germany, the **Bundesgerichthof** (Federal Supreme Court). This is where the most important postwar criminal trials have been held, including those of several of the Baader-Meinhof gang.

Karlsruhe's third Federal institution is the **Münze** (Mint) on Stephanienstrasse just to the west of the Kunsthalle. Weinbrenner's last building, this is still serving its original purpose, albeit on a much larger scale. Just down Karlstrasse is the **Prinz-Max-Palais**, a stolid Wilhelmine mansion now named after one of its former owners, who served a heady five-week stint in the autumn of 1918 as last chancellor of the Second Reich. In that time, he democratized the constitution, dismissed the military dictator Erich Ludendorff, began peace negotiations and announced the abdication of the Kaiser before the latter had consented; whereupon he himself resigned and vanished from the national stage. The top floor of the building now contains the **Stadtmuseum** (Tues, Wed, Fri & Sun 10am–6pm, Thurs 10am–8pm, Sat 2–6pm; free), with maps and prints, plus a model of how the city looked in 1834, when it was at its most splendid. Also exhibited is the *Draisienne*, first exhibited in Paris in 1818 by the Karlsruhe inventor **Karl von Drais**: decide for yourself whether or not it deserves its disputed title as the world's first bicycle.

Durlach

DURLACH, 5km east of the city centre, can be reached by train, or by tram #1 or #2. It was the original seat of the local margraves, and is hence described as the "mother town" of Karlsruhe, of which it now forms a part, while retaining its own quiet atmosphere. The focal point of Durlach is **Schloss Karlsburg**, an unfinished Baroque rebuild of the Gothic-Renaissance castle destroyed by the French in the War of the Palatinate Succession. Part of it now houses the **Pfinzgaumuseum und Karpatendeutsches Museum** (Tues 4–7pm, Wed 10am–noon, Sat 2–5pm, Sun 10am–5pm; free), the former focusing on Karlsruhe's hinterland, the latter on the folklore of the German communities in the Carpathians. A short walk to the east is the lower station of Germany's oldest functioning **rack railway**, the Turmbergbahn, which ascends to the summit of the Turmberg (mid-May to late Sept daily 10am–6/7pm, reducing gradually to weekends only in winter; DM1.50/€0.75 each way).

Eating, drinking and entertainment

Karlsruhe has many fine restaurants in addition to those in the hotels (see pp.347–348). For a university city, it's surprisingly quiet come the evening, though a few pockets – notably around Ludwigsplatz – do spring to life.

Restaurants

Africa, Kaiserpassage 18. Has a varied menu of North African food, and sometimes features live music.

Dudelsack, Waldstr. 79. Well known for its game and fish dishes, and has a pleasant terrace courtyard.

Goldenes Kreuz, Karlstr. 21a. Gaststätte of the local Hoepfner brewery, occupying an eighteenth-century building. Good-value set lunches are available.

Hansjakob Stube, Ständehausstr. 4. Cellar restaurant offering excellent *gutbürgerliche Küche*. Closed Sun evening & Wed.

Künsterlerkneipe zur Krone, Pfarrstr. 18, Daxlanden (☎07 21/57 22 47). A lovely old Weinstube with half-timbered courtyard whose walls are hung with paintings by late nineteenth- and early twentieth-century Black Forest artists. The food served is among the very best in the city, and reservations are advisable. Closed Sun & Mon; take tram #2 or #6 to Kirchplatz.

Oberländer Weinstube, Akademiestr. 7. Karlsruhe's oldest wine bar-restaurant has a truly *gemütlich* interior and garden courtyard; it also serves the best meals in the town centre. Closed Sun.

Rosa Bianca, Akademiestr. 23. Small, extremely popular Italian restaurant.

Schützenhaus, Jean-Ritzert-Str. 8, Durlach. Good Gaststätte with beer garden on top of the Turmberg. Closed Mon & Tues.

Bars and cafés

Café Feller, corner of Marktplatz and Kaiserstrasse. Traditional café which spills out into the square in summer.

Das Krokodil, Waldstr. 63. Café-bar which offers a good selection of salads and sometimes features live music.

Salmen, Ludwigsplatz. Animated café-bar much patronized by students.

Stephanie, Stephanienstr. 92. Trendy-bar-cum-Italian-restaurant which is particularly popular with artists and art students. Closed Sun.

Vogelbräu, Kapellenstr. 50. Hausbrauerei with beer garden, serving a cloudy unfiltered *Pils* and inexpensive meals and snacks.

Entertainment

The main **theatre** is the Badisches Staatstheater, Baumeisterstr. 11 (☎07 21/3 55 70 or 93 33 33), which presents opera, operetta, musicals, ballet and concerts in its main auditorium, plays in the smaller hall. Other venues for drama include Kammertheater, Karl-Friedrich-Str. 24 (☎07 21/2 31 11), and Die Insel, Wilhelmstr. 14 (☎07 21/3 55 74 50), while Marotte Figurentheater, Kaiserallee 11 (☎07 21/ 84 15 55), has puppet shows. Other concerts are held at the Stadthalle, Festplatz 4 (☎07 21/3 72 00), while **live jazz** is performed at Jubez, Am Kronenplatz (☎07 21/ 3 30 48). In June of even-numbered years, Karlsruhe hosts the *Internationales Trachten-und-Folklorefest*, a colourful **festival** featuring folk groups from all over Europe and beyond.

NORTHERN BADEN-WÜRTTEMBERG

The northern part of Baden-Württemberg consists of various territories which were only incorporated into the Grand Duchy of Baden and the Kingdom of Württemberg as a result of the Napoleonic redistribution of the map of Europe, and whose very different history and geography mean that they're best considered separately.

The fertile **Kraichgau** region, between the Rhine and the Neckar north of Karlsruhe, was particularly associated with the prince-bishops of Speyer, who established their resplendent new palatial headquarters at **Bruchsal** in the eighteenth century. Further north is the heart of the **Palatinate** (Pfalz or Kurpfalz), which was ruled by the Count Palatine of the Rhineland, the most senior official in the Holy Roman Empire and one of the seven Electors. The name of the old state lives on in the Land of Rhineland-Palatinate, but its original boundaries were very different. For five hundred years its capital was **Heidelberg** – a huge favourite with visitors, and a place which definitely warrants several days' stay. The planned town of **Mannheim**, now Baden-Württemberg's second city, was built as the new Palatine capital in the early eighteenth century, with **Schwetzingen** and its fantastical gardens used by the court in the summer months. Down the Neckar from Heidelberg is the well-preserved medieval town of **Bad Wimpfen**, for centuries a Free Imperial City.

Like Swabia, **Franconia** (Franken) was one of the five great provinces of medieval Germany. Under Napoleon, nearly all of this was incorporated into Bavaria, but the northwestern part – consisting of the **Hohenlohe** plain and part of the **Tauber valley** – was split off and used to beef up both Baden and Württemberg. This includes a section of the famous **Romantic Road**, which mostly lies in Bavaria.

Bruchsal

It was the first time I had seen such architecture. The whole of next day I loitered about the building; hesitating half-way up shallow staircases balustraded by magnificent branching designs of wrought metal; wandering through double doors that led from state room to state room; and gazing with untutored and marvelling eyes down perspectives crossed by the diminishing slants of winter sunbeams.

Patrick Leigh Fermor, *A Time of Gifts*

On his walk to Constantinople, Patrick Leigh Fermor struck it lucky at **BRUCHSAL**, staying as guest of the burgomaster in the resplendent Baroque **Schloss**. His description reflects the fact that this is no ordinary palace; indeed, it's a complete courtly town, comprising over fifty different buildings, which stands as an oasis in the midst of the ugly modern community which now surrounds it.

Construction work began in 1720 by order of the newly enthroned prince-bishop of Speyer, Cardinal Hugo Damian von Schönborn, who had fallen out with the local burghers and so decided to move his seat across the Rhine to what was then no more than a hamlet in the heart of the Kraichgau region. Several talented architects were recruited to carry out the work, and the great **Balthasar Neumann** was occasionally seconded from his employment at Würzburg to supply the bravura touches needed to lift the project into the artistic first division. The Schloss complex, whose cheerful yellow, red and white buildings have been restored to pristine condition following devastation in an air raid at the end of the war, stands on Schönbornstrasse, which leads north to Heidelberg. Along the eastern side of the street are a series of offices, with the chancellery centre-stage; an army of lackeys lived in the large edifice to the south. At the northern end of the street is the **Damianstor**, while a smaller triumphal arch gives access to the main courtyard. To the left is the **Hofkirche**, whose haughty onion-domed belfry towers over all the other buildings; the interior has unfortunately been modernized. On the opposite side is the **Kammerflügel**, where prestigious international **concerts** are often held.

The great reception rooms are all in the central *corps de logis*, now the **Schlossmuseum** (Tues–Sun 9.30am–5pm; DM6/€3). Facing you on entry is Neumann's ingenious monumental **staircase**. The lower section is laid out as a dark grotto, covered with antique-style frescoes; you then ascend via walls richly covered with stucco to the airily bright oval landing. Here a brilliant trompe l'oeil fresco – an integral part of the overall design – apparently reaches the height of the dome, extending a perspective into the open heavens. Painted by **Januarius Zick**, the most accomplished German decorative artist of the day, it eulogizes the history of the Speyer diocese. Neumann and Zick also collaborated on the two rooms off the staircase.

It's definitely worth paying the extra money to visit the **Museum Mechanischer Musikinstrumente** (guided tours Tues–Sun 9.30am–5pm; DM8/€4 including Schloss admission), which has been installed in some of the vacant rooms. Short demonstrations are given on a cross-section of the two hundred-odd exhibits, which were regarded as scientific miracles in their own time. Earliest of these are the musical clocks which were much in favour in eighteenth-century courts such as Bruchsal itself, and for which even the greatest composers were forced to prostitute their talents – Haydn wrote a delightful set of miniatures, while Mozart created several profound masterpieces, which have to be played on a full-sized organ for maximum effect. From the early twentieth century are examples of the piano-roll system pioneered by the German Firma Welte, which enables the accurate play-back of performances by famous pianists. This technique was later ambitiously adapted for the organ, and there's a marvellous instrument here which was formerly used to entertain guests in the *Hotel Excelsior* in Berlin.

Practicalities

Bruchsal's **Bahnhof** is a junction on the rail lines linking Stuttgart, Karlsruhe and Heidelberg. To reach the Schloss from there, turn left and continue straight on; you'll reach the gardens within a few minutes. Alternatively, turn right on arriving at Kaiserstrasse; this soon brings you to the end of Schönbornstrasse. The **tourist office** (Mon–Wed & Fri 8am–noon & 2–4pm, Thurs 8am–noon & 2–5pm; ☎ & fax 0 72 51/7 27 71, *www.bruchsal.de*) is in the huge modern shopping centre called Bürgerzentrum at Am Alten Schloss 2. **Hotels** include *Gasthof Graf Kuno*, Württemberger Str. 97 (☎0 72 51/20 13; ③), *Ratskeller*, Kaiserstr. 68 (☎0 72 51/7 12 30; ⑤), *Brauhaus Wallhall,* Kübelmarkt 8 (☎0 72 51/7 21 30; ⑥), and *Scheffelhöhe,* Adolf-Bieringer-Str. 20 (☎0 72 51/80 20; ⑦). There's a **campsite** and *Naturfreundehaus* at Karlsruher Str. 215 (☎0 72

51/1 51 06) to the south of the centre. All the hotels listed above have **restaurants**; another good place to eat is *Zum Bären*, within the Schloss complex at Schönbornstr. 28, which has the benefit of a beer garden.

Schwetzingen

There's nothing quite like the gardens of **SCHWETZINGEN**. This town, which lies on the rail line between Karlsruhe and Mannheim, some 12km west of Heidelberg, was of very minor significance until the 1740s, when the **Jagdschloss** (guided tours April–Oct Tues–Sun 9am–4pm; Nov–March Sat & Sun 11am–3pm; DM8/€4) was constructed as a summer residence for the Electors Palatine by the Heidelberg architect Johann Adam Breunig. The building itself is low-key; it's the **gardens** which get all the praise and all the visitors.

The Schlossgarten

The **Schlossgarten** (daily: March & Oct 9am–6pm; April–Sept 8am–8pm; Nov–Feb 9am–5pm; DM3.50/€1.75, but included in Schloss entrance) is a supreme triumph of the art of landscaping and of the Rococo style, representing a highly original escape into a world of pure fantasy. It took some thirty years to lay out the gardens and adorn them with a series of whimsical buildings. These aimed at capturing the atmosphere of various far-off civilizations; this fascination with the exotic marks out Schwetzingen as one of the precursors of the budding Romantic movement. Best time to see the gardens is late spring – the lilac, ivy and chestnut trees are a riot of colour in May, while the linden trees are at their most fragrant during June. High summer can be uncomfortably crowded; off-season, you might have the park to yourself, but, in addition to the absence of bloom, the pavilions are then kept locked.

The **Schlosstheater** (guided tours June–Sept daily at 11.30am, 2.15pm & 3.30pm; DM3/€1.50) was added to the main building by **Nicolas de Pigage**, an ingenious architect from Lorraine who arrived in Schwetzingen in 1750 and spent much of the next three decades constructing its garden buildings. In an individual confection, mixing Rococo with Neoclassicism, Pigage built a triple-tiered auditorium in the shape of a lyre, facing a deep stage harbouring complicated machinery underneath. It was originally intended for the performance of French comedies, and Voltaire, a personal friend of the Elector, was a regular visitor. With its grand dimensions, long vistas, straight avenues and symmetrical layout, the French-style **formal garden** is very much a product of the Age of Reason. It's richly endowed with fountains (which play daily in summer), mock-antique urns and a host of statues.

Just west of here is the **Tempel Apollos**, which served as an open-air auditorium. A sunken garden with sphinxes leads to an artificial mound crowned by a temple in the style of classical Rome, housing a statue of the god. This is the first in a row of buildings by Pigage; alongside is one of his finest works, the **Badhaus**. Its nine rooms are adorned with rosewood panellings, sculptures, landscape paintings and Chinese tapestries and silks. The marble bath repeats the elliptical shape of the central drawing room; its water pipes are artistically decorated, and the chamber itself adorned with mirrors and jewels. Next to the Badhaus is an arbour with a fountain of water-spouting birds; it's nicknamed "The End of the World" because of the trompe l'oeil perspective, which terminates in a painted diorama. Crossing the moat and continuing northwards, you come to the **Tempel der Botanik**, supposedly representing the trunk of an oak tree, and the **Römischer Wasserweg**, a spectacular fake of a fort and aqueduct, deliberately built as an ivy-covered ruin to enhance its illusory effect. Beyond here are the outer reaches of the park, laid out in the contrastingly untamed style of an English gar-

---

ELECTOR CARL THEODOR (1724-99)

Schwetzingen's stunning transformation from its long history of mediocrity was due to Elector Carl Theodor, who inherited the Palatinate from his childless uncle and later became a somewhat reluctant Elector of Bavaria as well, when another branch of the Wittelsbachs died out. As if by compensation, Carl Theodor started several aristocratic lines, ennobling such of his many mistresses as were not high-born; even today, there's a standing joke in the region that his bastard descendants can immediately be identified through having his distinctive nose. If Carl Theodor's ambitious political goals ultimately ended in failure (the Palatinate was carved up just two years after his death), his track record as a patron of the arts has proved far more enduring. The most important decision he took, alongside opening the great art treasures of the Alte Pinakothek in Munich to the public, was to make Schwetzingen his summer residence and to embellish it with the pleasure park he craved yet was unable to have in his fortified seat at Mannheim.

---

den. By following the path traversing this section, you can return to the main part of the park via the humpbacked **Chinesische Brücke**.

Pigage's remaining buildings are at the opposite end of the park. The **Tempel Merkurs** is reached via either of the paths along the side of the artificial lake. Originally, this monument was intended to be redolent of ancient Egypt, but ended up as a pastiche of the clifftop ruin of a European Romanesque castle, anachronistically adorned with scenes of the myth of Mercury. From here, there's a spectacular vista over a pond to the pink cupola and minarets of the **Moschee** (Mosque), the most original structure in the gardens and the last to be built. It's a unique translation of oriental forms into the language of eighteenth-century European architecture. Returning in the direction of the circular section of the garden, you come to the sixteen-columned **Tempel Minervas**, which goes back to the favourite source of inspiration, classical Rome. The goddess of wisdom is seated inside; she also appears in a frieze above the entrance, poring over a plan of the gardens of Schwetzingen, to which she gives her seal of approval.

Practicalities

The **Bahnhof** is five minutes' walk from the Schlossgarten down Carl-Theodor-Strasse. **Buses** to and from Heidelberg stop on Schlossplatz; services run every half-hour for most of the day. Although there's no particular reason for staying in Schwetzingen, it makes a good alternative base if Heidelberg is booked solid. Among the many **hotels** are *Gasthof Zum Ritter*, Schlossplatz 1 (☎0 62 02/93 3 00; ⑤), *Goldener Löwe,* Schloss-Str. 4 (☎0 62 02/2 80 90; ⑥–⑧), and *Adler-Post*, Schloss-Str. 3 (☎0 62 02/2 77 70; ⑥–⑧).

Asparagus has been cultivated in Schwetzingen for more than three centuries; in season (April–June) it can be sampled in any of the town's **restaurants**, including those in the hotels listed above. Each April and May, the Schlosstheater is the setting for an international **music festival**, often focusing on the works of Gluck. Another festival in September is devoted solely to Mozart; there are also regular musical and theatrical performances of all kinds throughout the year.

Mannheim

MANNHEIM was formerly considered one of the most beautiful cities in Germany. Writing in 1826, William Hazlitt called it "a splendid town, both from its admirable buildings and the glossy neatness of the houses. They are too fine to live in, and seem only made to be looked at." A mere stripling among German cities, it was founded in 1606

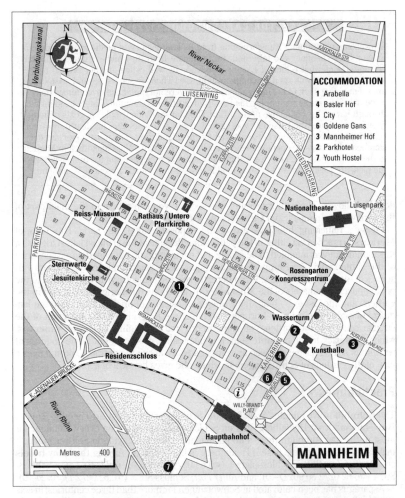

ACCOMMODATION
1 Arabella
4 Basler Hof
5 City
6 Goldene Gans
3 Mannheimer Hof
2 Parkhotel
7 Youth Hostel

MANNHEIM

as a fortress at the strategically important intersection of the rivers Rhine and Neckar. Its meteoric rise to prominence came with the return of the Counts Palatine to Catholicism; unable to establish a satisfactory relationship with the burghers of Heidelberg, Carl Philipp decided in 1720 to make Mannheim the main seat of his court. A daringly original **planned town** was laid out, which served as capital of the Palatinate for the next 57 years, becoming one of Europe's most celebrated centres of the performing arts. The nineteenth century saw heavy industrialization, centred on the harbour trade and shipbuilding, though its most prestigious feature was the automobile factory established by Carl Benz, who demonstrated his first vehicle here in 1886. Alas, the continued prominence of industry, coupled with heavy damage in the last war, means that the city's former glory has long since vanished. However, the highly esteemed **grid-plan** still survives.

THE CHESSBOARD TOWN

The construction of Mannheim was based on a **chessboard layout** on the strip of land between the Rhine and Neckar. Streets to the west of the central axis are designated A to K, moving northwards; proceeding in the same direction, those to the east are L to U. The street number indicates proximity to the axis, so that D7, for example, is to the far west, whereas R7 is at the extreme east. Obviously, each house then bears a second number, which indicates its position on the square. At first the system can be confusing, particularly when you arrive at the Hauptbahnhof, as the nearby blocks are of widely varying sizes. However, once you get the hang of it, there's really no other European city which it's so simple to find your way around.

Arrival, information and accommodation

Mannheim's **Hauptbahnhof** is just beyond the southeastern edge of the grid. The **tourist office** (Mon–Fri 9am–7pm, Sat 9am–noon; ☎06 21/10 10 11, fax 2 41 41, *www.tourist-mannheim.de*) is diagonally opposite at Willy-Brandt-Platz 3. **Mitfahrzentrale** is in the same building (☎06 21/1 94 44).

Hotels are overwhelmingly geared to the expense-account market, but there are a few budget choices as well. The **youth hostel** is at Rheinpromenade 21 (☎06 21/82 27 18, fax 82 40 73; DM22/€11 or DM27/€13.50); take the underground passageway at the back entrance of the Hauptbahnhof, then turn left; it's only a few minutes' walk away. **Camping** is possible (April–Sept only) on the banks of either of the city's two great rivers. The larger and cheaper site is at Neuostheim (☎06 21/41 68 40) on the Neckar to the east; the other is to the south on Strandbad in Neckarau (☎06 21/85 62 40); in spite of its name, it's located on a bend of the Rhine.

Hotels and Pensions

Arabella, M2, 12 (☎06 21/2 30 50, fax 1 56 45 27). The cheapest rooms in the city centre are in this apartment-block pension. ②.

Basler Hof, Tattersallstr. 27 (☎06 21/2 88 16, fax 15 32 92). One of several reasonably priced hotels on the street, a couple of minutes' walk north of the Hauptbahnhof. The rooms without facilities are particularly good value, not least on account of the huge buffet breakfasts. ③–⑤.

City, Tattersallstr. 20–24 (☎06 21/40 80 08, fax 44 99 48). The basic rooms are a bit more expensive than in the neighbouring hotels; those with facilities are around the same price and of comparable quality. ④.

Goldene Gans, Tattersallstr. 19 (☎06 21/10 52 77 or 42 20 20, fax 4 22 02 60). Good-value Gasthaus with Weinstube (closed Sun). A wonderful buffet breakfast is included in the price of a room. ③–⑤.

Mannheimer Hof, Augusta-Anlage 4 (☎06 21/4 00 50, fax 4 00 51 90, *www.steigenberger.com*). Classy hotel with restaurant, part of the Steigenberger chain, at the eastern edge of the city centre. ⑦–⑨.

Parkhotel, Friedrichsplatz 2 (☎06 21/1 58 80, fax 1 58 88 00, *www.maritim.de*). Now part of the Maritim chain, this deluxe century-old grand hotel with restaurant is nonetheless a place of real character. ⑧–⑨.

Zum Ochsen, Hauptstr. 70, Feudenheim (☎06 21/79 95 50, fax 7 99 55 33). This seventeenth-century Gasthof, the oldest in Mannheim, is situated north of the Neckar, 5km east of the city centre, near the terminus of tram #2. Its restaurant is among the best in the city for solid German fare, and it also has a shady beer garden. ⑥.

The City

Most of Mannheim's obvious sights are situated within or near the original grid. However, several notable technical attractions are a bit further afield in the green area adjacent to the Neckar.

The Residenzschloss

The pivot of the planned town is the horseshoe-shaped **Residenzschloss**, the most massive Baroque palace ever built in Germany. Soon after its completion, it became an expensive white elephant, as the court transferred to Munich when Carl Theodor inherited the Bavarian Electorate. The dignified exterior is heavily indebted to Palladianism; the interior was far more sumptuous, including rich stuccowork and ceiling frescoes by the Asam brothers. These were obliterated by wartime bombs; afterwards, the building was put to functional use to house the university, with only the outside restored in full.

However, as a real labour of love, the **Schlosskirche** (daily 9am–5pm) at the end of the western wing, plus the main reception rooms, nowadays designated the **Schlossmuseum** (guided tours April–Oct Tues–Sun 10am–1pm & 2–5pm; Nov–March same hours Sat & Sun only; DM5/€2.50) were re-created from old photographs. The success of this project is highly debatable, but at least the **Rittersaal**, reached via a monumental staircase, provides an effective concert hall, which is particularly appropriate as the Mannheim court's greatest achievements were in the field of music. Its orchestra, which pioneered the mellow tones of the clarinet, was regarded in the eighteenth century as the best in the world, while the symphony was developed here into the chief form of instrumental music.

The central part of the grid

On A5, just to the west of the Residenzschloss, is the **Jesuitenkirche**, deliberately constructed as the largest church in town to symbolize the Palatinate court's return to Catholicism; the grandiose facade and the central dome are the most striking features. Immediately to its rear is the **Sternwarte**, an observatory tower now used by artists.

Just to the north on C5 is the **Zeughaus**, erected in the penultimate year of Mannheim's period as Palatine capital. It now houses the **Reiss-Museum** (Tues & Thurs–Sat 10am–5pm, Wed 10am–9pm, Sun 10am–7pm; DM4/€2), with collections of Dutch and Flemish cabinet pictures, of decorative arts and of local history – look out for the old maps and prints which give an idea of the original dignified appearance of the grid-plan streets, something hardly even hinted at today. On the square directly in front of the Zeughaus is a brand-new building specially designed to house the most important section of the museum, the archeology department. This originated as the Elector's private cabinet of antiquities, and ranges from the Stone Age to the early medieval period. Also in the new museum are ethnological displays from Africa, the Islamic countries, India, China and Japan. There are usually important international loan exhibitions once or twice a year.

The **Marktplatz**, which occupies the square G1, is the scene of markets on Tuesday, Thursday and Saturday mornings. In the centre rises a large monument presented by Carl Theodor; originally representing the four elements, it was reworked into an allegorical composition in praise of Mannheim by the son of the original sculptor. On the south side of the square is a curious Siamese twin of a building, erected just before Mannheim became the seat of the court. Sharing a central tower, the eastern part serves as the **Rathaus**, while the western is the **Untere Pfarrkirche**; their physical union is supposed to symbolize the concord between Justice and Piety, between secular and sacred authority.

The fringe of the grid

The other main square, the Jugendstil **Friedrichsplatz**, is due east from here, just outside the central grid. It was laid out around the **Wasserturm**, which is some fifteen years older, and is the main example of a style which left a considerable mark all over the city. Another fine Jugendstil building is the **Kunsthalle** (Tues & Wed 10am–6pm,

Thurs–Sun 10am–7pm; DM4/€2, DM12/€6 during temporary exhibitions) on Moltkestrasse, the next street to the south. This contains one of the best collections of nineteenth- and twentieth-century painting and sculpture in Germany, and is now the city's most obvious single draw. Highlight of the collection is one of the great master-pieces of Impressionism, **Manet's** *Execution of Emperor Maximilian of Mexico*, the largest and most complete of the four versions he painted of this subject. Other notable works in the same room are **Cézanne's** *Pipe Smoker*, and still lifes by Renoir and Van Gogh. The German section was brutally pruned in the Nazi purges against "degener-ate art", but there's a room devoted to Romanticism, including several important exam-ples of **Feuerbach**. *Portrait of the Writer Max Herrmann-Neisse* is one of **George Grosz's** best canvases, while there's an outstanding array of modern German sculp-ture, with **Barlach** and **Lehmbruck** strongly represented, along with a host of avant-garde works. Major temporary exhibitions are frequently held in the gallery.

The banks of the River Neckar

At the northernmost end of the grid-plan the central axis road continues over the Neckar by the Kurpfälzbrücke. Moored close to the bridge is the 1920s passenger steamer *Mainz*, now designated the **Museumsschiff Mannheim** (Tues–Sun 10am–4pm; DM2/€1). Nearby is the departure point for **harbour cruises** (Easter & June–Aug; 40min trip DM5.50/€2.75; 1hr 30min voyage along the Neckar DM11/€5.50).

Eastwards along the river is the city's playground, the **Luisenpark** (daily 9am–dusk; March–Oct DM5/€2.50; Nov–Feb DM3.50/€1.75). This boasts various flower gar-dens, hothouses, an aquarium, a menagerie of farmyard animals and waterfowl, an open-air stadium for concerts, a gondola course and a watersports centre. There's also the TV tower or **Fernmeldeturm** (daily 10am–11pm; DM5/€2.50 including ascent by elevator), which offers a sweeping view of the region, but is unfortunately too far away from the grid to show its ground plan.

Just south of the park on Wilhelm-Varnholt-Platz is the **Planetarium** (showings Tues–Sun 3pm, also Tues 10am, Wed & Fri 8pm, Sat & Sun 4.30pm & 7.30pm; DM8/€4). Nearby, at Museumsstr. 1, is the **Landesmuseum für Technik und Arbeit** (Tues & Thurs 9am–5pm, Wed 9am–8pm, Sat 10am–5pm, Sun 10am–6pm, *www.landesmuseum-mannheim.de*; DM5/€2.50), housing a spectacular collection of historic machinery, including a steam locomotive which transports visitors through the grounds.

Eating, drinking and entertainment

Although Mannheim has no obvious concentration of good places to eat and drink, there's a varied assortment of recommendable establishments scattered throughout the city. The city also has a vibrant theatre tradition.

Restaurants

Andechser, N2, 10. Serves traditional Bavarian fare and beers from the monastic brewery of Andechs.

Augusta Giovanni, Augusta-Anlage 40. Moderately priced Italian restaurant.

Blass, Friedrichsplatz 12. Very formal and expensive restaurant with an international menu.

Da Gianni, R7, 34. One of Germany's most highly regarded Italian restaurants, the cooking show-ing *nouvelle* touches; predictably, it's very expensive. Closed Mon.

Eichbaum, Käfertaler Str. 168. Located just north of the Neckar, this is the Gaststätte of the epony-mous brewery, the largest in Mannheim. Its *Weizen* beers, both light and dark, are its most highly regarded products.

Heller's, N7, 13. Specialist vegetarian restaurant. Mon–Fri 11am–8pm, Sat 11am–4.30pm, Sun 11.30am–3pm.

Henninger's Gutsschänke, T6, 28. Excellent and fairly priced wine bar-restaurant. Evenings only.
Lao Thai, U5, 1. Claims to be Germany's only Laos speciality restaurant, though Chinese and Thai dishes are also offered. Evenings only, except Sun, when it's also open for lunch.
Martin, Lange Rötterstr. 53. This restaurant to the north of the Neckar is best known for its fish dishes, though it has a varied menu, including vegetarian options. Closed Sat lunchtime & Wed.
Skyline, Hans-Reschke-Ufer 2. Panorama restaurant in the Fernmeldeturm.

Bars and cafés
Café Kettemann, Willy-Brandt-Platz 11. Arguably the pick of the traditional cafés.
Flic Flac, B2, 12. Arty pub which features regular exhibitions and live music.
Mannheimer Hofbräu, Q4, 6–8. A beer hall with its own range of beers, though these are not brewed on the premises or even in Mannheim. Also serves full meals, including bargain lunches.
O'Reilly's, L15, 7–9. Genuine Irish pub, sometimes with live music.

Theatre and concerts
The main **theatre** is the Nationaltheater on Goetheplatz (☎06 21/1 68 01 50), the successor to the now-destroyed building near the Schloss which was associated with Schiller's youthful Sturm und Drang phase. Performances of plays, opera, ballet and musicals are presented, along with special shows for kids. Other venues are Klapsmühl' am Rathaus at D6, 3 (☎06 21/2 24 88), for cabaret and pantomime, and Puppenspiele, Collinistr. 26 (☎06 21/2 49 49), for puppets, while **concerts** are held at Rosengarten Kongresszentrum on Friedrichsplatz (☎06 21/4 10 63 03).

Heidelberg

When the Romantic movement discovered **HEIDELBERG** in the late eighteenth century, the city was very much a fallen star. Capital of the Palatinate for five hundred years, it had never fully recovered from two sackings at the hands of French troops in the previous century, and its rulers had abandoned their magnificent, crumbling Schloss in favour of the creature comforts of their new palace in Mannheim. Yet this wistful feeling of decay only enhanced the charms of the city, majestically set on both banks of the swift-flowing River Neckar between two ranges of wooded hills – a real-life fulfilment of the ideal German landscape, and a site known to be one of the earliest inhabited places in the world. To many of the rushed Grand-Tour-of-Europe coach parties of today, Heidelberg *is* Germany, the only place in the country they see – or, perhaps, want to see.

For English-speaking visitors, the distinguished roll-call of predecessors gives Heidelberg special claims on the attention. Earliest of these was the Scots-born princess, **Elizabeth Stuart**, daughter of the first monarch of the United Kingdom, James I. She arrived in 1613 as the 17-year-old bride of the Elector Palatine and presided over a spectacular court life for five years, before leaving for Prague and her ill-fated spell as the "Winter Queen". Heidelberg's greatest painter is also Britain's greatest: **J.M.W. Turner** first came to the city in 1836, and, in a series of oils and watercolours, captured its changing moods and magical plays of light in his own inimitable way. Among Americans, **Mark Twain** deserves pride of place: he began the hilarious travels round Europe recounted in *A Tramp Abroad* in Heidelberg in 1878, and his descriptions of the city have never been surpassed. By this time, Heidelberg was already a popular sojourn for Americans visiting Europe, though the numbers were a trickle in comparison with today. After World War II (in which, significantly, the city was spared from aerial bombardment), Heidelberg was chosen as the headquarters of the US Army in Europe, with the soldiers housed in the purpose-built Patrick Henry Village, to the south.

HEIDELBERG

ACCOMMODATION

4 Goldener Hecht
5 Hackteufel
2 Holländer Hof
9 Jeske
6 Kulturbrauerei
10 Perkeo
3 Schnookeloch
1 Schönberger Hof
8 Zum Ritter St Georg
7 Zum Sepp'l

Karlstor
Palais Weimar
Residenz
Schloss
Schlossgarten
Rathaus
Heiliggeistkirche
Dokumentations- und Kulturzentrum Deutscher Sinti und Roma
Haus Zum Ritter
Collegium Academicum
Jesuitenkirche
Alte Universität
Peterskirche
Universitätsbibliothek
Kurpfälzisches Museum
Theater der Stadt Heidelberg
Kongresshaus Stadthalle
Anatomie-Gebäude
Institut für Naturwissenschaft

River Neckar

N

Metres 0   200

ZIEGELHAUSER LANDSTR
HIRSCHGASSE
HÖLDERLINWEG
NECKARMÜNZPLATZ
AM HACKTEUFEL
MÖNCHGASSE
OBERE NECKARSTR
HAUPTSTR
KARLSPLATZ
KORNMARKT
MARKT PLATZ
FISCHMARKT
STEINGASSE
HASPELGASSE
KARL-THEODOR-BRÜCKE (ALTE BRÜCKE)
LAUERSTR
UNTERE STR
GROSSE MANTELGASSE
UNTERE FAULE PELZ
OBERE FAULE PELZ
BRUNNENGASSE
NEUE SCHLOSS-STR
NEUE SCHLOSS-STR
SCHLOSSBERG
BRAMTALWEG
UNIVERSITÄTS-PLATZ
GRABENGASSE
THEATERSTR
NECKARSTADEN
PLÖCK
HAUPTSTR
AKADEMIESTR
FRIEDRICH-EBERT-ANLAGE
FRIEDRICH-EBERT-ANLAGE
PHILOSOPHENWEG
NEUENHEIMER LANDSTR
ALBERT-ÜBERLE-STR

△ Hauptbahnhof and Post Office

HEIDELBERG VIEWPOINTS

It's the long-range views which have made Heidelberg so famous, and the city is a ready-made subject for picture-postcard **photography**; with its hilly setting, there are plenty of angles to choose from. If you take the trouble to go to the same vantage point at different times of day, you'll see the reason for Heidelberg's hold on painters: the red sandstone buildings change their hue with the movement of the sun, and the shafts of light make magical effects as they illuminate and cast into shadow different parts of the scene. "One thinks Heidelberg by day the last possibility of the beautiful," wrote Mark Twain, "but when he sees Heidelberg by night, a fallen Milky Way. . . he requires time to consider upon the verdict."

The best-known view is from the northern quays of the Neckar, where you get a full-frontal panorama of the Altstadt nestling snugly below the Schloss, itself sharply etched against the background of the wooded Königstuhl. The spectacle from street level is surpassed by climbing up the slopes of the Heiligenberg via the celebrated **Philosophenweg** (Philosopher's Walk), so called because of the stimulus it offered to the meditation of Heidelberg thinkers. It is best experienced late in the day, as the sun sets on the Schloss. A closer-range view of the Schloss and the Altstadt can be enjoyed from the tower of the Heiliggeistkirche (see p.366). For a completely different perspective, take the late nineteenth-century **funicular** (DM10/€5 return) from Kornmarkt to the *Molkenkur* hotel, which has a panorama terrace. Here you transfer to a second, slightly younger funicular, which continues up to the **Königstuhl**. This is crowned by the **Fernsehturm** (Television Tower; March–Oct daily 10am–6/7pm; DM2/€1), which commands a sweeping view over the Neckar valley and Odenwald.

Arrival and information

Heidelberg is best avoided in high summer: the students, who make such an essential contribution to the life of the city, clear out then and are replaced by hordes of tourists. Surprisingly, it's possible to cover all the essential sights fairly quickly, but you should certainly plan on staying for several days, in order to soak up the city's atmosphere. Be warned that first impressions of Heidelberg are likely to make you wonder what all the fuss is about: the **Hauptbahnhof** and **bus station** are situated in an anonymous quarter some 1.5km west of the centre, with a dreary avenue, Kurfürsten-Anlage, leading towards town. The often harassed **tourist office** is on the square outside (mid-March to mid-Nov Mon–Sat 9am–7pm, Sun 10am–6pm; rest of year closed Sun; ☎0 62 21/1 94 33 or 1 42 20, fax 1 38 81 11, *www.cvb-heidelberg.de*).

It's well worth investing in one of the rover tickets on the **public transport** network. The standard 24-hour pass costs DM10/€5, and provided it is not used before 9am on weekdays, it can be used by up to two adults and three children travelling together. Alternatively, there's the **HeidelbergCard**, which costs DM19.80/€9.90 for two days, and covers public transport in the city, free entry to nearly all the museums and sights and a host of miscellaneous reductions. The Altstadt is mostly pedestrianized; tram #1 takes you from the Hauptbahnhof to Bismarckplatz, at the western end of the long, straight Hauptstrasse. Alternatively, buses #11 and #33 travel all the way along the southern edge of the Altstadt, while buses #41 and #44 go to Universitätsplatz.

Accommodation

Heidelberg's popularity as a convention centre, as well as with tourists means that its **hotels** can be booked solid even out of high season. With this in mind it's worth reserving well in advance. If you want to look yourself, check out the board outside the tourist office which tells you where vacancies exist. The **youth hostel** is near the Zoo on the north bank of the Neckar, about 4km from the centre at Tiergartenstr. 5 (☎0 62 21/41 20 66, fax 40 25 59; DM24/€12 or DM29/€14/50); take bus #33. Both **campsites** are east of the city by the river, and reached by bus #35: *Heide* (☎0 62 23/ 21 11) is between Ziegelhausen and Kleingemünd; *Neckartal* (☎0 62 21/80 25 06) is in Schlierbach.

Hotels and pensions

Astoria, Rahmengasse 30 (☎0 62 21/40 29 29, fax 47 40 40). Very pleasant guesthouse in a quiet setting on the northern side of the Neckar, yet only a short walk from the Altstadt. ④.

Denner, Bergheimer Str. 8 (☎0 62 21/60 45 10, fax 60 45 30, *www.denner-hotel.de*). New hotel in the lively area just west of the Altstadt, with each bedroom individually decorated. It incorporates *Café Gecko*, which serves local and international dishes, and also offers Internet access. ⑤.

Elite, Bunsenstr. 15 (☎0 62 21/2 57 34, fax 16 39 49). Small budget hotel situated just south of the Altstadt. ④.

Goldener Hecht, Steingasse 2 (☎0 62 21/5 36 80, fax 53 68 99). Thanks to its location beside the Alte Brücke, this historic hotel with restaurant occupies a prominent position in the famous view of Heidelberg from across the Neckar. ⑥–⑧.

Hackteufel, Steingasse 7 (☎0 62 21/90 53 80, fax 9 05 38 11, *www.hackteufel.de*). A good-quality hotel and Weinstube on the same alley as *Goldener Hecht*. ⑥–⑧.

Hirschgasse, Hirschgasse 3 (☎0 62 21/45 40, fax 45 41 11, *www.hirschgasse.de*). This 500-year-old Gasthaus is one of Heidelberg's poshest hotels, with bedrooms decorated in modern designer style. It possesses the oldest duelling hall in Germany, one which features in Mark Twain's *A Tramp Abroad*. This is now one of the hotel's two restaurants, *Mensurstube*; although pricey, it's less expensive than the other, *Le Gourmet* (evenings only, closed Sun & Mon). ⑨.

Holländer Hof, Neckarstaden 66 (☎0 62 21/6 05 00, fax 60 50 60, *www.hollaender-hof.de*). Classy hotel beside the Alte Brücke, offering waterfront views. ⑦–⑨.

Jeske, Mittelbadgasse 2 (☎0 62 21/2 37 33). Basic pension in the heart of the Altstadt with what are by far the cheapest rooms in Heidelberg. It's regularly full, and is reluctant to take reservations, so the best strategy is to turn up as early as possible. Breakfast is not included. ①.

Kulturbrauerei, Leyergasse 6 (☎0 62 21/9 00 00, fax 90 00 99). Brand-new venture consisting of a hotel, a boutique brewery which produces two unfiltered and various seasonal beers, a restaurant housed in a splendid old hall, a beer garden, a jazz bar and an art gallery. ⑥.

Molkenkur, Klingenteichstr. 31 (☎0 62 21/60 08 94, fax 2 68 72). Stands on the site of the original Schloss, high above its successor, and is directly accessible by the funicular. The terrace commands a grandstand view of the city; there's also a fine restaurant. ⑥.

Perkeo, Hauptstr. 75 (☎0 62 21/1 41 30, fax 14 13 37). Comfortable hotel named in honour of the dwarf who was the custodian of the predecessor of the Grosses Fass (see p.365). It has an ideal location in the heart of the pedestrianized precinct. ⑥.

Schmitt, Blumenstr. 54 (☎0 62 21/2 72 96, fax 2 90 07). A decent budget hotel, one of a number located between the Hauptbahnhof and the Altstadt. ④.

Schnookeloch, Haspelgasse 8 (☎0 62 21/13 80 80, fax 1 38 08 13). Heidelberg's oldest surviving inn, dating back to 1407. Its tavern, which has a beer garden, is one of those which has long been associated with the student corps, and is covered throughout with graffiti. ⑥–⑧.

Schönberger Hof, Untere Neckarstr. 54 (☎0 62 21/1 40 60, fax 14 06 39, *www.romantik.de*). Upmarket hotel in a handsome Baroque palace facing the Neckar. ⑥.

Zum Ritter St George, Hauptstr. 178 (☎0 62 21/13 50, fax 13 52 30). Heidelberg's most magnificent mansion is now home to one of its most attractive hotels, a member of the Romantik group. It has a recommendable though fairly expensive restaurant. ⑥–⑨.

Zum Sepp'l, Hauptstr. 213 (☎0 62 21/1 43 30, fax 14 33 66). A luxury eight-roomed hotel has recently been established in this, the oldest of the famous Heidelberg taverns, one which has been used by the student corps continuously since 1634. It commodious dining room, decked out with bric-a-brac, is among the city's most celebrated tourist sights. ⑨.

The Schloss

Centrepiece of all the famous views of Heidelberg is the **Schloss**. A series of disparate yet consistently magnificent buildings of various dates, it somehow hasn't been diminished by its ruined condition; if anything, it has actually grown in stature. Enough remains (with the help of the plentiful pictorial records which exist) to give a clear idea of what it looked like in its prime, yet a new dimension has been added by the destruction, which reveals otherwise hidden architectural secrets and magnifies its relationship with the surrounding landscape.

The fortifications

The Schloss can be reached by the **funicular** from Kornmarkt (DM5.50/€2.75 return), but it's more fun to walk up via the Burgweg: that way, you can make a complete circuit of the exterior before entering. At the northwest corner is the sixteenth-century **Dicker Turm** (Fat Tower), now a semicircular shell, its outer wall, along with its top, having been blasted away. Behind the northern fortifications you get a glimpse of the Renaissance buildings and pass the **Zeughaus**, before coming to the **Redoute**, built just a few years before the Schloss was destroyed. Behind it stands the **Glockenturm** (Bell Tower), originally a single-storey defence tower, to which six residential levels were later added.

Continuing along the eastern side, you see the protruding **Apothekerturm**, an old defensive tower which was later converted into the apothecary's plus residential quarters. Between it and the Glockenturm is a superb oriel window, part of a now-vanished banqueting hall. At the southeastern corner you'll find the most romantic of the ruins, the **Pulver Turm** (Powder Tower), now generally know as the **Gesprengter Turm** (Blown-up Tower). Originally a gunpowder store, it was destroyed by miners who tun-

---

THE HISTORY OF THE SCHLOSS

The Schloss originally dates back to the first quarter of the thirteenth century. It was then that the title of **Count Palatine**, one of the great imperial offices of state, and one carrying the rank of an Elector, was bestowed on a Wittelsbach, Duke Ludwig of Bavaria, whose family retained the office right to the end of the Holy Roman Empire. The earliest significant portions of what can be seen today date from the following century, as the castle evolved into a sturdy medieval fortress capable of withstanding the most powerful siege weapons of the day. In the sixteenth century, the inner courtyard of the Schloss began to be embellished with sumptuous palatial buildings, as its role as a princely residence became of increasing importance; this gathered momentum mid-century when the Electors converted to Protestantism and began the construction of the most splendid **Renaissance buildings** in Germany.

Lutheranism was later jettisoned in favour of Calvinism, and the **Heidelberg Catechism** of 1562 remains the basic creed for many Reformed Churches. This took on an increasingly militant aspect when Elizabeth Stuart's youthful husband, **Friedrich V**, became nominal leader of the Calvinist League, which aimed to establish the irreversible supremacy of Protestantism in Germany and to topple the Habsburgs from their position of pre-eminence in the country's affairs. Friedrich's ham-fisted attempt was not only a personal disaster (he was defeated, exiled and stripped of his titles), but also led to the Thirty Years War, which devastated the country. However, it was French designs on the Palatinate in 1689 which led to the destruction of Heidelberg and its Schloss; although their claim on the territory was eventually withdrawn, the Electorship passed to a Catholic branch of the family. Unable to establish a rapport with the locals, they moved their seat; the planned rebuilding of the Schloss never occurred, and Heidelberg was left to vegetate.

nelled underneath and blew it up from the centre. This left a clean break in the now-overgrown masonry; the collapsed section still lies intact in the moat, leaving a clear view into the chambers of the interior, with their once-elegant central column supports.

From here, it's best to proceed to the western side of the Schloss, an artificial plateau formerly used as a gun battery but converted by Friedrich V into a pleasure garden. At its entrance is the graceful Roman-inspired **Elizabethpforte**, a gateway said to have been erected in a single night in 1615 as a surprise for the princess; the sober **Englischer Bau** adjoining the Dicker Turm was also built in her honour. At the western end of the garden is the semicircular **Rondell**, commanding a view over the rooftops of the city.

The Schlosshof

The **Schlosshof** (daily 8am–5.30pm; DM4/€2, but free access outside these hours; guided tours of apartments daily April–Oct 9am–4/5pm; check on noticeboard for times of departures in English; DM4/€2) is reached by a series of sixteenth-century defensive structures – the Brückenhaus, the bridge itself and the severe **Thorturm** (Gate Tower), the only part of the Schloss not blown up. Immediately to the left of the entrance is the Gothic **Ruprechtsbau**, where you can see two restored chambers, one with an elaborate chimneypiece. After the ruined library comes the **Frauenzimmerbau**, where the women of the court resided; its colossal ground-floor hall has been restored as a venue for concerts. Looking anti-clockwise from the entrance gate, you first of all see the Gothic **Brunnenhaus** (Well House), a loggia with a graceful star vault. Its marble columns were brought here from Charlemagne's palace, and had previously adorned a Roman building. This is followed by a series of functional buildings – the **Kaserne** (Barracks) and the **Oekonomiebau**, which housed offices and workshops; part of it has been converted to house the *Schlossweinstube* (see p.369).

What really catches your eye in the courtyard, however, is the group of Renaissance palaces on the north and east sides. Next to the Oekonomiebau is the mid-sixteenth-century **Ottheinrichsbau**, now just a shell but preserving its vigorous horizontal facade. The magnificent sculptural decoration has successive tiers of allegorical figures representing Strength, the Christian Virtues and the Planetary Deities. In the basement is the **Deutsches Apothekenmuseum** (daily 10am–5.30pm; included in Schlosshof entrance), an off-beat but worthwhile collection. Among the displays are several complete Baroque and Rococo workshops, an early seventeenth-century travelling pharmacy and a herbarium. You can also descend to the bowels of the Apothekenturm, which has been rigged out with a furnace and distilling apparatus in an attempt to re-create its old appearance.

The triple loggia of the earlier **Saalbau** forms a link to the celebrated late sixteenth-century **Friedrichsbau** built by Alsatian architect Johannes Schoch. A series of bucolic, larger-than-life statues is a pantheon of the House of Wittelsbach, beginning with Charlemagne (the alleged founder of the dynasty) and continuing right up to the ruling Elector. Those now on view are copies, but the originals can be seen inside, along with a number of restored rooms which have been decked out in period style. On the ground floor is the intact **Schlosskapelle**, which, in total contrast to the facade, harks back to the Gothic period; not surprisingly, in view of the photo opportunities outside, it's now a popular venue for weddings.

The **Fassbau** is reached down a passageway in front of the Schlosshof. It contains the celebrated **Grosses Fass** (Great Vat), said to be the largest wine barrel in the world with a capacity of over 50,000 gallons; this is crowned with a platform that did service as a dance floor. Made in the late eighteenth century, the vat is the third in a spectacular line; though a folly and long out of service, it's reputed to have been filled on at least one occasion, when there was a particularly good grape harvest in the Palatinate (whose Elector was entitled to claim a tithe). Facing the entrance, as a ploy to elicit a gasp from visitors when they turn the corner and see the real thing, is the so-called **Kleines Fass** (Little Vat), itself of ample proportions.

The Altstadt

The Altstadt, the historic centre of Heidelberg, is a largely pedestrianized area between the Schloss and the Neckar, bisected by an unusually long main street, Hauptstrasse. In comparison with the Schloss, its monuments can seem prosaic: although the old layout of the medieval city survives, the French devastation means that nearly all the buildings are eighteenth century or later, and are excessively sober in style. To many people, these are familiar from the Hollywood version of *The Student Prince* by the Hungarian-American composer Sigmund Romberg.

Marktplatz and the eastern Altstadt

The finest surviving buildings in the Altstadt are grouped on Marktplatz. In the middle is the Gothic red sandstone **Heiliggeistkirche**, founded just after the university at the end of the fourteenth century. Its lofty **tower** (Mon–Sat 10am–5pm, Sun 1–5pm; DM1/€0.50), capped by a Baroque dome, is one of the city's most prominent landmarks, and offers wonderful views in all directions. Note the tiny shopping booths between the buttresses, a feature ever since the church was built – this was a common practice in medieval times but has been frowned upon for so long that examples are now rare. The interior is light, airy and uncluttered, but was not always so, as the church was built to house the mausoleum of the Palatinate Electors. Only one tomb now remains – that of Ruprecht III, who became king of Germany in 1400, and his wife, Elizabeth von Hohenzollern. Formerly, the triforium gallery housed one of the great libraries of the world, the Bibliotheca Palatina; this was confiscated by Field Marshal Johann Tilly as war booty and presented to the pope. Some items were returned in the nineteenth century, but the finest books remain in the Vatican.

Facing the church is the only mansion to survive the seventeenth-century devastation of the town, the **Haus zum Ritter**, so called from the statue of St George dressed as a Knight which crowns the pediment. Built for a Huguenot refugee cloth merchant, it was clearly modelled on the Ottheinrichsbau in the Schloss to which, with its extravagant decoration of caryatids, scrollwork and fancy gables, it stands as a worthy competitor. Now an expensive hotel and restaurant, it completely outclasses its Baroque neighbours, among which is the **Rathaus** on the eastern side of the square.

On Bremeckgasse, a short walk south of Marktplatz, the new **Dokumentations- und Kulturzentrum Deutscher Sinti und Roma** (Tues 10am–8pm, Wed–Fri 10am–4.30pm, Sat & Sun 11am–4pm; free) is a belated act of atonement for the often overlooked atrocities committed by the Third Reich against Europe's Gypsy communities. A permanent exhibition documents the deportations and mass murders that were carried out, resulting, it is estimated, in around 500,000 deaths – a total that was only a fraction of that of the Jews, but on a comparable scale in proportionate terms. Temporary displays illustrate the culture of the two main German-based Gypsy peoples, the Sinti and the Roma.

East of Marktplatz, the imposing Baroque **Residenz** of the grand dukes of Baden, which now houses the German Academy of Sciences and Letters, can be seen on Karlspatz. Beyond, at Hauptstr. 235, is the **Palais Weimar**, now containing the **Völkerkunde-Museum** (Tues–Fri 3–8pm, Sun 1–8pm; DM5/€2.50), which has a wonderful group of artefacts from Asmat in western New Guinea, as well as good African collections. At the end of the street is the Neoclassical **Karlstor**, a triumphal arch in honour of Elector Carl Theodor, designed by his court architect, Nicolas de

Pigage. However, the most important structure this great artistic patron gave to his ancestors' capital is the **Alte Brücke** downstream. Dating from the 1780s, it's at least the fifth on this site. In the last war, it suffered the inevitable fate of being blown up but has been painstakingly rebuilt, including its fairy-tale gateway.

The university quarter

Much of the western half of the Altstadt is occupied by buildings of the **University**, officially known as the Ruperto-Carola, in honour of its two founders. It was established in 1386 by Elector Ruprecht I, which makes it the oldest university in what is now Germany, though German-speaking universities had preceded it in Prague and Vienna.

One side of Universitätsplatz, the Altstadt's second main square, is occupied by the **Alte Universität** (April–Oct Mon–Sat 10am–4pm; Nov–March Tues–Fri 10am–2pm; DM5/€2.50); like so many of the city's buildings, it dates back to the first quarter of the eighteenth century, and was designed by the local architect Johann Adam Breunig. The admission ticket gives access to a small museum documenting the university's history, and to the **Alte Aula**, the grand late nineteenth-century graduation hall on the first floor. It is also valid for the most celebrated university building, the former **Studentenkarzer** (Student Prison), on Augustinergasse to the rear. Between 1712 and 1914, this was used to detain students (a sizeable proportion, by all accounts) who had been convicted of an offence. Every available square centimetre of the walls of the otherwise spartan cells is covered with graffiti, with a black silhouette self-portrait of the prisoner the most popular motif.

The **Universitätsbibliothek** is down Grabengasse to the south of Universitätsplatz, with the entrance for temporary exhibitions round the corner on Plöck. In summer (normally 10am–7pm; free) there's generally a display centred on the treasures of the collection. Outstanding is the fourteenth-century *Codex Manesse*; apart from containing 137 beautiful miniatures, it ranks as the most important collection of Middle High German poetry. Opposite is the Gothic **Peterskirche**, which is now the university church, as well as a regular venue for vocal and choral concerts.

The **Jesuitenkirche**, tucked away just to the east of Universitätsplatz on Schulgasse, is in the sombre, classically inspired style favoured by this evangelizing order, who came here with the intention of recapturing Heidelberg for Catholicism, a mission which doesn't seem to have been particularly successful. Housed in its gallery and the adjoining monastery is a rather moderate **Museum für Sakralkunst** (June–Oct Tues–Sat 10am–5pm, Sun 1–5pm; Nov–May Sat 10am–5pm, Sun 1–5pm only; DM2.50/€1.25).

Following Plöck in a westerly direction, you come to the former **Institut für Naturwissenchaften** at the junction with Akadamiestrasse. Heidelberg's most famous scientist, **Robert Wilhelm Bunsen**, was based there for four decades. His name is familiar to school pupils all over the world for popularizing that staple gadget of the laboratory, the "Bunsen burner"; he was also the first to separate the colours of the spectrum.

The Kurpfälzisches Museum

Housed in the **Palais Morass** at Hauptstr. 97, an early eighteenth-century mansion built for a law professor, is the **Kurpfälzisches Museum** (Tues & Thurs–Sun 10am–5pm, Wed 10am–9pm; DM5/€2.50). The archeology department in the modern extension to the rear includes a cast of the jawbone of *Homo heidelbergiensis* (the original is owned by the university); this is estimated to come from the inter-glacial period 500,000 years ago, making it one of the oldest human bones ever discovered. There are also rooms devoted to excavations from the Roman and Merovingian periods. On the first floor of the Palais Morass itself is a section devoted to the history of the Palatinate. The intact

HEIDELBERG UNIVERSITY

Initially, Heidelberg university's fortunes were closely tied to that of the Palatinate Electors; it became a great centre of humanism and the Reformation, but fell into decline in the eighteenth century, to be revived in 1803 by Grand Duke Karl Friedrich as the first state university of Baden. One of its most lasting achievements came soon after: while still a student, Clemens Brentano and his brother-in-law Achim von Arnim put together the collection of folk poetry known as *Des Knaben Wunderhorn* (The Boy's Magic Horn) in the years 1805–08. This was to be a key influence on the future evolution of Romanticism, directly inspiring the researches of the Brothers Grimm, whose prose folk tales (being more amenable to translation) have gained a far wider international fame. However, the work of Arnim and Brentano has been spread by the composer Gustav Mahler, who gave the verses idiomatic tunes and cloaked them in succulent orchestral colours, with several finding their way into his symphonies.

In spite of the vicissitudes of German history in the last two centuries, Heidelberg has managed to preserve its academic reputation. It's one of the few universities largely exempted in criticism of the modern German higher educational system, which is generally seen as something of a failure. Heidelberg is particularly renowned in the natural sciences, where it has nurtured a stream of Nobel Prize winners. It was also here, under Max Weber, that sociology was developed as an academic discipline.

Of the many traditions associated with the university, the oddest was the fact that, until the present century, its students were not subject to civil jurisdiction. When a crime or breach of the peace was committed, the offender had to be dealt with by the university authorities. Moreover, when found guilty, the student did not need to serve his punishment immediately; he could do so at his leisure. Nor was there any stigma attached to imprisonment – indeed, it was seen as an essential component of the university experience. Nobody knows how this system came into being, but it presumably dates back to the times when most alumni were aristocratic and subject to the mores of *noblesse oblige*.

A second Heidelberg tradition – this time one which spread throughout Germany – was the *Mensur*, or fencing match. Students were divided into confraternities (*Verbindungen*) according to the region of their birth; the members wore a distinguishing cap and were forbidden from socializing with those belonging to other groups. At least three (in practice, far more) duels were held on two days of every week. Each bout lasted for fifteen minutes, excluding stoppages, unless it became dangerous to proceed; if the outcome was inconclusive, it had to be re-staged at a later date. The combatants wore goggles and every vital organ was padded, so that the risk of death was minimal. They were placed at arm's length from each other and fought by moving their wrists alone; to flinch or to step back were the ultimate disgraces. Wounds were frequent, particularly on the top of the head and left cheek; these were treated immediately by a surgeon or medical student. What was really bizarre was that the wounds became highly prized badges of courage; for optimum prestige, salt was rubbed into them, leaving scars which would remain for life. The anachronistic ideal of chivalry encapsulated in the Mensur staggers on to this day among right-wing toffs, while its effects can still be seen on elderly professorial brows.

Another tradition associated with the fencing corps was the Kneipe, a stag party where competition was confined within the group. The idea was to down as many mugs of beer as possible in a given space of time; the winner became the Bierkönig. As the rules were concerned solely with emptying the contents of the glass down the throat, and not about retaining the alcohol in the system, those who didn't mind the discomfort of consistently spewing up were able to accomplish prodigious totals of close to one hundred pints in an evening. Several taverns which were the scene of these bouts still exist (see opposite).

Schloss can be seen in a large documentary picture from the early seventeenth century; it also turns up in the background of Jan Brueghel's exquisite *Allegory of Summer*. There are also sensitive portraits of Elizabeth and her family by the Honthorst brothers, dating from her exile in Holland when she was extolled as "The Queen of Hearts" by a generation of gallants. The museum's prize possession is the limewood *Altar of the Twelve Apostles* by **Tilman Riemenschneider**, which was masked under a thick coat of polychrome for centuries, but has been returned to its original unpainted state.

Eating, drinking and entertainment

Hauptstrasse and the adjacent side-streets are jammed with places of entertainment to suit all tastes, and there's no better place for a pub crawl in all of Germany. The much-trumpeted **student taverns** (see also "Hotels" on p.363) are a must; they're perfectly genuine and are still patronized by the leftovers of the old fraternities, even if parties of tourists now make up the bulk of the clientele, particularly in summer. They're sights in themselves, with their faded photos and daguerreotypes, their trophies, swords, pads, helmets and miscellaneous paraphernalia.

To find out **what's on** in town, consult the monthly *Heidelberg aktuell* (*www.heidelberg-aktuell.de*; DM1/€0.50).

Restaurants

Abel's, Hauptstr. 133. Relaxed wine bar-cum-restaurant where you can sit outside.

Da Mario, Rohrbacher Str. 3. The best Italian restaurant in the city.

Essighaus, Plöck 97. Inexpensive Gaststätte serving traditional German food; also has a small beer garden.

Kalimera, Römerstr. 26. Good Greek restaurant, with a tiny sheltered garden to the rear.

Kurpfälzisches Museum, Hauptstr. 97. This wine bar is situated in the museum courtyard and serves excellent food.

Roter Ochsen, Hauptstr. 217. This rivals *Zum Sepp'l* (see p.363) for the right to be regarded as the most famous of Heidelberg's historic student taverns, and is on the itinerary of practically every tourist to the city. Its U-shaped interior has been patronized by the confraternities since it was built at the beginning of the eighteenth century and serves good, reasonably priced food. Closed Sun.

Schlossweinstube, Im Schlosshof. Classy and expensive wine bar-restaurant in the Schloss. Evenings only, closed Wed.

Schnizelbank, Bauamtsgasse 7. Another of the historic student taverns, and the only one where the drinking emphasis is on wine rather than beer.

Simplicissimus, Ingrimstr. 16 (☎0 62 21/18 33 36). High-class French restaurant. Very small, so reservations are obligatory. Evenings only, closed Tues.

Waves, Kurfürsten-Anlage 9. Vegetarian restaurant with a wide selection of dishes. Mon–Wed & Sat 11.30am–4pm, Thurs & Fri 11.30am–9pm.

Wilhelmsplatz, Kaiserstr. 30. This is well off the beaten tourist track, and a good place to meet locals; serves large, cheap meals. Closed Sun & Mon.

Wirtshaus zum Spreissel, Neckarstaden 66. Serves huge portions of traditional Baden, Alsatian and Swiss cuisine.

Zum Güldenen Schaf, Hauptstr. 115. Historic restaurant which serves both regional and international dishes and has a pleasant garden.

Zur Herrenmühle, Hauptstr. 239 (☎0 62 21/1 29 09). Heidelberg's best restaurant, occupying a fine seventeenth-century building with an inner courtyard. The cooking is innovative and therefore expensive; it's advisable to book in advance. Evenings only, closed Sun.

Cafés and bars

Biermuseum, Hauptstr. 143. Here you'll find the largest selection of beers in Heidelberg, with 101 varieties to choose from, ten of them on draught.

Café Journal, Hauptstr. 162. Best of the bistro-type cafés which are all the rage among present-day Heidelberg students. Has a wide selection of newspapers, and makes a good choice for breakfast.

Café Knösel, Haspelgasse 20. Heidelberg's oldest and most elegant café; its speciality is the Heidelberger Studentenkuss (Heidelberg Student Kiss), a dark chocolate filled with praline and nougat. Full meals also available. Closed Mon.

Café Schafheutle, Hauptstr. 94. Another old-world café, with its own garden and celebrated for its marzipan fancies. Closed Sun.

Café 7, Marktplatz 7. Serves good cakes and ice cream, plus Brazilian food.

Goldener Reichsapfel, Untere Str. 35. Popular student bar, one of several on the street.

Hemingway, Fahrtgasse 1. Student pub that sees very few tourists.

Max Bar, Marktplatz 5. French-style bistro that puts tables out onto the square in summer.

Palmbräuhaus, Hauptstr. 185. A modern re-creation of palm court days, with resident pianist.

Trinidad, Friedrich-Ebert-Anlage 62. The place to come for exotic cocktails.

Vetters Alt-Heidelberger Brauhaus, Steingasse 9. Hausbrauerei which makes *Pils*, *Weizen* and an extremely powerful *Bock*; also does good-value meals.

Zum Schwarzen Walfisch, Bahnhofstr. 27. *Szene* café-bar, which makes a good choice for breakfast.

Discos and live-music pubs

Cave 54, Krämergasse 2. Normally a nostalgic-style disco, except on Tues, when it's live jazz.

Doctor Flotte, Hauptstr. 130. Raucous bar playing both rock and jazz.

Fischerstübchen, Obere Neckarstr. 2. The favourite disco of the local students. Open Thurs–Sat.

Mata Hari, Oberbadgasse 10. Gay men's disco.

Schwimmbad Musik-Club, Tiergartenstr. 13. Has regular live gigs and discos Wed–Sat.

Ziegler, Bergheimer Str. 1b. Varied late-night spot, featuring a varied programme of jazz and rock concerts, cabaret and theatre.

Zigarillo, Bergheimer Str. 147. Crowded disco housed in an old factory.

Classical music, theatre and festivals

Classical music concerts are held in the modern Kongresshaus Stadthalle (☎0 62 21/80 90 80) overlooking the Neckar. The Heidelberger Kammerorchester is a Mozartean-sized band of good standing, even if its programmes tend to be conservative. The Heidelberger Sinfoniker is a full-sized symphony orchestra. At the main **theatre**, the Städtischen Bühnen, Theaterstr. 4 (☎0 62 21/58 35 23), there's a varied mixture of plays, opera, operetta, and performances by an experimental corps de ballet. Straight drama is also offered at the tiny Zimmertheater, Hauptstr. 118 (☎0 62 21/2 10 69), and the Taeter-Theater, Bergheimer Str. 147 (☎0 62 21/16 33 33). Productions for **kids** are performed at the Heidelberger Kinder und Jugendtheater, Zwingerstr. 3–5 (☎0 62 21/58 35 46). The Kulturbahnhof Karlstor, Am Karlstorbahnhof 1 (☎0 62 21/97 89 14), is a cultural centre with theatre, cinema and café.

Heidelberg's most spectacular **festivals** are those using the Schloss as a backdrop. On the first Saturdays of June and September, and the second in July, there are firework displays and historical pageants; these attract horrendously large crowds, but are highly enjoyable all the same. From late July until the end of August, there are open-air concerts and opera performances (inevitably, *The Student Prince* is included) in the Schlosshof at 8pm on most evenings (☎0 62 21/5 89 76 for tickets and information); in bad weather, they're transferred indoors. Throughout the year, various **fairs** are held on Karlsplatz – *Heidelberger Frühling* (early April), *Weindorf* (mid-Sept) and *Heidelberger Herbst* (late Sept). The climax of **Carnival** (variable Feb/March) is the Rose Monday parade; there's another procession through the streets on the third Sunday before Easter.

Listings

Bookshops The best ones are located around Sofienstrasse and Universitätsplatz.

Car rental Avis, Karlsruher Str. 43 (☎0 62 21/2 22 15); Hertz, Kurfürsten-Anlage 1 (☎0 62 21/2 34 34); InterRent, Bergheimer Str. 159 (☎0 62 21/2 08 45).

Cruises These leave from the quay beside the Stadthalle from mid-May to mid-Sept; they're run by Rhein-Neckar-Fahrgastschiffahrt (☎0 62 21/2 01 81) and Personenschiffahrt Hornung (☎0 62 21/48 00 64). A forty-minute local journey costs DM6.50/€3.25; the round trip to Neckarsteinach DM17.50/€8.75.

Cultural institute Deutsch-Amerikanisches Institut, Sofienstr. 12 (☎0 62 21/6 07 30).

Kids Märchenparadies on top of the Königstuhl (March–Oct daily 10am–6/7pm; DM5/€2.50, kids DM4/€2) is an adventure playground featuring fairy-tale characters and a miniature railway.

Markets on Marktplatz (Wed & Sat), and on Friedrich-Ebert-Platz (Tues & Fri).

Mitfahrzentrale Kurfürsten-Anlage 57 (☎0 62 21/2 46 46).

Post office Main branch with poste restante is beside the Hauptbahnhof; another is at Sofienstr. 6.

Shopping Untere Strasse is the trendiest street, featuring some amazing secondhand clothes shops, with quality ballgowns and hats available at knock-down prices. Flic-Flac, Untere Str. 12, is one of the best.

Sports The main swimming pool is beside the zoo on Tiergartenstrasse. The German Grand Prix motor race takes place at nearby Hockenheim each July.

Travel agencies American Express, Brückenkopfstr. 1–2 (☎0 62 21/9 12 70); HS Reisebüro, Hauptstr. 23 (☎0 62 21/9 77 00), does student deals.

Zoo Tiergartenstr. 3 (April–Sept daily 9am–7pm; Oct–March daily 9am–5pm; DM7/€3.50, kids DM3/€1.50).

Bad Wimpfen

BAD WIMPFEN, a pocket-sized town built high above a bend in the Neckar on one of the rail lines linking Heidelberg with Heilbronn, is a real visual treat, preserving a wonderful array of monuments as testament to its richly varied history. The site has been inhabited since prehistoric times; Romans, Frankish kings and the bishops of Worms were later rulers, prior to its choice, from around 1200, as a favourite **residence of the Staufian emperors**. Some 150 years later Wimpfen was made a Free Imperial City, an independence it retained, courtesy of the lucrative salt trade, until the advent of Napoleon, who allocated it to the Grand Duchy of Hesse-Darmstadt. After World War II, many locals hoped the town would become a detached southern enclave of the new Land of Hesse, but the American authorities placed it in an administrative district of Baden. Seven years later, it voted to switch allegiance to the other half of the new combined province of Baden-Württemberg, and has been part of the Heilbronn district ever since.

The **skyline** is immediately impressive and one of the most dramatic in Germany: it's best seen from the right bank of the Neckar, where the imperious towers, illuminated by night, give it the appearance of a miniature medieval Manhattan. Bad Wimpfen has two very distinct historic quarters. The upper town, **Wimpfen am Berg**, was originally built within the ruins of the Staufian palace and has the lion's share of the historic sights, though it is the lower town, **Wimpfen in Tal**, which possesses the dominant surviving monument, the Ritterstift.

Wimpfen am Berg

Hauptstrasse is the central street of the cobblestoned Wimpfen am Berg. About a third of the way up is the **Schwibbogen Tor**, which formerly gave access to the **Kaiserpfalz** (Imperial Palace). Substantial portions of the palace remain to this day, ranking among the most important of the relatively few surviving examples of Romanesque civil architecture in Europe. The austere riverside wall, which had the advantage of a formidable natural barrier behind, survives largely intact. At its southern end, it's guarded by the **Nürnberger Türmchen** and the **Roter Turm**, a gaunt box-like structure which was the last line of defence. From here, there's a fine view over the town and valley.

Further along is the **Pfalzkapelle** (April to mid-Oct daily 10am–noon & 2–4.30pm; DM1.50/€0.75, or DM5/€2.50 combined ticket to all three municipal museums), now containing a small collection of religious art. The gallery was reserved for the emperor who could, if necessary, make a quick getaway through a passage to the haven of the Roter Turm. Adjoining the chapel is the sole surviving part of the **Palast** itself – a weather-worn but still elegant row of arcades, each of whose paired columns is carved in a different manner.

Also from the Staufian epoch is the large **Steinhaus** (Stone House), which stands out among the later buildings, most of which are half-timbered. Originally the home of the castle commandant, it was modernized in the sixteenth century by the addition of Gothic gables. It's currently fitted out as the **Museum des Mittelalters** (April–Oct Tues–Sun 10am–noon & 2–4.30pm; DM2/€1), with exhibits from prehistoric times to the period of the Staufian emperors. Diagonally opposite is the symbol of Wimpfen and the most potent reminder of its days of power and glory, the **Blauer Turm** (Blue Tower; same hours as Museum des Mittelalters; DM2/€1), which can be ascended for a fine view over the town and the Neckar valley. Named after the tints of the limestone used in its construction, this watchtower was all but destroyed in a fire in 1848 and was only made fully secure in the 1980s. At noon on Sundays from April to September, the resounding strains of a trumpeter playing chorales from the top can be heard throughout the streets. On Obere Turmgasse just to the south is the town's most imposing half-timbered mansion, the **Bürgermeister-Elsässer-Haus**; it has a sixteenth-century core, though the large oriel window was only added until 1717.

The lower parts of the twin towers of the **Stadtkirche** are the last main features of the Romanesque part of Wimpfen's skyline; the rest of the building is a late Gothic hall church. Its interior boasts a spectacular cellular vault, and contains some notable furnishings, including a fifteenth-century *Christ on the Cross* with moving parts and human hair, and two early sixteenth-century retables. Behind the church is a large and emotional Crucifixion group similar to the one its sculptor, Hans Backoffen, made for his own tomb in Mainz. Close by is the **Wormser Hof**, part of which is also Staufian; it was the residence of the administrator in the service of the bishop of Worms, with a barn to store the tithe of agricultural produce he collected.

It's worth sauntering round the streets of the old town, which curve and plunge their way past half-timbered houses, Baroque mansions and quiet squares with Renaissance fountains. Among the many surprising vistas, that from the **Adlerbrunnen** (Eagle Fountain) at the junction of Hauptstrasse and Salzgasse is particularly fine. The best-preserved street is **Klostergasse**, one of whose mansions still preserves what was once a characteristic feature – an exterior gallery which served as a bath house. Down Bollwerkgasse is the **Bollwerk** or artillery bastion, built in the sixteenth century to designs by Dürer, no less. Nearby, the monumental half-timbered fifteenth-century **Spital** on Hauptstrasse has been restored to house the **Reichstädtisches Museum** (April–Oct Tues–Sun 10am–noon & 2–5pm; DM3/€1.50). This takes up the story of Wimpfen from the Middle Ages through to the nineteenth century; the original interiors themselves justify a visit.

Wimpfen in Tal

The lower town, known as Wimpfen in Tal, is built round the great **Ritterstift St Peter**. After a break of five centuries, the complex was repopulated in 1947 by Benedictine monks who had fled from Grüssau in Silesia, which had become the Polish town of Krzeszów. Try and catch a service to hear their wonderful Gregorian chant.

The fortress-like facade of the **Stiftskirche**, with a huge porch and a pair of octagonal towers, dates from the tenth century; the rest of the building is a masterly French-inspired Gothic design. This is generally attributed to the near-legendary mason **Erwin**

von Steinbach, who built part of Strasbourg Cathedral. Superb original sculptures can be seen on the south doorway and inside the chancel; the latter group includes the then recently deceased St Francis of Assisi. Also of note are some original stained-glass windows, a set of humorously carved choir stalls, and a poignant fifteenth-century terracotta *Pietà*. Access to the **cloister**, which has sections in each of the three phases of the Gothic style, is only allowed to groups who have booked in advance, but you can tag along with one of these (which are frequent during the summer, if not at other times) if you ask at the shop.

Practicalities

Bad Wimpfen still preserves its original **Bahnhof**, a rustic little building of 1868 at Carl-Ulrich-Str. 1 by the river in the lower part of town. The **tourist office** (Mon–Fri 9am–1pm & 2–5pm; Easter–Sept also Sat & Sun 10am–noon & 2–4pm; ☎0 70 63/9 72 00, fax 97 20 20, *www.badwimpfen.de*) is housed inside. Turn right outside to reach Hauptstrasse, or follow the main road to the left for ten minutes to reach Wimpfen in Tal. **Neckar cruises**, which run both upstream and down throughout the summer months, depart from the jetty beside the Neckarbrücke.

There are around a dozen private houses – scattered all over town – offering **rooms** (①–②). Wimpfen am Berg has one **pension**, *Traube*, Hauptstr. 1 (☎0 70 63/95 05 21; ④), plus several **hotels**. These include *Grüner Baum,* Hauptstr. 84 (☎0 70 63/2 94; ④), *Blauer Turm,* Burgviertel 5 (☎0 70 63/2 25 or 78 84; ④–⑤), *Weinmann,* Marktplatz 3 (☎0 70 63/85 82; ⑤), and *Sonne,* which occupies a lovely half-timbered building at Hauptstr. 87 (☎07063/2 45 or 96 11 60; ⑤). There are also two spa hotels, both with good bathing facilities, in the Kurgebiet at the northern end of town: *Am Kurpark*, Kirschenweg 16 (☎0 70 63/9 77 70; ⑤), and *Am Rosengarten*, Osterbergstr. 16 (☎0 70 63/99 10; ⑤).

The leading **restaurants** are those attached to the hotels *Rosengarten* and *Sonne*; the latter is run in tandem with *Weinstube Feyerabend*, Hauptstr. 87. The Vietnamese management of *Grüner Baum* have an Asian speciality restaurant, *Royal Orchid*, on the premises; this is particularly good value at lunchtime, when there are set menus. *Zum Kräuterweible*, Marktrain 5, is popular with locals for its chicken dishes; *Hohenstaufenpfalz*, Hauptstr. 34, is a long-established Gasthaus specializing in Swabian fare; *Dobel's*, Hauptstr. 61, serves over thirty different types of Maultaschen; while *Alt-Wimpfener Stuben* in the Bahnhof offers fish and vegetarian specialities plus a beer garden.

Wimpfen in Tal is the scene of one of Germany's oldest **popular festivals**: it's claimed the week-long *Talmarkt* in honour of SS Peter and Paul (June 29 to July 5) has been celebrated every year since 965. Nowadays, the end is marked by a spectacular fireworks display. Two more fairs dating back to the Middle Ages are held in the centre of Wimpfen am Berg: the *Zunftmarkt* for handicrafts at the end of August and the *Weihnachtsmarkt* in December, which is a cut above the imitative versions found in practically every German town. *Fasching* also has a long tradition here; highlights are the Sunday parade and the evening celebrations on Ash Wednesday.

Burg Guttenberg

Burg Guttenberg (daily March–Nov 9am–6pm; *www.burg-guttenberg.neckar.com*; DM5/€2.50), the best known of the many castles in the Neckar valley region, lies 8km north of Wimpfen am Berg and can be reached by buses bound for Neckarmühlbach, which can be picked up at the stop beside the Bollwerk. Impressively set on a hill, the fortress dates back to the Staufian epoch, but has been much altered; it became the seat of the barons of Gemmingen in 1449 and still remains in the possession of their descendants. The principal defensive features are an impressive curtain wall and the tall narrow keep. Inside, the main curiosity is the **Holzbibliothek**, a herbarium in which the flowers, fruit and leaves of nearly all the different local trees are stored in 93 wooden containers arranged to look like books. There's also an impressive tin-figure diorama of the Battle of Wimpfen, an early skirmish of the Thirty Years War.

However, the castle's main claim to fame is as the seat of the **Deutsche Greifenwarte**, Europe's largest station for **birds of prey**. Each day of the season (March & Nov at 3pm; April–Oct at 11am & 3pm; DM12/€6, DM14/€7 including admission to the Burg), there's an exhilarating demonstration by the station's founder, the ornithologist, falconer and traveller Claus Fentzloff, of several of the birds (usually including eagles and vultures) in free flight. Yet this is by no means just for show – there has been a highly successful programme for breeding endangered species, and an average of fifty birds per year are released back into the wild. There's also a good restaurant, the *Burgschenke*, set on a terrace commanding an extensive view over the valley.

The Tauber valley

At the extreme northeastern corner of Baden-Württemberg, the gentle **River Tauber** cuts through a lush, verdant landscape of undulating hills, often dotted with vineyards, which stands in sharp contrast to the rugged contours of the neighbouring Swabian Jura. It manages to preserve an agreeable atmosphere of rustic peace and quiet, at least outside those towns which are staging posts on the famous tourist route known as the **Romantic Road** (see box on p.213), which closely follows the entire length of the Tauber valley, with the exception of its northernmost stretch. Bad Mergentheim, Weikersheim and Creglingen all lie on the route while the equally popular Wertheim is just to the north. All except Creglingen are on the same rail line, the Taubertalbahn.

Wertheim

Situated at the point where the Tauber joins the westward-flowing Main, just a short journey away from Miltenberg in the Bavarian section of the Odenwald, **WERTHEIM** is the most northerly town in Baden-Württemberg. It's nicknamed "Little Heidelberg", and with some justification, as there are clear similarities between the two – the setting between the riverside and wooded slopes, the prevalence of superb and varied panoramic viewpoints, the twisting alleyways, the ruined castle looming high above. The original town was situated on the northern bank of the Main for fear of flooding, but it moved in the twelfth century when the local counts, realizing the strategic importance of the spit of land between the two rivers, used it as the basis for building up a territory between the two ecclesiastical principalities of Mainz and Würzburg. A precarious independence was maintained down the centuries from the prying hands of the bishops, whose unwelcome advances were a major factor in Wertheim becoming one of the earliest bastions of Protestantism.

The classic **view** of the town is obtained from the quay on the left bank of the Tauber, just south of the pedestrian bridge. Directly opposite are a number of old fishermen's houses and the **Kittsteintor**, a gateway which has a scale recording the high-water mark of each flood since 1595. Further up towards the Main is the **Spitzer Turm** (Pointed Tower), the original corner point of the fortifications erected around 1200. The streets immediately behind housed a large Jewish population right up until the days of the Third Reich.

At the heart of Wertheim is the **Marktplatz**, which is the setting for colourful markets on Wednesdays and Saturdays. The square is lined with half-timbered houses, and also features the **Engelsbrunnen**, an elaborately carved sixteenth-century fountain named after the figures of angels holding up the municipal coat of arms. The larger of the two Gothic churches is the fourteenth-century **Stiftskirche**, whose choir contains a series of ornate Renaissance tombs, the pantheon of the House of Wertheim. Diagonally opposite is the **Kilianskapelle**, a double chapel from the following century whose lower storey served as an ossuary.

A short walk down Mühlenstrasse is the **Glas-Museum** (April–Oct Tues–Sun 10am–noon & 2–4.30pm; DM3/€1.50, or DM5/€2.50 combined ticket with Grafschaftsmuseum), which occupies two old half-timbered houses. It features a comprehensive collection of historic glassware, as well as many impressive contemporary works, and incorporates a fully equipped workshop where the techniques of glass making are demonstrated. Alongside is the Baroque **Hofhaltung**, formerly the residential palace of the ruling family, nowadays the seat of the local administration.

On Rathausgasse to the north of Marktplatz, the former Rathaus and the half-timbered building opposite have been adapted to house the **Grafschaftsmuseum** (Tues–Fri 9.30am–noon & 2–4.30pm, Sat & Sun 2.30–5pm; DM3/€1.50), which is devoted to all aspects of the history of the former county of Wertheim. It includes sacred art, traditional costumes, ceramics and a wide range of objects associated with the local wine and fishing industries. One of the two main reception rooms of the Rathaus, which are both decorated with stuccowork, is hung with paintings of Wertheim by Otto Modersohn, the leading light of the artistic community at Worpswede in Lower Saxony (see p.634–635).

At the top of the town is the massive **Burg** (accessible at all times; DM1/€0.50 donation requested); this was left as a ruin after the Thirty Years War but still ranks among the most imposing medieval castles in Germany. From the twelfth-century fortress, the tall watchtower and part of the walls survive; later additions include the twin-towered barbican, the residential quarters and the formidable outer bulwarks. You can wander all round the walls and climb to the top of the tower, which offers an outstanding panoramic view encompassing the complex itself, the town, its two rivers, the Odenwald to the west and the wooded Spessart hills to the north.

Practicalities

Wertheim's **Bahnhof** is on the left bank of the Tauber, only a few minutes' walk from the centre. The **tourist office** (Mon–Fri 9am–1pm & 1.30–5pm, Sat 10am–noon & 2–5pm, Sun 2–5pm; ☎0 93 42/10 66, fax 3 82 77, *www.tourist-wertheim.de*) is on Wenzelplatz. There's a **youth hostel** in the hills at Alte Stiege 16 (☎0 93 42/64 51, fax 73 54; DM22/€11 or DM27/€13.50), and a **campsite** (☎0 93 42/8 31 11; closed mid-Nov to mid-March) at In der Christwiesen in the incorporated village of Bestenheid. In the town proper there are five **hotels**: *Bronnbacher Hof*, Mainplatz 10 (☎0 93 42/9 25 40; ③–⑤); *Löwensteiner Hof*, Bahnhofstr. 11 (☎0 93 42/12 59; ④); *Gasthof Wenzelstube*, Am Wenzelplatz 3 (☎0 93 42/3 90 75; ④); *Schwan*, Mainplatz 8 (☎0 93 42/9 23 30; ④); and *Am Malerwinkel*, Neuplatz 1 (☎0 93 42/2 16 28; ⑤). Of these, *Schwan* has the best **restaurant**; other good places to eat are *Bach'sche Brauerei*, Marktplatz 11, and *Burgschänke Schlossberg* in the Burg.

Bad Mergentheim

BAD MERGENTHEIM, some 36km up the river from Wertheim, is one of the most celebrated spas in the country. Judging from the evidence of excavations, which have led to the uncovering of a Celtic well, the presence of hot salt springs at this point was known to Bronze Age tribes. However, they lay forgotten for over two millennia, until their rediscovery in 1826 by a shepherd who noticed his flock crowding round a trickle of water close to the north bank of the Tauber. Three years later, the first hotel opened and the town has never looked back. The timing of the finding of the springs was fortuitous, as seventeen years before Mergentheim had lost the prestigious role it had held since 1525 – as seat of the **Order of Teutonic Knights** (see box opposite). Even if you normally find spas a turn-off, it's worth coming to see the old part of town, on which the Knights left a characteristic stamp. This is sharply differentiated from the cure facilities, and situated on the opposite side of the river.

The town centre

The whole of the eastern part of town is taken up by a gargantuan complex of buildings, most of it now used as offices. The Knights originally established themselves in the former Hohenlohe castle, which was expanded and rebuilt to form the enormous **Deutschordensschloss**. In accordance with the tenets of the order, the architecture is severely ascetic, with only the occasional touch of frivolity, as in the bright orange **Torbau** which forms the main entrance. At the corner of the main courtyard is the handsome Rococo **Schlosskirche**, in part the work of the two greatest German architects of the day – Balthasar Neumann designed the twin towers, and François Cuvilliés provided plans for the white stuccoed interior, whose vault is covered by a huge fresco glorifying the Holy Cross.

Opposite the facade of the church is the main range of the Schloss, approached by two Renaissance **staircases**: the northern one has an ingenious corkscrew shape and leads up to the **Deutschordensmuseum** (Tues–Sun 10am–5pm; DM6/€3). Apart from the Neoclassical **Kapitelsaal**, the rooms are surprisingly unostentatious and are used for displays on the history of the order, including valuable treasury items and portraits of all the Mergentheim Grand Masters.

The **Schlosspark** beyond, laid out in the English style, forms a south-bank counterpart to the **Kuranlage** opposite. Despite the presence of the railway line, which divides it horizontally, the latter is a beautifully manicured spa park, whose **Wandelhalle** (Pump Room) is a glass palace built in 1935 in a style which echoes both colonial architecture and the geometricity of the Bauhaus.

The spacious central Markt is divided in two by the step-gabled sixteenth-century **Rathaus**; the arms of the Grand Master who built it are borne by the hero Roland in the fountain in front. A colourful array of houses of various dates erected by vassals of the order lines the rest of the square. Immediately to the north of the square is the Gothic **Stadtkirche**, which was founded by another order of Crusaders, that of St John of Jerusalem. Beside it is the **Spital**, with a tiny Rococo chapel. South of Marktplatz is the **Marienkirche**, a former Dominican friary church. On the north wall of its nave is a magnificent Renaissance funerary monument to Grand Master Walter von Cronburg by Hans Vischer of Nürnberg. The chapel opposite has fourteenth-century frescoes of mystical scenes.

The outskirts

Now officially part of Bad Mergentheim, the village of **STUPPACH**, 8km southwest and served by occasional buses, possesses one of the supreme masterpieces of German Renaissance painting, **Grünewald's** *Virgin of the Snows*, in its otherwise unremarkable Pfarrkirche (daily: March & April 10am–5pm; May–Oct 9am–5.30pm; Nov–Feb 11am–4pm; DM2/€1). This is part of a triptych, one wing of which also survives and can be seen in the Augustinermuseum in Freiburg.

In the Katzenwald (Cats' Forest) 5km southeast of Bad Mergentheim on the main road to Crailsheim is the **Wildpark** (March–June, Sept & Oct daily 9am–6pm, July & Aug daily 9am–7pm; Nov–Feb Sat & Sun 9am–5pm; DM9.50/€4.75), the largest zoo in Europe where animals are kept in conditions close to their natural habitats. The best time to visit is in the afternoon, when there are successive feeding sessions, culminating in that of the pack of thirty wolves, which emerges and disperses with lightning speed.

THE TEUTONIC KNIGHTS

Originally founded as a hospitaller community in Palestine in 1190, the Order of Teutonic Knights (*Deutschritterorden*) quickly took on a religious and military character. It increasingly turned its attention towards the Christianization of Eastern Europe, pushing Germany's frontiers eastwards. By the early fourteenth century the Knights had exterminated the heathen Prussians, appropriating their name and controlling a powerful Baltic state from their fortress-headquarters at Marienburg (nowadays the Polish town of Malbork). They repopulated the territories with German peasants, and grew rich from the grain trade. Prosperity bred complacency, and in 1410, in the largest battle of the European Middle Ages, the Knights were defeated at Grunwald by the Poles and Lithuanians. As a result of the Thirteen Years War of 1454–66, in which the German settlers joined the alliance against them, they had to cede half their lands and re-establish themselves at Königsberg in East Prussia.

In 1525, Grand Master Albrecht von Hohenzollern converted to Protestantism and turned the territory into a secular duchy. Those of the order still loyal to Catholicism moved to Mergentheim. Although broken as a military force, the order retained great prestige, and its Grand Master belonged among the highest ranks of the German nobility. Mergentheim remained the Knights' base until they were disbanded by order of Napoleon in 1809; however, the order was reconstituted in Vienna 25 years later, where it remains active as a charitable body.

Practicalities

Bad Mergentheim's **Bahnhof** is conveniently situated between the medieval and spa parts of the town, on the same side of the Tauber as the former. The pavilion at Markt 3 contains the **tourist office** (Mon–Fri 9am–noon & 2.30–5pm, Sat 9am–noon; ☎0 79 31/5 71 31, fax 5 73 00, *www.bad-mergentheim.de*).

If you're looking for budget accommodation, the tourist office can supply a list of **private rooms** and small **pensions** (②–③). The cheapest **hotel** is *Gasthof Zum Wilden Mann,* Reichengässle 6 (☎0 79 31/76 38; ②). Good middle-range options are *Deutschmeister,* Ochsengasse 7 (☎0 79 31/96 20; ④–⑤), *Alte Münze,* Münzgasse 10 (☎0 79 31/56 60; ⑤), and *Bundschu,* Cronbergstr. 15 (☎0 79 31/93 30, *www. Hotel-Bundschu.de*; ⑥). Top of the range is *Victoria,* Poststr. 2–4 (☎0 79 31/59 30, *www.hotel-viktoria.de*; ⑦–⑨), which has a gourmet **restaurant**, *Zirbelstuben,* along with a more affordable Weinstube. All the other hotels listed above, except *Alte Münze,* also have restaurants. There's a **youth hostel** at Erlenbachtalstr. 44 (☎0 79 31/63 73, fax 5 27 95; DM24/€12 or DM29/€14.50) in the outlying village of Igersheim (which has its own Bahnhof) to the northeast. The **campsite** is 2km south of town at Willinger Tal (☎0 79 31/21 77). Bad Mergentheim's main **festival** is the *Stadtfest* in late June.

Weikersheim

WEIKERSHEIM, 11km due east of Bad Mergentheim, is the ancestral seat of the **House of Hohenlohe**, which first came to local prominence in the twelfth century. It subsequently split into various branches, which ruled for centuries over tiny tracts of territory between the Free Imperial Cities of Schwäbisch Hall, Heilbronn and Rothenburg ob der Tauber.

In 1586, when Count Ludwig II re-established Weikersheim as the family's main residence, he decided to replace the old moated castle with a magnificent new Renaissance **Schloss** (guided tours daily: April–Oct 9am–6pm; Nov–March 10am–noon & 1.30–4.30pm; DM7/€3.50). The Dutch architect Georg Robin chose a daringly original ground plan based on an equilateral triangle. Only one wing of this, characterized by six magnificent scrollwork gables, was built, as the Hohenlohes turned their money and attention to supporting the Protestant cause in the Thirty Years War. In the early eighteenth century the complex was completed in the Baroque style, though still retaining some parts of the medieval fortress. Unquestionably the highlight of the reception rooms is the **Rittersaal**, the most sumptuous banqueting hall ever built in Germany, whose decorations are a hymn of praise to the dynasty and its preoccupations. The huge coffered ceiling is painted with depictions of the glories of the hunt, the entrance doorway is carved with a scene of a battle against the Turks, and the colossal chimneypiece is adorned with a complicated allegory which illustrates the family motto, "God gives Luck". Flanking the fireplace are the reclining stucco figures of Count Ludwig and his wife, sister of William the Silent, above which are their respective family trees. Even more eye-catching are the life-sized stuccos of deer parading along the main walls, joined by an elephant, a beast the craftsmen had clearly never seen.

The **Schlossgarten**, which is contemporary with the later parts of the Schloss, is exceptionally well preserved. On the terrace immediately behind the palace is a series of sixteen caricature statues of members of the court, the only surviving set of the many inspired by the engravings of the Lorraine artist Jacques Callot. In the central pond is a representation of *Hercules Fighting the Hydra*; like many other petty German princes, the Hohenlohes fondly saw analogies between themselves and the great hero. Further evidence of their megalomania comes with the **Orangerie** at the end of the garden, which provides a theatrical backdrop to the Tauber valley beyond. Among the figures represented are the emperors of ancient Assyria, Persia, Greece and Rome whom they imagined to be their spiritual ancestors.

Weikersheim's planned central **Marktplatz** was laid out at the beginning of the eighteenth century as a processional way linking the Schloss with the **Stadtkirche**, which contains tombs of members of the Hohenlohe family. Also on the square is the **Tauberländer Dorfmuseum** (April–Oct Tues–Thurs 2–5pm, Fri–Sun 10am–noon & 2–5pm; DM3/€1.50), with folklore displays on rural life throughout Franconia.

Practicalities

Weikersheim's **Bahnhof** is just a few minutes' walk northeast of Marktplatz. The **tourist office** (April–Sept Mon–Fri 9am–noon & 2.30–5pm, Sat 9am–noon & 2–4pm; rest of year Mon–Fri only; ☎0 79 34/1 02 55, fax 1 02 58, *www.weikersheim.de*) is at Marktplatz 7. If you want to stay, there are a fair number of **private rooms** (①–③). The lowest-priced **hotel**, *Gasthof Krone,* Hauptstr. 14 (☎0 79 34/83 14; ③) is an excellent bargain. More expensive alternatives include *Grüner Hof,* Marktplatz 10 (☎0 79 34/2 52; ④), *Deutschherren-Stuben,* Marktplatz 9 (☎0 79 34/83 76; ④), and *Laurentius,* Marktplatz 5 (☎0 79 34/70 07; ⑤). There's a **youth hostel** on the bank of the Tauber at Im Heiligen Wöhr 1 (☎0 79 34/70 25, fax 77 09; DM24/€12 or DM29/€14.50).

You can indulge in a spot of **wine-tasting** of the local vintages at the *Gutskellerei* (Mon–Fri 8am–5pm, Sat 9am–5pm, Sun 11am–5pm) in one of the swaggering arcaded builidngs fronting the main entrance to the Schloss. Each of the hotels listed above has a **restaurant**: *Krone* is the best value; *Laurentius* has the most ambitious standards.

Creglingen

CREGLINGEN, 13km upstream from Weikersheim, and on the border with Bavaria, is an old-world village with half-timbered houses. Some of these are built directly over the former ramparts; another, the **Römschlössle**, has the dimensions of a Renaissance palace and now serves as a conference centre. After Creglingen, the Romantic Road crosses into Bavaria, the next stops being Detwang and Rothenburg ob der Tauber (see p.222 and p.217).

The village's renown is based on the isolated **Herrgottskirche** (April–Oct daily 9.15am–5.30pm; Nov–March Tues–Sun 10am–noon & 2–4pm; DM3/€1.50), a Gothic pilgrimage chapel founded in the fourteenth century after a ploughman had dug up a miraculous holy wafer in a nearby field. If you're travelling by Europabus, a stop is made here; otherwise the quickest and most pleasant way to come from Creglingen is via the path running alongside the brook named after the church.

The Herrgottskirche is architecturally unremarkable but houses the magnificent limewood altar of *The Assumption*, carved by **Tilman Riemenschneider** in about 1510. Set in a filigree shrine specially constructed in order to catch the day's changing light effects, the main scene ranks as the artist's masterpiece. The four reliefs of the life of the Virgin are of markedly lower quality and are presumably not the work of the master, who employed as many as twenty assistants in order to fulfil the flood of commissions which came his way. However, Riemenschneider certainly made the exquisite predella scenes of *The Epiphany* and *Christ Among the Doctors*; the calm, pensive central figure in the group of scholars is probably a self-portrait. A couple of decades after the retable was made, the chapel was given over to the Lutherans; its excellent state of preservation is due to the fact that, as the main scene was anathema to Protestant doctrine, it was closed off and not reopened until the nineteenth century.

Practicalities

Creglingen is no longer on a rail line; **buses** to Weikersheim and Rothenburg leave from the terminal on the town-centre side of the Tauber. There are three **hotels** in the town proper: *Gasthof Grüner Baum*, Torstr. 20 (☎0 79 33/6 18; ③); *Gasthof Herrgottstal*, Herrgottstal 13 (☎0 79 33/5 18; ③); and *Gasthof Krone*, Hauptstr. 12 (☎0 79 33/5 58; ④). Additionally, there are a few **private rooms** (①–③) and also a number of **farmhouses** offering bargain deals, the wackiest being the *Heuhotel Stahl* (☎0 79 33/3 78; ③) in the incorporated hamlet of Weidenhof to the northeast, where there's the option of sleeping on hay in the loft for DM30/€15, evening meal included. For more information about these, contact the **tourist office** (Mon–Fri 9am–5pm; ☎0 79 33/6 31, fax 7 01 30, *www.creglingen.de*), by the roadside on the main route out of town to the north, at An der Romantischen Str. 14. Beside the Münstersee some 3km away is a **campsite** (☎0 79 33/3 21), while there's a **youth hostel** on a hillside at the eastern end of Creglingen itself at Erdbacher Str. 30 (☎0 79 33/3 36, fax 13 26; DM24/€12 or DM29/€14.50).

travel details

Trains

Heidelberg to: Bad Wimpfen (hourly; 50min); Bonn (hourly; 2hr 20min); Bruchsal (every 30min; 20min); Cologne (hourly; 2hr 25min); Mainz (hourly; 1hr 5min); Mannheim (hourly; 10min).

Karlsruhe to: Baden-Baden (every 20min; 20min); Freiburg (every 30min; 1hr); Freudenstadt (hourly; 2hr); Mannheim (frequent; 30min); Schwetzingen (every 30min; 40min).

Stuttgart to: Cologne (hourly; 3hr 45min); Donaueschingen (hourly; 2hr); Esslingen (every 30min; 10min); Frankfurt (hourly; 2hr 5min); Freiburg (hourly; 2hr 45min); Hamburg (8 daily; 6hr 45min); Hannover (9 daily; 5hr 30min); Heidelberg (hourly; 1hr 10min); Heilbronn (hourly; 45min); Karlsruhe (every 30min; 1hr 10min); Konstanz (hourly; 2hr 40min); Ludwigsburg (frequent; 10min); Mainz (hourly; 2hr); Mannheim (hourly; 1hr 30min); Marbach (every 30min; 25min); Rottweil (hourly; 1hr 30min); Schwäbisch Gmünd (every 30min; 40min); Schwäbisch Hall (hourly; 1hr); Tübingen (every 30min; 1hr); Ulm (every 20min; 1hr).

Ulm to: Blaubeuren (hourly; 10min); Heidelberg (hourly; 2hr 15min); Mainz (hourly; 3hr 5min); Mannheim (hourly; 2hr 25min).

CHAPTER THREE

HESSE

O ccupying the geographical centre of Germany and manifesting elements of both north and south German culture, **Hesse** (Hessen) claims to be the very heart of the nation. Although one of the parts of the country least visited by foreigners, it's also, paradoxically, one which has created preconceived images of Germany more than any other. This is because of the worldwide familiarity of the folk-tales collected by the most famous Hessians, the **Brothers Grimm**, which are set in the darkly forested highlands, feudal castles and half-timbered towns so characteristic of the province.

Modern Hesse – flung together by the Americans as an administrative unit after World War II – represents an approximate revival of a territory founded in 1248 as an offshoot of Thuringia. It reached the height of its power and influence during the Reformation, when its ruler, Landgrave Philip the Magnanimous (Philipp der Grossmütige), was the undisputed champion of **political Protestantism**. On his death in 1567, however, Hesse was divided into four separate states. Within a short period, they had crystallized into two – Hesse-Kassel and Hesse-Darmstadt – and these formed the main basis of the region's division until modern times, though there were many other later fragmentations. The division proved to be particularly destructive during the Thirty Years War, in which much of Hesse was devastated.

During the eighteenth century the region's main export was mercenary soldiers, and a large press-ganged contingent helped Britain to lose the American War of Independence. The nineteenth century was a period of more conventional commercial activity, with the arrival of the Industrial Revolution and the founding of big concerns like Opel (originally a sewing machine factory) along the banks of the River Main. It was also a period of political wheeling and dealing as the local princes attempted to play Prussia and Austria off against each other. Hesse-Kassel, hitherto regarded as the senior province, backed the wrong side and was absorbed by the expanding Kingdom of Prussia in 1866. The wilier rulers of Hesse-Darmstadt were able to remain as independent grand dukes, and in this capacity joined the Second Reich five years later.

Today Hesse is one of the most prosperous of the German Länder, focused on the American-style dynamism of **Frankfurt**. Although traditional heavy industry still exists around the confluence of the Rhine and the Main, it's the serious money generated by

---

ACCOMMODATION PRICE CODES

All the pensions and hotels in this book have been graded according to the following price categories. The codes quoted are for the cheapest available double room, except for establishments which have rooms costing widely different rates, when the most expensive price is given as well. Exact charges are given for youth hostels; in the case of the official DJH (HI) establishments, this is the lowest available rate. When two figures are quoted for these hostels, the first applies to juniors (ie under 27 years of age), the second to seniors (27 and above).

① less than DM60/€30   ④ DM100–124/€50–62   ⑦ DM200–249/€100–124
② DM60–79/€30–39   ⑤ DM125–149/€63–74   ⑧ DM250–299/€125–149
③ DM80–99/€40–49   ⑥ DM150–199/€75–99   ⑨ upwards of DM300/€150

banking and modern communications-related industries in Frankfurt which provides the region's real economic base. The two former capitals, **Kassel** and **Darmstadt**, are likewise industrial. Both suffered heavily in the war, though both are worth visiting for the sake of their many reminders of past periods of artistic patronage. Otherwise, apart from occasional light industrial pockets, most of Hesse's inhabitants live from farming or tourism. By far the most beautiful city is modest-sized **Marburg**, Hesse's first capital and home to one of Germany's most prestigious universities; in conjunction with the other towns of the **Lahn** valley, it's a great place to spend a few days. The same can be said of the Baroque city of **Fulda**, still a major episcopal centre, which offers easy access to the **Vogelsberg** and **Rhön** hills. From a tourist point of view, the most popular part of Hesse is the **Rheingau**, a scenic stretch on the right bank of the Rhine, west of the Land capital **Wiesbaden**, a money-oriented playground and gambling centre.

Hesse is very accessible: Frankfurt has the busiest international airport in Europe and is easily reached by **rail** and **road** from the rest of Germany. There are good rail links between most of the major towns, although remoter areas like the Vogelsberg are best explored by car. **Accommodation** in the major cities is pricier than the national average, whereas the rural areas offer some of the best bargains in the country.

FRANKFURT AM MAIN

Straddling the River Main not long before it converges with the Rhine, **FRANKFURT AM MAIN** is the capital city Germany has never actually had, having been cheated on more than one occasion of the role to which its history and central geographical position would seem to entitle it. Yet that hasn't stopped it becoming the economic powerhouse of the country, a cut-throat financial centre which is home to hundreds of banks, including the Bundesbank and, since 1998, the European Central Bank. It's a modern international city, with over 28 percent of its residents – the highest proportion in Germany – being of foreign citizenship. Frankfurt is a major communications and transport centre, and consequently gives many travellers their first taste of the country. It's a place with a surprising amount to offer and it's worth spending at least a couple of days here rather than treating it as a mere transit point.

Over half of the city, including almost all of the centre, was destroyed during World War II and the rebuilders decided to follow a policy of innovation rather than restoration. The result is a skyline that smacks more of New York than the Federal Republic – appropriate enough in a city that has the reputation of being one of the most Americanized in Europe and whose most commonly used nickname is Mainhatten. It's also a surprisingly civilized metropolis which spends more per year on the arts than any other city in Europe, and whose inhabitants like nothing better than to spend an evening knocking back a few jugs of the local apple wine in the open-air taverns of the **Sachsenhausen** suburb.

Frankfurt has an energetic nightlife and is a thriving recreational centre for the whole of Hesse, with a good selection of theatres and galleries, and an even better range of museums, mostly concentrated along the south bank of the River Main. It comes across as a confident and tolerant city, and in the **Bockenheim** district there's a healthy "alternative" scene, not self-consciously institutionalized in the way that Berlin's has become.

Arrival, information and accommodation

Frankfurt **airport** (☎0 69/69 00) is one of the world's busiest, and is a major point of entry into Germany from abroad. There are regular rail departures from the airport

FRANKFURT AM MAIN

ACCOMMODATION

5	Admiral
9	Am Dom
8	Atlas
2	Backer
6	Diana
10	Frankfurter Hof
3	Glockshuber
11	Götz
13	Haus der Jugend (youth hostel)
7	Hessischer Hof
16	Kautz
15	Maingau
1	Palmenhof
14	Royal
4	Scala
12	Terminus
17	Wal

THE CAPITAL CITY THAT NEVER WAS

Frankfurt's **commercial tradition** goes back to Roman times, when its importance as a river crossing point and junction between north and south Germany was first recognized. Charlemagne had a fortress built on the old Roman site during the eighth century, and by the twelfth century Frankfurt was well established as a trading centre. This market evolved gradually into the Frankfurt fair which flourishes to this day, albeit in new premises just outside the centre. The stock exchange was opened in 1585 and Meyer Amschel Rothschild founded a financial dynasty here at the beginning of the nineteenth century. Frankfurt was also the main centre of the postwar German economic recovery. It was here that the Americans set in motion the currency reform that put the shattered nation back on its feet – overnight, on June 20, 1948, they introduced DM10.7 billion worth of new currency, printed in the US and delivered to Frankfurt under armed guard, to replace the vastly inflated *Reichsmark*. With the introduction of the euro as a replacement for some of the continent's most respected currencies, Frankfurt, as the headquarters of its central bank, is set to become a financial centre of ever-increasing importance.

The city's· **political role** has been similarly prominent, albeit with more variable results: its failure to establish itself as the nation's capital symbolizes the tragedy of German history, in which authoritarianism has so often triumphed. In 1356, Frankfurt gained permanent status as the place where the Electors met to choose the Holy Roman emperor, and in 1562 it supplanted Aachen as the scene of the imperial coronations. After the Napoleonic wars it was one of only four of the erstwhile Free Imperial Cities to preserve its status, and it was chosen as the seat of the National Assembly. However, hopes that it might provide neutral, liberal-minded leadership of a united Germany incorporating both Prussia and Austria were dashed in the aftermath of the revolutions of 1848–49. The city was annexed by Prussia in 1866 and has never been so much as a regional capital since. After World War II, it seemed to be the natural choice as capital of West Germany, but lost out on the casting vote of Chancellor Adenauer, who had campaigned in favour of Bonn, the city nearest his own home, in an alliance with Berliners who feared that Frankfurt would be strong enough to thwart Berlin's chances of ever regaining capital status.

Bahnhof which will enable you to reach most of Germany's cities fairly easily. Trains leave approximately once every ten minutes for Frankfurt's **Hauptbahnhof** (journey time 11min) from where there are even more comprehensive services covering Germany and beyond.

The regional **public transport** company (RMV) is responsible for bus, tram S-Bahn and U-Bahn services. A curiosity of the Frankfurt system is that single tickets are more expensive from 6–9am and 4–6.30pm on Mondays to Fridays. The 24-hour rover ticket costs DM8.20/€4.10, though it's usually better to invest in the **Frankfurt Card** (DM12/€6 for one day, DM19/€9.50 for two days), which includes half-price entry to virtually all the city's museums. (Bear in mind that these are free on Wednesdays.) An alternative to the latter is the two-day **Museumsufer Ticket**, which excludes public transport but covers the full costs of museum entry, and costs DM15/€7.50 for individuals, DM30/€15 for families.

From the Hauptbahnhof tram #11 goes right through the heart of the historic city centre; it takes about fifteen minutes to walk the same distance. One of the **tourist offices** is in the entrance hall of the Hauptbahnhof (Mon–Fri 8am–9pm, Sat & Sun 9am–6pm; ☎0 69/21 23 88 49, fax 21 24 85 12, *www.frankfurt-tourismus.de*); the other is in the heart of the city at Römerberg 27 (Mon–Fri 9.30am–5.30pm, Sat & Sun 10am–4pm; ☎0 69/21 23 87 08).

Accommodation is predictably pricey, thanks to the expense-account business people who come for the various Messen (trade fairs). It can also be quite difficult to find, and it's best to try and sort it out in advance – especially if you're arriving when one of the major fairs is on, such as the Book Fair, at the end of September/beginning of October. To do this via the tourist board, contact the administrative headquarters at Kaiserstr. 56 (☎0 69/21 23 08 08). Long-stay lets of apartments can be arranged via one of the **Mitwohnzentralen**: City, An der Staufenmauer 3 (☎0 69/1 94 30, *www.city-mitwohnzentrale.de*); Homecompany, Berger Str. 27 (☎0 69/1 94 45, *www.homecompany.de*); and Mainhattan, Fürstenberger Str. 145 (☎5 97 55 61, *mwz.mainhattan@topmail.de*).

Hotels and pensions

Predictably, budget hotels and pensions are scant, especially in the city centre. If you don't mind the sleazy environs, most of the few reasonably priced hotels cluster around the Hauptbahnhof, close to the Kaiserstrasse red-light district. There's also some in the more enticing location of the Westend district by the university. Expensive business-class hotels, on the other hand, are thick on the ground, though they still get booked out during the main trade fairs, when the normal prices are heavily marked up.

Admiral, Hölderlinstr. 25 (☎0 69/44 80 21, fax 43 94 02). For Frankfurt this is a good reasonably priced hotel, located beside the Zoo, a short distance east of the Altstadt. ⑥–⑧.

Am Dom, Kannengiessergasse 3 (☎0 69/28 21 41, fax 28 32 37). Scores for its location in a quiet Altstadt alley, with the museums and nightspots of Sachsenhausen only a short walk away over the Alte Brücke. ⑥–⑨.

Atlas, Zimmerweg 1 (☎0 69/72 39 46, fax 72 39 46). Small, homely hotel in an apartment block within easy walking distance of the Hauptbahnhof, yet away from the sleazier streets. ④.

Backer, Mendelssohnstr. 92 (☎ & fax 0 69/74 79 92). An excellent budget choice, this no-frills but well-maintained pension is located just round the corner from the U-Bahn Westend station. ③.

Diana, Westendstr. 83 (☎0 69/74 70 07, fax 74 70 79). Very pleasant Westend hotel on a quiet residential street. ⑥.

Frankfurter Hof, Am Kaiserplatz (☎0 69/2 15 02, fax 21 58 47, *www.steigenberger.de*). A flagship of the Steigenberger chain, this is the grandest of Frankfurt's grand hotels, occupying a palatial edifice from the time of the Second Reich. Of its restaurants, *Français* (closed Sat lunchtime, Sun & Mon) is a gourmet paradise ranking among the most prestigious in the country, while *Oscar's* has traditional German fare at more reasonable prices. ⑨.

Glockshuber, Mainzer Landstr. 120 (☎0 69/74 26 28, fax 74 26 29). Pleasant budget hotel just north the Hauptbahnhof, away from the sleazier streets. ④.

Gölz, Beethovenstr. 44 (☎0 69/74 67 35, fax 71 61 42). A good Westend pension, situated near the university. ⑤.

Hessischer Hof, Friedrich-Ebert-Anlage 40 (☎0 69/7 54 00, fax 7 54 09 24). Super-luxury hotel directly opposite the Messe buildings. It's beautifully furnished throughout, with a valuable porcelain collection in the restaurant. ⑨.

Kautz, Gartenstr. 17 (☎0 69/61 80 61, fax 61 32 36). One of surprisingly few options in Sachsenhausen, a short walk north of the S-Bahnhof Frankfurt-Süd. ⑥–⑧.

Maingau, Schifferstr. 38–40 (☎0 69/60 91 40, fax 62 07 90). The pick of the Sachsenhausen hotels, with the bonus of a fine restaurant. ⑥–⑧.

Palmenhof, Bockenheimer Landstr. 89–91 (☎0 69/7 53 00 60, fax 75 30 06 66, *Hotel-Palmenhof @t-online.de*). One of Frankfurt's most characterful hotels, a family-run concern in a tastefully furnished late nineteenth-century building near the Palmengarten. Its restaurant (closed Sat & Sun) serves top-class European fare. ⑧–⑨.

Royal, Wallstr. 17 (☎0 69/62 30 26, fax 61 16 92). Good-value hotel in the heart of Sachsenhausen, close to some of the well-known apple-wine taverns. ④–⑧.

Scala, Schäfergasse 31 (☎0 69/1 38 11 10, fax 28 42 34, *www.bestwestern.de*). A member of the Best Western group, this modern hotel has a convenient location in the heart of the shopping district. ⑦–⑨.

Terminus, Münchener Str. 59 (☎0 69/24 23 20, fax 23 74 11). Virtually facing the Hauptbahnhof, this is one of the best value in its price range. ④.

Wal, Stuttgarter Str. 9 (☎0 69/25 35 45, fax 72 12 56). Very basic but friendly pension, midway between the Hauptbahnhof and the Main. ③.

Youth hostel and campsite

Campingplatz Heddernheim, An der Sandelmühle 35 (☎0 69/57 03 32). In the northern suburb of Heddernheim; take U-Bahn #1, #2 or #3.

Haus der Jugend, Deutschherrnufer 12 (☎0 69/6 10 01 50, fax 61 00 15 99). The youth hostel is in Sachsenhausen, reached by bus #46 from the Hauptbahnhof. DM27/€13.50/DM34/€17 in large dorms, DM39.50/€19.75 (regardless of age) in four-bed dorms.

The City

Most of central Frankfurt can be covered on foot; almost all the main sights lie within the bounds of the old city walls, which have been turned into a stretch of narrow parkland describing an approximate semicircle around the city centre. From here it's an easy matter to cross the Main into Sachsenhausen, where most of the museums are conveniently located along the southern river bank.

The Altstadt

Until it was devastated in two massive air raids in 1944, Frankfurt had the largest and most complete Altstadt of any important German city. After the war, the most important monuments were carefully restored; other parts were hastily rebuilt in a modern manner. Even so, large gaps remained until the 1970s, when, after much debate, they were filled with a mixture of pastiche medieval buildings and ultra-modern public commissions.

The Römerberg

As good a point as any to begin your explorations is the **Römerberg**, the historical and, roughly speaking, geographical centre of the city. Charlemagne built his fort on this low hill, on the site of earlier Roman and Alemannic settlements, to protect the ford which gave Frankfurt its name – Frankonovurd (Ford of the Franks). Throughout the Middle Ages the Römerberg was Frankfurt's focal point, serving as marketplace, fairground, venue for every imaginable kind of *Volksfest* and, less frequently, for the celebrations associated with an imperial coronation. At the start of last century the Römerberg was still the heart of the city, an essentially medieval quarter ringed by half-timbered houses built by the rich merchants and bankers who had made Frankfurt one of Germany's richest centres – its "secret capital", according to Goethe.

At the western end of the Römerberg is the **Römer** itself, which maintains its historic function as the Rathaus. Its distinctive Gothic facade, with its triple-stepped gables, was more or less all that remained after the war, but the building has been restored with consummate skill. Its two upper storeys house the **Kaisersaal** (daily 10am–1pm & 2–5pm; DM3/€1.50), the former imperial coronation hall, which has 52 bombastic nineteenth-century portraits of the German emperors. The building fronts the Römerplatz, the market square, with the Mannerist **Gerechtigkeitsbrunnen** (Justice Fountain) in the middle. Facing the Römer, a row of seven half-timbered houses was built in the late 1970s using original plans and traditional construction methods.

On the southern side of Römerplatz stands the Gothic **Nikolaikirche**, originally the court chapel, now a Protestant parish church. It's a highly distinctive and lovingly restored little building, built on a virtually square ground plan. Opposite is the **Steinernes Haus**, a postwar reconstruction of one of the few stone-built houses of the Frankfurt Altstadt; it now houses a commercial art gallery (Tues–Sun 11am–8pm; DM8/€84).

Off the northern side of Römerplatz is the Neoclassical **Paulskirche** (daily 10am–5pm; free), built in the late eighteenth century as a Lutheran preaching hall.

However, it was soon taken over for secular purposes, and it was here that the ill-fated German National Assembly met during the revolutionary upheavals of 1848–49. The church still functions as a meeting hall and looks totally unecclesiastical inside. On the northern wall there's a monument to the victims of the Nazis.

Around the Römerberg

East of Römerplatz is the most controversial of the inner-city developments. At its core is the **Schirn Kunsthalle** (Tues & Sun 11am–7pm, Wed–Sat 11am–10pm; *www.schirn-kunsthalle.de*; variable entrance charges), a cultural centre consisting of a glass tunnel for exhibitions (which regularly attracts prestigious shows, particularly of archeological subjects, old master paintings and modern art) and a rotunda with more display space and a café. The centre also houses the **Struwwelpeter-Museum** (Tues–Sun 11am–5pm; free), which has displays of international editions of the eponymous children's classic, and documentary material on its creator, the nineteenth-century physician, psychiatrist and liberal politician, Heinrich Hoffmann. Locals have dubbed the Schirn the "Federal Bowling Alley", or, in their more fanciful moments, "Murder at the Cathedral", due to its proximity to the Dom. Whether you like it or not will probably depend on how you feel about Postmodernism, but in many ways it represents a brave attempt to re-create a sense of the Römerberg as the centre of Frankfurt. Running roughly parallel with it, and bounded to the south by Saalgasse, is a row of gabled townhouses which, though essentially modern in design and construction, echo the medieval past of the Römerberg.

Beyond is the **Historischer Garten**, where the foundations of some of the Roman, Carolingian and medieval buildings which previously occupied the site have been laid bare to form a little park. Diagonally opposite is the Gothic **Leinwandhaus** (Tues & Thurs 11am–6pm, Wed 11am–8pm, Fri–Sun 11am–5pm; variable charges), formerly a cloth hall. It now contains three galleries, one of which is used for international photography exhibitions. Just to the north, in Domstrasse, looms the **Museum für Moderne Kunst** (Tues & Thurs–Sun 10am–5pm, Wed 10am–8pm; *www.frankfurt-business.de*; DM10/€5, free Wed), looking like a hi-tech slice of cake. This has attracted a fair amount of criticism on the grounds that the collection is unworthy of its setting, though it does include some ambitious installations plus examples of such famous postwar artists as Beuys, Warhol and Lichtenstein.

The Dom

The most significant building in the Altstadt is the red sandstone church of **St Bartholomäus**, popularly if inaccurately referred to as the **Dom**, a courtesy title granted it by virtue of the fact that, being the venue for the election and coronation of the Holy Roman Emperors, it was far more important than most cathedrals. In essence, it's a Gothic hall church built in the thirteenth and fourteenth centuries. The two **portals** – and particularly that on the south side, which retains most of its original sculptures – are the finest features from this period. However, the outstanding part of the Dom is its 95-metre **tower** (April–Oct 9am–1pm & 2.30–6pm; DM3/€1.50), added in the early fifteenth century by the brilliantly idiosyncratic municipal architect **Madern Gerthener**, whose quirky genius left a profound mark on the city. The pinnacled summit is one of the most original creations of German Gothic and is a clear attempt to rethink earlier spires, such as those of Freiburg's Münster, in a more modern idiom. Before the construction of the modern skyscrapers, the tower was the tallest structure in the city, and even today, strict planning rules are enforced to preserve its dominance over the Altstadt, of which there's a marvellous **view** from the top.

The treasures of the spacious, light-filled interior include a monumental Crucifixion group on the west wall by the Mainz sculptor Hans Backoffen; the poignant fifteenth-century Maria Schlaf altar in the north transept chapel; the polychromed fourteenth-century tombstones directly opposite; and an intricately carved set of choir stalls of the same period. To the right of the choir is the relatively simple and unadorned **Wahlkapelle**, where the seven Electors used to make their final choice as to who would become emperor. Housed in the cloister is the **Dommuseum** (Tues–Fri 10am–5pm, Sat & Sun 11am–5pm; DM3/€1.50), which contains treasury items and historic ecclesiastical garments, plus precious artefacts recently unearthed from royal Merovingian graves during restoration work.

The southern Altstadt

Immediately south of Römerberg is the **Saalhof**, an amalgam of several architecturally diverse imperial buildings which also incorporates the Rententurm, one of the few surviving towers from the old city defences, and a Romanesque chapel, the **Saalkapelle**. The complex and its modern extensions house the excellent **Historisches Museum** (Tues & Thurs–Sun 10am–5pm, Wed 10am–8pm; DM8/€4, free Wed). Its newest gallery displays medieval and Renaissance artworks which formerly adorned the city's churches; these include the St Anne altar by the so-called **Master of Frankfurt**; the St Thomas altar, a co-operative venture which includes grisailles of St Cyriac and St Lawrence by **Grünewald**; and a *Baptism of Christ* triptych by **Baldung**. Upstairs, look out for the magnificent coloured woodcut, exhibited with part of the original block, showing a bird's-eye view of Frankfurt as it was during the siege of 1552; it's the masterpiece of one of the city's finest artists, **Conrad Faber von Kreuznach**. There's also an intriguing section on the seventeenth-century **Merian family**, who were responsible for the detailed topographic engravings of German cities which are such an ubiquitous feature of museums all over the country. Frankfurt's greatest painter, **Adam Elsheimer**, is represented by a tiny panel of *Tobias and the Angel*, displayed alongside a strong showing of the city's many highly accomplished still-life specialists. Another section of the museum offers belated homage to **Anne Frank**, the young Frankfurt-born Jewess who died at Belsen but who gained posthumous international fame through her intensely moving diaries.

A short distance to the west is the **Leonhardskirche**, originally a pilgrimage station on the well-trodden route to Santiago de Compostela in northern Spain. Surviving from this Romanesque church are the octagonal east towers and two beautiful portals, but the latter are now indoors as a Gothic aisle was built over them. At the end of this is the **Salvatorchörlein**, a chapel whose amazing pendant vault was considered the great sight of Frankfurt in the early days of tourism. The replacement chancel, built by Madern Gerthener, preserves most of its luminous stained-glass windows; to the side is a magnificent gilded altar from Antwerp.

A little to the northwest, entered from Münzgasse, is the **Karmeliterkloster** (Tues & Thurs–Sun 10am–6pm, Wed 11am–8pm; DM5/€2.50, DM8/€4 for combined ticket with the Museum für Vor-und Frühgeschichte, free Wed), a secularized late Gothic friary renowned for its marvellously idiosyncratic murals by the sixteenth-century painter and revolutionary leader **Jerg Ratgeb**. These were badly damaged in the war, but have been painstakingly restored: their faded condition is due in large part to their having been executed in tempera. The cycle in the cloisters forms a complete illustrated Bible; that in the refectory – which is nowadays used for temporary exhibitions of works by living artists – narrates the life of the prophet Elijah and the mission and martyrdom of Carmelite friars in the Holy Land.

The rest of the complex contains the **Museum für Vor- und Frühgeschichte** (Tues & Thurs–Sun 10am–5pm, Wed 10am–8pm; DM8/€4 including entry to the Karmeliterkloster, free Wed), and has a separate entrance on Karmelitergasse. This features archeological finds from the Near East and classical Greece and Rome, but is mainly dedicated to material excavated locally. In the transept of the former church are finds from a wide variety of prehistoric sites, the most notable being the contents of an

Iron Age warrior's grave. The nave is entirely devoted to the Roman period, with stone monuments, glass, ceramics, weapons and jewellery, much of it dug up in the settlement of Nida, which lies within the present-day boundaries of Frankfurt. Finally, the chapel alongside has rich hoards of valuables from Alemannic and Frankish graves, plus early medieval artefacts found underneath the city centre.

Further west, at Untermainkai 14–15, is the **Jüdisches Museum** (same hours; DM5/€2.50, free Sat), which recounts the history of Frankfurt's once powerful and wealthy Jewish community, the largest in Germany after that of Berlin.

The northern Altstadt

A few minutes' walk north of the Karmeliterkloster, at Grosser Hirschgraben 23, is the **Goethehaus und Goethe-Museum** (April–Sept Mon–Fri 9am–6pm, Sat & Sun 10am–4pm; Oct–March Mon–Fri 9am–4pm, Sat & Sun 10am–4pm; *www.goethehaus-frankfurt.de*; DM4/€2), the interior of which has been immaculately restored after being completely burned out during the war. This is where Goethe was born and raised, and the house has been made to look as much as possible like it did when he lived here. There are a few original objects which survived the war, while the well-stocked library has some autographed examples of his writings.

The **Katharinenkirche**, a little further along on Kleiner Hirschgraben, is where Goethe was baptized and confirmed. Opposite is the **Hauptwache**, an eighteenth-century Baroque building which used to be Frankfurt's biggest police station. These days it's a pricey city-centre café, while the station of the same name is a junction on nearly all of Frankfurt's S- and U-Bahn lines.

Nearby on the Liebfrauenberg stands the **Liebfrauenkirche**, a fifteenth-century church now belonging to a Capuchin friary. Look inside for the unusual Baroque altar, a huge alabaster and gilt affair which sits well in the dusky pink sandstone interior. Even finer is the original south doorway, now only visible from the inside; its gorgeous and still brightly coloured tympanum of *The Adoration of the Magi* is a masterpiece of the "Soft Style", and is thought to be the work of Madern Gerthener.

The **Markthalle** just behind the church is a hive of activity and sells the best fresh fruit and veg in town as well as fresh imported produce from Turkey. To the north, **Zeil** is one of Germany's most expensive and exclusive shopping streets, though the area around **Konstablerwache** has become notorious for its drugs pedlars: one downside of Frankfurt's prosperity is that it has become the undisputed drugs capital of Germany.

A little to the northwest of the Hauptwache is the **Börse**, Frankfurt's stock exchange. It's open to the public on application (Mon–Fri 10.30am–1.15pm). Appropriately enough two of the most expensive shopping streets in the city are just around the corner. **Goethestrasse** sells expensive jewellery and designer clothes, while **Grosse Bockenheimer Strasse**, known to the natives as Fressgasse (Guzzle Lane), is home to upmarket delicatessens and smart restaurants.

Both of these streets lead into Opernplatz, home of the grandiose **Alte Oper**, built in 1880 in imitation of, and as a rival to, the opera houses of Paris and Dresden. The present structure is the result of years of work to restore the damage of 1945 – the vestibule and first-floor café, all fake marble and colonnades, recapture something of the late nineteenth-century ambience. With its excellent acoustics, the Alte Oper is often used as a congress hall as well as playing host to classical musicians and stars of stage and screen. Oddly enough you won't see much opera here, apart from the occasional production which doesn't need elaborate staging.

The fringes of the Altstadt

For one of the best **views** of Frankfurt old and new, it's worth taking a walk through the **Taunusanlage** and the **Gallusanlage**, two narrow stretches of parkland running into each other that begin south of Opernplatz and curve round to the Main, following the line of the old city wall. With the Alte Oper to the north, the Hauptbahnhof to the west, the Römerberg to the southeast and all around you the ultra-modern high-rise office buildings which give the city its distinctive skyline, it's a great place to capture a view of the city. But – and it's a big but – this area is the favourite hangout of the city's junkies, and it's best to steer clear of the area at night.

A much more pleasant stroll from Opernplatz is in the opposite direction through the **Bockenheimer Anlage** and past a small lake to the **Nebbienisches Gartenhäuschen**, a playful little villa built in 1810 by a local publisher to mark his third marriage. At the end of the Bockenheimer Anlage rises the **Eschenheimer Turm**, the highest defensive tower in Germany. There were once 42 towers ringing the city and this is the most imposing of the survivors; its fantastical shape, peppered with oriels and turrets and looking like it was designed in the Hollywood dream factory, marks it out as the handiwork of the ever-resourceful Madern Gerthener. Look out for the nine holes in the shape of a figure 9 on the weather vane which, according to legend, were shot into it by a local poacher.

Nearby in Stephanstrasse is the **Petersfriedhof**, which for years was Frankfurt's most fashionable cemetery. In the adjacent school courtyard you can see the grave of Goethe's mother, "Frau Aja". About ten minutes' walk to the south, just off Fahrgasse, is a surviving stretch of the **Staufenmauer**, the twelfth-century city wall which was the grand daddy of all Frankfurt's subsequent defences. Just beyond here, a left turn into Berliner Strasse leads to Battonstrasse and the **Jüdischer Friedhof**, which was in use from 1462 to 1828 and contains the Rothschild family vault.

Sachsenhausen

If you want to escape from the centre of Frankfurt, or have a laid-back evening out, then head for **Sachsenhausen** on the south bank of the Main. Although it has been part of Frankfurt since 1318, this city-within-a-city retains a distinctive atmosphere. It's best known as the "apple wine quarter", in honour of its most famous product, which is served in practically every bar in the area, and it's here that you'll find Frankfurt's most civilized nightlife. In **Schweizer Strasse** there's every imaginable kind of speciality shop, while in the old **Schlachthaus** (slaughterhouse) on Deutschherrnufer (opposite the Flösserbrücke) there's a Flohmarkt (flea market) every Saturday morning.

The heart of the quarter

The best way to approach Sachsenhausen is over the **Eiserner Steg**, an iron footbridge which runs from just outside the Historisches Museum. Lazy alternatives, which cross via the Alte Brücke further to the east, are bus #46 from the Hauptbahnhof or, if you're feeling in the mood for a bit of tourist tack, the *Ebbelwei-Express*, an old-time tram with on-board apple wine and Bretzels (Sat & Sun at 1.30pm & 5.30pm; DM4/€2 inclusive). However you decide to get there, you'll be doing a lot of walking when you arrive as most the attractions are well spread out.

Just over the Alte Brücke, the road bridge east of the Eiserner Steg, is the **Deutschordenshaus**, a triple-winged eighteenth-century building formerly belonging to the Teutonic Knights, whose Baroque facade cunningly hides a Gothic church. A section of the conventual buildings has been adapted to house the **Ikonen-Museum** (Tues & Thurs–Sun 10am–5pm, Wed 10am–8pm; DM2/€1, but included on Museum für Angewandte Kunst ticket – see below; free Wed), a collection of icons concentrating on the eighteenth and nineteenth centuries. Overlooking the river just a couple of minutes' walk away is the **Kuhhirtenturm** (Cowherds' Tower): built in 1490 as part of the Sachsenhausen fortifications, it looks like an elongated fortified barn.

Most people go to Sachsenhausen to eat, drink and be merry in the restaurants and bars of **Alt-Sachsenhausen**, the network of streets around Affentorplatz to the south. The main attractions are the apple-wine houses – recognized by the Fichtekränzi (pine wreath) hanging outside – where drinkers sit at long wooden benches in an atmosphere that makes it easy to get into conversation (see p.395).

At the southernmost end of the quarter looms the 120-metre **Henninger Turm** (Mon–Sat 3–11pm, Sun 11am–11pm; DM5/€2.50) of the eponymous Frankfurt brewery. The entrance fee includes ascent by lift to the observation platform, which commands a fine view over Frankfurt. There are also a couple of top-notch restaurants, which are pricey, though not unreasonably so.

The eastern Museumsufer

Between the Eiserner Steg and the Friedensbrücke to the west is Schaumainkai, popularly known as the **Museumsufer**, as the best museums in Frankfurt, seven in all, are straddled along its bank. First up, at no. 15, is the **Museum für Angewandte Kunst** (Tues & Thurs–Sun 10am–5pm, Wed 10am–8pm; *www.mak.frankfurt.de*; DM8/€4, free Wed), which has one of the largest and best collections of applied art in Germany. It's housed in a discreetly innovative building designed by the American architect Richard Meier: all sloping ramps in place of stairs and glassless internal windows framing *objets d'art*. The museum is divided into four sections: European, featuring furniture, glassware and ceramics; Islamic, with some fine carpets; Far Eastern, with lots of jade and lacquerwork plus a liberal sprinkling of porcelain and sculptures; and finally a section devoted to books and writing. In a nineteenth-century villa at no. 29, the **Museum für Völkerkunde** (same hours; *www.voelkerkundemuseum.frankfurt.de*; DM6/€3, free Wed) is a small ethnographical museum with an extensive collection of masks and totems.

The **Deutsches Filmmuseum** (Tues, Thurs, Fri & Sun 10am–5pm, Wed 10am–8pm, Sat 2–8pm; *www.deutsches-filmmuseum.de*; DM5/€2.50, free Wed) at no. 41 is Germany's biggest and best on the subject, featuring a huge collection detailing the development of films and the film industry. A distinctly "hands-on" approach encourages visitors to get to grips with the various film-related items on display, which range from early bioscopes to modern movie cameras. On a larger scale, there's a reconstruction of the *Grand Café* in Paris where the Lumière brothers showed the first-ever public film, and of a Frankfurt cinema from 1912. There's also a good collection of film posters and a very extensive section on film music. Not surprisingly the museum has its own cinema (DM9/€4.50).

A passage leads from the Filmmuseum café to the **Deutsches Architekturmuseum** (Tues & Thurs–Sun 10am–5pm, Wed 10am–8pm; DM8/€4, free Wed) at no. 43, which is installed in a self-consciously avant-garde conversion of a nineteenth-century villa. The high point of the interior, which has been gutted and restyled in dazzling white, is the "house within a house", which dominates the museum like an oversized dolls' house. Most of the space is given over to changing exhibitions on architectural themes, though the top floor has a permanent display of miniature theatre sets presenting a potted history of world architecture.

More conventional in layout is the **Museum für Kommunikation** (Tues–Fri 9am–5pm, Sat & Sun 11am–7pm; *www.museumsstiftung.de*; free) at no. 53, which is devoted to postal and telecommunications history. The transport section features a postal coach of the 1890s and a post bus of 1925, while Frankfurt's claim to be regarded as the birthplace of the telephone is set out in an exhibition on Philipp Reis, who disputes with Alexander Graham Bell the right to be regarded as the inventor of the first prototype. The displays are enlivened by a number of thematically appropriate artworks, including Dali's *Lobster Telephone* and an amusing installation entitled *TribuT* by Jean Luc Cornec.

The Städelsches Kunstinstitut

Very much the star of the Museumsufer, the **Städelsches Kunstinstitut** or **Städel** (Tues & Thurs–Sun 10am–5pm, Wed 10am–8pm; *www.staedelmuseum.de*; DM10/€5, free Wed) at no. 63 ranks as one of the most comprehensive art galleries in Europe. Unlike the galleries of Munich and Berlin, it is not rooted in a royal collection – it was founded in the early nineteenth century by a local banker as an art college, with an assembly of old masters from which students could learn.

Chronologically, the layout begins on the top floor. Highlights of the German section include a naive but surpassingly beautiful *Garden of Paradise* by an unknown Middle Rhenish master of the early fifteenth century, the squeamish *Martyrdom of the Twelve Apostles* by the normally placid **Lochner**, *The Resurrection* by the **Master of the Housebook** and *Job on his Dungheap* by **Dürer**. Holbein the Elder's large *Passion Altar*, painted for the city's Dominican friary, is one of his finest works, with no quarter given in the representation of gruesome detail. **Cranach**'s *The Holy Kinship*, which incorporates portraits of some of the leading personalities of the day, is another major altarpiece from the eve of the Reformation. The idiosyncratic art of **Baldung** is represented by *Two Weather Witches*, while in **Altdorfer**'s opulent *Adoration of the Magi* the artist typically indulges his love of rich and elaborate detail. The outstanding *Portrait of Simon George of Cornwall* by **Holbein the Younger** is particularly intriguing for the fact that the subject was clean-shaven when the sittings began; the artist had to carry out a skilful modification in order to show the beard his patron subsequently grew.

One of the main strengths of the gallery is its wealth of paintings from the early Netherlandish School, dominated by the gem of the whole collection, **Jan van Eyck**'s *Lucca Madonna*, which shows his legendary precision at its finest. The first great painter of the school, now generally identified as **Robert Campin** but labelled here as the Master of Flémalle, is represented by several works, while his pupil **Rogier van der Weyden** features with a magnificent *Virgin and Child with SS Peter, John the Baptist, Cosmas and Damian*. There are also superbly observed male portraits by Memling and Massys, and one of **Bosch**'s earliest known works, *Christ Presented to the People*; though restrained by his standards, it already shows his penchant for caricature and facial distortions. The Madonna and Child, a frequent subject in the Netherlandish section, also dominates the Italian, where the outstanding treatment is the ethereal image by **Fra Angelico**. Versions by Verrocchio, Moretto da Brescia, Perugino, Bellini, Cima and Carpaccio make fascinating comparisons. Other highlights here are an *Annunciation* by **Carlo Crivelli**, *St Mark* by **Mantegna**, *An Ideal Female Portrait* by **Botticelli** and **Pontormo**'s *Lady with Lap-Dog*.

Pride of place among seventeenth-century paintings goes to Frankfurt's own **Adam Elsheimer**. The largest work ever painted by this master of the small-scale is the *Altarpiece of the Cross*, the seven panels of which have been patiently accumulated over the years. Also here are *The Great Flood* – a miracle of compression – and *The Dream of Joseph*. Poussin, Claude and Rubens, all admirers of Elsheimer, are on display in the next section, which also includes the most purely Baroque work in **Rembrandt**'s entire output, the violent *Blinding of Samson* – a striking contrast with the quiet dignity of his very early *David Playing the Harp before Saul*. There's a gloriously luminous **Vermeer**, *The Geographer*, and examples of most of the lesser artists of seventeenth-century Holland. Representation of the early eighteenth century is sparser, but there are two scenes from a *Horrors of War* series by **Goya**, the frothy *Isle of Cythera* by **Watteau** and examples of Tiepolo, Canaletto and Chardin.

Paintings from the late eighteenth century onwards occupy the first floor. Of the big French names, **Courbet** (a *View of Frankfurt*), **Degas** and **Monet** are the ones to look out for. However, German artists predominate. *Goethe in the Roman Campagna* by **Johann Heinrich Tischbein** is the most celebrated of the many Romantic portrayals of the writer. The Nazarene Brotherhood figures strongly, notably with paintings by

Philip Veit, once director of the Städel. If this isn't to your taste, you might prefer the realism of **Wilhelm Leibl**, whose *Unlikely Couple* is an update of a favourite Renaissance theme – mercenary love.

Until the days of the Third Reich, the Städel had perhaps the finest array of modern painting in Germany. However, over five hundred paintings were removed in the measures against "degenerate art", and the collection has never recovered, although it now has the benefit of being able to display loans from local industrialists and financial institutions. German highlights include **Liebermann's** *Amsterdam Orphanage Courtyard*, **Beckmann's** *The Synagogue*, **Dix's** unflattering *The Artist's Family*, **Ernst's** spooky *Nature in Morning Light* and **Kirchner's** *Nude Wearing a Hat*; the most notable foreign paintings are **Matisse's** *Still Life* and **Picasso's** *Portrait of Fernance Olivier*. Some avant-garde works, including several huge canvases by **Anselm Kiefer**, are also on view.

The Liebieghaus

Last but by no means least of the museums is the **Liebieghaus** (same hours; DM5/€2.50, free Wed) at no. 71. The villa which houses it can easily be identified by the bits and pieces of statuary on display in the garden, including *Ariadne on the Panther* by Johann Heinrich Dannecker. The collection is a step-by-step guide to the history of sculpture, and as such is the most important in the country. Sumerian, Egyptian, Greek, Roman and Coptic examples give a comprehensive overview of the classical world. German works predictably predominate in the later periods; look out in particular for the late fifteenth- and early sixteenth-century golden period, featuring important carvings by Nicolaus Gerhaert, Hans Multscher and Tilman Riemenschneider. There's also an illuminating section on Baroque altarpieces.

Westend and Bockenheim

Frankfurt's financial district, the **Westend**, developed as home to the commercial class during the nineteenth century. Until the Nazis came to power, many of the wealthier members of Frankfurt's Jewish community (the second largest in Germany) lived here – for example huge swathes of land between Bockenheimer Landstrasse and Reuterweg were owned by the Rothschild family until the city bought them out in 1938, for a "bargain" price. In the 1960s the property speculators moved in, forcing people out of their homes so the old buildings could be converted into offices or the sites used for skyscrapers. A rash of house occupations and squattings ensued, but caused only temporary delays to the process of redevelopment. The most impressive of the high-rise buildings which now dominate the Frankfurt skyline are the sleek **Deutsche Bank**, a little to the west of the Alte Oper, and the graceful **Messeturm** by the German-American Helmut Jahn, which provides a suitably dominant landmark for the vast complex of trade fair buildings north of the Hauptbahnhof.

Westend has its own stretch of greenery along its northern fringe. Starting from the east, there's the **Grüneburgpark**, a nineteenth-century English-style park which these days is popular with joggers and weekend footballers. Next is the **Botanischer Garten**, a good place to go for a walk as it has a sort of cultivated wildness to it. At the western end of the green belt is the wonderful **Palmengarten** (daily: March & Oct 9am–5pm; April–Sept 9am–6pm; Nov–Feb 9am–4pm; DM7/€3.50), where it's easy enough to while away several hours. The subtropical palms which give the garden its name can be seen in the majestic Palmenhaus, which was erected in 1869, while a host of tropical plants are grouped according to region in the Tropicarum, a complex of interconnected greenhouses. However, the attractions are by no means all indoors: there are separate manicured gardens for roses, rhododendrons, summer flowers, hardy perennials, cacti, rock plants, heath plants and meadow plants. The water garden, with its colourful whirling jets, adds a welcome lighter note.

Bockenheimer Landstrasse, once Frankfurt's millionaires' row, leads from Westend to **Bockenheim**, a predominantly working-class district which since the 1960s has been turned into the centre of Frankfurt's alternative scene by a big influx of students and arty types. The area also has a large *Gastarbeiter* population and is best thought of as a Frankfurt version of Berlin's Kreuzberg. Leipziger Strasse is the main shopping drag (on U-Bahn line #6 and #7) and there are plenty of good bars and restaurants around (see pp.396 & 397).

The university complex is at the southeastern edge of Bockenheim, which partly accounts for its popularity with students. In the vicinity, at Senckenberganlage 25, is the **Senckenbergmuseum** (Mon, Tues, Thurs & Fri 9am–5pm, Wed 9am–8pm, Sat & Sun 9am–6pm; *www.senckenberg.uni-frankfurt.de*; DM7/€3.50), one of the most important natural history museums in Europe. On the ground floor is a remarkable paleontology collection with an awe-inspiring array of dinosaur skeletons, including the only reasonably complete example of the *Edmontosaurus* yet discovered. One room is devoted to some of the spectacular fossils discovered at the shale pit of Messel (see also p.406), whose excavation is in the hands of scientists from the museum's research institute. Another shows skeletons of animals, such as elephants, sabre-toothed tigers, hippopotamuses and rhinorceroses, which inhabited the Rhine-Main region half a million years ago. The section on human evolution features the oldest and best-preserved skeleton of *Australopithecus afarensis*, a proto-human which still has many characteristics of an ape. On the upstairs floors, compendious collections of stuffed animals, birds, fishes and insects can be seen.

Höchst

Nowadays a western suburb of Frankfurt, **HÖCHST**, which can be reached by S-Bahn line #1 or #2 from the Hauptbahnhof or Hauptwache, is an ancient town in its own right, as well as being the home of the famous Hoechst chemical company. Although very much in the shadow of the chemical works, the small Altstadt rewards a quick look round. The **Balongaropalast** at Balongarostr. 109 is a Baroque town-house in whose gardens open-air theatre performances are occasionally held. A little further down the same street, in the **Dalberghaus** (no. 186), Höchst porcelain is once again being manufactured. On Schlossplatz to the south there's a Renaissance **Schloss** and the old **Zollturm** (Customs Tower). The latter houses the **Heimatmuseum** (daily 10am–4pm; free), which, having been sponsored by Hoechst, tends to dwell on the history of that company. East of here is the **Justiniankirche**, by far the oldest church in the Frankfurt conurbation. It preserves its Carolingian nave intact, though the chancel was replaced in the Gothic period.

Bus #54 from the Altstadt goes down Höchster Farben Strasse and to your left you'll see the huge chemical complex that is the **Hoechstwerk** stretching out down to the Main. The cathedral-like administrative offices of the factory were designed by the Jugendstil architect Peter Behrens and must be among the most aesthetically balanced industrial buildings anywhere. From there, the bus continues on to Zeilsheim, which in the immediate postwar years was the black market centre of Germany and where, around Coburger Strasse, you can still see the little cottages of the **Arbeiterkolonie Zeilsheim**, a turn-of-the-century model housing development for Hoechst workers.

Eating, drinking and nightlife

Not surprisingly, given its status as one of Germany's main urban centres, Frankfurt has a wealth of gastronomic possibilities. Whether it's vegan breakfast, Japanese afternoon tea or a gourmet Italian dinner you're after, you'll be able to find it somewhere. As for drink, the city is situated close to several famous wine-producing regions, and is itself an important beer centre. Binding is among the largest breweries in the country, while Henninger is a major exporter, and both produce a wide range of products. However, the city's favourite beverage is apple wine (Apfelwein; known as *Ebbelwei* or *Ebbelwoi* in the local dialect), a cider variant best sampled in the specialist taverns in Sachsenhausen.

Apple-wine taverns

The **apple-wine tavern** (*Apfelweinwirtschaft*) is as distinctive a Frankfurt institution as the Bierkeller is of Munich, or the Weinstube of Stuttgart. And in addition to the apple wine, they invariably offer hearty local **cuisine**, usually at very moderate prices. Although nearly all the best-known establishments are concentrated in Sachsenhausen, others are dotted all over the city. They're strongly traditional, a fact reflected in the surprisingly restricted opening hours many choose to operate.

Adolf Wagner, Schweizer Str. 71. One of the best of the taverns, with a lively clientele ranging from young to middle-aged. Frequently packed out. Open daily from 11am.

Atschel, Wallstr. 7. This offers a more extensive menu than many of its counterparts, and has bargain set lunches. There's a garden at the back. Closed Mon.

Klaane Sachsehäuser, Neuer Wall 11. A family place favoured by native Sachsenhauseners which has been run since 1886 by five generations of the same family. Open from 4pm, closed Sun.

Zu den Drei Stuebern, Dreieichstr. 28. Mainly patronized by locals; has a small bar-room and pleasant terrace at the rear. Open weekdays only from 3.30pm.

Zum Eichkatzerl, Dreieichstr. 29. An excellent traditional tavern which is particularly popular on account of its low-priced food. Open from 3pm, closed Mon.

Zum Feuerrädchen, Textorstr. 24. One of several traditional taverns on the street. Open from 3pm on weekdays, 11am at weekends, closed Mon.

Zum Gemalten Haus, Schweizer Str. 67. A bit kitschy with its oil-painted facade and stained-glass windows, yet quite intimate and lively, with long rows of tables outside. Open Wed–Sun from 10am.

Zur Buchscheer, Schwarzsteinkautweg 7. Set amidst the rose gardens on the southeastern edge of Sachsenhausen and very popular with walkers. Good home cooking and home-produced apple wine. Open from 3pm on weekdays, from 11am at weekends. Take S-Bahn #3 or #4 to Louisa.

Zur Eulenburg, Eulengasse 46. This Bornheim tavern, which has a predominantly middle-aged clientele, can rival any in Sachsenhausen for both food and *Ebbelwei*. Open Wed–Sun from 4pm. Take U-Bahn #4 to Seckbacher Landstrasse.

Zur Germania, Textorstr. 16. Another of the recommendable taverns on this street; nearly always crowded. Open daily from 4pm.

Restaurants

Many of the restaurants in the city centre are fast-food joints or credit-card rip-offs for unwary lunching business people, but you will find some of the best Thai, Mexican,

---

APPLE WINE

There's a theory that Europe has a cider belt separating the areas producing wine and beer, and that Frankfurt is the hub of this. This seems tenuous at best, as the apple-wine tradition here is historically a relatively recent one, having started in 1750. Made by the same process used in the production of ordinary wine, apple wine is bought in a blue-grey stone jug called *Bembel* and drunk from a *Schobbeglas*. There are four types: *Süsser*, sweet and fresh from the presses in autumn, and relatively weak; *Rauscher*, which will blow your head off if you don't treat it with respect; *Heller*, which is clear and smooth; and the hazy and golden *Altar*. Those in the know order *Handkäs mit Musik* (cheese served with onions and vinaigrette) or *Rippchen mit Kraut* (smoked pork chop with *Sauerkraut*) as a culinary accompaniment to their *Ebbelwei*.

Greek and Italian food here too. Other districts with good concentrations of restaurants are Sachsenhausen, Westend, Bockenheim and Bornheim, the inner suburb due north of the Altstadt. When there's a trade fair on, advance bookings are virtually mandatory, and most restaurants are open on the day or days they're normally closed.

The centre

Aubergine, Alte Gasse 14. Good French food, good service, reasonable prices (by central Frankfurt standards). Open for both lunch and dinner during the week, evenings only on Sat, closed Sun.

Avocado-Le Bistro, Hochstr. 27. Fine bistro fare, complemented by a carefully selected wine list. Closed Sun.

Buffalo, Kaiserhofstr. 18. City-centre steakhouse, much favoured by the American community. Also does good enchiladas and tacos. Closed Sun.

Eckstein, An der Staufenmauer 7. Very formal and expensive restaurant serving high-class European cuisine.

Fisch-Franke, Domstr. 9. Offers fresh fish dishes, with a choice of waitress- or self-service. Closed Sun.

Haus Wertheym, Fahrtor 1. A medieval Gaststätte on the Römerberg with *Bockbier*, traditional food and a friendly atmosphere. Closed Tues.

Iwase, Vilbeler Str. 31. Reasonably priced Japanese, with seating at the counter or the few tables. Evenings only, closed Mon.

Lalibela, Klingerstr. 2. An Ethiopian restaurant where you eat the food with your fingers. Low prices and plenty of vegetarian options. Closed Mon.

Sawadi, Grosse Friedberger Str. 34. Probably the best Thai place in Frankfurt; very popular, so you're not encouraged to linger. It has a bargain lunchtime menu. Closed Mon.

Tiger, Heiligkreuzgasse 20 (☎0 69/92 00 22 25). The restaurant attached to the Tigerpalast variety theatre presents some of the most creative and expensive cooking in Frankfurt. Evenings only, closed Mon. Reservations advisable.

Tse-Yang, Kaiserstr. 67. Frankfurt's leading Chinese restaurant, located just a stone's throw from the Hauptbahnhof. The business lunches are especially good value.

Westend and Bockenheim

Al Arischa, Leipziger Str. 108. A small family-run Lebanese place serving lamb and vegetarian dishes at reasonable prices. Evenings only, closed Sun.

Ban Thai, Leipziger Str. 26. Good, reasonably priced Thai restaurant, which also has a cheap Imbiss section.

Bistro Rosa, Grüneburgweg 25. The walls hung with pictures of pigs lend an element of kitsch, but the food is excellent. Evenings only, closed Sun.

Erno's Bistro, Liebigstr. 15 (☎0 69/72 19 97). Sublime mix of French and German cuisine that regularly wins top awards in the international dining guides. Closed Sat & Sun. Expensive. It's best to book in advance.

Golfo di Napoli, Leipziger Str. 16. Pricey Italian, popular with the Westend yuppies, but the food and atmosphere are good. Closed Sun.

Isoletta, Feldbergstr. 31. One of the more affordable Italian restaurants, popular with the nearby ad-agency types during the day.

Knoblauch, Staufenstr. 39. Friendly, intimate little place where everything comes liberally laced with garlic. Closed Sat & Sun.

Stars und Starlet, Friedrich-Ebert-Anlage 49. Located in the basement of the Messeturm, this American-style restaurant has wonderful fantasy decor by the designer Jordan Mozer. The set lunches are marvellous value, though the service is snail-paced. Closed Sat lunchtime & Sun.

Bornheim

Mesón la Paella, Habsburger Allee 43. Serves all the classic Spanish dishes, along with a good selection of wines. Evenings only, except on Sun, when it's also open for lunch.

Nibelungenschänke, Nibelungenallee 55. Typical Greek food at reasonable prices. The clientele is young and the place is usually open until 1am. Take U-Bahn #5 to Nibelungenallee.

Wolkenbruch, Rotlintstr. 47. No-smoking vegetarian restaurant serving everything from tofu burgers to wholemeal pizzas.

Sachsenhausen

Bistrot 77, Ziegelhüttenweg 1–3 (☎0 69/61 40 40). French restaurant with strong lines in game and fish. Has an outstanding selection of French wines, including some from the family's own vineyard in Alsace. Closed Sun. Booking essential.

Maaschanz, Färberstr. 75 (☎0 69/62 28 86). Small, congenial restaurant specializing in French cuisine, notably fish dishes, at affordable prices. Evenings only, closed Mon. It's best to book ahead.

Taj Mahal, Schweizer Str. 28. Popular Pakistani-run restaurant which has won an award as the city's best curry house. If offers bargain lunch dishes on weekdays.

Bars, cafés and café-bars

Sachsenhausen, with its cobbled streets and lively atmosphere, has many modern alternatives to its famous apple-wine taverns. As home to a large student population, Bockenheim has plenty of youthful, inexpensive cafés. In the city centre, there are a few gems which are well worth seeking out in preference to the many overcrowded and overpriced alternatives.

The centre

Altes Café Schneider, Kaiserstr. 12. This traditional café is one of the best places in town for *Kaffee und Kuchen*.

Bar Central, Elefantengasse 11. A long-established pillar of the Frankfurt *Szene*. Happy hour 8–9pm, and good music at all times.

Club Voltaire, Kleine Hochstr. 5. An eclectic clientele: political activists, artists, musicians, Greens, gays – you'll find them all here in one of Frankfurt's best-established meeting places. Also serves good bistro-type food at moderate prices.

CybeRyder, Töngesgasse 31. Frankfurt's first Internet café. Open Mon–Thurs 10am–11pm, Fri & Sat 10am–1am, Sun 2–11pm.

Deelight, Holzgraben 9. One of a number of gay hangouts in the area.

Dominicus, Brückhofstr. 1. A vaulted cellar establishment which draws a young crowd, particularly when there's live music on. Evenings only, closed Sun.

Helium, Bleidenstr. 7. Trendy bar which stays open late and serves night-time snacks. Daily 11am–4am.

Vinum, Kleine Hochstr. 9. Traditional cellar bar, serving some food, but it's expensive. Gets crowded, so arrive early to secure a table. Evenings only, closed Sun.

Volkswirt, Kleine Hochstr. 9. Located directly above *Vinum*, this has a pleasant summer garden at the front.

Zu den Zwölf Aposteln, Rosenberger Str. 1. Frankfurt's first Hausbrauerei, producing organically brewed light and dark beers. The ground-floor restaurant serves Balkan cuisine.

Zum Schwejk, Schäfergasse 20. This relaxed and unpretentious place offers a good way into the Frankfurt gay scene.

Westend and Bockenheim

Café au Lait, Am Weingarten 12. Among Bockenheim's trendiest meeting places, with a great selection for breakfast.

Laumer, Bockenheimer Landstr. 67. One of Frankfurt's oldest cafés, halfway up the Westend's main thoroughfare, now enjoying a new lease of life with a young arty clientele.

Plazz, Kirchplatz 8. Fun café offering a full repertoire of international breakfasts, including German, French, Italian and Russian. Attracts a mixed crowd.

Stattcafé, Grempstr. 21. Another place which does good breakfast. The emphasis is on healthy eating in an informal atmosphere – popular with the Bockenheim arty crowd. A real focal point, with work from Frankfurt artists on the walls.

Bornheim

Gegenwart, Bergerstr. 6. Spacious and very trendy hangout whose walls are a forum for avant-garde art. Serves the best coffee in town and imaginative breakfasts, lunches and dinners.

Harvey's, Bornheimer Landstr. 64. Slick, high-ceilinged colonnaded bar which in the evening hosts a mainly gay and lesbian crowd. Excellent breakfasts and daily specials.

Sachsenhausen

An Sibin, Wallstr. 9. One of Frankfurt's main Irish bars, popular with local expats and with Kilkenny, Guinness and Murphys on tap. Live music at weekends.

Irish Pub, Kleine Rittergasse 11–13. Frankfurt's original Irish pub, established in 1971 and still one of the best in the country, with regular live music sessions.

Lesecafé, Diesterwegstr. 7. Popular with would-be intellectuals, the gimmick here is that you read as you eat and drink. You can select a book from the neighbouring bookshop – or just admire the art on the walls.

Schwarzes Café, Schweizer Str. 14. This café has a distinctive black and mirrored decor which attracts a very hip clientele. Closed Sat lunchtime & Sun.

Sugar Hill, Frankensteiner Platz 25. Trendy bar with a wide choice of cocktails.

Tannenbaum, Brückenstr. 19. Friendly English pub-style place with beer garden and tasty food.

Zum Jodler, Klappergasse 14. Czech speciality place with *Budweiser Budvar* (the original) on tap. Evenings only.

Discos, nightclubs and live music

Not surprisingly Frankfurt's nightlife is pretty eclectic, and there's a wide range of live music on offer. The local disco scene is heavily dance music-oriented, with most venues serving up house/techno beats for predominantly young crowds. Places tend to stay open until 4am during the week and 5am or 6am at weekends. Entry starts at about DM10/€5. For details of events, the best magazines are *Prinz* (DM2/€1) and *Journal Frankfurt* (DM3.50/€1.75). Free magazines such as *Fritz* and *Strandgut*, which also cover other towns in central Hesse, are also useful.

Venues

Batschkapp, Maybachstr. 24. Live music or fairly up-to-the-minute DJ dance sounds. Daily 9pm–1am. Take S-Bahn #6 to Eschersheim.

Blue Angel, Brönnerstr. 17. Popular gay men's dance bar. Open daily from 11pm.

Brotfabrik, Bachmannstr. 2–4. One of the most innovative venues in the city, featuring live and disco music from all over the world, with salsa, African and Asian sounds particularly featured. Also has a café and a Spanish restaurant. Take U-Bahn #6 to Fischstein or U-Bahn #7 to Grosse Nelkenstrasse.

Cooky's, Am Salzhaus 4. Frankfurt's best-known and most popular disco. Dance music and chart stuff draws in a youthful crowd. On Mon there are usually live bands. Daily 10pm–4am, 6am on Fri & Sat.

Dorian Gray, Flughafen Terminal 1, Abschnitt C. Oddly located at the airport, one of the largest discos in Germany, and not always so easy to get into. Open Wed–Sun until 6am.

Jazzhaus, Kleine Bockenheimer Str. 12. Half-timbered house on Frankfurt's *Jazzgasse* (Jazz Alley), where many leading jazzers cut their musical teeth.

Jazzkeller, Kleine Bockenheimer Str. 18. Atmospheric cellar which is Frankfurt's premier jazz venue. Open 9pm–3am, closed Mon.

Sinkkasten, Brönnerstr. 5. This place has everything – pool room, cabaret stage, disco and, most importantly, a concert hall where they put on everything from jazz to avant-garde and indie stuff. Daily 9pm–2am.

The Cave, Brönnerstr. 11. Disco and live music club.

Culture

Frankfurt has a predictably lively performing-arts scene, with a wide range of choice in both music and theatre, and an established tradition of productions in English.

Venues

Alte Oper, Opernplatz (☎0 69/1 34 04 00). There are three halls here, of which the largest is used for orchestral concerts (the Radio-Sinfonie-Orchester-Frankfurt is the pick of the local bands), while the other two host chamber, instrumental and vocal recitals.

English Theater, Kaiserstr. 52 (☎0 69/24 23 16 20). Flourishing company which performs only in English.

Gallus-Theater, Kleyerstr. 15 (☎0 69/75 80 60 20). *Gastarbeiter* theatre which is arguably the most distinguished cultural institution of the immigrant community in the whole of Germany.

Jahrhunderthalle, Pfaffenwiese, Höchst (☎0 69/3 60 12 40, *www.jahrhunderthalle.de*). Modern concert hall offering similar fare to the Alte Oper.

Oper, Willy-Brandt-Platz (☎0 69/1 34 04 00, *www.frankfurt-oper.de*). Presents top-class performances of opera and ballet. The latter company has been directed since 1984 by the American choreographer William Forsythe, and has an unashamedly avant-garde repertoire.

Schauspielhaus, Willy-Brandt-Platz (☎0 69/21 23 79 99). The main civic theatre, offering drama old and new.

Die Schmiere, Seckbächer Gasse 2 (☎0 69/28 10 66). Satirical cabaret, housed in the Karmeliterkloster.

Theater am Turm, Eschenheimer Landstr. 2 (☎0 69/21 23 72 88). The Schauspielhaus's experimental offshoot.

Tigerpalast, Heiligkreuzgasse 16–20 (☎0 69/9 20 02 20, *www.tigerpalast.com*). The place to come for good old-fashioned variety shows, which are making something of a comeback in Germany.

Volkstheater, Grosser Hirschgraben 21 (☎0 69/28 85 98). Presents performances in the local dialect.

Listings

Airlines Air Canada, at the airport (☎0 69/2 71 51 11); British Airways, at the airport (☎0 18 03/25 06 30); Lufthansa, Am Hauptbahnhof 2 (☎0 69/2 55 45 11); Qantas, at the airport (☎0 18 03/34 03 40).

Bike rental Per Pedale, Leipziger Str. 4 (☎0 69/70 76 91 10).

Book Fair Held annually in Sept/Oct at the Messe Frankfurt to the northwest of the Hauptbahnhof, this is the largest book fair in the world. On the last day you can often pick up great bargains from the English and American stalls.

Bookstore British Bookshop, Börsenstr. 17 (☎0 69/28 04 92).

Car rental Avis, Mörfelder Landstr. 92 (☎0 69/61 07 07); Europcar, Hanauer Landstr. 334 (☎0 69/9 42 15 60); Hertz, Gutleutstr. 87 (☎0 69/24 25 26 27); Sixt, Allterheiligenstr. 52 (☎0 69/29 00 66). All the big companies, and some smaller ones, also have offices at the airport.

Consulates Australian, Gutleutstr. 85 (☎0 69/2 73 90 90); British, Bockenheimer Landstr. 42 (☎0 69/1 70 00 20); US, Siesmayerstr. 21 (☎0 69/7 53 50).

Cultural institute Amerika-Haus, Staufenstr. 1 (☎0 69/97 14 48 20).

Doctor ☎0 69/1 92 42.

Festivals Main folklore events are the *Waldchestag* at Whit weekend and the *Mainfest* in early August.

Mitfahrzentralen ADM, Baseler Str. 7 (☎0 69/1 94 40); Citynetz, Homburger Str. 36 (☎0 69/1 94 44).

Pharmacy Call ☎0 69/1 92 92 for details of late-opening pharmacies.

Post offices The main post office with poste restante is at Goetheplatz 2–4 (Mon–Fri 9.30am–8pm, Sat 9.30am–4pm); the longest hours are kept by the branch on the first floor of the Hauptbahnhof (Mon–Fri 6.30am–9pm, Sat & Sun 11am–6pm).

Women's centre Am Weingarten 25 (☎0 69/70 85 28).

Zoo Alfred-Brehm-Platz 16 (daily 8am–5/7pm; DM11/€5.50, kids DM5/€2.50). Take U-Bahn #6 or #7.

SOUTHERN HESSE

The southern part of Hesse includes the wooded heights of the **Odenwald** at the extreme tip of the province and the famous vine-growing **Rheingau** on the east bank of the Rhine. Although there are several outstanding small towns in the area, there are only two cities: the staid spa of **Wiesbaden** and the former ducal residence of **Darmstadt**, which is a place with more than a few surprises in store.

Darmstadt

A cursory inspection of **DARMSTADT**, some 30km south of Frankfurt, at the end of S-Bahn line #3, is unlikely to leave you with much of an impression. The only way it differs from any other prosperous German city rebuilt after the war is in the survival of the planned Neoclassical layout, with broad streets and spacious squares. Don't be discouraged, though; Darmstadt has a rich cultural heritage, traces of which have survived both the bombs and the planners.

During the second half of the eighteenth century the *Darmstädter Kreis* (Darmstadt Circle) flourished under the protection of Landgravine Karoline, numbering among its members Goethe, Martin Wieland and Johann Herder. The playwright Georg Büchner spent much of his short life in the city and wrote his great drama *Danton's Death* here in 1834, while under police observation for suspected revolutionary activities. It was at the turn of the last century, however, that the arts flourished most freely in Darmstadt when Grand Duke Ernst Ludwig (a grandson of Queen Victoria) supported the first and finest flowering of **Jugendstil**, the German form of Art Nouveau. The surviving monuments of this period are the most lasting and visible symbol of the city's support for artistic innovation.

Arrival, information and accommodation

If you arrive at the **Hauptbahnhof**, which is about 1km west of the city centre, you'll immediately get your first taste of the local Jugendstil heritage, as the station was a key part of the style's second phase in the second decade of the century. In a pavilion immediately outside is the **tourist office** (Mon–Fri 9am–6pm, Sat 10am–1pm; ☎0 61 51/13 27 82, fax 13 27 83, *www.darmstadt.de*). The **Darmstadt Card**, which costs DM9/€4.50 for one day, DM15/€7.50 for two days, covers all local **public transport** costs, and gives reduced entry to the museums and sights.

As for accommodation, the cheapest **hotels** are out in the suburbs, while the city centre has plenty of mid- and upper-range options. Darmstadt's **youth hostel** is at Landgraf-Georg-Str. 119 (☎0 61 51/4 52 93, fax 42 25 35, *Darmstadt@djh-hessen.de*; DM24/€12 or DM29/€14.50), right beside the open-air swimming pool at the Grosser Woog lake and also handily placed for visiting the Jugendstil buildings on Mathildenhöhe.

Hotels

Bockshaut, Kirchstr. 7–9 (☎0 61 51/9 96 70, fax 99 67 29). Good old-fashioned German inn with a convenient position in the very heart of the city. In summer, its restaurant offers alfresco eating in the inner courtyard. ④–⑤.

Hornung, Mornewegstr. 43 (☎0 61 51/92 66, fax 89 18 92). Located a couple of minutes' walk from the Hauptbahnhof, on the way to the city centre. ④.

Jagdschloss Kranichstein, Kranichsteiner Str. 261, Kranichstein (☎0 61 51/9 77 90, fax 97 79 20). Luxury hotel situated in the outbuildings of a Renaissance hunting lodge at the northeastern edge of Darmstadt. It has a daytime café-restaurant, *Kavaliersbau*, and a gourmet evening restaurant, *Der Grill*. ⑧–⑨.

Mathildenhöhe, Spessartring 53 (☎0 61 51/4 80 46, fax 49 84 50). This hotel is on the eastern side of the eponymous hill, ideally placed for visiting the city's Jugendstil heritage. ⑥.

Prinz Heinrich, Bleichstr. 48 (☎0 61 51/8 13 70, fax 81 37 13). On the western edge of the centre, with tasteful furnishings and a high-quality restaurant. ⑥.

Tonini, Frankfurter Landstr. 152, Arheilgen (☎0 61 51/37 10 51, fax 37 52 07). Budget hotel run in conjunction with a pizzeria in the far north of the city, directly opposite the terminus of trams #6, #7 and #8. ④.

Waldfriede, Friedrich-Naumann-Str. 8, Eberstadt (☎0 61 51/5 26 19, fax 5 34 81). Occupies a large old villa in the northern part of an incorporated town which lies due south of Darmstadt proper. Take tram #1, #6, #7 or #8. ⑤.

Weinmichel, Schleiermacherstr. 10–12 (☎0 61 51/6 04 04 44, fax 2 35 92). One of the best of the upmarket places and an adjunct to a celebrated wine restaurant. ⑧.

Weisser Schwan, Frankfurter Landstr. 190, Arheilgen (☎0 61 51/37 17 02, fax 37 78 84). Archetypal German hotel and restaurant in a northern suburb, only a few minutes' walk from either the S-Bahn station or the terminus of trams #6, #7 and #8. It's one of the few places in the city with reasonably priced single rooms. ④–⑤.

Zentral, Schuhardstr. 6 (☎0 61 51/2 64 11, fax 2 68 58). As central as its name suggests, located on a pedestrianized shopping street just off the east side of Luisenplatz. ④.

The City

Between 1567 and 1918, the city was capital of Hesse-Darmstadt, a Landgravate which was promoted to a Grand Duchy, with control over a large chunk of the Rhineland, during the Napoleonic period. The subsequent flurry of building activity to create a worthy capital meant that Darmstadt had its fair share of grand streets and squares, but most were destroyed on the night of September 11, 1944 when it was hit by 300,000 incendiary bombs and 700 high-explosive bombs. The resulting fire-storm, deliberately created following the tried and tested Hamburg pattern, killed 12,000 people. Darmstadt made a remarkably quick recovery, particularly in the cultural arena, but most of its historic quarter was gone forever.

The centre
At the centre of modern Darmstadt sprawls **Luisenplatz**, a windswept shopping plaza crisscrossed by tram and bus lines and notable only for the **Ludwigsmonument** (April–Sept first Sat of month 10am–4pm; DM2/€1) or Der Lange Lui, a 33-metre-high column crowned by a statue of Grand Duke Ludwig I. From here, Rheinstrasse leads east to Ernst-Ludwig-Platz, on which stands the **Weisser Turm** (April–Oct Wed 4–8pm, Sat 11am–6pm; DM2/€1), a fifteenth-century defensive tower which was later restyled in fashionable Baroque. Beyond is the spacious triangular Marktplatz, on whose southern side stands the gabled Renaissance **Rathaus**. Round the corner, the much-altered fourteenth-century **Stadtkirche** is mainly of note for the colossal Renaissance funerary monument to Landgrave Georg I and his wife Magdalena zur Lippe.

On the north side of Marktplatz is the **Schloss**, an extensive complex which developed gradually over seven hundred years. Reduced to a shell in the 1944 bombing raid, it has been diligently restored. The Baroque Neuschloss houses a library and the town archive, while the predominantly Renaissance Altschloss is home to a technical university and the **Schlossmuseum** (guided tours Mon–Thurs 10am–1pm & 2–5pm, Sat & Sun 10am–1pm; DM3.50/€1.75). Basically this is a typical example of the dreaded German *Heimatmuseum*, but it's redeemed by **Hans Holbein the Younger**'s *Madonna of Jacob Meyer*, painted in 1526, one of the supreme masterpieces of Renaissance painting. It's particularly intriguing in being the last Catholic altarpiece by any of the great German masters of the period, all of whom (including Holbein himself) became Protestant. The picture shows the former Burgomaster of Basel, accompanied by his living and deceased wives, asking the Virgin to intercede on behalf of his sickly baby son, whose features – bizarrely – duplicate those of the Christ Child.

The Hessisches Landesmuseum
Slightly to the north of the Schloss is the **Hessisches Landesmuseum** (Tues–Sat 10am–5pm, Wed also 7–9pm, Sun 11am–5pm; DM5/€2.50, free after 4pm), one of the best general museums in the country. Though there's a small **archeology** section, featuring an impressive Roman floor mosaic and jewellery from Frankish graves, most of the ground floor is given over to **applied art**. The medieval section is outstanding, highlights being a beautiful pair of tenth- or eleventh-century brooches found under the Dom in Mainz, and several masterly twelfth-century reliquaries from Cologne, including the domed *Darmstädter Kuppelreliquar*. In the basement, there's a glittering array of stained glass, notably a complete cycle from the Ritterstiftskirche in Bad Wimpfen, and a fragmentary ninth-century *Head of a Saint* from Kloster Lorsch. There's also an excellent Art Nouveau/Jugendstil section which sets Darmstadt's contribution in an international perspective. The first floor is devoted to **natural history**, and is dominated by a display of fossils found at the redundant open-cast shale pit at Messel in the outskirts of the city (see p.406).

However, the Landesmuseum's main claim to fame is as a picture gallery. In the ground floor's east wing is an outstanding collection of German Primitives, going back as far as a mid-thirteenth-century altar-table from Worms. **Lochner**'s gorgeous *Presentation in the Temple* shows the Cologne School at its mid-fifteenth-century peak, while the **Master of St Bartholomew**'s *Madonna and Child with SS Adrian and*

Augustine belongs to the final flowering of this movement a couple of generations later. Middle Rhenish painters closely followed Cologne's lead, and two of the finest products of this region are the works from which the **Master of the Ortenberg Altar** and the **Master of the Darmstadt Passion** derive their names. Several pictures by **Cranach** dominate the Renaissance section, including one of his greatest canvases, *Cardinal Albrecht von Brandenburg as St Jerome*.

Among the old masters on the second floor, the most important is the enigmatic *Magpie on the Gallows*, one of **Pieter Bruegel the Elder'**s last works. The evil-looking contraption for public executions strikes a menacingly discordant note in the sunny landscape, which forms the backdrop to a peasant dance. Highlights from the seventeenth century include pieces by Rubens, Domenichino and Domenico Feti, and a touching *Lamentation over the Dead Christ* by **Mathieu Le Nain**.

A number of canvases by the Swiss **Arnold Böcklin** dominate the Romantic section, which also includes *Iphigenia*, one of **Feuerbach'**s finest works. The rest of the floor is designated the **Beuys-Block** and contains some 300 works by the iconoclastic sculptor **Joseph Beuys**, the largest collection of his work in existence. The German avant-garde gets precedence in the galleries of the new extension, though many of the country's best-known twentieth-century artists, such as Corinth, Kirchner, Beckmann and Dix, are also represented.

The Herrngarten

Just behind the Landesmuseum is the **Herrngarten**, a spacious English-style park which contains the tomb of Landgravine Karoline and a Jugendstil monument to Goethe. At the northeastern end is the **Prinz-Georgs-Garten**, a formal Rococo garden. Its pavilion, the Prinz-Georg-Palais, houses the **Grossherzogliche Porzellansammlung** (Mon–Thurs 10am–1pm & 2–5pm, Sat & Sun 10am–1pm; DM5/€2.50), an extensive porcelain museum featuring examples from the local Kelsterbach factory and other leading German centres, and major pieces from England and Russia.

Mathildenhöhe

Mathildenhöhe, a unique artists' colony on the eastern edge of the city centre, is a living monument to Jugendstil. It's only a fifteen-minute walk along Erich-Ollenhauer-Promenade from just behind the Schloss; alternatively, take bus #F to Lucasweg. At the centre of the complex stands a building which fits in well with the Jugendstil buildings but pre-dates the colony itself – the **Russische Kapelle** (daily: April–Sept 9am–6pm; Oct–March 9.30am–5pm; DM1.50/€0.75). This heavily ornamented Russian Orthodox chapel crowned by two gilded domes was built in 1898 at the behest of the last czar of Russia, Nicholas II, who often spent the summer in Darmstadt with his Hessian wife. Serbian Orthodox services are regularly held here for Darmstadt's Balkan community.

Work on the Mathildenhöhe colony began in 1901 with the construction of the **Ernst-Ludwig-Haus**, designed by the Viennese architect Joseph Maria Olbrich for the *Dokument Deutscher Kunst 1901*, an exhibition whose aim was to encapsulate all aspects of the Jugendstil movement. Approached via a broad flight of steps, the building has something of the mausoleum about it, with its imposing portal flanked by monumental figures of Adam and Eve carved by Ludwig Habig. The **Museum Künstlerkolonie Darmstadt** (Tues–Sun 10am–5pm; DM5/€2.50) now occupies the interior, showing products made by the colony – ranging from stained-glass windows to furniture, jewellery, silverware and porcelain. These are grouped in sections corresponding to the four great exhibitions held during the life of the colony.

To complement the Ernst-Ludwig-Haus, Olbrich built seven houses as artists' residences immediately below on Alexandraweg and Mathildenhöhweg, also in 1901. Five survive in reasonably authentic shape: they vary in style and they all have unique and intricate design features which differentiate them from each other. Directly below the Ernst-Ludwig-Haus is the **Haus Olbrich**, a villa with a slightly subverted appearance where the architect spent the last years of his life. Directly facing it is the **Haus Habich**, which is almost Cubist in style, while further south is the smallest of the group, **Haus Deiters**, a striking reinterpretation of the English cottage style. Immediately west of Haus Habich are the **Kleines Glückerthaus**, which has an angular southern European look, and the **Grosses Glückerthaus**, which best represents the ethos of the original project. Next door to the latter is the **Haus Behrens**, designed by the Hamburg architect Peter Behrens, also in 1901. Its brick-framed white facade and red-tiled roof inject an element of Hanseatic sobriety into the colony, in deliberate contrast with Olbrich's more playful Mediterranean efforts. Only the door, decorated with swirling bronze appliqué work and flanked by rippling turquoise columns, has much in common with the neighbouring houses. Unfortunately, opportunities for viewing any of the interiors are far more limited than they were a few years ago. However, in the summer, on the first Sunday of each month, there are usually **guided tours** of the colony which include access to Haus Deiters and/or the Grosses Glückerthaus; ask at the tourist office or the Museum Künstlerkolonie Darmstadt for the latest details.

In 1908 work on the huge and gleaming **Austellungsgebäude** (Exhibition Hall; Tues–Sun 10am–6pm; variable entrance charge) at the top of Mathildenhöhe was completed. It's still in use, and the first-floor café is equipped with Jugendstil furnishings. Look out for the Olbrich-designed mosaic in the roof of the pavilion halfway up the entrance steps. Next to the Austellungsgebäude rises the **Hochzeitsturm** (Wedding Tower; March–Oct Tues–Sun 10am–6pm; DM3/€1.50) a 48-metre-high brick tower with a distinctive roof which, when seen head-on, looks like a hand facing palm outwards. It was presented to Grand Duke Ernst Ludwig and his bride by the city three years after their 1905 wedding and has become so popular that it's now Darmstadt's official emblem. A lift takes visitors to the top, though it's worth walking back down in order to glance into the two ornate reception rooms in the tower.

To the west is the **Platanenhain**, a formal garden of clipped plane trees first laid out in the 1830s, though its present appearance is a legacy of the colony's last exhibition in 1914, when it was adorned with symbolical sculptures and reliefs of the stages of life by Bernhard Hoetger. For the same exhibition, Albin Müller, who had taken over the leadership of the colony on Olbrich's death in 1908, designed the **Lilienbecken**, the fountain and basin immediately south of the Platanenhain, as well as the **Schwanentempel**, a garden pavilion beside the Russische Kapelle.

Rosenhöhe

Because most of the Mathildenhöhe buildings are now used by various design institutes and cultural organizations, Darmstadt's practising artists have moved to the nearby **Rosenhöhe** area. This is reached in about ten minutes from the Haus Olbrich by following Alexandraweg, turning right into Fiedlerweg, left into Seitersweg and then crossing the rail bridge. During the late 1960s a new artists' colony was established here in the **Rosenhöhe-Park**, whose original purpose was to provide a last resting-place for members of the ruling family of Hesse-Darmstadt. At the entrance to the park is the **Löwentor**, a gate comprising six Jugendstil lions standing on top of decorative brick pillars. Nearby is the **Ostbahnhof**, built in the style of a Russian country station at the request of Czar Nicholas II.

Jagdschloss Kranichstein

Set in its own extensive landscaped park in the northeast of the city, and served by regular buses, is **Jagdschloss Kranichstein** (April–Oct Wed–Sat 1–6pm, Sun 10am–6pm; Nov–March Wed–Sat 2–5pm, Sun 10am–5pm; DM5/€2.50), the former hunting lodge of the landgraves and grand dukes of Hesse-Darmstadt. Built in Renaissance style in the 1570s, it's one of few such structures of the era to have survived in reasonable condition, and has recently reopened following a decade-long restoration programme. The ground floor is laid out as a museum of the history of hunting from prehistoric times to the present day, and features a valuable collection of eighteenth-century air-guns. Upstairs, the chambers contain trophies, furnishings, tapestries and paintings, principally from the Baroque period, when the Jagdschloss was regularly used for courtly hunts and banquets.

Eating, drinking and nightlife

Darmstadt's nightlife is somewhat fragmented. Many of the best **restaurants** are in the hotels (see p.401), while there's also a good cluster of places to eat and drink just west of the Herrngarten. Most of the **Apfelwein** places are around the same park; this area is where many of the students live, and makes a good starting point for a pub crawl. There's also a wide range of **music** and **theatre** venues.

Restaurants

Alt-Hamburg, Landgraf-Georg-Str. 17. Cosy little restaurant specializing in game, fish and seafood. Closed Mon.

Braustüb'l, Goebelstr. 7–10. Offering a good range of local fare, this is the restaurant of the Darmstädter brewery, located right alongside, which makes no fewer than ten different styles of beer.

Las Palmas, Dieburger Str. 22. Good, inexpensive Spanish restaurant; also serves German food.

Lokales, Dieburger Str. 50. Specializes in inexpensive, mouth-watering Italian pizzas.

Oberwaldhaus, Dieburger Str. 257. This picturesque large house in the woods at the eastern edge of the city might have come straight out of a German fairy-tale. A popular weekend excursion destination, it offers a moderately priced menu of German and Balkan dishes and has a large beer garden. Take bus #F.

Orangerie, Bessunger Str. 44. One of Darmstadt's best restaurants, in a fine eighteenth-century park 1.5km south of Luisenplatz. Closed Mon.

Ratskeller, Marktplatz 8. Located on the ground floor of the Rathaus, rather than the usual cellars. It has its own Hausbrauerei, which makes light, dark and *Weizen* beers, plus a seasonal *Bock*.

Sitte, Karlstr. 15. The main Gaststätte of the local Pfungstädter brewery.

Bars and café-bars

Bembelsche, Irenenstr. 1. One of several apple wine taverns, in this case with a small front garden.

Café Chaos, Mühlstr. 36. Popular café-bar which also serves good pizzas and light meals.

Grohe, Nieder-Ramstädter Str. 1. Small Kneipe with beer garden alongside the tiny brewery of the same name, which makes a *Vollbier* and a *Bock*.

Pfungstädter Biergarten, Dieburger Str. 97. Beer garden worth checking out if the weather is good.

Petri, Ahrheilger Str. 50. Favourite haunt of hip youngsters, complete with beer garden. Evenings only.

Rem, Beckerstr. 22. Best place in town for exotic cocktails.

Sumpf, Kasinostr. 105. Studenty pub which does fairly cheap snacks. Daily from 8pm.

Live music pubs, clubs and discos

Eledil, Adelungstr. 9. Serves heavy-duty wholefood meals and features live music and discos.

Goldene Krone, Schustergasse 18. An amazing warren of a place, with several bars, games rooms and stages presenting live acts ranging from cabaret to various kinds of music. Entry is DM5/€2.50.

Jagdhofkeller, Bessunger Str. 84. Jazz bar featuring live sessions Wed–Sun at 9pm.

Kulturcafé, Hermannstr. 7. Vegetarian café featuring occasional theatre or live music.

Studentenkeller, Im Schlosshof. Enduringly popular student meeting-place, situated in the Schloss courtyard. Open daily from 9pm.

Tanzclub Huckebein, Heidelberger Str. 89a. Currently the city's hippest disco.

Culture

The main venue for **drama**, **opera** and formal **concerts** is the Hessisches Staatstheater on Georg-Büchner-Platz (☎0 61 51/2 81 12 11), which maintains Darmstadt's reputation for artistic innovation with three-quarters of its performances per season likely to be new productions. **Cabaret** is performed at halbNeun-Theater, Sandstr. 32 (☎0 61 51/2 33 30), and Tap, Bessunger Str. 125 (☎0 61 51/3 35 55), while adult **puppet** shows feature at Kikeriki, Heidelberger Str. 131 (☎0 61 51/96 42 66). Local **festivals** include the *Frühlingfest* in March or April, the *Heinerfest* for five days in early July and the *Herbstfest* in late September.

The Odenwald region

The **Odenwald** is a large upland forest area – which is designated as the *Naturpark Bergstrasse-Odenwald* – occupying almost all of the southernmost part of Hesse and stretching into both Bavaria and Baden-Württemberg. On its westernmost fringe is the misleadingly named **Bergstrasse** (Mountain Road): nowadays it's a tourist route running from Darmstadt to Heidelberg, but to the Romans – who called it the Strata Montana – it was a major military road. During the Middle Ages it developed as a trading route, and numerous castles sprang up along it to protect the merchants from outlaws lurking in the marshland around the Rhine. These days the area is known primarily for the fact that spring starts here earlier than anywhere else in Germany, and the best time to visit is in late March or early April, when the fruit trees that line it all suddenly come into bloom. Further east, the hilly countryside of the heart of the Odenwald, which is served by a branch rail line from Darmstadt, is punctuated by postcard-pretty half-timbered towns where traditional craft industries continue to flourish. At the northern edge of the Odenwald region, practically on Darmstadt's doorstep, is one of the most scientifically significant sites in the whole of Germany.

Messel

MESSEL, which likes to style itself the "Pompeii of Paleontology" lies just 3km east of Jagdschloss Kranichstein, on the Darmstadt–Aschaffenburg rail line. It's a village in two distinct parts, separated by an area of open countryside: to the north, Messel proper is a sleepy half-timbered village absolutely typical of rural Hesse, while **Grube Messel**, the area around the Bahnhof, grew up as an adjunct to the huge redundant **shale pit** – which measures 1km by 700m and is 70m deep – from which it takes its name. In 1900, just sixteen years after mining began, the pit was already responsible for 40 percent of Germany's crude oil. Together with the on-site carbonization furnaces, which produced petrol, diesel, highly refined paraffin and pure carbon used in paint manufacture, it remained an important industrial enterprise until it gradually succumbed to competition from petroleum mining. The furnaces were shut down in 1962; mining ended nine years later, though the vast slag heap continues to be used for making tennis courts and cinder running tracks.

Fossils from the Eocene period of 49 million years ago, when the pit was a lake surrounded by a tropical forest, were first discovered around the time that mining began. However, it is only since the site lost its industrial function that systematic scientific excavations have been undertaken. The fossils, which are extraordinarily well preserved, are of particular interest for showing animals at an early stage in their evolutionary process. Some, notably the horses, hardly resemble their modern-day counterparts, being no bigger than large dogs; others, such as the bats and crocodiles, are far more obvious ancestors. Such is the importance of the findings that the pit has gained inclusion on UNESCO's World Heritage List – the only natural wonder in Germany to be so honoured. Excavation work is still ongoing, and a grandstand view of this, and the pit itself, can be had from the **observation platform**, which is freely accessible at all times and reached by going 1km southwards along the main road from the Bahnhof, turning left down the signposted side road, then following the marked footpath. The only way the public can actually enter the pit is by booking one of the **guided tours** run by the Museumsverein Messel, Kohlweg 15 (☎0 61 59/2 56) well in advance.

Some of the fossils excavated at Messel are displayed in the Hessisches Landesmuseum in Darmstadt, the Senckenbergmuseum in Frankfurt and the Museum am Friedrichsplatz in Karlsruhe. Others can be seen in a half-timbered former school building in the centre of the village at Langgasse 2; which is now designated the **Fossilien- und Heimatmuseum** (May–Oct Tues–Sat 2–5pm, Sun 10am–noon & 2–4pm; Nov–April Sat 2–4pm, Sun 10am–noon & 2–4pm; *www.messel.de*; free).

Along the Bergstrasse

Although the Bergstrasse is best explored by car, it's easy enough to follow it by public transport, with most places lying on a rail line, and buses filling the gaps. In any case, the towns along the Hessian part of the route virtually run into one another, and are never more than a few kilometres apart. If pressed for time, the monastery at **Lorsch** and the palaces at **Auerbach** are the undoubted highlights.

Auerbach and Bensheim

First up is the little health resort of **AUERBACH**, now officially incorporated into the much larger town of **BENSHEIM**, which has a typical half-timbered centre. Set high above Auerbach, and reachable by road or by a winding footpath up the wooded slopes, is a thirteenth-century **Schloss** (Tues–Sun 10am–6pm or dusk; free). This was blown up by the French in the seventeenth century but remains an impressive ruin, the setting throughout the summer for open-air concerts and mock-medieval tournaments. Immediately to the south is the **Fürstenlager**, a beautiful English-style landscaped park planted with exotic trees, including Europe's oldest giant sequoia. Although most of the whimsical garden pavilions have not survived, the palatial eighteenth-century buildings which served as summer retreats for members of the Hesse-Darmstadt court can still be seen. One of these, the guesthouse or **Fremdenbau** (Mon–Fri 2–5pm, Sat & Sun 10am–5pm; DM2/€1), houses an exhibition on the park's history.

The Fremdenbau also has an information centre, but the main local **tourist office** (Mon–Fri 9am–noon & 2–5pm, Sat 10am–noon; ☎0 62 51/1 41 17, fax 1 41 23, *www .bensheim.de*) is at Rodensteinstr. 19 near Bensheim's Bahnhof. If you've the money to spare, Auerbach makes a wonderful overnight stop, as it has a couple of top-notch **hotels**: *Poststuben*, Schloss-Str. 28–30 (☎0 62 51/7 29 87; ⑤), and *Parkhotel Herrenhaus* (☎0 62 51/7 09 00, *www.parkhotel-herrenhaus.com*; ⑦) in the Fürstenlager's main building. Both of these have classy **restaurants**, though they face strong competition from *Burggraf-Bräu*, Darmstädter Str. 231, which offers a varied menu including plenty of vegetarian specialities, and also has a Hausbrauerei, brewing a *Pils*, a *Märzen*, a *Hefeweizen* and its own speciality, known as *Bensemer*.

Lorsch

From Bensheim, the Bergstrasse takes a short detour west to **LORSCH**, which lies on a small branch rail line linking the two parallel main lines between Frankfurt and Mannheim. Once again, the centre is half-timbered, but everything is completely overshadowed by the former Benedictine **Kloster** (free access at all times; guided tours of the interiors Tues–Sun 10am–5pm; *www.kloster-lorsch.de*; DM6/€3), a UNESCO-listed World Heritage Site. Founded in 764, the monastery was once among the most powerful in Germany, its abbot ranking as a secular prince answerable directly to the emperor. The extraordinary **Torhalle** (or **Königshalle**), which probably dates back to the ninth century, is the best-preserved monument to have survived from the Carolingian period. Its outline was clearly inspired by Roman triumphal arches, while the patterned stonework, arranged in the manner of a mosaic, is of outstanding quality. Inside, the upper storey, which functioned as a chapel, has a lively series of fourteenth-century frescoes. The only other intact part of the complex is the austere mid-twelfth-century **Vorkirche** which, despite its dimensions, was no more than the narthex of the main church, of which nothing other than the foundations can now be seen.

Lorsch's **tourist office** is in the finest of the half-timbered buildings, the Rathaus, Marktplatz 1 (Mon–Thurs 9am–noon & 2–4pm, Fri 9am–noon; ☎0 62 51/59 67 50, fax 59 67 60, *www.lorsch.de*). The town's **hotels** include *Gasthof Schillereck*, Schillerstr. 27 (☎0 62 51/5 23 01; ④), and *Jäger*, Bahnhofstr. 79 (☎0 62 51/5 22 44; ⑤). *Zum Schwannen*, Nibelungenstr. 52, is a renowned but expensive **restaurant**.

Michelstadt

MICHELSTADT, which celebrated its 1250th birthday in 1991, lies in the heart of the Odenwald. The late fifteenth-century **Rathaus**, which dominates the central Marktplatz, features on every tourist brochure to the region. With its characteristic half-timbering and spooky corner oriels crowned with sharp spires, it perfectly encapsulates the Romantic image of medieval Germany. Just to the south is the **Kellerei**, a courtyard formed by the half-timbered storage buildings of the former castle; it now houses the folklore collections of the **Odenwaldmuseum** (Easter–Oct Tues–Sun 10am–12.30pm & 2–5pm; Nov Sat & Sun 10.30am–12.30pm & 2–4pm; DM2/€1).

In the incorporated village of Steinbach, about 1km north of Marktplatz, is the **Einhardsbasilika** (Tues–Sun: April–May & Oct 10am–noon & 1–6pm; June–Sept 10am–noon & 1–7pm; Nov–March 10am–noon & 1–3pm; DM3.50/€1.75), a church dating back to 827, the year of its foundation by the local grandee Einhard, courtier to Charlemagne, and author of a fascinating biography of the emperor. Just to the east, **Schloss Fürstenau**, a moated thirteenth-century castle, is privately owned, but you're allowed to go into the courtyard and stroll in the extensive park.

Michelstadt's **Bahnhof** is midway between the Altstadt and Schloss Fürstenau. The **tourist office** is at Marktplatz 1 (Mon–Fri 8am–noon & 2–4pm; ☎0 60 61/7 41 46, fax 7 41 30, *www.michelstadt.de*). There are a number of private houses with **rooms** (①–②) to let. Centrally located **hotels** include the seventeenth-century *Gasthaus Zum Grünen Baum*, Grosse Gasse 17 (☎0 60 61/24 09; ③), *Wilder Mann*, Erbacher Str. 10 (☎0 60 61/25 93 or 9 42 50; ③), and *Drei Hasen*, Braunstr. 5 (☎0 60 61/7 10 17; ④). All of these have **restaurants**, with the one at *Drei Hasen* ranking as the best in town. Among the alternatives are *Zum Deutschen Haus*, Bahnhofstr. 20, which is the Gaststätte of the local Dörr brewery, and *Michelstädter Rathausbräu*, Mauerstr. 1–3, which brews a range of unfiltered beers on the premises. **Camping** is possible (May–Sept only) at *Odenwaldparadies*, Am Waldstadion (☎0 60 61/32 56). The town hosts a number of **festivals**, the most important being the ten-day *Bienenmarkt* at Whit.

Erbach

Virtually adjoining Michelstadt to the south is **ERBACH**. The town is completely dominated by the huge Baroque **Schloss** (guided tours March–Oct daily at 10am, 11am,

2pm, 3pm & 4pm; DM8/€4) of the counts of Erbach-Erbach. Its main reception rooms are the **Rittersaal**, which houses an important array of historic weapons, including the armour of King Gustavus II Adolphus of Sweden, and the **Hirschgalerie**, which is decked out with hunting trophies. Since the eighteenth century, Erbach has been the main German centre for ivory-carving, an art celebrated in the **Deutsches Elfenbeinmuseum** (March–Oct daily 10am–5pm; Nov–Feb Tues–Sun 10am–5pm; DM8/€4) at Otto-Glenz-Str. 1.

The **tourist office** is at Marktplatz 1 (Mon–Fri 9am–6pm, Sat & Sun 11am–5pm; ☎0 60 62/91 33 22, fax 91 33 22, *www.verkehrsverein-erbach.de*) and offers the usual provision of private **rooms** (①–③). Good-value **hotels** include *Gebhardt*, Jahnstr. 32 (☎0 60 62/32 86; ④), and *Gasthof Odenwälder Wappenstube*, Am Schlossgraben 30 (☎0 60 62/22 36; ⑤). The latter has one of the town's best **restaurants**; its main rival is *Zum Hirsch*, Bahnstr. 2. Erbach's **youth hostel** is at Eulbacher Str. 33 (☎0 60 62/35 15, fax 6 28 48, *Erbach@djh-hessen.de*; DM23.50/€11.75 or DM28.50/€14.25), while the **campsite**, *Camping Safari* (☎0 60 62/31 59), is in the suburb of Bullau to the southeast.

Wiesbaden

WIESBADEN, 40km west of Frankfurt, is the modern capital of Hesse, a role bestowed on it by the American occupying forces, in large part because – in contrast to all its possible rivals – it came through World War II virtually unscathed. Historically speaking, it does not even belong to the province and – its Roman origins notwithstanding – is very much a late developer. Indeed, it still had little more than two thousand inhabitants when, under the Napoleonic reforms, it became sole capital of Nassau, which was reunified and raised to the status of a duchy.

Strolling through the centre – complete with its grandiloquent Historicist architecture – it's not difficult to imagine how the city must have looked during its glory days as a nineteenth-century *Kurstadt*, when the aristocracy of Europe flocked to take the waters at the numerous thermal spas and to gamble away their fortunes in the famous casino. Today the Russian nobles who were once the main patrons have been replaced by wealthy Arabs and tanned, *nouveau-riche* Germans. Wiesbaden bears little resemblance to any other major German city and is a place you'll either love or loathe.

Arrival, information and accommodation

Wiesbaden's **Hauptbahnhof** is about fifteen minutes' walk south of the city centre, which can be reached by bus #1 or #8. The **tourist office** is at Marktstr. 6 (Mon–Fri 9am–6pm, Sat 9am–3pm; ☎06 11/1 72 97 80, fax 1 72 97 98, *www.tourist.wiesbaden.de*). **Hotels** in the city are predictably pricey, but if you're prepared to splash out a bit, you could take advantage of one of the excellent upmarket choices. Most of the budget options are out in the suburbs; the **youth hostel** is at Blücherstr. 66 (☎06 11/4 86 57, fax 44 11 19, *Wiesbaden@djh-hessen.de*; DM24/€12 or DM29/€14.50), best reached by bus #14 from the Hauptbahnhof.

Hotels

Am Landeshaus, Moritzstr. 51 (☎06 11/99 66 60, fax 9 96 66 66). Good medium-range hotel, just a short walk uphill from the Hauptbahnhof. ⑥.

Ambrosius, Alfred-Schumann-Str. 9, Schierstein (☎ & fax 06 11/2 23 24). A rare budget option in an incorporated village which is a train stop between Biebrich and Eltville. ②.

Bären, Bärenstr. 3 (☎06 11/30 10 21, fax 30 10 24, *www.hotelbook.com*). One of the least outrageously priced of the upmarket hotels in the city centre, notwithstanding the fact that it has its own thermal baths. ⑦.

Domäne Mechtildshausen, An der Airbase (☎06 11/73 74 60, fax 73 74 79). Wiesbaden's most unexpected hotel is an organic farm 4km southeast of the city centre. Its highly creative restaurant (closed Sun evening & Mon) is a popular excursion destination with locals. Take bus #28. ⑧.

Hansa, Bahnhofstr. 23 (☎06 11/3 99 55, fax 30 03 19, *www.info-wiesbaden.de/hansa-hotel*). Part of the Inter Europe chain, this classy hotel is conveniently located between the Hauptbahnhof and the centre. It has a good, reasonably priced restaurant, *Warsteiner Stube* (closed Sat lunchtime & Sun). ⑥.

Landhaus Diedert, Am Kloster Klarenthal 9 (☎06 11/1 84 66 00, fax 1 84 66 03). Country-house-style hotel with gourmet restaurant 5km northwest of the city centre. Take bus #12 or #A14. ⑦.

Meuser, Stettiner Str. 13, Biebrich (☎06 11/6 93 60, fax 69 36 88). Inexpensive hotel in Wiesbaden's most attractive suburb. ③.

Nassauer Hof, Kaiser-Friedrich-Platz 3 (☎06 11/13 30, fax 1 33 62, *www.nassauer-hof.de*). This is not only Wiesbaden's grandest hotel, but also among the most renowned and expensive in Germany, boasting every conceivable luxury, thermal baths included. Its principal restaurant, *Ente*, is no less celebrated, while the *Orangerie* is a leading exponent of *neue deutsche Küche*. ⑨.

Oranien, Platter Str. 2 (☎06 11/1 88 20, fax 1 88 22 00, *www.hotel-oranien.de*). Excellent, fully modernized nineteenth-century hotel with restaurant in the pedestrian zone. ⑦.

Ring, Bleichstr. 29 (☎ & fax 06 11/9 49 02 77). The nearest there is to a budget option in the city centre. ④–⑥.

The city centre

At the heart of Wiesbaden is the **Kurhaus**. Completed in 1906 in a Neoclassical style which would have been fashionable a hundred years previously, it's the self-conscious symbol of a city where appearances are everything. The building also houses the casino or **Spielbank** (daily 2.45pm–3am), which opened in 1949. However, gambling first started in earnest in 1771 and Wiesbaden's original casino was the inspiration for "Roulettenburg", in Dostoyevsky's novel *The Gambler*. Gambling was suspended between 1872 and 1949 as a result of a ban imposed by Kaiser Wilhelm I after his son, Crown Prince Friedrich III, had formed an "unsuitable" attachment to a woman gambler. The **Kurhauskolonnade** to the north, the longest pillared hall in Europe, contains the slot-machine section of the casino complex and a space for exhibitions. Opposite, the **Theaterkolonnade**, with its luxury boutiques, forms a front to the lavish neo-Rococo **Hessisches Staatstheater**, which was built at the end of the nineteenth century by Viennese architects. To the rear of the Kurhaus is the **Kurpark**, an English-style park. From there you can walk up into the wooded slopes of the Taunus, which rise to the north of the city.

Wilhelmstrasse, the main shopping street, runs past the Kurhaus into Friedrich-Ebert-Strasse and is full of expensive antique shops and glitzy designer stores. On Schlossplatz stands the **Stadtschloss**, built in the 1840s as the town residence of the dukes of Nassau. Nowadays, it's the Hesse state parliament. Facing the Stadtschloss is the seventeeth-century **Altes Rathaus**, the oldest building in the city. In front of it, on Marktplatz, where markets are held on Wednesdays and Saturdays, there's a small fountain topped by a playful-looking lion, one of the symbols of the city. The brick **Marktkirche** (Tues, Wed, Fri & Sat 10.30am–12.30pm, Thurs 4.30–5.30pm), which bristles with towers, steeples and turrets, bears the hallmarks of the pervasive influence of the English Gothic Revival style.

A few minutes' walk to the northwest, at Langgasse 38–40, is the most atmospheric and expensive of the city's thermal baths, the mock-Roman **Kaiser-Friedrich-Bad** (Mon–Thurs, Sat & Sun 10am–10pm, Fri 10am–midnight; DM31.50/€15.75), which dates back to 1913. The entry ticket is valid for four hours and includes a full Roman-Irish steam bath plus the use of the solarium. Note that Tuesdays are for women only; the other days are mixed. On Kranzplatz, not much more than a stone's throw to the north, is the **Kochbrunnen**, which has no fewer than fifteen different hot springs. You can sample the waters at the taps in the little Neoclassical temple. Despite their much-vaunted healing properties, the recommended maximum intake is one litre per day.

Many of finest of the grand villas so characteristic of Wiesbaden can be seen in the streets immediately south of the Kurhaus. Particularly notable is the **Villa Clementine** at the head of Frankfurter Strasse. Nowadays a cultural centre, it was the scene in 1888 of the abduction of Crown Prince Alexander of Serbia, who was forceably repatriated by his captors. Alongside is the mid-nineteenth-century Anglican church of **St Augustine of Canterbury**, which is still in regular use, thanks to the continued presence of a sizeable American community. Just to the south, at the top end of Friedrich-Ebert-Allee, is the **Museum Wiesbaden** (Tues 10am–8pm, Wed–Fri 10am–4pm, Sat & Sun 10am–5pm; *www.museum-wiesbaden.de*; DM5/€2.50). This possesses a large number of paintings by the Russian artist Alexej Jawlensky, a member of the Expressionist Der Blaue Reiter group who was a Wiesbaden resident for the last two decades of his life, and extensive collections of locally excavated Roman and early medieval antiquities.

The outskirts

On the northern edge of Wiesbaden looms the **Neroberg**, a 245-metre Taunus foothill commanding good views of the city. To get there take bus #1 to Nerotal and from there ascend by the water-powered funicular railway, the **Nerobergbahn** (April & Sept Wed & Sat noon–7pm, Sun 10am–7pm; May–Aug daily 9.30am–8pm; Oct Wed & Sat noon–6pm, Sun 10am–6pm; DM2.50/€1.25 single, DM3.50/€1.75 return), whose technology has remained unchanged since its inauguration in 1888. On the summit stand the Neoclassical **Neroberg-Tempel** and the **Opelbad** (May–Sept daily 9am–8pm), a Bauhaus-style open-air swimming pool. A short distance downhill is the **Russische Kapelle** (April–Oct daily 10am–5pm; Nov–March Sat noon–3pm, Sun 10am–4pm), a nineteenth-century Russian-style chapel instantly recognizable by its five gilded cupolas. It was built as a mausoleum for the Russian-born Duchess Elisabeth of Nassau, who died in childbirth at the age of nineteen. Nearby is the **Russischer Friedhof**, with the elaborate tombs of many Russian aristocrats and soldiers.

Northeast of the city centre, reached by bus #18 or #A32, is the **Kurzentrum Aukammtal**, the hub of the modern-day spa facilities. In addition to several clinics, there's the city's principal public baths, the **Thermalbad Wiesbaden** (Mon 12.30–10pm, Tues–Thurs 7.30am–10pm, Fri 7.30am–11pm, Sat & Sun 7.30am–7pm; day ticket DM10/€5, or DM 20/€10 including sauna and solarium).

It's also worth making a trip south to **Schloss Biebrich**, set on the Rhine in the suburb of the same name (take bus #3, #4, #13, #A3 or #A13). This eighteenth-century Baroque palace, the original Wiesbaden home of one of the lines of the Nassau dynasty, has a restrained elegance which puts the showy city centre to shame. Though the building itself is only open to the public for the occasional concert, you can stroll in the fine park. It's also the first embarkation point after Mainz for **cruises** down the Rhine (for more details on these, see box on p.487).

Eating, drinking and entertainment

Predictably enough, **eating** and **drinking** in Wiesbaden can be an expensive business. There are plenty of upmarket restaurants (see also "Hotels" on pp.409–10), but good cheaper places (including several run as adjuncts to food shops) do exist and there are some excellent centrally located pubs too.

Restaurants

Centro Italia, Wörthstr. 18. One of several notable Italian restaurants, distinguished by its range of Sicilian wines and speciality dishes. Closed Tues.

Feinkost Feickert, Wilhelmstr. 10. This elegant delicatessen has a bistro-restaurant open during shopping hours.

Frickel, Marktstr. 26. Daytime restaurant attached to a high-class fishmonger's shop that has been in existence since 1899.

Käfer's Bistro, Kurhausplatz 1. One of the best of Wiesbaden's upmarket restaurants, located in the Kurhaus. The cooking has a German accent, even though the decor is reminiscent of a Parisian bistro.

Rathsbräu, Schlossplatz 6. This is Wiesbaden's version of the inevitable Ratskeller, occupying the cellars of the Neues Rathaus. Its new name is a result of the addition of a Hausbrauerei, which produces organically brewed light and dark beers. Closed Sun.

Rheingold, Saalgasse 30. This is reckoned to be *the* place in Wiesbaden for *gutbürgerliche Küche*. Evenings only.

Schlossweinstube, Rheingaustr. 140, Biebrich. Wine bar-restaurant, the only part of Schloss Biebrich regularly open to the public.

Sir Winston Churchill, Taunusstr. 23. Long-established restaurant-cum-bistro-cum-café which starts serving breakfast at 8.30am and remains open till 4am. It aims to combine high culinary standards with the atmosphere and style of a British club.

Trüffel, Marktstr. 9. Located in one of the city's best delicatessens, this serves Italianate bistro food and is a lunchtime favourite with shoppers and office workers. Closed Sat evening and all day Sun.

Viva, Schützenhofstr. 3. Vegetarian and wholefood restaurant on a terrace above its own shop. It has a huge selection of dishes which you pay for by weight. Open Mon–Fri 9am–7.30pm, Sat 9am–4pm.

Weihenstephan, Armenruhstr. 6, Biebrich. A successful transplant of a Bavarian Bierkeller, serving good food (particularly fish dishes) and having the obligatory beer garden. Closed Sat.

Zum Dortmunder, Langgasse 34. Excellent traditional Gaststätte serving hearty cuisine and Dortmund beers.

Bars and cafés

Café Blum, Wilhelmstr. 44–46. The most prestigious of the many elegant coffee houses in the city centre.

Café Cicero, Citypassage. Tucked away on the first floor of a shopping centre, this *Kulturcafé* features regular artistic events, especially live jazz.

C/O, Moritzstr. 52. An alternative bar with a good atmosphere which also serves cheap meals.

Die Klappe, Nerostr. 20. Trendy café-bar with beer garden.

Irish Pub, Michelsberg 15. One of the better and more original of the new wave of Irish pubs which have sprung up all over Germany. There's often live music, and it's generally packed out by mid-evening.

Mo' Betta, Saalgasse 11. Trendy bar, much favoured by gays and lesbians, which sometimes features blues and jazz. Closed Fri; opens at 7pm every other day.

Park-Café, Wilhelmstr. 36. Extremely chic nightspot patronized by the beautiful set. Open Wed–Sun 9pm–4am.

Sächsische Konditorei, Langgasse 43. The café is an adjunct to the shop, which makes what are reckoned to be the best cakes and sweets in Wiesbaden.

Sherry & Port, Adolfsallee 11. The name of this bar, which combines English and Irish influences, is due to the large selection of sherries and ports on offer. Live jazz, folk and classical music sessions take place several times a week. Closed Sun.

Wirtshaus, Nerostr. 24. Another good student bar, still patronized by leftovers of the Sixties generation. Open daily from 8pm.

Culture

The Hessisches Staatstheater on Kurhausplatz (☎06 11/3 23 25) is the principal cultural venue; it presents **opera, operetta** and **ballet** in the plush main auditorium, **drama** on the two smaller, plainer stages. Classical **concerts** take place in the ornate Friedrich-von-Thiersch-Saal (☎06 11/1 72 99 30) in the Kurhaus. The main **cabaret** venues are Pariser Hoftheater, Spiegelgasse 9 (☎06 11/30 06 07), and Hinterhaus,

Karlsruher Str. 15 (☎06 11/37 95 48). The *Internationales Maifestspiel* throughout May is Wiesbaden's most important cultural **festival**, while the top popular event is the *Theatrium*, a huge street fair on Wilhelmstrasse on a weekend in early June.

The Rheingau

The Hessian side of the Rhine, running from Wiesbaden to the border with Rhineland-Palatinate at Lorchhausen, is known as the **Rheingau**. Sheltered from the elements by the gentle slopes of the Taunus, the region has developed into one of Germany's fore-most wine-producing districts, and its vineyards, ruined castles and drowsy little villages make it a favourite destination for coach parties and package tourists. Road B42, running from Wiesbaden to the Rhineland-Palatinate border and taking in all the little wine vil-lages, has been designated the **Rheingauer-Riesling-Route**, a special-interest stretch for wine fans, enabling them to stop off and do a spot of tasting and buying. There's also a walking route, the **Rheingauer-Riesling-Pfad**, which runs through the lower slopes of the **Rheingau-Gebirge** – the part of the Taunus which rises from the banks of the Rhine. Classical music buffs should make a point of visiting during the three months in summer when the *Rheingau-Musik-Festival* takes place, as it features of dozens of con-certs by international musicians of the highest rank. Though some performances are in Wiesbaden, the vast majority take place in the region's smaller towns and villages.

Eltville

The first stop out of Wiesbaden, just beyond its suburbs, is **ELTVILLE**, which lies on the main rail line north, and has plenty of bus connections into the surrounding coun-tryside. It's famous for its sparkling wines, for its 20,000 rose bushes which burst into a riot of colour in summer and for being the place where the urbane conman, Felix Krull, hero of Thomas Mann's comic novel, spent his youth. Overlooking the Rhine is the ruined **Burg** of the Archbishop-Electors of Mainz, now a shady promenade with rose garden. There are plenty of cute half-timbered houses, plus a Gothic **Pfarrkirche** with a fifteenth-century fresco of *The Last Judgement* and a font made in the workshop of the Mainz sculptor Hans Backoffen.

However, Eltville is above all a place for **eating** and, especially, **drinking**. Many of its **Weingüte** can be visited, and most serve food and drink. *Koegler*, at Kirchgasse 5, is of special note: it occupies the fifteenth-century Bechtermünzhof, the home and printing workshop of Gutenberg in his final years. Others to head for are *Diefenhardt'sches Weingut*, Hauptstr. 11, and *Krone*, Platz von Montrichard 1. There are also plenty of **wine-restaurants** where you can sample the local vintages – the best are *Weinhaus Weinpump*, Rheingauer Str. 3, and *Gelbes Haus*, Burgplatz 3. The town also has its own boutique brew-ery, Kleines Eltviller Brauhaus, Schwalbacher Str. 41–43, with an adjoining beer garden.

Eltville's **Bahnhof** is at the northern end of the town centre, while the **tourist office** is at Schmittstr. 2 (Mon–Fri 9.30am–noon & 2–5pm; ☎0 61 23/9 09 80, fax 90 98 90, *www.eltville.de*). Accommodation is in rather short supply, with only a few **private rooms** (②–③) and **hotels**; the latter include *Café Glockenhof*, Marktstr. 3 (☎0 61 23/6 11 41; ⑤), *Sonnenberg*, Friedrichstr. 65 (☎0 61 23/30 81; ⑥), and *Frankenbach-Mainzer Hof*, Wilhelmstr. 13 (☎0 61 23/90 40; ⑦). The big local **festival** is the *Biedermeier- und Sektfest* over five days in early July.

Kiedrich

From Eltville, it's only a 3km bus journey inland to **KIEDRICH**, a wine-growing village of half-timbered houses. Dominating it from the north is **Burg Scharfenstein**, a ruin since the seventeenth century, which commands a fine view over the region. In the centre of town is a walled close containing two imposing late Gothic churches. The smaller of these, the fifteenth-century **St Michaelskapelle**, has a tall lantern turret crowned with an openwork spire, an indication of its function as a funerary chapel. There are actually two chapels, the lower serving as the ossuary. Its counterpart above, which is generally kept open, is light and airy, with a graceful altar recess (or *Chörlein*) and an elaborate candelabra bearing a double-sided sculpture of the Madonna and Child. The external pulpit was used to address the epilepsy sufferers who once flocked to Kiedrich on pilgrimage.

Although it preserves parts of its predecessor, the **Pfarrkirche St Valentin** (March–Oct Mon–Sat 10.30am–12.30pm, Sun 2.30–4pm; Nov–Feb Sat 10.30am–12.30pm, Sun 2.30–4pm) is likewise predominantly fifteenth-century in date. Entry is via the main portal, which has an exquisite "Soft Style" polychromed **tympanum** with a combined scene of the Annunciation and Coronation of the Virgin. The interior is an extraordinary evocation of the Middle Ages, preserving as it does virtually all the original furnishings including the rood screen, pulpit, tabernacle, altars, choir stalls and the pews with their remarkable carved and painted vine motifs and Gothic script. Even more precious are the *Kiedrich Madonna*, a gorgeous fourteenth-century statue showing strong French influence, and what is claimed as the oldest largely intact church **organ** in the world still in working order. The latter, which preserves around eighty percent of its original pipework from around 1500, can be heard every Sunday morning at 9.30am, along with the local **choir**, the *Chorbuben*, who since 1333 have practised a unique form of singing Gregorian chant in Germanic dialect. Immediately after the service, their illuminated missals can be viewed in the parish house opposite.

Kiedrich has one large **pension**, *Ankermühle*, Eltviller Str. 6 (☎0 61 23/9 05 70; ⑤), and a couple of **hotels**, both with **restaurants**: *Goldene Krone*, Oberstr. 5 (☎0 61 23/9 05 60; ④), and *Nassauer Hof*, Bingerpfortenstr. 17 (☎06123/24 76; ⑥). Also recommended, whether for a meal or a glass of wine, is *Gutsschänke Schloss Groenesteyn*, Oberstr. 36; other possibilities are *Weinstube Zum Bur*, Oberstr. 3, and *Winzerhaus*, Kammstr. 3.

Kloster Eberbach

Several buses per day continue 5km westwards from Kiedrich to **Kloster Eberbach** (April–Sept daily 10am–6pm; Oct–March Mon–Fri 10am–4pm, Sat & Sun 11am–4pm; DM5/€2.50), one of the best-preserved medieval monasteries in Germany. It's situated at the lower end of the valley of the Kisselbach directly below the Taunus: exactly the sort of secluded setting favoured by the Cistercian order, who founded it in 1135. The Romanesque **Klosterkirche** is grandiosely austere, and devoid of decoration save for a few aristocratic tombs, the most notable being that in the chancel to a fourteenth-century archbishop of Mainz, Gerlach von Nassau. Behind the church are the leafy cloisters, surrounded by the former living quarters of the monks. Particularly outstanding is the upstairs **dormitory**, an immense vaulted room divided into two aisles, with a slight incline in its floor-level to make it seem even longer than it actually is. Built in the 1240s, it ranks among the supreme masterpieces of early Gothic architecture. Below it is the **Fraternei**, another impressive hall, which formerly contained the monastic workshops. In the **lay brothers' refectory** the huge wine presses once used by the monks are on display; some date back to the seventeenth century.

Wine production continued after the dissolution of the monastery in 1803, and the outbuildings are now used to press, ferment and store the produce of the Eberbacher Steinberg, the former monastic vineyard. Tasting sessions for groups are held in the **Hospital**, a magnificent Transitional-style building which is the only medieval monastic infirmary anywhere in Europe to have survived in its original form. Otherwise, you can buy the products at the shop, or drink them in the **restaurant** of the *Gästehaus Kloster Eberbach* (☎0 67 23/99 30; ⑤), an upmarket **hotel** which has been established in the monastery.

Rüdesheim

RÜDESHEIM, which is 17km from Eltville, claims the dubious distinction of being the most visited town in the region, attracting over three million sightseers a year. It's a favourite stopping-off point for coach parties and Rhine cruises as it conforms pretty well to the general conception of what a typical Rhine town should look like – all crooked narrow streets, half-timbered houses and souvenir shops, sloping down gently from the wooded hills and terraced vineyards above.

The big local attraction is the **Drosselgasse**, a street comprised entirely of taverns offering "traditional" German entertainment, which is crowded all day long with tourists being ripped off. The twelfth-century **Brömserburg**, a squat and angular fortress a few minutes' walk to the west, now houses the **Weinmuseum** (March–Oct daily 9am–6pm; DM5/€2.50). It contains 21 old presses and a vast collection of wine vessels, including some fine examples of vases that were used to store and transport wine from Roman times through to the Middle Ages. There's the bonus of a marvellous view over the town and the Rhine from the top of the keep.

The twelfth-century defensive tower called the **Boosenburg** just to the north and the circular late Gothic **Adlerturm** at the eastern end of the waterfront are further reminders of an era when this stretch of the Rhine was a turbulent and contested area. Lining Oberstrasse to the east of the Boosenburg are a number of nobles' houses, notably the **Brömserhof**, which has a picturesque half-timbered tower. It now houses **Siegfried's Mechanisches Musikkabinett** (guided tours March to mid-Nov daily 10am–6pm; DM9/€4.50), one of the largest collections of mechanical musical instruments in the country. Just off the central Marktplatz is another fine mansion, the **Klunkardshof**, which has a particularly well-preserved half-timbered facade.

The much-restored **Pfarrkirche Eibingen** at the extreme northeastern edge of Rüdesheim was formerly part of a convent established by the great mystic, poet and composer **Hildegard of Bingen** (see box on p.488). In the early years of the twentieth century, a new, considerably larger **Abtei St Hildegard** was built in neo-Romanesque style on the heights above. Wines from its vineyard, plus a couple of powerful spirits, can be purchased at its shop.

The main road just west of the abbey continues up to the **Niederwalddenkmal**, a bombastic statue of Germania built to mark the unification of Germany in 1871. This immense monument 225m above the town can be reached more directly by foot or by gondola (DM6.50/€3.25 single, DM10/€5 return) over the vineyards which swarm up the slopes behind Rüdesheim. Lower down, by one of the footpaths to Assmannshausen, are the undeniably romantic ruins of the thirteenth-century **Burg Ehrenfels**. This one-time toll castle was used in conjunction with the Mäuseturm, a tower built on a mid-river island, by the archbishops of Mainz to control traffic on the Rhine.

Practicalities

Ferries dock right by the town centre, whereas the **Bahnhof** lies a short distance further west. The **tourist office** (May–Sept Mon–Fri 8.30am–6.30pm, Sat 10am–5.30pm, Sun 11.30am–3.30pm; rest of year Mon–Fri only; ☎0 67 22/1 94 33, fax 34 85, *www .ruedesheim.de*) is at Rheinstr. 16.

There are plenty of **private rooms** (②–④) and **hotels** but they tend to be booked up during the high summer. A couple of inexpensive possibilities are *Gasthof Zur Guten*

Quelle, Katharinenstr. 3 (☎0 67 22/27 57; ③–⑥), and *Weinstube zur Lindenau*, Löhrstr. 10 (☎0 67 22/33 27; ④). If you want more luxury, try *Felsenkeller*, Oberstr. 39–41 (☎0 67 22/9 42 50, *www.ruedesheim-rhein.com*; ⑥), *Zum Bären*, Schmidtstr. 31 (☎0 67 22/10 91, *www.zumbaeren.de*; ⑥), *Central*, Kirchstr. 6 (☎0 67 22/91 20, *www.Centralhotel.net*; ⑥), or *Rüdesheimer Schloss*, Steingasse 10 (☎0 67 22/9 05 00, *www.ruedesheimer-schloss.com*; ⑥–⑧). The local **youth hostel** is set amidst the vines, a long walk from the town, at Am Kreuzberg (☎0 67 22/27 11, fax 4 82 84, *Ruedesheim@djh-hessen.de*; DM22/€11 or DM27/€13.50). There are two **campsites** in Rüdesheim: *Campingplatz am Rhein* (☎0 67 22/25 28 or 25 82) and *Ponyland* (☎0 67 22/25 18) near the Niederwalddenkmal.

All the hotels listed above have **restaurants**. Good **wine bars** include *Weingut Jakob Christ*, Grabenstr. 17, *Weingut Georg Breuer*, Grabenstr. 8, and *Weinhaus Fendel*, Marienthalerstr. 46. For something not so obviously typical of the region, try *Rüdesheimer Brauhaus*, Oberstr. 49, a Hausbrauerei which makes light, dark and *Weizen* beers.

At the beginning of July there's a firework display and in mid-August Rüdesheim has its *Weinfest*. During the latter it seems like all of those three million visitors have hit town at once and accommodation is impossible to find unless booked a very long time in advance.

Assmannshausen

Just out of Rüdesheim proper, the Rhine suddenly bends through ninety degrees to flow more or less south–north, and there follows a treacherous stretch of rapids called the **Binger Loch**. After 5km (one stop on the train or an enticing hour-long walk along the marked footpath) you arrive at **ASSMANNSHAUSEN**, a smaller and less touristy version of Rüdesheim, of which it now forms a part. In the terraced vineyards round about some of Germany's best red wines are produced from Spätburgunder grapes. A chairlift (DM6.50/€3.25 single, DM10/€5 return) runs up to **Jagdschloss Niederwald**, an eighteenth-century hunting lodge turned hotel (☎0 67 22/10 04; ⑧) near the Niederwalddenkmal, and commanding similarly good views of the Rhine.

Milberg, Am Rathaus 2 (☎0 67 22/29 45; ③), is a centrally located **pension**. The sixteenth-century *Krone*, Rheinuferstr. 10 (☎0 67 22/40 30, *www.Kroneas.de*; ⑧–⑨), ranks among the most exclusive **hotels** in the whole of the Rhineland, with a **restaurant** renowned for its fish and game specialities – and a remarkable wine list.

CENTRAL HESSE

The attractions of the central part of Hesse are diverse. To the west is the valley of the Lahn, a Rhine tributary, on whose banks stand two of Germany's most famous university towns, **Marburg**, a truly beautiful place, and **Giessen**, now rather a shadow of its prewar self. Further downstream are three very contrasting destinations: **Wetzlar**, with its distinguished legal and literary traditions, the Residenzstadt of **Weilburg** and the small cathedral city of **Limburg**. In the very heart of Hesse is the volcanic **Vogelsberg** range, with a number of pretty towns, most notably **Alsfeld**. Further east, at the edge of the Rhön, is **Fulda**, one of Germany's leading episcopal centres. South of the Vogelsberg are two wooded highland areas, the **Taunus** and **Spessart**.

The Taunus

The favourite playground of the citizens of Frankfurt, the **Taunus** is a hilly forest area bordered on three sides by the rivers Rhine, Main and Lahn. Much of it, notably the

High Taunus, is an unspoiled landscape ideal for hiking, though the undoubted high point is the spa town of **Bad Homburg** in the southern foothills.

The High Taunus

The thickly wooded slopes of the **High Taunus** (Hochtaunus) have been designated a *Naturpark*. On the whole, they're atmospheric and invigorating rather than breath-taking, and the most attractive part can be explored in a day's outing. The main peak, the **Grosser Feldberg** (880m), is the highest of any of the Rhineland schist massifs: from the summit there's a marvellous panorama of the region. In the nearby village of **OBERREIFENBERG**, the **youth hostel** at Limesstr. 14 (☎0 60 82/24 40, fax 33 05, *Oberreifenberg@djh-hessen.de*; DM23.50/€11.75 or DM28.50/€14.25) is the main local hiking base.

The area's principal town is **KÖNIGSTEIN IM TAUNUS**, which can be reached by train from Frankfurt or from Wiesbaden via Höchst. It boasts a striking ruined **Burg** (daily: March 9am–4.30pm; April–Sept 9am–7pm; Oct–Feb 9.30am–3/4pm; DM3/€1.50), whose keep commands a sweeping panorama over the region, with the main landmarks of Frankfurt visible on even a half-decent day. There are plenty of **hotels**, ranging from *Haus der Begegnung*, Bischof-Kaller-Str. 3 (☎0 61 74/30 61; ④) to the super-luxury *Sonnenhof*, Falkensteiner Str. 9 (☎0 61 74/2 90 80; ⑦–⑨). For a list of **private rooms** (②–④), contact the **tourist office**, Hauptstr. 21 (Mon, Tues, Thurs & Fri 9am–6pm, Wed 9am–1pm; ☎0 61 74/20 22 51, fax 29 08 75, *www.koenigstein.de*).

Bad Homburg vor der Höhe

BAD HOMBURG, reached by S-Bahn #5 from Frankfurt or bus #917 from Königstein, ranks second only to Baden-Baden as Germany's classiest spa. Following nearly two centuries as capital of the tiny state of Hesse-Homburg, it was annexed by Prussia in 1866 and quickly established itself as the favourite summer retreat of the Kaisers. It's very much a place of two faces: the historic centre, with its market-town air, is built on a steeply pitched hill, while the somnolent spa quarter is laid out on the low ground to the north.

The town centre

At the very top of the town, set in an extensive landscaped park, is the **Schloss** (guid-ed tours Tues–Sun 10am–4/5pm; DM7/€3.50). The predominantly Baroque exterior of the palace is largely due to Friedrich II, the hero of Kleist's play *Prince Friedrich of Homburg*. His **bust**, a masterly portrait by the Berlin sculptor Andreas Schlüter, stands in the entrance hall, while his famous wooden leg, known as the "Silver Leg" because of its silver joints, is one of the highlights of the tour. For the most part, the interiors are nineteenth century and reflect the taste of Empress Augusta: among the adorn-ments she ordered is one of the world's first telephone kiosks.

A second guided tour, run on Sundays only (at 11am, noon, 1pm, 2pm & 3pm; DM7/€3.50) goes round the **Englischer Flügel** (or **Elisabethenflügel**), which is named in honour of Princess Elizabeth, daughter of King George III of Great Britain, who married Landgrave Friedrich VI in 1818. She was a talented amateur artist, and many of her own creations, including some striking works in lacquer, are displayed throughout her apartments. This tour also takes in the galleried **Schlosskirche**, which contains the burial vault of the House of Hesse-Homburg. The tall **Weisser Turm** (White Tower; Tues–Sun 10am–4/5pm; DM1/€0.50) in the Schloss courtyard is the only reminder of the previous medieval castle. It can be ascended for an extensive panorama over the Taunus.

Opposite the Schloss, at the corner of Löwenstrasse and Dorotheenstrasse, is the **Sinclair-Haus** (Tues–Fri 3–7pm, Sat & Sun 10am–5pm; free), a Baroque mansion named after a prominent Homburg courtier. It's used for temporary art exhibitions, a mixture of ephemera and international blockbusters. Across the road is the **Erlöserkirche** (Church of the Redeemer), an extravagant Historicist building funded by Kaiser Wilhelm II.

The **Kurpark** is a huge and beautiful landscaped park designed by Peter Joseph Lenné. Along its main axis of Brunnenallee are no fewer than seven mineral springs, the most prestigious being the **Elisabethenquelle**, over which stands a handsome Neoclassical pavilion. At the heart of the park is the stolidly Wilhelmine building of the **Kaiser-Wilhelm-Bad**, which is still the main centre for therapeutic cures. Alongside, the **Spielbank** (daily 3pm–2.30am; DM5/€2.50) is the oldest casino in the world, founded in 1841 by the Frenchman François Blanc, who decamped to Monte Carlo when gambling was outlawed throughout Germany in 1872. It's essential to be respectably dressed in order to gain admission; minimum stakes are DM5/€2.50 for roulette, DM10/€5 for poker, DM20/€10 for blackjack.

Further east are the two main bathing complexes. The **Taunus-Therme** (Mon, Tues, Thurs & Sun 9am–11pm, Wed, Fri & Sat 9am–midnight; weekdays DM23/€11.50 for 2hr & DM45/€22.50 for the whole day, weekends DM26/€13 & DM49/€24.50) occupies a Japanese-style building with garden, and includes a Roman-Irish steam bath and a Finnish sauna among its facilities. Its more conventional neighbour, the **Seedammbad** (Mon 2–9pm, Tues–Fri 7am–9pm, Sat & Sun 8.30am–8pm; DM6/€3 for a two-hour swim, DM15/€7.50 for a sauna) likewise has indoor and outdoor sections. Also worth seeking out are a couple of exotic little turn-of-the century buildings: the **Russische Kirche** at the southern end of the park and the **Siamesischer Tempel** at the northwestern corner, the latter donated to the spa by one well-satisfied partaker of the waters, the king of Siam.

Practicalities

Bad Homburg's **Bahnhof** is on the south side of town. The **tourist office** (Mon–Fri 8.30am–7pm, Sat 9am–1pm; ☎0 61 72/17 81 10, fax 17 81 18, *www.bad-homburg.de*) is in the Kurhaus building in the heart of the town centre at Louisenstr. 58.

There's a huge range of accommodation to suit all pockets, including a **youth hostel** opposite the Schlosspark at Mühlweg 17 (☎0 61 72/2 39 50, fax 2 23 12, *Bad-Homburg @djh-hessen.de*; DM29.50/€14.75 or DM34.50/€17.25) and plenty of **private rooms** (②–④). Several of the city-centre **hotels** are surprisingly reasonable: try *Johannisberg*, Thomasstr. 5 (☎0 61 72/2 13 15; ③), *Zur Brücke*, Ritter-von-Marx-Brücke 2 (☎0 61 72/2 22 95; ④), or *Haus Fischer am Park*, Landgrafenstr. 12 (☎0 61 72/86 79 27; ④). *Villa Kisseleff*, Kisseleffstr. 19 (☎0 61 72/2 15 40 or 90 22 90; ⑤) is a good medium-range choice, while a couple of the less outrageously priced upmarket options are *Haus Dalheim*, Elisabethenstr. 42 (☎0 61 72/67 73 50; ⑥–⑧), and the Jugendstil *Villa am Kurpark*, Kaiser-Friedrich-Promenade 57 (☎0 61 72/1 80 00; ⑦–⑨). At the very top of the range is the *Steigenberger Bad Homburg*, Kaiser-Friedrich-Promenade 69–75 (☎0 61 72/18 10, *www.steigenberger.com*; ⑧–⑨), an Art Deco-style glass palace offering every conceivable luxury.

There's an equally wide variety of places to **eat** and **drink**, quite apart from the hotel restaurants. These include a vegetarian place, *Kartoffelküche*, Audenstr. 4. *Schreinerei Pfeiffer*, Audenstr. 6, has Hessian specialities, while *Isoletta*, Louisenstr. 80, is a good and not too expensive Italian. *Kofler* is a café-restaurant in the Schloss which does themed eat-as-much-as-you-can buffets on Thursday evenings. If you've plenty of money to spare, *Assmanns*, Kisseleffstr. 27, is a renowned exponent of *neue deutsche Küche*, while *Sänger's*, Kaiser-Friedrich-Promenade 85, is a gourmet restaurant with a national reputation.

Antidotes to the peace and quiet of the spa quarter are provided by Germany's oldest **dance-bar**, the *Tennis Bar* (Tues–Thurs 9pm–4am, Fri & Sat 9pm–5.45am, Sun 3pm–4am) at Kisseleffstr. 20, and by *Gambrinus* in the Fürstenbahnhof, the former royal terminal beside the Bahnhof, which has a **disco** or live music each evening. The Kulturzentrum Englische Kirche in the deconsecrated Anglican Christ Church on Ferdinandplatz (☎0 61 72/10 03 10) presents a varied programme of **cabaret, jazz** and **classical** music. Bad Homburg's churches host an international **organ** festival, *Fugato*, in the second half of September.

The Spessart

The **Spessart**, which is divided between Hesse and Bavaria, forms Germany's largest continuous upland forest area. Most of it has been dedicated as a *Naturpark*, though strung along the valley of the River Kinzig, which separates it from the Vogelsberg, are a number of towns, the most notable being **Gelnhausen**, a long-time Free Imperial City, and **Steinau**, of Brothers Grimm fame.

Gelnhausen

GELNHAUSEN lies 40km east of Frankfurt on the fast road and rail routes to Fulda, and is also the starting point for a branch rail line through the Vogelsberg to Giessen. One of the most atmospheric and picturesque small towns in Germany, it was a city-state for most of its history and exudes a grandeur which belies the fact that its population has never numbered more than a few thousand. It likes to call itself Barbarossastadt, a reference to its foundation in the twelfth century by **Frederick Barbarossa**, the emperor who was primarily responsible for moulding the feudal structure of the Holy Roman Empire. However, it's equally proud of being the birthplace of the seventeenth-century writer **Johann Jacob Christoffel von Grimmelshausen**, whose semi-autobiographical *Simplicissimus* is the first great German novel and one of the leading tragicomedies of European literature.

The ruins of Barbarossa's palace, the **Kaiserpfalz** (Tues–Sun 9am–4/5pm; DM3.50/€1.75), stand in what was formerly an island in the Kinzig, midway between the Bahnhof and the Altstadt, which clings to the steep hillside above. Substantial sections of the red sandstone masonry survive, including parts of the gateway, the tower and the chapel, though the most notable feature is a wall of the royal residence itself, featuring arcades adorned with beautifully carved Romanesque capitals. Above the palace portal is an enigmatic grotesque sculpture of a man, traditionally presumed to depict the red-bearded emperor himself.

The upper town is centred on two market squares, the Untermarkt and the Obermarkt, but the main feature of the skyline is the **Marienkirche** between the squares. Although built at various stages, it's a magnificent structure which graphically illustrates the transition from Romanesque to Gothic. Especially worthy of note are the four **towers**, which form an irresistibly photogenic ensemble, and the elaborately decorated interior of the chancel. This features a **rood screen** bearing highly expressive sculptures illustrating the Last Judgement, a gleaming set of stained-glass windows and a carved and painted high altar. In the vestry are two precious fifteenth-century tapestries, which the caretaker will show for a DM1/€0.50 donation. Immediately below the church, and nowadays serving as its hall, is the **Romanisches Haus**, which was built for the officials of Barbarossa's court.

Half-timbered buildings are otherwise predominant in the upper town, with the **Rathaus** on Obermarkt ranking as the most imposing. On Brentanostrasse, just west of Untermarkt, the **Synagoge**, now used as a cultural centre, retains some of its original Baroque decoration and furnishings, notably the Torah shrine. Much of the **Stadtbefestigung** enclosing the town also survives, including the picturesque **Hexenturm** on the southeast side, where supposed witches were imprisoned. It's well worth continuing uphill from here to the **Halbmondturm**, which commands a breathtaking view over the town and the valley.

Practicalities

Gelnhausen's **tourist office** (Mon–Fri 8am–noon & 2–4.30pm, Sat 9am–noon & 2–4.30pm, Sun 2–4.30pm; ☎0 60 51/83 03 00, fax 83 03 03, *www.gelnhausen.de*) is on the northern side of Obermarkt. Within the historic centre are one small **guesthouse**, *Kapellenweg*, Kapellenweg 23 (☎0 60 51/20 44; ③), and five **hotels**: *Schelm von Bergen*, Obermarkt 22 (☎0 60 51/27 55; ③), *Zur Burgschänke*, Burgstr. 19 (☎0 60 51/29 15; ⑤), *Grimmelshausen*, Schmidtgasse 12 (☎0 60 51/9 24 20; ⑤); *Stadt-Schänke*, Fürstenhofstr. 1 (☎0 60 51/1 60 51; ⑤), and *Burg-Mühle*, Burgstr. 2 (☎0 60 51/8 20 50; ⑤). Each of the hotels, except *Grimmelshausen*, has a **restaurant**; another good choice for a meal is the historic tavern *Zum Löwen*, Langgasse 28, which also has the benefit of a beer garden.

Steinau an der Strasse

The little half-timbered town of **STEINAU**, some 25km northeast of Gelnhausen on the main transport routes to Fulda, was the childhood home of the Brothers Grimm (see box on p.440), a connection resulting in a considerable volume of tourism these days. Focal point of the town is a large Renaissance **Schloss** (Tues–Sun 9am–5pm; DM4/€2 museum only, DM6.50/€3.25 including guided tour of the interiors), which contains period furnishings plus extensive documentation on the work of the brothers. There's more on the Grimms in the nearby **Amtshaus** (mid-March to mid-Dec daily 2–5pm; DM3/€1.50) at Brüder-Grimm-Str. 80, where they lived during the period of their father's service as the local magistrate. **Puppet performances** of some of their most famous stories are regularly performed at the Marionettentheater in the Schloss's former stables at Am Kumpen 4 (☎0 66 63/2 45).

Steinau's **Bahnhof** is at the northwestern fringe of town, a fifteen-minute walk from the centre. The **tourist office** is in the Rathaus, Brüder-Grimm-Str. 47 (Mon–Thurs 8.30am–noon & 1.30–4pm, Fri 8.30am–noon; ☎0 66 63/9 63 10, fax 96 31 33, *www.steinau.de*). There are several **hotels**, including *Landgasthof Grüner Baum*, Leipziger Str. 45 (☎0 66 63/97 40; ③–⑤), *Burgmannenhaus*, Brüder-Grimm-Str. 49 (☎0 66 63/9 64 00; ③–⑤), and *Gasthaus Weisses Ross*, Brüder-Grimm-Str. 48 (☎0 66 63/58 04, *bender-steinau@t-online.de*; ④).

The Lahn valley from Limburg to Giessen

The **River Lahn** forms a natural boundary dividing the upland forest areas of the Taunus and the Westerwald. Most of it lies within Hesse, but a small downstream stretch, shortly before it flows into the Rhine just south of Koblenz, is in Rhineland-Palatinate. A series of historic towns, each conveniently separated by intervals of approximately 20km, punctuate the Hessian section. Exploration is made easy by the road and rail line which closely follow the river for all but its uppermost stretch.

Limburg an der Lahn

The little episcopal city of **LIMBURG**, which lies hard by the Land border some 50km north of Wiesbaden, is beautifully situated on a rocky spur on the south bank of the Lahn. Compact enough to be seen in a short time, it's deservedly a popular destination with day-trippers from the Rhineland.

Limburg's **Dom** is built right at the top of the town and might at first sight appear to be a sacred counterpart to the fantasy castles erected all over Germany in the Romantic period. In fact, it's a perfectly genuine church from the first half of the thirteenth century, with an orange, white and yellow colour scheme and an exotic roofline comprising seven towers and spires. In essence the Dom belongs to the last phase of Romanesque, and, despite using some elements of the newly emerging Gothic style, it seems that the builders were unaware of the structural advantages of pointed arches and rib vaults, using them merely for novelty value and decorative effects. Just before the church was consecrated, it was endowed with a series of naive but vigorous **frescoes**, most of which survive; look out in particular for the striking depiction of Samson in the south transept. Two other furnishings from the same period can also be seen – the elaborate stone **font** in a south aisle chapel, and the **tomb** of the founder Conrad Kurzbold in the northern transept.

To the rear of the Dom, the **Schloss** of the local lords is another very picturesque jumble of buildings now used to house offices and the municipal archives. Down Domstrasse is the **Diözesanmuseum** (mid-March to mid-Nov Tues–Sat 10am–1pm & 2–5pm, Sun 11am–5pm; DM2/€1). This contains some stunning treasury items, notably the *Staurothek*, a Byzantine reliquary in the shape of a cross, which was brought back from the Crusades by a local Knight; the jewelled *Staff of St Peter*, made by a tenth-century goldsmith from Trier; and the eleventh-century lead reliquary from the high altar of the previous church on the site of the Dom.

The venerable houses of the Altstadt at the foot of the hill are predominantly half-timbered, with the cluster around **Fischmarkt** ranking among the oldest in the country. Here also is the **Historisches Rathaus**, which served as the town hall for exactly six centuries. To end your visit, cross over the **Alte Lahnbrücke**, a fourteenth-century bridge which preserves its original defensive tower. From here, or better still the opposite bank, you're rewarded with a wonderful **view** of the skyline.

Practicalities

Limburg's **Bahnhof** is just south of the Altstadt. The **tourist office** (April–Oct Mon–Fri 8am–12.30pm & 2–6pm, Sat 10am–noon; Nov–March Mon–Thurs 8am–12.30pm & 2–5pm, Fri 8am–12.30pm; ☎0 64 31/61 66, fax 32 93, *www.limburg.de*) is a couple of minutes' walk to the north at Hospitalstr. 2.

There's one inexpensive, but central **guesthouse**, *Zum Weissen Ross*, Westerwaldstr. 2 (☎0 64 31/87 76; ③). Around the Bahnhof are several **hotels**, including *Huss*, Bahnhofsplatz 3 (☎0 64 31/9 33 50; ⑤), *Martin*, Holzheimer Str. 2 (☎0 64 31/4 10 01 or 9 48 40; ⑤), and *Zimmermann*, Blumenröder Str. 1 (☎0 64 31/46 11; ⑥). Altstadt establishments include *Nassauer Hof*, Brückenstr. 1 (☎0 64 31/99 60; ⑥), and *Dom-Hotel*, Grabenstr. 57 (☎0 64 31/90 10; ⑥–⑧). There's a **youth hostel** at the extreme southern edge of town at Auf dem Guckucksberg (☎0 64 31/4 14 93, fax 4 38 73, *Limburg@djh -hessen.de*; DM23.50/€11.75 or DM28.50/€14.25); take bus #3. The **campsite** (☎0 64 31/2 26 10) is at Schleusenweg 16, at the northern end of town.

Both *Nassauer Hof* and *Dom-Hotel* have excellent **restaurants**; otherwise the best place to eat in Limburg is *St Georgsstube* in the Stadthalle, Hospitalstr. 4.

Weilburg

What **WEILBURG** lacks in size, it makes up for in visual appeal. Standing on a promontory surrounded on three sides by the River Lahn, its compact centre is grouped around the elegant sixteenth-century **Schloss** (guided tours Tues–Sun 10am–4/5pm; DM7/€3.50) which, together with its outbuildings and grounds, almost forms a town in itself. Once the residence of an offshoot line of the House of Nassau, the Schloss has a particularly beautiful central courtyard, offering an almost rustic interpretation of the

Renaissance style. In the eighteenth century, the complex was greatly expanded by the addition of the **Marstall** (stables) on the northern side, and by the laying out of the **Schlossgarten** as a series of terraces leading down to the Lahn. Within the latter is the curvaceous **Obere Orangerie** (same hours as Schloss; DM2/€1), which is used for temporary exhibitions of *objets d'art*, and the **Untere Orangerie**, now a café-restaurant. Alongside is the **Schlosskirche**, one of the finest Baroque churches in Hesse – its elaborate pillared altar, decorated with cherubs and sunbursts, has an almost Rococo feel to it.

Directly opposite the main entrance to the Schloss is the **Stadt- und Bergbaumuseum** (April–Oct Tues–Sun 10am–noon & 2–5pm; Nov–March Mon–Fri 10am–noon & 2–5pm; DM4/€2), whose main attraction is the Tiefe Stollen, a full-sized mock-up of a local mine. Upstairs, there's an early nineteenth-century pharmacy and the Weilburger Herbarium of 1842, which is still in its original display cabinets. In the middle of the adjacent Marktplatz is a heavily ornamented Renaissance fountain, the **Neptunbrunnen**.

North of the Schloss, the Lahn is crossed by the five-arched **Steinerne Brücke**, first erected in the 1760s. On either side of the peninsula, you can see the two entrances to the **Schiffstunnel**, the only such construction in Germany, which was dug in the middle of the nineteenth century to save ships from having to sail all the way round the town. It cuts beneath the **Kalvarienberg**, a hill with an unfinished sixteenth-century attempt at re-creating the Holy Places of Jerusalem.

Practicalities

Weilburg's **Bahnhof** is beside the Lahn, on the opposite bank from the Schloss. The **tourist office** is south of the Schloss at Mauerstr. 6 (Mon–Fri 9am–noon & 2–4.30pm, Sat 10am–noon; ☎0 64 71/76 71 or 3 14 67, fax 76 75, *www.weilburg.de*).

Zur Altstadt, Schulgasse 18 (☎0 64 71/3 91 86; ④), is a centrally located **pension**. Among the **hotels**, the most convenient are *Zum Weilburger Löwen*, Frankfurter Str. 27 (☎0 64 71/78 22; ④), *Villa im Park*, Frankfurter Str. 12 (☎0 64 71/9 38 30, *vip@weilburg.de*; ⑥), and *Schlosshotel*, which occupies the Marstall, Langgasse 25 (☎0 64 71/3 90 96; ⑧). There's a riverside **campsite** (☎0 64 71/76 20), but the **youth hostel** is a long walk from town, above the outlying village of Odersbach, 4km to the west, at Am Steinbühl (☎0 64 71/71 16, fax 15 42, *Weilburg@djh-hessen.de*; DM23.50/€11.75 or DM28.50/€14.25).

Weilburg has an abundance of good places to **eat** and **drink**. Predictably, the *Schlosshotel* has the best and most expensive restaurant. *Weilburger Hof*, Schwannengasse 14, is another good choice for traditional German dishes; *La Lucia*, Marktplatz 10, is a fine Italian restaurant; while *Zur Turmschmiede* on Turmgasse has a shady beer garden.

Wetzlar

The long-time city-state of **WETZLAR** occupies a hallowed place in the annals of German literature (see box opposite), which in turn was a consequence of its role from 1693 to 1803 as seat of the Reichskammergericht, the highest civil court of the Holy Roman Empire. These days it's a light industrial town, and is centred on a well-preserved Altstadt of half-timbered, grey-roofed houses precipitously clinging to the hillside above the Lahn.

Of the many steeply plunging squares in Wetzlar's Altstadt, the largest is Domplatz, named after the so-called **Dom**, a former collegiate church used for both Catholic and Protestant worship. It offers a fascinating insight into medieval building practices, as the Romanesque structure was demolished piece by piece to make way for a Gothic hall design. However, money ran out before completion, with the result that the old north tower and main entrance (the Heathens' Portal) still survive, the latter marooned

THE SORROWS OF YOUNG WERTHER

While working at the Reichskammergericht as a legal clerk, **Goethe** fell in love with Lotte Buff, the fiancée of a close friend. His response to this awkward situation was to run away from it. However, when another friend there, Karl Wilhelm Jerusalem, committed suicide over an unrequited love affair, he was inspired to fuse the two episodes by writing an epistolary novella, *The Sorrows of Young Werther*. It was an immediate sensation; before his twenty-fifth birthday, Goethe had become the most celebrated literary figure in Europe, inspiring a Romantic reaction against the Age of Reason and creating a continent-wide phenomenon of young men wearing blue coats and yellow breeches, suffering from melancholy and contemplating suicide.

behind its partly completed successor. The Gothic **south tower**, later capped with a Baroque belfry, is the symbol of the town and its most prominent landmark.

Just off the south side of Domplatz is the small Fischmarkt, on which stands the former **Rathaus**, later the seat of the Reichskammergericht and now a café. Following Pfaffengasse uphill from Domplatz brings you to the **Hof des Deutschen Ritterordens** (Court of the Teutonic Knights). Within the courtyard is the **Lottehaus** (Tues–Sun 10am–1pm & 2–5pm; DM3/€1.50, or DM8/€4 combined ticket for all the town's museums), the house where Lotte Buff lived with her parents and siblings. A must for Goethe aficionados, it has been turned into a small museum containing period furniture, pictures and books – with lots of first editions and translations of *Werther*. Next door is the **Stadt- und Industriemuseum** (same times and conditions), which details Wetzlar's history as a Free Imperial City and the development of its iron and optical industries. It was here that Oskar Barnack pioneered today's standard 35mm camera, and the town is home to Leitz, a leading camera manufacturer.

At the southeastern corner of the Altstadt, reached via the picturesque squares of Kornmarkt and Eisenmarkt, are three more small museums each well worth a visit. The pick of these is the **Sammlung Dr Irmgard von Lemmers-Danforth** (same times and conditions as the Lottehaus) at Kornblumengasse 1, which has a really lovely collection of Renaissance and Baroque furniture and decorative art from all over Europe, displayed in a handsome town mansion. A few paces away, at Hofstatt 19, is the **Reichskammergerichtsmuseum** (same times and conditions), detailing the history of the institution that brought Wetzlar its fame. Finally, just to the south at Schillerplatz 5 is the half-timbered **Jerusalemhaus** (same times and conditions), which has been restored to give a period feel of the time when it was the home of the lovelorn youth who was the inspiration for Goethe's Werther.

Practicalities

Wetzlar's **Bahnhof** is about 1km north of the Altstadt and on the opposite side of the Lahn. The **tourist office** is at Domplatz 8 (Mon–Wed & Fri 8am–noon & 2–4.30pm, Thurs 8am–noon & 2–5pm, Sat 9.30–11.30am; ☎0 64 41/9 93 38, *www.wetzlar.de*).

Hotels with a central location include *Domblick*, Langgasse 64 (☎0 64 41/9 01 60; ⑤), *Wetzlarer Hof*, Obertorstr. 3 (☎0 64 41/90 80; ⑥), *Bürgerhof*, Konrad-Adenauer-Promenade 20 (☎0 64 41/90 30; ⑥), and *Mercure*, Bergstr. 41 (☎0 64 41/41 70; ⑥). There are cheaper alternatives in the outlying villages, and the tourist office can help with these. Wetzlar's **youth hostel** is in a lovely secluded setting southeast of the Altstadt at Richard-Schirrmann-Str. 3 (☎0 64 41/7 10 68, fax 7 58 26, *Wetzlar@djh -hessen.de*; DM24.50/€12.25 or DM29.50/€14.75); take bus #12 to Sturzkopf. There are two local **campsites**: the first of these, *Niedergirmes*, is north of the Bahnhof (☎0 64 41/3 41 03); the other is at *Dutenhofener See* (☎06 41/2 32 20), about halfway to Giessen, near the Bahnhof Wetzlar-Ost.

The last three hotels listed above all have excellent **restaurants**. Otherwise, try *Zur Domtreppe*, Domplatz 5, which has a secluded beer garden, or head north of the Altstadt to *Häusler's*, Garbenheimer Str. 18, the evenings-only Gaststätte of the local Euler brewery.

Giessen

Before the war **GIESSEN** was as famous for its half-timbered houses as it was for its university, founded in the early seventeenth century. Unfortunately, it was severely battered by bombs, and the centre is now a bland postwar reconstruction. Giessen is also a US army garrison town and supply centre, but it's a lively place and, as it's a major rail junction, you may well find yourself passing through.

The skyline of the Altstadt is dominated by the disembodied Gothic tower that is all that remains of the **Stadtkirche**. Directly opposite, at Georg-Schlosser-Str. 2, is one of the few timber-framed buildings to have survived, the fourteenth-century **Burgmannenhaus**. Together with the adjoining building, it now contains the **Oberhessisches Museum** (Tues–Sun 10am–4pm; free), featuring the extensive archeology collections of the university, together with displays of regional history and folklore.

The other main concentration of historic sights is just to the east around Brandplatz. Here the **Neues Schloss**, a picturesque late Gothic half-timbered palace, is dwarfed by the adjacent **Zeughaus**, a Renaissance arsenal which houses part of the university. Opposite is the heavily restored fourteenth-century **Altes Schloss** (Tues–Sun 10am–4pm; free), now home to the art collection of the Oberhessisches Museum. Behind it is the **Botanischer Garten** (Mon–Fri 8am–3.30/8pm, Sat & Sun 8am–3.30/6pm; free), the oldest such institution in Germany, founded in 1609 for the purposes of scientific research. It's also a much-loved recreation spot, an oasis of calm in the heart of the city.

Just to the southwest of the Altstadt, at Liebigstr. 12, is the **Liebig-Museum** (Tues–Sun 10am–4pm; DM3/€1.50). Originally a guard house, the building was specially converted to serve as the teaching and research laboratory of the hugely influential nineteenth-century scientist Justus von Liebig (after whom the university is named) and is still preserved almost exactly as he knew it. Here Liebig pioneered a systematic approach to the study of chemistry, attracting students from all over Europe.

Some 6km southeast of the town centre is the **Schiffenbergkloster**, a walled monastery which began life as an Augustinian collegiate foundation, before being taken over by the Teutonic Knights. The rough-hewn Romanesque church is substantially intact, though it's open on the cloister side, which is now a huge beer garden. It's a favourite excursion goal at the weekends: all kinds of live music are performed on both days, while students conduct "secret" fencing matches at the crack of dawn on Sunday. Bus #6 runs out regularly from Berliner Platz, just beyond the southern edge of the Altstadt, on Sundays only.

Practicalities

Giessen's **Hauptbahnhof**, a grandly self-confident product of the golden era of rail travel, is a short walk southwest of the town centre. The **tourist office** (Mon–Wed & Fri 9am–1pm & 2–5pm, Thurs 9am–1pm & 2–8pm, Sat 9am–noon; ☎06 41/1 94 33, fax 7 69 57, *www.hessennet/giessen*) is at Berliner Platz 2.

Centrally located **hotels** include *An der Lahn*, Lahnstr. 21 (☎06 41/7 35 16; ④), *Am Ludwigsplatz*, Ludwigsplatz 8 (☎06 41/93 11 30; ⑤), *Köhler*, Westanlage 32–35 (☎06 41/97 99 90; ⑥), and *Steinsgarten*, Hein-Heckroth-Str. 20 (☎06 41/3 89 90; ⑦). The **youth hostel** is on the western side of town at Richard-Schirrmann-Weg 53 (☎06 41/6 58 79 or 7 10 68, fax 9 60 55 02, *Giessen@djh-hessen.de*; DM22/€11 or DM27/€13.50); take bus #7 to Untere Hardthöhe.

If you happen to find yourself in Giessen at night, head for Ludwigstrasse, which is known as Kneipenstrasse by the locals because it's full of **pubs**. Also worth checking out for occasional live music is *Ulenspiegel*, Seltersweg 53–55. The best **restaurants** are those in the last two hotels listed above, plus the *Schlosskeller* in the cellars of the Altes Schloss, Brandplatz 2. A varied **cultural** programme, including opera, ballet, musicals, concerts and drama, is performed at the Jugendstil Stadtheater on Berliner Platz (☎06 41/79 57 60).

Marburg

The cradle of Hesse and its original capital, **MARBURG** clusters up the slopes of the Lahn valley some 30km upstream from Giessen in a maze of narrow streets and medieval buildings. There are distinctive lower and upper towns, dominated respectively by two of Germany's greatest buildings, the Elisabethkirche and the Schloss. However, the whole ensemble is in many ways the most remarkable feature, as the town has been touched by war less than almost any other city in the country.

Marburg was one of the major pilgrimage centres of northern Europe on account of its patron **St Elisabeth** – a thirteenth-century Hungarian-born princess who had devoted herself to the poor – until the cult was abolished by her descendant, **Landgrave Philip the Magnanimous**, at the time of the Reformation. In 1527 he established the university, the first in the world to be subject to the new Protestant faith. Nowadays, nearly a quarter of the population is in some way associated with the university, and the presence of 15,000 students gives it a relaxed and lively atmosphere. Marburg has good rail and road links with Frankfurt, Kassel and Koblenz, and is worth going far out of your way to visit.

Arrival, information and accommodation

Marburg's **Hauptbahnhof** is on the right bank of the Lahn at the northern end of town, just five minutes' walk from the Elisabethkirche. The **tourist office** (April–Sept Mon–Fri 9am–6pm, Sat 10am–2pm; Oct–March Mon–Fri 9am–6pm; ☎0 64 21/9 91 20, fax 99 12 12, *www.marburg.de*) is at Am Pilgrimstein 26.

There's a surprising lack of **hotels** with a convenient location and it might be a good idea to enquire at the tourist office about places in outlying villages if you're after a budget deal. The **youth hostel** is at Jahnstr. 1 (☎0 64 21/2 34 61, fax 1 21 91, *Marburg@djh-hessen.de*; DM24.50/€12.25 or DM29.50/€14.75), a little to the southeast of the Altstadt; the *Lahnaue* **campsite** (☎0 64 21/2 13 31) is a bit further down the river at Trojedamm 47.

Hotels and guesthouses

Dammühle, Dammühlenstr. 1, Wehrshausen (☎0 64 21/9 35 60, fax 3 61 18, *hertel@scm.de*).Well worth considering if you've got your own transport, this occupies an old half-timbered water-mill, 5km west of the centre, and has a café-restaurant. ⑥.

Europäischer Hof, Elisabethstr. 12 (☎0 64 21/69 60, fax 6 64 04). This hotel, which has been in existence since 1834, has rooms of varying degrees of luxury and offers a good breakfast buffet. The restaurant, *Atelier*, has a predominantly Italianate menu. ⑤–⑨.

Hesse-Stübche, Untergasse 10 (☎0 64 21/2 58 87, fax 16 29 47). Typically German hotel with pub-restaurant in the heart of the upper town. ⑥.

Hostaria del Castello, Markt 19 (☎0 64 21/2 58 84, fax 12 32 25). Italian restaurant with a few rooms for rent. ⑤–⑦.

Müller, Deutschhausstr. 29 (☎0 64 21/6 56 59). Good-value guesthouse in the lower town, close to the Elisabethkirche. ④.

Schneider, Gladenbacher Weg 37 (☎ & fax 0 64 21/3 42 36). Inexpensive pension in the far south-western part of town. ③.

Tusculum, Gutenbergerstr. 25 (☎0 64 21/2 27 78, fax 1 53 04, *www.tusculum.de*). Hotel located just south of the upper town, with brightly painted rooms. ⑤.

Vila Vita, Rosenstr. 18–28 (☎0 64 21/6 00 50, fax 6 00 51 00, *www.vilavitahotels.com*). Marburg's newest and classiest hotel, beautifully furnished with antiques and with a gourmet restaurant and fitness centre. ⑨.

Waldecker Hof, Bahnhofstr. 23 (☎0 64 21/6 00 90, fax 60 09 59, *www.waldecker-hof-marburg.de*). The facilities at this hotel, which is conveniently close to the Hauptbahnhof, include a swimming pool, sauna, solarium and fitness room. ⑥–⑧.

Zur Sonne, Markt 14 (☎0 64 21/1 71 90, fax 17 19 40). This pretty half-timbered building, a Gasthaus since the sixteenth century, is the most atmospheric place to stay in Marburg. It also has a superb restaurant. ⑥.

The lower town

Although much of it is now taken up with functional modern buildings of the university and by a business and shopping district, the kernel of the lower town (*Unterstadt*) survives from the thirteenth century. It was then the property of the **Order of Teutonic Knights** (see p.377). Given their bellicosity, it's all the more ironic that they showed such dedication to St Elisabeth, whose life could hardly have presented a greater contrast.

The Elisabethkirche

No sooner had Elisabeth gained papal recognition as a saint in 1235, than the Teutonic Knights began the construction of the **Elisabethkirche** (April–Sept Mon–Sat 9am–6pm, Sun 12.30–6pm; Oct Mon–Sat 9am–5pm, Sun 12.30–5pm; Nov–March Mon–Sat 10am–4pm, Sun 12.30–4pm; DM3/€1.50 for admission to the chancel) on the site of her hospice, encasing her tomb in the process. The first purely Gothic building on German soil, it's also one of the most original and most beautiful, with the hall-church format (which necessitated heavy wall buttresses), and the trefoil or "clover leaf" plan for the east end adapted to the new style of architecture for the first time. The twin **towers**, with their relentless upward movement and tall pointed steeples, are also very Germanic and noticeably different from their more varied and elaborate French counterparts.

Inside, the church is full of statues and frescoes, mainly celebrating Elisabeth's piety. Curiously enough, her cult underwent a major revival just before the Reformation, and five magnificent winged **altars** were created by the local master carver Ludwig Juppe and the painter Johann von der Leyten. On the right as you enter is one of these, the Elisabeth altar, which vividly relates the saint's life. In an alcove to the other side is the tomb of **Paul von Hindenburg**, the *Reichspresident* who appointed Hitler Chancellor in 1933. His body was brought to this decidedly unsuitable location after the war by the Americans. At the opposite end of this aisle, a curvaceous **statue of Elisabeth** from about 1470 depicts her in a pose she would have despised – as a richly robed, crowned princess clutching a model of her church.

Just around the corner is the **Elisabeth-Chor**, as the northern part of the clover leaf plan is known. Its centrepiece is the towering **mausoleum** containing her coffin in its original location. Look out for the reliefs on the pedestal, which show her being mourned by beggars and cripples instead of the kings and bishops who normally occupied such a position. Among the **altars**, pride of place goes to that dedicated to the Virgin, in which Juppe skilfully incorporated a much-venerated older sculpture of the Pietà into the predella. A number of **murals** illustrating the saint's life, long covered up and only rediscovered last century, can also be seen.

The main choir, or **Hochchor**, still preserves its original thirteenth-century adornments – a curious high altar shaped like the narthex of a church, a complete set of stalls and stained-glass windows. Some of the windows have been mutilated, although an engagingly stylized series illustrating the Crucifixion remain. On the north side, the former sacristy now contains the church's most spectacular treasure, the resplendent mid-thirteenth-century **golden shrine** which contained the relics of Elisabeth until Philip the Magnanimous had them reinterred. Elisabeth's life is illustrated yet again on the reliefs on the lid.

Finally, the **Landgrafen-Chor**, the southern arm of the trefoil plan, serves as the **pantheon** of the rulers of Hesse. The first tomb in the eastern row is to Elisabeth's brother-in-law Conrad, while the fourth, artistically the finest of the group, commemorates Heinrich I, the first landgrave of Hesse. The only alabaster intruder among the stone tombs is Philip the Magnanimous's father Wilhelm II, who is gruesomely depicted as a decaying corpse.

The rest of the quarter

Grouped around the Elisabethkirche are several other buildings formerly belonging to the Teutonic Knights. Forming a sort of close around the church's east end are the thirteenth-century **Brüderhaus** and **Herrenhaus**, the fifteenth-century **Deutschordenhaus** and the sixteenth-century **Kornspeicher**. All are now used by the university: the Kornspeicher, formerly a corn store and bakehouse, now houses the **Mineralogisches Museum** (Wed 10am–1pm & 3–6pm, Thurs & Fri 10am–1pm, Sat & Sun 11am–3pm; free), which is more interesting than it sounds, with a glittering array of precious stones. Up a little hill to the west of the Elisabethkirche is the **Michaelskapelle**, a funerary chapel for the Knights and pilgrims to the shrine. St Elisabeth herself was buried in its peaceful little cemetery once the ban on her cult had been imposed.

Following Deutschhausstrasse southeastwards, then turning right into Biegenstrasse, at no. 11 you'll find the **Universitätsmuseum für bildende Kunst** (Tues–Sun 11am–1pm & 2–5pm; free), which has a Lucas Cranach the Elder portrait of Luther, a Klee, a Kandinsky and a Picasso, and works by German artists, notably the local painter Karl Bantzer.

The upper town

Other than its one supreme monument, the most remarkable feature of the upper town (*Oberstadt*) is its atmospheric appearance, with plunging streets, steep stairways, narrow alleys, secluded corners and surprising vistas. The most enticing way up is to follow the **Steinweg**, an old stepped street hemmed in by half-timbered buildings, from the Elisabethkirche.

Marktplatz and around

Heart of the Altstadt is the **Marktplatz**, with its St-Georg-Brunnen and an appealing line-up of golden half-timbered houses. During term-time the square is the focal point of Marburg's nightlife, but out of term it's very peaceful, except for the twice-weekly markets. Here you might see older women in the traditional costumes still sometimes worn in the area, a hangover from the days when Protestant and Catholic had to be able to tell each other apart – the Protestants wore black, dark brown, blue or green, while the Catholics wore bright colours with plaited hair. The **Rathaus**, a sixteenth-century Gothic building, has a gabled Renaissance staircase tower featuring another statue of Elisabeth by Ludwig Juppe, holding the arms of the landgraves of Hesse. The heraldic symbol is supposed to be a lion, but the sculptor mischievously made it look like a monkey.

South of the Markt is the **Kiliankirche**, Marburg's oldest church, but one which has been secularized since the sixteenth century. In the Nazi period it was appropriated for use as the local SS headquarters, and was also the final place to which Marburg's Jews were taken before deportation. Nowadays, it's the head office of the German Green Cross. Further south is the **Alte Universität**, which took over a Gothic Dominican friary, of which only the church (Tues–Sun 9am–5pm) now remains. The rest of the complex was rebuilt in a grandiose neo-Romanesque style, with the centrepiece being the **Aula**, a ceremonial hall adorned with frescoes depicting the history of the city.

Nicolaistrasse leads west from Marktplatz to the thirteenth-century **Marienkirche**, from whose terrace there's a good view out over Marburg and the Lahn. Just past here is a stairway called the Ludwig-Bickell-Treppe which provides the shortest route up to the top of the town. Alternatively, you can ascend the slower way to the northeast via the Renaissance **Kanzlei**, which now houses another university collection, the **Religionskundliche Sammlung** (Mon–Fri 10am–1pm; free), with material on the history of religions.

The Schloss

Towering above Marburg at a height of 102m above the Lahn is the **Schloss** (April–Oct Tues–Sun 10am–6pm; Nov–March Tues–Sun 11am–5pm; DM3/€1.50). There was a castle on this site as far back as the twelfth century, but the present structure was begun by order of Sophie of Brabant, daughter of St Elisabeth, to serve as the seat of the Landgraves of the new state of Hesse. Marburg lost its role as capital to Kassel at the beginning of the fourteenth century, but before then a substantial portion of the present Schloss had been built. This included the south wing, at the end of which is the **Schlosskapelle**. Inside, the lurid rose-coloured interior is quite striking; some original murals and part of the mosaic pavement also survive.

From the same period is the **Saalbau** on the northern side. This is notable for illustrating that this Schloss was primarily a residential palace, as opposed to the then standard fortified castle. Although the magnificent great hall, the largest structure of its kind in Germany, is known as the **Rittersaal**, it actually had no military function, instead being a venue for feasts and receptions. The most famous of these was the **Marburg Colloquy** of 1529, when Philip the Magnanimous failed to unite Protestantism.

The hall's two spectacular Renaissance inlaid-wood doorways are among the many additions and embellishments made to the Schloss during the fifteenth and sixteenth centuries, when Marburg periodically regained its position as capital of all or part of Hesse. At the eastern side of the complex, the **Wilhelmsbau**, linked to the main courtyard by a covered bridge, was the last significant part to be built. It now contains the miscellaneous archeology, applied art and local history displays of the **Museum für Kulturgeschichte**. From the terrace outside there's a wonderful aerial **view** over the Elisabethkirche and the lower town.

Eating and drinking

There's no shortage of places for eating and drinking in this student-dominated town. The best bars are among the half-timbered buildings on Hirschberg, the street leading off from the Markt, and on Untergasse.

Alter Ritter, Steinweg 44. Classy restaurant which offers bargain lunches and reasonably priced set dinners.

Babylon, Biegenstr. 23. Syrian and Lebanese speciality restaurant. Evenings only, except Sun, when it's also open for lunch.

Café Barfuss, Barfüsserstr. 33. Café-bar which serves a good selection of food, including its own pizza variant, *Fetizzo*.

Café Vetter, Reitgasse 4. A cross between a traditional café and a trendy café-bar, with its own panorama terrace.

Das Kleine Restaurant, Barfüssertor 25. Intimate little place serving some of the best cuisine in town. Closed Mon.

Hinkelstein, Markt 18. Cellar tavern with occasional live music, popular with students.

Kalimera, Lingelgasse 13a. Greek taverna with riverside garden, featuring a good choice of vegetarian options on its menu.

Milano, Biegenstr. 19. Highly regarded upmarket Italian restaurant.

Piscator, Stadthalle, Biegenstr. 15. A good traditional German restaurant and a worthy rival to the restaurant at *Zur Sonne* (see p.426).

Quodlibet, Am Grün 37. Good bar with billiard tables.

Roter Stern, Am Grün 28. Housed in a bookshop, this is where Marburg's coolest crowd hang out. Well known for its superb Nicaraguan coffee.

Weinlädele, Schlosstreppe 1. A cosy wine bar in a half-timbered building. Evenings only.

Entertainment

It's always worth checking up on **events** held on the Schlosspark's open-air stage. Otherwise, the principal highbrow **drama** and **concert** venue is the Stadthalle, Biegenstr. 15 (☎0 64 21/2 56 08); *KFZ*, Schulstr. 6 (☎0 64 21/1 38 98), is an alternative cultural centre featuring all kinds of live music, theatre and cabaret. The only **disco** as such is Kult-Lager, in the south of town at Terminstr. 9. Marburg's main **festival** is the bucolic *Marktfrühschoppen* on the first Sunday in July, while the *Elisabethmarkt* in mid-October is another good time to visit. **Boats** can be rented from *Bootsverleih*, Auf dem Wehr (☎0 64 21/2 68 64).

The Vogelsberg

The **Vogelsberg** is a quiet region of gently rolling hills, forests and small villages which has long been known to the weekend trippers of Hesse but remains relatively undiscovered by outsiders. A massive extinct volcano about 50km in diameter, the Vogelsberg rises to a maximum altitude of 774m at the **Taufstein** – not a dramatic landscape, but a good place for a bit of rustic recuperation. The heart of the range, the area known as the **High Vogelsberg** (Hoher Vogelsberg), has been designated a *Naturpark*. There are rail lines along the western and northern fringes of the range. Elsewhere bus connections run regularly between the small towns and villages on weekdays, but tend to dry up by midday on Saturdays.

Büdingen

BÜDINGEN lies at the southwestern edge of the Vogelsberg, on the rail line linking Giessen with Gelnhausen. Like the latter, which is little more than a fifteen-minute journey away, it dates back to the time of the Hohenstaufen emperors, and is chiefly worth visiting for its medieval survivals, though it's also a popular health resort. The Altstadt shelters behind a completely intact **Stadtmauer**, which is pierced with decorated Gothic gateways. There's also a **Schloss** (guided tours mid-March to mid-Dec Tues–Sun at 11.30am, 2pm, 3pm, 4pm & 5pm; *www.ysenburg.de*; DM6.50/€3.25), which still serves as the seat of the prince of Yburg-Büdingen. This is in two parts, with a Gothic **Vorburg** protecting the main **Kernburg**, a truly remarkable structure with thirteen sides. It was continuously rebuilt down the ages, so the component parts run the full gamut of architectural styles from the twelfth to seventeenth centuries. The late Gothic **Schlosskapelle**, with its elaborate network vaulting and richly carved stalls, is particularly outstanding.

Büdingen's **tourist office** is at Marktplatz 7 (Mon–Fri 9am–6pm, Sat 10.30am–2pm, Sun 10.30am–4pm; ☎0 60 42/9 63 70, fax 96 37 10, *www.buedingen.net*). There are several **hotels**, including *Stadt Büdingen*, Jahnstr. 16 (☎0 60 42/9 62 90; ⑥), and *Haus Sonnenberg*, Sudetenstr. 4–6 (☎0 60 42/30 51; ⑥). Additionally, there's a **youth hostel**, but it's on top of a hill 3km northwest of the town centre at Jugendherberge 1 (☎0 60 42/36 97, fax 6 81 78, *Buedingen@djh-hessen.de*; DM23.50/€11.75 or DM28.50/€14.25).

Alsfeld

ALSFELD, which lies at the northern fringe of the Vogelsberg, on the looping rail line between Giessen and Fulda, is so postcard-pretty that it once won a designation as a model town in a Europe-wide competition. Its buildings conform in the main to the half-timbered blueprint of the area, and many of them are so old that they seem ready to pitch forward into the cobbled streets. The slightly spooky-looking late Gothic **Rathaus**, one of the finest in the country, stands on the northern side of the Marktplatz, focal point of the Altstadt. Its arcaded lower storey formerly served as a covered market. On the eastern side of the square is the Renaissance **Hochzeitshaus**, a rare stone building originally constructed for the celebration of weddings and festivals.

Just off the southwest corner of Marktplatz, at Rittergasse 3–5, two showy Baroque mansions have been combined to house the **Regionalmuseum** (Mon–Fri 9am–5pm, Sat & Sun 10am–noon & 2–5pm; DM2/€1), with the usual displays on local archeology, history, trades, costumes and folklore. To the rear of the Rathaus is the **Walpurgiskirche**, a grey, geometrical church dating from the thirteenth century, but partly rebuilt in late Gothic style. Its Renaissance galleries are adorned with paintings illustrating Protestant doctrines, though plenty of pre-Reformation furnishings survive, notably the Romanesque font and the Gothic frescoes and high altar.

Alsfeld's **Bahnhof** lies a few minutes' walk to the west of the Altstadt. The **tourist office** is at Rittergasse 3 (Mon–Fri 9am–6pm, Sat 10am–1pm; ☎0 66 31/18 21 65, fax 18 22 10, *www.alsfeld.de*). There are four **hotels**, all capacious, centrally located and offering high standards in relation to the prices charged: *Krone*, Schellengasse 2–4 (☎0 66 31/40 41; ④), *Zur Erholung*, Grünberger Str. 26 (☎0 66 31/9 67 80; ④), *Zum Schwalbennest*, Pfarrwiesenweg 12–14 (☎0 66 31/50 61; ⑤), and *Klingelhöffer*, Hersfelder Str. 47 (☎0 66 31/20 73; ⑤). Each of these has a recommendable **restaurant**; otherwise the most appealing places to eat are a trio of old wine bars: *Marktkeller*, which is in the Hochzeitshaus, Marktplatz 7, *Ramsbeck's Weinkeller*, Marktplatz 9, and *Zum Brünnchen*, Untergasse 10. The main **festivals** are *Pfingstenfest* over the long Whit weekend and the *Stadt- und Heimatfest* on the first Saturday in August.

Schlitz

SCHLITZ, which boasts a well-preserved and strongly fortified Altstadt, is at the extreme northeastern fringe of the Vogelsberg; it is not on a rail line and is therefore best reached by bus from Fulda, which lies 15km to the southeast. The **Stadtmauer** is pierced by just two small gateways, yet ringed by no fewer than four castles of varying dates. At the highest part of town is the oldest and largest of these, the **Vorderburg**, which now houses the **Heimatmuseum** (April–Oct Tues–Sun 2–4pm; Nov–March Sat & Sun 2–4pm; DM2/€1), with displays of weapons, costumes and handicrafts. The thirteenth-century keep of the **Hinterburg** (April–Oct daily 9am–noon & 2–5/7pm; DM2/€1) can be ascended by lift for a fine panorama over the region. Neither of the other castles – the half-timbered **Schachtenburg** alongside the Hinterburg and the **Ottoburg**, a Baroque residential palace – had any defensive function. Within the Stadtmauer are many fine half-timbered houses, but the dominant monument is the **Stadtkirche**. Apart from the fifteenth-century steeple, the church is largely thirteenth-century in date, though some masonry survives from the original ninth-century basilica.

Two of the budget **hotels**, *Braustübchen*, Brauhausstr. 18 (☎0 66 42/10 18; ③), and *Gasthof Zum Auerhahn*, Untergasse 1 (☎0 66 42/50 31; ④) are named after the nearby *Auerhahn-Bräu*, which makes light and dark beers in its half-timbered nineteenth-century premises. Other hotels include *Guntrum*, Otto-Zinsser-Str. 5 (☎0 66 42/50 93; ④), and *Vorderburg*, An der Vorderburg 1 (☎0 66 42/50 41; ⑤). The main **festival** is the colourful *Schlitzerländer Heimat- und Trachtenfest*, held every other year on the second weekend of July.

Fulda

Lying in a narrow valley between the Vogelsberg and the Rhön, **FULDA** was best known throughout the Cold War as the weak point in NATO's front line (the so-called Fulda Gap) through which the massed tanks of the Warsaw Pact were supposedly most likely to pour into Western Europe. With that dubious threat now gone, the city can concentrate once more on its role as a major episcopal centre, the venue for the annual meetings of both the Catholic Bishops' Conference and the German Protestant Convention. Church affairs have dominated Fulda's history. Its roots go back to the eighth century when a small town grew up around the abbey founded by St Boniface, a monk sent from England to convert the Germans. After his martyrdom in 754, Fulda became a pilgrimage site, and over the years its abbey grew into one of the most important monasteries in Germany. It was here that a couple of monks transcribed the *Lay of Hildebrand*, one of the first recorded pieces of German literature. For centuries, the abbots doubled as secular princes, and on their promotion to the rank of bishops they transformed their seat into a Baroque vision of golden towers and crosses.

Arrival, information and accommodation

Fulda's **Hauptbahnhof** is at the northeastern end of the town centre. You'll find the **tourist office** within the Stadtschloss at Schloss-Str. 1 (Mon–Fri 8.30am–6pm, Sat 9.30am–4pm, Sun 10am–2pm; ☎06 61/10 23 46, fax 10 27 75, *www.fulda.de*). The main venue for **cultural** events is the Schlosstheater, Schloss-Str. 5 (☎06 61/1 02 14 83).

Fulda is quite well off for **hotels** in all price categories. There's a **youth hostel** at the southwestern edge of town at Schirrmannstr. 31 (☎06 61/7 33 89, fax 7 48 11, *Fulda@djh-hessen.de*; DM23.50/€11.75 or DM28.50/€14.25); the easiest way there is by bus #12 to Stadion.

Hotels and pensions

Brauhaus Wiesenmühle, Wiesenmühlenstr. 13 (☎06 61/92 86 80, fax 9 28 68 39, *www.fulda -online.de*). Occupying a converted fourteenth-century mill, this place has both an upmarket restaurant and a hugely popular bar and beer garden serving a range of inexpensive food. The Hausbrauerei brews a wide range of seasonally appropriate beers. ⑤.

Goldener Karpfen, Simpliziusbrunnen 1 (☎06 61/8 68 00, fax 8 68 01 00, *www.Hotel-Goldener -Karpfen.com*). Now a member of the Romantik group, and equipped with plenty of mod cons such as a sauna and solarium, this has long been Fulda's top hotel: Goethe was once a patron, writing much of the *Ost-West Divan* there. It has a distinguished wine bar-restaurant. ⑧–⑨.

Hodes, Peterstor 14 (☎06 61/7 28 62, fax 24 11 79). Bargain-price pension at the edge of the Altstadt. ②.

Kurfürst, Schloss-Str. 2 (☎06 61/8 33 90, fax 8 33 93 39, *www.kurfuerst.de*). Hotel and restaurant occupying an eighteenth-century palace opposite the Stadtschloss. ⑧.

Wenzel, Heinrichstr. 38–40 (☎06 61/7 53 35, fax 7 53 36). Homely pension, conveniently close to the Hauptbahnhof. ③.

Zum Bratwurstglöckle, Am Stockhaus 10–12 (☎06 61/7 28 75, fax 24 09 13). Located in the heart of the Altstadt, this is the epitome of a traditional Gasthof. Since the 1930s, its butcher's shop has been well known locally for its horsemeat, which features extensively (but not exclusively) on the restaurant menu. ③.

Zum Kronhof, Am Kronhof 2 (☎ & fax 06 61/7 41 47). Gasthof just to the rear of the Dom, offering some of the cheapest rooms in town. ②.

Zum Ritter, Kanalstr. 18–20 (☎06 61/25 08 00, fax 7 14 31, *www.hotel-ritter.de*). Grand nineteenth-century hotel modernized a few years back to a very high standard. Its restaurant is quite reasonably priced. ⑥.

The City

The city centre, dotted with open squares and areas of greenery, is still predominantly Baroque. There are very few older buildings and not too many modern eyesores either. Outside the centre are several other attractions well worth the detour, including the heights of the **Petersberg** and the magnificent **Schloss Fasanerie**.

The episcopal quarter

Fulda's imposing **Dom**, on the western edge of the town centre, is a classic early Baroque structure by Johann Dientzenhofer, the most accomplished member of a dynasty of architects, and is totally unlike any other German cathedral. The glory of the spacious and stuccoed interior is the high altar, depicting the Assumption of the Madonna in full-blown gilded splendour and flanked by six marble columns. Behind is a small and austere chapel where the monks used to assemble for prayer. St Boniface's tomb is in the crypt beneath the high altar – it's incorporated into a sepulchral black marble altar with carved reliefs depicting the saint's martyrdom and his resurrection on Judgement Day.

The **Dommuseum** (April–Oct Tues–Sat 10am–5.30pm, Sun 12.30–5.30pm; Nov, Dec, Feb & March Tues–Sat 10am–12.30pm & 1.30–4pm, Sun 12.30–4pm; DM4/€2) occupies the Dechanei (deanery) adjoining the northern transept. It contains Boniface's relics, which include his sword, his head and the book with which he vainly tried to fend off his murderers. There's also an impressive collection of ecclesiastical vestments, while the most important painting is Cranach's *Christ and the Woman Taken in Adultery*.

Next to the Dom is the Romanesque **Michaelskirche** (daily: April to mid-Oct 10am–6pm; mid-Oct to Dec & Feb–March 2–4pm), built in the shape of a Greek cross as a copy of the Church of the Holy Sepulchre in Jerusalem. It's among the very few significant buildings to have survived the wholesale conversion of Fulda to the Baroque. In comparison to the mighty Dom it's quite inconspicuous, but in some ways is more impressive than its larger neighbour, incorporating as it does the rotunda of an earlier church. Although this has been much altered, two of its eight columns date back to 822. Inside, look out for the fourteenth-century **stone tablet** in the Baroque chapel built onto the northern transept: it illustrates the Passion in an unusual graphic code for the benefit of the illiterate of the time.

Across from the Dom stands the former episcopal palace, the cream-coloured **Stadtschloss** (Mon–Thurs, Sat & Sun 10am–6pm, Fri 2–6pm; DM4/€2). Again the work of Johann Dientzenhofer, it's a huge building with several wings which has housed the municipal offices ever since it was acquired by the city in the nineteenth century. The most imposing chambers are the small **Spiegelsaal** (Mirror Room) and the main **Daalbergsaal**, which is painted with a quirky representation of the Four Seasons, with winter in the guise of a harlequin. There are also extensive displays of locally produced porcelain. The **tower** (same times; DM2/€1) can be ascended for a view over the city.

It's well worth taking a stroll in the **Schlossgarten**, a geometrical ornamental park which leads to the **Orangerie**, the best-looking of Fulda's secular Baroque buildings, nowadays a café. Inside, look out for the *Sauerkrautbild*, a ceiling painting showing Greek deities eating the favourite German meal of sausages with pickled cabbage. The **Floravase** in front of the Orangerie, named after the floral goddess whose statue crowns it, is a masterpiece of the art of garden sculpture. Opposite the Schlossgarten are two more Baroque showpieces, the **Paulustor**, an ornamental gateway, and the **Hauptwache**, the former guard house.

Elsewhere in the centre

In the heart of the pedestrianized town centre, reached from the Hauptwache via Friedrichstrasse, is the **Stadtpfarrkirche**, which pretty much conforms to Fulda house style, and the **Altes Rathaus**, which breaks the mould by having a half-timbered facade. Just to the south is the Jesuit Alte Stadtschule, now housing the **Vonderau-Museum** (Tues–Sun 10am–6pm; DM4/€2), a collection covering archeology, natural history and the arts. Among the exhibits is the Fuldamag, a locally produced three-wheeled car which was once a familiar sight on the streets of Britain as well as Germany. A short distance to the west is the **Abtei St Maria**, a seventeeth-century convent built in an archaic Gothic style. It's still active, and indeed is a flourishing centre of contemporary religious art. Finally, on Heinrich-von-Bibra-Platz, the eastern continuation of Schloss-Strasse, the **Hessische Landesbibliothek** (Mon & Fri 10am–noon, Tues–Thurs 10am–noon & 2–4pm; free) has a permanent exhibition featuring a Gutenberg Bible and some beautiful illuminated manuscripts.

Outside the centre

The **Petersberg**, a four-hundred-metre-high hill about 4km to the east of the centre and reached by bus #3, commands wonderful views of Fulda itself and across to the Vogelsberg and Rhön. The hill is crowned by the **Peterskirche** (April–Dec Tues–Sun 10–11.30am & 2.30–4pm; Feb & March Tues–Sun 2.30–4pm), the most significant of the four monastic churches grouped round the town in the symbolic shape of a cross. Its **crypt**, the burial place of St Lioba, a kinswoman of St Boniface, survives from the first building on the spot, and has precious if rather ghostly ninth-century frescoes. The main part of the church was rebuilt in the fifteenth century but preserves six outstanding **Romanesque reliefs** on and around its triumphal arch. On the western bank of the River Fulda, much closer to town, is the **Andreaskirche**, a former monastic church which has some more or less intact tenth- or eleventh-century frescoes in the crypt; these are currently the subject of a painstaking restoration programme.

Further delights await at **Schloss Fasanerie** (guided tours April–Oct Tues–Sun 10am–noon & 1–5pm; DM8/€4), about 6km southwest of the centre, and about fifteen minutes' walk beyond the Engelhelms terminus of bus #3. It was built at enormous expense in the eighteenth century as a hunting lodge and summer residence for the local prince-bishops. However, its original Baroque character was modified after it came into the possession of the Electors of Hesse-Kassel, with several of the main reception rooms refurbished to suit their penchant for the Neoclassical style. A stud farm occupies the subsidiary buildings, while the landscaped **Schlosspark** features Chinese and Japanese pavilions.

Eating and drinking

Some of the best places to eat and drink are in the hotels (see p.431), but there's a wide variety of other options.

Café Thiele, Mittelstr. 2. Perhaps the pick of several good traditional cafés in the town centre.

Da Mario, Bonifatiusplatz 2. Moderately priced Italian restaurant in the Hauptwache, serving tasty pizzas made in a wood-fired oven.

Dachsbau, Pfandhausstr. 7–9. Upwardly mobile types gravitate here to sample what's arguably the most creative cooking in Fulda. Closed Mon.

Felsenkeller, Leipziger Str. 12. Gaststätte of the Hochstift brewery, which is located alongside. It makes a fine dark beer, *Schwarzer Hahn*, as well as a *Pils*.

Krokodil, Karlstr. 31. Fairly upmarket café-bar, much favoured by the alternative set, which stays open until 1am.

Löhertor, Gerberstr. 9. A large complex which has several bars and restaurants plus a disco and cinema.

Schoppenkeller, Paulustor 6. Weinkeller with a very mixed clientele and quiet atmosphere. Closed Mon.

Waidesgrund, Esperantostr. 10. Vegetarian and wholefood restaurant, situated just to the rear of the Hauptbahnhof. Closed Mon.

Wirtshaus Zum Schwarzen Hahn, Friedrichstr. 18. Decked out with nostalgic bric-a-brac, this serves a range of regional specialities from all over Germany.

Zur Windmühle, Karlstr. 17. Popular traditional pub in a half-timbered building.

The Rhön and the Hessian Forest

East of Fulda stretches the **Rhön**, a volcanic region a little more wild and threatening than the Vogelsberg; indeed, it's distinctive enough to have gained inclusion on UNESCO's list of World Biosphere Reserves. It's split between Hesse, Bavaria and Thuringia, but Hesse has the highest and most attractive parts. These hills have become a big hang-gliding centre and there are plenty of good walking and cycling routes, best explored by using the small health resort of **Gersfeld** as a base. Immediately to the north of the Rhön is the **Hessian Forest** (*Waldhessen*), a low-lying rural area. This suffered throughout the Cold War era as a result of being a dead end right up against the barbed-wire frontier, but the principal town, the spa resort of **Bad Hersfeld**, successfully avoided any sense of blight.

Gersfeld

GERSFELD is the terminus of the Rhönbahn, a branch rail line from Fulda. In the Baroque **Pfarrkirche** in the town centre the altar, pulpit and organ are piled on top of one another in the approved Lutheran manner to great dramatic effect. The other dominant monument, situated in the nearby park, is the **Schloss**, which is likewise Baroque. Until a few years ago it was a museum but, in a reversal of the normal process, it was returned to private ownership and has been converted into offices.

The **Bahnhof** is a few minutes' walk south of the centre, while the **tourist office** is in the Kurverwaltung just off the Markt at Brückenstr. 1 (Mon–Fri 8am–12.30pm & 1.30–4.30pm, Sat 10am–noon; ☎0 66 54/17 80, fax 17 88, *www.gersfeld.de*). There's a **youth hostel** at Jahnstr. 6 (☎0 66 54/3 40, fax 77 88, *Gersfeld@djh-hessen.de*; DM22/€11 or DM27/€13.50), but most of the other accommodation in town costs little more: it includes **pensions** such as *Rhönlerche*, Hochstr. 34 (☎0 66 54/3 48; ②), and *Simon*, Am Kreuzgarten 12 (☎0 66 54/5 23; ②), as well as the **hotels** *Krone Post*, Marktplatz 30 (☎0 66 54/6 22; ③), and *Zur Sonne*, Amelungstr. 1 (☎0 66 54/9 62 70; ③), both of which have restaurants.

Within the municipality of Gersfeld is the **Wasserkuppe** (950m), the highest peak in the Rhön. It can be reached by road, or by the seven-kilometre-long footpath running almost due north from Fliegerstrasse. On the summit, which commands extensive views, are two **hotels**: *Deutscher Flieger* (☎0 66 54/3 81 or 70 07; ②) and *Peterchens Mondfahrt* (same ☎; ③–⑤). The latter has a fine restaurant, and bedrooms decorated in the styles of different countries.

Bad Hersfeld

BAD HERSFELD, which is situated some 45km north of Fulda and easily reached by train, acted decisively to counter the threat of isolation posed by the proximity of the GDR border. In 1951 it inaugurated an annual **drama festival**, the *Bad Hersfelder Festspiele*, which quickly established itself as one of the leading permanent fixtures in the German cultural calendar and remains so to this day. Lasting from mid-June to early August, it normally features five different plays, taking in both classical theatre (this is Germany's most celebrated Shakespeare stage) and modern works (typically one serious drama and one musical). A series of **concerts** of classical music runs concurrently with the drama festival, which is succeeded by a short **opera** season filling out the month of August.

All performances take place against the stirring backdrop of the **Stiftsruine** (March–Oct Tues–Sun 10am–noon & 2–5pm; DM3.50/€1.75), the remains of a Romanesque monastery which is the largest surviving example of its period anywhere in Europe. Although destroyed by French soldiers in 1761, its awesome proportions are still evident, and it retains impressive fragments, in particular the single-towered facade. The **Katharinenturm**, a detached belfry at the northeastern corner of the complex, houses the oldest bell in Germany, the 900-year-old Lullusglocke, named in honour of Archbishop Lullus of Mainz, who founded Hersfeld in 736. During the festival, the Stiftsruine can normally only be visited in conjunction with a performance; admission is also curtailed both beforehand and afterwards, to allow for the installation and dismantling of all the attendant apparatus. Only in spring and autumn is it possible to see the monument to full advantage, or to climb the west tower for a view over the town.

To the northeast of the Stiftsruine is the Altstadt, which presents the familiar half-timbered spectacle. There's a particularly fine group of houses on Kirchplatz, clustered around the Gothic **Stadtkirche**, whose tall tower dominates the skyline. A few paces away is the **Rathaus**, with an exterior in the cheery Weser Renaissance style. The peaceful **Kurpark** is on the opposite side of the Stiftsruine.

Practicalities

Bad Hersfeld's **Bahnhof** lies just outside the northeastern confines of the Altstadt, about fifteen minutes' walk from the Stiftsruine. The **tourist office** is at Am Markt 1 (June–Aug Mon–Fri 9am–12.30pm & 3–6pm Sat 10.30am–12.30pm; rest of year Mon–Fri 9am–12.30pm & 3–6pm; ☎0 66 21/20 12 74, fax 20 12 44, *www.bad-hersfeld.de*). Within the same building is the drama festival's **box office** (☎0 66 21/20 13 60, *www.bad-hersfelder-festspiele.de*), which should be contacted as far in advance as possible for tickets. Its counterpart for concerts and opera is at Nachtigallenstr. 7 (☎0 66 21/50 67 13, *www.oper-bad-hersfeld.de*). Another big annual event, the *St-Lullus-Fest*, which claims to be the longest-established **popular festival** in the country, takes place in the week which includes October 16.

Private rooms (①–③) can be booked via the tourist office, which has a separate phone number (☎0 66 21/1 94 33) for this service. The main concentration of **hotels** is just south of the Stiftsruine and west of the Kurpark. In this area, the lowest rates are at *Hakehaus*, Gerwigstr. 4 (☎0 66 21/7 45 61; ③), and *Haus Tanneck*, Stresemannallee 4 (☎0 66 21/5 03 50; ③). Excellent mid-range alternatives in the same district include *Wenzel*, Nachtigallenstr. 3 (☎0 66 21/9 22 00; ⑤), and *Schönewolf*, Brückenmüllerstr. 5 (☎0 66 21/9 23 30, *www.hotels-mit-herz.de*; ⑤), while the top address in town is the historic *Zum Stern*, Linggplatz 11 (☎0 66 21/18 90; ⑥–⑧). Each of the last three hotels has a recommendable **restaurant**, with *Wenzel* offering the unexpected pleasure of Swedish fare. Also worth a visit, whether for Hessian specialities or vegetarian dishes, is the half-timbered *Marktschänke*, Am Markt 22.

NORTHERN HESSE

Northern Hesse is, relatively speaking, well off the beaten tourist track. The only city is **Kassel**, which has one of the dullest centres in Germany, yet also boasts wonderful parks and fabulous art treasures. To the north lies the Reinhardswald, with the Baroque Huguenot settlement of **Bad Karlshafen**, while to the south is the outstanding medieval town of **Fritzlar**. Much of the western part of the area, known as the Waldeck, was for centuries a principality completely independent of Hesse. Here are the elegant spa of **Bad Wildungen**, the planned courtly town of **Bad Arolsen**, the **Edersee** reservoir of Dambusters fame, and, as a recent adjunct to the region, the half-timbered town of **Frankenberg**.

Kassel

Although nowadays chiefly famous for the *documenta*, the huge modern art exhibition held there once every five years (next held June–Sept 2002), **KASSEL** is basically an industrial city. Its big armaments industry ensured four-fifths destruction of its centre during the war, and consequently most of the buildings there are functional products of the 1950s. Despite the unenticing appearance of most of the centre, the city is one of the greenest in Germany, primarily due to the enormous **Wilhelmshöhe**. It also preserves plenty of reminders of its period of glory, which began in the late seventeenth century with the arrival of Huguenots expelled from France, continued throughout the following century with the acquisition of all the trappings of a capital city, and culminated in the years 1806–13, when it was the royal seat of the Kingdom of Westphalia.

Arrival, information and accommodation

Kassel has two main train stations. Express services, including *ICE* trains, tend to use the gleamingly modern **Bahnhof Wilhelmshöhe**, which is about 1km east of the Wilhelmshöhe park. The increasingly overshadowed **Hauptbahnhof**, 2.5km away at the northern edge of the city centre, is a dead end. To reverse its descent into seediness, it has been revamped as the Kulturbahnhof, with cinemas, bars and the Caricatura art gallery (the first in Germany to be devoted to comic art), while Jonathan Borofsky's *Man Walking to the Sky*, the most famous work from the 1992 *documenta*, has been re-erected in front of the main entrance. There are **tourist offices** in the city centre at Königsplatz 53 (Mon–Thurs 9.15am–6pm, Fri 9.15am–4.30pm; ☎05 61/70 77 07, fax 7 07 71 69, *www.kassel.de*) and in Bahnhof Wilhelmshöhe (Mon–Fri 9am–1pm & 2–6pm, Sat 9am–1pm; ☎05 61/3 40 54, fax 31 52 16). **Mitfahrzentrale** is at Friedrichstr. 18 (☎05 61/1 94 40).

Given the spread-out nature of the city, it's worth investing in the DM8.50/€4.25 **public transport** ticket, which covers any 24-hour period, or the entire weekend. An alternative to this is the **Kassel Service Card**, which additionally gives reduced entry to the museums and other attractions; for one person, it costs DM12/€6 for 24 hours, DM19/€9.50 for 72 hours, or DM22/€11 and DM29/€14.50 for the same periods for up to four people travelling together.

It's probably best to base yourself in Wilhelmshöhe, which has a wide variety of **hotels** – the budget end of the market is particularly well served here. There's another handy concentration on the southern half of Frankfurter Strasse (reached by tram #5, #6 or #9), just beyond the far end of the Karlsaue park; those in the city centre itself are mostly geared towards expense-account travellers. Kassel's **youth hostel** is a fifteen-minute walk west of the Hauptbahnhof at Schenkendorfstr. 18 (☎05 61/77 64 55, fax 77 68 32, *Kassel@djh-hessen.de*; DM24.50/€12.25 or DM29.50/€14.75), and there are **camping** facilities (closed Nov–Feb) at *Fulda-Camp*, on the banks of the Fulda just south of Karlsaue at Giesenallee 7 (☎05 61/2 24 33).

Hotels and guesthouses

Am Rathaus, Wilhelmsstr. 29 (☎05 61/97 88 50, fax 9 78 85 30). One of the more reasonably priced hotels in the city centre. ④.

Deutscher Hof, Lutherstr. 3–5 (☎05 61/9 18 00, fax 77 66 66). Located right in the centre of Kassel, this offers breakfast buffets and a good restaurant. ⑤.

Elfbuchen, Habichtswald (☎05 61/96 97 60, fax 6 20 43). Country-house hotel with café-restaurant in a peaceful woodland setting north of the Herkules. It has been run by the same family for well over a century. ⑦.

Gude, Frankfurter Str. 299 (☎05 61/4 80 50, fax 4 80 51 01, *www.hotel-gude.de*). By some way the classiest of the concentration of hotels on the street, with a highly regarded restaurant, *Pfeffermühle*. ⑥–⑧.

Kö 78, Kölnische Str. 78 (☎05 61/7 16 14, fax 1 79 82). The most obviously attractive of the city-centre hotels, a family-run concern in a late nineteenth-century building. ⑤.

Kurfürst Wilhelm I, Wilhelmshöher Allee 257 (☎05 61/3 18 70, fax 31 87 77). A member of the Best Western group, this very traditional hotel is right outside Bahnhof Wilhelmshöhe. Its restaurant, *Tavolo*, serves high-class Italian cuisine. ⑦.

Kurparkhotel, Wilhelmshöher Allee 336, Wilhelmshöhe (☎05 61/3 18 90, fax 3 18 91 24, *Kurparkhotel-Kassel@t-online.de*). One of the city's best hotels, with a fine restaurant and a health centre complete with swimming pool, sauna and solarium. It's on the route of tram #1. ⑦.

Lenz, Frankfurter Str. 176 (☎05 61/4 33 73, fax 4 11 88). Has some basic rooms which are among the cheapest in Kassel, along with others which are more luxurious. ③–⑤.

Neu Holland, Hüttenbergstr. 6, Wilhelmshöhe (☎05 61/3 32 29, fax 31 58 29). Small guesthouse and beer garden at the extreme western edge of Kassel, a short distance south of the Herkules; take bus #43 from the Druseltal terminus of tram #3. ④.

Neue Drusel, Im Druseltal 42, Wilhelmshöhe (☎05 61/3 20 56, fax 31 33 21). Medium-range hotel with café-restaurant at the edge of the Habichtswald, not far from a path leading up to the Herkules. ⑤.

Palmenbad, Kurhausstr. 27, Wilhelmshöhe (☎ & fax 05 61/3 26 91). A recommendable budget hotel in the residential part of Wilhelmshöhe; its restaurant (closed Sun evening & Mon lunchtime) has a good line in game dishes. The Brabanter Strasse stop of tram #3 is a stone's throw away. ③.

Schlosshotel Wilhelmshöhe, Schlosspark 8 (☎05 61/3 08 80, fax 3 08 84 28, *www.schlosshotel.com*). Luxurious modern hotel immediately north of the Schloss. The facilities include a high-class restaurant, a casino, a swimming pool, sauna and solarium. ⑧.

Wilhelmshöhe

It was Landgrave Carl, the same ruler who invited the Huguenots to settle in Kassel, who began the laying-out of the **Wilhelmshöhe**, a huge upland forest park which is the largest urban example of its kind in Europe. Situated at the western edge of the city, and reached by tram #1, it remains its most enduring permanent attraction. Although originally intended as a formal garden in the Italian Baroque manner, it was modified by Carl's successors in line with the eighteenth-century preference for the English approach to landscaping, with a predominantly "natural" appearance mingled with an assortment of hidden follies.

Bus #23 runs through the heart of the park, travelling between the Wilhelmshöhe terminus of tram #1 and the Brabanter Strasse stop of tram #3. From the Druseltal terminus of the last-named, bus #43 travels uphill to the Herkules via the main road on the park's western fringe.

The Schloss and the Gemäldegalerie Alte Meister

Curiously enough, the gargantuan **Schloss Wilhelmshöhe** was something of an after-thought, only begun in the 1780s. One of the finest Neoclassical buildings in Germany, it was designed and partly built by Simon-Louis du Ry, the last and most distinguished of a dynasty of local architects of Huguenot extraction. Its **Weissensteinflügel** is now designated the **Schlossmuseum** (guided tours Tues–Sun 10am–4/5pm; DM7/€3.50), and is decked out with opulent furniture, glassware, porcelain and other *objets d'art*, many from the time when Napoleon's brother Jérôme held court here as king of the puppet state of Westphalia. On the ground floor of the central block of the Schloss is the **Antikensammlung** (Tues–Sun 10am–5pm; DM5/€2.50), a collection of classical antiquities. Its prize possession is the *Kassel Apollo*, a Roman copy of an archetypal classical Greek bronze.

The rest of the building is occupied by the **Gemäldegalerie Alte Meister** (Old Masters Picture Gallery; same times and ticket as the Antikensammlung), which originated in the collection of Landgrave Carl's successor Wilhelm VIII, whose spell as governor of Breda and Maastricht fuelled a passion for the painting of the Dutch golden age. He accumulated what remains one of the world's finest collections of this period, supplemented by seventeenth-century paintings from elsewhere in Europe.

There are eleven masterpieces by **Rembrandt**, most notably the profoundly touching *Jacob Blessing his Grandchildren*. This rarely depicted subject shows the patriarch choosing to bless Joseph's second son Ephraim first, on the grounds he was destined for greater things – namely, to be the ancestor of the Gentiles. Rembrandt accordingly showed Ephraim as a fair-haired Aryan-type, in contrast to the dark features of the first-born, Manasseh. From roughly the same period comes one of his greatest portraits, *Nicolaes Bruyningh*, vividly conveying the sitter's animated personality. Two paintings from a decade earlier are unique in Rembrandt's oeuvre. *Winter Landscape* is his only nature study executed in bright colours, while the intimate *Holy Family with the Curtain* presents the scene in the manner of a tiny theatre set. *Profile of Saskia* is a demonstration of the young artist's virtuosity, with his first wife, gorgeously decked out in velvet and jewellery, depicted as an icon of idealized womanhood.

Hals's *Man in a Slouch Hat* is a late work, clearly showing the influence of Rembrandt married to his own talent for caricature, which can be seen more plainly in the earlier *Merry Toper*. Likewise from seventeenth-century Holland are paintings by Ter Brugghen and Jan Steen, and more than twenty works by **Philips Wouwerman**. In spite of Landgrave Wilhelm's strict Calvinism, which drew him to the Dutch School above all others, he assembled a magnificent group of Flemish paintings of the same period. There are some choice canvases by **Rubens**, notably *The Crowning of the Hero*, *The Madonna as a Refuge for Sinners*, the highly unflattering *Nicolas de Respaigne as a Pilgrim to Jerusalem* and a beautiful nocturnal *Flight into Egypt*. **Van Dyck** is represented by portraits drawn from all phases of his career, while the examples of **Jordaens** show his taste for the exotic on a large scale.

The seventeenth-century Dutch and Flemish collection takes up most of the first and second floors, but the end cabinets are devoted to small-scale fifteenth- and sixteenth-century paintings, mostly from Germany. **Cranach**'s early *Resurrection Triptych* is one of a number of highlights, others being **Dürer**'s *Elsbeth Tucher*, **Baldung**'s *Hercules and Antaeus* and an impassioned *Crucifixion*, set in a Danube landscape, by **Altdorfer**. On the top floor a group of Italian Renaissance pictures is dominated by a magnificent full-length *Portrait of a Nobleman* by **Titian**. But, once again it was the seventeenth-century masters who most appealed to the Hessian taste, and there are some spectacular examples of Italian Baroque, finest of which is **Preti**'s *Feast of Herod*. From Spain come outstanding canvases by **Murillo** and **Ribera**, while **Poussin**'s *Cupid's Victory over Pan* represents French art of this same period. **Schönfeld**'s *The Great Flood* is one of the finest of all seventeenth-century German paintings, while there are a couple of examples of the brilliant but short-lived **Johann Liss**: the enigmatic *Scene with Soldiers and Courtesans* and the effervescent *Game of Morra*, a work anticipatory of the Rococo style of a century later.

The rest of the park

Immediately to the north of the Schloss is the **Ballhaus** (April–Oct Tues–Sun 10am–5pm; DM3/€1.50), a neat little Neoclassical building which King Jérôme, Napoleon's brother, had built as a theatre in 1808 to plans by the young Leo von Klenze, who went on to design so much of Munich. Twenty years later it was turned into a ballroom with rich mock-Pompeian decoration and is nowadays used for temporary exhibitions. Alongside is the **Gewächshaus** (Jan–April daily 10am–5pm; DM2/€1), an impressive steel and glass hothouse built in 1822. On the other side of the lake is the **Löwenburg** (Tues–Sun 10am–4/5pm; DM7/€3.50), built in the late eighteenth century as a medieval-style ruin, complete with artifical portcullis and drawbridge. Among the 21 other follies scattered throughout the park are a huge aqueduct and the Teufelsbrücke (Devil's Bridge).

The **Bergpark**, the original Baroque ornamental garden, features a 250-metre-long, 885-tiered cascade. It's overlooked by the famous **Herkules** (mid-March to mid-Nov Tues–Sun 10am–5pm; DM3.50/€1.75), which might look like an eighteenth-century Michelin Man, but which commands a sweeping panoramic view, as well as being a source of great pride to the burghers of Kassel, who have made it the symbol of their town. The statue, by the Italian Giovanni Francesco Guerniero, lounges on top of a bizarre pyramidal structure, which is in turn set into a purely decorative castle called the **Oktogon**. At 2.30pm on Wednesdays, Sundays and holidays in summer, the floodgates at the foot of Herkules are opened and water pours down the cascade and over a series of obstacles, culminating about an hour later in a 52-metre-high jet of water spurting from the **Grosse Fontäne** in front of the Schloss.

Finally, at the park's eastern entrance, at Wilhelmshöher Allee 361, the Japanese-style **Kurhessen-Therme** (Mon, Tues, Thurs & Sun 9am–11pm, Wed, Fri & Sat 9am–midnight; DM21/€10.50 for 1hr 30min, DM47/€23.50 for the day) is an ultra-modern, open-plan spa complex complete with indoor and outdoor thermal pools, saunas, jacuzzis, cinema and restaurant.

The city centre

Kassel's half-timbered Altstadt has all but completely disappeared, while only a few isolated monuments remain from the Oberneustadt, the Baroque suburb of the Huguenots; these are now marooned among the postwar buildings of the business district which has engulfed the city centre. Nonetheless, there are several **museums** in this area well worth taking the trouble to see.

Museums on Brüder-Grimm-Platz and Schöne Aussicht

Starting from the west, the **Hessisches Landesmuseum** (Tues–Sun 10am–5pm; DM5/€2.50, free Fri) on Brüder-Grimm-Platz contains several collections, the most important being of applied arts. This features the exotic treasures accumulated by the counts of Katzenelnbogen, the *Kunstkammer* of the landgraves of Hesse-Kassel, some notable Gothic sculptures and a fine array of sixteenth-century Venetian glass. Restoration work means the department is likely to be closed until at least the latter part of 2001, with the exception of the twentieth-century sections housed in the adjacent **Torwache**, a Neoclassical guard house which was the home of the Brothers Grimm from 1814 until 1822. The extensive ethnological holdings, normally displayed in a series of changing exhibitions, are likewise in store at present. In the meantime, the main building offers displays on the pre- and early history of Hesse, plus the **Deutsches Tapetenmuseum** (German Wallpaper Museum), which adopts a generous interpretation of the word to cover all kinds of hangings, with exhibits from all eras and continents.

Directly across the street is the **Murhardsche Bibliothek**, whose most valuable books are displayed under conditions of the strictest security in the basement **Schatzkammer** (Mon, Wed & Fri 2–5pm; free); treasures include the ninth-century

THE BROTHERS GRIMM

One of the great inseparable partnerships, **Jacob Grimm** (1785–1863) and **Wilhelm Grimm** (1786–1859) were of an impeccable Hessian background. Born in Hanau, they were brought up in Steinau and educated in Marburg, before moving to Kassel, where they worked principally as court librarians. It was at Kassel that they put together their collection of tales, which they first published in 1812 under the title *Kinder- und Hausmärchen*. This was primarily a work of scholarship; the stories were all of folk origin and were taken straight down from oral sources. The book went through many editions, culminating in the definitive version of 1857, which contained two hundred tales. In the process, the desire of Jacob (the more gifted scholar of the two) to preserve the original unadorned version of the stories underwent increasing modification at the hands of Wilhelm, who had superior literary talents and favoured a certain amount of stylization and embroidering of the folk idiom.

The collection made the brothers celebrities, and such characters as Cinderella, Rumpelstiltskin, Hansel and Gretel, Snow White and Little Red Riding Hood became familiar to children all over the world. Yet this popular success did not interfere with their dedication to serious scholarship, particularly in their later years as professors at Göttingen (from which they were expelled for their liberal views) and Berlin. In 1854, they began to compile *Das Deutsche Wörterbuch* – the German equivalent of the *Oxford English Dictionary* – a task taken up by several subsequent generations of scholars and finally completed in 1961.

Hildebrandtlied, which features the earliest written occurrence of the word *Deutsch*, and also on view are a Gutenberg Bible and some beautiful illuminated manuscripts.

Only a couple of minutes' walk to the southeast, the **Neue Galerie** (Tues–Sun 10am–5pm; DM5/€2.50) at Schöne Aussicht 1 takes up the history of art where the Schloss Wilhelmshöhe collection leaves off. It contains a large number of works by the Tischbeins – in particular Johann Heinrich the Elder, the Kassel-based member of the dynasty – and by the members of the Willingshausen artists' colony, the first such in Germany. There's also a room devoted to the omnipresent Joseph Beuys.

Next door is **Schloss Bellevue**, a rare survivor of the Huguenots' Oberneustadt. Designed by Paul du Ry as an astronomical observatory, but later converted into a grand town-house, it now contains the **Brüder-Grimm-Museum** (daily 10am–5pm; DM3/€1.50). A model of its kind, with helpful translations into English, this documents the lives and times of the famous fairy-tale collectors and philologists (see box opposite) in a vivid and imaginative manner. Their own annotated manuscript version of the *Fairy Tales* takes pride of place among the displays of their publications, while the various personal artefacts, plus their appearances in many of the delightful water-colour paintings by their lesser-known younger brother Ludwig Emil, add a very human dimension to the presentation.

Friedrichsplatz and around

Along Frankfurter Strasse is the vast open space of Friedrichsplatz, on which stands the oldest purpose-built museum building in Europe, the **Museum Fredericianum** (variable times and prices; *www.documenta.de*), designed by Simon-Louis du Ry before he began work on Schloss Wilhelmshöhe. Nowadays, it's used for temporary exhibitions and is also the headquarters of the *documenta*, a retrospective of contemporary art inaugurated in 1955 which has become a multimedia event embracing everything from painting to video art. In effect, the whole city has become its venue, and many of the spectacular sculptures you see dotted throughout Kassel are leftovers from *documenta* events of previous years. One of the best known of these is the **Rahmenbau** at the opposite end of the square, which frames the views down to the Orangerie and beyond.

Across from the museum, at Steinweg 2, is the **Ottoneum**, constructed in the first decade of the seventeenth century as the first permanent theatre in Germany. Today it is home to the **Naturkundemuseum** (Tues–Sun 10am–5pm; DM3/€1.50), itself one of the oldest natural history collections in Europe. Among its curiosities are the sixteenth-century Ratzenberger Herbarium; the eighteenth-century Schildbach'sche Holzbibliothek, whose boxes are made from the wood of different trees and contain a leaf, fruit and flower from each; and the Goethe-Elefant, a stuffed elephant on which Goethe carried out pioneering researches.

If you follow Oberste Gasse or Mittelgasse north from here, you come to the **Martinskirche**. Like all the churches in the city centre, this was devastated during the war, and it has been rebuilt in a compromise style which makes no attempt to restore it to its original form. However, it's worth a quick visit to take a look at the huge Renaissance memorial to Landgrave Philip the Magnanimous, champion of Luther and founder of Marburg University.

The Karlsaue

The southeastern edge of the city centre, by the banks of the River Fulda, is taken up by another large Baroque park, the **Karlsaue**. In it stands the aforementioned **Orangerie**, a long, orange-coloured Baroque palace, which now houses the **Museum für Astronomie und Technikgeschichte** (Tues–Sun 10am–5pm; DM5/€2.50, free Fri). This contains a valuable collection of historic scientific instruments, notably those used in the then revolutionary observatory set up in the former Schloss in 1560 by Landgrave Wilhelm IV. There's also a **Planetarium** (introductory shows Tues & Sat at 2pm, Wed, Fri & Sun at 3pm, Thurs at 2pm & 8pm; DM7/€3.50). Alongside, and currently the subject of a long-term restoration programme, is the **Marmorbad**, an ornate bathing hall adorned with mythological statues and reliefs. At the far southern end of the Karlsaue is the **Blumeninsel Siebenbergen** (April to early Oct daily 10am–7pm; DM3.50/€1.75), a lovely island strewn with flowers, trees and exotic plants and shrubs.

Eating, drinking and entertainment

As with everything else in Kassel, the best places to **eat** and **drink** are scattered throughout the city. See also the hotels section on pp.437–8 for some of the leading restaurants.

Restaurants

Boccaccio, Queralle 36. Though prices are low and the decor decidedly minimalist, this serves some of the best Italian food in the city.

Calvados, Im Druseltal 12. Located near the tram #3 terminus, this offers both local specialities and international cuisine, with fish dishes prominent.

El Mesón, Oberste Gasse 2–8. Spanish restaurant with good food and wines, occupying part of the medieval Elisabeth-Hospital.

Gutshof, Wilhelmshöher Allee 347a, Wilhelmshöhe. High-quality Gaststätte with beer garden, located alongside the Kurhessen-Therme.

La Frasca, Jordanstr. 11 (☎05 61/1 44 94). The best restaurant in central Kassel, serving Italianate dishes. Fairly expensive; reservations advisable.

Odysseus, Mergellstr. 33, Kirchditmold. Long-established Greek restaurant in a half-timbered house with summertime courtyard. Take tram #8 to Teichstrasse.

Park Schönfeld, Bosestr. 13. Classy restaurant in an eighteenth-century Schloss near the Botanischer Garten in the south of the city. Take tram #5, #6, or #9, or bus #50. Closed Sun.

Bars and café-bars

Barranquilla, Friedrich-Ebert-Str. 14. Latin American dance bar which gets very crowded on Fri and Sat, yet is quiet at other times.

FES, Karthäuserstr. 17. A favourite meeting-place with the younger crowd.

Gleis 1, Bahnhofsplatz 1. Popular bar within the revamped Kulturbahnhof.

Holomed, Kurfürstenstr. 10. Vegetarian and wholefood self-service café, located just opposite the Hauptbahnhof. Open Mon–Thurs 11am–6pm, Fri 11am–4pm, Sat noon–3pm.

Irish Pub, Bürgermeister-Brunner-Str. 1. Features live music each evening, often with visiting foreign musicians.

Lohmann, Königstor 8. A long-standing Kassel institution; the bar itself is very small, but it has a summertime beer garden.

Mr Jones, Goethestr. 31. One of Kassel's hippest spots, a place for those who want to be seen; it serves good food, including late breakfasts and full meals. There's another branch at Goetheallee 8.

Festivals and entertainment

There are several worthwhile **festivals** in addition to the *documenta*. The *Zissel* in early August is a folklore event centred on the River Fulda, with processions, jousting and live music. On the first Saturday of September, the *Lichtfest* sees Wilhelmshöhe lit by a fireworks display and thousands of torchlights, with a large fair held earlier in the day. The beginning of November marks the *Kasseler Musiktage*, one of Europe's oldest festivals of classical music.

    Cruises on the Fulda are run by *Rehbein*, Weserstr. 5 (☎05 61/1 85 05), and *Söllner*, *Die Schlagd* (☎05 61/77 46 70). Most **concerts** are held in the *Stadthalle*, Friedrich-

Ebert-Str. 152 (☎05 61/7 88 20). The main **theatres** are the Hessisches Staatstheater, Friedrichsplatz 15 (☎05 61/1 09 42 22), which features **opera** as well as **drama**, and the Komödie, Friedrich-Ebert-Str. 39 (☎05 61/1 83 83).

Fritzlar

Some 30km southwest of Kassel, the market town of **FRITZLAR** presents one of the best-preserved medieval cityscapes in Germany. With its 450 half-timbered houses, it might seem at first sight to be archetypally Hessian, but it's actually very untypical of the province: having spent much of its history as an enclave of the Archbishop-Electors of Mainz, it has far more in common with the Rhineland. This is not only manifested in the architecture, but also in religious observance (despite having been part of Hesse for two centuries, about half the population is Catholic) and a vibrant tradition of popular festivals.

The Town

Built on a gentle slope on the north bank of the River Eder, Fritzlar's historic core is enclosed by the thirteenth-century **Stadtmauer**. This was actually built as a protection against the predatory designs of the landgraves of Hesse; the fabric remains substantially intact, with nine watchtowers and five bastions, though these are in varying states of repair. The wall encloses the Altstadt, with a separate extension around the tiny riverside Neustadt. A fine view of the ensemble can be had from the **Alte Brücke**, which you cross when approaching the town from the Bahnhof. An even better view is from the top of the **Grauer Turm**, the largest surviving watchtower in Germany, guarding the western entrance to the Altstadt. Though it doesn't have set opening times, there's generally a guardian on duty in summer; otherwise the key can be obtained from the tourist office (see p.444).

The Dom

Built at the securest point of the town's defences, the **Dom** has always been Fritzlar's principal building. The present building, a successor to one founded by the Englishman St Boniface, was begun in the picturesque late Romanesque style of the Rhineland. From this period belongs the mighty west end, with its twin towers and graceful "paradise" porch, though most of the rest of the church was constructed in the Gothic style.

The **Dommuseum und Domschatz** (May–Oct Sun & Mon 2–5pm, Tues–Sat 10am–noon & 2–5pm; Nov–April Mon–Thurs & Sun 2–4pm, Fri & Sat 10am–noon & 2–4pm; DM5/€2.50) occupy the buildings around the cloisters. There are some stunning treasury items, notably the reliquary of St Boniface, the jewelled cross of Emperor Heinrich IV and the oldest monstrance in Germany, dating back to 1320. Also included in the ticket is entrance to the two **crypts**, the larger of which contains the fourteenth-century tomb of St Wigbert, Fritzlar's first abbot, featuring an imaginary statue of him clasping a model of his church. Upstairs are the **Bibliothek**, with a valuable collection of printed books and manuscripts, and the festive **Musikzimmer**, whose walls are decorated with a lively cycle of fourteenth-century frescoes.

The rest of the town

Directly opposite the Dom is the **Rathaus**, one of the oldest town halls in Germany still used as such. Originally, it was in the style characteristic of Fritzlar's secular buildings – with a lower storey of stone and an upper one of half-timbering – but the latter was replaced in the nineteenth century with a tiled mansard roof. A block further north is

Marktplatz, on which stand some of the finest half-timbered mansions in town, the most imposing being a fifteenth-century guildhall, the **Gildehaus der Michaelsbruderschaft**, on the eastern side. In the middle of the square is the Renaissance **Rolandsbrunnen**, a rather more modest counterpart to the statues of the legendary hero found in the Hanseatic towns of the German coast.

On Burggraben west of Marktplatz is the most impressive of Fritzlar's half-timbered buildings, the **Hochzeitshaus**, built in the late sixteenth century to host weddings and civic receptions. Together with the patrician residence next door, it contains the unusually engrossing **Regionalmuseum** (Tues–Fri & Sun 10am–noon & 3–5pm, Sat 10am–noon; DM3/€1.50), which, in addition to the standard displays on archeology, history and folklore, has some nicely offbeat sections, including a collection of the painted roof tiles which are characteristic of the area, and a roomful of unusual inventions, many (including a sort of aerial bicycle) the brainchildren of a talented but totally eccentric local engineer.

Outside the perimeters of the Altstadt, there are only a couple of set-piece attractions. The Neustadt clusters round the **Ursulinenkloster**, a still-inhabited fourteenth-century convent whose church can be visited. It's also worth following Fraumünsterstrasse for about 1km east of the town centre to the **Fraumünster**, Fritzlar's oldest building, which stands in a walled garden just north of the Eder. Its stone walls date back to the Carolingian period, while the upper part adopts the Gothic half-timbering so typical of the town's mansions; inside is a cycle of Romanesque frescoes.

Practicalities

Fritzlar's **Bahnhof** is southeast of the centre, whereas the **bus station** is just outside the Stadtmauer, at the top end of Kasseler Strasse. If travelling by train, note that it's often necessary to change at Wabern, 6km to the east, which lies on the main Kassel–Marburg line. The **tourist office** (Mon 10am–6pm, Tues–Thurs 10am–5pm, Fri 10am–4pm, Sat & Sun 10am–noon; ☎0 56 22/98 86 43, fax 98 86 26, *www.fritzlar.de*) is next door to the Rathaus at Zwischen den Krämer 5.

There are four centrally sited **hotels**, all with **restaurants**: *Zur Post*, Giessener Str. 25 (☎0 56 22/91 64 03; ④), *Zur Spitze*, Marktplatz 25 (☎0 56 22/18 22; ④), the Greek-run *Kreta*, Neustädter Str. 9 (☎0 56 22/65 30; ④), and *Kaiserpfalz*, Giessener Str. 22 (☎0 56 22/99 37 70; ④–⑥).

Festivals include a Rhenish-style *Karneval* which reaches its climax on Rose Monday; the *Pferdemarkt*, a four-day-long horse fair beginning on the second Thursday in July; and the *Stadtfest* and *Mittelalterisches Fest*, held in alternate years on the third weekend of August.

The Waldeck

For more than seven centuries, the **Waldeck** (or Waldecker Land) was an independent territory within the German empire, first as a county, then as a principality. Despite its reputation as a rural backwater, it came to national prominence just before World War I with the construction of the huge **Edersee**, a reservoir created by flooding a large stretch of the valley of the Eder, the river flowing through the middle of the province. The Waldeck, however, did not long outlast the demise of the German aristocracy in 1918, being incorporated into Prussia eleven years later. It now forms an administrative region of Hesse and incorporates the area around the beautiful medieval town of **Frankenberg**. The two former capitals of the province make a fascinating pair: feudal **Waldeck** is now a popular recreation resort, while **Bad Arolsen** is a proud Baroque Residenzstadt. No less attractive is **Bad Wildungen**, one of Germany's leading spas.

Bad Wildungen

BAD WILDUNGEN, which was formed from the union of two previously separate communities, is set in wooded countryside just 10km west of Fritzlar. The present-day centre, originally the town of Niederwildungen, was a fortified settlement tightly packed on a small hill. Its skyline is dominated by the **Stadtkirche** (daily: April–Sept 10.30am–noon & 2–5pm; Oct–March 2–4pm), whose **winged altar** by the Westphalian **Conrad von Soest** ranks among the loveliest and best preserved of fifteenth-century German paintings, and one of the supreme masterpieces of the courtly International Gothic style. The thirteen panels narrate the life of Jesus in a markedly individual way, and are full of (often humorous) anecdotal detail, including the first representation of spectacles in northern European art. Likewise in the chancel are two swaggering Baroque **memorial monuments** to rulers of the House of Waldeck.

Immediately west of the centre is **Brunnenallee**, the spa quarter's main promenade. It terminates at the palatial **Fürstenhof**, an extremely self-confident Jugendstil building which has, throughout its history, maintained its position as the town's top sanatorium. Beyond is the **Kurpark**, a landscaped park merging seamlessly with the wooded hills above, with the **Wandelhalle**, a late Neoclassical pump room, at its far end.

On a much higher hill north of the centre is the former town of Altwildungen, dominated by one of the secondary residences of the Waldeck princes, **Schloss Friedrichstein** (Tues–Sun 10am–1pm & 2–4/5pm; DM5/€2.50). A Baroque rebuild of the original medieval castle, it's now a museum of hunting and weapons, including booty captured in the seventeenth- and eighteenth-century wars against the Turks, though it's equally of note for the wonderful view it commands over the surrounding countryside.

Practicalities

Bad Wildungen's **Bahnhof** lies at the eastern end of town, a ten-minute walk from the centre. It's now a dead end for passenger trains, except on summer Sundays, when excursion services are run along the otherwise disused line to Hemfurth. One of the **tourist offices** is in the Kurverwaltung, just beyond the end of Brunnenallee at Langemarckstr. 2 (Mon–Thurs 8am–4pm, Fri 8am–5pm, Sat 8am–noon; ☎0 56 21/7 89 00, fax 78 90 33, *www.bad-wildungen.de*); the other is in the Rathaus, Am Markt 1 (Mon–Wed 8am–4pm, Thurs 8am–6pm, Fri 8am–12.30pm, Sat 10am–noon; ☎0 56 21/70 13 20, fax 70 14 62).

Both places can book **private rooms** (①–③), of which there's an abundant supply. There are also plenty of good-value **guesthouses** and **hotels**, often in atmospheric old villas in the spa quarter. Look in particular on Hufelandstrasse, a block south of Langemarckstrasse, where you'll find *Villa Hügel* at no. 17 (☎0 56 21/25 14; ②), *Daheim* at no. 14 (0 56 21/27 16; ③), and *Villa Heilquelle* at no. 15 (☎0 56 21/23 92; ④). The two top hotels are *Quellenhof*, Brunnenallee 54 (☎0 56 21/80 70, *www.treff.de*; ⑦), and *Maritim Badehotel*, Dr-Marc-Str. 4 (☎0 56 21/79 99, *www.maritim.de*; ⑦).

There are plenty of **cafés** and **restaurants** all along Brunnenallee, though the best place for a meal, other than the two luxury hotels mentioned above, is the *Neues Kurhaus* in the Kurpark.

Frankenberg an der Eder

FRANKENBERG, which lies above the River Eder some 35km west of Bad Wildungen and a similar distance north of Marburg, is an archetypal Hessian town, with a well-preserved half-timbered centre. The Altstadt is centred on two market places, Untermarkt and Obermarkt, each of which is a wide rectangular space rather than the customary square. Between the two is the early sixteenth-century **Rathaus**, a cunning piece of design bridging the slope separating the two markets: indeed its lower storey serves both as a hall and a covered walkway linking them together. Partly half-timbered and partly slate-clad, the Rathaus boasts no fewer than ten spires, a German record. The humorous polychromed console carvings, showing fools sitting on the shoulders of burghers, are intended to proclaim the building's festive function.

Situated on the heights above the west end of the two markets is the **Liebfrauenkirche**, a thirteenth-century hall church modelled on Marburg's Elisabethkirche. It had to be partially rebuilt in the fifteenth century following a fire which destroyed most of the town, and many of the furnishings, plus the decorative paintings on the vault featuring the emblems of the guilds, date from this time. Built onto the south transept, but only accessible from outside, is the **Marienkapelle**, a tiny pentagonal pilgrimage chapel. A gem of fourteenth-century German architecture, it preserves some marvellous carvings, including the presumed self-portrait of master mason Tyle von Frankenburg in the tympanum, and irreverent console figures – the inspiration for those on the Rathaus – inside.

Below the northern side of the Altstadt, at Bahnhofstr. 8–10, is the **Zisterzienserinnenkloster** (Tues & Thurs 10am–noon, Wed & Sun 3–5pm; DM1/€0.50), a thirteenth-century Cistercian convent whose chapel, refectory and dormitory have been adapted to house the local museum, a surprisingly entertaining array of folklore and religious artefacts. Continuing west from here brings you to the **Museum Thonet** (Mon 10am–noon & 2–5pm, Wed & Fri 2–5pm; free) in the eponymous furniture company's headquarters on Michael-Thonet-Strasse. The display ranges from the mould-breaking bow-shaped chairs of the early years via the luxuriant Jugendstil adornments for Viennese coffee houses and the designs produced in collaboration with the staff of the original Bauhaus, to the very latest avant-garde models.

Practicalities

Frankenberg's **Bahnhof** is just to the northwest of the Altstadt; the only passenger rail link is south to Marburg, though the long-broken line northwards to Korbach, the present-day capital of the Waldeck, is slated to re-open in the near future. There's also a regular bus connection with Bad Wildungen. The **tourist office** (Mon–Thurs 8.30am–noon & 2–4pm, Fri 8.30am–12.30pm; ☎0 64 51/50 51 13, fax 50 52 03, *www.frankenberg.de*) is in the Stadthaus, Obermarkt 13.

There are a few **private rooms** (②–③), but only two excellent and pricey **hotels** – *Rats-Schänke*, Marktplatz 7 (☎0 64 51/7 26 60; ⑥), and *Sonne*, Marktplatz 2 (☎0 64 51/75 00; ⑥–⑧). These have the best **restaurants** in town; alternatively, try *Steinhaus*, which occupies a gabled thirteenth-century mansion at Pferdemarkt 20.

The Edersee

In the English-speaking world, the **Edersee**, a long, narrow artifical lake stretching for some 27km east to west, is best known because of its role in the Dambusters operation in World War II (see p.602) To Germans, however, it's a major holiday area, above all for watersports. From mid-May to late September, the **ferries** of the Personenschiffahrt Edersee (☎0 56 23/54 15) ply the lake, linking all the main resorts.

Waldeck

High above the northeastern end of the Edersee, some 15km northeast of Bad Wildungen and reached by regular buses, is the little town of **WALDECK**, the original home of the Waldeck dynasty. The hilltop **Burg**, although set below the present-day town, still commands the valley below in much the same way as it did in feudal times. It was abandoned in the seventeenth century and left to fall into ruin, but was later drastically restored, with one wing now serving as the area's plushest **hotel**. The most notable feature is the exhilarating **view** from the terrace over the Edersee and the surrounding hills. However, it's well worth visiting the **Burgmuseum** (April–Oct daily 9.30am–5pm; DM3/€1.50), in which the spartan main chambers look only relatively more comfortable than the dungeons below. There are displays on the history of Waldeck, including a fascinating photographic record of the construction of the Edersee and the drowning of villages that this entailed. Just to the north of the Schloss is the upper terminus of the Waldecker Bergbahn, a **cable lift** with open gondolas, which transports you down to the Edersee (DM5/€2.50 return). Just west of here, at Am Klippenberg, is the **youth hostel** (☎0 56 23/53 13, fax 53 51, *Waldeck@djh-hessen .de*; DM23.50/€11.75 or DM28.50/€14.25).

There are plenty of **hotels**, and even quite upmarket establishments in rustic surroundings with a view are not too prohibitively priced: *Belvedere*, Bahnhofstr. 2 (☎0 56 23/99 90; ⑥), and *Seeschlösschen*, Kirschbaumweg 4 (☎0 56 23/51 13; ⑥), especially. Highest rates are at the aforementioned *Burghotel Schloss Waldeck* (☎0 56 23/58 90; ⑨). **Private rooms** (①–③), which are plentiful, can be booked via the **tourist office** in the town centre at Sachsenhäuser Str. 10 (April–Oct Mon–Fri 8.30am–noon & 2–4.30pm; Nov–March Mon–Thurs 8.30am–noon, Fri 1–5pm; ☎0 56 23/9 99 80, *www.waldeck.de*).

Elsewhere on the lake

The famous dam, the **Edertalsperre**, is 2km south of Waldeck by the village of **EDER-SEE** at the eastern end of the reservoir. Capable of storing 202 million cubic metres of water, it remains an enormously important resource, and a major restoration project was completed only a few years ago. **HEMFURTH**, a further 1km south, stands at the head of a smaller lake, the Affolderner See. From here, an electric **rack rail line** (DM5/€2.50) ascends to the Peterskopf, which offers another stunning panorama.

Bad Arolsen

BAD AROLSEN, in the north of the Waldeck, 45km west of Kassel, is a planned town which the local princes began laying out in the early eighteenth century. It was intended as a miniature Versailles, though implementation of the project was forever dogged by a shortage of funds. Nevertheless, Bad Arolsen is in most respects the complete antithesis of Waldeck – except that it, too, is now a popular holiday resort and watersports centre, thanks to the creation a couple of decades ago of the **Twistesee** reservoir just to the east of town.

Towards the far eastern end of the town proper is the horseshoe-shaped **Residenzschloss** (guided tours May–Sept daily 10am–5pm; DM6/€3), where the descendants of the former ruling family still live. Outwardly, the debt to Versailles is obvious, though the interiors are far more modest in scale. Because of the financial constraints, these were created over a period of more than a hundred years, with the result that they form a virtual encyclopedia of changing tastes in interior design. The **Gartensaal** has rich Rococo stuccowork, whereas the main **Grosser Saal** exudes a stern Neoclassicism. Many of the private chambers are in the French Empire style, whereas the **Alhambrasaal**, which mimics the famous Granada palace, is a piece of Romantic kitsch.

The rest of the town centre bears all the hallmarks of having been planned in conjunction with the Schloss. Key buildings are the crescent-shaped **Marstall** (stables) across from the Schloss, and the **Stadtkirche**, which closes off the western end of Schloss-Strasse.

Practicalities

Following many years of closure, the **Bahnhof**, which is at the opposite end of town from the Schloss, has been returned to passenger use. There's a slow and circuitous service to Kassel, plus another south to Korbach, from where buses run to the other towns in the Waldeck. The **tourist office** is in the Kurverwaltung, just south of the Schloss at Landauer Str. 1 (May–Aug Mon–Fri 8am–4pm, Sat 10am–noon; Sept–April Mon–Fri 8am–4pm; ☎0 56 91/8 94 40, fax 51 21, *www.arolsen.de*).

There's a reasonably priced **hotel**, *Robitsch*, a few minutes' walk east of the Schloss at Wetterburgstr. 15 (☎0 56 91/37 44; ③), but for a bit more money, there are two special places in which you could stay – *Brauhaus*, a couple of blocks west of the Schloss at Kaulbachstr. 33 (☎0 56 91/8 98 60; ⑤), occupies the old court brewery, while *Residenzschloss*, Königin-Emma-Str. 10 (☎0 56 91/80 80; ⑦), is in part of the Schloss itself. Each of these last two has a top-class **restaurant**.

The Reinhardswald

The northernmost tip of Hesse lying immediately beyond Kassel is known as the **Reinhardswald** after the forest which covers much of its area. It has two major attractions in the Rococo **Schloss Wilhelmsthal** and the Baroque harbour town of **Bad Karlshafen**.

Schloss Wilhelmsthal

Just 10km north of Kassel, close to the village of Calden and reached by bus #46, is **Schloss Wilhelmsthal** (guided tours Tues–Sun 10am–4/5pm; DM7/€3.50), the summer residence of the landgraves, and later of King Jérôme. Due to the similarities with the famous Amalienburg in the Schlosspark Nymphenburg, it is thought to have been designed by François Cuvilliés, the great Rococo architect of Munich. However, he was not involved in the actual building, which was entrusted to Simon-Louis du Ry, whose first major commission it was, and who added the two side pavilions to the original plan. The interiors, though sumptuously decorated, are quite small and intimate; the most impressive is the **Schönheitsgalerie**, a gallery of court beauties painted by Johann Heinrich Tischbein the Elder, the Kassel-based member of the painting dynasty. There's also a fine English-style park which preserves a few follies, including an outlook tower and a grotto. In front of the latter is a basin with 370 tiny fountains, which play hourly in the summer.

Directly opposite the park gates is the *Schlosshotel* (☎0 56 74/8 48; ⑤), an excellent **hotel** with a café-restaurant.

Bad Karlshafen

BAD KARLSHAFEN is a Baroque town straddling the River Weser at the very northern tip of Hesse. It can be reached by rail from either Göttingen in Lower Saxony or Paderborn in Westphalia; from Kassel, the quickest approach is to take a train to Hofgeismar, then continue by bus. Now a spa and a popular tourist destination, the town was founded in 1699 by Landgrave Carl, who planned to build a canal from here to Kassel which would enable Hessian merchant ships to avoid the customs toll imposed at nearby Hann. Münden. Carl encouraged many of the Huguenot refugees to come and run the new harbour town, and Paul du Ry, grandfather of Simon-Louis, was responsible for drawing up the original plans. Although the scheme never came to fruition, Bad Karlshafen retains a unique ambience as a result of its intended role.

The most atmospheric part of town is the showpiece centre, the **Hafenbecken** (Harbour Basin), which is surrounded by delicately coloured gabled Baroque houses. Prominent among these is the arcaded **Rathaus**, built as Landgrave Carl's hunting lodge. Just to the north, occupying an old cigar factory, is the **Deutsches Hugenotten-Museum** (Tues–Sat 9am–1pm & 2–6pm, Sun 11am–6pm; DM4/E2), which provides comprehensive documentation on the role of the Huguenot immigrants in the development of the town and on their contribution to German culture. Set back from the Weser, about ten minutes' walk north of the harbour, is the **Kurpark**, which still preserves the remarkable wooden structure of the **Gradierwerk**, a simple but highly effective piece of technology which had the dual function of extracting salt from the town's saline springs and providing a healthy atmosphere for spa visitors, who today still stand underneath and breathe in the air.

Practicalities

The **tourist office** (Mon–Fri 9.30am–noon & 2–4/5.30pm, Sat 9.30am–noon; ☎0 56 72/99 99 24, fax 99 99 25, *www.weser.org/bad-karlshafen*) is in the Rathaus, Hafenplatz 8. **Cruises** run regularly in summer, both around the town and down the Weser to Hann. Münden and Bodenwerder.

There are any number of **rooms** (①–③) available in private houses and small guest-houses. Several of the town's **hotels** occupy wonderful old buildings: *Landgraf Carl*, Hafenplatz 2 (☎0 56 72/3 73; ③), *Hessischer Hof*, Carlstr. 13 (☎0 56 72/10 59; ⑤), *Alt Carlshaven*, Weserstr. 23 (☎0 56 72/92 51 00; ⑤), *Zum Weserdampfschiff*, Weserstr. 25 (☎0 56 72/24 25; ⑤), and *Zum Schwann*, Conradistr. 3–4 (☎0 56 72/10 44; ⑥). All of these also have good **restaurants**.

The **campsite** (☎0 56 72/17 70) is located by the bend in the Weser directly opposite the town centre, and the **youth hostel**, on the same side of the river, is just to the rear of the **Bahnhof** at Winnefelder Str. 7 (☎0 56 72/3 38, fax 83 61, *Bad-Karlshafen@djh-hessen.de*; DM22/€11 or DM27/€13.50).

travel details

Trains

Frankfurt to: Bremen (hourly; 4hr 20min); Cologne (hourly; 2hr 20min); Darmstadt (every 20min; 15min); Fulda (every 30min; 1hr); Giessen (hourly; 40min); Hannover (hourly; 3hr 15min); Kassel (every 30min; 2hr); Koblenz (hourly; 1hr 40min); Marburg (every 30min; 1hr); Trier (hourly; 2hr 45min); Wiesbaden (every 30min; 30min).

Kassel to: Freiburg (hourly; 1hr 35min); Fulda (hourly; 40min); Marburg (hourly; 1hr).

Wiesbaden to: Rüdesheim (hourly; 35min).

CHAPTER FOUR

RHINELAND-PALATINATE AND SAARLAND

O f all the German Länder, the **Rhineland-Palatinate** (Rheinland-Pfalz) is the one most overlaid by legend. The **River Rhine** is seen here at its majestic best, and there's hardly a town, castle or rock along this stretch which hasn't made a distinctive contribution to its mythology. This is the land of the national epic, the *Nibelungenlied*, an extraordinary tale of heroism, chicanery, dynastic rivalry, vengeance and obsession, which bites deep into the German soul. It's also the land of the deceptively alluring Lorelei, of the robber barons who presided over tiny fiefs from lofty fortresses and of the merchant traders who used the natural advantages of the river to bring the country to the forefront of European prosperity.

Nowadays, the Rhine's once treacherous waters have been tamed, enabling pleasure cruisers to run its length, past a wonderful landscape of rocks, vines, white-painted towns and ruined castles. Everything conforms perfectly to the image of Germany promoted by the tourist office; visitors swarm in, and people living on the trade do very nicely. Although the Rhine gorge is the bit most people want to write home about, the rest of the Land has plenty to offer. The **Mosel valley**, running all the way from France to its confluence with the Rhine at **Koblenz**, scores highly for scenic beauty and is not quite as over-subscribed and spoilt. Further north, the valley of the **River Ahr**, which flows into the Rhine near **Remagen**, rivals both of the larger rivers for spectacular

---

ACCOMMODATION PRICE CODES

All the pensions and hotels in this book have been graded according to the following price categories. The codes quoted are for the cheapest available double room, except for establishments which have rooms costing widely different rates, when the most expensive price is given as well. Exact charges are given for youth hostels; in the case of the official DJH (HI) establishments, this is the lowest available rate. When two figures are quoted for these hostels, the first applies to juniors (ie under 27 years of age), the second to seniors (27 and above).

① less than DM60/€30	④ DM100–124/€50–62	⑦ DM200–249/€100–124
② DM60–79/€30–39	⑤ DM125–149/€63–74	⑧ DM250–299/€125–149
③ DM80–99/€40–49	⑥ DM150–199/€75–99	⑨ upwards of DM300/€150

scenery. Only in the **Hunsrück** and the **Eifel**, the Rhineland-Palatinate's "mountain" ranges, do the otherwise ever-present vines give way to bare heathland and forest, creating landscapes that are at times almost desolate.

Industry exists only in isolated pockets, and **Mainz**, the state's capital and chief city, only just ranks among the forty largest in Germany. Its monuments, together with those of the two other Imperial cathedral cities of **Worms** (the font of Germany's once-rich Jewish culture) and **Speyer**, are of major importance, though the number one destination from the point of view of sights is **Trier**, which preserves the finest buildings of classical antiquity north of the Alps.

Trier's Roman survivals are a potent reminder of the area's illustrious **history**. The Rhine itself marked the effective limit of Roman power, and from that period onward the settlements along its western bank dominated national development. Throughout the duration of the Holy Roman Empire, the importance of this area within Germany can be gauged by the fact that two of the seven Electors were the archbishops of Mainz and Trier, while another was the *Pfalzgraf*, or Count Palatine of the Rhine. The last-named has provided the present Land, an artificial postwar construct, with its name, though the heart of his territory lay in the north of what is now Baden-Württemberg. Like the Romans, the French have often regarded the Rhine as the natural limit of their power, and their designs on the region – ranging from the destructive War of the Palatinate Succession launched in 1689, via the Napoleonic grand design, to the ham-fisted attempts to foster an independent state there after World War I – have had a profound impact on European history.

Adjoining Rhineland-Palatinate to the southwest is the miniature province of the **Saarland**. Long disputed between Germany and France because of its natural mineral wealth, it's predominantly an industrial region. From a tourist point of view, it's the least rewarding of all the German Länder, though it does have a few beauty spots, and a vibrant capital in **Saarbrücken**.

As far as **getting around** is concerned, this is one part of Germany where having your own transport is a definite benefit. Otherwise, buses tend to have the edge over trains for seeing the best of the scenery. Despite their associations with over-organized tour groups, the pleasure steamers which glide down the great rivers throughout the summer are certainly worth sampling. **Accommodation**, whether in hotels, youth hostels or campsites, is plentiful, but is best reserved in advance during the high season in the most popular areas.

THE WESTERN RHINELAND

Spaced out along the western bank of the Rhine are three of Germany's most venerable cities – **Mainz**, **Worms** and **Speyer** – which have all, at one time or another, played a key role in the country's history, the most potent reminder of their status being the mighty Romanesque Dom dominating each city. The distinctive size and shape of these three cathedrals reflects the curious power-sharing arrangement between civil and ecclesiastical powers – with each having an unusually large say in the other's affairs – that sustained the fragile structure of the Holy Roman Empire for so long. Further west lie the wooded uplands of the **Palatinate** and **Hunsrück**. They are little-known regions, particularly to foreigners, and thus ideal places to get away from it all. However, public transport services are comparatively sparse, and they are best explored by car or bike.

Mainz

"The capital of our dear Fatherland" was how Goethe styled **MAINZ**. However, this is a position this 2000-year-old city, situated by the confluence of the Rhine and Main, has never officially held, though its influential role throughout German history certainly gave it a far stronger claim for nomination as the postwar seat of government of the Federal Republic than Bonn. Mainz's importance developed in the mid-eighth century, thanks to the Englishman St Boniface, who raised it to the main centre of the Church north of the Alps. Later, the local archbishop came to be one of the most powerful princes in the Holy Roman Empire, holding Electoral status and having the official title of Archchancellor in addition to his ecclesiastical role as Primate of Germany. Further kudos was gained courtesy of Mainz's greatest son, the inventor **Johannes Gutenberg** (see box on p.456), whose revolutionary developments in the art of printing made a colossal impact on European civilization. Since the Napoleonic period – which saw

MAINZ

Schloss

Deutschhaus

Jupitersaule

St Peter
Zeughaus
Sautanz

Landesmuseum Mainz

Hauptbahnhof

Knebelscher Hof
Eiserner
Turm
Rathaus

Domus
Universitatis
Gutenberg-
Museum

Staatsheater
Mainz

Gutenberg-
Denkmal
Dom
Dom- und
Diözesanmuseum

Fastnachtbrunnen

St Stephan

ACCOMMODATION	
1 Austria	6 Schwan
2 Central Hotel Eden	5 Stadt Coblenz
8 Hof Ehrenfels	4 Terminus
3 Neubrunnenhof	7 Weinhaus Rebstock

Mainz for a time become the French city of "Mayence" – it has never managed to recover its former status, while its strategic location inevitably made it a prime target of World War II bombers. Nonetheless, it's now Land capital of the Rhineland-Palatinate and is an agreeable mixture of old and new.

Arrival, information and accommodation

Mainz's **Hauptbahnhof** is situated just beyond the northwestern edge of the Altstadt. The **tourist office** (Mon–Fri 9am–6pm, Sat 9am–1pm; ☎0 61 31/28 62 10, fax 2 86 21 55, *www.info-mainz.de*) is in the Brückenturm am Rathaus at the corner of Rheinstrasse. Here you can buy the **Mainz Card**, which costs DM10/€5 for one day or the whole weekend, and covers public transport costs, entry to museums and various other discounts, including a 10 percent rebate at selected hotels. If you're flying in or out of Frankfurt, Mainz makes a good alternative place to stay as the **airport** lies on the S-Bahn line between the two cities, with several services every hour and a journey time of less than thirty minutes. The stretch of the Rhine between Mainz and Koblenz is the most popular with tourists, and **steamers** depart from in front of the Rathaus (March–Oct only). You'll also find the K-D Linie offices here (☎0 61 31/2 45 11).

Mainz is a relatively expensive city for **accommodation**. There's a handy concentration of **hotels** around the Hauptbahnhof, but this is the most unsalubrious part of the city, and it's far pleasanter to stay in the Altstadt. Detailed information on all the city's hotels can be found on the tourist office Web site. The **youth hostel** (☎0 61 31/8 53 32, fax 8 24 22, *jh-mainz@djh-info.de*; DM30/€15 or DM39/€19.50) is situated 2km east of the centre at Otto-Brunfels-Schneise 4 in the wooded heights of Am Fort Weisenau; catch bus #61 or #62.

Hotels

Austria, Kaiserstr. 20 (☎0 61 31/27 02 70, fax 27 02 71 10). Newish and recommendable hotel with a conveniently central location. ⑥.

Central Hotel Eden, Bahnhofsplatz 8 (☎0 61 31/27 60, fax 27 62 76). Fine old hotel, now part of the Tulip Inn chain, directly facing the Hauptbahnhof. ⑦.

Favorite Parkhotel, Karl-Weiser-Str. 1 (☎0 61 31/28 89 90, fax 22 82 55). The most attractive of the city's luxury hotels, with a pleasant setting at the edge of the Stadtpark, just to the south of the Altstadt. It has an extensive bathing complex, a fine upmarket restaurant (closed Sun evening & Mon) and a beer garden. ⑧–⑨.

Hof Ehrenfels, Grebenstr. 5–7 (☎0 61 31/22 43 34, fax 23 79 10). Small hotel with Weinstube (evenings only) in an atmospheric Altstadt location. ④.

Moguntia, Nackstr. 48 (☎0 61 31/67 10 41, fax 67 10 58). Medium-range hotel, a ten-minute walk north of the Hauptbahnhof. ⑤.

Neubrunnenhof, Grosse Bleiche 26 (☎0 61 31/23 22 37, fax 23 22 40). This hotel has an excellent city-centre location, a stone's throw from the Landesmuseum. ⑦.

Schwan, Liebfrauenplatz 7 (☎0 61 31/14 49 20, fax 2 32 66 56). This new venture in a sixteenth-century building is an adjunct to Mainz's oldest wine bar, the *Alt-Deutsche-Weinstube* (evenings only), a popular establishment serving inexpensive daily dishes; *Specht*, the city's oldest Gaststätte (closed Mon lunchtime), which is right alongside at Rotekopfgasse 2, is under the same management. During the daytime, entry is usually via the back of the building. ⑥.

Stadt Coblenz, Rheinstr. 49 (☎0 61 31/22 76 02, fax 22 33 07). Hotel and restaurant in a grand Baroque building. The location would be excellent were it not for the fact that the front rooms face a major arterial road, and are subject to heavy traffic noise for all but a few hours of the day. ④.

Terminus, Alicenstr. 4 (☎0 61 31/22 98 76, fax 22 74 08). Moderately priced hotel diagonally opposite the Hauptbahnhof. ⑤.

Weinhaus Rebstock, Leichhofstr. 5 (☎0 61 31/23 03 17, fax 23 03 18). Occupying an old half-timbered building directly overlooking the Dom, this hotel is run in tandem with a wine bar-restaurant (evenings only, closed Sun & Mon). ④.

The City

Modern Mainz stretches over both sides of the Rhine, but the Altstadt, with all the important sights as well as the best bars and restaurants, is on the western bank. In line with the city's historic importance it occupies a considerable area, though the Dom provides a ready reference point.

The Dom

Rearing high above all the other buildings in the centre of Mainz are the six towers of the massive red sandstone **Dom** (or **Kaiserdom**). A few years ago it celebrated its 1000th anniversary, though little remains from this epoch other than the ground plan, some of the lower masonry and the bronze doors by the north entrance. Most of what can be seen today is twelfth-century Romanesque.

One of the Dom's most singular features – which is a deliberate ploy to emphasize its mass – is that it's completely surrounded by buildings, stuck right up against its walls. The present picturesque group of houses dates from the eighteenth century, but the **St-Gothard-Kapelle**, two storeys high and of a contrasting grey stone, is from the first half of the twelfth century. Once the archbishops' own chapel, it's now the area set aside for private prayer and is entered from the north transept. The Dom's status as an imperial cathedral, with a special area required for the emperor as well as the clergy, is apparent in the **choirs** at both ends of the building, each flanked by one large and two small towers. What's perhaps less immediately obvious, but a further emphasis of its historical importance, is that it follows the precedent of St Peter's in Rome in being oriented from east to west, the reverse of normal.

The solemn and spacious **interior** for the most part preserves its architectural purity. Above the nave's arcades is a cycle of murals of the life of Christ. Painted in the gentle Nazarene style – which aimed at recapturing the freshness and faith of medieval painting – they are a far more successful adornment than most such well-meaning nineteenth-century attempts at "improving" old churches. However, the interior is remarkable above all for serving as a very superior cemetery for the archbishops. These men were no shrinking violets, commissioning grandiose monuments to themselves which adorn the piers of the nave, forming an unrivalled panorama of sculpture from the thirteenth to nineteenth centuries.

Among the finest is the poignant late fifteenth-century **monument to Adalbert of Saxony**, third from the end on the north side; its youthful subject died before his consecration and is thus not shown in ecclesiastical robes. The same anonymous sculptor made the touching **Holy Sepulchre** in the Magnuskapelle. From early the following century are the most grandiose of all the tombs, those carved by **Hans Backoffen**, one of the outstanding crop of German sculptors of the period, whose work can be seen throughout the city centre. His masterpiece is the **monument to Uriel von Gemmingen**, on the last but one pillar of the north side of the nave; two others by him are directly opposite.

The **Bischöfliches Dom- und Diözesanmuseum** (Tues–Sun 10am–5pm; free), laid out in rooms opening off the cloisters, houses the greatest sculptures of all. These are fragments from the demolished rood screen, created around 1240 by the anonymous mason – one of the supreme artistic geniuses of the Middle Ages – known as the **Master of Naumburg** from his later work in the eastern German cathedral of that name. In his carvings here, such as the scenes of the Elect and the Damned, and above all in the *Head with Bandeau*, his uncanny realism and characterization are far in advance of any other sculpture of the time. The other great treasures of the museum are the late Gothic **tapestries**, which look wonderfully fresh following their recent restoration. In addition to seven mid-fifteenth-century courtly scenes of maidens, wild men and fabulous beasts, there's an early sixteenth-century *Tree of Jesse*, and two heraldic designs showing the arms of Cardinal Albrecht von Brandenburg.

The central squares

The spacious central **Markt** alongside the Dom is the scene of markets on Tuesday, Friday and Saturday mornings. Here also is the riotously colourful **Marktbrunnen**, the finest of Mainz's many fountains. A joyful Renaissance concoction, adorned with putti and topped by a statue of the Virgin and Child, it was made in the workshop of Hans Backoffen.

Adjoining the Markt to the east is Liebfrauenplatz, which has been a vast open space since the church from which it took its name was pulled down during the Napoleonic wars. On the north side of the square is the resplendent pink Renaissance facade of the **Haus zum Römischen Kaiser**, which houses the offices of the **Gutenberg-Museum** (Tues–Sat 9am–5pm, Sun 10am–5pm; *www.gutenberg.de*; DM6/€3); the actual displays are in a modern extension behind. It's a fitting tribute to the great inventor, making amends for the abysmal treatment he received at the hands of the authorities of his own day. Until 1978, Mainz had only the second volume of Gutenberg's most famous work, the **42-line Bible**. Printed in the 1450s, it's a gravely beautiful production employing

JOHANNES GUTENBERG (C. 1400–1468)

An illegitimate son of a canon of Mainz, Johannes Gutenberg dreamed of being able to reproduce manuscripts to the same standard of beauty and quality as that achieved by copyists, but without the painstaking physical labour that was involved. Although it's a myth that he invented printing as such – the Chinese had been able to do it for centuries – it was only through his pioneering development of moveable type that the mass-scale production of books became possible. His inventions were of tremendous significance, and were to survive without appreciable technological advancement right up to the twentieth century. However, they led to Gutenberg's personal ruin – his short-sighted creditors, interested only in making a quick profit, wrested his inventions from him by means of a lawsuit. Totally destitute, he thereafter had to rely on charitable handouts, latterly from the Electoral authorities, to continue his researches. His reward has come posthumously – the international exhibitions held in Mainz in 2000 hailed him, not without justification, as the "Man of the Millennium".

magisterial Gothic lettering. The city then managed to repatriate from America the last of the forty-odd surviving complete versions still in private hands, and this has pride of place in the strongroom on the second floor. The basement contains a mock-up of Gutenberg's workshop and printing machines of later dates; elsewhere there are displays of printed books from all around the world.

Across Schöfferstrasse from the Dom is Gutenbergplatz, with the red sandstone **Staatstheater Mainz** and the **Gutenberg-Denkmal**, which bears a statue of the inventor by the Danish Neoclassical sculptor, Bertel Thorwaldsen.

The central streets

Despite war damage, the centre of Mainz, especially around the Dom, contains many fine old streets and squares lined with examples of vernacular building ranging from half-timbered Gothic to Rococo. North of the Dom, the magnificent **Knebelscher Hof** is reminiscent of the Weser Renaissance style of northern Germany, while Kirschgarten and Augustinerstrasse to the south are particularly well preserved. Just off the end of the latter is the sumptuous church of **St Ignaz**, marking the transition from Rococo to Neoclassicism. Outside, a monumental Crucifixion group by Hans Backoffen stands over the sculptor's own tomb, which is even more imposing than those he had made for the archbishops. This marks the end of the historic quarter – beyond are the rare survivors of the sleazy red-light district that flourished until a few years ago. The former Markthalle on Holzhofstrasse a little further on is home to the **Museum für Antike Schiffahrt** (Tues–Sun 10am–6pm; free). Here you can watch ongoing restoration work on six Roman warships found under the city some years ago, and also see full-sized conjectural reconstructions.

Ludwigstrasse leads west from the Dom to Schillerplatz and Schillerstrasse, which are lined with impressive Renaissance and Baroque palaces, now offices. Here too is the elaborate modern **Fastnachtsbrunnen**, honouring the annual carnival festivities, whose celebration here ranks for spectacle second only to Cologne's. Up the hill by Gaustrasse is the fourteenth-century Gothic church of **St Stephan** (daily 10am–noon & 2–5pm). Although a pleasant enough building with a pretty cloister, it's chiefly remarkable for its impressive postwar windows. In 1976, the parish priest persuaded **Marc Chagall**, the great Russian Jewish artist long resident in France, to make a series of stained-glass windows. The theme chosen was reconciliation, symbolizing that between France and Germany, Christian and Jew. There are nine windows in all, luminously brilliant in their colouring and quite astonishingly vibrant for an artist in his nineties; they were finished in November 1984, just a few months before Chagall's death.

Along the Rhine

Most of Mainz's remaining monuments of interest are situated in close proximity to the **Rhine**. The quayside is dominated by the stark black and white lines of the 1970s **Rathaus**, designed by Arne Jacobsen and another impressive modern addition to the city's heritage. Across the road is the so-called **Eiserner Turm** (Iron Tower), once part of the medieval fortifications, now a commercial art gallery; the other surviving city gate, the **Holzturm** (Wooden Tower), is south down Rheinstrasse.

Continuing northwards up the same street, you come to the Baroque **Zeughaus**, behind which is its gabled Renaissance predecessor as the Electoral arsenal, the **Sautanz**; both buildings have been adopted to house the Staatskanzlei. The Zeughaus is also linked to the handsome sandstone **Deutschhaus**, which was built in the 1730s as a commandery of the Teutonic Knights, and since 1951 has been the seat of the Landtag, or state parliament. Opposite the entrance, a copy of the **Jupitersäule** – whose original is in the Landesmuseum (see below) – has been set up. The nearby church of **St Peter** has a Rococo interior more characteristic of Bavaria than the Rhineland.

On the opposite side of Grosse Bleiche is the **Schloss**, the enormous former palace of the Archbishop-Electors, a superbly swaggering late Renaissance building with a Baroque extension. The once-famous interiors were completely destroyed in the war; in their place is the **Römisch-Germanisches Museum** (Tues–Sun 10am–6pm; free), a rather confusing collection in which copies of famous antiquities mingle with original pieces.

The Landesmuseum Mainz

The **Landesmuseum Mainz** (Tues 10am–8pm, Wed–Sun 10am–5pm; DM5/€2.50, free Sat) occupies the old imperial stables directly down Grosse Bleiche from the Schloss. Its outstanding **archeology** department has some important Celtic items, including a dog made from coloured glass, but is principally renowned for its Roman antiquities. The largest of these are displayed in a hall dominated by the dismantled original parts of the Jupitersäule, the most important Roman triumphal column in Germany, and a triple-arched triumphal gate. In the **medieval** section, there are some fabulous treasures, notably a tenth-century ivory Madonna from Trier and an eleventh-century fibula in the shape of an eagle which once belonged to a German empress. The next hall displays spectacular fragments from demolished buildings, including the Liebfrauenkirche and the fourteenth-century trading hall, or Kaufhaus; the latter is one of only two German secular facades of the era to have survived intact. There are also several sculptures, notably the *Madonna of the Vines*, by an unknown early fifteenth-century local master with a distinctively florid style. The **Baroque** section which follows also has some impressive lapidary remains, as well as figures and sculptural models from the collection of the Electoral court sculptor, Johann Pfaff.

In the gallery at the southeast end of the ground floor are the most important German paintings. They include a cycle of nine canvases of the *Life of the Virgin* from the studio or circle of the mysterious, highly original fifteenth-century Middle Rhenish draughtsman known as **Master of the Housebook**. Also of note are copies of Dürer's celebrated *Adam* and *Eve* by his pupil **Baldung**, *St Jerome* by **Cranach** and an altar wing of *SS Andrew and Columba* by the **Master of St Bartholomew**, whose companion is in London's National Gallery. Works by an international cast of seventeenth-century artists, including Van Dyck, Jordaens, Guercino and Claude, can be seen in the adjoining rooms and their counterparts upstairs. The upper floors house a variety of other displays, including Jewish liturgical treasures saved from a short-lived prewar museum, ceramics, Expressionist and modern paintings, Jugendstil art (particularly glass) and local history.

Eating, drinking and nightlife

Mainz is unashamedly a **wine** city, boasting more vineyards within its boundaries than any other German municipality. If you fancy a wine crawl, you don't need to stray far from the vicinity of the Dom: there's an abundance of traditional **Weinstuben** on Liebfrauenplatz, Grebenstrasse, Augustinerstrasse, Kartäuserstrasse and Jakobsbergstrasse; see the hotels section on p.454 for additional recommendations. Some offer full menus, others only a limited range of snacks and hot dishes, though these are always chosen for their compatibility with the wines served. **Nightlife** is especially lively due to the large number of students in the city.

Weinstuben

Geberts Weinstuben, Frauenlobstr. 94. Family-run restaurant with excellent German cooking and a great choice of wines. Closed all day Sat & Sun lunchtime.

Haus des Deutschen Weines, Gutenbergplatz 3. High-quality and moderately priced restaurant with a huge range of wines from all over Germany.

Löschs Weinstube, Jakobsbergstr. 9. Tiny Weinstube which has a short menu, though the portions are generous and the prices low. Daily from 4pm.

Weinhaus Schreiner, Rheinstr. 38. Best of the Weinstuben for top-notch food at reasonable prices. Open Mon–Fri from 5pm, Sat from 3pm, closed Sun.

Weinhaus Zum Spiegel, corner of Heiliggrabgasse and Leichhofstrasse. One of the quieter options, occupying a fine old half-timbered house. Closed Sun.

Weinstube Bacchus, Jakobsbergstr. 7. Small establishment that frequently gets packed out. Evenings only, closed Sun.

Other restaurants

Augustinerkeller, Augustinerstr. 26. Something of a cross between a Weinstube and a Bierkeller, and very popular with business visitors and tourists.

Drei Lilien, Ballplatz 2 (☎0 61 31/22 50 68). Highly rated citadel of French *nouvelle cuisine*; very expensive, though set meals are available. Reservations advisable.

Heiliggeist, Rentengasse 2. The beautiful vaulted chambers of the thirteenth-century hospital now house a bistro with an international menu.

Incontro, Augustinerstr. 57. Good Italian restaurant in the heart of the Altstadt.

Zum Goldstein, Kartäuserstr. 3. Housed in a former brewery, so it's appropriate that it has the best beer garden in the city.

Zum Kartäuser Hof, Kartäuserstr. 14. Mainz's oldest inn, dating back to the twelfth century, serving German and international dishes.

Zum Salvator, Grosse Langgasse 4. Excellent Bavarian-style restaurant, an outstation of Munich's Paulaner brewery.

Zur Kanzel, Grebenstr. 4–6. Well-regarded Altstadt restaurant serving high-class, fairly pricey meals.

Cafés and bars

Altstadtcafé, Schönbornstr. 9. A favourite with local students, and a good choice for breakfast; closes at 8pm.

Café dell arte, Badergasse 18–22. Pleasant, modish café-bar on a quiet Altstadt street.

Caveau, Schillerstr. 11. Entered from the back of the Institut Français on Münsterstrasse, this friendly pub has live music on Tues and discos at the weekend.

Cuban Bar, Kötherhofstr. 2. Has the widest choice of cocktails – more than a hundred in all. Also serves Cuban and Mexican food.

Dom-Café, Am Markt 12–14. The oldest and best of the traditional cafés, occupying one of the Baroque pavilions built onto the Dom.

Eisgrub-Bräu, Weissliliengasse 1a. Hausbrauerei serving its own light and dark unfiltered beers. As well as full meals it does very good-value buffet breakfasts (9am–noon) and hot and cold lunches (12.15–4pm).

Irish Pub, Weissliliengasse 5. Always crowded in the evening, with live music regularly featured.

Kamin, Kapuzinerstr. 8. Has a big open chimney in the middle, and features an unusually wide choice of drinks, including no fewer than 23 Scotch whiskies.

Pieter van Amstel, An der Theodor-Heuss-Brücke, Kastel. Bar in a three-masted sailing ship moored to the right bank of the Rhine, offering a great view of the city-centre skyline.

Pomp, Grosse Bleiche 29. A favourite haunt of the in-crowd.

Discos and clubs

Jazzid, Malakoff-Center, Rheinstr. 4. New jazz club with a wide variety of music styles.

KUZ, Dagobertstr. 20b. Concert and theatre venue with a disco on Wed and at weekends.

L'Escalier, Am Winterhafen 19. Popular chart music disco.

Red Cat, Emmerich-Josef-Str. 13. Very much the in-venue at the moment, with music ranging from jazz to rock.

Terminus, Industriestr. 13, Mombach. Sparsely decorated warehouse, attracting clubbers from miles around.

Entertainment and festivals

The main **theatre** venue is the Staatstheater Mainz (☎0 61 31/2 85 10) on Gutenbergplatz; with other productions at the Mainzer Kammerspiele in the Malakoff-Center, Rheinstr. 4 (☎0 61 31/22 50 02), and the Forum Theater Unterhaus, Münsterstr. 5 (☎0 61 31/23 21 21). A cultural centre, Frankfurter Hof, Augustinerstr. 55 (☎0 61 31/22 04 38), is also worth checking out for music, dance and theatre. On the **classical music** front, look out for concerts by the Mainzer Kammerorchester, whose Mozart performances are particularly renowned.

Other than Carnival (here known as *Fastnacht* and using a far more intelligible dialect than in Cologne), the principal **popular festivals** are the *Johannisnacht* in mid-June, which includes fishermen's jousts and firework displays, and the *Weinmarkt* jamboree on the last weekend in August and the first in September.

Rhine-Hesse and the Palatinate

Between Mainz and the Land's southern border are two of Germany's most prestigious **wine** regions. **Rhine-Hesse** (Rheinhessen), the immediate hinterland of the city, is given a distinctive appearance by the *Trullos*, small conical white shelters for vineyard workers in among the vines. These are of a type only normally found in Apulia in Italy, and are said to have been built by Italian immigrants 150 years ago. In the **Palatinate** (Pfalz) further south there are around 230 square kilometres of vineyards and in some places the climate becomes almost sub-tropical, enabling farmers to grow lemons, figs and tobacco as well as vines.

Oppenheim

Rhine-Hesse's leading wine town is **OPPENHEIM**, midway along the rail line between Mainz and Worms. It has a hilly setting just back from the river, and is full of half-timbered houses set in narrow little streets. At its highest point is the **Katharinenkirche**, a grandiose church built over more than two centuries: the towers are Romanesque, the east end and transept early Gothic, the nave high Gothic. As an afterthought, the west chancel, which has the appearance and dimensions of a self-contained church in its own right, was added in late Gothic style. Inside, look out for the Oppenheimer Rose, a fourteenth-century stained-glass window with elaborate tracery, and for the many epitaphs to members of prominent local families. Immediately north of the church is the **Michaelskapelle**, which incorporates a charnel house containing the bones of some 20,000 citizens.

Oppenheim's **tourist office** (Mon–Fri 8am–noon; ☎0 61 33/7 06 99, fax 24 50, *www.stadt-oppenheim.de*) is in the Rathaus, Merianstr. 2. There are several **hotels**, including *Kurpfalz*, Wormser Str. 2 (☎0 61 33/9 49 40; ⑤), and *Oppenheimer Hof*, Friedrich-Ebert-Str. 84 (☎0 61 33/20 32; ⑤). These have the best **restaurants** in town; there are also plenty of Weinstuben where you can sample the local vintages.

The German Wine Road

The **German Wine Road** (Deutsche Weinstrasse), Germany's oldest designated tourist route, travels right through the heart of the Palatinate. Starting at Bockenheim, a small town about 50km south of Mainz and 14km west of Worms, it runs to Schweigen-Rechtenbach on the French border, some 80km away. As with most German tourist routes, it's meant for cars (look out for the bunch of grapes signposts), though you can follow most of it by train, resorting to buses to cover the occasional gap. All the towns and villages along the way have a plentiful supply of reasonably priced **accommodation** in pensions and private houses; the larger places also have hotels of every category.

The first main stop is **BAD DÜRKHEIM**, a spa with good rail connections to other towns in the Palatinate, as well as a cross-country tram link with Mannheim. It's particularly worth visiting on the second and third Sundays in September when it hosts a gargantuan **wine festival** called the *Wurstmarkt* (Sausage Fair). The **tourist office** is in the Rathaus, Mannheimer Str. 24 (Mon–Wed & Fri 8am–5pm, Thurs 8am–6pm, Sat 10am–noon; ☎0 63 22/93 51 56, fax 93 51 59, *www.bad-duerkheim.de*). There's plenty of **accommodation**, including a campsite – *Azur-Knaus*, Am Badesee (☎0 63 22/6 13 56) – numerous pensions (②–③) and some very classy hotels, such as *Gartenhotel Heusser*, Seebacher Str. 50 (☎0 63 22/93 00; ⑦), and *Kurparkhotel*, Schlossplatz 1 (☎0 63 22/79 70; ⑧), both of which have similarly upmarket restaurants.

Some 15km south at the foot of the Haardt hills (a branch of the Vosges) is the bustling commercial town of **NEUSTADT**, its well-preserved half-timbered centre peppered with inviting little Weinstuben. The town's sixteenth-century university building, the **Casimirianum**, is on Ludwigstrasse; on Marktplatz to the east is the handsome Gothic **Stiftskirche**, partitioned between Protestants and Catholics since 1708 by an internal wall. Neustadt has swallowed up the village of **HAMBACH** just to the south (reached by bus #502), whose neo-Gothic **Schloss** (March–Nov daily 10am–6pm; DM9/€4.50) sprang to fame in 1832 when a group of students, protesting against Germany's continued political fragmentation, raised the black, red and gold tricolour for the first time.

Buses run from Hambach to the **Kalmit** (673m) about 4km east, which commands incredible views across the plain as far as Speyer. From here head for **ST MARTIN**, a small village with narrow streets and vine-covered restaurants which makes a good place to break your journey. It's dominated by the **Kropsburg**, a ruined thirteenth-century fortress. A couple of kilometres to the south is **EDENKOBEN**. Signs direct you to **Schloss Villa Ludwigshöhe** (Tues–Sun 9am–5/6pm; DM6/€3), a nineteenth-century castle built for King Ludwig I of Bavaria, with some good wall and ceiling frescoes by Max Slevogt. Nearby is **RHODT**, a typical small wine town full of half-timbered *Winzerhäuser* (winehouses); look out for the arches of vines which grow on frames across some of the streets.

The last main stop is **BAD BERGZABERN**, which can be reached circuitously by train, or directly by bus from Landau, the next town south of Edenkoben. It was formerly a seat of the dukes of Zweibrücken, though their Schloss – Renaissance with Baroque additions – is completely overshadowed by their smaller residence, the **Gasthaus zum Engel**, unquestionably one of the finest Renaissance buildings in the Palatinate. Accommodation options include a **youth hostel** on Altenbergweg (☎0 63 43/83 83, fax 51 84; DM23/€11.50), lots of **pensions** (②–③) and some fine **hotels**, such as *Pfälzer Wald*, Kurtalstr. 77 (☎0 63 43/10 56; ⑤), and *Petronella*, Kurtalstr. 47 (☎0 63 43/10 75; ⑥).

Annweiler

ANNWEILER, which is some 20km northwest of Bad Bergzabern, and a similar distance west of Landau, with which it has a direct rail link, stands in the lee of the region's most famous castle, **Burg Trifels** (Tues–Sun 9am–5/6pm; DM6/€3). To get here you have to walk up a steep path to the jagged crag on which it stands, but it's well worth the trek. The Burg is one of the most venerable in Germany, dating back to the eleventh century, and was supposedly one of Frederick Barbarossa's favourite haunts. In 1193 Richard the Lionheart was imprisoned here and only released on payment of an enormous ransom. It subsequently served as an imperial treasury and then gradually fell into ruin after its abandonment in 1635, but a surprisingly effective rebuild was undertaken between 1938 and 1966. The **Burgkapelle** houses copies of the imperial crown jewels, while from the **Kapellenturm** there's a tremendous panoramic view of the surrounding area, including the ruins of Burg Anebos and Burg Scharfenberg to the south.

Worms

A rich web of fact and myth has been spun around **WORMS**, which lies on the left bank of the Rhine some 40km south of Mainz. Originally settled by Celtic tribes and then by the Romans, the city became the heart of the short-lived fifth-century Burgundian kingdom described in the *Nibelungenlied* (see box on p.463). It was a favoured seat of various subsequent royal dynasties, the scene of the weddings of both Charlemagne and Frederick Barbarossa and of the Concordat of 1122 which settled the power struggle between the papacy and the empire. In the Middle Ages Worms achieved great prosperity and was for a while a venue for sittings of the imperial parliament, or **Diet**, most famously that of 1521 at which Luther was declared an outlaw. Unfortunately, much of its magnificence was destroyed in successive wars against the French, but several outstanding monuments remain in the midst of the functional modern city centre which has grown up since World War II. As Worms was formerly home to a large **Jewish community**, earning the nickname "Little Jerusalem", it's appropriate that it preserves the most important reminders to be found in Germany of this once-rich heritage.

Arrival, information and accommodation

Worms' **Hauptbahnhof**, on the main line between Mainz and Mannheim, is northwest of the Altstadt; follow Wilhelm-Leuschner-Strasse straight ahead and you arrive in a few minutes at the Lutherdenkmal. The **tourist office** is at Neumarkt 14 (April–Oct Mon–Fri 9am–6pm, Sat 9am–noon; Nov–March Mon–Fri 9am–6pm; ☎0 62 41/2 50 45, fax 2 63 28, *www.worms.de*). For nine days in late August and early September, the city celebrates the *Backfischfest*, a wine **festival** where fried fish is the culinary speciality.

Worms is quite well off for **hotels**; most are reasonably priced for what they offer, but those in the city centre can get oversubscribed. There's a **youth hostel** handily located between the Dom and the Andreasstift at Dechaneigasse 1 (☎0 62 41/2 57 80, fax 2 73 94, *jh-worms@djh-info.de*; DM29/€14.50 or DM38/€19).

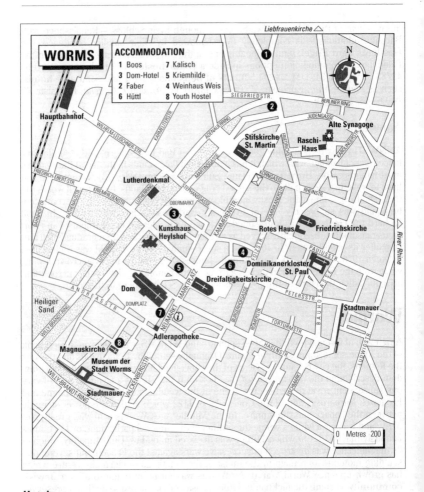

Hotels

Asgard, Gutleutstr. 4 (☎0 62 41/8 60 80, fax 8 60 81 00, *www.asgard-hotel.de*). Classy hotel in the southern part of the city. It serves good breakfast buffets, though no other meals. ⑥.

Bechtel, Pfälzer Waldstr. 98, Heppenheim (☎0 62 41/31 42, fax 3 47 45). A large converted farmhouse with balconies in an incorporated village on the western side of the city. ③.

Boos, Mainzer Str. 5 (☎0 62 41/94 76 39, fax 94 76 38). Budget hotel with restaurant, located a short walk north of the centre. ③.

Dom-Hotel, Obermarkt 10 (☎0 62 41/69 13, fax 2 35 15). Typical modern business-class hotel with restaurant. ⑥.

Faber, Martinspforte 7 (☎0 62 41/92 09 00, fax 92 09 09). Good medium-range hotel with restaurant (closed Mon lunchtime & Wed) at the northern edge of the Altstadt. ⑤.

Hüttl, Petersstr. 5–7 (☎0 62 41/9 05 90, fax 90 59 43). Pleasant, centrally sited hotel with an adjoining restaurant, *Marktstübchen*. ④.

Kalisch, Neumarkt 9 (☎0 62 41/2 76 66, fax 2 50 73). Moderately priced hotel whose back rooms directly face the Dom's east choir. ④.

Kraft-Hotel, An der Weidenmühle, Gundersheim (☎0 62 44/5 76 32, fax 5 74 32). This inexpensive American-style motel, 12km northeast of the city centre near the E31 exit on the A61 Autobahn, is well worth considering if you're travelling by car. It serves big breakfast buffets and hearty German and international meals in its restaurant, *Truck-Centre*. ③.

Kriemhilde, Hofgasse 2–4 (☎0 62 41/9 11 50, fax 9 11 53 10). Good-value hotel and restaurant (closed Sat) in a quiet location immediately north of the Dom. ④.

Weinhaus Weis, Färbergasse 19 (☎0 62 41/2 35 00). This small, no-frills hotel attached to a wine bar on an alley just east of the Dom charges the lowest rates in the city centre. ②.

The City

Given the present size of the city, the Altstadt is surprisingly extensive. The main Jewish monuments are at opposite ends, with the Dom providing the expected centre-piece. There are also a few places worth visiting outside the centre, notably the famous Liebfraumilch vineyards.

The Dom

Foremost among the survivors of Worms' bygone days of glory are the seven city-centre churches, not one of them built later than 1744. By far the largest and most imposing is the **Dom** (or **Kaiserdom**), a huge twelfth-century building which dominates the skyline even from a distance. From outside, it's highly distinctive in appearance, with its two domed choirs and four corner towers; it also displays great unity, with only a few Gothic additions having been made to the original late Romanesque structure.

The **east choir**, the first part to be built, was the prototype for what was to become a dis-tinctive trick of the local school of architecture – although the exterior walls are straight, they are rounded inside. Peering out from the arcades are statues of lions devouring their prey, their terrifying looks apparently intended to frighten off the devil; look out also for the enigmatic figure of a workman (thought to be a self-portrait of the master mason) with a monkey on his shoulder. Even more decorative is the **west choir**, the culmination of the building programme half a century later; with its rose windows, zigzag arcades and rich mouldings it ranks among the most imposing examples of all Romanesque architecture.

On the north side of the nave is the **Kaiserportal**, according to the *Nibelungenlied* the site where Kriemhild and her sister-in-law Brunnhild had a quarrel about just who had the right to enter the building first; this led to the murder of Siegfried and the even-tual collapse of the Burgundian nation. These days, however, it's the richly decorated Gothic **Südportal** – a veritable Bible in stone – which is the main entrance. Most unusually, the sculptures from its Romanesque predecessor weren't wasted, being placed on the wall immediately indoors.

THE NIBELUNGENLIED – GERMANY'S NATIONAL EPIC

Written at the end of the twelfth century, the **Nibelungenlied** describes the fall and vir-tual genocide of the Burgundian nation at the hands of King Etzel (Attila) the Hun. This was the culmination of the long vengeance planned by Etzel's wife, the Burgundian princess Kriemhild, in retribution for the murder of her first husband Siegfried, the famed dragon-slayer. The saga is actually a brilliant fusion, with a great deal of imagina-tive embroidering, of two quite separate episodes in Worms' colourful early history. The Burgundians, originally allies of the declining Roman Empire, settled in Worms in 413, but were driven out by Attila in 436 shortly after they had established their independence from Rome. At the turn of the seventh century, Worms was the residence of the Visigoth princess Brunichildis (the inspiration for Kriemhild's rival Brunnhild), one of two sisters who married kings of different parts of the Merovingian Empire; a subsequent quarrel led to a fratricidal war which claimed the lives of all four leading participants.

As you enter the Dom, the sight of Balthasar Neumann's huge Baroque **high altar** is truly stunning. It's an extravaganza in gilded wood and marble, featuring awe-inspiring statues of SS Peter and Paul with two angels pointing at the Madonna and Child, who seem to be coming straight towards you. Otherwise the Dom is relatively spartan, no more so than in the dark and eerie **crypt**, the last resting-place of five generations of the Salian dynasty, whose eight plain sarcophagi sit in oppressive silence. Off the south aisle is the **Niklauskapelle**, an elegant Gothic chapel divided down the middle by pillars, in the manner of a monastic refectory; it contains a font and a relief of three virgin martyrs. In the north aisle are five large late Gothic **tympana** of scenes from the life of Christ which formerly adorned the now-demolished cloister.

The western city centre

From the Dom, Dechaneigasse leads south to the **Magnuskirche**, the first church in this part of Germany to go over to Protestantism. It dates back to Carolingian times but has been repeatedly extended and altered. Across the square stands the former **Andreasstift**, now housing the **Museum der Stadt Worms** (Tues–Sun 10am–5pm; DM4/€2). The Romanesque church forms an appropriate setting for a collection of medieval sacred art; the collegiate buildings contain Roman and Frankish antiquities plus the Lutherzimmer, which details the events of the 1521 Diet and includes some of Luther's original writings. Just behind the Andreasstift is a surviving section of the **Stadtmauer**, with the still-intact **Andreastor**.

A modern ring road parallels the course of the wall. At its extreme southwest corner is the **Heiliger Sand**, the oldest Jewish cemetery in Europe and the most poignant reminder, in its leafy tranquillity, of the influential Jewish community of Worms (see box opposite). The **tombstones**, which have many beautiful inscriptions and carvings, date back as far as 1076. For reasons which have never been explained, they do not have the customary orientation to Jerusalem, the sole exception being that of the martyr Rabbi Meir von Rothenburg at the lowest point of the grounds. Although it's nothing less than a miracle that the cemetery survived the Third Reich, its situation outside the old walls and the neglected appearance of the twisted and sunken tombstones are not as sinister as they appear. Jewish tradition believed that contact with the dead, who should be allowed to rest in peace, caused impurity; hence they themselves chose to locate their cemetery at the opposite end of town from where they lived and to eschew the Gentile fashion for tending graves. The absence of tombstones later than 1940 likewise has nothing to do with Nazi depredations: by 1911, the cemetery had become so full that a new burial ground was created elsewhere, with only long-established families allowed to use the Heiliger Sand.

On the north side of the Dom, just up Lutherring from the Heiliger Sand, is the **Heylshofgarten**, occupying the site of the now-vanished imperial palace. In April 1521 this was the scene of the Diet at which Luther refused to renounce his views; he was forced to go into exile and the Reformation was set in motion. Within the park is the **Kunsthaus Heylshof** (May–Sept Tues–Sun 11am–5pm; Oct–April Tues–Sat 2–4pm, Sun 11am–4pm; DM5/€2.50), a foundation established by the leading family in Worms' nineteenth-century leather trade. Their exquisite collection of fine and applied arts includes a colourful array of medieval stained glass; a tender *Madonna and Child* by Rubens, along with several modellos by the same artist; a large number of seventeenth-century Dutch cabinet pictures; and a statue of *Adam* by the sixteenth-century Worms sculptor Conrad Meit, one of the few German artists to adopt the full-blooded Italian Renaissance style.

Across the Lutherring directly opposite is the nineteenth-century **Lutherdenkmal**, the largest-ever monument in honour of the Reformation. The bronze figure of Luther is flanked by Frederick the Wise of Saxony and Philip the Magnanimous of Hesse, the two powerful princes whose support made the Reformation a practical reality; behind stand the two scholars, Johannes Reuchlin and Philipp Melanchthon. The remaining male figures are the main precursors of Protestantism – Petrus Waldus, John Wycliffe, Jan Hus and Girolamo Savonarola; the seated women represent the first German cities to adopt the new faith.

The eastern city centre

On the eastern side of the Dom on Neumarkt is the **Adlerapotheke**, a Baroque town house and pharmacy which is one of the few surviving examples of the Baroque architecture which blossomed in Worms following its destruction in the War of the Palatinate Succession. Also from this period is the nearby **Dreifaltigkeitskirche**, but, although it preserves its handsome frontage, the interior was modernized after being burnt out in World War II. Following Kammerer Strasse northwards, you come to the Romanesque **Stiftskirche St Martin**, whose whitewashed walls and angular tower give it a decidedly singular appearance. St Martin was supposedly once imprisoned in a dungeon underneath this church.

Just east of here, centred on Judengasse, is the old Jewish quarter. The **Alte Synagoge** (daily: April–Oct 10am–12.30pm & 1.30–5pm; Nov–March 10am–noon & 2–4pm; free) was reduced to ruins on *Kristallnacht* and further damaged by World War II bombing, but was rebuilt using the old stones and rededicated in 1961; it's occasionally used for worship, mostly by the American army's Jewish personnel. The main part of the synagogue, in a late Romanesque style, was built in 1174–75, probably by the same masons as were then working on the Dom, and was for the use of men only. An extension for the use of women, featuring the new pointed arch, was added in 1212, at right angles to the existing structure. Adjoining the synagogue is the Talmudic teaching room known as the **Raschi-Kapelle**, while in the precincts is the underground **Tauchbad**, or ritual bath house (both same times; free). In the **Raschi-Haus**, a former school, meeting house and dance hall, is the **Jüdisches Museum** (Tues–Sun 10am–12.30pm & 1.30–5pm; DM3/€1.50), with an extensive collection detailing the history of the Jews of Worms.

Further along Judengasse is another well-preserved section of the city wall, with the **Raschiturm** and the **Friesenspitze**. South of here, Karolingerstrasse leads to the

---

LITTLE JERUSALEM

Jews are known to have settled in Worms by the year 1000, and quickly established what was to be one of their largest settlements in Germany for the next 940 years. A synagogue was built in 1034 and a Talmudic school was also established. The latter's leading luminary was Rabbi Salomo ben Isaak, known as **Raschi**, whose commentaries on the Torah and Talmud are works still cited by Hebrew scholars today. In 1096, the community suffered the first of its many trials when fanatical crusaders destroyed the entire Jewish quarter. Germany's most respected rabbi, **Meir von Rothenburg**, was imprisoned by King Rudolf von Habsburg in order to stifle the zeal for resettlement in Palestine; he died seven years later, without regaining his freedom. During the Great Plague of 1390 the Jews were attacked by their fellow townspeople who accused them of having poisoned local wells; and in 1615 social unrest among the rest of the populace once again meant persecution.

By the nineteenth century, matters had greatly improved. The ghetto to which the Jews had been restricted was opened up and from 1849 to 1852 Worms had a Jewish mayor, Friedrich Eberstadt. It wasn't until the Nazis came to power that Worms' ancient Jewish community was finally destroyed. In 1933 there were 1100 Jews in the city; by 1945 the Jews had ceased to exist here – all were either dead or had fled the country. Despite the rebuilding of the leading Jewish monuments as an act of postwar contrition, nobody returned, and the city's Jewish population currently consists of just two newcomers.

junction of Rheinstrasse and Römerstrasse, on which is the dignified Lutheran Baroque **Friedrichskirche**. Beside it stands the **Rotes Haus**, the only surviving Renaissance town-house in Worms. A couple of minutes' walk southwest brings you to the **Dominikanerkloster St Paul**, which has a rough sandstone Romanesque church. Although the present nave was rebuilt in the Baroque era, the building as a whole, and in particular the chancel and triple-towered westwork, is self-evidently a miniaturized version of the Dom. The exotic-looking dome appears to have been based on crusaders' descriptions of Middle Eastern architecture. Other surviving parts of the city walls, including the **Burgerturm**, the **Torturm** and **Lutherpförtchen**, are located just to the east. The **Nibelungenmuseum**, which will contain multimedia presentations on the great literary epic, is being built alongside and is due to open to the public in 2001.

Outside the centre

Because the centre lies about a kilometre inland, visitors to Worms often fail to realize that the city is actually on the banks of the Rhine. It's well worth walking along Rheinstrasse to the **Torturm**, a massive gateway which straddles the **Nibelungenbrücke** over the river. This Historicist extravaganza was built as recently as 1900, but coming into town by the B46 road gives the impression of entering some mysterious medieval world. Below the gateway, the bronze **Hagenstandbild** illustrates the scene from the *Nibelungenlied* when the villainous Hagen hurls the cursed treasure of the Nibelungen into the Rhine just after he has murdered Siegfried.

Just ten minutes' walk from the centre in the northern suburbs is the Gothic **Liebfrauenkirche**. The church, of cathedral-like dimensions, with multicoloured stonework and fantastical towers, is set in the **vineyards** from which *Liebfraumilch*, which was first produced here, takes its name. The wine's reputation has been tarnished by the sickly sweet derivatives that are hugely popular abroad, particularly in the UK. At its best, however, it is a product that fully justifies its official status as a quality wine: *Blue Nun* and *Madonna* are the best-known labels.

Eating and drinking

From a gastronomic point of view, Worms does not quite match Mainz or Speyer. Nonetheless, there's a wide choice of places to eat and drink.

Café Jux, Judengasse 3. Trendy café-bar with beer garden.

Hagenbräu, Am Rhein 3. Hausbrauerei directly overlooking the Rhine; it brews light, dark and various seasonal beers and serves full meals.

Kolb's Biergarten, Am Rhein 1. Cosy Gaststätte with beer garden located right alongside the above.

Kutscherschänke, Judengasse 2. Another lively bar in the old Jewish quarter. Closed Sun.

O'Shea, Rheinstr. 54. An absolutely genuine Irish pub, housed in a grand Romantic-era building between the centre and the Rheinbrücke.

Rôtisserie Dubs, Kirchstr. 6, Rheindürkheim. Worms' most creative restaurant, showing a strong French influence. It's located in an incorporated village by the Rhine, 9km north of the centre. Closed Sat evening & Tues.

Schmerker, Wilhelm-Leuschner-Str. 9. Worms' most elegant café and cake shop, well known for its *Wormser Nibelungenschätze*.

Stadtschänke, Kranzbühlerstr. 1. The best and priciest restaurant in the city centre. On Wed, it's open evenings only.

Tivoli, Adenauer-Ring 4. First-rate and not too expensive Italian restaurant. Closed Mon.

Zwiebel, Kämmererstr. 77. There's a bar on the ground floor, an Internet café upstairs.

Speyer

SPEYER, the final member of the triumvirate of imperial cathedral cities, is some 50km up the Rhine from Worms. It lies on a relatively minor rail line: there's a direct link with Karlsruhe in Baden-Württemberg, but from other points in the Rhineland-Palatinate it may be necessary to change trains at the sprawling industrial city of Ludwigshafen. In 1990, Speyer celebrated the 2000th anniversary of its foundation as a Roman infantry camp, and it's one of the few Rhenish towns to have come through World War II unscathed. Even though its role was once much grander, it stands today as an archetypal episcopal and market town, lively enough never to seem staid, yet not to the extent of spoiling its atmosphere of restrained dignity.

Speyer is a great culinary city with a really marvellous choice of restaurants. It also claims to have invented the Brezel, the crispy salted bread which is such a German favourite, and the main local **festival**, the *Brezelfest*, is held on the second weekend of July.

Arrival, information and accommodation

Speyer's **Hauptbahnhof** and **bus station** are about ten minutes' walk northwest of the centre, but most buses continue down Bahnhofstrasse to drop you opposite the Altpörtel. The **tourist office** is at Maximilianstr. 11 (Mon–Fri 9am–5pm, Sat 10am–noon; ☎0 62 32/14 23 92, fax 14 23 32, *www.speyer.de*).

There's a good choice of **hotels** in the heart of Speyer, some in attractive old buildings. The **youth hostel** is at Geibstr. 5 (☎0 62 32/6 15 97, fax 6 15 96, *jh-speyer@djh-info.de*; DM29/€14.50 or DM38/€19), on the banks of the Rhine a little south of the centre.

Hotels

Domhof, Im Bauhof 3 (☎0 62 32/1 32 90, fax 13 29 90, *www.domhof.de*). Stylishly designed new hotel in an old courtyard building just in front of the Dom. ⑥.

Goldener Engel, Mühlturmstr. 1a (☎0 62 32/1 32 60, fax 13 26 95). A modern designer touch has been applied to this historic hotel at the western edge of the city centre, creating a wonderfully distinctive environment. ⑤.

Graf's Löwengarten, Schwerdstr. 14 (☎0 62 32/62 70, fax 2 64 52, *www.graf-hotel.de*). Fine middle-range hotel just to the southwest of the city centre. Its wine bar-restaurant (evenings only, closed Sat & Sun) serves both local and international dishes. ⑤.

Grüne Au, Grüner Winkel 28 (☎0 62 32/7 21 96, fax 29 28 99). Rustic-looking, ivy-covered Gasthof in the north of the city centre. ③.

Kutscherhaus, Fischmarkt 5a (☎0 62 32/7 05 92, fax 62 09 22, *www.kutscherhaus-speyer.de*). Half-timbered old coaching inn with a top-notch restaurant (closed Wed) and a huge beer garden. ④.

Schlosser, Maximilianstr. 10 (☎0 62 32/7 64 33). Small budget hotel run in tandem with a café on Speyer's main street. ④.

Trutzpfaff, Webergasse 5 (☎0 62 32/29 25 29, fax 29 26 15). Has a central but quiet location, and an excellent Weinstube (closed Mon) which serves specialities of the Palatinate and vegetarian dishes. ⑤.

The City

The city itself is easily seen on foot as it has never grown very large; the focal point, as it always has been, is the Dom.

The Dom

Speyer rocketed to a prominent position in the second quarter of the eleventh century, when the Salian dynasty of emperors chose it, alongside Goslar, as their favourite seat.

They ordered the construction of a huge new **Dom** (or **Kaiserdom**) as their burial place. This regal building, in the purest Romanesque style, has dominated Speyer ever since; indeed, when it was finished, it was the largest church in the West. At the turn of the twelfth century it was partially rebuilt, notably with the erection of a new stone vault which was far higher than any ever previously attempted. The **towers** were also added, as were the **dwarf galleries** round the exterior which were to become such an essential feature of Rhineland churches. It's easy enough to distinguish the two building phases, as the smooth ashlar of the embellishments contrasts with the rough-hewn stonework of the original. The Dom was badly damaged by French troops in 1689, when Speyer was almost entirely destroyed; half the nave was left in ruins, but it was later brilliantly restored. Only the **westwork**, a romanticized nineteenth-century replacement for the one destroyed by the French, is a let-down, having taken its inspiration from the decorative late Romanesque style of Worms rather than the austere purity which is the hallmark of the rest of the building.

The interior has been all but stripped of furnishings, in order to focus attention on its awesome proportions. Its great glory is the **crypt**: although the earliest part to be built, it remains the largest in Germany, and is justifiably claimed as the most beautiful in the world. With its alternately coloured sandstone pillars and slabbed marble floor, it has an almost Middle Eastern quality. It's divided into three connected spaces and contains the coffins of four emperors and four kings, among them Rudolf von Habsburg (the first of the dynasty to become German king), who is depicted in a magnificently carved sepulchral slab displayed on the west wall of the burial vault.

In the nineteenth century, an English-style park, the **Domgarten**, was laid out around the Dom, meaning that there's an uninterrupted view of the great building from all sides. Particularly fetching is that from the **Heidentürmchen** (Heathens' Tower) to the east, one of the rare surviving sections of the medieval city wall; this formerly overlooked the Rhine, but the river has since been diverted to the east. Occupying the centre of the former cloisters on the south side is the sixteenth-century shrine of *Christ on the Mount of Olives*; however, the sculptures are pastiches of the originals, the sole survivors of which are kept under the northwest tower.

The Historisches Museum der Pfalz

Diagonally across Domplatz, housed in a triple-towered mock-medieval palace from the early years of the twentieth century, is the **Historisches Museum der Pfalz** (Tues & Thurs–Sun 10am–6pm, Wed 10am–8pm; *www.museum.speyer.de*; DM8/€4). Highlights of the outstanding archeology department are the so-called Golden Hat of Schifferstadt, a gold-plated Bronze Age cone named after the nearby town where it was found, and the contents of a Celtic prince's grave excavated in Bad Dürkheim. The Roman section includes the *terra sigillata* vessels from Rheinzabern, the largest surviving pieces of pottery of the period from north of the Alps, and a Mithras altar from Neustadt which was dedicated in 325, not long before the introduction of Christianity. Lapidary fragments from churches and Jewish buildings illustrate the medieval history of the region, while the paintings of the Speyer artists Anselm Feuerbach and Hans Purrmann dominate the section devoted to the modern Palatinate.

The building houses two other collections, both covered by the same ticket. In the **Weinmuseum**, every conceivable wine-related object is featured, including several historic presses and what is claimed to be the oldest bottle of wine in the world, dating from around 300 AD. The **Domschatzkammer** contains a wonderful array of treasures, the earliest being the Phrygian Omphaloschale from the sixth or seventh century BC, which is still used on special occasions. Other highlights are the burial crowns of four Salian monarchs, a Romanesque holy-water vessel from Mainz, the robe and shoes of King Philipp of Swabia and the jewelled Gothic staff of Bishop Johannes von Dalberg.

The rest of the city

Across Grosse Pfaffengasse, on the northern side of the museum, lies the enclosed heart of the former Jewish quarter, which can be entered from Judengasse. The east wall of the **Synagoge** still stands, but the main surviving monument is the **Judenbad** (April–Oct daily 10am–noon & 2–5pm; DM1.50/€0.75), a twelfth-century ritual bath-house for women. Seemingly built by the same masons who had recently completed the Dom, it's the oldest and best-preserved example in Germany and a poignant reminder of a vanished culture.

On the north side of the Dom are the fourteenth-century **Sonnenbrücke**, Speyer's only remaining old bridge, and the **Wirtschaft zum Halbmond**, a seventeenth-century half-timbered inn with a strange polygonal oriel window. On the other side of Hasenpfulstrasse is the **Kloster St Magdalena**, a Carmelite convent whose church has a tastefully understated Baroque interior. The now-canonized Jewish-born philosopher Edith Stein, whom the Nazis gassed at Auschwitz, was a nun here from 1923 to 1931.

Following Grosse Himmelsgasse from the Dom brings you to the **Dreifaltigkeitskirche**, a Protestant example of the many Baroque buildings built in Speyer after the devastation of 1689. Further west, along Korngasse, is **St Ludwig**, the church of a thirteenth-century Dominican priory. It contains the only surviving medieval altar front in the Palatinate and the winged late Gothic Bossweiler altar.

Speyer's main street, **Maximilianstrasse**, forms a dead-straight processional way right across the heart of the city to the Dom, widening towards the end to form a spacious square. Among the colourful Baroque and Rococo buildings which line it are the **Rathaus** (whose interior can usually be visited during normal working hours) and the **Alte Münze**, the former mint. Closing off the western end of the street is the **Altpörtel** (April–Oct Mon–Fri 10am–noon & 2–4pm, Sat & Sun 10am–5pm; DM1.50/€0.75), a craggy thirteenth-century gateway which is the only other surviving part of the city walls. A graceful arcaded gallery was built on top in the early sixteenth century, while the steep hip roof which finishes it off was added a couple of hundred years later. From the top, there's a wonderful **view** over Speyer and the Palatinate.

Down Gilgenstrasse and across Bartholomäus-Weltz-Platz is the **Gedächtniskirche der Reformation** (or **Retscherkirche**), a heavy neo-Gothic church built at the turn of the twentieth century in honour of the 1529 Diet of Speyer, at which supporters of Luther made their formal protest against the Edict of Worms, thus gaining the name "Protestants" for the first time. A large statue of the reformer dominates the porch; the interior blazes with a complete set of stained-glass windows. A few minutes' walk east at Allerheiligenstr. 9 is the **Feuerbachhaus** (Mon–Fri 4–6pm, Sun 11am–1pm; donation expected), the birthplace of the Romantic painter Anselm Feuerbach, who is chiefly remembered for his sweeping Italianate canvases of mythological scenes. The house is now a wine bar, but upstairs is an exhibition of his paintings and drawings.

Eating and drinking

Few small German cities offer such a variety of places to eat and drink, with the excellent hotel restaurants mentioned on p.467 rivalled by several other establishments.

Altpörtel-Café, Postplatz 2. Café with rooftop garden in the shadow of the eponymous gateway.

Anglerstubb, Zum Binsfeld 6a. Fish speciality restaurant which does its own smoking. Closed Mon.

Backmulde, Karmeliterstr. 11. Very classy restaurant offering innovative Mediterranean-style cooking. Closed Sun & Mon.

Café Schumacher, Wormser Str. 23. This long-established family-run concern is a good choice for *Kaffee und Kuchen* or a light meal. Closed Mon.

Domhof-Brauerei, Grosse Himmelgasse 6. Hausbrauerei run in association with the nearby hotel of the same name. It serves Palatinate speciality dishes and has a large beer garden.

Domnapf, Domplatz 1. Historic Gasthaus named after the old stone trough in front of the Dom. Its four dining rooms are all tastefully furnished; the food is of a high standard, the fish dishes especially, and the set lunch is a particular bargain. Closed Sun evening & Mon.

Maximilian, Korngasse 15. Extremely trendy bistro-cum-café, a good choice for breakfast or a snack.

Pfalzgraf, Gilgenstr. 26b. Fine traditional and quite moderately priced Gaststätte. Closed Wed evening & Thurs.

Wirtschaft zum Alten Engel, Mühlturmstr. 1a. Wonderfully atmospheric restaurant in a vaulted cellar decked out with antique furniture. The food is outstanding, and includes Alsatian as well as local dishes. Evenings only, closed Sun.

Zum Halbmond, Nikolausgasse 4. Authentic Hungarian dishes and wines are served up in Speyer's most picturesque half-timbered building.

The Hunsrück

The **Hunsrück**, which rises up between the rivers Mosel and Nahe, is one of the three huge volcanic schist massifs (the others are the Eifel and the Vosges) to the west of the Rhine. It's not well served by the rail network and the bus services are meagre in some places – this is a region best explored by car. Most of the Hunsrück is forested and dotted with small villages, with the occasional incongruous small industrial town rearing up out of the woods. In the past it was a big source of precious stones and metals, and even today quarrying and related industries are important to the economic life of the area.

One way of gaining a brief taste of the range is to take a ride on the Hunsrückbahn, Germany's **steepest standard-gauge** rail line. This departs from the Rhenish town of Boppard (see p.492), passing through five tunnels and over two viaducts in the spectacular ascent to Buchholz, climbing 300m in 8km. The train then continues for just one more stop, terminating at Emmelshausen.

Bad Münster am Stein-Ebernburg

The only other railway in the Hunsrück is that along the Nahe valley, the southern border of the range; this forms part of the main line between Mainz and Saarbrücken. As it flows towards its confluence with the Rhine at Bingen, the Nahe becomes broad and grand, assuming a truly spectacular aspect around the little town bearing the somewhat clumsy name of **BAD MÜNSTER AM STEIN-EBERNBURG**. Indeed, this landscape, a favourite subject with painters of the Romantic era, was once so famous that it was regarded as an obligatory stop on a Grand Tour of Europe. While it remains a popular destination with the Germans themselves, it has been all but forgotten by almost everyone else – though it is undoubtedly one of the country's most unusual and impressive beauty spots. Bad Münster am Stein-Ebernburg itself only came into existence in 1969, and a curiosity of their pre-twentieth-century history is that, despite many changes of ownership, the two constituent villages always belonged to different states.

No more than a cluster of houses until it was developed as a resort in the second half of the nineteenth century, Bad Münster is bordered on three sides by a loop of the Nahe, and faces the **Rheingrafenstein**, a dramatic cluster of red porphyry cliffs rising almost directly from the river. On top of one of these, at a height of 136m, is **Burg Rheingrafenstein**, the feudal seat of the lords of Stein, later the Rheingrafen or counts of the Rhine. Despite its seemingly impregnable position, the castle was captured and blown up by the French in 1689, and has remained a ruin ever since. To the rear is a 245m cliff, on top of which is an observation platform commanding a superb view of the town and valley. There is a **chained ferry** (daily: May–Aug 8am–8pm, reducing gradually in the off-season to 9am–6pm; DM1.30/€0.65 each way) from Bad Münster to the foot of the Rheingrafenstein, from where a path snakes up to the Burg and beyond. Boats are available for hire at the same jetty.

The **Kurpark**, which stretches almost as far as the waterfront, is a peaceful spot, enhanced by its whimsical spa buildings. These look particularly quaint when viewed from the north, where they appear dwarfed by the backdrop of the Rheingrafenstein. On either side of the manicured gardens are the **Salinen**, graduation towers which have existed since the first half of the eighteenth century, and are still used by guests for the original purpose of inhaling purified air. The **Kurverwaltung** at the southwestern corner is an eighteenth-century half-timbered building which was the administration office of the original salt industry, while the **Kurmittelhaus** alongside is an ingenious early twentieth-century structure which marries traditional timber frame architecture with Jugendstil design. Inside the latter is a pump room with fountains dispensing the local mineral waters, and a sunken former bathing hall.

The **Ebernburg**, the large fortress from which the left-bank part of the town takes its name, lies on top of a vineyard-clad hill on the opposite side of the Alsenz, a Nahe tributary, from the Rheingrafenstein. Thirteenth century by origin, it has been rebuilt on many occasions, and now serves as a family holiday home run under the auspices of the Protestant churches. Back across the Nahe, at the extreme northwestern edge of town, is the sheer-faced porphyry massif known as the **Rotenfels** (literally, "red cliffs"). A footpath runs along the top, offering yet more wonderful panoramic views.

Practicalities

The **Bahnhof**, a junction with direct connections to Bingen, Mainz and Saarbrücken as well as south through the Palatinate, lies towards the northeastern end of Bad Münster. A few minutes' walk to the southwest, at Berliner Str. 60, is the **tourist office** (Mon–Fri 8.30am–noon & 2–5pm, Sat 10am–noon; ☎0 67 08/39 93, fax 0 67 08 39 99, *www.bad-muenster-am-stein.de*). Bad Münster has plenty of **guesthouses** and **pensions**, including *Thomas*, Kurhausstr. 9 (☎0 67 08/6 30 00; ③), and *Rheingrafenblick*, Kapitän-Lorenz-Ufer 16 (☎0 67 08/14 16; ③). There are also several fine **hotels**: *Haus Lorenz*, Kapitän-Lorenz-Ufer 18 (☎0 67 08/18 41; ④); *Naheschlösschen*, Berliner Str. 69 (☎0 67 08/66 10 31; ⑤), *Am Kurpark*, Kurhausstr. 19 (☎0 67 08/62 90 00; ⑤), and *Krone*, Berliner Str. 73–75 (☎0 67 08/8 40; ⑥). All of these have **restaurants**, though the last two are for residents only. In Ebernburg, there are a couple of hotels run in tandem with **wine estates**: *Landhaus Rapp*, Schlossgartenstr. 100 (☎0 67 08/23 12; ③), and *Weinhotel Schneider*, Gartenweg 2 (☎0 67 08/20 43; ④). At both of these there are wine gardens where the vintages can be sampled.

Idar-Oberstein

The much larger double town of **IDAR-OBERSTEIN** lies some 45km up the Nahe from Bad Münster am Stein-Ebernburg. Formerly a mining centre for precious stones and minerals, Idar-Oberstein has remained, since the virtual exhaustion of the old lodes in 1870, a centre for stone-cutting and polishing, and for the manufacture of jewellery. Oberstein, crammed into the steeply wooded Nahe valley, is the historic part, while Idar, sprawling northwards up the narrow Idarbach valley, is more commercial in character.

From Oberstein's Marktplatz, 230 steps lead up to the late fifteenth-century **Felsenkirche** (daily: April–June & Sept 10am–6pm; July & Aug 9am–6pm; DM3/€1.50), a whitewashed late Gothic church set in a grotto about halfway up a steep rockface. According to legend, it was founded by a Knight in expiation for the murder of his brother in a quarrel over a woman; in reality, it was built in the 1480s on the site of a small fort by order of the local lord, Wyrich IV of Daun-Oberstein, whose portrait can be seen in one of the stained-glass windows. The font also dates from the time of construction, while the beautiful "Soft Style" **retable** of scenes from the life of Christ is older, painted around 1410 by an unknown Middle Rhenish master who has been dubbed the Master of the Oberstein Altar. Other features include a Baroque organ and a display cabinet of precious minerals, include a piece of agate from Brazil in the natural shape of a cross.

A path leads up from the Felsenkirche to two feudal castles, both of which command good views of Oberstein and the Nahe valley. **Burg Bosselstein** was built in 1196 by the lords of Stein-Oberstein, but was destroyed 38 years later and has remained as a ruin, now rather scanty, ever since. Further up is **Schloss Oberstein**, which replaced it in the early fourteenth century and remained substantially intact until suffering severe fire damage in 1855. Partially restored, it remains an impressive sight, with its south front seeming to grow organically out of the rockface.

On Marktplatz itself is the **Museum Idar-Oberstein** (daily 9am–5.30pm; DM7/€3.50), which details the development of the local precious stone and jewellery industry. It shows how stones were once cut and polished using *Schleifmühlen*, huge sandstone wheels powered by the waters of the River Nahe. Look out too for the translucent flakes of *Landschaftsachat*, fragments of agate on which patterns seem to take the form of ghostly landscapes.

Idar's centre is dominated by the ugly 22-storey office building on Schleiferplatz that houses the **Diamant-und-Edelsteinbörse**, Europe's only diamond and precious stone exchange. The **Deutsches Edelsteinmuseum** (daily 9am–5/6pm; *www.edelsteinmuseum.de*; DM8/€4), which occupies a grand late nineteenth-century villa at Hauptstr. 118, is full of precious stones with "before and after" examples of the stone-cutters' art. Bus #1 runs to the **Historische Weiherschleife** (mid-Feb to mid-March Mon–Fri 10am–4pm; mid-March to mid-Nov daily 9am-5pm; DM5/€2.50) at Tiefensteiner Str. 87 at the northern edge of Idar. There used to be over a hundred such water-powered jewel-cutting mills in the area, but this is the last to survive. Lying face down on wooden beams, cutters demonstrate the traditional techniques of sawing, grinding, sanding and polishing the stones.

At the far northwestern edge of Idar, reached by bus #3, is the **Edelsteinminen Steinkaulenberg** (guided tours mid-March to mid-Nov daily 9am–5pm; DM7/€3.50), the only gemstone mine in Europe accessible to the public. Not for the claustrophobic, this is a huge network of underground tunnels and chambers where agates, jasper and amethysts have been mined since Roman times. In addition to the tourist route, a miners' tunnel has been kept open for amateur treasure hunters. By booking a session in advance (☎0 67 81/4 74 00; mid-March to mid-Nov Mon, Tues & Thurs–Sat 9am–noon & 1–4pm; DM25/€12.50 per three-hour period) anyone over the age of 16 can try their luck and keep any finds.

Practicalities

The **Bahnhof** is in the middle of Oberstein, while the **tourist office** is a few minutes' walk along the Idarbach valley to the north at Georg-Maus-Str. 2 (☎0 67 81/6 44 21, fax 6 44 25, *www.idar-oberstein.de*). Here you can pick up a list of the various jewellers and craft workshops that are open to the public. Oberstein has a **pension**, *Trarbach*, Wüstlautenbachstr. 11 (☎0 67 81/2 56 77; ②), plus several good **hotels**, including *Schloss-Schenke*, Hauptstr. 442 (☎0 67 81/2 28 53; ④), *Edelstein*, Hauptstr. 302 (☎0 67 81/2 30 58; ⑤), and *City*, Otto-Decker-Str. 15 (☎0 67 81/5 05 50; ⑤). More upmarket than any of these is *Zum Schwann*, Hauptstr. 25 (☎0 67 81/9 44 30; ⑦) in Idar. The **youth hostel** is on the east side of Oberstein at Alte Treibe 23 (☎0 67 81/2 43 66, fax 2 67 12; DM27/€13.50 or DM33/€16.50).

At the end of June the main **festival**, the *Spiessbratenfest*, takes place, with pork and beef steaks marinaded according to a recipe brought back from South America by German agate miners during the nineteenth century, then barbecued outdoors over open fires. Most of Oberstein's **restaurants** offer the same dishes all year round, though they are usually cooked indoors: *Badischer Hof*, Hauptstr. 377, is a well-known practitioner. All the hotels mentioned above, with the exception of *City*, have restaurants, and these rank among the best in town.

THE MOSEL VALLEY

The **River Mosel** (better known in English under its French name, Moselle) rises in the foothills of the Vosges in France. In its German stretch, it flows between the Eifel and Hunsrück massifs, entering the Rhine at Koblenz. It's best known as a **wine-producing** area, and vineyards crowd the south-facing slopes, with more rugged terrain elsewhere. The combination of wine and scenery, plus castles and history, attracts a lot of visitors, and in high season hordes of organized tour groups turn the most popular destinations – such as **Cochem** – into real hellholes. However, there are still a few corners which have managed to fend off coach-trip attacks and retain some of the atmosphere which so impressed the **Romans**, on the edge of whose world the Mosel valley was. They've left their mark all along the valley, particularly in **Trier**, which has some of the best-preserved remains of classical antiquity in northern Europe.

Trier

"Trier existed 1300 years before Rome," exclaims the inscription on one of the city's historic buildings. In fact, this is a piece of hyperbole: although **TRIER** is the oldest city in Germany, it was actually founded by the Romans themselves. Once the capital of the Western Empire, Trier was also an important early centre of Christianity. This helped give it political clout throughout the Middle Ages and beyond, its archbishop ranking as one of the seven Electors. Nowadays, Trier has the less exalted role of regional centre for the upper Mosel valley, its relaxed air a world away from the status it formerly held. Despite a turbulent history, an amazing amount of the city's past has been preserved: it presents a veritable encyclopedia of European architectural styles, with pride of place going to the most impressive group of **Roman monuments** north of the Alps. These alone would be enough to put Trier in the rank of "must-see" German cities, and it's one place in the Rhineland-Palatinate deserving an unqualified recommendation.

Arrival, information and accommodation

The **Hauptbahnhof** is northeast of the centre, and it's about ten minutes' walk along Theodor-Heuss-Allee to the main entry-point to the Altstadt. Here, at An der Porta Nigra, is the **tourist office** (Jan & Feb Mon–Fri 9am–5pm, Sat 9am–3pm; March Mon–Sat 9am–6pm, Sun 9am–1pm; April–Oct Mon–Sat 9am–6.30pm, Sun 9am–3.30pm; Nov & Dec Mon–Sat 9am–6pm, Sun 9am–1pm; ☎06 51/97 80 80, fax 4 47 59, *www.trier.de*). It sells the **Trier-Card**, which costs DM19/€9.50 for one person, DM35/€17.50 for two adults and three children, and covers entrance to the museums and various other discounts over a three-day period. **Mosel cruises** operate from Zurlaubener Ufer in both directions (see box on p.482).

Trier has plenty of **accommodation** to suit all tastes and pockets. Although many of these are in the centre, some of the most enticing choices are in the outskirts.

TRIER

ACCOMMODATION
1 Casa Chiara   4 Weinhaus Haag
3 Kolpinghaus Jugendhotel   5 Wirtshaus Zur Glocke
3 Warsberger Hof   2 Zum Christophel

Hotels

Alte Villa, Saarstr. 133 (☎06 51/93 81 20, fax 9 38 12 12). Baroque villa, only converted into a hotel a few years back, in the southern part of the centre. It has a high-quality restaurant, and a pleasant garden terrace. ⑤–⑦.

Berghotel Kockelsberg, Kockelsberg 1 (☎06 51/8 24 80 00, fax 8 24 82 90, *www.mosel -guide.de/kockelsberg.htm*). An attractive option if you've got your own transport. The hotel commands a wonderful view over Trier from its position atop a hill on the left bank of the Mosel, 5km from the Altstadt. Its well-regarded restaurant is as reasonably priced as its rooms. ③–⑥.

Blesius-Garten, Olewiger Str. 135, Olewig (☎06 51/3 60 60, fax 36 06 33). Capacious hotel in the eighteenth-century premises of a former wine-producing estate. The facilities include mineral baths, a sauna, a solarium and a shady terrace with old trees and a spring-water fountain. The restaurant offers a predominantly French menu, a distinguished wine list and the products of its Hausbrauerei, Trier's only brewery. ⑤–⑦.

Casa Chiara, Engelstr. 8 (☎06 51/27 07 30, fax 2 78 81). Fine modern hotel in a quiet street close to the Porta Nigra. It serves large buffet breakfasts, but no other meals. ⑥.

Klosterschenke, Klosterstr. 10, Pfalzel (☎06 51/96 84 40, fax 9 68 44 30. Small hotel in a converted medieval convent in an incorporated village on the north bank of the Mosel, 7km east of the Altstadt. It has a fine restaurant with garden terrace. ⑥.

Maximin, Ruwerer Str. 12, Ruwer (☎ & fax 06 51/5 25 77). Very inexpensive, old-fashioned hotel with bar-restaurant in a northern suburb, a couple of kilometres beyond the Altstadt. ②.

Villa Hügel, Bernhardstr. 14 (☎06 51/3 30 66, fax 3 79 58). Occupies a 1914 villa set in a park above the Kaiserthermen. It has a sauna, swimming pool and a panorama terrace with a fine view over the city. ⑥.

Warsberger Hof, Dietrichstr. 42 (☎06 51/97 52 50, fax 9 75 25 40, *www.warsberger-hof.de*). Just off the Hauptmarkt and part of the Kolpinghaus complex, this offers cell-like but perfectly adequate rooms. ③.

Weinhaus Becker, Olewiger Str. 206, Olewig (☎06 51/93 80 80, fax 9 38 08 88, *www.weinhaus -becker.de*). Another of the Weinhäuser in this wine-producing suburb. There are often opportunities for cellar visits and wine tasting. ⑤.

Weinhaus Haag, Am Stockplatz 1 (☎06 51/97 57 50, fax 9 75 75 31). Budget hotel, centrally located in a pleasant square between the Porta Nigra and the Hauptmarkt, with a decent pizzeria, *Portofino*, on the ground floor. ③–⑤.

Wirtshaus Zur Glocke, Glockenstr. 12 (☎06 51/7 31 09). Traditional inn right in the heart of the Altstadt. The rooms are unmodernized and inexpensive; the restaurant serves gargantuan portions of hearty food. ②.

Zum Christophel, Simeonstr. 1 (☎06 51/7 40 41, fax 7 47 32). An old-fashioned hotel right beside the Porta Nigra with an excellent restaurant specializing in game and lamb dishes. ⑥.

Youth hostels and campsites

Jugendgästehaus, An der Jugendherberge 4 (☎06 51/14 66 20, fax 1 46 62 30, *jh-trier@djh-info.de*). Trier's official youth hostel is situated on the bank of the Mosel, near the lower station of the cable car. DM30/€15 or DM39/€19.50.

Kolpinghaus Jugendhotel, Dietrichstr. 42 (☎06 51/97 52 59, fax 9 75 25 40). The dormitory part of this complex costs DM24–28/€12–14 per bed. Private rooms are available in the *Warsberger Hof* part of the complex; see "Hotels", above.

Trier-City, Luxemburger Str. 81 (☎06 51/8 69 21, fax 8 30 79). Campsite situated on the western bank of the Mosel.

URANUS (☎ & fax 0 65 01/1 86 51). This is a ship which is moored in the Mosel between April and Oct; DM22/€11 for a dorm bed.

The City

Despite being relatively small in modern terms, some of Trier's sights are fairly far out, and two days is the minimum amount of time required to see everything, though there's a handy concentration in the centre if you've only a day to spare.

The Porta Nigra and Simeonstift

The **Porta Nigra** (Black Gate) retains its historic function as the main entry-point to the old city. By far the most imposing Roman building in northern Europe, it's also the biggest and best-preserved city gate of the classical period anywhere in the world and dates from the end of the second century. The massive sandstone blocks are held together by iron rods set in lead, and it has been weathered black by the passage of time (hence the name, bestowed in medieval times). Towering above the surrounding streets and buildings, it's an awesome symbol of Roman architectural skill and military might. Would-be attackers were trapped between inner and outer gates, enabling defenders to pour boiling oil and molten lead down from above; the gateway served its purpose well and was never breached.

The Porta Nigra owes its survival to the fact that, during the eleventh century, St Simeon, a Greek hermit who was a friend of the powerful Archbishop Poppo, chose the gloomy ground floor of the east tower as a refuge from the world. After his death in 1035 the Porta Nigra was transformed into the **Simeonstiftkirche**, a church in his honour. Various further additions were made, but in 1804 Napoleon ordered their removal, so that only the twelfth-century Romanesque choir and some slightly frivolous Rococo carvings remain from the post-Roman period.

TRIER UNDER THE ROMANS

Augusta Treverorum was founded, probably in 16 BC, as a crossing point on the junction between the imperial frontier along the Rhine and the Gallic-Belgic provinces. Its name, later shortened to Treveris (and the French form Trèves), signifies that it lay in the territory of the conquered Treveri tribe. The new settlement quickly developed into a major city, and remained so until it was sacked around 275 AD by the Alemanni. However, it was rebuilt shortly afterwards under **Emperor Diocletian**, who made it the headquarters of the western provinces stretching from Britain to Spain. Trier's prestige reached its height under **Emperor Constantine**, who lived there from 306 to 316: the time when he adopted Christianity, with Trier as the premier bishopric north of the Alps. The city then had 80,000 inhabitants – almost as many as it has today – and was adorned with spectacular new buildings. Decline began with the establishment of Constantinople as the overall imperial capital, though emperors continued to spend some of their time in Trier until the middle of the fourth century, when the administration of the western provinces was moved to Arles. Only its position as a major ecclesiastical centre saved it from falling into irreversible decline.

TRIER'S ROMAN MONUMENTS
Opening times for the Porta Nigra and the rest of Trier's Roman monuments, other than the Konstantinbasilika, are as follows: daily April–Sept 9am–6pm; Oct, Nov & Jan–March 9am–5pm; Dec 10am–4pm. The Barbarathermen are closed 1–2pm, all Dec, and on Mon throughout the year. Entry to individual sites is DM4/€2, or you can save by buying a ticket valid for all of them for DM9/€4.50.

Adjoining the western side is the **Simeonstift**, the collegiate foundation attached to the church. Its cloister, the *Brunnenhof,* is the oldest double cloister in Germany, and unusual in that the main walk is on the upper floor, which is supported by massive arcades below. Today the ground floor houses a restaurant (see p.480), with the **Städtisches Museum** (April–Oct daily 9am–5pm; Nov–March Tues–Fri 9am–5pm, Sat & Sun 9am–3pm; DM3/€1.50) above. This version of the inescapable *Heimatmuseum* is vastly better than usual, thanks to an anarchic layout and some outstanding exhibits, notably the original sculptures of some of the prominent structures on the Hauptmarkt: the Marktkreuz, the Steipe and the Petrusbrunnen. Also here is a good ancient history section, with Egyptian grave masks and paintings, hundreds of Roman terracotta lamps, a lot of Greco-Roman statuary and an important collection of Coptic textiles.

Simeonstrasse, the Hauptmarkt and beyond
From Porta Nigra, Simeonstrasse runs down to the Hauptmarkt, roughly following the route of an old Roman street. Today it's a busy shopping area, but boasts several medieval monuments. The most notable is the **Dreikönigenhaus** (House of the Magi), whitewashed but with garishly painted highlighting, which dates from the first half of the thirteenth century. An early Gothic dwelling tower of the kind found in Regensburg, this was a secure home in uncertain times for a rich merchant family. Then, the ground floor would not have opened onto the street at all: the original front door can be seen at first-floor level, high above the street. It was reached by a wooden staircase which could easily be dismantled in times of trouble, or by a ladder which could be pulled up from the street.

The **Hauptmarkt** remains a real focal point of the city, especially in summer: there are always a few stalls selling fruit and flowers, and Trier's kids and punks like to loll around the brightly coloured **Petrusbrunnen**, with its ornate replica Renaissance figures of the Four Cardinal Virtues. Alongside, atop a slender column, is a copy of the **Marktkreuz**, the original of which was placed here in the mid-tenth century. On the western side of the square is the late Gothic **Steipe**, the former banqueting hall of the town councillors, nowadays appropriately housing a café and pricey Ratskeller. Behind it is the stately Renaissance **Rotes Haus** (Red House), which bears the inscription about Trier being older than Rome. A few paces down Dietrichstrasse stands the **Frankenturm**, a Romanesque tower-house whose austere, unadorned stonework contrasts sharply with the tarted-up appearance of the Dreikönigenhaus.

At the southern end of Hauptmarkt a Baroque portal leads to the Gothic church of **St Gangolf**, which was built in the fifteenth century by the burghers of Trier in an attempt to outdo the Dom and wind up the archbishops, from whose temporal power they hoped to break free. The tower, added in 1507, actually made the church higher than the Dom, which angered the archbishop so much that he had one of the towers of his cathedral specially heightened to restore episcopal superiority. From here Fleischstrasse leads southwest to the Kornmarkt, in the centre of which is the ornate Baroque **Georgenbrunnen**.

Further on, at Brückenstr. 10, is the **Karl-Marx-Haus** (April–Oct Mon 1–6pm, Tues–Sun 10am–6pm; Nov–March Mon 2–5pm, Tues–Sun 10am–1pm & 3–6pm; DM3/€1.50). In this archetypally bourgeois Baroque mansion the famous revolutionary theoretician and economist (see box below) was born in 1818 to parents of Jewish extraction: his father was a respected lawyer who had converted to Protestantism, his mother a Dutchwoman who never mastered the German language. Unfortunately the displays here neglect the human angle, concentrating instead on detailed expositions of Marx's political theory. The museum is run by the SPD – something of an irony, as Marx did his best to scupper the party in its early days.

The Domfreihof

Up Sternstrasse from the Hauptmarkt is the **Domfreihof** (Cathedral quarter), which has a history as illustrious as that of Trier itself. St Helena, the mother of Constantine, supposedly donated the site of her palace for the creation of an immense double church, begun in 330 AD. It was one of the quartet of great churches founded more or

KARL MARX (1818–83)

The revolutions in Eastern Europe in 1989 and the collapse of central government in the Soviet Union in 1991 have dealt a crushing blow to the reputation of **Karl Marx**, a man who had been elevated to the status of a god throughout the Communist world. Yet, in his own lifetime, there were few hints of the heights to which he would posthumously rise. His career as a campaigning journalist in the Rhenish province of Prussia ended with his expulsion after the revolutionary failure of 1849; thereafter he lived in London and Paris, his subsequent writing activity – notably the vast tract *Das Kapital* – dependent on the charity of his well-heeled co-author Friedrich Engels.

Despite the fact that he rarely attended political meetings, disliked public speaking, was intellectually arrogant and usually expressed himself in prose of mind-numbing turgidity and verbosity, Marx held what Engels described as a "peculiar influence" on working-class and socialist movements – though at the time he was regarded as only one revolutionary prophet among many. His deification only came as a result of Lenin's adaptation of his theories before and after the Bolshevik Revolution of 1917, though there was a double irony here: not only had Marx predicted that the revolution would first occur in the industrialized West, he himself had what almost amounted to a racial prejudice against Russians, most manifest in his bitter struggles in the International against Mikhail Bakunin. Yet for seven decades attempts were made in Russia and its satellites to engineer Marx's prophecies of the classless society; it was only when these supposedly revolutionary regimes were themselves overthrown by popular revolutions that his powers as a seer finally became discredited.

less simultaneously by the emperor as the showpieces of the new imperial religion, the others being Old St Peter's in Rome, the Holy Sepulchre in Jerusalem and the Church of the Nativity in Bethlehem.

Some of the basilica's masonry survives in the present quadruple-towered **Dom**, which was started in 1030, though not finished until a couple of centuries later. However, the most tangible reminders of the original church are two granite pillars: one, the **Domstein**, can be seen in front of the southern portal, the other in the court-yard between the Dom and the Liebfrauenkirche. Save for the extension made to the southern tower to make it higher than St Gangolf, the Dom's austerely impressive facade has changed little since the eleventh century. Inside, there's an incredible sense of space, much enhanced by the ribbed vaulting of the ceiling. The most eye-catching items, such as the pulpit and the densely peopled All Saints' altar on the third pillar on the south side of the nave, were carved by **Hans Ruprecht Hoffmann**, an inventive local sculptor who was also responsible for the Petrusbrunnen on Hauptmarkt. The Dom's most important relic is the **Seamless Robe**, supposedly the garment worn by Christ when he was crucified: only occasionally displayed for veneration, it's kept in the raised **Heiltumskammer** at the east end, whose over-the-top Baroque decoration adds a rare jarring note. Also upstairs is the **Schatzkammer** (April–Oct Mon–Sat 10am–5pm, Sun 1.30–5pm; Nov–March Mon–Sat 11am–4pm, Sun 1.30–4pm; DM2/€1). This has examples of local goldsmiths' work, notably a bizarre tenth-century portable altar to hold a relic of the sandal of St Andrew.

From the airy **cloisters** you get a wonderful view of the ensemble of the Dom and the adjoining **Liebfrauenkirche**. The latter occupies the site of the southern section of Constantine's great double church, and thus continues the original idea of there being two separate places of worship in the complex. Begun in 1235, it was only the second church to be built in Germany in the Gothic style, of which it's a wonderfully pure example. The ground plan is highly original, taking the form of a rotunda with a cross superimposed on it; the vault is supported by twelve pillars representing each of the apostles. Now darkened by the insertion of modern stained-glass windows, the interior contains the Baroque marble tomb of the warlike Karl von Metternich.

Facing the north side of the Dom on Windstrasse is the **Bischöfliches Dom- und Diözesanmuseum** (April–Oct Mon–Sat 9am–5pm, Sun 1–5pm; Nov–March Tues–Sat 9am–1pm & 2–5pm, Sun 1–5pm; DM4/€2). The most important exhibit is the fourth-century **ceiling painting** from the palace which preceded the Dom. Also of special note is the ninth-century **fresco** from the vanished Carolingian church of St Maximin, although it wears its years less successfully. Upstairs is an important collection of **sculptures**, including most of the original statues from the facade of the Liebfrauenkirche, fragments of the Dom's rood screen and the refined **monument to Archbishop Jakob von Sierck** by Nicolaus Gerhaert von Leyden.

The Konstantinbasilika and the Palastgarten

From the Liebfrauenkirche, Liebfrauenstrasse leads past the ritzy Baroque Palais Kesselstadt to the **Konstantinbasilika** or **Aula Palatina** (April–Oct Mon–Sat 9am–6pm, Sun noon–6pm; Nov–March Tues–Sat noon–1pm & 3–4pm, Sun noon–1pm; free) on Konstantinplatz. This huge brick structure, once Constantine's throne hall, dates back to 310 AD, and is the most impressive of Trier's Roman remains after the Porta Nigra. Its dimensions are awe-inspiring: although 30m high and 75m long, it's completely self-supporting. Now a Protestant church and comparatively spartan, in Roman times it was richly decorated in accordance with its (albeit short-lived) role as seat of the Roman Empire. At 3pm on most days in summer, there are guided visits to the excavations below.

Next door is the seventeenth-century **Kurfürstliches Schloss**, once the residence of the Archbishop-Electors but now, more mundanely, a local government office. It's rather overshadowed by the adjoining **Rokoko-Palais der Kurfürsten**, which was built in 1756 for an archbishop who felt that the old Schloss wasn't good enough for him. Although it took some knocks over the next two hundred years, particularly in World War II, the facade survives and now sits in shockingly pink glory overlooking the **Palastgarten**, which is populated by Rococo statues.

At the southern end of the garden is the **Rheinisches Landesmuseum** (Tues–Fri 9.30am–5pm, Sat & Sun 10.30am–5pm; DM7/€3.50), which houses a fantastic collection of Roman relics – one of the best outside Italy. Prize exhibit, kept in the entrance hall, is the **Neumagener Weinschiff**, a stone sculpture found at Neumagen-Dhron in the Mosel valley, depicting a wine ship complete with crew. The following rooms have superb mosaics – among which the third-century **Rennführer Mosaik**, showing the charioteer Polydus and his four horses, is particularly outstanding. The **Igeler Säule**, the magnificent 23-metre-high column in the courtyard, however, is only a copy: the original can be seen in the centre of the village of Igel, 8km up the Mosel. An important recent addition to the collections is a hoard of **gold coins** unearthed in 1993, the largest ever found in the Roman Empire. Trier's illustrious post-Roman history is illustrated in the following rooms by jewellery and weapons from Merovingian graves, and by sculptural and architectural fragments from the early Middle Ages.

A couple of minutes' walk to the west at Weberbach 25 is the **Schatzkammer der Stadtbibliothek** (Easter–Oct Mon–Fri 10am–5pm; free). Displayed here are two of the world's most beautiful books: the ninth-century *Ada Evangelistary*, with an antique cameo of Constantine on the cover, and the tenth-century *Codex Egberti*, partly illuminated in Trier by the Master of the Registrum Gregorii.

The Kaiserthermen and the Amphitheater

Behind the Landesmuseum are the **Kaiserthermen**, the imperial baths built in the reign of Constantine. Although they haven't survived intact, the scale of what was once one of the largest bathing complexes in the Roman world is still apparent. Today only the ruined **Caldarium** (hot bath), with its distinctive strips of brick among the stonework, is visible above ground. The extensive underground heating system has also survived, and you can walk among the service channels and passages. By the Middle Ages local lords had turned the baths into a castle, which was incorporated into the **Stadtmauer**, surviving sections of which can still be seen nearby. An earlier ruined set of Roman baths, the **Barbarathermen**, lie at the opposite end of Südallee from the Kaiserthermen. Built in the second century, only the subterranean sections retain their original shape, a seemingly endless maze of passages, channels and chambers.

From the Kaiserthermen the route to the **Amphitheater** is well signposted. It was built into the slopes of the Petrisberg above the city in around 100 AD and is the oldest of the surviving Roman buildings in Trier. The structure has been exposed in most of its original glory, and you can sense the grandeur of the original, which had a seating capacity of 20,000. It's still possible to see some of the arched cage rooms where the animals were kept and take a look under the arena itself, which is partly supported by timber blocks and has an elaborate – and still functioning – drainage system cut into its base.

Outside the centre

The hills around Trier provide many marvellous panoramic views of the city and the Mosel valley. Easiest of access is the **Weisshaus**, which can be reached by **cable car** (Easter to mid-Nov Mon–Fri 9am–6pm, Sat & Sun 9am–7pm; DM4.50/€2.25 single, DM8/€4 return), leaving from Zurlaubener Ufer, a picturesque quayside lined with old fishermen's houses, many now converted into bars and restaurants.

Two contrasting churches are within easy walking distance of the centre. On the southern edge of town, about fifteen minutes' walk down Saarstrasse from Südallee, is the **Basilika St Matthias**. In 1127 crusaders brought back from the Holy Land relics of St Matthias (the apostle who replaced Judas Iscariot); this huge church was then built on the site of an existing one to provide sufficient space for the pilgrims who came here to venerate the only one of Jesus' followers to be buried north of the Alps. The whitewashed facade is startling, the original Romanesque modified by the addition of Baroque and Neoclassical features to create a truly sumptuous fricassee. The tomb of St Matthias is found at the intersection of the nave and transept; the burial place of the first two bishops of Trier, SS Eucharius and Valerius, to whom the previous church was dedicated, is two Roman sarcophagi in the crypt.

At the other end of town is **St Paulin**, designed by Balthasar Neumann. From the outside it looks moderately restrained, sober even, but the interior is an all-singing, all-dancing Rococo extravaganza of colour and light. The eye is assaulted by the complex ceiling frescoes and the ornate pillars, dripping with cherubs and scrollwork. It's all just as Neumann intended: his idea was that entering a church should be like entering heaven. Look out for the carvings on the high altar and the choir stalls by Ferdinand Tiez, which are some of the best Rococo decoration in the Rhineland-Palatinate.

Eating and drinking

Alongside several high-class traditional **restaurants** are plenty of central **bars** where you can get good and inexpensive food, thanks to the presence of a large and hungry student population. There are also numerous opportunities for wine tasting, if you want to sample the full range of the superb local vintages.

Restaurants

Am Ecken, Maarstr. 45. A big favourite with locals for its reasonably priced regional fare. Closed Sat & Sun.

Bagatelle, Zurlaubener Ufer 78. Although overshadowed by the neighbouring *Pfeffermühle*, this is nevertheless one of the best restaurants in Trier, particularly for *neue deutsche Küche*.

Brunnenhof, Im Simeonstift. Prone to be mobbed by tourists, but the food is of good quality, with the bonus of being able to sit outside in the historic cloister in fine weather.

Da Paolo, Neustr. 17. A reasonably priced pizzeria.

WINE TASTING

The tourist office's new Welcome shop (Mon–Sat 10am–7pm, Sun 10am–5pm) at Margaretengässchen 2a incorporates the *Vinothek* of the Weininformationen Mosel-Saar-Ruwer, which has fifty different still and sparkling wines from all over the region. Six different wine estates (Weingüte) within the city boundaries (four of them in the incorporated village of Olewig, which is east of the Amphitheater, and reached by bus #6) are open for a week at a time on a rotational basis throughout the year (daily 10am–6pm), except in early autumn and at Christmas. At these, you can sample four wines for DM6/€3, or eight for DM10/€5; check with the tourist office to find out which one is open during your stay. Two of Germany's most prestigious wine cellars are in Trier's Altstadt. The Reichsgraf von Kesselstatt Weinkeller, Liebfrauenstr. 10, occupies a total of 4300 square metres under the city. Alongside its prestigious restaurant, *Palais Kesselstatt* (see opposite), it has an informal bar, open until late in the evening, where wines from open bottles can be sampled in measures of 0.1 litre upwards. Bischöfliche Weingüter, a grouping of four estates of ecclesiastical origin, have their central cellar at Gervasiusstr. 1 (Mon–Fri 9am–5pm), part of which dates back to the sixteenth century. The wines are well known for their elegance and bouquet; nearly all are *Riesling*, and over half are dry or medium dry.

Hong-Kong-Haus, Georg-Schmitt-Platz 2. The best of the city's Chinese restaurants. Closed Tues.

Krim, Glockenstr. 6–7. Serves Mediterranean-style cuisine, including plenty of fish and seafood dishes. Breakfasts are also available, and there are bargain set lunch menus.

Palais Kesselstatt, Liebfrauenstr. 10 (☎06 51/4 02 04). Trier's most famous and upmarket restaurant, housed in a magnificent Baroque palace, and serving high-quality wines from its own Reichsgraf von Kesselstatt estates. Advance booking advisable; closed Sun & Mon.

Pfeffermühle, Zurlaubener Ufer 76 (☎06 51/2 61 33). Another celebrated, very intimate restaurant, serving French *haute cuisine*. Reservations usually necessary; closed all day Sun & Mon lunchtime.

Weisshaus, Weisshaus 1. Located right by the cable-car terminus with a wonderful view of Trier, though the food alone is worth the journey. Closed Mon.

Zum Domstein, Hauptmarkt 5. Trier's most innovative restaurant, offering adventurous vegetarian cuisine in addition to the standard *gutbürgerliche Küche*, while Roman-style dishes are served in the cellar. Bargain menus at lunchtime.

Bars and cafés

Astarix, Karl-Marx-Str. 11. Big, relaxed student bar serving an eclectic range of mountainous piles of cheap grub.

Blaues Blut, Treveris-Passage, Pferdemarkt. Bar where the "punk's not dead" crew congregate.

Brasserie, Fleischstr. 12. Housed in a handsome Baroque mansion with an attached winter garden, this is the Trier outpost of the Bitburger brewery in the Eifel, the largest and best-known beer producer in the wine stronghold that is the Rhineland-Palatinate.

Café Bley, Simeonstr. 19. Elegant traditional café in the Dreikönigenhaus.

En de Lauben, Zurlaubener Ufer 78. A pleasant traditional tavern, with good cider as well as wines. It has a garden pavilion overlooking the river, equipped with a heating system which enables it to be kept open all year round.

InFlagranti, Viehmarkt 13. One of the most popular student haunts; also serves light meals.

Mephisto, Kalenfelsstr. 3. Pub serving good-value food. There's a huge beer garden which gets packed out in summer.

Palais, Stockplatz. This bar-cum-disco is currently at the heart of the Trier *Szene*.

Styxx, Judengasse 2. Raucous cellar bar, one of several on the alley.

Zapotex, Pferdemarkt 1a. Hangout of the local fashion victims.

The Mosel Wine Road

From Trier you can follow the **Mosel Wine Road** (Mosel Weinstrasse) by bus or car to Koblenz, where the Mosel flows into the Rhine. The river meanders through innumerable wine villages and towns in a series of tortuous curves, the slopes of its valley lined with vineyards. This journey can also be accomplished by rail, but the line leaves the valley for substantial stretches and goes through relatively nondescript countryside, whereas the B53 road crisscrosses the Mosel and misses none of the splendid scenery along the route. An even more enticing way to travel, whether for all or just part of the way, is by **boat** – see the box on p.482 for details.

Bernkastel-Kues

Like many towns in the Mosel valley, **BERNKASTEL-KUES**, which is 50km downstream from Trier, was originally two completely separate communities facing each other across the river. It attracts its fair share of coach-tripping tourists and can get pretty busy in summer, but it well worth a visit, both for its sights and its wines.

In Bernkastel, on the south side of the Mosel, the main attraction is the half-timbered, gently sloping **Marktplatz**, which really does live up to tourist brochure hyperbole, with a stately coffee-and-cream-coloured Renaissance **Rathaus** as the focal point. Next door is the **Spitzhäuschen**, an absurdly narrow half-timbered building with

BOAT TRIPS ALONG THE MOSEL

Between May and early October, you can travel the length of the River Mosel from Trier to Koblenz, or just make short local trips; Eurail passes allow you to travel on the K-D Linie steamers without charge, while other rail passes bring reductions. The same company runs luxury cruises allowing you to see the best of both the Mosel and the Rhine: a three-day trip from Frankfurt to Trier or a two-day one from Trier to Cologne both cost upwards of DM400/€200, meals included.

FERRY COMPANIES AND ROUTES

Collée–Hölzenbein Rheinzollstr. 4, Koblenz (☎02 61/3 77 44)	Koblenz–Cochem
Gebruder Kolb Briedern (☎0 26 73/15 15)	Cochem–Trier
Gerhard Voss Goethestr. 15, Bernkastel-Kues (☎0 65 31/63 16)	Bernkastel-Kues–Leiwen
Hans Michelis Goldbachstr. 52, Bernkastel-Kues (☎0 65 31/68 97 or 82 22)	Bernkastel-Kues–Traben-Trarbach
K-D Linie Rheinwerft, Koblenz (☎02 61/3 10 30, *www.k-d.com*)	Koblenz–Cochem

a steep grey slate-pitched roof, which now houses a tiny Weinstube. In the middle of the vineyards above Bernkastel stands **Burg Landshut**, a thirteenth-century castle which went up in flames in 1693 and has been a ruin ever since, but from which you get panoramic views of the town and around.

In Kues, on the other side of the river, the bank is lined with the houses and villas of nineteenth-century vineyard owners. Fronting the river is the Gothic **St Nikolaus-Hospital** (Mon–Fri 9am–noon & 2–6pm, Sat & Sun 9am–noon; free; guided tours, subject to a minimum of five visitors, Tues 10.30am, Fri 3pm; DM5/€2.50), also known as the **Cusanusstift**, a poorhouse founded by the town's most famous son, the fifteenth-century theologian and philosopher Nikolaus Cusanus, who pursued a highly successful ecclesiastical career, latterly as a cardinal in Rome. The buildings were constructed to house 33 destitute old men – a symbolic figure representing each year of Christ's life – and have maintained the same function ever since. In the heavily ornate **Kapelle** there's a vivid mid-fifteenth century *Crucifixion* triptych by the Cologne narrative painter known as the Master of the Life of the Virgin. The **Bibliothek**, which contains 314 ninth- to fifteenth-century manuscripts collected by Cusanus, is considered one of the most valuable private libraries in the world, but is only accessible on the twice-weekly guided tours. Also within the complex is the **Mosel-Weinmuseum** (mid-April to Oct Tues–Sun 10am–5pm; Nov to mid-April Tues–Sun 2–5pm; DM3/€1.50), which features a large collection of wine presses, vessels and other related objects. There's also a *Vinothek* where local wines can be sampled and bought.

Practicalities

Bernkastel-Kues is not on a passenger rail line; the quickest way to reach it from Trier is to take a Koblenz-bound train as far as Wittlich, from where a connecting **bus** service covers the remaining 16km. The **tourist office** is at Am Gestade 5 (May–Oct Mon–Sat 8.30am–12.30pm & 1–5pm; Nov–April Mon–Fri 8.30am–12.30pm & 1–5pm; ☎0 65 31/40 23 24, fax 79 53, *www.bernkastel-kues.de*). There are dozens of **guesthouses** and **hotels**, but the town can still get full up because of the volume of summer traffic. There's a particularly enticing selection on the Bernkastel side, including

Kapuzinerstübchen, Römerstr. 35 (☎0 65 31/23 53; ③), *Römischer Kaiser*, Markt 29 (☎0 65 31/9 68 60; ④), *Binz*, Markt 1 (☎0 65 31/22 25; ④–⑤), *Doctor-Weinstuben*, in a seventeenth-century house with inner courtyard at Hebegasse 5 (☎0 65 31/60 81; ⑤), and *Zur Post*, Gestade 17 (☎0 65 31/9 67 00, *www.hotel-zur-post-bernkastel.de*; ⑤). In Kues try *Weinhaus St Maximilian*, Saarallee 12 (☎0 65 31/9 65 00; ③), or *Drei Könige*, Bahnhofstr. 1 (☎0 65 31/20 35; ⑤). There's a **youth hostel** uphill from Burg Landshut at Jugendherbergstr. 1 (☎0 65 31/23 95, fax 15 29, *jh-bernkastel-kues@djh-info.de*; DM23/€11.50), and a **campsite** at Am Hafen 2 (☎0 65 31/82 00) in Kues.

Not surprisingly, there are dozens of **cafés** and **restaurants** in Bernkastel-Kues and the general rule is that the ones in the quieter streets are less likely to be full of tourists being ripped off. All the Bernkastel hotels listed above can also be recommended as places to eat and drink, while the *Ratskeller*, Am Markt, and *Rotisserie Royale*, Burgstr. 19, are also particularly good. During the first weekend in September the biggest **wine festival** on the Mosel takes place here, when consumption of litres of the most famous local vintage, *Bernkasteler Doctor*, brings plenty of life to the streets.

Traben-Trarbach

Another double town, **TRABEN-TRARBACH**, is 24km downstream from Bernkastel-Kues, though only a fraction of that distance away as the crow flies. Traben, on the northern bank, was once a prime strategic site, as the two ruined fortesses above the town testify. **Schloss Grevenburg**, now reduced to a couple of walls, was blown up in 1697 in accordance with the terms of a recently signed peace treaty. In 1734 **Mont Royal**, built just 44 years previously by Louis XIV, suffered similar treatment, leaving the citizens free to get on with more peaceful pursuits like building half-timbered houses.

Most of these are actually in Trarbach on the opposite bank, where they rub shoulders with more substantial upper-middle-class villas from the nineteenth century. Also on the Trarbach side of the connecting bridge is the **Brückentor**, a monumental gateway designed by the Jugendstil architect Bruno Möhring, who created several other buildings in town in the same style, including the **Haus Huesgen**, Am Bahnhof 20, and the **Haus Breucker**, An der Mosel 7, both on the river bank in Traben.

Traben's **Bahnhof** is the terminus of a branch railway which connects with the main Trier–Koblenz line at Bullay. The **tourist office** is nearby at Bahnstr. 22 (July–Oct Mon–Fri 9am–noon & 2–5pm, Sat 10am–noon; Nov–June Mon–Fri 9am–noon & 2–4pm; ☎0 65 41/8 39 80, fax 83 98 39, *www.traben-trarbach.de*). On the Traben side the accommodation options include a **guesthouse**, *Germania*, Kirchstr. 101 (☎0 65 41/93 98; ②), and **hotels** such as *Krone*, An der Mosel 93 (☎0 65 41/8 38 70; ⑤), *Oase Moselschlösschen*, Neue Rathausstr. 12–16 (☎0 65 41/83 20; ⑤–⑦), and *Bellevue*, in a large Jugendstil building at Am Moselufer (☎0 65 41/70 30; ⑤–⑧). There is far less choice in Trarbach: the best address is *Moseltor*, Moselstr. 1 (☎0 65 41/65 51; ⑤). The **youth hostel** is at Hirtenpfad 6 (☎0 65 41/92 78, fax 37 59, *jh-traben-trarbach@djh-info.de*; DM27/€13.50 or DM33/€16.50), about fifteen minutes' walk from the Bahnhof on the same side of the river. Also in Traben are **camping** facilities at Rissbacher Str. 165 (☎0 65 41/31 11), while there's another site 2km down the road at Wedenhofstr. 25 (☎0 65 41/91 74) in Wolf. All the hotels listed above have recommendable **restaurants**, with that in *Krone* being particularly renowned. Traben-Trarbach's *Weinfest* is held during the last weekend in July; there's another on the last Sunday in June in Wolf.

Cochem

The next town of any size is **COCHEM**, which lies 55km downstream from Traben-Trarbach, and on the main Trier-Koblenz rail line. It's a place which has sold its soul to tourism and should be avoided like the plague in summer. The main attraction is the

Reichsburg (daily: mid-March to Oct 9am–5pm; first two weeks of Nov 9am–3pm; DM7/€3.50), one of the Rhineland-Palatinate's most famous replica castles. If it weren't a Romantic-era fake (the eleventh- to fourteenth-century original went up in smoke in 1689, assisted by enthusiastic French soldiers), the castle, which dominates the town with its cluster of towers and implacable walls, would be very impressive. Inside, it has been decorated in mock-medieval style, though there are some fine pieces of Renaissance furniture.

Cochem has a half-timbered **Marktplatz** with a sober Baroque **Rathaus**. Behind stands the **Martinskirche**, with a tower that looks like a Rococo soldier's helmet. It's a postwar rebuild of an original which dated back to the ninth century. Parts of the **Stadtmauer** are also still intact, including three chunky town gates. From one of them, **Enderttor**, you can take a chairlift ride (daily 9am–6pm; DM7/€3.50 single, DM9/€4.50 return) to the top of the **Pinnerkreuz** hill for the best view of the town and its environs.

Cochem's **Bahnhof** is at the northern end of town. The **tourist office** (April & Oct Mon–Thurs 9am–5pm, Fri 9am–6pm; May, June & Sept Mon–Thurs 9am–5pm, Fri 9am–6pm, Sat 9am–5pm; July & Aug Mon–Thurs 9am–5pm, Fri 9am–6pm, Sat 9am–5pm, Sun 9am–noon; Nov–March Mon–Fri 9am–1pm & 2–5pm; ☎0 26 71/6 00 40, fax 60 04 44, *www.cochem.de*) is at Endertplatz 1. Accommodation is plentiful and includes some **private rooms** (①–③), but it can get booked out at the height of the season. Among a couple of dozen **pensions** are *Lange*, Endertstr. 52 (☎0 26 71/71 73; ②), and *Café Becker*, Oberbachstr. 20–22 (☎0 26 71/72 24; ③). An even larger number of **hotels** includes *Karl Müller*, Moselpromenade 9 (☎0 26 71/13 33; ④–⑥), *Am Hafen*, Uferstr. 4 (☎0 26 71/9 77 20; ⑤), and *Lohspeicher*, Obergasse 1 (☎0 26 71/39 76; ⑥). All of these have good **restaurants**, with the palm going to the last-named. There's a **youth hostel** at Klottener Str. 9 (☎0 26 71/86 33, fax 85 68, *jh-cochem@djh-info.de*; DM24/€12) on the south side of the Mosel. The most convenient of the local **camp-sites** is *Freizeitzentrum*, Klottener Str. 17 (☎0 26 71/44 09).

Treis-Karden and around

From Cochem it's another 11km by road or rail to the little double town of **TREIS-KARDEN**. The dominant landmark in Karden, on the north side of the Mosel, is the **Stiftskirche St Kastor**, which was under construction for over three hundred years, marking the full transition from Romanesque to Gothic. Although small, its simple white lines make it one of the most visually appealing churches of the Mosel region. Inside, there's a fine early seventeenth-century side altar of *The Martyrdom of St Stephen* and a slightly faded wall-painting of Christ which looks startlingly modern. Built into the cliffs behind Treis on the south bank of the Mosel are two castles: the restored twelfth-century **Wildburg**, and **Burg Treis**, an eleventh-century ruin.

The **Bahnhof** is in Karden, where the **tourist office** (May–Oct Mon–Fri 9am–noon & 2–4/5pm, Sat 9am–noon; Nov–April Mon–Fri 9am–noon & 2–4/5pm; ☎0 26 72/61 37, fax 27 80, *www.treis-karden.de*) can be found at Hauptstr. 27. Most of the **hotels** are also in this part of town: the best are *Brauer*, Moselstr. 26 (☎0 26 72/12 11; ④), and *Schlosshotel Petry*, St-Castor-Str. 80 (☎0 26 72/93 40; ⑤); both have fine **restaurants**.

Burg Eltz

Karden is a gateway to the Mosel valley's greatest castle, **Burg Eltz** (guided tours daily April–Oct 9.30am–5.30pm; *www.burg-eltz.de*; DM9/€4.50), one of only three intact medieval fortresses in the Rhineland-Palatinate (the others are the Pfalzgrafenstein and the Marksburg – see pp.490 & p.493). It can be reached by car or bike from the village of Münstermaifeld to the north; there's no public transport, so the only other means of access are the steep footpaths from either Karden or (somewhat shorter) Moselkern, which can be reached by Koblenz-bound trains. Despite the relative difficulty of getting there, the place is prone to be swamped by tourists, and it's advisable to visit early, or during the early or late part of the season.

Burg Eltz seems to rise vertically straight out of the woods of the Elzbach valley and bristles with conical towers. It goes back at least as far as the twelfth century, developing over the next four hundred years as a defensive home for the various branches of the Eltz family, who managed to live there peaceably for a couple of hundred years until a run-in with Balduin, the Elector of Trier. This resulted in a two-year siege, during which **Burg Trutzeltz** was built by Balduin directly in front in order to lob rocks at the castle. After Burg Eltz fell the Eltz family were allowed to remain in possession as vassals of Balduin and peace returned. Most of what you see today was built during the fifteenth century: inside the walls are a number of residential towers crammed together round an inner courtyard, which escaped destruction by the French in 1689 only because a member of the Eltz family happened to be an officer in the French army.

The **interior** of the castle is more or less as it was during medieval times, complete with original furnishings, wall-hangings and paintings. Particularly impressive is the **Rübenacher Untersaal**, with sixteenth-century Flemish tapestries of unlikely-looking exotic animals and plants, and a number of panel paintings, including Cranach's *Madonna with Grapes*. The **Schatzkammer** (DM4/€2 extra), the only part of the interior which can be visited at leisure, is full of silver- and gold-ware, glass, porcelain, weapons and armour, including a suit of armour which belonged to Emperor Maximilian I.

Kobern-Gondorf

KOBERN-GONDORF is yet another little double town trailing out along the Mosel banks, 13km east of Treis-Karden. The most unusual local attraction is the **Goloring**, a prehistoric circular tomb complex dating from 1200 to 600 BC. In Kobern's Kirchstrasse is the **Abteihof**, the oldest half-timbered house in the Rhineland-Palatinate: built in 1321, it looks in remarkably good shape for its age. Also worth visiting is the castle complex. The **Niederburg** is an extensive pile of crumbling masonry with a more or less intact tower, while the **Oberburg** has the almost perfectly symmetrical Romanesque **Matthiaskapelle**, which once housed the remains of the Apostle Matthias (later transferred to the Matthiaskirche in Trier).

The **tourist office** (Mon–Thurs 3–5pm, Fri 2–5pm; ☎0 26 07/12 59, fax 40 45, *www.kobern-gondorf.de*) is on Kobern's Marktplatz. **Hotels** include *Gasthof Kastorschänke*, Bahnhofstr. 18 (☎0 26 07/12 59; ③), and *Simonis*, Marktplatz 4 (☎0 26 07/2 03; ⑥). For **eating** and **drinking**, try *Weingut Thomas Höreth*, housed in an old mill, complete with wine museum, at Mühlental 17. To get there, take the road up to the Matthiaskapelle, then turn down the road opposite the cemetery. There are restaurants in both the hotels mentioned above, and another well-regarded establishment, *Marais*, in the Oberburg. Kobern-Gondorf has a **wine festival** in late June and early July, another during the second weekend in September and a third in the second weekend in October.

THE RHINE GORGE

Beyond Mainz, the **Rhine** bends westwards and continues its hitherto stately but unspectacular journey. Suddenly, there's a dramatic change – the river widens and swings back to a northerly course, threatening the low banks on either side, while long wooded islands block the view ahead.

This marks the entrance to the spectacular **gorge**, which, though it's only a small part of the river's total length of 1320km, is the Rhine of popular imagination. The combination of the treacherous waters, whirlpools and rocky banks lining the sharp twists of the river poses a severe test of navigational skill. Nowadays, this has been considerably eased by the digging of channels to control the movement of the river, but it has inevitably thrown up legends of shipwrecks, sirens and mermaids. The lure of the castles of the medieval robber barons, the raw elemental beauty of the landscape itself and the famous wines made from the vines which somehow cling to the lower slopes make for one of Europe's major tourist magnets. Yet the pleasure steamers are still greatly outnumbered by the long, narrow commercial barges, a reminder of the crucial role the river has played in the German economy down the centuries.

The Rhine from Bingen to Koblenz

The first stretch of the gorge, up to the confluence with the Mosel, is undoubtedly the finest, lined with cute half-timbered towns and an extensive range of castles in various states of repair. In high season, this means a flood of organized tour parties, particularly from the UK, this being the one part of Germany the British have really taken to their hearts. If you must do this part of the Rhine in summer and are on a tight budget, then try and book your accommodation well in advance, or be prepared to commute from elsewhere. In addition to the hotels mentioned in the text, there's a reasonable – if not especially extensive – provision of **private rooms** (①–④), bookable via the appropriate local tourist office. Bearing in mind that the true identity of the region has been sacrificed to hard sell, you could do worse than take the **train** through this stretch and admire the best feature – the scenery – in comfort, but it's undeniably more fun to go by **boat**.

Spring and autumn are the best times to visit the area, and you could easily spend several days meandering around. Rail and road links lie on either side of the river and, although there are no bridges between Bingen and Koblenz, fairly frequent ferry links for passengers enable you to hop from one side of the river to the other without too much difficulty.

Bingen

Despite its imposing setting at the point where the Nahe joins the Rhine, **BINGEN** is generally regarded as something of a poor relation of Rüdesheim on the latter's opposite bank. Nonetheless, its star has been in the ascendant of late because of the burgeoning interest in one of the great female figures of the European Middle Ages, **Abbess Hildegard of Bingen** (see box on p.488).

The extensive programme of events marking the 900th anniversary of Hildegard's birth brought a permanent memorial in the form of a wide-ranging display on her life and career in the new **Historisches Museum am Strom** (Tues–Sun 10am–5pm; DM6/€3), which occupies a converted electricity station towards the western end of the town waterfront. Although presented in an informative manner, it suffers from a lack of any tangible objects associated with Hildegard herself. However, it has obtained

BOAT TRIPS ALONG THE RHINE

The imperious white vessels of the **K-D Linie** (Rheinwerft, Koblenz; ☎02 61/3 10 30, *www.k-d.com*; see also listings in Mainz, Bonn and Cologne) have several sailings daily during the June to September high season; the services thereafter progressively run down, and stop altogether at the end of October, to resume in a skeleton form at Easter or the beginning of April, whichever is the earlier. Although prices are lower than they used to be, they're still far from cheap (Bingen to Koblenz costs DM42.40/€21.20; Mainz to St Goar DM48/€24). However, day returns are available for only slightly more (DM44.80/€22.40 and DM54.60/€27.30 respectively in the case of the two examples quoted), and you travel free of charge if you can prove that it's your birthday. Eurail passes are valid, while other rail passes should bring a discount. In addition, a number of smaller companies offer much cheaper sailings along shorter stretches:.

FERRY COMPANIES AND ROUTES

Bingen-Rüdesheimer Fährgastschiffahrt Rheinkai 10, Bingen (☎0 67 21/1 41 40, *www.bingen-ruedesheimer.com*)	Bingen–St. Goar
Hebel Linie Rheinallee 35, Boppard (☎0 67 42/24 20, *www.boppard.com/Hebel-Linie*)	Boppard–Koblenz–Kobern–Gondorf
Hölzenbein Rheinzollstr. 4, Koblenz (☎02 61/3 77 44)	Koblenz–Bingen
Merkelbach Emster Str. 57, Koblenz (☎02 61/7 68 10)	Koblenz–Braubach
Rheinschiffahrt Goar (☎0 67 71/26 20)	St Goarshausen–St Goar

ABBESS HILDEGARD OF BINGEN (1098–1179)

The astonishing career of the multi-talented Hildegard of Bingen is quite unlike that of any other woman of her time. As the tenth child of a noble family, she was given to the Church as a tithe, and placed in the convent of Disibodenburg in the Nahe valley at the age of 8, becoming abbess in 1136. She went on to found two convents of her own – the Rupertsberg above Bingen in 1150 and Eibingen on the outskirts of Rüdesheim in 1165 – and is the only medieval woman who is known to have undertaken preaching tours, addressing clergy as well as laity. Between 1141 and 1151 she wrote her literary masterpiece *Scivias*, visionary descriptions of the world and the relationship between God and mankind. She also produced a two-volume tract on natural sciences and the art of healing. Yet it is arguable that her most lasting achievement was as a composer. Her legacy consists of the music drama *Ordo Virtutum*, the earliest-known morality play, plus 77 canticles, sequences and songs, in which she deploys a variety of devices, ranging from simple melodies to impassioned declamation, to enrich the vivid imagery of her own poetry.

In her lifetime she was regarded as a saint, and as early as 1227 a canonization process was instigated. This was never brought to completion, though in 1389 she was included in the *Martyrologicum Romanum*, the Roman Catholic Church's official register of saints. For several centuries, her reputation languished in obscurity, to undergo a spectacular revival in the second half of the twentieth century, when the rise of feminism and renewed interest in both holistic medicine and early music all helped to turn her into a proto-modern figure. In 1971, her feast day was added to the calendar of the dioceses of the German-speaking world, where she is commonly referred to as St Hildegard.

on loan from the Diözesanmuseum in Mainz two exquisite carvings of wild vines and hops by the Master of Naumburg, which are the earliest botanically accurate representations in Western art and postdate Hildegard by only a few decades. The museum also has a major archeological exhibit, a collection of 66 **surgical instruments** (many of them remarkably similar to those used nowadays) of a Roman army doctor of the second century AD, who was probably based at the fort in Bingen. It includes a complete set of implements for performing operations on the skull, as well as no fewer than thirteen scalpels.

The main historic monument in the town centre is the **Basilika St Martin** overlooking the Nahe, which is actually two churches in one: the original building, an early fifteenth-century collegiate church, and the **Barbarabau**, a double-aisled extension tacked on later the same century to serve for parish use. In addition, an eleventh-century **crypt** survives from a previous church on the site. The furnishings are remarkably disparate. In the main church, the side altars have beautiful statues of SS Barbara and Catherine which are contemporary with the architecture, while the pulpit and ciborium are Baroque, the high altar unashamedly avant-garde. The Barbarabau houses a touching Gothic relief of *The Lamentation* and a colourful Mannerist triptych of scenes from the life of the Virgin.

Towering high above Bingen is **Burg Klopp**, a former castle of the Archbishop-Electors of Mainz. The original fortress was destroyed in 1689 and the ruins were blown up in 1711, so that what can be seen today is very largely a nineteenth-century replica. Housed within the tower, which commands a marvellous view over the Rhine to the Taunus, is the **Heimatmuseum** (April–Oct Tues–Sun 9am–noon & 2–5pm; DM1/€0.50), which contains more local finds from the Roman era. Another good vantage point is the **Rupertsberg** above Bingerbrück, the suburb on the opposite side of the Nahe. This is the site of the **Kloster** where Hildegard was abbess, but unfortunately only the cellars plus scanty remains of the church still survive. Although rarely accessible to visitors, the town's best-known monument is the **Mäuseturm**, a former customs tower on an island in the Rhine immediately north of Bingerbrück in which, according to grisly legend, Archbishop Hatto of Mainz was devoured alive by mice after having burned all the local beggars during a famine.

Practicalities

Bingen's **Hauptbahnhof** adjoins the huge rail yards in Bingerbrück; the **Stadtbahnhof** is at the southern edge of the town centre. Close to the latter, at Rheinkai 21, is the **tourist office** (April–Nov Mon–Fri 9am–6pm, Sat 9am–12.30pm; Dec–March Mon–Fri 9am–4pm; ☎0 67 21/18 42 05, fax 1 62 75, *www.bingen.de*). A good range of **hotels** includes *Römerhof*, Rupertsberg 10 (☎0 67 21/3 22 48; ③), *Café Köppel*, Kapuzinerstr. 12 (☎0 67 21/1 47 70; ③), *Krone*, Rheinkai 19–20 (☎0 67 21/1 70 16; ④), *Martinskeller*, Martinstr. 1 (☎0 67 21/1 34 75; ⑤), and *Rheinhotel*, Hindenburganlage 1 (☎0 67 21/79 60; ⑦). There's a **youth hostel** at Herterstr. 51 (☎0 67 21/3 21 63, fax 3 40 12, *djh-bingen-bingerbrueck@djh-info.de*; DM22/€11) in Bingerbrück and a **campsite** (☎0 67 21/1 71 60) near the Hindenburgbrücke in the incorporated village of Kempten to the south. The town's leading **restaurants** are those in the hotels *Atlantis* and *Krone*, plus *Brunnenkeller*, Vorstadt 60. Adjoining the last-named, at Vorstadt 58, is *Brunnenstübschen*, a cosy little Weinstube; another good place to drink local vintages is *Weinhaus Zum Alten Rathaus*, Rathausstr. 28.

Trechtingshausen

Just before **TRECHTINGSHAUSEN**, the first village beyond Bingen, is one of the most photographed Rhine landmarks, **Burg Rheinstein** (March–Nov daily 9am–7pm; DM6/€3). Prince Friedrich Wilhelm of Prussia, influenced by the Romanticism that was then fashionable, had the ruined thirteenth-century fortress he had inherited in 1823 remodelled as a summer residence, so initiating what was to become a nineteenth-century mania for building replicas of the medieval castles of the Rhine valley. This is actually more tasteful than most: the **Burgkapelle** which was added is a fine example of the neo-Gothic style, while the castle retains some authentically medieval artefacts, including stained glass, arms, armour and furniture, as well as pastiche wall and ceiling frescoes.

Bacharach

BACHARACH, 10km downstream, was called Baccaracum by the Romans after an altar stone to Bacchus which once stood in the Rhine. This was blown up in 1850 to ease navigation of the river, but parts of the old town wall are still intact and there are plenty of half-timbered houses, particularly around Marktplatz and in Blücherstrasse. The thirteenth-century **Peterskirche** on Marktplatz has both late Romanesque and early Gothic features, and is one of the few medieval churches in Germany with an interior of four tiers. Above rises **Burg Stahleck**, a chunky-looking castle, dating back at least as far as the twelfth century, which was once a seat of the Counts Palatine of the Rhine. It still preserves its keep, battlements and a residential tract. From the overgrown and half-timbered Posthof square there's a good view of the **Wernerkapelle**, the red sandstone frame of a never-completed Gothic chapel.

The **tourist office** (Mon–Fri 8.30am–noon & 2–5pm, Sat 10am–noon; ☎0 67 43/29 68, fax 31 55, *www.bacharach.de*) is at Oberstr. 1. A wide choice of **hotels** includes *Im Malerwinkel*, Blücherstr. 41–45 (☎0 67 43/12 39; ②), *Gelber Hof*, Blücherstr. 26 (☎0 67 43/91 01 00; ④), *Altkölnischer Hof*, Blücherstr. 2 (☎0 67 43/13 39; ⑤), and *Parkhotel*, Marktstr. 8 (☎0 67 43/14 22; ⑤). All except the first of these have **restaurants**. The **youth hostel** is in Burg Stahleck (☎0 67 43/12 66, fax 26 84, *dj-bacharach@djh-info.de*; DM26/€13 or DM32/€16), while the **campsite** is at Strandbadweg (☎0 67 43/17 52).

Kaub

KAUB, a few kilometres north on the opposite bank of the Rhine, was another strong-hold of the Counts Palatine, who in 1277 purchased **Burg Gutenfels** above the town, together with the right to levy tolls on passing ships. The castle as you see it today is a late nineteenth-century rebuild of the original, and nowadays functions as a hotel (see below). Though you can't even enter the grounds unless you're a guest, it's worth following the footpath round the back, which leads to a vantage point offering a magnificent view over the Rhine.

It was at Kaub that Field Marshal Blücher, the Prussian commander who saved the day with his late arrival at the battle of Waterloo, crossed the Rhine during an earlier campaign against Napoleon by ordering the construction of a spectacular pontoon bridge. He's commemorated in the **Blüchermuseum** (April–Oct Tues–Sun 10am–noon & 2–4pm; Nov–March Tues–Sat 10am–noon, Sun 10am–noon & 2–4pm; DM4/€2) at Metzgergasse 6, the Baroque town-house he used as his headquarters. The rooms are decorated in grand Empire style and are full of military memorabilia from the Napoleonic wars and old Prussia.

From Kaub's waterfront promenade you get a great view of one of the most famous symbols of the Rhineland, the **Pfalzgrafenstein** or **Pfalz** (April–Sept Tues–Sun 9am–1pm & 2–6pm; Oct, Nov & Jan–April Tues–Sun 9am–1pm & 2–5pm; DM4/€2, plus DM3/€1.50 for the ferry; note that access is suspended when the river's water level is high). Construction of this white-walled toll fortress, which stands on an islet in the river like a permanently moored ship, was begun in 1326 by order of the Count Palatine Ludwig the Bavarian. Brought up to date in the seventeenth century by the provision of gun emplacements and look-out oriels, the Pfalzgrafenstein continued to serve as a toll-levying station until 1867.

Kaub's **tourist office** (Mon–Fri 8am–noon; ☎0 67 74/2 22, fax 82 30, *www.tal-der-loreley.de/ort.kaub*) is in the Rathaus, Metzgergasse 26. The cheapest of several reasonably priced **hotels** are *Weinhaus Bahles*, Bahnstr. 10 (☎0 67 74/2 58; ②), and *Deutsches Haus*, Schulstr. (☎0 67 74/2 66; ③), which also has a good restaurant. Top of the range in every sense is *Burg Gutenfels* (☎0 67 74/2 20; ⑦). There are **camping** facilities at *Am Elsleinband* on Blücherstrasse (☎0 67 74/5 60).

Oberwesel

OBERWESEL, back on the left bank just to the north, possesses the finest extant fortifications in the Rhineland, a three-kilometre-long **Stadtmauer** which still preserves sixteen of its towers from an original total of twenty-one. Unfortunately, the section guarding the riverfront is marred by the proximity of the railway, which runs directly alongside, but the whole ensemble is nonetheless impressive, not least at the hilly northwestern edge, where the fortified church of **St Martin** (popularly known, for obvious reasons, as the "white church") forms an integral part of the municipal defences. At the opposite end of town is a huge fortress, the **Schönburg**, which is now a ruin but still impressive. Below it stands the Gothic **Liebfrauenkirche** (which the locals call the "red church", after the huge red sandstone blocks used to build it). In its airy interior, look out for the St Nicholas altar, on which the saint is shown helping three Knights who have been sentenced to death for crimes they didn't commit, saving three sisters who have been forced into prostitution by their father and protecting passengers on board a ship.

The **tourist office** (July–Sept Mon–Fri 9am–1pm & 2–6pm, Sat 10am–noon; Oct–June Mon–Fri 9am–1pm & 2–6pm; ☎0 67 44/15 21, fax 15 40, *www.tal-der-loreley.de/ort.oberwesel*) is at Rathausstr. 3. There are a couple of **hotels** right alongside: *Weinhaus Weiler*, Marktplatz 4 (☎0 67 44/70 03; ④), and *Römerkrug*, Marktplatz 1 (☎0

67 44/70 91; ④). The best and most expensive place to stay in town is *Auf Schönburg* (☎0 67 44/9 39 30; ⑧–⑨) within the castle complex. All three of these have recommendable **restaurants**. There's a **campsite** (☎0 67 44/2 45) just off the B9 road to the north of town, while the **youth hostel** is by the castle at Auf dem Schönberg (☎0 67 44/9 33 30, fax 74 46, *jh-oberwesel@djh-info.de*; DM30/€15 or DM39/€19.50).

The Lorelei and St Goarshausen

Next stop is **ST GOARSHAUSEN**, 8km from Kaub, which trails along the eastern bank of the Rhine for a couple of kilometres. Just before the entrance to the town is the **Lorelei** (or **Loreley**), the famous outcrop of rock where, according to legend, a blonde woman used to sit combing her hair while she lured passing sailors to watery graves with her eerily compelling song. There's a naff statue at the water's edge to commemorate the legend. The rock itself has been over-hyped – it's impressive, but no more so than dozens of other cliffs in the Rhine gorge. However, there are outstanding views from the top, which, in accordance with a project undertaken in connection with EXPO 2000, has recently been made the focal point of a landscape park. In tandem with this, a brand-new multimedia visitor centre, the **Besucherzentrum Loreley** (daily: April–Oct 10am–6pm; Nov–March 11am–5pm; *www.besucherzentrum -loreley.de*; DM6/€3) has been built. This offers information on a range of topics, including the Lorelei legend and the literature it has inspired, as well as local geology, flora and fauna, Rhine tourism and shipping and the Rhenish wine industry. Also up here is the Loreley Freilichtbühne, an open-air stage that is frequently used for rock concerts.

Above St Goarshausen itself is **Burg Katz** (Cat Castle), the fourteenth-century fortress of the counts of Katzenelnbogen; it is currently being converted into what will become one of the leading luxury hotels in the region. It was built to rival another castle a few kilometres downstream, which belonged to the archbishops of Trier and earned the inevitable nickname **Burg Maus** (Mouse Castle) because of its relative puniness. This is now an eagle and falcon station, giving displays of bird flight (March–Oct Mon–Sat at 11am & 2.30pm, Sun 11am, 2.30pm & 4.30pm; DM12/€6).

There's an inexpensive **guesthouse**, *Winzerschänke*, on the way from St Goarshausen to the Lorelei at Forstbachstr. 38 (☎0 67 71/3 37; ②). **Hotels** include *Deutsches Haus*, Wellmicher Str. 7 (☎0 67 71/26 17; ③), *Colonius*, Am Rheinufer (☎0 67 71/26 04; ③), and *Pohl's Rheinhotel Adler*, Bahnhofstr. 6 (☎0 67 71/26 13; ⑥). The *Weinwoche* is during the second and third weeks in September, and there are other **wine festivals** at the end of September and during the third weekend in October.

St Goar

A ferry will take you back across to the west bank of the Rhine and **ST GOAR**, which is slightly prettier and more touristy than its counterpart. Looming above town is the enormous **Burg Rheinfels** (April–Sept daily 9am–6pm; Oct daily 9am–5pm; DM6/€3) which, until the French blew it up in 1797, was one of the most powerful fortresses on the Rhine. It was founded in 1245 by Count Dieter von Katzenelnbogen, who wanted to look after his Rhine toll-collecting racket, and just ten years later withstood a 9000-man siege by soldiers of the Alliance of Rhenish Towns. During the sixteenth and seventeenth centuries the landgraves of Hesse extended what was already a formidable castle into an enormous fortification complex which was to prove virtually impregnable: it was the only Rhineland castle that the French were unable to take during the War of the Palatinate Succession. In 1796 the castle surrendered to the troops of Napoleon without a shot being fired, and over the next three years the

French did their best to demolish it. Today, the medieval outline can still be seen and you can walk through the underground passages of the later battlements. Models in the **Heimatmuseum** (April–Sept 9.30am–noon & 1–5pm; admission included in Burg entrance fee), which is housed in a rebuilt section, show how the place looked before it was destroyed.

St Goar's **tourist office** is at Heerstr. 86 (May–Sept Mon–Fri 8am–12.30pm & 2–5pm, Sat 9.30am–noon; Oct–April Mon–Fri 8am–12.30pm & 2–4.30pm; ☎0 67 41/3 83, fax 72 09, *www.tal-der-loreley.de/ort.st-goar*). There are plenty of **hotels** in the town centre, including *Germania*, Heerstr. 47 (☎0 67 41/16 10; ③), *Zur Post*, Bahnhofstr. 3 (☎0 67 41/3 39; ③), *Zum Goldenen Löwen*, Heerstr. 82 (☎0 67 41/16 74; ③–⑥), and *Montag*, Heerstr. 128 (☎0 67 41/16 29; ④). If you want to splash out, try the *Schlosshotel* in the Burg Rheinfels complex (☎0 67 41/80 20; ⑦). All of these hotels also have **restaurants**. The **youth hostel** is just north of the town centre at Bismarckweg 17 (☎0 67 41/3 88, fax 28 69; *jh-st-goar@djh-info.de*; DM22/€11). Of the two **campsites**, *Friedenau* is west of town at Gründelbachstr. 103 (☎0 67 41/3 68), while *Loreleyblick* is directly across the Rhine from the Loreley at An der Loreley 29–39 (☎0 67 41/20 66).

Boppard

At **BOPPARD**, 14km downstream from St Goar, the Rhine gorge starts to level out and the valley landscape becomes a gentler one of rounded, vine-covered slopes. The town benefits enormously from an unspoiled and relatively quiet Rhine promenade running along its entire length, having forced the rail authorities to lay the tracks on the opposite side of the centre, instead of their customary position by the river.

Boppard's dominant building is the late Romanesque **Severuskirche** on Marktplatz. A twin-towered structure, brightly painted in white and yellow, it was built during the thirteenth century to house the remains of St Severus, Bishop of Ravenna. Contemporary with the church are the wall-paintings illustrating the life of the saint and a poignant triumphal cross. The squat Gothic **Karmelitenkirche**, near the Rhine quay, has elaborate fifteenth-century choir stalls, a couple of seventeenth-century altars and various tombs of local bigwigs. At the east entrance is a recess which houses the fourteenth-century *Traubenmadonna*. Traditionally, local vine growers place the first ripe bunch of grapes of the year by the statue and leave it there until it withers away.

At the end of Kirchgasse, which is just off Oberstrasse (Boppard's main street), are the remains of the Roman **Stadtmauer**, which has weathered the years remarkably well. Four watchtowers survive of the 28 which guarded the military camp of Baudobirga, laid out in the fourth century on the site of present-day Boppard. Remains of more recent fortifications can be seen at the end of Bingergasse. The **Binger Tor** was built during the Middle Ages and has survived more or less intact, bar the odd bit of crumbling here and there. Between Burgplatz and Rheinallee is the **Alte Burg**, a castle and residence built by the archbishops of Trier to consolidate their grip on the area. The central keep, with its apertures for the pouring of boiling oil, molten lead and the like, was built around 1327, while the more civilized-looking wings were added during the seventeenth century. These days the building houses the **Museum der Stadt Boppard** (April–Oct Tues–Sun 10am–noon & 2–5pm; free). Part of this is devoted to Michael Thonet, a son of Boppard, who, during the early nineteenth century, perfected the technique of laminating wood and earned himself a fortune for his highly distinctive furniture (see p.446), of which there is a fine collection on display.

At the northern end of town, a **chairlift** (DM7.50/€3.75 single, DM11/€5.50 return) ascends to the belvedere known as **Vierseenblick** (Four Lakes View) because the only parts of the Rhine which are visible are four seemingly separate stretches of water. A short waymarked walk away is another viewpoint, the **Rheinschleife**, which commands a magnificent panorama over the Rhine's most spectacular bend.

Practicalities

Boppard's **Bahnhof**, a terminus of the Hunsrückbahn (see p.470), is a few minutes' walk to the northwest of the town centre. The **tourist office** is in the Rathaus on Marktplatz (April–Sept Mon–Fri 8am–5.30pm, Sat 9am–noon; Oct–March Mon–Fri 8am–4pm; ☎0 67 42/38 88, fax 8 14 02, *www.boppard.de*). There are several inexpensive **hotels** in the town centre, the most recommendable being the Anglo-German *Ohm Patt*, Steinstr. 30 (☎0 67 42/23 66; ③), and *Weinhaus Sonnenhof*, Kirchgasse 8 (☎0 67 42/32 23; ③), which also has a good restaurant. Of the more upmarket waterfront hotels, best value is the American-owned *Günther*, Rheinallee 40 (☎0 67 42/8 90 90; ④–⑥), many of whose rooms have balconies offering grandstand views of the river. Alternatives are *Rheinvilla*, Rheinallee 51 (☎0 67 42/80 51 51; ⑤), and *Bellevue Rheinhotel*, Rheinallee 41 (☎06742/10 20; ⑦–⑨), which have the two leading **restaurants** in town. There are **camping** facilities at *Sonneck* (☎0 67 42/21 21), just north of town on the B9 right next to the Rhine.

Braubach

On the right bank of the Rhine and 12km downstream from Boppard is **BRAUBACH**. It's a typical Rhenish village with several **hotels**, including *Goldene Schlüssel*, Marktplatz 14 (☎0 26 27/3 40; ③), and the outstanding *Zum Weissen Schwanen*, Brunnenstr 4 (☎0 26 27/5 59; ④–⑥), a seventeenth-century Weinhaus with an attached fourteenth-century mill; note that the restaurant is open evenings only.

Set in the hills a good half-hour's walk above the town, the **Marksburg** (guided tours daily: Easter–Oct 10am–5pm; Nov–Easter 11am–4pm; DM8/€4) is the only medieval castle on this stretch of the Rhine, other than the Pfalzgrafenstein, to escape destruction by the French. Being an absolutely genuine original, it looks far more impressive than the often heavy-handed nineteenth-century reconstructions elsewhere in the valley. Most of the fortress, including the turreted sandstone keep, was built between the twelfth and fourteenth centuries with a few additional defensive features added in the seventeenth century. Inside there's a big collection of weapons from the Middle Ages, including some extremely unpleasant instruments of torture. The Marksburg also has the only preserved medieval botanic garden in Germany.

Lahnstein and Rhens

Next stop is **LAHNSTEIN**, on the right bank of the river, 4km downstream from Braubach and remarkable above all for its setting at the point where the River Lahn sweeps into the Rhine. Above the former is the only setpiece sight, the restored **Burg Lahneck** (guided tours April–Oct daily 10am–5pm; DM6/€3), in whose grounds is the local **campsite** (☎0 26 21/27 65). There are also plenty of **hotels**, such as *Jung*, Bahnhofstr. 54 (☎0 26 21/80 01; ④), *Strassburger Hof*, Koblenzer Str. 2 (☎0 26 21/9 69 10; ④), and *Bock*, Westallee 11 (☎0 26 21/26 61; ⑤), all of which have **restaurants**. In the Kurpark, high above the Lahn at the extreme eastern edge of town, is *Hof Aspich*, one of the hottest *Szene* venues in the Rhineland, numbering among its attractions a Hausbrauerei, a large beer garden and regular live music and cabaret performances. The **tourist office** (April–Sept Mon–Fri 8am–5pm, Sat 10am–noon; Oct–March Mon–Fri 8am–5pm; ☎0 26 21/91 41 71, fax 91 43 40, *www.tal-der-loreley.de/ort.lahnsein*) is in the Stadthallenpassage in the town centre.

From Lahnstein you can take the ferry (passengers only; if you're driving you'll have to go via the Koblenz road bridge) to the half-timbered village of **RHENS**, which preserves most of its medieval fortifications. The momentous-sounding **Königsstuhl** (Seat of Kings) on the heights above is a stone platform where the German Electors met from 1273 to 1400 to choose their king. In fact, like so many of the Rhine's "medieval" monuments, most of what can be seen today dates from as recently as 1842, inspired by the then fashionable vogue for resurrecting Germany's medieval past.

Koblenz

It's appropriate that the name of **KOBLENZ** derives from the Latin word for confluence, as it was the Romans who first recognized the favourable properties of the site at the point where the Mosel flows into the Rhine, establishing a settlement there in 14 AD. Nowadays, the town has become one of Germany's major tourist centres, profiting from its ready access to the two great river valleys and the hill ranges beyond. Koblenz itself polarizes opinion – some enjoy its relaxed, rather faded charm; others find it smug and boring. The connection with tourism actually has deep roots, as it was in Koblenz in 1823 that **Karl Baedeker** began publishing his famous series of guidebooks which aimed at saving travellers from having to depend on unreliable and extortionate local tour guides for information. Old editions of these (the one on *The Rhineland* itself is a good example) are still worth seeking out: their sententious prose evokes a vanished epoch, and their pull-out maps are wonderful to handle.

Arrival, information and accommodation

The **Hauptbahnhof** and **bus station** are side by side, to the southwest of the Altstadt. Close by, at Löhrstr. 141, is the **tourist office** (May–Sept Mon–Fri 9am–8pm, Sat & Sun 10am–8pm; Oct–April Mon–Fri 9am–6pm, Sat & Sun 10am–2pm; ☎02 61/3 13 04, fax 1 00 43 99, *www.koblenz.de*). The **ferry** to Ehrenbreitstein departs from Konrad-Adenauer-Ufer; its Mosel counterpart runs in summer only from the pier west of Deutsches Eck.

As you'd expect, Koblenz offers a huge choice of accommodation, with **hotels** in every category, most of them competitively priced in terms of what they offer. The **youth hostel** (☎02 61/97 28 70, fax 9 72 87 30, *jh-koblenz@djh-info.de*) in Festung Ehrenbreitstein – buses #7, #8 and #9 go closest – must rate as one of the most enticing in Germany. There's a campsite at Lützel, directly opposite Deutsches Eck (☎02 61/80 24 89; closed mid-Oct to March).

Hotels and pensions

Brenner, Rizzastr. 20–22 (☎02 61/91 57 80, fax 3 62 78). Elegant, beautifully furnished hotel with garden, located between the Hauptbahnhof and the Altstadt. ⑦.

Diehl's, Am Pfaffendorfer Tor 10, Ehrenbreitstein (☎02 61/9 70 70, fax 9 70 72 13). Koblenz's leading hotel is right by the Rhine, and commands wonderful views. Its facilities include thermal baths, a sauna and solarium, and there's a first-rate restaurant, *Rheinterrasse*. ⑦.

Im Stüffje, Hohenzollernstr. 5 (☎02 61/91 52 20, fax 9 15 22 44). A fine mid-range hotel with restaurant (Mon–Fri only), just round the corner from Brenner. ⑥.

Jan van Werth, Van-Werth-Str. 9 (☎02 61/3 65 00, fax 3 65 06). Good-value hotel between the Hauptbahnhof and Altstadt. ④.

Kleiner Riesen, Kaiserin-Augusta-Anlagen 18 (☎02 61/30 34 60, fax 16 07 25). Fine traditional hotel on the right-bank waterfront. ⑥.

Kornpforte, Kornpfortstr. 11 (☎02 61/3 11 74, fax 3 11 76). Medium-range hotel with Weinstube in the heart of the Altstadt. ⑤.

Sessellift, Obertal 22, Ehrenbreitstein (☎02 61/7 52 56). One of a number of inexpensive options in the right-bank suburb. ②.

The town centre

The place to begin a tour of Koblenz is the **Deutsches Eck**, where the Mosel flows into the Rhine. In 1897, a colossal equestrian monument in the heroic taste of the time was erected here to Kaiser Wilhelm I. It was destroyed in World War II, but the base, itself a pompous structure with over a hundred steps, was rebuilt and piously dedicated to the unification of Germany. After much soul-searching, a copy of the statue was re-erected in 1993 in belated celebration of the achievement of this.

Close by is the finest building in the city, the Romanesque collegiate foundation of **St Kastor**, largely twelfth century, whose imposing facade has twin towers with characteristic "bishop's mitre" roofs. A long-term project to restore the interior has left it looking wonderfully fresh. Look out for the elaborate **keystones** of the Gothic vault, especially the one showing the Madonna and Child in a boat. There's a good view of the church from the floral garden of the adjacent **Deutschherrenhaus** which now contains the **Ludwig-Museum** (Tues–Sat 10.30am–5pm, Sun 11am–6pm; DM5/€2.50), with an important collection of (predominantly French) modern art.

The Rhine bank is today largely given over to tourist facilities; the curious old crane, the **Rheinkran**, which is now converted into a pricey restaurant, is the only thing to catch the eye. Only a few monuments of medieval Koblenz's centre, which bordered on the Mosel, remain; they're rather over-restored in the romantic image of old Germany, with the exterior walls painted in bright colours, but are undeniably picturesque. You come first of all to the **Deutscher Kaiser**, a sixteenth-century tower-house which also is now a restaurant. Further on is the Florinsmarkt, with the Romanesque-Gothic **St Florin**, now a Protestant parish church, the **Schöffenhaus**, a pretty little orange building with corner turrets, and the **Altes Kaufhaus**. This last building now houses the **Mittelrhein-Museum** (Tues–Sat 10.30am–5pm, Sun 11am–6pm; DM5/€2.50), a fairly miscellaneous collection of paintings, sculptures and antiquities. The ground floor has a few German Primitives, including an *Adoration of the Magi* by the Augsburg painter **Jörg Breu** which unashamedly plagiarizes a portrait by his fellow citizen, Holbein the Elder, for the figure of one of the kings. Upstairs are many works by one of Germany's most accomplished Rococo painters, **Januarius Zick**, who eventually settled in Koblenz.

Further along the Mosel bank is the **Alte Burg**, altered to a Renaissance palace and now housing the municipal library, but originally constructed to defend the fourteenth-century **Balduinbrücke**. Turning away from the river, you come to **Münzplatz**, which still preserves the mint master's house. Also in the square is the mansion birthplace of the wily Habsburg statesman **Clemens von Metternich**, high priest of the theory (which was to dominate nineteenth-century politics) that the key to a peaceful Europe lay in maintaining a balance of power among the main states. His peak of influence came during his dominant hosting role at the Congress of Vienna in 1815, which laid down the structure of post-Napoleonic Europe; ironically, his native town was given to Prussia – arch-rival of his adopted Austria – as a result.

Down the pedestrian precinct at the intersection of Löhrstrasse and Markstrasse there's a fine grouping of four houses, each with ornamental oriel windows. Left from here is another large square, Plan, behind which are the exotic Baroque onion-shaped spires of the **Liebfrauenkirche**, a handsome if diffuse church with a galleried Romanesque nave and a Gothic chancel. Just beyond stands the **Rathaus**, incongruously housed in a cavernous former Jesuit college.

In the late eighteenth century, Koblenz was expanded to the south in the form of a planned Neoclassical town. The Archbishop-Electors of Trier moved their court here, centred on the huge **Schloss**; three years after its completion, the Elector fled in the wake of Napoleon's advance, never to return. The buildings were gutted during the last war and now serve as offices. A more lasting memento of the period is the stately **Theater** fronted by an obelisk on Deinhardplatz.

The outskirts

Across the Rhine lies **EHRENBREITSTEIN**, with the original **Residenz** of the Electors, designed by Balthasar Neumann. Looming high above is the vast **Festung** – one of the largest fortresses in the world – with an impressive set of defences which the Prussians painstakingly and quite needlessly rebuilt over a ten-year period after Koblenz passed into their hands. Commanding memorable panoramic views of the city and its two great rivers, the Festung is now home to the youth hostel and the **Landesmuseum Koblenz** (mid-March to Nov daily 9am–12.30pm & 1–5pm; DM6/€3). The latter contains displays on the local wine trade and other industries, but the star exhibit is the punningly named *Vogel Greif* (bird of prey), a **cannon** made for a sixteenth-century Archbishop-Elector of Trier, Richard von Greiffenklau. In season, there's an expensive **chairlift** (DM7/€3.50 single, DM10/€5 return) to the Festung; otherwise, follow the main road along the shore of the Rhine until you come to a path which snakes upwards.

At Koblenz's southernmost extremity, reachable by any bus travelling down the left bank of the Rhine, is **Schloss Stolzenfels** (April–Sept Tues–Sun 9am–5pm; Oct, Nov & Jan–March Tues–Sun 10am–noon & 2–4pm; DM5/€2.50), a Romantic-era fantasy designed by Karl Friedrich Schinkel to replace a thirteenth-century Burg which had gone up in smoke in 1688. The great Prussian architect let his imagination run riot, drawing inspiration not only from the old fortresses of the Rhineland – as evidenced by the main **Rittersaal** with its suits of armour and medieval weaponry – but from a variety of other historical sources, notably the Moorish palaces of Andalucia.

Eating and drinking

If not one of the Rhineland's more renowned gastronomic centres, Koblenz still has a decent choice of places to eat and drink.

Historischer Weinkeller, Mehlgasse 16. Cosy wine bar-restaurant in a vaulted medieval cellar. Closed Mon.

Irish Pub, Burgstr. 7. Has all the main Irish beers on tap, and features live music on Mon and Wed evenings.

Königsbacher, An der Königsbach 8. Capacious restaurant in the premises of the eponymous brewery, located in the south of town on the road to Schloss Stolzenfels. It makes an excellent bitter-tasting *Pils*, and also has a very fruity *Kölsch* named *Richmodis*, which is made by its subsidiary in Cologne.

Loup de Meer, Neustadt 12. Small speciality fish restaurant, located just to the west of the Schloss. May–Sept evenings only, closed Sun, Oct–April closed Sat & Sun.

Ratskeller, Am Plan 11. Typically reliable choice for *gutbürgerliche Küche*.

Salatgarten, Gymnasialstr. 14. Self-service vegetarian and wholefood restaurant. Closed Sun.

Stresemann, Rheinzollstr. 8. The bistro-style cooking here is among the most imaginative in town. Closed Tues (also Mon in winter).

Weindorf, Julius-Wegeler-Str. 2. A complex of four wine taverns, grouped together in the form of a village square. Although very tourist-oriented, it's a good place to sample the local *Riesling* and *Müller-Thurgau* vintages, and to eat typically Rhenish dishes. Closed all Nov.

Entertainment

The principal **cultural** venue is the abovementioned Theater der Stadt Koblenz on Deinhardplatz (☎02 61/1 29 28 40), whose programme of plays, opera and other events puts those of many larger cities to shame. Koblenz also boasts one of Germany's rare specialist **comedy** venues in Blaue Biwel, Entenpful 9 (☎02 61/3 55 77), where English-language acts are featured occasionally. The two main **festivals** are Carnival and *Der Rhein in Flammen*; the latter takes place on the second Saturday in August, and features fireworks and bonfires.

The Rhine from Andernach to Remagen

Soon after leaving Koblenz, the Rhine gorge opens out, cutting between the ranges of the Eifel and Westerwald. If this stretch doesn't quite match the grandeur of the preceding section, it's impressive nonetheless and well worth following by either boat or train. With exceptions, it also has the benefit of being less touristy.

Andernach

ANDERNACH, which lies 16km down the Rhine from Koblenz, can trace its history back further than almost any other German town. It celebrated its 2000th anniversary in 1988, commemorating the foundation of a Roman base for the campaigns against the tribes on the eastern side of the Rhine. Subsequently Andernach became a Franconian royal seat, before passing to the control of the Archbishop-Electors of Cologne, serving as the southern border of their territory until the Napoleonic invasion. Nowadays, it's an odd hybrid, having a fair amount of industry, yet taking advantage of its situation and monuments to double as a holiday resort.

If you're travelling along the Rhine by boat, it's definitely worth breaking your journey for a couple of hours in order to walk round the thirteenth-century **Stadtmauer**, which was laid out on the Roman foundations. The walls survive largely intact, making a solid back for many later buildings, including a well-concealed row of houses. Extra defence on the southern stretch was provided by the **Burg**, the most important town castle in the Rhineland. Blown up by French troops in 1688, a fair amount has nevertheless survived, notably the later embellishments such as the **Pulverturm** and residential palace wing.

Round to the north, overlooking the river, is the **Rheintor**, whose inner gate has weather-worn statues illustrating the best-known local legend, that of the Andernacher Bäckerjungen (baker boys of Andernach), who saved the town from occupation by letting loose their bees on the invading army. The most picturesque feature of Andernach's fortifications, however, is the fifteenth-century **Runder Turm** (key available from the tourist office) overlooking the Rhine on the northern side of town, whose octagonal upper storeys give it an exotic, oddly Moorish air. Thankfully, the French siege guns failed to penetrate its thick walls, but the enormous dent they made can still be seen clearly. Continuing down the river bank, there's the remarkable sixteenth-century **Alter Kran**, a crane whose original wooden mechanism remained in service into the twentieth century and is still in full working order.

Just to the west of the Runder Turm, the tall twin facade towers of the **Pfarrkirche Maria Himmelfahrt** rise majestically above the rest of the skyline. For the most part, it's an archetypal late Romanesque basilica with a pronounced Rhenish accent, though the northeastern belfry is in fact a survivor of the previous church on the site.

Andernach's main axis, Hochstrasse, runs from here to the Burg; about halfway down is the **Altes Rathaus**, occupying the site of the former ghetto. A **Mikwe** (Jewish ritual bath) was recently discovered underneath the session room; to see it, ask for the key at the tourist office (see p.498). On the adjacent Läufstrasse is the Gothic **Christuskirche**, a former Minorite friary church with a curiously lopsided interior. A little further down the street is the **Haus von der Leyen**, a Renaissance patrician mansion that now houses the **Stadtmuseum** (Tues–Fri 10am–noon & 2–5pm, Sat & Sun 2–4pm; DM2/€1). Lack of space means that only a small collection of antiquities is permanently on display, but the changing exhibitions (prominently featured on posters outside) are often surprisingly good.

Practicalities

Andernach's **Bahnhof** is on Kurfürstendamm; to reach the centre, walk straight ahead, then turn right under the rail bridge. **Buses** operate from Am Stadtgraben, the western range of the Stadtmauer. The **tourist office** is at Am Markt. 18 (Mon–Fri 8am–12.30pm & 1.30–5pm, Sat 9am–noon; ☎0 26 32/94 93 99, fax 94 93 96, *www .andernach.de*). In summer, the town is a popular overnight stop with tour coach operators; hence there are plenty of **hotels**, but many of these are often fully booked and anyway charge independent travellers inflated prices. Nonetheless, there are plenty of places worth trying, including *Andernacher Hof*, Breite Str. 83 (☎0 26 32/4 31 75; ③), *Villa am Rhein*, Konrad-Adenauer-Allee 3 (☎0 26 32/9 27 40; ⑤), *Alte Kanzlei*, Steinweg 30 (☎0 26 32/9 66 60; ⑥), and *Fischer*, Am Helmwartsturm 4–6 (☎0 26 32/49 20 47; ⑦). The last three places mentioned are also among the best places to **eat** and **drink**; *Alte Kanzlei* offers a particularly attractive ambience in its vaulted cellar and garden courtyard. Andernach hosts a number of **festivals**, including a medieval fair in the Burg (mid-July), *Die Tausenden Lichten* (The Thousand Lights), featuring fireworks and illuminations (first weekend in September), and, of course, Carnival.

Beyond Andernach

Immediately beyond Brohl, the train's second stop after Andernach, stands **Burg Rheineck**. This fortress, which was rebuilt in the nineteenth century, is no longer open to the public, but if you follow the path to the right, there's a belvedere commanding an impressive panorama. A further 3km on is **BAD BREISIG**, a popular spa and holiday resort, which makes a good base for exploring the area, thanks to a huge choice of **accommodation** in all categories, ranging from campsites via private guesthouses and riverside inns to luxury hotels.

From Bad Breisig, the rail line leaves the banks of the river for a spell, continuing to **SINZIG**, 6km away, which lies near the end of the valley of the Ahr. There's just one monument of note: the church of **St Peter**, one of the smallest but most original of the Romanesque basilicas of the Rhineland. Even more than usual, the impression is of a dream-like fantasy, an effect accentuated by the white and yellow paint covering the exterior walls. On the south side of the chancel is a chapel adorned with noble though fragmentary frescoes which are contemporary with the building, while the high altar has a brightly coloured late fifteenth-century *Passion* retable from Cologne.

Remagen

Back on the Rhine, 4km north of Sinzig, is **REMAGEN**, a town famous for a **bridge** which – apart from its support towers – no longer exists. The towers on the Remagen side have been converted into the **Friedensmuseum** (March–Oct daily 10am–5pm; DM3/€1.50), which chronicles the story of the bridge (see box opposite) by means of old photographs.

In the centre of town, the dominant building is the curious church of **St Peter und Paul**. At the turn of the century, it was decided that the original Romanesque-Gothic church was no longer sufficiently big for the town's expanding population; accordingly, a new church, imitating the style of the old but on a much larger scale, was tacked on to it at right angles. More directly appealing is the enigmatic **Pfarrhoftor**, a double

THE BRIDGE AT REMAGEN

Remagen's bridge was built during World War I to aid the movement of troops and supplies to the Western Front. On March 7, 1945, an advance regiment of the US Armoured Division reached this point, to find that the bridge – unlike all the others along the Rhine, Germany's most crucial natural defensive barrier – was still intact. The token Nazi force which had been left to guard it was quickly routed, enabling the Americans to establish a base on the opposite bank. Eisenhower declared the bridge to be "worth its weight in gold", while Hitler ordered the execution of four officers for their carelessness in failing to blow the bridge up. In retrospect, the importance of the Remagen episode seems exaggerated, as crossings were made by the Allies further up the Rhine the following week. Moreover, the bridge itself collapsed ten days later due to overloading, killing 28 American soldiers. However, it was symbolically a telling blow and has remained a popular subject for books, the best of which is Ken Hechler's *The Bridge at Remagen*.

gateway forming the entrance to the parish close. It's covered with carvings made by a Romanesque sculptor of limited technique but fertile imagination.

High above Remagen stands the mid-nineteenth-century **Apollinariskirche**, goal of a popular ten-day pilgrimage at the end of July. The church was built in tandem with the completion of the Dom in Cologne, and is a miniature version of it. Inside, the walls are covered with frescoes of the lives of Christ, the Virgin and St Apollinaris.

With its central location, Remagen is undoubtedly the best base for this part of the Rhine, and there's a **campsite**, *Goldene Meile* (☎0 26 42/2 22 22), right beside the river. The hotels beside the Bahnhof are geared to coach parties and are anyway best avoided, as thundering goods trains pass through all night. Far better to go for a room in a **private house** (②–③). For a full list, contact the **tourist office**, Kirchstr. 6 (Mon–Thurs 8.30am–noon & 2–4pm, Fri 8.30am–noon; ☎0 26 42/2 01 87, fax 2 01 27, *www.remagen.de*).

Rolandseck

ROLANDSECK, a further 6km north of central Remagen, has now been absorbed by Remagen. The train station building is now designated the **Künstlerbahnhof** (Tues–Sun 10am–5pm; DM5/€2.50), housing a notable collection of works by Hans Arp, along with changing exhibitions of contemporary art. More sculptures by Arp and by Henry Moore can be seen for free on the lawn outside.

One of the most famous Rhine legends is closely associated with the vicinity of Rolandseck. In the middle of the Rhine, just beyond the village, is the island of **Nonnenwerth**, occupied by a former convent. On hearing news of the death of Roland (Charlemagne's nephew) in an ambush in northern Spain, his betrothed is alleged to have come here, taking her final vows the moment before the hero, miraculously recovered from his wounds, arrived to claim her. Stricken by grief, he built the **Rolandsbogen** fortress on the hill above in order to catch occasional glimpses of her. Whatever the veracity of the story, it's well worth climbing up to the ruin, which commands one of the most extensive views of this part of the Rhine, with Bonn and the Siebengebirge (see pp.525 & p.532) immediately to the north.

THE EIFEL

Strictly speaking the mountains of the **Eifel** range – which are divided between the Rhineland-Palatinate and North Rhine-Westphalia – are little more than big hills. On the whole, they aren't desperately exciting, which probably accounts for the lack of mass tourism. However, in the part of the Eifel which lies in the Rhineland-Palatinate you'll find a gentle landscape of wooded hills and bare heathland, dotted with volcanic lakes and intersected by quiet, unspoiled valleys. The area is used to visitors, but most of them are Germans who spend their summer vacations abroad and come here for a second break in late spring or early autumn. This means that it's a good place to escape the crowds, particularly if you're otherwise concentrating on a nearby tourist area, such as the Rhine or Mosel. The only part of the region which has completely succumbed to tourism is the **Ahr valley** in the northeast where truly spectacular scenery brings hundreds of thousands of visitors during a season that lasts from May until late October. Otherwise much of the Eifel has a slightly sleepy air, its life revolving round the seasonal influxes of visitors and people coming to the various spa towns or *Luftkurorte*.

The Ahr valley

The valley of the **River Ahr** rates as one of the most scenic corners of western Germany. The landscape and most of the towns in this valley, which cuts through from the High Eifel to join the Rhine just outside Remagen, form a real Brothers Grimm landscape of ruined castles, forests and vineyards. Most unusually for Germany, the vineyards are known primarily for their red wines and, because of the relatively low yield, these are not easily obtainable outside the region. No effort has been spared when it comes to providing for mass tourism, and this is where the problems start. From May through to October all those idyllic little towns and villages are filled to overflowing with day-tripping German families, hikers, wine fans and British coach parties, and the only people who really benefit are the owners of tacky souvenir shops and the hotel-keepers who rack up their prices.

The best thing to do is to visit the area out of season when you can absorb the atmosphere of the place without the crowds. There really is a lot to take in: the countryside is magnificent once you hit the upper reaches of the valley (particularly around Altenahr), and many of the towns and villages look like they've hardly changed in centuries. The area is best explored by taking the branch railway, the Ahrtalbahn, from Remagen; at first the valley seems flat and nondescript but gradually vineyards start to crowd up to the rail line and the sides of the valley become steeper.

Bad Neuenahr-Ahrweiler

First stop is **BAD NEUENAHR-AHRWEILER**, which threads its way along the Ahr for a few kilometres just before the valley becomes narrower and the spectacular stuff begins. It's really two towns which have grown into each other: Bad Neuenahr is fairly modern and commercially oriented while Ahrweiler is so impossibly old-fashioned that it looks like a film set.

Bad Neuenahr

Though less attractive than its sister town, **BAD NEUENAHR** has a couple of things worth seeing: the **Williborduskirche** on Schweizerstrasse, with its Romanesque west tower and the usual melange of architectural details, and the **Beethovenhaus** on Beethovenstrasse, a Baroque town-house where the composer used to spend his holidays, probably to benefit from the town's thermal springs. Bad Neuenahr is still a well-known *Kurort*: the riverside **Kurgarten** (daily 7am–9.30pm; DM2.50/€1.25) and the classically elegant **Thermal Badehaus** are survivors from an era when wealthy families from all over Europe came here to enjoy the waters and hothouse social life. Another big attraction is the **Spielbank** in Casinostrasse, the largest casino in Germany. The roulette wheels start rolling daily at 2pm (DM5/€2.50 admission).

You'll find the **tourist office** at Hauptstr. 60 (late March to mid-Nov Mon–Fri 9am–6pm, Sat 10am–1pm, Sun 10.30am–4.30pm; rest of year Mon–Fri 8am–5pm, Sat 10am–1pm; ☎0 26 41/97 73 53, fax 2 97 58, *www.bad-neuenahr-ahrweiler.de*), next door to the **Bahnhof**. Among the huge range of **hotels** on offer, try *Zum Ahrtal*, Sebastianstr. 68 (☎0 26 41/2 69 69; ③), *Arabella*, Hauptstr. 45 (☎0 26 41/7 50 30; ⑤), or *Griffels Goldener Anker*, Mittelstr. 14 (☎0 26 41/80 40; ⑦–⑨).

Ahrweiler

The kernel of **AHRWEILER** dates back to the Middle Ages and seems wildly archaic with its narrow streets and half-timbered buildings. It's ringed by the **Stadtmauer**, built between the thirteenth and fifteenth centuries and still more or less intact despite numerous attempts to breach it during the Thirty Years War. Four gateways survive, including the **Niedertor**, which leads into Niederhutstrasse, the town centre's main commercial street, which has plenty of tacky souvenir shops, along with delicatessens and wine merchants.

Niederhutstrasse runs into the broad Marktplatz, on the north side of which is the thirteenth-century **Pfarrkirche St Laurentius**. Inside are fourteenth- and fifteenth-century frescoes and modern stained-glass windows, some of which have an almost Expressionist feel to them. At Altenbaustr. 3, just off the western end of Marktplatz, in a three-storey tower-house which was originally built in the thirteenth century but partially remodelled in Baroque style, is the **Museum der Stadt** (March–Dec Tues–Sun 10am–5pm; DM3/€1.50). It contains objects relating to the town and the Ahr valley area, including some fine medieval sculptures and a section on local wine-production methods through the centuries.

At the southern end of the centre the largest of the town gates, the **Ahrtor**, overlooks the River Ahr. From here you get a good view across to the **Ursulinenkloster Kalvarienberg**, which sits on the edge of town surrounded by vineyards. This imposing building, resembling a French chateau, houses a convent and girls' school.

Ahrweiler's **Bahnhof** is conveniently located just a few minutes' walk from the centre of town. The **tourist office** is at Marktplatz 21 (late March to mid-Nov Mon–Fri 9am–6pm, Sat 10am–3pm, Sun 10.30am–4.30pm; rest of year Mon–Fri 8am–5pm, Sat 10am–1pm; ☎0 26 41/97 73 62, fax 3 52 00, *www.bad-neuenahr-ahrweiler.de*). There's a fair provision of **private rooms** (①–③) and also many small **pensions**, including *Zur Erholung*, Schützenstr. 74 (☎0 26 41/3 49 36; ②), *Ippendorf*, Wolfgasse 7 (☎0 26 41/3 49 41; ②), and *Kronen*, Alveradisstr. 17 (☎0 26 41/3 42 02; ③). *Hohenzollern*, Silbergstr. 50 (☎0 26 41/97 30; ⑥), on the west side of town, is the best **hotel**. It also has a first-rate **restaurant**, though there are similarly good and much less expensive possibilities in the town centre, notably *Altes Zunfthaus*, Oberhutstr. 34, and *Eifelstube*, Ahrhutstr. 26. The **youth hostel** is at St-Pius-Str. 7 (☎0 26 41/3 49 24, fax 3 15 74, *djh-bad-neuenahr-ahrweiler@djh-info.de*; DM29.€14.50 or DM39/€19.50), about twenty minutes' walk from the Bahnhof along a well-signposted route. Ahrweiler's **campsite** is at Kalvarienbergstr. 1 (☎0 26 41/3 56 84), on the way out to the Ursulinenkloster.

Altenahr

The next stop after Ahrweiler is **ALTENAHR**, a town which can only be described as picturesque and whose population seems to increase tenfold in the summer. It's horrendously clogged up then, but if you go off-season you could easily spend a few days here using the town as a base to explore the surrounding area. The landscape is magnificent – the valley is so narrow at this point it almost becomes a gorge and the town is situated on a tortuous bend in the river. If you follow the river eastwards out of town precipitous rockfaces soar from the northern bank, and on the southern side steep forested slopes lead up to the craggy peaks of the **Voreifel**. By night, the whole place has an unearthly atmosphere.

In town there are plenty of suspiciously pristine half-timbered facades – and also plenty of souvenir shops and hotels. The best way to appreciate Altenahr's undeniable charms is to trek up to **Burg Are**, from whose ruined heights you get a tremendous view of the surrounding area. Burg Are itself was built around 1100 and the ruins have a romantic feel to them. Like most castles in this part of Germany it was destroyed by the French in 1690 after a nine-month siege. The whole town was once fortified but only a few remnants of the former wall and towers remain. There's also a Romanesque **Pfarrkirche** which, despite a few Gothic additions, retains very clear and simple lines.

Altenahr is a terminus of the Rotweinwanderweg, a 35km hiking trail waymarked with bunches of red grapes; additionally, there are fifteen signposted local **walking routes**. A number of paths lead up from the Bahnhof into the hills and to the nearby village of Altenburg. Look out for the **Teufelsloch**, a famous local landmark and view-point, where the elements have eroded a giant hole into the rock. From up here you gain a good view of the **Langfigtal Naturpark** and of the **Breite Ley**, a sheer volcanic rock formation which rises from the Ahr valley just outside town. There's also a chair-lift which runs from the bottom of Seilbahnstrasse to the 330-metre-high **Ditschardhöhe**, with a café and good views.

Altenahr's **tourist office** is housed in the Bahnhof building (Mon–Fri 10am–noon & 3–5pm, Sat 10am–noon; ☎0 26 43/88 48, fax 35 16). There are plenty of **private rooms** and small **pensions** (②), while a wide selection of **hotels** includes *Bahnhotel Hübel*, Altenburger Str. 3 (☎0 26 43/15 43; ③), *Gasthof Weiss*, Bahnhofstr. 36 (☎0 26 43/84 03; ③), and *Zur Post*, Brückenstr. 2 (☎0 26 43/93 10; ⑤). The local **youth hostel** (☎0 26 43/18 80, fax 81 36, *jh-altenahr@djh-info.de*; DM22/€11) is about thirty minutes' walk south of town down the unlit Langfigtal. **Camping** facilities are available just outside town near Altenburg (☎0 26 43/85 03). The leading **wine restaurant** is *Schäferkarre*, Brückenstr. 29.

The High Eifel

The **High Eifel** (Hohe Eifel), the central part of the range, is volcanic in origin, and still preserves many reminders of this in the form of basalt and tufa rocks, hot springs and crater lakes. There is only one railway – the branch line from Andernach to Mayen – but bus services are good in the main tourist areas.

Adenau

There are regular buses (approximately one an hour) from Altenahr to **ADENAU**, and the thirty-minute journey takes you through the upper reaches of the Ahr valley, via a succession of tiny villages, deep into the High Eifel. Adenau is a pretty little tourist town straggling along the river valley, notable mainly for the fifteenth- and sixteenth-century half-timbered houses which surround its **Markt**. These are actually the genuine article, as the occasional sagging roof or slightly buckled facade shows, but they have been prettified for the tourists and now house the usual range of cafés, bars and shops. There's also a venerable **Pfarrkirche** here that dates from the eleventh century, but which was altered in the thirteenth century.

The **tourist office** is at Kirchstr. 15 (☎0 26 91/3 05 16, fax 3 05 18, *www.adenau.de*). **Hotels** include *Poststübchen*, Hauptstr. 22 (☎0 26 91/25 89; ③), *Zum Wilden Schwein*, Hauptstr. 117 (☎0 26 91/91 09 20; ⑥), *Blaue Ecke*, in a sixteenth-century half-timbered house at Markt 4 (☎0 26 91/20 05; ⑥), and *Landhaus Sonnenhof*, Auf dem Hirzenstein

1 (☎0 26 91/70 34; ⑥–⑨). All of these have **restaurants**, with that in *Blaue Ecke* being outstanding.

Nürburg and the Nürburgring

From Adenau, regular buses run to the tiny health resort of **NÜRBURG**. This takes it name from the **Nürburg** (Tues–Sun 9am–1pm & 2–5/6pm; closed Dec; DM3/€1.50), which stands on one of the highest peaks in the Eifel range (678m). It was originally the site of a Roman fort, but the ruins you see today are of a twelfth-century castle destroyed by French soldiers after a long siege in 1690. There are a few **pensions** and **hotels**, including *Am Tiergarten*, Kirchweg 4 (☎0 26 91/9 22 00; ④–⑥), and *Zur Burg*, Burgstr. 4 (☎0 26 91/75 75; ⑤).

Easily reached from the village is the famous **Nürburgring** race track. This is in two parts, much the larger being the northern loop, which was laid out between 1925 and 1927. This was long regarded as the ultimate test in Grand Prix motor racing; not only is it an exceptionally long circuit, travelling some 23km through the forested High Eifel, it incorporates a fearsomely fast two-kilometre-long straight as well as numerous hills and bends. Jackie Stewart dubbed it "the green hell" and, following Niki Lauda's near-fatal crash in 1976, it was decided that it was too dangerous for Formula 1 races. Ever since, the German Grand Prix has been held at Hockenheim near Heidelberg. However, a new five-kilometre-long southern loop was opened in 1984, and this has since been used for both the Luxembourg and European Grand Prixs (the Nürburgring's next Formula 1 race will be the latter, on June 24, 2001). If you're travelling by car or motorbike you can take a spin round the northern loop yourself, at whatever speed you like and with no formalities other than paying the fee of DM20/€10 per lap; to check the opening times, which are subject to wide variation, phone ahead (☎0 26 91/30 26 00) or consult the Web site (*www.nuerburgring.de*). Alternatively, for DM150/€75 a professional racing driver will chauffeur a maximum of three passengers round this circuit in the so-called Renntaxi. It's advisable to book this in advance (☎0 26 91/30 21 78), as the number of trips per day is strictly limited.

Alongside the track is the brand-new **Erlebniswelt** (daily 10am–6pm; DM22.50/€11.25). The first of the four halls features both historic and present-day racing vehicles, the others a variety of motoring-related entertainments including simulators which enable you to take part in a Grand Prix race and test your reactions to a crash. There's also a luxury **hotel** with restaurant run by Dorint (☎0 26 91/30 90; ⑦–⑨).

Mayen

MAYEN, some 30km from Andernach at the end of the Eifel rail line, was almost completely flattened by the RAF on January 2, 1945 to prevent the Germans from using it as a staging post for troops during the Ardennes offensive. However, the rebuilding programme was carried out with a great deal of sensitivity and, apart from an ugly department store on the Marktplatz, no great architectural errors seem to have been made.

All that remains of the once 1600-metre-long Stadtmauer are the gateways at either end: **Brückentor** and the **Obertor**. From the former, Martkstrasse leads to the **Pfarrkirche St Clemens**, whose distinctive twisted steeple was caused by poor construction techniques and the influence of the weather. On Marktplatz itself is the Baroque **Altes Rathaus**, the only town-centre building to survive the war just about intact.

From the other end of the square the thirteenth-century **Genovevaburg** glowers over the town. Nowadays it houses the **Eifeler Landschaftsmuseum** (Tues–Fri 10am–12.30pm & 2–5pm, Sat & Sun 11am–5pm; DM6/€3), where a range of Eifel-related exhibits takes you from the Stone Age to modern times. Look out for the before-and-after pictures showing the war damage inflicted on the town.

Rising out of the wooded valley of the River Nette some 5km northwest of the town centre (buses depart from the stop between Im Möhren and Wittbende on the Habsburgring) is **Schloss Bürresheim** (April–Sept Tues–Sun 9am–6pm; Oct, Nov & Jan–March Tues–Sun 9am–5pm; DM5/€2.50), which is the epitome of the German fairy-tale castle. Begun as a fortress in 1220, it was turned into a residential palace during the sixteenth century, a change clearly reflected in its appearance, the grim stone walls of the original castle being topped by more fanciful Renaissance turrets.

From the **Westbahnhof**, the terminus of the rail line from Andernach, buses run to the Brückentor. Mayen's **tourist office** (Mon–Fri 9am–12.30pm & 1.30–5pm, Sat 9.30am–12.30pm; ☎0 26 51/90 30 04, fax 90 30 09, *www.mayen.de*) is in the Altes Rathaus, Am Markt. *Zum Alten Fritz*, Koblenzer Str. 56 (☎0 26 51/4 32 72; ②), is a good budget **hotel**, while the most expensive place to stay is *Maifelder Hof*, Polcher Str. 74 (☎0 26 51/9 60 40; ⑥); both have excellent restaurants. The **youth hostel** is some way out of the town centre at Am Knüppchen 5 (☎0 26 51/23 55, fax 7 83 78, *dj-mayen@djh-info.de*; DM23/€11.50); to get there walk down Göbelstrasse from Marktplatz, turn left onto Stehbachstrasse and then make an immediate right into Im Möhren and follow the road right up the steep hill.

Maria Laach

By far the most outstanding historical monument in the Eifel is the Benedictine **Abtei Maria Laach**, which lies in an isolated setting of forests, meadows and fields roughly 15km north of Mayen. Its name is derived from the adjacent **Laacher See**, which was formed by a volcanic cave-in, and which still has a raw primeval feel to it. Bus #6032 links Maria Laach with the nearest train station at Niedermendig and with Mayen, while bus #6031 runs there from Andernach.

The **Abteikirche** ranks as the most beautiful of all the great Romanesque churches of the Rhineland. Its sense of unity is all the more remarkable in that, although begun at the end of the eleventh century, it was not finished until well into the thirteenth century. One of its most distinctive features is its stonework – for the most part it's constructed from the local yellow-brown tufa, but dark basalt was used for architectural highlighting. Each end of the church is girded with an arrangement of three towers, presenting as varied and striking a silhouette as the Middle Ages ever produced.

Even more remarkable is the last part to be built, the **Paradise**, a courtyard placed in front of the building, enclosing the western choir. Apparently intended as a symbol of the innocence of the Garden of Eden, it's unique in Christian architecture, being suggestive of Islamic places of worship, an impression strengthened by the addition of the burbling Lions' Fountain in the middle. The capitals, showing a fabulous bestiary, were carved with a gossamer delicacy by a mason dubbed the Samson Master, who is also known to have worked at Andernach and Bonn.

After all this, the pure Romanesque sobriety of the interior comes as a surprise. However, the early Gothic **baldachin** at the high altar is again reminiscent of the art of Islam and is quite unlike any other such object in Europe. To see the **crypt**, the earliest part of the building, you have to join one of the regular guided tours (donation expected) conducted by the monks. It's worth catching one of the services to hear the Gregorian chant. Vespers are at 5.30pm, and finish in good time to catch the last bus.

The monastery has its own **hotel**, the *Seehotel Maria Laach* (☎0 26 52/58 40, *www.maria-laach.de/seehotel*; ⑦–⑨), which has an excellent restaurant, and there's a simple cafeteria alongside. You can also **camp** (☎0 26 36/24 85) on the shore of the Laacher See.

THE SAARLAND

The **Saarland**, taking its name from the River Saar which cuts through its length, is the poorest of the western German Länder, traditionally a big coalmining area which is now suffering from a bad case of post-industrial malaise. It's always been a political football; much of it belonged to France up until 1815, and wrangles continued into last century. After World War I the Saarland passed into League of Nations control, which effectively meant that the French took over, with the right to exploit local mines in compensation for damage done to their own mining industry during the war. In the January 1935 plebiscite 90 percent of Saarlanders voted for union with Nazi Germany. After World War II the Saar once again found itself in limbo, nominally autonomous but with the French government pushing for economic union. In November 1952 the population voted against reunion with Germany, but by January 1957 the increasing prosperity of the Federal Republic had convinced the Saarlanders that their future lay there, and they thus rejoined the fold – much to the chagrin of the French government.

The Land is modestly endowed in terms of tourist attractions, though it does have a surprising amount of pleasant, gently rolling wooded countryside. Moreover, the satanic mills of the industrial era which dominate many of the townscapes are now regarded as valuable parts of the heritage, particularly as this is one of the few parts of Western Europe where they have not already been demolished en masse. The French have left a small linguistic legacy in the shape of the greeting *Salü* which replaces the normal *Guten Tag* here. There's also been a marked French influence on local **cuisine**, traditionally a poor-man's fare based on innumerable potato variations, such as *Hooriche* (rissoles).

Saarbrücken

The Land capital **SAARBRÜCKEN** is a sizeable and predominantly modern industrial city which has generally been given a bad press. However, it is very much on the ascendant at the moment, its historical role as a melting-pot of German and French culture making it ideally placed to profit from the European Union's moves towards ever closer integration. It also has its fair share of visitor attractions, including a fine setting on a broad bend of the River Saar, a large array of handsome Baroque public buildings from its eighteenth-century heyday as a Residenzstadt, some good museums, a lively nightlife and – thanks in no small measure to the French connection – a distinguished culinary tradition.

Arrival, information and accommodation

Saarbrücken's **Hauptbahnhof** is at the northern end of the city centre. The **tourist office** (Mon–Fri 9am–8pm, Sat 10am–12.30pm; ☎06 81/93 80 90, fax 9 38 09 38, *www.kontour.de*) is directly opposite, in the front part of the SaarGalerie shopping centre, Reichsstr. 1. Here you can buy the **Saarbrücken Card**, which costs DM13/€6.50 for two days and covers travel on the local buses and entry to the museums and other attractions, as well as a wide range of discounts. For non-EU citizens, who may require visas to visit France, the **French consulate** is at Johannisstr. 2 (☎06 81/93 67 50). Saar **cruises** (DM12/€6 for a two-hour trip) are run from the landing stage on Berliner Promenade by Saarbrücker Personenschiffahrt Cornelius Hauck (☎06 81/3 40 84).

Hotels are mainly geared to business visitors, and correspondingly expensive, though there are some reasonably priced options. The **youth hostel** is at Meerwiesertalweg 31 (☎06 81/3 30 40, fax 58 00 03 03, *jh-saarbruecken@djh-info.de*), on the northeastern edge of town; take bus #49 or #69 (note that these do not run at weekends) to the Prinzenweiher stop. There are two **campsites**: *Saarbrücken* is at Am Spicherer Berg (☎06 81/5 17 80; closed Nov–Feb), near the Deutsch-Französischer Garten on the Franco-German border and reached by bus #42; *Burbach* is by the Saar on Mettlacher Strasse in the eponymous western suburb, served by buses #10, #17, #38 and #39.

Hotels

Am Triller, Trillerweg 57 (☎06 81/58 00 00, fax 58 00 03 03, *www.hotel-am-triller.de*). Upmarket hotel in the historic part of town; the facilities include a swimming pool, sauna, solarium, fitness room and garden. There's also a restaurant, *Galerie Marianne*, and a bistro-bar, *Palü*. ⑧.

Atlantic, Ursulinenstr. 59 (☎06 81/37 92 10, fax 37 45 03, *hotel-atlantic.de*). Good, moderately priced hotel, a short walk east of the Hauptbahnhof. ⑤.

Im Fuchs, Kappenstr. 12 (☎06 81/93 65 50, fax 9 36 55 36). This small hotel with restaurant is the only one actually located in the lively nightlife quarter of St Johann. ⑥.

La Résidence, Faktoreistr. 2 (☎06 81/3 88 20, fax 3 88 21 85, *www.la-residence.net*). High-class hotel, midway between the Hauptbahnhof and the River Saar. It also has a fine restaurant, *Casablanca* (closed Sat lunch & Sun). ⑦.

Madeleine, Cecilienstr. 5 (☎06 81/3 22 28, fax 37 47 04). Mid-range hotel located directly opposite the Rathaus. ⑤.

Schlosskrug, Schmollerstr. 14 (☎06 81/3 54 48, fax 37 50 22). Situated at the eastern edge of St Johann, this hotel with restaurant is the nearest Saarbrücken has to a budget option. ④.

Stadt Hamburg, Bahnhofstr. 71–73 (☎06 81/3 46 92, fax 3 7 43 30). Pleasant hotel on the upper floors of a building on the main pedestrianized shopping street, which means it's quiet at night. The room prices are very reasonable, including as they do a sizeable buffet breakfast. ⑤.

Victor's Residenz, Deutschmühlental (☎06 81/58 82 10, fax 58 82 11 99, *www.victors.de*). A French-style grand hotel alongside the Spielbank in the west of the city, not far from the border, and reached by bus #11. It offers a choice of individually decorated suites and has a fitness centre with sauna, solarium and massage. Local fare is served in the rustic *Victor's Stube*, Gallic cuisine in *Victor's Restaurant*, which is decked out in the style of a Paris brasserie. ⑧–⑨.

The City

The city is bisected by the Saar, with the original town, now known as **Alt-Saarbrücken**, on the left side of the bend in the river. Directly opposite is **St Johann**, a former fishing village which is now the main gastronomic and nightlife district. Immediately to its north, stretching towards the Hauptbahnhof, is the modern city centre, a largely pedestrianized area of shops and offices. Of the suburbs, the most notable from a historic point of view is the once separate town of **St Arnual** to the south.

Alt-Saarbrücken

The focal point of Alt-Saarbrücken is the sloping **Schlossplatz**, which was designed in a classically inspired Baroque idiom by **Friedrich Joachim Stengel**, the prolific court architect to the House of Nassau-Saarbrücken. Badly damaged in World War II, the **Schloss** at the top end of the square was remodelled in the early 1980s by Gottfried Böhm, who replaced the original central pavilion with an unashamedly avant-garde glass and steel structure which is guaranteed to startle the first-time viewer. The Schloss has long since lost all its historic interiors, but the basement, together with the modern annexe on the east side, contains the **Historisches Museum** (Tues–Sun 10am–6pm; DM5/€2.50), which has permanent exhibitions on Saarland under the Third Reich and in the uncertain times of the immediate postwar period, as well as temporary displays.

By far the most important of the three museums on the square is the **Museum für Vor- und Frühgeschichte** (Tues–Sat 9am–5pm, Sun 10am–6pm; free), which occupies the former parliament building on the east side. This contains a wide range of local archeological finds, the most notable being a major discovery of the Celtic period, the intact contents of a princess's grave from around 400 BC, which includes some beautiful jewellery and drinking vessels. On the north side of the square, the top floor of the **Altes Rathaus** houses the **Abenteuermuseum** (Tues & Wed 9am–1pm, Thurs & Fri 3–7pm, first Sat of month 10am–2pm; DM3/€1.50), which is devoted in roughly equal parts to the lives and cultures of "primitive" peoples and to the ego of its founder Heinz Rox-Schulz, who has spent most of his life travelling to far-flung corners of the world collecting and filming. Bizarre items from the collection include a 2000-year-old Peruvian mummy and some shrunken heads. Between Schlossplatz and the river is the fifteenth-century **Schlosskirche**, a Gothic church which is normally kept locked; it contains some tombs of the local counts.

From here head down Schlossstrasse and turn right into Eisenbahnstrasse. On the right is the plain white **Friedenskirche** (Peace Church) by Stengel, which is now used by Old Catholic and Russian Orthodox congregations. The former face eastwards to worship, and a single small crucifix is their altar's only adornment; the latter face west to their colourful iconostasis. Across the road is **Ludwigsplatz**, a masterly piece of late Baroque town planning, based on the French concept of a monumental *Place Royale*, which ranks as Stengel's greatest achievement. Its sides are lined with handsome urban palaces; that which closes it off to the west originally had the combined functions of poorhouse, orphanage, workhouse and prison. In the middle of the square stands the **Ludwigskirche** (Tues 3–5pm, Wed 10am–noon & 4–5.30pm, Sat 4–6pm, Sun 11am–noon; at other times only the vestibules are open), a highly original design with an unconventional tower placed over the opposite end of the building from the facade. The exterior, with its rich sculptural decoration, is unusually sumptuous for a Protestant church. In contrast, the gleaming white interior, whose four internal galleries have only recently been reinstated following war damage, is a classic example of Lutheran Baroque, not least in the tiered assemblage of altar table, pulpit and organ.

St Johann and the city centre

The pedestrianized **Alte Brücke**, which dates back to the sixteenth century but has been much altered since, crosses the Saar from the bank alongside the Schlosskirche. Just over the other side, the angular **Staatstheater**, a typical example of the kind of architectural thinking that went on in the Third Reich, can be seen to the right. Saarstrasse leads east to **St Johanner Markt**, an elongated old-world square with some elegant eighteenth-century houses and a Baroque fountain, all designed by Stengel. A block further east is the **Basilika St Johann**, another fine church by Stengel, this time in full Catholic pomp, with elaborate confessionals, balconies and high altar.

The **Saarland Museum** (Tues & Thurs–Sun 10am–6pm, Wed 10am–10pm; *www.saarlandmuseum.de*; DM3/€1.50) occupies two buildings at the southern end of St Johann. A short distance beyond the Staatstheater, at Bismarckstr. 11–19, is the **Moderne Galerie**, which contains art from the late nineteenth century until the present day. In the first hall, an excellent representation of the three leading German Impressionists, **Liebermann**, **Corinth** and **Slevogt**, is juxtaposed with a smaller group of works by their French counterparts, including Monet, Renoir and Sisley. The gallery owns the most important collection of works by **Albert Weisgerber**, an Expressionist who was one of many artistic talents to perish on the battlefields of Flanders during World War I. Though relatively little known, the works here, notably *Absalom* and *David and Goliath*, which both manage to convey a vivid sense of movement, show him to have been a highly original spirit. Other Expressionist masterpieces on view include

Bathers in a Room by **Kirchner** and *The Blue Horse* by **Marc**. There are also important paintings by Nolde, Jawlensky, Ernst, Dix and Beckmann, and sculptures by Barlach and Lehmbruck. Opposite, at Karlstr. 1, is the **Alte Sammlung**, which covers fine and applied art of earlier periods. Its main strength is a collection of medieval sculpture from not only the Saarland, but neighbouring Luxembourg and Lorraine as well. Appropriately enough, the highlight of the small array of old master paintings is a *Classical Landscape* by **Claude Lorraine**.

At the northern end of St Johann is the massive Historicist **Rathaus**, built in the last years of the nineteenth century by Georg von Hauberisser, who is best known for designing its equally pretentious Munich counterpart. A more aesthetically pleasing architectural curiosity is the **Bergwerksdirektion** (Mining Administration Headquarters) at the corner of Bahnhofstrasse and Reichsstrasse near the northern end of the large pedestrian precinct which forms Saarbrücken's commercial heart. Built in 1880, it resembles Schinkel's buildings of half a century earlier, which makes it seem all the odder that it was co-designed by the young Walter Gropius, founder of the revolutionary Bauhaus movement.

St Arnual

St Arnual, which can be reached by buses #20, #26 and #36, still preserves a village-like atmosphere, and seems a world away from downtown Saarbrücken, though it is in fact just 3km distant. Just off its market square, St Arnualer Markt, stands the Gothic **Stiftskirche**, nowadays the Protestant parish church. It was the favoured burial place of the House of Nassau-Saarbrücken, and contains several dozen tombs of family members. The most imposing is that in the middle of the choir to Elisabeth of Lorraine. A pioneering translator of French novels into German, she is depicted in the widow's outfit she wore on assuming the role of regent following the death of her husband in 1429. Most of the later memorials are placed upright against the walls; many are executed in a somewhat folksy version of the Renaissance style and still preserve their bright polychromy.

Eating, drinking and entertainment

Saarbrücken is one of Germany's leading gourmet cities, with many highly cosmopolitan **restaurants**, and also has a vibrant nightlife scene, thanks in no small part to the presence of a sizeable student population. A concentration of recommendable establishments is clustered on and around St Johanner Markt, though others can be found all over town, with some of the best restaurants being in the hotels (see p.506).

The Staatstheater, Tbilisser Platz 1 (☎06 81/3 09 20) is the main **cultural** venue, presenting opera, operetta, dance, drama and concerts. One unusual event is the *Perspectives du Théâtre* **festival** of young French theatre, held every May, which usually throws up a few avant-garde offerings. There's also the *Max-Ophüls-Preis* film festival held every January.

Restaurants

Bitburger Residenz, Dudweilerstr. 56. Well-regarded restaurant named after the Bitburger brewery in the Eifel, whose beer is available on draught. Closed Sat lunchtime.

Fröschengasse, Fröschengasse 18. One of the places to see and be seen, this two-tier restaurant with roof terrace serves high-class French and international cuisine, and has a wide-ranging wine list.

Hashimoto, Cecilienstr. 7. Quality Japanese restaurant which serves good-value set lunches. Closed Mon & Sat.

Kuntze's Handelshof, Wilhlem-Heinrich-Str. 17. One of Saarbrücken's leading gourmet addresses, serving both French and German cuisine. Closed Sun lunchtime & Mon.

Michelangelo, Rathausplatz 6. Italian restaurant decorated with pastiches of the heroic frescoes of the great Renaissance master.

tierlieb, Nassauer Str. 13. By German standards, this is an unconventional vegetarian restaurant, being open evenings only (except Sun, when it serves brunch) rather than during the daytime, and having a bistro-style ambience instead of the usual minimalism.

Weinhaus Hauck, St Johanner Markt 7. Wine bar-cum-wine merchant, with a large choice of local and international vintages and bistro-style food to match.

Zum Stiefel, Am Stiefel 2. This eighteenth-century Gasthaus is the flagship of the Bruch brewery, and has a menu with a good choice of local specialities. Closed Sun lunchtime.

Bars and cafés

Big Ben, Försterstr. 17. The heart of the local gay scene (both men and women).

Ein-und-Fünfzig (51), Am Schlossplatz. Trendy café with outside tables on Schlossplatz; it also serves light, Mediterranean-type cuisine.

Jazzkeller Giesskanne, Am Steg 3. The city's main jazz venue.

Kulturcafé, St Johanner Markt 24. Café attached to the Stadtgalerie; in the summer, there's a choice of sitting outside or surrounded by the artworks upstairs.

Schubert, Sulzbachstr. 2. Fine traditional coffee house.

Stamm-Kneipe, St Johanner Markt 11. The tap of the Neufangs brewery, whose best-known product is its *Grafenpils*.

Stiefelbräu, corner of Am Stiefel and Fröschengasse. Hausbrauerei which makes light and dark beers and serves cheaper and more basic meals than the restaurant next door.

Elsewhere in Saarland

Beyond Saarbrücken, the Saarland offers some major examples of industrial heritage, an important Roman site and a surprising amount of fine scenery, particularly along the banks of the Saar.

Völklingen

Few places can have experienced such dramatic swings of fortune in recent decades as the Land's third largest town, **VÖLKLINGEN**, which lies just 14km down the Saar from Saarbrücken. In the 1960s it was a thriving industrial community to which thousands of workers commuted every day. By the mid-1970s its heavy industry had gone into irreversible decline, and the town had become an economic blackspot. Yet twenty years later, it was propelled to the status of something that would have seemed totally implausible only a short time before – a tourist attraction of international stature.

This last development is a result of UNESCO's decision to include its redundant ironworks, the **Alte Völklinger Hütte** (late March to Oct Mon–Thurs, Sat & Sun 10am–6/7pm, Fri 10am–10pm; *www.voelklinger-huette.org*; DM9/€4.50, free Tues after 2pm), on the highly prestigious World Heritage List. This is frequently referred to as a "cathedral of the Industrial Age", though the description does not even begin to suggest the awesome size and extent of the buildings on the sixty-hectare complex, the only one of its type anywhere in the world to survive intact. Founded in 1873, the works were taken over by the Röchling family eight years later and remained in their hands until they were closed down in 1986, just two decades after the workface had peaked at 17,000. By the entrance is the **Gasgebläsehaus**, whose first-floor hall, now in regular service as a somewhat improbable concert venue, contains six huge gas compressors, all dating from just before World War I, which remained in operation right up until the day of closure. However, the most imposing feature of the works is the **Hochofengruppe**, a row of six huge blast furnaces erected between 1882 and 1916.

Although they look dramatic at any time, it's best to try and come on a Friday evening: an artistic light installation is switched on at dusk, and gradually envelops them in a kaleidoscope of colours. The **Hängebahn**, which transported coke to the blast furnaces, is a remarkable technical monument in its own right, using systems derived from both funiculars and hanging railways. Ironically, it was the presence of such technologically advanced features that was responsible for the ultimate demise of the Völklingen works, as it was less adaptable to modernization than competitors with more primitive equipment. Among the various exhibitions in the administration buildings, a photographic documentation on the life of the workers deals very honestly with the health problems that were endemic throughout the history of the works, due to the employees' constant exposure to heat, dust and dirt. It is small wonder that local emotions were mixed when production finally ceased.

Völklingen's **Bahnhof** is on the opposite side of the tracks from the ironworks. The **tourist office** (Mon–Fri 9am–5pm, Sat & Sun 10am–4pm; ☎0 68 98/2 11 00, fax 29 49 16, *www.voelklingen.de*) is right alongside, in the late nineteenth-century Alter Bahnhof, Rathausstr. 57. Although there's no real reason to stay the night, the town has a few **hotels**, including *Heidstock*, Gerhardstr. 124 (☎0 68 98/8 21 00; ④), and *Parkhotel Gegenbach*, Kuhlweinstr. 70 (☎0 68 98/91 97 00; ⑦). The latter's *Orangerie* is Völklingen's best and most expensive **restaurant**; the bistro in the abovementioned Alter Bahnhof is a good and much cheaper alternative.

Mettlach

Another 40km along the Saar from Völklingen is **METTLACH**, which ranks as one of Saarland's prettier towns, despite being a virtual fiefdom of the ceramics firm Villeroy & Boch, whose specialist factories dominate the townscape. The massive Baroque **Benediktinerabtei** overlooking the waterfront, which had fallen victim to the Napoleonic suppression, was taken over by Jean François Boch in 1809 to serve as the new headquarters of his family firm, founded in Lorraine back in 1748. This merged with the rival Villeroy works in 1836, and is still in the hands of the descendants. Part of the abbey complex is given over to a visitors' centre, **Keravision** (Mon–Fri 9am–6pm, Sat 9.30am–4pm; *www.villeroy-boch.com*; free), which features tableaux and explanatory material on the company. Its historical collection is housed in **Schloss Ziegelberg** (Tues–Sun 10am–5pm; DM4/€2) at the extreme northern edge of town, which was built in the 1870s in the style of a French Renaissance palace as the home of the Boch family.

On the western side of the Benediktinerabtei is a park in which stands the so-called **Alter Turm**, an octagonal chapel erected at the very end of the tenth century as a mausoleum for the town's founder, St Lutwinus, who was bishop of Trier at the turn of the eighth century. Some valuable treasures associated with him – a seventh-century bowl and bishop's ring, and a thirteenth-century triptych-reliquary – can be seen in the **Pfarrkirche St Liutwin**, a pretentious Historicist church high above the town centre on Freiherr-von-Stein-Strasse.

From the town's jetty, Mettlacher Personenschiffahrt (☎0 68 64/8 02 20) runs four **cruises** (DM12/€6 round trip) every day between March and October to the Saarland's best-known beauty spot, the **Saarschleife** (Saar Bend), a colossal loop in the river, between whose banks is a thickly wooded peninsula. However, this is not really seen at its best from water level; the famous view which features in all the tourist brochures is an aerial one from the **Cloef** belvedere. This is at the edge of the little health resort of **ORSCHOLZ**, which lies 6km northwest of Mettlach, of which it now forms a component part.

Bus #6300 runs between Mettlach and Orscholz from the former's **Bahnhof**, which is a short walk northeast of the town centre. The **tourist office** (Mon–Fri

8.30am–4.30pm; ☎0 68 64/83 84, fax 83 29, *www.mettlach.de*) at Freiherr-von-Stein-Str. 64 has a list of **private rooms** (①–③). Reasonably priced **hotels** in Mettlach itself include *Saarblick*, Freiherr-von-Stein-Str. 14 (☎0 68 64/5 83; ③), and *Zur Post*, Heinertstr. 17 (☎0 68 64/5 57; ④). More upmarket options are *Zum Schwan*, Freiherr-von-Stein-Str. 34a (☎0 68 64/72 79; ⑤), and *Saarpark*, Bahnhofstr. 31 (☎0 68 64/92 00; ⑦). In Orscholz, the best place to stay is *Zur Saarschleife*, Cloefstr. 44 (☎0 68 64/17 90; ⑥). There's a **youth hostel** at Herbergstr. 1 (☎0 68 68/27 0, fax 5 56, *jh-dreisbach@djh -info.de*; DM29/€14.50 or DM38/€19) in the incorporated village of Dreisbach to the west, which is also served by bus #6300. All the hotels listed have **restaurants**; another recommendable establishment is *Abtei-Bräu*, Bahnhofstr. 32, a Hausbrauerei with a large garden which makes an unfiltered beer and serves Saarland specialities.

Nennig

Bus #6300 also serves **NENNIG**, a small village in the Mosel valley, the only wine-growing part of the Saarland. Nowadays officially part of the town of Perl, 9km to the south, it boasts two notable historic monuments. The first of these is the **Römischer Mosaikfussboden** (April–Sept Tues–Sun 8.30–noon & 1–6pm; Oct, Nov & Jan–March 9–noon & 1–4pm; DM3/€1.50) at the southeastern edge of the village. The largest Roman mosaic ever found north of the Alps., it was unearthed, together with the huge villa to which it belonged, by a local farmer in 1852. It originally formed part of the villa entrance hall and includes vivid and detailed depictions of gladiatorial combat.

Schloss Berg, a twelfth-century *Wasserschloss*, has been refurbished as a luxury **hotel**, *Victor's Residenz* (☎0 68 66/7 90; ⑦–⑨), and its main **restaurant** is the Saarland's best-known gourmet address, though there is also a more affordable offshoot, *Die Scheune*. The village also has a couple of moderately priced hotels in *Schlossblick*, Berger Weg 9 (☎0 68 66/8 29; ②), and *Zur Traube*, Bübinger Str. 16 (☎0 68 66/3 49; ④).

travel details

Trains

Koblenz to: Andernach (hourly; 15min); Bingen (hourly; 45min); Boppard (hourly; 15min); Cologne (hourly; 1hr 30min); Rüdesheim (hourly; 1hr); Saarbrücken (8 daily; 2hr 25min); Trier (hourly; 1hr 20min).

Mainz to: Bonn (hourly; 2hr 15min); Cologne (hourly; 2hr 30min); Frankfurt (frequent; 30min); Idar-Oberstein (hourly; 1hr 20min); Karlsruhe (hourly; 1hr 5min); Koblenz (frequent; 1hr); Saarbrücken (8 daily; 2hr 30min); Worms (every 30min; 40min).

Saarbrücken to: Cologne (5 daily; 3hr 30min); Koblenz (8 daily; 2hr 25min); Trier (5 daily; 1hr 5min).

CHAPTER FIVE

NORTH RHINE-WESTPHALIA

North Rhine-Westphalia (Nordrhein-Westfalen) is only the fourth largest of the Länder in terms of area, but has, with seventeen million inhabitants, by far the largest population. As its double-barrelled name suggests, it's historically two distinct provinces whose separateness dates back to the very beginnings of German history, the North Rhine having belonged to the Franks, while Westphalia marked the beginning of Saxon territory. With the industrialization process in the nineteenth century, any lingering distinction between the two provinces – both of which had been absorbed by the expansionist Kingdom of Prussia – became hopelessly blurred with the mushroom growth of a vast built-up area around the mineral-rich valley of the River Ruhr. This formed a clearly recognizable unit, yet was divided almost exactly in half by the traditional boundaries. After World War II, it was decided to preserve the economic integrity of the **Ruhrgebiet**, as the area came to be known, by creating a single new Land out of the two old provinces.

Of the thirty-eight German cities registering a population of over 200,000, ten are in North Rhine and a further six in Westphalia. Many begin just as another ends, and the Ruhrgebiet is joined to a string of other cities stretching right to the southern border with Rhineland-Palatinate, making up the most densely populated area in Europe. In this conurbation, **Cologne** is by far the most outstanding city, managing to preserve much of the atmosphere and splendours of its long centuries as a free state, at times the most powerful in Germany. The Land's other city of top-class historical interest is **Aachen**, the original capital of the Holy Roman Empire. Next in line comes **Münster**, which would presumably be capital of Westphalia, if such a division still existed. As it is, the Land government meets in self-consciously cosmopolitan **Düsseldorf**, which inspires admiration and revulsion in roughly equal measure. At the southern end of the

---

ACCOMMODATION PRICE CODES

All the pensions and hotels in this book have been graded according to the following price categories. The codes quoted are for the cheapest available double room, except for establishments which have rooms costing widely different rates, when the most expensive price is given as well. Exact charges are given for youth hostels; in the case of the official DJH (HI) establishments, this is the lowest available rate. When two figures are quoted for these hostels, the first applies to juniors (ie under 27 years of age), the second to seniors (27 and above).

① less than DM60/€30
② DM60–79/€30–39
③ DM80–99/€40–49

④ DM100–124/€50–62
⑤ DM125–149/€63–74
⑥ DM150–199/€75–99

⑦ DM200–249/€100–124
⑧ DM250–299/€125–149
⑨ upwards of DM300/€150

Land is **Bonn**, capital of the West German state for its forty-year existence, and still one of the national seats of government. Never suited for the role it was so casually given in 1949, it's a place all too easily maligned.

In spite of the stranglehold heavy industry has traditionally held over North Rhine-Westphalia, much of the landscape is rural, with agriculture and forestry making key contributions to the economy. The **Eifel** in the Rhineland, and the **Sauerland**, **Siegerland** and **Teutoburg Forest** in Westphalia all offer varied scenery, and are popular holiday spots with the Germans themselves, being such obvious antidotes to urban life. In these areas are some wonderful small towns – **Monschau**, **Bad Münstereifel**, **Soest** and **Lemgo** – which can stand comparison with any in Germany. Their counterparts along the Rhine have been scarred by war, but **Brühl** and **Xanten** are still particularly worth visiting.

Sobriety is the keynote of the province's architecture; new styles were slow to develop, and there was far less readiness to replace buildings simply because they were old-fashioned than was the case further south. There is thus a legacy of **Romanesque architecture** which is unsurpassed in Europe. Gothic also took strong root, but the Renaissance barely made a mark, while the preferred form of Baroque was the dignified variety based on Roman models, which didn't lend itself to flowery Rococo offshoots.

Currently, North Rhine-Westphalia faces a number of **economic problems**. Its unemployment level is high, due to the recent need to scale down heavy industry, and it hasn't been as successful as other Länder in developing and attracting companies active in the new hi-tech fields. On the positive side, the Gastarbeiter have managed to integrate fairly well, with racism kept reasonably in check. The province's main cities are now as multicultural as Leicester or Bradford, Houston or Philadelphia, a fact tacitly acknowledged by the common practice of translating public notices into Greek, Turkish, Serbo-Croat, Italian and Spanish.

Getting around the province couldn't be simpler. There's an extensive **public transport** network, including two integrated systems of main-line and S-Bahn trains, trams and buses – one of these is based in Cologne and Bonn, the other in the Ruhrgebiet, Düsseldorf and the Lower Rhineland. You can therefore turn the claustrophobic character of the conurbation to your advantage: it's certainly never necessary to wait long for some form of transport from one city to another. Even the country areas have a generous allocation of buses, which are often hardly used by the locals. Transport enthusiasts, incidentally, will find two oddities worth making a detour to see – the Schwebebahn in **Wuppertal** and the Wasserstrassenkreuz in **Minden**. Prices for **accommodation** are well above the national average in the cities, but there's the usual extensive network of youth hostels and campsites, while rates in the countryside and smaller towns are generally excellent value.

THE RHINELAND–EIFEL REGION

The southwestern part of the North Rhineland is a mountainous region. The **Eifel range**, which forms a continuation of the Ardennes in Belgium, takes up the lion's share of this territory, while on the east bank of the Rhine the **Siebengebirge** are the last of the mountain ranges which give the river so much of its characteristic grandeur. At **Bonn**, the landscape adjacent to the Rhine flattens out, and here begins the enormous built-up conurbation which stretches, with hardly a break, all the way up to Dortmund. The prime attraction of this area, however, is undoubtedly the venerable city of **Aachen**.

Aachen

"In Aachen I saw all kinds of priceless treasures, the like of which no man has seen rarer," wrote Dürer following a visit there in 1560. His enthusiasm can still be echoed;

AACHEN possesses fabulous riches fit to be compared with those of Istanbul or Venice, as UNESCO duly recognized by choosing the magnificent Dom – which has since been superbly restored for its 1200th anniversary celebrations in 2000 – as one of the dozen global wonders which comprised the very first list of World Heritage Sites.

Now a frontier post – the municipal area includes stretches of border with both Belgium and the Netherlands – Aachen has metamorphosed from a far grander role. In the late eighth and early ninth centuries the city was seen as the successor to ancient Rome, the hub of the great Frankish empire of **Charlemagne** (Karl der Grosse) which comprised pretty well all of present-day Germany, France, the Benelux, Austria and Switzerland, as well as much of Italy and part of northern Spain. In 794, after 26 years of almost constant campaigning, Charlemagne established Aachen as the main seat of his court. The choice was made partly for strategic reasons, but also because of the presence of hot springs, over which the Romans had first built thermal baths. Exercising in these waters was one of the emperor's favourite pastimes, and his contemporaries rated him a swimmer without peer. The **spa** has continually given the city prestige and visitors, but its political power was short-lived, lasting only a generation after Charlemagne's death.

Arrival, information and accommodation

Aachen's **Hauptbahnhof** is just south of the city centre. Some buses stop outside, but others – including those to Monschau – leave from the **bus station** at the coner of Peterstrasse and Kurhausstrasse. The **tourist office** occupies the Atrium Elisenbrunnen on Friedrich-Wilhelm-Platz (Mon–Fri 9am–6pm, Sat 9am–2pm; ☎02 41/1 80 29 60, fax 1 80 29 31, *www.aachen-tourist.de*). **Mitfahrzentrale** have an office at Roermonder Str. 4 (☎02 41/15 20 17).

There's a large concentration of **hotels** near the Hauptbahnhof, but most of the genuine budget options are a long way out. The **youth hostel** is also out of the centre, situated on a little hill in a suburban park to the southwest, at Maria-Theresia-Allee 260 (☎02 41/71 10 10, fax 7 11 01 20; DM38.50/€19.25); take bus #2 direction Preuswald from the Elisenbrunnen and alight at Brüsseler Ring or Ronheide.

Hotels

Benelux, Franzstr. 21–23 (☎02 41/2 23 43, fax 2 23 45). The most characterful of the upmarket city-centre hotels. ⑥–⑧.

Brülls am Dom, Hühner Markt (☎02 41/3 17 04, fax 40 43 26). Medium-priced hotel with café in the handiest of locations. ⑥.

Burtscheider Markt, Burtscheider Markt 14–16 (☎02 41/60 00 00, fax 6 00 00 20). One of the city's best addresses – a true spa hotel with its own thermal baths. ⑥–⑧.

Buschhausen, Adenauerallee 215 (☎02 41/6 00 80, fax 60 28 30). Hotel-restaurant in the south of Burtscheid, with a wide choice of rooms. ③–⑦.

Drei Könige, Büchel 5 (☎02 41/4 83 93, fax 3 61 52). Run in conjunction with the *Pizzeria am Markt* by a truly international staff, this budget establishment is conveniently located just off the corner of the Markt. ④.

Dura, Lagerhausstr. 5 (☎02 41/40 31 35, fax 4 01 84 50). Cheapest of the many hotels clustered around the Hauptbahnhof. ③.

Göbel, Trierer Str. 546 (☎02 41/52 32 44, fax 56 46 10). Some 5km southeast of the centre, but a good-value option. Take bus #5, #15, #25, #35, #45, #55 or #65. ④.

Hansa-Haus, Von-Coels-Str. 42 (☎02 41/55 13 80, fax 55 13 50). Located 5km east of the centre on the route of buses #12 and #22, this offers the cheapest rooms in Aachen. ③.

Hesse am Marschiertor, Friedlandstr. 20 (☎02 41/47 05 40, fax 4 70 54 49). Good value, and also has a recommendable restaurant. ④.

Marx, Hubertusstr. 33–35 (☎02 41/3 75 41, fax 2 67 05, *www.hotel-marx.de*). Another fine middle-range choice, a little further west of the Hauptbahnhof. ④–⑤.

Quellenhof, Monheimsallee 52 (☎02 41/9 13 20, fax 9 13 21 00, *www.dorint.de/aachen*). Following several years of closure, Aachen's palatial old spa hotel has been refurbished to the highest standards by its new owners, the Dorint chain. It also has an outstanding restaurant. ⑨.

Stadt Koblenz, Leydelstr. 2 (☎02 41/47 45 80, fax 3 54 49). Run in tandem with the neighbouring *Am Bahnhof*, this offers decent rooms and ready access to the Hauptbahnhof. ③–⑤.

The city centre

Aachen's **Altstadt** lies ten minutes from the Hauptbahnhof along Bahnhofstrasse and then left into Theaterstrasse. It's small and compact, and can comfortably be seen in a day, though you'll need longer to take in more than a few of the city's varied and excellent **museums**. Badly damaged in World War II, Aachen was also devastated by a terrible fire in 1656. This accounts for the unusually large number of Baroque buildings by north German standards; their restrained, classically derived style is a world away from the wild fantasies which were then all the rage in Bavaria.

The Dom

Thankfully, although hardly anything else remains from Charlemagne's time, Aachen retains its crowning jewel in the former **Pfalzkapelle** (palace chapel). Now forming the heart and soul of the present-day **Dom**, its presence is enshrined in the French name for the city, Aix-la-Chapelle. A ninth-century monk-chronicler, Notker the Stammerer, relates how skilled workmen were brought from many lands in order that this edifice should surpass any previously erected, and concluded that it was "built by human hands, yet with the inspiration of God". Charlemagne's courtier Einhard, who must have watched the building's construction, attributed its splendour to the emperor's religious devotion, and fills in details of the decoration – "gold and silver, with lamps, and with lattices and doors of solid bronze". He also explained that marble columns were brought from as far as Ravenna, on whose basilica of San Vitale the chapel was largely modelled; indeed, the pope's letter authorizing Charlemagne to remove marbles and mosaics from the palace there still exists.

Even after such descriptions, you can't help being overwhelmed by its extraordinary symmetry, height and grandeur. Designed by **Odo von Metz**, it's an eight-sided dome, surrounded by a sixteen-sided ambulatory, above which is a two-tiered gallery with eight arcades of columns; the number eight is significant, representing perfection and harmony. The circumference of the octagon is 144 Carolingian feet – the cardinal number of the heavenly Jerusalem – and that of the outer polygon exactly twice that: an impeccable concord and order which are intended to symbolize Heaven. As a result of the cult of Charlemagne (he was canonized by an anti-pope in 1165) and the possession of the so-called Great Aachen Relics (allegedly the swaddling clothes and loin-cloth of Christ, the gown of the Virgin and the garb of St John the Baptist), pilgrims poured into the city in such numbers that the building needed to be expanded. An airily high and narrow **Gothic chancel** was therefore added, modelled on the Ste-Chapelle in Paris. Its original stained glass has been lost, but the replacements at least give the right effect. Also from this period is a series of two-storey chapels encircling the octagon. The one specially endowed for the use of Hungarian pilgrims was later replaced by an Italianate Baroque design, as successive generations sought to leave their mark on the Dom; another important addition was the western **tower**, which was under construction for several centuries.

Some of the **original furnishings** survive: in the vestibule alone you can see the bronze doors with lions' heads mentioned by Einhard, along with a pine cone which seems to have been a waterspout and an antique she-wolf. These are rather overshadowed by the costly embellishments with which Charlemagne's successors enhanced the Dom, making it positively drip with treasure. Adorning the main altar is the **Pala d'Oro**, an early eleventh-century altar front with ten embossed scenes of the Passion. Behind, and of similar date, is the **ambo**, a pulpit like no other, fashioned from gold-plated copper adorned with precious stones, reliefs of the Evangelists and ancient Egyptian ivories of profane subjects. Suspended from the dome by means of a mighty iron chain is the enormous twelfth-century **chandelier** given by Frederick Barbarossa. Regrettably, its weight quickly caused the mosaics to crack; those to be seen today are a nineteenth-century attempt at re-creating the effect of the originals. The gilded **shrine of Charlemagne** at the end of the chancel was finished in 1215, having been fifty years in the making. It contains the remains of the saint, who is depicted on the front, and also serves as a glorification of the Holy Roman Empire he founded, with portraits of his successors along the sides, instead of the normal biblical personages. Likewise in the chancel is the **shrine of St Mary**, which was made to house the Great Aachen Relics, but not started until the companion-piece to Charlemagne had at last been finished – a revealing illustration of how important his cult had become. Charlemagne's status is further emphasized by the early fifteenth-century statue of him on the pier behind his shrine, the only outsider in a cycle of the Virgin and Apostles.

In the gallery is the **imperial throne**, a marble chair with a wooden seat approached by six steps, in the manner of that in Solomon's temple; from here the emperor had a grandstand view of all that was happening below. Tests carried out in the 1960s suggested that the throne actually dated from the time of the coronation of Otto I, which initiated the tradition of emperors being crowned at Aachen, a practice which lasted until the sixteenth century. However, the most recent scientific examination has all but conclusively confirmed the traditional belief that it did indeed belong to Charlemagne. In order to see the throne (with an added bonus of a different perspective on the Dom and its furnishings) and enter the chancel you've no choice but to join a **guided tour**. These cost DM3/€1.50 and leave from the Schatzkammer, which has its own entrance on Klostergasse; there are at least a couple a day, with hourly departures at the height of the season.

The Schatzkammer

The **Schatzkammer** (Mon 10am–1pm, Tues, Wed & Fri–Sun 10am–6pm, Thurs 10am–8pm; DM5/€2.50), housed in chambers off the cloisters, is as much an essential sight as the Dom. Quite simply, it's the richest treasury in northern Europe, a dazzling feast for the eyes and an unashamed glorification of the wealth and power of the Church Triumphant. Prominent among its treasures is the greatest of all processional crucifixes, the late tenth-century **Lothar cross**, studded with jewels and bearing an antique cameo of Emperor Augustus; the Crucifixion is modestly engraved on the reverse. From the beginning of the following century come a **holy-water vessel**, carved from an elephant's tusk, and a **golden book cover** with an ivory of the Madonna and Child, which was made as an accessory to the Pala d'Oro in the decoration of the altar. The only items dating from the time of Charlemagne are a damaged **ivory diptych** and the Byzantine **Quadriga cloth**; the latter was used as his burial shroud, while the large **Roman sarcophagus** carved with a scene of the rape of Proserpine served as his improbable coffin from his death until his canonization.

Other priceless textiles include two associated with the coronation of Emperor Charles IV in 1349: the **Griffin cloth** and the so-called **Cappa Leonis**. Among many superb fourteenth-century **reliquaries**, note the idealized portrait head of Charlemagne and the two shaped like Gothic chapels. Gifts from such devotees as Margaret of York and Louis of Hungary show the international extent of the Aachen cult. The astonishing vibrancy of the local goldsmith tradition down the centuries is proved by the sixteenth-century work of **Hans von Reutlingen**, which stands comparison with any of the older masterpieces.

The Rathaus

Charlemagne's palace once extended across the Katschhof, now lined with ugly modern buildings, to the site of the present **Rathaus** (Mon–Fri 10am–5pm, Sat & Sun 10am–1pm & 2–5pm; DM3/€1.50). Fronting the Markt, which boasts the finest of the medieval houses left in the city, its facade is lined with the figures of fifty Holy Roman emperors – 31 of them crowned in Aachen. Above the entrance, Charlemagne shares a niche with Christ and Pope Leo III, who conducted his coronation ceremony in Rome on Christmas Day 800. Built in the fourteenth century on the palace foundations, and incorporating two of its **towers**, the Rathaus is a mix of attempts to restore its original Gothic form with the inevitable Baroque changes of later years. The finest feature of the interior is the much-restored **Kaisersaal**. Here the *Karlspreis* (Charlemagne Prize) is awarded annually to the citizen who is deemed to have made the largest contribution to European unity. A cycle of frescoes by the Düsseldorf artist Alfred Rethel gives a Romantic portrayal of scenes from Charlemagne's life, but your attention is more likely to be drawn by the crown jewels, dazzlingly displayed at one end. These are only reproductions, however; the originals have been kept in Vienna ever since the early nineteenth century, when they were commandeered by the Habsburgs (who had held

AACHEN'S FOUNTAINS

Seventeen fountains dot Aachen's streets. Most popular is the **Puppenbrunnen** (Dolls' Fountain), reached down Krämerstrasse; each doll – a rider, a market woman, a harlequin, a canon and a model – has moving limbs and represents a particular facet of Aachen life. In strong contrast is the stern Neoclassical solemnity of the **Elisenbrunnen**, a rotunda with two pavilions designed by Schinkel as the public drinking fountain, which lies due east. Plaques on the walls list the names of illustrious visitors to the springs, liberally augmented by many graffiti artists making their bid for immortality. The pervading smell is sulphuric, and the taste of the water – if you find its heat palatable – is hardly more appetizing.

a virtually hereditary stranglehold on the office of Holy Roman emperor in centuries) for their new role as emperors of Austria.

The rest of the centre

Southeast of the Markt is another square, the Hühner Markt, where livestock was formerly sold. Here stands the **Couven-Museum** (Tues, Wed & Fri–Sun 10am–5pm, Thurs 10am–1pm; DM2/€1), an elegant merchant-class home which has been named after a father-and-son team of architects who designed many of the city's Baroque buildings. It has been fitted out with mid-eighteenth- to mid-nineteenth-century furnishings gathered from houses of the Aachen-Liège region, giving an idea of the stylish if frivolous priorities of the local bourgeoisie. Look out for the complete pharmacy, a lavishly decorated first-floor living room with carved chimneypiece and the huge Advent crib in the attic. Before the construction of modern facilities, the hub of Aachen's spa life was the **Altes Kurhaus**, an ornate late eighteenth-century building by the younger Couven, situated east of the Markt at Komphausbadstr. 19.

In a house on Pontstrasse, which leads north of the Markt, **Paul Julius von Reuter** established his famous news agency, using carrier pigeons to circulate the reports. To commemorate this, the **Internationales Zeitungsmuseum** (May–Sept Tues–Fri 9.30am–1pm & 2.30–5pm, Sat 9.30am–1pm, Sun & Mon 2.30–5pm; rest of year closed Sun; free), with a collection of some 120,000 newspapers, has been established at no. 13 in the same street. An exhibition room has been set up to show by means of original editions how the press (German- and English-language examples dominate) reacted to great stories, from the 1848 revolutions via the two world wars to contemporary conflicts. If you're seriously interested, you can apply to see particular issues. At the end of Pontstrasse – which functions as the hub of the student nightlife scene – is the **Ponttor**, an awesome early fourteenth-century gateway which was formerly the strongest part of the city's fortification system. Of the ten other gates, the only survivor is the **Marschiertor**, just to the west of the Hauptbahnhof.

At the eastern edge of the centre, at Wilhelmstr. 18, is the **Suermondt-Ludwig-Museum** (Tue, Thurs & Fri 11am–7pm, Wed 11am–9pm, Sat & Sun 11am–5pm; DM6/€3, or DM10/€5 combined ticket with the Ludwig Forum and other museums). It has an excellent collection of northern European medieval sculpture, with an extensive array of Pietàs, Madonnas and Passions; these are almost exclusively anonymous and predominantly folksy in style, though some, such as the large Lower Rhenish *St Peter Altar*, achieve a rather more developed artistic sense. Also of special note are the Baroque fancies of **Dietrich von Rath**, the city's last important goldsmith, and the sculptures and stained glass by **Ewald Mataré**, an Aachen artist best known for his role in creating new works for German cathedrals and churches in the period of their restoration following war damage. There are also a number of old masters, including notable works by Joos van Cleve, Cranach, Van Dyck, Ribera and Zurbarán.

The suburbs

One of Aachen's two spa quarters is centred on **Monheimsallee** to the northeast of the Altstadt. At no. 52 is the city's main thermal bathing hall, the **Kurbad Quellenhof** (Mon–Sat 7am–9pm, Sun 7am–2pm; from DM17/€8.50), while the **Kurgarten** is the well-tended park you'd expect. However, Monheimsallee is best known for its **Casino** (Mon–Thurs & Sun 3pm–2am, Fri & Sat until 3am; minimum stake DM5/€2.50 at the cheapest roulette table), housed in a Neoclassical building with a glitteringly modernized interior. Note that the management want only the better class of visitor, with full evening dress the normal attire. If you strike it lucky at the tables, the excellent restaurant provides a tempting outlet for your winnings.

Just south of the quarter, housed in a Bauhaus-style former umbrella factory building at Jülicher Str. 97–109, is the **Ludwig Forum für Internationale Kunst** (Tues & Thurs 10am–5pm, Wed & Fri 11am–8pm, Sat & Sun 11am–5pm; DM6/€3). This is one of Germany's most vibrant centres for contemporary visual arts and while what's on display at any one time is obviously a lottery, all the big names of American painting and sculpture, including Roy Lichtenstein, Andy Warhol, Chuck Close and Duane Hanson, are well represented. Soviet and Eastern European art is another strength, with two large installations by the Ukrainian **Igor Kopytianskij** being particularly eye-catching. Also worth seeking out is a papier-mâché piece by a contemporary German-American sculptor, **Thomas Lanigan-Schmidt**, *A Rite of Passage – the Leprechaun*, which took eleven years to make; displayed alongside is his even more spectacular *Iconostasis*. **Jörg Immendorff**'s *Brandenburg Gate* is the highlight of an extensive representation of the German avant-garde.

About fifteen minutes' walk east of the Hauptbahnhof, at Bismarckstr. 68, is a moated medieval castle, **Burg Frankenberg** (Tues–Fri 10am–5pm, Sat & Sun 10am–1pm; DM2/€1). The interior has been restored to house the local history museum; though mainly of parochial appeal, this has interesting models which attempt to re-create the likely original form of Charlemagne's palace. Ceramic products from Aachen are displayed in the tower. On the opposite side of the rail tracks is the suburb of **Burtscheid**, the second spa quarter, which has a distinctive skyline, thanks to a handsome pair of churches built on its heights by the elder Couven. Again, it features thermal bathing facilities and sedate areas of parkland.

Eating, drinking and nightlife

Many of the best places to eat and drink are found in and around the Markt, while the most animated district is the student quarter, centred on Pontstrasse.

Restaurants

Aachener Brauhaus Degraa am Theater, Kapuzinergraben 4. The name of Aachen's now-defunct brewery lives on in this Gaststätte, which serves up huge portions of traditional fare, including bargain lunches Mon–Fri, in its wonderfully evocative galleried interior. By the entrance is a stand-up Kneipe, which claims to be the smallest bar in Europe.

Am Knipp, Bergdriesch 3. Finely appointed beer and wine restaurant, with a tradition dating back to 1698. Evenings only, closed Tues.

Da Salvatore, Bahnhofplatz 5. High-class but not unduly expensive Italian restaurant, whose menu features plenty of Sardinian specialities.

Elisenbrunnen, Friedrich-Wilhelm-Platz 14. Offers first-rate traditional German cooking in the elegant surroundings of one of Aachen's finest buildings.

Gala, Monheimsallee 44. The Casino's classy and very expensive restaurant (evenings only, closed Sun & Mon) is among the finest in the country. Less outrageously priced is its offshoot, *Palm-Bistro* (closed Sat lunchtime).

Goldener Schwan, Markt 37. Typical Gaststätte occupying a fine old mansion with a Gothic facade.

Postwagen, Krämerstr. 2. Unquestionably Aachen's most famous Gaststätte, and a sight in itself, both for its cheerful Baroque exterior tacked onto the Rathaus and the cramped and irregular rooms within.

Ratskeller, Markt 40. Housed in the Rathaus cellars, this features more innovative cooking than in most of its German counterparts.

Tradition, Burtscheider Str. 11–13. Very highly regarded restaurant located just west of the Hauptbahnhof, featuring fish specialities and other international dishes; on Mon & Thurs–Sat there's an extensive bargain menu at lunchtime. Closed Tues & Wed daytime.

Zum Goldenen Einhorn, Markt 33. Has an enormous and inexpensive menu with Italian and Greek cuisine as well as German, the speciality being thin fillets of veal with a huge choice of sauces.

Bars and cafés

Atlantis, Pontstr. 141–9. Attached to the cinema of the same name, this popular student pub was decorated by two Berlin artists in an evocaton of the lost continent.

Café Kittel, Pontstr. 39. Trendy café-bar with beer garden.

Café Middelburg, Rethelstr. 6. Traditional café which serves excellent cakes.

Domkeller, Hof 1. A genuine local, in spite of its location just off the Markt; always full, though it expands to the terrace outside in high summer.

Egmont, Pontstr. 1. French-style bistro featuring a range of live music including jazz, chansons, soul and funk as well as karaoke sessions.

Hauptquartier, Promenadenstr. 46. The city's most eccentric bar, a living testimony to the enduring popularity in Germany of all things punk.

Jakobshof, Stromgasse 31. Very trendy bar featuring live jazz and cabaret; also does full meals. Closed Mon.

Labyrinth, Pontstr. 156. Labyrinthine student bar with huge tables and minimalist decor. Serves Greek-style food.

Leo van den Daele, Büchel 18. Historic wood-panelled café with exquisite furnishings. Renowned for its huge rice cakes, it's also the best place to sample *Printen*, a spiced gingerbread which is the city's main claim to culinary fame.

Meisenfrei, Boxgraben 72. This café has a bewildering choice of games to entertain you.

Molkerei, Pontstr. 141. Bright and cheerful during the day, but lacks atmosphere in the evening.

Tangente, Pontstr. 141. Sharing a terrace with *Molkerei*, this is an elegant daytime café which transforms itself into a lively bar frequented by Aachen's younger residents at night.

Discos and clubs

Aoxomoxoa, Reihstr, 15. A big favourite with the in-crowd, featuring both live and recorded music. Open Mon–Thurs 10pm–3am, Fri & Sat 10am–5am.

B9, Blondelstr. 9. Aachen's top disco, with a bizarre range of music: funk on top of heavy metal via Europop to the jazz and soul played at the café next to the dance floor. Situated on the eastern side of town and best visited after midnight when the schoolkids have cleared off. Open Mon–Thurs 10pm–3am, Fri & Sat 10pm–5am.

Club Voltaire, Friedrichstr. 9. The only all-night joint worth mentioning; has a tiny dance floor, with music kept at conversation level. Open midnight–6am.

Odeon, Pontstr. 135. Very popular but rather poky disco in the student quarter.

Culture and festivals

The Eurogress centre next to the Casino at Monheimsallee 48 (☎02 41/9 13 10) is where both rock and classical **concerts** are held. More highbrow culture is available at the Theater Aachen on Theaterplatz (☎02 41/4 78 42 44); **drama** or **opera** is performed most evenings and standards are high – Herbert von Karajan first made his name as musical director there. Grenzlandtheater at Friedrich-Wilhelm-Platz 5/6 (☎02 41/4 74 61 11) offers modern fare, albeit with an emphasis on established playwrights.

The main **festivals** are Carnival, which is celebrated here with typical Rhenish enthusiasm; the *Karlspreis* in May; and the *Europamarkt der Kunsthandwerker*, a handicrafts fair held on the first weekend of September. *CHIO*, an international jumping and riding tournament in late June or early July, is the main sporting event.

The Northern Eifel

The German section of the **Eifel** massif is divided by the Land boundary between North Rhine-Westphalia and Rhineland-Palatinate; the former's share consists mainly of the **Hohes Venn**, an extensive plateau of impervious rocks which stretches into Belgium. Variation in the scenery is provided by the River Rur, which cuts a deep, winding valley, and by the vegetation of gorse, broom and cotton grass. The area is poor in natural resources: no cities have ever developed, and the nineteenth century saw mass emigration, much of it to the US. Nowadays, the principal industry is the provision of **activity holidays** – skiing in winter, hiking, angling and sailing in summer – punctuated by dead periods between the seasons.

Monschau

The Northern Eifel's other main draw is a series of well-preserved small towns, two of which rank among the finest in Germany. One of these is **MONSCHAU**, some 30km south of Aachen. It's only accessible by road, with slow but fairly frequent bus services; most of the Eifel rail lines have closed because of the high cost of maintenance and low usage levels, though excursion trains, often pulled by steam engines, run between Monschau and the Belgian town of Eupen on Sundays and holidays throughout the summer.

Monschau's main attraction is its dramatic setting deep in the Rur valley, with ruined fortresses – the **Burg** and the **Haller** (both with unrestricted access) – crowning two of the hills above. These offer some of the many superb **views** to be had in the area; others can be enjoyed from a belvedere just off the main road to Aachen, or from the commanding heights of the continuation of this road in the direction of Nideggen. The Burg, much the larger of the ruins, is the building from which Monschau developed. Its keep and gateway are Romanesque originals; the ring wall and parapets date from a strengthening of the defences in the fourteenth century, while the large **Eselsturm** (Asses' Tower), originally built in the same priod, was modified a couple of hundred years later, when the central **Palast** was added.

The lower part of Monschau is an almost completely preserved townscape, dominated by the magnificent **multistorey mansions** lining the Rur, whose slate roofs are sometimes pierced by two tiers of dormer windows. Though half-timbering is used extensively, these houses aren't as old as they might appear – they date from Monschau's main period of prosperity, centred on cloth production, which followed the Thirty Years War. The most ornate of all, the **Rotes Haus** (Red House; Good Friday to Nov Tues–Sun entry at 10am, 11am, 2pm, 3pm & 4pm; DM5/€2.50), adds a rare splash of colour to the town, which is otherwise so monochromatic that it seems to grow organically out of the landscape. Built by a merchant in the 1750s as a combined factory, office and house, it features a Rococo staircase with an elaborate iron railing, and is fully furnished in the same style. The nearby **Troistorff Haus** on Laufenstrasse, which is now used as municipal offices, is smaller, but has a fancier exterior and another fine stairway.

Practicalities
Monschau's **tourist office** (Easter–Oct Mon–Thurs 10am–4pm, Fri 10am–6pm, Sat & Sun 11am–3pm; rest of year Mon–Fri only; ☎0 24 72/33 00, fax 45 34, *www.monschau .de*) is at Stadtstr. 1 beside the main bridge.

Hotels are numerous and almost always good value. Right in the centre are *Eifeler Hof*, Stadtstr. 10 (☎0 24 72/50 46; ②), *Burghotel*, Laufenstr. 1 (☎0 24 72/23 32; ③), and *Royal*, Stadtstr. 4–6 (☎0 24 72/20 33; ③). High above the town and commanding a wonderful view is *Hubertusklause*, Bergstr. 45 (☎0 24 72/55 50 36; ⑤). There are two **youth hostels**, one located in the Palast, Auf dem Schloss 4 (☎0 24 72/23 14, fax 43 91; DM21.60/€10.80 or DM26.60/€13.30) and the other at Hargardsgasse 5 in Hargard (☎0 24 72/21 80, fax 45 27, *jh-monschau-hargard@t-online.de*; DM24/€12 or DM29/€14.50), some 3km away. **Private houses** (①–③) with rooms to let can be found mainly on Kirchstrasse, Laufenstrasse and Oberer Mühlenberg. There are **campsites** at Perlenau (☎0 24 72/6 36) and at Grünentalstr. 36 in the adjoining village of Imgenbroich (☎0 24 72/39 31).

The **cafés** and **restaurants** which crowd the town centre are mostly of high quality. Particularly outstanding are *Alte Herrlichkeit*, Stadtstr. 7, and *Remise*, Stadtstr. 14; the restaurant in the abovementioned *Hubertusklause* is also very fine. Try the products of the local Felsenkeller brewery; its speciality is *Monschauer Zwickelbier*, a dark, cloudy, bottom-fermented beer rich in vitamin B.

Bad Münstereifel

BAD MÜNSTEREIFEL, at the extreme eastern edge of the Eifel at the dead end of a branch rail line, is easiest reached from Bonn. For all its concealed position, deep in the valley of the River Erft, it's a place of considerable character, rivalling Monschau in quality; though not so homogeneous, nor so picturesquely sited, its monuments are more enjoyable. Prominent among these is the thirteenth- to fourteenth-century **Stadtmauer**, which survives intact. Straight ahead from the Bahnhof is the formidable northern gate, the **Werther Tor**; the corresponding position to the south is guarded by the **Orchheimer Tor**. To the east and west, the fortifications rise high into the hills, giving extra protection to the town huddled along the banks of the river. On the eastern side are the **Burg** (the only ruined feature) and the **Johannistor**; the western front now forms the boundary of the **Kurgarten** with its spa facilities, and is defended on its southern corner by the **Heisterbacher Tor**. You can walk freely along this stretch of rampart, which offers wonderful views over the town and the surrounding foothills of the Ahrgebirge (see pp.500–502). For a wholly different perspective, it's worth following the footpath round the walls.

Münstereifel (minster in the Eifel) derives its name from the fact that the town developed from a Benedictine monastery; this was founded in 830 and quickly became a popular place of pilgrimage through possession of the relics of the Roman martyrs Chrysanthus and Daria. The present **Stiftskirche** (named after the saints, whose graves are in the crypt) is a magnificently severe twelfth-century Romanesque church, which dominates the skyline of the lower town. Across the Kirchplatz is the striking red facade of the **Rathaus**, which began life in the mid-fourteenth century as a guild house. On Langenhecke to the rear of the church is the **Heimatmuseum** (Tues, Thurs & Fri 9am–noon, Wed 9am–noon & 2–4pm, Sat & Sun 1–4pm; DM2/€1). The building itself – once the home of a lay brother of the monastery – is more interesting than the local history displays inside. Dating back to 1167 and contemporary with the church, it's possibly the oldest intact house in Germany.

As well as these public buildings, Münstereifel offers one of the most satisfying townscapes in the region, enhanced by its rustic setting on the banks of the River Erft, which is never more than a stream; almost every street within the walls is worth exploring. Look out for the half-timbered mid-seventeenth-century **Haus Windeck** at Orchheimer Str. 23, the first floor of which is now a café. Also of interest is the seventeenth-century **Jesuitenkirche** facing the Markt, built in an anachronistic Gothic style.

Practicalities

Bad Münstereifel's **tourist office** is at Langenhecke 2 (Mon–Fri 9am–5pm, Sat 10am–noon & 2–4pm, Sun 10.30am–12.30pm; ☎0 22 53/50 51 82, fax 50 51 83, *www.bad -muenstereifel.de*). Private houses with **rooms** (①–③) to let can be found all over town – just look out for the *Zimmer frei* signs. Other reasonably priced options are a homely **guesthouse**, *Erftstiege*, Unnastr. 8–10 (☎0 22 53/89 00; ④), and a **hotel**, *Wolfsschlucht*, Orchheimer Str. 19 (☎0 22 53/9 20 30; ⑤); both serve excellent buffet breakfasts, while the latter has a good restaurant. There are also several spa hotels, including *Waldhotel Brezing*, Am Quecken 7–10 (☎0 22 53/95 30 30; ⑤), and *Amber Kurhotel*, Nöthener Str. 10 (☎0 22 53/5 40 00; ⑥). The **youth hostel** is high in the hills about 2km east of town at Herbergsweg 1–5 (☎0 22 53/74 38, fax 74 83; DM23/€11.50 or DM28/€14) just before the village of Rodert, while the **campsite** is to the south on the banks of the Erft (☎0 22 53/82 82). There are plenty of reasonably priced places to **eat** and **drink**, particularly along the main Wertherstrasse. Watch out for set menus, which are often tremendous bargains; this is particularly true of the *Burg-Restaurant* in the castle ruins. Among the cafés, the long-established *Café am Salzmarkt*, Orchheimer Str. 2, stands out.

Bonn

The name of **BONN** is indissolubly associated with the West German state, having served as its capital from the time the country was set up in 1949 until the unification of 1990, when Berlin was restored to its former role as Bundeshauptstadt (Federal Capital City). A year later, Bonn's tantalizingly narrow defeat in the bitter battle to retain its role as the main seat of government and parliament (see box on p.529) dealt an even more telling blow to the supreme self-confidence it had acquired. In some ways, this was no more than it deserved, as it was the most unlikely and unloved of European capitals: just "A Small Town in Germany" according to the title of John le Carré's spy thriller, or "The Federal Village" in the condescending eyes of the inhabitants of grander German cities. Yet Bonn subsequently confounded its critics by its stubborn refusal to lapse back into provinciality: in response to widespread fears about the dangers of Berlin becoming too dominant, it secured for itself, under the designation of Bundesstadt (Federal City), the status of a secondary governmental seat. Accordingly, seven federal ministries (including, significantly, defence and education), plus numerous other public bodies, will continue to have their headquarters there. Its official role aside, Bonn is a notable historic town, chiefly renowned, prior to its elevation as capital, as the birthplace of **Ludwig van Beethoven**.

Arrival, information and accommodation

The **Hauptbahnhof** lies plumb in the middle of the city, the central pedestrian area opening out immediately before it. To the right is the **bus station**, whose local services, along with the trams (which become the U-Bahn in the city centre), form part of a system integrated with that of Cologne. As the attractions are well spaced out, it's advisable to invest in one of the many runabout tickets on the **public transport** network. A 24-hour pass for the whole city costs DM9.60/€4.80; there's also a DM13.50/€6.75 mini-group ticket for up to five people travelling together as well as a three-day individual pass for DM24/€12. An enticing alternative to these is the **BonnCard**, which includes entrance to the city's museums. The one-day version of this is priced at DM24/€12 for individuals, DM32/€16 for families. Also shared with Cologne is the **airport**, which is linked with the city by bus #670 at least every thirty minutes. The **tourist office** (Mon–Fri 9am–6.30pm, Sat 9am–4pm, Sun 10am–2pm; ☎02 28/77 50 00, fax 77 50 77, *www.bonn.de*) is at Windeckstr. 9.

There are several good mid-range **places to stay** right in the centre of Bonn, but beware that the top hotels charge inflated rates. Those in Bad Godesberg tend to be better value and are far more enticing places to stay. The **youth hostel** is at Haager Weg 42 (☎02 28/28 99 70, fax 2 89 97 14, *JGH-Bonn@t-online.de*; DM39/€19.50) in the suburb of Venusberg, reached by bus #621. **Camping** is possible all year round at Im Frankenkeller 49 (☎02 28/34 49 49) in Mehlem, on the banks of the Rhine south of Bad Godesberg.

Hotels

Beethoven, Rheingasse 26 (☎02 28/63 14 11, fax 69 16 29). Modern hotel situated right by the Rhine; ask for a room with a view of the river. Also has a restaurant which serves bargain set lunches. ⑤.

Bergmann, Kasernenstr. 13 (☎02 28/63 38 91, fax 63 50 57). Small, good-value hotel just to the north of the Altstadt. ③.

Deutsches Haus, Kasernenstr. 19 (☎02 28/63 37 77, fax 65 90 55). A much larger and slightly more expensive alternative to its neighbour, *Bergmann*. Its restaurant is open weekday evenings only. ④.

Domicil, Thomas-Mann-Str. 24-26 (☎02 28/72 90 90, fax 69 12 07). Well-appointed designer hotel. ⑦–⑨.

Eden, Am Kurpark 5a, Bad Godesberg (☎02 28/95 72 70, fax 36 24 94). Classy hotel in the spa quarter. ⑥.

Godesburg, Auf dem Godesberg 5, Bad Godesberg (☎02 28/31 60 71, fax 31 12 18, *www .guennewig.de*). Modern hotel cunningly fitted into the ruins of the Burg, and commanding a great view over the Rhine and the Siebengebirge. It also has a fine restaurant (closed Sun evening and all day Mon). ⑥.

Mozart, Mozartstr. 1 (☎02 28/65 90 71, fax 65 90 75). On a quiet corner a few minutes' walk southwest of the Hauptbahnhof, this is among the best value in the centre. There's a Spanish restaurant, *Amadeo*, on the premises. ④–⑤.

Rheinhotel Dreesen, Rheinstr. 45–49, Bad Godesberg (☎02 28/8 20 20, fax 8 20 21 53, *www .rheinhoteldreesen.de*). This grandiose hotel with restaurant is set in its own park and offers wonderful views of the Rhine from its covered terrace. ⑧–⑨.

Savoy, Berliner Freiheit 17 (☎02 28/72 59 70, fax 69 68 99, *SavoyBonn@aol.com*). At the northern end of the city centre, this has large, spacious rooms. ⑤.

Schlosshotel Kommende, Oberkasseler Str. 10, Beuel (☎02 28/44 07 34, fax 44 44 00). In the district of Ramersdorf (reached by U-Bahn #62, #66 or #68), this occupies a neo-Gothic Schloss of the Teutonic Knights, with beautiful furniture and antiques. Also has a top-notch Italian restaurant. ⑥

Sternhotel, Markt 8 (☎02 28/7 26 70, fax 7 26 71 25, *www.sternhotel-bonn.de*). This fine old hotel has an ideal location in the heart of the Altstadt. ⑥–⑧.

Virneburg, Sandkaule 3a (☎02 28/63 63 66 or 65 61 65). Very basic Iraqi-run budget hotel. ②.

The City

Present-day Bonn is actually a federation of a host of formerly separate communities on both banks of the Rhine. The main attractions are far more spread out than in many much larger German cities, meaning that it isn't a place easily appreciated in a hurry.

The Altstadt

The small Altstadt is now predominantly a pedestrianized shopping area centred on two spacious squares. That to the east is named after the huge Romanesque **Münster**, whose central octagonal tower with its soaring spire is the city's most prominent landmark. Inside, it's airy and pleasing, the sensitive proportions reinforcing the feel of massive space. Below the chancel is a fine crypt, while there's an impressively severe and monumental **cloister** adjoining the southern side. The pink Rococo **Rathaus** adds a touch of colour to the other square, the Markt, which still hosts a market each weekday.

A couple of minutes' walk north of here, at Bonngasse 20, is the **Beethoven-Haus** (Mon–Sat 10am–5/6pm, Sun 11am–4pm; DM8/€4). This is one of the few old buildings in the centre to have escaped wartime devastation, and together with the more imposing house next door it contains an unfussy and intelligently presented museum dedicated to the great composer. Beethoven served his musical apprenticeship at the electoral court of his home town, but left it for good at the age of 22, though this has not deterred Bonn from zealously building up the best collection of memorabilia of its favourite son. There's a bunch of uncomfortable portraits of the tormented genius (who

---

LUDWIG VAN BEETHOVEN (1770–1827)

No composer has ever made a greater impact on the history of music than **Ludwig van Beethoven**. The successor to the Viennese classical tradition of Haydn and Mozart, he developed the three great forms of the period – the symphony, the string quartet and the piano sonata – to their ultimate limits. His work reflects his libertarian concerns and shows for the first time the ability of music to convey a humanitarian message without the aid of text, thus setting the scene for the Romantic composers of the next hundred years. From 1800, Beethoven had problems with his hearing, an affliction which was partly responsible for the transformations he wrought in orchestral sound; the menacing power of some of his symphonies was so different from anything previously composed that many contemporaries were – literally – physically scared of them. By the time he finished his *Ninth Symphony*, in which instrumental and choral music were woven into one for the very first time, he had become completely deaf, yet he continued to compose, notably five valedictory string quartets of awesome emotional intensity.

was a reluctant sitter), along with manuscripts and correspondence. The three instruments with which he was associated as a professional performer are shown in the form of the console of the destroyed organ on which he played as a youth, his last piano and his viola. Most poignant of all are the ear-trumpets which a friend made specially in order to combat his advancing deafness.

The Altstadt's second dominant building is the Baroque **Schloss**, an enormously long construction which was formerly the seat of the archbishop-electors of Cologne and is now used by the university. To the south, the Schloss is bounded by the open spaces of the Hofgarten, at whose far end is the **Akademisches Kunstmuseum** (Mon–Wed, Fri & Sun 10am–1pm, Thurs 10am–1pm & 4–6pm; DM1/€0.50), housed in a Neoclassical pavilion designed by Schinkel. This has an eerie collection of casts of famous antique sculptures, originally made for the benefit of art students.

The Rheinisches Landesmuseum

Despite the advent of a brand-new museum quarter, the pick of Bonn's collections is still the **Rheinisches Landesmuseum** (previously Tues, Thurs & Fri 9am–5pm, Wed 9am–8pm, Sat & Sun 10am–5pm; DM4/€2, but likely to be closed for reconstruction work until 2002) at Colmantstr. 14–16, behind the Hauptbahnhof. Star exhibit is the **skull of Neanderthal Man**, found in a valley near Düsseldorf (see p.568), and calculated to be some 60,000 years old. Highlights of the important Roman department are the tomb of Marcus Caelius, a set of arcades from Aachen and a mosaic dedicated to the sun. The medieval section includes the anguished sculpture known as the *Roettgen Pietà* and some lovely examples of the fifteenth-century Cologne School of painters, notably the delicate *Deposition* and *St Sebastian* by an anonymous artist who has been named **Master of the Bonn Diptych** as a result, and five panels by the painter known as **Master of the St Ursula Legend** after the dispersed series from which these came. Among later German paintings, a rare work by **Elsheimer**, *The Three Marys at the Sepulchre*, stands out. As long as restoration work is ongoing, many of the exhibits will be on view in other museums in the Rhineland, notably the Schnütgen-Museum in Cologne (see p.546).

Poppelsdorf and Kreuzberg

Also branching out from the Schloss is the kilometre-long avenue of chestnut trees which leads to **Poppelsdorf**, now a suburb of the city, where the Frenchman **Robert de Cotte**, who had undertaken modifications to the Schloss, was commissioned to build a second electoral residence. The resulting **Schloss Poppelsdorf** follows an ingenious trompe l'oeil design, its circular courtyard concealed within a rectangular ground plan. Again, the palace is now occupied by university departments, the grounds serving as the **Botanischer Garten** (April–Sept Mon–Fri 9am–6pm, Sun 9am–1pm; Oct–March Mon–Fri 9am–4pm; free). For a sociological as well as architectural stroll, wander in the **Südstadt**, the streets immediately to the east, such as Schloss-Strasse, Kurfürstenstrasse, Argelanderstrasse and Bismarckstrasse. These represent a remarkably complete picture of late nineteenth- and early twentieth-century town planning for the better-off sections of the middle classes.

To the other side of Schloss Poppelsdorf at Sebastianstr. 182 is the **Robert-Schumann-Haus** (Mon & Fri 10am–noon & 4–7pm, Wed & Thurs 10am–noon & 3–7pm; free), containing a collection of memorabilia of the Romantic composer. In spite of a blissful marriage to the pianist Clara Wieck, who inspired so many of his yearning, passionate song settings and virtuoso piano pieces, Schumann had a history of psychological instability, culminating in a complete mental breakdown and attempted suicide when he threw himself into the Rhine. At his own request, he spent the last two years of his life in Bonn confined to the sanatorium adjoining his house.

Continuing south from Poppelsdorf, a road leads uphill to the isolated pilgrimage church of **Kreuzberg**. The original seventeenth-century chapel was given the full

Rococo treatment a hundred years later, including the addition of the Holy Steps, an imitation in the lavishly ornate style of Balthasar Neumann of those now in Rome on which Christ allegedly ascended to receive Pilate's judgement.

The Regierungsviertel

Bonn's **Regierungsviertel** (government quarter) can be reached either by following Reuterstrasse from Poppelsdorf, or by taking Adenauerallee from the Hofgarten: the distance is about the same. Saddled with its "temporary status", it was not custom-built, but utilized a series of existing structures. Ironically enough, work had just started on new buildings when the sudden fall of Communism in East Germany in 1989 shook the city out of its complacent assumption that it was going to be a long-term capital.

Both the **Villa Hammerschmidt** and the **Palais Schaumburg** are pompous Empire buildings from the nineteenth century, once private dwellings of the mega-rich and later the official residences of the Federal President and Chancellor respectively. Further south, the **Bundeshaus** complex is in the Bauhaus style of the 1930s. More enticing than the buildings is the wonderful **view** over the Rhine and the Siebengebirge on the opposite bank.

Planned as a fitting cultural accompaniment to the government quarter at a time when Bonn seemed set for an indefinite stint at the heart of German political life, the **Museumsmeile** (Museum Mile) on its western edge only came to fruition after national unification had been achieved, by which time it already seemed an anachronism. Of the four institutions along its route, only the **Alexander-Koenig-Museum** (previously Tues–Fri 9am–5pm, Sat 9am–12.30pm, Sun 9.30am–5pm, but closed until 2002 for repairs; *www.uni-bonn.de/museumkoenig*; DM4/€2) at Adenauerallee 160 existed prior to 1992. One of the best natural history collections in the country, its displays are laid

---

THE STRUGGLES TO BECOME CAPITAL

When Germany was finally unified through Prussian military might in 1871, **Berlin** became the first official and undisputed capital the country had ever had. The partition of Berlin after World War II meant that the city could no longer fulfil its role, though the eastern sector became the official capital of the GDR. Meanwhile **Bonn** – hitherto a provincial university town – was chosen as capital of the West German state. In a sense, this was a deliberately crass choice in line with the "provisional" nature of the new country (see "The Historical Framework" in *Contexts*). Konrad Adenauer, the first Chancellor, lived nearby and championed its cause as a matter of personal convenience, forming an unholy alliance with West Berlin representatives, who were desperate to thwart the claims of **Frankfurt** (the only other city considered for the role), astutely realizing that the latter might be powerful enough to deny Berlin's reinstatement as capital.

For all the swiftness of the unification process when it finally happened, four decades of national partition had made the name of Bonn virtually synonymous with that of the new, responsible face of Germany. Thus, although Berlin was confirmed as capital in 1990, Bonn fought to remain the seat of government. The campaign was vitriolic: the Bonn lobby contrasted its proven record at the heart of a prosperous, democratic and peace-loving country with Berlin's tainted history as the successive headquarters of a militaristic absolute monarchy, then Nazi and Communist totalitarian dictatorships; the huge costs of making the move were also cited, as was the fact that, now that the Eastern Territories were accepted as lost forever, Berlin's geographical position was no longer sufficiently central. In retaliation, Berlin's supporters rubbished Bonn as a backwater inappropriately sited for the great challenge of rebuilding the shattered economy and society of eastern Germany. Chancellor Helmut Kohl, like Adenauer a native of the Rhineland, surprisingly endorsed Berlin, which in June 1991 won a narrow majority in the deciding parliamentary vote.

out on four floors with a true Germanic thoroughness. Next in line, at no. 250 on the same boulevard, is the **Haus der Geschichte der Bundesrepublik Deutschland** (Tues–Sun 9am–7pm; *www.hdg.de*; free), which traces the political, cultural, social and economic history of the Federal Republic. To non-Germans, its emphases might seem ephemeral, though the presentations are greatly enlivened by the extensive use of archive film, including John F. Kennedy's famous "Ich bin ein Berliner" speech.

At the head of Friedrich-Ebert-Allee, the continuation of Adenauerallee, is the **Kunstmuseum** (Tues & Thurs–Sun 10am–6pm, Wed 10am–9pm; DM5/€2.50), which contains the municipal gallery of modern art. Its main strength lies in its representation of the Expressionists, and in particular the brilliant **August Macke**, who spent part of his brief life in the city. The upper floor is devoted to the avant-garde, notably Joseph Beuys, Sigmar Polke and Anselm Kiefer. To the rear is the most attention-seeking of the three new museums, the **Kunst- und Ausstellungshalle der Bundesrepublik Deutschland** (Tues & Wed 10am–9pm, Thurs–Sun 10am–7pm; *www.kah-bonn.de*; variable charges), a space-age arts centre which can host up to five temporary exhibitions at one time. Already it has staged several blockbuster shows, including an ongoing series of loans from the great museums of the world, though the emphasis is firmly on diverse aspects of modern artistic creativity.

Bad Godesberg

When Bonn was officially expanded in 1969, it gobbled up a string of small villages, giving it a foothold on the eastern bank of the Rhine for the first time. It also annexed the old spa town of **BAD GODESBERG** (reached by U-Bahn #16 or #63, or main-line train) to the south, stretching its boundaries to the Land border. Bad Godesberg's character had already made it a favoured location for many of the diplomatic missions, who found its grandiose Empire-style villas just the sort of headquarters they were looking for. The town is also a famed conference centre, and has hosted at least two fateful events: the series of meetings between Chamberlain and Hitler in 1938, which paved the way for the Munich Agreement by which "peace in our time" was bought at Czechoslovakia's expense; and the 1959 conference of the Social Democrats, when the party, bidding to end a period of three decades in opposition, disavowed its earlier connections with Marxism, class warfare and anticlericalism, and became part of the post-war consensus rooted in acceptance of the idea of a "social market economy".

Rearing high over the town is the **Godesburg**, the most northerly of the great series of castles crowning promontories above the Rhine, built in the thirteenth and fourteenth centuries by the archbishops of Cologne and blown up in 1583. Today it's chiefly a hotel (see p.526), but the cylindrical **keep** is still intact and can be ascended (April–Oct Wed–Sun 10am–6pm; DM1/€0.50) for a panoramic **view**, including a distant glimpse of Cologne and the Siebengebirge. Views, indeed, are Bad Godesberg's major attraction; you'll find plenty more if you saunter down the **Rheinufer**, the promenade along the river bank. Otherwise, there are two spa parks in the town centre, separated by fashionable buildings, prominent among which is the late eighteenth-century **Redoute**, formerly the ballroom of the electors, now a prestigious function suite.

Schwarzrheindorf

The only one of Bonn's outer villages worth making a special detour to see is **SCHWARZRHEINDORF**, on the right bank of the Rhine to the extreme north, reached by bus #550 or #640. It boasts a relatively little-known but outstanding monument in the **Doppelkirche**, a former manorial church. Built in the mid-twelfth century, this offers an intriguing insight into the social and religious preoccupations of the medieval world. The exterior cleverly disguises the fact that it encases two separate chapels, the upper reserved for the lord, the lower for the use of the labourers. Apart from its architectural idiosyncrasies, the church has rare Romanesque **fresco** cycles. Turning on the light by the door reveals *The Vision of Ezekiel*, *The Transfiguration* and *The Crucifixion*, while upstairs the great visions of *The Apocalypse* were painted for their lordships' contemplation.

Eating, drinking and nightlife

Bonn has a fairly eclectic range of places to eat, its diplomatic status reflected in an unusually wide choice of **ethnic restaurants**. Most of the best bars are conveniently located in the Altstadt and the Südstadt.

Restaurants

Cassius Garten, Maximilianstr. 28d. Offers a mouth-watering choice of vegetarian food, which you pay for by weight. Closed Sun.

Don Quijote, Oxfordstr. 18. The most convenient of a surprising number of Spanish restaurants in the city. Evenings only.

Em Höttche, Markt 4. Good traditional Gaststätte which, in a previous incarnation, was patronized by the young Beethoven.

Grand' Italia, Bischofsplatz 1. The best of the city's many Italian restaurants.

Im Bären, Acherstr. 1–3. Excellent Gaststätte owned by the local Kurfürsten brewery.

Le Petit Poisson, Wilhelmstr. 23a. Expensive but very highly rated French restaurant. Evenings only, closed Sun & Mon.

Philoxenia, Clemens-August-Str. 34. One of Germany's few specifically Cypriot restaurants; also features dishes from other Mediterranean countries.

Redüttchen, Kurfürstenallee 1, Bad Godesberg. *Gemütlich* little restaurant in the former gardener's house beside the Redoute.

Salvator, In der Sürst 5–7. A Bavarian-style beer hall-restaurant, operated by Munich's Paulaner brewery.

Stadthalle, Koblenzer Str. 80, Bad Godesberg. Traditional German food at reasonable prices in the eastern of the two spa parks.

Weinhaus Jacobs, Friedrichstr. 18. Evenings-only wine bar-restaurant, which has been on the go since 1845. It offers a good choice of vintages from all over Germany.

Zur Lindenwirtin Aennchen, Aennchenplatz 2, Bad Godesberg. Historic student tavern with garden terrace, restored as an upmarket restaurant.

Bars and cafés

Aktuell, Gerhard-von-Are-Str. 8. Best known as the favoured haunt of journalists, a profession represented in Bonn in force. On Sun, it's only open in the evening.

Bla, Bornheimer Str. 20. A garishly decorated meeting-place of punk diehards.

Brauhaus Bönnsch, Sterntorbrücke 4. Hausbrauerei producing a distinctive blond ale known as *Bönnsch*, which is served in a curious horn-shaped glass. Also does good-value meals.

Jazz-Galerie, Oxfordstr. 24. Features live jazz sessions most evenings and a weekly jam session.

Kleimann, Rheingasse 16–18. Excellent traditional café. Closed Mon.

Namenlos, Bornheimer Str. 20. A less outlandish counterpart to the adjoining *Bla*, with minimalist decor.

StilArt, Friedensplatz 12. Exquisitely furnished café attached to a crafts shop. Closed Sun.

Südstadt-Kneipe, Königstr. 9. Laid-back pub reflecting the civilized air of the Südstadt area. Offers a selection of reasonably priced cocktails and food to a background of good music.

Zebulon, Stockenstr. 19. A big favourite with arts students, particularly for breakfast.

Zur Kerze, Königstr. 25. Subtitled *Künstlerkeller* (Artists' Cellar), this popular bar is open daily 7pm–5am. Bristling with alcoves and partitions, it's frequented by a mixed age range, and serves excellent (if fairly pricey) Italianate dishes.

Entertainment

Although not a national leader in any cultural field, Bonn offers a broad range of entertainment, with classical music – and in particular peformances of works by Beethoven – featuring strongly. The monthly *De Schnüss* (DM3.90/€1.95), available from newsagents, gives full listings of what's on.

Beethovenhalle, Wachsbleiche 26 (☎02 28/7 22 20, *www.beethovenhalle.de*). Bonn's principal concert hall, regularly featuring its own house orchestra, the Orchester der Beethovenhalle.

Biskuit-Halle, Wesselwerke (☎02 28/2 57 12 15). The main venue for visiting live bands.

Brotfabrik, Kreuzstr. 16, Beuel (☎02 28/42 13 10). Alternative arts centre which features theatre, exhibitions, cinema, readings and feminist events.

Euro Theater, Mauspfad (☎02 28/65 29 51). Small and intimate dramatic stage.

Haus der Springmaus, Frangasse 8 (☎02 28/79 80 81). The city's main cabaret venue.

Kammermusiksaal, Bonngasse 24–26 (☎02 28/77 80 00). This small hall adjoining the Beethoven-Haus is used for chamber, instrumental and vocal recitals.

Oper, Am Boeslagerhof 1 (☎02 28/9 81 75 15). Hosts not only opera, but also dance and drama.

Pantheon, Am Bundeskanzlerplatz (☎02 28/21 25 40). Cultural centre in the Regierungsviertel; it's best known for its satirical shows and also has weekend discos.

Listings

Airport ☎02 28/4 04 00 12 for flight information.

Bookstores There's a wide selection in and around Am Hof (behind the Schloss).

Embassies and consulates Britain, Argelanderstr. 108a (☎02 28/9 16 70); Canada, Friedrich-Wilhelm-Str. 18 (☎02 28/96 80); Ireland, Godesberger Allee 119, Bad Godesberg (☎02 28/95 92 90); US, Deichmanns Aue 29, Bad Godesberg (☎02 28/33 91).

Festivals Every year there's an international Beethoven festival in September. The main folklore event is the *Pützchensmarkt*, a colourful fair held annually on the first weekend of the same month in Beuel.

Markets Daily on the Markt; every third Sat of the month, there's a flea market on Rheinaue.

Mitfahrzentrale Herwarthstr. 11a (☎02 28/69 30 30).

Post office The main post office is at Münsterplatz 17 with a poste restante service.

Rhine cruises These depart from Brassentufer just south of Kennedybrücke: K-D Linie (☎02 28/63 21 34); Bonner Personenschiffahrt (☎02 28/63 63 63).

The Siebengebirge

The **Siebengebirge** (Seven Mountains), on the eastern bank of the Rhine just before the Land boundary with Rhineland-Palatinate, rank among the river's most suggestively grand stretches, steeped in the lore of legend and literature. According to one story, the mountains were created by seven giants clearing the dirt from their shovels. They're also often regarded as the site of the most famous of the Grimms' fairy-tales, *Snow White and the Seven Dwarfs*.

Despite the name, there are around thirty summits in this extinct volcanic range, which stretches for about 15km north to south and 5km east to west. From Bonn, six of the main peaks can be seen; the number seven, with its traditional mystical significance, applies only to those visible from a point further north. Of the group, **Drachenfels** (321m), **Wolkenburg** (325m) and **Lohrberg** (435m) are all of a mineral called trachyte; **Petersberg** (331m), **Nonnenstromberg** (336m) and **Grosser Ölberg** (461m) are of basalt, a later formation; while **Löwenburg** (455m) is of dolerite. For centuries, stone from these mountains was quarried to construct the great buildings of the Rhineland, notably the Dom in Cologne; this quarrying was brought to an end in 1889, when the whole area was designated as the first protected landscape in Germany. The

Siebengebirge are covered with thick woods, which means that views are very restricted most of the time, though all the more spectacular when you do reach a belvedere. This wasn't always so; old prints show the upper parts of the peaks free of trees, and generally crowned with a fortress.

Königswinter

Although the Siebengebirge make an easy day-outing from Bonn, to which they're connected by U-Bahn #66, the best bases for exploring them are the two holiday resorts which lie directly below them. The northerly one of the pair, **KÖNIGSWINTER**, has a relaxed, rather dated air. It offers a wide variety of **hotels**, ranging from moderately priced establishments such as *Wenzel*, Hauptstr. 457 (☎0 22 23/2 18 61; ③–⑤), and *Siebengebirge*, Hauptstr. 342 (☎0 22 23/2 13 59; ④–⑥), via the middle-bracket *Jesuiter Hof*, Hauptstr. 458 (☎0 22 23/2 26 50; ⑤), and *Rheinhotel Loreley*, Rheinallee 12 (☎0 22 23/92 50, *www.euro-hotel.de/rheinhotel-loreley.koenigswinter.de*; ⑥), to the top-of-the-range *Maritim*, Rheinallee 3 (☎0 22 23/70 70, *www.maritim.de*; ⑧–⑨). The last of these has the best and most expensive **restaurant** in town. There are also several enticing old Weinhäuser: one is the abovementioned *Jesuiter Hof*, which serves wines from its own estate; another is *Altes Fährhaus*, Rheinallee 4.

Königswinter's mainline **Bahnhof** lies at the northern end of town; the U-Bahn runs along the waterfront. The **tourist office** (Mon 10am–5pm, Tues–Fri 9am–5pm, Sat 10am–1pm; ☎0 22 23/91 77 11, fax 91 77 20, *www.koenigswinter.de*) is at Drachenfelsstr. 11. It's worth trying to time your visit to coincide with one of the numerous **festivals**, the most spectacular of which is *Der Rhein in Flammen*, a display of fireworks and illuminations held on the first Saturday in May; a week later, the cutting of the first crop of asparagus is celebrated. The main wine festival, the *Winzerfest*, takes place on the first weekend in October.

Bad Honnef

U-Bahn #66 containues down the Rhine to its terminus at **BAD HONNEF**. As befits a spa, this is somewhat more upmarket than its neighbour, and was the chosen residence of **Konrad Adenauer**, the first Chancellor of the Federal Republic. Its one setpiece attraction is his home at no. 8c in the street named after him in the northern suburb of Rhöndorf; this is now designated the **Stiftung Bundeskanzler-Adenauer-Haus** (guided tours Tues–Sun 10am–4.30pm; free), and contains material documenting his political achievements.

The mainline **Bahnhof** is just south of the U-Bahn terminus, while the **tourist office** (Easter–Oct Mon 10am–noon & 12.30–3.30pm, Tues–Thurs 8.30am–noon &

KONRAD ADENAUER (1876–1967)

A local government stalwart of the Catholic Centre Party during the Weimar Republic, **Konrad Adenauer** seemed to be merely a stop-gap leader when he finally entered the national stage at the age of 73. In the event, his impeccable record as an anti-Nazi (he had been deposed as mayor of Cologne) and his moderate right-wing politics happened to be exactly in tune with the country's mood in the postwar period, and he remained in power for fourteen years, only retiring when his coalition partners made this a condition of their continued support. Adenauer's high reputation rests on his twin achievements of the "Economic Miracle" and the international rehabilitation of Germany, though there's little doubt that his inflexible attitude towards the Russians was a contributory factor in cementing the division of the nation into two hostile states.

12.30–3.30pm, Fri 8.30am–1pm, Sat 9am–noon; Nov–Easter Mon–Fri only; ☎0 22 24/90 06 36, fax 7 96 87, *www.bad-honnef.de*) is at Hauptstr. 30. The town's **hotels** include *Bergischer Hof*, Hauptstr. 120 (☎0 22 24/21 35; ⑤), *Markt 3*, Am Markt 3 (☎0 22 24/9 33 20; ⑥), and *avendi*, Hauptstr. 22 (☎0 22 24/18 90, *www.avendi.de*; ⑦); the last two of these each has a top-notch **restaurant**. There's a **youth hostel** at Selhofer Str. 106 (☎0 22 24/7 13 00; DM22.50/€11.25 or DM27.50/€13.75) at the very southern end of town. Bad Honnef's *Weinfest* is held on the first weekend in September.

The mountains

Although the lowest of the mountains, **Drachenfels**, situated immediately behind Königswinter, is by far the most interesting, unfortunately it's also the most-climbed mountain in Europe, heavily tourist-oriented and even more heavily exploited. The Drachenfelsbahn, a **rack rail** line built in 1883 using a system pioneered in Switzerland, is an ingenious piece of engineering, rising 220 metres over a total length of 1.5km. However, the fare (DM11/€5.50 single, DM14/€7 return) is a bit of a rip-off, the more so as the footpath is paved and makes for a steep but easy ascent. About a third of the way up is the **Nibelungenhalle** (mid-March to mid-Nov daily 9am–6/7pm; rest of year Sat & Sun 11am–4pm; DM6/€3), a Jugendstil temple of honour to Richard Wagner, built in 1913 to commemorate the centenary of his birth. Along the walls of the interior of the rotunda is a cycle of twelve large Symbolist paintings illustrating scenes from *The Ring* by the academic artist Hermann Hendrich. The same ticket gives admission to the adjacent **Drachenhöhle**, which contains a thirteen-metre-long stone sculpture of the fearsome monster supposedly slain there by the hero Siegfried. By immediately immersing himself in its warm blood he gained a horny skin which would have rendered him invincible had a falling leaf not left a spot as vulnerable as Achilles' heel. From this legend comes the name of the wine, *Drachenblut* (dragon's blood), made from the grapes cultivated on these slopes, the most northerly vineyard in western Germany. Alongside the cave, and likewise included in the entrance fee, is a small zoo of live reptiles.

A short distance uphill is **Schloss Drachenburg** (guided tours April–Oct Tues–Sun 11am–6pm; DM4/€2, or DM1/€0.50 for entrance to the park only), which is a good example of the nineteenth-century German love of macabre Gothic fantasy. From the terrace there's a really spectacular **view**, though there's an even wider panorama from the Romanesque **Burg**, a ruin since the Thirty Years War, at the summit of the mountain. Apart from being able to trace the Rhine's path both upstream and down, you can see over the Eifel to the west, and get a different perspective on the Siebengebirge themselves; on an even half-decent day, the spires of Cologne can also be distinguished.

A series of well-marked hiking trails enables you to choose your own route round the rest of the range. **Petersberg** is probably the best known; its summit is occupied by a grandiose luxury hotel (☎0 22 33/7 40, *www.gaestehaus-petersberg.com*; ⑨), which was Chamberlain's base for his ill-fated talks with Hitler in Bad Godesberg. **Löwenburg** is allegedly haunted by a wild huntsman, doomed to an eternal chase as punishment for his cruelty when alive. **Grosser Ölberg** is the most enticing after Drachenfels, commanding the next best views. Although furthest from the Rhine of all the peaks, it has the advantage of being the highest, and of including panoramas over the Taunus to the east.

Kloster Heisterbach

From Grosser Ölberg, it's only a short descent to the area's sole great monument, the ruins of the early thirteenth-century Cistercian **Kloster Heisterbach**, which can also be reached by bus #520 or #521 from Königswinter. Like so many of this order's foundations, it was built in the Transitional style between Romanesque and Gothic. One of the first priors, Caesarius, was a chronicler of legends, which he collected in the *Dialogus Miraculorum*. The most famous of these – which was retold by Henry Longfellow – concerns a monk who, while out for his daily walk, was meditating disbelievingly on the text of Psalm 90, "a thousand years in thy sight are but as yesterday", on returning for vespers, he found that a whole century had elapsed since his departure. Heisterbach was pulled down at the beginning of the nineteenth century following the Napoleonic suppression, but the apse and its ambulatory were spared when the explosives failed to ignite. This tiny fragment had an impact on the Romantic imagination out of all proportion to its size; depictions of lonely, overgrown and crumbling abbeys set in wooded valleys, often illuminated by moonlight, became one of the favourite subjects of the movement's painters. Nowadays, the eighteenth-century monastic buildings are occupied by a convent of Augustinian nuns, who have built a modern church. They also run a café-restaurant, specializing in a huge choice of irresistible home-made gateaux.

Brühl

Midway between Bonn and Cologne, set inland from the Rhine, lies **BRÜHL**, a town which developed from a castle founded by the archbishop-electors in the thirteenth century. The eighteenth-century successor to this is the most sumptuous palace in the Rhineland, seemingly a little piece of Bavaria wafted mysteriously northwards. It makes the town one of the most interesting in the province, but the real reason two million people swarm here each summer is the hugely successful **Phantasialand** theme park.

The Town

From an aesthetic point of view, the most notable part of Brühl is the huge park with two palaces – both on the UNESCO World Heritage list – stretching southeast of the pedestrianized town centre. Phantasialand is at the southern fringe of Brühl, by the junction of the main roads to Trier and Aachen.

Schloss Augustusburg

In its own day Brühl's heart and soul, **Schloss Augustusburg** (guided tours Feb–Nov Tues–Sun 9am–noon & 1.30–4pm; DM6/€3) must have seemed as much of an extravaganza as Phantasialand does now. It's very much a personal creation of the eighteenth-century Archbishop-Elector **Clemens August**, a member of the Bavarian Wittelsbach dynasty. From an early age, he had been earmarked for an ecclesiastical career in order to advance the family's power base. In this, he was brilliantly successful, gaining no fewer than four prince-bishoprics in addition to the Cologne Electorate, and also becoming Grand Master of the Teutonic Knights. However, he showed no piety whatsoever, living a life of unashamedly pampered luxury and gaining a reputation as a womanizer – he was summoned to Rome by the pope to explain the presence of two particularly beautiful singers at his court, and his death came after he had danced the night away rather too energetically. He favoured Brühl as the seat of his court because of its ideal situation for his favourite hobby, falconry, and was determined to rebuild the medieval moated castle which had been destroyed by French troops in 1689.

Initially the design was in dignified Baroque by Johann Conrad Schlaun: building was later entrusted to **François Cuvilliés**, who eliminated all features reminiscent of a fortress and transformed the complex into a pleasure palace. As the final *pièce de résistance*, the greatest architect of the day, **Balthasar Neumann**, was recruited to draw up plans for the ceremonial **staircase** – a fricassee of marble and stucco, crowned by a fresco by Carlo Carlone glorifying the Virtues. The decorative scheme of this and the following **Wachenhalle** (Hall of Guards) and **Musikzimmer** (Music Room), which are almost equally sumptuous, is a complicated series of allegories in honour of the Wittelsbach dynasty. Facing the Schloss are the **Schlossgarten** and the **Jardin Secret**, two splendid French-style formal gardens seen at their best in the full bloom of summer.

The rest of the town centre

Adjoining the west front of the Schloss is the **Orangerie**; now housing a café-restaurant and an exhibition room, it forms a processional way to **St Maria zu den Engeln**. This was originally a Franciscan friary church, built in the simplest form of Gothic, but its interior was greatly pepped up for its new function as court chapel by the insertion of a lavish **high altar** – taking up the entire chancel – designed by Neumann. **Max Ernst**, the Dadaist and Surrealist painter, was born in Brühl, a fact commemorated by the **Max-Ernst-Kabinett** (Mon–Thurs 10am–5pm, Sun 2–5pm; DM4/€2) housed in his birthplace, a villa facing the northern wing of the Schloss at Bahnhofstr. 21. It has a few early oil paintings, but the bulk of the material is graphic work, displayed in a changing series of exhibitions.

Walking 2km east through the Schloss grounds takes you to the **Jagdschloss Falkenlust** (Feb–Nov Tues–Sun 9am–12.30pm & 1.30–4pm; DM4.50/€2.25), Clemens August's base for his falconry adventures, designed once again by Cuvilliés. It's intimate in scale, and this time you're allowed to explore it at your leisure. In the oval main Salon is a series of portraits of the Wittelsbachs in their hunting attire, but the most impressive rooms are the smallest – the **Lacquerkabinett**, reflecting the contemporary taste for chinoiserie, and the **Spiegelkabinett** directly above. Outside is the tiny **Kapelle**, a folly in imitation of a hermitage.

Phantasialand

Phantasialand (April–Oct daily 9am–6pm; *www.phantasialand.de*; adults DM38/€19, or DM56/€28 for a ticket valid on two consecutive days, children under 1.20m free) was the first amusement park in Europe to rival Disneyland in the States and a clear example of how strong the transatlantic influence had become in Germany. Laid out on the site of an open-cast mine at the extreme southern end of town, it can be reached by regular **bus** services from Brühl's Bahnhof. Attractions range from re-creations of prewar Berlin, a Wild West town and China of a thousand years ago, through rides on a Viking ship, an overhead monorail, the world's largest roller-coaster and a mock-up of outer space. Be warned that even the park's owners admit that there are uncomfortably large numbers of visitors on Sundays and throughout July and August.

Practicalities

Brühl's **Bahnhof** lies on the opposite side of the Schloss from the town centre. The **tourist office** (May–Oct Mon–Fri 9am–7pm, Sat 9am–4pm, Sun 1–5pm; Nov–April Mon–Fri 9am–7pm, Sat 9am–1pm; ☎0 22 32/7 93 45, fax 7 93 46, *www.bruehl.de*), at Uhlstr. 3, has a good list of private houses with **rooms** to let (②–③). Alternatively, there are a fair number of **hotels**: these include *Rheinischer Hof*, Euskirchner Str. 123 (☎0 22 32/3 4791; ④), *Mühlenhof*, Mühlenstr. 71 (☎0 22 32/41 98 03; ④), *Brühler Hof*, Uhlstr. 30 (☎0 22 32/4 27 11; ⑥), and *Treff Hansa*, Römerstr. 1 (☎0 22 32/20 40; ⑧). Places to **eat** include *Brühler Schlosskeller*, Kölnstr. 74, and the aforementioned *Orangerie*, Schloss-Str. 6, which functions as a café in the afternoon and a restaurant in the evening. **Concerts** by top international musicians in the Schloss are the main cultural attraction, while October sees a **festival** of international puppet theatre.

COLOGNE (KÖLN)

Although now in the political shadow of the neighbouring upstarts of Bonn and Düsseldorf, **COLOGNE** stands as a colossus in the vast urban sprawl of the Rhine-Ruhr conurbation, and is currently Germany's fourth largest city, with a population which crept over the million mark in the 1990s. The huge Gothic **Dom** is the country's most visited monument, while its assemblage of Roman remains and medieval buildings is unsurpassed and the museums bettered only by those in Berlin, Dresden and Munich. Cologne also ranks high as a **beer** centre: there are some two dozen breweries (more than in any other city in the world), all producing the distinctive *Kölsch*. Also of special note is one of Europe's most important popular celebrations, the annual **Carnival** in early spring.

Originally founded in 33 BC, Cologne quickly gained importance. It was the birthplace of Julia Agrippa, wife of Emperor Claudius, who in 50 AD raised it to the status of a colony (hence its name) with full rights as a **Roman city**. Subsequent development owed much to ecclesiastical affairs – a bishopric was founded in the fourth century and SS Severin, Gereon and Ursula were all martyred in the city; churches were soon dedicated to each and built over their graves. The **cult of St Ursula** was especially popular, being associated with the alleged death of her 11,000 virgin companions (the true figure was probably a more realistic eleven). In the twelfth century, Cologne forcibly acquired the relics of the Three Magi from Milan, thus increasing its standing as one of the greatest centres of **pilgrimage** in northern Europe.

Medieval Cologne, a Free Imperial City with 150 churches, became enormously prosperous because of its strategic situation on the Rhine at the intersection of trade routes. The largest city in Germany, it was one of the great European centres of learning and boasted a distinctive school of painters. Decline inevitably set in, but something of a comeback was made in the eighteenth century with a recipe imported from Italy, which involved distilling flower blossoms in almost pure alcohol. Although originally meant as an aphrodisiac, this was to achieve worldwide fame as a toilet water under the euphemism by which customers ordered it – water from Cologne, or *eau de Cologne*.

The modern city has reclaimed its old role as a major trade and business centre, and has also become Germany's radio and television metropolis. As a welcome contrast to the class-consciousness and frantic status-seeking of its neighbours, it has an openness about it similar to that of the city-states of Hamburg and Bremen. To this is added a general atmosphere of fun and irreverence more characteristic of the Mediterranean than Germany.

Arrival, information and accommodation

The **Hauptbahnhof** is right in the centre of the city, immediately below the Dom. Moving on is never a problem as some thousand trains per day stop here. The **bus station** is directly beside the rear exit. Cologne's **airport** is served by bus #170; there are departures approximately every twenty minutes, with a journey time of less than half an hour.

The **tourist office** is at Unter Fettenhennen 19, directly in front of the Dom (May–Oct Mon–Sat 8am–10.30pm, Sun & holidays 9am–10.30pm; Nov–April Mon–Sat 8am–9pm, Sun & holidays 9.30am–7pm; ☎02 21/1 94 33 or 22 13 33 45, fax 22 12 33 20, *www.koeln.de*). This is also a good place to try for a **hotel room**; a booking fee of DM5/€2.50 is charged, but last-minute deals at huge savings over normal prices are often available.

ACCOMMODATION

19 Altstadt
8 Antik-Hotel Bristol
5 Berg
6 Brandenburger Hof
9 Cristall
17 Das Kleine Stapelhäuschen
3 DomBlick

13 Dom-Hotel
14 Eden
12 Excelsior Hotel Ernst
10 Im Kupferkessel
20 Im Wasserturm
1 Jugendgästehaus Riehl
15 Jugendherberge Deutz

16 Lint
7 Madison am Dom
18 Rhein-Hotel St Martin
4 Rossner
11 Station Backpackers Hostel
2 Viktoria

COLOGNE

Cologne's **public transport** network uses a mixture of buses and trams; the latter become the U-Bahn around the centre. The system is shared with Bonn, and it's possible to take a stopping tram between the two cities – useful if you intend to leave from or arrive at somewhere which isn't central. Single ticket prices are high, making it better to invest in a **rover ticket**: those valid for 24 hours cost DM9.80/€4.90 for individuals, DM13.80/€6.90 for up to five people travelling together; there's also a three-day version of the former for DM24.6/€12.3. Another option is the DM30/€15 **KölnTourismus Card**, which includes entrance to all the municipally-owned museums plus reduced fares for Rhine cruises and other attractions.

Accommodation is plentiful, but it's scattered all over the city and mainly geared to the expense-account brigade attending the numerous trade fairs, the largest of which result in every room in the city being booked out. This does mean, however, that some of the better **hotels** offer cut-price rates of 50 percent or more at slack times. The tourist office (see above) is the best place to ask about special rates, but if you prefer to look yourself, the cheapest options lie just beyond the fringes of the Altstadt. By far the largest concentration of accommodation is to the rear of the Hauptbahnhof, where you'll find several streets of very similar hotels, though prices can vary a great deal from one to the other, and even within individual establishments. There are also three **hostels** and three **campsites** within the city. For **long-term stays**, contact the Mitwohnzentrale, Maximenstr. 2 (☎02 21/1 94 30), or Zeitwohnagentur März, Lindenstr. 77 (☎02 21/21 05 11).

Hotels and pensions

Altstadt, Salzgasse 7 (☎02 21/2 57 78 51, fax 2 57 78 53). On an alley not far from the Rhine, offering nicely furnished rooms and a sauna. ⑤.

Antik-Hotel Bristol, Kaiser-Wilhelm-Ring 48 (☎02 21/12 01 95, fax 13 14 95, *www.antik-hotel-bristol.com*). Quaintly appointed with old furniture and antiques; several of the rooms have four-poster beds. ⑦–⑨.

Berg, Brandenburger Str. 6 (☎02 21/12 11 24, fax 1 39 00 11, *www.hotel-berg.com*). One of a number of no-frills yet perfectly comfortable budget hotels immediately to the rear of the Hauptbahnhof. ②–⑦.

Brandenburger Hof, Brandenburger Str. 2–4 (☎02 21/12 28 89, fax 13 53 04). Another of the hotels behind the Hauptbahnhof; this one has the advantage of its own little garden. ③–⑦.

Cristall, Ursulaplatz 9–11 (☎02 21/1 63 00, fax 1 63 03 33). Fitted out in modern designer style and with a good location in one of the least touristed parts of the Altstadt. ⑥–⑨.

Das Kleine Stapelhäuschen, Fischmarkt 1–3 (☎02 21/2 57 78 62, fax 2 57 42 32). One of the most characterful hotels in the Altstadt, located in a pair of old houses at the corner of the square. Also has a cosy wine bar-restaurant. ⑤–⑦.

DomBlick, Domstr. 28 (☎02 21/12 37 42, fax 12 57 36). Good-quality hotel, one of the cluster to the rear of the Hauptbahnhof. ⑤–⑨.

Dom-Hotel, Domkloster 2a (☎02 21/2 02 40, fax 2 02 44 44, *www.lemeridien-hotels.com*). Splendid nineteenth-century luxury hotel whose restaurant terrace offers a stunning view of the south side of the Dom. ⑨.

Eden, Am Hof 18 (☎02 21/2 58 04 91, fax 2 58 04 95). Upmarket hotel next to the Ludwig Museum. ⑦.

Excelsior Hotel Ernst, Trankgasse 1–5 (☎02 21/27 01, fax 13 51 50). Cologne's top hotel for all the 130 years of its existence and ideally placed overlooking the north side of the Dom. It has two gourmet restaurants: *Hanse-Stube* and the slightly less expensive *Ambiance am Dom*. ⑨.

Hopper et cetera, Brüsseler Str. 26 (☎02 21/92 44 00, fax 92 44 06, *www.hopper.de*). This late nineteenth-century monastic building of the Brothers of Mercy has recently been converted into a stylish designer hotel, whose bedrooms feature parquet floors and cherrywood furniture. ⑥–⑨.

Im Kupferkessel, Probsteigasse 6 (☎02 21/13 53 38, fax 12 51 21). Renovated small hotel in the northwestern part of the Altstadt. ③–⑦.

Im Wasserturm, Kaygasse 2a (☎02 21/2 00 80, fax 2 00 88 88, *www.hotel-im-wasserturm.de*). Designer hotel in a nineteenth-century water-tower in the southeast part of the Altstadt. Its glass-topped eleventh-floor restaurant offers a fine view of the city. ⑨.

Jansen, Richard-Wagner-Str. 18 (☎ & fax 02 21/25 18 75). Situated just west of the Altstadt, this is a small and frequently oversubscribed pension. ④.

Lint, Lintgasse 7 (☎02 21/92 05 50, fax 9 20 55 55, *www.lint-hotel.de*). Recently refurbished small hotel on an Altstadt alley. ⑥–⑨.

Madison am Dom Ursulaplatz 10-12 (☎ & fax 02 21/13 29 91). Well-maintained modern hotel directly overlooking the Hauptbahnhof which sometimes offers bargain rates. There's also an Italian restaurant on the premises. ⑨–⑨.

Rhein-Hotel St Martin, Frankenwerft 31–33 (☎02 21/2 57 79 55, fax 2 57 78 75, *www.koeln -altstadt.de*). Good medium-range hotel whose front rooms directly face the Rhine. ④–⑦.

Rossner, Jakordenstr. 19 (☎02 21/12 27 03, fax 12 27 00). The homeliest and best value of the hotels behind the Hauptbahnhof. ③.

St Georg, Rolandstr. 61 (☎02 21/9 37 02 00, fax 93 70 20 11, *Gaestehaus.St.Georg@t-online.de*). A small guesthouse to the south of the Ring, run by the Boy Scout offices. ④–⑤.

Viktoria, Worringer Str. 23 (☎02 21/9 73 17 20, fax 72 70 67, *www.hotel-viktoria.com*). Fine century-old hotel right beside the Rhine to the north of the Altstadt. ⑦–⑨.

Youth hostels

Jugendgästehaus Riehl, An der Schanz 14 (☎02 21/76 70 81, fax 76 15 55, *jgh-koeln-riehl@t-online.de*). Located in the northern suburb of Riehl, this youth guesthouse has modern spacious rooms with lockers and a bar. Take U-Bahn #16 to Boltensternstrasse. DM39/€19.50.

Jugendherberge Deutz, Siegesstr. 5a (☎02 21/81 47 11, fax 88 44 25, *JH-DEUTZ@t-online.de*). The more central of the city's hostels, about a 15-min walk from the centre over the Hohenzollernbrücke, or just two blocks south of Bahnhof Deutz. DM33/€16.50 or DM38/€19.

Station Backpackers Hostel, Marzellenstr. 44–48 (☎02 21/9 12 53 01, fax 9 12 53 03, *station@t-online.de*). Privately owned hostel whose facilities include a laundry and Internet access. Dorm beds from DM27/€13.50, singles DM40/€20, doubles DM70/€35.

Campsites

Berger, Uferstr. 53a (☎02 21/39 22 11). Located in the right-bank suburb of Rodenkirchen by the Rodenkirchener Brücke and reached by U-Bahn #16 to Marienburg, then bus #130.

Städtischer Familienzeltplatz, Weidenweg (☎02 21/83 19 66). In the suburb of Poll to the south of Deutz, this convenient campsite is reached by U-Bahn #16 to Marienburg, after which it's just a short walk across the Rodenkirchener Brücke. Closed early Oct to April.

Waldbad, Peter-Baum-Weg (☎02 21/60 33 15). Located in the extreme northeastern suburb of Dünnwald.

The City

You don't need to walk very far to see the main attractions of Cologne – the **Dom** and the main **museums** are grouped conveniently together, with some of the traditional beer halls close by. Although most visitors venture no further, it would be a pity not to see something of the medieval **Altstadt**, which occupied an enormous area. Among the buildings to have survived are twelve Romanesque churches, much the finest collection anywhere. Don't expect to get more than a superficial impression in under two days, and a considerably longer period is needed to see everything. The best way to start your tour is to cross over to the right-bank suburb of Deutz – or at least to go some distance across either the Hohenzollernbrücke or the Deutzer Brücke – for the classic **view**, with the tall houses of the burghers lining the banks of the Rhine (crossed by no fewer than eight bridges within the city boundaries), and the chunky Romanesque tower of Gross St Martin providing an ideal counterfoil to the soaring openwork steeples of the Dom.

The Dom

...it was the most beautiful of all the churches I have ever seen, or can imagine. If one could imagine the spirit of devotion embodied in any material form, it would be in such a building.

Lewis Carroll's gushing tribute is typical of the extravagant praise which has been heaped upon Cologne's **Dom**. One of the most massive Gothic buildings ever constructed, it dominates the city in every sense. Its size reflects its power and status as "queen and mother of all German churches", whose archbishop was one of the seven Electors of the Holy Roman Empire.

Today, pollution has made it hard to distinguish between the medieval and nineteenth-century parts of the Dom, and the facade, of which you get a great uninterrupted view from the square in front, has an overwhelming, crushing power. Originally, the **spires** were, at 157m, the tallest structures in the world, but they were soon dwarfed by the Eiffel Tower and are no longer even the highest in Cologne. All the same, you need a fair bit of energy to climb up the south **tower** to the base of the steeple for a fine **panorama** over the city and the Rhine (daily: Jan, Feb, Nov & Dec 9am–4pm; March & April 9am–5pm; May–Sept 9am–6pm; DM3/€1.50, or DM8/€4 combined ticket with Schatzkammer).

The interior

Enter by the west door and your eye is immediately drawn down the great length of the building to the **high altar** with the shrine to the Magi, which illustrates the history of the world as described in the Bible, with Epiphany given due prominence. It's one of three artistic masterpieces to be found here; the others are in the chapels at the entrance to the ambulatory. On the north side is the ninth-century **Gero crucifix**, the most important monumental sculpture of its period. The corresponding chapel to the south has the greatest achievement of the fifteenth-century Cologne School of painters, the *Adoration of the Magi* triptych by **Stefan Lochner**. His refined, idealized style finds

---

THE HISTORY OF THE DOM

The history of the present Dom is an odd one, for, although the foundation stone was laid in 1248, the church was only completed in 1880. Most of what can be seen today was put up in two concentrated periods of activity separated by five centuries, yet in an almost identical architectural style. The impetus for the creation of a new cathedral came with the arrival of the alleged relics of the Magi and the subsequent increase in pilgrims. A spectacular **shrine** was commissioned to house the relics, begun in 1181 by **Nicholas of Verdun**, the greatest goldsmith of the day, and finished in 1220 by local craftsmen. What was then needed was a fitting palace to house this memorial to the kings. It was decided to adopt the ethereal new Gothic style of architecture for the cathedral, rather than the late Romanesque style still in vogue in the Rhineland, but to surpass earlier French models in size and splendour.

The chancel, designed by **Master Gerhard**, was completed in 1322, but thereafter the sheer ambitiousness of the plans began to take its toll. In 1560, the project was abandoned, with only the south tower and the lower parts of the nave and facade having been built. That might have been the end of the story, had it not been for the impact of the Romantic movement in the early nineteenth century, which led to a campaign for the completion of the cathedral, boosted by the discovery of two pieces of parchment which showed the medieval builders' designs for the facade. From 1842, in a remarkable act of homage from one age to another, the work was carried out in a style that would have been completely familiar to the original masons.

a perfect outlet in this truly gorgeous scene; the wings feature two of the Cologne martyrs, SS Ursula and Gereon, with their companions. Look out also for an elaborate sixteenth-century carved retable from Antwerp in the south transept, a colossal wooden St Christopher nearby, and (at the intersection of the north transept and the nave aisle) the fourteenth-century Clares altar. The whole **chancel** is outstanding, preserving an unparalleled set of furnishings contemporary with the architecture: choir stalls, painted wooden panels; vibrant statues of Christ, the Virgin and the Apostles, and a delicate altar front. To penetrate beyond the barrier for a marginally better view of these, you have to take one of the **guided tours** which leave from the main portal. English-language tours (DM7/€3.50) start at 10.30am and 2.30pm every day except Sunday, when they take place in the afternoon only.

Stained-glass windows are essential components of a Gothic cathedral, and Cologne has a marvellously varied assemblage. The oldest, dating from 1260, is in the axis chapel of the ambulatory and is a "Bible" window, pairing New Testament scenes with a parallel from the Old Testament; another is two chapels to the south. In a wholly different, far more monumental style is the late Gothic glass on the north side of the nave, designed by some of the leading local painters. These in turn contrast well with the brilliantly coloured nineteenth-century Bavarian windows opposite, a gift from King Ludwig I towards the Dom's completion. Between Easter and Corpus Christi each year, eight huge **tapestries** of *The Triumph of the Eucharist*, woven from designs by **Rubens** (whose childhood was spent in Cologne), are displayed in the nave. A magnificent panel of *The Crucifixion of St Peter*, which the same artist painted for the local church of St Peter, can currently be seen in the southern aisle.

The Schatzkammer and Diözesanmuseum

The **Schatzkammer** (daily 10am–5pm; DM6/€3) has recently moved to the cellars underneath the Dom, and is entered from the northern side of the building. It contains a few lovely Ottonian manuscripts plus a notable array of treasury items, including a crozier made to celebrate the consecration of the chancel and a fifteenth-century ceremonial sword symbolizing the status of the local archbishops as Electors of the Holy Roman Empire. Also on display are the sculptures which adorned the portal of the south tower, the only one dating from the medieval building period. Carved in the workshop of Michael Parler, they have been replaced *in situ* by faithful copies.

Just outside the Dom, at Roncalliplatz 2, is the **Erzbischöfliches Diözesanmuseum** (11am–6pm, closed Thurs; *www.kolumba.de*; free). A beautiful **Lochner**, *Madonna of the Violets*, forms the centrepiece, while in a glass case, and easily missed, is his little *Nativity*. Other highlights include: an eleventh-century crucifix which bizarrely uses an antique lapis lazuli of a woman as the head; the *St Severin Medallion* with a portrait of the saint; and two priceless textiles – a sixth-century Syrian silk illustrating a hunt, discovered in the shrine of St Kunibert, and a Byzantine cloth embroidered with lions.

Museums around the Dom

In addition to the Diözesanmuseum, there are two other notable museums right beside the Dom, housed in ultra-modern buildings which were designed to be prominent late twentieth-century contributions to the city skyline.

The Römisch-Germanisches Museum

Germany's most important collection of indigenous archeological finds, the **Römisch-Germanisches Museum** (Tues–Sun 10am–5pm; *www.museenkoeln.de*; DM10/€5) at

Roncalliplatz 4 is specially constructed around the star exhibit, the **Dionysos Mosaic**, excavated here in 1941. The finest work of its kind in northern Europe, it adorned the dining room of a patrician villa of about 200 AD. The mosaic is made from over a million pieces of limestone, ceramics and glass, covering an area of some 70 square metres, and depicts the inebriated Bacchus surrounded by Cupid, Pan, dancers, satyrs and vignettes of the delights of the table. Its astonishing state of preservation is due to the protective covering it received from the burnt-out remains of the building falling on it when sacked by a Germanic tribe in the fourth century.

The other main item is the **tomb of Poblicius**, a veteran who had served in the Fifth Legion. Dating from about 40 AD, this is an even more recent discovery. It stands about 15m high and has been re-erected beside the mosaic, although considerably more restoration has been necessary.

Otherwise, the museum is arranged thematically. The collection of **glass** is reckoned to be unsurpassed anywhere in the world. Among the early pieces is a tiny idealized portrait of Augustus Caesar made in 27 BC. From the second century, the Cologne workshops developed their own distinctive forms, with coloured serpentine threads used for decorative effects. This style culminated around 330 AD in the *diatreta* glass, decorated with a delicate network design. Perhaps of more general appeal is the dazzling array of **jewellery** on the first floor, most of which was found in Frankish graves. Also of special note are the fragments of the city's northern gateway, the Philosophers Mosaic of 260 AD and a spectacular array of over a thousand terracotta lamps.

The Museum Ludwig

Immediately to the east, at Bischofgartenstr. 1, is the second large museum building, which was erected in the 1980s to house the city's collection of paintings. It was subsequently decided to give the old masters a new home of their own, leaving most of the available display space here to the modern art holdings of the **Museum Ludwig** (Tues 10am–8pm, Wed–Fri 10am–6pm, Sat & Sun 11am–6pm; *www.museenkoeln.de*; DM10/€5).

This features a notable American section, including a large display of Pop Art which includes such favourite **Andy Warhol** subjects as Brillo boxes, Pepsi Cola and tins of Campbell's soup, as well as examples of Tom Wesselmann and Roy Lichtenstein. **Claes Oldenburg** is represented by *The Street,* which occupies a whole room. The many other eye-catching sculptures include the uncanny fibreglass creations of the Realists and **Ed Kienholz**'s *Portable War Memorial*, a devastating satire on his country's cultural values.

Among German works, there's a fine batch by **Kirchner**, notably a group portrait of *Die Brücke*; around it hang examples of these very painters. **Max Ernst** provided a similar memento of the Surrealists, including co-opted dead members, Raphael and Dostoyevsky. By the same artist is an iconoclastic ringing of the changes on the theme of the Madonna and Child; the furious mother administers a sound thrashing on the infant's buttocks while Ernst and friends look on. **Beckmann**, **Nolde** and **Kokoschka** are all strongly represented; look out for the latter's *View of Cologne*. There are three superb portraits by **Dix**, including one of himself, and a number of sculptures in various media by **Barlach**. Two rooms are devoted to **Picasso**, with sculptures and ceramics as well as paintings from most phases of his career. In contrast, there's only a single spectacular **Dalí**, *Perpignan Station*. Beside it hangs one of the most famous Surrealist canvases, *Presence of Mind* by **Magritte**. An impressive array of Russian paintings includes a large **Chagall**, *Moses Destroying the Tablets of the Law*.

A second museum in the premises, the **Agfa-Foto-Historama**, shows old photographic equipment and a changing selection of prints from the vast holdings of the famous company, whose headquarters are in nearby Leverkusen.

The Altstadt and the Romanesque churches

The vast area that was medieval Cologne suffered grievous damage in the last war. Much of it was rebuilt as quickly as possible, but in the case of the churches, time was allowed in order to undertake faithful restoration projects. What has been achieved is undoubtedly impressive – to realize this you only need to look at the photographs displayed in each church showing its state at the end of the war – although there's no denying that much has been irretrievably lost.

With that proviso, there's a lot to enjoy, and the **twelve Romanesque churches**, which range in date from the tenth to the thirteenth century, form one of the most coherent groups in a single architectural style to be found in any European city. The extraordinary St Gereon is the one that shouldn't be missed for its architecture, while St Maria im Kapitol has the finest furnishings, and Gross St Martin and St Aposteln have justifiably famous exteriors. The churches are generally open all day; some close at lunchtimes, which may last as long as noon till 3pm, though even then the vestibule may still be kept open.

From the Dom to the Rathaus

A short walk south of the Museum Ludwig is **Gross St Martin**, a former monastic church that was for long occupied by Benedictines from Scotland and Ireland. For nearly six hundred years its **tower**, surrounded by four turrets, was the dominant feature of the Cologne skyline, not being usurped by the Dom's spires until the late nineteenth century. The rest of the building seems rather truncated for such a splendid adornment, although the interior has been returned to its simple original form. Such old houses as remain are in the streets nearby; seen at close quarters, it's rather obvious that many are recent reproductions.

Just beyond is the Alter Markt, one of three large squares in the heart of the city. From here, you can see the irregular octagonal tower of the **Rathaus** (normally Mon–Thurs 7.30am–4.45pm, Fri 7.30am–2pm, but closed in 2000 for restoration; free), a building which is a real jumble of styles, yet with marvellous features. Its core is fourteenth-century Gothic; the following century the tower was added in a more flamboyant idiom, while in the 1570s a graceful loggia, a rare example of Renaissance architecture in the Rhineland, was provided as a frontispiece. Highlights of the interior include the **Hansa Saal** from the first building period, and the tower rooms with doorways of inlaid woods.

In front of the entrance to the Rathaus is a glass pyramid sheltering the **Mikwe**, a Jewish ritual bath house dating from about 1160, the only remnant of the ghetto which was razed soon after the expulsion order of 1424. It's officially open on weekends 11am–3pm, but from Monday to Friday you can ask for the key during office hours at the porter's desk in the Rathaus. More subterranean sights can be seen just a short distance away in the form of the foundations of the **Praetorium**, the Roman governor's palace, and the **Römischer Kanal**, a surprisingly elegant vaulted sewer some 100m long. The entrance to both of these is at Kleine Budengasse (Tues–Fri 10am–4pm, Sat & Sun 11am–4pm; DM3/€1.50).

The Wallraf-Richartz-Museum

A short walk to the south, at Martinstr. 39, are the strikingly angular new premises – the third home it has had in the last fifteen years – of the **Wallraf-Richartz-Museum** (Tues 10am–8pm, Wed–Fri 10am–6pm, Sat & Sun 11am–6pm; *www.museenkoeln.de*; DM10/€5) of old master paintings.

The first floor is devoted to the unique holdings of the fifteenth-century **Cologne School** (see p.1086), and it's worth looking out for the many intriguing backdrop depictions of the medieval city, often featuring the unfinished Dom. **Stefan Lochner** is the most admired artist of the school, and his *Last Judgement* is a major work, enormously inventive in its detail, gentle and fantastic in its view. More typical of his style is the exquisite *Madonna of the Rose Bower*, his artistic swansong. From the preceding generation, the **Master of St Veronica** is the most accomplished painter, represented here by two contrasting versions of the *Crucifixion*, one as delicately refined as an illuminated manuscript, the other with monumental figures. The most detailed vignettes of Cologne are by the **Master of the Glorification of the Virgin**, but the gems of the whole display are arguably the two large triptychs made for the Carthusians by the **Master of St Bartholomew**, who represented the final flowering of the school at the beginning of the sixteenth century. His figures are executed as if in imitation of sculpture and have a haunting, mystical quality. A major loan exhibition of works by this great but elusive artist will be held in the museum in the summer of 2001.

On the second floor are other German paintings, including a small **Dürer**, *Fifer and Drummer*, several typical examples of **Cranach** and *The Martyrdom of St Stephen* by **Elsheimer**. There are also a number of Flemish and Italian Primitives, among which a *Madonna and Child* by **Simone Martini** stands out. A good selection of **Rubens'** varied output includes two impressively large-scale canvases: *Juno and Argus* and *The Stigmatization of St Francis*. The latter was painted for the Capuchins of Cologne and makes for a fascinating comparison with *St Francis in the Porzincula Chapel* by the Spaniard **Murillo**, another of the great masters of the Counter-Reformation. A rich representation of seventeenth-century Dutch artists includes masterpieces by Hals, Ter Brugghen and Ruisdael, as well as what is probably the very last of **Rembrandt**'s great series of self-portraits, in which he depicted himself in the guise of a laughing philosopher (or perhaps the satirical painter Zeuxis) from ancient Greece.

The third floor is devoted to the nineteenth century, and includes a decent section on the French Impressionists. Among the German works of the same period are several examples of **Friedrich** and a large collection of the local artist **Wilhelm Leibl**, leader of the Realist movement.

The rest of the eastern Altstadt

The Wallraf-Richartz-Museum is built right up against the burnt-out church of **Alt St Alban**, which has been left as a war memorial. It in turn adjoins the **Gürzenich**, a much-rebuilt Gothic festive hall, best known as the home of the Carnival balls. A little further south is the tower which is all that survives of **Klein St Martin**.

Behind is **St Maria im Kapitol**, not seen to advantage from outside as it was built in a severe convent style and is now hemmed in by modern houses; however, it possesses a majestic interior complete with a full circuit for processions around the aisles. Originally constructed in the eleventh century, it pioneered the trefoil or clover-leaf chancel that became a staple feature of the churches of the Rhineland for the next two hundred years. Look out for the **wooden doors**, contemporary with the architecture and among the most precious works of their kind, depicting Christ's Nativity, teachings and Passion. The church has a magnificent monumental Renaissance **rood screen**, while the **cloisters**, unusually placed adjoining the facade, are the only ones left in Cologne.

Continuing in a southerly direction, Rheingasse leads to the **Overstolzenhaus**, the finest mansion in the city, a step-gabled patrician home contemporary with the later Romanesque churches. A short walk from here is the sailors' church of **St Maria in Lyskirchen**; their *Schöne Madonna* of about 1420 is one of several fine works of art. The vaults are covered with thirteenth-century frescoes of scenes from the Old and New Testaments and lives of saints, which are seen to best effect by climbing the stairs to the gallery. From here, head up Grosse Witschgasse and Georgstrasse to **St Georg**, an eleventh-century pillared basilica which resembles early Christian churches. The westwork, added the following century, looks squat and stumpy from without, but is impressively spacious when you're inside.

The southern Altstadt

From St Georg, it's a walk of some fifteen minutes due south to the **St Severin** quarter. The church itself is classified among the twelve Romanesque examples in Cologne, though only the twin-towered apse and part of the transept remain from that time, the rest being late Gothic. Now it's mainly of interest to archeology buffs, on account of the **Roman-Frankish graveyard** which has been found directly underneath; this can be visited on guided tours (Mon & Fri 4pm; DM2/€1). Just beyond the church is the **Severinstor**, part of the medieval fortifications which were largely demolished last century when the Ring was built. A short walk to the east, at Ubierring 45, is the **Rautenstrauch-Joest Museum** (Tues–Fri 10am–4pm, Sat & Sun 11am–4pm; DM5/€2.50). This large ethnological museum's particular strengths are Indo-China and Pre-Columbian America; West Africa, the Pacific and Indonesia are also well represented.

Following the ring road in a northwesterly direction, you pass the **Ulrepforte**, another turreted gateway. Further along, turn right at Waisenhausgasse for **St Pantaleon**, the oldest surviving church in the city, dating from the end of the tenth century. It's chiefly notable for its massive westwork with vestibule. Inside, there's an airy Flamboyant Gothic rood screen, crowned by a seventeenth-century organ in a Rococo case.

The western Altstadt

North up Poststrasse and Peterstrasse is the **Josef-Haubrich-Kunsthalle** (Tues 10am–8pm, Wed–Fri 10am–6pm, Sat & Sun 11am–6pm; *www.museen.koeln.de*; variable entrance charge), the city's main venue for temporary exhibitions, particularly of contemporary art. Immediately to the east stands **St Peter**, a Gothic church with gleaming stained-glass windows. Rubens painted the retable of its high altar, though for the past few years this has been displayed in the Dom.

Alongside is **St Cäcilien**, a Romanesque convent church which now houses the **Schnütgen-Museum** (Tues–Fri 10am–5pm, Sat & Sun 11am–5pm, first Wed of month 10am–8pm; *www.museenkoeln.de*; DM5/€2.50), a collection of religious art (except paintings) of the Rhineland. There are some wonderful ivories, notably a diptych which belonged to Charlemagne and the comb of St Heribert. Major pieces of Romanesque sculpture include the church's own tympanum, carved in a heavily antique style, the wooden crucifix from St Georg and the mysterious *Siegburg Madonna*. From the Gothic period the museum's most important possessions are some of the original carvings from the Dom's altar front and a polychrome console bust of a woman carved by a member of the Parler family. Many of the most important exhibits from the Rheinisches Landesmuseum in Bonn will be on display here until restoration work on its building is completed (see p.528).

Across the road and down Antongasse is the tiny Gothic **Antoniterkirche**, now a Protestant parish church, best known for housing one of the most famous of twentieth-century sculptures, **Barlach**'s *Memorial Angel*. This is a cast made from the plaster of the original, which was created for the 700th anniversary of the Dom in Güstrow but destroyed in the perverse Nazi measures against "degenerate art". Around the church is the main shopping centre; the streets follow the same plan as their Roman predecessors, but almost all the buildings are modern.

Up Herzogstrasse are the ruins of the Gothic **St Kolumba**, which wasn't restored after the war; instead Gottfried Böhm inserted a minute chapel within the shell in 1950.

Further down the same street is another Gothic church, the severe **Minoritenkirche**. It contains the tomb of John Duns Scotus, the Scots-born theologian who was the leading intellectual in early fourteenth-century Cologne. Ironically, he's the origin of the word "dunce": his defences of traditional religious orthodoxies so enraged his radical fellow countrymen at the time of the Reformation that they used his name as a personification of stupidity. Alongside the church is the **Museum für Angewandte Kunst** (Tues & Thurs–Sun 11am–5pm, Wed 11am–8pm; *www.museenkoeln.de*; DM5/€2.50), a comprehensive array of applied art from the Middle Ages to the present day. The Jugendstil section is particularly impressive, though the incongruous highlight of the museum is an exquisite little panel of *The Nativity* by **Memling**.

A short distance west of the Antoniterkirche lies Neumarkt. Housed in a bank at no. 18 is the **Käthe-Kollwitz-Museum** (Tues–Sun 10am–5pm; *www.kollwitz.de*; DM5/€2.50). It has a large display of graphics and a few sculptures by Käthe Kollwitz, one of the leading female artists of the twentieth century. Her preference for black-and-white media helps give her work an enormous pathos, evident in her variation on the Mother and Child theme, and her denunciations of the follies and sufferings of war.

The far end of Neumarkt is dominated by the majestic early thirteenth-century apse of **St Aposteln** (Holy Apostles – an unusual dedication outside the Orthodox world). This is an archetypal Rhenish basilica with all the characteristic features – clover-leaf chancel with dwarf-gallery, central octagon with turrets and, above all, the great western tower with its "bishop's mitre" roof. Despite its apparently homogeneous design, building actually began in the eleventh century; the interior is surprisingly plain. Nearby is another of the city gates, the **Hahnentor**, which resembles a castle's barbican.

The northern Altstadt

Due north of St Aposteln is **St Gereon**, the most idiosyncratic of the twelve Romanesque churches and a truly great building. Its kernel was an oval-shaped fourth-century chapel; in the eleventh and twelfth centuries a crypt, chancel and twin towers were added. Then, in the early thirteenth century, the Roman masonry was harnessed to form the basis of a magnificent four-storey decagon with ribbed dome vault, a work which has no parallel in European architecture. At this time, the adjoining baptistry was also built and adorned with frescoes. The decagon's interior seems more graceful and less massive than from outside; its modern stained glass is a controversial addition. In the crypt the original mosaic floor with Old Testament scenes is preserved.

From here, you can return towards the Dom, passing a fragment of Roman wall and the Zeughaus, which houses the **Kölnisches Stadtmuseum** (Tues 10am–8pm, Wed–Sun 10am–5pm; *www.museenkoeln.de*; DM5/€2.50). This focuses on the history of local trade and industry, along with sections on Carnival and eau de Cologne. Some good models show the city's building development. A little further east is **St Andreas**, which has a stately Romanesque nave preceded by a mighty westwork, an octagonal lantern tower and a Gothic chancel. Inside is the **Maccabeus shrine**, a piece of early sixteenth-century craftsmanship, doubtless inspired by the Dom's shrine to the Magi. Another casket contains the relics of St Albertus Magnus, the thirteenth-century scholar who was the star teacher at Cologne's renowned Dominican College; his pupils there included St Thomas Aquinas, later to develop into the greatest philosopher of his time and arguably of the entire medieval period. A short way along Marzellenstrasse is the pink exterior of **St Mariae Himmelfahrt**, a seventeenth-century Jesuit foundation and Cologne's only Baroque church of note. Its galleried interior, which surprisingly employs the long-out-of-favour Gothic pointed arch, is lavishly decorated – unusually for the Rhineland, where Bavarian excesses never caught on.

A bit further down the same street, turn left into Ursulaplatz, where **St Ursula**, with its prominent sturdy tower, still retains some Romanesque features, along with Gothic and Baroque accretions. Unless you're squeamish, try to get hold of the sexton, who will show you the **Goldene Kammer**, an ornate Baroque chamber gruesomely lined with reliquaries. He can be elusive, but is generally available during normal visiting hours, except at lunchtimes, Tuesdays and during the Sunday services. From here, the **Eigelsteintor**, another impressive survival of the medieval fortifications, is reached via the street of the same name. Dagobertstrasse then leads east to **St Kunibert**, the final fling of the Romanesque in the early thirteenth century, completed just as work began on the Dom. It was also the last church to be restored following war damage, with the nave and massive westwork having only been joined up a few years back. Inside, note the stained-glass windows in the apse, which are contemporary with the architecture. On the piers of the transept are the two dramatic polychrome figures of an *Annunciation* group, an important piece of Gothic carving by **Conrad Kuyn**, master mason at the Dom in the early fifteenth century.

Outside the centre

If you want to stray beyond the confines of the Altstadt, Cologne's suburbs offer a wide choice of **parks** and some of the most exciting **modern architecture** in Germany. In every way, the dominant building outside the centre is the **Fernsehturm** (telecommunications tower; daily 10am–10pm; DM5/€2.50, including ascent by elevator to the viewing platform), in the Stadtgarten west of the Ring. Completed in 1980, at 243m it's considerably higher than the Dom, and it's definitely worth going up for the breathtaking views over the city and the Rhine. Very close by, within the Stadtgarten, is **Neu St Alban**, one of several highly praised modern churches in Cologne. Also near the Ring, but to the north, is **St Gertrud** on Krefelder Strasse, with an amazing tapering tower. It's the work of **Gottfried Böhm**, whose father **Dominikus** was a pioneer of radical church design in the inter-war period. An example of the latter's 1930s Expressionism is **St Engelbert**, a centrally planned building of eight identical concrete shells, located very near the Jugendgästehaus on Riehler Gürtel. His **St Maria Königin**, in the southern suburb of Marienburg, is one of the most accomplished of a new generation of churches built to serve the needs of the residential quarters then being built.

From the Hahnentor, Aachener Strasse runs in a dead-straight line westwards to the outer suburbs. Just beyond the Ring, a short walk down Universitätstrasse brings you to the **Museum für Ostasiatische Kunst** (Tues, Wed & Fri–Sun 11am–5pm, Thurs 11am–8pm; *www.museenkoeln.de*; DM5/€2.50). Devoted to the arts of China, Japan and Korea, this is yet another of Cologne's collections which has been given specially designed modern premises, appropriately enough by a Japanese architect and with a traditional Japanese garden. It's arranged thematically, with leaflets in English available on each topic.

GREEN COLOGNE

Although there are few areas of green in the city centre, about a quarter of Cologne is given over to open spaces. Most popular is the **Rheinpark** in Deutz on the right bank of the Rhine, a legacy of large garden shows, with the Tanzbrunnen, round which concerts are held in summer. It's linked by the gondolas of the Rheinseilbahn (April–Oct daily 10am–6pm; DM7/€3.50 single, DM10/€5 return) over the Rhine to the **Flora- und Botanischer Garten** (summer 8am–9pm; winter 10am–dusk; free), near the Zoo and Aquarium (daily 9am–5/6pm; DM15/€7.50). Other parks are in the far suburbs. To the south are the recreational **Volksgarten** and a forestry reserve at **Rodenkirchen** (daily 9am–4/6/8pm according to season) with trees, plants and shrubs from around the world. The right bank has nature reserves at **Dünnwald**, **Brück** and **Porz**, the last featuring birds of prey (daily: April–Sept 9am–7pm; Oct–March 9am–5pm).

Further along Aachener Strasse at no. 1328, in the suburb of Weiden, is the city's final important Roman monument, the **Grabkammer** (Tues–Thurs 10am–1pm, Fri 10am–5pm, Sat & Sun 1–5pm; DM1/€0.50), a second-century burial chamber. It contains marble busts of a couple and a young woman which are contemporary with the building, and a sarcophagus from the following century with carvings of the seasons.

Weiden lies about halfway along the route to **BRAUWEILER**, reached by regular bus services. The village clusters around the **Abteikirche**, built as a Benedictine monastery in the twelfth and thirteenth centuries. There are no fewer than six towers, and inside the pillars of the nave are capped by sensual figurative capitals. The serene stone retable in the south apse is one of the masterpieces of German Romanesque sculpture, depicting St Nicholas, the church's patron, in a gathering around the Madonna and Child.

Eating and drinking

The gastronomy of Cologne is as distinctive and distinguished as that of any German city, with plenty of **local food specialities** in addition to the renowned *Kölsch* beer. With over three thousand restaurants, bars and cafés crammed into a relatively small area, there's certainly no shortage of choice, with the chic and trendy often standing cheek by jowl with the staid and traditional.

Beer halls, restaurants and cafés

The great Cologne institutions for both eating and drinking are the **Brauhäuser** (or *Weetschaften*, as they're known in the local dialect). Most of these brewery-owned beer halls date from the turn of the twentieth century, though they claim a much longer pedigree; a few of them still brew their *Kölsch* in-house, though most have moved production to larger premises elsewhere in the city. Whilst smaller than their Munich counterparts, they have similarly cavernous interiors with sparse decor. They're staffed by horribly matey *Köbes*, who all year round keep up the Carnival tradition of making insulting and corny jokes. These beer halls are often overrun with visiting businessmen and tourists, but they're definitely worth sampling as they offer some of the best-value food in the city, specializing in the local cuisine. Don't be misled by the dialect, however – *Halve Hahn* is not the half-chicken you'd expect but a rye roll with cheese, while *Kölsche Kaviar* is less of a bargain than it appears when you realize it's a black pudding, again with rye bread. The city has a varied range of ethnic **restaurants**, and is also amply endowed with **traditional cafés**.

Brauhäuser

Alt-Köln, Trinkgasse 7–9. This is a real one-off, its picturesque folly of an interior featuring a whole series of wooden alcoves and galleries which together represent a Romantic vision of a complex of

---

KÖLSCH

Kölsch beer is as much a piece of the local life of Cologne as the Dom or Carnival, and may only be produced in the breweries located in and around the city. It's clear, light, highly fermented and aromatically bitter, with a strong accentuation of hops. Invariably, it's served with a substantial head in a tall, thin glass (*Stange*) which holds only a fifth of a litre. This gives it a rather effete image among macho beer drinkers from elsewhere in Germany who tend to revile it, in contrast to the religious reverence it's accorded in Cologne.

old German taverns. The food is as good as the beer (Küppers), and very reasonably priced for a place which gets an outsized share of tourists.

Brauhaus Sion, Unter Taschenmacher 5. Though close to the Dom, the side-street location means that locals rather than visitors form the bulk of the clientele here. Serves generous portions of *gutbürgerliche Küche*; its *Kölsch* is notable for its strong bouquet and dry finish.

Früh am Dom, Am Hof 12–14. The most visited of the Brauhäuser, partly because of its wonderful location opposite the Dom, partly because of its excellent food, and above all because of the prestige of its delicately fruity *Cölner Hofbräu*, a classic *Kölsch*.

Gaffel-Haus, Alter Markt 20. The *Kölsch* served here is the driest and bitterest in Cologne; the food's pretty good too.

Haus Töller, Weyerstr. 96. Undoubtedly the cosiest of the Brauhäuser, occupying a fourteenth-century house that was one of the first in Cologne to be built of stone. Meals are good value; the beer is from Sion. Evenings only, closed Sun.

Hellers, Roonstr. 33. Modern Hausbrauerei which brews a *Weissbier*, a *Bock*, a *Doppelbock* called *No.33*, and a *Kölsch*. Evenings only.

Küppers Brauhaus, Altenburger Str. 157. Situated way beyond the Südstadt (take tram #15 or #16), but definitely worth a special trip. As well as the beer garden and tavern, reconstructed to resemble those in the city centre, there's the added attraction of Cologne's **Brauerei-Museum** (guided tours hourly every Sat 11am–3pm), which includes a re-creation of an old brewery, complete with historic equipment.

Päffgen, Friesenstr. 64. This traditional Hausbrauerei in the northwest Altstadt produces a *Kölsch* with a pleasingly hoppy finish. Also has a more centrally located branch at Heumarkt 62.

Peters Brauhaus, Mühlengasse 1. Though it looks as old as any of its competitors, this is a fairly recent addition, housed in the palatial premises of the long-defunct *Brauhaus Zum Kranz*.

Sünner im Walfisch, Salzgasse 13. Another relative newcomer, though it belongs to the oldest family-run brewery in the city. It occupies a beautiful half-timbered seventeenth-century house moved here from its original location.

Weiss-Bräu, Am Weidenbach 24. This was the first of Cologne's new-generation Hausbrauereien, established in a long-redundant brewery. It introduced locally produced *Weissbier* to the city, and also makes a *Kölsch* and a dark beer.

Zur Malzmühle, Heumarkt 6. A traditional Hausbrauerei, one whose name is reflected in the distinctly malty taste of its *Malzmühlenkölsch* and low-alcohol *Koch'sches Malzbier*.

Restaurants

Al Salam, Hohenstaufenring 22. Formal restaurant serving a wide range of Arab dishes to the accompaniment of Lebanese wines. Evenings only, except Sun, when it is only open for brunch.

Bei Barbara, Aachener Str. 22. Among the very few places in Germany serving authentic dishes from the country's Polish neighbour.

Bizim, Weidengasse 47. Turkish restaurants are now among the most ubiquitous features of German cities, but this is one of very few to aspire to *haute cuisine* status, and is correspondingly expensive. Closed Sun & Mon.

Daitokai, Kattenbug 2. Highly rated, if predictably expensive, Japanese restaurant. Closed all day Mon and Tues lunchtime.

Em Krützche, Am Frankenturm 1–3. Historic Gasthaus which is probably Cologne's best traditional restaurant, renowned for its game and fish specialities. Closed Mon.

Fischers, Hohenstaufenring 53. A truly creative restaurant whose weekday set lunches are quite exceptional value; set dinners are also available, but are more than twice the price. Closed Sat lunchtime and all day Sun.

Five Seasons, Brüsseler Str. 54. Vegetarian restaurant attached to a cookery school. It offers good-value set lunches.

Grande Milano, Hohenstaufenring 37. Arguably the best of a wide choice of Italian restaurants. It also has a moderately priced bistro, *Pinot di Pinot*. Closed Sun.

Haxenhaus zum Rheingarten, Frankenwerft 19. Located right on the Rhine promenade, this specializes in pork and lamb knuckles and metre-long sausages.

Jaipur, Marzellenstr. 50–56. Well-regarded, fairly upmarket Indian restaurant.

Le Moissonier, Krefelder Str. 25. Fine and authentically French bistro. Closed Sun & Mon.

Mandalay, Brüsseler Str. 53. Offers a rare chance to sample the little-known but delicious cuisine of Burma, which, logically enough, stands somewhere between that of India and China. Closed Tues.

Ratskeller, Rathausplatz 1. Like its counterparts throughout the country, this cellar restaurant offers good food and wine at high but far from extortionate prices; it also has the bonus of a pleasant inner courtyard. Note that, because of restoration work on the Rathaus, it will be subject to a temporary period of closure.

Sprössling, Mozartstr. 9. Good all-round veggie and wholefood specialist which stays open until late and has a courtyard garden. Closed Tues.

Tchang, Grosse Sandkaul 19. Perhaps the pick of Cologne's abundant supply of Chinese restaurants.

Traditional cafés

Cremer, Brückenstr. 1–3. An enduringly favourite rendezvous point with city-centre shoppers.

Fassbender, Bazaar de Cologne, Mittelstrasse. The location in a big central shopping precinct may seem unpromising, but this café enjoys a high reputation for its pralines and other handmade chocolates.

Reichard, Untere Fettenhennen 11. Cologne's best-known bastion of *Kaffee und Kuchen*, an elegant salon profiting from its situation hard by the Dom.

Bars and café-bars

There are four distinct quarters of Cologne with a recommendable concentration of nightspots. The most obvious is the area around Gross St Martin in the **Altstadt**; this tends to catch visiting tourists and businessmen, but the best places do manage to create their own distinctive atmosphere. In the **Südstadt**, or St Severin quarter, are some of the most stylish bars and cafés, as well as the biggest crowds. For once, it pays to follow them – it's their sheer exuberance that makes the place. Down the road from the university (in the southwestern part of the city), the **Quartier Lateng** is the place to mingle with the locals, even if it has lost some of its trendy edge. The more relaxed **Belgisches Viertel** (the streets around the Ring, just to the west of the centre) is nowhere near as packed or self-consciously trendy.

Altstadt

Biermuseum, Buttermarkt 39. A favourite haunt with tourists and correspondingly pricey; there are eighteen beers on tap.

Broadway Café, Ehrenstr. 11. At the entrance to the Broadway cinema; good breakfast from late morning onwards.

Corkonian, Alter Markt 49. Large Irish pub serving Guinness and Kilkenny, often featuring live Irish music. Packed out, especially at weekends.

Kännchen, Am Bollwerk 13. Tiny traditional pub with a riverside terrace whose *Kölsch* comes from the Gilden brewery.

Kauri, Auf dem Rothenberg 11. Conveniently sited cellar bar with good selection of jazz, funk and blues; free entry but drinks are extortionate.

Papa Joe's Em Streckstrumpf, Buttermarkt 37. Germany's oldest jazz bar, this is a cosier, smaller, equally good version of *Klimperkasten*; invariably standing-room only, with music beginning at 8.30pm and special Sun sessions at 11am.

Papa Joe's Klimperkasten, Alter Markt 50. The deservedly popular place to go for traditional live jazz, which is belted out to an appreciative audience from 8pm onwards. Very expensive drinks but young clientele at weekends; more businessmen at other times.

Südstadt

Bi Pis Bistro, Rolandstr. 61. In the unlikely setting of the Boy Scout offices; older, left-wing clientele and regular poetry readings.

Casa Blanc, Alteburger Str. 11. Very chic; like a French brasserie with bright lights and mirrors.

Chlodwig-Eck, Annostr. 1. Very trendy café-bar and restaurant.

Kurfürsten-Hof, Kurfürstenstr. 1. Café-bar offering salads, sandwiches and hot specials.

Opera, Alteburger Str. 1. Garishly coloured bar which attracts very young punters, particularly at weekends.

Spielplatz, Ubierring 58. More in the style of a beer hall, with a lot more character than some of its newer counterparts.

Zaff, Ubierring 22. In the forefront of the Südstadt scene with good music under subdued lights.

Quartier Lateng

Café Central, Jülicher Str. 1. Stylish café which is one of the best places for breakfast; good selection of newspapers; outside tables when the weather is fine.

Café Orlando, Engelbertstr. 9. Quiet café offering breakfast and health food; 1950s decor with old jukebox.

Casa dei Vini, Kyffhäuser Str. 47. As recommendable a place as any in Cologne for a glass of wine, with over forty varieties to choose from.

Filmdose, Zülpicher Str. 39. One of the most original fun pubs in Cologne when busy (particularly at weekends). It has a tiny stage for cabaret and also shows films in English.

Gilberts Pinte, Engelbertstr. 1. Notorious student dive, home to numerous *Stammtische*, but with plenty of atmosphere.

Peppermint Lounge, Hohenstaufenring 23. One of the most popular late-nighters, springing into action around midnight; also good for a late breakfast.

Santiago de Cuba, Zülpicher Str. 25. Has a long list of cocktails and also serves Latin American dishes.

Belgisches Viertel

Alabama, Antwerpener Str. 34. Cocktail bar-cum-American diner.

Alcazar, Bismarckstr. 39a. Snug and candlelit, with tasty if overpriced menu; somewhat older clientele.

Maxxim, Aachener Str. 59. Chaotic pub packed out with students; serves salads and other light meals.

Stadtgarten, Venloer Str. 40. Home of the Kölner Jazzhaus Initiative, so most of the jazz is modern and experimental. It also has a good restaurant, while in summer the park is used as a beer garden.

Velvet, Venloer Str. 33. Tiny corner street café-bar.

Entertainment

For music and theatre listings consult the billboards (which are found all over the city); the posters are changed every ten days. The tourist office publishes a comprehensive monthly programme, detailing important forthcoming events, *Köln-Monatsvorschau*, priced DM2/€1; commercial listings magazines include *Stadt Revue* (DM4/€2) and *Prinz* (DM2/€1). Advance **tickets** for most events can be purchased from KölnTicket on Roncalliplatz (☎02 21/28 01, *www.koelnticket.de*).

Discos and live rock music

Discos can be found throughout the four nightlife districts mentioned in the previous section, though the main venues for large-scale events are out in the suburbs.

Alter Wartesaal, Johannisstr. 11. The elegant former waiting room of the Hauptbahnhof is a die-hard of the Cologne nightlife scene. It serves full meals and plays music ranging from Europop to Gothic.

E-Werk, Schanzenstr. 37, Mülheim. Converted power station used for live rock concerts; also has discos on Fri & Sat.

Kölnarena, Willy-Brandt-Platz 1, Deutz. The main venue for big-name bands on tour.

Petit Prince, Hohenzollernring 90. Mainstream disco with different nights devoted to different sorts of music, including jazz, salsa and reggae.

Prime Club, Luxemburger Str. 40. Disco with a healthy mixture of dance music and chart stuff; also a popular live venue. Students' evening is on Wed.

Classical music

Cologne has its own **opera** company, plus two **symphony orchestras** – the Gürzenich-Orchester Kölner Phiharmoniker and the WDR Sinfonieorchester, the latter being attached to the national radio, whose headquarters are in Cologne. The radio studios were one of the pioneer centres of electronic music, being particularly associated with the work of Karlheinz Stockhausen, who is still a Cologne resident. As a contrast, look out for performances by Musica Antiqua Köln, Germany's leading **chamber ensemble** for Baroque music played on period instruments; its performance style is unashamedly astringent. There are any number of free concerts in the churches; these are all listed in a monthly programme which you can pick up in the venues themselves.

Venues

Funkhaus, Wallrafplatz (☎02 21/28 01). The radio studios host regular broadcast concerts by the WDR Sinfonieorchester and smaller ensembles.

Opernhaus, Offenbachplatz (☎02 21/22 12 84 00). Cologne's opera house, whose musical director is the American James Conlon, presents high-quality performances of works from the Baroque period to the present day.

Philharmonie, Bischofsgartenstr. 1 (☎02 21/28 01). Modern concert hall in the same building as the Museum Ludwig. Both local orchestras regularly perform there, as do soloists and chamber groups.

Theatre

Cologne's theatres cover a myriad of different types of theatrical experiences.

Atelier Theater, Roonstr. 78 (☎02 21/24 24 85). Offers varied programmes including mime, cabaret and musical theatre.

Comedia Colonia, Löwengasse 7–9 (☎02 21/3 99 60 10). Holds shows suitable for children and youths during the daytime, cabaret in the evenings.

Frei Kammerspiele, Thebäerstr. 17 (☎02 21/9 52 44 54). Presents both classical and contemporary plays.

Kaiserhof Theater, Hohenzollernring 92 (☎02 21/1 39 27 72). A comedy venue with large and small stages.

Kölner Künstler Theater, Stamstr. 8 (☎02 21/5 10 76 86). Children's and youth theatre.

Musical-Dome, Goldgasse 1 (☎02 21/5 15 25 30). Another of the recent prominent additions to the Cologne skyline, this is an appropriately brash venue for blockbuster musicals.

Puppenspiele der Stadt Köln, Eisenmarkt 2–4 (☎02 21/2 58 12 01). This celebrated marionette theatre has been on the go since 1802, but be warned that the unintelligible *Kölsch* dialect is used in its performances.

Schauspielhaus, Offenbachplatz (☎02 21/22 12 84 00). The flagship municipal theatre. Schlosserei is part of the same complex, but has a more experimental programme.

Senftöpfchen, Grosse Neugasse 2–4 (☎02 21/2 58 10 58). Specialist variety theatre.

theater der keller, Kleingedankstr. 6 (☎02 21/31 80 59). Tiny stage for intimate dramatic works.

Carnival

While there's no doubt that Cologne is worth visiting at any season, by far the best time to come is during **Carnival**. It's celebrated here with a verve normally associated with Mediterranean countries, and is a useful corrective to the common misapprehension that the Germans are an excessively serious and respectful people. For the *drei tollen Tage* ("three crazy days"– Thursday, Sunday and Monday of Carnival week), life in the city comes to a complete stop and everyone, from punks to grannies, dons make-up and costume, taking to the streets as clown, fool, harlequin or historical personality.

The present highly organized festival (here always known as *Karneval*, as opposed to *Fasching* or *Fastnet* in southern Germany) dates back to 1823, but its true origins go back a lot further. In part it derives from a pagan exorcism of evil spirits in the transition from one season to another, and in part from a Christian tradition of periods of fasting, which were invariably preceded by counterbalancing periods of merriment. This latter factor governs the timetable of the festival, which has moveable dates; the climax occurs in the week preceding Ash Wednesday, immediately before the stringencies of Lent. However, the Carnival season actually begins as early as "the eleventh of the eleventh", ie November 11, a date which was seen as having a foolish significance. From then on, Cologne holds both costume balls and *Sitzungen* (sessions); at the latter, speeches are made in rhyming couplets in the local *Kölsch* dialect (incomprehensible to outsiders, but fairly close to Dutch).

The festivities

The real business begins with **Weiberfastnacht** on the Thursday prior to the seventh Sunday before Easter. A ceremony in the Alter Markt, starting at 10am, leads to the official inauguration of the festival with the handing over of the keys of the city by the mayor at 11.11am precisely to *Prinz Claus III*, who assumes command for the "three crazy days". Whereas in other cities he's aided by a princess, in Cologne he has two companions, the peasant *Bauer Knut* and the virgin *Jungfrau Karla*, who is played by a man and is emphatically not his betrothed. The fun can then begin in earnest; in repentance for the chauvinism of earlier centuries, this particular day is now given over to the supremacy of women, who are allowed to take the liberties of their choice. At 3pm there's the first of the great **processions**, beginning at Severinstor, based on the **legend of Jan and Griet**. The former was Jan von Werth, a seventeenth-century cavalry officer who saved the city from ruin in the Thirty Years War. Griet was the Cologne girl who had spurned him, prompting him to assume a military career; they were not to meet again until she, as an ageing spinster, saw him enter the city as a general at the head of his troops. In the evening, the great series of **costume balls** begins, the most

---

HEINRICH BÖLL

Cologne and its Carnival form the setting for several novels and short stories by the local writer **Heinrich Böll**, notably *The Clown* and *The Lost Honour of Katharina Blum*, works which offer a trenchant examination of postwar West German society. Böll's earlier books, such as *And Where were You, Adam?* and *The Train was on Time*, give an equally penetrating analysis of the national psyche during World War II. His simple, direct style, refreshingly different from the intellectualization so often found in German literature, and the fearless way he bared the soul of his nation, brought him an international reputation as Germany's leading postwar writer – a status reflected in the award of the Nobel Prize for Literature in 1972. However, his work makes many Germans feel uncomfortable, and even now, some years after his death, he has not yet been honoured with a memorial museum.

prestigious being those in the Gürzenich. However, there are plenty of spontaneous bouts of singing, dancing and boisterous conviviality in the streets and taverns as an authentic alternative.

For the next two days, the city returns to relative normality during daylight hours, although fancy dress is still much in evidence, and on the Saturday morning there's the **Funkenbiwack**, featuring the *Rote und Blaue Funken* (Red and Blue Sparks), men dressed up in eighteenth-century military outfits; they disobey every order – a symbol of Cologne's long tradition of anti-militarism. The celebrations come to a climax with the two big costumed processions with floats; on Sunday the **Schull- un Veedleszög**, largely featuring children, forms a prelude to the more spectacular **Rosenmontagzug** (Rose Monday Parade). The latter is unquestionably the highlight of the celebrations, a riot of colour featuring over seven thousand people, half of them musicians, and three hundred horses; and costing some DM1 million to mount. This is only partly due to the costumes; a dominant feature is the fact that 40 tons of sweets, 100,000 chocolates, 100,000 packets of popcorn and innumerable bunches of flowers and containers of eau de Cologne are hurled into the crowd. The first part of the procession is a pageant on the history of the city; then comes the satirical section in which local, national and international politicians appear in effigy; finally there's the gala in honour of the Cologne Carnival, with the spectacular retinues of the peasant, the virgin and the prince bringing up the rear. It's all done with a proper sense of Germanic thoroughness, taking all of four hours to pass by. After this, the festival runs down; there are numerous smaller parades in the suburbs on Shrove Tuesday, while the restaurants offer special fish menus on Ash Wednesday.

Carnival practicalities

Although the city gets jam-packed with visitors during Carnival time, many are day-trippers and there's no problem finding **accommodation**, but bear in mind that both youth hostels are likely to be full at the weekend. A greater difficulty comes in deciding **where to stand** during the processions; if you want the backdrop of the Dom, make sure you come several hours before they start (12.30pm on Sun, noon on Mon) and choose a position on the elevated terrace. Alternatively, go somewhere towards the beginning or end of the route (the tourist office provides free maps), where the crowds are thinner. You could consider renting one of the grandstand **seats**, positioned all along the course of the route; these are expensive for the Rose Monday Parade, but good value on the Sunday. Remember to keep well wrapped up; even when the weather is sunny, it's likely to be cold. Don't expect to do anything else during the "three crazy days"; all the museums and most of the shops are closed, and even the Dom's doors are firmly locked except for the occasional service. Above all, join in the fun; it isn't essential to get dressed up (though it helps), and don't hesitate to follow the crowds, usually congregated round a big drum – it's the impromptu events as much as the setpieces which make this such a great festival. Note that there's a special deal allowing unlimited travel on the public transport network between Weiberfastnacht and Shrove Tuesday. For advance **tickets**, write to *Festkomitee des Kölner Karnevals*, Antwerpener Str. 55.

Listings

Airlines Lufthansa, Am Hof 30 (☎02 21/2 05 05 20).
Airport ☎02 21/40 4 0 01 for flight information.
Bookstores The streets circling Neumarkt have a dense concentration of bookstores; try also around the Dom, on Komödienstrasse or the area around the university. Specially recommended is Büchermarkt, Ehrenstr. 4, which stocks a huge range of cut-price titles on the arts, including many in English. Gleumes, Hohenstaufenring 45, is a specialist guidebook and map retailer.

Car rental Avis, Clemensstr. 29 (☎02 21/23 43 33); Condor, Wilhelm-Mauser-Str. 53 (☎02 21/58 10 55); Europcar, Wilhelm-Mauser-Str. 35 (☎02 21/9 58 44 10); Hertz, Bismarckstr. 19–21 (☎02 21/51 50 84). There's also a number of offices at the airport.

Cultural institutes Amerikahaus, Apostelnkloster 13–15 (☎02 21/20 90 10); British Council, Hahnenstr. 6 (☎02 21/20 64 40).

Doctor ☎02 21/1 92 92.

Festivals Everything else inevitably stands in the shade of Carnival (see pp.554–5). However, the Corpus Christi celebrations (variable date in May or June) are also impressive, featuring a barge procession along the Rhine, and another from the Dom through the streets of the Altstadt.

Markets The large squares in the Altstadt provide a fitting setting for frequent markets; there is a weekly one all day Fri in Alter Markt, and a flea market in the same location every third Sat. Special occasions are: the flower market in Alter Markt on weekends in late April and early May; the junk market in Neumarkt in mid-May and again in mid-Sept; the Weinwoche (actually nearer a fortnight) in Neumarkt in late May/early June; and the Weihnachtsmarkt in both locations throughout Advent.

Mitfahrzentrale ADM, Maximenenstr. 2 (☎02 21/1 94 40) Citynetz, Saarstr. 22 (☎02 21/1 94 44); there's also a Frauenmitfahrzentrale (along with a feminist bookstore) at Moltkestr. 66 (☎02 21/52 31 20).

Pharmacist ☎02 21/1 15 00 for information on late-opening pharmacies.

Post office The main office with poste restante is at Breite Str. 6–62 (Mon–Fri 8am–8pm, Sat 8am–4pm).

Rhine cruises K-D Linie at Frankenwerft 15 (☎02 21/2 08 83 18 or 2 58 30 11); Köln-Tourist-Personenschiffahrt at Konrad-Adenauer-Ufer (☎02 21/12 16 00); Colonia at Anleger Hohenzollernbrücke (☎02 21/2 57 42 25). Prices start at DM10/€5 for a 1hr round trip.

Shopping The pedestrian section of the Altstadt is the city's main shopping street. Eau de Cologne (*Kölner Wasser*) can be bought in innumerable stores. About twenty companies make the product: Farina, founded in 1709 and still in business today, is one of the original manufacturers; Mülhens is another firm with a long pedigree.

Sports The main outdoor ground is at Aachener Strasse in the western suburb of Müngersdorf; FC Köln play here, and there's an international athletics meeting in Aug. or early Sept. An ice rink and swimming stadium are at Lentstr. 30 in Riehl, and a huge *Sporthalle* for indoor events is at Mülheimer Strasse in Deutz.

Travel agencies Many are to be found in the vicinity of the Dom, including Thomas Cook at Komödienstr. 7 (☎02 21/20 20 80).

THE LOWER RHINELAND

The **Lower Rhineland** (Niederrhein) is the name given to the predominantly flat area north of Cologne; the great river thereafter offers no more dramatic scenery. Industrialization, though significant, is held in check most of the way up to **Düsseldorf**. Immediately beyond, however, begins the Ruhrgebiet, the most developed industrial region in the world. Although most of this forms part of Westphalia, the westernmost cities, **Duisburg** and **Essen**, belong to the North Rhine region, as do the corresponding towns across the river, including **Mönchengladbach**. After this, there's a dramatic change to a countryside very close in spirit to nearby Holland. There are no more cities, but a number of small historic towns, the most notable of which is **Xanten**.

North from Cologne

Immediately north of Cologne, making for easy excursions from the city, are some exciting destinations. On the left bank of the Rhine are the medieval customs post of **Zons** and the monastery of **Knechtsteden**. On the right bank, the area known as the Bergisches Land is punctuated by the bleak manufacturing towns that put Germany at the forefront of industrial development in the nineteenth century. It retains much green countryside, however, now designated a *Naturpark*, and shelters the great monastic church of **Kloster Altenberg**.

Zons

The curious village of **ZONS** lies 25km downstream from Cologne. It's now part of the municipality of Dormagen, an industrial town of no interest in itself, and is some 3km east of the latter's Bahnhof, to which it's connected by regular bus services (#875 and #882).

In 1372 the archbishop of Cologne, Friedrich von Saarwerden, decided to levy taxes on the profitable shipping route through his domain, and began the building of a walled town on the site of his predecessors' long-destroyed castle. For all Zons' history of bad luck – it's repeatedly been ravaged by fires and floods down the centuries – the original **Stadtbefestigung** remains largely intact. It ranks as one of the most important surviving examples of a medieval defensive system in Germany, though it now requires a bit of imagination to visualize the original setting, as silting means it's now some way back from the Rhine.

Zons is the sort of place you'd expect to be overrun by sightseeing coaches, but, on weekdays at least, it's remarkably quiet. You'll get the best views by walking around the outside of the circuit. Beginning at the bus stop, turn right and you come to the **Mühlenturm**, the upper section of which was converted into a windmill early in its history. From here, continue along the south side of the town, which has a double wall, the outer having been added for protection against flooding. At the corner are the ruins of **Schloss Friedestrom**, including the gateway, the chunky keep and a courtyard which forms a fitting setting for open-air theatre and pageants (every Sun afternoon mid-June to mid-Sept; also other random days). The eastern wall has two cylindrical defensive towers, along with an octagonal watchtower; at its far corner is the **Rheinturm**, the medieval entrance to the town and the place where customs dues were collected. Three watching posts pierce the northern wall, which terminates in the battlemented **Krötschenturm**. In the town centre there's one more tower, the round **Juddeturm**, which served as both prison and look-out. Around the Rheinturm are the few old houses which have survived the natural disasters; everything else is Baroque or later. The handsome **Herrenhaus** contains the **Kreismuseum** (Tues–Fri 2–6pm, Sat & Sun 10am–12.30pm & 2–5pm; DM4/€2), which mounts temporary exhibitions alongside its own collection of Jugendstil art.

Practicalities

Zons' **tourist office** (Mon, Wed & Fri 8.30am–noon, Tues 8.30am–noon & 2.15–4pm, Thurs 8.30am–noon & 2.15–5pm; ☎0 21 33/37 72 or 25 72 62, fax 25 74 61, *www.zons.de*) is at Schloss-Str. 37. **Hotels** include *Schloss Destille*, Mauerstr. 26a (☎0 21 33/4 76 58; ④–⑥); *Zum Feldtor*, Schloss-Str. 40 (☎0 21 33/2 45 90; ⑤) and *Schloss Friedestrom*, Parkstr. 2 (☎0 21 33/50 30; ⑦). All of these have **restaurants**, and there are plenty of other places in town where you can have a full meal or a snack. There are two **campsites** at Stürzelberg 1km to the north – *Strandterrasse* (☎0 21 06/7 17 17) and *Pitt-Jupp* (☎0 21 06/4 22 10).

Throughout the summer, regular daily **boat trips** (☎0 21 06/4 21 49 or 4 23 49) run to Benrath; there are very occasional sailings to Cologne.

Around Zons: Kloster Knechtsteden

Also within the municipality of Dormagen is the Romanesque **Kloster Knechtsteden**, built in the austere style favoured by its Premonstratensian founders, but enlivened by a central octagon flanked by twin towers. It stands in an isolated setting 3km west of the Bahnhof, connected by a frequent bus service (#876). As in the great imperial cathedrals, there's a choir at both ends of the building; the eastern one is a late Gothic replacement, while that to the west is adorned with mid-twelfth century **frescoes** showing Christ as Pantocrator, surrounded by angels and the symbols of the Evangelists, with portraits of the Apostles below. If you fancy a quiet night away from the cities, the *Klosterhof* (☎0 21 06/8 07 45; ④), just outside the monastery gate, has rooms along with a bar-restaurant.

Kloster Altenberg

Set in isolation in a wooded valley of the River Dhün about 15km northeast of Cologne is **Kloster Altenberg**, popularly known as the **Bergischer Dom**. In spite of this nickname, it's not a cathedral but a monastery built by the Cistercians, whose rule prescribed secluded settings of this kind. In 1133 the count of Berg moved his seat and donated his ancestral home, set on the hill above, to this reforming order of monks, who used the stones to construct their first church. What makes the present building, begun in 1255, particularly interesting is that it's contemporary with, and of similar stature to, the Dom in Cologne, only this time it was completed in just over a hundred years. In accordance with the austere Cistercian tradition there's no tower and little in the way of decoration. Nevertheless, it's still enormously photogenic, seeming to blend effortlessly into the landscape; the best view is from the hill to the east, where you see the choir with its corona of chapels (the earliest and finest feature) to best advantage.

Few buildings so perfectly encompass the basic tenets of the Gothic style: there are no grand gestures; everything is spacious, bright and harmonious, a visible manifestation of the order's quest for spiritual tranquillity. The chancel has wonderful original silvery-grey **stained-glass** windows which have geometric motifs only. This same type of glass, but with floral shapes, fills the big lights of the north transept, beaming down on the tombs of the counts (later dukes) of Berg. Relaxation of the normal Cistercian rejection of representational subjects is confined to the giant facade window, the largest in Germany: it depicts the Heavenly Jerusalem in predominantly golden tones, a particularly memorable sight when illuminated by the setting sun.

If you want to sample some of the atmosphere of rural peace, make sure you come on a weekday. On Sundays, Altenberg acts as a magnet for urban dwellers seeking their weekly retreat; a curiosity is that both Catholic and Protestant services are held. This was a condition laid down in the nineteenth century by the Prussian King Friedrich Wilhelm IV when he arranged for the church's repair and return to worship, after a period of disuse and decay following the Napoleonic suppression. The monastery – currently the subject of a major restoration programme that will last until 2004 – can be reached in an hour from the centre of Cologne, if you strike lucky with connections: take U-Bahn #16 to Wiener Platz, then bus #434.

Wuppertal

WUPPERTAL stands at the northernmost end of the Bergisches Land group of industrial towns, and some 30km east of Düsseldorf. The overriding justification for a detour is to see its public transport system – little recommendation, you would think, but the **Schwebebahn** (hanging rail line), a monorail suspension system without wheels, is genuinely unique. The city of Wuppertal didn't exist as such when the line was built between 1898 and 1900 to link the various towns strung along the valley of the River Wupper – **Barmen** and **Elberfeld** being the largest. These communities united in 1929, yet still preserve distinct identities; Wuppertal hasn't evolved a recognizable city centre.

THE SCHWEBEBAHN

The brainchild of **Carl Eugen Langen**, who failed to interest Berlin and Munich in his idea, the **Schwebebahn**, Wuppertal's creaking rail line, is suspended on high by a steel structure supported by 472 triangular girders. Between fifteen of its nineteen stations, it runs directly above the river, then passes over the main thoroughfares of Sonnborn and Oberwinkel to the west, leaving them permanently dank. It's well worth travelling along the whole route for a complete picture of the city; the Werther Brücke station, which preserves its original Jugendstil decoration, is a sight in itself. The sleek orange and blue cars are fourth generation; at weekends in summer one of the original models is run. This is the only gimmick associated with a genuine local facility which is both fast (it's all but immune from delays) and efficient (services run every few minutes). For nearly a century, it had the reputation of being the safest public transport system ever devised, one which had never had a serious accident, never mind a fatality. Tragically, that proud record came to an abrupt end in 1999, when a car which had not been properly reassembled after maintenance work plunged into the river, killing three passengers instantly. The accident caused massive dismay locally, but has made the authorities all the more determined to avoid even a single accident during the Schwebebahn's second century of operation.

Elberfeld

The centre of **ELBERFELD** is a vast pedestrian shopping precinct. At Poststrasse 11, look out for the watchmaker's shop whose incredible display is trumped by its own **Uhrenmuseum** (Mon–Fri 4–6pm, Sat 10am–1pm; DM5/€2.50). Here you can see over a thousand weird and wonderful timepieces, ranging from the earliest watch made in Germany to an eighteenth-century London fancy with an elephant and a rotating Chinese emperor's court.

Round the corner, at Turmhof 8, is the neo-Renaissance bulk of the former Rathaus, now containing the **Von-der-Heydt-Museum** (Tues, Wed & Fri–Sun 11am–6pm, Thurs 11am–8pm; DM6/€3), one of the country's finest galleries of nineteenth- and twentieth-century art. Centrepiece of the display is a group of some two dozen canvases by a local man, **Hans von Marées**, whose pronounced intellectual approach, marked Italianate influence and preference for a dark palette combine to make him one of Germany's most distinctive painters. Other artists particularly well represented are **Carl Spitzweg** (with five wonderfully humorous Biedermeier vignettes), **Max Beckmann** (notably self-portraits as a clown and as a World War I Red Cross worker), **Paula Modersohn-Becker** and **Alexej Jawlensky**, while individual highlights include **Kirchner**'s *Women in the Street*, **Dix**'s satirical *An die Schönheit* and **Schlemmer**'s *Twelve Figures in an Interior*. A good cross-section of French Impressionism is headed by a study for **Manet**'s seminal *Déjeuner sur l'Herbe*.

Barmen

At Engelsstrasse in **BARMEN** is a collection of more marginal interest, the **Museum für Frühindustrialisierung** (Museum of Early Industry; Tues–Sun 10am–1pm & 3–5pm; DM3/€1.50). In front stands the **Engels-Haus** (same times and ticket), an elegant late eighteenth-century building which belonged to a family of textile entrepreneurs. It now serves as a memorial to their celebrated black sheep **Friedrich Engels**, who was born nearby. As a young man, he was sent to England to work at the sister factory of Ermen & Engels in Manchester; there he became fascinated by the plight of the urban proletariat, and on his return to Barmen in 1845 wrote his celebrated *The Condition of the Working Class in England*. Soon afterwards, he began collaborating with Karl Marx, returning to work as a capitalist in Manchester in order to provide funds for their joint revolutionary writings. Though very much the junior partner in these, Engels always had a large input on matters concerning nationalities, diplomacy, the military and business practices – even in the books such as *Das Kapital* in which Marx appears as sole author.

Barmen really seems to relish its reputation as an anti-establishment town, as it was also the scene of the 1934 synod of the "Confessing Church", Protestant opponents of Hitler. At this meeting, the church declared its independence from state control, proclaiming itself the only true heir of the Lutheran tradition, in contrast to the bogus Reich Church most clergymen had been forced into joining. Its guiding force, **Pastor Martin Niemöller**, was later incarcerated in a concentration camp, but gained a reputation outside Germany as one of the most effective anti-Nazis, and survived to become a leading pacifist and international churchman after the war.

Practicalities

Wuppertal's **tourist office** (Mon–Fri 9am–6pm, Sat 9am–1pm; ☎02 02/1 94 33, fax 02 02/5 63 80 52, *www.wuppertal.de*) is just across from the Hauptbahnhof in Elberfeld at Am Döppersberg. There's a **Mitfahrzentrale** office at Emilstr. 55 (☎02 02/2 62 14 43).

Hotels are scattered all over the city. Those in Elberfeld tend to be on the expensive side; options there include *Astor*, Schlossbleiche 4–6 (☎02 02/45 05 11; ⑤), and *Zur Post*, Poststr. 4 (☎02 02/45 01 31; ⑤). Barmen also has a number of budget places, including *Wittenstein*, Wittensteinstr. 223 (☎02 02/25 55 60; ③–⑤), and *CVJM-Gästehaus* on Bundeshöhe (☎02 02/57 42 26; ④) to the south, while the small *Villa Christina*, set in a park to the east of town at Richard-Strauss-Allee 18 (☎02 02/62 17 36; ⑥), is perhaps the most attractive place to stay in Wuppertal. The **youth hostel** is at Obere Lichtenplatzer Str. 70 (☎02 02/55 23 72, fax 55 73 54; DM23/€11.50 or DM28/€14), a few minutes' walk to the south of Barmen's Bahnhof.

Reasonably priced places to **eat** and **drink** can be found all over the city, especially in the large pedestrian precinct in the centre of Elberfeld, though the best traditional restaurant is probably *Zum Futterplatz*, south of Barmen's Bahnhof at Obere Lichtenplatzer Str. 102.

The Schauspielhaus, near the tourist office at Bundesallee 260 (☎02 02/5 63 42 61 or 5 69 44 44), presents plays and operas, but is best known for Pina Bausch's *Tanztheater,* by some way Germany's leading **modern dance** company.

Düsseldorf

DÜSSELDORF disputes with Hamburg and Stuttgart the right to be regarded as Germany's richest city, and in many ways is the paragon of the postwar face of the Federal Republic – orderly, prosperous and self-confident. Few places can have a name so inappropriate to their present status: the "village on the Düssel" is now a thriving Land capital of 600,000 inhabitants on both banks of the Rhine, crossed here by no fewer than six bridges. Since the war, it has developed a cosmopolitan and strangely un-European character. Never as industrialized as its neighbours in the Ruhr, Düsseldorf has concentrated on its role as the region's financial and administrative centre, its skyline punctuated by the skyscrapers of innumerable multinational giants.

The extent to which you'll like or loathe Düsseldorf depends very much on your reaction to the way it has sold its soul to the corporate dream. If **luxury shops** are your scene, there are none more stylish between Paris and Berlin. The city likes to think of itself as Germany's leading fashion centre, with sartorial elegance and other displays of

ACCOMMODATION
1 Am Füchschen
4 Am Rathaus
5 Amsterdam
3 Breidenbacher Hof
9 Bristol
7 CVJM
12 Diana
10 Eden
11 Haus Hillesheim
6 Komet
8 Manhattan
2 Windsor

DÜSSELDORF

wealth serving as indicators of individual standing in its fiercely competitive high society. Even for a short visit, it's an expensive option, but there's no doubt that the
nightlife, at least, is one of the most varied and enjoyable in the country.

Arrival, information and accommodation

The **Hauptbahnhof** is situated in the southeast part of the city centre; from here, the
shopping streets begin to fan out. S-Bahn trains #1 and #7 leave at twenty-minute intervals for the underground terminal at the **airport** to the north, which now has a second
station on the main line to Duisburg. Note that, unlike neighbouring cities, most of
Düsseldorf's attractions are within walking distance of each other, so the DM10/€5 24-
hour ticket on the public transport network is really only of use if you specifically want
to see the outlying suburbs. A better alternative is the DM19/€9.50 **Welcome Card**,
which covers public transport costs for two days and gives reduced entry to museums
and other attractions. The **tourist office** (Mon–Fri 8.30am–6pm, Sat 9am–12.30pm;
room-booking counter Mon–Sat 8am–8pm, Sun 4–8pm; ☎02 11/17 20 20, fax 16 10 71,
www.duesseldorf.de) is at Immermannstr. 65b.

   Accommodation is overwhelmingly geared to the business traveller, and prices are
far above the national norm, even in the suburbs. The main concentration of hotels is
in the business district between the Hauptbahnhof and the Altstadt; several of the least
expensive options are in Friedrichstadt, the old suburb immediately south of the city
centre.

Hotels

Am Füchschen, Ratinger Str. 32 (☎02 11/86 79 60, fax 8 67 96 61, *RJonetat@t-online.de*). Small hotel in an Altstadt street which is well known for its bars and restaurants. ⑥–⑨.

Am Rathaus, Berger Str. 28 (☎02 11/32 65 56, fax 32 23 41). Another small Altstadt hotel, with a wonderful location in the very heart of the quarter. ⑤–⑦.

Amsterdam, Stresemannstr. 20 (☎02 11/8 40 58, fax 8 40 50). Good medium-priced city-centre choice. ④–⑨.

Breidenbacher Hof, Heinrich-Heine-Allee 36 (☎02 11/1 30 30, fax 1 30 38 30, *www.breidenbacherhof .de*). Without a doubt, the pick of the city's luxury hotels, with an ideal situation just off Königsallee. Has three separate restaurants, all of them prestigious. ⑨.

Bristol, Adersstr. 8 (☎02 11/37 07 50, fax 37 37 54). Surprisingly reasonable considering its location in the very north of Friedrichstadt, just south of the prestigious Königsallee. ④–⑤.

CVJM, Graf-Adolf-Str.102 (☎02 11/17 28 50, fax 1 72 85 44). Recently refurbished YMCA-run hotel by the Hauptbahnhof. Most of the bedrooms are grouped round an inner courtyard and are therefore well sheltered from street noise. ⑥–⑧.

Diana, Jahnstr. 31 (☎02 11/37 50 71, fax 3 85 00 70). Popular, moderately priced hotel in a quiet Friedrichstadt street. ③–⑥.

Eden, Adersstr. 29–31 (☎02 11/3 89 70, fax 38 97 77, *www.hotel-eden.de*). High-quality hotel with restaurant (closed Sun), a member of the Best Western group. ⑧–⑨.

Haus Hillesheim, Jahnstr. 19 (☎02 11/38 68 60, fax 3 86 86 33, *www.hotel-hillesheim.de*). Pleasant Friedrichstadt hotel that has been in existence since 1894. It has a quaintly furnished bar open to residents only. ③–⑦.

Komet, Bismarckstr. 93 (☎02 11/17 87 90, fax 1 78 79 50). A good medium-price recommendation in the city centre. ③–⑦.

Manhattan, Graf-Adolf-Str. 39 (☎02 11/37 11 38, fax 37 02 47). Reasonably priced hotel popular with young travellers. ④–⑥.

Windsor, Grafenberger Allee 36 (☎02 11/91 46 80, fax 9 14 68 40). The elegant furnishings mark this out as one of Düsseldorf's most appealing hotels. ⑦–⑨.

Youth hostel and campsites

Campingplatz Oberlörick, Niederkasseler Deich 305 (☎02 11/59 14 01). Located on the left bank of the Rhine; take U-Bahn #70, #74, #75, #76 or #77 to Belsenplatz, then bus #828. Closed Oct–March.

Campingplatz Unterbacher See (☎02 11/8 99 20 38). Düsseldorf's more tranquil campsite, at the eastern extremity of the city; take S-Bahn #7 to Eller, then bus #735.

Jugendherberge und Jugendgästehaus, Düsseldorfer Str. 1, Oberkassel (☎02 11/57 73 10, fax 57 25 13, *jgh-duesseldorf@t-online.de*). From the Hauptbahnhof, take bus #835 or walk down Graf-Adolf-Strasse and continue in a straight line, crossing the Rheinkniebrücke; it's the first building on the other side. DM38/€19.

The city centre

The **Altstadt**, close to the Rhine, reflects the meaning of Düsseldorf's name in its modest proportions. Never one of Germany's great cities from an architectural point of view, it's chiefly renowned today for its remarkable range of places of entertainment. Immediately to the east is a planned **green belt**, created by French landscape gardeners in the eighteenth century when Düsseldorf was a seat of the Electors Palatine, who succeeded the defunct line of the Dukes of Berg, the city's founders.

The Altstadt

Over two hundred restaurants, beer halls, wine cellars, bistros, snack bars, jazz centres and discos are crammed into the small area of the Altstadt, which pulsates with activity day and night. This fact tends to overshadow the historical sights, but two very contrasting churches do catch the eye. **St Lambertus**, a fourteenth-century brick building

HEINRICH HEINE (1797–1856)

One of Germany's most celebrated and intriguing men of letters, **Heinrich Heine** modified the traditional Romantic themes of his day by using a biting sense of irony. The recurring image of the *Doppelgänger* in his work reflects his lifelong feeling of isolation – as a poet in a family of merchants, a Jew and Protestant convert among Catholics, a Francophile who eventually settled in Paris yet remained German at heart, and as a revolutionary familiar with Marxism who kept faith with the bourgeois liberal tradition. His early *Buch der Lieder* provided the dying Schubert with the texts for his last songs, and was to be a similar source of inspiration for subsequent composers, notably Schumann, Brahms and Wolf. Later, his *Reisebilder*, combining factual descriptions, poems and political comment, initiated a new and much-imitated form of travel writing.

in the hall-church style, is easily recognizable because of its tall twisted spire, now ousted from its former physical and spiritual dominance over the city by the huge corporate skyscrapers. Inside, there's a graceful Gothic tabernacle, a fifteenth-century *Pietà*, and the spectacular late sixteenth-century marble and alabaster tomb of Duke Wilhelm V.

A short walk to the east is **St Andreas**, a Jesuit foundation of 1629 which is one of the chief reminders of the period when Düsseldorf was the seat of the Electors Palatine. Its galleried interior is ornately decorated with stucco; the **Mausoleum** (Mon–Fri 3–5.30pm) to the rear contains the surprisingly simple tin coffins of the electors. The most famous and genuinely popular of these rulers was Johann Wilhelm II, better known as **Jan Wellem**, who ruled from 1679 to 1716. He's commemorated in the huge open area named after him in the heart of the city, and by a masterly equestrian statue (the work of his Italian court sculptor Gabriel de Grupello), erected during his own lifetime outside the Renaissance **Rathaus**. In the square immediately to the north is the **Schlossturm**, the only remnant of the old fortifications; it has been restored to house the **Schiffahrtmuseum** (Wed & Sat 2–6pm, Sun 11am–6pm; DM5/€2.50), a small display of Rhineland navigation.

At Schulstr. 4, towards the southern end of the Altstadt, the former Palais Nesselrode now houses the **Hetjens-Museum** (Tues & Thurs–Sat 11am–5pm, Wed 11am–9pm; DM6/€3), which boasts of being the only one in Germany entirely devoted to the art of ceramics. The exhibits range over eight thousand years of history, and come from all over the world. International highlights include Mesopotamian grave objects from 3500 BC, painted vases from ancient Greece, figures from China's Tang dynasty period and a spectacular seventeenth-century Islamic cupola from Multan in Pakistan. There are also fine examples from most of the German porcelain manufactories; the largest collection of Rhenish stoneware in existence; and an exquisite Art Nouveau/Jugendstil section. The new extension is shared with the **Filmmuseum** (same times and ticket), which operates the Black Box, the city's most adventurous cinema. Nearby, at Bilkerstr. 14, is the **Heinrich-Heine-Institut** (Tue–Fri & Sun 11am–5pm, Sat 1–5pm; DM4/€2), a museum and research centre devoted to the great poet who is Düsseldorf's favourite son (see box above).

Overlooking the Rhine at the extreme southern end of the Altstadt is Peter Behrens' **Mannesmann-Gebäude**, a distinguished example of corporate architecture from the first decade of the twentieth century, but now dwarfed by the **Mannesmann-Haus**, the skyscraper which pioneered the postwar identification of Düsseldorf's appearance with the power of multinational companies. The quayside alongside is also named after the company, which lost its independence in 2000, when it succumbed to a hostile takeover – the first ever mounted in German business history – by the British mobile phone giant Vodaphone Airtouch. This was preceded by a long and bitter boardroom battle which traumatized the country's business and political communities, who were not only unused to the concept of hostile bids, but outraged that such a venerable company could fall victim to a relative upstart, and resulted in an ill-judged attempt at intervention by Chancellor Schröder. Just to the south is Düsseldorf's highest building, the **Rheinturm** (Mon–Fri 11am–11.30pm, Sat & Sun 10am–11.30pm; DM5.50/€2.75), a radio tower built between 1979 and 1982. You can ascend by high-speed lift to its observation platform for an absolutely stunning view over the city and the Rhine. Alongside is the **Landtag**, the state parliament of North Rhine-Westphalia.

The museum quarter

Housed in an ultra-modern gallery in Grabbeplatz just north of St Andreas is the **Kunstsammlung Nordrhein–Westfalen** (Tues–Thurs, Sat & Sun 10am–6pm, Fri 10am–8pm; *www.kunstsammlung.de*; DM5/€2.50, DM12/€6 when there's a loan exhibition). The genesis of this collection was a remarkable act of postwar contrition by the authorities. **Paul Klee**, the abstract painter, was a professor at the Düsseldorf Academy from 1930 until dismissed in the Nazi purges of 1933. In atonement for this, around ninety of his works were purchased from a private American source in 1960; shortly afterwards, a rapid acquisitions policy, of twentieth-century art only, was adopted. The Klee collection remains the obvious draw, although only about two-thirds of the works are on show at any one time. Even if you aren't attracted to this painter, there are many other highlights, such as one of **Picasso**'s most famous representational works, *Two Sitting Women*, **Léger**'s large *Adam and Eve*, **Kirchner**'s *Negro Dance*, **Modigliani**'s *Diego Rivera* and self-portraits by **Kokoschka** and **Chagall**. Already the collection resembles a who's who of modern art, and it continues to grow.

The **Kunstmuseum** (Tues–Sun 11am–6pm; *www.kunstmuseum-duesseldorf.de*; DM5/€2.50), directly north of the Altstadt at Ehrenhof 5, has extensive displays on three floors. This could very nearly have been one of Europe's finest art galleries, as the Electors owned a marvellous array of paintings which followed the court to Munich in 1806 and soon formed one of the bases of the Alte Pinakothek there. A **Rubens** masterpiece, an altarpiece of *The Assumption*, never made the journey because of its size; it now puts almost all the other old masters on the first floor completely in the shade. Among the few paintings not wholly outclassed are *Venus and Adonis* by the same painter, a *St Jerome* attributed to **Ribera** and *St Francis in Meditation* by **Zurbarán**. Also on this floor is a series of powerful lithographs by **Otto Pankok** called *The Passion*, though in fact Christ's whole life is depicted. Their gloomy, highly charged emotionalism, with hateful mobs and angst-ridden victims, directly reflects the contemporary horrors of the Holocaust. Upstairs, there's a modern section which complements that in the Kunstsammlung, along with an extensive show of the nineteenth-century historical painters of the **Düsseldorf Academy**. Now long out of fashion, they suffer from failing to find a sense of inspiration to match their undoubted technical skill. More pleasing is the sparkling **glass** section on the ground floor, dominated by Art Nouveau and Art Deco pieces from Germany, France and America.

The Königsallee and Hofgarten

The city's main thoroughfare, the **Königsallee**, laid out at the beginning of the nineteenth century, was the culmination of the transformation of Düsseldorf by the electors palatine into a city of parks, ponds and canals. It's one of Germany's most famous streets and is chic rather than beautiful; down one side are banks and offices, with expensive stores, representing all the trendiest names in international designer-made goods, lining the other. People shop here with an incredibly self-conscious air; in antithesis to the intended effect, the prevailing hallmark is one of vulgarity, and it's appropriate that the architectural setting is so mediocre. Only the late Jugendstil **Kaufhaus** by the Viennese Joseph Maria Olbrich has any merits as a building, though it has suffered from an interior modernization. Diagonally opposite its rear entrance is

Wilhelm-Marx-Haus erected in the 1920s, the earliest visible expression of Düsseldorf's infatuation with the New World.

The largest of the parks is the **Hofgarten**, shaped like a great stiletto-heeled shoe, and now incongruously cut in several places by busy streets. Towering over it is the **Thyssen-Haus**, by far the most arresting of the corporate structures which so altered the city skyline in the 1950s, offering a fascinating play of light on its three huge silvery-green slabs. Beside it, the daring white curves of the **Schauspielhaus**, built in 1970, provide an effective counterpoint, as well as a reminder that, in this city, the public structures stand very much in the shadow of big business.

At the far end of the Hofgarten is **Schloss Jägerhof**, a Baroque palace which sustained severe damage in the last war. Its interior decorations have been refitted as the **Goethe-Museum** (Tues–Fri & Sun 11am–5pm, Sat 1–5pm; DM4/€2), reckoned to be the best collection of memorabilia of the great poet and playwright after those in Frankfurt and Weimar. Unless you're an avid fan, the contents will seem fairly mundane, though it's worth glancing over the section on works of art inspired by his most celebrated drama, *Faust*. Just to the north of the Schloss is the city's finest modern church, **St Rochus**. Outside, it resembles a giant beehive; the interior is deliberately dark, in an attempt to re-create the old mysteries of religion.

Benrath

Of the towns which have been swallowed up by Düsseldorf, by far the most interesting is **BENRATH** to the south, best reached by S-Bahn #6. The **Schloss** (guided tours Tues–Sun 10am–5pm; DM7/€3.50) and its park were commissioned by Elector Carl Theodor (see box on p.355) in the mid-eighteenth century; the unusual harmony of the whole complex is due to the fact that the architect, the French-born **Nicholas de Pigage**, was also a landscape gardener. Its main block, in a style hovering between Rococo and Neoclassical, represents a very clever piece of trompe l'oeil construction – for all its seemingly small size, it contains eighty rooms. The tours take in the sumptuous reception and garden rooms on the ground floor, as well as some of the private apartments upstairs. Afterwards, you can stroll in the formal gardens and see the surviving building of the old palace.

Eating, drinking and nightlife

Walking through the Altstadt – "the longest bar in Europe" according to the tourist office – is an enjoyable activity in itself, especially on summer days when it's even more crowded than usual and virtually every bar and restaurant offers the opportunity for imbibing alfresco. This small quarter contains a large percentage of the city's most recommendable eateries, though there are, of course, plenty of alternatives elsewhere. Düsseldorf's multicultural make-up ensures a wide choice of ethnic cuisines; the best places for traditional local fare are the **Brauereigaststätten**, the restaurants cum beer halls of the local breweries, several of which still maintain the time-honoured tradition of brewing in-house. Their most popular product by far is the highly distinctive **Alt**, which is dark in colour and tending towards sweetness in some varieties, caused by the higher quantity of malt used than in lagers.

Brauereigaststätten

Brauhaus Johann Albrecht, Niederkasseler Str. 104, Oberkassel. A new-generation Hausbrauerei on the left bank of the Rhine. It brews a *Pils* and a dark beer, and serves good-value food.

Ferdinand Schumacher, Oststr. 123. Although located in the modern business district, this Hausbrauerei dates back to the mid-nineteenth century. It makes a delicate, fruity *Alt* and offers full meals.

Frankenheim, Wielandstr. 17. Another very traditional Brauereigaststätte, though the production of its tangy *Alt* has recently moved from the site to more modern premises in Neuss.

Heinrich-Heine-Stuben, Bolkerstr. 50. Cosy two-storey Gaststätte of the Schlösser brewery, which produces the sweetest-tasting *Alt*.

Im Füchschen, Ratinger Str. 28. Hausbrauerei producing a relatively bitter *Alt*, plus a wheat beer called *Silberfüchschen*. It also serves filling and inexpensive meals.

Im Goldenen Kessel, Bolkerstr. 44. Altstadt flagship of the Schumacher brewery, renowned for its reasonably priced food.

Im Goldenen Ring, Burgplatz 21. Traditional Gaststätte serving excellent food, including good-value set meals.

Zum Schiffchen, Hafenstr. 5. The Altstadt Gaststätte of the Frankenheim brewery offers slightly more upmarket cuisine than its competitors, and is therefore a little pricier. Closed Sun.

Zum Schlüssel, Bolkerstr. 45. Hausbrauerei producing a fairly malty *Alt*. High-quality local dishes are served in its cavernous and well-patronized interior.

Zum Uerige, Berger Str. 1. This nineteenth-century Hausbrauerei, one of the most famous in Germany, produces the ultimate in *Alt* beer, plus a good *Weizen*. It's primarily a drinking pub, though snacks are available from the sausage kitchen on the premises.

Other restaurants

Daitokai, Mutter-Ey-Str. 1. As Düsseldorf is the main European outpost of Japanese commerce, it's not surprising that the city is well endowed with Japanese restaurants, of which this is one of the very best.

Fischhaus, Berger Str. 3. Hugely popular fish restaurant.

Muschelhaus Benders Marie, Andreasstr. 13. As its name suggests, this is a specialist in mussels, though other seafood and fish dishes are also served.

Tante Anna, Andreasstr. 2. Historic wine bar-restaurant in a converted sixteenth-century chapel. There are 150 vintages to choose from. Closed Sun.

Zum Csikos, Andreasstr. 9. Highly rated but pricey Hungarian restaurant. Evenings only.

Bars and café-bars

Café Alte Bastion, Rathausufer 12. This genteel quayside café is a good place for *Kaffee und Kuchen*.

Café Bernstein, Oststr. 158. Stylish place for a nightcap, patronized by a distinctive Düsseldorf group – monied student couples.

Dr Jazz, Flingerstr. 11. Jazz hangout, with different bands each evening.

Front Page, Mannesmann-Ufer 9. Cosy piano bar.

g@rden, Rathausufer 8. Internet café-bar, one of several modish hangouts along the waterfront.

Irish Pub, Hunsrückenstr. 13. Genuine reminder of Hibernia, owned and staffed by expatriates, and with a long-established tradition. Such is the current German mania for all things Irish that it now has several competitors, one of them just three doors away.

Marktwirtschaft, Bernrather Str. 7. An excellent place to spend a quiet evening among the well-heeled youth of Düsseldorf.

Miles Smiles, Akademiestr. 6. Jazz bar which doubles as an Italian trattoria.

Ratinger Hof, Ratinger Str. 10. Germany's first and most notorious punk bar lives on, frequented by diehards of the cult and blasting out ear-splitting music.

Sassafras, Düsseldorfer Str. 90. Café-bar with a youthful and unpretentious clientele.

Schnabelewopski, Bolkerstr. 53. Literary café-bar housed in Heine's birthplace.

Weisser Bär, Bolkerstr. 33. Popular pub with raucous music frequented by a curious mixture of young Düsseldorfers and young tourists, and staffed by relics of the '68 generation.

ZAKK, Fichtenstr. 40. A bar with a difference, drawing visitors from neighbouring cities to its exhibitions, video showings and other arty events.

Zum Goldenen Einhorn, Ratinger Str. 18. An enduringly popular spot with the youth of the city, especially in summer when it opens its leafy little beer garden.

Clubs and discos

Bhaggy Disco, Graf-Adolf-Str. 87. Highly popular disco just a stone's throw from the Hauptbahnhof.

Soul Centre, Bolkerstr. 37. Of the two dozen discos in the Altstadt, one of only a couple deviating from playing standard modern fare.

Tor 3, Ronsdorfer Str. 143. South of the centre in the district of Bilk, this huge barn of a place is the city's leading disco. It has few concessions to comfort, but its customers are young, friendly and out to enjoy themselves with a vengeance.

Entertainment

Düsseldorf has a strong tradition in **classical music**, even if present standards are short of its nineteenth-century heyday when both Mendelssohn and Schumann did stints in charge of the city's musical affairs. It also offers a wide range of **theatrical** entertainments. To find out what's on, consult the listings magazines *Überblick* (DM4.50/€2.25), *Prinz* (DM2/€1) or the free *Coolibri*.

Capitol, Erkrather Str. 30 (☎02 11/7 34 40). A specialist venue for musicals.

Deutsche Oper am Rhein, Heinrich-Heine-Allee 16a (☎02 11/8 90 82 11). The city's opera house, which shares its company with neighbouring Duisburg.

Junges Theater in der Altstadt, Wilhelm-Marx-Haus, Kasernenstr. 6 (☎02 11/8 99 36 84). Presents alternative theatre programmes, many from abroad.

Kinder- und Jugendtheater, Münsterstr. 446 (☎02 11/61 26 86). An offshoot of the Schauspielhaus, staging shows for children and youths.

Kom(m)ödchen, Kay-und-Lore-Lorentz-Platz (☎02 11/32 94 43). This theatre with the bizarrely spelt name is one of Germany's best-known venues for political cabaret and satire, with the tradition established by founders Kay and Lore Lorentz still going strong under their son Kay.

Komödie, Steinstr. 23 (☎02 11/32 51 51). As its name suggests, this specializes in comedy dramas.

Marionettentheater, Bilkerstr. 7 (☎02 11/32 84 32). A well-regarded marionette theatre housed in the Baroque Palais Wittgenstein. It stages opera performances as well as the expected children's shows.

Philipshalle, Siegburger Str. 15, Overbilk (☎02 11/8 99 36 79). Huge hall hosting large-scale spectaculars, including pop concerts.

Puppentheater, Helmholtzstr. 48 (☎02 11/37 24 01). Puppet theatre mainly geared towards kids.

Robert-Schumann-Saal, Ehrenhof 4a (☎02 11/8 99 61 29). Small hall for instrumental, chamber and vocal recitals.

Roncalli's Apollo Variety, Haroldstr. 1 (☎02 11/8 28 90 90). New theatre for old-style variety shows.

DÜSSELDORF'S FESTIVALS

It's worth trying to time your visit to coincide with one of Düsseldorf's three main **popular festivals**. The **Carnival** celebrations (seven weeks before Easter) are ranked third in Germany, although those in nearby Cologne are the best of all. The celebrations are supposed to signify the end of winter; its beginning is heralded by **St Martin's Eve** on November 10, marked by an enormous procession of lantern-bearing children. In late July, the **Grosses Schützenfest** (riflemen's meeting) is an eight-day festival along the banks of the Rhine. Simultaneously, there's a huge funfair (claimed to be the largest of its type in the world) offering gut-churning rides on the Ferris wheel, the big dipper and other machines. The most celebrated local tradition is **cartwheeling** by local lads in the streets of the Altstadt. This is in honour of an urchin who saved the day when a wheel came loose on the popular Elector Palatine Jan Wellem's wedding coach, but the reason it survives is the less romantic one of extorting money from tourists. In spite of serving as an unofficial symbol of the city, you're unlikely to see any demonstrations out of season.

Schauspielhaus, Gustav-Grundgens-Platz 1 (☎02 11/36 99 11). One of Düsseldorf's most imposing modern buildings, this is the city's principal dramatic stage.

Tonhalle, Hofgartenufer (☎02 11/8 99 61 23). This converted planetarium is the main concert hall, featuring regular performances by the Dusseldorfer Symphoniker.

Listings

Airport ☎02 11/4 21 22 23 for flight information.

Consulates British, Yorckstr. 19 (☎02 11/9 44 80); Canadian, Prinz-Georg-Str. 126 (☎02 11/17 21 70).

Mitfahrzentralen ADM, Konrad-Adenauer-Platz 13 (☎02 11/1 94 40); Citynetz, Kruppstr. 102 (☎02 11/1 94 44).

Post office The main office is at Immermannstr. 1 with poste restante services.

Rhine cruises K-D Linie, Schlossufer (☎02 11/3 23 92 63).

Neanderthal and Neuss

It's easy enough to escape the cosmopolitan atmosphere of central Düsseldorf, and a couple of contrasting destinations just outside the boundaries of the city make for good half-day trips.

Neanderthal

One of the slowest trains in Germany wends its way up the River Düssel to Mettmann, stopping at **NEANDERTHAL** en route. This hamlet and the eponymous valley are named after the seventeenth-century Protestant poet **Joachim Neander**, who liked to meditate there. During his lifetime, the valley was a rugged canyon, not easily accessible; subsequently, the landscape was changed completely by limestone mining, and it was this that led to a sensational discovery which made Neanderthal famous. In 1856, workers dug up bones from the bottom of a cave; these were later identified as belonging to an earlier form of mankind than *Homo sapiens*, one still bearing a slight facial resemblance to the ape. The term **Neanderthal Man** has since been used to describe the tribes of humans who were wiped out by the last Ice Age. A game reserve established in the valley features animals such as bison which haven't evolved much since prehistoric times, but the landscape around is now irretrievably ruined, and the Düssel – little more than a ditch in the city – is nothing grander than a stream here.

In order to encourage more visitors to come to the site, a new **Neanderthal-Museum** (Tues–Sun 10am–6pm; *www.neanderthal.de*; DM10/€5) has been constructed as a replacement for its very modest predecessor. Symbolically laid out along a gently spiralling ramp, its interactive displays chart the entire course of human evolution. There are some original bones and artefacts from Neanderthal times, though not the famous skull itself, which is now in Bonn (see p.528).

Neuss

On the west bank of the Rhine, Düsseldorf's suburbs merge imperceptibly into **NEUSS**, officially a separate large industrial town with extensive dockyards; it's best reached by S-Bahn #8 or #11, as the fare is the same as for the trams. From the **Hauptbahnhof**, turn left and then left again into Krefelder Strasse, the start of the central shopping axis, which subsequently changes its name to Büchel, then Oberstrasse. About halfway down is the Markt, where you'll find the town's outstanding monument, the **Münster** or **St Quirinus**. It represents the apotheosis of the Rhineland

Romanesque style, built in the early thirteenth century at a time when Gothic was established elsewhere. There's all the exuberance characteristic of the end of an era – blind arcades are employed in playful patterns, and the clover-leaf shape favoured by Rhenish architects is used in the design of the windows as well as in the plan of the chancel. The dome provides a touch of almost oriental exoticism; together with its four turrets and the facade's belfry, it makes a memorable silhouette.

In complete contrast is the early twentieth-century **Dreikönigenkirche** to the south of the town centre at the junction of Jülicher Strasse and Dreikönigenstrasse. Following war damage, it was embellished with a wacky hanging vault by the father-and-son team of Dominikus and Gottfried Böhm. The church also has a complete set of stained-glass windows by the Dutch artist **Johan Thorn-Prikker**, one of the Jugendstil community based in Hagen; those in the chancel and transept are figurative and glow like jewels; the later geometric ones in the nave show his move to an abstract style. Neuss's only other building of note is the **Obertor** (part of the thirteenth-century fortifications), situated at the far end of the main shopping street. Along with a modern extension, it now houses the **Clemens-Sels-Museum** (Tues–Sun 11am–5pm; DM5/€2.50), an average local collection with some surprises, such as paintings by the Pre-Raphaelites and French Symbolists.

Neuss's **tourist office** (Mon–Fri 9.30am–6.30pm, Sat 10am–2pm; ☎0 21 31/27 32 42, fax 22 25 59, *www.neuss.de*) is in the First Reisebüro, Markt 4. There are plenty of **hotels**, ranging from the budget *Mara*, Krefelder Str. 27 (☎0 21 31/22 22 80; ④), to the luxurious *Swissotel*, Rheinallee 1 (☎0 21 31/77 00; ⑨). There's a **youth hostel** at Macherscheider Str. 113 (☎0 21 01/5 77 03 49, fax 5 77 03 50, *service-center@djh -rheinland.de*; DM24.50/€12.25 or DM29.50/€14.75) in the suburb of Uedesheim, reached by bus #851. Good traditional **restaurants** include the seventeenth-century *Em Schwatte Päd*, Büchel 50, and *Vogthaus*, Münsterplatz 10; the much more expensive *An der Poz*, Oberstr. 7, is a well-regarded practitioner of *neue deutsche Küche*. Neuss's big **festival** is the *Shakespearefest*, held throughout June in the *Globe-Theater* at An der Rennbahn (☎0 21 01/90 41 11), with performances of the Bard's plays in English and German.

Mönchengladbach

MÖNCHENGLADBACH, 30km west of Düsseldorf, is, like Bonn, an average-sized provincial town which was catapulted to prominence after World War II. The new role for this old textile and machine manufacturing community was the rather less enviable one of serving as NATO's operations base for Northern and Central Europe, and as the headquarters of the British Army on the Rhine. A purpose-built suburb was created at **Rheindahlen** to the west of the centre (reached by bus #7 or #17). This was a real Little Britain, whose colony, equipped as it was with cricket and rugby pitches, halls for Scout and Brownie packs and Anglican and presbyterian churches, did its utmost to forget that it was living on German soil. Now very depleted as a result of the end of the Cold War, this historical curiosity is unlikely to survive much longer.

The town centre

Though not the most obvious destination unless you're visiting a friend or relative, Mönchengladbach does have some notable attractions, including the most audacious publicly owned art gallery in Germany, the **Museum Abteiberg** (Tues–Sun 10am–6pm; *www.museum-abteiberg.de*; DM8/€4), an ultra-modern building right in the heart of the old part of the town. Inaugurated in 1982, it was intended from its conception a decade earlier to be a major piece of modern architecture. An architect who is also an artist, the Viennese **Hans Hollein**, was chosen to see the project through, and the acquisitions policy has eschewed nearly all the twentieth century's best-known artists, and supported the avant-garde in a big way. **Joseph Beuys**, who first sprang to fame following an exhibition in Mönchengladbach, is copiously represented. Other artists include Lucio Fontana, Cy Twombly, Richard Sella, Sigmar Polke and Arman Fernandez. If you're keen on the iconoclastic and experimental nature of modern art, this museum warrants a special trip; but if you've even a suspicion of allergy, best keep well away.

Directly behind is the **Münster**, successor to the tenth-century Benedictine abbey from which the town derives its name (*Mönchen* means monks). The present building was erected throughout the thirteenth century, straddling the late Romanesque and early Gothic periods and culminates in the chancel by **Master Gerhard**, who was also master mason at the Dom in Cologne. Its central "Bible" window, pairing fourteen New Testament scenes with episodes from the Old Testament which were believed to antic-ipate them, is the only surviving piece of original glass. Notwithstanding the fact that three of the bottom panes have had to be replaced, it ranks as one of the loveliest in Germany. The **Schatzkammer** (Tues–Sat 2–4pm, Sun 2–6pm; DM2/€1) displays the church's treasures, the most valuable of which is a twelfth-century portable altar from Cologne. You may have to ask to see the crypt and the sacristy: the former, unusually large for its time, is the oldest part of the church; the sacristy is a handsome Gothic room with delicately carved capitals and an amazingly well-preserved stone pavement.

Practicalities

Mönchengladbach's **Hauptbahnhof** is located fifteen minutes' walk from the old part of town: turn left at the exit and walk up Hindenburgstrasse, the main shopping street. The **tourist office** is in the First Reisebüro at Bismarckstr. 23–27, between the Hauptbahnhof and Alter Markt (Mon–Wed & Fri 9.30am–6.30pm, Thurs 9.30am–8pm, Sat 9.30am–1pm; ☎0 21 61/2 20 01, fax 27 42 22, *www.moenchengladbach.de*).

Central **hotels** include *Gladbacher Hof*, diagonally opposite the Hauptbahnhof at Hindenburgstr. 233 (☎0 21 61/2 21 28; ③), and *Burgund*, a short distance to the west at Kaiserstr. 85 (☎0 21 61/18 59 70; ⑤). There's also a handy concentration in the sub-urb of Hardt (bus #13 or #23), including *Kasteel-Scholl*, Vorster Str. 529 (☎ 0 21 61/55 96 94; ②), *Haus Faassen*, Vorster Str. 233 (☎0 21 61/55 91 82; ③); and *Lindenhof*, Vorster Str. 535 (☎0 21 61/55 93 40; ⑤), which also has a good restaurant. Also in Hardt, but a further 1km south in the woods, is the **youth hostel** at Brahmsstr. 156 (☎0 21 61/56 90 00, fax 55 64 64; DM26/€13 or DM31/€15.50). Its location is less isolated than it might appear as the Rheindahlen garrison is situated close by.

Mönchengladbach's best **restaurants** include *Haus Baues*, way to the west of the city centre at Bleichgrabenstr. 2, and the upmarket Italian *Michelangelo*, which is much more centrally placed at Lüpertzender Str. 133. At Alter Markt 21–22 is *Hannen Sudhaus*, the Gaststätte of the eponymous local brewery, which specializes in dark *Alt* beer. Nearby, at Waldhausener Str. 89, *Caspers am Grünewald* has a beer garden and a varied menu including many fish dishes. The same street is the epicentre of a fairly swinging **nightlife**, with a huge range of places of entertainment. Among them is *Dicker Turm*, a rebuilt tower which was formerly part of the fortifications; it now has snug little bars on three floors.

Borussia Mönchengladbach, whose ground is at Böklberg north of the centre, gave the city an additional claim to fame in the 1970s when, most improbably, it supplanted Bayern München as Germany's leading **football** club for several seasons. Its current status is less exalted: it was relegated from the top flight in 1999 and failed (albeit nar-rowly) to win back promotion the following year, though it did suceed in 2002.

Surprisingly, the favourite spectator sport is not soccer but horse-drawn wagon racing, a modern version of the Roman chariots, held at 6.30pm on Tuesdays at the Trabrennbahn stadium, An der Niersbrücke. The list of **festivals** is headed by Carnival, which is unusual in featuring its main parade on Shrove Tuesday, meaning you can move on to it after the main celebrations have finished elsewhere.

Duisburg

With **DUISBURG**, separated from Düsseldorf by just a few kilometres of open coun-tyside, the Ruhrgebiet begins with a vengeance. Until the early nineteenth century, this small walled town of about five thousand inhabitants had changed little since the great geographer Gerhard Mercator worked there in the sixteenth century. The Industrial Revolution saw it expand out of all recognition with the production of coal, iron and steel. Above all, it developed as a harbour for cargo, thanks to its key location at the point where the Ruhr enters the Rhine. It still ranks as the world's largest inland port, although recent years have seen a movement towards a post-industrial economy, with the closure of all but one of the seven pits, and steel production highly modernized. The city centre has been tidied up and largely given over to pedestrians, and a green belt has been created.

The City

Duisburg has little in the way of general attractions. The medieval city has almost com-pletely disappeared: the **Salvatorkirche**, a rather ordinary large Gothic church where Mercator is buried, is virtually the only reminder of time past. It's not a place you're likely to want to stay in for long, and the only reason for coming at all is if you're inter-ested in the river port or the museums.

Harbour cruises run from April to October and cost DM12/€6 for one hour, DM15/€7.50 for two. Be warned that the views are a world away from the legendary landscapes further up the Rhine: coal tips, scrap heaps, gaunt warehouses and belch-ing chimneys straight out of a Lowry painting are the order of the day. The two main departure points are the Schwanentor near the Salvatorkirche in the city centre (11am, 1pm & 3pm), and the Schifferbörse in the heart of the docklands at Ruhrort (12.15pm & 2.15pm). Bookings can be made at the offices at Harry-Epstein-Platz 10 (☎02 03/6 04 44 45). As a supplement, you can visit the **Museum der Deutschen Binnenschiffahrt** (Museum of German Inland Navigation; Tues & Fri–Sun 10am–5pm, Wed & Thurs 10am–4pm; DM3/€1.50), which occupies a converted Jugendstil swimming pool at Apostelstr. 84 in Ruhrort. Its exhibits include a medieval dug-out canoe plus a large collection of models; it also has an open-air section of his-toric vessels, which are moored in the adjacent Eisenbahnhafen.

The **Kultur- und Stadthistorisches Museum** (Tues & Thurs–Sat 10am–5pm, Wed 10am–4pm, Sun 11am–5pm; DM3/€1.50) on Johannes-Corputius-Platz, housed in a former mill and warehouse, is for the most part of average interest only, with the usual archeology and local history exhibits, including a series of models on how the city has developed. These are completely outclassed by the (German-only) display on the work of **Gerhard Mercator**, born in Flanders of German stock, who settled in Duisburg in 1552 and remained there until his death 42 years later. His most enduring legacy is the Mercator projection, still in use in a modified form today in both sea and air transport. It enabled maps to be drawn accurately on a flat surface and meant sailors could steer a course by plotting straight lines, instead of continually resorting to the compass. He was a prolific cartographer – several of his maps are shown – and it's from one of his collections that the term "atlas" has passed into use. The most eye-catching items here are the terrestrial globe of 1541 and its celestial counterpart of ten years later, works of art as much as science, whose beauty can be attributed to Mercator's early training in Antwerp as an engraver.

Modern art enthusiasts should overlook Duisburg's shortcomings in order to visit the **Wilhelm-Lehmbruck-Museum** (Tues–Sat 11am–5pm, Sun 10am–6pm; DM6/€3), Germany's premier collection of twentieth-century sculpture, situated in the Immanuel-Kant-Park. Its centrepiece is the legacy of the sculptor **Lehmbruck** himself, born to a Duisburg mining family, who committed suicide in 1919 at the age of 38. There are many examples here of his classically beautiful portrait busts, but it's his more ambitious compositions of elongated, writhing figures, such as *The Fallen One* (*Der Gestürzte*), *Mother and Child*, *Kneeling Woman* (*Kniende*) and *The Brooder* (*Sinnende*), which make a more lasting impression. There's also work by the most prestigious international sculptors of the twentieth century – Rodin, Barlach, Giacometti, Henry Moore, Archipenko, Marini, Lipchitz, Arp and Naum Gabo. An attractive feature is the way artists chiefly famous as painters are represented by their much rarer sculptures – the Fauvist **Derain** abandons his usual bright palette in *The Twin*; the Surrealists **Dalí** and **Magritte** provide two of the most memorable pieces in *Head of Dante* and *L'Avenir des Statues*; while their colleague **Max Ernst**'s *Un Ami Empressé* and *Objet Mobile* are shown alongside two of his canvases. The most spectacular exhibits include **Joseph Beuys'** *End of the Twentieth Century* and **Duane Hanson**'s *Vietnam War Piece*, a devastating attack on the folly of the conflict, with a horrifyingly real depiction of five American soldiers dead and dying in the mud. In contrast, there's the light-hearted *Das Märchenrelief* by **Jean Tinguely**, which needs to be set in motion for full effect; ask an attendant.

Practicalities

The **Hauptbahnhof** is at the eastern end of the city centre, reached from Immanuel-Kant-Park by Friedrich-Wilhelm-Strasse. Turning right from here is the beginning of Königstrasse, the main shopping street, where at no. 53 you'll find the **tourist office** (Mon–Fri 9am–6pm, Sat 10am–1pm; ☎02 03/2 85 44 11, fax 285 44 44, *www.duisburg.de*).

Hotel rooms in the centre are relatively expensive: lowest rates are at *Zum Buchenbaum*, Hohe Str. 14 (☎02 03/28 12 50; ④); and *Haus am Kantpark*, Gallenkampstr. 6 (☎02 03/28 28 90; ⑤); *Haus Friedrichs*, Neudorfer Str. 33–35 (☎02 03/35 57 37; ⑥) is a good medium-price choice, while top of the range is *Duisburger Hof*, Neckarstr. 2 (☎02 03/3 00 70; ⑨). Plenty of cheaper accommodation can be found in the suburbs; *Hof von Holland*, Bergiusstr. 46 (☎02 03/8 18 24; ③), in Ruhrort is worth trying. The **youth hostel**, Kalkweg 148 (☎02 03/72 41 64, fax 72 08 34, *jh.duisburg@usa.net*; DM24.50/€12.25 or DM29.50/€14.75), is in the suburb of Wedau, near the recreation parks; take bus #934, #943 or #944.

The city's best **restaurants** are *La Provence*, Hohe Str. 29, plus those in the Mercatorhalle on König-Heinrich-Platz and in the abovementioned *Duisburger Hof*. For more moderately priced fare, try one of the Hausbrauereien: *Brauhaus Schlacht 4/8*, which occupies a converted bank at Düsseldorfer Str. 21, or *Webster*, just north of Immanuel-Kant-Park at Dellplatz 13. Elsewhere, the obvious beer to sample is the locally produced *König Pils*, made in the largest brewery in Germany still in private hands. Concerts by the Duisburger Sinfoniker, among others, are held in the Mercatorhalle (☎02 03/30 50 50), while high-class **opera** and **drama** feature at the Theater der Stadt Duisburg, Neckarstr. 1 (☎02 03/3 00 91 00). The Musical Theater, Plessingstr. 20 (☎02 03/5 44 44) hosts blockbuster musicals.

Essen

Although its population has plummeted in recent years, **ESSEN** remains the largest city of the Ruhrgebiet, and the sixth in Germany. For centuries it was a small town under the control of its convent's abbesses, but it sprang to prominence as the steel metropolis in the nineteenth-century industrialization process, being effectively run by the most powerful of all Germany's commercial dynasties, the **Krupp** family. Essen is proud of its heritage, boasting northern Europe's oldest parish church, largest synagogue and tallest town hall; indeed, the city's publicity manages to make it sound a very enticing destination. While that's a somewhat exaggerated claim, Essen does nevertheless have a handful of worthwhile attractions – it's one Ruhr city that definitely merits a day or more of anybody's time.

Arrival, information and accommodation

Essen's **Hauptbahnhof** is situated bang in the city centre, only a couple of blocks south of the Münster. The **tourist office** (Mon–Fri 9am–5.30pm, Sat 10am–1pm; ☎02 01/20 11 94 33, fax 20 18 87 20 44, *www.essen.de*) is at Am Hauptbahnhof 2. **Mitfahrzentrale** is at Freiheit 4 (☎02 01/1 94 40).

Essen's **public transport** system is comprehensive, embracing buses, trams (some of which become the U-Bahn for part of their route) and the S-Bahn. Given the size of the place, a 24-hour ticket can be a good investment as it doesn't take many journeys to cover the DM10/€5 price.

As for **accommodation**, the **youth hostel** (☎02 01/49 11 63, fax 49 25 05; DM24/€12 or DM29/€14.50) is in Werden, at Pastoratsberg 2, a long way from the centre, but in a delightful location in the woods. To reach it, take the road passing uphill directly in front

THE KRUPP DYNASTY

The industrialist **Alfred Krupp** (1812–87) brought the dynasty to national prominence 250 years after his ancestors had established themselves as Essen's foremost family. He was in some respects a model employer, pioneering sick pay, free medical treatment, pensions and retirement homes for his workers. On the other hand, he also had a paranoid obsession for inventing ever more deadly weapons; he has appropriately been dubbed "the father of modern warfare" and his field guns were largely responsible for Prussia's victory over France in 1871 which sealed the unity of Germany. His son Fritz gave a hard business edge to this policy, developing an unrelenting cycle of inventing new offensive weapons, followed by defences against them, only to make these superfluous by the creation of even more powerful means of attack. These were sold to all and sundry in the arms race which reached its inevitable conclusion in World War I, and ensured international honours and fabulous riches for the family to offset the disappointment of German defeat. The next head of the clan, Gustav Krupp von Bohlen, provided Hitler with essential funding; he and his son Alfried were also enthusiastic participators in the Holocaust, making extensive use of concentration camp labour in producing new weapons for the Nazi onslaught on world civilization. Both were sentenced as war criminals at Nürnberg, but the Americans later took pity, and Alfried once more assumed command of an organization which continued to grow spectacularly, with his own personal fortune estimated at one thousand million dollars. Eventually he stretched his interests too far; the family lost control of their empire in 1967, but their name lives on in the corporation which succeeded it. In 1997, this merged with its longtime bitter rival, Thyssen.

of the abbey, and carry straight on; it lies well above the houses. Also in Werden, but on the opposite side of the river near the S-Bahn station, is one of the **campsites** (☎02 01/49 29 78). The other is on the south shore of the Baldeneysee in Fischlaken (☎02 01/40 20 07). A wide range of **hotels** can be found in all but the cheapest categories.

Hotels

Europa, Hindenburgstr. 35 (☎02 01/23 20 41, fax 23 26 56). Mid-range hotel in the southwest of the city centre. ⑥.

Kessing, Hachestr. 30 (☎02 01/23 99 88, fax 23 02 89). Moderately priced, in a handy location just west of the Hauptbahnhof. ④.

Lindenhof, Logenstr. 18 (☎02 01/23 30 31, fax 23 43 08). Budget place on the west side of the centre. ④.

Mövenpick, Am Hauptbahnhof 2 (☎02 01/1 70 80, fax 1 70 81 73). Fine old station hotel which was given a thorough refurbishment when it was taken over by the Swiss chain a few years back. Its restaurant is quite reasonably priced. ⑦–⑨.

Parkhaus Hügel, Freiherr-vom-Stein-Str. 209 (☎02 01/47 10 91, fax 44 42 07). Located right by Villa Hügel and boasting one of the very best restaurants in Essen. ⑥.

Schloss Hugenpoet, August-Thyssen-Str. 51 (☎0 20 54/1 20 40, fax 12 04 50). This is, without doubt, the best place to stay in Essen, a magnificent *Wasserschloss* in the suburb of Kettwig immediately south of Werden, 11km from the city centre. Its restaurant has an extensive wine list. ⑨.

Zum Deutschen Haus, Kastanienallee 16 (☎02 01/23 29 89, fax 23 06 92). In the northern part of the centre, with some of the least expensive rooms in the city. ④.

The city centre

The centre of Essen consists largely of an enormous shopping precinct. At the north-eastern end are two dominant features of which the tourist office is wildly proud, though in truth neither is much of an asset. The domed **Alte Synagoge** (Tues–Sun 10am–6pm; free) is a neo-Moorish monstrosity from the early twentieth century, remarkable mainly for having outlasted the Third Reich; it now houses a documentary centre on the suffering of the Jews under the Nazis. The other building, the **Rathaus**, a 1970s skyscraper, doesn't rate as one of the gems of modern architecture either.

In this setting, the **Münster** (or **Dom**) seems rather incongruous. A ninth-century foundation, it functioned as a collegiate church for aristocratic women until the Reformation. Since 1958, it has been the cathedral of a new diocese centred on the Ruhr. The west end is an eccentric tripartite eleventh-century structure apparently modelled on the Dom at Aachen; the rest of what must have been a magnificent building was destroyed by fire and replaced by a Gothic hall church. A stupendous collection of **treasures** by Ottonian craftsmen nonetheless makes the Münster a place of outstanding interest. Most prominent of these is the **Golden Madonna** of 965, the first known work of its kind. Housed in its own locked chapel beside the entrance to the crypt, it's highly venerated – at least as many people come to see it for devotional as for aesthetic reasons.

Also in the church is a large seven-branched candelabrum from about 1000, but the other star pieces are all in the **Schatzkammer**, housed in rooms off the south transept (Tues–Sat 10am–5pm, Sun 12.30–5pm; DM2/€1). Here are four dazzling **processional crosses** of the tenth and eleventh centuries; a gospel book cover with scenes carved in ivory; the crown of Otto III; and many other priceless items. Joined to the front of the Münster by means of an atrium is the **Johanniskirche**, a miniature Gothic baptismal church containing a double-sided altarpiece by Barthel Bruyn; whether you see the Christmas or Easter scenes depends on the time of year.

Between the Münster and the Hauptbahnhof, on the second floor of Rathenaustr. 2, is the **Deutsches-Plakat-Museum** (Tues–Sun noon–8pm; *www.plakatmuseum.de*; DM2/€1), a vast collection of artistic posters.

South from the centre

The main museum complex is at Goethestr. 41; to reach it, take Kruppstrasse westwards at the back of the Hauptbahnhof, turn left at Bismarckplatz into Bismarckstrasse and continue straight ahead. Here are two separate collections – the **Ruhrlandmuseum** and the **Museum Folkwang** (Tues, Wed & Fri–Sun 10am–6pm, Thurs 10am–9pm; *www.museum-folkwang.de*; combined ticket DM5/€2.50). The former has the usual local displays, with geology on the ground floor, customs, folklore and industries upstairs. Far more enticing is the Folkwang Museum, one of Germany's top galleries of nineteenth- and twentieth-century art. Two rooms are devoted to the French Impressionists and their followers, including versions of **Monet**'s favourite subjects, *Rouen Cathedral* and *Water Lilies*, an outstanding **Manet** of *Fauré as Hamlet* and four good examples each of **Gauguin** and **Van Gogh**. In the German section, two works by **Friedrich** stand out among the Romantics, while there are examples of all the main figures of the twentieth century, with **Nolde**, **Rohlfs** and **Kirchner** being particularly well represented; Kirchner's *Three Women in the Street* ranks as one of the key paintings in the development of the Expressionist movement.

Further south lies a surprising green belt. This begins with the **Gruga-Park** (April–Sept 8am–midnight; Oct–March 9am–dusk; DM4/€2), which incorporates the botanical gardens and large recreation areas. Beyond are extensive forests on both sides of the **Baldeneysee**, a long, narrow reservoir formed out of the River Ruhr. It's a popular leisure centre in summer, with watersports and walking trails. In this area are the grounds of the **Villa Hügel**, built for the **Krupp** family between 1868 and 1872, and serving as their home until 1945. You have to buy a ticket at the entrance to the park, just behind the S-Bahn station; it covers admission to both houses (Tues–Sun 10am–6pm; DM1.50/€0.75). This idyllic setting gives little clue to the significance of the family, who personify many of the tragedies of modern German history, their genius for both engineering and organization being channelled into the most destructive of ends.

The smaller of the houses has a Technicolor PR-type presentation of the achievements of the corporation; upstairs, the family history of the Krupps is described, with the darker episodes carefully glossed over. In the large house, to which it's linked by a pavilion, you can wander at leisure around some of the forbidding, high-ceilinged, wood-panelled rooms, hung with tapestries and portraits of the leading lights of the day, including the Kaisers, who were close friends. Every so often (generally June–Oct in even-numbered years) there's a blockbuster international **loan exhibition** on a major artistic theme.

Werden

South of Hügel and connected by S-Bahn lies **WERDEN**, officially a suburb of Essen but still preserving its small-town atmosphere. It's built round the **Abteikirche St Liudger**, one of the last of the great series of Romanesque basilicas in the Rhineland, dating from the end of the twelfth century. The exterior is especially impressive, with its massive westwork and central octagon, while an oddity is that the crypt, where St Liudger is buried, is an extension of the chancel, rather than being its lower storey. In a building behind the church is the **Schatzkammer** (Tues–Sun 10am–noon & 3–5pm; DM2/€1) containing many precious items, such as a fifth-century pyx, a ninth-century chalice, a bronze Romanesque crucifix and fragments of the saint's sarcophagus. Along Heckstrasse is the **Luciuskirche**, a daughter church of the abbey, but an even older building, which is claimed as the earliest parish church in northern Europe still in existence. It's been restored to its original and simple tenth-century form.

Eating and drinking

Many of Essen's best **restaurants** are in the luxury hotels, but there are a few others worth seeking out.

Bahnhof Süd, Rellinghauser Str. 175. Located south of the city centre, this is a favourite with the student crowd. Has a beer garden in the summer and a reasonably priced menu.

Brauhaus Graf Beust, Kastanienallee 95. One of a small chain of Hausbrauereien in the Ruhrgebiet. Its standard products are the blond *Gruben Gold* and *Mulvany's*, an Irish-style stout, but it brews other beers seasonally and also offers wholesome German fare.

Kockshusen, Pilgrimsteig 51. Located in the southeastern suburb of Rellinghausen, this outstanding restaurant occupies a half-timbered building from the seventeenth century, and has a garden terrace.

La Fontaine, III Hagen 47. Among the best of the city's Italian restaurants, located just west of Münsterplatz.

Rüttenscheider Hausbrauerei, Girardetstr. 2. Another boutique brewery with restaurant, situated in the Girardetshaus, not far from the Gruga Park.

Zodiac, Witteringstr. 41. Vegetarian specialist with an eclectic range of international fare. Evenings only, closed Thurs.

Entertainment

Essen is a vibrant cultural centre, with a wide variety of entertainment venues.

Aalto-Theater, Rolandstr. 10 (☎02 01/8 12 22 00, *www.theater-essen.de*). Named in honour of Alvar Aalto, the great Finnish architect who designed it, this is Essen's opera and dance stage.

Colosseum, Altendorfer Sr. 1 (☎01 80 54 44). Specialist venue for popular musicals.

GOP Varieté-Theater, Tottstr. 30 (☎2 47 93 93). Presents traditional variety shows.

Grillo-Theater, Theaterplatz (☎8 12 22 00, *www.theater-essen.de*). The principal municipally run dramatic stage.

Grugahalle, Norbertstr. 2 (☎02 01/7 24 42 90). Large hall used for pop concerts and other large-scale events.

Saalbau, Huyssenallee 53 (☎02 01/22 78 73 or 24 70 40, *www.theater-essen.de*). The city's main concert hall, featuring a regular series of performances by the Essener Philharmonie.

Satiricon, Girardetshaus, Girardetstr. 2 (☎79 75 39). Essen's main cabaret theatre.

Theater in Rathaus, Porscheplatz (☎2 45 55 55, *www.theater-in-rathaus.de*). Hosts comedy plays and celebrity shows.

Zeche Carl, Wilhelm-Nieswandt-Allee 100 (☎02 01/8 34 44 10). Has live music or discos two or three times per week.

Zeche Zollverein, Gelsenkirchener Str. 181 (☎02 01/83 03 60, *www.zollverein.de*). A Bauhaus-style mining complex in the north of the city (reached by tram #107) has recently been remodelled by Sir Norman Foster to serve as a multi-purpose cultural centre, featuring exhibitions and all kinds of live music.

Xanten

XANTEN, set just back from the Rhine some 40km downstream from Duisburg, is one of the oldest settlements in Germany. In about 100 AD Colonia Ulpia Traiana was founded as a residential town (the only one in the Rhineland other than Cologne) in succession to the nearby garrison of Vetera, centre of operations for the campaign to subdue the eastern Germanic tribes. It in turn was abandoned with the collapse of the empire, and followed by a new community built immediately to the south around the graves of Christians martyred in the fourth century during the last wave of purges. The graves were popularly but implausibly believed to contain St Victor and members of the Thebian Legion; the name given to the town is a contraction of the Latin *Ad Sanctos*

Martyres (To the Holy Martyrs). Writing at the end of the twelfth century, the anonymous poet of the Nibelungenlied, describing semi-mythical events centuries earlier, characterizes Xanten as "great", "splendid" and "far-famed", the birthplace and court of the invincible hero Siegfried, lord of the Netherlands, Norway and the mysterious Nibelungland, home of the fantastic gold treasure of the Rhine which was to form the basis of the very different version of the legend unfolded in Wagner's epic *Ring* cycle seven hundred years later.

The Town

Xanten is something of a Peter Pan, its current population of 16,000 little more than the probable size of the Roman town. It kept its medieval aspect until the last war, when it was badly bombed. Modern Xanten has successfully risen from the debris to appear once more as one of Germany's neatest country towns (the recipient of several prestigious conservation prizes), if one which is sometimes rather too crammed with day-trippers from the industrial hotbed to the south for its own good.

The Altstadt

The **Stadtbefestigung** survives in part, still defining the town's perimeter on the north and east sides. It's pierced by several towers, many of which have been converted into luxury flats, including the grandest of the group, the **Klever Tor**, whose double gateway formed the northwest entrance to the town. Just up Nordwall, the next tower underwent a more radical conversion in the eighteenth century, being reshaped to form a windmill. Immediately facing it is Brückstrasse, best preserved of the old streets.

Between here and the Markt is the **Propsteikirche St Viktor**, popularly known as the **Dom**, though it's only the seat of a suffragan bishop. It lies cocooned in its own close or "Immunity", so named from its status as a haven from external laws and taxes. From afar, the massive facade dominates the town; it was the only part of the Romanesque church spared when a sober Gothic replacement was put up in the late thirteenth century. Subsequent builders tampered with it right up until 1525, by which time the towers had been heightened considerably. On the exterior of the chancel is a polychrome fifteenth-century statue to the Dom's patron saint, St Victor. Whether one of the ancient tombs discovered in excavations of the crypt is really his burial place is a matter resolved more by faith than cold logic. The five-aisled **interior** gives a rare opportunity of sampling the genuine, cluttered feel of a medieval church, thanks to the extraordinary range of objects it has preserved – expressive pier statues of saints, a rood screen, choir stalls, a hanging *Double Madonna*, stained-glass windows and a crowd of altars. Particularly notable are the four carved and painted late Gothic winged **retables** in the aisles, one from Antwerp and three from nearby Kalkar; finest is that on the south side, with scenes from the life of the Virgin springing from a pyrotechnic *Tree of Jesse* by Henrik Douverman. The same sculptor made the reliquary busts for the high altar, which also incorporates the twelfth-century shrine of St Victor.

At the southwest corner of the close is the **Regionalmuseum** (Tues–Fri 9/10am–5pm, Sat & Sun 11am–6pm; DM9/€4.50 including entry to the Archäologischer Park and Grosse Thermen), which has extensive archeology and local history collections, but be warned that these are presented in an extremely didactic fashion, and that the most important finds from local excavations are housed in its parent museum, the Rheinisches Landesmuseum in Bonn. In the past, the museum has housed items from the Dom's **Schatzkammer**, whose treasures include: the *Achillespyxis*, a sixth-century pyx from Syria; the *Embriachi-Kästchen*, a fourteenth-century Venetian casket crowned a century later with a locally made crucifix; and many superb textiles, such as the twelfth-century chasuble of St Bernard of Clairvaux and the fourteenth-century *Almosentasche*, a French creation woven from costly gold thread. In 1999, the entire contents of the Schatzkammer began an ongoing tour of German towns, with the aim of raising funds for a new home.

From the close, you can pass out into the **Markt**, which is something of a hotchpotch of styles, with houses ranging from Gothic to Rococo. Running northwestwards from the square is **Karthaus**, a street named after the former Charterhouse whose Baroque facade is its dominant feature.

The Archäologischer Park and Grosse Thermen

From Karthaus, continue along Rheinstrasse; across the main road is the site of Colonia Ulpia Traiana, now the **Archäologischer Park** (daily: March–Nov 9am–6pm; Dec–Feb 10am–4pm; same ticket as for Regionalmuseum). Unlike many Roman towns in northern Europe, it was never built upon. That it subsequently disappeared is due to the fact that its stones were ideal building materials for later constructions, including the Dom. In the 1970s a proposal was made to develop the area into a recreation zone, but in return for sparing the site the authorities insisted that the excavations be given populist appeal. Thus, instead of merely uncovering ground plans, full-blooded conjectural reproductions of the main buildings of the town were attempted. The result is controversial to say the least, and purists will be horrified by the Disneyland touches. However, if you normally find archeological sites hamstrung by scholarly timidity, this will come as a revelation, giving a graphic picture of the true size and scale of a Roman town. Eventually, the aim is to go as far as re-creating the original riverside setting, which has now completely disappeared; at the moment, the **walls** with their massive fortifications, notably the **Hafentor** (Harbour Gate) at the very far end of the park, form the most impressive feature. Just inside the main entrance, an **inn** has been reconstructed; here the presentation goes outrageously over the top with toga-clad waiters serving the sort of meals it's alleged the Romans would have eaten. The **amphitheatre**, which is partly original, is now a venue for open-air theatrical performances; the **temple**, on the other hand, has been rebuilt only as a ruin.

Just west of the park are the **Grosse Thermen** (same times and ticket), a bathing complex thought to have been built on the personal orders of Emperor Hadrian. The excavated ruins have recently been covered by a protective glass structure whose appearance mirrors the likely form of the original building.

Practicalities

Xanten's **Bahnhof**, terminus of a branch line from Duisburg, is only a few minutes' walk from the town centre via either Hagenbuschstrasse or Bahnhofstrasse. Services on the line northwards to Kleve have been replaced by buses, which leave from the forecourt. The **tourist office** (Mon–Fri 9am–5pm, Sat 10am–4pm, Sun 1–5pm; ☎0 28 01/77 22 38, fax 77 22 09, *www.xanten.de*) is located in the Rathaus, Karthaus 2. Here you can pick up an accommodation list, which includes more than a dozen private houses with **rooms** (②–③) to let; you can choose a central location, or there are many in a more rural setting which are still within walking distance.

The least expensive of the **hotels**, all centrally situated, is *Galerie an de Marspoort*, Marsstr. 78 (☎0 28 01/10 57; ④), which doubles as an artists' gallery and café. Alternatives are *Nibelungen Hof*, Niederstr. 1 (☎0 28 01/7 80; ④–⑤), *Neumaier*, Orkstr. 19–21 (☎0 28 01/7 15 70; ⑤), *Hövelmann*, Markt 31–33 (☎0 28 01/7 18 18; ⑤), and the historic and luxurious *Van Bebber*, Klever Str. 12 (☎0 28 01/66 23; ⑦). The best **restaurants** are in the last two hotels; there's also an inexpensive Balkan eatery, *Dalmatien*, Markt 20. The town also has several good **cafés**, such as *Stadtcafé*, Markt 36–38, and *Café de Fries*, Kurfürstenstr. 8.

Kalkar, Kleve and Kevelaer

Of the many other historic towns in the Lower Rhineland, there are three which stand out. **Kalkar** has a Gothic parish church with some of the most remarkable furnishings in the country; **Kleve** is an old ducal seat with a nicely varied range of attractions; while **Kevelaer** ranks among Europe's most popular Marian shrines.

Kalkar (Calcar)

The little market town of **KALKAR** was built on a sandbank completely surrounded by an arm of the Rhine, but heavy silting has meant that it's now well inland. It lies midway between Xanten and Kleve, about 12km from either, and thanks to the presence of one of Germany's most remarkable churches, it rivals the former as the most interesting of the Lower Rhenish towns.

The central **Markt** lost much of its character to wartime bombs, but some old houses have been restored to provide fitting company for the **Rathaus**, a brick building with a prominent octagonal turret. Behind, a step-gabled merchant's residence, connected by a modern extension to the oldest house in the town, contains the **Stadtmuseum** (Tues–Sun 10am–1pm & 2–5pm; DM2/€1). This has an excellent collection of manuscripts and charters, along with the work of painters, most notably the Expressionist **Heinrich Nauen**, who lived in the town.

None of this prepares you for the splendours of **St Nicolai** (April–Oct Mon–Fri 10am–noon & 2–6pm, Sat 10am–noon & 2–4pm, Sun 2–6pm; Nov–March Mon–Fri & Sun 2–5pm, Sat 2–4pm; DM2/€1), built to the side of the Markt at the same time as the Rathaus. From the outside, it looks quite ordinary – a plain fifteenth-century brick building, enlivened only by its tall tower. The gleaming white interior is another matter altogether, bristling with such an astonishing array of **works of art** that it's now designated a "church-museum". It seems odd that what has never been more than a parish church in a town which has never been very large could have garnered such riches, but medieval Kalkar became wealthy through a cloth industry that used locally produced wool. The rich burghers showed their appreciation for this natural bounty by funding a school of woodcarving which flourished continuously for about a century from 1450, producing one great altarpiece after another, to illustrate the lives of Christ and the saints for the enlightenment of a largely illiterate congregation. Fifteen large retables and numerous other statues and paintings originally embellished the church; some were sold in the nineteenth century, but all the important pieces remain *in situ*.

It's worth taking time to examine the myriad details to be found in the big showpieces as all display an amazing level of technical virtuosity. **Henrik Douverman**, who made the altar of the *Seven Sorrows of the Virgin* in the south apse, the *Double Madonna* candelabrum in the middle of the nave and the superbly expressive *St Mary Magdalene* in the north aisle, has long been recognized as a highly individual artist, one who proved the continuing vitality of late Gothic forms well into the sixteenth century. However, many of his little-known predecessors, who were forced to submerge their artistic personalities in co-operative ventures, showed equal skill, nowhere more than in the crowded main *Passion* altar, begun by the founder of the school, **Master Arnt**, and continued by **Ludwig Jupan**. These carvers were also responsible respectively for the *St George* altar and the altar to the *Virgin* fronting the entrance to the chancel. Painted panels were added to many of the retables to fill out the story; particularly fine are the colourful scenes on **Jan Joest**'s *Passion* altar, which features a topographically accurate depiction of Kalkar's Markt as the backdrop to *The Raising of Lazarus*.

Practicalities

Buses between Xanten and Kleve (which run hourly Mon–Fri, spasmodically on Sat and not at all on Sun) conveniently stop on the Markt. Though there's no **tourist office** as such; leaflets can be picked up at the Stadtverwaltung, Markt 20 (☎0 28 24/13 11 20, fax 31 05, *www.kalkar.de*), during normal working hours.

There are three **hotels**, all bang in the centre: *Seydlitz*, Markt 25 (☎0 28 24/22 52; ⑤), *Stil(l)eben*, Wallstr. 10 (☎0 28 24/97 15 98; ⑤), and *Siekmann*, Kesselstr. 32 (☎0 28 24/9 24 50; ⑤). The best **restaurants** are the one in *Siekmann* and the excellent but pricey *Ratskeller*, Markt 20. There's also a pleasant **café-bar** in an old windmill, *Kalkarer Mühle*, just to the rear of the Stadtmuseum on Mühlensteg. Just north of Kalkar is the **Wisseler See**, a natural lake which is a watersports centre; it also has a **campsite** (☎0 28 24/66 13).

Kleve (Cleves)

Unusually for the area, **KLEVE** is built on hills, dominated by a cliff (which gives the town its name) crowned by the Schwanenburg (Swan Castle), which is closely associated with the legend of Lohengrin, Knight of the Holy Grail. It was the seat of the once-powerful local dukes, whose dynastic aspirations reached a climax in 1539 with the marriage of Anne of Cleves to Henry VIII of England – only to end in humiliation the following year when the "Flanders Mare", whom the king had disliked at first sight, was sent back home. The town's frontier position made it a prime target for aerial bombardment during World War II, and all that remains of the Altstadt are the main public buildings. These have lost much of their soul through heavy restoration, though a fine Baroque park and some notable works of art compensate. Kleve is linked to the commercial port of Emmerich on the opposite bank of the Rhine by the longest **suspension bridge** in Germany, an effortless structure spanning some 1300m.

The present **Schwanenburg** dates from the fifteenth century, but has had so many subsequent alterations it's difficult to categorize its style. Nowadays, it serves as law courts and local government offices, but you can ascend the **tower** (April–Sept daily 11am–5pm; Nov–March Sat & Sun only; DM2/€1), which also contains a small **Geologisches Museum**, for extensive views. Immediately opposite, the former stables house the town library, while behind is **St Mariae Himmelfahrt**, a large brick church similar to Kalkar's St Nicolai. In terms of artistic treasures, however, it's a poor relation, though its **high altar** was made by the star of the neighbouring town's school of woodcarving, Henrik Douverman. Little else remains of the old city, which has been transformed into a bland modern shopping centre.

Downhill at Kavarinerstr. 33 is **Haus Koekkoek** (Tues–Sat 2–5pm, Sun 11am–5pm; DM2/€1), the home of the Romantic artist Barent Koekkoek, many of whose works are on display. Also on show in the museum is a Book of Hours made in the workshop of the **Master of the Hours of Catherine of Cleves**, one of the most important illuminators of the late Middle Ages. The wonderful manuscript after which he's named became part of the transatlantic drain of works of art, and is now in the Pierpoint Morgan Library in New York. Another of the town's artists was **Joos van Cleve**, who settled in Antwerp, developing a style heavily indebted to the Italian Renaissance, but modified by a northern European brittleness. A *Male Portrait* by him has been placed on loan here by the federal government in order that his work may once more be seen in the place of his birth.

About 1km to the west via the street named after it is the **Tiergarten**, a terraced garden, laid out in 1656 in the Italian style by order of Johann Moritz of Nassau-Siegen, the erstwhile governor of Brazil. The garden features a rotunda, an amphitheatre, a canal and, as the centrepiece, a statue of Pallas Athene by the Amsterdam sculptor, Artus

Quellin. This is a copy, the original having been moved for preservation reasons to the nearby **Museum Kurhaus** (April–Oct Tues–Sun 10am–6pm; Nov–March Tues–Sat 11am–5pm, Sun 10am–5pm; DM6/€3). Occupying the long-redundant spa buildings, this museum is otherwise almost entirely devoted to modern art. It contains an important collection of works by the sculptor Ewald Mataré, as well as some spectacular installations such as *Plaza* by the Spaniard Juan Muñoz, with its super-realistic figures of Chinamen.

Practicalities

Kleves' **Bahnhof**, a dead end on a branch line from the industrial city of Krefeld to the northeast of Mönchengladbach, is a short walk east of the centre. There's no **tourist office** as such, but leaflets are available from the Rathaus (Mon & Wed 8.30am–12.45pm & 2–5pm, Tues & Thurs 8.30am–12.45pm & 2–3.30pm, Fri 8.30am–12.45pm; ☎0 28 21/8 42 67 or 8 44 22, fax 2 37 59, *www.stadt-kleve.de*).

The cheapest central **hotel** is *Zur Post*, Hagsche Str. 44 (☎0 28 21/2 45 79; ④), whose Balkan restaurant offers exceptionally good-value lunches. In the middle price range, there's *Heek*, Lindenallee 37 (☎0 28 21/7 26 30; ⑤), while the top address is *Cleve,* north of the centre at Tichelstr. 11 (☎0 28 21/71 70; ⑥), which has an expensive restaurant, *Lohengrin*, plus a more moderately priced bistro. The **youth hostel** is a fair distance west of the centre, at the top of a hill at St Annaberg 2 (☎0 28 21/2 36 71, fax 2 47 78; DM22/€11 or DM27/€13.50); take bus #57. A good alternative to the hotel **restaurants** is *Altes Landhaus zur Münze*, Tiergartenstr. 68, which has a beer garden overlooking the park.

Kevelaer

KEVELAER, which lies midway along the rail line between Kleve and Krefeld, is Germany's premier **place of pilgrimage**, drawing nearly a million believers each year in a "season" lasting from May to October. Just before Christmas 1641, a local pedlar, Hendrick Busman, heard voices charging him to build a chapel on the site. Shortly after, his wife had a vision of the chapel containing the image of *The Blessed Virgin of Luxembourg* which she had seen carried by two soldiers; this picture had been attributed with healing properties during a plague in Luxembourg. Within six months, Busman had built a simple shrine with his own hands, in which the miraculous icon was placed; the cult quickly grew, and three years later the far more substantial **Kerzenkapelle** (Chapel of the Candles) was built alongside in an archaic Gothic style to house the pilgrims. A decade later, Busman's construction was replaced by the elaborate hexagonal **Gnadenkapelle** (Chapel of the Favours), in which the image is displayed facing the square outside.

The fame of the pilgrimage spread so much in the nineteenth century that a vast neo-Gothic **Basilica** with a gaudily painted interior had to be built across the square to accommodate the crowds who flocked from all over the country. Ironically, much of the credit for the increased popularity of the shrine was due to a poem by Heine which most readers took at face value, failing to realize that its apparently mellifluous tone was actually a mocking one.

No doubt it's a reflection of the Germanic nature that Kevelaer lacks the sheer, unadulterated bad taste that's the hallmark of other leading Marian shrines in Europe, such as Lourdes, Fátima and Knock; unlike them, it can't really be recommended as worth seeing for shock value. Apart from the pilgrimage churches, the only other attraction is the **Niederrheinisches Museum für Volkskunde** (Lower Rhenish Museum of Folklore; Tues–Sun 10am–5pm; DM5/€2.50), just a stone's throw away at Hauptstr. 18. This contains a marvellous collection of toys from around the world, in addition to objects of local interest.

Practicalities

Kevelaer's **Bahnhof** is just east of the town centre. The **tourist office** (Mon–Thurs 7.30am–5.30pm, Fri 7.30am–12.30pm, Sat 10.30am–12.30pm; ☎0 28 32/12 21 51, fax 43 87, *www.kevelaer.de*) is in the Rathaus, Peter-Plümpe-Platz 12. There's a **youth hostel** at Am Michelsweg 11 (☎0 28 32/82 67, fax 89 94 32; DM22/€11 or DM27/€13.50). **Hotels** are scattered all over town and, being geared to the pilgrim market, are very reasonably priced – even upmarket options such as *Parkhotel*, Neustr. 3 (☎0 28 32/9 53 50; ⑤), and *Zur Brücke*, Bahnstr. 44 (☎0 28 32/23 89, *info@hotel-restaurant-zur-bruecke.de*; ⑥). These also have the two best **restaurants** in town.

WESTPHALIA

Westphalia (Westfalen) is named after one of the three main Saxon tribes, and by the early Middle Ages the term came to be used for all of Saxony west of the River Weser. Despite this long tradition as a definable part of Germany, it's never really been governed as a unit, and the boundaries have often been changed dramatically. The short-lived Kingdom of Westphalia, established by Napoleon for his brother Jérôme, consisted mostly of Hesse, while the present political division of the country has seen parts of the historic province transferred to Lower Saxony. Apart from the cities in the **Ruhrgebiet** which are traditionally Westphalian (including **Dortmund**, **Bochum**, **Hagen** and **Recklinghausen**), there are three distinct constituent parts – the fertile **Münsterland** plain to the north; the predominantly rural **Sauerland** and **Siegerland** to the south; and the depression to the east bounded by the vast stretch of the **Teutoburg Forest**. The last-named incorporates what was formerly one of the smallest states of the German Reich, the **Principality of Lippe**. Of the cities, the two largest, **Bielefeld** and **Münster**, could hardly be more different: the former is predominantly industrial whereas the latter is the epitome of middle-class prosperity. **Paderborn**, like Münster, is an important episcopal centre. However, many of the most memorable towns in the area – **Soest**, **Lemgo** and **Höxter** – are modest in size.

According to its tourist board, Westphalia is associated with "the solid and substantial things in life". In architecture, the characteristic features are moated castles, lofty hall churches and half-timbered farm buildings. Gastronomically, it's famous for hams, spit roasts, beer, schnapps and, above all, rye bread. It's an archetypal German province and a favourite holiday destination with the Germans themselves.

Münster

Northern Westphalia is dominated by **MÜNSTER**, one of the most varied and enticing of the cities spread across the flat German plain. It has an unusually rich architectural heritage, including examples of all the main styles from Romanesque to Baroque. Industry has been confined to the peripheries, and the chic shops crowding the centre are an unabashed celebration of the affluent consumerism enjoyed by a population which is overwhelmingly middle-class. The university is among the largest in Germany; one consequence of this is that the city has come firmly under the rule of the bicycle. However, the dominant influence on Münster has been the Church, its very name – the equivalent of the English word "minster" – deriving from the evangelizing monastery of **St Liudger**, who was consecrated bishop in 805 as part of Charlemagne's policy of converting the Saxon tribes to Christianity. Apart from the years 1534–35 when it was taken over by the fanatical Anabaptist sect, it has remained intensely loyal to Roman Catholicism, even during the Third Reich, when the city's bishop, **Clemens**

August von Galen, was one of the regime's most courageous and persistent opponents. In 1936, he organized a popular revolt which overturned an edict to remove crucifixes from school buildings – an apparently trivial incident, but one of the few occasions the Nazis gave in to domestic opponents. This defiance counted for nothing with the Allied bombing missions, which administered particularly brutal treatment to Münster, but the city recovered, adopting a much-praised rebuilding programme.

Arrival, information and accommodation

The **Hauptbahnhof** is directly to the east of the city centre, which is reached by heading straight down Windthorststrasse. **Bus services** both within the city and to other places in the province leave from the string of stops on both sides of Bahnhofstrasse. The main **tourist office** (Mon–Fri 9am–6pm, Sat 9am–1pm; ☎02 51/4 92 27 10, fax 4 92 77 43, *www.muenster.de*) is at Klemensstr. 9; there's also a branch within the Rathaus (Mon–Fri 9am–5pm, Sat 9am–4pm, Sun 10am–1pm; ☎02 51/4 92 27 24). **Mitfahrzentrale** is at Überwasserstr. 19 (☎02 51/4 04 00).

Münster has some splendid middle- and upper-range **hotels**, but relatively few inexpensive options. If you're on a tight budget, you might like to head out to the concentration of hotels in the outlying town of Hiltrup directly to the south, which are generally less expensive than in the city; take bus #1, #6 or #9. The **youth hostel** is at Bismarckallee 31 (☎02 51/53 24 70, fax 52 12 71, *jgh-muenster@t-online.de*; DM40.50/€20.25), in a good location by the right bank of the Aasee; take bus #10 or #34 to Hoppendamm. **Camping** is possible from mid-March to mid-October at Dorbaumstr. 35 (☎02 51/32 93 12), in the northeastern suburb of Handorf.

Hotels

Bockhorn, Bremer Str. 24 (☎02 51/6 55 10, fax 9 61 43 43). Somewhat old-fashioned budget hotel conveniently situated immediately to the rear of the Hauptbahnhof. ④–⑤.

Feldmann, An der Clemenskirche 14 (☎02 51/41 44 90, fax 4 14 49 10). Quality hotel at the eastern end of the Altstadt. It also has a fine restaurant (closed Sun & Mon). ⑤–⑦.

Haus von Guten Hirten, Mauritz Lindenweg 61, St Mauritz (☎02 51/3 78 70, fax 37 45 49). Church-run guesthouse offering some of the cheapest rooms in Münster. Situated in an inner suburb 2km east of the Hauptbahnhof; bus #14 goes closest. ④.

Hof zur Linde, Handorfer Werseufer 1, Handorf (☎02 51/3 27 50, fax 32 82 09). Classy hotel, part of the Romantik chain, in a seventeenth-century farmhouse 7km northeast of the centre; take bus #10. It also has a top-class if rather pricey restaurant. ⑦.

Krone, Hammer Str. 67 (☎ & fax 7 38 68). Small, reasonably priced Gasthof just south of the city centre. ④.

Lohmann, Mecklenbecker Str. 345, Mecklenbeck (☎02 51/7 15 25, fax 71 43 68). Guesthouse at the extreme southwest of the city, reached by bus #15. ④.

Schloss Wilkinghege, Steinfurter Str. 374 (☎02 51/21 30 45, fax 21 28 98). Münster's top hotel, complete with gourmet restaurant, occupies a sixteenth-century *Wasserschloss* in a landscaped park just off the B54 at the northwestern edge of the city. ⑧–⑨.

Wienburg, Kanalstr 237 (☎02 51/2 01 28 00, fax 2 01 28 15). In a park 2km north of the Altstadt, reached by bus #9 or #17, with a renowned restaurant (closed Mon). ⑥.

Windsor, Warendorfer Str. 177 (☎02 51/13 13 30, fax 3 99 16 10). Located east of the centre, reached by bus #2 or #10. Has a high-class Italian restaurant, *Il Cucchiaio d'Argento* (closed Sat lunchtime & Mon). ⑥.

Zum Schwan, Schillerstr. 27 (☎02 51/66 11 66, fax 6 76 81). Right behind the Hauptbahnhof, with a *Bierstube* offering reasonably priced meals. ⑥.

The City

Most of the city's main sights are, as ever, in the Altstadt, but it's worth venturing out of the centre to the green belt, particularly the area to the southwest.

Prinzipalmarkt

In the centre of the main street, **Prinzipalmarkt**, stands the magnificent Gothic **Rathaus**, scene of the signing in 1648 of the **Peace of Westphalia**, which brought to an end the multitude of religious, constitutional and dynastic conflicts known as the Thirty Years War. In honour of the treaty, the room where it was signed was renamed the **Friedensaal** (Peace Hall; Mon–Fri 9am–5pm, Sat 9am–4pm, Sun & holidays 10am–1pm; DM1.50/€0.75); it's filled with exquisite carving and is the one part of the Rathaus generally open to the public.

Next door, the **Stadtweinhaus**, a Renaissance building with an abutting Italianate portico, has also been returned to its former splendour. The rest of what must once have been one of the most handsome main thoroughfares in Europe is rather more of a compromise. Alongside faithfully rebuilt houses are some which are mere approximations, while others are deliberately modern reinterpretations using the old motifs.

At the end of Prinzipalmarkt is **St Lamberti**, a good example of the spacious hallchurch style characteristic of Westphalia. Its elegant openwork spire, one of the chief landmarks of the city, reflects the nineteenth-century German obsession with embellishing Gothic buildings. High up on the older part of the tower hang three wrought-iron cages; in them were displayed the bodies of the Anabaptist leader **Jan van Leyden** and his two principal lieutenants, following the crushing of their "Reich" by the princebishop's army in 1535. Apart from insisting on adult baptism, this sect believed in the common ownership of property and in heeding the biblical injunction to be fruitful and multiply – the leader himself took no fewer than sixteen wives. The iconoclastic tendencies of the Anabaptists led them to destroy the beautiful sculptural decoration which were key features of the city's medieval churches; one of the rare examples left *in situ* is the elaborate *Tree of Jesse* over St Lamberti's south doorway. Facing the church's apse on Alter Steinweg is the **Krameramtshaus**, a late sixteenth-century building in the Dutch style which is the oldest guildhall to have survived; nowadays it serves as the main public library.

Domplatz

The vast **Domplatz**, on which markets are held on Wednesdays and Saturdays, is just a short walk from Prinzipalmarkt down either Domgasse or Michaelisplatz. Almost any point on the square offers a superb view of the huge thirteenth-century **Dom**, built in less than forty years in a style bridging the transition from Romanesque to Gothic. The only entrance is via the porch (or "Paradise"), which is adorned on the inside with statues of Christ and the Apostles dating from the very beginning of the building period; the pier figure of St Paul, the Dom's patron, is from three hundred years later, the first of several subsequent additions to make up a full programme worthy of a Gate of Heaven, to which such doorways aspired.

The Dom's **interior** is highly unusual, the nave having just two bays of massive span. It's jam-packed with sculptural memorials and other works of art. What really catches your eye is the **astronomical clock**, made in the 1530s, in the southern arm of the ambulatory. Based on the most precise mathematical calculations available at the time, it shows the orbit of the planets and the movement of the fixed stars, as well as fulfilling the normal function of charting the course of the sun and the moon; the lowest section is a calendar. The leading Münster painter of the day, **Ludger tom Ring the Elder**, decorated the clock with the symbols of the Evangelists, delicate scenes of the Labours of the Months and a gallery of entranced spectators. If you brave the crowds at noon, you can hear the carillon and see the emergence of the Magi to pay tribute to the infant Christ.

At the far end of the cloisters the **Domkammer** (Tues–Sun 11am–4pm; DM2/€1) houses the treasury. Pride of place goes to the eleventh-century gold reliquary of St Paul, studded with jewels a couple of hundred years later; other outstanding pieces are the thirteenth-century processional cross and fourteen bust-reliquaries of the prophets.

The Westfälisches Landesmuseum

The Domplatz, which also contains several Baroque mansions, serves as the city's museum centre. The **Westfälisches Landesmuseum** (Tues–Sun 10am–6pm; DM5/€2.50) houses works of art of mostly Westphalian origin, but is of far more than parochial significance. On the ground floor is a really outstanding collection of **medieval sculpture**, including the original statues from the Überwasserkirche (see p.586). The massive group of *Christ's Entry into Jerusalem* originally adorned the upper part of the Dom's facade, destroyed in the war, and is the work of **Hinrik Brabender**, a long-forgotten name who now appears as one of the most individual of the remarkable group of late Gothic German sculptors. Also by him is a series of Passion scenes made for the Domplatz; despite their weary appearance – the Anabaptists smashed them only a few years after they were made – the wonderful dignity and characterization of the figures can still be appreciated. Also on display are examples of the quite different art of his son **Johann Brabender**, who was fully Renaissance in style and happiest on a small scale, as in sensitive and delicate works such as *Calvary* from the Dom's rood screen and *Adam and Eve* from the Paradise.

Upstairs, the history of Westphalian painting is traced, beginning with the "Soft Style" of **Conrad von Soest** and the **Master of Warendorf** in the early fifteenth century. From the next generation is **Johann Koerbecke**, whose masterpiece, the

Marienfeld Altar, contains background depictions of Münster. The Renaissance section is dominated by the diverse interests of the **tom Ring** family. Apart from the portraits for which they are best known, there are religious works by Hermann and pioneering still lifes by Ludger the Younger. On the second floor are two rooms of Expressionist paintings, with a good cross-section of the work of **Macke**.

The rest of the Altstadt

A short distance to the west of the Dom stands the **Liebfrauenkirche**, usually known as the **Überwasserkirche** (Church by the Water) since it stands beside the Aa, Münster's tiny river. Like St Lamberti, it's a fourteenth-century hall church, with a floridly decorated tower. Its superb sculptures proved particularly repugnant to the Anabaptists, who smashed and buried them; some 350 years later, they were dramatically rediscovered but were considered too fragile to return to their original location.

From here, Frauenstrasse leads to Schlossplatz with the resplendent eighteenth-century **Schloss** of the prince-bishops, its two side wings reaching out like embracing arms. The front facing the **Botanischer Garten** (daily 7.30am–5pm; free) is quite different, but the interior was completely destroyed in the war, and has been modernized for use by the university. Its architect, **Johann Conrad Schlaun**, was almost single-handedly responsible for making Münster the capital of north German Baroque, which was far more restrained than its southern counterpart. There are two other notable buildings by him at the opposite end of the city centre, reached from the Rathaus by following Klemensstrasse. The **Erbdrostenhof**, a nobleman's mansion, again shows his talent for the grand manner and has survived in better shape than the Schloss. Immediately opposite, the circular **Clemenskirche**, a former hospital church, presents a clever solution to the problem of building in a restricted space, and is richly decorated with a huge ceiling fresco glorifying the patron saint.

A couple of blocks further west, at the top end of Königsstrasse, two old town houses have been adapted to house the brand-new **Graphikmuseum Pablo Picasso** (Tues–Sat 10am–6pm, Sun 11am–5pm; *www.graphikmuseum-picasso-muenster.de*; DM9/€4.50). The first museum in Germany specifically devoted to the Spanish master, it contains the only complete collection of his lithographs, some 800 works in all. Thematic selections from this are shown in rotation; the rest of the display area is given over to temporary exhibitions on other aspects of the work of Picasso and his contemporaries.

Southwest from the centre

Heading southwest from the centre, the sausage-shaped **Aasee**, some 6km in circumference, is the most popular recreation area in the city, particularly at the weekend when the yachts and motorboats of prosperous locals crowd the water. At the lower end of the left bank is the **Mühlenhof** which, though small, is one of Germany's longest-established open-air museums (mid-March to mid-Oct daily 10am–6pm; mid-Oct to mid-March Tues–Sat 1–4.30pm, Sun 11am–4.30pm; DM5/€2.50; take bus #14). On a fine day, it's worth a plod round the twenty or so agricultural buildings from the province which have been re-erected here, the centrepieces being a trestle windmill of 1748 and an early seventeenth-century mill house, fitted out with authentic furnishings.

Eating, drinking and nightlife

One of Münster's greatest attractions is its wonderful choice of **bars**, **cafés** and **restaurants**. The most obvious place to begin is around the Prinzipalmarkt, but an equally notable nightlife area is the **Kuhviertel** just beyond the Überwasserkirche; this is usually described as the Latin quarter, but students no longer predominate. Look out for the amazing range of **beers** – *Pils, Alt, Hefeweizen, Malz, Leicht, Spezial* and the strong *Jubiläumsbier* – made by Pinkus Müller; although small, and the only one left in Münster, it's among the most highly regarded of all German breweries. *Alt*, whether from Pinkus or imported from Düsseldorf, is Münster's most popular drink and is generally mixed with syrup (*mit Schuss*) or with a punch of fresh raspberries and peaches (*Altbierbowle*).

Restaurants

Altes Brauhaus Kiepenkerl, Spiekerhof 45. Named after the statue of the pedlar outside, this has a ground-floor restaurant-cum-beer hall and an elegant upstairs café. Closed Tues.

Altes Gasthaus Leve, Alter Steinweg 37. This distinguished old restaurant, which has an elegant tiled interior, boasts of a tradition dating back to 1607. Closed Mon.

Fischbrathalle, Schlaunstr. 8. Fish restaurant which has been in existence since 1926. Lunchtimes only, closed Sun.

Kleiner Kiepenkerl, Spiekerhof 47. The food here is if anything superior to that served in its larger sister restaurant alongside. Closed Mon.

Kleines Restaurant im Oer'schen Hof, Königstr. 42. Expensive restaurant serving top-notch French cuisine and fish specialities. Closed Sun & Mon.

Pinkus Müller, Kreuzstr. 4–10. The brewery offers both a restaurant, *Altbierüche*, and a bar, *Biergalerie*. The former, which is decked out in traditional style, fills up heavily from mid-evening – notably with members of the American community. Not the cheapest, but arguably the best place in town for a traditional Westphalian meal. Closed Sun.

Torhaus, Mauritzstr. 27. Named after the Neoclassical guard house it occupies, this is the main local practitioner of *neue deutsche Küche*. Closed Mon & Tues.

Villa Medici, Ostmarkstr. 15. Rivals *Il Cuchiaio d'Argento* (see p.584) for the right to be regarded as Münster's best Italian restaurant. Closed Sun & Mon.

Cafés and café-bars

Café Kleimann, Prinzipalmarkt 48. Occupying one of the finest of the old guild houses, this is a good choice for *Kaffee und Kuchen*. Closed Sun.

Café Prutt, Bremer Str. 32. Vegetarian and wholefood specialist, situated just behind the Hauptbahnhof. Unusually for such institutions it stays open until late, and has its own little beer garden.

Café Vis a Vis, Hörsterstr. 11. Café-bar that's one of a number of popular meeting-places in this street in the eastern part of the city centre.

Palmen Café, Aegidiimarkt 1. Offers the best selection of teas in town. Closed Sun.

Bars

Bullenkopp, Alter Fischmarkt 24. Traditional Kneipe that still preserves its original nineteenth-century appearance. Closed Sun.

Cavete, Kreuzstr. 38. Popular bar with a young crowd, loud music and a selection of inexpensive pastas and puddings.

Das Blaue Haus, Kreuzstr. 16. A direct competitor of *Cavete* in every respect.

Der Bunte Vogel, Alter Steinweg 41. Another beer hall, though a bit trendier than usual.

Gambrinus, Königsstr. 34. Lively pub which does good-value schnitzels cooked in a score of different ways.

Kruse Baimken, Am Staatgraben 52. Located by the north bank of the Aasee, this is the place to come on a fine evening, when you may find close on a thousand people, including many of the beautiful set, relaxing in its beer garden.

Stuhlmacher, Prinzipalmarkt 6. The city's most celebrated pub, it has a wide selection of beers, and is ideal for a spot of people-watching, particularly in the early evening. However, the food is relatively expensive and you can eat better elsewhere.

Treibhaus, Steinfurter Str. 66. Less self-conscious alternative to *Kruse Baimken* further to the north; also does low-priced meals.

Ziege, Kreuzstr. 33. The smallest pub in Münster, with a truly *gemütlich* interior.

Clubs

Cascade, Berliner Platz 23. Offers different types of live music Fri & Sat from 10pm.
Elephant, Roggenmarkt 15. Situated in an arcade, this caters mainly for an older crowd.
Le Club, Roggenmarkt 11. In the basement of a clothes store, popular with young clubbers. Wed–Sat from 10pm.

Festivals and entertainment

The main **popular festival**, known as *Send*, is a fair held for five days at a stretch three times annually (March, June & Oct) in the Hindenburgplatz in front of the Schloss. Carnival is also celebrated, if not with the same gusto as in the Rhineland, while the *Lambertusfest*, beginning on September 17, is a festival for children. Münster's main **theatre** venue is the Städtische Bühnen, Neubrückenstr. 63 (☎02 51/41 46 71 00); **concerts** by the Symphonieorchester der Stadt Münster are also held there. Other venues are the Wolfgang-Borchert-Theater, Berliner Platz 23 (☎02 51/4 00 19), and Charivari, Körnerstr. 3 (☎02 51/52 15 00), which features puppet shows. The Halle Münsterland, Albertsloher Weg 32 (☎02 51/6 04 66), to the south of the centre, hosts large-scale events.

Münsterland

Münsterland is the name given to the large tract of Westphalia stretching from the Rhine to the Teutoburg Forest, bounded by the Netherlands and Lower Saxony to the north, and by the Ruhrgebiet to the south. Its rich soils are agriculturally highly productive, and it remains predominantly rural, with no large towns other than the capital. Being almost unrelievedly flat, it's emphatically not a province you visit for scenery, but it boasts over fifty **historic castles** surrounded by tracts of water (known as *Wasserburgen*; see box below), the nearest the country comes to rivalling the French Loire châteaux. The vast majority of these remain private dwellings, and are generally still in the hands of old aristocratic families. Few show much enthusiasm for the local tourist board's collective promotion of the castles as a means of enticing visitors to the region. Hence many of the *Wasserburgen* can only be seen from the outside – and, as often as not, large hedges and impenetrable gates make the view partial at best. That said, several of the most notable castles do offer reasonable public access, and are described in more detail below.

THE WASSERBURGEN

The **Wasserburgen** are so named because their most characteristic feature is a surrounding tract of water. This form was developed in the sixteenth century by local landlords for strongholds to protect their fiefdoms, and was necessitated by the lack of natural strategic points which more undulating countryside could provide; it superseded the earlier technique of building on artificial mounds, which had been rendered highly vulnerable by advances in gunpowder and firearms. A couple of centuries later, in more peaceful times, Baroque country houses were built in this countryside, some of them as replacements for their redundant predecessors, others completely new. These generally still included a moat, though now for aesthetic reasons only. Voltaire set the opening of his great satire *Candide* in one of these estates, lampooning the degenerate lifestyle of Baron Thunder-ten-tronckh and his twenty-five-stone wife and the intellectually bankrupt philosophy of the complacent tutor Dr Pangloss, who convinced everyone they were living "in the most beautiful and delightful of all possible mansions, in this best of all possible worlds".

As the timetabling of the local buses isn't ideal for castle-crawling, it's worth **renting a bike** to get around. The most convenient place to go is the underground Radstation, immediately in front of Münster's Hauptbahnhof, which charges DM11/€5.50 per day. Although there's plenty of accommodation in all the smaller towns, Münster itself is much the best base for exploring the area.

Around Münster

You don't need to venture far out of Münster for your first taste of these châteaux, as **Haus Rüschhaus** (guided tours March, April & Nov to mid-Dec Tues–Sun 11am–1pm & 2–4pm; May–Oct Tues–Sun 10am–1pm & 2.30–5.30pm; DM5/€2.50) stands just beyond the end of the built-up area, and can be reached by bus #5. The present building was designed and built from 1745 to 1748 by **Johann Conrad Schlaun** as a summer house for himself. It's quite an eccentric little construction, mostly homely in feel, but with touches of Baroque swagger, as in the sloping roofline and the sweeping facade which in fact fronts a fully practical barn, integrated into the house as was the norm in traditional local farmsteads. The Italian Room, named after the capriccio scenes on the handmade wallpaper from Paris, provides the only decorative note in the house. Originally Schlaun's bedroom, it was transformed to its present state by later owners, the family of Germany's leading woman author of the nineteenth century, **Annette von Droste-Hülshoff** (1797–1848), who lived here for twenty years from 1826, during which time she produced much of her finest work.

Best known for her charming poetic vignettes of nature, the writer spent the first three decades of her life in the original seat of her aristocratic family, **Haus Hülshoff** (mid-March to mid-Dec daily 9.30am–6pm; DM5/€2.50). Buses #563 and #564 go there from Münster, or you can walk from Rüschhaus in about half an hour by continuing straight ahead and turning left down the footpath just past the highway junction; don't follow the road, which adds a considerable distance to the journey. This castle is a classic example of the Renaissance *Wasserburg* design, the outer barrier (*Vorburg*) being a severe, low-lying building with square corner towers, the inner building (*Hauptburg*) an airy L-shaped dwelling in the Dutch style, to which a neo-Gothic chapel was added in the nineteenth century. There's also an attractive park, recently re-created after old designs. The *Hauptburg* features a suite of six rooms authentically furnished in the early nineteenth-century style familiar to the poet.

Burgsteinfurt

The town of **BURGSTEINFURT**, some 35km north of Münster on the main rail line to Gronau nowadays forms part of a larger municipality known as Steinfurt. It's still a seat of the House of Bentheim, which introduced the Calvinist faith to northern Germany, and the **Schloss** ranks as the most varied in Münsterland. Although the present duke is more generous with access than most private owners in the area, the organization of visits has been left in the hands of the **tourist office** (May–Sept Mon–Fri 9am–12.30pm & 2–5pm, Sat 9am–12.30pm; Oct–April Mon–Fri only; ☎0 25 51/13 83, fax 73 26, *www.steinfurt.de*) in the former Rathaus at Markt 2. It's advisable to make contact in advance to find out when these are: there are normally morning and afternoon tours on Saturdays, but on weekdays visits only take place if there is sufficient demand. The Schloss is a fascinating building, with all manner of fragments from diverse periods surviving in a ramshackle way, the courtyard alone serving as an encyclopedia of European architectural history. From the twelfth century there's a Romanesque double chapel, the lower of which remains in its simple original state, while the upper was adapted according to Protestant tenets. On the left-hand side, a Renaissance wing was built, centred on a superb two-storey oriel window. To the south is the **Bagno**, a spacious public park, which offers good distant views of the Schloss.

Lembeck

LEMBECK, about 50km southwest of Burgsteinfurt, can be reached by train from there or from Münster via Coesfeld. The **Schloss**, set back from the village, is also still in private hands, but the fact that part of it is now a **hotel** (☎0 23 69/7213; ⑥) and restaurant means that access is easier than normal (guided tours mid-March to Oct daily 10am–5pm; DM6.50/€3.25). In spite of the impressive severity of the exterior, conforming to the old *Wasserburg* design, it seems to be the first in the province to have been built more for pleasure than defence, a fact suggested by the exuberant helmets on the towers and by the very obvious vulnerability of the rear, connected by a small causeway to the gardens. Just to the east of Lembeck is the **Naturpark Hohe Mark**, a protected area of gently sloping forests, a veritable oasis in the midst of so much flatness.

Lüdinghausen

There's a choice of bus or train from Münster to **LÜDINGHAUSEN**, 30km south; the buses are better, as the rail route is circuitous and the Bahnhof is a long way out. The moated castle named after the town itself has been too messed about down the years to be of much interest, but **Burg Vischering** at the northern boundary is an archetypal *Wasserburg*, as well as the only one wholly given over to tourism, being designated the **Münsterland-Museum** (Tues–Sun 10am–12.30pm & 1.30–4.30/5.30pm; DM4/€2). Its *Hauptburg*, horseshoe in shape, with a singular octagonal tower in the centre of the courtyard, was beautified around 1620 by the addition of an abutting Renaissance section with an elegant oriel window. Directly facing this are the spreading branches of a trumpet tree, the most remarkable of several rare species planted in the grounds. As usual, the interiors are plain by comparison, but the **Rittersaal** with wooden beamed ceiling has been restored to good effect. There's an exhibition on life in the medieval castles of the region; other folklore displays, this time on the farms and the towns, are to be found in the *Vorburg*.

Nordkirchen

If you've only a day to spare on the castles, the best way to spend it is by combining a visit to Lüdinghausen and **NORDKIRCHEN**, 8km southeast. This redbrick giant is by far the largest and most spectacular **Schloss** of the group, a manifestation of the fantastic wealth of the Plettenberg dynasty of prince-bishops, who decided to replace their old fortress with a palace in the French manner. Every tourist brochure refers to it as the "Westphalian Versailles", a nickname it has had since its conception in 1703, when it referred to the older and much smaller palace at Versailles, on which Nordkirchen was directly modelled.

The complex is on one island only (instead of the two normally required for a *Wasserburg*), and exhibits all the sense of order characteristic of the Age of Reason. It's almost completely symmetrical and is specially designed to produce a spectacular main vista, an effect achieved by breaking up the main block into sections and preceding them with long, narrow pavilions. Behind, there's a formal garden with Baroque sculptures. Nowadays, Nordkirchen belongs to the Land government, which has adapted it as a college for financial studies; consequently there's free access at all times, and what you can see from outside definitely justifies a visit. Official opportunities for viewing the **interior** aren't generous (guided tours Sat & Sun 2–5pm; DM4/€2). However, there are many private visits on weekdays throughout the summer, with which you're allowed to tag along; consult the list posted in the porter's office or, better still, phone ahead (mornings only; ☎0 25 96/93 34 02). The rooms are less grandiose than you might imagine from outside, but have the full pomp of the Baroque in their rich stuccowork, ceiling paintings, wood panelling and plentiful furnishings.

There are no **buses** out of Nordkirchen on Sundays, and only one on Saturday afternoons (to Lüdinghausen), which entails taking the 2pm tour. The nearest train station, on a line with a very restricted weekend service, is at Cappel, 5km east.

Cappenberg

CAPPENBERG, 12km south of Nordkirchen, stands just outside the industrial town of Lünen, which marks the beginning of the Ruhrgebiet. There's been a **Schloss** (Tues–Sun 10am–5pm; free) here since the ninth century; the present building is Baroque, and now hosts temporary exhibitions of various kinds.

Far more significant is the **Stiftskirche** directly in front, founded by the brothers **Gottfried** and **Otto von Cappenberg** in atonement for the part they had played in helping Lothair of Saxony sack the city of Münster in 1121, destroying most of the Dom in the process. Their confessor, St Norbert, suggested that a fit form of repentance would be the establishment of a German headquarters for the Premonstratensian order he had recently founded in France. The plain architecture favoured by these monks, Romanesque with later Gothic additions, gives no hint of the riches within, which include two of the supreme masterpieces of German medieval art. Displayed in a safe in the south transept is the stunning **head-reliquary of Frederick Barbarossa**, the oldest surviving portrait of a German emperor made from life. Actually intended to contain a relic of St John the Evangelist, it's probably the work of an Aachen goldsmith of about 1160. In the choir is the early fourteenth-century **founders' memorial**, depicting them as rather jolly youths with virtually identical features clasping a model of the church. At around the same time, a tomb was made for the now-canonized Gottfried; it's kept in the south transept. Other important works of art are the polychrome Romanesque triumphal cross and the elaborately carved Gothic stalls (each of the misericords is worth looking at).

Below the castle complex is a privately owned **Wildpark** offering various nature trails. A further 2km on, actually within Lünen, lies the artificial boating lake named **Cappenberger See**. There's a **youth hostel** (☎0 23 06/5 35 46, fax 7 30 00, *jh-cappenberger.see@djh-wl.de*; DM22/€11 or DM27/€13.50) at Richard-Schirrmann-Weg on its northern shore.

Freckenhorst

FRECKENHORST, 25km east of Münster, and served by regular buses, also has an important Romanesque **Stiftskirche**. This time it's the architecture which is most striking, even if it's ruggedly impressive rather than beautiful. The massive solemn facade is particularly memorable, with two cylindrical corner towers huddling up against the great belfry. At the east end, a pair of square towers forms a perfect counterpoint. In the crypt is the thirteenth-century **tomb of Geva**, a memorial to the woman who founded the original convent in the ninth century. The most important work of art is the **baptismal font**; the upper register is adorned with masterly carvings of scenes from the life of Christ, with fantastic animals below. On the walls around are paintings from a dismembered "Soft Style" retable of about 1430 by the **Master of Warendorf**.

Recklinghausen

RECKLINGHAUSEN lies at the northern edge of the Ruhrgebiet, just before the vast built-up area gives way to the open spaces of Münsterland. Although small scale in comparison with the cities to the south, it does its best to appear distinctive. Originally founded as a royal seat by Charlemagne, it was a Hanseatic city in the Middle Ages, dominated by blacksmiths and cloth merchants. There are no major historic monuments, but you still get something of the feel of the old town amidst all the usual later accretions – certainly, there's more of a sense of continuous history here than is to be found anywhere else in the Ruhr.

Streets in the centre still follow the old twisting and turning pattern and there are a number of half-timbered houses, some fragments of the city wall and, as centrepiece, the **Petruskirche**, predominantly Gothic, but incorporating parts of its Romanesque predecessor as well as sundry modifications by subsequent builders. From the Baroque period, the **Engelsburg** on Augustinessenstrasse is a handsome mansion built round a courtyard. Round the corner on Geiststrasse is the **Gastkirche**, formerly an almshouse chapel, containing several striking altarpieces.

Recklinghausen's pride and joy, however, is its **Ikonmuseum** (Tues–Fri 10am–6pm, Sat & Sun 11am–5pm; DM5/€2.50) at Am Kirchplatz beside the Petruskirche. This isn't just another example of the seemingly inexhaustible German capacity for creating museums on the most abstruse of subjects – it really is the finest collection of this simple yet haunting and powerful art form outside the Orthodox world. The star piece is the huge late sixteenth-century Russian *Calendar Icon of the Year*, a *tour de force* illustrating the main stories of the Bible, as well as portraying hundreds of saints, arranged according to their feast day. From the following century come *The Credo*, executed using techniques reminiscent of Western manuscript illuminators, and a masterly *Enthroned Christ*, a signed work by the Cretan **Elias Moskos**. The earliest works, from the fifteenth-century Moscow and Novgorod schools, have perhaps the most overtly emotional appeal; among the finest are the symbolic *Christ the Unsleeping Eye* and *St Nicholas with Scenes from his Life*. In addition to over four hundred icons displayed by subject, there are extensive collections the decorative arts of the Orthodox and Coptic churches.

Practicalities

The **Hauptbahnhof** lies just to the east of the Altstadt. Recklinghausen has no **tourist office** as such, but you can pick up maps and leaflets at the Rathaus (☎0 23 61/50 15 51).

Among the **hotels**, *Kolpinghaus*, Herzogswall 38 (☎0 23 61/2 26 40; ②), offers budget rooms; the historic *Gasthof Albers*, Markt 3 (☎0 23 61/9 51 60; ⑤), is an excellent mid-range option; while the best address is *Parkhotel Engelsburg*, which occupies an early eighteenth-century palace at Augustinessenstr. 10 (☎0 23 61/20 10; ⑦). The last two hotels have fine **restaurants**, though strong competition comes from *Altes Brauhaus*, just east of the centre at Dortmunder Str. 16. A cheaper alternative is *Hausbrauerei Boente*, Augustinessenstr. 4, whose home brews can be sampled in its large beer garden.

Cultural life in Recklinghausen centres on the *Ruhrfestspiele*, a **festival** of concerts, plays, exhibitions and discussions held annually in May and June. The Festspielhaus, in the Stadtgarten to the west of the city centre, was opened in 1965 as the specially designed home for the festival.

Bochum

BOCHUM lies right at the heart of the Ruhrgebiet, sandwiched between the two giants of Essen and Dortmund. It boasts two of the best specialist **technical museums** on the achievements of German industry, but if these don't appeal, there's little else to justify a visit here, other than the remarkably vibrant **theatres**, which manage an improbable rivalry to the likes of Berlin and Munich. A pleasant if anonymous shopping area forms the centre, devoid of any sense of history bar the rather ghostly reminder provided by the **Propsteikirche**, a Gothic hall church now standing forlornly in its own grounds. In spite of the traditions in heavy industry, the leading employer is now the car plant of Opel, General Motors' European subsidiary.

The sixty-metre-high winding tower of the **Deutsches Bergbaumuseum** (German Mining Museum; Tues–Fri 8.30am–5.30pm, Sat & Sun 10am–4pm; DM8/€4) is a dominant feature of the skyline. Established in 1930, this claims to be the most important collection of its kind in the world, and is both exhaustive and inventive in scope. Budget at least two hours for a visit, as the ticket includes a 45-minute conducted tour around the demonstration pit in the bowels of the earth immediately below. It's also possible to ascend the tower.

The **Museum Bochum** (Tues & Thurs–Sat 11am–5pm, Wed 11am–8pm, Sun 11am–6pm; DM5/€2.50) is just round the corner on Kortumstrasse. The displays here, mounted in a series of changing exhibitions, are devoted to post-1945 art only. There's a branch at **Wasserburg Kemnade** (May–Oct Tues 9am–3pm, Wed–Fri 1–7pm, Sat & Sun 11am–6pm; Nov–April Tues–Fri 11am–5pm, Sat & Sun 10am–5pm; free), a moated castle at the far southeastern edge of the city, reached by bus #C31. Although heavily restored, a couple of ornate chimneypieces remain, and there's a large collection of historical musical instruments. Adjacent is the **Bauernhausmuseum** (Farmhouse Museum; May–Oct only, same times; free). Between here and the centre are the eye-catching futuristic buildings of the **Ruhr-Universität**, the largest of several institutions for technical education in the region. The **Botanischer Garten** is situated on the southern side (daily: April–Sept 9am–6pm; Oct–March 9am–4pm; free).

In the southern suburb of Dalhausen, which is served by S-Bahn, is the excellent **Eisenbahnmuseum** (Rail Museum; Wed & Fri 10am–5pm, Sun 10am–1/3pm; DM5.50/€2.75), which is run by the national preservation society. From the station, this is reached by turning left at the exit, then walking straight ahead for about 1.5km. Alternatively, take the museum's *Schiene-Strasse-Bus*, a bizarre hybrid which looks like a bus but is also equipped with wheels for travelling along rails. Vehicles like these were widely used in forest areas throughout Germany until the late 1960s. In the museum itself, some of the trains are in open yards, but most are grouped in two sheds. The first contains the locomotives themselves, with some real beauties, especially the oldest item, an imperious black and red monster from the 1920s. In the second hall are the passenger carriages, the comforts of the first class contrasting strongly with the hard benches in the third.

Practicalities

Bochum's **Hauptbahnhof** is at the eastern end of the centre. The **tourist office** (Mon–Fri 9am–5.30pm, Sat 10am–1pm; ☎02 34/96 30 20, fax 9 63 02 55, *www.bochum.de*) is in the front part of the station building on Kurt-Schumacher-Platz. There's a **Mitfahrzentrale** office at Ferdinandstr. 20 (☎02 34/3 77 94).

Hotels with a central location include *Wiesmann*, Castroper Str. 191 (☎02 34/59 10 65; ③), *Oberste-Ufer*, Nordring 30 (☎02 34/1 67 12; ③), *Antoni*, Flurstr. 1 (☎02 34/58 15 88; ④), *Plaza*, Hellweg 20 (☎02 34/1 30 85; ⑥), and *Excelsior*, Max-Greve-Str. 32 (☎02 34/9 55 20; ⑥). The nearest **campsite** is by the north bank of the Ruhr in the adjacent town of Hattingen (☎0 23 24/8 00 38).

There are abundant places to **eat** and **drink** in the city centre. Two local beers to try are *Vest* and *Fiege*; the *Stammhaus* of the latter brewery is at Bongardstr. 23, and is equally renowned for its food. *Mutter Wittig*, Bongardstr. 35, is another excellent traditional Gaststätte, while two establishments with a special ambience are *Altes Brauhaus Rietkökotter*, in a fine sixteenth-century house at Grosse Beckstr. 7, and *Luisenhof*, a Jugendstil bistro with beer garden at Luisenstr 14. *Oblomov*, Kurt-Schumacher-Platz 19, does cheap meals, while *Taufenbach*, Gerberstr. 19, is a Hausbrauerei which sometimes features live music. At Wasserburg Kemnade, there's a good restaurant in the castle itself.

Bochum has a high reputation for **theatre**, with a renowned repertory company based at the Schauspielhaus, Königsallee 15 (☎02 34/3 33 31 11). Puppet shows and **concerts** by the Bochumer Symphoniker, a highly rated orchestra whose current musical director is the American Steven Sloane, are also held at this venue. The Starlighthalle, Stadionring 24 (☎02 34/9 63 02 33) hosts large-scale musicals. Tarm-Center, Rombacher Hütte 6–8 (☎02 34/45 90 73 00), a huge **disco** with nightly laser shows, is always packed, as is Kulturzentrum Zeche, Prinz-Regent-Str. 50 (☎02 34/7 20 03), which has weekly discos and regular rock, pop and jazz concerts. Bahnhof Langendreer, a former station at the extreme east end of town at Wallbaumweg 108 (☎02 34/2 66 11 14), is an alternative-arts centre featuring music, theatre, cabaret and cinema. The city's main **festival** is *Bochum Total* in the second week of July.

Dortmund

The name of **DORTMUND** immediately brings **beer** to mind – it was first granted brewing rights in 1293, and even jealous rivals are forced to admit it's the national drink's number one city. In all, six million hectolitres are produced annually, a total surpassed in world terms only by Milwaukee. Much of it is for export, which has led to the word being used to categorize certain types of beer. Although many old labels live on, the number of breweries has declined markedly in the last few years – the venerable Kronen acquired both Thier and Stifts, then was itself taken over by DAB. As a result, all production is now concentrated in the hands of just two conglomerates, the aforementioned DAB and Union, the latter's name reflecting its late nineteenth-century origins as a union, of several breweries. Union's huge U logo is still one of the city centre's most prominent landmarks, though the building on which it stands has recently been converted into shops and flats, with operations transferred to a modern plant in the suburbs.

Alone among Ruhr cities, Dortmund was important in the Middle Ages when it was an active member of the Hanseatic League. This helps give it a rounded and distinctive character which all its neighbours somehow lack. Provided you're prepared to overlook the obvious limitations of a place where wartime bombs wreaked horrendous damage and where heavy industry is prominent, it's an interesting and enjoyable city in which to spend a day or two.

Arrival, information and accommodation

Dortmund's **tourist office** (Mon–Fri 9am–6pm, Sat 9am–1pm; ☎02 31/5 02 56 66, fax 16 35 93, *www.dortmund.de*) stands opposite the **Hauptbahnhof** at Königswall 20. The **Mitfahrzentrale** office is at Grüne Str. 3 (☎02 31/1 94 44).

There's a The **campsite** at Syburger Dorfstr. 69 (☎02 31/77 43 74), not far from the casino, the *Spielbank Hohensburg*; take bus #444. **Hotels** in every category can be found in the city centre.

Hotels and pensions

Atlanta, Ostenhellweg 51 (☎02 31/5 57 07 50, fax 5 86 00 54). Moderately priced hotel on one of the main streets of the pedestrian precinct. ⑤.

Carlton, Lütge-Brückstr. 5–7 (☎02 31/52 80 30, fax 52 50 20). No frills but fully acceptable budget hotel just a short walk from the Hauptbahnhof. ④.

Cläre-Fritz, Reinoldstr. 6 (☎02 31/57 15 23, fax 57 96 23). Small pension facing the Reinoldikirche. ④.

Europa Congresshotel, Lindemannstr. 88 (☎02 31/9 11 30, fax 9 11 39 99). Dortmund's most prestigious hotel is located in the south of the city, directly opposite the main congress centre, the Westfalenhallen. It also has a high-quality restaurant, which offers good-value lunchtime buffets. ⑦–⑨.

Königshof, Königswall 4–6 (☎02 31/5 70 41, fax 5 70 40). The most conveniently located of the mid-range hotels. ⑤.

Römischer Kaiser, Olpe 2 (☎02 31/54 32 00, fax 57 43 54). Part of the Holiday Inn chain, this is one of the best upmarket choices. It has a well-regarded restaurant offering budget menus. ⑥–⑨.

Stiftshof, Stiftstr. 5 (☎02 31/52 47 01, fax 52 4702). Another reasonably priced hotel in a good central location. ④.

The city centre

The inner ring road, whose sections all bear the suffix "wall", follows the line of the vanished thirteenth-century fortifications and thus defines the perimeter of the medieval city. Only a fraction of this area was left standing after the war, and not a single secular building from the Hansa days remains. The four civic churches, however, survived the onslaught in a battered condition, and a painstaking restoration programme which lasted into the 1980s has returned them to their former state. Although they're now marooned in a modern shopping centre, the layout of the old streets and squares has been followed. None of the churches is architecturally outstanding, but their assemblage of Gothic art treasures justifies a visit to the city – if the beer isn't a sufficient draw.

The churches

Directly facing the Hauptbahnhof is the **Petrikirche** (Tues–Fri 2–7pm, Sat 11am–2pm), boasting a colossal **Antwerp altar** from around 1520, which opens out to show expressively carved scenes of the *Passion* and *Legend of the Cross*, featuring no fewer than 633 separate figures. These can be seen between autumn and Whit; during the summer they're hidden behind the more modest painted section narrating the earlier part of Christ's life. A short walk down the central axis of Westenhellweg is the **Propsteikirche**, the one church retained by the Catholics when Dortmund embraced the Reformation. On the high altar is a colourful and crowded triptych from about 1490 by the Westphalian painter **Derick Baegert**, aided by his son **Jan**. Straddling the scenes of *The Holy Kinship*, *The Crucifixion* and *The Adoration of the Magi* is a view of a medieval town proudly girt with numerous towers and spires – the earliest-known depiction of Dortmund, and a poignant memorial to its long-lost splendours.

Continuing across Hansastrasse, Ostenhellweg leads to a large square overshadowed by the **Reinoldikirche**, named after the city's patron saint who was stoned to death in Cologne, whereupon his coffin is supposed to have rolled all the way to Dortmund under its own steam. He's depicted as a young Knight in a superb fourteenth-century wooden statue guarding the entrance to the chancel; the corresponding but later figure of a richly attired emperor is almost certainly Charlemagne. Unfortunately the choir area is fenced off, so you can only admire its abundant furnishings at a distance.

Immediately opposite is the **Marienkirche** (Tues–Fri 10am–noon & 2–4pm, Sat 10am–1pm), the oldest of the churches, with a nave which is still largely Romanesque. Its two masterpieces of International Gothic painting are the city's finest works of art. The high altar triptych dates from around 1420 and is by **Conrad von Soest**, a Dortmund citizen in spite of his name, and as endearing a painter as Germany ever produced. These panels of *The Nativity*, *The Dormition of the Virgin* and *The Adoration of the Magi* show the uniquely graceful and delicate "Soft Style" at its greatest, even though all were truncated in order to fit into a Baroque altar. The inner wings of *The Annunciation* and *The Coronation of the Virgin* have suffered such heavy paint loss that they're generally kept under cover, although the caretaker will open them if you ask. In the nave, the Berswordt Altar, a *Crucifixion* triptych, is about 25 years earlier, but has survived in much better shape. See also the late Gothic stalls – their irreverent carvings include, appropriately enough, a man downing a mug of beer.

The museums

The **Museum für Kunst und Kulturgeschichte** (Museum of Art and Cultural History; Tues, Wed, Fri & Sun 10am–6pm, Thurs 10am–8pm, Sat noon–6pm; DM4/€2), very near the Hauptbahnhof at Hansastr. 3, occupies an Art Deco building of the 1920s which was formerly a savings bank. Its highlight is a series of reassembled **interiors** – an eighteenth-century Westphalian pharmacy, the *Fliesensaal* (Tiled Room), with hunting scenes in Delft tiles, and a panelled music room from a bourgeois residence in Bremen. The most important of the rooms is *Der Raum als Gesamtkunstwerk* (The Room as a Complete Work of Art) by the Jugendstil architect-designer Joseph Maria Olbrich, in which every detail has been thought out in relation to its effect on the whole. Among the notable paintings is a stunning, sombre **Friedrich**, *Night on the Sea*. The archeology display is dominated by the *Dortmunder Goldschatz*, a hoard of fourth- and fifth-century gold coins found locally.

On the inner ring road is the **Museum am Ostwall** (Tues, Wed, Fri & Sun 10am–6pm, Thurs 10am–8pm, Sat noon–6pm; DM4/€2), devoted to the municipal collection of modern art, with changing exhibitions on the ground floor. Upstairs is a comprehensive display of Expressionism, dominated by what's arguably **August Macke**'s masterpiece, *Grosser Zoologischer Garten*, which experiments with the new Cubist forms in an anachronistic triptych format. Experimental sculpture includes several works by **Jospeh Beuys**, but the most eye-catching is **Wolf Vostell**'s *Thermo-Elektronischer Kaugummi* of 1970. Occupying a whole gallery, this has 13,000 forks and spoons grouped behind two barbed wire fences, and features 5000 pieces of chewing gum.

The **Mahn- und Gedenkstätte Steinwache** (Tues–Sun 10am–5pm; free), a short walk north of the Hauptbahnhof at Steinstr. 50, is housed in a building formerly used as a prison by the Gestapo. Between 1933 and 1945, thirty thousand opponents of the Nazi regime were detained here. Using original documents, photographs, personal effects and taped interviews, the exhibition comprehensively documents the rise of National Socialism, the resistance to it and the brutal persecution of its opponents. Some of the rooms have been returned to their former state as prison cells, giving an added edge to the overall atmosphere.

Eating and drinking

Inevitably, the **beer halls** are the focus for eating and drinking, and the city centre is ideal for a pub crawl. There's no need to move very far to sample the products of all the different breweries, and the Markt makes the obvious place to begin.

Bass, Münsterstr. 95. Jazz bar with regular live performances. Also serves food, including many vegetarian options, and has a small beer garden. Closed Sat & Sun.

Brauhaus Kronen am Markt, Betenstr. 1. Kronen has had an uninterrupted presence on this spot since 1430, an even longer pedigree than the Hofbräuhaus in Munich. It currently has a Hausbrauerei which produces *Wenkers Utrüb*, a blond ale top-fermented with plenty of yeast sediment left in.

Brinkhoffs No. 1, Markt 6. A flagship Gaststätte for the giant Union brewery, whose beers are milder, sweeter and maltier than those of the DAB group.

Café Hemmer, Ostenhellweg 62. If hardly typical for Dortmund, this genteel salon is a good place for the archetypally German fare of *Kaffee und Kuchen*.

FZW, Neuer Graben 167. *Szene* bar with regular discos and live rock.

Holzknecht, Hohe Str. 5. Offers Swabian as well as Westphalian dishes, and DAB beer.

Hövels Hausbrauerei, Hoher Wall 5. Occupying the old Thier brewery, the main product line here is the deceptively named *Bitterbier*, a malty bronze-coloured brew; various seasonal beers are also produced. There's the bonus of a beer garden, while the food on offer is among the best in the city.

La Table, Hohensyburgstr. 200. The casino's restaurant is a renowned gourmet address, generally regarded as by far the best in the city. Evenings only.

Pfefferkorn, Hoher Wall 38. Fine old Gaststätte of the Union brewery.

Zum Alten Markt, Alter Markt 3. Traditional Westphalian cooking and the full range of Thier beers, which include a very dry *Pils* as well as a typical *Export*.

Entertainment

Theatres include the Schauspielhaus and its Studio on Hiltropwall (☎02 31/16 30 41), while the Opernhaus is at Platz der Alten Synagoge (☎02 31/16 30 41). The huge Westfalenhalle (☎02 31/1 20 46 66) southwest of the centre is used for **sports** and big shows such as **jazz** and **pop concerts**. Live Station, Am Hauptbahnhof (☎02 31/16 17 83), presents **discos** and live music from Fridays to Sundays, while Luna Varieté und Theater, Harkortstr. 57a (☎02 31/77 31 96) in the suburb of Hombruch, is the place for cabaret and variety.

Hagen

Like nearby Wuppertal, **HAGEN** would be a characterless large town were it not for an imaginative and rather brilliant act of initiative around the turn of the last century. **Karl Ernst Osthaus**, a local industrialist and patron of the arts, was instrumental in persuading a group of talented international designers in the Art Nouveau style to come to Hagen. Prominent among them were the architects Peter Behrens of Hamburg, Henry van de Velde from Belgium and Mathiew Lauweriks from Holland, along with another Dutchman, the decorator Johan Thorn-Prikker. The artists' colony thus founded was a fitting successor to the one in Darmstadt, Germany's other main centre of **Jugendstil**, to which Behrens had also belonged. Nor were other styles shunned: the Expressionist painter Christian Rohlfs was summoned and stayed until he died in 1938, seventeen years after Osthaus's own premature death put an end to his ambitious plans for a complete garden city.

The Town

Your first glimpse of Hagen's legacy comes at the **Hauptbahnhof**. Illuminating the exit is a large stained-glass window by Thorn-Prikker, an allegory entitled *The Obeisance of the Crafts before the Artist*. From the square in front, turn right and then follow Elberfelder Strasse straight ahead, eventually taking any of the small side-streets to the right into the parallel Hochstrasse, where you'll find the **Karl-Ernst-Osthaus-Museum** (Tues, Wed & Fri–Sun 11am–6pm, Thurs 11am–8pm; free). The exterior is in the stolid late-nineteenth-century Wilhelmine style, but the interior, created a few years later by van de Velde, has all the sense of fantasy and romance characteristic of the best Art Nouveau. Originally this contained Osthaus's private art collection, the Folkwang Museum, which was hung in an unconventional thematic manner. After his death, it was sold *en bloc* by his heirs to the city of Essen, where it can still be seen. Since the acquisition of the building by the Hagen authorities in 1945, belated attempts have been made to re-create the original effect by acquiring works in line with Osthaus's tastes. There's a good representation of Expressionism and other twentieth-century German art, with several examples of **Rohlfs**, whose studio was housed here, along with works by **Macke** (*Women in Front of a Hat Shop*), **Dix** (the erotic *Artist and Muse*), **Kokoschka** (*The Actor Sommarunga*), Kirchner, Nolde, Beckmann and Schmidt-Rottluff.

To the east of the centre, reached by bus #522, is the projected garden suburb of **Hohenhagen**, of which only an incomplete crescent known as **Stirnband** was built. The nearer side of this consists of a row of houses by Lauweriks, homogeneous in style but each given its own identity. Still in private ownership, they are undoubtedly the ultimate residence within the Ruhrgebiet. Fronting the other entrance to the crescent is **Haus Cuno** by Behrens, now an academy of music. On weekdays it's worth sticking your head round the door to see the impressive stairwell. The rest of this street really forms a processional way to the vast **Hohenhof**, designed as Osthaus's own residence by van de Velde. This is one of the great achievements of the Art Nouveau movement, a dream home if ever there was one, and a building which seems to change dramatically from every angle of vision. Now owned by the city, it's a cultural centre, but the interior is generally only accessible on Saturdays between 2pm and 6pm. Try to come then to see the intricacies of its decorations, which include furniture designed by its architect, stained-glass windows by Thorn-Prikker and a huge canvas, *The Elect*, by the Swiss **Ferdinand Hodler**.

Hagen's other main attraction is the **Westfälisches Freilichtmuseum** (April–Oct Tues–Sun 9am–6pm; DM7/€3.50), south of the city in Selbecke; take bus #507. Laid out in the valley of the Mäckingerbach, this marks the point where the industrial Ruhrgebiet gives way to the rural Sauerland. There are some 65 traditional buildings, but it differs from other museums of the same type in that the emphasis is technical, rather than social or architectural. Horny-handed old sons of toil demonstrate all kinds of historical equipment, ranging from machinery for producing iron and steel, through printing and papermaking, spinning, weaving and dyeing, to baking and mustard production; it's possible to buy many of the products made here. There's also a windmill near the entrance but, as it's some distance from the other buildings, check first for the times when it's going to be put into action. Just to walk round the site takes quite a while, and you need to budget at least three hours for a visit – longer if you want to see all the crafts demonstrated.

Practicalities

Hagen's **tourist office** (Mon–Thurs 8am–5pm, Fri 8am–1pm; ☎0 23 31/2 07 33 83, fax 2 07 24 74, *www.hagen.de*) is in the Rathaus on Friedrich-Ebert-Platz. Given the fact that the sights of interest are so far apart, a day ticket on the **public transport** system, costing DM10/€5, is worth considering. There's a **Mitfahrzentrale** office at Södingstr. 3 (☎0 23 31/33 75 55).

Within a stone's throw of the Hauptbahnhof is a basic budget **hotel**, *Bürgerkrug*, Werdestr. 2–4 (☎0 23 31/2 67 79; ②). More upmarket possibilities are *Lex*, Elberfelder Str. 71 (☎0 23 31/3 20 30; ⑥), *Deutsches Haus*, Bahnhofstr. 35 (☎0 23 31/2 10 51 53; ⑥), *Central*, Dahlenkampstr. 2 (☎0 23 31/1 63 02; ⑥), and *Mercure*, Wasserloses Tal 4 (☎0 23 31/39 10; ⑧). The **youth hostel** is at Eppenhauser Str. 65a (☎0 23 31/5 02 54, fax 58 85 76, *jh-hagen@djh-wl.de*; DM23.40/€11.70 or DM28.40/€14.20), just a few minutes' from Stirnband and reached by bus #522 or #523. Although there's no **campsite** within the city boundaries, the one at Syburg (see p.594) is only a few kilometres away, reached by bus #544.

The best **restaurant** is in the *Mercure* hotel; cheaper alternatives are the *Ratskeller* on Friedrich-Ebert-Platz and *Alt-Nürnberg*, Elbersufer 10. **Concerts** by the Philharmonisches Orchester Hagen are usually held at the Stadthalle on Wasserloses Tal (☎0 23 31/32 65 13), while **drama**, **opera** and **ballet** all feature at the Jugenstil Theater Hagen, Elberfelder Str. 65 (☎0 23 31/2 07 32 18). For **live jazz**, go to Tubakeller, Hohenzollernstr. 10; the pub above, *Spinne*, has a beer garden.

Soest

SOEST, some 50km east of Dortmund, was a city of similar importance at the time of the Hanseatic League. Nowadays it's a whole world away in spirit, ranking as one of Germany's most delightful towns, yet it could so easily have been incorporated into the Ruhr conurbation. This proximity to the industrial heartland led to Soest being heavily bombed during the war, but restoration has been so deft that the scars have healed completely and there's scarcely a street within the fortifications which doesn't live up to the tourist-board image of Romantic Germany. All the main buildings were constructed from a local sandstone whose deep lime greens bestow a distinctive character on the town and are well offset against the many red-roofed and whitewashed half-timbered houses. The play of light on these surfaces produces such magical effects it's little wonder that Soest has nurtured more than its fair share of German artists.

The Town

The town has never expanded much beyond its walls, which survive minus their battlements, and it preserves a medieval air and layout, with a varied group of churches and secular buildings.

The Wiesenkirche and Hohnekirche

Rising majestically above the northern part of the Altstadt are the twin spires of the Gothic **Wiesenkirche** (Our Lady of the Meadows). This is a key building in German architectural history, when the favoured but problematic hall-church design finally acquired an elegance to match any other style of building. Although only a parish church, it's more like a cathedral in miniature, with an interior that's nothing short of stupendous.

Slender unadorned piers thrust effortlessly up to the lofty vault, and the walls seem to be made of nothing but dazzlingly brilliant **stained glass**. These were inserted over a period ranging from just after the church's construction in the fourteenth century to the early sixteenth century, when money ran out before the south side could be glazed. The masterpiece of this assemblage, placed over the north portal, is from the final period, showing *The Last Supper* with a Westphalian menu of beer, ham and rye bread. As a bonus, the church houses a richly varied collection of works of art, including three large triptychs; that in the right-hand apse chapel was painted by **Heinrich Aldegraver**, a resident of Soest and one of Dürer's most accomplished followers.

On higher ground to the rear stands the **Hohnekirche** (Our Lady on the Hill). The same Protestant congregation owns both this and the Wiesenkirche, taking refuge in the cosier surroundings of this squat, box-like structure for the winter months. It's a Romanesque attempt of about a century earlier at creating a hall church. The rather plain result was, however, greatly enlivened by a sumptuous fresco decoration, much of which has survived. Also here are a couple of fine works of art in the *Passion* altar by the late fifteenth-century Westphalian painter known as the Master of Liesborn, and the remarkable *Scheibenkreuz*, a four-metre-high triumphal cross from about 1200, adorned with delicate reliefs of the life of Christ.

The centre

The centre is soon reached from here by returning to Wiesenstrasse, continuing via an old water-mill up Am Seel. Dominating the skyline is the noble tower of **St Patrokli**, generally (if inaccurately) referred to as the **Dom**. This forms part of a resplendent Romanesque westwork, which is so grandiose a frontage that the rest of the building comes as an anticlimax, though it preserves the fine cycle of eleventh-century murals in the north transept apse.

Only a few yards in front stands the **Petrikirche**, towering over the square of the same name which also contains the **Rathaus**, the only significant Baroque addition to the city. Again with a westwork as its most notable feature, the Petrikirche is Romanesque with the addition of a Gothic chancel. On the third piers of the nave are two *Crucifixion* frescoes attributed to **Conrad von Soest**, a major figure of the fifteenth century, and one of the few early German masters known by name. An important painting which may also be by this artist, *St Nicholas Enthroned with SS Catherine, Barbara and the two Johns*, occupies the altar of the tiny Romanesque **Nicolaikapelle**, situated behind the east end of St Patrokli. In spite of an unprepossessing exterior, the inside of the chapel is a real gem, another variation on the hall-church theme, with rounded column shafts dividing the space into two equal aisles. It's generally locked (officially open 11am–noon on Tues, Wed, Fri & Sun); if so, ask for the key at the **Wilhelm-Morgner-Haus**, the local cultural centre based in a modern building directly in front (Mon–Sat 10am–noon & 3–5pm, Sun 10.30am–12.30pm; free). This is named after Soest's own Expressionist painter, whose short career overlapped with the presence in the city of two of the movement's leading lights, Christian Rohlfs and Emil Nolde. A number of Morgner's canvases can be seen on the first floor, revealing a versatile talent which was to end at the age of 26 on a Flanders battlefield. Also on view are a selection of Aldegraver's engravings, his favourite and most effective medium.

The rest of town

From here, follow Ulricher Strasse south, turning left into Burghofstrasse, and you'll come to a complex of buildings, including a rare Romanesque house and the **Burghof** (Tues–Sat 10am–noon & 3–5pm, Sun 11am–1pm; DM3/€1.50), a sixteenth-century mansion now housing the local history museum. The main feature is the **Festsaal** on the ground floor, whose walls are covered with white stuccowork; the biblical subjects are original, the battle scenes and emperors skilful modern pastiches. Another small museum is housed in the **Osthofentor** (April–Sept Tues–Sat 2–4pm, Sun 11am–1pm & 3–5pm; Oct–March Wed 2–4pm, Sun 11am–1pm; same ticket as Burghof), a stately Renaissance gateway which once formed the northeast entrance to the town, and a rare surviving adornment of the walls. The display here is mostly concerned with medieval warfare; what looks like a spectacular modern sculpture in the attic turns out to be a fancy arrangement of 25,000 crossbow bolts.

Practicalities

Both the **Hauptbahnhof** and the **bus station** are located just outside the northern stretch of the city walls. The **tourist office** (April–Oct Mon–Fri 9.30am–12.30pm & 2–4.30pm, Sat 10am–1pm, Sun 11am–1pm; rest of year closed Sun; ☎0 29 21/10 33 23, fax 3 30 39, *www.soest.de*) is at Am Seel 5. Soest is at its liveliest during the five-day-long *Allerheiligenkirmes*, which is claimed as the biggest town-centre **fair** in Europe; beginning on the Wednesday after All Saints' Day (Nov 1), it features a massive fairground, a horse market and fireworks displays. Other local festivals include the *Bördetag* on a weekend in May and the *Gauklertag* on a Saturday in September.

Within the Altstadt is a broad range of **hotels** of which the best budget choices are *Zum Amtsgericht*, Nöttenstr. 31 (☎0 29 21/1 33 03; ③), *Braustübl*, Thomästr. 53 (☎0 29 21/41 66; ③), and *Gasthof Drei Kronen*, Jakobistr. 37–39 (☎0 29 21/1 36 65; ④). More upmarket places include *Stadt Soest*, Brüderstr. 50 (☎0 29 21/3 62 20; ⑤), and the wonderful old *Pilgrim-Haus*, Jakobistr. 75 (☎0 29 21/18 28; ⑥), Westphalia's oldest inn with an uninterrupted tradition dating back to the fourteenth century. The **youth hostel**, Kaiser-Friedrich-Platz 2 (☎0 29 21/1 62 83, fax 1 46 23, *jh-soest@djh-wl.de*; DM22/€11 or DM27/€13.50), is just outside the southern section of the city wall. There's no **campsite**, but those around Möhnesee (see p.604) are just a few kilometres away and connected by regular bus services.

One consequence of the relentless flow of day-trippers from the Ruhr each weekend is an enormous choice of **restaurants** – over a hundred in all. Among the best are those in the last two hotels mentioned above. *Altes Gasthaus im Zuckerberg*, which occupies the oldest house in Westphalia at Höggenstr. 1, serves Italian cuisine; *Biermanns*, Thomästr. 47, offers expensive international dishes in designer premises; *Am Kattenturm*, Dasselwall 1, is of similar quality and more reasonably priced. *Brauhaus Zwiebel*, Ulrichstr. 24, is a Hausbrauerei producing both light and dark beers. Many traditional **cafés** – such as *Café Fromme*, Markt 1, and *Café am Dom*, Am Vreithof 2 – provide a relaxed atmosphere for *Kaffee und Kuchen*; while *Haus Sauerland*, Filzenstr. 4, is a café-restaurant which has been run by the same family for two centuries.

The food you should on no account miss is Soest's own contribution to culinary history, the famed **Pumpernickel**, a strongly flavoured rye bread popular throughout Germany at breakfast time. For the genuine article, go to *Wilhelm Haverland*; its factory at Markt 6 has been in operation since 1799, and you can choose from several different recipes in its side-street shop behind.

The Sauerland

The **Sauerland** forms an extensive part of eastern Westphalia, stretching from the eastern edge of the Ruhrgebiet across to the border with Hesse. Literally translated, the name means "Bitter Land", though it's unclear whether this comes from the fierce Saxon tribes who once inhabited the region and put up a doughty resistance to Charlemagne, or from the poor soils and hostile, rugged terrain. There's also the possibility that the name is a simple corruption of "South Land". It's rural, upland country, supposedly containing a thousand mountains; nowadays it serves as an obvious holiday

THE DAMBUSTERS

The importance of the Ruhr dams to the economy of the Third Reich was highlighted by the famous "**Dambusters**" episode of World War II (told in Paul Brickhill's book and in the popular film which, however, wasn't shot on location). At the time, these massive concrete structures would hardly have been grazed by existing explosives. In order to penetrate them, the inventor Barnes Wallis developed enormous ten-ton bombs which skipped across the water surface like a pebble, sinking behind the defensive nets and lodging themselves against the weakest point of the dams' walls. These "bouncing bombs" were dropped with devastating effect by the Lancasters of 617 Squadron, commanded by Wing Commander Guy Gibson, on May 17, 1943. Such havoc was caused by the ensuing flooding, which destroyed 123 factories, 25 bridges and 30 square kilometres of arable land, that it was estimated to have taken the equivalent of several months' work by 100,000 men to repair the damage – a telling blow to the whole Nazi war effort and a major propaganda coup. This, at any rate, is how the evidence has traditionally been presented. Latest research suggests that the claims were exaggerated, and that the Möhne dam, far from being wrecked, was eventually repaired. Fifty-six members of 617 Squadron were killed in the raid. "If only I'd known," Barnes Wallis said when he discovered the RAF losses, "I'd never have started this."

and recreation area for the teeming millions who live in the nearby cities of the Rhine-Ruhr conurbation. The Sauerland's attractions are quintessentially German – above all, it's good **hiking** country, with nearly 12,000km of marked footpaths, and four nature parks fall wholly or largely within its boundaries. Dotted with rivers and artificial lakes, it's also one of the country's main centres for **angling** and **activity holidays**, such as surfing, rowing, canoeing, sailing and hang-gliding, while riding in covered wagons Wild-West style has also been made into a regional speciality. Much of the Sauerland is of a surprisingly Alpine character for a place so far north, and **winter sports** help to keep its tourist trade going all year round.

On the surface, the Sauerland is the mirror opposite of the Ruhrgebiet. However, though there are no major cities, there are many medium-sized industrial towns. **Beer** is a leading product – the soft local spring water is a crucial ingredient. As a result, many aficionados rate Sauerland brews superior even to those of nearby Dortmund. Warsteiner, dubbed "the queen of beers" for its delicate taste, is currently being heavily promoted abroad; Veltins is popular throughout Germany, while Iserlohner and Hirsch are also very fine. Sauerland water, moreover, plays a key role in the economy of the Ruhrgebiet, and the great **dams** of the region are key features of the German inland waterway system.

Märkisches Sauerland

Furthest to the west of the region is the **Märkisches Sauerland**, corresponding to the old Duchy of Mark. This is sometimes taken to include Hagen itself; more logically, it begins with the incorporated town of Hohenlimburg, where the continuously built-up land of the Ruhrgebiet first gives way to open countryside. A scenic rail line follows the course of the River Lenne and continues all the way south to Siegen. On the east bank is the Lennegebirge range, which forms part of the **Naturpark Homert**; to the west begins the **Naturpark Ebbegebirge**.

Altena

ALTENA, 25km southeast of Hagen, is the obvious star of the Sauerland towns, thanks to its superb setting deep in the valley, high above which is its massive **Burg** (Tues–Fri 9.30am–5pm, Sat & Sun 11am–6pm; DM8/€4), one of the largest medieval castles in

Germany. Begun in the twelfth century, the buildings were erected at intervals up to the sixteenth century. The central keep is strongly protected by an outer bailey and no fewer than three consecutive gateways. The complex inevitably crumbled with disuse, and there were plans in the nineteenth century to rebuild it in a phoney Romantic style. Fortunately these were never carried out, and the present condition of the castle is due to a drastic restoration in the 1900s.

The world's **original youth hostel** (see box below) has been ossified as one of several museums in the castle. The day room is in the style of a traditional Westphalian farmstead; adjoining it is the area for groups, while downstairs is the spartan main dorm, its solid wooden bunks standing in triple tiers, and looking as if they could yet withstand many more years of service. Several of the rooms in the Burg have been restored in period style and equipped with impressive furniture. Highlights include the **Stadthalle** by the entrance, with its carved Renaissance chimneypiece; the **Grosser Saal**, with a notable collection of pewter; and the **Burgkapelle**, adorned with retables from Antwerp and Cologne, and a graceful fifteenth-century *Madonna and Child* made from Bamberg sandstone. Scattered throughout the rooms are important examples of **arms and armour**, reflecting the fact that the Sauerland was a major centre for their production.

There's a reasonable range of **hotels** including *Am Markt*, Kirchstr. 43 (☎0 23 52/2 29 05; ②), *Bahnhofshotel*, Bahnhofstr. 33 (☎0 23 52/2 28 88; ③), and *Alte Linden*, Hauptstr. 38 (☎0 23 52/7 12 10; ⑤). In the outer bailey of the Burg is what's rather cheatingly called the world's oldest functioning **youth hostel** (☎0 23 52/2 35 22, fax 2 63 30; DM20/€10 or DM25/€12.50); its location makes it the most attractive place to stay in town.

Iserlohn

ISERLOHN, the Sauerland's largest town, can be reached from Altena by either bus or train. Still a centre of the iron industry, it has a couple of moderately interesting churches, both with carved altars – Gothic **St Marien**, dominating the town from its hill, and the Romanesque **Bauernkirche**. Beside the latter is the **Stadtmuseum** (Tues, Wed & Fri–Sun 10am–5pm, Thurs 10am–7pm; free), housed in a ritzy Baroque mansion. The main local attraction, however, is the **Dechenhöhle** in the incorporated village of Lethmathe, arguably the most outstanding of several **stalactite caves** in the Sauerland (guided tours Jan Sat & Sun 10am–4pm; April–Oct daily 9am–5pm; Nov, Dec, Feb & March daily 10am–4pm; DM6/€3). Discovered last century when the rail line was being constructed, the geological formations are reckoned to be anything from 300 to 350 million years old. Inevitably, the cave's chambers have been given nicknames

---

THE BIRTH OF YOUTH HOSTELLING

In 1909, a teacher named **Richard Schirrmann** established the world's first-ever permanent **youth hostel** in the Burg at Altena, having previously operated from a schoolroom in town. Inspired by the simple idea of the need to provide low-cost accommodation for young travellers, Schirrmann's choice of Altena is explained by the fact that the countryside around is particularly good for hiking. In time, hundreds of hostels sprang up all over Germany, and have long been an established and important feature of national life. The idea was slow in catching on elsewhere (an international federation was only set up twenty years later), but eventually spread right around the world, to the gratitude of millions of travellers, not all of them young. Schirrmann's reward has been to have a plethora of streets named after him (usually the ones leading to the local hostel) – indeed, he's commemorated just as prolifically throughout Germany as Marx and Lenin once were in the GDR.

according to the shapes they supposedly resemble. Particularly impressive are the "Baumkuchen", with its single, tapering stem, and the "Kronleuchter", so called for looking like an abstract version of the famous Romanesque crown-shaped chandeliers in Aachen, Hildesheim and Comburg.

There are plenty of **hotels** in all price categories ranging from *Haus Schäfer*, Friedrichstr. 84 (☎0 23 71/6 03 16; ③), to the rustic *Vier Jahreszeiten*, Seilerwaldstr. 10 (☎0 23 71/97 20; ⑦–⑨). A full list is available from the **tourist office** at Theodor-Heuss-Ring 24 (Mon–Wed & Fri 10am–5pm, Thurs 10am–6pm, Sat 10am–1pm; ☎0 23 71/2 17 18 21, *www.iserlohn.de*).

Nordsauerland

Soest is sometimes counted as part of the **Nordsauerland**, an area centred on a ten-kilometre-long artificial lake, the **Möhnesee**. The northern bank has been developed as a holiday resort area for angling and watersports, and there are **campsites** all along this shore. **Cruises** depart from Günne, Delecke and Körbecke from April to October. Between these first two villages is the famous **dam** which, though not the largest, was the prime target of the "Dambusters" (see box on p.602), due to its proximity to the industrial centres. Controlling the flow of the River Heve into the River Ruhr, it's 650m long and 40m high; when it was breached, 134 million tonnes of water gushed out into the countryside. Now long repaired, it's one of four footbridges interspersed at fairly regular intervals allowing you to cross over to the opposite bank of the lake. This has been left in its natural state, and a southerly arm, the **Hevesee**, is a protected area for birdlife. The **youth hostel** (☎0 29 24/3 05, fax 27 88, *jh-moehnesee@djh-wl.de*; DM24/€12 or DM29/€14.50) lies directly across from Körbecke. Immediately beyond is the beginning of the **Arnsberg Forest** *(Arnsberger Wald)*, an upland *Naturpark* of beech, birch and larch, which stretches for some 30km east to west, and up to 15km north to south.

Hochsauerland

The **Hochsauerland** is much the largest of the four districts, beginning immediately beyond the Arnsberg Forest and continuing east to the boundary with Hesse and south to the Siegerland. As its name suggests, it has the highest mountains in the area.

Arnsberg and around

ARNSBERG itself is traditionally considered the "capital" of the Sauerland, and is the administrative centre for the whole region. It's built on a spur of land on a bend of the River Ruhr, rising neatly upwards in tiers. The southern part of the old town is dominated by the **Propsteikirche**, a Gothic church with Baroque furnishings, beside which stands the ornate **Hirschberger Tor**, a rare example of north German Rococo. Beyond is the **Neumarkt**, lined with a series of Neoclassical buildings erected when the Prussians took the town following the Napoleonic Wars and made it the regional capital. Particularly notable is the **Auferstehungskirche** (Church of the Resurrection), designed by Schinkel. Numerous half-timbered houses line the streets of the heart of the town, while the **Sauerland-Museum** (Tues–Fri & Sun 10am–5pm, Sat 2–5pm; DM2/€1) occupies the Renaissance **Landsberger Hof** at Alter Markt 26. Further uphill is the Schlossberg, with the ruins of the **Schloss**, which was destroyed in the Seven Years War. It's the setting for the nine-day-long *Ruinenfest* in late May and early June.

Arnsberg's **tourist office** is at Neumarkt 6 (Mon–Fri 9am–noon & 2–4pm; May–Oct also Sat 10am–noon; ☎0 29 31/40 55, fax 1 23 31, *www.arnsberg-info.de*). Two of the best hotels are *Zum Landsberger Hof*, Alter Markt 18 (☎0 29 31/8 90; ⑤), and *Menge*, Ruhrstr. 60 (☎0 29 31/5 25 20; ⑥), and both have high quality **restaurants**. There's a **youth hostel** at Rumbecker Höhe 1 (☎0 29 31/1 06 27, fax 1 35 89, *jh-arnsberg@djh-wl.de*; DM22/€11 or DM27/€13.50) on the east side of town, by the Arnsberg Forest.

The **Sorpesee**, another artificial lake, lies 10km south of Arnsberg. Again, it's a centre for angling and watersports; cruises run from May to September, departing from **LANGSCHEID** on the northern shore. There are a string of **campsites** and a **youth hostel** (☎0 29 35/17 76, fax 72 54, *jh-sorpesee@djh-wl.de*; DM24.50/€12.25 or DM29.50/€14/75) on the western bank. To the east and south of here is the bulk of the aforementioned **Naturpark Homert**; apart from its numerous trails, it's a good area for birdwatching, with some 450 resident species.

The Rothaargebirge

Further south is the **Naturpark Rothaargebirge** (Red-Haired Mountains), a range covered with conifers and deciduous woods, which separates the Sauerland from the Siegerland to the south. It's best known as wintersports country; the main resort, **WINTERBERG**, can be reached by train from Arnsberg via a branch line from Bestwig. As well as the pistes, Winterberg has an indoor skating rink, and bobsleigh and toboggan runs, while international dog-sleigh races are held each January. The town stands at the foot of the **Kahler Asten**, which at 841m is the highest peak in the Sauerland; it's covered with snow for about a third of the year, and the average winter temperature is freezing point. You can ascend to an observation platform (DM1/€0.50) for a huge panorama of the district. There's a **youth hostel** not far from the mountain in Astenberg (☎0 29 81/22 89, fax 5 69, *jh-winterberg@djh-wl.de*; DM24.50/€12.25 or DM29.50/€14.75). Winterberg itself has an abundant choice of **rooms** in private houses at only marginally higher rates, as well as **hotels** in all price categories. A full list is available from the **tourist office** (Mon–Fri 9am–5pm, Sat 10am–noon; ☎0 29 81/9 25 00, fax 92 50 24, *www.winterberg.de*) at Hauptstr. 1.

Südsauerland

At the heart of the **Südsauerland** is the largest of the reservoirs, the appropriately named **Biggesee**, which lies below the Ebbegebirge range. A branch of the main Hagen–Siegen rail line runs from Finnentrop down the western bank of the lake.

Attendorn

ATTENDORN, on the north shore, is an old Hanseatic town. Its fourteenth-century **Altes Rathaus**, apart from being the only remaining secular structure of its period in the entire region, is a striking building, with elaborate gables on both its short ends, and an open lower storey which was intended to serve as a market hall. It now houses the **Südsauerlandmuseum** (Tues–Fri 9am–1pm & 3–5pm, Sat 9am–1pm, Sun 11am–1pm; DM2/€1), which contains some fine examples of sacred art and a notable collection of tableaux of painted tin figurines. **St Johannes** is a fourteenth-century Gothic hall church incorporating the tower of its Romanesque predecessor. It's nicknamed the "cathedral of the Sauerland" due to its pre-eminence among the region's churches. Just to the north of town is the **Attahöhle** (guided tours May–Sept daily 9.30am–4.30pm; March, April & Oct daily 10am–4pm; Nov–Jan Tues–Sun 10.30am–3.30pm; DM8/€4), a particularly impressive stalactite cave. To the east is **Burg Schnellenberg**, the largest of the few surviving hilltop castles in Westphalia, part of which has been rebuilt as a luxury hotel.

The **tourist office** is in the Reisebüro am Rathaus at Kölner Str. 12a (Mon–Fri 9am–6pm, Sat 10am–noon; ☎0 27 22/6 42 29, fax 47 75, *www.attendorn.de*). There are plenty of **private rooms** (①–③) in which to stay. **Hotels** include *Rauch*, Wasserstr. 6 (☎0 27 22/9 24 20, fax 92 42 33; ⑤), *Zur Post*, Niederste Str. 7 (☎0 27 22/24 65; ⑥), and, for real style, the *Burghotel* (☎0 27 22/69 40; ⑦–⑨) in the castle. There's a **campsite**, *Hof Biggen*, 6km northeast of town at Finnetroper Str. 131 (☎0 27 22/9 55 30).

Festivals include the best Carnival celebrations in the Sauerland and various parades during Holy Week, while the first Saturday in August sees *Der Biggesee in Flammen* (The Biggesee in Flames), with fireworks and illuminations. **Cruises** are run on the lake between Easter and mid-October from both Attendorn and **OLPE**, the highly developed watersports resort on the southern bank, which is the terminus of the branch railline.

Siegerland-Wittgenstein

The Rothaargebirge range provides a horizontal dividing line separating the Sauerland from **Siegerland-Wittgenstein** to the south. This region is a somewhat bizarre mixture of a heavily industrialized valley (in many respects similar to South Wales) and a holiday resort area which, even more than the Sauerland, the Germans have reserved for themselves. It's a land of hills and mountains, cut right across the middle by the River Sieg which flows due west, entering the Rhine just north of Bonn.

Siegen

SIEGEN is the capital of this district and the only place within a radius of about 100km which can properly be called a city. Iron and steel production were the reasons for its development last century; relative isolation meant that its growth was checked, and even now its population is barely over 100,000. One of Siegen's main assets is its setting, rising from the banks of the river high into the hills above; this has been enhanced by the construction of a spectacular **viaduct** (the biggest in the country) which carries the A45 Autobahn – linking the Ruhrgebiet with Hesse – 104m above the Sieg.

The Town

A curiosity of Siegen is that it has two castles originally belonging to the Nassau-Siegen family, one at the top of the town, the other a few hundred metres below. This is due to the fact that the line split in 1623 over continued support for the Reformation; thereafter, the Catholic branch lived in the **Oberes Schloss**. The original fortified Burg has been much modified down the centuries and isn't particularly picturesque, but its ramparts command the best views over the town, while the gardens, in honour of the dynasty's intermarriage with the Dutch house of Orange, are planted with 60,000 tulips.

Part of the building has been adapted to house the **Siegerland-Museum** (Tues–Sun 10am–5pm; DM4/€2). This contains varied collections, including a realistic model of a mine fourteen metres under the courtyard. There's also a display of memorabilia on the **Busch** brothers, a remarkable twentieth-century Siegen family whose anti-Nazism gave further impetus to their international careers. Adolf and Hermann founded the Busch Quartet with two friends; their 78rpm recordings, particularly of Beethoven, have never been surpassed in terms of interpretation, and many can still be bought in modern remasterings. They also blazed a pioneering trail by championing the playing of Baroque music by authentic-sized chamber groups, instead of in the souped-up arrangements which had been the norm for the previous century. Fritz Busch was a leading conductor who was prominent in the establishment of opera at Glyndebourne in southeast England, while Willi was one of Germany's best actors.

However, the museum's main draw is its display on the art of **Peter Paul Rubens** (see box opposite) who, by a sheer fluke, can be counted a native of Siegen, though he

SIR PETER PAUL RUBENS (1577–1640)

Sir Peter Paul Rubens' father Jan, a Calvinist sympathizer, was forced to flee his native Antwerp, settling in Cologne, where he entered the service of Princess Anna of Saxony, second wife of William the Silent. Eventually he graduated from being her adviser and diplomatic agent to sharing her bed when her husband was at war. An untimely pregnancy led to his unmasking. Lucky to escape with his life, he was banished to Siegen, where the great painter was born in 1577. A year later, the family was allowed to return to Cologne; after Jan Rubens' death, they went back to Antwerp. Not only was the young artist quickly reconciled with Roman Catholicism, he was later one of the most ardent propagandists of the Counter-Reformation; he further went against his father in becoming a faithful diplomatic servant of the Spanish imperial power. A man who was almost indecently successful (he ran the equivalent of a picture factory, which churned out canvases by the hundred, all bearing the master's characteristic stamp even when he had contributed little to their actual execution), Rubens was an incorrigible social climber, a grovelling toady to all political and spiritual authority, and a shamelessly lustful male chauvinist. Yet it's a measure of his greatness as an artist that these offputting traits don't seem to matter – his works can be enjoyed for their phenomenal technical skill, carefully planned design, glorious colours and unabashed *joie de vivre*.

was in no sense a German. His qualities are all present in a late masterpiece here: somewhat pompously named *The Victorious Hero Seizes the Opportunity for Peace*, it's an allegory featuring Perseus with the head of Medusa, Minerva, Abundance, Opportunity and Time. From a decade earlier, *Roman Charity* illustrates the legend of Cimon, who was saved from starving to death in prison by being breast-fed by his daughter Pero. There's also a haughty *Self-Portrait* from about the same time, and five more original works.

The **Unteres Schloss**, the seat of the Protestant line, originally occupied an abandoned Franciscan friary. This was destroyed by fire in 1695 and replaced by the present extensive Baroque complex. It's now largely occupied by offices, but the royal crypt has survived. Between the two castles is the Markt, with the eighteenth-century Rathaus and the **Nikolaikirche**, one of the most distinctive of the extravagant series of late Romanesque churches founded in the Rhineland and around. The kernel of the building is a thirteenth-century galleried hexagon – the only example of this design in northern Europe. Two centuries later, the handsome red and white tower was added, forming a highly successful complement. Inside is a baptismal plate made in Peru, a legacy of the time when the Oranien-Nassau family, who used the Nikolaikirche as their court chapel, was playing an important role in the colonization of South America. Lower down the hill is the **Martinikirche**, the unremarkable late Gothic successor to one of the most important Ottonian churches in Germany, from which the mosaic pavement has been preserved.

Practicalities

The **tourist office** (Mon, Wed & Fri 8.30am–noon & 2–4pm, Thurs 8.30am–noon & 2–6pm; ☎02 71/4 04 13 16, fax 2 26 87, *www.siegen.de*) is in the Rathaus, Markt 2; leaflets are also available at the pavilion immediately in front of the **Hauptbahnhof**. To reach the Altstadt from here, walk right through the pedestrian precinct and turn left uphill at the end.

The best budget **hotels** are *Gasthof Rörig*, Eintrachtstr. 9 (☎02 71/33 15 33; ③), *Gasthof Meier*, St-Johann-Str. 3 (☎02 71/33 50 66; ③), *Schäfer*, Rosterstr. 111 (☎02 71/33 87 20; ④), and *Bürger*, Marienborner Str. 132–136 (☎02 71/6 25 51; ⑤). More upmarket choices include *Berghotel Johanneshöhe*, which commands a grandstand view over Siegen from its hillside location on the west side of town at Wallhausenstr. 1 (☎02 71/31 00 08; ⑥), and *Mercure*, which is south of the centre at Kampenstr. 83 (☎02 71/5 01 10; ⑧).

Siegen's top **restaurants** include those in the last two hotels, plus *Schloss-Stube* in the Oberes Schloss, and *Schwarzbrenner*, in an eighteenth-century house at Metzgerstr. 29. Local **beers** use the pure mountain water of the Siegerland; Krombacher is well known throughout Germany, whereas consumption of Irle and Urzquell is confined mainly to this district.

Freudenberg

FREUDENBERG, 11km northwest of Siegen, to which it's linked by very regular bus services, is an archetypal picture-postcard town which seems to feature on just about every German calendar. In 1660 the town was destroyed by fire for the second time in its 200-year existence; the streets built thereafter as replacements have survived almost intact – row upon row of black and white **half-timbered houses**, whose steeply pitched slate roofs bear witness to the harshness of the winter climate.

It's a popular recreation resort all year round, and has a couple of excellent **hotels**, both with restaurants: *Zum Alten Flecken*, Marktstr. 11 (☎0 27 34/2 76 80; ⑤), and *Zur Altstadt*, Orienstr. 41 (☎0 27 34/49 60; ⑥). There are also a few small **pensions** and **private rooms** (①–③); a full list is available from the **tourist office** (Mon–Fri 10am–4pm; ☎0 27 34/4 31 64, fax 4 31 15) at Krottorfer Str. 25.

Paderborn

The cathedral and market city of **PADERBORN** lies some 55km northeast of Soest, just before the North German plain gives way to the Teutoburg Forest. It's a characterful place, with a variety of archeological and artistic attractions to add to the geological curiosity from which it derives its name, meaning "source of the Pader". This, the country's shortest river at a mere 4km in length, rises in a park, the Paderquellgebiet, in the heart of the city. It's formed by the surfacing of more than two hundred warm springs, which pour out over five thousand litres of water per second. These originate as subterranean streams in the **Eggegebirge** range to the east; they're suddenly forced out into the open at this point by the abrupt change in topography from the plateau to a lowland whose soil contains an impermeable layer of marl.

The City

The **Paderquellgebiet**, right in the centre of the city, is an idyllic spot and makes the obvious place to begin any tour, offering as it does the best view of the city's two main churches – the twin-towered former **Abdinghof** monastery in the foreground, with the massive single steeple of the Dom rearing up behind.

During postwar rebuilding of the city, the foundations of the **Carolingische Kaiserpfalz**, the site of Charlemagne's momentous meeting with Pope Leo III in 799 which led to the foundation of the Holy Roman Empire, were discovered just to the north of the Dom; they had been hidden from view since a fire destroyed the building in the year 1000. Soon it became the most exciting archeological site in the country, and was excavated in the 1960s, revealing the ground plan of a sizeable complex which included a king's hall, a church, a monastery and courtyards. Also unearthed was an open-air throne, now under cover beneath the Dom's north portal; you can see it by peering in through the protective glass. To the rear was found the replacement **Ottonische Kaiserpfalz** (Tues–Sun 10am–6pm; DM2/€1), dating from immediately after the 1000 fire and itself desecrated by another fire in 1165. This time the controversial decision was taken to go beyond a routine excavation, and to try and re-create its original form in as scholarly a manner as possible. In 1976 the palace made its belated reappearance, its pristine stonework making an odd contrast with the venerable status of the design. It now houses the regional archeology museum, but interest centres on the structure itself, as no original palaces from this epoch survive. The vestibule lies through a subsidiary building; to the right is the two-storey Ikenbergkapelle, while to the left is the Great Hall, which takes up the lion's share of the complex. Standing on its own near the entrance is the only authentic remnant of the palaces, the tiny **Bartholomäuskapelle**. As the very first hall church erected in Germany, it can claim to be the initiator of what was to become the pre-eminent national architectural form. Despite a glum exterior, it's very dapper inside, a classically inspired design of three aisles of rounded pillars crowned with flowery Corinthian capitals.

In preparation for Pope Leo's visit, Charlemagne ordered the construction of a no-expense-spared church which was almost immediately raised to the status of a cathedral; ever since, the city's history has been dominated by its ecclesiastical role. The present **Dom** is a cavernous thirteenth-century Gothic hall church whose tower, slit by innumerable little windows, is a remnant of its Romanesque predecessor. It's entered by the southern **porch** (or "Paradise") whose portal is adorned with French-style figures. More refined carvings from a now vanished doorway can be seen on either side of the transept window; look out for the cartoon-like fables – a boar blowing a horn, a hare playing the fiddle, a crane removing a bone from a wolf's throat and a fox dressed as a scholar to receive his diploma. Inside, the Dom resembles a museum of seventeenth-century heroic sculpture to the glory of the prince-bishops, much of it by one of Germany's few Mannerists, **Heinrich Gröninger**. His masterpiece, almost facing you on entry, is the grandiose **monument to Dietrich von Fürstenberg**, complete with depictions of the buildings this bishop commissioned to transform the face of the city. The Dom's most enduring attraction returns to the animal theme and comes in the form of a puzzle, which you should try to work out in advance. Follow the signs marked *Hasenfenster* into the cloister garden; the tracery of one of the windows is the emblem of Paderborn, and a mason's trick which was celebrated in its day. This shows three hares running around in a circle, but, although each clearly has two ears of his own, it has only been necessary to carve one per creature.

The south side of the Dom faces the open space of the vast Markt, lined with tall Baroque houses and the Romanesque **Gaukirche**. In this setting, the lead-plated glass palace which houses a couple of shops, a café and the **Erzbischöflisches Diözesanmuseum** (Tues–Sun 10am–6pm; DM4/€2) creates a strident impact, the more so as it masks some of the wonderful views of the Dom. This brash modernist intrusion into the old city clearly had its supporters, as its architect was Gottfried Böhm, who immediately afterwards was asked to rebuild the Ottonian Kaiserpfalz. The interior, rising abruptly in tiers, is a cleverly thought-out design to provide a majestic setting for the museum. In the basement, the **Schatzkammer**'s most valuable pieces are two inlaid reliquary cabinets, made for the Dom and the Adinghof in about 1100, and the Baroque shrine of Paderborn's patron, St Liborius. The Dom's old bells are invitingly displayed with hammers, allowing you to indulge in a bit of instant campanology. Upstairs, pride of place is rightly given to the *Imad Madonna*, a mid-eleventh-century wooden statue named after its bishop donor.

The remaining sights can be covered by means of a short circular walk. Following Schildern at the southwest corner of the Markt, you come to the city's most handsome building, the **Rathaus**, bedecked with arcades, gables and oriel windows, and fronted by a zappy facade. Erected in the early seventeenth century in the Weser Renaissance style, it was modelled on the patrician **Heisingsches Haus** just down the street. Up the hill from here is the **Jesuitenkolleg** from the end of the same century, whose church, like the one in Cologne, has a vast galleried interior with anachronistic Gothic pointed arches.

Further along Kamp is the sober **Dalheimer Hof** by the Westphalian Baroque architect, Johann Conrad Schlaun. Going back downhill along Kasseler Strasse, you see the

Romanesque **Busdorfkirche**, whose main joy is its tiny cloister. A couple of minutes' walk down Heierstrasse, then left into Thisaut, is Hathumarstrasse, with the oldest remaining half-timbered house, **Adam-und-Eva-Haus**, now the local museum (Tues–Sun 10am–6pm; free). The most eye-catching exhibits are a couple of exquisite drawings of the city by Schlaun, and a display of engravings by **Heinrich Aldegraver**, a native of Paderborn who was one of Dürer's most faithful followers. From here, the Dom is back in view and only a few minutes' walk away.

Practicalities

The **Hauptbahnhof** is southwest of the centre, which is reached by turning right at the exit and continuing straight ahead. En route to the Markt you'll pass the **tourist office** at Marienplatz 2a (Mon–Fri 9.30am–6pm, Sat 9.30am–2pm; ☎0 52 51/88 29 80, fax 88 29 90, *www.paderborn.de*).

Centrally sited **hotels** include *Haus Irma*, Bachstr. 9 (☎0 52 51/2 33 42; ③), *Krawinkel*, Karlstr. 33 (☎0 52 51/2 36 63; ③), *Südhotel*, Borchener Str. 23 (☎0 52 51/7 80 05; ④), *Cherusker Hof*, Detmolder Str. 1 (☎0 52 51/5 55 34, *www.cherusker-hof.de*; ④–⑥), *Galerie Abdinghof*, Bachstr. 1a (☎0 52 51/1 22 40, *www.galerie-hotel.de*; ⑥), and *Arosa*, Westernmauer 38 (☎0 52 51/12 80, *www.arosa.bestwestern.de*; ⑧). For once, the **youth hostel** is conveniently sited, just a few minutes' walk from the main attractions at Meinwerkstr. 16 (☎0 52 51/2 20 55, fax 28 00 17, *jh-paderborn@djh-wl.de*; DM23.40/€11.70 or DM28.40/€14.20). The two **campsites** are both in the northern outreaches of the city – *Am Waldsee* at Husarenstr. 130 (☎0 52 51/73 72) and *Stauterrassen* at Auf der Thune 14 (☎0 52 51/45 04).

Among the best **restaurants** in the centre is that in the *Arosa* hotel. In addition, *Balthasar*, An der Alten Synagoge 1, presents genuinely creative cuisine, while the *Ratskeller* in the Rathaus offers both Westphalian dishes and *neue deutsche Küche*.

Pubs offering **live music** include *Tuba*, Kasseler Str. 26, *Das Treibhaus*, Detmolder Str. 21, and *Kukoz*, Tegelweg 3–5. Concerts, musicals, dance, opera and jazz are performed at the ultra-modern PaderHalle, Heiersmauer 45–51 (☎0 52 51/2 50 01). The main **popular festivals** occur in July, including a *Schützenfest* on the second weekend. There's also a beer week in October.

Bielefeld

BIELEFELD, some 35km north of Paderborn, clusters around the narrow middle strip of the Teutoburg Forest which runs right through the built-up areas. It's strongly reminiscent of the cities of the Ruhrgebiet in history, feel and appearance, and is the overwhelmingly dominant economic centre of eastern Westphalia. Founded in the thirteenth century by the Counts of Ravensberg, the town gained prosperity in the late Middle Ages through the linen trade. The nineteenth century saw a mushroom growth, due to the increased importance of this traditional industry, plus various new engineering products associated with it. Development was helped by the fact that nearby Minden, with a far more favourable geographical location, was preoccupied with its role as a garrison town.

The City

Right on the edge of the Teutoburg Forest, overlooking the southern end of the city centre, is Bielefeld's oldest building, the **Sparrenburg**, built between 1240 and 1250 as the seat of the counts of Ravensberg and strengthened in the sixteenth and seventeenth centuries by massive bastions conforming to the latest theories about military

Man Walking to the Sky sculpture, Kassel

The Dom, Limburg an der Lahn

Facade of the Ernst-Ludwig-Haus, Darmstadt

Burg Rheinstein, Trechtingshausen

The Alte Völklinger Hütte, Völklingen

BIELEFELD'S FESTIVALS

If Bielefeld is rather thin on historic monuments, its numerous **popular festivals** pro-vide a counterbalance. Best of these is the *Leineweber Markt* on the last weekend in May, which includes street theatre, jazz and rock concerts, as well as folklore displays. Open-air music of all kinds is played throughout the city during the summer, while every third Saturday from May to October sees a flea market; the location varies, but the Markt itself is regularly the venue. In mid-July, the *Sparrenburgfest* in the castle features tournaments and a medieval fair, while there's a week-long *Weinfest* in mid-September.

---

setting at Furtwänglerstr. 52 (☎05 21/9 21 10; ⑤). The tourist office can supply lists of generally cheaper alternatives in the suburbs: there's a whole clutch in Brackwede to the south. Bielefeld's spanking new **youth hostel** is in the heart of the city at August-Bebel-Str. 135 (☎05 21/9 51 40, fax 95 14 10, *jgh-bielefeld@djh-wl.de*; DM40.50/€20.25). A second hostel has an isolated location within the Teutoburg Forest 4km south of the centre at Oetzer Weg 25 (☎05 21/2 22 27, fax 2 51 96, *jh-bielefeld@djh-wl.de*; DM23.40/€11.70 or DM28.40/€14.20); take U-Bahn #2 to its terminus, then bus #118 to Waldkrug, but note that the latter stops running soon after the evening rush hour. There are also two **campsites**, both on the edge of the forest, at Vogelweide 9 (☎05 21/4 59 22 33) and Campingstr. 23 (☎0 52 03/44 53 38).

One of the city's best **restaurants** is *Sparrenburg* within the castle; another good choice is *Im Bültmannshof* in a fine half-timbered house at Kurt-Schumacher-Str. 17a. *Brauhaus Johann Albrecht*, Hagenbruchstr. 8, is a Hausbrauerei serving inexpensive meals.

The main **theatre** is the luxuriant Jugendstil Stadttheater, Niederwall 27 (☎05 21/17 70 77); drama is also performed at the Theater am Alten Markt (☎05 21/17 70 77), while Puppenspiele (puppet theatre) is at Ravensberger Str. 12 (☎05 21/6 63 44). **Concerts** are given at Rudolf-Oetker-Halle on Stapenhorststrasse (☎05 21/17 88 99). Bielefeld's most original venue, however, is the Alte Ravensberger Spinnerei, east of Jahnplatz at Heeper Str. 37 (☎05 21/51 65 26), a grandiose nineteenth-century linen mill, worth seeing in its own right as a rare survivor of the sort of factory which once dotted large German industrial towns. Lovingly restored, it's now a cultural centre, fea-turing exhibitions, films and music recitals.

Minden

MINDEN's strategic importance, at an easily fordable point of the River Weser, 30km northeast of Bielefeld, has meant that military affairs have dominated its history: the old ramparts were converted into a full-blown fortress by the Swedes during the Thirty Years War; it was the scene of a decisive battle in 1759 in which the British and Prussians defeated the French; and, during the Napoleonic wars, it was equipped with the latest defensive systems as a leading Prussian frontier town, a role it retained until the unification of Germany in 1871. The city kept its historic appearance until the last war, when its strategic importance inevitably led to severe aerial bombardment.

The Wasserstrassenkreuz

Minden's role as a fortress meant it could not expand and industrialize, but its favourable geographical position led to its development as the hub of the German inland water transport system, and it's from this function that its main present-day attraction derives. In the northern part of the city, you'll find the **Wasserstrassenkreuz** (Waterway architecture. The castle has a round **tower** (April–Oct daily 10am–6pm; DM1.50/ €0.75) which can be ascended for a panoramic view, and some 300m of underground **passageways** and **dungeons** (same times, but only accessible by joining a pre-booked group; DM2.50/€1.25). In the courtyard is a statue to Margrave Friedrich Wilhelm of Brandenburg, the man who established Bielefeld's prosperity by introducing the *Leinenlegge*, a quality control for linen.

Below the Sparrenburg to the north is the so-called Neustadt (New Town), grouped around the **Neustädter Marienkirche**, a handsome Gothic church built in the late thirteenth and early fourteenth centuries, and now standing, much in the manner of an English cathedral, in splendid isolation on a green. Its tall twin towers are crowned by unusually long and sharply pointed lead steeples; they look so venerable it's hard to believe they were devastated in an air raid and had to be rebuilt almost from scratch. The church, which contains outstanding **works of art**, is usually kept locked; ring at the door of the halls directly in front for the caretaker. On the high altar is a master-piece by the same Westphalian "Soft Style" artist who painted the Berswordt Altar in Dortmund. It shows the *Madonna and Child with Saints*, surrounded by a dozen small panels, mostly of scenes from Christ's life; the wings were cut up and sold in the nineteenth century, and are now in museums all over the world. A major but nameless fourteenth-century sculptor (whose works can also be seen in Cappenberg and Marburg) carved the frieze of apostles above the altar, which belonged to the former rood screen. He also created the magnificent **tomb** of Otto III von Ravensberg and Hedwig von Lippe, featuring a touching yet unsentimental portrayal of their previously deceased son. The other elaborate Ravensberg family monument is clearly modelled on this tomb, even though it was made over a century later.

On nearby Artur-Ladebeck-Strasse is the smooth red sandstone pile of the **Kunsthalle** (Tues, Thurs, Fri–Sun 11am–6pm, Wed 11am–9pm; DM8/€4). The building itself, erected in the 1960s, was intended to be a significant addition to the city's heritage; it was designed by **Philip Johnson**, Mies van der Rohe's principal American follower, who was himself one of the leading lights in propagating the International Style in architecture. Most of the Expressionists are represented, with good examples of Beckmann, Kirchner, Nolde and Macke; there are sculptures by Rodin, Barlach, Archipenko, Lipchitz, Caro and Moore (some inside, others in the garden), and several rooms of European and American abstract painting.

What remains of the Altstadt is just a short walk from the Kunsthalle – turn right into Obernstrasse at the end of Artur-Ladebeck-Strasse. The Markt is lined by the patrician houses originally built by the most prosperous linen merchants. Oldest of these is the late Gothic **Crüwellhaus** of 1530; the others are in the cheerful Weser Renaissance style of the following century. Round the corner on Postgang is the Gothic **Altstädter Nicolaikirche**, which contains a spectacular sixteenth-century altar from Antwerp, featuring some 250 figures in the carved depictions of the Passion. Behind the church is the **Leineweber-Denkmal**, depicting a linen weaver with the traditional characteristics of a long pipe and walking stick.

Practicalities

The **Hauptbahnhof** is immediately to the north of the city centre; directly opposite, in the Leinenmeisterhaus at Am Bahnhof 6, is the **tourist office** (Mon–Fri 9am–5.30pm, Sat 9am–1pm; ☎05 21/51 69 99, fax 17 88 11, *www.bielefeld.de*). There's a second branch in the Neues Rathaus, by the eastern edge of the centre at Niederwall 23 (same hours; ☎05 21/51 69 98). The **Mitfahrzentrale** office is at Siegfriedstr. 46 (☎05 21/13 00 88).

A wide range of centrally sited **hotels** includes *Kaiser*, Schildescher Str. 47 (☎05 21/6 19 84; ②–⑤), *Wiegmann*, Kronenstr. 11 (☎05 21/6 04 71; ③–⑤), and *Stadt Bremen*, Bahnhofstr. 32 (☎05 21/6 70 88; ⑥). *Waldhotel Brand's Busch* has a pleasant forest

Junction) which is unique in Europe. The most eye-catching feature is the surrealistic **Kanalbrücke** (Canal Bridge), a 375-metre-long aquatic flyover built between 1911 and 1914; it allows the **Mittlellandkanal** – which stretches right across north Germany, linking the Rhine with the Elbe – to pass directly over the Weser. The heart of the system is the fortress-like **Schachtschleuse** (Great Lock), which shifts 12,000 cubic metres of water while transferring ships from canal to river or vice versa in just seven minutes. Alongside is the exhibition hall (April–Oct Mon–Sat 9am–5pm, Sun 9am–6pm; DM2/€1), which explains the layout and working of the Wasserstrassenkreuz by means of models and diagrams. A series of paths enable you to explore the area on foot, but it's far more fun to take a **cruise**. Run by the Mindener Fahrgastschiffahrt (☎05 71/6 48 08 00), these leave from the jetty immediately opposite the Schachtschleuse. There's a choice of fifty-minute and one-and-half-hour trips, costing DM8/€4 and DM11/€5.50 respectively. The former departs six times daily in the high season (mid-May to mid-Sept), and three times daily for the six weeks before and after these dates. Though the longer cruise is the more enticing, taking in a short stretch of the Weser as well as the harbour, it only runs once daily (Mon–Sat at 2pm in low season, 3pm in high season, and Sun at 10.15am year round). It's also possible to sail for longer stretches up and down the Weser from here; check locally for details.

The rest of the city

The **Hauptbahnhof** is on the right side of the river; its situation, a good twenty minutes' walk from town, is explained by the fact that it was built as part of the Prussian fortifications. Along with the three small forts grouped in a semicircle around it, it's one of the few survivors of that period, as the citizens had no great love for their citadel, and dismantled it as soon as it was declared redundant.

The Altstadt is dominated by the **Dom**, whose massive westwork, with two subsidiary towers stuck like glue to the main belfry, is in the severest form of Romanesque. The main body of the building, however, is a hall church, erected in the late thirteenth century in a pure early Gothic style; this has a light and airy feel, thanks to the huge windows decorated with highly elaborate tracery. On the south transept wall is a frieze of Apostles, the remnant of a former Romanesque rood screen; from the same period is the bronze *Minden Crucifix*, the Dom's most important work of art. However, the one currently displayed here is a copy; the original is in the **Domschatz** in the Haus am Dom opposite (Tues, Thurs, Sat & Sun 10am–noon; Wed & Fri 3–5pm; free). Among many other valuable items, note the gilded twelfth-century reliquary of St Peter.

Just beyond lies the Markt, whose north side is taken up by the **Rathaus**. Its lower storey, featuring an arcaded passageway, is contemporary with the Dom; the upper part is late Renaissance. Continuing up the steps from here takes you to the best-preserved part of the Altstadt, centred on Martinikirchhof. On this square are two survivors of the Prussian garrison buildings, the **Körnermagazin**, where weapons were stored, and the **Martinihaus**, which served as the bakery. Also here is the **Schwedenschänke**, used by the Swedish troops as their refectory during the Thirty Years War. **St Martini** itself is the pick of Minden's gaunt and blackened parish churches, with a dignified interior housing notable furnishings – late Gothic stalls, Renaissance pulpit and wrought-iron font – and a magnificent organ, partly dating back to the sixteenth century.

Just off the square on Brüderstrasse is the **Alte Münze**, formerly the house of the master of the mint; today, it's a Greek restaurant. A rare example of Romanesque civil architecture, it owes its survival to the fact that it was subsequently embellished according to the tastes of the time (with a stepped gable in the Gothic period, and an oriel window in the Renaissance). Mansions in the characteristic Weser Renaissance style are dotted all over the quarter – the finest are on Bäckerstrasse, Am Scharn and Papenmarkt. The densest concentration, however, is on Ritterstrasse, where five houses have been adapted to contain the **Mindener Museum** (Tues–Fri 10am–1pm & 2.30–5pm, Sat 2.30–5pm, Sun 11am–6pm; free). Displayed in two courtyards are fragments of sculptural decoration from buildings such as these; see in particular a wonderful *Story of Samson*. Upstairs, along with the usual folklore displays, there's a room devoted to the **Battle of Minden**, a turning point in the Seven Years War.

Practicalities

Minden's **tourist office** is at Domstr. 2 (Mon–Fri 8am–1pm & 2–5pm, Sat 9am–1pm; ☎05 71/8 29 06 59, fax 8 29 06 63, *www.minden.de*). There are only a handful of conveniently located **hotels**. These include *Wappenkrug*, Marienstr. 121 (☎05 71/4 52 92; ③), *Altes Gasthaus Grotehof*, Wettinerallee 14 (☎05 71/5 40 18; ⑥–⑧), *Stadthotel Kronprinz*, Friedrich-Wilhelm-Str. 1–3 (☎05 71/93 40 80; ⑦), and *Silke*, Fischerglacis 21 (☎05 71/82 80 70; ⑦). Other cheaper options tend to be far out – such as *Gasthof Grashoff*, Bremer Str. 83 (☎05 71/4 18 34; ③), in the suburb of Todtenhausen, site of the Battle of Minden.

Among the best places to **eat** and **drink** are the *Ratskeller*, Markt 1, the vegetarian *Vita Table*, Simeonstr. 12, and the fish specialist *Zum Fishbäcker*, Obermarktstr. 34.

Lemgo

With its surprising vistas and architectural groupings, and the myriad delicate details on its buildings, **LEMGO**, 12km north of Detmold and 25km east of Bielefeld, would be a strong contender in any competition to find the prettiest town in northern Germany. It has escaped the ravages both of war and of mass tourism. Many of the buildings from its sixteenth-century Hanseatic heyday survive, and are now immaculately cared for, with the merchant class which built them from the profits of foreign trade now replaced by a mixture of retailers, wealthy commuters (over half the population works elsewhere) and public bodies.

The Town

The Altstadt, though more extensive than might be expected from the present modest size of the town, is easily explored on foot, and the two main sights outside its boundaries are just a short walk away.

The Hexenbürgermeisterhaus
Breite Strasse, the main axis linking the southern part of town with the central Markt, is one of Lemgo's finest thoroughfares, dominated by the spectacular **Hexenbürgermeisterhaus** (Witches' Burgomaster House) at no. 19. The facade, with its elegantly tapering gables, its *Fall of Man* over the doorway and its two quite different oriel windows (something of a Lemgo speciality) adorned with the Seven Cardinal Virtues, ranks as one of the supreme masterpieces of the Weser Renaissance style. It was built in 1571, three years after the completion of the rest of the house, by a local man, **Hermann Wulf**. Originally commissioned by a merchant family, the house's present curious name derives from an occupant in a later, more mordant period, the notorious **Hermann Cothmann**. He was burgomaster of Lemgo at the height of the hysterical campaign against supposed witches between 1666 and 1681, apparently sentencing some ninety women to death.

Inside, an above average **Städtisches Museum** (previously Tues–Sun 10am–12.30pm & 1.30–5pm; DM1.50/€0.75, but closed since 1999 for restoration) appropriately includes a room devoted to gruesome instruments of torture, from the

Junction) which is unique in Europe. The most eye-catching feature is the surrealistic **Kanalbrücke** (Canal Bridge), a 375-metre-long aquatic flyover built between 1911 and 1914; it allows the **Mittellandkanal** – which stretches right across north Germany, linking the Rhine with the Elbe – to pass directly over the Weser. The heart of the system is the fortress-like **Schachtschleuse** (Great Lock), which shifts 12,000 cubic metres of water while transferring ships from canal to river or vice versa in just seven minutes. Alongside is the exhibition hall (April–Oct Mon–Sat 9am–5pm, Sun 9am–6pm; DM2/€1), which explains the layout and working of the Wasserstrassenkreuz by means of models and diagrams. A series of paths enable you to explore the area on foot, but it's far more fun to take a **cruise**. Run by the Mindener Fahrgastschiffahrt (☎05 71/6 48 08 00), these leave from the jetty immediately opposite the Schachtschleuse. There's a choice of fifty-minute and one-and-half-hour trips, costing DM8/€4 and DM11/€5.50 respectively. The former departs six times daily in the high season (mid-May to mid-Sept), and three times daily for the six weeks before and after these dates. Though the longer cruise is the more enticing, taking in a short stretch of the Weser as well as the harbour, it only runs once daily (Mon–Sat at 2pm in low season, 3pm in high season, and Sun at 10.15am year round). It's also possible to sail for longer stretches up and down the Weser from here; check locally for details.

The rest of the city

The **Hauptbahnhof** is on the right side of the river; its situation, a good twenty minutes' walk from town, is explained by the fact that it was built as part of the Prussian fortifications. Along with the three small forts grouped in a semicircle around it, it's one of the few survivors of that period, as the citizens had no great love for their citadel, and dismantled it as soon as it was declared redundant.

The Altstadt is dominated by the **Dom**, whose massive westwork, with two subsidiary towers stuck like glue to the main belfry, is in the severest form of Romanesque. The main body of the building, however, is a hall church, erected in the late thirteenth century in a pure early Gothic style; this has a light and airy feel, thanks to the huge windows decorated with highly elaborate tracery. On the south transept wall is a frieze of Apostles, the remnant of a former Romanesque rood screen; from the same period is the bronze *Minden Crucifix*, the Dom's most important work of art. However, the one currently displayed here is a copy; the original is in the **Domschatz** in the Haus am Dom opposite (Tues, Thurs, Sat & Sun 10am–noon; Wed & Fri 3–5pm; free). Among many other valuable items, note the gilded twelfth-century reliquary of St Peter.

Just beyond lies the Markt, whose north side is taken up by the **Rathaus**. Its lower storey, featuring an arcaded passageway, is contemporary with the Dom; the upper part is late Renaissance. Continuing up the steps from here takes you to the best-preserved part of the Altstadt, centred on Martinikirchhof. On this square are two survivors of the Prussian garrison buildings, the **Körnermagazin**, where weapons were stored, and the **Martinihaus**, which served as the bakery. Also here is the **Schwedenschänke**, used by the Swedish troops as their refectory during the Thirty Years War. **St Martini** itself is the pick of Minden's gaunt and blackened parish churches, with a dignified interior housing notable furnishings – late Gothic stalls, Renaissance pulpit and wrought-iron font – and a magnificent organ, partly dating back to the sixteenth century.

Just off the square on Brüderstrasse is the **Alte Münze**, formerly the house of the master of the mint; today, it's a Greek restaurant. A rare example of Romanesque civil architecture, it owes its survival to the fact that it was subsequently embellished according to the tastes of the time (with a stepped gable in the Gothic period, and an oriel window in the Renaissance). Mansions in the characteristic Weser Renaissance style are dotted all over the quarter – the finest are on Bäckerstrasse, Am Scharn and Papenmarkt. The densest concentration, however, is on Ritterstrasse, where five houses have been adapted to contain the **Mindener Museum** (Tues–Fri 10am–1pm & 2.30–5pm, Sat 2.30–5pm, Sun 11am–6pm; free). Displayed in two courtyards are fragments of sculptural decoration from buildings such as these; see in particular a wonderful *Story of Samson*. Upstairs, along with the usual folklore displays, there's a room devoted to the **Battle of Minden**, a turning point in the Seven Years War.

Practicalities

Minden's **tourist office** is at Domstr. 2 (Mon–Fri 8am–1pm & 2–5pm, Sat 9am–1pm; ☎05 71/8 29 06 59, fax 8 29 06 63, *www.minden.de*). There are only a handful of conveniently located **hotels**. These include *Wappenkrug*, Marienstr. 121 (☎05 71/4 52 92; ③), *Altes Gasthaus Grotehof*, Wettinerallee 14 (☎05 71/5 40 18; ⑤–⑧), *Stadthotel Kronprinz*, Friedrich-Wilhelm-Str. 1–3 (☎05 71/93 40 80; ⑦), and *Silke*, Fischerglacis 21 (☎05 71/82 80 70; ⑦). Other cheaper options tend to be far out – such as *Gasthof Grashoff*, Bremer Str. 83 (☎05 71/4 18 34; ③), in the suburb of Todtenhausen, site of the Battle of Minden.

Among the best places to **eat** and **drink** are the *Ratskeller*, Markt 1, the vegetarian *Vita Table*, Simeonstr. 12, and the fish specialist *Zum Fishbäcker*, Obermarktstr. 34.

Lemgo

With its surprising vistas and architectural groupings, and the myriad delicate details on its buildings, **LEMGO**, 12km north of Detmold and 25km east of Bielefeld, would be a strong contender in any competition to find the prettiest town in northern Germany. It has escaped the ravages both of war and of mass tourism. Many of the buildings from its sixteenth-century Hanseatic heyday survive, and are now immaculately cared for, with the merchant class which built them from the profits of foreign trade now replaced by a mixture of retailers, wealthy commuters (over half the population works elsewhere) and public bodies.

The Town

The Altstadt, though more extensive than might be expected from the present modest size of the town, is easily explored on foot, and the two main sights outside its boundaries are just a short walk away.

The Hexenbürgermeisterhaus

Breite Strasse, the main axis linking the southern part of town with the central Markt, is one of Lemgo's finest thoroughfares, dominated by the spectacular **Hexenbürgermeisterhaus** (Witches' Burgomaster House) at no. 19. The facade, with its elegantly tapering gables, its *Fall of Man* over the doorway and its two quite different oriel windows (something of a Lemgo speciality) adorned with the Seven Cardinal Virtues, ranks as one of the supreme masterpieces of the Weser Renaissance style. It was built in 1571, three years after the completion of the rest of the house, by a local man, **Hermann Wulf**. Originally commissioned by a merchant family, the house's present curious name derives from an occupant in a later, more mordant period, the notorious **Hermann Cothmann**. He was burgomaster of Lemgo at the height of the hysterical campaign against supposed witches between 1666 and 1681, apparently sentencing some ninety women to death.

Inside, an above average **Städtisches Museum** (previously Tues–Sun 10am–12.30pm & 1.30–5pm; DM1.50/€0.75, but closed since 1999 for restoration) appropriately includes a room devoted to gruesome instruments of torture, from the inquisition stool with its seat of protruding nails, through thumb and leg screws, to less brutal items such as the barrel which formed a moveable stocks. There is also an exhibition on a more enlightened Lemgo citizen of the same period, **Engelbert Kämpfer**. A pioneering traveller in Russia, Persia, Java and Japan, Kämpfer had de luxe accounts of his journeys printed and published in his native town, which was then a leading centre of book production.

The Marienkirche, the Markt and around

Just off Breite Strasse down Stiftstrasse is the **Marienkirche**, the Gothic hall church of a convent which was suppressed when Lemgo went over to the Reformation. It has one of the richest musical traditions in Germany and there's a small international festival in the first week of June. The choir is celebrated, the **swallow's nest organ** even more so. Built between 1587 and 1613, initially by a Dutchman, and then by two brothers from Hamburg, the organ is rated amongst the sweetest-sounding instruments in Europe. If you aren't lucky enough to hear it, the woodwork is still an artistic treasure in its own right, although sadly stripped of its original bright polychromy. Also from the Renaissance is the **font**, the work of a local sculptor, **Georg Crossmann**, with unashamedly sensual figures of the Four Christian Virtues. Behind it are statues of the nobleman Otto Zur Lippe and his wife, masterpieces of late fourteenth-century funerary art.

Beyond the end of Breite Strasse, past a fine series of gabled houses, you reach the **Wippermannsches Haus**, the only one of the great merchant buildings in the extravagant late Gothic style. Just a few paces away is the **Markt**, lined with a wealth of superb structures from the fourteenth century onwards. The **Rathaus** complex on the east side represents the changing building fashions in its photogenic jumble of arcades, pinnacles and gables. Its northern corner, the old **Apothekenerker**, is still used as a pharmacy, and has a magnificent oriel window. The gossamer carvings, again the work of Crossmann, include a frieze of ten famous scientists, while the columns of the upper windows show the Five Senses.

The south side of the square is fronted by the early seventeenth-century **Ballhaus**; beside it is the sixteenth-century **Zeughaus**, whose rear wall is painted in psychedelic zigzags. The stately Renaissance edifices on the west side are flanked by two prize-winning buildings from the 1970s, Modernist, yet imbued with motifs from Lemgo's past, but perhaps rather too stridently self-confident. There can be no complaints, however, about the northern frontage of the square, which also forms part of Lemgo's central axis, Mittelstrasse. Appropriately, this is the street most evocative of the Hansa; half-timbering was used extensively, and some of the mansions have nicknames deriving from their decoration, such as **Planetenhaus** (House of the Planets) and **Sonnenuhrhaus** (Sundial House). The buildings to the right also have handsome backs, forming part of the close of the Gothic **Nikolaikirche**, whose twin towers were later varied by the addition of contrasting lead spires. Its interior, a characteristic hall design, has an assortment of works of art of various periods and styles, including another early Renaissance font by Crossmann.

The Junkerhaus and Schloss Brake

Continuing to the end of Mittelstrasse, then straight ahead down Bismarckstrasse to Hamelner Strasse, brings you to the remarkable **Junkerhaus** (previously mid-March to Nov Tues–Fri & Sun 10am–12.30pm & 1.30–5pm, Sat 10am–1pm; DM1.50/€0.75, but closed since 1999 for restoration). It's the obsessive single-handed creation of a totally eccentric local architect, painter and sculptor, **Karl Junker**, who was determined to bequeath his own vision of a dream house as a modern counterpart to the sixteenth-century mansions he knew so well. From the outside, it looks like the witch's cottage from *Hansel and Gretel*, while the interior is spookier than anything Hammer

House of Horror ever produced; the sinuous woodcarvings are the stuff of nightmarish fantasies.

Returning down Hamelner Strasse, a sharp left into Pagenhelle before the start of Bismarckstrasse takes you to **Schloss Brake** (Tues–Sun 10am–6pm; DM4/€2), a moated Renaissance palace of the counts of Lippe, whose striking six-storey tower has a secret stairway leading to the most private apartments. The palace now houses a museum of the Weser Renaissance, with extensive collections of paintings, sculptures, furniture and *objets d'art*. In the grounds are two old mills, the **Schlossmühle** and the **Ölmühle**, together with the miller's house, now fitted out as the **Mühlenmuseum** (Tues–Sun 10am–12.30pm & 2–5pm; free).

Practicalities

Lemgo's **Bahnhof**, on a branch line from Bielefeld, is just to the south of the historic kernel of the city; **buses** operate from the bays in front. The **tourist office** is at the corner of the Markt at Kramerstr. 8 (Mon–Fri 9am–1pm & 2–5pm, Sat 10am–1pm; ☎0 52 61/18 77 50, fax 18 90 35, *www.lemgo.de*).

Centrally located **hotels** include *Bahnhofswaage*, Am Bahnhof (☎0 52 61/35 25; ④), *Hansa*, Breite Str. 14 (☎0 52 61/9 40 50; ⑤), *Lemgoer Hof*, Detmolder Weg 14 (☎0 52 61/9 76 70; ⑥), and *Stadtpalais*, Papenstr. 24 (☎0 52 61/9 49 90; ⑥). Further out are several budget options, including *Gasthof Zum Landsknecht*, Herforder Str. 177 (☎0 52 61/6 82 64; ②), whose restaurant specializes in Swiss-style dishes, and *Zum Ilsetal*, Sommerhäuschenweg 45 (☎0 52 61/51 77; ③). The **campsite** *Alte Hansestadt Lemgo* (☎0 52 61/1 48 58) has a riverside setting at Regentorstr. 106, between Schloss Brake and the Altstadt.

The Altstadt abounds with places to **eat** and **drink**, including most of the usual ethnic varieties and several classy cafés, but the best restaurants are the one in the abovementioned *Stadtpalais* (weekday evenings only) and the cosy *Zur Neustadt*, Breite Str. 40.

Detmold and the Southern Teutoburg Forest

DETMOLD, capital of the former Lippe principality, makes the obvious base for seeing the varied attractions of the southern part of the **Teutoburg Forest** (Teutoburger Wald). If you're understandably baffled by the competing claims of Germany's innumerable forests, then this is one with a difference, adding extra natural, historical and artistic delights to the usual wooded trails.

The Town

An old jingle, quoted ad infinitum in tourist brochures and on billboards all over town, describes Detmold as *eine wunderschöne Stadt* (a wonderful town). That ranks as something of an exaggeration, but it's an agreeable place nonetheless, with a far more laid-back approach to life than is usual in Germany.

Lange Strasse, the Altstadt's main thoroughfare, and the streets around, such as Bruchstrasse, Schülerstrasse, Krumme Strasse and Exterstrasse, are lined with large **half-timbered houses**, interspersed with self-confident stone buildings of the Wilhelmine epoch. However, easily the most attractive street is the venerable and smaller-scale Adolfstrasse, running parallel to and east of Lange Strasse.

North of the Markt is a green area centred on the **Residenzschloss** (guided tours daily April–Oct at 10am, 11am, noon, 2pm, 3pm, 4pm & 5pm; Nov–March at 10am, 11am, noon, 2pm, 3pm & 4pm; DM6/€3), which is surrounded by water on three sides. The keep of the medieval fortress was incorporated into the present Renaissance structure, which was progressively shorn of its defensive features down the years. It remains in the possession of the descendants of the counts (later princes) of Lippe who built it. The interior is not what you'd expect from outside; its rooms were transformed in the eighteenth and nineteenth centuries according to the tastes of the time, but their most valuable adornment is a superb set of seventeenth-century Brussels tapestries of *The Life of Alexander the Great*, woven from cartoons made by the great French artist Charles Le Brun.

From here, the **Lippisches Landesmuseum** (Tues–Fri 10am–6pm, Sat & Sun 11am–6pm; *www.lippisches-landesmuseum.de*; DM4/€2) is reached down Ameide, to the rear of the Schloss. It's housed in two buildings, with natural history in one, archeology, local history and folklore in the other. The second building has a number of reconstituted period rooms and displays on the history of fashion and on local agriculture, incorporating a rebuilt tithe barn and granary.

The Landesmuseum makes a good prelude to the spectacular **Westfälisches Freilichtmuseum** (April–Oct Tues–Sun 9am–6pm; DM7/€3.50), the most important open-air museum in Germany, which is being laid out at the southern side of the town; to reach it, go in a straight line down the Allee, the continuation of Lange Strasse. When complete (which will not be for several years yet) it will comprise 168 redundant original buildings from rural Westphalia; currently around a hundred are in place. These are grouped together according to region, thus giving a clear picture of the different construction styles. As a centrepiece, there will be three complete simulated villages; other parts of the province are represented by a more modest selection, generally constructed round a large manor house. Apart from farmsteads and workshops of diverse kinds, you can see water-mills and windmills, humble privies, wayside chapels and a complete school. The whole way of life associated with these buildings is preserved as well – thus the traditional crafts of weaving, spinning, pottery, milling and forging are demonstrated, farmyard animals are reared, and the gardens are planted to give a practical yield of vegetables. Several hours are needed to do justice to the museum; reasonably priced lunches are available at the eighteenth-century inn *Zum Wilden Mann* on the main street of the Paderborn village, less substantial fare at *Tiergartenkrug* near the Tecklenburg and Minden group of houses.

Practicalities

Detmold's **Bahnhof**, on the line between Bielefeld and the important junction of Altenbeken, is situated next to the **bus station** just a short walk from the centre of town. Turn left along Bahnhofstrasse, then right into Paulinenstrasse and you'll reach the historic area down to the left. The **tourist office** (Mon–Thurs 9am–noon & 1–5pm, Fri 9am–noon/4pm; April–Oct also Sat 9am–noon; ☎0 52 31/97 73 27, fax 97 74 47, *www.detmold.de*) is in the Rathaus, Markt 5.

There are plenty of **private rooms** and small **pensions** (①–③) in the surrounding area (most of which are only practical if you've got your own transport), but only a couple in Detmold itself. The cheapest **hotels** in town are the English-owned *Meier*, Bahnhofstr. 22 (☎0 52 31/99 18 44; ③), which has a rustic-style restaurant, *Hinz und Kunz*, and its neighbour, *Brechmann*, Bahnhofstr. 9 (☎0 52 31/2 56 55; ④). In the middle range there's *Nadler*, Grabbestr. 4 (☎0 52 31/9 24 60; ⑤), whose *Café Stuck* serves good bistro-type meals. There are three excellent upmarket hotels in *Detmolder Hof*, Lange Str. 19 (☎0 52 31/9 91 20; ⑦), *Lippischer Hof*, Willy-Brandt-Platz 1 (☎0 52 31/93 60; ⑦), and *Residenz*, Paulinenstr. 19 (☎0 52 31/93 70; ⑧). All of these have top-notch **restaurants**, though they're rivalled by *Speisekeller im Rosental* in the Stadthalle, Schlossplatz 7. There's a **youth hostel** at Schirrmannstr. 49 (☎0 52 31/2 47 39, fax 2 89 27, *jh-detmold@djh-wl.de*; DM24.50/€12.25 or DM29.50/€14.75), right on the edge of town; from Paulinenstrasse, turn right into Freilingrathstrasse, then left into Brahmsstrasse, and follow its continuation, Schützenberg, to the end. A varied programme of **drama**, **music** and **dance** is presented at the Landestheater, Theaterplatz 1 (☎0 52 31/9 74 60, *www.landestheater-detmold.de*).

Around Detmold

Four of the **Teutoburg Forest**'s top sights are within 10km of Detmold; at a push, it's possible to see them all in a day, following a southerly route. Unless you've got your own transport, however, a fair amount of walking is necessary.

The Hermannsdenkmal

First, there's what can be regarded as Germany's equivalent of the Statue of Liberty, the **Hermannsdenkmal** (daily: April–Oct 9am–6.30pm; Nov–March 9.30am–4pm; *www.hermannsdenkmal.de*; DM2/€1), situated on the **Grotenburg** to the southwest of the town; two buses go out daily (mid-May to mid-Sept only), or it can be reached on foot by gently ascending paths from the suburb of Hiddesen. The monument commemorates **Arminius** (or "Hermann", see box below) and is placed near what was formerly thought to be the scene of his greatest victory (but see p.648). The completion of the project was entirely due to the single-minded dedication of the architect-sculptor **Ernst von Bandel**, who worked at it on and off from 1838 to 1875, according to the availability of funds. Resting on a colonnaded base, the monument is crowned with an idealized vision in copper of the hero brandishing his sword on high; the total height to the tip of the sword is 53m, and the figure weighs 76,865kg. From the platform there's a fine **view** over the whole range of the Teutoburg Forest.

The Vogel- und Blumenpark and Adlerwarte

Following Denkmalstrasse you descend in less than 2km to the first of two ornithological treats, the **Vogel- und Blumenpark** (Bird and Flower Park; daily variable date in March/April–Oct 9am–6pm; DM5/€2.50) with over two thousand varieties from all over the world, from miniature hens hardly bigger than insects to the large South American nandu. Particularly impressive is the collection of parrots and cockatoos, sufficiently domesticated to be left uncaged.

From here, you can follow the footpath to the right and continue in a straight line to the **Adlerwarte** (Eagle Watch; daily March to mid-Nov 9.30am–5.30pm; mid-Nov to Feb 10am–4pm; *www.adlerwarte-berlebeck.de*; DM7/€3.50) in Berlebeck. This eyrie, commanding a fine panorama over the forest, serves as a breeding station and clinic for birds of prey, with around ninety of these magnificent creatures kept here permanently. Displayed on chains or in cages are all kinds of eagles – imperial, golden, prairie, sea,

---

THE FIRST GERMAN HERO

Having served for three years in the imperial army, **Arminius**, a warrior prince of the Cherusci tribe, originally allies of the Romans, became wise to the fact that, by stealthy means, the Germanic peoples were in danger of being subjugated in the same way as the Gauls. In 9 AD he inflicted a crushing defeat on the Roman army in the Teutoburg Forest, using techniques akin to modern guerrilla warfare. He then tried to forge an alliance with the southern Germanic tribes, which might have spelt real disaster for the Romans, but was frustrated by their quisling leadership. Nevertheless, two more Roman campaigns to subdue Germania were repelled, leading them to abandon the attempt. The hero was murdered by his own in-laws in 21 AD and was forgotten for centuries, only to be rediscovered and eulogized by the Romantic movement, who saw him not only as a great liberator, but also (rather fancifully) as the first man with the vision of a united Germany, which was at long last to be achieved.

bald, martial, and the enormous and rare harpy – as well as falcons, hawks, kites, buzzards, vultures, condors, griffons and various breeds of owls. The site was specially chosen because of its suitability for **free flight**, and there are daily demonstrations (May–Sept 11am, 3pm & 4.30pm; Oct–April 11am & 3pm), except during the winter season.

The Externsteine

The **Externsteine**, a further 3km south just before the town of Horn-Bad Meinberg, is a jagged clump of sandstone rocks set by an artificial lake, a striking contrast to the wooded landscape to be found all around. It's one of Germany's most evocative sites, an enigmatic mixture of natural and man-made features, whose precise origin and significance has teased and baffled generations of scholars. Bus #782 passes nearby; a DM1.50/€0.75 charge is levied when the caretaker is on duty, but access is always free in the evening.

Adorning the bulky rock at the far right is a magnificent large **twelfth-century relief** of *The Descent from the Cross*, which was carved on the spot, making it quite unlike any other known sculpture of the period. Although Romanesque in style, it's imbued with the Byzantine spirit, one of the few German works of art, illuminated manuscripts apart, so influenced. Some limbs have been lost, but its state of preservation is otherwise remarkable. Directly below is a worn carving, probably representing Adam and Eve entwined around the serpent. To the side is a series of caves, now closed off; one of these bears an inscription saying it was consecrated as a chapel in 1115. There's also a stairway leading up to a viewing platform at the top. The next rock, fronted by an open-air pulpit, retains its natural peak, below which is a roofless chapel with a circular window exactly aligned to catch the sunrise on the summer solstice. It's too upright to accommodate a staircase, but you can ascend from the top of the stumpy rock to the left by means of a little bridge bent like a bow; from the ground it looks precarious, but it is totally secure. The fourth rock, bearing a plaque depicting the coat of arms of the counts of Lippe, is again crowned with apparent danger, in this case a large stone which seems ready to fall down, but which is actually fastened with iron hooks, following the repeated failure of attempts to dislodge it.

Many are convinced that the Externsteine served as a centre of pagan worship; others maintain that the site's religious origins go back no further than the twelfth century, and that it's a re-creation of the Holy Places of Jerusalem, inspired by crusaders' tales. What's known for sure is that it was an anchorite hermitage throughout medieval times, and that it then passed to the local counts, serving successively as a fortress, a pleasure palace and a prison, undergoing many alterations in the process, before being restored to its present form – assumed to be the original – in the early nineteenth century.

Höxter

HÖXTER, about 45km southeast of Detmold, is the easternmost town in Westphalia. Hamelin (see p.670), downstream along the River Weser, and Bad Karlshafen (see p.448), upstream, are just over the border in Lower Saxony and Hesse respectively. Höxter is principally of note for the venerable **Abtei Corvey**, though it also has a fine historic centre.

Höxter's Altstadt is dominated by the twin towers of the red sandstone **Kilianikirche**, a Romanesque building clearly modelled on Corvey; inside is a Renaissance pulpit adorned with fine alabaster reliefs. Otherwise, the town is notable for the prevalence of **half-timbered houses**, which include the mid-sixteenth-century **Küsterhaus** facing the church. Beyond is the **Rathaus**, a late Renaissance structure

DEUTSCHLAND ÜBER ALLES

Hoffmann von Fallersleben is best known for what soon became the national anthem of a united Germany, *Das Lied der Deutschen*, set to Haydn's stately and spacious *Emperor's Hymn*. Its opening line *Deutschland, Deutschland über alles* became notorious under the Nazis, who were unaware that the melody was based on a Croatian folk song, and was thus part of the hated and "inferior" Slav culture. In reality, there's nothing sinister about the words, which are liberal in sentiment. What might seem to be an assertion of national superiority is actually a clarion call to abandon the petty feuding of the old states in favour of German unity. The third stanza was retained by the West German state as its national anthem, and recently there were moves to reinstate the first verse to celebrate the unification of the two Germanies. However, the frontiers delineated – "from the Maas to the Memel" – are very out of date: the latter is now in Lithuania, with the entire length of Poland separating it from the nearest German territory.

from the following century, adorned with octagonal turret and oriel. It's rivalled in splendour by the earlier **Dechanei** (Deanery), an asymmetrical double house reached down Marktstrasse. Although it's the busiest street, Westerbachstrasse is astonishingly well preserved, offering a complete panorama of half-timbering down the centuries, from late Gothic (for example no. 43, Haus Ohrmann) to Neoclassical (no. 40). There's little doubt that the Renaissance buildings steal the show, particularly Tilly Haus (no. 33–37), Corveyer Hof (no. 29) and Altes Brauhaus (no. 28).

The main claim on your attention is the once powerful **Abtei Corvey** (April–Oct daily 9am–6pm; DM6.50/€3.25), just over 1km from the town centre, and reached by either following the river eastwards, or going in a straight line down Corbiestrasse. A ninth-century Carolingian foundation, it was a famous centre of scholarship, its greatest legacy being *The History of the Saxons*, written around 975 by the monk-chronicler **Widukind**. He gave the newly conquered barbarian race an appropriately grand origin in veterans of Alexander the Great's army, and vividly related their story right up to his own day. The **Abteikirche** (April–Oct 9am–1pm & 2–6pm; DM1/€0.50) actually retains the great westwork of the original building, one of the few pieces of architecture of this period to have survived anywhere in Europe. The towers and the gallery between them are twelfth-century modifications, but inside you can see the solemn entrance hall with the **Kaisersaal** above, surviving much as the early emperors would have known them, except that the organ now blocks the view downstairs. In any case, the church they looked down on was so badly ravaged in the Thirty Years War that it had to be replaced by a completely new building, which dates from 1667–71. Although normally described as Baroque, the architecture is Gothic in every respect, for all that this style was by then a total anachronism.

To the side of the church is the extensive complex of monastic buildings, built a generation later in the plain Baroque favoured in northern Germany. After the Napoleonic secularization it became a ducal **Schloss** and is now a museum. Temporary exhibitions are featured, and there are displays on folklore and local history, but you're likely to derive most pleasure simply from being allowed to roam loose through umpteen rooms. On the upper floor, the **Festsaal** forms an elegant setting for classical concerts by star international artists in May and June. In the adjacent rooms are displayed some of the eighty thousand volumes from the abbey's famous library. From 1860 until his death fourteen years later, the poet **Heinrich August Hoffmann von Fallersleben** (see box above) served as their custodian, and there's an exhibition on his work.

Practicalities

The **Bahnhof** is surnamed Rathaus with good reason; it's just a stone's throw from the centre, right beside the River Weser. Services on this branch line are slow; a pleasant alternative (late April to early Oct only) is to travel to Hamelin or Bad Karlshafen by **boat**; there's a departure point near the Bahnhof and another at Corvey. Höxter's **tourist office** is in the Rathaus, Weserstr. 11 (May–Sept Mon–Fri 8.30am–12.30pm & 2–6pm, Sat 10am–noon; Oct–April Mon–Fri 8.30am–12.30pm & 2–5pm; ☎0 52 71/1 94 33, fax 96 34 35, *www.hoexter.de*).

Hotels include *Zum Landsknecht*, Stummrigestr. 17 (☎0 52 71/24 77; ③), the above-mentioned *Corveyer Hof*, Westerbachstr. 29 (☎0 52 71/9 77 10; ④), *Weserberghof*, Godelheimer Str. 16 (☎0 52 71/9 70 80; ⑤), and *Niedersachsen*, Grubestr. 7 (☎0 52 71/68 80; ⑥–⑧). A number of rooms are also available in **private houses** (①–③); the tourist office has a complete list. The **campsite** (☎0 52 71/25 89) has a good location on the right bank of the Weser opposite the town. Alternatively, there's a **youth hostel** at An der Wilhelmshöhe 59 (☎0 52 71/22 33, fax 12 37, *jh-hoexter@djh-wl.de*; DM24.50/€12.25 or DM29.50/€14.75): from the far end of Westerbachstrasse, cross over to Gartenstrasse; after a couple of minutes' walk, turn left and follow the road to the end.

Höxter's best **restaurants** are in the last two hotels mentioned above. Other good places to eat and drink are the *Altes Brauhaus*, Westerbachstr. 28, and the *Schlossgaststätte* at Corvey.

travel details

Trains

Bielefeld to: Cologne (every 30min; 1hr 30min); Detmold (hourly; 1hr 15min); Dortmund (every 30min; 40min); Hanover (frequent; 1hr 30min); Lemgo (hourly; 1hr).

Cologne to: Aachen (every 20min; 45min); Bielefeld (every 30min; 1hr 30min); Bonn (every 15min; 20min); Dortmund (frequent; 1hr 10min); Düsseldorf (frequent; 25min); Essen (frequent; 50min); Hagen (every 30min; 50min); Hanover (frequent; 2hr 50min); Münster (frequent; 1hr 45min); Siegen (hourly; 1hr 35min); Soest (hourly; 2hr 20min); Wuppertal (hourly; 30min).

Dortmund to: Aachen (hourly; 1hr 50min); Bielefeld (every 30min; 40min); Bochum (frequent; 10min); Cologne (frequent; 1hr 10min); Düsseldorf (frequent; 1hr); Essen (frequent; 25min); Hagen (every 30min; 30min); Hanover (hourly; 2hr); Minden (hourly; 1hr 15min); Münster (hourly; 30min).

Düsseldorf to: Cologne (frequent; 25min); Dortmund (frequent; 1hr); Duisburg (frequent; 15min); Essen (frequent; 30min); Kleve (hourly; 1hr 25min); Mönchengladbach (frequent; 30min); Münster (frequent; 1hr 30min); Soest (4 daily; 1hr 20min); Wuppertal (every 30min; 40min).

Kleve to: Düsseldorf (hourly; 1hr 25min); Kalkar (hourly; 10min); Xanten (hourly; 40min).

Münster to: Bochum (frequent; 45min); Bremen (frequent; 1hr 15min); Cologne (frequent; 1hr 45min); Dortmund (hourly; 30min); Düsseldorf (every 30min; 1hr 20min); Essen (frequent; 55min); Hagen (hourly; 1hr 5min); Osnabrück (frequent; 25min); Wuppertal (hourly; 1hr 25min).

CHAPTER SIX

BREMEN AND LOWER SAXONY

Т**he Land of Lower Saxony** (Niedersachsen) only came into being in 1946, courtesy of the British military authorities. In forging this new province, the former **Kingdom of Hannover** – which had shared its ruler with Britain between 1714 and 1837, but which had later been subsumed into Prussia – was used as a basis. To it were added the two separate ex-duchies of (**Braunschweig**) and **Oldenburg**, plus the minute but hitherto seemingly indestructible principality of **Schaumburg-Lippe**. In spite of this diverse patchwork, the Land has strong historical antecedents, forming the approximate area inhabited by the Saxon tribes during the Roman period and the Dark Ages. In accordance with the general north–south divide, the Reformation took strong root in most of Lower Saxony.

Geographically, Lower Saxony is highly diverse. It contains much of Germany's sparse provision of **coastline** and **islands**, behind which stretches a flat landscape, at times below sea level. Further south is the monotonous stretch of the North German plain, but this gives way to the **Lüneburg Heath** to the east, and to highland countryside further south, in the shape of the hilly region around the **River Weser** and the gentle wooded slopes of the **Harz** mountains. Although it is the most extensive Land after Bavaria, it has a very low population density. None of its cities is as big as the old Hanseatic port of **Bremen**, an enclave within the province, but a Land in its own right, in continuation of its age-long tradition as a free state. Otherwise, there are just two cities with a population of over 200,000: the state capital, **Hannover**, which only came to prominence in the seventeenth century and is to be visited more for its museums and magnificent gardens than for its monuments; and the altogether more venerable **Braunschweig**, which still preserves considerable reminders of its halcyon period at the end of the twelfth century.

ACCOMMODATION PRICE CODES

All the pensions and hotels in this book have been graded according to the following price categories. The codes quoted are for the cheapest available double room, except for establishments which have rooms costing widely different rates, when the most expensive price is given as well. Exact charges are given for youth hostels; in the case of the official DJH (HI) establishments, this is the lowest available rate. When two figures are quoted for these hostels, the first applies to juniors (ie under 27 years of age), the second to seniors (27 and above).

① less than DM60/€30	④ DM100–124/€50–62	⑦ DM200–249/€100–124
② DM60–79/€30–39	⑤ DM125–149/€63–74	⑧ DM250–299/€125–149
③ DM80–99/€40–49	⑥ DM150–199/€75–99	⑨ upwards of DM300/€150

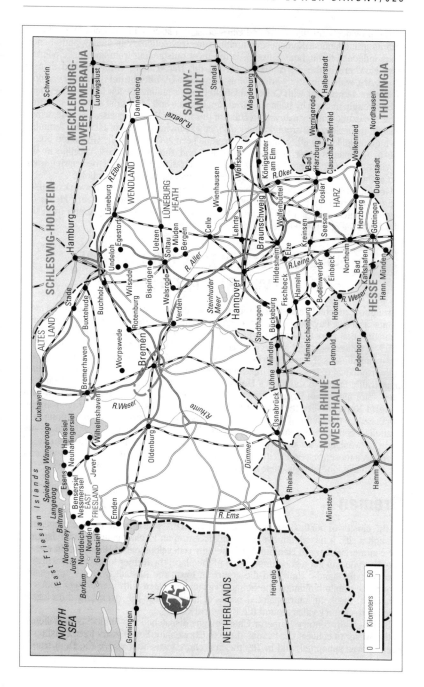

The province's smaller towns and cities present a fascinating contrast. **Hildesheim**, with its grandiloquent Romanesque architecture (revolutionary in its day, and of enormous influence throughout Europe), is the most outstanding from an artistic point of view. Nowhere is the mercantile heyday of the Hansa more vividly evoked than in **Lüneburg**, with its masterly brick Gothic showpieces. **Wolfenbüttel** is an early example of a planned town, and, with **Celle** and **Bückeburg**, is among the few places in Germany to be strongly marked by Italian-inspired Renaissance and Mannerist styles. Very different is the exuberantly ornate architecture of the archaic Weser Renaissance style, which reached its peak in and around the Pied Piper's stamping ground of **Hameln**. A mining town quite unlike any other in the world can be seen at **Goslar**, while **Göttingen** boasts one of Germany's most famous universities, and thus the liveliest nightlife in the province. **Einbeck**, home of *Bockbier*, is a reminder of the strength of the brewing tradition in these parts, and beer aficionados will find themselves spoilt for choice.

Getting around is seldom a problem, thanks to the usual efficient network of buses and trains. The only possible exceptions to this rule are in the Lüneburg Heath (in much of which there's a ban on fuelled transport) and in travelling to and from the islands off the coast, where ferry prices are relatively expensive.

BREMEN AND NORTHERN LOWER SAXONY

Throughout much of its past **Bremen** was governed not by the nobility, but by its merchants, as a free city state – a sharp contrast to the hundreds of German principalities, some tiny, that were run by feudal barons right into the nineteenth century. Those centuries of self-government and economic power have marked the character of the city and its inhabitants. There's a certain air of self-assuredness, superiority even, and pride in their political independence that marks out the Bremen people – a hangover that's inextricably linked to the town's **Hanseatic** past. Bremen still governs itself (and its deep-water harbour of **Bremerhaven**, 60km to the north) as the **smallest state in the Federal Republic**. It's the country's oldest and second largest port too, safe from the North Sea on the banks of the River Weser. Imports of commodities from far-flung destinations – cotton, coffee, tobacco, tropical fruits and cereals – coupled with the export trade in wool and wood have been the foundation of Bremen's status as one of Germany's most prosperous cities. The hinterland is entirely within Lower Saxony, and the city makes the obvious base for exploring the northern part of this province.

Bremen

Of the cluster of north German cities, it's **BREMEN** which is the most manageable. Though a city, it has an atmosphere reminiscent of an English country town, lacking the commercial buzz of Hamburg and the ugly redevelopment of Hannover. In one or two days you can get a good impression of the place: the former fortifications where a windmill still stands, almost in the centre of town; the Altstadt, with its impressive showpiece public buildings; the Schnoorviertel, crammed with the former homes of fisherfolk; the bold, mural-painted backs of houses near the river; and the elegant nineteenth-century villas around the Bürgerpark.

In the eighth century Emperor Charlemagne dispatched the Anglo-Saxon Willehad to the Weser to convert the Saxons there to Christianity. Seven years later a bishop of Bremen was appointed, and in 789 the first church was built where the Dom stands today. Two hundred years on, the city was granted free market status, giving independent merchants the same **trading rights** as those working on behalf of the Crown, a vital step for Bremen's economic expansion. By the eleventh century the city had also become an important centre for the Church, and over the centuries civic and ecclesiastical interests struggled for dominance. In 1358 Bremen joined the Hanseatic League, but the power of its prince-archbishops was not finally broken until the Reformation, when the city opted for Protestantism. Having survived a virtual cessation of trade during the Thirty Years War, it became a Free Imperial City in 1646.

Although very much a latecomer to the role of a city-state, Bremen was one of just four which preserved their independence after Napoleon dismantled the old structures of the Holy Roman Empire. This status was renewed in 1949 when Bremen, together with its deep-water port of Bremerhaven, was declared a Land of the Federal Republic of Germany. Since then, it's had a reputation for being the most politically radical part of the country, with the SPD having held power without a break. One of their most significant acts was the establishment of a university, which has set up an alternative, multi-disciplinary curriculum in opposition to the normal conservative, highly specialized bent of the country's higher education system.

Arrival, information and accommodation

The **Hauptbahnhof** is just to the north of the city centre. In a pavilion immediately outside on Bahnhofsplatz is the **tourist office** (Mon–Wed 9.30am–6.30pm, Thurs & Fri 9.30am–8pm, Sat & Sun 9.30am–4pm; ☎04 21/30 80 00 or 10 10 30, fax 3 08 00 30, *www.bremen-tourism.de*); there's a second, smaller branch at Liebfrauenkirchhof (same hours). The **airport**, which is 6km south of the city centre, is linked to the Hauptbahnhof by tram #6. A day ticket on the **public transport** network costs DM8.50/€4.25, but it's usually better value to invest in the the **TouristCARD Bremen**, available from the tourist offices. This covers all public transport plus a wide range of reductions in entry prices; for one adult plus one child it costs DM19.50/€9.75 for two days and DM26/€13 for three days; for up to five people travelling together it costs DM35/€17.50 and DM46/€23 respectively. There's also a **TouristCARD pur**, which omits the public transport element, and is priced at DM9.50/€4.75 per day for up to two adults and two children. Bremen is flat and therefore ideal for exploring by **bike**, which you can rent from the Fahrradstation by the entrance to the Hauptbahnhof. It charges DM15/€7.50 for one day, DM45/€22.50 for three days, with a DM50/€25 deposit on each bike.

The densest and most convenient cluster of **hotels** in the centre of town is near the Hauptbahnhof; not surprisingly, these are expensive. Budget accommodation is spread out all over the suburbs. Bremen's **youth hostel** is very well located in the western part of the Altstadt at Kalkstr. 6 (☎04 21/17 13 69, fax 17 11 02; DM30/€15 or DM35/€17.50) – take tram #1 or #8 to Am Brill. There's a good central **campsite**, *Internationaler Campingplatz Freier Hansestadt Bremen*, Am Stadtwaldsee 1 (☎04 21/21 20 02), on the north side of the Bürgerpark close to the university; bus #28 stops nearby.

Hotels and pensions

Bremer Haus, Löningstr. 16–20 (☎04 21/3 29 40, fax 3 29 44 11). Middle-range hotel in a convenient location slightly east of the Hauptbahnhof. It also has a good restaurant, *Löning* (closed Sun), complete with garden terrace. ⑥.

Enzensperger, Brautstr. 9 (☎04 21/50 32 24, fax 50 79 02). Small and basic budget hotel located a few minutes' walk from the Altstadt, on the opposite side of the River Weser. ②.

Haus Bremen, Verdener Str. 47 (☎04 21/43 27 20, fax 49 42 23). Good-quality pension ideally placed for the nightlife of the Ostertorviertel. ④.

Heinisch, Wachmannstr. 26 (☎04 21/34 29 25, fax 3 46 99 46). Small, moderately priced hotel by the southeast corner of the Bürgerpark, about a ten-minute walk from the Hauptbahnhof. ④.

Holiday Inn Crowne Plaza, Böttcherstr. 2 (☎04 21/3 69 60, fax 3 69 69 60). This is far from being a standard chain hotel, occupying as it does one of the wonderful fantasy buildings on Bremen's most famous street (see p.628). It serves a Swedish-style breakfast buffet, and has a fairly expensive main restaurant as well as a more reasonably priced alternative, *L'Oliva*. ⑦–⑨.

Landhaus Louisenthal, Leher Heerstr. 105 (☎04 21/23 20 76, fax 23 67 16). Country-house hotel in the northeast of the city which attracts large numbers of North American guests. ④–⑥.

Park, Im Bürgerpark (☎04 21/3 40 80, fax 24 43 43). This is by some distance Bremen's most luxurious and expensive hotel. In addition to its main restaurant, which features a notable wine list, there's the somewhat less expensive *La Fontana*. ⑨.

Peterswerder, Celler Str. 4 (☎04 21/44 71 01, fax 44 72 02). Guesthouse in the Ostertorviertel, offering rooms with and without facilities. ③–⑤.

Schaper-Siedenburg, Bahnhofstr. 8 (☎04 21/3 08 70, fax 30 87 88). A member of the Tulip Inn chain, this is another of the quality hotels close to the Hauptbahnhof. ⑥.

Überseehotel, Wachtstr. 27–29 (☎04 21/3 60 10, fax 360 15 55, *www.treff-hotels.de*). This hotel, part of the Treff chain, has an unbeatable location right at the edge of the Markt. ⑦.

Walter, Buntentorsteinweg 86–88 (☎04 21/55 80 27, fax 55 80 29). Functional guesthouse on the south side of the Weser, about a 10min walk from the Schnoorviertel. ③.

Weidmann, Am Schwarzen Meer 35 (☎ & fax 04 21/4 98 44 55). Pension in the Ostertorviertel; because of its limited capacity it's best booked well in advance. ③.

Weltevreden, Am Dobben 62 (☎04 21/7 80 15, fax 70 40 91). Good-value hotel excellently located about halfway between the city centre and the Ostertorviertel, heart of Bremen's nightlife. ④.

Zur Post, Bahnhofsplatz 11 (☎04 21/3 05 90, fax 3 05 95 91, *www.bestwestern.com*). This grand station hotel has a beauty salon and cosmetic studio, as well as a fitness centre with good bathing facilities, but is best known for its diverse culinary expertise. Its main restaurant, *L'Orchidée*, ranks as Bremen's top gourmet address; *La Dolce Vita* offers Italian cuisine; *Wabch* is an American-style diner and cocktail bar; while *Café Hauptmeier* serves home-made pastries and cakes. ⑦–⑨.

The City

Although more than half a million people live here, Bremen doesn't give the impression of being a large city – partly because the main area of historical interest is the compact **Altstadt** on the Weser's northeast bank. The former fortification that surrounded it, the **Wall**, is now an area of green park, with a zigzagging moat forming a curve around the perimeter of the old city. To the east, the **Ostertorviertel** (known as *das Viertel* – "the Quarter") was the first part of the city to be built outside those city walls, and is today the liveliest part of town, the area to head for at night. North of the Hauptbahnhof, the **Bürgerpark** and **Schwachhausen** areas are worthy of a stroll for their many streets of villas, each discreetly advertising Bremen's turn-of-last-century wealth. The Bürgerpark is twice the size of London's Hyde Park, and apart from being beautiful in itself, contains old wartime bunkers too sturdy to be blown up, which have been decorated by local artists and now sport political murals.

Sögestrasse

Bremen's main shopping street is **Sögestrasse** (Sow Street), along which swine used to be driven to the market. A life-size bronze of pigs, a swineherd and his dog marks its beginning, but as a standard Euro-shopping precinct, it's not particularly inspiring. The single place worth stopping off for is Bremen's bastion of *Kaffee und Kuchen*, **Café Knigge**, up on the right-hand side (see p.632). Just before Sögestrasse reaches the Markt is the **Liebfrauenkirche**, a hall church with contrasting Romanesque and Gothic towers. It's swathed by the flower market, which has a number of built-in booths around its walls.

The Markt

The **Markt** is dominated by the **Rathaus** (guided tours Mon–Sat at 11am, noon, 3pm & 4pm, Sun at 11am & noon; DM6/€3), whose highly ornate **facade** – rich in mouldings, life-size figures and bas-reliefs, and with the undersides of its large rounded arches set with enormous "jewels" – is in the Weser Renaissance style. It was added to the original Gothic structure between 1609 and 1612, two hundred years after the latter was first built. One of the most splendid of north Germany's buildings, it fortunately survived World War II unscathed. Inside, Bremen's civic pride is manifested in some splendidly decorated chambers, notably the main upstairs hall, the **Obere Saal**, and the small **Güldenkammer**, which has extravagantly carved Renaissance woodwork and allegorical paintings. Downstairs, the inevitable **Ratskeller** (guided tours, departing from the tourist office at Liebfrauenkirchhof, from early April to early Nov Fri at 4pm; DM15/€7.50 including a glass of wine; see also p.631) ranks as one of the most distinguished in the country, not least because of its cellar of over six hundred German vintages, some of which are stored in the eighteenth-century barrels which double as partitions. Bottles of these wines can also be bought from the shop to the rear of the Rathaus at Schoppensteel 1.

On the left as you face the Rathaus is a ten-metre-high stone statue of **Roland**, nephew of Charlemagne, who brandishes the sword of justice and carries a shield bearing the inscription (in the *Plattdeutsch* dialect): "Freedom do I give you openly." Erected by the burghers in 1404 as a symbol of Bremen's independence from its archbishop, he's the city's traditional protector; as long as Roland stands, they say, Bremen will remain free. Roland's pointy kneecaps were used as a medieval measurement-check by local housewives: the distance between the two is the exact length of one *Elle*, by which cloth was sold. In 1989 he was de-Nazified when a time capsule placed there in 1938, and containing Nazi documents, was removed. Poor Roland now spends his time staring at the much-disputed modern facade of the **Haus der Bürgerschaft** (Parliament Building), one of the ugliest edifices ever to disgrace a German town centre.

A happier postwar addition to the square is the bronze group of the **Bremer Stadtmusikanten** (Bremen Town Band) by the local sculptor, Gerhard Marcks. Rising like a pyramid, it shows a cock standing on a cat standing on a dog standing on a donkey, and is an illustration of an old folk-tale retold by the **Brothers Grimm**. In fact, this is the town band that never was: en route to the city, the animals arranged themselves in the way depicted and started to make music. In so doing, they frightened a group of robbers away from their hideout and took over the house for themselves, remaining there ever after.

Surviving buildings from Bremen's Hanseatic heyday are rare, but include the restored patrician houses lining much of the rest of the Marktplatz, and the **Schütting**, the ritzy, sixteenth-century Flemish-inspired mansion with contrasting gables, which was where the guild of merchants convened. Round the corner on Langenstrasse is the equally imposing step-gabled **Stadtwaage**, the municipal office for weights and measures.

The Dom

On a small rise beyond the Rathaus stands the twin-towered **Dom**, formerly the seat of one of medieval Germany's archbishops, but now a Protestant church. Any youngish men you see sweeping the steps are doing it because they have reached their 30th birthday without finding themselves a wife – this is the traditional penance (or, perhaps, a way of advertising their availability). The Dom itself has been restored recently, its brooding interior beautiful in architectural styles ranging from eleventh-century Romanesque to late Gothic. There are crypts at both ends of the building (one for the use of the emperor, the other for the archbishop), though that to the west had to be truncated when the huge twin-towered facade was erected in the thirteenth century. Just above the entrance is the early sixteenth-century **organ gallery**, adorned with statues, including Charlemagne and Willehad, by the Münster sculptor Hinrik Brabender. In the eastern crypt are more works of art, notably an eleventh-century *Enthroned Christ* and a magnificent thirteenth-century bronze **font**.

At the southeastern corner is the **Dommuseum** (May–Oct Mon–Fri 10am–5pm, Sat 10am–1.30pm, Sun 2–5pm; Nov–April Mon–Fri 11am–4pm, Sat 10am–1.30pm, Sun 2–5pm; DM3/€1.50), which features restored vestments and other treasures found in ecclesiastical graves. Entered from outside is the **Bleikeller** (Easter–Oct Mon–Fri 10am–5pm, Sat 10am–2pm, Sun 2–5pm; DM3/€1.50), where lead for the roofing was stored. It was opened up a number of years ago, and some bodies, perfectly preserved due to the lack of air, were discovered. Unusually, it's open to visitors, the "mummies" providing a popular – if macabre – attraction. Finally, it's possible to ascend one of the **towers** (same times; DM1/€0.50) for a view over the Markt and the city.

Böttcherstrasse

Off the south side of Marktplatz is a strange street which combines elements of neo-Gothic, Jugendstil, Expressionism and sheer fantasy: **Böttcherstrasse** or Coopers' Street. Once a humble alleyway in which barrel-makers lived and worked, it was transformed between 1923 and 1931 by the Bremen magnate **Ludwig Roselius**, who made much of his fortune from *Kaffee Hag*, the first-ever decaffeinated coffee. He commissioned local avant-garde artists, most notably **Bernhard Hoetger**, to effect the change. During the Nazi era, the whole street was to be demolished because it was considered corrupt art, but the charismatic Roselius persuaded the authorities to let it stand as a warning example, so to speak, of all that was considered bad in the arts.

The northern gateway to the street is guarded by gilded relief of *The Bringer of Light* by Hoetger. A short way down, at no. 6, is the only old house, a fourteenth-century stepgabled building with a sixteenth-century facade, that's now known as the **Roselius-Haus** (Tues–Sun 11am–6pm; DM8/€4). Though it gives an interesting opportunity to see the interior of a Hanseatic merchant's house, Roselius' collection of medieval art and furniture is not especially well displayed; the best works are paintings by Cranach the Elder and the Younger and an alabaster statue of *St Barbara* by Riemenschneider. Adjoining is the **Paula-Becker-Modersohn-Haus** (same hours and ticket), which contains a number of paintings by the artist, who lived and worked in the nearby village of Worpswede (see p.634). Upstairs in the same building is a display of sculptures by Hoetger.

At no. 3–5 on the street is the **Casino** (daily 3pm–3am), which offers a choice of roulette, blackjack, poker and gaming machines, with introductory films in German and English. Opposite, at no. 2, is the **Holiday Inn Crown Plaza**, which preserves some amazing decor, including a spectacular spiral staircase. Elsewhere on the street are boutiques, craft workshops, restaurants and the **Glockenspiel**; a carillon of Meissen porcelain bells in a revolving tower with ten wooden panels illustrating the history of transatlantic navigation, it chimes hourly (May–Dec noon–6pm; rest of year at noon, 3pm & 6pm, except during frosty spells).

The Schnoorviertel

Tucked away between the Dom and the river is a small, extraordinarily well-preserved area of medieval fisherfolks' houses known as the **Schnoorviertel**. Dating from the fifteenth century, this is Bremen's oldest surviving quarter. It's worth a wander through the small streets, far too narrow for modern traffic to pass, to see the variety of buildings and to get a feeling for the city's past. Predictably, in being preserved the area has been prettified and now houses pricey specialist shops selling antiques, crafts and toys, as well as many restaurants, cafés and bars and a couple of theatres (see p.633). Thankfully, it still manages to be a residential area too, avoiding a gentrification that would have left it soulless.

At the western edge of the quarter is the fourteenth-century **Propsteikirche St Johann**, a fine example of Gothic brickwork, whose towerless shape is a reflection of its original function as a mendicant friary church. The house at Schnoor 24 contains the **Spielzeugmuseum** (April–Dec Mon–Fri 11am–6.30pm, Sat 11am–6pm, Sun 11am–4pm; DM2/€1), a collection of historic toys. That at Wüstestätte 5 is known as the **Hochzeitshaus** (Marriage House), and has its origins in the custom that couples from the surroundings of Bremen who got married in the city had to spend one night there. It's now a "hotel" which can be rented by honeymooning couples – or anyone else for that matter. Another setpiece attraction is the **Packhaus St Jacobus**, the only historic warehouse in the city centre to have survived in its original form. It was restored in conjunction with EXPO 2000 and opened as an exhibition space.

The Kunsthalle

Just east of the Schnoorviertel at Am Wall 207 is the **Kunsthalle** (Tues 10am–8pm, Wed–Sun 10am–5pm; *www.kunsthalle-bremen.de*; DM8/€4, or DM10/€5 combined ticket with the Gerhard-Marcks-Haus), one of the oldest municipal art galleries in Germany. The ground floor is mostly given over to changing displays of modern art, but also contains a Jugendstil room containing valuable collections of graphic art. Most of the outstanding group of watercolours by **Dürer** were for long thought to have been destroyed in the war, but were actually confiscated by the Soviets as war booty; negotiations for their return are still ongoing. Meanwhile a small panel of *St Onofrio* by this artist can be seen in the first room upstairs, along with **Altdorfer**'s earliest surviving work, *The Nativity*, and several examples of **Cranach**. The adjacent galleries contain Dutch and Flemish paintings: *Noli Me Tangere* is a successful co-operative composition between **Rubens** (who painted the figures) and **Jan Brueghel** (who did everything else); there's also the striking full-length *Portrait of Duke Wolfgang Wilhelm of Pfalz-Neuburg* by **Van Dyck**, and a *Portrait of a Man* by **Rembrandt** or a member of his immediate circle. In the small cabinet rooms to the side are works by earlier European masters, notably Italians, of which the most important are *Madonna and Child* by **Masolino** (one of very few works by this artist to have left Italy) and *A Doctor* by **Moroni**.

However, the gallery's main draw is its superb array of nineteenth-century and early twentieth-century painting. Among the French School, there are five canvases by **Delacroix**, including *King Rodrigo*. A room is devoted to the Nabis: the most impressive works here are *Homage to Cézanne* by **Maurice Denis** and **Vuillard**'s designs for the decoration of the former Champs Elysées Theatre. Other highlights are an important early **Monet**, *Camille*, and **Manet**'s *Portrait of the Poet Zacharie Astruc*. Pick of the German works are **Beckmann**'s *Apache Dance* and *Self-Portrait with Saxophone*, **Kirchner**'s *Street Scene by Night* and a comprehensive representation of the Worpswede colony, with some forty examples of **Paula Modersohn-Becker** on view around the landing.

Next door to the Kunsthalle is the **Gerhard-Marcks-Haus** (Tues–Sun 10am–6pm; DM6/€3, or DM10/€5 combined ticket with the Kunsthalle) which contains sculptures, drawings and watercolours by the artist. Apart from the monument to the Bremen Town Band, Marcks is best known for the bronze doors and other works of art he made for a number of German cathedrals and churches to replace those lost in the war.

Out of the centre

Among several important museums outside the city centre is the **Neues Museum Weserburg** (Tues–Fri 10am–6pm, Sat & Sun 11am–6pm; DM8/€4), which occupies a group of converted warehouses on the peninsula formed by the two arms of the Weser due south of the Altstadt. Devoted to art of the last thirty-odd years only, it features extensive displays of most of the big guns, such as Warhol, Kienholz, Beuys, Fontana and Serra.

A short distance downstream, on the south bank of the Weser, is Germany's most internationally famous brewery, **Brauerei Beck & Co** (guided tours: in German Tues–Sat 10am–5pm, Sun 10am–3pm; in English same days at 1.30pm; DM5/€2.50). The visit takes in the brewhouse, where the brewmasters can be seen at work, the stables, with horses and wagons, as well as the museum, the cinema and the lounge, where a glass of beer is served at no extra charge. Although Bremen's brewers' guild, founded in 1489, is the oldest in the country, Beck is a comparative newcomer, having been founded in 1873. The ubiquitous *Premium Pilsener*, an amber-coloured brew in a green bottle, is made primarily for export, and sold in over a hundred different countries. Products bearing the *Haake-Beck* label are of superior quality and aimed at the home market; they include both a filtered and an unfiltered *Pils* (the latter known as *Kräusen*), as well as a dark beer.

Directly opposite the Hauptbahnhof at Bahnhofsplatz 13, the **Übersee-Museum** (Tues–Sun 10am–6pm; DM10/€5) celebrates Bremen's maritime tradition in a huge display of ethnographical objects from all the different countries with which local merchants traded. The latest addition to the city's ever-growing roster of museums is the **Universum Science Centre** (Mon, Tues & Thurs–Sun 10am–7pm, Wed 10am–9pm; DM16/€8), which opened in September 2000 in custom-built premises between Bürgerpark and the university, reached by taking tram #6 to Wiener Strasse. It's very much a hands-on experience, offering as it does more than two hundred interactive exhibits. Another new attraction is the visitor centre of **Astrium** (guided tours Fri at 5pm, Sat at 11am, 1pm & 3pm, Sun at 11.30am; DM29/€14.50), the headquarters of the German aeronautics and space administration. Beginning at the tourist office counter at the airport, the two-hour tour covers the exhibition hangar and part of the ISS International Space Station that is being assembled there, including demonstrations on how experiments in space are carried out by ground control.

The **Focke-Museum** or **Bremer Landesmuseum** (Tues 10am–9pm, Wed–Sun 10am–5pm; DM6/€3) is unfortunately rather a long way southeast of the centre at Schwachhauser-Heerstr. 240, though it's easily reached by tram #4. Laid out in an imaginative and informative manner, this traces the history of Bremen and its port, and has a collection of decorative arts. Among the most important exhibits are the original statues of Charlemagne and the seven electors from the Rathaus facade. If you're out this way, it's well worth continuing to the nearby **Rhododendronpark** (daily 7.30am–sunset) which, in May and June, is ablaze with some 680 different species of wild rhododendrons and azaleas, plus another thousand or so cultivated varieties.

Eating and drinking

In the gastronomic field, Bremen is renowned for its fish (particularly eel) specialities, best sampled in the *gemütlich* old restaurants of the Altstadt and Schnoorviertel. The city also has an excellently varied range of bistros and cafés. For drinking and nightlife, the place to head for is the Ostertorviertel, in particular along Ostertorsteinweg and in the short yard called Auf den Höfen, near the junction of Humboldtstrasse and Am Dobben.

Restaurants

Alte Gilde, Ansgaritorstr. 24. In the vaulted cellar of a seventeenth-century house, this is a good place for full meals, whether fish or otherwise.

Amtsfischerhaus, Schnoor 31. Fish speciality restaurant in the heart of the Schnoorviertel.

Beck's in'n Snoor, Schnoor 34–36. Fine Gaststätte of the eponymous brewery.

Flett, Böttcherstr. 3. In one of the fantasy houses in Bremen's most famous street (stained-glass windows and oriental carpets feature among the decor), this is another leading choice for fresh seafood dishes.

Friesenhof, Hinter dem Schütting 12. Excellent Gaststätte of the Jever brewery, serving Friesian specialities.

Kleiner Olymp, Hinter der Holzpforte 20. Another Schnoorviertel Gaststätte with a fish-based menu; it also has a good choice of beers, including the specially made *Schnoor-Bräu*, which is not available elsewhere.

Kleiner Ratskeller, Hinter dem Schütting 11. Offers solid, reasonably priced *gutbürgerliche Küche* along with one of the widest ranges of beer in town.

Knurrhahn, Schüsselkorb 32. One of the best and most inexpensive places for fresh fish. Open Mon–Wed 11am–7pm, Thurs & Fri 11am–8pm, Sat 11am–4pm.

Ratskeller, Am Markt. The most celebrated example of a great national institution, this offers a wide range of dishes which are fairly pricey, though not exorbitantly so. According to an old statute, it cannot serve beer, but has an extraordinary wine list of around 650 vintages, all of them German and some extremely rare.

Souterrain, Sielwall 50. Good, basic pizza place.

Bistros and cafés

Bistro Brasil, Ostertorsteinweg 83. Open all night, with a tropical atmosphere – at its best in the early hours of the morning.

Bistro Feinkost Hocke, Schüsselkorb 17. Expensive daytime bistro attached to Bremen's best delicatessen shop.

Café Engel, Ostertorsteinweg 31. Occupies a former pharmacy, whose furnishings it still preserves. If has good breakfasts and inexpensive daily specials, and has pleasant outdoor seating in summer.

Café Knigge, Sögestr. 44. Bremen's best (and best-known) traditional café.

Café Noir, Herdentorsteinweg 2. Open round the clock; it's near the Hauptbahnhof, so expect a very mixed crowd.

Café Stecker, Am Markt 11. Another recommendable place for *Kaffee und Kuchen*.

Café Tölke, Schnoor 23a. Serves a good range of teas, coffees and home-made cakes.

Kaffeemühle, Am Wall 212. Newly opened café in an old windmill; also serves full meals.

Kartoffelstube, Friedrich-Karl-Str. 11. Excellent for organic food, particularly the Swiss-style *Rösti*.

Schnoor Teestübchen, Hinter der Holzpforte 4. The ground-floor shop sells a huge variety of teas, which can be sampled in the cosy little café upstairs.

Bars

Brommy, Hemelinger Str. 7. One of the liveliest and most popular hangouts of the Ostertorviertel.

Gerken, Feldstr. 77. Another Ostertorviertel favourite.

Hegarty's, Ostertorsteinweg 80. Large Irish pub which serves good grub and often features live music.

Leierkasten, Pagentorner Heimweg 13. Tucked away between Staderstrasse and Friedrich-Karl-Strasse, this excellent pub has the bonus of a leafy beer garden.

Piano, Fehrfeld 64. Bustling bar in the Ostertorviertel which serves Mediterranean-style dishes.

Schüttinger, Hinter den Schütting 12–13. The only Hausbrauerei in the city centre; it makes a malty dark beer, a *Pils* and various seasonal brews, serves good-value meals and is frequently packed out at weekends.

Spitzen Gebetz, Hinter den Schütting 1. Tiny Kneipe directly opposite the entrance to Böttcherstrasse.

Wüstestätte, Wüstestätte 11. Schnoorviertel cellar bar offering live jazz and blues.

Entertainment

The best source of nightlife information is the tourist office, which is the city's main ticket-booking agency, and also publishes a free monthly **listings magazine**, *bremer umschau*. Also of use are two commercial magazines: *Prinz* (DM2/€1) and *Bremer* (DM4.50/€2.25). Bremen has a distinguished theatre tradition, and offers live performances of all kinds of music.

Discos and nightclubs

Aladin/Tivoli, Hannoversche Str. 11, Hemelingen. Has discos Wed & Sat from 10pm, live rock and blues at sundry other times.

Delight, Unser Lieben Frauen Kirchhof. Plays disco pap to an older clientele than the other clubs. On arrival, a card is issued on which your drinks are marked; minimum charge on exit is DM12/€6.

Modernes, Neustadtwall 28. A cinema during the week and a disco at weekends, playing half-hour snatches of all sorts of mainstream music; also has live rock, blues, soul and musical cabaret. Always busy and gets very hot, though there are periodic 5min breaks when the ceiling is opened for ventilation.

Stubu, Rembertiring 21. Has discos every evening from 9pm.

Music

In addition to the venues listed below, concerts and solo recitals frequently take place in Bremen's churches, most frequently in the Dom, which has a regular Thursday series at 7pm.

Die Glocke, Domsheide (☎04 21/33 66 99). Bremen's fine old concert hall has recently been well restored, and regularly hosts concerts by both of the city's orchestras. Of these, the Philharmonisches Staatsorchester is a full-sized symphony orchestra, while the Deutsche Kammerphilharmonie is an excellent chamber body with plenty of young musicians.

Schlachthof, Findorffstr. 51 (☎04 21/37 77 50). This converted slaughterhouse is now a cultural centre hosting world music events, as well as theatre and cabaret.

Stadthalle, Bürgerweide (☎04 21/3 50 53 30). The municipal hall behind the Hauptbahnhof is used for large-scale spectaculars and concerts by well-known pop soloists and bands.

Theater am Goetheplatz, Goetheplatz (☎04 21/3 65 30). Stages a mixed programme of operas, operettas, ballet and musicals.

Waldbühne, Bürgerpark (☎04 21/21 74 75). Open-air venue, complete with Bremen's largest beer garden, for Dixieland jazz and classic rock 'n roll.

Theatre

Brauhauskeller, Bleicherstr. 28 (☎04 21/3 65 33 33). The former brewery cellars to the rear of the Schauspielhaus are used for experimental drama projects.

Concordia, Schwachhauser Heerstr. 17 (☎04 21/3 65 33 33). Another experimental venue, featuring opera and dance as well as drama.

Musical-Theater Bremen, Richtweg 7–13 (☎04 21/5 54 43 21). New venue for Broadway-style musicals, currently staging *Jekyll & Hyde*.

Schauspielhaus, Ostersorsteinweg 57a (☎04 21/3 65 33 33). The city's principal mainstream dramatic stage.

Schnürschuh-Theater, Buntentorsteinweg 145 (☎04 21/55 54 10). Intimate historic playhouse with just 99 seats, offering a mixture of its own productions and visiting acts.

Theater am Leibnizplatz, Am Leibnitzplatz (☎04 21/50 03 33). The home of the bremer shakespeare company, the only theatre troupe in Germany to have ten of Shakespeare's plays in rep at any one time.

Theater im Schnoor, Wüstestätte 11 (☎04 21/32 60 54). A converted warehouse, used mainly for light comedies; it also has a specially fitted puppet theatre, with shows for both adults and children.

Theater Satyricon, Schildstr. 21 (☎04 21/7 40 07). Bremen's youth theatre.

Travestie-Theater im Schnoor Madame Lothär, Kopingstr. 9 (☎04 21/3 37 91 91). Old-fashioned variety theatre.

Waldau-Theater, Waller Heerstr. 165 (☎04 21/38 30 31). This long-established theatre is best known for its performances using the Low German dialect, though it does feature plays in standard High German as well.

Listings

Airport Information ☎04 21/5 59 50.

Festivals Leading folklore events are the *Eiswette* on Jan 6 (Epiphany), and the *Freimarkt* (or *Ischa Freimaak*) which begins with a procession in mid-Oct and lasts for seventeen days.

Harbour cruises Departures April–Oct at 11.45am, 1.30pm & 3.15pm from Martini–Anleger (☎04 21/32 12 29), through the pedestrian tunnel at the end of Böttcherstrasse. Tours last 1hr 15min and cost DM15/€7.50.

Markets Flea markets are held on Sat mornings on the north bank of the Weser from Wilhelm-Kaisen-Brücke and on Sun mornings on Bürgerweide.

Mitfahrzentrale Körnerwall 1 (☎04 21/1 94 40).

Post office The main post office is at the junction of An der Weide and Löningstrasse, beside the Hauptbahnhof, with poste restante services.

Sports SV Werder Bremen, one of the most successful football teams in the country in recent seasons, play at the Weserstadion in Osterdeich, on tram lines #2, #3 and #10. Indoor sporting events are held in the Stadthalle on Bürgerweide.

Swimming OASE im Weserpark, Hans-Bredow-Str. 17, which is reached by bus #25, is Europe's largest sauna and thermal baths complex.

Around Bremen

If you're staying in Bremen and want a trip out, the most obvious places to head for are the port of **Bremerhaven**, the former artists' colony of **Worpswede** and the old city of **Verden**, which is also a worthwhile stop-off if you're heading towards Hannover or the Lüneburg Heath.

Bremerhaven

Founded in 1827 as the deep-water harbour of Bremen, which lies 60km to the south, **BREMERHAVEN** is the Federal Republic's busiest fishing port. The pride of the town is the **Deutsches Schiffahrtsmuseum** (National Museum of Navigation; Tues–Sun 10am–6pm; DM6/€3) on Hans-Scharoun-Platz by the Alter Hafen, which lies between the modern commercial and fishing harbours. This traces the history of German sailing from prehistoric times to the present, and the star exhibit is a fourteenth-century Hanseatic log which was dredged up from the port of Bremen. Outside in the harbour is a wartime U-boat, the *Wilhelm Bauer* (April–Oct only; DM4/€2 extra), the only one of its kind still in existence.

The other main attractions are in the immediate vicinity. Just to the south are the **Kunsthalle** (Tues–Fri 2–6pm, Sat & Sun 11am–1pm; DM2/€1) which mounts temporary exhibitions, principally of modern art, and the **Radarturm** (Radar Tower; April–Sept Tues–Sun 10am–1pm & 2–6pm; Oct–March Sun 10am–1pm & 2–5pm only; DM2/€1) which commands a fine view over the harbours. To the north is the **Zoo am Meer** (daily 8am–5/7pm; DM4/€2), which has an aquarium plus a number of animals with an aquatic connection.

Bremerhaven's **Hauptbahnhof** is at the eastern end of town, about fifteen minutes' walk from the Alter Hafen. There are two **tourist offices**: at Van-Ronzelen-Str. 2 (May–Oct Mon–Fri 8am–6pm; Nov–April Mon–Fri 8am–4pm; ☎04 71/94 64 60, fax 9 46 46 51, *www.seestadt-bremerhaven.de*) and in the Columbus-Center, opposite the Schiffahrtsmuseum (Mon–Fri 9am–6pm, Sat 10am–1pm; ☎04 71/4 30 00, fax 4 30 80). Ask at either of these about **private rooms** (①–③). There are plenty of **hotels**; those with a central location include *Elbinger Platz*, Georgstr. 2 (☎04 71/92 44 30; ③), *Geestemünde*, Am Klint 20 (☎04 71/2 88 00; ④), *Comfort*, Am Schaufenster 7 (☎04 71/9 32 00; ⑥), *Haverkamp*, Prager Str. 34 (☎04 71/4 83 30; ⑤–⑨), and *Naber*, Theodor-Heuss-Platz 1 (☎04 71/4 87 70; ⑦–⑨). The **youth hostel** is at Gauss-Str. 54–56 (☎04 71/98 20 80, fax 8 74 26; DM24/€12 or DM29/€14.50); take bus #502 or #509 to Gesundheitsamt. Pick of the town's fish speciality **restaurants** is *Natusch*, Am Fischbahnhof 1. Worthy rivals are *Strandhalle*, at the Seebäderkaje by the northern end of Hermann-Heinrich-Meier-Strasse, and *Seute Deern*, a triple-masted barque in the Alter Hafen. Near the latter, at Van-Ronzelen-Str. 18, is *Koggen-Bräu*, a Hausbrauerei. Various harbour, river and sea **cruises** are available daily throughout the summer for around DM12/€6; there are also sailings to Heligoland (see p.766).

Worpswede

About 25km north of Bremen in the **Teufelsmoor** (the forbiddingly named "Devil's peat bog") is the intriguing village of **WORPSWEDE**. Back in the 1880s this was a simple farming village, where the inhabitants scraped together a living. The artists Fritz Mackensen and Otto Modersohn came here then, and over the next ten or so years Worpswede developed into an artists' colony, a movement run on roughly similar lines to the Pre-Raphaelites. The famous poet Rainer Maria Rilke was closely associated with them, as was his wife, Clara Westhoff. It was **Paula Becker**, who subsequently married Modersohn, who became the most significant of the set – her powerful, depressing pictures depicting the grim realities of peasant life, poverty and death stand out from the pretty, though comparatively facile, impressionistic scenes of the others.

Work by the first generation of Worpswede artists can be seen in a number of locations, notably the two main galleries in the heart of the village, the **Kunsthalle** (daily 10am–6pm; DM5/€2.50) at Bergstr. 17 and the **Grosse Kunstschau** (daily 10am–6pm; DM5/€2.50) round the corner at Lindenallee 3. The latter is among Worpswede's most significant buildings, one of several Expressionist masterpieces by Bernhard Hoetger. However, you're by no means limited to seeing the work of long-dead artists: the colony tradition is maintained to this day, and it's possible to visit – and, of course, to buy from – the workshops of a number of contemporary craftspeople.

Worpswede can be reached by bus #140 from Bremen's Hauptbahnhof; alternatively, there are infrequent boat services in summer. The **tourist office** (Mon–Fri 9am–1pm & 2–6pm; April–Oct Sat & Sun 10am–4pm; ☎0 47 92/95 01 21, fax 95 10 23, *www.worpswede.de*) at Bergstr. 13 has details of **private rooms** (①–③) and small **pensions** (①–④). Of the latter, the most intriguing is the *Haus im Schluh* (☎0 47 92/95 00 61; ④), run by the descendants of Worpswede artist Heinrich Vogeler, whose work is on display here. One of the town's highly distinctive stock of **hotels**, *Buchenhof*, Ostendorfer Str. 16 (☎0 47 92/9 33 90; ⑥), occupies the Jugendstil villa of another member of the colony, Hans von Ende. Other options are *Gasthof Zum Hemberg*, Hembergstr. 28 (☎0 47 92/12 84; ②), *Haar*, Hembergstr. 13 (☎0 47 92/9 32 50; ④), *Am Kunstcentrum*, Hans-am-Ende-Weg 4 (☎0 47 92/94 00; ⑤), *Waldhotel*, Hintern Berg 24 (☎0 47 92/9 31 80; ⑥), and *Eichenhof*, Ostendorfer Str. 13 (☎0 47 92/26 76; ⑦–⑨). There's a **youth hostel** a few minutes' walk west of the centre at Hammeweg 2 (☎0 47 92/13 60, fax 43 81; DM24/€12 or DM29/€14.50). Among an enticing array of **cafés** (which generally also serve full meals), *Kaffee Worpswede*, Lindenallee 1, housed in striking custom-designed premises by Hoetger, stands out, as does *Kaffeehaus Niedersachsen*, Am Thiergarten 2, which has original Worpswede furniture. The best **restaurants** are *Worpsweder Landhaus*, Findorffstr. 2, and those in the hotels *Am Kunstcentrum* and *Eichenhof*.

Verden

The former episcopal seat of **VERDEN**, some 28km southeast of Bremen on the main rail line to Hannover, nowadays christens itself Reiterstadt in honour of its status as Germany's equestrian capital, the setting for seven **horse markets** each year, of which those in mid-April and mid-October, with their attendant festivals, are the most important.

The compact Altstadt lies on the right bank of the River Aller. Much of it is now a bland pedestrianized shopping precinct, but towards the end of the latter is the impressive Gothic **Dom**. This imparts a surprising sense of unity, given that it was constructed over an unusually protracted period, and even then retains the tower and cloister of its Romanesque predecessor. The late thirteenth-century chancel is one of the earliest essays in the distinctively German hall-church style; although not finished until two hundred years later, the nave and transept dovetail perfectly with it.

In the shadow of the Dom is the Romanesque **Andreaskirche**, whose great treasure is the brass funerary slab – the oldest known example of its kind – of its founder Bishop Yso. Just north of the Dom at Untere Str. 13 is the **Domherrenhaus**, a timber-framed building from the early eighteenth century, which now houses the **Historisches Museum** (Tues–Sun 10am–1pm & 3–5pm; DM3/€1.50). Alongside the expected archeology, folklore, handicraft and local history displays is a wooden spear which is believed to be the oldest hunting weapon ever discovered. The main building in the northern half of the Altstadt is the **Johanniskirche** on Ritterstrasse, a Romanesque brick basilica transformed into a

Gothic hall church in the fifteenth century. It has well-restored cycles of medieval wall and ceiling frescoes and notable furnishings, including a relief of *The Last Judgement*.

On Holzmarkt, just to the east of the Altstadt, the former barracks have been converted to serve as the new home of the **Deutsches Pferdemuseum** (Tues–Sun 10am–5pm; *www.dpm-verden.de*; DM5/€2.50), a rather serious institution with a huge collection of equine artefacts and a valuable library of books on the same theme.

Verden's **Hauptbahnhof** is situated east of the Altstadt. Between the two, at Holzmarkt 15, is the **tourist office** (Mon–Fri 8.30am–5/6pm; Whit to Oct also Sat 10am–1pm; ☎0 42 31/1 23 17, fax 1 23 45, *www.verden.de*). The Niedersachsenhalle, scene of all the **equestrian events**, is situated in a park on the opposite side of the Hauptbahnhof from the town centre. In the suburb of Eitze, at the southeastern extremity of town, are a couple of budget **hotels**: *Der Oelfkenhof*, Im Dicken Ort 17 (☎0 42 31/6 29 63; ②), and *Eitzer Hof*, Walsroder Str. 42 (☎0 42 31/6 30 04; ③). Those with a more central location are far pricier; they include *Haag's Hotel Niedersachsenhof*, Lindhooper Str. 97 (☎0 42 31/66 60; ⑥), and *Höltje*, Obere Str. 13 (☎0 42 31/89 20; ⑦). The **youth hostel** is situated to the rear of the *Niedersachsenhalle* at Saumurplatz 1 (☎0 42 31/6 11 63, fax 6 81 21; DM25/€12.50 or DM30/€15). There are fine **restaurants** in each of the last two hotels, but the top gourmet address is *Pades*, Anita-Augspurg-Platz 7. Cheaper places to eat and drink include *Am Rathaus*, Grosse Str. 46, and *Annes Café*, Alte Bergstr. 16, which serves breakfast until 5pm.

Stade

Some 75km east of Bremerhaven, reachable by train via either Cuxhaven or Buxtehude, is the Elbe port of **STADE**. This old Hanseatic trading town, which was part of the Swedish Empire from 1645 to 1712, has flourished anew in recent decades, and its affluence has funded an ambitious restoration programme of its picturesque Altstadt of timber-framed brick houses, which is now in absolutely pristine shape; indeed, some would argue that it looks just a bit too polished for its own good.

The **Alter Hafen** at the northern end of the Altstadt functioned as a working port until 1966, but is nowadays an unashamedly showpiece area which has been regenerated by the introduction of museums, galleries, restaurants, cafés and bars where locals and tourists alike congregate. At the far end is the **Schwedenspeicher** (Swedish Warehouse; Tues–Fri 10am–5pm, Sat & Sun 10am–6pm; DM2/€1, or DM3/€1.50 combined ticket with the Kunsthaus and the Altländer Haus), which contains a distinguished archeological collection plus local history displays. Of particular note are the four **Stade wheels**, which were part of a late Bronze Age cart from around 700 BC; each weighs around 12kg, making them the largest of the period yet discovered.

The town's finest mansions line the western side of the Alter Hafen, which is known as Wasser West. By far the most spectacular is the **Bürgermeister-Hintze-Haus**, with its showy Renaissance facade. It's now a commercial art gallery, the Galerie Fündling. Alongside is the **Goebenhaus**, named in honour of the Prussian general August von Goeben who was born there in 1816. A little further along, the **Kunsthaus** (same times as the Schwedenspeicher; DM2/€1, or DM3/€1.50 combined ticket with the Schwedenspeicher and the Altländer Haus) displays a large number of works by the leading members of the original artists' colony at Worpswede (see p.634)

The central part of the Altstadt is dominated by the brick **Cosmaekirche**, which is Gothic in origin, though largely rebuilt after the disastrous town fire of 1659. From this period date the onion-shaped Baroque spire and a remarkable set of furnishings. These include a magnificent set of iron grilles, the high altar, the pulpit, the font, the chandeliers and the organ, which is in part an early work by the great Arp Schnitger. Regular recitals are held on it, including a Saturday morning series throughout the summer.

The **Rathaus** alongside is likewise Baroque, only the cellars having escaped destruction in the town fire.

On **Die Insel**, a small island just west of the Altstadt, is the **Freilichtmuseum** (free access at all times), with a group of redundant rural buildings from the Altes Land, the fertile agricultural countryside around Stade. Its centrepiece is the **Altländer Haus** (May–Sept Tues–Sun 10am–1pm & 2–5pm; DM2/€1, or DM3/€1.50 combined ticket with the Kunsthaus and the Schwedenspeicher), a large eighteenth-century farmstead.

Practicalities

Stade's **Bahnhof** lies a few minutes' walk south of the Altstadt. The **tourist office** (Mon–Fri 9am–6pm, Sat 9am–2pm; ☎0 41 41/40 91 70, fax 40 91 10, *www.stade.de*) is at Schiffertorstr. 6. Here you can ask about **private rooms** (①–③); there's also a small centrally sited **pension**, *Fleetenieker*, Bäckerstr. 22 (☎0 41 41/4 66 55; ③). **Hotels** include *Am Fischmarkt*, Fischmarkt 2 (☎0 41 41/4 49 62; ⑤), *Zur Einkehr*, Freiburger Str. 82 (☎0 41 41/23 25; ⑥), and *Herzog Widukind*, Grosse Schmiedestr. 14 (☎0 41 41/9 99 80, *www.treff-hotels.de*; ⑥). The **youth hostel** is at Kehdinger Mühren 11 (☎0 41 41/4 63 68, fax 28 17; DM25/€12.50 or DM30/€15).

Among many fine **restaurants**, *Knechthausen*, which occupies a lovely old building with back courtyard at Bungenstr. 20, stands out; it's expensive but does good-value set lunches. Only marginally less enticing are the *Ratskeller* in the Gothic cellars of the Rathaus at Hökerstr. 10, and the *Insel-Restaurant*, a fine old half-timbered *Gasthaus* transported to the Freilichtmuseum. *Cave*, Wasser West 9, is a trendy wine bar and bistro, while there are plenty of good cafés, such as *Im Goebenhaus*, Wasser West 21, and *Altstadtcafé*, Hökerstr. 29. The main **festival** is the *Schwedenwoche*, usually held in the second week of June.

WESTERN LOWER SAXONY

This area takes in points west of Bremen, as far as the border with The Netherlands – much of it is agricultural land, and the main area of interest is **East Friesia** (Ostfriesland). Over the centuries the Friesians have resolutely avoided complete absorption by their German neighbours, retaining their own language and cultural identity. They inhabit a low-lying, fertile province that was prey to constant inundation by the sea; it was a miserable sort of existence, as **Pliny** observed around 50 AD:

> *Here a wretched race is found, inhabiting either the more elevated spots or artificial mounds where they pitch their cabins. When the waves cover the surrounding area they are like so many mariners on board a ship, and when again the tide recedes their condition is that of so many shipwrecked men.*

Not surprisingly, the Friesians got pretty fed up with this sort of life, and as soon as the technology arrived began to build the dykes that have culminated in the sea barrier that extends right round the coast from **Emden** to **Wilhelmshaven**.

East Friesia may have poor weather and interminably flat countryside, but it has spawned an ingenious tourist subculture taking advantage of the "bracing maritime climate . . . that regenerates the blood and nerves", while "a walk along the foreshore will provide natural inhalation treatment", as a local tourist brochure put it. If you want more, you can pay for the privilege of being submerged in genuine North Sea mud in a number of large health spas, or join organized walks across the mudflats (the *Watt*) that encircle the coast – something you certainly shouldn't attempt on your own.

There are less esoteric alternatives: historic **towns** such as **Norden** and **Jever**; designated **nature reserves**; and two long-distance **footpaths** connecting Emden with

Wilhelmshaven. The first follows the Ems–Jade canal, the second the coastline, taking the name of Klaus Störtebeker, a fifteenth-century Friesian pirate and Robin Hood-type character whose name is much lauded locally. The **East Friesian islands**, with their long sandy beaches, lie just off the coast and are immensely popular holiday resorts. Outside East Friesia the main attractions are two cities: the former ducal seat of **Oldenburg** and the old episcopal centre of **Osnabrück**, which is also a major rail junction.

Most inland **travel** can be done by bus, though it's worth noting that services can be sparse on Sundays. **Ferry** details are listed in the text, though services can be erratic, dependent on the time of year and North Sea tides.

Oldenburg

OLDENBURG, a junction on the two rail lines between Bremen and the North Sea ports, is a good place to break a journey for a few hours or an overnight stop, even if it hardly ranks as a major destination in its own right. It has enjoyed an eventful history. Having fallen under Danish rule for a century, it made a spectacular comeback in 1773 as the seat of the independent duchy of Oldenburg-Holstein-Gottorp, which kept its place on the map (latterly as a grand duchy and then as a free state) until it fell victim to Hitler's centralization policies. Nowadays the capital of the Weser–Ems region, it's a busy inland port, market and shopping centre which usually teems with people from the neighbouring countryside. Although it was only minimally damaged in World War II, Oldenburg looks surprisingly modern, almost all its older buildings having been swept away in a huge fire in 1676.

Much of the moated Altstadt is a pedestrian precinct, with the main sights clustered together at the extreme southern end. Of these, the most important is the **Schloss**, an irregular horseshoe-shaped building begun in the early seventeenth century in a plain Renaissance style, but subsequently altered and enlarged. It now contains the **Landesmuseum für Kunst und Kulturgeschichte** (Tues, Wed & Fri 9am–5pm, Thurs 9am–8pm, Sat & Sun 10am–5pm; *www.landesmuseum-oldenburg.de*; DM4/€2), whose lure is a large collection of paintings and *objets d'art* set in period interiors. Particularly notable is the extensive array of the work of **Johann Heinrich Wilhelm Tischbein**, a friend of Goethe and the most accomplished member of one of Germany's best-known artistic dynasties. Duke Peter Friedrich Ludwig, an astute patron of the arts, brought him to the Oldenburg court in 1804, and he remained there for the last 25 years of his life. The large canvases, such as *Of Naked Men* and *Hector's Farewell to Andromache*, show his talent for the grand manner, but what really steals the show is the *Idyllen-Zyklus*, a cycle of 44 little mythological and pastoral scenes and landscapes, tree, bird and animal studies.

On the opposite side of Schlosswall is the **Schlossgarten**, originally a dairy and market garden for the court, but later remodelled into an English-style park. Nowadays, it also boasts hothouses, a rose garden and extensive patches of rhododendrons, and makes a good place to picnic or relax. Just across the moat on the corner of Elisabethstrasse and the Damm is a branch of the Landesmuseum, the **Augusteum** (same hours and ticket). It houses the modern parts of the collection: most of the leading Expressionists are represented, along with plenty of works by Franz Radzwill and other German Surrealists. Round the corner at Damm 40–44, the **Museum für Naturkunde und Vorgeschichte** (Tues–Thurs 9am–5pm, Fri 9am–3pm, Sat & Sun 10am–5pm; DM3/€1.50) features natural history displays laid out in the manner of nineteenth-century curio cabinets. There are also archeological finds from prehistoric times to the early Middle Ages, the most eye-catching being the 2400-year-old corpses found in Lower Saxon peat bogs.

A couple of minutes' walk north of the Schloss, the Markt is dominated by the **Lambertikirche**, whose brick Gothic exterior has repeatedly been rebuilt, giving it an incongruously modern sheen. Its interior was competely transformed in the 1790s by order of Duke Peter Friedrich Ludwig into a Neoclassical rotunda based on the Pantheon in Rome. The overall effect is astonishing – rather like a Wedgwood vase turned inside out. Alongside are the **Altes Rathaus**, a Historicist fantasy borrowing freely from the vocabulary of the Gothic and Renaissance, and the early sixteenth-century **Haus Degode**, the oldest surviving house in the city.

Practicalities

It's easy to get disoriented when arriving at the **Hauptbahnhof**, which is about fifteen minutes' walk northeast of the Altstadt. Following Bahnhofstrasse straight ahead, then turning left into Gottorpstrasse will take you in the direction of the Schloss. The **tourist office** (Mon–Fri 9am–6pm, Sat 9am–1.30/6pm; ☎04 41/1 57 44, fax 2 48 92 02, *www .oldenburg-tourist.de*) is at the extreme northwest corner of the Altstadt at Wallstr. 14.

The best budget **hotels** are *Mandel*, just west of the Hauptbahnhof at 91er-Str. 2 (☎04 41/2 58 64; ②), *Harmonie*, southeast of the Schloss at Dragonerstr. 59 (☎04 41/2 77 04; ③), and *Hegeler*, north of the Altstadt at Donnerschweer Str. 27 (☎04 41/8 75 61; ③). If you want to be more in the centre, try *Posthalter*, Mottenstr. 13 (☎04 41/21 90 80; ③–⑥), or *Antares*, Am Staugraben 8 (☎04 41/9 22 50; ⑦). The tourist office also has details of a few **private rooms** (②–③), while the **youth hostel** is about ten minutes' walk north of the Altstadt at Alexanderstr. 65 (☎04 41/8 71 35, fax 88 54 24 93; DM24/€12 or DM29/€14.50).

There are **restaurants** to suit all tastes. *Seewolf*, Alexanderstr. 41, specializes in fish dishes; the *Fürsten- und Jugendstilsaal* in the Hauptbahnhof serves *gutbürgerliche Küche* in surprisingly elegant surroundings; *Steffmann*, Kurwickstr. 23, is a typical Gaststätte; *Le Journal*, Wallstr. 13, is an upmarket French-style bistro; while *Die Stube*, Achternstr. 63, caters for vegetarians. *Leutbecher*, Schlossplatz 18, is the pick of the traditional **cafés**. If you're after a drink, there are plenty of **pubs** along Kurwickstrasse, or there's *Ulenspiegel*, Burgstr. 12, and *Hannen-Fass*, Baumgartenstr. 3, whose speciality is *Alt* beer, and which features live music on Wednesdays. Next door to the latter is *Sunup's*, a disco-café-bar.

Oldenburg has plenty of **festivals**, including the *Hafenfest* on the weekend after Whitsun, the *Altstadtfest* on the last weekend in August and the *Kramermarkt* for ten days in late September and early October. The main **theatre** is the Staatstheater, Theaterstr. 28 (☎04 41/2 22 51 11), while **concerts** are held at the Weser-Ems-Halle, Europaplatz 12 (☎04 41/8 00 30).

Emden and Greetsiel

The western gateway to East Friesia is the important seaport of **Emden**, which is easily accessible from Bremen or Oldenburg by train. Its hinterland includes the peninsula of Krummhörn, whose main draw is the old fishing village of **Greetsiel**. Buses connect Greetsiel with Norden and Emden, though Sunday services are poor.

Emden

Despite its modest size, **EMDEN** is the principal town of East Friesia, and has been a trading centre since the days of Charlemagne. It was becalmed when the River Ems changed its course in the seventeenth century, and only revived some three hundred years later with the digging of the Dortmund–Ems canal and the building of a new harbour. Heavily bombed in World War II, there's precious little of the old town left. Emden owes much of its present prosperity to Volkswagen, whose plant produces some thousand cars per day.

The main historic monument is the former **Rathaus** at Am Delft in the centre of town, a Flemish Renaissance civic showpiece modelled directly on its Antwerp counterpart. Nowadays, it houses the **Ostfriesisches Landesmuseum** (April–Sept Tues–Sun 10am–5pm; Oct–March Tues–Sun 11am–4pm; DM6/€3), which has a varied collection of items illustrating the history and culture of East Friesia, but which is notable mainly for the **Rüstkammer**, an arsenal containing one of the most impressive displays of sixteenth- and seventeenth-century arms and armour to be found anywhere in Europe.

Just outside, moored in the Ratsdelft canal, is the fireship *Deutsche Bucht*, which preserves its original machinery intact and is now open to the public as the **Museumsfeuerschiff** (April–Oct Mon–Fri 10am–1pm & 2.30–5pm, Sat & Sun 11am–1pm; DM2/€1). On either side, and accessible with the same ticket, are the herring trawler *AE7* (same times) and the lifeboat *Georg Breusing* (daily April–Oct 10am–1pm & 3–5pm). The **Bunkermuseum** (May–Oct Tues–Fri 10am–1pm & 3–5pm, Sat & Sun 11am–1pm; DM3/€1.50) east of the canal on Holzsägerstrasse is the only one of its type in Germany. It occupies six storeys of an air-raid shelter and contains documentation on the city during the Third Reich. The **Kunsthalle**, (Tues 10am–8pm, Wed–Fri 10am–5pm, Sat & Sun 11am–5pm; *www.kunsthalle-emden.de*; DM9/€4.50) on Hinter dem Rahmen 13 in the northern part of the town centre, ranks among the country's most distinguished collections of modern art. It has a particularly notable Expressionist section, in which Emil Nolde is copiously represented, while the new extension features a strong holding of the COBRA group.

Both the **Hauptbahnhof** and the **bus station** are on the west side of town, just a few minutes' walk from the centre. Emden's **tourist office** (May–Sept Mon–Fri 9am–6pm, Sat 10am–1pm, Sun 11am–1pm; Oct–April Mon–Fri 9am–1pm & 3–5.30pm, Sat 10am–1pm; ☎0 49 21/9 74 00, fax 9 74 09, *www.emden-touristik.de*), housed in a pavilion at Am Stadtgarten, can provide a list of **private rooms** (①–③). Among the **hotels** are *Haus Waage*, Hinne-Rhode-Str. 19 (☎0 49 21/2 26 00; ③), *Alt Emder Bürgerhaus*, Friedrich-Ebert-Str. 33 (☎0 49 21/2 42 41; ⑤), *Heerens*, Friedrich-Ebert-Str. 67 (☎0 49 21/2 37 40; ⑥), *Deutsches Haus*, Neuer Markt 7 (☎0 49 21/9 27 60; ⑥), and *Goldener Adler*, Neutorstr. 5 (☎0 49 21/9 27 30; ⑥). All but the first of these has a **restaurant**. Other places to eat include two of the docked ships: the aforementioned *Deutsche Bucht* and *Nautilus* further south at Am Alten Binnenhafen. The **youth hostel** is at An der Kesselschleuse 5 (☎0 49 21/2 37 97, fax 3 21 61; DM22/€11 or DM27/€13.50) on the eastern outskirts. In summer, daily **harbour cruises** (DM9/€4.50) operate from in front of the Rathaus.

Greetsiel

The strip of agricultural land to the west of Emden, known as the **Krummhörn**, was reclaimed from the sea between the wars. Near its northern tip is **GREETSIEL**, a shrimp-fishing village since the fourteenth century, with cobbled streets, hump-backed bridges, windmills and teashops, but – in season – definitely not for those with a low bus-party tolerance.

The **tourist office** at Zur Hauner Hooge 15 (☎0 49 26/9 18 80, fax 91 81 46, *www.greetsiel.de*) can arrange **private rooms** (①–③), of which there's a plentiful supply. **Hotels** include *Hohes Haus*, in a seventeenth-century building at Hohe Str. 1 (☎0 49 26/18 10; ⑥), and *Witthus*, Kattrepel 7 (☎0 49 26/9 20 00; ⑥). The **youth hostel** is at Kleinbahnstr. 15 (☎0 49 26/5 50, fax 14 73; DM22/€11 or DM27/€13.50), with **camping** fairly close by at Loquard (☎0 49 27/5 95). Both the hotels listed above have fine **restaurants**, while *Is Teetied* opposite the Pfarrkirche is an East Friesian-style old tea shop which also serves good food. Friesians may account for less than one percent of the population, but they drink a third of the nation's tea. They like it strong, poured over special giant sugar crystals (*Kluntjes*) and topped up with cream.

Norden

NORDEN, East Friesia's oldest town, lies some 30km north of Emden. A place with an individual if rather sleepy atmosphere, it's centred on a huge **Marktplatz**, half of which is grassed over and dominated by shady, mature trees, forming an odd (or at least unfamiliar) picture for this part of the world. The square is dominated by the medieval **Ludgerikirche**, which was built between the thirteenth and fifteenth centuries, and the tall, narrow freestanding bell tower alongside. Pride of the church is its **organ**, made in the 1680s by north Germany's greatest exponent of the craft, Arp Schnitger. Recitals take place, among other times, on Wednesdays at 8pm from mid-June to mid-September. Along the paved part of the Marktplatz, on which markets are held on Mondays and Saturdays, are three Renaissance houses known as the **Drei Schwestern** (Three Sisters), and several other fine facades. Also on Marktplatz is the **Heimat- und Teemuseum** (March–Oct Tues–Sat 10am–4pm; DM4/€2), which claims to be the first museum devoted to tea. It documents the history of the beverage in Europe, traces its cultural and commercial impact and shows an array of porcelain and other accessories.

There are plenty of **private rooms** (①–③) on offer. **Hotels** include *Das Smutje*, Neuer Weg 89 (☎0 49 31/9 42 50; ③), and *Reichshof*, Neuer Weg 53 (☎0 49 31/17 50; ⑤). Both of these have **restaurants**; alternatives range from *Die Alte Backstube*, a traditional Gaststätte opposite the museum at Westerstr. 96, via *Vesuvio*, a reasonably priced Italian restaurant in the Schöninghsches Haus, a magnificent Renaissance building at Osterstr. 5, to *Die Borke*, Brummelkamp 1, the favoured hangout of local hippies.

Norddeich

Norden incorporates the seaside resort of **NORDDEICH**, which is just 4km away, ten minutes by bus from Marktplatz. **Ferries** run from here to the islands of Juist and Norderney, and trains – which arrive from Amsterdam and Copenhagen as well as a range of German cities – are timetabled to coincide with the boats, going right up to the jetty of **Norddeich-Mole**. Buses also link up with appropriate trains to take passengers to Nessmersiel, the ferry port for Baltrum.

You could, of course, stop off in Norddeich itself, but it's an ugly, rambling place with precious little to recommend it. Almost every other house has **rooms** (②–④) to let (just look out for the *Zimmer frei* signs), but these are generally more expensive than in Norden. The **youth hostel** is in the middle of the resort at Strandstr. 1 (☎0 49 31/80 64, fax 8 18 28; DM22/€11 or DM27/€13.50), while the *Nordsee* **campsite** (☎0 49 31/80 73) is situated by the sea dyke 1.5km west of town. The **tourist office** (July & Aug Mon–Sat 9am–5pm, Sun 10am–noon; rest of year Mon–Thurs 9am–5pm, Fri 8.30am–4pm, Sat 10am–4pm; ☎0 49 31/98 62 00, fax 98 62 90, *www.norden.de*) for the whole of the municipality is at Dörper Weg 22.

The East Friesian islands

There are seven inhabited East Friesian islands: from west to east these are **Borkum**, **Juist**, **Norderney**, **Baltrum**, **Langeoog**, **Spiekeroog** and **Wangerooge**. They form part of the **Nationalpark Niedersächsisches Wattenmeer**, which also embraces the mainland coastline and was set up to protect the highly distinctive coastal ecosystem. Although they have been popular holiday destinations with the Germans themselves for the past century and a half, the islands are among the parts of the country least visited by foreign nationals. This is partly due to climatic factors, and partly to the fact that, while ideal for a restful vacation – the pace of life is very slow, with **cars banned** from all the islands except Borkum and Norderney – they are singularly ill suited to modern-day tourists who want and expect to cover a lot of ground in a short time. Indeed, it is something of an endurance test just to get to some of the islands, and touring around them all inevitably absorbs at least a week, and sometimes a considerably longer period, as weather and tides can both affect the frequency of **ferry** services, often making it impossible to visit an island and return to base on the same day. Moreover, with the exception of Juist and Norderney, which can both be reached from Norddeich Mole, each island is served by a different mainland port, where motorized vehicles have to be left, when appropriate, in large car parks. Although **bikes** can be taken to all of the islands, they are subject to a surcharge of up to DM20/€10 on the ferries. Smaller supplements are also levelled on large items of luggage on most routes.

Day-tickets on the ferries offer considerable savings over period returns, and many of the islands are in any case so small that they can easily be seen in a few hours. However, they are packed with **hotels** of all categories as well as **holiday homes** for self-catering and rooms in **private houses**, so it may be worth staying over. One peculiarity to note about all the island **youth hostels** is that they offer full-board terms only, with no reductions if meals are skipped. It is only at the very height of the season – when demand can easily exceed supply – that there is likely to be a problem finding accommodation, though it is advisable to contact the relevant tourist office in advance to make sure. The three westernmost islands are the easiest to access, and also have the most developed tourist facilities: Norderney in particular has some very grand hotels. The four easterly islands do not have this level of sophistication, and are characterized by sandy beaches to the north and mudflats to the south, modern settlements with something of a suburban air, and nature reserves.

Borkum

Borkum is the largest and most westerly of the East Friesian islands. It has all the usual facilities associated with seaside holidays, including a casino, an indoor swimming pool with sea water and artificial waves, a marina and long sandy beaches. In common with two of the other islands, it has its own small railway, which runs from the harbour of Reede (where the ferries dock) in the south to the village and bathing resort of Borkum in the north.

Ferries for Borkum leave from Emden's outer harbour (*Aussenhafen*), which lies south of the town and has its own Bahnhof, with direct links to many German cities. There are normally four daily departures in summer, two in winter; the journey takes two and a half hours and costs DM48/€24 for a return, DM25/€12.50 for a day trip. There's a DM15/€7.50 supplement for the catamaran, which cuts the travelling time to an hour. A ferry also runs between Borkum and the Dutch island of Eemshaven; tickets cost DM21/€10.50 for a day trip, DM38/€19 for a return (call ☎0 49 21/89 07 22 for timetable information).

Borkum's **tourist office** is close to the Bahnhof, at Am Georg-Schütte-Platz 5 (Mon–Fri 8.30am–12.30pm & 2–5.30pm; ☎0 49 22/93 31 08, fax 93 31 04, *www.borkum.de*). **Hotels** include *Graf Waldersee*, Bahnhofstr. 6 (☎0 49 22/91 26 00; ⑥), *Inselhotel Vierjahreszeiten*, Georg-Schütte-Platz 4 (☎0 49 22/92 00; ⑦), and *Nautic-Kurhotel Upstalboom*, Goethestr. 18 (☎0 49 22/30 40; ⑧). There's also a **youth hostel** at Reedestr. 231 (☎0 49 22/579, fax 71 24; DM42/€21 or DM47/€23.50).

Juist

Depending on the tides, between one and three ferries leave Norddeich Mole for **Juist** every day. The trip takes one hour and twenty minutes and costs DM30/€15 for a day trip, DM44/€22 for a period return. Juist is a narrow strip of land 17km long and a few hundred metres wide. A sandy, dune-fringed beach extends the entire length of its northern shore and even on hot summer days privacy is not hard to find. The only settlement is halfway along the island near the ferry terminal. It's a rather drab suburban affair, but at least it's not dominated by high-rise hotels and, best of all, there are no cars. Crisscrossed by foot and cycle paths, Juist has the full range of tourist facilities, with dozens of bars and restaurants, a large covered swimming pool and a nature reserve (the "Bill").

The **tourist office** (May–Sept Mon–Sat 8.30am–noon & 3–5pm; Oct–April Mon–Sat 8.30am–noon; ☎0 49 35/80 90, fax 80 92 23, *www.juist.de*) is at Friesenstr. 18. In addition to scores of **pensions** (②–④), there are **hotels** in all categories. Among the best are *Friesenhof*, Strandstr. 21 (☎0 49 35/80 60; ⑦), *Historisches Kurhaus Juist*, Strandpromenade 1 (☎0 49 35/91 60; ⑨), and *Achterdiek*, Wilhelmstr. 36 (☎0 49 35/80 40; ⑨). All of these also have excellent **restaurants** which, unlike some others on the island, are open to non-residents. The **youth hostel** is at Loogster Pad 20 (☎0 49 35/9 29 10, fax 82 94; DM38/€19 or DM43/€21.50). **Camping** is not permitted anywhere on Juist. For details of sailings to other islands a useful **travel agent** is Reisebüro Kiesendahl, Strandstr. 2 (☎0 49 35/91 40 80).

Norderney

According to the season, ferries make the fifty-minute journey from Norddeich Mole to **Norderney** between nine and thirteen times daily; a return – whether for one day or for a longer period – costs DM22.50/€11.25. The rugged lifestyle of its islanders in the first half of last century was graphically described in the second part of Heinrich Heine's *Travel Pictures*, and also inspired his cycle of poems, *The North Sea*. Today, the reality is very different, as Norderney does its utmost to cater for all kinds of holidaymakers. In the summer the bars are packed with serious drinkers, middle-aged couples tuck into apple strudels, and gamblers fill the casino with no time to eat or drink. Meanwhile earnest joggers trot round the myriad footpaths, families sunbathe on the long sandy beach, pensioners take the cures, and cyclists tour the nature reserve. If that's not enough, there are innumerable gourmet restaurants, a couple of small museums and the first-ever covered swimming pool to have sea water and artificial waves.

Slightly self-conscious, the town of **NORDERNEY** is the oldest bathing and health resort on the German North Sea coast, and was once a favourite royal holiday residence. The central square, with its manicured gardens, elegant cafés and Neoclassical buildings, has retained a certain nineteenth-century grace, though most of the town is a dull mixture of modern architectural styles. Its only surprise is a huge pyramid of stones piled up in the middle of an ordinary side-street. This is in fact a monument to Kaiser Wilhelm I and his achievement of German unification: 61 stones marked with their state of origin.

The **tourist office** (mid-May to Sept daily 9am–6pm; Oct to mid-May Mon–Fri 9am–12.30pm & 2.30–6pm, Sat 10am–12.30pm; ☎0 49 32/9 18 50, fax 8 24 94, *www .norderney.de*) is just off the main square at Bülowallee 5. It will find you a **room** in a pension or private house (②–④). Alternatively, there are plenty of **hotels**, particularly in the middle and upper ranges; these include *Friese*, Friedrichstr. 34 (☎0 49 32/80 20; ⑥), *Strandhotel an der Georgshöhe*, Kaiserstr. 24 (☎0 49 32/89 90; ⑥–⑨), *Strandhotel Pique*, Am Westrand 4 (☎0 49 32/9 39 30; ⑦), and *Kurhotel*, Weststrandstr. 4 (☎0 49 32/88 30 00; ⑦–⑨). All of these have recommendable **restaurants** open to non-residents.

There are two **youth hostels** (March–Oct only), which also fill up quickly in summer. The one at Südstr. 1 (☎0 49 32/24 51, fax 8 36 00; DM38/€19 or DM43/€21.50) can be reached by bus from the ferry, or else by a 35-minute walk via Zum Fahranleger and Deichstrasse. The alternative at Am Dünensender 3 (☎0 49 32/25 74, fax 8 32 66; DM38/€19 or DM43/€21.50) is way to the east of town, but has the advantage of attached **camping** facilities. There's another campsite, *Booken*, on the edge of town at Waldweg 2 (☎0 49 32/4 48).

The easternmost islands

Just 5km long, **Baltrum** is the smallest and quietest of the islands, whose houses are identified only by number, and not by streets. Three to six buses daily go from Norden's Bahnhof to the ferry port at Nessmersiel, arriving in time for ferry departures, though crossings may be delayed in rough weather. Period returns cost DM36/€18, though the DM24/€12 day-trip allows plenty of time to explore the island. The **tourist office** (March–Oct Mon–Fri 8.30am–noon & 2.30–5pm; Nov–Feb Mon–Fri 9am–noon; ☎0 49 39/91 40 03, fax 91 40 05, *www.baltrum.de*) by the harbour can help find a **private room** (①–④). Ask here for permission to use the sole **campsite**, at the edge of a nature reserve. **Hotels** include *Witthus* at no. 128 (☎0 49 39/99 00 00; ⑥), and *Strandhof* at no. 123 (☎0 49 39/8 90; ⑥).

Regular buses leave Norden for Esens, where you have to change for the connections (3–5 daily) to the port of Bensersiel, the departure point for **Langeoog**, the next island to the east. The ferry costs DM36/€18 period return, or DM30/€15 for a daytrip. It takes fifty minutes and synchronizes with the island's toy rail line to the somewhat dull main settlement. Far more enticing is Langeoog's main attraction, the **nature reserve** at the eastern end of the island, home to a colony of seabirds. The **youth hostel** (☎0 49 72/2 76, fax 66 94; DM38/€19 or DM43/€21.50; closed Oct–April), pleasantly set behind the Melkhörn sand dunes some 3km to the east of the village, is among the most atmospheric places to stay; it also has a **campsite** attached. Otherwise, check the noticeboard outside the **tourist office** (April–Sept Mon–Sat 9am–7pm, Sun 10am–2pm; Oct–March Mon–Fri 9am–5pm; ☎0 49 72/69 30, fax 69 31 16, *www .langeoog.de*) at Hauptstr. 28 for the current **room** (②–④) vacancies. There are several fine **hotels**, including *Lamberti*, Hauptstr. 31 (☎0 49 72/9 10 70; ⑦), and *Flörke*, Hauptstr. 17 (☎0 49 72/9 22 00; ⑦).

Another bus leaves Esens for Neuharlingersiel, from where two to four ferries per day sail to **Spiekeroog**. Tickets for the fifty-minute journey cost DM35/€17.50 period return, or DM30/€15 for a day-trip. This island has the oldest church on the islands, the late seventeenth-century **Inselkirche**. It contains wreckage from one of the ships of the Spanish Armada, which sank off the nearby coast in 1588. Spiekeroog's **tourist office** (Mon–Fri 9am–noon & 2–4pm, Sat 9am–noon; ☎0 49 76/9 19 30, fax 91 93 47, *www.spiekeroog.de*) at Noorderpad 25 supplies the usual information on **rooms** (②–④). The best **hotels** are *Zur Linde*, Noordloog 5 (☎0 49 76/9 19 40; ⑥), and *Inselfriede*, Süderloog 12 (☎0 49 76/9 19 20; ⑦). There's also a **youth hostel** within easy walking distance from the harbour at Bid' Utkiek 1 (☎0 49 76/3 29; DM38/€19 or DM43/€21.50; closed Nov to mid-March).

The easternmost of the East Friesian islands, **Wangerooge**, is one of the most attractive of the group, boasting all the usual tourist facilities, a railway, a small museum in the old lighthouse and several **bird sanctuaries**. It is reached via the port of Harlesiel, which is linked to both Esens and Wilhelmshaven by bus, though a change may be necessary at the inland harbour of Carolinensiel. Tickets for the ferry crossing cost DM56/€28 for a period return, DM29/€14.50 for a day-trip. The main settlement is in the middle of the island, connected by rail to the ferry terminal. A branch line also goes to the western tip where you'll find the Westturm, a stone tower now housing the **youth** hostel (☎0 44 69/4 39, fax 85 78; DM38/€19 or DM43/€21.50; closed Oct–March). As ever, the **tourist office** (April–Sept Mon–Sat 9am–noon & 2–5pm; Oct–March Mon–Fri 9am–noon; ☎0 44 69/9 48 80, fax 94 88 99, *www.insel-wangerooge.de*) on Strandpromenade can help with finding **rooms** (②–④). The leading **hotel** is *Strandhotel Upstalsboom*, Strandpromenade 21 (☎0 44 69/87 60; ⑤).

Jever

Situated some 60km from both Oldenburg and Emden, modest little **JEVER** is the most attractive town in Friesia. For more than four centuries the capital of a minute aristocratic territory, it reached its apogee in the sixteenth century under the last of its noble rulers, the energetic and gifted **Fräulein Maria**, who give it municipal rights, had the fortifications built, founded a school and commissioned several splendid works of art. Later, through marriage and conquest, Jever came under Russian, Dutch and French control, but it never developed into a place of significance, and remains something of a backwater to this day.

Jever's dominant monument is the rather magnificent pink **Schloss** (March–June & Sept to mid-Jan Tues–Sun 10am–6pm; July & Aug Mon 11am–5pm, Tues–Sun 10am–6pm; DM4/€2). Begun in the fifteenth century as a fortified castle, it was transformed by Fräulein Maria into a Renaissance palace. Highlight of the interior is the carved oak ceiling of the **Audienzsaal**, the work of the great Antwerp artist Cornelis Floris. Between May and September, it's possible to go up the **tower** (DM1/€0.50 extra) for a fine view over the skyline and the Schlosspark.

The town centre to the north is laid out round two squares. Neuer Markt is dominated by the **Stadtkirche**, which has been burned down and rebuilt at least nine times in its nine-hundred-year history. It last had a fire in 1959, when over half of the church was destroyed and replaced with a contemporary design. The enormous **funerary monument** by Floris that Fräulein Maria commissioned in honour of her father somehow survived, and can be seen in the remains of the Baroque church, which is now integrated into the new building. A work of architecture as much as sculpture, it's particularly remarkable for the extraordinary variety of materials used – wood, marble, sandstone and clay.

A few blocks further north, at Elisabethufer 17, is the distinctive silhouette of the **Friesisches Brauhaus zu Jever** (guided tours April–Oct Mon–Fri at 9.30am, 10am & 10.30am; Nov–March Tues & Thurs at 10.30am; advance booking essential, call ☎0 44 61/1 37 11; DM10/€5), which is claimed as the most modern brewery in Germany. Its *Pils* enjoys cult status as the bitterest-tasting beer made in the country. Other products are the low-alcohol, low-calorie *Light* and the drolly named *Fun*, which is alcohol-free. The price of the tour includes not only a visit to the production lines and the museum, but also a presentation glass, which can be filled up twice, with a *Brezel* to ward off any hunger pangs.

Practicalities

Jever's **Bahnhof** is situated some distance southwest of the centre. The **tourist office** (May–Sept Mon–Fri 10am–6pm, Sat 10am–2pm; Oct–April Mon–Fri 9am–5pm, Sat 9am–noon; ☎0 44 61/7 10 10, fax 93 92 99, *www.stadt-jever.de*) is at Alter Markt 18. Ask here about **private rooms** (①–③), which are in reasonable supply, both in the town itself and in the surrounding countryside. There are several budget **hotels**: *Schwarzer Adler*, Alter Markt 3 (☎0 44 61/55 32; ③), *Weisses Haus*, Bahnhofstr. 20 (☎0 44 61/68 39; ③), and *Stöber*, Hohnholzstr. 10 (☎0 44 61/55 80; ④). The classiest hotel in town is *Friesen*, to the south of the centre at Harlinger Weg 1 (☎0 44 61/93 40; ⑤). There's a

youth hostel (closed Nov–March), centrally sited at Mooshüttenweg 12 (☎0 44 61/35 90, fax 35 65; DM20/€10 or DM25/€12.50). Among the **restaurants**, the historic *Haus der Getreuen* deserves special mention; it's the Gaststätte of the brewery, situated across from it at Schlachstr. 1. Also very fine, albeit somewhat pricier, is *Alte Apotheke*, Apothekerstr. 1. Main **festivals** are the *Kiewittmarkt*, a spring market usually held at the end of March, and the *Altstadtfest* in mid-August.

Osnabrück

OSNABRÜCK, a major rail junction, lies close to the Land border, 105km south of Oldenburg. Geographically and historically, it really belongs to Westphalia, and it has many parallels with Münster (see pp.582–8), which is just 55km further south. Both owe their foundation to Charlemagne, and in the Middle Ages both were ruled by a prince-bishop, and were important trading centres. Subsequently, they shared the hosting of the long negotiations – regarded as the birth of modern diplomatic practices – which led to the signing of the **Peace of Westphalia** in 1648, bringing the Thirty Years War to an end. One curious agreement resulting from these talks was that Osnabrück was to be ruled in future by a Catholic and a Protestant bishop in turn. When the bishopric was secularized under Napoleon, the Hanoverians annexed its territories. Accordingly, Osnabrück joined the rest of Hannover in the new province of Lower Saxony after World War II.

Arrival, information and accommodation

Osnabrück's **Hauptbahnhof** is ten minutes' walk southeast of the city centre, which is reached by following Möserstrasse straight ahead, then crossing the River Hase. The **tourist office** (Mon–Fri 9.30am–6pm, Sat 9.30am–1pm; ☎05 41/3 23 22 02, fax 3 23 27 09, *www.osnabrueck.de*) is just off the Markt at Krahnstr. 58.

Osnabrück has a good choice of **hotels** in all price categories. There's a **youth hostel** to the south of town at Iburger Str. 183a (☎05 41/5 42 84, fax 5 42 94; DM25/€12.50 or DM30/€15); take bus #23 or #27 from Neumarkt, and alight at Kinderhospital. The *Niedersachsenhof* **campsite** (☎05 41/7 72 26) is in the northeast of the city at Nordstr. 109.

Hotels

Dom-Hotel, Kleine Domsfreiheit 5 (☎05 41/2 15 54, fax 20 17 39). Recommendable hotel right in the heart of the city. Also has a fine restaurant, open Mon–Thurs evenings only. ⑥.

Hohenzollern, Heinrich-Heine-Str. 17 (☎05 41/3 31 70, fax 3 31 73 51). Upmarket hotel close to the Hauptbahnhof on the way to the centre. ⑥.

Jägerheim, Johannistorwall 19a (☎05 41/2 16 35). Located on the southern inner ring road, this has the cheapest rooms in the city centre. ③.

Kulmbacher Hof, Schlosswall 65–67 (☎05 41/3 57 00, fax 35 70 20). Another good middle-range hotel with restaurant on the southwestern section of the inner ring road. ⑥.

Nord-Hotel, Hansastr. 31 (☎05 41/6 41 33, fax 6 41 22). Very good-value hotel a short distance beyond the Bahnhof Hasetor at the northern end of the Altstadt. Its restaurant serves huge portions at amazingly low prices, especially at lunchtime. ③.

Walhalla, Bierstr. 24 (☎05 41/3 49 10, fax 3 49 11 44). Despite occupying a seventeenth-century timber-framed house, this is a modern hotel with all the amenities, including sauna and solarium. Its restaurant is among the best in the city. ⑥.

Welp, Natruper Str. 227 (☎05 41/91 30 70, fax 9 13 07 34). Good medium-priced hotel with restaurant located just to the northwest of the Altstadt. ⑥.

The City

Much of the city is modern. Heavy damage was caused by bombing in World War II, and restoration has been less successful than in Münster. Some highly characterful streets and squares do remain, but it's a pity that more thought wasn't given to the planning of the bland shopping areas with which they're now intermingled.

The Dom

The **Dom** has a spacious setting in the middle of its own square in the heart of the city. Built in fits and starts between the twelfth and sixteenth centuries, its facade **towers** are a fascinating combination – the late Gothic one on the southern side is almost twice the width of its Romanesque neighbour. Inside, the Dom presents a pleasingly sober, predominantly Gothic appearance. Among a number of notable works of art, the early thirteenth-century bronze **font** and the exactly contemporary polychrome wood **triumphal cross** are outstanding. The latter's name is something of a misnomer, as Christ is here depicted as a pathetic, suffering, all-too-human figure. Wonderful gilded wrought-iron gates guard the entrance to the ambulatory, at the end of which is the *Margarethenaltar*, a limewood retable by the sculptor who also carved the *Madonna of the Rosary* in the north transept. The identity of this emotional artist, who was still working in the late Gothic style well into the sixteenth century, remains elusive: he's known simply as the **Master of Osnabrück**.

Further works by this carver can be seen in the **Diözesanmuseum** (Tues–Fri 10am–1pm & 3–5pm, Sat & Sun 11am–2pm; DM3/€1.50), housed in rooms above the cloister. The most eye-catching item here, however, is the gilded *Kapitelkreuz*, a **crucifix** made in the early eleventh century and studded with two pontifical rings, a couple of Roman cameos and a variety of coloured gems. The early seventeenth-century **confessional**, from a nearby convent, was made in the wake of the Tridentine reforms and is the earliest example in northern Europe of what was to become a very familiar structure.

The Markt

Just beyond the Dom is the other main square, the triangular-shaped **Markt**. Its colourful step-gabled mansions are modelled on the merchant houses of the Hanseatic ports, while in the centre there's a fountain which gushes with beer whenever there's a festival on. On the northern side of the square is the Gothic **Marienkirche**, which takes the hall-church design to its logical conclusion by omitting the transept. Inside are a fourteenth-century triumphal cross, a sixteenth-century *Passion* altar from Antwerp and numerous tombs – including that of Justus Möser, whose researches into Westphalian folklore in the eighteenth century were to serve as a trail-blazer for the Romantic movement. You can climb the **tower** on Sundays (11.30am–1pm; DM2/€1) for a view of the city. In the Stadtsbibliothek opposite there's a permanent exhibition **Remarque am Markt** (Tues–Fri 10am–1pm & 3–5pm, Sat 10am–1pm, first Sun in the month 11am–5pm; free), a documentary record of the career of the local author Erich Maria Remarque, whose novel *All Quiet on the Western Front* is the enduring German classic of World War I literature.

Closing the end of the Markt is the early sixteenth-century **Rathaus**, from whose steps the Peace of Westphalia was proclaimed. The present stairway dates from the nineteenth century, as do the large statues of German emperors, among which Kaiser Wilhelm I is lined up alongside his medieval predecessors. Inside, the wood-panelled **Friedenssaal** (Mon–Fri 8am–6pm, Sat & Sun 10am–1pm; free) features generally glum portraits of the representatives of Sweden and the Protestant German principalities, who deliberated here while their Catholic counterparts met in Münster. Ask at the porter's desk to see the **Schatzkammer**, which contains valuable documents and treasury items. Star piece is the magnificent fourteenth-century *Kaiserpokal*, a **goblet** adorned with coloured glass and figurines.

The rest of the city

Facing the rear of the Rathaus on Bierstrasse is the pretty half-timbered frontage of Osnabrück's most famous inn, **Walhalla**, which features extensively in Erich Maria Remarque's *The Black Obelisk*, a novel describing the traumatic hyperinflation of 1923. Most of Osnabrück's surviving **old houses** are nearby – on Marienstrasse, Hegerstrasse, Grosser Gildewartare, Krahnstrasse and Bierstrasse itself. The first three form a pedestrian precinct, where antique shops and bistros vie with each other for prominence. At the end of Bierstrasse is the former **Dominikanerkirche** (Tues–Fri 11am–6pm, Sat & Sun 10am–6pm; DM5/€2.50), now a cultural centre which regularly features temporary exhibitions of modern art. It also contains a weather-worn late Gothic statue of Charlemagne, the only survivor of the original cycle from the Rathaus facade. Beyond here, several fragments of the city wall can be seen round the ring road, including the Neoclassical **Heger Tor**, celebrating the victory at Waterloo.

Diagonally opposite is the **Kulturgeschichtliches Museum** (Tues–Fri 11am–6pm, Sat & Sun 10am–6pm; DM8/€4). Dominating the archeology section are the spectacular Roman finds from nearby Kaltkriese, which is now known to be the site of their defeat by the Cherusci under Arminius in 9 AD (see box on p.618). The local history collections are of interest for such fragments as the original medieval sculptures from the *Brautportal* of the Marienkirche. A new extension, the **Felix-Nussbaum-Haus** (same times and ticket), was built by Daniel Libeskind, the architect of the much-praised Judisches Museum in Berlin, in order that the large holdings of works by the local Jewish artist **Felix Nussbaum** could at last be displayed in their entirety. A member of the Neue Sachlichkeit art movement, which rejected Expressionism in favour of a starkly realistic form of representation, Nussbaum died in Auschwitz, aged 40, in 1944.

Continuing southwards along Heger-Tor-Wall, you soon see on the left the tall tower of the **Katharinenkirche**, a church broader than it is long. In the big square behind is Osnabrück's most original building, the **Leidenhof**. The sixteenth-century merchant owners converted their original fourteenth-century stone house into a miniature palace by the addition of a staircase tower and a new wing, whose facade resembles a gigantic cardboard cut-out. What really catches the attention, however, are the zigzags painted on the two Renaissance additions, making them look strangely modernistic. Opposite, set in its own fine park, is the huge yellow **Schloss** of the prince-bishops. Built in Italianate Baroque style, it nowadays houses part of the university.

Eating and drinking

Osnabrück is a lively city come the evening, and is well endowed with places to eat and drink.

Alte Gaststätte Holling, Hasestr. 53. Nowadays more a pub than a restaurant, though it does light meals. Evenings only except Sat, when it is open lunchtime.

Filmkneipe 8¹/2, Hasestr. 71. Trendy bar attached to a cinema. Games can be rented, and there are changing monthly art exhibitions.

Grüner Jäger, An der Katharinen Kirche 1. Hugely popular student Kneipe with minimalist decor and a glass-roofed beer garden.

Hermann's, Domhof 7b. Bistro serving an international menu, with good-value set lunches.

Pfannkuchenhaus, Lotter Str. 22. Specializes in wholemeal and buckwheat pancakes; also serves salads and pasta dishes. Evenings only except Sun, closed Mon.

Rampendahl, Hasestr. 35. Hausbrauerei which produces light and dark beer and a *Korn*. Also does full meals, including cheap set lunches.

Vital, Rosenplatz 23a. Vegetarian and wholefood restaurant open Mon–Fri 11.30am–7.30pm, Sat 11.30am–4pm.

EASTERN LOWER SAXONY

In the east of Lower Saxony, the landscape transforms itself from coastal plain to the rolling **Lüneburg Heath** (Lüneburger Heide), which contains the contrasting towns of **Lüneburg** and **Celle**, as well as several nature reserves. This extends eastwards to an area known as the **Wendland** that juts into the former GDR, and south towards the state capital of **Hannover** and the province's second city, **Braunschweig**. Continuing in a southerly direction, you soon come to more elevated land: **Hildesheim** stands in the foothills leading to the Harz, while there are fine rolling landscapes around **Hameln** in the valley of the River Weser further west.

Lüneburg

Of all the many medieval trading cities built by the Germans on and near the Baltic coast between Hamburg and Rīga, only **LÜNEBURG** has survived virtually unscathed. It was all but ignored by the World War II bombing missions which destroyed so much of northern Germany, having by then declined into economic insignificance. Yet in the Middle Ages the city was immensely wealthy, profiting from the fact that it was (literally) built on **salt** – then a rare and essential commodity, almost worth its weight in gold. At its peak, the Lüneburg saltworks had two thousand employees, which probably made it the largest commercial enterprise in Europe. The city's magnificent brick buildings were funded from exports of the salt to Scandinavia, Burgundy, Poland and Russia, and the other trading links which ensued. Gabled facades, from Gothic to Baroque, still line the streets of the centre. Many have a pronounced tilt, as a result of subsidence caused by disused mines. The salt deposits haven't been worked since 1980, leaving the saline springs of the spa quarter as the only active reminder of a tradition dating back to the tenth century.

Arrival, information and accommodation

Lüneburg's **Hauptbahnhof** has two terminals facing each other across Bahnhofsplatz. The quickest way to reach the centre is to go north along Lüner Weg, then turn left into Lünertor Strasse; this brings you to the Wasserviertel. Alternatively, turn right at the southern end of Bahnhofsplatz into Altenbrückertor Strasse, which takes you straight to Am Sande. Under the Rathaus's front arches is the municipal **tourist office** (May–Sept Mon–Fri 9am–6pm, Sat & Sun 9am–4pm; Oct–April Mon–Fri 9am–5pm, Sat & Sun 9am–2pm; ☎0 41 31/2 07 66 20, fax 2 07 66 44, *www.lueneburg.de*).

If you want to **rent a bike** to explore the area, go to *Laden 25* at Am Werder 25. Regular **cruises** on the River Ilmenau depart from the Wasserviertel; the office is at Im Wendischen Dorfe 3 (☎0 41 31/3 10 16). Lüneburg's main **festivals** are the *Bachwoche* in June, devoted to music by J.S. Bach, and the *Stadtfest* in July.

There's a **youth hostel** at Saltauer Str. 133 (☎0 41 31/4 18 64, fax 4 57 47; DM22/€11 or DM27/€13.50) well to the south of town, best reached by taking bus #11 to the Scharnhorststrasse stop. The **campsite**, *Rote Schleuse* (☎0 41 31/7 915 00), is by the bank of the River Ilmenau even further south; catch a bus towards Deutschevern. Lüneburg has a reasonable number of **private rooms** (①–④); contact the tourist office for a list.

Hotels

Alt-Lüneburger-Kutscherstube, Heiligengeiststr. 44 (☎0 41 31/44 11 34, fax 73 34 29). Small former coaching inn in the heart of the Altstadt. ④.

Bergström, Bei der Lüner Mühle (☎0 41 31/30 80, fax 30 84 99, *www.moevenpick-hotel.ch /lueneburg*). Part of the Mövenpick chain, Lüneburg's best hotel is beautifully situated in the Wasserviertel, and has both old and modern sections: the luxury suites are in a Gothic water-tower. There's also an excellent if pricey restaurant. ⑥–⑨.

Bremer Hof, Lüner Str. 12–13 (☎0 41 31/22 40, fax 22 42 24, *www.bremer-hof.de*). Characterful hotel in a former merchant's home. It has a good and not over-expensive restaurant whose menu features dishes of the distinctive sheep of the Lüneburg Heath. ⑤–⑦.

Das Stadthaus, Am Sande 25 (☎0 41 31/4 44 38, fax 40 41 98, *www.das-stadthaus.de*). A quaintly old-fashioned hotel, in business since 1880, directly opposite St Johannis. ⑤.

Parkhotel, Uelzener Str. 27 (☎0 41 31/4 11 25, fax 40 71 41). Occupies a villa in a quiet location near the Salztherme. ⑤.

Scheffler, Bardowicker Str. 7 (☎0 41 31/2 00 80, fax 20 08 20, *www.hotel-scheffler.de*). Long-established hotel and restaurant in a seventeenth-century half-timbered house just off the Markt. ⑥.

Zum Heidkrug, Am Berge 5 (☎0 41 31/2 41 60, fax 24 16 20). Small hotel in a brick Gothic mansion, run as an adjunct to the town's leading Italian restaurant. ⑤.

The Town

Today, Lüneburg is far from being the museum piece it might appear. Its population almost doubled in 1945 as a result of an influx of refugees from the confiscated Eastern Territories, and it has again become a lively regional centre.

The Markt

The **Markt** is the focus of the town's commercial life, particularly on Wednesdays and Saturdays, when markets are held. In the middle of the square is the sixteenth-century **Lunabrunnen**, a bronze fountain with a statuette of the moon goddess Luna, after whom Lüneburg is supposedly named.

The grandiose **Rathaus** (guided tours Tues–Sun at 11am, 12.30pm & 3pm; DM6/€3) occupies the west side of the Markt. Its Baroque facade is a mere frontispiece to the largest and most impressive medieval town hall in Germany. The **Grosser Ratssaal**, the old council chamber, is the most famous part. Originally from the fourteenth century, it was embellished a hundred years later with richly traceried windows bearing stained-glass portraits of nine great heroes. Another century later, it received its impressive wall and ceiling decoration, which included a scene of *The Last Judgement* in honour of its new function as the court of justice. Other highlights include the tiny **Körkammer**, where the burgomasters (four of whom are depicted in the windows) were elected, and the **Fürstensaal**, the former dance hall, with its fifteenth-century candelabra made from stags' antlers and seventeenth-century portraits of the local dukes. However, the finest room of all is the **Grosse Ratsstube**, which ranks as one of Germany's most important Renaissance interiors thanks to the pyrotechnic woodwork – benches, panelling and, most notably, the doorways – carved by Albert von Soest. At the end of the tour, you're allowed to linger over the municipal silverware, by far the finest collection in Germany. Unfortunately, what you see here are only replicas: the originals are now in the Kunstgewerbemuseum in Berlin.

Am Sande and St Johannis

Lüneburg's largest square is the elongated **Am Sande**, whose name reflects the fact that it was laid out on a sandy marsh. It lies almost due south of the Markt, and is reached along the partly pedestrianized Bäckerstrasse. On the way, take a peek inside the late sixteenth-century **Rathsapotheke**, whose orderly interior forms a perfect complement to the elaborate gable and portal outside. Am Sande itself has the finest group of burghers' mansions in town, illustrating the seemingly inexhaustible variations the local builders worked on the theme of the brick gable. The **Schwarzes Haus** (Black House) – so called from the colour of its glazed brickwork – is particularly impressive. Situated on the west side of the square, it was formerly an inn and brewery, and is now the seat of the local chamber of commerce.

The opposite end of Am Sande is closed off by the impressively large brick church of **St Johannis**. This was begun in the thirteenth century, but the tall tower (which leans a couple of metres out of true) was only erected in the early fifteenth century. The **organ** is celebrated – the case and some of the pipework are early eighteenth century, but it incorporates much of its mid-sixteenth-century predecessor, one of the oldest instruments in the country. It can be heard briefly each Friday at 5.30pm; from July to October, longer recitals are given on Tuesdays at 8pm. Almost equally precious is the **high altar**, a co-operative work by several fifteenth-century artists from Hamburg and Lübeck. Its reverse side, illustrating the lives of SS John the Baptist, Cecilia, George and Ursula, was painted by Hinrik Funhof with a delicacy worthy of comparison with the great Flemish masters of the period. Two more notable retables are housed in the chapels to either side; look out also for the *Madonna and Child* candelabrum in the north aisle, which has a marked similarity to those in the Rathaus.

The museums

From the rear of St Johannis, follow the River Ilmenau south for a couple of minutes, and cross over by Wandrahmstrasse, on which stand an old mill and the **Museum für das Fürstentum Lüneburg** (Tues–Fri 10am–4pm, Sat & Sun 11am–5pm; DM4/€2). This features a good collection of medieval artefacts, including the tomb of a local duke, along with the predictable folklore and local history displays. The most intriguing exhibit is a copy of the once-famous thirteenth-century map of the world from the near-by convent of Ebstorf; the original was destroyed in a bombing raid on Hannover.

Just off the western end of Am Sande, at Heiligengeiststr. 39, the **Kronen-Brauerei-Museum** (Tues–Sun 1–4.30pm; free) has been set up in the former premises of the only brewery left out of the eighty the town once had. A free English leaflet guides you round the four floors of equipment, enabling you to see every stage of the traditional beer-making process. The historic lobby and staircase of the front house are also open to view, and there's a permanent exhibition of old drinking vessels. You can end your tour in suitable style by enjoying the products of the modern brewery – the smooth *Lüneburger Pils* and the very dry *Moravia Pils* – in the beer hall, complete with garden.

Immediately to the rear, at Ritterstr. 10, is the **Ostpreussisches Landesmuseum** (Tues–Sun 10am–5pm; DM3/€1.50), which owes its existence to Lüneburg's large influx of refugees from the Baltic state of East Prussia, which in prewar years was the most far-flung part of Germany. In 1945, it was divided horizontally along the middle, with the southerly half allocated to Poland (to whom the whole territory had once belonged), while the remainder, including the capital city of Königsberg (which was renamed Kaliningrad), was made a province of Russia. The museum illustrates East Prussian history from the German viewpoint, in the process showing why bitterness at the Russian annexation remains so acute.

The rest of the Altstadt

At the edge of the Altstadt, several minutes' walk west of the Ostpreussisches Landesmuseum, is the site of the old saltworks. The surviving installations have been turned into the **Deutsches Salzmuseum** (Mon–Fri 9/10am–5pm, Sat & Sun 10am–5pm; DM6/€3), which tells you everything you are ever likely to want to know about the extraction, history, geology and economics of salt. In addition, you get to see the city's sole surviving saltpan, which is put into production each day in summer at

3pm. Continuing southwards, you come to the **Kurzentrum**, a modern spa complex set in an extensive park. The **Salztherme** (Mon–Sat 10am–11pm, Sun 8am–9pm), a thermal bathing complex, forms the centrepiece (DM13/€6.50 for 2hr, DM18/€9 for 4hr, DM22/€11 for a day-ticket).

In the opposite direction from the Salzmuseum is **St Michael**, another brick Gothic hall church, and the original home of the celebrated *Goldene Tafel* treasures, which are now divided between the Kestner-Museum and Landesgalerie in Hannover (see pp.663 & 664). It stands on J.S.-Bach-Platz, which is so named because the great composer was a pupil at the school established in the monastic buildings after secularization. From here, you can ascend **Kalkberg**, the low-lying hill to the west for a fine long-range view over Lüneburg and its surroundings. The best route back to the Markt is via Auf dem Meere, a street lined with old craftsmen's houses.

Following Bardowicker Strasse north from the Markt, you come to the fifteenth-century parish church of **St Nicolai**, where the sailors and artisans used to worship,. which is noted for its vertiginous, star-vaulted interior. Its **tower** (May–Sept daily at 3pm; DM2), a neo-Gothic replacement of the original, can be ascended for a view over the city. The old port or **Wasserviertel** lies just to the east along Lüner Strasse. With its peaceful riverside setting, trees, bridges, mills and other imperious buildings, it's the most evocative spot in town, creating a picture about as far removed from a modern-day harbour as it is possible to imagine. Formerly a herring warehouse, the **Altes Kaufhaus** had to be rebuilt after a fire in 1959, but still has its cheery Baroque facade. Opposite is the **Alte Krane** (old crane), which received its present form in the 1790s, though it dates back at least as far as the fourteenth century.

Kloster Lüne

Kloster Lüne (guided tours April to mid-Oct Mon–Sat 10am–12.30pm & 2.30–5pm, Sun 11.30am–5pm; DM5/€2.50, or DM7/€3.50 combined ticket with the Textilmuseum) lies 2km northeast of the Wasserviertel. The present complex dates largely from the late fourteenth and early fifteenth centuries, though the half-timbered outbuildings were added later. It became a Protestant convent at the Reformation, and has remained so to this day. Among the highlights of the tour are the church, with its intricately carved six-teenth-century altar and seventeenth-century organ, the frescoed winter refectory, the simple pre-Reformation cells and their painted Baroque equivalents from a few centuries later. The **Textilmuseum** (same times; DM5/€2.50, or DM7/€3.50 combined ticket with Kloster Lüne) displays under ultra-modern lighting conditions an astonishing col-lection of textiles, most of which were probably woven in the convent. Especially notable are the white embroideries from the thirteenth and fourteenth centuries, and the three huge, colourful tapestries from the early years of the sixteenth.

Eating and drinking

Some of the best restaurants are in the hotels, but there are plenty of other enticing places to eat and drink.

Camus, Am Sande 30. Does breakfasts until well into the afternoon, as well as pizzas cooked in a wood oven, meats grilled on lava stones and various vegetarian and bistro-type dishes.

Dialog, Am Stintmarkt 12. One of a row of lively waterfront pubs which are particularly attractive in summer, when tables are placed outside.

Kloster-Krug, Am Domänenhof 1. Gaststätte in a sixteenth-century timber-framed building direct-ly opposite Kloster Lüne.

Kronen-Brauhaus, Heiligengeiststr. 39. The beer hall-cum-restaurant of the local brewery, offer-ing typical North German cuisine.

Ratskeller, Am Markt 1. In the cellars of the Rathaus, fairly pricey but with a more imaginative menu than most of its counterparts in other German cities.

Stadtcafé, Untere Schrangenstr. 4. Good traditional café in a fine old town house.
Zum Alten Brauhaus, Groppengiesserstr. 11. Another fine Gaststätte, decked out in traditional style.

The Lüneburg Heath

Partly wooded, but mainly uncultivated open heathland, the **Lüneburg Heath** (Lüneburger Heide) between Lüneburg and Celle is grazed by large flocks of Heidschnucken, goaty-sheep descended from the Corsican mouflon. In late August the heather erupts in deep purple swathes, adding a mass of colour to the heath's otherwise subtle palette. Picturesque villages, with timber and brick houses and churches, are also dotted around, forming an idyllic backdrop for festivals, the annual coronation of the queen of the heath and shepherds who still wear their traditional green outfits. It was here, on May 4, 1945, that Field Marshal Montgomery received the unconditional German surrender. British troops still exercise on the heath, though their presence has been much reduced in recent years. This is one part of Germany where a car or bike is a distinct advantage, as public transport to and within the area is fiddly, serving the northern part of the heath from Lüneburg, the southern from Celle.

The Naturschutzpark Lüneburger Heide

The **Naturschutzpark Lüneburger Heide** is a 200-square-kilometre nature reserve in the northwest of the region, where the heathland and villages are least changed. Motor traffic is forbidden in much of this park, but there are networks of footpaths and cycle paths (renting a bike is easy in most towns) and horse-riding is another possibility. Bees buzz over the heather, and the local honey is renowned – as are the potatoes, oddly enough. Places to stay (mostly at low rates) abound, so you can normally rely on finding **accommodation** as you go, particularly as most towns have a tourist office.

The gateway to the park is the town of **SOLTAU**, a junction of several minor rail lines, including one from Hannover and another from Uelzen on the main line from Lüneburg to Celle. Buses run to **UNDELOH**, an attractive village in the heart of the park which boasts a half-timbered church going back to the twelfth century, and which has some two dozen hotels and pensions. From Undeloh, you can walk 4km south to ultra-quaint **WILSEDE**, along a road closed to traffic. An old farmhouse, **Dat Ole Huss** (Tues–Sun 10am–5pm; DM4/€2), has been opened as a museum illustrating the ways of the past. You can also climb up northern Germany's highest hill, the 169-metre **Wilseder Berg**, for all-round views of the heath. Because of their abundant accommodation, two other possible bases for exploring the area are the health resorts of **EGESTORF**, which lies just outside the western fringe of the park, and **BISPINGEN**, which is beyond the southern boundary. The latter is a particularly pretty village with a fourteenth-century church; it also has a **youth hostel**, at Töpinger Str. 42 (☎0 51 94/23 75, fax 0 51 94/77 43; DM22/€11 or DM27/€13.50).

Walsrode

The most popular destination in the Lüneburg Heath is **WALSRODE**, which lies on the direct rail line between Soltau and Hannover; it can be reached from Verden by bus, cycle path or by the very occasional excursion trains run on a privately owned rail line formerly used for the transportation of potash. The town itself is of scant appeal, but 3km north of the centre is the **Vogelpark Walsrode** (daily: March–Oct 9am–7pm; Nov–Feb 10am–4pm; *www.vogelpark-walsrode.de*; DM20/€10), with over five thousand indigenous and exotic birds representing some of the 850 different species on view in a beautifully manicured park which is the largest of its type in the world. There's a choice of three café-restaurants, and there's also a **hotel**, *Luisenhöhe* (☎0 51 61/9 86 20; ⑥).

Bergen

On the main road between Soltau and Celle is **BERGEN**, which has the misfortune to have its name immortalized in the name of one of the most infamous Nazi concentration camps, the **Konzentratsionslager Bergen-Belsen** (daily 10am–6pm; free), though this lies some 6km southwest of the town. Some fifty thousand people died there, many as a result of starvation and disease (this was the fate of the young diarist Anne Frank), or by the personal whim of the notorious camp commandant, Josef Kramer, the "Beast of Belsen". When the camp was liberated some thirteen thousand unburied bodies were found lying in heaps, and many of the thirty thousand survivors were on the point of death. The film made of the camp's liberation, which can be seen in the documentation centre, still appals: a number of Germans, who were forced to watch it and realize the atrocities that had been carried out in their name, subsequently committed suicide. In Britain the film was shown in every cinema in the country, revealing the horror of the "Final Solution" to the public for the first time. The camp buildings themselves were destroyed at the end of the war by the British, for fear of a typhus outbreak, but the mass graves remain, and a visit to the site of such horror is deeply disturbing. By **car**, the camp is 22km northwest of Celle on the B3; turn left when you reach Bergen. It's also reachable by turning off the main E4 route between Hannover and Hamburg at the Soltau-Süd junction. There up to three direct **buses** a day from Celle (but check locally, as this is subject to change), making it a feasible excursion, albeit one that will take up most of the day.

Because of the relative difficulty of access by public transport, it may be worth spending the night in Bergen. The town centre has a modest attraction of its own in the **Freilichtmuseum** (Mon–Thurs 9.30am–noon & 3–5pm, Fri 9.30am–noon; DM4/€2) at Am Friedenplatz 7, which brings together a number of old farm buildings from throughout the region. There's also a reasonable supply of accommodation, including **private rooms** (②–③) and **hotels** such as *Zum Schwan*, Bahnhofstr. 16 (☎0 50 51/51 51; ④), and *Kohlmann*, Lukenstr. 4–6 (☎0 50 51/9 87 60; ④–⑥).

Wienhausen

At the extreme southeastern edge of the Lüneburg heath, some 10km from Celle, to which it's connected by fairly regular buses, lies **WIENHAUSEN**, a village of half-timbered houses clustered around a remarkable **Kloster** (guided tours April to mid-Oct Mon–Sat at 10am, 11am, 2pm, 3pm, 4pm & 5pm, Sun at noon, 1pm, 2pm, 3pm, 4pm & 5pm; DM6/€3). Founded in 1231 by Agnes von Meissen, daughter-in-law of Henry the Lion, the convent became Protestant at the Reformation, and is still in use today. The severity of the brick buildings stands in contrast to the walls of the **nuns' chancel**, which are covered with a heavily restored cycle of fourteenth-century **frescoes** illustrating the life of Christ and the legend of the Holy Cross, along with secular subjects. In the centre of the chancel is a wooden **Holy Sepulchre**, complete with a figure of the dead Christ, which dates from the late thirteenth century.

The Kloster's most valuable treasures are its **tapestries**. Woven by the nuns in the fourteenth and fifteenth centuries, they rank among the greatest ever made. Also on view are some intriguing excavations, which include the implements used to weave the tapestries and the spectacles worn by their creators. For conservation reasons, the display is only open to the public for two weeks immediately after Whitsun each year (when the entry charge is raised to DM12/€6); check with the tourist office in Celle for the exact dates.

Celle

Despite being roughly the same size, having a closely connected history, and lying no more than 90km apart at opposite ends of the Lüneburg Heath, **CELLE** and Lüneburg seem to have come from different worlds. Celle has none of the massive brickwork public buildings which define the skyline of the Hanseatic trading cities of the north. For long a ducal Residenzstadt, it marks the transition to the timber-framed buildings so characteristic of central Germany. Like Lüneburg, it has been spared from serious war damage, and its centre retains whole streets of intact historic houses.

Arrival, information and accommodation

Celle's **Hauptbahnhof** is ten minutes' walk west of the town centre along Bahnhofstrasse. The **tourist office** (April–Oct Mon–Fri 9am–7pm, Sat 10am–4pm, Sun 11am–2pm; Nov–March Mon–Fri 9am–5pm, Sat 10am–1pm; ☎0 51 41/12 12, fax 1 24 59, *www.celle.de*) is in the Rathaus, Markt 14–16.

Celle has a particularly enticing range of **hotels**, many in wonderful old buildings. Alternatively, there's a **youth hostel** at Weghausstr. 2 (☎0 51 41/5 32 08, fax 5 30 05; DM22/€11 or DM27/€13.50); turn left on leaving the Hauptbahnhof and continue straight ahead for about 2km, or take bus #3. The **campsite**, *Silbersee* (☎0 51 41/3 12 23), is in Vorwerk, a suburb at the northern end of town, close to the terminus of bus #6.

Hotels

Am Landgestüt, Landgestütstr. 1 (☎0 51 41/21 72 19, fax 2 39 77). The cheapest hotel in Celle, with a decent location in a whitewashed house on a quiet street opposite the Landgestüt. ④.

Am Stadtgraben, Fritzenwiese 20–22 (☎0 51 41/10 91, fax 2 40 82). Luxury small hotel in an early twentieth-century villa containing many antiques. ⑧.

Celler Hof, Stechbahn 11 (☎0 51 41/2 0 11 40, fax 20 11 20, *www.residenzhotels.de*). Modernized Baroque palace in the handiest of settings directly across from the Schloss. ⑥–⑨.

Fürstenhof, Hannoversche Str. 55–56 (☎0 51 41/20 10; fax 20 11 20, *www.fuerstenhof.de*). Celle's most prestigious hotel occupies a seventeenth-century nobleman's palace a short distance south of the Altstadt. Its main restaurant, *Endtenfang*, is one of the best (and most expensive) in northern Germany; *Palio*, which serves Italian cuisine, is altogether more affordable. ⑧–⑨.

St Georg, St-Georg-Str. 25–27 (☎0 51 41/21 05 13, fax 21 77 25, *www.hotel-st-georg.de*). Another seventeenth-century building, this time a half-timbered house at the eastern edge of the centre. ⑥.

Schifferkrug, Speicherstr. 9 (☎0 51 41/70 15, fax 63 50). Medium-priced hotel with a particularly fine restaurant, midway between the Hauptbahnhof and the Schloss. ⑤.

Utspann, Im Kreise 13 (☎0 51 41/9 27 20, fax 92 72 52). Yet another restored half-timbered house, this time in the old Jewish quarter, with a good wine bar-restaurant. ⑥–⑧.

The Town

The Schloss dominates the town, much as it has always done, and the streets of the Altstadt, which lies to the east, run towards it with a gesture of subservience. These contain Celle's other outstanding feature, an array of 480 **half-timbered buildings**, many of which have been adapted successfully to commercial use.

The Schloss

Originally built in the late thirteenth century, the **Schloss** (guided tours April–Oct Tues–Sun at 10am, 11am, noon, 1pm, 2pm, 3pm & 4pm; Nov–March Tues–Sun at 11am & 3pm; DM5/€2.50) became the main residence of the dukes of Braunschweig-Lüneburg in 1371, when the independently minded burghers of Lüneburg flexed their collective muscle and chucked out their feudal overlords. In 1530, the building was completely rebuilt in the Renaissance style and the present whitewashed exterior, with its idiosyncratic corner towers, decorative gable and lofty, confined courtyard, dates almost entirely from this period.

Sole survivor of the medieval castle, and the highlight of the tour, is the **Schlosskapelle**, which was cleverly incorporated into the southeastern tower facing the town, its pointed Gothic windows being the only giveaway as to its presence there. Its architectural simplicity was obscured in the second half of the sixteenth century by an integrated programme of Mannerist decoration that's still stunningly fresh and vibrant. The cycle of 76 paintings, commissioned from the Antwerp artist **Marten de Vos** (once an assistant to Tintoretto in Venice), forms a complete illustrated Bible, in accordance with the new Protestant doctrines. The two galleries are adorned with portrait sculptures of Old and New Testament figures, and wacky pendants of varying shapes and sizes hang from the vault. Both the pulpit, with beautiful reliefs of the Passion, and the organ, with painted shutters, are intrinsic parts of the scheme.

Early in the eighteenth century the Duchy of Lüneburg was reunited with Hannover (which had split off the previous century) when Sophie Dorothea, daughter of the last duke of Lüneburg, married the future George I of Britain. Thereafter, Celle was no more than the second-string German residence of the Hanoverian dynasty, and a place where those who had fallen from grace could readily be dumped. In the 1770s the Schloss became home for a few years to an exiled queen, Caroline Mathilde of Denmark, who was banished following an indiscretion with a courtier. Her suite of rooms, the **Caroline-Mathilde-Räume** (Tues–Sun 10am–4.30pm; DM4/€2 including Bomann-Museum), contains a museum of the history of the Kingdom of Hannover.

An especially pleasant way to sneak a look inside other parts of the Schloss is to go to a performance at the **Schlosstheater** – dating back to 1674, it's the oldest one in Germany to have a resident company. Concerts and plays are performed throughout the year, except during July and August. Tickets and information are available from the box office in the Rathaus, Markt 14–16 (☎0 51 41/1 27 13, *www.schlosstheater-celle.de*). Unfortunately, you're unlikely to get near the handsome Baroque auditorium unless you're attending a performance.

The Altstadt

Every street in the Altstadt is a visual treat, and well worth including in a gentle stroll. The place to begin is Stechbahn (formerly a yard used for tournaments) which runs from the centre of Schlossplatz. Opposite the early sixteenth-century court pharmacy, the **Löwenapothek**, is the Gothic **Stadtkirche**, whose **tower** (April–Oct Tues–Sat 10am–noon & 3–4pm; DM2/€1), which was added as recently as 1913, commands the best view of the town. A trumpeter plays a chorale from here at 6.30am and 6.30pm every day. The interior of the church was transformed in the late seventeenth century by the addition of the Italianate stuccowork and painted galleries, another complete illustrated Bible. A whole series of elaborate Gothic, Renaissance and Baroque **tombs** of the local dukes line the walls of the chancel. Behind the Stadtkirche is the **Rathaus**, whose fourteenth-century Ratskeller is the oldest restaurant in northern Germany. Most of the building, however, is in the carefree Weser Renaissance style, and is distinguished by two beautifully contrasted oriel windows: one at street level, the other an extension of a gable.

The most outstanding half-timbered house in Celle is the **Hoppener Haus** at the corner of Rundestrasse and Poststrasse. Built for a courtier in 1532, it's richly carved with allegorical figures, monsters, scrollwork and scenes of rural life. The oldest dated house, at Am Heiligen Kreuz 26, states that it was built in 1526, though Neue Str. 32 (originally fifteenth century but with a Renaissance oriel) has the best claim to be regarded as the most venerable house in town. Look out for the corner of Nordwall and Bergstrasse, where someone built their home on top of a piece of the original city wall.

Among later Baroque stone buildings is the **Stechinellihaus** on Grosser Plan, named after an influential Italian architect and courtier who lived in a house on this site.

The **Bomann-Museum** (Tues–Sun 10am–5pm; DM4/€2 including Caroline-Mathilde-Räume), in a grandiose Jugendstil building at the corner of Schlossplatz and Stechbahn, is above average for a local collection. Its displays on regional trades, history and folklore feature several reconstructed farmhouses and (in the courtyard) a half-timbered house fully furnished in the Biedermeier style.

The rest of the town
Just outside the eastern edge of the Altstadt is the old ghetto, though the colourful Baroque half-timbered houses themselves hardly offer any clue to the area's former status. Within one of these houses, Im Kreise 24, is the **Synagoge** (Tues–Thurs 3–5pm, Fri 9–11am, Sun 11am–1pm). Its decoration was destroyed on *Kristallnacht*, but, most unusually, it wasn't burned down. After the war it was well restored, and it stands today as one of the very few historic Jewish temples left in Germany.

Not far from here, bounding the southern side of the Altstadt, is the **Französischer Garten** (French Garden), which was laid out in the seventeenth century and later adapted in the informal English manner. Beyond is the **Ludwigskirche**, a Neoclassical church built by local architects in close imitation of the style of Karl Friedrich Schinkel, who did so much to define the appearance of Berlin. The interior is a gem – a miniature, updated version of the columned basilicas of the Romans.

To the south, down Breite Strasse, is the **Niedersächsisches Landgestüt** (Lower Saxon Stud Farm), which was founded by King George II in 1735. It can be visited outside the season, when the 250 or so stallions are put out to stud (mid-July to mid-Feb Mon–Fri 8.30–11.30am & 3–4.30pm; free), but the best time to come is during the big autumn **festival**, the highlight of Celle's social calendar. Held on the last Sunday in September and the first in October (or, on occasions, the last two in Sept), plus the Wednesday preceding these, each programme lasts for three hours, and features a parade of the stallions, as well as a quadrille performed by coaches and ten.

Eating and drinking

As well as the restaurants in the hotels above, there are plenty of other good places to eat and drink in Celle.

Bier-Akademie, Weisser Wall 6. Traditional beer hall-cum-restaurant, with summer garden.

Café Kraatz, Piltzergasse 4–5. One of several good cafés in the Altstadt, particularly recommended for its cakes.

Café Kraemer, Stechbahn 7. Another fine coffee house, in a half-timbered building opposite the Stadtkirche.

Congress Union, Thaerplatz 1. Classy, municipally owned restaurant in a custom-built Jugendstil building with a winter garden. Bargain lunchtime menus and a mouth-watering cold table.

Hannen-Fass, Am Heiligen Kreuz 5. Perhaps the liveliest of the Altstadt pubs.

Ratskeller, Markt 14. Famous old cellar restaurant, among the best (and priciest) of its ilk in Germany.

Tiroler Stub'n, Altenoellertorstr. 9. As a change from standard German fare, this offers Austrian and Swiss specialities.

Hannover (Hanover)

HANNOVER, which lies some 50km southwest of Celle, was something of a late developer, only coming to the fore in the second half of the seventeenth century. Subsequently, it had the benefit of a long special relationship with Britain (see box on p.661), thanks to a quirk of fate which resulted in its ruling dynasty inheriting the British throne, and from

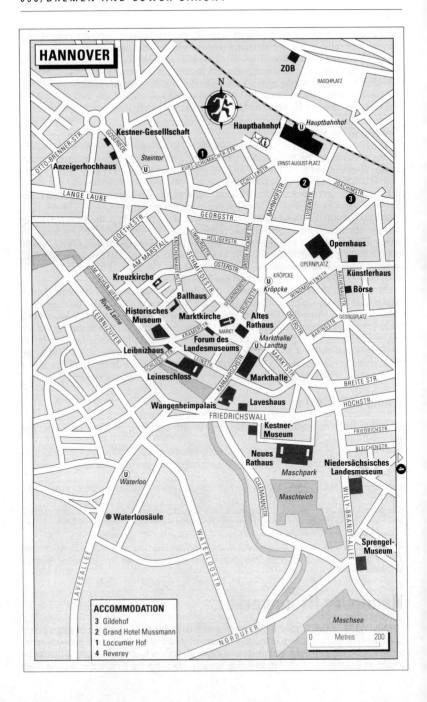

HANNOVER

ZOB

RASCHPLATZ

Kestner-Gesellllschaft

Hauptbahnhof   *Hauptbahnhof*

Anzeigerhochhaus   *Steintor*

OTTO-BRENNER-STR.   GOSERIEDE

LANGE LAUBE

ERNST-AUGUST-PLATZ

KURT-SCHUMACHER-STR.

GEORGSTR.

SCHILLERSTR.

BAHNHOFSTR.

LUISENSTR.

JOACHIMSTR.

HEILIGERSTR.

LIMBURGSTR.

KNOCHENHAUERSTR.

SCHMIEDESTR.

OSTERSTR.

GROSSE PACKHOF STR.

Opernhaus

OPERNPLATZ

Künstlerhaus

Börse

KRÖPCKE

Kröpcke

WINDMÜHLENSTR.

RATHENAUSTR.

GEORGSPLATZ

Kreuzkirche

Ballhaus

Historisches Museum

Marktkirche

Altes Rathaus

River Leine   LEIBNIZUFER   AM HOHEN UFER

Leibnizhaus

Forum des Landesmuseums

MARKT

Markthalle/ Landtag

OSTERSTR.

BARINSTR.

SELWINDERSTR.

GRUPENSTR.

KRAMERSTR.

SCHLOSS-STR.

LEINSTR.

MARKTSTR.

BREITE STR.

Leineschloss

Markthalle

HOCHSTR.

Wangenheimpalais

KARMARSCHSTR.

Laveshaus

FRIEDRICHSWALL

FRIEDRICHSTR.

Kestner-Museum

BLEICHENSTR.

Neues Rathaus

Maschpark

Niedersächsisches Landesmuseum

Waterloo

Maschteich

CULEMANNSTR.

WILLY-BRANDT-ALLEE

Waterloosäule

Sprengel-Museum

LAVESALLEE

WATERLOOSTR.

Maschsee

NORDUFER

ACCOMMODATION

3 Gildehof
2 Grand Hotel Mussmann
1 Loccumer Hof
4 Reverey

0   Metres   200

1815 to 1866 it was also a **royal capital city** in its own right. This status was suddenly lost when it fell victim to the expansionist policies of Prussia, and it was reduced to a marginal role until 1946, when it returned to prominence as capital of the new Land of Lower Saxony. Hannover's reputation as a dynamic, thrusting business centre was given a major boost when it was chosen to host **EXPO 2000**, the first World Exposition ever held in Germany, and the city hopes to profit from the legacy of this for many years to come.

Hannover suffers from the fact that it does not fit most people's perception of what a major historical metropolis should be like. It lacks a dominant architectural landmark, such as a great cathedral, castle or palace, and does not even have an obvious main thoroughfare or a grand public square. What it does have are really magnificent **gardens**. Those at Herrenhausen rank among the most impressive in Europe, preserving their spectacular original Baroque features almost intact. They now have a fitting modern complement in the EXPO site, which seem sure to become an important permanent tourist attraction. As the city also has a number of first-class **museums** and a vibrant cultural scene, it well warrants a visit of a couple of days at least.

Arrival, information and accommodation

Hannover's **Hauptbahnhof**, which preserves its nineteenth-century facade but is otherwise the most modern in the country, having been given an expensive makeover prior to EXPO 2000, is right in the centre of town; to the rear lies the **bus station** for

---

EXPO 2000

EXPO 2000, which attracted over eighteen million visitors (forty million were originally anticipated), was not only the first World Exposition to be held on German soil, but also the first to utilize an existing trade fair site, the 170-hectare **Messegelände** in the southeast of the city. This can be reached by mainline or S-Bahn train to Bahnhof Messe/Laatzen; alternatively U-Bahn #6 and #16 go to the east entrance, #8 and #18 to the north entrance. There were several other key differences from previous World Expositions: all participants were required to adhere to the single theme of "Mankind, Nature, Technology: A New World Arising"; the main event was accompanied by no fewer than 770 separate projects all around the world; international non-governmental organizations as well as individual countries were permitted to have a presence; and all pavilions had to use ecological construction techniques and reusable materials.

A number of the EXPO structures have already been removed from the site and re-located elsewhere. Far more still remain *in situ*, and although the exact future of many is still under discussion, it seems almost certain that the Messegelände will be preserved as a permanent showcase of international turn-of-the-millennium architecture. Whether or not any of the buildings will assume the same iconic status as previous World Fair showpieces – such as the Eiffel Tower in Paris and the Atomium in Brussels – remains to be seen. One possible candidate is Deutsche Post's **Postbox**, which at 46.5m in height is by far the largest post box in the world, complete with an observation platform offering a grandstand view of the grounds. Among the **national pavilions**, that of Bhutan, in the form of a traditional Buddhist temple, and of the United Arab Emirates, which imitated the appearance of a desert fort, imparted particularly exotic touches, and were correspondingly popular with visitors. The Venezuelan pavilion, with its roof of ten-metre-long petals which opened when the sun shone and closed when it threatened to rain, cleverly symbolized a living plant in a tropical forest; equally innovative was the pavilion of the Netherlands, which gained the nickname of the "Eco-Sandwich" because of the re-creations of five very different Dutch landscapes on each of its levels. Germany's pavilion, which has a prominent position on the central square, **EXPO-Plaza**, is an inward-curving transparent glass construction which is earmarked to play a prominent part in the future business and cultural life of Hannover.

long-distance routes. The **airport** is 10km northwest of the city and has a regular link to the Hauptbahnhof by S-Bahn #5.

Just outside the Hauptbahnhof, at Ernst-August-Platz 2, is the **tourist office** (Mon–Fri 9am–7pm, Sat 9.30am–3pm; ☎05 11/16 84 97 00, fax 16 84 97 07, *www.hannover.de*). Among the brochures you can pick up is *The Red Thread*, a horribly chatty but very useful booklet guiding visitors round the main sights via a painted red line which runs along the pavements, across roads and down subways.

There are only two fares on the city's **public transport** network, but if making more than one normal journey it is cost-effective to invest in a **day-ticket**, which costs DM6/€3 per person and DM12/€6 for a group ticket, allowing up to five people to travel together. Alternatively, there's the **HannoverCard**, which also includes entry to all the museums and costs DM14/€7 for one day, DM23/€11.50 for three days. Some trams stop on Ernst-August-Platz, while others go underground to form the U-Bahn in the city centre, with stops at the Hauptbahnhof and Kröpcke. Among the features of the city centre are the tram and bus stops decorated by contemporary artists.

Even before EXPO 2000, Hannover was well established as a flourishing centre of the lucrative trade fair industry (the April *Messe* is the largest in Europe). As a result, its hoteliers can afford to charge fancy prices, though a few reasonably priced establishments do exist. The tourist office charges a stinging DM10/€5 for its room-finding service. Its Web site contains detailed descriptions of many of the hotels.

Hotels

Am Funkturm, Hallerstr. 34 (☎05 11/3 39 80, fax 3 39 81 11). One of the more reasonably priced upmarket options, situated a few minutes' walk from the rear of the Hauptbahnhof. Also has an excellent Italian restaurant, *Milano*. ⑨–⑨.

Atlanta, Hinüberstr. 1 (☎05 11/3 38 60, fax 34 59 28). Good-quality hotel just to the east of the Hauptbahnhof, on the opposite side of the tracks from the city centre. ⑥–⑨.

Eden, Waldhausenstr. 30 (☎05 11/84 83 10, fax 8 48 31 44). Nicely furnished villa in the Waldhausen district south of the centre. With a good buffet breakfast included in the room price, it ranks as one of the best bargains in Hannover. Take U-Bahn #1, #2 or #8 to Döhrener Turm. ④.

Feuchers Lila Kranz, Berliner Allee 33 (☎05 11/85 89 21, fax 85 43 83). Although it has only five rooms, this is one of the city's best-known hotels, particularly for its restaurant, which offers creative local and international cooking and a huge wine list. ⑦.

Flora, Heinrichstr. 36 (☎05 11/38 39 10, fax 38 39 91 91). Located about a ten-minute walk northeast of the Hauptbahnhof, this Oststadt hotel has some of the lowest rates in central Hannover. ④–⑦.

Georgenhof, Herrenhäuser Kirchweg 20 (☎05 11/70 22 44, fax 70 85 59, *www.romantik.de*). Undoubtedly the most atmospheric place to stay in Hannover, this country-house hotel, part of the Romantik chain, is set in its own private park in the Nordstadt, not far from Herrenhausen. Its nationally renowned restaurant, *Stern*, has a very expensive à la carte menu, but also does set lunches at less than exhorbitant prices. ⑦.

Gildehof, Joachimstr. 6 (☎05 11/36 36 80, fax 30 66 44). Medium-priced hotel with restaurant, just a stone's throw from the Hauptbahnhof. ⑨.

Grand Hotel Mussman, Ernst-August-Platz 7 (☎05 11/3 65 60, fax 3 65 61 45). Fine old station hotel. ⑦–⑨.

Landhaus Ammann, Hildesheimer Str. 185, Waldenhausen (☎05 11/83 08 18, fax 8 43 77 49). Set in its own grounds just east of the Maschsee, this is another country-house style hotel, and again has a renowned gourmet restaurant. Take U-Bahn #1, #2 or #8 to Döhrener Turm. ⑨.

Loccumer Hof, Kurt-Schumacher-Str. 16 (☎05 11/1 26 40, fax 13 11 92). Classy establishment with equally good restaurant, conveniently close to the Hauptbahnhof. ⑦.

Reverey, Aegidiendamm 8 (☎ & fax 05 11/88 37 11). Medium-priced hotel just beyond the southeastern fringe of the Altstadt, handy for the Maschpark and the museums. ⑥.

Wülfeler, Hildesheimer Str. 380, Wülfel (☎05 11/86 50 86, fax 87 60 09). Situated in a southern suburb, and reached by U-Bahn #1 or #2 to Dorfstrasse, this is the hotel, Gaststätte and beer garden of the eponymous brewery, the third largest in Hannover. ③–⑧.

Hostels

Jugendherberge Hannover, Ferdinand-Wilhelm-Fricke-Weg 1 (☎05 11/1 31 76 74, fax 1 85 55). Hannover's youth hostel is 2km southwest of the centre: take U-Bahn #3 or #7 to Fischerhof, from where it's a five-minute walk to the left over the bridge. Alongside is a campsite. DM27/€13.50 or DM32/€16.

Naturfreundehaus in der Eilenriede, Hermann-Bahlsen-Allee 8 (☎05 11/69 14 93, fax 69 06 52). A good location on the edge of the wooded Eilenriede park; take U-Bahn #3 or #7 to Spannhagenstrasse. Beds in doubles or triples DM35/€17.50 per person.

The city centre

Hannover has had to reconstruct itself after being almost totally demolished by World War II bombing. The northern part of the city centre is a vast shopping area of mostly pedestrianized streets and arcades. Further south is the modest-sized Altstadt, beyond which is the inner ring road, the best museums and an attractive green belt.

HANOVERIAN HISTORY AND THE BRITISH CONNECTION

In the seventeenth century, the territories of the Welf House of Braunschweig-Lüneburg were split up, and the new Duchy of Braunschweig-Calenberg came into being. This was commonly known as **Hannover**, after the old Hanseatic market and brewing town which was its principal city. A new summer residence for the court was slowly laid out at the village of Höringehusen, a few kilometres from Hannover's Altstadt.

Ernst August, who acceded to the duchy in 1679, was a man of high ambition. He charged Gottfried Wilhelm Leibniz, the great philosopher and scientist who served as librarian and historian to the Welfs for forty years, with the task of proving that the House was descended from the Italian Este family. The successful conclusion of this entitled the duke to claim a new Electorate in the Holy Roman Empire, which was formally bestowed in 1692. Even more significant was Ernst August's marriage to **Sophie von der Pfalz**, daughter of Elizabeth Stuart, the "Winter Queen" (see p.360). In 1701, the English parliament passed the Act of Settlement, in order to cut off the Catholic "Old Pretender" and his heirs and ensure the continuation of a Protestant monarchy. Sophie was named as next in line to the throne after Princess (later Queen) Anne. In the event, Sophie died just before Anne in 1714, and her son **Georg Ludwig** became King George I of Great Britain and Ireland, the Act of Settlement having formed part of the 1707 Act of Union with Scotland. As well as a monarch, Britain gained one of the greatest composers of all time: anticipating the accession, the court director of music, **Georg Friedrich Händel**, was already well established in London by the time his employer took up residence.

Until 1837, Britain and Hannover shared the same ruler. At first, monarchs divided their residency between the territories (George I understandably so, as he never learned to speak English), but gradually they neglected their original seat. When William IV died without issue, however, the union came to an end. Salic Law, which excluded women from the succession in Hannover, meant that it was another Ernst August who ascended its throne (since 1814 it had been a kingdom in its own right), while his niece Victoria ascended the British throne. This led to another bright period in Hannover's history, during which the city was transformed in Neoclassical style by the court architect, **Georg Ludwig Friedrich Laves**. In the event, it turned out to be a false dawn. During the Seven Weeks War of 1866, the blind King Georg V opted to back neither Prussia nor Austria, and the rampaging Prussian victors responded by driving him into exile and annexing his kingdom. Hannover thereafter remained part of Prussia until 1946, when the old duchy became the main component of the newly created Land of Lower Saxony, with the city itself reinstated as a provincial capital.

Around the Hauptbahnhof

The view on arrival at the Hauptbahnhof, to the north of the centre, isn't exactly prepossessing, with a bland pedestrian precinct stretching ahead. Underneath runs the **Passarelle**; mostly under cover, but with sections in the open air, it's meant to be a sort of subterranean bazaar-cum-piazza. While the prime sites at the flashy end are occupied by expensive shops, towards the station it predictably becomes seedier; many shop sites are empty, and walking through at night is a little disconcerting.

Standing at Hannover's most popular rendezvous, the **Café Kröpcke**, slap bang in the middle of the precinct, the most imposing building in view is the **Opernhaus**, a proud Neoclassical design which is arguably the finest of the city's Laves-designed showpieces. On Sophienstrasse, the yellow- and red-brick **Künstlerhaus**, originally a museum, is now a lively arts centre, while the neo-Renaissance **Ständehaus**, built as a guild hall, houses the state treasury department. The **Börse** on Rathenaustrasse actually imitates the Tudor style – proof that British influence continued long after the end of the monarchical link.

If you're keen on modern architecture, make a detour along Georgstrasse to Goseriede to see the **Anzeigerhochhaus**. This newspaper office, made of brick-clad reinforced concrete and topped with a green copper dome, is an example of the 1920s Expressionism of Fritz Höger. Even if it's hardly the skyscraper it purports to be, and is less dramatic than the same architect's Chilehaus in Hamburg, it's nonetheless an arresting, balanced and well thought-out design. The dome now houses the city's most adventurous cinema. A little further up the same street, the **Kestner-Gesellschaft** (Mon–Wed & Fri–Sun 10am–7pm, Thurs 10am–9pm; variable entrance charges) mounts important temporary exhibitions, principally of contemporary art, in a converted swimming pool of the Jugendstil period.

The Altstadt

A few minutes' walk south of the Anzeigerhochhaus are a few streets of rebuilt **half-timbered houses**. These convey something of the impression of the medieval town, which had already been much altered before the devastation of World War II. Its form is easier to imagine if you've seen nearby Celle, which is preserved almost intact. The first major building in their midst is the fourteenth-century **Kreuzkirche** where there's a *Passion* triptych by Cranach at the high altar. One of the chapels is used by the local Serbian community, and is decorated with icons – a stark contrast with the Protestant sobriety of the rest of the church.

On Am Hohen Ufer to the south is the **Beginenturm**, the last surviving remnant of the city walls. It has been incorporated in the fabric of the modern building housing the **Historisches Museum** (Tues 10am–8pm, Wed–Fri 10am–4pm, Sat & Sun 10am–6pm; DM5/€2.50, free Fri), one of Germany's most imaginative local history museums. On the ground floor to the left are the four **state coaches** of the House of Hannover. These are still family property – even the gold carriage, adorned with Rococo paintings and carvings, which was made in London in 1783 and used for state openings of the Westminster parliament. Upstairs, there's a telling contrast to these in the form of the *Hanomag*, a tiny two-seater convertible developed in 1928, a sort of trial run for the Volkswagen "Beetle".

Just across the road is the **Ballhof**, a seventeenth-century half-timbered sports hall which is now the main repertory theatre. On nearby Holzmarkt (not its original location) the **Leibnizhaus** has been re-erected following its total destruction in the war. This magnificent Renaissance mansion was the home of **Gottfried Wilhelm Leibniz**. A historian by profession, Leibniz was active in a vast range of intellectual fields: he developed Pascal's calculating machine, arrived independently at the theory of differential calculus at the same time as Newton, charted the origins and migrations of mankind and made enormous contributions to the disciplines of jurisprudence, philosophy, theology, geology and linguistics.

The Altstadt's dominant building is the fourteenth-century **Marktkirche**, one of the most southerly of the series of brick hall churches characteristic of the Baltic lands. Its bulky tower, terminating in a spire of unusual design, has long been the emblem of the city. Originally, it was meant to be much higher, but an old chronicle reports that it was finished off quickly because "the masons had become tired and sick in the purse". The unadorned interior walls are now closer to how the building originally looked than has been the case for some three hundred years. There's a noble carved *Passion* retable, made around 1500, at the high altar; miraculously, the fourteenth- and fifteenth-century stained glass in the east windows has survived, and has recently been cleaned and restored.

Directly opposite is the high-gabled fifteenth-century **Altes Rathaus**, whose elaborate brickwork is enlivened with colourful glazed tiles. On the west side of the square is the **Forum des Landesmuseums** (Tues, Wed & Fri–Sun 10am–5pm, Thurs 10am–7pm; DM8/€4, or DM10/€5 combined ticket with Niedersächsisches Landesmuseum). Otherwise known as the Georg-von-Cölln-Haus, this five-storey nineteenth-century building, which uses iron as a key component in the construction, is the city's main venue for temporary exhibitions.

Friedrichswall and around

The line of the former city wall is now occupied by the inner ring road, forever seething with traffic. On Friederikenplatz stands the **Leineschloss**, which is now the Land parliament. Its dignified porticoes, modelled on the temples of ancient Greece, were added by Laves, who carried out a thorough transformation of the original structure. Immediately to the east, two more buildings by him – the **Wangenheim-Palais** and the **Laveshaus** – stand side by side; the latter was his own home. Down Lavesallee is yet another of his works, the **Waterloosäule**, a triumphal column commemorating the part played by the Hanoverian troops in the final defeat of Napoleon.

Opposite the Laveshaus is the **Kestner-Museum** (Tues & Thurs–Sun 11am–6pm, Wed 11am–8pm; *www.kestner-museum.de*; DM3/€1.50, free Fri). This compact decorative arts museum is named after its founder August Kestner, a Hanoverian diplomat in Rome. He was the son of Charlotte Buff, Goethe's first love and a central character in his novella *The Sufferings of Young Werther*. On the first floor, the medieval collection features treasures and textiles from Lower Saxon convents. Outstanding are surviving items from the *Goldene Tafel* of St Michael in Lüneburg, and the magnificent gilded bronze head-reliquary of an unknown saint, made around 1200 for Stift Fischbeck. The remaining galleries have an eclectic array of exhibits, ranging from Renaissance bronzes through eighteenth-century porcelain to a luxuriant selection of Art Nouveau *objets d'art* from America as well as Europe. Upstairs are examples of the ancient Greek, Etruscan, Roman and Cypriot civilizations, along with a more comprehensive Egyptian collection.

Next door is the **Neues Rathaus**, a gargantuan early twentieth-century Art Deco-cum-neo-Gothic fantasy, which is held into its marshy foundations by over six thousand piles of beechwood. It's definitely worth a peek inside; there are occasional guided tours but you can just wander round, up and down the spiral staircases. The **dome** (April–Oct daily 10am–12.45pm & 1.30–4.45pm; DM3/€1.50) offers the best views of the city, though the main attraction is the lift which takes you up – it follows an inclined path and is apparently one of only two in Europe like this. Look out for the models of Hannover at various stages of its history; the one of the bombed wartime city is a shocking record of the damage it suffered.

Directly behind the Neues Rathaus is the **Maschpark**, with a small artificial lake. Further on is a much larger man-made lake, the **Maschsee**, which serves as the locals' main playground. You can saunter down its tree-lined promenades, rent a rowing boat or canoe, or take a cruise on a pleasure steamer; the last-named are run by üstra-Reisen (☎05 11/70 09 50) and cost DM10/€5 for a round trip.

The Niedersächsisches Landesmuseum

The **Niedersächsisches Landesmuseum** (Tues, Wed & Fri–Sun 10am–5pm, Thurs 10am–7pm; *www.nlmh.de*; DM6/€3) occupies stolid-looking premises facing the east side of the Maschpark. Its main draw is the **Landesgalerie** on the second floor, which has an excellent collection of paintings from the Middle Ages to the early twentieth century. On the left are two rooms of Primitives, of which the most notable is a *Passion Altar* by the first German artist known by name, **Master Bertram**. Most of the other works are by his anonymous Saxon contemporaries and include the retables from which the **Master of the Golden Table** and the **Master of the Barfüsser Altar** get their names. Another highlight is the *SS Peter and Paul Altar* by the Hildesheim artist dubbed **Master of the Lambertikirche**; in a triumph of museum politics, all fourteen panels of this were reassembled here at the end of 2000, having previously been split among six different German collections. In the following rooms, the star painting is the tiny and exquisite *Portrait of Philipp Melanchthon* by **Hans Holbein the Younger**, displayed alongside its lid, which is one of the few surviving examples of Holbein's skill as a decorative artist. Hanging beside it is a lurid *Luther on his Deathbed* by **Cranach**, and a small *Christ Carrying the Cross* attributed to **Dürer**. A decent display of Italian Renaissance work includes pictures by Botticelli, Raphael, Pontormo and Bronzino.

The large *Bacchus and Venus* by the Antwerp Mannerist **Bartholomeus Spranger** is an allegory illustrating an old proverb: "Wine and women bring two sorrows to life." It's one of the most imposing paintings created in the erotic style cultivated at the turn of the seventeeth century at the court of Emperor Rudolf II in Prague – and in the tiny neighbouring principality of Schaumburg-Lippe. Pick of the seventeenth-century Flemish paintings are **Rubens'** *Madonna and Child*, **Van Dyck**'s *A Gentleman of Santander, the Governor of Antwerp*, and *Men Bathing by Moonlight* by **Michael Sweerts**; the last, characteristically for the artist, is a highly original subject, with wonderful luminous effects. There's a good cross-section of the Dutch school, including one of **Rembrandt**'s rare excursions into nature painting, *Landscape with the Baptism of the Eunuch*, another masterly exposition of light and shade. Also of special note is *A Woman in Profile* by his most talented pupil, the short-lived **Carel Fabritius**.

A comprehensive array of the varied styles practised in nineteenth-century Germany includes a set of four small canvases illustrating *The Times of Day* by **Friedrich**; **Leibl**'s haunting *Peasant Girl*; several humorous paintings by Spitzweg; and numerous examples of the Impressionists Liebermann, Corinth and Slevogt. A specially dimmed room shows the giant cartoons made by the members of the **Nazarene Brotherhood** for the decoration of the Casa Bartholdy in Rome.

On the first floor of the museum, the **archeology** department has as its showpiece the bodies of prehistoric men preserved naturally in the peat bogs of Lower Saxony. The varied contents of several excavated graves are another highlight, along with an array of Bronze Age jewellery. On the same floor is a **natural history** section with a wide variety of stuffed animals and a full-scale reconstruction of a dinosaur. Downstairs there's an **aquarium** with live fish from round the world and the **ethnography** department, with artefacts from Indonesia, Cameroon, Peru and the native tribes of North America.

The Sprengel-Museum

Further down the road, on Kurt-Schwitters-Platz, is the **Sprengel-Museum** (Tues 10am–8pm, Wed–Sun 10am–6pm; *www.sprengel-museum.de*; DM7/€3.50). Named after the chocolate magnate Bernhard Sprengel, whose gift of his private collection formed the basis of the museum, this ranks as one of the most exciting places in Germany in which to see modern art. Much of the display space is given over to changing exhibitions of photography, graphics and various experimental art forms, but there's also a first-rate permanent display of twentieth-century painting and sculpture.

Centrepiece of the museum is a huge range of the work of one of the twentieth century's most controversial and influential artists, Hannover's own **Kurt Schwitters**. His pleasing early landscapes and still lifes come as a surprise if you're only familiar with the famous Dadaist collages. The artist coined the term *Merz* to describe these, and set himself the target of creating a *Merzbau*, a work of art which would fill a house. Both completed versions of this were destroyed in the Nazi measures against "degenerate art", but an accurate reconstruction can be seen here.

Other highlights of the museum include a cross-section of **Picasso**'s work; complete rooms devoted to **Klee** and **Arp**; sculptures by Barlach and Henri Laurens; an updated *Prodigal Son* by **Beckmann**, along with self-portraits painted forty years apart; Surrealist paintings by Magritte, Tanguy and Ernst; and a huge range of Expressionists, with Munch, Nolde, Kirchner and Kokoschka all well represented.

Herrenhausen

The royal gardens of **Herrenhausen** (as Höringehusen came to be known) can be reached from the centre by U-Bahn #4 or #5. However, it's advisable to walk either there or back, as the route goes through two of the four gardens which make up the set. Before heading out, make sure you pick up the free tourist office leaflet which has an excellent plan of the complex.

The Welfengarten and the Georgengarten

Proceeding north from town along Nienburger Strasse, the least remarkable of the gardens – the **Welfengarten** – lies to the right, dominated by the huge neo-Gothic pile of the **Welfenpalais**, now occupied by the university. To the left, the dead-straight avenue of lime trees named Herrenhäuser Allee cuts through the **Georgengarten**. This is a *jardin anglais* of the type beloved by the Romantics, featuring trees arranged in an apparently natural setting, and an artificial lake, crossed by two graceful little bridges designed by Laves.

Also within this park is the Neoclassical **Georgenpalais**, home of the **Wilhelm-Busch-Museum** (Tues–Fri 10am–5pm, Sat & Sun 10am–6pm; *www.wilhelm-busch-museum.de*; DM8/€4). Local people flock to the temporary exhibitions on the ground floor, which centre on the work of artists who have made a significant contribution to satirical expression – Daumier, Doré and Cruickshank have all been featured in recent years, as well as contemporary cartoonists. Upstairs, there's a permanent display on **Wilhelm Busch**, who lived and worked in Hannover last century. He was a capable painter of landscapes and genre scenes, but gained worldwide popularity through his illustrated books, notably *Max and Moritz*. In these, he invented what has become a stock vocabulary for strip-cartoonists, using patterns of oscillation to express movement, and conventional signs to depict each emotion.

The Grosser Garten

The Georgengarten was created as a foil to the magnificence of the formal **Grosser Garten** (daily 8am–4.30/8pm; DM5/€2.50, free in winter), which is justifiably the city's pride and joy. It's best to time your visit to coincide with the playing of the **fountains** (May–Sept Mon–Fri 11am–noon & 3–5pm, Sat & Sun 11am–noon & 2–5pm) or when the **illuminations** are switched on (May–Sept Wed–Sun at dusk). Credit for the splendour of the layout goes to the Electress Sophie, who called them "my life", and her gardener, the Frenchman Martin Charbonnier, who transformed the modest garden into a spectacular showpiece which drew on elements of the French, Italian and Dutch traditions. Sadly the palace was totally destroyed by Allied bombing in the war, but the **Galerie**, a festive hall adorned with frothy frescoes of Virgil's *Aeneid*, and the **Orangerie** have survived.

Just inside the entrance gate is one of the most striking features, the **Gartentheater**. Temporary structures for music and drama were commonplace within royal gardens, but this one was permanent, featuring an auditorium in the form of an amphitheatre. The hornbeam hedges cleverly doubled as scenery and changing rooms, while a series of gilded statues on pedestals served as stage props. Plays by Molière and Racine, and music by Handel formed the staple repertoire of this theatre in its early days, and are still performed during the summer season. Immediately to the west is the **Grande Parterre**, whose eight sections are planted with geometric arrangements of flowers and shrubs. In front stands the Italianate **Grosse Kaskade**, belonging to the original garden, plus a sundial and grotto, while the maze is at the far end.

Behind the Grande Parterre is a modern embellishment: eight small plots have been laid out to illustrate different styles of landscape gardening down the centuries. Particularly notable is the **Renaissancegarten**, which reproduces a section of the now-vanished Hortus Palatinus in Heidelberg. East of here is the secluded **Boskettgarten**, used by courtiers for intrigues and romantic encounters. The rear section of the Grosser Garten consists of a series of radiating avenues bounded by hedges and trees, each ending at a fountain. As a centrepiece, there's the **Grosse Fontäne**, whose 82-metre water jet is the highest of any garden fountain in Europe.

The Berggarten and the Fürstenhaus

Across Herrenhäuser Strasse to the north of the Grosser Garten is the **Berggarten**, set up to tend rare and exotic plants. Its collection of orchids was considered the finest in Europe, and many are still cultivated in its hothouses. Behind these are a rock garden, a pergola garden and an iris garden; the last-named is in full bloom in April and May. Even more glorious is the central "Paradise" of rhododendrons. At the far end of the Berggarten stands the **Mausoleum** of the House of Hannover, a late work by Laves in the sternest Neoclassical manner. A graphic illustration of how the architect's style had developed is provided by the domed **Bibliothekspavilion** at the entrance, which he designed thirty years earlier in a carefree idiom still showing echoes of the Baroque.

Some compensation for the loss of the palace is provided by a number of courtly buildings to be found to the west along Herrenhäuser Strasse. The so-called **Fürstenhaus** (Tues–Sun 10am–5/6pm; DM6/€3) has been adapted as a sort of museum of the House of Hannover. There's one striking room entirely covered by a panorama of a hunt, and some fine portraits, including likenesses of King George III and Queen Sophie Charlotte by both Thomas Gainsborough and Johann Zoffany.

Eating, drinking and nightlife

As you'd expect in such a cosmopolitan city, there's a huge choice of places to eat and drink, with the Altstadt and the streets around being the liveliest area at night. Most of the gourmet restaurants are attached to hotels (see p.660). For a daytime **snack** or a quick lunch, head for the Markthalle on Karmarschstrasse, where the stallholders sell a host of different kinds of ethnic cooking. Hannover's **beer** tradition continues unabated: Gilde, the best-known local brewery, has operated uninterruptedly since 1546; its main rival is Herrenhausen. The city also has a predictably wide range of musical and theatrical venues.

Restaurants

Altdeutsche Bierstube, Lärchenstr. 4. Hannover's best traditional Gaststätte, situated northeast of the Hauptbahnhof.

Broyhan-Haus, Kramerstr. 24. Three-storey Gaststätte in the heart of the Altstadt, complete with historic cellars. It's named in honour of the sixteenth-century Hannover brewer who is credited with the invention of export beer.

Carmel-Wintergarten, Berliner Allee 34. Evenings-only kosher Jewish restaurant.

Gattopardo, Hainhölzer Str. 1. High-class and correspondingly expensive Italian restaurant to the north of the city centre. Evenings only.

Hiller, Blumenstr. 3. Speciality vegetarian and wholefood place on the eastern edge of the city centre, with inexpensive set lunches. Closed Sun.

Mandarin-Pavillon, Marktstr. 45. The city's best Chinese restaurant, with the usual bargain menus at lunchtime.

Mexcal in der Roneburg, Königsworther Str. 27. A decidedly unusual combination of a Mexican restaurant and a Hausbrauerei.

Patio, Schmiedestr. 3. Hannover here offers a modern re-interpretation of the traditional Ratskeller, with tables in the splendid main hallway of the Altes Rathaus and an international menu.

Rotisserie Helvetia, Georgsplatz 11. Top-notch Swiss speciality restaurant; it's a little on the pricey side, but not excessively so.

Seeterrassen, Arthur-Menge-Ufer 3. Housed in the decadent surroundings of the casino, this classy restaurant with views of the Maschsee is more affordable than might be expected.

Bars and cafés

Brauhaus Ernst August, Schmiedestr. 13. Hausbrauerei occupying the site of the original Broyhan brewery. One of the most popular spots in town, it serves reasonably priced meals and an excellent unfiltered *Pils*.

Café Safran, Königsworther Str. 39. Trendy café-bar with outside terrace which serves breakfasts until 4pm.

Cyberbar, Bahnhofstr. 4–6. The most convenient Internet café. Open Mon–Fri 9am–8pm, Sat 9am–4pm.

Doppelkorn, Limmerstr. 58. Café beside the Leinaustrasse stop on the route of tram #10, much favoured by alternative and arty types for its wholefood baking.

Expo-Café, Ständehausstr. 6. This looks as though it will be a permanent city-centre legacy of EXPO 2000. It offers a huge variety of coffees and often features live music in the evening.

Hannen-Fass, Knochenhauerstr. 36. Hugely popular Altstadt student bar which offers mountainous piles of cheap pub grub.

Kröpcke, Georgstr. 35. This famous café, now run by Mövenpick, is a real Hannover institution, one of its main landmarks.

Weinloch, Burgstr. 33. Liveliest of the several good pubs to be found in this street in the heart of the Altstadt.

Discos, nightclubs and live music venues

Faust, Zur Bettfedernfabrik 3, Linden. This former factory building by the River Leine is one of Hannover's major nightlife venues, with live music, parties, festivals and other events. There's also a beer garden and café-bar. Take U-Bahn #10 to Glocksee.

Jazz-Club, Lindener Berge 39. The main jazz venue, with regular sessions on Mon & Fri.

Osho, Raschplatz 7L. Bhagwan-run disco, patronized mainly by teenagers and twenty-somethings, in the "Bermuda Triangle" to the rear of the Hauptbahnhof.

Palo Palo, Raschplatz 8a. Small disco which plays funk and soul daily from 10pm.

Pavillon, Lister Meile 4. This multifunctional cultural centre in an old shopping mall is Hannover's main world music venue, with an annual festival, *Masala*. It also incorporates *Mezzo*, which is said to be the city's most patronized café.

UJZ Glocksee, Glockseestr. 35. A one-time squat having a new lease of life as a youth culture centre, with live music, discos and theatre. Take U-Bahn #10 to Glocksee.

Classical music and theatre

Many of the best **classical music** performances are to be heard in the Protestant churches; these are listed in a bi-monthly leaflet. The Knabenchor Hannover (Hannover Boys' Choir) is currently at least as good as its famous Viennese counterpart; in spite of the name it generally performs with adult male voices as well. There's also a female equivalent, the Mädchenchor Hannover.

Ballhof, Ballhofstr. 5 (☎05 11/1 68 61 42). Intimate theatrical stage in the heart of the Altstadt.

Funkhaus des NDR, Rudolf von Bennigsen Ufer 22 (☎05 11/98 80). Classical concerts are often held at the radio studios overlooking the Maschsee.

Künstlerhaus, Sophienstr. 2 (☎05 11/34 39 19). An arts centre with a strong line in experimental drama.

Opernhaus, Opernplatz 1 (☎05 11/32 11 33, *www.staatstheater-hannover.de*). In this Neoclassical masterpiece there are alternating opera and ballet performances, as well as occasional concerts by the Niedersächsisches Staatsorchester.

Schauspielhaus, Prinzenstr. 9 (☎05 11/16 84 67 01, *www.staatstheater-hannover.de*). This uncompromisingly modern building is the city's main dramatic stage.

Tanztheater im Hof, Lister Meile 33 (☎05 11/3 48 09 95). Small specialist venue for modern dance.

Theater am Aegi, Aegidientorplatz 2 (☎05 11/98 93 30). Another important venue for straight dramatic fare.

Listings

Airport ☎05 11/9 77 12 23 for flight information.

British Consulate Karl-Wiechert-Allee 50 (☎05 11/3 88 38 08).

Festivals Hannover's *Schützenfest* (marksmen's festival) for ten days in late June/early July is the most spectacular of the many held in northern Germany. It features processions with floats, fireworks and a considerable intake of alcohol, notably the *Lüttje-Lage*, in which you drink simultaneously from two glasses – one containing beer, the other schnapps – placed one inside the other.

Markets As well as the general markets on and around Am Markt, there's a flea market each Sat morning on Hohen Ufer.

Mitfahrzentrale Jakobistr. 15 (☎05 11/1 94 44).

Post office The main post office, with post restante services, is beside the Hauptbahnhof at Ernst-August-Platz 2.

Sports There's a huge *Sportpark* with indoor and outdoor stadiums and swimming pool on the west bank of the Maschsee.

Schaumburg

The tiny principality of **Schaumburg-Lippe** (formerly Holstein-Schaumburg) was one of the great survivors of imperial Germany. By skilful diplomacy it managed to avoid being swallowed up by unwelcome suitors, and kept its place on the map until 1946, when – shorn of its double-barrelled name – it became a part of Lower Saxony. Both of the towns which have served as its capital, **Stadthagen** and **Bückeburg**, lie on the main rail line between Hannover and Osnabrück. They're chiefly notable for having the finest Mannerist art and architecture on German soil, created by some of the same artists who worked at the famously eccentric court of Emperor Rudolf II in Prague.

Stadthagen

Situated some 45km west of Hannover, **STADTHAGEN** was the original capital of Schaumburg-Lippe, a role it regained after World War II. As an administrative as well as market centre, it's the more animated of the two towns, though it has less in the way of sights. The handsome Renaissance **Schloss** at the southern end of the town centre is now used as offices and can thus only be seen from outside. Focal point of the town is now the inevitable **Marktplatz**, which offers a palatial Renaissance Rathaus clearly modelled on the Schloss, several grandiose half-timbered burghers' houses and a deliberately over-the-top Rococo mansion.

Set in a close just off the square is **St Martini**, a rather gaunt Gothic hall church. This possesses an intricate fifteenth-century high altar and a Renaissance pulpit, but would be considered unremarkable were it not for the extraordinary seven-sided **Mausoleum** built onto the east end in the 1620s, in celebration of the promotion of the rulers of Schaumburg-Lippe from the rank of counts to princes of the Holy Roman Empire. The Dutchman **Adrian de Vries**, the most accomplished and least controversial of the imperial court artists of Prague, was commissioned to provide the sumptuous marble and bronze decorations. He responded with his masterpiece, the **Monument to Prince Ernst**, which occupies centre-stage. This features a superbly vivacious scene of the Risen Christ surrounded by angels, lions and sleeping guards, as well as the family coats of arms and a medallion portrait of the prince.

Stadthagen's **Bahnhof** is at the northern end of town, a twenty-minute walk from the centre. The **tourist office** (Mon–Fri 9am–12.30pm & 2–5pm; ☎0 57 21/92 50 65, fax 92 30 55, *www.stadthagen.de*) is at Am Markt 1. Among the **hotels** are *Oelkrug*, Waldsstr. 2 (☎0 57 21/80 25 25; ⑨;), *Gerber Hotel La Tannerie*, Echternstr. 14 (☎0 57 21/98 60; ⑥), *Zur Amtspforte*, Obernstr. 31 (☎0 57 21/98 40; ⑥), and *Parkhotel*, Büschingstr. 10 (☎0 57 21/9 72 70; ⑥). The city is very well off for **restaurants**. Of those in the hotels, *Gerber's Kleines Weinrestaurant* serves fine bistro cuisine, while *Zur Amtspforte* has a varied menu of Asian dishes. Other possibilities are the historic *Herrenhäuser* on Marktplatz, the fish specialist *Blanke*, Rathauspassage 5, and the high-class *Torschreiberhaus*, Krumme Str. 42.

Bückeburg

At the turn of the seventeenth century, the capital of Schaumburg-Lippe was moved 18km west to **BÜCKEBURG**, then a mere hamlet. This remains the seat of the former ruling family, who, like so many German aristocrats, are left with plenty of wealth and possessions as compensation for their loss of political power. It's worth bearing in mind that all the town's sights can be visited on Mondays – one of very few places in the country where this is so.

Set in its own extensive grounds at the edge of the town centre, the **Schloss** (guided tours daily 9am–noon & 1–5/6pm; *www.schloss-bueckeburg.de*; DM8/€4) was originally a fourteenth-century tower-house. It was transformed into a splendid Renaissance palace in the mid-sixteenth century, though one wing had to be rebuilt a couple of hundred years later following its destruction in a fire. Inside, the apartments are eclectic, to say the least, passing in quick succession from a grandiose Wilhelmine banqueting chamber with a huge Venetian-style fresco, through an intimate Rococo smoking room, to a Renaissance hall hung with superb Brussels tapestries. The **Schlosskapelle**, which was originally Gothic, was adapted in the Mannerist period for Protestant worship. As if to give the lie to the belief that the new faith was inimical to worldly beauty, it was decorated in the most extravagant manner possible. Every inch of the walls is covered with frescoes, and there's a complete set of gilded and carved furnishings. In the same period, the even more sumptuous **Goldener Saal** was built as a secular counterpart. Its doorway, rising to the full height of the room, is flanked by huge statues of Mars and Flora, with Mercury floating above in the company of cherubs and goddesses.

Also within the Schlosspark is a sombre neo-Romanesque **Mausoleum** (April–Oct daily 10am–5pm; DM4/€2), whose dome has what's apparently the largest mosaic in Germany. On the bridge over the moat which separates the park from the town proper are two writhing **bronzes**, *Venus and Adonis* and *The Rape of Proserpine*, both the work of Adrian de Vries.

The brothers Hans and Ebbert Wulf of Hildesheim, who had carried out the decoration of the Schlosskapelle and Goldener Saal, were afterwards commissioned to build Bückeburg's other focal building, the **Stadtkirche** (mid-April to mid-Oct Mon–Fri 10.30am–noon & 3–5pm, Sat 3–5pm; mid-Oct to mid-April Thurs & Sat 2–4pm), which lies at the top of the main Lange Strasse. This competes with Wolfenbüttel for the title of first full-scale Protestant church ever to be built. It's much the more unified building of the two, and is a real masterpiece of design, notwithstanding the Latin inscription running across the facade which declares that it is: "An Example of Piety, not of Architecture". Apart from its facade the exterior is a glum affair, but the **interior** is stunning. Massive Corinthian pillars shoot right up to the vault, and your eye is drawn to the gleaming gold case of the massive organ at the far end, at which Johann Christoph Friedrich Bach, son of J.S., presided for 45 years. In adapting the old hall-church formula to the Protestant emphasis on preaching, brightly painted galleries were added all round, and the **pulpit** placed in the centre. This pulpit is one of the most beautiful in the country, its base lined with gold-plated reliefs of the life of Christ. Even more impressive is Adrian de Vries's **font**, where the Holy Ghost, hooked up by wires, hovers above the Baptism of Christ.

Housed in a half-timbered house with a jarring modern extension on Sablé Platz, the pedestrian area between Lange Strasse and Bahnhofstrasse, is the **Hubschrauber-museum** (Helicopter Museum; daily 9am–5pm; *www.hubschraubermuseum.de*; DM6/€3), apparently the only one of its kind in the world. A reminder of the proximity of the German and British military bases, it incorporates an educational display on vertical flight technique, and is well labelled in English. Following a section on the history of man's attempts to fly, there are dozens of original machines, representing all the famous names in helicopter design.

Bückeburg's **Bahnhof** lies at the northern end of town; it's a straight ten-minute walk down Bahnhofstrasse to the Schloss. The **tourist office** (Mon–Fri 8am–12.30pm & 2–5pm, Sat 9–11am; ☎0 57 22/20 61 81, fax 20 62 10, *www.bueckeburg.de*) is at Marktplatz 4. Centrally located **hotels** are *Brauhaus*, Braustr. 1 (☎0 57 22/9 67 70; ④), *Bemfert*, Brauhausstr. 8 (☎0 57 22/47 21; ⑤), *Am Schlosstor*, Lange Str. 33 (☎0 57 22/9 59 90; ⑤), and *Ambiente*, Herminenstr. 11 (☎0 57 22/96 70; ⑥–⑧). The last-named has the best **restaurant** in town; cheaper alternatives are the Ratskeller in the Rathaus directly opposite the Schloss gates and the seventeenth-century *Zur Falle*, Lange Str. 13.

Hameln (Hamelin)

"A pleasanter spot you never spied" was how Robert Browning characterized the venerable town of **HAMELN**, situated on the River Weser 45km southwest of Hannover. His verse rendition of the **legend of the Pied Piper** has made the place one of the best-known towns in Germany as far as English-speaking people are concerned – and earned him the eternal gratitude of the local tourist board.

Inevitably, the Pied Piper legend – perhaps the most endurably fascinating of Germany's rich store of folk-tales – always looms large, which makes Hameln an ideal outing if you have kids. However, there are more serious attractions as well. Along with nearby Lemgo (see pp.614–16), it's the best place to see the distinctive **Weser Renaissance** style, a form of civil architecture which typically features large projecting bay windows, richly decorated gables ornamented with pyramids and scrollwork, ornamental fillets with coats of arms and inscriptions, and lavish grotesque carvings, many of which are appropriately dubbed *Neidköpfe* – envious "neighbours' heads". During the 1960s a comprehensive restoration programme was started, which has left Hameln looking in immaculate shape.

Arrival, information and accommodation

Hameln's **Bahnhof** is situated well to the east of the centre, which is reached via Bahnhofstrasse and Diesterstrasse. The **tourist office** (May–Sept Mon–Fri 9am–1pm & 2–6pm, Sat 9.30am–12.30pm & 3–5pm, Sun 9.30am–12.30pm; Oct–April Mon–Fri

---

THE PIED PIPER LEGEND

The **Pied Piper legend** was first chronicled in 1384, the exact centenary of when the event allegedly took place. A mysterious stranger dressed in a multicoloured coat appeared in Hameln and offered to rid the town of its plague of rats and mice. Upon promise of payment, he played on his pipe and lured the vermin to the Weser, where they all drowned. The ungrateful burghers reneged on the reward and sent the rat-catcher packing. He returned one Sunday morning when the adults were at church, dressed in a weird yellow and red huntsman's costume. This time it was the town's 130 children who answered the magnetic strains of his pipe, and they followed the stranger out of town and out of sight, apparently disappearing into a cavern, never to be seen again. The only children who were saved were a cripple and a deaf-mute.

Many **interpretations**, none of them conclusive, have been placed on this story. It may symbolize the plague epidemics that were a fact of life in medieval Europe – the term "children" of a town was often used in old chronicles as a synonym for "citizens". Alternatively, it's possible the piper was actually a land agent charged with finding settlers – the count of Schaumburg had a plantation in Moravia, while there are communities in Transylvania which claim descent from the children of Hameln. Another plausible theory is that the events were linked to the disastrous Children's Crusade of 1212, when youngsters from all over Europe joined in an attempt to conquer the Holy Land from the infidel by peace – something their seniors had failed to do by force. One of the two main leaders was a boy from Cologne called Nicolas, and it's quite likely that there were recruits to the cause from Hameln.

9am–1pm & 2–5pm; ☎0 51 51/9 57 80, fax 95 78 41, *www.hameln.de*) is in the Bürgergarten on Diensterallee just before the entrance to the Altstadt. There is also a branch in the Hochzeithaus (mid-April to mid-Oct Tues–Fri 11am–2pm & 2.30–4.30pm, Sat & Sun 10am–2pm).

During the tourist season, it's a good idea to spend the night in Hameln; that way you can see the town before or after the day-trippers have come and gone. There are surprisingly few **hotels**, and they're not particularly cheap. The **youth hostel** is well placed about five minutes' walk north of the Altstadt at Fischbecker Str. 33 (☎0 51 51/34 25, fax 4 23 16; DM22/€11 or DM27/€13.50), at the point where the Hamel (no more than a stream) flows into the Weser. On the latter's western bank is the **campsite** at Uferstr. 80 (☎0 51 51/6 11 67), which is open all year round. There are around a score of private houses, including some in the Altstadt, with **rooms** to let (①–③). Some of the hotels occupy fine old buildings.

Hotels

Altstadtwiege, Neue Marktstr. 10 (☎0 51 51/2 78 54, fax 10 45). Budget hotel and pub on a quiet Altstadt backstreet. ④.

An der Altstadt, Diensterallee 16 (☎0 51 51/75 91, fax 4 20 25). Fine old hotel which was modernized a few years back. ⑤.

Christinenhof, Alte Marktstr. 18 (☎0 51 51/9 50 80, fax 4 36 11). Upmarket hotel in an old half-timbered building with sauna and swimming pool. ⑦.

City, Neue Marktstr. 9 (☎0 51 51/72 61, fax 4 59 74). A marginally more expensive alternative to the *Altstadtwiege* next door. ④.

Jugendstil, Wettorstr. 18 (☎0 51 51/9 55 80, fax 95 58 66). Part of the Akzent chain, this occupies a huge terraced house in the Jugendstil quarter of the city immediately north of the Altstadt. ⑤.

Stadt Hameln, Münsterwall 2 (☎0 51 51/90 10, fax 90 13 33). The town's leading hotel, a palatial building with a modern extension. It has two restaurants, one on the terrace overlooking the river. ⑦.

Zur Krone, Osterstr. 30 (☎0 51 51/90 70, fax 90 72 17). Another upmarket hotel and restaurant, this time in a renovated half-timbered mansion on the main street. ⑥.

The Town

For centuries Hameln was no more than a small milling and market town, which lay within a heavily fortified circular **Stadtmauer**. In the wake of the Thirty Years War, its potential for growth was stunted by the strengthening of its defences by the Hanoverians, to the extent that it acquired the nickname of "the Gibraltar of the North". Napoleon ordered the demolition of the fortress so that the town could expand.

The only surviving sections of the Stadtmauer are two isolated medieval towers at the north end of town – the **Pulverturm** and the **Haspelmathsturm** – and the **Garnisonkirche**, now deconsecrated and used as a savings bank. It guards the entrance to **Osterstrasse**, the town's central axis – and one of Germany's finest streets. Facing the Garnisonkirche on the left is the **Rattenfängerhaus** (Rat-Catcher's House). Built for a local councillor at the beginning of the seventeenth century, its name is due solely to an inscription on the side wall documenting the legend. Its facade is one of the most original in Hameln, the delicacy of its ornamental details (which include plenty of "envious heads") standing in deliberate contrast to the massiveness of the overall design. The interior is only marginally less impressive; it now houses a restaurant (see opposite). Further up the street to the right is the **Leisthaus**, built about fifteen years earlier for a merchant by the local mason Cord Tönnies. The statue of Lucretia in a niche above the oriel window offers a profane contrast to the figures of the Seven Christian Virtues on the frieze below, a juxtaposition of sacred and secular that is typical of the German Renaissance. In this case inspiration was obviously provided by the carvings on the timber supports of the sixteenth-century **Stiftsherrnhaus** next door, which feature the planetary deities along with the Apostles and other biblical personages.

The rest of the Stiftsherrnhaus, along with all of the Leisthaus, is given over to the **Museum Hameln** (Tues–Sun 10am–4.30pm; DM3/€1.50). Among the collection of religious art on the first floor, the most striking items are a set of statues of the Apostles which formerly stood on the rood screen of the Münster, and the *Siebenlingsstein*. The latter commemorates another Hameln legend, that of the birth of septuplets to a local family in 1600. Though the parents and elder siblings are shown praying at the foot of a crucifix, there was again no happy ending, as all the babies died soon afterwards.

At the end of Osterstrasse is the huge **Hochzeithaus** (Wedding House), a festival hall erected in the early seventeenth century, whose main features are its high end gables and elaborate dormer windows, under each of which there is a doorway, which formerly led into a shop. On the side facing the Markt, a **carillon** has been installed. At 1.05pm, 3.35pm and 5.35pm each day, its figures enact the Piper's two visits to Hameln. Opposite is one of the most magnificent houses, the **Dempterhaus**, which was built a few years earlier for the burgomaster after whom it is named. The **Marktkirche** rather detracts from the scene; it was Hameln's only major loss to wartime air raids, and has been poorly rebuilt with smooth stones which clash with the remains of the original masonry.

Among many fine buildings on Bäckerstrasse, which begins off the left-hand side of the Markt, two stand out. The Gothic **Löwenapotheke**, still in use as a pharmacy, illustrates that the Weser Renaissance style sprang from quite plain origins – the basic form is similar, but there's almost no decoration, apart from the hexagonal star on the gable, which was intended to ward off evil spirits. Further along is the **Rattenkrug**, built by Cord Tönnies a couple of decades before the broadly similar Leisthaus. Originally the home of a burgomaster, it has long served as a Gaststätte.

Halfway down Wendenstrasse, a fine narrow street opposite the Löwenapotheke, is the **Lückingsches Haus**, whose profuse carvings mark it out as the best example of the revival of half-timbering which occurred in the mid-seventeenth century. Also worth seeing is Alte Marktstrasse, which joins Bäckerstrasse by the Rattenkrug. Its most notable building is **Kurie Jerusalem**, a large half-timbered store from about 1500 which was long derelict, but has been magnificently restored as a play-centre (where kids can be left if you want to go sightseeing without them in tow). Further down stands the **Redenhof**, the only remaining nobleman's mansion in Hameln. Dating from the mid-sixteenth century, it's surprisingly plain in comparison with the contemporary houses of the prosperous burgher families.

At the end of Bäckerstrasse, overlooking the Weser, is the **Münster**, successor to a Benedictine monastery founded around 800. It's something of a mix of styles – the eleventh-century crypt and the squat octagonal lantern tower survive from a Romanesque basilica which was converted into a Gothic hall church from the thirteenth century onwards, the austere belfry only being added some two hundred years later. Inside, the raised chancel is the most striking feature.

Eating, drinking and entertainment

Hameln is not a major gastronomic centre: it has few high-quality restaurants other than those in the last two hotels listed on p.671. Where it does score is in the range of highly distinctive eateries geared primarily to day-trippers and in many cases housed in premises which are sightseeing attractions in their own right. The Pied Piper legend is enacted in a **historical costume play** held in the town centre at noon every Sunday from mid-May to mid-September; performances last thirty minutes and are free. **Cruises** on the Weser (bear in mind that strong currents mean the upstream journeys are painfully slow) are run by Oberweser Dampfschiffahrt (☎0 51 51/93 99 99, *www.weserschiffahrt.de*), with departures from the jetty by the Münster; prices start at DM8/€4 for an hour-long round trip.

Restaurants and cafés

Kaffeestuben, Wendenstr. 9. Coffee house in an old bakery. A good choice for *Kaffee und Kuchen*; also does light meals.

Kartoffelhaus, Kupferschmiedstr. 13. Potato-based dishes predominate in this restaurant in the Bürgerhaus, one of Hameln's most ornate timber-framed houses.

Klütturm, Auf dem Klütberg. One of the town's very best restaurants, commanding a powerful view over the Weser valley from its hilltop position to the southwest.

Museums-Café, Osterstr. 8. Traditional café in the Stiftsherrnhaus, with outside tables in summer. Inevitably its speciality is called *Rattenfängertorte*.

Paulaner, Bäckerstr. 16. A Gaststätte of the celebrated Munich brewery is the current occupant of the Rattenkrug.

Pfannekuchen, Hummenstr. 12. There are some forty different pancakes – sweet and savoury, flour- or potato-based – on the menu in this cosy little restaurant in this delightful half-timbered house.

Rattenfängerhaus, Osterstr. 28. The cuisine here is predominantly *gutbürgerliche Küche*, though there are plenty of ice-cream-based dishes if you don't want a full meal.

The Weser country around Hameln

As a supplement to a visit to Hameln, it's well worth taking in some of the nearby sights in the Weser country. Three destinations in particular stand out; all are easy to reach, and needn't take up too much time. **Fischbeck** has an intriguing collegiate foundation; **Hämelschenburg** possesses one of Lower Saxony's most magnificent palaces; while **Bodenwerder** was the home town of Baron Münchhausen.

Fischbeck

Situated 8km north of Hameln and connected by buses #20, #25 and #26 (passenger trains no longer stop there), **FISCHBECK** is dominated by its **Stift** (guided tours Easter to mid-Oct Tues & Fri 9am–11am & 2–4pm, Wed, Thurs, Sat & Sun 2–4pm; *www.stift-fischbeck.de*; DM4/€2). This women's collegiate church was founded in 955, and has preserved an unbroken tradition ever since, having turned Protestant in the mid-sixteenth century. Today, five elderly canonesses keep up its charitable work, only taking their vows once they have retired from a professional career; their tasks include showing visitors round the complex. It's best to phone first (☎0 51 52/86 03), or check at Hameln's tourist office, to ensure admission; a tour in English can be arranged.

The **Stiftskirche** was built in the twelfth and early thirteenth centuries as a columned basilica. A drastic restoration a century ago removed most of the Baroque accretions, but some additions remain – such as the wooden balconies from where the canonesses, in true aristocratic manner, observe the services. Architecturally the finest part of the Stift is the **crypt**, whose capitals are all carved in a different manner. The **cloister** is a Gothic structure, with the houses of the canonesses on its upper storey.

Fischbeck has several outstanding works of art, but there's only a copy of the most famous, a gilded head-reliquary of a saint; the original is now in the Kestner-Museum in Hannover (see p.673). Earlier this century, the long-lost polychrome wood **statue of the foundress Helmburg** was discovered and placed in the chancel. Made around 1300, it's an imaginary, idealized portrait, showing her as a young woman, instead of the elderly widow she was when she founded the Stift, a story illustrated in a late sixteenth-century **tapestry** in the south transept. On a wooden beam high above the end of the nave is a thirteenth-century **triumphal cross**, while beside the pulpit there's an extraordinary wooden **seated Man of Sorrows** – carved around 1500, it radiates enormous pathos. According to legend, it was made for the Stift by an itinerant crafts-man in gratitude for having been cured there of the plague.

Hämelschenburg

If Hameln has given you a taste for the Weser Renaissance, it's well worth travelling the 12km south to the tiny village of **HÄMELSCHENBURG**, whose **Schloss** (guided tours April–Oct Tues–Sun 10am–noon & 2–5pm; *www.haemelschenburg.de*; DM8/€4) is arguably the most spectacular manifestation of the style. It was built between 1588 and 1613 for the Klencke family, in whose possession it still remains. The exterior, with its distinctive horseshoe shape, varied elevations and rich carvings, is particularly impressive. Inside are some splendid doorways and chimneypieces, along with a var-ied array of furniture, trophies, weapons and portraits. On the main road below the complex is the former **Schlosskirche**, now the parish church. Erected in 1563, it was the first freestanding church ever built for Protestant worship. The furnishings include a Gothic limewood group of the *Garden of Paradise*, a Renaissance epitaph to the Klencke family and a somewhat comical font with moving parts. Unfortunately the church is only open on Sunday mornings or when a pre-booked tour is visiting.

Hämelschenburg can be reached by bus #40 from Hameln; this runs several times a day during the week, but services dry up mid-morning on Saturdays, necessitating a 2.5km walk to Emmern, which has a rail link as well as a much more frequent bus ser-vice to Hameln.

Bodenwerder

BODENWERDER, 25km downstream from Hameln, is a good choice of destination if you want to take a short cruise on the Weser; it can also be reached by bus #520. Its

BARON MÜNCHHAUSEN

The real-life **Karl Friedrich Hieronymous von Münchhausen** was an eighteenth-century soldier of fortune who fought for the Russians against the Turks, before retiring to his ancestral seat, where he regaled credulous listeners with monstrously boastful tales of his adventures. These came to the attention of **Rudolph Erich Raspe**, himself a real rogue, who embroidered the stories further and published them under the Baron's name in Britain. For all his failings, Raspe was highly talented – he had been a protégé of Leibniz in his native Hannover – and the book is stylishly written, perfectly capturing the understated manner of a boring old raconteur launching every few minutes into yet another totally implausible anecdote. The Baron's numerous adventures included stranger travels than even Gulliver's – he made two trips to the moon (one of them unintentional), a journey all the way through the earth's crust and a voyage through a sea of milk to an island of cheese. In less far-flung parts, he shot a stag with a full-sized cherry tree between its antlers (thus obtaining haunch and sauce at the same time), served as a human cannonball in the war against the Turks and single-handedly saved Gibraltar from falling into Spanish hands by tossing the enemy's three hundred pieces of artillery into the sea. For all its spectacular special effects, Terry Gilliam's 1988 movie, *The Adventures of Baron Münchhausen*, is a leaden creation which flopped at the box office. Far more successful from an artistic point of view is the Goebbels-financed film of the same name – an incredibly futuristic wartime fantasy made in the UFA studios in Babelsberg.

name is synonymous with **Baron Münchhausen**, the King of Liars, who is one of Germany's most famous literary characters. Münchhausen's mansion, now the **Rathaus** (April–Oct daily 10am–noon & 2–5pm; DM2/€1), contains a small museum in his honour; its exhibits include the pistol with which he claimed to have shot down his charger from a church steeple. The ticket also gives admission to the **Heimatmuseum** (same times) next door, whose most notable exhibit is a fourteenth-century dugout canoe dredged up from the Weser. Outside is a fountain illustrating one of Münchhausen's most famous escapades (one that has always defeated the filmmakers) – stopping to water his prize Lithuanian horse, he found that the liquid was pouring out of its body, the rear end having been chopped off by a falling portcullis as he pursued the Turkish army into a walled town. Needless to say, the two parts of the steed were soon put back together again. On the first Sunday of each month between May and September, some of Münchhausen's exploits are re-enacted.

The **tourist office** (Mon–Fri 9am–12.30pm & 2.30–6pm, Sat 9am–noon; ☎0 55 33/4 05 41, fax 41 13, *www.bodenwerder.de*) is in the First Reisebüro, Weserstr. 3. There's an abundant range of **pensions** and **private rooms** (①–③), as well as a **youth hostel** in the hills to the east of town on Richard-Schirrmann-Weg (☎0 55 33/26 85, fax 62 03; DM22/€11 or DM27/€13.50), and a **campsite** at An der Himmelspforte (☎0 55 33/49 38). **Hotels** include *Königszinne*, Linser Str. 12 (☎0 55 33/9 72 40; ⑤), and *Deutsches Haus*, Münchhausenplatz 4 (☎0 55 33/39 25; ⑥). Both of these have good **restaurants**, though they face strong competition from *Münchhausen Stube*, Grosse Str. 5.

Hildesheim

HILDESHEIM, which lies 30km southeast of Hannover, stands unrivalled as Lower Saxony's premier city of art. Some of the finest buildings in all of Germany are to be found here, and its importance to European culture can hardly be exaggerated. During the eleventh-century Ottonian period, the **Romanesque style** – emerging hesitantly elsewhere – achieved a state of perfection here, not only in architecture, but in sculpture and

△ *Hauptbahnhof & Post Office*

N

ACCOMMODATION
2 Bürgermeisterkapelle
5 Klocke
4 Kurth
1 Le Meridien
3 Weisser Schwan

St. Michael
Knochenhaueramtshaus ❶
Rathaus ❷
Tempelhaus
Kaiserhaus
St. Andreas
❸
Roemer-Pelizaeus-Museum
Dom
Kreuzkirche
❹
Dom- und Diözesanmuseum
Lambertikirche
Kehswiederturm
Wernesches Haus
St. Godehard

0   Metres   200   ❺

HILDESHEIM

painting as well. Five hundred years later, the city was adorned with a multitude of **half-timbered buildings** whose sheer artistry far surpassed those of any other German city.

Because of this legacy, old guides used to consider Hildesheim as one of the "must" cities of Germany. Just a month before the German surrender in 1945, however, Hildesheim was bombed and the consequent fire, fuelled by the wooden buildings, caused damage which even some exemplary restoration cannot disguise, and left the surviving monuments marooned among typically bland, functional modern developments. For decades, the city was a shadow of its former self, until it made an astonishing comeback in the 1980s. Fortified by commercial prosperity, the local council made the bold decision to re-create what had hitherto been regarded as irretrievably lost. A fillip was given by UNESCO's decision to include the two main churches, both of which had been shattered in the war, on its World Heritage List.

Arrival, information and accommodation

Hildesheim's **Hauptbahnhof** is at the northern end of the city; the best way to reach the centre is to follow Bernwardstrasse, then Almstrasse, but be warned that these characterless shopping precincts make rather an inauspicious introduction. The **tourist office** (Mon–Fri 9am–7pm, Sat 9am–4pm; ☎0 51 21/1 79 80, fax 1 79 88, *www.hildesheim.de*) is in the Tempelhaus, Rathausstr. 18–20.

Hildesheim isn't well off for budget **hotels**, at least in the centre, though there's plenty of choice in the middle and upper ranges. The nearest **campsite** is way to the east of town, by the B6 at Derneburg (☎0 50 62/5 65, fax 87 85). Unfortunately, the **youth hostel** isn't much more convenient; it occupies a rustic location high in the wooded hills above Moritzberg at Schirrmannweg 4 (☎0 51 21/4 27 17, fax 4 78 47; DM24/€12 or DM29/€14.50), and is a good hour's walk from the centre. No bus goes anywhere near, though #1 and #4 will take you part of the way.

Hotels and pensions

Bürgermeisterkapelle, Rathausstr. 8 (☎0 51 21/1 40 21, fax 3 88 13). Modern hotel situated right behind the Rathaus. It incorporates a sixteenth-century Weinstube, the oldest in Lower Saxony, and a restaurant, *Strohmeyer's*. ⑥

Klocke, Humboldtstr. 11 (☎0 51 21/17 92 13, fax 1 79 21 40, *gaestehaus-klocke@t-online.de*). Long-established, fairly upmarket guesthouse at the southwestern edge of the Altstadt. ⑤.

Kurth, Küsthardtstr. 4 (☎0 51 21/3 62 72). This small pension is the cheapest option in the city centre. ④.

Le Meridien, Markt 4 (☎0 51 21/30 00, fax 3 00 04 44, *www.meridien-hildesheim.com*). Luxury modern hotel with restaurant, sauna and gym in a trio of reconstructed historic buildings. ⑥–⑨.

Marheinke, Peiner Landstr. 189, Drispenstedt (☎ & fax 0 51 21/5 26 67). Gasthof in the north of the city, reached by bus #1; it has rooms both with and without private facilities. ③–⑥.

Meyer, Peiner Landstr. 185, Drispenstedt (☎0 51 21/5 31 79, fax 5 31 07). Another Gasthof, offering very similar deals to its neighbour. ③–⑥.

Parkhotel Berghölzchen, Am Berghölzchen 1 (☎0 51 21/97 90, fax 97 94 00, *www.berghoelzchen.de*). Upmarket hotel with restaurant and beer garden up on the Moritzberg. ⑥–⑨.

Weisser Schwan, Schuhstr. 29 (☎0 51 21/1 67 80, fax 16 78 90). Mid-range city-centre hotel which has been run by the same family for over a century. ⑤.

The City

Hildesheim's attractions are well spaced out, and cannot comfortably be covered in a single day. To help guide visitors from one monument to another, a trail of white roses has been painted on the streets; a detailed brochure describing this, the *Hildesheimer Rosenroute*, is available from the tourist office.

Marktplatz

In 1983 work began on resurrecting the picturesque jumble of buildings around the central **Marktplatz**, which has now re-emerged, following its almost complete destruction in the war, as Germany's most imposing market square. Only two of the buildings are original: the early Gothic **Rathaus** at the eastern end, which was only partially destroyed and hurriedly rebuilt, and the fifteenth-century **Tempelhaus** at the southeast corner, which somehow remained intact while all its neighbours collapsed. The most likely explanation for the latter's puzzling name and distinctive shape is that it was inspired by a crusader's description of buildings he had seen in the Holy Land. Some softening of the rather spare, flat textures occurred with the addition of a late sixteenth-century oriel window bearing carvings of the Prodigal Son. Nowadays, the building houses a bookstore, as well as the tourist office, and the offices of the *Hildesheimer Allgemeine Zeitung*, the longest continually running daily newspaper in Germany. The Renaissance **Wedekindhaus** next door, the Baroque **Lüntzelhaus** and the part-Gothic, part-Baroque **Rolandstift** were restored by the local savings bank to serve as its headquarters. Directly opposite, the mid-seventeenth-century inn known as the **Stadtschänke**, along with the aptly named **Rokokohaus** and the early sixteenth-century **Wollenwebergildehaus** (Wool Weavers' Guild House), were rebuilt to serve collectively as a luxury hotel. The council themselves paid for a copy of the Renaissance

Marktbrunnen, which is topped by a figure of a Knight and has the municipal arms depicted on the basin.

As the culmination of the restoration project, the small **Bäckeramtshaus** (Bakers' Guildhall) of 1800 and the colossal early sixteenth-century **Knochenhaueramtshaus** (Butchers' Guildhall) on the west side of the square were re-created from scratch. The latter had earned for itself the title of "the most beautiful half-timbered house in the world", a title few would dispute on seeing its highly distinctive architecture and seemingly inexhaustible range of carvings on Christian, pagan and humorous subjects. Part of it now houses a restaurant, while the upper storeys contain the local history displays of the **Stadtgeschichtliches Museum** (Tues–Sun 10am–6pm; DM3/€1.50).

St Michael

Hildesheim's supreme building, the mould-breaking church of **St Michael**, is about ten minutes' walk west of the Marktplatz, reached via Michaelisstrasse. Perched on a little hill and girded with six towers, it's not too fanciful to see it as a depiction of the heavenly Jerusalem. Originally part of a Benedictine monastery, St Michael was very much a personal creation of **Bishop Bernward**. A confidant of Emperor Otto II and tutor to Otto III, this well-travelled, erudite man ruled the see of Hildesheim between 993 and 1022, and did much to foster the art and architecture of the city.

The nave forms the centrepiece of St Michael's meticulously thought-out design. An important innovation was the move away from the columned basilica of the Romans to a new system, subsequently known as the **Lower Saxon style**, whereby each bay is demarcated by a hefty square pillar, between which are placed two columns. These are topped by another new device, the cubiform capital, from which spring the arches, coloured in alternate white and red to impart a sense of rhythmic movement. The height of the roof is exactly twice the length of each bay of the nave. Shortly after Bernward was canonized in 1192, substantial embellishments were made in order that it should be a worthy resting-place for his relics. Seven capitals were carved for the nave, and in the west transept a **choir screen** was erected; only part of this remains, yet its stucco carvings rank among the masterpieces of German sculpture.

An even more spectacular addition was the **ceiling**, which is one of only two Romanesque painted wooden ceilings to have survived. Fortunately, it had been removed for safety during World War II, and its fresh state of preservation is remarkable – three-quarters of its 1300 separate oak panels are original. Executed in the style of contemporary illuminated manuscripts, its programme is based on the imagery of the tree, a decision prompted by the fact that the church's most sacred relic was a piece of the Holy Cross. In the first main scene, Adam and Eve are shown beside the Tree of Knowledge. Next comes the sleeping Jesse, from whose loins springs the rod which passes through descendants such as David and Solomon before arriving at the Virgin Mary and Christ himself.

St Bernward's body is interred in a stone sarcophagus in the ground-level **crypt** at the western end of the building. This necessitated a rebuilding to accommodate a raised chancel, which impaired the previously perfect architectural unity of the church. The Catholics were allowed to retain the crypt when St Michael became Protestant at the Reformation. It's only open for Mass, but you can peek in by opening the door to the left of the choir screen. Another later addition was the Gothic **cloister** to the north of the church, of which only one wing survives.

The Dom

The **Dom**, which is set in its own close and reached via Burgstrasse, is a poor relation of St Michael's, but its hauntingly romantic cloister and superb art treasures convinced UNESCO that it was an equally important piece of cultural heritage. The exterior is largely a fake, with prominent Gothic side chapels and a Romanesque facade and towers that are a modern guess at how the building might have looked before it was completely transformed in the Baroque epoch. Inside, the architecture has been restored to its original eleventh-century layout, a close adaptation of the forms pioneered at the great monastery fifty years before.

One of St Bernward's particular enthusiasms was the art of bronze-casting, and he established a foundry which was to flourish for centuries. Its first major product was a pair of **processional doors**, originally made for St Michael's, but moved a few years later to the Dom's main entrance, where they were installed on the inside. They tell the story of Adam and Eve on the left-hand side, and of Christ on the right. Soon afterwards, the craftsmen made the **triumphal column**, now in the southern transept. Rather more obviously inspired by Roman victory monuments, this illustrates the lives of Jesus and St John the Baptist in a manner akin to strip cartoons. Around 1065, the huge **wheel-shaped chandelier** was suspended from the vault of the nave. Mantled with alternate towers and gateways, it's yet another representation of the heavenly Jerusalem and was to serve as the prototype for the even more ornate candelabra in Aachen and Gross Comburg. In the baptismal chapel is the **font**, made in 1225, it rests on personifications of the four sacred rivers, while the basin and lid illustrate various biblical stories, mostly with a watery theme.

Most unusually, the **cloister** (April–Oct Mon–Sat 9.30am–5pm, Sun noon–5pm; DM0.50/€0.25) is built onto the transepts, forming a protective shield round the apse, on which grows the **thousand-year-old rosebush**, to which the legend of Hildesheim's foundation is inextricably tied. In 815, Ludwig the Pious, a son of Charlemagne, hung the royal chapel's relics of the Virgin on the tree while he was out hunting near *Hildwin's Heim*. When he tried to remove them, they would not budge; taking this to be divine instruction, he decided to endow the mother church of a new diocese on the very spot. Whether this is really the original bush is disputed, but it's certainly many centuries old, and does seem to lead a charmed life – it burst into flower not long after the air raid which had flattened most of the Dom itself, and has blossomed every year since. In the centre of the cloister garden is the **St-Annen-Kapelle**, a beautiful fourteenth-century miniaturization of a Gothic cathedral, with a set of gargoyles spouting from its walls. The sumptuous Renaissance **rood screen**, which fenced off the Dom's chancel until 1945, can be seen in the Antoniuskapelle off the cloister's southern walk.

On the south side of the Dom is the **Dom- und Diözesanmuseum** (Tues–Sat 10am–5pm, Sun noon–5pm; DM4/€2), one of the richest ecclesiastical treasuries in Germany. Among the highlights are several works dating from the time of St Bernward – the *Golden Madonna* (actually wooden but covered with gold leaf), a pair of candlesticks and two crucifixes named after the bishop himself. Equally imposing are various twelfth-century pieces – the cross of Henry the Lion, the shrine of St Godehard, three shield-shaped crucifixes and a set of enamel plates. The head-reliquary of St Bernward dates from the turn of the following century, while the eagle lectern was made around the same time as the font. Although it has no real connection with the bishop, the so-called chalice of St Bernward is an outstanding piece of goldsmith's work from around 1400.

The rest of the central Altstadt

Adjoining the north side of the Dom's close is the old Franciscan friary, which, together with its brand-new extension, now contains the **Roemer-Pelizaeus Museum** (Tues–Sun 9am–4.30pm; *www.roemer-pelizaeus-museum.de*; DM3/€1.50). Refreshingly different from the standard provincial museum, this hosts an international **loan exhibition** (daily 9am–5/6pm; DM12/€6) on a major archeological topic each year. What's on display is subject to change, but you're likely to be able to see part of the collection of **Egyptian antiquities**, which is one of the best in Europe and set attendance records for a touring display from Germany when it was shown in several North American cities at the end of the millennium. The most famous exhibit is the white limestone funerary monument of Hem-iunu from 2530 BC. Other outstanding sculptures include statuettes of Amenophis III and Teje (parents of Akhenaton), a statue of the fearsome half-man, half-jackal Anubis (the god of death) and the reliefs from the tomb of Seschem-nefer IV. The museum's other main strengths include a comprehensive collection of Chinese porcelain and a varied array of exhibits from the Peru of the Incas.

On Alter Markt, a short walk to the northeast, the heavily Italianate facade of Hildesheim's most celebrated Renaissance mansion, the **Kaiserhaus**, has recently been re-erected. Named after the statues and medallions of Roman emperors which adorn it, the facade has been placed in front of the headquarters of the **Hornemann-Institut**, the new scientific service centre of the Society for the Preservation and Conservation of World Cultural Heritage. Itself named in honour of one of Hildesheim's most famous sons, the pioneering Africa-explorer Friedrich Konrad Hornemann, the institute mounts a programme of temporary exhibitions (for up-to-the-minute information, call ☎0 51 21/40 81 74, or check the Web site: *www.hornemann-institut.de*) on global heritage themes in the Roemer-Pelizaeus Museum and elsewhere.

A little further to the east is the church of **St Andreas**. Within its exhilaratingly lofty Gothic interior, Luther's friend Johannes Bugenhagen converted the city to the Reformation. The church itself actually gained from the air raids – it was rebuilt according to the ambitious schemes of the original masons, which had never previously been fully put into effect. On the other hand, this hardly makes up for the almost complete loss of the square round the church, formerly regarded as a worthy rival to Marktplatz. For a fine view over the city, climb up the tall **tower** (April–Oct Mon–Sat 10am–5pm, Sun noon–5pm; DM3/€1.50).

The southern Altstadt

The southern part of Hildesheim was largely spared from war damage, and presents several streets of half-timbered houses as a reminder of what the whole of the old city once looked like. At the top end of Brühl, the nearest of these streets to the centre, the one surviving secular building from the time of St Bernward can be seen. Originally a fortified reception hall-cum-law court, it was converted into a collegiate foundation known as the **Kreuzkirche** in the late eleventh century, and now forms part of the otherwise Baroque parish church of the same name, making a truly odd combination. To the west of the southern section of Brühl runs the parallel Hinterer Brühl, an almost completely preserved old street. Look out for the early seventeenth-century **Wernersches Haus**, with its allegorical depictions of the Virtues and Vices, and representations of historical personalities.

At the end of the street is **St Godehard**, a former Benedictine monastery church built in the mid-twelfth century to commemorate the recent canonization of the man who had succeeded St Bernward as bishop of Hildesheim. Unusually well preserved, it boasts a pair of round towers on its facade, with a larger version of these over the transept. There is a delicate stucco relief over the north doorway showing Christ between St Godehard (holding a model of the church) and St Epiphanus. The interior proves the durability of the style pioneered at St Michael's, the only advance being the rich carvings on the capitals. The star piece of the church's rich treasury is a magnificent early twelfth-century psalter illuminated at the sister English monastery of St Albans; it is periodically kept here, but is also sometimes shown at the Diözesanmuseum.

East of St Godehard is another fine old street, Gelber Stern, among whose buildings is the mid-sixteenth-century **Haus des Waffenschieds**, the guild house of the armourers, decorated with carvings of the tools of the trade. At the end of the road, Lappenberg, which runs perpendicular to the south, has a complete row of craftsmen's homes. Nearby stands the **Kehrwiederturm**, the only surviving example of the gates which once surrounded the inner city. To the east is Kesslerstrasse, arguably the most imposing of the old streets, lined with impressive Renaissance and Baroque mansions. The largest and finest of these is the **Dompropstei** (Deanery) at no. 57, set in its own spacious yard. Just north of here is the **Lambertikirche**, which contains a lovely early fifteenth-century "Soft Style" retable painted by an unknown local master.

The suburbs

Another well-preserved old quarter is the **Moritzberg**, on a hill to the west of the city centre, and reached along Dammstrasse, Bergsteinweg and Bergstrasse. It's grouped round yet another Romanesque church, **St Mauritius**. Although dating from the second half of the eleventh century, this favoured the traditional format of a columned basilica, which is still evident despite the fact that the interior is now cloaked with Baroque decoration. The crypt and cloister, however, have been preserved in their original state. Unfortunately, there isn't much of a view from these heights; for that you have to go to the **Galgenberg**, at the opposite end of the city.

Eating, drinking and entertainment

Other than around Marktplatz, there's no obvious concentration of good places to **eat and drink** in Hildesheim, but there are plenty of possibilities dotted around the city which are well worth seeking out. A strong jazz tradition is the most distinctive feature of local cultural life.

Restaurants

Die Insel, Dammstr. 30. Named after its "island" setting among the canals at the western end of the Altstadt, this is a good choice for both full meals and *Kaffee und Kuchen*.

Knochenhaueramtshaus, Markt 7. The magnificent butchers' guildhall has eateries on four of its levels, offering everything from snacks to high-class cuisine.

Krehla, Moritzstr. 9. Up on the Moritzberg, this Weinstube with garden is a Hildesheim institution, having been run by the same family since 1853. Best known for its seven kinds of home-made fruit wines, it also serves inexpensive meals. Evenings only, closed Tues.

Kupferschmiede, Am Steinberg 6, Ochtersum (☎0 51 21/26 30 25). In a secluded forest setting 5km south of the Altstadt, this is one of the most famous restaurants in northern Germany, offering both *nouvelle cuisine* and hearty German fare. One for a splurge, although the set menus are far from extortionate. Closed Sun & Mon; reservations recommended.

La Gondola, Ostertorpassage, Osterstr. 41–44. Depsite its unprepossessing location in a shopping centre, this serves the best Italian food and wines in town.

Ratskeller, Markt 1. Far less expensive than its counterparts in most other cities (there are cheap daily specials at lunchtimes), yet it can rival them in quality. Closed Mon.

Schlegels Weinstube, Am Steine 4–6. Cosy, highly atmospheric little wine bar-restaurant in a half-timbered sixteenth-century building directly opposite the Roemer-Pelizaeus Museum. Evenings only; closed Sun.

Vier Linden, Alfelder Str. 55b. Part of a cultural centre which puts on cabaret and concerts, this has one of the most creative menus in Hildesheim, with plenty of vegetarian and wholefood dishes. Open Wed–Sun, evenings only.

Bars and cafés

Café Engelke im Bäckeramtshaus, Markt 8. Appropriately, the rebuilt bakers' guildhall houses a fine old-style café run by the municipal bakery.

Hildesheimer Brauhaus, Speicherstr. 9. Just a short walk from the Hauptbahnhof, this Hausbrauerei produces an organically brewed *Pils*; it also has a full menu and often features live music.

Il Giornale, Judenstr. 3–4. Internet café which also serves pizzas, salads and daily specials. Closed Sun.

Manhattan, Wollenweberstr. 78. Hildesheim is well known for its cocktail bars, and this is reckoned to be the coolest of the lot, with around two hundred different cocktails to choose from. Daily 8/9pm–4/5am.

Potters, Friesenstr. 17–18. Another very chic cocktail bar, one in which fresh fruit juices regularly feature among the mixes. Daily 5pm–2am, until 5am at weekends.

Spanier, Immengarten 5. Hildesheim's longest-established student Kneipe, offering a wide range of beers and inexpensive main courses. Open 8pm–2/3am, closed Sun.

Entertainment

Jazz fans should head for Hildesheim at Whit weekend, when the *Jazz-Time* festival presents the whole gamut of styles, both in formal concerts and impromptu open-air events. The regular year-round venue for live jazz is Bischofsmühle, Dammstr. 32. All kinds of **music** are featured along with **drama** in the varied programmes of the Stadttheater, Theaterstrasse 6 (☎0 51 21/3 31 64, *www.stadttheater-hildesheim.de*); there are also regular recitals and concerts in the Protestant churches. The main **popular festivals** are the *Frühlingsfest* for nine days in March, the *Weinfest* for a week in mid-May and the ubiquitous *Schützenfest* in mid-June.

Braunschweig (Brunswick)

Today **BRAUNSCHWEIG**, which lies 65km southeast of Hannover and 50km northeast of Hildesheim, is the epicentre of the most heavily industrialized part of Lower Saxony, but it preserves plenty of reminders of the far grander role it once played. During the twelfth century it was the chosen residence of **Henry the Lion** (Heinrich der Löwe), one of the most powerful princes in Europe, who commissioned innumerable monuments and works of art to grace his capital. Over the next few centuries the city became increasingly important as a commercial centre; its trade connections stretched into Russia, Scandinavia, Flanders and England, and the consequent wealth was put to use creating buildings worthy of the city's power and status. In the mid-eighteenth century Braunschweig had yet another brilliant period. The first technical university in the world, the Collegium Carolinum, was established here in 1745. When the local dukes took up residence again the following decade, having been absent for over three hundred years, their wonderful art treasures were put on public display and the city became a flourishing cultural centre.

Arrival, information and accommodation

Braunschweig's **Hauptbahnhof** is some distance to the southeast of the centre. It's quite a walk, so it's best to take tram #1, #2 or #5 to the "island" at the heart of the city. The main **tourist office** is at Vor der Burg 1 (Mon–Fri 9.30am–6pm, Sat 9.30am–2pm, Sun 9.30am–12.30pm; ☎05 32/27 35 50, fax 2 73 55 29, *www.braunschweig.de*); there's a branch in the entrance hall of the Hauptbahnhof (Mon–Fri 8.30am–5pm, Sat 9am–noon). **Mitfahrzentrale** have an office at Bohlweg 42–43 (☎05 32/1 40 41). The 24-hour **public transport tickets** are good value: within the city, they cost DM7/€3.50 for individuals, DM12/€6 for up to five people travelling together; these prices rise to DM10/€5 and DM16.50/€8.25 respectively if Wolfenbüttel and the surrounding area are included as well.

Braunschweig has a good range of **hotels** to suit all budgets, with several enticing upmarket options. The **youth hostel** is at Salzdahlumer Str. 170 (☎05 32/26 43 20, fax 2 64 32 70; DM28/€14 or DM32/€16) to the south of the city, reached by bus #11 or #19 to Krankenhaus, and has a few double rooms in addition to dormitories.

Hotels

Café am Park, Wolfenbütteler Str. 67 (☎05 32/7 30 79, fax 79 09 06, *www.hotel-cafeampark.de*). Very pleasant hotel and café at the eastern edge of the Bürgerpark, about ten minutes walk west of the Hauptbahnhof. Rooms with and without facilities are available. ④–⑥.

Deutsches Haus, Ruhfäutchenplatz 1 (☎05 32/12 00, fax 1 20 04 44 *www.ringhotels.de*). Fine old traditional hotel, part of the Ringhotel chain, at the corner of Burgplatz, to which it is linked by a picturesque "Bridge of Sighs". Its restaurant, *Zum Burglöwen*, is good and reasonably priced. ⑦.

Friedrich, Am Magnitor 5 (☎05 32/4 17 28, fax 2 40 77 43). Long-established Gasthof in the Magniviertel. It only has a few rooms, and is better known for its wine bar-restaurant, which has a huge vat with a capacity for storing ten thousand litres of wine. ②.

Haus zur Hanse, Güldenstr. 7 (☎05 32/24 39 00, fax 2 43 90 99, *www.haus-zur-hanse.de*). This hotel, which occupies a large half-timbered building, has one of the city's best restaurants, one which offers French-style cuisine as well as traditional German fare. ⑥.

Ritter St Georg, Alte Knockenhauerstr. 12–13 (☎05 32/1 30 39, fax 1 30 38, *www.ritter-st-georg.de*). A very attractive hotel in the oldest half-timbered house in the city, which dates back to 1346. The bedrooms are furnished in country-house style; the high-class, extremely expensive restaurant is beautifully appointed. ⑥.

Simoné, Celler Str. 111 (☎05 32/57 78 98, fax 57 43 13). Budget hotel a short distance to the north-west of the Altstadt, not far from the terminus of tram #1. ③.

Stadthotel Magnitor, Am Magnitor 1 (☎05 32/4 71 30, fax 4 71 34 99). Modern designer hotel in a fifteenth-century timber-framed building that was originally a storehouse. Its restaurant features both moderately priced and expensive dishes. ⑥–⑧.

Stadtpalais, Hinter Liebfrauen 1a (☎05 32/24 10 24, fax 24 10 25). Another designer hotel, this time in the whitewashed late eighteenth-century former orphanage. ⑦.

The City

The historic heart of the city is still completely surrounded by water – a man-made system based on the two arms of the River Oker – and contains several distinct medieval districts, which were formerly governed separately. Each of these quarters was centred on a market square and usually had its own parish church. Severe bomb damage in World War II means that the old buildings are now interspersed with plenty of ugly modern shops and offices, but it's still possible to visualize the medieval layout.

Burgplatz

To look at the city in chronological order, the **Burgplatz** in the middle of the "island" is the place to start. It's full of memories of Henry the Lion (see box below), who was at the peak of his power at the time the square was laid out. In 1166, he commissioned the **Burglöwe** (Lion Monument) to form its centrepiece. Perched high on a pedestal, this bronze statue, which was originally gilded, was the first freestanding sculptural monument to be made since the days of the Romans. Even though it has been replaced twice, the lion still stands as a potent reminder of the long centuries of power enjoyed by the Welfs.

In 1173 the **Dom** was begun, and was substantially complete before the end of the century. Its craggy, fortress-like external appearance (which seems to be another symbol of the power of the Welfs) is the prototype of a distinctive Braunschweig style, which was followed in all the other medieval churches of the city. Another feature copied throughout the city was the later insertion of a Gothic bell-gable between the two towers, which further increases the sense of the facade's massiveness. The interior is far lighter in feel. This is partly due to the well-preserved Romanesque **frescoes**, dating from around 1220, which were hidden behind plaster for centuries. The portraits

---

HENRY THE LION

Henry the Lion (1129/30–95) was born into the greatest of all dynastic feuds of the Middle Ages – that between his own family, the **Welfs**, and the **Hohenstaufens**, who then had a stranglehold on the office of Holy Roman emperor. His father, Henry the Proud, had been a major loser in this conflict, having been divested of his titles of duke of Saxony and Bavaria. By allying himself with his cousin, Emperor Frederick Barbarossa, "The Lion" quickly regained both duchies, and seemingly brought the feud to an end. His early career brought one success after another: he founded both the city of Munich and the port of Lübeck, and began the process of creating a strong Baltic state. However, he became too powerful for his own good, posing a threat to the feudal structure of the Holy Roman Empire. He fell out with Frederick over the price of his continued support of imperial policy in Italy and the Holy Land – his demand that the Free Imperial City of Goslar and its lucrative silver mines be made over to him was clearly excessive – and consequently was stripped of his titles and confined to his ancestral lands of Braunschweig-Lüneburg. The Welfs' feuding with the Hohenstaufens thereafter continued to bedevil medieval Germany – and dominated politics in Italy, where, under the names of the Guelphs and the Ghibellines, their followers championed the cause of papal and imperial power respectively. Nonetheless, the Welfs retained control over at least part of their heartland right up to the present century.

of saints in the nave, executed with the finesse of manuscript miniatures, are particularly fine. An even more crucial addition was the opening out of the north side of the Dom in the mid-fifteenth century by masons who seem to have been familiar with English Tudor architecture; the two new aisles are separated by a row of writhing **columns** which twist in alternate directions. On the end wall is the sole survivor of the previous cathedral which stood on this site, a Byzantine-inspired wooden *Crucifixion* signed by a certain Master Imerward. At the entrance to the choir a seven-branched **candelabrum,** donated by the founder, springs from a base of four crouching lions. In front is the limestone **tomb** of Henry the Lion and his second wife Matilda, daughter of Henry II of England. Memorials to other members of the Welf dynasty are housed in the crypt.

Facing the Dom is Henry's castle, **Burg Dankwarderode** (Tues & Thurs–Sun 10am–5pm, Wed 1–8pm; *www.museum-braunschweig.de*; DM5/€2.50 joint ticket with Herzog-Anton-Ulrich-Museum). Named in honour of the semi-mythical ninth-century founder of the city, it was constructed at the same time as the Dom. Its unusually complete appearance is mainly due to a nineteenth-century restoration, which follows the original form far more faithfully than most projects inspired by the Romantic reverence for the Middle Ages. From 10 to 11am (2.30–4pm on Wed) the showpiece **Rittersaal** on the first floor can be seen; for the remainder of the opening hours it is the museum of medieval art and artefacts on the ground floor which is on view. The star attraction of the latter is the **original Burglöwe**. Other highlights include an eighth- or ninth-century walrus-tooth casket, the eleventh-century arm-reliquary of St Blasius (patron of the Dom) and the cloak of Otto IV, son of Henry the Lion – and the only Welf to become Holy Roman Emperor.

The Burgplatz used to be a courtyard in its truest sense – the houses that stood around its edge belonged to the courtiers. Two half-timbered sixteenth-century successors to these survive – the **Von Veltheimsches Haus** and the **Huneborstelsches Haus** – and nowadays serve as the headquarters of the local chamber of commerce. The Neoclassical mansion in the opposite corner of the square was originally a publishing house, but now accommodates the **Braunschweigisches Landesmuseum** (Tues, Wed & Fri–Sun 10am–5pm, Thurs 10am–8pm; *www.landesmuseum-bs.de*; DM3/€1.50, or DM5/€2.50 combined ticket with Jüdisches Museum and the Abteilung Ur- und Frühgeschichte in Wolfenbüttel). This contains local history displays on the Braunschweig region; in the entrance hall is the second version of the Burglöwe.

Altstadtmarkt

The other significant cluster of Braunschweig's past is found in and around the **Altstadtmarkt** to the west. A corner of this is taken up by the former **Rathaus**, which ranks as one of the most beautiful and original secular buildings in Germany. Consisting of two wings arranged in an L-shape, its present form dates back to the early fifteenth century, when the open upper arcades, with their flowing tracery and statues of the Welfs, were added. The graceful lead **Marienbrunnen** in the middle of the square was made around the same time; it's topped by a shrine-like structure with the Virgin and Child and the four Evangelists.

Opposite stands the **Gewandhaus** (Drapers' Hall), its grandeur reflecting the importance of the medieval tailors. The facade is a Dutch-influenced Renaissance composition of extraordinary elaborateness, whose gable, shaped like an equilateral triangle, is crowned by a figure of Justice. Alongside is the half-timbered seventeenth-century **Zollhaus**, once used by customs officials and the military. Also on the square is the Baroque **Stechinellihaus**, designed by the Italian court architect after whom it's named, who was also responsible for many buildings in Celle.

St Martini, originally a twelfth-century basilica, stands at the far end of Altstadtmarkt. The finest and earliest of Braunschweig's parish churches, it follows a

---

TILL EULENSPEIGEL

One of Germany's most famous semi-historical characters, **Till Eulenspiegel** (the name means "Owl Mirror") was born of peasant stock in the village of Kneitlingen near Braunschweig around 1300. Disrespectful of all forms of authority and realizing the inherent foolishness of the human condition, he lived by his native wit, consistently putting points over on pompous aristocrats, merchants, churchmen and scholars with his practical jokes and punning sense of humour. Anecdotes about him were popular all over medieval Europe, and were first published in book form in the early sixteenth century. Oddly enough, it was not until 1995 that a complete and unbowdlerized English translation became available (see Contexts, p.1108). His name has since been enshrined in the German word for tomfoolery (*Eulenspiegelei*) and the French name for a rogue or scoundrel (*espiègle*). He has also inspired two major works of art – a brilliant orchestral showpiece by Richard Strauss and an epic poem by a winner of the Nobel Prize for Literature, Gerhart Hauptmann.

---

pattern repeated elsewhere in the city – it was initially modelled on the Dom, but was later altered internally to form a spacious hall. It also gained some fine sculptures in the fourteenth century, notably the group of the Wise and Foolish Virgins on the north doorway. Another addition is the Gothic chapel dedicated to St Anne, housing a Renaissance pulpit that shows St Martin dividing his coat in order to clothe a beggar.

The other historic quarters

North of Burgplatz, reached via Casparistrasse or Bohlweg, is the old district of Hagen, centred on Hagenmarkt. Its fountain bears a nineteenth-century statue of Henry the Lion carrying a model of the church of **St Katharinen**, which he also founded. Closely modelled on the Dom, St Katharinen's interior was later transformed into a spacious Gothic hall church. The same is true of **St Andreas** further to the west, which was the parish church of the Neustadt. Its south **tower** (May–Sept Mon, Wed & Fri 9am–noon & 2–4pm, Tues & Thurs 2–4pm, Sat 10am–noon; DM2/€1) can be ascended for a view over the city. Across from this church is the **Liberei**, a fifteenth-century library building which is the only example of Gothic brick architecture in the city. Further west, on Bäckerklimt, is the bronze **Eulenspiegelbrunnen**, commemorating the legendary jester Till Eulenspiegel (see box above). The owls and monkeys on the fountain represent the shapes into which he would work dough as an apprentice in a nearby bakery. The shop itself was bombed in 1944, but similar breads remain a local speciality to this day.

Raised above the old city on a slight hillock at its southern edge stands the former Benedictine monastery of **St Aegidien**, which incorporates the only church in Braunschweig built in a pure Gothic style. Its handsome pulpit retains the original late Gothic reliefs by Hans Witten, a sculptor who was the equal of the more famous Riemenschneider and Stoss, but whose reputation suffers from the fact that most of his work is in remote Saxon towns. The monastic buildings now house the **Jüdisches Museum** (Tues & Thurs–Sun 10am–5pm, Wed 10am–8pm; *www.landesmuseum-bs.de*; DM3/€1.50, or DM5/€2.50 combined ticket with Braunschweigisches Landesmuseum and the Abteilung Ur- und Frühgeschichte in Wolfenbüttel), which vividly illustrates German Jewish culture down the centuries. There's even a full-scale reconstruction, complete with all the original fittings, of a Baroque synagogue dismantled last century.

Braunschweig's other significant district is the Altewiek a few blocks further north. This is now usually known as the Magniviertel after the church of **St Magni** which forms its core. The few half-timbered streets in the city which completely escaped

destruction in the air raids are found around here, and the semicircular group immediately behind the church and the blind alley called Herrendorftwerte, just to the east,
are particularly evocative. This is also one of the liveliest areas at night, with a host of
pubs and restaurants.

The Herzog-Anton-Ulrich-Museum

North of the Magniviertel, on Museumstrasse, is the **Herzog-Anton-Ulrich-Museum**
(Tues & Thurs–Sun 10am–5pm, Wed 1–8pm; *www.museum-braunschweig.de*;
DM5/€2.50 joint ticket with Burg Dankwarderode). It's particularly intriguing in that
it reflects the personal artistic tastes of the duke after whom it's named, who was
responsible for building it up some three hundred years ago. The collection was
opened to the public in 1754, thus making it the first museum in Germany.

In the second-floor picture gallery, pride of place goes to the Dutch School, and in
particular to one of **Rembrandt**'s most psychologically acute works, *A Family Group*.
It was painted at the very end of his life, and shows his style at its most advanced and
daring, with its loose brushwork supplemented by extensive use of the palette knife, its
heavy chiaroscuro effects and the informal arrangement of its subjects. Rembrandt's
very personal vision of biblical stories is represented here by a tender nocturne of *The
Risen Christ Appearing to Mary Magdalene*. The dramatic *Landscape with
Thunderstorm*, bathed in warm golden hues, shows yet another side of his diverse
genius.

Vermeer's *Girl with the Wineglass* displays a level of technical virtuosity fully equal
to, but very different from, Rembrandt's. Probably executed with the help of a cam-
era obscura, it captures the three-dimensional space of the interior to uncanny effect.
Two other highlights of the Dutch collection include a subtly delicate late fifteenth-
century portable altar known as the *Braunschweig Diptych* and a sharply observed
Self-Portrait by the country's leading sixteenth-century artist, **Lucas van Leyden**.
Most of the specialist painters of the seventeenth century are represented; *The
Marriage of Tobias and Sara* by **Jan Steen** and three landscapes by **Jacob van
Ruisdael** are particularly notable. Among Flemish works of the same period are sev-
eral examples of **Rubens**, a fine **Van Dyck** and a fetching **Teniers**, *The Alchemist's
Workshop*.

The most important of the German works on view in the gallery is the *Portrait of
Cyriacus Kale* by **Holbein the Younger**. It was painted in London, where the
Braunschweig-born sitter worked at the Hansa trading headquarters, as the inscription
states. A strong representation of **Cranach** includes a lively workshop cycle of *The
Labours of Hercules*, and a *Hercules and Omphale*. The latter is by Cranach's hand alone,
as is the *Portrait of Albrecht von Brandenburg-Ansbach*, which depicts the cross-eyed
Hohenzollern who had been Grand Master of the Teutonic Knights. By the time this
picture was painted, Albrecht had converted to Protestantism, secularized his order's
holdings and thereby become Duke of Prussia – events which were crucial in his family's ultimately successful drive to win leadership of the German nation. A delicate
Morning Landscape by the short-lived **Elsheimer** rounds off this section.

Duke Anton Ulrich's taste in Italian painting seems to have been confined to the
sixteenth-century Venetians and the bombastic artists of the Baroque. The most fascinating work is what's labelled a *Self-Portrait* by the mysterious father-figure of Venice's
Renaissance, **Giorgione**. One of the few surviving paintings widely accepted as genuine, it's probably a cut-down version of a *David with the Head of Goliath*. Important
examples of the later Venetian Renaissance include works by Veronese, Tintoretto and
Palma il Vecchio.

In the **decorative arts** section on the top floor Italy features rather more extensively, with a notable array of bronzes and porcelain, plus a valuable onyx vase from

Mantua. Other particular strengths are Chinese lacquerwork, Limoges enamels and jewellery, ceramics and furniture from all over Europe.

Eating, drinking and entertainment

In addition to the excellent hotel restaurants mentioned above, Braunschweig has plenty of good places to eat and drink. There's a good concentration of these in the Altstadt, and another in the Uni-Viertel just to the north. Braunschweig has a strong **theatre** tradition; in the now demolished building on Hagenmarkt the first part of Goethe's *Faust* received its premiere in 1829.

Restaurants

Brodocz, Stephanstr. 1. Vegetarian and wholefood restaurant (it also serves fish dishes) in a pretty half-timbered courtyard. Closed Sun in winter.

Gewandhaus, Altstadtmarkt 1. High-quality restaurant in the Gothic cellars of the Gewandhaus. The menu includes several dishes in a dark sauce known as *Mumme*, named after a famous malt beer which was exported to England until the eighteenth century. Closed Sun.

Mutter Habenicht, Papensteig 3. This candlelit Gaststätte with beer garden has been going strong for well over a century. Closed Sun.

Rialto, Wendenring 1–4. Italian restaurant whose evening menu includes a selection of fresh fish displayed on a trolley. There's live music at weekends.

Rodizio Brazil, Kaiserstr. 8. Brazilian speciality restaurant which offers a DM35/€17.50 all-you-can-eat buffet, including ten different sorts of grilled meats on skewers.

Schalander, Stobenstr. 12. Serves very moderately priced *gutbürgerliche Küche*.

Stadtpark, Jasperallee 42. This late nineteenth-century half-timbered Gaststätte in the Stadtpark features both Swabian and local dishes, including freshly caught carp; it also has the city's largest beer garden. Closed Mon.

Tricolore, Güldenstr. 77. Occupying a fine historic house, this offers modern Italian cuisine and a good selection of Sicilian wines.

Cafés and bars

Anders, Am Magnitor 7. Trendy bar in the Magniviertel.

Bassgeige, Bäckerklimt 11. Bar which holds regular live jazz sessions.

Café L'Emigré, Rosenhagen 3. French-style brasserie.

Café Voigt, Friedrich-Wilhelm-Platz 6. The pick of the traditional cafés.

Die Schüssel, Konstantin-Uhde-Str. 4. Student Kneipe with beer garden; it has live jazz on Thurs, jam sessions on Fri.

Hermann's, Schleintstr. 18. Another popular bar in the Uni-Viertel; it serves a variety of food throughout the day, including huge baguettes. Open evenings only on Sat.

Schadt's, Höhe 28. Hausbrauerei which makes *Pils* and *Weizen* plus a seasonal *Märzen*; also serves full meals.

Zum Löwen, Waisenhausdamm 13. A larger offshoot of the above, housed in the same historic building as the *Stadtpalais* hotel.

Entertainment

The building where *Faust* was performed was replaced a few decades later by the Staatstheater (☎05 32/1 23 45 67) at Am Theater (between Museumpark and Theaterpark), which remains the leading venue for **opera** and **drama**. Shows with an alternative slant are presented at FreiBiZe, an old waterworks in the Bürgerpark (☎05 32/4 70 21 31). **Concerts** of all kinds are held at the modern Stadthalle on Leonhardplatz (☎05 32/7 07 70), not far from the Hauptbahnhof. There's a **festival** of modern chamber music each November, while the main annual folklore event is a medieval market held on Burgplatz at Whitsun.

Wolfenbüttel

Reached in just a few minutes from Braunschweig via the first state-owned rail line in Germany (opened in 1838), **WOLFENBÜTTEL** is a place which deserves to be far better known. One of the Welf duchies had its seat there from 1432 to 1754, and even today it preserves much of the layout and atmosphere of a ducal Residenzstadt. Indeed, it offers the most evocative example of the petty courts which once dotted the politically fragmented map of the Holy Roman Empire. When the local dukes moved back to Braunschweig, Wolfenbüttel seems to have fallen into a deep slumber. It came through World War II unscathed, and no fewer than six hundred historic half-timbered houses survive, as well as plenty of large public buildings.

The Town

Wolfenbüttel is the earliest example in Germany of a **planned town** – in fact, it evolved from several consecutive plans, all of whose outlines are still visible. At the western end is the spacious **Schlossplatz** with the main ducal showpieces, while beyond lies the **Alte Heinrichstadt**, the original centre. The subsequent planned suburbs lie further east.

Schlossplatz

On the western side of Schlossplatz is the huge, dazzlingly white **Schloss** (Tues–Sat 10am–5pm, Sun 10am–1pm; DM3/€1.50). Apart from the moat and some reused masonry, nothing remains of the medieval moated fortress, the present structure being a conflation of Renaissance and Baroque. The most distinguished feature is the Renaissance **tower**, whose unusual design includes a gabled clock-face on each side. It was built in the early seventeenth century by **Paul Francke**, who was responsible for many of the buildings in the first phases of the planning of Wolfenbüttel. This apart, the exterior of the Schloss dates from a century later and was designed by the highly inventive **Hermann Korb**. The upper arcades of the Palladian-style inner **courtyard** were originally open, following normal Italian practice; however, they were filled in soon after, when the incompatibility of open arcades and northern weather became apparent. Round the back of the Schloss, a troupe of English actors under Thomas Sackville established themselves as the first permanent theatre company in Germany in 1590.

THE WORLD'S MOST EXPENSIVE BOOK

Arguably the most sumptuous manuscript produced in the Romanesque period, Henry the Lion's *Evangelistary* or **Gospel book** was commissioned around 1180 for use in the Dom in Braunschweig. Among its 24 beautifully coloured full-page miniatures is a scene showing Christ crowning Henry and his English wife Matilda; the saints in paradise include Thomas à Becket, recently murdered as a result of a misunderstood remark made by his friend Henry II, Matilda's father. In the nineteenth century, the Welf family reacquired this heirloom, but sold it after World War II to a secretive private collector. In 1983, it was auctioned by Sotheby's in London; desperate to gain this key piece of their heritage, the Land government of Lower Saxony headed a consortium which splashed out £10 million, setting a world-record price for a work of art. Although this figure has been trumped many times, it was not until 1998 that a book (a copy of Audubon's *Birds of America*, which was paid for in US dollars) sold for a sum which could be said to be larger. However, when inflation is taken into account, the *Evangelistary* can still justly claim to be the most expensive book in the world.

This ushered in a golden era for the performing arts in Wolfenbüttel, but the opera house built there the following century has unfortunately not survived. The surprisingly modest **state apartments** give a good impression of how the dukes lived.

On the north side of Schlossplatz is the **Zeughaus**, again by Francke. Its cheerful crimson exterior, decorated with richly carved gables, hardly suggests its original function as an arsenal, whose cavernous lower floor once housed the biggest and most powerful cannons in Germany. Immediately behind is the grandest of Wolfenbüttel's half-timbered buildings, a huge mid-seventeenth-century storehouse.

Nowadays, the Zeughaus hosts temporary exhibitions from the pride of the town, the **Herzog-August-Bibliothek** (Tues–Fri 10am–4pm, Sat & Sun 10am–5pm; DM6/€3, including entry to the Lessinghaus), whose headquarters are the nineteenth-century pseudo-*palazzo* diagonally opposite. The dukes of Braunschweig-Wolfenbüttel were true bibliophiles and by the mid-seventeenth century the scholarly August the Younger had built up the largest library in Europe, consisting of 130,000 volumes, all catalogued by himself. Several rooms of the main library have been laid out as a museum, with changing selections from its holdings of rare books, as well as other specialities such as Renaissance maps and globes and twentieth-century artists' sketchbooks. A strongroom holds a display on the library's greatest treasure, the **Gospel book of Henry the Lion** (see box on p.689), but unfortunately the initial intention to put on permanent public display the original manuscript itself has not been honoured, though it is occasionally exhibited, usually in September.

The **Lessinghaus** (Tues–Fri 11am–5pm, Sat & Sun 10am–5pm; same ticket as the Herzog-August-Bibliothek) in front of the Bibliothek was the official residence of the librarian. A triple-winged summer house, it was finished just three years before the dukes decided to abandon Wolfenbüttel as a residence. Its present name comes from the second famous holder of the librarian's post, the hugely influential playwright **Gotthold Ephraim Lessing**, who spent the last eleven years of his life there; a collection of memorabilia pays tribute to him. The main work from his Wolfenbüttel years is *Nathan the Wise*, a piece particularly interesting in the light of subsequent German history – its wholly admirable hero is a Jew modelled on the famous philosopher Moses Mendelssohn.

Alte Heinrichstadt

East of Schlossplatz is the original late sixteenth-century planned town, the **Alte Heinrichstadt**. One of its focal points is the **Stadtmarkt**, a square lined with half-timbered buildings, in the centre of which is a bronze statue of Duke August the Younger, depicted leading his horse rather than riding it.

Off the north side of the square, on the street named after it, is the **Kanzlei** (Chancellery). Though somewhat messed about, it's notable as being the only surviving building by the Dutchman Hans Vredeman de Vries, the leading architectural theoretician of the Northern European Renaissance. The Kanzlei now houses the Braunschweigisches Landesmuseum's archeology department, the **Abteilung Ur- und Frühgeschichte** (Tues–Fri & Sun 10am–5pm; *www.landesmuseum-bs.de*; DM3/€1.50, or DM5/€2.50 combined ticket with Jüdisches Museum and the Braunschweigisches Landesmuseum in Braunschweig). Almost all the other streets around here are worth walking along; look out for **Klein-Venedig** (Little Venice), so named because it fronts a canal.

As a climax to the Alte Heinrichstadt, the **Hauptkirche** (Tues–Fri 10am–12.30pm & 2–4/5pm, Sat 10am–12.30pm & 2–4pm) was begun in 1608 by Paul Francke. Notwithstanding the dedication to Beatae Mariae Virginis, it was not only Lutheran from the outset, but was also the first parish church to be built specifically for the Protestant faith (although Bückeburg's Stadtkirche, started three years later, was actually finished first). It's an extraordinary confection, mixing late Gothic, Renaissance and

Mannerism, while the main portal – designed like a triumphal arch with statues of two of the dukes ensconced between Moses and Aaron below, and Christ at the summit – has all the swagger of the emergent Baroque style. On the long sides of the building are a series of profusely decorated gables, while on the facade and in the vestibule are hundreds of delicately carved reliefs of animals and demons. The church's light and spacious interior doubles as the ducal pantheon. Regular recitals are held on the early Baroque organ, first presided over by the composer **Michael Praetorius**, who is buried below. He's best known for his beguiling arrangements of over three hundred foot-tapping dance melodies, collectively known as *Terpsichore*.

The rest of the town

East of the Hauptkirche is the **Neue Heinrichstadt**, centred on the Holzmarkt; for the most part, its buildings faithfully follow the style of the earlier part of town. In the early eighteenth century, Hermann Korb finished off the square in an ingenious fashion by inserting the oval **Trinitatiskirche** (Tues 11am–1pm, Wed 11am–1pm & 2–4pm, Thurs 3–5pm Sat 11am–4pm) between the two redundant gateways at the far end, transforming the latter into a pair of towers for the church in the process.

Further east, across the Oker, a huge new town of manufacturing workshops called the **Juliusstadt** was once planned. However, it never got beyond a couple of streets. Instead, the far more modest craftsmen's suburb of **Auguststadt** was laid out at the opposite end of Wolfenbüttel, to the west of the Schloss. Its houses are remarkably similar to those in the "better" part of town, and the half-timbered **Johanniskirche**, set beside its detached belfry in a shady green, brings a touch of rusticity to the quarter.

Practicalities

Wolfenbüttel's **Bahnhof** is immediately south of the historic centre, on the opposite side of the River Oker. The **tourist office** (April–Oct Mon–Fri 10am–5pm, Sat 9am–1pm; Nov–March Mon–Fri 10am–5pm; ☎0 53 31/8 62 80, fax 8 64 44, *www.wolfenbuettel.de*) is at Stadtmarkt 9.

Many of the **hotels** occupy interesting old buildings. North of the Altstadt the half-timbered *Forsthaus*, Neuer Weg 5 (☎0 53 31/7 17 11; ③), was for thirty years the holiday home of the cartoonist Wilhelm Busch. *Gasthof Kaltes Tal*, to the rear of the Bahnhof at Goslarsche Str. 56 (☎0 53 31/4 38 28; ③), is an inn first documented in the seventeenth century. *Kronprinz*, Bahnhofstr. 12 (☎0 53 31/12 65; ④), has an inner courtyard and a winter garden, while *Altes Haus*, Enge Str. 25 (☎0 53 31/13 62; ④), and *Bayrischer Hof*, Brauergildenstr. 5 (☎0 53 31/50 78; ⑤), both occupy timber-framed buildings in the Altstadt. The most luxurious hotel is the modern *Parkhotel Altes Kaffeehaus* just beyond the southeastern fringe of the centre at Harztorwall 18 (☎0 53 31/88 80; ⑥). There's an unofficial **youth hostel** at Jägerstr. 17 (☎0 53 31/2 71 89, fax 90 24 45; DM24/€12 or DM30/€15).

The best **restaurants** are in the hotels listed above, especially the *Historisches Weingrotte* in the *Parkhotel Altes Kaffeehaus*, a reconstruction of the once celebrated but long-destroyed *Türkisches Kaffeehaus* of 1838. Main **festivals** are the open-air *Theaterfest* in June/July and the *Altstadtfest* in late August.

Königslutter and Wolfsburg

East of Braunschweig, on each of the two main rail routes into the former GDR, are a couple of very contrasting diversions, both well worth a visit. **Königslutter am Elm** is an adjunct to an imperial abbey, while **Wolfsburg** is the headquarters of one of Germany's most famous and successful enterprises, Volkswagen.

Königslutter am Elm

KÖNIGSLUTTER AM ELM lies some 20km away in the shadow of the beech forest of Elm. The one monument worth seeing here is the former **Abtei**, set at the opposite end of town from the Bahnhof. Founded by Emperor Lothar III in 1135, its earliest and finest parts were built by Romanesque masons from Lombardy. The small-scale and infinitely varied sculpture is an outstanding illustration of the thoughts and obsessions of the medieval mind. It can be seen on the exterior of the apse, adorned with grotesque human masks, imaginary beasts and hunting scenes, and on the north doorway, whose twisted columns are guarded by menacing lions. It's also present in the north walk of the cloister, each of whose columns is of a different shape and design from any other. The interior of the church is covered with frescoes – an over-enthusiastic nineteenth-century attempt, admittedly using some rather ghostly traces as a starting point, to re-create the original appearance.

Wolfsburg

WOLFSBURG, 30km further north, is an archetypal company town. As late as the 1930s, it was a hamlet of 150 souls; nowadays 130,000 people live here, almost exactly half of them employees of the giant **Volkswagenwerk** (guided tours usually Tues–Fri at 1.30pm; free; but phone ahead to confirm, on ☎0 53 61/92 42 70). The **Automuseum** (daily 10am–5pm; DM9/€4.50), east of the Hauptbahnhof on the opposite side of the tracks at Dieselstr. 35, displays around ninety different models produced in the course of the works' history, with examples by other German car makers. Other than this, Wolfsburg boasts significant examples of modern architecture. Right in the heart of town is the **Kulturzentrum** by the internationally acclaimed Finnish architect Alvar Aalto. The adjacent **Kunstmuseum**

THE PEOPLE'S CAR

The impetus behind the setting-up of the **Volkswagen** company (which was initially state-owned) came directly from Hitler, who wanted a small, reliable car that anyone could afford to buy and run. It was Ferdinand Porsche – a name indelibly associated with vehicles aimed at the very opposite end of the market – who in 1936 provided the design for the distinctive little machine whose hallmarks were its sloping bonnet, its rear engine and its starting crank, and which popularly came to be known as the Beetle. Two years later, the factory was built; it was destroyed during the war, whereupon the story might well have ended.

In the event, Volkswagen became a fairy-tale postwar success, and one of the linchpins of West Germany's "economic miracle". The Beetle's cheapness and durability made it a huge export hit, and up to 20 million were produced in a year. In 1961, 1.5 million small shareholders were given the chance to share in the profits when the government sold off its majority holding. However, the company ran into serious difficulties in the 1970s: no attempt had been made at diversification, and sales of the Beetle plummeted as increased general affluence led to a demand for more luxurious cars. To halt the decline, the drastic decision was taken to scrap the old faithful altogether (though it's still made under licence in Mexico), and to develop a new range of models, based on the more upmarket but still modest Golf. It was also decided to make extensive use of robots in the construction process. Finally, the CDU government, normally far less infatuated with privatization programmes than its Conservative counterpart in Britain, disposed of all its remaining shares in 1988. These measures have by and large been successful, even if the Midas-touch formula of the past is now accepted as having been lost for ever. In 1998, a new version of the Beetle was developed in California, this time with a front engine, giving the car a new lease of life for the new millennium.

(Tues 11am–8pm, Wed–Sun 11am–6pm; *www.kunstmuseum-wolfsburg.de*; DM7/€3.50) hosts permanent and temporary displays of modern art. Just to the southwest is the **Theater Wolfsburg**, a late work by one of Germany's leading twentieth-century designers, Hans Scharoun. About 1km south on Röntgenstrasse is Aalto's **Heilig-Geist-Kirche**.

SOUTHERN LOWER SAXONY

South of Wolfenbüttel, Lower Saxony's landscape soon makes a significant change to the gentle wooded slopes of the **Harz** mountain range. This was long a famous mining area, thanks to rich deposits of gold, silver and other less precious minerals, but these have, in the last century, become exhausted. At the edge of the mountains, the old imperial city of **Goslar** is the area's main draw, a place as evocative of medieval Germany as any you'll find. Nothing else within the Lower Saxon section of the Harz is of comparable quality, but just beyond the range are a number of impressive old half-timbered towns, such as **Einbeck**, the home of *Bockbier*, **Duderstadt** and **Hann. Münden**. As a complete contrast to these, there's the university city of **Göttingen**, which boasts the most exciting atmosphere of any town between Hannover and Frankfurt.

Goslar

The stereotype of a mining town immediately conjures up images of rows of grim identikit terraced houses paying obeisance to the gargantuan, satanic-looking machinery in whose shadow they lie. **GOSLAR**, which stands in an imposing location at the northern edge of the Harz, could not be more different. Admittedly, the mining here was always of a very superior nature – silver was discovered in the nearby six-hundred-metre-high **Rammelsberg** in the tenth century, and the town immediately prospered, soon becoming the "treasure chest of the Holy Roman Empire", and a favourite royal seat. As a Free Imperial City in the later Middle Ages, Goslar, though never very large, ranked as one of the most prosperous communities in Europe, with lead and zinc now added to the list of ready-to-hand mineral deposits. Despite two fires sweeping through the streets in 1800, much survives as a reminder of this heady epoch. The presence of a POW hospital during World War II helped to spare it from Allied bombing, ensuring that the entire town now enjoys the status of a protected monument. With just cause too, as Goslar claims to have more **old houses** (over 1500, with 168 dating from before 1550) than any other town in Germany.

Arrival, information and accommodation

Goslar's **Bahnhof** and **bus station** are at the northern edge of the Altstadt, just across from the Neuwerkkirche. It's only about ten minutes' walk to Marktplatz, where you'll find the municipal **tourist office** at no. 7 (May–Oct Mon–Fri 9.15am–6pm, Sat 9.30am–4pm, Sun 9.30am–2pm; Nov–April Mon–Fri 9.15am–5pm, Sat 9.30am–2pm; ☎0 53 21/7 80 60, fax 78 06 44, *www.goslarinfo.de*). The DM18/€9 **MuseumSpass** gives admissions to the main monuments and sights in the Altstadt.

There are around two dozen **private houses** (①–③) with rooms to rent; a full list is available from the tourist office. If travelling in a group and intending to stay for at least three days, it can be an even better deal to rent a **holiday home**; most atmospheric are the luxury apartments in *Burg im Zwinger*, Thomasstr. 2 (☎0 53 21/4 10 88 or 8 51 35, fax 410 61, *www.zwinger.de*; ③). The **youth hostel**, Rammelsberger Str. 25 (☎0 53 21/2 22 40, fax 4 13 76; DM22/€11 or DM27/€13.50), is at the foot of the mine, not too far from the centre, but a long trek from the Bahnhof. Nearest **camping** is the well-equipped *Sennhütte*, Clausthaler Str. 28 (☎0 53 21/2 24 98), in the Gose valley, along the B241 in the direction of Clausthal-Zellerfeld. Goslar is amply endowed with **hotels** and **guesthouses**, many of them in historic buildings.

Hotels and guesthouses

Der Achtermann, Rosentorstr. 20 (☎0 53 21/7 00 00, fax 7 00 09 99, *www.der-achtermann.de*). Goslar's most prestigious hotel, diagonally opposite the Bahnhof, is a huge rambling complex of various dates, with thermal and steam baths, sauna, solarium and romantic old-style restaurant. ⑦–⑨.

Das Brusttuch, Hoher Weg 1 (☎0 53 21/3 46 00, fax 34 60 99, *www.treff-hotels de*). Treff chain hotel in a famous sixteenth-century patrician mansion with salacious carvings on its facade. It has a restaurant and a Weinstube, and includes large breakfast buffets in the room price. ⑦–⑨.

Goldene Krone, Breite Str. 46 (☎0 53 21/3 44 90, fax 34 49 50, *www.kiekin-hotels.de/goldenekronegoslar*). Highly regarded hotel in a half-timbered house at the northeastern end of the Altstadt. Its restaurant specializes in local game dishes. ⑥.

Kaiserworth, Markt 3 (☎0 53 21/70 90, fax 70 93 45, *www.goslar.de/kaiserworth*). Another of Goslar's best-known buildings, a 500-year-old guildhall with a 1000-year-old cistern, through which you pass to reach the bar, the *Dukatenkeller*. Also has a wine bar, gourmet restaurant and pavement café. ⑥–⑧.

Möller, Schieferweg 6 (☎0 53 21/2 30 98) One of the best bargains in Goslar, this guesthouse is in a large Jugendstil villa few minutes' walk west of the Bahnhof. The buffet breakfasts, with lots of home-made goodies, are remarkable. ③.

Niedersächsischer Hof, Klubgartenstr. 1–2 (☎0 53 21/31 60, fax 31 64 44). Grand old station hotel, which has recently undergone a thorough modernization; many of the bedrooms have balconies. There's a good restaurant and a bistro, *Pieper's*. ⑥–⑨.

Verhoeven, Hoher Weg 12 (☎0 53 21/2 38 12, fax 4 66 53). Guesthouse with café in a slate and half-timbered house overlooking the Kaiserpfalz. ③.

Villa Berger, Obere Triftweg 6 (☎0 53 21/2 16 40, fax 4 22 06). Nicely furnished hotel with restaurant in a large villa high above the western side of the Altstadt, of which it has a fine view. ⑤.

Zur Alten Münze, Münzstr. 10 (☎0 53 21/2 25 46, fax 1 84 16). Mid-range hotel in a delightful 500-year-old timber-framed building in the heart of the Altstadt. ⑤.

Zur Börse, Bergstr. 53 (☎0 53 21/3 45 10, fax 1 84 37). Hotel and restaurant in a 400-year-old house with characteristic rosette decorations. ④–⑥.

The City

Few places in Germany so richly reward unguided wandering as Goslar, with the least visited corners often rivalling the obvious set pieces. Reckon on a couple of days to see everything.

Marktplatz

Although it hosts an attractive market with fish and pastry specialities on Tuesdays and Fridays, Goslar's **Marktplatz** is best seen empty to fully appreciate the gorgeous visual variety of its buildings, ranging from creamy-textured walls, via pretty half-timbering to sober red and grey slate. The rather comical-looking gold-plated **Reichsadler** (imperial eagle) sits perched on top of the fountain in the middle of the square. Sculpted in Romanesque style in the early thirteenth century, this is now the third copy, but, remaining completely faithful to the original, it still looks more like a cock uncertainly poised for take-off than a fearless bird of prey.

At 9am, noon, 3pm and 6pm, the modern **Glockenspiel** – rather appropriately housed on top of the municipal treasurer's building – explains how Goslar rose to be the richest town in Europe during the late Middle Ages. First to appear are a Knight and his horse; the latter, according to legend, pawed the ground of the Rammelsberg, and uncovered silver traces. When the boom began, the emperors moved in, and Otto I is presented here with a lump of silver by the Knight. The remaining groups show miners hacking their way from the Middle Ages through to the nineteenth century, finishing with their present-day counterparts proudly displaying their state-of-the-art equipment. It's a rather a sad twist, then, that due to depletion of the various ores, Europe's oldest mine – which had nearly three thousand employees – closed down for good in 1988.

Across the square is the **Rathaus** (guided tours daily: April–Oct 9am–5pm; Nov–March 10am–4pm; DM6/€3), whose **Huldigungssaal** (Hall of Homage) ranks as one of the best-preserved secular interiors of the Middle Ages. The name is rather misleading, as homage was actually paid in the great hall where the admission desk is now situated. Its gold-starred, marine-blue panelled ceiling dates from the original construction of the building in the latter half of the fifteenth century; the chandeliers, carved from antlers and carrying figures of the emperors, were transported from the

Dom a few decades later. The Huldigungssaal itself was the assembly hall of the city council from 1500 onwards and later used for the town's archives. Its richly decorated panels, painted by an unknown artist over four hundred years ago, show scenes from the life of Christ and portraits of various citizens of Goslar. Several valuable relics are hidden in altar niches and closets behind the panelling. Among them are a precious gold and silver tankard from the fifteenth century, elaborately embellished with mining and hunting scenes, and a facsimile of the **Goslarer Evangeliar** (Goslar *Evangelistary*), a thirteenth-century manuscript with exquisite Byzantine-inspired Romanesque miniature paintings. The **original Reichsadler** is also on view.

Opposite is the **Hotel Kaiserworth**, previously the guild house of tailors and cloth-makers. Here Baroque and Gothic tumble down on top of Renaissance arches, while the frontage bears eight statues of German emperors, with a corbel depicting a naked man excreting a gold coin thrown in for good measure. Just behind the Rathaus is the **Marktkirche**, dedicated to the Roman martyrs SS Cosmas and Damian, patrons of the medical profession. The architecture, a mix of Romanesque and Gothic, with twin towers and rough-hewn masonry, is typical of Goslar. Inside, look out for the cycle of stained-glass windows illustrating the saints' lives, and the bronze baptismal **font** created by a local artist, Magnus Karsten, in 1573: just about every major biblical event is represented on it in magnificent detail.

The southwestern quarters

Goslar's **half-timbered** beauty begins in earnest in the streets behind the Marktkirche. The styles to look out for are Gothic, Renaissance and Baroque, many homes having two and sometimes all of these: Gothic pointed arches are transformed into three-stepped inlays, usually dull red, gold and olive green in colour; sombrely brilliant rosettes cartwheel across the rafters of the Renaissance houses, while gaudily coloured Baroque devils lie like flattened gargoyles bereft of their power in their prisons of beam.

The oldest houses lie in the Bergstrasse and Schreiberstrasse areas; the **Siemenshaus** (Tues & Thurs 9am–noon; free), which was built by a forefather of what is today one of Germany's largest suppliers of medical equipment, electrical appliances and armaments parts, is conveniently situated on the corner of the two. Further down Schreiberstrasse, classic Gothic brick houses abound, the style exemplified by the early sixteenth century embodied at no. 10, with its lavishly decorated chimney passing through the two single-roomed storeys. From here, turn left into Frankenberger Strasse and continue down to Frankenberg Plan, on which stands the **Kleines-Heiliges-Kreuz**, set in spacious gardens where the old folk who retire there – and dozens of chickens – can amble about at their leisure.

Through the archway to the right, you can walk up to the **Frankenberger Kirche**, once the church favoured by miners for their weddings, which is situated in tranquil solitude on the little hill above. Built during the twelfth century as a Romanesque basilica, the later Gothic additions form part of the town's western ramparts. The gigantic Baroque carved wooden Passion altar verges on pastiche and could easily dominate the place until you begin to take in a few other details. Towards the back of the church, two fierce lions stand facing each other to absorb the evil believed to come from the west. Some faint thirteenth-century frescoes compete in vain for attention against an over-charged Baroque pulpit, and there's a strange **triumphal cross**, with a deathly white Christ macabrely topped with a wig of the artist's own hair, a device used frequently in the Harz area.

On Peterstrasse immediately to the east are some of the most intriguing of the town's houses: the **Kuhhaus** (Cow House) at no. 27 is named after its previous function, while the **Kürbishaus** (Pumpkin House) at no. 23 is named after its shape. In the **Klauskapelle** to the right and the **Schmiedhaus** (Blacksmith's House) opposite, the miners would respectively pray and collect their sharpened tools before beginning their daily trek up to the Rammelsberg.

The Kaiserpfalz

Dominating a spacious park at the southern end of the Altstadt is the **Kaiserpfalz** (daily: April–Oct 9am–5pm; Nov–March 10am–4pm; DM8/€4). By far the largest and most important Romanesque royal palace to have survived anywhere in Europe, its exterior is still a potent symbol of the power and wealth enjoyed by Germany's medieval rulers. Built at the beginning of the eleventh century to be home to a succession of greedy emperors enticed by the riches hidden in the Rammelsberg behind it, the Kaiserpfalz continued to flourish for nearly three hundred years, hosting important Imperial Diets and benefiting from Goslar's proximity to the crossroads of the two major trade routes of the Middle Ages – from Flanders to Magdeburg, and from Lübeck to Venice. A fire which gutted the palace in 1289 and a decline of interest around the same time by the emperors kept the building in a state of disrepair over the next few centuries, humbling it even to the point where it was used as a barn and stables during the seventeenth century. Kaiser Wilhelm I came to the rescue in 1868, paying for its reconstruction.

By present-day standards, the building seems over-restored. This is particularly true of the interior, where the vast **Reichsaal**, whose enormous arched window openings must have given birth to many a draughty Diet during the palace's heyday, was covered, floor to ceiling, with Romantic paintings. Various emperors are depicted being valiant (in battle), pious (distributing riches to the poor), conquering the earth and being blessed by heaven. On the southern side of the hall is the early twelfth-century **Ulrichskapelle**. This chapel, the most authentic part of the complex, is an ingenious piece of design: the ground plan is a Greek cross, but the upper storeys are shaped as a Byzantine-style octagon. In the centre stands the tomb of Emperor Heinrich III, though it contains only his heart: the rest of his body lies in Speyer.

Behind the palace, the *Goslar Warrior* by **Henry Moore** lies reclining with his shield on his toe; this is a legacy of the first of the annual prizes awarded by the city to a famous modern artist. Beyond it a pretty semi-walled rose garden, dotted about with firs and shady spreading trees, leads down to a small bridge, the Abzucht stream and a stone-walled tower.

Hoher Weg

On the opposite side of the Kaiserpfalz, facing the Hoher Weg, the enormous car park stretching below you was once the site of the eleventh-century **Dom** – more accurately, the **Stiftskirche St Simeon und Judas** – pulled down in 1822 due to lack of funds for restoration. Only the **Vorhalle** with its facade of stucco statues survived. Behind the protective glass door is the original part-bronze **imperial throne**; it was used symbolically at the opening assembly of the Second Reich in Berlin in 1871. Other relics from the church are housed in the Goslarer Museum (see below). The Dom's stones are now embedded in any number of houses, having been sold at the time of demolition to townsfolk who subsequently built their homes with them.

Directly in front of the Dom, Hoher Weg leads down to the **Grosses-Heiliges-Kreuz** (daily 11am–4/5pm; free) at no. 7, one of the oldest hospices in Germany, dating back to 1254. It has recently been beautifully restored, and has been given a new lease of life as a handicrafts centre. The magnificent main hall hosts several markets a year, and several small shops have been set up in the ground-floor cells. Further down the street is the **Musikinstrumente- und Puppenmuseum** (daily 11am–5pm; DM6/€3). On the first floor, an eclectic array of musical instruments from around the world features such oddities as a combined violin and trumpet, a cello with a keyboard and a sub-contrabass lute. What is thought to be the oldest musical instrument in Germany, a recently unearthed hurdy-gurdy from around 1500, is also on view. The second floor has a collection of rare old dolls.

Goslar's most famous mansion, the sixteenth-century **Brusttuch**, lies at the bottom of Hoher Weg, almost opposite the Marktkirche. It's an outstanding example of the "Wild Man" style, whose theme of "natural" unbridled sexuality was a great favourite with German Renaissance artists and craftsmen. The beams of the top storey are crammed with satirical carvings of figures from medieval life, folklore, religion and mythology: mischievous cherubs firing arrows at angels, dignified ladies perched on top of goats, and a carelessly suggestive dairymaid churning butter and squeezing her buttocks at the same time. Facing it across Marktstrasse is the **Bäckergildehaus** (Bakers' Guild House), a far more sober, yet equally imposing, example of half-timbering.

The northern quarters

Immediately north of the Marktkirche is the **Schuhhof**, the site of the former shoemakers' guildhall and market. Fires over the centuries have ravaged one part of the square, but the surviving side has three- and four-storey half-timbered houses from the seventeenth century. Münzstrasse on its western side contains more architectural beauties, including a seventeenth-century coaching inn, the **Weisser Schwan** at no. 11, where the **Zinnfigurenmuseum** (Tin Figure Museum; daily 10am–5pm; DM5/€2.50) depicts in miniature scenes from the history of Goslar and the Roman Empire.

At the end of the street, turn into Jakobistrasse, where, at no. 15, a Renaissance craftsman's house has been the subject of one of the most polished and professional pieces of restoration in Goslar. The **Mönchehaus Museum** (Tues–Sat 10am–1pm & 3–5pm, Sun 10am–1pm; DM5/€2.50) lies just beyond, at the corner with Mönchestrasse. A black and white half-timbered sixteenth-century building, it's the curious home to Goslar's permanent modern art exhibition, featuring works by recipients of the city's annual prize. The contrast works amazingly well indoors, with de Koonings, Tinguelys and Vasarelys hanging amidst the oak beams. The effectiveness of the huge metal sculptures parked in the garden is more debatable, but it's good to see something in Goslar with an experimental touch.

On the square at the eastern end of Jakobistrasse is the Catholic parish church, the **Jakobikirche**. Only the west wing remains from the original Romanesque structure, which was rebuilt in Gothic style. Inside, there's a moving Pietà by the great but elusive early sixteenth-century sculptor, Hans Witten. North along Rosentorstrasse, the **Neuwerkkirche** (Mon–Fri 10am–noon & 2.30–4.30pm, Sat 10am–noon) stands in a peaceful garden. It was built as a Cistercian convent church during the late twelfth and early thirteenth centuries; the most striking exterior features are the two polygonal towers, and the delicate late Romanesque carvings on the apse. Inside, there are works of art dating back to the period of construction, notably the choir screen and some rather clumsily retouched frescoes. The curious **stone handles** high up on the pillars of the nave are unique in the history of architecture and have a didactic purpose: those on the south have grotesque carvings and represent the temptations of the devil; the wreaths on the north symbolize the eternity for which the soul should strive. On the south side of the church is the recently planted **Romanischer Garten**, a re-creation, based on the writings of Hildegard of Bingen, among others, of a conventual garden of the period.

The Abzucht and the Stadtbefestigung

From Marktplatz, south along Worthstrasse, a fairly successful attempt at an artists' quarter has been constructed along and around the banks of the **Abzucht**, the tiny stream that passes through the southern part of Goslar. On the corner of Abzuchtstrasse and Königstrasse is the **Goslarer Museum** (April–Oct Tues–Sun

9am–5pm; Nov–March Tues–Sun 10am–4pm; DM5/€2.50). This contains the usual local history displays, including a section on mining in the Rammelsberg. However, the collection is taken out of the ordinary by some superb treasures from the Dom, including a couple of stained-glass windows and the exotic *Krodoaltar* – which looks more as if it were fashioned deep in the heart of Africa than in eleventh-century Europe. The original **Goslarer Evangeliar** is also on view, though only the cover can be seen. Another highlight is the seventeenth-century laboratory of the **Ratsapotheke**.

The Abzucht bubbles along the cobbles to occasionally bump into one of the handful of rickety water-mills still remaining of an original twenty-five; follow the red stones in the middle of the pathways to find the sites of the former mills, now replaced by houses. Look out for the **St-Annen-Stift** (Mon–Thurs 10am–noon & 2–4pm, Fri & Sat 10am–noon; knock at the door for entrance; free), a hospice dating from 1488, the oldest half-timbered building in Goslar. Inside, you can view the chapel with its medieval woodwork and seventeenth-century wall-paintings.

From here, it's a short walk down St Annenhöhe to see the best-preserved parts of the **Stadtbefestigung**. It takes about two hours to walk the complete circuit, which is interspersed with many stretches of greenery. If pressed for time, go down Zingerwall to see the **Zwinger** (March daily 10am–4pm; April to mid-Nov daily 9am–5pm; DM3.50/€1.75), an ivy-covered, thick-walled tower once used by the town's artillery. It commands a fine view over Goslar and the Harz; there's also a display of medieval weapons and a restaurant. The most imposing part of the town's fortifications is the bulky ensemble of the **Breites Tor** at the northeasternmost corner, the sight of which alone must have been enough to scare off any would-be invaders.

The Rammelsberg

Of the various walks in the vicinity of Goslar, the most interesting is the geological trail round the **Rammelsberg** (ask at the tourist office for a leaflet). A more pressing reason for visiting the mountain which provided the city with its wealth is the **Bergbaumuseum** (guided tours daily 9am–6pm; *www.rammelsberg.de*; DM21/€10.50 combined ticket for all three sections, see below for separate entry fees) which has been set up in the famous mine; bus #C runs to the entrance from the town centre. The visit begins in the hall-like changing room, now used as an exhibition explaining the historical background. Here you don a miner's overalls and helmet before descending into the bowels of the earth. Each of the three separate tours lasts between an hour and an hour and fifteen minutes. The first (DM9/€4.50) is a walk through the tunnels to see some of the old machinery, including the giant waterwheels; the second (DM13.50/€6.75) is a ride on the underground railway to the part of the mine that was the last to be exploited; while the third (DM9/€4.50) covers the equipment used for ore processing.

Eating and drinking

Goslar's food and drink scene is geared to the fact that many of the town's visitors are taking a relaxing holiday – hence the presence of so many cafés. Many of the best restaurants are in the hotels (see pp.694–5).

Barock-Café Anders, Hoher Weg 4. Best place in town for *Kaffee und Kuchen*; there's a Baroque room upstairs and a garden at the back with a leafy vista of the Harz.

Bistro Filou, Worthstr. 10. Offers creative Gallic-style cooking. Evenings only, closed Sun.

Brauhaus Wolpertinger, Marstallstr. 1. This Hausbrauerei, serving one dark and two light beers, revived Goslar's medieval brewing tradition after a long gap. It's one of several bars grouped round a courtyard which have collectively become the liveliest spot in town.

Butterhanne, Marktkirchhof 3. Located in a sixteenth-century hat-maker's shop, this café-restaurant specializes in home-made cakes and dishes using fresh game from the Harz.

Christall, Bäckerstr. 106. The long menu here features plenty of inventive vegetarian dishes.

Der Andechser im Ratskeller, Markt 1. Goslar's Ratskeller has recently been revamped as a Bavarian-style restaurant with beer from the monastic brewery of Andechs.

Digeridoo, Hoher Weg 13. Australian theme bar and restaurant serving kangaroo steaks and Foster's lager. Hugely popular with the locals.

Historisches Café, Markt 4. Another good choice for those with a sweet tooth, particularly when the weather is good and you can sit outside on the square.

Weisser Schwan, Münzstr. 11. Part of this famous old inn is given over to a Balkan grillroom that's a cut above the German norm.

Worthmühle, Worthstr. 4. Does excellent hot provincial cooking at very low prices.

The Harz mountains

Nowhere, other than in Berlin itself, was the reality of the postwar division of Germany more evident than in the **Harz mountains** (see map on p.907), the first barrier encountered by the icy winds which sweep across the North German plain. A popular holiday destination since the nineteenth century, the Harz were divided right through the middle by the notorious barbed-wire frontier. Most roads came to a dead end, and adjacent villages were completely cut off from each other, often to the ruin of local economies. Despite the many changes which have occurred since reunification – which have included the establishment of the **Nationalpark Harz** in the western part to match the Nationalpark Hochharz in Saxony-Anhalt – the differences between the two sides of the Harz remain a vivid illustration of the effects of four decades of national division. For one thing, many of the towns on the Lower Saxon side were converted into modern resorts which are characterless in comparison with their eastern counterparts. For another, the mountain steam rail lines which are still such an attraction in the former GDR were closed down here and replaced by buses: the only trains left are those running along the northern and western fringes of the range.

The range has a climate which is euphemistically described as "bracing". Although this means that there's lots of rain and fog, with heavy snowfall in winter, it doesn't deter hordes of mainly elderly holidaymakers who have earned the region the derisive sobriquet Rentnergebirge (pensioners' mountains). Perhaps they're drawn by the relatively gentle slopes of the mountains ("the skiing here is for babies," according to another insult) which make the Harz ideal for healthy but undemanding **walking** holidays.

Clausthal-Zellerfeld

The most direct route into the Harz from Goslar will take you to **CLAUSTHAL-ZELLERFELD**, some 20km to the southwest. If you're driving, it's best to take time to admire the scenery: the direct B241 road winds and climbs its way through dense forest flanked by a number of small, hidden lakes. Buses tend to follow a more circuitous route via Hahnenklee, a big winter-sports resort, now officially incorporated into Goslar, built round a Scandinavian-style stave church from the first decade of the twentieth century.

Two old towns merged into one, Clausthal-Zellerfeld is a characterful place where half-timbered houses are interspersed with those faced with coloured slate. It was the main mining centre of the Upper Harz, but the last pit shut down in 1931. The tradition is exhaustively documented in the excellent **Oberharzer Bergwerksmuseum** (daily 9am–5pm; DM7/€3.50) at Bornhardtstr. 16 in Zellerfeld, the northern part of the double town. Included in the entrance fee is a tour through the life-sized model of a pit which has been erected in the garden; make sure you ask for the English-speaking guide, as the language used is very technical. You can wander at your leisure round the other mining buildings, which have been moved here from their original locations. Star piece is the **Pferdegaipel**, a shaft which was worked by horses and is the only one of its kind in Germany.

Clausthal clusters around the **Marktkirche**, the largest wooden church in central Europe. Built in the first half of the seventeenth century, its main body is of fir, while the tower is made of oak. Inside are notable furnishings, of which many, including the double gallery, the retable and pulpit, are also fashioned from wood. Across the street is the **Technische Universität**, which grew out of the mining academy established here in the eighteenth century. Its **Mineraliensammlung** (Mon 2–5pm, Tues–Fri 9am–noon; DM1/€0.50) is reckoned to be one of the largest and best collections of minerals in the world.

Practicalities

The **tourist office** is in the old train station building in the gully between the towns at Bahnhofstr. 5a (Mon–Fri 9am–noon & 2–5pm, Sat 9am–noon; ☎0 53 23/8 10 24, fax 8 39 67, *www.clausthal-zellerfeld.de*). There are plenty of **private houses** with rooms to let (①–③). Among the **hotels** in Zellerfeld are *Zellefelder Hof*, Markstr. 13 (☎0 53 23/37 45; ④), *Der Kleine Prinz*, Goslarsche Str. 20 (☎0 53 23/9 66 10; ④), *Wolfs*, Gosalrsche Str. 60 (☎0 53 32/8 10 14; ⑤), and *Calvör*, Treuerstr. 6 (☎0 53 23/95 00; ⑤). In Clausthal the choice includes *Friese*, Burgstätterstr. 2 (☎0 53 23/9 38 10; ⑤), and *Goldene Krone*, Am Kronenplatz 3 (☎0 53 23/93 00; ⑥). The **youth hostel** is at the extreme eastern end of Clausthal at Altenauer Str. 55 (☎0 53 23/8 42 93, fax 8 38 27; DM22/€11 or DM27/€13.50), while the *Waldweben* **campsite** is at the northwestern fringe of Zellerfeld at Spiegeltaler Str. 31 (☎0 53 23/8 17 12). All of the hotels listed above have **restaurants**; the Gaststätte of the Bergwerksmuseum, which features game specialities, is another good place to eat, while the best **bar** is *Anno Tobak*, a student favourite at Osteroder Str. 4, diagonally opposite the Marktkirche.

Along the former border

The old border between East and West Germany has lost its barbed wire, and with it much of its fascination, but it remains well worth a visit for the scenery. The transport hub for the area is the plush spa of **BAD HARZBURG**, which has rail links to both Goslar (which is only ten minutes away) and Braunschweig. It also has plenty of accommodation to suit all pockets, from **private rooms** (①–③) to fine **hotels** such as *Parkblick*, Am Stadtpark 6 (☎0 53 22/78 09 70; ⑤), *Harzburger Hof*, Kurhausstr. 23 (☎0 53 22/78 20; ⑥), *Germania*, Berliner Platz 2 (☎0 53 22/95 00, *www.hotelgermania.de*; ⑦), and *Braunschweiger Hof*, Herzog-Wilhelm-Str. 54 (☎0 53 22/78 80; ⑦).

The fifteen-kilometre hiking trail from Bad Harzburg to the crossroads hamlet of **TORFHAUS** used to be one of the most prized Cold War thrills, passing as it did right alongside the Iron Curtain. Even now, it has an eerie fascination, as some ghostly watchtowers have been left standing. Torfhaus, which can also be reached by bus, offers the best views of the celebrated **Brocken** (see p.924), rendezvous of the witches on *Walpurgisnacht* (April 30), a festival celebrated in all the towns in the Harz. The path from here was reopened soon after the Berlin Wall came down, and makes an enticing alternative to the easier approach from Schierke. If you want to do some serious hiking in the area, Torfhaus's **youth hostel** (☎0 53 20/2 42, fax 2 54; DM24/€12 or DM29/€14.50) makes an obvious base. A further 5km south, there's another crossroads at the **Oder-Teich**, an artificial lake made in the eighteenth century, where you can take a swim.

Einbeck

EINBECK, which lies just to the west of the Harz, is something of a mecca for **beer** lovers, being the original home and the most authentic producer of Germany's famous strong brew, *Bockbier*. The town is almost equally well known for its half-timbered houses, characteristically painted in yellow, red, green and black – around 120 survive from the sixteenth century alone.

The hub of life in Einbeck is the **Marktplatz**, which is surrounded by well-kept and obviously genuine sixteenth-century houses. Look out for the **Brodhaus** and the **Ratsapotheke**, which stand next door to each other like two superannuated old men opposite the **Ratswaage** (Weigh House) and the vaguely sinister-looking **Rathaus**. The Rathaus could well have served as a model for the witch's house in the Hansel and Gretel story, thanks to three low conical spires which sprout out of the stairwell and the two sharply contrasted oriel windows. Dominating the square from its central position is the **Marktkirche**, a box-like Gothic hall church with a striking red sandstone Baroque facade.

Immediately to the west lies **Tiedexer Strasse**, the most impressive street in town, with a gloriously picturesque ensemble of half-timbered houses. However, the finest house of all is no. 13 in **Marktstrasse**, whose whole facade is covered with intricate allegorical carvings, drawing on Christian and Classical themes. Another handsome street, Steinweg, leads north to another red sandstone Gothic church, the **Stiftskirche St Alexandri** (Mon–Fri 10am–noon). Its set of choir stalls, bearing the date of 1288, is the oldest in Germany, though the main treasure is a magnificent Romanesque chandelier. At Steinweg 11, a fine patrician mansion has been adapted to contain the local history collections of the **Städtisches Museum** (Tues–Fri 10am–noon & 3–5pm, Sat & Sun 10am–noon; DM3/€1.50). The ticket also gives admission to the **Fahrradmuseum** (same times, but currently closed), a short walk south of Marktplatz at Pupenstr. 1–3, a collection of bikes which has everything from the wooden-wheeled boneshakers of 1817 to the very latest racers. It's also worth taking a walk round the surviving sections of the **Stadtmauer**; much of the fortification network is intact and you can stroll along the massive earthworks which were constructed to increase the protection afforded by the wall itself.

BOCKBIER

In the Middle Ages Einbeck boasted no fewer than seven hundred breweries – virtually all of which were tiny part-time operations run within the household. Many of the houses where beer was brewed can still be identified: two clues to look for are double doorways (one of which was used for rolling the barrels through), and dense groupings of dormer-like ventilation openings in the attic, where the raw ingredients were stored. Made from wheat and fermented from the top, what became known as *Einpöckisches Bier* was a strong brew designed for export, with fermentation taking place in the course of the journey to the customer. Its most famous historical appearance came at the Diet of Worms in 1521 when Luther used it to fortify himself during his heroic stand against the full might of the empire and the papacy. In time, the drink became known as **Bockbier** (after a corruption of the town's name); it was introduced into the Hofbräuhaus in Munich, and has long been as popular in Bavaria as in Lower Saxony. Two crucial differences between the modern and old versions are that it's now made from barley and fermented from the bottom. Nowadays, the Einbecker Brauerei is the only brewery left in the home town of this headily potent beer. It produces both light (*Hell*) and dark (*Dunkel*) varieties, as well as the special brown *Maibock*, available only in springtime. All of these have a smooth, dry and highly satisfying flavour. Curiously enough, locals tend to prefer its other, more conventional products: a *Brauherren-Pils* and a *Spezial*.

Einbeck's **Bahnhof** is 4km from the centre in the castle-crowned village of Salzderhelden. **Buses** have replaced the former branch rail line into the town, but note that these do not necessarily connect with the arrival and departure of trains. The **tourist office** is in the Rathaus (April–Sept Mon–Fri 9am–5.30pm, Sat 10am–1pm; Oct–March Mon–Thurs 9am–1pm & 2.30–5pm, Fri 9am–12.30pm; ☎0 55 61/91 61 21, fax 91 63 00, *www.einbeck-online.de*), Marktplatz 6–8.

Of the **hotels** with a central location, the most reasonably priced are *Zur Stadt Einbeck*, Benser Str. 27 (☎0 55 61/40 86; ④), and *Haus Joanna*, Bürgermeisterwall 8 (☎0 55 61/9 33 50; ④). For a bit more luxury, try *Der Schwann*, Tiedexer Str. 1 (☎0 55 61/46 09; ⑤), or *Gildehof*, Marktplatz 3 (☎0 55 61/79 00; ⑤). These also have two of the best **restaurants** in town – the former is the more expensive and is open evenings only – and are good places to sample the local beers. An alternative is *Zum Brodhaus*, which occupies a wonderful fourteenth-century building at Marktplatz 13. There are also several elegant **cafés**, including the exquisitely furnished *Antik Café*, Tiedexer Str. 42–44.

Göttingen

GÖTTINGEN is positively metropolitan in contrast to the surrounding area. It owes its exciting, buzzing atmosphere to its large student population (30,000 out of a total populace of 130,000), who have made sure that the **nightlife** here almost has a big-city feel to it. In fact, a lot of students come to Göttingen after studying in Berlin, and they seem to have brought some of the latter's pace with them. Things quieten down a little outside term time – but there's usually something going on.

Arrival, information and accommodation

Göttingen's **Hauptbahnhof**, a major rail junction, lies just to the west of the centre, which is reached by going straight ahead via the underpass, then along Goetheallee. The main **tourist office** (April–Oct Mon–Fri 9.30am–6pm, Sat & Sun 10am–4pm; Nov–March Mon–Fri 9.30am–1pm & 2–6pm, Sat 10am–1pm; ☎05 51/4 99 80 30, fax 4 99 80 10, *www.goettingen.de*) is on the first floor of the Altes Rathaus. There's another opposite the Hauptbahnhof at Berliner Str. 11 (Mon–Fri 9am–6pm, Sat 10am–2pm; ☎05 51/4 99 80 40, fax 4 00 29 98). **Mitfahrzentrale**'s office is at Burgstr. 7 (☎05 51/1 94 44).

The **youth hostel** is 3km east of the centre at Habichtsweg 2 (☎05 51/5 76 22, fax 4 38 87; DM27/€13.50 or DM32/€16); take bus #6 or #9 from Kornmarkt. Göttingen's centrally sited **hotels** tend to be on the pricey side, but there are plenty of bargains a bit further out.

Hotels

Berliner Hof, Weender Landstr. 43 (☎05 51/38 33 20, fax 3 83 32 32). Moderately priced hotel, handily placed for the university. ④.

Central, Jüdenstr. 12 (☎05 51/5 71 57, fax 5 71 05). The only hotel in the heart of the Altstadt. ⑥–⑧.

Gebhards, Goetheallee 22–23 (☎05 51/4 96 80, fax 4 96 81 10). Göttingen's leading hotel occupies a renovated eighteenth-century palace just across from the Hauptbahnhof on the way to the centre. It also has a fine restaurant, *Georgia-Augusta-Stuben*. ⑧–⑨.

Kasseler Hof, Rosdorfer Weg 26 (☎05 51/7 20 81, fax 7 70 34 29). Mid-range hotel a short distance southwest of the Altstadt. ④–⑥.

Landgasthaus Lockemann, Im Beecke 1, Herberhausen (☎05 51/20 90 20, fax 2 09 02 50). Offering very good value by Göttingen standards, this country-house style hotel with restaurant (closed Mon) is in an eastern suburb, reached by bus #10. ③.

Onkel Toms Hütte, Am Gewende 10–11 (☎05 51/7 20 36, fax 7 70 00 34). Very pleasant hotel with restaurant and beer garden in the southern outskirts, reached by bus #5 or #6. ④–⑥.

Stadt Hannover, Goetheallee 21 (☎05 51/4 59 57, fax 4 54 70). Good-quality hotel right alongside *Gebhards*. ⑤.

The Town

Most of Göttingen's sights are in the small Altstadt, particularly in and around the Markt. The famous university is spread out all over the town, though its most imposing buildings are found in the eastern part of the Altstadt, and around the green belt encircling the former fortifications.

The central Markt is dominated by the **Altes Rathaus**, a massive sandstone structure which has an almost Venetian feel to it, quite at odds with the half-timbered buildings nearby. Most of what you can see today dates back to the fourteenth and fifteenth centuries, when Göttingen was at the height of its commercial prosperity, but it was never completely finished, as resources had to be diverted to constructing the municipal fortifications. The only way of seeing much of the building is by taking a **guided tour** (Sun at 3pm; free). At other times, unless there's an exhibition on, you'll have to be content with viewing the medieval-looking frescoes and coats of arms painted on the inner walls; these are only a little over one hundred years old, having been commissioned by the authorities during the restoration of the building in the 1880s. When the weather is good the Rathskeller takes over part of the Markt and you can have a drink or a meal while looking at the **Gänseliesel**, "the most kissed girl in the world", a bronze

---

GÖTTINGEN'S ACADEMIC TRADITION

Göttingen was a decayed market town when King George II of Great Britain, in his capacity as elector of Hannover, founded the **University** in 1737. A free-thinking, liberal atmosphere was immediately promoted, in sharp contrast to the authoritarian traditions of Germany's other seats of learning. This enabled Göttingen to establish a high reputation very quickly, which it has maintained ever since. In its early days, it was particularly associated with poets, such as the group known as the Göttinger Hain-Bund, early Romantics who wrote on folklore, nature and homely themes, and **Gottfried August Bürger**, holder of the chair of aesthetics, whose ballads (especially *Leonore*, with its vivid image of Death) were enormously influential. The university's literary reputation continued in the nineteenth century with the appointment of the **Brothers Grimm** to professorships – while there Jacob wrote an exhaustive study, *Teutonic Mythology*, which was to inspire similar studies of national folklore all over Europe. Unfortunately, this tradition, along with Göttingen's liberal standing, was severely tarnished by the dismissal of the brothers and five colleagues in 1837 for failing to kowtow to the reactionary new constitution introduced into the Kingdom of Hannover.

Mathematics and science have, if anything, been even stronger academic specialities in Göttingen. In the eighteenth century, the leading figure was **Georg Christoph Lichtenberg**, who invented the prototype of the photocopying machine and the hot-air balloon. He was also a dedicated Anglophile and a brilliant satirical writer; his *Book of Aphorisms* (available in Penguin Classics) is a storehouse of worldly wisdom, whose clarity and precision puts all subsequent German philosophy to shame. Throughout the first half of the last century, **Carl-Friedrich Gauss** dominated the university's intellectual life. His name is given to a unit of the field of magnetic intensity, and, in partnership with Wilhelm Weber, he invented the electromagnetic telegraph. In the next generation, the chemist **Friedrich Wöhler**, best known for his pioneering work with aluminium, preserved the university's position at the forefront of world science. The last century saw a string of Nobel Prizes awarded to Göttingen professors. Since World War II, the town has been the headquarters of the fifty separate high-powered scientific research units of the **Max-Planck-Institut**, named in honour of the discoverer of quantum theory, who passed his last years here.

statue of a goose-girl erected at the beginning of last century, to whom, according to tradition, the students must give a few smackers when they pass their finals.

Behind the Altes Rathaus is the **Johanniskirche** (May–Oct daily 11am–noon), a twin-towered fourteenth-century Gothic church. Theological students are allowed free accommodation in one of the **towers**, but they have to endure the sound of the bells from the other tower and miserable living conditions (no running water or toilets), as well as granting admission on Saturdays between 2pm and 4pm to anyone wanting to climb up for a view of the town. Behind the church is the medieval **Johannesviertel**, more or less a slum district until the 1970s, when the city finally got round to tarting it up. At the point where Johanniskirchhof runs into Paulinerstrasse is the former **Paulinerkirche**, originally built by Dominican friars in 1331, which in 1529 was the scene of the first Lutheran church service in Göttingen. Used as the provisional home of the university when it first opened, the building now houses part of its library.

Following the pedestrianized main street, Weender Strasse, north from the Markt brings you to the **Jakobikirche** (May–Oct daily 11am–1pm), another Gothic church, dominated this time by a single octagonal tower which was designed by an associate of the famous Parler dynasty of masons. From Judenstrasse at the back of the church, turn right into Ritterplan, where the only aristocratic mansion left in the town has been refurbished to house the **Städtisches Museum** (Tues–Fri 10am–5pm, Sat & Sun 10am–5pm; DM3/€1.50). As you'd expect, this has a Göttingen bias, with a big collection of religious art and plenty of examples of locally produced glass and porcelain.

Finest of all the university buildings is the Neoclassical **Aula** on Wilhelmsplatz, a couple of blocks south of the Städtisches Museum and a similar distance east of the Markt; this graduation hall was built to celebrate the centenary of the university's foundation. Many of the departments have their own museum; unfortunately, these tend to be open only one day a week, or by appointment. One definitely worth trying to catch is the **Völkerkundliche Sammlung**, Theaterplatz 15 (Sun 10am–1pm; DM5/€2.50), which includes part of the collection assembled by Captain Cook in the South Seas and a bizarre array of four hundred fertility symbols and mother-god effigies.

Anybody who knows anything about German history won't be able to resist the **Bismarckhäuschen** (Tues 10am–1pm, Thurs & Sat 3–5pm; free), a small tower on the southern edge of the town centre which forms part of the old city wall. In 1833 this was home to the 17-year-old **Otto von Bismarck**, then a student in the city. The man who later became the "Iron Chancellor" and who finally realized, by a mixture of brute force and astute politicking, the long-established ideal of a united Germany, was forced to live here, having been banned from the city centre for drunkenness and "misbehaviour of various kinds".

North along Angerstrasse is the **Marienkirche**, which stands on what used to be the boundary between the Altstadt and the so-called Neustadt, built as a rival town outside the original city walls by a local nobleman in an attempt to challenge the increasingly powerful burghers. The citizens' response to this threat was an astute one. They waited until the nobleman went bankrupt and then bought the Neustadt from him, incorporating it into Göttingen itself. The Marienkirche looks quite unecclesiastical, which probably has something to do with the fact that its bell tower used to be one of the gateways to the Neustadt; the street still passes through an archway cut in it.

Eating, drinking and entertainment

Above all, Göttingen is a city where you can enjoy yourself. There are dozens of cafés, bars and restaurants which, thanks to the large student contingent, tend to be high on atmosphere and low in cost. All kinds of music and theatre are regularly performed in the town.

Restaurants and historic student taverns

Gauss am Theater, Obere Karspüle 22. Rivals the *Georgia-Augusta-Stuben*, in *Gebhards* hotel (see p.703) as the most distinguished restaurant in town. Evenings only, closed Sun.

Junkerschänke, Barfüsserstr. 5. Another of Göttingen's best restaurants, housed in a beautiful fifteenth-century half-timbered building; rather pricey, but worth it. Closed Mon.

Naturell, Lange-Geismar-Str. 40. Inventive vegetarian and wholefood restaurant. Open Mon–Fri 10.30am–7pm, Sat 10.30am–3pm.

Pfannkuchenhaus, Speckstr 10. A student favourite with a huge variety of sweet and savoury pancakes.

Rathskeller, Markt 9. Notwithstanding the anachronistic spelling, Göttingen's town-hall restaurant is archetypal, with food to rival any in Germany.

Taormina, Groner-Tor-Str. 28. Recommended pizzeria which stays open until 1.30am.

Zum Altdeutschen, Prinzenstr. 16. Göttingen's most famous student tavern, even if these days its clientele seems to be dominated by tourists.

Zum Schwarzen Bären, Kurze Str. 12. Romantic Gaststätte dating back to the sixteenth century, complete with stained-glass windows and cosy little alcoves; the food is first class and fairly reasonable in price. Closed Sun evening & Mon.

Zum Szültenbürger, Prinzenstr. 7. Another celebrated student tavern, with basic dishes such as *Schmalzbrot* as an alternative to full meals.

Bars and cafés

Blue Note, Wilhelmsplatz 3. Slightly upmarket jazz/blues bar which seems to be favoured by medical and law students.

Chups, Kornmarkt 9. A chrome-decor basement café, which, thanks to its cheap baguettes and live music in an animated atmosphere, is highly popular with undergraduates.

Cron & Lanz, Weender Str. 25. Celebrated traditional café with roof terrace; it makes wonderful cakes, chocolate and marzipan.

Kaffeehaus Zindel, Kornmarkt 4. Popular coffee house which spills out onto the square in the summer.

KAZ-Keller, Hospitalstr 6. Trendy pub with beer garden; also does light meals.

Nörgelbuff, Groner Str. 23. Favourite haunt of the more bohemian members of the student community; features occasional live music and theatre.

Teehaus Klunje, Lange-Geismar-Str. 34. Has the best selection of teas in town.

Entertainment

Göttingen's main **cultural** venues are the Deutsches Theater, Theaterplatz 11 (☎05 51/49 69 11), and the Stadthalle, Albaniplatz 2 (☎05 51/4 97 00 20), which face each other across Theaterplatz, and the more experimental Junges Theater, Hospitalstr. 6 (☎05 51/5 51 23). Each June, Göttingen celebrates the music of Handel in the *Händelfest*, one of Europe's best and most adventurous celebrations of the work of a single composer; many long-forgotten masterpieces have been dusted down here and successfully brought back into the repertoire.

Duderstadt

DUDERSTADT lies just over 30km east of Göttingen in the upper part of the remote **Eichsfeld** region. Most of this area became part of the GDR; in thanks for being spared this fate, Duderstadt styled itself the centre of Die Goldene Mark (The Golden Borderland). As a result of the success of Willi Brandt's *Ostpolitik*, the town was chosen as one of the places where the hitherto impenetrable border could be crossed.

For much of its history, Duderstadt was an enclave belonging to the archbishop-electors of Mainz. The **half-timbered houses** (some 550 in all) have a unique subtlety which somehow stands out from that of all the other towns in the area. Typically, they're brightly coloured and decorated with carvings (including many impressive figures) and inscriptions, messages from the past which still have an uncanny vitality. The best examples are in **Hinterstrasse**, where there's a rich mix of architectural styles, reflecting phases in the town's history of partial destruction followed by intense reconstruction.

Duderstadt's central axis, **Marktstrasse**, widens to form a square at each end. Untermarkt to the west is dominated by the Protestant parish church of **St Servatius**, which was given a Jugendstil look inside after being burned out in 1915. On Obermarkt, its Catholic counterpart, **St Cyriakus**, is a handsome Gothic hall church with impressive Baroque furnishings inside, notably the tall candelabra with figures of angels, which are often carried on religious processions. Between the two churches is the **Rathaus** (April–Oct Mon–Wed & Fri 9am–4.30pm, Thurs 9am–7pm, Sat & Sun 9.30am–12.30pm & 2.30–4.30pm; Nov–March closed weekend afternoons; DM2.50/€1.25), whose thirteenth-century kernel can be appreciated from inside, though the exterior has been masked behind such superb embellishments as the late Gothic turrets and half-timbering, and the elaborate Renaissance balcony and stairwell. Outside the Rathaus stands the **Mariensäule**, a sandstone statue of the Virgin Mary set on top of a tall pillar whose base is flanked by palm trees, creating an incongruously Mediterranean atmosphere.

The other main sight is the **Westertorturm**, the original northwestern gateway to the town. Its high, narrow roof has, over the years, gradually turned on its own axis and taken on a characteristic spiral appearance. This makes the best point to begin a walk round the surviving parts of the fortifications, from where there are many surprising views of the town.

Practicalities

Duderstadt is not on a rail line, but there are frequent **bus** connections with Göttingen; some leave from the station below the Westertorturm, but others depart from Untermarkt. The **tourist office** is in the Rathaus, Marktstr. 66 (April–Oct Mon–Wed & Fri 9am–4.30pm, Thurs 9am–7pm, Sat & Sun 9.30am–12.30pm & 2.30–4.30pm; Nov–March closed weekend afternoons; ☎0 55 27/84 12 00, fax 84 12 01, *www .duderstadt.de*), and this is the best place to ask about **private rooms** (①–③).

There are four **hotels** in the town centre. *Deutsches Haus*, Hinterstr. 29 (☎0 55 27/40 52; ③), *Budapest*, Marktstr. 99 (☎0 55 27/9 86 30; ③), and *Zum Halben Mond*, Haberstr. 17–19 (☎0 55 27/26 98; ④), all occupy half-timbered buildings; but top of the range is *Zum Löwen*, Marktstr. 30 (☎0 55 27/30 72, *www.hotelzumloewen.de*; ⑧–⑨), in a splendid town palace. Each of these hotels has a **restaurant**: *Budapest* predictably offers Hungarian as well as German dishes, while *Zum Löwen* has the best kitchen in town, serving two restaurants, a cellar wine bar and a café with winter garden and terrace. Outside the hotels the best place to eat is the inevitable *Ratskeller*, Am Gropenmarkt.

The unofficial **youth hostel** is at Adenauerring 23 (☎0 55 27/9 84 70, fax 98 47 77; DM35/€17.50 or DM47/€23.50). **Camping** facilities are available at *Campingplatz Forsthaus Nesselröder Warten* (☎0 55 08/3 64) in Nesselröde, which lies on the Duderstadt–Göttingen road. Duderstadt's main **festival** is the *Schützenfest* on the second weekend in July.

Hann. Münden

Playing the time-honoured game of listing the Seven Wonders of the World, the great German traveller-scholar Alexander von Humboldt – who had seen a fair bit of the globe for himself – listed **HANN. MÜNDEN** as ranking among the top seven most beautifully sited towns. Even if this judgement seems tinged by excessive patriotism, there can be no doubt about the charm of the setting, below thickly wooded hills at the point where the **River Weser** is formed by the merging of the **Fulda** and **Werra**. The town's odd name, by the way, is the official contraction of "Hannoversch Münden", the name it assumed when it was part of the Kingdom of Hannover.

Hann. Münden has even more **half-timbered houses** than Duderstadt – over seven hundred in all. Separated by some six centuries of history, they completely dominate the face of the town, and their main attraction lies in the effect of the overall ensemble – individually, they're less impressive than their counterparts elsewhere. Look out, however, for no. 34 on the main street, Lange Strasse. This was the home of the town's most celebrated citizen, **Johann Andreas Eisenbart**, an eighteenth-century doctor whose controversial medical techniques gained him a reputation as a miracle-worker. A statue of him stands outside, while his life is the subject of an open-air costume play held each Sunday between mid-May and the end of August.

Curiously enough, Hann. Münden's few set pieces are all of a more solid stone construction. The most impressive of these is the **Rathaus.** This dates back in part to the fourteenth century, but the side facing the Markt was rebuilt at the turn of the seventeenth century in the cheerful Weser Renaissance style by Georg Crossmann, the creator of many similar buildings in Lemgo. The facade is masterly, with the ornate gables, resplendent doorway and the obligatory two-storey oriel window all competing for pre-eminence. During working hours, the interior, including the elaborate main **Festsaal**, is freely accessible. Across Kirchplatz is **St Blasius** (May–Sept Mon–Fri 11am–12.30pm & 2–5pm, Sat 11am–12.30pm, Sun 2–5pm), an unusual-looking Gothic hall church with a hexagonal tower and a very steeply pitched roof of red slate. It contains a couple of masterpieces of late fourteenth-century bronzework in the font and the door of the sacrament niche.

The other major monument is the **Schloss** (Wed–Fri 10am–noon & 2.30–5pm, Sat 10am–noon & 2.30–4.30pm, Sun 10am–12.30pm; DM2/€1), an "L"-shaped Renaissance palace overlooking the Werra from which one branch or other of the Welf family ruled the town for most of its history. It now houses the standard local history displays, but of more interest are the fresco cycles dating from soon after the time of the building's construction, among the few in Germany from this period. However, these can only be seen on group guided tours, bookable at the tourist office.

Behind the Schloss is the **Werrabrücke**, a bridge which dates back at least as far as the fourteenth century. From here, you can cross over to **Doktorwerder**, an island with a sculpture garden. Of the other islands around the confluence, the largest is **Unterer Tanzwerder**, a popular recreation area. Here also are the landing stage for cruise boats, a swing bridge over the Fulda and the **Weserstein**, a stone marking the birth of the great river at the point where, according to the rather trite inscription, "the Fulda and Werra kiss". Encircling the town centre are several towers, the remnants of the dismantled medieval **Stadtmauer**.

To appreciate the beauty of Hann. Münden's setting, and the harmonious layout of the town with its sea of red roofs, you really need to see it from above. One possibility is to cross over the Werrabrücke and follow the signs up to the **Weserliedanlage** belvedere. For a really magnificent bird's-eye view, at its best in the late afternoon or evening, cross the Fulda by the Pionierbrücke, and climb up to the nineteenth-century tower known as the **Tillyschanze** (March–Oct Mon 1–8pm, Tues–Sun 9am–8pm; Nov–Feb Mon 1–4pm, Tues–Sun 11am–4pm; DM2/€1).

Practicalities

Hann. Münden lies on the express rail line between Göttingen and Kassel, 35km from the former, 23km from the latter; the **Bahnhof** is ten minutes' walk east of the town centre. The **tourist office** (May–Sept Mon–Fri 9am–1pm & 2–5pm, Sat 9am–1pm; Oct–April Mon–Thurs 9am–1pm & 2–4pm, Fri 9am–1pm; ☎0 55 41/7 53 13, fax 7 54 04, *www.hann.muenden.de*) is in the Rathaus. After closing time, an information point is kept open daily until 8pm or 9pm according to season.

In addition to an abundant supply of **private rooms** (①–③), there are a trio of relatively inexpensive and centrally sited **hotels**: *Gasthaus im Anker*, Bremer Schlagd 18 (☎0 55 41/49 23; ③), *Aegidienhof*, Aegidienstr. 7–9 (☎0 55 41/9 86 40, *www.fahrrad-hotel.de*; ④), and *Rathausschänke*, Ziegelstr. 12 (☎0 55 41/88 66; ④). There are also more upmarket options in *Schlosschänke*, Vor den Burg 3–5 (☎0 55 41/7 09 40; ⑥), and *Alter Packhof*, Bremer Schlagd 10–14 (☎0 55 41/9 88 90; ⑥–⑧). Two enticing alternatives lie high above town on the left bank of the Fulda: *Schmucker Jäger*, Wilhelmshäuser Str. 45 (☎0 55 41/9 81 00; ③–⑤), and *Berghotel Eberburg*, Tillyschanzenweg 14 (☎0 55 41/50 88; ⑥). The **youth hostel** is way to the north of town at Prof-Oelkers-Str. 10 (☎0 55 41/88 53, fax 7 34 39; DM22/€11 or DM27/€13.50), while you can **camp** at a handier location on an island in the River Fulda. Excellent **restaurants** can be found in the hotels *Schlosschänke*, *Schmucker Jäger* and *Eberburg*. other good places to eat are the Ratskeller in the Rathaus, which offers international and fish dishes, and the *Waldgaststätte* below the Tillyschanze. In summer, several companies run daily **river cruises** from Unterer Tanzwerder; as well as local round trips, there are services downstream to Bad Karlshafen and upstream to Kassel. For contact details for all the cruises, see p.673

travel details

Trains

Bremen to: Bremerhaven (hourly; 50min); Emden (hourly; 2hr); Hannover (every 30min; 1hr); Norddeich (hourly; 2hr 50min); Oldenburg (every 30min; 35min); Osnabrück (hourly; 2hr).

Hannover to: Braunschweig (every 30min; 50min); Bremen (hourly; 1hr); Celle (every 20min; 25min); Einbeck (hourly; 1hr); Goslar (hourly; 1hr 20min); Göttingen (every 20min; 1hr); Hameln (hourly; 50min); Hann. Münden (hourly; 2hr); Hildesheim (every 20min; 25min); Lüneburg (every 30min; 1hr 20min), Wolfenbüttel (every 30min; 1hr 10min).

Ferries

Bensersiel to: Langeoog (3–5 daily; 50min).

Emden to: Borkum (summer 4 daily, winter 2 daily; 2hr 30min).

Harle to: Wangerooge (summer 2–3 daily, winter 1 daily; 1hr 10min).

Nessmersiel to: Baltrum (2–4 daily; 30min).

Neuharlingersiel to: Spiekeroog (2–4 daily; 50min).

Norddeich Mole to: Juist (1–3 daily; 1hr 20min); Norderney (9–13 daily; 50min).

CHAPTER SEVEN

HAMBURG AND SCHLESWIG-HOLSTEIN

J utting up between the Baltic and North Sea, and stretching as far as the Danish border, **Schleswig-Holstein** is the northernmost of Germany's Länder. It's about as far removed as is possible to imagine from the stereotyped image of the country – there are no mountains, cute fairy-tale towns or back-slapping dances, and a Bavarian would surely feel less at home than someone from Britain. Both geographically and culturally, Schleswig-Holstein might seem to belong more naturally to Scandinavia. Indeed, for most of its history it was quasi-independent, suspended nebulously between Germany and Denmark.

As the name suggests, Schleswig-Holstein was originally two separate territories, divided horizontally by the River Eider. The duchy of Schleswig was a fief of the Danish Crown, whereas Holstein was a county of the Holy Roman Empire. However, in 1386 the two came together under the same ruler, and in 1459 the king of Denmark was accepted as the perpetual overlord, even though this meant that the predominantly German-speaking Holstein had dual loyalties. Subsequently, the united duchy was partitioned among different branches of its ruling family, blurring the division between the two original component parts. This arrangement lasted until the nineteenth century when, under the impact of the nationalist fervour gripping Europe, both Denmark and the emerging German nation set their sights on absorbing at least "their" part of the territory. Because of the threat it posed to international peace and security, the so-called **Schleswig-Holstein Question** was a major preoccupation of chancelleries throughout the continent. The exasperation felt about finding a solution was summed up in 1864 by the British Prime Minister Lord Palmerston, who declared: "Schleswig-Holstein's history is so complicated that only three people have ever understood it. One of them, Prince Albert, is already dead. Another is myself,

---

ACCOMMODATION PRICE CODES

All the pensions and hotels in this book have been graded according to the following price categories. The codes quoted are for the cheapest available double room, except for establishments which have rooms costing widely different rates, when the most expensive price is given as well. Exact charges are given for youth hostels; in the case of the official DJH (HI) establishments, this is the lowest available rate. When two figures are quoted for these hostels, the first applies to juniors (ie under 27 years of age), the second to seniors (27 and above).

① less than DM60/€30	④ DM100–124/€50–62	⑦ DM200–249/€100–124
② DM60–79/€30–39	⑤ DM125–149/€63–74	⑧ DM250–299/€125–149
③ DM80–99/€40–49	⑥ DM150–199/€75–99	⑨ upwards of DM300/€150

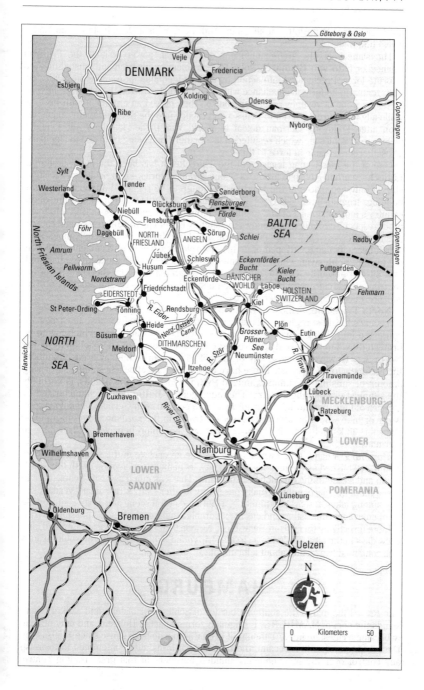

but I have already forgotten it all again. And the third is a Danish statesman, and it drove him mad."

The same year, the arch-manipulator of European power politics, the Prussian Chancellor **Otto von Bismarck**, solved the problem by his tried and trusted method of brute force. Precipitated into action by an ill-judged attempt to integrate Schleswig into Denmark, he formed an alliance with Austria which wrested the whole of the united duchy from all vestiges of Danish control, then picked an argument with his erstwhile ally to ensure it passed to Prussia and thence into the Second Reich established soon after. Following German defeat in World War I, the victorious Allies held a plebiscite in Schleswig which resulted in its northern half being returned to Denmark. These borders remain in force to this day.

One of the rare lasting legacies of the Third Reich has been the incorporation of **Lübeck** – a proud city-state for the previous seven centuries – into Schleswig-Holstein. One of only two places in the Land large enough to be regarded a city, its legacy of buildings from its heyday as Germany's premier mercantile port constitutes one of the country's most magnificent and distinctive monumental ensembles. In this, and many other respects, it totally overshadows the slightly larger city of **Kiel**, the somewhat surprising choice as capital of the modern Land and the starting point of the famous canal which bears its name. Stripped of its historic role as a seat of government, the lovely old town of **Schleswig**, which first came to prominence under the Vikings, has sunk into blissful obscurity. On the other hand, **Flensburg**, hard by the Danish border, remains a bustling port which has made a spectacularly successful adaptation of its well-preserved centre to modern needs.

North Friesland, Schleswig-Holstein's northwestern corner, has a reputation as Germany's bleakest region – a landscape of marshes and bogs whose few trees are contorted into strange shapes by the constant onshore winds, and which has to be protected by a network of dykes from the constant danger of encroachment by the North Sea. However, it's also one of the nation's favourite holiday areas, thanks to the archipelago off its coast. These have mile upon mile of beaches and a surprising amount of sunshine in summer; indeed **Sylt**, the largest of the islands, is normally the sunniest place in the country. The much gentler **Baltic coast**, characterized by a series of long, narrow inlets or fjords, is also popular with German holidaymakers. A car or bike would be a definite asset for **travel** in the rural areas, though public transport links between the main centres are as comprehensive as elsewhere in Germany.

Hamburg, a Land in its own right, exists like an enclave in the south of the state. Firmly established as the nation's second city, its name is synonymous with the prostitution and sleaze of the infamous Reeperbahn. That's as much as many people care to know about the place, but it actually has plenty to offer – an extraordinary verdant setting among lakes, a sparkling nightlife, a vibrant cultural scene and a city centre made up of enjoyably contrasting and easily explorable neighbourhoods. It's possible to travel there directly by **ferry** from Harwich or Newcastle on the east coast of England, and a few days in the city coupled to a circular trip round Schleswig-Holstein would make a well-contained trip lasting about a fortnight.

HAMBURG

The River Elbe marks the southern border of Schleswig-Holstein, and 120km inland stands the port of **HAMBURG**. It originally formed part of Holstein, and only officially became a city-state in 1770, though it been this in a de facto sense since 1459, as the Danish kings, who then became the nominal overlords, never attempted to exercise any control over the independently minded burghers of this great trading centre.

Exhilaratingly different from any other German metropolis, it officially bears the title of "Freie und Hansestadt" (Free and Hanseatic City) to this day.

During World War II Hamburg was massively bombed by the Allies. As the first city that bombers flying from England would pass over on the North Sea route into central Germany, Hamburg was often attacked. But on July 28, 1943 it became the first city to suffer a **firestorm**, when the combination of high explosives and incendiary bombs turned 21 square kilometres of the centre into one huge conflagration, with winds the speed of hurricanes uprooting trees and sucking people into the inferno. On that night, over 42,000 civilians were killed.

Hamburg's wealth enabled it to recover quickly in the postwar years, and although its reputation is tainted by tales of the **red-light area**, that's only a small part of what the city is about. It's a stylish media centre, a huge modern seaport, a scene of radical protest and home of the latest generation of a long-standing merchant class. Unless you arrive at one of the coastal ports, Hamburg is also where you're likely to begin your travels around Schleswig-Holstein. Allow two or three days to explore the centre and suburbs, and as many nights as your pocket (and constitution) will stand to soak up its **nightlife**.

In spite of the vast proportions of the city's outline, only one third is actually built up. The rest is either **parks**, **lakes** or tree-lined **canals** – the city boasts that it has more **bridges** than Venice. To cycle around, you'd never believe you were in one of Germany's major industrial cities, the largest after Berlin. Municipal policy dictates that two thousand new trees have to be planted each year, and the result is a very pleasing effect, with almost every road lined with trees, keeping the city green and the air cleaner.

Arrival and information

Hamburg's huge **Hauptbahnhof** lies at the eastern edge of the city centre. Arriving there can be a disorienting experience: the platforms are well below ground level, with staircases leading up to the walkways at the north and south ends of the building, each of which has an exit at either corner. Many express trains also stop at **Bahnhof Dammtor**, which is just beyond the northern end of the centre, while **Bahnhof Altona** in the west of the city and **Bahnhof Harburg** in the south are the starting or finishing point for many more services than the Hauptbahnhof itself. The **bus station**, which has a wide range of international as well as local routes, is just to the southeast of the Hauptbahnhof, between Adenauerallee and Kurt-Schumacher-Allee.

Ferries from England arrive at **Fischerhafen** in Altona. Cruise ships from other countries dock at **St Pauli Landungsbrücken** further to the east, which has a combined S- and U-Bahn station attached. The **airport** is in the north of the city, and linked at ten-minute intervals by an express bus to the S- and U-Bahn station of Ohlsdorf.

Hamburg's **tourist office** (☎0 40/30 05 13 00 or 30 05 13 51, fax 30 05 13 33, *www.hamburg-tourism.de*) operates three branches. There's one by the Kirchenalle exit in the Hauptbahnhof (daily 7am–11pm); another between bridges 4 and 5 of the St Pauli-Landungsbrücken (daily: April–Sept 10am–7pm; Oct–March 10am–5.30pm); and a third in terminal 4 of the airport (daily 6am–11pm).

Public transport around the city is quick and efficient by the integrated network of buses and S- and U-Bahn trains. The so-called **day-ticket**, which is actually only valid for nine hours from the time of validating, costs DM8/€4 and can be used by one adult accompanied by up to three children under 11; the group version of this, covering five people of any age, is priced at DM13.80/€6.90. However, it's usually much better value to invest in the **HamburgCARD**, which also gives free entry to the municipally owned museums (or reduced entry when they have a special exhibition on, as it normally the case) plus substantial reductions on a number of other attractions, including lake and harbour cruises. Current prices are DM12.80/€6.40 for a day (which can be used from

HAMBURG

ACCOMMODATION

6 Alameda
21 Alte Wache
2 Amsterdam
10 Annenhof
3 Backpacker Hostel Instant Sleep
7 Baseler Hof
6 Bei der Esplanade
13 Frauenhotel Hanseatin
19 Fürst Bismarck
11 Helga Schmidt
22 Jugendherberge auf dem Stintfang
8 Kempinski Hotel Atlantic
17 Kieler Hof
16 Kronprinz
15 Lilienhof
18 Nord
9 Sarah Petersen
4 Schanzenstern
12 Steens
1 Sternschanze
20 Terminus
14 Vier Jahreszeiten
5 Wedina

6pm the day before) and DM26.50/€13.25 for three days (valid from the first day until midnight on the last). Families or up to five people travelling together can buy inclusive tickets: these cost DM24.50/€12.25 for one day, DM43/€21.50 for three days.

Accommodation

In spite of a good variety of types of accommodation, it can be difficult to find somewhere easily affordable if you don't want to use the **youth hostels** or **campsites**. It's true that there are plenty of cheapish **hotels** in the St Georg quarter, next to the Hauptbahnhof, but in Bremer Reihe and the adjacent streets the unsuspecting will as likely as not end up in a brothel: it's impossible to tell them apart from "normal" hotels. To avoid this happening, choose one of those described below, or one which features on the much longer approved list published by the tourist office; alternatively, pay the DM6/€3 fee the latter charges for making a reservation. For long-term stays in furnished or unfurnished apartments or shared flats, contact one of the **Mitwohnzentralen**: HomeCompany, Schulterblatt 112 (☎0 40/1 94 45) in the Schanzenviertel, or Die Mitwohnzentrale, Lobuschstr. 22 (☎0 40/1 94 30) in Altona.

Hotels and pensions

Alameda, Colonnaden 45 (☎0 40/34 40 00, fax 34 34 39). This hotel has a handy location in the shopping area, just west of the Binnenalster. ④–⑥.

Alte Wache, Adenauerallee 21–27 (☎0 40/2 84 06 60, fax 2 80 17 54). Good-quality hotel close to the Hauptbahnhof. ⑦.

Amsterdam, Moorweidenstr. 34 (☎0 40/4 41 11 10, fax 45 68 20, *www.hotelamsterdam.de*). One of several mid-range hotels in the Dammtorpalais, a huge red-brick building at the southern end of the Univiertel. ⑤–⑦.

Annenhof, Lange Reihe 23 (☎0 40/24 34 26, fax 24 55 69). Friendly, good-value hotel in a sturdy old tenement building to the east of the Hauptbahnhof, well away from any sleaziness. ④.

Baseler Hof, Esplanade 11 (☎0 40/35 90 60, fax 35 90 69 18). Very highly regarded hotel with a location equally handy for the city centre, the Univiertel and the Alster lakes. Its restaurant, *Kleinhuis*, offers bargain lunches. ⑦.

Bei der Esplanade, Colonnaden 45 (☎0 40/35 50 11 70, fax 35 50 11 99, *www.hotel-bei-der-esplanade.com*). Occupies the upper floors of the same building as the *Alameda*, offering broadly similar rates. ⑤.

Frauenhotel Hanseatin, Dragonerstall 11 (☎0 40/34 13 45, fax 34 58 25). Women-only hotel just west of the city centre, near the Gänsemarkt U-Bahn. It incorporates the *Frauencafé endlich* (see box on p.733). ⑦.

Fürst Bismarck, Kirchenallee 49 (☎0 40/2 80 10 91, fax 2 80 10 96). One of a clutch of hotels directly facing the main entrance to the Hauptbahnhof. ⑦.

Helga Schmidt, Holzdamm 14 (☎0 40/2 80 21 19, fax 24 37 05). Homely pension between the Hauptbahnhof and the Alster lakes. ⑥.

Kempinski Hotel Atlantic, An der Alster 72–79 (☎0 40/2 88 80, fax 24 71 29, *www.kempinski.com*). Opened in 1909, this imperious grand hotel with a wonderful setting overlooking the Aussenalster was intended for passengers of transatlantic ocean liners, and its whitewashed architecture readily evokes the golden age of the great cruise ships. It has a wide range of facilities, including swimming pool, sauna, solarium, massage, garden terrace and two restaurants. ⑨.

Kieler Hof, Bremer Reihe 15 (☎0 40/24 30 24, fax 24 37 05). Basic budget hotel just east of the Hauptbahnhof. ④.

Kronprinz, Kirchenallee 46 (☎0 40/24 32 58, fax 2 80 10 97). Renowned for its restaurant, the top-notch *Schifferbörse*, though the accommodation is also of a good standard. ⑤.

Lilienhof, Ernst-Merck-Str. 4 (☎0 40/24 10 87, fax 2 80 18 15). Decent if somewhat functional modern hotel by the Hauptbahnhof. ④–⑥.

Nord, Bremer Reihe 22 (☎ & fax 0 40/28 05 17 33). Despite some very dubious neighbours, this hotel is respectable, and reasonably priced. ④.

Sarah Petersen, Lange Reihe 50 (☎ & fax 0 40/24 98 26). Small pension named after the artist who runs it. Has a certain celebrity status, so advance booking is advisable. ⑥–⑨.

Steens, Holzdamm 43 (☎0 40/24 46 42, fax 2 80 35 93). Charmingly located hotel in a quiet, pretty corner of St Georg. ⑥.

Sternschanze, Schanzenstr. 101 (☎0 40/43 33 89, fax 4 30 51 65). In the heart of the bohemian Schanzenviertel, and one of the best bargains in Hamburg. ③.

Terminus, Steindamm 5 (☎0 40/2 80 31 44, fax 24 15 18). Conveniently close to the Hauptbahnhof, and a regular choice for foreign budget travellers. ③–⑤.

Vier Jahreszeiten, Neuer Jungfernstieg 9–14 (☎0 40/3 49 40, fax 34 94 26 00, *www.hjv.de*). This top-notch luxury hotel beside the Binnenalster has been in business for a century. It is elegantly furnished with antiques, and some of the rooms overlook the lake. There are three restaurants: *Haerlin* (closed Sat lunch, Sun & Mon) is the most upmarket; *Jahreszeiten Grill* is the grillroom its name suggests; while *Doc Cheng's* (closed Sun evening & Mon) has a mixed European and Asian menu and is, relatively speaking, quite reasonably priced. ⑨.

Wedina, Gurlittstr. 23 (☎0 40/24 30 11, fax 2 80 38 94). Set on the southeastern edge of the Aussenalster, this nicely renovated hotel with a garden and swimming pool is undoubtedly one of the pleasantest places to stay in central Hamburg. ⑥.

Youth hostels

Backpacker Hostel Instant Sleep, Max-Brauer-Allee 277 (☎0 40/43 18 23 10, fax 43 18 23 11, *www.instantsleep.de*). New independent hostel in the lively Schanzenviertel. It offers cooking and washing facilities, and Internet access. Take S-Bahn #3 or #21 or U-Bahn #3 to Sternschanz. Dorm beds from DM29/€14.50, singles DM49/€24.50, doubles DM80/€40, triples DM108/€54.

Jugendgästehaus Horner Rennbahn, Rennbahnstr. 100 (☎0 40/6 51 16 71, fax 6 55 65 16, *jgh-hamburg@t-online.de*). Slightly the more expensive and appealling of the two official hostels. Situated in a light, airy modern building next to the horse-racetrack in the eastern suburb of Horn, it's peaceful enough when there isn't a race on. Take U-Bahn #3 to Horner Rennbahn. DM30/€15 or DM36/€18.

Jugendherberge auf dem Stintfang, Alfred-Wegener-Weg 5 (☎0 40/31 34 88, fax 31 54 07, *jh-stint-fang@t-online.de*). The other official hostel has an excellent location, not just for the city's attractions, but also because it's perched on a steep incline above the port, with panoramic maritime views. It's reached by S-Bahn #1, #2 or #3 or U-Bahn #3 to Landungsbrücken. DM27/€13.50 or DM32/€16.

Schanzenstern, Bartelsstr. 12 (☎0 40/4 39 84 41, fax 4 39 34 13, *www.schanzenstern.de*). Another privately run hostel in the Schanzenviertel, complete with a restaurant serving wholefood and organically produced drinks. Dorm beds from DM33/€16.50, singles DM60/€30, doubles DM90/€45, triples DM110/€55, quads DM140/€70.

Campsites

Buchholz, Kieler Str. 374 (☎0 40/5 40 45 32, fax 5 40 25 36). Year-round campsite located in a northern suburb, a short walk from the zoo. Take U-Bahn #2 to Hagenbecks Tierpark or S-Bahn #3 or #21 to Stellingen.

Blankenese, Falkensteiner Ufer 101 (☎0 40/81 29 49). Situated directly on the Elbe. Take S-Bahn #1 or #11 to Blankenese, then bus #189.

Schnelsen-Nord, Wunderbrunnen 2 (☎0 40/5 59 42 25, fax 5 50 73 34). In the far north of the city. Take U-Bahn #2 to Niendorf Markt, then bus #291. Closed Nov–Feb.

The City

Central Hamburg is neatly recognizable on any map, as it's bordered by large roads which trace the original city's fortifications. It has a semicircular shape, with its base facing the River Elbe and Hamburg's massive **port**, while the rest of the city fans out around the centre's rounded contours. Bulging out to the northeast are the city's glamorous **Alster lakes**, lined by some of the poshest quarters in town. To the west of the centre lie the quarters of **St Pauli** and **Altona**, and just north of these the **Univiertel** (university quarter), which together form the heartland of Hamburg's best nightlife. Finally, there are some famous **suburbs** worth visiting, chiefly Blankenese, Oevelgönne and Neuengamme.

Most of the **centre** of Hamburg was consumed in a great fire in 1842: the flames ran out of control for several days, which is why you don't find many buildings dating from before that period. Add to that the British "Operation Gomorrah" in 1943, when half of the city was destroyed by bombs, and it's a wonder there's anything over fifty years old left to see at all. But there are a great many nineteenth- and early twentieth-century buildings remaining, tucked in between prize-winning modern developments, and hidden within this central mêlée you'll also find the sole surviving seventeenth-century houses of the city.

The Altstadt

The centre arches in a great semicircle over the baseline of the Ost-West-Strasse, about 2km long. This semicircle is then loosely divided by the slanting Alsterfleet canal, which separates the original Altstadt quarter from the later Neustadt on the other side of the water. Most maps no longer record this difference, since nowadays they have melted into one, but the division is still useful for visitors to the city.

The historic core

The oldest part of Hamburg is around the ruined tower of **St Nikolai**, formerly one of Germany's finest neo-Gothic churches, designed by Sir George Gilbert Scott, only to be flattened by his countrymen about a hundred years later. Today its blackened stump stands as an anti-war memorial. Close by is the **Trostbrücke**, which connected the old city with the Neustadt, the "new" quarters west of the Alsterfleet canal, which developed in the early Middle Ages. The two statues on the bridge are of St Ansgar, Hamburg's first archbishop, and Count Adolf III, founder of the new quarters and, more importantly for the city's future development, instrumental in the signing of the imperial decree which gave Hamburg the right to tax-free import of goods and transport of passengers from the sea to its port, 120km inland along the River Elbe. Thus the city's future as one of Europe's largest and most important commercial ports was sealed as early as the twelfth century. Today the bridge appears somewhat incongruous, surrounded as it is by modern office buildings.

Following the canal south, crossing the busy Ost-West-Strasse at Holzbrücke you'll find the remaining eighteenth-century merchant homes, with their grand facades facing the street and the red-brick, gabled backs facing the canal, where goods were directly hoicked into the merchant's attic store rooms. The most famous examples are the row of houses along **Deichstrasse**, which is also where the Great Fire broke out. Seven rooms within no. 37, which is now designated the **Alt-Hamburg Bürgerhaus**, have been decked out with period furnishings, each of a different style or era. All of these can be rented for dinners or functions, and although the building is not a regular tourist sight it's usually possible to take a peek inside. The best place to see the crooked backs of the Deichstrasse houses is the Hohe Brücke to the east. Further along the canal front is the Gothic church of **St Katharinen**, which was badly damaged in the war but sympathetically restored. Its tower, like those of the other historic churches, remains a prominent feature of the skyline.

The eastern Altstadt

Heading northeast along the Dovenfleet, with the waterfront warehouses on your right, you come to the U-Bahn station Messberg, and directly opposite, the remarkable

Chilehaus. Built with the traditional red bricks of north German architecture, this unconventional house was created in the early 1920s and remains one of the most original works of the period. It was designed by the Expressionist architect Fritz Höger, whose idea it was to mirror Hamburg's ocean-going ships in this large office block. As you wander around the outside of it – ideally from the other side of the road for the best views – you begin to recognize the contours of a great ship, the staggered balconies high above recalling the various decks, and the sharp corner of its eastern extremity representing a ship's bow. If the name seems incongruous, that's because it has nothing to do with the building, but recalls the country in which the architect originally made his fortune.

North American readers might care to know that nearby, at Steinstr. 7, is the **Historic Emigration Office** (Tues & Thurs 9.30am–5.30pm; *www.hamburg.de/ LinkToYourRoots/english/welcome.htm*; ☎0 40/30 05 12 82), which has the most comprehensive archives in existence of emigration to the New World. For the years 1850–1934, there are complete records of name, age, sex, occupation and place of origin of each and every one of the 5.8 million emigrants from all over Europe who departed from Hamburg. If you want to find your ancestors' records, all you need to know is the name and year of emigration, and the staff will conduct a search for a US$75 fee. Eventually, all the documentation will be published on the Internet: indeed, this has already been done for the years 1890–93.

Across the Burchardsplatz and up the Mohlenhofstrasse is another of central Hamburg's five church towers, which traditionally characterize its skyline. This is **St Jakobi**, which contains the precious treasure of Arp Schnitger's seventeenth-century **organ**, which ranks among the greatest instruments ever made and is still in frequent use. Unfortunately, postwar rebuilding did not attempt to re-create the original architecture, so the interior is in drab 1950s style, with only the outside recalling the building's former glory.

Directly behind St Jakobi lies **Mönckebergstrasse**, which is the main artery of the city's commercial shopping. Follow this street west, and you're heading to the hub of the city centre, which clusters around the grandiose Rathaus. On the way you pass **St Petri**, originally the oldest of the city's churches, believed to have its origin in an eleventh-century chapel. Destroyed in the Great Fire and then again in 1943, it nevertheless retains much of its nineteenth-century neo-Gothic architecture and boasts Hamburg's oldest surviving piece of craftwork, the fourteenth-century bronze **doorknocker** on the central western portal.

Around the Rathaus

A stone's throw away from here, the **Rathaus** sits heavily in all the boastful splendour of the German neo-Renaissance. Built to display the superior quality of Hamburg's civil parliament, there is something faintly self-conscious about the building's style. Perhaps they were trying a little too hard to create the proper symbolism, with both the city's patron saints and maritime images lined up alongside each other around its rooftop rim. When the city's parliament isn't in session, guided tours around its stately rooms offer an instructive view of Hamburg's uniquely glamorous municipal headquarters (tours in English hourly Mon–Thurs 10.15am–3.15pm, Fri–Sun 10.15am–1.15pm; in German every 30min Mon–Thurs 10am–3pm, Fri–Sun 10am–1pm; DM2/€1).

In front of the Rathaus, the **Rathausmarkt** is usually teeming with tourists and shoppers alike, sampling goodies from the variety of stalls, while the elegant **Alsterarkarden** and its expensive stores lead out onto the **Binnenalster**, which is the petite forerunner of the larger **Aussenalster** lake, beyond the city centre. The arcades were built to echo those on Venice's Piazza San Marco, though it's pretty evident that a few arcades don't make up a Venetian square. If you're interested in seeing the **Börse**, Germany's first stock market and Hamburg's financial heart, then head along the arcades away from the lakes, and you'll soon find yourself round the back of the Rathaus on the Adolphsplatz. Founded in 1558, the stock market reflected the fact that Hamburg's cosmoplitan world of trade and commerce was bilingual, in those days commonly using both German and Dutch. The present building is a restored version of the Neoclassical one built in the mid-nineteenth century, and extended in the early part of the twentieth century.

The Neustadt

Hamburg's Neustadt is a "new town" only in the relative sense – although founded 378 years after the Altstadt, it celebrated its 800th birthday back in 1988.

Around Jungfernstieg

Turning away from the Rathaus and towards the Binnenalster, you cross the **Reesendammbrücke**, which has been there in some form or other since the thirteenth century. The present version was built in the 1840s, but in the early Middle Ages this was the site of a corn-mill, which dammed the River Alster's water to turn its wheel. From then onwards, there's always been a small lake here – the larger one beyond created a few hundred years later – and Hamburg's high society, then as now, delighted in promenading around its edges. The finest and most expensive promenade is traditionally the **Jungfernstieg**, named after the young women who used to twirl their umbrellas here. Head north, along the Neuer Jungfernstieg, and you'll find the splendid houses of the city's bankers and businessmen, as well as Hamburg's best address: the **Hotel Vier Jahreszeiten**, which boasts of being one of the leading hotels in the world, and charges accordingly. The least expensive way to sample it is to go for a coffee in its lovely Biedermeier café, *Conti*.

If you're tempted by any of the **boat trips** offered along the Jungfernstieg, the best is undoubtedly the two-hour Kanal-Fahrt (late March to late April & early to late Oct daily at 9.45am, 12.45pm & 3.45pm; late April to early Oct daily at 9.45am, 11.45am, 12.45pm, 2.45pm, 3.45pm & 5.45pm; DM22/€11). This tour will take you round both the Alster lakes, and also along the River Alster itself, passing many of the city's finest villas and sailing clubs, and presenting a view of Hamburg otherwise impossible to see.

The Hanseviertel

The streets spreading out behind the Jungfernstieg, towards the Gänsemarkt and down Neuer Wall, Grosse Bleichen and ABC-Strasse, are collectively known as the **Hanseviertel**, an area of offices and the city's flashest shopping arcades. The city's renowned opera and ballet house, the **Hamburgische Staatsoper**, is on the Dammtorstrasse nearby.

Heading southwest from the Hanseviertel you enter a more residential area on the other side of Kaiser-Wilhelm-Strasse. Streets worth strolling along are Breiter Gang or Wexstrasse, where you'll not only find attractive houses, but also the odd bar or restaurant you might fancy. **Grossneumarkt**, in particular, is a favourite haunt for inner-city eating and drinking. Not far from here, the **Peterstrasse** is one of Hamburg's most beautiful streetscapes, a small stretch of completely restored eighteenth-century townhouses, built in traditional red-brick style, with gabled tops tapering towards the sky. Walking along this street gives you an idea of what most of the city must once have looked like. If you're interested in musical heritage, head to the **Johannes-Brahms-Museum** (Tues & Thurs 10am–1pm, first Sun of month 11am–2pm; DM4/€2), at Peterstr. 39, which has documentation on the life and work of the composer, who was born in Hamburg and spent many unsuccessful years here.

Immediately to the west is Holstenwall, which marks the boundary between the Neustadt and St Pauli. At no. 24 the **Museum für Hamburgische Geschichte** (Mon

1–5pm, Tues–Sun 10am–6pm; DM10/€5) will tell you everything you could possibly want to know about Hamburg's origins and history, its people and times. There are meticulous miniaturized re-creations of historic quarters, and a large variety of model boats through the ages. An intriguing and unexpected section on the Reeperbahn dwells not on the commercial sex which makes it notorious these days, but on its original role as home to the rope-makers who supplied the giant ropes used by the port's ships.

St Michaelis and the Krameramtswohnungen

A few minutes' walk to the southeast stands Hamburg's city symbol and finest church: **St Michaelis**. Seated on a small hill, its copper-plated tower is visible from most parts of the city. The church was originally built between 1649 and 1661, but has burned down no fewer than three times since then: once after it was struck by lightning in the eighteenth century, again in 1906, and lastly in the World War II firebombing of the city. Happily, this is the one Hamburg church that has not only been rebuilt on the outside, but also on the interior, so that you can still marvel at its superb northern Baroque elegance. Inside, you find the typically Lutheran design, which directs the congregation's eyes not to the altar, but to the pulpit. The best bird's-eye **view** of the city is from the tower's 82-metre-high **look-out platform** (mid-March to Sept, Mon–Sat 9am–6pm, Sun 11am–6pm; Oct to mid-March Mon–Sat 10am–5pm, Sun 11am–5pm; DM5/€2.50). The **vaults** (same times; DM2.50/€1.25, or DM6/€3 combined ticket with tower) are also worth a look; they contain the grave of the composer Carl Philipp Emanuel Bach, son of J.S. and pioneer of the symphonic form, and an exhibition about the history of the church. There is also a **multimedia show**, Multivision Hamburg (Thurs–Sun 12.30pm, 2.30pm & 3.30pm; DM5/€2.50, or DM9/€4.50 combined ticket for all three). If your German is up to it, this is an accessible introduction to the city's history and development, with many famous names and events portrayed with a vivid slide show, and suitably dramatic music – and even if you don't speak German, it makes an interesting moving picture gallery.

A rather touristy but nevertheless worthwhile visit is to the **Krameramtswohnungen** (Tues–Sun 10am–5pm; DM2/€1), round the corner from St Michaelis at Krayenkamp 10. This tiny backyard of seventeenth-century housing is the last remaining in the city. It was built as retirement homes for the widows of storekeepers, who were forbidden to carry on their husband's trade after his death and were housed here by the guild. They were still in use until the early 1960s, but now all but the one preserved as a museum have been turned into trinket shops or art galleries.

The port: from Fischmarkt to Speicherstadt

The best time and place to begin an exploration of the length of Hamburg's harbour is to go to the **Fischmarkt**, not far from St Pauli Landungsbrücken, early on a Sunday morning. In the early morning (April–Nov 5am–10am; Oct–March 7–10am), the former fishmarket hall and a large part of the waterfront around it are given over to a weekly circus of shopping and selling, where you can buy anything from fish to live ducks, potted palms, clothes or tacky trinkets. The bars and Imbiss stands in the vicinity open for the occasion, filled with shoppers and late-night survivors alike, all tucking in to the sounds of early morning jazz and stall-holders bellowing out their wares. If you can make it, it's a spectacle worth seeing, though be prepared for crowds. By 10am, the market is supposed to end, in accordance with an old law that was to ensure that trade didn't compete with Sunday church services. In fact, it lingers on for a good hour more, but many of the most colourful traders have sold out by then, no longer performing their crowd-drawing sales pitches. The short stretch of waterfront road that connects the Fischmarkt with the Landungsbrücken is the infamous **Hafenstrasse**, for long a fiercely disputed spot between developers and squatters.

HAMBURG'S PORT

Hamburg's **port**, founded in the late twelfth century, was the making of the city. Today it's one of Europe's four major ports, and the world's largest depot for oriental carpets, as well as Germany's leading market for coffee, tea and spices from all over the world. Ever since Emperor Frederick Barbarossa granted free trade and a customs exemption for all goods brought in by ship in 1189, wealth and municipal status have been assured. These days, of course, the port's significance is tempered by the worldwide recession in ocean-going trade, as well as the decline in related industries such as shipbuilding. The authorities have tried to make their wharfs competitive by cutting labour and mechanizing the handling of containerized cargo, but the human cost of these measures has been great, and unemployment is higher here (and in the north generally) than in most other parts of the country.

The port's workforce has a history of powerful organization, and there were systemized strikes as early as the 1840s. In the 1880s came the longest strike the city has seen, when 18,000 harbour workers went out for ten weeks, in protest against the massive rehousing that was necessitated by the demolition of their homes to make way for the Speicherstadt, the port's tax-free warehouses. In the turmoil immediately following World War I, there was more action: a sailors' revolt in November 1918, two days after the one in Kiel. In 1923 came the **Hamburg uprising**, with fighting on the streets at the height of the postwar crisis of inflation and hunger. In recent times, the embattled Hafenstrasse has been at the heart of present-day conflict with the authorities.

Back down by the **Landungsbrücken**, many bridges lead to the floating pontoon lined with expensive Imbiss stands and restaurants, and there are plenty of boats offering hour-long **harbour tours** (*Hafenrundfahrten*) for about DM15/€7.50. Make sure you go on one of the small ferries and not the large double-decker, since only the small ones take in the canals of the Speicherstadt as well as the port itself. If you want to see the hulls of mighty container ships close up, then this is the tour for you. **Tours in English** go from Brücke 1 (March–Nov daily at 11.15am; DM15/€7.50).

The distinctive green-hulled **Rickmer Rickmers** (daily 10am–5.30pm; DM6/€3) is moored opposite the S-Bahn station. Built in 1896, this three-masted, ocean-going barque had a history of international sailing before it was impounded by the British in 1916. They used it as part of their maritime war effort, and once World War I was over, gave it to the Portuguese. Eventually, some Hamburg businessmen found the boat mouldering away off the coast of Portugal, brought it back in 1987, restored it to its original beauty, and now it's regarded as one of the city's most important treasures. There's also a gourmet restaurant on board. A little to the east, at Überseebrücke, lies the **Cap San Diego** (daily 10am–6pm; DM6/€3). This typical 1960s freighter is now an impressive museum. Visitors can walk all over the ship, from the engine room to the bridge, gaining a vivid impression of the sailors' living and working conditions. There's a restaurant on board here too.

A brisk fifteen minutes' walk further along the waterfront will take you to the separate world of the nineteenth-century **Speicherstadt**. The world's largest self-contained warehouse complex, complete with canals and cobblestone streets, it was built between 1885 and 1910 in the beautiful red-brick style of local architecture. Sacks of coffee can be seen piled high, thousands of oriental carpets lie rolled up, scents of teas and spices waft out of open doors, and men can be seen heaving goods by the traditional hooks used a hundred years ago. All the buildings are under protection, so there are no lifts or other machinery to assist present-day workers. Goods can be stored here over many years tax-free, until the merchant thinks he'll get the best price.

The Speicherstadt contains three unusual museums: the **Hot Spice Gewürzmuseum** (Tues–Sun 10am–5pm; DM4/€2), with displays on the spice trade; at Am Sandtorkai 32;

the **Speicherstadtmuseum** (same times; DM5/€2.50) at St Annenufer 2, with exhibits on the working life of the old warehouse quarter; and the **Zollmuseum** (same times; free), Alter Wandrahm 16, devoted to customs and smuggling.

The museum quarter

Hamburg's **museums** are scattered all over the city, but the two which are of world-class importance – the **Kunsthalle** and the **Museum für Kunst und Gewerbe** – are to be found on either side of the Hauptbahnhof. Nearby are several temporary exhibition venues, the most important being the **Deichtorhallen** (Tues–Fri 11am–6pm, Sat & Sun 10am–6pm; *www.deichtorhallen.de*; variable entrance charges) on Deichtorstrasse to the south. These wrought-iron and glass structures, which formerly served as the fruit and veg market halls, were restored some years ago as an important addition to the municipally owned stock of art galleries.

The Kunsthalle
Immediately north of the Hauptbahnhof on Glockengiesserwall is the renowned **Kunsthalle** (Tues, Wed & Fri–Sun 10am–6pm, Thurs 10am–9pm; *www.hamburger -kunsthalle.de*; DM12/€6). Its collection of paintings and sculpture ranges from medieval to contemporary, and is often augmented by special exhibitions, in which case there's a compulsory supplement to the entrance fee. A pillared hall at the back of the building houses *Café Liebermann*, Hamburg's grandest **café**, and it's well worth scheduling a stop there for *Kaffee und Kuchen* or a light lunch. Starting upstairs to the right with the earliest works, the collection is arranged in a broadly chronological fashion.

One room is entirely devoted to three retables by **Master Bertram**. An important figure in German art, he was the country's first painter identifiable by name, and worked for most of his life in Hamburg. His masterpiece is the huge folding altarpiece, mixing paintings and sculpture, which was made for St Petri. The panel showing *The Creation of the Birds and Beasts* is outstanding; the characterization of each creature is delightfully fresh, but a prophetic warning note is struck – already the polecat has attacked a sheep. In the next room is part of the dismembered *St Thomas à Becket* altar piece by Bertram's successor, **Master Francke**. Painted for the league of merchants who traded with England, it's in a very different style – the figures are more monumental, the structure tauter, the mood more emotional. The most interesting work here from the Renaissance period is **Cranach**'s *The Three Electors of Saxony*. This uses the religious format of the triptych, with a continuous landscape background, in order to show the deceased Electors, Frederick the Wise and John the Fearless, alongside the then ruler, John Frederick the Magnanimous.

The Flemish section begins with a tiny house altarpiece by **Isenbrandt** and includes a mature religious masterpiece by **Van Dyck**, *The Adoration of the Shepherds*. Most of the specialist painters of seventeenth-century Holland are represented, but they're rather overshadowed by two examples of **Rembrandt**. *The Presentation in the Temple* is one of his earliest surviving works: he was only 21 when he painted it, yet there's no sign of immaturity or lack of confidence. From five years later, when Rembrandt was established as a fashionable society portraitist, comes *Maurits Huyghens*.

Highlights among the display of seventeenth- and eighteenth-century European painting are: **Claude**'s *Dido and Aeneas at Carthage*; a pair of **Tiepolos**, *The Agony in the Garden* and *The Crowning with Thorns*; **Canaletto**'s *Capriccio with a View of Padua*; **Bellotto**'s *Ideal View with Palace Steps*; **Goya**'s *Don Tómas Pérez Estala*; and *The Creation of Eve* by the eccentric Swiss artist **Heinrich Füssli**, whose sensationalism makes a fascinating contrast with the paintings of Bertram from four hundred years earlier. There is one outstanding sculpture from this period – a bust of a cardinal by **Bernini**.

The nineteenth-century German section is one of the museum's main strengths. Of a dozen works by **Caspar David Friedrich**, three rank among his most haunting and original creations. *Wanderer above the Mists* shows an isolated figure with his back to the viewer, contemplating an eternity of sky and clouds; overpowering and intimate at the same time, it stresses the awesome, unfathomable power of the natural world. This same theme is present to even greater effect in *Eismeer*; inspired by the voyages of polar exploration, which were then beginning, it depicts a ship half-submerged against a cracked iceberg. It also has political significance, since the picture symbolizes lost hopes after the 1848 Revolution. In contrast, *The First Snow of Winter* imparts a dimension of grandeur to a quite ordinary landscape scene.

Another German artist with a distinctive vision of the world was the short-lived **Philipp Otto Runge**, most of whose best work can be seen here. His most arresting images are portraits of children (usually his own). Chubby-cheeked, over life-size and bursting with energy, they're placed at eye level to face the viewer head-on. Very different, but equally effective, is the realist approach of **Wilhelm Leibl**, the German equivalent of Courbet. *Three Women at Church*, with its phenomenal detail, super-smooth texture and uncanny evocation of the rapt concentration of the subjects, is rightly considered his masterpiece.

The German Impressionists, **Max Liebermann** and **Lovis Corinth**, are each allocated a room, close to a choice collection of their French counterparts, including a version of **Manet**'s *Fauré as Hamlet* which is less finished but livelier than the one in Essen. Among the Expressionists, look out for two masterpieces by **Munch**: *Girls at the Seaside* and *Girls on the Bridge*. The twentieth-century section includes a large group of works by the Surrealist **Richard Oelze**; other highlights are **Otto Dix**'s *Der Krieg* triptych, a powerful anti-war statement, and **Paul Klee**'s translucent *Goldfish*, an abstract composition with a rare sense of poetry.

Directly adjacent to the Kunsthalle, and connected to it by an underground passageway, is the shining new modernist cube of the **Galerie der Gegenwart** (Gallery of Contemporary Art; same times and ticket), which is devoted to art from the 1960s to the present, with much of the display space given over to installations. A large collection of American Pop Art, including examples by Andy Warhol, Robert Rauschenberg, Claes Oldenburg, George Segal, Tom Wesselmann, Larry Rivers and Jim Dine, can be seen in the basement alongside works by their German contemporaries, such as Joseph Beuys. The first floor features young German artists; recent art from America, beginning with Bruce Nauman, can be found on the second; while the top floor is host to some of the established contemporary stars of the German art world: Georg Baselitz, Gerhard Richter, Sigmar Polke and Markus Lüpertz.

The Museum für Kunst und Gewerbe

On Steintorplatz, facing the southern side of the Hauptbahnhof, is the **Museum für Kunst und Gewerbe** (Museum of Arts and Crafts; Tues, Wed & Fri–Sun 10am–6pm, Thurs 10am–9pm; *www.mkg-hamburg.de*; DM12/€6). The European displays are arranged chronologically, and begin to the left of the entrance with an important **medieval** section. Among its most notable treasures are a twelfth-century bronze reliquary chest by one of the craftsmen who made the famous bronze doors of the church of San Zeno in the Italian city of Verona; a gilded and bejewelled silver reliquary of St George attributed to the late fifteenth-century Lübeck master Bernt Notke; carvings of the *Madonna and Child* by two of the great German sculptors of the late Gothic period, Nicolaus Gerhaert von Leyden and Tilman Riemenschneider; and a magnificent Easter embroidery woven at the beginning of the sixteenth century by the nuns of Kloster Lüne in Lüneburg (displayed in odd-numbered years only for conservation reasons).

The **Renaissance** section which follows contains bronzes by Peter Vischer the Younger and Hubert Gerhard; a spectacular inlaid doorway from the now-destroyed

Schloss of the dukes of Prussia in Königsberg; and many notable examples of the work of German goldsmiths and silversmiths, including the ceremonial *Wilkomm* of Hamburg's coopers' guild. Many more luxury items can be seen in the **Baroque** department, which features some outstanding pieces made in Augsburg, including a very early example of an enamel tea set and a toilet service commissioned by the Mecklenburg court. There are also collections of porcelain from most of the leading German manufactories. The **nineteenth-century** displays which complete the ground-floor circuit include two interiors from Hamburg mansions, one of them a curious little chamber modelled on a ship's cabin.

On the first two floors of the brand-new glass extension which has been discreetly built in one of the courtyards is one of the world's finest collections of **historic keyboard instruments**, including many items of real beauty. Some of the instruments are demonstrated every Saturday at 3pm, while a more extensive event, culminating in a concert, takes place at the same time on the first Sunday of the month. The first floor of the main museum building has a wonderful **Art Nouveau/Jugendstil** section featuring several intact interiors, including two rooms purchased from the Paris World Exhibition of 1900 plus others designed by Henry van de Velde and Josef Hoffmann. Further highlights are a complete set of furniture made for a house in Hagen by Hamburg's own Peter Behrens; a tapestry of *The Adoration of the Magi* by William Morris and Edward Burne-Jones; and a stained-glass window by Charles Rennie Mackintosh.

Likewise on the first floor are displays of modern crafts and design, of antiquities from Egypt, Greece and Rome, of the art of the Islamic world and of the decorative arts of East Asia. The last-named includes a **Japanese tea house**, where ceremonies are occasionally held. A far more regular culinary attraction on the same floor is the museum's **café-restaurant**, *Destille*, which is decorated in the style of a Hamburg Gaststube of the turn of the twentieth century, and offers a superb Scandinavian-style cold table. The second floor is largely devoted to **photography**, and regularly features special exhibitions.

The Alster lakes and the river

The Alster lakes, in the heart of Hamburg, make up the main recreational area of the city. Whether with ice-skating in winter or sailing and boating in summer, the large **Aussenalster** is always a busy place, while the smaller **Binnenalster** is frequented mainly by commercial boats and pedestrians promenading around its shores. Together, the two lakes encompass an area of about three square kilometres with no fewer than nine thousand boats licensed to use them. All around the shore of the Aussenalster there are operators renting out sailing and rowing boats to visitors. The shoreline around both lakes is open to the public, and the footpaths along it are incorporated into park landscapes.

Walking all the way around the lakes takes about three hours, and the route leads past many of the city's finest villas, clubs and consulates, especially along the **western shore**, where the rich have traditionally built their lakeside homes. The areas known as **Rotherbaum** and **Harvestehude** are two of the most exclusive residential parts of Hamburg, and if you enjoy nineteenth-century and Jugendstil architecture, it's worth exploring some of the streets around here: especially those branching off from the Klosterstern, such as Harvestehuder Weg and its side-streets. Around Pöseldorfer Weg and Milchstrasse, parallel with Harvestehuder Weg, is an area known locally as **Pöseldorf**. This has become a particularly trendy and upmarket spot, where media types hang out in expensive cafés and pose in the similarly pricey restaurants. The **eastern shore** presents an equally well-heeled facade. However, immediately beyond are the sleazy streets of **St Georg**, the quarter best known for its budget hotels and brothels, though its dominant landmark is the huge red-brick **Dom**, which was built in the 1890s on the model of its counterpart in Bremen. In 1995, it became the seat of the revived Roman Catholic archbishopic of Hamburg, which had been defunct since the Reformation. Further to the northeast, the area by the Aussenalster becomes respectably residential, gradually meeting up with the exclusive villas spilling over from Harvestehude.

The course of the **River Alster** stretches for a good 50km further, heading first north, through Hamburg's suburbs, and then twisting and turning its way westwards to **Henstedt**. There's a marked footpath (yellow triangles) that follows the course of the river, but the trip to Henstedt is not something you could manage in one day, unless you go by bike and are very energetic. However, for countrified bike excursions, you don't need to go too far out. The 18km stretch from the tip of the Aussenalster to the Wohldorf lock runs through shady park landscapes as well as past river scenes little changed for centuries. There's no need to retrace your route back into the city either, since public transport is available at various points. For example, the U-Bahn stops Ohlsdorf or Klein Borstel are not far from the Fuhlsbüttel lock; 6km further on is the Poppenbüttel S-Bahn stop; and not far from the Wohldorf lock is the Ohlstedt U-Bahn stop. Maps of the entire route are available from the tourist office, in the brochure entitled *Die Alster*.

The inner suburbs

Beginning along the shore of the River Elbe and curving northeast towards the base of the Aussenalster, the four quarters of St Pauli, Altona, Schanzenviertel and Univiertel embrace the western curve of the city centre's traditional edge. St Pauli and Altona are the southernmost part, melting smoothly into each other, while the Schanzenviertel and Univiertel sit compactly north of St Pauli. Collectively, they form the main stomping ground for night-time revellers of all kinds, and contain Hamburg's red-light district, centred on the infamous Reeperbahn.

St Pauli

St Pauli, defined by the River Elbe, the Holstenstrasse towards Altona and the rail tracks to the north, is nearest to the city centre, and was originally home to Hamburg's sea-related trades and crafts. The **Reeperbahn**, for example, was where the ropemakers once lived; and the Grosse and Kleine Freiheit (Big Freedom and Little Freedom) are streets so-named not because of the live sex shows you see there today, but because in medieval times craftsmen were free to practise their trade here. To a large extent, St Pauli is a working-class, residential area to this day, with the sex industry confining itself to the very small area of the Reeperbahn and short streets running off either side, especially those leading towards the port. Lately, St Pauli has been infiltrated by a new set of after-dark revellers, since many bars and clubs have been taken over by avant-garde theatre operators and entrepreneurs. In the middle of the Reeperbahn, for example, is one of the city's trendiest alternative cabaret and theatre bars, *Schmidt*. For detailed listings of local bars see pp.731–2.

Altona

Heading west, **Altona**, which was only incorporated into Hamburg in 1937, follows directly on from St Pauli. Like its neighbour, it has its share of river, partly lined with industrial fish-processing plants, but also with the leafy environs of the **Palmaille** and **Elbchaussee**, grand avenues lined with nineteenth-century villas. Its western border is roughly defined by Fischersallee, while to the north it spreads almost as far as Fruchtallee. Although much of Altona is unremarkable for the visitor, it has had an

THE BEATLES IN HAMBURG

I was raised in Liverpool, but I grew up in Hamburg.

John Lennon

Hamburg is inextricably bound up with the early career of **The Beatles**, who made five separate visits to the city between 1960 and 1962. During this period, they took up residence at four different clubs, and although these have long been closed, you can still see the original buildings in St Pauli. You'll get a good idea of the seedy environment the band found themselves in and you can visit all the sites in a matter of minutes as they are within a stone's throw of each other.

The fab five – **John Lennon**, **Paul McCartney**, **George Harrison**, bass player **Stuart Sutcliffe** and drummer **Pete Best** – first arrived in Hamburg on August 16, 1960. Thinking they were appearing at the Kaiserkeller nightclub, the lads were dismayed to find themselves booked at the Indra (Grosse Freiheit 34), a well-known strip club instead. They played four and a half hours a night every Tuesday to Friday and six hours every Saturday and Sunday. After seven weeks, the club was closed down, owing to complaints about the noise, and the group did make their debut at the *Kaiserkeller* (Grosse Freiheit 36) on October 4. Unfortunately, the next month, George was deported for being under age at 17. The others decided to stay but a few days later both Paul and Pete were arrested and told to leave Hamburg for allegedly attempting to set fire to their lodgings at the back of the Bambi Kino, a small cinema at Paul-Roosen-Str. 33.

On their second visit, The Beatles were booked to play at the more prestigious Top Ten Club (Reeperbahn 136) and things started to pick up for them. Stuart wasn't so enchanted, however, and decided to leave the group. He'd already fallen in love with local photographer, **Astrid Kirchherr**, and decided to settle in Hamburg and concentrate on his painting. Tragically, his artistic career was cut short – when The Beatles made their third visit to Hamburg on April 11, 1962, they were met by Astrid with the news that Stuart had died following a convulsion the day before. The band had little time to come to terms with the terrible news; their seven-week residence at the Star Club (Grosse Freiheit 39) started just two days later. Despite the traumatic circumstances, it became a popular venue with the group and on the two further visits they made to Hamburg later that year, it was to the Star Club that they returned.

The **influence of Hamburg** on The Beatles' musical career cannot be overstated. Bruno Koschmider, the owner of the Indra, was not impressed by the band's static performance and demanded they "make a show". Within weeks they had transformed their act, and began talking to the audience and fooling around on stage. The famous **Moptop haircut** was undoubtedly copied from the "mushroom" style (*Pilzkopf*) adopted by the Exis, Hamburg's young existentialists. Astrid Kirchherr first cut Stuart Sutcliffe's hair in this style and, despite initial reservations, the other band members soon followed suit. And it was in Hamburg in 1960 that The Beatles first met the drummer for Rory Storm and the Hurricanes – **Ringo Starr**.

interesting history. Originally a Danish settlement on the edges of German Hamburg, it has always been a haven of free-thinkers and religious tolerance. It was a place of racial tolerance too, and as maritime trade brought more and more foreigners to the area, many chose to settle in Altona. A legacy of those times are the many excellent and cheap Portuguese restaurants near the harbour. In the twentieth century, Altona became a favoured home for the Turkish, Greek and Arabic "guestworkers" of the city, hence the many kebab shops and takeaway kiosks around Bahnhof Altona, especially along Ottenser Hauptstrasse. To find out more about the quarter's history, and in particular its Dutch heritage, the **Altonaer Museum** (Tues–Sun 10am–6pm; DM8/€4), just south of the Bahnhof at Museumstr. 23, has displays on the entire region, concentrating on trades such as boat-building, farming, fishing and the many different crafts associated with ships and the sea.

Traditionally, Altona's residents were not much more upmarket than St Pauli's. But the developers have slowly been moving in on the beautiful but decaying nineteenth-century buildings, and certain areas are rapidly becoming rather chic with prices to match. One such street is **Friedensallee**: this is still unremarkable at its northwestern end but stroll along the short stretch beginning near Bahnhof Altona, and ritzy, neon-lit stores cluster among sophisticated restaurants and bars. Nearby Barnerstrasse is also home to one of the city's most favoured and enduring live music venues, Fabrik (see p.734).

Schanzenviertel and Univiertel

Northeast of Altona is another popular entertainments quarter, the **Schanzenviertel**. One of its main streets, **Schulterblatt** (near the Sternschanze S- and U-Bahn stop), is home to several popular student Kneipen, as well as excellent cheap restaurants. A very different atmosphere prevails around here, not so much trendy as relaxed and unpretentious. The **Schanzenstrasse**, which splits away from Schulterblatt, is also worth checking out, and for all bar and café listings, see pp.731–3. On Lagerstrasse at the far northeastern edge of the quarter is Hamburg's highest building, the **Fernsehturm** (daily 9/10am–10/11pm; DM6.50/€3.25 including ascent by lift), which commands sweeping panoramic views of the city.

Immediately to the north lies the **Univiertel**. The streets of most interest are **Grindelhof** and **Rentzelstrasse**: this is where you'll find the largest variety of reasonably priced restaurants and café-bars. Also here is the city's most popular "alternative" cinema, the Abaton, which has a large bar-restaurant upstairs, and is regularly packed. There's not much life except on these two streets, but for choice and variety it's the best place to be for relaxed eating and drinking, where dress code and image are of little significance.

Just beyond is the **Hamburgisches Museum für Völkerkunde** (Tues, Wed & Fri–Sun 10am–6pm, Thurs 10am–9pm; DM7/€3.50) at Rothenbaumchaussee 64. Here Hamburg's maritime associations with Africa, the South Pacific, the Americas and Russia are on display. It's particularly refreshing that the museum tries to avoid pandering to voyeuristic attitudes, by showing the cultures as present-day societies with present-day concerns, rather than as exotic curiosities. The effects of tourism on the Pacific is just one display that stimulates fresh attitudes.

The outer suburbs

Heading west along the Elbe from Altona, a road and then a path lead first to **Oevelgönne** and then to **Blankenese**. Both were originally suburbs which housed fishermen and sea captains in beautiful, tiny houses. Today, these areas are among the most popular with the well-heeled, who pay silly prices to squeeze themselves into the "quaint" houses with wide views across the river. The route along the water is very pleasant, with plenty of sandy beaches along the way, and both can easily be visited within the space of a morning's relaxed cycling. Alternatively, catch a boat from St Pauli as far as Neumühlen, or one station further to Teufelsbrück, using the HADAG Niederelbedienst (the Lower Elbe boat service run by HADAG shipping), which will take your bicycle for a half-fare. Bus #112, from Bahnhof Altona, will also take you to Oevelgönne, or you can go by S-Bahn #1 or #11 to Blankenese.

A particular attraction of Oevelgönne is the **Museumshafen**, where around twenty old-time working boats are moored. Each one has been lovingly restored, from early twentieth-century fire brigade boats to nineteenth-century wooden fishing trawlers and double-masted freighters. It's a private museum, run by enthusiasts, who willingly show visitors around if they happen to be there. Blankenese, a twenty-minute cycle ride further along the river, is remarkable chiefly because it is situated on a small yet steep hill, a great rarity in this flat part of Germany. Long gone are the times when it was home to retired fishing folk, who watched the constant flow of ships sailing by. Now, villas squeeze tightly in alongside the older houses, and steep roads and stairway paths wind in among them. It's very picturesque, and down by the beach of beautiful white sand, refined cafés and restaurants cater to your every need. Nearby, there's also a fragrant park of ancient trees, now home to many deer; the woods conceal many cafés as well.

Bergedorf, on the other side of Hamburg, towards its eastern edge, is reached by S-Bahn #2 or #21. Its thirteenth-century red-brick **Schloss** (Tues–Thurs, Sat & Sun 10am–5pm; DM5/€2.50) was situated on an important medieval trade route, and its role was primarily as a tax-collecting point rather than a noble residence. Inside is a local museum, which concentrates on regional folklore and costumes, as well as traditional rural arts and crafts.

The Nazi concentration camp **KZ-Gedenkstätte Neuengamme** (Tues–Fri 10am–5pm, Sat & Sun 10am–5/6pm; free), which can be reached from Bergedorf by bus #227 or #327, is now a political education centre. It has an exhibition of photos and documents that re-creates the horrors of the past and records the story of resistance. Hamburg's other concentration camp was at Fuhlsbüttel (near the airport); some fifty thousand people, including over six thousand Hamburg Jews, died in these two camps.

Eating and drinking

When it comes to choosing where to eat and drink in Hamburg, it's worth looking further afield than the city centre: though there are plenty of recommendable options there, the choice and variety is greater, and the prices lower, if you head to the nearby **Univiertel** or **Schanzenviertel**. For Imbiss-type food, the stalls in the St Georg area near the Hauptbahnhof offer cheap snacks, as do those in the Reeperbahn in St Pauli. Another place for quick snacks is the pedestrian area outside Bahnhof Altona. The most famous fast food of them all, though, the **hamburger**, is not especially popular in its "home" town – invented in the mid-nineteenth century and introduced to America by German immigrants, the popular snack takes its name from the city.

Restaurants

Traditional Hamburg Gaststätten, including many specializing in **fish dishes**, can be found throughout the city. There are two **local specialities** to try. *Aalsuppe*, generally made with plums and mixed vegetables as well as eels, is one of the most outstanding soups you'll encounter in Germany. *Labskaus*, a traditional sailors' dish, is more controversial, not to say indigestible; it's a hash which typically contains pickled corned beef, herring, beetroot, mashed potato, onions and gherkins, all topped with a fried egg. The city also has plenty of restaurants offering **international fare**, as well as a quite amazingly diverse range of **ethnic cuisines**, including a large number of Portuguese restaurants (which are seldom encountered elsewhere in Germany) and some real rarities.

German cuisine

Aalkate, Ost-West-Str. 47. Housed on the fourth floor of the Gröninger Haus, which contains two other eateries, this specializes in home-smoked eel and other fish dishes. Evenings only, closed Sun.

Ahrberg, Strandweg 33, Blankenese. Located down by the river, this ranks among the city's best German/fish restaurants, with carp a speciality.

Alt Hamburger Aalspeicher, Deichstr. 43. One of the best places to sample *Aalsuppe*. It's not cheap, but is always excellent. Try to avoid the place during lunch hour when hordes of businessmen descend.

Anno 1750, Ost-West-Str. 47. Gaststätte on the ground floor of the Gröninger Haus, with a pedigree dating back to 1750, as its name suggests. Closed Sat lunchtime & Sun.

But'n Dammdoor, Mittelweg 27. In existence for well over a century, this is favoured by a number of prominent Hamburgers, but nevertheless offers good, reasonably priced meals: its sauté potatoes are said to be the best in the city.

Das Kontor, Deichstr. 32. Serves high-quality German cuisine, and has a good selection of organic wines from around the world.

Fischerhaus, St-Pauli-Fischmarkt 14. Offers no-nonsense fish dishes down by the Fischmarkt, not necessarily at cheap prices.

Fischküche, Kajen 12. This Neustadt restaurant serves some of the best fish dishes in the city, and has a different business-lunch menu every weekday. Closed Sat lunchtime & Sun.

Franziskaner, Grosse Theaterstr. 9. A Bavarian-style beer hall and garden, a real rarity in these northerly climes. Closed Sun.

Landhaus Scherrer, Elbchaussee 130, Altona (☎0 40/8 80 13 25). Located in the Othmarschen district in the west of Altona, this very expensive restaurant has long been considered Hamburg's premier gourmet address, raising traditional German cooking to unexpected levels of excellence. Reservations advisable. Closed Sun.

Nikolaikeller, Cremon 36. Claims to have the longest and best menu of herring dishes in Germany. There are bargain lunches on weekdays and outside seating at the back, overlooking the canal.

Old Commercial Room, Englische Planke 10. Touristy but recommendable restaurant facing St Michaelis which has the decor and ambience of an English club but serves very traditional Hanseatic cuisine. Its guest book reads like an international who's who.

Ratsweinkeller, Grosse Johannisstr. 2. As is hinted by its longer-than-usual name, Hamburg's version of the inevitable town-hall cellar restaurant is posher – and better – than most. Closed Sun.

Weinkeller Alt-Hamburg, Cremon 33–34. Wine bar-restaurant with bargain lunchtime menus.

International cuisine

Cölln's Austernstuben, Brodschrangen 1 (☎0 40/32 60 59). The city centre's foremost restaurant, particularly for fish dishes; its lunch menus are surprisingly reasonable in price. It's ideal for discreet discussions, as the dining area is divided into individually decorated compartments which seat between two and twelve people. Reservations usually necessary. Closed Sat lunchtime & Sun.

Deichgraf, Deichstr. 23. Elegantly furnished restaurant with an upmarket menu of traditional international dishes. Closed Sat lunchtime & Sun.

Le Canard, Elbchaussee 139, Altona (☎0 40/8 80 50 57). Located directly across the street from *Landhaus Scherrer*, this is another of Hamburg's very best restaurants, with some quite moderately priced options at lunchtime. Reservations advisable. Closed Sun.

Monopoly, Stadthausbrücke 1. Equally well known for its wacky decor and its eclectic menu of European and Asian dishes. Closed Sun.

Nil, Neuer Pferdemarkt 5. Extremely trendy St Pauli restaurant, popular with artists and media types. On weekdays, it serves very good-value set lunches; it's open evenings only at the weekend.

Petit Delice, Grosse Bleichen 21. Small restaurant in the classy Galleria shopping arcade, offering creative cooking and a well-chosen wine list.

Ethnic cuisines

A Hereford Beefstouw, Schopenstehl 32. Danish grill in a handsome old Baroque house. Open evenings only Sat & Sun.

Arkadasch, Grindelhof 17. Offers a large choice of Turkish dishes at very affordable prices.

At Nali, Rutschbahn 11. Turkish restaurant with a large menu and friendly atmosphere.

A Varinha, Karpfangerstr. 16. Excellent Portuguese restaurant; good food at good prices. Two people could easily share one of these tremendous portions.

Balutschi, Grindelallee 33. Pakistani food in authentic surroundings; leave your shoes at the door before sitting on the floor at one of the low tables.

Cuneo, Davidstr. 11. Long-established Italian, particularly recommendable for pasta dishes. Evenings only, closed Sun.

Le Fouta, Eimsbütteler Chaussee 121. African speciality restaurant run by a family from Sierra Leone.

Le Plat du Jour, Dornbusch 4. Excellent and fairly priced French restaurant.

Matsumi, Colonnaden 96. Japanese restaurant with sushi and sashimi bars. Closed Sun.

Medded, Bahrenfelder Chaussee 140. Egyptian food that's a bargain at the price. Evenings only.

New York Deli, Levantehaus, Mönckebergstr. 7. Although tucked away on the upper floor of a shopping centre, plenty of American visitors seem to find their way to this daytime diner, to gorge themselves on hero sandwiches, hamburgers, bagels and Ben & Jerry ice cream.

Pasadena, Kirchenallee 19. The location alongside the Hauptbahnhof looks unpromising, but it serves decent Tex-Mex cooking.

Peking Enten Haus, Rentzelstr. 48. As the name suggests, the house speciality is Peking duck: the poultry served is specially reared, and is prepared by chefs from the Chinese capital. Evenings only, except Sun, when it's also open for lunch.

Sagres, Vorsetzen 42. One of the many Portuguese eating houses around the harbour, this is a homely place, popular with Portuguese dock workers – which means giant portions.

Saidal, Mittelweg 25. Inexpensive Afghan restaurant, with plenty of vegetarian options.

Sala Thai, Brandsende 6. Thai restaurant featuring folk-dancing on Wednesday evenings and specializing in seafood grills. Bargain lunches are offered on weekdays.

Saliba, Leverkusenstr. 54, Altona. Well-regarded, fairly pricey Syrian restaurant. Closed Sat lunchtime & Sun.

San Michele, Englische Planke 8. Classic Italian restaurant in the shadow of St Michaelis – the food is pricey but very good.

Shalimar, Dillstr. 16. Arguably the city's best Indian restaurant, specializing in Mughal cuisine. Evenings only.

Tibet, Harkorstieg 4, Altona. Tibetan restaurant with a wide-ranging menu, including vegetarian dishes. Evenings only, closed Mon.

Tre Fontane, Mundsburger Damm 45. Cosy and well-priced Italian.

Ukamau, Beckstr. 17. Germany's only Bolivian restaurant, often featuring live performances of Andean music, is in the Schanzenviertel. Evenings only, closed Tues.

Vegetarian cuisine

Goldene Oase, Eppendorfer Baum 34. Serves both German and Indian vegetarian and wholefood cuisine at moderate prices.

Suryel, Thadenstr. 1. Good all-round veggie specialist in St Pauli.

Thymaro, Stellinger Weg 47, Eimsbüttel. This restaurant goes against the usual hairshirt image of vegetarianism, offering an attractive menu including some fine home-made desserts. Evenings only.

Zorba the Buddha, Karolinenstr. 7, Eimsbüttel. Bhagwan restaurant and meditation centre, with a surprisingly good selection of wines.

Bars

Hamburg's **bars** regularly move in and out of favour, but the following make up the heart of the city's nightlife. These days it centres around the St Pauli area and many places don't open before 10pm. Popular student bars, which are drinking haunts as well as good for cheap meals, can be found in the **Univiertel** and the **Schanzenviertel**. In the former, Grindelhofstrasse, Rentzelstrasse and Grindelallee are particularly good streets to explore.

St Pauli

Blaue Nacht, Gerhardstr. 16. This is the one that started the trend into St Pauli in the mid-1980s. These days its popularity is waning, but it's not dead yet.

Christiansen, Pinnasberg 60. The drinks list here features some five hundred spirits, including over a hundred whiskies.

Kurhaus, Beim Grünen Jäger 1. Tiny bar that is currently one of the hottest spots of the Hamburg *Szene*.

Mary Lou's, Hans-Albers-Platz 3. Red lighting notwithstanding, a hangout favoured by the new set of St Pauli.

Molotow, Spielbudenplatz 5. Post-punk background music in this increasingly popular haunt.

Prinzenbar, Kastanienallee 20. Stuccoed angles and chandeliers are the setting for drinking, with good soul sounds as well as occasional live shows.

Tempelhof, Hamburger Berg 12. Very popular seedy bar, which retains its swivel chairs and lowered lights. Party troopers mix with red-light customers.

Schanzenviertel, Univiertel and Altona

Abaton, Grindelhof 14a. Has an innovative cinema attached, and is a large and noisy place that gets very busy with students at night.

Down Under, Grindelallee 1. Australian theme bar.

Eisenstein, Friedensallee 9, Altona. Situated in an old factory, bare stone walls and a high ceiling are the setting for people to show just how important they are, or at least how good they are at looking like it. Excellent pizzas.

Erika's Eck, Sternstr. 98. The favoured haunt of late-night drinkers who work in the nearby slaughterhouse. Open 1am–2pm, serving one of the best breakfasts in the city.

Filmhauskneipe, Friedensallee 7, Altona. Popular with creative types and media people. The interior is plain, with simple wooden tables and chairs comfortable enough for a whole night's drinking. The food is good, though the atmosphere gets very smoky.

Frank und Frei, Schanzenstr. 93. A big, slow-paced favourite with students.

Limerick, Gridenallee 18. Wonderful beer bar with wooden interior, offering good meals at good prices. Favourite with students.

Luxor, Max-Brauer-Allee 251. Something of a hybrid between a bar and a restaurant, with good cocktails and international cuisine showing Asian influences.

Oma's Apotheke, Schanzenstr. 85. A big student favourite, with rustic-style decor and food that is, by German standards, spicier than normal.

Vienna, Fettstr. 2. Tries to create the atmosphere of a bistro-cum-sitting room.

Elsewhere in the city

Bambus, Brüderstr. 15. Long-established Neustadt bar, with four hundred different cocktails to choose from.

Gröninger Braukeller, Ost-West-Str. 47. This Hausbrauerei in the cavernous cellars of the Gröninger Haus brews an amber-coloured *Pils* and a wheat beer; it also serves full meals.

Souterrain, Papenhuder Str. 26. Popular, even though it is over on the eastern edge of the Aussenalster (Mundsburg is the nearest U-Bahn stop).

Cafés and café-bars

Most **café-bars** have food as well, most notably excellent breakfasts and snacks (expect to pay around DM8–12/€4–6). Each reflects the area it's in: you can expect places like Pöseldorf to be pricey and full of yuppies, while the Univiertel and Schanzenviertel are more studenty; and Altona is unpretentious, with mixed crowds.

City centre and St Georg

Café Gnosa, Lange Reihe 93. Lovely 1930s café with good food. It's popular with the gay community – it advertises itself as being friendly to those who are HIV-positive – but has heterosexual habitués as well.

Café Koppel, Koppel 66. Best known for its delicious chocolate cake; also serves vegetarian and wholefood dishes, and has a summer garden.

Café Schöne Aussichten, Gorch-Fock-Wall 1. Situated in the middle of the park, this is an excellent summertime place, with a tree-shaded terrace.

Café Urlaub, Lange Reihe 63. Serves good breakfasts and salads and baguettes at other times.

GAY HAMBURG

Not surprisingly, Hamburg has a lively **gay scene**. Other than talking to people in bars and cafés, the best way to find out what's on is from the city's free gay magazine *hinnerk*, which is available in most gay bars. Good starting points for **men** are *Café Gnosa* (see opposite); and the current favourite rendezvous, *Baluga Bar*, Lincolnstr. 6, St Pauli. For **women**, the best place to find out what's on and where to go around town is probably the *Frauenbuchladen*, Bismarckstr. 98 (☎0 40/4 20 47 48), which also runs a café. Other women's cafés, not necessarily exclusively lesbian, are *Café Meg Donna*, Grindelallee 43, *Frauenkneipe*, Stresemannstr. 60, and *Frauencafé endlich*, which is now part of the *Frauenhotel Hanseatin* on Dragonerstall (see p.716). A **women-only disco** worth checking out is *Camelot*, Hamburger Berg 12, St Pauli.

Geel Haus, Koppel 76. Evenings-only café-bar, sometimes with live jazz.

Gestern & Heute, Kaiser-Wilhelm-Str. 55. Legendary for the variety of its breakfasts, this place is open around the clock.

Loft, Grosse Bleichen 21. Exclusive daytime café for monied people. Located in the Galleria shopping arcade.

Max und Consorten, Spadenteich 7. Situated on a deceptively pretty square, whose trees shade daytime prostitutes.

Elsewhere in the city

Amphore, Hafenstr. 140. *Szene* café-bar in St Pauli.

Café Backwahn, Grindelallee 148. Univiertel café offering a choice of set breakfasts from around DM8/€4.

Café Stenzel, Schulterblatt 61. A traditional *Kaffee und Kuchen* establishment in the heart of the Schanzenviertel.

Café Treibeis, Gaussstr. 25, Altona. Alternative hangout, and a good place for weekend breakfasts.

Fun Club, Fischers Allee 78, Altona. Internet café.

Maybach, Heussweg 66, Altona. On the northern edges of the quarter, this has a beer garden too, a rarity in these parts.

Strandperle, Am Schulberg, Oevelgönne. Situated by the beach, this is a favourite summertime hangout with the in-crowd.

Witthüs, Elbchaussee 499a, Blankenese. Idyllic manor house which functions as a café in the afternoons (and on Sun morning), a *nouvelle cuisine* restaurant in the evenings.

Entertainment

Hamburg is renowned for its discos and nightclubs, boasts just about the best jazz scene in Germany, and attracts a good range of visiting international bands. For those with more highbrow tastes, its traditions in classical music and theatre are of the highest class. To find **what's on**, consult the magazines *Szene Hamburg* (DM5/€2.50) or *Prinz* (DM2/€1), or the more abbreviated listings in the tourist office's free *Hamburg Führer*.

Discos and nightclubs

Angie's Nighclub, Spielbudenplatz 27–8. One of the best-known clubs in Germany, and a favourite celebrity haunt. Open Wed–Sat from 10pm.

Grünspan, Grosse Freiheit 58. Long-established late-closing hard rock disco. Fri & Sat 10pm–7am.

Kaiserkeller, Grosse Freiheit 36. Part of *Grosse Freiheit* (see live music venues, below) and one of the city's largest discos. Daily 9pm–4am.

Kontor, Altstädter Str. 1. Altstadt disco particularly favoured by young locals. Thurs–Sat from 10pm.

Madhouse, Valentinskamp 47. Much the liveliest of the city's discos on weekdays. Daily 10pm–4am.
Mojo Club, Reeperbahn 1. Hugely popular disco and acid jazz venue. Wed & Thurs from 10pm, Fri & Sat from 11pm.

Live music venues

Birdland, Gärtnerstr. 122, Eimsbüttel. Prestigious jazz venue; the music varies from avant-garde experimentation to trad Dixieland.

Cotton Club, Alter Steinweg 10. Traditional jazz club, with live music Mon–Sat at 8.30pm.

Docks, Spielbudenplatz 19. Worth checking out, but the acoustics here are dodgy, and it can get very stuffy.

Fabrik, Barnerstr. 36, Altona. One of the longest-enduring live music venues in Hamburg, this place is always worth a visit.

Grosse Freiheit, Grosse Freiheit 36. The city's main venue for rock/contemporary live music, with big-name bands mostly playing at weekends. The admission charge depends on who's performing.

Logo, Grindelallee 5. Mainly English and American underground bands.

Werkstatt 3, Nernstweg 32, Altona. This is a centre for alternative projects which often acts as a stage for Third World bands. Fri & Sat evenings are tropical dance nights.

Classical music

Hamburg's musical tradition can match that of any city in the world. There are three full-sized **orchestras** – the Philharmonisches Staatsorchester, the Hamburger Symphoniker and the NDR-Sinfonie-Orchester (the house orchestra of the locally based radio station). Of these, the last-named has gained international cult status in recent years for its performances and recordings under the baton of its veteran conductor laureate Günter Wand, one of the very last surviving members of the old school of autocratic maestros. Thanks to his insistence on the most meticulously detailed rehearsals, it can be relied upon for absolutely definitive renditions of the central German classics, such as the symphonies of Beethoven and Brahms. Hamburg also has a high reputation for its **opera**, **ballet**, **choral** and **organ** music. It's always worth looking out for concerts and recitals in the city's **churches**, especially St Jakobi.

Venues

Allee Theater, Max-Brauer-Allee 76 (☎0 40/30 05 16 60). The home of the Hamburger Kammeroper, which stages a wide range of operas, with a particular emphasis on rarities. The performances, regardless of the original language, are in German.

Hamburgische Staatsoper, Dammtorstr. 28 (☎0 40/35 17 21). Located not far from the famous but now vanished old building on the Gänsemarkt that was once run by Telemann, this has long ranked among the top ten opera houses in the world, even if it has strong competition for supremacy within Germany from both Munich and Stuttgart. The ballet company attached to the house, run by the American John Neumeier, enjoys a particularly high reputation.

Forum der Hochschule für Musik und Theater, Harvestehuder Weg 12. Hamburg's music academy features regular concerts and recitals by established professional orchestras and soloists as well as students.

Musikhalle, Johannes-Brahms-Platz (☎0 40/34 69 20). This building from the early years of the twentieth century contains two concert halls. The larger one is used for symphonic concerts by the three local orchestras, among others; the smaller for chamber, vocal and instrumental music.

Theatre

More than any other city in the country, Hamburg has caught the national craze for British and American **musicals**, which are translated into German and performed for years on end in the same (often custom-built) venue. However, there's also a long and distinguished tradition of serious **drama**, while traditional **variety** also has a strong hold.

Venues

Deutsches Schauspielhaus, Kirchenallee 39 (☎0 40/24 87 13). This is one of Germany's leading dramatic theatres. It's the successor to the Nationaltheater, one of whose first employees was the great eighteenth-century playwright and critic Gotthold Ephraim Lessing.

English Theatre of Hamburg, Lerchenfeld 14 (☎0 40/2 27 70 89). Performs predominantly light fare, such as comedies and thrillers, in English.

Hamburger Kammerspiele, Hartungstr. 9 (☎0 40/44 33 44 44). Small avant-garde stage.

Hansa-Theater, Steindamm 17 (☎0 40/24 14 14). On the go for well over a century, this presents old-fashioned variety and circus-type shows.

Kampnagel, Jarrestr. 20–26 (☎0 40/2 70 94 90). Experimental theatre which has an open-air season in summer.

kömodie winterhuder fährhaus, Hudtwalckerstr. 13 (☎0 40/30 05 19 00). Specialist light comedy venue.

Musicaltheater, Norderelbstr. 6 (☎0 40/30 05 11 50). Tent-like theatre alongside the St Pauli Landungsbrücken that has been playing *Buddy* (the story of Buddy Holly) since it opened in 1994.

Neue Flora, Stresemannstr. 159a (☎0 40/30 05 13 50). Another specialist venue for musicals, which has staged Andrew Lloyd Webber's *The Phantom of the Opera* continuously since 1990.

Ohnsorg-Theater, Grosse Bleichen 23 (☎0 40/30 05 15 50). Hamburg's version of the Volkstheater performs plays in the *Plattdeutsch* dialect.

Operettenhaus, Spielbudenplatz 1 (☎0 40/30 05 13 50). Theoretically this is a specialist operetta theatre, but since 1986 it has been monopolized by the Lloyd Webber musical *Cats*.

St-Pauli-Theater, Spielbudenplatz 29 (☎0 40/31 43 44). Hosts musicals by British and American touring companies.

Schmidt, Spielbudenplatz 24 (☎0 40/30 05 14 00). Cabaret and variety venue.

Thalia-Theater, Alstertor (☎0 40/30 05 17 50). Intimate galleried theatre, founded in 1834, with a high reputation and a wide-ranging programme.

Theater für Kinder, Max-Brauer-Allee 76 (☎0 40/38 25 38). Specialist children's theatre.

Listings

Airport information ☎0 40/5 07 50.

American Express Ballindamm 39 (☎0 40/30 39 38 11).

Car rental Hertz, Kirchenallee 34–36 (☎0 40/2 80 12 01); Sixt Budget, Im Hauptbahnhof (☎0 40/32 24 19); Topcar, Gertrudenstr. 2 (☎0 40/33 59 98). All of these companies have desks at the airport.

Consulates British, Harvestehuder Weg 8a (☎0 40/4 48 03 20); Irish, Feldbrunnenstr. 43 (☎0 40/44 18 62 13); New Zealand, Domstr. 19 (☎0 40/4 42 55 50); US, Alsterufer 28 (☎0 40/41 17 10).

Cultural Institutes British Council, Rothenbaumchaussee 34 (☎0 40/44 60 57).

Doctor ☎0 40/22 80 22.

Festivals are by no means a Hamburg speciality, but the *Übersee Tag* on May 7 celebrates the founding of the port in 1189. A funfair, the *Dom*, is held on the Heiligengeistfeld, close to the St Pauli U-Bahn station, with separate spring, summer and autumn sessions.

Mitfahrzentrale Lobuschstr. 22 (☎0 40/39 17 21), Gotenstr. 19 (☎0 40/1 94 44), Ernst-Merck-Str. 8 (☎0 40/1 94 40).

Pharmacies Internationale Apotheke, Ballindamm 39 (☎0 40/3 09 60 60); Senator Apotheke, Hachmannplatz 14 (☎0 40/32 75 27).

Post office For the main post office with poste restante facilities, take the Kirchenallee exit out of the Hauptbahnhof.

Sports Hamburger SV, one of Germany's best football teams, plays in the Volksparkstadion in Altona. Sailing regattas are frequently held on the Aussenalster, and there are various international events, such as a tennis championship in late May and an equestrian event in early June.

Swimming The beautiful baths at Bismarckbad in Altona are the city's most luxurious, and have women-only days. For outdoor swimming the smaller lakes around Hamburg (such as the Grossensee, Mönchsteich and Bredenbeker Teich) are the best, but getting to them by public transport is tricky.

Taxis ☎0 40/21 12 11, 22 11 22 or 66 66 66.

Zoo Hagenbecks Tierpark (daily 9am–6pm or dusk; DM21/€10.50) in the north of the city (take U-Bahn #2 to the station of the same name) is generally regarded as one of the world's leading zoos, pioneering the modern practice of simulating the animals' natural habitat, rather than keeping them caged up.

SCHLESWIG-HOLSTEIN

A land between two seas, **Schleswig-Holstein** is chiefly an agricultural region, with large areas of forest and moorland. There's little heavy industry, and only two major cities. **Kiel**, destroyed in the war and drably rebuilt, is the capital of the Land and seat of its only fully fledged university. For most of its history, it has lain in the shadow of **Lübeck**, once northern Europe's leading merchant city and the undoubted highlight of a visit to the province. Of the other towns, **Flensburg** is another highly atmospheric trading port, **Husum** is an attractive old fishing harbour, while **Schleswig**, the province's historic capital, is incongruously rich in treasures for a place so small.

Schleswig-Holstein has two very contrasting coastlines: the gently lapped and undulating **Baltic shore** and the flat, windblown **North Sea coast**, off which lie the **North Friesian islands**, providing a relaxing, if uneventful, break from the mainland. Hot tea and stiff alcohol are the traditional means of making the long, cold and dark winters pass. In summer, though, the landscape vibrates with blues and greens, the corn dotted with poppies and cornflowers, the fields burning with the bright yellow of rapeseed. It's beautiful countryside to meander through by any means, most perfectly by cycling, and along the coast frequent local boat services provide enjoyable alternatives.

The most obvious **route** to take, assuming that you're coming from and returning to Hamburg, is a circular one up the Baltic and down by the North Sea coast – though with so many ferries heading off to Scandinavia, it's also a good point for moving on. It's worth knowing that **bikes** can be rented on a daily basis during summer months for about DM15/€7.50 per day from the stations at Büsum, Flensburg, Meldorf, Niebüll and Schleswig.

Lübeck

In medieval times, **LÜBECK** was one of Europe's most important merchant cities, dominating the highly lucrative trading routes along the Baltic. Although long overshadowed by the North Sea harbours of Hamburg and Bremen, which replaced it as international seaports, the city proudly displays the magnificent architectural wealth of its mercantile heyday – Germany's oldest town hall still in use, beautiful merchants' houses, fine Gothic brick-built churches and quaint old charitable institutions – many of which employ a highly decorative form of brickwork. Indeed, Lübeck's leadership in the artistic sphere was as pronounced as it was in commerce, influencing the appearance of cities along the entire length of the northern European coast, from Amsterdam to Tallinn. The importance of Lübeck's heritage was given official recognition in 1987 by UNESCO's decision to place its entire Altstadt on the list of the world's most significant monuments – the first place in northern Europe to be so honoured. This award

LÜBECK

0 Metres 200

Wallhafen

Hansahaven

Wakenitz

Burgtor ❶

Burgkloster

Heiligen-Geist-Hospital

Haus der Schiffergesellschaft ❷

Jakobikirche

Theater Lübeck

Behnhaus & Drägerhaus ❸

Musik- und Kongresshalle

Schabbelhaus ❹

Buddenbrookhaus

Katharinenkirche

Marienkirche ❺ ⓘ

Hauptbahnhof ⓘ

Rathaus

ZOB ▪

Holstentor ⓘ

Konditorei-Café Niederegger

Petrikirche ❻
Museum für Figurentheater ⓫

Salzspeicher

Aegidienkirche

St-Annen-Museum

Dom ⓬

N

WALLSTR

Mühlenteich

Kanal-Trave

❶③

ACCOMMODATION

4	Alter Speicher
2	Am Dom
9	baltic
11	CVJM Sleep-In
8	Excelsior
6	Jensen
5	Jugendgästehaus
13	Kaiserhof
2	Klassik Altstadt Hotel
10	Petersen
3	Rucksackhotel Backpackers
7	Stadt Lübeck
1	Zum Goldene Anker

was not only a tribute to the past, but also to the skill and efficacy of modern German restoration techniques: the city was severely bombed in World War II, with a quarter of the centre completely destroyed, but what little evidence of this survives today has mostly been left as a deliberate reminder.

In the Cold War years, Lübeck was the only important city to be sited alongside the notorious barbed-wire frontier. Paradoxically, this stimulated a revival in its fortunes after a long period of decline. Nearly 100,000 refugees came to settle, not only from the lost Eastern Territories, but also from the GDR itself, before the frontier was finally sealed. Even if its days of glory are no more than a memory, it's still a vibrant city with a wide range of attractions which merits a visit of at least a couple of days – longer if you want to spend some time in the deepwater port-cum-seaside resort of **Travemünde**, which lies 20km north of the city centre, yet has been an integral part of Lübeck since the fourteenth century.

LÜBECK AND THE HANSEATIC LEAGUE

In the eleventh century, a small Wend settlement had been established at the point where the Trave is joined by the Schwartau. It was destroyed by a rival Slav tribe in 1138, to be replaced five years later by a trading town owing allegiance to the Counts of Holstein. This move was none too popular with **Henry the Lion**, the powerful Duke of Saxony, whose own economic situation was adversely affected by the success of the new Baltic port. After it had burned to the ground in 1157, he forced the count to hand the site over to him, re-establishing it as a city and harbour two years later, and as a bishopric the year after that. He gave it special privileges, whereby the merchants ran the town council independently of ducal control and administered their own system of justice. The so-called **statutes of Lübeck** were later adopted by over a hundred other Baltic towns, and set the trend for medieval German cities being far freer in outlook and atmosphere than the feudalistic principalities. In 1226 Lübeck was officially recognized as a Free Imperial City of the Holy Roman Empire and grew quickly in wealth and trading power. Within a century of its birth, it had become the richest city in Germany and the Baltic's premier port.

In 1243, Lübeck formed a trading alliance with Hamburg; this in time, under the name of the **Hanseatic League**, extended to nearly all other ports along the Baltic, as well as to inland cities such as Braunschweig, Lüneburg, Magdeburg and Cologne. A fairly informal grouping, it was initially inspired by the need for mutual protection against pirates, and as an instrument to settle disputes and squabbles among the member towns – matters which Germany's weak central authority was unable to influence. However, in time the Hanseatic League developed into the equivalent of a cartel, excluding non-members from any share in the lucrative Baltic trade and opening a network of trading centres abroad, the most important being in London, Bruges, Bergen and Novgorod. Lübeck was accepted as the leader and spokesman of the League, though it began to lose its supremacy to Danzig (now Gdańsk) in the latter half of the fifteenth century. Throughout the following century, the League itself declined, as valuable herring stocks diminished. The balance of power in Europe shifted, as the Dutch – with their superior vessels and forward-looking philosophy of free trade – began to bite deeply into the old monopoly, and as trading routes changed due to the discovery of the Americas and new shipping routes to the east. The Thirty Years War, which drained energy and resources and left the powerful nation-states of Sweden and the emergent Brandenburg-Prussia in control of much of the Baltic, finally killed it off. Down to just nine members, the League met for the last time in Lübeck in 1669. However, Lübeck, along with Hamburg and Bremen, remained a significant port and trading centre. It was only in 1937 that it lost its status as a free city and was incorporated into Schleswig-Holstein.

Arrival, information and accommodation

Lübeck's **Hauptbahnhof** lies just a few minutes' walk west of the Altstadt. A branch line runs to Travemünde, which has three stations – the **Bahnhof Skandinavienkai** serves the ferries, the **Hafenbahnhof** the town centre and harbour, while the **Strandbahnhof** is close to the beach. **Mitfahrzentrale** (☎04 51/1 94 40) has a kiosk beside platform #20 of the **bus station**, which is almost immediately east of the Hauptbahnhof.

Three different organizations operate **tourist offices** within the city. Lübeck und Travemünde Tourist-Service has its head office at Breite Str. 62 (Mon–Fri 9.30am–7pm, Sat 10am–4pm, Sun 10am–3pm; ☎0 18 05/88 22 33, fax 1 22 54 19, *www.luebeck -tourismus.de*), and a branch in the Aqua Top building at Strandpromenade 1b in Travemünde (May–Sept Mon–Fri 9.30am–6pm, Sat 10am–5pm, Sun 10am–3pm; Oct–April Mon–Fri 9.30am–5pm, Sat & Sun 10am–2pm). Fremdenverkehrsverein Lübeck has its office in the Holstentor-Passage, Holstenstr. 20 (Mon–Fri 10am–6pm,

Sat 10am–2pm; ☎04 51/6 13 07 07, fax 6 13 07 12, *www.luebeck.de*), while Lübecker Verkehrsverein operates an office inside the Hauptbahnhof (Mon–Fri 10am–6pm, Sat 10am–2pm; ☎04 51/86 46 75, fax 86 30 24, *www.luebecker-verkehrsverein.de*).

All sell the **LübeckCard**, which costs DM9/€4.50 for one day, DM18/€9 for three days, and covers travel on the municipal buses and on the branch rail line to Travemünde, plus a range of discounts. These apply not only to museums and monuments, but also to the **cruises** run by several competing companies. Maak-Linie (☎04 51/7 06 38 59, *www.maak-linie.de*) and Quandt-Linie (☎04 51/7 77 99) both offer round trips through the city's canals and harbour (DM12/€6); the former departs from Untertrave, the latter from Moltebrücke. KuFra Schiffahrtslinien (☎04 51/2 80 16 35) sails between Untertrave and Travemünde (DM12/€6 single, DM20/€10 return). Wakenitzschiffahrt Quandt (☎04 51/79 38 85) and Personenschiffahrt Reinhold Maiworm (☎04 51/3 54 55, *www.maiworm-schiffahrt.de*) both run trips from Moltebrücke along the River Wakenitz to Rothenhusen on the Ratzeburger See, with the option of making a connection onwards to Ratzeburg itself; the former charges DM12/€6 single, DM20/€10 return, the latter DM14/€7 single, DM24/€12 return. See p.747 for more details of this journey.

Hotels are clustered mainly around the Hauptbahnhof or within the Altstadt; there are also some enticing options in Travemünde. Although only a few rooms are available in **private houses** (②–④), it's worth asking one of the tourist offices about these, as some have enticing locations in the Altstadt. Lübeck is a good place for budget travellers, with a wide choice of **dormitory** accommodation.

Hotels

Alter Speicher, Beckergrube 91–93 (☎04 51/7 10 45, fax 70 48 04). A converted warehouse in the Altstadt fitted out with all the mod cons. ⑥–⑧.

Am Dom, Dankwartsgrube 43 (☎04 51/7 02 02 51, fax 7 88 86). Reasonably priced hotel with restaurant on a quiet street near the Dom. ⑤.

baltic, Hansestr. 11 (☎04 51/8 55 75, fax 8 38 31, *www.baltic-hotel.de*). One of several inexpensive hotels immediately to the rear of the bus station. It has small basic singles which cost less than half the price of any of the doubles. ④.

Bed & Breakfast, Chasotstr. 25, Marli (☎04 51/61 05 81 fax 6 41 69). Lübeck's cheapest hotel, in a suburban setting 2km east of the Altstadt; take bus #4 or #14. Despite its name, breakfast is an optional extra. ②.

Excelsior, Hansestr. 3 (☎04 51/8 80 90, fax 88 09 99). Capacious hotel located just beside the bus station, with large breakfast buffets a definite plus. ⑥.

Jensen, Obertrave 4–5 (☎04 51/70 24 90, fax 7 33 86, *www.hotel-jensen.de*). A member of the Ringhotel group, this occupies a modernized old mansion with a waterside view. It also has a good fish speciality restaurant, *Yachtzimmer*. ⑥.

Kaiserhof, Kronsforder Allee 11–13 (☎04 51/70 33 01, fax 79 50 83, *www.kaiserhof-luebeck.de*). Nicely furnished upmarket hotel located in a pair of former patrician mansions just to the south of the Altstadt. ⑥–⑧.

Klassik Altstadt Hotel, Fischergrube 52 (☎04 51/70 29 80, fax 7 37 78, *www.klassik-hotel.com*). Elegant hotel in Neoclassical premises in the heart of the Altstadt. It serves good breakfast buffets, but no other meals. ⑤–⑦.

Koglin, Kottwitzstr. 39, Marli (☎04 51/62 24 32, fax 6 10 16 65). This pension has slightly more expensive rooms than its neighbour, *Bed & Breakfast*; take bus #4 or #14. ③.

Kurhaus, Ausenallee 10, Travemünde (☎0 45 02/88 10, fax 7 44 37). Very traditional seaside hotel with restaurant and good bathing and sports facilities, set in its own park. ⑤–⑨.

Maritim Strandhotel, Trelleborgallee 2, Travemünde (☎0 45 02/8 90, fax 89 20 20). This gargantuan tower-block hotel dominates the beachfront, offering wonderful views from its upper storeys. It also has a good if pricey restaurant. ⑦–⑨.

Petersen, Hansestr. 11a (☎04 51/8 45 19, fax 86 45 92). Another of the budget hotels by the bus station, offering a choice of rooms with and without facilities. ③–⑤.

Siemer, Mecklenburger Landstr. 36, Travemünde (☎0 45 02/24 08). Travemünde's cheapest rooms are in this pension in Priwall on the south side of the Trave, which can be reached by ferry from the centre of the resort. ③.

Stadt Lübeck, Am Bahnhof 21 (☎04 51/8 38 83, fax 86 32 21). Somewhat old-fashioned hotel whose location directly opposite the Hauptbahnhof is much quieter than might be expected. ③–⑤.

Strandperle, Kaiserallee 10, Travemünde (☎0 45 02/8 66 00, fax 86 60 18). Good-value middle-range hotel by the beach; it has a fine restaurant serving Italian and international dishes. ⑥.

Zum Goldenen Anker, Grosse Burgstr. 9 (☎04 51/7 16 92, fax 7 16 97). Lübeck's oldest Gasthaus, with a tradition dating back to 1439. It preserves much of its Wilhelmine decor and has a tea salon in addition to a restaurant, which has cask wine as well as beer on tap. ③.

Campsites and youth hostels

Campingplatz Schönböcken, Steinrader Damm 12 (☎04 51/89 30 30). Lübeck's campsite is in a western suburb, reached by bus #7.

CVJM Sleep-In, Grosse Petersgrube 11 (☎04 51/7 19 20, fax 7 89 97, *www.cvjm-luebeck.de*). A YMCA hostel in a renovated historic house in the middle of the Altstadt, offering the cheapest beds in the city, from DM17/€8.50.

Jugendgästehaus, Mengstr. 33 (☎04 51/7 02 03 99, fax 7 70 12). This official youth hostel likewise has an excellent Altstadt location. DM29/€14.50 or DM37/€18.50.

Jugendherberge Gertrudenkirchhof, Am Gertrudenkirchhof 4 (☎04 51/3 34 33, fax 3 45 40). Located just outside the Altstadt: go through the Burgtor, then bear left for about 200m. DM28/€14 or DM33/€16.50.

Jugendherberge Travemünde, Mecklenburger Landstr. 69, Travemünde (☎0 45 02/25 76, fax 46 20). Located by the beach on the Priwall side of the Trave, which is reached by ferry from the resort centre. There are also several campsites in the immediate vicinity. DM22/€11 or DM27/€13.50; closed mid-Oct to March.

Rucksackhotel Backpackers, Kanalstr. 70 (☎04 51/70 68 92, fax 7 07 34 29). A privately owned hostel charging upwards of DM24/€12 for dorm beds; also has doubles (DM80/€40). It's located at the eastern edge of the Altstadt.

The Altstadt

Almost everything worth seeing in Lübeck is in the **Altstadt**, an egg-shaped island still surrounded by the water defences of the Trave and the city moat. Its streets, while not conforming to a pre-arranged plan, are nevertheless arranged very symmetrically, so it's easy to find your way around. For a general view of the magnificent skyline, walk northeast from the Hauptbahnhof to the Marienbrücke: better still, take one of the cruises round the harbour area (see p.739).

The Holstentor, the Petrikirche and around

Entry to Lübeck was once through, but is now along the side of, the **Holstentor** (Holstein Gate; Tues–Sun 10am–4/5pm; DM5/€2.50), whose two sturdy circular towers with turret roofs, joined by a gabled centre section, form the city's emblem. Built in 1477, it leans rather horrifyingly these days, but that shouldn't put you off calling in at its small historical museum, which provides a useful introduction to the city and Hanseatic history. On the waterfront to the right of the Holstentor is a row of lovely old gabled buildings, the **Salzspeicher** (salt warehouses). They were built in the sixteenth and seventeenth centuries to store precious salt, extracted in Lüneburg and destined for Scandinavia.

Straight ahead over the bridge and up Holstenstrasse, the first church on the right (just down a side-street) is the Gothic **Petrikirche**, one of the many buildings to suffer during the massive Allied bombing of March 29, 1942. It no longer functions as a place of worship; instead, the whitewashed, five-aisled interior is put to use for changing exhibitions of contemporary art. A lift goes to the top of the **tower** (March–Dec daily

10am–4/6pm; DM3.50/€1.75), and Lübeck's centre is compact enough for this to be very useful for getting to grips with the layout of the city.

In the shadow of the church, at Kolk 16, is the **Museum für Puppentheater** (daily 10am–6pm; DM6/€3), which claims to be the world's largest collection of puppet-theatre material, with examples from all over Europe, Asia and Africa. Special matinees for kids are staged daily (except Mon) at 3pm in the adjoining Marionettentheater (DM8/€4); performances for adults are held on Fridays and Saturdays at 7.30pm (DM13–16/€6.50–8). The next street along, **Grosse Petersgrube**, ranks as one of the finest in the city, with an impressive array of mansions showing all the different ver-nacular styles from Gothic to Neoclassical.

The Rathaus

Across Holstenstrasse from the Petrikirche is the Markt, two sides of which are occu-pied by the imposing **Rathaus**, which illustrates Lübeck's characteristic brickwork – with alternating rows of red unglazed and black glazed bricks – at its most inventive. The north wing, which dates from the mid-thirteenth century, has a high super-structure with spire-topped turrets and two huge holes to lessen wind resistance; its side facing the Markt was further enlivened by the addition of a Renaissance loggia made of very white-coloured stone from the city's old trading partner, the Swedish island of Gotland. At the turn of the fourteenth century, the east wing, with an arcade leading to Breite Strasse behind, was added. Its extension, the **Neue Gemach**, was begun around 1440 and is the finest part of all, providing a highly refined variation on the earlier theme of windbreaks and corner turrets, with the bonus of coats of arms embedded in the brickwork. On the Breite Strasse side, it was further embellished with an extremely elaborate stone staircase in the Dutch Renaissance style and an oriel window.

Guided tours (Mon–Fri at 11am, noon & 3pm; DM4/€2) go round some of the inte-riors, though it has to be said that these don't quite match what you see from outside. The most notable rooms are the late Baroque **Audienzsaal**, with its allegorical paint-ings and Renaissance doorway, and the neo-Gothic **Bürgerschaftssal**. Leaving by the north side, you get a good view of the original thirteenth-century building, and can also see the **Kanzleigebäude**, the chancellery building tacked on in the fifteenth century.

The Marienkirche

Rearing up behind the north wing of the Rathaus is the city's largest and finest church, the **Marienkirche**. It's certain that the two buildings were intended to be seen as a coherent architectural group, as the Marienkirche was where the city's richest citizens worshipped – and they planned from the outset that it should overshadow the bishops' Dom not only by its prominent situation, but in its architectural splendour as well. Built at a leisurely pace between the early thirteenth and mid-fourteenth centuries, it's a tall, soaring building in the French Gothic style – but in brick, rather than stone, which gives it a very different and authentically German appearance. Its twin square **towers** are topped by spires to a height of 185m, while the nave is supported by flying but-tresses that rise from the verdigris roofs of the side aisles. In the 1942 bombings the Marienkirche was severely damaged and burnt out – an exhibition inside shows pho-tographs of the devastation and also of the restoration. Even more dramatically, the bells in the southern tower chapel have been left smashed on the ground, the way they fell during the bombing. War damage was a mixed blessing. The roof timbers and spires were destroyed, threatening the whole structure; both organs and many other items, including the chancel screen and much other fine woodwork, were lost. On the other hand, original Gothic **wall-paintings** which had been covered for centuries were revealed and restored – indeed the entire interior was laid bare for a restoration to its original simplicity.

Today the interior is very light, with a feeling of great loftiness. Detail of the fine ribbing and vaulting is picked out against the pale grey chalk wash in the old terracotta and grey-green colours. All this makes a good backdrop for the church's **art treasures**. The fifteenth-century high altar, in front of which is a pretty fourteenth-century font, is of modest dimensions, but a number of impressive works, dating from the late fifteenth and early sixteenth centuries, can be seen in the ambulatory. These include a life-size carving of St John the Evangelist (unfortunately only partly restorable after war damage), a series of powerful Passion reliefs by the Münster sculptor Hinrik Brabender and a beautiful locally made gilded tabernacle. In the axial chapel is a magnificent carved and painted altarpiece from Antwerp in a gilded wood frame, depicting the life of the Virgin Mary, while in the Alenkapelle, the chapel adjoining the northern transept, is a grave slab of a merchant cast by Lübeck's greatest artist, Bernt Notke. Before leaving, have a look inside the **Briefkapelle** at the southwestern end of the nave, a masterly miniature church which is used by the congregation during the winter.

Mengstrasse and Breite Strasse

On the north side of the Marienkirche is **Mengstrasse**, which is lined with an impressive row of patrician houses. At no. 4 is the Baroque **Buddenbrookhaus** (daily 10am–5pm; *www.buddenbrookhaus.de*; DM8/€4), which was where the famous literary brothers Heinrich and Thomas Mann (see box opposite) grew up. Recently converted into a memorial museum in their honour it takes its name from the latter's youthful novel of mercantile life in the city. Further up the street, nos. 48 and 50 are together designated the **Schabbelhaus**. It's now one of several restaurants in the city that are regarded as sightseeing attractions in their own right, crammed as it is with antiques.

Another of these is the **Konditorei-Café Niederegger** (Mon–Fri 9am–7pm, Sat 9am–6pm, Sun 10am–6pm), facing the Rathaus across Breite Strasse, whose **marzipan** is internationally renowned. This is the oddest hangover from the city's trading heyday: the confection was first produced in Lübeck in the Middle Ages from fine almonds imported from Italy. The Niederegger family perfected the art in 1806, and the mind-boggling range on sale in the shop is the result of the uninterrupted continuation of the business. On the second floor is a display on the history of marzipan. At the opposite, northern end of Breite Strasse are two impressive Renaissance halls – the **Haus der Kaufmannschaft**, the offices of the local chamber of commerce, and the **Haus der Schiffergesellschaft**, the former sea captains' guild house. The latter is another of the city's best-known restaurants, and is decked out inside with all sorts of seagoing paraphernalia; predictably, it's on the programme of every tour group.

Across the street stands the **Jakobikirche**, traditionally the parish church of the seafaring community. In comparison with the Marienkirche, it's modest in scale, the only obvious point of similarity being the Gothic wall-paintings on its square pillars. Nonetheless, it's rich in works of art, the finest being the **Brömbse Altar** in the chapel to the right of the entrance, which features a carving of the *Crucifixion* by Hinrik Brabender and delicate little Flemish-style paintings. The carved oak **organ lofts** are also impressive; a beautifully worked spiral staircase leads up to the large Baroque organ in the west gallery, though its smaller counterpart in the transept, dating back in part to the fifteenth century, is the more precious instrument of the two.

Grosse Burgstrasse and Königstrasse

Guarding the extreme northern end of the Altstadt, but unlike the Holstentor still on the island itself, is the formidable-looking **Burgtor**, a square tower topped by a bell-shaped roof. The side buildings of the gateway were originally used for stabling the horses of people arriving in the city at this point. On Hinter der Burg just to the south is the **Burgkloster** (Tues–Sun 10am–4/5pm; DM5/€2.50), a thirteenth-century

THE MANN LITERARY DYNASTY

One of the giants of modern European literature, **Thomas Mann** (1875–1955) was equally adept at writing short stories and epic novels. He made his name with *Buddenbrooks*, the saga of a Lübeck merchant dynasty's decline. In *The Magic Mountain*, which won him the Nobel Prize, the inmates of a Swiss TB sanatorium present a microcosm of a sickened Europe sleepwalking towards World War I. Another favourite theme, the conflict between the artist and society, is superbly expressed in his most famous story, *Death in Venice*. Mann's opposition to Nazism, expressed in the story *Mario and the Magician*, led him to leave Germany voluntarily in 1933. He settled in the US, where he wrote of biblical exile in the vast trilogy, *Joseph and his Brothers*. Mann's later works include *Doktor Faustus*, a terrifying allegory of Germany's pact with Nazism, in which the narrator – writing as Allied bombs reduce city after city to rubble – records the intellectual arrogance and descent into madness of his composer friend. Never really happy in the New World, Mann settled after the war in Switzerland, where he wrote his last works, including *The Confessions of Felix Krull, Confidence Man*, one of the few great comic novels in the German language.

Heinrich Mann (1871–1950) was initially preoccupied with similar themes, albeit with the addition of a good deal of erotic fantasy. However, he was given to more direct social and political comment than his soul-searching younger brother, and many of his novels are clear statements of his socialist views. His most famous work is his devastating attack on reactionary German pedagogy, *Professor Unrat*, which was filmed as the Marlene Dietrich classic, *The Blue Angel*. Its scope was widened in his best novel, *Man of Straw*, which lays bare the true nature of the political and business ethics of the Second Reich.

Three of Thomas Mann's children became writers, and the short-lived **Klaus Mann** (1906–49) is increasingly regarded as a major literary figure in his own right. He tackled the Faust theme before his father did in *Mephisto*, a thinly veiled attack on his former brother-in-law, an actor who sold out to the Nazis. His early work, *The Pious Dance*, is a graphic portrayal of the decadent homosexual underworld of Berlin in the days of the Weimar Republic.

Dominican friary which served after secularization as a poorhouse, then as a court and prison, and is now a cultural centre which is Lübeck's main venue for temporary artistic exhibitions.

Following Grosse Burgstrasse back towards the city centre, you come to the thirteenth-century **Heiligen-Geist-Hospital** (Tues–Sun 10am–4/5pm; free), one of the earliest and best-preserved hospices of the medieval period, whose rhythmic facade is characterized by its gables and tall pepperpot turrets. Inside, the vaulted chapel is richly decorated with frescoes, retables and a Gothic rood screen bearing delicate paintings telling the story of St Elizabeth. The tiny chambers leading off the main hall were built in the nineteenth century as an improvement on the previous communal space which you can glimpse through the gateway.

Königstrasse, the southern continuation of Grosse Burgstrasse, is dominated by stately mansions of the Baroque period and later. The **Gemeinnützige Gesellschaft** at no. 5 was another charitable institution; some of its elegant interiors are now used as a restaurant. Two patrician homes, the **Drägerhaus** at no. 9 and the **Behnhaus** at no. 11, have been combined to form the **Museum für Kunst und Kulturgeschichte** (Museum for Art and Cultural History; Tues–Sun 10am–4/5pm; DM5/€2.50, free first Fri of the month). It's surprising to see how large these houses are inside, compared with the narrow street frontage; tax was formerly paid on a building's width rather than its overall size, which led to houses being built long and narrow. The Drägerhaus has impressive interiors with original nineteenth-century furniture, clocks, porcelain and other *objets d'art*. A gallery of nineteenth- and early twentieth-century paintings occupies the Behnhaus. This includes a room devoted to Lübeck's own **Johann Friedrich Overbeck**, founder and guiding light of the influential Nazarene movement (see Contexts p.1095). There's also a lovely *Coastal Landscape by Evening Light* by Friedrich, and fine examples of the Expressionists Kirchner and Munch.

At the corner of the next block is the **Katharinenkirche** (April–Sept Tues–Sun 10am–1pm & 2–5pm; free), formerly the church of a Franciscan convent – the city's only monastic foundation from the days of the Hansa to have survived intact. In the niches of the facade are nine life-size figures. The first three on the left (*Woman in the Wind, The Beggar* and *The Singer*) are by **Ernst Barlach**: he was commissioned to make the series in the early 1930s, but these were all he had completed by 1932, when his work was banned by the Nazis. The other six were added after the war by **Gerhard Marcks**: you can have a closer look at them in Schloss Gottorf in Schleswig (see p.755), where another set of terracotta castings from the same moulds is exhibited. Inside, the main peculiarity is the two-storey chancel, the lower of which functioned as a crypt, even though it's at ground level. On the west wall is a large altarpiece of *The Raising of Lazarus* by **Tintoretto**, brought from Venice by a Lübeck merchant. Nearby stands a cast of Bernt Notke's masterpiece, a spectacular group of *St George and the Dragon*, the original of which is in Stockholm.

The eastern quarters

Down Glockengiesser Strasse to the side of the Katharinenkirche, you can step through what appear to be doors in the wall into two of Lübeck's finest courtyards, whose small almshouses were built by seventeenth-century benefactors. The **Füchtings-Hof** at no. 23 was built for the widows of sea captains and merchants; the slightly earlier **Glandorps-Gang** and **Glandorps-Hof** further down at no. 39 were intended for the widows of craftsmen. Another attractive example is the **Haasenhof**, a couple of blocks to the south at Dr-Julius-Leber-Str. 37. At the junction of this street with Königstrasse is the **Löwen-Apotheke**, the oldest remaining house in the city. Two groups of Gothic almshouses can be seen in streets further south – **Von-Höveln-Gang** at Wahmstr. 73–77 and **Dornes-Hof** at Schlumacher Str. 19.

Presiding over the quiet, village-like streets of the southeastern quarter (an area into which few tourists venture) is the handsome single tower of the **Aegidienkirche** (Tues–Sat 10.30am–noon & 2–3pm), Lübeck's smallest parish church, whose congregation was made up of craftsmen, smallholders and the less affluent merchants. There was a strong musical tradition here, and the early Baroque organ can rival any in Lübeck. What really catches the eye, however, is the richly decorated Renaissance **choir gallery** which shuts off the chancel from the nave. A Protestant variant on the old Catholic idea of the rood screen, its very positioning emphasizes the importance of music in Lutheran worship, while its paintings interpret biblical stories in line with the doctrines of the new faith.

Round the corner, the **St-Annen-Museum** (Tues–Sun 10am–4/5pm; DM5/€2.50, free first Fri of the month) is housed in the surviving parts of the late Gothic St-Annen-Kloster, an Augustinian convent which burned down in the nineteenth century. It has a first-rate collection reflecting domestic, civic and religious art and history from the thirteenth to the eighteenth century. The star piece is the magnificent *Passion* triptych which **Memling** painted for the Dom. There's also a room full of retables commissioned by the various guilds for their chapels; the finest, predictably enough, is that made for the artists' own guild of St Luke, which has attractive paintings illustrating the life of their patron by the leading Lübeck master of the late fifteenth century, **Hermen Rode**. The courtyard, surrounded by very Dutch-looking buildings, is one of the most restful spots in the city; its garden contains many imposing monumental Baroque statues, including the original figures from the Puppenbrücke, the bridge leading from the Hauptbahnhof to the Holstentor.

The Dom

At the extreme southern end of the Altstadt is the only surviving reminder of Henry the Lion's city, the huge brick-built **Dom**. It was completed in 1230, with its two 120-metre towers, as a Romanesque basilica. A couple of decades later, the pure early Gothic porch or "Paradise" was added on the south side to serve as the main entrance. Soon after, work began on replacing the original chancel with a spacious Gothic hall. The whitewashed interior is dominated by an enormous **triumphal cross**, the first important work of **Bernt Notke**, who was a celebrity throughout the Baltic lands in the late fifteenth and early sixteenth centuries. Probably a painter as well as a sculptor, he specialized in the grandiose, making highly original works to adorn churches in Denmark, Sweden and Estonia. This one is a complicated allegory on the salvation offered by the Cross, which rests on an elaborate beamed structure bearing marvellously expressive figures of saints and angels. Notke was also responsible for the carvings on the **rood screen** behind, to which an astronomical clock was appended in the seventeenth century. Among the Dom's numerous other adornments, look out for the ornate Renaissance pulpit in the main nave, the fifteenth-century *Müllerkrone* candelabrum in the north aisle, the winged retables in the transept, and, in the chancel, the memorials to bishops and noblemen, which range from simple Gothic tombs to commemorative chapels in the swankiest Baroque.

Travemünde

Despite having been part of Lübeck for nearly seven centuries, **TRAVEMÜNDE** is so far from the city centre that it seems like a separate town. Its initial importance was as an outer harbour, and the fishing and shipping quays retain their dominant positions. However, Travemünde has also become a rather glamorous seaside resort. Go there in winter and you might find the odd playful seal on the fine sandy beach. In summer, though, it is hardly the place to go to get away from it all. The beach is packed full of busy *Strandkörbe* (hooded basket-seats rented out like deck chairs to keep off the breeze), sailing boats and windsurfers ply the water, and the fashionable **Casino** makes fat profits (not least on its terrace, *the* place to sit for cool drinks and ice cream). By the southern end is a large indoor bathing complex, **Aqua Top** (daily 10am–9pm). From the beach it's odd to watch large ships apparently sailing right onto land – they're actually entering the mouth of the Trave. If you walk northwards up the beach, it eventually peters out and is replaced by cliffs, the Brodtener Ufer. This is the place to get a rare view of the Baltic from above sea level.

Eating, drinking and entertainment

Lübeck's attractions are far from being only historical: the city is also a renowned gastronomic and musical centre, and there is plenty of nightlife. The tourist office publishes a free monthly brochure, *Lübeck Heute*, with details of current events.

Restaurants

You'll pass many of Lübeck's most prestigious restaurants – from the point of view of both food and setting – on a tour around the Altstadt. All are pricey, though less expensive menus are often available at lunchtimes. However, the city has plenty of cheaper alternatives, many of them of comparable quality.

Aubergine, Hüxstr. 57. Vegetarian and wholefood restaurant. Closed Sun.

Das Kleine Restaurant, An der Untertrave 39. The menu here includes a ten-course gourmet set dinner. Evenings only, closed Sun.

Die Gemeinnützige, Königstr. 5–7. A really classy restaurant, with beautifully furnished interiors plus a garden terrace. Closed Sun evening.

Historischer Weinkeller, Koberg 8. Wine bar-cum-restaurant in the cellars of the Heiligen-Geist-Hospital. Its offshoot, *Kartoffelkeller*, serves potato-based dishes. Closed Tues.

Ratskeller, Markt 13. Among the best of its ilk, with hearty *gutbürgerliche Küche*, some vegetarian options and a good wine list.

Roberto Rossi im Schabbelhaus, Mengstr. 48–52. Upmarket restaurant in a sixteenth-century merchant's house with courtyard, serving Italian and international dishes. Closed Sun.

Schiffergesellschaft, Breite Str. 2. Famous old seaman's tavern, often overrun by tour groups, but serves excellent food and is not unduly expensive. Closed Mon.

Schmidt's, Dr-Julius-Leber-Str. 60–62. Inexpensive restaurant in the heart of the student quarter, with an eclectic menu of salads, pasta, pizzas, tandoori and vegetarian dishes. Evenings only.

Stadtrestaurant, Am Bahnhof 2–4. Despite its unpromising-looking setting on the first floor of the Hauptbahnhof, this serves food of a standard rivalling many of the city's most famous restaurants.

Tipasa, Schlumacher Str. 14. A great student favourite, featuring a large, ever-changing and reasonably priced menu of bistro-type dishes, plus wonderful pizzas and bread. If you're pressed for time, it has a fast takeaway service next door.

Wullenwever, Beckergrube 71 (☎04 51/70 43 33). Occupying a sixteenth-century mansion, this is currently Lübeck's most prestigious gourmet address, with fish and duck dishes the main specialities. Evenings only, closed Sun & Mon. Reservations advisable.

Zimmermann's Lübecker Hanse, Kolk 3–7. Housed in a beautiful old building by the Petrikirche, this excellent if pricey restaurant features French cuisine as well as German dishes. Mon–Fri only, except in Nov & Dec, when it's also open Sat.

Cafés and bars

Amadeus, Königstr. 26. Good place for rolls and salads – and for finding out what's on in town.

Brauberger, Alfstr. 36. Hausbrauerei serving low-cost meals and its own unfiltered beer. Evenings only.

Café Affenbrot, Im Werkhof, Kanalstr. 70. Vegetarian café with summer terrace and winter garden; it serves changing daily lunchtime specials and organically produced beer and wine.

Café Art, Kapitelstr. 4–8. Café-bar with a large summer garden which serves breakfasts until 3pm.

Café Maret, Markt 17. Traditional café claiming a pedigree dating back to 1786.

Café Niederegger, Breite Str. 89. The celebrated marzipan shop has an elegant backroom café, plus a first-floor dining room; there's a wide choice of breakfasts, plus good-value set lunches. Another branch can be found at Vorderreihe 56, Travemünde.

Charly Rivel's Sohn, Glockengiesser Str. 91. Café-bar frequented by Lübeck's artistic set.

Im Alten Zolln, Mühlenstr. 93. The most atmospheric of the city's traditional Kneipen; also does meals and sometimes has live music.

Discos and live music venues

Body and Soul, Auf dem Boot, corner of Kanalstrasse and Höhe Glockengiesserstrasse. Located on a boat, this disco as its name suggests – concentrates on soul music. Mon–Thurs & Sun 9pm–3am, Fri & Sat 9pm–5am.

Dr Jazz, An der Untertrave 1. A popular live jazz venue.

Queen's Club, Falkenstr. 45. Housed in a huge converted factory. Fri & Sat from 9pm.

Tiffany, Kreuzweg 5. Conveniently close to the Hauptbahnhof, this is for the real night owls. Mon–Thurs 8pm–3am, Fri–Sun 8pm–5am.

Culture and festivals

No German city is better known for its **organ recitals** – a tradition dating back to the early seventeenth century, when the Danish composer Diderik Buxtehude became one of the first musicians to achieve fame as a virtuoso solo instrumentalist, drawing huge crowds to his improvisatory recitals at the Marienkirche (see p.741). The Marienkirche's two modern organs (one of which is the biggest mechanical musical instrument in the world) are used alternately for recitals each Saturday at 6.30pm, while one or other of the Jakobikirche's historic organs is played on Saturdays at 5pm.

Concerts by the Philharmonisches Orchester der Hansestadt Lübeck are held at the Musik- und Kongresshalle, Willy-Brandt-Allee 10 (☎04 51/7 90 44 00). Other classical music can be heard at the Musikhochschule, Grosse Petersgrube 17–29 (☎04 51/1 50 51 05). The Theater Lübeck, Beckergrube 10–14 (☎04 51/7 45 52, *www.theater.luebeck .de*) stages **opera** in its Grosses Haus, **drama** in the Kammerspeile.

Lübeck's main **festivals** are *Markt Anno Dazumal*, an old-time fair held in the Rathausmarkt for ten days in May; a two-week *Volksfest* in mid-July; and the *Altstadtfest* on the second weekend in Sept (even-numbered years only). The Advent celebrations are a cut above the norm, thanks to the setting of the *Kunsthandwerker-Weihnachtsmarkt* in the Heiligen-Geist-Hospital, and the fairyland displays of the *Weichnachtsmärchenwald* outside the Marienkirche.

Ratzeburg

The idyllic town of **RATZEBURG** lies some 23km from Lübeck, towards the southern end of the **Ratzeburger See**, the largest of the forty or so lakes punctuating the wooded countryside through which the notorious border with the GDR used to run. Its picturesque if vulnerable-looking Altstadt is built on a small island linked by causeways to the modern suburbs on either bank.

Towards the northern tip of the Altstadt is the **Dom** which, like Lübeck's, was founded by Henry the Lion. The main external features of this Romanesque brick basilica are its massive west tower and porticoed southern porch. Inside, the triumphal cross and choir stalls remain from the original furnishings. Gothic additions include the pew used by the dukes of Saxony and the stone **Passion altar** in the chancel, an outstanding example of the Westphalian "Soft Style". The Renaissance pulpit, with its elaborate sounding board, is the most prominent of the post-Reformation embellishments. Also within the Dom are many tomb slabs to local bishops and dukes.

Back towards the commercial centre, the **A. Paul-Weber-Museum** (Tues–Sun 10am–1pm & 2–5pm; DM3/€1.50) at Domhof 5 displays the work of a satirical artist best known for his attacks on the Nazis. A few doors down at Domhof 12 is the **Kreismuseum** (Tues–Sun 10am–1pm & 2–5pm; DM3/€1.50), which has displays on the archeology and history of the town and the surrounding district. A few minutes' walk further south, the **Ernst-Barlach-Haus** (March–Nov Tues–Sun 10am–noon & 2–5pm; DM5/€2.50) on Barlachplatz to the rear of the Markt commemorates an even more celebrated artistic opponent of the Third Reich, the sculptor who created the figures on the facade of Lübeck's Katharinenkirche. Barlach spent part of his youth in this house, which now contains examples of his wonderful Expressionist carvings and graphic work. It's also worth crossing over to the eastern side of the lake to ascend the **Aussichtsturm** (May–Sept Tues–Sun 10am–5pm; DM2/€1), which commands fine views over the town and the Ratzeburger See.

Cruises on the lake are run by Schiffahrt Ratzeburger See, Schlosswiese 6 (☎0 45 41/79 00). A round trip costs DM12/€6, but it's well worth sticking to the water all the way between Ratzeburg and Lübeck, whether as a single journey (DM18/€9), or as a day return (DM29/€14.50). This is a combination ticket: the leg between Ratzeburg and Rothenhusen at the northern end of the lake is with Schiffahrt Ratzeburger See, the stage along the **River Wakenitz** is with Wakenitz Schiffahrt Quandt (see p.739). Because of the proximity of the border, this voyage was impossible throughout the four decades of German division, and the impenetrability of the area meant that it remained marvellously unspoiled. Even if not exactly the "Amazon of the North" it is billed as in publicity material, the beautiful swampy forest landscape is now a protected nature reserve inhabited by a rich variety of birdlife, notably herons, cormorants and kingfishers.

Practicalities

Ratzeburg's **Bahnhof**, on the line between Lübeck and Lüneburg, lies at the extreme western fringe of town. If time is of the essence, it's better to make the 25-kilometre journey from Lübeck by **bus**, as this takes you right into the Altstadt. The **tourist office** (May–Sept Mon–Thurs 9am–5pm, Fri 9am–6pm, Sat, & Sun 10am–4pm; Oct–April Mon–Fri 9am–5pm; ☎0 45 41/80 00 81, fax 85 85 65, *www.ratzeburg.de*) is just to the west of the Altstadt at Schlosswiese 7. Here you can book **private rooms** (①–③); the other budget option is the **youth hostel** at Fischerstr. 20 (☎0 45 41/37 07, fax 8 47 80; DM22/€11 or DM27/€13.50), which has the benefit of an Altstadt setting with lakeward views.

Alternatively, *Haus Betzinger*, Dermin 2a (☎0 45 41/8 34 30; ③), is a small **pension** on the west side of town. Within the Altstadt are several **hotels**, including *Seegarten*, Theaterplatz 5 (☎0 45 41/73 77; ④), *Wittler's*, Grosse Kreuzstr. 11 (☎0 45 41/32 04; ⑤), and *Der Seehof*, Lüneburger Damm 1–3 (☎0 45 41/86 01 00, *www.derseehof.de*; ⑥–⑧). The terrace **restaurant** at *Der Seehof* is the best place to eat in town; *Wittler's* is another good choice, as is the sixteenth-century *Askanier-Keller*, Töpferstr. 1, which serves local specialities.

Kiel

The naval port of **KIEL**, Schleswig-Holstein's capital, lies some 90km northwest of Lübeck at the head of the Kieler Förde, a typical Baltic coast fjord (though nothing like as dramatic as the Norwegian variety). Long overshadowed by Lübeck, the city's fortunes soared with the opening in 1895 of what is still the world's biggest and busiest man-made shipping lane. This is always known in English as the **Kiel Canal**, though its German title of Nord-Ostsee-Kanal is a more accurate designation of its status as the link between the North Sea and the Baltic. In 1918, it was a mutiny by the sailors of Kiel which sparked off the German Revolution, leading to the abdication of the Kaiser and the birth of the Weimar Republic. As the main **U-boat centre** in World War II, it was a prime target for Allied bombing missions, and much of it subsequently had to be rebuilt from scratch. Consequently, there's not much point in looking for charm amid its sober 1950s three- and four-storey blocks: from a sightseeing point of view, Kiel is one of Germany's least rewarding cities. Nonetheless, it attracts hordes of visitors in the last full week of June for the *Kieler Woche*, Germany's premier annual **regatta**.

Arrival, information and accommodation

Kiel's **Hauptbahnhof** and **bus station** are located together at the southern end of the central shopping area. The **tourist office** (May, Aug & Sept Mon–Fri 9am–6.30pm, Sat 9am–4.30pm; June & July Mon–Fri 9am–8pm, Sat 9am–4.30pm, Sun 9am–2pm; Oct–April Mon–Fri 9am–6.30pm, Sat 9am–1pm; ☎04 31/67 91 00, fax 6 79 10 99, *www.kiel-tourist.de*) is a short walk away at Andreas-Gayk-Str. 31. If you're intending to visit the outskirts, it makes sense to invest in the **Kieler Karte**, a runabout ticket on the public transport system: this costs DM12/€6 for 24hr, DM17/€8.50 for three days or DM27/€13.50 for a week. In the summer, there are regular **cruises** round the harbour, across the Kieler Förde, and down the Kiel Canal. It's also worth noting that **ferries** run to various Danish destinations from here, as well as to Oslo and Göteborg.

Bear in mind that accommodation of any kind is likely to be very difficult to come by during the *Kieler Woche*. **Hotels** in all categories are scattered throughout the city. Kiel's **youth hostel** is at Johannesstr. 1 (☎04 31/73 14 88, fax 73 57 23; DM28/€14 or

DM33/€16.50) in the suburb of Gaarden on the right bank of the Kieler Förde; take bus #11 or #12 or walk over via the pedestrian bridge. The **campsite**, *Falckenstein*, is in the far northern suburbs at Palisadenweg 171 (☎04 31/39 20 78), and not a very practical option unless you've got your own transport. **Mitfahrzentrale** is at Sophienblatt 54 (☎04 31/1 94 40).

Hotels

Berliner Hof, Ringstr. 6 (☎04 31/6 63 40, fax 6 63 43 45). Good medium-range hotel just west of the Hauptbahnhof. ⑥.

Kieler Yacht-Club, Hindenburgufer 70 (☎04 31/8 81 30, fax 29 28 69). This yachting enthusiasts' haunt occupies a lovely waterside setting only a short distance north of the city centre, with wonderful views over the Kieler Bucht. It also has a well-regarded restaurant. ⑧–⑨.

Parkhotel Kieler Kaufmann, Niemannsweg 102 (☎04 31/8 81 10, fax 8 81 11 35, *www.ringhotels .de*). A member of the Ringhotel chain, this has a pleasant park setting just north of the city centre, and also boasts a fine restaurant. ⑧–⑨.

Rendsburger Hof, Rendsburger Landstr. 363, Russee (☎04 31/69 01 31, fax 69 17 41). Budget hotel in a suburban setting 2km southwest of the centre. ③.

Runge, Elisabethstr. 16, Gaarden (☎04 31/73 33 96, fax 73 19 92). Located in a right-bank suburb, this good-value hotel offers a choice of rooms with and without facilities. ③–⑤.

Schweriner Hof, Königsweg 13 (☎04 31/6 14 16 or 6 26 78, fax 67 41 34). The cheapest hotel with a central location. ④–⑥.

Steigenberger Conti-Hansa, Schlossgarten 7 (☎04 31/5 11 54 44, fax 29 28 13, *www.steigenberger .de*). Kiel's most luxurious hotel has an ideal location at the northern fringe of the centre. Its restaurant, *Jakob*, is among the best in the city. ⑨.

Waffenschmiede, Friedrich-Voss-Ufer 4, Holtenau (☎04 31/36 96 90, fax 36 39 94). Good-value hotel directly overlooking the north side of the Kiel Canal, just to the west of the Schleusen. The restaurant is moderately priced and has a garden terrace. ⑤.

The City

The dominant building of the centre of Kiel is the huge Jugendstil **Rathaus** (guided tours May–Sept Wed & Sun at 9.30am & 10.30am; DM2/€1) on Rathausstrasse, whose tower commands an extensive panorama of the city and its fjord. A few minutes' walk to the northeast is the Alter Markt, on which stands the **Nikolaikirche**, a Gothic church partially restored and remodernized following war damage. Inside are a few notable furnishings, such as a fourteenth-century font and a fifteenth-century altar and triumphal cross, while outside stands an imposing sculpture by Barlach, *Der Geistkämpfer* (literally, "The Fighter for the Spirit").

A few paces away, at Dänische Str. 19, the **Warleberger Hof**, one of the few surviving old mansions, now houses the **Stadtmuseum** (mid-April to mid-Oct daily 10am–6pm; rest of year Tues–Sun 10am–5pm; DM2/€1), with changing exhibitions on the city's history. A little further along, set in gardens overlooking the promenade, is the exceedingly modest **Schloss**, part of which contains the **Stiftung Pommern** (Tues–Fri 10am–5pm, Sat & Sun 2–6pm; DM2/€1), a collection of paintings which includes works by seventeenth-century Dutch masters as well as examples of German art from Romanticism to Impressionism.

The old fish market hall just opposite at Wall 65 has been adapted as the **Schiffahrtsmuseum** (mid-April to mid-Oct daily 10am–6pm; rest of year Tues–Sun 10am–5pm; free), documenting local maritime history. During the summer months, you can also look round the three sailing craft moored outside – the steamship *Bussard*, the lifeboat *Hindenburg* and the fireship *Kiel*. A few minutes' walk further north, at Düsternbrooker Weg 1, is the **Kunsthalle** (Tues & Thurs–Sun 10.30am–6pm, Wed 10.30am–8pm; *www.uni.kiel.de/kunsthalle*; DM6/€3), which has a large array of predominantly modern art plus a collection of classical antiquities. At no. 20 on the same street, the **Aquarium im Institut für Meereskunde** (daily: April–Sept 9am–7pm; Oct–March 9am–5pm; DM2.50/€1.25) is home to seals and large aquaria of Baltic fish.

The **Schleusen** (locks) at the eastern end of the Kiel Canal are among the most interesting parts of the waterway; to reach them, take bus #11 from the bus station to the terminus at Wik. There are raised platforms on both banks; to cross over to the northern side, walk west for a few minutes to catch one of the regular free ferries.

At Molfsee, some 6km southwest of the centre (take a bus bound for Flintbek), is the **Schleswig-Holsteinisches Freilichtmuseum** (April–Oct daily 10am–6pm; Nov–March Sun & holidays 11am–4pm in fine weather only; DM7/€3.50). Here around thirty sixteenth- to nineteenth-century farmsteads and barns from throughout Schleswig-Holstein have been reassembled in regional groups to give a comprehensive picture of rural life down the ages. A pottery, bakery, four mills, a forge and a dairy are all worked in the old ways, and their products are on sale. Many of the houses have tiny cabin beds in which whole families used to sleep: in winter they slept sitting up and huddled together against the cold.

Eating, drinking and entertainment

Many of the best **restaurants** are in the hotels, but Kiel has a reasonable range of other places to eat and drink. The main **cultural** venues are the Opernhaus, Rathausplatz 4 (☎04 31/90 12 88 01), where opera and ballet are performed, and the Schauspielhaus, Holtenauer Str. (☎04 31/9 01 39 20), which is principally used for straight drama.

Restaurants

Dratenhof, Hamburger Landstr. 99, Molfsee. This converted eighteenth-century farmhouse by the Freilichtmuseum serves excellent, fairly priced food. Closed Sun evening & Mon.

Friesenhof, Rathausplatz 1. Located in the Rathaus, this is the ubiquitous Ratskeller masquerading under another name.

Im Schloss, Wall 80. This is generally regarded as Kiel's leading restaurant, and is expensive, though not excessively so. Closed Sat evening & Mon lunchtime, plus all day Sun & Mon in July & Aug.

Klosterbrauerei, Alter Markt 9. Hausbrauerei which produces an unfiltered dark beer and a *Bock*; also serves inexpensive meals.

Oblomow, Hansastr. 82. A longstanding student favourite which does good cheap food.

Seeburg, Düsternbrooker Weg 2. Café-restaurant handy for the museums, with the bonus of a view over the fjord.

Zauberlehrling, Lutherstr. 24. Has a good vegetarian menu, though it also caters for carnivores.

Around Kiel

Within easy reach of Kiel are a wide variety of enticing destinations making good full- or half-day trips; some of them are also possible stopovers on the way to or from Lübeck, Flensburg or Schleswig. Places to head for include **Rendsburg**, where the most interesting features of the Kiel Canal can be seen, the former ducal residence of **Eutin**, and the beach resorts of **Laboe** and **Eckernförde**.

Laboe

The Kieler Förde has a number of fine beaches, none better than that at **LABOE**, a popular resort some 18km from the city, reachable in well under an hour either by bus #100 or #101 or by one of the regular ferries which ply the inlet in summer. The waterfront is dominated by the celebrated 85-metre **Marine-Ehrenmal**, a memorial to sailors of all nationalities who died in the two world wars. Part of this now contains the **U-Boot-Museum** (daily 9.30am–4/6pm; DM5/€2.50), which tells you all you're likely to want to know about German submarines. As a supplement, you can visit **U-Boot 995** (same hours; DM3.50/€1.75), which is moored alongside.

Laboe has plenty of **pensions** (②–③), plus an excellent **hotel**, *Seeterrassen*, Strandstr. 86 (☎0 43 43/60 70; ⑤). Full information about accommodation is available from the **tourist office**, Strandstr. 25 (May–Sept Mon–Fri 10am–noon & 1–4pm, Sat & Sun 10am–3.30pm; April & Oct daily 10am–2pm; Nov–March Mon–Fri 10am–2pm; ☎0 43 43/42 75 53, fax 17 81, *www.laboe.de*).

Eutin

EUTIN, which likes to style itself "Rosenstadt" (the town of roses), lies almost exactly midway along the road and rail lines linking Lübeck and Kiel. It's the most attractive of the many *Kurorte* in **Holstein Switzerland**, an area which contains no mountains and so presumably owes its nickname to the presence of a multiplicity of lakes, some 140 in all.

The town's focal point is the **Schloss** (guided tours March–Oct Tues–Sun at 10am, 11am, noon, 2pm, 3pm & 4pm; DM5/€2.50), which is set in a fine park with both French and English sections. It has its origins in a fortified castle of the prince-bishops of Lübeck, who were forbidden to reside within the boundaries of the city-state itself; later, it became one of the residences of the dukes of Holstein-Gottorf-Oldenburg, and was rebuilt in the Baroque period. Inside, there are apartments decorated in late Baroque, Regency and Neoclassical styles. They contain a series of large **ship models** donated by Czar Peter the Great of Russia and a collection of portraits by Goethe's friend **Johann Heinrich Wilhelm Tischbein**, who resided in Eutin as court painter for 21 years. The former stables (**Marstall**) of the Schloss now house the **Ostholstein-Museum** (April–Sept Tues, Wed & Fri–Sun 10am–1pm & 2–5pm, Thurs 10am–1pm & 2–7pm; DM3/€1.50). This is primarily devoted to evoking the town's golden era in the early nineteenth century, and displays yet more paintings by Tischbein as well as memorabilia of **Carl Maria von Weber**, the founding father of musical Romanticism, who was born in Eutin in 1786. Weber's compositions are the mainstay of the *Eutiner Festspiele*, a **festival** held in the Schloss in July and August.

Eutin's **tourist office** (Mon–Fri 9am–5pm; ☎0 45 21/7 09 70, fax 70 97 20, *www.eutin.de*) is at Bleekergang 6. The town has some very pleasant **hotels**: *Uklei Fährhaus*, which is by the Kellersee, 5km north of the centre at Eutiner Str. 7 in the incorporated village of Sielbeck (☎0 45 21/24 58; ④); *Am See – Der Redderkrug*, which lies 3km northeast of town at Am Redderkrug 5 (☎0 45 21/22 32; ⑥); and *Voss-Haus*, which occupies a beautiful eighteenth-century building at Vossplatz 6 (☎0 45 21/7 07 70; ⑥). There's a **youth hostel** overlooking the town, at Jahnhöhe 6 (☎0 45 21/21 09; DM22/€11 or DM27/€13.50). All of three hotels listed above have good **restaurants**. Other enticing places to eat are *Schlossterrassen*, which occupies the former ducal riding hall in the stables, and *L'Etoile*, Lübecker Landstr. 36, one of Schleswig-Holstein's foremost gourmet addresses, which runs a moderately priced bistro as an adjunct.

Eckernförde

There are two rail lines linking Kiel with Flensburg. The first crosses the Kiel Canal immediately north of the city before passing through the area known as the Dänischer Wohld, where there are quite high cliffs along the coastline. Further on, about 30km from Kiel, the beach and health resort of **ECKERNFÖRDE** is at the head of the next major inlet, the Eckernförder Bucht. Despite having some typically bland modern *Kurzentrum* facilities tacked on, the old part of town is pretty enough, and the

Nicolaikirche is worth looking into for its carved dark oak and beautifully painted choir ceiling and altar. The fifteenth-century **Rathaus** on Rathausmarkt now houses the **Heimatmuseum** (July & Aug Mon 3–5pm, Tues–Sun 10am–5pm; rest of year Tues–Sat 3–5pm, Sun 10am–5pm; DM3/€1.50), which is mainly devoted to life in the first half of the twentieth century. There's a typical *Flüchtungszimmer*, or refugee room, with an array of simple belongings and mementoes brought on a long odyssey from the east. It's a reminder that, just after the war, Schleswig-Holstein became the new home of many **refugees** who left behind most of their worldly goods and trekked for weeks or months to avoid having to live in the Soviet sector.

The **tourist office** (mid-May to Aug daily 8am–6pm; Sept to mid-May Mon–Fri 9am–noon & 1–5pm, Sat & Sun 10am–noon; ☎0 43 51/7 17 90, fax 62 82; *www.ostseebad-eckernfoerde.de*) is at Am Exer 1. **Hotels** include *Park*, Preusserstr. 24 (☎0 43 51/54 11; ③), *Seegarten*, Berliner Str. 73 (☎0 43 51/50 22; ⑥), *Seelust*, Preusserstr. 3 (☎0 43 51/7 27 90; ⑥), and the luxurious *Stadthotel*, Am Exer 3 (☎0 43 51/7 27 80; ⑦). The **youth hostel**, towards the southern edge of town at Sehestedter Str. 27 (☎0 43 51/21 54, fax 36 04; DM22/€11 or DM27/€13.50), has views over the sea. Many of the best **eating** possibilities are concentrated around Frau-Clara-Strasse, though the top restaurant is definitely the Ratskeller in the Rathaus.

Rendsburg

The alternative rail line from Kiel to Flensburg first travels westwards for 35km to the garrison town of **RENDSBURG**. It's well worth going here for the ride alone, the last part of which is one of the most spectacular in Germany, as the rail line has to perform some extraordinary gymnastics in order to cope with crossing the Kiel Canal high enough for shipping to pass underneath, yet get back to ground level again for the **Bahnhof** at the southeastern edge of the town centre, only a few hundred metres ahead. The solution is ingenious – having traversed the bridge, the **Schwebefähre Hochbrücke**, the train descends via a gently sloping **loop**, which circles for a good 2km all the way round the inner suburb of Scheleife. Bizarrely, this trip offers one of the best views of Rendsburg: when there's a train approaching in the opposite direction, the effect is positively surreal. Other impressive feats of transport engineering in town are the four-lane **road tunnel** taking road traffic beneath the canal, and Europe's longest **escalator**, which takes pedestrians down to it.

The main historic buildings are clustered together around the Altstädter Markt, a few minutes' walk north of the Bahnhof. Here the timber-framed sixteenth-century **Altes Rathaus** is notable for the archway cut through it, allowing the street to pass underneath. Nearby is the brick **Marienkirche**, which dates back to the thirteenth century and is the oldest building in town.

In the opposite direction from the Bahnhof, at Prinzessinstr. 8, the handsome nineteenth-century **Synagoge** (Tues–Sat 11am–1pm & 4–6pm, Sun 3–6pm; DM5/€2.50) has been restored to house a museum of Jewish life and culture. Just to the west is the spacious Paradeplatz, on which stands the late seventeenth-century **Christuskirche**, which was specially designed so that the garrison's entire contingent of two thousand men could all attend services at the same time.

Rendsburg's **tourist office** (July & Aug Mon–Fri 10am–noon & 3–5pm, Sat 10am–noon; rest of year Mon–Fri only; ☎0 43 31/2 11 20, fax 2 33 69, *www.rendsburg.de*) is in the Altes Rathaus. There are plenty of **hotels**, such as *Deutsche Eiche*, Herrenstr. 12 (☎0 43 31/5 80 20; ③–⑤), *Tüxen*, Lancasterstr. 44 (☎0 43 31/2 70 99; ⑤), *Hansen*, Bismarckstr. 26 (☎0 43 31/5 90 00; ⑤), and *Pelli-Hof*, a fine eighteenth-century mansion at Materialhofstr. 1 (☎0 43 31/2 22 16; ⑥). The **youth hostel** is 1km west of the Altstadt at Rotenhöfer Weg 48 (☎0 43 31/7 12 05, fax 7 55 21; DM22/€11 or DM27/€13.50). Most of the best **restaurants** are in the abovementioned hotels. A cheaper alternative is *Niewarker* on Paradeplatz, a Hausbrauerei which makes both a bottom-fermented light beer and a top-fermented dark beer.

Schleswig

Though well off the tourist track, **SCHLESWIG**, which lies 25km north of Rendsburg, is worth going far out of your way to see. Nowadays an administrative centre with a sleepy, civil-servant pace, it dozes gently on the banks of a beautiful fjord, the Schlei, and could easily trick you into thinking that nothing had ever happened there. It did, though – for three centuries from after around 800 the **Vikings**, whose trade routes stretched from the Black Sea to Greenland, had their main northern European trading centre here, the shortest crossing point between the Baltic and North Sea. Following their demise, the town was re-established on the opposite side of the Schlei. This subsequently became a Danish royal residence, and then, after the partition of Schleswig-Holstein in 1544, the seat of one of its lines, the House of Gottorf. This illustrious history has bequeathed a marvellous legacy of monuments, making Schleswig one of the most outstanding small towns in all of Germany.

Arrival, information and accommodation

Schleswig's **Bahnhof** is over 1km south of Schloss Gottorf, and about 3km from the centre. Local buses #1 and #2 run from there via Schloss Gottorf to the **bus station**, which is located just to the north of the Altstadt. A couple of minutes' walk south of here, at Plessenstr. 7, is the **tourist office** (May–Sept Mon–Fri 9am–12.30pm & 1.30–5pm, Sat 9am–noon; Oct–April Mon–Thurs 9am–12.30pm & 1.30–5pm, Fri 9am–12.30pm; ☎0 46 21/98 16 16, fax 98 16 19, *www.schleswig.de*). Here you can buy the **SchleswigCard**, which costs DM13/€6.50 for individuals, DM29/€14.50 for families, and gives three days' travel on the local buses and entrance to all the museums.

Bikes and **boats** can both be rented at the Stadthafen during the summer months, when various companies also run **cruises** on the Schlei. The **folklore** tradition of Holm continues in the *Holmer Beliebung* held two weeks after Whitsun and featuring processions, music and a ball in which the minuet and fandango are performed; another big annual event is the *Twiebakken-Regatta* in late August.

Schleswig offers a good choice of **hotels**; the best are listed below. The **youth hostel** is at Spielkoppel 1 (☎0 46 21/2 38 93, fax 2 07 96; DM22/€11 or DM27/€13.50); from the Bahnhof, take a bus as far as the Theater (ie before the bus station), then walk up the steps known as the Lollfusstreppe. There's a **campsite** (☎0 46 21/3 24 50) at Haddeby, near the Wikinger Museum.

Hotels

Dom-Hotel, Domziegelhof 6 (☎0 46 21/2 43 13, fax 2 38 36). Moderately priced hotel with restaurant, just to the west of the Altstadt. ④.

Olschewski, Hafenstr. 40 (☎0 46 21/2 55 77, fax 2 21 41). Small hotel overlooking the Schlei at the edge of the Altstadt, attached to the best restaurant in town. ⑤.

Schleiblick, Hafengang 4 (☎ & fax 0 46 21/2 34 68). The most atmospheric of the cheaper hotels, located in an old fishermen's house in the Altstadt. To book in person, it may be necessary to go to the *Friesenstube* restaurant, Fischbrückstr. 15 (at the end of the same street). ④.

Stadt Hamburg, Lollfuss 108 (☎0 46 21/90 40, fax 90 42 22). Hotel with restaurant in a huge whitewashed building between the Schloss and the Altstadt. ⑤.

Strandhalle, Strandweg 2 (☎0 46 21/90 90, fax 90 91 00, *www.ringhotels.de*). A member of the Ringhotel group, this hotel with restaurant is located alongside its own yachting marina just to the west of the Altstadt. ⑥.

Waldschlösschen, Kolonnenweg 152 (☎0 46 21/38 30, fax 38 31 05, *www.hotel-waldschloesschen .de*). Schleswig's best hotel lies 2km southwest of the centre in a rustic woodland setting where the dukes of Gottorf used to go hunting. It has a swimming pool, whirlpool, steam baths, saunas and an excellent restaurant, *Adam Olearius*. ⑦.

Zum Stadtfeld, Stadtfeld 2a (☎0 46 21/2 39 47). Located to the north of the bus station, this bargain hotel is run as an adjunct to a Gaststätte. ③.

The Town

Despite a present-day population that barely tops the 25,000 mark, Schleswig possesses a sense of grandeur to match its past, not least in the way it sprawls over a large area. Its attractions are well spread out, meaning that it's a place not easily seen in a hurry, but all the sights are served by city buses.

The Dom

Schleswig's skyline, best viewed from across the Schlei, is dominated by the **Dom**, and in particular its oversized late nineteenth-century tower, which, close up, looks even more modern than it is, due to a re-facing of its brickwork in the 1950s. The main body of the building is essentially a Gothic hall church, though the imposing south **portal** and the transepts are Romanesque. Inside, the vaults of the latter, plus the triumphal arch of the choir, are covered with precious thirteenth-century **frescoes**, the most notable being *The Saviour of the Rainbow*. On the south wall is another of the Dom's early adornments, a lovely polychromed **retable** to the Three Magi, carved around 1400.

However, your attention is most likely to be drawn to the twelve-metre-high **Bordesholm altar** in the choir, one of Europe's most astonishing pieces of woodcarving. Carved from oak between 1514 and 1521, and originally commissioned for the Augustinian Kloster of Bordesholm south of Kiel, it shows some four hundred figures on a background so delicate it resembles filigree. The Passion scenes appear to be based on woodcuts by Dürer, and are certainly the closest sculptural equivalent to the work of Germany's most famous artist. Yet the creator of this long-celebrated masterpiece, one **Hans Brüggemann** of Husum, remains a shadowy figure about whom little else is known, though one of his earlier works is the remarkable elongated **statue of St Christopher** by the transept entrance. Legend has it that the jealous monks of Bordesholm fed him with a potion which caused him to go blind, ensuring that he could never create an altar to rival their own.

In the northern ambulatory is the magnificent **tomb of King Friederick I**, carved in the 1550s by the Antwerp sculptor-architect **Cornelis Floris**. Its pure Renaissance style, with classically inspired Virtues and mourning angels bearing the reclining effigy of the deceased monarch, shows how tastes changed in the generation after Brüggemann. Nearby hangs the **Kilmannseck altar**, an elaborate Baroque epitaph with an allegorical painting by the local painter **Jürgen Ovens**, a student of Rembrandt and the only German artist to take up the style of the great Dutch master. He was also responsible for *The Blue Madonna* on the pillar of the end bay of the nave.

The rest of the Altstadt and Holm

Everything else in the Altstadt stands very much in the shade of the Dom. There are plenty of grand mansions of various dates, but the only other setpiece attraction is the **Graukloster** on Rathausmarkt immediately to the east. This former Franciscan friary is the unlikely looking headquarters of the local administration, and is linked to the **Rathaus** proper, a plain Neoclassical structure. You're free to wander around during working hours; at weekends, only the ground floor of the cloister is left open.

A couple of minutes' walk beyond the eastern end of the Altstadt brings you to the formerly separate fishing village of **Holm**, whose name (meaning "surrounded by water") reflects the fact that it was an island until 1935. These days, there are only some twenty fishermen still eking a living from the eel- and herring-catches of the Schlei, instead of the three hundred or so in Holm's heyday. Nonetheless, the quarter preserves the appearance of a tightly knit community. The immaculately tended circular **Friedhof** (cemetery), with a rustic nineteenth-century chapel as its bull's-eye, provides the unexpected centrepiece. The houses around it are notable for their two-piece doorways (the so-called "chatting doors") and for their bay windows, which give views in three directions.

At the eastern edge of Holm is the fascinating **Adeliges St-Johannis-Kloster**, a one-time Benedictine convent which has been a Protestant collegiate foundation since the Reformation. The canonesses, who only come here on retirement from their normal careers, live in the splendid Baroque houses grouped round the courtyard. Call at the home of the prioress at no. 8, or, better still, phone in advance (☎0 46 21/2 42 36), for a **guided tour** (DM2/€1) round the complex, taking in the church, cloister and refectory.

Schloss Gottorf

On a little moated island in the Bergsee, a lake close to the head of the Schlei, about 1.5km west of the Altstadt, stands **Schloss Gottorf**, a truly regal palace whose facade, one of the finest achievements of northern European Renaissance architecture, masks what's actually an extremely disparate structure, incorporating older defensive features as well as many later additions. Together with its dependencies, it's home to the **Schleswig-Holsteinisches Landesmuseum** (March–Oct daily 9am–5pm; Nov–Feb Tues–Sun 9.30am–4pm; DM9/€4.50). Note that the ticket gives admission to several separate collections, which in total warrant at least half a day, and that it's best to avoid Mondays, when only some parts are open.

A wide range of artefacts are displayed chronologically in the finest interiors of the Schloss itself. At the entrance, the **Königshalle**, a stately Gothic hall, houses Gothic paintings and sculptures, though the finest pieces are in the small rooms beyond. These include a gorgeous *Nativity* by the Lübeck painter **Hermen Rode** and a small retable of *The Holy Kinship* by **Brüggemann**; the latter postdates the Bordesholm altar, thereby suggesting that the story of the sculptor's blinding is a myth. Important later paintings are *Frederick the Wise* by **Cranach** and a wonderfully luminous *Cain and Abel* by **Johann Liss**. Passing through the re-erected interior of a seventeenth-century Weinstube from Lübeck, you come to a suite of rooms decorated in Baroque style, of which the finest, the **Blauer Saal** (Blue Room), makes an elegant backdrop for a number of canvases by **Ovens**. Beyond is the **Schlosskirche**, a perfectly preserved Renaissance gem complete with painted gallery, an ornate ducal oratory and a still-functioning sixteenth-century organ. Adjoining this is the most spectacular chamber of all, the main festive hall, known as the **Hirschsaal** because of the life-sized, startlingly realistic polychrome stuccoes of deer on the walls. Finally, there's a first-class **folklore** collection upstairs, complete with a series of reconstructed interiors from rural houses.

On the west side of the Schloss, the modern **Nydamhalle** is visually rather jarring, but its contents, which illustrate the pre- and early history of the region, are themselves sufficient reason for a visit to Schleswig. The major treasure is the huge **Nydamboot**, an oak rowing boat from around 350 AD. This is the single most important object to have survived from the era of the Germanic tribes who eventually came to form the German nation. There are other impressive sailing craft on show as well, including one from Roman times. Another highlight is the grisly display of *Moorleichen*, **peat-bog** corpses reckoned to be around two thousand years old. Most shocking are the facial expressions, ranging from the beatific look of one who seems to have died in peace, to the utter anguish of another, whose fate can only be imagined.

The **Kreuzstall**, a cross-shaped stables building on the other side of the Schloss, is home to a fine array of twentieth-century German art. On the ground floor, particular works to look out for are the second set of castings of the figures on the facade of the

Katharinenkirche in Lübeck by **Gerhard Marcks** and the cartoons by **Kokoschka** for the destroyed mosaic he made for St Nikolai in Hamburg. Many of the other big names, such as Kirchner, Nolde, Macke, Rohlfs and Barlach are also well represented. Upstairs are more modern pieces, of which the most eye-catching is the brightly coloured set of 33 scenes by **Hap Grieshaber** illustrating Thomas Mann's biblical epic, *Joseph and his Brothers*.

The inclusive ticket also gives admission to the **Reithalle**, the riding hall immediately east of the Kreuzstall, where temporary exhibitions are held, and the **Kutschensammlung**, a collection of old coaches kept in the building behind the Nydamhalle. A display on local crafts and industries, the **Volkskundliche Sammlung** (same times; DM3/€1.50) has recently been relocated from another of the Schloss outbuildings to a former Prussian army storehouse about 1km to the northeast on Hesterberg.

The Städtisches Museum

Just south of Schloss Gottorf runs Friedrichstrasse, the main thoroughfare of the suburb on the opposite side of the Schlei. It's predominantly modern, but has a few older survivals, notably **Von Günderotscher Hof**, an intact seventeenth- and eighteenth-century manor house with dependencies, grouped round a courtyard. The main building now contains the **Städtisches Museum** (Tues–Sun 10am–5pm; DM4/€2), whose disparate exhibits include finds from the recent excavations of the Altstadt, an overview of local history which includes a surprisingly extensive and candid documentation of life during the Third Reich and an excellent collection of historic children's toys. Periodically, demonstrations are held in the **Druckerei**, which has a room dedicated to composing by hand with old typesetting and printing equipment.

Haithabu

Haithabu, the site of the original Viking settlement, is about 4km from the Altstadt by road. It can be reached by any bus going in the direction of Kiel, but in summer there's the far more atmospheric option of reaching it by a small boat across the Schlei which leaves the Stadthafen just south of the Dom. The earthwork ramparts of the otherwise vanished town have survived, and the extensive excavations yielded by the site are now kept in the **Wikinger Museum** (April–Oct daily 9am–5pm; Nov–March Tues–Sun 10am–4pm; DM5/€2.50), a bold modern design constructed, Viking-fashion, like a series of upturned boats. The main discovery has been a **longship**, now partially reconstructed to its original state and exhibited alongside models illustrating how it was built. Elsewhere, there are informative displays (English translations are available) on all aspects of Viking life; look out in particular for some wonderful jewellery and for the runic stones, one of which is engraved with a lurid orange script.

Eating and drinking

Many of the best places to eat are in the hotels, though there are several other enticing possibilities.

Asgaard, Königstr. 27. The restaurant of Schleswig's only brewery, which is located on site. A relative newcomer, it has quickly established a high reputation for its dry, fruity premier product, known simply as *Asgaard*, as well as its *Pils* and *Weizen*.

Holm Café, Süderholmstr. 15. Cosy little daytime café in Holm, serving home-made cakes and a good selection of teas and coffees.

Panorama, Plessenstr. 15. The varied menu includes pizzas baked in a wood-fired oven, as well as noodle, vegetarian and fish dishes. There are inexpensive daily specials at lunchtime.

Ringelnatz, Fischbrückstr. 3. Serves good-value food, teas and beer in a series of intimate little rooms, each quite different from the other.

Schleimöwe, Süderholmstr. 8. Fish speciality restaurant in Holm, offering dishes prepared from seasonal catches in the Schlei.

Senatorenkroog, Rathausmarkt 9–10. Serves fairly upmarket *gutbürgerliche Küche*.

Stadt Flensburg, Lollfuss 102. Handily located near Schloss Gottorf, this intimate restaurant occupies a house built in 1699 and presents both local and international dishes. Closed Wed.

Flensburg

There's a quite astonishing contrast in feel between Schleswig and its larger near neighbour **FLENSBURG**, a bustling commercial port and border town just over 30km to the north. Once the richest mercantile city under the Danish Crown, Flensburg has continued to prosper in spite of having lost much of its hinterland to Denmark in the wake of the 1920 plebiscite, when it opted to remain part of Germany. Standing at the head of the gentle Flensburger Förde, the town has expanded from its original waterside location up into the hills on either side of the inlet. Until the 1980s, it looked rather scruffy, but its Altstadt, which was surprisingly little touched by war, has gradually been restored to pristine shape as a result of an extremely imaginative urban regeneration programme.

The Town

Flensburg's pride and joy is its central axis, a pedestrian precinct successively known as Holm, Grosse Strasse and Norderstrasse, which stretches for well over a kilometre along the entire length of the Altstadt from the Südermarkt to the Nordertor. Along its length are a series of **Höfe**, former merchants' courtyards (see box below). These have no counterpart anywhere else in Germany, and are illuminating documents of social history, as well as the main contributory factor to the town's indubitably distinctive appearance.

The Südermarkt, on which markets are held on Wednesdays and Saturdays, is dominated by the **Nikolaikirche**, whose massive late sixteenth-century steeple, a very tardy example of Gothic, had to be reconstructed in the nineteenth century following fire damage. The rest of the building, which is in the traditional hall-church style, belongs to an earlier phase of Gothic. Inside, the most important adornment is the Renaissance **organ**, the largest in Schleswig-Holstein, which preserves its original case, a loving piece of craftsmanship by the sculptor Heinrich Ringerinck, who probably also made the pulpit. Also of note is the late fifteenth-century bronze **font** with its picturesque Baroque canopy.

Proceeding up Holm, look out for nos. 19–21, a courtyard dating back to the sixteenth century, and for house no. 10 opposite, which has a well-restored facade. At the

---

THE FLENSBURG HÖFE

Most of Flensburg's courtyards are laid out according to a clear pattern. Facing the main street is the showpiece home of the merchant, with his offices often incorporated as well. The two side wings typically have the stables and workshops where the imported raw materials were turned into finished products, while the far end is normally closed off by a large warehouse building with an entrance gateway and crane. For obvious reasons of convenience, most of these back directly onto the harbour, which is only one block to the east. Therefore, the western side of Flensburg's main axis was left to those of lesser means and was populated mainly by craftsmen, whose modest houses stand in stark contrast to the courtyards directly opposite.

back of no. 24 on Grosse Strasse is the **Westindienspeicher** (West Indies Warehouse), a late eighteenth-century "skyscraper" which stands as a reminder of the importance of the rum and sugar trade to the local economy. Like many of the other historic buildings it has, following restoration, been converted into a mixture of offices and apartments. On the left-hand side further up Grosse Strasse is the **Heiliggeistkirche**, a fourteenth-century chapel which has been the main place of worship of the local Danish-speaking community since 1588.

Just beyond is Nordermarkt, on which stands the **Neptunbrunnen**, which gushes out the famous spring water used for rum-making. Also here is the **Marienkirche**, a Gothic hall church with impressive frescoes from about 1400 in its northern aisle and a fine set of Renaissance furnishings – altar, pulpit and font. Alongside are the **Schrangen**, covered arcades where traders' stalls have stood since the sixteenth century. Kompagniestrasse goes down to the right to the **Kompagnietor**, the former mariners' guildhall, where a plaque reveals something of the northern mercantile philosophy that behaving justly will, with the help of God, always bring large profits.

Continuing onwards, the **Künstlerhof** at no. 22 Norderstrasse is a courtyard of half-timbered houses which have been restored as artists' studios. The central axis terminates at the **Nordertor**, a step-gabled Renaissance gateway which has become the symbol of the town. It bears the coats of arms of both Flensburg and King Christian IV of Denmark. Facing the harbour at Schiffbrücke 39, only a couple of minutes' walk from Nordertor, a warehouse which was still in use as late as the 1970s has been adapted to contain the **Schiffahrts- und Rum-Museum** (Tues–Sun 10am–4/5pm; DM5/€2.50, including entry to the Städtisches Museum). The main part of this is devoted to the history of the port and its trade, including many fetching models of ships made by sailors. In the basement, a new section focuses on the local rum business; at the last count, there were 58 different varieties being produced in Flensburg.

Returning to Norderstrasse, the stone stairway known as the Marientreppe leads up some 150 steps to the **Schlosswall**, the site of the former castle, from where there's a good view across the harbour to the opposite and traditionally less salubrious side of town. Also on the heights, a bit further south on Lutherplatz, and reached via Rathausstrasse from the junction of Grosse Strasse and Holm, is the vast neo-Renaissance bulk of the **Städtisches Museum** (same times and ticket at Schiffahrts- und Rum-Museum). Its displays include some fine medieval artefacts, a series of interiors from rural farmsteads and a collection of watercolours by Emil Nolde.

Finally, it's worth crossing eastwards from Südermarkt to reach the oldest part of the town, grouped round the **Johanniskirche**, a rustic little twelfth-century church. Viewed from inside, the building almost seems to sag under the weight of its wacky sixteenth-century vault, which is covered with what is, for the most part, a decidedly unecclesiastical decorative fresco scheme.

Practicalities

Flensburg's **Hauptbahnhof** is about fifteen minutes' walk due south of the centre; the **bus station** is south of the harbour, on the opposite side of the busy Süderhofenden from the Altstadt. The **tourist office** (June–Sept Mon–Fri 9am–6pm, Sat 10am–1pm; rest of year Mon–Fri only; ☎04 61/9 09 09 20, fax 9 09 09 36, *www.flensburg.de*) is housed in a converted warehouse at Spiecherlinie 40. There are plenty of **private rooms** (①–③) on offer, plus an inexpensive **pension**, *Ziesemer*, right beside the bus station at Wilhelmstr. 2 (☎04 61/2 51 64; ③). **Hotels** include: *Handwerkerhaus*, Augustastr. 2 (☎04 61/14 48 00; ④); *Am Rathaus*, Rote Str. 32–34 (☎04 61/1 73 33 35; ⑤); *Am Wasserturm*, Blasberg 13 (☎04 61/3 15 06 00; ⑥); *Flensburger Hof*, Süderhofenden 38 (☎04 61/14 19 90; ⑥); and the top-of-the-range *Europa Comforthotel*, Norderhofenden 6–9 (☎04 61/8 41 10; ⑦). Well to the northeast of town, reached by

Glücksburg-bound buses, is the **youth hostel**, Fichtestr. 16 (☎04 61/3 77 42, fax 31 29 52; DM22/€11 or DM27/€13.50).

The Altstadt has a nicely varied selection of places to **eat** and **drink**. Liveliest place is *Hansens*, Grosse Str. 83, which includes a tramcar among its furnishings and has changing hot and cold buffets, but is mainly of note as a Hausbrauerei brewing its own *Pils* and *Alt*. This marks a bold challenge to the renowned *Pilsener* of the Flensburger brewery, which holds sway in most of the other bars and restaurants – and whose distinctive flip-top bottles have helped make it something of a cult drink elsewhere in Germany, notably Berlin. *Das Kleine Restaurant*, Grosse Str. 73, has a varied menu including good pastas and salads, while the *Vegetarisches-Vollwert Restaurant*, Marienstr. 29, is, as its name suggests, a vegetarian and wholefood specialist. *Alt-Flensburger Haus*, Norderstr. 8, occupies one of the town's finest mansions, while *Borgerforeningen*, Holm 17, serves arguably the best meals of all. The *Galerie-Musikkneipe*, Holm 66, features live bands and food, and *Kunstwerk*, Norderstr. 107–109, is the best café-bar, serving breakfast until well into the afternoon.

A varied programme of **drama** and **music** is held at the Landestheater, Nordergraben 2–6 (☎04 61/14 10 00). To find out **what's on** here and elsewhere, pick up the monthly *Flensburger Programm* from the tourist office, or the alternative magazine called *Hallimasch*. **Boat trips** are run by Förde-Reederei, Norderhofenden 20 (☎04 61/86 40).

Around Flensburg

The obvious excursion from Flensburg is to nearby **Glücksburg**, whose Schloss is among the finest in Schleswig-Holstein. A little further afield is **Angeln**, with its impressive old village churches, while to the west, **Niebüll** is gateway to the North Friesian islands and home to two notable art collections.

Glücksburg

A few kilometres along the fjord from the end of the built-up part of Flensburg lies **GLÜCKSBURG**, a fairly typical little *Kurort* offering parks, beaches, forest walks and a first-rate sea-water swimming pool. It also has a late sixteenth-century **Schloss** (April–Sept daily 10am–6pm; Oct Tues–Sun 10am–6pm; Nov–March Sat & Sun 10am–5pm; *www.schloss-gluecksburg.de*; DM7.50/€3.75), which is still the seat of the Sonderburg-Glücksburg line of the Schleswig-Holstein duchy. Set in a small lake, it now looks a little austere – it was shorn in the nineteenth century of its original decoration, which closely resembled the ebullient Weser Renaissance style – but is nonetheless impressive, especially when floodlit. Unusually, it is constructed not on the normal wooden piles, but on a massive granite base sunk into the bed of the lake. Its interior is equally singular, with each floor featuring a long central hallway with four rooms leading off on either side and a further room in each of the corner turrets. The decoration of the **Schlosskapelle** is a classic example of Lutheran Baroque, while the festive rooms have a marvellous array of **tapestries** and **leather wall-hangings**.

Angeln

The land to the east of the rail line between Flensburg and Schleswig is **Angeln**, home of the Angles who came to Britain in the fifth century. They must have felt at home there as Angeln's slightly hilly landscape, with clusters of woodland and fields divided by hedgerows and pocked with marshes is far more reminiscent of England than of most of Germany. The larger villages here have some unimpressive modern buildings,

---

INTO DENMARK

From both Flensburg and Niebüll it's very easy to get across the border into **Denmark**. Boats run regularly from Flensburg to Sønderborg, and there are regular bus connections. It's definitely worth making a short trip by bus from either Flensburg or Niebüll to **TØNDER**, the oldest market town in Denmark, first mentioned in the twelfth century. The semicircular old town has at its heart the lovely **Kristikirk**, with **small gabled houses** round about. Some, such as in the Uldgade, are so tiny you can touch the roof. On the last weekend of August Tønder hosts a large international **jazz and blues festival**, but all through the summer there are music performances in the market place. The extremely helpful **tourist office** (they speak excellent English – proof that you're in Scandinavia) is at Ostergade 2a (☎45/74 72 12 20), right in the centre of the old town.

---

but in the smaller hamlets, and along the lanes, you come across plenty of **traditional farmhouses**. Unique to Angeln are the **early churches** built of enormous blocks of granite – the oldest, with a thirteenth-century font, is in **SÖRUP**, roughly 20km south and east of Flensburg. Husby, Norderbrarup, Eggebek, Munkbrarup, Oeversee and Struxdorf all have thirteenth-century Romanesque churches too. Many small areas are designated nature reserves, such as the peat bog of **Satrupholmer Moor**. The **Torsberger Moor** is the site of major archeological finds of early Germanic settlements, though the best place to find out more and actually see anything of this is Schloss Gottorf in Schleswig.

Getting around this area is not exactly straightforward: trains will take you from Flensburg to Sörup and on either to Schleswig or via Süderbrarup to Eckernförde. Buses, however, are notoriously rare. The best way to explore the countryside is under your own steam – rent a bike in Flensburg or Schleswig and you can explore the coastline (beaches and campsites all the way along) as well as the villages with their Danish-sounding names. Flensburg tourist office (see p.758) has a cycle map called *Rad- und Wanderwege*, indicating touring routes in this area. Most of the roads are pretty quiet, and there are some special routes, such as the old rail line from Tarp to Süderbrarup.

Niebüll

A one-horse town in Schleswig-Holstein's farthest-flung northwest corner isn't top of anyone's list of places to visit, but **NIEBÜLL**, which lies in the bleak North Friesian landscape 40km west of Flensburg, has one or two surprises. First, it's from here that the train runs across that thin strip of land to the island of Sylt. Secondly, there are two terrific museums dedicated to artists who fell foul of the Third Reich – Emil Nolde and, less famously, Richard Haizmann.

The **Richard-Haizmann-Museum** (Tues–Fri 11am–4.30pm, Sat 10am–noon, Sun 2–5pm; DM3/€1.50) in the Rathaus on Rathausplatz is dedicated to the artist's sculpture, pottery and pictures. Haizmann was exiled to Schleswig-Holstein in what was termed "inner emigration", following the banning of his work by the Nazis. Some of it had been displayed in the famous 1930s Berlin exhibition of so-called degenerate art and was subsequently destroyed. Haizmann's work bears the influence of oriental and African art, and is beautifully displayed in a museum created by the curator and the artist's widow, who struggled for many years to open a museum, achieving her ambition only days before her death. Elsewhere in the town centre, the only place of interest is the **Friesisches Heimatmuseum** (daily June–Sept 2–6pm; DM2/€1) at Osterweg 76, an old farmhouse decked out in seventeenth-century style.

The **Nolde-Museum** (daily: March–Oct 10am–6pm; Nov 10am–5pm; DM7/€3.50) stands alone in the countryside at Seebüll, some 5km from the town centre, in the house and gallery that Emil Nolde built in the 1950s. These were the years when Nolde could be acknowledged again after his work had been condemned by the Nazis. A novel by postwar author Siegfried Lenz, *The German Lesson*, has as a main character an artist, painting in secret during the war, who was based on Nolde. The museum can be very full in summer, but if you are there on a quiet day you may have the luxury of enjoying Nolde's vibrant colours on your own. His Expressionistic paintings have some brutal themes; the brilliant flower and landscape series are simpler, but powerful nonetheless. In accordance with Nolde's wishes, the shop sells books and postcards, but no reproductions. A bus runs out to the museum from Niebüll, and the way is clearly signposted if you are travelling by car or bike.

Niebüll's **tourist office** (Mon, Wed & Fri 8am–noon, Tues 8am–noon & 2–4pm, Thurs 8am–noon & 2–6pm; ☎0 46 61/6 01 90, *www.niebuell.de*) is in the Rathaus. You can ask here about **private rooms** (①–③), though the town's **hotels** are all quite reasonably priced. They include *Insel-Pension*, Gotteskoogstr. 4 (☎0 46 61/21 45; ④), *Zum Morgenstern*, Deezbüller Str. 70 (☎0 46 61/42 04; ④), *Zur Alten Schmiede*, Hauptstr. 27 (☎0 46 61/42 18; ④), and *Stadt Tonder*, Hauptstr. 70 (☎0 46 61/9 66 00; ⑤). There's also a **youth hostel** at Deezbülldeich 2 (☎0 46 61/87 62, fax 2 04 57; DM22/€11 or DM27/€13.50). Note that, whereas there are ample trains passing through on the Hamburg–Sylt line, the cross-country route to Flensburg is served only by **buses**.

The North Friesian Islands

The **North Friesian Islands** lie scattered off the coast, storm-battered for centuries and until recently the home of a small population of fisherfolk and farmers eking out a fragile existence. Today tourism is by far the biggest source of income. The land is so flat directly offshore that the sea retreats to reveal large areas of mudflat – the **Watt** – which have their own sensitive ecosystem, including masses of birdlife. In order to ensure their protection, the islands and adjacent coastline have been declared the **Nationalpark Schleswig-Holsteinisches Wattenmeer**. The main islands are **Föhr**, **Amrum** and **Sylt**, which, although little more than a strip of land running north–south, is touristically the most developed and sophisticated. They are all family-holiday centres, with holiday homes and riding, tennis and windsurfing facilities. In season, all are likely to be very busy.

Sylt

Sylt is an altogether different kettle of fish from the other homely islands. It's a favourite among monied Germans, who visit to mix business with pleasure and impress their guests with second homes in the sun. As a result, the island is heavily populated during the major holidays (including Christmas and Easter), and prices for both eating out and accommodation can be high. Such is the demand for **accommodation**, which is available in all price categories, that unless you have booked a couple of months in advance – regardless of when you visit – you could be unlucky. To add to complications, there's no central tourist office – each resort on the island has its own agency.

WESTERLAND is Sylt's main town and the hub for bus and train connections. It's considered rather chic and glamorous: a place to dress up for an evening in the **Casino** on Andreas-Nilsen-Strasse rather than stomp around in boots. Outside of Westerland the island is quieter (though full of holiday houses). Above all there's plenty of fine **sandy beach** here. The island is shaped rather like a T on its side – Westerland is on the stalk (west side) and the cross-stroke runs north to south for about 40km in a narrow strip, under 1km wide, lined with beaches, dunes and small cliffs (Rotes Kliff) which make for a good hiking route.

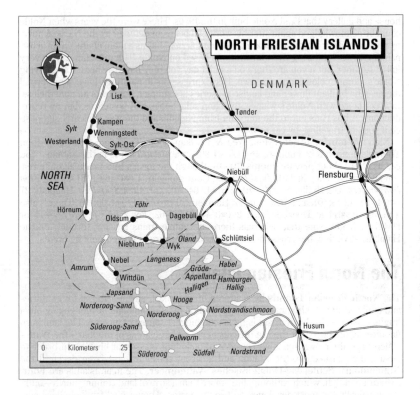

North of Westerland is **KAMPEN**, an exclusive enclave of 650 monied inhabitants. Formerly a place of inspiration for the writers Thomas Mann and Carl Zuckmayer and the painter Emil Nolde, its tiny streets are today packed with antique stores, gourmet restaurants and expensive clothes stores. It's doubtful whether such a large amount of luxury is spread so thick on so small an area anywhere else in Germany.

Further north is Sylt's most famous stretch of beach, **Buhne 16**, a haven for naked (but gold-dripping) sun-worshippers. After sunset the place to be is *Gogärtchen* on the strip known as "Whiskystrasse". Beyond lies **LIST**, which has Germany's largest expanse of sand dune around it. The village has a small harbour from which ferries run daily to the port of Havenby on the Danish island of Rømø.

Practicalities

A regular **bus service** runs between Westerland, Kampen and List. Sylt is joined to the mainland at Niebüll by a narrow causeway along which **trains** run – if you want to take a car, it has to be loaded onto the train first. A cheaper option is to take a **ferry** to List from Rømø in Denmark. Ferries to the islands of Föhr and Amrum leave from Hörnum at the southern tip of Sylt.

Accommodation is best found through the Westerland **tourist office** (Mon–Sat 9am–6pm, Sun 10am–6pm, reduced hours out of season; ☎0 46 51/99 88, fax 99 81 00, *www.westerland.de*), which is right beside the Bahnhof at Am Bundesbahnhof. This town is particularly well endowed with upmarket **hotels**, ranging from the small *Jörg Müller*,

Süderstr. 8 (☎0 46 51/2 77 88; ⑨), via the medium-sized *Atlantic*, Johann-Möller-Str. 30 (☎0 46 51/9 88 00; ⑨), to the resort's most prestigious address, the capacious *Stadt Hamburg*, Strandstr. 2 (☎0 46 51/85 80; ⑨). Still in Westerland, a good choice for traditional German **food** is *Alte Friesenstube*, Gaadt 4, which is housed in one of the oldest buildings on the island. More upmarket fare can be found in the hotel restaurants: of those mentioned above, *Stadt Hamburg* has a reasonably priced bistro in addition to its expensive main dining room, while *Jörg Müller* is of true gourmet stature.

One of the island's two **youth hostels** is in an isolated setting outside List (☎0 46 51/87 03 97, fax 87 10 39; DM24/€12 or DM29/€14.50). The other is at Friesenplatz 2 (☎0 46 51/88 02 94, fax 88 13 92; DM24/€12 or DM29/€14.50) in Hörnum.

Föhr

Föhr is Sylt's nearest neighbour, but quite different in character. Outside of a few bars and cafés nightlife is non-existent, and accommodation is reasonably easy to come by. Ferries from Dagebüll on the mainland arrive at **WYK**, the island's main town. It's a peaceful old place with a thirteenth-century church, a harbour and precious little else. Depending on finances you can either take a **taxi** and go for a one-hour ride around the island, or **rent a bike** (from one of the numerous shops displaying a *Fahrrad Verleih* sign; around DM10/€5 per day). First place to cycle to should be the village of **NIEBLUM** to the west, an exceptionally quaint and picturesque place of old gabled and thatched cottages along cobbled streets, with a thirteenth-century church. Listen to the local dialect: a mixture of *Plattdeutsch*, *Hochdeutsch* and Friesian, the last of which is itself a mix of Danish, Dutch and English.

There's a **youth hostel** in Wyk at Fehrstieg 41 (☎0 46 81/23 55, fax 55 27; DM24/€12 or DM29/€14.50); alongside is a **campsite**. Other accommodation can be arranged via the **tourist office** (☎0 46 81/30 40, fax 30 68, *www.wyk.de*) at Hafenstr. 23.

Amrum

Amrum is a less exciting prospect than the previous islands. Ferries land at the town of **WITTDÜN**, where, if you're not careful, you'll find yourself stuck since ferries and local buses aren't synchronized. The village has a one-horse feel, though you can rent bikes and there's a **tourist office** (☎0 46 82/9 40 30, *www.wittduen.de*) at Mittelstr. 34. on the edge of the harbour car park. Walks, beaches, sea birds and sports are the order of the day here, and the bracing breeze becomes quite enjoyable in the end. Most visitors book into **hotels** and **pensions** for a week or more, so it is easiest to ask the tourist office about vacancies. The **youth hostel** is at Mittelstr. 1 (☎0 46 82/20 10, fax 17 47; DM24/€12 or DM29/€14.50).

It is possible – tides permitting and only under the supervision of an experienced guide – to **walk across the Watt** from Amrum to Föhr. For more information and details of tours, contact the Schutzstation Wattenmeer in Hörnum on Sylt (Tues–Sun 10am–noon & 3–5pm; ☎0 46 51/88 10 93).

The Halligen

Smaller, and almost at sea level, is another, distinct group of undyked islands – the **Halligen**. These last remnants of land are scarcely above sea level; as you approach them by ship all you see are a few houses apparently sitting on the waves. Once you set foot on dry land you discover that these houses are built on specially constructed hummocks that stay dry when the rest of the land is washed over by winter storms. The land is really good only for grazing sheep, and bed and breakfast is a major source of income for the Hallig inhabitants nowadays. Even more than on the mainland, few young people are interested in staying on to maintain old ways of life, and the Halligen seem set for a slow but sure period of decline.

The main Halligen are inhabited, but the tiny **Hallig Habel** is a nature reserve, with just one family present in summer; the even smaller **Norderoog** is a **bird-breeding sanctuary**, and also just has a summertime warden. The main islands, **Nordstrand** and **Pellworm** (together with **Hamburger Hallig** and **Nordstrandischmoor**), used to form a larger island known as **Alt-Nordstrand**, or just Strand, with five quays and some fifty-nine churches and chapels – a major settlement in its time. A tidal wave in 1634 created today's geography. Nordstrand is now connected to the mainland by a narrow causeway, as are Nordstrandischmoor and Hamburger Hallig; the latter has become a virtual peninsula because of silting up on both sides of its link with the mainland. **Hallig Langeness** is similarly connected to **Hallig Oland**, which in turn has a mainland connection.

Pellworm and **Hallig Hooge**, however, are reached by peak-season **ferries** running from the mainland ports of Dagebüll and Schlüttsiel (run by WDR lines) and from Nordstrand (Kurt Paulsen). **Pellworm**, to the southeast of Amrum, has thirteenth- and seventeenth-century churches bearing witness to its history, and hardly anything else. Its future may be anticipated by a huge **solar collector** (it's one of Germany's sunniest places, which bodes well for visitors), generating 280,000 kilowatt hours per year. A small **Wattmuseum** (Mon–Thurs 8am–noon & 2–4/6pm, Fri 8am–noon; DM2/€1) holds the former local postman's lifetime collection of finds from the Watt. The **tourist office** is at Uthlandestr. 1 (π0 48 44/1 89 40, fax 1 89 44).

All the tourist offices and some train stations have leaflets and posters with details of ferries. It doesn't take long to look round a Hallig – so unless you feel like communing with wind and water, the few hours between boats may be all the time you want to spend there.

Husum and around

HUSUM, some 40km south of Niebüll and 35km west of Schleswig, is by far the most attractive town in North Friesland. Its character is defined by the small harbour right in the centre, which must have given welcome shelter to generations of fishermen returning from the perils of the North Sea. As a town, it's a mixture of small-scale grandeur and workaday simplicity, filled with fishy smells that waft in from the harbour, and with a sufficient smattering of interesting buildings to catch the imagination. In summer, it serves as a jumping-off point for the Halligen islands and for Helgoland (see below), though it's at its picturesque best during the springtime bloom.

Husum is perhaps best known in association with the name of **Theodor Storm**, a nineteenth-century novelist, poet and civil figure (it was he who gave the town its rather unfair title *Die graue Stadt am Meer* – "the grey town by the sea") who was especially active in Schleswig-Holstein's struggle to remain out of the clutches of the expansionist state of Prussia. His name crops up all over the town: you may even find yourself staying in the hotel or youth hostel named after him.

The Town

The main axis of the town centre is the broad **Gross-Strasse**, which opens out into the **Markt**. Both of these are lined with large houses, mainly eighteenth- and nineteenth-century (though there are one or two beautiful seventeenth-century gabled buildings reminiscent of Lübeck), most of which have stores on the ground floor. Here too is the step-gabled fourteenth-century **Herrenhaus**, the oldest building in town, albeit with sandstone pillars and a doorway added in the seventeenth and eighteenth centuries. On the north side of the square stands the seventeenth-century **Rathaus**.

Turning northwards from here, you come to the Schlossgang, a narrow walkway leading past small houses, a couple of cafés and craft-giftshops to the **Schloss** (April–Oct Tues–Sun 11am–5pm; DM5/€2.50). Over to the left, the **Torhaus**, the former gatehouse, is actually more attractive than the main building. It has retained some ornate Renaissance features, whereas the Schloss itself, built at the same time, underwent extensive later modifications, giving it a Baroque interior with fine sandstone and alabaster fireplaces. The **Schlosspark**, which contains a memorial to Theodor Storm, turns into a great sea of mauve crocuses in spring. These were originally planted in the Middle Ages by monks who had a monastery on the site.

About 100m south of Gross Strasse is the **Schiffbrücke**, an inner harbour busy with fishing boats; it's also the place where the ferry takes shelter in winter. One famous catch landed here is *Husumer Krabben* – not crabs, confusingly, but tasty little brown shrimps. They're found in abundance on local menus, especially in the form of *Husumer Krabbensuppe*, a soup that often comes topped with whipped cream. In summer, there's a shrimp stall on Hafenstrasse, towards the outer harbour, selling the freshly boiled catch.

Up Wasserreihe, the narrow street to the right, is the **Theodor-Storm-Haus** (April–Oct Mon, Sat & Sun 2–5pm, Tues–Fri 10am–noon & 2–5pm; Nov–March Tues, Thurs & Sat 2pm–5pm; DM4/€2), the home of the writer between 1866 and 1880, when he was at the height of his career. With many original documents, and as the headquarters of the Theodor Storm society, it's obviously chiefly of interest to his fans. However, the house is worth catching as an example of nineteenth-century middleclass lifestyle in this area, as the rooms still have original furnishings. Storm's woodpanelled study, where he produced about twenty of his novels, has a display of correspondence with the Russian novelist Turgenev and other literary figures. The Wasserreihe itself is a characterful street, with several typical fisherfolk houses.

A couple of blocks further north, at Nordhusumer Str. 13, is the **Ostenfelder Bauernhaus** (April–Oct Tues–Sun 10am–noon & 2–5pm; DM3/€1.50), a reconstructed seventeenth-century farmhouse. At the southern end of the town centre, in the Nissenhaus at Herzog-Adolf-Str. 25, is the **Nordfriesisches Museum** (April–Oct daily 10am–5pm; Nov–March Tues–Fri & Sun 10am–4pm; DM5/€2.50). This was founded in the early 1930s by local-boy-made-good Ludwig Nissen, who amassed a fortune in the United States. It's especially good on the geological background of the area, flood control and town history.

Practicalities

Both the **Bahnhof** and the **bus station** are just a short walk from the town centre, which is reached via Herzog-Adolf-Strasse. The **tourist office** (June to mid-Sept Mon–Fri 9am–6pm, Sat 10am–1pm; rest of year Mon–Thurs 9am–noon & 2–4pm, Fri 9am–noon & 2–3pm; ☎0 48 41/8 98 70, fax 89 87 70, *www.husum.de*) is in the Altes Rathaus, Gross-Str. 27.

At the tourist office you can pick up the extensive list of **private rooms** (①–③). There's a good range of **hotels** in every category. At the lower end are *Rödekrog*, Wilhelmstr. 10 (☎0 48 41/37 71; ③), and *Wohlert*, Markt 30 (☎0 48 41/22 29; ④). In the medium range, *Zur Grauen Stadt am Meer*, overlooking the harbour at Schiffbrücke 8–9 (☎0 48 41/8 93 20; ⑤), is a lovely place, with an excellent restaurant serving local fish specialities; an alternative in this category is *Osterkrug*, Osterende 56 (☎0 48 41/28 85; ⑤). Moving up the scale, the inevitably named *Theodor Storm*, Neustadt 60 (☎0 48 41/8 96 60; ⑦), has a restaurant serving hot and cold buffets every day, plus its own Hausbrauerei. Top of the range is *Altes Gymnasium*, which occupies a historic school building at Süderstr. 6 (☎0 48 41/83 30; ⑨) and has wonderful bathing facilities plus two prestigious restaurants, *Wintergarten* and *Eucken*. Husum's **youth hostel** is at the far northwestern end of town at Schöbuller Str. 34 (☎0 48 41/27 14, fax 8 15 68; DM24/€12 or DM29/€14.50), while the **campsite** is well located right by the beach to the west of the centre at Dockkoog (☎0 48 41/6 19 11).

Quite apart from the hotel restaurants, Husum is well off for places to **eat** and **drink**. *Dragseth's Gasthof* at Zingel 11, a sixteenth-century house with a small gallery and teashop, offers a good selection of food including vegetarian dishes. *Anna*, in the basement of Stadtpassage, Schiffbrücke 16, also does good vegetarian (as well as other) food. *Friesenkroog*, Kleikuhle 6, has a fine selection of fresh fish. *Café Schöneck* at Schiffbrücke, whose rooms are crammed with old Friesian furniture, has good soups, a vast array of warming alcoholic drinks, and Danish pastries far surpassing those normally found south of the border. *Husumer Speicher*, a converted warehouse at Hafenstr. 17, is the local place for **live music** and entertainment.

Ferries to Heligoland (DM55/€27.50) leave from the Eidersperrwerk; those to the Halligen (upwards of DM19/€9.50) leave from Nordstrand. There's a bus link (included in the cost of the ticket) to both terminals from Husum Aussenhafen; information is available from Schiffsmakler Schmidt (☎0 48 41/20 14). There's also a bus from the Bahnhof to the island of Nordstrand.

Friedrichstadt

FRIEDRICHSTADT, 15km south of Husum on the rail line to Hamburg, is a small corner of Holland transported to North Friesland. It was built in the 1620s by Dutch settlers with the encouragement of Duke Friedrich III of Schleswig-Holstein-Gottorf, who hoped it would develop into a major commercial centre. It didn't, but the little town, complete with its canals, bridges, step-gabled houses and public buildings such as the **Alte Münze** (Old Mint), remains a gem of Dutch Renaissance architecture in an unlikely setting. A seventeenth-century merchant's residence at Am Mittelburgwall 4 has been expertedly restored as the *Holländische Stube* (☎0 48 81/9 39 00; ⑥), a **hotel** with a highly regarded **restaurant**. It has several competitors, including *Holsteinisches Haus*, Eiland 1–3 (☎0 48 81/2 09; ④), and *Aquarium*, Am Mittelburgwall 4 (☎0 48 81/9 30 50, *www.hotel-aquarium.de*; ⑥). The **youth hostel** is at the eastern edge of town at Ostdeutsche Str. 1 (☎ & fax 0 48 81/79 84; DM20/€10 or DM25/€12.50).

Helgoland (Heligoland)

There are no fewer than fifteen possible starting points for a trip to Germany's most isolated corner, the red limestone island of **Helgoland**, which is about a square kilometre in area and stands isolated in the North Sea, 70km from the mouth of the Elbe. From the west coast of Schleswig-Holstein, there are sailings from, among others, Husum, Hornüm, Wyk and Wittdün; other places to catch a boat include Hamburg, Bremen, Bremerhaven and the Lower Saxon ports of Cuxhaven and Wilhelmshaven. Between April and October, there are daily departures from many of these harbours, but the frequency of service falls sharply during the winter months. Period returns on normal boats cost in the region of DM70/€35, day-trips about DM55/€27.50; the snag with the latter is that they only allow three or four hours on the island – roughly the same time as it takes to get there. However, in 2000 Reederei Warrings (☎9 44 64/9 49 50, *www.reederei-warrings.de*) introduced a daily summer service, departing from Bremen at 8am, with the catamaran *MS Speedy*. This always halts in Bremerhaven, but thereafter goes by several different routes. On the days designated for the direct passage, it only takes an hour and a half to reach Helgoland from Bremerhaven, allowing a halt of five and a half hours before the return journey, which costs DM80/€40 from Bremerhaven, DM95/€47.50 from Bremen. On other days, the timetabled halt is just three hours, and the journey itself correspondingly longer.

Once an important naval base and coaling station, Helgoland was long occupied by the British, and only came into German hands in 1890, when it was swapped for Zanzibar. Bombarded during World War II, its inhabitants were forcibly evacuated in 1947, and the remaining fortifications were blown up. For five years it served as a bombing target for the RAF, until finally returned to Germany in 1952. Reconstruction began immediately and Helgoland has become a popular holiday resort with all the usual facilities, plus the added advantage of **duty-free** status – which, due to a legal loophole, still exists here, despite its abolition throughout the rest of the EU. This is undoubtedly the main reason it attracts so many visitors, though the presence of dramatic craggy **cliffs** mean that it is scenically far superior to any of Germany's other North Sea islands. There's also a setpiece attraction in the **Aquarium Biologische Anstalt** (May–Oct daily 10am–4.30pm; DM5/€2.50) on Kurpromenade, which is devoted to the fish and plant life of the North Sea.

If you decide you would like to stay over, it would be advisable to contact the **tourist office** (May–Sept Mon–Fri 9am–5pm, Sat & Sun 11.30am–5pm, reduced hours out of season; ☎0 47 25/81 37 11, fax 81 37 25, *www.helgoland.de*) at Lung Wai 28 to arrange this in advance. Alternatively, you could book directly with the **youth hostel** (☎0 47 25/3 41, fax 74 67; DM25/€12.50 or DM30/€15; closed Nov–March), which is only a shortish walk from the harbour, or with one of the **hotels**. Of the latter, there are several classy establishments, usually with fine fish and seafood **restaurants** attached; they include: *Helgoland-Schwan*, Am Südstrand 16 (☎0 47 25/8 15 30; ⑥), *Seehotel*, Lung Wai 23 (☎0 47 25/8 13 10; ⑥), and *Atoll*, Lung Wai 27 (☎0 47 25/80 00; ⑨).

travel details

Trains

Hamburg to: Flensburg (every 2hr; 1hr 45min); Husum (hourly; 2hr); Kiel (hourly; 1hr 15min); Lübeck (hourly; 40min); Rendsburg (every 2hr; 1hr 10min); Schleswig (every 2hr; 1hr 30min).

Kiel to: Flensburg (hourly; 1hr 10min); Husum (hourly; 1hr 30min); Lübeck (hourly; 1hr 10min); Rendsburg (hourly; 30min); Schleswig (hourly; 50min).

Ferries

Dagebüll to: Amrum (winter 5 daily; summer 8 daily; 2hr); Föhr (winter 7 daily; summer 10 daily; 45min).

Hamburg to: Harwich (every 2 days; 20hr 30min); Newcastle Tynemouth (May to early Sept every 4 days; 24hr).

Nordstrand to: Pellworm (winter 3–5 daily; summer 5–7 daily; 35–40min).

Schlüttsiel to: Amrum (1 daily; 2hr 30min); Hallig Hooge (summer 2 daily; winter very irregular; 1hr 15min); Hallig Langeness (same times and boat as to Hallig Hooge; 1hr 50min).

CHAPTER EIGHT

MECKLENBURG-LOWER POMERANIA

Mecklenburg-Lower Pomerania (Mecklenburg-Vorpommern) is eastern Germany's maritime province. The tideless Baltic Sea laps at the slim coastline of some 370km, while the rivers Elbe and Oder form natural borders to the west and east; to the south is a spacious lakeland which is the most thinly populated part of Germany. The Land is something of a compromise creation, most of its territory once belonging to two separate grand duchies; the remainder is the German rump (not deemed to be viable as a Land in its own right) of the ancient and much-disputed province of Pomerania, the greater part of which was ceded to Poland in 1945.

From **Wismar**, the incongruously large-scale medieval townscape at the western end of the province, the coastal landscape gradually changes from flat indented shores to the windswept dunes behind **Rostock**, the chief port and largest city. Further east, within the surviving German part of Pomerania, is **Stralsund**, whose grand Hanseatic buildings look across a narrow channel to **Rügen**, Germany's largest island, characterized by dramatic landscapes of battered headlands and chalky cliffs rising steeply from the sea. Beyond here, the coast curves southeastwards via the university city of Greifswald and the Pomeranian ducal capital of **Wolgast** towards the sandy island of **Usedom** and the Polish border. During the summer the coast is overrun by holiday-makers, but for the rest of the year the region returns to a peaceful emptiness, and a Sunday afternoon atmosphere descends on even the larger towns.

Inland, the great **Mecklenburg Lake Plateau** tilts gently south, with few major towns disturbing the rural landscape before Berlin, about 300km away. This, eastern Germany's granary, is a real backwater and has changed relatively little since debt-

---

ACCOMMODATION PRICE CODES

All the pensions and hotels in this book have been graded according to the following price categories. The codes quoted are for the cheapest available double room, except for establishments which have rooms costing widely different rates, when the most expensive price is given as well. Exact charges are given for youth hostels; in the case of the official DJH (HI) establishments, this is the lowest available rate. When two figures are quoted for these hostels, the first applies to juniors (ie under 27 years of age), the second to seniors (27 and above).

① less than DM60/€30	④ DM100–124/€50–62	⑦ DM200–249/€100–124
② DM60–79/€30–39	⑤ DM125–149/€63–74	⑧ DM250–299/€125–149
③ DM80–99/€40–49	⑥ DM150–199/€75–99	⑨ upwards of DM300/€150

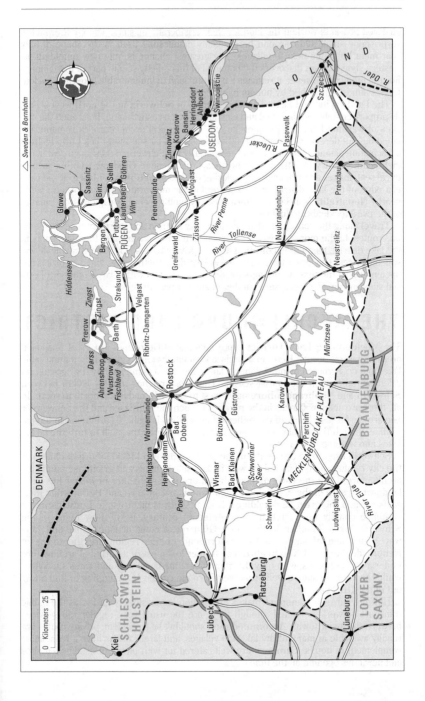

enslaved peasants worked the land for their aristocratic masters. The GDR era left a surprisingly small mark around here, mainly manifesting itself in the shape of ugly apartment buildings next to villages. The greatest change is only now unfolding, as western-style tourism discovers the potential of this quietly scenic part of the country. For the moment, however, it remains a beautiful land of innumerable lakes and ancient forests almost untouched by human habitation.

The Land capital and former ducal residence of **Schwerin** in the northwest seems disproportionately sophisticated and elegant in such a rustic region. It escaped the ravages of wartime bombs – its Baroque and Neoclassical architecture is romantically faded but not derelict as in so many other places. Not far southwest lies **Ludwigslust**, a fascinating planned town which was temporarily the Schwerin dukes' main seat in the eighteenth century. A little further northeast, picturesque **Güstrow**, another former ducal seat, makes an ideal base for exploring the lakes. **Neubrandenburg**, at the eastern edge of the lake district, retains a spectacular medieval defensive system, while nearby **Neustrelitz** is a Baroque town specially built to serve as capital of the smaller of the two Mecklenburg duchies.

Travel along the coast and inland is fairly easy by train and there are many regional bus routes. In the more touristy areas, such as the Baltic coast and the main spots in the lake district, plentiful **accommodation** in private rooms is readily available at reasonable prices. The larger towns are also well equipped with hotels, and new places are opening up all the time. Camping shouldn't be a problem with a large number of official sites and an ever-increasing number of smaller private ones.

THE MECKLENBURG LAKE DISTRICT

The **Mecklenburg Lake District** represents one of Germany's last great unspoiled areas of natural beauty. Here, in a landscape of endless fields dotted by innumerable lakes and crisscrossed by quiet country lanes, life is still dominated by the agricultural calendar rather than the tourist season. The area stretches roughly l00km between **Schwerin** and **Neubrandenburg** on its west to east axis, and 80km north to south. In all, there are about 650 lakes in the region, of which the Müritzsee and the Schweriner See are the largest. Many of the hitherto undisturbed lakeshores are home to unique wildlife, though these habitats are now being disturbed by the rush to turn the larger lakes into watersports resorts.

Schwerin used to be the capital of the larger of the two Mecklenburg duchies and the city retains some of its old air with its lakeside Schloss and grandiose municipal architecture. Until the early nineteenth century it was a centre of *Junker* life – the landowning elite of the era dividing their time between here and Berlin while their serfs worked the great land-holdings. Not far south is picturesque **Ludwigslust**, a complete courtly town built in the eighteenth century as the new home of the Schwerin dukes. Another destination is **Güstrow**, a noted artistic centre and gateway to a chain of lakes. At the eastern end of this region are the towns of Neubrandenburg and **Neustrelitz**. The former lost most of its original architecture under a hail of bombs, with only the magnificent medieval wall and gates surviving, while the latter, despite a well-preserved Baroque centre, is struggling to find a way out of the GDR era.

Having your own **transport** makes exploration immeasurably easier, as the public transport network is limited, though there are the usual very regular rail services between the major towns. **Accommodation** shouldn't be a problem: private rooms are readily available in many of the lakeside villages, and larger towns have a reasonable complement of hotels. **Campers** are well catered for with plenty of established sites and new ones opening all the time.

Schwerin

SCHWERIN, situated amid a chain of lakes 65km east of Lübeck, was the winner of the tussle to become capital of Mecklenburg-Lower Pomerania. Revelling in its role, it has become one of the ex-GDR's most go-ahead cities, and is undoubtedly among the most rewarding to visit, helped enormously by the fact that it is relatively unencumbered with Communist-era eyesores. Founded in 1160 by Henry the Lion (see p.684), Schwerin is the oldest town in the province, though little remains of its early heritage. Its glory period began in 1837, when Grand Duke Paul Friedrich of Mecklenburg-Schwerin decided to demote Ludwigslust to a secondary residence and to reinstate his dynasty's original base as the main seat of his court. This led to the creation of a monumental nineteenth-century cityscape which remains largely extant to this day; a vibrant cultural life was also introduced then, and has been of significance ever since.

Water is an omnipresent feature of Schwerin: the city is built around no fewer than ten lakes (the largest being the **Schweriner See** to the east), while the constituent parts of the centre – the **Altstadt**, the Baroque **Schelfstadt** and the nineteenth-century **Paulusstadt** – each border a different side of the pond known as the **Pfaffenteich**.

Arrival, information and accommodation

Schwerin's **Hauptbahnhof** is in the Paulusstadt, two blocks west of the Pfaffenteich, and a ten-minute walk from the Altstadt. The **tourist office** is at Am Markt 11 (Mon–Fri 10am–6pm, Sat 10am–2/6pm; ☎03 85/5 92 52 12, fax 55 50 94, *www.schwerin.de*).

There are now plenty of **hotels** in Schwerin, including several highly imaginative conversions of old buildings. It's also worth considering staying in the suburbs, where there are a number of enticing establishments in attractive surroundings. As for **private rooms** (②–③), there are a fair few available through the tourist office. The **youth hostel** is in a lakeside setting at Waldschulweg 3 (☎03 85/3 26 00 06, fax 3 26 03 03; DM25/€12.50 or DM30/€15); it's near the terminus of bus #14, though a pleasanter means of access is to take the ferry to the jetty at Zippendorf, from where it's only a few minutes' walk northwards. Along the banks of the Schweriner See are a number of **campsites**, the most convenient being *Seehof* (☎03 85/51 25 40) in the village of the same name just north of the city, which is reached by bus #8.

Hotels

Alt Schweriner Schankstuben, Schlachtermarkt 9 (☎03 85/59 25 30, fax 5 57 41 09). Traditional Altstadt hotel with wine bar-restaurant. ⑤.

Am Hauptbahnhof, Grunthalplatz 11–12 (☎03 85/56 57 02, fax 557 42 96). Hotel with restaurant and Bierstube on the square directly facing the Hauptbahnhof. ④.

An den Linden, Franz-Mehring-Str. 26 (☎03 85/51 20 84, fax 51 22 81). Fine medium-range hotel in a late Neoclassical building; its facilities include a sauna and a winter garden. ⑥.

Arte, Dorfstr. 6, Krebsförden (☎03 85/6 34 50, fax 6 34 51 00). Occupies a converted brick farmstead in a southern suburb, close to the Ostorfer See. Its restaurant, *Fontane*, serves high-quality local dishes. ⑦.

Elephant, Goethestr. 39–41 (☎03 85/5 30 70, fax 5 30 71 55, *www.hotel-elefant.de*). An elegant hotel preserving Wilhelmine and Jugendstil features from its former lives, firstly as a cigarette factory, then as the home of a wealthy brewer. The restaurant, the top-lit *Elefantensaal*, is from the former period, the ballroom from the latter. ⑥.

Hospiz am Pfaffenteich, Gauss-Str. 19 (☎03 85/56 56 06, fax 5 69 61 2). Pleasant, reasonably priced establishment in the Schelfstadt, directly overlooking the Pfaffenteich. ④.

Niederländischer Hof, Karl-Marx-Str. 12–13 (☎03 85/59 11 00, fax 59 11 09 99, *www.niederlaendischer-hof.de*). A grand hotel and restaurant, stylishly furnished throughout, on the west side of the Pfaffenteich. ⑦.

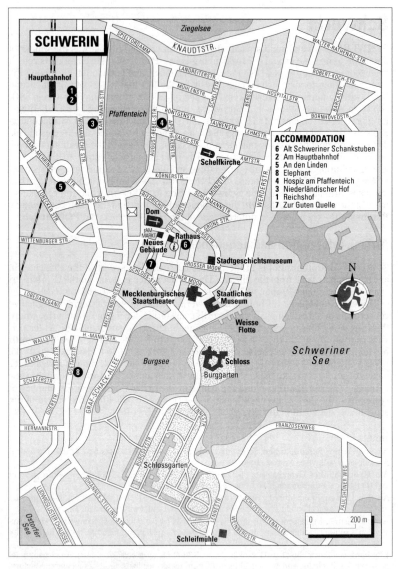

Reichshof, Grunthalplatz 15–17 (☎03 85/56 57 98, fax 56 57 98). The cheapest of the cluster of hotels by the Hauptbahnhof. ④.

Seehotel Frankenhorst, Frankenhorst 5, Wickendorf (☎03 85/55 50 71, fax 55 50 73, *www.seehotel -best-western.de*). Located in a lovely landscaped park at the northern tip of the Ziegelsee, in the far north of the city. The restaurant, *Bootshaus*, has a terrace overlooking the lake. ⑦.

Speicher am Ziegelsee, Speicherstr. 11 (☎03 85/5 00 30, fax 5 00 31 11, *www.speicher-hotel.de*). A large grain storehouse of 1939 towards the southeastern edge of the Ziegelsee, just north of the

Schelfstadt, has been converted into a high-quality hotel. It has a terrace overlooking the lake, a bistro-café, a piano bar and a restaurant, *aurum*. ⑦.

Strand-Hotel, Am Strand 13, Zippendorf (☎03 85/20 83 80, fax 2 00 22 02). Hotel with café-restaurant named after the small beach it overlooks. ④.

Zur Guten Quelle, Schusterstr. 12 (☎ & fax 03 85/56 59 85, fax 56 59 85). Small hotel with restaurant in a half-timbered building in the heart of the city. ⑥.

The City

Although there's a concentration of sights in the city centre, a stay of at least two days is required in order to cover everything, as there are several worthwhile attractions in the outskirts.

The centre

The only significant medieval building left in Schwerin is the **Dom**, whose massive bulk rises high above the rest of the centre. It was one of four cathedrals founded by Henry the Lion, but, unlike the others, was completely rebuilt a century later in Gothic style. The **tower** (Mon–Fri 11am–noon & 2–3pm, Sat 11am–noon & 2–4pm, Sun noon–3pm; DM1/€0.50), which was only added in the nineteenth century, gives a fine view over the city. Inside, the architectural details are picked out in orange and green against a whitewashed background. The most remarkable furnishing is the gilded fifteenth-century **triumphal cross**, a work of enormous poignancy and pathos brought here after the war from the destroyed Marienkirche in Wismar. It rather overshadows the beautiful but undersized **high altar** below, carved later the same century in a Lübeck workshop. In the north transept are some splendid brasses in honour of fourteenth-century bishops, while a varied range of **funerary monuments** to aristocrats can be seen in the ambulatory and its chapels. Particularly outstanding are those to Helena von der Pfalz by the great Nürnberg bronze-founder Peter Vischer and to Duke Christopher of Mecklenburg and his consort Elizabeth of Sweden.

To the rear of the Dom is the **Markt**, the hub of the city's commercial life. On its eastern side, the mock-Tudor facade of the **Rathaus** is typical of the city's nineteenth-century architecture. Altogether grander, the **Neues Gebäude** on the north side, an imperious Neoclassical building with a columned portico, is used for temporary art exhibitions. Most of the rest of the Altstadt is a pedestrianized shopping centre with a fair number of surviving half-timbered houses.

The far more atmospheric **Schelfstadt** immediately to the northeast was founded at the beginning of the eighteenth century but not integrated into Schwerin until well over a hundred years later; it has street after street of old houses, and is a good place for strolling at leisure. At the heart of the quarter is the **Schelfkirche**, a Baroque parish church with a strikingly emphatic cruciform design, including entrance portals on each wing. Across the Pfaffenteich are the strait-laced buildings of the **Paulusstadt**, the most notable being the huge **Arsenal**, which again mimics the architectural tastes of Tudor England.

Directly east of the Markt, Grosser Moor leads down towards the Schweriner See. At no. 38 on this street is the **Stadtgeschichtsmuseum** (Tues–Sun 10am–6pm; DM3/€1.50), which has both permanent and temporary exhibitions on the history of the city. With luck, you'll be able to see the superb and much-prized aerial photographs of Schwerin shot during the Third Reich.

The Staatliches Museum

At the foot of Grosser Moor, on a square named Alter Garten, stands the stern Neoclassical premises of Schwerin's pride and joy, the **Staatliches Museum** (Tues 10am–8pm, Wed–Sun 10am–5/6pm; *www.museum-schwerin.de*; DM7/€3.50). One of

Germany's most engaging art galleries, it's imbued with a pronounced collector's instinct, this being a legacy of the tastes of the local ducal family which was responsible for most of the acquisitions. The displays on the main floor begin with a section on early German painting, including official portraits by **Cranach** of Luther and his wife Katharina von Bora and of King Ferdinand, the brother and successor of Emperor Charles V. However, most of the rest of the floor space is given over to a marvellous array of works illustrating the full diversity of the art of seventeenth-century Holland. **Hals** is represented by an enchanting pair of roundels of laughing boys, while there are several examples of the highly polished genre scenes of Rembrandt's collaborator **Gerrit Dou**, plus a rare masterpiece, *The Guard*, by his most talented pupil, the short-lived **Carel Fabritius**. Another painter who died very young, the animal specialist **Paulus Potter**, is represented by some of his best works, notably *The Milkmaid*. **Ter Brugghen**'s *St Peter Liberated from Prison* is one of the finest examples of Dutch Tenebrism, while the same artist's *Flautist* and *Violinist* are perceptive character studies.

One gallery is devoted to still-life specialists, including a number of canvases by the Haarlem artist **Jan de Heem**. Equally fascinating are the compositions of the little-known **Otto Marseus van Schrick**, which typically feature reptiles or butterflies among the flowers and fruit. At the opposite end of the building, there's a selection of the museum's copious holdings of the works of **Jean-Baptiste Oudry**, court painter to King Louis XV of France; these include several of his familiar hunting scenes and trophies, though the keenly observed animal studies, such as *The Antelope* and *The Leopard*, make a more lasting impression. In the same room is a magnificent full-length portrait of a British queen, the former Princess Charlotte of Mecklenburg-Strelitz, by **Gainsborough**. The nineteenth-century section includes a *Winter Landscape* by **Friedrich** and canvases by Liebermann, Corinth and Franz von Stuck. A large group of works by the Frenchman **Marcel Duchamp**, only recently acquired, is the centrepiece of the displays of modern art in the basement.

The Schloss and its gardens

A few paces south of here, a bridge leads over to Schwerin's vast neo-Renaissance apparition of a **Schloss** (Tues–Sun 10am–5/6pm; *www.museum-schwerin.de*; DM8/€4), which occupies the same site as Henry the Lion's original castle, an island in the Schweriner See. Gloriously over the top, it was modelled on the famous château of Chambord in France's Loire valley. Plans were originally drawn up by the Dresden architect Gottfried Semper, though only the main tower was built according to his design. The rest is the work of two pupils of Schinkel, Georg Adolph Demmler and Friedrich August Stüler, who between them were responsible for most of Schwerin's showpiece nineteenth-century buildings.

On the first floor, highlights are the wood-panelled **Speisezimmer** and the circular **Teezimmer** next door, with its ornate white stuccowork. Upstairs, the **Ahnengalerie** is hung with (mostly imaginary) portraits of all the Mecklenburg dukes, while the gilded **Thronsaal**, like the Schloss itself, is of a scale and splendour more appropriate for a powerful kingdom than a tiny duchy. There's also a gallery devoted to local painters, of whom the most notable are **Carl Malchin**, with his evocative nineteenth-century landscapes, and **Erich Venzmer**, who specialized in stark views of sodden Mecklenburg flatlands.

The remainder of the island is occupied by the **Burggarten**, which is a fine example of nineteenth-century landscape gardening. It makes a fascinating comparison with the much larger **Schlossgarten** to the south, which is in the formal Baroque style and features a set of statues (now replaced by copies) of classical gods by the great sculptor of Baroque Dresden, Balthasar Permoser. At the far end, about fifteen minutes' walk from the Schloss, is the **Schleifmühle** (April–Nov Fri–Sun 10am–5pm; DM3/€1.50). This half-timbered water-mill, the only one of its kind in Europe still in full working order, dates back to 1705 but was rebuilt fifty years later for grinding down the precious stones needed to make the furnishings for the Mecklenburg palaces. The actual process, which is painfully slow but highly effective, is demonstrated to visitors.

The Schweriner See

No trip to Schwerin is complete without a **cruise** on the **Schweriner See**: this is *the* way of seeing the city's skyline to best effect. Boats, run by Weisse Flotte (☎03 85/55 77 70), depart from the jetty on the north side of the Schloss. From April until October, round trips (DM12.50/€6.25 for 1hr, DM20/€10 for 2hr) run every day, leaving every thirty minutes at the height of summer. A good alternative is the ferry service which runs back and forth from May to October down the lake to the beach at **Zippendorf** (DM5/€2.50) and the idyllic island nature reserve of **Kaninchenwerder** (DM9/€4.50).

Set back from the lake at Crivitzer Landstr. 13 in the suburb of Muess, a twenty-minute walk east of Zippendorf, is the **Mecklenburgisches Volkskundemuseum** (May–Oct Tues–Sun 10am–6pm; DM3/€1.50), an open-air museum which features eighteenth- and nineteenth-century buildings brought here from all over rural Mecklenburg.

Eating, drinking and entertainment

The centre of Schwerin is well endowed with good places to eat and drink, with many of the best establishments being in the hotels (see pp.771–3). Since the nineteenth century, the city has kept up a distinguished tradition in the performing arts.

Restaurants

Friedrich's, Friedrichstr. 2. Pleasant restaurant in a villa at the southeastern edge of the Pfaffenteich.

Gewölbe-Restaurant, Am Markt 1. Gaststätte offering typical examples of *gutbürgerliche Küche*.

Lukas, Grosser Moor 5. The main fish specialist.

Michelangelo, Grosser Moor 36. The city's leading Italian restaurant.

Pück, Puschkinstr. 37. High-class restaurant, a worthy rival to those in Schwerin's top hotels. Closed Sat lunchtime & Sun.

Ratshof Zum Goldenen Reiter, Puschkinstr. 44. Offers an eclectic menu of international dishes.

Weinhaus Uhle, Schusterstr. 15. A superemely elegant wine bar-restaurant housed in fine Rococo premises; it's attached to a wine merchant's shop which has been in business since 1751.

Cafés and bars

Café Prag, Schloss-Str. 17. As its name suggests, this is a café in the Central European style. As well as cakes and pastries, it also serves light meals.

House of Whiskey, Arsenalstr. 14. This bar has over a hundred kinds of whisky, as well as eight beers on tap; it also serves snacks and meals, and often features live music.

Schlosscafé, Lennéstr. 1. Good place for *Kaffee und Kuchen*, located in the Schloss itself.

Schlossgartenpavillon, Am Kreuzkanal. Café in the grounds of the Schloss.

Wallenstein, Werderstr. 140. This café with terrace is located right alongside the jetty of the Weisse Flotte cruise ships, and offers good lakeside views. It also serves full meals.

Entertainment

The liveliest **nightspots** are on Wittenberger Strasse; the Achteck disco at no.120 is particularly trendy, while the Sport- und Kongresshalle at no.118 (☎03 85/76 19 00) is the main venue for large-scale pop concerts. Highbrow cultural events, including drama, opera and concerts, are staged in the main **theatre**, the Neoclassical Mecklenburgisches Staatstheater, opposite the Staatliches Museum at Alter Garten (☎03 85/5 30 01 23, *www.theater-schwerin.de*). In summer, the courtyard of the Schloss is used for the open-air performances of the *Schlossfestspiele* (☎03 85/5 30 01 27).

Ludwigslust

LUDWIGSLUST, which lies 35km south of Schwerin, was founded in 1756 on the site of a hunting lodge as the residence of the local dukes, remaining as such until 1837, when the court moved back to the original capital. In accordance with the taste of the time, it's a planned town with a generous complement of green spaces, and it remains almost completely intact. Under the GDR regime, Ludwigslust's all-too-obvious feudalist overtones meant that it was allowed to fall into decay, but an enormous amount of reconstruction work has already been carried out, and the whole town should soon be in immaculate shape. As such, it makes a fascinating contrast with Neustrelitz, its direct counterpart in the other former Mecklenburg duchy. The story of the construction of Ludwigslust is dogged by a yawning gap between the ambition of its rulers and the finances available to them. This meant that all kinds of cost-cutting measures were adopted, the most immediately obvious being the use of plain, ordinary bricks for the construction of almost all the buildings.

The outsized **Schloss** (Tues–Sun 10am–5/6pm; *www.museum-schwerin.de*; DM6/€3) in the heart of the town, which was not even begun until sixteen years after Ludwigslust's foundation, provides the clearest evidence of the crafty measures taken to skimp on money. Outwardly, it looks very imposing indeed, its show frontage revealing the first stirrings of Neoclassicism while retaining the full pomp of late Baroque. However, the resplendent stonework is a facade in both senses of the word, masking the brickwork from which the palace is actually built. An even cleverer trick is played in the **Goldener Saal**, the main reception hall of the interior. Glittering with mirrors and gilt, adorned with golden vases, columns and figures of cherubs, it makes a stunning setting for concerts. Almost everything, however, is fashioned from a form of papier-mâché known as *Ludwigsluster Carton*, which was specially developed here to produce such trompe l'oeil effects. The rest of the interior, which served as the home of the deposed ducal family until it was appropriated in 1945, subsequently suffered from the depredations of the Red Army and its use as offices. However, a number of smaller rooms have also been restored and refurnished in period style.

To the north and west stretches the enormous **Schlosspark**, a masterly exercise in English-style landscaping by the ubiquitous Peter Joseph Lenné. Its varied delights include a canal, fountains, cascades, a beautiful stone bridge, two Neoclassical mausolea, a neo-Gothic chapel, a grotto and a bizarre funeral monument to a horse.

South of the Schloss is a large oval-shaped green, down the sides of which are the modest little cottages built for the estate workers. Another, this time rectangular, area of greenery separates the axial road from the second main focal point of the town, the **Stadtkirche**. Designed, like the Schloss and most of the rest of Ludwigslust, by the local architect Johann Joachim Busch, it ranks as one of the most distinctive and unexpected Protestant churches in Germany. The monumental facade is like a great classical Roman temple, though the rest of the exterior is completely plain. Inside, everything is pure theatre, from the ornate ducal loft at one end to the vast mural of *The Adoration of the Shepherds* at the other. In the latter, the church's organ, most of which is hidden from view, appears to be played by one of the angels in the heavenly apparition above.

Practicalities

Ludwigslust's **Bahnhof**, which is on the main line between Schwerin and Stendal in Saxony-Anhalt, lies at the far northern end of town, a fifteen-minute walk from the centre. The **tourist office** (Mon–Fri 10am–12.30pm & 1.30–4pm; ☎0 38 74/5 26 25, fax 52 61 09, *www.stadt-ludwigslust.de*) is at Schloss-Str. 36. Here you can book **private rooms** (②–③), which are in reasonable supply and noticeably cheaper than in Schwerin. There's also a small **pension**, *Schwarzenberg*, Am Seminargarten 4 (☎0 38 74/2 24 38; ③). The local **hotels**, however, are fairly pricey, though this is justified by the refurbishments all have undergone. Between the Bahnhof and the centre, good choices are *Park*, Kanalstr. 19 (☎0 38 74/2 20 15; ④), *Stadt Hamburg*, Letzte Str. 4–6 (☎0 38 74/41 50; ④), and *Erbprinz*, Schweriner Str. 38 (☎0 38 74/4 71 74; ⑤). In the heart of town, occupying a ritzy mansion at Schloss-Str. 15, *Landhotel de Weimar* (☎0 38 74/41 80; ⑥) is the best and most expensive of the lot. All of these hotels have recommendable **restaurants**.

Güstrow

About 60km northeast of Schwerin lies **GÜSTROW**, formerly the capital of one of the Mecklenburg duchies, which was for a short time ruled by the mercurial and inscrutable military genius Alfred von Wallenstein, supreme commander of the imperial forces in the Thirty Years War. When the ruling house died out in 1695, however, it was reduced to the status of a second-string residence of the dukes of Mecklenburg-Schwerin, and has remained pretty provincial ever since, a fact which enabled it to escape the attentions of wartime bombers. Before the war it was the home and workplace of **Ernst Barlach**, the greatest German sculptor of the twentieth century, and the important collections of his work here are a prime tourist draw. Güstrow is also the birthplace of **Uwe Johnson**, a GDR author who went into exile in 1959 following conflict with the authorities. His novels deal with the psychological shock of Germany's division and the development of fear and distrust on opposite sides of the border between the two states.

The Town

Mostly pedestrianized, the **Altstadt** is still the heart of the modern town. Its predominantly eighteenth- and nineteenth-century buildings retain many original features such as brass shop signs and elaborately carved doors. Güstrow's other highlight is the gorgeous surrounding countryside, with easy access to lakes such as the Inselsee and Sumpfsee on the outskirts of the town, and the much larger Krakower See to the south.

The central Markt is built up in the middle on the central European model, with the secular and the sacred, in the shape of the Baroque **Rathaus** and Gothic **Pfarrkirche**, given equal billing centre-stage. The church contains a marvellous array of furnishings, dominated by a magnificent early sixteenth-century **high altar** made in Brussels. When open, it shows delicately carved and polychromed oak scenes of the Passion by the sculptor Jan Borman; when closed, the brightly coloured paintings of the life of the Virgin by Barent van Orley, court painter to the Habsburgs, are on view.

A couple of blocks away, at the southern end of the Altstadt, is the huge sixteenth-century **Schloss** (Tues–Sun 9am–5pm; *www.museum-schwerin.de*; DM6/€3). From the outside, it's one of the most impressive Renaissance palaces anywhere in Germany, providing a classic example of how Italianate forms could be ever so subtly modelled to suit these more northerly climes. Unfortunately, it fell into disrepair on the demise of the local duchy, and was only regularly used again in 1811 when Napoleon's troops set up a field hospital here on their way to Russia. The Nazis transformed it into a prison, destroying much of what was left of the furniture and decor. Nonetheless, some fine original interiors remain, notably in the south wing. There's also a decent representation of German, Italian and Dutch art of the sixteenth century.

Hidden away unassumingly at the southwestern corner of the Altstadt is the **Dom**, another brick Gothic church which was first a collegiate foundation, then the court chapel, rather than the cathedral its name would suggest. The architecture is almost totally overshadowed by some extraordinary furnishings, which include a gilded high altar by the fifteenth-century Hamburg carver Hinrik Bornemann, and a vibrant series of apostles on the pillars of the nave by the sixteenth-century Lübeck sculptor, Claus Berg. Even more arresting are the Renaissance **funerary monuments** in the choir by the Dutchman Philipp Brandin. Look out in particular for the two largest – to the Dom's founder Heinrich Borwins II, and to the sculptor's patron Duke Ulrich with his two wives – each of which has an elaborate armorial background. In the northern aisle of the nave are three **Barlach sculptures**, including the famous *Flying Angel*, which is suspended above an ornate Renaissance grille. The original of this, a memorial to the dead of World War I, was melted down in 1938 as part of the Nazi measures against "degenerate art". Fortunately, a cast had previously been taken, enabling the work to be re-created after the war.

The stature of Ernst Barlach continues to rise, and few would now dispute his right to be regarded among last century's most significant artists. His bronzes and wood-carvings, borrowing techniques from the medieval and Renaissance German masters, show a warm humanity and a haunting sense of pathos; he also carried his Expressionism over into other media, being a fine graphic artist and an accomplished playwright. There are two museums in Güstrow devoted to him; between them they contain the largest collection of his work in existence. The museum in the **Gertrudenkapelle** (March–Oct Tues–Sun 10am–5pm; Nov–Feb Tues–Sun 11am–4pm; *www.barlach-stiftung.de*; DM3/€1.50), a little Gothic chapel set in its own grounds just over the ring road from the northwestern side of the Altstadt, is the obvious destination, particularly if you're pressed for time, as it contains original versions of many of his finest works. The **Atelierhaus** (same hours; DM3/€1.50), Barlach's house and workshop, lies in the narrow strip of land between the Inselsee and the wooded Heidberg; it's about 4km south of the Altstadt, and can be reached by bus #4. Here you can see the sculptures left unfinished at his death in 1938, along with casts of his other work in a variety of different media.

Practicalities

Güstrow's **Bahnhof**, which has regular services on the lines to Schwerin, Rostock and Neubrandenburg, is five minutes' walk from the northern end of the Altstadt. The **tourist office** (May–Sept Mon–Fri 9am–6pm, Sat & Sun 9.30am–1pm; Oct–April closed Sun; ☎0 38 43/68 10 23, fax 68 20 79, *www.guestrow.de*) is at Domstr. 9.

Plenty of **private rooms** (①–③) are available through the tourist office. The **youth hostel** is near the Barlach Atelierhaus at Heidberg 33 (☎0 38 43/84 00 44, fax 84 00 45, *jh-guestrow@t-online.de*). There's a centrally sited pension, *Villa Camenz*, Lange Stege 13 (☎0 38 43/21 49 93; ③), plus several **hotels**: *Rubis*, Schweriner Str. 89 (☎0 38 43/6 93 80; ⑤), *Altstadt*, Baustr. 8–10 (☎0 38 43/68 60 03; ⑥), *Am Güstrower Schloss*, Schlossberg 1 (☎0 38 43/76 70; ⑥), and *Stadt Güstrow*, Pferdemarkt 58 (☎0 38 43/78 00; ⑥). With the exception of *Altstadt*, all these hotels have **restaurants**, and they rank among the best in town, though strong competition comes from *Barlach-Stuben*, Hagebócker Str. 9, which features typical Mecklenburg dishes. Reliable alternatives include the *Ratskeller*, Markt 10, and *Marktkrug*, Markt 14, while *Jägerstübschen*,

Schloss-Str. 1, offers game specialities. The best place for *Kaffee und Kuchen* is the long-established *Café Küpper*, Domstr. 15.

Festivals include the *Stadtfest* in June, the *Schlossfest* in July and the *Inselseefest* on the first weekend of August; the main year-round **cultural** venue is the Neoclassical *Ernst-Barlach-Theater* on Franz-Parr-Platz (☎0 38 43/68 41 46).

Neubrandenburg

At the eastern end of the Mecklenburg lake district, about 75km southeast of Güstrow, is **NEUBRANDENBURG**, an important rail junction, especially for routes into Poland. Like so many places in the former GDR, it offers the dichotomy of historic monuments of the highest class co-existing with the most painful of eyesores. As the main sights can be seen in a few hours, it's best viewed as a stop-off en route to or from the Baltic coast, 100km to the north, or the lakes to the west.

The town was founded in 1248 by Margrave Johann I of Brandenburg (hence its name), but was incorporated into Mecklenburg early the following century. From this period dates the extraordinary 2.5-kilometre-long **Stadtmauer** – one of the most impressive municipal fortification systems anywhere in Europe – encircling the Altstadt. Miraculously, it came through World War II virtually intact, though the rest of the town was almost completely destroyed. Subsequently, the Altstadt was filled with the concrete architecture beloved of the GDR regime, with the fifteen-storey **Haus der Kultur und Bildung** (House of Culture and Education) placed smack in the middle. The building's one saving grace is the **view** from the platform at the top, which can be reached by lift (DM1/€0.50).

To appreciate the Stadtmauer to the full, you need to walk round it twice – once on the inside, once on the outside. It's pierced by four colossal gateways, whose patterned brickwork is of a scale or delicacy more in keeping with a great civic church or town hall than a defensive system. Earliest of these is the **Friedländer Tor**, the northeastern entrance to the town, which has inner and outer gateways linked by a stretch of fortified wall, plus a semicircular tower, known as the Zinger, as a first line of defence. Today it's a café and commercial art gallery. Only slightly less formidable-looking is the **Treptower Tor** (Tues–Sun 10am–5pm; DM2/€1) on the western side of town, which now houses the local archeology museum. The most elaborately decorative brickwork of all is found on the southern gateway, the **Stargarder Tor**, whose inner face is adorned with nine enigmatic, highly stylized female figures. Eight more statues in the same vein can be seen on the **Neues Tor** to the east, which is distinguished by enormous finger-shaped gables. Another curiosity of Neubrandenburg is the presence of 26 (out of an original total of 56) half-timbered houses, known as **Wiekhäuser**, which are conversions of the bastions built directly onto the Stadtmauer. Not surprisingly, they're the most sought-after properties in town; several are now craft shops.

Two large brick Gothic churches are the only setpiece attractions within the walls. The modest architecture of the **Johanniskirche** at the northern end of the Altstadt is a reflection of its original function as a Franciscan friary: the church itself is now a Protestant parish, while the refectory is used as local government offices. Altogether grander is the **Marienkirche** a few minutes' walk to the south, which forms a clear ecclesiastical counterpart to the four gateways. Grievously damaged in the war, it's undergoing a comprehensive restoration process and will reopen in due course as a concert hall.

Practicalities

Neubrandenburg's **Bahnhof** is just beyond the northern confines of the Altstadt, separated from it only by the width of Friedrich-Engels-Ring, which follows the perimeter of the Stadtmauer. The **tourist office** (Mon–Fri 9am–6pm, Sat & Sun 10am–2pm; ☎03 95/1 94 33, fax 5 82 22 67, *www.neubrandenburg.de*), which is right in the heart of the Altstadt at Marktplatz 1, can arrange **private rooms** (②–③). A fair number of **hotels** can be found just outside the perimeters of the Stadtmauer. These include *Jahnke*, Rostocker Str. 12 (☎03 95/58 17 00; ④), *St Georg*, St Georg 6 (☎03 95/5 44 37 88; ⑤), *Weinert*, Ziegelbergstr. 23 (☎03 95/58 12 30; ⑤), and *Andersen*, Grosse Krauthöfer Str. 1 (☎03 95/55 60; ⑤). Both *St Georg* and *Andersen* have good **restaurants**, and the former has the benefit of a beer garden. Food of comparable quality is served at *Fritz Reuter*, at Friedländer Str. 2a in the Altstadt; other restaurants with a cosy atmosphere are *Wiekhaus 45* and *Mudder-Schulten-Stuben*, both on 4-Ringstrasse, and *Zur Lohmühle*, Am Stargarder Tor 4, a converted mill with a wine and beer garden. A varied **cultural** programme is presented at the Schauspielhaus, Pfaffenstr. 22 (☎03 95/2 22 26 17); the town is also home to a full-sized symphony orchestra, the Neubrandenburger Philharmonie.

Neustrelitz

About 35km south of Neubrandenburg by road or rail is the odd town of **NEUSTRELITZ**, which was founded in 1732 as the custom-built capital of Mecklenburg-Strelitz, the smaller of the two duchies into which Mecklenburg was divided in 1701. It's a fascinating example of a planned Residenzstadt built to a strict geometric plan around a small hunting lodge transformed into a grand ducal palace. Streets of sober Baroque buildings radiate out from a central square to striking effect, and the town slopes down towards the tree-lined shores of the Zierker See. Though it initially prospered from its position on trade routes between the coast and Berlin, it never rose above sleepy backwater status, as the absence of significant post-eighteenth-century development testifies. It was allowed to decay in the GDR period, and has struggled in recent years to come to terms with post-unification realities. Nonetheless, it benefits from its setting between the two constituent parts of the **Nationalpark Müritz**, which was established a few years ago to protect a section of the Mecklenburg Lake District particularly rich in flora (especially orchids) and bird life. Much the larger of the two parts lies immediately west of town, and stretches all the way to the eastern bank of the Müritzsee.

The focal point of Neustrelitz itself is the central **Markt**, which is a perfect square measuring 120 metres on each side. For several years after the *Wende*, a huge Soviet war memorial stood in the grassy area in the middle. Although it has now been removed, the square has not yet followed the normal eastern German pattern of being reclaimed for commerce. The one setpiece now left is the Baroque **Stadtkirche**, which was built according to plans drawn up by a doctor in the service of one of the local dukes.

From the Markt, the streets radiate outwards in eight directions. Head down Schloss-Strasse to the **Schlosspark**, a lakeside ornamental garden laid out in the English style by the great Berlin landscape gardener, Peter Joseph Lenné. The Schloss itself was destroyed in 1945 and no traces now remain, though its **Orangerie**, built in 1755 as a winter home for plants, still survives. Its previously bare interior was transformed in the 1840s by two more leading lights of the Berlin art world – the architect Karl Friedrich Schinkel and the sculptor Christian Daniel Rauch. Together they created three highly ornate interiors for festive purposes, each dominated by a particular colour scheme and decorated in a pseudo-Pompeian style.

Schinkel's very personal and visionary neo-Gothic manner was the inspiration for the architecture of the nearby **Schlosskirche**, though he was not involved in the actual construction. At the northwestern end of the Schlosspark, just past the small Neoclassical **Tempel**, the **Zierker See** begins. Its shores are wonderful for strolling; you can also **rent boats**, and there are **cruises** during the summer months.

Practicalities

Neustrelitz's **Bahnhof** is only about ten minutes' walk from the Markt along Strelitzer Strasse. The **tourist office** (April & Oct Mon–Fri 9am–noon & 1–4.30pm; May–Sept Mon–Fri 9am–5pm, Sat & Sun 10am–1.30pm; Nov–March Mon–Thurs 9am–noon & 1–4.30pm, Fri 9am–1pm; ☎0 39 81/25 31 19, fax 20 54 43, *www.neustrelitz.de*) is at Markt 1. Chances are that you won't want to stay overnight, but there are plenty of **private rooms** (②–③) available here, plus several **hotels** which are generally better value than normal by eastern German standards. These include *Gasthof Zur Klause*, Strelitzer Str. 53 (☎0 39 81/20 05 70; ③), *Haegert*, Zierker Str. 44 (☎0 39 81/20 03 05; ③), *Pinus*, Ernst-Moritz-Arndt-Str. 55 (☎0 39 81/44 53 50; ④), *Schlossgarten*, Tiergartenstr. 15 (☎0 39 81/24 50 00; ⑤), and *Park Hotel Fasanerie*, Karbe-Wagner-Str. 59 (☎0 39 81/44 36 00; ⑥). With the exception of *Pinus*, each of these has a **restaurant**. An alternative place for a meal is the *Inselgaststätte Helgoland*, on an islet linked to the shore by a footbridge; it's near the town's harbour area, just north of the Schlosspark. The Neoclassical Landestheater Neustrelitz, Friedrich-Ludwig-Jahn-Str. 14 (☎0 39 81/27 70), is the main venue for both **drama** and **music**.

THE BALTIC COAST

The towns of the Baltic coast had their heyday in the Middle Ages. At that time **Wismar**, **Rostock**, **Stralsund** and **Greifswald** were important centres of merchant trading, forming a vital link on northern Europe's east–west shipping routes. They became so rich that they could override traditional domination by the aristocracy, instead joining the **Hanseatic League**, a federation of towns along the entire German coast that represented their economic interests nationally and abroad. But once merchant shipping spread to the Americas and the Far East, the Baltic Sea routes lost their importance and the coastal towns went into decline. The final nail in the coffin was the disastrous Thirty Years War, which resulted in this entire stretch of coast going to the Swedish empire. Wismar and Stralsund, in particular, were turned into Swedish garrison towns and exploited for all they were worth, though little evidence of this period remains today.

The medieval townscapes took a battering during the later stages of World War II, and suffered from lack of attention in the immediate postwar years, when aesthetics took a back seat to rehousing the population in soulless modern estates. However, restoration work is well under way in the historic showpieces, and the entire city centre of Stralsund, which has the richest architectural heritage, had already had a preservation order placed on it by a diligent GDR government department. Rostock, home to the former GDR's merchant navy and shipbuilding industry, is the region's gateway to the world, and its port is now open for passenger services as well as freight traffic. Like Greifswald, it's also among the oldest university cities in Germany, and the continued presence of large numbers of students ensures a lively atmosphere for at least half the year.

Wismar

History has not always been kind to **WISMAR**, the first Hanseatic city east of Lübeck, the dominant force in the great trading alliance. During the League's golden age, it was a rich and influential port, but after it was taken over by the Swedes in 1648, the city was regarded as a vital defensive bulwark against Denmark and turned into a strong fortress. In 1803, it was mortgaged to the Duke of Mecklenburg-Schwerin on a hundred-year lease, but not reclaimed. Wismar has remained a modest-sized town ever since, the monumentality of the Hanseatic buildings in its Altstadt seeming completely out of scale with its modern status. Badly neglected in the GDR epoch, Wismar is now making a determined comeback: it takes tourism very seriously indeed, and its beautiful centre deservedly draws plenty of day-trippers from Hamburg, Lübeck and the Baltic resorts.

The Altstadt

The **Altstadt**, set just back from the Wismarbucht, a sheltered Baltic bay, was quite badly damaged during World War II, though its sense of faded grandeur was if anything increased by the fact that key monuments were left as ruins. In the past few years, however, ambitious restoration projects have been initiated, and within a few years the town should look in immaculate shape once more.

The hundred-square-metre **Marktplatz**, one of the largest in Germany, has regained its commercial function since the fall of Communism. Showpiece of the square, though sometimes rather obscured by all the stalls, is the **Wasserkunst**, a domed wrought-iron pavilion in the Dutch Renaissance style which shelters the municipal well, the town's only source of drinking water until 1897. Opposite is a mansion misleadingly known as the **Alter Schwede**: the oldest surviving house in town, dating back to 1380, it's a fine example of the brick Gothic architecture typical of the Baltic. In contrast to the gabled east and south sides of the square, the northern end is dominated by the slate-blue of the Neoclassical **Rathaus**.

Standing forlorn in the middle of the Marienkirchhof, the next square to the west, is the disembodied tower of the **Marienkirche**, the rest of which was destroyed in the war; sadly, this seems to be the one building accepted as being past meaningful restoration. At the square's southeastern corner is the **Archdiakonat**, a fine example of black and red brickwork from the fifteenth century.

Kellerstrasse leads west to Wismar's most distinctive building, the **Fürstenhof**, a mid-sixteenth-century palace constructed in a Baltic adaptation of the Italian Renaissance style. It's adorned with beautiful friezes: the lower is of limestone and depicts the Trojan War on the street facade, the story of the Prodigal Son on the courtyard side; the upper is of terracotta and has portrait medallions of personalities of the day intermingled with heroes of the classical world. The magnificent portal bears the coat of arms of the Mecklenburg dukes.

Beyond is the hefty torso of the **Georgenkirche**, Wismar's largest church, a highly decorative example of Gothic brickwork which, in the days of the Hansa, was the place of worship of the craftsmen and tradesfolk. Left as a roofless shell in 1945, it's currently the subject of the town's most ambitious restoration project, with the aim of reconstructing it completely, a task which will take many more years.

On Lübsche Strasse, a block north of Marktplatz, the **Heiligen-Geist-Spital** (daily 10am–4pm; free), ranks second to Lübeck's as the best-preserved old hospital in Germany. Originally fifteenth-century Gothic, it was partially remodelled a couple of hundred years later in late Renaissance style. The most notable feature from the latter period is the painted wooden ceiling of the church, whose medallions illustrate Old Testament scenes. Look out also for some notable older furnishings, including a pair of processional candelabra and a regal stone group of the Adoration of the Magi.

Further north, the Altstadt is bisected by the **Grube**, the oldest landscaped canal in any German city, and lined with recently restored buildings. On its southern bank, alongside Schweinsbrücke, is the **Schabbellhaus** (May–Oct Tues–Sun 10am–8pm; Nov–April Tues–Sun 10am–5pm; DM3/€1.50), a ritzy mansion in the Dutch Renaissance style built as the home and workplace of a local brewer and town councillor. Today, it contains an excellent museum on the history of Wismar. There's a gory section on medieval torture, with the grisliest exhibit being two shrivelled human hands preserved in a bowl. These came from a murder victim and were used to confront the perpetrator in court – an accusing finger from the grave, so to speak, successfully used to extract a confession. Other, more aesthetic, highlights are the bronze doorknocker from the Georgenkirche, the drinking horn of the wool weavers' guild and the original figures from the Wasserkunst. A small archeology department features the so-called Wismar Horn from 1200 BC.

Directly opposite stands the **Nikolaikirche**, the only one of the three brick Gothic churches to remain intact in 1945. As with Marktplatz, its monumental proportions seem highly exaggerated for this small town: indeed, its dizzying 37-metre-high interior makes it the tallest church in the whole of the former GDR. The lofty sense of space conveyed is undoubtedly the most memorable feature, though there are a few fine works of art, notably in the chapel beside the sacristy, which has a fourteenth-century bronze font and the fifteenth-century retable of the mariners' guild.

Just to the northwest is the **Wassertor**, the only one of the five medieval gateways to have survived. It guarded the entrance to the harbour, the **Alter Hafen**, which these days still buzzes with fishing boats.

Practicalities

Wismar's **Hauptbahnhof** lies just outside the northeastern confines of the Altstadt. The **tourist office** (daily 9am–6pm; ☎0 38 41/1 94 33, fax 25 18 19, *www.wismar.de*) is in the Stadthaus, Am Markt 11.

Some **private rooms** (①–③) are available through the tourist office, while the **youth hostel** is at Juri-Gagarin-Ring 30a (☎0 38 41/3 26 80, fax 32 68 68; DM29/€14.50 or DM34/€17); take bus #D to the Frauenklinik stop. There are several centrally located medium- and upper-range **hotels**, including *Altes Brauhaus*, Lübsche Str. 33 (☎0 38 41/28 32 23; ⑤), *Reingard*, Weberstr. 18 (☎0 38 41/28 49 72; ⑥), *Alter Speicher*, Bohrstr. 12 (☎0 38 41/21 17 46; ⑥), and *Stadt Hamburg*, Am Markt 24–25 (☎0 38 41/23 90; ⑥). The **restaurants** of the last two hotels are among the best in town. Other places to eat and drink include: *Alter Schwede*, Am Markt 22, which lives up to its name by offering Swedish as well as German cuisine; the historic *Zum Weinberg*, Hinter dem Rathaus 3; and the fish specialists *Seehase*, Altböterstr. 6, and *Hanse Keller*, Lübsche Str. 22. A good choice for *Kaffee und Kuchen* is *Caféhaus 15*, Lübsche Str. 15, while *Brauhaus am Lohberg*, Lohberg 15, is a Hausbrauerei.

You'll find the nearest stretch of reasonable Baltic **beach** on the island of **Poel**, about 10km north of town. Its best section is at Schwarzer Busch – but don't expect too much, as it's only a very thin strip of land that gets very crowded. Local buses regularly run over the causeway to Poel; in summer there are also ferries, which sail from Alter Hafen, passing the bird sanctuary on the isle of Walfisch en route.

Bad Doberan and the beach resorts

Between Wismar and Rostock lie a number of holiday resorts which have begun to reclaim the prestigious status they held before the GDR brought them firmly downmarket. Prominent among these, and an excellent touring base for the whole region, is the spa town of **Bad Doberan**, which lies 50km northeast of Wismar. It now forms a joint municipality with nearby **Heiligendamm**, the oldest seaside resort in Germany, while just to the west is an even bigger beachcomber's paradise, **Kühlungsborn**. An added attraction is that the three towns are linked by one of eastern Germany's celebrated narrow-gauge rail lines.

Bad Doberan

BAD DOBERAN, the one-time summer residence of the grand dukes of Mecklenburg-Schwerin, began life as an adjunct to one of the country's most powerful Cistercian monasteries. Of this, the **Münster**, the former monastic church, still survives at the eastern edge of the centre. It incorporates a fragment of the original Romanesque building, but is otherwise a peerless example of the brick Gothic architecture characteristic of the Baltic lands. Although the graceful pillars and vaulting provide the most imposing features of the interior, there are a number of impressive adornments, including the winged fourteenth-century high altar and the tall tabernacle. Just to the northeast of the church is a curious octagonal structure in a similar style; known as the **Beinhaus**, it used to serve as an ossuary.

To the west, the **Kamp**, formerly a common, was transformed into an English-style park when Doberan came into favour with the Schwerin court. On the east side of August-Bebel-Strasse, which bisects the park from north to south, are a number of grand Empire buildings from the same period, among them the ducal **Palais**, which has been converted into a hotel (see below). Amid the greenery to the west are two whimsical garden pavilions in the Chinese style: the smaller **Roter Pavillon** is a commercial art gallery, while the larger **Weisser Pavillon** is a café.

Northwest of here lies **Goethestrasse**, with its eighteenth- and nineteenth-century mansions now under reconstruction following decades of shameful neglect. The Molli, the **narrow-gauge railway** linking Bad Doberan with the two coastal resorts, begins its fifteen-kilometre journey by running right along the middle of this street before chugging through a forest nature reserve towards the nearby beaches.

Bad Doberan's **Bahnhof** is located at the southern end of the town centre. The **tourist office** (May–Sept Mon–Fri 9am–6pm, Sat 10am–4pm; Oct–April Mon & Wed–Fri 9am–5pm, Tues 9am–6pm; ☎ & fax 03 82 03/6 21 54, *www.bad-doberan.de*) at Goethestr. 1 has plenty of **private rooms** (①–③) on its books. The **youth hostel** on the western side of town at Am Tempelberg (☎03 82 03/6 24 39, fax 6 22 28; DM23/€11.50 or DM29/€14.50). There are also several **pensions**, including *Am Fuchsberg*, Am Fuchsberg 7 (☎03 82 03/6 34 74; ④), but the only **hotel** as such is *Friedrich-Franz Palais*, August-Bebel-Str. 2 (☎03 82 03/6 30 36; ⑦). This also has the best **restaurant** in town, though the *Ratskeller*, August-Bebel-Str. 3, is a reliable and cheaper alternative.

Heiligendamm and Kühlungsborn

The first main stop on the Molli (see Bad Doberan, above) is **HEILIGENDAMM**, a grand remnant of Germany's aristocratic past. Founded in 1793 by Duke Friedrich Franz I, this was the first place in Germany where the well-heeled came to enjoy the newly fashionable pastime of swimming in the sea. Throughout the GDR period, its palatial white buildings served as holiday homes for manual workers, but these are gradually being restored as hotels and sanatoria.

For a bit more life and bustle, continue to the Molli's terminus of **KÜHLUNGSBORN**, one of the Baltic's largest holiday resorts. Here there are dozens of **hotels**, particularly along the seafront. Many are in elegant Wilhelmine and Jugendstil buildings; among the most attractive are *Poseidon*, Hermannstr. 6 (☎03 82 93/71 82; ⑤), *Villa Patricia*, Str. des Friedens 2 (☎03 82 93/85 40; ⑥), *Westfalia*, Ostseeallee 17 (☎03 82 93/1 21 95; ⑥), and *Neptun*, Strandstr. 37 (☎03 82 93/6 30; ⑦). There's also a **youth hostel** at Dünenstr. 4 (☎03 82 93/1 72 70, fax 1 72 79, *jh-kuehlungsborn @t-online.de*; DM26/€13 or DM31/€15.50). Further information about accommodation can be had from the **tourist office**, Ostseeallee. 19 (☎03 82 93/8 49 20, fax 8 49 30, *www.kuehlungsborn.de*).

Rostock

ROSTOCK, 17km east of Bad Doberan, is well served by ferry routes, but approaching by boat you'd never guess you were heading for the German Baltic's largest port. Instead, the fishing village of Warnemünde presents its sandy beach, and tugs are the largest boats around. However, you then swing round to the River Warnow's wide estuary, with its vast deep-sea port; Rostock itself stands a few kilometres further down, on the southern river bank. It presents an intriguing architectural mix – medieval and 1950s architecture in the centre, nineteenth-century villas in the suburb of Steintor-Vorstadt and modern housing estates for the rest.

The city has had a tough time coming to terms with the consequences of German unification, which brought to a speedy end its postwar role as the shipbuilding metropolis of the Communist bloc, resulting in mass unemployment. A vicious neo-Nazi attack on an immigrants' hostel in 1992, which was captured on film and broadcast round the world, has brought it a notoriety it is still finding hard to shake off.

Arrival, information and accommodation

Rostock's **Hauptbahnhof** is situated well to the south of the Altstadt, and connected to the town centre by trams #11 or #12. **Ferries** (including catamarans and jetfoils) dock at the **Überseehafen** on the right bank of the Warnow by the S-Bahn terminus Seehafen-Nord, and at the **Fährhafen** beside Warnemünde's Bahnhof. International

ACCOMMODATION
2 Courtyard by Marriott
4 Mecklenburger Hof
3 Nordland
1 Sonne

△ *Hauptbahnhof*

services run to and from Trelleborg in Sweden, Gedser in Denmark, Helsinki in Finland and Tallinn in Estonia. Harbour **cruises** are run by several competing companies from Alter Strom in Warnemünde and from the Stadthafen on the west side of the city centre. **Mitfahrzentrale** is at Am Kabutzenhof 21 (☎03 81/4 93 44 38).

The main **tourist office** (May–Sept Mon–Fri 10am–6pm, Sat & Sun 10am–2.30pm; Oct–April Mon–Fri 10am–5pm, Sat 10am–2.30pm; ☎03 81/1 94 33 or 3 81 22 22, fax 3 81 26 01, *www.rostock.de*) is at Neuer Markt 3. There's another in Warnemünde at Am Strom 59 (May–Aug Mon–Fri 10am–7pm, Sat & Sun 10am–4pm; Sept–April Mon–Fri 10am–6pm, Sat & Sun 11am–4pm; ☎03 81/54 80 00, fax 5 48 00 30). Both sell the **RostockCard**, which costs DM15/€7.50 for 48 hours, and covers all public transportation costs within the city boundaries, plus a wide variety of reductions, ranging from museum entry to leisure facilities and restaurant meals.

Accommodation in **private homes** (①–④) is plentiful in Warnemünde and the coastal villages between Rostock and Bad Doberan, but the tourist office does have some city-centre rooms on its books. There's a **youth hostel** in a museum-ship, the *Traditionsschiff* (☎03 81/71 62 24, fax 71 40 14; DM28/€14 or DM39/€19.50), in the suburb of Schmarl; take the S-Bahn to Lütten-Klein, from where it's a twenty-minute walk. Another is at Parkstr. 46 (☎03 81/54 81 70, fax 5 48 17 23; DM26/€13 or DM31/€15.50) in Warnemünde. Most **hotels** in the city centre are geared to business visitors and priced accordingly; Warnemünde, which has plenty of seaside pensions, is an altogether happier hunting ground for anyone on a budget.

Hotels and pensions

Alabama, Alexandrinenstr. 80, Warnemünde (☎03 81/54 82 50, fax 5 48 25 33). Run in tandem with a Wirtshaus, this is one of a number of moderately priced pensions in picturesque old houses in the heart of Warnemünde. ④.

Am Alten Strom, Am Strom 60, Warnemünde (☎03 81/54 82 30, fax 54 82 34 44). Large hotel with restaurant, picturesquely located by the old harbour. ⑤.

Am Bahnhof, Konrad-Adenauer-Platz 1 (☎03 81/3 63 31, fax 4 93 46 79). Medium-range hotel with restaurant directly opposite the Hauptbahnhof. ④–⑤.

Bellevue, Seestr. 8, Warnemünde (☎03 81/5 43 33, fax 5 43 34 44). Good old-fashioned seaside hotel with restaurant. The front rooms have balconies directly overlooking the beach. ⑤.

Courtyard by Marriott, Schwaansche Str. 6 (☎03 81/4 97 00, fax 4 97 07 00, *www.courtyard.com*). Although part of the eponymous chain, this is among the most characterful of the city-centre hotels. It has a relatively quiet Altstadt setting and one of Rostock's best restaurants. ⑥.

Fischerhus, Alexandrinenstr. 124, Warnemünde (☎03 81/54 83 10, fax 5 19 10 41, *www.all-in-all.com*). Pleasant hotel with café in the historic quarter of the seaside village. It also offers apartments in an old fisherman's cottage further down the street. ⑤.

Mecklenburger Hof, August-Bebel-Str. 111 (☎03 81/4 92 23 01, fax 4 92 23 03). City-centre hotel run in tandem with a fish restaurant, *Gastmahl des Meeres*. ④.

Neptun, Seestr. 19, Warnemünde (☎03 81/77 70, fax 5 40 23, *www.hotel-neptun.de*). This behemoth of a hotel enjoys a certain notoriety, both because of its GDR origins and its over-prominent position. However, it has been well refurbished and retains its status as one of the most luxurious addresses on the entire Baltic coast. It also has a fine restaurant. ⑨.

Nordland, Steinstr. 7 (☎ & fax 03 81/4 92 37 06). Another good central choice; it has a reasonably priced restaurant, *7 Türme*. ⑤.

Sonne, Neuer Markt 2 (☎03 81/4 97 30, fax 4 97 33 51, *www.hotel-sonne-rostock.de*). A member of the Arkona chain, this hotel in a modernized gabled mansion is now the best and most expensive in the city centre. It also has a top-notch restaurant. ⑦–⑨.

The city centre

Although much of Rostock's Altstadt was destroyed in the war, its boundaries are still clearly marked by significant suriving sections of the **Stadtmauer**, including three gateways. Between here and the Hauptbahnhof is the Steintor-Vorstadt, a nineteenth-century inner suburb of residential villas.

Neuer Markt is the city's main square, where the fifteenth-century Gothic **Rathaus**, which had a Baroque facade slapped on it in the eighteenth century, stands opposite slim, gabled Renaissance houses. The area between here and the Warnow was all but razed by wartime bombs, and almost everything you see now has been built during the last fifty-odd years. **Lange Strasse**, which leads off the square to the west, was intended to be the showpiece of socialist rebuilding, but its only notable quality is its size: overwide, and lined by large red-brick buildings, it dwarfs the people and cars below.

Perched on a little hill to the east is the original Altstadt, which became a working-class neighbourhood as the city expanded. Its twisting cobblestoned streets display the names of many former trades like leather-dyeing, fishing and milking. Less honourable occupations get a look in too – Diebstrasse means "thief street". The **Petrikirche** on the Alter Markt is a wonderfully peaceful spot. Its tall spire, by which ships would navigate their way to harbour, was blown off during the war, and only replaced in 1994. The **viewing platform** (May–Sept Mon–Fri 9am–5pm, Sat & Sun 11am–5pm; DM2.50/€1.25, or DM3/€1.50 by lift) commands a good view over the Warnow and the city.

Just to the northwest of Neuer Markt is the Altstadt's overwhelmingly dominant monument, the **Marienkirche** (Mon–Sat 10am–5pm, Sun 11.15am–noon; DM2/€1), a late Gothic church built with the red bricks characteristic of north German architecture. It was intended to rival its counterpart in Lübeck, but the nave collapsed, leaving only two bays extant, and a long hall transept had to be added to stabilize the structure. The result is a building of strange yet striking proportions, both inside and out. From the **tower** there's another fine view of the city. Among the furnishings, look out for the Baroque **organ** and the late thirteenth-century bronze **font**. However, the prize feature is the **astronomical clock**, the only one of its kind left in Europe. Originally made in 1472, it's been running continuously since 1643, when it was modernized in accordance with the latest scientific knowledge. Its upper clock-face is divided into 24 hours, as well as rings showing monthly star signs and the work associated with each one. The lower, older face consists of thirteen concentric circles showing time and planetary movements.

To the west of Neuer Markt, Kröpeliner Strasse cuts through the pedestrianized heart of the city. Look out for the **Spitalpfarrhaus** at no. 82, the finest brick gabled Gothic house remaining in the city; formerly belonging to the medieval hospital, it's now the public library. Beyond lies **Universitätsplatz**, where people loll around the Brunnen der Lebensfreude (Fountain of Happiness), playing music and drinking, surrounded by market stalls and open-air cafés. Around here are the main buildings of the university, founded in 1419, the first in northern Germany. Although nothing remains from this period – most of the structures are examples of the varied but heavy-handed Historicist tastes of the nineteenth century – there's a fine **Barocksaal** on the east side of the square, which is regularly used as a concert hall. Across from it is the **Blücherdenkmal**, erected in 1819 immediately after the death of the city's most illustrious son, the Prussian Field Marshal Gebhard Leberecht von Blücher. Both the statue and the bas-reliefs were carved by the great Berlin Neoclassical sculptor Johann Gottfried Schadow; the latter depict Blücher's most important victories, among them Waterloo.

Just to the west of Universitätsplatz is the **Kloster zum Heiligen Kreuz**, a former Cistercian monastery whose Gothic interiors now house the **Kulturhistorisches Museum** (Tues–Sun 10am–6pm; DM4/€2). Its ground-floor exhibits include eighteenth-century travelling trunks and fourteenth- and fifteenth-century religious artefacts and retables. On the first floor are works from both before and after World War II from the artists' colony in nearby Ahrenshoop (see p.789). The second floor covers paintings of the late nineteenth- and early twentieth-century period, during which Ahrenshoop was first "discovered".

At the end of Kröpeliner Strasse stands the **Kröpeliner Tor** (Wed–Sun 10am–6pm; DM4/€2), the most impressive of the city's gateways. Its lower part dates back to the late thirteenth century, while the more elegant upper storey was added around 1400. Inside is the local history museum. From here, you walk southeastwards through the landscaped Wallangen, laid out alongside a well-preserved segment of the medieval walls. Between here and the **Steintor** is a rose garden, while immediately to the east of the latter is another surviving section of wall, including the **Kuhtor**, the oldest of the gates.

A couple of minutes' walk south of the Steintor, at August-Bebel-Str. 1, the **Schiffahrtsmuseum** (Tues–Sun 10am–6pm; DM4/€2) is mainly concerned with the region's seafaring history. It contains collections of model boats and sailing craft from the days of the Hanseatic League to the battleships of Kaiser Wilhelm II.

The outskirts

WARNEMÜNDE, now Rostock's seaside suburb but still preserving the distinctive feel of a separate town, is best reached by S-Bahn. Unlike the rest of the city, it has profited enormously from the demise of the GDR, and has undergone a spectacular visual transformation, with many of its villas returned to their nineteenth-century splendour. On either side of the picturesque old harbour, **Alter Strom**, small fishermen's houses stand sideways to the sea to avoid biting winds, and along the seafront a boulevard stretches for about a kilometre, with cafés on one side and a white sandy beach on the other. It's not exactly St Tropez – the ugly **Hotel Neptun**, a five-star monstrosity built to obtain hard currency from westerners, disfigures the far end of the seafront – but it's still one of the country's favourite holiday spots. For a view over the harbour, climb up the hundred-year-old **Leuchtturm** (May–Sept daily 10am–7pm; DM3/€1.50). If you'd like to see what the old fishermen's homes looked like inside, visit the doll's house of a **Heimatmuseum** at Alexandrinenstr. 30–31 (Wed–Sun 10am–6pm; DM3/€1.50).

In Schmarl, midway between Warnemünde and the centre of Rostock, the **Traditionsschiff** (Tues–Sun 10am–6pm; DM4/€2) is an old merchant navy vessel moored just over 1km east of S-Bahn stop Lütten-Klein. Walking around the ship's engine room is the best feature unless you're fascinated by the history of shipbuilding and the tools and parts of the trade.

Eating, drinking and entertainment

As you'd expect, Rostock's main strength in the food and drink field lies in the many **fish restaurants**, though there are plenty of other recommendable establishments as well; see also the hotels section on p.786.

Restaurants

Braukeller, Doberaner Str. 27. The main Gaststätte of the Rostocker brewery, nowadays a subsidiary of the famous Beck's of Bremen.

Fischerklause, Am Strom 123, Warnemünde. Speciality fish restaurant located right by the harbour where the catch is landed.

Gartenlaube, Anastasiastr. 24, Warnemünde. One of the city's best and most inventive restaurants.

Il Ristorante, Am Strom 107, Warnemünde. Excellent but pricey Italian restaurant overlooking the harbour. Evenings only.

Ratskeller, Neuer Markt 1. Typically reliable choice for *gutbürgerliche Küche*.

Zur Kogge, Wokrenterstr. 27. Historic seamen's tavern that's cosy in an obvious, tourist-catering sort of way.

Zur Troika, Alte Warnemünder Chaussee 42. Russian speciality restaurant.

Bars and cafés

Am Windspiel, Schnickmannstr. 7. Hip hangout which puts on regular art exhibitions.

Grand Café Wagner, Universitätsplatz 5-7. The best choice for *Kaffee und Kuchen*.

riz mediencafé, Wismarsche Str. 44. Internet café which also features films and live music.

Studentenkeller, Universitätsplatz. The best-known student rendezvous, functioning as a café in the daytime and a bar with live music and discos in the evening.

Zum Alten Fritz, Warnowufer 65. Hausbrauerei which makes an unfiltered beer and also serves inexpensive meals.

Culture, nightlife and festivals

The main **cultural** venue is the *Volkstheater*, Doberaner Str. 134/5 (☎03 81/24 40, *www.rostock.de/volkstheater*), which puts on a varied programme of drama, opera and ballet, plus orchestral concerts by the Norddeutsche Philharmonie. **Discos** include Bel Air, St-Petersburger Str. 18b, and Speicher, Am Strande 3a. Local **festivals** tend to be dominated by the nautical theme: these include the *Warnemünder Woche* in early July and the *Hanse Sail* in early August.

Fischland, Darss and Zingst

Seen on a map, the peninsula of **Fischland, Darss** and **Zingst** looks like a crooked finger hooking itself around the mainland coast midway between Rostock and Stralsund. Bounded to the north by the Baltic and to the south by a series of shallow bays, or *Bodden*, this isolated area makes a good destination either as a day-trip or overnight stop. Like the whole Baltic coast, the peninsula gets crowded, but isn't invaded in summer in the same way that the holiday islands of Rügen and Usedom are – probably because the beaches are less sandy, the scenery a little more rugged and communications sparser.

Fischland

The isthmus of **Fischland** is the most rewarding part of this area. From Rostock travel by rail to Ribnitz-Damgarten, from where buses cover the whole area. First stop is **WUSTROW**, a sleepy little settlement overlooking the **Saaler Bodden**. Just past the village entrance it's worth climbing the tower of the **Dorfkirche**, built on the remnants of Slavonic defences, which offers expansive views of the whole island (if the doors are locked the key is available from the parish house in the first street on the right after the church itself). Otherwise simply wander the streets taking in the reed-roofed houses, an architectural characteristic of the area. From the village's small harbour behind the church a **cruise boat** plies the Bodden chain. There's a small **tourist office** at Sandstr. 10 (☎03 82 20/2 51, fax 2 53, *www.wustrow.de*). Among the **hotels** are *Sonnenhof*, Strandstr. 33 (☎03 82 20/61 90; ⑥), and *Dorint*, Strandstr. 46 (☎03 82 20/6 50; ⑥), the latter renowned for its bathing facilities.

North from Wustrow the windswept cliffs of the **Hohes Ufer** lead to the quiet resort of **AHRENSHOOP**, which developed into an artists' colony at the turn of the twentieth century. Artistic overpopulation and the realization that the area only offered a limited number of themes later led the painters to decamp in search of new inspiration. However, the tradition has revived, and exhibitions can be seen in the village's four commercial **galleries**: *Kunstkaten*, Strandweg 1; *Bunte Stube*, Dorfstr. 24; *Dünenhaus*, Am Schifferberg; and *Kunsthaus Guttenberg*, Feldweg 3. The local beach, just 100m north of Dorfstrasse, is narrow and a little stony, protected from the Baltic waves by a series of groynes.

Ahrenshoop's **tourist office** is in the Kurverwaltung, Kirchnersgang 2 (Mon, Wed & Fri 9am–4pm; Tues & Thurs 9am–noon; June–Sept Sat & Sun 9am–3pm; ☎03 82 20/2 34, fax 3 00, *www.ahrenshoop.de*). Among the **hotels** are *Möwe*, Schifferberg 16–17 (☎03 82 20/60 80; ⑥), *Fischerwiege*, Schifferberg 2 (☎03 82 20/60 60; ⑥), and *Haus am Meer*, Dorfstr. 37 (☎03 82 20/8 08 16; ⑦). All of these have good **restaurants**; *Café Namenlos* in *Fischerwiege* is particularly well regarded. Also recommendable is *Café Buhne*, Grenzweg 12, an arty place overlooking the sea at the head of the Hohes Ufer.

Darss

Darss, which marks the traditional transition from Mecklenburg to Pomerania, is a heavily forested area, jutting out into the sea north of Fischland. Much of it lies within the **Nationalpark Vorpommersche Boddenlandschaft**, which stretches via Darss to the west coast of Rügen. From Ahrenshoop the main road snakes around the edge of the Darss forest, passing through the traditional fishing villages of Born and Wieck.

About 3km northeast of Wieck is the resort of **PREROW**, a little place protected from the Baltic by a line of sand dunes. Prerow doesn't really have a centre, it just straggles along two streets, Strandstrasse and Waldstrasse, which lead off Wiecker Weg, the main road into town. The **beach** is about 300m north of Waldstrasse along Im Schuning, its "entrance" marked by a cluster of cafés and kiosks.

Other attractions are the **Darss-Museum**, Waldstr. 48 (May–Sept daily 9am–5pm; Oct daily 9am–4pm; DM2/€1), devoted to the history of Darss and the seafaring past of its people, and the eighteenth-century **Seemannskirche** (Seamen's Church) on the Zingst road heading west out of town. This modest church has a surprisingly elaborate Baroque altar, and its graveyard is littered with simple monuments that form a sociological history in stone. As with other villages on the peninsula, wandering the sidestreets can be rewarding, with lots of unusual architectural features – colourfully painted doors, carved window frames and ornate weathercocks – adorning the reed-bedecked wooden houses. From Prerow there are a number of walking possibilities: a woodland path marked by posts with horizontal red lines leads from Bernsteinerweg (opposite Küsters Allee) on the northwest corner of town through the woods to **Darsser Ort** headland with its isolated lighthouse, while another path traverses the sand dunes west of town in the direction of Zingst.

Prerow's **tourist office** is at Gemeindeplatz 1 (Mon–Fri 10am–6pm; ☎03 82 33/61 00, fax 6 10 20). There are a few **pensions** (②–④) catering for those who wish to stay. The leading **hotel** is *Waldschlösschen*, Bernsteinweg 4 (☎03 82 33/61 70; ⑥), which is also the best place for a meal.

Zingst

The village of **ZINGST**, just over 5km east of Prerow, is notable mainly for its **beach**, which stretches for 10km, with fine yellow sand, backed by high dunes. Otherwise, the only setpiece attraction is the **Heimatmuseum** (mid-May to Sept Tues–Sat 9am–noon & 1–4pm; Oct to mid-May Tues, Fri & Sat only; DM2/€1), in a sea captain's house at Strandstr. 19. The wooded eastern end of Zingst is home to numerous rare plants and birds, and at the end of the road there's a small exhibition house hidden away in the woods behind the car park.

Zingst's **tourist office** at Klosterstr. 21 (☎0 82 32/8 15 24, fax 8 15 25, *www.zingst.de*) has information on the whole region and can arrange accommodation. **Hotels** include *Boddenhus*, Hafenstr. 9 (☎03 82 32/1 57 13; ⑥), and *Am Strand*, Birkenstr. 21 (☎03 82 32/1 56 00; ⑥), both of which have **restaurants**. There's a **youth hostel** at Glebbe 14 (☎03 82 32/1 54 65, fax 1 22 85; DM24/€12 or DM29/€14.50).

Stralsund

Pomerania's westernmost city is **STRALSUND**, which lies 70km along the coast from Rostock. It's far more provincial than its neighbour, but is also far more attractive, and is undoubtedly one of the best places to stay along the coast, particularly as it's possible to make day-trips to the holiday island of Rügen (see p.794), to which it's linked by a causeway carrying both road and rail traffic. First impressions of the city don't flatter, as it's ringed by horrid concrete suburbs, but the Altstadt, despite four decades of neglect under the GDR, is wonderfully evocative of its Hanseatic past, preserving a wealth of outstanding buildings. Life in Stralsund has always been tied closely to the fisheries trade: the German Baltic's main fishing fleet is based here, and the local shipyard specializes in building trawlers. These activities help to ensure that the town is in no danger of mothballing into a museum piece.

Arrival, information and accommodation

From the **Hauptbahnhof**, the Tribseer Damm traverses the isthmus leading directly into the Altstadt. The **tourist office** (May–Sept Mon–Fri 9am–7pm, Sat 9am–2pm, Sun 10am–2pm; Oct–April Mon–Fri 10am–5pm, Sat 10am–2pm; ☎0 38 31/2 46 90, fax 24 69 49, *www.stralsund.de*) is at Alter Markt 9. Weisse Flotte, Fährstr. 16 (☎0 38 31/26 81 16) runs regular **ferry** services across to Altefähr on Rügen; the same company offers harbour cruises (DM8/€4) twice daily from May to September. In summer, Reederei Hiddensee (☎0 38 31/26 81 38) runs three services per day to Hiddensee.

Plenty of **private rooms** (②–③) are available at the tourist office (☎0 38 31/24 69 69 for advance reservations), but these tend to be booked out well in advance in midsummer. There are two **youth hostels**: one has an ideal position in a half-timbered building with a courtyard at Am Kütertor 1 (☎0 38 31/29 21 60, fax 29 76 76, *jh-stralsund @sunddata.de*; DM25/€12.50 or DM30/€15); the other is 8km from the Altstadt in the seaside suburb of Devin at Strandstr. 21 (☎0 38 31/49 02 89, fax 49 02 91, *jh-devin@sunddata.de*; DM22/€11 or DM27/€13.50) – take bus #3. The medium-priced range of the **hotel** market is very well served, but there are only a few small **pensions** to cater for the budget end.

Hotels and pensions

Herwig's, Heilgeiststr. 50 (☎0 38 31/29 39 54 or 2 66 80, fax 26 68 23). Medium-range hotel with an atmospheric cellar restaurant. ⑤.

Im Grünen, Rostocker Chaussee 28a (☎0 38 31/49 48 68, fax 49 48 68). Capacious pension offering some of the cheapest rooms in town. The drawback is its suburban location, 3km southwest of the centre. ③.

Klabautermann, Am Querkanal 2 (☎0 38 31/29 36 28, fax 28 06 12). Small hotel directly overlooking the harbour. ⑤.

Norddeutscher Hof, Neuer Markt 22 (☎ & fax 0 38 31/29 31 61). Pleasant hotel in the very heart of the Altstadt. ⑤.

Regenbogen, Richtenberger Chaussee 2a (☎0 38 31/49 76 74, fax 49 48 46). This pension is one of the rare budget options. It's situated in the Tribseer Vorstadt, a ten-minute walk west of the Hauptbahnhof. ③.

Royal Am Bahnhof, Tribseer Damm 4 (☎0 38 31/29 52 68, fax 29 26 50). Palatial station hotel with a very reasonably priced restaurant, *Esprit*. ⑥.

Stralsund, Heinrich-Heine-Ring 105 (☎0 38 31/36 70 or 39 03 30, fax 36 71 11). Located in the Kneiper Vorstadt, 2km north of the centre. Its restaurant, *Herwig's*, is among the best in Stralsund. ⑤.

Zur Post, Tribseer Str. 22 (☎0 38 31/20 05 00, fax 20 49 99). Very pleasant and traditional hotel and restaurant just off Neuer Markt. ⑥.

The Altstadt

The Altstadt stands on what is almost an island, with the sea and two natural ponds – the **Frankenteich** and the **Kneiper Teich** – forming a kind of moat. The skyline, framed by the towers of the great brick Gothic churches, is best seen from the southern shore of the willow-lined Frankenteich. As Stralsund was one of only a handful of places the GDR authorities placed under a total protection order, there remains a wonderful legacy of Gothic architecture from the Hansa days, and Baroque from the two centuries of Swedish rule.

Neuer Markt and the central streets

Crossing the isthmus via Tribseer Damm, Tribseer Strasse leads to Neuer Markt, one of the two town squares. Here stands Stralsund's largest church, the late fourteenth-century **Marienkirche**, the main local rallying point for opposition groups during the *Wende*. It's a good idea to start your tour by ascending the original medieval wooden staircase of its single **tower** (July & Aug Mon–Sat 9am–6pm, Sun 11.30am–6pm; rest of year Mon–Sat 10am–4/5pm, Sun 11.30am–4/5pm; DM2/€1), part of a massive westwork which has undergone repeated alterations down the centuries. From the top, there's a marvellous view of the medieval townscape, as well as of Rügen a couple of hundred metres across the straits. The scrubbed interior of the church is notable for its vertiginous elevation; the most spectacular vaults are in the narthex, which are fashioned into a dazzling variety of star shapes. Of the many Baroque adornments, pride of place goes to the **organ**, one of the most celebrated in the country, which was made by the Lübeck master, Friedrich Stellwagen, in the 1650s. During the summer months, it can normally be heard at 11am each day, except on Thursdays, when there's a full-scale recital at 8pm on alternate weeks.

On Mönchstrasse just north of Neuer Markt, the **Katharinenkloster**, the former Dominican priory, has been converted to contain the city's two main museums. The church itself contains what has long been the most popular sightseeing attraction in the whole of the former GDR, the **Deutsches Museum für Meereskunde und Fischerei** (daily: July & Aug 9am–6pm; rest of year 10am–5pm; *www.meeresmuseum.de*; DM8/€4, DM5/€2.50 for kids). Much loved by kids, but also a serious scientific institute, it focuses on all aspects of life under the sea. On the ground floor is an aquarium full of all kinds of tropical fish, while the upper floors focus on evolution and on the fishing trade. The most spectacular exhibit is the skeleton of a finback whale washed up on Rügen in 1825.

Next door, occupying the conventual buildings, is the **Kulturhistorisches Museum** (Tues–Sun 10am–5pm; DM6/€3). Its medieval artefacts are beautifully displayed in a series of elegant Gothic halls, but unfortunately only facsimiles are on view of the glittering hoard of tenth-century treasure dug up on the nearby island of Hiddensee. Another highlight is the wonderful collection of eighteenth- and nineteenth-century dolls' houses and other children's toys. On Böttcherstrasse immediately to the south, the museum has opened an extension in a splendidly grand old warehouse, or **Speicher** (same hours and ticket); this is devoted to the folklore, costumes and lifestyle of the rural communities of the Baltic coast.

At the end of the same street is the **Jacobikirche**, the youngest of the three brick Gothic parish churches; it's under restoration and isn't yet open for visits. From here, follow Jacobiturmstrasse north to **Badenstrasse**, Stralsund's finest street, lined with mansions ranging in style from Gothic to Neoclassical.

The Alter Markt, the Nikolaikirche and around

Towards the northern end of the Altstadt is the **Alter Markt**, the original main square, one clearly modelled on its Lübeck counterpart. The focal point is the **Rathaus**, whose showpiece late fourteenth-century facade, crafted from delicately glazed bricks and bristling with fantastical gables, ranks as one of the greatest masterpieces of Gothic civil architecture. Very different in style is the Baroque southern portal on Ossenreyerstrasse, which bears the royal coat of arms of Sweden. Another important legacy of Stralsund's era as a Swedish town is the **Commandanten-Hus** at no. 14 on Alter Markt, the mansion of the local governor. It stands in stark contrast to the city's finest Gothic house, the **Wulflamhaus** at no. 5, named after the mayor who commissioned it as his residence.

Behind the Rathaus is the **Nikolaikirche**, which was built virtually in tandem with it. In design, above all in its twin towers (one of which is now capped by a Baroque helmet and spire), it's clearly modelled on the Marienkirche in Lübeck, which pioneered the Hanseatic format of pairing the main civic church with the town hall. Inside are a number of outstanding furnishings, including two **high altars** – the one in the choir itself has a carved *Passion* retable made around 1500, while that in front of the screen is a frilly Baroque creation designed by the great Berlin sculptor, Andreas Schlüter. The **astronomical clock** in the ambulatory is dated 1394 and is thus one of the oldest in Europe. However, the most intriguing adornment is the **Novgorod stall** in the southern aisle, named after the Russian city which was the easternmost outpost of the Hanseatic League. Its reliefs depict Russians hunting for animal skins, and taking honey and wax from bees, products which they then sell to a German merchant.

To the north and west of the Alter Markt are **Fährstrasse**, **Schillstrasse** and **Mühlenstrasse**, which together contain many of Stralsund's finest medieval townhouses. Mühlenstr. 3 is particularly worth seeking out: as it's now an exhibition hall, you can go inside and see the interior of this typical Hanseatic trader's residence. There are no partitioning walls, only three open-plan levels, which were used as combined living and storage quarters. At the southern end of the same street is the **Kütertor**, one of two surviving city gates. From here, it's worth following the course of the old fortifications, passing along the shore of the Kneiper Teich, then continuing via the **Kneiper Tor** to the **Johanniskloster** (early May to mid-Oct Tues–Sun 10am–6pm; DM3/€1.50). Although this former Franciscan friary was badly damaged in the war, some parts still survive, including the remarkable **Räucherboden** and the Baroque **Bibliothek**. The ruined church serves as an occasional open-air theatre.

Eating, drinking and entertainment

Many of the fine old buildings in Stralsund's Altstadt have been taken over for gastronomic purposes. Some of the best restaurants are in the hotels listed on p.791.

Café Lütt, Alter Markt 12. Good traditional coffee house.

Galerie Café Art, Badenstr. 44. Artists' café, serving light meals and staging regular exhibitions. Closed Sun.

Hansekeller, Mönchstr. 48. Cellar restaurant offering inexpensive local dishes.

Nur Fisch, Heilgeiststr. 92. Inexpensive fish specialist. Open Mon–Wed & Fri 10am–6pm, Thurs 10am–7pm, Sat 11am–2pm.

Scheelehaus, Fährstr. 23. One of Stralsund's best restaurants, this occupies a lovely gabled Gothic mansion and has a grand hall-like dining room.

Speicher-Café, Katharinenberg 34. Popular youthful hangout in a converted warehouse. Often has live music or discos in the evening.

Torschliesserhaus, Am Kütertor 1. Trendy bar next door to the youth hostel which does bistro-type food.

Wulfcronas Bier- und Weinstube, Heilgeiststr. 30. Period-piece bar which still looks much as it did when it was founded in the heady days of the Weimar Republic. Closed Sun.

Zum Alten Fritz, Greifswalder Chaussee 84–5. This is the parent of a small chain of Hausbrauereien in the northern half of the former GDR. It produces a *Zwickelbier* and various seasonal brews, and serves full meals.

Zur Kogge, Tribseer Str. 26. Has a traditional Gaststätte on the ground floor and a bar-disco in the basement.

Culture and festivals

The main **cultural** venue is the Theater Stralsund on Olaf-Palme-Platz (☎0 38 31/29 54 91). Stralsund was quick to launch or reinstate a number of **festivals** in the immediate aftermath of the demise of the GDR. These include: the *Stralsunder Segelwoche* in July, a regatta round Rügen and Hiddensee; and the *Wallensteintage* for several days around July 24, a commemoration of the city's successful defence during the Thirty Years War against the siege mounted by the imperial forces under Alfred von Wallenstein.

Rügen

Rügen is Germany's largest island and has been a favourite summer destination since bathing first became fashionable during the nineteenth century. Its long, sandy beaches and airy forests make it an ideal family holiday destination and even in GDR days Rügen drew over a million visitors a year. Since then, many of the crumbling old villas and faded grand hotels have undergone expensive refurbishments as the islanders have striven to re-establish Rügen as a fairly upmarket holiday destination. **Accommodation** is virtually unobtainable during the months of July and August without advance booking, and you should certainly consider visiting off-season. Rügen is particularly atmospheric and empty in winter when the Baltic often freezes over to create an eerie ice-scape.

Geographical divisions split the island into four distinct areas: **South Rügen** with the best, and most heavily populated, stretches of beach; **Jasmund** with its forested national park and chalk cliffs overlooking the Baltic; windswept **Wittow** in the north; and **West Rügen**, a gentle landscape of farmland and woods. The last-named is generally taken to embrace the island of **Hiddensee**, an isolated strip of land a few kilometres offshore with a landscape of surprising contrasts and an idyllic, car-free atmosphere. Also not to be missed are wind-battered **Kap Arkona** at the northeastern corner of Wittow with its Schinkel-designed lighthouse and, nearby, the secluded fishing village of **Vitt**. Equally spectacular are the **Stubbenkammer** cliffs, the most famous of Jasmund's chalk faces. Of Rügen's towns, the main places to head for are in South Rügen: **Binz** and **Sellin** are archetypal resorts with tree-lined boulevards and grandiose villas, many of which are now in use as hotels, while **Putbus** is, in effect, a giant Neoclassical folly built during the early 1800s to the greater glory of a local prince. Island capital **Bergen** provides the nearest there is to an urban atmosphere, while **Sassnitz** in Jasmund is a bustling port offering ferry services to Sweden and the Danish island of Bornholm.

Getting to Rügen poses no problems as the island is linked to Stralsund by a causeway (opened five times daily to let ships pass through) which takes both road and rail traffic. The quickest approach is by **train** – there are very frequent services on the line from Stralsund to Sassnitz via Bergen, a fair number of which originate in Berlin or even further afield. There's a regular local **bus** link between Stralsund and Altefähr on Rügen's southern coast, a route also served by ferries which leave at approximately two-hour intervals.

Island **transport links** are fairly good, with various branch rail lines leading from the main line on the eastern half of the island, and bus links to more out-of-the-way destinations. Travelling around the island is considerably easier if you have your own car; cycling is a possibility but Rügen is hilly and roads are often potholed or cobbled.

South Rügen

South Rügen offers a relaxing landscape of fields and woods, but the main attraction is its kilometres of fine beach. The best stretches are on either side of **Binz**, and there are further strands between the resorts of **Sellin** and **Thiessow**. Island capital **Bergen** isn't really a resort, but is a communications junction most visitors will pass through at least once. **Putbus**, the other main inland town and starting point of the island's narrow-gauge rail line, is well worth a visit, as is the incorporated harbour village of **Lauterbach** from where cruises run to the nature-reserve isle of **Vilm**.

Bergen

Rügen's capital, **BERGEN** is a small market town and hub of the island's communications. It's built on a pronounced incline, at the top of which is the **Marienkirche**. This church, originally Romanesque but with substantial Gothic additions, is the oldest on the island, dating back to the days when its inhabitants were Slavs. Embedded in its western wall is a **Slavonic gravestone**, blurrily depicting a bearded man; inside are some fine but faded old frescoes.

Bergen's **Bahnhof** is at the southern edge of town, with the **bus station** a couple of minutes' walk to the north along Friedenstrasse. The municipal **tourist office** is at Markt 11 (mid-May to mid-Oct Mon–Fri 10am–8pm, Sat 10am–2pm; mid-Oct to mid-May Mon–Fri 10am–6pm; ☎0 38 38/25 60 95, fax 25 60 96); that for the whole of Rügen is at Markt 4 (☎0 38 38/8 07 70, fax 25 44 40, *www.insel-ruegen.de*). It might be worth enquiring about **private rooms** (②–③) here if you're stuck for accommodation, though even Bergen fills up during the summer. The most attractive **hotel** is *Kaufmannshof*, Bahnhofstr. 6 (☎0 38 38/8 04 50; ⑦), which also has a good restaurant.

Putbus

About 8km south of Bergen by rail or bus is the little town of **PUTBUS**, built as a planned Neoclassical Residenzstadt by local grandee Prince Wilhelm Malte during the early nineteenth century. Under the GDR it fell into a decaying and melancholic state, but has since staged a recovery. With its attractive layout and architecture, based on plans originally drawn up by Karl Friedrich Schinkel, it's the artistic highlight and cultural hub of Rügen.

At the heart of it all is the **Circus**, a large roundel with a plain pillar at its centre commemorating the founding of the town. Around are grand houses, most of which have been converted into apartments and defaced by satellite dishes. Alleestrasse runs southwest from the Circus past the **Theater**, the only one on Rügen. Its flamboyant exterior, bedecked with an exaggerated portico and pseudo-classical friezes showing poets, lyre-players and assorted Muses, belies its present status as a venue for light classical concerts and farces. Next to it is the **Marktplatz**, ringed by stolid nineteenth-century buildings, with a monument at its centre commemorating Prussia's military triumphs over Austria, Denmark and France.

On the other side of Alleestrasse, the **Schlosspark** is bisected from north to south by the chestnut-tree-lined Kastanienallee. The Schloss itself was demolished in 1962, just before a visit to the area by Walter Ulbricht, the then GDR leader. Allegedly, the local party bosses hoped to score points with the SED top brass by eradicating this symbol of the feudal past. Fortunately, some fine-looking ancillary buildings remain, and the leafy lanes of the park and the banks of the **Schwanenteich**, a small lake with adjacent ruined stables, make for good strolling. At the western end is the **Christuskirche**, which has been the parish church for the past century, but was built fifty years before as the dining room, games room and ballroom for visitors on recuperative holidays. Towards the eastern end of the park (just off Kastanienallee) is the **Orangerie**, once a winter refuge for exotic plants from the park, and now housing exhibition rooms.

Some 3km southeast of Putbus, but still within its municipality, is the small fishing and sailing port of **LAUTERBACH**. It's the terminus of the branch rail line from Bergen, and is also served by buses from the Circus. Lauterbach was chosen as the site of Wilhelm Malte's very own purpose-built resort, and his opulent colonnaded Neoclassical **Badehaus** still stands on the eastern outskirts. The large wooded park behind it is the beginning of a pleasant coastal walking route.

Lauterbach is the starting point for boat trips around the island of **Vilm**, which was inaccessible to the public during the GDR period. Then, its designation as a nature reserve served mainly to camouflage its role as an exclusive holiday island for the SED hierarchy (revelations in the press about "Erich Honecker's private island" served further to discredit the SED chief after his fall from power). Vilm was opened to the public after the *Wende* but then closed again, since it was felt that indigenous rare animal and plant species were being harmed by the renewed tourist traffic. Access was then reinstated, albeit on a strictly limited basis, and most cruises simply circumnavigate the island. To find out about whether there's any possibility of making a landing, contact Fahrgastreederei Lenz, Alleestr. 9 (☎03 83 01/6 18 96) in Putbus or the Agentur Rolf Kempe (see below).

Putbus's **Bahnhof** is at the eastern edge of town, downhill from the Circus; this is a terminus of Rasender Roland, a **narrow-gauge steam railway** that runs from here to Binz, Sellin and Göhren, the main resorts on Rügen's southeastern coast. The **tourist**

office (July & Aug Mon–Fri 8am–noon & 1–6pm; rest of year Mon & Wed–Fri 8am–noon & 1–4pm, Tues 8am–noon & 1–6pm; ☎03 83 01/4 31, *www.putbus.de*) is at August-Bebel-Str. 1. Another useful contact for accommodation and other services is the privately run Agentur Rolf Kempe, Bahnhofstr. 2 (Mon–Fri 9am–6pm, Sat 10am–2/4pm; ☎03 83 01/6 05 13). Although there are a fair number of **private rooms** (②–③), the only **hotel** is *Koos*, Bahnhofstr. 7 (☎03 83 01/2 78; ⑥). For **eating** and **drinking**, the *Rosencafé*, on the eastern side of Kastanienallee, serves Italian dishes, while the *Kurhaus* at the western end of Alleestrasse has a good German menu; another possibility is the *Jägerhütte*, just beyond the Tierpark in the Schlosspark, which specializes in game. In Lauterbach, reasonably priced fish dishes can be had at *Hafenklause*, Dorfstr. 1. The Theater, Markt 13 (☎03 83 01/80 80), is the hub of Rügen's **cultural** life.

Binz

In common with the rest of the Baltic coast, Rügen's main beach resorts preface their names with the official designation Ostseebad. Biggest of these is **BINZ**, which lies 14km northeast of Putbus by road or the narrow-gauge rail line. It's been in business since the days of the Kaisers and retains much of its nineteenth-century atmosphere. The town's tree-shaded streets are lined by solid mansions with wrought-iron balconies and fancy gables. These houses were originally built as holiday residences for wealthy families, and most were confiscated by the GDR government for use as workers' rest homes. They have since been sold off for conversion into hotels and apartments, ventures which promise to be lucrative, given the heavy volume of summer visitors.

At the end of Hauptstrasse, the main shopping street, is Binz's extensive sandy **beach**, scattered with *Strandkörbe*. Nearby stands the impeccably grand **Kurhaus**, whose terrace looks out over the Baltic. The beach stretches north for about 10km to the cranes of Neu Mukran, while in the opposite direction it curves southeast for a kilometre or so before disappearing at the foot of tree-covered cliffs. At the southern end of the beach a sewage-polluted stream flows into the sea; from here, a path leads through the cliff-top woods to the headland viewpoints of **Silvitzer Ort** and **Granitzer Ort**.

The **Jagdschloss Granitz** (May–Oct daily 9am–6pm; Nov–April Tues–Sun 10am–4pm; DM5/€2.50), another Wilhelm Malte folly, built on top of the 107-metre Tempelberg, now lies within the municipality of Binz; the easiest means of access is to take the narrow-gauge rail line to Haltepunkt Jagdschloss. Again designed by Schinkel, it's in the heavily romanticized neo-Gothic style the great architect favoured for his fantasy castles. Within, a vertiginous cast-iron staircase leads up the viewing tower to a prospect of Binz and the Jasmunder Bodden freshwater lake to the west, and the island of Vilm. The Jagdschloss also houses a small hunting museum, plus portraits of Malte's ancestors.

Older vestiges of the past can be found near the village of **LANCKEN-GRANITZ** (reached by taking the narrow-gauge rail line to Haltepunkt Granitz and walking south for about 1km, or by direct bus from Binz). Turn right at the signpost marked *Ziegensteine* at the southwestern edge of the village; after about 1km there's a car park from where a path leads across the fields to a number of prehistoric grave sites. The first, under a massive oak tree, dates back to 2300 BC and consists of two huge stone slabs laid over uprights to create a grave chamber. Nearby are a couple of similar but less well-defined examples, and the surrounding fields and woods hide a number of grave mounds and indeterminate piles of stone.

Binz's **Bahnhof**, which lies to the north of the centre, its the terminus of the branch railway up the coast which connects with the main line between Bergen and Sassnitz. Southeast of the centre is **Bahnhof Binz-Ost**, which is used only by the Rasender Roland service. The **tourist office** (Jan–March, Nov & Dec Mon–Fri 9am–4pm; April,

May, Sept & Oct Mon–Fri 9am–6pm, Sat 10am–1pm; June–Aug Mon–Fri 9am–8pm, Sat 10am–1pm & 2–5pm, Sun 2–5pm; ☎03 83 93/3 06 75, fax 3 06 76, *www.binz.de*) is in the Kurverwaltung, Heinrich-Heine-Str. 7. Most of the **hotels** have recently been refurbished and are consequently on the pricey side. In the town centre are *Vineta*, Hauptstr. 20 (☎03 83 93/3 90; ⑥), and *Central,* Hauptstr. 13 (☎03 83 93/3 47; ⑥). There are more options down by the seafront, with *Villa Schwanebeck*, Margaretenstr. 18 (☎03 83 93/20 13; ⑥), and *Binzer Hof*, Lottumstr. 15 (☎03 83 93/23 26; ⑥), both just a block away from the beach. Directly on the Strandpromenade are most of the top addresses, including *Villa Salve* at no. 41 (☎03 83 93/22 23; ⑧), *Strandhotel Lissek* at no. 33 (☎03 83 93/38 10; ⑧), and *Arkona Strandhotel* at no. 59 (☎03 83 93/5 70; ⑧–⑨). The **youth hostel** is at Strandpromenade 35 (☎03 83 93/3 25 97, fax 3 25 96, *jugendherberge-binz@t-online.de*; DM36/€18 or DM44/€22), while the **campsite** (☎03 83 93/51 41) is just north of town at Prora in the woods between the main road and the beach. Alternatives to the excellent **restaurants** in all the hotels listed above are the fish specialist *Poseidon*, Lottumstr. 1, *Dünenhaus* at Strandpromenade 23, which has a pleasant terrace, and *Strandhalle*, Strandpromenade 5.

Sellin

About 4km east of Lancken-Granitz, and reached by a narrow-gauge rail connection from Haltepunkt Granitz or by bus, is **SELLIN**, another fine example of *fin-de-siècle* holiday-making grandeur. The main street here is the dignified **Wilhelmstrasse** (from the Bahnhof follow Ostbahnstrasse and then turn left into Granitzer Strasse), which slopes up in some style to the top of low cliffs overlooking the beach. The street is lined by wonderful late nineteenth-century edifices, many of which are in use as hotels and pensions. Steps lead down to the beach, which, though littered with *Strandkörbe*, is marginally less crowded than that at Binz.

The **tourist office** is at Warmbadstr. 4 (Mon–Fri 9am–5pm, Sat 10am–noon; ☎03 83 03/16 11, fax 8 72 05, *www.sellin.de*). There's a wide range of family **pensions** such as *Tatjana*, Wilhelmstr. 28 (☎03 83 03/14 50; ④), *Villa Elisabeth*, Wilhlemstr. 40 (☎03 83 03/8 70 44; ④), and *Petri*, Ostbahnstr. 5 (☎03 83 03/89 10; ⑤). **Hotels** include *Villa Subklew*, Warmbadstr. 1 (☎03 83 03/8 59 87; ⑥), and *Bernstein*, Am Hochufer 8 (☎03 83 03/17 17; ⑦). Sellin also boasts one of the ex-GDR's premier luxury hotel complexes in *Cliff*, Siedlung am Wald 22a (☎03 83 03/84 84; ⑨). Here, party bosses enjoyed holidays in style, taking full advantage of their own tennis courts, cinema and private beach (served by an elevator). All these hotels and pensions have **restaurants**; that in Tatjana serves Russian cuisine. An alternative place to eat is *Berliner Hof*, Granitzer Str. 48.

The Mönchgut peninsula

Rügen's southeastern extremity is the **Mönchgut**, a jagged, three-pronged peninsula of gentle hills and sheltered bays. Straddling an exposed headland on the east coast of the peninsula is the windswept little resort of **GÖHREN**. Just offshore is the **Buskam**, a glacier-deposited rock, once used as an altar by the Slav inhabitants of the island. The name is derived from the old Slavonic *bogis kamien*, meaning "God's Stone", and it's the biggest of Rügen's many *Findlinge* – rocks left by the passage of Ice Age glaciers. At the junction of Strandstrasse and Poststrasse is the **Mönchguter Museum** (July & Aug daily 10am–6pm; rest of year Tues–Sun 10am–4/5pm; DM4/€2, including entry to the Museumshof Rookhus and Museumsschiff luise), a mildly diverting display of local folk costumes and material about the development of tourism and other indigenous industries like fishing and piloting. A few doors down on the same street is the **Museumshof** (same times and ticket), essentially an old barn crammed with diverse and improbable-looking agricultural implements. There's another museum, the **Rookhus** (May, June & Sept Tues–Sun 10am–5pm; July & Aug 10am–6pm; same ticket as for the Mönchguter Museum), a seventeenth-century fishing cottage, on the road to Lobbe. Just out of town, off the main road in the dunes of the southern beach, is the **Museumsschiff Luise** (May, June & Sept Tues–Sun 10am–5pm; July & Aug daily 10am–6pm; same ticket as for the Mönchguter Museum), an old beached freighter.

Göhren's **Bahnhof**, the southern terminus of the Rasender Roland steam service, is close to the seafront. The **tourist office** (May–Sept daily 9am–7pm; Oct–April Mon–Sat 10am–5pm; ☎03 83 08/2 59 10, fax 2 59 11, *www.goehren.de*) is at Schulstr. 8. In addition to **private rooms** (②–③), there are numerous **hotels**, including *Albatros*, Ulmenallee 5 (☎03 83 08/54 30; ⑥), *Waldhotel*, Waldstr. 7 (☎03 83 08/5 05 00; ⑦), and *Nordperd*, Nordperdstr. 11 (☎03 83 08/70; ⑦). The **campsite** (☎03 83 08/21 22; closed Nov–March) is hidden away in the woods a stone's throw from the sea, just northeast of the Bahnhof; with a capacity of four thousand, it's the largest on the island but can still get overrun in high season. Inexpensive alternatives to the hotel **restaurants** are *Kaiser's Hofkneipe*, Waldstr. 11, and *Zur Muschel Bar* on Strandweg, a fish specialist.

South of Göhren, sandy beaches fringed with stones run all the way to the southern end of the peninsula. However, the presence of a massive **campsite** (☎03 83 08/23 14; closed Oct–Easter) just south of Lobbe and innumerable holiday homes means that these are often vastly oversubscribed. One way of escaping the crowds is to take a left turn off the main road about a kilometre south of Lobbe, and make for the tiny, one-street village of **GROSS ZICKER**. A path beyond the car park at the western end of the settlement ends at a stretch of isolated, sandy beach which, though popular, seems empty after the crowds on the eastern beaches. From Gross Zicker there's also access to the 66-metre **Bakenburg**, Mönchgut's highest point, with correspondingly good views.

At the southern end of Mönchgut, the low-lying village of **THIESSOW** lives mainly from fishing, with a little tourism on the side. Local seamen also act as pilots for vessels sailing through the shallows separating Rügen from the mainland. To reach the nearest stretch of beach, cut through the woods just north of the village. Though there are no hotels, about three dozen private houses on Hauptstrasse and Strandstrasse have **rooms** (①–③) to rent. There's a **campsite** just west of the main road on the way into town (☎03 83 08/82 26; closed Nov to mid-Dec). The *Strandcafé* on the northern beach does excellent ice cream, while *Mönchguter Fischerklause*, towards the southern end of the village at Hauptstr. 69, has good fish dishes.

The absolute end of the road is the village of **KLEIN ZICKER**, just under 2km west of Thiessow. Crammed into the space at the foot of a hill on an odd blob of land sticking out into the sea, the place is a mecca for watersports enthusiasts, particularly surfers.

Jasmund

Rügen's most striking scenery is to be found in **Jasmund**, an area of undulating woods and fields jutting out into the Baltic on the island's northeastern shore. The celebrated white cliffs of **Stubbenkammer** have become Rügen's unofficial symbol, partly because of the romanticized paintings of Caspar David Friedrich. Running back from the coast is the forested pocket of **Stubnitz**, where easy walking routes crisscross a woodland landscape more reminiscent of Europe's centre than its northern coast.

Sassnitz

The large port of **SASSNITZ**, Jasmund's only town of any size, is the terminus of Rügen's main rail line. Before World War II, it was the most popular seaside resort in Rügen, but during the GDR epoch this function played second fiddle to the fish-processing industry. Now, the crumbling old villas are gradually being restored as hotels and guesthouses, and tourism looks set to regain its prominent role within the local economy.

The **tourist office** (April–Oct Mon–Fri 8am–7pm, Sat & Sun 3–7pm; Nov–March Mon–Fri 8am–5pm; ☎03 83 92/6 69 45, fax 6 69 47, *www.sassnitz.de*) at Hauptstr. 27 offers the usual booking service for **private rooms** (②–③). **Hotels** include *Waterkant*, Walterstr. 3 (☎03 83 92/5 08 44; ⑤), and *Villa Aegir*, Mittelstr. 5 (☎03 83 92/30 20; ⑥). Overlooking the harbour on Strandpromenade are several **fish restaurants**, including *Gastmahl des Meeres* and *Zur Mole*; another good place to eat is *Köpi-Eck*, Hauptstr. 26.

Ferries run regularly from Sassnitz to the Danish island of Bornholm and the Swedish port of Trelleborg; there are also **cruises** up the coast, giving a sea view of the famous cliffs to the north.

The Nationalpark Jasmund

Unless Scandinavia-bound, your best bet is to pass straight through Sassnitz and head for the area's real attraction, the **Nationalpark Jasmund**, with the famous **Stubbenkammer** chalk cliffs of the coast and the surrounding **Stubnitz** forest. There are two ways to do this. The most obvious option is to head direct to Stubbenkammer by bus, a pleasant hilly ride through the woods. The alternative is to follow the coastal path from the northern end of Sassnitz; allow at least three hours for this. Mostly it's a cliff-top walk, but occasionally the route dips down into steep-sided stream valleys. The *Gaststätte Waldhalle*, a few kilometres beyond the edge of Sassnitz, is a handy place to interrupt your journey. Adjacent is the **Wissower Klinken**, first of the really large chalk blocks, best appreciated from the cliff-top viewpoint on the **Ernst-Moritz-Arndt-Sicht**, just to the north.

The path continues for several kilometres to the **Kleine Stubbenkammer** with the best views of the mighty **Königsstuhl**, a vast pinnacle of chalk standing free from the main cliff-face. Königstuhl means "king's seat", and legend has it that in days of yore whoever could climb the seaward side of the 117-metre cliff would become king of Rügen and occupy a stone throne at the top. These days the place swarms with visitors, most of whom choose an easier means of access via the narrow footbridge (DM2/€1) from the car park at the head of the road from Sassnitz. The view from the Königstuhl is, inevitably, splendid though you may have to fight for a space by the rail at the summit. In summer, the lines of parked cars along the approach road usually stretch back for several kilometres and the army of day-trippers is served by a Gaststätte, a couple of Imbiss stands and souvenir shops. From the Königstuhl footbridge a precipitous path meanders down to the beach, which stinks and is strewn with seaweed. The last couple of metres are descended by ladder.

Shortly before the Königstuhl, a track branches off into the forest from the main road. A path leads from this junction to the mysterious **Herthasee**, a dark lily-bedecked pool hidden in the woods, said to have been the bathing place of the Germanic goddess Hertha, who rewarded the efforts of local farmers with rich harvests. According to the tale, after bathing Hertha would drown her mortal servants, and their spirits gather on the shore each night. North of the Herthasee is the **Herthaburg,** a small hill with a large stone block nearby, which is thought to have served Rügen's early Slav inhabitants as a sacrificial altar.

Glowe

At the western end of Jasmund is **GLOWE**, distinguished by the transmitting masts of Radio Rügen, broadcasting mainly for the benefit of ships at sea and monitoring distress frequencies in the Baltic. Glowe is the gateway to the **Schaabe**, a sandy isthmus planted with Scots pine, separating the Grosser Jasmunder Bodden from the sea, with superb beaches along the Baltic side. In addition to **private rooms** (②–③), there are two excellent **hotels**: *Alt Glowe*, Hauptstr. 37a (☎03 83 02/5 30 59; ⑤), and *Meeresblick*, Hauptstr. 128 (☎03 83 02/74 40; ⑥). Both of these have fine **restaurants**, though there's also a renowned fish specialist, *Fischerhus*, Hauptstr. 58.

Wittow

Wittow is Rügen's northern extremity, wind-battered and sparsely populated, with the headland of **Kap Arkona** and the hidden village of **Vitt** as its main tourist pulls. The area has some decent stretches of beach but these tend to be more exposed and generally less hospitable than those elsewhere on the island. Fish figures highly on local menus and is well worth sampling.

Breege-Juliusruh and Altenkirchen

Wittow begins at the western end of the Schaabe with the twin village of **BREEGE-JULIUSRUH**, reached by bus from Stubbenkammer and Glowe. It's largely given over to holiday camps, and the only real reason to stop here is to take advantage of the beaches, a continuation of the Schaabe strands to the south. With your own transport, Breege, overlooking the Breeger Bodden inlet, is just about worth a quick diversion from the main road to look at the thatched *Kapitänshäuser*, eighteenth- and nineteenth-century fisher houses lining the main street, and to stop off for a bite at the *Fischerstube*, a fish speciality place (eels mainly – grilled, jellied and in soup) on the harbour. If you want to stay, choice is between *Gasthof zum Breeger Bodden*, Dorfstr. 55 (☎03 83 91/5 38; ④), and *Am Wasser*, Dorfstr. 79 (☎03 83 91/40 20; ⑤).

En route from Breege-Juliusruh to Kap Arkona you'll pass the village of **ALTENKIRCHEN**, whose thirteenth-century **Pfarrkirche** is one of the most venerable churches on the whole Baltic coast, richly decorated with thirteenth-century frescoes, only uncovered during the late 1960s.

Kap Arkona

At the northern end of Wittow is **Kap Arkona**, whose cliff-top lighthouses and Slavonic fort draw streams of visitors. Buses run from Altenkirchen to **PUTGARTEN**, an inoffensive little place from where the Kap Arkona lighthouses are clearly visible.

Just north of the village is a large parking lot for visitors to the cape. Here also is the **tourist office** (daily 10/11am–5/7pm according to season; ☎03 83 91/41 90), which can help find **private rooms** (②–③) in the area. The **Neuer Leuchtturm** (New Lighthouse), dating from the turn of last century and looking very business-like with its orange and black stripes, is the first to assert itself. Moving closer, the **Alter Leuchtturm** (Old Lighthouse), designed by the ubiquitous Schinkel in 1826, doesn't really look much like a lighthouse at all, but this three-storey red-brick building, with its inset windows and verdigris-dusted dome, does justice to its creator.

Vitt

The small fishing port of **VITT** lies hidden in the trees about 1km southeast of Putgarten at the end of a rudimentary concrete road. This is out of bounds to visitors' cars, so the best approach is to walk from Kap Arkona, though multi-seated horse-drawn carriages run to and from Putgarten. At the village entrance is the small thatched **Dorfkapelle** with an octagonal ground plan (the hand of Schinkel once again). The interior is almost bare with only naive wall-paintings of fishing-village life as decoration. From the chapel a path leads down into a small valley and the village itself, a cluster of improbably well-preserved and unspoiled thatched cottages. Vitt survives almost unchanged since the nineteenth century, seemingly oblivious to the tourists who flock here to wonder at its unique atmosphere, which owes much to the absence of cars, supermarkets and other facets of modern life. Its **beach** is stony and not particularly attractive, but it's quiet, the water is fairly clean and there's not a *Strandkorb* in sight.

Vitt's justly famous *Gasthof zum Goldenen Anker* is one of the best **restaurants** around, serving up wonderful fish and seafood dishes (particularly eel). Inside it's intimate and a model of *gemütlichkeit,* while outside you can sit on benches in good weather. The chances of finding somewhere **to stay** in Vitt are practically nil, at least in summer. There are no pensions or hotels; what few rooms do exist are privately rented, usually to long-standing regular visitors, but should you wish to try your luck head for the small craft shop at Vitt no. 8, which may be able to find accommodation. **Rowing boats** can be rented from the small harbour or you can let a local sea dog do the work for you in a motorboat.

Hiddensee

Another artist's holiday destination of long standing is the idyllic car-free island of **Hiddensee**, a sixteen-kilometre-long finger of land that stands like a barrage between Rügen and the Baltic. Hiddensee experiences a heavy volume of visitors, but with a little legwork or pedalling it's not difficult to escape the crowds. Despite its small size, the island has a startling variety of landscapes. The northern **Dornbusch** area is a plug of high ground topped by scrubby fields and sandy woods, while the central part of the island, focusing on the **Dünenheide**, is low-lying heath, giving way to a tapering strip of ever-shifting sand dunes called **Gellen**. Hiddensee has only 1300 inhabitants, most of whom are concentrated in the villages of **Kloster**, **Vitte** and **Neuendorf**, though these numbers swell considerably during the summer. Kloster is easily the most appealing of the Hiddensee villages, and the best way to explore the rest of the island is to rent a bike here (around DM10/€5 per day) and pedal your way around. Most visitors come to Hiddensee as day-trippers, and the relatively small number of available beds means that, as elsewhere on Rügen, it's effectively impossible to find somewhere to stay during July and August without a reservation made far in advance.

From the thirteenth century onwards life on Hiddensee was dominated by the Cistercian order of monks, who, while the island's lay inhabitants plundered grounded ships, were not averse to mixing it with mainland fishermen for the prize of exclusive rights to the island's waters. The Reformation ended all that and the island later passed into Swedish hands until Prussia took over in 1815. Not to be left out of the general nineteenth-century tourism boom, Hiddensee used its superior natural charms to lure a better class of visitor, and the island attracted its share of artists and writers.

Ferries to the island are run by Reederei Hiddensee, Diek 4, Vitte (☎03 83 00/2 10). The nearest port of access is Schaprode on the west coast of Rügen, from where there are several daily sailings throughout the year; these cost DM21/€10.50 return to Neuendorf, DM24/€12 return to Vitte or Neuendorf. In summer, there are normally three sailings each day from Stralsund (DM24 return to Neuendorf, DM26/€13 to Vitte or Neuendorf) and one from Zingst (DM33/€16/50 return to any of the villages). A flat DM10/€5 charge is levied for transporting a bike.

Kloster

Hiddensee's most popular destination is the little village of **KLOSTER**, which straddles the northern end of the island. It's incredibly unspoilt, and is at its best when the daytime crowds have disappeared. There's easy access from the village to the west coast of the island which basically forms an eight-kilometre-long beach.

From the small harbour where ferries from the mainland dock a lane leads into Kloster. A left turn at the village pond leads along Hauptstrasse, the nearest thing the town has to a main street. To the north of Hauptstrasse is the **Inselkirche** (Island Church), in whose graveyard **Gerhart Hauptmann** (1862–1946) is buried. Hauptmann, one of the many writers and artists who moved to Rügen in the nineteenth century, belonged to the Naturalist movement of the 1880s, and his dramas focused mainly on the lives and struggles of ordinary people. The realism of his most famous play *Vor Sonnenaufgang* (Before Sunrise), a "social drama" dealing with the human impact of industrialization, caused a sensation at its premiere, and though his earlier works remain his most famous Hauptmann's influence on modern German drama has been extensive. Signposts point the way to the **Gerhart-Hauptmann-Haus** (daily: May–Oct 10am–5pm; Nov–April 11am–4pm; DM3/€1.50), which the writer bought with the money he received from winning the Nobel Prize for Literature. It's also known more picturesquely as *Haus Seedorn* and is now packed with photos, manuscripts and theatre posters, though some of the rooms have been left as they were when the playwright lived and worked in them.

A little further along Hauptstrasse, just before the beach, is the **Museum der Insel Hiddensee** (April–Oct daily 10am–4pm; Nov–March Fri–Sun 11am–3pm; DM4/€2), the island museum, packed with archeological bits and pieces and ceramics. The **beach**, protected by blocks of rock, can be windswept and wave-battered, but on a good day it's perfect, and if you're willing to walk you can soon leave your fellow visitors behind as the sands stretch south for a good 8km. To the north the beach rounds a headland, continuing for several kilometres at the base of the steepish cliffs of the Dornbusch.

The most obvious **accommodation** possibilities in Kloster are *Haus Wieseneck*, Kirchweg 18 (☎03 83 00/316, *www.wieseneck.de*; ③), and *Hitthim*, Hafenweg 8 (☎03 83 00/66 60; ⑥), which also has a good fish restaurant. For **bike rental** try *Fahrradverleih Gerhard Wannewitz*, Leuchtturmweg 5, reached by heading straight on at the village pond rather than turning left.

The Dornbusch

The gentle hills of the **Dornbusch** area to the north of Kloster are the most appealing part of Hiddensee and are dominated by a lighthouse that warns ships of the island's presence. It's a good region to explore by bike: take the road north to the minuscule hamlet of **GRIEBEN**, where *Zum Enddorn* (☎03 83 00/3 04; ⑥) and its large garden entice thirsty cyclists. A little further along is *Hella's Eiscafé*, an ice-cream place in a thatched cottage. From the "main" road – in reality a crudely concreted track – there are a couple of turnings in the direction of the **Leuchtturm**, reached after a steep climb, but worth the effort for the excellent views of the island. Adjacent to the lighthouse is a military installation and signs warn of the risk of being shot if you approach. Skirting the edge of the nearby woods leads to a clearing and *Zum Klausner* (☎03 83 00/2 15; ④), one of the island's best eating and drinking places with outside tables during summer. In addition to its own double rooms, it also has rustic-looking twin-bedded bungalows for rent. From here a steep path leads back down into Kloster.

Vitte and Neuendorf

A kilometre or so south of Kloster is **VITTE**, Hiddensee's biggest settlement and a kind of island capital. Despite this there's not much here, local builders having been less than discriminating in their efforts, though the **Blaue Scheune**, an old fisher-house painted completely blue, is worth a look for occasional art exhibitions. The **tourist office** (for the whole island) is at Norderende 162 (July & Aug Mon–Fri 8am–5pm, Sat & Sun 10am–noon; rest of year Mon–Fri 8am–5pm; ☎03 83 00/6 42 26, fax 6 43 33, *www.insel-hiddensee.de*). There are several **hotels**, including *Godewind*, Süderende 53 (☎03 83 00/23 51; ④), *Zum Hiddenseer*, Wiesenweg 22 (☎03 83 00/4 19; ⑤), and *Post Hiddensee*, Wiesenweg 26 (☎03 83 00/64 30; ⑥). *Zum Hiddenseer* has the best **restaurant** on the island. **Bike rental** is available from *Fahrradverleih Ludwig Müller* near the *Kaufhalle* supermarket opposite the harbour.

South of Vitte is the **Dünenheide**, an area of heathland which is at its best in August when the abundant heather blooms purple. A road leads across it via the *Heiderose*, In den Dünen 127 (☎03 83 00/6 30; ⑦), a pleasant **hotel** with restaurant; it also has holiday bungalows for rent.

Southernmost of the island's three villages is **NEUENDORF**, a quiet little place which makes a good starting point for wandering the **Gellen**, a sandy spit jutting out south towards the mainland. This is the island's most peaceful part, and the place to head to avoid the crowds. On the western shore, just south of Neuendorf, is a bathing beach, though on the Gellen itself you're restricted to marked paths, as the whole area is a nature reserve. *Am Meer* (☎03 83 00/2 01; ⑥), a GDR-era luxury **hotel** with a swanky restaurant, is the only accommodation option. An alternative place for drinks and light snacks is the *Strandcafé*. For **bike rental** enquire at the *Freizeitcenter Neuendorf*, Neuendorf no. 20.

Greifswald

GREIFSWALD, the final member of the province's quartet of old Hanseatic trading cities, lies 30km south of Stralsund on the fast rail line to Berlin. Founded in the thirteenth century by the Cistercian monks of Kloster Eldena, it became the seat of a university in 1456, and retains a distinct academic atmosphere to this day.

The Altstadt

In contrast to its Hanseatic neighbours, the Altstadt of Greifswald lies 3km inland from the Baltic. Both in terms of individual monuments and overall appearance, it seems rather small-scale in comparison with the others. Substantial parts of the **Stadtbefestigung** which ringed the original town survive intact, and the area around them has been transformed into a shady promenade.

Greifswald's skyline was immortalized in a number of paintings by the town's favourite son, the Romantic artist Caspar David Friedrich. The dominant building, then as now, is the **Dom**, a typical example of Gothic brickwork, which lies close to the middle of the Altstadt. Its most remarkable feature is the mighty **tower** (May–Sept Mon–Fri 10am–4pm, Sat 10am–2pm, Sun 11am–noon; DM3/€1.50), whose four turrets, octagonal upper storeys and onion-domed Baroque spire combine to produce a memorable silhouette. A medieval wooden staircase leads to the viewing platform, which commands a fine panorama over the Altstadt to the Baltic. The Dom's interior was given a romanticized neo-Gothic remodelling in the nineteenth century, with most of the walls covered with a coat of whitewash. However, a precious series of **frescoes**, painted around 1400 in the manner of manuscript illuminations, still adorns some of the south side chapels.

Diagonally opposite the west front of the Dom are the buildings of the **Ernst-Moritz-Arendt-Universität**. Most of these are in the bloated Historicist styles of the nineteenth century, but the main block is a fine example of the dignified Baroque so characteristic of northern Germany. Its **Aula** is a fittingly splendid graduation hall, but unfortunately neither this nor other parts of the complex – such as the graffiti-covered student prison, which is reminiscent of its renowned counterpart in Heidelberg – are as yet regular tourist sights, so it's pot luck whether you find anything open.

A couple of minutes' walk to the east of the Dom is the **Markt**, a bustling square lined with a variety of well-restored buildings. Principal among these is the **Rathaus**, originally Gothic, but nowadays with a rather composite appearance as the result of various alterations. On Brüggstrasse just to the north, the **Marienkirche** is the town's oldest surviving church, unmissable with its distinctive square tower. It lacks a chancel, a fact which gives it striking dimensions, both inside and out. Look out for the humorous frescoes in the entrance hall, and for the Renaissance pulpit with its portraits of the reformers Luther, Melanchthon and Bugenhagen.

When complete, the new **Pommersches Landesmuseum** (Tues–Sun 10am–6pm; *www.pommersches-landesmuseum.de*; DM5/€2.50) will occupy a group of historic buildings in the vicinity of the Markt. The first part of the project, the **Gemäldegalerie** in the late Neoclassical **Quistorp-Gebäude**, opened in 2000. It contains a couple of oils plus a number of drawings by Caspar David Friedrich, as well as paintings by Hals, Runge, Van Gogh and Liebermann, among others. The museum headquarters, together with the archeology, history and folklore displays, will be housed in the **Graues Kloster**, the former Franciscan friary which until recently was home to the now-defunct Museum der Stadt. However, this is unlikely to be ready before 2004.

Wieck and Eldena

Greifswald's most famous sights are not in the centre, but in two incorporated villages by the River Ryck (which also forms the northern boundary of the Altstadt), just before it disgorges itself into the Baltic. They can be reached by bus #40 from the Hauptbahnhof or from Wolgaster Strasse immediately beyond the eastern boundary of the Altstadt.

WIECK is a fishing village of the active rather than tourist variety, as the smell of herring wafting from the harbour testifies. Here the river is traversed by the photogenic **Hubbrücke**, a Dutch-style wooden drawbridge restored to pristine condition a few years ago in celebration of its centenary. On the northern side of the river, take a stroll along Dorfstrasse, where there are a number of old fishermen's cottages.

A few minutes' walk south of Wieck is **ELDENA**, whose ruined **Kloster**, directly facing Wolgaster Strasse, was home to a wealthy Cistercian congregation which exercised an enormous influence on the surrounding area. It was a favourite subject of Caspar David Friedrich, and thus became at least the indirect inspiration for the vogue depictions of lonely, overgrown and crumbling monasteries in secluded settings produced by so many painters of the Romantic movement. Founded in the twelfth century by Danish monks, the Kloster was destroyed by Swedish soldiers, who carted off most of its bricks as building material. Only skeletal remains survive, but the arched doorways and empty windows of the ruin are undeniably romantic, and, more prosaically, make a good spot for a picnic.

Practicalities

Greifswald's **Hauptbahnhof** lies immediately below the southwestern corner of the Stadtbefestigung, only a few minutes' walk from the Dom. A block east of the Markt, at Schuhhagen 22, is the **tourist office** (May–Sept Mon–Fri 9am–6pm, Sat 9.30am–12.30pm; Oct–April Mon–Fri 9am–5pm; ☎0 38 34/52 13 80, fax 52 13 82, *www.greifswald.de*).

There are a fair number of **private rooms** (①–③) available. In Wieck there's also an inexpensive **pension**, *Schipp in*, Am Hafen 3 (☎0 38 34/84 00 26; ③), plus several **hotels**, including *Zur Fähre*, Fährweg 2 (☎0 38 34/84 00 49; ④), *Maria*, Dorfstr. 45 (☎0 38 34/84 14 26; ⑤), and *Ryckhotel*, Rosenstr. 17b (☎0 38 34/8 33 00; ⑥). Among the options in town are *Alter Speicher*, Rossmühlenstr. 25 (☎0 38 34/7 77 00; ⑥), *Am Dom*, Lange Str. 44 (☎0 38 34/7 7 50; ⑥), and *Kronprinz*, Lange Str. 22 (☎0 38 34/79 00; ⑥). All these hotels have **restaurants**; other good choices are *Zur Hütte*, Am Markt 12, which does everything from *Kaffee und Kuchen* to light meals, and *Zum Alten Fritz*, Am Markt 13, a Hausbrauerei with beer garden.

Wolgast

The relaxed little harbour town of **WOLGAST** lies 24km southeast of Greifswald on the southern shore of the Peene Strom, the narrow sound separating the German mainland

and the holiday island of Usedom. Best viewed as a stopover of a few hours en route to Usedom, Wolgast was for centuries a residence of the dukes of Lower Pomerania, developing into an important trade centre during the eighteenth and nineteenth centuries. Much of its old fabric survives in the network of narrow streets that slope down to the harbour from the central square, and the town remains important as a port with a large working shipyard.

On the main square, **Rathausplatz**, is the pretty little **Rathaus**, with a fluid Baroque facade which looks almost like an upturned boat. A fountain in front is decorated with scenes depicting the town's history. Also on the square is Wolgast's oldest secular building, the half-timbered **Kaffeemühle** ("Coffee Grinder") – so called because of its distinctive shape. It now houses the **Stadt- und Kreismuseum** (June–Aug Tues–Fri 10am–6pm, Sat & Sun 10am–2pm; Sept–May Tues–Fri 10am–5pm, Sat 10am–2pm; DM5/€2.50), a local history museum which also includes a small section on the development of the V2 at nearby Peenemünde (see opposite), plus changing exhibitions by local artists.

Wolgast's main sight is the nearby **Petrikirche**, a huge, angular Gothic structure whose tall **tower** (mid-May to mid-Sept Mon–Sat 10.30am–noon & 1.30–3pm, Sun 1.30–3pm; DM3/€1.50) dominates the town's skyline. It was the court church of the dukes of Lower Pomerania and is the last resting-place of nine of them. The most notable interior decorative feature is the action-packed *Totentanz* (Dance of Death) frieze, depicting Death in various guises from soldier to well-dressed noblewoman.

On Kronwiekstrasse overlooking the harbour is the **Philipp-Otto-Runge-Haus** (June–Aug Tues–Fri 10am–6pm, Sat & Sun 10am–2pm; Sept–May Tues–Fri 10am–5pm, Sat 10am–2pm; DM6/€3), the birthplace of the eponymous artist, an important figure in the early Romantic school and contemporary of Caspar David Friedrich. A large number of his graphic works are on view. To the north of the harbour is a bridge leading across to **Schlossinsel**, a small island between the mainland and Usedom which was once the site of Wolgast's castle. From here, the **Brücke der Freundschaft**, which can be used by vehicles and pedestrians, spans the sound across to Usedom. In 2000, it was joined by the new **Klappbrücke**, which reinstated the rail link for the first time since its destruction in 1945.

Practicalities

Wolgast's **Hauptbahnhof** is at the southwestern edge of town, but it's better to alight at **Wolgast-Hafen**, the harbour terminal; the next stop, **Wolgast-Fähre**, is on Usedom. Note that not all trains from Greifswald travel direct to Wolgast; some require a change at Züssow. The **tourist office** (June–Aug Mon–Fri 9am–6pm, Sat 10am–2pm; Sept–May Mon–Fri 9am–5pm; ☎0 38 36/25 12 15, fax 60 01 18, *www.wolgast.de*) in the Kaffeemühle at Rathausplatz 6 can book **private rooms** (①–③) in the town or in Usedom. Otherwise, there are a few **pensions** – including *Peene-Ufer*, Rathausplatz 8 (☎0 38 36/20 26 73; ⑤), and *Kirchstein*, Schützenstr. 25 (☎0 38 36/2 72 20; ⑤) – plus a couple of **hotels**: *Zur Insel*, Str. der Freundschaft 54 (☎0 38 36/26 10 77; ⑤), and *Pennebrücke*, Burgstr. 2 (☎0 38 36/2 72 60, *www.hotel-peenebruecke.de*; ⑥). For **eating** and **drinking**, the Ratskeller in the Rathaus is excellent, and, most unusually, offers Italian as well as German cuisine. Best choice for *Kaffee und Kuchen* is *Café Biedenweg*, Lange Str. 15.

Usedom

Just offshore from Wolgast is **Usedom**, Germany's second largest island. It has some fine beaches but is very much in the shadow of Rügen as a Baltic holiday destination, lacking the latter's variety of landscape. Fifty kilometres in length and at times only a kilometre wide, the island has a random shape, like the pattern of spilled liquid, and is separated from the mainland by the Peene Strom, which, though little more than a narrow channel for most of its length, expands suddenly and takes a big bite out of the southern shore as the **Achter Wasser** bay. At its eastern end Usedom is abruptly cut off by the border with Poland, leaving a tiny sliver of its area, including the port of **Świnoujście** (formerly German Swinemünde), in Polish hands.

Before the war Usedom was the haunt of Europe's rich and its resorts ranked among Germany's most fashionable. In the GDR period, it catered primarily to working-class holiday-makers, but since the *Wende* it has gradually moved upmarket again, with many of the grand old Wilhelmine hotels having undergone expensive refurbishments. Much fine Baltic shorefront architecture, and some of the ambience that drew the prewar glitterati, can be experienced in the trio of resorts – **Bansin**, **Heringsdorf** and **Ahlbeck** – which are virtually contiguous and collectively styled the "Kaiserbäder", though each retains a distinct identity. Further west are the finest stretches of beach, at **Zinnowitz** and **Koserow**, and the island's only historic site of note, the rocket research station of **Peenemünde**. As everywhere on the Baltic coast, there's little chance of being able to find a room in July or August without booking in advance. Usedom is fairly flat and so well suited to cycling, although the volume of car traffic in summer is heavy. It is also well served by **public transport**. The railway, the **Usedomer Bäderbahn**, was slated for closure after the demise of the GDR, but subsequently enjoyed such a spectacular revival in popularity that in 2000 it was extended in both directions, so that it now runs from Wolgast over the Peene Strom and along the entire length of the island to the Polish border. There are also buses serving the main destinations.

Peenemünde

At the extreme northwestern tip of Usedom, at the end of a branch rail line, lies **PEENEMÜNDE**, a former restricted-access military village which is a world away in spirit from the nearby beach resorts. The army arrived in 1936 to build the research centre at which the long-range liquid-fuel rocket known as the V2 was developed under Werner von Braun, and successfully launched in October 1942. The following August, the base suffered massive damage in an RAF raid, but the V2 was eventually put into production and first used in an attack on London in September 1944. After the war, the base was taken over by the Red Army, later passing to the GDR's Volksarmee, and remained operational until 1990. The **Historisch-Technisches Informationszentrum** (Tues–Sun 9am–4/6pm; DM6/€3), housed in the control bunker of the research station's red-brick power station, documents the base's wartime role, somewhat disingenuously advertising itself as the "Birthplace of Space Travel" – a claim founded on von Braun's subsequent career in the United States as chief designer of the Apollo rocket that put man on the moon, and on the fact that the October 1942 launch was the first time a flying object had left the earth's atmosphere.

Zinnowitz and Koserow

Leaving all this and heading southeast brings you to a string of seaside towns. First up after rejoining the main road, and connected by bus and train to Wolgast and Peenemünde, is **ZINNOWITZ**, Usedom's largest resort, which has a two-kilometre-long beach and a wide promenade. Many of its grandiose-looking **hotels** were converted into factory and trade-union holiday centres during the GDR period, but those currently open to the general public include *Kastaninehof*, Ahlbecker Str. 14 (☎03 83 77/49 30; ④), *Dünenschloss*, Neue Sandstr. 27 (☎03 83 77/7 90; ⑤), *Asgard*, Dünenestr. 20 (☎03 83 77/46 70; ⑦), and *Parkhotel Am Glienberg*, Glienbergweg 10 (☎03 83 77/7

20, *www.parkhotel-am-glienberg.de*; ⑦). **Private rooms** (①–③) can be booked at the **tourist office** (June–Sept Mon–Fri 9am–6pm, Sat 10am–2/3pm, Sun 10am–3pm; rest of year closed Sun; ☎03 83 77/49 20, fax 4 22 29, *www.zinnowitz.de*) at Neue Sandstr. 30. There's a **campsite**, *Pommernland* (☎03 83 77/4 03 48), just off the main road on the northern edge of town.

KOSEROW lies a few kilometres to the southeast of Kinnowitz. At first sight this village of modern houses straggling along the road seems to have little to offer. However, beyond the pine-covered slope rising above it is a wonderful stretch of sandy beach backed by low cliffs. If you're contemplating spending any time on Usedom, Koserow makes an excellent base; there's virtually nothing to see here, but the beach (nudist for substantial stretches) has a delightfully secluded feel, and the volume of visitors, though heavy, is not unbearable. The **tourist office** (June & Sept Mon–Fri 9am–6pm, Sat 9am–noon; July & Aug Mon–Fri 9am–6pm, Sat 9am–noon, Sun 9am–noon; reduced hours the rest of the year; ☎03 83 75/2 04 15, fax 2 04 17, *www.koserow.de*) at Hauptstr. 34 can book **private rooms** (①–②). Other options include a **pension**, *Herkules*, Karlstr. 9 (☎03 83 75/2 01 43; ⑤), and a **hotel**, *Hanse-Kogge*, Hauptstr. 22 (☎03 83 75/26 00; ⑥). There's also a handy **campsite** at Hauptstr. 15 (☎03 83 75/3 59). For **eating and drinking** try *Kelch's*, Karlstr. 9, which does decent fish dishes. At the other end of town, at the foot of the sixty-metre Streckelsberg (Usedom's highest elevation), is *Zum Streckelberg,* Meinholdstr. 25, good for a post-beach ice cream or beer.

Bansin

BANSIN, a short distance to the southeast, is very much a family holiday destination with an excellent, but inevitably crowded, sandy beach. There's otherwise not much to detain you, though Seestrasse, the town's main drag, running from station to beach, is lined by impressive turn-of-the-century houses in brilliant white with wrought-iron balconies. The street terminates at a small square with a clock which marks the main entrance to the beach.

The **tourist office** (April–Oct Mon–Fri 9am–5/6pm, Sat & Sun 10am–1/3pm; Nov–March Mon–Fri 9am–4pm, Sat & Sun 10am–noon/1pm; ☎03 83 78/4 70 50, fax 47 05 15, *www.bansin.de*) is in the Haus des Gastes on Strandpromenade. As well as **private rooms** (①–③), there are plenty of **hotels**, including *Villa Ingeborg*, Bergstr. 25–26 (☎03 83 78/2 92 47; ④), *Admiral*, Strandpromenade 36 (☎0 38 78/6 60; ⑦), *Zur Post*, Seestr. 5 (☎03 83 78/5 60; ⑦), and *Strandhotel Atlantic*, Strandpromenade 18 (☎03 83 78/6 05; ⑧). The **restaurants** of these hotels are the best places for full meals.

Heringsdorf

The most attractive of the Kaiserbäder triumvirate is **HERINGSDORF**, which retains something of its prewar atmosphere to complement its near-impeccable looks. Described by Baedeker as "the most fashionable of the Baltic sea-bathing places", Heringsdorf is the oldest resort on Usedom and at one time enjoyed international fame, attracting aristocratic and wealthy holiday-makers from all over Europe, despite its rather unprepossessing name – "Herring Village" – a leftover from its origins as a small fishing port.

Its central square, **Platz des Friedens**, is disfigured by an enormous residential/shopping complex, but elsewhere the town's architecture is mostly in the familiar Baltic-resort style of abundant white facades and attractive balconies. The new **Seebrücke** is the longest in Germany, its imposing dimensions being a direct tribute to its celebrated predecessor, which was demolished by the Communists. Heading west, the **Strandpromenade**, decked out with well-regimented flowerbeds, leads past the **Kunstpavillon**, an odd structure looking like a futurist bandstand enclosed by glass, that plays host to temporary art exhibitions.

At the western end of Strandpromenade, a sharp left into Strandstrasse, followed by a right turn, leads you into Maxim-Gorki-Strasse. Here, at no. 13, is the **Maxim-Gorki-Gedenkstätte** (daily 9am–noon & 1–4pm; DM2/€1), a small museum devoted to Maxim Gorky and the time he spent in Heringsdorf in 1922. It's housed in the former *Pension Irmgard*, where the author stayed, a period in which he wrote the autobiographical volume *My Universities*. Returning to Platz des Friedens via Badstrasse and Kulmstrasse offers a chance to appreciate Heringsdorf at its best; quiet leafy streets straggle up a hill, flanked by small villas with flaking facades set in little gardens.

The **tourist office** (April–Oct Mon–Fri 9am–5/6pm, Sat & Sun 10am–1/3pm; Nov–March Mon–Fri 9am–4pm, Sat & Sun 10am–noon; ☎03 83 78/24 51, fax 24 54, *www.heringsdorf.de*) is at Kulmstr. 33. There are plenty of **private rooms** (①–③). Most **hotels** are of high quality and consequently expensive; among the most attractive are *Wald und See*, Rudolf-Breitscheid-Str. 8 (☎03 83 78/3 14 16; ⑥), *Pommerscher Hof*, Seestr. 41 (☎0 3 83 78/610; ⑦), *Strandhotel Ostseeblick*, Kulmstr. 28 (☎03 83 78/5 40; ⑦), and *Oasis*, Puschkinstr. 10 (☎03 83 78/26 50; ⑦–⑨). All these hotels have **restaurants**; other possibilities for eating and drinking are *Zur Klause*, Strandstr. 6, which does a reasonable selection of inexpensive dishes, and *Terrassencafé*, Kulmstr. 29, which has a good sea view.

Ahlbeck

AHLBECK, which follows on closely from Heringsdorf, is another good-looking town with some ornate villas and grand hotels, and there's a pleasant promenade and sandy beach. Its **Seebrücke**, which is graced with four corner towers, is by far the most picturesque on the island. At the far eastern end of town is the border with Poland, around which is an informal market with plenty of inexpensive goods on offer from Polish traders.

The **tourist office** (April–Oct Mon–Fri 9am–5/6pm, Sat & Sun 10am–1/3pm; Nov–March Mon–Fri 9am–4pm, Sat & Sun 10am–noon; ☎03 83 78/2 44 97, fax 2 44 18) is at Dünenstr. 45. There's the usual supply of **private rooms** (①–③) and plenty of **hotels**, particularly at the upper end of the market. Among the best are *Seeperle*, Dünenstr. 38 (☎03 83 78/25 50; ⑥), *Ostseehotel*, Dünenstr. 41 (☎03 83 78/6 00; ⑦), *Villa Auguste Viktoria*, Bismarckstr. 1 (☎03 83 78/24 10; ⑦), *Strandhotel*, Dünenstr. 19 (☎0 38 78/5 20; ⑦), *Ostende*, Dünenstr. 24 (☎03 83 78/5 10; ⑦), and *Ahlbecker Hof*, Dünenstr. 47 (☎03 83 78/6 20; ⑧–⑨). All of these have fine **restaurants**.

travel details

Trains

Bergen to: Lauterbach (via Putbus; 9 daily; 40min); Lietzow (for Binz; 12 daily; 10min); Sassnitz (10 daily; 45min).

Greifswald to: Berlin (13 daily; 2hr 30min); Stralsund (frequent; 25min); Wolgast (11 daily; 25min).

Lietzow to: Binz (12 daily; 20min).

Neubrandenburg to: Berlin (10 daily; 2hr 10min); Güstrow (8 daily; 2hr); Neustrelitz (17 daily; 45min); Stralsund (10 daily; 1hr 50min).

Neustrelitz to: Berlin (frequent; 1hr 30min); Neubrandenburg (frequent; 45min); Rostock (13 daily; 1hr 40min); Stralsund (10 daily; 2hr 30min).

Putbus to: Göhren (Rasender Roland narrow-gauge line via Binz, Jagdschloss Granitz, Sellin and Baabe; 9 daily; 1hr 10min).

Rostock to: Bad Doberan (16 daily; 25min); Berlin (12 daily; 3hr); Güstrow (frequent; 40min); Magdeburg (9 daily; 4hr); Neubrandenburg (13 daily; 2hr 30min); Neustrelitz (13 daily; 2hr); Sassnitz (15 daily; 1hr); Schwerin (12 daily; 1hr 15min); Stralsund (15 daily; 1hr 20min);

Warnemünde (frequent; 25min); Wismar (11 daily; 1hr 45min).

Sassnitz to: Rostock (via Bergen: 2 daily; 3hr 30min); Stralsund (via Bergen: 11 daily; 1hr).

Schwerin to: Berlin (7 daily; 3hr); Bützow (for Güstrow; 12 daily; 1hr); Ludwigslust (hourly; 30min); Magdeburg (6 daily; 3hr); Rostock (15 daily; 2hr 30min); Wismar (11 daily; 1hr).

Stralsund to: Berlin (17 daily; 4hr 30min); Neubrandenburg (10 daily; 1hr 50min); Neustrelitz (7 daily; 2hr 30min); Rostock (15 daily; 1hr 20min); Sassnitz (10 daily; 1hr 10min).

Wismar to: Rostock (12 daily; 1hr 45min); Schwerin (12 daily; 1hr).

Wolgast to: Ahlbeck (12 daily; 1hr 30min); Züssow (for Greifswald and Stralsund; 10 daily; 30min).

CHAPTER NINE

BERLIN AND BRANDENBURG

Berlin is something of a weather-vane of modern European history, yet its rise to national prominence was a long and slow process. Founded in the thirteenth century, it is little more than a third of the age of Cologne or Augsburg. It did not achieve the early growth and economic development of other medieval foundations, such as Hamburg, Lübeck, Frankfurt or Nürnberg; it was not even the capital of a substantial feudal duchy, as Munich and Stuttgart were. Instead, it belatedly became the capital of **Brandenburg**, a marshland territory at the very eastern extremity of the Holy Roman Empire. This province was founded as a Margravate, or frontier district, by **Albert the Bear** (Albrecht der Bär) in 1157 from land bequeathed to him by Pribislav-Heinrich, a Slav king who had converted to Christianity.

In 1411, Brandenburg was made a hereditary possession of the **Hohenzollern** family, and four years later the Margravate was raised to the status of an Electorate of the Holy Roman Empire. However, for all the dynasty's lofty ambitions, Berlin remained little more than a village until the seventeenth century, by which time it had still not played any significant part in German history. The first important step towards a grander role came in 1618, when Elector Johann Sigismund inherited the Baltic duchy of **Prussia**, and merged it with his family's heartlands to form the new state of Brandenburg-Prussia, which quickly established itself as an expansionist miltary force on the European stage. Named after the exterminated tribe that had inhabited it in the early Middle Ages, Prussia lay outside the Holy Roman Empire and thus was not subject to any of its rules. In 1701, Elector Friedrich III circumvented one of the most important of these – the ban on the assumption of royal status – by crowning himself King Friedrich I of Prussia. Thereafter, the Hohenzollern state, although still centred on Berlin, went under the misleading designation of Prussia. It became ever more

ACCOMMODATION PRICE CODES

All the pensions and hotels in this book have been graded according to the following price categories. The codes quoted are for the cheapest available double room, except for establishments which have rooms costing widely different rates, when the most expensive price is given as well. Exact charges are given for youth hostels; in the case of the official DJH (HI) establishments, this is the lowest available rate. When two figures are quoted for these hostels, the first applies to juniors (ie under 27 years of age), the second to seniors (27 and above).

① less than DM60/€30
② DM60–79/€30–39
③ DM80–99/€40–49

④ DM100–124/€50–62
⑤ DM125–149/€63–74
⑥ DM150–199/€75–99

⑦ DM200–249/€100–124
⑧ DM250–299/€125–149
⑨ upwards of DM300/€150

predatory in its policy of territorial acquisition, eventually stretching all the way west to the French border.

When the Prussians finally forged a unified Germany for the first time ever in 1871, Berlin was the only possible choice for the new role of **national capital**. Hitler intended to take this a stage further by transforming it into a world capital named Germania. Instead, the city found itself **partitioned** among the victors after World War II, and quickly became a microcosm of the Cold War era. While the Soviet-occupied eastern sector – which included the historic city centre – duly became the capital of the rump state that was the GDR, the larger part of the city was left as the stranded enclave of West Berlin, a place with an ambiguous status (it was never formally merged into the Federal Republic) propped up by vast outside subsidies, with a declining population only kept in check by an influx of immigrants (principally from Turkey), draft-dodgers and seekers of alternative lifestyles. From 1961, the two parts of the city were physically separated by the **Berlin Wall**, the first frontier in history built to keep its own citizens in, rather than an invader out.

After the Wall fell in 1989, Berlin's status as capital of Germany (which it had never officially lost) was reconfirmed. However, it faced determined opposition from Bonn in its desire to re-establish itself as the national **seat of government**. Although Berlin eventually emerged triumphant from this argument, it was only able to gain the major share of the spoils, as it was decided to keep several key ministries and other public bodies in Bonn. This was a calculated measure designed to ensure that Berlin – with its deeply tainted historical record – does not become too powerful and dominant within Germany. Thus, the vast rebuilding and redevelopment that the city is currently undergoing is something of a delicate balance. There is a clear need to increase the population (which had fallen by more than a million from its prewar level), and to create a city that is a worthy capital of Europe's most powerful nation, yet at the same time to ensure that it does not become a direct German counterpart of London or Paris.

One unintended consequence of Berlin's postwar division is that it has belatedly become a city-state, with the rest of the old Margravate of Brandenburg now an entirely separate Land of the Federal Republic. Though there were hopes that the two Länder would eventually merge, that now seems a distant prospect at best, having been flatly rejected by the latter in a referendum. **Potsdam**, Brandenburg's present-day capital, forms a virtually seamless whole with Berlin. Once the great cultural showpiece of the Prussian kingdom, it has wonderful palaces and parks which easily outdo those of its larger neighbour. Elsewhere in the province are time-warped towns such as **Neuruppin**, **Rheinsberg** and **Brandenburg** itself. There is also a highly distinctive scenic area, the water-strewn **Spreewald**.

BERLIN

The division of **BERLIN** into zones of occupation in 1945, although seemingly arbitrary, followed exisiting local government boundaries, and the dual profile which emerged was by no means solely a product of the Cold War. In his famous interwar collection of short stories, *Goodbye to Berlin*, Christopher Isherwood wrote:

> *Berlin is a city with two centres – the cluster of expensive hotels, bars, cinemas, shops around the Memorial Church, a sparkling nucleus of light, like a sham diamond, in the shabby twilight of the town; and the self-conscious civic centre of buildings around the Unter den Linden, carefully arranged.*

The latter, the political and cultural core of the Imperial German capital, duly became the heart of East Berlin and of the GDR, while the former quickly adapted itself to the makeshift role of city centre. Because of the decades of division, the reunited city found itself with two of almost everything, but the rationalization process has already reduced the duplication quite markedly, and will eliminate it almost entirely over the course of the next decade.

Although never a conventionally beautiful city, Berlin has much fine architecture, as well as an extraordinary spread of **museums** which collectively rank among the very richest on the planet. It also has a wide range of **bars** and **restaurants**, a vibrant **nightlife** and strong traditions in the **performing arts**. Because it occupies a vast geographical area, one interrupted by a plethora of parks, forests and lakes, Berlin is not a place that is appreciated easily or quickly.

Arrival and information

Most scheduled and charter **flights** arrive at **Tegel** airport, from where buses #X9 and #109 run every five to fifteen minutes to Bahnhof Zoo (see below), while JetExpressBus TXL goes to Unter den Linden. Alternatively, take bus #109 to Jakob-Kaiser-Platz or bus #128 to Walter Schreiber Platz and transfer to the U-Bahn system

ACCOMMODATION

7 Adler
16 Alpenland
   Altberlin am
24 Potsdamer Platz
33 Am Anhalter Bahnhof
27 Am Lehniner Platz
12 art'otel Berlin Mitte
   artist Hotelpension
5 Die Loge
28 Bogota
31 Brandenburger Hof
35 Bregenz
22 Charlot
8 Circus Hostel
21 Columbus
17 Cortina
30 Dittberner
10 Forum
36 Frauenhotel Artemisia
29 Funk
34 Grossbeerenkeller
21 Imperator

13 Intermezzo
14 Jugendgästehaus am Zoo
19 Jugendgästehause Berlin
37 Jugendgästehaus Central
   Jugendgästehause
25 Deutsche Schreberjugend
1 Kastanienhof
18 Kempinski Hotel Bristol
20 Kettler
15 Luisenhof
6 Märkischer Hof
26 Meineke
3 Merkur
2 Meyer's Hotel
4 Novalis
32 Pariser Eck
39 Schöneberg
9 Sorat Hotel Spreebogen
23 Sylter Hof Berlin
38 Transit
11 Unter den Linden

(the bus ticket is valid for the U-Bahn journey; opposite). Taxis cost DM30–40/ €15–20 to Bahnhof Zoo, covering the distance in about half the time. Berlin's second airport, **Schönefeld**, lies just beyond the southeastern edge of the city, and mainly serves eastern Europe and the Middle and Far East. Take bus #171 from the terminal building to S-Bahnhof Flughafen Schönefeld, from where S-Bahn #9 provides a direct link to the city centre. **Tempelhof**, the closest airport to the city centre, to which it is linked by bus #119, is used mainly by German domestic carriers and scheduled flights by very small operators. The Platz der Luftbrücke U-Bahn station is just outside.

Trains from western European destinations generally stop at both **Bahnhof Zoologischer Garten** (shortened to **Bahnhof Zoo**, or **Zoo Station**) and **Ostbahnhof**; some also halt at Wannsee or Spandau. **Bahnhof Lichtenberg**, which is easily accessible by S-Bahn from all other stations, is the main terminus for trains to and from eastern Europe. The **Lehrter Stadtbahnhof** is currently being developed as Berlin's first-ever central rail terminal, though it is unlikely to be operational before 2005. International **buses** and those from other German cities mostly use the **Zentraler Omnibus Bahnhof** or **ZOB** on Masurenallee near the Funkturm. Bus #149 and U-Bahn #2 from Kaiserdamm link it with the centre.

The headquarters of the **tourist office**, Berlin Tourismus Marketing, at Am Karlsbad 11 (information ☎0 30/01 90 75 40 40, reservations 25 00 25, fax 25 00 24 24, *www.btm.de* or *www.berlin-info.de*) is not open to the public, but deals with all written and telephone enquiries. Its main branch for personal callers is in the Europa-Center on Budapester Strasse (Mon–Sat 8.30am–8.30pm, Sun 10am–6.30pm); there's another in the south wing of the Brandenburger Tor (daily 9.30am–6pm) and smaller information points in the KaDeWe department store, Tauentzienstr. 24–24 (Mon–Fri 9.30am–8pm, Sat 9am–4pm), and at Tegel airport (daily 5am–10.30pm). The very helpful **EurAide** office in the hallway of Bahnhof Zoo (daily: June–Sept 8am–noon & 1–6pm; Oct–May 8am–noon & 1–4.30pm; *www.euraide.de*) exists specifically to dispense help and advice to English-speaking travellers.

Berlin has two essential **listings magazines** – *Tip* (DM4.70/€2.35; *www.tip*) and *Zitty* (DM4/€2; *www.zitty.de*) – which come out on alternate weeks. A free magazine, *030*, is another useful source on nightlife, with good club, music and film listings. Berlin's diverse arts scene is well covered by *Artery Berlin* (DM3.50/€1.75), a monthly English/German publication. Another monthly, the *Berlin Programm* (DM3/€1.50; *www.berlin-programm.de*), has more condensed listings, alongside information on opening times, and national and international train, bus and plane timetables.

Getting around

Berlin is a large, sprawling city, and sooner or later you'll need to use its efficient, if expensive, public transport system. The fastest part of this is the **S-Bahn**, which shares with mainline trains the distinctive elevated tracks which cut right through the heart of the city. There are also some underground stretches in the centre, while in the outskirts it runs at ground level. As its name implies, the **U-Bahn**, whose stations are generally much closer together, is predominantly an underground system, but also has some elevated track. Free coloured **maps** of Berlin's **Schnellbahnnetz** (the entire network of S-Bahn, U-Bahn and mainline trains) can be picked up from the cubicle outside Bahnhof Zoo, and from the kiosks on station platforms. **Buses** cover most of the areas which cannot be reached by train, and also provide handy linkages: #100 and #200, which run between Bahnhof Zoo and Alexanderplatz, are particularly useful for sightseeing purposes. Eastern Berlin's **tram** network survives from prewar days, and has been extensively modernized in the last few years.

Tickets and passes

Tickets are valid on all forms of transport within the system, including regional mainline trains, and can be bought from the orange-coloured machines at the entrances to all U- and S-Bahn stations, and from manned kiosks at the larger stations. The network is divided into three tariff zones which are colour-coded on maps, and journeys which entail travelling in all three are slightly more expensive than others.

Single tickets (*Normaltarif*) cost DM3.90/€1.95 and are valid for two hours, though journeys of up to three train stops or six bus stops are covered by a *Kurzstrecke*, or short-trip ticket, priced DM2.50/€1.25). It's usually better to invest in a **day-ticket** (*Tageskarte*), costing DM7.80/€3.90 for two zones, DM8.50/€4.25 for three zones. You can also buy a **seven-day ticket** (*Sieben-Tage-Karte*) for DM42–52/€21–26, depending on the zones through which you travel, or a **monthly ticket** (*Monatskarte* or *Umweltkarte*) for DM105–130/€52.50–65. A **premium monthly ticket** (*Umweltkarte Premium*), costing DM120–150/€60–75, allows unlimited travel through all three tariff zones and for one adult and up to three children to travel with you free after 8pm, all day Saturday and Sunday and on public holidays. Note that, although monthly tickets offer considerable savings, their validity commences on the first of each month, not on the date of purchase. Another option, available from tourist offices and hotels as well as ticket kiosks, is the **Berlin Welcome Card**, which costs DM35/€17.50 for three days, giving unlimited travel across the system for an adult and up to three children, plus reduced entry to many museums and attractions.

Accommodation

Berlin offers a wide variety of **accommodation**, at widely varying costs. At the lowest end of the scale, there are several campsites and a wide choice of youth hostels, most of which are privately run. There are also several bed and breakfast agencies offering private rooms at moderate prices, while the long-stay specialists, the *Mitwohnzentralen*, can almost always locate a suitable room or flat, generally for a minimum stay of a week, at reasonably short notice. The number and quality of hotels in the city have increased considerably in the last few years, and finding a free room is a bit easier than it used to be, particularly in the middle and upper ranges. Nevertheless, it's advisable to book well ahead, particularly during trade shows or for special events such as the Love Parade (early July), the Berlin Marathon (first Sunday in October) and the Berlin International Film Festival (February).

Hotels and pensions

Although a clutch of new establishments have opened on the eastern side of the city in the past couple of years, moderate and budget hotels and pensions continue to be found in much greater numbers in the west. Even if it is not so well endowed as it was before unification, the area around Kurfürstendamm and Savignyplatz remains a fruitful hunting ground for reasonably priced rooms.

Mitte

Adler, Friedrichstr. 124 (☎0 30/2 82 93 52, *www.berliner-zimmerreservierung.de*). This pension, which has spartan but bearable rooms, is about as central as you're likely to get at the price. ②.

artist Hotelpension Die Loge, Friedrichstr. 115 (☎ & fax 0 30/2 80 75 13, *die-loge@t-online.de*). Small pension in a prewar building just steps away from the Scheunenviertel. ④.

art'otel Berlin Mitte, Wallstr. 70–73 (☎0 30/24 06 20, fax 24 06 22 22, *www.arthotel.de*). Prestigious designer hotel, partly in the historic Ermelerhaus, partly in a modern extension. It has two restaurants – the expensive *Im Ermelerhaus* (evenings only, closed Sun & Mon) and the quite moderately priced *Raabe-Diele*. ⑧–⑨.

Forum, Alexanderplatz (☎0 30/2 38 90, fax 23 89 43 05, *forumberlin@interconti.com*). A big, ugly block dominating Alexanderplatz, but its one thousand en-suite rooms are pleasant enough in a bland way, with unbeatable views over the city. It also has a decent restaurant. ⑦–⑨.

Intermezzo, An der Kolonnade 14 (☎0 30/22 48 90 96, *www.hotelintermezzo.de*). Very simply furnished and inexpensive pension for women, within walking distance of Potsdamer Platz and Unter den Linden. Breakfast not included. ②.

Kastanienhof, Kastanienallee 65–66 (☎0 30/44 30 50, fax 44 30 51 11). Well-appointed rooms at reasonable prices, and handy for the nightlife of nearby Prenzlauer Berg. ⑥–⑧.

Luisenhof, Köpenicker Str. 92 (☎0 30/2 41 59 06, fax 2 79 29 83). This nineteenth-century coaching company building has converted into a very tastefully appointed hotel and restaurant. ⑧–⑨.

Märkischer Hof, Linienstr. 133 (☎0 30/2 82 71 55, fax 2 82 71 55; *hotelmh@t-online.de*). Centrally located hotel with restaurant, a stone's throw from Oranienburger Strasse and within easy strolling distance of Unter den Linden. ⑤.

Merkur, Torstr. 156 (☎0 30/2 82 82 97, fax 2 82 77 65). Pension within easy walking distance of city-centre attractions and local nightlife. ④–⑥.

Novalis, Novalisstr. 5 (☎0 30/2 82 40 08, fax 2 83 37 81). Quiet, small hotel not far from Oranienburger Tor S-Bahn station. ⑥.

Unter den Linden, Unter den Linden 14 (☎0 30/23 81 10, fax 23 81 11 00). A survivor of the GDR, simply furnished but comfortable mid-range place at the junction of Friedrichstrasse and Unter den Linden. ⑥.

The West End

Alpenland, Carmerstr. 8 (☎0 30/3 12 39 70, fax 3 13 84 44). Unpretentious hotel with a restaurant serving local specialities. It has both basic and en-suite rooms and thus attracts a fairly broad clientele. ④–⑥.

Altberlin am Potsdamer Platz, Potsdamer Str. 67 (☎0 30/2 61 29 99, fax 2 61 46 37). Large pension just a few minutes' walk from the Tiergarten museums, recently refurbished with *fin-de-siècle* trappings. ⑥.

Am Lehniner Platz, Damaschkestr. 4 (☎0 30/3 23 51 00, fax 3 23 93 59). Tiny and economical pension in the middle of an area that's lively at night. ④.

Bogota, Schlüterstr. 45 (☎0 30/8 81 50 01, fax 88 33 58 87, *hotelbogota@t-online.de*). Pleasant large hotel in a nineteenth-century buiding, offering a choice of rooms of varying degrees of luxury. ④–⑥.

Brandenburger Hof, Eislebener Str. 14 (☎0 30/21 40 50, fax 21 40 51 00). A member of the Relais & Chateaux group, this occupies a grand Wilhelmine palace with Bauhaus interior decoration. One of its restaurants, *Die Quadriga* (weekday evenings only) ranks among Berlin's top gourmet addresses. ⑨.

Bregenz, Bregenzer Str. 5 (☎0 30/8 81 43 07). Small pension ten minutes' walk from Kurfürstendamm. ④.

Charlot, Giesebrechtstr. 17 (☎0 30/3 23 40 51, fax 3 24 08 19). Efficient and friendly hotel in a neatly restored Jungendstil building; it's near Adenauerplatz and good value for this area. ④.

Columbus, Meinekestr. 5, (☎ & fax 0 30/8 81 50 61). Quiet and comfortable pension in a tenement just off the Ku'damm. ④–⑥.

Cortina, Kantstr. 140 (☎0 30/3 13 90 59, fax 3 13 73 96). Reasonable rooms in an ideal location for exploring the West End and Savignyplatz. ④.

Dittberner, Wielandstr. 26 (☎0 30/8 84 69 50, fax 8 85 40 46). Old-fashioned finery in this large, comfortable pension; all rooms have en-suite facilities. ⑥.

Frauenhotel Artemisia, Brandenburgische Str. 18 (☎0 30/8 73 89 05, *Frauenhotel-Berlin@t-online.de*). A popular women-only hotel, with a roof garden and exhibitions. Fills up quickly, so book well in advance. ⑥.

Funk, Fasanenstr. 69 (☎0 30/8 82 71 93, fax 8 83 33 29). Approached via a marble stairway with antique lift, this pension just off Ku'damm still preserves many of the design features of the time when it was the home of Danish silent-movie star Asta Nielsen. It has some basic rooms, as well as more luxurious ones which are all individually furnished. ④–⑥.

Imperator, Meinekestr. 5 (☎0 30/8 81 41 81, fax 8 85 19 19). Good-value, intimate hotel, situated in the same building as *Columbus*. Rooms are spacious and stylishly decorated. ⑤–⑦.

Kempinski Hotel Bristol, Kurfürstendamm 27 (☎0 30/88 43 40, fax 8 83 60 75, *www.kempinski.com*). For many years this ranked as the city's most famous luxury hotel, and, despite being challenged by a host of newcomers, still ranks among the very best. It has two prestigious restaurants – the very expensive *Kempinski Grill* (closed Mon) and the more reasonably priced *Kempinski-Eck*. ⑨.

Kettler, Bleibtreustr. 19 (☎0 30/8 83 49 49). A tiny and charming pension on a lively, café-lined street. ④.

Meineke, Meinekestr. 10 (☎0 30/8 86 7 81 90). Old-fashioned, typical Berlin hotel, with an amiable atmosphere, a minute's walk from the Ku'damm. ⑥.

Pariser Eck, Pariser Str. 19 (☎0 30/8 81 21 45, fax 8 83 63 35). Adequate pension in a pleasant, leafy backstreet; it's a ten-minute walk from the Ku'damm and has some classy cafés nearby. ④.

Sorat Hotel Spreebogen, Alt-Moabit 99 (☎0 30/39 92 00, fax 39 92 09 99, *www.sorat-hotels.com*). A gleaming modern hotel directly overlooking the Spree, offering very high overall standards. It also has a fine if expensive restaurant (closed Sun evenings). ⑥.

Sylter Hof Berlin, Kurfürstenstr. 116 (☎0 30/2 12 00, fax 2 14 28 26, *info@sylterhof-berlin.de*). Well-appointed large hotel close to Wittenbergplatz and the Ku'damm. It also has a good restaurant (closed Sun). ⑧–⑨.

Elsewhere in the city

Am Anhalter Bahnhof, Stresemannstr. 36 (☎0 30/2 51 03 42, fax 2 51 48 97, *www.hotel-anhalter-bahnhof.de*). This hotel has a good location south of Potsdamer Platz and the Kulturforum, although don't expect peace and quiet, as it faces a major thoroughfare. ④–⑥.

Am Weissen See, Parkstr. 78 (☎0 30/9 78 90 10). Tiny pension out in leafy Weissensee, but with reasonable public transport access to the centre. ④.

Brauhaus in Spandau, Neuendorfer Str. 1 (☎0 30/3 53 90 70, fax 35 39 07 11). A charming, if slightly kitsch, small hotel in Spandau, at the far western edge of the city. Its Hausbrauerei brews a *Pils* and various seasonal brews, serves moderately priced meals, often features live music and has a beer garden. ⑥.

Greifswald, Greifswalder Str. 211 (☎0 30/4 42 78 88, fax 4 42 78 98, *www.hotel-greifswald.de*). A casual, familiar atmosphere reigns in this pension, tucked away in a quiet rear courtyard not far from Alexanderplatz and the nightlife in Prenzlauer Berg. ⑥.

Grossbeerenkeller, Grossbeerenstr. 90 (☎0 30/7 42 49 84). Family-run pension that's better known for its ancient bar of the same name in the cellar. ⑥.

Haus Acksel, Belforter Str. 21 (☎0 30/44 33 76 33, fax 4 41 61 16). Small hotel with flair in the midst of the lively Prenzlauer Berg scene. Breakfast not included. ③.

Meyer's Hotel, Metzer Str. 26 (☎0 30/44 01 40). A new hotel, simply but tastefully furnished, in the quiet courtyard of a renovated late nineteenth-century building. ⑨.

Schöneberg, Hauptstr. 135 (☎0 30/7 80 96 60, fax 7 88 10 20, *www.hotel-schoeneberg.de*). Pleasant hotel bordering leafy suburban Friedenau to the south of the city centre. Has some no-smoking rooms. ⑨–⑦.

Transit, Hagelberger Str. 53–54 (☎0 30/7 89 04 70, fax 78 90 47 77, *welcome@Hotel-Transit.de*). Converted factory in a quiet courtyard that attracts a young clientele. ④.

Mitwohnzentralen and Bed and Breakfast

bed & breakfast privatzimmervermittlung, Mehringdamm 66, Kreuzberg (☎0 30/78 91 39 71, fax 78 91 39 72, *www.bed-and-breakfast.de*). Part of a national chain, offering B&B accommodation ranging from simple to luxurious. Mon–Fri 9am–6pm.

Bed & Breakfast in Berlin, Belforter Str. 21, Prenzlauer Berg (☎0 30/44 05 05 82, fax 44 05 05 83, *www.bed-and-breakfast-berlin.de*). Single and double rooms starting at about DM65/€32.50 a night. Mon–Fri 9am–6.30pm.

Fine + Mine, Neue Schönhauser Str. 20, Mitte (☎0 30/2 35 51 20, fax 23 55 12 12, *www.fineandmine.de*). International *Mitwohnzentrale* offering long- and short-term rooms and apartments. English spoken. Mon–Fri 10am–6pm.

Home Company, Joachimstaler Str. 17, Charlottenburg (☎0 30/1 94 45, fax 8 82 66 94, *www.homecompany.de*). A long-established *Mitwohnzentrale*, and thus offering lots of listings. Mon–Fri 9am–6pm, Sat 11am–2pm.

Mitwohnagentur Streicher, Immanuelkirchstr. 8, Prenzlauer Berg (☎0 30/4 41 66 22, fax 4 41 66 23). Helpful agency with rooms and apartments all over the eastern part of the city. English spoken. Mon–Fri 11am–2pm & 3pm–6pm.

Wohnagentur am Mehringdamm, Mehringdamm 66, Kreuzberg (☎0 30/7 86 20 03, fax 7 85 06 14, *www.wohnung-berlin.de*). This *Mitwohnzentrale* has a particularly good selection of rooms and apartments in Kreuzberg and Schöneberg. Mon–Fri 10am–6pm.

Zimmervermittlung Dentler (☎0 30/5 66 78 40, *www.zimmer-berlin.de*). Rooms for short-term stays all over the city, starting from about DM60/€30, without breakfast. No visitable office, but phonecalls are answered Mon–Fri 8am–6pm.

Youth hostels

Berlin's three **DJH youth hostels**, which all require a current HI card, are used extensively by school and sporting parties, and are frequently booked out: consequently it's always advisable to phone ahead to check about vacancies. Beds at all three can be reserved two weeks or more in advance of a visit via the special phone and fax numbers of the hostel at Kluckstr. 3 (☎0 30/2 62 30 24, fax 2 62 95 29). Requests at shorter notice should be directed to a specific hostel. In general, the ever-growing number of **privately run hostels** are run in a more informal fashion, dispensing with traditional hostelling practices such as surcharges for older guests, lock-outs and curfews.

Circus Hostel, Rosa-Luxemburg-Str. 39–41, Mitte (☎0 30/28 39 14 33, fax 28 39 14 84, *www.circus-berlin.de*). Plain but light-filled rooms with high ceilings and big windows, located near the attractions of the east; take U-Bahn #2 to Rosa-Luxemburg-Strasse. Dorm beds DM25/€12.50, singles DM50/€25, doubles DM80/€40. Breakfast is not included.

Globetrotter Hostel Odyssee, Grünberger Str. 23, Friedrichshain (☎0 30/29 00 00 81, *www.hostel-berlin.de*). Imaginatively decorated rooms, a young staff and hard by the emerging scene in Friedrichshain; take U-Bahn #5 to Frankfurter Tor. Dorm beds DM24/€12, doubles DM72/€36.

Jugendgästehaus am Wannsee, Badeweg 1, Zehlendorf (☎0 30/8 03 20 35, fax 8 03 59 08, *jh-wannsee@jugendherberge.de*). This DJH hostel is very pleasantly located, with plenty of woodland walks on hand near the beaches of the Wannsee lakes, but it's far from the city centre. Take S-Bahn #1 or #7 to Nikolassee. DM34/€17 or DM42/€21.

Jugendgästehaus am Zoo, Hardenbergerstr. 9a, Charlottenburg (☎0 30/3 12 94 10). Extremely popular, thanks to an excellent western location. Singles DM47/€23.50, doubles DM85/€42.50, quads DM140/€70.

Jugendgästehaus Berlin, Kluckstr. 3, Tiergarten (☎0 30/2 61 10 97, fax 2 65 03 83, *jh-berlin@jugendherberge.de*). This is the most conveniently located of the DJH hostels, being just a few minutes' walk from the Kulturforum and Potsdamer Platz. Take U-Bahn #1 to Kurfürstenstrasse, or bus #129 to the Gedenkstätte Deutscher Widerstand stop. DM34/€17 or DM42/€21.

Jugendgästehaus Central, Nikolsburger Str. 2–4, Wilmersdorf (☎0 30/8 73 01 88, *www.jugendgaestehaus-central.de*). Institutional and plain, but clean and very well located on a quiet street south of Bahnhof Zoo; take U-Bahn #9 to Güntzelstrasse. Beds in two- to six-bed rooms for DM39/€19.50 including breakfast, DM43/€21.50 half-board and DM45/€22.50 full board.

Jugendgästehaus Deutsche Schreberjugend, Franz-Künstler-Str. 4–10, Kreuzberg (☎0 30/6 15 10 07). Offers easy access to hot spots in both eastern and western areas of the city; take U-Bahn #1 to Hallesches Tor. Beds in doubles or triples DM38.50/€19.25, including breakfast.

Jugendherberge Ernst Reuter, Hermsdorfer Damm 48–50, Reinickendorf (☎0 30/4 04 16 10, fax 4 04 59 72, *jh-ernst-reuter@jugendherberge.de*). Situated so far from town that it's the least popular of the DJH hostels and therefore least likely to fill up in summer, despite being by far the smallest. Take U-Bahn #6 to Alt-Tegel, then bus #125 towards Frohnau. DM28/€14 or DM35/€17.50.

Lette'm Sleep 7, Lettestr. 7, Prenzlauer Berg (☎0 30/44 73 36 23, fax 44 73 36 25, *www.backpackers.de*). Spare but comfortable rooms just steps away from the nightlife of Prenzlauer Berg; take U-Bahn #2 to Eberswalder Strasse. Beds in small dorms DM30/€15, doubles DM90/€45. Breakfast is not included.

Campsites

None of Berlin's **campsites** is close to the centre: each requires time and effort to reach. All are inexpensive – prices are a uniform DM7.40/€3.70 per tent plus DM9.90/€4.95 per person per night – and well run.

Am Krossinsee, Wernsdorfer Str. 38, Köpenick (☎0 30/6 75 86 87, fax 6 75 91 50). The only site in the erstwhile GDR, pleasantly located in the woods and with easy access to local lakes. There are also bungalows for rent. Take S-Bahn #8 to Grünau, then tram #68 to Schmöckwitz, then bus #463.

Dreilinden, Albrechts-Teerofen, Wannsee (☎0 30/8 05 12 01). Close to the former border in the southwest of the city, this is only really an option if you have your own wheels. By public transport, take U-Bahn #1 to Oskar-Helene-Heim, then bus #118 bus (direction Kohlhasenbrück) to Katchenweg; from there it's a 2.5-kilometre walk. Closed mid-Oct to mid-March.

Gatow, Kladower Damm 207–213, Spandau (☎ & fax 0 30/3 65 43 40, 36 80 84 92). New camping ground not far from the long-established Kladow site. Take U-Bahn #7 to Rathaus Spandau, then bus #134 or #X34 to Flugplatz Gatow.

International Jugendcamp, Ziekowstrasse 161, Reinickendorf (☎0 30/4 33 86 40). Basic facilities only open to those aged between 14 and 26; a sleeping mat and blanket are provided. Take U-Bahn #6 to Alt-Tegel then bus #222 (direction Alt-Lübars) to Titusweg. Open June 26 to Aug 31 only. DM10/€5 per night, breakfast DM3/€1.50.

Kladow, Krampnitzer Weg 111–117, Spandau (☎0 30/3 65 27 97, fax 3 65 12 54). Friendly campsite on the western side of the Havelsee, with the best facilities of all the campsites, including a free crèche, bar, restaurant and shop. Six-week maximum stay. Take U-Bahn #7 to Rathaus Spandau, followed by bus #134 to Alt-Kladow, and finally bus #234, alighting when it swings off Krampnitzer Weg; the site is then a short walk to the west.

Kohlhasenbrück, Neue Kreis Str. 36, Zehlendorf (☎ & fax 0 30/8 05 17 37). Has all the basic facilities, plus a children's playground and a restaurant. Take S-Bahn #7 to Greibnitzsee, from where it's a ten-minute walk. Closed mid-Oct to mid-March.

The eastern centre

Berlin's historic heart is the **Mitte** district, which the Hohenzollern rulers developed into the showpiece centre of their capital. Throughout the life of the GDR, it enacted a similar role, though this was one for which it was decidedly ill suited, not only from a practical point of view – it protruded so far to the west that it was bounded on three sides by sectors held by the British and Americans – but also because of the ever-present imperialistic and militaristic associations. The Communist authorities never really came to grips with this conundrum. They demolished some key buildings which were seen as embarrassments, notably the huge royal palace, the Stadtschloss, but restored and redeployed others; they also tried to give parts of the district a "socialist" face by erecting grand new public buildings as well as identikit apartment blocks and huge offices for the state bureaucracy. A great deal of restoration work on the historic buildings has been carried out since the *Wende*, but the debate about how far this should go still rages on. There is a vocal lobby in favour of re-creating as much as possible of the imperial legacy, and erasing the visual reminders of the GDR, and an equally determined body of opinion which wants to retain the present mix.

The central axis

Since the fall of the Wall, the broad boulevard of **Unter den Linden** ("Beneath the Lime Trees") has been restored to its position as the city's main east–west artery. Originally a bridle path linking the Stadtschloss with the hunting grounds of the

EASTERN CENTRAL BERLIN

Volksbühne
MOLLSTR.
WADZECKSTR.
OTTO-BRAUN-STR.
KARL-LIEBKNECHT-STR.
WEYDINGERSTR.
KARL-MARX-ALLEE
KARL-LIEBKNECHT-STR.
ALEXANDERSTR.
Jannowitzbrücke
S U
HOLZMARKTSTR.
BRÜCKENSTR.
ROSA-LUXEMBURG-STR.
MAX-BEER-STR.
MÜNZSTR.
Weinmeisterstr. U
ROSENTHALER STR.
HACKESCHE HÖFE
Hackescher Markt S
Alexanderplatz S
ALEXANDERPLATZ
U S
Fernsehturm
Marienkirche
Alte Nationalgalerie
ROCHSTR.
LITTENSTR.
Rotes Rathaus
Klosterstr. U
STRALAUER STR.
ROLANDUFER
INSELSTR.
Märkisches Museum
Märkisches Museum U
Neue Synagoge
ORANIENBURGER STR.
Monbijou Park
Pergamonmuseum
Neues Museum
Altes Museum
Dom
SPANDAUER STR.
KARL-LIEBKNECHT-STR.
HEILIGGEISTSTR.
NIKOLAIVIERTEL
MÜHLENDAMM
BREITE STR.
Neue Marstall
Fischerinsel
GERTRAUDENSTR.
NEUE GRÜNSTR.
Spittelmarkt U
SEYDELSTR.
Bodemuseum
Zeughaus
Kronprinzenpalais
Palast der Republik
Schinkel-Museum
Staatsrat
NIEDERWALLSTR.
KURSTR.
0   200 m
Maxim-Gorki-Theater
Staatsoper
Neue Wache
Humboldt-Universität
ROSENTHALER STR.
UNTER DEN LINDEN
OBERWALLSTR.
WERDERSTR.
St Hedwigs-Kathedrale
FRANZÖSISCHE STR.
Schauspielhaus
Hausvogteiplatz U
JERUSALEMER STR.
Admiralspalast
Staatsbibliothek
Deutsche Guggenheim
Königliche Bibliothek
Hugenottenmuseum &
Französische Friedrichstadtkirche
Französische Str.
Deutsche Kirche
Stadtmitte U
FRIEDRICHSTR.
GLINKASTR.
CHARLOTTENSTR.
LEIPZIGER STR.
KRONENSTR.
KRAUSENSTR.
SCHÜTZENSTR.
N
Friedrichstr. S
U
Friedrichstr.
DOROTHEENSTR.
Berliner Ensemble
REINHARDTSTR.
SCHIFFBAUERDAMM
Deutsches Theater
LUISENSTR.
Bundestag (Reichstag)
Brandenburger Tor
PARISER PLATZ
Unter den Linden S
Russische Botschaft
BEHRENSTR.
WILHELMSTR.
MAUERSTR.
TAUBENSTR.
Mohrenstr. U
Museum für Kommunikation
Former course of the Wall
Haus am Checkpoint Charlie
JÄGERSTR.
Site of Führerbunker
WILHELMSTR.
Topographie des Terrors
Martin-Gropius-Bau
Luftfahrtsministerium
ZIMMERSTR.
NIEDERKIRCHNER STR.
STRESEMANNSTR.
Potsdamer Platz U S
POTSDAMER PLATZ
EBERTSTR.
STR. DES 17 JUNI
Sowjetisches Ehrenmal
River Spree
Former course of the Wall
PAUL-LÖBE-STR.
LEIPZIGER STR.

THE BERLIN WALL

After the war, Berlin was split between its conquerors, as Stalin, Roosevelt and Churchill had agreed at Yalta. Each sector was administered by the relevant country, and was supposed to exist peacefully with its neighbour under a unified city council. But almost from the outset, antagonism between the Soviet and other sectors was high. Only three years after the war ended the Soviet forces closed down the land access corridors to the city from the Federal Republic, in what became known as the **Berlin Blockade**. It was successfully overcome by a massive Western **airlift** of food and supplies that lasted nearly a year. This, followed by the 1953 uprising, large-scale cross-border emigration (between 1949 and 1961, over three million East Germans – almost a fifth of the population – fled to the Federal Republic) and innumerable "incidents", led to the building of what was known in the GDR as the "Anti-Fascist Protection Wall".

Erected overnight on August 13, 1961, to cordon off the Soviet sector and corral the British, American and French sectors of the city some 200km inside the GDR, the Wall underlined the city's schizophrenia and frenzy and marked the city's *raison d'être* – the "stabilization of the impossible". The Wall followed the Soviet sector boundary implacably, cutting through houses, across squares and rivers with its own cool illogicality. One oddity about the Wall was that it was actually built a few metres inside GDR territory; the West Berlin authorities therefore had little control over the **graffiti** that covered it like a static New York subway car. The Wall was an ever-changing mixture of colours and slogans, with the occasional burst of bitterness: "*My friends are dying behind you*"; humour: "*Last one out please turn off the lights*"; "*Why not jump over and join the Party?*"; and stupidity: "*We shoulda nuked 'em in '45*".

Over the years, around two hundred people were **killed** endeavouring to cross the Wall. Initial escape attempts were straightforward and often successful – hollowing out furniture, ramming checkpoint barriers and simple disguise brought many people over. However, the authorities quickly rose to the challenge, and would-be escapees became more resourceful, digging tunnels, constructing gliders and one-man submarines, building their own hot-air balloons. By the time the Wall came down, every escape method conceivable seemed to have been used – even down to passing through Checkpoint Charlie in the stomach of a pantomime cow – and those who were desperate to get out of the GDR preferred the long wait and complications of applying to leave officially to the risk of being gunned down by a border guard. The guards, known as *Grepos*, were under instructions to shoot anyone attempting to scale the Wall, and to shoot accurately: any guard suspected of deliberately missing was court-martialled, and his family could expect severe harassment from the authorities.

Late in 1989 the East German government, spurred by Gorbachev's *glasnost* and confronted by a tense domestic climate, realized it could keep the impossible stable no longer. To an initially disbelieving and then jubilant Europe, travel restrictions for GDR citizens were lifted on November 9, 1989 – effectively, the Wall had ceased to matter, and pictures of Berliners, East and West, hacking away at the detested symbol filled newspapers and TV bulletins around the world. Today, especially in the city centre, it's often hard to tell exactly where the Wall ran: odd juxtapositions of dereliction against modernity, or an unexpected swathe of erstwhile "death strip" are in many cases all that's left of one of the most hated borders the world has ever known. The few sections of the Wall that remain are protected from the tourist chisels by barbed wire and by its official status as an "historic landmark".

Tiergarten, it was beautified after the Thirty Years War by the planting of lime and walnut trees. These were axed by the Nazis to allow room for processions, but replanted by the Communists. The street is closed off at its western end by **Pariser Platz**, a square which was the most exclusive address in the city in the 1930s. Devastated by bombs in World War II, it was left as a closed-off wasteland during the GDR era, but has since been the subject of a highly exclusive redevelopment programme.

The Brandenburger Tor

Although restoration work means that it is likely to be covered by a shroud until early 2002, the **Brandenburger Tor** (Brandenburg Gate) at the far end of Pariser Platz is so dense with meaning and historical significance that it is the obvious place to begin a tour of Berlin. Built as a city gate-cum-triumphal arch between 1788 and 1791, it was designed by Carl Gotthard Langhans on the model of the Propylaea, the entrance to the Acropolis, thereby symbolizing Berlin's self-image as a modern Athens. Guarding as it did the city's grandest thoroughfare, the gate became the backdrop for many epic events. It was where Prussian troops celebrated their great victories of 1815 and 1871, which saw the demise of Napoleon and the belated achievement of Germany unity. Nazi storm troopers held torch-lit marches there to celebrate Hitler's assumption of power in 1933, while on August 13, 1961, it was the first place to be sealed off as construction work on the Berlin Wall began. Inaccessible to the general public for 28 years, it was the scene of the first euphoric chipping-away at the hated frontier on November 9, 1989, and of the gargantuan celebrations on the last day of the same year and on October 3 the following year, when the two Germanies were united. These events were captured on film and broadcast to a huge international audience, with the result that the Brandenburger Tor is now one of the world's most famous monuments.

Atop the gate is the **Quadriga**, a huge bronze group of the goddess Nike on her chariot by Johann Gottfried Schadow. Napoleon removed this to Paris as war booty in 1806. On its return, Karl Friedrich Schinkel transformed Nike into a personification of German Victory, bearing the new military decoration, the Iron Cross, and wearing a wreath with the Prussian eagle. These attributes were removed when the Quadriga was recast in the 1950s, but reinstated during repair work carried out following damage sustained in the 1989 celebrations.

From Pariser Platz to the Humboldt-Universität

On the first block of the south side of Unter den Linden is the **Russische Botschaft** (Russian Embassy), the pivotal building of the GDR-era diplomatic quarter. Constructed for the use of Soviet diplomats in the early 1950s, it mixes the debased form of Neoclassicism favoured by Stalin with some Cubist elements, which are most evident in the lantern tower. At the end of the following block is the intersection with another of Berlin's most important axes, the 3.5-kilometre-long **Friedrichstrasse**, which was formerly partitioned by the Wall.

Further on, at the corner of Unter den Linden and Charlottenstrasse, is the **Deutsche Guggenheim Berlin** (during exhibitions daily 11am–8pm; *www.deutsche-guggenheim-berlin.de*; DM8/€4, free Mon). Housed in a former bank building, it's a far cry from the institution's architectural landmarks in New York and Bilbao, though its modest galleries are well laid out and effectively lit. There are no permanent displays, but a rolling exhibition programme (separated by periods of closure) featuring the work of leading contemporary artists from around the world.

Standing in the middle of Unter den Linden a little further to the east is the **Denkmal Friedrich II**, a large mid-nineteenth-century memorial to the most influential and successful of the Prussian kings, Frederick the Great. An updated version of the bronze equestrian monuments of classical antiquity, it was sculpted by Christian Daniel Rauch, Schadow's most talented follower. On the pyramid-shaped base are scenes from the monarch's life and portraits of members of his entourage: soldiers and statesmen feature most prominently, with writers and artists confined to the short end below the rear of the horse.

To the north is the main building of the **Humboldt-Universität**, which was originally the town palace of Frederick the Great's younger brother Heinrich. It was designed in a classically inspired Baroque style by the court architect **Georg Wenzeslaus von Knobelsdorff**, one of the key figures in the development of both

Berlin and Potsdam, and erected by the Dutchman Johann Boumann. On either side of the entrance are marble statues of the university's founder, the educational reformer Wilhelm von Humboldt, and his even more influential younger brother Alexander, a natural scientist best known for his Latin American explorations and researches into the cosmos. The institution's most internationally celebrated teachers were Jacob and Wilhelm Grimm, who ended their careers there, preoccupied with compiling the definitive German dictionary, the *Deutsches Wörtebuch*, which was finally completed a century after their deaths. Alumni of the university include Karl Marx, Friedrich Engels and Karl Liebknecht.

August-Bebel-Platz

Directly opposite is a spacious square, built between 1741 and 1780, which is the only completed part of Frederick the Great's ambitious plans for a latter-day Roman forum. The GDR authorities renamed it **August-Bebel-Platz** in honour of the joint founder of the Social Democratic Workers' Party; the old name of Opernplatz has not been reinstated, largely because of its association with the infamous **book-burning ceremony** of May 10, 1933. Under the supervision of Hitler's propaganda minister, Joseph Goebbels, thousands of publications went up in smoke, including the works of "un-German" authors such as Erich Maria Remarque, Heinrich and Thomas Mann, Stefan Zweig and Erich Kästner (who was an eye-witness to the event), along with volumes by countless foreign writers, H.G. Wells and Ernest Hemingway among them. The most fitting comment on this episode was made with accidental foresight by the poet Heinrich Heine during the previous century: "Where they start by burning books, they'll end by burning people." A recent and intriguing memorial to the book-burning incorporates these words on a plaque: go to the middle of the square and look through the glass pane set in the ground.

Opernplatz took its name from the first part to be built, the **Staatsoper** on the east side, whose porticoed facade faces Unter den Linden. Knobelsdorff used Palladio's famous Villa Rotonda near Vicenza as his model, giving the structure four separate projections. As a freestanding theatre, rather than a part of a complex, it was a revolutionary design for its day. Another unusual feature was that the stalls of the auditorium could be raised and the space used for balls and receptions. Although it has been damaged by fire and bombs and subject to internal modifications, it remains a magnificent performance space.

Knobelsdorff also drew up the plans for **St-Hedwigs-Kathedrale** on the south side of the square. This was the first permanent place of worship for Berlin's Roman Catholic minority, whose numbers had swelled as a result of Prussia's annexation of most of the erstwhile Austrian province of Silesia, and hard-nosed political calculations were behind the decision of Frederick the Great – an agnostic member of a staunchly Protestant dynasty – to sponsor its construction. According to tradition, the king wanted the church to be in the shape of an upturned teacup with handle. However, it is more likely that he was having his own private joke by choosing the pagan Roman Pantheon as a model, particularly as its centralized plan is totally unsuited to the Catholic liturgy. Badly damaged in World War II, the building was belatedly restored with a modernized interior.

On the western side of the square is the **Königliche Bibliothek**, a former royal library known colloquially as the **Kommode** ("chest of drawers") because of its curvaceous Baroque facade. Its design was a plagiarization of an unbuilt plan made half a century earlier by Fischer von Erlach for an extension to the Hofburg in Vienna. As such, it was another conscious piece of one-upmanship on the Austrians, and in particular on Frederick's bitter rival, Empress Maria Theresia. Its contents were transferred shortly before World War I to the new Staatsbibliothek on the opposite side of Unter den Linden, and it is now used by the university.

The eastern end of Unter den Linden

Immediately east of the Staatsoper are four statues by Christian Daniel Rauch to the Prussian heroes of the Napoleonic wars: Gerhard von Scharnhorst is on Unter den Linden itself, August von Gneisenau, Gebhard von Blücher and Ludwig Yorck von Wartenburg are on the lawn behind. Beyond is the **Kronprinzenpalais** (10am–6pm, closed Wed; *www.dhm.de*; free), a Baroque palace which was once the Berlin residence of the Prussian crown princes. It is currently hosting temporary exhibitions of the Deutsches Historisches Museum (see below), and will continue to do so until the latter reopens in its permanent home. There are future plans for it to serve as a national portrait gallery, which will make it the first such institution outside the English-speaking world.

Another key element in the ambitious plans for the reordering of Berlin's state-owned museums over the next decade (see also box opposite) is the vacant plot alongside the Kronprinzenpalais, which was formerly occupied by the strikingly angular **Bauakademie**, the masterpiece of **Karl Friedrich Schinkel**, the nineteenth-century architect who gave Berlin its distinctive Neoclassical stamp. Damaged in the war but eminently restorable, this was razed by the Communists and replaced by the ugly Aussenministerium (Foreign Ministry), which was in turn bulldozed in 1995. At some point in the next decade, the Bauakademie is likely to make a phoenix-like return to its original location to serve as an architectural museum.

Diagonally opposite the Kronprinzenpalais is one of Schinkel's most famous surviving buildings, the **Neue Wache**. It was built between 1816 and 1818 to serve both as a guardhouse and a memorial to the Prussian casualties of the Napoleonic wars, and the architecture mirrors both functions, having the plan of a Roman fort, with the addition of a Doric portico to impart a sense of spirituality. In 1931 it was converted into a memorial to the military dead of World War I, and it was rededicated in 1957 to the "Victims of Fascism and Militarism". Since 1993, it has been the official national memorial to "Victims of War and Tyranny".

Just east of the Neue Wache is one of Berlin's greatest buildings, the old arsenal or **Zeughaus**, whose size and splendour reflect the dominant role played by militarism in the rise and expansion of Brandenburg-Prussia. The state's predilection for warfare goes some way to explaining why this Baroque masterpiece was built by outsiders: it was begun in 1695 by the Dutchman Johann Arnold Nering, who was succeeded three years later by a partnership of Jean de Bodt, a Huguenot refugee from France, and Andreas Schlüter, a native of the city-state of Danzig (now Gdańsk). Adorning the ground floor of the exterior are 76 keystones of military trophies carved in the workshop of de Bodt and Schlüter. The attic decoration, consisting of huge groups of Mars and Minerva with their entourages, plus a further 44 trophies, is the work of another Huguenot, Guillaume Hulot. For all their splendour, these sculptures are eclipsed by those of the **Schlüterhof**, the wonderfully harmonious inner courtyard. Here Schlüter carved the 22 keystones known as the *Dying Warriors*, a deeply moving and highly individualistic pictorial record of death. In a highly controversial move inspired by the success of his Louvre pyramid in Paris, the Chinese-American architect Ieoh Ming Pei has been commissioned to cover the Schlüterhof with a glass roof. He has also been entrusted with adding an extension to the Zeughaus, which will be used for temporary exhibitions of the **Deutsches Historisches Museum** (*www.dhm.de*). The institution's permanent collection, illustrating the entire history of the German nation, is due to go on display in Zeughaus itself in 2002, and the interior of the building will be closed to the public until then.

The southern districts

Friedrichswerder, the first Baroque extension to the medieval city of Berlin, lay to the southeast of Unter den Linden. Another Baroque suburb, the much larger Friedrichstadt, was later laid out to a grid pattern immediately to the west.

THE STAATLICHE MUSEEN BERLIN

Despite heavy wartime losses, the state-run museums of Berlin, the **Staatliche Museen Berlin**, rival those of London (which are concentrated in a far smaller number of much larger institutions) for the right to be regarded as the finest and most wide-ranging in the world. During the decades of German division, their treasures were split between East and West Berlin, and the task of putting them back together again is a massive undertaking which is unlikely to be completed before 2010. Until then, entire collections are liable to be closed for several years at a time – though they are not necessarily wholly inaccessible to the public, often being sent abroad as touring exhibitions.

For the forseeable future, the museums will be spread among four main locations – Museumsinsel, the Tiergarten Kulturforum, Charlottenburg and Dahlem – though other institutions can be found elsewhere. In the longer term, it is hoped that most will be concentrated in Museumsinsel and the area around, with a key role being given to the Stadtschloss, if it is indeed rebuilt. A **day-ticket** valid for all the Staatlichen Museen (the Web address for all sites is: *www.smb.spk-berlin.de*) costs DM8/€4; this is the same as the entry charge to most of the individual museums, though the fee for others is DM4/€2. There's also a **three-day ticket**, costing DM16/€8. Entry to all the museums is **free** on the first Sunday of each month.

Friedrichswerder

Nothing remains of the original settlement of Friedrichswerder, but its name lives on in the **Friedrichswerdersche Kirche**, which was built by Schinkel to face its market square, Werderscher Markt. Although nowadays an open space, the area was then a dense and irregular network of streets, and the great architect decided that a church in a medieval idiom would dovetail far better with these surroundings than one in the Neoclassical style he favoured for most of his Berlin commissions. Because of the restricted site, he eventually settled on a design modelled on the chapels of the Oxbridge colleges, though the twin towers, each of two identical superimposed cubes, are in his own very personal vein. Now deconsecrated, the church is designated the **Schinkel-Museum** (Tues–Sun 10am–6pm; DM4/€2; *www.smb.spk-berlin.de*). The gallery running all the way round the interior displays documents and plans from throughout Schinkel's career; the main body of the church houses works by the leading Neoclassical sculptors of Berlin, notably Schadow, Rauch and Christian Friedrich Tieck.

Gendarmenmarkt

Friedrichstadt was centred on **Gendarmenmarkt**, the most imposing square in Berlin. It was first laid out in the late seventeenth century, but only given its showpiece character a hundred years later, when Frederick the Great decided to turn it into a monumental public square on the model of the Piazza del Popolo in Rome.

Dominating the square are two churches, which at first sight seem identical, but are actually very different. On the north side is the **Französische Friedrichstadtkirche**, which was built at the very beginning of the eighteenth century for the influential Huguenot community, whose descendants still worship there. One of their number, the military engineer Jean Louis Cayart, was entrusted with the design, which he modelled on the destroyed "mother church" of the Huguenots at Charenton in the Paris outskirts. In 1780, Frederick the Great commissioned one of his favourite architects, Carl von Gontard, to build an extension, known as the **Turmbau**, to the plain and severe original building. This grandiose domed edifice is crowned by a cupola and fronted by three great pedimented porticos, which are profusely decorated with sculptures made from designs provided by two artists who successively served as directors of Berlin's academy, Daniel Nikolaus Chodowiecki and Christian Bernard Rode. It completely dwarfs the actual church, and the curious dual structure has popularly if inaccurately been known as the Französischer Dom (French Cathedral) ever since. Within the Turmbau is the **Huguenotten-Museum** (Tues–Sat noon–5pm, Sun 11am–5pm; DM3/€1.50), which details the history of the Huguenots in France and Brandenburg. A longish spiral stairway leads to the **viewing platform** (daily 10am–6pm; DM3/€1.50) below the tower, which offers good views over the surrounding construction sites.

At the southern end of the square is the **Deutsche Kirche**, otherwise known as the Deutscher Dom, which served the German and Swiss citizens of Friedrichstadt of both Lutheran and Calvinist persuasions. The church itself was built to a more elaborate design than its neighbour, but Gontard's Turmbau is an almost identical twin, differing only in the subjects of its sculptural programme. Nothing remains of the original interior, which is now used to house a permanent exhibition, **Fragen an die Deutsche Geschichte** (Questions on German History; Tues–Sun 10am–6pm; free). This contains some good archive footage, but the German-only text suffers from the common fault of trying to smooth over the most calamitous events in the nation's not-so-distant past.

Between the two churches is the **Schauspielhaus**, which Schinkel built as a replacement for Langhans's fire-damaged Nationaltheater, whose Doric portico, approached by a broad flight of steps, was incorporated into the new design. Schinkel himself designed the pediment reliefs, while the bronze sculptural group of Apollo in his chariot on the roof of the building was made by Rauch. A month after its opening, the playhouse premiered Weber's *Der Freischütz*, which is nowadays generally considered the first opera of the Romantic era. Since 1984, the building has been used as a concert hall rather than a theatre, and is generally known as the **Konzerthaus Berlin** (see p.864). Outside stands the **Schillerdenkmal**, an elaborate commemorative monument, unveiled in 1871, to the Enlightenment-era poet and playwright Friedrich Schiller.

Leipziger Strasse and Potsdamer Platz

From Gendarmenmarkt, Charlottenstrasse continues south to **Leipziger Strasse**, once a main Berlin shopping street running from Alexanderplatz to Potsdamer Platz. Towards the western end of the street, at the junction with Mauerstrasse, is the former imperial postal ministry, now the home of the **Museum für Kommunikation Berlin** (Tues–Fri 9am–5pm, Sat & Sun 11am–7pm; *www.museumsstiftung.de*; free). Its exhibits include a complete set of German stamps from 1849 to the present day, as well as equipment ranging from a prototype of the telephone to the latest computers.

At the next junction to the west, Leipziger Strasse bisects Toleranzstrasse, the prewar Wilhelmstrasse, which was then the heart of the government quarter. Here can be found one of the most prominent surviving buildings of the Third Reich, the **Luftfahrtministerium** (Air Ministry). Its head, Hermann Göring, rashly promised Berliners that not a single bomb would fall on the city during the war, declaring that, should his confidence prove misplaced, he would change his name to the Jewish one of Meyer. In the GDR era, the building served as the Haus der Ministerien (House of Ministries), and afterwards became the headquarters of the Treuhandanstalt, the agency responsible for the privatization of the state-owned enterprises which made up the greater part of its economy. In its latest incarnation, it houses the Bundesministerium der Finanzen (Federal Finance Ministry).

Beyond, Leipziger Strasse runs into **Potsdamer Platz**, which was once the heart of Berlin and a prewar hub of the city's transport and nightlife. It was made desolate by wartime bombing, and for fifty years after the war remained wasteland: the Berlin Wall wrapped around it and incorporated the once busy quarter into the death strip, ensuring that it would remain undeveloped. The dismantling of the Wall produced one of Europe's most valuable lots, and for several years the area, sporting a thicket of huge cranes and dominated by the near-incessant sound of building, was touted as "Europe's largest construction site".

Daimler-Benz and the Sony Corporation each bought a huge chunk of Potsdamer Platz and have built large commercial complexes. Designed by Renzo Piano, the **Daimler-Benz-Areal** includes several restaurants, a stage theatre, a movie multiplex, a 3-D big-screen movie theatre and the obligatory shopping mall. **Sony-Center**, designed by Helmut Jahn, consists of several similar glass-sheathed buildings grouped around a capacious, tented circular courtyard. It has the same touristy pulls as its neighbour, but also includes a couple of additional attractions. The **Filmmuseum Berlin** (Tues–Sun 10am–6pm; *www.filmmuseum-berlin.de*; DM12/€6) contains an excellent presentation on the history of the movies, concentrating on the German film industry, and also has a large collection, occupying three rooms, of Marlene Dietrich artefacts. The **Music Box** (Mon–Thurs & Sun 10am–8pm, Fri & Sat 10am–10pm; DM15/€7.50) is an interactive mutimedia museum allowing visitors to experience music in various ways: you can, for example, "conduct" an orchestral peformance, or experiment with different drum sounds.

East of Potsdamer Platz, and just above An der Kolonnade, is the site of the **Führerbunker**, where Hitler spent his last days, issuing meaningless orders as the Battle of Berlin raged above. Here he married Eva Braun and wrote his final testament: he personally was responsible for nothing; he had been betrayed by the German people, who had proved unequal to his leadership and deserved the future he could now envisage ahead of them. On April 30, 1945, he shot himself, and his body was hurriedly burned by loyal officers. In the wrangles after the war to prove his death, the Soviet Army apparently came up with Hitler's teeth, which they had managed to retrieve from the charred remains and have verified by the Führer's dentist.

Fischerinsel and Museumsinsel

Immediately east of Unter den Linden is a large island in the Spree. This was the site of the fishing village of Cölln, which was first documented in 1237 – seven years before the earliest mention of Berlin, which was originally confined to the east bank of the river. Although the two communities built a joint town hall in 1307, they did not formally merge until 1432. Cölln's name subsequently fell into disuse, though the larger part of the island is known as **Fischerinsel** (Fishermen's Island) in its honour. The peninsula at the northern end, once a swampy marsh, is called **Museumsinsel** (Museum Island), as it is entirely given over to a group of publicly owned museums housed in suitably grand and palatial premises.

Schlossplatz and the Lustgarten

At the eastern end of Unter den Linden, the Spree is spanned by the Schinkel-designed **Schlossbrücke**. The eight marble groups which line the sides of the bridge each depict a goddess of war accompanied by a mythological hero, while the wrought-iron railings are in the shapes of dolphins and tritons. The bridge leads to **Schlossplatz**, formerly the site of the **Stadtschloss**, the old imperial palace. Renaissance by origin, it was given a Baroque facelift by Schlüter, and further modified by Schinkel and his pupil August Stüler, who added a huge Neoclassical dome. Despite strong international protests, the huge bomb-damaged building which had for centuries been Berlin's pivotal landmark was razed by the Communist authorities in 1950–51.

Two decades later, the vacant space was occupied by the **Palast der Republik**, which housed a number of different institutions, including the Volkskammer, the GDR's rubber-stamp parliament. Irreverently dubbed Ballast der Republik, this huge angular building with its bronzed, reflecting windows was completed in less than a thousand days, and was a source of great pride to the Honecker regime. The hundreds of lamps hanging from the ceiling of the main foyer gave rise to its other nickname, Erichs Lampenladen – "Erich's lamp shop". Shortly before reunification an asbestos hazard was discovered in the building, and following October 3, 1990, it was closed indefinitely. Today it stands empty, an unmissable reminder of the old GDR and an embarrassment to the new Germany, its future – indeed its existence – uncertain. Its demolition would certainly be necessary were the Stadtschloss to be rebuilt, as now seems quite likely, despite widespread public concerns about the astronomical costs of such an ambitious undertaking.

The one significant surviving portion of the Stadtschloss is the portal incorporated in the 1960s **Staatsrat** on the south side of the square. It was designed by Schlüter and decorated with carvings by Balthasar Permoser, the leading sculptor of Baroque Dresden, but its preservation had nothing to do with its artistic qualities, rather with the fact that it incorporates the balcony from which Karl Liebknecht proclaimed the establishment of the German Socialist Republic in 1918. Immediately to the east of the Staatsrat is the **Neue Marstall**, a derivative late nineteenth-century construction built to house the hundreds of royal coaches and horses. Nowadays, it is used for exhibitions, especially those related to large public projects.

Immediately north of Schlossplatz is the **Lustgarten**, which, since 1999, has reverted to its original function as a garden, having served a variety of functions in the interim, such as being a parade ground for the Prussian army and the setting for some of the Nazis' most infamous propaganda exercises. At its far northern end is the **Granitschale**, which was made in 1830 from a single Ice Age granite block. Formerly considered one of the wonders of Berlin, it is now perpetually vandalized and popularly referred to as the "soup bowl".

On the eastern side of the Lustgarten stands the hulking pile of the **Dom**, which was built in a pompous Historicist style at the beginning of the twentieth century as a replacement for its much smaller predecessor, a Baroque building remodelled by Schinkel. Ever since it was built, it has attracted widespread scorn, though it's worth going inside to see the magnificent **tombs** of the Hohenzollern dynasty in the transepts. The most notable are of Elector Johann Cicero, which was cast in one of the great foundries of the Renaissance era, the Vischer workshop in Nürnberg, and those of King Friedrich I and Queen Sophie Charlotte, both of which were carved by Schlüter. An aerial view of the vast central space can be obtained from the balcony at the top of the **Kaiserliches Treppenhaus**, a marble staircase at the southwest corner of the building.

The Altes Museum and the Neues Museum

Museumsinsel is deemed to begin at the **Altes Museum** (Tues–Sun 10am–6pm; *www.smb.spk-berlin.de*; DM8/€4), which faces the northern end of the Lustgarten. It's arguably Schinkel's most impressive surviving work, and is the most extreme example of his classicizing manner, though its carefully calculated architectonic relationship to the previous Dom and the Stadtschloss is now irretrievably lost. Externally, the main feature is the **portico** of eighteen Ionic columns, which gives the impression that the building is of one storey rather than two. Inside, the central **rotunda**, with its elaborate coffered vault, offers a modern variant of the Pantheon in Rome, and has been returned to its original function as a showcase for classical sculptures.

Until late 2001, a selection from the holdings of the Alte Nationalgalerie (see p.832) will be on display upstairs, while part of the **Antikensammlung**, a collection of Greek and Roman antiquities, is exhibited in the ground-floor rooms around the rotunda. In due course, the latter will take over the whole building, which is scheduled to be closed altogether between 2002 and 2005 in order that the necessary reconstruction work be carried out. The Antikensammlung houses the finest collection of **Attic vases** in the world, the star piece being the so-called *Berlin Amphora*, which dates from around 490BC and came from Vulci in Etruria. It also has a distinguished array of Greek sculpture, ranging from Cycladic figures of 2200 BC to first-century clay statuettes found in the excavations of Priene in Asia Minor. Of special note is one of the few surviving life-sized bronzes of the antique era, the third-century BC *Praying Boy* from Rhodes. There are also two treasury chambers, devoted to gold and silver arefacts respectively. The former includes a Scythian horde of around 800 BC excavated at Vetterfelde in south-eastern Brandenburg; the latter is dominated by the **Hildesheim Silver**, a trove of seventy magnificent pieces from the first century BC and the first century AD, named after the Lower Saxon city where they were found.

As Berlin's collections grew too large for the Altes Museum, August Stüler was commissioned to build the **Neues Museum** (*www.smb.spk-berlin.de*) immediately to its rear. This was almost totally destroyed in World War II, and left as a ruin by the GDR authorities, but is now being rebuilt to plans by the London architect David Chipperfield. When complete (around 2008), it will once again house Berlin's famous Ägyptisches Museum, plus another collection which is likewise currently on display in Charlottenburg, the Museum für Vor- und Frühgeschichte.

The Pergamonmuseum

Immediately to the north is the **Pergamonmuseum** (Tues–Sun 10am–6pm; *www.smb.spk-berlin.de*; DM8/€4), a massive interwar structure in the style of a Babylonian temple. It was specially designed in order to display to best effect what are undoubtedly some of the most spectacular exhibits to be found in any museum anywhere in the world – a series of huge architectural showpieces unearthed by German archeologists from various ancient civilizations.

The museum is divided into three sections, the best known being the large-scale exhibits of the **Antikensammlung**. These are centred on a hall containing the structure which gives the museum its name, the **Pergamon Altar**, which formerly stood on the acropolis of the eponymous town in Asia Minor, the present-day Bergama in Turkey. Dating from 180 to 160 BC, it ranks as the supreme masterpiece of late Hellenistic art. In the centre of the hall is a conjectural full-scale reconstruction of the altar, while around the walls are the originals of its reliefs. The main **frieze**, the second largest monumental sculpture to have survived from ancient Greece, vividly depicts the battle between the giants and the gods, whose victory was achieved with the help of the mortal Hercules, father of Telephus, founder of Pergamon. Telephus's life is told in a smaller frieze in somewhat lower relief from a subsidiary altar. In the room to the north are more Greek architectural fragments, including the Temple of Athena from Pergamon, which predates the altar by a century. Dominating the Roman room to the south is the colossal Market Gate of Miletus; the Orpheus Mosaic comes from the same city.

The **Vorderasiatisches Museum**, also on the main floor, is laid out around the spectacular reconstruction, based on original excavated materials, of the parts of the fabulous **Palace of King Nebuchadnezzar II of Babylon**. Dating from around 600 BC, they are made from specially durable baked and glazed bricks. Although they look awesome, they are miniaturizations of the originals: the **Processional Way**, with its parade of lions set between geometric borders and rosette friezes, was six times longer and six times broader, while the **Ishtar Gate**, with its symbolic bulls and dragons, was not only taller but also no more than a front to a much larger structure. Parts of the facade of the **Throne Room**, which shows lions below highly stylized depictions of palm trees, are also on view. The smaller rooms contain many impressive artefacts excavated at other sites in the Near East, notably the Sumerian city of Uruk, the Assyrian courts of Nineveh and Nimrud, and King Darius of Persia's royal palace at Susa.

Pride of place in the **Museum für Islamisches Kunst** on the first floor goes to the exquisitely carved facade of an eighth-century caliph's palace from M'schatta in present-day Jordan, which was presented to Kaiser Wilhelm II by the Sultan of Turkey. Other highlights are the prayer niches from two thirteenth-century mosques, and a room with mixed Arab and Western decoration from the seventeenth-century house of a Christian merchant of Aleppo in Syria. There are also many small-scale exhibits from all over the Islamic world, including miniature paintings, carpets, ceramics, leather-work and wooden and ivory carvings.

The Bodemuseum and the Alte Nationalgalerie

At the northeastern tip of Museumsinsel is the **Bodemuseum** (*www.smb.spk-berlin.de*), housed in an intimidating, triangular-shaped neo-Baroque building. Before the war it was known as the Kaiser-Friedrich-Museum and contained the city's magnificent hold-ings of old master paintings; in the GDR era it was renamed in honour of a former direc-tor of the Berlin museums, Wilhlem Bode, and displayed the rumps of several divided collections. It is presently closed (probably until 2005) for structural repairs. When it reopens, it will house the reunited **Skulpturensammlung**, an excellent collection of sculpture particularly strong in the work of German masters of the fifteenth and six-teenth centuries, including major figures such as Nicolaus Gerhaert, Michel Erhart, Hans Multscher and Tilman Riemenschneider. Also finding a home here will be the **Museum für Spätantike und Byzantinische Kunst**, which has a wonderful range of artefacts from the pre-medieval eastern Mediterranean, including some notable sculp-tures from Constantinople and a monumental sixth-century mosaic from Ravenna.

Also closed at the time of writing, but due to reopen at the end of 2001, is the **Alte Nationalgalerie** (*www.smb.spk-berlin.de*), which stands just to the north of the Neues Museum and is likewise the work of Stüler, who offered a somewhat exaggerated re-interpretation of a Corinthian temple. It will house the nineteenth-century section of Berlin's state art collection, including the contents of the Galerie der Romantik in Charlottenburg (see p.847). Highlights from the later parts of its collection are cur-rently on display at the Altes Museum (see p.830). There's a fine group of works by the Berlin artist **Adolph Menzel**, ranging from detailed historical scenes of the life and times of Frederick the Great to *The Iron Rolling Mill*, a seminal documentary record of the dawn of the Industrial Age. Also of particular note is *The Story of Joseph*, an intact co-operative venture by the members of the **Nazarene Brotherhood**, which was paint-ed for the house of the German consul in Rome. The late Romantic artists Anselm Feuerbach and Hans von Marées are well represented, as is their Swiss counterpart, Arnold Böcklin. There are also a few works by Impressionist and Post-Impressionist artists, including examples of Monet, Degas and Van Gogh.

The medieval centre

The original settlement of Berlin lay on the east side of the Spree, immediately opposite Cölln. A few medieval buildings still stand as a reminder of the city's early life, but although some remain prominent landmarks they are engulfed by later surroundings, this being a part of the city which still bears strong visible evidence of the Communist years.

From Schlossplatz to Alexanderplatz

Karl-Liebknecht-Strasse, the axial link between Schlossplatz with Alexanderplatz, is in effect an eastern continuation of Unter den Linden. On its south side is the **Marx-Engels-Forum**, a small park with a lumpen bronze representation of the founders of Communism at its heart. Beyond, on the other side of Spandauer Strasse, is an open space on which stands the **Neptunbrunnen**, a large late nineteenth-century fountain showing the sea god surrounded by creatures from his kingdom. Across Rathausstrasse to the southeast is the **Rotes Rathaus**, the seat of the united Berlin city government since October 1991. It's a grand Historicist building of the 1860s, influ-enced by Italian, Flemish and North German medieval architecture. A terracotta frieze above the ground-floor windows illustrates the history of the city in 36 panels.

To the north of Neptunbrunnen is medieval Berlin's most significant surviving build-ing, the **Marienkirche**. It's a typical example of a Gothic hall church, begun in the mid-thirteenth century, but extensively rebuilt following a fire in 1380. The tower dates from the following century, except for the upper storeys, which were added at the end of the eighteenth century by Langhans. In the porch is a **frieze** of the Dance of Death, painted by an unknown artist soon after the plague of 1484. Among the notable furnishings in the main body of the church are a fifteenth-century bronze **font** resting on dragons; the **tomb** of Field Marshal Otto Christoph von Sparr, which was executed by the Antwerp sculptor Artus Quellinus while the subject was still alive; and the magnificent **pulpit** by Schlüter, which is exceptionally ornate by Protestant standards. The **organ** by the Baroque master Joachim Wagner is both visually and tonally splendid; recitals are normally given at 4.30pm on Saturdays.

Along with every other building in the vicinity, the Marienkirche is overshadowed by the gigantic TV tower, or **Fernsehturm** (daily: March–Oct 9am–1am; Nov–Feb 10am–midnight; *www.berlinerfernsehturm.de*; DM10/€5). This 365-metre transmitter is the second highest structure in Europe and dominates the eastern Berlin skyline like a displaced satellite sitting on top of a huge factory chimney. There's a tremendous **view** (40km on a rare clear day, although the summit is often shrouded in cloud) from the observation platform, which is reached by a very fast lift. Immediately above is the *Tele-Café*, which revolves on its own axis twice an hour. When the sun shines on the globe of the tower, the reflected light forms a cross visible even in western Berlin, much to the chagrin of the old GDR authorities and amusement of the locals, who dubbed it the "Pope's Revenge", or, in a sarcastic reference to the then dictator Walter Ulbricht, "St Walter".

To the east is the open space of **Alexanderplatz**, popularly known as "Alex". It acquired its present name after Czar Alexander I visited Berlin in 1805, and it was made famous beyond the city by Alfred Döblin's epic novel of low life in the Weimar era, *Berlin Alexanderplatz*. This windswept pedestrianized plaza has figured prominently in city upheavals ever since revolutionaries (including the writer Theodor Fontane) set up barricades here in 1848. More recently, it was the focal point of the million-strong city-wide **demonstration** of November 4, 1989, which formed a prelude to the events of November 9. Hundreds of thousands of people crammed into the square to hear opposition leaders speak. Veteran writer Stefan Heym summed up the mood in his speech to the crowd: "Power belongs not to one, not to a few, not to the party and not to the state. The whole people must have a share." Nonetheless, Alexanderplatz remains an unmistakable product of the old East Germany, having been remodelled as the showpiece centre of a modern "Socialist" capital city. The only older structures to have survived are the labyrinthine S- and U-Bahn station, and the angular **Berolinahaus** and **Alexanderhaus** at nos. 1 and 2 on the square, which are both late works by Peter Behrens, the one-time Jugendstil architect who latterly concentrated on industrial and commercial design, strongly influencing the founders of the Bauhaus.

The Nikolaiviertel and Am Köllnischen Park

Slightly to the southwest of the Rotes Rathaus lies the **Nikolaiviertel**, a showpiece GDR development carried out in the run-up to Berlin's 750th anniversary celebrations of 1987. Not only did this restore the main monuments of Berlin's oldest quarter, complete with its medieval layout, it also re-erected there replicas of historic buildings from elsewhere in the city which didn't make it through to the postwar era, such as *Zum Nussbaum* (see p.856), a convincing enough re-creation of a celebrated sixteenth-century Wirtshaus, as well as stylized buildings not based on anything in particular, but striving for an "old Berlin" feel.

At the centre of it all is the Gothic **Nikolaikirche** (Tues–Sun 10am–6pm; *www.stadtmuseum.com*; DM5/€2.50 combined ticket with Knoblauchhaus and Ephraim-Palais, free Wed), a brickwork hall church. Now deconsecrated, it is often given over to temporary exhibitions. Among the furnishings are Schlüter's monument to the court goldsmith Daniel Mannlich, which can be seen above a mock doorway on the west wall.

Nearby, at Poststr. 23, is the Rococo **Knoblauchhaus** (same times and ticket), one of only four houses from the prewar Nikolaiviertel to have survived. At the end of the street, facing Mühlendamm, is the rebuilt **Ephraim-Palais** (same times and ticket), a rather more splendid Rococo mansion built for Frederick the Great's court jeweller and mint master, Nathan Veitel Heine Ephraim. It contains displays of Berlin artworks of the period.

South of the Spree is the former suburb of Neukölln am Wasser, nowadays known as Am Köllnischen Park. Its dominant monument is the **Märkisches Museum** (Tues–Sun 10am–6pm; *www.stadtmuseum.com*; DM8/€4), an early twentieth-century building in the style of a medieval monastery. The displays are devoted to the history of Berlin and the province of Brandenburg from prehistoric times to the present day. Among the highlights are a beautiful Gothic sculpture known as the *Spandau Madonna*; the horse's head from Schadow's original casting of the Quadriga on the Brandenburger Tor; and the Panorama, a late nineteenth-century rotating drum which shows a series of fascinating 3-D photos of old Berlin.

The northern quarters

North of Unter den Linden lies another of Berlin's Baroque quarters, **Dorotheenstadt**, which postdates Friedrichswerder but predates Friedrichstadt. It was later joined by several other inner suburbs which are full of fascinating corners which nevertheless lie off the well-worn tourist track.

North from Bahnhof Friedrichstrasse

From **Bahnhof Friedrichstrasse**, a 1920s terminal that was once the most important border crossing between East and West Berlin, Friedrichstrasse itself runs north across the River Spree over the wrought-iron **Weidendammbrücke**. Immediately to the left on Bertolt-Brecht-Platz is the late nineteenth-century building of the **Berliner Ensemble**, Berlin's "Brecht theatre", complete with a statue of the playwright himself in front.

A little way further north is Oranienburger Tor, beyond which is the **Dorotheenstädtische Friedhof** (daily: April–Sept 8am–7pm; Oct–March 8am–4pm), eastern Berlin's VIP cemetery. Here are the graves of, among others, Brecht and his actress wife Helene Weigel, the architect Schinkel, the sculptors Schadow and Rauch, the philosophers Hegel and Fichte, the novelist Heinrich Mann and the Dadaist artist John Heartfield. Just beyond the cemetery, at Chausseestr. 125, is the **Brecht-Haus** (guided tours Tues, Wed & Fri 10am–noon, Thurs 10am–noon & 5pm–7pm, Sat 9.30am–2pm, Sun 11am–6pm; DM4/€2), a two-storey tenement flat where the poet and playwright lived for the last three years of his life. The most unexpected feature is the large collection of English-language crime novels, which he liked to read in the original.

Continuing northwestwards along Chausseestrasse, a left turn into Invalidenstrasse leads to the **Museum für Naturkunde** (Tues–Sun 9.30am–5pm; DM5/€2.50) at no. 43. In the top-lit central hall are five reasonably complete 150-million-year-old dinosaur skeletons unearthed during a paleontological expedition of 1909–13 to German East Africa (present-day Tanzania); these include the *Brachiosaurus brancai*, the largest and most spectacular yet discovered. The museum also has a fine collection of minerals, including a number of meteorites, and some charming 1920s dioramas, the first to be made outside the US.

Oranienburger Strasse

Since the *Wende*, **Oranienburger Strasse**, which runs southeast from Oranienburger Tor, has become a trendy spot, lined with many stylish watering-holes. The revitalization of the street began with **Tacheles**, a group of young international artists who took over a spectacularly ruined building on the southern side of the street, just beyond the Oranienburger Tor junction, in early 1990. The exterior is usually festooned with works in progress, and the building has become home and workplace to an ever-changing band of painters, sculptors, kindred spirits and hangers-on.

The presence of the grand **Neue Synagoge** (Mon–Thurs & Sun 10am–6pm, Fri 10am–2pm; free, except for special exhibitions) halfway down Oranienburger Strasse is a reminder that this area was, before the war, Berlin's main Jewish quarter. Designed by two prominent non-Jewish architects, Eduard Knoblauch and August Stüler, in an exotic idiom combining Moorish and Byzantine elements, the synagogue was inaugurated in the presence of Bismarck in 1866. Partially burned on *Kristallnacht* and further damaged by bombing during World War II, it stood derelict for many years, a silent reminder of the savagery of Nazi rule. On November 9, 1988, the 50th anniversary of *Kristallnacht*, work began on restoration of the facade and the reconstruction of the gilded dome, and this was completed seven years later, though it was decided not to re-create the main body of the temple, whose ground plan is marked out in the rear garden. The front rooms now serve as the **Centrum Judaicum**, a Jewish cultural centre.

At the eastern end of Oranienburger Strasse, turn left into Grosse Hamburger Strasse, where on the immediate right is the **Alter Jüdischer Friedhof**, Berlin's oldest Jewish cemetery, established in 1672. Most of the headstones were smashed by the Nazis, and the space was subsequently grassed over, though a monument to Moses Mendelssohn, the Enlightenment-era philosopher and grandfather of composer Felix, was re-erected after the war. Alongside is the site of the first Jewish old people's home to be founded in the city. The Nazis used this as a detention centre, and 55,000 Jews were held here before being shipped off to the camps. A memorial tablet, on which people, following the traditional Jewish practice, have placed pebbles, and a sculpted group of haggard-looking figures representing deportees, mark the spot where the home stood.

Continuing along the street, past late nineteenth-century neo-Baroque apartment buildings with shrapnel-pitted facades, brings you to the entrance gateway of the **Sophienkirche**. Built at the beginning of the eighteenth century, this closely resembles Wren's London churches, though the tower is modelled on Schlüter's design for the Münzturm of the Stadtschloss, which collapsed due to weak foundations. It was the only central Berlin church to survive the war more or less undamaged.

The western centre

The centre of the artificially created city of West Berlin, a pocket of western capitalism kept alive by interested parties in the heart of Soviet-occupied territory, consisted of the district of **Tiergarten**, which takes its name from the former hunting grounds at its core, as well as part of the sprawling district of **Charlottenburg**, which was a separate municipality until 1920 and therefore had a clearly defined town centre. Since losing its *raison d'être* with the reunification of the city, some of the lustre has worn off the old western centre. However, it remains home to a world-class cultural complex, the **Kulturforum**, while in the evening the area awakens into a **nightlife** that ranks among the best in Europe. The bars here are by turn raucous, shady, stylish and promiscuous, the discos and clubs blast their stuff well into the early hours; restaurants are excellent, cheap and of great variety.

The commercial heart

If you come to Berlin by train, or on the bus from Tegel airport, chances are you'll arrive at **Bahnhof Zoologischer Garten** (Zoo Station). Despite the lack of a large

WESTERN CENTRAL BERLIN

lobby or grand entry portal, it's an atmospheric place to end a journey, its elevated glass-covered platforms conjuring up memories of the steam trains which called there when it was built in the run-up to the 1936 Olympics. In recent years, it has been smarted up quite a bit, and although there's still a retinue of urban casualties permanently posted by the entrance, it has changed markedly from a decade ago, when it was a marketplace for heroin dealing and child prostitution.

Step out east from Bahnhof Zoo and you're in the centre of the west end's maelstrom of bright lights, traffic and high-rise buildings. Another block south is the eastern end of **Kurfürstendamm** (universally known as the **Ku'damm**), a 3.5-kilometre strip of ritzy shops, cinemas, bars and cafés that homes in on the centre like the spoke of a broken wheel.

The major landmark here is the **Kaiser-Wilhelm-Gedächtniskirche** (Kaiser Wilhelm Memorial Church), built at the end of the nineteenth century and destroyed by British bombing in November 1943. Left as a ruin, it's a strangely effective memorial, the crumbling tower providing a hint of the old city. The narthex, or **Gedenkhalle** (Mon–Sat 10am–4pm; free), features a mosaic of Hohenzollern rulers, as well as a small exhibit showing wartime destruction and a "before and after" model of the city centre. Adjacent, a 1960s concrete and glass chapel contains the tender, sad *Stalingrad Madonna*, while at the back the blue glass campanile from the same period has gained the nickname of the "Lipstick" or the "Soul-Silo"; its base contains a shop selling Third World gifts. The area around the church is a magnet for vendors, caricaturists and street musicians.

Breitscheidplatz marks the beginning of Tauentzienstrasse, with the **Europa-Center**, a huge shopping centre that contains the main tourist office on its northern side. There's nothing much of interest in this rather generic mall, which was built in the 1960s as a capitalist showcase for West Berlin, topped by a huge, rotating Mercedes Benz symbol. Further down Tauentzienstrasse, and claiming to be the largest store on the continent, is the **KaDeWe**, an abbreviation of Kaufhaus Des Westens – "the Department Store of the West". It's an impressive statement of the city's standard of living, and the sixth-floor food hall is a mouthwatering inducement to sample the many exotic snacks sold there.

There's little to do on Ku'damm other than spend money, and there's only one cultural attraction, the **Käthe-Kollwitz-Museum** (11am–6pm, closed Tues; *www.kaethe-kollwitz.de*; DM8/€4) at Fasanenstr. 24. The drawings and prints of Käthe Kollwitz are among the most moving works from the first half of the twentieth century. Born in 1867, she lived for almost all her life in Prenzlauer Berg in the eastern part of Berlin, where her work evolved a radical left-wing perspective. Following the death of her son in World War I, her woodcuts, lithographs and prints became explicitly pacifist, often dwelling on the theme of mother and child. When her grandson was killed in World War II her work became even sadder and more poignant. The museum's comprehensive collection of her work makes it possible to trace its development, culminating in the tragic sculptures on the top floor.

By the time you reach **Adenauerplatz**, the slick showrooms of the Ku'damm have died out and the bars become affordable: although the clientele tends to consist of loud and brash teenagers, it's not a bad starting point for a bar crawl. Best of all for eating, drinking and nightlife, though, is the squashed rectangle of streets south and west of Bahnhof Zoo, roughly bordered by Kantstrasse, Hardenbergstrasse and Leibnizstrasse, and centred on **Savignyplatz**.

The Zoologischer Garten and the Tiergarten

Back in the centre, the **Zoologischer Garten** (daily 9am–5/6.30pm; DM14/€7, or DM22.50/€11.25 combined ticket with Aquarium; kids DM7/€3.50 & DM11.50/€5.75

respectively) was laid out in the 1840s at the southern end of the Tiergarten. It is beautifully landscaped with trees and flowers, and offers many framed views of the landmarks of the city centre. For the most part, the animals are kept out of cages and allowed to roam freely in re-creations of their natural habitats, though some spend part of their time in the whimsical garden pavilions – the elephants in a mock-Burmese pagoda, the antelopes in an imitation mosque, the zebras in a pseudo-Arab fort.

The **Tiergarten** proper was transformed into an English-style park in the 1830s by Peter Joseph Lenné, the most celebrated German landscape designer of the century, and a man who played a defining role in the creation of the Berlin landscape. The park was destroyed during the Battle of Berlin in 1945 – though so successful has its replanting been that these days it's hard to tell it's not original. You can wander through the park, tracing the course of the **Landwehrkanal**, an inland waterway off the River Spree. Near the Corneliusbrücke, a small, odd sculpture commemorates the radical leader **Rosa Luxemburg**, co-founder of the short-lived Socialist Republic of 1918, whose body was dumped in the canal at this point by the militia group who had kidnapped her. **Karl Liebknecht**, her co-conspirator, was gunned down while "attempting to escape", and thrown into a nearby lake, the Neuer See.

The broad avenue cutting through the Tiergarten is the **Strasse des 17 Juni**, whose name commemorates the day in 1953 when workers in East Berlin rose in revolt against the occupying Soviet powers, demanding free elections, the removal of all borders separating the two Germanys and the release of political prisoners. Soviet forces were quickly mobilized, and between two and four hundred people died; the authorities also ordered the execution of twenty-one East Berliners and eighteen Soviet soldiers – for "moral capitulation to the demonstrators".

At the centre of the avenue is the **Siegessäule** (daily 9.30am–5.30/6.30pm; DM2/€1), a column commemorating Prussia's military victories over Denmark, Austria and France in the period 1864–71. In 1938 the column was shifted to this spot on Hitler's orders from what is today the Platz der Republik. Though the boulevard approaches exaggerate its size, it's still an eye-catching monument: 67m high and topped with a colossal gilded and winged statue of Victory that symbolically faces France. The viewing platform, approached via a spiral stair of 585 steps, offers good distant views. At the base of the column are mosaics illustrating the main consequence of the victories, the unification of the German peoples into one nation for the first time ever.

Strasse des 17 Juni terminates at the Brandenburger Tor; a little further north, albeit still on the western side of the former wall, is the **Reichstag** (or **Bundestag**, as it is now officially known). This late nineteenth-century parliament building, inscribed with the words *Dem Deutschen Volke* ("To the German People"), has witnessed many dramatic events. In November 1918 the German Republic was declared from its balcony by the Social Democrat Philipp Scheidemann, while Karl Liebknecht was proclaiming a Socialist Republic down the road from a window of the Stadtschloss. The Reichstag was seriously damaged by fire in 1933, an event Hitler used as a pretext for his seizure of power. For decades, the building stood as a symbol of national unity hard by the border that underlined its division, and was belatedly restored in a simplified form to host occasional plenary sessions of parliament. In 1990, the new all-German parliament held its first session there, and when Berlin was later confirmed as the national capital and main seat of government, preparations began on equipping it for a resumption of its former role, which it duly assumed in 1999. During the intervening period, the interior was completely gutted and refashioned, and a new glass **dome** was place on top. Designed by British architect Sir Norman Foster, the dome, controversial when proposed, has proven a hugely popular success. A circular ramp winds up the glass cupola to a **viewing deck** (daily 8am–10pm; free) that offers a stunning view of the city; be warned that there are often very long queues for admission.

By the river bank at the northeastern corner of the Reichstag is one of several small cemeteries close to the Berlin Wall commemorating those, many of them unknown, who died trying to escape. Southwest of the Reichstag is the **Sowjetisches Ehrenmal** (Soviet War Memorial) to the Red Army troops who died in the Battle of Berlin. Built from the marble of Hitler's destroyed Berlin HQ, the Reichskanzlei, it's flanked by two tanks that were supposedly the first to reach the city.

The Kulturforum

Immediately west of Potsdamer Platz is the Kulturforum, a group of museums and other cultural institutions that could easily fill several days of your time. It's almost entirely a postwar development: the only older building is Stüler's **Matthäikirche**, though even that has a modernized interior. The **tower** (Wed–Sun noon–6pm; DM2/€1) commands a fine general view over Berlin, and in particular over the brand-new buildings of Potsdamer Platz.

The Gemäldegalerie

Inaugurated in 1998 as the culmination of the Kulturforum project, the **Gemäldegalerie** (Picture Gallery; Tues–Fri 10am–6pm, Sat & Sun 11am–6pm, *www.smb.spk-berlin.de*; DM8/€4), ranks as one of the world's most comprehensive collections of old masters. Originally housed in the prewar Kaiser-Friedrich-Museum, the paintings were stashed in various locations for safekeeping during the war years. The lion's share of the collection was held in the west, and was eventually displayed in less than ideal conditions at Dahlem; only the much smaller and less distinguished part held in the Soviet sector returned to its renamed former home. Although only opened in 1998, the current premises were originally conceived for the Dahlem works only and many fine paintings have had to be banished to a densely hung study section in the basement in order that the reunited collection can be displayed in full. It is therefore likely that part of the collection will move back to the Bodemuseum when it reopens, and there is a longer-term plan to build a new and much larger gallery in the vicinity of Museumsinsel.

Arranged in chronological order, and subdivided geographically, the displays begin on the north side of the building with German works of the Middle Ages and Renaissance. Highlights include the large *Wurzach Altar* of 1437, made in the workshop of the great Ulm sculptor **Hans Multscher**; its exaggerated gestures and facial distortions mark it out as an distant precursor of Expressionism. An interesting contrast is offered by the far more subtle *Solomon before the Queen of Sheba*, painted in the same year by **Konrad Witz**, while the exquisite *Nativity* by **Martin Schongauer** is the most important surviving panel by the father-figure of the German Renaissance.

Of the brilliant generation who followed, **Altdorfer** is represented by several canvases – *Allegory of Beggary Sitting on the Train of Pride* is the most individualistic – which show his love of lush lundscapes and exotic architecture. His works are hung alongside those of **Dürer**, by whom there are some penetrating portraits, notably of two future mayors of Nürnberg – *Hieronymous Holzschuher* and *Jacob Muffel*. Among an impressive group of works by Dürer's eccentric pupil **Hans Baldung** is an exotic *Adoration of the Magi* triptych. **Holbein the Younger** is represented by five superbly observed portraits, the most celebrated being *The Danzig Merchant Georg Gisze*, with a still-life background that's a real *tour de force* of artistic virtuosity. Notable among the many examples of **Cranach** are his tongue-in-cheek *The Fountain of Youth* and his free reinterpretation of Bosch's famous triptych *The Garden of Earthly Delights*.

In the Netherlandish section, **Jan van Eyck**'s beautifully lit *Madonna in the Church* is crammed with architectural detail, with the Virgin lifted in the perspective for gentle emphasis. **Petrus Christus** is thought to have been a pupil of Van Eyck, and certainly knew his work, as *The Virgin and Child with St Barbara and a Carthusian Monk* reveals: in the background are tiny Flemish houses and street scenes, the artist carefully locating the event in his native Bruges. **Dieric Bouts's** figures tend to be rather formalized, but his *Christ in the House of Simon the Pharisee* is filled with gesture, expression and carefully drawn detail. **Rogier van der Weyden** developed the Eyckian technique to a warmer, much more emotional treatment of religious subjects, and the figures in his *Middelburg Altar* reveal a delicacy of poise and an approachable humanity that was to greatly influence German painting in the fifteenth century. *Etienne Chevalier with St Stephen,* a rare panel by the great French illuminator **Jehan Fouquet,** makes for a fascinating comparison with the Flemish works; it depicts the Treasurer of France accompanied by his patron saint.

The Dutchman **Albert van Ouwater** was another influential artist, although *The Raising of Lazarus* is his only complete work to have survived; it's a daring picture, the richly dressed merchants on the right contrasting strongly with the simplicity of the Holy Family on the left. **Geertgen tot Sint Jans** was Ouwater's pupil, but his *St John the Baptist* is quite different from his master's painting – the saint sits almost comically impassive against a rich backdrop of intricately constructed landscape. Among the gallery's most prized possessions are two of the few surviving altarpieces by **Hugo van der Goes.** *The Adoration of the Magi* has a superbly drawn realism that marks a new development in Netherlandish art, carrying precision over into a large-scale work with a deftly executed, complex perspective; *The Adoration of the Shepherds* (painted when the artist was in the first throes of madness) displays an exalted sense of religious fervour, especially in the dramatic device of Old Testament prophets drawing back a curtain to unveil the scene. *St John the Evangelist on Patmos* is a typically unconventional composition by **Hieronymus Bosch,** while **Pieter Bruegel the Elder's** *Netherlandish Proverbs* is an amusing, if hard-to-grasp, depiction of over a hundred sixteenth-century maxims.

The final rooms in this wing are devoted to seventeenth-century Flemish and Dutch paintings, beginning with the fleshy canvases of **Rubens** – whose *Child with a Bird,* a portrait of his nephew, gives a rare glimpse of a more intimate vein – and several grand portraits of Genoese nobility by **Van Dyck.** *Kitchen Scene with View of the Last Supper* by **Joachim Wtewael** is a virtuoso example of Dutch Mannerism, while **Frans Hals** is represented by several portraits, among which the satirical *Malle Babbe* stands out. In total contrast are two enchantingly luminous examples of the very distinctive art of **Vermeer:** *Woman with a Pearl Necklace* and *Man and Woman Drinking Wine.*

Formerly, Berlin boasted of owning 25 paintings of **Rembrandt** – the largest collection in the world – but the exhaustive research carried out on the painter in recent years has reduced this figure markedly. Controversy still surrounds the authorship of some of the canvases, but one that has been conclusively proved to be a member of the studio is the most famous picture here, *The Man in the Golden Helmet,* though this does little to detract from the elegance and power of the portrait, its reflective sorrow relieved by the bright helmet. Works definitely by the master himself include the luxuriantly Baroque *Rape of Prosperine; The Mennonite Preacher Anslo and his Wife,* one of the finest achievements of his middle period; and two visionary late masterpieces – *Jacob Wrestling with the Angel* and *Moses Destroying the Tables of the Law.*

The galleries on the southern side are largely devoted to Italian paintings, with the Florentine School figuring strongly. Of the early works, pride of place is taken by **Giotto's** largest surviving panel, *The Dormition of the Virgin.* **Fra Angelico's** *The Last Judgement* is a radiant Dantesque vision, while *The Adoration in the Forest* by his pupil **Fra Filippo Lippi** is a mystical image of unusual grace and beauty, rightly one of the most admired paintings of the period. A gorgeously coloured tondo of *The Adoration of the Magi* is one of the tantalizingly few surviving panels by **Domenico Veneziano.** Finest of several **Botticelli** masterpieces is a large altarpiece, *The Madonna and Child Enthroned with the two St Johns.* From elsewhere in Italy are masterpieces by

Mantegna, Bellini, Raphael, Titian and **Correggio**, whose playfully suggestive *Leda with the Swan* so offended an eighteenth-century religious fanatic that he hacked it to pieces.

In the following rooms, paintings by seventeenth-century Italian masters are hung alongside works by their Latin contemporaries. Particularly celebrated are **Caravaggio**'s *Cupid Victorious*, heavy with symbolism and homoeroticism, and **Poussin**'s *Self-Portrait*, one of only two purely figurative works in his entire oeuvre. The displays end with eighteenth-century paintings from all over Europe, including canvases by Tiepolo and Canaletto, and three Watteaus which once belonged to Frederick the Great. There is also a surprisingly good representation of British portraiture, including characteristic examples of Gainsborough, Reynolds, Lawrence and Raeburn.

The Kupferstichkabinett and the Kunstgewerbemuseum

Two further collections of European art can be found in buildings interlinked with the Gemäldegalerie. The **Kupferstichkabinett** (Engraving Cabinet; Tues–Fri 10am–6pm, Sat & Sun 11am–6pm; *www.smb.spk-berlin.de*; DM8/€4), holds an extensive array of manuscripts, prints, drawings, watercolours and engravings, selections from which are shown to the public in a series of temporary exhibitions. Its most famous possessions are 84 exquisite drawings by Botticelli illustrating scenes from Dante's *Divine Comedy*.

The **Kunstgewerbemuseum** (Museum of Applied Arts; Tues–Fri 10am–6pm, Sat & Sun 11am–6pm, *www.smb.spk-berlin.de*; DM4/€2), is an encyclopedic collection, whose displays begin with the medieval section on the ground floor. Some of the earliest items come from the Westphalian town of Enger; these include an eighth-century purse-shaped reliquary which belonged to Duke Widikund, leader of the Saxon resistance to Charlemagne. There are dazzling groups of treasures from the Dom in Braunschweig (including a crucifix, a reliquary and a book cover, all donated by the Welf family) and from the Münster in the Swiss city of Basel. In the following rooms are many magnificent examples of Renaissance silverware, notably the 32-piece set made for ceremonial municipal use in Lüneburg. At the entrance to the top floor are the surviving parts of the Pommersche Kunstschrank, an ebony cabinet of curios formerly in the Stadtschloss; the following galleries illustrate changing artistic tastes from Rococo to Jugendstil and Art Deco. In the basement is a small assembly of Bauhaus furniture, glittering contemporary jewellery and a display on the evolution of product design.

The Scharoun buildings

Opposite the Kunstgewerbemuseum is the **Philharmonie**, home of the Berlin Philharmonisches Orchester, which has for long enjoyed an unmatched reputation in the musical world, being distinguished for its richness and precision of tone, and its supreme artistic discipline. The distinctive gold-plated building, an irregular pentagon with a tent-shaped roof, was designed in the early 1960s by Hans Scharoun, who was also responsible for the general plan of the Kulturforum. Its interior arrangement is unconventional, with terraced seating around a central orchestral podium, yet this ensures that every member of the audience enjoys a clear view as well as excellent acoustics. Just over two decades later, the **Kammermusiksaal**, a venue for smaller-scale groups, was added alongside. Again the design is Scharoun's, though it was built by his pupil Edgar Wisniewski.

The same architectural team was also responsible for the **Musikinstrumenten-Museum** (Tues–Fri 9am–5pm, Sat & Sun 10am–5pm; DM4/€2, free first Sun of month) on the north side of the Philharmonie. This has a fine collection of historic musical instruments, including some pretty Rococo musical clocks and two full-sized organs – one from early nineteenth-century England, the other a Mighty Wurlitzer. Recordings of appropriate short pieces of music have been made using many of the instruments, and these can be heard via the headphones placed throughout the museum. There are also regular live performances at 11am on Sundays.

Across Potsdamer Strasse is the **Staatsbibliothek** (Mon–Fri 10am–8pm, Sat 10am–7pm; free), which has over three and a half million books, occasional exhibitions, a small concert hall, a reasonable café and a wide selection of British newspapers. The Staabi's most recent claim to fame came when it was used as an important backdrop in Wim Wenders' poetic film elegy to the city, *Wings of Desire*.

The Neue Nationalgalerie

At the southern end of the Kulturforum is the **Neue Nationalgalerie** (Tues–Fri 10am–6pm, Sat & Sun 11am–6pm; *www.smb.spk-berlin.de*; DM8/€4), a black-rimmed glass box that seems almost suspended above the ground, its clarity of line and detail having all the intelligent simplicity of the Parthenon. It was designed by Mies van der Rohe in 1965 and the ground-floor section is used for temporary exhibits, often of contemporary art, while the underground galleries contain paintings from the beginning of the twentieth century onwards. There's a notable array of paintings by the Expressionist Die Brücke group, including **Kirchner**'s *Potsdamer Platz* of 1914, though it might as well be in another country instead of just down the road. Another work with a Berlin setting is **Grosz**'s *The Pillars of Society*, a savage attack on the hypocrisy endemic in the power structures of the Weimar Republic. Cubism is represented by examples of **Braque**, **Gris** and **Picasso** (though the last-named is seen in greater number and to better effect in the Berggruen-Sammlung in Charlottenburg). There are also works by, among others, Klee, Dix, Beckmann and Feininger.

Paintings and sculptures of more recent decades are exhibited in the Neue Nationalgalerie's annexe, the **Hamburger Bahnhof** (Tues–Fri 10am–6pm, Sat & Sun 11am–6pm; *www.smb.spk-berlin.de*; DM8/€4) in the northern district of Moabit, one of the early working-class suburbs of the city. The building itself dates from the 1840s and is the only remaining example of the first generation of Berlin rail terminals, though it has not been used as a train station for nearly a century.

The Bendlerblock and the Bauhaus-Archiv

On Stauffenbergstrasse, a block west of the Kulturforum proper, is the **Bendlerblock**, a huge building where the one nearly successful attempt on Hitler's life, the Bomb Plot of July 1944, was hatched, and where the conspirators were subsequently executed. The rooms on the second floor have been designated the **Gedenkstätte Deutscher Widerstand** (Memorial to the German Resistance; Mon–Fri 9am–6pm, Sat & Sun 10am–6pm; free), and contain a fascinating documentary record on the many groups and individuals who actively opposed the Third Reich, despite the risk of death or imprisonment that was the automatic consequence. It thus serves as a useful corrective to the all-too-commonly expressed view that all Germans were Nazis, though it does little to help explain why the opposition was unco-ordinated and ineffective, or why so many prominent anti-Nazis – including Count Claus Schenk von Stauffenberg, the hero of the Bomb Plot – were initially prepared to serve Hitler quite loyally.

Further west, occupying a quayside setting at the junction of Klingelhöferstrasse and Von-der-Heydt-Strasse, is the **Bauhaus-Archiv** (10am–5pm, closed Tues; *www.bauhaus.de*; DM5/€2.50). The building was designed in 1964 by Walter Gropius, the first director of the Bauhaus, and was originally conceived for a hilly site in the Hessian city of Darmstadt. However, this project failed to come to fruition, and it was not until seven years later (by which time Gropius was already dead) that a modified version could be built on this flat location. Unless displaced by a temporary display, the exhibition halls inside display some of the classics of Bauhaus design, such as Marcel Breuer's tubular steel chair, Marianne Brant's tea and coffee set, and László Moholy-Nagy's *Light-Space Modulator*. There are also paintings by Klee, Kandinsky, Feininger and Schlemmer.

The western suburbs

The western suburbs of Berlin are nothing if not diverse, ranging as they do from densely populated inner-city districts such as **Kreuzberg** and **Schöneberg**, each of which has been through a self-consciously trendy period, to the vast rural landscapes of the **Grunewald** and the **Havel lakes**. From a historic point of view, **Schloss Charlottenburg** is a particular highlight, and its park is a wonderful place to spend a lazy afternoon. In the immediate vicinity are some important public museums; yet another group can be found in the peaceful, village-like setting of **Dahlem**. While **Plötzensee** offers one of the most chilling reminders of the brutality of the Third Reich, the **Olympia-Stadion** is one of the few monuments of that era still regarded with a certain amount of affection – largely because the Games for which it was built did not entirely go according to script.

Kreuzberg

Kreuzberg, which lies south of Mitte, is famed for its large immigrant community and self-styled "alternative" inhabitants, nightlife and goings-on. Effectively there are two Kreuzbergs: the **west**, the area bounded by Friedrichstrasse, Viktoriapark and Südstern, is a richer, fancier, more sedate area than its neighbour to the **east**, which is sometimes referred to as **SO 36** after its old postal code. East Kreuzberg is western Berlin's "happening" quarter, a mix of punks and old hippies, and the place to hang out and hit the raucous nightspots.

West Kreuzberg

Southeast of Potsdamer Platz is the **Martin-Gropius-Bau** (variable times and prices). Designed in 1877 by Martin Gropius, a pupil of Schinkel and the uncle of Walter, the building was, until its destruction in the war, home of the Kunstgewerbemuseum. In recent years it has been rebuilt and refurbished, and now houses changing exhibitions of art, photography and architecture. Alongside is the **Topograpie des Terrors** (Tues–Sun 10am–6pm; *www.topographie.de*; free). This consists of an outdoor exhibition in a grassy field, for nothing is left of the buildings that once stood here: the Reich Security offices, including the headquarters of the Gestapo and SS. In buildings along here Himmler planned the Final Solution, the deportation and genocide of European Jews, and organized the Gestapo, the feared secret police. A numbered series of noticeboards with photographs and English texts indicate the sites of the most important Nazi buildings in the area and reveal just how massive a machine the Nazi organization became.

From here it's a ten-minute walk down Wilhelmstrasse, then along Kochstrasse, to the site of **Checkpoint Charlie**, one of the most famous names associated with Cold War-era Berlin. This Allied military post on Friedrichstrasse marked the border between East and West Berlin until July 1990, when it was removed. While it stood it was one of Berlin's more celebrated landmarks and the building lent its name informally to the adjacent GDR border crossing (official title *Grenzübergang Friedrichstrasse*), which, with its dramatic sign "YOU ARE NOW LEAVING THE AMERICAN SECTOR", (a replica of which can still be seen) and unsmiling border guards, used to be the archetypal movie-style Iron Curtain crossing.

Tangible evidence of the trauma the Wall caused is still on hand at the **Museum Haus am Checkpoint Charlie** at Friedrichstr. 44 (daily 9am–10pm; *www.mauer -museum.com*; DM8/€4). Here the history of the Wall is told in photos of escape tunnels and with the home-made aircraft and converted cars by which people attempted, succeeded and sometimes tragically failed to break through the border. Films document the stories of some of the over 230 people murdered by the East German border guards, and there's a section on human rights behind the Iron Curtain, but it's a scruffy, rather dated collection, and not quite the harrowing experience that some visitors seem to expect.

It's only a short walk south, cutting down Stresemannstrasse, from the Martin-Gropius-Bau to the remains of the **Anhalter Bahnhof**, a sad reminder of misguided civic action that some would term civic vandalism. The Anhalter Bahnhof was once one of the city's (and Europe's) great rail termini, forming Berlin's gateway to the south. Completed in 1870, it received only mild damage during World War II and was left roofless but substantial in 1945. Despite attempts to preserve it as a future museum building, it was blown up in 1952 – essentially because someone had put in a good offer for the bricks. Now only a fragment of the facade stands, giving a hint at past glories. The patch of land that the station once covered is today devoted to a park and, from November 2001, a sports and concert hall, the **Tempodrom**, a popular venue for concerts of touring bands and world music.

A brisk twenty-minute walk east from here, through streets levelled during wartime bombing, takes you to another Kreuzberg high spot, the **Jüdisches Museum Berlin** at Lindenstr. 14 (*www.jmberlin.de*), housed in a stunning "deconstructivist" building designed by Daniel Libeskind. The building is an extraordinary creation: shaped like a compressed lightning bolt, sheathed in polished metallic facing, with windows, mere thin angular lines, that trace geometric patterns on the exterior. The inside is just as unusual, manifesting Libeskind's ideas about sculptural and symbolic architecture: an empty and inaccessible diagonal shaft, signifying loss and emptiness, cuts through the building; three long intersecting corridors, each symbolic of an element of the Jewish experience comprise the basement – the "axis of continuity", leading to the exhibition space, an "axis of exile," which leads outside to a garden of steles, and an "axis of the Holocaust", which leads to the Holocaust Tower, dimly lit and, again, completely empty. Set to open in October 2001, the museum will portray the history and culture of German-speaking Jewry and its relation to German history in general, not necesarily an easy task, given the country's sensitivities.

A fifteen-minute walk south from the Martin-Gropius-Bau, down Stresemannstrasse and Möckenstrasse, leads to the **Deutsche Technikmuseum** (Tues–Fri 9am–5.30pm, Sat & Sun 10am–6pm; *www.dtmb.de*; DM5/€2.50, kids DM2/€1)at Trebbiner Str. 9. This is one of the city's most entertaining museums – a children's and button-pushers' delight. The technology section has plenty of experiments, antiquated machinery and computers to play with, alongside some elegant old cars and planes. The transport museum, a superb collection of ancient steam trains and carriages, is even more impressive; the polished behemoths have been brought to rest in what was once the goods depot of the old Anhalter Bahnhof.

Reaching the **Viktoriapark** (the "Kreuzberg", as it's popularly known) from here means a half-hour's walk, retracing your steps to the U-Bahn and heading south down Grossbeerenstrasse. On the slopes of a hill, the park is one of the city's most likeable, a relaxed ramble of trees and green space with a pretty brook running down the middle. To one side is the *Golgotha Café* and disco (see "Cafés and bars", p.860), packed on summer evenings; on another side is what claims to be Germany's northernmost vineyard; and atop the hill is the **Kreuzberg** itself, the monument from which the district takes its name. More correctly known as the **Befreiungsdenkmal** (Liberation Memorial), this huge neo-Gothic cast-iron spire, crowned with Prussia's highest military honour, the Iron Cross, is the only completed part of Schinkel's ambitious scheme for a series of monuments to commemorate the victory over Napoleon.

The well-restored streets around the hill, along with Yorckstrasse to the north, have a scattering of cafés, their tone and clientele reflecting the residents of the neighbourhood, who are on the whole slightly older than those of East Kreuzberg. Between Hagelbergerstrasse and Yorckstrasse, **Riehmer's Hofgarten** is an impressive *fin-de-*

siècle bourgeois residential building, though the steel and glass Yorck Cinema doesn't fit well in the ensemble.

South and east of the Viktoriapark, the housing fades away to the flatlands containing **Flughafen Tempelhof** (not actually in Kreuzberg but in the neighbouring *Bezirk* of Tempelhof). The airport was open in the 1920s and was once Germany's largest; the present complex was built in 1936–41 and is one of the best surviving examples of Nazi architecture. Today it handles only a light load of small carrier flights. Sadly, the airport is scheduled to close in a few years' time; what will become of the land is a matter for heated debate. It was to Tempelhof that the Allies flew in supplies to beat the **Berlin Blockade** of 1948–49: an act that was to strengthen anti-Soviet feeling among West Berliners and increase the popularity of the occupying forces. At the height of the airlift a plane landed here every minute and the **Luftbrückendenkmal**, a memorial at the entrance to the airport, commemorates the seventy airmen and eight ground crew who died in crashes while attempting to land. The memorial represents the three air corridors used, and forms half of a bridge: the other half, "joined by air", is in Frankfurt.

East Kreuzberg ("SO 36")

Despite its reputation as a hotbed of radical protest and alternative lifestyles (a leftover from the days when West Germany's disaffected youth came to Berlin, since those living in the city were exempt from military service), you don't need any interest in revolution or city machinations to enjoy Kreuzberg. The **nightlife** here is among the city's wildest and it's an enjoyable area to wander through by day, stopping off at one of the innumerable Turkish snack bars for a kebab, breakfasting on a 9am vodka-and-beer special at a café (see p.860), or just taking in the feel of the place – which is much like an Istanbul market than an Eastern Bloc housing development.

Catching U-Bahn line #1 to **Kottbusser Tor** or Schlesisches Tor is a good introduction to eastern Kreuzberg. The area around the former is typical: a scruffy, earthy shambles of Turkish street vendors and cafés, the air filled with the aromas of southeast European cooking. Cutting through Dresdener Strasse, past the Babylon cinema, takes you to Kreuzberg's main strip, **Oranienstrasse**, which from Moritzplatz eastwards is lined with café-bars, art galleries and clothes shops, and in a way forms an "alternative" Kurfürstendamm. Stop off at any of the bars along here for a taste of what the locals call a *Szene* place – somewhere that's in and happening.

The Landwehrkanal runs south of Oranienstrasse, and below that the broad path of Hasenheide-Gneisenaustrasse marks the transition from east to west Kreuzberg. Around the Südstern (which has a convenient U-Bahn station) is another clutch of café-bars, and Gneisenaustrasse has some good restaurants; but the flavour of east Kreuzberg has gone, and things feel (and are) a lot tamer.

Schöneberg

Like Kreuzberg, **Schöneberg** was once a separate suburb, one that was swallowed up by Greater Berlin as the city expanded in the late eighteenth and nineteenth centuries. Blown to pieces during the war, it's now a mostly middle-class residential area, stretching below the Tiergarten and sandwiched between Kreuzberg to the east and Wilmersdorf to the west. Things to see are few, but what is here is both fascinating and moving.

From the middle of Potsdamer Strasse, it's a short detour west along Bulow Strasse to **Nollendorfplatz**, which, on its southern side, holds the proto-Deco **Metropol-Theater**, and down Maassenstrasse, which leads on to Nollendorfstrasse, where, at no. 17, stands the building in which **Christopher Isherwood** lived during his years in pre-war Berlin, a time that was to be elegantly recounted in perhaps the most famous collection of stories about the city ever written – *Goodbye to Berlin*.

Schöneberg has since been reborn as a fancy, even chic neighbourhood; the would-be Isherwoods of the moment hang out in East Kreuzberg, or Prenzlauer Berg (see p.852) in eastern Berlin. At night, this part of Schöneberg, particularly the area around **Winterfeldtplatz**, is good for eating and especially drinking: tidily bohemian, less sniffy than Savignyplatz and much more middle-of-the-road than East Kreuzberg. On Wednesday and Saturday mornings the square holds an excellent **market**.

Schöneberg's most famous attraction actually has the least to see: the **Rathaus Schöneberg** on Martin-Luther-Strasse, the penultimate stop on U-Bahn line #4. Built just before World War I, the Rathaus became the seat of the West Berlin parliament and senate after the last war, and it was outside here in 1963 that **John F. Kennedy** made his celebrated "Ich bin ein Berliner" speech on the Cold War, just a few months after the Cuban missile crisis. What the president hadn't realized as he read from his phonetically written text was that he had actually said "I am a small doughnut", since *Berliner* is a name for jam doughnuts; to convey his intended meaning, he should have omitted the word "ein". The day after Kennedy was assassinated, the square in front of the Rathaus was given his name – a move apparently instigated by the city's students, among whom the president was highly popular.

If you've time and interest you can climb the Rathaus tower (daily 10am–5pm) and see the replica **Liberty bell** donated to the city by the US in 1950, though it's more pleasant, and certainly less strenuous, to take a stroll in the small **Volkspark**, a thin ribbon of greenery that runs southwest from here.

Plötzensee

Berlin sometimes has the feel of a city that has tried, unsuccessfully, to sweep its past under the carpet of the present. When concrete reminders of the Third Reich can be seen, their presence in today's postwar city becomes all the more powerful. Nowhere is this more true than in the buildings where the Nazi powers brought dissidents and political opponents for imprisonment and execution – what is today the **Gedenkstatte Plötzensee** (daily: March–Sept 8.30am–6pm; Oct & Feb 8.30am–5.30pm; Nov & Jan 8.30am–4.30pm; Dec 8.30am–4pm; free). This stands in the northwest of the city, on the border between the boroughs of Charlottenburg and Wedding. To get there, take bus #123 from Tiergarten S-Bahn station to the beginning of Saatwinkler Damm (ask for the "Gedenkstatte Plötzensee" stop; the journey takes 30min), and walk away from the canal along the wall-sided path of Hüttigpfad.

The former prison buildings have been refurbished as a juvenile detention centre, and the memorial consists of the buildings where the executions took place. Over 2500 people were hanged or guillotined here between 1933 and 1945, usually those sentenced in the Supreme Court of Justice in the city. Following the July Bomb Plot, 89 of the 200 people condemned were executed here in the space of a few days. Hitler ordered the hangings to be carried out with piano wire, so that the victims would slowly strangle rather than die from broken necks, and spent his evenings watching movie footage of the executions. Today the execution chamber has been restored to its wartime condition: on occasion, victims were hanged eight at a time, and the hanging beam, complete with hooks, still stands. Though decked with wreaths and flowers, the atmosphere in the chamber is chilling, and in a further reminder of Nazi atrocities an urn in the courtyard contains soil from each of the concentration camps. Perhaps more than at any other wartime site in Berlin, it is at Plötzensee that the horror of senseless, brutal murder is most palpably felt.

Charlottenburg: the Schloss and museums

The district of **Charlottenburg** stretches north and west of the centre of town, reaching as far south as the forests of the Grunewald. The most significant attraction here, one that needs half a day at least to cover, is the **Schloss Charlottenburg and museum complex** on Spandauer Damm. The nearest U-Bahn stations are five to ten minutes away by foot: Richard-Wagner-Platz on the #7 line or Sophie-Charlotte-Platz on the #2 line. The nearest bus routes are #X21, #X26, #109, #110 and #145.

Schloss Charlottenburg

Schloss Charlottenburg (Tues–Fri 9am–5pm, Sat & Sun 10am–5pm; *www.spsg.de*; DM15/€7.50 combined ticket for all sections except the Galerie der Romantik and Museum für Vor- und Frühgeschichte; separate tickets priced individually below) comes as a surprise after the unrelieved modernity of the city streets. Commissioned as a country house by the future Queen Sophie Charlotte in 1695 (she also gave her name to the district), the Schloss was expanded and added to throughout the eighteenth and early nineteenth centuries to provide a summer residence for the Prussian kings. Approaching through the main courtyard, you're confronted with Andreas Schlüter's **Denkmal des Grossen Kurfürsten**, an equestrian statue of Friedrich Wilhelm, the Great Elector, cast as a single piece in 1700. It's in superb condition, despite (or perhaps because of) spending the war years sunk at the bottom of the Tegeler See for safekeeping.

Immediately behind is the entrance to the oldest part of the Schloss, now known as the **Nering-Eosanderbau** (lower floor DM8/€4, upper floor DM3/€1.50) in honour of the two architects (the Dutchman Johann Arnold Nering and the Swede Johann Eosander von Göthe) who designed it. The ground floor, containing the main state apartments, can only be seen via a German-language guided tour. Highlights are the **Porzellan-Zimmer**, which is packed to the ceiling with china, and the **Schlosskapelle**, which is exceptionally extravagant for a Protestant chapel, and includes a portrait of Sophie Charlotte as the Virgin ascending to heaven. The upper floor has a suite of rooms refurbished in the nineteenth century for King Friedrich Wilhelm IV, but is mainly of note for the Hohenzollern family collections of porcelain and silver, plus miscellaneous heirlooms, of which the oldest are the Florentine Renaissance sword and scabbard of Margrave Albrecht III Achilles. Also on view are the **regalia** used at the 1701 ceremony where Elector Friedrich III crowned himself King Friedrich I, so raising Prussia to the rank of a kingdom. The two crowns and the imperial seal were specially made for the event, where they were used in conjunction with a sixteenth-century sword and a seventeenth-century sceptre and imperial apple.

Frederick the Great's eastern extension to the Schloss is known as the **Knobelsdorff-Flügel** (DM5/€2.50), again in honour of its architect. Six rooms on the garden side have been restored to their original appearance, and are hung with portraits by Frederick's court painter **Antoine Pesne**: the vivacious *La Barberina*, which immortalizes an Italian dancer, stands out from the formality of the others. On the front part of the ground floor are the quarters of Friedrich Wilhelm III; here can be seen **Jacques Louis David**'s famous heroic image of *Napoleon Crossing the Alps*, which Blücher took as war booty from Paris following his victory over the French dictator at Waterloo. The eastern section of the upper floor contains the main reception rooms – the **Weisser Saal**, whose ceiling paintings have been replaced by witty contemporary pastiches; and the **Goldene Galerie**, which ranks among Knobelsdorff's finest interiors. The small chambers beyond contain part of Frederick's personal collection of French paintings. These include several masterpieces by **Watteau**, notably *The Embarcation for Cythera*, a delicate Rococo frippery tinged with sympathy and sadness, and *The Shop Sign*, an astonishingly original mixture of reality and illusion, which the dying artist painted in eight mornings for an art dealer friend.

Downstairs, the Knobelsdorff-Flügel currently contains the **Galerie der Romantik** (Tues–Fri 10am–6pm, Sat & Sun 11am–6pm; *www.smb.spk-berlin.de*; DM4/€2), a collection of nineteenth-century paintings from the German Romantic, Classical and

Biedermeier movements. The gallery is soon to be integrated into the collection of the Alte Nationalgalerie on Museumsinsel, which is scheduled to reopen in Dec 2001 (see p.832). Most dramatic are the works of **Caspar David Friedrich**, all of which express a powerful elemental and religious approach to landscape, particularly *Morning in the Riesengebirge* and *The Watzmann*. Comparably memorable are the visionary compositions of **Karl Friedrich Schinkel**, even although he was never more than an occasional painter. His works here are meticulously drawn Gothic fantasies, often with sea settings: *Gothic Church on a Seaside Bluff* is the most moodily dramatic. Look out, too, for the topographical paintings of **Eduard Gaertner**, which show the Berlin of the early nineteenth century – and make for a fascinating comparison with the present day.

The final addition to the main structure of the Schloss was Carl Gotthard Langhans's Neoclassical **Theaterbau** at the far western end. Its modernized interior now contains the **Museum für Vor- und Frühgeschichte** (Museum of Pre- and Early History; Tues–Fri 10am–6pm, Sat & Sun 11am–6pm; *www.smb.spk-berlin.de*; DM4/€2), a miscellaneous collection of archeological finds from both the Berlin area and abroad. Some artefacts from the Schliemann excavations of Troy are on view, though the most precious items (some represented here in reproductions) are in Russia, having been carted away as spoils of war. Delicate negotiations for the return of the Schliemann treasures continue, and the Germans hope that they will have them back in Berlin by the time this collection moves to the Neues Museum on Museumsinsel in 2008.

The Schlossgarten

The **Schlossgarten** is a mixture of different elements of landscaping styles. Closest to the Schloss is a formal Baroque garden; the rest was transformed by Lenné into an English-style landscaped park in which water plays a key role, the Spree being complemented by a series of ponds and canals spanned by graceful little bridges. Just a few metres away from the northeastern corner of the Schloss is the **Schinkel-Pavillon** (Tues–Sun 10am–5pm; *www.spsg.de*; DM4/€2), which was built as a Neapolitan-style retreat for Friedrich Wilhelm III. Schinkel designed the interior down to the minutest detail, and some of his drawings and paintings have since been added. Also on view are more topographical paintings by Gaertner, including views of Paris and Moscow as well as the remarkable hexagonal *Panorama from the Friedrichswerdersche Kirche*.

Much deeper into the gardens, on the north side of the carp pond, is the **Belvedere** (April–Oct Tues–Sun 10am–5pm; Nov–March Sat & Sun only noon–4pm; *www.spsg.de*; DM3/€1.50), built by Langhans as a combined outlook tower, teahouse and chamber music venue. It now houses a historical display of Berlin-made porcelain. On the western side of the gardens a long tree-lined avenue leads to the hushed and shadowy **Mausoleum** (April–Oct Tues–Sun 10am–5pm; *www.spsg.de*; DM2/€1), where Friedrich Wilhelm III is buried, his sarcophagus, carved by Christian Daniel Rauch, making him seem a good deal younger than his 70 years. Friedrich Wilhelm had commissioned the mausoleum to be built thirty years earlier for his wife, Queen Luise, whose own delicate sarcophagus, likewise by Rauch, depicts her not dead but sleeping. Later burials here include Kaiser Wilhelm I, looking every inch a Prussian king.

The Charlottenburg museums

Facing the Schloss across Spandauer Damm are two domed barracks built by Stüler in the 1850s for the royal guard. The eastern of these houses the **Ägyptisches Museum** (Tues–Fri 10am–6pm, Sat & Sun 10am–6pm; *www.smb.spk-berlin.de*; DM8/€4), which displays the fruits of innumerable German excavations in Egypt from the early part of the twentieth century. The museum's pride and joy is the **bust of Nefertiti** on the first floor, a treasure that has become a symbol for the city as a cultural capital. There's no questioning its beauty – the queen has a perfect bone structure and gracefully sculpted lips – and the history of the piece is equally interesting. Created around 1350 BC, the bust probably never left the studio in Akhetaten in which it was created, acting as a model for other portraits of the queen (its use as a model explains why the left eye was never drawn in). When the studio was deserted, the bust was left there, to be discovered some three thousand years later in 1912. In the last few days of the war, the bust was "removed" from the Soviet sector of Berlin, and wrangles continued over its return for the entire duration of the Cold War. Elsewhere in the museum, atmospheric lighting focuses attention on the exhibits, which are of a uniformly high standard. Look out for the astonishingly modern-looking **Green Man** of the Ptolemaic period, and the **Kalabsha Monumental Gate**, given to the museum by the Egyptian government in 1973.

The corresponding building directly opposite contains the latest addition to the roster of Berlin's state museums, the **Berggruen-Sammlung** (Tues–Fri 10am–6pm, Sat & Sun 11am–6pm; *www.smb.spk-berlin.de*; DM8/€4), which was initially placed on loan by the private collector Heinz Berggruen, but recently acquired for the city at a knockdown price. It contains what is by far the largest array of paintings by **Picasso** to be seen anywhere in Germany, with examples from all periods of his career. There are also rooms devoted to Matisse and Klee, plus a few works by Cézanne and Van Gogh.

Just to the south is the **Bröhan-Museum** (Tues–Sun 10am–6pm; DM6/€3), which is devoted exclusively to the Jugendstil and Art Deco movements. The walls are hung with paintings of the Berlin Secession, notably the luxuriant landscapes of Karl Hagenmeister; many of the other artworks – ceramics, furniture, glass, tapestries, ivories, goldware and silverware – are grouped together as simulated interiors of the period.

Western Charlottenburg

West of Charlottenburg is the **Funkturm**, a skeletal transmission mast inspired by the Eiffel Tower; to reach it, take U-Bahn #2 to Kaiserdamm, then travel one stop south on bus #204, or catch bus #149 from Bahnhof Zoo. The Funkturm was built in 1928 as a radio and, eventually, a TV transmitter. One of Goebbels's lesser-known achievements was to create the world's first regular TV service in 1941. Transmitted from the Funkturm, the weekly programme could only be received in Berlin; the service continued until just a few months before the end of the war. Today the Funkturm only serves police and taxi frequencies, but the mast remains popular for the toe-curling views from its 126-metre-high **observation platform** (daily 10am–11pm; DM6/€3). With the aluminium-clad monolith of the **Internationales Congress Centrum** lying

THE 1936 OLYMPICS

Hitler used the international attention the **1936 Olympics** attracted to show the "New Order" in Germany in the best possible light. Anti-Semitic propaganda and posters were suppressed in the city, German half-Jewish athletes were allowed to compete, and when the Olympic flame was relayed from Athens, the newsreels and the world saw the road lined with thousands wearing swastikas and waving Nazi flags. To the outside world, it seemed that the new Germany was rich, content and firmly behind the *Führer*.

Though the Games themselves were stage-managed with considerable brilliance – a fact recorded in Leni Riefenstahl's poetic and frighteningly beautiful film of the events, *Olympia* – not everything went according to official National Socialist doctrine. Black American athletes did supremely well in the games, **Jesse Owens** alone winning four gold medals, disproving the Nazi theory that blacks were "subhuman" and the Aryan race all-powerful. But eventually Germany won the most gold, silver and bronze medals (there's a memorial at the western end of the stadium), and the games were deemed a great success.

immediately below, it's possible to look out across the S-Bahn tracks to the gleaming city in the distance – a sight equally mesmerizing at night.

Three stops to the west by U-Bahn #2 is the largest Nazi-era building in the city, the **Olympia-Stadion**, which was purpose-built for the 1936 Olympic Games (see box on p.849), and remains very much in use. Whatever your feelings about that year's Games, the building in which they took place is still impressive, the huge pseudo-Neoclassical space a deliberate rejection of the modernist architecture then prevalent elsewhere. If you cut south and west around the stadium, down the road named after Jesse Owens, and take a right onto Passenheimer Strasse, you reach the bell tower, or **Glockenturm** (April–Oct daily 9am–6pm; DM4/€2). Rebuilt after wartime damage, it's chiefly interesting for the stupendous view it gives, not only over the stadium but also north to the natural amphitheatre that forms the Waldbühne, an open-air concert site, and across the beginnings of the Grunewald to the south. Also easy to spot is the **Teufelsberg** (Devil's Mountain), a massive mound that's topped with a faintly terrifying fairy-tale castle that used to be a US signals and radar base. The mountain itself is artificial: at the end of the war, the mass of debris that was once Berlin was carted to several sites around the city. Beneath the poplars, maples and ski runs lies the old Berlin, about 25 million cubic metres of it, presumably awaiting the attention of some future archeologist. In the meantime, it's popular as a place for weekend kite-flying and for skiing and tobogganing in winter.

Spandau

Spandau, situated at the confluence of the Spree and Havel, about 10km northwest of the city centre, is Berlin's oldest district – it was granted a town charter in 1232, and preserved its municipal independence until 1920. Its name immediately brings to mind the name of its jail's most famous – indeed in later years only – prisoner, **Rudolf Hess**, Hitler's former deputy who flew to Scotland in 1941 on a bizarre peace mission, and who hanged himself there in 1989.

However, there's little connection between Hess and Spandau itself. The jail, 4km away from the centre on Wilhelmstrasse, was demolished to make way for a supermarket for the British armed forces, and the chief reason to come here today is to escape the city centre, wander Spandau's village-like streets, and to visit the **Zitadelle** (Tues–Fri 9am–5pm, Sat & Sun 10am–5pm; DM4/€2), a fort established in the twelfth century and greatly strengthened in the second half of the sixteenth, when it was equipped with high-walled bastions on the Italian model which were believed to be impregnable. From the round **Juliusturm**, the only surviving part of the original castle, there's a good view over the complex and the surrounding countryside.

Spandau's Altstadt, which occupies a small island at the confluence of the rivers, is centred on the **Nikolaikirche**, a typical example of Gothic brickwork. At the quiet north end of the island is a well-restored medieval street, **Kolk**. Nearby, at Neuendorfer Str. 1, is the **Brauhaus in Spandau**, a nineteenth-century brewery that produces beer to a medieval recipe, and has tours explaining the brewing process. It's also possible in the summer months to catch **boats** from Spandau to Tegel, Wannsee and elsewhere.

Dahlem

The suburb of **Dahlem**, which is served by U-Bahn #1, lies to the southwest of central Berlin in the district of Zehlendorf. It's a neat village-like enclave that feels a world away from the technoflash city centre. Mostly residential, it's home to the Free University, the better-off bourgeoisie and a large museum complex, the **Staatliche Museen Dahlem** (Tues–Sun 10am–6pm; *www.smb.spk-berlin.de*; DM8/€4), which has

STEVE BENBOW

The inner port, Hamburg

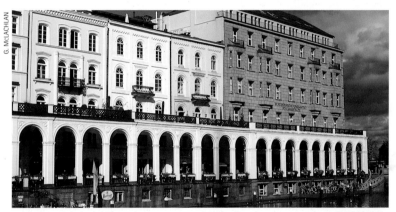

G. MCLACHLAN

The Alsterarkaden, Hamburg

E. NÄGELE

The North Friesian island of Amrun

Stralsund with the island of Rügen in the background

Strandkörbe (beach shelters) at Heringsdorf on the island of Usedom

The Neue Synagoge, Berlin

The Bundestag, Berlin

The Haus der Kulturen der Welt in the Tiergarten, Berlin

Schloss Sanssouci, Potsdam

The Wartburg, Eisenach

The Krämerbrücke with acrobats, Erfurt

Karl-Marx-Denkmal, Chemnitz

One of the Baroque atlantes in the Zwinger, Dresden

entrances on Arminallee and Lansstrasse. Until 1998 it contained the greater part of the Gemäldegalerie; when this moved to the Tiergarten, a huge amount of extra display space became available for the three museums which are likely to remain there for the foreseeable future.

The largest of these is the **Museum für Völkerkunde**, a wide-ranging ethnographic collection. When founded in 1873, it was a pioneering institution for the study of the cultures of non-European peoples, and its early acquisitions, mostly from the German colonies, brought so-called "Primitive" art to the attention of a Western audience, and later had a profound impact on the country's own Expressionist movement. Its **African** section is of special note, including as it does magnificent sculptures from two of the continent's greatest artistic centres, the Nigerian cities of **Ife** and **Benin**. The twelfth-to fifteenth-century terracotta heads from the former are the only examples to be seen outside Nigeria; the more widely disseminated bronze tradition of the latter is represented by some wonderfully characterized portrait heads of the fifteenth century and elaborate plaques from the following two centuries. Even when there was the competing draw of the old masters, the **Oceanic** department was hugely popular with visitors to Dahlem. It vividly evokes the island societies of the South Seas in a display of sailing craft, a complete clubhouse building, several totem poles, and an array of masks and cult objects. After a gap of more than fifty years, the **North American Indian** department is back on public view, complete with artefacts looted by the Red Army and only recently returned. Other sections of the museum are devoted to Ancient America, East Asia, South Asia and musical ethnology.

The name of the **Museum für Indische Kunst** is something of a misnomer, as it includes objects from China, Nepal, Tibet, Burma, Thailand, Cambodia, Indonesia and Afghanistan as well as the Indian subcontinent. Particularly outstanding are the **Buddhist cave paintings** from the famous Silk Road; dating from the fifth to the eleventh centuries, they were excavated by German archeologists in several expeditions just before World War I. The **Museum für Ostasiatische Kunst** concentrates on the art and calligraphy of China and Japan. Normally the objects are displayed in rotation, most being too fragile for permanent display.

The Grunewald, Havel and Wannsee

Few people associate Berlin with walks through dense woodland or swimming from crowded beaches, though that's just what the **Grunewald** and the Havel lakes have to offer. The Grunewald is 32 square kilometres of mixed woodland between the suburbs of Dahlem and Wilmersdorf, and the Havel lakes to the west; it's popular with Berliners for its bracing air and walks. Seventy percent of the Grunewald was cut down in the postwar years for badly needed fuel, and subsequent replanting has replaced pine and birch with oak and ash, making it all the more popular.

One possible starting point is the **Jagdschloss Grunewald** (mid-May to mid-Oct daily 10am–5pm; mid-Oct to mid-May Sat & Sun only 10am–4pm; *www.spsg.de*; DM4/€2), a royal hunting lodge built in Renaissance style in the sixteenth century by Caspar Theyss, who was also responsible for the Stadtschloss. Inside are several paintings by Cranach, as well as a fascinating series of portraits commissioned by the House of Orange of the first twelve Roman emperors. Each of these was entrusted to a different artist: for example, Rubens was responsible for *Julius Caesar*, Ter Brugghen for *Claudius*.

Just southeast of the Jagdschloss, the **Brücke-Museum** (Mon & Wed–Sun 11am–5pm; DM7/€3.50) at Bussardsteig 9 houses a collection of works by the Expressionist artistic group known as Die Brücke (The Bridge), who worked in Dresden and Berlin from 1905 to 1913. There is a generous representation of each of the five regular members (Kirchner, Heckel, Schmidt-Rottluff, Pechstein and Müller), as well as of Nolde, who was only affiliated for a brief period.

An alternative approach to the Grunewald, and to the start of a strip of **beaches**, is to take S-Bahn #1 or #7 to Nikolassee, from where it's a ten-minute walk or a quick bus ride to **Strandbad Wannsee**, a kilometre-long strip of pale sand that's the largest inland beach in Europe, and one which is packed as soon as the sun comes out. From here it's easy to wander into the forests. Travel one station further on the S-Bahn, to Wannsee, and you can catch one of several **ferries** that leave from nearby. It's possible to sail across the lake to Kladow on the F#10 (your S-Bahn ticket is valid, otherwise it's DM4/€2) or south to Potsdam and north to Spandau by other seasonal (or private) services.

Another possible destination is the **Pfaueninsel** (Peacock Island; daily: April & Oct 9am–5pm; May–Sept 8am–6pm; Nov–Feb 10am–4pm; *www.spsg.de*; ferry DM2/€1). Its **Schloss** (April–Oct Tues–Sun 10am–5pm; DM4/€2), a folly in the form of a ruined medieval castle, was built for the mistress of King Friedrich Wilhelm II. Inside, almost all the original decoration and furniture still survive; particularly intriguing is the **Tahitikabinett** in the northern tower, which is painted to resemble the interior of a bamboo hut. Equally enjoyable are the gardens, which were landscaped by Lenné so as to provide as many surprising vistas as possible. No cars are allowed on the island (nor, incidentally, are dogs, ghetto-blasters or smoking), which has been designated a conservation zone and is home to a flock of peacocks.

The eastern suburbs

In the ten years since the *Wende*, rebuilding has significantly changed the face of the **eastern suburbs** of Berlin and is changing them still. There's much to see, including some decidedly offbeat attractions, and the experience of these eastern districts, or *Bezirke*, is an important part of understanding the true identity of Berlin.

Your first goal should be the streets of **Prenzlauer Berg**, a part working-class, part bohemian district that fans out northeast of the city centre, and has long been a centre of "alternative" culture and lifestyle. This area is also home to some of the best cafés, bars and nightlife in the eastern part of the city. **Friedrichshain**, immediately to the east of the centre, has some fascinating examples of GDR architecture, and one of the city's oldest and best parks. It has become, in the last few years, the new frontier for the city's clubbers and bar-hoppers. If you've enough time, head out southeast to **Treptow** and its massive Soviet war memorial and riverside parks or even farther out to **Köpenick**, which has the atmosphere of a small village rather than a district of Berlin.

Prenzlauer Berg

The old working-class district of **Prenzlauer Berg** radiates out from the city centre in a network of tenement-lined cobbled streets, and has for all intents and purposes usurped Kreuzberg's role as home of the Berlin *Szene*. In GDR days it was a uniquely vibrant and exciting corner of East Berlin, home to large numbers of artists and young people who chose to live here on the edge of established East German society (literally as well as figuratively – the western boundary of Prenzlauer Berg was marked by the Berlin Wall). Since 1989 countless new bars, restaurants and boutiques have opened, particularly in the streets around Kollwitzplatz, thriving partly because the area's original inhabitants have been joined by an influx of people (often students) drawn from the west. The forces of gentrification are on the move, but the area still preserves a sense of freshness and energy. The quickest way to get there is to take the U-Bahn #2 to either Eberswalder Strasse or Schönhauser Allee. For a more atmospheric approach, take tram #1 from Hackescher Markt, which, going up Prenzlauer Allee, is the most direct route to the Kollwitzplatz area, or try tram #13 or #53, which will take you through some of eastern Berlin's lesser-known backstreets.

Schönhauser Allee is Prenzlauer Berg's main drag and cuts through Senefelder Platz. A stone's throw from here, at Schönhauser Allee 23–25, is the **Jüdischer Friedhof** (Mon–Thurs 10am–4pm, Fri 10am–1pm), which contains over twenty thousand Jewish graves. In 1943, most of the gravestones were smashed, but today many of the stones have been restored and repositioned, and a memorial stone near the cemetery entrance entreats visitors: "You stand here in silence, but when you turn away do not remain silent."

Beyond the junction of Schönhauser Allee, Danziger Strasse, Kastanienallee and Eberswalder Strasse, Schönhauser Allee assumes its true identity as an old-fashioned shopping street with cobbles and narrow shop facades. Just to the southeast of Schönhauser Allee U-Bahn station, at the intersection of Stargarder Strasse and Greifenhagener Strasse, is the **Gethsemenekirche**, which was an important focal point for reformist activities during the summer 1989 exodus from the GDR. Turning left onto Oderbergerstrasse leads you to Kastanienallee, which has become a lively area of bars and shops, or continue along Oderbergerstrasse to hit an active strip featuring a variety of eating and drinking spots. On the other hand, you can turn right into Sredzkistrasse from Schönhauser Allee and find the former **Schultheiss-Brauerei**, an 1890s brewery built in the pseudo-Byzantine style much favoured by Berlin's architects during the late nineteenth century. Its grounds have been transformed into the **KulturBrauerei**, a cultural centre with an alternative slant.

Retracing your path down Knaackstrasse and past Sredzkistrasse leads to **Kollwitzplatz**, named after the artist **Käthe Kollwitz**, who lived in nearby Weissenburgerstrasse (now called Kollwitzstrasse) from 1891 to 1943. An unflattering statue of the artist sits in the little park at the centre of the square. Her work, which embraced political and pacifist themes, is best appreciated in the Käthe-Kollwitz-Museum (see p.837). Running north from Kollwitzplatz is **Husemannstrasse**, now home to a lively restaurant and bar scene.

Friedrichshain and Lichtenberg

Spreading out east from the city centre, **Friedrichshain** is mainly residential in the north, but given over to extensive goods yards and moribund industry around the Ostbahnhof and down towards the River Spree in the south. It has earned notoriety of late as the new frontier for the city's clubbers and bar-hoppers. The kind of eclectic bar scene that sprang up in Prenzlauer Berg and Mitte in the early 1990s still blooms in Simon-Dach-Strasse and around Boxhagener Platz, as well as to the north around Rigaer Strasse.

The district's longest-established attractions are the Stalinist architecture of **Karl-Marx-Allee**, and the **Volkspark Friedrichshain**, resting-place of the victims of the 1848 revolution. Since 1989 these have been augmented by the **East Side Gallery**, a surviving stretch of Wall that has been transformed into a unique open-air art gallery. Running along Mühlenstrasse, between the Ostbahnhof and the Oberbaumbrücke in the south of the district, it's been daubed with various political/satirical images, some imaginative, some trite and some impenetrable. Take the U-Bahn #1 to Schlesisches Tor and walk across the Oberbaumbrücke for the best approach.

Another recent attraction, in the neighbouring district of **Lichtenberg**, is the former headquarters of the *Stasi*, the GDR's all-pervasive secret police. Part of the complex (Ruschestr. 103, Haus 1), is now designated the **Forschungs- und Gedenkstätte Normannenstrasse** (Normannenstrasse Research and Memorial Centre; Tues–Fri 11am–6pm, Sat & Sun 2–6pm; *www.Stasi-Museum.de*; DM5/€2.50). This incorporates the stained wood offices of Erich Mielke, the GDR's all-too-real Big Brother, as well as displays of the surveillance apparatus used by the *Stasi* to monitor real or imagined opponents of the regime.

Treptow

The only real reason to come to **Treptow** is to see the huge and sobering **Sowjetisches Ehrenmal**, Berlin's main Soviet war memorial. Standing in the Treptower Park, a well-known interwar assembly point for revolutionary workers about to embark on demonstrations, it commemorates the Soviet soldiers killed during the Battle of Berlin in April and May 1945, and is burial place to five thousand of the Soviet Union's estimated 305,000 casualties during the Battle of Berlin. To get there, take S-Bahn #6, #8, #9 or #10 to Treptower Park: from there it's just a few hundred metres to the memorial's arched entrance on the south side of Puschkinallee. A little way to the south of the entrance is a sculpture of a grieving woman representing the Motherland, to the left of which a broad concourse slopes upwards towards a viewing point flanked by two vast triangles of red granite, fashioned from stone bought from Sweden by the Nazis to furnish Berlin with projected victory monuments. From the viewing point the vista is dominated by a vast symbolic statue, a typically Soviet piece of gigantism fashioned out of marble from Hitler's Chancellery. Over 11m high and set on top of a hill, it shows an idealized Russian soldier clutching a saved child and resting his sword on a shattered swastika. Inside the plinth is a memorial crypt with a mosaic in true Socialist Realist style, showing Soviet citizens honouring the dead. In the long sunken park area which leads up to the statue are the mass graves of the Red Army troops, lined by sculpted frescoes of stylized scenes from the Great Patriotic War.

Köpenick

Köpenick is one of eastern Berlin's more pleasant *Bezirke*, located on the banks of the River Spree towards the southeast edge of the city, and easily reached by S-Bahn #3. At the southern end of the Altstadt, a footbridge leads to the Schlossinsel, an island at the confluence of the Spree and the Dahme, on which stands the **Schloss**, which was built in the late seventeenth century for the Great Elector Friedrich Wilhelm. For the past few years the building has been undergoing refurbishment in order that it can once again house part of the **Kunstgewerbemuseum** (*www.smb.spk-berlin.de*), and is due to reopen in 2002. It will display interior decorations from the sixteenth to eighteenth centuries, including the most important surviving furnishing from the Stadtschloss – the Berlin Silver Buffet, which was made by Augsburg silversmiths to designs by Andreas Schlüter.

Eating and drinking

You can spend as much or as little as you like on food in Berlin; it's one item, at least, that won't break the bank. The city's compressed, cosmopolitan nature means that it has **restaurants** offering a whole gamut of cuisines from around the globe. Indeed, ethnic eateries – many of which serve full meals for under DM15/€7.50. – are at least as ubiquitous as traditional German Gaststätten. And nowhere is more than a stone's throw from a **bar**, at least in the western part of the city. Just about every street corner has a small Kneipe, ranging from lugubrious beer-swilling holes to slick, upscale hangouts for Berlin's night people. Most stay open later than elsewhere in Germany: it's quite feasible to drink around the clock here, the result of a law that requires bars to close only for an hour a day for cleaning. It's worth bearing in mind that many are excellent (and inexpensive) choices for food, especially breakfast, which may be served till afternoon – or later.

The city's most distinctive drink is *Berliner Weisse*, a top-fermented, very pale-coloured wheat **beer** with a low alcohol content (usually around 2.5 percent). It has an acidic taste when drunk neat, but it's normally pepped up with a shot of fruity syrup, or *Schuss*, and served in a large bowl-shaped glass as a summer refresher. Ask for it *mit grün* and you get a dash of woodruff, creating a greeny brew with a strong herby taste; *mit rot* is a raspberry-flavoured kiddy drink that works wonders at breakfast time. The city's two large breweries, Kindl and Scultheiss, both make *Berliner Weisse*, in addition to their own version of *Pils*. A broader portfolio of beers is available from an ex-GDR brewery, Berliner Bürgerbräu, whose products include a dark *Bock* and an even darker *Schwarzbier*.

Restaurants

The more established restaurants are in the west, but in the last few years the eastern districts of the city have experienced a restaurant boom. Generally speaking, these eastern establishments cater to a young and savvy crowd and emphasize *nouvelle* and ethnic menus. Particularly in Mitte and Prenzlauer Berg, there are now plenty of choices and excellent food to be had.

German and Austrian

Austria, Bergmannstr. 30, Kreuzberg. Dark rustic surrounds and solid wood tables serving generous portions of excellent Austrian food.

Café Jolesch, Muskauerstr. 1, Kreuzberg. Noisy, smoky and very popular Austrian restaurant, particularly renowned for its desserts.

Die Krahe, Kollwitzstrasse 86, Prenzlauer Berg. Inventive, fresh and seasonal, with a mixed German and French menu.

Florian, Grolmanstr. 52, Charlottenburg. A leading light of the *neue deutsche Küche* movement, this is as much a place to be seen as to eat in. The food, similar to French *nouvelle cuisine*, is light, flavourful – and expensive.

Gugelhof, Knaackstr. 37, Prenzlauer Berg. Inventive German, French and Alsatian food, beautifully presented.

Henne, Leuschnerdamm 25, Kreuzberg (☎0 30/6 14 77 30). Pub-style restaurant with the best chicken in Berlin. The interior here is original – it hasn't been changed, the owners claim, since 1905. Reservations essential.

Historische Weinstuben, Poststr. 23, Mitte. A reasonable little wine restaurant in the basement of the Knoblauchhaus in the Nikolaiviertel.

Honigmond, Borsigstr. 28, Mitte. Understated and tastefully appointed dining rooms serving well-prepared fresh cuisine, both traditional and modern.

Kellerrestaurant im Brechthaus, Chausseestr. 125, Mitte. Atmospheric restaurant, decorated with Brecht memorabilia, including models of his stage sets, in the basement of the poet's old house. Serves Viennese specialities from recipes supposedly dreamed up by his wife Helene Weigel.

Kulisse, Friesenstr. 14, Kreuzberg. Reasonably priced Swabian specialities, though imagination sometime exceeds skill here.

Medici, Lausitzer Str. 25, Kreuzberg (☎0 30/6 18 68 26). Presents *neue deutsche Küche* in stylish surroundings. Trendy, so book ahead. Evenings only, closed Thurs.

November, Husemannstrasse 15, Prenzlauer Berg. Imaginative daily specials and the best weekend brunch in Prenzlauer Berg.

Offenbach-Stuben, Stubbenkammerstr. 8, Prenzlauer Berg (☎0 30/4 45 85 02). A near-legend even in GDR days and one of the best places in Prenzlauer Berg, with all kinds of unexpected specialities on the menu. Theatrical decor and intimate seating niches great for late-night conversation. Booking essential.

Restauration 1900, Husemannstr. 1, Prenzlauer Berg. Another Prenzlauer Berg culinary highlight, serving traditional German dishes that spring a few surprises.

Riehmers, Hagelberger Str. 9, Kreuzberg. Husband-and-wife-run restaurant with a comfortable ambience and outstanding food and service. In summer, there's outdoor seating in the historic Riehmer's Hofgarten.

Slobo's, Heimstr. 8, Kreuzberg (☎0 30/6 93 09 00). One of Berlin's smallest restaurants, creating imaginative dishes with a French/German slant. Booking advisable; closed Wed.

Weltrestaurant Markthalle, Pücklerstr. 34, Kreuzberg. Spacious restaurant with long communal tables offering German food in hearty portions. Popular with a young crowd.

Wirtshaus Schildhorn, Str. am Schildhorn 4a, Grunewald. Housed in an attractive old Wirtshaus on the edge of Lake Havel, this is an ideal spot if you've spent the day exploring the area.

Zum Nussbaum, Am Nussbaum 3, Mitte. A convincing copy of a destroyed prewar Wirtshaus once patronized by the artists Heinrich Zille and Otto Nagel. It serves typically hearty Berlin fare.

Zur Letzten Instanz, Waisenstr. 14–16, Mitte. One of the city's oldest Gaststätten, with a wonderfully evocative interior, complete with tiled oven, and a beer garden. Reasonably priced traditional dishes all have legal-themed names, a reminder of the days when people used to drop in on their way to the nearby courthouse.

Other cuisines

Angkor Wat, Paulstr. 22, Tiergarten. Wonderful, subtle Cambodian food that is often surprising and always pleasing. There's another branch at Seelingstr. 34–36, Charlottenburg.

Aroma, Hochkirchstr. 8, Schöneberg (☎0 30/7 82 58 21). Inexpensive, yet well above average Italian with photo gallery and Italian films on Tues nights. It's advisable to book after 8pm.

Asia Inn, Knaackstr. 45, Prenzlauer Berg. Serves a range of regional Chinese cusines, including Mongolian, Cantonese and Szechuan.

Carib, Motzstr. 31, Schöneberg. Offers moderately priced Caribbean cuisine and friendly service from the Jamaican owner.

Cenone, Marienburger Str. 48, Prenzlauer Berg. Northern Italian kitchen with a huge wine list. Fresh breads, Italian delicacies and sandwiches can be bought from the associated shop. Open Mon–Fri 11am–8pm, Sat 11am–4pm.

Chez Maurice, Botzowstr. 39, Prenzlauer Berg (☎0 30/4 25 05 06). A little out of the way but worth it for the totally authentic food and theatrics of the eponymous French chef. Service can be slow; reservations recommended. Open daily 7pm–2am.

Cour Carrée, Savignyplatz 5, Charlottenburg. Deservedly popular French restaurant with *fin-de-siècle* decor and garden seating.

Der Ägypter, Kantstr. 26, Charlottenburg. This Egyptian restaurant, run in tandem with a jewellery shop, is an adventurous alternative to the safe bets around Savignyplatz. It serves spicy, filling meals, including good vegetarian selections.

Edd's, Lutzowstr. 81, Schöneberg (☎0 30/2 15 52 94). Huge portions of superbly cooked fresh Thai food make this a popular place any day of the week. Reservations essential.

La Rustica, Kleine Presidenenstr.4, Mitte. Serves wonderful gourmet pizza and excellent pasta and antipasto.

Los Cucarachas, Oranienburger Str. 38, Mitte. Very popular and spirited Tex-Mex place that fills up just about every night. Offers burritos and tacos from the Mexican side of the border; hamburgers and fried chicken from the Texas side.

Lusiada, Kurfürstendamm 132a, Charlottenburg. Boisterous, moderately priced Portuguese place renowned for its fish dishes.

Merhaba, Hasenheide 39, Kreuzberg. Highly rated Turkish restaurant that's usually packed with locals. A selection of the starters here can be more interesting than a main course.

Naan, Oderbergerstr. 49, Prenzlauer Berg. Authentic and inexpensive Indian, a favourite of the local art and student crowd in Prenzlauer Berg.

Osteria No. 1, Kreuzbergstr. 71, Kreuzberg (☎0 30/7 86 91 62). Classy, inexpensive and therefore highly popular Italian, run by a collective. Booking essential.

Pasternak, Knaackstr. 24, Prenzlauer Berg. Authentic, intimate Russian restaurant in the thick of the bustling local *Szene.*

Sapporo-Kan, Schlüterstr. 52, Charlottenburg. Japanese restaurant that's a popular lunchtime spot: admire the wax culinary creations in the window, then eat the real thing inside.

Storch, Wartburgstr. 54, Schöneberg. Rustic eatery serving cuisine from the Alsace region in what was once – they claim – a brothel. The excellent, reasonably priced food is served at long communal tables, so don't come for an intimate chat.

Tuk-Tuk, Grossgörschenstr. 2, Schöneberg. Amiable Indonesian near Kleistpark U-Bahn. It's advisable to enquire about the spiciness of your dish before ordering.

Vietnam, Suarezstr. 61, Charlottenburg. One of the city's most popular Vietnamese restaurants, quietly situated in a street of junk shops.

Viva Mexico, Chausseestr. 36, Mitte. A real rarity this side of the Atlantic – a Mexican restaurant that is actually run by a Mexican family. The food is very reasonably priced and absolutely authentic; if you take a table at the front you can watch your meal being prepared.

Zlata Praha, Meinekestr. 4, Charlottenburg. Moderately priced yet high-quality Czech speciality restaurant, with the original *Budweiser Budvar* on tap.

Vegetarian and kosher

Abendmahl, Muskauerstr. 9, Kreuzberg. A magnificent restaurant in every respect: excellent food (especially the soups – try the *Kürbis* or pumpkin), a busy but congenial atmosphere and reasonable prices.

Arche Noah, Fasanenstr. 79, Charlottenburg. Fine kosher restaurant in the Jüdisches Gemeindehaus.

Café Oren, Oranienburger Str. 28, Mitte. Next door to the Neue Synagoge, offering light vegetarian (and kosher-esque) dishes in a stylish interior.

Hakuin, Martin-Luther-Str. 1, Schöneberg. Excellent Japanese vegetarian-macrobiotic, run by a Buddhist order, featuring tofu and tempura dishes, often complemented by a seaweed salad.

Little Shop of Food, Kollwitzstr. 90, Prenzlauer Berg. Never disappointing, the kitchen turns out a wonderful and ever-changing selection of soups, entrées and freshly baked goods. Open noon–10pm, closed Sat.

Thymian, Gneisenaustr. 57, Kreuzberg. Somewhat austere and self-conscious vegetarian place, but with an inventive menu.

Snack bars

The cheapest places for a meal are the **Mensas** of the Technical University on Ernst-Reuter-Platz and at Hardenbergstr. 34, which are officially for university students only and open Mon–Fri 11.15am–2.30pm. In addition to these, there is a wide variety of inexpensive **snack stands** and stand-up eateries in Berlin. In fact, there seems to be a Turkish fast-food stand, Italian pizzeria, or a Chinese or Thai takeaway on just about every corner, but separating the good from the ugly can be a bit hit or miss. The following are recommended.

Al Rai, Grosse Hamburger Str. 20/21, Mitte. A spacious, informal place where you can linger long over your tea. It offers Arab specialities such as couscous and shish kebab.

Brooklyn, Oranienstr. 176, Kreuzberg. Wonderful, inexpensive American-style hero sandwiches, cheesecake and brownies.

Duy Thai Snack, Prenzlauer Allee 226, Prenzlauer Berg. Inexpensive and tasty Thai cookery including many vegetarian and noodle dishes.

Soup Kultur, Kurfurstendamm 224, Charlottenburg. Soup kitchen with changing daily specials and take-away service. Mon–Fri noon–8pm. Sat noon–4pm.

Hausbrauereien

Berlin has supplanted Munich in the leading role in the national enthusiasm for new-generation Hausbrauereien, where beer is brewed in the bar-cum-restaurant where it is served. In addition to those listed below, one other can be found in the hotels section on p.819.

Alter Fritz, Karolinenstr. 12, Reinickendorf. A popular excursion destination in the north of the city, this is set in a huge and leafy beer garden. Its speciality is a malty, copper-coloured beer; it also brews a *Bock* and a *Weizen*.

Aschinger, Kurfürstendamm 26, Charlottenburg. Old-fashioned underground Bierkeller, first established in 1892. Nowadays with a large tourist clientele, it brews a range of unfiltered beers and serves inexpensive traditional German food.

Brauhaus Georgbräu, Spreeufer 4, Mitte. This riverside Hausbrauerei in the historic heart of the city makes light and dark beers and its own powerful *Korn*; it also has a menu of hearty old-style Berlin cuisine.

Brauhaus in Rixdorf, Glasower Str. 27, Neukölln. Berlin's closest relative to the British village pub, this is crammed full of knick-knacks and beer-related paraphernalia.

Lemke, S-Bahn arch 143 by Hackescher Markt, Mitte. Always has three varieties of the house beer on tap: *Export, Bock* and *Festbier*. Serves, incongruously, Japanese food.

Leopold's Brauhaus, Karl-Liebknecht-Str. 13, Mitte. Despite its unpromising location in a modern shopping centre, this makes a good attempt at re-creating the ambience of a Bavarian beer hall. It makes an excellent *Zwickelbier* as well as various seasonal brews, and has a good menu, particularly of poultry dishes.

Luisenbräu, Luisenplatz 1, Charlottenburg. Large, bustling Hausbrauerei within sight of Schloss Charlottenburg. You can watch the light and dark beers being brewed; they're served in 0.2 litre glasses to ensure maximum freshness. The food is inexpensive, particularly at lunchtime, when there are changing daily specials; live music is performed several evenings per week.

Traditional cafés

Berlin is exceptionally well endowed with elegant old-world cafés serving delicious *Kaffee und Kuchen* in an unhurried environment.

Café Bilderbuch, Akazienstr. 28, Schöneberg. Classy yet cosy Viennese-style *Kaffeehaus* with delicious spiked coffee drinks. Various kinds of live music (with dancing Thurs 7–8.30pm & Sun 4–7pm) are performed several times a week in the back room.

Café Einstein, Kurfürstenstr. 58, Schöneberg. Housed in an old villa with a fine garden, this is as close as you'll get to the ambience of a prewar Berlin *Kaffeehaus*. International newspapers are available, and breakfast is served 10am–2pm. There's also a branch at Unter den Linden 42, Mitte.

Café Hardenberg, Hardenbergstr. 10, Charlottenburg. Large, old-fashioned café with excellent and cheap food that draws in local students.

Café Möhring, Kurfüstendamm 215, Charlottenburg. Founded in 1898, this is probably Berlin's best-known traditional café, offering a changing daily selection of some two dozen cakes, plus a range of main courses, ice creams and fresh fruit cocktails. An offshoot can be found at Charlottenstr. 55, Mitte.

Kaffeestube, Poststr. 19, Mitte. A Nikolaiviertel café that tries to recreate the atmosphere of a Biedermeier coffee house.

Operncafé, Opernpalais, Unter den Linden 5, Mitte. Located in a former royal palace, this café successfully evokes the atmosphere of imperial Berlin. Coffee and amazing cakes make it a recommended place for a break while visiting the many sights and museums in the vicinity.

Tadschikische Teestube, Palais am Festungsgraben 1, Mitte. Housed in an eighteenth-century palace, this is a convincing re-creation of a Tadzhik tea room, where you take off your shoes on entry, then recline or sit on cushions placed around the floor. As well as a range of speciality teas, light meals of Russian and Tadzhik origin are available. Open Mon–Fri 5pm–midnight, Sat & Sun 3pm–midnight.

Wintergarten, Fasanenstr. 23, Charlottenburg. Occupying a handsome villa in a quiet garden, this is part of the Literaturhaus, an institution devoted to poetry readings and other bookish events. Breakfast is served from 10am.

Bars and café-bars

Berlin's bar and café-bar scene is focused on a number of distinct areas. Both drinking and eating are generally best done away from the obvious tourist strips like Unter den Linden and Kurfürstendamm, where standards tend to be lower and prices higher. The **Scheunenviertel**, just north of the city centre, and the inner-city district of **Prenzlauer Berg** today boast the city's most eclectic possibilities. **Friedrichshain**, a district characterized by working-class neighbourhoods and former squats, seems poised to offer refuge to those disenchanted with increasingly chi-chi Prenzlauer Berg or Mitte. Meanwhile, the institutionalized anarchy of **Kreuzberg** – for so long the area to be after hours – is starting to feel slightly shopworn, though it would be quite easy to spend a few weeks bar-crawling here before you even began to exhaust the possibilities. Adjacent **Schöneberg** tends to be a little smarter and a little more sedate; you'll find a scattering of slick cafés alongside corner Kneipen, but none of the extremities of its neighbour.

Scheunenviertel

Aufsturz, Oranienburger Str. 67. Not as hip as some of the local hangouts but comes into its own on those occasional broiling summer days, thanks to outdoor seating on the shady side of the street. An additional attraction is the extensive range of bottled beers, taking in everything from erstwhile GDR premium beer *Radeberger* to cherry-flavoured Belgian arcana.

Café Ici, Auguststr. 61. By day pipe-smoking aesthetes sit composing poetry amid the venerable furnishings of this pleasantly soporific café-gallery, and though things tend to liven up a bit in the evening it's a good place to escape the Scheunenviertel crowds. Open until 3am.

Obst und Gemüse, Oranienburger Str. 48. Always crowded, always chaotic, in many ways this is the quintessential Scheunenviertel bar, although it is past its hipness zenith. You can wait a while to get served but, as the place attracts quite a lot of tourists, at least you'll be waiting in company.

Reingold, Novalisstr. 11. Sophisticated Art Deco cocktail lounge with a clientele in their 20s and 30s.

Strandbad Mitte, Kleine Hamburger Str. 16. At the end of a small street off the beaten tourist track, this inviting café and bar make a good retreat when it all becomes too much. Excellent breakfasts served 9am–4pm.

The Pips, Auguststr. 84. Sophisticated cocktail bar and dance club. Fills up fast and stays that way through the night.

Webtimes, Chausseestr. 8. Internet café at the quarter's northern periphery.

Prenzlauer Berg

Akba Lounge, Sredzkistr. 64. Very popular, so the narrow bar gets uncomfortably crowded very fast. The adjoining club plays lounge and house music.

Alpha, Dunckerstr. 72. Internet café, open daily 3pm to midnight.

Café Anita Wronski, Knaackstr. 26–28. This smart Wasserturm café-bar is an excellent place to start local wanderings, though it can get very crowded. Good breakfasts 10am–3pm.

Café Manatees, Lychener Str. 64. A new bar catering to a somewhat younger crowd. The distinguishing feature here is a Sunday breakfast that starts at 5am.

Prater, Kastanienallee 7–9. A traditional beer garden, built in the nineteenth century and recently renovated. In summer you can swig beer, feast on *Bratwurst*, *Eisbein* or other native food and listen to German rock from the 1970s. A true Berlin experience.

Sevilla Bar, Rykestr. 54. A little north of the action around the Wassertum, this narrow little cocktail bar gets missed by most tourists, meaning you can enjoy the cocktails and tapas in relative peace.

Times, Husemannstr. 10. The kitchen here is open until 6am – handy if you're on a long pub crawl in the neighbourhood.

Friedrichshain

Astro Bar, Simon-Dach-Str. 40. With its 1970s sci-fi trappings and DJs most nights a week, this is spearheading Friedrichshain's campaign to be the next boho borough.

Supamolly, Jessnerstr. 41. A holdover from Friedrichshain's turbulent squatter days shortly after the fall of the Wall, this cheap bar is still popular with the alternative set.

Tagung, Wühlischstr. 29. Friendly bar with GDR kitsch and memorabilia. Cellar hosts Cube Club disco.

Savignyplatz and around

CUT, Knesebeckstr. 16. Over three hundred cocktails in a black cocoon, and certainly a cut above the rest pricewise.

Hegel, Savignyplatz 2. Tiny Russian-themed café on the southeastern side of Savignyplatz that attracts an older crowd. Gregarious fun when someone starts up on the piano.

Schwarzes Café, Kantstr. 148. The best young, chic hangout on the street, with a relaxed atmosphere, good music and food (like all-day breakfast and a "Black Special" of black coffee, a Sobranie Black Russian cigarette and black bread). Dated perhaps, but still a classic. Open round the clock, except Tues when it's open 8am–8pm.

Wirtshaus Wuppke, Schlüterstr. 21. Old-fashioned Kneipe without the sleaze.

Zillemarkt, Bleibtreustr. 48a. Wonderful if shabby bar that attempts a *fin-de-siècle* feel. Unpretentious and fun, and a good place to start Savignyplatz explorations – it's by the S-Bahn station. Breakfast 10am–4pm.

Kreuzberg

Ankerklause, corner of Kottbusser Damm and Maybachufer. A sleepy, nautically themed pub overlooking a canal has been transformed into a hip bar playing techno and easy listening. Usually packed by 11pm.

Bierhimmel, Oranienstr. 183. Candlelit bar with a cosy 1950s cocktail lounge out back (open Wed–Sun from 10pm). Great atmosphere, and a second home to many locals. Cocktail bar.

Café Adler, Friedrichstr. 206. Small café whose popularity came from the fact that it is next to the site of the Checkpoint Charlie border crossing. Serves breakfasts and meals.

Golgotha, Viktoriapark. Enormous, hugely popular open-air café and disco (summer only), perched near the top of Kreuzberg's hill. Breakfast served 11am–3pm.

Würgeengel, Dresdener Str. 122. Named after the Buñuel film *El angel exterminator* and next to the Babylon movie theatre, this is a popular hangout for cineastes.

Schöneberg and around

Bar am Lützowplatz, Lützowplatz 7. Distinguished in having the longest bar in the city, this also has Berlin's best selection of whiskies (63) and a superb range of moderately priced cocktails.

E & M Leydicke, Mansteinstr. 4. This claims to be the oldest Kneipe in western Berlin, and has been run by the same family for well over a century. It's best known for its home-made fruit wines.

Green Door, Winterfeldtstr. 50. Somewhat snooty cocktail bar, attracting a well-dressed crowd of young professionals and party-goers. Once you're past the pretension, though, the place can be fun, and they mix an awfully good cocktail.

Kumpelnest 3000, Lützowstr. 23. Carpeted walls and a mock-Baroque effect attract a rough-and-ready crew of thirtysomethings to this erstwhile brothel. Gets going around 2am. The best place in the area. Normally standing room only.

Mister Hu, Goltzstr. 39. Cool blue cocktail bar with a great offering of drinks and some of the city's best bartenders.

Mutter, Hohenstaufenstr. 4. Large café and bar of indirect lighting and loud music. Quite popular and usually crowded. Sushi available.

N N Train, Hauptstr. 162. Two subway cars converted into a long, thin cocktail bar. Inside it's buoyant and not as kitschy as you'd think.

Pinguin Club, Wartburgstr. 54. Tiny and cheerful bar with 1950s and 1960s America supplying its theme and background music. Well worth a visit.

Elsewhere in western Berlin

Blisse 14, Blissestr. 14, Wilmersdorf. Café-bar designed especially, but not exclusively, for disabled people. A good meeting-place.

Café am Neuen See, Lichtensteinallee 1, Tiergarten. Smack in the middle of the Tiergarten park, this upmarket venue has slick Italian food in a beautiful lakeside setting. Summer outdoor eating is especially pleasant.

Website, Joachimstaler Str. 41. Internet café conveniently close to Bahnhof Zoo.

Zur Weissen Maus, Ludwigkirchplatz 12, Charlottenburg. Chic 1920s-style bar with reproductions of Otto Dix and Max Beckmann reflected in the mass of mirrors. Popular with older artists and has good, if expensive, cocktails. Opens around 10pm.

Gay bars

The most concentrated area of gay bars is between Wittenbergplatz and Nollendorfplatz, south of Kleiststrasse. For more detailed listings, pick up a free copy of either *Siegessäule* or *Serjei*, available from most bars.

Anderes Ufer, Hauptstr. 157, Schöneberg. Opened at the tail end of the first gay movement heyday in the late 1970s, this classic is still going strong, attracting a mixed gay and lesbian crowd. Regular art and photography exhibitions.

Berlin Connection, Martin-Luther-Str. 19, Schöneberg. Modern café-bistro, strewn with palms and mirrors, which attracts a young to late-30s crowd. Second corner bar, and terrace in summer.

Café Anal, Muskauer Str. 15, Kreuzberg. Long-established alternative bar in east Kreuzberg and a second home for gay punks. Gets lively after 11pm.

Die Busche, Mühlenstr. 11–12, Friedrichshain. This holdover from the East Berlin gay scene still attracts a fun-loving gay and lesbian crowd with music ranging from ABBA to German schlager.

Schoppenstube, Schönhauser Allee 44, Prenzlauer Berg. The best-known gay place in the east. In reality this is two very different bars: a pleasant wine bar upstairs, and a steamy, cruiser's haven downstairs. Knock for entry and if the doorman likes the look of you you're in.

Tom's Bar, Motzstr. 19, Schöneberg. Dark, sweaty and wicked cruising bar with a large back room. Possibly Berlin's most popular gay bar, and a great place to finish off an evening.

Twilight Zone, Welserstr. 24, Schöneberg. Candlelit basement bar underneath Connection disco. On Wed, Thurs and Sun it's leather, rubber or uniforms only. Fairly macho/heavy. Closed Mon & Tues.

Women's cafés and bars

Many of Berlin's women-only bars have a strong lesbian following, though straight women are welcome everywhere.

Begine, Potsdamer Str. 139, Schöneberg. Stylishly decorated bar-bistro/gallery with inexpensive food. Hosts films, readings and concerts.

Café Seidenfaden, Dircksenstr. 47, Mitte. Alcohol-free café, open only until 9pm.

Die Zwei, Am Wasserturm, Spandauer Damm 168, Charlottenburg. The city's tackiest best, a determinedly (non-exclusive) lesbian bar, popular particularly among older women, with music from Marlene via Iron Butterfly to Madonna.

Offenbar, Schreinerstr. 5, Friedrichshain. Lesbian hangout in alternative Friedrichshain.

Roses, Oranienstr. 187, Kreuzberg. Gay bar but with a strong lesbian presence. Currently one of the locales of choice.

Music, nightlife and entertainment

Since the time of the Weimar Republic, and even through the lean postwar years, Berlin has had a reputation for having some of the best – and steamiest – nightlife in Europe, an image fuelled by the cartoon-like drawings of George Grosz and films like *Cabaret*. Among the big draws today are the **clubs** that have grown up out of the city's techno scene. In a remarkably short space of time these places, many housed in abandoned buildings on or around the former no-go area of the East-West border strip, have spawned a scene that ranks among the most exciting in Europe. If manic dance music is not your thing, then check out the city's wide range of more traditional clubs and discos, ranging from slick hangouts for the trendy to raucous punky dives.

Berlin's reputation as a leader of the avant-garde is also reflected in the number of small, often experimental **theatre** groups working here. The scene is an active one, though bear in mind that many theatre companies take a break in July and August. **Classical music** has long been dominated by the world-class Berlin Philharmonic, though several other orchestras and three opera companies are based in the city. Vanishing subsidies have cast a shadow over theatres, orchestras and opera houses in the city, which, as a legacy of the decades of division, currently has a surplus of such institutions. Though some rationalization is inevitable in the coming years, it's likely that all the big names will weather current storms.

Theaterkassen (ticket offices) are usually the easiest – and occasionally the only – way of buying tickets for all major music, theatre and dance events. Open during normal working hours, they take credit-card bookings and charge a hefty commission (up to 17 percent of the ticket price). The best place to try, especially for fringe theatre, more obscure classical concerts and dance, is **Hekticket**, Rathausstr. 1, Mitte (☎0 30/24 31 24 31). Other good bets are **Box Office**, Nollendorfplatz 7, Schöneberg (☎2 15 54 63), **Wertheim**, Kurfürstendamm 231, Charlottenburg (☎0 30/8 82 25 00), and **Ko Ka 36**, Oranienstr. 29, Kreuzberg (☎0 30/6 15 88 18, *www.icf.de/koka36*).

The way to find out exactly **what's on** and where is to look in the listings magazines *Tip* and *Zitty* (see p.816), in *Berlin Programm* or on the innumerable flyposters about town.

Discos and clubs

Berlin's clubs and discos are smaller, cheaper and less exclusive than their counterparts in London or New York – and fewer in number. You don't need much nous to work out that the places along the Ku'damm are tourist rip-offs: the real all-night sweats take place in the newer **dance-music clubs** that have opened up, mainly in the former East Berlin, where glitz is out and raving is in. For the slightly older, post-punk crowd, Schöneberg and Kreuzberg tend to be where it's happening. Don't bother turning up until midnight at the earliest, since few places get going much before then. Admission is often free – when you do pay, it shouldn't be much more than DM15/€7.50. Some of the ravey places have strict door policies, but if you look the part you'll probably get in. Like most cities, Berlin's turnover in nightspots is rapid: expect the following listings to have changed at least slightly by the time you arrive – this applies particularly to the newer places on the east side of town.

Casino, corner of Saarbrücker Strasse and Prenzlauer Allee, Prenzlauer Berg. Housed on grounds of a former baked-goods factory, Casino is the rave joint *du jour*, with star DJs like Paul Van Dyk packing them in.

El Barrio, Potsdamer Str. 84, Tiergarten. An irresistable salsa/lambada disco precedes weekend bands.

Knaack-Club, Greifswalder Str. 224, Prenzlauer Berg. Rock (David Byrne to Nirvana) in the cellar and dance on the first floor of a big old club building in a Prenzlauer Berg courtyard, drawing a young, mainly East Berlin crowd. Nightly from 10pm.

Kurvenstar, Kleine Präsidentenstr. 3, Mitte. Beautifully decorated retro Seventies club with a front bar and dancefloor in the back. Caters now to a young, not very gregarious hip-hop crowd on Wednesdays and Saturdays, although other nights feature drum'n'bass or triphop.

Ostgut, Mühlenstr. 26-30 (entrance Rummelsburger Platz), Friedrichshain. Generous space for raves, often featuring big name DJs such as Westbam. Also home of Lab.oratory gay fetish evenings.

Soda, Knaackstr. 97, Prenzlauer Berg. Recently opened club in the newly renovated KulturBrauerei cultural centre located on the grounds of a former brewery. The eclectic club-cum-literary salon-cum-restaurant concept is still finding its feet. Check out the GDR rock disco Fridays at the neighbouring Alte *Kantine*.

WMF, Ziegelstr. 22, Mitte. Legendary post-Wall club now at its fifth location, still worth checking out if you're into any flavour of house.

Live rock and pop music

In the big venues, you should book well in advance for anything even vaguely popular. Invariably you can't buy tickets from the places themselves, but need to go to one of the ticket offices listed opposite. It's also worth remembering that, in addition to the places listed below, many bars and cafés put on live music.

Arena, Eichenstr. 4, Treptow (☎0 30/5 33 73 33, *www.arena-berlin.de*). Located almost in the middle of nowhere, this medium-sized hall usually offers rappers, teenie groups and other popular bands for a young audience. The adjacent *Glashaus* hosts regular Sunday morning house breakfasts and hip-hop jams.

ColumbiaFritz, Columbiadamm 9–11, Tempelhof (☎0 30/69 81 28 28). A former US-army movie theatre, this place now serves as a snug though smoky venue for local and (minor) international rock and punk bands.

Columbiahalle, Columbiadamm 13–21, Tempelhof (☎0 30/6 98 09 80). Right across the street from the Tempelhof airport, this venue hosts crowd-pleasing international acts.

Eierschale Zenner, Alt-Treptow 14–17, Treptow (☎0 30/5 33 73 70). A large and popular beer garden by the shore of the River Spree, with 1950s and 1960s rock and roll and other summery music.

ICC Berlin, Messedamm 26, Charlottenburg (☎0 30/3 03 81). Vast, soulless hall for trade fairs that often hosts gigs.

Knaack, Greifswalderstr. 224, Prenzlauer Berg (☎0 30/4 42 70 60, *www.knaack-berlin.de*). Mostly local rock bands, plus the odd visiting post-punk legend.

Kesselhaus@KulturBrauerei, Knaackstr. 97, Prenzlauer Berg (☎0 30/4 41 92 69). Sharing space in a nineteenth-century brewery with an arts and cultural centre, this club offers local and mid-level bands.

Tacheles, Oranienburger Str. 53–56, Mitte (☎0 30/2 81 61 19, *www.tacheles.de*). Concerts from around 10pm. The performers are likely to be pretty eclectic, ranging from guitar bands to industrial noise merchants.

Tempodrom, Str. der Pariser Kommune 8, Friedrichshain (*www.tempodrom-berlin.de*). Tent venue hosting mid-level rock and world-music acts. Hosts a free music festival each summer.

Tränenpalast, Reichstagsufer 17, Mitte (☎0 30/2 38 62 11). A former waiting room at the border between east and west is now a medium-sized hall featuring rock, soul and jazz.

Velodrom, Paul-Heyse-Str. 29, Prenzlauer Berg, (☎0 30/44 30 44 30). Home of mega sports events such as the six-day bicycle race, this is also the place to go to see the likes of Britney Spears or Janet Jackson.

Waldbühne, Glockenturmstrasse, Charlottenburg (☎0 30/3 04 06 76). Open-air spot in a natural amphitheatre near the Olympia-Stadion that features movies, bands, classical concerts and other entertainments. Great fun on summer evenings, but arrive early as it often gets crowded.

Jazz and world music

Berlin offers a good range of live jazz venues, and is an important centre for the burgeoning world music movement. Some of the venues in the list above also feature these kinds of music.

A-Trane, Bleibtreustr. 1, Charlottenburg (☎0 30/3 13 25 50). Presents up-and-coming and well-known jazz artists in a comfortable, intimate setting. Weekends from 10pm.

b-flat, Rosenthaler Str. 13, Mitte (☎0 30/2 80 63 49). Small jazz club with live groups on weekends and a serious audience – don't talk during sets. Open from 10pm.

Flöz, Nassauische Str. 37, Wilmersdorf (☎0 30/8 61 10 00). Basement club that's the meeting point for Berlin's jazz musicians and a testing ground for the city's new bands. Also offers occasional salsa and cabaret. Can be wild.

Haus der Kulturen der Welt, John-Foster-Dulles-Allee 10, Tiergarten (☎0 30/39 78 71 75, *www.hkw.de*). The city's number one venue for world music. Always worth checking out.

Pfefferberg, Schönhauser Allee 176, Prenzlauer Berg (☎0 30/44 38 31 10). A converted East Berlin industrial space offering world-music-themed concerts and club nights. Grooving to non-European sounds in the summer beer garden takes you away from hectic atmosphere of Berlin.

Podewil, Klosterstr. 68–70, Mitte (☎0 30/24 74 96, *www.podewil.bkv.org*). Contemporary jazz, world music and occasional classical concerts. Less lively than some other venues but dedicated to the music.

Quasimodo, Kantstr. 12a, Charlottenburg (☎0 30/3 12 80 86). Berlin's best jazz spot, with nightly programmes starting at 10pm. A high-quality mix of international (usually American) stars and up-and-coming names. Small, with a good atmosphere. Often free on weekdays.

Classical music

For centuries, Berlin's standing in the musical world lagged well behind that of other major German cities such as Leipzig, Dresden, Munich and Hamburg. That situation began to change with the foundation in 1882 of the Berliner Philharmonisches Orchester, which established a position of global pre-eminence in the field of large-scale **orchestral** music under its principal conductor Hans von Bülow and his successors Arthur Nikitsch, Wilhelm Fürtwängler and Herbert von Karajan. The current incumbent, Claudio Abbado, will be succeeded in 2002 by the Englishman Sir Simon Rattle, who secured the appointment on the basis of the extraordinary rapport he had built up with the players during his appearances as a guest conductor. Of the other full-sized symphony orchestras based in the city, the oldest is the Rundfunk-Sinfonieorchester Berlin, which was until recently directed by the Spaniard Rafael Frühbeck de Burgos; being attached to the local radio station, it tends to have a more adventurous repertoire than its rivals. The Deutsches Symphonie-Orchester built up a formidable reputation under the directorship of the Russian-born pianist-conductor Vladimir Ashkenazy, who has now been succeeded by the American Kent Nagano. East Berlin's old orchestra, the Berliner Sinfonie-Orchester, has likewise just had a change of conductor, with Eliahu Inbal replacing Michael Schønvandt. The city also has numerous smaller orchestras, usually specializing in music of a particular period: they include the Akademie für Alte Musik Berlin, the Berliner Bach-Akademie, the Barock Orchester Berlin, the Haydn-Ensemble Berlin, the Kammerorchester Berlin and the Neues Berliner Kammerorchester.

As a legacy of the decades of division, Berlin still operates three **opera houses**. This is probably one more than it needs, and the downside is that several other German cities have houses which currently enjoy higher critical standing than any of the trio in the capital. Although none has yet come close to demise, the first steps towards rationalization are due to take place in 2001, with the projected merger of the ballet companies formerly attached to each house into one ensemble, Berliner Ballett. The city is home to several highly distinguished **choirs**, two of the finest being those attached to the Protestant and Catholic cathedrals, the Dom and St-Hedwigs-Kathedrale, where their liturgical contributions are supplemented by regular concerts. Among the many **chamber music** groups based in Berlin are the Berliner Oktett and one of the world's leading string quartets, the Brandis-Quartett.

Venues

In addition to the main venues listed below, concerts and recitals are regularly held in the city's churches and other historic buildings, while the Musikinstrumenten-Museum (see p.841) hosts a weekly series at 11am on Sundays.

Deutsche Oper Berlin, Bismarckstr. 35, Charlottenburg (☎0 30/3 43 84 01, *www.deutsche-oper.berlin.de*). This is a modern building, which was built to give West Berlin the opera house it would otherwise have lacked, and has an established tradition of attracting star international singers and conductors with Christian Thielemann the current musical director.

Komische Oper, Behrenstr. 55–57, Mitte; box office at Unter den Linden 41, Mitte (☎0 30/20 26 03 60, *www.komischeoper.line.de*). In contrast to its two rivals, this is a repertory company which eschews expensive jet-set soloists; tickets therefore cost around half the price. The Viennese-style neo-Baroque interior stages a wider range of operas than its name would suggest, being suitable for all but the grandest examples of the genre.

Konzerthaus Berlin (Schauspielhaus), Gendarmenmarkt, Mitte (☎0 30/2 03 09 21 01, *www.konzerthaus.de*). Although the acoustics of the Grosser Saal – which hosts regular concerts by the

Berliner Sinfonie-Orchester, among others – are not absolutely ideal, the architectural splendour of the converted playhouse by Schinkel more than makes amends. On the top floor of the southern wing is the delectable little Kammermusiksaal, Schinkel's original concert hall, which is used for vocal, instrumental and chamber recitals.

Philharmonie, Herbert-von-Karajan-Str. 1, Tiergarten (☎0 30/2 61 43 83, *www.berlin.philharmonic .com*). The custom-built home of the Berliner Philharmonisches Orchester was specially designed to give the best possible acoustic effects. Tickets for the orchestra's concerts are not as hard to come by as is often supposed, as the same programme is often performed on three consecutive evenings. Concerts by visiting orchestras take place frequently, while the adjoining Kammermusiksaal, a daring and versatile venue in the round, is used by soloists and smaller groups of all types, including contemporary music specialists.

Staatsoper, Unter den Linden 5–7, Mitte (☎0 30/20 35 45 55, *www.staatsoper/berlin.org*). This is undoubtedly one of the most beautiful opera houses in the world. It has a distinguished performing tradition: among the predecessors of the present musical director, the Israeli pianist-conductor Daniel Barenboim (who is due to vacate the position shortly), were the composers Giacomo Meyerbeer and Richard Strauss. Be warned, however, that the cheapest seats in the main auditorium have only a partial view of the stage. Chamber operas, predominantly of the Baroque era, and concerts by the house orchestra, the Staatskapelle Berlin, are usually performed in the Apollo-Saal.

Theatre

Throughout the first three decades of the twentieth century, Berlin's theatrical life enjoyed an unparalleled international reputation, thanks in large measure to the inspired tutelage of the seemingly omnipresent figure of Max Reinhardt. He emigrated on the eve of the Nazi takeover of power, which soon led to the collapse of the proud tradition he had built up. However, after the war another prominent exile, Bertolt Brecht, returned to settle in East Berlin, and his celebrity status – he was then almost universally regarded as the most influential playwright of the century – ensured that theatre played a prominent role in the cultural life of the GDR capital. It retained a privileged status right up to the regime's demise, by which time Brecht's own standing, at least in the dramatic field, had suffered a huge posthumous slump. Nowadays, Berlin's theatres face a tough task living up to the heady golden eras of the not so distant past. Within Germany, however, their standing remains generally high, and the city is a major venue not only for the performance of established classics, but also for experimental work. That said, English-speakers often find much of the favoured repertoire, as well as the production and performance styles, rather heavy going.

Venues

Berliner Ensemble, Bertolt-Brecht-Platz 1, Mitte (☎0 30/2 82 31 60, *www.berliner-ensemble.de*). Recently privatized, Brecht's old theatre (like the man himself) polarizes opinion, with many now regarding it as a cultural dinosaur. Brecht still forms the staple fare here, though the productions are a little livelier and less reverential than in GDR days. There are also occasional experimental productions on the Probebühne (rehearsal stage).

Berliner Figurentheater, Yorckstr. 59, Kreuzberg (☎0 30/7 86 98 15). The pick of several puppet theatres in the city: geared mainly towards children, it stages innovative productions with superbly crafted dolls.

Deutsches Theater, Schumannnstr. 13a, Mitte (☎0 30/28 44 12 21, *www.deutsches-theater .berlin.net*). Good, solid productions taking in everything from Schiller to Mamet make this one of Berlin's best theatres. Also includes a second theatre, the Kammerspiele des Deutschen Theaters, and Die Baracke, an experimental stage.

Freunde der Italienischen Oper, Fidicinstr. 40, Kreuzberg (☎0 30/6 91 12 11). Tiny courtyard theatre specializing in fringe productions performed in English.

Grips Theater, Altonaer Str. 22, Tiergarten (☎0 30/39 74 74 77). Specialist children's and young people's theatre, with most performances improvised.

Hebbel-Theater, Stresemannstr. 29, Kreuzberg (☎0 30/25 90 04 27, *www.hebbel-theatre.de*). Hosts short runs of European and American theatre and dance.

Maxim-Gorki-Theater, Am Festungsgraben 2, Mitte (☎0 30/20 22 11 15). Offers consistently good productions of modern works by established playwrights. More experimental fare is staged on the Studiobühne.

Schaubühne am Lehniner Platz, Kurfürstendamm 153, Wilmersdorf (☎0 30/89 00 23, *www.schaubuehne.de*). Erich Mendelsohn's Expressionist-style cinema of the 1920s was converted into a state-of-the-art theatre half a century later for Peter Stein's brilliant theatrical troupe. It stages both classics and experimental pieces; the new directorship installed in 2000 promises an infusion of young energy and more of an accent on dance.

Schiller-Theater-Werkstatt, Bismarckstr. 110, Charlottenburg (☎0 30/3 12 65 05). The Schiller-Theater no longer exists as a serious theatre venue, but its experimental group lives on.

Stella Musical Theater, Marlene-Dietrich-Platz 1, Tiergarten (☎0 18 05/44 44). New venue for blockbuster musicals.

Studiotheater der Hochschule für Schauspielkunst (BAT), Belforter Str. 15, Prenzlauer Berg (☎0 30/4 42 79 96). Originally a "workers' and students' theatre", founded in 1975, this one can usually be relied on to come up with challenging experimental offerings, including theatre-student graduation projects.

Stükke, Palisadenstr. 48, Friedrichshain (☎0 30/71 58 11 43). Hosts an international selection of contemporary theatre and performance works.

Theater Am Halleschen Ufer, Hallesches Ufer 32, Kreuzberg (☎0 30/2 51 06 55). Venue for a variety of theatre, performance and dance, sometimes in English. Puts up the large-scale shows of Freunde der Italienischen Oper and Tanzfabrik.

Theater des Westens, Kantstr. 12, Charlottenburg (☎0 30/8 82 28 88, *www.theater-des-westens.de*). Housed in a beautiful *fin-de-siècle* building, this features classic musicals, operettas and the odd Broadway-type show.

Volksbühne, Rosa-Luxemburg-Platz, Mitte (☎0 30/2 47 67 72). Under director Frank Castorf, this has become one of Berlin's most adventurous and interesting theatres. He has gone all out to bring in young audiences, with the result that performances are often highly provocative – nudity and throwing things at the audience crop up fairly regularly and there's a statistically high chance of witnessing a partial audience walkout.

Zaubertheater Igor Jedlin, Roscherstr. 7, Charlottenburg (☎0 30/3 23 37 77). Jedlin's long-established one-man magic shows usually take place Thurs–Sun 3.30pm for kids, 8pm for adults.

Cabaret, variety and dance

Sadly, Berlin's legendary prewar cabaret scene is little more than a memory. However, a few establishments gamely strive to keep alive the tradition of political satire, while old-style variety shows have made something of a comeback in the city (as elsewhere in Germany) in the past decade. In addition to the ballet companies attached the opera houses (see above), a number of high-quality dance groups are based in the city.

Ballhaus Naunynstrasse, Naunynstr. 27, Kreuzberg (☎0 30/25 88 66 44). Renovated former ballroom in the heart of Kreuzberg. Repertoire of events includes mixed-media performances and fringe theatre as well as dance.

BKA (Berliner Kabarett Anstalt), Mehringdamm 32, Kreuzberg (☎0 30/2 51 01 12). Cabaret and one-person shows, often dealing with political themes and current events.

Friedrichstadtpalast, Friedrichstr. 107, Mitte (☎0 30/23 26 24 74). Big flashy variety theatre with leggy chorus girls, but the real stuff is to be found in their small café-theatre.

Tanzfabrik Berlin, Möckernstr. 68, Kreuzberg (☎0 30/786 58 61). Attached to Berlin's biggest contemporary dance school, this place stages experimental and modern works.

Varieté Chamäleon, Rosenthaler Str. 40–41, Mitte (☎0 30/2 82 71 18). Cabaret and variety theatre. Check out the *Mitternachtshow* at midnight on Friday and Saturday.

Wintergarten, Potsdamer Str. 96, Tiergarten (☎0 30/23 08 82 30). A glitzy attempt to re-create the Berlin of the 1920s, with acts from all over the world – cabaret, musicians, dance, mime, etc. Much the most expensive venue in town.

Listings

Airline offices Air France, Tegel Airport (☎0 18 05/ 83 08 30); British Airways, Tegel Airport (☎0 18 05/ 26 65 22); Deutsche BA, Postst. 4–5, Mitte (☎0 30/2 47 36 80); KLM, Tegel Airport (☎0 18 05/ 21 42 01); Lufthansa, Kurfürstendamm 220, Charlottenburg (☎0 30/88 75 88).

Airports Schönefeld, Tegel and Tempelhof all share the same info number: ☎0 18 05/00 01 86.

Bike rental Fahrradstation, with branches at Bahnhof Friedrichstrasse (☎0 30/20 45 45 00), Bergmannstr 9, Kreuzberg (☎0 30/2 15 15 66), and Auguststr 29a, Mitte (☎0 30/28 59 56 61). Prices start at DM20/€10 for an ordinary bike for a day.

Bookstores The best selections of English paperbacks and books on the city can be found at British Book Shop, Mauerstr. 83–84, and Kiepert, Hardenbergstr. 4–5.

Car rental ACS Rent a Car, Albrechtstr. 117, Schöneberg (☎0 30/7 92 00 15); City Trans, Wönnichstr, 100, Lichtenberg (☎0 30/5 12 71 14), and C. Nagel, Bundesallee 176, Wilmersdorf (☎0 30/8 54 30 00) are among the cheapest. International firms (which also have offices at Tegel airport) include Avis, Budapester Str. 43, Charlottenburg (☎0 30/2 30 93 70), Hertz, Spandauer Str. 5, Mitte (☎0 30/2 42 44 40), and National, Witzlebenstr. 26, Charlottenburg (☎0 30/8 85 72 70).

Cultural centre British Council, Hackescher Markt 1, Mitte (☎30 30/1 10 99 10; *www.britcoun.de*).

Dentist ☎0 30/89 00 43 33.

Disabled travel Movado, Langhansstr. 64, Weissensee (☎0 30/4 71 51 45, *www.movado.de*), has a great wealth of information on hotels and restaurants that are wheelchair-accessible, city tours for disabled travellers and transportation services.

Doctor ☎0 30/31 00 31.

Embassies Britain, Wilhelmstr. 70/71 (☎0 30/20 18 40, *www.britischebotschaft.de*); Canada, Friedrichstr. 95 (☎0 30/20 31 20, *www.kanada-info.de*); Ireland, Friedrichstr. 200 (☎0 30/22 07 20); US, Neustadtische Kirchstr. 4–5 (☎0 30/2 38 51 74), visa section, Clayallee 170 (☎0 30/8 32 92 33, *www.usembassy.de*).

Mitfahrzentralen Citynetz, Joachimstaler Str. 17 (☎0 30/6 93 60 95); Mitfahrzentrale am Zoo, Zoologischer Garten U-Bahn #2 platform direction Pankow (☎0 30/1 94 44); Frauenmitfahrzentrale, Potsdamer Str. 139 (☎0 30/2 15 31 65).

Pharmacies Apotheke im Bahnhof Zoo (Mon–Fri 7.30am–8pm, Sat 8.30am–4pm; ☎0 30/31 50 33 61). When it's closed, check the list on the door of this, or any other *Apotheke*, for the nearest place open.

Post office Bahnhof Friedrichstrasse (Mon–Fri 6am–10pm, Sat 8am–10pm); Joachimstaler Str. 7 (Mon–Sat 8am–midnight, Sun 10am–midnight).

Sports Now in its seventh decade, the Olympia-Stadion remains the main venue for spectator sports, including the home matches of the city's only top-flight football team, Hertha Berlin.

Taxis Outside KaDeWe, on Savignyplatz; by Bahnhof Zoo; at the northern entrance to Friedrichstrasse station; the entrance to Alexanderplatz S-Bahn station; and in front of the nearby *Forum Hotel*. To book, call ☎ 0 30/21 01 01 or 0 30/26 10 26.

Travel agents Autopia Reiseladen, Kurfürstenstr. 153, Schöneberg (☎0 30/2 61 18 21, *www.autopia-reise.de*); United Planets, Greifswalder Str. 29, Prenzlauer Berg (☎0 30/42 80 78 54, *www.united-planets.de*).

BRANDENBURG

Brandenburg is geographically the largest of Germany's five new Länder, though it has a very low population density, largely because it is now shorn of Berlin, its epi-centre and traditional capital. Its landscape consists in the main of undulating farmland and sandy forests which are unexpectional but by no means unattractive. In lieu of Berlin, the old royal residence of **Potsdam** on its outskirts has taken over as Land cap-ital, and its outstanding assemblage of Baroque and Rococo palaces and parks is the province's prime tourist draw. West of here lies the long-overshadowed city of

Brandenburg which, despite the ravages of war and pollution, preserves an important medieval heritage. The only other major towns, **Frankfurt an der Oder** and **Cottbus**, are similarly scarred, though the latter has the good fortune to lie close to the province's one area of outstanding natural beauty, the water-strewn **Spreewald**, which is still inhabited by the Sorbs, Germany's only indigenous Slav minority.

Potsdam

"The first fine day should be devoted to Potsdam, without which a complete impression of Berlin can scarcely be obtained," intoned the prewar *Baedeker*, a nod to the fact that **POTSDAM**, although not officially part of Berlin, was the natural completion of the Hohenzollern capital, forming an almost seamless extension of its western suburbs. Although founded as far back as 993, Potsdam was of little significance until 1660, when Friedrich Wilhelm, the Great Elector, decided to built a new residence there. His successors – most notably Frederick the Great, who made it the main seat of his court – oversaw a stunning triumph of man over nature, whereby the swampy marshland of the Havel and its lakes was gradually transformed into the proudest adornment of the Prussian kingdom, a glorious planned townscape replete with palaces, parks and gardens. It was precisely because Potsdam was such a national showpiece that the "Big Three" of the United States, the United Kingdom and the Soviet Union held their victorious conference there after World War II, showing the Germans in the most unambiguous way possible that they had been totally and utterly defeated, and thus eliminating any possibility of a repetition of the "stab in the back" legend which had quickly gained currency after World War I.

Potsdam's **Altstadt**, notwithstanding grievous losses in the war and the hamfisted attempt by the GDR regime to give parts of it a "socialist" makeover, is a fine example of a Baroque and Neoclassical town, even if it is overshadowed by the nearby parks. Of these, the wondrous **Park Sanssouci** is rightly the most famous and visited, but there are two other splendid areas of landscaped greenery in the **Neuer Garten** and **Park Babelsberg**. Nor is Potsdam resting on its laurels with regard to its distinctive heritage. The bi-annual national garden show, the **Bundesgartenschau**, is to be held there from April 21 to October 7, 2001 (the main venue is the Bornstädter Feld, a former military area immediately north of Park Sanssouci), and promises to bequeath a legacy of new gardens, squares and promenades throughout the city.

Arrival, information and accommodation

Potsdam's **Hauptbahnhof**, which is just a short walk across Lange Brücke from the town centre, is linked to Berlin's Bahnhof Zoo and Bahnhof Friedrichstrasse by S-Bahn #7 and mainline trains. Alternatively, bus #116 from S-Bahnhof Wannsee will deposit you on the Potsdam side of the Glienicker Brücke, from where tram #93 runs to the central Platz der Einheit. A more atmospheric approach is provided by the cruise **boats** from Wannsee (see p.852).

Just south of the Platz der Einheit, at Friedrich-Ebert-Str. 5, is the **tourist office** (April–Oct Mon–Fri 9am–8pm, Sat 9am–6pm, Sun 9am–4pm; Nov–March Mon–Fri 10am–6pm, Sat & Sun 10am–2pm; ☎03 31/27 55 80, fax 2 75 58 99, *www.potsdam.de*). There's also a smaller office in the Hauptbahnhof (daily 9am–8pm; ☎03 31/2 70 91 50). Another useful source of **information** is Sanssouci's **visitor centre**, at the northern edge of the park at An der Historischen Mühle (daily: April–Oct 8.30am–5pm; Nov–March 9am–4pm; ☎03 31/9 69 42 00, fax 9 69 41 07, *www.spsg.de*). This sells day-tickets covering all the park's monuments (DM20/€10, or DM25/€12.50 family ticket).

POTSDAM

0 ___ 500 m

N

Jungfernsee

Glienicker Brücke

Schloss Babelsberg

Gerichtslaube

Matrosenhaus

Flatowturm

Park Babelsberg

Bahnhof Babelsberg

Telegrafenberg & Einsteinturm

BERLINER VORSTADT

Tiefer See

Schloss Cecilienhof ❷

Neuer Garten

Heiliger See

Marmorpalais

Orangerie

Königliche Bibliothek

Französische Kirche

Rathaus

Nikolaikirche

St-Peter- und-Paul Kirche

Belvedere

Pomonatempel

Pfingstberg

Jüdischer Friedhof

Russische Kirche Hl Alexander Newsky

Russische Kolonie Alexandrowka

NIEDLITZER STR

Nauener Tor ❸

Jägertor ❹

Filmmuseum ❼

Brandenburger Tor

River Havel

Ruinenberg

Bildergalerie

Grosse Fontäne

Neptungrotte

Schloss Sanssouci

Historische Mühle

Marlys Garten

Friedenskirche

Lustgarten

Dampfmaschinenhaus

Bahnhof Charlottenhof

Neue Kammern

Orangerie

Drachenhaus

Sizilianischer Garten

Chinesisches Teehaus

Park Charlottenhof

Römische Bäder

Schloss Charlottenhof

Antikentempel

Belvedere

Neues Palais

Communs

Bahnhof Wildpark

ACCOMMODATION

1 Apartment-Hotel
8 Bornimer Hof
9 Froschkasten
4 Mercure
4 Reinhold
10 Schiffspension Luise
7 Schlossgarten
6 Schloss Cecilienhof
2 Siebenschläfer
3 Voltaire
5 Zum Hummer

Private rooms (②–④) can be booked via the tourist office. There's an unofficial **youth hostel**, *Siebenschläfer*, at Lotte-Puewka-Str. 43 (☎03 31/74 11 25; DM25/€12.50 or DM31/€16.50), almost directly across the River Nuthe from the Hauptbahnhof, and on the route of bus #695. The nearest **campsite**, *Sanssouci-Gaisberg*, is at An der Pirschheide 1 (☎ & fax 0 33 27/5 56 80) on the bank of the Templiner See; it's a short walk south of Bahnhof Pirschheide, which is linked to the town centre by tram #94 and buses #631 and #695, the last of which goes via the Maulbeerallee in Park Sanssouci.

Hotels and pensions

Apartment-Hotel Bornimer Hof, Rückerstr. 31 (☎03 31/54 96 60, fax 5 49 66 15). In a very quiet wooded setting north of town, offering suites, some quite spacious, of widely ranging prices. ③–⑦.

art'otel potsdam, Zeppelinstr. 136 (☎03 31/9 81 50, fax 9 81 55 55). A bright and colourful designer hotel, partly within a warehouse building by Ludwig Persius, partly in a gleaming modern extension. ⑦.

Babelsberg, Stahnsdorfer Str. 68, Babelsberg (☎03 31/7 88 89, fax 70 76 68). An old-fashioned, value-for-money hotel in the villa district by the Filmpark. ③–⑤.

Filmhotel Lili Marleen, Grossbeerenstr. 75, Babelsberg (☎03 31/74 32 00, fax 7 43 20 18). Inaugurated in 1996, this is a theme hotel and restaurant, geared at cinema fans visiting the nearby Filmpark. Bus #692 from the centre stops outside. ⑤.

Froschkasten, Kiezstr. 3–4 (☎ & fax 03 31/29 13 15). Pension attached to a recommendable Gaststätte in one of the Altstadt's most atmospheric streets. ③–⑤.

Mercure, Lange Brücke (☎03 31/27 22, fax 29 34 96). The notorious *Stadt Potsdam*, an all-too-prominent GDR-era behemoth, has been successfully revamped by the Mercure chain. It also has a good restaurant. ⑥.

Reinhold, Dortusstr. 8 (☎03 31/28 49 90, fax 2 84 99 30, *www.hotel.reinhard.de*). Comfortable small hotel with restaurant in the heart of the Altstadt. ⑤.

Schiffs Pension Luise, Heinrich-Mann-Allee 1 (☎03 31/2 70 62 29). A boat moored by the Lange Brücke offering five small rooms with very close-up views of the Havel. ①.

Schloss Cecilienhof, Neuer Garten (☎03 31/3 70 50, fax 29 24 98, *www.castle-cecilienhof.com*). Housed in a wing of Schloss Cecilienhof, this was the most prestigious address of the entire GDR hotel network, and is still of high standing, though it now has several rivals for the title of best hotel in Potsdam. Its restaurant serves both hearty Brandenburg specialities and high-quality lighter fare. ⑧–⑨.

Schlossgarten, Geschwister-Scholl-Str. 41a (☎03 31/97 17 00, fax 97 17 04 04). Plain but pleasant new hotel near Bahnhof Wildpark, at the southwestern edge of Park Sanssouci. ⑤.

Voltaire, Friedrich-Ebert-Str. 88 (☎03 31/2 31 70, fax 2 31 71 00). Luxury hotel, decked out with modern artworks, in Palais Brühl, a splendid old Altstadt palace. Its facilities include: a fitness centre; a gourmet restaurant, *Hofgarten*, with garden terrace; and a lively pub, *Potsdamer Bierstange*. ⑦–⑨.

The Altstadt

Potsdam's Altstadt is unfortunately shorn of two of its most important buildings, the Stadtschloss and the Garnisonkirche, which were damaged in the war and erased by the Communists as unwanted reminders of the city's royal and militaristic traditions. Baroque, Rococo and Neoclassical masterpieces are now intermingled with ugly highrise blocks from the Communist era. This situation seems likely to persist, though there are still hopes that the prewar appearance of the city will eventually be re-created.

The southern Altstadt

On the main square, Am Alten Markt, stands the stately **Nikolaikirche** (Mon 2pm–5pm, Tues–Sat 10am–5pm, Sun noon–5pm), which the Communists were unable to displace from its dominant position on the Potsdam skyline. One of the indisputably great churches of the nineteenth century, it is the artistic testament of **Karl Friedrich Schinkel**, who designed not only the building itself, but every detail of its decoration.

Ironically, he took no part in the actual construction, which was entrusted to his disciples Friedrich August Stüler and Ludwig Persius, and did not live to see the raising of the great **dome**. This was one of his most audacious projects, the four slender corner towers being necessary to counteract the otherwise unsustainable pressure the dome exerts on the body of the church. It is as impressive from inside as from out, being adorned with fourteen statues of Old Testament figures and gigantic paintings of the four major prophets: Isaiah, Jeremiah, Ezekiel and Daniel.

In front of the church is the **Obelisk** by Georg Wenzeslaus von Knobelsdorff, while the eastern side of the square is dominated by the **Altes Rathaus**, the work of another of Frederick the Great's favourite architects, the Dutchman Johann Boumann, to a design (though one never used) by the last great master of the Italian Renaissance, Andrea Palladio. Until 1875 the circular tower, on top of which a gilded Atlas bears the world on his shoulders, served as the town jail. The Rathaus lost its municipal function in 1885, and was taken over by a bank. In the GDR era it became an arts centre, a role it retains.

To the south is the **Freudschaftsinsel**, a leafy Havel island with a number of gardens, the most recent of which, specially planted for the Bundesgartenschau, is the only one in Germany specifically devoted to herbaceous perennials. West of Am Alten Markt are Yorckstrasse and Wilhelm-Staab-Strasse, which both boast a number of fine **Baroque houses**. Am Neuen Markt, just to the south of Yorckstrasse, also has a couple of good-looking survivors – including, on the west side (behind the *Waage* restaurant), some improbably grand (but decrepit) eighteenth-century coaching stables with an entrance in the form of a triumphal arch, which are now home to a haulage firm. At Am Neuen Markt 1 is the **Kabinetthaus**, a small mansion that was the birthplace of Friedrich Wilhelm II, the only member of the Hohenzollern family actually born in Potsdam.

A little further south, at Schloss-Str. 1, is the former **Marstall**, or royal stables, which now houses the **Filmmuseum** (Tues–Sun 10am–6pm; *www.brandenburg.de/filmmuseum*; DM4/€2, DM10/€5 for special exhibits). Drawing on material from the UFA studios in nearby Babelsberg (later DEFA, the GDR state film company), the museum presents both a technical and artistic history of German film from 1895 to 1980. There's a vaguely hands-on feel, with a few visitor-operated Bioscopes and numerous screens playing clips. The museum **cinema** is the best in Potsdam and there's also a good café.

From here it's worth making a quick detour down **Kiezstrasse**, where a number of eighteenth-century Rococo houses have been beautifully restored. In the midst of the high-rises to the west is the **Dampfmaschinenhaus** (guided tours mid-May to mid-Oct Sat & Sun 10am–5pm, *www.spsg.de*; DM4/€2), the most imaginative pump-house in Germany. The architect, Ludwig Persius, designed it to resemble a mosque, with the chimney taking the form of a minaret. However, it is no Romantic-era folly: it belatedly solved the problem of the supply of water to Park Sanssouci, at last enabling the Grosse Fontäne to function effectively.

The northern Altstadt

North of Am Alten Markt are two more large squares. The first of these is the Platz der Einheit, dominated by the neo-Baroque mass of the **Postamt**. Immediately to the north, a plaque marks the site of the **Synagoge**, which was wrecked on *Kristallnacht* and later demolished. Beyond is Bassinplatz, at the southeastern corner of which is the oval **Französische Kirche**, which was erected in the 1750s by Boumann to plans by Knobelsdorff for the Huguenot community. Dating from just over a century later, the much larger **St Peter und Paul** was the first major church to be built for Roman Catholic worship in this staunchly Protestant town.

To the west of here, on and around **Brandenburger Strasse**, Potsdam's pedestrianized main shopping street, are many ornate Baroque houses, which were built between 1732 and 1742, with slight variations in detail to avoid monotony, for trades-people in the then rapidly expanding town. At the end of the street is the **Brandenburger Tor**, one of three surviving gateways from the 1730s fortifications system. Four decades after it was built, it was transformed by Carl von Gontard into triumphal arch, adorned with Rococo carvings which give it a playful character wholly lacking in its Berlin namesake. The only one of the gates to have survived in something like its original form is the **Jägertor** (Hunter's Gate) at the end of Lindenstrasse to the northeast, which is surmounted by a sculpture of a stag succumbing to a pack of baying hounds. Further east along Hegelallee is the **Nauener Tor**, which was rebuilt in the 1750s as the first German essay in the English Gothick style, which had brought the pointed arch back into favour.

Between here and Bassinplatz is the **Holländisches Viertel** (Dutch quarter), the earliest of several settlements in Potsdam established for specific immigrant communities. It was Boumann's first major Prussian commission, built 1732–42, and he adhered closely to the vernacular architecture of his native Amsterdam, using brick instead of stone, and building elaborately gabled houses, numbering 134 in all, arranged in terraces. Unfortunately, relatively few Dutch settlers took up the invitation to settle there, and many of those who did returned home when the promised employment dried up. During the GDR era, some of the houses fell into dereliction, but a number of excellent restored examples can be found along **Mittelstrasse**, particularly at the junction with Benkertstrasse. Mittelstrasse has now been gentrified to a large extent, with a number of trendy shops and cafés.

Park Sanssouci

Park Sanssouci, Frederick the Great's fabled retreat, stretches out for 2km west of the Altstadt, and its gardens and palaces are what draw most visitors to the town. In 1744 Frederick, who had no great love for his capital, Berlin, or his queen, Elizabeth Christine, ordered the construction of a residence where he could live "without cares" – or *sans souci*, in the French spoken at court. Huge teams of craftsmen, led by the finest German architects, sculptors, painters, decorators and landscape gardeners of the day, were employed to turn the king's whims into reality. The plan adopted was an original one, abandoning the traditional Baroque format of a grandiose palace as the park's centrepiece. Instead, there are a host of buildings: the earliest of these are modest in scale, though Frederick himself later initiated the trend towards adding larger structures that was also favoured by the most artistically minded of his successors, Friedrich Wilhelm IV. The park is at its most stunning in autumn, when it erupts into a blaze of colour worthy of New England, but springtime, when the trees are in leaf and the flowers in bloom, is also delightful. These days, it's all too often overrun by tourists; to avoid the crowds, visit on a weekday, preferably outside summer, when you'll be better able to appreciate the place.

The eastern park

The main entrance to the park is the **Obeliskpforte** by Knobelsdorff at the eastern end, which features two clusters of pillars flanked by statues of the goddesses Flora and Pomona by Friedrich Christian Glume. It is named after the nearby **Obelisk**, which is covered with Egyptian-style hieroglyphs, though these are purely decorative, predating the first modern decipherment of the ancient script.

Just to the south is the Italianate **Friedenskirche** (Peace Church; mid-May to mid-Oct daily 10am–6pm), which was built to plans by Persius to commemorate Sanssouci's centenary. With its 39-metre campanile and lakeside setting, it conjures up the southern European atmosphere that Friedrich Wilhelm IV was striving to create when he ordered the construction of the church using the San Clemente basilica in Rome as a model. The shape and measurements of the building were predetermined by the magnificent apse mosaic which the king had acquired from Murano in the Venetian lagoon. With the exception of the damaged example owned by Berlin's Bodemuseum, this is the only intact Byzantine mosaic to be found north of the Alps. Adjoining the church is a domed Hohenzollern mausoleum containing the tombs of Friedrich Wilhelm IV, Friedrich III and their wives.

Immediately west of the Friedenskirche is **Marlys Garten**, a kitchen garden transformed by Peter Joseph Lenné into a *jardin anglais*. On the opposite side of Hauptallee, the avenue running straight through the middle of the park, is the playful Rococo **Neptungrotte**, Knobelsdorff's last work. Further along the main axis is the **Grosse Fontäne**, a huge water jet in a circular basin. It's surrounded by statues of mythological figures, some of which – notably the figures of Venus and Mercury by the Frenchman Jean Baptiste Pigalle – rank among the great masterpieces of garden sculpture. Immediately to the north is a tiered vineyard, one of the most northerly in Europe, known as the **Weinbergterrassen**. In 1991, the uppermost level of this was the setting for a midnight ceremony attended by many prominent national figures, at which Frederick the Great was finally laid to rest in his favoured place alongside his greyhounds. Deeming this an unsuitable grave for a king, his heirs had him interred in the now-demolished Garnisonkirche, from where his coffin was spirited away at the end of World War II to his ancestral seat of Burg Hohenzollern near the Swabian town of Hechingen. On the same terrace is an ornate trellis pavilion sheltering the statue of a deity.

Schloss Sanssouci

Schloss Sanssouci (guided tours April–Oct Tues–Sun 9am–5pm; Nov–March Tues–Sun 9am–4pm; DM10/€5) is a relatively modest single-storey palace whose fragility has led to the imposition of strict quotas on the number of visitors allowed on any one day. It's therefore advisable to arrive as early as possible to secure a ticket: if desired, the actual visit can be postponed until a set time later on. The building was constructed by Knobelsdorff from drawings by Frederick the Great himself, who had very clear ideas as to what he wanted. Externally, the main feature is the **garden front**, which has a truly festive air, with a protruding domed central section and a superb series of 36 **caryatids**, each individually characterized, by Friedrich Christian Glume. The entrance facade, which is fronted by a colonnaded *cour d'honneur*, commands a fine view up to the Ruinenberg, a hill crowned with mock classical ruins and the reservoir supplying the park's fountains.

All but one of the Schloss's dozen rooms are included on the tour; they are decorated in archetypal Rococo style, with coloured marble, stuccowork, gilded wood, ceiling frescoes, specially made furniture and both real and imitation antique statues. There are also many French paintings of the period, including several canvases by Watteau which have only recently returned, having spent the decades of German division at Schloss Charlottenburg in Berlin. The most impressive chamber is the central **Marmorsaal**, which is fashioned with marble from the famous quarries of Carrara. Also of special note is the **Konzertzimmer**, with its murals by Antoine Pesne illustrating Ovid's *Metamorphoses*; this was where Frederick staged his musical soirées, at which he himself often played the flute. His other favourite haunt was the tiny circular **Bibliothek**, whose bookcases, which are set into the walls, are largely devoted to French publications.

The Schloss was little used between the time of Frederick the Great's death and the accession of Friedrich Wilhelm IV. However, the latter commissioned an appropriately modest-looking western extension, known as the **Damenflügel** (mid-May to mid-Oct Sat & Sun 10am–5pm; DM3/€1.50) for the use of ladies-in-waiting and kitchen staff.

The Bildergalerie and the Neue Kammern

On the eastern side of Schloss Sanssouci, overlooking the ornamental **Holländischer Garten** (Dutch Garden), is the **Bildergalerie** (Picture Gallery; mid-May to mid-Oct Tues–Sun 10am–5pm; DM4/€2), a restrained Baroque design of 1755 by Johann Gottfried Büring. Generally considered to be the first building in mainland Europe to be erected specifically as a museum, it contains a single festive hall with a cabinet at the far end for the smaller works. All the paintings are hung closely together in the traditional but now unfashionable manner. The most celebrated work is **Caravaggio's** *Incredulity of St Thomas*; there's also a wonderful *Supper at Emmaus* by his most talented Dutch follower, **Ter Brugghen**. **Rubens** and **Van Dyck** are both well represented. The most important canvases by the former are *St Jerome in his Study* and *The Four Evangelists*. Among the works by the latter are portraits of members of the British court, plus a couple of mythological works: *Venus in Vulcan's Workshop* and *Rinaldo and Armida*.

On the opposite side of the Schloss, steps lead down to a very similar-looking building to the Bildergalerie, known as the **Neue Kammern** (early April to mid-May Sat & Sun 10am–5pm; mid-May to mid-Oct Tues–Sun 10am–5pm; DM5/€2.50). Originally an orangery, it was transformed in the 1770s into a plush guesthouse for visiting dignitaries. The interiors, appropriately enough, are slightly less grand than those of the Schloss; they include the **Ovidgalerie** – with reliefs illustrating scenes from Ovid's *Elegies* – and the oval **Bankettsaal**. Below the Neue Kammern is a peaceful rose garden, to the west of which is the **Sizilianischer Garten** (Sicilian Garden), which Lenné laid out according to the formal patterns of the Italian Renaissance.

The northern park

There are several notable buildings on the northern side of **Maulbeerallee** (Mulberry Alley), a road open to traffic which cuts right through Park Sanssouci. Starting from the east, the first is the **Historische Mühle** (April–Oct daily 10am–6pm; Nov–March Sat & Sun 10am–4pm; DM3/€1.50), an old windmill which was one of just two park buildings to suffer extensive damage in the 1945 air raid on the town. It was only restored to working order as part of the 1993 celebrations of Potsdam's millennium. Immediately to its west is another Lenné creation, the **Nordischer Garden** (Nordic Garden).

Further west is the **Orangerie** (mid-May to mid-Oct Tues–Sun 10am–5pm; DM5/€2.50), a bombastic 1850s building by Persius and Stüler whose dimensions – the facade is 330-metres long – are wholly at odds with the original conception of the park. The western wing is still used as a refuge for tropical plants in winter, and during the summer it's possible to ascend its **tower**. In the central block is the **Raphaelsaal**, whose walls are hung with specially commissioned nineteenth-century copies of paintings thought to be by Raphael, then regarded as the greatest artist of all time. These include not only some of his most familiar masterpieces, but also works now known to be by his master Perugino, or by pupils such as Giulio Romano.

From the western wing of the Orangerie, the arrow-straight **Krimlindenallee**, lined with lime trees, leads up towards the Rococo **Belvedere** by Georg Christian Unger, the last of the park pavilions to be built under Frederick the Great. It received a direct hit in World War II and has only recently been restored. A couple of hundred metres short of the Belvedere, a path branches off left towads the **Drachenhaus**, which Gontard modelled on the Chinese pagoda in London's Kew Gardens. Today there's a genteel café inside, an ideal point to interrupt your wanderings.

The Neues Palais

At the far western end of Park Sanssouci is the **Neues Palais** (April–Oct Mon & Wed–Sun 9am–5pm; Nov–March Mon–Thurs, Sat & Sun 9am–4pm; DM8/€4), built between 1763 and 1769 to celebrate the end of the Seven Years War, which had seen Prussia oust Austria from its centuries-long role as the dominant power in German affairs. The scale of the three-storey palace, which marked a radical departure from the intimate single-level buildings that had previously been constructed in the park, was intended as a deliberate triumphalist statement. Büring drew up the original plans, but was replaced early in the construction process by Gontard. A huge team of craftsmen was recruited to carve the rich programme of **statuary** adorning the balustrade and gardens. The most striking external feature, however, is the massive windowless central **dome** over the central block.

Inside, the **Grottensaal** makes for a startling introduction: its walls are encrusted with marble, shells, fossils, precious stones, glass and corals, all dimly lit to enhance the sense of mystery. Alongside, the **Marmorgalerie**, which is modelled on the halls of mirrors characteristic of the French royal palaces, has walls and floor of white marble and red jasper and ceiling frescoes of morning, noon and evening by Christian Bernard Rode. Upstairs, directly above the Grottensal, is the **Marmorsaal**, the principal festive hall. The adjacent **Obergalerie**, which corresponds to the Marmorgalerie below, is hung with canvases by seventeenth-century Italian painters, including Guido Reni and Artemesia Gentileschi. In the southern wing are Frederick's apartments and the **Schlosstheater**, a delectable Rococo auditorium where the king enjoyed Italian opera and French plays. A francophile to the point of near mania, Frederick believed that the Germans were philistines incapable of producing great art. It was said that he'd "rather a horse sang him an aria, than allow a German in his opera".

Facing the front entrance of the Neues Palais are the **Communs**, a couple of porticoed and domed structures linked by a curved colonnade. They look grandiose, but their purposes were mundane: they housed serving and maintenance staff, and blocked off what would otherwise have been an unsightly view of the marshland beyond. Likewise by Gontard are two small temples just east of the palace's garden front, on either side of Hauptallee. The **Antikentempel** is a domed rotunda built to house Frederick the Great's collection of antiquities, but was later converted to serve as the last resting-place of a number of Hohenzollerns, including the Empress Auguste Victoria, and Hermine, the woman Wilhelm II married in exile, who came to be known as the "last Empress". The circular **Freundschaftstempel** is a memorial to Frederick's elder sister, Margravine Wilhelmine of Brandenburg-Bayreuth, one of the few women for whom the great misogynist showed the slightest affection.

The Rehgarten and Park Charlottenhof

Another long straight avenue, Ökonomieweg, leads eastwards through the **Rehgarten** (Deer Garden), the former court hunting ground, to Sanssouci's kitschest yet most endearing pavilion, the **Chinesisches Teehaus** (mid-May to mid-Oct Tues–Sun 10am–5pm; DM2/€1). Built by Büring in the 1750s, it was based on descriptions provided by contemporary visitors to China. Eerily lifelike statues of oriental figures drinking tea and coffee and playing musical instruments are grouped around the exterior. Inside, the main hall and the adjoining cabinets are used to display Chinese and Meissen porcelain.

South of Ökonomieweg is **Park Charlottenhof**, which now forms a seamless whole with the much larger Park Sanssouci, though it was originally a separate estate. This was acquired by the future Friedrich Wilhelm IV, and transformed by Lenné into a *jardin anglais* of lawns, hillocks and artificial stretches of water. Schinkel was commissioned to design two buildings for the park. Of these, the **Römische Bäder** (mid-May to mid-Oct Tues–Sun 10am–5pm; DM3/€1.50, or DM7.50/€3.75 for combined ticket with Schloss Charlottenhof), which was actually built by Persius, consists of a tea pavilion, a Renaissance-style villa and a suite of rooms in the manner of a Roman house, including the bathroom from which the whole building takes its name. Further south is **Schloss Charlottenhof** (same times), a Neoclassical villa which is clearly modelled on its Roman predecessors, yet never resorts to slavish imitation.

The northern quarters

Potsdam has several rewarding corners which lie well off the beaten tourist track of the Altstadt and Sanssouci, and the quarters north of the Altstadt are particularly well endowed with often surprising sights.

Alexandrowka

About ten minutes' walk north of the Nauener Tor is **Alexandrowka**, the only surviving example of the once common Russian military villages, and the only one built outside Russia. Its origins lie in the capture of five hundred czarist soldiers by the Prussians in 1812, from whom 62 were selected to form a choir to entertain their captors. These men remained in Prussian service after the erstwhile enemies became allies. By 1825, only a dozen of the singers were still alive, and it was decided to reward them with a permanent home in Potsdam that would remind them of their native land. The settlement was laid out along two avenues in the form of a St Andrew's cross, with the homes of the twelve singers placed along the axes, and the residence of the Prussian overseer in the middle. The houses, with their distinctive balconies and ornamental gables, give the appearance of genuine Russian log cabins, but in reality they are half-timbered with wooden facing. Each has at least one nameplate in Cyrillic script, showing the name of the first occupant. When that is all that is shown, the house remains in the hands of a direct descendant of one of the choristers; those which have been relet also show the name of the present tenant.

As an adjunct to Alexandrowka, the **Russische Kirche Hl Alexander Newsky** was built on the wooded Kapellenberg immediately above. The plans for its construction were drawn up at the St Petersburg court, and it has an archetypally Russian appearance, with a central onion-domed tower surrounded by four smaller domes. Inside, the iconostasis has some icons painted in Russia at the same time as construction work was under way, as well as others of later date. The church has remained in constant use by the émigré community (which nowadays mostly consists of Belarussians), which in 1986 won back, after a long gap, the right to have its own priest.

The Pfingstberg

Immediately to the north of the Kapellenberg is the wooded **Pfingstberg**, at the foot of which is the walled **Jüdischer Friedhof** (Jewish Cemetery). Only organized visits are possible, every Sunday at 10am – enquire at the tourist office in town for details. The cemetery was given by the town to Potsdam's growing Jewish population in 1763; until then, they had had to bury their dead in Berlin. As recently as 1933 the Jewish community of Potsdam numbered several hundred, of whom just two returned after the war.

At the top of the hill is the **Belvedere**, a vast and improbable-looking Italianate folly designed to provide sweeping views over Potsdam, the Havel and its lakes. Although virtually undamaged by the war, it was allowed to collapse into ruin by the GDR authorities, who had no intention of allowing their citizens a bird's-eye view over the barbed-wire frontier separating them from the West. It remains in a highly dangerous condition, but is currently under renovation. The small building just to the southeast is the **Pomonatempel**, Schinkel's first-ever finished building, constructed in 1800 when he was a 19-year-old student.

The Neuer Garten

East of the Pfingstberg is another large park complex, the **Neuer Garten**, which was laid out from 1786 onwards by order of Friedrich Wilhelm II, the immediate successor of Frederick the Great. As an antidote to the geometric formality of Sanssouci, it marked the Potsdam debut of the naturalistic English style of landscape gardening. At the northernmost tip of the park, in an area that was out of bounds in GDR days, is the **Meierei**, which was built by Carl Gotthard Langhans as a farmhouse with cowsheds and a workshop, but later remodelled by Persius, who gave it its present castellated appearance. It subsequently became Potsdam's second idiosyncratic pump-house, but was badly damaged in 1945 and is still awaiting restoration.

A short walk to the south, and reachable from the town centre by bus #694, is **Schloss Cecilienhof** (Tues–Sun 9am–4/5pm; DM6/€3), which looks like a mock-Tudor mansion transplanted from suburban England. Building work on this, the last palace to be commissioned by the Hohenzollerns, began in 1913 and was completed in 1917, the war apparently having done nothing to change the owners' architectural tastes. Cecilienhof would only rate a mention in passing, were it not for the fact that it was the setting for the **Potsdam Conference** of July 17, to August 2, 1945. This confirmed the decisions made earlier that year at Yalta about the postwar European order, and formally set the limit of German territory at the Oder-Neisse Line, thereby confiscating well over 100,000 square kilometres of the prewar Reich. The **Konferenzsaal**, where the Allied delegates worked out the details of the division of Europe at a huge round table specially made in Moscow, still looks as it did in 1945. Much the same can be said of the chambers used by the delegates: the Soviets had the music room and parlour; the Americans the smoking and living rooms; the British the library and reading room.

Further south, directly beside the Heiliger See, is the **Marmorpalais** (Marble Palace; April–Oct Tues–Sun 10am–5pm; Nov–March Sat & Sun 10am–4pm; DM6/€3), which is actually mainly built of brick. The central pavilion, with its graceful belvedere on top, was built by Gontard and Langhans in a hybrid Rococo and Neoclassical style. In addition to many notable furnishings, including a distinguished Wedgwood collection, it has some highly individual interiors, notably the **Grottensaal** and the upstairs **Konzertsaal** and **Orientalisches Kabinett**, the last of which mimics the appearance of the tents used by the Turks in their seventeenth-century campaigns against Christian Europe. The palace's wings were only completed in the 1840s, and their interior decoration consequently reflects quite different artistic tastes.

Further on, the **Holländisches Etablissement**, Potsdam's second Dutch-style settlement, was built for the palace's servants, on the model of the distinctive almshouses of Holland. Behind them is the **Orangerie** by Langhans, the facade of which, in a curious juxtaposition of Egyptian and Greek motifs, features a sphinx seated on a portico of Doric columns. The same architect built the **Königliche Bibliothek** (Royal Library) at the southern tip of the Heiliger See. This time it is Neoclassical and neo-Gothic elements that are mixed in an unusual design of two single-room storeys, with the upper surrounded by a viewing platform.

Berliner Vorstadt

On the opposite shore of the Heiliger See to the Neuer Garten is the **Berliner Vorstadt**, formerly an elegant Potsdam suburb, whose crumbling villas were given over to various party and social institutions under the SED regime. Here, too, were numerous imperial army barracks, housing elite units like the Garde du Corps and Hussars, which until the summer of 1994 were in Russian hands. At the end of Berliner Strasse, leading back to Berlin, is the **Glienicker Brücke**, the famous spy-swap bridge which inspired many a Cold War film scene. Here, in 1962, U-2 pilot Gary Powers was traded for a Soviet agent, while in 1986 Jewish dissident Anatoly Scharansky was freed into the West in an early manifestation of Gorbachev's *glasnost*. The bridge was reopened to normal traffic at the beginning of 1990, and today there are few reminders of the era when people living in the immediate vicinity needed special permits simply to come and go from their own homes.

The southern quarters

On the opposite side of the Havel from Potsdam's Altstadt are several more suburbs, including the formerly separate town of Babelsberg.

The Teltower Vorstadt

Directly facing the Altstadt is the hilly suburb known as the **Teltower Vorstadt**. Crossing over by the Lange Brücke from Potsdam, it's hard not to notice a square tower rising up out of the trees on the **Brauhausberg** above. This is the former local SED headquarters or **Kreml** (Kremlin), to give it its local nickname. Originally built as a military college at the beginning of the twentieth century, it later served as a state archive building – a dark oval patch on the side of the tower marks where the SED symbol used to be.

Albert-Einstein-Strasse leads up the western side of the Brauhausberg to the **Telegrafenberg**. This was the site chosen in 1832 for a telegraph station, one of a whole network positioned between Berlin and Coblenz to relay messages by means of mechanical signals. Soon after, other scientific institutes were set up on the hill, notably the **Astrophysicalisches Observatorium**, a triple-domed observatory built of bricks insterspersed with ceramic tiles.

A path leads onwards to the nearby **Einsteinturm**, a twenty-metre-high observatory tower – the product of a chance meeting between the architect Erich Mendelsohn and the astrophysicist Erwin Finlay-Freundlich, who wanted to commission a structure where he could test Einstein's theory of relativity by means of practical experiments. The resultant building, the most famous architectural product of the Expressionist movement, looks like an element from a Dalí dreamscape and seems astonishingly futuristic for something erected as long ago as 1920. Although the initial tests carried out there were inconclusive and regarded as a failure, scientific work continues there today with research into the sun's magnetic field.

Babelsberg

East of the Teltower Vorstadt is the formerly separate town of **BABELSBERG**. Just north of the S-Bahn station of the same name is another intriguing example of town planning, the settlement of **Nowawes**, which was established by Frederick the Great in 1750 as a home for Protestant weavers and spinners fleeing religious persecution in Bohemia. It was shortly afterwards extended to accommodate craftsmen from southern Germany and Switzerland who came to work on the Neues Palais. Unfortunately, none of the original single-storey semi-detached houses around the triangular-shaped Weberplatz survives in an absolutely authentic shape, though many give a fair impression of how they all once looked. Rather better preserved is the rustic double-galleried **Friedrichskirche** in the centre of Friedrichsplatz.

North of Nowawes is Potsdam's third major landscape garden, the often-overlooked **Park Babelsberg**, which is also easily accessible from the Berlin side of the Glienicker Brücke. Its focal point is **Schloss Babelsberg** (April–Oct Tues–Sun 10am–5pm; Nov–March Sat & Sun 10am–4pm; DM4/€2), a neo-Gothic architectural extravaganza built by Schinkel and Persius for the future Kaiser Wilhelm I. Their main source of inspiration was the recent extension to England's Windsor Castle, and the contrast in style with the duo's Nikolaikirche – which was under construction at the same time –

could hardly be starker. Inside, the most striking rooms are the two-storey **Tanzsaal** inside the great octagon; the **Teesalon**, with its star-shaped ceiling; and the **Bibliothek**, with its distinctively English fan vault. A couple of nineteenth-century architectural oddities lurk in the park: the **Flatowturm** (April to mid-Oct Sat & Sun 10am–5pm; DM3/€1.50), an improbable-looking neo-Gothic guesthouse and lookout tower; and the **Matrosenhaus**, a gabled house built for the crews of the royal boats. The park is also home to the Gothic **Gerichtslaube**, Berlin's original town hall and law-court, which was brought here in 1872 after being displaced by the Rotes Rathaus.

At the eastern end of Babelsberg, reached by buses #690 and #692, is the **Filmpark Babelsberg** (mid-March to Oct daily 10am–6pm; *www.filmpark.de*; DM29/€14.50, kids DM26/€13), a huge complex of 430,000 square metres entered from Grossbeerenstrasse. Production began here in 1912, though its halcyon years coincided with those of the Weimar Republic. Under the name of UFA, it rivalled Hollywood as a centre of cinematic innovation, producing over a thousand films. These included Robert Wiene's Expressionist masterpiece *Das Kabinett des Dr Caligari* ("The Cabinet of Dr Caligari"), Fritz Lang's *Metropolis* and *Der Blaue Engel* ("The Blue Angel") starring the young Marlene Dietrich. During the Third Reich, the studios were taken over by Goebbels' Ministry of Propaganda, whose most notorious production was *Jud Süss*, which corrupted Lion Feuchtwanger's pro-Jewish novel into an anti-Semitic tirade. Against all the odds, the war years produced a masterpiece in the special-effect-laden colour epic *Münchhausen*, which was scripted by Erich Kästner, who wrote under a pseudonym in order to circumvent the Nazi ban on him as a supposedly subversive writer. Renamed as DEFA, the studios were the heavily subsidized centre of the East German film industry, which produced some fine children's films, such as *Little Muck*, but which didn't last much longer than the GDR itself. Since the *Wende*, Babelsberg has reinvented itself as a film theme park, and visitors can wander through the costume and props departments and watch technicians going through the motions of shooting film scenes for their bene-fit. In addition, there are carnival-type rides, several featuring cartoon characters familiar to German kids, and animal shows. It's also possible to visit the hangar-like studio where Fritz Lang is believed to have filmed *Metropolis* and admire a reproduction of his futuris-tic set. It takes several hours to see the whole site, which makes a good day-trip in itself.

Eating, drinking and nightlife

Potsdam has a good selection of **restaurants**, some of the best of which are to be found in the hotels (see p.870). The most convenient concentration of places to eat and drink is along Brandenburger Strasse, although it pays to go a little further afield.

Restaurants

Hafthorn, Friedrich-Ebert-Str. 90. Large and lively restaurant offering Swabian specialities for sur-prisingly little money.

Juliette, Jägerstr. 39. High-quality and very expensive French restaurant.

Kleines Schloss, Park Babelsberg. A traditionally minded lakeside place serving standard German dishes far from the hubbub of the city. Open Wed–Sun 11am–9pm.

Luise, Luisenplatz 6. Mid-priced German and continental food in casual surroundings, the perfect place to eat before tackling Sanssouci, just up the road.

Villa Kellermann, Mangerstr. 34. Potsdam's best Italian restaurant occupies a villa on the eastern bank of the Heiliger See.

Waage, Am Neuen Markt 12. Serves inventive dishes with local ingredients, though it's a little on the pricey side.

Zum Laubenpieper, Am Pfingstberg 25. Rustic restaurant offering huge servings of traditional German food. Its hill-top beer garden is open during the summer.

Zur Linde, Lindenstr. 50. Personable and relaxing restaurant with typical German food.

Cafés

Arco, corner of Friedrich-Ebert-Strasse and Kurfürstenstrasse. Occupying the east wing of the Nauener Tor, this small café, which has outdoor seating in summer, serves excellent continental food.

Babette, Brandenburger Str. 71. Pleasant little café, also open as a cocktail bar Wed–Sun until 1am.

Café im Filmmuseum, Schloss-Str. 1. One of Potsdam's best cafés, and a good place to take a break while visiting the museum.

Café Galerie Mittelstrasse, Mittelstr. 18. An arty but friendly café, bar and gallery in a venerable Dutch house. It serves cheap food, and has an outdoor barbecue in summer.

Café Lapis Lazuli, Benkertstr. 21. Hippie-ish café with old wooden tables and candles. Light snacks only.

Deli Frizz, Friedrich-Ebert-Str. 35. Alternative bistro and natural food store.

Drachenhaus, Maulbeerallee. A pleasant and genteel little café in Park Sanssouci, housed in a pagoda-style building once used by royal vintners. You can also eat well here.

La Leander Benkertstr. 1. In the Holländisches Viertel, a dark and relaxing café with a short menu.

Bars

Brauerhaus, Kurfürstenstr. 52. In a restored Freemasons' building, this moderately priced Hausbrauerei features German food and its own brew.

pub à la pub, Breite Str. 1. A student hangout in a classic GDR concrete building adorned with a Socialist Realist mosaic.

Seerose, Breite Str. 24. Housed in a bizarre-looking modern building, this popular bar offers good views across the Neustädter Havelbucht.

Souterrain, Allee nach Sanssouci 4. Away from the centre on the road to Sanssouci, this lively café-bar is worth dropping into.

Entertainment

Cruises on the Havel and its lakes are run by Weisse Flotte (☎03 31/2 75 92 10, *www.weisse-flotte-potsdam.de*), departing from Lange Brücke. If you prefer to pilot yourself, **boats** can be rented at Grosse Fischer 11 (☎03 31/61 90 26).

Potsdam's main venue for **drama** is the Hans-Otto-Theater, Zimmerstr. 10 (☎03 31/2 30 38). The Schlosstheater (☎03 31/27 57 10) in the Neues Schloss is an ideal stage for small-scale **operas**, and those by Mozart feature regularly; it is also sometimes used for **concerts**. The town's **cabaret**, Kabarett Obelisk, is at Schopenhauerstr. 27 (☎03 31/29 10 69).

For **nightlife** the best bet is Lindenpark, Stahnsdorfer Str. 76–78 (☎03 31/74 79 70) in Babelsberg, with regular "alternative" discos and live bands. Also recommendable is the Waschhaus, Schiffbauergasse 1 (☎03 31/2 71 56 26, *www.waschhaus.de*), just off Berliner Strasse on the way into town from the Glienicker Brücke, a large complex with live music, parties, galleries and an open-air cinema. At the same address is Fabrik (☎03 31/2 80 03 14), a theatre for contemporary dance and new music. The Altes Rathaus (☎03 31/29 20 79) offers local live bands on occasional weekends, while the *Art Speicher* disco, Zeppelinstr. 136 (☎03 31/9 81 50, *www.artspeicher.de*), is open Thursday to Saturday from 9pm.

Brandenburg and around

BRANDENBURG, the city from which the province takes its name, lies on the main Berlin–Hannover rail line just over 30km west of Potsdam. For all its illustrious past – it was founded by the Slavs in the sixth century, made the seat of a precarious missionary German bishopric in the tenth century, before becoming the capital of the Margravate established by Albert the Bear in 1157 – its more recent history has been a catalogue of misfortunes. These began when the Nazis chose it as the site of a concentration camp; future GDR dictator Erich Honecker served twelve years there, and among those murdered were 10,000 victims of a compulsory euthanasia programme for the mentally handicapped. The Nazis turned Brandenburg's industry – hitherto based on the production of bikes and motor vehicles – over to military purposes, ensuring the city was a prime target for Allied bombers. It was further damaged by the Red Army in 1945, when the defenders mounted a futile last-ditch resistance. After the war, the Communists made it the metropolis for the steel industry their dogma demanded; as a result, the medieval skyline was disfigured by the addition of sixteen smoking chimneys and drab apartment buildings to accommodate its workers. Many historic buildings were left as ruins, while others rotted under the impact of some of the worst air pollution in Europe. Despite all this, Brandenburg still has a great deal to offer, including some magnificent examples of north German brick architecture, and a beautiful natural setting at a point where the broad course of the Havel fashions a wondrous lake-strewn landscape.

The City

Brandenburg's historic centre is divided into three distinct parts – the **Dominsel**, the **Altstadt** and the **Neustadt** – each of which is situated on its own island in the Havel.

The Neustadt

Closest to the Hauptbahnhof, the first of the three island quarters is the **Neustadt** or New Town. It's new only in a relative sense, having been founded as the commercial quarter at the end of the twelfth century, a generation after the previously Slav Altstadt had been re-established as a German town. Despite conspicuous gaps left by the war, its narrow streets retain much of their old feel. The first building in view is the cylindrical **Steintor** (Tues–Fri 9am–5pm, Sat & Sun 10am–5pm; DM4/€2), one of four surviving gateways out of the ten that the two settlements once possessed. There's a small museum inside showing special exhibitions on the city's history. Northeast of here is the **Paulikloster**, a thirteenth-century Dominican friary left in ruins during World War II, though some reconstruction work has been carried out since the *Wende*.

Right in the middle of the island is the Neustädtischer Markt, now returned to its age-old role as a market square. It's dominated by the **Katharinenkirche**, a Gothic pile from the turn of the fifteenth century. Outside, the walls are crammed with spouting gargoyles and frilly gables tacked on for purely decorative effect, with the varied colouring and positioning of the bricks helping to transform the surface effects yet further. The fantastical interior design tends to overshadow the church's treasures, which include a finely carved fifteenth-century altar and a fourteenth-century stained-glass window in the choir which was fortuitously removed from the Paulikloster in 1942.

The Altstadt

Hauptstrasse runs northwestwards over the Havel into the **Altstadt**, which occupies only a small portion of a much larger island. Immediately over the river is the **Johanniskirche**, another brick Gothic church still remaining in the burnt-out state it was left in at the end of the war. Further along, at Hauptstr. 96, is the **Freyhaus** (Tues–Fri 9am–5pm, Sat & Sun 10am–5pm; DM4/€2, free first Sun of month), a Baroque mansion which now houses the district museum. This array of local ephemera is more interesting than you might expect, particularly the displays on the archeology of the Havelland, the graphic art section and a fascinating toy collection.

At the end of Ritterstrasse, the continuation of Hauptstrasse, Plauer Strasse leads north to the Altstädtischer Markt, over which looms the fourteenth-century **Altstädtisches Rathaus**, whose facade is topped with an unusual stepped gable. In front of it stands a mighty five-metre-high **statue of Roland**, medieval symbol of Brandenburg's status as a market town. He previously stood guard in front of the Neustädtisches Rathaus opposite the Katharinenkirche, but was brought here after its destruction in World War II.

Continuing northwards, you come to the parish church of the Altstadt, the **Gotthardtkirche**. Its facade is in the austere Romanesque style of the Premonstratensian monks, but behind it stands a light and airy Gothic hall church erected in the fifteenth century. Inside, look out for the thirteenth-century font and the lovely Burgundian tapestry showing the hunting of the unicorn. On the square facing the church is the **Schulhaus**, a half-timbered former school building from the sixteenth century.

The Dominsel

The **Dominsel**, the smallest of the three islands on which the historic quarters of Brandenburg are built, escaped the worst of the bombing and is by far the most visually pleasing part of town. From the Gotthardtkirche, you have to approach it circuitously via yet another island, occupied mainly by sports fields, to the north; there's a more direct approach along Mühlendamm from the Neustädtischer Markt. Taking the latter approach, the first monument you come to is the **Petrikapelle**, a thirteenth-century chapel given a spectacular interior transformation three hundred years later, with the addition of the intricate late Gothic cellular vault resting on hexagonal pillars.

The **Dom** was begun around 1165 as a Romanesque basilica, and slowly converted to Gothic in the fourteenth and fifteenth centuries, though many parts of the old structure were retained, notably the arcades of the nave. The most atmospheric part is the **crypt**, where you can see the poignant original **triumphal cross**, supplanted *in situ* by a more monumental Gothic group. Even more eye-catching are the **capitals**, whose carvings of fabulous beasts and eerie half-human creatures show the vivid flights of imagination of which the medieval mind was capable. A contrastingly sombre note is struck by a series of metal plates, each accompanied by an appropriate biblical quotation, commemorating local clergymen murdered by the Nazis. It's a fitting reminder of the high-profile political role the Dom has played, most recently during the *Wende* of 1989 when the church was regularly filled for recitals given on the magnificent Baroque **organ**, attracting large financial donations for the democratic cause in the process. In the south transept is a beautifully carved and painted **Bohemian altar** from around 1375, whose radiantly joyous saints mark a refreshing change from the anguished figures normally found in religious art. This was originally the high altar, but it was displaced in favour of a large retable brought here when Kloster Lehnin (see opposite) was secularized after the Reformation. In front of the latter stands a delicately modelled fourteenth-century **font**, with scenes from the childhood of Christ on its basin, and more fantastic animals on the base. On the north side of the choir, look out for the appropriately named **Bunte Kapelle** (Painted Chapel), another survivor from the Romanesque period.

The **Dommuseum** (Mon–Fri 10am–5pm, Sat 10am–6pm, Sun 11am–6pm; DM5/€2.50) occupies the conventual buildings of the Premonstratensian collegiate foundation which moved here from the Gotthardtkirche. There's a superb array of medieval textiles, including a *Hungertuch* of 1290, made to cover the altar during Lent. Even finer is the collection of manuscripts, of which the star piece is the **Brandenburg Evangelistary**, a sumptuous late Romanesque Gospel book adorned with colourful miniatures. The original is displayed with one page open; a facsimile of the whole book is kept for examination at leisure.

Practicalities

Brandenburg's **tourist office** (Mon–Wed & Fri 9am–7pm, Thurs 9am–8pm, Sat 10am–2/4pm; ☎ & fax 0 33 81/22 37 43, *www.stadt-brandenburg.de*) is at Hauptstr. 51; as usual, it can arrange **private rooms** (①–③). Among the **pensions** are some with a central location, such as *Zum Birnbaum*, Mittelstr. 1 (☎0 33 81/5 27 50; ④), and *Engel*, Grosse Gartenstr. 37 (☎0 33 81/20 03 93; ④). There are only a handful of **hotels** within the city: *Gerono*, Magdeburger Str. 12 (☎0 33 81/3 40 90; ④); *City*, Grosse Gartenstr. 2 (☎0 33 81/52 26 92; ④); *Axxon*, Magdeburger Landstr. 288 (☎0 33 81/32 10; ⑤); *Am St Gotthard*, Mühlentorstr. 56 (☎0 33 81/5 29 00; ⑥); and *Sorat*, Altstädtischer Markt 1 (☎0 33 81/59 70; ⑧). The most convenient of the **campsites** by the lakes around the city is *Seecamp Malge* (☎0 33 81/66 31 34) on the Breitlingsee, which also has bungalows for rent. Two more can be found on the nearby islands; yet another, the *Margaretenhof* (☎0 33 81/40 32 27), is on the peninsula jutting into the Plauensee.

With the exception of *Gerona*, the hotels listed above all have recommendable **restaurants**. Another good place to eat is the *Ratskeller* in the Altstädtisches Rathaus. The *Stadtcafé*, Hauptstr. 26–28, is typical of the vogue for trendy western-style **cafés** in the ex-GDR, but isn't bad for all that. **Cruises** (DM10/€5) for a two-hour round trip, are run by *Bollmann Flotte* (☎0 33 81/22 39 59), and depart from Salzhofufer on the Altstadt side of the river.

Lehnin

About 20km southeast of Brandenburg, and equally accessible from Potsdam, the timewarp village of **LEHNIN** clusters round its huge **Kloster** (May–Oct Mon–Sat 9am–5pm, Sun 11am–5pm; *www.stift-lehnin.de*; DM6/€3), which was founded in 1180 by Cistercian monks on what was then a swampy marsh deep in a forest populated mainly by heathen and hostile Slavs. Despite many vicissitudes, the **Klosterkirche** survives intact and offers a graphic illustration of the way the Romanesque style of the east end – the first part to be built – had given way to the Gothic by the time the building was completed in 1260. Although the simple majesty of the elevation is the most impressive feature, there are also a few notable works of art, including a Romanesque triumphal cross and the tomb slab of Margrave Otto IV, son-in-law of Emperor Rudolf von Habsburg, the founder of medieval Europe's most powerful dynasty. Within the monastic complex is a **guesthouse** (☎0 33 82/76 80; ⑤); the village also has a good **hotel** with restaurant, *Markgraf*, Friedensstr. 13 (☎0 33 82/76 50; ⑤).

Oranienburg

About 20km northwest out of Berlin at the terminus of S-Bahn #1 is **ORANIENBURG**, a drab-looking place set apart from dozens of other towns around the capital by a monument that recalls the grimmest chapter in German history – the **Konzentrationslager Sachsenhausen**.

This concentration camp, now officially known as the **Gedenkstätte und Museum Sachsenhausen** (Tues–Sun: April–Sept 8.30am–6pm; Oct–March 8.30am–4.30pm; free) is in the northern suburb of Sachsenhausen. It's reached from S-Bahnhof Oranienburg by bus #273 or on foot after a twenty-minute walk. A tree-lined road leads to a **museum** devoted to the history of the camp and special exhibitions. Just north of here is **Turm A**, the gatehouse entrance to the camp proper with a stretch of the original electrified camp fence running either side of it.

Beyond Turm A is the **Apellplatz**, or parade ground, where the prisoners were gathered together for roll call and often kept standing for hours on end or forced to witness

THE HISTORY OF SACHSENHAUSEN CAMP

Opened as a memorial on April 23, 1961 by the GDR government, **Sachsenhausen Concentration Camp** is an inevitably sobering place: as the official guidebook puts it, "Every footstep of this earth is soaked with the blood and death-sweat of tens of thousands of martyrs from many different nations." The camp was originally opened in July 1936 (replacing an earlier ad hoc camp housed in a local brewery from 1933 to 1935) as a *Schutzhaftlager* ("Protective Custody Camp"), specifically to house opponents of the Nazi regime – mainly Communists, Socialists and trade unionists. New categories of prisoner were added with every year of Nazi rule: people convicted of "antisocial" behaviour, homosexuals and finally Jews, six thousand of whom were brought to Sachsenhausen after the brutal *Kristallnacht* attacks of November 9–10, 1938. The war years saw thousands of new internees arrive from the occupied countries and the beginning of organized mass murder, as opposed to the relatively arbitrary killings and executions of the 1930s.

At the end of the war the SS evacuated the camp, moving 33,000 prisoners north towards the Baltic where it was intended to herd them aboard boats which would then be sunk. Known as the **Todesmarsch** (Death March), this pitiless forced-march across northern Germany claimed the lives of six thousand prisoners, most of whom died by the roadside (today plaques across the region commemorate them). Fortunately, the survivors fell into Allied hands before the SS could put the final stage of their plan into effect. A further three thousand prisoners, most of them only barely alive, were found in the camp hospital when the liberating Soviet army arrived at Sachsenhausen on April 22, 1945.

In August of that year the MVD, the military branch of the Soviet secret police, reopened Sachsenhausen as **MVD Special Camp No. 7**. Originally for war criminals, former Nazis and *Wehrmacht* officers, it gradually filled with people who were simply opponents of the occupying regime including, after 1946, large numbers of Social Democrats who had protested about the forced merger of their party with the Communist Party. Among all these prisoners were a few who had previously been interned here by the Nazis. By the time the camp was finally closed on March 10, 1950, about sixty thousand prisoners had passed through, of whom some twenty thousand died, mainly of hunger and lung diseases. In a postscript to this episode, mass graves containing the bodies of Germans executed by the MVD were unearthed in nearby woods in the spring of 1990.

executions on the camp **gallows**. Behind the gallows, in four semicircular rows, were the **barrack buildings**, originally intended to hold 130 prisoners in cramped conditions but each filled by the end of the war with up to 500 men. Only two remain: one now houses a **museum**, the other is a memorial hall where documentaries are regularly shown. The museum itself dates from the GDR and very much reflects the Communist viewpoint of that country; after unification, it was decided to retain the exhibition within as a part of the camp's history. The positions of the other barracks are marked with granite blocks. Beyond them is an open space leading to the stylized camp **memorial**.

Many of the victims commemorated by the memorial died nearby at **Station Z**, where the Germans turned the process of executing Soviet prisoners of war into an almost industrial one, dispatching tens of thousands of men with shots to the back of the neck. At the opposite side of the camp are two surviving barrack blocks used to house **Jewish inmates**, with a special exhibition devoted to their sufferings. In September 1992, these barracks were set on fire by young right-wing radicals, and the burnt walls remaining have been incorporated into the exhibit. Just beyond here are **cells** where prominent prisoners, mainly workers' leaders and patriots from the occupied countries, were held in isolation, usually pending execution. One of the inmates best known to posterity is the anti-Nazi cleric, **Pastor Martin Niemöller**, who was one of the few to survive incarceration here. At the northeast end of the grounds is an exhibition devoted to the history of Sachsenhausen after 1945, when it was used as a special camp by the Soviets.

Neuruppin

Reached easily by road or rail from Oranienburg, the lakeside town of **NEURUPPIN** is the birthplace of the writer Theodor Fontane and the architect Karl Friedrich Schinkel. It's a predominantly eighteenth-century town, whose historic centre is all the more appreciable for being slightly faded.

The town is laid out on a grid-like pattern around three large squares: a result of carefully planned reconstruction following a great fire in 1787. From the Hauptbahnhof access to the town is via Bahnhofstrasse, which leads into Schinkelstrasse and ends at the large square of **Kirchplatz** on which sits the **Pfarrkirche St Marien**, a tatty-looking Baroque-influenced church from the early nineteenth century. Karl Friedrich Schinkel's father was superintendent of the Pfarrkirche's predecessor and behind the church is the **Schinkel-Denkmal**, a monument to his famous son. Schinkel was born in 1781 and lived in Neuruppin through the time of the great fire and rebuilding, something that may have influenced his later choice of profession. In his adolescence he was sent to school in Berlin, and, having studied architecture, entered the Prussian civil service as a surveyor, later rising to take overall control of the Prussian building office. The mark he left on Berlin is tremendous. He completely transformed the old capital, doing much to give the city its predominantly Neoclassical feel, best exemplified by buildings along and around the Unter den Linden like the Neue Wache and the Altes Museum. Lesser works by the architect crop up all over north Germany, and there seems to be hardly a town in the region untouched by his hand.

Not far from the Schinkel monument is the **Fontanehaus**, the pharmacy with a stone lion above its doorway at Karl-Marx-Str. 84, which was the birthplace of Neuruppin's other famous son, the author Theodor Fontane – though these days there's little about the building to betray its past. A few steps along Karl-Marx-Strasse from the Fontanehaus is Neuruppin's Neoclassical **Gymnasium**, the school attended by both Schinkel and Fontane, now containing a commercial art gallery. A similarly grandiose edifice is the **Heimatmuseum** (Tues–Fri 10am–5pm, Sat & Sun 10am–4pm; DM5/€2.50) at August-Bebel-Str. 14–15. This building was one of the first in Germany to be erected specifically as a museum (the Bildergalerie in Potsdam came first) and contains, naturally enough, extensive material about Neuruppin and its surroundings, as well as sections devoted to Schinkel and Fontane. Just behind is the **Tempelgarten**, a park where Frederick the Great often retreated from his duties as commander of a local army regiment, after being sent here as a young crown prince by his father. The

THEODORE FONTANE 1818–98

Fontane was born in Neuruppin in 1819 to a couple of Huguenot descent. Before publishing his first work he was employed as a pharmaceutical dispenser, later serving as a war correspondent during the Austro-Prussian War of 1866 and the Franco-Prussian War of 1870–71. He wrote a couple of books describing his war experiences and four volumes about his travels in the Mark of Brandenburg, plus two others on his visits to Scotland and England. His career as a writer of fiction did not begin until the age of 57 when he penned the Napoleonic epic *Before the Storm*. He subsequently published a further seventeen novels, mostly with a contemporary setting, which collectively stand as the summit of late nineteenth-century German literature. His best-known work is *Effi Briest*, published in 1895, the story of an upper-class Prussian woman drawn into an adulterous affair with predictably tragic consequences. Fontane, by his sympathetic portrayal of the protagonists, turns what could easily have become a rather trite reworking of the *Madame Bovary* story into a thinly veiled critique of the inflexible social mores of Prussian society of the time and their devastating effect on the individual.

park is named after its circular Neoclassical temple, the first work of the architect Georg von Knobelsdorff. Towards the southwestern end of Karl-Marx-Strasse is **Bernhard-Brasch-Platz**, a bleak parade ground previously known as Königsplatz, around which large numbers of attractive Baroque buildings survive. At the very end of the street is the **Fontane-Denkmal**, a bronze statue of Fontane surveying the main road into town.

A few hundred metres south of Karl-Marx-Strasse lies **Seeufer**, a broad lakeside promenade on the shores of the **Ruppiner See**, the lake that threads south of town for about 10km. Overlooking Seeufer, the thirteenth-century **Klosterkirche** (daily noon–6pm) offers clear views of the lake and town and, most prominently, a huge seventeen-metre polished steel statue entitled *Parzival am See*, perched over the lake since 1999.

Practicalities

Neuruppin's **tourist office** at Karl-Marx-Str. 1 (Mon–Fri 9am–6pm, Sat 10am–2pm; ☎0 33 91/45 54 60, fax 45 46 66; *www.neuruppin.de*) can arrange accommodation in any of the dozens of **private houses** (①–③) with rooms for rent. There's also a reasonable choice of **hotels**: *Berliner Hof*, Karl-Marx-Str. 96 (☎03 3 91/35 86 62; ④); *Ruppiner Spiesegaststätte*, August-Babel-Str. 36–37 (☎0 33 91/29 44; ④); *Zum alten Siechenhospital*, Siechenstr. 4 (☎0 33 91/39 88 44; ⑤); and *Altes Kasino*, Seeufer 11 (☎0 33 91/30 59; ⑤). The last two hotels have the best **restaurants**; otherwise try *Fehrbelliner Hof*, Karl-Marx-Str. 63, or *Café Huth*, Karl-Marx-Str. 85. Between May and September, **cruises** are run on the Ruppiner See, departing from Seeufer.

Rheinsberg

About 20km northeast of Neuruppin, and the dead end of a branch rail line from Herzberg to the east, is **RHEINSBERG**, a small resort at the southern end of a network of lakes, dotted with campsites and watersports facilities. It's a pleasant, predominantly eighteenth-century town, best known for its associations with Frederick the Great, mouldering quietly on the shore of the Grienericksee, the southernmost end of the Rheinsberger See.

The main sight is the lakeside **Schloss** (April–Oct Tues–Sun 9.30am–5pm; Nov–March Tues–Sun 10am–3.45pm; DM5/€2.50), a three-winged building in smudged white at the southwestern edge of the centre. An earlier building on the same site was the residence of Frederick the Great from 1736 until he acceded to the throne in 1740. He spent his time in Rheinsberg in the study of science and art, later claiming it as the happiest period of his life. His favourite architect, Georg Wenzeslaus von Knobelsdorff, was commissioned to design the present structure as a palace for Frederick's younger brother Heinrich, who spent sixty years there, enjoying the company of attractive young men and redesigning the gardens. Highlight of the Schloss's interior is an allegorical ceiling painting *Day Drives Away the Night*. This shows a barn owl (representing the unloved "Soldier King", Friedrich Wilhelm I) retreating before the advance of Aurora (Frederick and/or Heinrich).

Part of the Schloss is designated as a memorial to the Berlin writer **Kurt Tucholsky** (1890–1935), who immortalized the town in *Rheinsberg – A Picture Book for Lovers*, a tender, ironic idyll about two sweethearts paying a weekend visit. It's very untypical of the author's output as a whole, which is mostly made up of short, devastatingly witty satires. Like his nineteenth-century precursor Heinrich Heine, Tucholsky was a Jew who abandoned Judaism and became a vociferous critic of Germany's Jewish community, yet who never really adopted an alternative faith or value system. With the advent of Nazism, he fled to Denmark, where he took his own life.

The **Schlosspark** is dotted with a number of odd monuments including, just to the west of the Schloss itself, the red-brick **Pyramide** to Prince Heinrich. Near the lakeshore is one of his own creations, the strange **Steingrotte**, a grotto containing a jumble of urns and statue pediments. The **Obelisk** on the opposite shore to the Schloss celebrates the Prussian generals who fell in the Seven Years War.

Practicalities

Rheinsberg's **tourist office** is in the Kavalierhaus on the Markt (Mon–Sat 10am–4pm, Sun 10am–2pm; ☎ & fax 03 39 31/20 59; *www.rheinsberg.de*). There are plenty of good-value **private rooms** (①–②), and also several **pensions**: *Zu den Vier Jahreszeiten*, Rhinstr. 4 (☎03 39 31/24 24; ④); *Holländer Mühle*, Schwanower Str. (☎03 39 31/23 32; ④); and *Am Rheinsberger Schlosspark*, Fontaneplatz 2a (☎03 39 31/3 92 71; ⑤). The only **hotels** are *Goldener Stern*, Mühlenstr. 4 (☎03 39 31/21 79; ④), *Der Seehof*, Seestr. 18 (☎03 39 31/40 30; ⑤), and *Schlosshotel Deutsches Haus*, Seestr. 13 (☎03 39 31/3 90 59; ⑥). Nearest **campsite** is at Warenthin, two and half kilometres from the town (☎03 39 31/3 82 92). *Schlosshotel Deutsches Haus* is the town's leading **restaurant**; its counterpart in *Der Seehof* is also very fine, as is the *Ratskeller*, Markt 1. Rheinsberg's main annual event is the *Kammeroper Schloss Rheinsberg*, a summer **opera festival** (for information and tickets call ☎03 39 31/3 92 96) which offers both indoor and outdoor performances. The former are staged in the recently restored Schlosstheater in the Schloss, which was built for Prince Heinrich in 1774, and is now a year-round venue for **concerts** by the local music academy; the latter on the picturesque lakeside terrace outside.

The Schorfheide

The largest area of protected landscape anywhere in Germany is the **Schorfheide** to the northeast of Berlin, which occupies a total of almost 1300 square kilometres. Nearly half of this is forest; there are also some 250 lakes, plus moorland, wetland and farmland. Although the Schorfheide is distinctive enough to have gained inclusion on the UNESCO list of World Biosphere Reserves, it's better known for its set-piece attractions, which include the magnificent ruined Kloster at **Chorin** and what is surely the most visually impressive technical monument in the country, the Schiffshebewerk at **Niederfinow**. These are easily combined in a day-trip from Berlin by train, though when travelling between the two it's necessary to change at Eberswalde-Finow, a rather nondescript industrial town 50km from the capital.

Chorin

Sixty kilometres from Berlin, on the main rail line to the Polish city of Szczecin, is the tiny village of **CHORIN**. Alight at Bahnhof Kloster Chorin, the first of the two train stations, to see the evocatively ruined Cistercian **Kloster** (daily: mid-March to Oct 9am–6pm; Nov to mid-March 9am–4pm; DM5/€2.50), which, in accordance with the ideals of its founders, is in a secluded setting in the middle of the woods by a small lake, the Amtssee. To reach it, walk all the way through the village, bearing right, then follow the forest path. Established on this site in 1273, the Kloster was constructed over the following sixty years, and is an example of Gothic brick architecture at its most daringly inventive. In the nineteenth century, Schinkel carried out major structural repairs on the long-abandoned monastery, then in danger of collapse. Both the church and the monastic quarters are substantially intact, though the former now gapingly opens out directly onto the cloister – helping create a much expanded auditorium for the **concerts** which are regularly held throughout the summer months. Architecturally, the finest feature is the highly idiosyncratic **facade**, the last part of the church to be built. A dazzling exercise in patterned brickwork, it contrasts sharply but effectively with the solemn grandeur of the structure behind. Also of special note are the gabled **brewery** by the entrance and the **kitchen** to its rear.

There are two **hotels** in Chorin: *Landgasthaus Zur Kroneiche*, Bahnhofstr. 1 (☎03 33 66/2 80; ④), and *Haus Chorin*, Neue Klosterallee 10 (☎03 33 66/5 00; ⑤). Both of these have **restaurants**; an alternative is *Alte Klosterschänke*, Am Amt 9.

Niederfinow and the Schiffshebewerk

Ten kilometres east of the Eberswalde rail junction, at **NIEDERFINOW**, is one of the area's more unexpected sights, the **Schiffshebewerk**, a barge-lift of titanic proportions on the Havel–Oder canal. It can be reached by bus from Niederfinow's Bahnhof, although it's a pleasant enough walk of only a couple of kilometres: cross the bridge near the station and head north.

The Schiffshebewerk is used to transport barges from the western upland section of the canal down into the Oder valley and vice versa, replacing an antiquated system of locks. It was opened in 1934, and at the time of its construction was the largest structure of its kind in the world: 94m long, 27m wide and an amazing 60m high. Subsequently it became an important staging post on the canal network linking Germany and Poland, reducing the time taken to lower and raise vessels from several painstaking hours to about fifteen minutes. The lift is basically an enormous steel trough capable of accommodating a thousand-tonne barge, raised and lowered by an electric-powered system of counterweights, within a casing of steel girders.

For a closer look at how it works, follow the crowds up the steps on the western side of the road. These will bring you to the upper canal level and a walkway that runs around the outside of the barge-lift (daily 9am–6pm or dusk; DM2/€1, although this is often waived). The structure attracts its fair share of visitors and there's a large car park with souvenir shop and Imbiss stands in the shadow of its massive girders. If you want something more substantial to eat or drink, head back along the main road towards the Bahnhof, where there are a couple of Gaststätten and a plush modern **hotel**, *Am Schiffshebewerk* (☎03 33 62/7 00 99; ⑤).

Frankfurt an der Oder

Some 90km east of Berlin lies the border town of **FRANKFURT AN DER ODER**. Like so many communities along the course of the River Oder, it was split in two in 1945, with the Altstadt on the west bank remaining in German hands, while the east bank suburb became the Polish town of Słubice. As Frankfurt was almost totally destroyed during the war, it's mainly of interest now as a stopover point on journeys to and from Poland. Nonetheless, it's a place with a long and distinguished history, dating back to the thirteenth century, when German merchants founded a settlement and built a wooden bridge over the Oder. Subsequently, the town developed as an important trade centre.

Today the **Marktplatz** remains the focal point of the centre. On its southern side is the **Marienkirche**, the biggest of all Germany's brick Gothic hall churches. It was reduced to a roofless ruin following a bombing raid, and remained in this forlorn state throughout the GDR epoch. Restoration work has been in progress since the *Wende*; it now has a roof once again, and for the time being at least, the enormous interior is devoted to temporary exhibitions. Directly opposite, forming a deliberate juxtaposition of the sacred and secular, is the **Rathaus**, another exercise in virtuoso brickwork, which ranks among the most impressive town halls in Germany.

HEINRICH VON KLEIST (1777–1811)

Born into an old Prussian military family, **Heinrich von Kleist** began his career as a soldier, but resigned his commission and adopted a wandering lifestyle. Despite taking his own life at the age of 34 in a bizarre suicide pact with a woman dying of cancer, he bequeathed an astonishingly varied body of literature, which speaks more forcefully to the modern reader than that of any other great German writer of his time. His plays range from *The Broken Jug*, a comedy in which a crooked village judge tries a case in which he is the real culprit, via *Penthesilea*, a tragi-comic mythological spoof, to *Prince Frederick of Homburg*, in which Prussia's Great Elector appears as Justice and Mercy personified. In contrast to the emotional tone of the plays, Kleist's short stories are narrated with detached objectivity. Often set in exotic locations, they characteristically feature dramatic twists of plot, with scenes of lyrical intensity alternating with episodes of savage brutality.

Between Marktplatz and the river is the **Kleist-Museum** (Tues–Sun 11am–5pm; DM4/€2), which is devoted to the life and works of the town's favourite son, the dramatist and short-story writer **Heinrich von Kleist** (see box above). At C.-P.-E.-Bach-Str. 11 is the **Museum Viadrina** (Tues–Sun 11am–5pm; DM4/€2), a grandiose Prussian *Junker* house containing displays on the history of Frankfurt and the surrounding region. The building will be under renovation until 2003, but a small temporary exhibition is on view from May 2001.

Further north, beyond the bridge to Poland, is the **Konzerthalle C.P.E. Bach**, the main concert hall of a town with a strong musical tradition, as is reflected by the presence of the academy alongside. The building, an intact Gothic hall church, is named in honour of Carl Philipp Emmanuel Bach – son of J.S. and one of the most bizarrely idiosyncratic composers of musical history – who spent part of his life in the town. Finally, at the southern end of the Altstadt, the curious two-storey **Gertraudkirche** (Mon–Fri 8am–4.30pm) contains the treasures formerly kept in the Marienkirche, including two outstanding fourteenth-century pieces: a tall candelabra and a font adorned with 44 reliefs of Old and New Testament scenes.

Practicalities

Frankfurt's **Hauptbahnhof**, itself a border crossing point, occupies an elevated position about ten minutes' walk southwest of the Altstadt. The **tourist office** (Mon–Fri 10am–6pm, Sat 10am–12.30pm; ☎03 35/32 52 16, fax 2 25 65, *www.frankfurt-oder.de*) lies just west of Marktplatz at Karl-Marx-Str. 8a.

Though there's no particular reason to stay over, you can book **private rooms** (②–③) at the tourist office. There are three **hotels** in the town centre: *Gallus*, Fürstenwalder Str. 47 (☎03 35/5 61 50; ③); *Zur Alten Oder*, Fischerstr. 32 (☎03 35/55 62 20; ⑤); and *City Park,* Lindenstr.12 (☎03 35/5 53 20; ⑥). All the hotels have **restaurants**, though the best place to eat is the *Ratskeller* in the historic cellars of the Rathaus, which includes vegetarian dishes on its menu. There's also a restaurant, *Turm 24*, atop the town's lone skyscraper at Logenstr. 8, which, although a bit pricey, affords wonderful views of the surrounding greenery.

The Spreewald

The **Spreewald**, a unique forest area bisected by the River Spree, which lies 100km southeast of Berlin, is by far the most beautiful landscape in the Land of Brandenburg, although its atmosphere can be marred by the sheer volume of visitors. It falls into two parts: the **Unterspreewald** and **Oberspreewald**, north and south of the town of Lübben respectively. Although the Unterspreewald, east of Schlepzig, is pleasant enough, the real attraction is the Oberspreewald, a 500-square-kilometre area of deciduous woodland. The woods, which are broken up in places by land given over to market gardening – the cucumbers produced here are renowned – are watered by three hundred channels (fed by the River Spree) known as *Fliesse*, and crisscrossed by man-made canals, creating an environment that Theodor Fontane described as "Venice as it might have been 1500 years ago".

Most of the local populace are Slavic **Sorbs** (also known as **Wends**; see box below) with their own language and traditions, and Sorbish street signs add more than a hint of exotica to an already unusual region. Unfortunately, the Spreewald was discovered a long time ago and tourists flock here in unbelievable numbers during the summer, overrunning the local Gaststätten and block-booking seats on the **punts** that ferry visitors around the area (motorized craft are banned), charging on average DM5/€2.50 per hour for trips which can last from anything between an hour and a half to ten hours. Nevertheless, the Spreewald really does live up to tourist-brochure hyperbole. **Walking** is just as good a way of getting around as taking a punt, but it's essential to get hold of the local *Wanderkarte*, as it's all too easy to get lost or disoriented. The provision of **accommodation** has mushroomed since the *Wende*, but it's still advisable to book in advance during the summer months.

Lübben (Lubin)

LÜBBEN, which is easily reached by rail from Berlin, is the first major town in the Spreewald and from its harbour it's possible to take punt trips into both the Unter- and Oberspreewald. The town also has a sixteenth-century church, the **Paul-Gerhardt-Kirche**, which is named in honour of the religious poet buried there, and a **Schloss**. Within the latter, whose address is Ernst-von-Houwald-Damm 15, is the **tourist office** (April–Oct daily 10am–6pm; Nov–March Mon–Fri 10am–4pm; ☎0 35 46/30 90, fax 25 43, *www.luebben.com*), where you can book **private rooms** (②–③). There are also several small **pensions**, the most convenient being *Am Markt*, Hauptstr. 5 (☎0 35 46/32 72; ③). **Hotels** include *Spreeblick*, Gübbener Str. 53 (☎0 35 46/23 20; ④), *Spreeufer*, Hinter der Mauer 4 (☎0 35 46/2 72 60; ⑤), and *Stephanshof*, Lehnigksberger Weg 1 (☎0

THE SORBS

A West Slav tribe whose language resembles both Czech and Slovak, the **Sorbs** have lived throughout their history in the province known as **Lusatia** (*Lausitz*), which still maintains a tenuous position on maps of Germany. In the fifteenth century it was divided into Upper Lusatia (*Oberlausitz*) and Lower Lusatia (*Niederlausitz*): the former is now in Saxony; the latter (of which the Spreewald forms the northern part) is in Brandenburg. As many as 100,000 Sorbs still live throughout the region. There were nationalist stirrings in the nineteenth century, leading in 1912 to the formation of the *Domowina* (a word equivalent to the German *Heimat*, or "homeland", a cultural and political organization which is still the main vehicle for Sorbist aspirations.

They were particularly persecuted under the Nazis when Göring proposed expelling them to turn the Spreewald into a gigantic game hunting park stocked with elk and bison. Things improved under the GDR, when the Sorbs were allowed a degree of cultural autonomy, with their language given equal status with German. However, they were mercilessly exploited for tourist purposes: their vivid costumes and popular **festivals** added a much-needed dash of colour to that grey puritanical land. The latter include the *Vogelhochzeit* (Marriage of the Birds) on January 25, Carnival, horseback Easter processions and, on April 30, the *Hexenbrennen*, a variant of the witches' *Walpurgisnacht*.

35 46/2 72 10; ⑤). The **youth hostel** is at the southern edge of town at Zum Wendenfürsten 8 (☎ & fax 0 35 46/30 46; DM19/€9.50 or DM24/€12). The **campsite** is across the Spree from the Schloss at Am Burglehn (☎0 35 46/70 53; closed Nov to mid-March). The hotels mentioned above have good **restaurants**, though the best place to eat is the *Historischer Weinkeller*, Ernst-von-Houwald-Damm 14.

Lübbenau (Lubnjow)

Perhaps a better starting point for exploring the Oberspreewald is the slightly larger town of **LÜBBENAU**, a fifteen-kilometre train journey southeast of Lübben. It gets incredibly crowded, though, giving the impression that all of the one million visitors who come here each year are passing through at once. Lübbenau's origins are also Slavonic, and it was defended by a wooden wall, later destroyed by the Germans who built a castle here. The original castle was in turn replaced by the Neoclassical **Schloss** visible today, which was built just after the Napoleonic wars by Count Lynar. The Lynar family owned much of the area until 1945, after which their castle became a school; they returned to claim their seat after the *Wende*, converting it into a hotel. At the **Spreewaldmuseum** at Topfmarkt 12 (April to mid-Sept Tues–Sun 10am–6pm; mid-Sept to Oct Tues–Sun 10am–5pm; DM6/€3), you'll find details of the history of the town and area.

Punt trips run from either of the **harbours**, the Grosser Hafen and Kleiner Hafen. It's best to be there as early as possible (around 8/8.30am) as there are bound to be very heavy crowds during the tourist season. The **tourist office** at Ehm-Welk-Str. 15 (March–Oct Mon–Fri 9am–6pm, Sat & Sun 10am–6pm; Nov–Feb Mon–Fri 9am–4pm; ☎0 35 42/36 68) can book **private rooms** (②–③). Among many **pensions** are *Höhn*, Dammstr. 38 (☎0 35 42/4 57 22; ③), *Zum Brauhaus*, Brauhausgasse 2 (☎0 35 42/21 26; ③), and *Lübbenauer Hof*, Ehm-Welk-Str. 20 (☎0 35 42/8 31 62; ⑤). There are also three upmarket **hotels**: *Turm*, Nach Stottof 1 (☎0 35 42/8 91 00; ⑥); *Spreewaldeck*, Dammstr. 31 (☎0 35 42/8 90 10; ⑥); and *Schloss Lübbenau*, Schlossbezirk 6 (☎0 35 42/87 30; ⑥–⑧). For **eating and drinking**, try any of the hotels or *Zum grünen Strand der Spree*, a reasonable though often packed riverside Gaststätte.

Lehde (Ledy)

One way to escape the crowds is to walk (rather than take a punt) to the incorporated village of **LEHDE**, which will take about thirty minutes. Until 1931 the village could only be reached by water transport or by crossing the ice of the frozen channels in winter. Lehde's **Freilandmuseum** (daily: April to mid-Sept 10am–6pm; mid-Sept to March 10am–5pm; DM6/€3) is packed with information about the area's history and customs. Farmhouses typical of the region have been brought here from other parts of the Spreewald and you can see how they were constructed: the foundations were built on large stones which in turn rested on timber poles driven deep into the marshy ground. Inside, examples of furniture (look out for the large beds designed to accommodate a whole family) and household objects offer an impression of how the Sorbish populace lived during the last century.

Good places to **eat** in Lehde are *Café Venedig* or *Zum Fröhlichen Hecht*. If you don't mind paying much more than you would for similar facilities in Lübbenau, there are a couple of **pensions** where you can stay: *Hirschwinkel* (☎0 35 42/899 9 50; ⑤) and *Quappenschänke* (☎0 35 42/899 9 60; ⑤).

Cottbus (Chośebuz)

At the southern end of the Spreewald stands **COTTBUS**, formerly the capital of one of the three *Bezirke* into which Brandenburg was divided in GDR days. It has a long industrial tradition, the twin pillars of the local economy being the textile industry, established by Dutch settlers in the Middle Ages and later developed by Huguenot refugees, and coalmining, which was the chief cause of the city's rapid growth in the nineteenth century. Because of this pedigree, Cottbus was seen by the Communists as something of a role model for the rest of the country, though its mixture of crumbling old tenements and Stalinist-style apartment buildings was not one that many others found attractive. Since the *Wende*, however, the city has done much to make itself more appealing, and has added a new dimension to its existence by becoming the seat of a technical university.

The heart of the town is the **Altmarkt**, which is lined with an impressive series of Baroque mansions, dating from immediately after one of the many disastrous fires which have ravaged the town. At no. 24 is the **Niederlausitzer Apothekenmuseum** (guided tours Tues–Fri 11am & 2pm, Sat & Sun 2pm & 3pm; DM4/€2), a pharmacy which has functioned continuously since 1573 and contains a number of historic interiors. A block to the south, at Mühlenstr. 12, is the **Wendisches Museum** (Tues–Fri 8.30am–5pm, Sat & Sun 2–6pm; DM4/€2), which has extensive displays on the history and culture of the Sorbs. Just north of Altmarkt is the Gothic **Klosterkirche**, whose tower is, most unusually, placed at the east end. A later and more visually impressive Gothic church, the **Oberkirche**, stands northeast of the Altmarkt. Its high altar, fashioned in marble, wood, alabaster and sandstone, is a hymn of late Renaissance extravagance.

Between here and the Spree is the **Münzturm**, where the town's first coins were minted. It's one of three towers surviving from the old fortifications: the others are the **Lindenpforte**, through which the path from the Stadtpromenade to the Altstadt leads, and the **Spremberger Turm**, at the far end of Spremberger Strasse, which goes south from the Altmarkt. On Schillerplatz, just outside the confines of the Altstadt, is the impressively large Jugendstil **Staatstheater Cottbus**.

Cottbus's star attraction, however, is **Schloss Branitz** (April–Oct Tues–Sun 10am–6pm; Nov–March Tues–Sun 10am–5pm; DM6/€3) at the southeastern edge of town. This was the custom-built seat of one of the great characters of nineteenth-century Germany, Prince Hermann von Pückler-Muskau, who was the worthy successor to Lenné as landscape gardener to the Prussian court, as well as a writer, world traveller and landowning aristocrat in his own right. The Schloss itself, designed by the Dresden architect Gottfried Semper in a tardy Baroque idiom, contains displays on the life of the prince, who himself designed the wonderful **Schlosspark**. This features a whimsical series of buildings, including a pergola, grandiose stables in the English neo-Gothic style and, at the western end, a curious series of mock-Egyptian pyramids, one of which serves as his own mausoleum.

Practicalities

Cottbus's **Hauptbahnhof** is situated well to the southwest of the centre in a particularly unsalubrious neighbourhood, so it's worth taking tram #1 to Stadtpromenade, then walking east along Marktstrasse to the Altmarkt. The **tourist office** is at the western edge of the city centre at Karl-Marx-Str. 68 (Mon–Fri 9am–6pm, Sat 9am–2pm; ☎03 55/2 42 54, fax 79 19 31, *www.cmt-cottbus.de*).

As an overnight stop, Cottbus is less enticing than the smaller towns of the Spreewald, but **private rooms** (②–③) can be booked via a special number at the tourist office (☎03 55/2 42 55). There are also plenty of **pensions**, among which *Aarian*, Karlstr. 22a (☎03 55/79 12 29; ③) is conveniently central, while *Café Pücklerstube*, Menzelstr. 4 (☎03 55/71 57 31; ④), is close to the Schlosspark. Among the many **hotels** are *Zum Schwan*, Bahnhofstr. 57 (☎03 55/7 82 00 or 795 3 35; ④), *Zur Sonne*, Taubenstr. 7–8 (☎03 55/3 81 88 01; ④), and *Ostrow*, Wassenstr. 4 (☎03 55/78 00

80; ⑤). There's also a **youth hostel**, occupying an old half-timbered house at Klosterplatz 2 (☎03 55/2 25 58, fax 2 37 98; DM21/€10.50 or DM26/€13). The choice of **restaurants** and **cafés** is also good: *Wendisches Café*, August-Bebel-Str. 82, serves Sorb dishes; *Lipa*, Wendenstr. 1, does regional specialities; *Paulaner Bräu*, Sandower Str. 57, is a Bavarian-style beer hall; while *Café Altmarkt*, Altmarkt 10, is best for *Kaffee und Kuchen*. **Nightlife** possibilities include: *Stadtwächter*, a cosy tavern in an old watchman's house attached to the Stadtmauer; *Molle*, Stadtpromenade 10, with nine different beers on tap; and *Clou Nachtbar*, Oberkirchplatz 10, a bar with a dancefloor. The Staatstheater Cottbus, Schillerplatz 1 (☎03 55/7 82 40), presents a varied programme of **theatre** and **music**.

travel details

Trains

Berlin-Zoologischer Garten/Ostbahnhof to: Brandenburg (frequent; 1hr); Cottbus (hourly; 1hr 45min); Dessau (15 daily; 2hr); Dresden (every two hours; 2hr 10min); Hamburg (hourly; 2hr 40min); Hannover (hourly; 2hr 50min); Leipzig (hourly; 2hr 20min); Lübbenau (17 daily; 1hr 10min); Munich (15 daily; 7hr 20min); Potsdam (frequent; 30min).

CHAPTER TEN

SAXONY-ANHALT

After the fall of the GDR, there was much talk about the reinstatement of the five "historic" Länder in the east. In the case of **Saxony-Anhalt** (Sachsen-Anhalt), the description was a complete misnomer: the province had first come into existence, courtesy of the Soviet military authorities, in 1947. Five years later it was abolished in line with the GDR's policy of concentrating power in the centre. Despite its dubious pedigree, there was genuine popular demand that this somewhat artificial Land should be revived, and it has duly taken its place on the new political map of the country.

The "**Saxony**" in the Land's title is a throwback to the old Prussian province of that name. It came into existence after the 1815 Congress of Vienna forced the Kingdom of Saxony to cede about half of its territories as a punishment for having supported Napoleon; these were then united with a number of secularized bishoprics Prussia had acquired after the Thirty Years War. **Anhalt** was a duchy founded by descendants of Albert the Bear, the first Margrave of Brandenburg. For centuries it was splintered into a number of petty principalities; these finally united in 1863, and the province served as a constituent state of Germany up to World War II.

Given its diverse make-up, it's hardly surprising that Saxony-Anhalt is the most varied of the new German Länder. The northernmost tract is the **Altmark**, the first piece of Slav territory taken over by the Germans in the great drive to the east they launched in the early medieval period. It's a varied landscape, with stretches of heath and sandy marshes in addition to farmland. The **River Elbe** defines its eastern border; the same river washes the **Börde**, the plain to the south. This has some of Germany's richest and most productive soils, and the otherwise monotonous agricultural countryside is punctuated by **Magdeburg**, the state capital and one of only two major cities in the Land.

Continuing southwards, the **Harz**, Germany's northernmost mountain chain, is approached via gentle foothills. Thickly covered with forests, the Harz proper is by far the best-known part of the Land. The home of the *Walpurgisnacht* legend, it's archetypally German in character, containing some outstanding scenery plus a clutch of well-preserved old towns. Beyond here, eastern Germany's largest area of heavy industry can be found in and around **Halle**, the Land's largest city, and **Dessau**, the historical capital of Anhalt. Further up the valley of the **Saale**, at the southern end of the province, the scenery becomes more rustic, the towns smaller.

Because the early history of the territories which make up Saxony-Anhalt is closely associated with missionary activity directed at heathen Slavs, the Land is unusually rich in medieval cathedrals and monasteries. The archbishops' Dom in Magdeburg ranks among the finest in all of Germany, yet its counterparts (all demoted to parish churches long ago) in **Halberstadt**, **Havelberg**, **Merseburg** and especially **Naumburg** are worthy rivals. For all the impact these had on the history of Germany, their influence pales beside that of **Wittenberg**, the little university town from where Martin Luther launched the Protestant Reformation. Two other modest-sized places, **Quedlinburg** and **Tangermünde**, had short spells as the capital of Germany; each retains a striking medieval appearance, and respectively has some of the best half-timbered and brick architecture to be found in the country.

Travel throughout the region presents few problems; the transport network itself is one of the main draws of the Harz, which retains the most comprehensive network of **narrow-gauge steam rail lines** to be found anywhere in Europe. The popularity of this with foreigners in GDR days is one reason the tourist facilities are so much better here than anywhere else in the Land.

THE ELBE-HAVEL REGION

The highlights of northern Saxony-Anhalt are thinly spread. In the Börde, **Magdeburg** is the only destination of note; as well as its Dom, it boasts a range of historical and technical monuments. The Altmark's chief town, **Stendal**, has reclaimed its role as a bustling market centre, though its monuments are rather overshadowed by those of nearby **Tangermünde**, which, but for a twist of fate, might have developed into a great metropolis. East of the Altmark lies a thin strip of land around the confluence of the Elbe and the Havel that was controversially allocated to Saxony-Anhalt rather than to Brandenburg; this includes the outstanding yet little-known town of **Havelberg**.

Magdeburg

Thanks to its pivotal position on the key communications network between Berlin and Hannover, **MAGDEBURG** received strong West German backing in its acrimonious tussle with Halle for the status of capital of Saxony-Anhalt just before reunification. This support proved crucial; had Magdeburg lost out, it would have been one more reverse in what had been a long run of bad luck. Its first calamity came in the Thirty Years War: during the Catholic siege and occupation of 1631, over two-thirds of the population perished, and the city was burnt to the ground. It made a spectacular recovery after the Peace of Westphalia, but the grandiose Baroque centre which then emerged suffered a similar fate to its medieval predecessor in the Anglo-American air raids of 1945.

Under Communism, Magdeburg had the reputation of being the greyest of grey cities. The surviving historic monuments in the centre – with the partial exception of the imperious Dom, the largest church in eastern Germany – were engulfed by new buildings in the brutalist style favoured by the Stalinist regime; the antiquated infrastructure of heavy industry was retained with no thought for the environment or for the future. However, the city, buoyed by its new role as a regional capital, has undergone an astonishingly swift transformation, developing a vibrant get-up-and-go atmosphere wholly at odds with its recent past. The worst Communist eyesores have been demolished; the more palatable "wedding cake" buildings of the same period have been given colourful makeovers; and the surviving Baroque mansions and grand Wilhelmine tenements gradually restored.

Arrival, information and accommodation

The **Hauptbahnhof** is situated just a few minutes' walk west of the city centre. There are also several suburban stations on the small S-Bahn network which can be useful if you're staying far out or intending to visit some of the outlying sights. The **tourist office** (Mon–Fri 10am–6pm, Sat 10am–1pm; ☎03 91/5 40 49 03, fax 5 40 49 10, www.magdeburg .de) is at Alter Markt 12.

A large number of **hotels** have opened since the *Wende*; the majority cater to business people and are priced accordingly. However, there are some bargains to be had, and in

MAGDEBURG

Theater der Landeshauptstadt

Lukasturm

Hauptbahnhof

Magdeburger Reiter

Rathaus

Johanniskirche

Kloster Unser Lieben Frauen

St. Sebastian

Landtag

Kulturhistorisches Museum

Dom

Stadthalle

Aussichtsturm

Adolf-Mittag-See

Kulturpark

River Elbe

ACCOMMODATION

3 InterCity
2 Maritim
1 Ratswaage
4 Youth Hostel

0 Metres 200

addition plenty of **private rooms** (②–③) can be booked via the tourist office. The **youth hostel** is just a short walk from the Hauptbahnhof at Leiterstr. 10 (☎03 91/5 32 10 10, fax 5 32 10 20, *Jugendherberge Magdeburg@gmx.de*; DM34/€17 or DM39/€19.50). There's a **campsite** (☎03 91/50 32 44) on the banks of the Barleber See at the extreme northern end of the city; take the S-Bahn to the station of the same name.

Hotels and Pensions

Alt Prester, Alt Prester 102, Prester (☎03 91/8 19 30, fax 8 19 31 18). Excellent mid-range hotel located in a southeastern suburb on the right bank of the Elbe. Its inexpensive restaurant with beer garden is a popular excursion destination with locals. ⑥.

Bildungshotel, Lorenzweg 57 (☎03 91/2 51 5065, fax 22 34 30). Functional and no-frills yet very modern hotel just north of the city centre. ③.

Eberlein, Letzlinger Str. 6 (☎03 91/5 61 73 97). Budget pension in the Neustadt, near the S-Bahn station of the same name, and within walking distance of the centre. ③.

Geheimer Rat von G., Goethestr. 38 (☎03 91/7 38 03, fax 7 38 05 99). Good-quality hotel about 1km west of the Altstadt. Its restaurant serves evening meals to residents only. ⑥.

InterCity, Bahnhofstr. 69 (☎03 91/5 96 20, fax 5 96 24 99). Large business-class hotel with restaurant directly opposite the Hauptbahnhof. ⑦.

Maritim, Otto-von-Guericke-Str. 87 (☎03 91/5 94 90, fax 5 94 99 90, *www. maritim.de*). Gleaming new hotel whose facilities include a restaurant, *Sinfonie*, and a swimming pool. ⑧.

Parkhotel Herrenkrug, Herrenkrugstr. 194 (☎03 91/85 08 00, fax 8 50 85 01). Magdeburg's most prestigious hotel occupies a mansion located in an Elbe-side park designed by the doyen of German landscape gardeners, Peter Joseph Lenné. Its two restaurants, *Eiskeller* (evenings only, closed Sun & Mon) and *Die Saison* (which has original Jugendstil decor), are among the very best in the city. ⑧.

Ratswaage, Ratswaageplatz 1–4 (☎03 91/5 92 60, fax 5 1 96 5). Luxury modern hotel with restaurant, part of the Upstalboom chain, located on the square immediately north of Alter Markt. ⑦.

Residenz Joop, Jean-Burger-Str. 16 (☎03 91/6 26 20, fax 6 26 21 00). One of the city's most attractive hotels, occupying a nineteenth-century villa, about ten minutes' walk southwest of the Dom. ⑦.

The City

The Dom overshadows everything else in Magdeburg, but there's a variety of other sights well worth seeking out. These are scattered all over the city, with an attractive group on and around the banks of the Elbe.

The Dom

Through all Magdeburg's tribulations, the **Dom** has somehow managed to survive with little damage to its fabric. The present building is the immediate successor to the monastic foundation which Emperor Otto the Great raised in 962 to be the seat of a prince-archbishop. It's one of the country's most impressive cathedrals, its lofty Gothic architecture complemented by a truly dazzling array of **sculpture** spanning an entire millennium. There's also the bonus of a picturesquely landscaped setting above the Elbe and, as the Dom stands in isolation, there are several wonderful vantage points. One is from the vast **Domplatz**, two sides of which are lined with dignified Baroque buildings which have been refurbished to house the Land parliament and ministries. Even more spectacular is the view from the Dom's own south-side **cloister**, one wing of which is a survivor of Otto's original monastery.

Construction of the present Dom began in the early thirteenth century with the building of the ambulatory and its chapels in a primitive Gothic style still showing Romanesque influence. Soon after, the masons who had built the Swabian monastery of Maulbronn took over the construction of the main part of the chancel, introducing more refined and progressive architectural forms. They in turn were succeeded by architects who built the transepts and nave in the High Gothic manner of the great French cathedrals, doubling the length of the bays to create an impression of space, and designing large traceried windows which flood the building with light. With the addition of the north transept **porch** (or Paradise) in the mid-fourteenth century, the body of the Dom was substantially complete. However, work on the facade, whose distinctive **towers**, with their spire-crowned octagonal turrets, are such a feature of the city's skyline, wasn't concluded until 1520. Later that century, the prince-archbishop was ousted in favour of a Protestant bishop, as Magdeburg became one of the stoutest promoters of the Reformation.

The ambulatory, whose capitals are inventively carved with depictions of fabulous beasts, luxuriant foliage and contorted human heads, contains a number of notable **tombs**. Oldest of these are the bronze monuments to two twelfth-century archbishops. There's also a touching stone memorial to a fourteenth-century successor to these, Otto of Hesse, the great-grandson of St Elisabeth, and a highly elaborate Flamboyant Gothic cenotaph belatedly honouring Empress Edith, wife of Otto the Great.

The last-named contrasts with the plain, box-like tomb of the emperor himself, which sits in solemn grandeur in the middle of the choir. Also surviving from his original cathedral are the **Easter candlestick** in front of the high altar and the beautiful coloured **marble columns** from Ravenna, which were reused to support the statues of saints placed high up between the piers of the tribune gallery. These figures, together with the unique little scenes in the niches below, belong to the period in the mid-thirteenth century when the Magdeburg workshop, along with its counterparts in Bamberg and Naumburg, was producing some of the greatest sculpture of the Middle Ages. The most arresting figure made here is the **statue of St Maurice**, placed on a pedestal on the south side of the choir; although now truncated, the masterly originality of what was probably the first representation of a black African in Western art is still very apparent. Only marginally less fine are the companion figure of St Catherine, the Dom's other patron, directly opposite, and the Annunciation group on the pillar behind. The fourteenth-century oak **choir stalls** and the fifteenth-century **rood screen** illustrate the way the Gothic style evolved over the following two hundred years.

A more substantial production of the earlier Magdeburg sculptors is the inner **portal** of the Paradise, which features superbly dramatic portrayals of the Wise and Foolish Virgins, and the enlightened Church and blindfolded Synagogue, along with a tympanum of the Death of the Virgin. Just indoors, in the northern transept, is a masterpiece of twentieth-century sculpture, the haunting *Monument to the Victims of World War I* by **Ernst Barlach**. It forms a surprisingly effective counterfoil to the idealized beauty of the late thirteenth-century *Madonna and Child*, formerly believed to have miracle-working powers, in the other transept.

The most intriguing feature of the nave is the freestanding **sixteen-sided chapel**, whose original function is an enigma. It contains thirteenth-century statues of a seated royal couple, leading to speculation that it's another memorial to Otto the Great and Edith, though it's more likely to be an allegorical representation of Christ as ruler of the world, with the Church as his bride. Behind it is the most significant adornment of the Protestant era, the elaborate alabaster Renaissance **pulpit** by the Thuringian sculptor Christoph Kapup. At the far end of the nave is the oldest furnishing, a porphyry **font** which belonged to Otto's cathedral, but which is thought to have originated in ancient Egypt or Assyria. Finally, under the western porch is the **Ernstkapelle**, a memorial chapel to Archbishop Ernst of Saxony, whose decision to honour himself in such a way has meant that the Dom's main entrance has been blocked up for the past five centuries, an act of megalomania partially mitigated by the sheer magnificence of the tomb, cast by the great Nürnberg bronze-founder, Peter Vischer the Elder. The chapel contains two other notable examples of late Gothic art: a seven-branched candelabrum and an alabaster statue, this time intact, of St Maurice.

The Kulturhistorisches Museum

A couple of minutes' walk west of the Dom, at Otto-von-Guericke-Str. 68–73, is the **Kulturhistorisches Museum** (Tues–Sun 10am–6pm; DM4/€2). This suffered heavy losses in World War II – partly, it now seems, as a result of Soviet looting – and never recovered during the GDR era. Of late, virtually the entire collection – which ranges from an important archeology section to local history, arts and crafts and paintings by Cranach and Friedrich, among others – has been packed away while restoration work on the building is carried out. Indeed, the only one of the permanent exhibits left on view in 2000 was its star possession, the original of the **Magdeburg Rider** (*Magdeburger Reiter*), a secular product of the mid-thirteenth-century Dom workshop, which disputes with its Bamberg counterpart the right to be regarded as the first equestrian statue since classical antiquity. This time, it's quite likely that the mounted figure is an idealized portrait of Otto the Great, accompanied by two maidens. A major, much-touted exhibition on this emperor will be held in the museum from August 20 until December 2, 2001, and it is hoped that at least some of the collection will be back on display by then.

St Sebastian and the Kloster Unser Lieben Frauen

Immediately north of the museum is the former monastic church of **St Sebastian**, itself a cathedral nowadays, being the seat of the local Catholic bishop. Outwardly unprepossessing, it has a light late Gothic interior, with slender, twisting columns.

Magdeburg's oldest surviving building, the **Kloster Unser Lieben Frauen** (Tues–Sun 10am–6pm; DM4/€2), lies just beyond the northern end of Domplatz. Badly damaged during the war, this severe-looking former Premonstratensian monastery has been patiently restored to serve as a museum and cultural centre. The **Klosterkirche**, now the city's main concert hall, has a highly unusual interior, the original Romanesque forms having been clad with Gothic overlay and vaulting at around the same time as work began on the Dom. However, the most impressive part of the monastery is the **cloister**, and in particular its picturesque well chapel, nicknamed the *Tonsur*. Housed in the conventual buildings is a nationally owned collection of **small sculptures**, divided into a medieval section of mostly anonymous devotional works and a more extensive gallery of modern pieces, with examples of Rodin, Barlach and Lehmbruck, plus examples of the Socialist Realism fostered by the GDR state.

The Alter Markt

Ten minutes' walk to the north, the **Alter Markt** has regained since the fall of Communism its former role as the hub of day-to-day trading activity, with markets every day except Sunday. Sadly, the square itself is a shadow of its former self, with only the Baroque **Rathaus** restored to its prewar state. Fragments from burnt-out buildings have been stuck up on the side wall of the tourist office as a reminder of past splendours, while a bronze replica of the Magdeburg Rider has been set up under the Baroque canopy which once housed the original. There is also a memorial to Otto von Guericke (see below), while the Gothic **Johanniskirche** rears up behind. Burnt out in 1945, the shell of this hall church was turned into a war memorial, but the post-unification fever for overturning decisions made in the Communist epoch led to it being rebuilt.

Along the River Elbe

From 1680, when it was incorporated into Brandenburg-Prussia, until just before World War I, Magdeburg was one of the most strongly fortified cities in Germany. Fragments of the Prussian-built **Festungsanlagen** can be seen all along the banks of the Elbe; the most impressive bits are those incorporating parts of the medieval city walls, which include the two towers immediately to the rear of the Dom and the section north of the Johanniskirche. The latter terminates at the **Lukasturm** (Tues–Sun 10am–5pm; DM2/€1), a brick-built fifteenth-century tower now housing a special display on the inventions of **Otto von Guericke**, inventor of the "Magdeburg hemispheres" that first demonstrated the power of the vacuum in the seventeenth century.

For a better perspective on these, it's well worth crossing over to the **Kulturpark Rotehorn**, a large park laid out in the 1920s between two branches of the Elbe, utilizing a smaller central arm as a boating area. Overlooking the main course of the Elbe towards the southern end of the park, across from the striking **Pferdetor** (a row of columns topped by stylized sculptures of horses), is the Bauhaus-influenced **Aussichtsturm** (Tues–Sun 10am–6pm; DM2/€1), which you can ascend by lift for a fine panoramic view. By the river is the **SS Württemberg** (daily 10am–4pm; DM2/€1), a paddle steamer built at the beginning of the twentieth century, which has been preserved as a reminder of the sort of vessels used at the time Elbe shipping was at its peak; it also houses a decent restaurant. Immediately north is the city's most remarkable industrial monument, the **Hubbrücke**. This was built in the 1840s as a rail bridge on the line to Potsdam and was equipped with a turning central mechanism to allow ships to pass through. Some fifty years later, it was converted into a lift bridge, before being transformed to its present appearance in the 1930s.

Eating, drinking and nightlife

Even if Magdeburg still lags well behind comparable western German cities in the gastronomic field, it's relatively well off by ex-GDR standards. Many of the best restaurants are in the hotels (see p.898).

Restaurants, cafés and bars

Bötelstube, Alter Markt 11. Basic but serviceable Gaststätte which offers the cheapest full meals available in the city centre.

Café am Dom, Breiter Weg 214. Traditional café which is a popular rendezvous point.

Damm-Mühle, Alt Prester 1, Prester. Cosy restaurant on three floors of a converted mill in the southeast of the city. Closed Mon.

Le Cochon, Hegelstr. 39. French-style bistro, one of several new eateries in the government quarter.

Mausefalle, Breiter Weg 224. Student pub serving salads, pasta and steaks grilled on lava stones.

Orangerie am Theater, Erzbergerstr. 2. High-quality restaurant attached to a delicatessen. Closed Sat lunchtime & Sun.

Otto von Guericke, Otto-von-Guericke-Str. 104. Pleasant city-centre Gaststätte with beer garden.

Ratskeller, Alter Markt 13. Historic restaurant under the Rathaus, with similar standards and prices to its western counterparts.

Savarin, Breiter Weg 226. High-quality restaurant in the southern part of the centre. Closed Sun & Mon, though the attached pub, *Schalander*, remains open.

SS Württemberg, Heinrich-Heine-Platz. Restaurant located in Magdeburg's museum ship. Evenings only, except at weekends; closed Tues.

Tucher-Stube, Breiter Weg 19. New venture offering Franconian cuisine and beer from the eponymous Nürnberg brewery.

Zum Paulaner, Einsteinstr. 13b. Eastern outpost of the eponymous Munich brewery, serving typically hearty food.

Entertainment

Elbe **cruises** are run by Weisse Flotte (☎03 91/5 43 39 26) from the Petriförder landing stage near the Lukasturm. The main **theatre**, with a varied programme of drama, opera, operetta and ballet, is the Theater der Landeshauptstadt, Universitätsplatz 13 (☎03 91/5 40 64 64); other venues include the cabaret Kugelblitze, Breiter Weg 200 (☎03 91/5 40 64 64), the Städtisches Puppentheater, Warschauer Str. 25 (☎03 91/4 04 24 29), and the Freie Kammerspiele, Otto-von-Guericke-Str. 64 (☎03 91/5 40 63 63).

Concerts by the Magdeburgische Philharmonie are held at the aforementioned Theater der Landeshauptstadt; while the Kloster Unser Lieben Frauen (☎03 91/5 65 02 32) is used by smaller ensembles, and for vocal and choral music. The latter regularly features works by the most prolific composer of all time, the Magdeburg-born **Georg Philipp Telemann**, who in his lifetime was considered at least the equal of his great contemporaries, Bach and Handel. Even today, his reputation within Germany is only slightly lower than theirs, though he is an under-appreciated figure elsewhere. This is despite the fact that his finest compositions have great spiritual depth, while he was also one of the most consistently adept humourists in musical history.

Stendal

STENDAL, which lies 60km north of Magdeburg, is an important rail junction on the main route to the Baltic with the second-string line between Berlin and Hannover. It has maintained its historic role as the main town of the Altmark, and, despite its modest size, is positively cosmopolitan in comparison with the rest of this rural backwater.

The Town

The Altstadt comprises a surprisingly large proportion of the present-day town and retains two medieval gateways. The **Tangermünder Tor**, on Bahnhofstrasse in the southern Altstadt, has a stone lower storey dating back to Stendal's thirteenth-century origins; the upper part, with its characteristically fancy brickwork, is from a hundred years later. Just across the street, occupying the former Katharinenkloster, is the **Altmärkisches Museum** (Tues & Sat 1–5pm, Wed, Thurs & Fri 10am–noon & 2–5pm, Sun 11am–6pm; DM5/€2.50), which documents the history of Stendal and the Altmark region, and includes a collection of medieval religious art.

Set, in the manner of many an English cathedral, in splendid isolation in the spacious green to the west of here is the **Stiftskirche St Nikolaus**, popularly if inaccurately known as the **Dom**. It's the largest of the town's medieval churches – which display a remarkable degree of similarity with one another, reducing the favoured north German format of the brick hall church to the barest essentials, with fortress-like towers and a minimum of surface decoration. A rare touch of extravagance, however, was allowed in the north transept, with its elaborate gable and bricks patterned into a false rose window and six-sided stars. Pride of the interior is one of the most impressive sets of **stained-glass windows** in Germany – 23 in all, each dating from the fifty-year period in the middle of the fifteenth century when the church itself was erected. The twelve windows in the choir use sombre colours in a deliberate attempt to create a mystical atmosphere in the holiest part of the building; those in the nave and transepts, in contrast, sparkle like jewels. Of similar vintage are the **choir stalls**, whose misericords are vivid illustrations of the humour of the day. Also of special note are the **reliefs** of the life of Christ on the back of the rood screen, masterly Romanesque carvings retained from the church which previously stood on the spot.

From the north side of the Dom, follow Am Dom to the east, then turn right into Hallstrasse, which eventually leads to the central **Markt**. Guarding the picturesquely gabled Renaissance **Rathaus** is a weather-worn statue of Roland, almost as big as its celebrated counterpart in Bremen. However, it's only a replica of the sixteenth-century original, which was destroyed by a hurricane in 1972. Rising up behind the Rathaus is the main parish church, the **Marienkirche**, whose similarities with the Dom even extend to having Romanesque carvings adorning the Gothic rood screen. However, the main treasure is the painstakingly reconstructed sixteenth-century **astronomical**

clock. It's set underneath the organ gallery, whose frieze of paintings of the life of Christ, along with part of the instrument itself, are from the same epoch.

Breite Strasse leads north from here to the oldest quarter of town, which is dominated by the **Jacobikirche**. This church has another magnificent array of stained glass in the chancel; this time some of the windows date back to the fourteenth century. At the end of Breite Strasse, Altes Dorf leads west to the symbol of the city, the **Uenglinger Tor** (May–Sept Sat & Sun 10am–noon & 3–5pm; DM2/€1). Incredible as it seems, this lovingly crafted masterpiece of fifteenth-century patterned brickwork was built for a purely defensive role; nowadays it provides something of an obstacle for traffic – as well as the best view of the town.

Just south of here, at Winckelmannstr. 36, the **Winckelmann Museum** (Tues–Sun 10am–noon & 1–5pm; DM5/€2.50) has been set up in the half-timbered house where Johann Joachim Winckelmann, connoisseur and art historian, the son of the local shoemaker, was born in 1717. The rooms are devoted to displays on the life and work of the man whose writings, based on exhaustive research during a twelve-year stay in Rome, set the study of archeology and art history on a rigorous scientific footing and provided the most potent stimulus for the great flowering of German classicism in Weimar.

Practicalities

Stendal's **Hauptbahnhof** is situated just beyond the southern edge of the Altstadt. The **tourist office** (May–Sept Mon–Fri 8.30am–noon & 12.30–5pm, Sat 9.30am–3pm; rest of year Mon–Fri only; ☎0 39 31/65 11 90, fax 65 11 95, *www.stendal.de*) is in the Rathaus, Markt 1. There's now a reasonable provision of **private rooms** (②–③). **Hotels** with a central location are *Am Uenglinger Tor*, Moltkestr. 17 (☎0 39 31/68 48 01; ④), *Postamt 3*, Hallstr. 64 (☎0 39 31/21 35 11; ⑤), *Altstadt*, Breite Str. 60 (☎0 39 31/6 98 90; ⑥), and *Am Bahnhof*, Bahnhofstr. 30 (☎0 39 31/71 55 48; ⑥). Both of the last two hotels have **restaurants**; other good places to eat are the *Ratskeller*, in the vaulted former merchants' hall under the Rathaus, and *Altstadt-Bierstube*, Mittelstr. 6.

Tangermünde and around

Towns languishing in centuries-long decay are a common enough feature of the Mediterranean lands, but are a rarity in Germany. **TANGERMÜNDE**, which lies at the confluence of the rivers Tanger and Havel 10km southeast of Stendal, is an exception – and a truly spectacular exception at that. When Charles IV, King of Bohemia and the most astute and successful Holy Roman Emperor of the later medieval period, acquired the Margraviate of Brandenburg in 1373, he chose this prosperous market town, a midway point on the trade routes between the Baltic and central Europe, as the second-string royal residence to Prague. Tangermünde's planned development into a national capital received a setback with the emperor's death five years later, though it continued to prosper for another hundred years, whereupon its star rapidly waned. At the beginning of the twentieth century, it became the Altmark's only industrial centre other than Stendal. The GDR regime's ideology kept it in a time warp, its skyline presenting an endearing juxtaposition of magnificent but crumbling medieval brick buildings and outdated factories.

The Town

Tangermünde's **Stadtmauer** is one of the most complete and impressive municipal defences to have survived in Germany. The north side, the first you see if you arrive in town by public transport, has been laid out as a park and is relatively unforbidding, save for the bleak cylindrical **Schrotturm** which guards the northwestern corner. Altogether more arresting is the **Neustädter Tor** on the west side. Its elaborately patterned tower is a stylistic twin of the Uenglinger Tor in Stendal and was the work of the same builders; in addition, there's a sturdy barbican, adorned with coats of arms.

The defences were particularly strong along the harbour side, in case of attack from the river; to see them to best advantage, it's well worth crossing over to the rustic pathway laid out on the opposite bank. Towards the far end of this section is another fine gateway, the **Elbtor**; the part-brick, part-timber extension suspended above its archway on the side facing the town was the home of the watchman. Subsequent expansion of the town has partially obscured the eastern side of the walls, though the oldest gateway, the **Hünendorfer Tor**, survives as a marker at the opposite end of Lange Strasse from the Neustädter Tor.

Charles IV's **Burg** was built overlooking the Elbe just outside the confines of the Stadtmauer. It was successively occupied by the Danes and the imperial forces during the Thirty Years War, and was all but destroyed in 1640 during an ultimately successful siege by the Swedes. At the beginning of the present century, the ruins were made into a shady public park, to which there's free access at all times. In addition to the main gateway and two very picturesque towers, the **Kanzlei**, which formerly served as a festive hall still survives.

Set in its own close just to the east of the Hünendorfer Tor is the fourteenth-century **Stephanskirche**, whose mighty westwork looks more like a fortress than any of the far more decorative towers of the fortification system. Most of the rest of the exterior is equally austere, though there are occasional deft touches, such as the patterned double doorway. The hall interior, with its graceful pillars, is altogether lighter in feel. After its conversion to Protestant worship, it gained a number of intriguing adornments, including a Baroque altar which has an unusual depiction of Christ in the guise of the Lion of Judea. The early seventeenth-century **organ** is by one of the greatest-ever masters of the craft, the Hamburg builder Hans Scherer, and is especially valuable for being his only instrument to have survived relatively intact. Recitals are held at 4.30pm on Saturdays from mid-May to late October.

Tangermünde's other setpiece is the **Rathaus**, which was built on the central Markt in the 1430s, the period when the town was at its commercial peak. Its fantastical eastern facade, bristling with pinnacles and gables, and pierced by ornate open and false rose windows, is one of the great pieces of secular Gothic architecture. The vaulted basement is given over to the **Heimatmuseum** (Tues–Sun 10am–5pm; DM2/€1), a small local history collection; you can also see the two upstairs halls, the **Festsaal** and the **Standesamt**, upon request.

Close to the harbour, the streets are cobblestoned and still medieval in aspect. In the centre, on the other hand, are large numbers of **half-timbered houses** from the seventeenth and eighteenth centuries, some with elaborate doorways. The reason for this new building activity was that much of Tangermünde was destroyed by fire in 1617; a woman by the name of Grete Minde was made the scapegoat and burned as a witch. Over 250 years later, she became the eponymous heroine of a novel by Theodor Fontane, who used the incident to write one of his many powerful indictments of the moral injustices suffered by women.

Practicalities

Tangermünde is linked to Stendal by a branch rail line and by buses, which alternate at approximately two-hour intervals throughout the day; both arrive and depart from the **Bahnhof**, which is a couple of blocks north of the Altstadt. The **tourist office** (April–Oct Mon–Fri 10am–6pm, Sat & Sun 11am–4pm; Nov–March Mon–Fri 10am–5pm, Sat 1–4pm; ☎03 93 22/37 10, fax 4 37 70, *www.tangermuende.de*) is at

Marktstr. 13. Here you can book **private rooms** (①–②) of which the town has a reasonable number.

There are also several **pensions**, including *Am Schrotturm*, Lindenstr. 5 (☎03 93 22/9 76 50; ③), *Zur Guten Stube*, Luisenstr. 38 (☎03 93 22/7 35 40; ③), and *Zur Altstadt*, Lange Str. 40 (☎03 93 22/25 18 or 9 85 00; ③). Likewise on Lange Strasse are three **hotels**: *Alte Brauerei* at no. 34 (☎03 93 22/4 41 45, *www.hotel-alte-brauerei-de*; ④); *Stars Inn* at no. 47 (☎03 93 22/98 70; ④); and *Schwarzer Adler* at no. 52 (☎03 93 22/23 91; ⑥).

The *Schwarzer Adler* has the best **restaurant** in town; other possibilities are *Galerie Ludwig*, Stendaler Str. 54, *Zur Post*, Lange Str. 4, and *Störtebeker*, a ship moored outside the Burg. Reederei Kaiser (☎03 93 22 421 8162) runs a variety of **cruises**, mostly short round trips, but also weekly sailings to both Magdeburg and Havelberg.

Jerichow

JERICHOW, 8km southeast of Tangermünde, is strictly speaking outside the Altmark, the Elbe having formed the natural eastern border of the old province. Its biblical-sounding name seems a fitting reflection of its role as an important missionary centre in the early Middle Ages, though in fact this is pure coincidence, being a slight corruption of the title of the Slav settlement which preceded it. At the northern end of the village is the huge **Klosterkirche** (guided tours April–June, Sept & Oct Mon–Fri at 2pm, Sat & Sun at 11am & 2pm; July & Aug daily at 11am & 2pm; DM2/€1). It's the oldest significant building in the area, its typically plain brick architecture Romanesque in style with a few later Gothic touches like the twin towers. Highlight of the interior is the **crypt** underneath the choir, whose columns bear immaculately carved stone capitals. The separately run **Klostermuseum** (April–Oct daily 10am–5pm; Nov–March Tues–Fri 10am–noon & 1–4pm; DM2/€1), in the attractive monastic buildings grouped round the cloister, displays important archeological finds from the cloister garden along with documentation on the history of the monastery.

Havelberg

HAVELBERG, which lies just shy of the confluence of the Havel with the Elbe some 45km north of Jerichow, is another medieval gem as yet barely touched by overzealous restoration, or by the invasion of foreign visitors. Founded in 968 by Otto the Great as a missionary bishopric, in what was then heathen Slav territory, it proved impossible to defend and was abandoned for nearly a century and a half before being resettled by Premonstratensian monks. The town subsequently became a fishing port, even managing to establish a monopoly on fish sales on the Hamburg–Berlin trading route. When it fell to Brandenburg-Prussia after the Thirty Years War, it was developed into a major shipbuilding centre.

Dominating the town from its hillside location above the north bank of the Havel, the **Dom** is no more than a Protestant parish church nowadays. The lower part of its gaunt, fortress-like **westwork** probably belongs to the original Ottonian cathedral, which the Premonstratensians restored and expanded in the twelfth century. This building in turn was ravaged by fire a hundred years later; the subsequent reconstruction features Gothic vaulting and false arcades superimposed on the Romanesque framework. Also from this period are the monumental triumphal cross, the choir stalls and the three large column-shaped candelabra. However, the most imposing work of art is the fourteenth-century **choir screen**, which ranks among the masterpieces of monumental German sculpture. In the manner of a poor man's Bible, it bears statues of saints and twenty large reliefs illustrating the Passion of Christ, carved by a workshop familiar with both the "Soft Style" of Prague and the more realistic Netherlandish masters. The refined spirituality of the most accomplished of the sculptors contrasts sharply with the boisterous and patently anti-Semitic approach of one of his colleagues, who favoured an expressionistic idiom, with exaggerated mannerisms and facial contortions. Contemporary with the screen are two **stained-glass windows** at the end of the northern aisle, unusual grisailles with depictions of vine, acorn and ivy leaves.

Adjoining the south side of the Dom is a complex of part-Romanesque, part-Gothic brick monastic buildings, which bear more than a passing resemblance to their counterparts in Jerichow. The upper storeys now contain the **Prignitz-Museum** (Wed–Sun 10am–noon & 1–5/6pm; DM2/€1), which details the history of Havelberg and the vicinity from prehistoric times to the nineteenth century. Clustered around the Dom's close are a number of formerly dependent buildings such as the school, the deanery and the houses of the canons; these are now put to an imaginative variety of uses, ranging from the local police headquarters to a small clothing factory.

At the foot of the Dom's hill is the **Annenkapelle**, a small octagonal Gothic brick chapel with a strikingly pointed roof. From here, the Steintorbrücke leads to the compact little **Altstadt**, which occupies an island in the Havel; an alternative approach is by the Dombrücke, directly below the Dom. Crooked old houses once occupied by fisherfolk and farmers line the banks of the river; even today, smallholdings and market gardening are clearly in evidence. The main attraction of the Altstadt is its constantly changing range of watery panoramic views. However, it's well worth walking all round the tightly packed little streets: look out for the late fourteenth-century **Beguinenhaus**, whose portal has a lintel of *The Crucifixion* carved in a similar style to the Dom's choir screen. Towering above the rest of the island is the Gothic **Stadtkirche St Laurentius**, whose vivid ceiling frescoes were recently discovered when the wooden vaulting which had concealed them for over a century was removed.

Practicalities

Havelberg is no longer on a rail line, but there's a reasonable **bus** link with Stendal via Tangermünde; the best place to alight or embark is at the stop by the Annenkapelle. The sole **hotel** is *Am Schmokenberg*, Schönberger Weg 6 (☎03 93 87/8 91 77; ④). Otherwise, there are a few small **pensions**, including *Elb-Havel*, Genthiner Str. 5 (☎03 93 87/8 93 79; ②), and plenty of **private rooms** (①–②). Bookings can be made at the **tourist office** (April–Sept Mon–Fri 9am–6pm, Sat 10am–3pm, Sun 1–3pm; Oct–March Mon–Fri 9am–5pm, Sat 10am–3pm; ☎03 93 87/8 82 24, fax 8 80 42, *www.havelberg.de*) at Salzmarkt 1. The town's best **restaurants** are the one in *Am Schmokenberg*, plus *Güldene Pfanne*, Lehmkule 2, and *Harmonie*, Hinter der Kirche 3.

On the first weekend in September, Havelberg takes on a wholly different appearance with the arrival of over a hundred thousand visitors – most of whom end up camping or sleeping in their cars – for the *Pferdemarkt*, one of the biggest **festivals** in the former GDR. As its name suggests, it was originally a horse market, but now spawns a flea market in which anything and everything is bought and sold, a handicrafts bazaar, a giant funfair, sports events, dancing and beer tents.

THE HARZ REGION

The **Harz** mountains were formerly divided right through the middle by the notorious barbed wire frontier separating the two German states. Uniquely, comparisons between the two (the border itself apart) were almost entirely in the East's favour – it inherited the best of the scenery, several gorgeous unspoiled old towns and an extensive network of **narrow-gauge steam rail lines**. Until the 1970s, it was almost impossible for Westerners to stay, though it was one of the main holiday areas for East Germans

themselves, with a vast provision of trade union holiday homes. Restrictions were subsequently relaxed, because the growing number of train buffs wanting to visit was seen as a useful source of hard currency. Since the fall of the Wall, the Harz has become one of the most desirable areas in the east in which to travel, not least because the tourist facilities are better and more extensive than almost anywhere else.

In the northern foothills of the Harz are the impressive old cathedral city of **Halberstadt** and the half-timbered towns of **Osterwieck** and **Quedlinburg**, both of which have comprehensive preservation orders. Similarly protected are **Blankenberg** and **Wernigerode** on the edge of the mountains, **Stolberg** in the very heart of the range and **Eisleben** in its eastern foothills. Wernigerode is also the starting point of the Harzquerbahn, the longest of the narrow-gauge rail lines; another of these, the Selketalbahn, leaves from **Gernrode**, a village with one of Germany's most distinctive churches. Scenically, the finest landscapes are to be found in the **Bode valley**, particularly around **Thale**, though the legendary **Brocken**, rendezvous of the witches on *Walpurgisnacht*, is an equally irresistible destination, accessible by the third narrow-gauge railway, the Brockenbahn.

Halberstadt

Set in the gentle foothills of the Harz **HALBERSTADT**, about 55km southwest of Magdeburg, is one of the oldest cities in eastern Germany, having been established as a bishopric by Charlemagne at the turn of the ninth century. It also used to be considered one of the most beautiful, but was devastated by an Anglo-American air raid in the closing days of World War II. The Communists restored some showpieces, but demolished the ruins of others which interfered with the creation of a new Stalinist-style commercial centre. Unification has heralded a face-lift: Halberstadt was one of five cities granted special government funds for restoration, and has used this for an extensive programme of cleaning its old buildings, and for erecting copies of key landmarks lost in the war.

Arrival, information and accommodation

Halberstadt's **Hauptbahnhof** is situated well to the east of the centre; best take tram #1 or #2 as the walk is boring. There are also a couple of suburban stations, including one for Spiegelsberge. The **bus station** is about midway between the Hauptbahnhof and the Markt, while the **tourist office** is at Hinter den Rathause 6 (Mon–Fri 9am–1pm & 2–6pm, Sat 10am–1pm; ☎0 39 41/55 18 15, fax 55 10 89, *www.halberstadt.de*).

There's now a reasonable choice of **hotels** and **pensions**, thanks to the opening of a number of new establishments. Otherwise, you should be able to find a **private room** (①–③) via the tourist office. The **campsite**, *Campingplatz am See*, is on the right bank of the Halberstädter See at the northeastern edge of the city at Warmholzberg 70 (☎0 39 41/60 93 08, fax 57 07 91).

Hotels and Pensions

Abtshof, Abtshof 27a (☎0 39 41/6 88 30, fax 68 83 68). This new guesthouse in a half-timbered Altstadt house offers really excellent value at the price asked. ④.

Am Grudenberg, Grudenberg 10 (☎0 39 41/6 91 20, fax 69 12 69). Another fairly recent venture, this hotel is again in a half-timbered building, and includes a sauna and fitness room among its facilities. ④–⑤.

Antares, Sternstr. 6 (☎0 39 41/60 02 50, fax 60 02 49). New, custom-built business-class hotel with restaurant (closed Sun evening) in the west of town. ⑤.

Halberstädter Hof, Trillgasse 10 (☎0 39 41/2 70 80, fax 2 61 89). High-class hotel and restaurant in a renovated half-timbered building. ⑥.

Heimliche Liebe, Robert-Koch-Str. 25 (☎ & fax 0 39 41/44 23 93). Small pension with restaurant, just to the southeast of the Altstadt. ④.

Heine, Kehrstr. 1 (☎0 39 41/3 14 00, fax 3 15 00). Brand-new hotel, with restaurant and Hausbrauerei, located close to the Hauptbahnhof. ⑤.

Jagdschloss, In den Spiegelsbergen (☎0 39 41/5 82 31 53). The hunting lodge in the Spiegelsberge has long housed a restaurant; a small hotel has recently been established there as well. ④.

Parkhotel Unter den Linden, Klamrothstr. 2 (☎0 39 41/60 00 77, fax 60 00 78, *www.parkhotel -halberstadt.de*). Halberstadt's top hotel, now part of the Romantik chain, occupies a villa built according to the principles of the British Arts and Crafts movement. Its restaurant is also the best in town. ⑤.

The City

Most of Halberstadt's prime attractions are grouped together on the spacious elliptical **Domplatz**. It suffered as much from bomb damage as the rest of the city, but monopolized the postwar restoration funds and ranks among the country's most impressive squares. Below it is the lower town whose half-timbered houses are gradually reappearing in pristine shape after restoration. Another attractive corner is the **Spiegelsberge** hill range at the extreme southern edge of the city.

The Dom

Halberstadt's **Dom** is the only one in Germany to conform to the pure Gothic forms established in the great French cathedrals. The only exception to this is the facade: its lower storeys were built in the early thirteenth century by the same team of masons engaged on the archbishop's Dom in Magdeburg, while the current look of the towers is the result of a neo-Gothic remodelling at the very end of the nineteenth century. There was a long lull before work on the main body of the building got under way, and the whole project took the better part of three hundred years to complete.

Placed proudly atop its rood screen is the Dom's greatest work of art, a wooden **triumphal cross** from the very end of the Romanesque period. Elsewhere, the pillars are adorned with unusually characterful **statues** of saints and biblical figures, the most eye-catching being the unashamedly sensual pair of Adam and Eve in the transept. The ensemble of **stained-glass windows** in the choir and the ambulatory is among the most complete in the country; the earliest and finest are the five large lancets in the apsidal Marienkapelle, which date from 1330. Also of special note is that in the south ambulatory illustrating the life of Charlemagne, the Dom's original founder.

One of the richest treasuries in Germany, the **Domschatz** (guided tours April–Oct Mon–Fri at 10am, 11.30am, 2pm & 3.30pm, Sat at 10am & 2pm, Sun at 11.30am & 2.30pm; Nov–March Mon–Sat at 10am & 2pm, Sun at 11.30am & 2.30pm; donation expected) is housed in the cloister and its dependencies; entrance is via the doorway on the southeast side. The most valuable items are the textiles, and in particular three twelfth-century **tapestries** which are among the oldest in existence. One tells the story of the patriarch Abraham, another is dedicated to the Apostles, while the third shows Charlemagne with philosophers of classical antiquity. From the same period are two outstanding pieces of **woodcarving** – *The Seated Madonna*, which was probably made in the same workshop as the great triumphal cross, and a cupboard painted with a depiction of the Visitation. The **treasury** items include the fourth-century *Consular Diptych* from Rome and the Byzantine *Weihbrotschale*, a magnificent gilded silver dish for consecrated bread which was brought here by a crusader. Also included on the tour is a visit to the **Kapitelsaal**, the only surviving part of the Romanesque Dom.

The Kurien

The two long sides of Domplatz are lined with the **Kurien**, the houses of the members of the Dom chapter. Oldest of these is the **Dompropstei**, the elegant Renaissance mansion in the middle of the south side, which marries two very disparate styles in its Italianate arcaded lower storey and archetypally German half-timbered upperwork.

A similar architectural mix is found in the **Gleimhaus** (Mon–Fri 9am–4/5pm, Sat & Sun 10am–4pm; DM5/€2.50, including admission to the Städtisches Museum, the Heineanum and the Museum Bürgerlicher Wohnkultur um 1900) at the far northeast corner of the square. It was the home of the eighteenth-century poet **Johann Wilhelm Ludwig Gleim**, who served as secretary to the Dom for 56 years, and it has been preserved as one of the earliest – and best – literary museums in the country. A prolific letter-writer, he maintained contact with almost all the great and good in a German society of his day. To celebrate his range of contacts, he hit upon the idea of creating a **Freundschaftstempel** (Temple of Friendship), commissioning 150 portraits, which are hung throughout the first-floor rooms.

Next door, the stately Baroque **Domdechanei** is now a medical school. The slightly more modest palace next door houses the **Städtisches Museum** (Tues–Fri 9am–5pm, Sat & Sun 10am–5pm; same ticket as the Gleimhaus), which documents the history of the town, including material on the buildings lost in the bombings. However, the exhibits in the main building are overshadowed by those in the garden extension, the **Heineanum** (same hours and ticket). Greeting you on entry are two spectacular dinosaur skeletons, thought to be up to 220 million years old, found during excavations in the town. The rest of the collection is devoted to ornithology, with stuffed birds of the Harz region on the ground floor and an international display upstairs.

The Liebfrauenkirche

Forming a counterbalance to the Dom at the western end of Domplatz is the Romanesque **Liebfrauenkirche**, formerly an Augustinian collegiate church. The main feature of the exterior is the roofline, with the two octagonal towers with pointed spires at the east end forming a contrast with the pair of "bishops' mitres" on the facade. Inside are two more products of the school of sculptors active here in the early thirteenth century. Suspended on high is another **triumphal cross**, with a youthful-looking Christ in a strikingly classical pose. Even more impressive is the **choir screen**, a rare work in stucco which still preserves its original polychromy; it features realistic portraits of Christ, the Virgin and the Apostles, plus decorative friezes carved with a gossamer sense of delicacy. Look out also for the **Barbarakapelle**, whose walls are covered with a cycle of late fourteenth-century frescoes.

Set in an idiosyncratic position in front of the church, the Gothic **cloister** (Mon–Fri 9am–4pm; free) has been made into a small open-air museum, with decorative fragments from some of the many half-timbered houses destroyed in 1945. Adjoining it to the south is the **Petershof**, the massive former bishops' palace, entered via a handsome Renaissance portal.

The rest of the centre

The **lower town** (Unterstadt) on the north side of Domplatz has a confusingly mazy layout, with some of the streets following quasi-circular routes. This quarter, which has most of the surviving **half-timbered houses**, fell into shocking disrepair in the 1970s, eventually taking on the appearance of a ghost town as the inhabitants were evacuated to ugly new apartment buildings nearby. Soon after the revolution, private citizens began buying up the properties, and many have already been turned into dream homes. A few showpieces had previously been restored by the GDR state, prominent among them being the mansion at Voigtei 48. Its courtyard wing, now the **Museum Bürgerlicher Wohnkultur um 1900** (Museum of Middle-Class Living Conditions around 1900; Tues–Sun 10am–4pm; same ticket as the Gleimhaus), formerly the home of a wealthy burgher family, was bequeathed to the city as a time capsule of life at the turn of last century.

Another half-timbered building well worth seeking out is the **Johanniskirche**, which lies in a peaceful garden just off Westendorf, the busy street immediately to the south of Domplatz. This rustic-looking church, built for a Protestant congregation at the end of the Thirty Years War, has a disarmingly artless appearance from the outside, with its barn-like roof and stumpy detached belfry. Inside, however, it's surprisingly dapper, the coffered ceiling, galleries and pulpit all finely carved in late Renaissance style.

To the east of Domplatz lies the **Markt**. The ruined buildings on this square, including the Gothic **Rathaus**, were bulldozed after the war in favour of a windswept piazza which had no apparent function until open-air markets returned after the fall of Communism. In 1998, after a building period lasting just sixteenth months, the Markt became a fully fledged square once again, complete with a reproduction of the demolished Rathaus. The sole original building is the severe Gothic **Martinikirche**, which was the local rallying point during the *Wende* of 1989 – an appropriate choice, as it had been built by the citizens as a deliberate statement of civic pride in opposition to the prince-bishops' Dom across the road. Indeed, the two towers, linked by a lookout gallery, were a key part of the city's defences, with the huge fifteenth-century **statue of Roland** underneath as a good luck charm. The church's furnishings include an elaborate Renaissance **pulpit** and an early fourteenth-century bronze **font** resting on symbolic representations of the four rivers of Paradise and adorned with brightly coloured scenes from the life of Jesus.

The Spiegelsberge

At the southern edge of the city, reached by tram #1 or #2, is the range of hills known as the **Spiegelsberge**. Following a visit to the famous gardens of Wörlitz, the poet Gleim had the idea of creating something similar in Halberstadt. The result was the construction here of a number of follies which, while falling short of their great model, nevertheless make for a pleasing diversion. Centrepiece of the complex is the **Jagdschloss**, now a hotel and restaurant (see p.909). Ask to see inside the cellars, whose Renaissance doorway and great vat – the second largest in Germany – were brought here from the former country house of the defunct bishopric. Other attractions include a mausoleum, a grotto, a memorial column and the **Belvedere**, an observation tower (free access) built against a romanticized rocky backdrop, which commands a fine distant view of the city.

Eating and drinking

As with the hotels, the gastronomic situation has shown marked improvement over the past few years.

Alt Halberstadt, Voigtei 17–19. Café-restaurant with beer garden offering local speciality dishes. Closed Mon.

Alt Westendorfer Hanse Haus, Westendorf 16. Large complex of eateries including a bistro, a café, a beer bar and a cellar restaurant which offers "medieval" dishes.

Am Kühlinger Tor, Kühlingerstr. 24. Good traditional Gaststätte.

Galerie Café 1580, Lichtengraben 15. Recommendable place for *Kaffee und Kuchen*, with the bonus of exhibitions of contemporary art on the walls.

Kreuzgang, Domplatz 5. The eclectic menu here includes plenty of vegetarian dishes.

Museumscafé, Domplatz 36. Pleasant café with garden which offers inexpensive light meals.

Osterwieck

The entire town centre of **OSTERWIECK**, which lies between two arms of the River Ilm 25km northwest of Halberstadt, is under a protection order, and with good reason:

it has some four hundred historic **half-timbered houses**, many of them of outstanding quality. It's an archetypal example of a place stuck in a time warp: the number of inhabitants has remained virtually unchanged for hundreds of years, despite extensive industrialization in the nineteenth century, which saw the town become a leading centre for the manufacture of gloves. The GDR's penchant for outdated technology has left it as a wonderful period piece, but one consequence of this was that many of the houses were allowed to fall into a terrible state of decay – a situation that is now gradually being remedied.

On the small central Markt, the **Altes Rathaus** (Tues–Thurs & Sun 10am–noon & 1–4pm; DM2/€1) has been converted into a museum of the town's history; it also serves as the nearest thing to a local tourist office and keeps the keys to the **Stephanikirche** (otherwise Sat & Sun 2–4pm only) in the close behind. The church's fortress-like facade, crafted from rough stonework, dates from the first half of the twelfth century, with the steeples added four hundred years later. The main body of the church is built in a florid late Gothic style, its vault bearing elaborate keystones showing the crests of prosperous local families. Among the diverse furnishings are a Romanesque font, a Renaissance pulpit and many fine epitaphs.

Two of the finest half-timbered houses are on the L-shaped Schultenstrasse, which wends its way round the back of the Markt. The **Alte Voigtei** at no. 3 started a local trend for having a frieze of coloured rosettes for decoration, while the **Eulenspiegelhaus** at no. 8 is the best example of those favouring a richer decoration, with lots of small, symbolic carvings. Kapellenstrasse, the main street into town from the east, has another fine group; no. 4 here is the oldest in Osterwieck, dating back to 1480. Following Hagen north from here, you come to one of the largest of the buildings, the **Hospital St Bartholomäus**. The other main setpiece is the **Bunter Hof**, a huge manor on Rössingstrasse at the southeastern end of the old town.

Practicalities

Osterwieck is at the end of a branch rail line; it's usually necessary to change at Heudeber if coming from Halberstadt. The **Bahnhof** is to the east of the centre, though trains continue on to the terminus, **Osterwieck-West**. Between the former and the Markt is the **bus station**, a halt on the Halberstadt–Goslar route, and with other services into the Harz.

Accommodation options are limited to the odd **private house** (①–②) and two quality **hotels**: *Brauner Hirsch*, Stephanikirchgasse 1–2 (☎03 94 21/6 96 10; ⑤), and *Waldhaus*, 1km north of the centre at Am Fallstein 1 (☎03 94 21/7 22 32; ⑤). Both of these have good **restaurants**; otherwise the best place to eat is the *Ratsweinstube* on the Markt.

Quedlinburg

QUEDLINBURG, 14km southeast of Halberstadt, is one of the most remarkable places in all of Germany – over 1600 of its buildings are listed as being of historic interest, and the entire town has been declared a World Heritage Site by UNESCO. Although the big setpieces are all hewn out of a whitish sandstone which has taken on a grey patina, the town's character is defined by the **half-timbered houses** which line almost all its streets. The full diversity of this quintessentially German architectural form is on view, with examples ranging from the fourteenth to the nineteenth century. Thankfully, the GDR authorities saw Quedlinburg as a great national asset. The factories the state's dogma deemed essential were confined to the outskirts and have caused only a modest degree of pollution. This has helped to ensure that Quedlinburg is the ideal combination of a genuine, living community in a stunning visual setting, which has avoided the fate – suffered by so many of its western German counterparts – of becoming over-reliant on tourism.

Quedlinburg owes its distinctive silhouette to the buildings on the **Burgberg**, the larger of the two hills at the southern end of town. In the early part of the tenth century this became the headquarters of the German nation when the expansionist drive to the east was begun by the Saxon king, **Henry the Fowler** (Heinrich der Vogler). He built a palace here, which on several occasions hosted meetings of the Imperial Diet. On his death in 936, his widow **Mathilde** established a collegiate foundation for aristocratic women, which survived until the Napoleonic suppression. Its abbesses effectively controlled the town which grew up in the valley below; when it attempted to assert municipal independence by joining the Hanseatic League in the fifteenth century, the abbesses succeeded in re-establishing ecclesiastical dominance – hence the reason Quedlinburg never developed into a major city.

Arrival, information and accommodation

Quedlinburg's **Bahnhof** and **bus station** are side by side to the east of town. The Neustadt lies just over the Bode, while the Altstadt is a ten-minute walk away straight ahead along Bahnhofstrasse, then left into August-Wolf-Strasse. However, the most atmospheric approach to the town is to follow the Bode upstream towards the Burgberg; many picturesque panoramic views open up en route. The **tourist office** (March, April & Oct Mon–Fri 9am–6pm, Sat & Sun 10am–3pm; May–Sept Mon–Fri 9am–7pm, Sat & Sun 10am–4pm; Nov–Feb Mon–Fri 9am–5pm; ☎0 39 46/90 56 24, fax 90 56 29, *www.quedlinburg.de*) is at Markt 2.

For accommodation, there's a plentiful supply of **private rooms** (①–③) on the tourist office books, as well as a good stock of **hotels**, many in fine old buildings. The **youth hostel** has a central location at Nuendorf 28 (☎0 39 46/28 81, fax 9 16 53; DM24/€12 or DM29/€14.50).

Hotels and Pensions

Am Brühl, Billungstr. 11 (☎0 39 46/9 61 80, fax 9 61 82 46, *www.hotelambruehl.de*). Classy hotel in a historic building that was formerly a barn, then a spirits factory. Appropriately, a home-made liqueur, *Harzgeist*, can be ordered in its Weinstube (closed Sun), one of the best restaurants in town. ⑥.

Am Dippeplatz, Breite Str. 16 (☎0 39 46/70 50 22, fax 70 50 22). Moderately priced hotel in the heart of town. ④.

Schlossmühle, Kaiser-Otto-Str. 28 (☎0 39 46/78 70, fax 78 74 99, *www.schlossmuehle.de*). Quedlinburg's leading hotel occupies a grandiose old mill, and boasts two restaurants, a bar, library and fitness centre. ⑥.

Theophano, Markt 13–14 (☎0 39 46/9 63 00, fax 96 30 36, *www.hoteltheophano.de*). Offers an absolutely ideal location, nicely furnished rooms and a fine vaulted Weinkeller which serves some of the best food in Quedlinburg. ⑥.

Villa Klara, Am Schiffbleek 11a (☎0 39 46/70 52 95, fax 70 52 94). Bargain-priced pension, well located just below the Schlossberg. ④.

Zum Bär, Markt 8–9 (☎0 39 46/77 70, fax 70 02 68). This eighteenth-century inn was for long the top address in town, and was the only place Westerners were allowed to stay in GDR days. It then suffered a huge slump in its reputation because of its *Stasi* connections, but is now making a comeback. ⑥.

Zur Goldenen Sonne, Steinweg 10–11 (☎0 39 46/9 62 50, fax 96 25 30, *www.hotel-qlb.de*). Occupies a magnificent example of Baroque half-timbering, complete with oriel window and saddle roof. The restaurant serves reasonably priced specialities of the Harz. ⑤.

Zum Schloss, Mühlenstr. 22 (☎0 39 46/33 33 or 70 74 83, fax 70 74 84). Small hotel with restaurant in a seventeenth-century half-timbered building by the Stiftskirche. ⑤.

The Town

The original medieval layout of the town is preserved intact: the River Bode divides the Altstadt, the merchants' quarter on the right bank, from the Neustadt, where the small-holders lived, while at the southern end of the former are the two hills where monastic life was centred.

The Schloss

The present **Schloss** complex on the Burgberg is predominantly Renaissance, though the plain exterior walls below the frilly gables are evidence of the original defensive function. Access from the town is via the **Torbau**, a much-modified medieval gateway, beyond which are a number of half-timbered service buildings and a terrace commanding a sweeping view.

Apart from the Stiftskirche, the two main buildings on the courtyard are the **Residenzbau**, the palace of the abbesses, and the L-shaped **Wohntrakt**, which contained the apartments of the other canonesses, the kitchen, bakery, pharmacy and workshops. The former now contains the **Schlossmuseum** (daily 10am–5pm; DM5/€2.50), a rambling, old-fashioned display which ranges through Ice Age fossils, a hoard of Bronze Age treasure and a comprehensive array of medieval instruments of torture, to regional costumes and sections on the history of the town. However, the main attraction is being able to wander through the building itself, whose rooms are surprisingly modest – even in the elegantly furnished Baroque extension which replaced a redundant part of the fortifications.

The Stiftskirche St Servatius

The **Stiftskirche St Servatius** (Tues–Sat 10am–4/6pm, Sun noon–4/6pm; DM6/€3) is the eleventh- and twelfth-century successor to Mathilde's original church. Apart from the twin towers, which are nineteenth-century pastiches, and the Gothic apse, it's a very pure example of Romanesque architecture. The **capitals**, together with the friezes above, provide the only decoration; carved with supreme delicacy by Lombard craftsmen, they show animal, plant and geometric motifs. Another fine group can be seen in the **crypt**, the last resting-place of Henry and Mathilde. Their plain sarcophagi are overshadowed by those of the abbesses, which are placed upright against the south wall, a position which helps endow the life-size effigies with a Byzantine sense of hierarchy.

In the northern transept is the fabulous **Schatzkammer**, now intact once more, following the return in 1993 of a number of long-lost items which turned out to have been pilfered by the American lieutenant put in charge of their safety in 1945. The glittering twelfth-century **reliquary** of the church's patron, St Servatius, is outstanding, with its vibrant ivory carvings of the Apostles and its encrusted diamonds and enamels. The gilded **casket** dedicated to St Catherine, though more orthodox, is equally beautiful. Another highlight is an early thirteenth-century **bridal chest**, decorated with 31 different coats of arms, which rank as the earliest surviving heraldic symbols in Germany. Of the recently returned pieces, the finest are two Gospel books and the so-called **comb of Heinrich I**, an elaborate ivory creation perhaps dating back as far as the seventh century. Housed in the transept opposite is the church's most valuable treasure, the oldest **tapestry** north of the Alps; woven around 1200, it shows the marriage of Mercury to Philology, the Queen of Knowledge.

The Klopstockhaus and neighbouring museums

At no. 12 on Schlossberg, the street of half-timbered houses below the Schloss, is the **Klopstockhaus** (Tues–Sun 10am–5pm; DM5/€2.50), the boyhood home of the eighteenth-century poet **Friedrich Gottlieb Klopstock**. Founder of the classicizing tendency in German literature, Klopstock self-consciously regarded himself as a Christian Homer, devoting much of his life to the composition of a huge twenty-part epic, *The Messiah*; he also wrote odes on typical Enlightenment themes such as man and nature, the fatherland, peace and liberty. Though his reputation is somewhat in eclipse, his verses have gained a wide audience through Mahler's settings, notably in the hugely popular *Resurrection Symphony*. The museum also contains memorabilia of two other influential Quedlinburgers of the same epoch: **Dorothea Christiana Erxleben**, the first German woman to gain the title of doctor, in 1754, and **Johann Christoph GuthsMuths**, the founding father of school gymnastics – and thus the unwitting begetter of the somewhat sinister role sport has played in German society, from Prussian militarism via the Nazis to the GDR.

To the rear of here, in a heavy *fin-de-siècle* building at Finkenherd 5a, is the **Lyonel-Feininger-Galerie** (Tues–Sun 10am–5/6pm; DM6/€3), devoted to the German-American Cubist, a key member of staff of the Bauhaus during its Weimar and Dessau periods. A large selection of his woodcuts, engravings, lithographs, drawings and watercolours is on display in specially dimmed galleries; there are also a few oil paintings, including an early *Self-Portrait*.

A couple of minutes' walk northwest of here, on the bank of an arm of the Bode at Wordgasse 3, is the **Fachwerkmuseum Ständerbau** (May–Sept Mon–Wed & Fri–Sun 11am–5pm; DM4/€2). The building itself, which probably dates from the early fourteenth century, is the earliest surviving timber-framed house in Germany and a good 150 years older than any other in Quedlinburg. Inside, the displays illustrate how the different styles of half-timbering evolved.

The Markt and around

The spacious triangular **Markt** was the subject in the 1970s of the sort of thorough restoration programme characteristic of western Germany. The buildings are a varied mix – no. 5 and nos. 13/14 were the sixteenth-century guild houses of the weavers and tanners respectively; the music school at no. 2 occupies a large Baroque palace, while the Neoclassical **Zum Bär** is a celebrated hotel whose reputation is tainted because of *Stasi* patronage. At the far end stands the **Rathaus** (guided tours daily at 1.30pm; DM4/€2), most of which, including the graceful portal, is Renaissance. Outside the Rathaus is a puny-looking **statue of Roland**, erected as a symbol of municipal independence when Quedlinburg was a member of the Hansa – and removed as soon as the abbesses re-established full authority.

To the rear of the Rathaus, and set in an unusual semicircular close, is the **Marktkirche St Benedikti**. Its fortress-like facade shows the transition from Romanesque to early Gothic; the rest of the structure was rebuilt at the end of the Gothic period. Entrance is via the Kalandskapelle on the north side, whose walls are hung with Renaissance memorials to local dignitaries. The main body of the church is of particular interest for the furnishings dating from after its conversion to Protestant worship, in particular the Mannerist wooden pulpit and the sober Baroque high altar. A more effusive form of Baroque was employed in the burial chapel of the Gebhardt family, which stands outside the church.

Breite Strasse, the long street leading north from here, has some superb half-timbered buildings, notably no. 33, which is Gothic, and no. 39, the Renaissance **Gildehaus zur Rose**, which is generally regarded as the most beautiful house in Quedlinburg. East of here, at Klink 11, is the **Freihaus**, another outstanding Renaissance mansion of almost palatial dimensions.

The Neustadt

Across the Bode from the Freihaus is Steinweg, the main east–west axis of the Neustadt, with the best examples of half-timbering to be found in the quarter.

Particularly notable are the Baroque **Zur Goldenen Sonne** at no. 11, which has been immaculately restored and returned to its historic role as a hotel (see p.913), and the late Renaissance **Zur Börse** at no. 23, which boasts an ingenious corner oriel. Due south of here, on Hinter der Mauer, are the best-preserved fragments of the **Stadtmauer**, including a couple of watchtowers.

The **Nikolaikirche**, the Gothic parish church of the Neustadt, is principally of note for its wonderful setting in the middle of a close of truly monumental grandeur. Outwardly, the two towers, one somewhat broader than the other, tend to overwhelm the rest of the building, an impression confirmed by the squat appearance of the hall interior, whose most notable furnishings are the elaborately Baroque high altar and pulpit and a touchingly naive statue of St Godehard.

The Münzenberg and the Wippertikirche

The **Münzenberg**, the hill just to the west of the Burgberg, was formerly crowned by a convent founded in Quedlinburg's tenth-century heyday. This was dissolved at the Reformation, whereupon a community of artisans, minstrels and travelling folk settled here, reusing its stones in the construction of their modest little houses. Even now, the quarter has an engagingly quiet, run-down feeling, and the view of the Burgberg from here alone justifies the trek up.

In the valley to the south, a large cemetery has grown up around the **Wippertikirche** (guided tours daily May–Oct, usually at 11am; DM6/€3), a former monastic church whose simple architecture rather resembles that of a barn – which is exactly the function it performed throughout most of last century. Its crypt dates back to the tenth century and is the only surviving monument from Quedlinburg's period as the German capital, while the Romanesque north portal, with its exquisite columns and weather-worn carvings, was brought here from the destroyed convent on the Münzenberg.

Eating and drinking

It's a measure of Quedlinburg's tourist appeal that the choice of places to **eat** and **drink** has always been wide by eastern German standards.

Am Finkenherd, Schlossberg 15. Good traditional coffee house.

Boulevard-Café, Markt 1. Another option for *Kaffee und Kuchen*, particularly recommendable in summer, when tables are placed out on the square.

Brauhaus Lüdde, Blasiistr. 14. This was one of the first home-brew pubs to open in the former GDR. It makes a *Pils* and an *Alt* as well as various seasonal beers, and also serves full meals.

Münzenberger Klause, Pölle 22. Fine traditional Gaststätte. Closed Thurs.

Ratskeller, Markt 1. Offers really splendid *gutbürgerliche Küche*, and as such is a worthy rival to any of the hotel restaurants. Closed Wed.

Schlosskrug, Schlossberg 1. Restaurant with a handy location in the Schloss complex. Closed Mon, and at 8pm on other days.

Word-Haus, Im Wasserwinkel 4. Occupying an example of nineteenth-century half-timbering, this serves regional specialities and has a good wine list.

Zun Roland, Breite Str. 2–8. Café-restaurant occupying no fewer than seven historic houses

Gernrode and the Selke valley

The recuperative health resort of **GERNRODE**, situated 9km south of Quedlinburg on the fringe of the Harz mountains, clusters round one of Germany's oldest and most remarkable churches. For the most part it's a somnolent little place – except around the Bahnhof to the north of the town proper, where the shed and freight yards of the

THE SELKETALBAHN

The **Selketalbahn** (*www.hsb-wr.de* for timetables and fares), the narrow-gauge rail line which runs the 35km between Gernrode and Stiege, is named after the peaceful valley of the **River Selke**, which defines part of its route. Gernrode itself does not lie in the valley, which is reached by the most atmospheric part of the journey, a steep climb past a couple of secluded lakes, then through wooded countryside unpenetrated by roads. Built in 1887, the line is plied by a number of antique locomotives, among them a *Mallet* of 1897, the oldest still-functioning locomotive in Germany; unfortunately, (relatively) modern diesels have been introduced as well. Alone among eastern Germany's surviving narrow-gauge passenger lines, freight carriages are attached – proof that this is no tourist trap.

The River Selke is reached at Mägdesprung, 10km south of Gernrode. A couple of stops further on is **ALEXISBAD**, a curious little resort whose spa buildings are an illustration of the Romantic movement's infatuation with chinoiserie. From here there's a three-kilometre branch line (served by six trains a day) to **HARZGERODE**. For several decades this town was the capital of a minute principality of the House of Anhalt – hence the late Renaissance Schloss, which, with the half-timbered Rathaus and slate-towered Marienkirche, gives the place an air of grandeur wholly inconsistent with its size.

Three trains a day go all the way to **STIEGE**, where the link with the Harzquerbahn (see box on p.922), which fell into disuse after World War II, was reinstated in 1984. Here you can choose between continuing on the two through trains to the Harzquerbahn's southern terminus at Nordhausen; going as far as Eisfelder Talmühle, then changing to the service north to Wernigerode; taking the five-kilometre-long branch line to Hasselfelde; or returning with the train to its shed in Gernrode.

Selketalbahn, the oldest **narrow-gauge steam rail line** in the region, stand directly opposite the main line.

Gernrode's history goes back to the mid-tenth century, when a women's collegiate church, the **Stiftskirche St Cyriakus**, was founded. This is substantially the same building as the one which can be seen today, with the exception of the west choir and towers and the double-storey cloister, all of which were added a couple of hundred years later. By far the best preserved of any church of its date, it exhibits most of the characteristics associated with Romanesque, the first original architectural style indigenous to northern Europe. The nave's triforium gallery was the first ever built north of the Alps, and suggests a certain Byzantine influence – a connection explained by the fact that the dowager Empress Theophanu, a native of Greece, was then living in Quedlinburg. Another innovation pioneered at Gernrode – alternating columns and pillars – became a hallmark of churches throughout the Saxon lands.

In the southern aisle stands a **Holy Sepulchre**, the oldest German reproduction of Christ's tomb in Jerusalem, which probably dates back to the late eleventh century. Unfortunately, it's somewhat mutilated, but the high quality of its carvings can still be seen on two of its sides, one showing Jesus appearing to Mary Magdalene after the Resurrection, the other with a wonderfully delicate frieze – a sort of carved version of an illuminated manuscript – featuring prophets, fantastic animals, foliage and a decorative border. Other highlights of the interior are the retouched frescoes in the east choir, the twelfth-century font and the late Gothic monument in honour of Margrave Gero.

The survival of the steam rail line ensured a steady stream of foreign visitors in GDR days, but, as they were forced to stay elsewhere, tourist facilities are underdeveloped in comparison with other parts of the Harz. Now, however, there are a fair number of **private rooms** (①–②); a **pension**, *Bückemuuhle*, Am Bückeberg 3 (☎03 94 85/4 19, *www.bueckemuehle.de*; ③), which is attached to a freshwater fish speciality restaurant; and a **hotel**, *Gasthof zum Bären*, Marktstr. 21 (☎03 94 85/54 50, *www.urlaubstip.de*; ④), which likewise has a restaurant. The **tourist office** (Mon–Fri 9am–4pm; ☎03 94 85/4 78) is on Suderoder Strasse.

The Bode valley

Before reaching Quedlinburg, the **River Bode** travels a mazy route right through the Harz mountains. Not only is it, at 169km, the longest river in the range, it also offers by far the most beautiful scenery the region has to offer, seen at its best under the menacingly dramatic skies the uncertain climate so often brings – making it easy to understand why such a rich store of supernatural folklore has grown up in association. The Bode has stirred the imagination of the literati to an extent unmatched by any other beauty spot in the country: Goethe, Herder, Klopstock, Eichendorff, Heine and Fontane all sang its praises.

Thale and around

German unification has meant that **THALE**, which lies right on the edge of the Harz 10km southwest of Quedlinburg, must look to tourism for its future, as its ironworks – the bedrock of the local economy for over five hundred years – have been reduced to a relatively minor operation. The town itself is of scant interest, the only monument of note being the **Wendhusenturm**, a tower-house (perhaps dating back as far as the tenth century) in the old quarter north of the Bode. However, the surroundings are marvellous; with 150km of marked trails in the vicinity, Thale is unquestionably one of the best **hiking** bases in eastern Germany. Nor should the unenergetic be put off: the best of the scenery starts to unfold just beyond the Friedenspark, the park across from the Bahnhof, terminus of a branch line from Quedlinburg.

Hexentanzplatz and Rosstrappe

Guarding the southern entrance to Thale are two rocky crags, both known to have been sites of pagan worship and commanding superb views over the valley and beyond. On the right bank, 454m above the valley, is the vertiginous **Hexentanzplatz** (Witches' Dancing Place), so named because it was where the local witches supposedly had their initial rendezvous on *Walpurgisnacht* (see p.924), before flying off to the main celebration on the Brocken. The lazy way to reach it is by **cable car** (DM5/€2.50 single, DM8/€4 return); the station for this is on the opposite side of the Bode, just over the bridge at the end of Friedenspark. There's also a road up from the southeastern end of Thale, plus several pathways, quickest and most convenient being the steps of the Hexenstiege, which lead to the belvedere via the **Harzer Bergtheater**, a fine natural amphitheatre where plays are staged regularly during the summer months. Alongside is the **Walpurgishalle** (daily May–Oct 9am–5pm; DM3/€1.50), an exhibition hall with displays on the *Walpurgisnacht* legend.

Directly across the river, at a height of 437m, is the **Rosstrappe** (Horse's Clip-Clops). There were once plans to make a direct transport link with the Hexentanzplatz, but instead a **chair lift** was built just north of the valley terminus of the cable car (DM4/€2 single, DM6/€3 return). Alternative ways up are the looping main road from the centre of Thale, and a walking trail, the Präsidentenweg. From the plateau-like summit, you can descend to a curious group of rocks poised directly above the river; here can be seen a natural indentation closely resembling that of a horse's hoof. According to legend, this was made by the mighty steed being ridden by a princess called Brunnhilde, who was being chased through the Harz by a lustful Knight by name of Bodo. Coming to this point, she spurred her mount on to make a successful leap across to Hexentanzplatz. Bodo, however, plunged into the chasm, where he was turned into a hound, compelled forever to guard the crown of Brunnhilde which had fallen into the river in her wake.

Up the valley

The classic walk from Thale is the 10km route along a path (identified by signs marked with blue triangles) that closely follows the course of the Bode; contrary to what you'd expect, the views from the valley floor surpass those from the heights. If you don't want to walk the whole way, the best of the scenery can be seen in the first 3km, around the **Teufelsbrücke** (Devil's Bridge), from where you can make a detour up to the Rosstrappe via a belvedere-punctuated trail named the Schurre. Beyond the Teufelsbrücke, the main path climbs high above the river, affording wonderful views back to the Rosstrappe and of the spectacular **Bodekessel** below, a gorge in which steep granite cliffs rise directly from the foaming waters with their angry whirlpools. You then descend to a more placid landscape, which is chiefly notable for its richly varied flora and fauna. Orchids, daphnes, Turk's-cap lilies and hart's-tongues are among the plants here; some of the trees are hundreds of years old, while the large numbers of waterfowl make this stretch a magnet for birdwatchers.

TRESEBURG, the terminus of the walk, is a scattered village of grand houses picturesquely spaced out along the banks of the Bode, with a very ruinous castle crowning the hill above. It's beginning to develop its potential as a resort, with guesthouses and holiday homes springing up, though it's being upstaged in this by **ALTENBRAK**, a somewhat larger village 4km upstream, which has taken to the new opportunities afforded by tourism like a duck to water.

Practicalities

Thale's **tourist office** (May–Oct Mon–Fri 9am–6pm, Sat & Sun 10am–3pm; Nov–April Mon–Fri 9am–5pm; ☎0 39 47/25 97, fax 22 77, *www.thale.de*) is in the pavilion directly facing the Bahnhof at Rathausstr. 1. Here you can get a list of the numerous **private houses** (①–②) with rooms to rent. **Pensions** include *Kleiner Ritter*, Markt 2 (☎0 39 47/25 70; ②), *Schröder*, Karl-Marx-Str. 10 (☎0 39 47/23 92; ④), and *Am Steinbach*, Poststr. 9 (☎0 39 47/6 38 83; ④). There are **hotels**, both with restaurants, on the summits of the two mountains: *Berghotel Rosstrappe* (☎0 39 47/30 11; ④) and *Berghotel Hexentanzplatz* (☎0 39 47/47 30; ⑤). The **youth hostel** (☎0 39 47/28 81; DM24/€12 or DM29/€14.50) occupies an ideal position for a hiking centre, on the right bank of the Bode just beyond the Hexenstiege.

Rübeland and around

A few kilometres upstream from Altenbrak, the waters of the Bode and its tributaries have been harnessed to create an eight-kilometre-long reservoir, the **Rappbodetalsperre**, whose hilly eastern bank is another attractive walking area. The large dam at the northern end, built in the 1950s, was one of the GDR's proudest technological achievements, particularly as various prewar projects to build it had come to nought. A much smaller second reservoir, the **Talsperre Wendefurth**, was built in the 1960s, principally as a protection against flooding.

RÜBELAND, another old iron-smelting town, lies a couple of kilometres northwest of here, clustering round a remarkable group of stalactite caves. Oldest of these, formed some 600,000 years ago, is the **Baumannshöhle** (guided tours May–Oct daily 9.30am–5.30pm; Nov–April alternately with the Hermannshöhle 9.30am–3.30/4.30pm; DM7/€3.50). It was inhabited by prehistoric bears, some of whose skeletons, which are between 20,000 and 40,000 years old, are on display; much later, Stone Age peoples also made it their home. Discovered in the early sixteenth century, the Baumannshöhle already had the status of a famous tourist attraction when Goethe paid three visits here in the last quarter of the eighteenth century. In his honour, the magnificent natural auditorium at the heart of the complex has been named the Goethesaal, and is occasionally used as a theatre.

If anything, the stalactite formations are even finer in the only other cave open to the public, the triple-tiered **Hermannshöhle** (same hours; DM7/€3.50). Although this lies directly opposite, its existence remained unknown until a workman engaged on the construction of the main road stumbled across it in the nineteenth century. A far more diverse range of skeletons of prehistoric mammals has been found here, while thirteen sorts of salamander still inhabit its underground lake. From the Hermannshöhle, you can walk up to Rübeland's only other attraction, the ruined **Burg Birkenfeld**, from where there's a fine panoramic view over the region.

Rübeland can be reached by regular **buses** from Thale and the other villages of the Bode valley. It also lies on a branch rail line from Halberstadt via Blankenburg; the **Bahnhof** is right beside the entrance to the Baumannshöhle.

Blankenburg and around

BLANKENBURG, which lies on the edge of the Harz, 10km northeast of Rübeland and 13km west of Quedlinburg, is a quiet health resort and residential town, which, at the turn of the seventeenth century, briefly found itself at the forefront of European power politics. In 1690, Ludwig Rudolf, a younger son of the Welf House of Braunschweig-Wolfenbüttel, made Blankenburg into the resplendent capital of a new principality. He also brought off an amazing double dynastic coup by marrying one of his daughters to the future Holy Roman Emperor Charles VI, and another to the son of Czar Peter the Great of Russia. Four decades later, he inherited his family's main duchy – and relegated the town he had himself built up to a second-string residence.

Despite the brevity of its period of glory, Blankenburg acquired two Baroque palaces. The smaller and prettier of these is the **Kleines Schloss** (Tues–Sat 10am–5pm, Sun 2–5pm; DM2/€1) just east of the centre, which houses a better-than-average local museum. Its curvaceous northern facade overlooks a fine French-style formal garden, in which stand an over-the-top grotto dedicated to Neptune and a copy of the celebrated Burglöwe (Lion Monument) of Braunschweig.

From here, Marktstrasse leads west to the Renaissance **Rathaus**, above whose door are the coats of arms of both Blankenburg and Braunschweig. Steps lead up to the **Bartholomäuskirche**, a Gothic hall church containing the tombs of members of the local rulers. East of here, Burgstrasse is lined with seventeenth-century **half-timbered houses**; others can be seen in the streets west of the Rathaus. At the very top of the town is the main **Schloss**, which was allowed to fall into a poor state of repair in the GDR era, and is currently under restoration.

Just to the north of the historic part of town is the spa quarter, centred on two large areas of greenery, the **Kurpark** and the **Thiepark**. At the edge of the latter is the **Teufelsbad**, which offers a wide range of facilities, the speciality of the house being mud baths.

Practicalities

Blankenburg lies on the rail line from Halberstadt to Rübeland; the **Bahnhof** and **bus station** are both at the northern end of town. The **tourist office** (May–Oct Mon–Fri 9am–7pm, Sat 9am–noon; Nov–April Mon–Fri 9am–6pm; ☎0 39 44/28 98, fax 6 31 02, *www.blankenburg.de*) is right in the centre at Lange Str. 17.

There are dozens of **private rooms** (①–②) for rent. Similar rates are available at a couple of **pensions** – *Wegner*, Friedrich-August-Str. 2 (☎0 39 44/30 75; ②), and *Klaus*,

Lindestr. 12 (☎0 39 44/24 23; ②). An excellent range of **hotels** includes *An der Teufelsmauer*, Timmenröder Str. 2 (☎0 39 44/36 41 00; ③), *Kurhotel Fürstenhof*, Mauerstr. 9 (☎0 39 44/9 04 40; ⑤), and *Viktoria Luise*, Hasselfelder Str. 8 (☎0 39 44/9 11 70, *www.hotel.viktoria-luise.de*; ⑥). The last two of these have the best **restaurants** in town.

Around Blankenburg

Blankenburg, being set in particularly attractive surroundings, makes a good walking base. From a scenic point of view, the best excursion is the four-kilometre circular path which leads southeast from the Kleines Schloss to the **Teufelsmauer** (Devil's Wall), a row of huge, heavily fissured sandstone boulders believed to have been formed some 90 million years ago. Near the beginning of the circuit are the **Grossvaterfelsen** (Grandfather Rocks), from where there's a wonderful view over the town.

Another walking trail leads 3km north from the Bahnhof to the fascinating labyrinthine ruins of **Burg Regenstein** (May–Oct daily 9am–6pm; Nov–April Wed–Sun 9am–4pm; DM3/€1.50). The original twelfth-century Romanesque castle, partly carved out of the living rock, was the first seat of the local counts. It was badly damaged in feudal wars against the combined might of the bishop of Halberstadt, the count of Wernigerode and the burghers of Quedlinburg, who joined together to prevent Blankenburg establishing regional dominance. In 1670, the castle was taken over by the Prussians, although it lay outside the boundaries of their state; they enlarged the old fortifications to create a modern military stronghold.

Wernigerode and around

Known as "the colourful town in the Harz" because of the kaleidoscopic paintwork on its half-timbered buildings, **WERNIGERODE** has by far the most animated atmosphere to be found in the region. In part, this is due to the fact that it's no stranger to international tourism – in GDR days, it was the only place in the Harz where Westerners were encouraged to stay. This led to an influx of steam-train buffs from all over the world, who came to ride the Harzquerbahn, the longest and most scenic **narrow-gauge rail line** in the country. Wernigerode is its northern terminus, and the sight of antiquated locomotives puffing their way through the streets before beginning their ascent into the mountains remains the most enduring image of a town plentifully endowed with picturesque corners.

The Town

The town clusters along the valleys of the Holtemme and Zillerbach, with the Altstadt lying just to the east of their confluence. From the streets of the Altstadt, the striking silhouette of the Schloss, perched high on a hill at the southern end of town, can often be seen looming in the background. Immediately beyond the Schloss, the thickly wooded slopes of the Harz mountains begin to unfold, and even within the boundaries of the town there are marked walking trails which give a good idea of the characteristic scenery and vegetation of the range.

Wernigerode's pride and joy is the **Rathaus** on Marktplatz, a building of stridently pictorial qualities that could belong in no country but Germany. The bright orange facade, with sharply pointed lead steeples sprouting from resplendent double-storey oriels, represents the final phase of Gothic in the mid-sixteenth century. This formed part of an ingenious building programme whereby the Rathaus was crafted out of two existing structures – the former theatre-cum-gymnasium which forms the core, and the

THE HARZQUERBAHN

The **Harzquerbahn** (*www.hsb-wr.de* for timetables and fares), one of Europe's most memorable rail lines, travels the 60.5km between Wernigerode and Nordhausen in Thuringia. Up to five trains per day make the complete trip; many others cover shorter stretches. Most of the locomotives used are steam trains built in the 1950s, but diesels, to the horror of purists, were introduced in 1988. A *Mallet* of 1898 – the same year as the line was inaugurated – is brought out of storage for occasional excursion trips, for which advance booking is necessary. Although the Harzquerbahn has been something of a tourist attraction since its inception, it has always been used for the movement of goods, as well as providing a genuine public transport service to the villages in the remotest part of the Harz. It accounts for nearly half the length of the surviving narrow-gauge network in the region, which is now all linked up again, and also includes the Selketalbahn (see box on p.917) and the Brockenbahn (see p.924).

The first stop, Westerntor, a station designed by Fritz Höger, architect of notable Expressionist buildings in Hamburg and Hannover, is located just outside the eponymous medieval gateway at the western end of the Altstadt; it's a handy place to pick up the train if you don't want to trail down to the Hauptbahnhof. There are two more stations within Wernigerode itself, before the train passes through its only tunnel in the course of its exhilarating climb – maintaining an almost constant one in thirty gradient – to its highest point at **Drei Annen Hohne**. Here is the junction with the Brockenbahn; it's also the place to alight if you want to follow the 10km trail up the other main mountain in the area, the Hohneklippen (908m).

The Harzquerbahn then descends to the villages of **Elend** and **Sorge**, whose names ("Misery" and "Sorrow") seemed particularly appropriate in GDR days, when they found themselves right up against the notorious frontier between the two Germanys. Indeed, the train used to travel within a few metres of the electrified barbed wire on this stretch, and guards kept a wary eye on passengers' behaviour. Only the markings on the trees now indicate where the border used to be. After climbing again to the little resort of **Benneckenstein**, the train begins its rapid descent to Nordhausen. The junction with the Selketalbahn is at **Eisfelder Talmühle**, which is just over the boundary with Thuringia. At around 6.30pm each day, three passenger steam trains travelling in different directions have to wait for each other here, before proceeding in their separate directions – a sight which can no longer be seen anywhere else in the world.

municipal weigh house to the south west. The exterior of the latter, with its painted corbels of saints and Carnival characters, can be seen by walking down Klintgasse.

On the western side of the Markt is the **Gothisches Haus**, another richly decorated building, originally the home of a wealthy fifteenth-century burgher family. Since the middle of the nineteenth century, it has been a restaurant, and latterly a hotel as well. At no. 5 on Klintgasse is the **Teichmühle**, a seventeenth-century mill popularly known, for obvious reasons, as "The Leaning House of Wernigerode". The Neoclassical mansion at no. 10 on the same street houses the **Harzmuseum** (Mon–Sat 10am–4/5pm; DM3/€1.50), which features displays on the town's half-timbered houses and their construction, as well as on the history, geology, flora, fauna and industries of the Harz region.

Just south of here is the **Silvestrikirche**, the parish church of the Altstadt, but far more remarkable than the church itself is its peaceful close, the **Oberkirchhof**, which is lined with a beautiful and varied group of houses that range from two to four hundred years old. Particularly outstanding is no. 13, the **Gadenstedtsches Haus**, a late Gothic half-timbered construction to which was added a spectacularly protruding upper-storey oriel in High Renaissance style.

On **Kochstrasse**, at the southernmost end of the Altstadt, can be seen the more modest dwellings of the local craftsmen. Notwithstanding its three storeys, no. 43 is the smallest house in town; sandwiched between the low-ceilinged kitchen and minute attic bedroom is the "main" level, consisting of a single room with a floor space of just 10 square metres. Another street worth seeking out is **Hinterstrasse**, a block north of the Markt, which has the oldest houses in town, some of which date back to the 1400s.

Much the most imposing street, however, is **Breite Strasse**, the pedestrianized main shopping thoroughfare leading east from the Markt. Despite some losses in a 1944 air raid, it preserves an almost uninterrupted array of high-quality vernacular architecture. Oldest house is the late sixteenth-century merchant's residence at no. 4, which was given an improbable but effective Jugendstil interior refit as a Viennese-style café. Even more eye-catching is the **Krummelsches Haus** at no. 72, whose half-timbering is all but obscured by the exuberant Baroque carvings which cover almost all its facade. At no. 95 is the **Krell'sche Schmiede** (Wed, Thurs, Sat & Sun 1–4pm; Fri 10am–3pm; DM3/€1.50), decorated with horseshoes and a horse's head to indicate its function as a smithy – which it remains today, an uninterrupted tradition dating back over three hundred years.

The **Schloss** (May–Oct daily 10am–6pm; Nov–April Tues–Fri 10am–4pm, Sat & Sun 10am–6pm; *www.schloss-wernigerode.de*; DM8/€4), a Romantic fantasy which almost completely replaced the original fortress, was the brainchild of Count Otto of Stolberg-Wernigerode, one of Bismarck's closest cronies. Although the architecture is pseudo-Gothic and Renaissance in style, there's nothing fake about the furnishings, which include valuable pieces ranging from the thirteenth to the nineteenth centuries, many of them brought from the former count's first-string residence of Stolberg. Especially notable are two works in the **Schlosskapelle** – an embroidery dedicated to St Mary Magdalene that was woven around 1250 and the late fifteenth-century retable carved by Ulrich Mair. The other big attraction is the **view** over Wernigerode and the Harz from the ramparts.

Practicalities

Wernigerode's **Hauptbahnhof** – which, in addition to being the terminus of the Harzquerbahn, has mainline services to Magdeburg via Halberstadt – lies about fifteen minutes' walk north of the town centre. Alongside is the **bus station**. The **tourist office** (Mon–Fri 9am–5/6pm, Sat & Sun 10am–3pm; ☎0 39 43/63 30 35, fax 63 20 40, *www.wernigerode.de*) is at Nicolaiplatz 1. There's the usual **private room** (①–②) booking service, though this has competition from the Zimmervermittlung agency at Breite Str. 70 (daily 10am–8pm; ☎0 39 43/60 60 00, fax 60 61 61, *www.t-online.de/home /schlossbahn*).

Among many good-value **pensions** are *Oberbeck*, Hilleborchstr. 4 (☎0 39 43/63 26 62; ③), *Zur Neuen Quelle*, Friedrichstr. 129 (☎0 39 43/63 27 25; ③), *Hasseröder Hof*, Amtsfeldstr. 33a (☎0 39 43/63 25 06; ④), and *Harzkrone*, Nöschenröder Str. 42–46 (☎0 39 43/2 32 56; ⑤). There's a wide choice of **hotels**, mostly in grand half-timbered buildings, including *Zur Tanne*, Breite Str. 57–59 (☎0 39 43/63 25 54; ③–⑤), *Schossblick*, Burgstr. 58 (☎0 39 43/63 20 04; ⑤), *Zur Post*, Marktstr. 17 (☎0 39 43/6 90 40, *www.hotel-zurpost-wernigerode.de*; ⑥), *Weisser Hirsch*, Am Markt 5 (☎0 39 43/60 20 20, *www.ringhotels.de*; ⑥–⑧), and *Gothisches Haus*, Am Markt 2 (☎0 39 43/67 50, *www .travelcharme.com/gothisches-haus*; ⑥–⑨). The local **youth hostel** is at Am Eichberg 5 (☎0 39 43/60 61 76, fax 60 61 77; DM28/€14 or DM33/€16.50) in the incorporated village of Hasseröde.

All the recommended hotels have **restaurants**, though they face strong competition from the *Ratskeller* under the Rathaus, which is as good as any in eastern Germany. *Café Wien*, Breite Str. 4, is the obvious place to go for ice cream or coffee. Wernigerode's Hasseröder **beer** ranks fairly high by eastern standards; its premium product is called *Pilsator*. The town has a number of **festivals**, including the *Weintage* towards the end of May, the *Rathausfest* in late June and the *Schützenfest* in mid-July.

The Brocken

Southwest of Wernigerode, the **Nationalpark Hochharz** is centred on the celebrated peak of the **Brocken** (1142m), meeting-place of the witches on *Walpurgisnacht* (April 30), an event vividly described in the first part of Goethe's *Faust*. The legend seems to have arisen at least partly as a result of the so-called "spectre of Brocken" – when the sun is low, it casts magnified silhouettes from the peak onto clouds hanging around the lower neighbouring mountains. *Walpurgisnacht* is somewhat oddly named after St Walburga, an eighth-century English-born missionary whose name is evoked as a protection against evil spirits; however, it seems she gained this role through her name having been confused with that of Waldborg, the pagan goddess of fertility.

Throughout the entire history of the GDR, the Brocken's mystique was increased by the fact that it was a restricted military area used for border surveillance activities, with Westerners forbidden to come anywhere near it. Such is its impact on the German consciousness, however, that it was made accessible to walkers within a month of the fall of the Berlin Wall. Soon afterwards work began on restoring the Brockenbahn, the **narrow-gauge railway** (*www.hsb-wr.de* for timetables and fares) that branches off from the Harzquerbahn, and the full 19km of this, from Drei Annen Hohne to the summit of the mountain, was put back in operation. Near the terminus, the **Brockenmuseum** (daily 10am–4pm; DM2.50/€1.25) has displays on the geology, history and legends of the peak.

Of the many other paths up the mountain, the most atmospheric is that from Torfhaus (see p.701), which offers the best views of the peak. Another favourite hiking base is **SCHIERKE**, which has a station on the Brockenbahn line, and which can also be reached from Wernigerode in about forty minutes by bus. This resort village is amply endowed with **private rooms** and **pensions** (①–③). There are also several **hotels**, including *König*, Kirchberg 15 (☎03 94 55/3 83 or 5 10 56, *www.harz-hotel-koenig.de*; ④), *Brockenscheideck*, Brockenstr. 49 (☎03 94 55/2 68 or 5 10 37, *www.harz-hotel-brockenscheideck.de*; ④), and *Waldschlösschen*, Hermann-Löns-Weg 1 (☎03 94 55/6 70, *www.waldschloesschen-schierke.de*; ⑤). A full accommodation list is available from the **tourist office** (Mon–Fri 9am–noon & 1–4/5pm, Sat 10am–noon; ☎03 94 55/3 10) at Brockenstr.10.

Stolberg

It's not without justification that **STOLBERG** styles itself as "the pearl of the southern Harz", as this tiny former county capital occupies a secluded setting bestriding beautiful hills and valleys. Although a centre for silver, iron and copper mining for much of its history, it's had the status of a *Kurort* since 1945. Formerly it used this as a prefix to distinguish it from other towns of the same name, but, just before the *Wende* of 1989, this was replaced with the designation "Thomas-Müntzer-Stadt", in celebration of the 500th anniversary of the birth here of the most radical figure of the Reformation period. Müntzer's leadership of the Peasants' War of 1525 was regarded by the GDR authorities as the first precursor of Communist rule, and he came close to rivalling Marx in the state's roll call of heroes.

At first sight, the painted sundial seems to be the only remarkable feature of the half-timbered **Rathaus** on the Markt. A closer inspection shows that it's actually a real architectural curiosity – there are no interior stairways, access to each upper storey only being possible from the steps which serve as the public footpath up the hill. Formerly, there was a second peculiarity, in that the number of windows equalled the number of weeks in the year and the number of panes equalled the number of days in the year, but these tidy calculations have been spoiled by subsequent remodelling.

At the top of the steps is the gaunt late Gothic church of **St Martini**, where, at the height of the Peasants' War, Luther – who regarded Müntzer as a dangerous upstart liable to undo all the achievements of the Reformation – dared to come to preach against the town's famous son. At the top of the hill is the late seventeenth-century **Schloss**, the former seat of the counts of Stolberg-Stolberg. Most of its interiors – which are currently inaccessible because of restoration work – are decorated with Baroque stuccowork, though two were remodelled by Schinkel in Neoclassical style.

The town's finest houses can be seen along Niedergasse, which leads south from the Markt. Best of all is the brightly coloured **Alte Münze** (Tues–Sat 10am–12.30pm & 1–5pm, Sun 10am–12.30pm & 1.30–5pm; DM2/€1) at no. 19. Inside, you can see a reconstruction, complete with original equipment, of the workshop of the mint formerly housed here; there are also sections on the other craft industries and on mining. The top floor is a memorial to Müntzer: the four sixteenth-century console figures are all that remain of the house on this street where he was born, which was destroyed by fire in the nineteenth century. Finally, while all the hills around which Stolberg is built offer fine views, the best of the town itself are from the belvedere known as the **Lutherbuche**, almost due west of the Markt.

Stolberg is an excellent hiking centre, with a wide variety of marked trails in the vicinity. The most popular destination is the **Josefskreuz** (May–Oct daily 9am–6pm; Nov–April Tues–Sun 9am–dusk; DM2/€1), 6km to the northeast. This huge iron double cross was erected at the end of the nineteenth century to replace its Schinkel-designed wooden predecessor, which had been destroyed by lightning. You can ascend the platform for a sweeping panoramic view stretching from the Brocken to the Kyffhäuser; there's also a Gaststätte (same hours) offering full meals or snacks.

Practicalities

Stolberg's **Bahnhof** is at the southern end of town; note that trains only go southwards to the rail junction of Berga-Kelbra in Thuringia, but that there are good **bus** connections from here – and from the stop on the Markt – to other towns in the Harz. The **tourist office** (Mon–Fri 9am–12.30pm & 1–6pm; ☎03 46 54/4 54 or 8 01 50, fax 7 29, *www.stadt-stolberg.de*) is at Markt 2. Here you can also book a room in a **private house** (①–②), of which the town has an abundant supply.

Stolberg also has several attractive **hotels**, all of which are very good value considering their quality: *Weisses Ross*, Rittergasse 5 (☎03 46 54/4 03 or 6 00, *www.stolberg.purespace.de*; ③); *Zum Kanzler*, Markt 8 (☎03 46 54/2 05 or 2 39, *www.harz-hotelvereinigung.de*; ④); *Stolberger Hof*, Markt 6 (☎03 46 54/3 20; ④); and *Zum Bürgergarten*, Thyratal 1 (☎03 46 54/81 10, *www.akzent.de*; ④). All these also have reasonably priced **restaurants**, with the last-named perhaps having the edge on the others. An even cheaper alternative is the *Ratskeller* on the ground floor of the Rathaus.

Eisleben

Mansfelder Land, the Landkreis encompassing the eastern foothills of the Harz, takes its name from Mansfeld, a small county that survived as a constituent state of the Holy Roman Empire until 1780, when it was subsumed into Saxony. While not its historic capital, **EISLEBEN**, which lies midway along the rail line from Berga-Kelbra to Halle, has always been its principal town, and is the administrative centre of the present-day district. Since 1946, its official name has been Lutherstadt Eisleben, in honour of its indelible association with **Martin Luther**, the man whose impact on German society and culture has arguably been more profound and long-lasting than that of any other individual. The scourge of the papacy and the Holy Roman Empire, the founder of Protestantism and – almost as a by-product – of modern written German, was born there in 1483 to parents who had been brought up on humble peasant farms in Thuringia. Although his family moved to the nearby town of Mansfeld the following year, Eisleben remained a place for which Luther retained a special affection, and it was where he spent the last few weeks of his life, dying there in 1546. These connections led to the town becoming a pioneer of heritage tourism long before the concept was invented: indeed, the first steps to ensure the preservation of its Luther memorials were taken as far back as 1689, in the wake of a fire which caused widespread destruction.

The Town

Despite never growing very large, Eisleben preserves a sizeable historic core, consisting not only of the usual Altstadt, which dates back to the tenth century, but also three suburbs, all founded in the twelfth century, plus an early sixteenth-century Neustadt which was for long a separate town in its own right.

The Petriviertel

Luther was a native of Eisleben's southern suburb, the Petriviertel (or Brückenviertel). His father, Hans Luder (the reformer himself altered the surname), had been excluded from the family farm by local inheritance laws, and moved to the county of Mansfeld, where he pursued a career in the copper mines and the associated smelting industry, eventually becoming the owner of several foundries. He rented part of a half-timbered house in the Petriviertel's Lange Gasse (nowadays Lutherstrasse), and it was there that Luther was born. Opened to the public in 1693 as the first memorial museum in Germany, it now goes under the name of **Luthers Geburtshaus** (Luther's Birth House; April–Oct daily 10am–6pm; Nov–March Tues–Fri 10am–4pm, Sat & Sun noon–4pm; *www.MartinLuther.de*; DM4/€2, or DM6/€3 combined ticket with Luthers Sterbehaus). In preparation for the opening, the main room on the first floor was transformed into a festive hall, the **Schöner Saal**, which is decorated with a large ceiling painting of an angel, full-length portraits of Luther, his close colleague Philipp Melanchthon and the electors of Saxony, and a statue of a swan, one of the metaphorical symbols associated with the Reformation. A medieval kitchen can be seen on the ground floor, though this was probably used by the landlord rather than the Luders. There are also various books and works of art from the time of Luther's childhood, including a German-language Bible with coloured woodcuts which was printed in Nürnberg the year he was born. Across the courtyard, and included in the entry price, is an early nineteenth-century school for the poor, the **Lutherarmenschule**, displaying minerals and fossils from the Harz region, plus the presses used by the Eisleben-born Friedrich Koenig, whose printing works, founded in 1818, are still in business today.

Just a few steps south of the house is **St Peter und Paul** (Mon–Fri 10am–noon & 2–4pm, Sat 11am–4pm, Sun 11am–1pm), the parish church of the Petriviertel, and the place where Luther was baptized. Architecturally, it's a somewhat gaunt Gothic hall church, but it contains two beautiful Gothic **retables**, the one at the high altar being in honour of St Anne, the miners' patron saint. On the walls are four imposing examples of an art form that flourished during the early Protestant period, the **painted epitaph**. That to the Heidelberg family is of particular note, as it features a distant view of Eisleben, with Luther and his associates conversing in the middle ground, as the backdrop to an allegorical depiction of the doctrine of Redemption and portraits of eighteen members of the clan.

The Altstadt

The heart of Eisleben's Altstadt is the sloping **Markt**, which is lined with relatively plain Renaissance and Baroque burghers' mansions. In the middle of the square is the

Lutherdenkmal, a Romantic-era statue of Luther on a plinth adorned with bas-reliefs of scenes from his life.

Directly above the square is **St Andreas** (Mon–Fri 10am–noon & 2–4pm, Sat 11am–4pm, Sun 11am–1pm), another somewhat stern-looking Gothic hall church, albeit one with a distinctive silhouette, with the slender pair of octagonal towers over the facade offset by their massive single counterpart on the north side. The **pulpit**, still preserved in its original early sixteenth-century form, has gained independent renown as the place from which Luther preached his last four sermons. It was formerly draped with a fine stumpwork **embroidery**, which is now displayed in a glass case on the south wall. Despite its modest dimesions, the **high altar** – and in particular the reverse side, whose delicate panels were painted in a Nürnberg workshop – is a distinguished example of late Gothic art. The church served as the mausoleum of the House of Mansfeld, and contains several notable **funerary monuments**, the most spendid being the bronze and sandstone tomb of Count Hoyer VI in the north apse, carved in full Renaissance pomp by Hans Schlegel of Halle. In 1817, in celebration of the 300th anniversary of the Reformation, the **busts** of Luther and Melanchthon were commissioned from the great Berlin Neoclassical sculptor Johann Gottfried Schadow, who used contemporary painted portraits by Cranach as his models.

On the south side of Andreaskirchplatz, the square around the church, is the **Luther Sterbehaus** (Luther Death House; April–Oct daily 9am–5pm; Nov–March Tues–Fri 10am–4pm, Sat & Sun noon–4pm; *www.MartinLuther.de*; DM4/€2), where the reformer spent his last weeks, having been drawn back to the town of his birth by the need to settle some disputes concerning his family's business interests. The wood-panelled front-facing rooms have been restored to their original, wonderfully evocative, late Gothic appearance. Luther did not die in the room with the bed, as might be supposed, but in the adjacent chamber, where his death mask and the original wooden pall for his coffin can be seen. The perpendicular courtyard wing contains a display on the history of the Reformation, including a beaker, which is thought to have belonged to Luther, and the gilded Communion cup he presumably used at St Andreas. The building opposite, for which the same ticket is valid, is home to the **Regionalgeschichtliches Museum**, an entertaining array of artefacts associated with the Mansfeld region, ranging from a Bronze Age boat to a 90-piece dinner set painted with local views. The latter was made in the nineteenth century at Berlin's royal porcelain factory.

The Neustadt

Adjoining the Altstadt to the west is the Neustadt, which was specifically built to house the families who worked in the mines on which the town's prosperity rested for a total of 800 years. This tradition is commemorated by a polychromed statue of an Eisleben miner, popularly known as **Kamerad Martin**, in the heart of the quarter.

Uphill is **St Annen**, which was built in the second decade of the sixteenth century to serve both the Neustadt parishioners and a small eremitical community of Luther's own order, the Augustinians, whose members lived in the picturesque row of gabled houses alongside. (The present occupants take it in turns to open the church to visitors: if shut, a notice tells you which doorbell to ring for admission.) In 1523, with only the chancel in place, the church became the first in Mansfeld county to embrace Protestantism. Impetus towards completing the building came in 1585 from the widowed Countess Margarete, who commissioned the remarkable **Steinbilder-Bibel** from the Münster sculptor Hans Uttendrup. A work with no obvious parallel anywhere in Europe, this consists of a set of 39 sandstone reliefs, arranged in the format of a poor man's Bible, placed in front of the choir stalls. With the exception of the first two scenes of the Passion, and the four Evangelical symbols at the end, they illustrate the Old Testament only. However, the New Testament is given due prominence in the slightly later polychromed stuccowork **pulpit** alongside, in which a jolly sense of humour is apparent. The church's nave is a classic example of the Lutheran Renaissance style, being a spacious hall designed primarily for preaching. It boasts a spectacular coffered **ceiling**, whose central section features paintings of the Trinity and the Apostles.

Practicalities

Eisleben's **Bahnhof** is in the southeastern part of town; the quickest way to the centre is to go sharp left along Bahnhofsring, then right into Bahnhofstrasse. The **tourist office** (Mon & Wed–Fri 10am–5pm, Tues 10am–6pm, Sat 9am–noon; ☎0 34 75/60 21 24, fax 60 26 34, *www.stadt-lutherstadt-eisleben.de*) is at Bahnhofstr. 36.

In addition to a reasonable supply of **private rooms** (②–③), there a few **pensions**, the most convenient being *Neuber*, Bucherstr. 2 (☎0 34 75/6 54 63; ③), and *Morgenstern*, Hallesche Str. 18 (☎0 34 75/60 28 22; ③). Among the **hotels** are *Parkhotel*, Bahnhofstr. 12 (☎0 34 75/9 27 30; ③), *Alter Simpel*, Glockenstr. 7 (☎0 34 75/69 65 07; ④), and *Mansfelder Hof*, Hallesche Str. 33 (☎0 34 75/66 90; ⑤). The last of these has the town's leading **restaurant**; another good place to eat and drink is *Brauhaus Zum Reformator*, Friedensstr. 12, a Hausbrauerei which makes light and dark beers, bakes bread, smokes eels and serves "medieval" dishes as well as the normal traditional fare.

In September the town hosts the largest **popular festival** in Saxony-Anhalt, the *Eisleber Wiese*.

THE ELBE-SAALE REGION

As in the north of Saxony-Anhalt, the main tourist draws in the south of the province are found in the basin of the Elbe and one of its major tributaries, in this case the Saale. Of the old Anhalt princely capitals, **Bernburg** is particularly attractive, while **Köthen**, despite pollution, also has its points. **Dessau**, on the other hand, was devastated in the war, but is worth a visit for its wonderful heritage of Bauhaus architecture; it's also the hub of an eighteenth-century scheme of landscaped gardens which reached its climax at nearby **Wörlitz**. Not far from here is **Wittenberg**, the unlikely-looking university town which, during its spell as the capital of Saxony, was the main setting for the Reformation. **Halle** is of note as a major city which still evokes the nation's vanished prewar existence; nearby **Merseburg** preserves reminders of its time as a missionary bishopric, though its Dom is overshadowed by that of **Naumburg** further up the Saale, which lies close to the river's most picturesque stretch around **Bad Kösen**.

Bernburg and Köthen

Until it was finally united in 1863, with Dessau as its capital, Anhalt had had an almost continuous history of political fragmentation, with each branch of the same family ruling a tinpot principality from its own Residenzstadt. Apart from Dessau itself (the only one which developed into a city), **Bernburg** and **Köthen** both served as courtly towns for extended periods and preserve reminders of their heady days – which contrast sharply with their present provincial status.

Bernburg

By far the most attractive of the Anhalt capitals is **BERNBURG**, which spreads across both banks of the River Saale, just east of the Harz range and about 30km south of Magdeburg. A curiosity of the town is that it's a place whose centre has shifted. The

Talstadt, or lower town, on the north bank of the Saale is the oldest part: here are a couple of Gothic churches and a spacious but incongruously quiet Marktplatz lined with Renaissance and Baroque houses. Far more memorable than any of these, however, is the **waterfront**, where a lock and several museum-piece mills make a picturesque foreground to the wonderful view of the **Bergstadt**, or upper town, on the opposite bank.

Completely dominating the Bergstadt, which has become the modern commercial centre, is the **Schloss**, by origin a medieval fortress but converted into a magnificent Renaissance palace in the mid-sixteenth century. It has a richly varied skyline of towers, turrets and gables, with the defensive features of the old castle softened with decorative adornments. The courtyard is also impressive, particularly the showpiece northern facade with its two double-storey oriels adorned with colourful carvings, grotesque heads and heraldic emblems. A small part of the complex houses the **Schlossmuseum** (Tues 9am–1pm & 2–6pm, Wed & Thurs 9am–1pm & 2–4.30pm, Fri 9am–1pm, Sat & Sun 10am–1pm & 2–5pm; DM3/€1.50), with the expected archeology and local history displays, plus an extensive section on the local mills. There's also a surprisingly good lapidary department, with sculptures from the Romanesque period onwards: look out for the relief portraits, which formerly decorated the exterior of the Schloss, of seven princes of the Reformation period. On summer weekends, you can ascend the Romanesque keep, the **Eulenspiegelturm**, for a panorama over the town and the valley.

Bernburg's **Bahnhof** is at the eastern end of the Bergstadt, while the **bus station** is right in the centre. The **tourist office** (Mon–Fri 9am–6pm; ☎0 34 71/37 20 30, fax 37 20 32, *www.bernburg.de*) is at Rheineplatz 4. Between March and October, you can take a **cruise** on the Saale from the landing stage below the Schloss; the boats sail from here as far as Halle. In addition to the **private rooms** (①–②), which can be booked at the tourist office, there's a selection of relatively expensive **hotel** options, including *Kammerhof*, Breite Str. 62 (☎0 34 71/35 39 45; ⑤), *Ulmer Spatz*, Heinrich-Zille-Str. 2 (☎0 34 71/2 40 21; ⑤), *City*, Lindenstr. 1c (☎0 34 71/2 21 70; ⑤), and *Askania*, Breite Str. 2–3 (☎0 34 71/35 40; ⑥). The **youth hostel** is to the west of the Talstadt at Krumbholzallee 2 (☎ & fax 0 34 71/35 20 27, *jh_bbg@t-online.de*; DM24/€12 or DM29/€14.50) and a **campsite** at the extreme southwestern edge of town at Am Stadtbad (☎0 34 71/2 23 34). Bernburg's best **restaurants** are *Alter Markt*, Markt 26, in the Talstadt and the *Haus des Handwerks*, Karlsplatz 34, in the Bergstadt.

Köthen

KÖTHEN, which lies 20km east of Bernburg, stands at the northern end of the notorious industrial region centred on Halle. This led to severe pollution problems during the GDR era, but it has been cleaned up over the past decade. The town holds an honoured place in musical history as a result of **Johann Sebastian Bach**'s period of service as court *Kapellmeister* from 1717 to 1723, and an equally distinguished position in the field of ornithology as the home town of the German Audubon, **Johann Friedrich Naumann**, whose work is commemorated in a gem of a museum.

At the northeastern end of the town centre is a typically outsized **Schloss**. Its southern wing, the **Ludwigsbau**, was built in Renaissance style at the turn of the seventeenth century, when the principality of Anhalt-Köthen was first established. Now designated the **Schlossmuseum** (Tues–Fri 9am–5pm, Sat 2–5pm, Sun 10am–noon & 2–5pm; DM4/€2), its historic interiors include two which are regularly used for concerts: the **Schlosskapelle**, which has a splendid Baroque organ, albeit one postdating Bach's stay, and the Neoclassical throne room, the **Spiegelsaal**. The museum also houses the **Bach-Gedenkstätte**, a large collection of memorabilia of the great composer, whose Köthen years occupy a special place in his career. As his patron, Prince

Leopold, was a Calvinist, Bach was freed from his usual obligation to produce a continuous stream of church music. Inspired by the virtuosity of the eighteen-strong court orchestra, he wrote a host of instrumental masterpieces, including the *Brandenburg Concertos*, the first part of *The Well-Tempered Clavier* and the extraordinary works for solo violin and cello, which occupy unique places in the repertoire of their respective instruments.

Across the courtyard, the Neoclassical **Ferdinandsbau**, erected by the last ruler of Anhalt-Köthen, houses the **Naumann-Museum** (Tues–Fri 9am–4.30pm, Sun 10am–noon & 2–5pm; DM3/€1.50). A series of Biedermeier display cabinets contain the collection of stuffed birds instituted by the great nineteenth-century ornithologist, one of the pioneers of taxidermy and author of a definitive thirteen-volume study of the bird life of Germany. Naumann was a highly talented artist who made all the illustrations for his publications, and the highlight of the museum is a display of original watercolours that served as the basis for these.

The three town-centre churches make for a fascinating contrast. On Springstrasse, to the west of the Schloss, is the Neoclassical **Marienkirche**, which Duke Ferdinand erected to mark his conversion to Catholicism. Just to the west, on Stiftstrasse, is **St Agnus**, a plain Baroque building that was built at the behest of Prince Leopold's mother, Princess Gisela Agnes, for her fellow Lutherans. Bach was a member of this church, whose most notable adornments are an altarpiece of *The Last Supper* by Cranach the Younger in which the disciples flanking Christ bear the features of Luther and Melanchthon, and a portrait of the foundress in mourning gear attributed to Antoine Pesne, court painter to Frederick the Great. Much the largest and oldest of the churches is the gaunt Gothic **Jakobskirche**, which dominates the central Marktplatz. Its sparsely adorned interior is a testament to the long era when Calvinism held sway in the town.

Köthen's **Bahnhof**, an important junction offering good connections to Magdeburg, Halle and Dessau, is about ten minutes' walk east of the centre. The **tourist office** (May–Sept Mon–Fri 9am–12.30pm & 1–5pm, Sat 10am–2pm; rest of year Mon–Fri only; ☎ & fax 0 34 96/21 62 17, *www.stadt-koethen.de*) is housed in a tower that survives from the medieval fortifications, the Hallesches Turm at Hallesche Str. 10. As well as a few **private rooms** (②), there are numerous **pensions** such as *Feldner*, Hallesche Str. 53–54 (☎0 34 96/21 36 13; ③), *Zum Rüdesheimer*, Friedrich-Ebert-Str. 48 (☎0 34 96/21 30 26; ③), and *Zur Schlachteplatte*, Lindenstr. 1 (☎0 34 96/21 24 98; ③). There are also three **hotels**: *Stadt Köthen*, Friedrich-Ebert-Str. 22 (☎0 34 96/55 61 06; ③), *Am Hubertus* on Fasanerieallee (☎0 34 96/57 40; ④), and *Anhalt*, Ludwigstr. 53 (☎0 34 96/55 00 11; ⑤). There are **restaurants** attached to each of the last two pensions and the first two hotels listed above; other options are *Troika*, Holzmarkt 8, and the *Ratskeller* in the Rathaus on Marktplatz.

Dessau

DESSAU, the historic capital of Anhalt, lies 60km southeast of Magdeburg. These days, it's a bleak industrial city that has suffered from all the worst aspects of modern Germany – with post-unification blight the latest sorry episode in a list which began with horrendous wartime damage followed by drab Stalinist rebuilding. All of which is a pity, as Dessau had previously maintained a highly distinguished cultural tradition. In the late eighteenth century, its pastoral-type setting between the Elbe and Mulde rivers was put to full use in its transformation into a garden city, with parks and palaces laid out all around its environs. Even more significantly, it was home to the **Bauhaus**, the most influential architecture and design movement of the twentieth century, during its most exciting and innovative period between 1925 and 1932. The survival of a large number of buildings from this time means that Dessau is a place no modern architecture buff should miss.

The City

There are plenty of delights to be found amid the prefabricated concrete jungles – but this requires time and patience given that the sights are very scattered. Curiously the city centre is fairly low on sights, but there are important clusters of Bauhaus buildings in both the northern and southern quarters, plus several lovely areas of greenery.

The Bauhausgebäude and the Meisterhäuser

The **Bauhausgebäude** (guided tours mid-Feb to Oct Mon–Fri at 11am & 2pm, Sat & Sun at 11am, 2pm & 4pm; Nov to mid-Feb daily at 11am & 2pm; *www.bauhaus-dessau.de*; DM11/€5.50), one of the seminal buildings of the twentieth century, stands just west of the Hauptbahnhof on Gropiusallee, and can be reached in about five minutes from the rear exit via Schwabestrasse and Bauhausstrasse. A striking-looking structure even today, it was a sensation when the Bauhaus director, **Walter Gropius**, designed it in 1925 as the new custom-built headquarters for the school on its move here from Weimar (see p.958). Built according to the very latest methods around a steel and concrete skeleton with much use of light-admitting glass, it was the forerunner of architectural styles that would not come into their own until the 1950s and 1960s. There are actually three interconnected structures – one with the classrooms, a second with the workshops, the third the student residence. Following a comprehensive restoration programme in the 1970s (the Bauhausgebäude was damaged in World War II and not properly restored), an art and design college was re-established here. The workshop wing – whose starkly Cubist appearance has inspired countless buildings around the world – houses the **Bauhausmuseum** (Tues–Sun 10am–5/6pm; DM5/€2.50). This contains an enormous collection of furniture, ceramics, graphics and photographs detailing the work done here, with background information about the Germany of the 1920s.

Ten minutes' walk north of the Bauhausgebäude itself, at the beginning of Ebertallee, are the **Meisterhäuser**, a collection of seven houses built for the senior staff of the school. Gropius, who was again responsible for the design, lived in the first house in the scheme, which was later occupied in turn by the subsequent directors, Hannes Meyer and Mies van der Rohe; the others were the homes of Moholy-Nagy, Feininger, Muche, Schlemmer, Kandinsky and Klee. These angular buildings were revolutionary for 1926, though the passing of years and familiarity with styles of architecture derived from Gropius and others lessens their impact today. Following their recent restoration, the **Kandinskyhaus** and the **Kleehaus** (both Tues–Sun 10am–5pm; *www.meisterhaeuser.de*; DM8/€4) have been made accessible to the public. The **Feiningerhaus** (same times and ticket) is now home to the **Kurt-Weill-Zentrum**, a display on the work of the Dessau-born composer. Best known for *The Threepenny Opera* and other collaborations with Bertolt Brecht, Weill was one of the twentieth century's most versatile and distinctive musicians, with a legacy ranging from symphonies to Broadway musicals.

About fifteen minutes' walk north of here, overlooking a horseshoe bend in the Elbe, is the **Kornhaus**, a restaurant-cum-dance hall by Carl Fieger, one of Gropius's assistants. With the fine views over the river from its terrace, it makes a good spot for a relaxing break from sightseeing.

The Georgium and the city centre

Immediately to the northwest of the Hauptbahnhof is the **Georgium**, the most accessible of the eighteenth-century parks to be found in and around the city. At its heart stands the modest-sized and graceful Neoclassical **Schloss Georgium** (Tues–Sun

10am–5pm; DM5/€2.50) by Friedrich Wilhelm von Erdmannsdorff, who is best known for his work at nearby Wörlitz. The collection of old masters inside includes works by Cranach, Rubens, Hals and Dou; there are also a large number of official portraits of members of the ruling house, many by J.F.A. Tischbein. It's worth walking through the shady park itself, which is dotted with pools and artificial ruins. At its eastern end, just across Georgenallee, is the **Lehrpark**, planted with 125 different kinds of tree and home to numerous semi-captive small animals.

The few surviving old buildings in the city centre are the **Stadtbibliothek**, which lies just north of Schlossplatz, and, on the square itself, the *fin-de-siècle* **Rathaus** and the **Marienkirche**. Although the last of these, the most southerly of the brick Gothic churches so characteristic of northern Germany, was badly damaged in the war and left as a ruin throughout the entire GDR era, it has now been rebuilt. Its **tower** (April–Oct Sat & Sun 10am–5pm; DM4/€2) contains a small local history display and can be climbed for a view over the city. However, the **Schloss** itself is probably too far gone for any kind of meaningful restoration: the fragment known as the Johannbau is all that remains of what must once have been a splendid Renaissance palace.

A few minutes' walk west of here, on August-Bebel-Platz, is Gropius's **Arbeitsamt**, an employment office designed at the end of the 1920s, nowadays a health centre. The building consists of a semicircular hall, well lit by glass skylights, joined to a two-storey administration building. It was built to achieve maximum efficiency, serving job-seekers as quickly as possible – something that was to become an urgent necessity after the start of the Depression in 1929.

The outskirts

A few kilometres south of town, reached by tram #1 from the Hauptbahnhof or the centre to Damaschkestrasse, is the suburb of **Törten**, a purpose-built settlement designed under the direction of Gropius to provide decent living conditions for Dessau's working-class population. The earliest buildings include the large **Konsumgebäude** in the middle of the scheme and the rows of houses along Klein Ring, Mittel Ring and Doppel Reihe; a second phase, constructed to designs by Hannes Meyer, added the **Laubenganghäuser**, the monumental apartment buildings on Peterholzstrasse. Unfortunately, the Bauhaus buildings are now somewhat engulfed by later developments. Nevertheless, fans of the school should definitely come out here to see two of its finest products – the austere, appropriately named **Stahlhaus** (Steel House) by Georg Muche, and the futuristic **Haus Fieger**, built by Carl Fieger as his own home. Both are among the detached houses standing in their own gardens at the southern end of Südstrasse.

In the outer fringes of Dessau are two more palace-park complexes. The older of these is **Schloss Mosigkau** (guided tours Tues–Sun 11am–5/6pm; DM8/€4) in the western suburb of the same name, which can be reached by bus #D or #L or mainline train. Designed by Georg von Knobelsdorff, court architect to Frederick the Great, it contains a fine array of *objets d'art* and seventeenth-century Dutch and Flemish paintings, including works by Rubens and Jordaens and Van Dyck's *Portrait of Wilhelm II of Oranien-Nassau*.

Schloss Luisium (guided tours Tues–Sun 10am–4/5pm; DM8/€4), set in an English-style park with fake ruins, grottoes and sculpture at the northeastern extremity of the city near the terminus of bus #G, is another small Neoclassical summer palace by Erdmannsdorff. The ground-floor **Festsaal** is adorned with reliefs, stucco and paintings; the upper chambers are contrastingly intimate in character.

Practicalities

Dessau's **tourist office** is at Zerbster Str. 2c (Mon–Fri 9am–6/7pm, Sat 9/10am–1pm; ☎03 40/24 14 42, fax 2 04 11 42, *www.dessau.de*). Here you can buy the **DessauCard**, which costs DM15/€7.50 for three days, and covers local transportation costs plus entry to many of the sights.

There's a reasonable provision of **private rooms** (①–③). Alternatively, there are several **pensions**, including *Bürgerhaus*, Mendelssohnstr. 43 (☎03 40/2 20 45 28; ③), *Süd*, Heidestr. 181 (☎03 40/8 82 51 84, *www.pension-sued.de*; ④), and *An der Sieben Säulen*, Ebertallee 66 (☎03 40/61 96 20; ④). The main central **hotels** are *Astron*, Zerbster Str. 29 (☎03 40/2 51 40; ④), and *Steigenberger Avance* on Friedensplatz (☎03 40/2 51 50; ⑦–⑨), which is decked out in Bauhaus style. An enticing alternative to these is *Zum Kleinen Prinzen*, Erich-Weinert-Str. 16 (☎03 40/51 70 71; ⑤) in Mosigkau. Dessau also has a **youth hostel** at Waldkaterweg 11 (☎ & fax 0340/61 94 52; DM21/€10.50 or DM26/€13); take bus #K from the Hauptbahnhof for four stops. The **campsite** is at An der Adria 1 (☎03 40/2 16 09 45) in the eastern lakeside suburb of Mildensee, reached by bus #B or #G.

There are recommendable **restaurants** in each of the three hotels listed above. Alternatives for a full sit-down meal are *Dessauer Bierstuben*, Hobuschgasse 2, *Restaurant am Museum*, Franzstr. 90, and the *Ratskeller* in the Rathaus. Just south of Törten is *Jägerklause*, Alte Leipziger Str. 76, which specializes in game dishes. The *Kornhaus*, Kornhausstr. 146, is the obvious destination when visiting the Bauhaus buildings (see p.931). In the Bauhausgebäude itself, there's a **café** serving coffee, cakes and snacks; while the *Teehäuschen* in the Stadtpark at the western edge of the city centre is a tea house which also serves full meals.

A varied **cultural programme**, encompassing opera, musicals, dance, drama and concerts by the Anhaltische Philharmonie, is performed at the Anhaltisches Theater, Friedensplatz 1a (☎03 40/2 51 10).

Wörlitz

WÖRLITZ, which lies 18km east of Dessau, seems a world away in spirit: there's no sign of industrial blight here, just a quiet rural village destined to prosper as one of eastern Germany's greatest tourist magnets. For that, it can thank Leopold Friedrich Franz of Anhalt-Dessau, an enlightened despot who commissioned Friedrich Wilhelm von Erdmannsdorff, Anhalt's court architect, to upgrade his family's old hunting seat into the crowning showpiece of the principality's group of landscaped gardens. In the village itself are a number of buildings by Erdmannsdorff, including the central Markt with the Rathaus, a brewery and a farm.

The **Schlosspark** seems to grow seamlessly out of the village, an embryonic relationship inspired by the then revolutionary intention that the public should be free to enjoy the park at all times – hence the lack of entrance barriers. The layout of the park, with its carefully planned axes and perspectives, was strongly influenced by the spirit of the Age of Reason and the theoretical writings of Rousseau and Winckelmann. It's a very conscious act of homage to England, then in the first throes of the Industrial Revolution, which had made a great impression on both Prince Leopold and Erdmannsdorff when they travelled there together. In particular, it copies the very English idea of a country house with a working estate, a concept then completely foreign to Germany, where the aristocracy retained a far greater degree of feudalistic political power and hence generally resided in urban palaces, creating gardens for purely private recreational use.

To further emphasize the narrowing of the gap between rulers and ruled, the pristine white **Schloss** (guided tours March–Oct Mon 1–5/6pm; Tues–Sun 10am–5/6pm; DM8/€4) was built right beside the village, at the edge rather than the middle of the park. Strongly influenced by the neo-Palladian stately homes of England, it marked the German debut of full-blooded Neoclassicism. Inside, there's none of the bombast normally found in German palaces; instead, everything is on an intimate scale. There are a number of impressive antique statues, the most important being the *Amazon of Wörlitz*, a Roman copy of a lost Greek original. Pick of a choice group of old master paintings is Rubens' *Alexander the Great Crowning Roxana*.

To the rear of the Schloss is the elliptical **Wörlitzer See**, the largest of the park's four lakes, which are interconnected by means of canals. It's overlooked by the circular **Synagoge**, which, in a sad reversal of the original ideals of Wörlitz, had its interior burnt out on *Kristallnacht*. To reach the main gardens you have to take a ferry over the lake from here, but you can avoid the expense by making a detour east to the least visited but perhaps the most attractive part of the park. At the **Grotto der Egeria**, which stands opposite the **Stein**, an island with a number of fake Roman ruins, the path swings north, passing over a miniature version of the Industrial Revolution's symbol, the Iron Bridge in Shropshire, to the lakeside **Pantheon**, a mini-version of its great Roman counterpart.

West of here, on the northern shore of the Wörlitzer See, the central **Schochs Garten** is dotted with mock-classical statues, urns and sarcophagi, plus temples to Flora and Venus. The wider Historicist sympathies marking the beginnings of Romanticism are shown by the inexhaustible types of **bridges** – chain, swing, stepped, floating and arched being just some of the varieties. An even clearer indication of this trend comes with the second of the palaces, the **Gotisches Haus** (guided tours as for Schloss; DM5/€2.50), which presents a somewhat squat, dreamlike vision of the long-neglected Gothic style. The interior furnishings cunningly mix the genuine and the pastiche; among the former are a roomful of paintings by Cranach. At the southernmost end of the park are a number of islands. Largest of these is **Neumarks Garten**, which features a labyrinth, a pergola, a library and an exhibition building.

Practicalities

To see Wörlitz properly, you really need the best part of a day: it takes several hours just to walk round the entire length of the park – and there are surprises in even the most far-flung corners. If possible, avoid weekends and holidays, when an uncomfortably large number of people throng the immediate vicinity of the Schloss. Unfortunately, the most atmospheric way to approach the village – on the Wörlitzer Eisenbahn, a **train** which leaves from its own station just north of Dessau's Hauptbahnhof – is only possible on Wednesdays, Saturdays and Sundays between Easter and October; two return journeys are made each day, and historic locomotives are sometimes used. Otherwise, there's a very regular **bus** link with Dessau and a somewhat less frequent one with Wittenberg.

The **tourist office** (April–Oct daily 9am–6pm; Nov–March Mon–Fri 9am–4pm; ☎ & fax 03 49 05/2 02 16, *www.woerlitz.de*) is at Neuer Wall 103, just south of the park. There are more than a dozen **private houses** (①–②) in the village with rooms to rent. Additionally, there are three very fine **hotels**: *Parkhotel*, Erdmannsdorffstr. 62 (☎03 49 05/2 03 22; ⑤); *Zum Stein*, Erdmannsdorffstr. 228 (☎03 49 05/5 00; ⑥); and *Wörlitzer Hof*, Markt 96 (☎03 49 05/41 10; ⑥). All of these have **restaurants** and beer gardens.

Wittenberg

It's seems hard to believe such a small and unassuming town as **WITTENBERG**, which lies 35km east of Dessau on the main Berlin–Halle rail line, played a pivotal role in the history of Europe. Although the capital of Electoral Saxony, it stretched for no more than 1.5km along a sandbank on the north side of the Elbe and had a population of just 2500 at the time when **Martin Luther** formulated his 95 theses attacking the corrupt trade in indulgences and so launched the Protestant Reformation.

LUTHER'S 95 THESES

Luther, then an Augustinian monk, came to give philosophy lectures in 1508 at the University of Wittenberg, settling permanently in the town three years later, whereupon he was appointed to the chair of biblical studies and quickly established a reputation as its star teacher. The subsequent course of the Reform movement was directed by Luther and his associates from Wittenberg, earning it the nickname of "the Protestant Rome".

The issue which finally triggered the Reformation was the trade in **indulgences**, a blatantly corrupt practice used by the Church for raising revenues. Their purchase enabled the buyer to gain some form of remission of sin. Many of the great medieval cathedrals were largely funded from this racket; ironically enough, Wittenberg University was itself financially dependent on cash raised from indulgences sold at the Schlosskirche on All Saints' Day each year.

Luther's theses were conceived in reaction against the campaign mounted in 1517 by the most renowned and skilful indulgence salesman, the Dominican friar **Johann Tetzel**. One of the main beneficiaries was the luxury-loving Pope Leo X, who required extra money for the rebuilding of St Peter's in Rome. Luther was incensed on two counts – from a political point of view he saw his beloved Germany being bled dry by Italian popes; and from the perspective of a devout monk he regarded the whole trade as outright blasphemy. In formulating his theses, he mounted an audacious attack on both these fronts; by pinning them to the door of the Schlosskirche, he was following the accepted practice for initiating a scholarly dispute. The matter at first seemed a monkish quarrel, bound up in the long-running rivalry between the Augustinians and Dominicans, and Tetzel retaliated by formulating 122 antitheses. However, Luther's theses were translated into German, and gained immediate and powerful popular support. He broadened his attack on indulgences to a more general repudiation of the religious and political status quo. Within a couple of years, Luther was regarded as the veritable champion of the nation – the "German Hercules".

Nowadays bearing the official designation of Lutherstadt Wittenberg, the town shows few signs of the usual GDR-era neglect. This is because a comprehensive restoration programme was carried out in 1983 to mark the 500th anniversary of Luther's birth, an event preceded by a stealthy political rehabilitation of the reformer, hitherto regarded as a great historical villain for his opposition to the Peasants' War of 1525. However, further restoration work, which is still ongoing, has been necessary, in part because of the increased volume of tourism which has ensued since Wittenberg was given a joint UNESCO World Heritage listing with Eisleben in 1997.

The Town

All Wittenberg's historic sights are within the confines of the Altstadt. Although the university at which Luther taught was shut down in 1815 and incorporated into that of Halle, there has been a renewal of academic life revolving around a theology faculty which is a leading centre of Protestant thought.

Collegienstrasse

At the eastern end of Wittenberg's main street, Collegienstrasse, is the **Luthereiche**, an oak planted on the exact spot where, in December 1520, Luther burned the papal bull threatening him with excommunication if he failed to retract his views.

About halfway down the street, at no. 54, is the **Augusteum**, the former medical faculty building of the university. On the southern side of its courtyard stands the **Lutherhalle** (previously April–Sept Tues–Sun 9am–6pm; Oct–March Tues–Sun 10am–5pm; *www.MartinLuther.de*; DM7/€3.50; currently closed for restoration), which was originally the Augustinian monastery that Luther entered on arriving in Wittenberg. When this was dissolved at the beginning of the Reformation, part of it was made into a hall of residence for students, while the rest was given to Luther as a home for himself and his family. Entry to the latter is via the ornate **Katharinenportal**, a birthday gift to Luther from his wife, the former Cistercian nun Katharina von Bora, in 1540. Of the interiors, particularly intriguing is the **Lutherstube**, a grand hall with a coffered wooden ceiling and Renaissance tiled oven. The Lutherhalle contains the world's most important collection of objects related to the history of Reformation. However, only a small part of this has been on view in the past, and the main purpose of the current restoration work is to double the previous display area. Reopening is scheduled for October 2002, the 500th anniversary of the foundation of Wittenberg University. In the meantime, selections from the museum's holdings can be seen in the Rathaus and the Cranachhaus (see below).

A couple of doors down from the Lutherhaus at Collegienstr. 60 is the **Melanchthonhaus** (April–Sept Tues–Sun 9am–6pm; Oct–March Tues–Sun 10am–5pm; DM5/€2.50, or DM10/€5 including the temporary exhibitions in the Rathaus and Cranachhaus), a Renaissance mansion with a gable that resembles fingers rising above an outstretched palm. It was the home of Luther's closest lieutenant and the greatest scholar of the Reformation period, **Philipp Schwarzerd** – who is generally known as **Melanchthon** – from 1536 until his death in 1560. Melanchthon came to Wittenberg as professor of Greek in 1519, when aged just 21, and soon found himself caught up in the dramatic events which had begun there two years previously. Though he lacked Luther's self-assuredness, he possessed a sharper intellect and was primarily responsible for the precise articulation of the new Protestant doctrines: the Augsburg Confession, the definitive statement of the Lutheran faith, is chiefly his work. The displays, which have recently been revamped using modern presentation techniques, commemorate his life and career.

Marktplatz

Collegienstrasse terminates at the **Marktplatz**, on which stand memorials to the two great Reformers. The **Lutherdenkmal** was erected in 1821, with a statue by the great Berlin Neoclassical sculptor Johann Gottfried Schadow topped with a cage-like canopy designed by Schinkel. The similarly styled **Melanchthondenkmal** was not added until 1860.

Prominent among the imposing Renaissance buildings lining the square is the former **Rathaus**, an august gabled edifice with a richly decorated portal adorned with allegorical figures. Until September 15, 2002, it will host an exhibition (same times and ticket as for the Melanchthonhaus) of many of the key items of Lutherabilia normally displayed in the Lutherhalle, including the originals of Luther's own desk and the pulpit from which he normally preached, as well as first editions of his books. Also on the square is the recently restored **Cranachhaus** (same times and ticket), which belonged to one of Luther's immediate circle, **Lucas Cranach the Elder**, court painter to the Electors of Saxony. Cranach had an astonishingly successful career in Wittenberg, not only as a prolific artist who ran a picture workshop, but also as a local businessman and politician, who was for several years the mayor of the town. The exhibition from the holdings of the Lutherhalle, which runs for the same period as that in the Rathaus, will concentrate on Cranach's role as chief pictorial propagandist for the Reformation, and include his celebrated didactic painting illustrating *The Ten Commandments*.

Rising high above the row of houses at the eastern end of Marktplatz is the **Stadtkirche St Marien**. This twin-towered Gothic church is Wittenberg's oldest surviving building; the choir dates back to around 1300, though work on the rest went on until 1470, while the distinctive octagonal turrets were only added after the Reformation. Luther, who often preached in the church, was married there in 1525, while each of his six children were baptized in the magnificent late Gothic **font**, which was made by Hermann Vischer, founder of the renowned Nürnberg dynasty of bronze-casters. The church's walls are hung with a splendid series of carved and painted **epitaphs**, the finest being that to Lucas Cranach the Younger. However, the most eye-catching decorative feature is the large and complex **Reformation altar** by Cranach the Elder. In the central scene of *The Last Supper*, Luther is shown as the disciple receiving the cup; in the predella he preaches on the theme of the crucified Christ; while other leading figures of the Reformation, including Melanchthon and Elector Frederick the Wise, are featured on the wings.

The Schlosskirche and the Residenzschloss

Schloss-Strasse leads west from Marktplatz to the far end of the Altstadt, and the **Schlosskirche**, which is late Gothic by origin, but extensively remodelled in the nineteenth century. The famous wooden **doors** where Luther nailed his theses on October 31, 1517, were destroyed during the Seven Years War; their heavy bronze replacements were installed in 1858 to commemorate the 375th anniversary of Luther's birth, and have the Latin texts of the 95 theses inscribed on them. More or less opposite the doorway of the church are the simple tombs of Luther and Melanchthon. The rest of the interior is a riot of statues, reliefs, portraits and epitaphs of local worthies. Look out for the bronze epitaph to Frederick the Wise, and the pair of large alabaster statues of the same Elector and his heir, John the Steadfast. You can also ascend the **tower** (Mon–Fri 2–4pm, Sat & Sun 10am–noon & 2–4pm; DM1/€0.50) for a view over the town.

The Schlosskirche is part of the **Residenzschloss**, though this once-resplendent Renaissance palace is but a shadow of its former self, having been repeatedly ravaged by fire and war. These days, it houses a youth hostel, reached via an unusual exterior staircase in the western wing. The same wing is also home to the **Museum für Natur- und Völkerkunde** (Tues–Sun 9am–5pm; DM2/€1), which has natural history and ethnography collections.

Practicalities

Wittenberg's **Hauptbahnhof** is a few minutes' walk east of the Altstadt; some west-bound slow trains also stop at **Bahnhof Elbtor**, just south of the Markt. The **tourist office** is at Schlossplatz 2 (March–Oct Mon–Fri 9am–6pm, Sat 10am–3pm, Sun 11am–4pm; Nov–Feb Mon–Fri 10am–4pm, Sat 10am–2pm, Sun 11am–3pm; ☎0 34 91/49 86 10, fax 49 86 11, *www.wittenberg.de*).

In addition to the **youth hostel**, with its enticing location in the Residenzschloss (☎ & fax 0 34 91/40 32 55; DM21/€10.50 or DM26/€13), there are plenty of **private rooms** (①–③) for rent. Budget rates are also available at a number of **pensions**, some of which are in the Altstadt, including *Central*, Mittelstr. 20 (☎0 34 91/41 15 72; ③), and *Zur Elbe*, Elbstr. 4a (☎0 34 91/41 90 24; ③). Wittenberg also has a good choice of **hotels**. Those with a central location are *Acron*, Am Hauptbahnhof 3 (☎0 34 91/4 33 20; ④), *Am Schwanenteich*, Töpferstr. 1 (☎0 34 91/41 10 34; ⑤), *Art*, Puschkinstr. 15 (☎0 34 91/46 73 10; ⑤), and *Park Inn*, Neustr. 7–10 (☎0 34 91/46 10; ⑥–⑧). There are also a couple of enticing options in the outskirts: *Klabautermann*, 3km west of the centre at Dessauer Str. 93 (☎0 34 91/66 21 49; ④), and *Grüne Tanne*, 2km northwest at Am Teich 1 (☎0 34 91/62 90; ④–⑥).

The last three hotels listed above all have good **restaurants**, with *Klabautermann* being well known for its fish specialities. Other options include: *Haus des Handwerks*, Collegienstr. 53a, which offers tasty no-nonsense Teutonic cuisine at reasonable prices; the swanky *Schlosskeller*, Schlossplatz 1; and the gimmicky *Schlossfreiheit*, which offers Reformation-era dishes, at Coswiger Str. 24 just off the Markt.

Halle

When the Land of Saxony-Anhalt was created in 1947, the old market town and salt-producing centre of **HALLE** was chosen as capital. It recommended itself to the authorities on account of its position at the heart of one of eastern Germany's largest industrial belts and its distinguished Socialist pedigree. Communist favour, however, proved a severe disadvantage when it competed with Magdeburg to become capital of the resurrected Land in 1990. In compensation, it became the Land's largest city by the incorporation of Halle-Neustadt (the most important new town built during the GDR period) on the opposite side of the Saale, and still holds this status, despite suffering heavy depopulation over the past decade. Relatively little damaged in World War II, Halle ranks, along with Erfurt, as the German city most reminiscent of its prewar self. It has been racked by pollution, but still preserves a nicely varied roster of sights.

Arrival, information and accommodation

Halle's **Hauptbahnhof** is just beyond the southeastern edge of the city centre. From there, a pedestrian underpass leads under Riebeckplatz, a monumental Stalinist-style square-cum-highway intersection, to Leipziger Strasse, the main shopping street. The **tourist office** (May–Sept Mon–Fri 10am–6pm, Sat & Sun 10am–2pm; Oct–April closed Sun; ☎03 45/2 02 33 40, fax 50 27 98, *www.halle-tourist.de*) is in the Roter Turm, Marktplatz 1.

Private rooms (②–④) can be booked via the tourist office's special phone number (☎03 45/2 02 83 71). The **youth hostel** occupies a Jugendstil villa in the northern part of the Uni-Viertel at August-Bebel-Str. 48a (☎03 45/2 02 47 16, fax 2 02 51 72; DM24/€12 or DM29/€14.50). A dramatic increase in the number of **hotels** in the past few years means that the middle and upper ranges are very well served, whereas budget choices are still quite scarce.

Hotels and Pensions

Am Alten Markt, Schmeerstr. 3 (☎03 45/5 21 14 11, fax 5 23 29 56). Centrally located pension in a renovated nineteenth-century tenement. ④.

Ankerhof, Ankerstr. 2a (☎03 45/2 32 32 00, fax 232 32 19). Fine new hotel and restaurant in a converted nineteenth-century warehouse. ⑥.

Apart, Kohlschütterstr. 5 (☎03 45/5 29 50, fax 5 25 92 00, *www.apart-hotels.de*). Located midway between the city centre and Giebichenstein, this is the most luxurious of several new hotels set up in Jugendstil buildings, with a sauna, solarium and whirlpool among the facilities. ④–⑥.

Bergschänke, Heidestr. 1, Nietleben (☎03 45/64 74 53, fax 8 05 76 53). Moderately priced hotel with café-restaurant on the edge of the heathland in the northwestern outskirts of Halle, not far from the S-Bahn terminus of Dölau. ④.

Dessauer Hof, Paracelsusstr. 9 (☎03 45/2 90 90 28, fax 2 90 90 20). Well-maintained pension near the Jugendstil Wasserturm at the northeastern edge of the city centre. It's an adjunct to Halle's oldest restaurant, *Gasthaus Zum Tagelöhner*, which serves inexpensive traditional fare, being well-known locally for its gargantuan portions of spare ribs. ③.

Kaffeehaus Sasse, Geiststr. 22 (☎03 45/23 33 80, fax 2 83 63 55). This hotel and café occupy a renovated Jugendstil apartment block just north of the centre. ⑤.

Martha-Haus, Adam-Kuckhoff-Str. 5–8 (☎03 45/5 10 80, fax 5 10 85 15). Run under the auspices of the Protestant churches, this immaculate hotel occupies a handsome old house in a quiet central street. ⑥.

Rotes Ross, Leipziger Str. 76 (☎03 45/2 92 92 20, fax 2 92 92 22; *www.kempinski.de*). Part of the Kempinski chain, this stylishly furnished luxury hotel on the main street boasts a fitness centre with whirlpool, sauna, solarium and steam baths. ⑧.

Saaletal, Fischerweg 3, Lettin (☎03 45/5 50 86 18, fax 5 50 86 18). One of the cheapest places to stay in the city, this pension lies 7km north of the centre on the route of bus #21. ②.

HALLE

ACCOMMODATION
4 Am Alten Markt
3 Ankerhof
2 Martha-Haus
5 Roles Ross
6 Schweizer Hof
1 Youth Hostel

Schweizer Hof, Waisenhausring 15 (☎03 45/2 02 6392, fax 50 30 68). Among the most characterful of the upmarket hotels in the centre. Its restaurant (closed Sun evening & Mon lunchtime) is one of the best in the city. ⑨.

The City

The boundaries of Halle's **Altstadt** are clearly defined by the inner ring road, which follows the course of the fortifications, the only surviving parts of which are some fragments of wall plus a single gateway, the **Leipziger Tor**. Somewhat unusually, several of the most important historic monuments lie outside this compact central area, and it really requires at least a couple of days to cover all the principal sights.

Marktplatz

Halle's **Marktplatz**, which is surveyed by a pensive statue of the city's favourite son, the composer **George Frideric Handel** (see box below), immediately impresses by virtue of its monumental dimensions and its many-towered skyline. Unfortunately, the square's beauty is impaired by mass of tram rails and cables. A far less excusable eyesore is the gallery, now housing the tourist office, which was added in the 1970s to the **Roter Turm** (Red Tower), a freestanding late Gothic belfry topped by an engagingly fantastical spire with little corner turrets. Outside is a **statue of Roland**, an eighteenth-century stone copy of the wooden original, erected when Halle was a member of the Hansa as an assertion of the city's desire for independence from its feudal overlords, the Magdeburg archbishops.

The **Marktkirche Unser Lieben Frauen** (Mon, Tues & Thurs–Sat 10am–noon & 3–6pm, Wed 3–6pm, Sun 11am–noon) opposite is a real oddity, which owes its existence to Cardinal Albrecht von Brandenburg, Archbishop of Magdeburg and Mainz, who planned to turn Halle into a showpiece Catholic city to spearhead a counter-attack on the Wittenberg-led Reformation. Originally, the **Hausmannstürme** (Watchman's Towers) to the east, which can be ascended (Mon–Sat at 3.30pm; DM5/€2.50) for a view over the city, and the **Blaue Türme** (Blue Towers) to the west, belonged to two different Romanesque churches. These were demolished in 1529 and the two pairs of towers linked up by a brand-new hall church in the Flamboyant Gothic style. An unknown follower of Cranach, dubbed the Master of Annaberg, painted its **high altar**, which immodestly features a large portrait of Cardinal Albrecht flanked by SS Mary

---

GEORGE FRIDERIC HANDEL (1685–1759)

The career of the man born as Georg Friedrich Händel differs starkly from that of any previous German musician. Unattracted by the musician's normal, very provincial existence as *Kapellmeister* to a court, or *Kantor* in a large church (roles which occupied his contemporary J.S. Bach throughout his entire life), Handel embarked on a dazzling peripatetic career as a virtuoso keyboard player and composer. Notwithstanding his devout Protestant faith, he was lionized during his long sojourn in Italy, and successfully blended the showy Italianate forms with solid German counterpoint into a unique musical language of his own. On his return to Germany, he had a spell as musical director to the court at Hannover.

Anticipating the succession of his patron to the British throne, he moved to London, where he stayed for the rest of his life. There he found his true spiritual home – he abandoned his previously footloose existence altogether, changing both his name and nationality – and entered his most productive creative phase, in which his favoured format increasingly became oratorios set to English texts. Of these, the sublime *Messiah* has become one of the great setpieces of Protestant culture, whose annual performance is a ritual performed by choirs, both amateur and professional, all round the world.

Magdalene, John the Evangelist and Catherine; he also turns up at the far right of the predella in the group of saints adoring the Madonna and Child. A few years after the Marktkirche was completed, Halle adopted the Reformation; the church was then converted to Protestant use. A later adornment was the tiny Baroque **organ**, on which Handel received lessons; it can be heard on Tuesdays and Thursdays at 4pm.

The small Renaissance palace at no. 13 on the square, the **Marktschlösschen**, has a commercial gallery on the ground floor, while the upstairs rooms house the **Musikinstrumenten-Ausstellung** (Wed–Sun 1–5pm; DM3/€1.50), a notable collection of all kinds of historical musical instruments.

The northern Altstadt

Immediately north of Marktplatz is a maze of run-down but nonetheless evocative old streets. At Grosse Nikolaistr. 5 is the **Händelhaus** (Mon–Wed & Fri–Sun 9am–5.30pm, Thurs 9am–7pm; DM5/€2.50, free Thurs), the large Baroque mansion where the great composer was born. It contains extensive documentation on his life and times, and you can listen on headphones to many of Handel's most famous works.

A couple of minutes' walk west of the Händelhaus is the **Dom** (June–Oct Mon–Sat 2–4pm). This was built as the church of a Dominican friary, and the basic structure employs the simple, unadorned forms favoured by the preaching orders. Its present eccentric appearance, however, is largely due to a remodelling commissioned by Cardinal Albrecht, who took it over to serve as his court church. A curious gabled upper storey in brick, one of the earliest Renaissance constructions in central Germany, was tacked onto the old building; the entrance portal and interior staircase are also in this style. Most of the lavish interior decorations have been dispersed, though seventeen over-life-sized **statues of saints** by Peter Schroh remain *in situ*. A later Baroque transformation, carried out after the Dom became a Protestant parish church, brought the high altar and the organ, at which Handel presided as a teenager.

On the south side of the Dom is the **Neue Residenz**, a Tuscan-style *palazzo* which the cardinal hoped to develop into the Catholic answer to Wittenberg University, but which, in a neat twist of fate, is used by the institution now known as the Martin-Luther-Universität Halle-Wittenberg. Part of the building is given over to the **Geiseltalmuseum** (Mon–Fri 9am–noon & 1–5pm; also second and fourth Sat & Sun of the month 9am–1pm; free), a fascinating collection of fossils, reckoned to be fifty million years old, found perfectly preserved in the brown coal region of the Geisel valley just south of the city.

A couple of blocks north of the Dom is the **Moritzburg**, constructed as a citadel against the rebellious burghers by Archbishop Ernst at the end of the fifteenth century, but converted into a palace a generation later under Cardinal Albrecht. Some splendid Renaissance chambers, which have not been accessible to the public for a very long time, are currently under restoration and should open in the near future, possibly in 2002. A satirical cabaret and a student club occupy the east tower, while the former palace chapel, the **Magdalenenkapelle**, has been taken over by a Calvinist congregation. The south and west wings are home to the **Staatliche Galerie** (Tues 11am–8.30pm, Wed–Sun 10am–6pm; *www.moritzburg.halle.de*; DM5/€2.50, free on Tues). In the vaulted cellars is a good decorative arts section, the most notable pieces being statues from demolished buildings. Elsewhere, the emphasis is on painting and sculpture of the nineteenth and twentieth centuries: Klimt, Kirchner, Marc, Munch, Beckmann and Barlach are among those represented.

The southern Altstadt

From the Marktplatz, Schmeerstrasse leads to the **Alter Markt**, the elongated original square with the **Eselbrunnen** (Donkey Fountain) in the centre, which was used for markets until supplanted by its much larger successor. **Rannische Strasse**, which leads south from the intersection of Schmeerstrasse and Alter Markt, boasts a superb array of Renaissance, Baroque and Rococo mansions, among which nos. 10, 17, 20 and 21 are particularly outstanding.

Beyond the western end of Alter Markt is the fifteenth-century **Moritzkirche**, the Catholic parish church. From outside, it presents an austere picture, an appearance accentuated by the fact that it's built directly onto one of the surviving sections of the medieval walls. The hall interior, in contrast, is light and spacious, with elaborate star and network vaults and limpid sculptures by Conrad von Einbeck, the church's master mason; these include a poignant *Man of Sorrows* and a sharply characterized *Bust of a Man*, traditionally assumed to be a self-portrait.

The Franckesche Stiftungen

Immediately south of the Altstadt, across the ugly ring road, is Halle's most singular sight, the vast complex of buildings – forming what is in effect a complete township – known as the **Franckesche Stiftungen**. The greatest single legacy of the evangelical Pietist movement, it's named in honour of its founder, **August Hermann Francke**, who came to Halle in 1692 to serve both as Professor of Greek and Oriental Languages and as pastor of the rundown parish of Glaucha. On Easter Day 1695, an anonymous donation placed in his church poor box inspired Francke to set up a school for needy children. Three years later, he established an orphanage as well, and in due course his foundation spawned several educational institutions, a prestigious public library and a number of workshops. Living quarters were also built, and by the time of Francke's death in 1727, his "town within a town" had a population of almost 3000. New buildings were added right up until 1914, but the foundation was dissolved by the Communists in 1946. Although taken over by the university, the complex was thereafter allowed to fall into a state of semi-dereliction, and was in a perilous state by the time of the *Wende*. In 1991, however, the foundation was reconstituted, and is active once again in the social and educational spheres.

Although reconstruction work on the complex will take many years, the **Hauptgebäude** (Tues–Sun 10am–5pm; *www.francke-halle.de*; DM5/€2.50), a huge U-shaped structure in the plainest possible Baroque style, has already been beautifully restored. On the ground floor are an exhibition on the life of Francke and the **Cansteinsche Bibelkabinett**, a chronological display of the products of the foundation's printing workshop, which for more than two centuries was the principal Bible press in the German-speaking world. The attic contains the truly astonishing **Kunst- und Naturalienkammer**, an eighteenth-century variant on the princely cabinet of curiosities, though in this case the objects were intended not for amusement, but for pedagogic instruction. Exhibited in the centre of the room are the largest pieces: a model of the geocentric world system, flanked by globes of the earth and the heavens; an apothecary's table, with individual compartments for each drug; and models of buildings and a sailing ship. The colourful display cabinets around the walls contain an amazingly disparate array of items, including stuffed animals, preserved plants, shells, stones, weapons, coins, masks, clothes, paintings, sculptures, religious objects, mechanical models and ethnographic artefacts from around the world.

Francke's library, established in 1698, was opened to the public ten years later, and grew so quickly as a result of donations and bequests that a separate structure to house it, the **Bibliothekgebäude**, was built immediately east of the Hauptgebäude in the 1720s. The oldest secular library building in Germany, it still preserves its historic core, the so-called **Kulisse Bibliothek** (Scenery Library; Tues–Sun 10am–noon & 2–4pm; free) on the first floor. The library is named for its floor plan: the bookshelves, which are closed off by a graceful wooden gate, are arranged in the manner of a theatre set.

Elsewhere in the city

Francke, in common with many of the most notable figures from Halle's past, is buried in the **Stadtgottesacker**, which lies just to the northeast of the Altstadt, beyond the Leipziger Tor. Founded by Cardinal Albrecht, the cemetery was converted by Nickel Hoffmann into a grand galleried necropolis in the manner of the Campo Santo in Pisa. It is the only one of its type in Germany.

Likewise just beyond the confines of the Altstadt is the old saltworks, now the **Technisches Halloren- und Salinenmuseum** (Tues–Sun 10am–5pm; DM4/€2), which are set on an island formed by two arms of the Saale. It can be reached on foot in about ten minutes from either the Moritzkirche or the Neue Residenz, with the tall brick chimney which rises above the half-timbered buildings providing a useful pointer. If you come on a Sunday, you can see the last surviving saltpan being used to produce an excellent coarse-grained salt – which is on sale at the shop. At other times, you'll have to be content with seeing the machinery and the associated historical documentation.

To the north of the city centre, at Richard-Wagner-Str. 9, is the **Landesmuseum für Vorgeschichte** (Tues–Fri 9am–5pm, Sat & Sun 10am–6pm; DM4/€2), which contains an important collection of Stone, Bronze and Iron Age artefacts found in the Halle area. To get to the museum, it's best to take tram #7, which continues on to **Burg Giebichenstein** (also served by tram #8 from the centre). There are actually two castles here, both of which were destroyed in the Thirty Years War. The lower, or **Unterburg**, was first constructed in the tenth century under King Henry the Fowler, although the oldest surviving portions are mid-fifteenth-century. It was rebuilt in the Baroque period, and now serves as a school of arts and crafts. The fourteenth-century **Oberburg** (April–Oct Tues–Fri 9am–6pm, Sat & Sun 9am–6.30pm; DM4/€2), perched on the cliff above, has been left in an appropriately ruinous and overgrown state, but it's worth climbing for the sake of the sweeping view over the Saale valley.

Eating, drinking and entertainment

Halle has developed into one of the best places in the former GDR for **food** and **drink** (see "Hotels and Pensions", p.938, for further recommendations) and has by far the liveliest nightlife in Saxony-Anhalt.

Restaurants

Atlantic, Ankerstr. 3. The main fish speciality restaurant. Open Mon–Sat 3pm–midnight, Sun 11am–3pm.

Baba Jaga, Moritzzwinger 11. Serves both Russian and Ukrainian cuisine.

Barfüss, Barfüsserstr. 15. Pleasant restaurant in a newly renovated half-timbered building with inner courtyard.

Gildenhaus St Niklaus, Grosse Nikolaistr. 9–11. Traditional Gaststätte whose menu includes dishes made according to old recipes of the local saltworkers.

Mönchshof, Talamtstr. 6. Directly overlooking the Marktkirche, this is among Halle's best restaurants, yet is very moderately priced. Closed Sun evening.

Quinoa, Ludwigstr. 37. Vegan and vegetarian restaurant, about 1km south of the Altstadt.

Wirtshaus Alt Halle, Kleine Ulrichstr. 32–33. Cosy Gaststätte in a sixteenth-century timber-framed building which offers many local specialities. Evenings only; closed Fri.

Zum Mohr, Burgstr. 72. Historic inn below Burg Giebichenstein; it serves fine traditional dishes and has a summer beer garden.

Bars, cafés and café-bars

Café Austria, Kleiner Berlin 2. This new venture aims to recreate the ambience of a Viennese coffee house.

Café Nöö, Grosse Klausstr. 11. Café-bar much patronized by the alternative set; serves light meals and sometimes features live music.

Kaffeeschuppen, Kleine Ulrichstr. 11. *Szene* café-bar whose clientele includes artists, students and foreign construction workers.

Malzgarten, Grosse Brauhausstr. 5. Large beer garden alongside the Stadtmauer, with a wood-fired grill for cooking steaks and sausages.

Objekt 5, Seebener Str. 5. Student bar with live music and other artistic events.

Pierrot, Grosser Sandberg 10. Bar-disco at the forefront of the local gay scene.

Weiberwirtschaft, Robert-Franz-Ring 22. Feminist café-bar.

Zur Apotheke, Mühlberg 4a. Popular theme bar, decked out with all sorts of pharmaceutical paraphenalia.

Entertainment

The main **theatre** venues are the Opernhaus, Universitätsring 24 (☎03 45/51 10, *www.opernhaus.halle.de*), which features opera and dance; the neues theater, Grosse Ulrichstr. 50 (☎03 45/2 05 02 22), which presents wide-ranging dramatic fare; and the Steintor Varieté, Am Steintor 10 (☎03 45/2 08 02 05), which offers variety shows. There's also a Puppentheater at Mühlweg 12 and a satirical cabaret, Die Kiebitzensteiner, in the Moritzburg (both ☎03 45/5 23 35 28). **Concerts** by the Philharmonisches Staatsorchester Halle are normally held in the new Georg-Friedrich-Händel-Halle, Salzgrafenplatz 1 (☎03 45/2 92 90); smaller ensembles often play at the Händelhaus (☎03 45/50 09 00); while the Konzerthalle Ulrichskirche, a deconsecrated Gothic church at Kleine Brauhausstr. 26 (☎03 45/2 21 30 21) is generally favoured for choral music. Among the trendiest **nightspots** are the Studentenclub Turm in the Moritzburg (free admission with student ID) and Capitol, Lauchstädter Str. 1a.

Festivals include the *Händel-Festspiele* in June, featuring the music of Handel; the *Lanternenfest* on the last weekend of August; and the *Drachenfest* in October. **Cruises** on the Saale, run by Reederei Riedel (☎03 45/2 83 20 70), depart daily in summer from the landing stage immediately below Burg Giebichenstein.

Merseburg

MERSEBURG, the most venerable of the towns in the region, was a favourite royal seat in the tenth century but is now a virtual satellite of Halle. It has the misfortune to be sandwiched between two giant chemical plants, Buna-Werke and Leuna-Werke; these are nowadays operating at a very reduced capacity, but their incessant burning of lignite throughout the GDR period left the historic monuments badly scarred. Nonetheless, the upper town still retains its arresting medieval skyline, which is seen to best advantage from the bridge spanning the Saale.

Set high above the river, the **Dom** (Mon–Sat 9am–noon & 1–4/6pm, Sun 1–4/6pm; DM6/€3) was founded as a missionary bishopric in the early eleventh century, though only the crypt survives from this time. Of the thirteenth-century Transitional-style rebuilding there remain the choir, transepts and westwork, whose pair of octagonal towers contrasts well with their cylindrical counterparts at the east end. A Flamboyant Gothic hall nave was substituted in the sixteenth century. The most eye-catching furnishings are the **funerary monuments**. Look out in particular for the hauntingly hierarchical bronze memorial in the choir to the eleventh-century royal pretender Rudolf of Swabia, and the Renaissance epitaph in the north transept, cast by Hermann Vischer of Nürnberg, to Bishop Thilo von Trotha. A chapel in the cloisters houses the mid-thirteenth-century memorial to the Knight Hermann von Hagen, carved with a sense of characterization clearly inspired by the famous workshop of nearby Naumburg.

Adjoining the north side of the Dom is the stately **Schloss**, originally the residence of the prince-bishops, later of the secular dukes. Its wings range in style from Flamboyant Gothic to Baroque, though Renaissance predominates, with the superb portal and oriel being the most distinguishing features. The peace of the courtyard is constantly disturbed by the squawkings of the caged **raven**, the latest in a line dating back to the late fifteenth century. Its presence is explained by the fact that, when Bishop Thilo von Trotha's most precious ring was stolen, an innocent man was charged with the crime, tried and executed. After his death, the missing ring was found in a raven's nest, whereupon the guilty bird was imprisoned in a cage for the rest of its life, with its sin ever after being visited on a member of the same species. Most of the Schloss is used as offices, but a small part contains the **Kulturhistorisches Museum** (Tues–Sun 9am–5pm; DM2/€1), with the standard archeology and local history displays.

Practicalities

Merseburg's **Bahnhof** lies at the western edge of the town centre. The **tourist office** (Mon–Fri 9am–1pm & 2–6pm, Sat 10am–4pm; ☎0 34 61/21 41 70, fax 21 41 77) is at Burgstr. 5. There are several budget **pensions** on the opposite side of the Bahnhof from the centre: *Leisner*, Klobikauer Str. 58 (☎0 34 61/21 06 95; ③); *Elisa*, August-Bebel-Str. 23 (☎0 34 61/20 24 35; ③); *Am Park*, Gutenbergstr. 18 (☎0 34 61/21 54 72; ③); and *Luise*, Gutenbergstr. 4 (☎0 34 61/21 34 29; ③). Centrally sited **hotels** include *C'est la Vie*, König-Heinrich-Str. 47–49 (☎0 34 61/20 44 20; ⑤), and *Dessauer Hof*, Dammstr. 2–4 (☎0 34 61/2 11 45; ⑤). The best **restaurant** is the *Ratskeller*, Ölgrube 1.

Naumburg

Before the war, **NAUMBURG**, which is set on heights overlooking the Saale valley 20km upstream from Merseburg, was considered one of Germany's most beautiful and distinctive towns, thanks mainly to its peerless Dom, which shows medieval architecture and sculpture at their highest peak. Although it suffered minimal bomb damage, Naumburg fell off tourist itineraries in the GDR period and became the headquarters of a large Soviet garrison. Since the *Wende* the town has made giant steps in scraping off the grime which had smothered its buildings and is well on the way to reappearing at its best.

The Town

Naumburg was founded at the beginning of the eleventh century by Margrave Ekkehardt of Meissen. Originally a fortress, it soon afterwards became the seat of a prince-bishopric transferred from nearby Zeitz. By the beginning of the thirteenth century, the town had prospered as a market centre, and it was decided to replace the original cathedral with a spectacular new structure – the present Dom. This has dominated the skyline ever since, leaving everything else in its shadow, though most of the Altstadt is quietly attractive.

The Dom
Naumburg's **Dom** (Mon–Sat 9am–4/5/6pm, Sun noon–4/5/6pm; DM6/€3) is among the country's greatest buildings, above all for its wondrous sculptural decoration. Yet, although it was built as one of Germany's showpiece cathedrals, with choirs at both ends of the building to emphasize its imperial status and a monastery-like range of ancillary buildings, it's been no more than a Protestant parish church since 1564, when

the bishopric was suppressed following the reign of the first and last Lutheran incumbent.

Because the Dom was built at a time of rapidly changing architectural tastes, it exhibits a variety of different yet compatible styles – despite having been substantially completed in the relatively short period of fifty years. The original masons began by erecting the **east choir**, complete with its almost oriental-looking **towers**, according to florid late Romanesque principles; the cupolas added in the Baroque period further add to the exotic appearance. The transepts and the nave are Transitional in approach, whereas the marvellously harmonious **west choir**, with its polygonal apse (a replica of which was added to the east choir the following century), adopts the pure High Gothic of the great French cathedrals. Nonetheless, its towers help give it a distinctively German accent, though only the northern one dates back to this time. Its stylistic twin was added, in accordance with the original plans, at the end of the nineteenth century, as a result of the Romantic movement's frenzied enthusiasm for all things Gothic which inspired the belated completion of so many important German churches.

Pride of the interior is the assemblage of sculptures in the west choir, which rank among the all-time masterpieces of the art. They were carved by a workshop led by the so-called **Master of Naumburg**, by far the most idiosyncratic and original of all the masons who created the great European cathedrals: his ideas and techniques were at least 150 years ahead of their time, anticipating both the Renaissance and the Reformation. Though it's reasonable to suppose that he was a German, he was trained in France, after which he worked at the Dom in Mainz, where a few carvings by him can still be seen.

The polychrome **rood screen**, illustrating the Passion, is unlike anything previously found in religious art. Each of the life-sized figures of the crucified Christ, the Virgin and St John radiates an enormous sense of suffering and pathos – but recognizably human, not other-worldly. On the upper frieze, the small scenes unfold like a great drama, with plenty of anecdotal detail and a wonderfully rhythmic sense of movement imparted in the gestures and groupings of the figures. Sadly, the last two of these were destroyed by fire, and replaced by Baroque pastiches, whose feebleness serves to emphasize the Master's genius. Plants, flowers and fruits are featured on a second frieze, and on the capitals and keystones; carved with a matchless sensitivity, these are, apart from their fragmentary counterparts in Mainz, the earliest botanically accurate depictions in western art.

Very different from the rood screen, but recognizably the product of the same humanistic mind, are the twelve large **statues of the founders**, again still preserving much of their original colouring, which are placed on pedestals within the west choir. The granting of such prominent positions of honour to lay personages was, to say the least, unusual, but what is even more remarkable, given that they were long dead, is that each is given a highly distinctive and noble characterization. Particularly outstanding are the imperiously serene couple **Ekkehardt II and Uta**, who stand together on the first pillar on the north side of the apse; they've become the most famous statues in the country, symbolizing the Germans' own romantic view of their chivalrous medieval past.

Inevitably, the east choir is overshadowed by the west, though it's equally well preserved. It also has a **rood screen** – this is the only medieval church in Europe to have two – in this case a simple Romanesque structure adorned with a cycle of retouched frescoes. Ascending to the intimate **high choir**, with its elaborate late Gothic stalls, its fourteenth-century high altar and its gleaming stained-glass windows, is like eavesdropping on the past, as it can hardly have changed in centuries. Here also are two more works from the celebrated sculptural workshop – the statue of a deacon and the tomb of Bishop Dietrich II.

The rest of the town

Steinweg and its continuation Herrenstrasse – each of which has its fair share of fine houses – lead eastwards from the Dom to the central **Markt**. Dominating the square is the **Rathaus**, late Gothic by origin but remodelled in Renaissance style in the sixteenth century, when it received the huge curved gables which clearly served as a model for other mansions in the city. The Mannerist portal, a later addition, strikes a supremely self-confident note, but the building's most endearing feature is the polychrome capital at the northeastern corner, showing two dogs fighting over a bone – this symbolizes the conflict between the ruling prince-bishops and the increasingly self-confident burghers.

At no. 18 on the square is **Hohe Lilie**, a late Gothic mansion incorporating a Romanesque tower-house which is of the same vintage as the Dom. It has recently been restored in order to serve as the new home of the **Stadtmuseum** (Tues–Sun 10am–5pm; *www.museumnaumburg.de*; DM4/€2), an entertaining local history display whose star exhibit is the *Ratstrinkhorn*, the elegant late fourteenth-century municipal **drinking horn**. Also of note is the house's own **Prunkstube**, with its pair of console figures bearing the date 1526. Of the other houses on the Markt, the most imposing are the **Schlösschen** at no. 6, which was built for the one Protestant bishop, and the **Alte Residenz** at no. 7, three houses knocked together to serve as the temporary palace for Duke Moritz of Saxony while he waited for Schloss Moritzburg outside Dresden to be completed.

Rising behind the south side of the Markt is the curiously elongated **Stadtkirche St Wenzel**, which was the burghers' answer to the prince-bishop's Dom. In the Baroque period, this late Gothic church was given an interior face-lift, including the provision of an organ, highly praised by Bach, built by Zacharias Hildebrand, a pupil of the great Silbermann. Also of note are two paintings by **Cranach** – *The Adoration of the Magi* and *Christ Blessing Children*. The single **tower** (Wed–Sun 10am–5pm; DM3/€1.50), which was deliberately built higher than those of the Dom, commands a magnificent panorama over the city and the Saale valley.

More fine mansions can be seen on Jacobstrasse, which leads eastwards from the Markt. Also well worth seeing is the **Marientor** (daily 10am–5pm; free) at the northeastern edge of the inner ring road. This double gateway, one of the best preserved in the country, is the only significant reminder of the fifteenth-century fortifications which, on this evidence, must have presented a formidable obstacle to would-be invaders. In summer, the courtyard is used as a puppet theatre. At the southeastern edge of the Altstadt, at Weingarten 18, is the **Nietzsche-Haus** (Tues–Fri 2–5pm, Sat & Sun 10am–4pm; DM3/€1.50), the philosopher's home throughout his childhood and youth. Nietzsche was one of the GDR's all-time bogeymen, and it was not until well after the *Wende* that the house was restored to serve as a memorial museum.

Practicalities

Naumburg's **Hauptbahnhof**, which has good rail links with Halle, Leipzig and Weimar, is below and northwest of the historic centre, which is reached by heading along Bahnhofstrasse, then up Bergstrasse. The **tourist office** (March–Oct Mon–Fri 9am–1pm & 2–7pm, Sat 10am–4pm; Nov–Feb Mon–Fri 9am–1pm & 2–5pm; ☎0 34 45/20 16 14, fax 26 60 47, *www.naumburg.de*) is at Markt 6.

In addition to **private rooms** (①–③), there are a number of small **pensions**: *Hentschel*, Lindenhof 16 (☎0 34 45/20 12 30; ③); *St Othmar*, Othmarsplatz 7 (☎0 34 45/20 12 13; ③); *Zum Alten Krug*, Lindenring 44 (☎0 34 45/20 04 06; ④); and *Caféhaus Kattler*, Lindenring 36–37 (☎0 34 45/20 28 23; ④). There's also a good range of **hotels**: *Deutscher Hof*, Franz-Ludwig-Rasch-Str. 10 (☎0 34 45/70 27 34 or 70 61 34; ③); *St*

Marien, Marienstr. 12 (☎0 34 45/2 35 40; ④); *St Wenzel*, Friedrich-Nietzsche-Str. 21 (☎0 34 45/7 17 90; ⑤); *Zur Alten Schmiede*, Lindenring 36 (☎0 34 45/2 43 60; ⑥); and *Stadt Aachen*, Markt 11 (☎0 34 45/24 70; ⑥). The **youth hostel** is way to the south of the centre at Am Tennisplatz 9 (☎ & fax 0 34 45/70 34 22; DM24/€12 or DM29/€14.50).

With the exception of *St Marien*, all the hotels listed above have **restaurants**, with *Carolus Magnus* in *Stadt Aachen* perhaps having the edge over the others. However, it faces strong competition from the *Ratskeller* in the Rathaus, Markt 1, and *Domklause*, Herrenstr. 8. The main local **festivals** are the *Kirschfest* (Cherry Festival) on the last weekend in June and the *Weinfest* at the end of August.

Bad Kösen

By far the best base for exploring the Saale region is the spa town of **BAD KÖSEN**, which lies in the most beautiful part of the valley, 7km upstream from Naumburg, and one stop away by train. It's a quiet and restful place to stay, with a wide choice of accommodation; it also has the advantage of having excellent transport connections into the neighbouring provinces of Saxony and Thuringia – Leipzig, Jena, Weimar and Erfurt can all be reached within an hour or so.

Bad Kösen presents a rare case of the GDR state's penchant for outdated technology being a cause for thanks rather than criticism. The side of town on the southern bank of the Saale is dominated by an extraordinary set of very primitive-looking wooden structures erected in 1730 for the extraction and production of **salt**, which survived in full working order until 1945, when they were electrified. There are four separate parts to the system. Right by the river is the **Wasserrad** or waterwheel. From here, the **Kunstgestänge**, a double set of drill stems, travels to the **Soleschacht**, a well dug to a depth of 175m for the extraction of brine. The Kunstgestänge then continues up the hill to the huge 320-metre-long **Gradierwerk**, where the salt was crystallized. When the town became a spa in the middle of the nineteenth century, the Gradierwerk doubled as part of the cure facilities, because of its unusually healthy air.

Overlooking the Wasserrad is the **Romanisches Haus** (May–Sept Tues–Fri 10am–noon & 1–5pm, Sat & Sun 10am–5pm; Oct–April Tues–Fri 9am–noon & 1–4pm, Sat & Sun 9am–4pm; DM4/€2), which dates back to about 1140 and is thus the oldest surviving house in central Germany. It now contains a small museum, with displays on the history of local salt production, plus carved fragments from, and documentary material about, the Cistercian monastery of Kloster Pforta 3km to the south of the town. Also on this side of the river is the **Loreleypromenade**, which is well worth walking along for views over the town and the river. On the opposite bank is the shady **Kurpark**, in which you'll find exotic trees, floral gardens and the Neoclassical spa buildings.

From the landing pier by the Kurpark, you can take a motorboat cruise (DM4/€2 single, DM7/€3.50 return) up the Saale to two feudal castles which both date back to the twelfth century. You're deposited below the first and larger of the two, the **Rudelsburg**, which was sacked by the citizens of Naumburg in 1348 and subsequently rebuilt. Although ruinous, a great deal of masonry survives, and the layout of the defensive Vorburg and residential Kernburg is still obvious. The latter now contains a restaurant, open daily 10am–6pm, when there's free and unrestricted access to the castle, though you're expected to make a DM1/€0.50 donation if you want to climb the keep, which commands a superb view over the valley.

It's only a few minutes' walk to **Burg Saaleck** (May to mid-Oct Wed–Sun 9am–5pm; DM2/€1), of which only the two keeps and the lower sections of the curtain wall remain. One of the keeps can be ascended for a view of the valley with the Rudelsburg in the picture. The other was the hiding place of the men who assassinated the German

foreign minister, Walther Rathenau, in 1922. It now contains a display on the background to that event, which brought home the strength and determination of the anti-democratic forces ranged against the infant Weimar Republic.

Practicalities

Bad Kösen's **Bahnhof** is at the southern end of the Kurpark; the main bus stop lies slightly to the west. The **tourist office** (Mon–Fri 10am–6pm, Sat & Sun 10am–4pm; ☎03 44 63/2 82 89, fax 2 82 80; *www.bad-koesen.de*) is on Loreleypromenade. There are numerous **private houses** (①–②) with rooms to let.

Centrally sited **hotels** (which are also the best places to eat and drink) include *Loreley*, Loreleypromenade 8 (☎03 44 63/2 87 88; ④), *Zum Wehrdamm*, Loreleypromenade 3 (☎03 44 63/2 84 05; ④), *Schöne Aussicht*, Ilskeweg 1 (☎03 44 63/2 73 67; ④), and *Villa Ilske*, Ilskeweg 2 (☎03 44 63/3 66 20; ⑤). The last two command fine views over the valley, though best of all is from *Berghotel Wilhelmsburg*, Eckartsbergaer Str. 20 (☎03 44 63/36 70; ⑤), 2.5km to the northwest. There's also a **youth hostel** at Bergstr. 3 (☎03 44 63/2 75 97; DM19/€9.50 or DM24/€12) and a **campsite** (☎03 44 63/2 87 05) by the Saale at the western edge of town.

travel details

Trains

Dessau to: Bernburg (frequent; 1 hr); Köthen (frequent; 30min); Wittenberg (frequent; 30min).

Halberstadt to: Blankenburg (frequent; 30min); Quedlinburg (frequent; 30min); Thale (frequent; 45min); Wernigerode (frequent; 40min).

Halle to: Dessau (frequent; 45min); Eisleben (hourly; 40min); Halberstadt (8 daily; 1hr 45min); Merseburg (frequent; 15min); Naumburg (12 daily; 30min); Wittenberg (frequent; 45min).

Magdeburg to: Dessau (frequent; 1hr 45min); Halberstadt (hourly; 1hr 15min); Halle (frequent; 1hr 30min); Köthen (frequent; 1hr); Stendal (frequent; 1hr).

CHAPTER ELEVEN

THURINGIA

Of all the Länder, east or west, it's **Thuringia** (Thüringen) which comes nearest to encapsulating the nation's soul – and to providing an insight into the Germany of old, which elsewhere has largely been swept away by one or other of the dramatic events of the twentieth century. In many ways, it stands apart from the other eastern provinces – for one thing, it has been German since the Dark Ages, rather than land won from Slavs; for another, it suffers relatively little from industrial blight, thanks to being predominantly rural in character, with a vast forest accounting for a considerable proportion of its area.

Despite having been one of the five original provinces of early medieval Germany, Thuringia became defunct as a political entity in the thirteenth century. Most of it fell to the powerful **House of Wettin**, who amalgamated it with their Saxon holdings; smaller tracts were held by the dynasties of **Schwarzburg** and **Reuss**. In the sixteenth century, the Wettin possessions began to fragment into a series of tiny duchies (identified in English by the prefix "Saxe-"), while Schwarzburg and Reuss were also partitioned. Despite many subsequent amalgamations, there were still eight separate Thuringian principalities among the 25 states which came together to form the Second Reich in 1871. It took German defeat in World War I to bring this feudalistic situation to an end: the aristocracy was forced to follow the Kaiser's lead in resigning political power and Thuringia made a phoenix-like return to the map, having managed to preserve a definite regional identity throughout this long history of political fragmentation.

The most visible expression of Thuringia's past is the unparalleled number of **castles** and **palaces**, many of which turned what would otherwise have been villages into proud capital cities, and which should now help ensure that the Land has a secure future in the tourism stakes. Yet these are by no means always empty expressions of the vanity of Ruritanian princes – some of the courts were vibrant cultural centres which have made an impact on the nation out of all proportion to their size. Indeed, **Weimar** was the main driving force behind the German Enlightenment, and its overall contribution to the country's development far surpasses that of most of its major cities. Nearby **Jena** has maintained a strong academic tradition, particularly in the sciences,

---

ACCOMMODATION PRICE CODES

All the pensions and hotels in this book have been graded according to the following price categories. The codes quoted are for the cheapest available double room, except for establishments which have rooms costing widely different rates, when the most expensive price is given as well. Exact charges are given for youth hostels; in the case of the official DJH (HI) establishments, this is the lowest available rate. When two figures are quoted for these hostels, the first applies to juniors (ie under 27 years of age), the second to seniors (27 and above).

① less than DM60/€30	④ DM100–124/€50–62	⑦ DM200–249/€100–124
② DM60–79/€30–39	⑤ DM125–149/€63–74	⑧ DM250–299/€125–149
③ DM80–99/€40–49	⑥ DM150–199/€75–99	⑨ upwards of DM300/€150

while **Eisenach**, which likewise belonged to the same duchy for a considerable period, has also made a huge mark on the national consciousness.

The capital of modern Thuringia is **Erfurt**. Although its population is less than a quarter of a million, it's by far the largest city in the province and a place very different from the former courtly towns, the well-preserved historic core evoking its past as a major episcopal centre. Walled **Mühlhausen** is, if anything, even more suggestive of the Middle Ages, while **Schmalkalden** offers plenty of reminders of its heyday during the Renaissance and Reformation. In contrast, **Gera**, the province's second city, has shrugged off its past as a Residenzstadt to become a bustling modern community; of the other princely capitals, **Altenburg** and **Gotha** have (in common with Weimar, Jena and Eisenach) become medium-sized towns, whereas all the others remain engagingly provincial. In terms of scenery, the attractions are fairly low key, though the **Thuringian Forest** has its fair share of beauty spots, as does the valley of the **Saale** at its far end, while at the far north of the province are the **Kyffhäuser**, a miniature mountain chain.

Travel in Thuringia is rendered particularly easy by the small distances separating most of the major attractions; at a pinch, it would even be possible to cover much of the province from a single centrally sited base, such as Weimar, Erfurt or Gotha. Tourist **facilities** are, on the whole, much better than average for eastern Germany; this is particularly true of the Thuringian Forest, which has a glut of accommodation, though it also applies to the main towns, which are used to a heavy volume of visitors.

CENTRAL THURINGIA

The central part of Thuringia, in which lie four outstanding historic cities, is the part most tourists come to see. It's also the most easily assimilated – only 80km separates **Weimar**, which lies just beyond the Saxony-Anhalt border, from **Eisenach**, near the former East–West German frontier. The two are linked by one of eastern Germany's main express rail lines; en route are **Erfurt** and **Gotha**.

Weimar

If Heidelberg is the German city foreigners are most prone to drool over, then **WEIMAR** is the one the Germans themselves hold dearest. Despite its modest size, its role in the development of national culture is unmatched. Above all, it was here that the German Enlightenment had its most brilliant flowering, when it was home to the writers Friedrich Schiller, Johann Gottfried Herder, Christoph-Martin Wieland and, most significantly, **Johann Wolfgang von Goethe** (see box on p.957), whose name is commemorated all over the town. Prior to this, Weimar's roll call of famous citizens had included Lucas Cranach and J.S. Bach; it would later number Franz Liszt, Richard Strauss, Friedrich Nietzsche and the architects and designers of the Bauhaus school. Later, the name of Weimar became synonymous with the republic established after defeat in World War I, which marked the birth of German democracy. Its inglorious failure, culminating fifteen years later with the Nazis gaining power by largely legal means, brought a sad twist to the town's cultural reputation, as it was the birthplace of the Hitler Youth movement and the site of one of the most notorious concentration camps.

Arrival, information and accommodation

Weimar's **Hauptbahnhof** is well to the north of the main sights. From here, Carl-August-Allee leads straight ahead to Theaterplatz; to get to the Schloss, turn left at

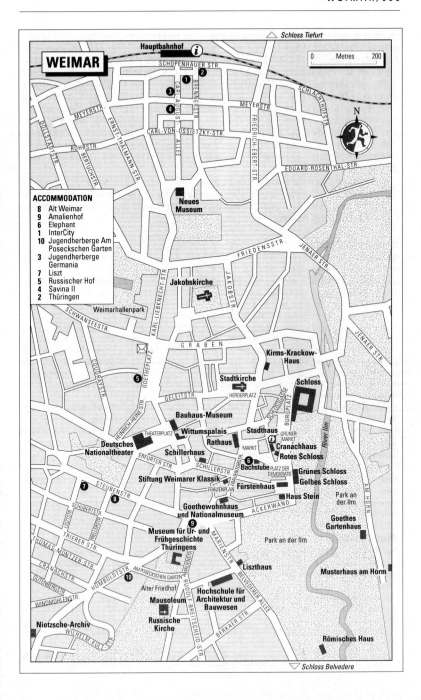

WEIMAR

Hauptbahnhof

SCHOPENHAUER STR.

Schloss Tiefurt

0 Metres 200

N

SCHLACHTHOFSTR.

MEYERSTR.

CARL AUGUST ALLEE

BRENNERSTR.

FRIEDRICH-EBERT-STR.

MEYERSTR.

CARL-VON-OSSIETZKY-STR.

EDUARD-ROSENTHAL-STR.

ERNST-THÄLMANN-STR.

DÖLLSTÄDTSTR.

ROHRSTR.

BERTUCHSTR.

Neues Museum

FRIEDENSSTR.

JENAER STR.

JAKOBSTR.

ACCOMMODATION

8 Alt Weimar
9 Amalienhof
6 Elephant
1 InterCity
10 Jugendherberge Am Poseckschen Garten
3 Jugendherberge Germania
7 Liszt
5 Russischer Hof
4 Savina II
2 Thüringen

Jakobskirche

KARL-LIEBKNECHT-STR.

Weimarhallenpark

SCHWANSEESTR.

COUDRAYSTR.

GOETHEPLATZ

G R A B E N

JENAER STR.

Kirms-Krackow-Haus

Stadtkirche

HERDERPLATZ

GELEITSTR.

HEINRICH-HEINE-STR.

Schloss

SCHLOSSGASSE

BURGPLATZ

River Ilm

Bauhaus-Museum

Wittumspalais

THEATERPLATZ

Deutsches Nationaltheater

Rathaus

ERFURTER STR.

Schillerhaus

SCHILLERSTR.

Stiftung Weimarer Klassik

STEUBENSTR.

SCHUBERTSTR.

PRELLERSTR.

TRIERER STR.

THOMAS-MÜNTZER-STR.

CRANACHSTR.

GUTENBERGSTR.

WINDMÜHLENSTR.

Nietzsche-Archiv

WILHELM-KÜLZ-STR.

Stadthaus

GRÜNER MARKT

MARKT

Cranachhaus

Rotes Schloss

Bachstube

PLATZ DER DEMOKRATIE

FRAUENTORSTR.

Fürstenhaus

FRAUENPLAN

Grünes Schloss

Gelbes Schloss

Haus Stein

Park an der Ilm

Goethewohnhaus und Nationalmuseum

ACKERWAND

Museum für Ur- und Frühgeschichte Thüringens

AM POSECKSCHEN GARTEN

HUMBOLDTSTR.

MARIENSTR.

Park an der Ilm

Goethes Gartenhaus

Liszthaus

Musterhaus am Horn

AM HORN

Alter Friedhof

Mausoleum

Russische Kirche

RUDOLF-BREITSCHEID-STR.

Hochschule für Architektur und Bauwesen

BELVEDERER ALLEE

BERKAER STR.

Römisches Haus

Schloss Belvedere

the first main junction into Friedenstrasse, then right into Jakobstrasse. The **tourist office** (April–Oct Mon–Fri 9.30am–6pm, Sat 9.30am–5pm, Sun 9.30am–4pm; Nov–March Mon–Fri 10am–6pm, Sat & Sun 10am–2pm; ☎0 36 43/2 40 00 or 1 94 33, fax 24 00 40, *www.weimar.de*) is in the Stadthaus at Markt 10; there's also a branch in the entrance hall of the Hauptbahnhof (daily 10am–8pm). Another useful **information office** is that of the Stiftung Weimarer Klassik (which administers Thuringia's literary sites) at Frauentorstr. 3 (daily: April–Oct 10am–5.30pm; Nov–March 9am–4pm; ☎0 36 43/54 51 02, *www.weimar-klassik-de*). It is well worth investing in the **Weimar Card**, which gives unlimited travel on the town's buses as well as admission to most (though not all) of the museums and sights; it costs DM20/€10 for three consecutive days and an extra DM10/€5 for a three-day extension to this.

You can book **private rooms** (①–③) at the tourist office. The plentiful provision of these is a real boon, given that there's a shortage of budget **hotels** (although there are now plenty of options in the middle and upper ranges). Weimar also has no fewer than four DJH/HI **youth hostels**.

Hotels and Pensions

Alt Weimar, Prellerstr. 2 (☎0 36 43/8 61 90, fax 86 19 10, *www.alt-weimar.de*). Characterful hotel and restaurant at the southern edge of the centre. ⑥.

Am Berkaer Bahnhof, Peter-Cornelius-Str. 7 (☎0 36 43/20 20 10). Small pension located just north of the suburban station after which it is named, reached by bus #3 from Goetheplatz. ③.

Amalienhof, Amalienstr. 2 (☎0 36 43/54 90, fax 54 91 00, *www.vch.de/amalienhof*). Hotel with Church affiliations, occupying an Enlightenment-era palace. ⑥.

Dorotheenhof, Dorotheenhof 1, Schöndorf (☎0 36 43/45 90, fax 45 92 00, *www.dorotheenhof.com*). Located 4km north of the centre on the route of bus #7, this hotel with restaurant, a member of the TOP Hotel chain, was formerly the manor house of a cavalry officer, and is set in its own park. ⑦.

Elephant, Markt 19 (☎0 36 43/80 20, fax 6 53 10, *www.weimar.de/kempinski*). Weimar's most famous hotel dates back to 1696, but the interior is predominantly Art Deco. It has a gourmet restaurant, *Anna Amalia* (evenings only except at weekends), plus the surprisingly affordable *Elephantenkeller* (closed Sun evening). ⑨.

InterCity, Carl-August-Allee 17 (☎0 36 43/23 40, fax 23 44 44). Modernized mid-nineteenth-century hotel, complete with winter garden restaurant, right opposite the Hauptbahnhof. ⑤–⑦.

Liszt, Lisztstr. 1–3 (☎0 36 43/5 40 80, fax 54 08 30). A good mid-range hotel in a quiet area just south of the centre. ⑥.

Russischer Hof, Goetheplatz 2 (☎0 36 43/77 40, fax 77 48 40, *www.deraghotels.de*). A grand, beautifully furnished hotel with restaurant with a tradition dating back to 1805. ⑦–⑨.

Savina II, Meyerstr. 60 (☎0 36 43/8 66 90, fax 86 69 11, *www.weimar.de/pensionsavina*). Pension situated a few minutes' walk south of the Hauptbahnhof. ③–⑤.

Thüringen, Brennerstr. 42 (☎0 36 43/90 36 75, fax 90 36 76). Medium-price hotel and restaurant diagonally opposite the Hauptbahnhof. ⑥.

Youth Hostels

Am Ettersberg, Ettersberg-Siedlung (☎0 36 43/42 11 11, fax 42 11 12). Rustic hostel in the Prinzenschneise nature reserve north of the city, a five-minute walk from the Obelisk stop on the route of bus #6. Advance bookings should be made via the Maxim Gorki hostel. DM26/€13 or DM31/€15.50.

Am Poseckschen Garten, Humboldtstr. 17 (☎0 36 43/85 07 92, fax 85 07 93). The most central of the hostels, located close to the Alter Friedhof; take bus #6 to Humboldtstrasse. DM25/€12.50 or DM30/€15.

Germania, Carl-August-Allee 13 (☎0 36 43/85 04 90, fax 85 04 91). Located just a few paces south of the Hauptbahnhof. DM25/€12.50 or DM30/€15.

Maxim Gorki, Zum Wilden Graben 12 (☎0 36 43/85 07 50, fax 85 07 49). This lies 5km south of the centre, reached by bus #8 to Rainer-Marie-Rilke-Strasse. DM26/€13 or DM31/€15.50.

The Town

If you aren't interested in its literary and artistic associations, Weimar can seem a provincial sort of place. But its great merit is that it uncannily preserves both the appearance and atmosphere of its heyday as the most influential of the hundreds of capitals of pint-sized independent states which once littered the map of Germany. A rather tatty place in GDR days, it underwent a frantic programme of restoration in preparation for 1999, when it celebrated the 250th anniversary of Goethe's birth and served as European City of Culture.

The Schloss

Set by the River Ilm at the eastern edge of the town centre, Weimar's **Schloss** (Tues–Sun: April–Oct 10am–6pm; Nov–March 10am–4.30pm; *www.kunstsammlungen-weimar.de*; DM6/€3) is of a size more appropriate for ruling a great empire than a duchy whose population never rose much above 100,000. The complex is mostly in the Neoclassical style typical of the town: only the tall tower and the portal at the southwest corner remain of the original Renaissance palace of John Frederick the Magnanimous of Saxony, who established Weimar as the capital of his truncated duchy in 1547, following the loss of Wittenberg in the Schmalkaldic Wars.

On the ground floor there are notable collections of Thuringian medieval sculpture, fifteenth- to nineteenth-century Russian icons, and old master paintings. The last of these is dominated by important examples by the **Cranach** family, who followed the erstwhile elector here from Wittenberg. Pick of the works by Lucas the Elder are *Luther as Junker Jörg* (showing him in the disguise he adopted when in hiding at the Wartburg), *John Frederick the Magnanimous and Sybille von Cleve* (a pair of official bridal portraits), *Samson and the Lion*, and the erotically suggestive *Age of Silver*, illustrating the favourite Renaissance theme of a battle between "wild men". Other highlights are **Dürer's** *Hans and Elspeth Tucher* (a pair of portraits of a prominent Nürnberg patrician couple), and a typically idiosyncratic canvas by his pupil **Baldung**, *The Sacrifice of Marcus Civitius*.

On the first floor, some fine original interiors can be seen, the most imposing being the huge main **Festsaal** and the **Grosse Galerie**. There are also memorial chambers devoted to each of the four great Weimar poets; these are decorated with murals illustrating their main works. Also here are seventeenth-century Dutch school still lifes and German painting from the Age of Enlightenment to the present day; look out for **Friedrich's** haunting *Tomb of Hutten*, **Runge's** touching *Portrait of Louise Perthes* and **Moritz von Schwind's** colourful *Seven Ravens*.

The second floor displays works by painters of the Weimar School, including a good selection of canvases by **Christian Rohlfs**, among which *The Ilm Bridge at Buchfart* stands out.

Herderplatz, Jakobstrasse and beyond

Just west of the Schloss on Herderplatz is the **Stadtkirche St Peter und Paul** (April–Oct Mon–Sat 10am–noon & 2–4pm, Sun 11am–noon & 2–3pm; Nov–March daily 11am–noon & 2–3pm), a much-remodelled Gothic church usually known as the **Herderkirche** in honour of the poet, folklorist and literary theorist who was its chief pastor for three decades. Inside, the eye is drawn to the large **triptych** at the high altar, which is usually described as the artistic swan song of the elder Cranach, but was almost certainly painted as a memorial by his son, as it features the aged painter and his friend Luther as the main spectators at a Crucifixion scene arranged as a propaganda statement of the new Protestant doctrine of salvation. On the wings, John Frederick can be seen in the company of his wife and children. Also in the choir are a number of elaborate **tombstones**, including that of the elder Cranach and members of the ducal family; Herder is commemorated by a plain tablet under the organ loft.

Up Jakobsstrasse at the northeast corner of the square is the **Kirms-Krackow-Haus** (Tues–Sun: late March to mid-May & early Sept to late Oct 9am–6pm; mid-May to early Sept 9am–7pm; late Oct to late March 9am–4pm; DM4/€2). This mansion, now a literary centre with a regular programme of events, belonged to a rich bourgeois family and preserves a suite of rooms furnished according to early nineteenth-century taste. Its courtyard of wooden galleries is particularly characteristic of the domestic architecture favoured in Weimar's glory days.

Further up the street is the **Jakobskirche**, a plain Baroque church with a Neoclassical interior. In 1806, it was the scene of the wedding of Goethe to Christiane Vulpius, with whom he had been living for eighteen years in a relationship that had scandalized many influential figures in Weimar society. Christiane lies buried in the peaceful cemetery surrounding the church, as does Cranach, whose original tombstone has been replaced here by a copy.

Further north on Carl-August-Allee, the long-derelict Grossherzogliches Museum was recently renovated to house the **Neues Museum** (Tues–Sun: April–Oct 10am–6pm; Nov–March 10am–4.30pm; *www.kunstsammlungen-weimar.de*; DM5/ €2.50). This displays changing selections from the international avant-garde collection of Paul Maenz, who for two decades ran a highly successful commercial gallery in Cologne. A strong American showing includes examples of Carl Andre, Donald Judd, Dan Flavin and Sol LeWitt; another feature is the Italian section, in which Giulio Paolini and Piero Manzoni are particularly well represented.

The Markt and the Platz der Demokratie

South of Herderplatz is the **Markt**, lined by an unusually disparate jumble of buildings. Most eye-catching is the green and white gabled **Stadthaus** on the eastern side. Beside it is the **Cranachhaus**, where the artist spent his final years; directly opposite stands the neo-Gothic **Rathaus**. On the south side is the **Hotel Elephant**, the setting for all but the last chapter of Thomas Mann's novel about the town in Goethe's day, *Lotte in Weimar*. The historic inn was much favoured by Hitler, and it was just about the only place Westerners were allowed to stay during the GDR period, when it swarmed with *Stasi* agents; subsequently it has reclaimed its former position as one of Germany's leading hotels. Adjoining it are two more old hostelries and the **Bachstube**, where the composer lived during his years as leader of the court orchestra and organist from 1708 to 1717. This ended with a month-long imprisonment, following his fury at being passed over for the musical directorship, whereupon he left for a new position at the much smaller court of Köthen.

Beyond is an even larger square, the **Platz der Demokratie**, lined by a colourful series of palaces, over which an equestrian statue of Grand Duke Carl August presides. On the north side is the **Rotes Schloss** (Red Palace), a Renaissance building with Neoclassical additions, while to the south the grand Baroque **Fürstenhaus** is where Goethe was received on his arrival in Weimar. It now houses the Liszt-Hochschule, a prestigious academy of music. The east side of the square is closed by the **Grünes Schloss** (Green Palace). The finest of the group, it contains the **Herzogin-Anna-Amalia-Bibliothek** (April–Oct Mon–Sat 11am–12.30pm; DM4/€2), one of the most important collections of German literature in the world, with an exquisite central **Rokokosaal**. Beside it stands the more modest **Gelbes Schloss** (Yellow Palace), while further south is the **Haus Stein**, the former ducal stables, which the stablemaster, Baron Friedrich von Stein, converted into a house. His wife Charlotte was Goethe's first great Weimar love, notwithstanding the fact that she was seven years the poet's senior and the mother of seven children.

Schillerstrasse, Theaterplatz and Frauenplan

Schillerstrasse snakes away from the southwest corner of the Markt to the **Schillerhaus** (9am–4/5pm, closed Tues; DM5/€2.50), the home of Friedrich Schiller

JOHANN WOLFGANG VON GOETHE (1748–1832)

Often regarded as the last of the great universal geniuses, **Johann Wolfgang von Goethe** produced a vast and diverse literary output – ranging from lyric to philosophic poetry, via comic and tragic dramas, to novels, short stories, travelogues, artistic criticism and scientific tracts – even though he was never truly a full-time writer. Despite his youth, he had already gained a Europe-wide literary reputation before his appointment to the Weimar court, thanks largely to the epistolary novel *The Sorrows of Young Werther*. His first decade in Weimar furnished him with a broad range of practical experience which he would later put to full use, but it left him little time for writing. By undertaking a long Italian sojourn in 1786, his creative spark was rekindled, though the play *Torquato Tasso* is a thinly veiled exposition of the frustration he felt at having to operate in the environment of a small court. His major prose work, *Wilhelm Meister*, is a cycle of six novels written over a period of five decades which, in common with much of his output, is a close reflection of his own personal development. A similarly protracted process attended the writing of his supreme masterpiece, the two-part drama *Faust*, completed just before his death, which symbolically examines the nature of Western man, his errors and ultimate salvation. The reverence accorded Goethe in Germany and the academic industry which has grown up around him are almost as extensive as those surrounding Shakespeare in the English-speaking world.

for the last three years of his life, following his resignation of his academic chair at Jena. Here he wrote his last two dramas on great historical personalities, *The Maid of Orleans* (the story of Joan of Arc) and *William Tell*; and the rooms are furnished as he knew them. The modern extension behind contains the **Schillermuseum** (same times and ticket), with extensive documentation on his life and work.

Beyond lies **Theaterplatz**, in the centre of which is a large monument to Goethe and Schiller. The **Deutsches Nationaltheater** on the west side of the square was founded and directed by Goethe, though the present building, for all its stern Neoclassical appearance, is a pastiche, the facade from the beginning of the twentieth century, the rest from a rebuilding necessitated by its almost complete destruction in World War II. Apart from having seen the premieres of many of the greatest plays in the German language, the theatre was also the venue for the National Assembly's sittings in 1919 and saw the adoption of the constitution of the Weimar Republic.

Opposite is the **Wittumspalais** (Tues–Sun: late March to mid-May & early Sept to late Oct 9am–6pm; mid-May to early Sept 9am–7pm; late Oct to late March 9am–4pm; DM6/€3), a large Baroque palace built as the retirement home of Regentess Anna Amalia, Weimar's great patron of the arts. Even as a dowager duchess, she continued to play a leading role in the town's intellectual life, organizing "Round Table" sessions here at which Goethe presided each Friday. The interiors are among the finest in Weimar, with the main **Festsaal** a design based on Goethe's ideas. There's also a large array of mementoes of Christoph-Martin Wieland, now a rather neglected figure, but then regarded as the leading theoretician of the Enlightenment, as well as a major poet and philosopher.

Also on the square is the Kunsthalle, which has been converted to house the **Bauhaus-Museum** (Tues–Sun: April–Oct 10am–6pm; Nov–March 10am–4.30pm; *www.kunstsammlungen-weimar.de*; DM5/€2.50). The main gallery displays works produced by artists of the Bauhaus during its early years in Weimar. One of the two small rooms is devoted to its forerunner, the Belgian Art Nouveau architect Henry van de Velde's Kunstgewerbeschule, founded in 1900 in an attempt to revive Weimar as a major artistic centre. The other room documents the successor to the Bauhaus, Otto Bartning's Staatliche Bauhochschule.

On Frauenplan south of the Markt is the excellent **Goethewohnhaus und Nationalmuseum** (Tues–Sun: late March to mid-May & early Sept to late Oct

9am–6pm; mid-May to early Sept 9am–7pm; late Oct to late March 9am–4pm; DM8/€4). As its name suggests, it's in two parts. The more rewarding of these is the large Baroque mansion where the titan of German literature resided for some fifty years until his death in 1832. It's been preserved exactly as he knew it, and still has a lived-in feel to it, particularly the study with the desk where he sat dictating works to his secretary (he only composed poems with his own hand), and the little chamber where he died. In the adjoining museum the full range and versatility of his achievement is chronicled with typically Teutonic attention to detail.

The Südstadt

Most of the remaining sights are found in the **Südstadt**, the southern part of town. From the Goethewohnhaus, continue down Marienstrasse to the **Liszthaus** (Tues–Sun: late March to mid-May & early Sept to late Oct 9am–6pm; mid-May to early Sept 9am–7pm; late Oct to late March 9am–4pm; DM4/€2), the garden house of the great Austro-Hungarian composer Franz Liszt. His move to Weimar in 1848, where he spent eleven years as director of the local orchestra and opera company, marked a sea change in his career away from his earlier preoccupation with barnstorming virtuoso piano music towards richly scored programmatic orchestral pieces – the most ambitious being the Goethe-inspired *Faust Symphony* – which in turn cast a strong spell over his son-in-law, Richard Wagner. Despite having left in a huff over the town's narrow-minded tastes, he returned in 1869, staying at this house for each of the remaining seventeen summers of his life.

A couple of minutes' walk to the west down Geschwister-Scholl-Strasse is Henry van de Velde's custom-built home for the Kunstgewerbeschule, the **Hochschule für Architektur und Bauwesen**. In 1919, Walter Gropius established the original **Bauhaus** – which was to have such a profound impact on the subsequent course of modern architecture and design throughout the world – in this college. However, it only remained here for six years before its move, prompted by hostility from reactionary elements in the town, to the more liberal climate at Dessau. The building still functions as an art college (one raised in 1993 to university status), and isn't a regular tourist sight, though you're free to wander in and look at any exhibitions that may be on.

Further to the west, at Amalienstr. 6, is the **Museum für Ur- und Frühgeschichte Thüringens** (Museum of Ancient and Early Thuringian History; Mon–Fri 9am–5pm, Sat & Sun 10am–5pm; DM3/€1.50), the most important archeological museum in the province. It charts the history and prehistory of the area from the Stone Age to the Thuringian tribes of the early medieval period. Highlights include Bronze Age jewellery from Schwarza, imaginatively displayed on reconstructed period dresses; the contents of a Germanic princess's grave unearthed at Hassleben; and the spectacular hoard of jewellery from the time of the fifth-century Thuringian kingdom found at nearby Ossmanstedt.

Immediately south of here is the **Alter Friedhof** (Old Cemetery), complete with a poignant array of carved tombstones and the Neoclassical **Fürstengruft** (daily: late March to mid-May & early Sept to late Oct 9am–1pm & 2–6pm; mid-May to early Sept 9am–1pm & 2–7pm; late Oct to late March 9am–1pm & 2–4pm; DM4/€2). Originally, this was intended for the Grand Ducal family, but it now has the tombs of Goethe and Schiller as well, following Carl August's decision that he wanted to be buried beside the two brightest stars of his court – though this necessitated reinterring the latter's corpse. Built onto the rear of the Mausoleum is the tiny **Russische Kirche** (Mon, Wed–Sun, 9am–4.45pm; free), built for the Grand Duchess Maria Pavlova, daughter-in-law of Carl August, who insisted on remaining loyal to the Orthodox faith of the Russian royal family to which she belonged.

Further to the southwest, at Humboldtstr. 36, is the Villa Silberblick, where the philosopher Friedrich Nietzsche, by then mentally ill, spent the last three years of his life. His sister commissioned Henry van de Velde to remodel the ground floor as a memorial and study centre, the **Nietzsche-Archiv** (Tues–Sun: late March to mid-May & early Sept to late Oct 9am–6pm; mid-May to early Sept 9am–7pm; late Oct to late March 9am–4pm; DM4/€2). This has now reopened, having been closed by the GDR authorities who used the villa as an official guesthouse.

The Park an der Ilm

The **Park an der Ilm** is a large English-style park, complete with ruined follies, a statue of Shakespeare and a cemetery for Soviet soldiers killed in World War II, stretching southwards on both sides of the Ilm from the Schloss to the southern edge of town. At the western fringe of the park, close to the Liszthaus, a stairway leads down to the **Parkhöhle Weimar** (Wed–Sun: April–Oct 9am–6pm; Nov–March 10am–4pm; DM6/€3). As their appearance indicates, these subterranean chambers have had an eventful history: originally used by the court as an ice cellar, they later became the focus of scientific interest, on account of the minerals and prehistoric fossils discovered there, and in World War II served as an air-raid shelter.

Almost due east, though on the opposite bank, is **Goethes Gartenhaus** (Tues–Sun: late March to mid-May & early Sept to late Oct 9am–6pm; mid-May to early Sept 9am–7pm; late Oct to late March 9am–4pm; DM4/€2), where the writer stayed when he first came to Weimar; later, it served as his summer retreat. A few years ago, it was the subject of a drastic and highly controversial restoration, which has led to the banishment of all the furniture which had been acquired since Goethe's time, leaving the interiors looking very bare. Further south and back on the west side of the Ilm is the Neoclassical ducal summer house, known as the **Römisches Haus** (Tues–Sun: late March to mid-May & early Sept to late Oct 9am–6pm; mid-May to early Sept 9am–7pm; late Oct to late March 9am–4pm; DM4/€2), whose ground-floor apartments are adorned with mock-Pompeian murals. In the basement is a (German-only) documentary exhibition on the history of the park.

Overlooking the east side of the Park an der Ilm is one of Weimar's most exclusive streets, Am Horn. Among its many grand villas is one seemingly incongrous intruder, the **Musterhaus am Horn** (Wed, Sat & Sun 10am–6pm; DM3/€1.50) at no. 61. This was designed by Georg Muche for the first Bauhaus exhibition in 1923, and was intended to be the prototype for a complete garden city, but ended up as the only true Bauhaus building ever erected in the movement's birthplace. Belatedly recognized as a classic of twentieth-century architecture, it has gained inclusion on UNESCO's World Heritage List.

The outskirts

Another villa only recently made accessible to the public is Henry van de Velde's own custom-built home, the **Haus Hohe Pappeln** (House Under the Tall Poplars; Tues–Sun 10am–6pm; DM5/€2.50) at Belvederer Allee 58 in the incorporated village of Ehringsdorf; it can be reached by bus #1 or #12 to Papiergraben. Designed in the shape of an upturned boat, the upper floor and attic were intended as living quarters, and remain as such today, with the ground floor used for changing exhibitions.

Bus #12 continues onwards to the extreme south of town and the full-blown summer palace, **Schloss Belvedere** (April–Oct Tues–Sun 10am–6pm; *www.kunstsammlungen -weimar.de*; DM5/€2.50). Its light and airy Rococo style and its collections of porcelain form a refreshing contrast to the Neoclassical solemnity of so much of the town. The **Orangerie** (April–Oct Tues–Sun 10am–1pm & 2–6pm; DM1/€0.50) contains a dozen historic coaches which served the Weimar court, while the surroundings were transformed under Goethe's supervision into another park in the English manner.

Schloss Tiefurt (Tues–Sun: late March to mid-May & early Sept to late Oct 9am–6pm; mid-May to early Sept 9am–7pm; late Oct to late March 9am–4pm;

DM6/€3), situated northeast of the town centre and reached by bus #3 or #4, is a far more modest palace, more like a small manor house in fact. It was created for the Dowager Duchess Anna Amalia, who transferred her "Round Table" meetings here during the summer months. Again, there's a fine park with plenty of small follies and retreats.

The **Konzentrationslager Buchenwald** (May–Sept Tues–Sun 9.45am–6pm; Oct–April Tues–Sun 8.45am–5pm; free) is to the north of Weimar on the Ettersberg heights, and can be reached by bus #6, which runs hourly from the Hauptbahnhof. Over 240,000 prisoners were incarcerated in this concentration camp, with 56,000 dying here from starvation, torture and disease, but despite the high number of deaths – averaging two hundred a day – Buchenwald was never an extermination camp. Among the prisoners killed here was the interwar leader of the German Communist Party, **Ernst Thälmann**. This gave the place a special significance for the GDR authorities, but the official state propaganda was tarnished by the discovery in 1990 of mass graves in the nearby woods, which provided conclusive proof that the Soviets used the camp after the war to round up and eliminate former Nazis and other political opponents. A documentary centre on the history of the camp has been set up in the former storehouse. The crematorium, disinfection chambers and prisoners' canteen are the other main buildings which may be visited.

Eating and drinking

Many of Weimar's best **restaurants** are in the hotels (see p.954), though there are plenty of good alternatives.

Bratwurstglöck'l, Carl-August-Allee 17a. Just a stone's throw from the Hauptbahnhof, this delightful little half-timbered Gasthaus with front beer garden has been in existence since 1870.

Eckermann, Brauhausstr. 13. A genuine Hungarian restaurant, specializing in fiery, freshly made goulashes, with a good selection of wines as accompaniments.

Felsenkeller, Humboldtstr. 37. Thuringia's first Hausbrauerei, set among the villas of the Südstadt, brews light and dark beers known as *Deinhardt* and also serves reasonably priced meals.

Frauentor, Schillerstr. 2. Serves both *Kaffee und Kuchen* and bistro-type meals.

Gastmahl des Meeres, Herderplatz 16. Fish speciality restaurant.

Ratskeller, Markt 10. Typically German cellar restaurant, though it's opposite rather than underneath the Rathaus.

Residenz-Café, Grüner Markt 4. Coffee house with a 150-year-old tradition; a good choice for breakfast.

Sommers Weinstuben, Humboldtstr. 2. Wine bar-cum-restaurant which has been run by the same family, save for a short interregnum during the GDR period, for five generations. It's decked out in nineteenth-century style and has a small garden to the rear. Closed Sun evening and Mon lunchtime.

Theater-Café, Theaterplatz 1a. Offers late breakfasts, vegetarian and *vom heissen Stein* dishes, with regular live music sessions.

Zum Weissen Schwan, Frauentorstr. 23. Historic Gasthaus whose praises were sung by Goethe. It's still among the best in town, with the game dishes particularly recommendable.

Entertainment

The liveliest **nightspot** is the Studentenklub Kasseturm, Goetheplatz 1, which is no longer exclusively for students. Weimar's main **theatre** venue is the Deutsches Nationaltheater, Theaterplatz 2 (☎0 36 43/75 53 34), which regularly features plays by Goethe and Schiller alongside touring productions and cabaret, as well as opera and concerts. **Festivals** include the *Bachtage* at the end of March, the *Liszttage* in October and the *Zwiebelmarkt* (Onion Market) on the second weekend of October.

Erfurt

Of all Germany's large cities, it's the the Thuringian capital of **ERFURT**, which lies 20km west of Weimar, that's most redolent of its prewar self. Although it lost several impor- tant monuments in the air raids of 1944 and 1945, the damage to the overall historic fab- ric was relatively slight, while the many streets of stately turn-of-the-century stores were saved by the Communist interregnum from the developers who would have demolished them had the city lain on the other side of the Iron Curtain.

In 1970, Erfurt was the scene of the meeting between West German Chancellor Willy Brandt and East German Premier Willi Stoph which marked the beginning of the for- mer's **Ostpolitik** and the end of the GDR's status as an international pariah. During the *Wende*, the city again provided a national lead by being the first place where the *Stasi* offices were stormed, thus preventing the destruction of incriminating files. Erfurt cele- brated its 1250th birthday in 1992 with a year-long programme of events. The culmina- tion was the re-establishment of the **University**, which was founded in 1392; it was once one of the largest and most prestigious in northern Europe, numbering Martin Luther among its graduates, but had been dormant since the Prussians suppressed it in 1816.

Arrival, information and accommodation

Erfurt's **Hauptbahnhof** is situated at the southeastern corner of the city centre. The **tourist office** (Mon–Fri 9am–6/7pm, Sat & Sun 10am–4pm; ☎03 61/6 64 00, fax 6 64 02 90, *www.erfurt-tourist-info.de*) is at Benediktsplatz 1. Here you can buy the **Erfurt Card** (DM12/€6 for 24hr, DM25/€12.50 for 72hr), which covers travel on the local trams and buses, plus entry to all the municipally owned museums and sights.

The **youth hostel** is at Hochheimer Str. 12 (☎03 61/5 62 67 05, fax 5 62 67 06, *jugendherberge-erfurt@t-online.de*), southwest of the centre; take tram #5 to the Steigerstrasse terminus. **Private rooms** can be booked in advance via the tourist office's special numbers (☎03 61/6 64 01 10, fax 6 64 02 80). **Hotels** are overwhelm- ingly geared toward the upper and middle range of the market, though the scarcity of inexpensive options is compensated for by the presence of numerous small **pensions**.

Hotels and Pensions

Daberstedt, Buddestr. 2 (☎03 61/3 73 34 61). Budget hotel a short distance south of the Hauptbahnhof, near the route of trams #3 and #6. ②.

Erfurtblick, Nibelungenweg 20 (☎03 61/22 06 60, fax 2 20 66 20). Green-belt hotel, reached by tram #1. As its name suggests, it commands a fine view of the city. ⑤.

Excelsior, Bahnhofstr. 35 (☎03 61/5 67 00, fax 5 67 01 00, *www.excelsior.bestwestern.de*). Upmarket modern hotel behind a Jugendstil facade on the way from the Hauptbahnhof to the city centre. ⑦.

Gartenstadt, Binderslebener Landstr. 212 (☎03 61/2 10 45 12 or 2 25 60 50, fax 210 45 13). Excellent middle-range hotel and restaurant not far from the ega grounds (see p.966), reached by tram #1. It has a sauna and solarium and serves good buffet breakfasts. ⑤.

Haus zum Pfauen, Marbacher Gasse 12–13 (☎03 61/2 11 11 00). Characterful old inn in the Altstadt. In its courtyard is what is claimed to be the world's smallest brewery, which makes light (*Pfauenbräu*) and dark (*Der Schluntz*) beers to a recipe of 1587. ③.

Malluche, Kartäuserstr. 32 (☎03 61/2 22 07 87, fax 2 25 42 51, *www.hotel-on-line.de/malluche*). Pension in a half-timbered Jugendstil villa not far from the centre. ④.

Nikolai, Augustinerstr. 30 (☎03 61/59 81 70, fax 59 81 71 20). Fine mid-range hotel by the River Gera at the northern end of the Altstadt. It has a good restaurant (evenings only, except at week- ends) with garden terrace. ⑤.

Scheel, Paulinzeller Weg 23 ☎03 61/41 38 38). Homely pension in a quiet street in the southern sub- urbs; there are several alternatives in the near neighbourhood. Take tram #3 or #6 to Blücherstrasse. ③.

ERFURT

ACCOMMODATION
5 Excelsior
2 Haus zum Pfauen
1 Nikolai
3 Sorat
4 Zumnorde

Sorat, Gotthardstr. 27 (☎03 61/6 74 00, fax 6 74 04 44; *www.sorat-hotels.com*). New designer hotel built alongside, and incorporating, the historic *Zum Alten Schwan* restaurant. ⑦–⑨.

Zumnorde, Anger 50 (☎03 61/5 68 00, fax 5 68 04 00). Classy hotel with spacious bedrooms, a restaurant, bar and roof terrace. ⑦.

The City

Dominating the historic heart of Erfurt from its western side are two hills, the **Domhügel** and the **Petersberg**. The former is the city's episcopal centre, crowned by two highly distinctive churches. A monumental flight of steps leads up to the Domhügel from **Domplatz**, a vast open space formed as the result of a fire in 1813, now used as a site for markets, fairs and other entertainments. It's worth wandering through almost any street in the centre of Erfurt, which preserves a superb range of buildings evoking all the different periods of its past, and whose open, expansive layout offers the bonus of a whole range of surprising vistas.

The Domhügel and the Petersberg

On the southern side of Domhügel is the **Dom**, the larger of the two churches. The lower parts of its north and south **towers** are Romanesque and belonged to the previous church on the site, but otherwise it's a masterly Gothic construction which uses its sloping site to full advantage. From the first building period at the end of the thirteenth century are the central tower and the massive, fortress-like substructure known as the **Kavaten**. The choir and transepts, in a pure High Gothic style, were perched on top of the latter in the mid-fourteenth century, followed by the flamboyantly decorative **triangular porch**. A century later, the building was completed with the spacious hall nave, whose very German appearance is in marked contrast to the French influence manifested elsewhere.

Inside is one of the most impressive sets of **stained-glass windows** to be found in Germany, but the Dom's most valuable treasures are the two mid-twelfth-century masterpieces in the south transept – a **candelabrum** in the shape of a man, popularly known as *Wolfram*, and the stucco **altar** of *The Enthroned Madonna with Saints*. Among the adornments of the nave are a small altar of *The Madonna and Child with SS Catherine and Barbara* by **Cranach**, and the **tomb** of the supposedly bigamous Count of Gleichen and his wives. The central tower houses the **Gloriosa**, the largest bell cast during the Middle Ages. Guided tours (April–Oct Thurs 9am–1pm, Fri & Sun 1–4pm, Sat 11am–4pm; DM4/E2) to see it were introduced in 1997 in commemoration of its 500th anniversary, but note that the bell chamber does not offer a view over the city.

Alongside the Dom is the **Severikirche**, whose distinctive triple-towered east end, sheltering a disarmingly small choir, acts as a perfect foil to its neighbour. The five-aisled hall nave has an impressively lofty feeling considering its relatively modest size. It contains the monumental **tomb of St Severus**, carved out of a soft pink sandstone by a sensitive mid-fourteenth-century sculptor, now dubbed the Master of St Severus, who also made the statue of the saint over the entrance doorway. Both of the other important furnishings – **the alabaster relief** of *St Michael* on the south wall, and the **font** with its spectacular fifteen-metre-high canopy – date from the year 1467.

Behind the Domhügel is a much larger hill, the **Petersberg**, which lies off the well-worn tourist trail. It was likewise once a centre of religious life, as the site of a Benedictine abbey, the **Peterskirche**, which five times hosted the imperial Reichstag in the days of Emperor Frederick Barbarossa. The church still survives, now cocooned within the **Zitadelle**, one of the finest surviving examples of Baroque military architecture anywhere in Europe. As a bonus, there's a wonderful view over the city, with the spires on the Domhügel in the foreground.

Marktstrasse and Fischmarkt

Marktstrasse, which leads eastwards from Domplatz, was once on the trade route that linked Frankfurt and Leipzig with the Russian city of Novgorod. These days, it seems a tad narrow for a major thoroughfare, particularly given the greatly increased volume of traffic since the *Wende*. It's worth making detours off it south down Grosse Arche, and north along Allerheiligenstrasse. At no. 11 on the latter is one of the city's finest houses, **Zum Roten Stern**, the late Gothic home, complete with oriel window, of one of the city's many distinguished printers.

Given that it was trade and commerce which made Erfurt rich in the Middle Ages, the central **Fischmarkt** is of unassuming dimensions. The statue of Roland in the middle was built as a symbol of defiance against the feudal overlords, the archbishop-electors of Mainz, though Erfurt never managed to gain the status of a Free Imperial City. On the north side of the square is a showy Renaissance mansion, **Zum Breiten Herd**, which rivals the less demonstrative, more classically balanced **Zum Roten Ochsen** (Wed & Fri–Sun 11am–6pm, Thurs 11am–10pm; DM3/€1.50) on the west side for the title of best building on the square. The latter is now a gallery, often featuring major temporary exhibitions of modern art.

Directly opposite is the bulky nineteenth-century **Rathaus**, which is primarily of note for the heroically Romantic fresco cycles inside, depicting scenes from the lives of legendary and historical figures with a Thuringian connection. To its rear, on Stadtmünze, is the **Kleine Synagoge** (Tues–Sun 11am–6pm; free), a small Neoclassical building which has recently been restored to house a permanent exhibition on the Jews of Erfurt.

The Krämerbrücke and Michaelisstrasse

Just east of Fischmarkt is Erfurt's most singular sight, the **Krämerbrücke**, which adds a welcome dash of colour to a city which, for all its grandeur, can appear rather monochrome. Walking along, you have the illusion of entering a narrow medieval alley; the fact that this is actually a bridge lined with shops in the manner of the Ponte Vecchio in Florence is concealed at street level and only becomes obvious if you go down to the banks of the River Gera. The Krämerbrücke is known to have existed in the early twelfth century, but the history of the present structure begins with the stone rebuilding of 1325. In the Middle Ages, there were over sixty little shops on it, mostly associated with the trade in silk, spices, sugar and paper; their larger half-timbered replacements currently number thirty-two and contain a mixture of boutiques, antique dealers and commercial art galleries. The far end of the Krämerbrücke is framed by the **Aegidienkirche**, a small upstairs church used by a German Methodist congregation. Its **tower** (variable opening times; DM2/€1) commands a marvellous view over the city.

Shortly before the western end of the Krämerbrücke, the **Michaelisstrasse** – the heart of the old university quarter, but now one of the quietest parts of the city – stretches northwards. Just off it lies Waagegasse, a picturesque alley lined with sixteenth- and seventeenth-century storehouses. At the junction with Allerheiligenstrasse is the **Michaeliskirche**, an early Gothic church which was the main place of worship of the academic community. Its Renaissance high altar doubles as a memorial to a local councillor, while the **Dreifaltigkeitskapelle**, added at the turn of the sixteenth century, boasts a prominent oriel window, an embellishment rarely found in ecclesiastical architecture. The galleried courtyard is one of the most peaceful spots in Erfurt.

Across the street is the imposing Flamboyant Gothic portal of the **Collegium Majus**; the rest of this, the main university building, was a casualty of World War II bombs and is only now being reconstructed. Its outstanding collection of old manuscripts, the **Amploniana**, survived and is currently kept in the nineteenth-century science library behind.

East of the River Gera

Across the river is the **Augustinerkloster** (guided tours April–Oct Tues–Sat at 10am, 11am, noon, 2pm, 3pm & 4pm, Sun at 10.45am; Nov–March Tues–Sat at 10am, noon & 2pm, Sun at 10.45am; *www.augustinerkloster.de*; DM6/€3), the monastery where Luther lived between 1505 and 1511, first as a novice, then as a monk and priest. The complex was badly damaged in the war and has only been partially restored. A visit to a reconstruction of Luther's cell forms part of the tour, which also includes the cloister and the typically austere church, now used by Protestants. It's enlivened by some of Erfurt's most beautiful stained-glass windows, including one depicting the life of the order's founder, St Augustine.

A few blocks to the south, not far from the eastern end of Krämerbrücke, is the **Schottenkirche** (Scottish Church), so called from the nationality of the monks who lived here in the Middle Ages. The Baroque facade masks a simple pillar basilica which is one of the few Romanesque buildings left in Erfurt.

To the east is the north–south Johannesstrasse, the longest street in the Altstadt, lined with some of its most impressive Renaissance mansions. Particularly striking is the **Haus zum Stockfisch** at no. 169, which has a rusticated facade reminiscent of an Italian *palazzo*, with a carving of a dried cod above the door which gives the house its name. The interior now contains the local history displays of the **Stadtmuseum** (Tues–Sun 10am–6pm; DM3/€1.50). Further east, the Juri-Gagarin-Ring marks the boundary of the medieval city. Across it, at no. 140a, is the sixteenth-century **Hospital**, now housing the **Museum für Thüringer Volkskunde** (Tues–Sun 10am–6pm; DM3/€1.50), a folklore collection focusing on the province's traditional lifestyles (re-created in a number of interiors), festivals, costumes, crafts and industries.

Anger and around

Johannesstrasse terminates at the **Kaufmannskirche** (Merchants' Church), with a memorial to Luther outside. This also marks the beginning of **Anger**, which starts off as a square but continues westwards as one of the main shopping streets, lined with the most opulent mansions in the city. It's worth making a short detour down Bahnhofstrasse to see the **Reglerkirche**, another Augustinian collegiate church, whose high altar has the best of the large carved and painted retables which were an Erfurt speciality in the fifteenth century.

Straddling Bahnhofstrasse and Anger is an ornate Baroque palace built as a weigh house and repository. It's now the **Angermuseum** (Tues–Sun 10am–6pm; DM3/€1.50), an excellent collection of fine and decorative arts. The highlight is the medieval section, which features the painted shields which formerly adorned the ceiling of the demolished fourteenth-century Rathaus, and several works – a *Crucifixion*, a *Pietà* and a *St Michael* – by the Master of St Severus. From the Renaissance period are paintings by Cranach and Baldung, while the usual range of nineteenth- and twentieth-century German paintings is supplemented by a chamber frescoed by the Expressionist Erich Heckel.

Further down Anger, you pass the **Bartholomäusturm**, the only surviving part of the court church of the counts of Gleichen. At the far end of the street, there's a fork; the northern branch, Regierungsstrasse, leads to the **Statthalterei**, a magnificent Baroque palace built by Maximilian von Welsch, court architect to the archbishops of Mainz, to serve as the headquarters of the city's government. A room on the first floor was the scene in 1808 of one of history's famous meetings – that between Goethe and Napoleon, who conversed knowledgeably about the former's plays.

The Barfüsserkirche and the Predigerkirche

Just north of here is the **Barfüsserkirche** (April–Oct Tues–Sun 10am–1pm & 2–6pm; DM3/€1.50), a vast, austere Franciscan friary church which was the most serious casualty of World War II bombs. Its nave has been left as a shell, but the choir has been restored to house a small branch of the Angermuseum's medieval collection. The stained-glass windows, which include a depiction of the life of St Francis, have been restored to their original position; some of them date back to the early thirteenth century.

On the other side of the river is the **Predigerkirche**, formerly the Dominican priory but since the Reformation the city's main Protestant church. Its exterior takes plainness to an extreme, but the interior is a masterpiece of spacial harmony in the purest Gothic style, and has preserved its layout and furnishings intact. The church was constructed in the thirteenth century when Master Eckhart, Germany's most celebrated mystic, was a monk there; he later became prior and vicar of Thuringia, in spite of holding pantheistic beliefs which many regarded as heresy. On the **rood screen**, which you can ascend for a rare aerial view, is a beautiful mid-fourteenth-century group of *The Annunciation*; the niches of the **choir screen** behind shelter a number of works of the same date. Elsewhere in the church are many elaborate epitaphs, a fifteenth-century carved and painted high altar and some lovely thirteenth-century stained glass made up of floral motifs.

To the rear of the church at Schlösserstr. 25a is the **Neue Mühle** (guided tours hourly Tues–Sun 10am–6pm; DM3/€1.50), the last still-functioning water-mill in the city.

Cyriaksburg

For the past three decades, the ample grounds of the **Cyriaksburg** (daily April–Sept 9am–6pm; Oct–March 10am–4pm; DM5/€2.50), a castle southwest of the city centre at the terminus of tram #2, have been given over to the **Internationale Gartenbauausstellung** (commonly known as ega), a vast garden show. It's best visited in spring, when the eye-swimming plantations of flowers are in full bloom. However, there are plenty of other attractions, notably the **Gartenbaumuseum** (Tues–Sun 10am–4/6pm; included in entrance ticket) in the Cyriaksburg itself, which traces the history of gardening. There are also several restaurants, exhibition halls, a look-out tower and hothouses displaying orchids, cacti and other tropical plants.

Eating and drinking

Under Communism, Erfurt had a noticeable shortage of places to eat and drink, but the situation, although still more fluid than in most eastern German cities, is improving every year.

Alboth's, Futterstr. 15. Located in part of an elegant eighteenth-century building known as the Kaisersaal (Imperial Hall) because it hosted the 1808 meeting of Napoleon and Czar Alexander I, this is currently Erfurt's best and most expensive restaurant.

Bärenkeller, Andreasstr. 26. Offers Thuringian specialities and *vom heissen Stein* dishes.

Café Rommel, Johannesstr. 34. Very traditional café, founded in 1912 and still preserving its original Viennese-style decor.

Erfurter Brauhaus, Anger 21. New Hausbrauerei which makes light, dark and various seasonal beers, and also serves hearty local cuisine.

Kaffeemühle, Schlösserstr. 25a. Café in the Neue Mühle, with riverside garden. Open till 1am, closed Mon.

Kleines Café, Anger 19–20. Good choice for breakfast or *Kaffee und Kuchen*.

Paganini in Gildehaus, Fischmarkt 13. An upmarket Italian restaurant now occupies the ground floor of Zum Breiten Herd and its neo-Renaissance extension, the Gildehaus.

Rathaus-Arcade, Fischmarkt 1. Smart new restaurant in the ground floor of the Rathaus.

Wirtshaus Christoffel, Michaelisstr. 41. This "medieval" theme restaurant is one of a number of lively new ventures in the former university district.

Zum Güldenen Rade, Marktstr. 50. Located in an old tobacco mill, this offers a wide-ranging menu, Köstritzer beer (see p.997), and a back garden with chestnut trees.

Entertainment

Erfurt's principal **festival**, the *Kramerbrückenfest*, takes place in the latter part of June and features a medieval market and all kinds of music. The city also maintains a varied cultural life throughout the year.

Theatre and concert venues

Kaisersaal, Futterstr. 15 (☎03 61/5 68 81 23).Though this still sometimes serves its original purpose as a ballroom, it is also used for concerts of all kinds of music.

KuppelTheater, An der Thüringerhalle; box office at Dalbergsweg 2 (☎03 61/2 23 31 55). This new tent-like construction has taken over the staging of opera, musicals and dance since the Neoclassical Opernhaus was condemned as a fire hazard in 1997.

Schauspielhaus, Klostergang; box office at Dalbergsweg 2 (☎03 61/2 23 31 55). The main municipal theatre, with large and small stages.

Theater die Schotte, Schottenstr. 7 (☎03 61/6 43 17 22). The other venue for straight plays.

Waidspeicher, Grosse Arche; box office at Domplatz 18 (☎03 61/5 98 29 24). Hosts the puppet shows of the Puppentheater and the satirical cabaret, Die Arche.

Clubs and live music

Centrum, Anger 7. Plays a variety of music (hip-hop, techno, pop and rock) several evenings per week from 9pm.

Jazzkeller, Fischmarkt 13–16. The city's premier jazz venue, with live music Thurs & Fri at 8.30pm.

Museumskeller, Juri-Gagarin-Ring 140a. Features live bands Fri & Sat at 10.30pm, and the rest of the time is a hip-hop club.

Studentenclub Engelsburg, Allerheiligenstr. 20. The liveliest dance club in the city, with events most evenings.

Gotha

GOTHA, which lies 25km west of Erfurt, is a handsome market town and main gateway to the popular holiday area of the Thuringian Forest. In the English-speaking world, it is indelibly associated with the **House of Saxe-Coburg-Gotha**, the name of the British royal family until they changed it to Windsor for patriotic reasons at the outbreak of World War I. The end of the war saw the dissolution of this united duchy, with the citizens of Coburg plumping for union with Bavaria rather than joining all the region's other petty states in the revived province of Thuringia. Gotha also holds an honoured place in the pantheon of the German left, as it was here in 1875 that the Socialist Workers' Party of Germany – renamed the **Social Democratic Party** fifteen years later, and still one of the country's main political forces – was formed.

The Town

Almost the whole of the southern half of central Gotha is taken up by the **Schlosspark**, whose spacious effect is slightly marred by being divided by two main thoroughfares – through the middle by Parkallee, and down the eastern fringe by Friedrichstrasse. After the park, the rest of Gotha is for the most part an anticlimax, though the Hauptmarkt is a highly original square.

Schloss Friedenstein

Schloss Friedenstein, which lies towards the northwestern end of the Schlosspark, is a U-shaped palace with massive square corner towers, built in sober early Baroque style. Its historical apartments and art collections are together designated the

Schlossmuseum (Tues–Sun 10am–4/5pm; DM8/€4, or DM10/€5 for inclusive ticket covering all the museums in the Schlosspark). Despite the plain exterior, it's highly elaborate inside, forming a visual encyclopedia of changing tastes in interior design, ranging from the heavy Baroque stuccowork of the main **Festsaal** to the **Dichter-Zimmer** (Poets' Chamber), adorned with Romantic landscapes, including **Friedrich's** *Cross in the Mountains*, a variant of one of his favourite themes. The **Kunstkammer** is a typical princely curio cabinet, whose dazzling if slightly frivolous treasures include a gilded elephant by the great Dresden goldsmith Dinglinger.

The picture gallery's star attraction is the hauntingly enigmatic *Pair of Lovers*, the most important of the few surviving paintings by the mysterious Rhenish draughtsman dubbed the **Master of the Housebook**. No less striking are the little boxwood figures of *Adam and Eve* by **Conrad Meit**, which rank among the greatest carvings of the German Renaissance. A marvellous group of works by **Cranach** includes several known to be by the master's own hand, rather than the more usual products of his workshop. *The Adoration of the Magi* is the masterpiece of his middle period, while a rare self-portrait of the artist can be seen at the far left corner of *Judith at the Table of Holofernes*, a story continued in the companion *Death of Holofernes*. A diptych of *The Fall and Salvation of Man* is a complicated tract illustrating the theological teachings of Melanchthon. Another, albeit far less sophisticated work inspired by the new Protestant doctrines, is a folding altar painted by **Heinrich Füllmaurer** with 157 scenes full of anecdotal details on German life of the day. There's also an array of paintings from the Low Countries; look out for a brilliant pair of **Rubens** sketches for the ceiling of the Jesuit church in Antwerp.

The southwest tower of the Schloss contains the **Ekhof-Theater** (same hours as the Schlossmuseum; DM3/€1.50, but part of inclusive ticket), a perfectly preserved Baroque gem, which is still in regular use. It is named in honour of Conrad Ekhof, a theatrical reformer who between 1774 and 1778 directed here the first company in Germany staffed by fully professional actors. Upstairs is the **Museum für Regionalgeschichte und Volkskunde** (same hours and ticket as Schlossmuseum), with the usual local history and folklore displays.

The **Schlosskirche** (April–Sept Tues–Sat 9am–4pm) is tucked away in the eastern part of the north wing, with no clue as to its presence from outside. Its interior is a fine example of courtly Lutheran Baroque: at the east end, the altar, pulpit and organ are all piled on top of one another; while the ceiling is covered with stuccowork and allegorical paintings, the one in the nave being a glorification of the wise regime of the House of Saxe-Gotha.

Around the Schlosspark

Facing the Schloss across Parkallee is a heavy neo-Renaissance pile built to house the Kunstkammer, but now containing the **Museum der Natur** (Tues–Sun 10am–5pm; DM4/€2, but part of inclusive ticket). Should you be intending to visit the Thuringian Forest, it's worth coming here to see the displays on its flora and fauna – including creatures such as the wolf and the lynx now extinct there. In addition, there's a section on the Thüringer Waldbahn, the forest tramway (see p.974). Elsewhere in the southern half of the Schlosspark are a large boating lake and the **Dorischer Tempel**, designed by Friedrich Wilhelm von Erdmannsdorff, creator of the gardens of Wörlitz. East of Schloss Friedenstein is the so-called **Teeschlösschen**, a folly, long used as a kindergarten, built in imitation of an English church. Beyond are the two pavilions of the **Orangerie**, one of which is a library, the other a café.

The rest of the town

The **Hauptmarkt** is built on a pronounced incline, which sweeps majestically up to Schloss Friedenstein. Standing in splendid isolation in the middle is the Renaissance

Rathaus, whose **tower** (daily 10am–4pm; DM1/€0.50) can be ascended for a view over the town. Also on the square are a Baroque fountain and a number of colourful houses, among them the **Lucas-Cranach-Haus** at the top end, which is known to have belonged to the painter, though the facade is much later. From here, Lucas-Cranach-Strasse leads to the Rococo **Frankenbergsches Gartenhaus**, which stands in its own pretty courtyard down a little alley.

A few minutes' walk southwest of the Hauptmarkt, at Cosmarstr. 10, is the **Haus Tivoli**, where the Socialist Workers' Party of Germany was founded in 1875. In the past, it was open as a memorial, though it posed something of a problem for the Communist authorities, as Marx had bitterly opposed the new party, which he regarded as a sell-out; indeed, his scathing *Critique of the Gotha Programme* was rated by Lenin as one of his three seminal texts. At present, the building is under restoration.

Practicalities

Gotha's **Hauptbahnhof** is at the southern end of town and trams #1, #2 and #4 will all take you in the direction of the centre; the last of these is actually the Thüringer Waldbahn. The **tourist office** is situated west of the Hauptmarkt at Blumenbachstr. 1–3 (Mon–Fri 9am–5pm, Sat 9am–noon; ☎36 21/85 40 36, fax 22 21 34, *www.gotha.de*). As ever, it can book **private rooms** (②–③).

The **youth hostel** is handily located just east of the Schlosspark and north of the Hauptbahnhof at Mozartstr. 1 (☎ & fax 0 36 21/5 40 08; DM21/€10.50 or DM26/€13). There are also plenty of conveniently located **pensions**, including *Am Schloss*, Bergallee 3a (☎0 36 21/85 55 32 06; ②), *Gaa*, Kleine Fahnenstr. 6 (☎0 36 21/75 58 90; ③), *Café Suzette*, Bebelstr. 8 (☎0 36 21/85 67 55; ④), and the much larger *Regina*, Schwabhäuser Str. 4 (☎0 36 21/40 80 20; ④). Among several good medium-priced **hotels** are *St Gambrin*, Schwabhäuser Str. 47 (☎0 36 21/3 09 00; ⑤), which also has a fish speciality restaurant (*Da Bruno*), and *Waldbahn*, Bahnhofstr. 16 (☎0 36 21/23 40; ⑥), whose amenities include a sauna, solarium, beer garden and reasonably priced restaurant. At the top of the range is *Am Schlosspark*, Lindenauallee 20 (☎0 36 21/44 20, *www.hotel-am-schlosspark.de*; ⑦), which features Roman-style baths and two classy restaurants.

Other good places to **eat** and **drink** are the *Pagenhaus* in the Schloss, the historic *Weinschänke*, Gartenstr. 28, and *Tanne*, Burgeraue 3. The wackily decorated *Firlefansz*, Klosterstr. 5, serves Swiss-style dishes, while the *König-Sahl*, Brühl 7, is an evenings-only Hausbrauerei which makes light and dark beers and serves full meals. There are several excellent traditional **cafés**: close to the Hauptbahnhof is the abovementioned *Suzette*, while in the centre are *Loesche*, Buttermarkt 6, and *Junghans*, Hauptmarkt 42.

Eisenach

EISENACH, 28km west of Gotha, grew up as an appendage to the **Wartburg**, the original seat of the landgraves of Thuringia, which overlooks it from the fringe of the Thuringian Forest to the south. Though foreigners may prefer the fantasy creations of King Ludwig II of Bavaria, the Wartburg's rich historical associations make it the castle the Germans themselves most treasure, and its proximity to the hated postwar border has made it something of a symbol of the united nation.

Arrival, information and accommodation

Eisenach's **tourist office** (Mon 10am–6pm, Tues–Fri 9am–6pm, Sat & Sun 10am–2pm; ☎0 36 91/7 92 30 or 1 94 33, fax 79 23 20, *www.eisenach-tourist.de*) is at Markt 2. There is also a separate information centre for the Wartburg in the town centre at Schlossberg

2 (April–Oct Mon–Fri 9am–5pm, Sat 9am–4pm; Nov–March Mon–Fri only; ☎0 36 91/7 70 73). The main **festivals** are the folkloric *Sommergewinn* on the Saturday three weeks before Easter, and the concerts of the *Thüringer Bachtage* around Easter. A varied **cultural programme** is presented all year round at the Thüringer Landestheater, Theaterplatz 4–7 (☎0 36 91/25 62 19).

Eisenach's **youth hostel** is at Mariental 24 (☎0 36 91/74 32 59, fax 74 32 69), on a road which branches off Wartburger Allee. There is the usual supply of **private rooms** (①–③) bookable via the tourist office. The town also has a wide range of **hotels** and **pensions**, including many in fine old buildings.

Hotels and Pensions

Am Bachhaus, Marienstr. 7 (☎0 36 91/2 04 70, fax 2 04 71 33). Newly refurbished town-centre hotel with restaurant and Musikkeller, the latter decked out with elaborate murals. ④.

Auf der Wartburg (☎0 36 91/79 70, fax 79 71 00, *www.wartburghotel.de*). Luxury hotel with restaurant in the Wartburg itself. ⑧–⑨.

Burgfried, Marienstr. 60 (☎0 36 91/21 42 21, fax 21 42 24, *www.flairhotel.com*). Good old-fashioned hotel, now part of the Flair group, in a large villa at the southern edge of the centre. ④–⑤.

Haus Hainstein, Am Hainstein 16 (☎0 36 91/24 20, fax 24 21 09, *www.vch.de/hainstein.eisenach*). Church-run hotel with café-restaurant in the green belt directly below the Wartburg. ⑤.

Kaiserhof, Wartburgallee 2 (☎0 36 91/21 35 13, fax 20 36 53, *www.romantik.de*). The top hotel in the town centre, part of the Romantik group. Has two restaurants – the *Weinrestaurant Trumschänke* is archetypically Thuringian, whereas *Der Zwinger* is in the style of a Bavarian Bierkeller. ⑥.

St Peter, Am Petersberg 7 (☎0 36 91/89 04 01, fax 87 28 31). Century-old Gasthaus in the southern part of town. ③.

Schlosshotel, Markt 20 (☎0 36 91/21 42 60, fax 21 42 59). New hotel in the converted buildings of the former Franziskanerkloster; also has a good wine bar-restaurant. ⑥.

Storchenturm, Georgenstr. 43 (☎0 36 91/21 52 50, fax 73 32 65). New Gasthof tucked away in a courtyard behind its street address, with plain but exceptionally good-value rooms and a restaurant in a renovated barn. ③.

Villa Anna, Fritz-Koch-Str. 12 (☎0 36 91/2 39 50, fax 23 95 30). Charming small hotel in a Jugendstil villa with tasteful modern furnishings in the southern part of town. ④–⑤.

Villa Kesselring, Hainweg 32 (☎0 36 91/73 20 49, fax 74 42 90, *www.wartburgkreis-info.de*). Pension in an extravagant Romantic-era villa in a very quiet setting just south of the centre, near one of the paths up to the Wartburg. ③.

The Town

For all its modest size, Eisenach is so rich in monuments and museums that it warrants an unhurried visit. It's best to proceed systematically southwards, perhaps leaving the Wartburg, the undoubted climax, for a second day.

The fortifications and the Markt

From the Hauptbahnhof, it's only a couple of minutes' walk along Bahnhofstrasse to the **Nikolaitor**, a massive gateway erected in the second half of the twelfth century. Above its arch are two sculptures, one presumed to be of Ludwig I, founder of the Ludowingian dynasty which first ruled Thuringia, the other the province's heraldic lion. A few decades later, the **Nikolaikirche** was built directly onto the Nikolaitor to serve both as a parish church and as a convent for Benedictine nuns. One other significant section of the **Stadtmauer**, including a couple of towers, survives; it can be seen at the northern end of town, just beyond Jakobsplan.

Heading diagonally across Karlsplatz brings you to Karlstrasse, leading to the bright orange **Rathaus**, many times rebuilt, which faces onto the Markt. On the north side of the square is the **Stadtschloss**, a compact Rococo palace begun in 1741 as the second residence of the newly united House of Saxe-Weimar-Eisenach. Previously the elegant interiors housed a museum of Thuringian decorative arts, but at present the building is closed indefinitely for restoration.

In the middle of the Markt stands the **Georgenkirche**, cathedral of the Protestant diocese of Thuringia. It is the late Gothic successor to the church where Landgrave Ludwig IV married the Hungarian princess now known as St Elisabeth (see also pp.425–427) in 1221, and where Luther, whose mother was a native of the town, sang as a choirboy. Soon after its construction, it was adapted to the needs of Protestant worship, notably by the erection of the tiered galleries. J.S. Bach was baptized here in 1685, and the church maintained its reputation as a place of destiny by being a key meeting place of opposition groups in the 1989 *Wende*. On the walls are a number of fourteenth-century carved epitaphs commemorating the Ludowingian rulers. Outside is the mid-sixteenth-century **Marktbrunnen**, showing the church's patron, St George, in his familiar dragon-slayer role.

The Thüringer Museum, the Lutherhaus and the Bachhaus

Just off the eastern side of the Markt is the **Predigerkirche**, built in the simple and austere Gothic style favoured by the Dominicans whose friary church it was. For the past century it has been home to the **Thüringer Museum** (Tues–Sun 9am–5pm; DM5/€2.50), an outstanding collection of wood sculpture, an art form in which Thuringia excelled throughout the Middle Ages. The earliest pieces are from the twelfth century, and include a *St John the Evangelist* of enormous tragic pathos, and range through a whole series of *Madonnas*, *Pietàs* and *Crucifixions* from the various phases of Gothic, to the large winged altars produced in Erfurt and Saalfeld in the years immediately before the Reformation. However, the most intriguing exhibit is the thirteenth-century **statue of Heinrich Raspe**, carved under the realist influence of the Naumburg School. As the crown on his head indicates, Raspe, the brother-in-law of St Elisabeth, usurped the German throne, though he was subsequently accorded the status of an "anti-king". He was also the last Landgrave of Thuringia, his death without issue leading to a war which saw the end of the province as a unit.

JOHANN SEBASTIAN BACH (1685–1750)

Although popular imagination has turned Mozart into the supreme composer touched by a flawless genius, most practising musicians would, if pressed, be far more likely to accord this honour to **Johann Sebastian Bach**. What makes this particularly remarkable is the fact that the defining feature of his career was its sheer provinciality. Born into a long-standing Thuringian musical family, he followed their tradition of salaried employment, serving as a church organist in Arnstadt and Mühlhausen, and as a court musician in Weimar and Köthen, before spending the last 27 years of his life as *Kantor* in Leipzig. Bach's vast output includes well over two hundred cantatas, the entire kernel of the organist's repertoire and most of the greatest music written for solo violin, cello and harpsichord. Although associated primarily with music of intense spirituality – of which the heart-rending *St Matthew Passion* is the supreme expression – Bach was a peerless practitioner of dance rhythms, as the *Orchestral Suites* show, and even adept at humorous effects, as in the *Coffee Cantata*.

Strangely, his reputation during his lifetime was based primarily on his prowess as a virtuoso performer. Few contemporaries appreciated the unique genius of his music, which, because it brought the Baroque age to a glorious climax rather than breaking new ground, was quickly forgotten after his death, not to be revived until Mendelssohn exhumed it a century later. Bach ensured the continuity of the family musical tradition by fathering twenty children, of whom at least two, the waywardly eccentric Carl Philipp Emmanuel and the elegantly refined Johann Christian, who brought the *galant* style to London, deserve to be considered as important composers in their own right.

Off the southwestern corner of the Markt is Lutherplatz, on which stands the **Lutherhaus** (daily: April–Oct daily 9am–5pm; Nov–March 10am–5pm; DM5/€2.50), in actual fact the home of the Cotta family, with whom Luther boarded as a schoolboy. The present house, predominantly a half-timbered structure of the sixteenth and eighteenth centuries, encloses the original, which preserves the two rooms used by the famous lodger. Inside are displays on his two periods in Eisenach, plus a large collection of Reformation books and other archive material.

A few minutes' walk south of the Lutherhaus is Frauenplan, with the **Bachhaus** (April–Sept Mon noon–5.45pm, Tues–Sun 9am–5.45pm; Oct–March Mon 1–4.45pm, Tues–Sun 9am–4.45pm; *www.bachhaus.de*; DM5/€2.50), a large Baroque house presumed to be the birthplace of J.S. Bach. Inside, an attempt has been made at re-creating the sort of bourgeois interiors typical of the composer's childhood. There's also extensive documention on his career and a valuable collection of historical musical instruments. To round off the visit, it's worth waiting for one of the demonstrations given by a member of staff, who puts a harpsichord, clavichord and chamber organ through their paces in performances of short pieces by Bach.

Elsewhere in the centre

Just east of the Bachhaus is Marienstrasse, where at no. 45 is the **Goldener Löwe** (Mon–Fri 9am–4pm; free), the former inn where August Bebel and Wilhelm Liebknecht set up their revolutionary socialist party in 1869, only to amalgamate it with its more moderate rival six years later in Gotha. Unlike most such memorial museums, it has reopened following a period of closure after the *Wende*. At the end of Marienstrasse, Reuterweg leads west to the **Reutervilla** (Tues–Sun 10am–5pm; DM4/€2), home of the nineteenth-century Low German writer Fritz Reuter, and still furnished as he knew it. Of more general appeal is the huge array of Wagner memorabilia, including his death mask. These were bought to commemorate the composer's sojourn in Eisenach, where he came to find inspiration for his opera *Tannhäuser*, which is set in and around the Wartburg, fusing into an imaginary, romanticized whole two true episodes from the castle's history.

Housed in temporary premises in the savings bank building at Rennbahn 6–8, a short walk west of the Hauptbahnhof on the opposite side of the tracks from the town centre, is the **Automobilbaumuseum** (Tues–Sun 10am–5pm; DM4/€2). This collection of historic vehicles celebrates Eisenach's tradition, dating back to 1898, as a leading centre of the German car industry. One of the earliest exhibits, the Dixi, was capable of the then mind-boggling speed of 60km per hour – it initiated a reputation for quality products which continued with the flashy BMW sports cars of the 1930s. From the postwar period are examples of the different versions of the Wartburg, the flagship of GDR car production. Unlike the ridiculous Trabant, with which it was often unfairly bracketed, it was a respectable motor and – like the Rolls-Royce – one of very few which had the body fitted to the chassis by hand. To local dismay, the factory, which lay immediately behind the bank, was closed down as unprofitable in 1991, though many of the workers were able to find alternative employment with BMW and Opel, who have both set up plants here. On the site, it is hoped to build a new museum that will be capable of displaying the entire collection instead of just the small selection currently on view.

The Wartburg

From the Reutervilla, it's a steep thirty-minute ramble through the woods to the **Wartburg** (daily: March–Oct 8.30am–8pm; Nov–Feb 9am–6pm; *www.wartburg-eisenach.de*; DM6/€3) – a far more atmospheric approach than the circuitous main road. Alternatively, the castle can be reached from the Hauptbahnhof by bus #10 or #13. If at all possible, avoid visiting at weekends or holiday periods, and arrive first thing: tourism here has soared since the *Wende*, often approaching bursting point.

THE HISTORY OF THE WARTBURG

The Wartburg was founded by Count Ludwig I in 1067. His descendants, promoted to the status of Landgraves, presided over a cultured court, patronizing some of the greatest Minnesänger (German troubadours), including Wolfram von Eschenbach, who wrote part of his epic *Parzifal* here, and Walter von der Vogelweide, the finest lyric poet of the day.

The most significant event in the Wartburg's history began in May 1521 when **Martin Luther**, having been declared an outlaw by the Diet of Worms, was kidnapped by order of Elector Frederick the Wise and taken to this safe haven. During his ten-month stay, the hitherto tonsured and clean-shaven monk disguised himself under a head of hair and beard, passing as a minor landowner by name of Junker Jörg (Farmer George). In a frenzy of activity, he translated the New Testament from Erasmus' Greek into the vernacular language spoken by the people of his day, so creating the foundations of modern written German.

In 1817 the Wartburg was the rallying place of the **Burschenschaften**, idealistically minded students protesting at the continued division of Germany, even after the Congress of Vienna, into a host of tinpot principalities.

Given its richly varied history, it's perhaps appropriate that the Wartburg is a melange of several different epochs, unfolding like a great picture book of German architecture. The oldest and most imposing part is the late twelfth-century **Palas** at the left-hand end of the second courtyard, one of Europe's few surviving examples of a Romanesque palace. A number of structures – including the **Torhalle** between the courtyards, the cross-crowned **Bergfried**, or keep, and the **Neue Kemenate** adjoining the Palas – were added in Romantic style in the nineteenth century, when the whole castle was given a thorough, albeit over-enthusiastic, restoration. The entrance ticket entitles you to climb the **Südturm**, from where there's a good view over the complex and the dense tracts of the Thuringian Forest beyond.

To see the interior of the Palas, you have to take a **guided tour** (April–Oct 8.30am–5pm; Nov–March 9am–3.30pm; additional DM5/€2.50). In all the Palas has around two hundred carved **capitals**, a third of them original, highly stylized masterpieces of late Romanesque carving. The finest are those on the central columns which are a distinguishing feature of most of the rooms, including the fourteenth-century **Burgkapelle**. To the modern eye, it's a matter of regret that there are so many Romantic embellishments, though these are often beautiful works in their own right, notably the three fresco cycles by **Moritz von Schwind** illustrating the life of St Elisabeth, the Minnesänger contest and the history of the castle. Rather more over the top are the Jugendstil mosaics in the saint's bedroom, and the colossal coffered vault of the main **Festsaal**, where the Burschenschaften met.

The museum in the Neue Kemenate is largely devoted to artefacts from around the time of the Reformation, including paintings, sculptures, weapons, furniture and tapestries. Among several works by **Cranach**, look out for the pendants of *Hans and Margarete Luder*, the parents of the great reformer.

From here, you cross the courtyard to the beamed interior of the Wehrgang (sentry walk), which leads round to the **Lutherstube**, the simple wood-panelled room where the German translation of the Bible was made. In the glass case is a copy of the original *Lutherbibel*, while on the walls hang portraits of Luther and Melanchthon, plus an engraving of Luther as Junker Jörg, all by Cranach. There was once a blot on the wall by the stove which, according to tradition, was made when Luther threw an inkpot at an apparition of the Devil, but souvenir hunters chipped away at it so much that there's now nothing but a hole going right through to the bare masonry.

Eating and drinking

Many of the best restaurants and cafés are in the hotels listed above, but there are plenty of others elsewhere.

Alt Eisenach, Karlstr. 51. Offers Thuringian specialities plus *Kaffee und Kuchen*.

Brunnenkeller, Markt 10. Restaurant in cellars formerly used by the local court.

Café Moritz, Bahnhofstr. 7. Long-established café, complete with summer terrace.

Lackner, Johannisstr. 22. Another traditional café, good for breakfast though it also does full meals.

Residenzkeller, corner of Esplanade and Markt. Cosy little restaurant with a shady beer garden. Evenings only, except at weekends.

Rheinischer Hof, Clemensstr. 15. Inexpensive Gaststätte to the rear of the Hauptbahnhof. In the past it has brewed its own beer, but is not doing so at present.

SOUTHWESTERN THURINGIA

The **Thuringian Forest** (Thüringer Wald), a typical central European highland area of densely wooded hills and valleys, covers almost the entire southwestern part of the province. In GDR days, it rivalled the Baltic coast as the main national holiday area, and its resorts had the advantage that they could function all year round, thanks to the suitable conditions for skiing and other winter sports. However, it's as a hiking area that the forest is best known, and it offers some of Germany's finest walks, notably in the countryside around **Friedrichroda**, **Suhl** and **Ilmenau**. Nor are the attractions purely scenic; there are several fine historic towns, including **Schmalkalden** in the heart of the forest, and **Meiningen** and **Arnstadt** on its fringes. Because of the nature of the terrain, communications can be difficult, yet public transport services are as excellent as ever.

Friedrichroda and around

It isn't necessary to stray far from Thuringia's central belt in order to see some of the best of the forest, as nowhere was more popular or developed during the GDR era than the area centred on **FRIEDRICHRODA**, just 20km from Gotha. Thanks to the super-abundance of cheap accommodation possibilities, this makes an excellent place for either a quiet break or some serious hiking – the only way to see the best of the forest.

Friedrichroda can be reached by the branch rail line from Fröttstädt, on the main line between Eisenach and Gotha. However, the best approach is by the **forest tramway**, the Thüringer Waldbahn, which runs from Gotha Hauptbahnhof to an interchange at the small industrial town of Waltershausen, whereupon it climbs steeply up to Friedrichroda before veering westwards to its terminus at the neighbouring resort of Tabarz. It's painfully slow – the 23-kilometre journey often takes longer than the hour for which it is timetabled – but it's the easiest way to see the scenery in comfort. Before the war, rural tramways were common throughout Germany: now the only other remaining is a much shorter one in Saxon Switzerland.

On leaving Friedrichroda, the Waldbahn stops outside the Thuringian Forest's most important natural curiosity, the **Marienglashöhle** (guided tours daily 9am–4/5pm; DM7/€3.50). This is the largest crystalline cave in Europe, complete with underwater lake; its name comes from the fact that, in times past, its products were used for making jewels to adorn statues of the Virgin Mary. The most pleasant part of Friedrichroda itself is the northern **Reinhardsbrunn** suburb, which has its own station and Waldbahn stop. Here an English-style park has been laid out around the medieval monastery which was converted into a grand neo-Gothic **Schloss** in the nineteenth century. It subsequently became a hotel, and is likely to become so again once restoration work is complete.

Hikes around Friedrichroda

By far the most popular hike in the area is the ascent of the Thuringian Forest's third highest and best-known peak, the **Grosser Inselberg** (916m), which lies just to the southwest of Tabarz. Unfortunately, the summit itself is disfigured by an ugly TV tower and a number of other buildings, including a couple of restaurants and a **youth hostel** (☎03 62 59/6 23 29, fax 6 23 29; DM18/€9 or DM23/€11/50). In compensation, there's a truly sweeping view, which is often given added drama by fickle microclimatic conditions. It isn't necessary to expend much energy getting to the top – taking the Friedrichroda to Brotterode bus to the Grenzwiese stop leaves only a short walk up. The same place marks the convergence of several other trails; among these is the **Rennsteig** (see box below), one of Germany's oldest and finest long-distance wilderness footpaths.

Another recommended area for walks is the vicinity of **FINSTERBERGEN**, a small resort 4km southeast of Friedrichroda. Its name means "Dark Mountains", and the forest around here is unusually dense and seen at its best under lowering skies. The village itself is attractive, with an unassuming-looking **Dorfkirche** whose interior, complete with double galleries, painted ceiling and organ, is a perfectly preserved example of the rustic interpretation of the Baroque style.

Practicalities

If you want help in finding accommodation in Friedrichroda, the **tourist office** is in the Kurverwaltung, Marktstr. 13–15 (Mon–Thurs 9am–5pm, Fri 9am–6pm, Sat 9am–noon; ☎0 36 23/3 32 00, fax 33 20 29, *www.friedrichroda.de*). There are dozens of **private rooms** (①–③), while **hotels** include *Im Grund*, Im Grund 3 (☎0 36 23/3 04 58 83; ④), and *Kavaliershaus* in the Schlosspark Reinhardsbrunn (☎0 36 23/30 42 53; ⑦). There's also a **youth hostel** at Waldstr. 25 (☎0 36 23/30 44 10, fax 30 50 03, *jugendherberge_friedrichroda@t-online.de*; DM21/€10.50 or DM26/€13).

Schmalkalden

Some of the buses which pass the Grosser Inselberg continue south to the lively market town of **SCHMALKALDEN**, 18km southwest of Friedrichroda. The town's name is associated above all with the Reformation, in which it played a key role; the Schmalkaldic League, formed here in 1531, was an alliance of Protestant princes and Free Imperial Cities determined to protect their independence against the renewed threat of the

---

THE RENNSTEIG

The 168-kilometre-long **Rennsteig** cuts right through the heart of the Thuringian Forest, from Hörschel, west of Eisenach, all the way to Blankenstein by the border with the Czech Republic. In the Dark Ages, it served as the frontier between the Thuringians and the Franks; later, it was used to demarcate the limits of the province's petty principalities, and a number of boundary stones, some dating back as far as the sixteenth century, survive as a reminder of this. When hiking became a popular pastime in the nineteenth century, the Rennsteig was laid out as a marked footpath, identified by signs bearing a large R. Five or six days is the normal time needed for the complete walk. Hostels, campsites and refuges lie directly on the trail, though there are also plenty of resorts on the way – Brotterode, Oberhof, Neustadt, Neuhaus and Steinbach – which make obvious places for an overnight stop. If you don't want to do the complete route, plenty of small sections make for satisfying walks in their own right.

reimposition of centralized political and religious authority posed by Emperor Charles V. The Schmalkaldic Wars, which broke out just after Luther's death in 1546, led to a disastrous defeat for the Protestants and the occupation of Wittenberg, but they staged such a spirited recovery that by 1555 their aim of a decentralized Germany with each state free to choose its own religion had been enshrined in the Peace of Augsburg.

Schmalkalden's main square, the Altmarkt, is dominated by the **Stadtkirche St Georg** (May–Oct Mon–Sat 10am–noon & 2–4pm), a late Gothic hall church whose clock-face shows Death claiming a young girl. Among the many notable old houses are the half-timbered **Lutherhaus** on Luthermarkt (formerly the potters' market), where the reformer stayed during his visits to the town; the **Heiliggrabesbehausung**, a huge sixteenth-century tenement on Weidebrunner Gasse; and the **Hessenhof** on Neumarkt. Preserved under the last-named, but not open to the public, is a Romanesque cellar with some of the oldest secular frescoes in Europe, depicting scenes from *The Iwein Saga* by the troubadour Hartmann von der Aue.

Standing proudly on its hill at the eastern end of town is the whitewashed **Schloss Wilhelmsburg** (Feb–Oct Tues–Sun 9am–5pm; Nov–Jan Tues–Sun 10am–4pm; DM6/€3), built in the 1580s as a summer residence and hunting seat for the landgraves of Hesse-Kassel, who had recently won complete control of the town. One of the best-preserved Renaissance palaces in Germany, its interior now houses exhibits outlining the town's complicated history, but these are overshadowed by the reception rooms themselves, most of which have elaborate coffered ceilings and huge decorative wall-paintings. Particularly outstanding is the **Riesensaal** (Hall of Giants), with Landgrave Wilhelm intruding among the portraits of Old Testament and mythological heroes. Another room contains copies of the frescoes under the Hessenhof.

However, the most striking and significant part of the building is the **Schlosskirche**, the earliest surviving church to adhere faithfully to the design tenets of Protestantism. Taking up most of one wing, the only clue to its presence from outside is the small tower. Inside, each of the three tiers has, grouped vertically one above the other, the three essential props of Protestant worship – the plain marble **altar table**, here resting on the four Evangelical symbols; the **pulpit**, whose basin is carved with a depiction of Pentecost; and the **organ**, which has wooden pipes and is adorned with painted shutters. The last-named is still in fine working order, and is regularly used for recitals. Otherwise, the rich stucco vault provides the only extravagant touch.

Practicalities

Schmalkalden's **Bahnhof** is a short walk west of the town centre. The **tourist office** (April–Oct Mon–Fri 9am–1pm & 2–5pm, Sat 10am–1pm & 2–5pm; Nov–March Mon–Fri 9am–1pm & 2–5pm, Sat 10am–1pm; ☎0 36 83/40 31 82, fax 60 40 14, *www.schmalkalden.de*) is at Mohrengasse 2. Plenty of **private rooms** (①–③) can be booked there.

Centrally sited accommodation options include a **pension**, *Noblesse*, Rötweg 8 (☎0 36 83/8 83 01; ④), and two **hotels**: *Teichhotel*, Teichstr. 21 (☎0 36 83/40 26 61; ⑤), and *Stadthotel Patrizier*, Weidebrunner Gasse 9 (☎0 36 83/60 45 14; ⑥). There are a couple of enticing alternatives in the outskirts: *Jägerklause*, Pfaffenbach 45 (☎0 36 83/60 45 11; ④), and *Henneberger Haus*, Notstr. 33 (☎0 36 83/6 50 00; ⑥). All the hotels listed above have good **restaurants**, though they're rivalled by the *Ratskeller*, Altmarkt 2.

Meiningen and around

On the banks of the River Werra at the extreme southwestern corner of the Thuringian Forest, some 25km from Schmalkalden, lies **MEININGEN**, an old ducal capital with a very distinctive tradition in the performing arts. In the latter half of last century, under the enterprising rule of Duke Georg II, it became one of Germany's leading centres for both theatre and music, with a resident orchestra, the Meininger Hofkapelle, which was among the most celebrated in the world, and one of the first to undertake global concert tours. Today Meiningen is a purely provincial town with a population of little more than 25,000, but it's an agreeable place with beautiful surroundings and an interesting Schloss, and warrants a stay of a day or two.

The Town

Meiningen's dominant building is **Schloss Elisabethenburg** (Tues–Sun 10am–4.45/6pm; DM6/€3), which stands in its own park at the northern end of the Altstadt, this combined area being separated from the rest of the town by a narrow canal system linked to the Werra. The Schloss was built in the late seventeenth century, immediately after the foundation of the duchy of Saxe-Meiningen, and is in the plainest possible Baroque style; indeed its geometric austerity seems strangely anticipatory of the Bauhaus, with the red-and-white colour scheme providing one of the few surface distractions. However, its ground plan is highly unusual, featuring an enclosed courtyard as a result of the addition of the so-called **Rundbau** (Round Building) to the orthodox palace format. Most of the **interiors** were remodelled according to the Historicist tastes of Duke Georg, and evoke the whole gamut of European architectural styles. They house three separate permanent exhibitions. That devoted to the fine arts includes notable examples of Gothic wood sculpture, plus an eclectic display of old masters whose star piece is *Lot and his Daughters* by Ribera. There are also displays on the Hofkapelle's **music directors**, who included Hans von Bülow — one of the first virtuoso conductors — and the composers Richard Strauss and Max Reger.

Part of the **Theatermuseum** (same hours and ticket), which features some spectacular stage sets plus a number of sketches for costume designs by Duke Georg himself, is still displayed in the Schloss itself, but the main part of the collection has been moved to the former riding hall, the Reiterhalle. On the top storey of the Schloss's central tower is the ornate **Hessensaal**, one of the few original interiors to have survived; it now houses the museum café (open from 1pm). The only other Baroque interior which can be visited is the former **Schlosskirche** in the southern wing, which has been converted, albeit with the retention of all its furnishings, into a concert hall.

Just across from the entrance to the Schloss, at Burggasse 22, is one of the town's finest half-timbered constructions, the **Baumbachhaus** (same times and ticket as the Schloss, otherwise DM2/€1). This houses a small museum on literary figures who have stayed in or near the town, among them Schiller and Jean Paul; the latter was the most popular and influential German novelist of the late eighteenth and early nineteenth centuries.

A few minutes' walk south, in the very heart of the Altstadt, is the spacious rectangular Markt. It's dominated by the **Stadtkirche St Marien** whose eccentrically fantastical twin spires help create a memorable silhouette. Although by origin late Gothic, the church's present appearance, both inside and out, is yet another manifestation of the artistic tastes of Duke Georg.

East of the Altstadt is Bernhardstrasse, a stately boulevard lined with several imposing buildings, notably the **Meininger Theater**. Despite its uncompromising Neoclassicism, above all in the porticoed facade, it only dates from the first decade of the twentieth century, and is a replacement for its fire-damaged predecessor. It retains the services of a full-sized orchestra, now rechristened the Orchester des Meininger Theaters, and presents ambitious programmes of music, opera, ballet and drama (☎0 36 93/45 12 22). Behind is the town's second important park, the Englischer Garten.

Practicalities

Meiningen's **Bahnhof** directly overlooks the Englischer Garten, and is just a few minutes' walk from the centre. The **tourist office** (April–Oct Mon–Fri 9am–6pm, Sat 10am–3pm; Nov–March Mon–Fri 9am–5pm; ☎ 36 93/4 46 50, fax 045 65 44, *www.meiningen.de*) at Bernhardstr. 6 performs the usual booking service for **private rooms** (②–③), which are fairly numerous.

There are several small **pensions**, including *Zum Bratwurstglöckle*, Untere Kaplaneistr. 8 (☎0 36 93/47 65 28; ③), *Pelzer*, Georgstr. 8 (☎0 36 93/4 42 10; ④), and *Sonnengarten*, Gartenstr. 14 (☎0 36 93/82 99 61; ④). Town-centre **hotels** include *An der Kapelle*, Anton-Ulrich-Str. 19 (☎0 36 93/4 49 20; ⑤), *Schlundhaus*, Schlundgasse 4 (☎0 36 93/81 38 38; ⑥), and *Sächsischer Hof*, Georgstr. 1 (☎0 36 93/45 70; ⑦). However, the most enticing place to stay has to be *Schloss Landsberg*, a medieval castle rebuilt in the nineteenth century in neo-Gothic style; it's situated 4km northwest of the centre at Landsberger Str. 150 (☎ 0 36 93/4 40 90; ⑦).

The best places to **eat** and **drink** are the hotels (all those listed have recommendable restaurants), or there's the *Schlossgaststätte* in the Rundbau of the Schloss, which offers Hungarian as well as traditional German dishes.

Walldorf and Wasungen

Immediately north of Meiningen, the first two stops on the rail line to Eisenach are a couple of contrasting small towns which are both well worth a visit. The first of the two is **WALLDORF**, from where there's a fine view of the abovementioned Schloss Landsberg. At the western edge of town are the **Sandstein- und Märchenhöhle** (guided tours daily: March–May, Sept & Oct 9am–5pm; June–Aug 9am–6pm; DM5/€2.50), a series of stalactite caves which have been made specially attractive for kids by being fitted out with three dozen scenes illustrating fairy tales and sagas. Nearby, set atop a rock, is the highly idiosyncratic **Kirchenburg**, a plain Renaissance church erected within the ruins of a twelfth-century fortress.

WASUNGEN, a few kilometres beyond, was one of the rare towns the GDR authorities placed under a total preservation order. Rightly so, as this is a distinctive little place, tightly packed in the restricted area between the Werra and the hills above. Its run-down appearance only adds to the charm, and the backstreet alleys present an undisturbed medieval picture. There are many outstanding half-timbered buildings, typically with a lower storey of stone, two of the best examples being the **Rathaus** and the **Damenstift**, both on the main street. High above the town, commanding a grandstand view over the Thuringian Forest, is **Burg Marienluft**, a ruined medieval castle whose later outbuildings house a **hotel** (☎03 69 41/47 80; ⑤) and restaurant.

Suhl and around

About 30km northeast of Meiningen, on the mazy rail and road routes to Erfurt, lies **SUHL**, the largest town within the Thuringian Forest, and one primarily of note for offering easy access to some of its finest scenery. However, it also has a certain curiosity value as a place which was heavily moulded in the GDR image. In 1951, it was chosen as the capital of one of the fifteen *Bezirke* into which the country was divided; thereafter, its population grew rapidly, and it was developed according to the "Socialist" method of planning, with the tiny historic centre ringed by skyscraper-lined boulevards, with suburbs of massive concrete apartment buildings which look wholly incongruous in their surroundings.

The main attraction in Suhl itself is the **Waffenmuseum** (April–Oct Tues–Sun 9am–5pm; Nov–March Tues–Sat 9am–4pm, Sun 10am–4pm; DM5/€2.50), housed in the Malzhaus, an impressively long half-timbered construction on Friedrich-König-Strasse on the northern fringe of the Altstadt. This celebrates Suhl's pre-eminence in weapons manufacture. In the sixteenth century, the town established itself as the armaments-producing capital of Europe, and the industry remains an important local employer to this day, specializing in hunting and sporting guns. Given that shooting was a favourite pastime among the GDR leadership, it's not too fanciful to see this being the reason they lavished their favours on Suhl. The museum offers a typically comprehensive documentary history of local production, with plenty of examples from other manufacturing centres for comparison.

The best vantage point within the town boundaries is the **Domberg** to the north: it's accessible by car, but is otherwise a long and steep walk through the forest. At the top are a Gaststätte (closed Wed) and an outlook tower, which is freely open during the summer months.

Practicalities

Suhl's **Hauptbahnhof**, at the rear of which is the **bus station**, is at the western end of the town centre; it's about ten minutes' walk to Marktplatz. The **tourist office** (Mon–Fri 10am–6pm, Sat 10am–4pm, Sun 10am–2pm; ☎ & fax 0 36 81/72 00 52; *www.suhl.de*) is in the Congress Centrum, Friedrich-König-Str. 42.

There's a wide provision of **private rooms** (①–③) in the town and its surroundings, while *Am Markt*, Pfarrstr. 20 (☎0 36 81/3 97 50; ④) is a conveniently central **pension**. Among the **hotels** are *Simson-Villa*, Dombergsweg 7 (☎0 36 81/2 24 83; ⑤), and the GDR-era showpieces, *Stadt Suhl*, Bahnhofstr. 25 (☎0 36 81/78 20; ⑥), and the all-too-prominent *Ringberg*, occupying a commanding hilltop position above the town, about 7km east by road, at Ringberg 10 (☎0 36 81/38 90; ⑥).

In addition to the hotel **restaurants**, good places for a meal are *Tivoli*, Rimbachstr. 24, which does Italian and German cuisine equally well, and *Gastmahl des Meeres*, Steinweg 15, which offers the expected fish dishes.

The Vesser valley

The finest hiking area around Suhl lies to the east; the easiest means of access is to take any Ilmenau-bound bus for about 10km to the Wegscheide stop, which marks the convergence of several marked trails. Of these, the most popular is that following the entire course of the **Vesser valley**, a lovely and undemanding thirteen-kilometre walk. It's 1km from the Wegscheide to the source of the river, reached by following the signs marked "Vesserquelle". The Vesser initially tumbles gently downhill through the trees before cutting across open meadows to **VESSER**, a sleepy village grouped around a half-timbered Pfarrkirche. Hitherto no more than a stream, its character changes rapidly in its lower stage, as it cleaves a deep valley through the forest. The trail ends with the Vesser's confluence with the Breitenbach at the village of the same name, from where it's 1km to St Kilian, which has rail and bus links with Suhl.

Schleusingen

Rather than return directly from St Kilian to Suhl, it's worth continuing a further 6km south to **SCHLEUSINGEN**, the terminus of the branch rail line, and also the starting point for a line to Ilmenau. This little town is dominated by one of the most outwardly imposing castles in Thuringia, **Schloss Bertholdsburg** (May–Sept Tues–Fri 9am–5pm, Sat & Sun 10am–6pm; Oct–April Tues–Sun 9am–5pm; DM5/€2.50). The seat of the counts of Henneberg, this dates back to the thirteenth century, but was rebuilt three hundred years later, with some picturesque half-timbered sections, in a hybrid late Gothic and Renaissance style. Most of the interior is given over to a museum on the geology and natural history of the region, though the last room is covered with impressive monochrome trompe l'oeil paintings made around 1600. Additionally, you can climb the tower for a view over the town and the Thuringian Forest.

Ilmenau and the Goethe trail

The old glass-making and procelain-producing town of **ILMENAU** lies on the River Ilm some 30km northeast of Suhl by a circuitous road, and also has a direct rail link with both Schleusingen and Arnstadt. It's a place with an unexpectedly youthful presence, being the seat of several colleges, including the recently founded Technical University. However, its name is associated above all with **Goethe**, who declared it to be a place where he was always happy; his administrative work on behalf of the Duchy of Saxe-Weimar meant that he was a regular visitor. The main reason for visiting Ilmenau is to walk one of Germany's best-known **footpaths**, *Auf Goethes Spuren*. While primarily of interest to literary buffs, it also offers an excellent overview of the scenery of the Thuringian Forest, and along the route are several excellent country Gaststätten offering wholesome German cooking.

The starting point for the walk is the **Amtshaus** (daily: May–Oct 9am–noon & 1–4.30pm; Nov–April 10am–noon & 1–4pm; DM2/€1), the administrative building at the top end of the Markt. This houses a small museum with period interiors containing mementoes of Goethe, who lived and worked there during his sorties to the town, and examples of local porcelain.

Practicalities

Ilmenau has two stations – the **Hauptbahnhof** is east of the town centre and marginally closer to the Markt than the **Bad-Bahnhof** to the south. The latter is more useful if you want to take the direct trail to the Kickelhahn. It's also closer to the **tourist office**

THE GOETHE TRAIL

The famous footpath, **Auf Goethes Spuren** (In Goethe's Footsteps), takes in a number of places connected with the poet in the course of an 18.5-kilometre route from Ilmenau. The terrain is fairly demanding, with many steep uphill stretches; allowing for regular sightseeing stops, it's likely to take up a full day. It's very well signposted by means of a G monogram copied from Goethe's own handwriting.

From the Markt in the centre of Ilmenau, the route travels westwards to the village of Manebach, from where it ascends the celebrated **Kickelhahn** (861m), which can also be reached directly by a much shorter path from the southern end of Ilmenau. On this mountain are an outlook tower, which commands an extensive panorama over Ilmenau and the Thuringian Forest, and a replica of the long-destroyed **Goethehäuschen**, the little wooden hideaway, where the poet composed one of his most quoted poems, *The Wayfarer's Night Song II*.

About fifteen minutes' walk further along the route is the **Jagdhaus Gabelbach** (Wed–Sun: April–Oct 9am–5pm; Nov–March 10am–4pm; DM4/€2), a hunting lodge containing a museum devoted to Goethe's studies in natural history, a subject which preoccupied him during his visits to this region. From here, the trail continues south to its terminus at the village of **STÜTZERBACH**, where the **Goethehaus** (same times; DM4/€2) preserves rooms where Goethe stayed and worked, and also features displays on the local glass industry.

(Mon–Fri 9am–6pm, Sat 9am–noon; ☎0 36 77/20 23 58, fax 20 25 02, *www.ilmenau.de*), which is just over the Ilm at Lindenstr. 12.

You can book **private rooms** (①–③) at the tourist office. There are also a few small **pensions**, including *Melanie*, just south of the Bad-Bahnhof at Heinrich-Heine-Str. 3 (☎0 36 77/67 01 45; ③). The one budget **hotel**, *Zum Elephant*, is right in the heart of town at Marktstr. 16 (☎0 36 77/20 24 41; ③); the alternatives, all much more expensive, are *Tanne*, Lindenstr. 38 (☎0 36 77/65 90; ⑥), *Zur Sonne*, Am Markt 3 (☎0 36 77/88 87 77; ⑥), and *Lindenhof*, Lindenstr. 7–11 (☎0 36 77/6 80 00; ⑥). Also worth considering is the *Berg- und Jagdhotel Gabelbach*, situated 2km from the town near the Jagdhaus at Waldstr. 23a (☎0 36 77/86 00; ⑥). All the hotels have good **restaurants**. The **youth hostel** is in the southeastern part of town at Am Stollen 49 (☎0 36 77/88 46 81, fax 88 46 82, *jh-ilmenau@t-online.de*; DM25/€12.50 or DM30/€15).

Arnstadt

First documented in 704, **ARNSTADT**, which lies just beyond the fringes of the Thuringian Forest, 22km north of Ilmenau and 18km southwest of Erfurt, has the best claim to be regarded as the oldest town in eastern Germany. Its well-preserved historic centre of narrow alleys and half-timbered houses evokes the sort of timeless provincial air that has all but vanished from the western Länder and may not last for much longer here; it also has the advantage of being surrounded by a typically Germanic landscape of woods and hills.

Arnstadt's layout is characteristic of the feudal pattern of Thuringia with the princely palace occupying a green area, now known as the Stadtpark, at the edge of the town centre. The tower and a few other scanty fragments are all that remain of the sixteenth-century **Schloss Neideck**, the original seat of the House of Schwarzburg-Arnstadt. Before it fell into disrepair, a second palace, the **Neues Palais** (May–Sept Tues–Sun 8.30am–noon & 1–4.30pm; Oct–April Tues–Sun 9.30am–4pm; DM3.50/€1.75), was built to the south in the early eighteenth century. Its main attraction is **Mon Plaisir**, a collection of over four hundred dolls arranged into 82 scenes, depicting the life of all social classes of the day. This is far more profound than it at first appears – far from being intended as playthings for children, these scenes were commissioned over half a century by Princess Augusta Dorothea as a serious artistic enterprise. As well as the figures, the clothes, utensils and furniture are all precisely crafted, and constitute a valuable documentary source on social conditions in the period. The palace is also renowned for its seventeenth- and eighteenth-century porcelain, some of which is ingeniously displayed on gilded tables in the **Spiegelkabinett**.

A few minutes' walk to the west is the Markt, where the Renaissance **Rathaus** springs a surprise in its uncompromising imitation of Dutch-style architecture. The church opposite was once known as the Neue Kirche. In 1703, the 18-year-old J.S. Bach gained his first major professional appointment as organist here; as a result, it's now officially called the **Bachkirche**, and the organ on which he played still survives. Unfortunately, the Arnstadt congregation failed to appreciate his genius as either a composer or performer and, stung by criticism of his revolutionary improvisatory style, he left four years later for Mühlhausen. The Bach theme is taken up in the Renaissance-Baroque **Haus zum Palmbaum** (Mon–Fri 8.30am–12.30pm & 1–5pm, Sat & Sun 9.30am–5pm; DM4/€2) at Markt 3, which contains the local history museum. Among the memorabilia of the composer, the most striking is the original console of his organ, which had to be removed when the instrument's action was modernized.

Beyond the far end of the Markt is the **Liebfrauenkirche**, whose architecture, and in particular the two magnificent west towers, is loosely based on the Dom in Naumburg. The chapel on the north side of the choir served as the mausoleum of the counts of Schwarzburg and contains the beautiful double **tomb** of Günther XXV and his wife Elisabeth, thought to have been carved in the famous workshop of Peter Parler in Prague. Also of note are the **stained-glass windows** in the nave aisles, and the **high altar** of *The Coronation of the Virgin*, a fine example of fifteenth-century Thuringian woodcarving. Alongside the church is one of the town's oldest half-timbered houses, the **Alte Mühle**, which began life as the corn mill of a convent.

Practicalities

Arnstadt's **Hauptbahnhof** is situated at the northern end of town., while the **tourist office** (Mon–Fri 10am–6pm, Sat 10am–4pm, Sun 10am–2pm; ☎0 36 28/60 20 49, fax 74 57 48, *www.arnstadt.de*) is in the centre, at Rankestr. 11. The best times to visit are during the **musical festivals**, the *Bachtage* at the end of March and the *Orgelsommer* in June and July.

As well as the **private rooms** (①–③) which can be booked at the tourist office, there are **hotels** to suit most pockets. At the budget end of the scale are *Goldene Sonne*, Ried 3 (☎0 36 28/60 27 76; ③), and *Riedschenke*, Vor dem Riedtor 6 (☎0 36 28/60 23 74; ③); while *Brauhaushotel*, Brauhausstr. 3 (☎0 36 28/60 74 00; ④) is an excellent new middle-range choice. The most luxurious options are *Krone*, Am Bahnhof 8 (☎0 36 28/7 70 60; ⑥), and *Anders*, Gehrener Str. 22 (☎0 36 28/74 53; ⑥).

There are fine **restaurants** in each of the last two hotels, while the *Brauhaushotel* is part of a complex centred on the Stadtbrauerei, which brews a distinctive black *Weizen* (it is claimed that *Hefeweizen* was invented in Arnstadt in 1617) and serves excellent food. It has a covered winter garden and a summer beer garden, while alongside are Schalander, a live music and cabaret cellar, and the Stadthalle (☎0 36 28/60 77 06), where concerts and large-scale events take place.

NORTHERN THURINGIA

The northern part of Thuringia is, in comparison with the central belt, little touched by tourism. Here are two towns, **Mühlhausen** and **Nordhausen**, which went against the regional grain in the medieval period by functioning as city-states. Though Nordhausen is now a shadow of its former self, the centre of Mühlhausen looks much as it has done for centuries. The other main draws in the north are the often-overlooked princely seat of **Sondershausen** and the hills of the **Kyffhäuser** range.

Mühlhausen

Even within Thuringia, there are few places which conjure up the past so vividly as **MÜHLHAUSEN**, which dates back at least as far as Charlemagne. Its historic core has almost completely intact medieval walls, inside which is a maze of alleys lined with half-timbered houses and six Gothic churches, with a further four standing just outside the fortifications. As a Free Imperial City throughout the Middle Ages, Mühlhausen was a rare island of independence in this part of the country, which explains why it became the headquarters of the ill-fated Peasants' War of 1525, led by the town's firebrand pastor, **Thomas Müntzer** (see box opposite). To the GDR authorities, this was the first great social revolution in German history; accordingly, Müntzer became one of the state's supreme heroes, regarded as a Moses-like precursor of Marx. In 1975, to mark the 450th anniversary of the event, the town was officially renamed "Thomas-Müntzer-Stadt-Mühlhausen", and two of the churches were made over as memorials to him. The latter have survived the post-*Wende* re-evaluations, though the town's forename has been discarded.

THOMAS MÜNTZER AND THE PEASANTS' WAR

By far the most controversial, not to say sinister, figure of the Reformation, **Thomas Müntzer** has a significance far beyond the distorted one promoted by the GDR – he can be regarded as the father of all the myriad forms of sectarian Protestantism which retain such an influence to this day. As vitriolic about Luther (whom he dismissed as "Dr Pussyfoot" and "Dr Easychair") as about Catholicism, Müntzer believed that the Bible had to be reinterpreted by a second Daniel (needless to say, himself) who would lead the elect in a crusade against the ungodly. His electrifying preaching gained him a huge popular following, but his bloodthirsty message so alarmed the authorities of electoral Saxony that he was expelled from the territory.

On his appointment at Mühlhausen, he hitched his cause to that of the peasants who were already in revolt against their feudal masters over their economic plight. In reality, Müntzer was primarily interested in them for religious reasons, though he was the only leading churchman of the day who understood that faith among the common people was not nourished by starvation. Incensed by Müntzer's actions, Luther was inspired to write a pamphlet condemning the peasants, and backed the princely armies which crushed his rival's untrained forces at Frankenhausen. Müntzer was captured in the battle and brought back to Mühlhausen, where he was tried, tortured and executed.

The Town

The best introduction to Mühlhausen is to walk all the way round the outside of the 2.7-kilometre-long **Stadtmauer**, which still preserves six towers and two gateways. It's at its most impressive around the main western entrance, the **Inneres Frauentor**. Here a small section has been opened to the public, enabling you to go along part of the sentry walk and ascend the **Rabenturm** (Tues–Sun: May, June, Sept & Oct 1–5pm; July & Aug 10am–noon & 1–5pm; DM2/€1).

On Holzstrasse, the northern of the two streets leading to the centre, you pass the thirteenth-century **Hospital** and a number of fine houses, of which the most notable is no. 1, which began life as the town-house of Kloster Zella before becoming a post office in the period of the Thurn und Taxis monopoly. Herrenstrasse to the south also has fine buildings, though the parish house at the far end is a replacement of the one where Müntzer lived, which was destroyed by fire.

Both streets terminate at the **Marienkirche** (daily 10am–4.30pm; DM3/€1.50), where Müntzer served as pastor during the three fateful months he lived in Mühlhausen. The church itself has a distinctive triple-towered **facade** in which the massive Flamboyant Gothic central tower, crowned with a bravura nineteenth-century steeple, is flanked by its two modest counterparts, one late Romanesque, the other early Gothic. No less idiosyncratic is the **south portal**: although some of its original statuary – carved by the Parler school of Prague – was destroyed as a result of the iconoclasm fomented by Müntzer, the balcony with the peering figures of Emperor Charles IV, Empress Elisabeth and two courtiers survives intact. Inside, the most impressive feature is the soaring architecture of the five-aisled hall nave with its elaborate vault. The **furnishings** include a number of fine retables (the high altar to the Virgin Mary was made during the brief return to Catholicism following Müntzer's demise), and the grand white Ratsstuhl, where councillors sat during services.

Following Ratsstrasse south from here brings you to the **Rathaus** (Sat & Sun 10am–5pm; DM1/€0.50) complex, which dates back to about 1300 but which grew in size to such an extent down the centuries that it straddles the street, with the two parts linked by a covered passageway. In the **Ratsstube**, adorned with Gothic wall-paintings, Müntzer held his daily *Ewig Rat* (Perpetual Council); the **Archiv**, with its complete set of Renaissance furniture and documents pertaining to Mühlhausen's period as a city-state, is also worth a look.

A couple of blocks south on Kornmarkt is the **Barfüsserkirche** (Tues–Sun 10am–4.30pm; DM2/€1), a barn-like former Franciscan friary church given over to a museum on the Peasants' War. Further south on Johann-Sebastian-Platz is the **Divi-Blasii-Kirche**, a former church of the Teutonic Knights, whose place in musical history is assured as a result of the year Bach spent there as organist following his departure from Arnstadt. Despite the shortness of his tenure, he drew up the specification for a new organ, a much-prized instrument still reguarly used for recitals. The twin towers are a good illustration of the way late Romanesque passed seamlessly into Gothic; the rest of the building is, like the Marienkirche, a fourteenth-century hall church.

Practicalities

Mühlhausen's **Bahnhof**, which has regular services to both Gotha and Erfurt, is three blocks beyond the easternmost part of the Stadtmauer. The **tourist office** (May–Oct Mon–Fri 9am–5pm, Sat 10am–noon; Nov–April Mon–Fri only; ☎0 36 01/45 23 35, fax 45 23 16, *www.muehlhausen.de*) is at Ratsstr. 20; there's a separate phone number (☎0 36 01/45 23 20) for booking **private rooms** (①–③).

The **youth hostel** is in the outskirts of town at Auf den Tonberg 1 (☎0 36 01/81 33 18, fax 81 33 20; DM21/€10.50 or DM26/€13); take bus #5 or #6 to Blobach. There are many **pensions**, some of them centrally located, such as *Schilling*, Erfurter Str. 30 (☎0 36 01/81 28 83; ②), *Höfler*, Kuttelgasse 23 (☎0 36 01/4 46 99 09; ③), and *Adams*, Allerheiligengasse 2 (☎0 36 01/44 24 18; ③). **Hotels** include *Gasthof Bundschuh*, Jüdenstr. 43 (☎0 36 01/4 62 30; ④), *Stadt Mühlhausen*, Untermarkt 18 (☎0 36 01/45 50; ④), *An der Stadtmauer*, Breitenstr. 5 (☎0 36 01/4 65 00; ⑤), *Ammerscher Bahnhof*, Ammerstr. 83–85 (☎0 36 01/87 31 32; ⑤), *Mirage*, Karl-Marx-Str. 9 (☎0 36 01/43 90; ⑥), and *Brauhaus Zum Löwen*, Kornmarkt 3 (☎0 36 01/47 10; ⑥).

There's a surprisingly good choice of **restaurants**; among the best is *Zum Nachbarn*, just east of the Marienkirche at Steinweg 65, which specializes in poultry dishes. Strong competition comes from several of the hotel restaurants, particularly *Brauhaus Zum Löwen*, which brews its own beer, and *An der Stadtmauer*.

Mühlhausen was one of the few places in the GDR which kept up much of a tradition in **festivals**, of which the most important is the *Kirmes*, a fair held at the end of August.

Nordhausen

NORDHAUSEN lies just to the south of the Harz mountains, at the fringe of the fertile plain known as the Goldene Aue (Golden Meadow), about 45km northeast of Mühlhausen. It's predominantly an industrial town, best known for its production of spirits (a mouth-burning *Korn* has been made here since the early sixteenth century) and tobacco (especially *Kautabak*, or "chewing tobacco"). Unfortunately, this rather overshadows its historical role as a former Free Imperial City, the more so as a large number of monuments were destroyed in 1945, during the severest bombing raid carried out on any Thuringian town. Nonetheless, there are a few sights well worth stopping to see if you happen to find yourself here – Nordhausen is the southern terminus of the narrow-gauge steam rail line through the Harz, the Harzquerbahn (see box on p.922).

The **Stadtmauer** was among the monuments damaged in the war, though 1.5km of the circuit still remain, the most impressive section being the set of double fortifications around Jüdenstrasse, about halfway up the hill between the Hauptbahnhof and the Markt. Following the wall northwards, you can see the **Finkenburg**, one of the oldest and finest of the few half-timbered houses spared by the bombs, at An der

Wassertreppe. East of here is the Markt, whose late Renaissance **Rathaus**, outside which stands the inevitable statue of Roland, was rebuilt from wartime ruins.

Further up, the skyline is dominated by the so-called **Dom**, more correctly the **Kloster zum Heiligen Kreuz**, the successor to a nunnery founded by Empress Mathilde in 963. The present church is an architectural jumble – the towers, the cloister and the crypt are Romanesque, the choir early Gothic, the lofty hall nave Flamboyant Gothic. Inside, the finest feature is the group of six late thirteenth-century statues in the choir, clearly modelled on their counterparts in Naumburg.

The more modest **Blasiikirche** just to the east exhibits a remarkably similar architectural mix, though one of its two octagonal towers has a truncated aspect since its damage in a seventeenth-century fire. Barfüsserstrasse, which leads north from here, is the least damaged of Nordhausen's old streets, with a number of half-timbered houses, of which no. 6, now a library, was the town's first theatre.

In 1943, a subsidiary concentration camp of Buchenwald, under the name of **Dora**, was set up at the foot of the Kohnstein at the northernmost fringe of Nordhausen. The following year, renamed **Mittelbau**, it became a full-blown camp in its own right. Some sixty thousand prisoners from twenty-one different countries were interned here, engaged on the secret production of V1 and V2 missiles, working underground in a network of tunnels and caverns. Nearly a third of them died here; in their honour, the site has been turned into a memorial, the **Gedenkstätte Mittelbau-Dora** (April–Sept daily 10am–4/6pm; free), with documentary displays on the conditions they suffered. The easiest way to get here is to take the Harzquerbahn to Krimderode, then follow the main road round to the west.

Practicalities

Nordhausen's **Hauptbahnhof** lies south of the Altstadt, on the opposite side of the River Zorge; the Harzquerbahn's terminus, misleadingly designated Nordhausen-Nord, is just across Bahnhofsplatz. The **tourist office** (Mon–Fri 7.30am–6.30pm, Sat & Sun 8.30am–4.30pm; ☎0 36 31/90 21 55, *www.nordhausen.de*) at Bahnhofsplatz. 3a can book **private rooms** (①–③).

The town has few **hotels**, the best being *Zur Sonne*, Hallesche Str. 8 (☎0 36 31/60 21 10; ④), *Avena*, Hallesche Str. 13 (☎0 36 31/60 20 60; ⑤), and *Handelshof*, Bahnhofstr. 13 (☎0 36 31/62 50; ⑥). There's also a **youth hostel** at Parkallee 2 (☎0 36 31/90 23 91, fax 90 23 93, *rothleinmühle@t-online.de*; DM25/€12/50 or DM30/€15) near the Stadtpark; take bus #6 to Altentor.

Nordhausen doesn't score highly for **eating** and **drinking**, but try *Café Altstadt*, Kranichstr. 19, or the *Ratskeller*, Markt 1. The main local **festival** is the *Rolandfest* on the second weekend in June.

Sondershausen

SONDERSHAUSEN, which lies 20km south of Nordhausen in a pretty setting in the valley cut by the River Wipper between two groups of wooded hills, the Hainleite and the Windleite, is a place which deserves to be far better known. Formerly the capital of the county of Schwarzburg, and later of the principality of Schwarzburg-Sondershausen, its main attraction is as one of the courtly towns so characteristic of Thuringia. However, it's far less soporific than most of its counterparts. The huge winding tower (now preserved as a technical monument) which greets you on arrival at the Hauptbahnhof is a reminder that Sondershausen has for centuries been a major centre of potash production, while the historic heart of the town has regained its former role as a market and trading centre.

A typically oversized **Schloss** (April–Sept Tues–Fri 10am–5pm, Sat & Sun 10am–6pm; Oct–March Tues–Sun 10am–4pm; DM6/€3) is Sondershausen's overwhelmingly dominant building. It can be approached from the west via its rustic park, or from the Markt by the monumental steps to the side of the Neoclassical guard house, the Alte Wache. The north wing dates back to the sixteenth century, while the seventeenth century saw the beginning of a massive extension programme, including the addition of a Baroque tower and south wing. A late Rococo palace, subsequently modified in Neoclassical style, was then added at an angle of 45 degrees to the original, creating an almost triangular courtyard. The wonderfully eclectic interior graphically conjures up the real-life fantasy world of a petty German court. In the original palace is the most individual chamber, the Mannerist **Wendelstein**, which boasts a dazzlingly brilliant stucco vault showing the Elements, the Seasons, the Virtues, putti and mythological characters. The main reception room is the Baroque **Riesensaal** (Giants' Hall), so called from the sixteen over-life-sized statues of classical deities; it also boasts a superb coffered vault with ornate stucco trophies and paintings illustrating Ovid's *Metamorphoses*. In its Rococo counterpart, the turquoise **Festsaal**, the antique theme is continued with the story of Jupiter and Calypso. Two other highlights are the **Liebhabertheater** (Conoisseurs' Theatre), a Biedermeier gem which is one of the smallest theatres in Germany, and the gilded **state coach**.

In the park west of the Schloss is the **Karussel** or **Achteckiges Haus**, a tall, eccentric-looking octagon with interior galleries and a fresco of *The Triumph of Venus*. Built at the beginning of the eighteenth century to serve as the main venue for court entertainments, it's occasionally used for concerts by the Loh-Orchester.

It's also worth taking a walk in the **Hainleite**, the hills to the south of Sondershausen; they're best reached by following Possenallee straight ahead from the town centre. From here, it's an easy ascent to the **Rondell**, a belvedere commanding a fine view of the valley. A couple of kilometres further south brings you to the **Jagdschloss zum Possen**, the former hunting lodge of the court, which is now a recuperative centre with a wildlife park alongside. There's also a tall half-timbered **Aussichtsturm** (daily 10am–6pm; DM1/€0.50) dating from the very end of the eighteenth century, which you can climb for the most extensive panorama of the whole region.

Practicalities

Sondershausen's **Hauptbahnhof** is about fifteen minutes' walk west of the centre; the Haltepunkt Sondershausen-Süd below the Hainleite is actually slightly nearer the Markt and the Schloss. The **tourist office** (Mon–Fri 9am–12.30pm & 1.30–5pm, Sat 9–11am; ☎0 36 32/78 81 11, fax 60 03 82, *www.sondershausen.de*) is in the Alte Wache, Markt 9.

In addition to a **youth hostel**, which has a conveniently central location at Güntherstr. 26–27 (☎0 36 32/60 11 93, fax 78 22 59; DM18/€9 or DM23/€11.50), there are plenty of **private rooms** (①–③) for rent. Alternatively, there are a few **pensions**: *Zur Sonne*, Conrad-Röntgen-Str. 11 (☎0 36 32/60 24 86; ②), *Schweizer Haus*, Im Loh 1a (☎0 36 32/60 11 11; ③), and *Haus Waldheim*, Erfurter Str. 29 (☎0 36 32/75 87 79; ④). However, there are just two **hotels**: *Zum Erbprinzen*, Im Loh 1 (☎0 36 32/75 03 36; ⑤), and *Thüringer Hof*, Hauptstr. 30–32 (☎0 36 32/65 60; ⑥). The best **restaurants** are the one in *Thüringer Hof* (which serves Italian cuisine), the *Ratskeller*, Markt 7, and the *Schlossrestaurant* in the Schloss.

The Kyffhäuser

The **Kyffhäuser**, a small group of wooded sandstone mountains, form a virtual southern continuation of the Harz, which they closely resemble – except for the fact that they're virtually uninhabited. Despite their modest dimensions – they occupy less than 60 square kilometres, while the peaks are all under 500m – they have a grandeur that belies their actual size. In addition, they hold a special place in the national consciousness, being the seat of one of the great imperial castles of early medieval Germany and the place where, according to legend, Emperor Frederick Barbarossa (the country's real-life counterpart of King Arthur) lies slumbering, awaiting his second coming. For the GDR state, the Kyffhäuser had the additional allure of being where the first German revolution, the Peasants' War of 1525, came to its untimely end.

Bad Frankenhausen

The gateway to the Kyffhäuser, and the obvious base for a visit, is the small spa town of **BAD FRANKENHAUSEN**, which lies at their southern edge, 20km east of Sondershausen, just below the **Schlachtberg** (Battle Hill) where Thomas Müntzer's peasant army was routed by vastly superior forces loyal to the nation's rulers.

In the late sixteenth century, Frankenhausen became the capital of one of the four counties into which Schwarzburg was divided, an event which necessitated the building of the modest little **Schloss** (Tues–Sun 10am–5pm; DM3/€1.50) at the southern end of the old quarter, about five minutes' walk from the Bahnhof. It's now a museum devoted to the Kyffhäuser region, with displays on its flora, fauna, archeology, history, arts and crafts, with the highlight being a diorama of the battle of 1525. Just north of the Schloss is the Markt, with a Neoclassical Rathaus; from here, Kräme, a pedestrianized shopping street, leads to **Anger**, the spacious main square, which boasts a few half-timbered houses. Uphill lies the best-preserved section of the thirteenth-century fortification system, centred on the impressive **Hausmannsturm**.

Much further up, crowning the top of the Schlachtberg, is the white rotunda housing the **Bauernkriegs-Panorama** (guided tours: April–June & Sept Tues–Sun 10am–6pm; July & Aug Mon 1–6pm, Tues–Sun 10am–6pm; Oct–March Tues–Sun 10am–5pm; DM10/€5). Claimed as the largest painting in the world, this huge, vividly coloured panoramic picture of the battle was unveiled in 1989 to celebrate Müntzer's 500th anniversary, and the 40th birthday of the GDR. Begun twelve years previously, it was commissioned as a co-operative work by a team of artists, on the model of the many nineteenth-century panoramic battle pictures, a once-popular art form which, until then, seemed to have been killed off by the cinema. As work progressed, the Leipzig professor **Werner Tübke** assumed an increasingly dominant role, eventually taking over the project completely. Over 70 percent of the painting is by him, with much of the rest being detail provided by specialists. Both politically and artistically the end result is controversial, though neither critical derision nor the inflated entrance fee deters the crowds who flock here, often queuing for hours during the main holiday periods because of the restricted admissions policy.

Practicalities

The **tourist office** (May–Sept Mon–Fri 9am–6pm, Sat 10am–3pm, Sun 10am–noon; Oct–April Mon–Fri 9am–5pm, Sat 10am–noon; ☎03 46 71/7 17 16, fax 7 17 19, *www.bad-frankenhausen.de*) is at Anger 14, the oldest half-timbered house in town. You can book a **private room** (①–③) here, though they're easy enough to find on your own if you look for the *Zimmer frei* signs.

For a bit more luxury, there are several **hotels**: *Grabenmühle*, Am Wallgraben 1 (☎03 46 71/7 98 82; ④), *Bellevue*, Goethestr. 13 (☎03 46 71/6 30 68; ⑤), *Reichental*, Rottleber Str. 4 (☎03 46 71/6 80; ⑥), and *Residence Frankenburg*, Am Schlachtberg 3 (☎03 46 71/7 50; ⑥). All of these also have good, reasonably priced **restaurants**.

The mountains

The Kyffhäuser are combed with marked walking trails, and it's easy enough to devise your own circular routes. Easiest hike is to the **Barbarossahöhle** (guided tours daily

9am–5/6pm; DM6/€3), 5km to the west and just north of Rottleben, the next stop on the rail line to Sondershausen. Discovered during mining operations in the nineteenth century – whereupon it immediately became coupled to the Barbarossa legend – this is, with a total length of 800m, one of Europe's largest gypsum caves, featuring some amazing vaults and tiny lakes with crystal-clear waters.

For the more energetic, there's a ten-kilometre path from Bad Frankenhausen which travels right through the heart of the Kyffhäuser to its highest summit, the **Kulpenberg** (477m). This is crowned by a television tower whose observation platform was formerly open to the public, but is currently closed.

A few kilometres east of here, and linked by a direct trail to Bad Frankenhausen, is the **Kyffhäuserdenkmal** (daily 9am–5/6pm; DM6/€3). This Historicist monstrosity, which commands another sweeping view over the region, was erected at the end of the nineteenth century in honour of the recently deceased Kaiser Wilhelm I, the first emperor of the Second Reich and thus the man seen as something of a reincarnation of Frederick Barbarossa, an early champion of German unity. In order to build it, a substantial portion of the surviving fragments of the upper fortress of the famous Romanesque **Reichsburg**, one of the strongholds of the Hohenstaufen emperors, had to be demolished – an act of vandalism uncharacteristic of the time. Thankfully, the ruins of the lower fortress, including a well some 176m deep, survive to give an idea of the scale and appearance of the original.

EASTERN THURINGIA

The easternmost part of Thuringia has a natural border in the form of the middle reaches of the valley of the River Saale, on whose banks lie the university city of **Jena**, and the former courtly towns of **Rudolstadt** and **Saalfeld**. Further east lie **Gera** and **Greiz**, the capitals of the two old principalities of Reuss, while jutting into Saxony, and only recently returned to its traditional Thuringian homeland, is a strip of territory centred on **Altenburg**.

Jena and around

JENA, which is just 20km southeast of Weimar, lies at the point where the Saale valley is at its grandest, surrounded by red sandstone and chalk hills, which have a climate mild enough for the growing of vines. The **University** is among the most famous in Germany; founded in 1558 with the help of Melanchthon, it was closely associated with the great flowering of Classicism in Weimar, to which Jena then belonged, following its own short-lived period as capital of an independent duchy. In the nineteenth century, it played a leading role in scientific research, and had strong links with the world-renowned optics company, the Carl-Zeiss-Stiftung, whose works are still a prominent feature of the skyline.

Sadly, the city was exceptionally badly bombed in World War II and still bears the scars of this. Nevertheless, there's still plenty to see – particularly if you are at all of a scientific bent – while the atmosphere is the liveliest, and the choice in eating, drinking and nightlife by far the best in Thuringia.

Arrival, information and accommodation

Jena has two main train stations. The **Saalbahnhof** in the north of the city is on the express Berlin-Munich line, with local services northwards to Dornburg and Naumburg, and southwards to Rudolstadt and Saalfeld; the **Westbahnhof** to the southwest of the centre is on the line linking Erfurt and Weimar with Gera. Many of the trains to and from the Saalbahnhof stop at the **Paradiesbahnhof**, which is at the southern fringe of the centre; slightly to the north of here is the **bus station**.

The **tourist office** (Mon–Fri 9am–6pm, Sat 9am–2pm; ☎0 36 41/80 64 04 or 1 94 33, fax 80 64 09, *www.jena.de*) is at Johannisstr. 23. **Private rooms** (②–③) can be booked, as usual, through them. The **youth hostel** is at Am Herrenberge 3 (☎0 36 41/68 70; DM26/€14 or DM31/€15.50) in the suburb of Lichtenhain southwest of the centre, reached by bus #10, #13 or #40. **Hotels** and **pensions** are scattered all over the city, with something to suit all pockets.

Hotels and Pensions

Adria Grill, Wenigenjenaer Ufer 15 (☎0 36 41/44 55 72, fax 89 00 50). Small pension run as an adjunct to a Balkan restaurant. ④.

Esplanade, Carl-Zeiss-Platz 4 (☎0 36 41/80 00, fax 80 01 50, *www.steigenberger.de*). Jena's most prestigious hotel, part of the exclusive Goethe-Galerie shopping centre. Its restaurant *Rotunda* occupies a hexagonal tower with a panorama terrace. ⑥–⑧.

Jembo Park, Rudolstädter Str. 93, Göschwitz (☎0 36 41/68 50, fax 68 52 99, *www.jembo.de*). Thuringia's first motel, located on the B88 just a short distance north of Bahnhof Göschwitz, 4km south of the centre. Has bungalows as well as hotel rooms, a restaurant and an English-style pub. ⑤.

Jenaer Hof, Bachstr. 24 (☎0 36 41/44 38 55, fax 44 38 66). Small hotel with café in a Jugendstil building right in the city centre. ④.

Papiermühle, Erfurter Str. 102 (☎0 36 41/4 59 80, fax 45 98 45). An old paper mill on the west side of the city has been converted to house this combined hotel, restaurant and *Bockbier* brewery. ⑤.

Schwarzer Bär, Lutherplatz 2 (☎0 36 41/40 60, fax 40 61 13, *www.schwarzer-baer-jena.de*). Hotel with a tradition dating back some five hundred years at the northwestern corner of the Altstadt, not far from the Saalbahnhof. Its restaurant is very reasonably priced. ⑤.

Thüringer Hof, Westbahnhofstr. 8 (☎0 36 41/2 92 90, fax 29 9 99, *www.jenanet.de/thueringerhof*). Recently upgraded hotel near the Westbahnhof. It has a bistro, *Louis*, and a beer garden. ⑤.

Zur Noll, Oberlauengasse 19 (☎ & fax 0 36 41/44 15 66). Gasthof in the very heart of the Altstadt, with restaurant, beer garden and exhibition gallery. Often hosts different types of live music. ⑤.

Zur Schweiz, Quergasse 15 (☎0 36 41/5 20 50, fax 5 20 51 11). Another good central Gasthof, with a particularly recommendable restaurant and a beer garden. ⑤.

Zur Weintraube, Rudolstädter Str. 70, Winzerla (☎0 36 41/69 57 70, fax 60 65 83). Eighteenth-century inn on the B88, 3km south of the centre. Its excellent, moderately priced restaurant offers many Thuringian specialities. ⑤.

The City

Given its size, Jena's attractions are fairly spread out. However, most of what you're likely to want to see is concentrated in a few easily assimilated areas and can be covered comfortably on foot.

Eichplatz

Dominating the centre of Jena from the middle of the spacious Eichplatz, dwarfing even the Carl Zeiss buildings just to the west, is the **Universitätshochhaus**, a 120-metre-high cylindrical tower inaugurated in 1972. Though by no means the worst example of the GDR school of brutalist architecture, it's distinctly unloved locally: irreverent students were quick to dub it *Phallus Jenensis*, and this has since passed into the cruder vernacular form of *Jenaer Pimmel* (Jena's Willie). The demise of the GDR inevitably led to calls for its demolition, but although the university has since moved out, it now seems certain to be spared, a massive cleaning and reconstruction programme having been started in 2000.

In order to build the tower, many of the surviving historical buildings on Eichplatz and the streets around had to be razed, and it was only as a result of a protest campaign that the original university, the **Collegium Jenense**, which stands just to the south on

Collegienstrasse, was spared. Originally a Dominican friary, it's a marvellously ramshackle array of bits and pieces from various epochs, which evoke the cloistered tranquillity of academe. The most arresting feature is the bravura Renaissance carving in the courtyard of the coat of arms of the Ernestine line of the House of Wettin, the university's original patrons. Just east of the Collegium is the ruined **Anatometurm**, one of the three towers surviving from the fourteenth-century fortification system.

The Markt and around

Separating Eichplatz from the much smaller Markt is the **Rathaus**, a simple Gothic structure crowned with a miniature Baroque belfry housing the *Schnapphans*, a mechanism which strikes the hours. In the middle of the square stands the **statue of Hannfried**, this being the nickname given locally to the university's founder, John Frederick the Magnanimous.

Such few old houses as Jena possesses can be found mostly on the Markt itself and in the two alleys, Oberlauengasse and Unterlauengasse, immediately to the east. The finest of these, at Markt 7, is now the **Stadtmuseum Göhre** (Tues & Thurs–Sun 10am–5pm, Wed 10am–6pm; DM5/€2.50). It contains displays on local arts and crafts, wine-making, religious art, the so-called "Seven Wonders of Jena" and the history of the university (including a reproduction of the Studentenkarzer, or prison, with its characteristic graffiti). There's also a reconstruction of a nineteenth-century café if you need a bit of light refreshment.

Despite its name, Unterm Markt, which stretches to the west, is a street rather than a square. At no. 12a is the large Baroque mansion which was formerly the home of Johann Gottlieb Fichte, one of a host of renowned philosophers (Hegel, Schelling, the Schlegels and the Humboldts were others) based in Jena during the Romantic period. Now designated the **Romantikerhaus** (Tues & Thurs–Sun 10am–5pm, Wed 10am–6pm; DM5/€2.50), it's decked out with period furnishings, and also has a small art gallery.

The Stadtkirche and around

Behind the Markt rises the Gothic **Stadtkirche St Michael**. Outside, the main features are the Brautportal (Bridal Doorway) on the south side, and the remarkable street passageway under the chancel, the best-known of the "Seven Wonders", the more so as there's not the slightest hint of its presence in the brightly painted hall interior, whose light and lofty feel is achieved by means of slender pillars which shoot directly up to the vault. The church's most celebrated treasure is the original bronze **tombstone of Luther** – with a full-length portrait cast from designs provided by Cranach – on the north wall. It was brought here for safekeeping because of the threat of desecration from the imperial forces occupying Wittenberg, but was never returned.

From the Stadtkirche, Johanniskirche leads west along the northern side of Eichplatz; no. 12, the **Haus zur Rosen**, is a Baroque mansion whose cellars contain a renowned student club. At the end of the street is the **Johannistor**, the only gateway remaining from the city's fortifications; just to the north is the most impressive of the surviving towers, the battlemented **Pulverturm**.

The Botanischer Garten

Across Goetheallee is the **Botanischer Garten** (daily 9am–5/6pm; DM2/€1), which was first created for growing medicinal herbs; it was then turned into a pleasure park before assuming its current function, which is primarily one of scientific research. The **Inspektorhaus** on the street side was designed by Goethe and was his favourite residence during his many sojourns in Jena, which he found to be a more amenable working environment than Weimar. Here he completed many of his literary projects; he also undertook a great deal of scientific research and produced the rather odd work he himself considered his masterpiece, *The Theory of Colours*. Part of the building is now designated the **Goethe-Gedenkstätte** (April–Oct Wed–Sun 11am–3pm; free) and contains memorabilia of his stays here.

On the eastern fringe of the garden is the domed **Zeiss-Planetarium**, which, when it was built in 1925, was the first such structure in the world. Now as then, it utilizes the technology of the Carl Zeiss works; there are several sessions each day, costing DM8/€4, except Mondays. There are occasional showings in English for groups, so it would also be worth checking here or at the tourist office to see if any are scheduled.

The Carl-Zeiss-Stiftung

The factory buildings of the **Carl-Zeiss-Stiftung**, mostly dating from the first two decades of the twentieth century, stand immediately to the west of Eichplatz; among them is a tower which is claimed as Germany's earliest skyscraper. **Carl Zeiss** was a mechanic who established himself in Jena in 1846, and attempted to develop microscopes of improved optical performance. Having failed to make the desired progress within twenty years, he formed what proved to be a spectacularly fruitful partnership with the physicist **Ernst Abbe**. Their company soon became the world leader in the field of optics, and has maintained this position ever since, though its post-1945 history was sullied by the existence of rival companies in the two Germanys, which have recently come together again.

The **Optisches Museum** (Tues–Fri 10am–5pm, Sat 1–4.30pm, Sun 9.30am–1pm; DM8/€4) on Carl-Zeiss-Platz is in two parts. In the first, there's a re-creation of the 1866 workshop of Zeiss and Abbe; the second contains a huge collection of historic spectacles, microscopes, telescopes and other instruments. Outside stands the imposing **Ernst-Abbe-Denkmal**, a shrine-like memorial by Henry van de Velde, inside which are four bronze reliefs of working-class life by Constantin Meunier.

Ernst-Haeckel-Haus and Schillers Gartenhaus

A few minutes' walk to the south is Ernst-Haeckel-Strasse, where, at the corner with Berggasse, is the **Ernst-Haeckel-Haus** (guided tours Tues–Fri at 8.30am, 10am, 11.30am, 2pm & 3.30pm, Sat at 8.30am, 10am, 11am & 2pm; DM2). Haeckel, the leading Continental protagonist of Darwin's theories of evolution, dominated intellectual life at Jena around the turn of last century. He was also a talented artist, and his watercolour landscapes are the highlight of the displays in the villa where he lived. Just to the south, at Am Paradiesbahnhof, is the **Phyletisches Museum** (daily 9am–4pm; DM1/€0.50), which Haeckel founded in 1907. It's a natural history collection with a difference, concentrating on how each species developed.

For a time Haeckel lived in the house at Schillergässschen 2, which is now known as **Schillers Gartenhaus** (April–Oct Tues–Sun 11am–3pm; Nov–March Tues–Sat 11am–3pm; DM2/€1) in honour of a previous occupant, the poet and dramatist **Friedrich Schiller**, after whom the university is now named. As professor of history, he lived in Jena for ten years, the longest he spent in any one place. The conditions in which he worked have been lovingly re-created; particularly evocative is the upstairs room in the garden pavilion, his favourite work place.

Eating, drinking and nightlife

Undoubtedly one of the prime attractions of Jena is its wide variety of places to eat, drink and socialize; indeed, within the former GDR it offers a better choice than almost anywhere outside the three largest cities.

Restaurants, bars and cafés

Alt Jena, Markt 10. Upmarket wine bar, offering nearly a hundred different vintages, plus a good range of food, including plenty of fish dishes.

Fiddler's Green, Sophienstr 10. The local Irish pub, often with live music. Daily 5pm–1am.

Fuchsturm, Turmgasse 26. Traditional Gaststätte in a tower on top of the Hausberg, a hill on the west side of the Saale. Closes 10pm during the week, midnight on Sat, 7pm on Sun.

Grüne Tanne, Karl-Liebknecht-Str. 1. Historic Gasthaus with a courtyard beer garden, serving hearty yet inexpensive traditional cuisine. Evenings only, closed Sun & Mon.

Kleine Quelle, Johannisstr. 11. Trendy cocktail bar-cum-disco. Mon–Sat 9pm–4am.

Marktmühle, Saalstr. 23. Pub with a good selection of whiskies, plus Irish and English beers.

Rosenkeller, Johannisstr. 13. By far the most popular student club, set in cavernous cellars. Often features live music; even out of term, it has an animated atmosphere. Free admission with student ID, otherwise you'll have to pay around DM4/€2 to get in.

Saaltor, Saalstr. 8. Thuringia's first-ever Chinese restaurant; the food is authentic, and the set lunches are particularly good value.

Talschänke, Pennickental 44, Wöllnitz. Hausbrauerei in an incorporated village on the east bank of the Saale, south of the city centre. It brews a mild *Weissbier* and serves freshly-caught trout.

Zum Roten Hirsch, Holzmarkt 10. Offers cheap but decent food, with a fast lunchtime service.

Dornburg

The one unmissable excursion from Jena is to **DORNBURG**, 15km down the Saale. From the Bahnhof, it's a steep twenty-minute climb up to the three palaces lining the terrace which has been laid out on a precipitous ninety-metre-high rock perched directly above the valley, of which there's a stunning view. Entry to the park is by the **Renaissanceschloss** (Wed–Sun: April–Oct 9am–6pm; Nov–March 10am–4pm; DM2/€1) at the southern end, a grand country house with frilly gables and prominent stair turret. Built at the turn of the seventeenth century by a high official of the Duchy of Saxe-Weimar, this was one of Goethe's favourite retreats. The three rooms he used are furnished and decorated according to the tastes of Weimar Classicism, and contrast strongly with the splendours of the **Kaminzimmer**, the one chamber to have survived in something like its original form.

The **Rokokoschloss** (same times; DM4/€2, but closed in 2000 for restoration) in the middle of the terrace was commissioned as a summer retreat for the Weimar dukes; it's decorated with stuccowork, porcelain and period furniture, though the show is stolen by the magnificent garden. Beyond it is the **Altes Schloss**, by origin an imperial fortress of the Romanesque period, though most of what you see today dates from the mid-fifteenth century, when it belonged to the electors of Saxony. At the time of writing, it was under restoration, but will open to the public in due course.

Rudolstadt and the Schwarza valley

Some 40km upstream from Jena is **RUDOLSTADT**, set in a picturesque stretch of wooded and hilly countryside, near the point where the Saale is joined by the **River Schwarza**, which cuts a particularly beautiful valley to the southwest. For three and a half centuries it was the capital of the county, later principality, of Schwarzburg-Rudolstadt, then, for the decade before its abolition after World War I, of the united province of Schwarzburg, and it still preserves both the authentic appearance and the languid atmosphere of a rural county town.

The Town

Perched high on a hill above Rudolstadt is the vast bulk of **Schloss Heidecksburg** (Tues–Sun 10am–6pm; DM6/€3). The previous Renaissance Schloss was so badly damaged by fire in 1735 that Friedrich Anton, who also wanted to celebrate his earlier promotion from count to a fully fledged prince of the Holy Roman Empire, decided to commission an extravagant new building in the Dresden Rococo style. In lieu of the great Pöppelmann, who was too ill to accept, the plans were drawn up by the most talented Dresden architect of the next generation, Johann Christoph Knöffel, while the work was completed by another native of that city, Gottfried Heinrich Krohne.

The former **Schlosskapelle** in the west wing has been stripped of all religious connotations and now houses a collection of porcelain, much of it of local manufacture. This is the departure point for the **guided tours** round the ornate state apartments. Highlights are the galleried main **Festsaal**, with its huge ceiling fresco of Mount Olympus, the gorgeous **Spiegelkabinett**, with its striking inlaid floor and mock oriental touches and the highly original **Bänderzimmer**, whose medallion portraits give a foretaste of the forthcoming Neoclassical style. At the end of the tour, you're free to wander round the art gallery at leisure; the star piece is Friedrich's brooding *Morning Mist in the Mountains*. The north wing of the Schloss, which still preserves the brightly painted double Renaissance portal with statues of the Virtues, now houses the **Schlossmuseum**. On the ground floor is a particularly outstanding arsenal, containing weapons from the fifteenth to the nineteenth centuries. The upstairs displays on local history are more prosaic, but include the *Schwarzenburger Willkomm*, a fine piece of late sixteenth-century goldsmithery.

In the town centre, the main building is the **Stadtkirche St Andreas** at its eastern end, which in its own way evokes the local courtly tradition as vividly as the Schloss itself. By origin an unexceptional Gothic hall church, it was progressively beautified down the years to create the present sumptuous effect. From the Renaissance period are the fantastical portal with its fake door knockers and resplendent coat of arms, and the monumental marble and alabaster epitaph to the Schönefeld family on the end wall of the nave. A burst of creative activity after the Thirty Years War brought a host of Baroque embellishments, including the eccentric sculptures of angels suspended from the vault, plus the princes' loft and burial chamber, the pulpit and the organ.

Rudolstadt's only other attraction is the **Volkskundemuseum Thüringer Bauernhäuser** (Wed–Sun 9am–noon & 1–4/5pm; DM2/€1) in the Stadtpark to the rear of the Bahnhof. One of Germany's oldest open-air museums, this brings together two redundant farmhouses from the region, complete with their furnishings. The larger, standing alongside its original barn, dates back to the 1660s; the other, which is a few decades younger, houses a complete village apothecary's shop.

Practicalities

Rudolstadt's **tourist office** (Mon–Fri 9am–6pm, Sat 9am–noon; ☎0 36 72/42 45 43, fax 43 12 86, *www.rudolstadt.de*) is at Marktstr. 57; there's the usual booking service for **private rooms** (①–③). As yet, there are only a few **hotels**, including *Schwarzposle*, Schwarzburger Str. 31 (☎0 36 72/35 31 20; ③), *Zur Pilsener Schenke*, Mörlaer Str. 8 (☎0 36 72/42 23 43; ③), *Thüringer Hof*, Bahnhofsgasse 3 (☎0 36 72/41 24 22; ④), and *Adler*, Markt 17 (☎0 36 72/44 03; ⑤). Overlooking Rudolstadt, some 3km to the southeast, is the *Panoramahotel Marienturm*, Marienturm 1 (☎0 36 72/4 32 70; ⑥). The best **restaurants** are in the last three hotels. Rudolstadt's main **festival** is the *Tanz- und Folkfest* in July.

The Schwarza valley

The **Schwarza valley** is at its most imposing in the ten-kilometre canyon between Bad Blankenburg and Schwarzburg, the original seat of the princely dynasty. This stretch also has an exceptionally rich indigenous flora, including Turk's-cap lilies, columbines, akelei and liverworts. Although there's a road linking the two towns, you really need to follow the footpath, which is liberally endowed with belvederes, to appreciate the landscape to the full. The wonderfully scenic rail line, the Schwarzatalbahn from Rudolstadt, does not follow the Schwarza at this point, instead travelling along its tributary, the Rottenbach, to the town of the same name, a junction on the line to Arnstadt. From Schwarzburg, however, it hugs the bank of the Schwarza all the way along the remaining 20km of its route to the terminus at Katzhütte.

About halfway along this last stage is **OBSTFELDERSCHMIEDE**, the valley station of one of Germany's great transport curiosities, the Oberweissbacher Bergbahn. This is the world's steepest **cable rail line** on which normal carriages can run: it ascends 323m in the 1.4-kilometre-long track to **LICHTENHAIN**, a journey which takes eighteen minutes. At the summit, passengers transfer to a tiny diesel train, which takes a further eight minutes to cover the journey through meadows to **CURSDORF**, a pretty resort village of slate-faced houses.

Saalfeld

The old mining town of **SAALFELD**, 10km south of Rudolstadt, marks the transition between the middle and upper parts of the Saale valley; beyond lie the Schiefergebirge (Slate Mountains), now a popular recreational area of wooded hills and artificial lakes with watersports facilities. Saalfeld itself has reclaimed its former status as a tourist resort – apart from its value as an excursion base, it possesses one of Germany's most strangely beautiful natural wonders and has a historic centre which will look very striking once it has been tidied up.

The Town

The **Hauptbahnhof** lies on the east bank of the Saale; Bahnhofstrasse leads over the two arms of the river to the **Saaltor**, one of three surviving medieval gateways. From here, there's a choice of routes. The right-hand fork, Puschkinstrasse, follows the former course of the fortifications past two more gates, beyond which lies the largest remaining stretch of the walls. Saalstrasse, to the left, leads straight to the Markt, but it's worth making a small detour to the south up Am Hügel to see the Renaissance **Schlösschen Kitzerstein** (now the music school), with its stylized, Dutch-looking gable, and the ruins of the **Hoher Schwarm**, a feudal castle of the type characteristic of the Saale.

At the southeastern corner of the Markt, returned once more to its original function, is the pristine white **Rathaus**. It's a quintessential building of the German Renaissance with its lingering Gothic feel, its protruding stairwell, its prominent gables and its two strongly contrasted oriel windows. Opposite is the partially Romanesque **Marktapotheke**, which dates back to the town's twelfth-century origins, though it's been altered repeatedly down the centuries.

Towering above the northern side of the Markt, and fronting Blankenburger Strasse, the pedestrianized main shopping street, is the Gothic **Johanniskirche**. Its exterior is richly decorated with late fourteenth-century sculptures of the Parler school; the west portal tympanum of *The Last Judgement* is particularly fine. The most startling feature of the hall interior is the bright red colouring of the vault – a symbolical reference to the blood of Christ. It reaches its climax in the elaborate network design in the chancel, which is painted with a recently uncovered vision of the path to Heaven.

Up Brudergasse is the former Franciscan friary, now housing the **Thüringer Heimatmuseum** (Tues–Sun 10am–5pm; DM3.50/€1.75), a good-quality regional collection featuring displays on mining, folklore and arts and crafts, the highlight being examples of the local Gothic school of woodcarvers.

Between 1680 and 1735, Saalfeld was capital of the duchy of Saxe-Saalfeld, which was then subsumed into Saxe-Coburg. The inevitable legacy of this period is a large Baroque **Schloss**, situated a few minutes' walk north of the confines of the Altstadt along Schloss-Strasse, then right into Schlossberg. It's now used by the municipality as offices, but you can wander in and have a look round, particularly at the showpiece staircase; ask to see the ornate **Schlosskapelle**, which is regularly used for concerts in summer. Extravagantly decorated with stuccowork and trompe l'oeil frescoes, its unorthodox design features an irregular octagon within a rectangular ground plan.

The **Feengrotten** (Fairy Grottoes; guided tours March–Oct daily 9am–5pm; Nov Sat & Sun 10am–3.30pm; Dec–Feb daily 10am–3.30pm; *www.feengrotten.de*; DM8/€4), Saalfeld's chief attraction, lie about 1.5km southwest of the town centre, and can be reached by bus #13. Geologically formed 400 million years ago, the present astonishing appearance of this site is the result of a fluke caused by the interaction of natural and human forces. From the mid-sixteenth century, there was a mine here, which was exploited for its alum slate and vitriol. This functioned until the 1840s, when it was run down and closed as stocks moved towards exhaustion and demand from the chemical industry slumped. In 1910, waters rich in mineral resources were found pouring out of the abandoned mine; an investigation of its interior revealed that oxidization had turned the galleries into a natural drip-water cave, with stalactites and stalagmites formed from iron phosphate, and the walls cloaked in an astonishing kaleidoscope of colours. Artificial lighting further enhances the effect, seen at its best in the Märchendom (fairy-tale cathedral), also known as the Gralburg (Holy Grail castle) because of its uncanny resemblance to a Wagnerian theatre set.

Practicalities

Saalfeld's **tourist office** (Mon–Fri 9am–6pm, Sat 9am–noon; ☎ & fax 0 36 71/3 39 50, *www.saalfeld.de*) is at Blankenburger Str. 4. There are plenty of **private rooms** (①–③) available.

In the town centre there are a couple of small budget **hotels**: *Weltrich,* Saalstr. 44 (☎0 36 71/27 32; ③), and *Fisherman's Friend,* Sonneberger Str. 44 (☎0 36 71/53 06 12; ③). More upmarket options are *Tanne,* Saalstr. 35 (☎0 36 71/82 60; ⑤), *Am Hohen Schwarm,* Schwarmgasse 18 (☎0 36 71/28 84; ⑤), and *Anker,* Markt 25–26 (☎0 36 71/59 90; ⑥). A good-value alternative in the outskirts is *Asterra,* high above the town to the east at Sperberhölzchen 34 (☎0 36 71/51 74 40; ④), whose **restaurant** serves innovative local specialities. The best place to eat, however, has to be *Zum Güldenen Gans,* a historic cellar restaurant in the *Anker* hotel.

Gera and around

Thuringia's second largest city is **GERA**, which lies 45km east of Jena in the hilly countryside of the Weisse Elster valley. For nearly four centuries it was the capital of one of Germany's smallest states, the junior of the two Reuss principalities. However, it's totally different from the province's other courtly residences, being predominantly an industrial town, with a long tradition in the production of textiles and musical instruments. Indeed, during the Second Reich it was one of the richest places in Germany, and the multitude of industrialists' villas which can still be seen in its inner suburbs is a reminder of this heady epoch. Despite heavy wartime damage, it's a surprisingly agreeable place, generally recognized as being the one and only town in the GDR where postwar planning was carried out with sensitivity and good taste. The result is a lively city which offers a balanced mixture of old and new.

The City

Gera's compact historical centre lies on a gentle incline about fifteen minutes' walk southeast of the Hauptbahnhof. Its exemplary preservation is marred only by the loss of the huge Baroque palace of the Reuss princes which stood above. This was damaged by bombs in the last days of the war and subsequently razed by the Communists, though may yet make a phoenix-like return.

At the heart of the Altstadt is the **Markt**, whose good looks compensate for its modest dimensions. In the centre burbles the **Simsonbrunnen**, showing the Old Testament hero Samson wrestling with the lion; this is a modern replica of the waterworn late seventeenth-century original. The whitewashed Renaissance **Rathaus**, the town's finest building, stands proudly to the northeastern corner. Designed by Nicol Gromann, the Saxon court architect, it boasts a dignified off-centre octagonal tower and a riotously decorative portal with busts, grotesque figures, inscriptions and brightly painted coats of arms. A similar style can be seen on the oriel of the **Stadt-Apotheke** at the opposite end of the square; apart from heraldic motifs, its carvings show the Apostles and the Four Seasons. Kleine Kirchstrasse leads to a vast open square, Zentraler Platz, whose handsome red Baroque palace standing in splendid isolation was once the town orphanage. Nowadays it houses the local history displays of the **Stadtmuseum** (10am–5pm, closed Fri; DM4/€2).

Uphill from the Markt, Grosse Kirchstrasse – which is lined with a number of fine mansions, now mostly stores – leads to the **Salvatorkirche**, a large Baroque church with Jugendstil furnishings perched at the top of a monumental stairway. On its northern side stands the **Schreiberhaus**, the late seventeenth-century mansion of a rich merchant. It is now the **Museum für Naturkunde** (Tues–Sun 10am–5pm; DM4/€2), with displays on the natural history and geology of the Gera region, including the skeleton of a prehistoric rhinoceros. The interior itself is at least as good a reason for a visit, however. At the back of the house is the entrance to the town's most unusual attraction, the **Geraer Höhle** (guided tours Mon–Fri at 11am & 3pm, Sat at 11am, 2pm & 3pm, Sun at 10am, 11am, 2pm & 3pm; DM4/€2), a network of caverns and tunnels used in the seventeenth and eighteenth centuries as workshops, and as a place where homebrewed beer could mature in cool conditions.

To the rear of the Hauptbahnhof is the Küchengarten, a pleasant park at whose far end stands the Rococo **Orangerie** (Tues 1–8pm, Wed–Fri 10am–5pm, Sat & Sun 10am–6pm; DM2/€1). Inside is a collection of paintings and sculptures from the Middle Ages to the present day. Mohrenplatz, just to the west over the Weisse Elster, is the finest square in Gera after the Markt, and is dominated by the Romanesque-Gothic **Marienkirche**. At no. 4 on the square is the **Otto-Dix-Haus** (Tues–Fri 10am–5pm, Sat & Sun 10am–6pm; DM4/€2), birthplace of one of the most highly regarded German artists of the twentieth century, the leading light of the Neue Sachlichkeit movement. In addition to a huge number of drawings and graphics, displayed in rotation, there are a couple of dozen canvases, the pick of which is *St Christopher*, an allegorical work inspired by the emigration from Germany under the Nazis.

Schlossbergstrasse leads up from Mohrenplatz to the site of **Schloss Osterstein**, now occupied by a terrace café-restaurant The restored Romanesque **tower** survives from the original castle of the Reuss dynasty, and on the afternoons of summer weekends and holidays it may be ascended (DM1/€0.50) for a view over the town.

Practicalities

Gera's **tourist office** (Mon–Fri 9am–8pm, Sat 9am–2pm; ☎03 65/61 93 01, fax 61 93 04, *www.gera.de*) is a short walk from the Hauptbahnhof at Ernst-Toller-Str. 14. There is a good selection of **hotels** in town. At the budget end of the scale are *Burgkeller*, Schuhgasse 2 (☎03 65/8 38 16 91; ③), and the huge *Am Galgenberg*, Laasener Str. 108 (☎03 65/8 37 26 77; ④). The best mid-range establishments are *An der Elster*, Südstr. 12 (☎03 65/7 10 61 61; ⑤), and *Galerie*, Leibnizstr. 21 (☎03 65/2 01 50; ⑤); the latter is in the western suburb of Untermhaus and – as its name implies – incorporates an art gallery. Pick of the upmarket options is the centrally located and beautifully furnished *Schillerhöhe*, Schillerstr. 9 (☎03 65/83 98 80; ⑥).

The best **restaurant** for traditional Thuringian dishes is *Ritterhof*, Rittergasse 6, while the *Ratskeller* at Markt 1 offers many fish specialities and *Paulaner Keller*, Clara-Zetkin-Str. 14, represents the burgeoning Bavarian influence. Among the ethnic eateries, *Trajika*, Altenburger Str. 16, offers a rare chance to sample Bulgarian cuisine, while *Royal*, Sorge 19, presents high-quality French cuisine. *Riebeck's Braustüb'l*, Braustr. 2, is the tap of the local brewery.

The main venue for **drama** and **concerts** is the Jugendstil Theater Gera (☎03 65/8 27 91 01), immediately to the rear of the Hauptbahnhof at Küchengartenallee 2. There's also a Puppentheater on Gustav-Henning-Platz (☎03 65/2 47 07), and a satirical cabaret, Fettnäppchen, in the cellars of the Rathaus (☎03 65/2 37 31).

Bad Köstritz

A more congenial base than Gera itself is the little spa of **BAD KÖSTRITZ**, which lies 8km to the north, on the rail line to Leipzig. Its name is synonymous with the rich, smooth, coal-black beer produced in the **Köstritzer Schwarzbierbrauerei**, a monumental early twentieth-century complex at Heinrich-Schütz-Str. 6 in the centre of the village. This, the former princely brewery of Reuss, was one of the few permitted to maintain a distinctive production line during the Communist epoch, and its speciality is one of the rare success stories of the post-GDR economy, ranking as Germany's best-selling dark beer, with a near-mythical status akin to that enjoyed by *Guinness* in the English-speaking world.

The name of the street on which the brewery stands is a reminder of Bad Köstritz's other claim to fame, as the birthplace of **Heinrich Schütz** (1585–1672), the father-figure of the great German musical tradition. The house where he was born, at no. 1 on the same street, is designated the **Heinrich-Schütz-Haus** (Tues–Fri 10am–5pm, Sat & Sun 1–5pm; DM2.50/€1.25) and contains documentary material on the composer's long and productive career, which began with a period of study in Venice, and ended at the Dresden court. Schütz was responsible for introducing Italian-style declamation and instrumental writing to Germany; his works include the first German opera (though this is now lost), a host of resplendent psalm settings and motets, and Passions and oratorios which served as direct models for Bach a century later.

The **Schlosspark**, in which stands a small Neoclassical temple, lies between the town centre and Bad Köstritz's **Bahnhof**, which is 1km to the east. There are a couple of exceptionally good-value **pensions** in *Pufe*, Schulstr. 22 (☎03 66 05/25 23; ②), and *Elstertal*, Bahnhofstr. 98 (☎03 66 05/22 39; ③). Alternatively, there are two upmarket **hotels**: *Schlosshotel*, Julius-Sturm-Platz 9 (☎03 66 05/3 30; ⑤), and *Goldener Loewe*, Heinrich-Schütz-Str. 5 (☎03 66 05/3 80; ⑦). Both the hotels, and *Elstertal*, have recommendable **restaurants**; an alternative place to eat is the rustic *Gasthaus Zum Frosch*, alongside the brewery at Am Mühlgraben 1.

Greiz

The smallest of the 25 states which formed the Second German Reich was the senior of the Reuss principalities, whose capital was **GREIZ**, which lies 30km up the Weisse

Elster valley from Gera. Since 1875, the two Reuss capitals have been linked by the Elstertalbahn, a railway which continues on to the Saxon town of Plauen. While this beautiful line is less obviously spectacular than those in the neighbouring Vogtland (see p.1021), the awkward nature of the terrain posed severe challenges to the engineers, the most difficult being the 270-metre-long tunnel which had to be cut through the Schlossberg, the hill overlooking the centre of Greiz. The town itself has been dogged by ill-luck: it has repeatedly been destroyed by fire down the ages, and is suffering notably from post-GDR blight, which has seen the end of its 500-year-old textile tradition. Yet it's an extraordinarily attractive place nonetheless, with a glorious natural setting and a fine ensemble of buildings from the late eighteenth to the early twentieth century, a period when it basked in true Ruritanian prosperity.

The Town

By far the oldest surviving building is the **Oberes Schloss** (guided tours April–Oct Mon–Fri at 10am & 2pm, Sat & Sun at 10am, 2pm & 4pm; DM3/€1.50) atop the Schlossberg. This dates at least as far back as the thirteenth century, and was the residence of Heinrich II of Plauen, who in 1306 founded the dynasty and county of Reuss, a name derived from his marriage to a Russian princess. Relatively little medieval masonry survives, the complex being a jumble of Renaissance, Baroque and Rococo buildings. Since the nineteenth century, many of these have been used as houses, though the residents are now gradually moving out. The local archive, which currently occupies the elaborately stuccoed reception rooms, is due to move to new premises in 2001, and it is hoped that these interiors will thereafter form part of the tour. In the meantime, the highlight is the sweeping view from the top of the seventeenth-century **Schlossturm**.

A group of monumental Neoclassical buildings dominate the town centre's waterfront. The most prominent is the **Unteres Schloss**, a direct replacement for its predecessor, which was destroyed in the most serious of Greiz's fires, that of 1802. It now houses a music academy, various municipal offices, a café and two museums. Of these, the **Heimatmuseum** (10am–12.30pm & 1–5pm, closed Fri; DM2/€1) occupies a suite of Beidermeier rooms overlooking the river, including the externally prominent winter garden. It contains the expected local history displays, including a lovingly crafted model of the town as it was in 1899. Across the courtyard, the **Schauwerkstatt** (same times; DM2/€1) documents Greiz's textile tradition, featuring a number of historic looms as well as others which were recently still in service.

Adjoining the Unteres Schloss, and likewise rebuilt after the great fire, is the former court church, now the **Stadtkirche St Marien**. Its galleried interior contains the tomb of the most celebrated of the Reuss rulers, the military hero Heinrich VI, who died in combat against the Turks at the Battle of Zenta in 1697. Other notable buildings from the same period are the former guard house, the **Alte Wache**, to the rear, and the former **Lyzeum**, now the public library, to the side. The Neoclassical ensemble is completed by a somewhat later building, the huge **Gymnasium** to the east. Otherwise, the town centre is characterized by the presence of a large number of **Jugendstil houses**, which were erected in the wake of two fires in the first decade of the twentieth century. The best examples are to be seen on Thomasstrasse and Burgstrasse, with the most eye-catching being that at the corner of the latter and Marktstrasse, which has a facade mosaic of a goldsmith at work.

On the opposite side of the Oberes Schloss from the town centre is the town's greatest joy, the **Greizer Park**. Originally a kitchen garden, then a formal Rococo garden, it was extended and transformed into a Romantic-era landscape park in the English style, assuming its definite appearance as late as the 1870s. It's a wonderful place for a stroll, with its long and often unexpected vistas, and its spectacular array of imported trees and shrubs, including some not found elsewhere in Europe, which erupt into a riot of colour in autumn. There are also several picturesque garden buildings, including the late eighteenth-century **Rotunde** at the eastern edge, which was built to house the princely porcelain collections but was later converted into a chapel and then a war memorial, and the half-timbered **Schwanenhaus** on the islet in the large artificial lake. From here, there's a sweeping view upwards to two popular vantage points – the **Weisses Kreuz** (White Cross) and the **Pulverturm** (Powder Tower).

At the southern end of the Greizer Park is the **Sommerpalais** (Tues–Sun 10am–4/5pm; DM2/€1), a French-inspired building in an early Neoclassical style still showing lingering Rococo influence. It was begun in 1779 as a summer pleasure palace for the ruling family, which had gained promotion to princely status the previous year. The extravagantly stuccoed **Gartensaal** on the ground floor is used for temporary exhibitions, including the *Triennale*, the tri-annual (next in June–Oct 2003) national festival of caricatures, cartoons and satiric art. In the handsome suite of reception rooms on the first floor are a selection of books and engravings from the foundation established by the Reuss family after its abdication from power. This includes a valuable library of French Enlightenment works, still displayed in the original bookcases, plus a collection of eighteenth-century **British political cartoons**, the only one of its type on the Continent. Amassed by Princess Elizabeth, the future Landgravine of Hesse-Homburg (see p.417), who bequeathed it to her niece, Princess Caroline of Reuss, the latter features examples of the work of Thomas Rowlandson and James Gillray, among others. Exhibitions from the holdings of **Satiricum**, the satirical art collection somewhat improbably established by the GDR – a regime which offered a host of ready-made targets for cartoonists – are staged on the top floor.

Practicalities

Greiz's **Bahnhof** lies just to the southwest of the town centre. The **tourist office** (Mon–Fri 9am–6pm, Sat 9am–noon; ☎0 36 61/68 98 15 or 1 94 33, fax 70 32 91, *www.greiz.de*) is in the Unteres Schloss on Burgplatz.

There's a very good-value **pension**, *Krug zum Grünen Kranz*, right beside the Greizer Park at Parkgasse 7 (☎0 36 61/67 28 88; ③), plus a budget riverside **hotel**, *Haus Friedensbrücke*, Carolinenstr. 1–3 (☎0 36 61/22 21; ③). The more expensive alternatives are *Ambiente*, Bahnhofstr. 7 (☎0 36 61/67 20 54; ⑤), and *Schlossberg*, Marienstr. 1–5 (☎0 36 61/62 21 23, *www.schlossberghotel-greiz.de*; ⑤). Greiz's **youth hostel** is high above the town at Amselstieg 12 (☎0 36 61/21 76, fax 68 78 08; DM21/€10.50 or DM26/€13).

Among the places to **eat** and **drink** are the taps of the two local breweries, *Grüne Linde*, Grüne Linde 2, and *Feldschlösschen*, Feldschlösschenstr. 4. However, they're now somewhat overshadowed by *Zapfwerk 1/3*, due west of the Greizer Park at Zeulenrodaer Str. 6, an evenings-only entertainment complex which claims to have the largest number of beers on draught (eighty in all, with half from Germany, half from the rest of the world) of any hostelry in Europe.

Altenburg

ALTENBURG, 40km northeast of Gera, dubs itself Skatstadt in honour of the fact that *Skat*, Germany's most popular card game, has both its main production centre and governing headquarters here. Its name is relatively little known abroad, though it's one of the most worthwhile of Thuringia's old courtly towns. Lying in the easternmost part of the Land, close to the borders with both Saxony and Saxony-Anhalt, Altenburg makes an excellent base for forays into three provinces; alternatively, it can be used as a stopover if travelling on the main rail route south from Leipzig.

The Town

Although the town centre of Altenburg is pleasant enough, it's totally overshadowed by the two main attractions – the **Schloss** which overlooks it from the north, and the unexpectedly rich **Lindenau-Museum** further to the northeast.

The Schloss

The vast hilltop **Schloss** complex, which features just about every European architectural style, has to be entered from the southern end of its park. Despite its long spell as a ducal residence, it still preserves part of its medieval defences, among which the round tower known as the **Flasche**, built into the northern walls, dates back as far as the eleventh century. Nearby is a freestanding tower of uncertain vintage, the **Hausmannsturm** (Tues–Sun 9.30am–5pm; DM1/€0.50), which can be ascended for a fine view over the Schloss and the town. Across the courtyard, in the centre of which is a Mannerist fountain to Neptune, lies the main palace block, now designated the **Schloss- und Spielkarten Museum** (same times; DM5/€2.50). Predictably, the main emphasis is on the history of playing cards throughout the last five centuries, and in particular of *Skat*. Other highlights are a display of medieval weapons, and Bernhard von Lindenau's collections of oriental and Meissen porcelain.

From the museum, **guided tours** are run round the state apartments of the Schloss, which are slowly being restored. They're a surprising mixture: the **Goldsaal** is elegantly Baroque, while the main **Festsaal** is a nineteenth-century Historicist extravaganza in red, white and gold, with frothy ceiling frescoes by the Munich Romantic artist Karl Mossdorf depicting stories from Apuleius' *The Golden Ass*. It's occasionally used for concerts, as is the more intimate **Bachsaal**, an early twentieth-century pastiche of its fire-destroyed Renaissance predecessor.

Included in the tour is a visit to the sumptuous **Schlosskirche**. This is otherwise only open for services and for the summer weekend recitals on the eighteenth-century **organ**. The church itself is predominantly late Gothic, with a magnificent star vault. However, the general appearance owes much to a mid-seventeenth-century interior transformation, which added the ducal loft at the west end, the galleries with their statues of saints and Old Testament figures, and the theatrical high altar.

The Lindenau-Museum

The rusticated neo-Renaissance *palazzo* containing the **Lindenau-Museum** (Tues–Sun 10am–6pm; DM7/€3.50) is at the northeastern edge of the Schlosspark. Its cosmopolitan displays, originating in the private collections of Bernhard von Lindenau, a nineteenth-century statesman and Italophile, are a world away from those normally found in small German towns. On the ground floor, an important group of Greek and Roman vases is kept in one wing, changing selections of modern art in the other. Upstairs, the old masters department includes choice examples of Gothic and Renaissance paintings from Florence and Siena. Small panels from dispersed polyptychs predominate – look out for a rare pair by **Masaccio** of *The Agony in the Garden* and *St Jerome in the Desert,* and for **Fra Angelico**'s exquisite *Three Dominicans* and *St Francis's Trial by Fire*. Of the larger works, the star pieces are *Catherina Sforza as St Catherine* by **Botticelli**, *St Helena* and the *Blessed Filippo Benizzi* by **Perugino**, and a tondo of *The Holy Family* by **Beccafumi**.

The rest of the town

The townscape south of the Schloss is dominated by the **Rote Spitze** (Red Points), the two brick towers of a twelfth-century Augustinian collegiate church. To the west, across the busy Wallstrasse, lies the old merchant quarter, centred on two squares. Much the larger of these, the Weibermarkt, has become the modern commercial heart of town.

It's overlooked by the handsome Renaissance **Rathaus**, with its dignified portal and showpiece corner oriel. Further north is the Alter Markt, with the Baroque **Seckendorff'sche Palais** and a fin-de-siécle fountain that honours the game of *Skat*. Just off the square is the main parish church, the **Bartholomäikirche**, whose kernel is Gothic, but whose most notable features are the tapering octagonal Renaissance tower and the graceful little Romanesque crypt.

Practicalities

Altenburg's **Hauptbahnhof** is in the northern part of town. The **tourist office** (Mon 9am–3pm, Tues, Wed & Fri 9am–5pm, Thurs 9am–6pm, Sat 9am–1pm; ☎0 34 47/1 94 33 or 59 41 74, fax 59 41 79, *www.stadt-altenburg.de*) is at Moritzstr. 21, with the entrance on Kornmarkt. You can ask here for **private rooms** (②–③), which are in plentiful supply, and small **pensions** (②–④).

The town has a good cross-section of **hotels**, including *Treppengasse*, Treppengasse 5 (☎0 34 47/31 35 49; ④), *Altenburger Hof*, Schmöllnsche Landstr. 8 (☎0 34 47/58 40; ④–⑥), *Am Rossplan*, Rossplan 8 (☎0 34 47/5 66 10; ⑤), *Astor*, Bahnhofstr. 4 (☎0 34 47/58 70; ⑥), and *Parkhotel*, August-Bebel-Str. 16–17 (☎0 34 47/58 30; ⑥).

Each of the hotels, except *Treppengasse*, has a **restaurant**; other good places to eat are the *Ratskeller* in the Rathaus, Markt 1, and *Die Villa*, Friedrich-Ebert-Str. 14. Altenburg manages to maintain an ambitious **cultural** programme centred on the Landestheater, Theaterplatz 19 (☎0 34 47/58 51 61).

travel details

Trains

Erfurt to: Arnstadt (frequent; 25min); Eisenach (frequent; 1hr); Gera (11 daily; 2hr); Gotha (frequent; 30min); Jena (frequent; 45min); Meiningen (14 daily; 2hr 30min); Mühlhausen (11 daily; 1hr); Nordhausen (10 daily; 1hr 30min); Sondershausen (10 daily; 1hr 30min–2hr); Suhl (14 daily; 2hr); Weimar (frequent; 15min).

Gera to: Saalfeld (frequent; 1hr 15min–2hr); Greiz (hourly; 40min).

Gotha to: Friedrichroda (frequent; 35min); Mühlhausen (frequent; 1hr).

Jena to: Gera (frequent; 1hr); Rudolstadt (frequent; 1hr); Saalfeld (frequent; 1hr 20min); Weimar (frequent; 30min).

CHAPTER TWELVE

SAXONY

Saxony (Sachsen) is the most enigmatic of Germany's Länder. Its identity appears very secure and well defined, yet it has only the most nebulous connection with the tribes and territories after which it's named. Seemingly so archetypally German, it occupies land which originally belonged to the Slavs, while much of its scenery has more in common with the neighbouring Czech Republic than anywhere in Germany, and many of its towns bear the distinctive central European hallmark of a diversity of cultural influences. Other than Berlin, all three of the ex-GDR's largest cities are here, yet the Land is politically by far the most right-wing in all of Germany. Whereas at least two of the major cities should slot into the new economic framework without too much disruption, other parts of Saxony seem to belong to a bygone age, trying to maintain the same industries that have supported them for centuries. The list of contradictions seems endless.

Like Thuringia, Saxony's history is closely tied to that of the **Wettin** family, whose original early medieval power base was as **Margraves of Meissen**, charged with securing the Holy Roman Empire's eastern frontier and pushing it deeper into Slav territory to the east and south. The name of "Saxony" only came to be associated with the territory when it became the heartland of the **Albertine** line of the dynasty, which usurped the rival **Ernestine** line from the prized Electorate of the Holy Roman Empire in 1547 and thereafter built up a strong, centralized state. Descendants also gained the crown of Poland on three separate occasions, but failed to make it a hereditary possession. Compensation came in 1806, when Napoleon proclaimed Saxony a **kingdom** in its own right; a heavy price had to be paid for this nine years later, when Prussia made huge territorial annexations, although the royal status was retained until 1918.

Dresden, the capital since the foundation of the Albertine line in 1485, is nowadays chiefly associated with the terrible Anglo-American bombing raid of 1945 which obliterated one of Europe's greatest artistic and cultural centres. Its remarkable comeback has gathered pace since the *Wende*, the ultimate aim being to return it to its former appearance. The similarly sized city of **Leipzig** is basking in the glory of having provided the leadership of the revolution which overthrew totalitarian rule. **Chemnitz**, the third major city, is a place only the most dedicated of travellers will include on their itinerary, but is of special interest for the remarkable insights it offers into the preoccupations of the GDR period. The one

---

ACCOMMODATION PRICE CODES

All the pensions and hotels in this book have been graded according to the following price categories. The codes quoted are for the cheapest available double room, except for establishments which have rooms costing widely different rates, when the most expensive price is given as well. Exact charges are given for youth hostels; in the case of the official DJH (HI) establishments, this is the lowest available rate. When two figures are quoted for these hostels, the first applies to juniors (ie under 27 years of age), the second to seniors (27 and above).

① less than DM60/€30
② DM60–79/€30–39
③ DM80–99/€40–49

④ DM100–124/€50–62
⑤ DM125–149/€63–74
⑥ DM150–199/€75–99

⑦ DM200–249/€100–124
⑧ DM250–299/€125–149
⑨ upwards of DM300/€150

other place large enough to be regarded as a city is **Zwickau**, whose attraction of a well-preserved centre is overshadowed by a reputation as home of the infamous Trabi car.

Of the smaller towns, the undoubted star is **Meissen**, the original political heart of the region, and the place where the first European porcelain was manufactured. **Freiberg** and **Annaberg-Buchholz** are the most notable of the mining towns which reached the height of their prosperity in the sixteenth century, a period commemorated in the dazzlingly rich interiors of their churches. **Bautzen** is the main cultural centre of the Sorbs, the Slav people who have remained in the area throughout a millennium of German rule, while **Görlitz** is another place with a richly diverse historical tradition. **Torgau** is best known to English-speaking people for its wartime connections, though it's the little town of **Colditz** which brings back the most vivid memories of that era. **Saxon Switzerland**, the rocky and wooded countryside round the Elbe south of Dresden, is deservedly the best-known scenic part of the Land, though the raw mountain landscapes around **Zittau** and in the **Erzgebirge** range have their attractions, as does the somewhat gentler scenery of the **Vogtland** further west.

Travel throughout the area presents few problems; a comprehensive rail network includes numerous narrow-gauge lines, some of which have only recently been put back into operation. For **accommodation**, the multitude of private houses recently opened up for tourism often offer a valuable lifeline as several towns are noticeably short of hotels.

WESTERN SAXONY

The northwestern part of Saxony is a flat plain, with nothing of interest other than the vibrant city of **Leipzig**. Bounding it on the east is a beautiful but little-known valley, that of the **Zwickauer Mulde**, which is dotted with a number of enticing little towns, among them **Colditz**, home of the famous prisoner-of-war camp. Upstream, **Zwickau** itself, along with the large industrial city of **Chemnitz** and the old mining town of **Freiberg** to the east, stands in the foothills of the **Erzgebirge**, a windswept highland region whose mineral wealth was responsible for such former boom towns as **Schneeberg** and **Annaberg**. To the extreme southwest lies the plateau of the **Vogtland**, an area of spa resorts and craft industries centred on the lace-making town of **Plauen**.

Leipzig

Pictures from **LEIPZIG** filled the world's television screens in the autumn of 1989, as the GDR's second city assumed leadership of the *Wende*, the peaceful revolution that toppled the Communist dictatorship and ushered in the elections which led to national unification a year later. Having traditionally been one of Germany's most dynamic cities, it was perhaps inevitable that Leipzig was the place where the frustration of GDR citizens about their postwar lot reached breaking point. Its **trade fairs** (the only ones in Europe with an uninterrupted tradition dating back to the Middle Ages) remained of importance during the Communist interregnum: for all the difficulties the authorities had in squaring these with their ideology, the lure of promoting and developing the GDR as the economic success story of Eastern Europe, with Leipzig as its commercial heart, proved too difficult to resist. This did mean, however, that the city never suffered the sense of isolation from outside influences experienced by so many places behind the Iron Curtain.

In Goethe's *Faust*, Leipzig is described as "Little Paris". That was always an exaggeration – it has never been considered one of Germany's more visually appealing cities – and the analogy seemed very far-fetched indeed during the Communist era, when a legacy of eyesores and pollution was added to the destruction wrought by wartime bombs. However, huge advances have been made in the past decade. The general appearance of the centre has changed, almost out of recognition, by a combination of restoration work (which has allowed many architectural gems to re-emerge from the grime that had obscured them), demolition and new building, while the state-of-the-art trade-fair site opened in 1996 in the northern suburb of Wiederitzsch should ensure the city's future economic prosperity. Through all the upheavals of the past century, one factor that has remained constant is Leipzig's importance as a cultural centre, particularly in the field of **music**, where the great tradition of Bach, Mendelssohn, Schumann and Wagner is jealously maintained.

Arrival, information and accommodation

Leipzig's vast **Hauptbahnhof** is at the northeastern end of the Ring (ring road), which encircles the Altstadt; by the eastern side is the **bus station**. Some local trains, particularly from Zwickau, use the **Bayerischer Bahnhof**, which is a few minutes' walk south of the Ring. The **airport** (✆03 41/2 24 11 55 for flight information), the most important in the former GDR, is linked to the Hauptbahnhof by buses which run approximately every thirty minutes.

Directly opposite the Hauptbahnhof, at Richard-Wagner-Str. 1, is the main **tourist office** (Mon–Fri 9am–7pm, Sat 9am–4pm, Sun 9am–2pm; ✆03 41/7 10 42 60, fax 7 10 42 76, *www.leipzig.de*). It's well worth investing in the **Leipzig Card**, which covers all public transport in the city, and gives reduced entry prices to the museums. For individuals, it costs DM9.90/€4.95 a day, DM21/€10.50 for three days; for a family ticket, covering two adults and up to three children of 14 or under, it's DM21/€10.50 and DM34/€17 respectively. **Mitfahrzentrale** is at Goethestr. 7–10 (✆03 41/1 94 40).

Leipzig is exceptionally well endowed with **hotels** geared to expense-account travellers and priced accordingly; these are scattered all over the city, with only a minority in the centre. There's also a much smaller provision of accommodation in small hotels and **pensions**, which are likewise spread over the entire urban area. **Private rooms** (③–④) can be booked via the tourist office (✆03 41/7 10 42 54 or 7 10 42 55 for advance reservations); many of these are in Communist-era apartment blocks in the city centre, which at least means that they are convenient, though the trade-fair business results in prices being higher than might be expected for the facilities on offer. Alternative budget options are two **youth hostels** and a **campsite**.

Hotels and pensions

Accento, Tauchaer Str. 260, Portitz (✆03 41/9 26 20, fax 9 26 21 00, *www.accento-hotel.de*). Leipzig's first – and, as yet, only – hotel in the modern designer style, located 6km northeast of the city centre, very close to the A14. It also has a fine restaurant (evenings only). ⑤–⑧.

Am Nordplatz, Nordstr. 58 (✆03 41/9 60 31 43, fax 5 64 98 71). Small budget hotel about 1km northwest of the Hauptbahnhof. ④.

Christin, Kochstr. 4 (✆ & fax 03 41/2 32 93 66). No-frills pension in the southern inner suburbs, just west of the Bayerischer Bahnhof. ③.

De Saxe, Gohliser Str. 25, Gohlis (✆03 41/5 93 80, fax 5 93 82 99). Well-regarded hotel, part of the Akzent chain, located just north of the Zoo; take tram #4 to Menckestrasse. It has a high-quality yet reasonably priced restaurant. ⑥.

Galerie Hotel Leipziger Hof, Hedwigstr. 1–3 (✆03 41/6 97 40, fax 6 97 41 50, *www.leipziger-hof.de*). Situated just over 1km east of the Hauptbahnhof, this hotel is given a distinctive character by the presence throughout of art works, some by established names, others by unknowns. It also has a restaurant with beer garden. ⑥.

Im Sachsenpark, Walter-Köhn-Str. 3, Wiederitzsch (✆03 41/5 25 20, fax 5 25 25 28, *www .sachsenparkhotel.de*). Modern business hotel with restaurant situated right alongside the new trade-fair grounds in the north of the city, by the terminus of tram #16. ⑥–⑧.

Kempinski Hotel Fürstenhof, Tröndlinring 8 (✆03 41/14 00, fax 1 40 37 00, *www.kempinski.com*). Leipzig's top address is a late eighteenth-century patrician palace transformed internally when it became a hotel a century later. Long dormant, it was restored at enormous expense by the Kempinski chain, with the addition of modern facilities, including a fitness centre. There's also a top-notch restaurant. ⑦–⑨.

Merseburger Hof, Merseburger Str. 107, Lindenau (✆03 41/4 77 44 62, fax 4 77 44 13, *www .merseburger-hof.de*). Located in a western suburb, reached by S-Bahn #1 or by tram #8 or #15. Its facilities include a fitness centre and a restaurant with beer garden. ④–⑥.

prima, Dresdner Str. 82 (✆03 41/6 88 34 81). A medium-sized pension directly on the main east-bound road, about 2km from the Ring; take tram #4 or #7 to Reudnitz. ②.

Ratskeller Plagwitz, Weissenfelser Str. 10, Plagwitz (✆03 41/48 75 80, fax 4 87 58 20). Fine traditional hotel and restaurant in a western suburb; reached by S-Bahn #2 or tram #14. ⑥.

Seaside Park, Richard-Wagner-Str. 7 (☎03 41/9 85 20, fax 9 85 27 50, *www.seaside-hotels.de*). The new name of this Art Deco hotel directly facing the Hauptbahnhof may be incongruous, but it has been refurbished to a very high standard and is a very convenient place to stay. There's a recommendable restaurant (evenings only, closed Sun) on the premises. ⑥–⑧.

Victor's Residenz, Georgiring 13 (☎03 41/5 00 35 32, fax 5 00 34 48, *www.victors.de*). Another of the clutch of grand hotels around the Hauptbahnhof; it has likewise undergone a makeover and has a good restaurant. ⑥–⑨.

Völkerschlachtdenkmal, Prager Str. 153, Reudnitz (☎03 41/26 99 00, fax 9 90 20 99, *www .voelkerschlacht.com*). Rustically decorated hotel in the south of the city, founded, like the eponymous nearby monument, in 1913 and still in the hands of the same family. It has a good restaurant and a large beer garden. ⑤.

Weisses Ross, Ross-Str. 20 (☎03 41/9 60 59 51). Small budget hotel just south of the Ring, run in conjunction with a traditional *Gaststätte* which is open weekdays only. ③.

Campsite and hostels

Campingplatz am Auensee, Gustav-Esche-Str. 5, Wahren (☎03 41/4 65 16 00, fax 4 65 16 17). Leipzig's campsite is 5km northwest of the city-centre reached by tram #10. It also has bungalows for rent – an extremely economical option for families or small groups.

Hostel Sleepy Lion, Käthe-Kollwitz-Str. 3, Lindenau (☎03 41/9 93 94 80, *www.hostel-leipzig.de*). A privately run hostel in the west of the city; take tram #1 to Gottschedstrasse. Dorm beds from DM27/€13.50, singles DM45/€22.50, doubles DM70/€35.

Jugendherberge Leipzig-Centrum, Voksgartenstr. 24, Schönefeld (☎03 41/2 45 70 11, fax 2 45 70 12, *servicecenter@djh-sachsen.de*). Its name notwithstanding, the DJH hostel is situated in an eastern inner suburb, take tram #1 to Löbauer Strasse. DM25/€12.50 or DM30/€15.

The City

Leipzig is easy to get to grips with: the historic buildings lie mostly within the Altstadt, whose boundaries are defined by the Ring, or just outside. The only sights beyond immediate walking distance are conveniently grouped near to each other southeast of the centre.

The Hauptbahnhof, Ring, Nikolaikirche and Alte Nikolaischule

The **Hauptbahnhof** is a masterpiece of early twentieth-century rail architecture and deserves to be considered one of the main sights of Leipzig – especially now that the sad decline into which it had been allowed to fall in GDR days has now been decisively reversed by a thorough restoration and the addition of an underground shopping mall. It's the largest dead-end passenger station in the world and covers a site formerly occupied by four small terminals. A curiosity is that it has two entrance halls and two levels, as until centralization was introduced under the Third Reich, the Prussian and Saxon authorities each ran their own half of the station as a separate concern. The top-lit **Wartessal** is by far the grandest waiting room in a country whose major stations all too often lack this useful facility.

Now busy with a far heavier volume of traffic than it had in GDR days, the **Ring** is familiar from news footage as the place where the famous Monday demonstrations against totalitarian abuses of power took place. It's therefore particularly appropriate that the **Runde Ecke** (Wed–Sun 2–6pm; free), the former *Stasi* headquarters building at Dittrichring 24, now contains a permanent exhibition on the organization entitled *Macht und Banalität* (Power and Banality). As well as documentary material, you can see examples of the different types of surveillance equipment used, as well as massive piles of confiscated mail.

Following Nikolaistrasse (the street immediately facing the Hauptbahnhof's entrance) due southwards brings you to the **Nikolaikirche**, one of the two main civic churches, and one which has gained an honoured place in the national consciousness. Not only was it the local key rallying point during the *Wende*, but the Monday meetings and prayers which had been held there since 1982 entitle it to be considered as the true fountainhead of the revolution. Although a sombre medieval structure from outside, the church's interior is a real eye-opener, thanks to an audacious late eighteenth-century transformation which flirts between Rococo and Neoclassical. The double-galleried nave is particularly striking: its coffered vault is supported by fluted Corinthian columns with capitals sprouting out in the shape of palm trees.

Opposite the church is its former school, the **Alte Nikolaischule**. It's now used by the university, with one floor given over to the **Antikenmuseum** (Tues–Thurs, Sat & Sun noon–5pm; DM3/€1.50), an important collection of classical antiquities only returned to public view a few years ago after several decades of closure. The main highlights are a fine array of Attic vases and the so-called *Leipzig Alexander*, a marble head of Alexander the Great carved in Roman-occupied Egypt around 150 BC.

The heart of the Altstadt

A couple of blocks to the west of the Nikolaikirche is the open space of the Markt, whose eastern side is entirely occupied by the city's finest building, the **Altes Rathaus** (Tues–Sun 10am–6pm; DM5/€2.50, free first Sun in month). Designed by **Hieronymous Lotter**, who also served as the mayor of the city, it's in the grandest German Renaissance style, with elaborate gables, an asymmetrical clock tower – and the longest inscription to be found on any building in the world. The ground floor retains its traditional function as a covered walkway with shops; the upper storeys, long abandoned as the town hall, now house the local history museum. However, the main reason for going in is to see the 53-metre-long **Festsaal** on the first floor, with its ornate chimneypieces and haughty full-length portraits of the local mayors and Saxon Electors. Also on view is the only likeness of J.S. Bach painted during his lifetime.

On the north side of the Markt is another handsome public building by Lotter, the old weigh house, or **Alte Waage**; only its sundial-crowned facade was restored following its destruction in the war. A survivor of the Baroque period is **Barthels Hof**, just off the west side of the square. This is the only extant example of the courtyards where trading used to take place – a distinctive feature is that it also opens out onto Kleine Fischergasse behind, in order that carriages bearing goods for sale did not have to turn. As the trade fair grew in the early years of the twentieth century, many historic buildings nearby were demolished to make way for the functional modern structures which now predominate, a fate the Altes Rathaus escaped through the casting vote of the mayor. Another survivor is the **Alte Börse** (Old Exchange), the joyous little Baroque building immediately to its rear.

Another distinctive legacy of Leipzig's commercial tradition is the presence of a number of covered shopping malls, of which the largest is the partially modernized **Specks Hof**, entered from Reichsstrasse, a block to the east of the Markt. A better-preserved example is the **Mädler-Passage** at the head of Grimmaische Strasse, just off the Markt's southeastern corner. Tucked away underneath its boutiques is **Auerbachs Keller**, a tavern founded in 1525 which is the setting for the famous scene in Goethe's *Faust* when Mephistopheles tricks the local topers with optical illusions before vanishing into the air on a barrel. This, along with other scenes from the play, is depicted in the murals now adorning the cellar.

Following Barfussgässchen off the western side of the Markt brings you to Kleine Fleischergasse and Leipzig's other celebrated refreshment house, the cheerful Baroque **Zum Arabischen Coffe Baum**. Leipzig was one of the main centres of the craze for coffee which followed the Turkish invasion of central Europe in the late seventeenth century, a theme satirized by Bach in the *Coffee Cantata*. Above the doorway is a delightful relief showing a small cherub proffering a cup to a Turk reclining under a coffee tree. Following many years of closure for restoration work, the whole building has been opened up to the public for the first time ever. In addition to a series of restaurants and cafés (see p.1012), it houses the **Museum Coffe Baum** (daily 11am–7pm; free), whose second-floor entrance is guarded by an early eighteenth-century polychromed statue of the "coffee god". Its fifteen rooms illustrate the history of coffee culture in Europe, with a particular emphasis on Saxony. On display are works of art inspired by the beverage, as well as all kinds of coffee-making equipment and coffee sets, including some beautiful examples of Meissen porcelain.

The Museum der Bildenden Künste
Since 1998, the **Handelshof** (an early twentieth-century trade-fair hall) at Grimmaische Str. 1 has been the temporary home of the **Museum der Bildenden Künste** (Tues & Thurs–Sun 9am–5pm, Wed 1–9.30pm; DM5/€2.50), an eclectic collection of paintings and sculptures from the Middle Ages to the present day, which was previously housed in the Reichsgerichts (see below), its original premises having been lost to wartime bombs. The museum has some fine early German works, notably a *Man of Sorrows* by Hamburg's **Master Francke** and an erotic allegory, *The Magic of Love*, by an unknown Lower Rhenish painter. There are also a few outstanding Netherlandish panels of the same period, among which *The Visitation* by **Rogier van der Weyden** and *The Institution of the Rosary*, attributed to the very rarely encountered **Geertgen tot Sint Jans**, stand out. German painting of the Renaissance is dominated by several examples of **Cranach**, among which *Nymph at the Well* is outstanding, and **Baldung**, whose *Seven Ages of Woman* is one of his most inspired compositions. Highlights of a broad range of seventeenth-century works from across Europe are *The Mulatto* by **Hals**, *The Miracle of St Walburga* by **Rubens** and *The Annunciation* by **Murillo**. From a strong display of Romantic painting, *The Steps of Life* by **Friedrich**, the marvellously comic *The Knight Kuno von Falkenstein* by **Moritz von Schwind** and the celebrated *Isle of the Dead* by **Böcklin** stand out. There are also many works by the versatile Leipzig artist **Max Klinger**, who was equally proficient at painting, engraving and sculpture, and who is increasingly being seen as a figure of some stature.

A new museum, consisting of a central building surrounded by four L-shaped blocks, is currently under construction on Sachsenplatz, immediately north of the Markt. Scheduled for completion at the end of 2002, it will hopefully transform this square, one of the worst eyesores of the Communist era, as well as provide much-needed extra display space for the collection. In the meantime, the **Info-Pavillon** (Tues–Sun 1–6pm; free) at the edge of the building site displays a model of the museum, along with information on its progress. If current plans are implemented, the ground floor will be devoted to the twentieth century (including, significantly, a section on the GDR period), the second floor to the nineteenth century, and the middle floor to works of earlier periods.

The Thomaskirche and the southwestern quarter
A short distance southwest of the Markt is the **Thomaskirche**, the senior of the two big civic churches and the place where **Johann Sebastian Bach** (see also box on p.971) served as *Kantor* for the last 27 years of his life, composing a vast body of choral works for use in its services. Originally part of an Augustinian monastery, the church is predominantly Gothic but has been repeatedly altered down the centuries. Its single **tower** can normally be ascended on summer weekends (DM3/€1.50) for a view over the city. The main features of the interior are the galleries added by Hieronymous Lotter in line with the Protestant emphasis on preaching, the Gothic winged altarpiece, the Renaissance font and the many elaborate epitaphs. However, the most remarkable feature of the church is its musical tradition, and its **choir**, the Thomanerchor, which Bach once directed, can usually be heard on Fridays at 6pm, Saturdays at 3pm and at the Sunday service at 9.30am.

Outside the southern entrance to the church is the **Bach-Denkmal**. Across from it, at Thomaskirchhof 16, the **Bosehaus** contains a small concert hall, a satirical cabaret and the **Bach-Museum** (daily 10am–5pm; *www.bach-leipzig.de*; DM6/€3), which has an extensive show of mementos of the great composer, along with a collection of musical instruments of his time. Facing the opposite side of the church is the **Commerzbank**, the most imposing of Leipzig's historic bank buildings, not least for its huge gold figures, which positively glitter when the sun is shining. Almost due south of the Thomaskirche is Burgplatz, on which stands the **Neues Rathaus**. This

Historicist monstrosity from the turn of the twentieth century employs elements of just about every European architectural style, even incorporating a "Bridge of Sighs" to link the main building to its extension.

South across the Ring is Georgi-Dimitroff-Platz and the supreme court of prewar Germany, the **Reichsgerichts**, a bulky neo-Renaissance palace. The opulent main courtroom and its ancillary chambers on the first floor were the setting for the famous trial on the Reichstag fire – the event which served as a pretext for the Nazis' clampdown on the activities of their political opponents. During the trial, one of those accused of starting the fire, Georgi Dimitroff, the Bulgarian head of the Communist International, completely outwitted Hermann Göring, the chief prosecutor. This was celebrated with relish in GDR days, when the building served as a museum. However, restoration work has been under way for several years in preparation for a return to judicial use: the Bundesverfassungsgericht is due to transfer here from Karlsruhe in 2002. As a result, it will probably not be readily accessible again.

Augustusplatz and the university quarter

East of the Markt is a vast square, returned to its old name of Augustusplatz, which serves as the main focus of both academic and musical life in the city. On its northern side is the **Oper Leipzig**, whose sombre pseudo-Neoclassical form recalls the architecture of the Third Reich, though it was actually built under Communism. Very different is the **Neues Gewandhaus** opposite, an avant-garde building inaugurated in 1981 as the new home of the famous Gewandhausorchester, the oldest and largest orchestra in the world.

Rising high up from the centre of the square is the 34-storey **Universitätshochhaus**, begun in 1968 as a prestige project of the then dictator of the GDR, Walter Ulbricht, a native of Leipzig. In order to build this new home for the university, which was founded back in 1409, a number of historic buildings were demolished, including the Universitätskirche. Only a Schinkel-designed gateway on the west side remains, looking hopelessly forlorn against the skyscraper, which is shaped to resemble an open book. In recent years, it seemed to be a potential candidate for demolition, but is currently the subject of an ambitious reconstruction project. The **Moritzbastei** to the rear, another Lotter creation, is the only surviving part of the fortifications, and has found a new lease of life as the focal point of the student social scene. To the west, at Schillerstr. 6, the **Ägyptisches Museum** (Tues–Sat 1–5pm, Sun 10am–1pm; DM3/€1.50) has a surprisingly good collection of Egyptian antiquities from nineteenth-century excavations by university archeologists.

Just across the Ring from the Moritzbastei, the late Neoclassical tenement building at Goldschmidtstr. 12 contains the **Mendelssohn-Haus** (daily 10am–6pm; *www.mendelssohn-stiftung.de*; DM5/€2.50), the flat where Felix Mendelssohn Bartholdy spent the last two years of his short life, dying there in 1847. He lived in Leipzig for twelve years in all, and, in addition to his compositional activities, he directed the Gewandhausorchester, founded the Conservatory and revived the long-forgotten music of his great predecessor J.S. Bach. The apartments are furnished in the Biedermeier style the composer would have known: indeed, his work room is an accurate reconstruction based on a contemporary watercolour. Elsewhere, a number of watercolours by Mendelssohn himself, who was a talented amateur painter, can be seen. There are also some original documents and possessions, including the wood and leather travelling trunk with a view of *Ye George Inn* presented to him during his triumphant British tour of 1840; a piano he is known to have played is also on display.

The Grassi-Museum

On Täubchenweg, a short walk to the northeast, is the Grassi-Musuem, a vast Bauhaus complex. Badly damaged during the war, it remained in partial use until 2001, when it closed for reconstruction work that will last several years. Of the three museums it normally contains, the **Musikinstrumentenmuseum** (previously Tues–Sat 10am–5pm, Sun 10am–1pm; DM5/€2.50), the university's collection of historical musical instruments, has yet to be allocated a temporary home. However, some of the holdings of the **Museum für Völkerkunde** (Tues–Fri 10am–6pm, Sat & Sun 10am–5pm; DM4/€2) are now on view in the Mädlerpassage, in rooms directly above Auerbachs Keller. The ethnology displays range across Russia and the other states of the former Soviet Union, Africa (including a distinguished group of bronze sculptures from the Nigerian city of Benin), Peru, Persia, China, India, Australia and the South Seas.

A selection of artefacts from the **Museum für Kunsthandwerk** (previously Tues & Thurs–Sun 10am–6pm, Wed noon–8pm; DM5/€2.50), one of Europe's finest collections of decorative arts, ranging from the Carolingian era to the Bauhaus, is on show from 2001 just around the corner, at Neumarkt 20. Particular highlights are several Renaissance goldsmiths' pieces from the municipal treasure, the *Leipziger Ratsschatz*; the ivory, bronze, copper and wood *Triumph of the Cross* by the Dresden Baroque sculptor Balthasar Permoser; the gem cabinet from the Stadtbibliothek; and a group of sketches for Meissen chinoiserie.

South of the centre

Rail buffs should make the trek south of the Altstadt to see the **Bayerischer Bahnhof**, the oldest functioning train station in Europe. The grand Neoclassical structure erected in the 1840s was virtually flattened during World War II, and only the facade has been restored. Just a handful of services still run from here, suggesting it's kept open principally for the sake of preserving its record.

A few other worthwhile sights lie south of here on the route of tram #21; they can also be reached by tram #15 from elsewhere. On Deutscher Platz is the **Deutsche Bücherei**, the largest German-language library in the world. Part of it is given over to the **Deutsches Buch- und Schriftmuseum** (Mon–Sat 9am–4pm; free), which traces the history of books during the past five thousand years. Just to the east is the **Russische Gedächtniskirche St Alexij**, a striking pastiche of the churches of Novgorod, decorated inside with original eighteenth-century icons. It was built in 1913 to commemorate the 22,000 Russian soldiers who died in the **Battle of the Nations** a hundred years previously.

The actual site of this conflict, in which the Russians combined with the Prussians, Austrians and Swedes to defeat Napoleon, lies just to the south, on the opposite side of the old trade-fair site. Subsequently, the French dictator was banished to exile in Elba. A colossal and tasteless monument, known as the **Völkerschlachtdenkmal** (daily: April–Oct 10am–6pm; Nov–March 10am–4pm; DM6/€3), was erected to commemorate the centenary of the victory. It can be ascended for an extensive if unexciting view over the city and the flat countryside around, and is increasingly in use as a cultural venue (see p.1013). The new **Forum 1813** (same times; DM4/€2) alongside contains several hundred artefacts associated with the battle. These include the personal effects of the most famous casualty, the Polish marshal Prince Józef Poniatowski: his defeat and death meant that hopes for the revival of Poland's independence, lost in 1795, were laid to rest, not to be revived for another century. There is also a large diorama of the Battle of Probstheida which took place a few days later, completing Napoleon's defeat.

Eating and drinking

Leipzig rivals and indeed surpasses most western German cities in its choices for eating and drinking, offering a wide range of traditional German taverns, ethnic restaurants, cafés and bars. Many of the best places are conveniently close to the Markt; there are also some particularly recommendable establishments in the northern suburb of Gohlis.

Restaurants

Apels Garten, Kolonnadenstr. 2. Although moderately priced, this is one of the very best restaurants in Leipzig. Featured on the menu are several dishes made according to recipes from the *Leipziger Kochbuch* of 1706. Closed Sun from 3pm.

Auerbachs Keller, Mädler-Passage, Grimmaische Str. 2–4. This restaurant's fame makes it a must, and the food served is of high quality. Except when there's a fair on, there's seldom any problem getting a table in either the cavernous main cellar, the *Grosser Keller* (which serves beers from the out-of-town Krostitz brewery) or in the smaller and more upmarket *Historische Weinstuben* (evenings only, closed Sun) on the other side of the stairway.

Barthels Hof, Hainstr. 1. Restaurant and wine bar in a celebrated Renaissance courtyard. The house specialities are the *Eintopf* dishes, which are available as either starters or main courses.

Coffe Baum, Kleine Fleischergasse 4. On the ground floor are three cosy little dining rooms serving rustic local fare and beers from the Krostitz brewery; these include the *Schumannzimmer*, which is named after one-time regular, the composer Robert Schumann. Directly above is *Lusatia* (evenings only), which presents somewhat more expensive and upscale cuisine.

Gohliser Schlösschen, Menckestr. 23, Gohlis. This beautiful little late Baroque palace, the only building of its type in Leipzig, houses a restaurant serving French and Saxon dishes.

Gosenschenke Ohne Bedenken, Menckestr. 5, Gohlis. Just down the road from the above, this nineteenth-century Gaststätte is decked out in period style and has a spacious beer garden to the rear. It serves hearty meals and has revived production of *Gose*, a fruity, acidic brew similar in character to the Belgian *Gueuze* – though in German terms it's technically not a beer, as it contains spices banned under the *Reinheitsgebot*.

Hopfenspeicher, Oststr. 38, Reudnitz. The Gaststätte of the Reudnitzer brewery, Leipzig's largest, with a wider than usual product range for the former GDR.

Kaiser Maximilian, Neumarkt 9. Fairly pricey restaurant serving a variety of Mediterranean cuisines.

Kubanische Speisebar Varadero, Barfussgässchen 8. Popular and genuine Cuban restaurant, a hardy survivor of the GDR era, specializing in grills and cocktails. On Mon, it's only open in the evening.

Leipziger Brauerei, Thomaskirchhof 3–5. A somewhat unexpected combination of an Italian restaurant, serving moderately priced pizzas, pasta and other typical food, and a Hausbrauerei which brews light, dark and various seasonal beers.

Medici, Nikolaikirchhof 5. The city's leading Italian restaurant, presenting upmarket cuisine in very formal surroundings. Closed Sun.

Paulaner, Klostergasse 3. The city-centre Gaststätte of the eponymous Munich brewery offers both Bavarian and Saxon dishes and has firmly established itself as one of Leipzig's most popular eateries.

Paulaner im Mückenschlösschen, Waldstr. 86, Gohlis. The company's other Leipzig venture is a restaurant, bistro and bar in an imposing Wilhelmine-era palace in the Rosental park. It also has Leipzig's biggest beer garden.

Ratskeller, Lotterstr. 1. Typically reliable cellar restaurant in the Neues Rathaus; because of its situation well away from the Markt, it's less than usually prone to be full of tourists. Closed Sun evening.

Stadtpfeiffer, Augustusplatz 8. Highly rated, rather pricey restaurant of the Neues Gewandhaus, serving an international menu. Closed Sun in July & Aug.

Sylter Stube, Markt 9. Fish and seafood speciality restaurant, with fresh produce from the North Sea.

Thüringer Hof, Burgstr. 19. Leipzig's oldest surviving Gaststätte, with a pedigree dating back to 1454. It has a rambling layout of rooms and a glass-covered inner courtyard, and is the best-value choice in the Altstadt for a hearty German meal.

Zur Neuberin, Grosse Fleischergasse 2. Cosy wine bar-restaurant on four floors of a fifteenth-century timber-framed house. Evenings only, closed Sun.

Cafés and bars

Boomerang, Waldstr. 29. Australian theme bar, serving wines, beers and rum from Down Under.

Café am Brühl, Richard-Wagner-Platz 1. Traditional café in an elegant Rococo mansion with garden; it's also the home of the Leipziger Brettl cabaret.

Café Vis à Vis, Rudolf-Breitscheid-Str. 33. Café-bar whose predominantly youthful clientele contains a large proportion of gays and lesbians; open round the clock.

Coffe Baum, Kleine Fleischergasse 4. There are two new cafés on the second floor of this famous old coffee house: one French in style, the other Viennese. A third is decked out in the Arabian manner, but has a purely decorative function.

Gohliser Schlösschen, Menckestr. 23, Gohlis. The aforementioned palace also contains a café; the best time to come is between 3pm and 5pm on Sun, when *Kaffee und Kuchen* is served in the Orangerie to the accompaniment of music played by a salon ensemble whose members are drawn from the ranks of the Gewandhausorchester.

Kaffehaus Riquet, Schumachergässchen 1. Viennese-style coffee house and wine cellar in a wacky Jugendstil shop building.

Kandler, Thomaskirchhof 11. This has a huge range of teas, which are stored in large jars, and home-made pralines.

Kulturcafé, Nikolaikirchhof 1. Offers breakfast from 10am, organic wines, beers from the Reudnitzer brewery, and regular live music sessions in the evening.

le bit, Kohlgartenstr. 2. One of several Internet cafés in the city.

Moritzbastei, Universitätstr. 9. Complex of student clubs, bars and a disco which offers a choice of live entertainments most evenings.

Podium, Naschmarkt 1–3. One of several Irish pubs to have sprung up in the city since the *Wende*.

Spizz, Markt 9. Live music bar, with jazz the most regular feature; there's also a disco in the basement.

Culture

Leipzig occupies a hallowed place in the musical world, and hosts performances of the highest standards in several different genres all year round – a remarkable achievement for a city of its size. It also has a strong theatrical tradition, not least in the field of cabaret. Full listings of **what's on** can be found in the free magazine *Fritz*.

Classical music

The **Thomaskirche** (see p.1009) continues to play a very prominent role in Leipzig's musical life, with regular organ recitals and choral concerts (by the Thomanerchor and others), to which there's often free admission. As in Bach's lifetime, the **Nikolaikirche** (see p.1007) is an important secondary venue for performances of sacred music. In the **orchestral** field, the Gewandhausorchester, which is renowned for the clean, beautifully balanced sound it produces, remains one of the world's best, the tradition of Felix Mendelssohn, Arthur Nikisch, Wilhelm Furtwängler and Bruno Walter having been maintained by Kurt Masur (who also played a key role in the *Wende*) and current music director, Herbert Blomstedt. The local radio orchestra, the MDR-Sinfonieorchester, is also of good standing, while the associated MDR-Chor and MDR-Kinderchor are among Europe's best large mixed-voiced and children's **choirs** respectively.

Bosehaus, Thomaskirchhof 16 (☎03 41/96 44 10, *www.bach-leipzig.de*). The hall here is used primarily for performances of Baroque music.

Mendelssohn-Haus, Goldschmidtstr. 12 (☎03 41/1 27 02 94, *www.mendelssohn-stiftung.de*). In honour of a tradition established by Mendelssohn himself, recitals of chamber music or lieder are held every Sun at 11am.

Neues Gewandhaus, Augustusplatz 8 (☎03 41/1 27 00, *www.gewandhaus.de*). In addition to the main concert hall, the home of the Gewandhausorchester, there's also a smaller room, the Mendelssohn-Saal, for chamber, instrumental and vocal music.

Oper Leipzig, Augustusplatz 12 (☎03 41/1 26 12 61, *www.leipzig-online.de/oper*). Presents a varied programme of opera and ballet, including a generous number of contemporary works.

Völkerschlachtdenkmal, Prager Str. 210 (☎03 41/8 61 71 20). A venue of true curiosity value, whose own choir performs regular concerts under quite extraordinary acoustic conditions: the echo lasts up to twenty seconds.

Theatre

academixer, Kupfergasse 6 (☎03 41/9 60 48 48). Founded by local students in the 1960s, this cabaret in an Art Deco-style cellar is still going strong.

Haus Dreilinden, Dreilindenstr. 30 (☎03 41/12 61 19). Specialist venue for musicals and musical comedies.

Krystallpalast Varieté, Magazingasse 4 (☎03 41/14 06 60, *www.krystallpalastvariete.de*). Presents old-style variety shows.

Leipziger Funzel, Nikolaistr. 6–10 (☎03 41/9 60 32 32). Venue for satirical cabaret.

Leipziger Pfeffermühle, Thomaskirchhof 16 (☎03 41/9 60 31 96, *www.kabarett-leipziger-pfeffermuehle.de*). Long-established cabaret venue.

LOFFT, Lindenauer Markt 21 (☎03 41/9 61 76 15, *www.leipzig-online.de/lofft*). Offers a wide variety of alternative and experimental theatre.

Neue Szene, Gottschedstr. 16 (☎03 41/1 26 81 68). Focuses on modern plays and other contemporary art forms.

Puppentheater Sterntaler, Talstr. 30 (☎03 41/9 61 54 35, *www.projeckt-sterntaler.de*). Leipzig's puppet theatre.

SanftWut, Mädler-Passage, Grimmaische Str. 2–4 (☎03 41/9 61 23 48, *www.sanftwut.de*). Cabaret with a strong musical emphasis.

Schauspielhaus, Bosestr. 1 (☎03 41/1 26 81 80, *www.schauspielhaus-leipzig.de*). The main municipally run stage for dramatic fare.

Theater der Jungen Welt, Lindenauer Markt 21 (☎03 41/48 66 00). Germany's most venerable youth theatre.

Festivals

Leipzig now has a wide variety of festivals throughout the year. The twice-yearly *Honky Tonk* (in May and early November) is billed as Europe's largest **bar festival**, with around a hundred different acts performing in nearly as many different venues. The Markt is the setting for various **markets**, notably the nine-day-long *Ostermesse* at Easter. Of the annual **cultural** events, the ten-day *Bachfest* centred on Ascension Day (variable date in May/June) celebrates the music of J.S. Bach; the *Leipziger Kulturwochen* in the first half of October offers a varied programme of concerts; the *Lachmesse* in mid-October is a festival of humour and satire centred on the cabaret venues listed above; while the *Dokfest* in mid-November features documentaries and short films.

Torgau

TORGAU, a former residence of the Saxon Electors, stands on the banks of the Elbe 50km to the northeast of Leipzig; it can be reached in an hour or less by the regular trains on the fast line to Cottbus. Beside the road bridge is a memorial commemorating the fact that it was at this spot, in the closing days of World War II, that the advancing Soviet and American armies finally met up.

The town centre is built on a cliff high above the river, and centred on a typically spacious Markt with a handsome Renaissance **Rathaus**. Directly overlooking the river is the **Marienkirche**, a Gothic church containing the tombstone of Katharina von Bora, wife of Luther, who died in the town, and a panel of *The Fourteen Helpers in Need* by Cranach. This was part of his early masterpiece, *The Holy Kinship*, whose central panel is now in the Städel in Frankfurt.

Frederick the Wise, the man of power who made the Reformation possible, was born in **Schloss Hartenfels**, the large castle which dominates the town. It dates back to the tenth century, but in its present form is predominantly a residential palace; entry is over a moat with a bear pit, into which brown bears have been reintroduced. The **Albrechtsbau** at the southeastern corner is one of the earliest Renaissance buildings in Germany; its **tower** (Tues–Sun 9.30am–noon & 1–4pm; DM1/€0.50) can be ascended for a fine view over the town and the complex. An altogether grander style is present in the **Johann-Friedrich-Bau** which forms the east wing of the courtyard, and its exterior spiral staircase, the *Grosse Wendelstein*, is the Schloss's most arresting feature.

Part of the north wing is given over to the **Kreismuseum** (Tues–Sun 9.30am–noon & 1–4.30pm; DM2/€1), which houses a collection of medieval arms and armour, together with displays on the history of the town. Far more intriguing is the **Schlosskapelle** alongside, which was consecrated by Luther in 1544, and thus has the best (though disputed) claim to be regarded as the first building designed specifically for Protestant worship. In line with the ideals of the Reformation, the architecture is plain and simple, adopting a rectangular format with no apse. The galleries introduced here became a standard feature of Protestant buildings, while the elaborate vaulting was also favoured in early Lutheran churches.

Practicalities

Torgau's **Bahnhof** is ten minutes' walk northwest of the centre. The **tourist office** (April–Sept Mon–Fri 10am–6pm, Sat & Sun 11am–4pm; Oct–March Mon–Fri 10am–5pm; ☎0 34 21/71 25 71, fax 71 02 80, *www.torgau.de*) at Schloss-Str. 11 can book **private rooms** (②–③). Additionally, there are a few **pensions**: *Haus am Stadtpark*, north of the centre at Reditzer Weg 1 (☎0 34 21/90 34 32; ③); *Zum Eisbären*, southwest of the centre at Lassallestr. 1 (☎0 34 21/70 84 50; ③); and *Am Markt*, Bäckerstr. 12 (☎0 34 21/71 13 79; ④). The town's three **hotels** are *Torgauer Brauhof*, in the north of town at Warschauer Str. 7 (☎0 34 21/7 30 00; ⑤), *Goldener Anker*, Markt 6 (☎0 34 21/90 387 4; ⑥), and *Central*, Friedrichplatz 8 (☎0 34 21/71 00 26; ⑥). All these hotels have **restaurants**. Alternatively, try *Restaurant im Kulturhaus*, Rosa-Luxemburg-Str. 16, the cosy little *Bärenschenke*, Schloss-Str. 25, or the inevitable *Ratskeller*, Markt 1.

In May 1994, Torgau revived one of prewar Germany's biggest **folk festivals**, the biennial *Auszugfest*, which combines a horseback procession in sixteenth-century costume with a marksmen's fair. The main annual event is the *Elbe Day* on April 25, commemorating the meeting of the American and Soviet forces and featuring Dixieland performers from around the world.

Colditz and the Zwickauer Mulde valley

Mention the name of **COLDITZ** to most Germans and you're likely to be met with a blank stare. This is the one place in the country that, because of **Oflag IVC**, the wartime maximum security camp for prisoners of war, is far better known abroad than at home. The main reason for this is that the GDR regime, embarrassed about the fact that the camp had been on their territory and unable to make any pro-Communist propaganda out of it (as they could with the concentration camps, where many of their own number had been incarcerated), chose to suppress its very existence. No references to it could be found in the official English-language guide to the country, while the 64-page German booklet on the town gave it just one paragraph. Although a fair number of English-speaking visitors used to travel the 48km south from Leipzig out of curiosity, they were unable to visit the site of the camp, which reverted to its psychiatric status as a psychiatric hospital, while Colditz itself went back to being a sleepy rural community. Since the *Wende*, there has been a positive encouragement of visitors and a willingness to make a dispassionate examination of the past.

The Town

On its own merits, Colditz is a surprisingly pretty town in attractive surroundings; add in the wartime connection and it's easy to see why the potential for tourism is very real.

OFLAG IVC

Schloss Colditz was chosen as the site of **Oflag IVC**, the Third Reich's most secure prisoner-of-war camp, principally because of its geographical position – it was 700km to any border not controlled by the Nazis. The nature of the castle itself, with its secure medieval defences and situation above a small, isolated town, was another factor. **Major Pat Reid**, who wrote a trilogy of books about his Colditz experiences, recorded his initial impression of it as "beautiful, serene, majestic and yet forbidding enough to make our hearts sink into our boots". According to the Nazi authorities, Colditz castle was impossible to escape from, but in all, 31 men performed the feat, aided by the fact that the main qualification for being sentenced to the castle – that of having attempted to escape before – gave the prisoners a rich fund of experience and ingenuity, which they gladly pooled.

In 1941, **Peter Allan** became the first Briton to escape, by hiding in a sack which was taken away in a delivery van; however, on reaching Vienna, he was recaptured and sent back. Following a number of successful getaways by French prisoners, **Airey Neave** (who later led the campaign to make Margaret Thatcher the Conservative Party leader, five years before he was blown up by the IRA) made the first of the eleven British "home-runs" early in 1942, dressed in the uniform of a German officer; Reid was among the others who accomplished the feat that same year. The latter's books are the best source for an insight into life in the camp; for a completely different perspective, see *Colditz – the German Story* by Reinhold Eggers, the official in charge of security.

The streets, laid out in a ramshackle old pattern, are full of historic half-timbered houses, while the main **Markt** is a highly distinctive sloping cobblestoned square. At the top is a handsome gabled **Rathaus** in the ebullient style of the German Renaissance.

From the foot of Marktplatz, there's a great view of the huge **Schloss** (guided tours Tues–Sun 10am–5pm; DM9/€4.50), the former Oflag IVC, which completely dominates the town from its cliff-top site. There's been a fortress here since the eleventh century, and it came into the possession of the Wettins, the Saxon ruling house, in 1404. In the middle of the following century, Elector August rebuilt it as a Renaissance palace, though retaining its medieval format of defensive *Vorburg* protecting the main *Hauptburg*. The magnificent armorial decoration above the second gateway shows his own coat of arms, alongside that of his wife. Under Augustus the Strong (see box on p.1034), the Schloss was used as a hunting lodge, but it was abandoned by later Saxon rulers in favour of more modern palaces. In 1800, it became the local poorhouse, later becoming one of Germany's first psychiatric hospitals. It was specially chosen in World War II as the place to house men who had escaped from less secure confinements and subsequently been recaptured, and for *Prominenten*, prisoners who were specially prized because of their high rank or important connections.

Currently, its future is uncertain. The Land government moved out the psychiatric patients and put it up for sale in 1994, hoping to find a foreign buyer prepared to turn it into a hotel or conference centre but have subsequently assumed responsibility for its restoration, opening a documentary exhibition centre, the **Fluchtmuseum**, in the old guard house. The exhibits include a large number of photographs taken during World War II plus a fascinating display of some of the ingenious devices the prisoners used in planning their escapes, including a typewriter which could be taken to pieces to prevent its discovery, a razor transformed into a saw and a home-made sewing machine, along with false identification papers and German banknotes. You can also see inside the galleried **Schlosskapelle** and descend to the 44-metre-long **tunnel** which the French prisoners dug over an eight-month period. They intended this to be the means of a mass escape, but it was discovered before it could be used.

To join one of the tours, go first to the **Städtisches Museum** (same hours and ticket; DM2/€1 for separate ticket), which occupies a fine Baroque house at Tiergartenstr.

1, just uphill from the church near the entrance to the Schloss. It's a decent local history museum in its own right; the exhibits include the original sculptures from the Schlosskapelle and the Rathaus's eighteenth-century clock.

Practicalities

Colditz lies on a minor rail line; to get there from Leipzig, it's normally necessary to change at Grossbothen, though there's a direct bus service as an alternative. The **tourist office** is at An der Kirche 1 (Mon–Fri 9am–5pm; ☎03 43 81/4 35 19, *www.colditz.de*). Accommodation options are limited: there's a **youth hostel** just below the Schloss at Haingasse 42 (☎03 43 81/4 33 35, fax 4 11 40; DM19/€9.50 or DM24/€12); a few **private rooms** (②–③); a **pension**, *Zur Alten Stadtmauer*, Am Graben 5–7 (☎03 43 81/4 31 79; ③); and, at the edge of town, a **hotel**, *Waldhaus*, Lausicker Str. 60 (☎03 43 81/4 33 71; ③). In the village of Zschadrass a couple of kilometres to the northeast is another hotel – *Gildehof Zschadrass*, Hauptstr. 4 (☎03 43 81/80 20; ③). The best places to **eat** and **drink** are the *Schloss-Café* (a traditional Gaststätte, in spite of its name) and the *Marktstübl*, both on the Markt, and *Ponydiele*, Schulstr. 15.

The Zwickauer Mulde valley

Upstream along the **Zwickauer Mulde** from Colditz lies a really lovely secluded valley, which is often surprisingly deep, considering the modest scale of the river itself. Along its banks are several outstandingly picturesque towns and villages, all linked by a scenic rail line.

Rochlitz

ROCHLITZ, 11km upstream from Colditz, is a junction of three rail lines. From the Bahnhof at the northern end, the line along the Zwickauer Mulde departs from the river's snaking course to run right down the length of the town, passing over a viaduct before traversing the river. At this point, there is briefly a dramatic view of the large fifteenth- and sixteenth-century **Schloss** (Tues–Sun 10am–5pm; DM3/€1.50), the former headquarters of the local counts, with its picturesque silhouette of church-like towers and palace buildings with huge sloping roofs. It's currently the subject of a long-term restoration project, and part of it is occupied by a rehabilitation centre for those suffering from lung diseases. However, you can visit the small museum of local history and climb one of the towers for a view over the valley. The town centre, with its two market squares, has recaptured its old county town atmosphere and is worth a quick stroll. Varied perspectives on the Schloss can be had from the pedestrian footbridge, and from the hills above, which are dotted with marked trails.

The **youth hostel** is just up from the footbridge at Sassnitzer Str. 1 (☎0 37 37/42131, fax 14 90 53; DM19/€9.50 or DM24/€12). There are also two reasonably priced **hotels**, *Bayrische Bierstube*, Markt 23 (☎0 37 37/4 22 20; ④), and *Goldener Löwe*, Markt 3 (☎0 37 37/4 24 38; ④), plus a plentiful number of **private rooms** (①–③) – look out for *Zimmer frei* signs.

Wechselburg

Set high above the valley a further 9km south is **WECHSELBURG**, formerly one of the seats of another aristocratic dynasty, the counts of Schönburg. In contrast to Rochlitz, it's a quiet village sleeping in rural obscurity, with its Renaissance **Schloss** now functioning as a children's home.

The other dominant monument is the Romanesque **Stiftskirche**, which, in line with the faith of the former aristocratic masters, is Catholic – one of the few such historic churches in eastern Germany. Its extraordinary **rood screen**, made around 1235, is a masterpiece of both architecture and sculpture. One of the most remarkable things about it is that it was reassembled a couple of decades ago; for the previous three hundred years, its constituent parts were scattered throughout the building: the section above the archway, with its relief of Christ in Majesty, served as the pulpit. The six niche figures of Old Testament characters – particularly the large statue of Melchizedek to the far right – and the triumphal cross group at the summit, are brilliant pieces of carving. Look out also for the **tomb** of the founders, Count Dedo and his wife Mechthila.

Rochsburg
Another 8km upstream is **ROCHSBURG**, entered via a spectacular double viaduct over the river. The village is, if anything, even more soporific than Wechselburg, and is similarly set on lofty heights. It takes its name from the **Rochsburg** (April–Oct Tues–Sun 10am–5pm; Nov–March Tues–Sun 9am–4pm; DM3/€1.50) whose silhouette rears up proudly above the wooded slopes. Originally built as a feudal castle by an offshoot of the counts of Rochlitz, it was acquired by the Schönburgs in the sixteenth century and skilfully transformed, after a fire, into the present Renaissance palace, which has the best of both worlds by retaining many of the old defensive features. The interiors, though fairly low-key, have some impressive doorways and Renaissance furniture.

Zwickau

ZWICKAU, Saxony's fourth largest city, is a major rail junction and gateway to both of the rural areas in the south of the province, the Vogtland and the Erzgebirge. It's about 90km south of Leipzig, and can be reached directly by express services via the Thuringian town of Altenburg, or more picturesquely by the line along the Zwickauer Mulde. For the foreseeable future, Zwickau's name will be irrevocably associated with the Trabant (popularly known as the Trabi), the wretched but now rather celebrated "people's car" of the GDR, which was manufactured here. However, in spite of its industrial tradition, it's an agreeable city of broad parks, with a historic centre which came through World War II almost entirely unscathed.

The City

Zwickau grew up as a market town trading in minerals mined in the Erzgebirge. Its Altstadt occupies a roughly circular area inside the busy inner ring road, Dr-Friedrichs-Ring, with the Zwickauer Mulde forming a second boundary to the east. Because of earlier wars, only a few monuments from the Middle Ages remain; instead, there's a varied assemblage, with plenty of grand nineteenth- and early twentieth-century offices and stores. Largely pedestrianized, it's quickly developing into a modern commercial city centre on the western German model. Several other worthwhile attractions lie to the north of the centre.

The Altstadt
At the southwestern corner of the central Hauptmarkt is the **Robert-Schumann-Haus** (Tues–Sat 10am–5pm; DM5/€2.50), birthplace of German music's purest Romantic spirit. It documents all phases of his career, from his early days as a virtuoso pianist in Leipzig (which were brought to an end after his fingers were damaged in a hand-

THE TRABI

Because it swiftly became a common sight on western German streets (from which it was previously banned on environmental grounds), the Trabi is, perversely, the most potent symbol of the unification of Germany. The earliest version of the Communist answer to the Volkswagen was first built in 1955 in the former Horch and Audi works; two years later, it was put into mass production under the name of Trabant. Three million vehicles were subsequently manufactured, repeating the original formula almost exactly, apart from a few changes introduced in 1964. With its plastic bodywork and two-cylinder, two-stroke engine, the Trabi was hopelessly antiquated even in its early days. It was also a major contributor to the GDR's pollution, belching out five times as much carbon monoxide and nine times as much hydrocarbon as the average Western car. Though it was the cheapest and most readily available car in the GDR, it wasn't easy to obtain – twelve years was about the normal waiting time. Its lawnmower-like noise was an omnipresent feature on GDR streets, while it's the only car ever built capable of coming off the worse in a collision with a pedestrian.

The most popular of the many Trabi jokes – the suggestion that you could double its value by filling it up with petrol – suddenly came true in the summer of 1989, when East Germans escaping to the West via Hungary gladly exchanged their Trabis for the price of the petrol in its tank. Production ended in 1990, when Volkswagen moved back to Zwickau, but the Trabi will be a familiar sight for a while yet, as its one strong point was its remarkable longevity.

stretching machine), to his sad final years, during which he was racked by mental instability. There's similarly extensive material on his devoted wife, **Clara Wieck**, who inspired his vast outpourings of passionate, heart-on-sleeve piano pieces and songs. As the leading pianist of her day and an accomplished composer in a style derived from her husband's, she was herself a substantial figure.

In the middle of the south side of the square is the **Rathaus**, whose showy facade masks a medieval structure. Further along is the Renaissance **Gewandhaus**, built in the early sixteenth century as the market hall and guild house of the drapers. Now serving as the town's main theatre, its most notable feature is the amazing five-tiered gable.

Just off the western side of Hauptmarkt is the main civic church, the **Marienkirche** (now designated as the **Dom**, though it's never been a cathedral). Its decorative late Gothic hall-church format, and the profusion of furnishings from the same period, are typical of the Erzgebirge region. Many of the present sumptuous exterior adornments, including the large south porch with its depiction of the Wise and Foolish Virgins, and the now very blackened figures on the buttresses, were only added a century ago in a flush of Romantic over-enthusiasm. The **tower**, whose lead helmet with double cupola is a Baroque embellishment, can be ascended for a view over the Hauptmarkt and the city (Mon–Fri at 3.30pm; DM2/€1). Inside, the main adornment is the magnificent **high altar**, made in the Nürnberg workshop of **Michael Wolgemut**, the teacher of Dürer. It can be opened to reveal any of three sections, though only one of these is visible at a time. Normally the carved part, with life-size gilded figures of the Madonna and Child surrounded by eight female saints, is on view, but the cycles of paintings illustrating the Nativity and the Passion are shown during their respective seasons. Also in the chancel is a **Holy Sepulchre**, carved in filigree style in the manner of a Flamboyant Gothic chapel, and adorned with figures of sleeping Knights. The other work of art of special note is the *Pietà* in a north aisle chapel, the masterpiece of **Peter Breuer**, a local man who is one of the brilliant group of German sculptors straddling the late Gothic and early Renaissance eras.

Just south of the Marienkirche, on the triangular site formed by the pointed intersection of Domhof and Münzstrasse, is Zwickau's most eccentric building, the **Schiffchen-Haus**, a late fifteenth-century house shaped like the prow of a ship. The Altstadt's remaining sights are all north of the Hauptmarkt. The semicircular Nicolaistrasse loops round via the back of the **Pulverturm** (Powder Tower), the only remaining part of the city walls, to the **Katharinenkirche**, another late Gothic hall church, which formerly belonged to a Benedictine monastery. Inside are a high altar made in Cranach's workshop and a statue of *The Risen Christ* by Breuer. Opposite is the Renaissance **Posthalterei**, which was built as the home of a wealthy cloth manufacturer and merchant, later serving as a coaching house, before becoming a top-class restaurant. At the extreme northern end of the Altstadt is an even grander Renaissance structure, **Schloss Osterstein**, a former residence of the Electors of Saxony. Alongside is the late fifteenth-century **Kornhaus**, one of the largest and oldest grain stores in the country.

The rest of the city

Between the Altstadt and the Hauptbahnhof to the west is the extensive **Stadtpark**, which provides welcome peace in the middle of the city. It's centred on a huge artificial boating lake; other attractions are an open-air theatre, a music pavilion and an aviary, though it's fun enough just to wander through and watch the locals at play. About ten minutes' walk to the north, via Crimmitschauer Strasse, is Lessingstrasse, on which stands the **Städtisches Museum** (Tues, Thurs & Sun 10am–6pm, Wed 10am–8pm, Sat 1–6pm; DM3/€1.50), a rambling, old-fashioned collection in a specially designed domed building from the end of the Jugendstil epoch. Its exhibits range from medieval sculpture, including a triptych and a *Crucifixion* by Breuer, via displays of locally produced porcelain and official portraits of the Saxon Electors, to the minerals and mining history of the Erzgebirge.

From here, it's just a short walk north to the **Automobilmuseum August Horch** at Walter-Rathenau-Str. 51 (Tues–Thurs 9am–5pm, Sat & Sun 10am–5pm; *www.trabant.de*; DM5/€2.50), which celebrates Zwickau's role as a leading centre of car production. As the exhibits show, the Trabi (see box on p.1019) was the unworthy and improbable inheritor of a distinguished tradition dating back via the prewar Audi to the Horch factory of 1904. Another ten minutes' walk to the northeast brings you to Leipziger Strasse, the city's north–south arterial road. At no. 182, set in a small park by the Zwickauer Mulde, is **Neue Welt** (New World), a Jugendstil complex built for concerts and dances. Part of it now houses a restaurant; a door on the north side is usually kept open, allowing you to peek in at the ornate main hall.

Practicalities

Zwickau's **Hauptbahnhof** is about fifteen minutes' walk west of the Hauptmarkt. The **tourist office** (Mon–Fri 9am–6.30pm, Sat 10am–4pm; ☎03 75/1 94 33 or 29 37 13, fax 03 75/29 37 15, *www.zwickau.de*) is right in the heart of town at Hauptstr. 6, and can arrange **private rooms** (②–④). There's a good choice of middle-range **hotels**: *Merkur*, Bahnhofstr. 58 (☎03 75/29 42 86; ⑤), *Sachsenring*, Leipziger Str. 160 (☎03 75/21 62 51; ⑥), *Achat*, Leipziger Str. 180 (☎03 75/87 20; ⑥), *Airport*, Olzmannstr. 57 (☎03 75/5 60 20; ⑥), and *Park Eckersbach*, northeast of the Altstadt near the terminus of tram #1 at Trillerplatz 1 (☎03 75/47 55 72; ⑥). Top of the range is *Holiday Inn*, Kornmarkt 9 (☎03 75/2 79 20; ⑦).

There are **restaurants** in each of the last four hotels, and these rank among the best in town; their main rival is *Drei Schwäne*, Heinrich-Heine-Str. 69, very near Neue Welt. Other good places to eat and drink are *Posthalterei*, Katharinenstr. 27, *Goldener Anker*, Hauptmarkt 6, *Zur Grünhainer Kapelle*, Peter-Breuer-Str. 3, and *Ringkaffee*, Dr-Friedrichs-Ring 21a.

Plauen

PLAUEN, which lies 48km southwest of Zwickau, is the only major town in the **Vogtland**, a region whose name has lingered on from the Middle Ages, when it was governed on behalf of the Holy Roman emperor by administrators known as Vogts. For the most part, the Vogtland is a high plateau, but the landscape is far from monotonous – it's cut by many rivers and streams which often cleave surprisingly deep valleys. The journey from Zwickau to Plauen via a stretch of the Leipzig–Nürnberg rail line is one of Germany's most spectacular train rides – the viaducts, and in particular the triple-tiered **Göltzschtalbrücke** just beyond Mylau, are triumphs of mid-nineteenth-century engineering. Although Plauen itself was devastated in World War II, with much of its centre rebuilt in an uncompromisingly modern style, it has many attractive features, not least its imposing **setting** in the hills above the Weisse Elster and Syra rivers and the profusion of **Jugendstil houses** scattered all over the town.

At the heart of Plauen is the Alter Markt, now revived as an outdoor market. On its northern side is the **Altes Rathaus**, dwarfed by its monstrous early twentieth-century replacement behind. The facade facing the square is a handsome building, complete with curly gables, a resplendent clock and a balcony with a double stairway. The ground floor still preserves an elegant Gothic hallway, which, together with the adjoining rooms, is home to the **Museum Plauener Spitzen** (Mon–Fri 10am–5pm; Sat 9am–2pm; DM1.50/€0.75). This traces the history and production methods of **Plauen lace**, with plenty of examples of the town's most celebrated product.

Southeast of Alter Markt is the **Johanniskirche**, fronted by the twin Romanesque towers of the original building, which are now capped with Baroque cupolas. The rest of the structure is a hall church of the 1550s, one of the last major buildings in Germany to be built in the Gothic style. By this time the Reformation had been adopted in Plauen, so it was constructed with the Renaissance galleries characteristic of Lutheran churches. An expressive winged altar stands in the choir.

East across the broad expanse of Syrastrasse is the **Schloss** of the Vogts; apart from the Roter Turm (Red Tower), which survives intact, it has been left as a ruin following its destruction in World War II. From here, you can descend to the Weisse Elster, which can be crossed on foot via the **Alte Elsterbrücke**, a bridge known to date back at least as far as the thirteenth century. Uphill from the Schloss, the **Nonnenturm** (Nuns' Tower) is the only remaining part of the medieval fortifications, now standing forlorn in the large open square created during postwar reconstruction of the town. Just to the west is the **Lutherkirche**, which has a late fifteenth-century retable from Erfurt with emotional carvings of scenes from the Passion.

Plauen's most imposing street is **Nobelstrasse**, a block west of the Markt. Here three adjacent merchants' houses of the late eighteenth century have been converted to contain the **Vogtland-Museum** (Tues–Sun 10am–4pm; DM1.50/€0.75), which documents the folklore, arts, crafts and history of the region, but is mainly of interest for a captivating series of period interiors, some re-created, others original to the buildings themselves. Among the latter is the very French-looking **Festsaal**, decorated in the full-blown Louis XVI style, whose rich stuccowork includes wall-panels symbolizing the months of the year.

West of here is the **Friedensbrücke** over the Syra, which was the world's largest arched stone bridge at the time of its construction at the beginning of last century, a distinction it kept until 1945. An equally impressive technical monument is the **Syratalbrücke** further to the west, which the Upper Vogtland rail line crosses on its journey south towards the Czech border.

Practicalities

Plauen has two train stations, each for separate lines. The **Oberer Bahnhof** at the top of the town, reached from the centre straight along Bahnhofstrasse, is on the Leipzig–Nürnberg route, and is the start of the line to the Czech city of Plzeň via the Upper Vogtland. The **Unterer Bahnhof**, on the south bank of the Weisse Elster, has services along that valley to the Thuringian towns of Greiz and Gera. Plauen's **tourist office** (Mon–Fri 9am–6pm, Sat 9am–noon; ☎0 37 41/2 91 10 27, fax 2 91 11 09, *www.plauen.de*) in the Rathaus, Unterer Graben 1, can book the usual range of **private rooms** (①–③).

Additionally, there are a number of good-value small **pensions**, such as *Fritsche*, Fritz-Reuter-Str. 9 (☎0 37 41/52 60 00; ②), *Lochbauer*, Pfaffengutstr. 30 (☎0 37 41/52 66 41; ③), and *Fischer*, Thiergartner Weg 81 (☎0 37 41/22 77 20; ③). **Hotels** include *Echo*, Alte Pausaer Str. 169 (☎0 37 41/52 21 01; ④), *City*, Neundorfer Str. 23 (☎0 37 41/1 52 30; ⑤), *Alexandra*, Bahnhofstr. 17 (☎0 37 41/22 14 14; ⑥), and *Parkhotel*, Rädelstr. 18 (☎0 37 41/2 00 60; ⑥). There's also a **youth hostel** at Reusaer Waldhaus 1 (☎0 37 41/47 28 11, fax 47 28 12; DM22/€11 or DM27/€13.50); take tram #4 to Schloss Reusa, from where it's a fifteen-minute walk.

The best **restaurants** are in the hotels listed above. Otherwise, try *Roma*, Oberer Steinweg 8, which offers Italian food and wines. Just to the south, at Alter Teich 9, is the *Malzhaus*, an eighteenth-century maltings which is now a lively bar and arts centre. Each June, Plauen hosts a major **popular festival**, the *Spitzenfest*.

The Erzgebirge

The **Erzgebirge** (Iron Ore Mountains) occupy most of southern Saxony, stretching from the Vogtland to just before the Elbe. They take their name from the rich mineral deposits found there in the Middle Ages which were of crucial importance to the wealth of the Saxon state and in turn to its high-profile political role within the Holy Roman Empire. As the mines became exhausted, the inhabitants turned to cottage industries, notably lace-making, woodcarving and the production of children's toys.

The landscapes of the Erzgebirge are stark and often bleak, while the climate is decidedly raw – these conditions are exacerbated by the fact that much of the range is an environmental disaster area. In particular, a huge percentage of its trees are suffering from *Waldsterben* as a result of smog blown here from lignite-burning factories in the Czech Republic. Despite this, the Erzgebirge is a popular tourist area, both in summer and winter – this being a rare part of Germany where snow is virtually guaranteed. Another plus is that it's one of the few parts of eastern Germany which has retained much of a tradition in **popular festivals**; it also has a couple of historic towns which are well worth a detour in their own right.

Schneeberg

The old silver-mining town of **SCHNEEBERG** lies on a ridge high above the valley of the Zwickauer Mulde, 18km southeast of Zwickau. It's rich in old traditions and is particularly worth visiting during the run-up to Christmas, when there are a whole series of events, including the *Fest des Lichtes und der Freude* (Festival of Light and Joy) in the second week of Advent. At this time, the town (in common with others in the region) is decorated with huge illuminated wooden pyramids adorned with figures of miners. Another big annual event is the *Streittag* on July 22, featuring a costumed procession of mining guilds.

Focal point of most of Schneeberg's festivities is the sixteenth-century **Stadtkirche St Wolfgang** at the top of the town. Outwardly plain, it has a highly original hall interi-

---

THE NARROW-GAUGE RAILWAYS OF THE ERZGEBIRGE

There are no fewer than four narrow-gauge rail lines in the Erzgebirge, two of which have functioned continuously since they were built in the late nineteenth century. The **Fichtelbergbahn** (or Erzgebirgsbahn), opened in 1897, was the last such railway to be built in Germany. Its 17.4km route links Cranzahl with **Kurort Oberwiesenthal**, and did much to stimulate the development of the latter's tourist industry. In the course of its journey, it climbs 238 metres, passing through the valleys of the Sehma and Pöhlbach before traversing a 110-metre-long iron viaduct shortly before reaching its terminus.

The **Weisseritztalbahn** (or Osterzgebirgsbahn), which takes its name from the river whose valley it follows, is the longest-running narrow-gauge service in Germany, having been in operation since 1883. It begins at **Freital-Hainsberg**, on the main line between Freiberg and Dresden. From there, it skirts the eastern edge of the Erzgebirge all the way to its terminus at **Kurort Kipsdorf**, 26km away. This unassuming little health resort has by far the largest narrow-gauge station in Germany, a sight in itself with its eight running lines. However, the highlight of the journey comes 5km before at **Schmiedeberg**, where the train passes high above the village on a stone viaduct.

Until it was closed and dismantled in 1984, the **Pressnitztalbahn** was considered by rail buffs to be the most enjoyable of all eastern Germany's narrow-gauge railways. Beginning at **Wolkenstein**, on the main line between Annaberg-Buchholz and Flöha, it climbed 293 metres and crossed 52 bridges in the course of its 23km-long journey south along the River Pressnitz to the winter-sports resort of **Jöhstadt** on the Czech border. Since the *Wende*, the final 7.8km of this line have been reinstated, and it is hoped that more will be reopened in due course.

Finally, at **Schönheide** in the southwest of the Erzgebirge, 4km of a narrow-gauge railway (one which formerly served nearly fifty different commercial enterprises) have been put back into operation, and there are plans to re-lay the entire route.

---

or whose galleries, most unusually, go all the way round the church, including the chancel. Its suspiciously fresh look is due to the fact that restoration, following destruction in the closing days of World War II, was only recently completed. The main treasure is the huge *Passion* altar, a mature masterpiece by **Cranach**.

Down on the **Markt** is an assemblage of handsome Baroque, Rococo and Neoclassical mansions. Just off the western side, on Obere Zobelgasse, the **Museum für Bergmännische Volkskunst** (Tues–Sun 9.30am–5pm; DM4/€2) illustrates the crafts and costumes of the local miners.

Schneeberg is one of the few places of any size in the former GDR to have lost its rail link – the nearest station is in the adjacent town of Aue, which lies across the valley, but there are regular **bus** connections with Zwickau, departing from just off the Markt. The **tourist office** is in the Rathaus, Markt 1 (Mon, Wed & Fri 9am–12.15pm & 12.45–4pm, Tues & Thurs 9am–12.15pm & 12.45–6pm, Sat 9am–1pm; ☎0 37 72/2 03 14, fax 2 23 47, *www.schneeberg.de*). Here you can book **private rooms** (①–③), which are in plentiful supply. There are also several small **pensions**, including *Drei Tannen*, Eibenstocker Str. 3 (☎0 37 72/32 60 80; ②), and *Sabine*, Hartensteiner Str. 13 (☎0 37 72/2 10 36; ②). The only **hotels** are *Berghotel Steiger*, high above town at Am Mühlberg (☎0 37 22/3 94 90; ④), and the small *Büttner*, Markt 3 (☎0 37 72/35 30; ⑤). Both have **restaurants**, with the latter's being of gourmet status.

Annaberg-Buchholz

In the early sixteenth century, the largest town in Saxony was **ANNABERG**, which grew up alongside the range's richest silver mines. It's now the northern half of a double town set high above the two sides of the Sehma valley and in the lee of the commanding heights of the Pöhlberg, 35km east of Schneeberg and 30km south of Chemnitz. Although nowadays very provincial in feel, it remains the undoubted star of the Erzgebirge, possessing the finest artistic and technical monuments in the region.

Occupying the dominant position in town, the **Stadtkirche St Annen** was erected during the town's short-lived heyday in the first quarter of the sixteenth century. Crafted from rough masonry, the exterior's only feature of note is the tower, shaped like the keep of a castle with an octagonal superstructure; the rest is little more than a shell covering one of Germany's most dazzlingly brilliant interiors. Ribs spring in all directions from the slender columns, forming an intricate star vault adorned with fancy keystones and elaborate little carved figures. The rich and colourful furnishings are contemporary with the architecture. There are two masterpieces by **Hans Witten**, whose reputation has suffered from the fact that most of his work is found in the relative obscurity of the Erzgebirge region. The **Schöne Pforte** (Beautiful Doorway) at the facade end of the northern aisle shows the Holy Trinity adored by the angelic host, with SS Francis and Clare looking on. Witten's **font** is another extraordinary creation, strangely foreshadowing the productions of Fabergé. Both the **pulpit** and the **gallery** were carved by his colleague Franz Maidburg; the latter forms an illustrated Bible in one hundred scenes. The **high altar**, by the Augsburg sculptor Adolf Daucher, shows the Tree of Jesse, its cool Renaissance poise standing in contrast to the late Gothic sumptuousness of the other works.

Just across from the Stadtkirche, at Grosse Kirchgasse 16, is the **Erzgebirgsmuseum** (Tues–Sun 10am–5pm; DM4/€2), which has some fine displays on the folk art of the region. There's also a roomful of medieval sculptures, plus sections on mining and the guilds.

In the valley below the town is the **Frohnauer Hammer** (guided tours daily 9–11.45am & 1–4pm; DM4/€2). The visit has three separate parts, beginning with the hammer-mill itself, the only one of its kind left in Europe. In the fifteenth century it was a grain mill with four millstones, but was rebuilt at the turn of the seventeenth century for iron and copper production, worked by three huge hammers which each weigh nearly six hundredweight. After this has been demonstrated, you cross over the road to see another collection of local crafts, before touring the Baroque **Herrenhaus**, the half-timbered mansion of the mill-owner.

Practicalities

Annaberg-Buchholz has three train stations, the most useful being the **Unterer Bahnhof**, which lies about ten minutes' walk east of the Frohnauer Hammer, and immediately below the town centre. The **bus station** is at the western end of the upper part of town. Among the centrally sited accommodation options are a **pension**, *Clärchen*, Buchholzer Str. 21 (☎0 37 33/2 49 55; ③), and three **hotels**: *Alt Annaberg*, Farbegasse 4 (☎0 37 33/2 72 52 or 1 83 10; ③), *Goldene Sonne*, Adam-Ries-Str. 11 (☎0 37 33/2 21 83; ⑤), and *Wilder Mann*, Markt 13 (☎0 37 33/14 40; ⑥). Down in the valley, choice is between *Gasthof Zur Schmiede*, Sehmatalstr. 8 (☎0 37 33/2 30 19; ④), and *Parkhotel Waldschlösschen*, Waldschlösschenpark 1 (☎0 37 33/6 45 81; ⑥). As usual, there are plenty of **private rooms** (①–③), though these are often inconveniently situated; they can be booked at the **tourist office** (Mon–Fri 9am–6pm, Sat 10am–noon; ☎0 37 33/42 51 39, fax 42 51 38, *www.annaberg-buchholz.de*) in the Rathaus, Markt 1.

The best **restaurants** are in the hotels *Waldschlösschen*, *Goldene Sonne* and *Wilder Mann*; the last-named has a beautiful dining room covered by a sixteenth-century wooden ceiling. Other possibilities are the *Ratskeller* in the Rathaus and the *Frohnauer Hammer* in the Herrenhaus. Annaberg is host to the biggest **festival** in the Erzgebirge, the *Rät*, which has been going since 1520, and begins on the Saturday after Trinity Sunday (variable date in May/June).

Kurort Oberwiesenthal

The main resort in the Erzgebirge is **KURORT OBERWIESENTHAL**, which lies hard by the Czech border, 27km south of Annaberg. It's most easily reached by bus, but it's far more fun to take a mainline train to Cranzahl, then transfer to the **narrow-gauge** Fichtelbergbahn (see box on p.1023), which terminates in the very centre of the village. If you want **to stay**, there should be no problem in finding accommodation – in addition to the big Alpine-style hotels, geared mainly to the skiing market (and priced accordingly), practically every other house seems to have rooms (①–③) to let.

Oberwiesenthal, itself the highest village in the former GDR, stands at the foot of its highest mountain, the **Fichtelberg** (1214m). A fairly straight hiking path leads to the summit, or you can ascend in five minutes by cable car, which costs DM5/€2.50 single, DM6/€3 return. Even by the standards of the Erzgebirge, the Fichtelberg has a depressing climate – it's said to have fog on an average of 270 days each year and storms on 150 days. On the rare clear days, the view is extensive, but, because the whole range is so high above sea level, the individual peaks have little sense of grandeur.

Chemnitz and around

When the GDR authorities looked for a place to be renamed in honour of Karl Marx, their choice fell on **CHEMNITZ** (pronounced "Kemnitz"), their fourth largest city, set in the northern foothills of the Erzgebirge, at a pivotal point on the main communications network between Zwickau and Dresden. Thus, between 1953 and 1990, the city became "Karl-Marx-Stadt", with its real name expunged altogether – though the West Germans insisted on retaining it as a suffix. As a city which was rebuilt after the war in a deliberately Soviet-influenced style, Chemnitz has a special curiosity value. In GDR days, its broad boulevards, with their creaking trams and Stalinist-style high-rise offices and tenements, looked and felt quite unnervingly like Russia rather than Germany, and the illusion to some extent persists, despite the heavy volume of traffic.

The city

Chemnitz's main north–south axis is Strasse der Nationen. Towards its southern end is the **Versteinerter Wald**, the remains of a petrified forest, with tree stumps reckoned to be 250 million years old. Behind stands the huge pile of the **König-Albert-Museumsbau**, which contains two separate collections. Much the more interesting is the **Kunstsammlungen Chemnitz** (Tues, Thurs, Sat & Sun 11am–5pm, Wed 11am–7.30pm, Fri noon–5pm; DM4/€2), which features a large number of works by the local painter Karl Schmidt-Rottluff, the most abstract member of the Die Brücke group of Expressionists; the furnishings from a Jugendstil villa, Haus Esche, designed by Henry van de Velde (it's aimed to restore the original house as a museum in due course); and several galleries of twentieth-century art. The **Museum für Naturkunde** (Tues, Thurs & Fri 9am–noon & 2–5pm, Wed 9am–noon & 2–7.30pm, Sat & Sun 11am–5pm; DM4/€2, DM6/€3 combined ticket with the Kunstsammlungen Chemnitz) is mainly of note for its explanatory displays on the Versteinerter Wald.

Turning right at the next junction, previously Karl-Marx-Allee, now Brückenstrasse, you come to the Soviet-made **Karl-Marx-Denkmal**, which consists of a huge bronze head of the founder of Communism and a plaque bearing his famous dictum, "Working men of all countries, unite!", in several languages. After the *Wende*, there were plans to tear this monument down, but it's been decided to retain it as a reminder of the "culture" of the GDR years. Across the road is a park containing the Stadthalle and the **Roter Turm** (Red Tower), a survivor from the medieval city wall.

Further south the Markt, the historic part of the city centre, is once more the scene of market stalls. The whitewashed **Altes Rathaus** is entered via a portal bearing statues of Judith and Lucretia. Behind is the **Hoher Turm** (High Tower) and the *fin-de-siècle* Neues Rathaus. This incorporates a few Jugendstil features, but a better example of the style is the facade which was added to the Gothic **Jakobikirche** alongside. The house at no. 20, with its frilly Rococo facade, seems something of an anomaly in this city, though all the more welcome for that.

At the far northern end of the centre is a park focused on a large artificial lake, the Schlossteich. On the hill above is the **Schlosskirche**, a late Gothic hall church with a stumpy neo-Gothic tower, incorporating some of the masonry from a former twelfth-century monastery. Inside are two masterpieces by **Hans Witten** – a typically idiosyncratic carved group of *Christ at the Column* at the high altar, and the church's original north portal, carved with the help of Franz Maidburg, which now stands against the south wall. This has a tympanum showing the Holy Trinity, along with carvings of the church's founders, Emperor Lothar and Empress Richenza.

A Renaissance **Schloss** for the Electors of Saxony supplanted the former monastic buildings. In commemoration of the 500th anniversary of the birth of Georgius Agricola, Chemnitz's favourite son and four times burgomaster, and an early pioneer in the sciences of mineralogy and metallurgy, it was restored to serve as home to the local history displays of the **Schlossbergmuseum** (May–Sept Tues–Fri 11am–5pm, Sat & Sun 10am–6pm; DM4/€2).

In the far north of Chemnitz, standing in a disarmingly rustic setting in open fields and served by bus #40, is the **Stiftskirche Ebersdorf** (if shut, get the key from the parish house at the back of the close). This was a popular pilgrimage spot in the late Middle Ages, the goal being the beautiful Marienkapelle, the star-vaulted chapel on the south side. The whole interior bristles with works of art, notably of the late Gothic period, including several by Witten – a *Crucifixion*, statues of an angel and a deacon and the tomb of Dietrich von Harras, which bears a startlingly realistic effigy of the dead Knight.

At the western extremity of the city, reached by tram #3, is the **Schaubergwerk Felsendome Rabenstein** (guided tours Mon 10am–4pm, Wed–Sun 9am–5pm; DM5/€2.50), an underground limestone quarry where the atmospheric conditions since the cessation of mining have caused the walls to take on subtly luminous effects. Alongside is the former limekiln, a half-timbered eighteenth-century structure which has an exhibition outlining the history of the works. About twenty minutes' walk west of here, connected to the city centre by bus #47, is **Burg Rabenstein** (May–Oct Tues–Sun 9am–noon & 1–6pm; DM2/€1), the tower and residential block of a large feudal castle, the rest of which has disappeared. Inside are a few Renaissance murals, and a display of *objets d'art*.

Practicalities

Chemnitz's **bus station** lies just off the western side of Strasse der Nationen, while the **Hauptbahnhof** is a block to the east. The **tourist office** (Mon–Fri 9am–6pm, Sat 9am–1pm; ☎03 71/69 06 80, fax 6 90 68 30, *www.chemnitz.de*) is at Bahnhofstr. 6. There are plenty of **private rooms** (②–④) on offer, though many are in distant suburban locations. **Hotels** are geared almost exclusively to business visitors. Those with a central location include *Europa*, Str. der Nationen 56 (☎03 71/68 11 29; ⑤), *Elisenhof*, Mühlenstr. 102 (☎03 71/47 16 90; ⑨), *Mercure*, Brückenstr. 19 (☎03 71/68 30; ⑥), and *Chemnitzer Hof*, which occupies an original Bauhaus building of the 1920s at Theaterplatz 4 (☎03 71/68 40; ⑦). In the suburbs, by far the most attractive place to stay is *Burghotel Rabenstein*, Grünaer Str. 2 (☎03 71/85 65 02; ⑥). Chemnitz's **youth hostel** is out in the southeastern suburbs, at Augustusburger Str. 369 (☎ & fax 03 71/7

13 31; DM25/€12.50 or DM30/€15) – take bus #T245, or tram #1 or #6 to Pappelhain and then walk the remaining 1.5km.

Each of the last three hotels listed above has an excellent **restaurant**; another good choice is *Metropolitan*, An der Alten Post 1. Vegetarians should head for *Café Henrie* in the basement of the Umweltzentrum, Henriettenstr. 5. There are homely Gaststätten outside both the Schaubergwerk Felsendome and Burg Rabenstein.

Chemnitz maintains a lively **cultural** scene, with concerts at the Luxorpalast, Hartmannstr. 11 (☎03 71/69 04 90), puppet shows at the Puppentheater, Hartmannstr. 9 (☎03 71/6 44 67 51), operas at the Opernhaus, Theaterplatz 2 (☎03 71/4 88 46 71), and plays at the Schauspielhaus in the Park der Opfer des Faschismus (☎03 71/4 88 43 15).

Augustusburg

The most obvious excursion from Chemnitz is to the village of **AUGUSTUSBURG** 14km to the east. Augustusburg clusters below its cliff-top Renaissance **Schloss** (daily: April–Oct 9am–6pm; Nov–March 10am–5pm; *www.augustusburg-schloss.de*; DM10/€5 combined ticket with the Jagdtier- und Vogelkundemuseum, Motorradmuseum and Kutschenmuseum, otherwise separate tickets required for each section), built as the hunting lodge of the Saxon Electors by the Leipzig architect, Hieronymous Lotter, though its colossal dimensions suggest an altogether grander function.

Guided tours (DM5/€2.50) take you to the **Brunnenhaus**, a deep well still preserving its original wooden machinery, the historic apartments of the **Lindenhaus** and the **Schlosskapelle**, a beautiful galleried Renaissance chapel. The last-named is among the earliest buildings designed specifically for Lutheran worship. It features a tiny historic organ on which recitals are occasionally given, an altarpiece by Cranach the Younger showing Elector Augustus and his wife with fourteen children, and a pulpit adorned with paintings of scenes from the life of Christ by the same artist.

Other parts of the Schloss can be visited independently. They include the **tower** (DM2/€1), which not only commands a fine view, but also houses an art gallery. The **Hasenhaus** (DM5/€2.50) contains the **Jagdtier- und Vogelkundemuseum**, which has displays on the animal and bird life of the Erzgebirge region, but is mainly of note for the rooms themselves, adorned with monumental trompe l'oeil murals, including the humorous depictions of hares in the guise of humans which give the wing its name. Within the Küchenhaus is the **Motorradmuseum** (DM5/€2.50), Germany's most impressive museum of bicycles and motorbikes, with a collection ranging from a Laurin-Klement from the end of the nineteenth century, through the many productions of NSU to the latest roadsters. The **Marstall** (DM3/€1.50), or stables, houses the **Kutschenmuseum**, a collection of historic coaches including those used by the postal services. Finally, the **Adler- und Falkenhof** (DM10/€5) has a wide variety of birds of prey, some of which take part in the free-flight demonstrations at 11am and 3pm.

To get to Augustusburg, alight at Erdmannsdorf, on the main rail line between Chemnitz and Annaberg-Buchholz; from here the **Drahtseilbahn** (DM4/€2 single, DM6/€3 return), a funicular built in 1911, ascends directly to the Schloss. There's a really top-notch **restaurant**, the *Augustuskeller* (closed Sun evening and Mon) within the Schloss, which also houses a **youth hostel** (☎03 72 91/2 02 56, fax 63 41; DM22/€11 or DM27/€13.50). The village has several **hotels**, including *Morgensonne*, Morgensternstr. 2 (☎03 72 91/2 05 08; ④), and *Café Friedrich*, Hans-Planer-Str. 1 (☎03 72 91/66 66; ⑤). A full accommodation list is available from the **tourist office** (Mon–Fri 9am–noon & 1–5pm, Sat 9am–2pm; ☎03 72 91/3 95 50, fax 3 95 55, *www.augustusburg.de*) in the Rathaus, Marienberger Str. 24.

Freiberg

Exactly halfway along the eighty-kilometre-long rail line between Chemnitz and Dresden is **FREIBERG**, whose town centre looks, by eastern German standards, startlingly immaculate. Somehow the town came through World War II completely undamaged, and thereafter its long history as a mining community so endeared it to the GDR authorities that they had all the historic buildings cleaned and spruced up in the 1980s. The mining tradition is enshrined in the town's name, "Free Mountain", which is a reference to a twelfth-century imperial decree allowing anyone to come to the area to prospect for minerals and keep all the proceeds. In 1765, the Bergakademie, the world's first college of mining, was founded here; now raised to university status, it's a centre of metallurgical training and research of international repute, imparting a degree of sophistication to what might otherwise now be a very provincial town indeed.

The Town

Freiberg is centred on two market squares, Obermarkt and Untermarkt. From the outside the most remarkable feature is the assemblage of old buildings, but the overall highlight is the interior of the Dom, the town's principal monument.

The Dom

The **Dom** (guided tours May–Oct Mon–Sat at 10am, 11am, 2pm, 3pm & 4pm, Sun at 11am, 2pm, 3pm & 4pm; Nov–April daily at 11am, 2pm & 3pm; DM3/€1.50), as the Marienkirche is officially designated despite never having been a bishop's seat, is outwardly unassuming and doesn't even have a prominent position, being stuck at the back of the lower of the two main squares, the Untermarkt. However, in sheer richness and variety of interior decoration (a legacy of the patronage of the Saxon Electors, and of the wealth brought by the mines), it's unsurpassed by any of the country's cathedrals.

Two important survivors of the original building, destroyed by fire in the late fifteenth century, were incorporated in the airily light hall church that replaced it. One is the **Goldene Pforte** (Golden Doorway – a reference to its original gilding), which formed the main entrance, but is now placed on the south side. Dating from the 1230s, it's one of the few German counterparts of the great figure portals characteristic of the Gothic cathedrals of France; it's a symbolical vision of a heavenly paradise, centred on a tympanum showing *The Adoration of the Magi*. Similar in date, though still Romanesque in spirit, is the anguished **triumphal cross** group placed high up on a beam above the entrance to the choir. Below it is an early example of a Protestant **high altar**; painted by a follower of Cranach, it incorporates suitably modest-sized figures of a host of local burghers as spectators at the Last Supper.

In the nave, your eye is drawn to the extraordinary writhing, twisting forms of the most precious adornment from the time of the church's construction, the **Tulpenkanzel** (Tulip Pulpit) by **Hans Witten**. Even judged against his own prodigious originality, it's a singular work, being an allegory of the Church as the flower in the garden of God. Resting at the foot is the figure of a local miner in the guise of Daniel in the lions' den, a theme developed in the second pulpit alongside, accordingly known as the **Bergmannskanzel** (Miners' Pulpit), which was made just over a century later. The chancel was transformed to serve as the **mausoleum** of the Albertine line of the House of Wettin. The huge tomb of Elector Moritz occupies centre stage, though the double memorial to two princesses by Balthasar Permoser, the Baroque sculptor of Dresden, is no less imposing. Another addition from this period is the **ducal loft** on the north side of the nave, designed by the Dresden architect Pöppelmann.

However, the church's most significant Baroque adornments are the two **organs**, both the work of **Gottfried Silbermann**, a friend of Bach and one of the first manufacturers of pianos. The ringing, silvery tones of the larger of these, which many organists regard as the greatest instrument ever made, can be heard on the 11am Sunday tour, and at the recitals held each Thursday from May to October at 8pm.

The rest of the town

At the corner of Am Dom and Untermarkt, a number of late Gothic houses have been knocked together to contain the **Stadt- und Bergbaumuseum** (Tues–Sun 10am–5pm; DM4/€2), which explains the history of mining in the area in a surprisingly illuminating way, with plenty of large-scale models. Untermarkt itself has a fine assemblage of mansions, including examples of Gothic, Renaissance and Baroque, as does Kirchgasse, the western continuation of Am Dom. If you want to pursue the mineralogical connection, visit the **Mineralogische Sammlung der Bergakademie** (Wed–Fri 9am–noon & 1–4pm, Sat 9am–4pm; free), just off the northwestern corner of Untermarkt at Brenhausgasse 14, which has a valuable collection drawn from all round the world.

A block to the north, at the edge of the historic part of town, is **Schloss Freudenstein**, a much-restored Renaissance palace of the Saxon Electors; there's free access to the courtyard, but otherwise nothing much to see. From here Burgstrasse, which is lined with a number of superb Renaissance and Baroque houses, leads to the harmonious-looking main square, the **Obermarkt**, where local youths loll around the central fountain with its statue of Emperor Otto the Rich, the town's founder. The late Gothic **Rathaus** stands on the east side, with the (for once) separate **Ratskeller**, entered via a handsome Renaissance portal, to the north. Just to the west of Obermarkt, set in its own peaceful close, is the Gothic **Petrikirche**, proud possessor of another Silbermann organ.

Practicalities

Freiberg's **Hauptbahnhof** is located about fifteen minutes' walk south of Obermarkt, while the **bus station** is about halfway between the two, just before the inner ring road. The **tourist office** (Mon–Fri 9am–5/6pm, Sat 9am–noon; ☎0 37 31/2 36 02, fax 27 32 60, *www.freiberg.de*) at Burgstr. 1 offers the usual booking service for **private rooms** (①–③).

There are also plenty of inexpensive **pensions**; those with a central location include *Gemeiner*, Schöne Gasse 6 (☎0 37 31/35 67 94; ③), *Heidi*, Lange Str. 46 (☎0 37 31/3 46 81; ④), and *Bräustübel*, Donatsgasse 3 (☎0 37 31/2 64 80; ④). The town is also well supplied with characterful **hotels**. *Gasthof Brauhof*, Körnerstr. 2 (☎0 37 31/2 32 81 or 3 53 30; ④), is a particular bargain; it serves excellent meals and also has a beer garden. *Mauck'sches Gut*, Hornstr. 20 (☎0 37 31/3 39 78; ⑤), occupies an old farmstead just outside the Altstadt, *Am Obermarkt*, Waisenhausstr. 2 (☎0 37 31/3 43 61; ⑥), has an ideal location plus a fine café and cellar restaurant, *Alekto*, Am Bahnhof 3 (☎0 37 31/79 40; ⑥–⑧), is a grand station hotel with a distinguished Italian restaurant, while *Silberhof*, Silberhofstr. 1 (☎0 37 31/2 39 70 or 2 68 80; ⑦), occupies a Jugendstil mansion on a quiet inner suburban street and has a fine evenings-only restaurant.

Other good **restaurants** include the *Ratskeller*, Obermarkt 16, *Zum Alten Brennmeister*, Kesselgasse 30, a specialist in game dishes, and the wine bars *Weinstube St Nikolai*, Kesselgasse 24, and *Weinhaus Blasius*, Burgstr. 26. Also recommended is a long-established **café**, *Hartmann*, Peterstr. 1a. A varied programme of **music** and **drama** is presented at the late eighteenth-century Mittelsächsisches Theater, Borngasse 3 (☎0 37 31/35 82 30). The main **festival** is the *Bergstadtfest* in late June, a celebration of local mining tradition.

EASTERN SAXONY

In GDR days, the eastern part of Saxony was jokingly referred to as the "Valley of the Clueless", on the grounds that most of the area, unlike everywhere else in the country, was unable to receive West German television and hence unable to hear a non-Communist view of the outside world. The end of the Erzgebirge range is marked here by the valley of the **River Elbe**, one of the most beautiful parts of Germany, particularly the area immediately before the Czech border known as **Saxon Switzerland**. Downstream lies the state capital of **Dresden** which, despite its wartime losses, still has some of Europe's greatest buildings, museums and theatres. The former capital of **Meissen**, a short distance beyond, is also one of eastern Germany's most attractive towns, preserving its medieval appearance almost intact.

To the east is **Upper Lusatia** (Oberlausitz), one of the two main homelands of the Sorbs, the original Slav inhabitants of the region (see p.890). It's had a turbulent history, having frequently changed hands, though the two finest towns, **Bautzen** and **Görlitz**, along with **Zittau**, the gateway to the mountain region to the south, all came through the last war with relatively little damage.

Dresden

The name of **DRESDEN** stands alongside Hiroshima as a symbol of the horrendously destructive consequences of modern warfare. What was generally regarded as Germany's most beautiful large city – the "Baroque Florence" – survived World War II largely unscathed until the night of February 13 and 14, 1945. Then, in a matter of hours, it was reduced to a smouldering heap of ruins in the most savage **saturation bombing** ever mounted by the British and American air forces against civilian targets

---

THE BOMBING OF DRESDEN

The **bombing of Dresden** has attracted far more criticism of British and American methods during World War II than any other event – even though it was in reality merely the culmination of a deliberately destructive bombing policy, operational since 1940, in which civilians and historic buildings were regarded as legitimate targets. However, the sheer extent of the damage and the fact that thousands of innocent people, who were themselves victims of Nazism, perished in the raids, put it in a different class from all previous such attacks.

The greatest tragedy of Dresden is that it remains unclear exactly why the raids were carried out at all. The genesis seems to have been a nebulous decision taken in 1944 to carry out a saturation raid on some city (none was specified) which had hitherto not been bombed, as a means of breaking the German resolve once and for all. Although the Soviets specifically requested this tactic, they later distanced themselves from it completely, using it during the Cold War period as a useful propaganda tool against the West. (They were responsible for the casualty estimate of 135,000, which is now believed to have been a deliberate exaggeration.) Winston Churchill, who certainly authorized the attack, also tried to feign ignorance almost immediately afterwards, leaving most of the opprobrium to fall on **Sir Arthur Harris**, the controversial head of Bomber Command. After the war, Harris was denied the peerage which all other service chiefs received, and was shunned by the British establishment, while his forces, who had suffered appalling casualties throughout the war, were refused a campaign medal. The posthumous reassessment of his reputation, culminating in the decision to honour him with a statue in central London, drew widespread official protests from Dresden and other bombed cities.

(see box on p.1030). At least 35,000 people died – though the total may have been considerably higher (according to one estimate, by as much as 100,000), as the city was packed with refugees fleeing from the advancing Red Army. With this background, it's all the more remarkable that Dresden has adapted to the economic framework of the reunited Germany better than anywhere else in the former GDR. Like Berlin, it's an exciting place to be in at the moment: be prepared for striking visual changes as the post-Communist authorities put into effect their policy of restoring all the historic buildings left as ruins.

By origin a Slav fishing village, Dresden stood in the shadow of nearby Meissen until it was made capital of the Albertine line of the House of Wettin in 1485. Its glory period came in the early eighteenth century, when Elector **Augustus the Strong** gathered round him a brilliant group of artists and architects who transformed the city into a great European capital built in a distinctive, highly decorative Baroque style. At the same time, the court collections were organized into outstanding public **museums**. The city built on its already distinguished musical tradition during the Romantic period, becoming one of Europe's leading performance centres, a position it has retained to this day.

Arrival, information and accommodation

Dresden has two major train stations – the **Hauptbahnhof** is south of the Altstadt, while **Bahnhof Neustadt** is at the northwestern corner of the "new town" (which in fact is eighteenth century) on the opposite bank of the Elbe, and only slightly further away from the main sights, which are grouped close to the river. Between the two, alongside Yenidze, an old cigarette factory built in the shape of a mosque, is the unmanned **Bahnhof Mitte**, but, in spite of its name, it's no more convenient than the others. The **airport** in the far north of the city is linked to the Hauptbahnhof by City Liner **buses**, though an S-Bahn link will open in due course. **Mitfahrzentrale** is at Antonstr. 41 (☎03 51/1 94 40).

Undoubtedly the most atmospheric way to arrive in Dresden is by **boat**. All services run by Sächsische Dampfschiffahrt, Hertha-Lindner-Str. 10 (☎03 51/86 60 90, *www.saechsische-damfschiffahrt.de*), which operates the world's oldest and largest fleet of paddle steamers, dock at the landing stage at Terrassenufer in the very heart of the city. There are trips downstream to Meissen and upstream to Saxon Switzerland, as well as shorter cruises within the city.

Dresden's **tourist office** (☎03 51/49 19 20, fax 49 19 21 16, *www.dresden-tourist.de*) operates two branches. One is in a pavilion just a couple of minutes' walk from the Hauptbahnhof at Prager Str. 10 (Mon–Fri 9am–7pm, Sat 9am–4pm); the other is in the Schinkelwache on Theaterplatz (Mon–Fri 10am–6pm, Sat & Sun 10am–4pm). Both sell the **Dresden City-Card**, which costs DM27/€13.50 for 48 hours, and covers public transport costs, entry to the main museums and sundry discounts; there's also a **Dresden Regio-Card**, costing DM45/€22.50 for 72 hours, which extends the coverage to the surrounding region, including Moritzburg, Meissen, and Saxon Switzerland. Otherwise, a 24-hour public transport ticket within the city costs DM8/€4 for individuals, DM12/€6 for up to two adults and four children; a day-ticket for the museums is DM12/€6 per person.

Nowhere is the recent revitalization of Dresden more manifest than in the improvement in its stock of **hotels**, which can rival that of any German city, at least in the middle and upper ranges. Any deficiency at the budget end of the market is remedied by small suburban **pensions** and a plentiful supply of **private rooms** (②–④), which can be booked at either tourist office (☎03 51/49 19 22 22 for advance reservations) or the independently run Zentraler Zimmernachweis (Mon–Fri 9am–8pm, Sat 9am–7pm, Sun 10am–3pm; ☎03 51/4 71 61 21) just inside the entrance to the Hauptbahnhof. Dresden is well equipped with **youth hostels** and also has a campsite.

Hotels and pensions

Am Birkenhain, Barbarastr. 76, Pieschen (☎03 51/8 51 40, fax 8 51 41 00). Moderately priced hotel with restaurant in a suburban area northwest of Neustadt, close to the S-Bahn station Pieschen. ④.

art' otel, Ostra-Allee 33 (☎03 51/4 92 20, fax 4 92 27 77, *www.artotel.de*). Trendy Modernist venture whose distinctively arty appearance is the joint work of a local painter and a Milanese designer. Its restaurant, *Factory*, serves high-quality Californian-style food. ⑦–⑨.

Bastei, Prager Strasse (☎03 51/48 56 66 61, fax 4 95 40 76). One of a trio of huge GDR-era concrete boxes (the others are *Königstein* and *Lilienstein*) on this street, all now part of the ibis chain. They're worth trying for their geographical convenience and for the special deals which are often available, though solo travellers get, at best, just a small discount on the price of a double. With over 300 rooms in each hotel, there are usually vacancies. ④.

Bellevue, Grosse Meissner Str. 15 (☎03 51/80 50, fax 8 05 16 09, *www.westin-bellevue.com*). Before the *Wende*, this modern hotel incorporating a Baroque palace was Dresden's flagship address. Despite losing this status, it still offers the advantage of a marvellous Neustadt location right by the Elbe, and has a fine restaurant. ⑨.

Bülow Residenz, Rähnitzgasse 19 (☎03 51/8 00 30, fax 800 3100, *www.buelow-residenz.de*). Exclusive hotel in a renovated Baroque palace in Neustadt with a handsome interior courtyard. Its restaurant, *Caroussel*, currently ranks as Dresden's top gourmet address. ⑨.

City-Herberge, Lingnerallee 3 (☎03 51/4 85 99 00, fax 4 85 99 01, *www.city-herberge.de*). Large modern hotel just east of the Altstadt, which is somewhat institutional in feel but succeeds in its aim of offering modern facilities at bargain rates. The room price includes a large buffet breakfast. ④.

Gewandhaus, Ringstr. 1 (☎03 51/4 94 90, fax 4 94 94 90, *www.radisson.com*). Occupying the former cloth hall, this was a medium-range hotel in GDR days, but has been refurbished to five-star standard by the Radisson chain. It has a similarly pricey restaurant. ⑨.

Hotelschiff Florentina, Terrassenufer (☎03 51/4 59 01 69, fax 4 59 50 36, *www.hs.florentina.de*). This hotel-ship with restaurant is moored in the Elbe just east of the Carolabrücke and is one of the least expensive city-centre options. ⑤.

Loschwitz, Grundstr. 40 (☎03 51/2 68 77 85, fax 2 67 87 75). Bargain-priced pension in the valley between the Standseilbahn and the Bergschwebebahn. ③–⑤.

Martha Hospiz, Nieritzstr. 11 (☎03 51/8 17 60, fax 8 17 62 22, *www.vch.de/marthahospiz.dresden*). Century-old Church-affiliated Neustadt hotel modernized to a high standard. Its cellar houses the *Kartoffelkeller*, where potato-based dishes predominate. ⑥.

Schloss Eckberg, Bautzener Str. 134, Loschwitz (☎03 51/8 09 90, fax 8 09 91 99, *www.schloss -eckberg.de*). English-style neo-Gothic stately home set in its own lovely park high above the north bank of the Elbe, linked to the centre by tram #11. Its restaurant serves reasonably priced menus at lunchtime. ⑦.

Taschenberg-Palais, Taschenberg 3 (☎03 51/4 91 20, fax 4 91 28 12, *www.kempinski-dresden.de*). This magnificent palace alongside the Residenzschloss was built by Augustus the Strong for one of his mistresses, Countess Kosel. Left as a burnt-out shell for four decades, it was restored according to the original plans by the Kempinski chain and is now easily the best hotel in town, with every conceivable luxury including swimming pool, sauna and solarium. Surprisingly, its *Paulaner* restaurant is moderately priced, and is an ideal place for lunch; the *Sophienkeller* in the basement is somewhat more expensive, and often has live folk music. ⑨.

Villa Emma, Stechgrundstr. 2, Weisser Hirsch (☎03 51/26 48 10, fax 2 64 81 18). Beautifully restored Jugenstil villa in Dresden's poshest suburb, reached by tram #11. It also has a high-quality and fairly expensive restaurant (evenings only). ⑧.

Wenotel, Schachthofring 24 (☎03 51/4 97 60, fax 4 97 61 00, *www.wenotel.de*). Located a short distance northwest of the Altstadt, this hotel offers modern standards and facilities at a relatively low cost. Although large, it has double rooms only, with just a small discount for single occupancy. ④.

Zur Pillnitzer Schlossfähre, Hosterwitzer Str. 22, Kleinzschachwitz (☎03 51/2 00 93 03, fax 2 00 93 04). Budget pension with café at the extreme southeastern edge of the city, close to the terminus of trams #9 and #14 and to the ferry to Schloss Pillnitz from which it takes its name. ③.

Youth hostels and campsite

Campingplatz Mockritz, Boderitzer Str. 30, Mockritz (☎03 51/4 71 52 50). Has bungalows to rent as an alternative to pitching a tent. Take bus #76 from the Hauptbahnhof.

CVJM-Jugendschiff, Leipziger Str. 15c (☎03 51/3 17 92 97, fax 3 36 10 88, *www.cvjm-sachsen.de*). A YMCA-run hostel on a ship moored on the Neustadt side of the Elbe, in the harbour just north of the bridges. Dorm beds from DM35/€17.50 for those under 18 only; otherwise singles DM60/€30, doubles DM100/€50.

Herbergesschiff Pöppelmann, Leipziger Str. 15 (☎03 51/8 40 09 81). Another hostel-ship, docked immediately to the north of the above. Beds from DM25/€12.50.

Jugendgästehaus, Maternistr. 22 (☎03 51/49 26 20, fax 4 92 62 99, *servicecenter@djh-sachsen.de*). The DJH youth guesthouse, by far the largest of the city's hostels, is in a modern tower block just a few minutes' walk southwest of the main Altstadt sights. DM33/€16.50 or DM38/€19.

Jugendherberge Rudi Arndt, Hübnerstr. 11 (☎03 51/4 71 06 67, fax 4 72 89 59, *servicecenter@djh-sachsen.de*). Municipally run hostel located just to the south of the Hauptbahnhof. DM25/€12.50 or DM30/€15.

Jugendhotel Die Boofe, Louisenstr. 20 (☎03 51/8 01 33 61, fax 8 01 33 62, *www.boofe.com*). A youth hotel-cum-hostel in Neustadt. Dorm beds from DM25/€12.50, singles DM50/€25, doubles DM79/€39.50.

Mondpalast, Katharinenstr. 11–13 (☎ & fax 03 51/8 04 60 61, *www.mondpalast.de*). Another privately owned Neustadt hostel, just a block south of the above. Dorm beds from DM25/€12.50, singles DM37/€18.50, doubles DM62/€31.

The city centre

Central Dresden consists of two distinct districts, the Altstadt and the Neustadt, which lie south and north of the Elbe respectively. The former contains the lion's share of sights, but both have Baroque masterpieces from the city's golden age. Both also have plenty of Communist-era concrete buildings.

The southern Altstadt

If you arrive at the Hauptbahnhof, you see the worst of modern Dresden first, as the **Prager Strasse**, which leads to the historic part of the city, is an example of Stalinist

---

AUGUSTUS THE STRONG (1670–1733)

The irony behind Dresden's magnificent Baroque heritage is that it was commissioned by, and for the greater glory of, **Augustus the Strong** (August der Starke), who, even by the standards of the Age of Absolutism, was an exceptionally loathsome character. He came to power in 1694 as Elector Friedrich August I of Saxony, and three years later won the contest to become King of Poland, assuming the title Augustus II. As if to disprove the false maxim that religion and politics do not mix, Augustus converted to Catholicism in order to qualify for the latter election, thus reversing the stance of his ancestors who had backed Luther against the papacy and the empire, in the process strengthening their own political position. His nickname derives partly from his great physical strength – he could allegedly break a horseshoe with his bare hands – but mainly from his sexual prowess, which is said to have included the siring of a child for each day of the year. This may have been a scurrilous exaggeration put about by his estranged wife, a member of the Hohenzollern family, but he certainly did keep a bevy of mistresses, many of them prominent figures in their own right, such as Countess Aurora of Königsmark, abbess of the imperial convent in Quedlinburg. But if he was popular in bed, Augustus was an inept political operator, whose reign was an unmitigated disaster for Poland, which plummeted from its position as Europe's premier military power to being a client state of Russia, a position from which, it could be argued, it has only recently managed to escape. Deposed by the Poles in 1706, he was reinstated with Russian help four years later, but was no more than a puppet ruler for the remaining 23 years of his reign. Saxony also suffered financially by being tied to an old nation in terminal decline – but in compensation gained a gloriously beautiful capital.

town planning on the grand scale – a spacious pedestrian precinct containing the standard cocktail of high-rise luxury hotels, public offices, box-like apartment, soulless cafés and restaurants catering mainly for organized tour groups, with a few fountains and statues thrown in for relief. It was here that masses of people congregated in October 1989, hoping to be able to jump aboard the special trains laid on for the East Germans who had sought refuge in the West German embassy in Prague.

At the far end, beyond the inner ring road, is the **Altmarkt**, which was much extended after its wartime destruction; the only building of note which remains is the **Kreuzkirche**, the Protestant cathedral. The present structure mixes a Baroque body with a Neoclassical **tower** (April–Sept Mon, Tues, Thurs & Fri 10am–5.30pm, Wed & Sat 10am–4.30pm, Sun noon–4.30pm; Oct–March Mon–Fri 10am–4.30pm, Sat 10am–3.30pm, Sun noon–4.30pm; DM2/€1) and a modernized interior impressive in its starkness and loftiness. On Saturdays at 6pm and at the 9.30am Sunday service you can usually hear the Kreuzchor, one of the world's leading church choirs, which is especially renowned for its performances of the seventeenth-century Dresden composer Heinrich Schütz, father-figure of Germany's rich musical tradition.

Behind stands the heavy bulk of the **Rathaus**, built in the early twentieth century in a lumbering Historicist style complete with a belfry which rises well above that of the church. Further east is the late eighteenth-century **Gewandhaus**, the old cloth hall, which has been transformed into a hotel. Across the wide Wilsdruffer Strasse from here is the contemporaneous **Landhaus**, home to the local history collections of the **Stadtmuseum** (10am–6pm, closed Fri; DM3/€1.50), which are presented in a far more interesting manner than usual.

The Zwinger
North of Wilsdruffer Strasse lies the palace quarter. At its western end is the great glory of Baroque Dresden, the joyous pleasure palace known as the **Zwinger**, built for festivals and tournaments. It was badly damaged in the war, but quickly rebuilt and is now once more the subject of a major restoration programme. The building was designed by **Matthaeus Daniel Pöppelmann**, one of the most original architects Germany ever produced, and the plan he chose here is appropriately daring: a vast open space with fountains surrounded by a single-storey gallery linking two-storey pavilions, and entered from exuberantly grandiose gateways. The effect is further enhanced by the marvellously expressive decoration by the sculptor **Balthasar Permoser**, though much of this has had to be replaced by copies. Unfortunately, the northern wing was never built because funds ran out.

The main entry to the courtyard is via the **Kronentor**, which guards the moat on the western side; shaped like a triumphal arch, it takes its name from the huge carving of the Polish royal crown which stands on top. An alternative way in is via the **Glockenspielpavillon** at the southwest corner, which has a carillon of forty bells crafted out of Meissen porcelain. At the opposite end of the courtyard is the most beautiful pavilion, the lantern-shaped **Wallpavillon**, astride which rises a heroic figure of Hercules carrying the world on his shoulders. Behind it is the **Nymphenbad**, an elaborate sculptured fountain which ranks as Permoser's most ornate creation.

The Zwinger contains several museums. In the southeastern pavilion, entered from Sophienstrasse, is the **Porzellansammlung** (closed until 2002 for restoration; previously Mon–Wed & Fri–Sun 10am–6pm; *www.staatl-kunstsammlungen-dresden.de*; DM5/€2.50). Products from the famous Meissen factory are featured extensively, making a fascinating comparison with examples drawn from the two-thousand-year-old history of Chinese porcelain manufacture. A small natural history display, the **Staatliches Museum für Tierkunde** (9am–6pm, closed Tues; DM6/€12), is housed in the southern gallery. The southwestern pavilion is known as the **Mathematisch-Physikalischer Salon** (9.30am–5pm, closed Thurs; *www.staatl-kunstsammlungen-dresden.de*; DM3/

€1.50), which is a good deal more interesting than it sounds, offering a fascinating array of old globes, clocks and scientific instruments.

The Rüstkammer

The open space on the north side of the Zwinger was filled by the **Semperbau**, which is named in honour of its architect Gottfried Semper, who was responsible for many of the city's finest nineteenth-century buildings. Exhibited in an elegant columned hall on its ground floor is a selection of pieces from the Saxon armoury, or **Rüstkammer** (Tues–Sun 10am–6pm; *www.staatl-kunstsammlungen-dresden.de*; DM3/€1.50), which has a really magnificent collection of historic arms and armour from around the world. The focal point of the display is a dazzling Renaissance suit of armour for a man and a horse, adorned with engravings of scenes of the Labour of Hercules and the Trojan War, which was made in Antwerp in the 1560s by Eliseus Libaerts. Other highlights include the sword commissioned by Duke Moritz of Saxony to celebrate his promotion to the rank of Elector; the tournament armour of Elector August; tiny suits of armour made for the children of the court; the coronation robes of Augustus the Strong (see box on p.1034); and various ornate artefacts used in the pageants held in the Zwinger.

The Gemäldegalerie Alte Meister

The **Gemäldegalerie Alte Meister** (Tues–Sun 10am–6pm; *www.staatl-kunstsammlungen -dresden.de*; DM7/€3.50) is also within the Semperbau, except for the early Netherlandish and German paintings, which are displayed in an interconnected chamber in the Baroque Zwinger. Although it has had almost no additions made to it in the past century, the collection of old masters built up by the Saxon Electors still ranks among the dozen best in the world.

The Gemäldegalerie contains some of the most familiar of all Italian Renaissance paintings, of which the star is **Raphael's** *Sistine Madonna*, a wondrous vision of the Virgin and Child among the clouds, adored by SS Sixtus (who bears the features of the warrior pope Julius II) and Barbara. Almost equally celebrated is the *Holy Night* by **Correggio**, which interprets one of the most ubiquitous artistic subjects in a completely fresh manner, stressing the nocturnal element ignored by so many other painters. The *Sleeping Venus* by **Giorgione** is one of the most sensual nudes of western art, and among the few paintings almost universally accepted as being by this short-lived father-figure of the Venetian Renaissance. It's documented as having been unfinished at the time of his death by plague and was completed by his friend **Titian**, who is represented here by several of his own finest works, including *Young Woman with a Fan* and the deeply psychological *Christ and the Pharisees*. Among several typically resplendent works by **Veronese** is one of his famous banquet scenes, *The Marriage at Cana*, while **Tintoretto** is represented by a diverse group of works, the most memorable being the vividly sketched *St Michael*.

Antonello da Messina's *St Sebastian* is a composition of startling audacity, using an unorthodox low vantage point and incorporating plenty of anecdotal detail in the background, to which the eye is irresistibly drawn. Other Renaissance works to look out for are the sumptuous *Annunciation* by the rarely seen Ferrarese painter **Francesco del Cossa**; the disarmingly simple *Portrait of a Boy* by **Pinturicchio**; and the consciously theatrical *Scenes from the Life of St Zenobius* by **Botticelli**. A distinguished group of seventeenth-century Italian pictures includes **Annibale Carracci's** *The Genius of Fame* and **Guercino's** arresting *Ecstasy of St Francis*. However, the gems are the series of the Parables – including many rarely depicted scenes – which rank as the masterpieces of the short-lived **Domenico Feti**; the wonderfully simple *Parable of the Lost Coin* is particularly memorable. From the eighteenth century, the brilliantly detailed views of Dresden, then at its most resplendent, by the court painter **Bernardo Bellotto** (often known as Canaletto, after his more celebrated uncle) particularly merit attention, not least for the poignance they have acquired since the wartime destruction of the city. Several of his views of Pirna are also on show.

Among the German pictures are two masterpieces by **Holbein the Younger** – *Thomas and John Godsalve* presents, in its unusual diagonal poses, a successful solution to the particularly tricky art of the double portrait, while *Le Sieur de Morette* is executed with stunning virtuosity of technique. Very different is the almost abstract style apparent in the pendants *Duke Henry the Pious* and *Duchess Anna of Mecklenburg* by **Cranach**, which are among the earliest full-length portraits ever painted. The same artist's *Martyrdom of St Catherine* was painted for the Schlosskirche in Wittenberg, as was the so-called *Dresden Altarpiece* by **Dürer**, who is also represented by *The Seven Joys of the Virgin* and *Portrait of a Young Man*. Among later paintings, there's a striking *Rape of Proserpine* by **Josef Heintz**, a Swiss Mannerist who worked at the imperial court in Prague, and a large number of works by the highly influential Neoclassicist **Anton Raffael Mengs** and other painters of the Dresden school.

The Gemäldegalerie has few early Netherlandish works, but the *Madonna and Child* triptych by **Van Eyck**, executed with a miniature-like precision, is unquestionably one of its supreme treasures. Pick of the many works by **Rubens** is *Bathsheba Receiving King David's Letter*, a subject which provided him with an excuse to paint a suggestive portrait of his youthful second wife. **Van Dyck** is represented by one of the variants of his *The Three Children of King Charles I*, and by a superbly characterized *Man in Armour*. The most famous of the **Rembrandt** canvases here is *Self-Portrait with Saskia*, in which he somewhat enigmatically shows himself with his new and clearly not overjoyous wife in the guise of the Prodigal Son carousing in an inn. His interpretation of *The Rape of Ganymede* is also highly unconventional – instead of showing the handsome young boy being carried off to become the cupbearer to the gods by the jealous Jupiter disguised as an eagle, he chose to depict an infant being dragged by his shirt tail, stricken with fear and urinating in desperation. There are two canvases by **Vermeer** – *Girl Reading a Letter* is a typical work, set by a window, and concentrating on the subtle play of light and shade, while the painting known as *The Procuress* is a mysterious composition whose exact meaning is unclear.

Among the French paintings, **Poussin**'s vivacious mythological scenes, such as *The Kingdom of Flora* and *Pan and Syrinx*, make a fascinating contrast with the coolly classical approach favoured by **Claude** in works like *Landscape with Acis and Galatea*. In the eighteenth-century section, **Watteau**'s frilly *Conversation in a Park* stands out. Though the Spanish section is modest, it shows no fall-off in quality, with **El Greco**'s *Christ Healing the Blind* (which actually dates from his Venetian years), **Ribera**'s *St Agnes in Prison* and **Zurbarán**'s *St Bonaventure Kneeling before the Papal Crown* being particularly outstanding. The final room is devoted to eighteenth-century pastels, and contains a huge collection of portraits by the Venetian **Rosalba Carriera**, fittingly displayed alongside the work she herself considered the greatest of all pastel paintings, *The Chocolate Girl* by the Swiss **Liotard**.

The Residenzschloss

Across from the Zwinger is the colossal main palace of the Electors and kings of Saxony, the predominantly Renaissance **Residenzschloss** (Tues–Sun 10am–5pm; *www.staatl-kunstsammlungen-dresden.de*; DM5/€2.50). This was horribly destroyed in the war, and, although the GDR authorities paid lip service to the ideal of restoring it, in practice they did little more than employ two or three workmen to ensure that the ruins, which were kept fenced off, remained upright. The rebuilding programme which has been under way since the *Wende* is a massive task, which will cost an estimated DM500/€250 million; the projected completion date of 2006 (the city's 800th anniversary) seemed optimistic when it was set, but now looks achievable. A good view of the bulding site, and the city beyond, can be had from the top of the **Hausmannsturm** (April–Oct only; included in entry ticket).

At some point in the next few years the famous **Grünes Gewölbe** (Green Vault), one of the richest and most dazzling treasuries in the world, will be returned to its original location in the **Spiegelzimmern** (Mirror Rooms), which miraculously survived the bombing but are not currently accessible to the public. Although the best-known pieces are still in their long-time temporary home, the Albertinum (see opposite), most of the earlier works, including some wonderfully elaborate creations of sixteenth-century Nürnberg goldsmiths, have been moved to the exhibition rooms in the Schloss's **Georgenbau**. They are displayed in the mirrored wall from the Pretiosensaal and the reconstructed display cabinet from the Bronzenzimmer, thus giving a foretaste of what the whole collection will look like when it is finally returned to its original location and appearance. In 2000, the recently restored **Perlfiguren**, which had not been on public view for many years, were also put on display (but may be moved temporarily to the Albertinum). These 57 little grotesques, which are made of misshapen pearls (hence their name) plus gold, enamel and precious stones, are among the most distinctive productions of Dresden Baroque. Based on the famous engravings of the Lorraine artist Jacques Callot, they were made over a period of several decades by Johann Heinrich Köhler, one of Augustus the Strong's court jewellers, and a Huguenot goldsmith from Berlin, Jean Louis Girardet. The exhibition rooms also contain some notable artefacts connected with the **history of the Schloss**, including the armour of Elector Moritz; lapidary fragments from the Schlosskapelle; the audience chair of the Electors; and the court silverware collection. Additionally, there are normally two or three temporary thematic displays each year.

The Hofkirche

At the end of this street is the **Hofkirche** (also known as the **Kathedrale**, as it is now the seat of a Roman Catholic bishop), the largest church in Saxony. It was commissioned by Friedrich August II, the only legitimate son of Augustus the Strong, who succeeded him as Elector of Saxony and, after a short interregnum, as King of Poland as well. To emphasize its Catholic allegiance in what was otherwise a staunchly Protestant province, the Italian architect Gaetano Chiaveri was imported to draw up plans. He responded with a highly original design, featuring advancing and receding walls topped by numerous theatrical statues, the whole rounded off with a flourish by an elegant campanile. The gleaming white interior has an elliptical central space surrounded by large chapels. Some of these are normally fenced off; to see them, and the crypt with its tombs of members of the Wettin dynasty, you have to take a **guided tour** (Mon–Thurs at 11am & 2pm, Fri & Sat at 1pm & 2pm, Sun at 1pm; donation expected).

At the **high altar** is a large canvas of *The Ascension* by Anton Raffael Mengs, who had been appointed court artist in Madrid by the time he finished the work. The side altar of *The Immaculate Conception* and *The Dream of Joseph* are by the same artist. Balthasar Permoser made the wonderfully frilly limewood **pulpit**, which was later given an extravagant canopy; he also made the marble font, and the huge statues of SS Ambrose and Augustine under the gallery. The immaculately voiced **organ** (on which recitals are given on summer Saturdays at 4pm) is the artistic testament of the doyen of the craft, Gottfried Silbermann.

Theaterplatz, the Johanneum, the Frauenkirche and the Kasamatten

Facing the Hofkirche across Theaterplatz is the **Italienisches Dörfchen** (Italian Village), whose name recalls that it was the site of the huts of the Italian masons who built the church. Since its immaculate restoration a few years ago, it houses a trio of restaurants (see p.1042). Opposite is the plush **Sächsische Staatsoper**, now usually known as the **Semperoper** in honour of its architect. Its tradition is second to none, having seen the premieres of Wagner's *The Flying Dutchman* and *Tannhäuser* and Richard Strauss's *Elektra, Salome* and *Der Rosenkavalier*. **Guided tours** (DM9/€4.50) of the interior take place throughout the year, except for two months in mid-summer; check the noticeboard for details. Tickets for performances are hard to come by – the box office for this and other musical events is in the **Schinkelwache**, a sternly Neoclassical guard house designed by Karl Friedrich Schinkel.

Augustusstrasse snakes southeast from the Hofkirche between the **Landtag**, the parliament building, and the back of the **Johanneum**, the former stables. Along the wall of the latter can be seen a huge early twentieth-century Meissen porcelain frieze, the *Fürstenzug*, showing a procession of all the ruling members of the Wettin dynasty. On the other side of the complex is the **Lange Gang** (Long Walk), an arcaded late sixteenth-century courtyard in Florentine Renaissance style, and the **Schöne Pforte** (Beautiful Gateway). Part of the building is given over to the **Verkehrsmuseum** (Transport Museum; Tues–Sun 10am–5pm; DM4/€2), with exhibits ranging from trams to aeroplanes.

The entrance to the museum is on Neumarkt, which was formerly dominated by the **Frauenkirche**, a domed church by Georg Bähr, the most talented Dresden Baroque architect after Pöppelmann. One of the finest ever built for Protestant worship, it was designed as both a foil and rival to the Hofkirche. As it was reduced to a heap of rubble in the war with only a fragment of wall left standing, the Communists decided to leave it in this condition as a permanent war memorial. It became the focus for annual peace meetings to mark the anniversary of the wartime bombing raids, and was an important rallying point during the *Wende*. After a fierce controversy, the decision was taken in 1991 to rebuild it completely, and work, thanks in no small part to a successful international fundraising drive, is proceeding at a steady pace: indeed it may well be finished before the target date of 2006. The very latest computer technology is being utilized to make this the most faithful reconstruction project ever undertaken: not only are the original stones being reused, they are actually being put back in their original positions, with little more than 10 percent of the total masonry being new. Several **guided tours** (free, but donation expected) are run round the building site every day; the **crypt** is fully operational and a regular concert venue.

North of Neumarkt, a spacious promenade, the Brühlsche Terrasse, runs along the bank of the Elbe. Here are the **Kasamatten** (guided tours daily 10am–4/5pm; DM6/€12), the underground sections of the municipal fortification system, which were built in the mid-sixteenth century according to the most advanced principles of Renaissance military architecture.

The Albertinum

Also on Brühlsche Terrasse is the **Albertinum** (10am–6pm, closed Thurs; *www.staatl -kunstsammlungen-dresden.de*; DM7/€3.50), a huge Historicist building which houses many of Dresden's most celebrated art treasures, grouped in several collections.

Taking centre stage is the major part of the **Grünes Gewölbe**, exhibited in display cabinets which make a good stab at re-creating the original effect of the Spiegelzimmern. The most fetching works are the extraordinarily elaborate fancies created by the chief jeweller at the court of Augustus the Strong, **Johann Melchior Dinglinger**, a highly original craftsmen who was strongly influenced by Asian art. His first important commission was a gold and enamel **coffee set**, one of the earliest manifestations of the craze for what was, for Europeans, a brand new beverage. After its completion, Dinglinger and his brothers, together with a host of apprentices, worked for the next seven years on a depiction of the **Court of Delhi** on the birthday of the Great Moghul Aurungzebe. This is a real *tour de force*, featuring 137 gilded and enamelled figures studded with 3000 diamonds, emeralds, rubies and pearls; its glorification of an absolute monarch is a thinly veiled allegory in praise of Augustus the Strong.

Many of Dinglinger's smaller pieces were made in collaboration with Balthasar Permoser – the pick of these are the riotously ornate *Bath of Diana* and the *Moor with a Basket of Emeralds*. By Permoser himself are a number of dainty little ivories, notably the *Hottentot Couple*. Of the nine **jewellery sets**, those made from sapphires and cornelians are the products of Dinglinger's workshop. All the others are slightly later in date; among them is a set of brilliants with a 41-carat green diamond, the world's largest.

The Albertinum's second main collection is the **Gemäldegalerie Neue Meister**, which features nineteenth- and twentieth-century paintings and sculptures. It begins with German Romantic paintings, among which the dozen or so canvases by **Friedrich** stand out. These include one of his most famous and haunting works, *The Cross in the Mountains*, a purely secular subject framed to resemble an altarpiece and originally used as such in a private chapel. The Saxon **Ludwig Richter**, better known as a book illustrator, is well represented, while the Biedermeier style is seen at its best in the humorous compositions of **Spitzweg**. Realist masterpieces include several striking works by **Menzel**, but the portraits – including **Lenbach**'s *Paul Heyse* (the Nobel Prize-winning writer) and *Wilhelm Busch* (the cartoonist), and **Leibl**'s *Baron von Stauffenberg* – steal the show. Works by most of the French Impressionists and their German contemporaries, including Liebermann and Corinth, precede a section devoted to the Expressionist artists of Die Brücke, the artistic group founded in Dresden. Of the later pictures, look out for two pacifist works in an anachronistic triptych format: *War* by **Otto Dix** and the Bosch-like *The Thousand Year Reich* by **Hans Grundig**, a local artist who spent four years in a concentration camp.

Likewise in the Albertinum, and covered by the same entry ticket, are the **Münzkabinett** with its displays of coins and medallions, and the **Skulpturensammlung**, which is particularly strong on the classical period, with Roman copies of lost Greek originals.

The Neustadt

The Neustadt across the Elbe was a planned Baroque town, and its layout is still obvious, even if few of the original buildings survive. In the centre of the Markt rises the **Goldener Reiter**, a gilded equestrian statue of Augustus the Strong. The only Baroque building to have been rebuilt here is the **Blockhaus**, a guard house designed by Zacharias Longuelune, a Frenchman who worked closely with Pöppelmann. Just to the east of the square, on Köpckestrasse, is the seventeenth-century **Jägerhaus**, now housing the **Museum für Sächsische Volkskunst** (Tues–Sun 10am–6pm; *www.staatl-kunstsammlungen-dresden.de*; DM3/€1.50), a collection of folklore objects from throughout Saxony.

The Neustadt's central axis, Hauptstrasse, is a pedestrian precinct lined with a host of restaurants and cafés. It's something of a compromise between the old and the new. Although it in some ways resembles Prager Strasse, a number of Baroque houses have been preserved, among them the **Kügelgenhaus** at no. 13, now decked out with early nineteenth-century furnishings as the **Museum zur Dresdner Frühromantik** (Wed–Sun 10am–6pm; DM3/€1.50). Beyond stands the Neustadt's parish church, the **Dreikönigskirche**, which was designed by Pöppelmann and built by Georg Bähr. Only recently restored following war damage, it is now an ecumenical centre, and the interior of the church, which has been rebuilt in a reduced form, is currently home to the huge carved Renaissance frieze of *The Dance of Death* which formerly adorned a gateway to the Residenzschloss. From the top of the **tower** (Mon–Sat 10am–6pm, Sun noon–6pm; DM2/€1) there's a fine view across the Elbe to the Altstadt.

In the park overlooking the river is the most esoteric creation of Dresden Baroque, the **Japanisches Palais**, in which most of the city's leading architects had a hand. It now contains the **Landesmuseum für Vorgeschichte** (Tues–Sun 10am–5pm;

DM4/€2), a turgid archeological museum, and the rather more rewarding **Staatliches Museum für Völkerkunde** (Tues–Sun 10am–6pm; DM4/€2), a collection of ethnographic objects from around the globe. There's free access to the courtyard, a fantasy inspired by the eighteenth-century infatuation with chinoiserie.

Another whimsical attraction is **Pfund's Molkerei** at Bautzner Str. 79 at the eastern end of Neustadt. Long derelict, its tiled Jugendstil decoration, a mixture of grotesque motifs and picture-book scenes, has been lovingly restored, and its claim to be regarded as "the most beautiful dairy shop in the world" is surely justified. It sells a marvellous selection of cheeses from around the world, and makes a good spot for lunch – whether in the stand-up section in the shop itself, or in the café-restaurant upstairs (see p.1043).

The outskirts

In stark contrast to the centre, some of the suburbs of Dresden sustained very little damage in the 1945 air raids. Although off the beaten tourist track, they contain some of the city's most rewarding sights, and are well worth a day of anyone's time.

The villa quarters

During Dresden's period as capital of the Kingdom of Saxony, it grew to be Germany's fourth largest city, with a population far in excess of its present-day level. In the process, it spawned a whole series of new suburbs, the most prosperous of which consisted largely of exclusive custom-built **villas** commissioned by the most affluent members of society. Collectively they form an important and distinctive feature of the cityscape; although many have fallen into decay, others have been restored and some now serve as hotels and restaurants (see pp.1033 & 1042).

The densest and most architecturally distinguished group of villas is to be found in **Blasewitz** on the left bank of the Elbe 3km east of the centre; as a result, the entire district has been given the status of a protected monument. To get there, take tram #1 from the Altstadt, or tram #6 from Neustadt. One of Germany's most famous bridges, the so-called **Blaues Wunder** (Blue Wonder) links Blasewitz with **Loschwitz**, a villa suburb on the opposite side of the river. Opened in 1893 after a two-year construction period, this steel suspension bridge was a revolutionary design for its day, and was subsequently much imitated.

In Loschwitz there are two impressive transport curiosities from the time of the Second Reich; it costs DM3/€1.50 for a single ticket for either, though they're free with the Dresden Card, and half-price with the 24-hour public transport ticket. Just up from the Blaues Wunder is the valley station of the **Drahtseilbahn**, a funicular railway which runs to the former spa of **Weisser Hirsch**. Instituted in 1895, the funicular was given a thorough overhaul and modernization in preparation for its centenary. A couple of minutes' walk to the south is the rather less orthodox **Bergschwebebahn** (Hanging Mountain Railway), which ascends to Oberloschwitz, the upper part of the quarter. It was put into operation in 1901, and thus postdates its much larger counterpart in Wuppertal, though it was the first of its type in the world built to negotiate a gradient.

At Grundstr. 26, in the valley between the Drahtseilbahn and the Bergschwebebahn, is one of the most spectacular villas, the **Leonhardi-Museum** (Tues–Fri 2–6pm, Sat & Sun 10am–6pm; DM1.50/€0.75). This mock-medieval mansion was the home and studio of Edouard Leonhardi, a landscape painter of the late Romantic period who was a professor at the Dresden Academy. Several of his huge, luxuriantly detailed canvases are on view; regular exhibitions of the work of contemporary artists are also featured. A stone's throw south of the Bergschwebebahn station is Loschwitz's parish church, now known as the **Georg-Bähr-Kirche** in honour of its architect. Left as a shell after the war, it has only recently been rebuilt.

Schloss Pillnitz

Schloss Pillnitz, which lies up the Elbe at the extreme edge of the city boundary, is a Pöppelmann creation inspired by the mystique of the Orient. He built two separate summer palaces: the **Wasserpalais** (late April to late Oct 9.30am–5.30pm, closed Tues; *www.staatl-kunstsammlungen-dresden.de*; DM3/€1.50) directly above the river contains a museum of applied arts; the **Bergpalais** (late April to late Oct Tues–Sun 9.30am–5.30pm; DM3/€1.50) across the courtyard is an almost exact replica, although this time you get to look round the apartments. However, what can be seen inside is of small account in comparison with the exteriors, whose main inspiration seems to have been the palaces of Moghul India, despite the painted Chinese scenes under the eaves. Between the two palaces is a formal garden, while the **Neues Schloss** at the far end is a Neoclassical replacement for its burnt-out Renaissance predecessor, which Pöppelmann retained as the focus of his design. In addition, there's a fine park laid out according to the aristocratic tastes of the time, with sections in both the English and Chinese styles.

Pillnitz can be reached from Blasewitz or Loschwitz by bus #85, or from the city centre by taking tram #9 or #14 to the terminus at Kleinzschachwitz, then crossing the Elbe by ferry. More enjoyably, it's a stop on the route of the Sächsische Dampfschiffahrt cruise ships which sail from the Terrassenufer in the heart of the city down into Saxon Switzerland.

Eating and drinking

Dresden's gastronomic scene has changed out of all recognition over the past decade. Although some of the better establishments from the GDR era still remain in business, they're now heavily outnumbered by more recent ventures. Consequently, there's a wide choice of places to eat and drink in both the Altstadt and the Neustadt, as well as several worthwhile destinations in the suburbs, some of which lie conveniently close to sight-seeing attractions. At night, the liveliest areas are the outer fringes of the Neustadt, and the Univiertel to the south of the Hauptbahnhof.

Restaurants

Am Thor, Hauptstr. 35. A worthy survivor from GDR days, this small Gaststätte serves tasty food, with changing daily specials, and a small but good selection of draught beers.

bremNessel, Schützengasse 18. Dresden's best vegetarian restaurant, presenting creative, freshly prepared dishes in a bar-type setting.

Drachen, Bautzner Str. 72. Founded in 1919 by the former court butcher to the Saxon kings, and still in the hands of his descendants, this restaurant presents changing seasonal dishes and a fine view of the Elbe, whether from the cosy little *Turmzimmer* or the terrace and beer garden outside.

Feldschlösschen Stammhaus, Budapester Str. 32. The Gaststätte of the eponymous brewery, which used to be located alongside, but has moved to new premises in the outskirts: it's best known for a black beer, *Schwarzer Steiger*. Inexpensive *Eintopf* dishes are available Mon–Fri lunchtimes.

Fischgalerie, Maxstr. 2. High-quality, very expensive fish speciality restaurant whose decor is inspired by aquatic themes. Closed Sun, open evenings only Mon & Sat.

Im Kulturpalast, Schloss-Str. 2. Classy second-floor restaurant, serving both local and international dishes, in the main arts centre.

Italienisches Dörfchen, Theaterplatz 3. This historic building with a terrace overlooking the Elbe has been refurbished to house three fairly upmarket restaurants. The *Kurfürstenzimmer* and *Weinzimmer* both serve German fare; *Bellotto* presents upscale Italian cuisine.

Kö 5, Königstr. 5. *Gutbürgerliche Küche* is served in several tastefully furnished rooms of this restored Baroque building with a pretty inner courtyard.

König Albert, Königstr. 26. Upmarket restaurant with a truly international menu. Closed Sat lunchtime and Sun.

Kügelgenhaus, Hauptstr. 13. Atmospheric restaurant, with a Bierkeller underneath, in a fine Baroque building.

Mandarin, Gewandhausstr. 5. Dresden's best Chinese restaurant, tucked away on a quiet square behind the Gewandhaus.

Maximius, Maxstr. 5. Art Deco-style café-restaurant with beer garden. It has an international menu, and is open 9am–3am.

Narrenhäusel, Grosse Meissner Str. 3. Spacious restaurant specializing in Swabian dishes with a large terrace overlooking the Elbe.

Opernrestaurant, Theaterplatz 2. Modern, expensive restaurant and bar right beside the opera house.

Ratskeller, Dr-Kulz-Ring 19. Cavernous cellar restaurant decorated in the German Romantic manner, serving typically hearty fare, some to old local recipes.

Schillergarten, Schillerplatz 9, Blasewitz. Nineteenth-century half-timbered restaurant right beside the Blaues Wunder, with a winter garden directly overlooking the river.

Szeged, Wilsdruffer Str. 4. The local Hungarian restaurant.

Villa Marie, Fährgässchen 1, Blasewitz. Located opposite *Schillergarten*, this Italian-inspired villa appropriately houses a restaurant specializing in Tuscan cuisine.

Yenidze, Weisseritzstr. 3. New restaurant, with a menu of local and international fare, in the dome of one of Dresden's most prominent landmarks, the Moorish-style former cigarette factory beside Bahnhof Mitte. It also has a terrace beer garden, which has the bonus of fine views.

Zur Eule, Grundstr. 100, Loschwitz. Historic Gasthaus, serving typical Saxon dishes, with a tradition dating back to 1378.

Cafés and café-bars

Café B. liebig, Liebigstr. 24. Café-bar in the heart of the Univiertel, with a good selection of food and wines.

Café Kästner, Alaunstr. 1. Neustadt café-bar named in honour of Erich Kästner, author of the children's classic *Emil and the Detectives*, who was born nearby.

Café Kreuzkamm, Am Altmarkt 18. Dresden's best-known coffee house, founded in 1823, has returned to its genteel traditions since the fall of Communism.

Café Schinkelwache, Theaterplatz 1. *Kaffee und Kuchen* establishment occupying part of the Altstädter Wache. In summer, when tables are put out on the square, some of Dresden's finest views can be enjoyed while imbibing.

La Vie en Rose, Alaunstr. 64. French-style café and bistro with Jugendstil decor.

Internetcafé-Spielforum, Leipziger Str. 172. Offers a choice of games plus the opportunity to surf the Net.

Müllers Café, Bergstr. 78. A big student favourite, situated right by the entrance to the University campus.

Pfund's, Bautzner Str. 79. Although a relatively recent venture, this aims to re-create the appearance and atmosphere of a prewar Dresden coffee house. Some of the items on the menu come from the famous dairy shop downstairs (see p.1041).

Bars

Alte Schankwirtschaft, Am Schiesshaus 19. A real old-world German tavern, located just west of the Altstadt.

Die 100, Alaunstr. 100. This wine bar is a stalwart of the Neustadt *Szene*.

Hausbräu im Ballhaus Watzke, Kötzschenbroder Str. 1, Mickten. Lamplit Hausbrauerei, which makes an unfiltered *Pils*, in the cellars of a late nineteenth-century ballroom. Its beer garden commands a fine view up the Elbe to the Altstadt, from which it can be reached by tram #4 or #5.

Linie 6, Schaufuss-Str. 24, Blasewitz. Award-winning theme bar containing a host of paraphernalia associated with tram cars. Its cellar, inevitably named *U6*, hosts late-night cabaret sessions Thurs–Sat. As you'd expect, it lies on the route of tram #6 (and #4 and #10 as well); the nearest stop is Ludwig-Hartmann-Strasse.

Peaches, Antonstr. 29. Cocktail bar situated directly opposite Bahnhof Neustadt.

Plantwirtschaft, Louisenstr. 20. Has one of Dresden's largest and most popular beer gardens, and is a good choice for breakfast.

Raskolnikov, Böhmische Str. 34. One of the city's trendiest watering-holes, offering Russian food and a large selection of vodkas in minimalist surroundings. Evenings only.

Waldschlösschen, Am Brauhaus 8b. Hausbrauerei and cocktail bar in the administration building of what was once a full-sized brewery.

Culture and nightlife

Dresden now has quite an adventurous nightlife, though this is still overshadowed by more highbrow cultural offerings, for which the city has a world-class reputation. To find out **what's on**, there's no real need to look further than a couple of free monthly magazines: *Fritz* has comprehensive daily listings, while the tourist office's *Kulturkalender* gives fuller information on theatre, concerts and art exhibitions.

Discos and clubs

Bärenzwinger, Brühlscher Garten 1. Student club with a varied nightly programme of discos, films, folk music, jazz and dancing.

Dance Factory, Bautzner Str. 118. Huge disco and live music stage. Open Thurs–Sun.

Down Town, Katharinenstr. 11–13. Disco which plays a varied daily mixture of indie, soul, rap and funk. Upstairs is a rock bar, *Groove Station*.

Jazzclub Tonne, Am Brauhaus 3. The main jazz venue in the city. Live music on Fri, Sat and Sun at 8.30pm.

Mowtown Club, St-Petersburger-Str. 9. Open as a café-bar during the week, a live music club with international acts at weekends.

Scheune, Alaunstr. 36–40. Arts centre in Neustadt with live music, theatre and a cinema. Its café serves Indian food, including plenty of vegetarian dishes, and has a beer garden.

Yenidze, Weisseritzstr. 3. Disco in the basement of the former cigarette factory.

Theatre and classical music

Dresden has two international-class symphony **orchestras**, the Staatskapelle Dresden (which is renowned for its silky sound) and the Dresdner Philharmonie, plus an excellent chamber-sized body, the Virtuosi Saxoniae. The last-named is directed by Germany's leading trumpeter, Ludwig Güttler, who has been a key figure in raising money for the restoration of the Frauenkirche. Tickets for the Sächsische Staatsoper and Schauspielhaus are available from the booking office in the Schinkelwache on Theaterplatz (☎03 51/49 19 22 33); unsold tickets can be bought at the venue immediately before each performance. It's also well worth checking up on the regular musical events in the city's churches.

bebe, Clara-Zetkin-Str. 44 (☎03 51/4 12 13 75). Fifty-seater theatre presenting cabaret and avantgarde shows.

Dresdner Brettl, Terrassenufer 17 (☎03 51/4 96 94 50). The best-known cabaret stage in the city.

Komödie, Freiberger Str. 39 (☎03 51/86 64 10). Venue for comedies and musicals, housed in the new World Trade Centre building.

Kulturpalast, northern end of Altmarkt (☎03 51/48 66 66). A large arts centre with a concert hall used for all kinds of music, including a regular series by the Dresdner Philharmonie.

Sächsische Staatsoper, Theaterplatz 2 (☎03 51/4 91 17 05, *www.semperoper.de*). One of the city's finest buildings, this stages a wide-ranging operatic programme plus concerts by its house orchestra, the Staatskapelle Dresden.

Schauspielhaus, Ostra-Allee 3 (☎03 51/4 91 35 55, *www.staatschauspiel-dresden.de*). The city's main venue for classical drama.

Staatsoperette, Pirnaer Landstr. 131 (☎03 51/2 07 99 29). Dresden's home of operetta and light opera, located in the southeast of the city. Take tram #6, #9, #12 or #14 to Altleuben.

Theater Junge Generation, Meissner Landstr. 4 (☎03 51/42 91 20). Children's and youth theatre.

Festivals

Dresden's main annual **folklore festival** is the Advent market, here known as the *Striezelmarkt*. It features a medieval-style market in the courtyard of the Residenzschloss, plus food and handicrafts stalls in the streets and squares of Neustadt. There is copious consumption of *Christstollen*, the German Christmas cake that is now a firm international favourite; the earliest recipe for this dates back to the mid-fifteenth century and is preserved in Dresden's Stadtmuseum. One day of the market is designated the *Stollenfest*, and features a procession in which a giant *Christstollen* is carried from the Zwinger to the Altmarkt. In mid-April Dresden hosts a **film** festival, centred on the celebrated Rundkino on Prager Strasse. A big **jazz** event, the *International Dixieland Festival*, is held each May/June; around the same time, there's a **classical music** festival, the *Dresdner Musikfestspiele*.

Moritzburg and Gross-Sedlitz

Two undamaged examples of the work of the great Baroque architects of Dresden can be seen just outside the city boundaries in **Moritzburg** and **Gross-Sedlitz**. Both of these make enjoyable half-day outings; as a bonus, the journey to the former can be an experience in itself.

Moritzburg

The small village of **MORITZBURG**, 15km north of Dresden, is connected with the Hauptbahnhof by bus #326, but it's far more fun to take the **narrow-gauge railway**, the Lössnitztalbahn. This starts from the Ostbahnhof at Radebeul, on the S-Bahn line between Dresden-Neustadt and Meissen, and takes about an hour to cover the 17km to its terminus at Radeburg. No fewer than seventeen bridges are crossed in the course of the journey along the Lössnitz valley, which is mostly a pastoral landscape with fields, meadows and ponds; Moritzburg is about halfway along.

At the edge of the village is the **Schloss** (April–Oct daily 10am–5.30pm; Nov–March Tues–Sun 10am–4pm; DM7/€3.50). It was founded as a hunting lodge in 1542 by Duke Moritz of Saxony, but was almost completely rebuilt in the 1720s for Augustus the Strong using designs provided by Pöppelmann – only the **Schlosskapelle** (an addition of the 1660s), the **corner towers** and foundations were retained. A large artifical lake, fashioned out of several small ponds, was created round the Schloss, giving it an appearance akin to the great French châteaux of the Loire. As with them, the interior does not quite match up to the exterior, though there are some fine rooms, notably the **Audienzsaal** with its grand mythological paintings, the **Zimmer mit Damenbildnissen**, featuring portraits of court beauties (including some of Augustus's mistresses) and the **Speisesaal**, which was used both as a dining room and a theatre and is adorned with a large number of hunting trophies.

It's also worth taking a stroll in the vast English-style **Schlosspark**. Towards its western end is the **Fasanenschlösschen** (previously April–Oct Tues–Sun 9.30am–4pm, but currently closed for restoration), a small gaming lodge of the 1780s, which is normally home to a collection of stuffed birds. Nearby, at the side of the lake, are two follies – the **Mole** (pier) and the **Leuchtturm** (lighthouse).

Between the wars, Moritzburg was the main home of the Wettin family, who had recently been stripped of royal status. In 1944, Prince Ernst Heinrich invited the great Berlin sculptress and graphic artist Käthe Kollwitz, whose home had been bombed, to settle at Meissner Str. 7 in the village, and she spent the last year of her life there. Now designated the **Käthe-Kollwitz-Gedenkstätte** (April–Oct Tues–Fri 11am–5pm, Sat & Sun 10am–5pm; Nov–March Tues–Fri noon–3pm, Sat & Sun 11am–4pm; DM3.50/€1.75), it contains displays of her work.

Moritzburg's **tourist office** (April–Oct Mon–Fri 9am–6pm, Sat & Sun noon–4pm; Nov–March Mon–Fri 10am–4pm; ☎03 52 07/8 54 10, fax 8 54 20) is at Schlossallee 3b. In addition to **private rooms** (①–②), there's a **pension**, *Schlossallee*, Schlossallee 35 (☎03 52 07/8 16 90; ④), and several **hotels**, including *Eisenberger Hof*, Kötzschenbrodaer Str. 8 (☎03 52 07/8 16 73; ⑤), *Landhaus*, Schlossallee 37 (☎03 52 07/8 16 02; ⑥), and *Waldschänke*, an eighteenth-century hostelry in a wooded setting off Grosse Fasanenstrasse (☎03 52 07/86 00; ⑥). All of these have fine **restaurants**.

Gross-Sedlitz

A short walk from the S-Bahn station of **GROSS-SEDLITZ**, on the line linking Dresden with Saxon Switzerland, is the **Barock-Garten** (daily: April–Sept 7am–8pm; Oct–March 8am–6pm; DM2/€1), a masterpiece of landscape gardening by Pöppelmann and two of his closest associates, Zacharias Longuelune and Johann Christoph Knöffel. Modelled on the gardens of Versailles, it contains a small palace, the **Friedrichschlösschen**, plus two orangeries, and a double staircase with fountains known as **Stille Musik**. Statues from the workshop of Balthasar Permoser are placed throughout the formally arranged gardens, which are in bloom for much of the year. In summer, open-air concerts are often held.

Meissen

Regular S-Bahn trains take around 45 minutes to cover the 25km between Dresden and **MEISSEN**, although you can also take the slow scenic route by boat down the Elbe. Meissen is associated in most people's minds with "Dresden china", yet the famous porcelain factory is only one of the attractions of this photogenic and unspoiled old city. In total contrast to Dresden, it came through World War II almost unscathed; it suffered quite badly from pollution under the GDR, but is steadily being cleaned up, having been one of five towns selected to receive special Federal restoration grants.

Arrival, information and accommodation

Meissen's **Hauptbahnhof** is on the right bank of the Elbe directly across the river from the city centre. The **tourist office** (May–Sept Mon–Fri 9am–6.30pm, Sat & Sun 9am–4pm; Oct–April Mon–Fri 10am–6pm, Sat & Sun 10am–3pm; ☎0 35 21/4 19 40, fax 41 94 19, *www.meissen.de*) is at Markt 3.

Following several years of total flux in the accommodation situation, Meissen now has a decent number of **pensions** and **hotels** in most price categories, as well as **private rooms** (②–④) bookable via the tourist offfice.

Hotels and pensions
Burkhardt, Neugasse 29 (☎0 35 21/45 81 98, fax 45 81 97). Pension with an ideal location in the heart of the Altstadt. ③.

Goldgrund, Goldgrund 14 (☎0 35 21/4 79 30, fax 47 93 44). Fine medium-range hotel with restaurant in a very quiet woodland setting at the southern edge of town, a few minutes' walk from the Staatliche Porzellan-Manufaktur. ⑤.

Im Kleinen Haus, Leinewebergasse 3 (☎0 35 21/45 30 18, fax 45 10 90). Small pension in a half-timbered Altstadt house. ④.

Landhaus Nassau, Nassauweg 1 (☎0 35 21/73 81 60, fax 73 81 69). Good-value hotel and restaurant set at the edge of a nature reserve at the extreme eastern edge of town, reached by bus #D. ④.

Parkhotel Pannonia, Hafenstr. 27–31 (☎0 35 21/7 22 50, fax 72 29 04, *www.pannonia-hotels.com*). Meissen's leading hotel occupies a large Jugendstil villa in a park by the right bank of the Elbe. Its facilities include a fine restaurant, a summer terrace and a whirlpool. ⑦.

Ross, Grossenhainer Str. 9 (☎0 35 21/5 10, fax 75 19 99). Grand, well-refurbished late nineteenth-century hotel with restaurant close to the Hauptbahnhof. ⑤–⑦.

Schweizerhaus, Rauhentalstr. 1 (☎0 35 21/45 71 62, fax 45 71 62). Pension with restaurant in a half-timbered chalet opposite the Staatliche Porzellan-Manufaktur. ③.

Tagungszentrum Domherrenhof, Freiheit 10 (☎0 35 21/46 09 40, fax 46 09 49). A small hotel occupies part of this former canons' residence. Its café-restaurant has a summer terrace which commands a wonderful view over the Altstadt to the Burgberg. ⑤.

The City

Never having grown into a major city, Meissen is compact and ideal for exploration on foot. Even from afar, its feudal layout is apparent, with the houses of the **Bürgerstadt** clustered in the valley under the **Burgberg**, which is crowned by the buildings of the joint rulers, the margrave and the bishop. The city centre lies on the left bank of the Elbe, but it is from the right bank (where you will arrive if you come by train) that the strategic significance of the site can be appreciated more easily. You're also rewarded with the best of the many breathtaking panoramas the town has to offer.

The Albrechtsburg

Centrepiece of all the views is the commandingly sited **Albrechtsburg** (daily 10am–5/6pm; *www.albrechtsburg-meissen.de*; DM6/€3). This isn't the original castle of the margraves of Meissen, but a late fifteenth-century replacement commissioned by Elector Ernst of Saxony and his brother Duke Albrecht, who jointly ruled the combined Wettin territories. It retains the medieval requirement for a military fortress, but combines this, for the first time in Germany, with the new demands of Renaissance princes for a residential palace. It's the masterpiece of one of the most prolific and accomplished builders of the time, **Arnold von Westfalen**. To appreciate the ingenuity of his design, it really needs to be viewed from afar: that way, you can see how the architect was forced to use the contours of the rocky, sloping site, solving the problem by building in huge blocks of six storeys, the first two being essentially to support the superstructure. While work was under way, the heirs of the two brothers split into two hostile factions, with Meissen becoming the seat of the Albertines, the junior of the two lines. Soon after completion, the court decamped to Dresden, leaving the Albrechtsburg as something of a white elephant. In 1710, it was given a wholly new function as the headquarters of the original porcelain factory, the first in Europe.

As it stands directly above the valley, the Albrechtsburg has to be approached from the rear, where it's guarded by a bridge and gateway leading into a vast courtyard. The underuse of the palace largely explains the somewhat bare feeling of most of its **interior**, which overenthusiastic nineteenth-century Romantic painters tried to liven up by adding cycles of heroic historical frescoes, with decidedly dubious consequences. Nonetheless, it's worth paying to go inside just to see the truly spectacular, almost crazy, **vaulting**, which was something of a speciality of Arnold von Westfalen. There's a seemingly inexhaustible range of variations, those with deep pyramidal niches between their ribs being the most original. The other highlight of the visit is the ascent of the beautiful **external staircase**, the *Grosser Wendelstein*, the main feature of the castle's courtyard exterior. Housed in the last few rooms on the visitors' circuit is the medieval section of the state sculptural collection, the rest of which is in Dresden.

The Dom

Cocooned within the Albrechtsburg courtyard is the **Dom** (April–Oct Mon–Fri & Sun 9am–6pm, Sat 9am–5.30pm; Nov–March daily 10am–4pm; DM3.50/€1.75), along with its subsidiary buildings, such as the bishop's palace and the houses of the canons, most of which have been altered repeatedly down the years. For the most part, the Dom itself is a pure High Gothic structure, begun in the mid-thirteenth century by the same workshop of masons that had built the famous west choir in Naumburg, though the relative decline in quality suggests that its director, the so-called Master of Naumburg, had died in the interim. However, the somewhat eccentric facade long remained unfinished: Arnold von Westfalen added the third storey in Flamboyant Gothic style, but the florid openwork spires, which soar above the rest of Meissen's skyline, only date from the early 1900s.

Entry is via the **Fürstenkapelle**, which was tacked onto the facade in the fifteenth century to serve as a mausoleum for members of the Wettin family. It contains a number of resplendent bronze memorials, sometimes using designs by Dürer and Cranach. The richly sculptured **portal** behind was made the previous century as the main entrance to the Dom; its archway is cleverly used as a frame for the depiction of Christ in Majesty. Just to the right of here is the **Georgenkapelle**, the private memorial chapel of Duke George the Bearded, entered via a strikingly Italianate Renaissance doorway. At the far end of the south nave aisle is the **Achteckbau** (Octagon); it opens directly outside, and contains three fine statues by the Naumburg carvers.

The same men were also responsible for the **rood screen**, except for its Flamboyant upper storey, added in the sixteenth century as a choir gallery; and for the statues of the founders and patron saints in the choir. The central **stained-glass window**, showing Old and New Testament scenes in pairs, dates back to the thirteenth century, while *The Adoration of the Magi* **triptych** is by an unknown Netherlandish painter of the turn of the sixteenth century. From here you can exit via the **cloister**, off which is the **Magdalenenkapelle**, where the original statues of the south portal have been brought for conservation reasons.

The Bürgerstadt

The Bürgerstadt is laid out as a series of twisting and meandering streets between the Burgberg and the Elbe. More impressive as an ensemble than for any outstanding highlights, it's ideal for an aimless stroll. Centrepiece is the Markt, dominated by the **Rathaus**, in which the dying flickers of Flamboyant Gothic are fused with the new spirit of the Renaissance. At no. 8 on the square is the Fachgeschäft, the porcelain factory's shop, which is well worth a visit even if you aren't intending to buy. Next door, at no. 9, the Küfertheke, is one of the places where you can try local wines.

On its own small square to the side is the Flamboyant Gothic **Frauenkirche** (May–Oct daily 10am–12.30pm & 1–4pm), whose carillon, with the first bells in the world to be fashioned from porcelain, can be heard six times daily. The pride of the interior is the retable of *The Coronation of the Virgin*, made around 1500, while the **tower** (same hours; DM2/€1) commands a superb view over the city and the Elbe. On the terrace above the church is the celebrated **Gasthaus Vincenz Richter**, an old half-timbered tavern which preserves an early eighteenth-century wine press. The wines served here have the reputation of being the best in eastern Germany, though that's less of a claim than it might appear, as the area around is one of only two significant parts of the former GDR with a climate mild enough for growing grapes.

The Staatliche Porzellan-Manufaktur Meissen

The **Staatliche Porzellan-Manufaktur Meissen** lies about 1.5km south of the Markt, and is most easily reached by going down Fleischer Gasse, then continuing straight along Neugasse; it also lies close to the S-Bahn terminus, Meissen–Triebischtal. This is the latest factory to manufacture "Dresden china", whose invention had truly bizarre origins. Augustus the Strong imprisoned the alchemist **Johann Friedrich Böttger** in Festung Königstein in Saxon Switzerland, charging him with what was then believed to be a feasible task, the production of gold. Instead, he invented the first true European porcelain, according to a formula which remains a jealously guarded secret – its products are identified by the trademark of crossed blue swords.

   Guided tours (daily 9am–5/6pm; DM5/€2.50) are run round the workshops, enabling you to see all the different stages of the production process. Be aware that this is on the itinerary of just about every tour group visiting eastern Germany and in summer you can be faced with a horrendous wait unless you arrive early. No such problems beset the **Schauhalle** (same hours; DM9/€4.50), which in any event is of far more immediate appeal: it contains the largest collection of Meissen porcelain in existence, and shows how the style of the factory has developed from the beginning to the present day. Highlight is the display of the gloriously over-the-top Rococo fripperies created by the most talented artist employed here, **Joachim Kaendler**.

   If you're walking between the town centre and the factory, it's worth stopping off at the **Nikolaikirche** (May–Sept Tues–Thurs & Sun 2–4pm), a little Romanesque church set in the Stadtpark. Inside, forming a poignant memorial to the fallen of World War I, are the largest porcelain figures ever made, two groups of mothers with children, each of which is 2.5m high and 300kg in weight.

Eating and drinking

Few ex-GDR towns are as well equipped gastronomically as Meissen, whose wine bar-restaurants represent its main strength in this field.

Bahrmanns Brauereikeller, Webergasse 2. Large cellar restaurant, warmed by a huge open fire, in the nineteenth-century premises of a former brewery.

Café Schönitz, Neugasse 22. French-style café-bistro which often features live music.

Café Zieger, Rote Stufen 5. Traditional coffee house which has been run by the same family for over 150 years. Its speciality is a puff pastry known as the *Meissner Fummel*.

Domkeller, Domplatz 9. Meissen's oldest restaurant, with a tradition dating back to 1520. It serves Saxon specialities and has a terrace offering a fine view over the town.

Monasterium, Freiheit 13. Daytime café-restaurant in the chapel and cloisters of the former Kloster St Afra. Open 11am–5pm, closed Wed.

Vincenz Richter, An der Frauenkirche 12. This sixteenth-century Weinschänke is one of the essential sights of Meissen. Although the menu is short, the food served is arguably the best in town. Open Tues–Fri 4–11pm, Sat 3pm–midnight, Sun noon–6pm.

Weinprobierestube der Sächsischen Winzergenossenschaft, Bennoweg 9. Historic wine restaurant in the northeast of town, offering local dishes served on Meissen porcelain, and regular sampling sessions. Evenings only.

Zur Seemannsruhe, Uferstr. 12. Restaurant in a late sixteeenth-century house directly on the left bank of the Elbe offering Bohemian cuisine and a variety of fish dishes.

Saxon Switzerland

The area between Dresden and the Czech border 50km south is popularly known as **Saxon Switzerland** (Sächsische Schweiz), though this nickname, first coined by artists of the Romantic movement, is misleading. Now designated the **Nationalpark Sächsische Schweiz**, the landscape, far from looking Swiss, is archetypally Middle European, with the meandering **River Elbe** cutting a grand valley through dense forests interrupted by outcrops of rock welded into truly fantastic shapes. There's no better **hiking** country in all of Germany, and some walking is essential if you want to see the best of the scenery. If pressed for time, the S-Bahn line down the left bank offers a good overview of the region, and, even on a day-trip from Dresden, it should be possible to combine this with a visit to a couple of the main set-piece attractions. A good alternative is to take a **cruise** with the Sächsische Dampfschiffahrt ships: there are two or three departures daily from Dresden throughout the season (see p.1032). However, given that there's abundant and inexpensive **accommodation** in all the resorts mentioned below, it would be a pity not to stay for a few days.

Pirna

PIRNA, 17km south of Dresden, is the gateway to Saxon Switzerland. Untouched in World War II, this old market town has been spruced up in line with its new role as a major tourist centre. Set on a hill overlooking the town is **Schloss Sonnenstein**, now mainly used as offices, though it does have a terrace restaurant. The central **Markt** is lined with a variety of handsome mansions, while the Rathaus stands on its own in the middle of the square.

Between the Schloss and the Markt is the **Stadtkirche St Marien**, a flamboyant Gothic hall church similar to those in the Erzgebirge region, with all interest concentrated inside. Here, it's the stupendous star and network **vaulting** that steals the show – at times the ribs erupt into audacious flights of fancy, notably in the chancel, where they take on the form of a tree trunk. A curiosity of the church's building history is that it was begun at the turn of the sixteenth century as a Catholic parish church, but was appropriated for Protestant use before its completion. This change was immediately given visible expression in the painted decoration which was added to the vault: two of the Evangelists are depicted with the features of Luther and Melanchthon.

The **tourist office** (Mon–Fri 9am–6pm, Sat 9.30am–1pm; ☎ & fax 0 35 01/52 84 97, *www.pirna.de*) is at Markt 7. Here you can book **private rooms** (①–③) in the town and in other places in Saxon Switzerland. The wide range of **hotels** includes: *Weisse Taube*, Arthur-Thiermann-Str. 58 (☎0 35 01/52 41 20; ③); *Schwarzer Adler*, Dohnaischer Platz 2 (☎0 35 01/52 86 10; ④); *Sächsicher Hof*, Gartenstr. 21 (☎0 35 01/44 75 51; ⑤); and, both situated in old buildings, *Pirna'scher Hof*, Am Markt 4 (☎0 35 01/4 43 80; ⑤), and *Deutsches Haus*, Niedere Burgstr. 1 (☎0 35 01/44 34 40; ⑥). There's also a **youth hostel**, situated on the opposite side of the Elbe from the centre in the incorporated village of Copitz at Birkwitzer Str. 51 (☎0 35 01/44 56 01, fax 44 56 02; DM25/€12 or DM30/€15). The best **restaurants** are in the last three hotels listed above.

Kurort Rathen and Hohnstein

If visiting Saxon Switzerland on a day-trip, one place you should definitely make for is **KURORT RATHEN**, a small health resort on the east bank of the Elbe, linked by regular ferries to its Bahnhof, which is 12km and three stops on from Pirna. Should you want to stay, there are ample accommodation possibilities on both sides of the river, including plenty of **private rooms** (①–③). The best hotel is *Erbgericht* (☎03 50 34/7 04 54; ⑥), with a terrace overlooking the Elbe.

High above the village, about thirty minutes' walk away, is the **Bastei** (daily 9am–6pm; DM2/€1, but free access outside these times). Even the unfortunate siting of the GDR-era *Berghotel* (☎03 50 24/7 04 06; ⑥) cannot detract from the grandeur of this natural belvedere of strangely shaped rocks, which is not only astonishing in itself – seemingly fashioned by some great divine sculptor – but also commands really stunning views, both over the Elbe and into the forest. As a bonus, there are the ruins of **Felsenburg Neurathen**, a thirteenth-century castle ingeniously juxtaposed among the rocks. Lower down, the setting has been put to a more peaceful use by the creation of a spectacular open-air theatre.

Another walk well worth making is the hour-long trail along the Knotenweg to **HOHNSTEIN**, the most picturesque of the villages set away from the riverside, with a hilly site which affords a wide range of perspectives. The **Schloss** (free access to court-yard; interiors daily March–Oct 9am–5pm; DM2/€1), itself a fine vantage point, hous-es an attractive *Naturfreunde* **hostel** (☎03 59 75/8 12 02). There are a number of fine Baroque buildings on and around the Markt, notably the **Georg-Bähr-Kirche**, a rustic-looking church named in honour of its architect, one of the key figures of Dresden Baroque.

Königstein

From Rathen, the train follows the loops of the Elbe round to the small country town of **KÖNIGSTEIN**, 6km away. It's of no interest in itself, but the colossal fortress above, **Festung Königstein** (daily: May–Sept 9am–8pm; Oct 9am–6pm; Nov–April 9am–5pm; DM7/€3.50), rivals the Bastei as the most impressive sight in Saxon Switzerland. It takes a steep climb of thirty or forty minutes to reach it, though a tourist "train" has been introduced for the benefit of the better-heeled visitors who now visit the region. Once a virtually impregnable frontier post of the Saxon state, the fortress was continu-ally strengthened right up until the Napoleonic period, so that it forms a virtual ency-clopedia of changing defensive techniques. Long before this it had ceased to have much strategic value, and its main function was as Saxony's most secure prison. Johann Friedrich Böttger, the inventor of Meissen porcelain, was incarcerated here by Augustus the Strong; the same fate later befell the nineteenth-century Socialist leader August Bebel, and a number of prominent anti-Nazis. It also proved a secure home in World War II for the moveable art treasures of Dresden. The most remarkable struc-ture is the sixteenth-century **Tiefer Brunnen** (Deep Well), which is 152m deep and took a group of miners from Freiberg six years to dig. Also of note are the cellars, the barracks and the two arsenals, both containing an array of historic weapons. However, there's no doubt that the view – even finer than that from the Bastei – is the prime draw.

To see Königstein itself at reasonably close range, there's a choice of vantage points – the **Pfaffenstein** to the south, or the **Lilienstein** on the opposite side of the Elbe. Ferries run across to the latter from Königstein; it's then a walk of about an hour to the summit.

In town, there are plenty of **private rooms** (①–③) bookable via the **tourist office**, just off the central Markt at Schreiberberg 2 (April–Oct Mon, Tues, Thurs & Fri 9am–5.30pm, Wed 1–5.30pm, Sat 9am–noon; Nov–March same times, except closed Sat; ☎03 50 21/6 82 61, fax 6 88 87). There's a small, centrally sited **guesthouse**, *Schrägers*, Kirchgasse 1 (☎03 50 21/6 83 52; ③), plus three **hotels** in the outskirts: *Vogelsberg*, Elbhäuser Weg 20 (☎03 50 21/6 82 32; ④); *Panoramahotel Lilienstein*, Ebenheit 7 (☎03 50 21/5 30; ⑤); and *Lindenhof*, Gohrischer Str. 2 (☎03 50 21/6 82 43; ⑥).

Bad Schandau and around

Next stop, a further 5km on, is the spa of **BAD SCHANDAU**, the chief resort of the area and a wonderful base for hikes. It's also the border post, having swallowed up all the villages before the frontier. The best view over the area is from the tall platform tower of the iron lift, or **Personenaufzug** (daily 9am–6pm; DM4/€2), which was built at the southern end of town in 1904. Also worth a look is the **Johanniskirche** just off the Markt, a Gothic church remodelled in the Baroque period, which contains two notable Renaissance furnishings in the pulpit and the high altar.

From the park in the centre of Bad Schandau, the Kirnitzschtalbahn, one of only two surviving examples of the once-ubiquitous **rural tramways**, creaks along the banks of the River Kirnitzsch to the **Lichtenhainer Wasserfall** 7km northeast. (If driving along this stretch, take extra care, as the tram travels on the main road most of the time, making overtaking extremely hazardous.) From the terminus, where there's a restaurant, it's a gentle uphill signposted walk to the **Kuhstall** (Cow Stall), one of Saxon Switzerland's most picturesque rock groupings and a fine vantage point over the wooded countryside away from the Elbe. Overlooking the river, a couple of hours' walk from here or Bad Schandau, are the **Schrammsteine**, the most extended group of rock formations in the area and a favourite haunt of daredevil climbing enthusiasts.

Bad Schandau's **Bahnhof** is on the west side of the Elbe; regular **ferries** run from there to the town centre on the opposite bank. The **tourist office** (April–Oct Mon–Fri 9am–7pm, Sat 9am–4pm, Sun 2–6pm; Nov–March Mon–Fri 9am–6pm; ☎03 50 22/9 00 30 33, fax 9 00 34, *www.bad-schandau.de*) at Markt 12 provides the normal booking service for **private rooms** (①–③). There's also a homely **pension** in *Café Menge*, Badallee 12 (☎03 50 22/58 30; ④). The town has many fine **hotels**, such as *Zum Roten Haus*, Marktstr. 10 (☎03 50 22/4 23 43; ④), *Elbterasse*, Markt 11 (☎03 50 22/4 85 60; ⑤), *Lindenhof*, Rudolf-Sendig-Str. 11 (☎03 50 22/48 90; ⑤), and *Parkhotel*, Rudolf-Sendig-Str. 12 (☎03 50 22/5 20; ⑥). All of these have **restaurants**. There's a **campsite** at Ostrauer Mühle on the Kirnitzsch (☎03 50 22/4 27 42), and a **youth hostel** at Rudi-Hempel-Str. 14 (☎03 50 22/4 24 08, fax 4 24 09; DM25/€12.50 or DM30/€15) in the village of Ostrau.

Bautzen (Budyšin)

Some 60km east of Dresden is **BAUTZEN**, the cultural capital of the Sorbs, Germany's only indigenous Slav minority, whose homeland is divided between Upper Lusatia in Saxony and Lower Lusatia in Brandenburg (see p.890). They settled in this area as far back as the sixth century, and have remained ever since; the bilingual signs and the two official forms of the city's name, impart a touch of exoticism, though in Bautzen itself (as opposed to some of the outlying villages) you're unlikely to hear the language spoken in the streets. Bautzen is potentially a really beautiful town: it occupies a compact site high above the still young River Spree, which looks wild and untamed, although it's harnessed to form a reservoir immediately beyond the northern suburbs. In 2002, it will celebrate its own millennium with an extensive programme of events. The centrepiece will be an extended version of its main **festival**, the *Bautzener Frühling*: this will run from May 17 to 26 and feature medieval spectacles, folklore groups from all over Europe and the usual side attractions.

The Town

The silhouette of Bautzen, dotted with towers of all shapes and sizes, looks magnificent when seen from a distance. Closer up, it's not quite so impressive, the GDR period having bequeathed a legacy of pollution and tattiness, though it is gradually being cleaned up in preparation for the 1000th birthday celebrations.

A good way to begin your tour is by climbing the **Reichenturm** (daily April–Oct 10am–5pm; DM1/€0.50), which lies at the top end of Kornmarkt at the eastern edge of the Altstadt. The original defensive tower dates back to the late fifteenth century, and was subsequently adorned with a relief portrait of Bautzen's then overlord, Emperor Rudolf II, ruler of the famously degenerate court at Prague. When an over-large Baroque lantern was added in the early eighteenth century, a pronounced tilt immediately occurred – hence the nickname of "the leaning tower of Bautzen". After World War II there were plans to demolish it for safety reasons, but it was decided to secure the foundations instead. From the top, you get a good overview of the layout of the town.

The busy pedestrianized **Reichenstrasse**, lined with Baroque houses built after one of the many fires that have ravaged the town throughout its history, leads from the Reichenturm to the **Hauptmarkt**, where markets are held on Tuesdays, Thursdays and Saturdays. This is separated from a second market square, Fleischmarkt, by the **Rathaus**, a classically inspired Baroque building whose most pleasing feature is the tall tower, Gothic by origin, but neatly remodelled to harmonize with the rest of the structure. Opposite is the **Gewandhaus**, a neo-Renaissance replacement of the old trading hall and weigh house, whose handsome vaulted cellars, now the *Ratskeller* restaurant, survive underneath.

Fleischmarkt's top end is closed by the very parochial-looking **Dom**, whose late Gothic architecture reduces the hall church to its simplest format. It's chiefly of note for two peculiarities. First, as can be seen from the outside, but far more noticeably within, the body of the church is built with a very pronounced curve, possibly symbolic of the body of Christ on the Cross, but more likely to be due to the restrictions of the site. The second curiosity is that this is a *Simultankirche*, one used by Protestants and Catholics alike. Immediately the Reformation was introduced, it was divided in two, the Catholics taking the choir and the Protestants the nave, a situation that persists to this day, with only a small iron barrier separating the two congregations. The very different sets of furnishings immediately betray which part you're in; the Catholics have the star piece in the large *Crucifixion* by Balthasar Permoser, a donation from the sculptor himself.

To the rear of the Dom is the **Domstift**, a triple-winged Baroque palace entered via a cheerful gateway adorned with statues inspired by Counter-Reformation theology. Inside, the ecclesiastical treasures of the **Domschatzkammer** (Mon–Fri 10am–noon & 1–4pm; free) are on view. All around this area are twisting little alleys of peeling houses which are marvellously evocative of days gone by, but desperately in need of restoration.

The Reichenturm also makes a good jumping-off point for a walk round the fortifications, of which many portions survive. Immediately to the north is the **Wendischer Turm**, whose name signifies that it presided over the quarter where the Wends (the alternative name for the Sorbs) lived. Long used as a prison, it was saved from demolition through the ingenuity of Gottfried Semper, who incorporated it into the castellated **Kaserne** (barracks) he was commissioned to build on the site. This rather wonderful neo-Gothic fantasy itself became redundant, but has found a new lease of life as municipal offices.

The L-shaped alley known as Gickelsberg leads from here to the **Schülerturm**, beyond which is Am Zwinger, a rustic-looking potholed road leading west past the **Gerberbastei** (now the youth hostel) to the **Nikolaiturm**. Alongside the latter is **Nikolaikirche**, once the church of the Catholic Sorbs, but a ruin since its destruction in the Thirty Years War. It's a peaceful spot, now used as a cemetery, commanding a fine view over the Spree.

An even better vantage point is the terrace of **Schloss Ortenburg** further west. The present castle, replacing a much earlier stronghold of the margraves of Meissen, was erected in the late fifteenth century by order of Matthis Corvinus, King of Hungary and Bohemia, who is depicted seated between crown-bearing angels in the nine-metre-high memorial on the entrance gateway. Later additions include the playful Renaissance gables and the plain Baroque wing now housing the **Sorbisches Museum** (daily 10am–4/5pm; DM3/€1.50), documenting the festivals, costumes and literature of the Sorbs. If you've got time to spare, it's well worth descending to the Spree and crossing the footbridge to a belvedere offering a view of the Schloss and the town.

Following Osterweg southwards, you pass the **Mühlenturm** en route to the **Michaeliskirche**, the parish church of the Sorb Protestants, which forms a picturesque corner in conjunction with the **Alte Wasserkunst** (daily April–Oct

10am–5pm; DM2/€1), a mid-sixteenth-century water-tower which was operational until 1963. Inside is a small museum outlining the technical particulars of its machinery, while the viewing platform at the top offers yet another outlook on the valley. On the bank of the Spree below is the **Hexenhäuschen** (Witches' House), the only old fisherman's house to have withstood all the fires which destroyed its counterparts – the belief that the inhabitants must therefore have been possessed of magical powers led to its present nickname. Finally, the wonderful full-frontal view of Bautzen that appears in all the tourist brochures can be seen for real by walking a short distance south to **Friedensbrücke**.

Practicalities

Bautzen's **Hauptbahnhof** is about fifteen minutes' walk south of the Altstadt, which is reached via Bahnhofstrasse and Karl-Marx-Strasse. The **tourist office** (April–Oct Mon–Fri 10am–6pm, Sat & Sun 10am–3pm; Nov–March Mon–Fri 10am–5pm, Sat 10am–3pm; ☎35 91/4 20 16, fax 53 43 09, *www.bautzen.de*) is at Hauptmarkt 1. There's a reasonable number of **private rooms** (①–③) on its books. The **youth hostel** is located in an old bastion at Am Zwinger 1 (☎0 35 91/4 03 47, fax 4 03 48; DM19/€9.50 or DM24/€12). There are several conveniently sited **pensions**, such as *Fischer*, Löhrstr. 19 (☎0 35 91/60 71 85; ②), *Lausitz*, Bahnhofstr. 16 (☎0 35 91/3 78 10; ④), and *Le Petit*, Steinstr. 35 (☎0 35 91/4 35 98; ④). Centrally located **hotels** include *Alte Gerberei*, Uferweg 1 (☎0 35 91/30 10 11, *www.hotel-alte-gerberei.de*; ④), *Schloss-Schänke*, Burgplatz 5 (☎0 35 91/30 49 90; ④–⑥), *Holiday Inn*, Wendischer Graben 20 (☎0 35 91/49 20, *www.bautzen-touristik.de*; ⑤–⑦), and *Goldener Adler*, Hauptmarkt 4 (☎0 35 91/4 86 60; ⑥).

Each of the hotels listed above has a **restaurant**. For more exotic fare, head to either of the Sorb eateries: *Sorbisches Café*, Postplatz 2, or *Wjelbik*, Kornstr. 7. Another oddity is *Zum Haseneck*, just east of the Reichenturm at Kurt-Pchalek-Str. 1, whose menu largely consists of different sorts of rabbit dishes. Most unusually, the *Ratskeller*, Innere Lauenstr. 1, is now an Italian restaurant. The Deutsch–Sorbisches Volkstheater, Seminarstr. 12 (☎0 35 91/58 40), is the only bilingual **theatre** in the country, with performances in Sorb alternating with German. A folklore group, the Sorbisches National-Ensemble, is also based in the town, and regularly performs there.

Zittau and the Zittau mountains

Some 65km from Bautzen, near the meeting point of the frontiers with the Czech Republic and Poland at the extreme southeastern corner of Saxony, is **ZITTAU**. Despite its industrial infrastructure, it's a well-preserved historic town, but is best known as the gateway to a wooded upland area, the **Zittau mountains** (*Zittauer Gebirge*). This wild countryside, characterized by dramatic rock formations, was part of the old kingdom of Bohemia, with Zittau itself having been founded in the early thirteenth century by one of its monarchs, Otakar I.

The Town

Zittau's Altstadt is a circular area bounded by green boulevards which have replaced the dismantled fortifications. With its spacious squares and innumerable fountains, it has a vaguely Mediterranean look to it, which seems more than a little incongruous, given its volatile central European climate.

The central **Markt** features a fountain dedicated to Mars, an old pharmacy and a number of Baroque and Rococo mansions. To the east, it merges seamlessly with

Rathausplatz, dominated by the **Rathaus** itself, a Schinkel-designed reinterpretation of an Italian Renaissance *palazzo*. Beyond lies Neustadt, an enormous elongated open space. It has no fewer than three fountains: from south to north these respectively depict the Good Samaritan, Hercules and a group of swans. The **Marstall** in the middle of the square was originally a sixteenth-century warehouse for storing salt, but was transformed into stables a couple of centuries later, when the colossal mansard roof was added.

To the north of the Markt is the **Johanniskirche**, whose present sombre Neoclassical aspect, with a grand facade and a high, flat-ceilinged interior, is due to plans provided by Schinkel. Its **tower** (May–Oct Mon–Fri noon–5pm, Sat & Sun 1–5pm; DM3/€1.50) commands a fine view over the town. Across from the church stands the oldest of the town's surviving houses, the sixteenth-century **Dornspachhaus**, named after the burgomaster who lived there.

Further to the northeast is Klosterplatz, named after the Franciscan friary that now houses the **Stadtmuseum** (Tues–Sun 10am–noon & 2–5pm; DM3/€1.50). The cellars, with an intact drinking well and a frightening display of torture instruments, are the highlight of the displays. On the same square are the town's finest fountain, the **Grüner Born**, which shelters under an imposing wrought-iron canopy, and a gabled Renaissance mansion, the **Heffterhaus**.

At the extreme northeastern edge of the Altstadt is the **Kreuzkirche**, a fine example of the distinctive Bohemian Gothic style. This is the new home of the town's greatest artistic treasures, two **Lenten embroideries** which, until their recent restoration, had not been on public view for over sixty years. Woven for the medieval Johanniskirche, the larger dates from 1472 and forms a complete illustrated Bible with ninety different scenes; the smaller was made 101 years later.

Practicalities

The **Hauptbahnhof** lies due north of the centre, and Bahnhofstrasse and Bautzener Strasse will lead you towards the Markt via the Johanniskirche. Zittau's **tourist office** (Mon–Fri 8am–6pm, Sat 9am–1pm, Sun 10am–1pm; ☎0 35 83/75 21 37, fax 75 21 61, *www.zittau.de*) is in the Rathaus, Markt 1. Here you can book a **private room** (①–②) in town or in a nearby village. Alternatively, there are several **hotels**, including: *Bergschlösschen*, Kummersberg 8 (☎0 35 83/51 07 17; ③); *Riedel*, Friedensstr. 23 (☎0 35 83/68 60; ③); *Dresdner Hof*, Äussere Oybiner Str. 9 (☎0 3583/5 73 00; ④); *Schwarzer Bär*, Ottokarplatz 12 (☎0 35 83/55 10; ④); *Zum Weberhof*, Äussere Weberstr. 46 (☎0 35 83/5 73 70; ④–⑥); and *Drei Ländereck*, Bautzner Str. 9 (☎0 35 83/55 00; ⑤). Each of these hotels has a reasonably priced **restaurant**. Other places to eat are *Klosterstübl*, Johannisstr. 4, *Stadtkrug*, Markt 8, *Zum Schwaben*, Innere Weberstr. 11, and *Gewandhauskeller*, Rathausplatz 14.

Into the Zittau mountains by steam train

Most visitors to Zittau come to ride the Bimmelbahn, a **narrow-gauge steam rail line** which travels from the Hauptbahnhof into the mountains to the south. This was earmarked for closure a few months before the *Wende*, as a seam of lignite, the GDR's favourite but most environmentally damaging fuel, was discovered in the area. National unification won it a reprieve.

After 9km, there's a fork in the Bimmelbahn at Bertsdorf; one part of the train continues a further 3km south to **KURORT OYBIN**, a quiet little health resort centred on the **Bergkirche**, a perfectly preserved example of Baroque at its most rustic. Towering above the village is **Berg Oybin** (daily: May–Aug 9am–6pm; Sept–April 9am–4pm; DM4/€2), on which stand a ruined castle and monastery founded by Emperor Charles

IV in his capacity as king of Bohemia, and built by masons of the great Parler workshop of Prague, but destroyed by lightning in the sixteenth century. A great deal of the monastic church still survives; given its semi-overgrown appearance and theatrical backdrop, it's hardly surprising that it was a favourite subject with painters of the Romantic movement. There are plenty of **private rooms** (①–②) in the village, plus a fine **hotel**, *Zum Berg Oybin*, Friedrich-Engels-Str. 34 (☎03 58 44/73 20; ⑤), which also has a good restaurant. Another possibility is *Zum Hochwaldblick*, Kammstr. 13 (☎03 58 44/71 60; ⑤), in the incorporated village of Lückendorf, just over 1km to the east.

The other section of the Bimmelbahn branches 4km southwest from Bertsdorf to **KURORT JONSDORF**. It's far less attractive than its neighbour but has a pretty open-air theatre, and is an equally good base for **hiking** in the range, which is peppered with marked trails. There's a wide choice of **private rooms** (①–②), and a **youth hostel** at Hainstr. 14 (☎03 58 44/7 21 30, fax 7 21 31; DM22/€11 or DM27/€13.50).

Gross-Schönau

The lovely village of **GROSS-SCHÖNAU** lies in the valley of the River Mandau immediately below the Zittau mountains; it's about 9km northwest of Jonsdorf and can be reached by mainline train from Zittau. For centuries, weaving was the foundation of the local economy, with the production of damask a speciality. A surprisingly entertaining **Damask- und Heimatmuseum** (May–Oct Tues–Sun 9am–noon & 2–5pm; Nov–April Mon–Fri 9am–4pm; DM4/€2) has been set up in the early nineteenth-century mansion of a factory owner overlooking the river at Schenaustr. 3. In addition to demonstrations of the old looms (with explanations in English on request), you can also see displays on the folklore of the region.

Gross-Schönau has a fine ensemble of historic houses, including the best examples of a vernacular style of building peculiar to Upper Lusatia, a hybrid between half-timbering and wood panelling known as an *Umgebindehaus*. The Gaststätte next to the museum is a recommendable place to **eat**. **Private rooms** (①–②) are particularly cheap here, while the only **campsite** (☎03 58 41/24 93) in the Zittau mountains is located by an artificial lake a couple of kilometres out of town on the road to Jonsdorf.

Görlitz

GÖRLITZ, the largest town of Upper Lusatia and Germany's easternmost point, lies 45km east of Bautzen and 34km north of Zittau. Travelling by train from the latter has a certain curiosity value: the line threads its way along the Neisse valley, skipping from one bank to the other and therefore in and out of Poland. One of the consequences of the Oder–Neisse border was that Görlitz found itself divided between two countries – the historic part of the city lies on the west bank and therefore remained German, while the suburbs opposite became the Polish town of Zgorzelec.

Perhaps that's an appropriate fate for a true central European city which doesn't easily fit into any nationalist framework. Slav by origin, Görlitz has been dominated by Germans since the thirteenth century, but belonged to Bohemia for much of its history. It fell to Saxony in the Thirty Years War; following its annexation by Prussia in 1815, it was incorporated into Silesia, and now stands as one of the few reminders of a province that the Germans have finally accepted is lost to them forever.

The Town

Wartime damage to Görlitz, whose ensemble of Renaissance and Baroque houses is unsurpassed in Germany, was minimal. The Communist authorities put the entire city centre under a preservation order; thus, though it has suffered badly from pollution, it will no doubt soon be restored to its original beauty.

Marienplatz at the southern end of the Altstadt is dominated by the very blackened **Frauenkirche**, the late Gothic church of the former hospital and poorhouse, whose most notable feature is the double portal topped by an Annunciation group. Close by is the **Karstadt-Warenhaus**, a large Jugendstil department store which survives as an intact period piece, both in its statue-lined exterior, and in its steel-framed galleried interior. Just to the north, the **Dicker Turm** (Fat Tower) is a cylindrical structure of the early fourteenth century, adorned with a prominent sandstone relief of Görlitz's coat of arms and crowned by a graceful Renaissance cupola.

Following either of the alleys to the left, you come to Demianiplatz, the first in a row of three squares at the heart of the town. On the south side is the Neoclassical **Gerhard-Hauptmann-Theater**, which takes its present name from the Nobel Prize-winning Realist writer. His intense early drama *The Weavers*, set against the background of a heroic but inevitably futile mid-nineteenth-century uprising by the Silesian weavers against the mill owners, was a theatrical sensation, gaining its reputation as the first "Socialist" play by having a collective rather than a single hero.

The west side of the square is framed by the **Kaisertrutz** (May–Oct Tues–Sun 10am–5pm; DM3/€1.50), a circular double bastion from the mid-nineteenth century, encasing its fifteenth-century predecessor. Inside is part of the local museum, including sections on medieval religious art, Upper Lusatian painters of the last two centuries and the history of the city, though the curious building is itself the main attraction. The original formed a defensive pair with the tall **Reichenbacher Turm** (same hours, DM3/€1.50) opposite, whose lower storey, culminating in the sentry gallery, dates back to the fourteenth century. The cylindrical upper section was added a hundred years later, and the whole finally topped off with a Baroque turret. A collection of arms and armour is housed inside; you can also climb to the summit for a fine view over the city.

Demianiplatz opens out to the east into the long oblong **Obermarkt**, the main market square, which is lined with a colourful array of Baroque houses. At the northeastern corner stands the **Dreifaltigkeitskirche**, formerly the church of a Franciscan friary. Its splendidly musty interior has several fine late Gothic furnishings, including a set of richly carved choir stalls, a touching *Holy Sepulchre* and a carved retable to the Virgin. Underneath the **Mönch** (Monk), as the church's tall, curiously thin-looking tower is popularly known, is the **Kunstbrunnen**, a Renaissance figure bearing the arms of electoral Saxony. Bruderstrasse, which prolongs the Obermarkt to the east, is lined with some of the town's finest mansions, including the **Schönhof** at no. 8, the work of Wendel Roskopf, the leading local architect of the Renaissance period.

Downhill is the **Untermarkt**, one of Germany's most imposing squares, which is built up in the middle, on the normal central European model. Best of the many mansions are nos. 2–5, late Gothic and early Renaissance, along the south side, which are collectively known as the **Lange Laube**. They belonged to the richest merchants and officials, and characteristically have bright vaulted entrance halls. It's particularly worth peeking into no. 5, whose original murals have survived. Also of special note are the Renaissance **Ratsapotheke** at no. 24, with its elaborate sundial; the **Flüsterbogen** (Whispering Arch) at no. 22; the large **Waage** (Weigh House) in the central block; and the early Baroque **Alte Börse**, the merchant's hall.

The **Städtisches Museum** (Tues–Sun 10am–5pm; DM3/€1.50) occupies a Baroque mansion just off the east side of Untermarkt at Neiss-Str. 30. It displays fine and decorative arts from the Renaissance to Biedermeier, along with material on Upper Lusatian folklore, and documentation on **Jakob Böhme**, the city's most distinguished son, the man regarded as both the first true German philosopher and the last of the medieval mystics and alchemists. Alongside at no. 29 is one of Görlitz's most unusual buildings, the **Biblisches Haus**; it dates from about 1570 and is adorned with little reliefs of scenes from the Old and New Testaments – a sure sign that the Reformation had taken root here, as religious depictions had hitherto been banned from secular buildings. Peterstrasse, which leads north from Untermarkt, is another impressive street; take a look inside no. 14, whose amazing stairway seems to defy gravity.

At the end of Peterstrasse is the **Peterskirche**, a five-aisled Flamboyant Gothic hall church with whitewashed exterior walls, a sturdy pair of towers crowned by fantastical nineteenth-century steeples, and a crypt which is itself of church-like dimensions. To the south side, the thirteenth-century **Renthaus** is the oldest house in the city; the terrace beyond preserves remnants of the former walls and commands a view over the Neisse to Poland. A few minutes' walk to the northeast lies the **Nikolaifriedhof**, a hillside cemetery with many elaborate tombstones, including that of Jakob Böhme.

East along Steinweg, you come to Görlitz's most intriguing sight, the **Heiliges Grab** (guided tours normally Wed, Sat & Sun at 11.30am, but it's advisable to enquire first at the tourist office; donation expected). The only complete and reasonably authentic medieval reproduction of the Holy Places of Jerusalem, it was built by Georg Emmerich, a rich young citizen of Görlitz. Prevented from marrying the girl of his choice, he went on pilgrimage to the Holy Land, where he made plans of the biblical sites which he commissioned Conrad Pflüger, the architect of the Peterskirche, to build on a site meant to resemble the Garden of Gethsemane. The visit begins with the **Kapelle zum Heiligen Kreuz**, a two-storey chapel whose crypt is named in honour of Adam, the upper part after Golgotha, symbolizing the tradition that Christ was crucified on the site of Adam's grave. Alongside is the tiny **Salbhaus**, behind whose wrought-iron gates is a sculpture of the Virgin Mary lamenting over Jesus' dead body. Finally comes the **Grabkapelle**, which is of special interest as being a far more accurate, if miniaturized, version of the original, than its much-altered counterpart in Jerusalem. It's an elegant building in its own right; particularly outstanding is the turret, a skilful fusion of European and Middle Eastern architecture.

Practicalities

Görlitz's **Hauptbahnhof** lies southwest of the Altstadt; from there, it's only a ten-minute walk straight ahead to Marienplatz. The **tourist office** (Mon–Fri 10am–6pm, Sat 10am–4pm, Sun 10am–1pm; ☎0 35 81/4 75 70, fax 47 57 27, *www.goerlitz.de*) occupies a handsome Baroque mansion at Obermarkt 29.

There are plenty of **private rooms** (②–③) on offer. Additionally, there are several inexpensive **pensions**, including three with a central location: *Drehscheibe*, Landeskronstr. 26 (☎0 35 81/31 41 49; ③); *Haus Wiesbaden*, Schulstr. 7 (☎0 35 81/42 08 50; ③); and *Destille*, Nikolaistr. 6 (☎40 53 02; ④). A good spread of **hotels** can likewise be found in the heart of town: *Goldener Engel*, Hugo-Keller-Str. 1 (☎0 35 81/40 33 37; ④); *Zum Klötzelmönch*, which occupies a Baroque palace at Fleischerstr. 3 (☎0 35 81/4 75 80; ⑤); and *Sorat*, in a Jugendstil mansion at Struvestr. 1 (☎0 35 81/40 65 77, *www.sorat-hotels.com*; ⑦). In the Südstadt, on the opposite side of the rail tracks from the city centre, are two more grand hotels: *Silesia*, Biesnitzer Str. 11 (☎0 35 81/4 81 00; ⑤), and *Zum Grafen Zeppelin*, Jauernicker Str. 15–16 (☎0 35 81/40 52 12; ⑥). Also in this area is the **youth hostel**, which occupies a spectacular Jugendstil villa at Goethestr. 17 (☎ & fax 0 35 81/40 65 10; DM22/€11 or DM27/€13.50).

Restaurants can be found in all the hotels listed above, with *Goldener Strauss* in the *Sorat* being perhaps the pick of the bunch. Also very fine, and very traditional, is the one attached to the *Destille* pension. The main **cultural** venues are the abovementioned Gerhard-Hauptmann-Theater, Demianiplatz 2 (☎0 35 81/47 47 47), which puts on a varied programme of drama, ballet, opera and musicals, and the Stadthalle, Am Stadtpark 1 (☎0 35 81/4 75 00), where concerts are held.

travel details

Trains

Chemnitz to: Annaberg-Buchholz (10 daily; 2hr); Freiberg (every 30min; 50min); Rochlitz (5 daily; 1hr 15min); Zwickau (hourly; 1hr).

Dresden to: Bad Schandau (every 30min; 1hr); Bautzen (hourly; 1hr); Chemnitz (hourly; 1hr 30min); Freiberg (every 30min; 50min); Görlitz (hourly; 2hr); Leipzig (hourly; 2hr); Meissen (every 30min; 45min); Pirna (every 30min; 30min); Zittau (10 daily; 2hr).

Görlitz to: Bautzen (hourly; 1hr); Zittau (10 daily; 1hr).

Leipzig to: Chemnitz (15 daily; 1hr 30min/2hr); Colditz (10 daily; 1hr 20min); Plauen (15 daily; 2hr); Rochlitz (10 daily; 1hr 40min); Torgau (frequent; 1hr); Zwickau (hourly; 1hr 30min).

Zwickau to: Plauen (hourly; 1hr).

THE
CONTEXTS

THE HISTORICAL FRAMEWORK

To think of a continuous German history is impossible, since there was no single nation called Germany until 1871, and even then it was not strictly speaking a country, but an empire made up of a number of sovereign states. Nevertheless, a recognizable German culture can be traced through the history of a large and disparate group of territories and traditions.

THE BEGINNINGS

From around the eighth century BC, the bulk of present-day Germany was inhabited by **Celtic peoples**, who established the first permanent settlements. Warlike, nomadic **Germanic tribes** gradually appeared further north and began pushing their way into the Celtic lands. Their loose structure later made them awkward opponents of the expanding **Roman Empire**, which decided to use the natural boundaries of the rivers Rhine and Danube as the limit of their territory: attempts to push eastwards were finally abandoned after a crushing defeat in the Teutoburg Forest in 9 AD.

A number of towns founded by the Romans – Trier, Regensburg, Augsburg, Mainz and Cologne – were to be the main bases of urban settlement for the next millennium. **Christianity** was introduced under Emperor Constantine, and a bishopric (the first north of the Alps) was established in Trier in 314.

At the beginning of the fifth century Germany was overrun by the Huns, an action which precipitated the indigenous Saxons into invading England. Gradually the **Franks**, who had been based in what is now Belgium, began to assert themselves over the other Germanic peoples, particularly towards the end of the fifth century under King Clovis, who established the **Merovingian** dynasty and built up a powerful Rhenish state. In time, the Merovingians were supplanted by their former henchmen, the **Carolingians**, with the help of papal support. The new dynasty was bent on expansion, and saw the benefits of involving the Church in its plans. Missionaries – the most influential of whom was the English-born St Boniface – were recruited to undertake mass conversion campaigns among rival tribes.

Under **Charlemagne**, who succeeded to the throne in 768, the fortunes of the Franks went from strength to strength. A series of campaigns saw them stretch their power base from the North Sea to Rome, and from the Pyrenees to the River Elbe. In the context of Western Europe, only Britain plus the southern parts of Spain and Italy lay beyond their control. A power-sharing structure for Europe, in which the pope and the king of the Germans would be the dominant forces, was agreed. On Christmas Day 800, Charlemagne was anointed emperor in Rome, giving him the official status of heir to the Caesars. Though the name was only coined much later, this brought into existence the concept of the **Holy Roman Empire of the German Nation**, which was to last for the next thousand years. This gave the German king considerable power over Italian internal affairs, while the Church's influence in matters of state was similarly assured.

When Charlemagne died, however, the empire began to crack because of its very size. In 843, by the **Treaty of Verdun**, it was split into a Germanic Eastern Europe and a Latin Western Europe, thus sharply delineating the French and Germans for the first time. The first king of the newly formed German eastern empire was **Ludwig the German**. Under his rule the Germanic people became more closely defined, with a specific culture of their own – still with many disparate regions but recognizably made up of the same peoples. When the last of Charlemagne's descendants died in 911, rulership passed to the Saxon King Henry the Fowler, bringing the Carolingian era to an end.

THE BUILDING OF A NEW EMPIRE

In the mid-tenth century the second Saxon monarch, **Otto the Great**, was faced with the problem of the growing power of the hereditary duchies which posed a threat to the unity of the empire. In order to curb this, he strengthened his alliance with the papacy. The Church was given grants of land, coupled with temporal powers of jurisdiction over them, thus creating the basis for subsequent ecclesiastical dominance over much of the country by a large number of prince-bishoprics and imperial monasteries and convents. In 962, he was crowned **Holy Roman Emperor**, firmly establishing himself as the main ruler in the Christian world. In many respects, this marks a second foundation of the curious dichotomy that characterized the Holy Roman Empire; from then on, only kings of Germany could gain the title of Roman Emperor, and it was only the pope who could grant this title.

Following a series of bitter **power struggles** between the papacy and the emperors, imperial interference in Church affairs was severely curtailed. So too was the centralized power of the emperor, as the nobility were released by the pope from their vows of allegiance to any secular authority. They soon made their own demands, the most important of which was that emperors should no longer be hereditary rulers, but elected by a council of princes.

By the twelfth century, most of the powerful **dynasties** which were to dominate German politics at both local and national level for hundreds of years to come had appeared. There was an intense feud between the two most powerful, the **Hohenstaufens** and **Welfs**, which was to continue for centuries, particularly in Italy. The Hohenstaufens, until they died out, managed to keep the upper hand, holding onto the office of Holy Roman Emperor for well over a century. **Frederick Barbarossa**, best known as an enthusiastic crusader in the Holy Land, was their most successful ruler.

By the mid-thirteenth century the nation's boundaries began to be pushed increasingly eastwards, following a policy begun by Otto the Great. Impetus for this came from many sources, being particularly associated with the **Knights of the Teutonic Order**, who turned their attentions towards the Christianization of

Eastern Europe. By the early fourteenth century, they had conquered much of the Baltic (notably the area known as Prussia) and repopulated the land with German peasants. Subsequently, they grew rich on their control of the highly profitable grain trade.

THE MIDDLE AGES

In the fourteenth century, a number of significant changes were made to the structure of the Holy Roman Empire. The **Golden Bull** of 1356 finally established the method for choosing the monarch. This fixed the electoral college at the traditional number of seven, with three **Electors** drawn from the ecclesiastical sphere (the archbishops of Cologne, Mainz and Trier) and four from different ranks of the nobility (the King of Bohemia, the Duke of Saxony, the Margrave of Brandenburg and the Count Palatine of the Rhine).

From then on, these seven princes were tremendously powerful grandees – they had the right to construct castles, mint their own coinage, impose tolls and act as judges in all disputes, with no right of appeal. Oddly enough, the title of emperor almost invariably went to a candidate outside this group. Increasingly, it was conferred on a member of the **Habsburg** dynasty, who had built up Austria into the most powerful of the German states.

The papacy's residual power over internal German affairs was killed off by the **Great Schism** of 1378–1417, when rival popes held court in Rome and Avignon. By this time, the social structure was undergoing changes that had far-reaching effects. The most important was the growth of **towns** at strategic points and along important trading routes. Initially, these were under patrician control. However, merchants and craftsmen organized themselves into guilds which gradually wrested control of civic life and laid the foundations for a capitalist economy.

Most important towns gained the status of **Free Imperial City**, which meant they were independent city-states, responsible only to the emperor. Their prosperity was greatly enhanced by the ruinous Hundred Years War between France and England, which enabled them to snap up diverted trade to and from the Mediterranean. Though in many ways in competition with each other, the leadership of the towns realized they also had common cause.

This led to the foundation of various trading and defence leagues. Of particular importance was the north German **Hanseatic League**, founded in Lübeck, which successfully combated piracy, and led not only to German economic domination of the Baltic and North Sea, but to increased political power as well, with the establishment of German communities in Scandinavia and all along the opposite coast as far as Estonia.

The **bubonic plague** swept Europe in the fourteenth century, wiping out a quarter of the German population. In all probability, the plague was introduced by merchants returning from Asia, but a different scapegoat had to be found, and the **Jews**, who lived in segregated settlements around the towns, readily fitted the bill. Jews had lived in Europe since the tenth century, but their place had never been an easy one, with their close-knit and separate communities giving rise to popular suspicion and prejudice. Excluded from guilds and trades, they took up the only occupation forbidden to Christians: money-lending – a service that did nothing to endear them to the locals. **Pogroms** therefore frequently occurred.

The fifteenth century saw the Habsburgs establish themselves firmly as the driving force in high politics, holding onto the office of Holy Roman Emperor almost continuously from 1432 until its abolition nearly four hundred years later. **Maximilian I** acceded to the title in 1493, and embarked on a policy of making his family the most powerful not just in Germany, but in all of Europe. His own wedding to Mary of Burgundy gained him the Netherlands; a series of astute dynastic marriages involving his relatives led to Spain, Hungary and Bohemia all coming under Habsburg control. However, he antagonized the members of the Swiss Confederation, which broke away from the empire to become a separate state in 1499.

THE REFORMATION AND AFTER

In order to cash in on popular fear, the Church demanded money from the faithful to ensure salvation of their souls, and a lucrative trade in **indulgences** was established, whereby people could buy absolution of their sins. Bishops across the land acted as agents, and the papal coffers filled up to finance the building of St Peter's in Rome and many other great sacred buildings. Discontent with the Church was par-

ticularly widespread in Germany, given the Church's dual role within society and the fact that territories under the control of religious office-holders tended to be particularly harshly run. Thus it was hardly surprising that it was here that the full-frontal assault on the Church's traditional powers began.

The attack was led by a man of burning religious convictions, the Augustinian monk **Martin Luther**, who had been appointed Professor of Theology at the University of Wittenberg. Believing that the Church was corrupt and had lost its way totally, Luther focused his attentions on the problem of **salvation**, finding in the Bible that Man justifies himself by faith alone. This meant that he could play no part in his own salvation; therefore the trade in indulgences was a total fraud. On the eve of All Saints' Day, 1517, he nailed his **95 theses** to the door of the Schlosskirche in Wittenberg. This was in fact the normal way of inviting academic discussion, but it was seen as a deliberately provocative act and is now considered the official **beginning of the Reformation**.

In time Luther widened his attack, denouncing the centralized power of the pope, the privileged position of priests as intercessors between God and the faithful, and the doctrine of transubstantiation, which maintained that the bread and wine used in the sacrament of the Eucharist physically turned into Christ's body and blood.

However, Luther's arguments might have had as little impact as any other scholarly dispute, or led to his immediate execution as a heretic, had not the curious power structure in Germany dealt him an amazing piece of good fortune. The death of Maximilian I in 1519 led to a bizarre **Europe-wide power struggle** for the crown of the Holy Roman Empire. Francis I of France decided to stake a claim for the title, in order to stop the unhealthy concentration of power which would ensue if victory went to the Habsburg candidate, Charles I of Spain. In order to stop this interference from abroad, the pope had to keep the Electors sweet, even suggesting one of their number, Luther's patron Elector Frederick the Wise of Saxony, as a compromise candidate.

After much bribery by the two main contenders, the Spanish king won the election unanimously and took office as Emperor Charles V. However, he immediately became embroiled in a war with France. As a result, the powerful princes of the Holy Roman Empire seized this chance to establish a far greater degree of independence. Many of them saw the religious struggle as a convenient cloak for their ambitions. Luther was excommunicated in 1520, but still had the right, as a citizen of the empire, to have a hearing before an Imperial Diet. This was hastily convened at Worms the following year, and, though Luther was branded an outlaw and his books were ordered to be burned, he was given a safe haven at the Wartburg outside Eisenach, under the protection of Elector Frederick. There he **translated the Bible into German**, thus making it accessible to the common man for the first time; this work is also seen as the foundation stone of the modern German language.

Luther's ideas spread like wildfire throughout society, greatly aided by the fact that books could now be produced cheaply and quickly, thanks to the printing revolution launched by the German inventor **Johannes Gutenberg** during the previous century. They found a ready market among the oppressed classes, who took the attacks on Church authority as invitations to attack authority in general.

This formed one of the causes of the **Peasants' War** of 1524–25, which brought wholesale destruction of monasteries and castles. Poorly armed, organized and led, it was brutally crushed by the princely armies. To the dismay of the rebels, Luther aligned himself on the side of worldly authority, arguing that it was God's will that there should be different strata in society; equality was only for the hereafter. Thus, the Reformation progressed as a revolution controlled from above, setting the tone for German history for centuries to come.

In 1529, the representatives of six principalities and fourteen Free Imperial Cities which supported Luther met at Speyer, where the name **Protestant** came to be used for the first time. The following year, Charles V convened a Diet at Augsburg in an attempt to defuse the growing crisis. However, he was confronted by a closely argued definition of the Reformers' position, thereafter known as the **Confession of Augsburg**, which was drawn up by Luther's lieutenant, the brilliant scholar Philipp Melanchthon. This set the seal not only on the division of the Western Church, but also on the effective division of Germany into a multitude of small states.

So many states had joined the Protestant cause by 1555 that Charles V had to admit defeat, abdicating in order to retire to a Spanish monastery. He was succeeded by his brother Ferdinand, who almost immediately signed the **Peace of Augsburg**, a historic agreement that institutionalized religious tolerance, leaving the decision as to the form of religion practised in each state firmly in the hands of its secular rulers. Though a measure of considerable significance, it was in effect a carve-up between the Catholics and Lutherans at the expense of more radical Protestant groups.

THE STRUGGLE FOR RELIGIOUS SUPREMACY

After Luther's death in 1546, the Catholics began to make something of a comeback after the reforms thrashed out at the Council of Trent launched the **Counter-Reformation**. Radical Protestantism was also given a fillip by Melanchthon's shift away from central Lutheran doctrines to more extreme solutions. Inevitably, one of the political goals of Protestantism was to gain control of the imperial electoral college, and oust the Catholic Habsburgs from their long tradition of pre-eminence.

Bavaria's annexation of the predominantly Protestant free city of Donauwörth in 1608 led to the formation of the **Protestant Union**, an armed alliance under the leadership of the Palatinate. The **Catholic League** was set up in opposition by the Bavarians the following year, meaning that there was now a straight division of the country into two hostile camps. Meanwhile, the way central authority in Germany had collapsed was cruelly exposed by the weak 36-year reign of Rudolf II, who chose to govern from Prague, at the very fringe of the empire. There he presided over a bizarre court filled with astrologers and alchemists, until his growing insanity led to his deposition in 1611.

As it happened, this same city was to see the beginning of the great trial of strength between the two faiths. In 1618, the youthful Count Palatine Friedrich V usurped the crown of Bohemia, which itself was an elected office, thus seemingly ensuring a Protestant majority in the next imperial election. Unfortunately for him, he lost both his titles a year later, and had by then set in train the complicated series of religious and dynastic conflicts commonly known as the **Thirty Years War**.

Much of the German countryside was laid waste, towns were pillaged, and there was mass rape and slaughter, at the end of which the total population of the country may have been reduced by as much as a third. Initially, the Catholic League, commanded by the brutal Johann Tilly, held the upper hand, but first Denmark, then Sweden intervened, fearing for both their independence and their Protestant faith. The Swedes, led by King Gustavus II Adolphus, had their greatest moment of triumph on the European stage, defeating Tilly and over-running the country, thus rising to the rank of a major power. Spain intervened on behalf of its Habsburg cousins, while Catholic France supported the Protestants, on the grounds that their faith was a lesser evil than the threatened Habsburg hegemony.

From 1643, concerted attempts were made to end the war, with the Catholics meeting in Münster, the Protestants in Osnabrück. The negotiations are generally seen as the beginnings of modern diplomacy; they culminated five years later in the signing of the **Peace of Westphalia**. While the ending of the messy conflicts was a major achievement in itself, for Germany the peace treaty was as disastrous as the war itself; the Holy Roman Empire was killed off in all but name, with the emperor reduced to a figurehead.

Real power was diffused among a **plethora of states**, numbering some three hundred principalities, plus over a thousand other territories, some of them minute — a system which could hardly have been better designed to waste resources and stunt economic and political development. Germany ceased to be a factor of importance on the European stage.

THE RISE OF PRUSSIA

In the course of the late seventeenth and eighteenth century, almost all the petty German princes adopted an **absolutist** system of government, based on the divine right of rulers. They spent a vast amount of their revenue building palaces on a scale out of all proportion to their needs, to create at least the visual pretence that they were mighty monarchs. Only a few managed to rise above the general level of mediocrity; one of these was the House of Welf, which made an astonishing comeback after centuries of confinement to its Lower Saxon heartlands. As a result of clever politicking, the

Hanoverian branch of the family gained the British crown in 1714 and maintained a royal union until 1837.

Within the Holy Roman Empire itself, **Austria** at first maintained her dominance, with the Habsburgs holding on to the imperial title, for what it was worth. The country received a severe jolt when the Turks reached the gates of Vienna in 1683, but after the enemy was beaten back, the way was cleared for Austria to build up an empire in the Balkans. As German-speaking influence spread eastwards, so the western flank became vulnerable. The **French**, like the Romans before them, saw the Rhine as the natural limit of their territory. They formally annexed Alsace and Strasbourg in 1681, then laid claim to the Palatinate in a series of bloody campaigns between 1688 and 1697.

By then, a new power had arisen in northeastern Germany in the shape of **Brandenburg-Prussia**. In 1411, the old frontier district of Brandenburg was given to the ambitious **Hohenzollern** family, whose attempts to gain power at the heart of the empire had met with no success. Since 1525, the family had also held the Baltic territory known as Prussia, which lay outside the Holy Roman Empire and thus was not subject to any of its rules. One of these forbade princes from promoting themselves to royal titles: in 1701, Friedrich III defied this with impunity by having himself crowned as King of Prussia. The Habsburgs duly turned a blind eye to this in order to gain Hohenzollern support in the **War of the Spanish Succession**, which broke out as a result of rival Austrian and French claimants for the throne of Spain.

Throughout the eighteenth century, Prussia was built up as a strongly centralized state, based in Berlin. There was a tight administrative structure, but it became associated above all with **militarism**. It was a second Sparta, described with some justification as not a state with an army, but an army with a state: at times, two-thirds of national revenue was spent on the military. The other dominant force in society was the **Junker** class, landowners who ran huge estates in which the labourers were treated as little more than serfs.

Prussia's rise to the rank of a major European power was achieved under **Frederick the Great**, who came to the throne in 1740. A Francophile and epitome of the enlightened despot, Frederick softened his country's rough-hewn image by introducing a few liberal reforms at home, and developed a cultured courtly life. However, his main concern was expansion by military force, and he used an old Brandenburg claim on one of the tiny Silesian principalities to extract most of Silesia from Austria. In revenge, the Habsburgs launched the Seven Years War in 1756, thereby hoping to annihilate Prussia as a potential rival; in this, they had the full military backing of the two other great continental powers, France and Russia, whereas Frederick had only the tacit support of Britain and Hannover to fall back on.

Within three years, the highly rated Prussian troops seemed to have overreached themselves. They were given an unexpected reprieve when the Austrians and Russians fell out; new recruits were thrown into the conflict, eventually achieving an incredible turn-around in fortunes, in the process establishing Prussia as a force of the first rank. By annexing much of Poland in the partition of 1772, Frederick achieved his aim of establishing a north German version of Austria.

THE NAPOLEONIC PERIOD AND ITS AFTERMATH

Ironically, the first steps towards unifying Germany came as a result of the expansionist aims of revolutionary France. By the War of the First Coalition of 1792–97, the left bank of the Rhine fell under French control. However, it was only with the advent of the dictator **Napoleon Bonaparte** that radical changes were made. Following the defeat of Austria in 1802 in the War of the Second Coalition (in which Prussia tactfully remained aloof), he decided to completely reorder the German map, which he rightly saw as anachronistic. All but four of the free cities (Frankfurt, Bremen, Hamburg and Lübeck), and every single one of the ecclesiastical territories, were stripped of their independence, which in many cases went back five or six centuries.

Napoleon created a series of buffer states: Bavaria, Württemberg and Saxony were raised to the rank of kingdoms, while Baden and Hesse-Darmstadt became grand duchies. In 1806, during the War of the Third Coalition, the Holy Roman Empire was officially abolished with the Habsburgs consoling themselves for suffering yet another defeat by promoting themselves from archdukes to emperors of Austria,

deciding thereafter to concentrate their energies on preserving their Balkan lands. Gradually the German satellite states began to remove economic, religious and servile restrictions, developing into societies which were liberal by German standards.

The same year, Prussia suffered a series of humiliating defeats; Berlin was occupied and the country forced to sign away half its territory and population. Thereafter, it was made to mend its ways: serfdom was abolished, and its cities were allowed to develop their own municipal government. In the event, Prussia's humiliation was short-lived, and it soared in international prestige as a result of its key role at the **Battle of Waterloo** in 1815, when Napoleon's overambitious plans for the total subjugation of Europe were finally put to rest.

The **Congress of Vienna**, which met the same year to determine the structure of post-Napoleonic Europe, established Prussian dominance in German affairs. Westphalia and the Rhineland were added to its territories, meaning that it now stretched all the way from the French border to the River Memel, interrupted only by a few enclaves. Otherwise, much of the Napoleonic reorganization of the Holy Roman Empire was ratified, with Hannover added to the list of kingdoms. In all 39 independent states were left – still far too many, but a major step forward nonetheless. A German Confederation was established, with each state represented in the Frankfurt-based Diet, which, however, had no effective power.

TOWARDS GERMAN UNIFICATION

Whereas the main political forces in German society in the aftermath of the Congress of Vienna were still staunchly conservative, the accelerating **Industrial Revolution** was resulting in radical economic and social changes. This closely followed the British lead, but profited by learning from the pioneering country's mistakes. The first German railway was established in 1835, and industrial production advanced in leaps and bounds. Thanks to its rich mineral deposits, the dominant centre for industry was the Rhine-Ruhr area, which had recently been allocated to Prussia. In 1834, Prussia's increasingly dominant role within the German nation was underlined by the establishment of a customs union, known as the **Zollverein**.

The Industrial Revolution led to a whole **new social order**, with wage-earning workers and an emergent bourgeoisie. Both groups were quick to agitate for their interests – the workers for better working conditions and the bourgeoisie for political representation. Meanwhile the large peasantry was still living in abject poverty and under almost feudal conditions, which pressed hard during the failed harvests of the late 1840s. Social unrest was inevitable, and violence erupted both in the countryside and the cities, causing ever more reactionary policies from the landowning elite with the political power.

In 1848, there were uprisings all over Europe. This forced the Prussian king to allow elections to the **National Assembly** in Frankfurt, thereby hoping to nip republican and socialist aspirations in the bud. For the first time, an opportunity was presented to found a liberal tradition in the country, but it was completely muffed. The bourgeois members of the Assembly were much too keen to establish the new-found status of their own social groups to attempt any far-reaching political reforms, and they certainly posed no threat to the existing order. Thus, when armed rebellions broke out in 1849, the National Assembly was exposed as an ineffective talking shop, easily disbanded in the face of the revolutionary emergency. Any steps towards constitutional rule were wiped out by the combined forces of the Prussian army and battalions from other German kingdoms and principalities.

The 1850s saw political stagnation, but the increasing success of the Industrial Revolution meant that the creation of a single internal German market, preferably accompanied by a political union, was of paramount importance. By now, Prussia had manoeuvred itself into a position of such power that it was the only possible agent for enforcing such a change.

In 1862, **King Wilhelm I** chose as his chancellor the career diplomat **Otto von Bismarck**, a member of the Junker class who had already gained a reputation as an operator of a rare sharpness. In order to win over the Prussian liberals, Bismarck backed the concept of universal male suffrage. He also played the nationalist card immediately: seeing that the chancellor was bent on creating a united Germany, the liberals muted their opposition and backed his plans for a thorough modernization of the army.

In 1864, Bismarck lured Austria into supporting him in a war against Denmark to recapture the lost duchies of Schleswig and Holstein. Having achieved an easy victory, he then provoked a disagreement over the spoils: the result was the **Seven Weeks War** of 1866, in which the superior Prussian weapons and organization achieved a crushing victory. Not only was Austria forced out of Germany's affairs, but those states which had remained neutral, including Hannover and Hesse-Kassel, were incorporated into Prussia. The German Confederation was dissolved, to be replaced by one covering the north of the country only, which was totally under Prussian domination.

To complete the jigsaw, Bismarck still needed to woo the southern states. His tactic was an original one: to provoke a war against the old enemy, France. In 1870, having carefully prepared the diplomatic ground to ensure that no other power would intervene to support the French, he goaded them by proposing that a Hohenzollern should succeed to the vacant throne of Spain. The French emperor, Napoleon III, managed to force the Prussians to withdraw, but foolishly sent a telegram asking for an apology. Bismarck doctored this to make it seem worse than it was, giving the excuse to begin the **Franco-Prussian War**.

By January 1871, the Prussian field guns had helped chalk up yet another easy victory. A united German empire, which once more included the long-disputed provinces of Alsace and Lorraine, was proclaimed in Versailles. King Wilhelm I of Prussia was the inevitable choice as Kaiser; three other kings were among the rulers who were henceforth subjugated to him. The new empire became known as the Second Reich, in honour of the fact that it had revived the German imperial tradition after a gap of 65 years.

THE SECOND REICH

In his domestic policy for the united Germany, Bismarck indulged in a series of **liberal reforms**. Uniform systems of law, administration and currency were introduced, an imperial bank was set up, restrictions on trade and movement of labour were lifted, and cities were given municipal autonomy.

By such measures, Bismarck aimed to control the opposition parties in the Reichstag and to keep power in the hands of the elite. The darker side of his nature came out in the **Kulturkampf**, which aimed at curbing the power of the Catholic Church, whose power and influence was anathema to the Protestant aristocracy of Prussia. However, this met with spirited opposition, which led to Bismarck making a rare retreat, though not until he had exacted his price: the Catholics were forced to support protectionist agricultural measures, designed to subsidize the large, outdated Junker estates. By then, a formidable new opposition had arisen in the shape of the **Social Democratic Party** (SPD), founded in 1875. In order to take the wind out of its sails, Bismarck introduced a system of welfare benefits for workers, a system belatedly copied in many other industrialized countries.

Bismarck's **foreign policy** involved a complicated set of jugglings. He set up the Dreikaiserbund, an alliance of the three great imperial powers of Germany, Austria and Russia; indulged in a Mediterranean naval alliance with Britain in order to check Russian designs on the Balkans; yet initiated a bit of colonial rivalry with the British.

Bismarck's awesome reputation for political sure-footedness meant that Germany's internal and external stability seemed completely safe in his hands. However, Friedrich III, who succeeded his father Wilhelm I in 1888, died after only a few months on the throne. His son, **Wilhelm II**, was a firm believer in the divine right of kings. He was of a generation which did not feel beholden to Bismarck, and strongly disliked the veteran politician. Two years later, he removed the chancellor from office – a move compared to dropping the pilot from a ship – and thereafter relied on a series of ineffective kowtowing men to lead his government.

Britain, which had hitherto been a natural ally of Germany as a result of dynastic ties and mutual suspicion of France, was increasingly seen as the main rival. A notorious telegram sent by the Kaiser in support of the Boers in 1896 signalled the beginning of a severe deterioration in relations between the two countries. This was fuelled by an **arms race**, affecting all of Europe, in which the Krupp armaments factory played a crucial role. Nowhere was the attempt to establish supremacy more evident than in the naval sphere, where the Germans set out to usurp Britain's long period of supremacy, achieving parity by 1909.

By this time, the major powers of Europe were divided into **two nervous alliances**. Bismarck's successors failed to maintain his two-faced foreign policy. As a result, Germany was bound up once more with Austria, whose eastern empire was tottering under the nationalist aspirations of the many ethnic groups contained within it; Italy was a somewhat reluctant partner. Ranged against them were France and Russia, drawn together by mutual fear of the ever-increasing power of the German-speaking countries. Britain, while maintaining its time-honoured policy of trying to preserve an effective balance of power in Europe, was increasingly drawn towards the latter alliance.

WORLD WAR I

Everybody expected that war would come sooner or later, and master strategies were carefully planned. The Germans developed the **first-strike theory**, which envisaged a quick knockout blow against both France and Russia, as a prelude to a tougher struggle against the more formidable British. Public opinion in the country was easily won over by the bogus theory that the Fatherland was under threat from the "iron ring" which surrounded it. Even the Social Democrats were persuaded of the necessity and desirability of a war.

The spark which lit the inferno happened to come in **Austria's unwieldy empire**. In 1914, the crown prince, Archduke Franz Ferdinand, was assassinated in Sarajevo by a Bosnian nationalist. Austria sent the independent neighbouring state of Serbia a threatening ultimatum, although no connection between the Serbian government and the conspirators was ever proved. This inevitably provoked the Russians, who had an agreement to protect their fellow Slavs from any threat. The German generals saw this as a golden opportunity to put their first-strike theory into operation. As soon as the Russians mobilized, German troops were sent to attack France. The quickest route was through Belgium, thus violating its neutrality, which was guaranteed by Britain. So fast did events move that the Kaiser sent a telegram ordering withdrawal, but this was ignored. **World War I** was thus under way.

The German High Command believed the French would capitulate within six weeks, the Russians within six months. They were soon proved hopelessly wrong, and found themselves with what they had been most anxious to avoid – a war on two fronts. Even then, they could hardly have anticipated the Armageddon which was unleashed. After rapidly advancing towards Paris, they were forced to retreat at the first Battle of the Marne in September, and dig **trenches** all across northern France and Belgium. This gave rise to a wholly new form of warfare, with casualties quite unlike any that had previously been known. In 1916, an attempt to exhaust the French at the four-month-long Battle of Verdun proved to be self-defeating, and the same year the British proved their continued mastery of the seas at the Battle of Jutland.

As a result of these setbacks, the Kaiser handed over effective military and political power to the dual leadership of Field Marshal **Paul von Hindenburg**, and his quartermaster-general, **Erich Ludendorff**; though the latter was nominally the junior partner, he became the effective dictator of the country. In January 1917, it was decided to introduce unrestricted submarine warfare. This was a complete disaster, its barbarity prompting the United States to enter the war. A reprieve was gained as a result of the revolution in Russia that autumn, which ended the fighting on the eastern front. This allowed the Germans to transfer large numbers of troops to the west, break through the Allied lines in February 1918, and advance deep into France.

THE END OF THE WAR; FAILURE OF THE GERMAN REVOLUTION

The euphoria of this triumph soon faded, however: the German lines became hopelessly overextended; captured Allied supply dumps showed the German troops how poorly provisioned they were by comparison; many soldiers from the east had acquired Communist views and were agitating against the war; and American troops were at last beginning to arrive in substantial numbers. On August 8, 1918 – the "Black Day of the German Army" – the Allies broke the German offensive and turned it into a rout. Finally convinced that the war was lost, Ludendorff looked about for ways to minimize the High Command's loss of face. He seized on the idea of letting a parliamentary government handle the **peace negotiations**; it would be likely to secure more lenient terms, and would also be a useful scapegoat in the event of a harsh treaty. Furthermore, it would

help counteract the far more horrifying alternative of a Bolshevik-style revolution, an only too real prospect once the German people realized the extent to which their leaders had been deceiving them.

Accordingly, he persuaded the Kaiser to appoint the liberal monarchist **Prince Max von Baden** as chancellor. A full parliamentary democracy was proclaimed; the cabinet was drawn from the ranks of the Reichstag, with Social Democrats included for the first time. On October 3, Prince Max sued for peace. Ludendorff, sensing that the Allies were going to drive a hard bargain, subsequently resigned; Hindenburg offered to do likewise, but was allowed to remain at his post.

Towards the end of the month, Admiral Scheer decided to mount a futile last-ditch offensive; his crews mutinied, refusing to lay down their lives so unnecessarily. This revolt spread throughout northern Germany and might well have developed into the full-scale revolution Ludendorff had been conniving to avert, had it not been for the bitter **division of the political left-wing** into three factions.

The SPD had previously split into two separate parties over the war; the pacifist group, the USPD, was now frustrated by the tepid nature of their erstwhile colleagues' socialism, which embraced constitutional monarchy and a bourgeois social order. In turn, their politics were seen as too tame by the Spartakist League, a Marxist group who aimed to follow the example of their Russian mentors by seizing power in Berlin. **Friedrich Ebert**, leader of the SPD, decided to forestall them by calling a general strike to demand the Kaiser's abdication. Prince Max took matters into his own hands by announcing this without the monarch's consent, and then himself resigned in favour of Ebert. Matters were still delicately poised with the news that **Karl Liebknecht** of the Spartakists intended to proclaim the establishment of a socialist republic on November 9.

In order to wrest the initiative, Ebert's lieutenant **Philipp Scheidemann** made an impromptu declaration of a free German Republic from the Reichstag balcony, thus bringing the regime of the Kaisers to an abrupt end. Two days later, an armistice was signed, as Ebert realized that either a collapse of military discipline, or the spread of Bolshevism, would lead to an Allied invasion. As part of his plans, he made a pact with the High Command, which provided him with an army to protect the state against internal left-wing opponents, but at the price of allowing it almost complete autonomy.

This policy paid immediate dividends for him, as the military was used to crush an attempted revolution by the Spartakists in January, a last-ditch attempt at a Communist seizure of power before the elections for the new National Assembly later in the month. The brutal behaviour of the army – Liebknecht and his co-leader Rosa Luxemburg were among those murdered – was to have disastrous long-term consequences for the fledgling republic, which should have made a purging of the anti-democratic and war-crazed officer class one of its most urgent priorities.

THE WEIMAR REPUBLIC

The elections confirmed the SPD as the new political leaders of the country, with 38 percent of the vote; as a result, Ebert was made president, with Scheidemann as chancellor. Initially, **Weimar**, the small country town which had seen the most glorious flowering of the German Enlightenment, was chosen as the seat of government in preference to Berlin, which was tinged by its monarchical and militaristic associations.

A **new constitution** was drawn up, hailed as the most liberal and progressive in the world. While on the surface an admirable document, this constitution was hopelessly idealistic for a people so unfamiliar with democratic practice and responsibilities. No attempt was made to outlaw parties hostile to the system; this opened the way for savage attacks on the republic by extremists at both ends of the political spectrum. The use of proportional representation, without any qualifying minimum percentage of the total vote, favoured a plethora of parties promoting sectional interests. This meant that the Weimar governments were all unwieldy coalitions, whose average life was about eight months and which often pursued contradictory policies in different ministries.

Two months before the constitution was ratified in July 1919, Germany had been forced to accede to the **Treaty of Versailles**. In contrast to the Habsburg Empire, which was broken up into a series of successor states, German territorial integrity was largely preserved, but the losses were painful ones – the industrially productive Saarland and Alsace-Lorraine went to France, while the resurrected country of Poland was given Upper Silesia plus a corridor to the sea, which left East Prussia cut off from the rest of the country. All overseas colonies were confiscated, the Rhineland was declared a demilitarized zone, the navy limited to six light battleships, and the army to a hundred thousand men with conscription prohibited. Germany and her allies were found guilty of having started the war, and, as a result, were landed with an enormous **reparations bill**, which would have taken over half a century to pay.

In all, this amounted to a pretty stiff settlement, albeit one considerably less harsh than the Germans had recently enforced on the Russians at Brest-Litovsk. So incensed were the military leaders with this humiliating Diktat that they toyed with the idea of resuming hostilities. As this was not a feasible option, they contented themselves with inventing the **"stab in the back" legend**, maintaining that the army, undefeated in the field, had been betrayed by unscrupulous politicians – a preposterous distortion accepted all too easily by gullible sections of the public.

The treaty spelled the beginning of the end for the Social Democratic republic. Scheidemann immediately resigned as chancellor, and, following gains by the two political extremes in the 1920 elections under the new constitution, the party, though still the largest in the Reichstag, withdrew from government altogether, leaving power in the hands of minority administrations drawn from liberal and moderate conservative parties. Right-wing extremism flourished in a series of political murders and attempted putsches, which were barely punished by a judiciary which rivalled the army in its contempt for the republic.

The reparations bill crippled the economy, to the extent that payments began to be withheld. This gave the French the excuse to occupy the Ruhr in 1923; they were met by a policy of passive resistance. As no work was done, galloping **inflation** – the most catastrophic ever known in world history – quickly ensued, causing the ruin of the entire middle class as the currency became utterly worthless. The Weimar Republic seemed irretrievably doomed, but it made an astonishing comeback, largely due to the political skills of the new chancellor, **Gustav Stresemann**. He was an unlikely saviour, an old-fashioned conservative who had begun his career as Ludendorff's mouthpiece in the Reichstag, and whose precise commitment to the republic is still disputed. A supreme pragmatist, he realized the danger of economic collapse and the futility of confrontation with the Allies. Therefore he ended passive resistance and negotiated huge American loans to rebuild the economy. This was so successful that by October 1924 money had regained its former value; (nearly) full employment and general prosperity soon followed.

Although Stresemann's government broke up long before these effects were felt, he subsequently served as foreign minister for six years in a variety of coalitions, achieving **Germany's rehabilitation on the world stage**. By the 1925 Locarno Pact, he gained *rapprochement* with France and guarantees that there could be no further threat of foreign occupation. Reparation payments were scaled down, and further American aid given. It seemed that the republic was set for a secure future, even if the political immaturity of the German people was still apparent, most notably in the presidential election of 1925. This was won by the 78-year-old Hindenburg, a wily operator basking in an undeserved military reputation, vocal exponent of the "stab in the back" legend and an embarrassing reminder of times past.

THE RISE OF NAZISM

The **National Socialist German Workers' Party** was founded in 1918 by a locksmith by the name of Anton Drexler, but only gained momentum when he was ousted three years later by **Adolf Hitler**, a failed artist and ex-corporal from Austria. It was a rag-bag group of fanatics and misfits whose views, as the party name suggests, were an odd mixture of the extreme right and left. They modelled their organization on the Communists and the Italian Fascisti, adopting their own uniform and slogans, and developing a private army, the brown-shirted **SA** (*Sturmabteilung*, or "Storm Troopers"). Such limited success as the party enjoyed was at first confined to Bavaria, where a botched attempt at a putsch was made in 1923; following this, Hitler was arrested and convicted of high treason.

The leniency shown by the judiciary to right-wing opponents of the republic – aided by the fact that he had involved Ludendorff in the plot – meant that Hitler only served nine months in prison, during which he set out his ideology and political programme in his autobiography, *Mein Kampf*. This consists of verbose rantings and ravings, drawing from all the nastiest and most reactionary theories of the day, but is an important source, as it sets out unequivocally what Hitler genuinely believed, and was to serve as his blueprint for power.

Racism forms the keynote: the so-called Aryans were the earth's rightful masters, while inferior peoples such as the Slavs were fit only to serve them. All ills could ultimately be laid at the door of the Jews, who were stealthily conspiring for world dominance. The German Volk had been betrayed by socialism, democracy and the traitors who had signed the Versailles Treaty. A new German Reich must be created under the direction of an all-powerful *Führer*, uniting with Austria and gaining living space (*Lebensraum*) to the east; to this end, France had to be subdued and Russia crushed.

Sales of the book – in spite of its ready captive market in the ranks of the party faithful – failed to reach 10,000 in the first year, and declined steadily for the next five. Nazi representation in the Reichstag also decreased from twenty-five in 1924 to just twelve after the 1928 elections, making it the ninth and smallest party, and one widely regarded as something of a joke. Only the extraordinarily mesmeric personality of Hitler held it together; having learnt from past mistakes, he was now determined to gain power by strictly legal means.

Stresemann died in October 1929, exhausted by overwork and by persecution from his former right-wing allies. Three weeks later came the **Wall Street crash** in America, whose repercussions swiftly destroyed the new German order he had created. Wholesale withdrawal of credit – on which the economy was totally dependent – led to another bout of escalating unemployment and inflation, to which there was no ready-made solution, as there had been in 1923. The coalition partners quarrelled over what measures to take; as a result, the SPD, who had only recently returned to government following eight years voluntarily out of office, once more abdicated the responsibility of leadership. A minority government was set up under **Heinrich Brüning** of the Catholic Centrists; frustrated by having to rely on rule by presidential decree, he took a gamble by asking Hindenburg to dissolve the Reichstag.

The elections, held in September 1930, offered a golden opportunity for the political extremes, with their formulas for righting all wrongs. The Nazi rise was meteoric, taking even Hitler by surprise – they gained 6.4 million votes and became the second largest party. This support was overwhelmingly from the disaffected ranks of the unemployed (particularly the young) and the ruined petty bourgeoisie. Though a significant breakthrough, it was far from being a decisive one, and there was still no inevitability about the Nazi triumph, which was only achieved because of the **short-sightedness and greed of the traditional right wing**.

In Hitler, they at last found their Kaiser-substitute, a man who could deliver the broad mass of support they could not otherwise muster and who would return Germany to its traditions of hierarchical authoritarian rule at home and military glory abroad. Leading figures in industry and politics latched onto Hitler and gave him respectability; by acting as his financiers and power brokers, they believed they would be able to control his excesses. Nazi coffers were swelled by contributions from many of the giant corporations, following a lead given some years before by the steel magnate Fritz Thyssen. The army began to abandon its role above party politics, overlooking its earlier aversion to the paramilitary SA.

Hitler offered a clue as to the naivety of these hopes by standing against the revered Hindenburg in the 1932 presidential election, only just managing to secure German citizenship in time to be eligible. The desperate straits into which the republic had fallen were shown by the fact that the ancient soldier, teetering on the verge of senility, was supported by the SPD and all the other democratic parties, who abstained from fielding a candidate of their own in the belief that there was no other way of beating Hitler.

In the event, Hindenburg only just failed to obtain an outright majority on the first ballot, and comfortably won the second, with the Communists trailing a very poor third. Fresh hope was provided by the remarkable success of Chancellor Brüning, still dependent on presidential decree, who was developing into a worthy successor to Stresemann. His sensible economic programme alleviated the worst hardships, and he was on the verge of pulling off a tremendous double success in foreign affairs,

with the end of reparations and the return of Germany's right to equality of armaments in sight. An attempt at reforming the outdated pattern of land ownership proved to be Brüning's undoing; the aristocracy howled with rage at this alleged crypto-Bolshevism, and Hindenburg was left with no alternative but to ditch him.

That marked the last attempt to make the republic work; power passed to a small coterie of traditional conservatives close to the president, who would bear the final responsibility for Hitler's assumption of power. The next two chancellors – the bumbling intriguer **Franz von Papen** and the far more astute fixer **General Kurt von Schleicher**, who had elaborate plans for using Hitler and then destroying him – had no taste for democracy, and were content to play courtier-style politics.

Two elections held in 1932 were inconclusive; in the first, following a campaign of mass terror by the SA, the Nazis gained nearly fourteen million votes and became the largest party, but were still well short of a majority. As Hindenburg's hand-picked cabinet failed to secure the support of the Reichstag, new elections had to be called; these saw the Nazis lose two million votes, as the party's true aims and methods became clearer. However, having been toppled by von Schleicher, it was von Papen – a figure seemingly escaped from a comic opera, now centre-stage in one of the world's greatest-ever tragedies – who entered into a disastrous plot with Hitler which brought the end of the republic.

Von Papen persuaded Hindenburg to make Hitler chancellor, with himself as deputy, of a coalition able to command a Reichstag majority. As the Nazis would only be given two other cabinet seats, von Papen assumed that he would retain the real control for himself. Hitler was therefore sworn in on January 30, 1933, having achieved with ease his objective of coming to power by constitutional means.

THE THIRD REICH

Once in power, **Hitler acted swiftly to make his position absolute**; he had no intention of being beholden to anyone, least of all a fool and political amateur such as von Papen. New elections were arranged for March; this time, the Nazis had the advantage of being able to use the full apparatus of the state to back up their campaign of terror. In this, they were greatly aided by the fact that **Hermann Göring**, one of the Nazis in the cabinet, was Prussian minister of the interior and thus in control of the police.

On the night of February 27, the **Reichstag** was burned down; a simple-minded Dutch Communist was arrested for this, though the fire was almost certainly the work of the Nazis themselves. At any rate, it gave them the excuse to force Hindenburg into declaring a state of emergency. Thereafter, opponents could be gagged legally, and Communists persecuted. The Nazis duly were elected with over seventeen million votes, just short of an absolute majority.

An **Enabling Bill** was laid before the Reichstag, which was effectively asked to vote itself out of existence. By the arrest of the Communist deputies and some of the SPD, and with the support of the traditional right, Hitler was only just short of the two-thirds majority he needed to abolish the Weimar Republic quite legally. The SPD salvaged some self-respect by refusing to accede to this, but the Catholic Centrists failed to repeat their act of defiance against Bismarck, meekly supporting the measure in return for minor concessions.

Now officially the country's dictator, Hitler immediately put into effect the remainder of his **policy of co-ordination** (*Gleichschaltung*), by which society was completely Nazified. With breathtaking speed, every institution surrendered. The Länder were stripped of their powers, making Germany a centralized state for the first time. All political parties except the Nazis were forced to dissolve, and free trade unions were banned. Purges were carried out in the police, judiciary and professions, to ensure that each was in the control of party loyalists.

Many of the vicious features for which Nazism became notorious soon made their appearance. **Jews were ostracized and persecuted**; their businesses were boycotted and they were banned from the professions; two years later, they were stripped of citizenship and forbidden to marry Germans. Fifty or so **concentration camps** were set up for political opponents, who were sadistically tortured and often cold-bloodedly murdered. Conformity was ensured by networks of informers under the control of the secret police, the **Gestapo**. The educational system was perverted in order to indoctrinate the great "truths" of Nazi ideology.

Recognizing the importance of controlling young minds at all times, membership of the **Hitler Youth** and League of Young German Women was made compulsory. Cultural life virtually collapsed, as "degenerate" forms of expression were suppressed. These ranged from virtually all modern art to books and plays with a liberal or socialist slant; it even affected music, as the performance of works by composers with Jewish blood was outlawed. Soon the main threat to the regime lay within the Nazi Party itself, with the original socialist wing, backed by the SA, pressing for a second revolution.

On June 30, 1934, the "**Night of the Long Knives**", hundreds of potential Nazi opponents were assassinated, notably the leading left-winger Gregor Strasser and the SA chief Ernst Röhm. The SA was stripped of its powers and put under the control of **Heinrich Himmler**'s black-shirted **SS** (*Schutzstaffel*), originally no more than Hitler's bodyguard. This measure also had the benefit of laying to rest the one remaining threat, that of intervention by the army; with their potential usurpers out of the way, they quickly came to terms with Nazism. When Hindenburg died a few weeks later, Hitler combined the offices of president and chancellor into that of an all-powerful *Führer*, a measure he had ratified by a plebiscite in which he was endorsed by 90 percent of those eligible to vote.

The genuine **popular support** Hitler enjoyed is one of the most striking and disturbing features of what became known as the Third Reich, the successor to the empires of Charlemagne and Bismarck. Although many of the most talented people, especially in the arts and sciences, fled the country, and many others tenaciously defied it from within, the level of opposition was negligible.

However, there's no doubt that the economic policies Hitler pursued were popular on both sides of industry. Full employment was restored, and, although industrial and agricultural workers were effectively reduced to the status of serfs, there was no question of starvation or total financial ruin. Business leaders were pleased for a different reason – when it came to profits, the totalitarian state stopped short of its normal all-embracing function.

One by one, the terms of Versailles were breached – reparation payments were stopped, the formerly secret rearmament was stepped up and made open, with conscription reintroduced; the Rhineland was reoccupied; and Austria was forced into becoming part of the Reich. The German-speaking people in the Sudetenland part of Czechoslovakia, who had never previously been a source of discontent, were used as an excuse to begin the policy of *Lebensraum*; the matter escalated into an international crisis in 1938, in which the British and French made a humiliating climb-down by an agreement signed at Munich, in which they sacrificed Czech territorial integrity for what they believed would be world peace.

Hitler was encouraged by this show of weakness to launch one of his most cherished ambitions the following year – the elimination of Poland. It's probable he believed there would be a similar collapse of will by the western powers, the more so as he first pulled off the spectacular coup of signing a non-aggression pact with his ultimate enemy, the Soviet Union, thus ensuring there would not be a war on two fronts. However, this was a miscalculation; two days after the invasion began on September 1, Britain and France, realizing that the earlier promises of an end to German expansion in Eastern Europe were a sham, decided to honour their treaty obligations. Thus **World War II** began.

WORLD WAR II

At first, the war went well for the Nazis, aided by the fact that Germany was the only country properly prepared, by reason of the massive arms build-up that it had semi-secretly been instigating since 1930. Poland was routed and the Low Countries soon fell, leading to the British evacuation from Dunkirk in May 1940. Within a month, France had signed an armistice, and a puppet government was installed. A quick invasion would probably then have accounted for Britain, but Hitler delayed in favour of an aerial bombardment in which the Luftwaffe was repulsed by the RAF. Rather than prolong this approach, German sights turned eastwards again. The Balkans were subdued, and in June 1941 plans were hatched for the largest military operation in history – the invasion of the Soviet Union. This period also marks the beginnings of the worst **concentration camps**, in which Nazi racial theories were put fully into practice. Inmates from the conquered

territories were used as slave labour, and horrendous experiments in the name of Nazi "science" were carried out, followed by an attempt at the "final solution" of the Jewish "problem". Over six million (about a third of the population of world Jewry) perished as a result; a similar number of other "undesirable" peoples were massacred in addition.

On December 7, 1941 Hitler's Japanese allies (courted in the hope they would attack the USSR from the east) attacked Pearl Harbor, an action which almost immediately **brought the US into the war**, the very reverse of German intentions. In any event, Nazi Germany had hopelessly overreached itself; defeats in North Africa in 1942 were followed by **the turning-point at Stalingrad** the following year when the Russian winter and the vast size of the country combined, not for the first time, to repulse a foreign invader. German losses rivalled those sustained in World War I, and a crushing blow was dealt to morale, as this ranked as the most disastrous defeat in the country's military history.

From then onwards, the story is one of Nazi retreat on all fronts. A **German resistance movement** sprang up under the leadership of senior army officers. Various attempts were made to assassinate Hitler, and he had several extraordinary escapes, most notably in the carefully hatched plot of July 20, 1944, when a planted bomb killed several people sitting alongside him. Yet, bad luck apart, the conspiratorial groups were handicapped by their excessive concern to secure in advance lenient terms for a defeated but democratic Germany; they also had no firm base of popular support, nor a detailed plan of campaign for what to do once Hitler had been killed.

As it turned out, the country's ultimate collapse was drawn out, and did not occur before nearly all major German cities and innumerable small towns had been ruthlessly bombed. Eventually, the Allies occupied the entire country and on April 30, 1945, marooned in his Berlin bunker, Hitler committed suicide, so bringing the "thousand-year Reich" to an inglorious end.

THE DIVISION OF GERMANY

The Allied powers, determined not to repeat the mistakes of Versailles, now had to decide **what to do with Germany**. At Potsdam in August, the country was partitioned into four zones of occupation, corresponding to an agreement made earlier in the year at Yalta when the war was still in progress; Berlin was similarly divided. The eastern frontier of Germany was redrawn at the Oder–Neisse line, meaning that East Prussia and most of Pomerania and Silesia passed to Poland, in compensation for territory annexed by the Soviet Union.

Initially, there was a great deal of co-operation amongst the Allies. All the leading Nazis who had survived were brought to **trial in Nürnberg** for war crimes or crimes against humanity, and the civil service was purged of the movement's sympathizers. Relief measures were taken against the terrible famine sweeping the country, refugees from the former Eastern Territories were given help to begin a new life, and the first steps were made towards rebuilding destroyed cities and the shattered economy.

Germany's internal **political life** was relaunched under the leadership of prominent anti-Nazis. The right of the spectrum was occupied by a new and moderate party, the **Christian Democrats** (CDU), in which the Catholic Centrists were joined by Protestants who held similar social views. Left-wing politics were still marred by the legacy of bad blood between the SPD and the Communists. In the Russian zone, the SPD took the lead in forming a new group, the **Socialist Unity Party** (SED), which was intended to be Marxist but not Marxist-Leninist; the Communists only tagged along under Russian pressure after the poor showing of the party in the Austrian elections. This new grouping was not repeated in the other zones.

Inevitably, **strains developed among the Allies**; the zones began to develop in different ways, mirroring the societies of their conquerors. Frustrated by Russian stalling, the Western powers began a currency reform in their zones in 1948, soon extended to West Berlin. This gesture was regarded as highly provocative by the Soviets, who retaliated by cutting off western access to the divided city in the **Berlin Blockade**. Another world war could have ensued, but the beleaguered western zones were saved by the success of **air lifts** bringing essential supplies, forcing the Russians to abandon the blockade within a year.

By this time, two different societies were emerging on German soil: the Russians enforced massive nationalization and collectivization; in contrast, the Western powers allowed even those industrialists most associated with the Nazis, such as Thyssen and the Krupps, to return to their businesses with minimal punishment. Rocked by the independent line taken by Tito in Yugoslavia, the Russians transformed the SED into a Soviet-style party led by a Politburo into which the erstwhile SPD members were trapped, while a Parliamentary Council was set up in the west to draft a new constitution. The logical conclusion of these events – the creation of two rival states – soon followed. In May 1949, the three western zones amalgamated to form the **German Federal Republic**; four months later, the Russians launched their territory as the **German Democratic Republic**.

THE FEDERAL REPUBLIC

Like the Weimar Republic, the new West German state was founded on **liberal democratic principles**, only this time the constitution was much tighter. The power of the president was sharply reduced, giving him a role not unlike that of the British monarch. A true federal structure was created, in which the Länder were given considerable powers over all areas of policy except defence, foreign affairs and currency control. Proportional representation was retained, but with a 5 percent qualifying minimum, and elections were fixed for every four years. A constitutional court was established to guarantee civil and political liberties, and anti-democratic parties were outlawed.

Konrad Adenauer became the first chancellor following elections in which his Christian Democrats emerged as the largest party, though far short of a majority. Aged 73 and with no experience of national politics – he had been mayor of Cologne until removed by the Nazis – he bore the look of a temporary leader, though as an elder statesman with an untainted past he fitted the precise needs of the time exactly.

In the event, the evening of his career was a prolonged one; he remained in power for fourteen years, during which time he developed an aura of indispensability at home and appeared as a figure of substance abroad. Much of this success was due to the **"Economic Miracle"** masterminded by **Ludwig Erhard**, in which the wrecked economy made a spectacular recovery, with high-quality products fuelling an export boom. An annual growth rate of 8 percent was achieved; within a decade West Germany ranked as the most prosperous major European country. In many ways, this was due simply to disciplined hard work by the bulk of the population, but it was also aided by the fact that a fresh start had to be made. Industry was relaunched with the most modern equipment, and in a sensible atmosphere of partnership between management and just seventeen large trade unions which eliminated the class-based fear and inter-union rivalry which continued to dog other countries. Erhard also promoted the concept of the "social-market economy", giving due emphasis to the development of a welfare state.

In foreign affairs, priority was given to **ending the long era of enmity with France**; the two countries formed the European Coal and Steel Pact in 1951, serving as a prelude to the creation of the European Economic Community six years later. The Federal Republic's integration into the Western alliance was cemented by admission to **NATO**, and the adoption of a hard-nosed attitude towards the Soviet Union and her satellites.

By the **Hallstein Doctrine**, the Federal Republic claimed to be the legitimate voice of all Germany, arguing that it was the only part properly constituted. Not only did it fail to recognize the GDR, it successfully ostracized its neighbour by refusing to establish diplomatic relations with any country who did.

THE GERMAN DEMOCRATIC REPUBLIC

Meanwhile the inappropriately styled German Democratic Republic rapidly evolved a **centralized system of government on the Soviet model**. The Christian Democratic and Liberal parties were forcibly subordinated to the SED, and two further bourgeois groups were created from above. Elections were still held, but a single list of candidates was drawn up which the voters had to accept *en bloc*. The only method of protest was to reject it outright, which had to be done publicly, making it a dangerous as well as a futile gesture. Police, education and management of the economy were all put under SED control. Real power was centralized in the hands of party secretary **Walter Ulbricht**, a hard-line Stalinist who had spent almost the

entire Nazi period ensconced in the Soviet Union.

At first, the Russians were ambivalent about their rump state. They administered punitive reparations, stripping it of much of its industry and shipping valuable plants and machinery to the Soviet Union; they were worried about the GDR's long-term viability and may even have been prepared to sacrifice it altogether in their own defensive interests. Stalin was on record as saying in 1944, "Communism fits Germany as a saddle fits a cow", and it's doubtful if he was ever particularly keen on a separate GDR. In 1952, he made **an offer to establish a unified and neutral Germany on a democratic basis**, which was rejected out of hand in the West as mere bluff.

The **GDR began life unpromisingly**, exploited by its parent, having no historical or economic rationale, unloved by the vast majority of its populace, thousands of whom emigrated to the West, and seemingly wanted only by its leaders who had had power handed to them on a plate. A second industrial revolution had to be launched, simply to meet reparation commitments; the existing infrastructure included very little heavy industry (which was now developed apace, though more for ideological reasons than out of necessity), and was now deprived of access to its commercial hinterland. The pressure of this caused the first revolt in the Soviet satellite states, a series of **workers' strikes** in 1953, put down by Russian tanks. The following year, reparations were ended and the country began to develop as a key member of the bloc, becoming one of the founder members of the **Warsaw Pact**.

In spite of many problems – access to Western markets was hindered by the lack of a convertible currency, trade with the Soviet Union was conducted on unfavourable terms, and imbalances were caused by the ideological imperative to give massive subsidies to basic necessities – the 1950s saw an **economic recovery** which in its own way was as extraordinary as West Germany's. Once again, the people showed their legendary ability to adapt to any kind of regime; they were in any event now well attuned to totalitarian life. If West Germans felt a sense of superiority in their far more advanced lifestyle, the comparison was hardly a fair one: they had received munificence from their conquerors, not retribution; they had also started with the enormous benefit of being in possession of the Ruhr and other areas of rich natural resources and advanced industry. At the 1958 Party Congress, Ulbricht was rash enough to predict that, within a few years, the country would overtake its neighbour in terms of per capita income, thus proving the inherent superiority of the Communist system.

THE BERLIN WALL

This optimism proved short-lived, as the late 1950s saw the beginning of a period of **unprecedented West German prosperity and economic expansion**. A shortage of labour meant that workers had to be imported; the unskilled labourers tended to come from Turkey, Greece, Yugoslavia, Italy and Spain. For the better-qualified positions, industry looked to East Germany and a flood of **emigration** started.

Quickly realizing that he could not afford to lose so many professionals, engineers, intellectuals and craftsmen, Ulbricht was forced into drastic action. The loophole was the western sector of Berlin; if it could be sealed off, the problem would disappear. Having failed at a second attempt to make the Allies evacuate the city, Ulbricht persuaded the Soviets of the necessity of constructing the **Berlin Wall**, erected on August 13, 1961. It was immediately patrolled by armed guards under instructions to shoot to kill, and the main boundaries of the country were also greatly strengthened. A visual and moral affront to humanity, it was justified as the "Anti-Fascist Protection Wall", a label it retained until its demolition.

In the Federal Republic, Adenauer was finally forced into retirement in 1963, to be succeeded by Erhard, who proved far less successful as the country's leader than he had been as economic guru. The liberal Free Democrats (FDP), who had served as the CDU's junior coalition partners for all but a short period of the Federal Republic's history, went into opposition in 1966. A "**Grand Coalition**" was established with the SPD, who thus returned to government for the first time since 1930. To rid itself of its tarnished image, the party had undergone a substantial reform (or sell-out, according to many) at its 1959 conference, disavowing its roots in Marxism and class conflict and its traditional anticlericalism, embracing instead the CDU's

"social-market economy", but with a stronger emphasis on the social side of the equation.

The chancellor, the CDU's Kurt Georg Kiesinger, was remarkable mainly for being a reformed Nazi – a rather uncomfortable indicator as to how far West Germans were prepared to forget the past. It was hardly surprising that the period of the Grand Coalition saw the first simmerings of disenchantment with the cosy form of consensus politics which had dominated the country's postwar history, with the Communists re-formed as a counterweight to the neo-Nazi NPD; neither party, however, gained much of a following. More serious were the beginnings of what became a persistent feature of West German life, **extra-parliamentary opposition**. This first came to the fore with the 1968 student revolt under Rudi Dutschke. Grievances initially centred on unsatisfactory conditions in the universities but spread to wider discontent with society and the new materialistic culture.

OSTPOLITIK

A more positive feature of the Grand Coalition was the rise of **Willy Brandt**, the dynamic leader of the SPD, who assumed the foreign affairs portfolio. A former Resistance journalist, he had been mayor of West Berlin throughout the period of crisis leading up to the building of the Wall, and was determined to take a new tack on the problem. His **Ostpolitik** began in earnest, helped by a general thawing of the Cold War, when he became chancellor in 1969, at the head of a SPD–FDP coalition, itself something of a mould-breaker. Treaties were signed with the Soviet Union and Poland in 1970, recognizing the validity of the Oder–Neisse line; West Berlin's special status was guaranteed by the Four Power Agreement the following year; and in 1972 a Basic Treaty was signed between the two Germanys which at last normalized relations.

This stopped short of full diplomatic recognition of the GDR, but the Federal Republic recognized its frontiers and separate existence, abandoning the Hallstein Doctrine. In return, West Germans were allowed to visit family and friends over the border, though movement the other way was confined to pensioners and the disabled. One consequence of Ostpolitik was the **fall of Ulbricht** in 1971; he wanted to drive a harder bargain than suited the Soviets, who were in any case tired of his constant lectures to them on ideological purity. His replacement was **Erich Honecker**, who, although regarded as a comparative liberal, had first come to prominence as construction supremo of the Berlin Wall.

With the mirage of reunification now cleared, the two German societies were able to continue developing in their separate ways. **The GDR began to clarify and modify its image**; in 1974, the country was given yet another new constitution, which omitted previous references to overcoming the division of Germany, and stated the country was "forever and irrevocably" allied with the USSR. The GDR was characterized as a "developed socialist society", in which different divisions existed. This had the twin benefits of justifying both the inequality which was still clearly manifest (though less extreme than in the West) and the continued leadership role of the SED – along with all the attendant privileges for its elite.

To counterbalance this, a "**social contract**" was made with the population, which curbed arbitrary use of police powers, effectively meaning that only active dissidents were persecuted. Honecker cultivated an avuncular image for himself which came as a refreshing change after the austere authoritarianism of his predecessor. **Sports** – or at least those with a high profile in the Olympic Games, such as athletics, swimming and skiing – were increasingly used as the chief means of gaining international prestige, and the results proved stunningly successful, catapulting the country to the dizzy heights of the improbable third "super-power" in these events. **Economic performance** became ever more impressive, and was easily the best in the Soviet bloc; full employment was preserved as much out of necessity as principle. However, in comparison with West Germany the economic mix looked hopelessly outdated, and the average earner was little more than half as well off in real terms, with the gap widening rather than narrowing. As well as all the old problems, there were frequent shortages (often caused by sudden opportunities to sell stocks to gain hard currency) and a lack of consumer goods for which the demand was growing apace.

Boosted by the success of both his Ostpolitik and his welfare programmes, Brandt led his coalition to victory in 1972, with the SPD winning more votes than the CDU for the first time.

In view of the reconciliatory nature of his approach to the GDR, it was ironic that Brandt's downfall occurred two years later as a result of the unmasking of one of his closest aides as an East German spy.

Staying on in the influential role as SPD chairman (until 1987, when another scandal, this time over a bizarre choice of a young CDU-sympathizing Greek woman as party spokesperson, caused his retirement), Brandt was succeeded by **Helmut Schmidt**, an able pragmatist who increasingly came to be seen as something of a right-winger, though this was in part due to the nature of the problems he faced. The quadrupling of OPEC oil prices in 1974, and the stagnation in world trade which ensued, posed particular difficulties for the export-led and growth-geared German economy. These were tackled more successfully than in most countries, but **unemployment** became an issue for the first time since Hitler.

Extra-parliamentary opposition had by now taken on a fearsome and anarchic character. In the early 1970s, there had been a spate of kidnappings and armed bank robberies by the Baader-Meinhof gang. These had no sooner been quelled than there arose a far more organized and ruthless offshoot, the **Red Army Faction**, which assassinated a number of public figures. The turning point in the government's campaign against them came with the hijacking of a Lufthansa plane in 1977, and a threat to kill the hostages if the remaining members of the gang were not released from prison.

On personal instructions from Schmidt – on which he was prepared to stake his chancellorship – the aircraft was successfully stormed; within three years, most of the terrorist leaders had been arrested and imprisoned. Peaceful extra-parliamentary opposition proved to have a far more potent significance. This was inspired above all by fears that divided Germany would serve as the stage for a future nuclear war. NATO's 1979 decision to install medium-range American nuclear missiles in West Germany was a particular source of protest, but there was also **increased general concern about the environment**, especially pollution of the beloved forests.

These issues then served as a focus for the many who were dissatisfied with a society which had become over-competitive and too obsessed with consumerism, and out of an amorphous collection of pressure groups active in these areas the **Green Party** was born. Schmidt's backing of the bases alienated the SPD's left wing, but he was still able to lead his coalition to victory in 1980. In this he was aided by the CDU's recurrent leadership problem, which reached its nadir at this point with the fielding of **Franz-Josef Strauss**, who had last held federal office under Adenauer, as chancellor candidate. Longstanding leader of the CSU, the separate and exclusively Bavarian counterpart of the CDU, this blatant careerist and strident right-winger unsurprisingly proved to be a major electoral liability.

THE 1980S

Despite this lifeline, the long period of SPD domination was coming to an end. Schmidt's tough economic policies under the influence of another round of drastic oil price increases further widened the party's divisions, leading the FDP to lose confidence and withdraw from the government in September 1982. The CDU, now revived under **Helmut Kohl**, gambled on a "constructive vote of no confidence" – the only way round the fixed-term parliaments enshrined in the constitution. Having won this, they formed a new government with the FDP and called for fresh elections. Fears that the FDP would fail to surmount the 5 percent threshold (having damaged themselves by their rather dubious stance) proved unfounded, and Kohl was able to continue as before.

Kohl was something of a departure, the first German leader drawn from a generation too young to have Nazi associations of any kind. He remained in power for sixteen years, unexpectedly seeing Germany through its biggest upheaval since World War II. Initially, his government was rather unexciting, cutting back on the state's very modest role in economic intervention, but making **further strides in Ostpolitik**. Since Brandt, this had become low-key, and depended very much on the climate of superpower relations. The new developments were in many cases cynical – massive **interest-free loans** were given to the GDR in return for allowing greater numbers of its citizens to emigrate, and football-style transfer fees were paid for its political prisoners.

Honecker was keen to **set the seal of legitimacy on the GDR** by paying an official visit to the Federal Republic; two attempts were abandoned in the face of Soviet pressure before he finally made it in September 1987. It was the high point of his career and seemed to provide its justification as, amid much publicity, he was received in a way just below that for a head of state. However, by this time his regime was already beginning to be undermined by the new policies of *glasnost* and *perestroika* introduced in the Soviet Union under **Mikhail Gorbachev**, and somewhat desperate attempts were made to insulate GDR citizens from the seemingly inexorable move towards reform in the eastern bloc.

As it transpired, the initial impetus for the astonishing and rapid transformation of Germany (what Germans call *die Wende*), came from outside the country. On May 2, 1989, the Hungarian authorities began taking down the barbed wire along their border with Austria, creating **a hole in the Iron Curtain**. Many East Germans headed there, ostensibly for their holidays, and by August around two hundred were **crossing into Austria** every night; additionally, about twenty thousand GDR refugees were being housed in the West German embassy in Budapest and in Hungarian holiday camps, awaiting their chance for an official emigration to the West. On September 10 the Hungarian government finally **gave the East Germans leave to depart**. Now forbidden to travel to Hungary, would-be GDR refugees instead made for Prague, swamping the West German embassy. On September 30 they too were allowed to leave, the result of a special deal announced by West German foreign minister Hans-Dietrich Genscher.

In the GDR **opposition groups** such as Neues Forum were starting to emerge. Popular unrest came to a head at the **October 7** celebration of the 40th anniversary of the GDR. Guest Mikhail Gorbachev stressed the need for dialogue and openness to new ideas, while Erich Honecker responded with a clichéd speech praising the status quo. A vainglorious official parade of military hardware was followed by angry **demonstrations** which were brutally suppressed by the police. There were also demonstrations in Leipzig and Dresden, and open popular unrest spread across the country over the following weeks despite widespread fears of an armed crackdown by the authorities. The expected violence never materialized and on October 18 Erich Honecker was suddenly replaced by **Egon Krenz**, his long-time heir apparent, a man widely regarded as a neo-Stalinist hardliner.

To everyone's surprise Krenz **expressed a desire for dialogue** with opposition groups. The exodus of GDR citizens continued but there was now a feeling that change might be possible. On November 4 one million people gathered in the centre of East Berlin, in **the biggest anti-Communist demonstration** since the workers' uprising of 1953. Three days later most of the old government resigned and **Hans Modrow**, the former Dresden SED chief, a man regarded as a liberal, was appointed prime minister. By now two hundred thousand East Germans had left the GDR since the start of the year.

The **opening of the Berlin Wall** was announced almost casually. On the evening of Thursday, November 9, Berlin party boss Günter Schabowski told a press conference that East German citizens were free to leave the GDR with valid exit visas which were henceforth to be issued without delay. Events immediately took on a momentum of their own. TV stations broadcast the announcement and citizens began heading for the nearest border crossings. All along the frontier border guards began letting through the masses, and people on both sides of the city flocked to the Wall. Huge crowds converged on the Brandenburger Tor where an impromptu street party broke out celebrating an event that many Germans had never imagined they would see. Over the days that followed **East Germans poured across the border**: 2,700,000 exit visas were issued in the first weekend after the Wall was opened, and the two Germanys rediscovered each other at breakneck speed.

On December 1 the East German parliament passed a motion ending the leading role of the SED and **free elections were promised** for the following May. The SED repackaged itself as the supposedly voter-friendly PDS – Partei des Demokratischen Sozialismus or "Democratic Socialist Party". A more significant event for the future of Germany was Chancellor Helmut Kohl's visit to Dresden on December 19 when he declared to cheering crowds that his ultimate goal was a **united Germany**.

GERMANY SINCE 1990

With the new decade things progressed rapidly. The GDR elections, brought forward to March 18, resulted in a **victory for a right-wing alliance dominated by the CDU** under Lothar de Mazière. This really represented a victory for Chancellor Helmut Kohl, the self-proclaimed champion of reunification.

Almost immediately the new East German government set about dissolving the GDR. An agreement with the West Germans about **economic union** was hammered out and put into effect on July 1. The next step was to work out a formula for political reunification. This was effectively left to Helmut Kohl and Mikhail Gorbachev (who at this stage still had the final say); between them during a July summit in the Caucasus, they worked out a mutually acceptable agreement which was quickly rubber-stamped by the GDR parliament.

October 3, 1990 was the date of **German reunification**, an event which did not see a repeat of earlier celebrations. For many people in the east, dazed by the rapid economic collapse of the GDR and subsequent social dislocation, reunification seemed to offer little, other than the prospect of unemployment and uncertainty. Nonetheless, Kohl remained determinedly upbeat, maintaining that no German would lose out as a result of unification. His opportunistic masterminding of events meant that the SPD was forced into making penny-pinching complaints about costs, thereby inviting the charge that it was not up to dealing with the great historical challenge facing the nation. Now that the two states had formally merged, Kohl's fast-track approach to a fully integrated economy and society offered no more risks than the slower methods advocated by his opponents, and it was therefore no surprise that the **CDU-led coalition scored a landslide victory** in the first united German elections, held in December 1990.

The rosy picture painted by Kohl of the country's economic prospects was not mere optimistic posturing. He rashly calculated that an initial spending spree would be unleashed in the east as a result of the introduction of the Deutschmark, and that the natural capacity of Germans to work hard, coupled with the fact that a large percentage of women in the former GDR were in gainful employment, would thereafter fuel a major boom which would spread to the west as well.

The essential weakness in this prognosis was that it failed to anticipate the speed and totality of the **collapse of the Soviet Union** in the wake of its satellites. This spelt absolute ruin for whole sectors of the economy of the former GDR, which were suddenly left without markets for their products. Worse, the logistics of central planning meant that entire towns, dependent on a single industry, found themselves facing a desperate future, with half or more of the local population out of work at a single stroke.

Not only did the government's standing plummet in the east, it also nose-dived in the west when vastly unpopular **tax increases** were introduced in 1991 for the specific purpose of funding the unification process. The CDU paid the electoral penalty in the state elections in the Rhineland-Palatinate soon afterwards, losing to the SPD what had always been considered a sure-fire stronghold, the place where Chancellor Kohl had built his original power base. Similar humiliations befell the party in subsequent elections in other Länder.

One of the beneficiaries of the government's discomfiture was the **far right**, which had hitherto failed to make much of an impact on postwar Germany. Playing heavily on the political immaturity of the eastern German Electorate, and on the fears and resentments building up in the west, the far right, in the shape of the outwardly respectable Republican Party, made some unexpectedly strong showings in these local elections, leading many at home and abroad to voice fears that Germany might yet again embrace Nazism.

The far right concentrated on the issues of **unemployment and immigration**, making a direct and largely bogus connection between the two. Violent racist attacks on foreigners, sometimes resulting in deaths, soon became commonplace, particularly in the former GDR, where a number of shocking incidents of mob hatred were captured on film and broadcast round the world. The official response to this was a review of Germany's exceptionally liberal immigration laws, introduced as an atonement for the crimes of the Third Reich, and these were eventually repealed in 1993.

While the government was widely condemned for what looked like a weak-kneed reaction to the problem of racist violence, it was also possible to see its response as a pragmatic one to a situation that was otherwise in danger of getting out of hand, particularly when political refugees from the disintegrating

Yugoslavia started to arrive in force to swell the ranks of the mainly economic refugees from the former Soviet bloc. It certainly seemed to help put the advance of the far right firmly into reverse, though it failed to touch on a key issue of race relations – the lack of citizenship rights of the large *Gastarbeiter* population, which now includes an entire generation who were born in Germany and have lived their whole lives there.

By 1992, it was clear that the economy was in **recession**. Defeat for the CDU in the fixed-term general elections set for October 1994 looked inevitable, but the SPD's massive lead in the opinion polls was gradually whittled away by its seemingly perennial crisis over its choice of chancellor candidate, while an economic upturn rallied CDU support. Meanwhile, the PDS profited from the renewed sympathy for reformed Communists expressed throughout Eastern Europe. Kohl's biggest worry was the very real prospect that his coalition partners in the FDP would fail to get the 5 percent of votes necessary to gain parliamentary representation – a scenario which would virtually ensure the accession of some form of left-wing coalition. In the event, the FDP achieved the qualifying minimum with a bit to spare, and the **Kohl government continued in office**, albeit with its majority slashed to just ten seats.

Kohl's fourth term in office was dominated by the drive towards **European Monetary Union**, for which he lobbied energetically in the face of the misgivings of many of Germany's European partners. After announcing that the 1998 election would mark his retirement, he changed his mind and decided to run for an unprecedented fifth term, in the grandiose belief that, having achieved German unification, he was the only living statesman with the necessary clout to pull off the task of delivering full European integration. However, the performance of the domestic economy did not bode well for electoral success: the austerity measures demanded by the need to meet the convergence criteria for EMU exacerbated problems that remained unsolved in the wake of reunification; the Deutschmark was at its lowest for decades, while **unemployment** had reached almost five million – its highest since 1933. It was therefore no surprise that Kohl went down to a comprehensive defeat at the hands of an alliance of the SPD and Greens, bringing the latter into national government for the first time.

The new chancellor, **Gerhard Schröder**, had modelled himself quite closely on Britain's Tony Blair, though in one key area of difference – his reputation as a serial bridegroom – he faced the problem of a question mark against his trustworthiness. Moreover, the corporate style of leadership favoured by the SPD during their years in opposition meant that it was initially unclear who was really in charge of the government – Schröder or the maverick 1990 chancellor-candidate Oskar Lafontaine, who assumed the portfolio of Finance Minister in addition to his duties as party chairman. This issue was, however, soon resolved conclusively in favour of the former, as Lafontaine was ousted from both roles, to be replaced by the chancellor himself in the latter.

The Schröder government has continued to pursue Kohl's enthusiastically pro-European policies. Despite its left-wing credentials, it has placed its faith in large-scale tax cuts for securing new investment from abroad and a reduction in unemployment at home. Its hopes for re-election in 2002 have been given a massive boost by the financial scandals which have plagued the CDU ever since Kohl was personally incriminated in allegations of fraudulent fundraising. In the foreign press, these have often been presented as the total ruination of his carefully cultivated reputation as one of the seminal figures of German history, though it seems highly unlikely that future historians will judge these misdemeanours so harshly. Nonetheless, the scandals have already claimed the scalp of his anointed successor, Wolfgang Schäuble, leading to the unopposed election of Angela Merkel, a former GDR citizen with only a decade of political experience, as the leader of the CDU.

PAINTING AND GRAPHICS

Germany's artistic history is marked more by solid and sustained achievement than by the more usual pattern of pre-eminence followed by decline. As in Italy, the fragmentation of the nation into a multitude of tiny states led to the development of many important centres of art, often of a very distinctive character.

The country's geographical position has meant that it has been a melting pot for influences from Italy, France and the Low Countries, although, with several notable exceptions, the work of German painters never managed to gain the same international esteem. This, however, is mainly because the vast majority of German paintings have remained within the German-speaking countries, a consequence of the fact that many of the petty princes were great art collectors, and also because of the Romantic movement, which fostered a sense of awareness of the national heritage. As a result, important **museums** existed all over the country by the mid-nineteenth century.

German **graphic work**, being by its nature for dissemination, is perhaps more immediately familiar; the stark contrasts enforced by the media of woodcut, engraving and etching obviously proved temperamentally ideal for the country's artists, whose legacy in these fields far surpasses that of anywhere else in Europe.

THE BEGINNINGS

German painting has its roots in the ninth-century Carolingian epoch. **Illuminated manuscripts** were created in the scriptoria of the court and the monasteries; these typically featured vibrant figures in flowing draperies, charged with movement and set in elaborate architectural surrounds. This art form was refined and developed in the subsequent Ottonian period, most notably in Trier, which in the late tenth century boasted the first great German artist in an illuminator now dubbed **Master of the Registrum Gregorii**. A number of manuscripts by him have been identified; they show a new, more plastic style based on an understanding of classical antiquity, solving the problems of space and form which baffled all the other illuminators of the time. He built up a highly influential fund of forms which was imitated in the other great places of book production – Fulda, Hildesheim and Bavaria – although there were also more conservative centres, particularly those on the island of Reichenau, favouring an expressive linear form.

Fresco cycles were the other chief form of painting, and were often more closely related to the art of the book than might be supposed from the contrasting nature of the two forms. One of the best early examples to have survived is again from Trier; probably dating from the end of the ninth century, it originally adorned the crypt of St Maximin, but has been removed to the Bischöfliches Museum. From the following century, there is an important cycle still in situ at St Georg in Oberzell on Reichenau, along with one in the Andreaskirche in Fulda. Belonging more obviously to international Romanesque currents are the later fresco cycles of the Lower Rhineland and Regensburg. The former – St Gereon in Cologne, Schwarzrheindorf and Knechtsteden – are all influenced by Byzantine concepts of form, style and iconography; regrettably, their quality has been impaired by over-enthusiastic nineteenth-century restorers who indulged in far too much speculative retouching.

Later Romanesque illuminated manuscripts tend to follow rather than develop the Ottonian forms, although there was something of a revival in the late twelfth century, with such de luxe products as the *Gospels of Henry the Lion*, now in Wolfenbüttel. Roughly contemporary is a survival which is unique of its kind, the painted **wooden ceiling** illustrating the *Tree of Jesse* which adorns the vault of St Michael in Hildesheim.

THE EARLY GOTHIC PERIOD

The earliest Gothic **panel paintings** to have survived in Germany date from around 1300. Throughout the fourteenth century, religious themes retained their monopoly, and the most active workshops were in Cologne and Westphalia. The former was the dominant city of medieval Germany, and maintained its own strong and characteristic traditions right up until the early sixteenth century, assimilating varied foreign influences yet remaining rooted in tradition. Painting there was based on a strict **guild system**, which imposed stiff tests of skill on would-be applicants and even stipulated the quality of materials which had to be employed. Among the most important productions of this school in the fourteenth century were the monumental paintings on the backs of the Dom's stalls, the *Clares altar*, again in the Dom, and some very ruinous frescoes for the Rathaus which have been attributed to a somewhat legendary figure named **Master Wilhelm**.

The first German artist about whom much information has survived is **Master Bertram** (c.1345–1415), a Westphalian who worked in Hamburg. He seems to have been influenced by the art of Bohemia, which was part of the Holy Roman Empire and far in advance of fourteenth-century Germany in terms of the achievements of its painters. Bertram favoured narrative cycles of little panels grouped round pieces of sculpture; his major work is the *Grabow altar* of 1379 in Hamburg, which displays prodigious and original imaginative powers, particularly in the charming scenes of the Creation. From about a decade later is the *Passion altar* in Hannover, while the *Buxtehude altar*, again in Hamburg, is from ten years later; both are remarkably consistent in style.

Another Westphalian was the **Master of the Berswordt Altar** (active late fourteenth century), named after a triptych still *in situ* in the Marienkirche in Dortmund; he also painted a polyptych for the Neustädter Marienkirche in Bielefeld. The influence of French and Burgundian manuscripts is apparent, and he was an early representative of the courtly and idealized International Gothic style which was to spread all over Europe. In Germany, this is usually referred to as the **"Soft Style"**, and is found in sculpture as well as painting. Its greatest exponent was **Conrad von Soest** (active c.1394–1422), one of the most immediately appealing of all German painters, who may even have been the son of the previous artist. His panels are refined and beautiful, executed in glowing colours and including a fair amount of amusing anecdotal detail. The late high altar triptych of the Marienkirche in his native Dortmund shows his art at its peak, but is sadly truncated. The triptych in Bad Wildungen, however, has survived in remarkable shape. Another major painter in this style was **Master Francke** (active c.1405–25), who succeeded Bertram in Hamburg and could conceivably have been his pupil; his reputation rests largely on the *St Thomas à Becket altar* which was commissioned by the local merchants who traded with England. Also active at this time were the **Master of the Virgin of Benediktbeuern** in Bavaria and various artists in Lower Saxony, most of whose works are now in Hannover.

THE FIFTEENTH-CENTURY COLOGNE SCHOOL

The entire fifteenth century was an outstandingly brilliant artistic period for Cologne. Although the artists still mostly remain anonymous, their styles became far more contrasted than in former times, and art historians have been able to group bodies of work under pseudonyms based on the names of their major masterpieces, which are now mostly housed in the city's Wallraf-Richartz Museum, or in the Alte Pinakothek in Munich. As well as large-scale commissions to adorn the plethora of churches and monasteries, there's increasing evidence of the burgeoning of the merchant class in the number of small altarpieces (obviously intended for private devotion) which have survived. The symbolic depiction of the Madonna and Child in the Garden of Paradise was enduringly popular; another vogue subject (the two were sometimes combined) was the Holy Kinship, depicting the extended family of Christ. First to develop a distinctive style was the **Master of St Veronica** (active c.1400–20), named after *St Veronica with the Sudarium*, now in Munich. The monumental faces in this work, mirrored elsewhere in his output, give evidence of influence from

Bohemia, but that he had also understood the lessons of Burgundian miniatures is proved by the crowded *Calvary* in Cologne. His workshop may have been taken over after his death by the **Master of St Lawrence** (active c.1415–30), whose main work is a retable made for the demolished church of St Lorenz, parts of which survive in the museums of Cologne and Nürnberg.

These artists were surpassed by **Stefan Lochner** (c.1400–51), a Swabian who settled in the city and perfectly assimilated its traditions, along with innovations from Flanders. His soft, gentle and painstakingly detailed panels are among the peaks of the entire International Gothic movement, and he appears to have been something of a celebrity, which accounts for his name surviving the oblivion into which his rivals have plunged. His masterpiece is the *Epiphany* triptych now in Cologne's Dom, originally painted for the Rathaus, a far more monumental work than was usual in Cologne. It has been criticized for a failure to characterize the figures, but that is to miss the point – Lochner's art is quite consciously ethereal in spirit. If anything, the later *Presentation in the Temple*, now in Darmstadt, is even more sumptuous, while his last work, *Madonna of the Rose Bower* in Cologne, takes the art of the small altar to a level beyond which it could not progress. Even with gruesome subjects, such as *The Last Judgement* in Cologne and its reverse, *Martyrdoms of the Apostles*, now in Frankfurt, Lochner did not depart from his essential gentleness, always drawing the optimistic lesson from the subject; if that can be counted as a failing, his extraordinary inventive powers amply compensate.

The following generation moved away from static and decorative effects to a lively narrative style, clearly modelled on the great contemporary Netherlanders. Rogier van der Weyden's late *St Columba* triptych (now in Munich) was painted for a church in Cologne, and must have made an enormous impact, although the more rounded and less emotional style of Dieric Bouts is the obvious source for the leading artist of the group, the **Master of the Life of the Virgin** (active c.1460–85), so named from a cycle of eight panels, seven of which are also now in Munich. He displays all the qualities of a great storyteller, the figures strongly drawn and richly clad, standing out in sharp relief from

the background, with plenty of subsidiary anecdotal detail including exquisite still lifes. This artist's later work includes portraits of merchants, which mark the end of the ecclesiastical monopoly over art. Three other painters closely associated with him are the **Master of the Lyversberg Passion**, the **Master of the St George Legend** and the **Master of the Bonn Diptych**; they may even have shared the same studio. Slightly later is the **Master of the Glorification of the Virgin** (active c.1475–95) who is less overtly Flemish in spirit; his backgrounds include accurate depictions of Cologne and its surrounding countryside.

Among the final generation of Cologne painters, the **Master of the Holy Kinship** (c.1450–1515) takes his name from the most spectacular version ever painted of the favourite Cologne subject, which shows acquaintance with the very latest Flemish innovations; otherwise, he seems to have been more adept on a smaller scale, his larger canvases betraying the use of inexperienced assistants. His contemporary, the **Master of the St Ursula Legend** (active c.1490–1505), developed the narrative tradition in a now dispersed series, partly preserved in the museums of Cologne, Bonn and Nürnberg. This artist displays far more interest in integrating the backgrounds with the action, and his handling of space and perspective shows a sizeable advance, while his technique of rapid brushstrokes is quite different from the smooth layered approach of his predecessors. He influenced the **Master of St Severin** (active c.1490–1510), a prolific and uneven painter, with whom he probably shared a studio.

Ultimately, the Cologne School simply burned itself out, but it did come to a fitting climax with the **Master of the St Bartholomew Altar** (active c.1470–1510), whose highly idiosyncratic compositions display all the sense of freedom and mannerism which so often characterize the final fling of an artistic style. He was trained in Utrecht and may have been Dutch; at first he worked as a manuscript illuminator. His earlier panels are rather hesitant, but by about 1495 he was painting with ever-increasing confidence, using bright, enamel-type colours. Invariably his figures are executed as if in imitation of sculpture, and some of his paintings, such as the eponymous work in Munich and the *Crucifixion* triptych in Cologne, appear as trompe l'oeil versions of carved retables. Even more bizarre are canvases such as the *St Thomas altar* in Cologne, where the highly realistic figures are made to float quite illogically in space.

GOTHIC ELSEWHERE IN GERMANY

In the early fifteenth century, Cologne unquestionably held the artistic lead in Germany; a gorgeous *Garden of Paradise* preserved in Frankfurt by an unknown Upper Rhenish master from about 1420 is a clear case of the hegemony this style enjoyed. The equally beautiful *Ortenberg altar* in Darmstadt, painted the following decade by an anonymous Middle Rhenish artist, is likewise imbued with the idealized forms characteristic of Cologne, though it has a greater sense of monumentality.

As the century wore on, however, it was Swabian painters who pioneered moves towards more realistic forms, and thus paved the way to the Renaissance. First of these was **Lucas Moser**, probably a stained-glass designer by training, whose sole known work is the outside of the triptych still *in situ* in Tiefenbronn, dated 1431. Although the execution is still very soft and beautiful, an attempt is made at diminishing perspectives, while the water in the sea has both ripples and reflections. Very different is the *Wurzach altar* of six years later, now in Berlin, which was made in the workshop of the great Ulm sculptor **Hans Multscher** (c.1400–67), though it's unresolved as to whether it was executed by the master himself, or by an unknown assistant who specialized in the painting side of the business. The figures in these Passion scenes are made deliberately crude, with exaggerated theatrical gestures, and seem to have been modelled on real-life peasants; they are about as far away from the contemporary work of Lochner as it is possible to get.

A far more refined realist painter was **Konrad Witz** (c.1400–46) of Rottweil, who spent his working life in Switzerland. His surviving legacy consists of about twenty panels taken from three separate retables; Basel and Geneva have the best examples, but others are in Berlin and Nürnberg. In them, he successfully resolved the new realism with traditional forms and grappled with such problems as perspective and movement. His figures have a sculptural quality and are treated as masses,

not as means of portrayal; the rich and luminous colours employed are also an important feature. Most enduring of all was his contribution to landscape painting, being the first to introduce topographically accurate views of scenery, as opposed to cities, into his pictures. Witz's influence is discernible in the few surviving works of the **Master of the Darmstadt Passion**, who was active mid-century in the Middle Rhine region. **Friedrich Herlin** (c.1435–1499) of Nördlingen, who painted grave, severe figures, was another to follow his example; he in turn was succeeded by **Bartholomäus Zeitblom** (c.1455–1520) of Ulm.

Among Bavarian painters of this period, the **Master of the Tegernsee Altar** (active c.1430–50) was somewhat archaic in style but capable of highly dramatic effects, notably the curious *Crucifixion* in his native Munich, which is set within elaborate Gothic architecture. Also working in this city was the **Master of the Polling Panels** (active c.1434–50), who retained the International Gothic style, whilst injecting it with a dose of realism. In the same period, Nürnberg boasted the **Master of the Imhoff Altar** and the **Master of the Tucher Altar**; the latter's work is characterized by strongly drawn thick-set figures, prominent still lifes and attempts at perspective. They were succeeded by **Hans Pleydenwurff** (c.1420–72), who showed a thorough knowledge of Netherlandish artists such as Bouts in colour, figure modelling and background cityscapes, often with small subsidiary scenes; he was also a notable portraitist. After his death, his workshop was taken over by **Michael Wolgemut** (1434–1519). **Rueland Frueauf** (c.1440–1507) founded the Danube School of painting in Passau and Salzburg; although few works by him survive, the *Man of Sorrows* in Munich is an arresting masterpiece, achieved by great economy of means. His son of the same name (c.1470–1545) carried on his style.

The late Gothic period also saw something of a revival in Westphalia. In Münster, **Johann Koerbecke** (active 1446–90) gave a more forceful treatment to facial expression than his Cologne contemporaries. A sensitive touch is revealed in the work of the **Master of Liesborn** (active late fifteenth century); whilst **Derick Baegert** (c.1440–1515) imbued his paintings with a rugged dramatic quality.

Jan Joest of Kalkar (c.1455–1519) sub-merged himself in the art of the nearby Netherlands; he appears to have had a remark-able career, travelling as far afield as Spain, where he painted a retable for Palencia cathe-dral which remains *in situ.* Two north German practitioners of the new Netherlandish-influ-enced realism were **Hinrik Funhof** (c. 1435–85), whose masterpiece is in St Johannis in Lüneburg, and Lübeck's **Hermen Rode** (active 1485–1504).

THE RISE OF THE GRAPHIC ARTS

Gutenberg's printing revolution sounded the death knell for illuminated manuscripts and gave an enormous stimulus to the black and white arts, with the traditional woodcut being followed by the new techniques of line engrav-ing and drypoint, which appeared in the 1440s. At first, the forms were dominated by obscure figures from the Mainz area – the two pioneers were the so-called **Master of the Playing Cards**, whose reputation rests on an elaborate card deck, and **Master ES**, whose creations include a fantastic alphabet. Another engraver known only by his initials is **Master LCZ** of Bamberg, by whom some expressive panels also survive.

A more rounded personality appears in the **Master of the Housebook** (active c.1470–1500), around whom a sizeable body of work has been gathered; many attempts have been made to equate him with **Erhard Reuwich**, who executed a series of woodcuts for a book on a journey to the Holy Land. His pseudonym derives from an extraordinary book of drawings in a private collection; it was the manual of a master of munitions at a princely court, and contains elaborate astrological groupings as well as scenes of warfare. Even finer are his delicate drypoints, which depict with both humanity and humour the everyday life of the time, from the fashions and fantasies of the small courts to the earthy pastimes of the peasantry. The draughtsman's technique is also evident in the linear form of his few paintings, which include two retables, one in Mainz, the other dispersed in the museums of Freiburg, Berlin and Frankfurt.

An equally great but very different graphic artist was **Martin Schongauer** (c.1450–91) of Colmar, which was then very much a German city. He has always been a revered figure, as he

marks the transition from the late Gothic to the Renaissance, and is thus the founding father of the short but glorious period when the German visual arts reached the highest peaks of their achievement. Over a hundred surviving engrav-ings show his successful fusion of realism and expressionism from northern artists with the exotic interests and technical innovations of space, form and perspective which characterize the Italian Renaissance. They were to serve as a model and an inspiration to the succeeding generation, who increasingly came to realize that the print was an important new democrat-ic art form closely in tune with the spirit of the age, with potential for reaching a far wider pub-lic than had ever been possible before. Schongauer's surviving paintings are tantaliz-ingly few but always of very high quality – they include the large *Madonna of the Rose Bush* in his native city, some damaged frescoes of *The Last Judgement* in nearby Breisach, and several little panels of *The Nativity*, the finest of which is in Berlin.

THE TRIUMPH OF THE RENAISSANCE

The most dominant personality in the history of German art was **Albrecht Dürer** (1471–1528), who trained under Wolgemut in his native Nürnberg. Dürer was a true man of the Renaissance, gaining a broad range of experi-ences in antithesis to the painstaking workshop traditions which were the lot of the medieval artist. He undertook travels to Italy, Switzerland, Alsace and the Low Countries, assimilating their traditions, and gained mastery in all artis-tic media, yet also found time to write and engage in mathematical and scientific research as well as to be involved in the Reformation, ending up excommunicated for Lutheran sympa-thies. Surprisingly, canvas painting does not always show Dürer at his best – he was at times rather conservative in his earlier religious panels, but increased in confidence with time, as can be seen in his valedictory *Four Apostles* in Munich. His portraits from life, however, are almost uniformly superb, laying bare the soul of the subject in penetrating psychological obser-vations, as in *Jacob Muffel* and *Hieronymus Holzschuher*, both now in Berlin. With the woodcut, Dürer was in a class of his own; while still in his twenties he created an *Apocalypse* series of quite menacing power and profound imagination, which he printed and published himself. This was followed by two *Passion* series, a lovely *Life of the Virgin* and the stupendous *Triumphal Arch* commissioned by Emperor Maximilian; he also made many memorable engravings, often deeply overlaid with symbolic meaning. Dürer was also the first artist to realize the possibilities of watercolour, executing beautiful landscapes and plant and animal studies. The originals of these are now rarely exhibited for conservation reasons, yet such works as *Young Hare* and *Blade of Grass* rank among the most familiar images in Renaissance art.

Hans Wertinger (c.1465–1533), who worked primarily in Landshut and Freising, was an ambitious and versatile artist who is nowadays remembered principally for his tiny, highly detailed paintings of the months and seasons, which were intended to adorn domestic interiors. In Munich, the Polish-born **Jan Polack** (active c.1480–1519) painted mannered altarpieces featuring emotional figures clad in swirling draperies, along with portraits more obviously imbued with the new Renaissance outlook.

A far more significant artistic centre was Augsburg, a seat of the Habsburg court. **Hans Holbein the Elder** (c.1465–1524) showed increasing Renaissance influence in his prolific output of retables, although he was never entirely able to free himself from the old forms. His brother-in-law **Hans Burgkmair** (1473–1531) was more successful, benefiting from a spell as Schongauer's assistant; he particularly delighted in the most luxuriant Italianate features, which he skilfully synthesized into his altars. This decorative talent was given full rein by Emperor Maximilian I, who commissioned him to supervise the overall programme of the huge series of woodcuts of his *Triumphal Procession*; many of the leading German artists, including Dürer, contributed, although the success of the project was due to the relish shown by Burgkmair. **Jörg Breu** (c.1475–1537) was another fine retable painter resident in the city, while **Bernhard Strigel** (c.1460–1528), who served as court portraitist, developed family groups as an independent art form.

By far the greatest painter Augsburg produced was **Hans Holbein the Younger** (1497/8–1543), but he left while still in his teens, and spent the rest of his career in Switzerland and England. He first settled in Basel (which retains by far the best collection of his art), where he was enormously productive in all kinds of media – portraits, altarpieces, decorative schemes of many types (now mostly lost) and woodcuts, including the celebrated *Dance of Death*. One of his masterpieces from this period, and one of the few works by him actually in Germany, is the *Madonna of Burgomaster Mayer* in Darmstadt Schloss, which combines sharply characterized portraits and a devotional theme. He subsequently concentrated almost exclusively on portraiture, developing a cool, detached style based on absolute technical mastery, and frequently incorporating amazingly precise still lifes based on the paraphernalia of the sitter's occupation; *The Danzig Merchant Georg Gisze*, now in Berlin, is an outstanding example. On his second visit to England, he became court painter to Henry VIII, and left a haunting series of drawings of that magnificent but tragic circle, though sadly few of the finished paintings have been preserved.

Lucas Cranach the Elder (1472–1553) was the earliest great Saxon painter. The first thirty years of his life are obscure; he is first known as a mature artist playing a dominant role in the Danube School, painting portraits and religious scenes set in lush and suggestively beautiful verdant landscapes. His masterpiece of this period is *The Three Crosses* in Munich, which uses a blatantly eccentric vantage point in order to emphasize the artist's technical control. Whereas these works have consistently been admired, Cranach's long second phase at Wittenberg in the service of the Electors of Saxony is far more controversial. He ran the equivalent of a picture factory, often repeating the same subjects ad infinitum with only minor variations; the style is mannered with imperfections in drawing and subjects placed in wholly unrealistic relationships. Yet these were surely deliberate traits by a great humorist and individualist, whose sinuous nudes and erotic mythological scenes added a dimension to German painting which had previously been lacking. He seems to have invented the full-length portrait as a genre, and excelled at characterization. As a personal friend of Luther and Melanchthon, he created the definitive images of the leaders of the Reformation and made propaganda woodcuts on their behalf, but was not averse to accepting traditional commissions from the Catholics as well. His son **Lucas Cranach the Younger** (1515–86) took over the workshop and continued its tradition faithfully.

Albrecht Altdorfer (c.1480–1538) of Regensburg became the leading master of the Danube School; his luxuriant landscape backgrounds assume even greater significance than with Cranach, and at times the ostensible subject is quite unimportant, as with *St George and the Dragon* in Munich. Fantastic buildings also feature in several of his works, reflecting the fact that he was also a practising architect. When the figures do matter, they are integrated with their surroundings and given highly expressive tendencies, achieved by deliberate anatomical imprecisions and exaggerated gestures. Light is often an important feature, with unnaturally colourful effects; unorthodox aerial perspectives further distinguish his paintings. The largest group of Altdorfer's work, in which all these features appear, is still mostly *in situ* in the Austrian monastery of St Florian. However, his masterpiece is the *Battle of Darius and Alexander* in Munich; commissioned as part of a war series, each by different artists, it makes all the others look like the work of bumbling amateurs. The actual battle is depicted with all the skill of a miniaturist, yet it is set within a spectacular cosmic perspective in what ranks as one of the most formidable displays of sheer pyrotechnics in the history of painting. His chief follower was **Wolf Huber** (c.1490–1553) of Passau, who was rather more restrained in his effects.

The extreme tendency towards expression in German painting is found in the work of the painter known as **Grünewald**, although his real name was **Mathis Gothardt Neithardt** (c.1470/5–1528), who is almost a direct opposite of Dürer. Fully proficient in the new Renaissance developments of space and perspective, he used them as mere adjuncts to his sense of drama; he was also the only great German artist of his time who seems to have had no interest in the print. Even in an early work such as *The Mocking of Christ* in Munich, Grünewald's emotional power is evident. No artist ever painted Passion scenes with anything like the same harrowing intensity; in the words of the nineteenth-century French novelist Huysmans, "he promptly strikes you dumb with the fearsome nightmare of a Calvary". His huge

folding polyptych, the *Isenheim altar*, represents the majority of his surviving work. Though its panels are of uneven quality, its moods – ranging from a tender *Madonna and Child* to the blazing triumphant glory of *The Resurrection* – are of such variety that it deserves its reputation as the ultimate masterpiece of German painting; ironically, its Colmar home is now French territory.

Grünewald's art is so individual and overpowering that he had no successors. However, **Jerg Ratgeb** (c.1480–1526) must have come under his influence as his few works – fresco cycles in Frankfurt and Maulbronn, and the *Herrenberg altar* in Stuttgart – have an even rawer expressiveness, which might have developed had he not been executed for his leading role in the Peasants' War.

Of the younger generation of Renaissance artists, by far the most interesting is **Hans Baldung Grien** (1484/5–1545), a flawed genius who studied under Dürer and eventually settled in Strasbourg. Colour and volume play a large part in his pictures, but his fascination with the bizarre is the most obvious recurring element, with moralistic fantasies being among his finest works. Baldung's main religious works are two altars for Freiburg Münster, but there is no concentration of his output, which is now spread among many museums. The late engravings such as *Wild Horses* and *Bewitched Stable Boy* are quite unlike the work of any other artist, and arguably rank as his greatest achievements.

Hans Süss von Kulmbach (c.1480–1522) and **Hans Leonard Schäuffelein** (c.1483–1539/40) were loyal followers of Dürer's example, but their productions ultimately lack his inspired touch; the specialist engravers, the brothers **Hans Sebald Beham** (1500–50) and **Barthel Beham** (1502–40), and the Westphalian **Heinrich Aldegraver** (1502–60) were arguably more successful at capturing his spirit. The **Master of Messkirch** (active c.1530–45) added a personal expressive sense to the Düreresque idiom.

The early sixteenth century also saw a mushrooming of talented provincial portraitists who were able to satisfy the ever-increasing demand from the rising middle classes; they often painted religious and mythological subjects as well, but with less success. In Nürnberg, **Georg Pencz** (c.1500–50), possibly another pupil of

Dürer, was strongly influenced by Venetian models. Augsburg at this time had **Ulrich Apt** (c.1460–1532) and **Cristoph Amberger** (c.1500–61/2), who was more associated with the court. The portraits of Frankfurt's **Conrad Faber von Creuznach** (c.1500–53) are particularly felicitous, with the sitters placed against landscapes reminiscent of the Danube School; he also executed a magnificent woodcut of the siege of his home city. **Barthel Bruyn** (1492/3–1555) was the first Cologne painter to break away from two centuries of tradition; in spite of several diverse influences, the city's great heritage seems to have made little impression on his art. In Münster, **Ludger tom Ring the Elder** (1496–1547) founded a dynasty which specialized in slightly crude portraits and altars for both Protestant and Catholic use. His style was continued by his sons **Hermann tom Ring** (1521–96) and **Ludger tom Ring the Younger** (1522–84); the latter seems to have been the first German artist to treat still life as an independent form. **Hans Mielich** (1516–73) dominated artistic life in Munich for several decades, though his panel paintings are rather stiff and formal in comparison with his exquisite manuscript illuminations.

MANNERISM AND THE EARLY BAROQUE

Mannerism is already evident in the work of the generation after Dürer, but only appears in a full-blooded way with **Hans von Aachen** (1552–1616), who particularly excelled at sensual mythological subjects, and who played a leading role in the highly distinctive erotic style fostered at the court of Emperor Rudolf II in Prague. **Johann Rottenhammer** (1564–1625) travelled extensively in Italy, before returning to his native Augsburg. He came under the spell of Paolo Veronese's huge decorative works filled with figures; his response was to reduce such compositions onto little copper panels, adding an extra degree of luminosity into the landscapes.

This highly skilled technique was developed by his pupil, **Adam Elsheimer** (1578–1610), who settled in Rome and achieved a remarkable synthesis of diverse influences which gives his works a stature that belies their small size. Elsheimer drew on Altdorfer's heritage in creating a union between the subjects and nature, which Rottenhammer left as rather disparate

features. He also seemed to share the earlier master's genius for light effects, and was particularly adept at night scenes and at strong contrasts of brightness and shadow derived from Caravaggio. A slow and deliberate worker, Elsheimer died early, so his legacy is numerically modest, but it was to influence such contrasting great successors as Rubens, Rembrandt and Claude. The largest assemblage of his work is *altar of The Holy Cross*, whose panels have been painstakingly reassembled over the years in his native Frankfurt; many of his best paintings are in Britain, due to the esteem in which he was held by the aristocrats of the Grand Tour.

Unfortunately, there was no great German successor, although his style was continued with varying success long after his death by **Johann König** (1586–1642). Elsheimer's influence is also evident in the legacy of **Gottfried Wals** (c.1595–1638), best known as the teacher of Claude, but a distinctive artist in his own right, specializing in small copper roundels of landscapes with figures bathed in light.

The other main German painter of the early seventeenth century, **Johann Liss** (1597–1629), was constantly on the move, leaving his native Holstein for the Low Countries and then Italy, absorbing their diverse traditions. One vein of his work, the small arcadian landscapes, reveals the impact of Elsheimer or at least his Roman followers, but his best canvases are far more monumental in scale, swaggering in the full pomp characteristic of the new Baroque age. These religious and mythological scenes, sometimes featuring sumptuous banquets, are executed with fluid brushwork in daringly unorthodox colours.

Liss was also to occupy a premature grave, and it seems as if German painting in the seventeenth century was to be jinxed, in contrast to its richness and diversity in this period over the rest of Europe. The Thirty Years War, which so exhausted and preoccupied the country, acted as a massive restraint on artistic activity at the time, but was to fuel a long-standing vogue for depictions of battles and genre scenes of military life evidenced in the work of **Matthias Scheits** (c.1630–1700) and **Georg Philip Rugendas** (1666–1742), though these tend to follow the decorative Dutch manner, rather than convey the true horrors the country suffered. An increased religious fervour as a result of the war is mirrored in the emotional cycles of canvases and frescoes by the Catholic convert **Michael Willmann** (1630–1706), the best of which are in the monasteries in Silesia (now part of Poland).

The Moravian-born **Georg Flegel** (1566–1638) was the first German artist to specialize exclusively in still life, initiating a vogue for this genre in his adopted home city of Frankfurt. Equally precise and detached, the works of the last major Frankfurt master of still life, **Abraham Mignon** (1640–79), are altogether lusher in effect, typically showing ripe fruit and flowers in full bloom. Other specialist painters of the period include **Wolfgang Heimbach** (c.1613–78), a deaf-mute who created small scenes of middle-class life and used nocturnal lighting to good effect; and the animal artists **Carl Andreas Ruthart** (c.1630–73) and **Philipp Peter Roos** (1655–1706).

Far more versatile than any of these was **Johann Friedrich Schönfeld** (1609–84), whose output is rather uneven due to an excessive number of changes of style in response to the diversity he encountered on his Italian travels. His best paintings are colourful history scenes with elaborate backgrounds, painted under the influence of the classically derived compositions of Poussin which held sway in Rome, but tempered by the more light-hearted Neapolitan approach. The only German artist to fall under the spell of Rembrandt was **Jürgen Ovens** (1623–78), who spent part of his career in Amsterdam in the circle of the great Dutch master, before returning to his native Schleswig-Holstein, where he produced portraits and history scenes in his teacher's most Baroque vein.

However, the most significant art works produced in mid-seventeenth-century Germany were the detailed engravings of towns, known as *Topographia Germaniae*, started by **Matthäus Merian** (1593–1650), and continued by his sons. In due course, the appearances of some two thousand German communities – a unique pictorial record – were preserved for posterity.

LATE BAROQUE, ROCOCO AND NEOCLASSICISM

The best late Baroque German painting is not to be found in any museum, but on the walls of the ornate pilgrimage churches of Bavaria and Baden-Württemberg. These buildings, which aimed at fusing all the visual arts into a coher-

ent synthesis, are among the most original creations in the country. Their rich interior decoration formed an intrinsic part of the architecture from the outset, and was often the work of the same masters.

One of the most accomplished of these was **Cosmas Damian Asam** (1686–1739), who formed a team with his sculptor brother, Egid Quirin Asam. At first they decorated existing churches, such as the Dom in Freising, but later moved on to undertaking the entire programme themselves. They trained in Rome and were for the most part loyal to its dignified High Baroque, rather than to the more frivolous Rococo derivatives favoured by their fellow countrymen. C.D. Asam's ceiling frescoes fall into two separate categories – the trick device of diminishing perspective in the manner of the Italian Jesuit Andrea Pozzo, and a more conventional spatial format of open heavens.

Johann Baptist Zimmerman (1680–1758), in contrast, is fully Rococo; he did not design buildings himself, but enjoyed a particularly close relationship with two of the leading architects of the time: François Cuvilliés, with whom he collaborated on the Munich Residenz and Schloss Nymphenburg; and his own younger brother Dominikus, with whom he worked at Steinhausen and the Wieskirche. Two other major fresco painters were **Johann Georg Bergmüller** (1688–1762) and **Matthäus Günther** (1705–88), who successively directed the Augsburg Academy.

By this time, Prussia had arisen as a major power in European affairs, and was by far the dominant German state. Frederick the Great was a major patron of the arts, but he was also a Francophile whose court painter was the Parisian-born **Antoine Pesne** (1683–1757). This artist was commissioned to paint allegorical and mythological decorative schemes for the royal palaces, but his realistic portraits, very much in the French manner of the time with rich colours and subtle lighting effects, were more successful and ultimately highly influential, serving as the model for later Berlin artists. His most important pupil was **Bernhard Rode** (1725–97), who was also involved in the work on the palaces, but who is seen at his best in quietly observed genre scenes. For the last period of his life, he directed the Berlin Academy, one of several founded in the major cities in order to foster a theoretical approach to painting. Another of this circle was **Daniel Nikolaus Chodowiecki** (1726–1801), although his talent was best suited to vignette etchings, mostly to illustrate books. A later Berlin artist, **Asmus Jakob Carstens** (1754–98) was also at his finest in black and white media, executing large chalk cartoons of classical subjects.

One of the guiding lights of the movement was **Anton Raffael Mengs** (1728–79), son of the court painter in Dresden, who had ruthlessly prepared him for artistic fame from a very early age. Mengs was to have an amazingly successful career in Germany, Italy and particularly Spain. He was a key theorist and guru of the new Neoclassicism; his works are enormously skilful technically, but emotionally cold. The Swiss-born **Anton Graff** (1736–1835) was also a leading academic portraitist in Dresden. This same city was home to a succession of landscape painters throughout the century, whose work foreshadows the far more arresting compositions of the Romantics; **Johann Alexander Thiele** (1685–1752) was the first and most accomplished of these.

A strict Neoclassical style was adopted at the Kassel Academy under **Johann Heinrich Tischbein** (1722–89). This was modified by his nephews **Johann Friedrich August Tischbein** (1750–1812) and **Johann Heinrich Wilhelm Tischbein** (1751–1829), who introduced the greater warmth found in English and French works of the time, though both remained loyal academicians. The latter's *Goethe in the Campagna* in Frankfurt is the most celebrated work of the dynasty.

Another family of painters had as by far its most accomplished member **Januarius Zick** (1730–97), who turned his back on his academic training. He was a theatrical but effective frescoist in the grand manner, as can be seen in the cycles in Wiblingen and Bruchsal. In contrast, his canvases are often of modest size, achieving an original synthesis of the light effects usually found in Rembrandt's deeply intimate small-scale works with the airy Rococo grace of Watteau.

ROMANTICISM

The Romantic movement, a reaction against the rigidity of Neoclassicism but with the same Roman roots, was particularly strong in Germany; the rich outpourings of music and literature make it one of the supreme high points in the country's cultural history. Although there was not the same depth of talent in painting, the haunting and highly original landscapes of **Caspar David Friedrich** (1774–1840) form a fitting visual counterpart to the works of the great poets and composers of the time. Friedrich created a new spiritual way of looking at the scenery: it was always the immensity and majesty of Nature that he sought to convey, often using the technique of enormously long perspectives. Unlike his great predecessor Altdorfer, he did not stress the unity of man and landscape, but rather the unconquerable power of the latter. Where figures are introduced, they are typically seen from the back, contemplating the wonders before them; in the more common absence of humans, the evidence of Man's presence tends to stress his fragility and ephemeral status – as in the famous *Eismeer* in Hamburg, or the many scenes with classical temples and Gothic abbeys – in comparison with the omnipotent changelessness of the surroundings.

The influence of Friedrich's way of looking can sometimes be detected in the canvases of **Karl Friedrich Schinkel** (1781–1841), who was forced by financial considerations to turn to painting, where he abandoned the Neoclassicism of his buildings in favour of vast panoramas and architectural fantasies. **Leo von Klenze** (1794–1864), the other great architect of German Neoclassicism, was likewise a gifted occasional painter, producing romanticized views of the ruins of Greece and Rome. More orthodox followers of Friedrich include **Carl Gustav Carus** (1787–1869) and **Ernst Ferdinand Oehme** (1797–1855).

Philipp Otto Runge (1777–1810) might have developed into Friedrich's figurative counterpart had he lived longer. He had enormously grandiose ideas, aiming to recover the lost harmony of the universe through the symbolism of colours and numbers, and began a project called *The Times of Day*, of four panels over 8m in height, which he aimed to install in a specially designed building in which poetry and music would be performed. That he managed to persuade Goethe to co-operate in this suggests that there was genuine substance to this apparently utopian dream, but it was never executed and only studies survive, leaving Runge's reputation to rest largely on his portraits, particularly the oversized ones depicting children.

Johann Friedrich Overbeck (1789–1869) was another Romantic with original convictions, settling in Rome where he founded the **Nazarene Brotherhood** of painters who lived like monks in a deconsecrated monastery. They produced two large co-operative fresco cycles: *The Story of Joseph*, now in the Alte Nationalgalerie in Berlin, and another, still *in situ*, of scenes taken from Italian Renaissance literature. These detailed works emphasized theme and content at the expense of form.

Whereas Overbeck remained in Italy, his collaborators **Peter von Cornelius** (1783–1867), **Philipp Veit** (1793–1877), **Julius Schnorr von Carolsfeld** (1794–1872) and **Wilhelm Schadow** (1788–1862) returned to Germany where they pursued careers in the academies. Cornelius had spells in charge of the two most dominant, Düsseldorf and Munich, and aimed to establish a tradition of monumental historical painting to rival the great frescoes of Italy. Although both influential and genuinely popular in its day, this style of painting has, for the past century, attracted nothing but critical scorn, appearing as an empty display of bombastics. It can still be seen all over the country, often desecrating the walls of great medieval buildings; among the better efforts are the cycles by **Alfred Rethel** (1816–59) in the Aachen Rathaus and by the Austrian-born **Moritz von Schwind** (1804–71) in Karlsruhe's Kunsthalle, and the Wartburg near Eisenach. The latter was the most refined illustrator of the Romantic view of the German Middle Ages, whose ethos he captured in numerous beautifully coloured and detailed canvases, such as *The Knight Kuno von Falkenstein* in Leipzig. **Ferdinand Olivier** (1785–1841) painted narrative canvases in the Nazarene style, as well as more conventional Romantic landscapes.

Standing somewhat apart are the expansive, open-ended fresco views painted in Munich by Ludwig I's court artist **Carl Rottmann** (1797–1850). Other Munich artists took the grand academic manner to its most extreme. Prominent among them were **Wilhelm von Kaulbach** (1805–76), a pupil of Cornelius, who produced monumental designs for the decoration of the Neue Pinakothek, and **Karl von Piloty** (1826–86), whose huge, highly theatrical history paintings were intended to evoke patriotic sentiment.

Romanticism in one form or another flourished throughout the nineteenth century. The brothers **Andreas Achenbach** (1815–1910) and **Oswald Achenbach** (1827–1905) continued in Friedrich's manner; the former was particularly successful at evocative northern scenery, whereas the latter added popular scenes to his pictures. **Carl Blechen** (1798–1840) also began in this style, but his later works, following a visit to Paris, became more consciously realist. **Anselm Feuerbach** (1829–80) pursued a heavily Italianate form of Romanticism in his portraits and densely crowded mythological scenes. There is a highly personal mixture of the Neoclassical and Romantic in **Hans von Marées** (1837–87), who achieved his masterpiece in his one commission for monumental frescoes, the Aquarium in Naples. For long out of critical favour, his canvases have recently begun to attract a great deal of interest. The inconsistent **Hans Thoma** (1839–1924) tried many styles in his time; his Romantic views of the Black Forest are by far the most successful.

OTHER NINETEENTH-CENTURY STYLES

Although many different trends were current in nineteenth-century German painting, none of them can match the vitality of the best Romantic work. A style which was largely confined to the country and its immediate neighbours from about 1815 to 1848 was Biedermeierstil, a bourgeois-inspired classicism which drew on the pleasant aspects of living. **Carl Spitzweg** (1808–85) was its principal exponent; his homely pictures of the middle classes are injected with a touch of humour mocking the complacency that was all too apparent. **Franz Krüger** (1797–1857) chronicled Berlin life of the time in a more straight-laced vein, particularly in his ceremonial scenes and architectural views; **Eduard Gaertner** (1801–77) executed more felicitous topographical views of Berlin, while the Prussian court painter **Carl Graeb** (1816–84) produced exquisitely detailed little works of the same city and of the palaces and gardens of nearby Potsdam. Though he sometimes worked in the Düsseldorf academic manner, **Georg Friedrich Kersting** (1785–1847) was at his best in small-scale interiors, in which he showed his interest in everyday objects and activities as matters of beauty in their own right. The Dresden artist **Ludwig Richter** (1804–83) was a fine landscape painter, but again his true métier lay in a quite different field, in this case his illustrations of legends for children's books. His pupil **Edouard Leonhardi** (1825–1905) specialized in highly detailed, meticulously executed forest scenes.

In contrast to this movement, there was a continued demand for official portraitists; one of the most accomplished was **Franz von Lenbach** (1836–1904), who painted Bismarck eighty times. **Franz Xaver Winterhalter** (1805–73) had the most dazzling career of all, progressing round all the main European courts, leaving behind unremittingly flattering portrayals of smug monarchs.

Standing in total contrast is the versatile **Adolph Menzel** (1815–1905), who complemented his superb technique with meticulous background research on his subject-matter. He painted wonderfully characterized portraits throughout his long life; few of these are in oil, as he preferred to use chalk, pencil, pastel or gouache for portraiture. Among his most hauntingly distinctive compositions are small paintings of unoccupied interiors, but he adopted the grand manner for his history scenes (predominantly of the life of Frederick the Great), which nonetheless eschew the heroic idealized imagery then fashionable in favour of a psychological approach. In the second half of his career, Menzel devoted much of his energy to documenting contemporary life, and his masterpiece, *The Iron Rolling Mill* in the Alte Nationalgalerie in Berlin, was the first painting to offer a detailed and accurate picture of the realities of working life in the Industrial Age.

Germany's other leading Realist was **Wilhelm Leibl** (1844–1900), who aimed to recreate the technical skill of the old masters. To this end he conducted such experiments as reviving tempera to create an enamel-like surface, and painting with the attention to detail of a miniaturist, as in *Three Women in Church* in Hamburg. Much of his finest work was done in the 1870s, when he lived in rural Bavaria, and used peasants as real-life models. **Wilhelm Trübner** (1851–1917) was another practitioner of Realism, one who undertook a broad mix of subjects.

Impressionism was very slow to catch on, and never seems to have suited the German temperament, but three major artists adopted it at some point in their careers. Of these, **Max Liebermann** (1847–1935), originally favoured the sombre colours of the French Barbizon School and the Realists, and it was in the latter vein that he executed his many large, highly detailed canvases of life in Dutch orphanages, schools and old peoples' homes. Following his Impressionist phase, he ended his long working life as the most sought-after society portraitist of the Weimar Republic. **Lovis Corinth** (1858–1925) painted an unusually wide range of subjects; his religious and mythological canvases often exude a sense of raw emotional power and menace, yet he also produced sun-filled interior views and highly erotic nudes. Among his most distinctive compositions are the late views of the Walchensee in Bavaria, executed in cold colours; these postdate a stroke which had left his painting hand paralysed. **Max Slevogt** (1868–1932) was also a book illustrator and, late in life, a painter of monumental frescoes.

Liebermann was the leading figure in the Berlin section of the **Secession movement** which began in the 1890s; this was a reaction by the avant-garde against the stultifying power wielded by the academies. Prominent members of the earlier Munich group were **Fritz von Uhde** (1848–1911), who painted intimate genre scenes and strikingly original reinterpretations of biblical stories in contemporary dress, and **Franz von Stuck** (1863–1928), an artist of violent mythological scenes, humorous drawings and large-scale decorative work. Based in the artistic backwater of Leipzig, the painter, sculptor and engraver **Max Klinger** (1857–1920) cut a somewhat solitary figure; although his output is very uneven in quality, he was capable, particularly in his graphic work, of real emotional power.

The most successful of several artists' colonies was that at Worpswede near Bremen, which was founded by **Fritz Mackensen** (1866–1953) in 1889. It survives to this day, though much of the best work done there was in its early years, when Mackensen and his friends **Otto Modersohn** (1856–1943), and **Hans am Ende** (1864–1918) produced a stream of canvases illustrating the bleakness of the local landscape and the harshness of life for its inhabitants.

EXPRESSIONISM

Much as the early part of the nineteenth century saw the dominance of Romanticism in

German painting, so the first decades of the twentieth century came under the sway of Expressionism, a new and largely indigenous style, which aimed to root modern painting firmly in the tradition of the old German masters, and to establish it on an equal footing with France, for some time the dominant force in world art. Because of the entrenched power of existing interests, artists found they had to bind themselves into **groups** in order to make an impact; the early history of Expressionism is particularly associated with two of these.

Although its members were younger, **Die Brücke** (The Bridge) was first to be founded, in 1905. Its initial personnel, **Ernst Ludwig Kirchner** (1880–1938), **Erich Heckel** (1883–1970) and **Karl Schmidt-Rottluff** (1884–1976), were architectural students in Dresden who felt constrained by the inability of their subject to capture the immediate freshness of inspiration. Consequently, they turned to painting, in which none had much experience; they were shortly joined by **Max Pechstein** (1881–1955) and **Otto Müller** (1874–1930). They valued colour as a component in its own right, and later strove to enhance its surface effect as well. Their devotion to the country's artistic heritage was shown in the emphasis they placed on feeling, and on their revival of the woodcut as a valid alternative to oils.

The group moved to Berlin, where they turned away from their original preoccupation with landscapes to the depiction of city life. Kirchner developed into the leader and best artist of the group. *Three Women in the Street*, now in Essen, is a key work; its strong sense of line shows the impact made by the arts of primitive peoples, then being appreciated in Europe for the first time. The group broke up in 1913, and thereafter each artist pursued an independent career. Kirchner turned to decorative design in the 1920s, working on embroideries and tapestries; his later paintings show a stronger sense of abstraction. Heckel's work is closest to Kirchner's, though he was later to add a greater sense of realism to his pictures. Pechstein, at the time regarded as the most important Expressionist of all, has since suffered a slump in reputation; he was the most loyal to naturalistic representation and thus stands furthest removed from the path followed by Schmidt-Rottluff. Gypsy culture features strongly in Müller's work; he seems to have felt

a genuine affinity with it, and spent much of the 1920s travelling among Balkan communities.

The second group of artists was **Der Blaue Reiter** (The Blue Rider), a strongly intellectual movement originating in Munich which aimed at uniting all the arts. Its name is taken from its magazine, which appeared only once (in 1912); it was very loosely structured and far more diverse than Die Brücke, with the lead being taken by two contrasting artistic personalities. The Russian-born **Wassily Kandinsky** (1866–1944) was a pioneer of pure abstraction, using fluid and soft forms, but strong and vibrant colours; he was also a noted writer and used words as the starting points for his images. **Franz Marc** (1880–1916), on the other hand, always retained at least a partial form of representation in his compositions. He was devoted to nature, and animals are a recurrent theme in his art; he regarded them as noble and uncorrupted, the complete antithesis to Man. At first they appear detached in the foreground; from 1913, when he adopted more abstract methods, they are more closely integrated with their surroundings. Geometry was always important to Marc, and he favoured prismatic colours, to which he attached a mystical significance. His development was cut short by the outbreak of war, and he died in combat.

This fate also befell an even younger member of the group, **August Macke** (1887–1914). Although Macke was clearly influenced by the new Cubist movement, his works are always representational, and he ranks as the most poetic and gentle of all the Expressionists. The figures are unmistakeable; slim and column-like, they glide across the picture surface, taking their Sunday stroll in the park, or indulging in a bit of window-shopping. More often than not, they wear a hat, which serves to distinguish them, as their facial features are never included. Strong colours are used, but they are never strident; they rather add to the happy and relaxed atmosphere.

Paul Klee (1879–1940), born in Switzerland but having German nationality as well, was the fourth main member of the group. He never concerned himself with any of the social, political or psychological problems of the age, but preferred to construct his own abstract language in which he aimed to recapture the mystery and magic of the universe. To this end, he developed a series of fractured and fragmented forms –

arcs, forks and bars – which were usually painted black against a coloured background. In the
1920s, when they worked at the Bauhaus, he
and Kandinsky formed **Die Blauen Vier** (The
Blue Four) as a successor to Der Blaue Reiter.

The other members were **Alexej
Jawlensky** (1864–1941), also of Russian birth,
who specialized in characterful portrait heads;
and **Lyonel Feininger** (1871–1956), who was
born and died in New York, but who can be
regarded as the most loyal German Cubist,
being most notable for his architectural and
marine scenes. Russian influence is apparent in
the paintings of **Heinrich Campendonk**
(1889–1957), the youngest member of *Der
Blaue Reiter*, although his preferred medium
was the woodcut.

A number of Expressionists unattached to
either group were active in the Rhine-Ruhr area,
where Macke also spent much of his life.
Throughout a very long career, **Christian
Rohlfs** (1849–1938) tried many different styles;
he clearly came under the influence of the
Impressionists but never fully adopted their
manner. His true artistic personality did not
emerge until his Expressionist phase, particularly the architectural paintings he made in Soest
and Erfurt, and the very late flower pieces.
Rohlfs clearly inspired **Wilhelm Morgner**
(1891–1917), another war casualty. **Heinrich
Nauen** (1880–1940) was one of several
Expressionists who were quite overt about following French leads, in his case Matisse and
the Fauves, whose bright colours form an important feature of his hybrid style.

Hans Purrmann (1880–1966) was
Matisse's most loyal German disciple, while
Fauvism, particularly the classically inspired
works of Derain, heavily influenced **Carl Hofer**
(1878–1955). Primitive art as filtered through
Gauguin made a strong impression on **Paula
Modersohn-Becker** (1876–1907), the most
talented artist of the colony at Worpswede.
Whether or not she is really an Expressionist is
debatable, as she did not concern herself with
drama or emotions, though her favourite
Mother and Child theme has achieved a certain
poignancy as she later died in childbirth.

The most individualistic Expressionist of all,
even though he had a spell as a member of Die
Brücke, was **Emil Hansen** (1867–1956), generally called **Nolde** after his birthplace. In his
depictions of the rugged North Sea coastline

that was his home, he can be regarded as the
successor to Friedrich. However, there's no
sense of romance in Nolde's landscapes, which
convey the harsh and forbidding nature of the
terrain and its climate, emphasized in the way
he captured its special colours and light effects
by means of rich, strong and violently contrasting tones. Flowers and garden scenes provide a
lighter note, but he also revived the somewhat
lost art of religious painting, in which he aimed
to recreate something of the intensity of
Grünewald, along with the simple devotion he
found in primitive art.

Ludwig Meidner (1884–1966) was dubbed
the most Expressionist of the Expressionists, as
a result of the powerful apocalyptic visions he
painted before the war, which stand at the
opposite extreme to the primitive trends in the
movement. The union of all the arts sought by
so many found its best individual manifestation
in the work of **Ernst Barlach** (1870–1938).
Primarily a sculptor, he was also a talented
graphic artist, illustrating his own plays and
travel writings. Another sculptor, **Käthe
Kollwitz** (1867–1945) achieved great emotional power in her pacifist woodcuts, engravings
and lithographs of wartime horrors.

OTHER TWENTIETH-CENTURY MOVEMENTS

Expressionism, in spite of its dominance, does
not by any means cover the entire richness of
German art in the early part of the twentieth
century. The nihilistic Dada movement, which
grew up during the war, included **Kurt
Schwitters** (1887–1948), who took the concept
of non-art to its extreme, experimenting with
collages incorporating pieces of torn-up paper
before moving on to using rubbish as his basic
component. He dubbed his art *Merz* after the
letters from one of the pieces of paper he used,
and intended his life's work to be a huge composition which would fill a house, but the first
two completed versions were destroyed, and
his last attempt, in exile in England, was unfinished at his death. **Hannah Höch** (1889–1978)
and the Austrian-born **Raoul Hausmann**
(1886–1944) were two rather milder Dadaists.

George Grosz (1893–1959) also began in
this style, but his later works were more representational. A committed Communist, he was a
savage satirist, particularly in his humorous
drawings, ruthlessly attacking the corrupt and

decadent vested interests of the Weimar Republic. Ironically, he was entranced by America and emigrated there just before the Nazi rise to power. Another prominent Dadaist and left-winger was **John Heartfield** (1891–1968), who adopted an anglicized form of his original name, Helmut Herzfeld, in protest at German xenophobia. Best known as the inventor of the photomontage, which he used to devastating effect to attack the Nazis from his exile in Czechoslovakia and Britain, he settled in the GDR after World War II, where his work, in the service of the state, lost much of its sharpness.

Inevitably, there grew a tendency which stood in polar opposition to Expressionism: **Neue Sachlichkeit** (New Objectivity), a term first used in 1923 to describe trends already apparent. This can be thought of as an updated form of Realism, which aimed at depicting subjects in a straightforward and detailed way. Some of Grosz's work belongs to this style, but its finest practitioner was **Otto Dix** (1891–1969), who had been profoundly affected by the war. This formed a persistent subject of his work, although he used it to depict Man's suffering as opposed to any directly political overtone. He aimed to recapture the actual technique of the old masters, and his portraits show larger-than-life characters under a rich sheen of paint. In spite of the overt eroticism of many of his canvases, he was also drawn to the Passion, on which he placed a humanitarian and allegorical interpretation.

The former Dadaist **Christian Schad** (1894–1982) represents a more extreme form of Dix's style, with many explicit scenes drawn from the bohemian world he himself inhabited; **Rudolf Schlichter** (1890–1955) had similar preoccupations. In contrast, there was a romantically inclined wing of this movement, exemplified by **Georg Schrimpf** (1898–1938). The Jewish artist **Felix Nussbaum** (1900–1944), another member of Neue Sachlichkeit, is best known for his sombre late works depicting the Auschwitz concentration camp where he died.

Max Beckmann (1884–1950) defies classification, lying somewhere between Expressionism and Neue Sachlichkeit. He believed it was the artist's duty to express Man's spiritual condition. To this end, he used the self-portrait as a means of expressing his changing reaction to world events, making himself appear in different guises, whether as clown, convict, king or hero. The symbolism associated with Carnival and the circus is a recurring theme in his work, as are the use of gesture to reveal character and the manipulation of space. To express opposition to the Nazis, he took to the anachronistic format of the triptych.

Max Ernst (1891–1976) was another who began as a Dadaist, producing first collages and then frottages. However, he is best known as one of the leading Surrealist painters, a style he turned to on Surrealism's foundation in 1924, and for which his early interest in psychology and the creative works of the mentally ill made him most suitable. To what extent he can be considered a German artist is debatable, as he left his native country in 1922, taking first American then French nationality. The most accomplished Surrealist who can definitely be classed as German is **Edgar Ende** (1901–66), whose compositions are directly comparable with those of the Italian Giorgio de Chirico. **Wolfgang Lettl** (b. 1919) keeps the tradition alive in a distinctive manner, in which humour is very much to the fore.

Oskar Schlemmer (1888–1943) was one of the most varied German painters of the century, touched by seemingly every style; he also practised both decorative and functional art. Among the practitioners of abstraction following Kandinsky and Klee, **Willi Baumeister** (1889–1955), **Ernst Wilhelm Nay** (1902–68) and **Alfred Wolfgang Schulze** (1913–51), better known as **Wols**, acquired the greatest reputations.

Apart from Heartfield, leading luminaries of the GDR artistic establishment in its early years included **Otto Nagel** (1894–1967), who had established his reputation before the war as a chronicler of proletarian life in Berlin, and Dresden's **Hans Grundig** (1901–58), whose powerful visionary images show an obvious debt to medieval and Renaissance predecessors. For most of its life, however, the state fostered a particularly sterile form of Socialist Realism as the only acceptable form of artistic activity; artists who rebelled against this, such as **Roger Loewig** (b.1930), faced persecution and eventual expulsion. Few products of the state-sponsored style still survive on public display, except as mere historical curiosities. An exception is the most spectacular commission granted by the regime, the controversial

Panorama in Bad Frankenhausen in honour of the Peasants' War, painted by Leipzig professor **Werner Tübke** (b. 1929).

In the postwar Federal Republic, avant-garde artistic activity flourished, thanks to generous subsidy levels by all tiers of government. How many of the painters whose work currently lines the walls of the country's many museums of modern art will prove to be of lasting significance remains a moot point. Among those who have gained international standing, **Georg Baselitz** (b.1940) paints figuratively but groups the differ-

ent components of his works in a deliberately arbitrary way. **Sigmar Polke** (b.1941) can be seen as something of a disciple of Dadaism in the objects he tacks onto his canvases, mirroring his interest in German society's obsession with kitsch. **Anselm Kiefer** (b.1945) has been concerned with the German psyche in its historical context, focusing on gestures, symbols and myths. **Jörg Immendorff** (b.1945) and **Bernd Koberling** (b.1938) have taken an overtly left-wing political stance in their work, with ecological themes also being associated with the latter.

BOOKS

Publishers are detailed below in the form of British publisher/American publisher, where both exist. University Press is abbreviated to UP and Oxford University Press to OUP.

TRAVEL

Heinrich Heine *Deutschland: A Winter's Tale* (Angel; also included in the *Complete Poems*). This magisterial verse travelogue describes Heine's journey from exile in Paris to his family home in Hamburg. It's full of insight into the places he passed through, and contains devastating exposés of mid-nineteenth-century German society. The *Harz Journey* (*Selected Prose*, Penguin) is one of the author's *Travel Pictures* – much imitated travelogues featuring inserted poems within the narrative.

Patrick Leigh Fermor *A Time of Gifts* (Penguin). The author set out to walk from Rotterdam to Constantinople in 1933, travelling along the Rhine and Danube valleys en route. Written up forty years later in luscious, hyperrefined prose, it presents the fresh sense of youthful discovery distilled through considerable subsequent learning and reflection. Prewar Germany is shown suffering from all the schizophrenic influences of the era, yet the country's enduring beauty is also captured.

Claudio Magris *Danube* (Harvill). Absorbing, searching exploration of the great river and the places along it from the Black Forest to the Black Sea, mixing travelogue with all manner of scholarly diversions; not the easiest of reads, but rewards the effort.

Mark Twain *A Tramp Abroad* (Penguin). The early, German-based part of this book, particularly the descriptions of Heidelberg, show Twain

on top form, by turns humorous and evocative. There's an over-the-top appendix entitled "The Awful German Language", which mercilessly pillories the over-complexity of "this fearsome tongue".

HISTORY

Roland Bainton *Here I Stand* (Lion/NAL). The best and liveliest biography of Martin Luther, one of the undisputed titans of European history.

Geoffrey Barraclough *Origins of Modern Germany* (Blackwell/Norton). The most easily digestible general introduction to the country's history, tackling the medieval period better than any more specialized book.

Volker Berghahn *Germany and the Approach of War in 1914* (Macmillan/St Martin's Press). An instructive general picture of Germany before World War I. It chronicles the political, economic and social pressures, and succeeds in giving plausible explanations for the apparently inevitable.

Owen Chadwick *The Reformation* (Penguin). Traces the German origins of the biggest-ever rupture in the fabric of the Church, and follows their impact on the rest of Europe.

Einhard and Notker the Stammerer *Two Lives of Charlemagne* (Penguin). Einhard was a leading courtier in the service of the founder of the Holy Roman Empire, and provided a beautifully written, all-too-short biography of his master. Written a century later, Notker's book is a series of monkish anecdotes, many no doubt apocryphal, which help flesh out the overall portrait of Charlemagne.

Mary Fulbrook *A Concise History of Germany* (Cambridge UP). "Concise" is the key word for this post-unification history, whose brevity is simultaneously its strength and its weakness.

Sebastian Haffner *The Rise and Fall of Prussia* (Phoenix). A short study of the legend behind the remarkable state which forged German unity in 1871, yet vanished from the map in 1947.

Friedrich Heer *The Holy Roman Empire* (Phoenix). Comprehensive account of the thousand-year history of the First German Reich.

Golo Mann *The History of Germany Since 1787* (Pimlico). Written by the son of Thomas Mann, this comprehensive study traces not only the politics but also the intellectual and cultural currents of the period.

Nancy Mitford *Frederick the Great* (Penguin). Lively biography of the man who brought Prussia to the forefront of German affairs, and to a place among the great powers of Europe.

Detlev Pleukert *The Weimar Republic* (Penguin). Trenchant dissection of the endlessly fascinating but fundamentally flawed state – until recently the only experiment at a united and democratic Germàn nation – which survived for just fourteen years.

Alexandra Richie *Faust's Metropolis* (HarperCollins). The most detailed history of Berlin in English, with the emphasis placed firmly on the momentous events of the twentieth century.

Tacitus *The Germania* (Penguin). Brilliant series of concise analyses of each of the warlike Germanic tribes, which are often compared favourably with the author's native Rome. Some of the observations about German character are startlingly prophetic.

A.J.P. Taylor *Bismarck: The Man and the Statesman* (Penguin/Random House). Britain's most controversial historian here provides a typically stirring portrait of the ruthless schemer who forged (reluctantly, in the author's view) the nineteenth-century unification of Germany.

Veronica (C.V.) Wedgwood *The Thirty Years War* (Methuen/Routledge). Easily the most accomplished book on the series of conflicts which devastated the country and divided the continent in the first half of the seventeenth century.

Andrew Wheatcroft *The Habsburgs* (Penguin). Wide-ranging history of the extraordinary dynasty which not only dominated German affairs for several centuries, but controlled much of the rest of Europe as well.

NAZISM AND WORLD WAR II

Alan Bullock *Hitler: A Study in Tyranny* (Penguin). Ever since it was published, this scholarly yet highly readable tome has ranked as the classic single-volume biography of the failed Austrian artist and discharged army corporal whose evil genius fooled a nation and caused the deaths of millions.

Joachim Fest *The Face of the Third Reich* (Penguin). Mainly of interest for its biographies

of the gallery of rogues surrounding the *Führer* – Göring, Goebbels, Hess, Himmler, Speer et al.

Klaus P. Fischer *Nazi Germany* (Constable/Continuum). Offers a well-balanced general history of the Third Reich and its origins.

Daniel Jonah Goldhagen *Hitler's Willing Executioners* (Abacus). One of the most important recent contributions to the history of the Third Reich, this controversial tome sets out to prove that guilt for the implementation of the Holocaust lies with a far broader constituency than the Nazi elite.

Adolf Hitler *Table Talk* (OUP/Knopf). Hitler in his own words: Martin Bormann, one of his inner circle, recorded the dictator's pronouncements at meetings between 1941 and 1944. The early *Mein Kampf* (Pimlico/Noontide), a series of rambling, irrational and hysterical outbursts on every subject under the sun, is also of interest, as it genuinely constituted Hitler's blueprint for power.

Ian Kershaw *Hitler* (Penguin). A well-nigh definitive new two-volume biography of Hitler, the first part covering the years up to 1936, the second the last nine years of his life.

Claudia Koonz *Mothers in the Fatherland* (Methuen/St Martin's Press). Perceptive study of the role of women in Nazi Germany. Includes a rare and revealing interview with the chief of Hitler's Women's Bureau, Gertrud Scholtz-Klink.

William Shirer *The Rise and Fall of the Third Reich* (Mandarin/Simon & Schuster). This makes a perfect complement to Bullock's book: Shirer was an American journalist stationed in Germany during the Nazi period. Notwithstanding the inordinate length and excessive journalese, this book is full of insights and is ideal for dipping into, with the help of its exhaustive index.

James Taylor and Warren Shaw *A Dictionary of the Third Reich* (Penguin). The handiest reference book of the period.

Hugh Trevor-Roper *The Last Days of Hitler* (Macmillan/Chicago UP). A brilliant reconstruction of the closing chapter of the Third Reich, set in the Berlin bunker. Trevor-Roper subsequently marred his reputation as the doyen of British historians by authenticating the forged *Hitler Diaries*, which have themselves been the subject of several books.

POSTWAR SOCIETY AND POLITICS

John Ardagh *Germany and the Germans* (Penguin). The most comprehensive English-language characterization of the country and its people, taking into account its history, politics and psyche, and covering almost every aspect of national life, revised after unification. Its approach is always lively, yet remains scrupulously unbiased.

David Childs *The GDR: Moscow's German Ally* (Unwin Hyman/Routledge). The best book on the GDR period, fully revised the year before *Die Wende*, when the regime still seemed fully secure. Obviously now dated, but still of considerable interest for its detailed descriptions and explanations.

David Childs and Richard Popplewell *The Stasi* (Macmillan/New York UP). In-depth academic study of the huge parasitical ministry that was the East German secret police.

W.A. Coupe *Germany Through the Looking-Glass* (Berg). The author presents the period 1945–1986 via a collection of German political cartoons, adding his own analysis of the issues in each case. Opinionated and subjective, the book introduces German humour and a German view of the country's postwar development.

Ian Derbyshire *Politics in Germany* (Chambers). Survey of the German political scene, with *Die Wende* and the subsequent elections fully documented.

Timothy Garton Ash *The File* (Flamingo). Following the opening of the *Stasi* archives, the author traced all those who had spied on him, and lays bare the informer society that was the GDR.

Stuart Parkes *Understanding Contemporary Germany* (Routledge). Sympathetic examination – with a broadly optimistic conclusion – of the political, economic and social structures of post-unification Germany.

Peter Schneider *The Germany Comedy* (I.B. Tauris/Farrar, Straus & Giroux). Discussion of the myriad problems caused by unification, with many wry descriptions and observations of the bizarre contradictions and anomalies that ensued.

Günther Wallraff *Lowest of the Low* (Methuen/Freundlich). In 1983, Wallraff spent two years labouring among Turkish and other immigrant workers, finding out about the under-side of German affluence. The book was a political bombshell when it came out, painting a picture of exploitation and malpractice rarely discussed in Germany. Unfortunately, it now seems that the author was guilty of fabricating some of the evidence, thus diminishing its long-term impact. *The Undesirable Journalist* (Pluto Press) is a collection of short but similarly shocking pieces exposing some of the nastier aspects of the country's postwar prosperity.

Alan Watson *The Germans: Who are they now?* (Mandarin/Edition Q). A guide to German identity and the way it is shaping for the future. Each of the eight chapters attempts to provide an answer to one strand of the question posed in the title.

GERMANY IN ENGLISH-LANGUAGE FICTION

Elizabeth von Arnim *Elizabeth and her German Garden* (Virago), *Elizabeth in Rügen* (Virago). Although billed as novels, these are effectively autobiographical works by Katherine Mansfield's cousin, an Australian who married a German aristocrat and went to live on his Pomeranian estates.

Sybille Bedford *A Legacy* (Penguin). Semi-autobiographical novel about two German families – one Berlin, Jewish and mercantile, the other rural, Catholic and aristocratic – improbably united by marriage. Full of sparkling dialogue and richly comic episodes.

Erskine Childers *The Riddle of the Sands* (Wordsworth). Set against the background of the Great Naval Race in the run-up to World War I, this is generally regarded as the first modern spy novel. The authentic descriptions of the Friesian islands give it a strong local colour.

Daniel Defoe *Memoirs of a Cavalier* (OUP). The first half of this novel is set in the Germany of the Thirty Years War, and offers vivid descriptions of some of the key battles: indeed the book is so lifelike that Defoe was able to pass it off as a true autobiography of a soldier of fortune.

Thomas de Quincey *Klosterheim* (Woodbridge Press). The only novel by the celebrated opium eater, this spooky Gothic fantasy again uses the backdrop of the Thirty Years War, but (in contrast to Defoe) is told from the point of view of the Catholic side.

Richard Hughes *The Fox in the Attic, The Wooden Shepherdess* (Harvill). The most taciturn of writers, Hughes established an enormous literary reputation on a handful of works, including these first two parts of an unfinished trilogy about an Anglo-German family in the years following World War I. Focusing heavily on the fatal attraction of the Nazis, each mixes fictional episodes with vivid descriptions of real-life events, including Hitler's Beer Hall Putsch and the Night of the Long Knives.

Christopher Isherwood *Mr Norris Changes Trains, Goodbye to Berlin* (Methuen/Norton). Set in the decadent atmosphere of the Weimar Republic, these stories brilliantly evoke the period and bring to life some classic Berlin characters; they subsequently formed the basis of the films *I Am a Camera* and *Cabaret*. See also *Christopher and his Kind* (Methuen), a fairly dire autobiographical product of the author's declining years which is nonetheless of interest for describing the true-life events and people on which the stories were based.

Jerome K. Jerome *Three Men on the Bummel* (Penguin). Sequel to the (deservedly) more famous *Three Men in a Boat*, this features the same trio of feckless English travellers taking a cycling holiday through Germany at the turn of the twentieth century. The second half of the book features plenty of entertaining anecdotes, with opinions bandied about on every conceivable subject. *Diary of a Pilgrimage* (Alan Sutton) is an account of the same author's visit to see the Oberammergau Passion Play.

John Le Carré *A Small Town in Germany* (Coronet/Dell). Vintage spy novel set in 1960s Bonn. The then recently built Berlin Wall is the setting for both the beginning and ending of *The Spy Who Came in from the Cold* (Coronet), Le Carré's best-known Cold War fiction.

Katherine Mansfield *In a German Pension* (Penguin). One of the author's earliest works, this is a collection of short stories set in early twentieth-century Bavaria. Funny but often acerbic too.

Robert Muller *The World That Summer* (Sceptre). A beautifully written novel based on the author's own experience as a half-Jewish boy growing up in Hamburg during the Third Reich, with all the inevitable conflicts that involved.

Rudolph Erich Raspe *The Adventures of Baron Munchausen* (Dedalus/Hippocrene). The outrageously exaggerated humorous exploits of the real-life Baron Münchhausen were embroidered yet further by Raspe and first published in English. Copies with the classic nineteenth-century engravings of Gustave Doré can often be found in remainder and secondhand shops.

Stephen Spender *The Temple* (Faber & Faber). Set in Hamburg and the Rhineland during the Weimar Republic years, this makes a fascinating comparison with the closely related works of Isherwood, who is actually one of the main characters. Because of its explicit homosexuality, it could not be published at the time, and remained in draft manuscript until a few years ago.

Anthony Trollope *Linda Tressel* (OUP). One of the Victorian master novelist's shorter full-length works, a powerful psychological study, set against the backdrop of Nürnberg, of the crushing of a young woman's spirit by her bigoted aunt.

GERMAN FICTION CLASSICS

Theodor Fontane *Before the Storm* (OUP). Set in Prussia during the period of the Napoleonic wars, this epic is the greatest German historical novel of the second half of the nineteenth century, dealing with the conflict between patriotism and liberty. The much shorter *Effi Briest* (Penguin) focuses on adultery in the context of the social mores of the age. *Cécile* (Angel) likewise deals with moral dilemmas and ends tragically, while *Two Novellas* (Penguin) demonstrate the author's mastery of the small-scale.

Johann Wolfgang von Goethe *The Sorrows of Young Werther* (Penguin). An early epistolary novella, treating the theme of suicide for the first time ever. *Wilhelm Meister: The Years of Apprenticeship* and *Wilhelm Meister: The Years of Travel* (both John Calder/Riverrun Press) is a huge, episodic and partly autobiographical cycle of novels. *Tales for Transformation* (City Lights) is a series of short stories, showing Goethe's interest in the supernatural.

Johann Jacob Christoffel von Grimmelshausen *Simplicius Simplicissimus* (Dedalus). This massive, brilliantly witty semi-autobiographical novel, at long last available in a reliable translation, is one of the high points of seventeenth-century European literature. Set against the uncertainties of the Thirty Years

War, it charts the story of its hero from boyhood to middle age.

Gerhart Hauptmann *Lineman Thiel and Other Stories* (Angel). These three remarkable stories, written towards the end of the nineteenth century, anticipate Freud in their psychological penetration, and the techniques of the cinema in their use of strong visual symbols.

Johann Peter Hebel *The Treasure Chest* (Penguin). A wonderful collection of moral tales, anecdotes, jokes, reports of murders, disasters and mysteries, all originally written for inclusion in a popular religious almanac.

Ernst Theodor Amadeus Hoffmann *Tales of Hoffmann* (Penguin), *The Best Tales of Hoffmann* (Dover). These selections of work by the schizophrenic master of fantasy and the macabre overlap slightly, but each features only one of his two greatest masterpieces; Penguin has *Mademoiselle de Scudéry*, the world's first detective story, while Dover includes the nightmarish allegory, *The Golden Pot*, in Thomas Carlyle's inspired translation. *The Life and Opinions of the Tomcat Murr* (Penguin) is a full-scale novel on the author's favourite theme of two juxtaposed stories, in this case the supposed memoirs of a cat and a musician clearly modelled on Hoffmann himself.

Heinrich von Kleist *The Marquise of O and Other Stories* (Penguin). Like Hoffmann, who was only one year older, Kleist was one of the all-time greats of short-story writing. His eight tales range in length from three to one hundred pages, but they're all equally compelling.

Frank G. Ryder (ed.) *German Romantic Stories* (Continuum). A marvellous anthology which includes three of the classic novellas of German Romanticism: *Memoirs of a Good-for-Nothing* by Joseph von Eichendorff, *Undine* by Friedrich de la Motte Fouqué and *The Strange Story of Peter Schlemihl* by Adelbert von Chamisso.

Jeffrey L. Sammons (ed.) *German Novellas of Realism* (Continuum). Another fine collection, including two exquisite prose idylls by writers better known as poets: *The Jew's Beech* by Annette von Droste-Hülshoff and *Mozart on the Way to Prague* by Eduard Mörike.

Theodor Storm *The Dykemaster* (Angel). Powerful short novel, set against the bleak western coastline of Schleswig-Holstein, about the inventor of a new type of dyke who is demonized by the self-centred community which opposes him. *Hans and Heinz Kirch* (Angel), a novella about a father–son conflict in a family of Baltic merchants, is the lead title in an anthology which includes two of the author's finest short stories.

GERMAN FICTION SINCE 1900

Heinrich Böll *The Lost Honour of Katharina Blum* (Minerva/Penguin). Winner of the Nobel Prize for Literature in 1972, Heinrich Böll is the most popular postwar German novelist – at least with non-Germans. This is the harrowing story of a young woman whose life is ruined by the combined effects of a gutter-press campaign and her accidental involvement with a wanted terrorist. *The Clown* (Marion Boyars/Penguin) again uses the backdrop of Cologne for a more detailed critique of modern German society. *And Where Were You, Adam?* (Minerva/Northwestern UP) is set in 1944, chronicling the effect of war and Nazism on ordinary German people.

Bertolt Brecht *Short Stories* (Methuen/Routledge). A highly entertaining collection, proving that this side of Brecht's output has been unfairly neglected. In contrast, his single large-scale prose work, *The Threepenny Novel* (Penguin), a much-expanded version of the *Opera*, is stultifyingly verbose.

Alfred Döblin *Berlin-Alexanderplatz* (Ungar). A prominent socialist intellectual during the Weimar period, Döblin went into exile shortly after the banning of his books in 1933. *Berlin-Alexanderplatz* is his weightiest and most durable achievement, an unrelenting epic of the city's underclass.

Hans Fallada *Little Man, What Now?* (Libris/Academy Chicago Publishers). A once-famous but now unjustly neglected masterpiece, describing with style, humour and tenderness the story of a young couple struggling against the spiralling inflation of the final Weimar years. The German psyche on the eve of the Nazi takeover is captured and distilled far more effectively than in any history book.

Günter Grass *From the Diary of a Snail*, *The Flounder*, *The Tin Drum* (all Minerva/Random House). Grass, the Nobel Laureate of 1999, is one of Germany's best-known postwar personalities, concerned to analyse and come to terms with his country's awful recent heritage. His highly political novels are all studies of the German character, concentrating on how Nazism found a foothold among ordinary Germans and on postwar guilt, but also on postwar materialism and spiritual poverty.

Hermann Hesse *Narziss and Goldmund* (Penguin/Holt). A beautifully polished novel, set in medieval Germany and narrated in the picaresque vein, about two monks, one a dedicated scholar, the other a wanderer, artist and lover. *Steppenwolf* (Penguin/Holt) is a bizarre fantasy about schizophrenia, while *The Glass Bead Game* (Picador/Henry Holb) is a monumental utopian novel, set in a future where an elite group develops a game which resolves the world's conflicts.

Georg Heym *The Thief and Other Stories* (Libris). These seven Expressionist stories, notable for their rich imagery and relentlessly grim subject-matter, comprise the entire prose output of the author, who was already a well-established poet at the time of his death in a skating accident at the age of 25.

Stefan Heym *The King David Report* (Northwestern UP). Heym was one of the many Marxist writers who chose to settle in the GDR, but he quickly became disillusioned and for decades functioned as a one-man opposition to the regime. This is his best novel, a devastatingly witty send-up of modern totalitarianism by means of a biblical allegory.

Gert Hofmann *The Parable of the Blind* (Minerva/Fromm), *Our Conquest* (Minerva). Hofmann was a latecomer to fiction, but quickly established himself among the most original contemporary German writers. *The Parable of the Blind* is an imaginative rendering of the story behind Brueghel's enigmatic painting, while *Our Conquest* offers a child's-eye view of the aftermath of defeat in World War II.

Ernst Jünger *The Glass Bees* (Noonday Press), *Eumeswill* (Quartet), *Aladdin's Problem* (Quartet). Jünger is the most controversial German writer of the twentieth century, mainly because, although never a Nazi, he was an avowed right-winger who willingly served as a soldier in World War II. His novels belong to the genre of utopian fiction and are multi-layered in approach, offering critiques which can be taken to apply to Germany in particular or to modern society in general.

Wolfgang Koeppen *Pigeons on the Grass* (Holmes & Meier). A collage-like novel describing through a score of different characters the events in a single day in an occupied German city after World War II. It's part of an informal trilogy which also includes *Death in Rome* (Penguin), a ruthless dissection of the various component parts of the German soul as manifested through four members of the same family.

Siegfried Lenz *The German Lesson* (New Directions). A classic German novel about World War II, focusing on the clashes between a father and son, and between duty and personal loyalty. *The Lightship* (Methuen) examines similar themes in a very different setting.

Heinrich Mann *Man of Straw* (Penguin). The best novel by Thomas Mann's more politically committed elder brother, here analysing the corrupt nature of political and business life under the Second Reich.

Klaus Mann *The Pious Dance* (Gay Men's Press), *Mephisto* (Penguin). The erotic novels of Thomas Mann's son were long banned; he now appears as a remarkable individual voice in his own right. His vivid descriptions of the Berlin underworld in the former strongly influenced Isherwood, while *Mephisto* is a striking *roman à clef* about an actor who sells his soul to the Nazi party.

Thomas Mann *The Magic Mountain* (Minerva/Random House). Generally considered the author's masterpiece, this is a weighty novel of ideas discussing love, death, politics and war through a collection of characters in a Swiss sanatorium, whose sickness mirrors that of European society as a whole. *Buddenbrooks* (Minerva/Random House) is the story of a merchant dynasty in the author's native Lübeck; *Confessions of Felix Krull, Confidence Man* (Minerva/Random House) is the great comic novel of German literature; *Lotte in Weimar* (Minerva/Random House) is a brilliant evocation of Weimar in the era of Goethe; while *Doctor Faustus* (Minerva/Random House) updates the Faust legend through the story of a twentieth-century German composer.

Erich Maria Remarque *All Quiet on the Western Front* (Picador/Fawcett). The classic German novel of World War I, focusing on the traumatic impact of the conflict on the life of an ordinary soldier. *Three Comrades* (Fawcett

Columbine) explores the theme of friendship in the uncertain atmosphere of late 1920s Germany.

Herbert Rosendorfer *The Architect of Ruins* (Dedalus). This, the first and best novel of one of Germany's most admired contemporary writers, is an amusing, dreamlike work consisting of a series of stories within stories. *The Night of the Amazons* (Minerva) is a black comedy about Nazi Germany, while *Stephanie* (Dedalus) narrates a German housewife's trips back in time to her previous existence as an eighteenth-century Spanish duchess.

Bernhard Schlink *The Reader* (Phoenix/Pantheon). The most widely praised German-language novel of recent years, this is a Holocaust book with a difference, based around the postwar love story of the narrator and an older woman. Written in spare, taut prose, it deals with the great themes of guilt, atonement, redemption, forgiveness and conscience with extraordinary power and economy of means.

Peter Schneider *The Wall Jumper* (Allison & Busby/Pantheon). A series of vignettes about the Berlin Wall: about those who crossed it (in both directions), and about the two different states of mind it induced. Although billed as fiction, much of it is clearly autobiographical and factual, albeit larded with a few hoaxes.

W.G. Sebald *The Emigrants* (Harvill). Billed as a work of fiction – notwithstanding the inclusion of numerous old photographs as evidence of its factual basis – this is a haunting lament for the vanished Jewish culture of Germany, illustrated through the lives of four exiles.

Anna Seghers *The Seventh Cross* (Monthly Review Press). Now rather a neglected figure, Seghers was one of the literary stalwarts of the GDR. This, her best-known novel, is a stirring wartime adventure story about a Communist on the run from the Nazi prison camps.

Kurt Tucholsky *Germany? Germany!* (Carcanet). A reader drawn from the writings of the sharpest German satirist of the century. The outrageously witty monologues of the complacent Jewish businessman Herr Wendriner are chillingly prophetic.

Jakob Wassermann *Caspar Hauser* (Penguin). A masterly exposition of the theme of innocence betrayed, this novel is the finest of the many books inspired by the true story of the famous foundling. *The Maurizius Case* (Carroll

& Graf) is a weighty novel about the pursuit of justice.

Christa Wolf *A Model Childhood* (Virago/Farrar, Straus & Giroux). The author gained a reputation for literary integrity, despite her loyalty to the GDR. This book is a fictionalized account of her own youth in Bavaria in the 1930s, providing an excellent portrait of a child's confrontation with Nazi ideas and the shattering disillusionment that came from facing the truth as an adult.

POETRY

Anon *Carmina Burana* (Penguin). A wonderful collection of (originally) dog-Latin songs and poems from thirteenth-century Bavaria. In spite of their monastic origin, the texts are often bawdy and erotic. Many were used by Carl Orff in his choral showpiece named after the manuscript.

Bertolt Brecht *Poems* (Eyre Methuen/Time Warner). Brecht's poems have worn far better than his plays. They sound even more inspired when heard in the musical settings provided by Kurt Weill and the more ideologically inspired Paul Dessau and Hans Eisler. Many recordings are available of these – the best are by Lotte Lenya (CBS), Ute Lempe (Decca) and, in English, Robyn Archer (EMI).

Leonard Forster (ed.) *The Penguin Book of German Verse* (Penguin). Best of the anthologies, representing all the big names (and many more) from the eighth century to the present day, with folk songs, ballads and chorales added for good measure.

Johann Wolfgang von Goethe *Selected Poems* (John Calder/Princeton UP), *Selected Verse* (Penguin), *Epigrams and Poems* (Anvil). Varied anthologies drawn from Goethe's prodigious output. *Roman Elegies and The Diary* (Libris) couples two of Goethe's most accessible poetic works.

Heinrich Heine *Complete Poems* (OUP/Gordon Press), *Selected Verse* (Penguin). Heine's works, with their strong rhythms and dramatic, acerbic thrusts, translate far better into English than those of any of his contemporaries; he was also the favourite poet of the great Romantic composers.

Friedrich Hölderlin *Selected Verse* (Anvil). Hölderlin's poetry, with its classical metres and vivid imagery, is notoriously difficult to translate, but this anthology makes a successful stab at the thankless task. Another selection (Chicago UP) also includes some of the very different lyric poetry of Eduard Mörike.

Novalis (Georg Philipp von Hardenberg) *Hymns to the Night* (Enitharmon). Fine new translation of the great mystic masterpiece of German Romanticism, accompanied by an illuminating essay.

DRAMA

Bertolt Brecht *Plays* (Eyre Methuen/Random House). Brecht's short but fruitful collaboration during the Weimar Republic with the composer Kurt Weill – *The Threepenny Opera, The Rise and Fall of the City of Mahagonny* and *The Seven Deadly Sins* – show him on top form, though the music is an essential component in these works. Of his other plays, the "parables" – *The Caucasian Chalk Circle* and *The Good Woman of Setzuan* – are generally more successful than those with a more overtly political tone.

Georg Büchner *Complete Plays* (Penguin). Büchner died in 1837 at the age of 23. Two of his three plays are masterpieces – *Danton's Death* is a political statement about the French Revolution, while the astonishing unfinished *Woyzeck*, a tragedy based on the life of an insignificant soldier, must be the tersest drama ever written, with not a word wasted in the telling. This anthology also includes his only major prose work, the unfinished novella *Lenz*.

Johann Wolfgang von Goethe *Faust Part One* (Penguin/OUP), *Faust Part Two* (Penguin/OUP). Goethe made the completion of this vast drama – which examines the entire gamut of preoccupations of European civilization – the major task of his life, and he duly finished it just before his death, having worked at it for around sixty years. All his other important works for the stage are collected together in *Early Verse Drama and Prose Plays* (Princeton UP) and *Verse Plays and Epics* (Princeton UP).

Georg Kaiser *Plays Vol. 1, Plays Vol. 2* (John Calder/Riverrun). These contain a selection of the vast output of the leading dramatist of the Expressionist movement, typically using very stark language and stressing ideas at the expense of characterization – the players are typically denoted by their worldly function, rather than their name. Another piece by Kaiser

features in *Seven Expressionist Plays* (John Calder/Riverrun), which also contains works by two dramatists better known as artists – Ernst Barlach and Oskar Kokoschka.

Heinrich von Kleist *Five Plays* (Yale UP). Ranges over Kleist's varied output, from German theatre's finest comedy, *The Broken Jug*, to the patriotic drama, *Prince Frederick of Homburg*.

Gotthold Ephraim Lessing *Nathan the Wise, Minna von Barnhelm and Other Plays* (Continuum). The first of these plays is unusual in German literature in having a Jew as the hero; the second is one of German theatre's earliest examples of middle-class comedy, using contemporary eighteenth-century events as a backdrop.

Friedrich Schiller *The Robbers, Wallenstein* (Penguin). This pairs an early Sturm und Drang drama (which established Schiller as the leader of that movement) with one of his later historical plays, set against the background of the Thirty Years War. *William Tell* (Chicago UP) is the playwright's last work.

Ottmar Weiss and Alois Daisenberger *Oberammergau: A Passion Play* (Dedalus). A complete translation of the classic nineteenth-century text of the play.

LEGENDS AND FOLKLORE

Anon *The Nibelungenlied* (Penguin). Germany's greatest epic was written around 1200 by an unknown Danubian poet; the story varies greatly from Wagner's *Ring*, which draws equally heavily on Nordic sources of the legend. It's here given a highly entertaining prose translation.

Anon *Till Eulenspiegel* (OUP). The first complete and uncensored English translation of the adventures of Germany's most famous folk hero, the roguish jester who fought pomposity in all its many manifestations.

Francis G. Gentry (ed.) *German Medieval Tales* (Continuum). Includes most of the best-known German legends with a medieval origin, notably the *Historia and Tale of Doctor Johannes Faustus*, which became one of European literature's most fertile sources.

Jakob and Wilhelm Grimm *Complete Grimms' Tales* (Gollancz/Doubleday). The world's most famous collection of folk-tales, meticulously researched by the Brothers Grimm, has stories to appeal to all age ranges. A selection of the tales (Penguin) has the ingenious idea of rendering some of them in Scots and Irish, thus capturing something of the dialect flavour of the originals, which is otherwise lost in translation.

Jennifer Russ *German Festivals* (Oswald Wolff/ Ungar). Rather a pity it's not a bit longer, but this book provides useful background information on all the main annual folklore celebrations.

Frank G. Ryder (ed.) *German Literary Fairy Tales* (Continuum). An anthology of elaborate reworkings of folk-tales made by Goethe, Novalis, Eichendorff, Mörike, Storm and others.

Lewis Spence *Germany: Myths and Legends* (Bracken). Narrates the rich store of legends associated with the Rhine, arranged in the form of a journey down the great river.

Gottfried von Strassburg *Tristan* (Penguin), **Wolfram von Eschenbach** *Parzifal* (Penguin). Two more epic masterpieces from early thirteenth-century Germany, both based on the Grail legends.

THE VISUAL ARTS

Peter Adam *The Arts of the Third Reich* (Thames & Hudson). Engrossing and well-written account of the officially approved state art of Nazi Germany – a subject that for many years has been ignored or deliberately made inaccessible. Includes over three hundred illustrations, many reproduced for the first time since the war.

Jost Amman *The Book of Trades* (Dover). The 114 woodcuts illustrate the trades and crafts practised in early sixteenth-century Germany; each is accompanied by a poem by the most famous Meistersinger, Hans Sachs.

Michael Baxendall *The Limewood Sculptors of Renaissance Germany* (Yale UP). Examines the work of Tilman Riemenschneider, Veit Stoss and many other lesser-known artists in their social and political context. A lavish series of photographs accompanies the text.

Wolf-Dieter Dube *The Expressionists* (Thames & Hudson). A general introduction to Germany's most distinctive contribution to twentieth-century art.

Albrecht Dürer *The Complete Woodcuts* (Dover), *The Complete Etchings, Engravings and Drypoints* (Dover). These two books enable you to own, at minimal cost, a complete set of the graphic work of one of the world's greatest-ever

masters of the art. The book of woodcuts is particularly recommended.

William Vaughan *German Romantic Painting* (Yale UP). A good introduction to many of Germany's best nineteenth-century artists.

Frank Whiteford *Bauhaus* (Thames & Hudson). Introduction to the twentieth century's most influential art and design movement, tracing its development during its early years in Weimar, Dessau and Berlin.

GUIDEBOOKS

Karl Baedeker *The Rhineland, Northern Germany, Southern Germany, Berlin* (Baedeker). The old Baedekers, all long out of print, are still indispensible classics. They covered a Germany which was considerably more extensive than today, stretching all across Poland into Lithuania and Russia. Look out for the editions dating from the early years of the twentieth century, immensely learned and full of now-untenable opinions. The glossy, modern successors to these (Automobile Association) are not in the same class.

Grant Bourne and Sabine Kröner-Bourne *Walking in the Bavarian Alps* (Cicerone). A recommendable hiking guide to Germany's most spectacular scenic region.

Jack Holland and John Gawthrop *The Rough Guide to Berlin* (Rough Guides). Companion volume to the book you're holding, this gives the full lowdown on the sights, culture and nightlife of one of Europe's most exciting cities.

Graham Lees *Good Beer Guide to Munich and Bavaria* (CAMRA). Impressively wide-ranging guide to the myriad brews of the world's premier beer region, and to the best places to sample them.

Gordon McLachlan *Berlin* (Odyssey). Recently updated, this is predominantly a cultural guide, lavishly illustrated with both archive and commissioned photographs. The main text is accompanied by a wide selection of literary excerpts. *Germany's Romantic Road* (Cicerone) is a detailed guide, with special reference to walkers and cyclists, to the country's most popular tourist route.

Fleur and Colin Speakman *Walking in the Black Forest, King Ludwig Way, Walking in the Harz Mountains* (all Cicerone). Three guides for specific hikes in Germany.

LANGUAGE

German is a very complex language and you can't hope to master it in a short time. As English was a compulsory subject in the West German school curriculum, many people have some familiarity with it, which eases communication a great deal. English is now compulsory in schools throughout Germany.

Nonetheless, a smattering of German does help, especially in out-of-the-way rural areas, or in the former East, where Russian was more commonly taught in schools. Also, given the long-standing and continued presence of American and British forces who make little effort to integrate into local communities or learn German, people are particularly sensitive to presumptuous English-speakers. On the other hand, most will be delighted to practise their English on you once you've stumbled through your German introduction.

Should you be interested in **studying the language** during your stay, the best places to enrol in are the Goethe-Instituten, which can be found in most major cities. The German Tourist Board or local information offices have all relevant addresses.

PRONUNCIATION

English-speakers find the complexities of German grammar hard to handle, but **pronunciation** isn't as daunting as it might first appear. Individual syllables are generally pronounced as they're printed – the trick is learning how to place the stresses in the notoriously lengthy German words.

VOWELS AND UMLAUTS

a as in f**a**ther

e as in d**ay** or as in w**e**t

i as in l**ee**k

o as in b**o**ttom or as in r**o**se

u as in b**oo**t

ä is a combination of a and e, sometimes pronounced like **e** in b**e**t (eg Länder) and sometimes like **ai** in p**ai**d (eg spät)

ö is a combination of o and e, like the French eu

ü is a combination of u and e, like tr**ue**, only sharper in sound

VOWEL COMBINATIONS

ai as in l**ie**

au as in h**ou**se

äu as in **oi**l

ie as in fr**ee**

ei as in h**ei**ght

eu as in **oi**l

CONSONANTS

Consonants are pronounced as they are written, with no silent letters. The differences from English are:

r is given a dry throaty sound, similar to French

j pronounced similar to an English y

s pronounced similar to, but slightly softer than an English z

v pronounced somewhere between f and v

w pronounced same way as English v

z pronounced ts

The German letter ß, the Scharfes S, sometimes replaces ss in a word: pronunciation is identical.

CONSONANT COMBINATIONS

ch is a strong back-of-the-throat sound as in the Scottish loch

sp (at the start of a word) is pronounced shp

st (at the start of a word) is pronounced sht

GENDER

German words can be one of three genders: masculine, feminine or neuter. Unfortunately, the designation of these can appear very illogical: for example, a train is masculine, a cat (even a tomcat) is feminine, and a girl is neuter. Each has its own definite article (respectively der, die, das); as with qualifying adjectives, these decline according to the case used.

GERMAN WORDS AND PHRASES

BASICS

ja, nein	yes, no	*gross, klein*	large, small
bitte	please, you're welcome	*mehr, weniger*	more, less
bitte schön	a more polite form of *bitte*	*wenig*	a little
		viel	a lot
danke, danke schön	thank you, thank you very much	*billig, teuer*	cheap, expensive
		gut, schlecht	good, bad
wo, wann, warum?	where, when, why?	*heiss, kalt*	hot, cold
wieviel?	how much?	*mit, ohne*	with, without
hier, da	here, there	*rechts*	right
geöffnet, offen, auf	all mean "open"	*links*	left
geschlossen, zu	both mean "closed"	*geradeaus*	straight ahead
da drüben	over there	*oben*	above
dieses	this one	*unten*	below
jenes	that one		

GREETINGS AND TIMES

Guten Morgen	Good morning	*Übermorgen*	the day after tomorrow
Guten Abend	Good evening	*Tag*	day
Guten Tag	Good day	*Nacht*	night
Grüss Gott	Good day (in southern Germany)	*Mittag*	midday
		Mitternacht	midnight
Gute Nacht	Good night	*drei Uhr*	three o'clock
Wie geht es Ihnen?	How are you? (polite)	*viertel nach drei*	quarter past three
Wie geht es dir?	How are you? (informal)	*halb vier*	half past three (ie half to four)
Lass mich in Ruhe	Leave me alone		
Hau ab	Get lost	*viertei vor vier*	quarter to four
Geh weg	Go away	*Woche*	week
Auf Wiedersehen	Goodbye	*Wochenende*	weekend
Tschüs	Goodbye (informal)	*Monat*	month
jetzt, später	now, later	*Jahr*	year
früher	earlier	*am Vormittag/ vormittags*	in the morning
Heute	today		
Gestern	yesterday	*am Nachmittag/ nachmittags*	in the afternoon
Morgen	tomorrow		
Vorgestern	the day before yesterday	*am Abend/abends*	in the evening

DAYS, MONTHS AND DATES

Montag	Monday	*Januar*	January
Dienstag	Tuesday	*Februar*	February
Mittwoch	Wednesday	*März*	March
Donnerstag	Thursday	*April*	April
Freitag	Friday	*Mai*	May
Samstag	Saturday	*Juni*	June
Sonnabend	Saturday (in northern Germany)	*Juli*	July
		August	August
Sonntag	Sunday	*September*	September

continued overleaf

continued from previous page

Oktober	October	*Ferien*	holidays
November	November	*Feiertag*	bank holiday
Dezember	December	*Montag, der erste*	Monday, the first of
Frühling	Spring	*April*	April
Sommer	Summer	*der zweite April*	the second of April
Herbst	Autumn	*der dritte April*	the third of April
Winter	Winter		

QUESTIONS AND REQUESTS

All enquiries should be prefaced with the phrase *Entschuldigen Sie bitte* (Excuse me, please). Note that *Sie* is the polite form of address to be used with everyone except close friends, though young people and students often don't bother with it. The older generation will certainly be offended if you address them with the familiar *Du*, as will all officials.

Sprechen Sie Englisch?	Do you speak English?	*Wann fährt der nächste Zug?*	When does the next train leave?
Ich spreche kein Deutsch	I don't speak German	*Um wieviel Uhr?*	At what time?
Sprechen Sie bitte langsamer	Please speak more slowly	*Wieviel Uhr ist es?*	What time is it?
		Sind die Plätze noch frei?	Are these seats taken?
Ich verstehe nicht	I don't understand	*Die Rechnung bitte*	The bill please
Ich verstehe	I understand	*Ist der Tisch frei?*	Is that table free?
Wie sagt man das auf Deutsch?	How do you say that in German?	*Die Speisekarte bitte*	The menu please
Können Sie mir sagen wo … ist?	Can you tell me where… is?	*Fräulein…!*	Waitress…! (for attention)
Wo ist…?	Where is…?	*Herr Ober…!*	Waiter…! (for attention)
Wie komme ich nach …?	How do I get to (a town)?	*Haben Sie etwas billigeres?*	Have you got something cheaper?
Wie komme ich zur/zum…?	How do I get to (a building, place)?	*Haben Sie Zimmer frei?*	Are there rooms available?
Wieviel kostet das?	How much does that cost?	*Wo sind die Toiletten bitte?*	Where are the toilets?

Ich hätte gern dieses I'd like that one
Ich hätte gern ein I'd like a room for two
 Zimmer für zwei

Ich hätte gern ein I'd like a single room
 Einzelzimmer
Hat es Dusche,Bad, Does it have a shower,
 Toilette...? bath, toilet...?

SOME SIGNS

Damen/Frauen	Women's toilets	*Notausgang*	Emergency exit
Herren/Männer	Men's toilets	*Baustelle*	Building works
Eingang	Entrance	*Ampel*	Traffic light
Ausgang	Exit	*Krankenhaus*	Hospital
Ankunft	Arrival	*Polizei*	Police
Abfahrt	Departure	*Nicht rauchen*	No smoking
Ausstellung	Exhibition	*Kein Eingang*	No entrance
Autobahn	Motorway	*Drücken*	Push
Einfahrt	Motorway entrance	*Ziehen*	Pull
Ausfahrt	Motorway exit	*Frei*	Vacant
Geschwindigkeit	Speed limit	*Besetzt*	Occupied
Begrenzung		*Verboten, Untersagt*	Prohibited
Umleitung	Diversion	*Zoll*	Customs
Achtung!	Attention!	*Kasse*	Cash desk
Vorsicht!	Beware!	*Grenzübergang*	Border crossing

NUMBERS

1	*eins*	12	*zwölf*	30	*dreissig*
2	*zwei, zwo*	13	*dreizehn*	40	*vierzig*
3	*drei*	14	*vierzehn*	50	*fünfzig*
4	*vier*	15	*fünfzehn*	60	*sechzig*
5	*fünf*	16	*sechszehn*	70	*siebzig*
6	*sechs*	17	*siebzehn*	80	*achtzig*
7	*sieben*	18	*achtzehn*	90	*neunzig*
8	*acht*	19	*neunzehn*	100	*hundert*
9	*neun*	20	*zwanzig*	1000	*tausend*
10	*zehn*	21	*ein-und-zwanzig*	1999	*neunzehn-hundert-*
11	*elf*	22	*zwei-und-zwanzig*		*neun-und-neunzig*

GLOSSARIES

ART AND ARCHITECTURE

AISLE part of church to the side of the nave.

AMBULATORY passage round the back of the high altar, in continuation of the aisles.

APSE vaulted termination of the east (altar) end of a church.

ART DECO geometrical style of art and architecture prevalent in 1930s.

ART NOUVEAU sinuous, highly stylized form of architecture and interior design; in Germany, mostly dates from period 1900–15 and is known as Jugendstil.

BALDACHIN canopy over an altar or tomb.

BAROQUE expansive, exuberant architectural style of the seventeenth and early eighteenth centuries, characterized by ornate decoration, complex spatial arrangements and grand vistas. The term is also applied to the sumptuous style of painting of the same period.

BASILICA church in which nave is higher than the aisles.

BAUHAUS plain, functional style of architecture and design, originating in early twentieth-century Germany.

BIEDERMEIERSTIL simple, bourgeois style of painting and decoration practised throughout first half of the nineteenth century.

CAPITAL top of a column, usually sculpted.

CHANCEL part of the church in which altar is placed; normally at east end, though some German churches also have one at the west.

CHOIR part of church in which service is sung, usually beside the altar.

CRYPT underground part of a church.

EXPRESSIONISM emotional style of painting, concentrating on line and colour, extensively practised in early twentieth-century Germany; term is also used for related architecture of the same period.

FRESCO mural painting applied to wet plaster, so that colours immediately soak into the wall.

GOTHIC architectural style with an emphasis on verticality, characterized by pointed arch, ribbed vault and flying buttress; introduced to Germany around 1235, surviving in an increasingly decorative form until well into the sixteenth century. The term is also used for paintings of this period.

GRISAILLE painting or stained glass window executed entirely in subdued monochrome.

HALF-TIMBERED style of building in which the walls have a framework of timber interspersed with either bricks or plaster.

HALL CHURCH (*Hallenkirche*) church design much favoured in Germany, in which all vaults are of approximately equal height.

LAVABO well-house in a cloister.

MANNERISM deliberately mannered style of late Renaissance art and architecture.

MODELLO small version of a large picture, usually painted for the patron's approval.

NAVE main body of a church, generally forming the western part.

NEOCLASSICAL late eighteenth- and early nineteenth-century style of art and architecture returning to classical models as a reaction against Baroque and Rococo excesses.

ORIEL projecting bay window.

PARADISE (*Paradies*) richly sculpted porch forming the entrance to some cathedrals.

POLYPTYCH carved or painted altarpiece on several joined panels.

PREDELLA lowest part of an altarpiece, with scenes much smaller than in main sections.

RENAISSANCE Italian-originated movement in art and architecture, inspired by the rediscovery of classical ideals.

RETABLE altarpiece.

ROCOCO highly florid, light and graceful eighteenth-century style of architecture, painting and interior design, forming the last phase of Baroque.

ROMANESQUE solid architectural style of late tenth to mid-thirteenth centuries, characterized by round-headed arches and a penchant for horizontality and geometrical precision. The term is also used for paintings of this period.

ROMANTICISM late eighteenth and early nineteenth-century movement, particularly strong in Germany, rooted in adulation of the natural world and rediscovery of the achievements of the Middle Ages.

ROOD SCREEN screen dividing nave from chancel (thus separating laity and clergy), originally bearing a rood (crucifix).

SOFT STYLE (*Weicher Stil*) delicate style of painting and sculpture pioneered in fourteenth-century Bohemia, which dominated German art to the mid-fifteenth century.

STUCCO plaster used for decorative effects.

TABERNACLE a freestanding canopy or ornamental recess designed to contain the Holy Sacrament.

TRANSEPT arm of a cross-shaped church, placed at ninety degrees to nave and chancel.

TRANSITIONAL architectural style between Romanesque and Gothic in which the basic shapes of the older style were modified by the use of such new forms as the pointed arch and ribbed vault.

TRIPTYCH carved or painted altarpiece on three panels.

TROMPE L'OEIL painting designed to fool the viewer into believing the image is three-dimensional.

TYMPANUM sculptured panel above a doorway.

WESER RENAISSANCE archaic, highly elaborate style of secular Renaissance architecture cultivated in and around the Weser valley in Hesse, Lower Saxony and Westphalia.

WESTWORK (*Westwerk*) grandiose frontage found on many German medieval churches, traditionally reserved for the use of the emperor and his retinue.

GERMAN TERMS

ABTEI abbey.

ALTSTADT old part of a city.

AUSKUNFT information.

AUSLÄNDER foreigner; the word has come to be a pejorative term for any non-white non-German.

AUSSTELLUNG exhibition.

AUSWEIS identity document.

BAD spa (before the name of a town), bath.

BAHNHOF station.

BAU building.

BEFESTIGUNG fortification.

BERG mountain, hill.

BERGBAHN funicular.

BIBLIOTHEK library.

BIERGARTEN beer garden.

BIERKELLER beer cellar; beer hall.

BOTSCHAFT embassy.

BRÜCKE bridge.

BRAUEREI, BRAUHAUS brewery.

BRUNNEN fountain, well.

BUNDESKANZLER Federal Chancellor (Prime Minister).

BUNDESRAT Upper House of German Parliament.

BUNDESTAG Lower House of German Parliament.

BURG castle, fortress.

BÜRGERMEISTER mayor.

CAROLINGIAN (*Karolingisch*) dynasty founded by Charles Martel in the early eighth century which ruled Germany until the last quarter of the ninth century. The term is particularly associated with the reign of Charlemagne (768–814).

DENKMAL memorial.

DIET Parliament of Holy Roman Empire.

DOM cathedral.

DONAU River Danube.

DORF village.

EASTERN TERRITORIES (*Ostgebiete*) lands to the east of the Oder–Neisse line, occupied by German-speaking peoples since the Middle Ages, but forcibly evacuated, and allocated to Poland and the Soviet Union after World War II.

EINBAHNSTRASSE one-way street.

ELECTOR (*Kurfürst*) sacred or secular prince with a vote in the elections to choose the Holy Roman Emperor. There were seven for most of the medieval period, with others added later.

EVANGELISCHE KIRCHE federation of Protestant churches, both Lutheran and Reformed.

FACHWERKHAUS half-timbered house.

FAHRSTUHL lift, elevator.

FASCHING name given to Carnival, especially in Bavaria.

FASTNET name given to Carnival, especially in Baden-Württemberg.

FEIERTAG holiday.

FEST festival.

FESTUNG fortress.

FLUGHAFEN airport.

FLUSS river.

FRANCONIA (*Franken*) historical province of central Germany, stretching as far west as Mainz; name later became associated only with the eastern portion of this territory, most of which is now incorporated in Bavaria.

FREE IMPERIAL CITY (*Freiereichstadt*) independent city-state within the Holy Roman Empire.

FREIHERR baron.

FREMDENZIMMER room for short-term let.

FÜRST prince.

FUSSGÄNGERZONE pedestrian area.

GASSE alley.

GASTARBEITER (guest worker) anyone who comes to Germany to work.

GÄSTEHAUS guesthouse.

GASTHAUS pub, inn.

GASTHOF inn.

GASTSTÄTTE restaurant serving traditional German cuisine.

GEDENKSTÄTTE memorial museum.

GEMÄLDE painting.

GEMÜTLICH snug or cosy.

GRAF count.

GRÜNEN, DIE (The Greens) political party formed from environmental and anti-nuclear groups.

HABSBURG the most powerful family in medieval Germany, operating from a base in Austria. They held the office of Holy Roman Emperor almost continuously from 1452 to 1806, and by marriage, war and diplomacy acquired territories all over Europe.

HAFEN harbour, port.

HANSEATIC LEAGUE (*Hansebund*) medieval trading alliance of Baltic and Rhineland cities, numbering about one hundred at its fifteenth-century peak. Slowly died out in the seven-teenth century with competition from Baltic nation-states and rise of Brandenburg-Prussia.

HAUPTBAHNHOF main train station in a city.

HAUPTBURG central, residential part of a castle.

HAUPTSTRASSE main street.

HEIDE heath.

HEIMAT (homeland) often given a mystical significance and used emotively in connection with Germans displaced from the Eastern Territories.

HERZOG duke.

HOF court, courtyard, mansion.

HOHENSTAUFEN Swabian dynasty who held office of Holy Roman Emperor from 1138 to 1254.

HOHENZOLLERN dynasty of Swabian origin, who became margrave-Electors of Brandenburg in 1415, and slowly built up their territorial base. In the nineteenth century they ousted the Habsburgs from their pre-eminent place in German affairs, forging the Second Reich in 1871 and serving as its emperors until 1918.

HÖHLE cave.

HOLY ROMAN EMPIRE (*Heiliges Römisches Reich*) title used to describe the First German Reich, established in 800. Despite its weak structure, it survived until 1806, when the ruling Habsburgs, in response to the Napoleonic threat, began building up a more solid empire from their Austrian base.

IMBISS snack bar.

INNENSTADT inner city.

INSEL island.

JAGDSCHLOSS hunting lodge.

JUGENDHERBERGE youth hostel.

JUGENDSTIL German version of Art Nouveau.

JUNKER Prussian landowning class.

KAISER emperor.

KAMMER room, chamber.

KAPELLE chapel.

KARNEVAL term used for Carnival, especially in Rhineland.

KAUFHAUS department store.

KINO cinema.

KIRCHE church.

KLOSTER monastery, convent.

KNEIPE drinking pub.

KÖNIG king.

KREUZGANG cloister.

KUNST art.

KURHAUS assembly rooms in a spa.

KURORT health resort.

KURVERWALTUNG reception building in spa resorts.

LAND (pl. **LÄNDER**) name given to the constituent states of the Federal Republic; first introduced in Weimar Republic.

LANDGRAVE (*Landgraf*) count in charge of a large province.

LEUCHTTURM lighthouse.

MARGRAVE (*Markgraf*) count in charge of a Mark (March; later Margraviate), a frontier district established at the time of Charlemagne.

MARKT market, market square.

MAUER wall.

MEER sea.

MEROVINGIAN Frankish dynasty established by Clovis in 481; ruled until the early eighth century.

MIKWE Jewish ritual bath.

MÜNSTER minster, large church.

NATURPARK area of protected countryside.

NEUES FORUM umbrella group for political opposition organizations within the former GDR.

NEUSTADT New part of the city.

ODER–NEISSE LINE eastern limit of German territory set by victorious Allies in 1945.

OSTPOLITIK West German policy of détente towards the GDR.

OTTONIAN (*Ottonisch*) epoch of Otto I and his two eponymous successors. Term is used in connection with the early Romanesque art forms pioneered in this and the subsequent Salian epoch (mid-tenth to mid-eleventh century).

PALAS, PALAST residential part of a castle.

PALATINATE (*Pfalz*) territory ruled by the Count Palatine, a high-ranking imperial official. The present Land is only the western part of the historical province, whose original centre is now part of Baden-Württemberg.

PFARRKIRCHE parish church.

PLATZ square.

PRINZ prince; since 1918, used in a less grandiose way as a courtesy title for aristocrats in place of the plethora of now-defunct titles.

PRUSSIA (*Preussen*) originally, an eastern Baltic territory (now divided between Poland and the Russian Federation). In 1525 it became a duchy under the control of the Hohenzollerns, who merged it in 1618 with their German possessions to form Brandenburg-Prussia (later shortened to Prussia); this took the lead in forging the unity of Germany, and was thereafter its dominant province. The name was abolished after World War II because of its monarchical and militaristic connotations.

QUITTUNG official receipt.

RASTPLATZ picnic area.

RATHAUS town hall.

RATSKELLER cellars below the Rathaus, almost invariably used as a restaurant serving *gutbürgerliche Küche*.

REICH empire.

REISEBÜRO travel agency.

RESIDENZ palace.

RESIDENZSTADT courtly town.

RITTER Knight.

ROMANTISCHE STRASSE ("Romantic Road") scenic road in Bavaria and Baden-Württemberg, running between Würzburg and Füssen.

RUNDGANG way round.

SAAL hall.

SALIAN dynasty of Holy Roman Emperors, 1024–1125.

SAMMLUNG collection.

SÄULE column.

S-BAHN commuter railway network operating in and around conurbations.

SCHATZKAMMER treasury.

SCHICKIE or **SCHICKIE-MICKIE** yuppie.

SCHLOSS castle, palace (equivalent of French château).

SCHMALSPURBAHN narrow-gauge railway.

SEE lake, sea.

SEEBRÜCKE pier.

SEILBAHN cable car.

SESSELBAHN chair lift.

STADT town, city.

STADTMITTE town or city centre.

STAMMTISCH table in a pub or restaurant reserved for regular customers.

STANDSEILBAHN funicular.

STASI (*Staatssicherheitsdienst*) former "State Security Service" or secret police of the GDR.

STAUFIAN pertaining to the epoch of the Hohenstaufen.

STAUSEE reservoir.

STIFTSKIRCHE collegiate church.

STIFTUNG foundation.

STRAND beach.

STRANDKORB wicker beach chair with hood.

STRASSENBAHN tram.

SWABIA (*Schwaben*) name used for the south-western part of Germany from the eleventh century onwards; after the ruling Hohenstaufen dynasty died out, became politically fragmented.

SZENE trendy bar or club.

TAL valley.

TALSPERRE dam.

TANKSTELLE petrol station.

TOR gate, gateway.

TRABI conversational shorthand for the now-famous Trabant, East Germany's two-cylinder, two-stroke car.

TURM tower.

U-BAHN network of underground trains or trams.

VERKEHRSAMT, VERKEHRSVEREIN tourist office.

VIERTEL quarter, district.

VOLK people, folk; given mystical associations by Hitler.

VORBURG outer, defensive part of a castle.

VORSTADT suburb.

WALD forest.

WALDSTERBEN (dying forest syndrome) term used to describe the environmental pollution which has decimated Germany's forests.

WALLFAHRT pilgrimage.

WASSERBURG castle surrounded by a moat.

WECHSEL exchange.

WEIMAR REPUBLIC (*Weimarische Republik*) parliamentary democracy established in 1918 which collapsed with Hitler's assumption of power in 1933.

WEINGUT wine-producing estate.

WEINSTUBE wine bar.

WELF dynastic rivals of Hohenstaufens in Germany and Italy. Descendants became Electors of Hannover, and subsequently kings of Great Britain.

WENDE literally "turning point" – the term used to describe the events of November 1989 and after.

WETTIN dynasty chiefly responsible for pushing Germany's frontiers eastwards from the tenth century, becoming Electors of Saxony in 1423 and ruling the province and the Thuringian principalities until 1918. The Saxe-Coburg line provided monarchs for several countries; renamed as Windsor, one branch is the current British royal family.

WIESE field, meadow.

WILHELMINE (*Wilhelminisch*) pertaining to the epoch of the Second Reich (1871–1918).

WIRTSCHAFT, WIRTSHAUS tavern.

WITTELSBACH dynasty which ruled Bavaria from 1180 to 1918; a branch held the Palatinate Electorate, while the family often held several bishoprics, notably the archbishop-Electorate of Cologne.

ZAHNRADBAHN rack railway.

ZEITSCHRIFT magazine.

ZEITUNG newspaper.

ZEUGHAUS arsenal.

ZIMMER room.

ACRONYMS

BRD (*Bundesrepublik Deutschlands*) official name of West German state (1949–90) and of the unified Germany since 1990.

CDU (*Christlich Demokratische Union*) Christian Democratic Party.

CSU (*Christlich Soziale Union*) Bavarian-only counterpart of CDU, generally more right-wing in outlook.

DB (*Deutsche Bahn*, formerly *Deutsche Bundesbahn*) national rail company retaining the logo of its West German predecessor under a modified name.

DDR (*Deutsche Demokratische Republik*) the Communist East German state, 1949–90.

DJH (*Deutsches Jugendherbergswerk*) German Youth Hostel Association.

FDP (*Freie Demokratische Partei*) Free Democratic Party.

GDR (*German Democratic Republic*) English version of DDR.

NSDAP (*National Sozialistische Deutsche Arbeiterpartei*, "National Socialist German Workers' Party") official name for the Nazis, totalitarian rulers of Germany in the Third Reich, 1933–45.

PDS (*Partei des Demokratischen Sozialismus*) repackaged former SED.

SED (*Sozialistische Einheitspartei Deutschlands*) Socialist Unity Party of Germany, the permanent governing party of the GDR, formed in 1946 as a union of the SPD and Communists in the Russian zone of occupation.

SPD (*Sozialdemokratische Partei Deutschlands*) Social Democratic Party.

ZOB (*Zentral-Omnibus-Bahnhof*) main bus station.

INDEX

around the world

in twenty years

London Mini Guide ★ London Restaurants ★ Los Angeles ★ Madeira ★ Madrid ★ Malaysia, Singapore & Brunei ★ Mallorca ★ Malta & Gozo ★ Maui ★ Maya World ★ Melbourne ★ Menorca ★ Mexico ★ Miami & the Florida Keys ★ Montréal ★ Morocco ★ Moscow ★ Nepal ★ New England ★ New Orleans ★ New York City ★ New York Mini Guide ★ New York Restaurants ★ New Zealand ★ Norway ★ Pacific Northwest ★ Paris ★ Paris Mini Guide ★ Peru ★ Poland ★ Portugal ★ Prague ★ Provence & the Côte d'Azur ★ Pyrenees ★ The Rocky Mountains ★ Romania ★ Rome ★ San Francisco ★ San Francisco Restaurants ★ Sardinia ★ Scandinavia ★ Scotland ★ Scottish Highlands & Islands ★ Seattle ★ Sicily ★ Singapore ★ South Africa, Lesotho & Swaziland ★ South India ★ Southeast Asia ★ Southwest USA ★ Spain ★ St Lucia ★ St Petersburg ★ Sweden ★ Switzerland ★ Sydney ★ Syria ★ Tanzania ★ Tenerife and La Gomera ★ Thailand ★ Thailand's Beaches & Islands ★ Tokyo ★ Toronto ★ Travel Health ★ Trinidad & Tobago ★ Tunisia ★ Turkey ★ Tuscany & Umbria ★ USA ★ Vancouver ★ Venice & the Veneto ★ Vienna ★ Vietnam ★ Wales ★ Washington DC ★ West Africa ★ Women Travel ★ Yosemite ★ Zanzibar ★ Zimbabwe

also look out for our maps, phrasebooks, music guides and reference books

ROUGH GUIDES TWENTY YEARS